YOUR Window TO History

Reading like a Historian

Historians use paintings, like *Washington Crossing the Delaware,* to help understand the past. As you study United States history, you too will learn how to use different historical sources to **Read like a Historian.**

To find out more about reading like a historian and the historical sources that follow, visit go.hrw.com More Online KEYWORD: HISTORIAN

By Frances Marie Gipson
Secondary Literacy Coordinator
Los Angeles Unified School District, Los Angeles, California

How to Analyze a Political Cartoon

In 1871, Thomas Nast published this cartoon—"Who Stole the People's Money?"—poking fun at corruption in politics. As you study political cartoons in this textbook, use the following helpful tips and questions.

- List the parts of the political cartoon and the importance of each part.
- Describe the focus or significance of the political cartoon.
- Do the captions and call-out boxes clarify the political cartoon's purpose?
- Does the cartoon help me understand the information that I am studying in my textbook better?

TEACHER'S EDITION

HOLT

CALIFORNIA SOCIAL STUDIES

United States History

Independence to 1914

William Deverell

Deborah Gray White

HOLT, RINEHART AND WINSTON

A Harcourt Education Company

Orlando • Austin • New York • San Diego • Toronto • London

Authors

William Deverell

William Deverell is Professor of History at the University of Southern California and Director of the Huntington-USC Institute on California and the West. He is the author of *Railroad Crossing: Californians and the Railroad, 1850-1910* and *Whitewashed Adobe: The Rise of Los Angeles and the Remaking of the Mexican Past.* He is the editor of the *Blackwell Companion to the American West.* With Greg Hise, he co-authored *Eden by Design: The 1930 Olmsted-Bartholomew Plan for the Los Angeles Region* and co-edited *Land of Sunshine: The Environmental History of Metropolitan Los Angeles.* He is the former chairman of the California Council for the Humanities and was the 2002-2003 Fellow of the John Randolph Haynes and Dora Haynes Foundation of Los Angeles.

Deborah Gray White

Deborah Gray White, a former New York City school teacher, is Distinguished Professor of History at Rutgers University in New Brunswick, New Jersey. A specialist in American history and the history of African Americans, she is the author of several books including: *Ar'n't I A Woman? Female Slaves in the Plantation South, Two Heavy a Load: Black Women in Defense of Themselves, 1894-1994,* and *Let My People Go, African Americans 1804-1860,* volume 4 in the *Young Oxford History of African Americans.*

For acknowledgments, see page R100, which is an extension of the copyright page.

Printed in the United States of America

ISBN 0-03-041224-2

1 2 3 4 5 6 7 8 9 048 11 10 09 08 07 06 05

Program Consultants

Contributing Author

Kylene Beers, Ed.D.
Senior Reading Researcher
School Development Program
Yale University
New Haven, Connecticut

General Editor

Frances Marie Gipson, Ph.D.
Secondary Literacy
Los Angeles Unified School District
Los Angeles, California

Senior Literature and Writing Specialist

Carol Jago
English Department Chairperson
Santa Monica High School
Santa Monica, California

Consultants

Martha H. Ball, M.A.
Religion Consultant
Utah 3Rs Project Director
Utah State Office of Education
Salt Lake City, Utah

John Ferguson, M.T.S., J.D.
Senior Religion Consultant
Assistant Professor
Political Science/Criminal Justice
Howard Payne University
Brownwood, Texas

Rabbi Gary M. Bretton-Granatoor
Religion Consultant
Director of Interfaith Affairs
Anti-Defamation League
New York, New York

J. Frank Malaret
Senior Consultant
Dean, Downtown and West Sacramento Outreach Centers
Sacramento City College
Sacramento, California

Kimberly A. Plummer, M.A.
Senior Consultant
History-Social Science Educator/Advisor
Holt, Rinehart & Winston
California Consultant Manager

Andrés Reséndez, Ph.D.
Senior Consultant,
Assistant Professor
Department of History
University of California at Davis
Davis, California

California Specialists

Ann Cerney, M.A.
Middle School History Teacher
San Dieguito Union High School District
Solana Beach, California

Julie Chan, Ed.D.
Director, Literacy Instruction
Newport-Mesa Unified School District
Costa Mesa, California

Gary F. DeiRossi, Ed.D.
Assistant Superintendent
San Joaquin County Office of Education
Stockton, California

Fern M. Sheldon, M.Ed.
Curriculum Specialist
Rowland Unified School District
Rowland Heights, California

California Program Advisors

The California program consultants and reviewers included on these pages provided guidance throughout the development of Holt California Social Studies: *United States History: Independence to 1914*. As the map below demonstrates, their valuable contributions represent the viewpoints of teachers throughout California.

Educational Reviewers

Sally Adams
Garden Grove High School
Garden Grove, California

Michael Bloom
Ross School
Ross, California

Ann Cerney, M.A.
Middle School History Teacher
San Dieguito Union High School District
Solana Beach, California

Julie Chan, Ed.D.
Director, Literacy Instruction
Newport-Mesa Unified School District
Costa Mesa, California

Gary F. DeiRossi, Ed.D.
Assistant Superintendent
San Joaquin County Office of Education
Stockton, California

Charlyn Earp
Mesa Verde Middle School
San Diego, California

Charles Fluty
Victorville, California

Tim Gearhart
Daniel Lewis Middle School
Paso Robles, California

Frances Marie Gipson, Ph.D.
Secondary Literacy
Los Angeles Unified School District
Los Angeles, California

Robert Hayes
Retired
Mission Viejo, California

Carol Jago
English Department Chairperson
Santa Monica High School
Santa Monica, California

Noma Lemoine, Ph.D.
Director, Academic English Mastery
Los Angeles Unified School District
Los Angeles, California

J. Frank Malaret
Senior Consultant
Dean, Downtown and West Sacramento Outreach Centers
Sacramento City College
Sacramento, California

Janet Mulder
Jamul/ Dulzura Union School District
Jamul, California

Kristen Oliveira
Clovis West High School
Fresno, California

Kimberly A. Plummer, M.A.
Senior Consultant
History-Social Science Educator/ Advisor
Holt, Rinehart & Winston
California Consultant Manager

Andrés Reséndez, Ph.D.
Senior Consultant,
Assistant Professor
Department of History
University of California at Davis
Davis, California

Vera Roberts
Lynwood Middle School
Los Angeles, California

Fern M. Sheldon, M.Ed.
Curriculum Specialist
Rowland Unified School District
Rowland Heights, California

Field Test Teachers

Raul Barragan
James Madison Middle School
North Hollywood, California

Kathryn Gallego
John Muir Middle School
Burbank, California

Barbara Jacobs
AP Giannini Middle School
San Francisco, California

Academic Reviewers

Albert Camarillo, Ph.D.
Department of History
Stanford University

Larry Conyers, Ph.D.
Department of Anthropology
University of Denver

Willard Gatewood, Ph.D.
Emeritus Alumni Distinguished Professor, Department of History
University of Arkansas

Christopher Hendricks, Ph.D.
Department of History
Armstrong Atlantic State University
Savanna, Georgia

Skip Hyser, Ph.D.
Department of History
James Madison University
Harrisonburg, Virginia

Yasuhide Kawashima
Department of History
University of Texas at El Paso

Brenda E. Stevenson, Ph.D.
Department of History
UCLA
Los Angeles, California

David Switzer, Ph.D.
Department of Social Studies
Plymouth State University

Jessica Wang, Ph.D.
Department of History
UCLA
Los Angeles, California

Nan Woodruff, Ph.D
Department of History
Pennsylvania State University

Craig Yirush, Ph.D.
Department of History
UCLA
Los Angeles, California

California Teacher's Edition

Contents

Contents

California Standards

History–Social Science

7.7 Students compare and contrast the geographic, political, economic, religious, and social structures of the Meso-American and Andean civilizations.

7.11 Students analyze political and economic change in the sixteenth, seventeenth, and eighteenth centuries (the Age of Exploration, the Enlightenment, and the Age of Reason).

Analysis Skills

HR 1 Frame questions that can be answered by historical study and research.

History's Impact Video Series
Exploration of North America

UNIT 2 A New Nation

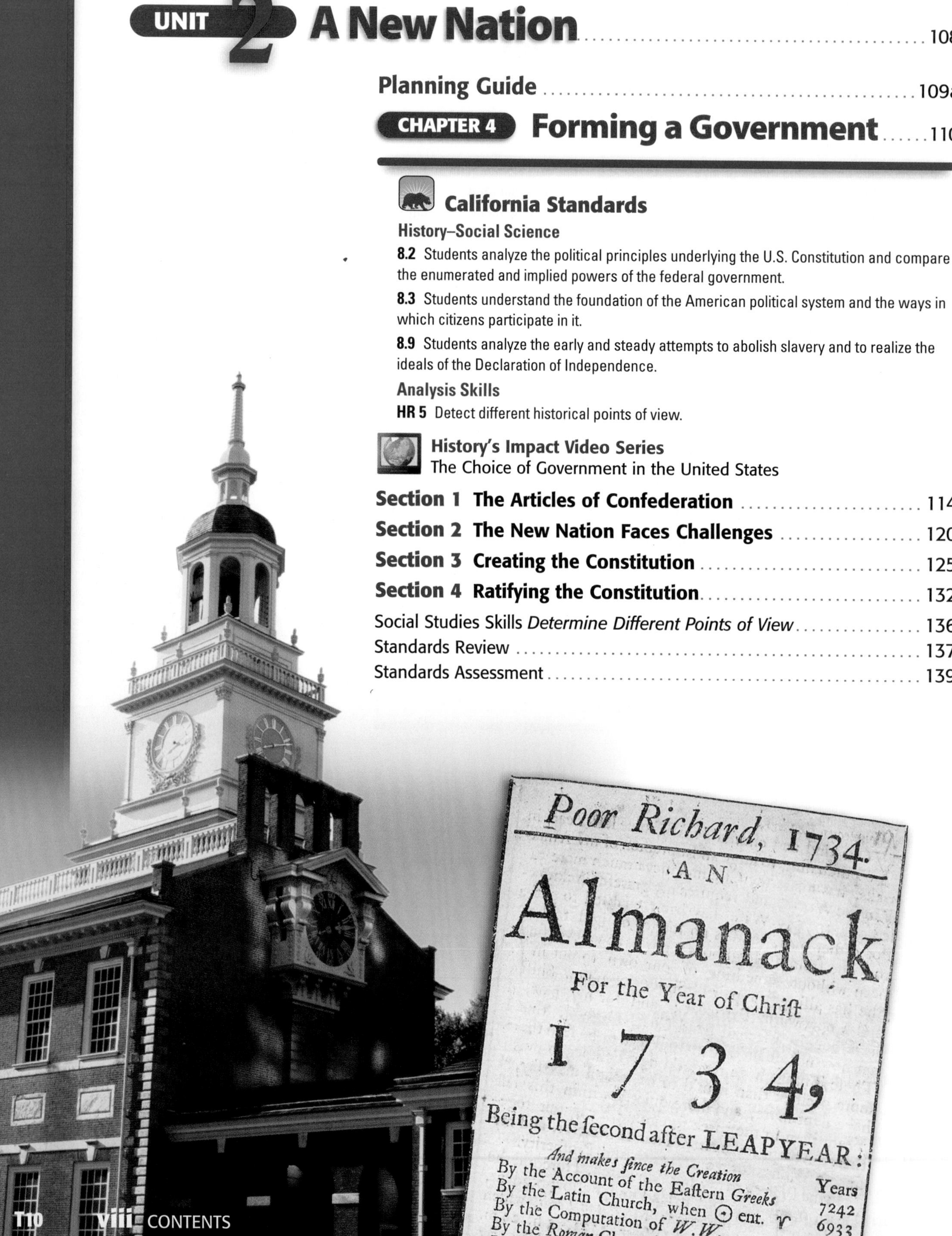

Poor Richard, 1734.
AN
Almanack
For the Year of Chrift
1734,
Being the fecond after LEAPYEAR:
And makes fince the Creation
Years
By the Account of the Eaftern Greeks 7242
By the Latin Church, when ☉ ent. ♈ 6933
By the Computation of W.W.
By the Roman Chronology 5743

California Standards

History–Social Science

8.2 Students analyze the political principles underlying the U.S. Constitution and compare the enumerated and implied powers of the federal government.

8.3 Students understand the foundation of the American political system and the ways in which citizens participate in it.

Analysis Skills

HR 5 Detect different historical points of view.

History's Impact Video Series
The Constitution and Citizens of the United States

California Standards

History–Social Science

8.1 Students understand the major events preceding the founding of the nation and relate their significance to the development of American constitutional democracy.

8.3 Students understand the foundation of the American political system and the ways in which citizens participate in it.

8.4 Students analyze the aspirations and ideals of the people of the new nation.

8.5 Students analyze U.S. foreign policy in the early republic.

History's Impact Video Series
Washington's Presidency

California Standards

History–Social Science

8.4 Students analyze the aspirations and ideals of the people of the new nation.

8.8 Students analyze the divergent paths of the American people in the West from 1800 to the mid-1800's and the challenges they faced.

8.10 Students analyze the multiple causes, key events, and complex consequences of the Civil War.

History's Impact Video Series
Andrew Jackson and the New Nation

California Standards

History–Social Science

8.8 Students analyze the divergent paths of the American people in the West from 1800 to the mid-1800's and the challenges they faced.

8.9 Students analyze the early and steady attempts to abolish slavery and to realize the ideals of the Declaration of Independence.

Analysis Skills

CS 3 Use a variety of maps and documents to identify physical and cultural features of neighborhoods, cities, states, and countries.

History's Impact Video Series
Conflict and Settlement in the West

California Standards

History–Social Science

8.6 Students analyze the divergent paths of the American people from 1800 to the mid-1800's and the challenges they faced, with an emphasis on the Northeast.

8.9 Students analyze the early and steady attempts to abolish slavery and to realize the ideals of the Declaration of Independence.

History's Impact Video Series
Individual Beliefs in Society

California Standards

History–Social Science

8.9 Students analyze the early and steady attempts to abolish slavery and to realize the ideals of the Declaration of Independence.

8.10 Students analyze the multiple causes, key events, and complex consequences of the Civil War.

Analysis Skills

HR 3 Distinguish relevant from irrelevant information.

HR 4 Assess the credibility of primary and secondary sources and draw sound conclusions about them.

History's Impact Video Series
The States' Rights Debates and National Unity

The Nation Breaks Apart

California Standards

History–Social Science

8.10 Students analyze the multiple causes, key events, and complex consequences of the Civil War.

History's Impact Video Series
The Civil War in America

California Standards

History–Social Science

8.10 Students analyze the multiple causes, key events, and complex consequences of the Civil War.

8.11 Students analyze the character and lasting consequences of Reconstruction.

Analysis Skills

HR 3 Distinguish relevant from irrelevant information.

HI 4 Recognize the role of chance, oversight, and error in history.

History's Impact Video Series
Impact of Reconstruction in the South

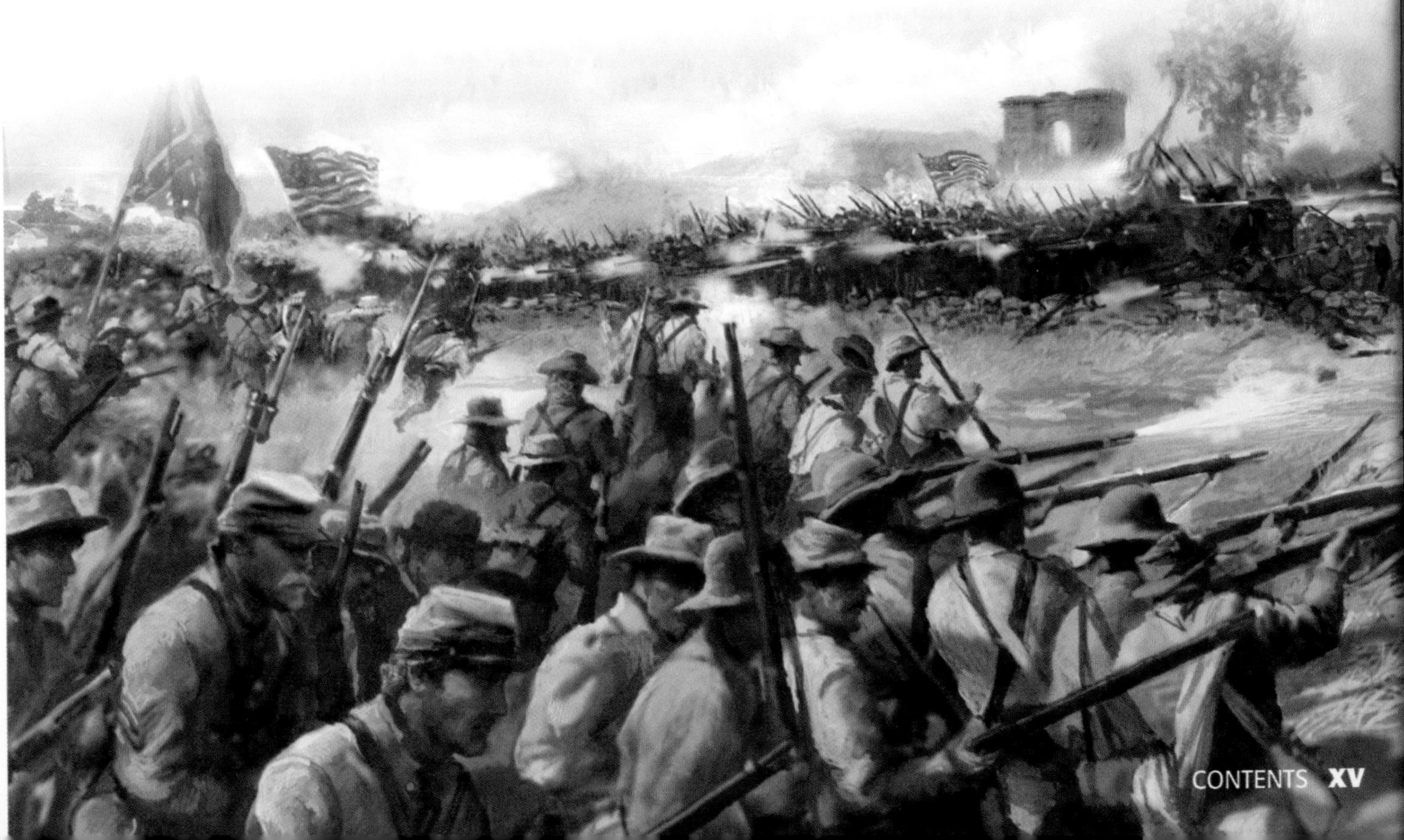

California Standards

History–Social Science

8.12 Students analyze the transformation of the American economy and the changing social and political conditions in the United States in response to the Industrial Revolution.

Analysis Skills

HI 2 Understand and distinguish cause, effect, sequence, and correlation in historical events.

HR 2 Distinguish fact from opinion in historical narratives.

History's Impact Video Series
Progressivism in Government and Society.

California Standards

History–Social Science

8.12 Students analyze the transformation of the American economy and the changing social and political conditions in the United States in response to the Industrial Revolution.

Analysis Skills

HI 3 Explain the sources of historical continuity and how the combination of ideas and events explains the emergence of new patterns.

History's Impact Video Series
Imperialism and U.S. Expansion

Features

History and Geography

Explore the relationships between history and geography.

Literature in History

Learn about the beliefs and experiences of people who lived in other times and places in excerpts from literature.

Biographies

Meet the people who have influenced history and learn about their lives.

Charts, Graphics, and Time Lines

Analyze information presented visually to learn more about history.

CHARTS

INFOGRAPHICS

TIME LINES

QUICK FACTS

Examine key facts and concepts quickly and easily with graphics.

History Close-up

See how people lived and how places looked in the past by taking a close-up view of history.

LINKING TO TODAY

Link people and events from the past to the world you live in today.

Points of View

See how different people have interpreted historical issues in different ways.

Historic Documents

Examine key documents that have shaped U.S. history.

Political Cartoons

Interpret political cartoons to learn about U.S. history.

Social Studies Skills

Learn, practice, and apply the skills you need to study and analyze history.

Reading Social Studies

Learn and practice skills that will help you read your social studies lessons.

Writing Workshop

Learn to write about history.

Focus on Writing and Speaking

Use writing and speaking skills to study and reflect on the events and people who made history.

Supreme Court Decisions

Study the impact of Supreme Court decisions on U.S. history.

Interdisciplinary Connections

Learn history through connections to other disciplines.

Primary Sources

Relive history through eyewitness accounts, literature, and documents.

CHAPTER 11

CHAPTER 12

CHAPTER 13

CHAPTER 14

CHAPTER 15

CHAPTER 16

CHAPTER 17

CHAPTER 18

CHAPTER 19

CHAPTER 20

Maps

Interpret maps to see where important events happened and analyze how geography has influenced history.

 Standards Overview: Grade 6

Standards — Chapters:	1	2	3	4	5	6	7	8	9	10	11	12	13	14	15
6.1 Students describe what is known through archaeological studies of the early physical and cultural development of humankind from the Paleolithic era to the agricultural revolution.															
1. Describe the hunter-gatherer societies, including the development of tools and the use of fire.		•													
2. Identify the locations of human communities that populated the major regions of the world and describe how humans adapted to a variety of environments.		•													
3. Discuss the climatic changes and human modifications of the physical environment that gave rise to the domestication of plants and animals and new sources of clothing and shelter.		•													
6.2 Students analyze the geographic, political, economic, religious, and social structures of the early civilizations of Mesopotamia, Egypt, and Kush.															
1. Locate and describe the major river systems and discuss the physical settings that supported permanent settlement and early civilizations.			•	•											
2. Trace the development of agricultural techniques that permitted the production of economic surplus and the emergence of cities as centers of culture and power.			•	•											
3. Understand the relationship between religion and the social and political order in Mesopotamia and Egypt.			•												
4. Know the significance of Hammurabi's Code.			•												
5. Discuss the main features of Egyptian art and architecture.				•											
6. Describe the role of Egyptian trade in the eastern Mediterranean and Nile valley.				•											
7. Understand the significance of Queen Hatshepsut and Ramses the Great.				•											
8. Identify the location of the Kush civilization and describe its political, commercial, and cultural relations with Egypt.					•										
9. Trace the evolution of language and its written forms.			•	•											
6.3 Students analyze the geographic, political, economic, religious, and social structures of the Ancient Hebrews.															
1. Describe the origins and significance of Judaism as the first monotheistic religion based on the concept of one God who sets down moral laws for humanity.								•							
2. Identify the sources of the ethical teachings and central beliefs of Judaism (the Hebrew Bible, the Commentaries): belief in God, observance of law, practice of the concepts of righteousness and justice, and importance of study; and describe how the ideas of the Hebrew traditions are reflected in the moral and ethical traditions of Western civilization.								•							
3. Explain the significance of Abraham, Moses, Naomi, Ruth, David, and Yohanan ben Zaccai in the development of the Jewish religion.								•							

Standards — Chapters:	1	2	3	4	5	6	7	8	9	10	11	12	13	14	15
4. Discuss the locations of the settlements and movements of Hebrew peoples, including the Exodus and their movement to and from Egypt, and outline the significance of the Exodus to the Jewish and other people.								•							
5. Discuss how Judaism survived and developed despite the continuing dispersion of much of the Jewish population from Jerusalem and the rest of Israel after the destruction of the second Temple in AD 70.								•							
6.4 Students analyze the geographic, political, economic, religious, and social structures of the early civilizations of Ancient Greece.															
1. Discuss the connections between geography and the development of city-states in the region of the Aegean Sea, including patterns of trade and commerce among Greek city-states and within the wider Mediterranean region.									•						
2. Trace the transition from tyranny and oligarchy to early democratic forms of government and back to dictatorship in ancient Greece, including the significance of the invention of the idea of citizenship (e.g., from Pericles' Funeral Oration).									•						
3. State the key differences between Athenian, or direct, democracy and representative democracy.									•						
4. Explain the significance of Greek mythology to the everyday life of people in the region and how Greek literature continues to permeate our literature and language today, drawing from Greek mythology and epics, such as Homer's Iliad and Odyssey, and from Aesop's Fables.									•						
5. Outline the founding, expansion, and political organization of the Persian Empire.										•					
6. Compare and contrast life in Athens and Sparta, with emphasis on their roles in the Persian and Peloponnesian Wars.										•					
7. Trace the rise of Alexander the Great and the spread of Greek culture eastward and into Egypt.										•					
8. Describe the enduring contributions of important Greek figures in the arts and sciences (e.g., Hypatia, Socrates, Plato, Aristotle, Euclid, Thucydides).										•					
6.5 Students analyze the geographic, political, economic, religious, and social structures of the early civilizations of India.															
1. Locate and describe the major river system and discuss the physical setting that supported the rise of this civilization.						•									
2. Discuss the significance of the Aryan invasions.						•									
3. Explain the major beliefs and practices of Brahmanism in India and how they evolved into early Hinduism.						•									
4. Outline the social structure of the caste system.						•									
5. Know the life and moral teachings of Buddha and how Buddhism spread in India, Ceylon, and Central Asia.						•									
6. Describe the growth of the Maurya empire and the political and moral achievements of the emperor Asoka.						•									
7. Discuss important aesthetic and intellectual traditions (e.g., Sanskrit literature, including the Bhagavad Gita; medicine; metallurgy; and mathematics, including Hindu-Arabic numerals and the zero).						•									

Standards Chapters:	1	2	3	4	5	6	7	8	9	10	11	12	13	14	15
6.6 Students analyze the geographic, political, economic, religious, and social structures of the early civilizations of China.															
1. Locate and describe the origins of Chinese civilization in the Huang-He Valley during the Shang Dynasty.							•								
2. Explain the geographic features of China that made governance and the spread of ideas and goods difficult and served to isolate the country from the rest of the world.							•								
3. Know about the life of Confucius and the fundamental teachings of Confucianism and Taoism.							•								
4. Identify the political and cultural problems prevalent in the time of Confucius and how he sought to solve them.							•								
5. List the policies and achievements of the emperor Shi Huangdi in unifying northern China under the Qin Dynasty.							•								
6. Detail the political contributions of the Han Dynasty to the development of the imperial bureaucratic state and the expansion of the empire.							•								
7. Cite the significance of the trans-Eurasian "silk roads" in the period of the Han Dynasty and Roman Empire and their locations.							•								
8. Describe the diffusion of Buddhism northward to China during the Han Dynasty.							•								
6.7 Students analyze the geographic, political, economic, religious, and social structures during the development of Rome.															
1. Identify the location and describe the rise of the Roman Republic, including the importance of such mythical and historical figures as Aeneas, Romulus and Remus, Cincinnatus, Julius Caesar, and Cicero.											•				
2. Describe the government of the Roman Republic and its significance (e.g., written constitution and tripartite government, checks and balances, civic duty).											•				
3. Identify the location of and the political and geographic reasons for the growth of Roman territories and expansion of the empire, including how the empire fostered economic growth through the use of currency and trade routes.											•	•			
4. Discuss the influence of Julius Caesar and Augustus in Rome's transition from republic to empire.												•			
5. Trace the migration of Jews around the Mediterranean region and the effects of their conflict with the Romans, including the Romans' restrictions on their right to live in Jerusalem.													•		
6. Note the origins of Christianity in the Jewish Messianic prophecies, the life and teachings of Jesus of Nazareth as described in the New Testament, and the contribution of St. Paul the Apostle to the definition and spread of Christian beliefs (e.g., belief in the Trinity, resurrection, salvation).													•		
7. Describe the circumstances that led to the spread of Christianity in Europe and other Roman territories.													•		
8. Discuss the legacies of Roman art and architecture, technology and science, literature, language, and law.												•			

Analysis Skills Standards — Chapters:	1	2	3	4	5	6	7	8	9	10	11	12	13	14	15
Chronological and Spatial Thinking															
1. Students explain how major events are related to one another in time.					●						●				
2. Students construct various time lines of key events, people, and periods of the historical era they are studying													●		
3. Students use a variety of maps and documents to identify physical and cultural features of neighborhoods, cities, states, and countries and to explain the historical migration of people, expansion and disintegration of empires, and the growth of economic systems.			●					●	●			●			
Research, Evidence, and Point of View															
1. Students frame questions that can be answered by historical study and research.	●														
2. Students distinguish fact from opinion in historical narratives and stories.							●								
3. Students distinguish relevant from irrelevant information, essential from incidental information, and verifiable from unverifiable information in historical narratives and stories.															●
4. Students assess the credibility of primary and secondary sources and draw sound conclusions from them.							●								
5. Students detect the different historical points of view on historical events and determine the context in which the historical statements were made (the questions asked, sources used, author's perspectives).													●		
Historical Interpretation															
1. Students explain the central issues and problems from the past, placing people and events in a matrix of time and place.			●												
2. Students understand and distinguish cause, effect, sequence, and correlation in historical events, including the long- and short-term causal relations.				●		●									
3. Students explain the sources of historical continuity and how the combination of ideas and events explains the emergence of new patterns.								●							
4. Students recognize the role of chance, oversight, and error in history.										●				●	
5. Students recognize that interpretations of history are subject to change as new information is uncovered.		●													
6. Students interpret basic indicators of economic performance and conduct cost-benefit analyses of economic and political issues.									●			●			

 Standards Overview: Grade 7

Standards	1	2	3	4	5	6	7	8	9	10	11	12	13	14	15	16	17
7.1 Students analyze the causes and effects of the vast expansion and ultimate disintegration of the Roman Empire.																	
1. Study the early strengths and lasting contributions of Rome (e.g., significance of Roman citizenship; rights under Roman law; Roman art, architecture, engineering, and philosophy; preservation and transmission of Christianity) and its ultimate internal weaknesses (e.g., rise of autonomous military powers within the empire, undermining of citizenship by the growth of corruption and slavery, lack of education, and distribution of news).		•															
2. Discuss the geographic borders of the empire at its height and the factors that threatened its territorial cohesion.		•															
3. Describe the establishment by Constantine of the new capital in Constantinople and the development of the Byzantine Empire, with an emphasis on the consequences of the development of two distinct European civilizations, Eastern Orthodox and Roman Catholic, and their two distinct views on church-state relations.		•															
7.2 Students analyze the geographic, political, economic, religious, and social structures of the civilizations of Islam in the Middle Ages.																	
1. Identify the physical features and describe the climate of the Arabian peninsula, its relationship to surrounding bodies of land and water, and nomadic and sedentary ways of life.			•														
2. Trace the origins of Islam and the life and teachings of Muhammad, including Islamic teachings on the connection with Judaism and Christianity.			•														
3. Explain the significance of the Qur'an and the Sunnah as the primary sources of Islamic beliefs, practice, and law, and their influence in Muslims' daily life.			•														
4. Discuss the expansion of Muslim rule through military conquests and treaties, emphasizing the cultural blending within Muslim civilization and the spread and acceptance of Islam and the Arabic language.				•													
5. Describe the growth of cities and the establishment of trade routes among Asia, Africa, and Europe, the products and inventions that traveled along these routes (e.g., spices, textiles, paper, steel, new crops), and the role of merchants in Arab society.				•													
6. Understand the intellectual exchanges among Muslim scholars of Eurasia and Africa and the contributions Muslim scholars made to later civilizations in the areas of science, geography, mathematics, philosophy, medicine, art, and literature.				•													
7.3 Students analyze the geographic, political, economic, religious, and social structures of the civilizations of China in the Middle Ages.																	
1. Describe the reunification of China under the Tang Dynasty and reasons for the spread of Buddhism in Tang China, Korea, and Japan.							•										
2. Describe agricultural, technological, and commercial developments during the Tang and Sung periods.							•										
3. Analyze the influences of Confucianism and changes in Confucian thought during the Sung and Mongol periods.							•										
4. Understand the importance of both overland trade and maritime expeditions between China and other civilizations in the Mongol Ascendancy and Ming Dynasty.							•										
5. Trace the historic influence of such discoveries as tea, the manufacture of paper, woodblock printing, the compass, and gunpowder.							•										
6. Describe the development of the imperial state and the scholar-official class.							•										
7.4 Students analyze the geographic, political, economic, religious, and social structures of the sub-Saharan civilizations of Ghana and Mali in Medieval Africa.																	
1. Study the Niger River and the relationship of vegetation zones of forest, savannah, and desert to trade in gold, salt, food, and slaves; and the growth of the Ghana and Mali empires.					•												
2. Analyze the importance of family, labor specialization, and regional commerce in the development of states and cities in West Africa.					•												

Standards	1	2	3	4	5	6	7	8	9	10	11	12	13	14	15	16	17
3. Describe the role of the trans-Saharan caravan trade in the changing religious and cultural characteristics of West Africa and the influence of Islamic beliefs, ethics, and law.						●											
4. Trace the growth of the Arabic language in government, trade, and Islamic scholarship in West Africa.						●											
5. Describe the importance of written and oral traditions in the transmission of African history and culture.						●											
7.5 Students analyze the geographic, political, economic, religious, and social structures of the civilizations of Medieval Japan.																	
1. Describe the significance of Japan's proximity to China and Korea and the intellectual, linguistic, religious, and philosophical influence of those countries on Japan.								●									
2. Discuss the reign of Prince Shotoku of Japan and the characteristics of Japanese society and family life during his reign.								●									
3. Describe the values, social customs, and traditions prescribed by the lord-vassal system consisting of shogun, daimyo, and samurai and the lasting influence of the warrior code in the twentieth century.								●									
4. Trace the development of distinctive forms of Japanese Buddhism.								●									
5. Study the ninth and tenth centuries' golden age of literature, art, and drama and its lasting effects on culture today, including Murasaki Shikibu's Tale of Genji.								●									
6. Analyze the rise of a military society in the late twelfth century and the role of the samurai in that society.								●									
7.6 Students analyze the geographic, political, economic, religious, and social structures of the civilizations of Medieval Europe.																	
1. Study the geography of the Europe and the Eurasian land mass, including its location, topography, waterways, vegetation, and climate and their relationship to ways of life in Medieval Europe.									●								
2. Describe the spread of Christianity north of the Alps and the roles played by the early church and by monasteries in its diffusion after the fall of the western half of the Roman Empire.									●								
3. Understand the development of feudalism, its role in the medieval European economy, the way in which it was influenced by physical geography (the role of the manor and the growth of towns), and how feudal relationships provided the foundation of political order.									●								
4. Demonstrate an understanding of the conflict and cooperation between the Papacy and European monarchs (e.g., Charlemagne, Gregory VII, Emperor Henry IV).										●							
5. Know the significance of developments in medieval English legal and constitutional practices and their importance in the rise of modern democratic thought and representative institutions (e.g., Magna Carta, parliament, development of habeas corpus, an independent judiciary in England).										●							
6. Discuss the causes and course of the religious Crusades and their effects on the Christian, Muslim, and Jewish populations in Europe, with emphasis on the increasing contact by Europeans with cultures of the Eastern Mediterranean world.										●							
7. Map the spread of the bubonic plague from Central Asia to China, the Middle East, and Europe and describe its impact on global population.										●							
8. Understand the importance of the Catholic church as a political, intellectual, and aesthetic institution (e.g., founding of universities, political and spiritual roles of the clergy, creation of monastic and mendicant religious orders, preservation of the Latin language and religious texts, St. Thomas Aquinas's synthesis of classical philosophy with Christian theology, and the concept of "natural law").										●							
9. Know the history of the decline of Muslim rule in the Iberian Peninsula that culminated in the Reconquista and the rise of Spanish and Portuguese kingdoms.										●							
7.7 Students compare and contrast the geographic, political, economic, religious, and social structures of the Meso-American and Andean civilizations.																	
1. Study the locations, landforms, and climates of Mexico, Central America, and South America and their effects on Mayan, Aztec, and Incan economies, trade, and development of urban societies.														●	●		

Standards — Chapters:	1	2	3	4	5	6	7	8	9	10	11	12	13	14	15	16	17
2. Study the roles of people in each society, including class structures, family life, warfare, religious beliefs and practices, and slavery.														•	•		
3. Explain how and where each empire arose and how the Aztec and Incan empires were defeated by the Spanish.														•	•		
4. Describe the artistic and oral traditions and architecture in the three civilizations.														•	•		
5. Describe the Meso-American achievements in astronomy and mathematics, including the development of the calendar and the Meso-American knowledge of seasonal changes to the civilizations' agricultural systems.														•	•		
7.8 Students analyze the origins, accomplishments, and geographic diffusion of the Renaissance.																	
1. Describe the way in which the revival of classical learning and the arts fostered a new interest in humanism (i.e., a balance between intellect and religious faith).											•						
2. Explain the importance of Florence in the early stages of the Renaissance and the growth of independent trading cities (e.g., Venice), with emphasis on the cities' importance in the spread of Renaissance ideas.											•						
3. Understand the effects of the reopening of the ancient "Silk Road" between Europe and China, including Marco Polo's travels and the location of his routes.											•						
4. Describe the growth and effects of new ways of disseminating information (e.g., the ability to manufacture paper, translation of the Bible into the vernacular, printing).											•						
5. Detail advances made in literature, the arts, science, mathematics, cartography, engineering, and the understanding of human anatomy and astronomy (e.g., by Dante Alighieri, Leonardo da Vinci, Michelangelo di Buonarroti Simoni, Johann Gutenberg, William Shakespeare).											•						
7.9 Students analyze the historical developments of the Reformation.																	
1. List the causes for the internal turmoil in and weakening of the Catholic church (e.g., tax policies, selling of indulgences).												•					
2. Describe the theological, political, and economic ideas of the major figures during the Reformation (e.g., Desiderius Erasmus, Martin Luther, John Calvin, William Tyndale).												•					
3. Explain Protestants' new practices of church self-government and the influence of those practices on the development of democratic practices and ideas of federalism.												•					
4. Identify and locate the European regions that remained Catholic and those that became Protestant and explain how the division affected the distribution of religions in the New World.												•					
5. Analyze how the Counter-Reformation revitalized the Catholic church and the forces that fostered the movement (e.g., St. Ignatius of Loyola and the Jesuits, the Council of Trent).												•					
6. Understand the institution and impact of missionaries on Christianity and the diffusion of Christianity from Europe to other parts of the world in the medieval and early modern periods; locate missions on a world map.												•					
7. Describe the Golden Age of cooperation between Jews and Muslims in medieval Spain that promoted creativity in art, literature, and science, including how that cooperation was terminated by the religious persecution of individuals and groups (e.g., the Spanish Inquisition and the expulsion of Jews and Muslims from Spain in 1492).												•					
7.10 Students analyze the historical developments of the Scientific Revolution and its lasting effect on religious, political, and cultural institutions.																	
1. Discuss the roots of the Scientific Revolution (e.g., Greek rationalism; Jewish, Christian, and Muslim science; Renaissance humanism; new knowledge from global exploration).													•				
2. Understand the significance of the new scientific theories (e.g., those of Copernicus, Galileo, Kepler, Newton) and the significance of new inventions (e.g., the telescope, microscope, thermometer, barometer).													•				
3. Understand the scientific method advanced by Bacon and Descartes, the influence of new scientific rationalism on the growth of democratic ideas, and the coexistence of science with traditional religious beliefs.													•				

Standards — Chapters:	1	2	3	4	5	6	7	8	9	10	11	12	13	14	15	16	17
7.11 Students analyze political and economic change in the sixteenth, seventeenth, and eighteenth centuries (the Age of Exploration, the Enlightenment, and the Age of Reason).																	
1. Know the great voyages of discovery, the locations of the routes, and the influence of cartography in the development of a new European worldview.																●	
2. Discuss the exchanges of plants, animals, technology, culture, and ideas among Europe, Africa, Asia, and the Americas in the fifteenth and sixteenth centuries and the major economic and social effects on each continent.																●	
3. Examine the origins of modern capitalism; the influence of mercantilism and cottage industry; the elements and importance of a market economy in seventeenth-century Europe; the changing international trading and marketing patterns, including their locations on a world map; and the influence of explorers and map makers.																●	
4. Explain how the main ideas of the Enlightenment can be traced back to such movements as the Renaissance, the Reformation, and the Scientific Revolution and to the Greeks, Romans, and Christianity.																	●
5. Describe how democratic thought and institutions were influenced by Enlightenment thinkers (e.g., John Locke, Charles-Louis Montesquieu, American founders).																	●
6. Discuss how the principles in the Magna Carta were embodied in such documents as the English Bill of Rights and the American Declaration of Independence.																	●

Analysis Skills Standards — Chapters:	1	2	3	4	5	6	7	8	9	10	11	12	13	14	15	16	17
Chronological and Spatial Thinking																	
1. Students explain how major events are related to one another in time.							●										
2. Students construct various time lines of key events, people, and periods of the historical era they are studying.							●										
3. Students use a variety of maps and documents to identify physical and cultural features of neighborhoods, cities, states, and countries and to explain the historical migration of people, expansion and disintegration of empires, and the growth of economic systems.		●	●		●										●	●	
Research, Evidence, and Point of View																	
1. Students frame questions that can be answered by historical study and research..	●																
2. Students construct various time lines of key events, people, and periods of the historical era they are studying.				●													
3. Students distinguish relevant from irrelevant information, essential from incidental information, and verifiable from unverifiable information in historical narratives and stories.									●								
4. Students assess the credibility of primary and secondary sources and draw sound conclusions from them.											●						
5. Students detect the different historical points of view on historical events and determine the context in which the historical statements were made (the questions asked, sources used, author's perspectives).										●							
Historical Interpretation																	
1. Students explain the central issues and problems from the past, placing people and events in a matrix of time and place.								●									
2. Students understand and distinguish cause, effect, sequence, and correlation in historical events, including the long- and short-term causal relations.												●					
3. Students explain the sources of historical continuity and how the combination of ideas and events explains the emergence of new patterns.													●				●
4. Students recognize the role of chance, oversight, and error in history.								●									
5. Students recognize that interpretations of history are subject to change as new information is uncovered.						●								●			
6. Students interpret basic indicators of economic performance and conduct cost-benefit analyses of economic and political issues.		●													●	●	●

 Standards Overview: Grade 8

Standards — Chapters:	1	2	3	4	5	6	7	8	9	10	11	12	13	14	15	16	17	18	19	20
8.1 Students understand the major events preceding the founding of the nation and relate their significance to the development of American constitutional democracy.																				
1. Describe the relationship between the moral and political ideas of the Great Awakening and the development of revolutionary fervor.		•																		
2. Analyze the philosophy of government expressed in the Declaration of Independence, with an emphasis on government as a means of securing individual rights (e.g., key phrases such as "all men are created equal, that they are endowed by their Creator with certain unalienable Rights").			•						•											
3. Analyze how the American Revolution affected other nations, especially France.			•			•														
4. Describe the nation's blend of civic republicanism, classical liberal principles, and English parliamentary traditions.				•																
8.2 Students analyze the political principles underlying the U.S. Constitution and compare the enumerated and implied powers of the federal government.																				
1. Discuss the significance of the Magna Carta, the English Bill of Rights, and the Mayflower Compact.		•																		
2. Analyze the Articles of Confederation and the Constitution and the success of each in implementing the ideals of the Declaration of Independence.				•																
3. Evaluate the major debates that occurred during the development of the Constitution and their ultimate resolutions in such areas as shared power among institutions, divided state-federal power, slavery, the rights of individuals and states (later addressed by the addition of the Bill of Rights), and the status of American Indian nations under the commerce clause.				•																
4. Describe the political philosophy underpinning the Constitution as specified in the Federalist Papers (authored by James Madison, Alexander Hamilton, and John Jay) and the role of such leaders as Madison, George Washington, Roger Sherman, Gouverneur Morris, and James Wilson in the writing and ratification of the Constitution.				•																
5. Understand the significance of Jefferson's Statute for Religious Freedom as a forerunner of the First Amendment and the origins, purpose, and differing views of the founding fathers on the issue of the separation of church and state.					•															
6. Enumerate the powers of government set forth in the Constitution and the fundamental liberties ensured by the Bill of Rights.					•															
7. Describe the principles of federalism, dual sovereignty, separation of powers, checks and balances, the nature and purpose of majority rule, and the ways in which the American idea of constitutionalism preserves individual rights.				•	•															
8.3 Students understand the foundation of the American political system and the ways in which citizens participate in it.																				
1. Analyze the principles and concepts codified in state constitutions between 1777 and 1781 that created the context out of which American political institutions and ideas developed.				•																

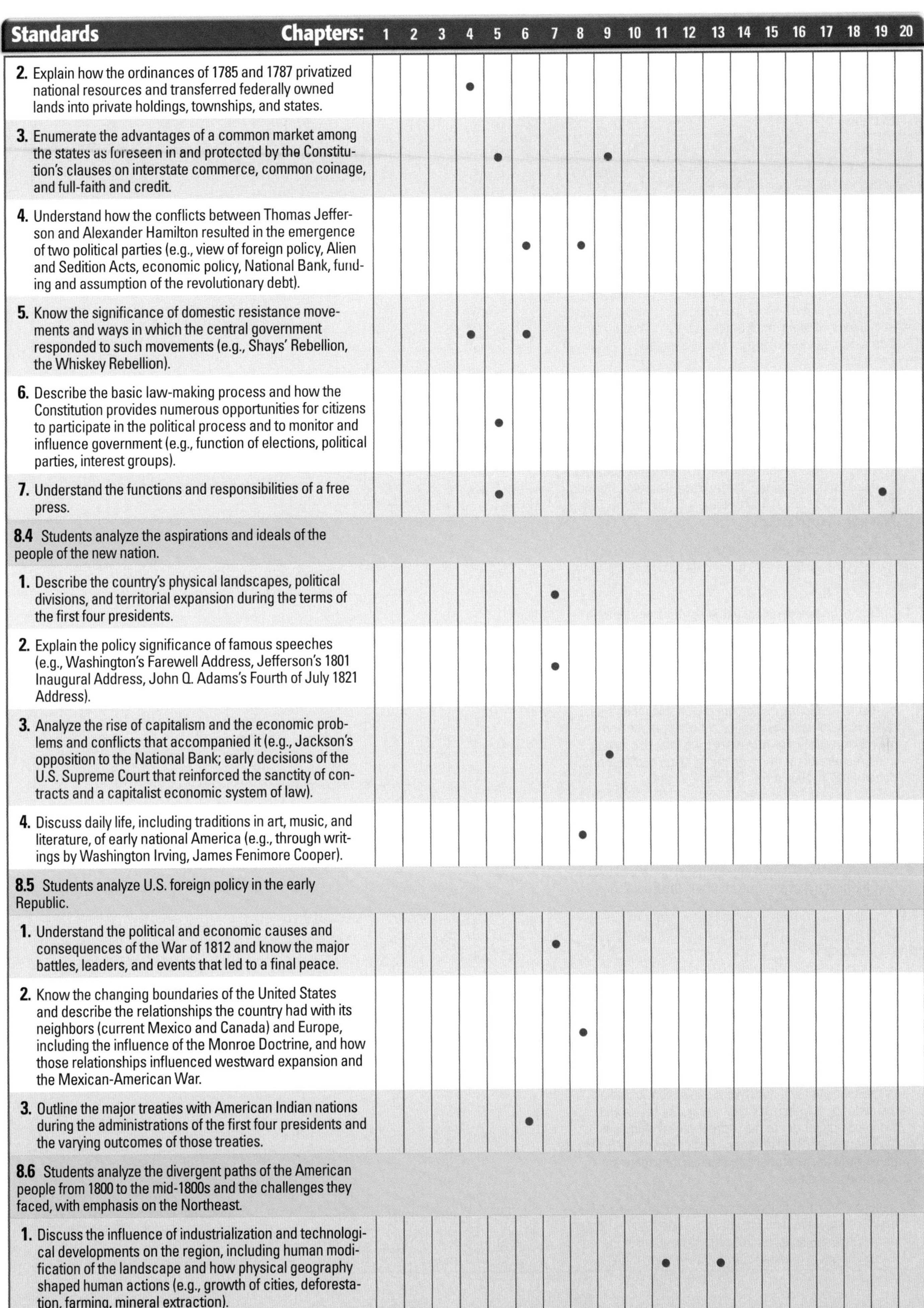

Standards	Chapters: 1	2	3	4	5	6	7	8	9	10	11	12	13	14	15	16	17	18	19	20
2. Explain how the ordinances of 1785 and 1787 privatized national resources and transferred federally owned lands into private holdings, townships, and states.				•																
3. Enumerate the advantages of a common market among the states as foreseen in and protected by the Constitution's clauses on interstate commerce, common coinage, and full-faith and credit.					•				•											
4. Understand how the conflicts between Thomas Jefferson and Alexander Hamilton resulted in the emergence of two political parties (e.g., view of foreign policy, Alien and Sedition Acts, economic policy, National Bank, funding and assumption of the revolutionary debt).						•		•												
5. Know the significance of domestic resistance movements and ways in which the central government responded to such movements (e.g., Shays' Rebellion, the Whiskey Rebellion).				•		•														
6. Describe the basic law-making process and how the Constitution provides numerous opportunities for citizens to participate in the political process and to monitor and influence government (e.g., function of elections, political parties, interest groups).					•															
7. Understand the functions and responsibilities of a free press.					•														•	
8.4 Students analyze the aspirations and ideals of the people of the new nation.																				
1. Describe the country's physical landscapes, political divisions, and territorial expansion during the terms of the first four presidents.							•													
2. Explain the policy significance of famous speeches (e.g., Washington's Farewell Address, Jefferson's 1801 Inaugural Address, John Q. Adams's Fourth of July 1821 Address).							•													
3. Analyze the rise of capitalism and the economic problems and conflicts that accompanied it (e.g., Jackson's opposition to the National Bank; early decisions of the U.S. Supreme Court that reinforced the sanctity of contracts and a capitalist economic system of law).									•											
4. Discuss daily life, including traditions in art, music, and literature, of early national America (e.g., through writings by Washington Irving, James Fenimore Cooper).								•												
8.5 Students analyze U.S. foreign policy in the early Republic.																				
1. Understand the political and economic causes and consequences of the War of 1812 and know the major battles, leaders, and events that led to a final peace.							•													
2. Know the changing boundaries of the United States and describe the relationships the country had with its neighbors (current Mexico and Canada) and Europe, including the influence of the Monroe Doctrine, and how those relationships influenced westward expansion and the Mexican-American War.								•												
3. Outline the major treaties with American Indian nations during the administrations of the first four presidents and the varying outcomes of those treaties.						•														
8.6 Students analyze the divergent paths of the American people from 1800 to the mid-1800s and the challenges they faced, with emphasis on the Northeast.																				
1. Discuss the influence of industrialization and technological developments on the region, including human modification of the landscape and how physical geography shaped human actions (e.g., growth of cities, deforestation, farming, mineral extraction).											•		•							

Standards	Chapters: 1	2	3	4	5	6	7	8	9	10	11	12	13	14	15	16	17	18	19	20
2. Outline the physical obstacles to and the economic and political factors involved in building a network of roads, canals, and railroads (e.g., Henry Clay's American System).								•												
3. List the reasons for the wave of immigration from Northern Europe to the United States and describe the growth in the number, size, and spatial arrangements of cities (e.g., Irish immigrants and the Great Irish Famine).													•							
4. Study the lives of black Americans who gained freedom in the North and founded schools and churches to advance their rights and communities.													•							
5. Trace the development of the American education system from its earliest roots, including the roles of religious and private schools and Horace Mann's campaign for free public education and its assimilating role in American culture.													•							
6. Examine the women's suffrage movement (e.g., biographies, writings, and speeches of Elizabeth Cady Stanton, Margaret Fuller, Lucretia Mott, Susan B. Anthony).													•							
7. Identify common themes in American art as well as transcendentalism and individualism (e.g., writings about and by Ralph Waldo Emerson, Henry David Thoreau, Herman Melville, Louisa May Alcott, Nathaniel Hawthorne, Henry Wadsworth Longfellow).													•							
8.7 Students analyze the divergent paths of the American people in the South from 1800 to the mid-1800s and the challenges they faced.																				
1. Describe the development of the agrarian economy in the South, identify the locations of the cotton-producing states, and discuss the significance of cotton and the cotton gin.												•								
2. Trace the origins and development of slavery; its effects on black Americans and on the region's political, social, religious, economic, and cultural development; and identify the strategies that were tried to both overturn and preserve it (e.g., through the writings and historical documents on Nat Turner, Denmark Vesey).												•								
3. Examine the characteristics of white Southern society and how the physical environment influenced events and conditions prior to the Civil War.												•								
4. Compare the lives of and opportunities for free blacks in the North with those of free blacks in the South.												•								
8.8 Students analyze the divergent paths of the American people in the West from 1800 to the mid-1800s and the challenges they faced.																				
1. Discuss the election of Andrew Jackson as president in 1828, the importance of Jacksonian democracy, and his actions as president (e.g., the spoils system, veto of the National Bank, policy of Indian removal, opposition to the Supreme Court).									•											
2. Describe the purpose, challenges, and economic incentives associated with westward expansion, including the concept of Manifest Destiny (e.g., the Lewis and Clark expedition, accounts of the removal of Indians, the Cherokees' "Trail of Tears," settlement of the Great Plains) and the territorial acquisitions that spanned numerous decades.							•			•							•			
3. Describe the role of pioneer women and the new status that western women achieved (e.g., Laura Ingalls Wilder, Annie Bidwell; slave women gaining freedom in the West; Wyoming granting suffrage to women in 1869).										•										

Standards	1	2	3	4	5	6	7	8	9	10	11	12	13	14	15	16	17	18	19	20
4. Examine the importance of the great rivers and the struggle over water rights.										•										
5. Discuss Mexican settlements and their locations, cultural traditions, attitudes toward slavery, land-grant system, and economies.										•										
6. Describe the Texas War for Independence and the Mexican-American War, including territorial settlements, the aftermath of the wars, and the effects the wars had on the lives of Americans, including Mexican Americans today.										•										
8.9 Students analyze the early and steady attempts to abolish slavery and to realize the ideals of the Declaration of Independence.																				
1. Describe the leaders of the movement (e.g., John Quincy Adams and his proposed constitutional amendment, John Brown and the armed resistance, Harriet Tubman and the Underground Railroad, Benjamin Franklin, Theodore Weld, William Lloyd Garrison, Frederick Douglass).														•						
2. Discuss the abolition of slavery in early state constitutions.				•																
3. Describe the significance of the Northwest Ordinance in education and in the banning of slavery in new states north of the Ohio River.				•																
4. Discuss the importance of the slavery issue as raised by the annexation of Texas and California's admission to the union as a free state under the Compromise of 1850.										•				•						
5. Analyze the significance of the States' Rights Doctrine, the Missouri Compromise (1820), the Wilmot Proviso (1846), the Compromise of 1850, Henry Clay's role in the Missouri Compromise and the Compromise of 1850, the Kansas-Nebraska Act (1854), the Dred Scott v. Sandford decision (1857), and the Lincoln-Douglas debates (1858).														•						
6. Describe the lives of free blacks and the laws that limited their freedom and economic opportunities.												•								
8.10 Students analyze the multiple causes, key events, and complex consequences of the Civil War.																				
1. Compare the conflicting interpretations of state and federal authority as emphasized in the speeches and writings of statesmen such as Daniel Webster and John C. Calhoun.														•						
2. Trace the boundaries constituting the North and the South, the geographical differences between the two regions, and the differences between agrarians and industrialists.									•					•						
3. Identify the constitutional issues posed by the doctrine of nullification and secession and the earliest origins of that doctrine.									•					•	•					
4. Discuss Abraham Lincoln's presidency and his significant writings and speeches and their relationship to the Declaration of Independence, such as his "House Divided" speech (1858), Gettysburg Address (1863), Emancipation Proclamation (1863), and inaugural addresses (1861 and 1865).														•	•					
5. Study the views and lives of leaders (e.g., Ulysses S. Grant, Jefferson Davis, Robert E. Lee) and soldiers on both sides of the war, including those of black soldiers and regiments.															•					
6. Describe critical developments and events in the war, including the major battles, geographical advantages and obstacles, technological advances, and General Lee's surrender at Appomattox.															•					

Standards	Chapters: 1	2	3	4	5	6	7	8	9	10	11	12	13	14	15	16	17	18	19	20
7. Explain how the war affected combatants, civilians, the physical environment, and future warfare.															•	•				
8.11 Students analyze the character and lasting consequences of Reconstruction.																				
1. List the original aims of Reconstruction and describe its effects on the political and social structures of different regions.																•				
2. Identify the push-pull factors in the movement of former slaves to the cities in the North and to the West and their differing experiences in those regions (e.g., the experiences of Buffalo Soldiers).														•						
3. Understand the effects of the Freedmen's Bureau and the restrictions placed on the rights and opportunities of freedmen, including racial segregation and "Jim Crow" laws.																•				
4. Trace the rise of the Ku Klux Klan and describe the Klan's effects.																•				
5. Understand the Thirteenth, Fourteenth, and Fifteenth Amendments to the Constitution and analyze their connection to Reconstruction.																•				
8.12 Students analyze the transformation of the American economy and the changing social and political conditions in the United States in response to the Industrial Revolution.																				
1. Trace patterns of agricultural and industrial development as they relate to climate, use of natural resources, markets, and trade and locate such development on a map.																		•		
2. Identify the reasons for the development of federal Indian policy and the wars with American Indians and their relationship to agricultural development and industrialization.																	•			
3. Explain how states and the federal government encouraged business expansion through t.ariffs, banking, land grants, and subsidies.																				•
4. Discuss entrepreneurs, industrialists, and bankers in politics, commerce, and industry (e.g., Andrew Carnegie, John D. Rockefeller, Leland Stanford).																		•		
5. Examine the location and effects of urbanization, renewed immigration, and industrialization (e.g., the effects on social fabric of cities, wealth and economic opportunity, the conservation movement).																		•	•	
6. Discuss child labor, working conditions, and laissez-faire policies toward big business and examine the labor movement, including its leaders (e.g., Samuel Gompers), its demand for collective bargaining, and its strikes and protests over labor conditions.																		•	•	
7. Identify the new sources of large-scale immigration and the contributions of immigrants to the building of cities and the economy; explain the ways in which new social and economic patterns encouraged assimilation of newcomers into the mainstream amidst growing cultural diversity; and discuss the new wave of nativism.																		•		
8. Identify the characteristics and impact of Grangerism and Populism.																	•			
9. Name the significant inventors and their inventions and identify how they improved the quality of life (e.g., Thomas Edison, Alexander Graham Bell, Orville and Wilbur Wright).																		•		

Analysis Skills Standards — Chapters:	1	2	3	4	5	6	7	8	9	10	11	12	13	14	15	16	17	18	19	20
Chronological and Spatial Thinking																				
CS1 Students explain how major events are related to one another in time.				●																
CS2 Students construct various time lines of key events, people, and periods of the historical era they are studying.		●																		
CS3 Students use a variety of maps and documents to identify physical and cultural features of neighborhoods, cities, states, and countries and to explain the historical migration of people, expansion and disintegration of empires, and the growth of economic systems.																	●			
Research, Evidence, and Point of View																				
HR1 Students frame questions that can be answered by historical study and research.	●															●				
HR2 Students distinguish fact from opinion in historical narratives and stories.																			●	
HR3 Students distinguish relevant from irrelevant information, essential from incidental information, and verifiable from unverifiable information in historical narratives and stories.																●				
HR4 Students assess the credibility of primary and secondary sources and draw sound conclusions about them.														●	●					
HR5 Students detect the different historical points of view on historical events and determine the context in which the historical statements were made (the questions asked, sources used, author's perspectives).				●																
Historical Interpretation																				
HI1 Students explain the central issues and problems from the past, placing people and events in a matrix of time and place.								●			●									
HI2 Students understand and distinguish cause, effect, sequence, and correlation in historical events, including the long- and short-term causal relations.				●							●								●	
HI3 Students explain the sources of historical continually and how the combination of ideas and events explains the emergence of new patters.																				●
HI4 Students recognize the role of chance, oversight, and error in history.																●				
HI5 Students recognize the interpretations of history are subject to change as new information is uncovered.			●		●															
HI6 Students interpret basic indicators of economic performance and conduct cost-benefit analyses of economic and political issues.																		●		

HOLT CALIFORNIA SOCIAL STUDIES

provides integrated **practice** and **review** for every California standard

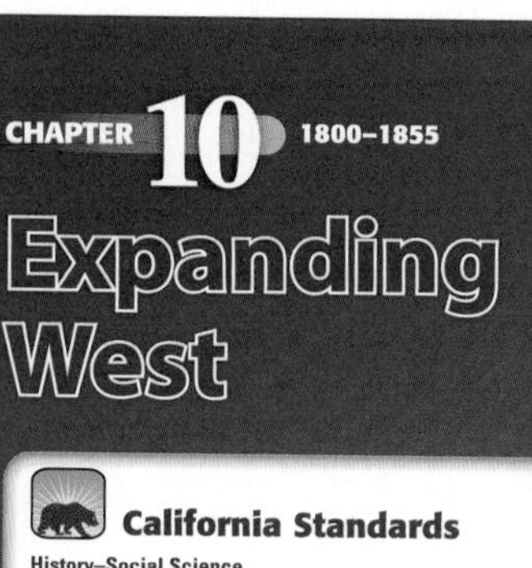

HOLT History's Impact
▶ video series
Watch the video to understand the impact of conflict on settlement in the West.
What You Will Learn...
In this chapter you will learn about how the United States expanded west. The country acquired vast amounts of territory in a short time. Lured by land and gold, hundreds of thousands of Americans followed trails west in search of a better life. However, many Californio families, like the one pictured here, had already lived in California for generations.
UNITED STATES
1811 John Jacob Astor founds the fur-trading post Astoria on the Columbia River.
1810
1820
1827 The United States and Great Britain agree to continue joint occupation of Oregon Country.
1830
1846 The United States declares war against Mexico.
1840
1848 Gold is discovered in California on January 24.
1850
1821 Mexico wins its independence from Spain.
1838 Californios revolt unsuccessfully against the Mexican government.
1842 China gives Great Britain control of the island of Hong Kong.
1854 Commodore Matthew Perry negotiates a trade treaty with Japan.
EXPANDING WEST 305

California Standards

History–Social Science

8.8 Students analyze the divergent paths of the American people in the West from 1800 to the mid-1800s and the challenges they faced.

8.9 Students analyze the early and steady attempts to abolish slavery and to realize the ideals of the Declaration of Independence.

Analysis Skills

CS 3 Students use a variety of maps and documents to identify physical and cultural features of neighborhoods, cities, states, and countries.

English–Language Arts

Writing 8.2.1.c Employ narrative and descriptive strategies.

California History-Social Science, Historical Analysis and Social Science Skills, and Language Arts Standards are provided at the beginning of every chapter to help prepare students for learning.

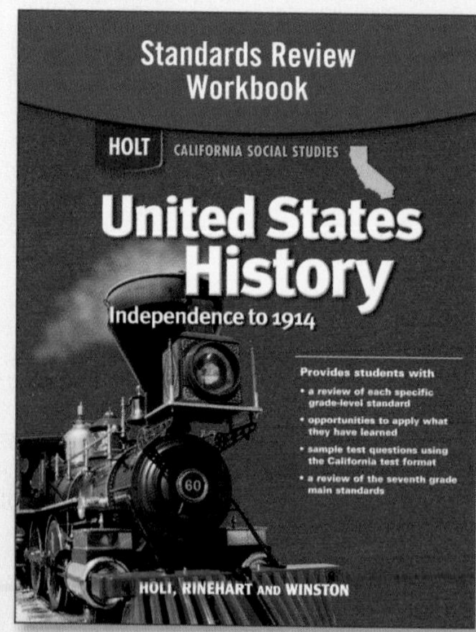

Standards Review Workbook
HOLT CALIFORNIA SOCIAL STUDIES
United States History
Independence to 1914
Provides students with
• a review of each specific grade-level standard
• opportunities to apply what they have learned
• sample test questions using the California test format
• a review of the seventh grade main standards
HOLT, RINEHART AND WINSTON

The *Standards Review Workbook* provides students with a quick review and test preparation for every standard.

SECTION 3

What You Will Learn...

Main Ideas

1. Many Americans believed that the nation had a manifest destiny to claim new lands in the West.
2. As a result of the Mexican-American War, the United States added territory in the Southwest.
3. American settlement in the Mexican Cession produced conflict and a blending of cultures.

The Big Idea

The ideals of manifest destiny and the outcome of the Mexican-

In the *Teacher's Edition,* **Teach the Big Idea: Master the Standards** provides teachers with strategies and activities that help students grasp the big ideas and master the standards for each section.

Teach the Big Idea: Master the Standards

Standards Proficiency

The Mexican-American War HSS 8.8.6; HSS Analysis Skills: CS 1, HI 1

1. **Teach** Ask students the Main Idea questions to teach this section.
2. **Apply** Have students work as a class to help you list the main events and issues in this section. Then have students write a news headline for each event or issue. **LS Verbal/Linguistic**
3. **Review** As you review the section's main ideas, have students share their headlines. Encourage feedback and discussion of headlines.
4. **Practice/Homework** Have each student select one of their headlines—or assign students a headline or topic—and create a political cartoon to go with it. Students should provide short captions explaining their political cartoons. Have volunteers share their cartoons with the class. **LS Visual/Spatial**

Alternative Assessment Handbook, Rubrics 27: Political Cartoons; and 42: Writing to Inform

In the *Teacher's Edition,* **Standards Focus** helps teachers respond to students' questions by telling them what the standard **means** in relation to the section content and why the standard **matters.**

Students also see the **Standards** at the beginning of every section in the *Student Edition.*

HSS 8.8.6 Describe the Texas War for Independence and the Mexican-American War, including territorial settlements, the aftermath of the wars, and the effects the wars had on the lives of Americans, including Mexican Americans today.

316 CHAPTER 10

Standards Focus

HSS 8.8.6

Means: Describe the main events of the Mexican-American War and explain how it affected Americans' lives, including the lives of Mexican Americans today.

Matters: The Mexican-American War had a significant and far-reaching effect on life in the American Southwest.

316 CHAPTER 10

HOLT CALIFORNIA SOCIAL STUDIES

includes standards assessment to monitor students' progress effectively

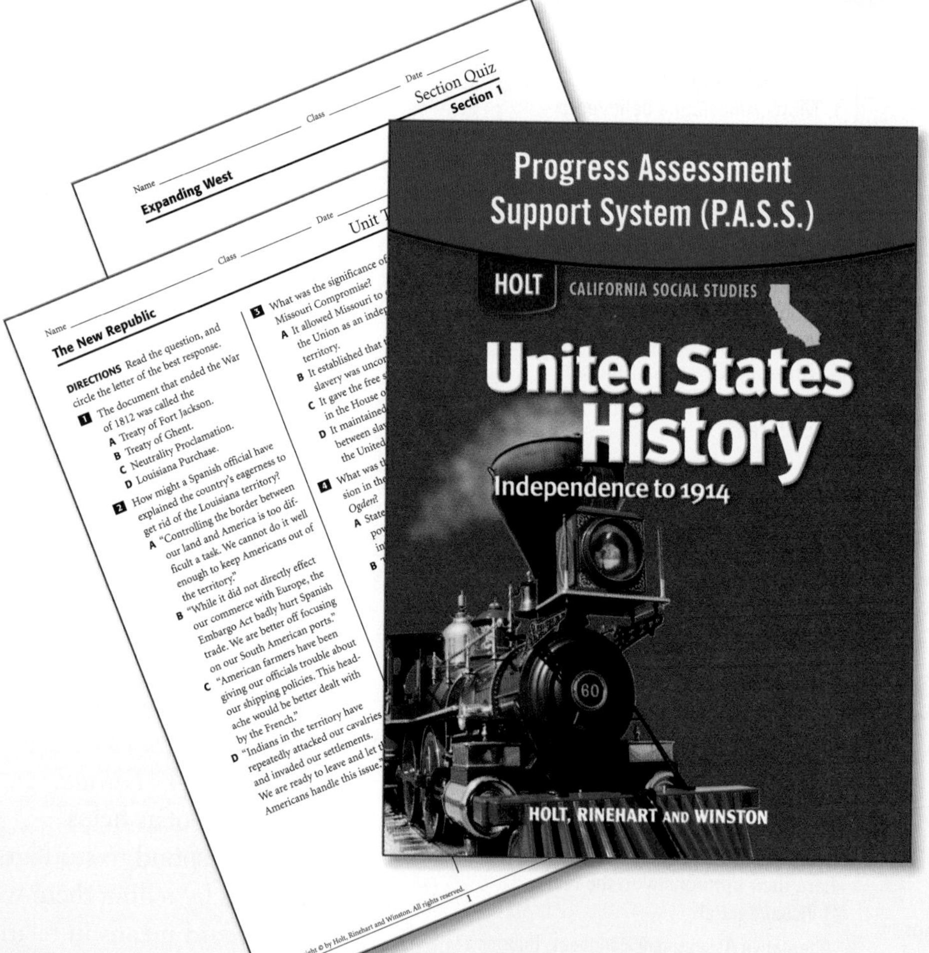

Holt's new *Progress Assessment Support System (P.A.S.S.)* includes all the assessment for every chapter and unit and helps teachers monitor students' progress.

P.A.S.S. includes

- **Section Quizzes**
- **Chapter Tests**
- **Diagnostic Pretest**
- **Benchmark Tests**
- **Summative End-of-the-Year Test**
- **Assessment Rubrics**

Every test on the **ExamView® Test Generator,** on the ***One-Stop Planner® CD-ROM,*** is also correlated to the California Standards, making it easy to reteach and offer more support to those students who need it.

A new technology, **Holt Online Assessment,** helps teachers assess students' mastery of the standards.

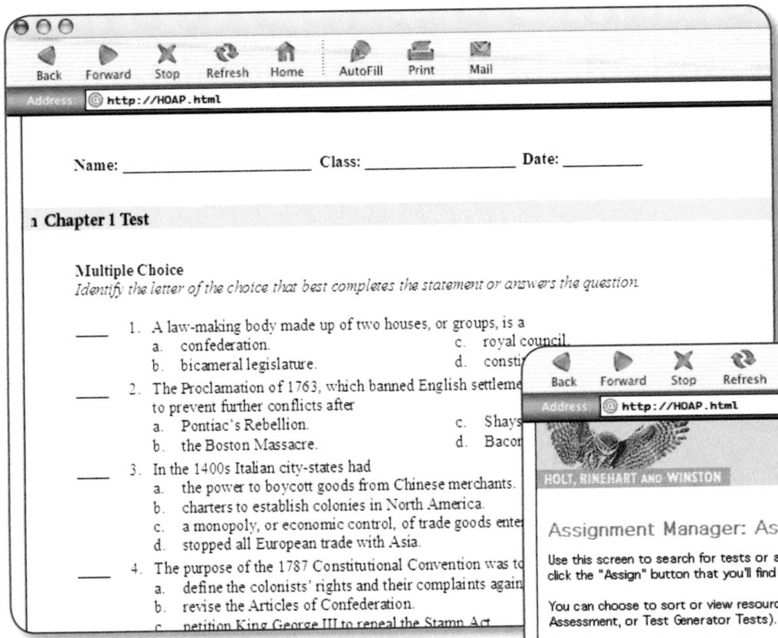

Back Forward Stop Refresh Home AutoFill Print Mail

Address: http://HOAP.html

Name: ____________ Class: ____________ Date: ________

1 Chapter 1 Test

Multiple Choice
Identify the letter of the choice that best completes the statement or answers the question.

____ 1. A law-making body made up of two houses, or groups, is a
a. confederation.
b. bicameral legislature.
c. royal council.
d. consti

____ 2. The Proclamation of 1763, which banned English settleme to prevent further conflicts after
a. Pontiac's Rebellion.
b. the Boston Massacre.
c. Shays
d. Bacon

____ 3. In the 1400s Italian city-states had
a. the power to boycott goods from Chinese merchants.
b. charters to establish colonies in North America.
c. a monopoly, or economic control, of trade goods ente
d. stopped all European trade with Asia.

____ 4. The purpose of the 1787 Constitutional Convention was to
a. define the colonists' rights and their complaints again
b. revise the Articles of Confederation.
c. petition King George III to repeal the Stamp Act

▲ STEP 1
Create a test

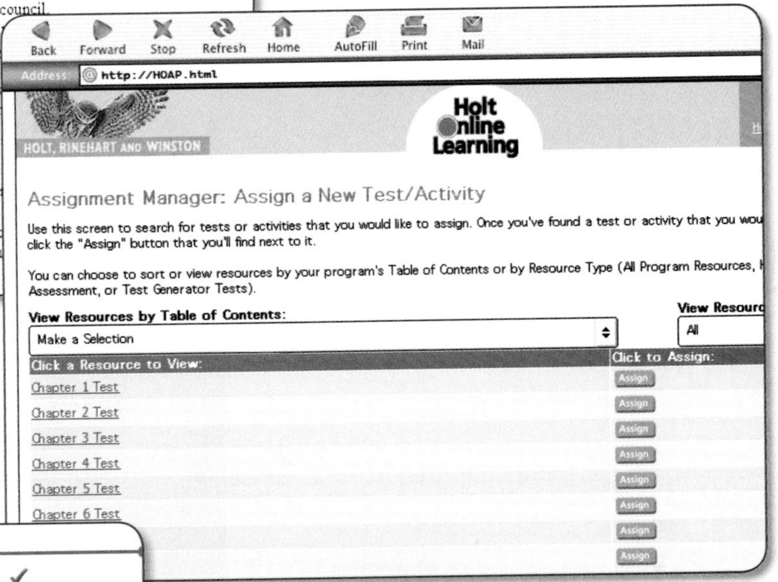

Back Forward Stop Refresh Home AutoFill Print Mail

Address: http://HOAP.html

HOLT, RINEHART AND WINSTON

Holt Online Learning

Assignment Manager: Assign a New Test/Activity

Use this screen to search for tests or activities that you would like to assign. Once you've found a test or activity that you wou click the "Assign" button that you'll find next to it.

You can choose to sort or view resources by your program's Table of Contents or by Resource Type (All Program Resources, Assessment, or Test Generator Tests).

View Resources by Table of Contents: Make a Selection

View Resourc All

Click a Resource to View:	Click to Assign:
Chapter 1 Test	Assign
Chapter 2 Test	Assign
Chapter 3 Test	Assign
Chapter 4 Test	Assign
Chapter 5 Test	Assign
Chapter 6 Test	Assign
	Assign
	Assign

▲ STEP 2
Assign a test

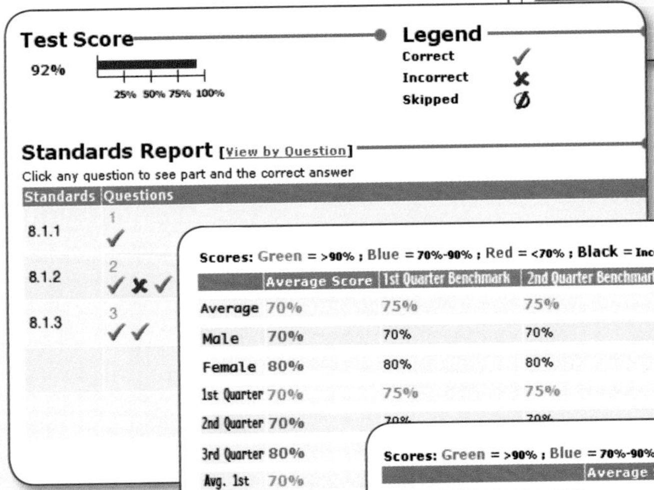

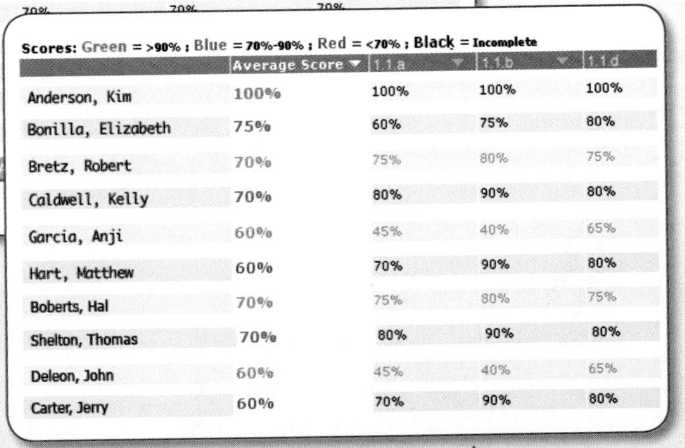

Test Score
92%
25% 50% 75% 100%

Legend
Correct ✓
Incorrect ✗
Skipped Ø

Standards Report [View by Question]
Click any question to see part and the correct answer

Standards	Questions
8.1.1	1 ✓
8.1.2	2 ✓ ✗ ✓
8.1.3	3 ✓ ✓

Scores: Green = >90% ; Blue = 70%-90% ; Red = <70% ; Black = Incomplete

	Average Score	1st Quarter Benchmark	2nd Quarter Benchmark	3rd Quarter Benchmark
Average	70%	75%	75%	75%
Male	70%	70%	70%	70%
Female	80%	80%	80%	80%
1st Quarter	70%	75%	75%	75%
2nd Quarter	70%	70%	70%	70%
3rd Quarter	80%			
Avg. 1st	70%			
Avg. 2nd	70%			
Avg. 3rd	80%			

Print Export Save A

Scores: Green = >90% ; Blue = 70%-90% ; Red = <70% ; Black = Incomplete

	Average Score	1.1.a	1.1.b	1.1.d
Anderson, Kim	100%	100%	100%	100%
Bonilla, Elizabeth	75%	60%	75%	80%
Bretz, Robert	70%	75%	80%	75%
Caldwell, Kelly	70%	80%	90%	80%
Garcia, Anji	60%	45%	40%	65%
Hart, Matthew	60%	70%	90%	80%
Boberts, Hal	70%	75%	80%	75%
Shelton, Thomas	70%	80%	90%	80%
Deleon, John	60%	45%	40%	65%
Carter, Jerry	60%	70%	90%	80%

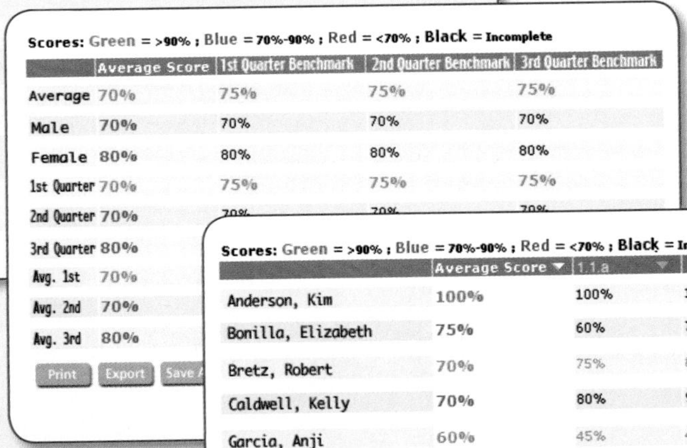

▲ STEP 3
View Reports

HOLT CALIFORNIA SOCIAL STUDIES involves students in the study of history and helps them discover a story well told

Stunning visuals put students into the context of the time period, bringing people, places, and concepts to life.

History Close-up
Ranch Life
Spanish and Mexican *vaqueros*, or cowboys, were expert horseriders. They used their horses to herd cattle on the ranches of the Spanish Southwest.
Vaqueros were known for their specially designed hats.
Leather chaps protected riders from dust and scrapes.
Saddles like these were highly prized by *vaqueros*.
ANALYSIS SKILL ANALYZING VISUALS
What features of the *vaqueros'* life are shown in this painting?
318 CHAPTER 10

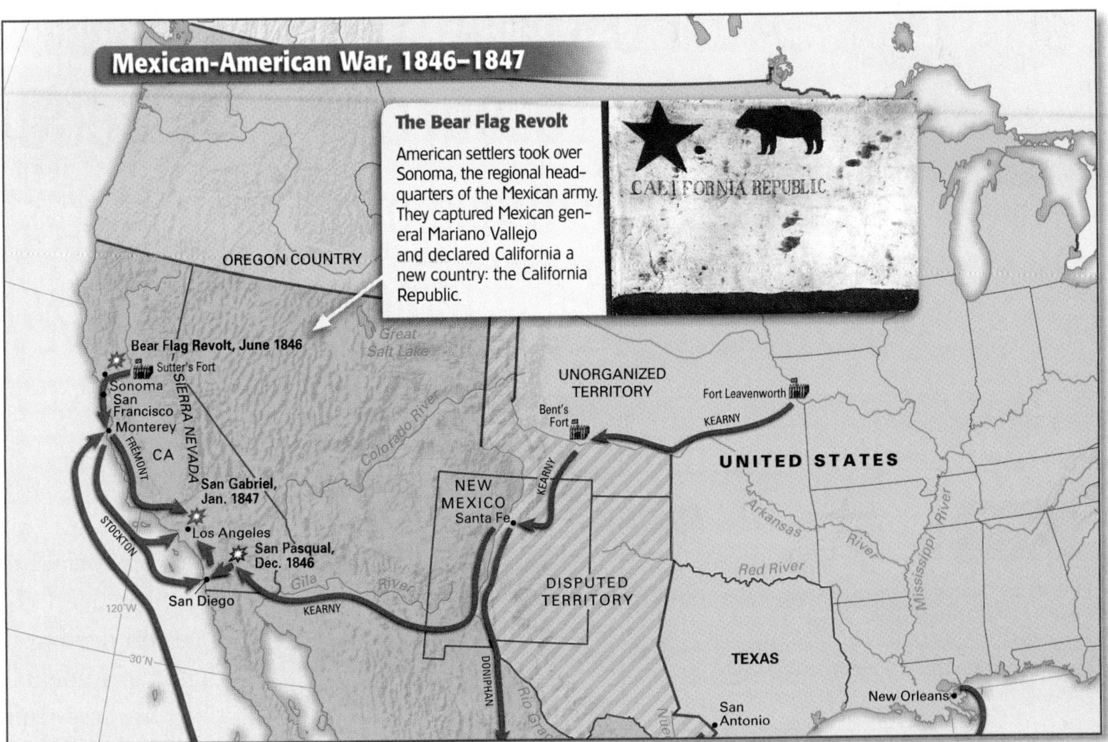

Holt's unique maps offer another way to engage students, showing them the connections between geography and history. Online Interactive Maps provide activities that develop map skills.

The California Gold Rush

If YOU were there...

You are a low-paid bank clerk in New England in early 1849. Local newspaper headlines are shouting exciting news: "Gold Is Discovered in California! Thousands Are on Their Way West." You enjoy having a steady job. However, some of your friends are planning to go West, and you are being influenced by their excitement. Your friends are even buying pickaxes and other mining equipment. They urge you to go West with them.

Would you go west to seek your fortune in California? Why?

If You Were There, introducing each section, challenges students with a provocative question designed to make the history presented in that section come alive.

HOLT

History's Impact

▶ video series

Watch the video to understand the impact of conflict on settlement in the West.

History's Impact Video Program helps students connect history to events in the current world (available on VHS, DVD, and the Online Textbook).

HOLT CALIFORNIA SOCIAL STUDIES

integrates **research-based reading instruction** and offers support so students understand and remember what they learn

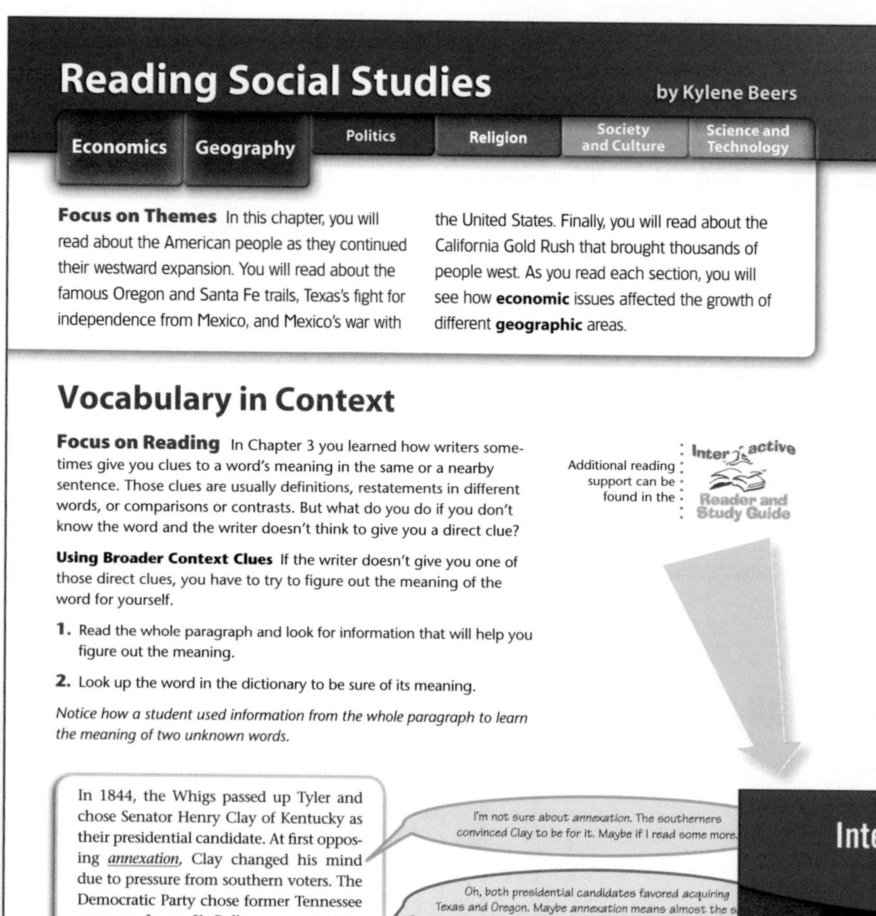

Reading Social Studies

by Kylene Beers

Economics | Geography | Politics | Religion | Society and Culture | Science and Technology

Focus on Themes In this chapter, you will read about the American people as they continued their westward expansion. You will read about the famous Oregon and Santa Fe trails, Texas's fight for independence from Mexico, and Mexico's war with the United States. Finally, you will read about the California Gold Rush that brought thousands of people west. As you read each section, you will see how **economic** issues affected the growth of different **geographic** areas.

Vocabulary in Context

Focus on Reading In Chapter 3 you learned how writers sometimes give you clues to a word's meaning in the same or a nearby sentence. Those clues are usually definitions, restatements in different words, or comparisons or contrasts. But what do you do if you don't know the word and the writer doesn't think to give you a direct clue?

Additional reading support can be found in the Interactive Reader and Study Guide

Using Broader Context Clues If the writer doesn't give you one of those direct clues, you have to try to figure out the meaning of the word for yourself.

1. Read the whole paragraph and look for information that will help you figure out the meaning.
2. Look up the word in the dictionary to be sure of its meaning.

Notice how a student used information from the whole paragraph to learn the meaning of two unknown words.

In 1844, the Whigs passed up Tyler and chose Senator Henry Clay of Kentucky as their presidential candidate. At first opposing *annexation*, Clay changed his mind due to pressure from southern voters. The Democratic Party chose former Tennessee governor James K. Polk to oppose Clay. Both candidates strongly favored *acquiring* Texas and Oregon, but Polk was perceived as the *expansionist* candidate. *(p. 317)*

I'm not sure about *annexation*. The southerners convinced Clay to be for it. Maybe if I read some more.

Oh, both presidential candidates favored *acquiring* Texas and Oregon. Maybe *annexation* means almost the s thing as *acquiring*. I'll check the dictionary.

The dictionary definition is "to add or attach." That's close. Now what about *expansionist*? I know one mea of *expand* is similar to *add*. An *expansionist* was probably so who wanted to add to or expand the country.

306 CHAPTER 10

Reading Social Studies lessons in every chapter focus on reading strategies that help students develop skills to successfully access information and master content.

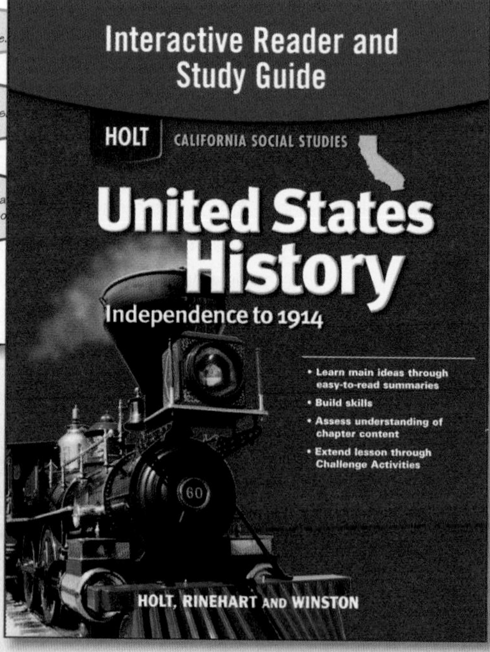

Interactive Reader and Study Guide
HOLT CALIFORNIA SOCIAL STUDIES
United States History
Independence to 1914
• Learn main ideas through easy-to-read summaries
• Build skills
• Assess understanding of chapter content
• Extend lesson through Challenge Activities
HOLT, RINEHART AND WINSTON

The *Interactive Reader and Study Guide* provides **all** students with additional support to master content and standards through strategies and review.

Live Ink Online Reading Help is an online tool that displays the text of the *Holt California Social Studies Online Editions* in a format that has been proven to improve comprehension and increase test scores.

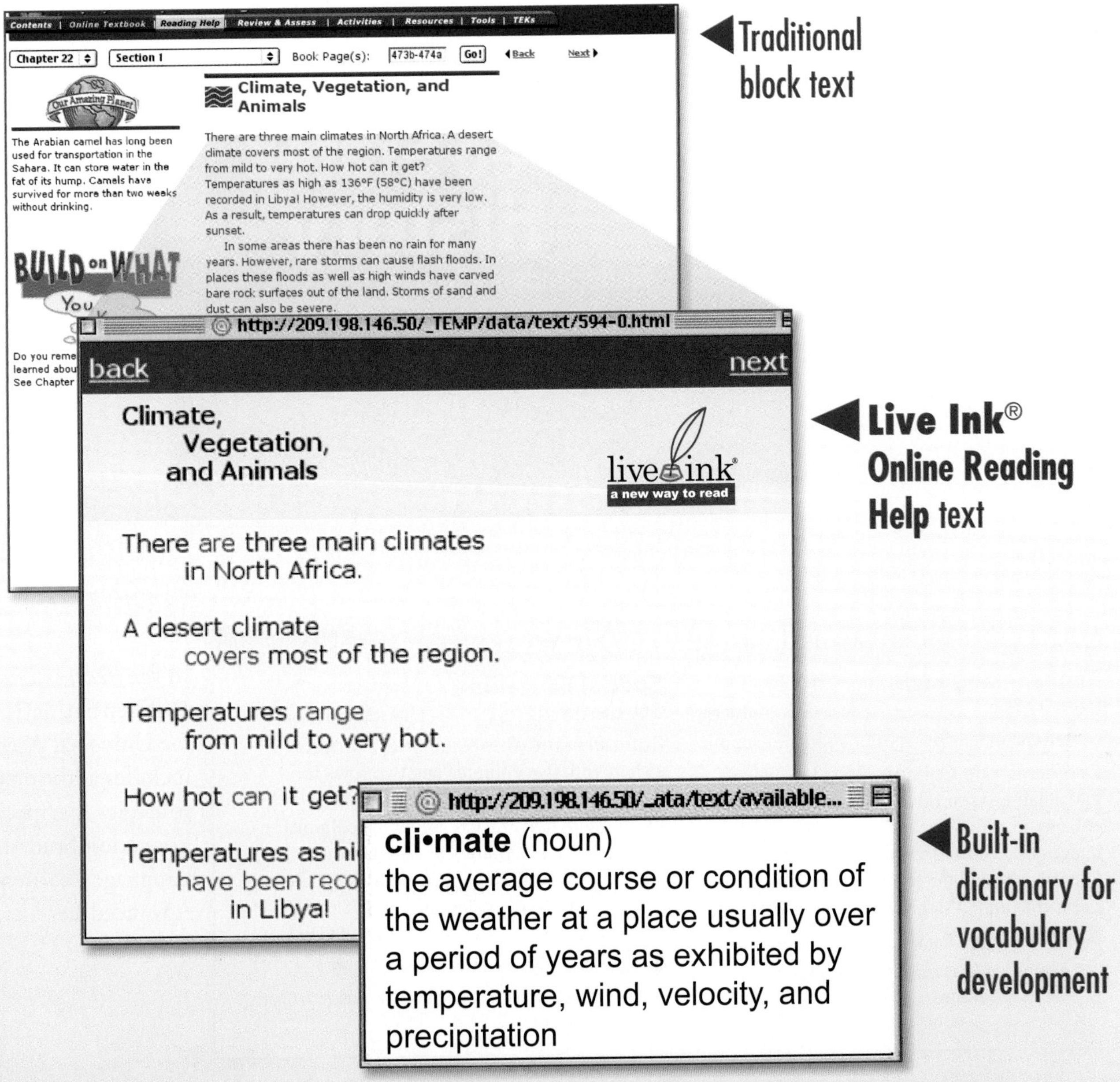

Contents | Online Textbook | Reading Help | Review & Assess | Activities | Resources | Tools | TEKs

Chapter 22 | Section 1 | Book Page(s): 473b-474a | Go! | Back | Next

Our Amazing Planet

The Arabian camel has long been used for transportation in the Sahara. It can store water in the fat of its hump. Camels have survived for more than two weeks without drinking.

BUILD on WHAT You

Do you reme... learned abou... See Chapter

Climate, Vegetation, and Animals

There are three main climates in North Africa. A desert climate covers most of the region. Temperatures range from mild to very hot. How hot can it get? Temperatures as high as 136°F (58°C) have been recorded in Libya! However, the humidity is very low. As a result, temperatures can drop quickly after sunset.

In some areas there has been no rain for many years. However, rare storms can cause flash floods. In places these floods as well as high winds have carved bare rock surfaces out of the land. Storms of sand and dust can also be severe.

◀ Traditional block text

http://209.198.146.50/_TEMP/data/text/594-0.html

back next

Climate,
Vegetation,
and Animals

live ink
a new way to read

There are three main climates
in North Africa.

A desert climate
covers most of the region.

Temperatures range
from mild to very hot.

How hot can it get?

Temperatures as hi...
have been reco...
in Libya!

◀ **Live Ink®** **Online Reading Help** text

http://209.198.146.50/_ata/text/available...

cli•mate (noun)
the average course or condition of the weather at a place usually over a period of years as exhibited by temperature, wind, velocity, and precipitation

◀ Built-in dictionary for vocabulary development

HOLT CALIFORNIA SOCIAL STUDIES ensures Universal Access for all students

Holt's award-winning *One-Stop Planner* provides easy-to-use print and technology resources that allow teachers to maximize their effectiveness and save time in planning, teaching, and assessing each lesson.

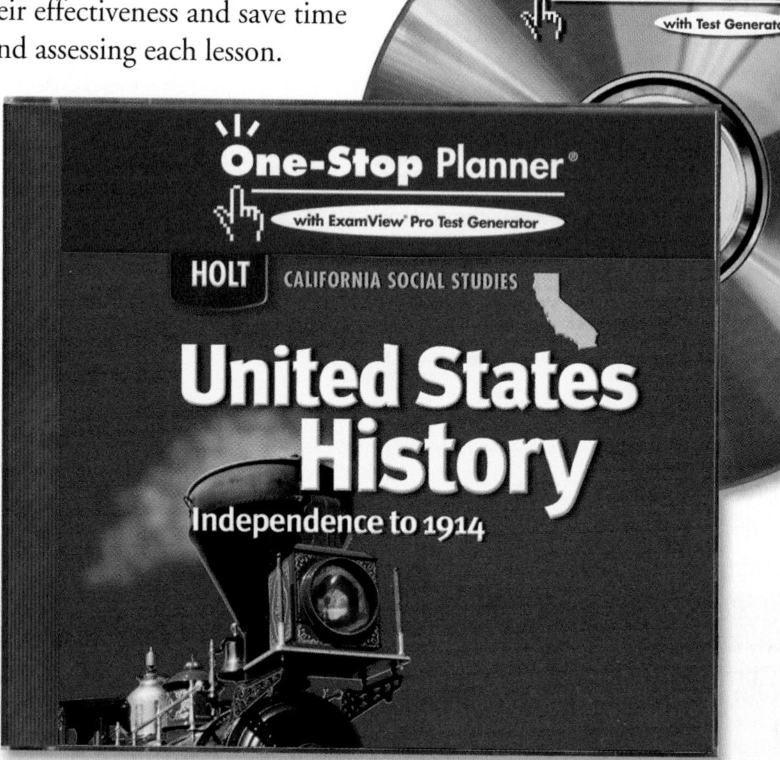

Differentiating Instruction for Universal Access

English-Language Learners

Prep Required

Standards Proficiency

Materials: magazines, poster board, art supplies

California Life Collage Organize students into small groups. Have each group create a collage, in which one half of the collage shows images related to life in California under Spanish rule and the other half depicts life in California under Mexican rule. **LS Visual/Spatial**

HSS 8.8.5; **HSS Analysis Skills:** CS 1, HI 1

Alternative Assessment Handbook, Rubric 8: Collages

Special Education Students

Reaching Standards

Compare-and-Contrast Chart Create a chart with two columns and two rows for students to see. Title the chart *California under Spain and Mexico.* Label the columns *Similarities* and *Differences* and the rows *Spanish Rule* and *Mexican Rule.* Have students work in pairs to complete the chart. Then discuss the answers as a class. **LS Visual/Spatial**

HSS 8.8.5; **HSS Analysis Skills:** CS 1, HI 1

Alternative Assessment Handbook, Rubric 7: Charts

In the *Teacher's Edition,* Differentiating Instruction for Universal Access includes additional strategies for Special Education Students, English-Language Learners, and Advanced Learners/GATE.

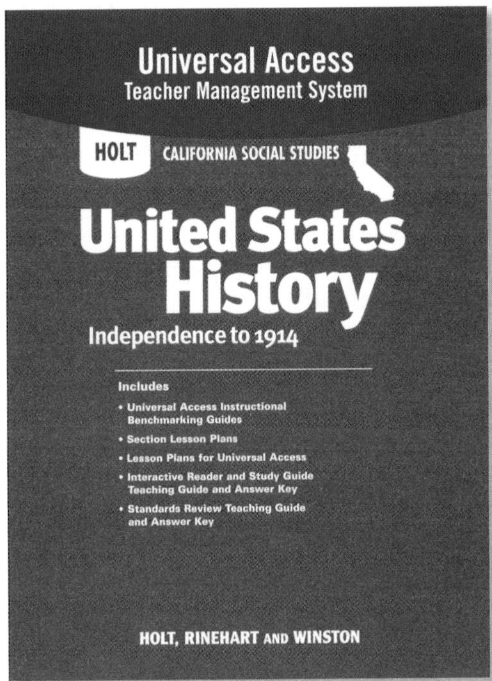

Holt's *Universal Access Teacher Management System* offers a wide variety of planning and instructional strategies.

The system includes:

- **Section Lesson Plans**
- **Lesson Plans for Universal Access**
- **Instructional Benchmarking Guides**
- **Interactive Reader and Study Guide Teaching Guide**
- **Standards Review Workbook Teaching Guide**

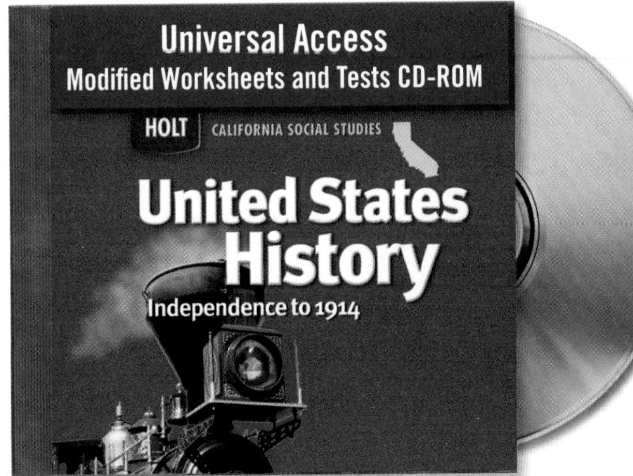

The *Universal Access Modified Worksheets and Tests CD-ROM* provides key resources modified to meet the specifications for students' **Individualized Education Plans (IEPs).**

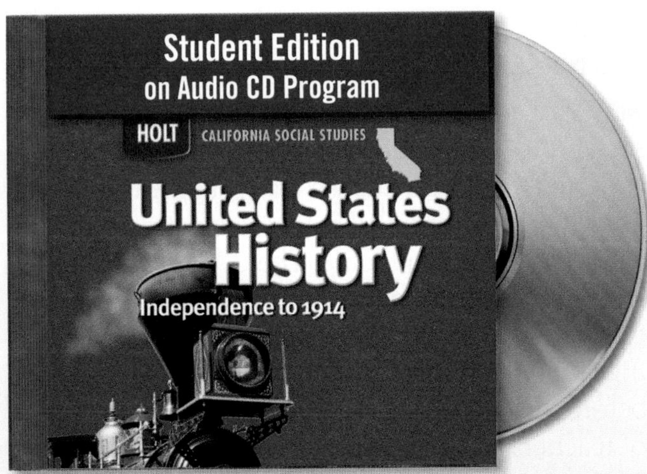

Student Edition on Audio CD Program is a direct read of the *Student Edition,* providing extra support for auditory learners, English-language learners, and reluctant readers. Also available is the ***Spanish Chapter Summaries Audio CD Program.***

English–Language Arts Standards and the Social Studies Teacher

by Carol Jago

Carol Jago teaches English at Santa Monica High School and directs the California Reading and Literature Project at UCLA. She is the author of *Cohesive Writing: Why Concept Is Not Enough.*

Q: Why should a social studies teacher have to teach to English–Language Arts Standards?

A: With a full set of standards of their own, many social studies teachers wonder why they should be expected to address English–Language Arts standards as well. In California all students must pass an exit exam in order to graduate. The CAHSEE (California High School Exit Exam) measures student competency in reading, writing, and mathematics. Preparing students to meet this challenge begins long before high school and is the shared responsibility of teachers across the subject areas. The English–Language Arts standards assessed on the CAHSEE are in many cases closely aligned with the social studies curriculum, for example Standard 2.8: "Evaluate the credibility of an author's argument or defense of a claim by critiquing the relationship between generalizations and evidence, the comprehensiveness of evidence, and the way in which the author's intent affects the structure and tone of the text (e.g., in professional journals, editorials, political speeches, primary source materials). Teaching to such standards will not only help students pass the exit exam but also help them learn history.

Q: What does research say about writing in social studies curriculum?

A: The National Commission on Writing in America's Schools and Colleges issued a report titled "The Neglected 'R'" calling for a writing revolution. NAEP research shows that only 50 percent of students meet "basic" levels of performance in writing and only one in five can be called "proficient." One student in five produces completely unsatisfactory prose. The 2003 report recommends that writing be incorporated into all state standards and that writing be required in every curriculum at all grade levels. "Very few things are more important to improving student achievement than restoring writing to its proper place in the classroom," said Commission Vice-Chair Arlene Ackerman, San Francisco superintendent of schools. "Writing is how we can teach students complex skills of synthesis, analysis, and problem solving." Given the controversial nature of so many topics in their curriculum, social studies teachers are uniquely positioned to help students develop these skills through persuasive writing.

Q: But how am I supposed to grade all those papers?

A: It isn't possible for teachers to work any harder. We need to work smarter. One method for assessing student writing effectively is to use rubrics. When the features of each numerical rubric score are laid out alongside a writing task, it is possible to assign a number to each student paper with confidence and, if not ease, efficiency. Social studies teachers needn't feel that they must teach the mechanics of correctness. Language arts teachers recognize that this is their primary responsibility. By assigning writing, social studies teachers reinforce the lessons learned in English–Language Arts.

Sample Scoring Rubric: Persuasive Essays

4 The Writing

- Clearly addresses all parts of the writing task
- Authoritatively defends a position with precise and relevant evidence
- Demonstrates a clear understanding of purpose and audience
- Maintains a consistent point of view, focus, and organizational structure, including the effective use of transitions
- Includes a clearly presented central idea with relevant facts, details, and/or explanations
- Includes a variety of sentence types
- Contains few, if any, errors in the conventions of the English language

3 The Writing

- Addresses all parts of the writing task
- Generally defends a position with relevant evidence and addresses the reader's concerns, biases, and expectations
- Demonstrates a general understanding of purpose and audience
- Maintains a mostly consistent point of view, focus, and organizational structure, including the effective use of some transitions
- Includes a central idea with relevant facts, details, and/or explanations
- Includes a variety of sentence types
- Contains some errors in the conventions of the English language

2 The Writing

- Addresses only parts of the writing task
- Defends a position with little, if any, evidence and may address the reader's concerns, biases, and expectations
- Demonstrates little understanding of purpose and audience
- Maintains an inconsistent point of view, focus, and organizational structure, which may include ineffective or awkward transitions that do not unify important ideas
- Suggests a central idea with relevant facts, details, and/or explanations
- Includes little variety of sentence types
- Contains several errors in the conventions of the English language

1 The Writing

- Addresses only one part of the writing task
- Fails to defend a position with any evidence and fails to address the reader's concerns, biases, and expectations
- Demonstrates no understanding of purpose and audience
- Lacks a point of view, focus, organizational structure, and transitions that unify important ideas
- Lacks a central idea but may contain marginally relevant facts, details, and/or explanations
- Includes no sentence variety
- Contains serious errors in the conventions of the English language

Scoring rubrics help social studies teachers assess student writing efficiently and effectively.

Q: With so much history to read, why are we asking students to read literature?

A: Literature helps bring history to life, animating historical events and allowing students to walk in the shoes of those who have lived long ago in places distant from their own experience. Good literature is also disturbing. It forces readers to examine the lives of others from the inside out, exposing young people to the complexity of the world they live in. Literature doesn't offer simple solutions. While reading fiction is not a vaccine for small-mindedness, it does make it difficult to think only of one's self. If one purpose of public education is to prepare students for the complex responsibilities of citizenship, I can think of no better preparation for these responsibilities than reading the work of authors such as Stephen Crane, Jack London, Frank Norris, Theodore Dreiser, and Upton Sinclair. Literature creates empathy and without empathy there can be little hope of a civilized society.

Standard English Learners

Language Acquisition as a Scaffold to Social Studies Curricula

by Dr. Noma LeMoine

Dr. Noma Lemoine, Ph.D., is a nationally recognized expert on issues of language variation and learning in African American and other students for whom Standard English is not native. She is Director of Academic English Mastery and Closing the Achievement Gap Branch for the Los Angeles Unified School District. She is a member of the National Citizen's Commission on African American Education, an arm of the Congressional Black Caucus Education Brain Trust. Dr. LeMoine is also the author of *English for Your Success: A Language Development Program for African American Students.*

Standard English Learners arrive at school in kindergarten as competent users of the language of their home but demonstrating limited proficiency in the language of school, that is, Standard American English. They are generally classified as English Only on school language surveys even though many of the rules that govern their home language are based in languages other than English. Because of their designation as English Only, these students' need for structured programs that support their acquisition of standard and academic English is often overlooked.

Who are Standard English Learners?

Standard English Learners (SELs) are students for whom standard English is not native or whose home language—the language acquired between infancy and five years of age—structurally does not match the language of school. Standard English Learners include African American, Hawaiian American, Mexican American, and Native American students that have in common a linguistic history grounded in languages other than English. Prior to coming in contact with English their ancestors spoke African languages, Hawaiian languages, Latin American Spanish, or Native American languages. In each case these "involuntary minorities"—people who were enslaved, colonized, conquered, or otherwise subordinated in the context of America—combined English vocabulary with their native language and fashioned new ways of communicating in their new environments. These language forms, African American Language (often referred to as Black English); Hawaiian American Language (referred

SEL Administrative Support Strategies

- Provide ongoing, comprehensive professional development for teachers and paraeducators including "literature circles" centered around the literature on the culturally and linguistically responsive instruction.
- Support the development of cooperative learning communities at the school site that engage teachers in review of the research, lesson study, peer coaching, and analysis of student work as a condition necessary for effectively educating SELs.
- Infuse information on the origin and historical development of standard and non-standard languages into the instructional curriculum.

to as Hawaiian Pidgin English); Mexican American Language (referred to as Chicano English); and Native American Language (sometimes referred to as Red English) incorporate English vocabulary, but differ in structure and form from standard American English.

Language Variation and Learning in SELs

In order for culturally and linguistically diverse Standard English Learners to succeed academically they must acquire the language, culture, and literacies of school. They must become literate in the forms of English that appear in newspapers, magazines, textbooks, voting materials, and consumer contracts. How best to facilitate this learning in Standard English Learners (SELs) has proven elusive for most American public educational institutions and minimal emphasis has been placed on identifying instructional methodologies that scaffold SELs' access to core curricula. Learning is viewed as a social phenomenon and knowledge is recognized as a social construction that is influenced by the cultural and linguistic experiences, perspectives, and frames or references both students and teachers bring to the learning environment. For Standard English Learners this suggests that an instructional model, which validates and builds on prior knowledge, experiences, language and culture while supporting the acquisition of school language through content learning is an appropriate pedagogy.

The History–Social Science curriculum is perhaps the best vehicle for creating learning opportunities in both content and language acquisition areas. Opportunities to engage in critical thinking and participate in knowledge building abound in the History–Social Science curriculum. As teachers help students develop skills as historians who re-create and share knowledge, students can also be provided opportunities to develop skills as speakers, readers, and writers.

SELs must be provided opportunities to add school language and literacy to their repertoire of skills using instructional approaches that build on the culture and language they bring to the classroom. In order for SELs to experience greater success in accessing core curricula, teachers will need to construct learning environments that are authentic, culturally responsive, support language acquisition, and build upon the experiences, learning styles, and strengths of SELs.

SEL Instructional Support Strategies

- Incorporate contrastive analysis strategies (linguistic, contextual, situational, and elicited) into the daily instruction of SELs to facilitate mastery of academic language.
- Incorporate applicable SDAIE (Specially Designed Academic Instruction in English) strategies into instruction including utilization of visuals, manipulatives, graphic organizers, media and other tools to explain concepts.
- Provide continuous and varied opportunities for students to use language to interact with each other and the content through instructional conversations.
- Provide 30 to 45 minutes per day of Mainstream English Language Development (MELD) instruction that promotes the development of listening, speaking, reading, and writing skills in standard and academic English.
- Establish classroom libraries that include culturally relevant books and provide opportunities for SELs to be read to and to engage in free voluntary reading (FVR) on a daily basis.
- Encourage student/classroom development of a personal thesaurus of conceptually coded words to support the acquisition of academic vocabulary.
- Convey knowledge on ancient Africa, Mexico, Hawaii, and North America; their cultures and history.
- Convey knowledge of the impact of diverse cultures on the modern world with an emphasis on historical and contemporary achievers.
- Make connections to students' prior knowledge, experiences, and cultural funds of knowledge to support learning and retention of learned concepts.

Making History–Social Science Accessible to English Learners

by Dr. Julie Chan

Dr. Julie Chan, Ed.D., is Director of Literacy Instruction in the Newport-Mesa Unified School District, located in Costa Mesa, California. She is a member of the California Reading and Literature Project (CRLP), UCI/Orange County region, and serves on the state level CRLP Secondary Academic Literacy Toolkit (SALT) development team. Dr. Chan also teaches graduate courses on "The Sociocultural Contexts of Literacy and Learning" in the Masters of Reading program at CSU Fullerton and "Linguistics in Action in the Multicultural Classroom" at Concordia University.

As increasing numbers of English Language Learners (ELLs) enter California's secondary schools each year, it is incumbent upon all of us to help each student fully access the History–Social Science curriculum.

History–Social Science instruction relies heavily on language—oral language (listening/speaking) and written language (reading/writing). Because of their limited—but developing—proficiency in the English language, ELLs have a difficult time grasping the information presented orally by the teacher, as well as struggling when reading the printed text in History–Social Science textbooks.

Chamot and O'Malley (1994) identified six areas where teachers can support ELLs: (1) conceptual understanding, (2) vocabulary, (3) language functions and discourse, (4) structures, (5) academic language skills, and (6) study skills and learning strategies. Here are some ways that teachers can make History–Social Science accessible to English Language Learners.

Conceptual Understanding While all students need to develop the concepts of time, chronology, distance, and differing ways of life, some ELLs may have never studied world history or geography and History–Social Science can be one way to learn about the United States. Teachers could approach unfamiliar concepts and content through what the *History–Social Science Framework* calls "a story well told" by reading aloud trade books to build background knowledge and/or to provide a mental model at the beginning of a unit of study.

Vocabulary Students need to learn the specialized and technical terminology of History–Social Science in order to discuss and report on the ideas studied. As students move up through the grades, the academic vocabulary of History–Social Science becomes increasingly difficult because of the complexity of the concepts it represents. Thus, knowing which words and how and when to introduce them is critical.

Language Functions and Discourse According to the California Content Standards, middle school students are expected to analyze, compare, contrast, and make judgments about social studies information. In contrast to the narrative discourse of ELD texts, social studies textbooks feature expository discourse across six text structures. By using graphic organizers that match each of the text structures, teachers can make abstract ideas, concepts, and content visible and concrete for ELLs.

Differentiating Instruction for Universal Access

English-Language Learners HSS 8.2.6; HSS **Analysis Skills:** HI 1 **Standards Proficiency**

1. Review with students important terms from this section with which they may not be familiar: *apportionment, concurrent powers, delegated powers, distinct, dual sovereignty, elastic clause, executive orders, federal system, impeach, pardons, representative democracy, reserved powers, veto.*
2. Draw a tic-tac-toe diagram (nine-square grid) for students to see. Divide the students into two groups: Xs and Os.
3. Determine which group will go first, then select one student in that group to answer a question. Given one of the vocabulary words, students are to define the term and use it in a sentence. Upon answering correctly, that group puts their mark in the square of their choosing. The first group to get three in a row wins. LS **Verbal/Linguistic**

Alternative Assessment Handbook, Rubric 11: Discussions

CRF: Vocabulary Builder Activity, Section 1

Lessons designed to support instructions for English-Language Learners can be found throughout the Teacher's Editions.

Structures Oral and written language structures present special challenges to ELLs. When teachers use research-based effective strategies to support oral and written language as well as published text structures, they can nudge their ELLs toward thinking, talking, reading, and writing like historians.

Academic Language Skills Students typically learn History–Social Science through the receptive modes of listening and reading. In contrast, they "show what they know" through the productive modes of class discussion, oral presentations and written products such as projects, reports, and expository/analytical essays. When the academic vocabulary of the content/concept to be studied is explicitly taught, ELLs can be more productive and therefore more successful at showing what they know.

Study Skills and Learning Strategies Chamot and O'Malley (1994) note that study skills, thinking skills, and social skills are also important aspects of the History–Social Science curriculum. ELLs may not have, as yet, developed the learning strategies essential to these three skill areas. Thus, teachers should help ELLs develop these skills so they can be better prepared to cope with the growing amount of new and abstract information found in grade-level History–Social Science classrooms, textbooks, and primary source documents.

Teachers who use research-based best practices in the areas of (1) conceptual understanding, (2) vocabulary, (3) language functions and discourse, (4) structures, (5) academic language skills, and (6) study skills and learning strategies will be better prepared to support growing numbers of ELLs in their History–Social Science classes, regardless of each student's proficiency level in English. Whether a teacher has regular History–Social Science classes or a sheltered section (also known in California as SDAIE, or Specially Designed Academic Instruction in English), the result will be ELLs who have greater access to the History–Social Science curriculum and who will experience greater success as learners moving into the mainstream.

Chamot, Anna Uhl and J. Michael O'Malley (1994). *The CALLA Handbook: Implementing the Cognitive Academic Language Learning Approach.* Reading, MA: Addison-Wesley Publishing Company.

The History-Social Science Framework for California Public Schools, Kindergarten through Grade Twelve (2000). Sacramento, CA: The California Department of Education.

ELL Instructional Support Services

- Use graphic organizers to teach abstract ideas.
- Teach specialized History–Social Science vocabulary and usage.
- Promote development of study skills, thinking skills, and social skills.
- Read aloud content-related materials to help students build background knowledge.

Professional Resources and Bibliography

Professional References

This section provides information about resources that can enrich your U.S. History class. Included are addresses of guest speakers, museum visits, electronic field trips, nonprofit organizations, and many others. Since addresses change frequently, you may want to verify them before you send your requests. You may also want to refer to the HRW Web site at http://www.hrw.com for current information.

GUEST SPEAKERS

National Council for History Education
Speakers' Bureau
26915 Westwood Rd., Suite B-2
Westlake, Ohio 44145

MUSEUM VISITS

American Association of Museums
1575 Eye Street NW. Suite 400
Washington, DC 20005

ELECTRONIC FIELD TRIPS

Library of Congress/Congressional Server
thomas.loc.gov/

E3 Electronic Field Trips
Teachers College (TC 1008)
Ball State University
Muncie IN 47306
866-279-8716
Web: http://www.bsu.edu/eft

eFieldTrips.org
2960 W. Player Dr.
Snowflake, Arizona 85937
928-536-4954

NONPROFIT ORGANIZATIONS

Constitutional Rights Foundation
601 South Kingsley Drive
Los Angeles, CA 90005
213-487-5590; Fax: 213-386-0459
www.crf-usa.org

Center for Civic Education
5145 Douglas Fir Road
Calabasas, CA 91302-1440
Tel: 818-591-9321
Fax: 818-591-9330
www.civiced.org

National Council for the Social Studies
8555 Sixteenth Street
Silver Spring, MD 20910
301-588-1800
www.socialstudies.org

National Trust for Historic Preservation
1785 Massachusetts Ave. NW
Washington, DC 20036

National History Day
University of Maryland
at College Park
0121 Caroline Hall
College Park, MD 20742

American Association for State and Local History
172 Second Avenue North, Suite 202
Nashville, TN 37201

American Bar Association
Division for Public Education
321 North Clark Street
Chicago, IL 60610
312-988-5000
www.abanet.org

PERIODICALS

Cobblestone: The History Magazine for Young People
Cobblestone Publishing, Inc.
30 Grove St.
Peterborough, NH 03458

American Spirit Magazine
DAR Magazine Office
Attn: New Subscriptions
1776 D Street NW
Washington, DC 20006-5303

American History
Primedia History Group
PRIMEDIA Special Interest Publications
6405 Flank Drive
Harrisburg, PA 17112
www.thehistorynet.com

Magazine of History
Organization of American Historians
P.O. Box 5457
Bloomington, IN 47408-5457
812-855-9851
www.oah.org

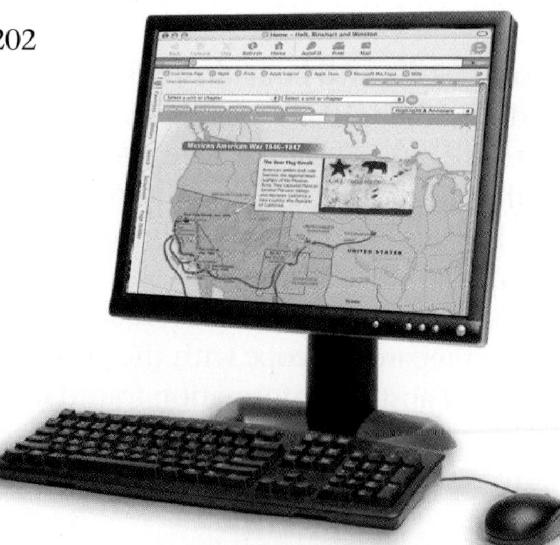

GOVERNMENT RESOURCES

National Park Service
Office of Public Inquiries
Washington, DC 20013-7127

National Register of Historic Places
Interagency Resources Division
National Park Service
P.O. Box 37127
Washington, DC 20013-7127

U.S. Department of Education
400 Maryland Ave., SW
Washington, D.C. 20202-0498
800-USA-LEARN
www.ed.gov/teachers/landing.jhtml?src=fp

Smithsonian Institution
Smithsonian Information
P.O. Box 37012
SI Building, Room 153, MRC 010
Washington, DC 20013-7012
202-357-2700
www.si.edu

The Library of Congress
01 Independence Ave, SE
Washington, DC 20540
202-707-5000
www.loc.gov/homepage/lchp.html

SUBSCRIPTION SERVICES

Magazines.com Inc.
P.O. Box 682108
Franklin, TX 37068
800-929-2691
www.magazines.com

MISCELLANEOUS

Educational Resources Information Center (ERIC)
2277 Research Blvd.
Rockville, MD 20852
800-538-3742

K-12 WebSite for Busy Teachers
http://www.ceismc.gatech.edu/busyt/hers.shtml

A Bibliography for the Social Studies Teacher

This bibliography is a select compilation of resources available for professional enrichment.

SELECTED AND ANNOTATED LIST OF READINGS

Social Studies and Language Arts

Burke, Jim. *Writing Reminders: Tools, Tips, and Techniques*
Portsmouth, NH: Heinemann, 2003
Burke offers a collection of strategies for teaching writing, complete with the instructional tools for implementing the strategies.

Jago, Carol. *Cohesive Writing: Why Concept Is Not Enough*
Portsmouth, NH: Heinemann, 2002
This book provides a coherent roadmap for teaching students how to write in each of the writing types required for the STAR assessment: summary, narrative, response to literature, and persuasion.

Social Studies and Standard English Mastery

LeMoine, N. and Los Angeles Unified School District. *English for Your Success: A Language Development Program for African American Students. Handbook of Successful Strategies for Educators.*
New Jersey: The Peoples Publishing Group, 1999
English for Your Success provides lessons using proven strategies for facilitating language acquisition and learning in African American Standard English Learners.

Ornstein-Galicia, J. *Form and Function in Chicano English*
Malabar, FL: Krieger Publishing Co., 1988
This text address issues of language and learning in Mexican American Standard English Learners (SELs) who speak mainly Chicano English.

Social Studies and English Learners

Billmeyer, Rachel and Mary Lee Barton. *Teaching Reading in the Content Areas: If Not Me, Then Who?* Second Edition
Aurora, CO: Mid-Continent Regional Educational Laboratory (McREL), 1998
These 40 strategies help students of all ages expand their vocabularies, understand different types of texts, and discuss what they have read.

Buehl, Doug. *Classroom Strategies for Interactive Learning,* Second Edition.
Newark, DE: International Reading Association, 2001
More than 40 literacy strategies for middle school and high school educators outside the reading field.

Readance, John, Thomas W. Bean and R. Scott Baldwin. *Content Area Literacy: An Integrated Approach.* Eighth Edition
Dubuque, IA: Kendall/Hunt Publishing Company, 2000
The authors provide strategies for helping students read, understand, and enjoy nonfiction. A CD accompanies this widely used text.

Mapping the Earth

A **globe** is a scale model of the earth. It is useful for showing the entire earth or studying large areas of the earth's surface.

A pattern of lines circles the globe in east-west and north-south directions. It is called a **grid**. The intersection of these imaginary lines helps us find places on the earth.

The east-west lines in the grid are lines of **latitude**. Lines of latitude are called **parallels** because they are always parallel to each other. These imaginary lines measure distance north and south of the **equator**. The equator is an imaginary line that circles the globe halfway between the North and South Poles. Parallels measure distance from the equator in **degrees**. The symbol for degrees is °. Degrees are further divided into **minutes**. The symbol for minutes is ´. There are 60 minutes in a degree. Parallels north of the equator are labeled with an N. Those south of the equator are labeled with an S.

The north-south lines are lines of **longitude**. Lines of longitude are called **meridians**. These imaginary lines pass through the Poles. They measure distance east and west of the **prime meridian**. The prime meridian is an imaginary line that runs through Greenwich, England. It represents 0° longitude.

Lines of latitude range from 0°, for locations on the equator, to 90°N or 90°S, for locations at the Poles. Lines of longitude range from 0° on the prime meridian to 180° on a meridian in the mid-Pacific Ocean. Meridians west of the prime meridian to 180° are labeled with a W. Those east of the prime meridian to 180° are labeled with an E.

Lines of Latitude

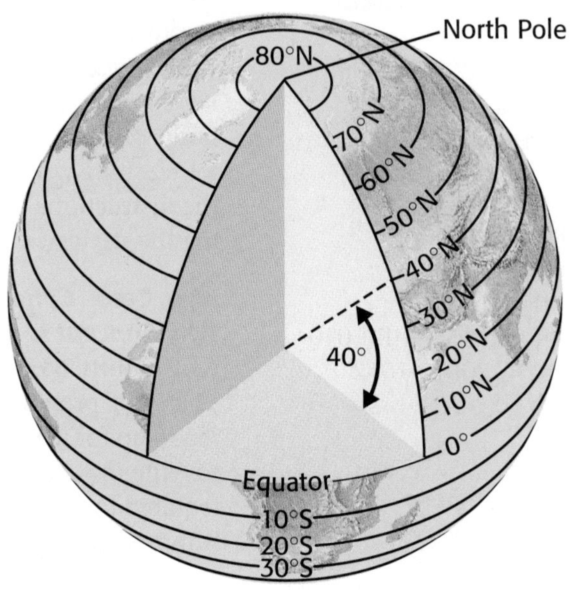

Lines of Longitude

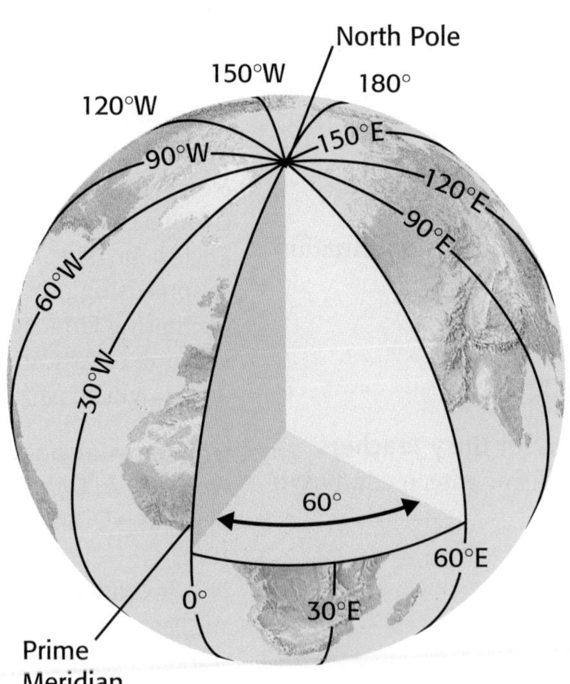

The equator divides the globe into two halves, called **hemispheres**. The half north of the equator is the Northern Hemisphere. The southern half is the Southern Hemisphere. The prime meridian and the 180° meridian divide the world into the Eastern Hemisphere and the Western Hemisphere. However, the prime meridian runs right through Europe and Africa. To avoid dividing these continents between two hemispheres, some mapmakers divide the Eastern and Western hemispheres at 20°W. This places all of Europe and Africa in the Eastern Hemisphere.

Our planet's land surface is divided into seven large landmasses, called **continents**. They are identified in the maps on this page. Landmasses smaller than continents and completely surrounded by water are called **islands**.

Geographers also organize Earth's water surface into parts. The largest is the world ocean. Geographers divide the world ocean into the Pacific Ocean, the Atlantic Ocean, the Indian Ocean, and the Arctic Ocean. Lakes and seas are smaller bodies of water.

Northern Hemisphere

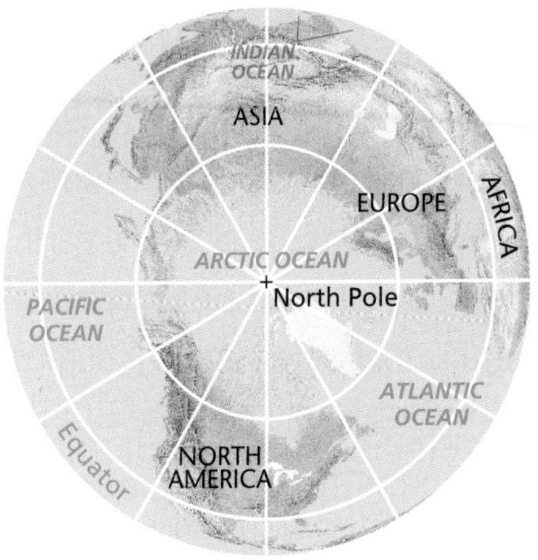

Southern Hemisphere

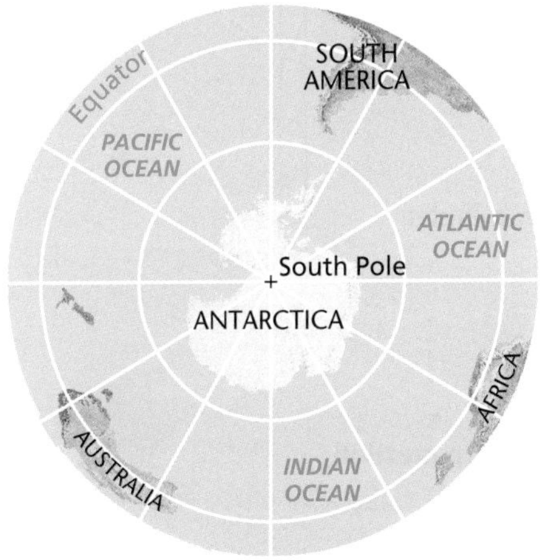

Western Hemisphere

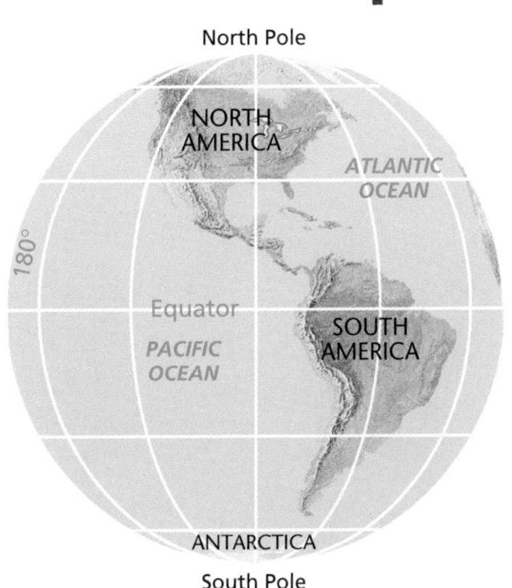

Eastern Hemisphere

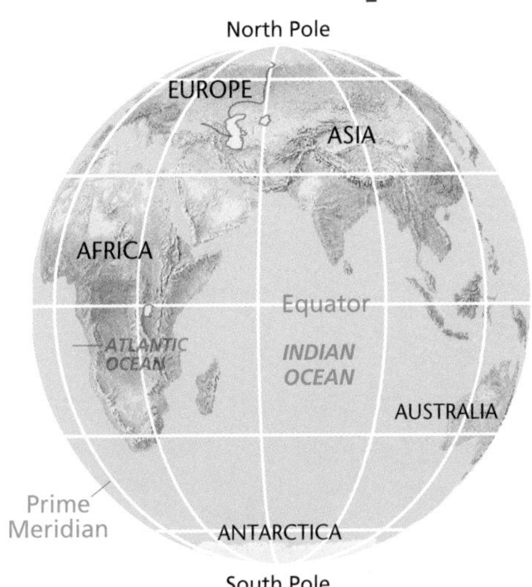

Mapmaking

A **map** is a flat diagram of all or part of the earth's surface. Mapmakers have created different ways of showing our round planet on flat maps. These different ways are called **map projections**. Because the earth is round, there is no way to show it accurately in a flat map. All flat maps are distorted in some way. Mapmakers must choose the type of map projection that is best for their purposes. Many map projections are one of three kinds: cylindrical, conic, or flat-plane.

Cylindrical Projections

Cylindrical projections are based on a cylinder wrapped around the globe. The cylinder touches the globe only at the equator. The meridians are pulled apart and are parallel to each other instead of meeting at the Poles. This causes landmasses near the Poles to appear larger than they really are. The map below is a Mercator projection, one type of cylindrical projection. The Mercator projection is useful for navigators because it shows true direction and shape. However, it distorts the size of land areas near the Poles.

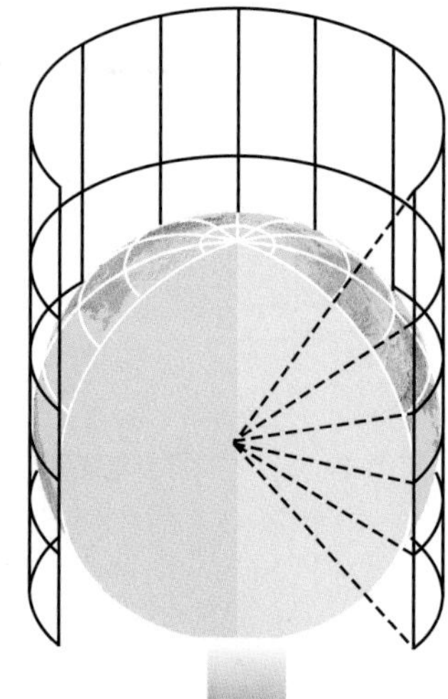

Paper cylinder

Mercator projection

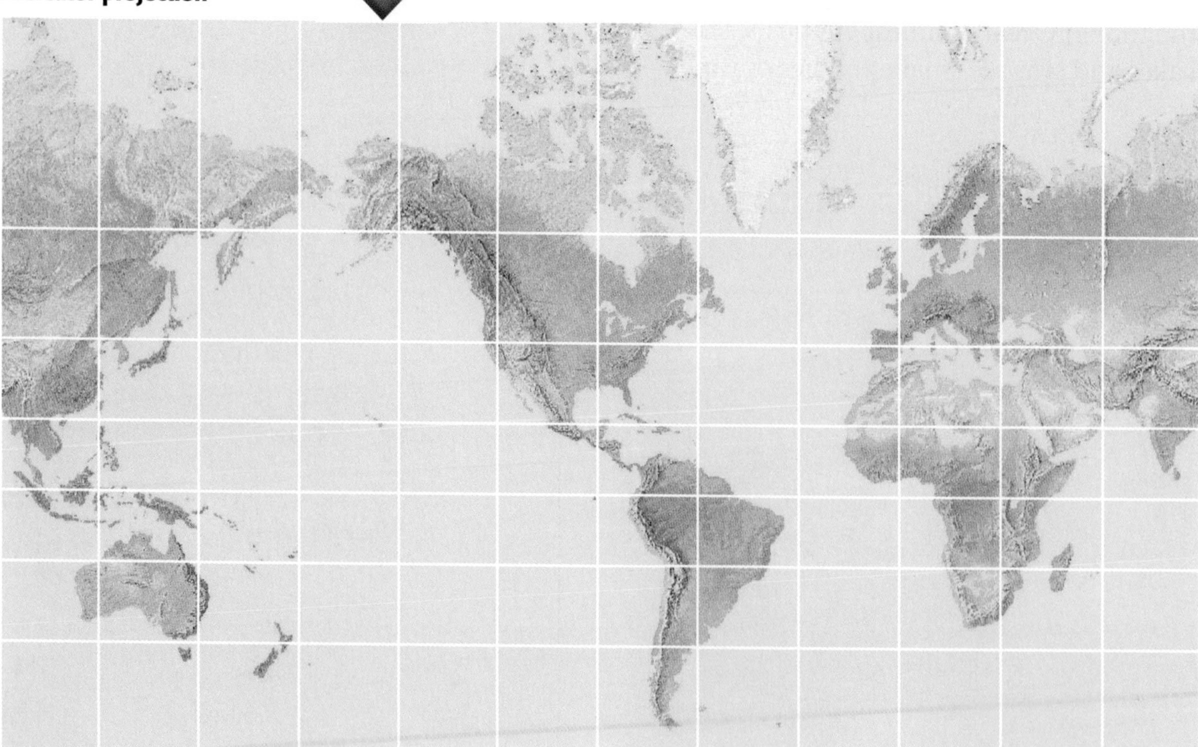

Conic Projections

Conic projections are based on a cone placed over the globe. A conic projection is most accurate along the lines of latitude where it touches the globe. It retains almost true shape and size. Conic projections are most useful for showing areas that have long east-west dimensions, such as the United States.

Paper cone

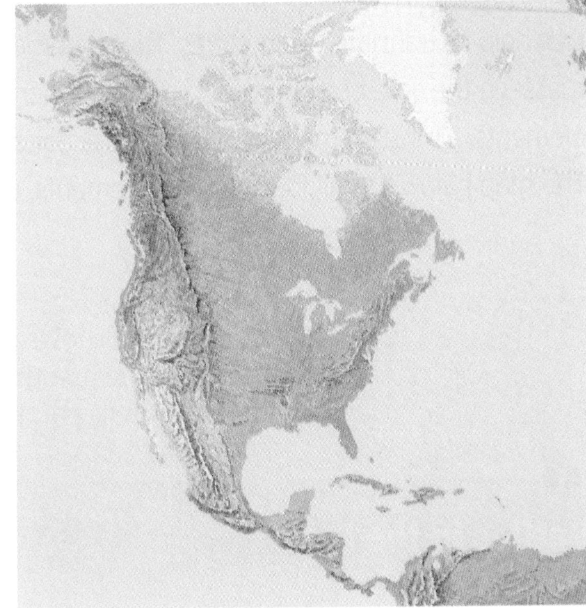

Conic projection

Flat-plane Projections

Flat-plane projections are based on a plane touching the globe at one point, such as at the North Pole or South Pole. A flat-plane projection is useful for showing true direction for airplane pilots and ship navigators. It also shows true area. However, it distorts the true shapes of land massess.

Flat plane

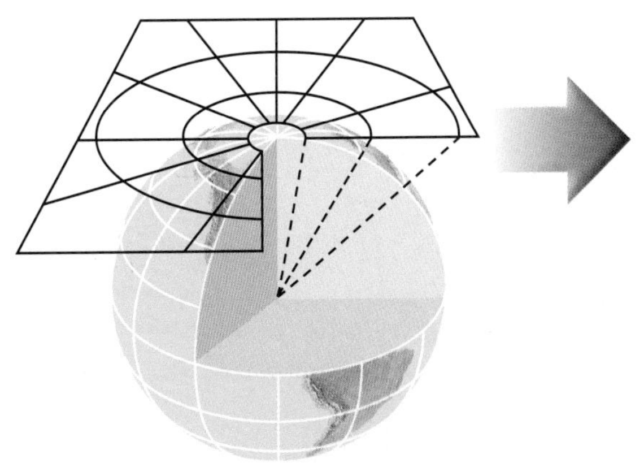

Flat-plane projection

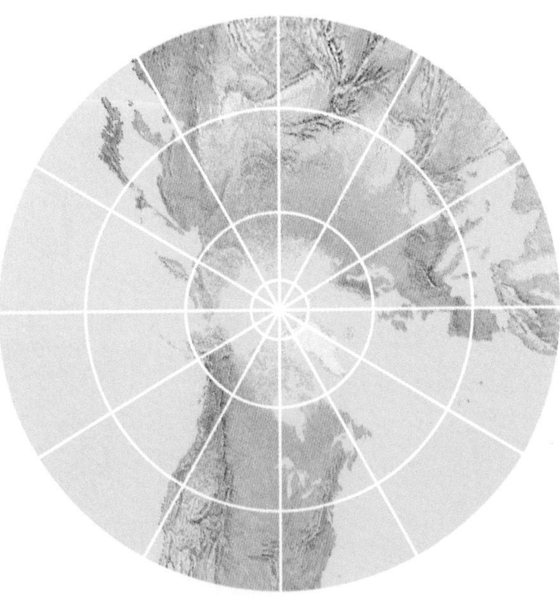

Map Essentials

Maps are like messages sent out in code. Mapmakers provide certain elements that help us translate these codes. These elements help us understand the message they are presenting about a particular part of the world. Of these elements, almost all maps have titles, directional indicators, scales, and legends. The map below has all four of these elements, plus a fifth—a locator map.

❶ Title

A map's **title** shows what the subject of the map is. The map title is usually the first thing you should look at when studying a map, because it tells you what the map is trying to show.

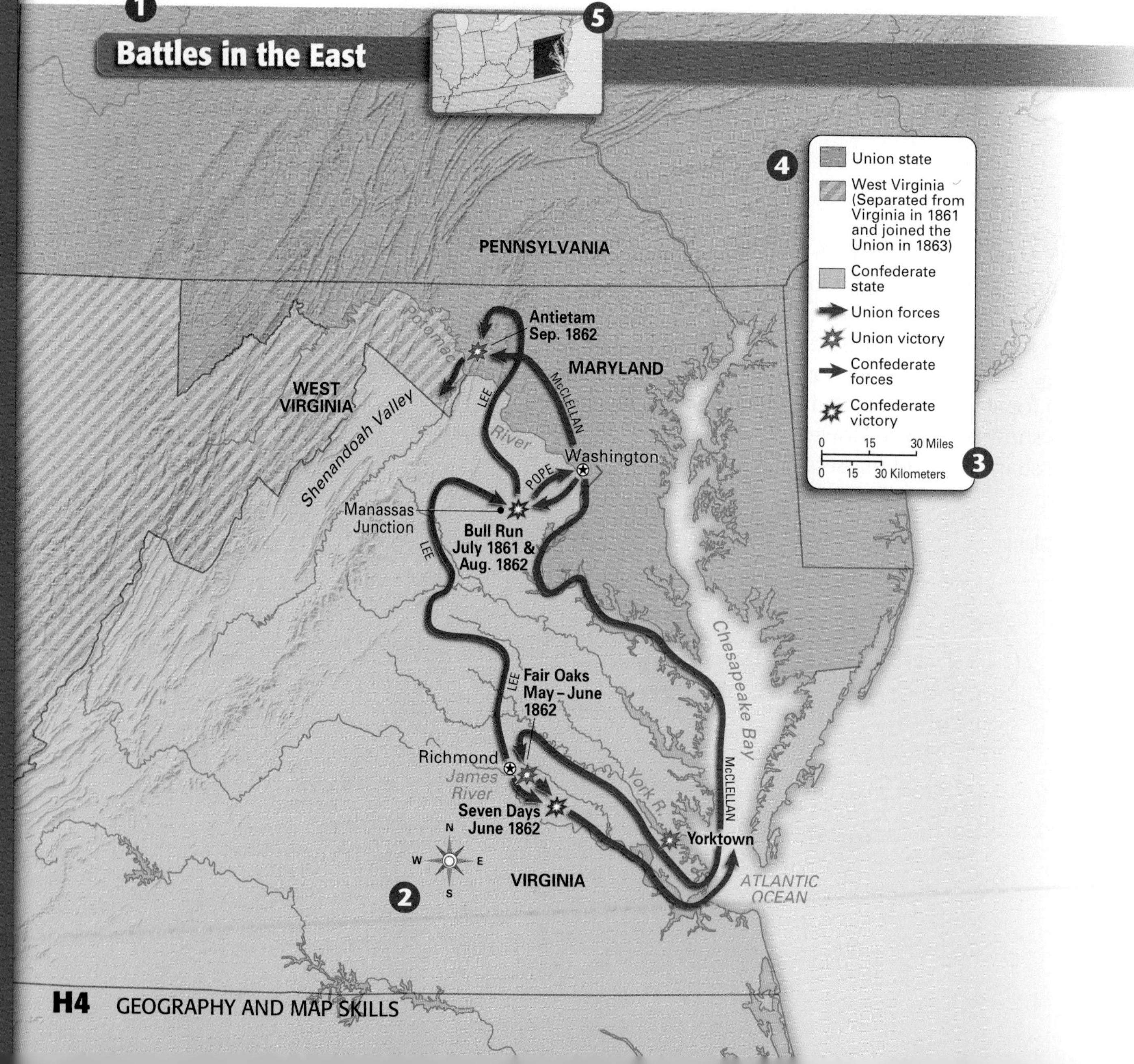

❷ Compass Rose

A directional indicator shows which way north, south, east, and west lie on the map. Some mapmakers use a "north arrow," which points toward the North Pole. Remember, "north" is not always at the top of a map. The way a map is drawn and the location of directions on that map depend on the perspective of the mapmaker. Most maps in this textbook indicate direction by using a compass rose. A **compass rose** has arrows that point to all four principal directions, as shown.

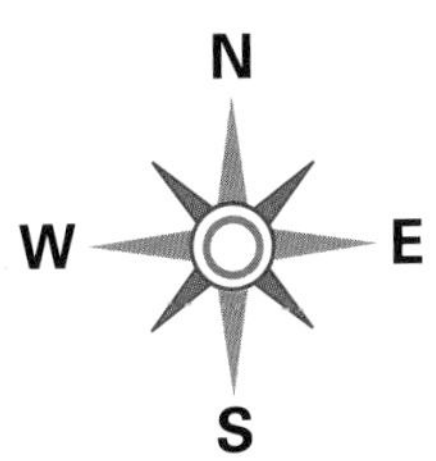

❸ Scale

Mapmakers use scales to represent show the distances between points on a map. Scales may appear on maps in several different forms. The maps in this textbook provide a bar **scale**. Scales give distances in miles and kilometers.

To find the distance between two points on the map, place a piece of paper so that the edge connects the two points. Mark the location of each point on the paper with a line or dot. Then, compare the distance between the two dots with the map's bar scale. The number on the top of the scale gives the distance in miles. The number on the bottom gives the distance in kilometers. Because the distances are given in large intervals, you may have to approximate the actual distance on the scale.

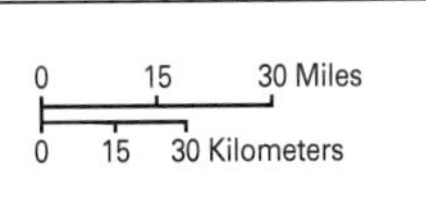

❹ Legend

The **legend**, or key, explains what the symbols on the map represent. Point symbols are used to specify the location of things, such as cities, that do not take up much space on the map. Some legends, such as the one shown here, show colors that represent certain elevations. Other maps might have legends with symbols or colors that represent things such as roads. Legends can also show economic resources, land use, population density, and climate.

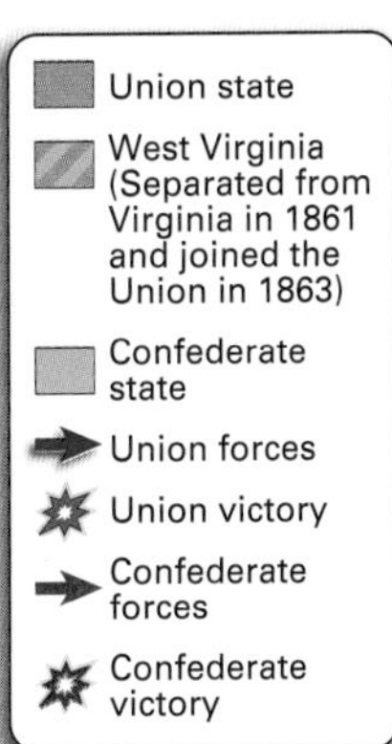

❺ Locator Map

A locator map shows where in the world the area on the map is located. The area shown on the main map is shown in red on the locator map. The locator map also shows surrounding areas so the map reader can see how the information on the map relates to neighboring lands.

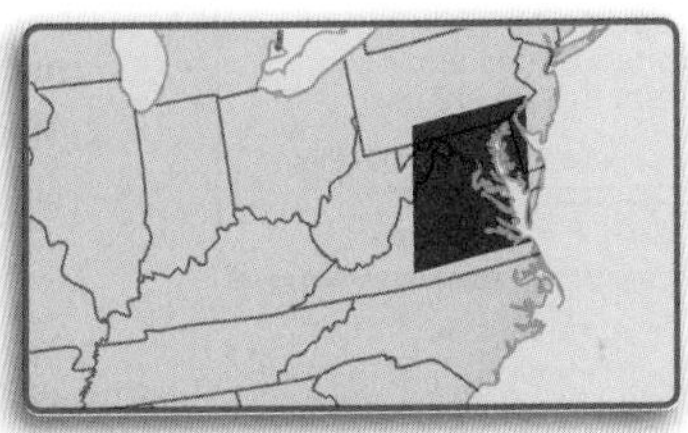

GEOGRAPHY AND MAP SKILLS

Working with Maps

The Atlas at the back of this textbook includes both physical and political maps. Physical maps, like the one you just saw, show the major physical features in a region. These features include things like mountain ranges, rivers, oceans, islands, deserts, and plains. Political maps show the major political features of a region, such as countries and their borders, capitals, and other important cities.

Historical Map

In this textbook, most of the maps you will study are historical maps. Historical maps, such as this one, are maps that show information about the past. This information might be which lands an empire controlled, where a certain group of people lived, what large cities were located in a region, or how a place changed over time. Often colors are used to indicate the different things on the map. Be sure to look at the map title and map legend first to see what the map is showing. What does this map show?

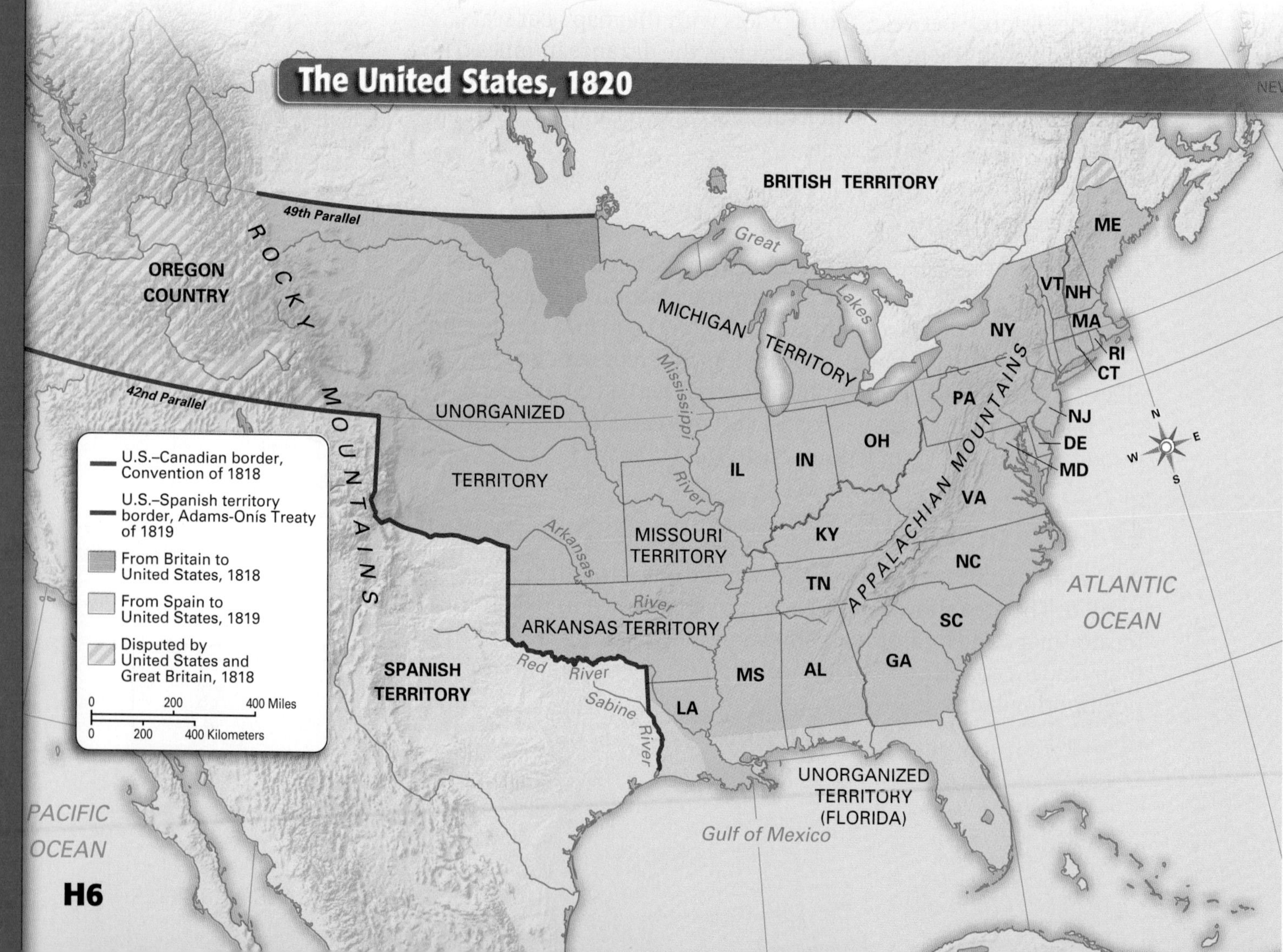

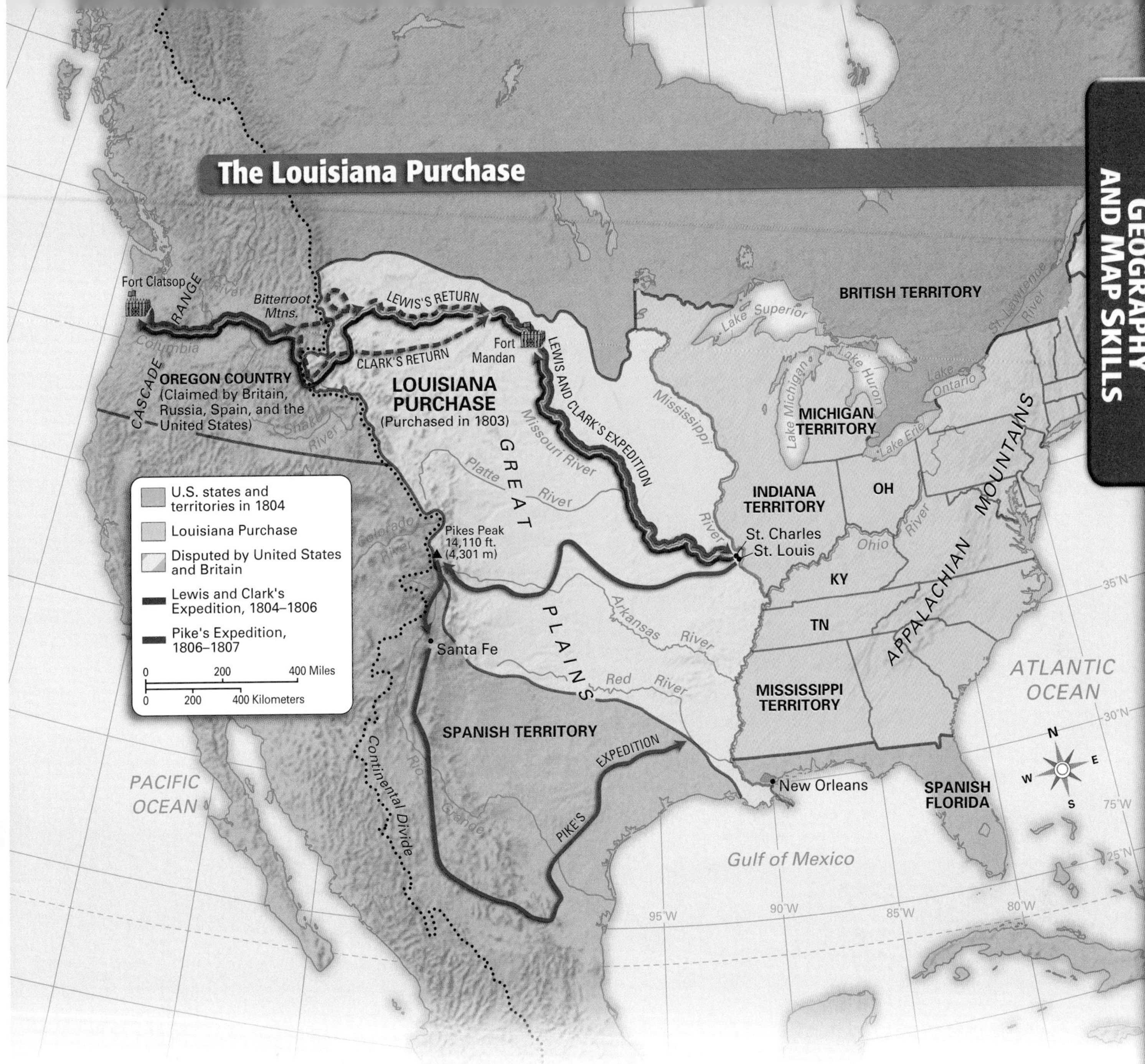

The Louisiana Purchase

Route Map

One special type of historical map is called a route map. A route map, like the one above, shows the route, or path, that someone or something followed. Route maps can show things like trade routes, invasion routes, or the journeys and travels of people. The routes on the map are usually shown with an arrow. If more than one route is shown, several arrows of different colors may be used. What does this route map show?

The maps in this textbook will help you study and understand history. By working with these maps, you will see where important events happened, where empires rose and fell, and where people moved. In studying these maps, you will learn how geography has influenced history.

GEOGRAPHY AND MAP SKILLS

Geographic Dictionary

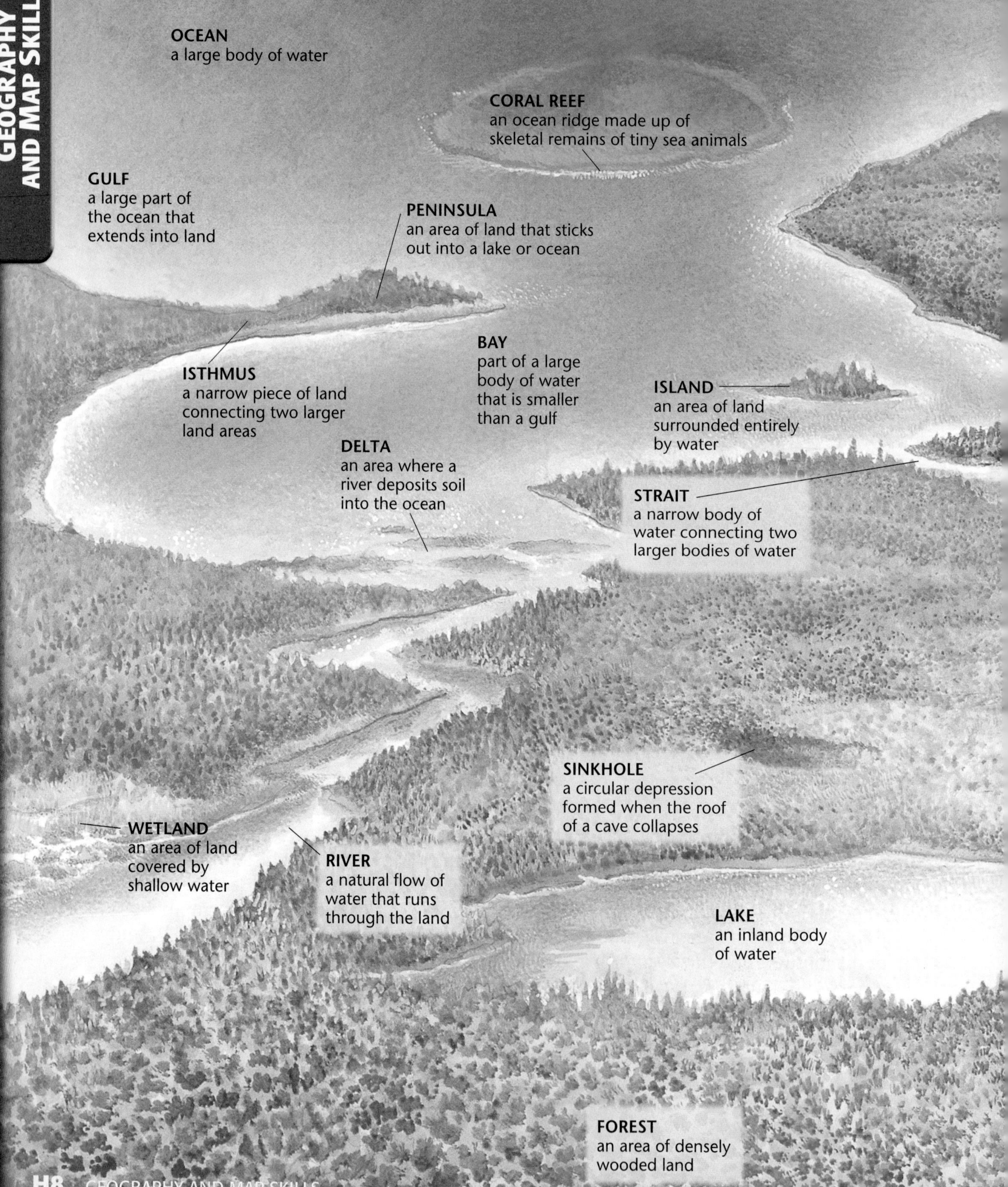

OCEAN
a large body of water

CORAL REEF
an ocean ridge made up of skeletal remains of tiny sea animals

GULF
a large part of the ocean that extends into land

PENINSULA
an area of land that sticks out into a lake or ocean

BAY
part of a large body of water that is smaller than a gulf

ISTHMUS
a narrow piece of land connecting two larger land areas

ISLAND
an area of land surrounded entirely by water

DELTA
an area where a river deposits soil into the ocean

STRAIT
a narrow body of water connecting two larger bodies of water

SINKHOLE
a circular depression formed when the roof of a cave collapses

WETLAND
an area of land covered by shallow water

RIVER
a natural flow of water that runs through the land

LAKE
an inland body of water

FOREST
an area of densely wooded land

COAST
an area of land near the ocean

MOUNTAIN
an area of rugged land that generally rises higher than 2,000 feet

VALLEY
an area of low land between hills or mountains

GLACIER
a large area of slow-moving ice

VOLCANO
an opening in Earth's crust where lava, ash, and gases erupt

CANYON
a deep, narrow valley with steep walls

HILL
a rounded, elevated area of land smaller than a mountain

PLAIN
a nearly flat area

DUNE
a hill of sand shaped by wind

OASIS
an area in the desert with a water source

DESERT
an extremely dry area with little water and few plants

PLATEAU
a large, flat, elevated area of land

GEOGRAPHY AND MAP SKILLS

The Five Themes of Geography

Geography is the study of the world's people and places. As you can imagine, studying the entire world is a big job. To make the job easier, geographers have created the Five Themes of Geography. They are: **Location, Place, Human-Environment Interaction, Movement,** and **Region**. You can think of the Five Themes as five windows you can look through to study a place. If you looked at the same place through five different windows, you would have five different perspectives, or viewpoints, of the place. Using the Five Themes in this way will help you better understand the world's people and places.

1 Location The first thing to study about a place is its location. Where is it? Every place has an absolute location—its exact location on Earth. A place also has a relative location—its location in relation to other places. Use the theme of location to ask questions like, "Where is this place located, and how has its location affected it?"

2 Place Every place in the world is unique and has its own personality and character. Some things that can make a place unique include its weather, plants and animals, history, and the people that live there. Use the theme of place to ask questions like, "What are the unique features of this place, and how are they important?"

3 Human-Environment Interaction People interact with their environment in many ways. They use land to grow food and local materials to build houses. At the same time, a place's environment influences how people live. For example, if the weather is cold, people wear warm clothes. Use the theme of human-environment interaction to ask questions like, "What is this place's environment like, and how does it affect the people who live there?"

4 Movement The world is constantly changing, and places are affected by the movement of people, goods, ideas, and physical forces. For example, people come and go, new businesses begin, and rivers change their course. Use the theme of movement to ask questions like, "How is this place changing, and why?"

5 Region A region is an area that has one or more features that make it different from surrounding areas. A desert, a country, and a coastal area are all regions. Geographers use regions to break the world into smaller pieces that are easier to study. Use the theme of region to ask questions like "What common features does this area share, and how is it different from other areas?"

1
LOCATION
The United States is located in the Western Hemisphere. Forty-eight of the states are located between Mexico and Canada. This location has good farmland, many resources, and many different natural environments.

2
PLACE
New York City is one of the most powerful cities in the world. The people of New York also make the city one of the most ethnically diverse places in the world.

3
HUMAN-ENVIRONMENT INTERACTION
People near Las Vegas, Nevada, transform the desert landscape by building new neighborhoods. Americans modify their environment in many other ways—by controlling rivers, building roads, and creating farmland.

5
REGION
The United States is a political region with one government. At the same time, smaller regions can be found inside the country, such as the Badlands in South Dakota.

4
MOVEMENT
People, goods, and ideas are constantly moving to and from places such as Seattle, Washington. As some places grow, others get smaller, but every place is always changing.

Become an Active Reader

by Dr. Kylene Beers

Did you ever think you would begin reading your social studies book by reading about reading? Actually, it makes better sense than you might think. You would probably make sure you learned some soccer skills and strategies before playing in a game. Similarly, you need to learn some reading skills and strategies before reading your social studies book. In other words, you need to make sure you know whatever you need to know in order to read this book successfully.

Tip #1
Use the Reading Social Studies Pages

Take advantage of the two pages on reading at the beginning of every chapter. Those pages introduce the chapter themes; explain a reading skill or strategy; and identify key terms, people, and academic vocabulary.

Themes

Why are themes important? They help our minds organize facts and information. For example, when we talk about baseball, we may talk about types of pitches. When we talk about movies, we may discuss animation.

Historians are no different. When they discuss history or social studies, they tend to think about some common themes: Economics, Geography, Religion, Politics, Society and Culture, and Science and Technology.

Reading Skill or Strategy

Good readers use a number of skills and strategies to make sure they understand what they are reading. These lessons will give you the tools you need to read and understand social studies.

Key Terms, People, and Academic Vocabulary

Before you read the chapter, review these words and think about them. Have you heard the word before? What do you already know about the people? Then watch for these words and their meanings as you read the chapter.

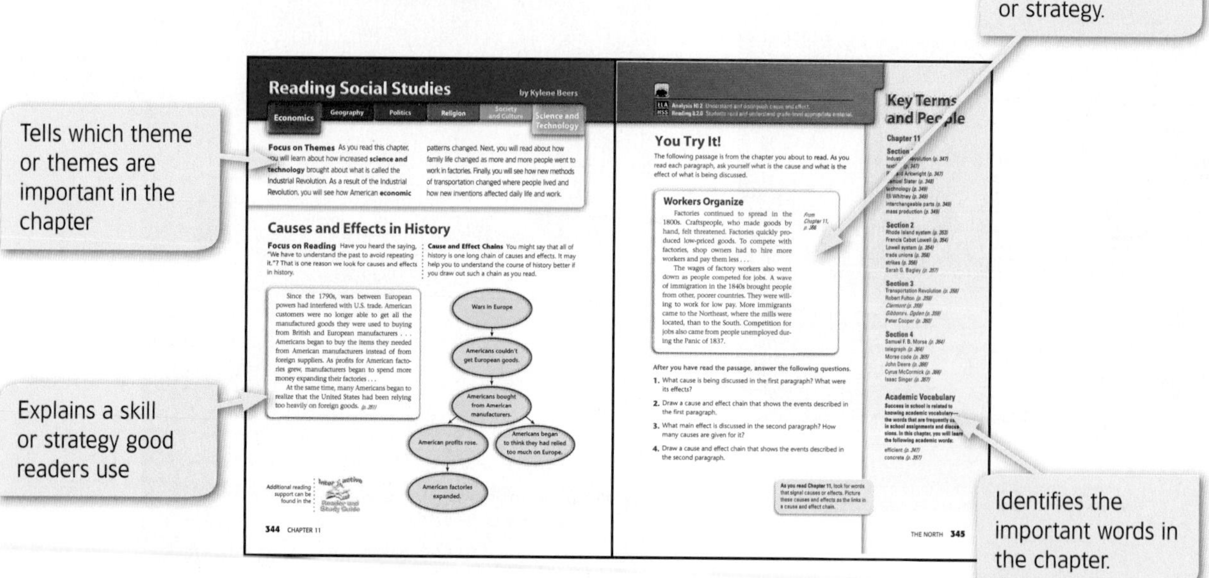
Gives you practice in the reading skill or strategy.
Tells which theme or themes are important in the chapter
Explains a skill or strategy good readers use
Identifies the important words in the chapter.
Reading Social Studies
Causes and Effects in History
You Try It!
Workers Organize
Key Terms and People

Tip #2

Read like a Skilled Reader

You will never get better at reading your social studies book—or any book for that matter—unless you spend some time thinking about how to be a better reader.

Skilled readers do the following:

- They preview what they are supposed to read before they actually begin reading. They look for vocabulary words, titles of sections, information in the margin, or maps or charts they should study.
- They divide their notebook paper into two columns. They title one column "Notes from the Chapter" and the other column "Questions or Comments I Have."
- They take notes in both columns as they read.
- They read like **active readers**. The Active Reading list below shows you what that means.
- They use clues in the text to help them figure out where the text is going. The best clues are called signal words.

Chronological Order Signal Words: *first, second, third, before, after, later, next, following that, earlier, finally*

Cause and Effect Signal Words: *because of, due to, as a result of, the reason for, therefore, consequently*

Comparison/Contrast Signal Words: *likewise, also, as well as, similarly, on the other hand*

READING SOCIAL STUDIES

Active Reading

Successful readers are **active readers**. These readers know that it is up to them to figure out what the text means. Here are some steps you can take to become an active, and successful, reader.

Predict what will happen next based on what has already happened. When your predictions don't match what happens in the text, re-read the confusing parts.

Question what is happening as you read. Constantly ask yourself why things have happened, what things mean, and what caused certain events.

Summarize what you are reading frequently. Do not try to summarize the entire chapter! Read a bit and then summarize it. Then read on.

Connect what is happening in the part you're reading to what you have already read.

Clarify your understanding. Stop occasionally to ask yourself whether you are confused by anything. You may need to re-read to clarify, or you may need to read further and collect more information before you can understand.

Visualize what is happening in the text. Try to see the events or places in your mind by drawing maps, making charts, or jotting down notes about what you are reading.

Reading Social Studies

Tip #3

Pay Attention to Vocabulary

It is no fun to read something when you don't know what the words mean, but you can't learn new words if you only use or read the words you already know. In this book, we know we have probably used some words you don't know. But, we have followed a pattern as we have used more difficult words.

Key Terms and People

At the beginning of each section you will find a list of key terms or people that you will need to know. Be on the lookout for those words as you read through the section.

...pped after 1783.
..., Britain forced American mer-
... high **tariffs**—taxes on imports
... tariffs applied to goods such

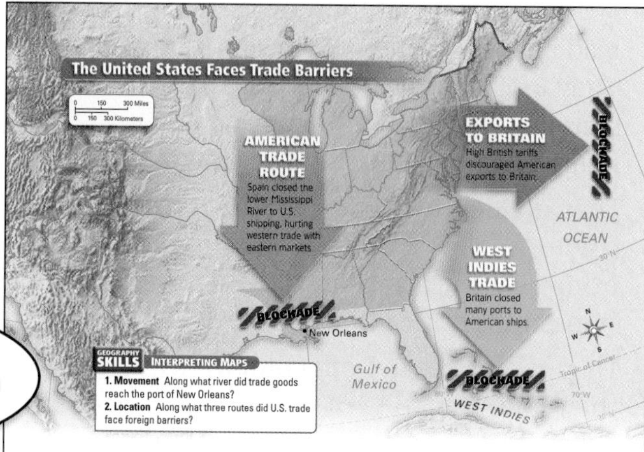

AMERICAN TRADE ROUTE

EXPORTS TO BRITAIN
High British tariffs discouraged American exports to Britain.

GEOGRAPHY SKILLS Interpreting Maps

1. **Movement** Along what river did trade goods reach the port of New Orleans?
2. **Location** Along what three routes did U.S. trade face foreign barriers?

Trade with Britain

The United States also faced problems trading with Great Britain. After the signing of the Treaty of Paris, Britain closed many of its ports to American ships. Before the Revolutionary War, colonial ships had traded a great deal with the British West Indies and stopped there on their way to other destinations. This travel and trading stopped after 1783.

In addition, Britain forced American merchants to pay high **tariffs**—taxes on imports or exports. The tariffs applied to goods such as rice, tobacco, tar, and oil that were grown or mined in the United States and then sold in Britain. Merchants had to raise prices to cover the tariffs. Ultimately, the costs would be passed on to customers, who had to pay higher prices for the goods. The economic condition of the country was getting worse by the day.

Trade with Spain

In 1784 Spanish officials closed the lower Mississippi River to U.S. shipping. Western farmers and merchants were furious because they used the Mississippi to send goods to eastern and foreign markets. Congress tried to work out an agreement with Spain, but the plan did not receive a majority vote in Congress. The plan could not be passed. As a result, Spain broke off the negotiations.

Many state leaders began to criticize the national government. Rhode Island's representatives wrote, "Our federal government is but a name; a mere shadow without substance [power]." Critics believed that Spain might have continued to negotiate if the United States had possessed a strong military. These leaders believed that the national government needed to be more powerful.

FORMING A GOVERNMENT 121

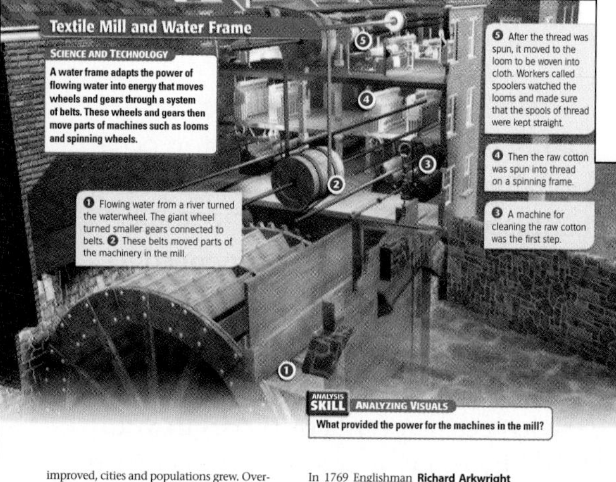

Textile Mill and Water Frame
Science and Technology
A water frame adapts the power of flowing water into energy that moves wheels and gears through a system of belts. These wheels and gears then move parts of machines such as looms and spinning wheels.
1 Flowing water from a river turned the waterwheel. The giant wheel turned smaller gears connected to belts. 2 These belts moved parts of the machinery in the mill.
3 A machine for cleaning the raw cotton was the first step.
4 Then the raw cotton was spun into thread on a spinning frame.
5 After the thread was spun, it moved to the loom to be woven into cloth. Workers called spoolers watched the looms and made sure that the spools of thread were kept straight.

ANALYSIS SKILL Analyzing Visuals

What provided the power for the machines in the mill?

improved, cities and populations grew. Overseas trade also expanded. Traditional manufacturing methods did not produce enough goods to meet everyone's needs.

People began creating ways to use machines to make things more efficient. These changes led to the **Industrial Revolution**, a period of rapid growth in using machines for manufacturing and production that began in the mid-1700s.

Textile Industry

The first important breakthrough of the Industrial Revolution took place in how **textiles**, or cloth items, were made. Before the Industrial Revolution, spinning thread took much more time than making cloth. Several workers were needed to spin enough thread to supply a single weaver.

In 1769 Englishman **Richard Arkwright** invented a large spinning machine called a water frame. The water frame could produce dozens of cotton threads at the same time. It lowered the cost of cotton cloth and increased the speed of textile production.

The water frame used flowing water as its source of power. Merchants began to build large textile mills, or factories, near rivers and streams. The mills were filled with spinning machines. Merchants began hiring people to work in the mills.

Additional improvements also speeded up the spinning process. Britain soon had the world's most productive textile manufacturing industry.

Academic Vocabulary
efficient productive and not wasteful

READING CHECK **Drawing Conclusions** How did machines speed up textile manufacturing?

THE NORTH 347

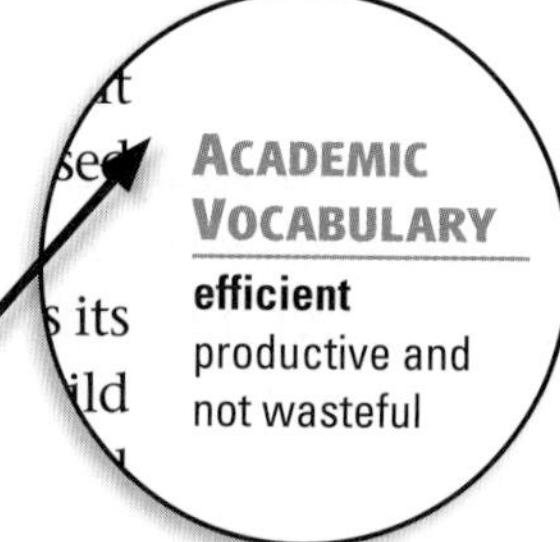

Academic Vocabulary

When we use a word that is important in all classes, not just social studies, we define it in the margin under the heading Academic Vocabulary. You will run into these academic words in other textbooks, so you should learn what they mean while reading this book.

Social Studies Vocabulary

We know that some words are special to this particular topic of social studies, United States history. As you read this book, you will be more successful if you know the meaning of the words in the following list.

Social Studies Words to Know

Time	
AD	refers to dates after Jesus's birth
BC	refers to dates before the birth of Jesus of Nazareth
BCE	refers to "Before Common Era," dates before the birth of Jesus of Nazareth
CE	refers to "Common Era," dates after Jesus's birth
century	a period of 100 years
decade	a period of 10 years

The Earth and Its Resources	
climate	the weather conditions in a certain area over a long period of time
geography	the study of the earth's physical and cultural features
physical features	the features on the land's surface, such as mountains and rivers
region	an area with one or more features that make it different from surrounding areas
resources	materials found on the earth that people need and value

People and the Way They Live	
civilization	the culture of a particular time or place
culture	the knowledge, beliefs, customs, and values of a group of people
custom	a repeated practice; tradition
economy	the system in which people make and exchange goods and services
society	a group of people who share common traditions
trade	the exchange of goods or services

Politics and Government	
civil	having to do with the citizens of a country
democracy	governmental rule by the people, usually on a majority rule principle
independence	freedom from forceful rule
monarchy	governmental rule by one person, a king or queen
North	the region of the United States sometimes defined by the states that did not secede from the Union during the Civil War
rebellion	an organized resistance to the established government
South	the region of the United States sometimes defined by the states that seceded from the Union to form the Confederate States of America

Academic Words

If only . . .

If only reading in school was like reading a letter from your best friend.

If only reading in History was like reading *Harry Potter.*

It can be . . .if you learn the language!

There is a reason that you feel uncomfortable with reading academic textbooks. Common words in these books account for less than 2% of the words in your favorite novels. No wonder reading in school seems so different!

Academic vocabulary refers to words that are used in most of your school subjects. The Holt Social Studies program has identified Academic Words that will be highlighted throughout this textbook. The Holt program provides structured practice to help support student proficiency with this specialized vocabulary.

Grade 6 Academic Words

acquire	to get
agreement	a decision reached by two or more people or groups
aspects	parts
authority	power, right to rule
cause	the reason something happens
classical	referring to the cultures of ancient Greece or Rome
contract	a binding legal agreement
develop/ development	creation
distribute	to divide among a group of people
effect	the results of an action or decision
establish	to set up or create
ideal	ideas or goals that people try to live up to
impact	effect, result
method	a way of doing something
neutral	unbiased, not favoring either side in a conflict
primary	main, most important
principle	basic belief, rule, or law
process	a series of steps by which a task is accomplished
purpose	the reason something is done
rebel	to fight against authority
role	a part or function
strategy	a plan for fighting a battle or war
vary/various	to be different

Grade 7 Academic Words

affect	to change or influence
aspects	parts
authority	power, right to rule
classical	referring to the cultures of ancient Greece or Rome
develop/ development	the process of growing or improving
efficient/ efficiency	productive and not wasteful
element	part
establish	to set up or create
features	characteristics
impact	effect, result
influence	change, or have an effect on
innovation	a new idea or way of doing something
logic/logical	reasoned, well thought out
policy	rule, course of action
principle	basic belief, rule, or law
procedure	a series of steps taken to accomplish a task
process	a series of steps by which a task is accomplished
rebel	to fight against authority
role	assigned behavior
strategy	a plan for fighting a battle or war
structure	the way something is set up or organized
traditional	customary, time-honored
values	ideas that people hold dear and try to live by
vary/various	of many types

Grade 8 Academic Words

abstract	expressing a quality or idea without reference to an actual thing
acquire	to get
advocate	to plead in favor of
agreement	a decision reached by two or more people or groups
aspects	parts
authority	power, right to rule
circumstances	surrounding situation
complex	difficult, not simple
concrete	specific, real
consequences	the effects of a particular event or events
contemporary	existing at the same time
criteria	rules for defining
develop/ development	the process of growing or improving
distinct	separate
efficient/ efficiency	productive and not wasteful
element	part
establish	to set up or create
execute	to perform, carry out
explicit	fully revealed without vagueness
facilitate	to bring about
factor	causes
function	use or purpose
implement	to put in place
implications	effects of a decision
implicit	understood though not clearly put into words
incentive	something that leads people to follow a certain course of action
influence	change, or have an effect on
innovation	a new idea or way of doing something
method	a way of doing something
motive	a reason for doing something
neutral	unbiased, not favoring either side in a conflict
policy	rule, course of action
primary	main, most important
principle	basic belief, rule, or law
procedure	a series of steps taken to accomplish a task
process	a series of steps by which a task is accomplished
reaction	a response
role	assigned behavior
strategy	a plan for fighting a battle or war
vary/various	of many types

History–Social Science Content Standards

Students in grade eight study the ideas, issues, and events from the framing of the Constitution up to World War I, with an emphasis on America's role in the war. After reviewing the development of America's democratic institutions founded on the Judeo-Christian heritage and English parliamentary traditions, particularly the shaping of the Constitution, students trace the development of American politics, society, culture, and economy and relate them to the emergence of major regional differences. They learn about the challenges facing the new nation, with an emphasis on the causes, course, and consequences of the Civil War. They make connections between the rise of industrialization and contemporary social and economic conditions.

8.1 Students understand the major events preceding the founding of the nation and relate their significance to the development of American constitutional democracy.

1. Describe the relationship between the moral and political ideas of the Great Awakening and the development of revolutionary fervor.
2. Analyze the philosophy of government expressed in the Declaration of Independence, with an emphasis on government as a means of securing individual rights (e.g., key phrases such as "all men are created equal, that they are endowed by their Creator with certain unalienable Rights").
3. Analyze how the American Revolution affected other nations, especially France.
4. Describe the nation's blend of civic republicanism, classical liberal principles, and English parliamentary traditions.

8.2 Students analyze the political principles underlying the U.S. Constitution and compare the enumerated and implied powers of the federal government.

1. Discuss the significance of the Magna Carta, the English Bill of Rights, and the Mayflower Compact.
2. Analyze the Articles of Confederation and the Constitution and the success of each in implementing the ideals of the Declaration of Independence.
3. Evaluate the major debates that occurred during the development of the Constitution and their ultimate resolutions in such areas as shared power among institutions, divided state-federal power, slavery, the rights of individuals and states (later addressed by the addition of the Bill of Rights), and the status of American Indian nations under the commerce clause.
4. Describe the political philosophy underpinning the Constitution as specified in the *Federalist Papers* (authored by James Madison, Alexander Hamilton, and John Jay) and the role of such leaders as Madison, George Washington, Roger Sherman, Gouverneur Morris, and James Wilson in the writing and ratification of the Constitution.
5. Understand the significance of Jefferson's Statute for Religious Freedom as a forerunner of the First Amendment and the origins, purpose, and differing views of

the founding fathers on the issue of the separation of church and state.

6. Enumerate the powers of government set forth in the Constitution and the fundamental liberties ensured by the Bill of Rights.
7. Describe the principles of federalism, dual sovereignty, separation of powers, checks and balances, the nature and purpose of majority rule, and the ways in which the American idea of constitutionalism preserves individual rights.

8.3 Students understand the foundation of the American political system and the ways in which citizens participate in it.

1. Analyze the principles and concepts codified in state constitutions between 1777 and 1781 that created the context out of which American political institutions and ideas developed.
2. Explain how the ordinances of 1785 and 1787 privatized national resources and transferred federally owned lands into private holdings, townships, and states.
3. Enumerate the advantages of a common market among the states as foreseen in and protected by the Constitution's clauses on interstate commerce, common coinage, and full-faith and credit.
4. Understand how the conflicts between Thomas Jefferson and Alexander Hamilton resulted in the emergence of two political parties (e.g., view of foreign policy, Alien and Sedition Acts, economic policy, National Bank, funding and assumption of the revolutionary debt).
5. Know the significance of domestic resistance movements and ways in which the central government responded to such movements (e.g., Shays' Rebellion, the Whiskey Rebellion).
6. Describe the basic law-making process and how the Constitution provides numerous opportunities for citizens to participate in the political process and to monitor and influence government (e.g., function of elections, political parties, interest groups).
7. Understand the functions and responsibilities of a free press.

8.4 Students analyze the aspirations and ideals of the people of the new nation.

1. Describe the country's physical landscapes, political divisions, and territorial expansion during the terms of the first four presidents.
2. Explain the policy significance of famous speeches (e.g., Washington's Farewell Address, Jefferson's 1801 Inaugural Address, John Q. Adams's Fourth of July 1821 Address).
3. Analyze the rise of capitalism and the economic problems and conflicts that accompanied it (e.g., Jackson's opposition to the National Bank; early decisions of the U.S. Supreme Court that reinforced the sanctity of contracts and a capitalist economic system of law).
4. Discuss daily life, including traditions in art, music, and literature, of early national America (e.g., through writings by Washington Irving, James Fenimore Cooper).

8.5 Students analyze U.S. foreign policy in the early Republic.

1. Understand the political and economic causes and consequences of the War of 1812 and know the major battles, leaders, and events that led to a final peace.
2. Know the changing boundaries of the United States and describe the relationships the country had with its neighbors (current Mexico and Canada) and Europe, including the influence of the Monroe Doctrine, and how those relationships influenced westward expansion and the Mexican-American War.
3. Outline the major treaties with American Indian nations during the administrations of the first four presidents and the varying outcomes of those treaties.

8.6 Students analyze the divergent paths of the American people from 1800 to the mid-1800s and the challenges they faced, with emphasis on the Northeast.

1. Discuss the influence of industrialization and technological developments on theregion, including human modification of the landscape and how physical geography shaped human actions (e.g., growth of cities, deforestation, farming, mineral extraction).
2. Outline the physical obstacles to and the economic and political factors involved in building a network of roads, canals, and railroads (e.g., Henry Clay's American System).
3. List the reasons for the wave of immigration from Northern Europe to the United States and describe the growth in the number, size, and spatial arrangements of cities (e.g., Irish immigrants and the Great Irish Famine).
4. Study the lives of black Americans who gained freedom in the North and founded schools and churches to advance their rights and communities.
5. Trace the development of the American education system from its earliest roots, including the roles of religious and private schools and Horace Mann's campaign for free public education and its assimilating role in American culture.
6. Examine the women's suffrage movement (e.g., biographies, writings, and speeches of Elizabeth Cady Stanton, Margaret Fuller, Lucretia Mott, Susan B. Anthony).
7. Identify common themes in American art as well as transcendentalism and individualism (e.g., writings about and by Ralph Waldo Emerson, Henry David Thoreau, Herman Melville, Louisa May Alcott, Nathaniel Hawthorne, Henry Wadsworth Longfellow).

8.7 Students analyze the divergent paths of the American people in the South from 1800 to the mid-1800s and the challenges they faced.

1. Describe the development of the agrarian economy in the South, identify the locations of the cotton-producing states, and discuss the significance of cotton and the cotton gin.
2. Trace the origins and development of slavery; its effects on black Americans and on the region's political, social, religious, economic, and cultural development; and identify the strategies that were tried to both overturn and preserve it (e.g., through the writings and historical documents on Nat Turner, Denmark Vesey).
3. Examine the characteristics of white Southern society and how the physical environment influenced events and conditions prior to the Civil War.
4. Compare the lives of and opportunities for free blacks in the North with those of free blacks in the South.

8.8 Students analyze the divergent paths of the American people in the West from 1800 to the mid-1800s and the challenges they faced.

1. Discuss the election of Andrew Jackson as president in 1828, the importance of Jacksonian democracy, and his actions as president (e.g., the spoils system, veto of the National Bank, policy of Indian removal, opposition to the Supreme Court).
2. Describe the purpose, challenges, and economic incentives associated with westward expansion, including the concept of Manifest Destiny (e.g., the Lewis and Clark expedition, accounts of the removal of Indians, the Cherokees' "Trail of Tears," settlement of the Great Plains) and the territorial acquisitions that spanned numerous decades.

3. Describe the role of pioneer women and the new status that western women achieved (e.g., Laura Ingalls Wilder, Annie Bidwell; slave women gaining freedom in the West; Wyoming granting suffrage to women in 1869).
4. Examine the importance of the great rivers and the struggle over water rights.
5. Discuss Mexican settlements and their locations, cultural traditions, attitudes toward slavery, land-grant system, and economies.
6. Describe the Texas War for Independence and the Mexican-American War, including territorial settlements, the aftermath of the wars, and the effects the wars had on the lives of Americans, including Mexican Americans today.

8.9 Students analyze the early and steady attempts to abolish slavery and to realize the ideals of the Declaration of Independence.

1. Describe the leaders of the movement (e.g., John Quincy Adams and his proposed constitutional amendment, John Brown and the armed resistance, Harriet Tubman and the Underground Railroad, Benjamin Franklin, Theodore Weld, William Lloyd Garrison, Frederick Douglass).
2. Discuss the abolition of slavery in early state constitutions.
3. Describe the significance of the Northwest Ordinance in education and in the banning of slavery in new states north of the Ohio River.
4. Discuss the importance of the slavery issue as raised by the annexation of Texas and California's admission to the union as a free state under the Compromise of 1850.
5. Analyze the significance of the States' Rights Doctrine, the Missouri Compromise (1820), the Wilmot Proviso (1846), the Compromise of 1850, Henry Clay's role in the Missouri Compromise and the Compromise of 1850, the Kansas-Nebraska Act (1854), the *Dred Scott* v. *Sandford* decision (1857), and the Lincoln-Douglas debates (1858).
6. Describe the lives of free blacks and the laws that limited their freedom and economic opportunities.

8.10 Students analyze the multiple causes, key events, and complex consequences of the Civil War.

1. Compare the conflicting interpretations of state and federal authority as emphasized in the speeches and writings of statesmen such as Daniel Webster and John C. Calhoun.
2. Trace the boundaries constituting the North and the South, the geographical differences between the two regions, and the differences between agrarians and industrialists.
3. Identify the constitutional issues posed by the doctrine of nullification and secession and the earliest origins of that doctrine.
4. Discuss Abraham Lincoln's presidency and his significant writings and speeches and their relationship to the Declaration of Independence, such as his "House Divided" speech (1858), Gettysburg Address (1863), Emancipation Proclamation (1863), and inaugural addresses (1861 and 1865).
5. Study the views and lives of leaders (e.g., Ulysses S. Grant, Jefferson Davis, Robert E. Lee) and soldiers on both sides of the war, including those of black soldiers and regiments.
6. Describe critical developments and events in the war, including the major battles, geographical advantages and obstacles, technological advances, and General Lee's surrender at Appomattox.
7. Explain how the war affected combatants, civilians, the physical environment, and future warfare.

8.11 Students analyze the character and lasting consequences of Reconstruction.

1. List the original aims of Reconstruction and describe its effects on the political and social structures of different regions.
2. Identify the push-pull factors in the movement of former slaves to the cities in the North and to the West and their differing experiences in those regions (e.g., the experiences of Buffalo Soldiers).
3. Understand the effects of the Freedmen's Bureau and the restrictions placed on the rights and opportunities of freedmen, including racial segregation and "Jim Crow" laws.
4. Trace the rise of the Ku Klux Klan and describe the Klan's effects.
5. Understand the Thirteenth, Fourteenth, and Fifteenth Amendments to the Constitution and analyze their connection to Reconstruction.

8.12 Students analyze the transformation of the American economy and the changing social and political conditions in the United States in response to the Industrial Revolution.

1. Trace patterns of agricultural and industrial development as they relate to climate, use of natural resources, markets, and trade and locate such development on a map.
2. Identify the reasons for the development of federal Indian policy and the wars with American Indians and their relationship to agricultural development and industrialization.
3. Explain how states and the federal government encouraged business expansionthrough tariffs, banking, land grants, and subsidies.
4. Discuss entrepreneurs, industrialists, and bankers in politics, commerce, and industry (e.g., Andrew Carnegie, John D. Rockefeller, Leland Stanford).
5. Examine the location and effects of urbanization, renewed immigration, and industrialization (e.g., the effects on social fabric of cities, wealth and economic opportunity, the conservation movement).
6. Discuss child labor, working conditions, and laissez-faire policies toward big business and examine the labor movement, including its leaders (e.g., Samuel Gompers), its demand for collective bargaining, and its strikes and protests over labor conditions.
7. Identify the new sources of large-scale immigration and the contributions of immigrants to the building of cities and the economy; explain the ways in which new social and economic patterns encouraged assimilation of newcomers into the mainstream amidst growing cultural diversity; and discuss the new wave of nativism.
8. Identify the characteristics and impact of Grangerism and Populism.
9. Name the significant inventors and their inventions and identify how they improved the quality of life (e.g., Thomas Edison, Alexander Graham Bell, Orville and Wilbur Wright).

Historical and Social Sciences Analysis Skills

The intellectual skills noted below are to be learned through, and applied to, the content standards for grades six through eight. They are to be assessed *only in conjunction* with the content standards in grades six through eight.

In addition to the standards for grades six through eight, students demonstrate the following intellectual reasoning, reflection, and research skills:

Chronological and Spatial Thinking

1. Students explain how major events are related to one another in time.
2. Students construct various time lines of key events, people, and periods of the historical era they are studying.
3. Students use a variety of maps and documents to identify physical and cultural features of neighborhoods, cities, states, and countries and to explain the historical migration of people, expansion and disintegration of empires, and the growth of economic systems.

Research, Evidence, and Point of View

1. Students frame questions that can be answered by historical study and research.
2. Students distinguish fact from opinion in historical narratives and stories.
3. Students distinguish relevant from irrelevant information, essential from incidental information, and verifiable from unverifiable information in historical narratives and stories.
4. Students assess the credibility of primary and secondary sources and draw sound conclusions from them.
5. Students detect the different historical points of view on historical events and determine the context in which the historical statements were made (the questions asked, sources used, author's perspectives).

Historical Interpretation

1. Students explain the central issues and problems from the past, placing people and events in a matrix of time and place.
2. Students understand and distinguish cause, effect, sequence, and correlation in historical events, including the long- and short-term causal relations.
3. Students explain the sources of historical continuity and how the combination of ideas and events explains the emergence of new patterns.
4. Students recognize the role of chance, oversight, and error in history.
5. Students recognize that interpretations of history are subject to change as new information is uncovered.
6. Students interpret basic indicators of economic performance and conduct cost-benefit analyses of economic and political issues.

How to Make This Book Work for You

Studying U.S. history will be easy for you using this textbook. Take a few minutes to become familiar with the easy-to-use structure and special features of this history book. See how this U.S. history textbook will make history come alive for you!

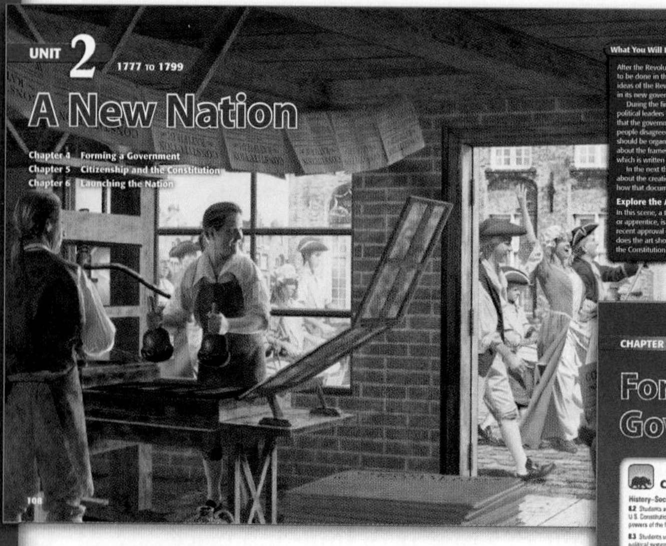

Unit

Each chapter of this textbook is part of a Unit of study focusing on a particular time period. Each unit opener provides an illustration showing a young person of the period and gives you an overview of the exciting topics that you will study in the unit.

Chapter

Each Chapter begins with a chapter-opener introduction where the California History-Social Science Standards and Analysis Skills are listed out, and ends with Standards Review pages and a Standards Assessment page.

Reading Social Studies These chapter-level reading lessons teach you skills and provide opportunities for practice to help you read the textbook more successfully. Within each chapter there is a point of reference *Focus on Reading* note in the margin to demonstrate the reading skill for the chapter. There are also questions in the Standards Review activity to make sure that you understand the reading skill.

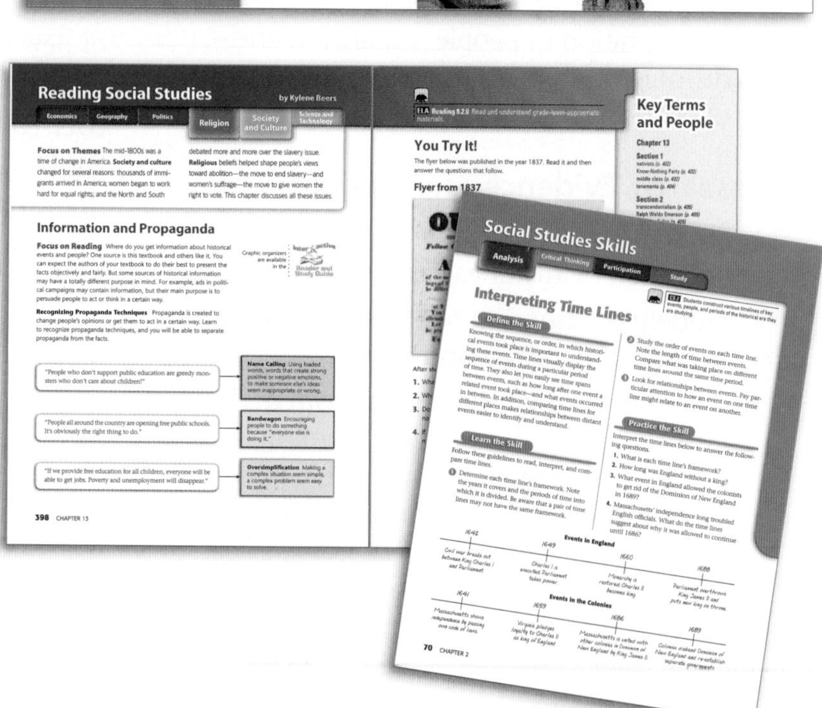

Social Studies Skills The Social Studies Skills lessons, that appear at the end of each chapter, give you an opportunity to learn and use a skill that you will most likely use again while in school. You will also be given a chance to make sure that you understand each skill by answering related questions in the Standards Review activity.

Section

The Section opener pages include: Main Idea statements, an overarching Big Idea statement, and Key Terms and People. In addition, each section includes the following special features.

If You Were There . . . introductions begin each section with a situation for you to respond to, placing you in the time period and in a situation related to the content that you will be studying in the section.

Building Background sections connect what will be covered in this section with what you studied in the previous section.

Short sections of content organize the information in each section into small chunks of text that you should not find too overwhelming.

The California History-Social Science Standards for 8th grade that are covered in each section are listed on the first page of each section of the textbook.

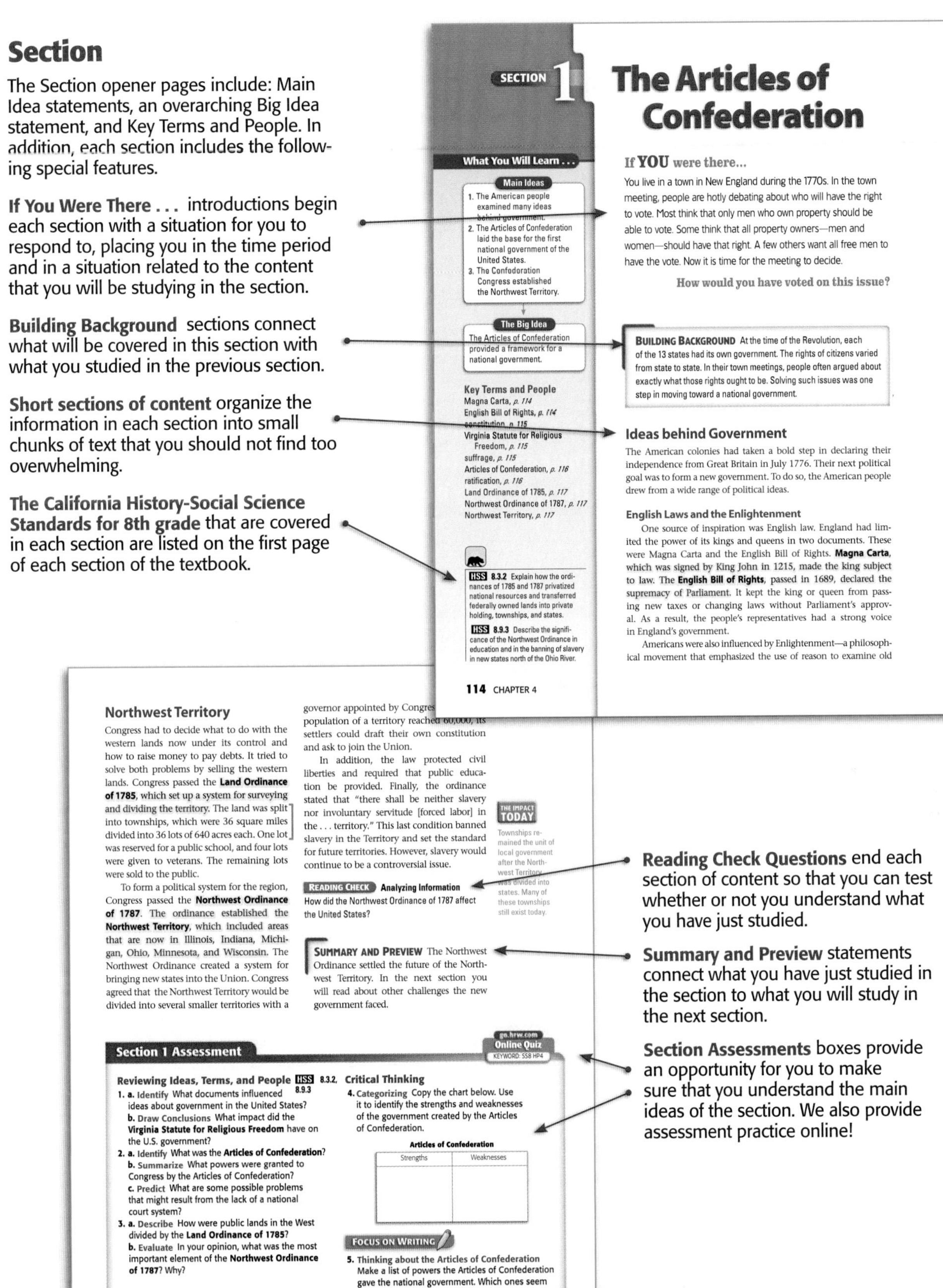

SECTION 1

The Articles of Confederation

What You Will Learn . . .

Main Ideas

1. The American people examined many ideas behind government.
2. The Articles of Confederation laid the base for the first national government of the United States.
3. The Confederation Congress established the Northwest Territory.

The Big Idea

The Articles of Confederation provided a framework for a national government.

Key Terms and People

Magna Carta, *p. 114*
English Bill of Rights, *p. 114*
constitution, *p. 115*
Virginia Statute for Religious Freedom, *p. 115*
suffrage, *p. 115*
Articles of Confederation, *p. 116*
ratification, *p. 116*
Land Ordinance of 1785, *p. 117*
Northwest Ordinance of 1787, *p. 117*
Northwest Territory, *p. 117*

HSS 8.3.2 Explain how the ordinances of 1785 and 1787 privatized national resources and transferred federally owned lands into private holding, townships, and states.

HSS 8.9.3 Describe the significance of the Northwest Ordinance in education and in the banning of slavery in new states north of the Ohio River.

If YOU were there...

You live in a town in New England during the 1770s. In the town meeting, people are hotly debating about who will have the right to vote. Most think that only men who own property should be able to vote. Some think that all property owners—men and women—should have that right. A few others want all free men to have the vote. Now it is time for the meeting to decide.

How would you have voted on this issue?

BUILDING BACKGROUND At the time of the Revolution, each of the 13 states had its own government. The rights of citizens varied from state to state. In their town meetings, people often argued about exactly what those rights ought to be. Solving such issues was one step in moving toward a national government.

Ideas behind Government

The American colonies had taken a bold step in declaring their independence from Great Britain in July 1776. Their next political goal was to form a new government. To do so, the American people drew from a wide range of political ideas.

English Laws and the Enlightenment

One source of inspiration was English law. England had limited the power of its kings and queens in two documents. These were Magna Carta and the English Bill of Rights. **Magna Carta**, which was signed by King John in 1215, made the king subject to law. The **English Bill of Rights**, passed in 1689, declared the supremacy of Parliament. It kept the king or queen from passing new taxes or changing laws without Parliament's approval. As a result, the people's representatives had a strong voice in England's government.

Americans were also influenced by Enlightenment—a philosophical movement that emphasized the use of reason to examine old

114 CHAPTER 4

Northwest Territory

Congress had to decide what to do with the western lands now under its control and how to raise money to pay debts. It tried to solve both problems by selling the western lands. Congress passed the **Land Ordinance of 1785**, which set up a system for surveying and dividing the territory. The land was split into townships, which were 36 square miles divided into 36 lots of 640 acres each. One lot was reserved for a public school, and four lots were given to veterans. The remaining lots were sold to the public.

To form a political system for the region, Congress passed the **Northwest Ordinance of 1787**. The ordinance established the **Northwest Territory**, which included areas that are now in Illinois, Indiana, Michigan, Ohio, Minnesota, and Wisconsin. The Northwest Ordinance created a system for bringing new states into the Union. Congress agreed that the Northwest Territory would be divided into several smaller territories with a governor appointed by Congres[s] ... population of a territory reached 60,000, its settlers could draft their own constitution and ask to join the Union.

In addition, the law protected civil liberties and required that public education be provided. Finally, the ordinance stated that "there shall be neither slavery nor involuntary servitude [forced labor] in the . . . territory." This last condition banned slavery in the Territory and set the standard for future territories. However, slavery would continue to be a controversial issue.

THE IMPACT TODAY

Townships remained the unit of local government after the Northwest Territory was divided into states. Many of these townships still exist today.

READING CHECK **Analyzing Information** How did the Northwest Ordinance of 1787 affect the United States?

SUMMARY AND PREVIEW The Northwest Ordinance settled the future of the Northwest Territory. In the next section you will read about other challenges the new government faced.

Section 1 Assessment

go.hrw.com
Online Quiz
KEYWORD: SS8 HP4

Reviewing Ideas, Terms, and People HSS 8.3.2, 8.9.3

1. a. Identify What documents influenced ideas about government in the United States?
   b. Draw Conclusions What impact did the **Virginia Statute for Religious Freedom** have on the U.S. government?
2. a. Identify What was the **Articles of Confederation**?
   b. Summarize What powers were granted to Congress by the Articles of Confederation?
   c. Predict What are some possible problems that might result from the lack of a national court system?
3. a. Describe How were public lands in the West divided by the **Land Ordinance of 1785**?
   b. Evaluate In your opinion, what was the most important element of the **Northwest Ordinance of 1787**? Why?

Critical Thinking

4. Categorizing Copy the chart below. Use it to identify the strengths and weaknesses of the government created by the Articles of Confederation.

Articles of Confederation

Strengths	Weaknesses

FOCUS ON WRITING

5. **Thinking about the Articles of Confederation** Make a list of powers the Articles of Confederation gave the national government. Which ones seem strong? Can you think of any important powers that are missing?

FORMING A GOVERNMENT 117

Reading Check Questions end each section of content so that you can test whether or not you understand what you have just studied.

Summary and Preview statements connect what you have just studied in the section to what you will study in the next section.

Section Assessments boxes provide an opportunity for you to make sure that you understand the main ideas of the section. We also provide assessment practice online!

Unit Preview

Introduce the Unit

Share the information in the chapter overviews with students.

Chapter 1 According to many scholars, humans migrated to the Americas across a land bridge from Asia during the last Ice Age. As they spread throughout the Americas, humans developed varied cultural groups and in time formed civilizations. During the 1400s, European explorers were searching for direct trade routes to Asia. This search led to the European discovery of the Americas. The event changed life around the world. Soon, Europeans were competing to colonize the Americas, with Spain leading the way.

Chapter 2 In 1607 a group of colonists established the first permanent English settlement in the Americas. Soon, thirteen English colonies lined the Atlantic Coast. Varied ways of life developed across these colonies as settlers adapted to different environments. Settlers also came into conflict with Native Americans and French settlers. These tensions led to the French and Indian War, which Great Britain won in 1763. Taxes to pay for this war angered colonists, though, who began protesting against British laws.

Chapter 3 Colonial tensions with Great Britain heightened and the Revolutionary War broke out in April 1775. On July 4, 1776, colonial *(continued on p. 2)*

Standards Focus

For a list of the overarching standards covered in this unit, see the first page of each chapter.

UNIT 1 BEGINNINGS TO 1783

Connecting with the Past: Our Colonial Heritage

Unit Resources

Planning

- Universal Access Teacher Management System: Unit Instructional Benchmarking Guides
- One-Stop Planner CD-ROM with Test Generator: Holt Calendar Planner
- Power Presentations with Video CD-ROM
- A Teacher's Guide to Religion in the Public Schools

Standards Mastery

- Standards Review Workbook
- At Home: A Guide to Standards Mastery for United States History

Differentiating Instruction

- Universal Access Teacher Management System: Lesson Plans for Universal Access
- Pre-AP Activities Guide for United States History
- Universal Access Modified Worksheets and Tests CD-ROM

Enrichment

- **CRF 1:** Economics and History: Mercantilism: Government Control of Trade
- **CRF 1:** Interdisciplinary Project: What Will You Take on Your Sea Voyage?
- Civic Participation
- Primary Source Library CD-ROM

Assessment

- Progress Assessment Support System: Benchmark Test
- OSP ExamView Test Generator: Benchmark Test
- go.hrw.com Holt Online Assessment Program (in the Premier Online Edition)
- Alternative Assessment Handbook

The **Universal Access Teacher Management System** provides a planning and instructional benchmarking guide for this unit.

What You Will Learn...

North and South America were populated by Native American societies before Europeans arrived and began to colonize them. During the colonial period, Europeans came to the Americas to make new homes and gain wealth. As England's colonies in North America became more successful, they began to have conflicts with neighboring colonies, Native American people, and the British government. In the first three chapters, you will learn about native people meeting the Europeans, and about the English colonists that created the United States.

Explore the Art

In this picture, Spanish teenager Hernando d'Escalante Fontaneda washes ashore in Florida after a shipwreck. How does the picture show what life was like before Europeans came to North America?

Democracy and Civic Education

Standards **Proficiency**

Authority: Reasons for Government

1. Organize students into small groups. Have each group discuss the need for school rules. Each group should create a chart listing the costs and benefits of school rules. How well would the school function without rules? What would happen if students did not obey school rules or authority figures? Have each group share its chart with the class.
2. Explain that societies, like schools, need governments and laws. Have each group create a second chart listing the costs and benefits of government. The groups should then use their charts to identify what they think the purposes of government should be.
3. Have each group share its findings. Conclude by explaining that the purpose of government in the United States is to protect individual rights and to promote the common good.

LS Interpersonal, Verbal/Linguistic

Alternative Assessment Handbook, Rubrics 7: Charts; and 14: Group Activity

Civic Participation

Unit Preview

Unit Overview *continued*

leaders approved the Declaration of Independence, creating the United States of America. American forces, aided by France and Spain, fought many hard battles and faced numerous hardships before winning the war. In 1783, Britain recognized U.S. independence.

Connect to the Unit

Activity Simulation Role-Play

Provide students with the following scenario: A multinational space expedition has made contact with a nonhostile civilization on another planet. Communication has been slow but is occurring.

Ask students to predict how life on Earth might change as a result of this new contact. Have students work in pairs or in small groups to create hypothetical conversations between people on Earth discussing the event and its possible effects. Ask for volunteers to act out their conversations for the class.

LS Interpersonal, Verbal/Linguistic

Explore the Art

Hernando d'Escalante Fontaneda spent 17 years living among Native Americans along the edge of the Everglades. Fontaneda was just one of many Europeans who would soon come to the Americas. The changes that resulted from contact between Europeans and Native Americans would have far-reaching effects.

About the Illustration

This illustration is an artist's conception based on available sources. However, historians are uncertain exactly what this scene looked like.

Answers

Explore the Art *shows the type of dress, ornamentation, and crafts that some Native Americans used*

Chapter 1 Planning Guide

Early Exploration and Settlement

Chapter Overview	Reproducible Resources	Technology Resources
CHAPTER 1 **pp. 2–31** **Overview: In this chapter, students will learn about the discovery and exploration of the Americas and the results of those events.** See p. 2 for the California History–Social Science standards covered in this chapter	**Universal Access Teacher Management System:*** • Universal Access Instructional Benchmarking Guides • Lesson Plans for Universal Access **Interactive Reader and Study Guide:*** Chapter Graphic Organizer **Chapter Resource File*** • Focus on Writing Activity: Writing a Letter • Social Studies Skills Activity: Framing Historical Questions • Chapter Review Activity	**One-Stop Planner CD-ROM:** Calendar Planner **Student Edition Full-Read Audio CD-ROM** **Universal Access Modified Worksheets and Tests CD-ROM** **Power Presentations with Video CD-ROM** **History's Impact: American History Video Series (VHS/DVD):** Early Exploration and Settlement*
Section 1: **The Earliest Americans** **The Big Idea:** Native American societies developed across Mesoamerica and North America. 7.7.1	**Universal Access Teacher Management System:*** Section 1 Lesson Plan **Interactive Reader and Study Guide:*** Section 1 Summary **Chapter Resource File*** • Vocabulary Builder, Section 1 • History and Geography Activity: Migration • Primary Source Activity: Iroquois Creation Legend	**Daily Bellringer Transparency:** Section 1* **Map Transparency:** Migrations of Early Peoples* **Map Transparency:** Native American Culture Areas*
Section 2: **The Age of Exploration** **The Big Idea:** As trade routes developed across the globe, European explorers crossed the Atlantic Ocean to the Americas. 7.11.1, 7.11.2	**Universal Access Teacher Management System:*** Section 2 Lesson Plan **Interactive Reader and Study Guide:*** Section 2 Summary **Chapter Resource File*** • Vocabulary Builder, Section 2 • Biography Activity: Queen Isabella • Primary Source Activity: The Journal of Christopher Columbus • Literature Activity: Karlsefni Goes to Vinland • Interdisciplinary Project: What Will You Take on Your Sea Voyage?	**Daily Bellringer Transparency:** Section 2* **Map Transparency:** Trade Routes, 1200s to 1400s* **Map Transparency:** European Exploration of the Americas* **Map Transparency:** The Columbian Exchange* go.hrw.com **Internet Activity:** Columbus Cause-and-Effect Chart
Section 3: **Spanish America** **The Big Idea:** Spain established an empire in the Americas. 7.7.3	**Universal Access Teacher Management System:*** Section 3 Lesson Plan **Interactive Reader and Study Guide:*** Section 3 Summary **Chapter Resource File*** • Vocabulary Builder, Section 3 • Biography Activities: Explorers; Malintzin • Primary Source Activity: The Aztecs See Horses • Economics and History Activity: Mercantilism	**Daily Bellringer Transparency:** Section 3*
Section 4: **The Race for Empires** **The Big Idea:** Other European nations challenged Spain in the Americas. 7.9, 7.11.1	**Universal Access Teacher Management System:*** Section 4 Lesson Plan **Interactive Reader and Study Guide:*** Section 4 Summary **Chapter Resource File*** • Vocabulary Builder, Section 4	**Daily Bellringer Transparency:** Section 4* **Map Transparency:** Empires in North America c. 1765* go.hrw.com **Internet Activity:** Map of Settlements in North America

SE Student Edition | Print Resource | Audio CD | Video
TE Teacher's Edition | Transparency | CD-ROM | DVD
go.hrw.com | CA Standards Mastery | **LS** Learning Styles
OSP One-Stop Planner CD-ROM | * also on One-Stop Planner CD

Review, Assessment, Intervention

- **Standards Review Workbook***
- **Quick Facts Transparency:** Early Exploration and Settlement Visual Summary*
- **Online Chapter Summaries in Six Languages**
- **Progress Assessment Support System (PASS):** Chapter Test*
- **Universal Access Modified Worksheets and Tests CD-ROM:** Modified Chapter Test
- **One-Stop Planner CD-ROM:** ExamView Test Generator (English/Spanish)

- **PASS:** Section 1 Quiz*
- **Online Quiz:** Section 1
- **Alternative Assessment Handbook**

- **PASS:** Section 2 Quiz*
- **Online Quiz:** Section 2
- **Alternative Assessment Handbook**

- **PASS:** Section 3 Quiz*
- **Online Quiz:** Section 3
- **Alternative Assessment Handbook**

- **PASS:** Section 4 Quiz*
- **Online Quiz:** Section 4
- **Alternative Assessment Handbook**

California Resources for Standards Mastery

INSTRUCTIONAL PLANNING AND SUPPORT

- **Universal Access Teacher Management System***
- **One-Stop Planner CD-ROM with Test Generator: Teacher Management System with Interactive Teacher's Edition**

STANDARDS MASTERY

- **Standards Review Workbook***
- **At Home: A Guide to Standards Mastery for United States History**

Holt Online Learning

To enhance learning, Internet activities are available for a Columbus Cause-and-Effect Chart and a Map of Settlements in North America.

KEYWORD: SS8 TEACHER

- **Teacher Support Page**
- **Content Updates**
- **Rubrics and Writing Models**
- **Teaching Tips for the Multimedia Classroom**

KEYWORD: SS8 US1

- **Current Events**
- **Document-Based Questions**
- **Holt Grapher**
- **Holt Online Atlas**
- **Holt Researcher**
- **Interactive Multimedia Activities**
- **Internet Activities**
- **Online Chapter Summaries in Six Languages**
- **Online Section Quizzes**
- **American History Maps and Charts**

HOLT PREMIER ONLINE STUDENT EDITION

Complete online support for interactivity, assessment, and reporting

- **Interactive Maps and Notebook**
- **Standardized Test Prep**
- **Homework Practice and Research Activities Online**

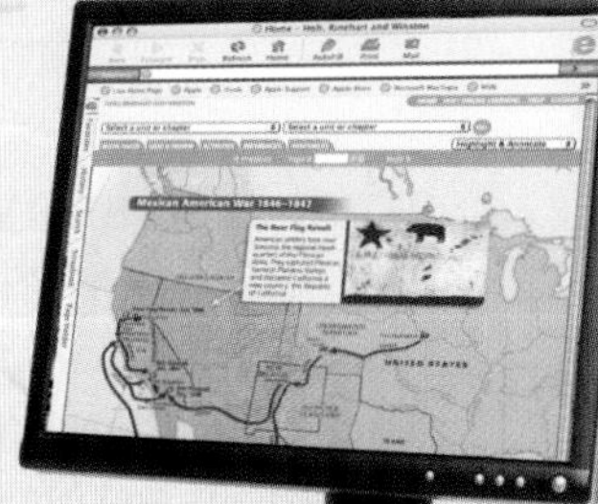

Mastering the Standards: Differentiating Instruction

Reaching Standards	Basic-level activities designed for all students encountering new material
Standards Proficiency	Intermediate-level activities designed for average students
Exceeding Standards	Challenging activities designed for honors and gifted-and-talented students
Standard English Mastery	Activities designed to improve standard English usage

Frequently Asked Questions

INSTRUCTIONAL PLANNING AND SUPPORT

Where do I find planning aids, pacing guides, lesson plans, and other teaching aids?

Annotated Teacher's Edition:
- Chapter planning guides
- Standards-based instruction and strategies
- Differentiated instruction for universal access
- Point-of-use reminders for integrating program resources

Power Presentations with Video CD-ROM

Universal Access Teacher Management System:
- Year and unit instructional benchmarking guides
- Reproducible lesson plans
- Assessment guides for diagnostic, progress, and summative end-of-the-year tests
- Options for differentiating instruction and intervention
- Teaching guides and answer keys for student workbooks

One-Stop Planner CD-ROM with Test Generator: Teacher Management System with Interactive Teacher's Editon:
- Calendar Planner
- Editable lesson plans
- All reproducible ancillaries in Adobe Acrobat (PDF) format
- ExamView Test Generator (English & Spanish)
- Game Tool for ExamView
- PuzzlePro
- Transparency and video previews

DIFFERENTIATING INSTRUCTION FOR UNIVERSAL ACCESS

What resources are available to ensure that Advanced Learners/GATE Students master the standards?

Teacher's Edition Activities:
- The Medicis, p. 13
- Life in Spanish Settlements, p. 22

Lesson Plans for Universal Access

Primary Source Library CD-ROM for United States History

What resources are available to ensure that English Learners and Standard English Learners master the standards?

Teacher's Edition Activities:
- Questions and Maps, p. 7
- Mapping Native American Culture Groups, p. 9

Lesson Plans for Universal Access

Chapter Resource File: Vocabulary Builder Activities

Spanish Chapter Summaries Audio CD Program

Online Chapter Summaries in Six Languages

One-Stop Planner CD-ROM:
- PuzzlePro, Spanish Version
- ExamView Test Generator, Spanish Version

What modified materials are available for Special Education?

Teacher's Edition Activities:
- Trade and Exploration Graphic Organizer, p. 14

The *Universal Access Modified Worksheets and Tests CD-ROM* provides editable versions of the following:

Vocabulary Flash Cards

Modified Vocabulary Builder Activities

Modified Chapter Review Activity

Modified Chapter Test

HOLT **History's Impact**
▶ video series
Early Exploration and Settlement

What resources are available to ensure that Learners Having Difficulty master the standards?

Teacher's Edition Activities:
- Mapping Native American Culture Groups, p. 9
- European Explorers Quiz Game, p. 17
- Challenges to Spain Graphic Organizer, p. 25

Interactive Reader and Study Guide

Student Edition Full-Read Audio CD

Quick Facts Transparency: Exploration and Settlement Visual Summary

Standards Review Workbook

Social Studies Skills Activity: Framing Historical Questions

Interactive Skills Tutor CD-ROM

How do I intervene for students struggling to master the standards?

Interactive Reader and Study Guide

Quick Facts Transparency: Exploration and Settlement Visual Summary

Standards Review Workbook

Social Studies Skills Activity: Framing Historical Questions

Interactive Skills Tutor CD-ROM

PROFESSIONAL DEVELOPMENT

What teacher training resources are available to help me grow professionally?

- In-service and staff development as part of your Holt Social Studies product purchase
- Quick Teacher Tutorial Lesson Presentation CD-ROM
- Intensive tuition-based Teacher Development Institute
- *Teaching American History* Online 2 Module Professional Development Course
- Convenient Holt Speaker Bureau face-to-face workshop options
- PRAXIS™ Test Prep (#0089) interactive Web-based content refreshers*
- 24/7 *Ask A Professional Development Expert* at http://www.hrw.com/prodev/

* PRAXIS is a trademark of Educational Testing Service (ETS). This publication is not endorsed or approved by ETS.

Information Literacy Skills

To learn more about how History–Social Science instruction may be improved by the effective use of library media centers and information literacy skills, go to the Teacher's Resource Materials for Chapter 1 at **go.hrw.com**, keyword: SS8 MEDIA.

The following materials were developed by the Division for Public Education of the American Bar Association. These materials are part of the **Democracy and Civic Education** supplement.
- Constitution Study Guide
- Supreme Court Case Studies

• Chapter Preview •

Standards Focus

Standards by Section
Section 1: HSS 7.7.1
Section 2: HSS 7.11.1, 7.11.2
Section 3: HSS 7.7.3
Section 4: HSS 7.11.1

Teacher's Edition
HSS **Analysis Skills:** CS 1, CS 2, CS 3, HR 1, HR 3, HR 5, HI 1, HI 2

Preview Grade 11 Standards
HSS **11.3** Students analyze the role religion played in the founding of America, its lasting moral, social, and political impacts, and issues regarding religious liberty.

Focus on Writing
The **Chapter Resource File** provides a Focus on Writing worksheet to help students write their letters.

CRF: Focus on Writing Activity: Writing a Letter

CHAPTER 1 BEGINNINGS–1700

Early Exploration and Settlement

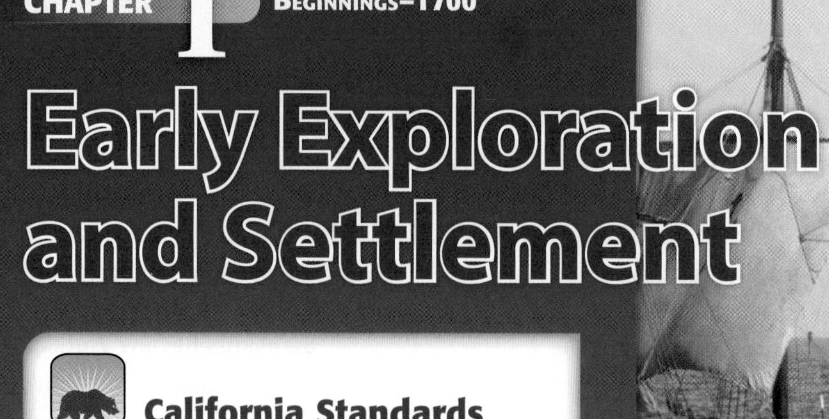

California Standards

History–Social Science

7.7 Students compare and contrast the geographic, political, economic, religious, and social structures of the Meso-American and Andean civilizations.

7.11 Students analyze political and economic change in the sixteenth, seventeenth, and eighteenth centuries (the Age of Exploration, the Enlightenment, and the Age of Reason).

Analysis Skills

HR1 Students frame questions that can be answered by historical study and research.

English–Language Arts

Writing 8.2.1.a Relate a clear, coherent incident, event, or situation by using well-chosen details.

Reading 8.1.0 Students recognize specialized vocabulary.

FOCUS ON WRITING

Writing a Letter In this chapter, you'll learn about many different groups of people struggling to make a home for themselves in the Americas. Imagine that one of these is a French trader named Jacques working in America in the early 1700s. After you read this chapter, you'll write a letter from Jacques to his family in France. You'll tell them about life and people in early America.

c. 38,000–10,000 BC Paleo-Indians migrate to the Americas.

c. 5000 BC Communities in Mexico cultivate corn.

Introduce the Chapter

Standards Proficiency

Focus on Exploration and Contact

HSS **Analysis Skills:** HR 5, HI 1

1. Ask students how they think sailors leaving on voyages of discovery might have felt as they pulled away from European shores. Write students' responses for the class to see.
2. Next, ask students how they think Native Americans might have felt the first time they saw European explorers. Again, write students' responses for the class to see.
3. Then have students compare and contrast the feelings and points of view of Native Americans and early European explorers. Use the activity to remind students that different groups have had different points of view on historical events.
4. Tell students that in this chapter they will learn about early exploration and settlement in the Americas. These events involved groups of people coming into contact with one another for the first time. The effects of these events would be dramatic and far-reaching for all involved. LS **Intrapersonal, Logical/Mathematical**

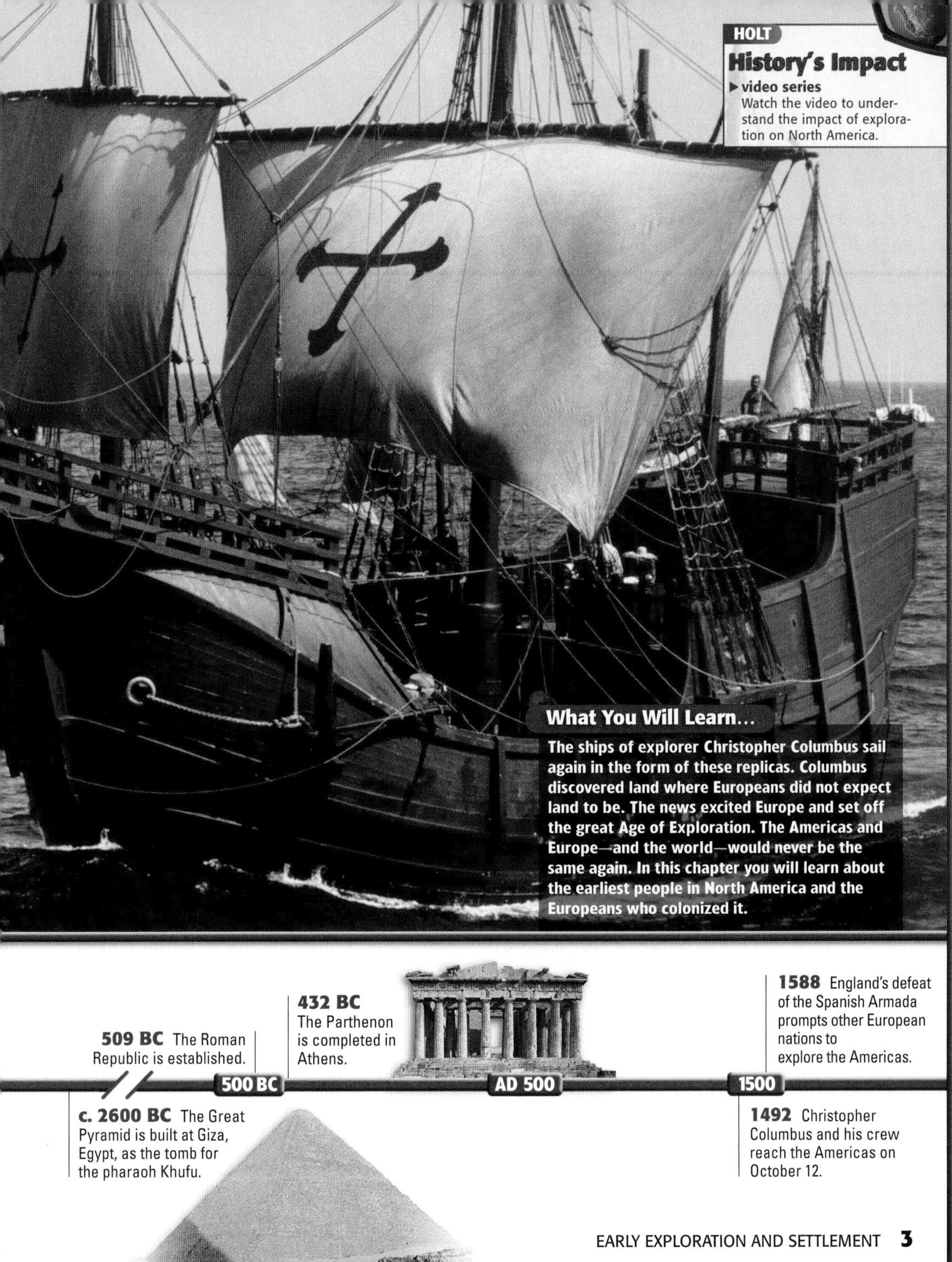

What You Will Learn...

The ships of explorer Christopher Columbus sail again in the form of these replicas. Columbus discovered land where Europeans did not expect land to be. The news excited Europe and set off the great Age of Exploration. The Americas and Europe—and the world—would never be the same again. In this chapter you will learn about the earliest people in North America and the Europeans who colonized it.

c. 2600 BC The Great Pyramid is built at Giza, Egypt, as the tomb for the pharaoh Khufu.

509 BC The Roman Republic is established.

500 BC

432 BC The Parthenon is completed in Athens.

AD 500

1500

1492 Christopher Columbus and his crew reach the Americas on October 12.

1588 England's defeat of the Spanish Armada prompts other European nations to explore the Americas.

• Chapter Preview •

HOLT
History's Impact
▶ **video series**
See the Video Teacher's Guide for strategies for using the chapter video **Early Exploration and Settlement**.

Chapter Big Ideas

Section 1 Native American societies developed across Mesoamerica and North America. HSS 7.7.1

Section 2 As trade routes developed across the globe, European explorers crossed the Atlantic Ocean to the Americas. HSS 7.11.1, 7.11.2

Section 3 Spain established an empire in the Americas. HSS 7.7.3

Section 4 Other European nations challenged Spain in the Americas. HSS 7.11.1

Explore the Picture

Sailing into the Unknown On his initial voyage, Columbus set sail with some 100 men, most of them experienced sailors. At first, he struggled to find crew members because of people's fears of the unknown. The Spanish government helped by offering to free any convicts who joined the crew.

Analyzing Visuals Ask students how this photograph makes them feel about Columbus's voyage. *Answers will vary, but students might consider feelings of fear of the unknown, excitement, the thrill of adventure, and amazement over how small the ships were.*

Explore the Time Line

1. Based on this time line, how would you describe Paleo-Indian migration to the Americas? *over a long period of time*
2. How many years between the initial migration to the Americas and when corn was first cultivated in Mexico? *33,000 years*
3. How long had there been communities in the Americas before Christopher Columbus's arrival in 1492? *about 7,000 years*
4. How long after Columbus's voyage was the English defeat of the Spanish Armada? *96 years*

HSS **Analysis Skills:** CS 1

Info to Know

Development of Farming Around 5000 BC groups in what is now Mexico began planting and growing corn. The development of farming changed life in the Americas. No longer were early Americans dependent on fishing, hunting, and searching for food. Farming enabled early people to settle in one place, to support larger populations, and to focus on things other than finding food. These changes, in turn, enabled the great Olmec, Maya, Aztec, and Inca civilizations to develop.

go.hrw.com
Online Resources
Chapter Resources:
KEYWORD: SS8 US1
Teacher Resources:
KEYWORD: SS8 TEACHER

Reading Social Studies

Understanding Themes

Tell students that there are many themes that are repeated throughout history. Point out to students the themes listed across this page. Ask students to explain what each theme means and how it relates to the study of history. Then introduce to students the two themes of this chapter—economics and geography. Lead students in a discussion of the roles that geography and economics played in the settlement and exploration of the Americas. Write down students' suggestions for the class to see

Specialized Vocabulary of Social Studies

Focus on Reading Explain to students that every field develops its own specialized vocabulary to meet its needs. Ask for examples of these types of words. If students have trouble, remind them of words they use or hear every day, especially those from computer technology, such as *spam*. Organize students into groups of three or four. Each group should pick a field, such as science or computers, that interests them. Students should then compile a list of specialized terms used in that field. Ask groups to share their lists with the class.

Standards Focus

ELA Reading 8.1.0

Reading Social Studies

Economics | Geography | Politics | Religion | Society and Culture | Science and Technology

Focus on Themes This chapter explains the discovery and early development of Mesoamerica and North America. You will read about early explorers from Europe, learn about the early settlements, and discover why the Spanish, the English, and the French all wanted a part of this new land. As you read the chapter, you will see how **geography** affected exploration and will learn about the **economic** issues that influenced growth and settlements.

Specialized Vocabulary of Social Studies

Focus on Reading If you flipped through the pages of this book, would you expect to see anything about square roots or formulas? How about Petri dishes or hypotheses? Of course you wouldn't. Those are terms you'd only see in math and science books.

Specialized Vocabulary Words that are used in only one field are called specialized vocabulary. Like most subjects, social studies has its own specialized vocabulary. The charts below list some terms you may encounter as you read this book.

Terms that deal with time	
Decade	a period of 10 years
Century	a period of 100 years
Era	a long period marked by great events, developments, or figures
BC	a term used to identify dates that occurred long ago, before the birth of Jesus Christ, the founder of Christianity; it means "before Christ." BC dates get smaller as time passes, so the larger the number the earlier the date.
AD	a term used to identify dates that occurred after Jesus's birth; it comes from a Latin phrase that means "in the year of our Lord." Unlike BC dates, AD dates get larger as time passes, so the larger the number the later the date.
BCE	another way to refer to BC dates; it stands for "before the common era"
CE	another way to refer to AD dates; it stands for "common era"

Terms that deal with government and society	
politics	the art of creating government policies
economics	the study of the creation and use of goods and services
movement	a series of actions that bring about or try to bring about a change in society
campaign	an effort to win a political office, or a series of military actions
colony	a territory settled and controlled by a country

Reading and Skills Resources

Reading Support

- Interactive Reader and Study Guide
- Student Edition on Audio CD
- Spanish Chapter Summaries Audio CD Program

Social Studies Skills Support

- Interactive Skills Tutor CD-ROM

Vocabulary Support

- **CRF:** Vocabulary Builder Activities
- **CRF:** Chapter Review Activity
- Universal Access Modified Worksheets and Tests CD-ROM:
  - Vocabulary Flash Cards
  - Vocabulary Builder Activity
  - Chapter Review Activity

OSP Holt PuzzlePro

ELA Reading 8.1.0 Students determine the meaning of specialized vocabulary.

You Try It!

The following passage shows you how some specialized vocabulary is defined in context.

Migration to the Americas

Different environments influenced the development of Native American **societies**— groups that share a culture. **Culture** is a group's set of common values and traditions. These include language, government, and family relationships.

Like all societies, Native American groups changed over time. They learned to domesticate, or breed, wild plants and animals.

From Chapter 1, p. 7

Using the clues to understand meaning.

1. Find the word *societies.* The phrase after the dash is the definition. Often in this book, specialized vocabulary words are defined after a **dash**. So be on the lookout for dashes.
2. The word *domesticate* is defined in the fifth sentence. The clue to finding this definition is the **comma** followed by the word **or**. Look at what the comma does in that sentence:

   They learned to domesticate or breed wild plants . . .

   They learned to domesticate, or breed, wild plants . . .

   Without the comma, the sentence is saying that Native American groups did two things to wild plants—domesticate and breed. But with the comma before the word or, you understand that "breed" is the definition of "domesticate."
3. In the first and second sentences, you see a term that is in boldface print. You should recognize that **word** from seeing it on the section opener. The definition is **highlighted**. Why do you think some specialized vocabulary words are in boldface print while others are not?

As you read Chapter 1, keep track of the specialized vocabulary you learn in your notebook.

Key Terms and People

Chapter 1

Section 1
Paleo-Indians *(p. 6)*
migration *(p. 6)*
hunter-gatherers *(p. 6)*
environments *(p. 7)*
societies *(p. 7)*
culture *(p. 7)*
totems *(p. 10)*
Iroquois League *(p. 11)*

Section 2
capital *(p. 13)*
joint-stock companies *(p. 13)*
Christopher Columbus *(p. 15)*
Ferdinand Magellan *(p. 17)*
Northwest Passage *(p. 17)*
Columbian Exchange *(p.18)*

Section 3
conquistadors *(p. 20)*
Hernán Cortés *(p. 20)*
Moctezuma II *(p. 20)*
Francisco Pizarro *(p. 21)*
Junípero Serra *(p. 22)*
encomienda system *(p. 22)*
Bartolomé de Las Casas *(p. 23)*
plantations *(p. 23)*

Section 4
Protestant Reformation *(p. 25)*
Protestants *(p. 25)*
printing press *(p. 25)*
Spanish Armada *(p. 25)*
inflation *(p. 25)*
charter *(p. 27)*

Academic Vocabulary

Success in school is related to knowing academic vocabulary—the words that are frequently used in school assignments and discussions. In this chapter, you will learn the following academic words:

method *(p. 8)*
develop *(p. 10)*

Reading Social Studies

Key Terms and People

Preteach the key terms and people from this chapter by having students create a Four-Corner FoldNote. Instruct students to fold a sheet of paper to create eight separate boxes. Then have students unfold the paper and cut the outside boxes like the diagram below. Have students write the terms for each section on a separate flap. As students read each section, have them define or identify each key term or person. Encourage students to review their definitions regularly. **LS Kinesthetic, Verbal/Linguistic**

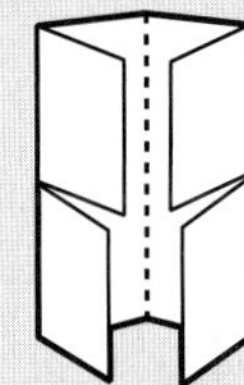

Focus on Reading

See the **Focus on Reading** questions in this chapter for more practice on this reading social studies skill.

Reading Social Studies Assessment

See the **Standards Review** at the end of this chapter for student assessment questions related to this reading skill.

Teaching Tip

To help students learn the meaning of words that are frequently used, but are not part of the specialized vocabulary of history, instruct students to review the academic vocabulary terms in each chapter. Point out to students that these words are an important part of their academic vocabulary—words that they are expected to know in any subject.

Answers

You Try It! 3. *possible answer—Some words are in bold face print to show that they may be words that are important words that relate to the section. Other specialized vocabulary words are not in bold face because they are used often.*

Preteach

Bellringer

If YOU were there . . . Use the **Daily Bellringer Transparency** to help students answer the question.

Daily Bellringer Transparency, Section 1

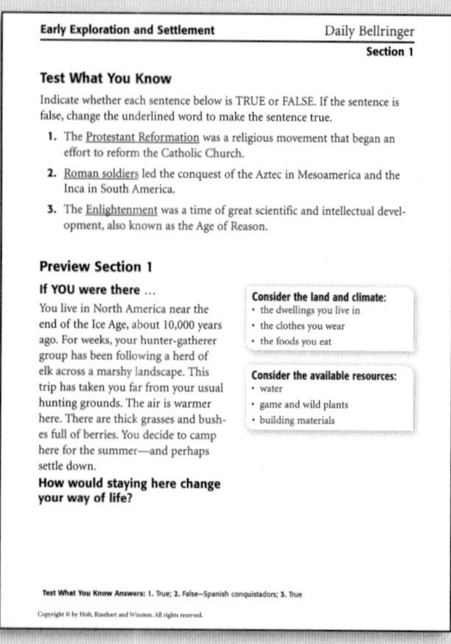

Early Exploration and Settlement — Daily Bellringer

Section 1

Test What You Know

Indicate whether each sentence below is TRUE or FALSE. If the sentence is false, change the underlined word to make the sentence true.

1. The Protestant Reformation was a religious movement that began an effort to reform the Catholic Church.
2. Roman soldiers led the conquest of the Aztec in Mesoamerica and the Inca in South America.
3. The Enlightenment was a time of great scientific and intellectual development, also known as the Age of Reason.

Preview Section 1

If YOU were there ...

You live in North America near the end of the Ice Age, about 10,000 years ago. For weeks, your hunter-gatherer group has been following a herd of elk across a marshy landscape. This trip has taken you far from your usual hunting grounds. The air is warmer here. There are thick grasses and bushes full of berries. You decide to camp here for the summer—and perhaps settle down.

How would staying here change your way of life?

Consider the land and climate:
- the dwellings you live in
- the clothes you wear
- the foods you eat

Consider the available resources:
- water
- game and wild plants
- building materials

Test What You Know Answers: 1. True; 2. False—Spanish conquistadors; 3. True

Academic Vocabulary

Review with students the high-use academic terms in this section.

develop the process of growing or improving (p. 10)

method a way of doing something (p. 8)

CRF: Vocabulary Builder Activity, Section 1

Standards Focus

HSS 7.7.1

Means: Understand the effects of geography and climate on the people who lived in the Americas.

Matters: Geography and climate have affected the development of all societies, both in the past and today.

SECTION 1

The Earliest Americans

What You Will Learn...

Main Ideas

1. Climate changes allowed people to migrate to the Americas.
2. Early societies existed in Mesoamerica and North America.
3. Cultures in North America were influenced by the environment.

The Big Idea

Native American societies developed across Mesoamerica and North America.

Key Terms and People

Paleo-Indians, *p. 6*
migration, *p. 6*
hunter-gatherers, *p. 6*
environments, *p. 7*
societies, *p. 7*
culture, *p. 7*
totems, *p. 10*
Iroquois League, *p. 11*

HSS 7.7.1 Study the locations, landforms, and climates of Mexico, Central America, and South America and their effects on Mayan, Aztec, and Incan economies, trade, and development of urban societies.

If YOU were there...

You live in North America near the end of the Ice Age, about 10,000 years ago. For weeks, your hunter-gatherer group has been following a herd of elk across a marshy landscape. This trip has taken you far from your usual hunting grounds. The air is warmer here. There are thick grasses and bushes full of berries. You decide to camp here for the summer—and perhaps settle down.

How would staying change your way of life?

BUILDING BACKGROUND The first settlers in the Americas probably came in small groups from Asia over thousands of years. Over time, they moved into nearly every region of North and South America. They encountered many different types of land and climate.

Migration to the Americas

Many scientists believe that people first arrived in North America during the last Ice Age. At the start of the Ice Age, Earth's climate grew colder. Large amounts of water froze into huge, moving ice sheets called glaciers. As a result, ocean levels dropped more than 300 feet lower than they are today. When the water level fell, a land bridge appeared between northeastern Asia and present-day Alaska. Geographers call this the Bering Land Bridge. Although no one knows exactly when or how people crossed into North America, evidence suggests that people called **Paleo-Indians** crossed this bridge into Alaska between 38,000 and 10,000 BC.

This **migration**—a movement of people or animals from one region to another—took place over a long time. The Paleo-Indians are thought to have traveled into present-day Canada, the United States, and Mexico in search of animals to hunt. Over time, their descendants went as far as the tip of South America. Paleo-Indians were **hunter-gatherers** who lived by hunting animals and gathering wild plants.

6 CHAPTER 1

Teach the Big Idea: Master the Standards

Standards Proficiency

The Earliest Americans HSS 7.7.1; HSS Analysis Skills: HI 1

1. **Teach** Ask students the Main Idea questions to teach this section.
2. **Apply** Create a three-column table for students to see. Label the columns *Culture Area, Land and Climate,* and *Major Characteristics of Groups in this Area.* Help students fill in the first two columns of the table. Leave the last column blank for students to complete on their own. **LS Verbal/Linguistic**
3. **Review** Using the information in this section, ask students to describe the geography and climate of each culture area and how it affected the people living there.
4. **Practice/Homework** Have students copy the table and complete the third column. **LS Verbal/Linguistic**

Alternative Assessment Handbook, Rubric 13: Graphic Organizers

Migrations of Early Peoples

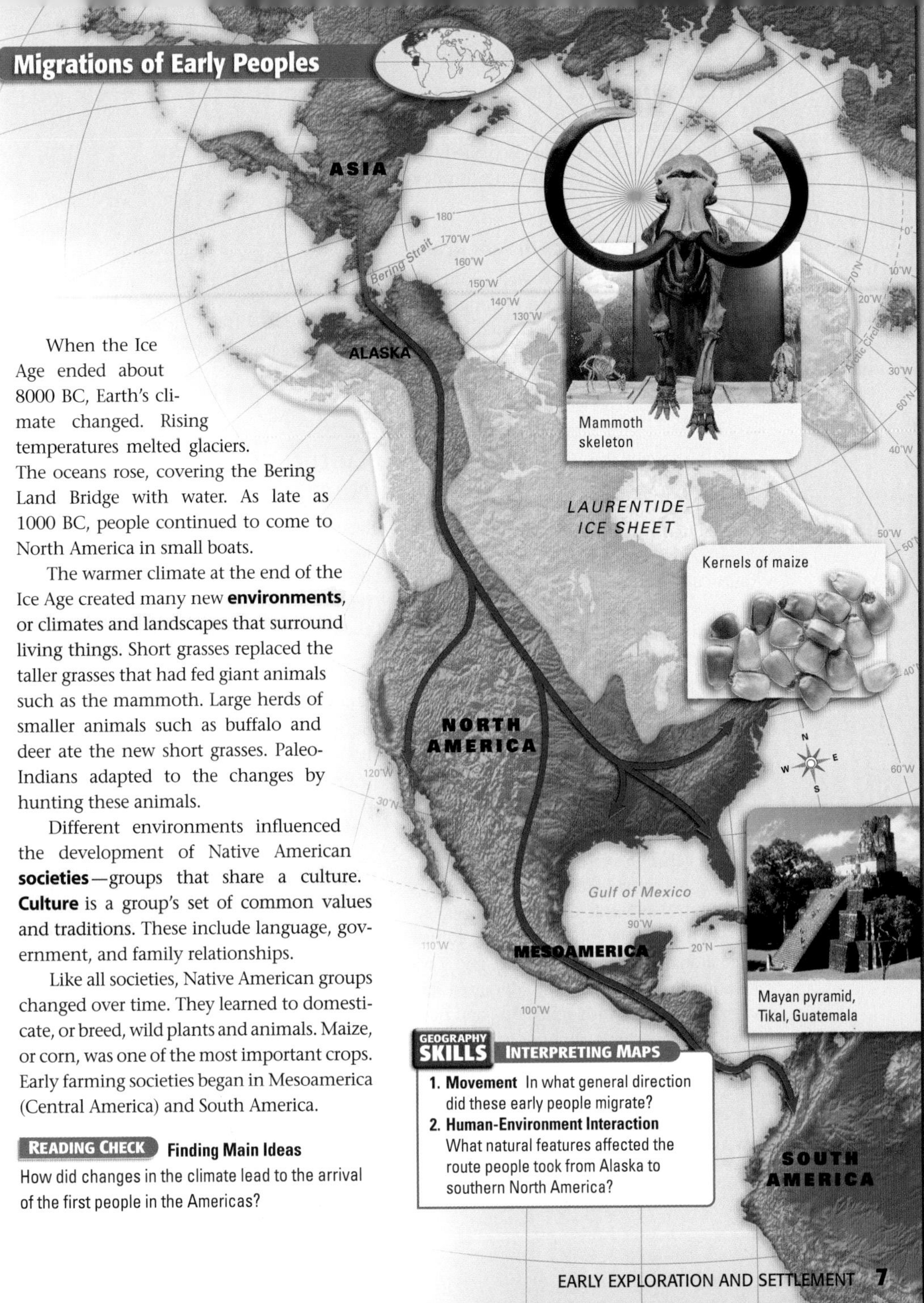

Mammoth skeleton

Kernels of maize

Mayan pyramid, Tikal, Guatemala

When the Ice Age ended about 8000 BC, Earth's climate changed. Rising temperatures melted glaciers. The oceans rose, covering the Bering Land Bridge with water. As late as 1000 BC, people continued to come to North America in small boats.

The warmer climate at the end of the Ice Age created many new **environments**, or climates and landscapes that surround living things. Short grasses replaced the taller grasses that had fed giant animals such as the mammoth. Large herds of smaller animals such as buffalo and deer ate the new short grasses. Paleo-Indians adapted to the changes by hunting these animals.

Different environments influenced the development of Native American **societies**—groups that share a culture. **Culture** is a group's set of common values and traditions. These include language, government, and family relationships.

Like all societies, Native American groups changed over time. They learned to domesticate, or breed, wild plants and animals. Maize, or corn, was one of the most important crops. Early farming societies began in Mesoamerica (Central America) and South America.

READING CHECK **Finding Main Ideas**
How did changes in the climate lead to the arrival of the first people in the Americas?

GEOGRAPHY SKILLS **INTERPRETING MAPS**

1. **Movement** In what general direction did these early people migrate?
2. **Human-Environment Interaction** What natural features affected the route people took from Alaska to southern North America?

Direct Teach

Main Idea

1 Migration to the Americas

Climate changes allowed people to migrate to the Americas.

Recall What is the name of the early people who migrated to the Americas, and how did they arrive? *Paleo-Indians; crossed the Bering Land Bridge*

Identify Cause and Effect How did the end of the Ice Age affect the Americas? *created new environments that supported herds of smaller animals, which Paleo-Indians began hunting*

Make Inferences Why do you think different Native American societies developed in different parts of the Americas? *Different environments led people to rely on different foods, building materials, and ways of life.*

CRF: History and Geography Activity: Migration to the Americas

Map Transparency: Migrations of Early Peoples

HSS 7.7.1; **HSS Analysis Skills:** HI 1, HI 2

Linking to Today

New Theories on Migration to the Americas Scientists have dated Monte Verde, an archaeological site in Chile, as being at least 12,500 years old. Because Monte Verde is located some 10,000 miles south of the Bering Strait, some scientists think the first Americans may have come from Asia by boat and sailed south along the coast.

Differentiating Instruction for Universal Access

English-Language Learners

Reaching Standards

Materials: blank outline maps of the Americas and eastern Asia

1. Organize students into pairs. Have partners ask each other questions about the first Americans. Questions should focus on the following:
   - where the first Americans came from *(Asia)*
   - how they got to the Americas *(by land over the Bering Land Bridge; later in small boats)*
   - where they settled *(present-day Canada, United States, Mexico; over time, to tip of South America)*
   - how geography affected their movements, and how they lived. *(They traveled south to warmer areas; each group ate foods available locally.)*
2. Provide outline maps of the Americas. Have pairs draw the migration of early people.
   LS Verbal/Linguistic, Visual/Spatial

HSS 7.7.1; **HSS Analysis Skills:** CS 3, HI 1

Alternative Assessment Handbook, Rubric 20: Map Creation

Answers

Interpreting Maps **1.** *south and east;* **2.** *ice sheets, mountains, rivers*

Reading Check *ice formed, dropping the water level and forming the Bering Land Bridge, over which people crossed from Asia to North America*

Direct Teach

Main Idea

❷ Mesoamerican and North American Societies

Early societies existed in Mesoamerica and North America.

Define What are glyphs? *symbols that represent ideas in a system of writing*

Recall What were some of the accomplishments of the Maya? *They built stone temples, palaces, and bridges; created calendars; and studied mathematics and astronomy.*

Generalize What did the Anasazi, Hopewell, and Mississippian societies have in common? *were all farming cultures*

HSS 7.7.1; **HSS Analysis Skills:** HI 1

Info to Know

Inca Road System Across their empire, the Inca built a network of thousands of miles of roads. These roads let armies and official messengers move quickly throughout the empire. Later, Spanish conquistadors would use these same roads to move their armies through the empire.

A Mississippian Game The Mississippians often played games, including a game called chunkey. This game involved one player rolling a stone disk down a court, while other players threw poles at the spot where they thought the stone would stop. The player whose pole landed closest to where the stone stopped scored points.

Mesoamerican and North American Societies

Some of the earliest American civilizations developed in Mesoamerica, also called Central America. The Olmec society was one of the first.

Mesoamerica and South America

ACADEMIC VOCABULARY
method a way of doing something

The Olmec society developed along the Mexican Gulf coast between about 1200 and 400 BC. Olmec priests created complex number and calendar systems. They also developed a method of writing using glyphs, or symbols that represent ideas.

The Maya civilization thrived in southeastern Mesoamerica from about AD 300 to 900. The Maya built large stone temples, palaces, and bridges. They created calendars and studied mathematics and astronomy.

About AD 1200, Aztec invaders came south and occupied the central valley of Mexico. At the same time, the Inca of South America created their own civilization in the Andes Mountains. Eventually, the Inca Empire stretched from present-day Ecuador to central Chile.

North American Societies

Although less populated than South America and Mesoamerica, North America had several farming cultures. One of these, the Anasazi (ah-nuh-SAH-zee), lived in the Four Corners region, where present-day Arizona, Colorado, New Mexico, and Utah meet.

The Hopewell, another farming culture, lived along the Mississippi, Ohio, and lower Missouri River valleys. They supported their large populations with agriculture and trade. They built large burial mounds to honor their dead. The Mississippians lived along the Ohio and Mississippi rivers. They, too, farmed, traded, and built large burial mounds.

READING CHECK **Summarizing** What early societies existed in Mesoamerica and North America?

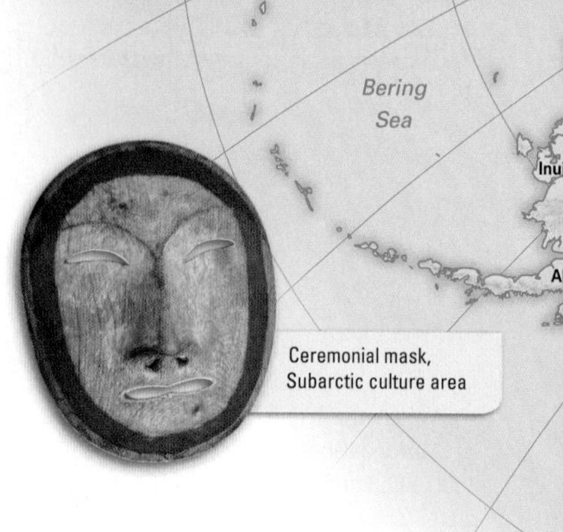

Ceremonial mask, Subarctic culture area

Cultures in North America

Researchers use culture areas—the geographic locations that influenced societies—to help them describe ancient Native American peoples. North America is divided into several culture areas.

Far North

The Far North of North America is divided into the Arctic and Subarctic culture areas. Both regions have long, cold winters and short summers. Few plants grow in the Arctic because the ground is always frozen beneath a thin, top layer of soil. The Inuit peoples adapted to these harsh conditions in present-day northern Alaska and Canada. The Aleut lived in western Alaska. The two groups shared many cultural features, including language. Both survived by fishing and by hunting large mammals. They also depended on dogs for many tasks, such as hunting and pulling sleds.

South of the Arctic lies the Subarctic, home to groups such as the Dogrib and Montagnais peoples. While following the seasonal migrations of the deer, they lived in temporary shelters made of animal skins. At other times they lived in villages made up of log houses.

Collaborative Learning

Standards Proficiency

Early American Societies Flash Cards

HSS 7.7.1; **HSS Analysis Skills:** HR 1, HI 1

Materials: seven blank note cards per student

1. Give each student seven blank note cards.
2. Ask students to label each of the cards with one of the following: *Olmec, Maya, Aztec, Inca, Anasazi, Hopewell,* and *Mississippians.*
3. On each card, have students write one question about an aspect of the labeled early society. Have students write the answers on the back of the cards.
4. Pair students and have partners use their cards to quiz each other. **LS Interpersonal**
5. **Extend** Organize students into groups and have each group conduct research on one of these Native American societies and the ways in which geography influenced it. Have groups report their findings to the class. **LS Verbal/Linguistic**

Alternative Assessment Handbook, Rubric 30: Research

Answers

Reading Check *Mesoamerica—Olmec, Maya, Aztec; North America—Anasazi, Hopewell, Mississippian*

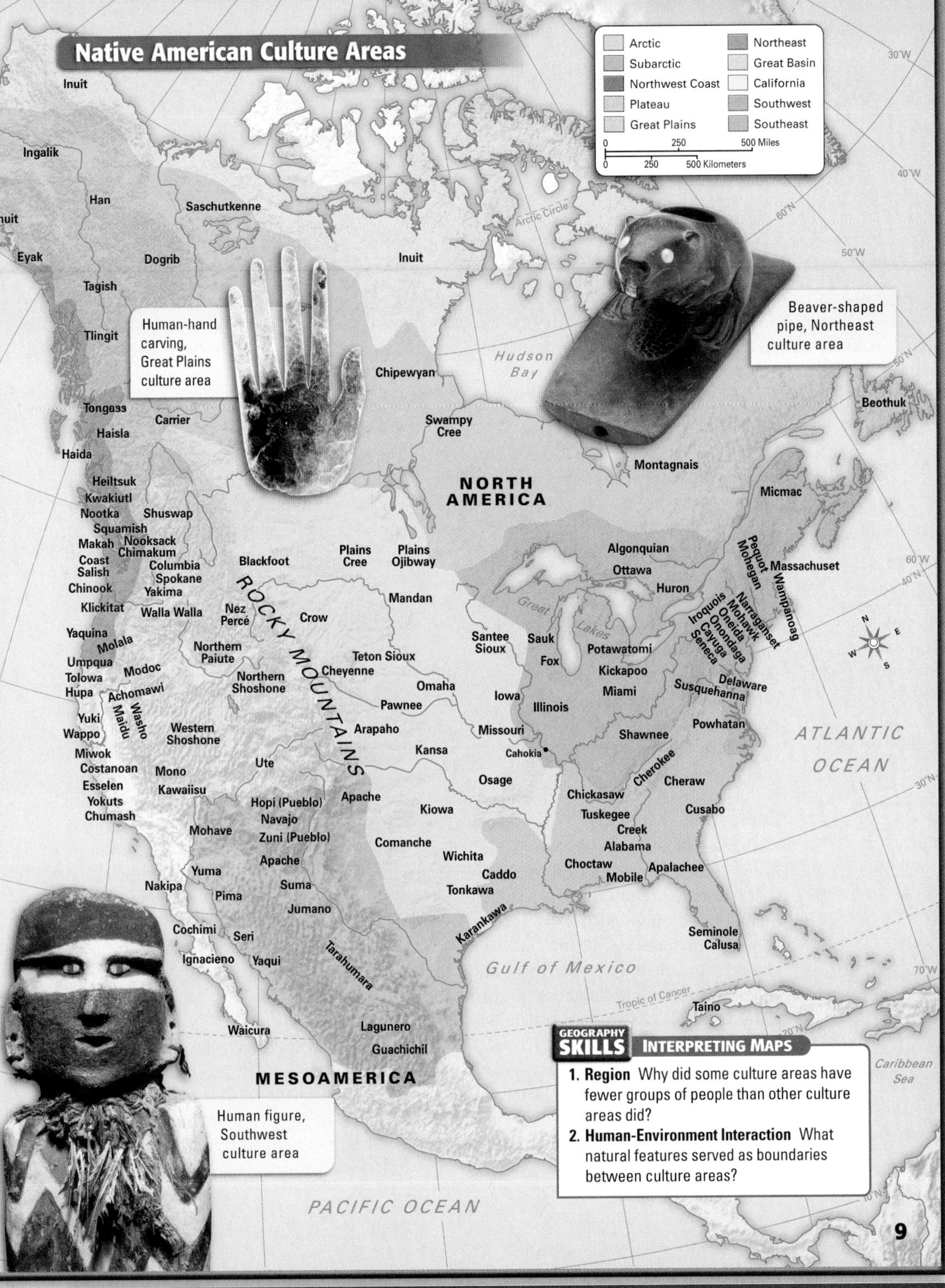

Human-hand carving, Great Plains culture area

Beaver-shaped pipe, Northeast culture area

Human figure, Southwest culture area

GEOGRAPHY SKILLS INTERPRETING MAPS

1. **Region** Why did some culture areas have fewer groups of people than other culture areas did?
2. **Human-Environment Interaction** What natural features served as boundaries between culture areas?

Direct Teach

Main Idea

❸ Cultures in North America

Cultures in North America were influenced by the environment.

Define What is a culture area? *a geographic location that influenced the society living there*

Contrast What was the main difference between the Inuit and the Aleut? *The Inuit lived in present-day northern Alaska and Canada, while the Aleut lived in western Alaska.*

Draw Inferences Why did Subarctic peoples live in different types of shelter at different times? *When following the seasonal migrations of deer, these peoples needed shelters they could move easily. The rest of the time, they could live in more permanent dwellings.*

CRF: Primary Source Activity: Iroquois Creation Legend

Map Transparency: Native American Culture Areas

HSS 7.7.1; HSS **Analysis Skills:** HI 1

Info to Know

Getting Around in the Far North In addition to dogsleds, the Inuit and Aleut used kayaks, or one-person canoes covered with skins. Kayaks enabled the Inuit to cross icy waters in the Arctic.

Summarize How did the Inuit and Aleut adapt their methods of travel to their harsh environment? *traveled by sled to cross over snow easily and by kayaks to cross icy waters*

Social Studies Skills: Creating Maps

Reaching Standards

Mapping Native American Culture Groups

HSS 7.7.1; HSS **Analysis Skills:** CS 3

Materials: colored pencils, blank outline maps of North America

1. Have students examine the above map, "Native American Culture Areas."
2. Have students label the following on blank maps of North America:
   - Native American culture areas and groups covered in this section
   - three distinguishing features about each culture area, such as methods of obtaining food, types of shelter, types of government, and religious rituals
   - major geographical features, such as mountain ranges and bodies of water.
3. Maps should also include a title and a legend.
4. Have students refer to their maps as you review how the environment influenced cultures in North America. LS **Visual/Spatial**

Alternative Assessment Handbook, Rubric 20: Map Creation

Answers

Interpreting Maps 1. *because some culture areas were less suitable for habitat because of harsh climates or a lack of food or water sources;* **2.** *rivers, lakes, mountain ranges, deserts*

Direct Teach

Main Idea

3 Cultures in North America

Cultures in North America were influenced by the environment.

Find Main Ideas How did the environment influence food sources for Native Americans in the Pacific Coast and California regions? *Mild climate allowed for many food sources, which meant large populations could develop without the need for farming.*

Summarize What different methods did Native American groups of the Southwest use to adapt to their dry climate? *irrigated crops, hunted game; some raided other groups*

Compare and Contrast What were some similarities and differences between Native American cultures in the Great Plains and the East? *similarities—farming, hunting, gathering, importance of women; differences—buffalo vital on Plains; temporary shelters on Plains, fixed shelters in the East, Iroquois League in the East*

HSS 7.7.1; HSS **Analysis Skills:** HI 1

Connect to Civics

Authority and the Iroquois The Iroquois formed the Iroquois League in part to promote "peace, civil authority, righteousness, and the great law." One of the laws of the league was that members should cast aside self-interest and look after the welfare of their people.

Northeast Indians such as the Iroquois lived in longhouses made of the bark of trees. The drawing shows how the longhouses were arranged in one Iroquois village.

Why do you think a fence was placed around the longhouses?

Pacific Coast

Unlike the Far North, the Pacific Coast had a mild climate. The area had a rich supply of game animals, sea life, and wild plants. These resources allowed large populations to develop without the need for farming.

ACADEMIC VOCABULARY
develop: the process of growing or improving

People in the Northwest like the Kwakiutl and the Chinook built wooden houses and carved images of **totems**—ancestor or animal spirits—on tall, wooden poles. People showed their wealth and earned social standing by holding special events called potlatches. At these gatherings hosts gave away most of their belongings to gain respect.

California

Farther south along the coast was the California region. Native Americans living in this area had many food sources available year-round, so farming was not necessary. One major plant food was acorns, which were ground into a flour. People in the California region also fished and hunted deer and other game. Most Native Americans here lived in isolated groups of families. Each of these groups had a small population of only 50 to 300 people. Among these Native American groups, including the Pomo, Hupa, and Yurok, more than 100 different languages were spoken.

West and Southwest

The West and Southwest of the present-day United States received less rain than the Pacific Coast and California regions did. To survive, Native Americans fished, hunted, and gathered plants. Groups in the West (which is divided into the Great Basin and Plateau regions) and Southwest included the Modoc and Nez Percé.

Native Americans of the West adapted to the drier climate by gathering seeds, digging roots, and trapping small animals for food. Most groups in this region, including the Paiute, Shoshone, and Ute, spoke the same language.

Native Americans of the Southwest also adapted to a dry climate. Southwestern culture groups included the Apache, Navajo, and Pueblo. The Pueblo irrigated their land to grow crops. Pueblo religion focused on two key areas of Pueblo life—rain and maize. The Apache hunted game and raided the villages of the Pueblo and others.

Great Plains

The huge Great Plains region stretches south from Canada into Texas. This culture area is bordered by the Mississippi Valley on the east and the Rocky Mountains on the west. The Plains were mainly grassland, on which millions of buffalo and other game grazed

Critical Thinking: Finding Main Ideas

Standards Proficiency

Native Americans and the Environment

HSS 7.7.1; HSS **Analysis Skills:** HI 1, HI 2

1. Remind students that the environment influenced the ways in which each Native American culture developed.
2. Write the following culture areas for students to see: *Arctic, Subarctic, Pacific Coast, California, West, Great Basin, Southwest, Great Plains, Southeast,* and *Northeast.* Save the list.
3. Have each student list the culture areas and indicate for each one at least one way in which people in that area adapted to their environment.
4. Ask volunteers to share some of their answers with the class. Write the responses for students to see next to the culture areas you listed at the start of the activity.
5. **Link to Today** Have students identify the culture area that existed where they live. Then have students compare and contrast their lives to the lives of ancient Native Americans who lived in their area. LS **Verbal/Linguistic**

Alternative Assessment Handbook, Rubric 11: Discussions

Answers

Iroquois Longhouse *for protection and defensive purposes* in herds. Groups like the Mandan and the Pawnee grew beans, maize, and squash. Like some other Native American groups, Pawnee society was matrilineal. This means that people traced their ancestry through their mothers, not their fathers.

People on the southern Plains hunted buffalo on foot and gathered berries, nuts, and vegetables. The Arapaho, Blackfoot, and Comanche lived on the borders of the Plains. Hunters from these groups killed buffalo by chasing the animals over steep cliffs, driving them into corrals, or trapping them with a ring of fire.

East

Eastern North America was rich in sources for food and shelter. Most southeastern groups, including the Cherokee, Creek, and Seminole, lived in farming villages governed by village councils.

The Algonquian and Iroquois people were the two main groups of the Northeast. Algonquian peoples, whose territory extended to the Far North region, survived by hunting and gathering plants. Those in the south farmed, hunted, gathered plants, and fished.

To the east of the Algonquian lived the Iroquois. The Iroquois were farmers, hunters, and traders. They lived in longhouses, or rectangular homes made from logs and bark that housed 8 to 10 families.

The Iroquois also developed the **Iroquois League**. This political confederation was established by the Cayuga, Mohawk, Oneida, Onondaga, and Seneca nations. The League waged war against and made peace with non-Iroquois peoples. Its goal was to strengthen the alliance against invasion. Women selected the male members of the League council. Women could overrule council decisions and could remove its members. The League helped the Iroquois become one of the most powerful peoples in North America.

READING CHECK **Generalizing** How did the environment influence Native American cultures in North America?

SUMMARY AND PREVIEW In this section you learned about the first people in North and South America. In the next section you'll read about European exploration that led to the discovery of the Americas.

Section 1 Assessment

go.hrw.com
Online Quiz
KEYWORD: SS8 HP1

Reviewing Ideas, Terms, and People HSS 7.7.1

1. **a. Describe** How did people migrate to the Americas?
   b. Analyze How did the warmer climate affect the environment in which Paleo-Indians lived?
2. **a. Identify** What farming cultures existed in North America?
   b. Sequence In what order did Mesoamerican civilizations arise?
3. **a. Recall** What was the **Iroquois League**?
   b. Draw Conclusions Why were Native Americans who practiced agriculture more likely than hunter-gatherers to establish permanent homes?

Critical Thinking

4. **Identifing Cause and Effect** Using a chart like the one at right, show how the environments of the Far North, the Southwest, and the East affected the cultures of the Native Americans who lived in each area.

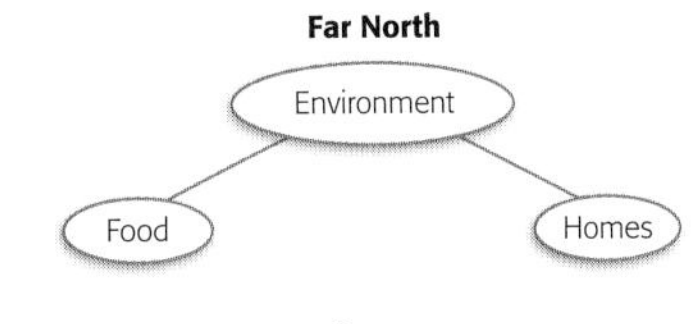

FOCUS ON WRITING

5. **Taking Notes on Native American Groups** As you read this section, take notes on each group of Native Americans discussed. Make sure to note how they lived and what was unique about their cultures.

Direct Teach

What about Horses? When reading about Native Americans of the Great Plains, some students may picture scenes from movies or television showing Plains Indians on horses. Point out to students that horses did not exist in North America at this time. Explain that European explorers brought horses to the Americas.

Review & Assess

Close

Briefly review the development of early Mesoamerican and North American societies. Remind students of each group's location and characteristics.

Review

Online Quiz, Section 1

Assess

SE Section 1 Assessment

PASS: Section 1 Quiz

Alternative Assessment Handbook

Reteach/Classroom Intervention

California Standards Review Workbook

Interactive Reader and Study Guide, Section 1

Interactive Skills Tutor CD-ROM

Section 1 Assessment Answers

1. **a.** on foot across the Bering Land Bridge; later in small boats
   b. created new environments, shorter grasses replaced taller grasses, herds of smaller animals developed, and Paleo-Indians hunted these animals
2. **a.** Anasazi, Hopewell, and Mississippians
   b. Olmec, Maya, Aztec
3. **a.** a powerful political confederation formed by the Cayuga, Mohawk, Oneida, Onondaga, and Seneca nations to strengthen their alliance against invasion and to make war and peace
   b. Farmers settled in one place to cultivate their crops; hunter-gatherers moved frequently to follow the herds.
4. Far North—food: fishing, hunting; homes: temporary shelter, log homes; Southwest—food: crops, hunting; homes: villages; East—food: hunting, gathering, farming; homes: longhouses, villages
5. Students should identify and describe the Native American societies and culture areas in this section.

Answers

Reading Check *possible answers—if there was little water, cultivating crops became difficult; groups near the oceans could easily obtain seafood; warmer climates provided abundant food.*

Preteach

Bellringer

If YOU were there . . . Use the **Daily Bellringer Transparency** to help students answer the question.

Daily Bellringer Transparency, Section 2

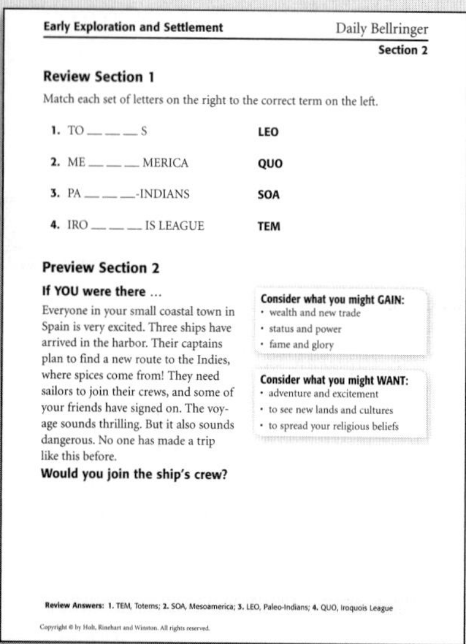

Early Exploration and Settlement Daily Bellringer

Section 2

Review Section 1

Match each set of letters on the right to the correct term on the left.

1. TO __ __ __ S	**LEO**
2. ME __ __ __ MERICA	**QUO**
3. PA __ __ __-INDIANS	**SOA**
4. IRO __ __ __ IS LEAGUE	**TEM**

Preview Section 2

If YOU were there ...

Everyone in your small coastal town in Spain is very excited. Three ships have arrived in the harbor. Their captains plan to find a new route to the Indies, where spices come from! They need sailors to join their crews, and some of your friends have signed on. The voyage sounds thrilling. But it also sounds dangerous. No one has made a trip like this before.

Would you join the ship's crew?

Consider what you might GAIN:
- wealth and new trade
- status and power
- fame and glory

Consider what you might WANT:
- adventure and excitement
- to see new lands and cultures
- to spread your religious beliefs

Review Answers: **1.** TEM, Totems; **2.** SOA, Mesoamerica; **3.** LEO, Paleo-Indians; **4.** QUO, Iroquois League

Building Vocabulary

Preteach or review the following terms:

immunity natural resistance (p. 19)

monopoly sole economic control (p. 14)

CRF: Vocabulary Builder Activity, Section 2

Standards Focus

HSS 7.11.1

Means: Know the great voyages of exploration and their routes, and explain how mapmaking changed Europeans' view of the world.

Matters: Exploration connected people and expanded their views and knowledge of the world.

HSS 7.11.2

Means: Discuss the exchange of goods, animals, and ideas among the Americas, Africa, Asia, and Europe during the 1400s and 1500s, and how this exchange affected each continent.

Matters: The exchange of plants, animals, diseases, and ideas between the "Old World" and the "New World" had dramatic and lasting effects.

SECTION 2

The Age of Exploration

What You Will Learn...

Main Ideas

1. Economic growth in Europe led to new ways of thinking.
2. Trade with Africa and Asia led to a growing interest in exploration.
3. Many European nations rushed to explore the Americas
4. The Columbian Exchange affected the Americas, Africa, Asia, and Europe.

The Big Idea

As trade routes developed across the globe, European explorers crossed the Atlantic Ocean to the Americas.

Key Terms and People

capital, *p. 13*
joint-stock companies, *p. 13*
Christopher Columbus, *p. 15*
Ferdinand Magellan, *p. 17*
Northwest Passage, *p. 17*
Columbian Exchange, *p. 18*

HSS 7.11.1 Know the great voyages of discovery, the locations of the routes, and the influence of cartography in the development of a new European worldview.

7.11.2 Discuss the exchanges of plants, animals, technology, culture, and ideas among Europe, Africa, Asia, and the Americas in the fifteenth and sixteenth centuries and the major economic and social effects on each continent.

If YOU were there...

Everyone in your small coastal town in Spain is very excited. Three ships have arrived in the harbor. Their captains plan to find a new route to the Indies, where spices come from! They need sailors to join their crews, and some of your friends have signed on. The voyage sounds thrilling. But it also sounds dangerous. No one has made a trip like this before.

Would you join the ship's crew?

BUILDING BACKGROUND Europeans had many reasons for exploring the world in the late 1400s. One was curiosity about unknown lands—part of the adventurous spirit of the Renaissance. Also, changes in trade and the economy encouraged merchants to take chances on overseas ventures.

Economic Growth in Europe

Europe's wealth and population grew steadily during the late Middle Ages. Then in the mid-1300s, Europe suffered a terrible blow when a deadly disease called the Black Death swept through Europe. Brought by merchants ships carrying infected rats from Central Asia, the disease killed millions of people. Eventually Europe recovered from the Black Death and the shortage of workers it created.

In the 1200s Europe had begun to experience the Commercial Revolution, a great change in the European economy. During this time, the way people did business changed dramatically. Many cities grew rich, often from specializing in certain crafts. For example, the Italian city of Florence became famous for dyeing cloth. Venice and many other cities also began dealing in rare goods brought from faraway lands. In this way they became rich trading centers.

Wealth became more important in European society. More than ever before, increasing one's wealth became the best way to gain greater status and power.

Teach the Big Idea: Master the Standards

Standards Proficiency

The Age of Exploration HSS 7.11.1, 7.11.2; HSS Analysis Skills: HI 1, HI 2

Materials: poster board (optional)

1. **Teach** Ask students the Main Idea questions to teach this section.
2. **Apply** Have each student create a flow chart by writing the section's main ideas on a piece of paper and drawing a large box below each main idea. Then have students enter supporting details about each main idea into the boxes. Last, have students write statements on their charts explaining how each main idea leads into or relates to the next main idea. **LS Visual/Spatial**
3. **Review** As you review the section, have students share the information in their flow charts and discuss the cause-and-effect connections among the section's main ideas.
4. **Practice/Homework** Have students create poster-size, illustrated versions of their flow charts. **LS Visual/Spatial**

Alternative Assessment Handbook, Rubrics 13: Graphic Organizers; and 28: Posters

Trade in Venice

Venice was a prosperous center of trade and business in 1494 when this picture was painted. The bridges of Venice were often lined with shops along both sides, where merchants sold cloth, jewelry, spices, and other goods from far away. People used small boats called gondolas to make their way through the canals.

How does this painting show the wealth of Venice?

Merchant families in Europe wanted to get **capital**—money or property that is used to earn more money. During the late 1300s the Medici (MED-ee-chee) family of Florence opened banks that gave loans. The borrowers repaid these loans with extra money called interest, which earned more money for the bankers. The Medici and other bankers gained influence in Europe.

Merchants also created **joint-stock companies**, or businesses in which a group of people invest together. The investors share in the companies' profits and losses. Forming joint-stock companies allowed investors to share all profits and also all losses. Therefore, a single investor would lose less than he or she would as a sole owner of a company.

READING CHECK **Analyzing** How did economic growth in Europe in the 1200s and 1300s lead to changes in business?

Trade with Africa and Asia

Much of the wealth of the Commercial Revolution was made through trade. The greatest profits came from trading with distant continents such as Africa and Asia. From Africa came gold, ivory, salt, and slaves. Salt was used to preserve foods. From Asia came silk and spices. Skilled European tailors used silk fabric to sew fancy clothing. Cooks used expensive spices to flavor food.

Overland Trade

Goods usually traveled long overland routes to reach Europe. The Silk Road, for example, stretched thousands of miles westward from China. These journeys were very dangerous for traders because of harsh conditions and possible attacks from bandits. Still, many merchants risked the trip because they could earn huge profits. Each merchant raised the price of the goods when selling to the next trader. By the time the goods arrived in Europe, their prices had risen greatly.

THE IMPACT TODAY

Many modern-day banking practices developed during the Commercial Revolution, including the bill of exchange. Like a check, the bill of exchange allowed traders to pay for goods on their routes without having to carry gold.

Direct Teach

Main Idea

1 Economic Growth in Europe

Economic growth in Europe led to new ways of thinking.

Identify What was the Commercial Revolution? *a great change in the European economy in the 1200s, during which the way people did business changed dramatically*

Draw Conclusions Why did wealth become more important in European society during this time? *Increasing one's wealth became the best way to gain status and power.*

Elaborate Why do you think banks developed as a way to provide capital? *Merchants required capital, and banks could charge interest.*

HSS Analysis Skills: HI 1, HI 2

Analyzing Visuals

Trade in Venice

Based on the image, why do you think that people in Venice built shops along bridges? *because land and space on which to build was limited*

Did you know . . .

Europeans used salt from Africa and spices from Asia to preserve their foods. Because Europeans lacked modern sanitation and refrigeration, salt and spices were important to their daily lives.

Differentiating Instruction for Universal Access

Advanced Learners/GATE

Exceeding Standards | Research Required

1. Explain to students that during the Renaissance, powerful families began to control the individual Italian trading cities. Explain that the Medici family of Florence was one example.
2. Have students conduct research on the Medici family. The research should cover not only how the family became wealthy but also what they did with their wealth.
3. Have each student write a report describing the rise of the Medici family and how they used their wealth and power to support the arts and education. The report should include a time line showing important events related to the Medici family. **LS Verbal/Linguistic**

HSS 7.11.2; **HSS Analysis Skills:** CS 1, CS 2, HI 1, HI 2

Alternative Assessment Handbook, Rubrics 30: Research; and 42: Writing to Inform

Answers

Trade in Venice *The many gondolas, the people's attire, and the crowded walkways give the scene an air of busy prosperity.*

Reading Check *Wealth became more important, cities became rich trading centers, and banking and investing grew.*

Direct Teach

Main Idea

❷ Trade with Africa and Asia

Trade with Africa and Asia led to a growing interest in exploration.

Define What is a monopoly? *sole economic control of something*

Find Main Ideas Why did European merchants want to find a sea route to Africa and Asia? *Overland trade routes had become less reliable, and merchants wanted direct access to African and Asian goods so they could bypass Italy and increase profits.*

Identify Cause and Effect Why did the Portuguese become leaders in exploration? *had the best mapmakers, sailors, shipbuilders, and financial support from Prince Henry*

Map Transparency: Trade Routes, 1200s to 1400s

HSS 7.11.1; **HSS Analysis Skills:** HI 1, HI 2

Biography

Marco Polo (1254–1324) Marco Polo was a teenager when he journeyed with his father and uncle to China. About 25 years later when he returned to Italy, he wrote *A Description of the World*. The tales of his travels in the East astonished Europeans. Here, Polo describes the splendor of Kublai Khan's great palace: "The walls of the halls and chambers are all covered with gold and silver and decorated with pictures of dragons and birds."

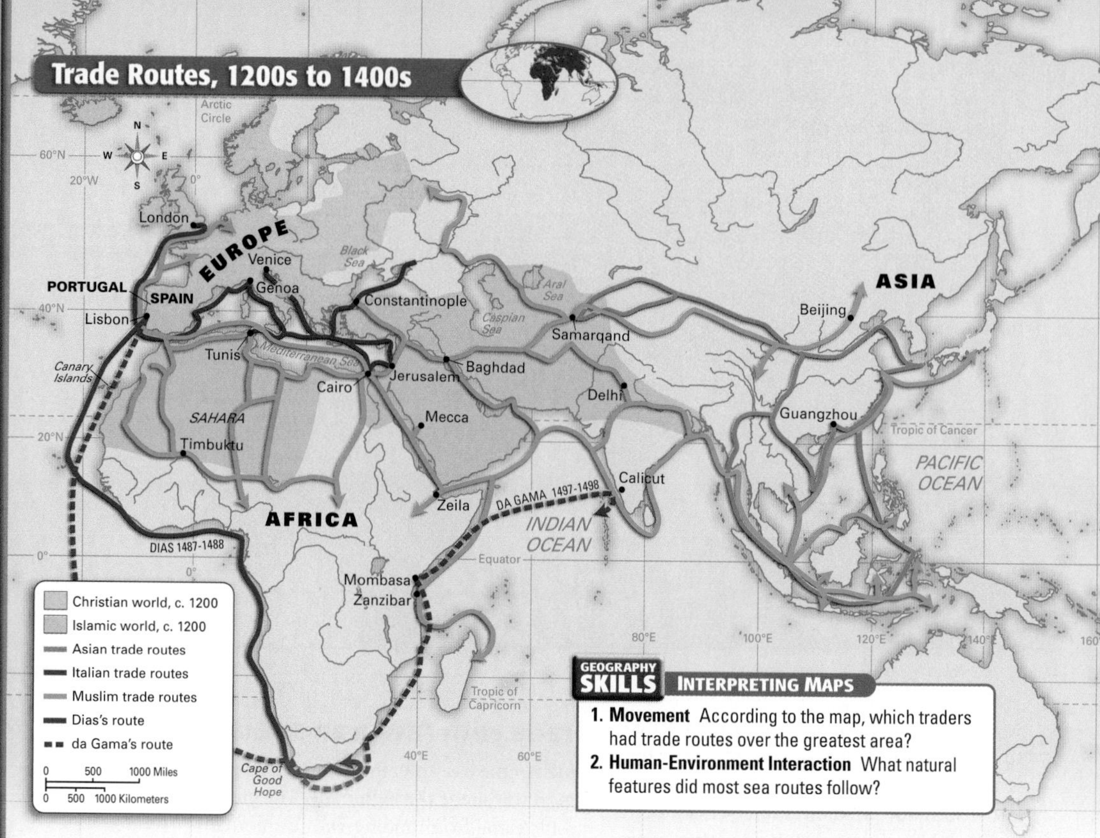

GEOGRAPHY SKILLS INTERPRETING MAPS

1. **Movement** According to the map, which traders had trade routes over the greatest area?
2. **Human-Environment Interaction** What natural features did most sea routes follow?

Search for New Routes

By 1400 many of the overland trade routes had become less reliable. At the same time, ship designs had improved. European merchants began to search for a sea route to Africa and Asia. They wanted direct access to the goods in these regions to increase their profits. They hoped to bypass merchants in Venice, who had a monopoly on, or sole economic control of, the Asian products that reached the Mediterranean. Merchants elsewhere wanted to make their own money from the trade.

Meanwhile, many educated Europeans had become interested in Asian cultures. Explorer Marco Polo's book about his travels in Asia remained popular in Europe long after his death in 1324. Many Europeans hoped to learn more about Asia and spread Christianity. All of these factors encouraged Europeans to explore the Atlantic Ocean in search of new trade routes to Asia and Africa.

Advances in Technology

New technology also led to exploration. Sailors began to use tools such as the magnetic compass and the astrolabe. The astrolabe allowed navigators to learn their ship's location by charting the position of the stars. Better charts and instruments let sailors travel the open sea without landmarks to guide them.

Finding sea routes to Africa and Asia meant crossing the Atlantic Ocean. However, no one knew the actual size of the ocean. Some people claimed that more than 10,000

Differentiating Instruction for Universal Access

Special Education Students **HSS** 7.11.1; **HSS Analysis Skills:** HI 1, HI 2

1. To help students identify the main reasons for increased European exploration in the 1400s, draw the graphic organizer here for students to see. Omit the blue, italicized answers.
2. Have each student copy the graphic organizer. Then as you discuss each topic, help students complete the graphic organizer.
LS Verbal/Linguistic, Visual/Spatial

Alternative Assessment Handbook, Rubric 13: Graphic Organizers

Trade with Africa and Asia
- *overland trade routes unreliable*
- *wanted direct trade access to increase profits*

Advances in Technology
- *better ship designs*
- *better navigation tools (magnetic compass, astrolabe)*

↓

Increased European Exploration of the Seas

Answers

Interpreting Maps 1. *the Muslims;* 2. *coastlines*

miles separated Europe from the Indies—the European name for Asia. Traveling such a long distance seemed impossible.

Portuguese Explorations

Portugal became a leader in exploration in the early 1400s. Prince Henry, known as the Navigator, greatly helped Portugal's efforts. Henry gathered together the finest mapmakers, sailors, and shipbuilders. His designers developed the caravel, a small ship that moved quickly and handled well. Henry also paid for expeditions to explore the west coast of Africa.

In 1488 Portuguese navigator Bartolomeu Dias led an expedition southward along the African coast. A storm blew the ships around the southern tip of Africa. This point became known as the Cape of Good Hope. Dias wanted to continue the voyage, but his men did not. Supplies were also low, so Dias returned to Portugal.

King Manuel of Portugal sent another explorer, Vasco da Gama, on an expedition around the Cape of Good Hope. Da Gama left Lisbon in July 1497 and arrived in southwestern India the next year. Two Muslim traders greeted da Gama when he sailed into the port of Calicut. They cried out in Portuguese, "A lucky venture, a lucky venture! Plenty of rubies, plenty of emeralds! You owe great thanks to God, for having brought you to a country holding such riches!" One of da Gama's crew members wrote, "We never expected to hear our language spoken so far away from Portugal."

The Portuguese soon learned that the Indians had been trading with Muslim and Italian merchants for many years. Da Gama made two more trips back to India. He governed a small Portuguese colony there. Portugal had won the European race for a sea route to the wealth of Asia.

READING CHECK **Finding Main Ideas** What was the most important result of da Gama's explorations?

Exploring the Americas

Stories of fabulous kingdoms and wealth in the Indies captured the imagination of **Christopher Columbus**, a sailor from Genoa, Italy. Columbus was convinced that he could reach Asia by sailing west across the Atlantic Ocean.

Christopher Columbus Sails West

Columbus persuaded King Ferdinand and Queen Isabella of Spain to pay for his expedition across the Atlantic. Some of their advisers were against the plan because they thought the globe was larger than Columbus said it was. For this reason, the king and queen allowed Columbus to have only three ships. They ordered him to bring back any items of value and to claim for Spain any lands he explored.

On August 3, 1492, Columbus's three ships set sail. The *Niña* and the *Pinta* were caravels. Columbus sailed in the larger *Santa María*. The ships carried some 90 sailors and a year's worth of supplies. They made a stop in the Canary Islands and then resumed their journey on September 6. After more than a month with no sight of land, the crew grew restless. "Here the people could stand it no longer, and complained of the long voyage," wrote Columbus in his journal. The crew threatened to rebel, so Columbus promised that if they did not find land soon, they would return to Spain.

Just a few days later, the crew saw signs of land—birds and tree branches. Columbus promised a reward "to him who first sang out that he saw land." On October 12, 1492, a lookout cried, "Land! Land!," ending the 33-day journey from the Canary Islands. Columbus thought he had landed in Japan. He believed he had circled the world and found a western route to Asia. It would be some time before he realized that the royal advisers had been right, and that the world was bigger than he thought.

Direct Teach

Main Idea

3 Exploring the Americas

Many European nations rushed to explore the Americas.

Identify and Explain Who was Christopher Columbus, and why are his voyages of exploration significant? *Italian sailor who led a 1492 voyage; historically significant for reaching the Americas, a continent then unknown to Europeans*

Make Inferences What dangers do you think Columbus and his crew faced during their voyage in 1492? *possible answers—sailing uncharted waters, storms, running out of supplies, unrest and fear*

Evaluate Do you think Columbus's voyages were a success or a failure? *success—He reached lands unknown to Europeans; failure—he did not reach the Indies or find any riches, which had been his goals.*

CRF: Biography Activity: Queen Isabella

CRF: Primary Source Activity: The Journal of Christopher Columbus

HSS 7.11.1; HSS **Analysis Skills:** HI 1

Info to Know

Sailors' Logs Before the time of Prince Henry, sea captains rarely wrote down what they did on their voyages. Prince Henry required his sailors to record notes of their journeys, however. He then collected these logs and had a cartographer use them to create maps. These maps helped Portugal dominate the seas.

Critical Thinking: Finding Main Ideas

Standards Proficiency

Financing Columbus's Journey

HSS 7.11.1; HSS **Analysis Skills:** HI 1, HI 2

Materials: posterboard, art supplies

1. Ask students why a sponsor might have been skeptical about funding Columbus's journey. *(possible answers—the high cost; no one had reached Asia by sailing west)*
2. Have students create an advertisement in which Columbus seeks financial backers for his voyage. Students' ads should explain why Columbus thought a voyage west across the Atlantic Ocean was a good idea, what he hoped to find, and what backers could hope to receive in return for their investment.
3. Encourage students to make the ads attractive and attention-grabbing while keeping them historically accurate. Students may want to include images, such as a ship, in their ads.
4. Have volunteers share their ads with the class. Then have students describe Columbus's voyages of exploration and discuss their influence on European worldviews.

LS Verbal/Linguistic

Alternative Assessment Handbook, Rubric 2: Advertisements

Answers

Reading Check *Portugal won the European race for a sea route to the wealth of Asia.*

Direct Teach

Interpreting Maps

European Exploration of the Americas

Activity Explorers Award Ceremony Organize students into five groups and assign each group one of the countries or explorations listed in the map legend. Ask students to imagine that they are creating plaques for a European explorers award ceremony. Have each group create a plaque acknowledging the exploration accomplishments of its assigned country or explorer. Then hold a mock award ceremony. **LS Interpersonal**

Info to Know

The Taino The name *Taino* came from a Native American word meaning "good" or "noble." Columbus described the Taino as gentle and loving, but he did not consider them as advanced as Europeans. He pointed out that the Taino had no knowledge of iron or weaponry. When they were first handed swords, they grabbed them by the blade and cut their hands. Although they used paint to prevent sunburn, they did not wear as much clothing as Europeans did. Such instances shaped the views of Columbus and other Europeans.

go.hrw.com
Online Resources
KEYWORD: SS8 US1
ACTIVITY: Columbus Cause-and-Effect Chart

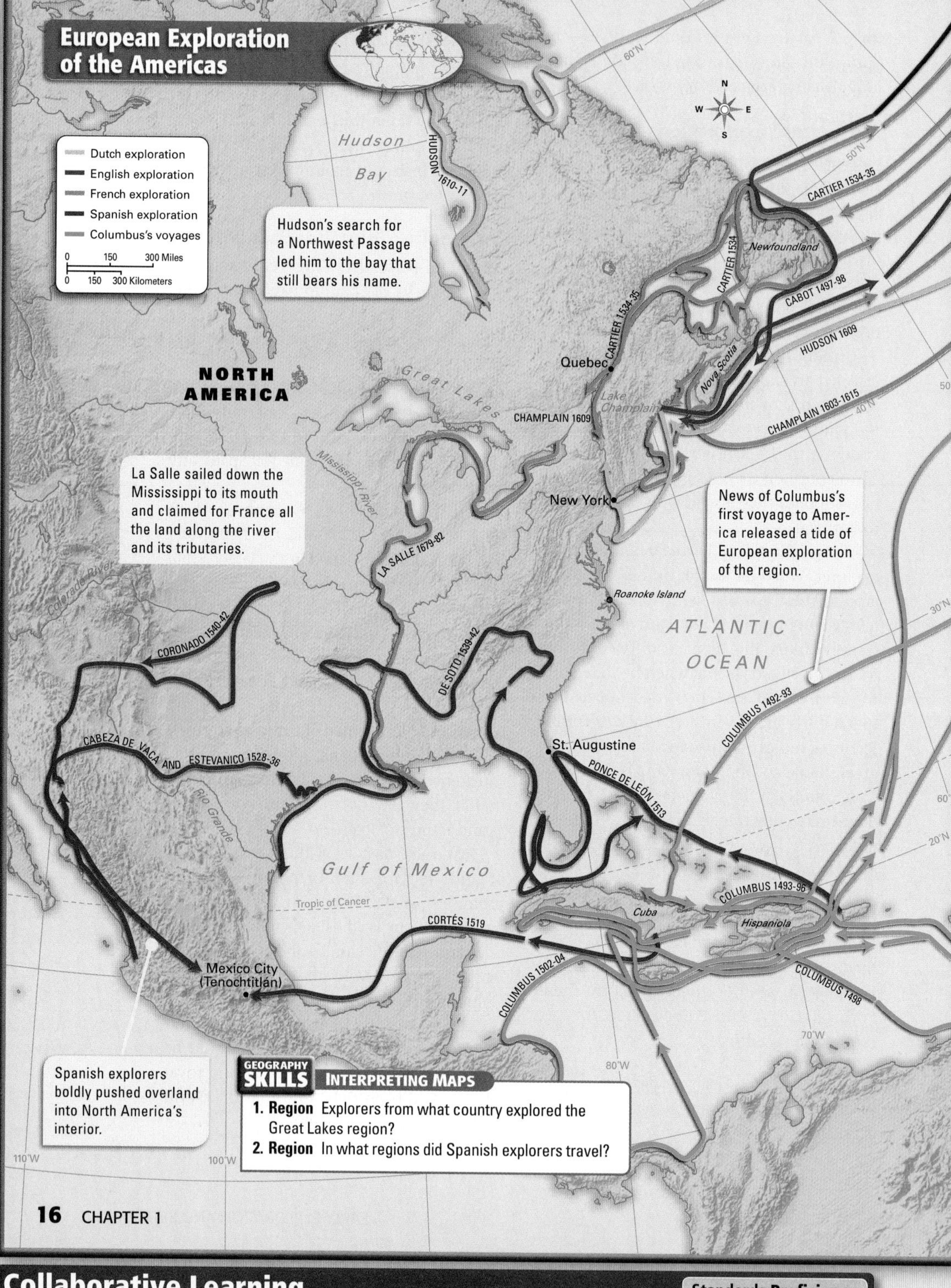

GEOGRAPHY SKILLS INTERPRETING MAPS

1. **Region** Explorers from what country explored the Great Lakes region?
2. **Region** In what regions did Spanish explorers travel?

Collaborative Learning

Standards Proficiency

Explorers Museum

HSS 7.11.1; HSS **Analysis Skills:** CS 1, CS 2, CS 3, HI 2 — Research Required

Materials: art supplies, poster board or butcher paper

1. Organize students into small groups and assign each group one of the following explorers—Bartolomeu Dias, Vasco da Gama, Christopher Columbus, Amerigo Vespucci, Vasco Núñez de Balboa, Ferdinand Magellan, Jacques Cartier, Samuel de Champlain, Henry Hudson.
2. Ask students to imagine that they are planning a museum exhibit on their assigned explorer.
3. Each group's "exhibit" should provide a summary of the explorer's achievements, an annotated time line of his travels, and a map of his travels. Encourage students to also include "artifacts," drawings, models, and additional information.
4. Have the groups display their exhibits for the class to view. **LS Interpersonal, Visual/Spatial**

Alternative Assessment Handbook, Rubrics 14: Group Activity; and 29: Presentations

Answers

Interpreting Maps **1.** *France;* **2.** *by sea into the Gulf of Mexico; overland into the southwestern and southeastern parts of North America*

Two Cultures Meet

The ships landed on an island in the Bahamas. Columbus called the island San Salvador, which means "Holy Savior." Columbus also visited an island he called Hispaniola. There he met the Taino (TY-noh). He called these Native American people Indians because he believed that he had landed in the Indies.

The Taino lived in small, peaceful farming communities. In his journal, Columbus wrote that the Taino were "so generous . . . that no one would believe it who has not seen it." However, Columbus and his crew were interested in discovering gold, not in Taino culture. After two months of exploring and collecting exotic plants and animals, Columbus decided to return to Spain.

In all, Columbus made three voyages to the West Indies. In 1504 he returned to Spain in poor health and out of favor with the Spanish throne. In 1506 he died. It would be years before Europeans realized the impact of Columbus's travels on their world.

BIOGRAPHY

Christopher Columbus

1451–1506

Christopher Columbus began his career at sea at age 14, and he quickly became an experienced sailor. He eventually ran his own ships and explored islands off the western coast of Africa for Portugal. While doing so, he learned much about sailing in the Atlantic Ocean. But he could not know just how large the ocean was. When he set off with Spain's support to cross the Atlantic, he and his crew sailed into the unknown. His bold explorations changed the world forever.

Summarizing What experiences helped Columbus prepare for the journey across the Atlantic?

Other Explorers Set Sail

In 1501 Italian explorer Amerigo Vespucci (vuh-SPOO-chee) led a Spanish fleet to the coast of present-day South America. A German mapmaker, or cartographer, labeled the continents across the ocean America in honor of Vespucci. Europeans began using the names North America and South America.

In a new settlement in present-day Panama, explorer Vasco Núñez de Balboa (NOON-yays day bahl-BOH-uh) heard stories from local Indians about another ocean. Balboa set out to find it. For weeks he and his men struggled through thick jungle and deadly swamps. In 1513 they reached the top of a mountain. From there Balboa saw a great blue sea—the Pacific Ocean—stretching as far as the eye could see.

In 1519 a Portuguese captain, **Ferdinand Magellan** (muh-JEL-uhn), set out with a Spanish fleet to sail to Asia across the "Southern Ocean." Three years later, only one of his five ships returned to Spain. Magellan had been killed during the expedition, and only 18 members of the original crew survived. These sailors were the first people to sail completely around the world, a 40,000-mile journey. They had finally found the western route to Asia.

Search for a Northwest Passage

While Spain and Portugal were exploring Central and South America, other European nations turned to North America. They hoped to find a **Northwest Passage** through North America that would let ships sail from the Atlantic to the Pacific.

Jacques Cartier (kahr-TYAY), a French sailor, led a major exploration of North America. He made two trips to present-day Canada in 1534 and 1535. He sailed into the St. Lawrence River and traveled all the way to present-day Montreal. Some 70 years later, French sailor Samuel de Champlain explored the St. Lawrence River and visited the Great Lakes, led by Indian guides. Champlain founded a small colony on the St. Lawrence

FOCUS ON READING

Be sure to notice that the highlighted definition of a vocabulary term is near the boldfaced term itself.

Direct Teach

Main Idea

❸ Exploring the Americas

Many European nations rushed to explore the Americas.

Locate Where did Columbus first land, and where did he meet the Taino people? *on an island in the Bahamas that he called San Salvador; on the island of Hispaniola*

Recall How did the Americas get their name? *A mapmaker labeled them America in honor of explorer Amerigo Vespucci, who led a Spanish voyage to South America.*

Make Inferences Why do you think explorers such as Columbus and Henry Hudson (described on the next page) sailed for countries other than their native ones? *possible answer—Their own countries may not have had the desire or the money to fund their explorations.*

- **CRF:** Literature Activity: Karlsefni Goes to Vinland
- **CRF:** Interdisciplinary Project: What will You Take on Your Sea Voyage?
- Map Transparency: European Exploration of the Americas
- HSS 7.11.1; HSS **Analysis Skills:** HI 1

Linking to Today

Native American Views of Columbus

While some Americans regard Columbus as a hero for his achievements, many Native Americans consider Columbus Day a day of mourning. They view his arrival in the Americas as the start of many problems for Indians.

Collaborative Learning

Reaching Standards

European Explorers Quiz Game

HSS 7.11.1; HSS **Analysis Skills:** CS 3, HI 1 Prep Required

Materials: 20 questions about European explorers in this section

1. Organize students into two or more teams. Tell them they are going to play a game about European explorers. Give students a day to prepare.
2. Prepare 20 questions about the explorers in this section. Questions should focus on where they went, when they traveled, what they found, and the lasting significance of their travels. In addition, some of the questions should have students refer to one of the maps in the section.
3. Play the game. Select a team to go first. Ask that team a question. If the team misses the question, give another team a chance to answer it. Award each team one point for each correctly answered question, but emphasize the fun of the game rather than who wins.

LS Interpersonal

Alternative Assessment Handbook, Rubric 14: Group Activity

Answers

Biography *his experience sailing, commanding his own ships, and exploring and sailing the Atlantic Ocean*

Direct Teach

Main Idea

4 Columbian Exchange

The Columbian Exchange affected the Americas, Africa, Asia, and Europe.

Summarize How did Native Americans use European animals such as cattle, horses, and pigs? *for transportation; to improve their diet*

Analyze What was a negative effect of the Columbian Exchange? *Diseases introduced from Europe killed hundreds of thousands of Native Americans who had no immunity to the diseases.*

Map Transparency: The Columbian Exchange

HSS 7.11.1; HSS **Analysis Skills:** HI 1, HI 2

Info to Know

Quebec In 1608, French explorer Samuel de Champlain and 32 settlers founded the colony of Quebec. The colony was located along the St. Lawrence River in what is now Canada. The first winter was hard, and only Champlain and eight other settlers survived it. The arrival of more colonists and the fur trade helped the struggling colony, though. By the time of Champlain's death in 1635, Quebec had expanded to both shores of the St. Lawrence River.

River that he named Quebec. His explorations helped France claim much of Canada.

The Dutch hired English captain Henry Hudson to enter the race to find a Northwest Passage. Hudson first sailed to present-day New York in 1609. The following year, he reached a strait that he hoped would lead to the Pacific Ocean. Instead, it led into a huge bay, later named Hudson Bay.

Neither Cartier, Champlain, nor Hudson ever found a Northwest Passage. Their explorations, however, increased European interest in North America.

READING CHECK **Finding Main Ideas**
Why did European explorers seek a Northwest Passage, and how successful were their efforts?

Columbian Exchange

Explorers brought plants, animals, and diseases to the "New World" of the Americas. They also brought back plants and animals to the "Old World"—Asia, Africa, and Europe. This transfer of plants, animals, and diseases became known as the **Columbian Exchange** because it resulted from Columbus's explorations. The Columbian Exchange dramatically changed the world.

European explorers in North and South America found many plants and animals that were unlike any seen back home. Many of these plants, including corn, tomatoes, potatoes, tobacco, and cocoa, proved valuable.

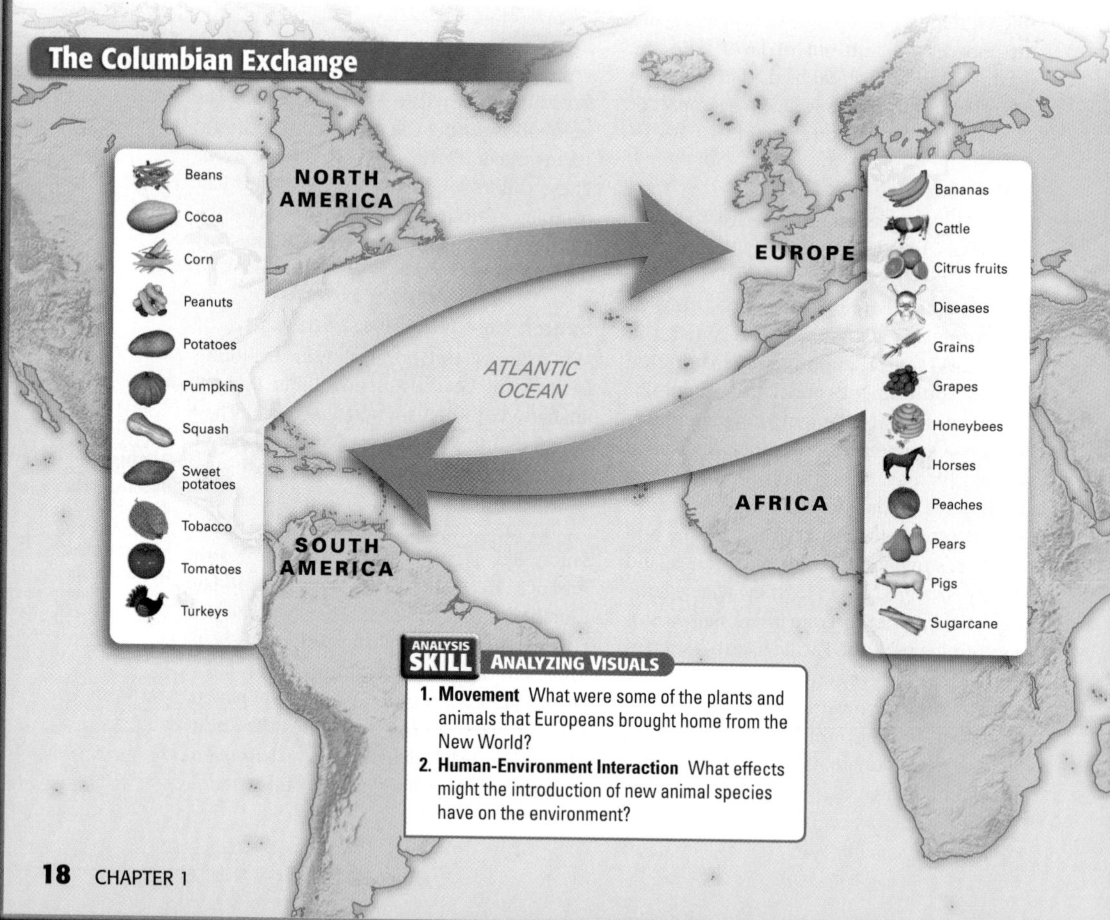

ANALYSIS SKILL **ANALYZING VISUALS**

1. **Movement** What were some of the plants and animals that Europeans brought home from the New World?
2. **Human-Environment Interaction** What effects might the introduction of new animal species have on the environment?

Critical Thinking: Finding Main Ideas

Standards Proficiency

Ad for "New World" Products

HSS 7.11.2; HSS **Analysis Skills:** HI 1

1. Ask students to imagine that they are merchants in a large European city in the early 1500s. They have just received a shipment of goods from the Americas. Have each student create a print advertisement promoting these goods.
2. Students' ads should have a picture of the goods, describe them, and encourage people to buy the new goods.
3. Display students' advertisements around the classroom. LS **Visual/Spatial**
4. **Extend** Have students discuss the exchange of goods, ideas, and information in the world today. What foods do students eat that come from other countries? What products do they use that are made elsewhere? How are ideas and information spread around the world? Help students see how the exchange of goods and people's views of the size of the world have changed since the 1500s. LS **Verbal/Linguistic**

Alternative Assessment Handbook, Rubrics 2: Advertisements; and 11: Discussions

Answers

Analyzing Visuals **1.** *See the list in the map;* **2.** *They might harm or destroy other animals or plants, multiply in large numbers, cause disease, and so on.*

Reading Check *They still hoped to find a shorter sea route to Asia by passing through North America. They were not successful.*

Explorers introduced maize to Europe for use as animal food. Many Europeans began to cook with tomatoes, particularly in Mediterranean countries. In the late 1600s some Europeans began to grow potatoes, which were from South America. Potatoes became a common food source for Europeans. Later, European settlers introduced potatoes to North America. Meanwhile, tobacco and cocoa became luxury items in Europe.

Settlers and explorers also brought plants and animals to the American continents. European horses, cattle, and pigs soon ran wild. American Indians came to use these animals for transportation and to improve their diet. They also started to farm European grains such as wheat and barley. These grains grew well in cool climates. Europeans also introduced rice from West Africa.

Without intending to do so, the explorers also introduced deadly diseases. Measles, smallpox, and typhus were common in Europe. As a result, most adult Europeans had developed immunity, or natural resistance, to them. American Indians, however, had never been exposed to such diseases. They had no immunity to them. Many Native Americans became terribly sick after the first encounters with Europeans took place.

No one knows exactly how many Indians died from European diseases, but the loss of life was staggering. Hundreds of thousands of American Indians are believed to have died after catching these diseases. Spanish historian Fernández de Oviedo wrote in 1548 about the destruction of the American Indians of Hispaniola. Of the estimated 1 million American Indians who had lived on the island in 1492, "there are not now believed to be at the present time . . . five hundred persons [left]."

There is still debate about whether any diseases traveled from the New World to the Old World. Although historians cannot prove that any did, there was not a large population decline in Europe, Asia, and Africa as in the Americas.

READING CHECK **Drawing Inferences** How did Europeans benefit from the Columbian Exchange?

SUMMARY AND PREVIEW In this section you learned about the European exploration that led to the discovery of the Americas. In the next section you'll read about the Spanish exploration of North and South America.

Section 2 Assessment

go.hrw.com
Online Quiz
KEYWORD: SS8 HP1

Reviewing Ideas, Terms, and People

HSS 7.11.1, 7.11.2

1. a. **Describe** How did **joint-stock companies** work?
   b. **Explain** How did Europe's economy change?
2. a. **Recall** Why were Europeans eager to trade with Africa and Asia?
   b. **Evaluate** Do you think trading with Asia and Africa was worth the difficulty? Explain.
3. a. **Identify** List the European explorers who journeyed to the Americas.
   b. **Analyze** How was Europe affected by **Christopher Columbus's** expedition to the West?
4. a. **Describe** What was the **Columbian Exchange**?
   b. **Elaborate** What item introduced to the Americans in the Columbian Exchange do you think was most important? Why?

Critical Thinking

5. **Sequencing** Using a chart like the one below, put the explorations in the section in the order in which they occured.

Year	Explorer	Lands Explored

FOCUS ON WRITING

6. **Taking Notes on Early Explorers** Take notes on each of the explorers discussed in this section. What countries did they come from? Why did they come? How did they interact with Native Americans?

Section 2 Assessment Answers

1. a. enabled several people to invest in a company and share the profits as well as the risks
   b. became more focused on wealth and capital
2. a. because of potential wealth from trade if direct sea routes to Asia and Africa were found
   b. possible answer—yes, because of high profits
3. a. See answer to Question 5.
   b. gained new goods, sent explorers to Americas
4. a. transfer of new animals, plants, and diseases between the Americas and Africa, Asia, Europe
   b. introduced valuable plants and animals to the Americas, Africa, Asia, Europe; spread diseases to the Americas; dramatically changed the world
5. 1488, Dias, African coast; 1492 to 1504, Columbus, West Indies; 1497–98, Gama, African coast to India; 1501, Vespucci, South American coast; 1513, Balboa, Central America, Pacific coast; 1519–22, Magellan, started round-the-world voyage; 1534, 1535, Cartier, North America; early 1600s, Champlain, St. Lawrence River, Great Lakes; 1609–10, Hudson, present-day New York, Hudson Bay
6. Students should take notes on the above explorers.

Direct Teach

Did you know . . .

Did you know that for many years some Europeans thought tomatoes were poisonous? It's true! Tomatoes originated in South America and later spread to Mesoamerica. They were first brought to Europe by Spanish explorers. Northern Europeans grew tomato plants for decoration but were not sure they were safe to eat. In Italy and Spain, however, people soon began cooking with tomatoes. Many years later, Europeans brought tomatoes back across the Atlantic to North America.

Review & Assess

Close

Divide the class in half. Have one half of the students list positive results of European exploration. Have the other half list negative results. Then have students share items on their lists as you create a master list for the class to see.

Review

- Online Quiz, Section 2

Assess

- SE Section 2 Assessment
- PASS: Section 2 Quiz
- Alternative Assessment Handbook

Reteach/Classroom Intervention

- California Standards Review Workbook
- Interactive Reader and Study Guide, Section 2
- Interactive Skills Tutor CD-ROM

Answers

Reading Check *New plants and animals that proved valuable were introduced to the Americas, Africa, Asia, and Europe.*

Preteach

Bellringer

If YOU were there . . . Use the **Daily Bellringer Transparency** to help students answer the question.

Daily Bellringer Transparency, Section 3

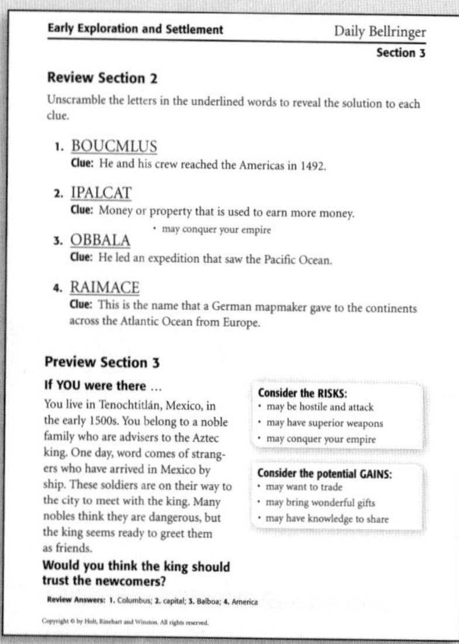
Early Exploration and Settlement — Daily Bellringer, **Section 3**

Review Section 2

Unscramble the letters in the underlined words to reveal the solution to each clue.

1. BOUCMLUS
 Clue: He and his crew reached the Americas in 1492.
2. IPALCAT
 Clue: Money or property that is used to earn more money.
3. OBBALA
 Clue: He led an expedition that saw the Pacific Ocean.
4. RAIMACE
 Clue: This is the name that a German mapmaker gave to the continents across the Atlantic Ocean from Europe.

Preview Section 3

If YOU were there ...

You live in Tenochtitlán, Mexico, in the early 1500s. You belong to a noble family who are advisers to the Aztec king. One day, word comes of strangers who have arrived in Mexico by ship. These soldiers are on their way to the city to meet with the king. Many nobles think they are dangerous, but the king seems ready to greet them as friends.

Would you think the king should trust the newcomers?

Consider the RISKS:
- may be hostile and attack
- may have superior weapons
- may conquer your empire

Consider the potential GAINS:
- may want to trade
- may bring wonderful gifts
- may have knowledge to share

Review Answers: **1.** Columbus; **2.** capital; **3.** Balboa; **4.** America

Building Vocabulary

Preteach or review the following terms:

missions settlements established by the Catholic Church to convert Native Americans to Catholicism (p. 22)

presidios military bases (p. 22)

pueblos trading posts and sometimes centers of government (p. 22)

CRF: Vocabulary Builder Activity, Section 3

Standards Focus

HSS 7.7.3

Means: Explain where the Aztec and Inca empires were located and how they were conquered by the Spanish.

Matters: The Spanish established an empire in much of the Americas and had a lasting influence on the region's culture.

SECTION 3

Spanish America

What You Will Learn...

Main Ideas

1. Spanish armies explored and conquered much of the Americas.
2. Spain used a variety of ways to govern its empire in the Americas.

The Big Idea

Spain established an empire in the Americas.

Key Terms and People

conquistadors, *p. 20*
Hernán Cortés, *p. 20*
Moctezuma II, *p. 20*
Francisco Pizarro, *p. 21*
Junípero Serra, *p. 22*
encomienda system, *p. 22*
Bartolomé de Las Casas, *p. 23*
plantations, *p. 23*

HSS 7.7.3 Explain how and where each empire arose and how the Aztec and Incan empires were defeated by the Spanish.

If YOU were there...

You live in Tenochtitlán, Mexico, in the early 1500s. You belong to a noble family who are advisers to the Aztec king. One day, word comes of strangers who have arrived in Mexico by ship. These strangers are on their way to the city to meet with the king. Many nobles think they are dangerous, but the king seems ready to greet them as friends.

Would you think the king should trust the newcomers?

BUILDING BACKGROUND The voyages of the Age of Exploration opened up new lands to Europeans. The Spanish and Portuguese took the lead in exploring these new lands. For the Spanish, one important goal was the gold and silver to be found in the Americas. Soon their armies conquered two great Native American empires.

Spanish in the Americas

Spanish **conquistadors** (kahn-kees-tuh-DAWRS) were soldiers who led military expeditions in the Americas. The governor of Cuba sent conquistador **Hernán Cortés** to present-day Mexico in 1519. Cortés heard of a wealthy land to the west ruled by a king named **Moctezuma II** (mawk-tay-soo-mah).

Conquest of the Aztec Empire

Moctezuma ruled the Aztec Empire. His capital, Tenochtitlán (tay-naweh-teet-LAHN), was a large city with temples and buildings on an island in the middle of a lake. The Aztec had thousands of warriors. In contrast, Cortés had only 508 soldiers, around 100 sailors, 16 horses, and some guns. Cortés hoped that his superior weapons would bring him victory. Cortés also received help from an Indian woman named Malintzin (mah-LINT-suhn) and enemies of the Aztec.

At first Moctezuma believed Cortés to be a god and welcomed him. Cortés then took Moctezuma prisoner and seized control of

Teach the Big Idea: Master the Standards

Standards Proficiency

Spanish America

HSS 7.7.3; **HSS Analysis Skills:** CS 1, HI 1

Materials: posterboard, colored pencils

1. **Teach** Ask students the Main Idea questions to teach this section.
2. **Apply** Organize students into five groups. Assign each group one of the following topics: (1) Conquest of the Aztec; (2) Conquest of the Inca; (3) Spanish Rule and Settlement; (4) Spanish in California; and (5) Spanish *Encomienda* System. Ask students to imagine that they are planning a documentary of their assigned topic. Have each group create a five-scene storyboard. Each panel should combine text and images. **LS Interpersonal, Visual/Spatial**
3. **Review** As you review the section, have each group explain its storyboard to the class.
4. **Practice/Homework** Have each student write a short summary for each of the five topics listed in Step 2. **LS Verbal/Linguistic**

Alternative Assessment Handbook, Rubrics 14: Group Activity, and 29: Presentations

For Gold and Glory

The Spanish came to the Americas in search of fortune and to claim lands to expand Spain's empire. They brought with them many aspects of Spanish life including the Catholic religion.

What do you think the Aztec thought when they first met the Spanish conquistadors?

Tenochtitlán. Later, however, while Cortés was away, the Aztec drove the Spanish from their city. Moctezuma died during the fighting. Despite heavy losses, Cortés refused to accept defeat. He gathered thousands more allies and attacked Tenochtitlán again. When the fighting ended, the city lay in ruins. Smallpox and other diseases brought by the Spanish quickened the fall of the Aztec Empire.

Pizarro's Conquest of the Inca

Another conquistador, **Francisco Pizarro** (puh-ZAHR-oh), heard rumors of the Inca cities in the Andes of South America. The Inca ruled over a large territory that stretched from present-day Chile to Colombia. But, like the Aztec, the Inca had no weapons to match the conquistadors' swords and guns. The Spanish killed the Inca ruler, and by 1534 Pizarro and his American Indian allies had conquered the Inca Empire. The second great empire of the Americas had fallen.

Other Spanish Explorers

Many other Spanish explorers came to North America. In 1513, Juan Ponce de León searched present-day Florida in vain for a magical Fountain of Youth. Hernando de Soto traveled through Florida and North Carolina in 1539. The next year, Francisco Vásquez de Coronado began exploring an area stretching from present-day New Mexico to Kansas without finding the cities of gold for which he was searching. In 1542, Juan Rodríguez Cabrillo (kah-BREE-yoh) sailed 1,200 miles along the coast of what is now California. Cabrillo failed to find wealth, but his journey gave Spain a claim to the Pacific coast of North America.

READING CHECK **Contrasting** How did the expeditions of Cortés and Pizarro differ from those of other Spanish explorers in the Americas?

Direct Teach

Main Idea

❶ Spanish in the Americas

Spanish armies explored and conquered much of the Americas.

Identify and Locate What two Native American empires did Spanish conquistadors conquer, and where were these empires located? *Aztec Empire in present-day Mexico; Inca Empire in the Andes of South America*

Draw Conclusions How were small bands of Spanish conquistadors able to defeat the large and powerful Aztec and Inca empires? *because the Spanish had superior weapons*

Evaluate Why do you think Cortés destroyed the Aztec capital and killed the Aztec leader? *possible answer—to weaken Aztec resistance to Spanish rule*

Activity **Explorers' Routes** Give students blank outline maps of the Americas and have students draw the routes of at least three of the explorers discussed in this section.

- **CRF:** Biography Activities: Explorers, Malintzin
- **CRF:** Primary Source Activity: The Aztecs See Horses for the First Time
- **HSS** 7.7.3; **HSS** **Analysis Skills:** HI 1, HI 2

Did you know . . .

At the center of Tenochtitlán stood a large pyramid topped by two stone temples: one to the Aztec sun god (also the war god) and the other to the Aztec rain god.

Critical Thinking: Identifying Points of View

Standards Proficiency

An Aztec Journal

HSS 7.7.3; **HSS** **Analysis Skills:** HR 5, HI 1

Background Some Aztec believed that Cortés was actually the god Quetzalcoatl. This belief was based on Aztec legends that said Quetzalcoatl would return from beyond the sea and would have pale skin and dark hair.

1. Ask students to imagine that they are young Aztecs at the time of the arrival of Spanish forces.
2. Have students write several journal entries in which they describe the arrival of the Spanish and the events that followed through to the fall of the Aztec Empire. At a minimum, students should describe the Spaniards' dress, weapons, horses, and actions.
3. Close by having students compare and contrast Aztec and Spanish points of view about the events covered here. **LS** **Verbal/Linguistic**

- Alternative Assessment Handbook, Rubric 15: Journals
- **CRF:** Primary Source Activity: The Aztecs See Horses for the First Time

Answers

For Gold and Glory *possible answer—They were frightened of the conquistadors.*

Reading Check *Cortés and Pizarro conquered large, wealthy empires, whereas other explorers found little to conquer and little wealth.*

Direct Teach

Linking to Today

Origins of Hispanics in the United States

Have students discuss the various ways in which Hispanic culture has influenced life in the United States. *Answers will include architecture, food, music and dance, language, and religion.*

Main Idea

❷ Spanish Empire

Spain used a variety of ways to govern its empire in the Americas.

Describe How did Spain rule its American empire? *through a system of royal officials, with the Council of the Indies at the top and overseeing two viceroys, one for New Spain and one for Peru*

Summarize How did the Spanish settle New Spain? *by establishing pueblos, missions, and presidios connected by a network of roads called El Camino Real*

Defend Provide arguments against Spain's use of the encomienda system. *Students should discuss how the harsh treatment of Indian labor killed many Native Americans and led to a labor shortage.*

CRF: Biography Activity: Junípero Serra

CRF: Economics and History Activity: Mercantilism

HSS Analysis Skills: HI 1

Answers

Analyzing Information 1. *Mexico;* 2. *13 percent (4 percent in Cuba + 9 percent in Puerto Rico = 13 percent)*

LINKING TO TODAY

Origins of Hispanics in the United States

Today about 33 million people in the United States are of Hispanic origin. They account for more than 12 percent of the U.S. population—about 1 in 8 Americans. Hispanic Americans trace their roots to various countries.

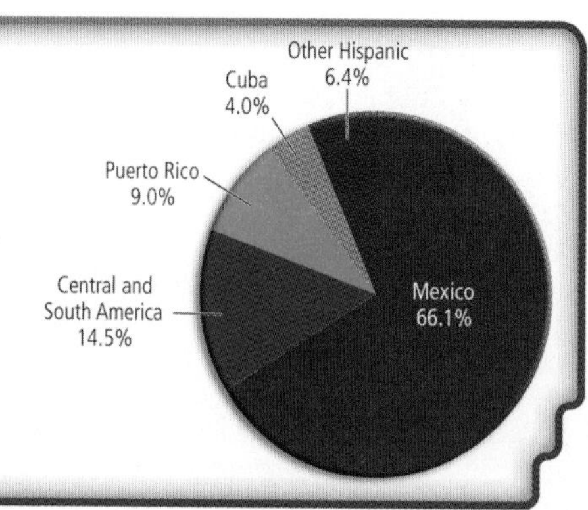

ANALYSIS SKILL ANALYZING INFORMATION

1. To what country do the largest percentage of Hispanic Americans trace their roots?
2. According to the graph, what percentage of Hispanic Americans trace their roots to Cuba and Puerto Rico?

Spanish Empire

THE IMPACT TODAY Roman Catholicism is still the most commonly practiced religion in Latin America. More than 80 percent of the population is Catholic.

Spain's American colonies helped make it very wealthy. From 1503 to 1660, Spanish treasure fleets carried 200 tons of gold and 18,600 tons of silver from the former Aztec and Inca empires to Spain. Mexico and Peru also grew food to help support Spain's growing empire.

Ruling New Spain

Spain ruled its large American empire through a system of royal officials. At the top was the Council of the Indies, formed in 1524 to govern the Americas from Spain. The Council appointed two viceroys, or royal governors. The Viceroyalty of Peru governed most of South America. The Viceroyalty of New Spain governed Central America, Mexico, and the southern part of what is now the United States.

Life in Spanish America

The Spanish established three kinds of settlements in New Spain. Pueblos served as trading posts and sometimes as centers of government. Priests started missions to convert local American Indians to Catholicism. The Spanish also built presidios, or military bases, to protect towns and missions.

The Catholic Church played an important part in ruling New Spain. The Spanish king commanded priests to teach the local people about Christianity. Some Native Americans combined Spanish customs with their own. Others rejected Spanish ideas completely.

To connect some of the scattered communities of New Spain, Spanish settlers built El Camino Real, or "the Royal Road." This network of roads ran for hundreds of miles, from Mexico City to Santa Fe. The roads later stretched to settlements in California.

The Spanish in California

California was one of the last borderland areas settled by the Spanish. In 1769 missionary **Junípero Serra** (hoo-NEE-pay-roh SER-rah) traveled to California to spread Christianity. Serra founded San Francisco and eight other missions along the Pacific coast. Most Spanish settlers saw better opportunities in Mexico and Peru, however. By 1790 fewer than 1,000 Spaniards had settled in California.

Spain's Effect on Native Americans

To reward settlers for their service to the Crown, Spain established the **encomienda** (en-koh-mee-EN-duh) **system.** It gave settlers the right to tax local Native Americans or to make them work. In exchange, these

Critical Thinking: Analyzing Information

Exceeding Standards

Life in Spanish Settlements

HSS **Analysis Skills:** HR 1, HR 3, HI 1

Research Required

1. Review with students the three basic types of settlements in New Spain: pueblos, missions, and presidios. Tell students that they will be conducting research on one type of settlement.
2. Have students create a list of questions they want to answer in their research. For example, if researching pueblos, questions might include: How were pueblos organized? What were some trade goods? What was life like in pueblos?
3. Have students conduct research to answer their questions. Each student should then use the answers to create a short report or presentation. Remind students to evaluate the validity of their sources.
4. Encourage students to include maps and illustrations in their reports. **LS Verbal/Linguistic**

Alternative Assessment Handbook, Rubrics 29: Presentations; 30: Research; and 42: Writing to Inform settlers were supposed to protect local American Indians and convert them to Christianity.

Most Spanish treated the Indians like slaves. They forced them to grow crops, to work in mines, and to herd cattle. The working conditions were hard, and many American Indians died. Some settlers spoke out against this poor treatment. **Bartolomé de Las Casas** was a Spanish priest who defended American Indians' rights.

So many Native Americans died of disease and exhaustion that, in 1501, the Spanish started bringing enslaved Africans to New Spain. Thousands of slaves worked on **plantations**, large farms that grew just one kind of crop and made huge profits for their owners. The African slave trade continued despite protests.

READING CHECK **Analyzing** How did the encomienda system strengthen Spanish rule?

SUMMARY AND PREVIEW In this section you read about the Spanish exploration of the Americas. In the next section you'll learn about developments in Europe that led to colonies in North America.

Primary Source

BOOK

Brief Account of the Devastation of the Indies

Bartolomé de Las Casas, a Catholic priest in New Spain, encouraged better treatment of American Indians.

"When they [Spaniards] have slain all those who fought for their lives or to escape the tortures they would have to endure, that is to say, when they have slain all the native rulers and young men (since the Spaniards usually spare only the women and children, who are subjected to the hardest and bitterest servitude [slavery] ever suffered by man or beast), they enslave any survivors. With these infernal [devilish] methods of tyranny they debase and weaken countless numbers of those pitiful Indian nations."

–Bartolomé de Las Casas,
from *Brief Account of the Devastation of the Indies*

ANALYSIS SKILL **ANALYZING POINTS OF VIEW**

How did Las Casas's view of the treatment of Indian groups differ from the views of other Spaniards?

Section 3 Assessment

go.hrw.com
Online Quiz
KEYWORD: SS8 HP1

Reviewing Ideas, Terms, and People HSS 7.7.3

1. a. **Identify** Who was **Moctezuma II**?
   b. **Analyze** How was **Cortés** able to conquer the Aztec Empire?
   c. **Predict** How might Juan Cabrillo's explorations affect later settlements in California?
2. a. **Summarize** What types of settlements did the Spanish create in New Spain?
   b. **Analyze** How did the **encomienda system** affect American Indians?

Critical Thinking

3. **Categorizing** Using a chart like the one on the right, identify and describe the impact Spain had on the Americas.

Spanish America	
government	
religion	
labor	

FOCUS ON WRITING

4. **Taking Notes on the Spanish Empire** Think about the section you just read. What can you tell Jacques' French family about the Aztec and the Spanish? Jot down some dates about people, places, and events.

Direct Teach

Primary Source

Brief Account of the Devastation of the Indies

In *The Conquest of America* by Tzvetan Todorov, Las Casas states, "The natural laws and rules and rights of men are common to all nations . . . whatever their sect [religious faith], law, state, color, and condition, without any difference."

Analyzing Points of View Paraphrase this statement in modern English and then explain Las Casas's point of view.

HSS **Analysis Skills:** HR 5

Review & Assess

Close

Have students summarize the Spanish conquest of the Americas from the viewpoints of both the Spaniards and Native Americans.

Review

Online Quiz, Section 3

Assess

SE Section 3 Assessment

PASS: Section 3 Quiz

Alternative Assessment Handbook

Reteach/Classroom Intervention

California Standards Review Workbook

Interactive Reader and Study Guide, Section 3

Interactive Skills Tutor CD-ROM

Section 3 Assessment Answers

1. a. ruler of the Aztec empire; taken prisoner by Hernán Cortés and later killed by the Spanish
   b. had superior weapons and armor, help from other Native Americans, and diseases weakened the Aztec population
   c. Settlements would likely be Spanish.
2. a. pueblos, missions, and presidios
   b. Native Americans became virtual slaves to the Spanish, were treated harshly, and many died.
3. government—conquered parts of the Americas and made them a part of Spain's empire, created the viceroyalties of Peru and New Spain, established pueblos; religion—taught Native Americans about Catholicism; established missions to convert Indians to Catholicism; labor—developed the encomienda system, which forced Indians to work for Spanish settlers; began importing African slaves in 1501
4. Notes should include that Spanish conquistadors led by Hernán Cortés landed in present-day Mexico in 1519 and went on to conquer the Aztec Empire.

Answers

Analyzing Points of View *He showed sympathy for the plight of Native Americans and urged better treatment for them; many other Spaniards did not care.*

Reading Check *gave Spanish settlers the right to tax local Native Americans or to make them work, which gave the Spanish control over Native Americans and a free labor force*

Preteach

Bellringer

If YOU were there . . . Use the **Daily Bellringer Transparency** to help students answer the question.

Daily Bellringer Transparency, Section 4

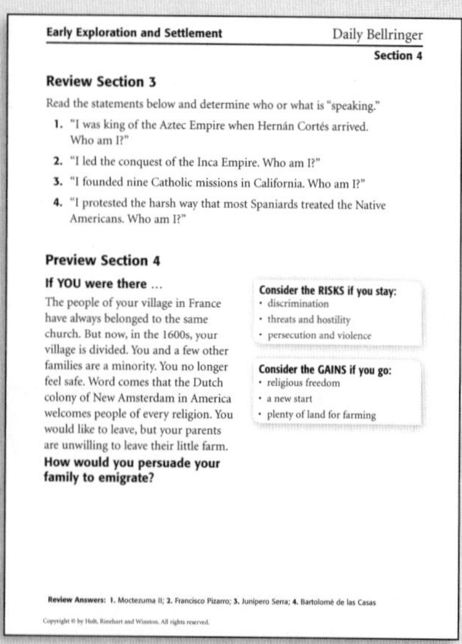

Early Exploration and Settlement — Daily Bellringer — **Section 4**

Review Section 3

Read the statements below and determine who or what is "speaking."

1. "I was king of the Aztec Empire when Hernán Cortés arrived. Who am I?"
2. "I led the conquest of the Inca Empire. Who am I?"
3. "I founded nine Catholic missions in California. Who am I?"
4. "I protested the harsh way that most Spaniards treated the Native Americans. Who am I?"

Preview Section 4

If YOU were there ...

The people of your village in France have always belonged to the same church. But now, in the 1600s, your village is divided. You and a few other families are a minority. You no longer feel safe. Word comes that the Dutch colony of New Amsterdam in America welcomes people of every religion. You would like to leave, but your parents are unwilling to leave their little farm.

How would you persuade your family to emigrate?

Consider the RISKS if you stay:
- discrimination
- threats and hostility
- persecution and violence

Consider the GAINS if you go:
- religious freedom
- a new start
- plenty of land for farming

Review Answers: **1.** Moctezuma II; **2.** Francisco Pizarro; **3.** Junipero Serra; **4.** Bartolomé de las Casas

Building Vocabulary

Preteach or review the following terms:

Huguenots French Protestants (p. 25)

sea dogs sailors that raided ships (p. 25)

CRF: Vocabulary Builder Activity, Section 4

Standards Focus

HSS 7.11.1

Means: Describe French, Dutch, Swedish, and English exploration and settlement in North America.

Matters: These groups had a lasting influence on the settlement and culture of North America.

SECTION 4

The Race for Empires

What You Will Learn...

Main Ideas

1. The Protestant Reformation led to conflict in Europe in the 1500s.
2. Conflict between Spain and England affected settlement of North America.
3. European nations raced to establish empires in North America.

The Big Idea

Other European nations challenged Spain in the Americas.

Key Terms

Protestant Reformation, *p. 25*
Protestants, *p. 25*
printing press, *p. 25*
Spanish Armada, *p. 25*
inflation, *p. 25*
charter, *p. 27*

HSS 7.11.1 Know the great voyages of discovery, the locations of the routes, and the influence of cartography in the development of a new European worldview.

If YOU were there...

The people of your village in France have always belonged to the same church. But now, in the 1600s, your village is divided. You and a few other families are a minority. You no longer feel safe. Word comes that the Dutch colony of New Amsterdam in America welcomes people of every religion. You would like to leave, but your parents are unwilling to leave their little farm.

How would you persuade your family to emigrate?

BUILDING BACKGROUND During the 1500s arguments over religion threw much of Europe into turmoil. In some places religious conflicts and political rivalries led to long-lasting wars. At the same time, several European nations were also competing for land and influence overseas. Political and religious conflicts in Europe affected settlements in the Americas.

Protestant Reformation

On October 31, 1517, a priest named Martin Luther nailed an important paper to the door of Castle Church in Wittenberg, Germany. The paper listed Ninety-five Theses, or viewpoints, about the Catholic Church. Luther charged that the church was too wealthy. He also thought the church abused its power.

Key Events in European History
c. 1450
Johann Gutenberg develops his moveable-type printing press.

Teach the Big Idea: Master the Standards

Standards Proficiency

The Race for Empires HSS 7.11.1; HSS Analysis Skills: HI 1

1. **Teach** Ask students the Main Idea questions to teach this section.
2. **Apply** Tell students they will learn how other European nations challenged Spain in the Americas. Write the text of the Big Idea (listed above) for students to see. Above it, write *Causes.* Have students list the factors that led to increased European exploration and settlement in the Americas *(Protestant Reformation, English defeat of the Spanish Armada, economic problems in Spain).* Below the Big Idea, write *Results.* Have students describe the results *(French, Dutch, Swedish, and English exploration and settlement).* **LS Verbal/Linguistic**
3. **Review** Have the class review the causes and effects of the challenges to Spain.
4. **Practice/Homework** Have each student write a one-paragraph summary of the section. **LS Verbal/Linguistic**

Alternative Assessment Handbook, Rubrics 13: Graphic Organizers; and 37: Writing Assignments

Martin Luther became well known for protesting the policies of the Catholic Church. His actions led to the **Protestant Reformation**. This religious movement began as an effort to reform the Catholic Church and spread through German towns in the 1520s and then to other parts of Europe. The reformers became known as **Protestants** because they protested the Catholic Church's practices. Many Protestants believed that the Bible intended religion to be simple. They disagreed with many of the Catholic Church's rules. They also thought the pope had too much power.

The **printing press**—a machine that produces printed copies—helped spread the ideas of the Reformation. Protestants printed large numbers of Bibles as well as short essays explaining their ideas. This let more people read and think about the Bible on their own, rather than relying on the teachings of a priest.

Conflict between Catholics and Protestants took place throughout Europe, often leading to civil war. During the late 1500s French Catholics fought French Protestants, known as Huguenots (HYOO-guh-nahts). Many Huguenots eventually emigrated to the Americas in search of religious freedom.

In 1534 King Henry VIII founded the Church of England, or the Anglican Church. By making himself the head of the church, Henry defied the authority of the pope and angered Catholics.

READING CHECK **Identifying Cause and Effect** What major religious change occurred in Europe, and what effect did it have?

Conflict between Spain and England

In the late 1500s King Philip II used Spain's great wealth to lead a Counter-Reformation against the Protestant movement. Standing in his way was English queen Elizabeth I and her sea dogs. Sea dogs were sailors who raided Spanish treasure ships. The most successful sea dog was the daring Sir Francis Drake.

Philip was angered by English attacks and began gathering the Spanish Armada, a huge fleet of about 130 ships and some 27,000 sailors and soldiers. The **Spanish Armada** was launched to invade England and overthrow Queen Elizabeth and the Anglican Church. In July 1588, however, the much smaller English fleet defeated the Armada in a huge battle.

The Armada's defeat shocked the Spanish. In addition to the naval defeat, Spain's economy was in trouble. The gold and silver that Spain received from the Americas caused high inflation. **Inflation** is a rise in the price of goods caused by an increase in the amount of money in use. Economic problems, combined with England's defeat of the Spanish Armada, led countries such as England, France, and the Netherlands to challenge Spanish power overseas.

READING CHECK **Analyzing** What led to the decline of the Spanish Empire?

1517
Martin Luther nails his Ninety-five Theses to the door of a church in Wittenberg, Germany.

1588
The English defeat the Spanish Armada. The loss greatly weakens Spain, allowing other European countries to claim land in North America.

Direct Teach

Main Idea

1 Protestant Reformation

The Protestant Reformation led to conflict in Europe in the 1500s.

Recall How did Protestants come to be called by that name? *because they protested the policies of the Catholic Church*

Analyze Explain the role of technology in the spread of the Protestant Reformation. *development of the printing press helped spread the ideas of the Protestant Reformation*

HSS **Analysis Skills:** HI 1

Main Idea

2 Conflict between Spain and England

Conflict between Spain and England affected settlement of North America.

Identify Who were sea dogs? *English sailors encouraged by Queen Elizabeth to raid Spanish treasure ships*

Draw Conclusions How did the defeat of the Spanish Armada affect European settlement of North America? *Other European nations challenged Spain by setting up their own colonies in the Americas.*

HSS 7.11.1; HSS **Analysis Skills:** HI 1

Differentiating Instruction for Universal Access

Learners Having Difficulty

Reaching Standards

1. To help students understand the factors that led other nations to challenge Spain in the Americas, draw the graphic organizer here for students to see. Omit the blue, italicized answers.
2. Have students copy and complete the graphic organizer. Pair students who are having difficulty with students who have mastered the content. LS **Visual/Spatial**

HSS **Analysis Skills:** HI 1, HI 2

Cause:	Cause:
England's defeat of the Spanish Armada in 1588	*Economic problems in Spain because of inflation*

↓

Spain's power declines. Other nations race to challenge Spain in the Americas.

Answers

Reading Check (left) *The Protestant Reformation occurred, resulting in religious and political conflict and the formation of the Anglican Church in England.*

Reading Check (right) *Protestant Reformation, economic problems in Spain as a result of inflation, and the English defeat of the Spanish Armada*

Direct Teach

Main Idea

❸ European Empires

European nations raced to establish empires in North America.

Recall What did the French call their North American territory, and where was it located? *New France; upper northwest Canada, along the Great Lakes and Mississippi River*

Contrast How did the way the French treated Native Americans differ from the way other Europeans treated them? *The French treated Native Americans with more respect, learning their languages and ways of life and trading with them.*

Evaluate Which nation do you think was most successful in challenging Spain in the Americas—France, the Netherlands, Sweden, or England? *Answers will vary, but students should exhibit an understanding of each nation's American settlement.*

Map Transparency: Empires in North America c. 1765

HSS 7.11.1; HSS **Analysis Skills:** HI 1

Linking to Today

Explorers' Legacies Many cities in the United States are named after early explorers. Balboa, California, and Joliet, Illinois are two examples. Ask students if they can name others.

go.hrw.com

Online Resources

KEYWORD: SS8 US1
ACTIVITY: Map of Settlements in North America

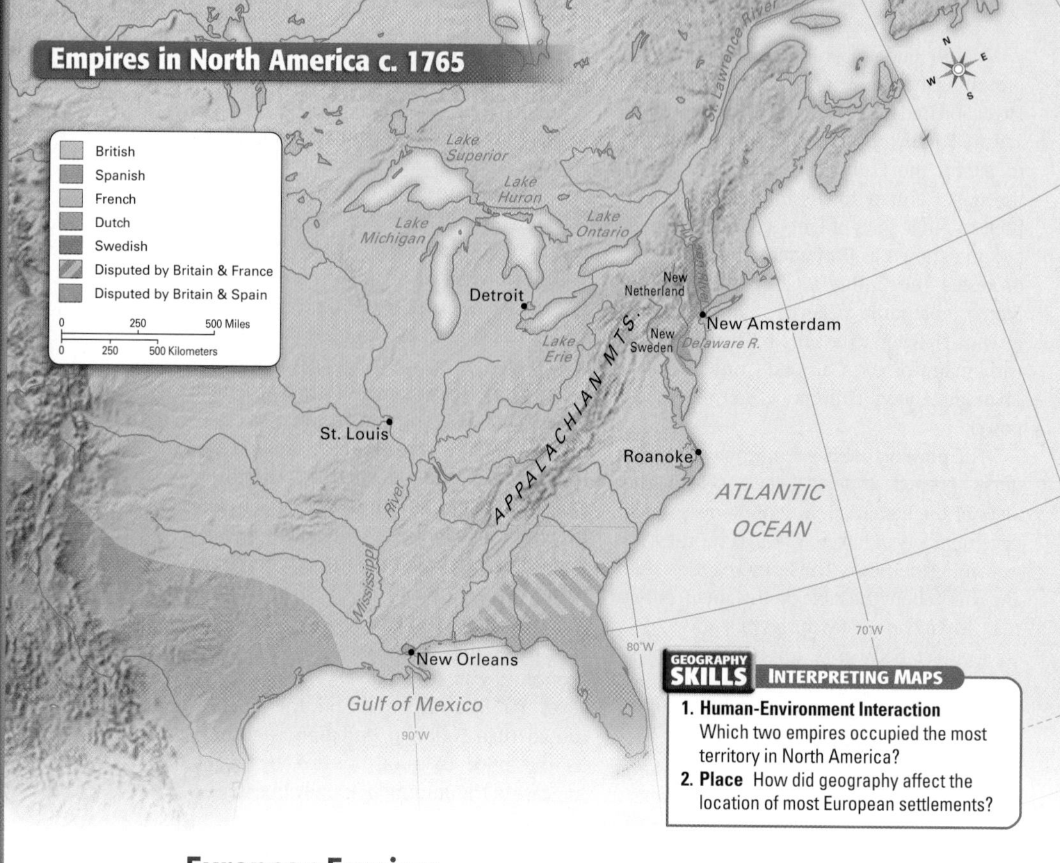

GEOGRAPHY SKILLS INTERPRETING MAPS

1. **Human-Environment Interaction** Which two empires occupied the most territory in North America?
2. **Place** How did geography affect the location of most European settlements?

European Empires

In the late 1600s the French began spreading out from the St. Lawrence River. Calling their North American territory New France, French fur traders, explorers, and missionaries were all on the move.

In the 1650s French missionaries reported stories about "a beautiful river, large, broad, and deep." In 1673 explorer Louis Jolliet (jahl-ee-ET) and missionary Jacques Marquette set out to find this great river, the Mississippi. They reached it and traveled down it as far as present-day Arkansas.

Nine years later René-Robert de La Salle followed the Mississippi River to the Gulf of Mexico. He claimed the Mississippi Valley for King Louis XIV of France. To honor the king, La Salle named the region Louisiana.

Starting in the early 1700s, the French built new outposts. These included Detroit on the Great Lakes and Saint Louis and New Orleans along the Mississippi River. Most towns in the French territory were small. By 1688 there were only about 12,000 French settlers in New France. Its small population and the value of the fur trade led French settlers to ally and trade with local American Indians.

Because of their close trading relationships, the French treated American Indians with more respect than did some other European settlers. Many French settlers learned American Indian languages and adopted their ways of life. In time, these close relationships would aid the French in claiming large amounts of land in their North American empire.

Collaborative Learning

Standards Proficiency

Interviewing an Explorer HSS 7.11.1; HSS **Analysis Skills:** HI 1

1. Organize students into pairs and assign each pair one of the explorers covered in this section.
2. Have each pair create a skit in which one student plays the role of an interviewer and the other student plays the role of the assigned explorer.
3. Partners should work together to write questions and answers for an interview of the explorer and his achievements, including where he went and when, and the significance of the explorations. Encourage students to use their historical imaginations to enliven their interviews. If time allows, have students conduct research to learn more about their explorers.
4. Have students rehearse their interviews and then present them before the class.

LS **Interpersonal, Verbal/Linguistic**

Alternative Assessment Handbook, Rubric 33: Skits and Reader's Theater

Answers

Interpreting Maps 1. *France and Great Britain;* **2.** *Rivers, lakes, and mountain ranges served as common boundaries between nations' territories, and settlements tended to be located along rivers and lakes or near coastlines.*

New Netherland and New Sweden

The Dutch, who had merchant fleets around the world, came to America in search of trade. Explorer Henry Hudson's first voyage to North America gave the Dutch a claim to the land between the Delaware and Hudson rivers. He called it New Netherland. In 1624 the newly formed Dutch West India Company sent about 30 families to settle in New Netherland. Two years later Peter Minuit bought Manhattan Island from local American Indians and founded the town of New Amsterdam. To attract colonists, the Dutch practiced religious toleration.

Minuit also helped Swedish settlers found New Sweden along the Delaware River. Swedish settlers were among the first in North America to build log cabins. Like the Dutch and French, they traded with Native Americans and trapped animals for fur. The Swedish settlement was small, but the Dutch felt that it threatened Dutch lands and fur trading. The two sides fought a series of battles. Finally the governor of New Netherland, Peter Stuyvesant (STY-vi-suhnt), conquered New Sweden in 1655.

English Settlement

In the late 1500s England decided to start its own American colony in order to establish a presence in the New World. Sir Walter Raleigh received a **charter,** a document giving permission to start a colony. He sent an expedition that landed in present-day Virginia and North Carolina. Raleigh named the entire area Virginia.

In 1585 Raleigh sent another group to found a colony on Roanoke Island. The English colonists found life hard. They fought with local American Indians and had trouble finding and growing food. In 1586, Sir Francis Drake arrived and offered to take the remaining settlers home to England.

John White resettled the Roanoke colony in the spring of 1587. White's granddaughter, Virginia Dare, was the first English colonist born in North America. White went back to England to get more supplies, but when he returned he found the colony's buildings deserted. No one is certain what happened to the colony, though the name of a Native American group was carved into a nearby tree.

READING CHECK **Drawing Conclusions** Were the first colonies in North America successful? Why or why not?

SUMMARY AND PREVIEW In this section you learned about events in Europe that led to settlements in North America. In the next chapter you will learn more about English colonies in North America.

Section 4 Assessment

go.hrw.com Online Quiz KEYWORD: SS8 HP1

Reviewing Ideas, Terms, and People HSS 7.11.1

1. a. **Identify** What was the **Protestant Reformation**?
   b. **Explain** What role did the **printing press** play in the Protestant Reformation?
2. a. **Explain** Why did Spain try to invade England?
   b. **Make Inferences** How did the defeat of the **Spanish Armada** affect European settlement of North America?
3. a. **Identify** In which parts of North America did the French settle?
   b. **Summarize** What problems did the Dutch, Swedish, and English experience?
   c. **Evaluate** Which of the European empires in North America do you think was most successful? Why?

Critical Thinking

4. **Summarizing** Using a diagram like the one below, list the European nations that established colonies in North America during the 1500s and 1600s. Include the location of these colonies.

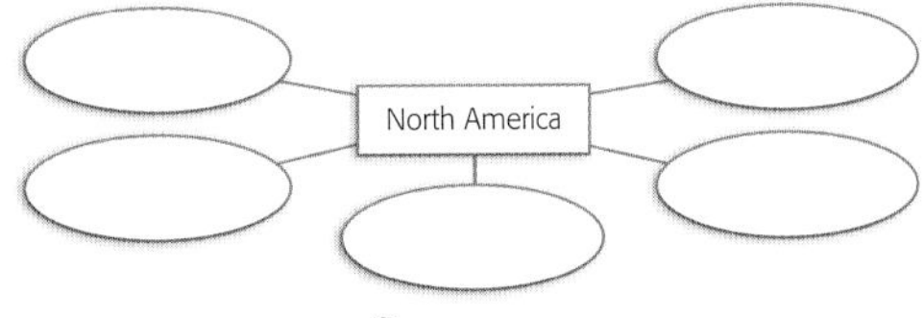

FOCUS ON WRITING

5. **Taking Notes on the French Empire and Other Settlements** What would you include in Jacques' letter about the French, Dutch, Swedish, and English people who settled in America. Why did they come? What did they want and need in their new home?

Direct Teach

Info to Know

England and Colonization Although explorers for England traveled in North America during the 1500s, the English made no serious attempt to establish colonies there for nearly 100 years. England's first attempt at colonization instead began with its neighbor, Ireland, in the late 1500s.

Review & Assess

Close

Draw a three-column chart for students to see and label the columns *Dutch and Swedish, English,* and *French.* Have students summarize each group's exploration and settlement in North America.

Review

Online Quiz, Section 4

Assess

SE Section 4 Assessment

PASS: Section 4 Quiz

Alternative Assessment Handbook

Reteach/Classroom Intervention

California Standards Review Workbook

Interactive Reader and Study Guide, Section 4

Interactive Skills Tutor CD-ROM

Section 4 Assessment Answers

1. a. a religious movement that began as an effort to reform the Catholic Church
   b. It helped spread the ideas of the Reformation.
2. a. to stop English sea dogs from attacking Spanish ships, and to overthrow England's Queen Elizabeth.
   b. Other European nations began to challenge Spain in the Americas.
3. a. inland along the St. Lawrence River, Great Lakes region, along Mississippi River
   b. Dutch and Swedes—fought over territory; English—Native Americans conflicts; food shortages
   c. Answers will vary but should reflect an understanding of each nation's American settlement.
4. France—see Question 3a answer; Netherlands—between Delaware and Hudson rivers; Sweden—along Delaware River; England—along Atlantic coast and around Hudson Bay; Spain—southeast and southwest regions of North America
5. Students' notes should accurately describe these groups' exploration and settlement in North America.

Answers

Reading Check *Some were more successful than others; French established successful trading posts, Dutch established successful settlements; Swedish settlements survived but were conquered by the Dutch, English settlement failed.*

Social Studies Skills

Framing Historical Questions

Activity Evaluating Questions Ask students to imagine that a friend of theirs has just witnessed a crime taking place. Ask students what sorts of questions they would ask their friend to learn more about the event. Then ask students to imagine that their friend has just won an award. What sorts of questions might they ask to learn more about the award and why their friend received it? Write students' suggested questions for the class to see and then evaluate each question. Point out questions that are too broad or that might be biased. Then assign students a topic from the chapter and have students practice the skill by writing five questions that would be effective in helping them conduct research on the topic. **LS Verbal/Linguistic**

Alternative Assessment Handbook, Rubric 37: Writing Assignments

HSS Analysis Skills: HR 1

Social Studies Skills

Analysis | Critical Thinking | Participation | Study

HR1 Students frame questions that can be answered by historical study and research.

Framing Historical Questions

Define the Skill

One of the most valuable ways that people gain knowledge is by asking effective questions. An effective question is one that obtains the kind of information the person asking the question desires. The ability to frame, or construct, effective questions is an important life skill as well as key to gaining a better understanding of history. Asking effective historical questions will aid you in studying history and in conducting historical research.

Learn the Skill

Effective questions are specific, straight-forward, and directly related to the topic. When we do not obtain the information we want or need, often it is because we have asked the wrong questions. Asking effective questions is not as easy as it seems. It requires thought and preparation. The following guidelines will help you in framing effective questions about history and other topics as well.

1. Determine exactly what you want to know.
2. Decide what questions to ask and write them down. Having written questions is very important. They will help guide your study or research and keep you focused on your topic and goal.
3. Review each of your questions to make sure it is specific, straight-forward, and directly related to your topic.
4. Rewrite any questions that are vague, too broad, or biased.

Questions that are vague or too broad are likely to produce information not directly related to what you want to know. For example, if you wanted to know more about trade and the voyages of exploration that are discussed in Chapter 1, "What were the voyages of exploration?" may not be a good question to ask. This question is too broad. Its answer would not give you the information you want.

Asking "Why was trade the most important cause of the voyages of exploration?" would not be an effective question either. This question is biased because it *assumes* trade was the main reason for the voyages, when that might not have been true. Good historical investigation assumes nothing that is not known to be fact. A more effective question, which would get the information you want, is: "Were trade and the voyages of exploration connected, and, if so, in what ways?". Do you see now why wording is so important in asking effective questions and why you should write out and review your questions beforehand?

Practice the Skill

Reread the information about Cortés and the Aztec on pages 20–21, then complete the activities below.

1. Suppose you wanted to learn more about Cortés's defeat of the Aztec. Decide whether each of the following would be an effective question to ask about this topic. Explain why or why not.
   - **a.** What happened when the Aztec and the Spanish met?
   - **b.** Why did other Indians betray the Aztec?
   - **c.** What resources did Cortés have that helped him conquer the Aztec?
2. Frame five questions that would be effective in helping you to learn more about this topic.

Answers

Practice the Skill 1. *(a) too broad; (b) biased because of use of word* betray; *(c) well framed question;* **2.** *Students' questions will vary but might include some of the following: What events led to conflict between Cortés and the Aztec? What events led up to Cortés's defeat of the Aztec? Where and when did Cortés's defeat of the Aztec take place? How did the weapons and armor of the Aztec compare to those of Cortés and his soldiers? What other resources did Cortés have that helped him defeat the Aztec?*

Social Studies Skills Activity: Framing Historical Questions

5W-How Questions

HSS Analysis Skills: HR 1 — Standards Proficiency

1. Write the *5W-How* questions for students to see: *Who? What? When? Where? Why?* and *How?*
2. Explain that these questions can help students frame historical questions to guide their learning and research.
3. Provide students with a topic from the chapter. Write the topic for the class to see. Have students practice as a class using the *5W-How* questions to frame historical questions about the topic. Provide guidance.
4. Then assign a second topic and have students work independently to use the *5W-How* questions to frame five historical questions about the topic. Have volunteers share their questions with the class. Give other students a chance to evaluate each question. Correct students as needed. **LS Verbal/Linguistic**

Alternative Assessment Handbook, Rubric 37: Writing Assignments

CHAPTER 1

Standards Review

Visual Summary

Use the visual summary below to help you review the main ideas of the chapter.

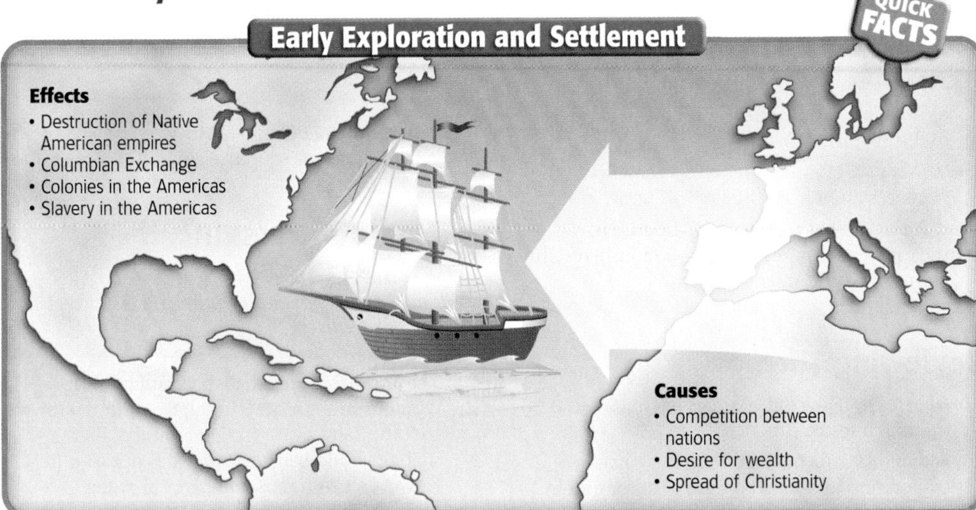

QUICK FACTS
Early Exploration and Settlement
Effects
• Destruction of Native American empires
• Columbian Exchange
• Colonies in the Americas
• Slavery in the Americas
Causes
• Competition between nations
• Desire for wealth
• Spread of Christianity

Reviewing Vocabulary, Terms, and People

Complete each sentence by filling in the blank with the correct term or person.

1. The first voyage to sail completely around the world was headed by _________ _________.
2. _____________ are people who survive by eating animals that they have caught or plants they have collected.
3. Sir Walter Raleigh founded the colony of Virginia after receiving a _________, or a grant to set up a colony, from the queen of England.
4. Large farms that specialize in growing one type of crop for profit, or _________, were common in Spanish America.
5. One of the most important European explorers was _______ _________, who was the first person to claim lands in the Americas for Spain.

Comprehension and Critical Thinking

SECTION 1 *(Pages 6–11)* **HSS 7.1.1**

6. **a. Describe** How did the first people migrate to the Americas?
   b. Compare and Contrast In what ways were societies in North America similar to and different from those in Mesoamerica and South America?
   c. Elaborate In which culture area of North America would you have preferred to live? Why?

SECTION 2 *(Pages 12–19)* **HSS 7.11.1, 7.11.2**

7. **a. Recall** Why was Columbus's discovery important?
   b. Analyze What factors led Europeans to begin their voyages of exploration?
   c. Evaluate In your opinion, did the Columbian Exchange improve or worsen life in the Americas? Explain your answer.

Answers

Visual Summary

Review and Inquiry Use the visual summary to review the chapter's main ideas. Ask students to explain or to provide examples for each of the causes and effects listed.

Quick Facts Transparency: Early Exploration and Settlement Visual Summary

Reviewing Vocabulary, Terms, and People

1. Ferdinand Magellan
2. Hunter-gatherers
3. charter
4. plantations
5. Christopher Columbus

Comprehension and Critical Thinking

6. **a.** by crossing the Bering Land Bridge during the last Ice Age
   b. similar—farming, trade, some large populations, religion; different—Mesoamerica and South America: advanced civilizations, larger population; North America: more varied culture areas, less populated
   c. Answers will vary but should reflect an understanding of the main characteristics of each culture area.

Review and Assessment Resources

Review and Reinforce

- SE Standards Review
- **CRF:** Chapter Review Activity
- California Standards Review Workbook
- Quick Facts Transparency: Early Exploration and Settlement Visual Summary
- Spanish Chapter Summary Audio CD
- Online Chapter Summaries in Six Languages
- OSP Holt PuzzlePro; GameTool for ExamView
- Quiz Game CD-ROM

Assess

- SE Standards Assessment
- PASS: Chapter Test, Forms A and B
- Alternative Assessment Handbook
- OSP ExamView Test Generator, Chapter Test
- Universal Access Modified Worksheets and Tests CD-ROM: Chapter Test
- Holt Online Assessment Program (in the Premier Online Edition)

Reteach/Intervene

- Interactive Reader and Study Guide
- Universal Access Teacher Management System: Lesson Plans for Universal Access
- Universal Access Modified Worksheets and Tests CD-ROM
- Interactive Skills Tutor CD-ROM

go.hrw.com
Online Resources
Chapter Resources:
KEYWORD: SS8 US1

Answers

7. **a.** It expanded the European view of the world and began a tide of European exploration and settlement in the Americas.
b. desire to make money by finding safer, faster, and more direct trade routes to Asia and Africa; interest in Asian culture; desire to spread Christianity; advances in technology, such as better ship designs, magnetic compass, and astrolabe
c. Answers should exhibit an understanding that the Columbian Exchange introduced many new goods to the Americas, while also leading to the conquest of some civilizations and the death of many Native Americans.

8. **a.** southern North America, Central America, much of South America
b. superior weapons and armor, horses, help from some Native Americans, harmful effects of European diseases on Native Americans
c. provided Spanish settlers with a tax system and free labor

9. **a.** It shocked Spain, weakened their power overseas, and led other countries to challenge Spain in the Americas.
b. French settlements—located in many areas of North America, mainly outposts for fur trade, treated Native Americans with respect; English settlements—located along Atlantic Coast, experienced many difficulties building colonies, had problems with Native Americans
c. possible answer—Conflicts might arise among them as they vie for land, control, and power.

Reviewing Themes

10. The last Ice Age lowered sea levels, which exposed land over which people crossed from Asia to North America.

11. Many were attempts to find better trade routes to Asia and Africa.

12. They adapted by hunting new animals such as buffalo and deer, and by developing societies in response to their environments.

SECTION 3 *(Pages 20–23)* **HSS 7.7.3**

8. **a. Identify** What territories in the Americas did Spain control?
b. Analyze What factors enabled the Spanish to defeat the Aztecs and Incas?
c. Evaluate Why was the encomienda system important to Spanish settlers?

SECTION 4 *(Pages 24–27)* **HSS 7.11.1**

9. **a. Describe** What were the results of the defeat of the Spanish Armada?
b. Contrast How did French settlements in the Americas differ from the English settlements?
c. Predict What problems might arise between the different empires that had established settlements in North America?

Reviewing Themes

10. **Geography** How did changes in climate lead to migration to the Americas?
11. **Economics** In what way were the voyages of exploration motivated by the wish for money?
12. **Religion** What role did religion play in the conflict between England and Spain?

Using the Internet

13. **Activity: Compare and Contrast** What causes large groups of people to migrate? Factors that influence why people migrate can be labeled as "push" and "pull." Poor climate and lack of resources was one of the things that "pushed" Paleo-Indians to North America. This activity will help you understand factors of migration. Enter the activity keyword, then compare and contrast push-pull factors involved in Paleo-Indian migration with the factors influencing immigration to the United States today. Create an illustrated chart to display your research.

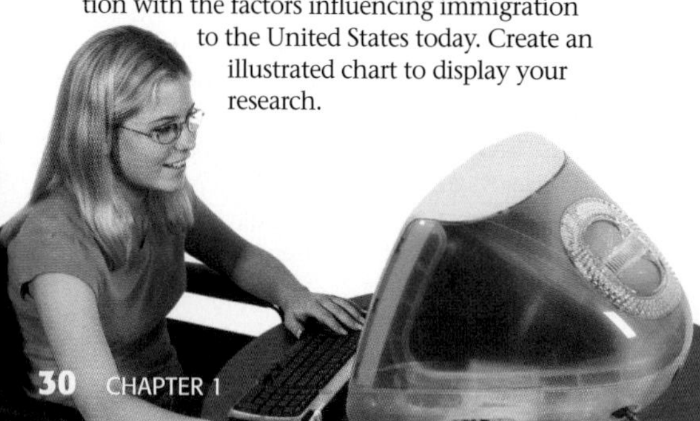

Reading Skills

Understanding Specialized Vocabulary *Use the Reading Skills taught in this chapter to answer the question about the reading selection below.*

> Merchant families in Europe wanted to get capital—money or property that is used to earn more money. *(p. 13)*

14. What is the definition of the word *capital* according to the sentence above?

Social Studies Skills

Framing Historical Questions *Use the Social Studies Skills taught in this chapter to answer the question about the reading selection below.*

> The Taino lived in small, peaceful farming communities. In his journal, Columbus wrote that the Taino were "so generous . . . that no one would believe it who has not seen it." However, Columbus and his crew were interested in discovering gold, not in Taino culture. *(p. 17)*

15. Which question is answered by the above passage?
a. What kind of clothing did the Taino wear?
b. In what kind of towns did the Taino live?
c. Did Columbus and his crew discover gold?
d. Did Columbus and the Taino fight each other?

FOCUS ON WRITING

16. **Writing Your Letter** First, review your notes and decide how Jacques feels about all the different groups of people who live in America. Remember that he has Native American friends, but he also takes advantage of America's opportunities. Then write a letter from Jacques to his family in France. Tell his family about some of the people Jacques has met in America, as well as some of the interesting things that are happening. End with a sentence about Jacques's hopes and fears for the future of the Americas and its people.

30 CHAPTER 1

Using the Internet

13. Go to the HRW Web site and enter the keyword shown to access a rubric for this activity.

KEYWORD: SS8 TEACHER

Reading Skills

14. money or property used to earn more money

Social Studies Skills

15. b

Focus on Writing

16. **Rubric** Students' letters should:
- begin with a main idea
- describe Jacques's feelings about the different groups living in America
- describe at least three people and three events from early America
- use correct grammar, punctuation, spelling, and capitalization

Standards Assessment

DIRECTIONS: Read each question and write the letter of the best response.

1

> "I came to get gold, not to till the soil like a peasant."

Which person would have been *most* likely to have made such a statement?

A Spanish conquistador Hernán Cortés
B Aztec ruler Moctezuma II
C French missionary Jacques Marquette
D Spanish priest Bartolomé de Las Casas

2 Before the arrival of the first Europeans, the most advanced Native American societies were located in what is now

A California.
B the eastern United States.
C the American Southwest.
D Mexico.

3 All of the following established colonies in North America *except*

A the Portuguese.
B the Dutch.
C the English.
D the French.

4 Which of the following *best* illustrates the process known as the Columbian Exchange?

A Christopher Columbus sailed west to reach Asia and encountered the Americas.
B Corn and tomatoes were introduced to Europe from America.
C Asian goods moved long distances along the Silk Road to reach Europe.
D Advances in technology allowed sailors to better navigate on the open seas.

5 How did the Reformation in Europe affect European settlement of the Americas?

A It caused Spain to abandon its New World colonies.
B It resulted in Protestants conquering Mexico.
C It created religious tensions in Europe that some people fled to America to escape.
D It led to freedom of worship in most European colonies in the Americas.

Connecting with Past Learnings

6 Indians in Spain's encomienda system in the Americas were *most* similar to the

A skilled European tailors who used silk fabric.
B serfs on manors in medieval Europe.
C samurai who served masters in feudal Japan.
D heretics persecuted by the Spanish Inquisition.

7 In Grade 7 you learned about inventions that aided explorers. The compass, which helped Europeans make the voyages that brought them into contact with Native American peoples, was first developed

A in Italy during the Renaissance.
B by Islamic scholars in North Africa.
C by the Polish scientist Copernicus.
D in early China.

Answers

1. A
Break Down the Question Tell students to consider what they know about each person listed and what he did before selecting an answer.

2. D
Break Down the Question This question requires students to recall that the Aztec society in Mexico was the most advanced Native American society before Europeans arrived.

3. A
Break Down the Question This question requires students to recall factual information. Refer students who miss the question to the coverage of American colonization in Sections 3 and 4.

4. B
Break Down the Question Point out that the italicized word *best* means that more than one answer may be correct and that students are to choose the one that provides the most complete answer.

5. C
Break Down the Question This question requires students to identify cause and effect. Refer students who miss the question to the Protestant Reformation material in Section 4.

6. B
Break Down the Question This question requires students to recall information covered in Grade 7.

7. D
Break Down the Question This question requires students to recall information covered in Grade 7.

Intervention Resources

Reproducible

- Interactive Reader and Study Guide
- Universal Access Teacher Management System: Lesson Plans for Universal Access

Technology

- Quick Facts Transparency: Chapter Visual Summary
- Universal Access Modified Worksheets and Tests CD-ROM
- Interactive Skills Tutor CD-ROM

Tips for Test Taking

Master the Question Have you ever said, "I knew the answer, but I thought the question asked something else"? Be certain that you **know** what each test question is asking. Remind students to read a question at least twice before reading the answer choices. Have students watch for words such as *not* and *except* that affect the meaning of the question and signal that they should look for the opposite of something.

Standards Review

Have students review the following standards in their workbooks.

- California Standards Review Workbook: HSS 7.7, 7.11

Chapter 2 Planning Guide

The English Colonies

Chapter Overview	Reproducible Resources	Technology Resources
CHAPTER 2 **pp. 32–73** **Overview: In this chapter, students will learn about the English colonies in North America and the tensions that developed there over British tax policies.** See p. 32 for the California History–Social Science standards covered in this chapter.	**Universal Access Teacher Management System:*** • Universal Access Instructional Benchmarking Guides • Lesson Plans for Universal Access **Interactive Reader and Study Guide:*** Chapter Graphic Organizer **Chapter Resource File*** • Focus on Writing Activity: Writing an Infomercial • Social Studies Skills Activity: Interpreting Time Lines • Chapter Review Activity **Pre-AP Activities Guide for United States History:*** Categorizing Information	**One-Stop Planner CD-ROM:** Calendar Planner **Student Edition Full-Read Audio CD-ROM** **Universal Access Modified Worksheets and Tests CD-ROM** **Power Presentations with Video CD-ROM** **History's Impact: United States History Video Program (VHS/DVD):** The English Colonies* **A Teacher's Guide to Religion in the Public Schools***
Section 1: **The Southern Colonies** **The Big Idea:** Despite a difficult beginning, the southern colonies soon flourished. 8.1	**Universal Access Teacher Management System:*** Section 1 Lesson Plan **Interactive Reader and Study Guide:*** Section 1 Summary **Chapter Resource File*** • Vocabulary Builder, Section 1 • Biography Activity: Pocahontas • History and Geography Activity: Agriculture in the Colonies	**Daily Bellringer Transparency:** Section 1* **Map Transparency:** Jamestown Colony* **Map Transparency:** Early Slave Populations* **Internet Activity:** Jamestown Graph
Section 2: **The New England Colonies** **The Big Idea:** English colonists traveled to New England to gain religious freedom. 8.2.1	**Universal Access Teacher Management System:*** Section 2 Lesson Plan **Interactive Reader and Study Guide:*** Section 2 Summary **Chapter Resource File*** • Vocabulary Builder, Section 2 • Literature Activity: American Colonial Poetry **Political Cartoons Activities for United States History,** Cartoon 1: *The Mayflower**	**Daily Bellringer Transparency:** Section 2* **Quick Facts Transparency:** Church and State*
Section 3: **The Middle Colonies** **The Big Idea:** People from many nations settled in the middle colonies. 8.1	**Universal Access Teacher Management System:*** Section 3 Lesson Plan **Interactive Reader and Study Guide:*** Section 3 Summary **Chapter Resource File*** • Vocabulary Builder, Section 3 • Primary Source Activity: Sarah Kemble Knight	**Daily Bellringer Transparency:** Section 3* **Quick Facts Transparency:** Characteristics of the Middle Colonies*
Section 4: **Life in the English Colonies** **The Big Idea:** The English colonies continued to grow despite many challenges. 8.1.1, 8.2.1	**Universal Access Teacher Management System:*** Section 4 Lesson Plan **Interactive Reader and Study Guide:*** Section 4 Summary **Chapter Resource File*** • Vocabulary Builder, Section 4 • Primary Source Activity: Jonathan Edwards	**Daily Bellringer Transparency:** Section 4* **Map Transparency:** The Thirteen Colonies* **Map Transparency:** Triangular Trade* **Map Transparency:** North American Empires before and after the Treaty of Paris* **Internet Activity:** The Courts and Freedom of the Press
Section 5: **Conflict in the Colonies** **The Big Idea:** Tensions developed as the British government placed tax after tax on the colonies. 8.1.1, 8.2.1	**Universal Access Teacher Management System:*** Section 5 Lesson Plan **Interactive Reader and Study Guide:*** Section 5 Summary **Chapter Resource File*** • Vocabulary Builder, Section 5 • Biography Activities: Samuel Adams; Crispus Attucks; Patrick Henry **Political Cartoons Activities for United States History,** Cartoon 2: No Taxation without Representation*	**Daily Bellringer Transparency:** Section 5* **Quick Facts Transparency:** The Road to Revolution*

SE Student Edition | Print Resource | Audio CD | Video
TE Teacher's Edition | Transparency | CD-ROM | DVD
go.hrw.com | CA Standards Mastery | LS Learning Styles
OSP One-Stop Planner CD-ROM | * also on One-Stop Planner CD

Review, Assessment, Intervention

- **Standards Review Workbook***
- **Quick Facts Transparency:** The English Colonies Visual Summary*
- **Spanish Chapter Summaries Audio CD Program**
- **Online Chapter Summaries in Six Languages**
- **Progress Assessment Support System (PASS):** Chapter Test*
- **Universal Access Modified Worksheets and Tests CD-ROM:** Modified Chapter Test
- **One-Stop Planner CD-ROM:** ExamView Test Generator (English/Spanish)
- **Alternative Assessment Handbook**

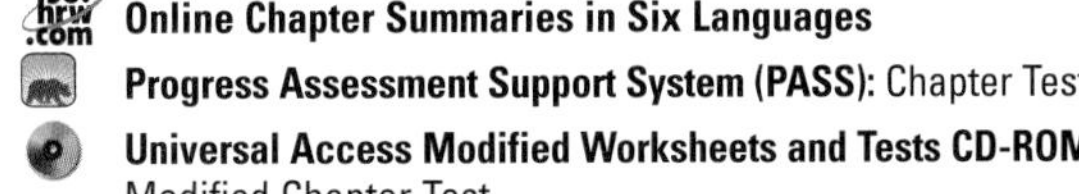

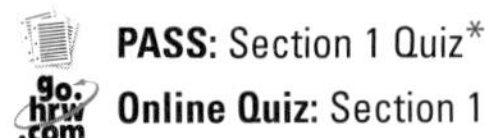

- **PASS:** Section 1 Quiz*
- **Online Quiz:** Section 1
- **Alternative Assessment Handbook**

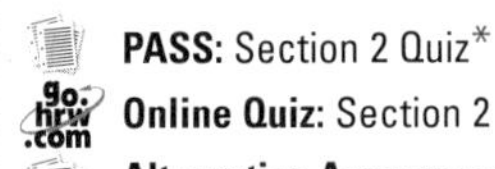

- **PASS:** Section 2 Quiz*
- **Online Quiz:** Section 2
- **Alternative Assessment Handbook**

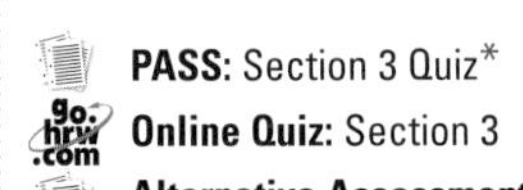

- **PASS:** Section 3 Quiz*
- **Online Quiz:** Section 3
- **Alternative Assessment Handbook**

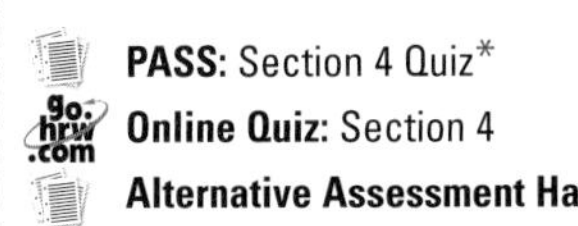

- **PASS:** Section 4 Quiz*
- **Online Quiz:** Section 4
- **Alternative Assessment Handbook**

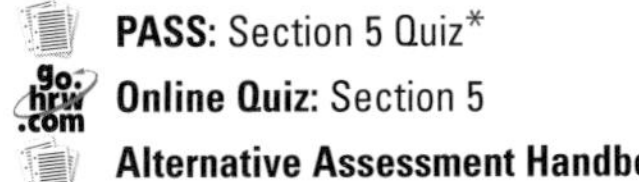

- **PASS:** Section 5 Quiz*
- **Online Quiz:** Section 5
- **Alternative Assessment Handbook**

California Resources for Standards Mastery

INSTRUCTIONAL PLANNING AND SUPPORT

- **Universal Access Teacher Management System***
- **One-Stop Planner CD-ROM with Test Generator: Teacher Management System with Interactive Teacher's Edition**

STANDARDS MASTERY

- **Standards Review Workbook***
- **At Home: A Guide to Standards Mastery for United States History**

Holt Online Learning

To enhance learning, Internet activities are available for a Jamestown Graph and The Courts and Freedom of the Press.

KEYWORD: SS8 TEACHER

- **Teacher Support Page**
- **Content Updates**
- **Rubrics and Writing Models**
- **Teaching Tips for the Multimedia Classroom**

KEYWORD: SS8 US2

- **Current Events**
- **Document-Based Questions**
- **Holt Grapher**
- **Holt Online Atlas**
- **Holt Researcher**
- **Interactive Multimedia Activities**
- **Internet Activities**
- **Online Chapter Summaries in Six Languages**
- **Online Section Quizzes**
- **American History Maps and Charts**

HOLT PREMIER ONLINE STUDENT EDITION

Complete online support for interactivity, assessment, and reporting

- **Interactive Maps and Notebook**
- **Standardized Test Prep**
- **Homework Practice and Research Activities Online**

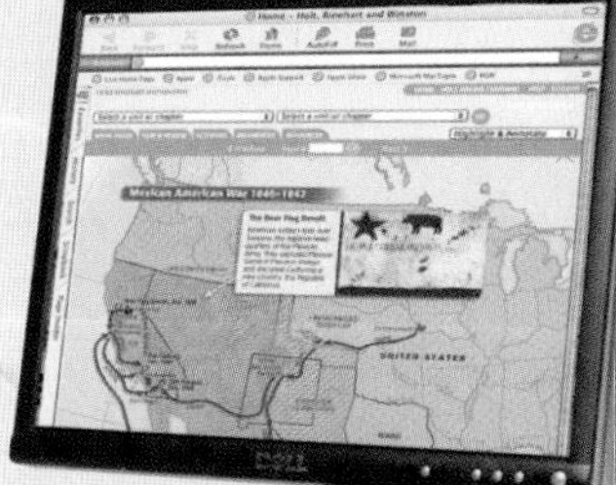

Mastering the Standards: Differentiating Instruction

Reaching Standards	Basic-level activities designed for all students encountering new material
Standards Proficiency	Intermediate-level activities designed for average students
Exceeding Standards	Challenging activities designed for honors and gifted-and-talented students
Standard English Mastery	Activities designed to improve standard English usage

Frequently Asked Questions

INSTRUCTIONAL PLANNING AND SUPPORT

Where do I find planning aids, pacing guides, lesson plans, and other teaching aids?

Annotated Teacher's Edition:
- Chapter planning guides
- Standards-based instruction and strategies
- Differentiated instruction for universal access
- Point-of-use reminders for integrating program resources

Power Presentations with Video CD-ROM

Universal Access Teacher Management System:
- Year and unit instructional benchmarking guides
- Reproducible lesson plans
- Assessment guides for diagnostic, progress, and summative end-of-the-year tests
- Options for differentiating instruction and intervention
- Teaching guides and answer keys for student workbooks

One-Stop Planner CD-ROM with Test Generator:
- Calendar Planner
- Editable lesson plans
- All reproducible ancillaries in Adobe Acrobat (PDF) format
- ExamView Test Generator (English & Spanish)
- Game Tool for ExamView
- PuzzlePro
- Quiz Game CD-ROM
- Transparency and video previews

DIFFERENTIATING INSTRUCTION FOR UNIVERSAL ACCESS

What resources are available to ensure that Advanced Learners/GATE Students master the standards?

Teacher's Edition Activities:
- Decision-making in the Southern Colonies, p. 39
- Mayflower Compact Simulation, p. 43
- Alternative Labor Proposals, p. 57

Lesson Plans for Universal Access

Pre-AP Activities Guide for United States History: Categorizing Information

Primary Source Library CD-ROM for United States History

What resources are available to ensure that English Learners and Standard English Learners master the standards?

Teacher's Edition Activities:
- Terms and Definitions, p. 37
- Guide to Massachusetts Bay, p. 45
- Colonial Trade Posters, p. 57

Lesson Plans for Universal Access

Chapter Resource File: Vocabulary Builder Activities

Spanish Chapter Summaries Audio CD Program

Online Chapter Summaries in Six Languages

One-Stop Planner CD-ROM:
- PuzzlePro, Spanish Version
- ExamView Test Generator, Spanish Version

What modified materials are available for Special Education?

Teacher's Edition Activities:
- Taxation Talk, p. 65

The ***Universal Access Modified Worksheets and Tests CD-ROM*** provides editable versions of the following:

Vocabulary Flash Cards

Modified Vocabulary Builder Activities

Modified Chapter Review Activity

Modified Chapter Test

What resources are available to ensure that Learners Having Difficulty master the standards?

Teacher's Edition Activities:
- Labor in Virginia Venn Diagram, p. 38
- Map of the Colonies, p. 40
- Connecticut and Rhode Island, p. 46
- Colonial Governments Chart, p. 55
- Frontier Conflicts Time Line, p. 60

Interactive Reader and Study Guide

Student Edition Full-Read Audio CD

Quick Facts Transparency: The English Colonies Visual Summary

Standards Review Workbook

Social Studies Skills Activity: Interpreting Time Lines

Interactive Skills Tutor CD-ROM

How do I intervene for students struggling to master the standards?

Interactive Reader and Study Guide

Quick Facts Transparency: The English Colonies Visual Summary

Standards Review Workbook

Social Studies Skills Activity: Interpreting Time Lines

Interactive Skills Tutor CD-ROM

PROFESSIONAL DEVELOPMENT

What teacher training resources are available to help me grow professionally?

- In-service and staff development as part of your Holt Social Studies product purchase
- Quick Teacher Tutorial Lesson Presentation CD-ROM
- Intensive tuition-based Teacher Development Institute
- *Teaching American History* Online 2 Module Professional Development Course
- Convenient Holt Speaker Bureau face-to-face workshop options
- PRAXIS™ Test Prep (#0089) interactive Web-based content refreshers*
- 24/7 *Ask A Professional Development Expert* at http://www.hrw.com/prodev/

* PRAXIS is a trademark of Educational Testing Service (ETS). This publication is not endorsed or approved by ETS.

Information Literacy Skills

To learn more about how History–Social Science instruction may be improved by the effective use of library media centers and information literacy skills, go to the Teacher's Resource Materials for Chapter 2 at **go.hrw.com**, keyword: SS8 MEDIA.

The following materials were developed by the Division for Public Education of the American Bar Association. These materials are part of the **Democracy and Civic Education** supplement.
- Constitution Study Guide
- Supreme Court Case Studies

Chapter Preview

Standards Focus

Standards by Section
Section 1: HSS 8.1
Section 2: HSS 8.2.1
Section 3: HSS 8.1
Section 4: HSS 8.1.1, 8.2.1
Section 5: HSS 8.1.1, 8.2.1

Teacher's Edition
HSS **Analysis Skills:** CS 1, CS 2, CS 3, HR 5, HI 1, HI 2, HI 3
ELA Writing 8.2.4.b; Reading 8.1.3

Preview Grade 11 Standards
HSS **11.1** Students analyze the significant events in the founding of the nation and its attempts to realize the philosophy of government described in the Declaration of Independence.
11.1.1 Describe the Enlightenment and the rise of democratic ideas as the context in which the nation was founded.
11.1.2 Analyze the ideological origins of the American Revolution, the Founding Fathers' philosophy of divinely bestowed unalienable natural rights, the debates on the drafting and ratification of the Constitution, and the addition of the Bill of Rights.
11.3 Students analyze the role religion played in the founding of America, its lasting moral, social, and political impacts, and issues regarding religious liberty.

Focus on Writing
The **Chapter Resource File** provides a Focus on Writing worksheet to help students write their infomercials.

CRF: Focus on Writing Activity: Writing an Infomercial

CHAPTER 2 1605–1774

The English Colonies

California Standards

History–Social Science

8.1 Students understand the major events preceding the founding of the nation and relate their significance to the development of American constitutional democracy.

8.2 Students analyze the political principles underlying the U.S. Constitution and compare the enumerated and implied powers of the federal government.

Analysis Skills

CS 2 Students construct various time lines of key events, people, and periods of the historical era they are studying.

English–Language Arts

Writing 8.2.4.b Present detailed evidence, examples, and reasoning to support arguments.

Reading 8.1.3 Use word meanings within the appropriate context.

FOCUS ON WRITING

Writing an Infomercial What if television had been invented during the time that the English colonies were being founded in North America? Instead of relying on printed flyers and word of mouth to attract settlers, the founders of colonies might have made infomercials. In this chapter you will read about life in the American colonies during different times. You will choose one time period and colony and write an infomercial encouraging English citizens to settle in the colony of your choice.

UNITED STATES

1620 The Pilgrims sign the Mayflower Compact.

1620

WORLD

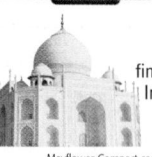

1648 Work is finished on India's Taj Mahal.

Mayflower Compact courtesy of the Pilgrim Society, Plymouth, Massachusetts.

32 CHAPTER 2

Introduce the Chapter

Standards Proficiency

Focus on Reasons for Colonization

HSS 8.1; HSS **Analysis Skills:** HI 1

1. Write the following scenario for students to see. *The U.S. government has decided to found a colony on another planet. What do you think the government hopes to gain from the colony? What conditions might make you move to this distant colony? What challenges might you and other settlers face at this colony?*
2. Give students time to consider and discuss the scenario and questions. List students' answers for the class to see. Encourage students to explain their reasoning and opinions.
3. Review with students what they learned in the last chapter about European colonies in North America. *(Remind students that England, France, the Netherlands, Spain, and Sweden had all founded American colonies.)* What did these countries hope to gain from their colonies, and what challenges did colonists face?
4. Tell students that in this chapter they will learn about the thirteen colonies that England founded in North America, which would later become the United States. LS **Verbal/Linguistic**

HOLT
History's Impact
▶ **video series**
Watch the video to understand the impact of English settlement on North America.

What You Will Learn...

Plymouth Colony thrives again in this highly accurate re-creation. The original colonists came to North America in 1620 in search of religious freedom. By 1627, the year this scene re-creates, the colonists were well established. Their success encouraged others. In this chapter you will learn about English settlements that dotted the east coast of North America.

1670

1681 William Penn establishes the colony of Pennsylvania.

1682 Peter the Great becomes czar of Russia.

1720

1763 Pontiac, an American Indian, leads a rebellion on the western frontier.

1768 British explorer James Cook sets sail on his first trip to the South Pacific, meeting people like this Sandwich Islander.

1770

1773 Patriots stage the Boston Tea Party.

THE ENGLISH COLONIES **33**

• Chapter Preview •

HOLT
History's Impact
▶ **video series**
See the Video Teacher's Guide for strategies for using the chapter video **The English Colonies.**

Chapter Big Ideas

Section 1 Despite a difficult beginning, the southern colonies soon flourished. **HSS** 8.1

Section 2 English colonists traveled to New England to gain religious freedom. **HSS** 8.2.1

Section 3 People from many nations settled in the middle colonies. **HSS** 8.1

Section 4 The English colonies continued to grow despite many challenges. **HSS** 8.1.1, 8.2.1

Section 5 Tensions developed as the British government placed tax after tax on the colonies. **HSS** 8.1.1, 8.2.1

Explore the Picture

Plymouth Colony The Pilgrims and other members of the Mayflower named their colony Plymouth after the last English port the ship stopped at on its journey. Plymouth Colony was built on the site of a former Native American town. Many of the town's inhabitants, the Wampanoag, had died from disease, most likely brought by European fishers and traders. The survivors had moved to other villages.

Analyzing Visuals What can you tell from this picture about the types of homes in the Plymouth Colony? *possible answers—built of wood with thatched roofs; had fireplaces (from chimneys); were small and set close together*

go.hrw.com
Online Resources
Chapter Resources:
KEYWORD: SS8 US2
Teacher Resources:
KEYWORD: SS8 TEACHER

Explore the Time Line

1. How long after the Pilgrims signed the Mayflower Compact was the Boston Tea Party? *153 years*
2. What colony did William Penn found, and when? *Pennsylvania, in 1681*
3. Based on the time line, what themes are addressed in this chapter? *political and economic themes of colonization and conflict*

HSS Analysis Skills: CS 1

Info to Know

English Workers In the early 1600s, English laborers were paid very little. Several able London workers reported that even though they and their families wore themselves out working long hard hours, they still only earned just enough to keep themselves alive.

Draw Conclusions Why might some English workers at the time have moved to a colony in North America? *in hopes of finding a better life for themselves*

Reading Social Studies

Understanding Themes

The themes of economics and politics are presented in this chapter. Ask students to imagine that their families have decided to move to a foreign country to seek new opportunities. Guide students in a discussion of reasons why their families might have chosen to leave their home countries. Have students identify the difficulties they think their families might face in their new country and how they might try to overcome them. Emphasize issues related to economics and politics, such as trade and government. Write students' responses for everyone to see. Tell students that as they study this chapter, they will learn about the problems early settlers in America faced, and how they worked to overcome them.

Vocabulary Clues

Focus on Reading Organize the class into pairs. Then have each pair go through one of their textbooks. Ask students to look for sentences where a word is explained using context clues. Ask students to find five sentences that use vocabulary clues to define a term. Then have students make a list of the different ways in which the meaning of a word is given in the context of the text. Answers might include clue words or punctuation.

Reading Social Studies

by Kylene Beers

Economics | Geography | Politics | Religion | Society and Culture | Science and Technology

Focus on Themes In this chapter you will read about the people who settled the early colonies of North America. You will learn about the problems they faced as they felt the tug between their homeland and their new land. You will see how they settled political differences (sometimes peacefully, other times not) and learned how to trade goods and grow crops to establish a thriving economy. You will discover that the **economy** often influenced their **politics**.

Vocabulary Clues

Focus on Reading When you are reading your history textbook, you may often come across a word you do not know. If that word isn't listed as a key term, how do you find out what it means?

Using Context Clues Context means surroundings. Authors often include clues to the meaning of a difficult word in its context. You just have to know how and where to look.

Clue	How It Works	Example	Explanation
Direct Definition	Includes a definition in the same or a nearby sentence	In the late 1600s England, like most western European nations, practiced mercantilism, *the practice of creating and maintaining wealth by carefully controlling trade.*	The phrase "the practice of creating and maintaining wealth by carefully controlling trade" defines *mercantilism.*
Restatement	Uses different words to say the same thing	The British continued to keep a standing, *or permanent,* army in North America to protect the colonists against Indian attacks.	The word *permanent* is another way to say *standing.*
Comparisons or Contrasts	Compares or contrasts the unfamiliar word with a familiar one	*Unlike legal traders,* smugglers did not have permission to bring goods into the country.	The word *unlike* indicates that smugglers are different from legal traders.

Graphic organizers are available in the

Reading and Skills Resources

Reading Support

- Interactive Reader and Study Guide
- Student Edition on Audio CD
- Spanish Chapter Summaries Audio CD Program

Social Studies Skills Support

- Interactive Skills Tutor CD-ROM

Vocabulary Support

- **CRF:** Vocabulary Builder Activities
- **CRF:** Chapter Review Activity
- Universal Access Modified Worksheets and Tests CD-ROM:
  - Vocabulary Flash Cards
  - Vocabulary Builder Activity
  - Chapter Review Activity

OSP Holt PuzzlePro

Standards Focus

ELA Reading 8.1.3

ELA Reading 8.1.3 Show ability to verify word meanings by definition, restatement, example, comparison, or contrast.

You Try It!

The following sentences are from this chapter. Each uses a definition or restatement clue to explain unfamiliar words. See if you can use the context to figure out the meaning of the words in italics.

Context Clues Up Close

From Chapter 2

1. In 1605 a company of English merchants asked King James I for the right to *found*, or establish, a settlement. *(p. 36)*
2. The majority of these workers were *indentured servants*. These servants signed a contract to work four to seven years for those who paid for their journey to America. *(p. 38)*
3. In New England, the center of politics was the *town meeting*. In town meetings people talked about and decided on issues of local interest, such as paying for schools. *(p. 55)*

Answer the questions about the sentences you read.

1. In example 1, what does the word *found* mean? What hints did you find in the sentence to figure that out?
2. In example 2, where do you find the meaning of *indentured servants*? What does this phrase mean?
3. What is the definition of *immigrants* in example 3? What kind of context clues did you find in that sentence?
4. In example 4, you learn the definition of *town meeting* in the second sentence. Can you combine these two sentences into one sentence? Try putting a dash after the word *meeting* and replacing "In town meetings" with "a place where . . ."

As you read Chapter 2, look for context clues that can help you figure out the meanings of unfamiliar words or terms.

Key Terms and People

Chapter 2

Section 1
Jamestown *(p. 36)*
John Smith *(p. 37)*
Pocahontas *(p. 37)*
indentured servants *(p. 38)*
Bacon's Rebellion *(p. 38)*
Toleration Act of 1649 *(p. 39)*
Olaudah Equiano *(p. 41)*
slave codes *(p. 41)*

Section 2
Puritans *(p. 42)*
Pilgrims *(p. 42)*
immigrants *(p. 42)*
Mayflower Compact *(p. 43)*
Squanto *(p. 43)*
John Winthrop *(p. 45)*
Anne Hutchinson *(p. 46)*

Section 3
Peter Stuyvesant *(p. 49)*
Quakers *(p. 50)*
William Penn *(p. 50)*
staple crops *(p. 51)*

Section 4
town meeting *(p. 55)*
English Bill of Rights *(p. 55)*
triangular trade *(p. 57)*
Middle Passage *(p. 58)*
Great Awakening *(p. 58)*
Enlightenment *(p. 59)*
Pontiac *(p. 61)*

Section 5
Samuel Adams *(p. 63)*
Committees of Correspondence *(p. 63)*
Stamp Act of 1765 *(p. 64)*
Boston Massacre *(p. 65)*
Tea Act *(p. 66)*
Boston Tea Party *(p. 66)*
Intolerable Acts *(p. 67)*

Academic Vocabulary

In this chapter, you will learn the following academic words:

authority *(p. 37)*
factors *(p. 38)*

Reading Social Studies

Key Terms and People

Challenge students to create a matching game using the key terms and people from this chapter. Organize the class into pairs, then assign each pair a term or person from the list. Have each group write a description or definition for their term on one index card and the word or name on a separate card. Collect all the index cards and place them in a basket. Have each student draw a card from the basket. Then have students try to find the person whose word or name matches the description on their card. Challenge the students even more by not allowing any talking while they match terms and descriptions!
LS Interpersonal, Verbal/Linguistic

Focus on Reading

See the **Focus on Reading** questions in this chapter for more practice on this reading social studies skill.

Reading Social Studies Assessment

See the **Standards Review** at the end of this chapter for student assessment questions related to this reading skill.

Teaching Tip

Point out to students that there are usually hints that indicate when a word is defined in the context of the sentence. One of these hints is the use of punctuation. Commas and dashes often are used to set off phrases from the rest of the sentence. These phrases often define or restate the unfamiliar word. Another hint is the use of signal words and phrases. Phrases are often used to indicate a definition or restatement. Remind students to look for words and phrases such as *which means, which is, in other words, or, called,* and *that is.*

Answers

You Try It! 1. *establish; a restatement of the word was used;* **2.** *in the second sentence; servants who signed a contract to work a number of years for those who paid for their journey to America;* **3.** *In New England, the center of politics was the town meeting—a place where people talked about and decided issues of local interest, such as paying for school.*

Preteach

Bellringer

If YOU were there . . . Use the **Daily Bellringer Transparency** to help students answer the question.

Daily Bellringer Transparency, Section 1

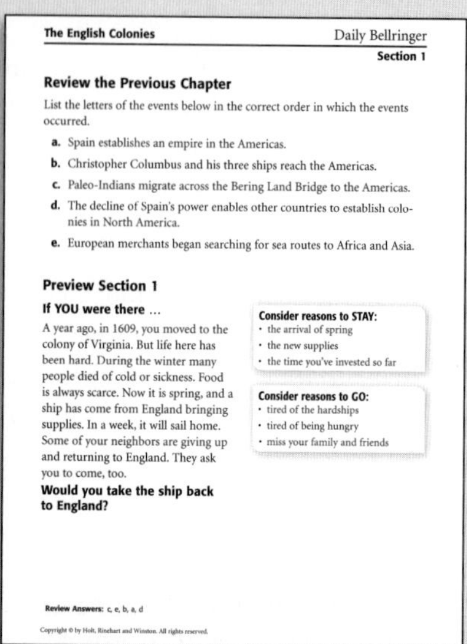

The English Colonies Daily Bellringer

Section 1

Review the Previous Chapter

List the letters of the events below in the correct order in which the events occurred.

a. Spain establishes an empire in the Americas.
b. Christopher Columbus and his three ships reach the Americas.
c. Paleo-Indians migrate across the Bering Land Bridge to the Americas.
d. The decline of Spain's power enables other countries to establish colonies in North America.
e. European merchants began searching for sea routes to Africa and Asia.

Preview Section 1

If YOU were there ...

A year ago, in 1609, you moved to the colony of Virginia. But life here has been hard. During the winter many people died of cold or sickness. Food is always scarce. Now it is spring, and a ship has come from England bringing supplies. In a week, it will sail home. Some of your neighbors are giving up and returning to England. They ask you to come, too.

Would you take the ship back to England?

Consider reasons to STAY:
- the arrival of spring
- the new supplies
- the time you've invested so far

Consider reasons to GO:
- tired of the hardships
- tired of being hungry
- miss your family and friends

Review Answers: c, e, b, a, d

Academic Vocabulary

Review with students the high-use academic terms in this section.

authority power, right to rule (p. 37)

factors causes (p. 38)

CRF: Vocabulary Builder Activity, Section 1

Standards Focus

HSS 8.1

Means: Students understand the major events that led up to the founding of the United States, such as the development of the thirteen colonies.

Matters: The thirteen colonies became the first states in the nation.

SECTION 1

The Southern Colonies

What You Will Learn...

Main Ideas

1. The settlement in Jamestown was the first permanent English settlement in America.
2. Daily life in Virginia was challenging to the colonists.
3. Religious freedom and economic opportunities were motives for founding other southern colonies, including Maryland, the Carolinas, and Georgia.
4. Farming and slavery were important to the economies of the southern colonies.

The Big Idea

Despite a difficult beginning, the southern colonies soon flourished.

Key Terms and People

Jamestown, *p. 36*
John Smith, *p. 37*
Pocahontas, *p. 37*
indentured servants, *p. 38*
Bacon's Rebellion, *p. 38*
Toleration Act of 1649, *p. 39*
Olaudah Equiano, *p. 41*
slave codes, *p. 41*

HSS 8.1 Students understand the major events preceding the founding of the nation and relate their significance to the development of American constitutional democracy.

If YOU were there...

A year ago, in 1609, you moved to the colony of Virginia. But life here has been hard. During the winter many people died of cold or sickness. Food is always scarce. Now it is spring, and a ship has come from England bringing supplies. In a week it will sail home. Some of your neighbors are giving up and returning to England. They ask you to come, too.

Would you take the ship back to England?

BUILDING BACKGROUND Several European nations took part in the race to claim lands in the Americas. Their next step was to establish colonies in the lands that they claimed. The first English colonies were started in the late 1500s but failed. Even in successful colonies, colonists faced hardships and challenges.

Settlement in Jamestown

In 1605 a company of English merchants asked King James I for the right to found, or establish, a settlement. In 1606 the king granted the request of the company to settle in a region called Virginia.

Founding a New Colony

The investors in the new settlement formed a joint-stock company called the London Company. This allowed the group to share the cost and risk of establishing the colony. On April 26, 1607, the first 105 colonists sent by the London Company arrived in America. On May 14, about 40 miles up the James River in Virginia, the colonists founded **Jamestown**, the first permanent English settlement in North America.

A lack of preparation cost a lot of the colonists their lives. Most of the men who came to Jamestown were adventurers with no farming experience or useful skills such as carpentry. Jamestown was surrounded by marshes full of disease-carrying mosquitoes. By the time winter arrived, two-thirds of the original colonists had died.

Teach the Big Idea: Master the Standards

Standards Proficiency

The Southern Colonies HSS 8.1; HSS Analysis Skills: CS 3, HI 1

Materials: five blank index cards per student

1. **Teach** Use the Main Idea questions to teach this section.
2. **Apply** Have students create colonial picture postcards. Give each student five blank index cards, one for each of the southern colonies. On the front of the postcards, have students create "I am Here" maps showing the location of the colony, the date it was founded, and its main settlements. On the backs, have students list facts about the colonies.
   LS Visual/Spatial
3. **Review** Have students share some of the facts they listed. Write the list for students to see.
4. **Practice/Homework** Have each student select one southern colony and imagine that he or she has moved there. Each student should write a letter home to England describing the colony, life there, and the challenges that he or she is facing.
   LS Verbal/Linguistic

Alternative Assessment Handbook, Rubric 41: Writing to Express

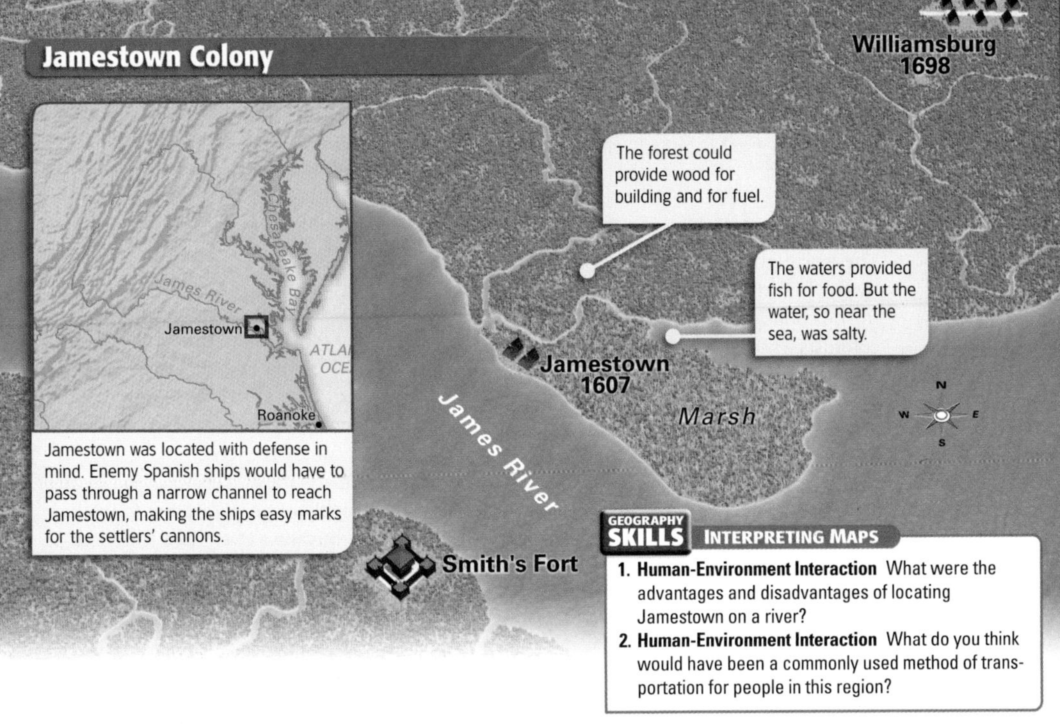

Jamestown was located with defense in mind. Enemy Spanish ships would have to pass through a narrow channel to reach Jamestown, making the ships easy marks for the settlers' cannons.

GEOGRAPHY SKILLS INTERPRETING MAPS

1. **Human-Environment Interaction** What were the advantages and disadvantages of locating Jamestown on a river?
2. **Human-Environment Interaction** What do you think would have been a commonly used method of transportation for people in this region?

Powhatan Confederacy

The situation in Jamestown temporarily improved after **John Smith** took control of the colony in September 1608. He forced the settlers to work harder and to build better housing by creating rules that rewarded harder workers with food. The Jamestown colonists received help from the powerful Powhatan Confederacy of Indians after Smith made an agreement with them. The Powhatan brought food to help the colonists, and then taught them how to grow corn.

In 1609 some 400 more settlers arrived in Jamestown. That winter, disease and famine once again hit the colony. The colonists called this period the starving time. By the spring of 1610, only 60 colonists were still alive. Jamestown failed to make a profit until colonist John Rolfe introduced a new type of tobacco that sold well in England.

War in Virginia

John Rolfe married **Pocahontas**, daughter of the Powhatan leader, in 1614. Their marriage helped the colonists form more peaceful relations with the Powhatan. However, Pocahontas died three years later in England, which she was visiting with Rolfe.

In 1622, colonists killed a Powhatan leader. The Powhatan responded by attacking the Virginia settlers later that year. Fighting between the colonists and the Powhatan continued for the next 20 years. Because the London Company could not protect its colonists, the English Crown canceled the Company's charter in 1624. Virginia became a royal colony and existed under the **authority** of a governor chosen by the king.

ACADEMIC VOCABULARY
authority power, right to rule

READING CHECK **Finding Main Ideas** What problems did the Jamestown colonists face?

Direct Teach

Main Idea

1 Settlement in Jamestown

The settlement in Jamestown was the first permanent English settlement in America.

Recall When was Jamestown founded, and where was it located? *1607; on the James River in Virginia*

Summarize Briefly describe the changing nature of the relationship between the Jamestown settlers and the Powhatan Indians. *At first, relations were good, strengthened by a marriage between John Rolfe and Pocahontas, but conflict erupted after settlers murdered a Powhatan leader.*

CRF: Biography Activity: Pocahontas

Map Transparency: Jamestown Colony

HSS 8.1; **HSS Analysis Skills:** HI 1, HI 2

Info to Know

Smith and Pocahontas Powhatan Indians captured Captain John Smith at one point. Smith wrote in his *Generall Historie of Virginia* that they were preparing to kill him when the 13-year-old Pocahontas threw herself over him, saving his life. Not all historians believe Smith's story, though.

go.hrw.com
Online Resources
KEYWORD: SS8 US2
ACTIVITY: Jamestown Graph

Differentiating Instruction for Universal Access

English-Language Learners

Standards Proficiency | Standard English Mastery

1. Write the following terms and names for students to see: London Company, joint-stock company, Jamestown, adventurers, mosquitoes, John Smith, Powhatan Confederacy, winter, John Rolfe, tobacco, Pocahontas, peaceful, fighting, and royal colony.
2. Have students work as a class to define each term as it is used in the text on the above pages. Ask volunteers to use each term in a sentence. Help students to improve their use of standard English.
3. Then pair students and have each pair use the list of words to write a summary of the portion of the text titled "Settlement in Jamestown."
4. **English Learners Having Difficulty** Write the summary yourself and provide blanks for the words in the list. Have students fill in the blanks. **LS Verbal/Linguistic**

HSS 8.1; **HSS Analysis Skills:** CS 1, HI 1, HI 2

Alternative Assessment Handbook, Rubric 37: Writing Assignments

Answers

Interpreting Maps **1.** *advantages—fishing, water transportation; disadvantages—mosquitoes in nearby marsh, possible flooding;* **2.** *boats or canoes*

Reading Check *lack of preparation, disease-carrying mosquitoes, famine, conflict with Native Americans*

Direct Teach

Main Idea

❷ Daily Life in Virginia

Daily life in Virginia was challenging to the colonists.

Recall What was the main cash crop in Virginia? *tobacco*

Analyze Why did the plantation system develop in Virginia? *in part because of the headright system, under which colonists who paid their way received 50 acres of land plus 50 more for each person they brought*

Contrast How were indentured servants different from slaves? *Indentured servants worked voluntarily under a contract for a specified number of years; slavery was an involuntary and permanent condition.*

HSS 8.1; HSS Analysis Skills: HI 1

Primary Source

A Note from Virginia

Interpret What does John Pory hope might become some future means of making money in Virginia? *vineyards, cattle*

Connect to Economics

The Slave Trade in the Early 1600s

Initially, farmers in Virginia did not use much slave labor, in part because England did not share in the African slave trade. In the early 1600s the Dutch, Portuguese, and Spanish controlled much of the slave trade out of West Africa.

Daily Life in Virginia

In early Virginia, people lived on scattered farms rather than in towns. Tobacco farmers soon began establishing large farms called plantations.

Headright System

These plantations were made possible in part by the headright system, which was started by the London Company. Under this system, colonists who paid their own way to Virginia received 50 acres of land. A colonist could earn another 50 acres for every additional person brought from England. Rich colonists who brought servants or relatives to Virginia gained large amounts of land.

ACADEMIC VOCABULARY
factors causes

Labor in Virginia

Colonists in Virginia faced a hard life. They suffered very high death rates, which led to labor shortages in the colony. The majority of workers were **indentured servants**, people who received a free trip to North America by agreeing to work without pay for a period of years.

Expansion of Slavery

Not all laborers in Virginia came from Europe. A Dutch ship brought the first Africans to Virginia in 1619. Some Africans were servants; others had been enslaved. Some African servants became successful farmers when their contracts ended.

The demand for workers was soon greater than the supply of people willing to work as indentured servants. Over time, the cost of slaves fell. These **factors** led some colonists to turn to slave labor. By the mid-1600s most Africans in Virginia were being kept in lifelong slavery.

Bacon's Rebellion

As plantations grew, the economy of Jamestown began to expand. Soon, colonial officials began to ask for more taxes. During the mid-1600s poor colonists protested the higher taxes. They were also upset about the governor's policies toward Native Americans. They thought the colony was not well protected against attack from Indians. In 1676 a group of former indentured servants led by Nathaniel Bacon attacked some friendly American Indians. Bacon opposed the governor's policies promoting trade with American Indians. He also thought the colonists should be able to take the Indians' land. When the governor tried to stop him, Bacon and his followers attacked and burned Jamestown in an uprising known as **Bacon's Rebellion**.

At one point, Bacon controlled much of the colony. He died of fever, however, and the rebellion soon ended.

READING CHECK **Analyzing** What factors led to the increased use of slave labor in Virginia?

Primary Source

LETTER

A Note from Virginia

In this 1619 letter, the secretary of the Virginia colony, John Pory, encouraged people to move to Virginia.

"As touching the quality of this country, three things there be, which in few years may bring this colony to perfection; the English plow, vineyards, & cattle . . . All our riches for the present do consist in tobacco, wherein one man by his own labor has in one year, raised to himself to the value of 200 pounds sterling; and another by the means of six servants has cleared at one crop a thousand pound English. These be true, yet indeed rare examples, yet possible to be done by others."

—from *The Power of Words*, edited by T. H. Breen

ANALYSIS SKILL ANALYZING PRIMARY SOURCES

How does this letter indicate the importance of tobacco in Virginia?

Critical Thinking: Comparing and Contrasting

Reaching Standards

Labor in Virginia Venn Diagram

HSS 8.1; HSS Analysis Skills: HI 1, HI 2

1. Draw the Venn diagram for students to see. Omit the blue, italicized answers.
2. Have students copy the diagram and list words and phrases that describe each type of labor. In the overlapping area, students should list words and phrases that describe both types of labor.
3. Review students' answers as a class. Then discuss the factors that led to the increased use of slave labor in Virginia. LS Visual/Spatial

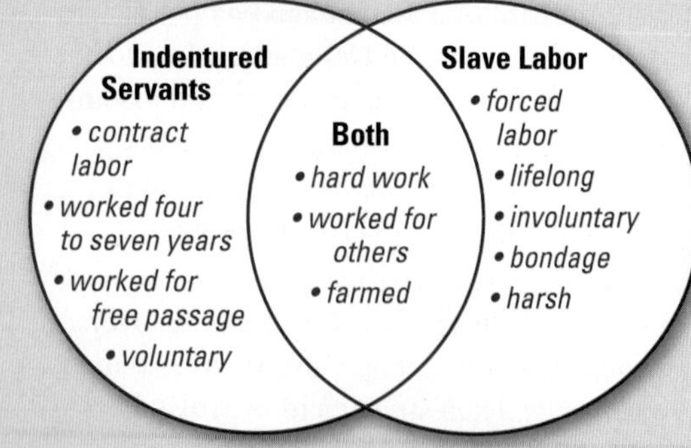

Answers

Analyzing Primary Sources *It lists tobacco as the colony's main cash crop and means of support.*

Reading Check *Demand for labor outpaced the supply of people willing to work as indentured servants, and the cost of slaves fell.*

Southern Wealth

Colonists overcame tough beginnings to create large and wealthy settlements like this one in Virginia. Churches were often the first major buildings in a growing town.

How does the large church in the picture show Virginia's wealth?

Colonial Williamsburg Foundation

Other Southern Colonies

As Jamestown was developing in Virginia, new groups of colonists began planning their move to America. Many English Catholics came to America to escape religious persecution. English Catholics had long been against England's separation from the Roman Catholic Church. For this reason they were not allowed by the Church of England to worship freely. English leaders also feared that English Catholics would ally with Catholic countries such as France and Spain in conflicts.

Maryland

In the 1620s George Calvert, the first Lord Baltimore, asked King Charles I for a charter establishing a new colony in America for Catholics. In 1632 Charles issued the charter to Calvert's son, Cecilius, who took over the planning of the colony. Cecilius, known as the second Lord Baltimore, named the colony Maryland in honor of England's queen, Henrietta Maria. It was located just north of Virginia in the Chesapeake Bay area. Calvert intended for the colony to be a refuge for English Catholics. It would also be a proprietary colony. This meant that the colony's proprietors, or owners, controlled the government.

In 1634 a group of 200 English Catholics came to Maryland. Included in the group were wealthy landowners, servants, craftspeople, and farmers. Settlers in Maryland benefited from the lessons learned by the Jamestown colonists. They spent their time raising corn, cattle, and hogs so that they would have enough to eat. Before long, many colonists also began growing tobacco for profit.

Although Catholics founded Maryland, a growing number of Protestants began moving there in the 1640s. Soon, religious conflicts arose between Catholics and Protestants in the colony. To reduce tensions, Lord Baltimore presented a bill to the colonial assembly that became known as the **Toleration Act of 1649**. This bill made it a crime to restrict the religious rights of Christians. This was the first law supporting religious tolerance passed in the English colonies.

The Toleration Act did not stop all religious conflict. However, it did show that the government wanted to offer some religious freedom and to protect the rights of minority groups.

Direct Teach

Main Idea

❸ Other Southern Colonies

Religious freedom and economic opportunities were motives for founding other southern colonies, including Maryland, the Carolinas, and Georgia.

Explain Why did English Catholics settle in the colony of Maryland? *to escape religious persecution*

Contrast How was the colony of Maryland different than Jamestown? *Jamestown—founded to make a profit; joint-stock company colony then a royal colony; faced many years of hardship and loss of life; most early settlers were adventurers; Maryland—founded to provide English Catholics with religious freedom; proprietary colony; most settlers were farmers willing to work hard.*

HSS 8.1; HSS **Analysis Skills:** HI 1

Info to Know

Colonial Death Rates Death rates were high for early colonists in the Chesapeake region. During the 1600s, some 40 percent of colonists died within two years of their arrival from diseases such as typhoid and malaria.

Did you know . . .

Cecilius Calvert, also known as Lord Baltimore, never visited Maryland, although he founded the colony.

Critical Thinking: Analyzing Information

Exceeding Standards

Decision-making in the Southern Colonies

HSS 8.1; HSS **Analysis Skills:** HI 1

1. Discuss with students the ways in which royal and proprietary colonies differed. Focus on who made decisions in each type of colony.
2. To start, discuss with students Maryland's Toleration Act of 1649. Mention that Lord Baltimore presented the bill to the colonial assembly. Have students discuss this process as an example of how a decision was made in a proprietary colony. To address a royal colony, discuss Georgia with students.
3. Then have students contrast how decisions were made in Virginia, Maryland, and Georgia. Have each student write a short summary of the differences among the types of colonies.

LS **Verbal/Linguistic**

Alternative Assessment Handbook, Rubrics 11: Discussions; and 37: Writing Assignments

Answers

Southern Wealth *The church is large enough and the architecture elaborate enough to have cost a large sum at the time it was built.*

• Direct Teach •

Main Idea

❸ Other Southern Colonies

Religious freedom and economic opportunities were motives for founding other southern colonies, including Maryland, the Carolinas, and Georgia.

Recall Why did the Carolina colony separate into North and South Carolina? *The settlements in the colony were far apart, making them hard to govern together.*

Analyze How did James Oglethorpe hope to make Georgia different from the other colonies? *He hoped Georgia would not have large plantations owned by a few wealthy people. Instead, he wanted to give the poor and debtors a fresh start, so he originally outlawed slavery and kept land grants small.*

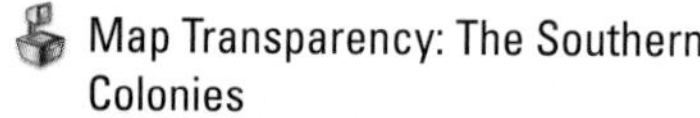

Map Transparency: The Southern Colonies

HSS 8.1; HSS **Analysis Skills:** HI 1

Interpreting Maps

Early Slave Populations

Place What foreign territory did Georgia border? *Spanish Florida*

Identify Cause and Effect Why did South Carolina develop such a large population of enslaved Africans? *The colony's system of large land grants encouraged plantation owners to bring in large numbers of slaves.*

Answers

Interpreting Charts *1700—about 35,000; 1750—about 230,000*

Reading Check *to escape religious persecution, to farm, to get a fresh start*

The Southern Colonies

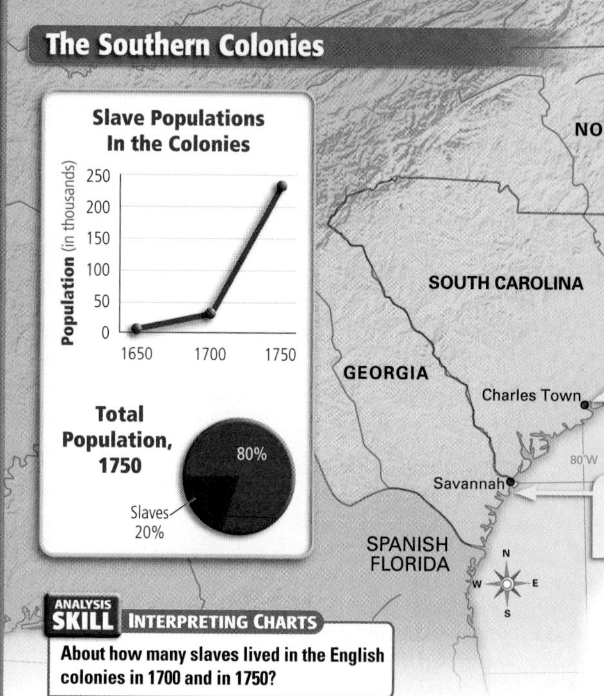

Charles Town was founded in 1670. South Carolina's large land grants encouraged plantation owners to bring in thousands of slaves.

James Oglethorpe tried to prevent slavery in Georgia. But slaves soon provided the labor for the colony's many rice plantations.

ANALYSIS SKILL INTERPRETING CHARTS

About how many slaves lived in the English colonies in 1700 and in 1750?

Carolinas and Georgia

Colonies were also established south of Virginia. In 1663 the English king, Charles II, gave much of the land between Virginia and Spanish Florida to eight of his supporters. At first Carolina was a single colony. However, the settlements were far apart, and it was hard to govern them. In 1712 the colony separated into North and South Carolina.

Most of the colonists in North Carolina were farmers who had moved south from Virginia. Colonists primarily from Europe settled South Carolina. Those who paid their own way received large grants of land, and some brought enslaved Africans with them. By 1730 about 20,000 enslaved Africans were living in the colony, compared to some 10,000 white settlers.

South Carolina's proprietors managed the colony poorly, and the British government bought it in 1719. The Crown then purchased North Carolina in 1729, making it a royal colony as well.

In 1732 King George II granted a charter to James Oglethorpe and other trustees to found Georgia. The king hoped that Georgia would shield Britain's other colonies from Spanish Florida. Oglethorpe wanted the new colony to be a place where debtors, who had been jailed for their debts in England, could make a new start. In 1733 Oglethorpe and 120 colonists, mostly from England, founded the city of Savannah.

Oglethorpe did not want Georgia to have large plantations owned by a few wealthy individuals. He wanted many small farmers. To reach this goal, Oglethorpe outlawed slavery and limited the size of land grants. Soon, however, the settlers grew unhappy with Oglethorpe's strict rules. In 1752 the British government made Georgia a royal colony with new laws. Coastal Georgia was soon filled with large rice plantations worked by thousands of slaves.

READING CHECK **Finding Main Ideas** What were some of the reasons colonists came to the southern colonies?

Differentiating Instruction for Universal Access

Learners Having Difficulty

Reaching Standards | Prep Required

Materials: outline maps of eastern United States

1. To help students learn where each colony was in relation to the others, give students blank outline maps of the eastern United States.
2. Display a master outline map as well. As you begin your discussion of each colony, draw in the basic borders of that colony on the master map.
3. Have students follow your example by adding each colony's borders to their maps in turn. Briefly discuss the location of each colony, its location in relation to the other colonies, and how its location influenced life in the colony.
4. Have students write the names of the founders of each southern colony and the date the colony was founded on the map. Continue the activity through Sections 2 and 3. (For a map of the thirteen colonies, see p. 55.)

LS Visual/Spatial

HSS 8.1; HSS **Analysis Skills:** CS 3, HI 1

Alternative Assessment Handbook, Rubric 20: Map Creation

Economies of the Southern Colonies

The economies of the southern colonies depended on agriculture. They also exported materials for building ships, such as wood and tar. Some colonies traded with local Indians for deerskins to sell.

The colonies had many small farms and some large plantations. Farms did well because the South enjoyed a warm climate and a long growing season. Many farms grew cash crops that were sold for profit. Tobacco, rice, and indigo—a plant used to make blue dye—were the most important cash crops.

The southern colonies' cash crops required a great deal of difficult work to grow and harvest. This meant a large workforce was needed. By the 1700s enslaved Africans, rather than indentured servants, had become the main source of labor.

Slavery was a viciously brutal condition for many inhabitants of the southern colonies. One former slave named **Olaudah Equiano** recorded his experiences.

> "Tortures, murder, and every other imaginable barbarity ... are practiced upon the poor slaves with impunity [no punishment]. I hope the slave-trade will be abolished."
>
> —Olaudah Equiano, from *The Interesting Narrative of the Life of Olaudah Equiano, or Gustavus Vassa, the African*

Most of the southern colonies passed **slave codes**, or laws to control slaves. Colonies with large numbers of slaves had the strictest slave codes. For example, South Carolina's slaveholders feared that slaves would revolt. As a result, South Carolina's code said slaves could not hold meetings or own weapons. Some colonies did not allow slaveholders to free their slaves.

READING CHECK **Summarizing** What role did slavery play in the southern plantation economy? How was it regulated?

SUMMARY AND PREVIEW In this section you read about life in the southern colonies. In the next section you will learn about the New England colonies.

Section 1 Assessment

go.hrw.com
Online Quiz
KEYWORD: SS8 HP2

Reviewing Ideas, Terms, and People HSS 8.1

1. a. **Describe** How did **John Smith** improve conditions in Jamestown?
   b. **Explain** What events led to a conflict between the **Jamestown** settlers and the Powhatan Confederacy?
2. a. **Recall** Why were **indentured servants** necessary in Virginia?
   b. **Evaluate** What do you think was the most serious problem faced by settlers in Virginia? Why?
3. a. **Identify** Which colony was the first to promote religious tolerance?
   b. **Analyze** Why did more enslaved Africans live in South Carolina than did white settlers?
   c. **Predict** How might the colony of Georgia have been different if Oglethorpe's plan had succeeded?
4. a. **Recall** What was the purpose of **slave codes**?
   b. **Analyze** Why were slaves in high demand in the southern colonies?

Critical Thinking

5. **Contrasting** Using a chart like the one below, identify when and why each of the southern colonies was founded.

Colony	Year Founded	Reason for Establishment

FOCUS ON WRITING

6. **Gathering Some Ideas** As you read this section, take notes on the early colonies of Virginia, Maryland, the Carolinas, and Georgia. Be sure to note what advantages they offered to settlers and what difficulties settlers faced. Start to think about the people who would be most likely to settle in the southern colonies.

Section 1 Assessment Answers

1. a. forced the colonists to work harder and improve conditions; obtained help from Powhatan
   b. Some colonists killed a Powhatan leader, and in response the Powhatan attacked the settlers.
2. a. High death rates led to labor shortages.
   b. Answers will vary, but problems included lack of preparation, disease, famine, and conflicts with Native Americans.
3. a. Maryland
   b. Large land grants there encouraged plantation owners to bring in many enslaved Africans.
   c. Answers will vary, but students should show an understanding of Oglethorpe's plan to emphasize small farms and help debtors.
4. a. to control slaves
   b. main cash crops required lots of labor
5. Virginia—1607; profit; Maryland—1634; religious freedom for Catholics; Carolinas—1663; profit; Georgia—1733; fresh start for poor and debtors
6. Students should note advantages such as the South's warm climate and long growing season and disadvantages such as high death rates.

Direct Teach

Main Idea

4 Economies of the Southern Colonies

Farming and slavery were important to the economies of the southern colonies.

Identify What were the main cash crops in the southern colonies, and how did they contribute to the use of slavery? *tobacco, rice, and indigo; required lots of work and a large workforce to grow and harvest*

Evaluate Why was the geography of the southern colonies suitable for farming? *The South enjoyed a warm climate and a long growing season.*

CRF: History and Geography Activity: Agriculture in the Colonies

HSS 8.1; HSS **Analysis Skills:** HI 1, HI 2

Review & Assess

Close

Have students compare and contrast the southern colonies and why they were founded.

Review

go.hrw.com Online Quiz, Section 1

Assess

SE Section 1 Assessment

PASS: Section 1 Quiz

Alternative Assessment Handbook

Reteach/Classroom Intervention

California Standards Review Workbook

Interactive Reader and Study Guide, Section 1

Interactive Skills Tutor CD-ROM

Answers

Reading Check *Slavery provided the main workforce for the labor-intensive cash crops grown on the region's large plantations. Most colonies passed laws to control slaves.*

Preteach

Bellringer

If YOU were there . . . Use the **Daily Bellringer Transparency** to help students answer the question.

 Daily Bellringer Transparency, Section 2

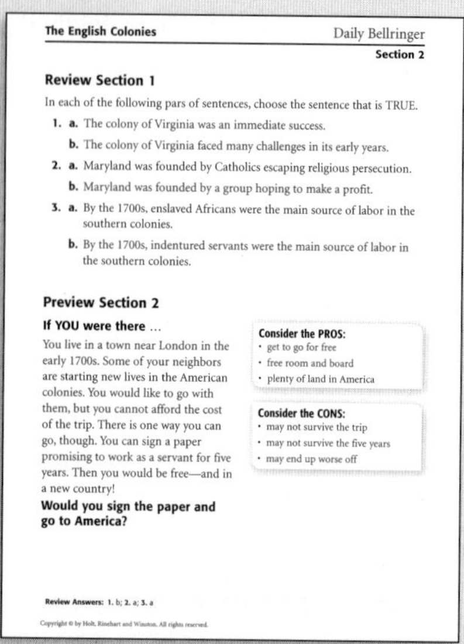

The English Colonies — Daily Bellringer

Section 2

Review Section 1

In each of the following pars of sentences, choose the sentence that is TRUE.

1. **a.** The colony of Virginia was an immediate success.
   b. The colony of Virginia faced many challenges in its early years.
2. **a.** Maryland was founded by Catholics escaping religious persecution.
   b. Maryland was founded by a group hoping to make a profit.
3. **a.** By the 1700s, enslaved Africans were the main source of labor in the southern colonies.
   b. By the 1700s, indentured servants were the main source of labor in the southern colonies.

Preview Section 2

If YOU were there ...

You live in a town near London in the early 1700s. Some of your neighbors are starting new lives in the American colonies. You would like to go with them, but you cannot afford the cost of the trip. There is one way you can go, though. You can sign a paper promising to work as a servant for five years. Then you would be free—and in a new country!

Would you sign the paper and go to America?

Consider the PROS:
- get to go for free
- free room and board
- plenty of land in America

Consider the CONS:
- may not survive the trip
- may not survive the five years
- may end up worse off

Review Answers: 1. b; 2. a; 3. a

Building Vocabulary

Preteach or review the following terms:

bicameral two houses (p. 45)

congregation church members (p. 46)

covenant promise (p. 44)

dissenters people who disagree with official opinions (p. 44)

Protestant Reformation religious movement that began in the 1520s as an effort to reform the Catholic Church (p. 42)

radical extreme (p. 46)

CRF: Vocabulary Builder Activity, Section 2

Standards Focus

HSS 8.2.1

Means: Discuss why the Mayflower Compact was important in U.S. history.

Matters: The Mayflower Compact was one of the first attempts at self-government in the English Colonies.

SECTION 2

The New England Colonies

What You Will Learn...

Main Ideas

1. The Pilgrims and Puritans came to America to avoid religious persecution.
2. Religion and government were closely linked in the New England colonies.
3. The New England economy was based on trade and farming.
4. Education was important in the New England colonies.

The Big Idea

English colonists traveled to New England to gain religious freedom.

Key Terms and People

Puritans, *p. 42*
Pilgrims, *p. 42*
immigrants, *p. 42*
Mayflower Compact, *p. 43*
Squanto, *p. 43*
John Winthrop, *p. 44*
Anne Hutchinson, *p. 46*

HSS 8.2.1 Discuss the significance of the Magna Carta, the English Bill of Rights, and the Mayflower Compact.

If YOU were there...

You live in a town near London in the early 1700s. Some of your neighbors are starting new lives in the American colonies. You would like to go with them, but you cannot afford the cost of the trip. There is one way you can go, though. You can sign a paper promising to work as a servant for five years. Then you would be free—and in a new country!

Would you sign the paper and go to America?

BUILDING BACKGROUND England's first successful colonial settlements were in Virginia. They were started mainly as business ventures. Other colonists in North America had many different reasons for leaving their homes. Many, like the Pilgrims and Puritans, came to have freedom to practice their religious beliefs. Others, like the person above, simply wanted a new way of life.

Pilgrims and Puritans

Religious tensions in England remained high after the Protestant Reformation. A Protestant group called the **Puritans** wanted to purify, or reform, the Anglican Church. The Puritans thought that bishops and priests had too much power over church members.

Pilgrims on the Move

The most extreme English Protestants wanted to separate from the Church of England. These Separatists formed their own churches and cut all ties with the Church of England. In response, Anglican leaders began to punish Separatists.

The **Pilgrims** were one Separatist group that left England in the early 1600s to escape persecution. The Pilgrims moved to the Netherlands in 1608. The Pilgrims were **immigrants**—people who have left the country of their birth to live in another country.

The Pilgrims were glad to be able to practice their religion freely. They were not happy, however, that their children were learn-

Teach the Big Idea: Master the Standards

Standards Proficiency

The New England Colonies HSS 8.2.1; HSS Analysis Skills: CS 3, HI 1

1. **Teach** Ask students the Main Idea questions to teach this section.
2. **Apply** Draw a web graphic organizer for students to see. In a central circle, write *The New England Colonies.* In circles radiating out from this central circle, write the labels *Pilgrims, Puritans, Religion and Government, Economy,* and *Education.* Have each student copy the graphic organizer and enter five or more facts in each of the circles. **LS Visual/Spatial**
3. **Review** As you review the section's main ideas, have volunteers share the information they listed. Enter students' answers into the version of the graphic organizer that you drew.
4. **Practice/Homework** Have each student create a map of the New England colonies, label each colony, and note when it was founded and where the Pilgrims and Puritans settled. **LS Visual/Spatial**

Alternative Assessment Handbook, Rubrics 13: Graphic Organizers; and 20: Map Creation ing the Dutch language and culture. The Pilgrims feared that their children would forget their English traditions. The Pilgrims decided to leave Europe altogether. They formed a joint-stock company with some merchants and then received permission from England to settle in Virginia.

On September 16, 1620, a ship called the *Mayflower* left England with more than 100 men, women, and children aboard. Not all of these colonists were Pilgrims. However, Pilgrim leaders such as William Bradford sailed with the group.

The Mayflower Compact

After two months of rough ocean travel, the Pilgrims sighted land far north of Virginia. The Pilgrims knew that they would thus be outside the authority of Virginia's colonial government when they landed. Their charter would not apply. So, they decided to establish their own basic laws and social rules to govern the colony they would found.

On November 21, 1620, 41 of the male passengers on the ship signed the **Mayflower Compact**, a legal contract in which they agreed to have fair laws to protect the general good. The Compact represents one of the first attempts at self-government in the English colonies.

In late 1620 the Pilgrims landed at Plymouth Rock in present-day Massachusetts. The colonists struggled through the winter to build the Plymouth settlement. Nearly half of the tired Pilgrims died during this first winter from sickness and the freezing weather.

Primary Source

HISTORICAL DOCUMENT

The Mayflower Compact

In November 1620, Pilgrim leaders aboard the Mayflower *drafted the Mayflower Compact. This excerpt from the Mayflower Compact describes the principles of the Pilgrim colony's government.*

We whose names are underwritten . . . having undertaken, for the glory of God, and advancement of the Christian faith, and the honour of our King and country, a voyage to plant the first colony in the northern parts of Virginia, do by these presents solemnly and mutually in the presence of God, and one of another, covenant and combine ourselves together into a civil body politic for our better ordering and preservation and furtherance of the ends aforesaid; and by virtue hereof, to enact, constitute, and frame such just and equal laws, ordinances, acts, constitutions, and offices . . . as shall be thought most meet and convenient for the general good of the colony unto which we promise all due . . . obedience.

The Pilgrims describe the reasons they want to form a colony in North America.

The Pilgrims promise to obey laws that help the whole colony.

by these presents: by this document
covenant: promise
civil body politic: group organized to govern
aforesaid: mentioned above
virtue: authority
ordinances: regulations
meet: fitting

ANALYSIS SKILL **ANALYZING PRIMARY SOURCES**

1. **Why do you think the colonists felt the need to establish a government for themselves?**
2. **How do you think the Mayflower Compact influenced later governments in America?**

Pilgrims and Native Americans

In March 1621 a Native American named Samoset walked boldly into the colonists' settlement. He spoke in broken English. Samoset had learned some English from the crews of English fishing boats. He gave the Pilgrims useful information about the peoples and places of the area. He also introduced them to a Patuxet Indian named **Squanto**. Squanto had at one time lived in Europe and spoke English as well.

From Squanto the Pilgrims learned to fertilize the soil with fish remains. Squanto also helped the Pilgrims establish relations with the local Wampanoag Indians. Conditions in the Plymouth colony began to improve.

The Pilgrims invited Wampanoag chief Massasoit and 90 other guests to celebrate their harvest. This feast became known as the first Thanksgiving. For the event, the Pilgrims killed wild turkeys. This event marked the survival of the Pilgrims in the new colony.

Direct Teach

Main Idea

❶ Pilgrims and Puritans

The Pilgrims and Puritans came to America to avoid religious persecution.

Explain What factors led the Pilgrims to leave England and settle in America? *religious persecution in England; desire to preserve English traditions*

Elaborate What role did chance play in the aid the Pilgrims received from Native Americans? *a large one because there just happened to be friendly Native Americans living nearby who could speak English*

Political Cartoons Activities for United States History, Cartoon 1: The Mayflower

HSS 8.2.1; HSS **Analysis Skills:** CS 1, HI 1, HI 2, HI 4

Primary Source

Reading Like a Historian

The Mayflower Compact Help students practice reading the document like historians. Ask the following:

- Who wrote the Mayflower Compact? What viewpoints and beliefs did the authors hold?
- How does this document fit into a time and place in history?

HSS 8.2.1; HSS **Analysis Skills:** HR 4, HR 5, HI 1

Teaching Tip

Remind students of the difference between immigrants and emigrants.

Critical Thinking: Analyzing

Exceeding Standards

Mayflower Compact Simulation

HSS 8.2.1; HSS **Analysis Skills:** HI 1, HI 2

1. To help students understand the importance of government, ask them to imagine what society would be like without laws. What might occur if there were no speed limits or traffic signals?
2. Then organize students into small groups. Ask them to imagine that they were planning to found a space colony on Planet Virginia. Their spaceship has gone off course, though, and they have landed on an unknown planet, which they have named Planet Plymouth. Have each group create a list of rules to govern its colony. Students should refer to the Mayflower Compact and discuss what the "greater good" is and how to determine it.
3. Ask representatives to share some of their group's rules with the class.
4. Conclude by having students discuss why Pilgrim leaders drafted the Mayflower Compact and the significance of the document.
   LS **Verbal/Linguistic**

Alternative Assessment Handbook, Rubric 11: Discussions

Answers

Analyzing Primary Sources 1. *They were outside the authority of Virginia's colonial government and wanted to maintain a rule of law to protect the public good.* **2.** *encouraged continued support of self-government*

Direct Teach

Main Idea

1 Pilgrims and Puritans

The Pilgrims and Puritans came to America to avoid religious persecution.

Describe What was family life like for the Pilgrims? *Families were the center of religious life, health care, and community well-being; all family members worked; women did household duties; men worked in the fields.*

Identify Points of View How did the Pilgrims view women and children? *Evidence suggests that they valued them, because Pilgrim families traveled together to North America, children were educated, and women had more legal rights than in England.*

Identify Cause and Effect What factors led to the Great Migration, and why is it significant? *economic hardship, political crisis, and religious persecution of Puritans in England; led Puritans to found English colonies in New England*

HSS Analysis Skills: HR 5, HI 1

Info to Know

How the Pilgrims Got Their Name William Bradford gave the name Pilgrims to the group aboard the *Mayflower.* Bradford took the word from the Christian Bible. In his journal, later published under the title *Of Plymouth Plantation,* he explained that the people seeking religious freedom knew they were Pilgrims.

Activity Have students look up the word *pilgrim* in a dictionary and discuss its meaning.

Pilgrim Community

Although the Pilgrims overcame many problems, their small settlement still struggled. Most Pilgrims became farmers, but the farmland around their settlement was poor. They had hoped to make money by trading furs and by fishing. Unfortunately, fishing and hunting conditions were not good in the area. Some colonists traded corn with American Indians for beaver furs. The Pilgrims made little money but were able to form a strong community. The colony began to grow stronger in the mid-1620s after new settlers arrived and, as in Jamestown, colonists began to have more rights to farm their own land.

The Pilgrims' settlement was different from Virginia's in that it had many families. The Pilgrims taught their children to read and offered some education to their indentured servants. Families served as centers of religious life, health care, and community well-being.

All family members worked together to survive during the early years of the colony. Women generally cooked, spun and wove wool, and sewed clothing. They also made soap and butter, carried water, dried fruit, and cared for livestock. Men spent most of their time repairing tools and working in the fields. They also chopped wood and built shelters.

Women in the Colony

In Plymouth, women had more legal rights than they did in England. In England women were not allowed to make contracts, to sue, or to own property. In America, Pilgrim women had the right to sign contracts and to bring some cases before local courts. Widows could also own property.

From time to time, local courts recognized the ways women helped the business community. Widow Naomi Silvester received a large share of her husband's estate. The court called her "a frugal [thrifty] and laborious [hardworking] woman."

Puritans Leave England

During the 1620s England's economy suffered. Many people lost their jobs. The English king, Charles I, made the situation worse by raising taxes. This unpopular act led to a political crisis. At the same time, the Church of England began to punish Puritans because they were dissenters, or people who disagree with official opinions. King Charles refused to allow Puritans to criticize church actions.

Great Migration

These economic, political, and religious problems in England led to the Great Migration. Between 1629 and 1640 many thousands of English men, women, and children left England. More than 40,000 of these people moved to English colonies in New England and the Caribbean. In 1629, Charles granted a group of Puritans and merchants a charter to settle in New England. They formed the Massachusetts Bay Company.

In 1630 a fleet of ships carrying Puritan colonists left England for Massachusetts to seek religious freedom. They were led by **John Winthrop**. The Puritans believed that they had made a covenant, or promise, with God to build an ideal Christian community.

A New Colony

The Puritans arrived in New England well prepared to start their colony. They brought large amounts of tools and livestock with them. Like the Pilgrims, the Puritans faced little resistance from local American Indians. Trade with the Plymouth colony helped them too. In addition, the region around Boston had a fairly healthful climate. Thus, few Puritans died from sickness. All of these things helped the Massachusetts Bay Colony do well. By 1691, the Massachusetts Bay Colony had expanded to include the Pilgrims' Plymouth Colony.

READING CHECK **Summarizing** What role did religion play in the establishment of the Massachusetts Bay Colony?

Collaborative Learning

Standards Proficiency

First Thanksgiving News Report

HSS Analysis Skills: HI 1, HI 2

1. Organize students into small groups and ask them to imagine that they are TV reporters covering the first Thanksgiving in Plymouth Colony.
2. Have each group create a script for its on-the-spot news report. Group members should assign roles for a news anchor, an on-the-spot reporter, writers, and copy editors.
3. The group's news reports should explain who the Pilgrims are, why they founded Plymouth Colony, the struggles they have faced, how Native Americans have helped them, and why they are holding a Thanksgiving feast. **LS Interpersonal, Verbal/Linguistic**
4. **Extend** Have each group conduct research on what the Pilgrims ate and drank in the 1620s and then create a "menu" for the first Thanksgiving meal. **LS Verbal/Linguistic**

Alternative Assessment Handbook, Rubrics 14: Group Activity; 30: Research; and 37: Writing Assignments

Answers

Reading Check *Religious persecution contributed to the Great Migration; Puritans believed they had a covenant with God to establish an ideal Christian community.*

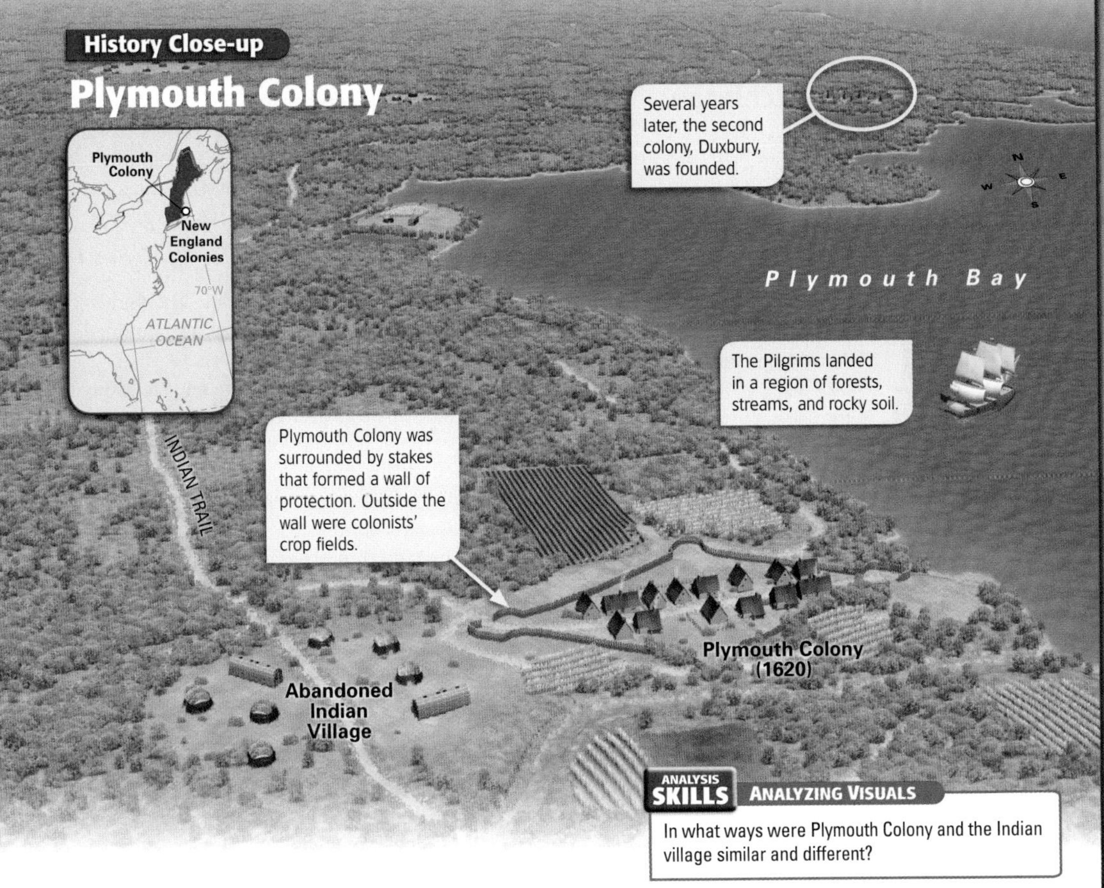
History Close-up
Plymouth Colony
Plymouth Colony
New England Colonies
70°W
ATLANTIC OCEAN
Several years later, the second colony, Duxbury, was founded.
Plymouth Bay
The Pilgrims landed in a region of forests, streams, and rocky soil.
Plymouth Colony was surrounded by stakes that formed a wall of protection. Outside the wall were colonists' crop fields.
INDIAN TRAIL
Plymouth Colony (1620)
Abandoned Indian Village

ANALYSIS SKILLS ANALYZING VISUALS

In what ways were Plymouth Colony and the Indian village similar and different?

Religion and Government in New England

Massachusetts Bay Colony had to obey English laws. However, its charter provided more independence than did the royal charter of Virginia. For example, it created a General Court to help run the Massachusetts colony.

The Puritan colonists turned this court into a type of self-government to represent the needs of the people. Each town sent two or three delegates to the Court. After John Winthrop served as the colony's first governor, the General Court elected the governor and his assistants. In 1644 the General Court became a two-house, or bicameral, legislature.

Politics and religion were closely linked in Puritan New England. Government leaders were also church members, and ministers often had a great deal of power in Puritan communities. Male church members were the only colonists who could vote. Colonists became full members in the church by becoming what the Puritans called God's "elect," or chosen. Reaching this status was a difficult process. Individuals had to pass a public test to prove that their faith was strong.

Direct Teach

Main Idea

❷ Religion and Government in New England

Religion and government were closely linked in the New England colonies.

Recall What was the function of the General Court in the Massachusetts Bay Colony? *Each town in the colony sent delegates to the Court, which served as a governing body.*

Analyze How was religion connected to government in the New England colonies? *Government leaders had to be church members, ministers often had a great deal of power, and only male church members could vote.*

HSS Analysis Skills: HI 1

Teaching Tip

Pilgrims and Puritans

Some students may have trouble understanding the difference between Pilgrims and Puritans. Help students by explaining that they were each Protestant groups that disagreed with aspects of the Anglican Church. The Puritans wanted to purify the Church of England; the Pilgrims wanted to separate from it.

Differentiating Instruction for Universal Access

English-Language Learners

Standards Proficiency — Prep Required

Materials: paper, colored pencils, art supplies

1. Lead students in a discussion of what new settlers arriving in Massachusetts Bay Colony would need and like to know about life there. *(For example, information about the climate, the governing body, and so on.)* Make a list for students to see.
2. Organize students into small groups. Assign each group related items from the list, such as geography, government, religion, and so on.
3. Provide each group with paper and art supplies. Have each group create three to five pages for an illustrated *Guide to Massachusetts Bay.*
4. Each group should present its work to the class. Then bind all the pages to make a class guide. **LS Interpersonal, Visual/Spatial**

HSS Analysis Skills: HI 1

Alternative Assessment Handbook, Rubrics 3: Artwork; and 14: Group Activity

Answers

Analyzing Visuals *similar—located in same area in the midst of woods and near streams; small; different—Plymouth was closer to the bay, surrounded by fields of crops, and had different types of dwellings and protective stakes.*

Direct Teach

Main Idea

❷ Religion and Government in New England

Religion and government were closely linked in the New England colonies.

Explain How was Connecticut's government distinctive? *Connecticut had the Fundamental Orders of Connecticut, which allowed men who were not church members to vote and made the government more democratic.*

Compare What did Roger Williams and Anne Hutchinson have in common? *both forced to leave Massachusetts because of their religious views; formed new settlements in what became the colony of Rhode Island*

Make Inferences What effect do you think the witch trials had on Puritan communities? *possible answers—harmed community trust; created fear and anxiety; led some to unite against those they distrusted*

Quick Facts Transparency: Church and State

HSS **Analysis Skills:** HI 1, HI 2

Answers

Biography *Her ideas differed from theirs, and she undermined their religious authority.*

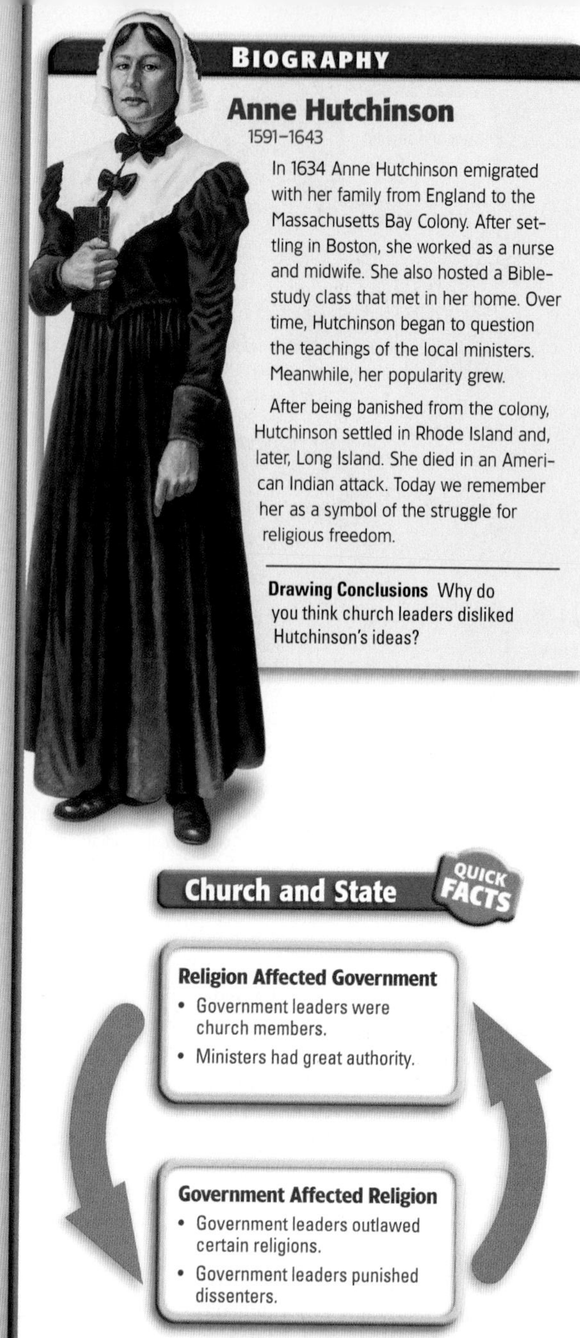

BIOGRAPHY

Anne Hutchinson
1591–1643

In 1634 Anne Hutchinson emigrated with her family from England to the Massachusetts Bay Colony. After settling in Boston, she worked as a nurse and midwife. She also hosted a Bible-study class that met in her home. Over time, Hutchinson began to question the teachings of the local ministers. Meanwhile, her popularity grew.

After being banished from the colony, Hutchinson settled in Rhode Island and, later, Long Island. She died in an American Indian attack. Today we remember her as a symbol of the struggle for religious freedom.

Drawing Conclusions Why do you think church leaders disliked Hutchinson's ideas?

Church and State QUICK FACTS

Religion Affected Government
- Government leaders were church members.
- Ministers had great authority.

Government Affected Religion
- Government leaders outlawed certain religions.
- Government leaders punished dissenters.

In 1636 minister Thomas Hooker and his followers left Massachusetts to help found Connecticut, another New England colony. In 1639 Hooker wrote the Fundamental Orders of Connecticut. This set of principles made Connecticut's government more democratic. For example, the Orders allowed men who were not church members to vote. As a result, some historians call Hooker the father of American democracy. The Fundamental Orders of Connecticut also outlined the powers of the general courts.

Not all Puritans shared the same religious views. Minister Roger Williams did not agree with the leadership of Massachusetts. He called for his church to separate completely from the other New England congregations. Williams also criticized the General Court for taking land from American Indians without paying them.

Puritan leaders worried that Williams's ideas might hurt the unity of the colony. They made him leave Massachusetts. Williams took his supporters to southern New England. They formed a new settlement called Providence. This settlement later developed into the colony of Rhode Island. In Providence, Williams supported the separation of the church from the state. He also believed in religious tolerance for all members of the community.

In Boston, an outspoken woman also angered Puritan church leaders. **Anne Hutchinson** publicly discussed religious ideas that some leaders thought were radical. For example, Hutchinson believed that people's relationship with God did not need guidance from ministers.

Hutchinson's views alarmed Puritans such as John Winthrop. Puritan leaders did not believe that women should be religious leaders. Puritan leaders put Hutchinson on trial for her ideas. The court decided to force her out of the colony. With a group of followers, Hutchinson helped found the new

Differentiating Instruction for Universal Access

Learners Having Difficulty

Reaching Standards  HSS **Analysis Skills:** HI 1

1. To help students identify the key people, events, and issues related to the colonies of Connecticut and Rhode Island, draw the graphic organizer for students to see. Omit the blue, italicized answers.
2. Have each student copy and complete the graphic organizer. Review students' answers as a class. **LS Visual/Spatial**

Alternative Assessment Handbook, Rubric 13: Graphic Organizers

Connecticut	Rhode Island	
Thomas Hooker: *minister; left Massachusetts with followers in 1636 to found Connecticut* **Fundamental Orders of Connecticut, 1639:** *set of principles that made colonial government more democratic*	**Roger Williams:** • *called for his church to separate; criticized taking land from Native Americans without payment* • *forced to leave Massachusetts* • *founded settlement of Providence*	**Anne Hutchinson:** • *Her religious views alarmed Puritan leaders.* • *put on trial; then forced out of Massachusetts* • *founded settlement of Portsmouth on Aquidneck Island*

colony of Portsmouth, later a part of the colony of Rhode Island.

Perhaps the worst community conflicts in New England involved the witchcraft trials of the early 1690s. The largest number of trials were held in Salem, Massachusetts. In Salem a group of girls had accused people of casting spells on them. The community formed a special court to judge the witchcraft cases. The court often pressured the suspected witches to confess. Before the trials had ended, the Salem witch trials led to 19 people being put to death.

READING CHECK **Identifying Cause and Effect** What led to religious disagreements among the Puritans, and what was the result?

New England Economy

Connecticut, Massachusetts, New Hampshire, and Rhode Island were very different from the southern colonies. The often harsh climate and rocky soil meant that few New England farms could grow cash crops. Most farming families grew crops and raised animals for their own use. There was thus little demand for farm laborers. Although some people held slaves, slavery did not become as important to this region.

Merchants

Trade was vital to New England's economy. New England merchants traded goods locally, with other colonies, and overseas. Many of them traded local products such as furs, pickled beef, and pork. Many merchants grew in power and wealth, becoming leading members of the New England colonies.

Fishing

Fishing became one of the region's leading industries. The rich waters off New England's coast served as home to many fish, including cod, mackerel, and halibut. Merchants exported dried fish. Colonists also began hunting for whales that swam close to shore. Whales were captured with harpoons, or spears, and dragged to shore. Whaling provided valuable oil for lighting.

Shipbuilding

Shipbuilding became an important industry in New England for several reasons. The area had plenty of forests that provided materials for shipbuilding. As trade—particularly in slaves—in the New England seaports grew, more merchant ships were built. The fishing industry also needed ships. New England shipyards made high-quality, valuable vessels. Ship owners sometimes even told their captains to sell the ship along with the cargo when they reached their destination.

Skilled Craftspeople

The northern economy needed skilled craftspeople. Families often sent younger sons to learn skilled trades such as blacksmithing, weaving, shipbuilding, and printing. The young boys who learned skilled trades were known as apprentices.

Apprentices lived with a master craftsman and learned from him. In exchange, the boys performed simple tasks. Apprentices had to promise the craftsmen that they would work for them for a set number of years. They learned trades that were essential to the survival of the colonies. Apprentices received food and often clothing from the craftsmen. Gabriel Ginings was an apprentice in Portsmouth, Rhode Island. He received "sufficient food and raiment (clothing) suitable for such an apprentice," as his 1663 contract stated.

After a certain amount of time had passed, apprentices became journeymen. They usually traveled and learned new skills in their trade. Eventually they would become a master of the trade themselves.

READING CHECK **Categorizing** What types of jobs were common in the New England colonies?

THE IMPACT TODAY

Fishing remains an important industry in New England, earning hundreds of millions of dollars each year.

Direct Teach

Main Idea

❸ New England Economy

The New England economy was based on trade and farming.

Recall What class of people gained power and wealth from trade in the New England colonies? *merchants*

Identify Cause and Effect How did the climate and terrain of New England make slavery unpopular in this area? *There was little demand for farm labor because few New England farms grew cash crops.*

Evaluate What is your opinion of the apprentice system? *Answers will vary but should reflect an understanding of the roles of apprentices and skilled craftspeople in the New England economy.*

 **Analysis Skills:** HI 1, HI 2

World Events

The European Witch Hunt At the same time that the Salem witchcraft trials were taking place, a vicious witch hunt was taking place in Europe. The European witch-hunt began in the early 1500s and lasted until the late 1700s. During this time, judges in Europe tried more than 100,000 people as witches and warlocks. More than half of the trials took place in German lands in the Holy Roman Empire.

Collaborative Learning

Standards Proficiency

New England Colonial Trade Ads

HSS **Analysis Skills:** HI 1

Materials: art supplies, poster board (optional)

1. Organize students into small groups. Assign each group one of the following New England colonial trades: fur trader, meat merchant, fisher, whaler, shipbuilder, blacksmith, printer, or weaver.
2. Provide art supplies and paper. Have each group create a flyer advertising its assigned trade. Group members should combine text and illustrations to create their advertisements.
3. Have each group present its flyer to the class. Display the flyers in the classroom. **LS Interpersonal, Verbal/Linguistic**
4. **Extend** Have each student create a want ad for a colonial apprentice. Ads should list the apprentice's duties and desired characteristics. Have volunteers share their want ads with the class. **LS Verbal/Linguistic**

Alternative Assessment Handbook, Rubrics 2: Advertisements; and 28: Posters

Answers

Reading Check (left) *Different views on religion, on mixing government and religion, and on relations with Native Americans; forced to leave, dissenters established new settlements in New England.*

Reading Check (right) *merchants selling trade goods, fishing and shipbuilding jobs, skilled craftspeople*

Direct Teach

Main Idea

❹ Education in the Colonies

Education was important in the New England colonies.

Recall What was the first college in New England, and why was it founded? *Harvard College; to ensure educated ministers for the future*

Contrast How did education in the New England colonies differ from that in Virginia? *New England—Many communities provided public schools to ensure that children could read the Bible; Virginia—Parents or private tutors taught children, and fewer people learned to read and write.*

CRF: Literature Activity: American Colonial Poetry

HSS Analysis Skills: CS 1, HI 1

Review & Assess

Close

Briefly review how and why the Plymouth, Massachusetts Bay, Connecticut, and Rhode Island colonies were formed.

Review

go.hrw.com Online Quiz, Section 2

Assess

SE Section 2 Assessment

PASS: Section 2 Quiz

Alternative Assessment Handbook

Reteach/Classroom Intervention

California Standards Review Workbook

Interactive Reader and Study Guide, Section 2

Interactive Skills Tutor CD-ROM

Education in the Colonies

Education was important in colonial New England. Mothers and fathers wanted their children to be able to read the Bible. The Massachusetts Bay Colony passed some of the first laws requiring parents to provide instruction for their children.

Public Education

To be sure that future generations would have educated ministers, communities established town schools. In 1647 the General Court of Massachusetts issued an order that a school be founded in every township of 50 families.

THE IMPACT TODAY Public schools remain the primary source of education for most U.S. children. Total enrollment today is around 50 million students.

Schoolchildren often used the *New England Primer,* which had characters and stories from the Bible. They learned to read at the same time that they learned about the community's religious values.

The availability of schooling varied in the colonies. There were more schools in New England than in the other colonies where most children lived far from towns. These children had to be taught by their parents or by private tutors. Most colonial children stopped their education after the elementary grades. Many went to work, either on their family farm or away from home.

Higher Education

Higher education was also important to the colonists. In 1636 John Harvard and the General Court founded Harvard College. Harvard taught ministers and met the colony's need for higher education. The second college founded in the colonies, William and Mary, was established in Virginia in 1693.

By 1700 about 70 percent of men and 45 percent of women in New England could read and write. These figures were much lower in Virginia, where Jamestown was the only major settlement.

READING CHECK **Analyzing** Why was education important to the New England colonies?

SUMMARY AND PREVIEW In this section you learned about the role that religion played in the New England colonies. In the next section you'll learn about New York, New Jersey, and Pennsylvania.

Section 2 Assessment

go.hrw.com Online Quiz KEYWORD: SS8 HP2

Reviewing Ideas, Terms, and People HSS 8.2.1

1. **a. Recall** Why did the **Pilgrims** and **Puritans** leave Europe for the Americas?
   b. Elaborate Do you think the Pilgrims could have survived without the assistance of **Squanto** and the Massasoit? Explain your answer.
2. **a. Describe** What role did the church play in Massachusetts?
   b. Analyze Why did some colonists disagree with the leaders of Massachusetts?
3. **a. Identify** Describe the economy in the New England colonies.
   b. Analyze Why do you think New England merchants became leading members of society?
4. **a. Describe** What steps did the Massachusetts Bay Colony take to promote education?
   b. Predict What are some possible benefits that New England's emphasis on education might bring?

Critical Thinking

5. **Categorizing** Copy the chart below and use it to identify the characteristics of the New England colonies.

Role of Church	Economic Activities	Education

FOCUS ON WRITING

6. **Comparing Colonies** Take notes on the early New England colonies. Be sure to note what advantages they offered to settlers and what difficulties settlers faced. Put a star beside the colony or colonies you might use in your infomercial.

Section 2 Assessment Answers

1. **a.** to escape religious persecution
   b. Answers should show knowledge of the ways in which Native Americans aided the Pilgrims.
2. **a.** Religion was closely tied to government, ministers had a great deal of power, and only male church members could vote.
   b. They disagreed about different aspects of religion and how to treat Native Americans.
3. **a.** little reliance on cash crops; focus on trade, fishing, shipbuilding, and skilled crafts
   b. because they became wealthy and powerful
4. **a.** required parents to educate children, established town schools and colleges
   b. possible answers—well educated colonists, well run government, attracted more settlers
5. possible answer: Role of Church—important, influential; Economic Activities—fishing, shipbuilding, craftspeople, merchants; Education—promoted or required
6. Students should include notes on the Pilgrims and Puritans and the Plymouth, Massachusetts Bay, Connecticut, and Rhode Island colonies.

Answers

Reading Check *Parents wanted their children to be able to read the Bible and to ensure that future generations had educated ministers.*

SECTION 3

The Middle Colonies

If YOU were there...

You are a farmer in southern Germany in 1730. Religious wars have torn your country apart for many years. Now you hear stories about a place in America where people of all religions are welcome. But the leaders of the colony—and many of its people—are English. You would not know their language or customs. Still, you would be free to live and worship as you like.

How would you feel about moving to a country full of strangers?

BUILDING BACKGROUND The middle section of the Atlantic coast offered good land and a moderate climate. Several prominent English people established colonies that promised religious freedom. To people like the settler above, these colonies promised a new life.

What You Will Learn...

Main Ideas

1. The English created New York and New Jersey from former Dutch territory.
2. William Penn established the colony of Pennsylvania.
3. The economy of the middle colonies was supported by trade and staple crops.

The Big Idea

People from many nations settled in the middle colonies.

Key Terms and People

Peter Stuyvesant, *p. 49*
Quakers, *p. 50*
William Penn, *p. 50*
staple crops, *p. 51*

New York and New Jersey

The Dutch founded New Netherland in 1613 as a trading post for exchanging furs with the Iroquois. The center of the fur trade in New Netherland was the town of New Amsterdam on Manhattan Island. Generous land grants and religious tolerance soon brought Jews, French Huguenots, Puritans, and others to the colony. Director General **Peter Stuyvesant** (STY-vuh-suhnt) led the colony beginning in 1647.

Peter Stuyvesant was forced to surrender New Amsterdam to the English in 1664.

HSS 8.1 Students understand the major events preceding the founding of the nation and relate their significance to the development of American constitutional democracy.

Preteach

Bellringer

If YOU were there . . . Use the **Daily Bellringer Transparency** to help students answer the question.

Daily Bellringer Transparency, Section 3

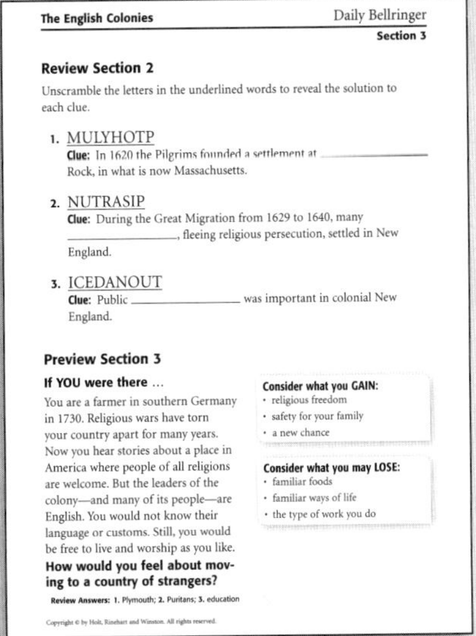

The English Colonies — Daily Bellringer — Section 3

Review Section 2

Unscramble the letters in the underlined words to reveal the solution to each clue.

1. MULYHOTP
Clue: In 1620 the Pilgrims founded a settlement at ____________ Rock, in what is now Massachusetts.
2. NUTRASIP
Clue: During the Great Migration from 1629 to 1640, many ____________, fleeing religious persecution, settled in New England.
3. ICEDANOUT
Clue: Public ____________ was important in colonial New England.

Preview Section 3

If YOU were there ...

You are a farmer in southern Germany in 1730. Religious wars have torn your country apart for many years. Now you hear stories about a place in America where people of all religions are welcome. But the leaders of the colony—and many of its people—are English. You would not know their language or customs. Still, you would be free to live and worship as you like.

How would you feel about moving to a country of strangers?

Consider what you GAIN:
- religious freedom
- safety for your family
- a new chance

Consider what you may LOSE:
- familiar foods
- familiar ways of life
- the type of work you do

Review Answers: 1. Plymouth; 2. Puritans; 3. education

Building Vocabulary

Preteach or review the following terms:

diverse varied (p. 50)

Huguenots Protestants in France (p. 49)

midwives women who helped deliver babies (p. 51)

CRF: Vocabulary Builder Activity, Section 3

Teach the Big Idea: Master the Standards

Standards Proficiency

The Middle Colonies HSS 8.1; HSS Analysis Skills: CS 1, CS 3, HI 1

1. **Teach** Ask students the Main Idea questions to teach this section.
2. **Apply** Create a chart with four columns for students to see. Label the columns *New York, New Jersey, Pennsylvania,* and *Delaware*. Have students copy the chart and list in each column some of the important facts about the settlement of each colony, including key dates, people, events, and issues. **LS Verbal/Linguistic, Visual/Spatial**
3. **Review** To review the section's main ideas, have students share the facts they listed. Use the facts to complete the master chart that you drew.
4. **Practice/Homework** Have each student create a map of the middle colonies that labels each colony, when it was founded, and where the main settlements were located. **LS Visual/Spatial**

Alternative Assessment Handbook, Rubrics 7: Charts; and 20: Map Creation

Standards Focus

HSS 8.1

Means: Students understand the major events that led up to the founding of the United States, such as the development of the thirteen colonies.

Matters: The thirteen colonies became the first states in the nation.

Direct Teach

Main Idea

❶ New York and New Jersey

The English created New York and New Jersey from former Dutch territory.

Recall What was the population of New Jersey like? *diverse, with Dutch, Swedes, Finns, and Scots*

Draw Conclusions Why did New York have a Dutch influence? *The Dutch founded the settlement that later became the colony of New York.*

CRF: Primary Source Activity: Journal of Sarah Kemble Knight

Quick Facts Transparency: Characteristics of the Middle Colonies

HSS 8.1; **HSS Analysis Skills:** CS 1, HI 1

Main Idea

❷ Penn's Colony

William Penn established the colony of Pennsylvania.

Identify What was the capital of Pennsylvania, and what did its name mean? *Philadelphia; "the city of brotherly love"*

Summarize What beliefs did Quakers hold? *equality of men and women before God, religious tolerance, non-violence*

HSS 8.1; **HSS Analysis Skills:** HI 1

Characteristics of the Middle Colonies (QUICK FACTS)

Social	Economic
• New York: Dutch influence • New Jersey: diverse population • Pennsylvania: founded by Quakers	• Farming of staple crops • Slaves and indentured servants important sources of labor • Trade

In 1664 an English fleet captured the undefended colony of New Amsterdam without firing a single shot. New Netherland was renamed New York, and New Amsterdam became New York City.

THE IMPACT TODAY

Today New York City is the largest city in the United States, with more than 8 million people.

Soon after the English conquest in 1664, the Duke of York made Sir George Carteret and Lord John Berkeley proprietors of New Jersey. This colony occupied lands between the Hudson and Delaware rivers. It had a diverse population, including Dutch, Swedes, Finns, and Scots. The fur trade was important to the economies of New York and New Jersey through the end of the 1600s.

READING CHECK **Comparing** How were New York and New Jersey similar?

BIOGRAPHY

William Penn

1644–1718

William Penn was born in London as the son of a wealthy admiral. Penn joined the Quakers in 1666 and became an active preacher and writer of religious works. He supported toleration of dissenters.

In 1681 he received a charter to establish a new colony called Pennsylvania. There, Penn put his beliefs into practice. He insisted on fair dealings with local American Indians, welcomed immigrants, and promised religious toleration.

Making Generalizations How did Penn's ideas influence the rules of the colony?

Penn's Colony

The Society of Friends, or the **Quakers**, made up one of the largest religious groups in New Jersey. Quakers did not follow formal religious practices and dressed plainly. They believed in the equality of men and women before God. They also supported nonviolence and religious tolerance for all people. At the time, many Quaker beliefs and practices shocked most Christians. As a result, Quakers were persecuted in both England and America.

One proprietor of the New Jersey colony was a Quaker named **William Penn**. Penn wished to found a larger colony under his own control that would provide a safe home for Quakers. In 1681 King Charles II agreed to grant Penn a charter to begin a colony west of New Jersey.

Penn's colony, known as Pennsylvania, grew rapidly. Penn limited his own power and established an elected assembly. He also promised religious freedom to all Christians. His work made Pennsylvania an important example of representative self-government— a government that reflects its citizens' will— in the colonies.

Penn named the capital of his colony Philadelphia, which means "the city of brotherly love." In 1682 the Duke of York sold Penn a region to the south of Pennsylvania. This area, called Delaware, remained part of Pennsylvania until 1776.

READING CHECK **Finding Main Ideas** Why did William Penn establish Pennsylvania, and how did he influence its government?

Answers

Biography *In keeping with his beliefs, he supported religious tolerance, immigrants, and fair dealings with Native Americans.*

Reading Check (left) *Both had diverse populations and were middle colonies; fur trade was important.*

Reading Check (right) *to provide a safe place for Quakers and religious freedom for all Christians; established an elected assembly to govern the area, which served as an example of representative self-government*

Critical Thinking: Analyzing Information

Exceeding Standards

European Influence in the Middle Colonies

HSS Analysis Skills: HI 1 — Research Required

Background Many Dutch settlers remained in New York after it became an English colony. Their influence can still be seen today. For example, the Dutch contributed words such as *boss, cookie* (from the Dutch word *koekje*), and *stoop* to the English language.

1. Discuss with students the diversity of the people who settled the middle colonies. Ask students to identify some of the different groups who settled in the middle colonies during the early and mid-1600s.
2. Next, have students conduct research on the region of the middle colonies today to find current examples of early European influence. For example, students might look for place-names, words, or foods that show the influence of different groups of early colonists.
3. Have students make a list of their findings. Ask volunteers to share some of the items on their lists with the class.

Alternate Assessment Handbook, Rubric 30: Research

Economy of the Middle Colonies

The middle colonies combined characteristics of the New England and southern colonies. With a good climate and rich land, farmers there could grow large amounts of **staple crops** — crops that are always needed. These crops included wheat, barley, and oats. Farmers also raised livestock.

Slaves were somewhat more important to the middle colonies than they were to New England. They worked in cities as skilled laborers, such as blacksmiths and carpenters. Other slaves worked on farms, onboard ships, and in the growing shipbuilding industry. However, indentured servants largely filled the middle colonies' growing labor needs. Between 1700 and 1775 about 135,000 indentured servants came to the middle colonies. About half of them moved to Pennsylvania. By 1760 Philadelphia had become the largest British colonial city. Other cities in the middle colonies, such as New York City, also grew quickly.

Trade was important to the economy of the middle colonies. Merchants in Philadelphia and New York City exported colonial goods to markets in Britain and the West Indies. These products included wheat from New York, Pennsylvania, and New Jersey.

Throughout the colonies, women made important contributions to the economy. They ran farms and businesses such as clothing and grocery stores, bakeries, and drugstores. Some women also practiced medicine and worked as nurses and midwives. However, colonial laws and customs limited women's economic opportunities.

Most colonial women worked primarily in the home. Married women managed households and raised children. Sometimes they earned money for their families by selling products like butter. They also made money through services such as washing clothes.

FOCUS ON READING You can tell **staple crops** means "crops that are always needed" because of the dash between the vocabulary term and the definition.

READING CHECK **Finding the Main Idea** On what were the economies of the middle colonies based?

SUMMARY AND PREVIEW In this section you learned about the middle colonies. In the next section you will read about colonial government, the slave trade, and conflicts that arose in the English colonies.

Section 3 Assessment

go.hrw.com **Online Quiz** KEYWORD: SS8 HP2

Reviewing Ideas, Terms, and People HSS 8.1

1. a. **Describe** Name the middle colonies. Where were they located?
   b. **Draw Inferences** What led to the diverse populations of New York and New Jersey?
2. a. **Identify** Who are the **Quakers**?
   b. **Analyze** How did **William Penn** attempt to create a colonial government that would be fair to all?
3. a. **Describe** What different types of jobs did slaves in the middle colonies hold?
   b. **Evaluate** In what ways were women essential to the middle colonies?

Critical Thinking

4. **Sequencing** Copy the time line below. Complete the time line by listing, in order, the events in the establishment of the colonies of New York and New Jersey.

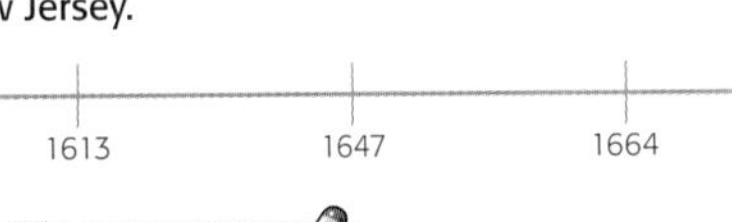

FOCUS ON WRITING

5. **Comparing Colonies** You've just read about early colonies in New York, New Jersey, and Pennsylvania. Think about the advantages they offered to settlers and what difficulties settlers faced. In your notes, put a star beside one of the colonies you might use in your infomercial.

Section 3 Assessment Answers

1. a. New York—Manhattan Island and former colony of New Netherland; New Jersey—between Hudson and Delaware rivers; Pennsylvania—west of New Jersey
   b. religious tolerance, generous land grants
2. a. a religious group known as the Society of Friends, which supported religious tolerance, non-violence, and equality of men and women
   b. He limited his own power, established an elected assembly that reflected the citizens' will, and provided religious freedom to all Christians.
3. a. worked as skilled laborers, farm laborers, and on board ships and in the shipbuilding industry
   b. ran farms and businesses, practiced medicine, earned money for their families by selling goods
4. 1613—Dutch found New Netherland as a trading post; 1647—Peter Stuyvesant leads the colony of New Netherland; 1664—English capture the colony and rename it New York; soon after, English colony of New Jersey is founded
5. Students may note advantages such as diversity, religious freedom, good farmland, and trade.

Direct Teach

Main Idea

3 Economy of the Middle Colonies

The economy of the middle colonies was supported by trade and staple crops.

Summarize How did women contribute to the middle colonies' economy? *ran farms and businesses, practiced medicine, worked as nurses and midwives*

Make Inferences Why do you think the middle colonies depended more on indentured servants than slaves for labor? *possible answers—Many colonists, such as Quakers, may have opposed slavery for religious or other reasons; indentured servants may have been easier to obtain and less expensive.*

HSS 8.1; HSS **Analysis Skills:** HI 1

Review & Assess

Close

Discuss why people from many nations settled in the middle colonies and how they supported themselves.

Review

Online Quiz, Section 3

Assess

SE Section 3 Assessment

PASS: Section 3 Quiz

Alternative Assessment Handbook

Reteach-Classroom Intervention

California Standards Review Workbook

Interactive Reader and Study Guide, Section 3

Interactive Skills Tutor CD-ROM

Answers

Reading Check *trade, staple crops*

History and Geography

Activity **Interpreting Maps** Have students describe how physical features influenced colonial settlement patterns. *Ports, rivers, and mountains influenced the location of early colonial settlements.* Then have students examine the maps in Section 4. Have students compare the locations of early French settlements and forts to those of the English colonies and discuss reasons for the differences. *(Early French exploration, waterways, and trade shaped early French settlement along the St. Lawrence River, Great Lakes, and Mississippi River.)*
LS Visual/Spatial

HSS 8.1; HSS **Analysis Skills:** CS 3

Connect to Geography

The Appalachians The Appalachian Mountains extend in a series of almost continuous mountain ranges from the Canadian province of Newfoundland to central Alabama. Although long, the Appalachian chain is quite narrow, rarely exceeding 100 miles in width. The range's highest peak—Mount Mitchell in North Carolina—reaches 6,684 feet above sea level. Its lowest areas are in Massachusetts and Connecticut.

Linking to Today

The Appalachian Trail While early pioneers struggled through dense forests and over rugged land in the Appalachians, today hikers walk the Appalachian Trail for fun. This footpath runs some 2,100 miles from Mount Katahdin in Maine to Springer Mountain in Georgia. The longest continuous footpath in North America, the Appalachian Trail runs through 14 states, seven national forests, and four national parks.

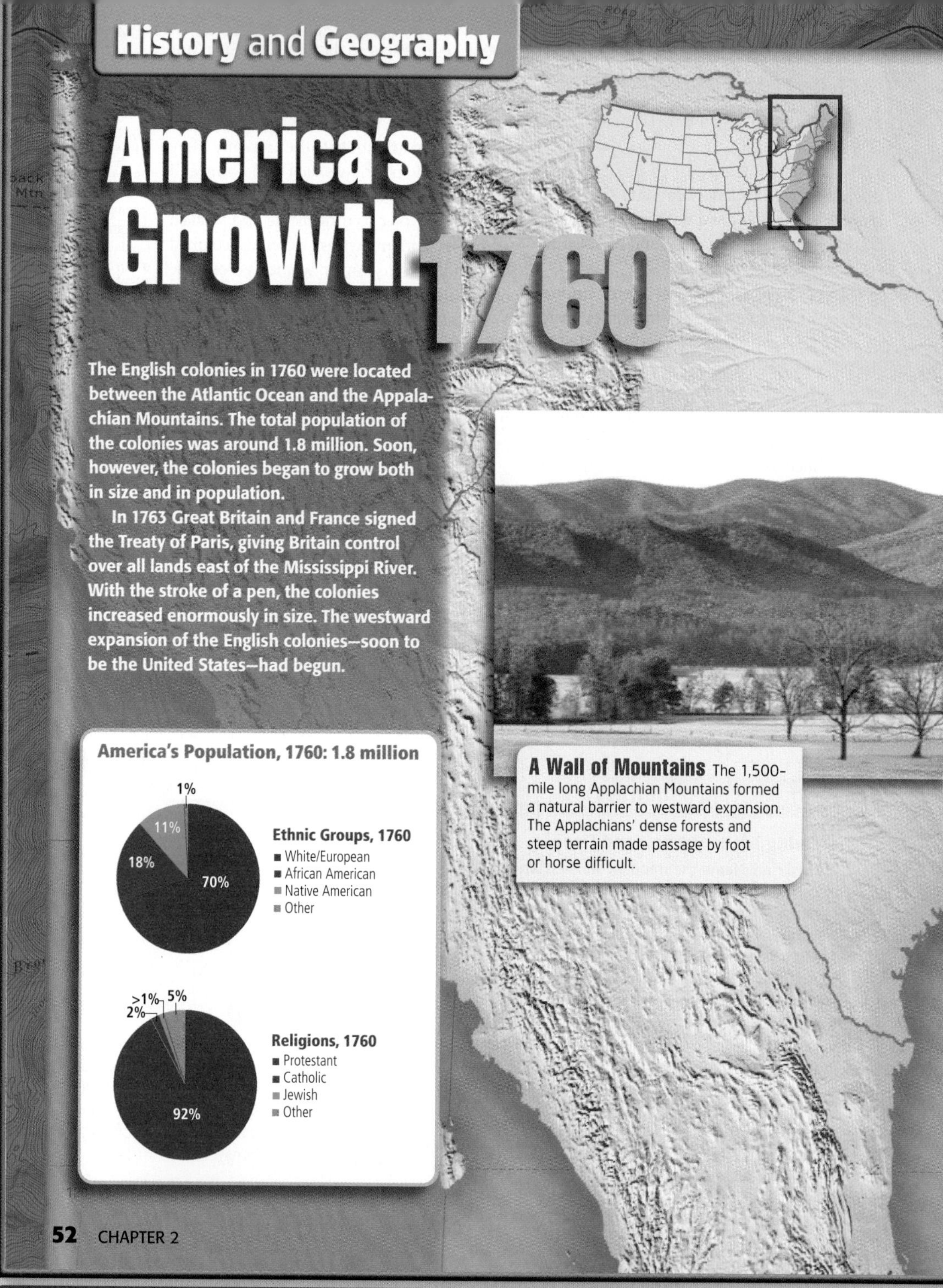

The English colonies in 1760 were located between the Atlantic Ocean and the Appalachian Mountains. The total population of the colonies was around 1.8 million. Soon, however, the colonies began to grow both in size and in population.

In 1763 Great Britain and France signed the Treaty of Paris, giving Britain control over all lands east of the Mississippi River. With the stroke of a pen, the colonies increased enormously in size. The westward expansion of the English colonies—soon to be the United States—had begun.

America's Population, 1760: 1.8 million

A Wall of Mountains The 1,500-mile long Applachian Mountains formed a natural barrier to westward expansion. The Applachians' dense forests and steep terrain made passage by foot or horse difficult.

Social Studies Skill: Interpreting Maps

Standards Proficiency

U.S. Cities Today

HSS 8.1; HSS **Analysis Skills:** CS 3

Research Required

Materials: outline maps of the United States

1. Have students conduct research on the 10 most populous U.S. cities today.
2. Give students blank outline maps of the United States or have them draw their own. Have students mark the locations and populations of the 10 cities.
3. Then have students use their maps and the above map to answer the following questions:
   - What are the three largest U.S. cities today? *New York, Los Angeles, Chicago*
   - What are some possible reasons these three cities are so populated? *possible answers—available jobs, resources, trade and business, culture and lifestyle*
   - How do the locations of these cities differ from the locations of the three largest cities in 1760? *They are spread across the continent instead of all being located on the East Coast.*

LS Visual/Spatial

Alternative Assessment Handbook, Rubrics 20: Map Creation; and 21: Map Reading

Standards Focus

HSS 8.1 Students understand the major events preceding the founding of the nation and relate their significance to the development of American constitutional democracy.

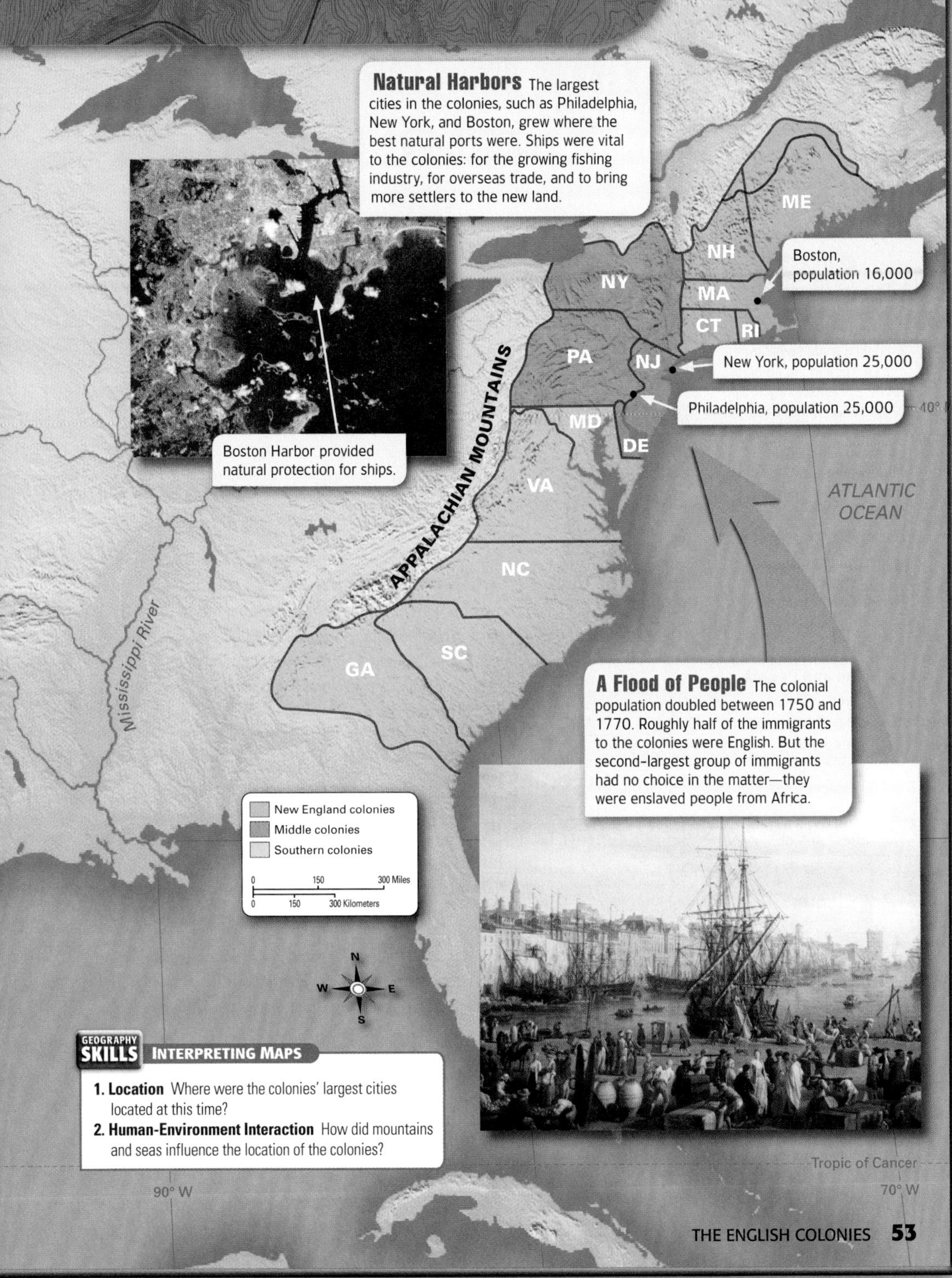

Natural Harbors The largest cities in the colonies, such as Philadelphia, New York, and Boston, grew where the best natural ports were. Ships were vital to the colonies: for the growing fishing industry, for overseas trade, and to bring more settlers to the new land.
Boston Harbor provided natural protection for ships.
ME
NH
MA
CT
RI
NY
PA
NJ
MD
DE
VA
NC
SC
GA
APPALACHIAN MOUNTAINS
Mississippi River
Boston, population 16,000
New York, population 25,000
Philadelphia, population 25,000
ATLANTIC OCEAN
A Flood of People The colonial population doubled between 1750 and 1770. Roughly half of the immigrants to the colonies were English. But the second-largest group of immigrants had no choice in the matter—they were enslaved people from Africa.
New England colonies
Middle colonies
Southern colonies
0 150 300 Miles
0 150 300 Kilometers
N
S
E
W
40° N
Tropic of Cancer
90° W
70° W

GEOGRAPHY SKILLS INTERPRETING MAPS

1. **Location** Where were the colonies' largest cities located at this time?
2. **Human-Environment Interaction** How did mountains and seas influence the location of the colonies?

History and Geography

Info to Know

Westward Expansion As the map shows, early European colonists settled mainly along the East Coast. West of the Appalachians, fur traders and a few forts were the only signs of Europeans. By the 1750s, however, European pioneers were moving into the Ohio River valley. Pioneers found that the valley provided fertile soil for farming and plenty of wild game. After the French and Indian War, pioneers began crossing the Appalachians in greater numbers. The Proclamation of 1763, which prohibited settlement west of the Appalachians, had little effect. The Proclamation proved difficult to enforce, and pioneers ignored it. The lure of the West proved irresistible.

Linking to Today

New York City As the map shows, New York was one of the largest cities in the English colonies in 1760. Today the city is the nation's largest, with a population of more than 7 million. New York City serves as a cultural and economic center and is one of the most culturally diverse cities in the United States. The city now consists of five boroughs—the Bronx, Brooklyn, Manhattan, Staten Island, and Queens.

Making Inferences Why do you think New York City has remained a major population center? *possible answer—Its strategic location serves as a gateway for incoming immigrants and trade. It has also become a center for many major American industries.*

Critical Thinking: Analyzing Information

Standards Proficiency

Pioneer Letter

HSS 8.1; HSS **Analysis Skills:** CS 3, HI 1

1. Ask students to imagine that they live in the English colonies in 1760. Their families have recently joined a group of pioneers and settled west of the Appalachian Mountains in the Ohio River valley.
2. Have students write letters to relatives or friends in Philadelphia describing why their families have moved west and some of the hardships they faced during the trip. If time allows, have students conduct research to learn more about pioneers and westward expansion in the 1770s.
3. Have volunteers read their letters to the class.
4. **Extend** Have students conduct research on Daniel Boone and his role in westward expansion during this period. Each student should write a biographical sketch of Boone. **LS Verbal/Linguistic**

Alternative Assessment Handbook, Rubrics 4: Biographies; and 25: Personal Letters

Answers

Interpreting Maps 1. *along the mid- and northern Atlantic coast;* **2.** *Immigrants arrived in North America by boat and landed on the East coast, so many colonists settled along the coast; the Appalachian Mountains formed a barrier to westward movement and settlement.*

Preteach

Bellringer

If YOU were there . . . Use the **Daily Bellringer Transparency** to help students answer the question.

Daily Bellringer Transparency, Section 4

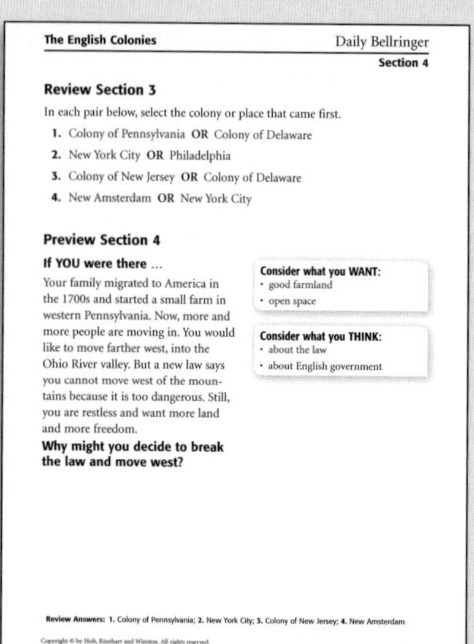

The English Colonies Daily Bellringer **Section 4**

Review Section 3

In each pair below, select the colony or place that came first.

1. Colony of Pennsylvania **OR** Colony of Delaware
2. New York City **OR** Philadelphia
3. Colony of New Jersey **OR** Colony of Delaware
4. New Amsterdam **OR** New York City

Preview Section 4

If YOU were there ...

Your family migrated to America in the 1700s and started a small farm in western Pennsylvania. Now, more and more people are moving in. You would like to move farther west, into the Ohio River valley. But a new law says you cannot move west of the mountains because it is too dangerous. Still, you are restless and want more land and more freedom.

Why might you decide to break the law and move west?

Consider what you WANT:
- good farmland
- open space

Consider what you THINK:
- about the law
- about English government

Review Answers: **1.** Colony of Pennsylvania; **2.** New York City; **3.** Colony of New Jersey; **4.** New Amsterdam

Building Vocabulary

Preteach or review the following terms:

backcountry thinly settled rural area (p. 61)

casualties captured, injured, or killed soldiers (p. 60)

dominion an area governed by a ruler (p. 55)

Privy Council a council or group that advises a ruler (p. 54)

revivals religious gatherings where people came together to hear sermons (p. 58)

CRF: Vocabulary Builder Activity, Section 4

Standards Focus

HSS 8.1.1

Means: Describe how the Great Awakening led to revolutionary fervor.

Matters: The Great Awakening raised ideas about political equality.

HSS 8.2.1

Means: Describe the significance of the English Bill of Rights.

Matters: The English Bill of Rights enabled more representative forms of government to develop in the colonies.

SECTION 4

Life in the English Colonies

What You Will Learn...

Main Ideas

1. Colonial governments were influenced by political changes in England.
2. English trade laws limited free trade in the colonies.
3. The Great Awakening and the Enlightenment led to ideas of political equality among many colonists.
4. The French and Indian War gave England control of more land in North America.

The Big Idea

The English colonies continued to grow despite many challenges.

Key Terms and People

town meeting, *p. 55*
English Bill of Rights, *p. 55*
triangular trade, *p. 57*
Middle Passage, *p. 58*
Great Awakening, *p. 58*
Enlightenment, *p. 59*
Pontiac, *p. 61*

HSS 8.1.1 Describe the relationship between the moral and political ideas of the Great Awakening and the development of revolutionary fervor.

8.2.1 Discuss the significance of the Magna Carta, the English Bill of Rights, and the Mayflower Compact.

If YOU were there...

Your family migrated to America in the 1700s and started a small farm in western Pennsylvania. Now, more and more people are moving in. You would like to move farther west, into the Ohio River valley. But a new law says you cannot move west of the mountains because it is too dangerous. Still, you are restless and want more land and more freedom.

Why might you decide to break the law and move west?

BUILDING BACKGROUND When they moved to America, the English colonists brought their ideas about government. They expected to have the same rights as citizens in England. However, many officials in England wanted tight control over the colonies. As a result, some colonists, like this family, were unhappy with the policies of colonial governments.

Colonial Governments

The English colonies in North America all had their own governments. Each government was given power by a charter. The English monarch had ultimate authority over all of the colonies. A group of royal advisers called the Privy Council set English colonial policies.

Colonial Governors and Legislatures

Each colony had a governor who served as head of the government. Most governors were assisted by an advisory council. In royal colonies the English king or queen selected the governor and the council members. In proprietary colonies, the proprietors chose all of these officials. In a few colonies, such as Connecticut, the people elected the governor.

In some colonies the people also elected representatives to help make laws and set policy. These officials served on assemblies. Each colonial assembly passed laws that had to be approved first by the advisory council and then by the governor.

Teach the Big Idea: Master the Standards

Standards Proficiency

Life in the English Colonies **HSS** 8.1.1, 8.2.1; **HSS Analysis Skills:** CS 1, HR 3, HR 5, HI 1, HI 2

1. **Teach** Ask students the Main Idea questions to teach this section.
2. **Apply** Organize students into four groups and assign each group one of this section's subsections, indicated by the blue heads. Have each group develop a detailed outline of its subsection. Then ask each group to exchange its outline with another group and write five questions and answers about the information in that outline. **LS Verbal/Linguistic**
3. **Review** Collect students' questions and use them to review the section and quiz the class.
4. **Practice/Homework** Ask students to predict how the British colonists reacted to the Proclamation of 1763. Then have students imagine that they are colonists and write letters to the editor of a colonial newspaper expressing their views on the new law. **LS Verbal/Linguistic**

Alternative Assessment Handbook, Rubrics 37: Writing Assignments; and 41: Writing to Express

Established in 1619, Virginia's assembly was the first colonial legislature in North America. At first it met as a single body, but it was later split into two houses. The first house was known as the Council of State. The governor's advisory council and the London Company selected its members. The House of Burgesses was the assembly's second house. The members were elected by colonists.

In New England the center of politics was the **town meeting**. In town meetings people talked about and decided on issues of local interest, such as paying for schools.

In the southern colonies, people typically lived farther away from one another. Therefore, many decisions were made at the county level. The middle colonies used both county meetings and town meetings to make laws.

Political Change in England

In 1685 James II became king of England. He was determined to take more control over the English government, both in England and in the colonies.

James believed that the colonies were too independent. In 1686 he united the northern colonies under one government called the Dominion of New England. James named Sir Edmund Andros royal governor of the Dominion. The colonists disliked Andros because he used his authority to limit the powers of town meetings.

English Bill of Rights

Parliament replaced the unpopular King James and passed the **English Bill of Rights** in 1689. This act reduced the powers of the English monarch. At the same time, Parliament gained power. As time went on, the colonists valued their own right to elect representatives to decide local issues. Following these changes, the colonies in the Dominion quickly formed new assemblies and charters.

READING CHECK **Finding Main Ideas** How did the English Bill of Rights affect the colonists?

The Thirteen Colonies

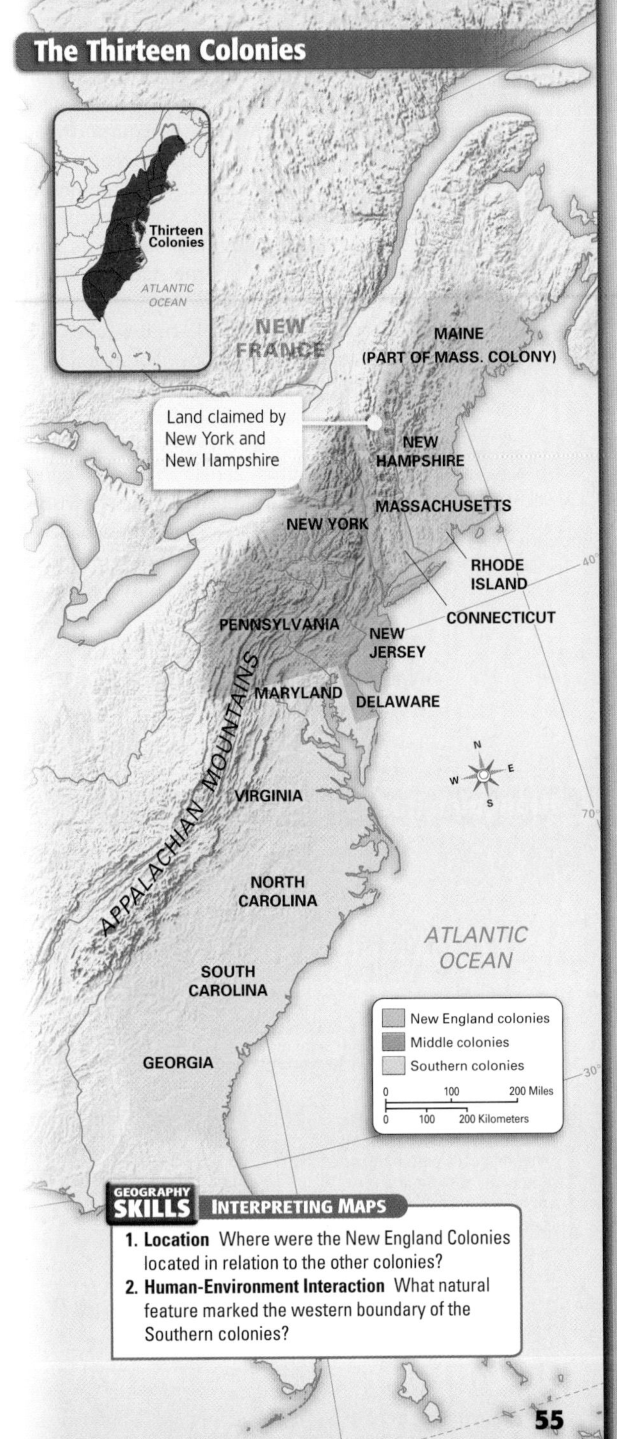

GEOGRAPHY SKILLS **INTERPRETING MAPS**

1. **Location** Where were the New England Colonies located in relation to the other colonies?
2. **Human-Environment Interaction** What natural feature marked the western boundary of the Southern colonies?

Direct Teach

Main Idea

1 Colonial Governments

Colonial governments were influenced by political changes in England.

Recall What served as the center of politics in New England? *town meetings, in which people decided local issues*

Analyze What forms of representative government did the English colonists begin to develop? *Some colonies had elected legislative assemblies, such as Virginia's House of Burgesses.*

Draw Conclusions What opinion do you think colonists in New England had of the Dominion of New England? *Most of them probably disliked it because the dominion limited the powers of town meetings.*

Map Transparency: The Thirteen Colonies

HSS 8.2.1; HSS **Analysis Skills:** CS 1, HI 1

Answers

Interpreting Maps 1. *to the north;* 2. *Appalachian Mountains*

Reading Check *They formed new assemblies and charters and increasingly valued their right to elect representatives to decide local issues.*

Differentiating Instruction for Universal Access

Learners Having Difficulty

Reaching Standards  HSS 8.2.1; HSS **Analysis Skills:** HI 1

1. To help students compare and contrast the different forms of colonial government, draw the graphic organizer. Omit the blue answers.
2. Have students copy and complete the graphic organizer. Review the answers as a class.
3. Then have students discuss how the English Bill of Rights affected colonial government. **LS Verbal/Linguistic, Visual/Spatial**

Alternative Assessment Handbook, Rubric 13: Graphic Organizers

Monarch	*ultimate authority over all English colonies*
Privy Council	*royal advisors; set English colonial policies*
Governors	*appointed by Crown or proprietors, or elected by people; served as head of colonial government; assisted by advisory councils*
Assemblies	*elected representatives; assisted in making laws and setting policies; had to get approval from advisory council and governor*
Town Meetings	*center of politics in New England; decided local issues*
Courts	*provided control over local affairs; protected individual freedoms*

Direct Teach

Main Idea

❷ English Trade Laws

English trade laws limited free trade in the colonies.

Define What is mercantilism? *creating and maintaining wealth by carefully controlling trade and the balance of imports to exports*

Explain How did the Navigation Acts limit colonial trade? *restricted colonial trade to England and imposed duties on some trade goods*

Identify Points of View How did colonists view the trade laws that England set? *Some colonists respected and obeyed the laws, while others considered them too restrictive and smuggled to get around them.*

Make Inferences Why do you think that British officials rarely carried out the Molasses Act? *possible answers—probably was hard to enforce; made the products from the West Indies cheaper for them to buy; did not agree with the law*

Map Transparency: Triangular Trade

HSS **Analysis Skills:** HR 5, HI 1, HI 2

go.hrw.com
Online Resources
KEYWORD: SS8 US2
ACTIVITY: The Courts and Freedom of the Press

Colonial Courts

Colonial courts made up another important part of colonial governments. Whenever possible, colonists used the courts to control local affairs. The courts generally reflected the beliefs of their local communities. For example, many laws in Massachusetts enforced the Puritans' religious beliefs. Laws based on the Bible set the standard for the community's conduct.

Sometimes colonial courts also protected individual freedoms. For example, in 1733 officials arrested John Peter Zenger for printing a false statement that damaged the reputation of the governor of New York. Andrew Hamilton, Zenger's attorney, argued that Zenger could publish whatever he wished as long as it was true. Jury members believed that colonists had a right to voice their ideas openly and found him not guilty.

THE IMPACT TODAY
The Zenger case was the first major case establishing freedom of the press in British North America. Today this is an important right of all Americans.

READING CHECK **Analyzing Information** Why were colonial assemblies and colonial courts created, and what did they do?

English Trade Laws

One of England's main reasons for founding and controlling its American colonies was to earn money from trade. In the late 1600s England, like most western European nations, practiced mercantilism, a system of creating and maintaining wealth through carefully controlled trade. A country gained wealth if it had fewer imports—goods bought from other countries—than exports—goods sold to other countries.

To support this system of mercantilism, between 1650 and 1696 Parliament passed a series of Navigation Acts limiting colonial trade. For example, the Navigation Act of 1660 forbade colonists from trading specific items such as sugar and cotton with any country other than England. The act also required colonists to use English ships to transport goods. Parliament later passed other acts that required all trade goods to pass through English ports, where duties, or import taxes, were added to the items.

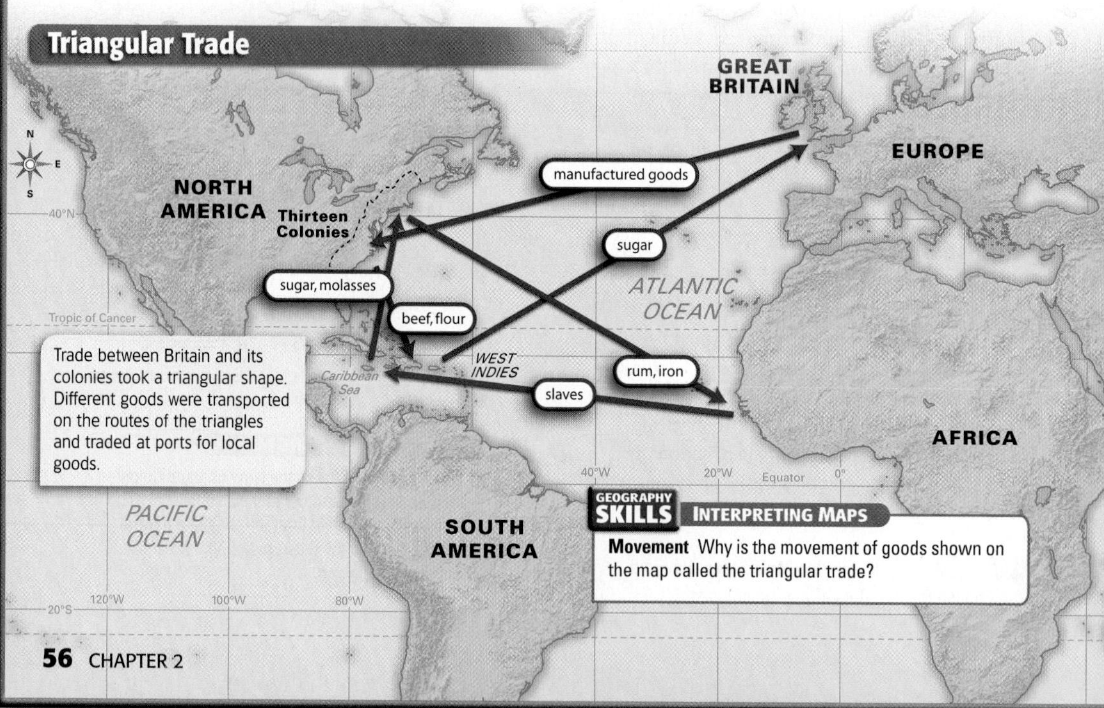

Trade between Britain and its colonies took a triangular shape. Different goods were transported on the routes of the triangles and traded at ports for local goods.

GEOGRAPHY SKILLS **INTERPRETING MAPS**

Movement Why is the movement of goods shown on the map called the triangular trade?

Cross-Discipline Activity: Government

Standards Proficiency

Reporting the Zenger Trial

HSS **Analysis Skills:** HI 1

Background On November 5, 1733, John Zenger published his first issue of the *New York Weekly Journal*, in which he criticized New York's colonial governor, John Cosby. As publisher, Zenger was legally responsible for the newspaper's contents. The paper's attacks on Cosby continued for a year, and in November 1734, Zenger was arrested for libel.

1. Provide students with the background of the Zenger trial.
2. Have each student write a headline and a newspaper article about the Zenger trial. In their articles, students should stress the importance of freedom of the press.
3. Have volunteers share their headlines and articles with the class. Have students discuss why freedom of the press continues to be an important right. LS **Verbal/Linguistic**

Alternative Assessment Handbook, Rubric 42: Writing to Inform

Answers

Interpreting Maps *because trade routes among Africa, Europe, the West Indies, and North America were roughly triangular*

Reading Check *to provide colonists with some control over local affairs through setting policies, making laws, and protecting freedoms*

England claimed that the Navigation Acts were good for the colonies. After all, the colonies had a steady market in England for their goods. But not all colonists agreed. Many colonists wanted more freedom to buy or sell goods wherever they could get the best price. Local demand for colonial goods was small compared to foreign demand.

Despite colonial complaints, the trade restrictions continued into the 1700s. Some traders turned to smuggling, or illegal trading. They often smuggled sugar, molasses, and rum into the colonies from non-English islands in the Caribbean. Parliament responded with the Molasses Act of 1733, which placed duties on these items. British officials, however, rarely carried out this law.

By the early 1700s English merchants were trading around the world. Most American merchants traded directly with Great Britain or the West Indies. By importing and exporting goods such as sugar and tobacco, some American merchants became wealthy.

Triangular Trade

Trade between the American colonies and Great Britain was not direct. Rather, it generally took the form of **triangular trade** —a system in which goods and slaves were traded among the Americas, Britain, and Africa. There were several routes of the triangular trade. In one route colonists exchanged goods like beef and flour with plantation owners in the West Indies for sugar, some of which they shipped to Britain. The sugar was then exchanged for manufactured products to be sold in the colonies. Colonial merchants traveled great distances to find the best markets.

BIOGRAPHY

Olaudah Equiano

1745–1797

Olaudah Equiano was born in Africa in present-day Nigeria. In 1756 he was sold into slavery. Equiano survived the Middle Passage, traveling in a slave ship across the Atlantic. After arriving in the colonies, a Virginia planter purchased him and again sold him to a British naval officer. While working as a sailor, Equiano eventually earned enough money to purchase his own freedom in 1766. Equiano later settled in England and devoted himself to ending slavery.

Analyzing Information How did Equiano gain his freedom?

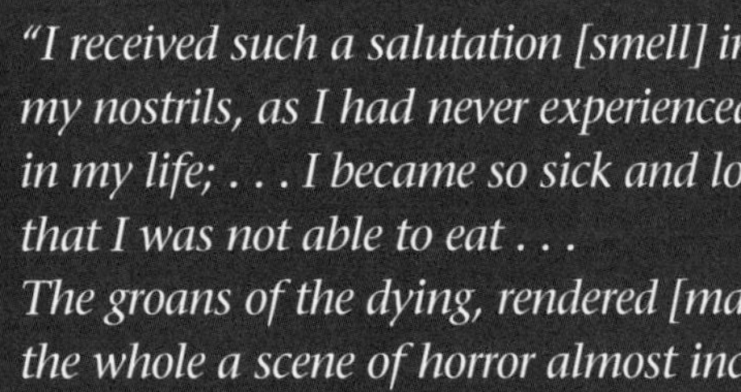

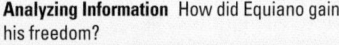

"I received such a salutation [smell] in my nostrils, as I had never experienced in my life; . . . I became so sick and low that I was not able to eat . . .
The groans of the dying, rendered [made] the whole a scene of horror almost inconceivable [unbelievable]."

—Olaudah Equiano, from *The Interesting Narrative of the Life of Olaudah Equiano, or Gustavus Vassa, the African*

Differentiated Instruction for Universal Access

English-Language Learners — Standards Proficiency

Colonial Trade Posters Organize students into small groups of mixed ability. Have each group create a poster illustrating the various types of goods traded in the English colonies. Students' posters will vary but should include depictions of common trade items, the triangular trade, and reactions to trade restrictions such as smuggling. **LS Interpersonal, Visual/Spatial**

HSS Analysis Skills: HI 1, HI 2

Advanced Learners/GATE — Exceeding Standards

Alternative Labor Proposals Have students write a proposal that suggests ways the English colonies could have developed without relying on slave labor. Students' proposals should address the reasons that farming colonies, in particular, participated in the slave trade. Have volunteers share their proposals with the class.
LS Verbal/Linguistic

HSS Analysis Skills: HI 1, HI 2

Direct Teach

Connect to Economics

The Hat Act One of the more unusual restrictive acts that the British government passed was the Hat Act, which prohibited the sale of hats among the colonies and required a seven-year apprenticeship for anyone who wished to become a hat maker. Parliament passed this act in response to pressure from London felt makers who wanted to protect their industry from competition.

Biography

Olaudah Equiano (c. 1745–1797)
After purchasing his freedom, Olaudah Equiano traveled to the Mediterranean, the Arctic, and Central America. However, he was never able to return to Africa, the land of his birth and childhood, despite strong efforts to do so.

Did you know . . .

The Vermont Constitution of 1777 was the first document in the United States to abolish slavery. The United States, however, did not end slavery until after the Civil War, nearly 100 years later.

Checking for Understanding

Multiple Choice Select the best answer for each of the following:

1. The Zenger case was the first major case establishing
   a. freedom of religion
   b. freedom of assembly
   c. *freedom of the press*
   d. right to trial by jury
2. England controlled trade in the colonies through the practice of
   a. colonialism
   b. *mercantilism*
   c. triangular trade
   d. navigation

HSS Analysis Skills: HI 1

Answers

Biography *by saving money and purchasing his freedom*

Direct Teach

Main Idea

❸ Great Awakening and Enlightenment

The Great Awakening and the Enlightenment led to ideas of political equality among many colonists.

Define Describe the Great Awakening in your own words. *A religious movement that swept through the colonies in the 1730s and 1740s.*

Draw Conclusions How did John Locke's beliefs influence colonial society? *His ideas about natural rights, such as equality and liberty, began to influence colonial leaders.*

CRF: Primary Source Activity: Sinners in the Hands of an Angry God

HSS 8.1.1; **HSS Analysis Skills:** HI 1

Biography

George Whitefield (1714–1770)

George Whitefield was born in Gloucester, England, and educated at Oxford. He experienced a strong religious awakening during his high school and college years, which he called a "new birth." He believed that every truly religious person needs to experience a rebirth in Jesus Christ, and preached this message throughout America and Great Britain.

The Great Awakening

George Whitefield gives a powerful sermon during the Great Awakening. Ministers like Whitefield emphasized personal religious experiences over official church rules. They also allowed ordinary church members—whatever their race, class, or gender—to play a role in services. The value placed on individuals of all types during the Great Awakening helped shape American political ideas about who should have a say in government.

How do you think religious freedom led to political freedom?

Middle Passage

One version of the triangular trade began with traders exchanging rum for slaves on the West African coast. The traders then sold the enslaved Africans in the West Indies for molasses or brought them to sell in the mainland American colonies.

The slave trade brought millions of Africans across the Atlantic Ocean in a voyage called the **Middle Passage**. This was a terrifying and deadly journey that could last as long as three months.

Enslaved Africans lived in a space not even three feet high. Slave traders fit as many slaves as possible on board so they could earn greater profits. Thousands of captives died on slave ships during the Middle Passage. In many cases, they died from diseases such as smallpox. As farmers began to use fewer indentured servants, slaves became even more valuable.

READING CHECK **Identifying Cause and Effect** What factors caused the slave trade to grow? How did this affect conditions on the Middle Passage?

Great Awakening and Enlightenment

In the early 1700s revolutions in both religious and nonreligious thought transformed the Western world. These movements began in Europe and affected life in the American colonies.

Great Awakening

After years of population growth, religious leaders wanted to spread religious feeling throughout the colonies. In the late 1730s these ministers began holding revivals, emotional gatherings where people came together to hear sermons.

Many American colonists experienced "a great awakening" in their religious lives. This **Great Awakening** —a religious movement that swept through the colonies in the 1730s and 1740s—changed colonial religion. It also affected social and political life. Jonathan Edwards of Massachusetts was one of the most important leaders of the Great Awakening. His dramatic sermons told

Critical Thinking: Finding Main Ideas

Standards Proficiency

Great Awakening and Enlightenment **HSS** 8.1.1; **HSS Analysis Skills:** HI 1, HI 2

1. Discuss with students the significance of the Great Awakening and the Enlightenment.
2. Create a chart with two columns. Label one column *Great Awakening* and the other column *Enlightenment*. Have students copy the chart.
3. In the columns, students should write their own definitions of the movements and identify one or more of their key figures.
4. Next, have students list examples of how each movement affected political and social views in the English colonies.
5. Review students' answers as a class. Conclude by having students discuss the effects of the Great Awakening and the Enlightenment.

LS Verbal/Linguistic

Alternative Assessment Handbook, Rubric 7: Charts

Answers

The Great Awakening *Sermons about spiritual equality led to some demands for more political equality.*

Reading Check *As farmers began to rely less on indentured servants, they needed more slaves to work their farms. Slave traders placed as many slaves on ships as possible to increase profits, which created the terrifying and deadly conditions of the passage.*

sinners to seek forgiveness for their sins or face punishment in Hell forever. In 1739 British minister George Whitefield made the second of his seven trips to America. He held revivals from Georgia to New England.

The Great Awakening drew people of different regions, classes, and races. Women, members of minority groups, and poor people often took part in services. Ministers from different colonies met and shared ideas with one another. This represented one of the few exchanges between colonies.

The Great Awakening promoted ideas that may also have affected colonial politics. Sermons about the spiritual equality of all people led some colonists to begin demanding more political equality. Revivals became popular places to talk about political and social issues. People from those colonies with less political freedom were thus introduced to more democratic systems used in other colonies.

Enlightenment

During the 1600s Europeans began to re-examine their world. Scientists began to better understand the basic laws that govern nature. Their new ideas about the universe began the Scientific Revolution. The revolution changed how people thought of the world.

Many colonists were also influenced by the **Enlightenment**. This movement, which took place during the 1700s, spread the idea that reason and logic could improve society. Enlightenment thinkers also formed ideas about how government should work.

Some Enlightenment thinkers believed that there was a social contract between government and citizens. Philosophers such as John Locke thought that people had natural rights such as equality and liberty. Eventually, ideas of the Scientific Revolution and the Enlightenment influenced colonial leaders.

READING CHECK **Summarizing** How did the Great Awakening and the Enlightenment influence colonial society?

The French and Indian War

By the 1670s tensions had arisen between New England colonists and the Wampanoag. Metacomet, a Wampanoag leader also known as King Philip, opposed the colonists' efforts to take his people's lands. In 1675 these tensions finally erupted in a conflict known as King Philip's War. The colonial militia—civilians serving as soldiers—fought American Indian warriors. Both sides attacked each other's settlements, killing men, women, and children. The fighting finally ended in 1676, but only after about 600 colonists and some 3,000 Indians had been killed, including Metacomet.

Native American Allies

Some Native Americans allied with the colonists to fight against Metacomet and his forces. These Indians had developed trade relations with colonists. They wanted tools, weapons, and other goods that Europeans could provide. In exchange, the colonists wanted furs, which they sold for large profits in Europe. As a result, each side came to depend upon the other.

French colonists traded and allied with the Algonquian and Huron. English colonists traded and allied with the Iroquois League. This powerful group united American Indians from six different groups. Many American Indians trusted the French more than they did the English. The smaller French settlements were less threatening than the rapidly growing English colonies. No matter who their allies were, many Indian leaders took care to protect their people's independence. As one leader said:

> "We are born free. We neither depend upon [the governor of New France] nor [the governor of New York]. We may go where we please . . . and buy and sell what we please."
>
> —Garangula, quoted in *The World Turned Upside Down*, edited by Colin G. Calloway

Direct Teach

Main Idea

❹ The French and Indian War

The French and Indian War gave England control of more land in North America.

Describe Describe the main events of King Philip's War. *Conflict broke out in 1675 between the Wampanoag, led by Metacomet (also known as King Philip) and colonists who wanted Indian lands; ended in 1676, with the death of many colonists and Native Americans, including Metacomet.*

Identify Points of View Why did some Native Americans trust the French more than the English? *French settlements were smaller and less threatening than the rapidly growing English colonies.*

Analyze Why did some Native Americans join Europeans in wars against other Native Americans? *to protect trade alliances on which different groups of Native Americans had become dependent*

HSS HR 5, HI 1, HI 2

Connect to Science

The Scientific Revolution It was during the Scientific Revolution that Sir Isaac Newton developed his three laws of motion, the basic principles of modern physics.

Critical Thinking: Identifying Points of View

Standards Proficiency

Native American, English, and French Relations

HSS Analysis Skills: CS 3, HR 5, HI 1

1. Write the following three labels for students to see: *Native Americans, English colonists,* and *French traders and settlers.*
2. Ask students to describe how these three groups interacted in North America, and write students' responses under the correct headings.
3. Then lead a discussion further exploring how Native Americans and settlers in the English colonies viewed each other. **LS Verbal/Linguistic**
4. **Extend** Have students conduct research on Native American groups in the region of the English colonies. Then have each student create a map showing the locations of various Native American groups and English settlements. Conclude with a class discussion on how the locations of different groups affected their viewpoints.

Alternative Assessment Handbook, Rubrics 7: Charts; 11: Discussions; and 30: Research

Answers

Reading Check *They led to the desire for political equality and encouraged discussion about political and social issues.*

Direct Teach

Main Idea

❹ The French and Indian War

The French and Indian War gave England control of more land in North America.

Recall Why did fighting break out in the Ohio River valley between British colonists and the French? *British colonists wanted to settle in the region, which the French opposed because such settlement might harm their valuable fur trade.*

Identify Cause and Effect What caused the French and Indian War, and how did it affect North America? *cause—France captured a British fort; effects—Britain gained Canada, all French lands east of the Mississippi, and Spanish Florida*

Elaborate How did the war change the balance of power in North America? *Great Britain and Spain controlled most of North America and vied for power there.*

 Map Transparency: North American Empires before and after the Treaty of Paris

HSS Analysis Skills: HI 1, HI 2

Interpreting Maps

North American Empires before and after the Treaty of Paris

Regions What happened to the amount of unclaimed land between 1754 and 1763? *decreased in size, with Spain taking some and the rest disputed by Britain, Russia, and Spain*

Place Who lived in this "unclaimed" region? *Native Americans*

HSS Analysis Skills: CS 3

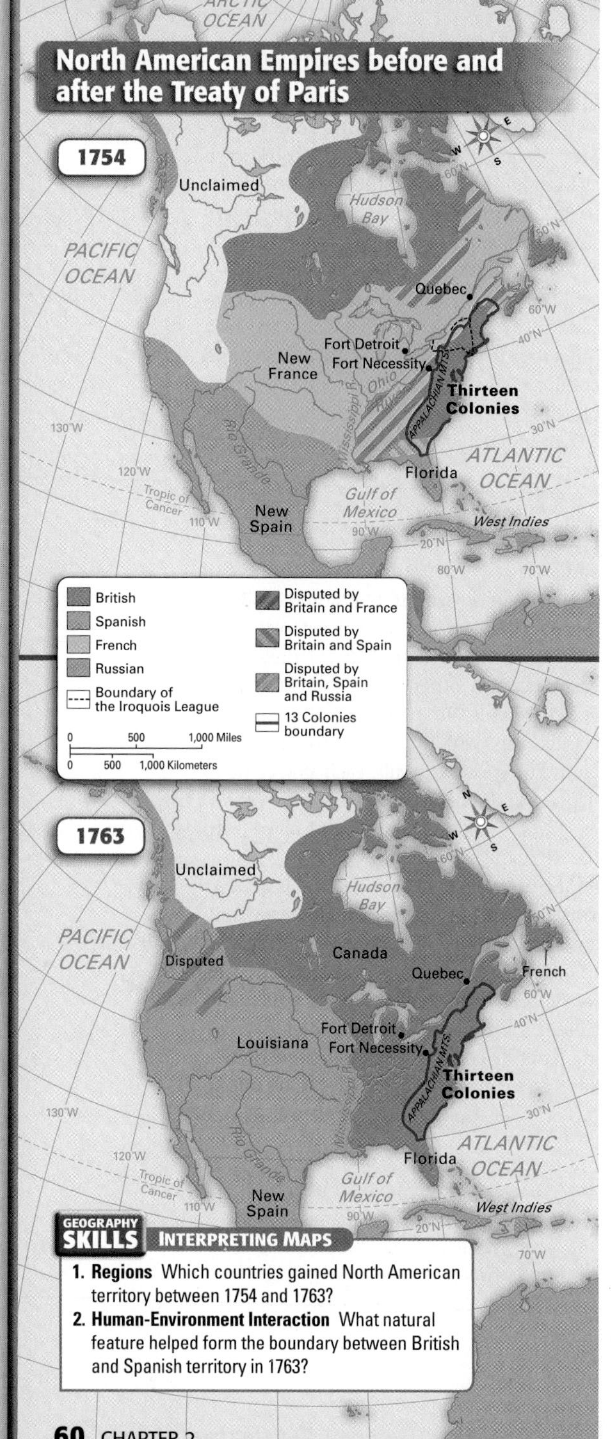

GEOGRAPHY SKILLS INTERPRETING MAPS

1. **Regions** Which countries gained North American territory between 1754 and 1763?
2. **Human-Environment Interaction** What natural feature helped form the boundary between British and Spanish territory in 1763?

60 CHAPTER 2

War Erupts

During the late 1600s to mid-1700s, France and Great Britain struggled for control of territory in North America. British colonists wanted to settle in the Ohio River valley, where they could take advantage of the valuable fur trade and also have room for their colonies to expand. The French believed this settlement would hurt their fur trade profits. A standoff developed in the Ohio Valley where the French had built three forts. Fighting erupted in 1753 as the British military moved to take over the valley.

When a young Virginian named George Washington arrived with more soldiers, he found the area under French control. Washington and his troops built a small, simple fort that he named Fort Necessity. After his troops suffered many casualties—captured, injured, or killed soldiers—Washington finally surrendered. His defeat in 1754 was the start of the French and Indian War. Meanwhile, in 1756 fighting began in Europe, starting what became known as the Seven Years' War.

Treaty of Paris

The turning point of the war came in 1759. That year British general James Wolfe captured Quebec, gaining the advantage in the war. However, the war dragged on for four more years. Finally, in 1763 Britain and France signed the Treaty of Paris, officially ending the war.

The terms of the treaty gave Canada to Britain. Britain also gained all French lands east of the Mississippi River except the city of New Orleans and two small islands in the Gulf of St. Lawrence. From Spain, which had allied with France in 1762, Britain received Florida. In an earlier treaty, Spain had received Louisiana, the land that France had claimed west of the Mississippi River. The Treaty of Paris changed the balance of power in North America. Soon British settlers began moving west to settle new lands.

Social Studies Skills Activity: Interpreting Time Lines

Frontier Conflicts Time Line

Reaching Standards

1. Have students create time lines of key dates and events related to King Philip's War, the French and Indian War, and Pontiac's Rebellion.
2. Instruct students to illustrate and annotate their time lines with related drawings and facts.
3. Have students share their time lines with the class. As they do, create a master time line for the class to see. Point out significant cause-and-effect relationships as you create the time line.
4. Lead students in a guided discussion of the significance of these frontier conflicts for the British colonists, the French, and the Native Americans in North America. Then ask students to predict how the British colonists responded to the Proclamation of 1763. **LS Verbal/Linguistic, Visual/Spatial**

HSS Analysis Skills: CS 1, CS 2, HI 1, HI 2

Alternative Assessment Handbook, Rubric 36: Time Lines

Answers

Interpreting Maps 1. *Britain and Spain;* **2.** *Mississippi River*

Western Frontier

Most colonial settlements were located along the Atlantic coast. Colonial settlers, or pioneers, slowly moved into the Virginia and Carolina backcountry and the Ohio River valley.

Indian leaders like Chief **Pontiac** opposed British settlement of this new land. Pontiac's Rebellion began in May 1763 when his forces attacked British forts on the frontier. Within one month, they had destroyed or captured seven forts. Pontiac then led an attack on Fort Detroit. The British held out for months.

British leaders feared that more fighting would take place on the frontier if colonists kept moving onto American Indian lands. To avoid more conflict, King George III issued the Proclamation of 1763. This law banned British settlement west of the Appalachian Mountains. The law also ordered settlers to leave the upper Ohio River valley.

READING CHECK **Summarizing** Why did George III issue the Proclamation of 1763?

BIOGRAPHY

Pontiac

1720–1769

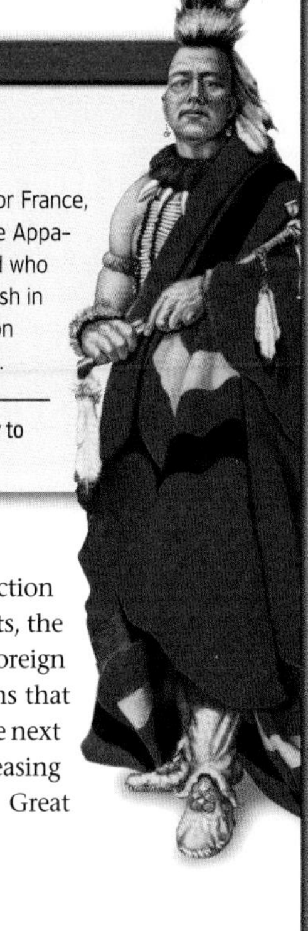

Pontiac, an Ottawa chief who had fought for France, tried to resist British settlement west of the Appalachians. Calling them "dogs dressed in red who have come to rob us," he attacked the British in the Ohio country in 1763. Pontiac's rebellion was put down, and he surrendered in 1766.

Analyzing Information How did Pontiac try to stop the British?

SUMMARY AND PREVIEW In this section you read about colonial governments, the slave trade, and the conflicts with foreign countries and with Native Americans that the colonies faced as they grew. In the next section you'll learn about the increasing tension between the colonies and Great Britain that led to independence.

Section 4 Assessment

go.hrw.com **Online Quiz** KEYWORD: SS8 HP2

Reviewing Ideas, Terms, and People HSS 8.1.1, 8.2.1

1. a. **Describe** How were colonial governments organized?
   b. **Analyze** How did political change in England affect colonial governments?
2. a. **Explain** What is **mercantilism**?
   b. **Analyze** How did the Navigation Acts support the system of mercantilism?
   c. **Evaluate** Did the colonies benefit from mercantilism? Why or why not?
3. a. **Identify** What was the **Great Awakening**?
   b. **Compare** How was the **Enlightenment** similar to the Great Awakening?
4. a. **Explain** What caused the French and Indian War?
   b. **Evaluate** Defend the British decision to ban colonists from settling on the western frontier.

Critical Thinking

5. **Identifying Cause and Effect** Copy the graphic organizer below and use it to list the causes and effects of the Great Awakening.

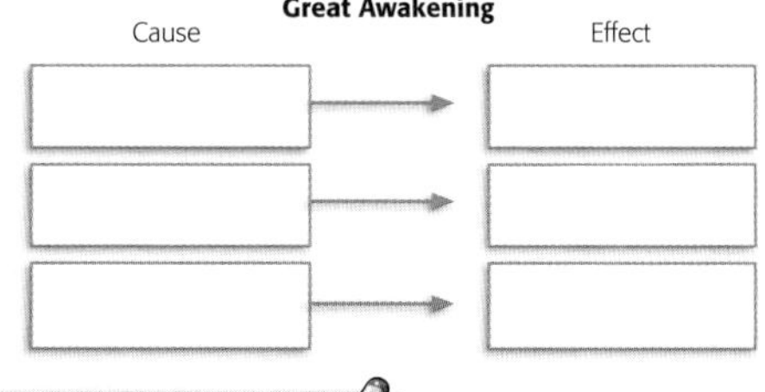

FOCUS ON WRITING

6. **Reviewing the Information** This section focused on what life was like in all the English colonies discussed so far. Does this information give you any new ideas about the colony you'll use in your infomercial?

Direct Teach

Info to Know

Colonial Muskets Could you stand still while people shot at you? That is how the British and other Europeans fought during the 1600s and 1700s. The muskets soldiers used at the time were not very accurate. As a result, officers told soldiers to get close to the enemy, stand in one place, and shoot as quickly as possible. Sometimes, dozens of shots were required to hit one target!

Review & Assess

Close

Briefly review the challenges that British colonists faced during this period, and how colonists dealt with these challenges.

Review

Online Quiz, Section 4

Assess

SE Section 4 Assessment

PASS: Section 4 Quiz

Alternative Assessment Handbook

Reteach/Classroom Intervention

California Standards Review Workbook

Interactive Reader and Study Guide, Section 4

Interactive Skills Tutor CD-ROM

Section 4 Assessment Answers

1. a. governor and advisory council; some also had elected assemblies or held town meetings
   b. Crowning of King James II led to loss of some political control; his removal and English Bill of Rights led to more representative government.
2. a. practice of creating and maintaining wealth by carefully controlling trade
   b. allowed colonists to trade only with England, giving England a guaranteed market for exports
   c. Answers will vary, but many colonists did not see mercantilism as a benefit.
3. a. religious movement in the 1730s and 1740s that affected colonial social and political life
   b. both raised ideas of political equality
4. a. British and French tensions over the Ohio River valley; French capture of a British fort
   b. possible answer—would promote peace
5. causes—desire to spread religious feeling; effects—changed colonial religion and social and political life, raised ideas of political equality
6. Students should provide notes about the selected colony's government, social life, and conflicts.

Answers

Biography *by leading American Indian attacks on British settlers who were invading Indian lands*

Reading Check *to stop the fighting between colonists and Native Americans*

History and Geography

Activity Geographic Forces Chain-of-Events Chart Ask students to use the map to trace the steps and routes involved in the Atlantic slave trade. Then have students work either individually or in pairs to create chain-of-events charts showing the geographic factors that led to the growth of slavery in the English colonies. A sample chart is shown below. **LS Visual/Spatial**

HSS 8.7.2; HSS **Analysis Skills:** CS 3

The climate of the southern colonies was suited to certain crops such as cotton, tobacco, and sugarcane.

↓

These crops required large amounts of labor.

↓

Other sources of labor, such as indentured servants, were not able to fill labor needs.

↓

Colonists turned to enslaved Africans to fill labor needs.

Connect to Economics

Social Classes in Colonial America

Colonial America had several socioeconomic classes. Large landowners, wealthy merchants, and professional workers ranked at the top of society. Free wage earners ranked below the top group. These people were unskilled laborers or skilled workers, such as cabinetmakers or tailors. Farmers with small amounts of land were usually considered on the same level of society as these urban workers. At the bottom were people who were not free—white indentured servants and enslaved Africans.

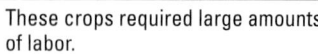

Standards Focus

HSS 8.7.2 Trace the origins and development of slavery; its effects on black Americans and on the region's political, social, religious, economic, and cultural development.

History and Geography

The Atlantic Slave Trade

The slave system that arose in the American colonies was strongly influenced by geographic forces. The climate of the southern colonies was suited to growing certain crops, like cotton, tobacco, and sugarcane. These crops required a great deal of labor to grow and to process. To meet this great demand for labor, the colonists looked to one main source—enslaved Africans.

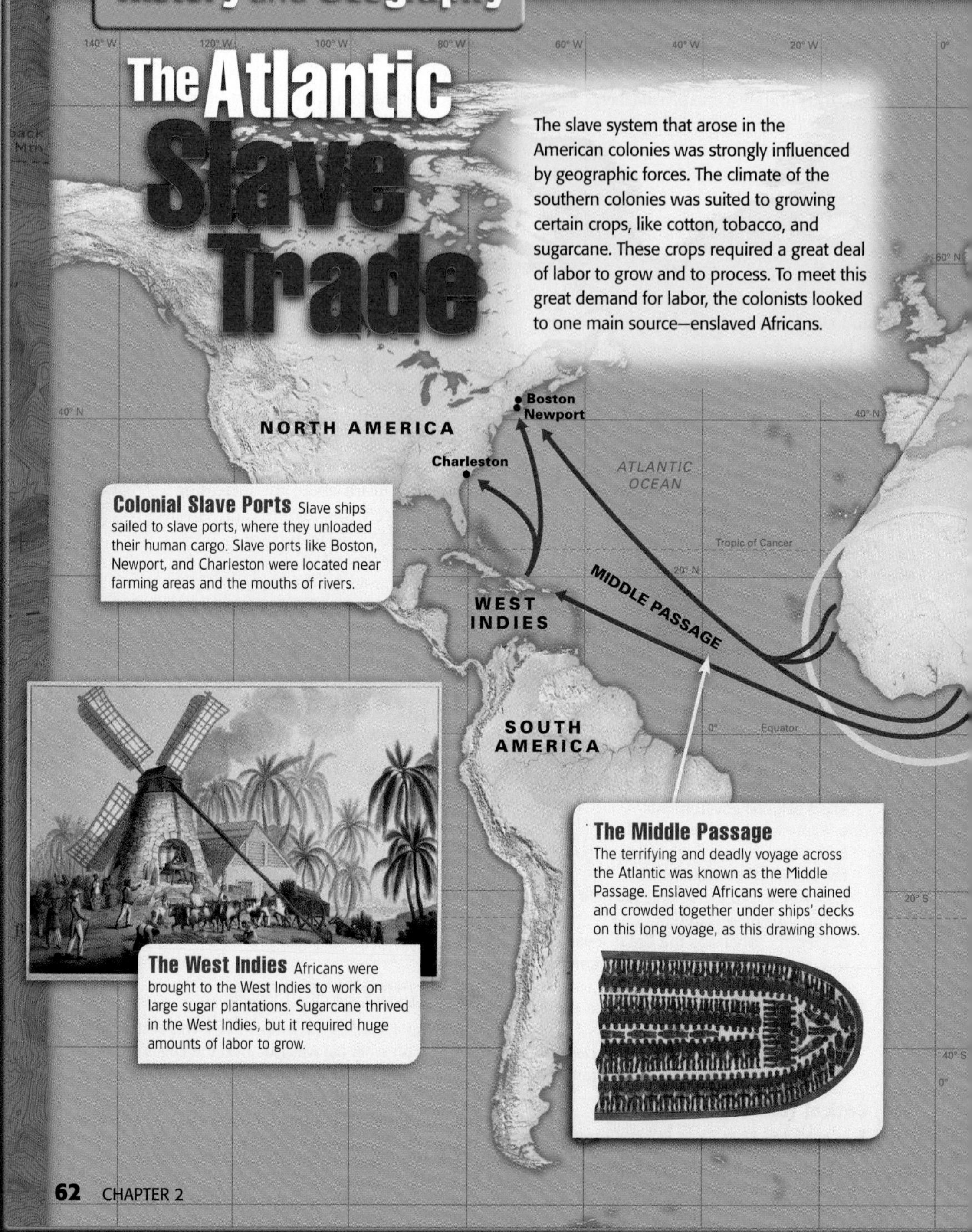

NORTH AMERICA
Boston
Newport
Charleston
ATLANTIC OCEAN
WEST INDIES
MIDDLE PASSAGE
SOUTH AMERICA
Tropic of Cancer
Equator

Colonial Slave Ports Slave ships sailed to slave ports, where they unloaded their human cargo. Slave ports like Boston, Newport, and Charleston were located near farming areas and the mouths of rivers.

The West Indies Africans were brought to the West Indies to work on large sugar plantations. Sugarcane thrived in the West Indies, but it required huge amounts of labor to grow.

The Middle Passage The terrifying and deadly voyage across the Atlantic was known as the Middle Passage. Enslaved Africans were chained and crowded together under ships' decks on this long voyage, as this drawing shows.

Differentiating Instruction for Universal Access

Reaching Standards

Learners Having Difficulty

HSS 8.7.2; HSS **Analysis Skills:** CS 3

1. Review inset maps with students. Then have students identify the region shown in the inset map above. Explain that most enslaved Africans came from West Africa. Next, have volunteers read aloud the captions about the slave forts. Then discuss the primary source.
2. Have a volunteer read aloud the caption about the Middle Passage. Ask students to suggest adjectives to describe the Middle Passage.
3. Ask students to identify the destinations of the Atlantic slave trade. Next, have volunteers read aloud the Colonial Slave Ports and West Indies captions. Ask students to identify the geographic forces that led to the slave system.
4. Have students interpret the bar graph. Ask students to discuss reasons for the increase in the number of slaves over time. **LS Visual/Spatial**

Alternative Assessment Handbook, Rubric 21: Map Reading

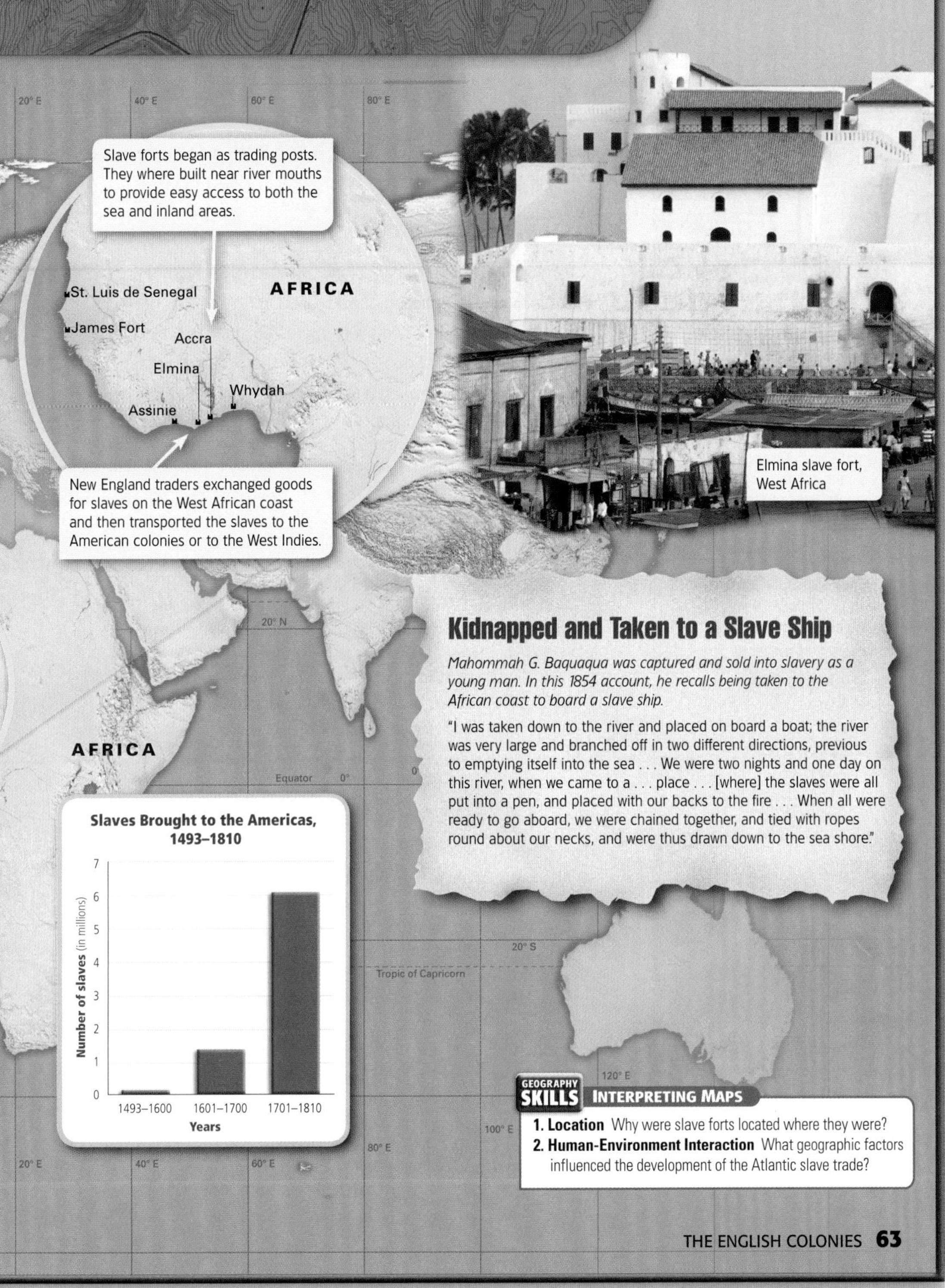
Slave forts began as trading posts. They where built near river mouths to provide easy access to both the sea and inland areas.
AFRICA
St. Luis de Senegal
James Fort
Accra
Elmina
Whydah
Assinie
New England traders exchanged goods for slaves on the West African coast and then transported the slaves to the American colonies or to the West Indies.
AFRICA
Equator
Tropic of Capricorn
Slaves Brought to the Americas, 1493–1810
Number of slaves (in millions)
1493–1600
1601–1700
1701–1810
Years

Elmina slave fort, West Africa

Kidnapped and Taken to a Slave Ship

Mahommah G. Baquaqua was captured and sold into slavery as a young man. In this 1854 account, he recalls being taken to the African coast to board a slave ship.

"I was taken down to the river and placed on board a boat; the river was very large and branched off in two different directions, previous to emptying itself into the sea . . . We were two nights and one day on this river, when we came to a . . . place . . . [where] the slaves were all put into a pen, and placed with our backs to the fire . . . When all were ready to go aboard, we were chained together, and tied with ropes round about our necks, and were thus drawn down to the sea shore."

GEOGRAPHY SKILLS INTERPRETING MAPS

1. **Location** Why were slave forts located where they were?
2. **Human-Environment Interaction** What geographic factors influenced the development of the Atlantic slave trade?

History and Geography

World Events

Captives of War About half the Africans sold to traders were captives of war. African kingdoms, like those elsewhere in the world, fought each other for power and wealth. Some of these kingdoms sold war captives into slavery. These kingdoms traded slaves for European goods. As a result of the slave trade, native populations in some parts of Africa greatly decreased. These population losses had disastrous effects on Africa's development.

Info to Know

African Languages and Gullah Africans arriving in the Americas often spoke different languages. In time a number of pidgin languages developed based on English, French, Spanish, and Portuguese. One of these languages that has survived to this day is Gullah. This language is still spoken in parts of Georgia and in the Sea Islands of South Carolina.

Differentiating Instruction for Universal Access

English-Language Learners

Reaching Standards

1. Pair students and have partners take turns explaining the information above. Students should define words they do not understand.
2. Read the primary source aloud to students. Have each student create an image based on the excerpt. **LS Visual/Spatial**

HSS 8.7.2; **HSS Analysis Skills:** CS 3, HR 4

Alternative Assessment Handbook, Rubrics 3: Artwork; and 21: Map Reading

Advanced Learners/GATE

Exceeding Standards

Research Required

1. Have students conduct research on the Middle Passage. Instruct students to take notes on the conditions, perils, and death rates on slave ships.
2. Have students work in pairs to create a script for a voice-over for the opening scenes of a documentary on the Middle Passage. **LS Interpersonal, Verbal/Linguistic**

HSS 8.7.2; **HSS Analysis Skills:** HI 1

Alternative Assessment Handbook, Rubrics 30: Research; and 37: Writing Assignments

Answers

Interpreting Maps **1.** *Slave forts were located on the coast so that captives could be transported by ship to the Americas, and near rivers to provide easy access to inland areas.* **2.** *See the graphic organizer in the side column on the previous page.*

Preteach

Bellringer

If YOU were there . . . Use the **Daily Bellringer Transparency** to help students answer the question.

Daily Bellringer Transparency, Section 5

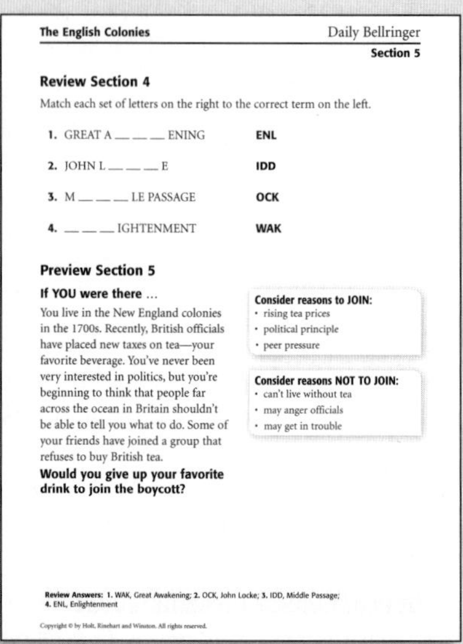

The English Colonies Daily Bellringer
Section 5

Review Section 4

Match each set of letters on the right to the correct term on the left.

1. GREAT A ___ ___ ___ ENING	**ENL**
2. JOHN L ___ ___ ___ E	**IDD**
3. M ___ ___ ___ LE PASSAGE	**OCK**
4. ___ ___ ___ IGHTENMENT	**WAK**

Preview Section 5

If YOU were there ...

You live in the New England colonies in the 1700s. Recently, British officials have placed new taxes on tea—your favorite beverage. You've never been very interested in politics, but you're beginning to think that people far across the ocean in Britain shouldn't be able to tell you what to do. Some of your friends have joined a group that refuses to buy British tea.

Would you give up your favorite drink to join the boycott?

Consider reasons to JOIN:
- rising tea prices
- political principle
- peer pressure

Consider reasons NOT TO JOIN:
- can't live without tea
- may anger officials
- may get in trouble

Review Answers: **1.** WAK, Great Awakening; **2.** OCK, John Locke; **3.** IDD, Middle Passage; **4.** ENL, Enlightenment

Building Vocabulary

Preteach or review the following terms:

boycott refusal to buy a particular good or service (p. 65)

coercive forceful (p. 68)

intolerable unbearable (p. 68)

propaganda a story giving only one side in an argument (p. 67)

repeal do away with (p. 66)

resolutions something to be voted on (p. 66)

revenue money earned (p. 66)

CRF: Vocabulary Builder Activity, Section 5

Standards Focus

HSS 8.1 .1

Means: Describe how the ideas of the Great Awakening helped lead to revolutionary fervor.

Matters: The Great Awakening raised ideas about political equality.

HSS 8.2.1

Means: Describe the significance of the English Bill of Rights.

Matters: The English Bill of Rights enabled more representative forms of government to develop in the colonies.

SECTION 5

Conflict in the Colonies

What You Will Learn...

Main Ideas

1. British efforts to raise taxes on colonists sparked protest.
2. The Boston Massacre caused colonial resentment toward Great Britain.
3. Colonists protested the British tax on tea with the Boston Tea Party.
4. Great Britain responded to colonial actions by passing the Intolerable Acts.

The Big Idea

Tensions developed as the British government placed tax after tax on the colonies.

Key Terms and People

Samuel Adams, *p. 65*
Stamp Act of 1765, *p. 66*
Boston Massacre, *p. 67*
Tea Act, *p. 68*
Boston Tea Party, *p. 68*
Intolerable Acts, *p. 68*

HSS 8.1.1 Describe the relationship between the moral and political ideas of the Great Awakening and the development of revolutionary fervor.

8.2.1 Discuss the significance of the Magna Carta, the English Bill of Rights, and the Mayflower Compact.

If YOU were there...

You live in the New England colonies in the 1700s. Recently, British officials have placed new taxes on tea—your favorite beverage. You've never been very interested in politics, but you're beginning to think that people far across the ocean in Britain shouldn't be able to tell you what to do. Some of your friends have joined a group that refuses to buy British tea.

Would you give up your favorite drink to join the boycott?

BUILDING BACKGROUND As the British colonies grew and became prosperous, the colonists got used to running their own lives. Britain began to seem very far away. At the same time, officials in Britain still expected the colonies to obey them and to earn money for Britain. Parliament passed new laws and imposed new taxes. But the colonists found various ways to challenge them.

Great Britain Raises Taxes

Great Britain had won the French and Indian War, but Parliament still had to pay for it. The British continued to keep a standing, or permanent, army in North America to protect the colonists against Indian attacks. To help pay for this army, Prime Minister George Grenville asked Parliament to tax the colonists. In 1764 Parliament passed the Sugar Act, which set duties on molasses and sugar imported by colonists. This was the first act passed specifically to raise money in the colonies.

British officials also tried harder to arrest smugglers. Colonial merchants were required to list all the trade goods they carried aboard their ships. These lists had to be approved before ships could leave colonial ports. This made it difficult for traders to avoid paying duties. The British navy also began to stop and search ships for smuggled goods.

Teach the Big Idea: Master the Standards

Standards Proficiency

Conflict in the Colonies

HSS 8.1.1, 8.2.1; **HSS Analysis Skills:** CS 1, HR 5, HI 1, HI 2

Materials: construction paper, art supplies

1. **Teach** Ask students the Main Idea questions to teach this section.
2. **Apply** To help students understand why tensions increased over taxes in the colonies, have each student draw a colonial storefront. On their drawings, have students list the acts that Britain passed and draw the products it taxed, such as tea. On each product, have students draw a price tag with the word *Tax* on it. **LS Visual/Spatial**
3. **Review** As you review the section's main ideas, have students discuss the colonists' reactions to Britain's actions and taxes, and the British reactions to the colonists' protests.
4. **Practice/Homework** Have each student design a version of the stamp, or seal, the British forced colonists to buy and then a flyer listing the items that require the stamp. **LS Visual/Spatial**

Alternative Assessment Handbook, Rubric 3: Artwork

Voice of Protest

Leaders like Patrick Henry made speeches that encouraged colonists to protest the British government. Here, Henry is shown protesting the Crown's control of religion in front of a Virginia court.

Why were public speeches so important to protesting British rule?

Parliament also changed the colonies' legal system by giving greater powers to the vice-admiralty courts. These courts had no juries, and the judges treated suspected smugglers as guilty until proven innocent. In regular British courts, accused persons were treated as innocent until proven guilty.

Taxation without Representation

Parliament's actions upset many colonists who had grown used to being independent. Merchants thought the taxes were unfair and hurt business. Many believed that Great Britain had no right to tax the colonies at all without their consent.

James Otis argued that the power of the Crown and Parliament was limited. Otis said they could not "take from any man any part of his property, without his consent in person or by representation." No one in Britain had asked the colonists if they wanted to be taxed. In addition, the colonists had no direct representatives in Parliament. Colonial assemblies had little influence on Parliament's decisions.

At a Boston town meeting in May 1764, local leader **Samuel Adams** agreed with Otis. He believed that Parliament could not tax the colonists without their permission. The ideas of Otis and Adams were summed up in the slogan "No Taxation without Representation," which spread throughout the colonies.

Adams helped found the Committees of Correspondence. Each committee got in touch with other towns and colonies. Its members shared ideas and information about the new British laws and ways to challenge them.

A popular method of protest was the boycott, in which people refused to buy British goods. The first colonial boycott started in New York in 1765. It soon spread to other colonies. Colonists hoped that their efforts would hurt the British economy and might convince Parliament to end the new taxes.

Direct Teach

Main Idea

1 Great Britain Raises Taxes

British efforts to raise taxes on colonists sparked protest.

Explain Why did Great Britain pass the Sugar Act? *to help pay for the French and Indian War and to support a standing army in the American colonies*

Identify Cause and Effect How did the laws Parliament passed increase British control in the American colonies? *tax and currency regulations; crackdown on smugglers; use of vice-admiralty courts*

Make Judgments Do you think Parliament had the right to tax the colonists without their consent? Explain. *Answers will vary but should indicate an understanding of the arguments on both sides of the issue.*

Activity No Taxation Flyer Have each student create a "No Taxation without Representation" flyer that explains the colonists' complaints and urges other colonists to take action.
LS Verbal/Linguistic

- Alternative Assessment Handbook, Rubric 2: Advertisements
- **CRF:** Biography Activity: Samuel Adams
- Political Cartoons Activities for United States History, Cartoons 2: No Taxation without Representation

HSS Analysis Skills: HR 5, HI 1, HI 2

Differentiating Instruction for Universal Access

Special Education Students

Reaching Standards

1. Write the following question for students to see: *What would you do if your favorite drink suddenly cost three times as much as it last did?* Give students time to share their reactions.
2. Next, ask students if they can identify any items that they buy that are taxed. Discuss with students the purpose of taxes and how the U.S. government uses tax money. Explain that the British placed taxes on the colonists to pay for the costs of fighting the French and Indian War.
3. Then explain that elected public officials now vote on taxes. Contrast today's situation with that of the colonists. Write the slogan "No Taxation without Representation" for students to see. Help students understand that the American colonists were angry because they did not have a political say in whether they were taxed. **LS Verbal/Linguistic**

HSS Analysis Skills: HR 5, HI 1

Alternative Assessment Handbook, Rubric 11: Discussions

Did you know . . .

The British required American colonists accused of violating the Sugar Act to go to Halifax, Nova Scotia, to face trial.

Answers

Voice of Protest *They provided the colonists with a means of voicing and debating their opinions.*

Direct Teach

Main Idea

1 Great Britain Raises Taxes

British efforts to raise taxes on colonists sparked protest.

Identify What items were taxed under the Stamp Act? *paper items, including legal documents, licenses, newspapers, pamphlets, and playing cards*

Contrast How did the Stamp Act and the Townshend Acts differ? *The Stamp Act required colonists to pay for an official stamp to buy various paper items; the Townshend Act placed duties on imported glass, lead, paints, paper, and tea.*

Make Inferences Why do you think American colonists chose to boycott British goods as a way to protest taxes? *possible answer—because not buying British goods would hurt the British economy and perhaps persuade Parliament to change the unpopular laws or give colonists representation*

CRF: Biography Activity: Patrick Henry

HSS Analysis Skills: HI 1

Info to Know

Taxes Taxes have existed since ancient times. Ancient Rome issued property and sales taxes. Most taxes are used either to pay for government spending, to promote economic growth, or to help spread wealth. Taxes can also be used to encourage or discourage certain activities.

Stamp Act

The British government continued to search for new ways to tax the American colonies, further angering many colonists. For example, Prime Minister Grenville proposed the **Stamp Act of 1765**. This act required colonists to pay for an official stamp, or seal, when they bought paper items. The tax had to be paid on legal documents, licenses, newspapers, pamphlets, and even playing cards. Colonists who refused to buy stamps could be fined or sent to jail.

Grenville did not expect this tax to spark protest. After all, in Britain people already paid similar taxes. But colonists saw it differently. The Stamp Act was Parliament's first attempt to raise money by taxing the colonists directly, rather than by taxing imported goods.

Protests against the Stamp Act began almost immediately. Colonists formed a secret society called the Sons of Liberty. Samuel Adams helped organize the group in Boston. This group sometimes used violence to frighten tax collectors. Many colonial courts shut down because people refused to buy the stamps required for legal documents. Businesses openly ignored the law by refusing to buy stamps.

In May 1765 a Virginia lawyer named Patrick Henry presented a series of resolutions to the Virginia House of Burgesses. These resolutions stated that the Stamp Act violated colonists' rights. In addition to taxation without representation, the Stamp Act denied the accused a trial by jury. Henry's speech in support of the resolutions convinced the assembly to support some of his ideas.

Repealing the Stamp Act

In Boston the members of the Massachusetts legislature called for a Stamp Act Congress. In October 1765, delegates from nine colonies met in New York. They issued a declaration that the Stamp Act was a violation of their rights and liberties.

Pressure on Parliament to repeal, or do away with, the Stamp Act grew quickly. A group of London merchants complained that their trade suffered from the colonial boycott. Parliament repealed the Stamp Act in 1766.

Members of Parliament were upset that colonists had challenged their authority. Thus, Parliament issued the Declaratory Act, which stated that Parliament had the power to make laws for the colonies "in all cases whatsoever." The Declaratory Act further worried the colonists. The act stripped away much of their independence.

Townshend Acts

In June 1767 Parliament passed the Townshend Acts. These acts placed duties on glass, lead, paints, paper, and tea. To enforce the Townshend Acts, British officials used writs of assistance. These allowed tax collectors to search for smuggled goods. Colonists hated the new laws because they took power away from colonial governments.

The colonists responded to the Townshend Acts by once again boycotting many British goods. Women calling themselves the Daughters of Liberty supported the boycott. In February 1768 Samuel Adams wrote a letter arguing that the laws violated the legal rights of the colonists. The Massachusetts legislature sent the letter to other colonies' legislatures, who voted to join the protest.

At the same time, tax collectors in Massachusetts seized the ship *Liberty* on suspicion of smuggling. This action angered the ship's owner and the Sons of Liberty. They attacked the houses of customs officials in protest. In response, the governor broke up the Massachusetts legislature. He also asked troops to restore order. British soldiers arrived in Boston in October 1768.

READING CHECK **Sequencing** What series of events led to the arrival of British troops in Boston in 1768?

Collaborative Learning

Standards Proficiency

Colonial Tax Trivia Game HSS Analysis Skills: CS 1, HI 1, HI 2

1. Organize students into three teams. Assign each team either the Sugar Act, the Stamp Act, or the Townshend Acts. Have each team write five questions and answers related to its topic.
2. Review each team's questions and answers to make certain the questions are clear and relevant and the answers are correct.
3. Have the teams participate in a game of Colonial Tax Trivia. Select a team to ask the first question. The first person on either of the other teams to raise his or her hand gets to answer the question. If the answer is correct, that person's team receives a point. If the answer is incorrect, give the other team a chance to answer the question.
3. Have each team ask a question in turn. Repeat this process until all the questions have been asked. The team with the most points at the end wins. **LS Interpersonal, Verbal/Linguistic**

Alternative Assessment Handbook, Rubric 14: Group Activity

Answers

Reading Check *Parliament passed the Townshend Acts; colonists boycotted many British goods; tax collectors seized the ship* Liberty *on suspicion of smuggling; Sons of Liberty attacked houses of customs officials; the governor broke up the Massachusetts legislature and asked for British troops to restore order.*

Primary Source

NEWSPAPER ARTICLE

The Boston Massacre

An account of the Boston Massacre appeared in the Boston Gazette and Country Journal *soon after the event.*

"The People were immediately alarmed with the Report of this horrid Massacre, the Bells were set a Ringing, and great Numbers soon assembled at the Place where this tragical Scene had been acted; their Feelings may be better conceived than expressed; and while some were taking Care of the Dead and Wounded, the Rest were in Consultation what to do in these dreadful Circumstances.

But so little intimidated were they [Bostonians], notwithstanding their being within a few Yards of the Main Guard, and seeing the 29th Regiment under Arms, and drawn up in King street; that they kept their Station and appeared, as an Officer of Rank expressed it, ready to run upon the very Muzzles of their Muskets."

—*Boston Gazette and Country Journal*, March 12, 1770

ANALYSIS SKILL **ANALYZING PRIMARY SOURCES**

Why do you think the people described were not intimidated by the soldiers?

Boston Massacre

Many Bostonians saw the presence of British troops as a threat by the British government against its critics in Massachusetts. Some colonists agreed with Samuel Adams, who said, "I look upon [British soldiers] as foreign enemies." The soldiers knew that they were not welcome. Both sides resented each other, and name-calling, arguments, and fights between Bostonians and the soldiers were common.

The tension exploded on March 5, 1770. A lone British soldier standing guard had an argument with a colonist and struck him. A crowd gathered around the soldier, throwing snowballs and shouting insults. Soon a small number of troops arrived. The crowd grew louder and angrier by the moment. Some yelled, "Come on you rascals . . . Fire if you dare!" Suddenly, the soldiers fired into the crowd, instantly killing three men, including sailor Crispus Attucks. "Half Indian, half negro, and altogether rowdy," as he was called, Attucks is the best-remembered casualty of the incident. Two others died within a few days.

Samuel Adams and other protesters quickly spread the story of the shootings. They used it as propaganda—a story giving only one side in an argument—against the British. Colonists called the shootings the **Boston Massacre**. Paul Revere created an elaborate color print titled "The Bloody Massacre perpetrated in King Street" (above).

The soldiers and their officer, Thomas Preston, were charged with murder. Two Boston lawyers, Josiah Quincy and John Adams—Samuel Adams's cousin—agreed to defend the soldiers. They argued that the troops had acted in self-defense. The Boston jury agreed, finding Preston and six soldiers not guilty. Two soldiers were convicted of killing people in the crowd by accident. These men were branded on the hand and released. The trial helped calm people down, but many were still angry at the British.

READING CHECK **Analyzing** What was the significance of the Boston Massacre?

Direct Teach

Main Idea

❷ Boston Massacre

The Boston Massacre caused colonial resentment toward Great Britain.

Describe How did the Boston Massacre begin? *An argument between a British soldier and a colonist drew a crowd, and escalating taunting and violence between colonists and soldiers led to shooting.*

Analyze How did Samuel Adams and other colonial protesters use the shooting as propaganda? *They spread a one-sided story about the shooting, which they called the Boston Massacre to make it seem unjustified.*

Draw Conclusions Why do you think the trial of the British soldiers helped calm people down? *because the jury ruled that the soldiers were acting in self-defense but punished two of them for the accidental deaths*

CRF: Biography Activity: Crispus Attucks

HSS Analysis Skills: CS 1, HR 5, HI 1, HI 2

Primary Source

Reading Like a Historian

The Boston Massacre Help students practice reading the article like historians. Ask the following questions:

- Do you think the author of this article supported or opposed the British government's actions?
- What words and phrases indicate the author's viewpoint? *opposed; "horrid Massacre," "tragical Scene," "dreadful Circumstances"*

HSS Analysis Skills: HR 4, HR 5

Critical Thinking: Identifying Points of View

Standards Proficiency

Boston Massacre Broadsides

HSS Analysis Skills: HR 5, HI 1

Materials: poster board or construction paper, colored markers, art supplies

1. Lead a guided discussion of the significance of the Boston Massacre.
2. Divide the class in two. Have the students in one half create broadsides describing the Boston Massacre from the colonial protesters' point of view. The broadsides should explain what has happened and call for colonists to unite.
3. Have the students in the other half of the class create broadsides describing the Boston Massacre from the British point of view. The broadsides should explain what has happened and call for colonists to remain calm and loyal to Britain.
4. Ask volunteers to share their work with the class. **LS Verbal/Linguistic, Visual/Spatial**

Alternative Assessment Handbook, Rubric 28: Posters

Answers

Analyzing Primary Sources *They were angry and in a frenzied state.*

Reading Check *further increased tensions between American colonists and the British government*

Direct Teach

Main Idea

❸ The Boston Tea Party

Colonists protested the British tax on tea with the Boston Tea Party.

Recall What was the purpose of the Tea Act? *allowed the British East India Company to sell tea directly to the colonies in hopes that cheaper tea might stop colonial smuggling of tea*

Analyze Why did colonists oppose the Tea Act? *Colonial merchants feared the British East India Company's cheap tea would put them out of business.*

Identify Cause and Effect What was the significance of the Boston Tea Party? *enraged British officials and led Parliament to punish Boston by passing the Coercive Acts, which colonists called the Intolerable Acts*

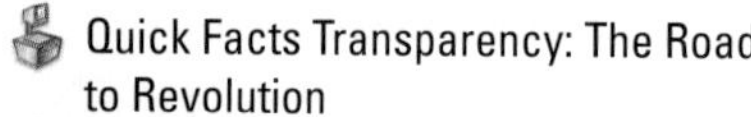

Quick Facts Transparency: The Road to Revolution

HSS **Analysis Skills:** CS 1, HR 5, HI 1, HI 2

Reading Time Lines

The Road to Revolution

- What year did Great Britain begin taxing paper products in the colonies? *1765*
- When did Great Britain close Boston Harbor? *1774*

Quick Facts Transparency: The Road to Revolution

The Road to Revolution

QUICK FACTS

Colonists reacted to British laws with anger and violence. Parliament continued to pass tax after tax.

	1764 The Sugar Act	1765 The Stamp Act
British Actions	The Sugar Act is passed to raise money from the colonies for Britain.	The Stamp Act taxes newspapers, licenses, and colonial paper products.
Colonists' Reactions	Samuel Adams founds the Committees of Correspondence to improve communication among the colonies.	A series of resolutions is published stating that the Stamp Act violates the rights of colonists.

The Boston Tea Party

To reduce tensions in the colonies, Parliament repealed almost all of the Townshend Acts. However, it kept the tax on tea. British officials knew that the colonial demand for tea was high despite the boycott. But colonial merchants were smuggling most of this imported tea and paying no duty on it.

The British East India Company offered Parliament a solution. The company had huge amounts of tea but was not allowed to sell it directly to the colonists. If the company could sell directly to the colonists, it could charge low prices and still make money. Cheaper tea might encourage colonists to stop smuggling. Less smuggling would result in more tax money.

Parliament agreed and passed the **Tea Act** in 1773, which allowed the British East India Company to sell tea directly to the colonists. Many colonial merchants and smugglers feared that the British East India Company's cheap tea would put them out of business. As a result, colonists united against the Tea Act.

Three ships loaded with tea from the British East India Company arrived in Boston Harbor in 1773. The Sons of Liberty demanded that the ships leave. But the governor of Massachusetts would not let the ships leave without paying the duty. Unsure of what to do, the captains waited in the harbor.

On the night of December 16, 1773, colonists disguised as Indians sneaked onto the three tea-filled ships. After dumping over 340 tea chests into Boston Harbor, the colonists headed home to remove their disguises. This event became known as the **Boston Tea Party**. Soon the streets echoed with shouts of "Boston harbour is a teapot tonight!"

READING CHECK **Summarizing** What factors led to the Boston Tea Party?

The Intolerable Acts

Lord North, the new British prime minister, was furious when he heard about the Boston Tea Party. Parliament decided to punish Boston. In the spring of 1774 it passed the Coercive Acts. Colonists called these laws the **Intolerable Acts**. The acts had several effects.

1. Boston Harbor was closed until Boston paid for the ruined tea.
2. Massachusetts's charter was canceled. The governor decided if and when the legislature could meet.
3. Royal officials accused of crimes were sent to Britain for trial. This let them face a more friendly judge and jury.

Collaborative Learning

Standards Proficiency

Colonial Protest Rallies

HSS **Analysis Skills:** CS 1, HR 5, HI 1

Materials: art supplies, butcher paper, poster board, sticks, string, scissors, colored markers

1. Review with students the series of events covered in this section and how the colonists and the British government responded to them.
2. Organize students into five groups and assign each group one of the following: Sugar Act, Stamp Act, Townshend Acts, Tea Act, or Intolerable Acts.
3. Ask students to imagine that their group is planning a colonial rally to protest its assigned act. Have each group create a banner, slogans, and picket signs for its rally.
4. Hold the rallies in the order in which the acts were passed. Give each group time to present its message. **LS Interpersonal, Kinesthetic**

Alternative Assessment Handbook, Rubrics 14: Group Activity; and 34: Slogans and Banners

Answers

Reading Check *passage of the Tea Act in 1773; colonial merchants' fears that the act would put them out of business; colonial and British reactions to the arrival of British East India ships in Boston Harbor*

1770 The Boston Massacre

British soldiers fire into a crowd of colonists, killing five men.

Colonists protest and bring the soldiers to trial.

1773 The Boston Tea Party

The Tea Act is passed, making British tea cheaper than colonial tea.

Colonists protest by dumping shipments of British tea into Boston Harbor.

1774 The Intolerable Acts

Boston Harbor is closed, and British troops are quartered.

Colonists' resentment toward Britain builds.

ANALYSIS SKILL ANALYZING VISUALS

In what year did the conflict between Britain and the colonists turn violent?

4. General Thomas Gage became the new governor of Massachusetts.

The British hoped that these steps would bring back order in the colonies. Instead they simply increased people's anger at Britain.

READING CHECK **Analyzing** What was the purpose of the Intolerable Acts?

SUMMARY AND PREVIEW In this section you learned about the increasing dissatisfaction between the colonists and Great Britain. In the next chapter you'll learn about the result of these conflicts—the American Revolution.

Section 5 Assessment

go.hrw.com
Online Quiz
KEYWORD: SS8 HP2

Reviewing Ideas, Terms, and People HSS 8.1.1, 8.2.1

1. a. **Explain** Why did Great Britain raise taxes in its American colonies?
   b. **Evaluate** Which method of protesting taxes do you think was most successful for colonists? Why?
2. a. **Describe** What events led to the **Boston Massacre**?
   b. **Elaborate** Why do you think John Adams and Josiah Quincy agreed to defend the British soldiers that were involved in the Boson Massacre?
3. a. **Recall** What was the purpose of the **Tea Act**?
   b. **Draw Conclusions** What message did the **Boston Tea Party** send to the British government?
4. a. **Explain** Why did Parliament pass the Intolerable Acts?
   b. **Draw Conclusions** Why do you think the colonists believed that these laws were "intolerable"?

Critical Thinking

5. **Identifying Cause and Effect** Copy the graphic organizer. Use it to identify the laws passed by the British Parliament between 1764 and 1774 and the result of each law.

Law	Result
1.	
2.	
3.	
4.	
5.	

FOCUS ON WRITING

6. **Gathering Information** Now you have some information about the political situation in Boston in the late 1700s. Why might someone from Britain want to immigrate to Boston at this time? Would you consider the city of Boston, rather than a whole colony, for the subject of your infomercial?

Section 5 Assessment Answers

1. a. to pay for the French and Indian War and the cost of defending the colonies
   b. Answers will vary but should show a knowledge of the forms of protest the colonists used.
2. a. arguing, taunting, and fighting between colonists and British soldiers led to shots being fired
   b. Answers will vary but should exhibit an understanding that the trial helped calm the colonists.
3. a. to raise revenue and stop colonial smuggling
   b. that the colonists would act to defend their rights
4. a. to punish Boston for the Boston Tea Party
   b. laws were unreasonable; took power away from colonial governments
5. Sugar Act—colonial protests; boycotts; Stamp Act—boycotts; Stamp Act Congress; act repealed; Towshend Acts—boycotts; tensions increased; Boston Massacre; most repealed; Tea Act—Boston Tea Party; Intolerable Acts—Boston Harbor closed; Massachusetts charter canceled
6. Students' notes should describe the situation in Boston at the time.

Direct Teach

Main Idea

4 The Intolerable Acts

Great Britain responded to colonial actions by passing the Intolerable Acts.

Recall What was the result of the Intolerable Acts? *They increased the colonists' anger toward Great Britain.*

Evaluate Which one of the Intolerable Acts do you think most angered colonists, and why? *Answers will vary but should reflect an understanding of how each act likely affected life in the colonies.*

HSS **Analysis Skills:** HR 5, HI 1

Review & Assess

Close

Use the time line on these pages to review the growing tension, anger, and violence between the American colonies and the British government during the 1760s and early 1770s.

Review

Online Quiz, Section 5

Assess

SE Section 5 Assessment

PASS: Section 5 Quiz

Alternative Assessment Handbook

Reteach/Classroom Intervention

California Standards Review Workbook

Interactive Reader and Study Guide, Section 5

Interactive Skills Tutor CD-ROM

Answers

Analyzing Visuals *1770*

Reading Check *to punish the citizens of Boston for the Boston Tea Party*

Social Studies Skills

Interpreting Time Lines

Activity Examining the Chapter Time Line Have students examine the time line at the beginning of the chapter. Ask students to identify the two categories of events that the time line shows *(U.S. events on the top and world events on the bottom)*. Next, ask students what dates the time line spans *(1620 to 1773)*. Then ask students to identify any relationships among events shown on the time line. For example, the 1620 and 1681 events both involve English colonization. The expansion of English colonization then contributed to Pontiac's Rebellion in 1763. Finally, have students skim the chapter and find three events that could be added to the chapter time line. Ask for volunteers to share their events and to indicate where they would go on the time line. Challenge students to think of other world events to add to the time line as well. **LS Visual/Spatial**

- Alternative Assessment Handbook, Rubric 36: Time Lines
- Interactive Skills Tutor CD-ROM, Lesson 3: Interpret and Create a Time Line and Sequence Events

HSS Analysis Skills: CS 2

Social Studies Skills

Analysis | Critical Thinking | Participation | Study

CS 2 Students construct various timelines of key events, people, and periods of the historical era they are studying.

Interpreting Time Lines

Define the Skill

Knowing the sequence, or order, in which historical events took place is important to understanding these events. Time lines visually display the sequence of events during a particular period of time. They also let you easily see time spans between events, such as how long after one event a related event took place—and what events occurred in between. In addition, comparing time lines for different places makes relationships between distant events easier to identify and understand.

Learn the Skill

Follow these guidelines to read, interpret, and compare time lines.

1. Determine each time line's framework. Note the years it covers and the periods of time into which it is divided. Be aware that a pair of time lines may not have the same framework.
2. Study the order of events on each time line. Note the length of time between events. Compare what was taking place on different time lines around the same time period.
3. Look for relationships between events. Pay particular attention to how an event on one time line might relate to an event on another.

Practice the Skill

Interpret the time lines below to answer the following questions.

1. What is each time line's framework?
2. How long was England without a king?
3. What event in England allowed the colonists to get rid of the Dominion of New England in 1689?
4. Massachusetts' independence long troubled English officials. What do the time lines suggest about why it was allowed to continue until 1686?

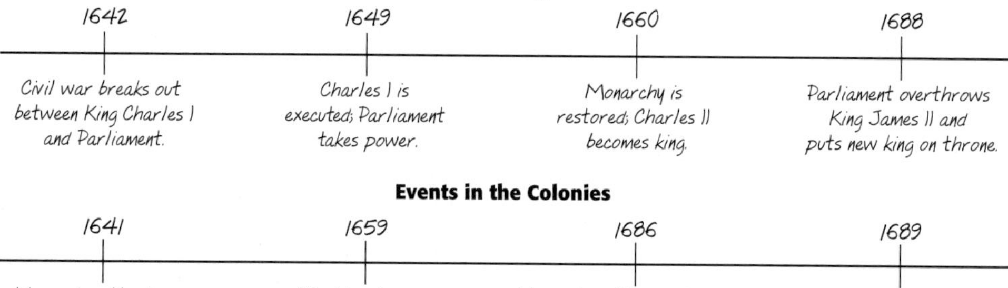

Events in England
1642
Civil war breaks out between King Charles I and Parliament.
1649
Charles I is executed; Parliament takes power.
1660
Monarchy is restored; Charles II becomes king.
1688
Parliament overthrows King James II and puts new king on throne.
Events in the Colonies
1641
Massachusetts shows independence by passing own code of laws.
1659
Virginia pledges loyalty to Charles II as king of England.
1686
Massachusetts is united with other colonies in Dominion of New England by King James II.
1689
Colonies disband Dominion of New England and re-establish separate governments.

Social Studies Skills Activity: Interpreting Time Lines

English Colonies Time Line

HSS Analysis Skills: CS 2

Standards Proficiency

Materials: art supplies, butcher paper, colored markers

1. Have students work as a class to create a large time line on butcher paper of the events covered in this chapter.
2. Organize students into groups and assign each group a specific part of the time line to complete. Start by having students copy the events from the time line that appears at the beginning of the chapter. Either tell students to leave off the world events or to keep the U.S. and world events separate, as they are on the chapter time line.
3. Have groups complete the time line by adding events from the chapter. Each group should also add photos, images, drawings, and quotes to illustrate its part of the time line. **LS Interpersonal, Visual/Spatial**

- Alternative Assessment Handbook, Rubric 36: Time Lines

Answers

Practice the Skill 1. *top time line—spans 1642 to 1688; bottom time line—spans 1641 to 1689;* **2.** *11 years;* **3.** *Parliament's removal of King James II in 1688;* **4.** *England was experiencing political turmoil and leaders probably did not have the time to focus on Massachusetts.*

CHAPTER 2

Standards Review

Visual Summary

Use the visual summary below to help you review the main ideas of the chapter.

QUICK FACTS

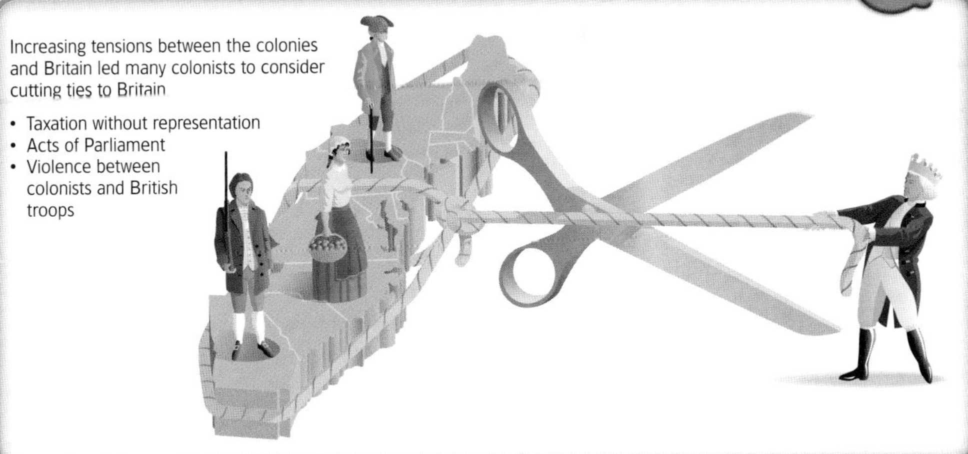

Increasing tensions between the colonies and Britain led many colonists to consider cutting ties to Britain
• Taxation without representation
• Acts of Parliament
• Violence between colonists and British troops

Reviewing Vocabulary, Terms, and People

Match the words in the left column with the correct definition in the right column.

1. Committees of Correspondence
2. Jonathan Edwards
3. mercantilism
4. immigrants
5. indentured servants
6. William Penn
7. Pocahontas
8. Quakers
9. staple crops
10. town meeting

a. colonists who received free passage to North America in exchange for working without pay for a certain number of years

b. created in Massachusetts, these groups helped towns and colonies share information about resisting the new British laws

c. crops that are continuously in demand

d. daughter of Powhatan chief whose marriage to colonist John Rolfe eased tensions between the Powhatan and the colonists

e. one of the leaders of the Great Awakening, he urged sinners to seek forgiveness

f. Protestant sect founded in England that believed salvation was available to all people

g. people who move to another country after leaving their homeland

h. political gathering at which people make decisions on local issues

i. Quaker leader who established a colony with the goal of fair government for all

j. system of creating and maintaining wealth through controlled trade

Answers

Visual Summary

Review and Inquiry Have students use the visual summary to explain the factors that led the colonists to want to cut ties with Great Britain.

Quick Facts Transparency: The English Colonies Visual Summary

Reviewing Vocabulary, Terms, and People

1. b
2. e
3. j
4. g
5. a
6. i
7. d
8. f
9. c
10. h

Comprehension and Critical Thinking

11. **a.** lack of preparation, disease and starvation, conflicts with Native Americans
b. first law in the English colonies that promoted religious tolerance
c. Answers will vary but should indicate an understanding that a reliance on slave labor could lead to slave rebellions and an unwillingness to change the system.

Review and Assessment Resources

Review and Reinforce

SE Standards Review

CRF: Chapter Review Activity

California Standards Review Workbook

Quick Facts Transparency: The English Colonies Visual Summary

Spanish Chapter Summary Audio CD Program

Online Chapter Summaries in Six Languages

OSP Holt PuzzlePro; GameTool for ExamView

Quiz Game CD-ROM

Assess

SE Standards Assessment

PASS: Chapter Test, Forms A and B

Alternative Assessment Handbook

OSP ExamView Test Generator, Chapter Test

Universal Access Modified Worksheets and Tests CD-ROM: Chapter Test

Holt Online Assessment Program (in the Premier Online Edition)

Reteach/Intervene

Interactive Reader and Study Guide

Universal Access Teacher Management System: Lesson Plans for Universal Access

Universal Access Modified Worksheets and Tests CD-ROM

Interactive Skills Tutor CD-ROM

go.hrw.com
Online Resources
Chapter Resources:
KEYWORD: SS8 US2

Answers

12. a. fishing, shipbuilding, trade
b. similar—both in New England, sought religious freedom, brought families to settle, faced little resistance from American Indians, emphasized education; different—Pilgrims: received assistance from American Indians, established the Mayflower Compact; Puritans: close link of church and state, experienced dissent
c. Answers will vary but should indicate that those who disagreed with the church often left.

13. a. staple crops such as wheat, barley, and oats
b. large land grants and religious tolerance drew a variety of settlers
c. religious tolerance, active trade, diverse population, reliance on indentured servants

14. a. political shifts in England, trade restrictions, conflict with Native Americans and the French, desire to settle in the western frontier
b. introduced political ideas of equality and liberty
c. Answers will vary but should indicate that both events encouraged a greater demand for political equality in the colonies.

15. a. to pay for the French and Indian War and for keeping a standing army in North America
b. increased tensions, violence, and anger between the colonists and the British government
c. Answers will vary but should show an understanding that the Intolerable Acts only further angered the American colonists.

Comprehension and Critical Thinking

SECTION 1 *(Pages 36–41)* **HSS 8.1**

11. a. Explain What problems did the settlers of Virginia face?
b. Draw Conclusions Why was Maryland's Toleration Act of 1649 important?
c. Predict How might the southern colonies' reliance on slave labor eventually cause problems?

SECTION 2 *(Pages 42–48)* **HSS 8.2.1**

12. a. Describe On what was the economy of the New England colonies based?
b. Compare and Contrast How were the Pilgrim and Puritan colonies similar and different?
c. Evaluate Explain why you think the close ties between church and state in Massachusetts helped or hurt their government.

SECTION 3 *(Pages 49–51)* **HSS 8.1**

13. a. Identify What types of crops were grown in the middle colonies?
b. Draw Conclusions Why did the middle colonies have a more diverse population than either New England or the South?
c. Elaborate What are some possible reasons why immigrants would have chosen to live in the middle colonies?

SECTION 4 *(Pages 54–61)* **HSS 8.1.1, 8.2.1**

14. a. Identify What challenges did the English colonies face?
b. Analyze What effect did the Great Awakening and the Enlightenment have on the colonies?
c. Evaluate Explain which you think had a greater impact on colonial government—the passage of the English Bill of Rights or the Great Awakening.

SECTION 5 *(Pages 64–69)* **HSS 8.1.1, 8.2.1**

15. a. Recall Why did the British believe it was necessary to raise taxes on the American colonists?
b. Draw Conclusions How did the Boston Massacre and the Boston Tea Party affect relations between Great Britain and the colonies?
c. Evaluate Did the British government overreact to colonial protests by issuing the Intolerable Acts? Why or why not?

Reviewing Themes

16. Politics What political influences shaped the governments of the British colonies?

17. Economics How did mercantilism affect the economies of Great Britain and the American colonies?

Reading Skills

Understanding Words through Context Clues *Use the Reading Skills taught in this chapter to answer the question about the reading selection below.*

> A popular method of protest was the boycott, in which people refused to buy British goods. (p. 65)

18. According to the reading section above, what is the best definition of *boycott*?
a. a popular method
b. buying British goods
c. people refusing
d. protest in which people refuse to buy goods

Social Studies Skills

Interpreting Time Lines *Use the Social Studies Skills taught in this chapter to answer the questions about the time lines on page 70.*

19. How many years after the English Civil War did Parliament overthrow King James II?

20. How many years did the Dominion of New England last?
a. 41
b. 18
c. 3
d. 6

Focus on Writing

21. Writing Your Infomercial Choose a colony and time period. Review your list of reasons why English citizens might want to live there. Then write an infomercial with at least four scenes. Each scene should have video and a voice-over telling one of the reasons for immigrating.

Reviewing Themes

16. influences of Magna Carta, the English Bill of Rights, and ideas from the Great Awakening and the Enlightenment

17. benefited the economy of Great Britain, but hampered the economies of the colonies

Reading Skills

18. d

Social Studies Skills

19. 46 years

20. c

Focus on Writing

21. Rubric Students' infomercials should:
- include four scenes that clearly explain the benefits of living in the colonies
- include voiceovers that explain the video images
- be persuasive and enthusiastic
- use correct grammar and spelling

Standards Assessment

DIRECTIONS: Read each question and write the letter of the best response.

1

The red box on this map indicates which early colonial settlement?

- **A** Plymouth
- **B** Massachusetts Bay
- **C** New Amsterdam
- **D** Jamestown

2 The most common economic activity throughout the early English and Dutch colonies in North America was

- **A** whaling.
- **B** farming.
- **C** manufacturing.
- **D** mining.

3 Ideas about spiritual, social, and political equality arose in the colonies in the 1700s in a religious movement called

- **A** Separatism.
- **B** the Enlightenment.
- **C** the Great Awakening.
- **D** Puritanism.

4 How did Parliament's passage of the English Bill of Rights in 1689 affect England's North American colonies?

- **A** Colonists became more interested in being governed by representatives they elected.
- **B** Several colonies decided to unite and formed the Dominion of New England.
- **C** The Great Awakening took place.
- **D** A movement to end slavery developed.

5 What was the central issue in the dispute between Britain and its American colonies?

- **A** the restrictions Parliament placed on trade
- **B** the presence of British troops in the colonies
- **C** the colonists' right to religious freedom
- **D** the power to tax the colonists

Connecting with Past Learnings

6 Life on an English colonial plantation in the early 1700s was most like life

- **A** in Great Britain during the same time.
- **B** on the Iberian Peninsula under Muslim rule.
- **C** on a medieval manor in western Europe.
- **D** in the Inca Empire before Europeans arrived.

7 In Grade 7 you learned about the Enlightenment, which shaped how some colonial leaders thought about individual rights. The Enlightenment had its origins in what earlier event in Europe?

- **A** the Renaissance
- **B** the colonial era
- **C** the *Reconquista*
- **D** the Crusades

Answers

1. D
Break Down the Question Remind students to read all the labels on the map and to identify geographic features before choosing an answer.

2. B
Break Down the Question This question requires students to synthesize information from the first three sections. Help students by having them first answer the question for each region of the thirteen colonies.

3. C
Break Down the Question Some students may confuse the Great Awakening and the Enlightenment. Have students look up the glossary definition for each term, if needed.

4. A
Break Down the Question This question requires students to identify cause and effect. Refer students who miss the question to the text titled "Colonial Governments" in Section 4.

5. D
Break Down the Question Point out to students that the word *central* means that they should select the main or most important issue.

6. C
Break Down the Question This question requires students to recall information covered in Grade 7.

7. A
Break Down the Question This question requires students to recall information covered in Grade 7.

Intervention Resources

Reproducible

- Interactive Reader and Study Guide
- Universal Access Teacher Management System: Lesson Plans for Universal Access

Technology

- Quick Facts Transparency: The English Colonies Visual Summary
- Universal Access Modified Worksheets and Tests CD-ROM
- Interactive Skills Tutor CD-ROM

Tips for Test Taking

Track Your Time Use all the time allowed for a test to avoid making errors. Use these **checkpoints** to help monitor your time:

- How many questions should you have answered when one quarter of the time is gone?
- What should the clock read when you are halfway through the questions?
- If you find yourself behind, speed up. If you are ahead, you can—and should—slow down.

Standards Review

Have students review the following standards in their workbooks.

- California Standards Review Workbook: HSS 8.1.1, 8.2.1

Chapter 3 Planning Guide

The American Revolution

Chapter Overview	Reproducible Resources	Technology Resources
CHAPTER 3 pp. 74–105 **Overview: In this chapter, students will learn about the events that occurred during the American Revolution.** See page 74 for the California History–Social Science standards covered in this chapter.	**Universal Access Teacher Management System:*** • Universal Access Instructional Benchmarking Guides • Lesson Plans for Universal Access **Interactive Reader and Study Guide:*** Chapter Graphic Organizer **Chapter Resource File*** • Focus on Speaking Activity: Giving an Oral Report • Social Studies Skills Activity: Understanding Historical Interpretation • Chapter Review Activity **Pre-AP Activities Guide for United States History:*** Analyzing Primary Sources	**One-Stop Planner CD-ROM:** Calendar Planner **Student Edition Full-Read Audio CD-ROM** **Universal Access Modified Worksheets and Test CD-ROM** **Interactive Skills Tutor CD-ROM** **Primary Source Library CD-ROM for United States History** **Power Presentations with Video CD-ROM** **History's Impact: United States History Video Program (VHS/DVD):** The American Revolution*
Section 1: **The Revolutionary War Begins** **The Big Idea:** The tensions between the colonies and Great Britain led to armed conflict. 8.1	**Universal Access Teacher Management System:*** Section 1 Lesson Plan **Interactive Reader and Study Guide:*** Section 1 Summary **Chapter Resource File*** • Vocabulary Builder, Section 1 • History and Geography Activity: Early Battles Around Boston • Primary Source Activity: Patrick Henry	**Daily Bellringer Transparency:** Section 1* **Map Transparency:** British Retreat From Boston*
Section 2: **Declaring Independence** **The Big Idea:** The colonies formally declared their independence from Great Britain. 8.1.2	**Universal Access Teacher Management System:*** Section 2 Lesson Plan **Interactive Reader and Study Guide:*** Section 2 Summary **Chapter Resource File*** • Vocabulary Builder, Section 2 • Biography Activity: John Hancock	**Daily Bellringer Transparency:** Section 2* go.hrw.com **Internet Activity:** Patriots vs. Loyalists Essay
Section 3: **Dark Hours for the Revolution** **The Big Idea:** Patriot forces faced many obstacles in the war against Britain. 8.1.3	**Universal Access Teacher Management System:*** Section 3 Lesson Plan **Interactive Reader and Study Guide:*** Section 3 Summary **Chapter Resource File*** • Vocabulary Builder, Section 3 • Biography Activities: Phillis Wheatley, Haym Salomon, Bernardo de Gálvez • Literature Activity: Thomas Paine • Primary Source Activity: Benjamin Rush's Letter	**Daily Bellringer Transparency:** Section 3* **Map Transparency:** Battles in the Middle Colonies* **Map Transparency:** The Battle of Saratoga*
Section 4: **The Patriots Gain New Hope** **The Big Idea:** The war spread to the South, where the British were finally defeated.  8.1	**Universal Access Teacher Management System:*** Section 4 Lesson Plan **Interactive Reader and Study Guide:*** Section 4 Summary **Chapter Resource File***  • Vocabulary Builder, Section 4 • Primary Source Activity: General Nathanial Greene  **Political Cartoons Activities for United States History,** Cartoon 3: American Independence*	**Daily Bellringer Transparency:** Section 4*  **Map Transparency:** Battle of Yorktown* **Map Transparency:** North America after the Treaty of Paris of 1783* go.hrw.com **Internet Activity:** Revolutionary Battle Site Tourist Brochure

SE Student Edition  Print Resource · Audio CD · Video
TE Teacher's Edition · Transparency · CD-ROM · DVD
go.hrw.com · CA Standards Mastery · LS Learning Styles
OSP One-Stop Planner CD-ROM · * also on One-Stop Planner CD

Review, Assessment, Intervention

- **Standards Review Workbook***
- **Quick Facts Transparency:** The American Revolution Visual Summary*
- **Spanish Chapter Summaries Audio CD Program**
- **Online Chapter Summaries in Six Languages**
- **Quiz Game CD-ROM**
- **Progress Assessment Support System (PASS):** Chapter Test*
- **Universal Access Modified Worksheets and Test CD-ROM:** Modified Chapter Test
- **One-Stop Planner CD-ROM:** ExamView Test Generator (English/Spanish)
- **Alternative Assessment Handbook**

- **PASS:** Section 1 Quiz*
- **Online Quiz:** Section 1
- **Alternative Assessment Handbook**

- **PASS:** Section 2 Quiz*
- **Online Quiz:** Section 2
- **Alternative Assessment Handbook**

- **PASS:** Section 3 Quiz*
- **Online Quiz:** Section 3
- **Alternative Assessment Handbook**

- **PASS:** Section 4 Quiz*
- **Online Quiz:** Section 4
- **Alternative Assessment Handbook**

California Resources for Standards Mastery

INSTRUCTIONAL PLANNING AND SUPPORT

- **Universal Access Teacher Management System***
- **One-Stop Planner CD-ROM with Test Generator: Teacher Management System with Interactive Teacher's Edition**

STANDARDS MASTERY

- **Standards Review Workbook***
- **At Home: A Guide to Standards Mastery for United States History**

Holt Online Learning

To enhance learning, Internet activities are available for a Patriots vs. Loyalists Essay and a Revolutionary Battle Site Tourist Brochure.

KEYWORD: SS8 TEACHER

- **Teacher Support Page**
- **Content Updates**
- **Rubrics and Writing Models**
- **Teaching Tips for the Multimedia Classroom**

KEYWORD: SS8 US3

- **Current Events**
- **Document-Based Questions**
- **Holt Grapher**
- **Holt Online Atlas**
- **Holt Researcher**
- **Interactive Multimedia Activities**
- **Internet Activities**
- **Online Chapter Summaries in Six Languages**
- **Online Section Quizzes**
- **American History Maps and Charts**

HOLT PREMIER ONLINE STUDENT EDITION

Complete online support for interactivity, assessment, and reporting

- **Interactive Maps and Notebook**
- **Standardized Test Prep**
- **Homework Practice and Research Activities Online**

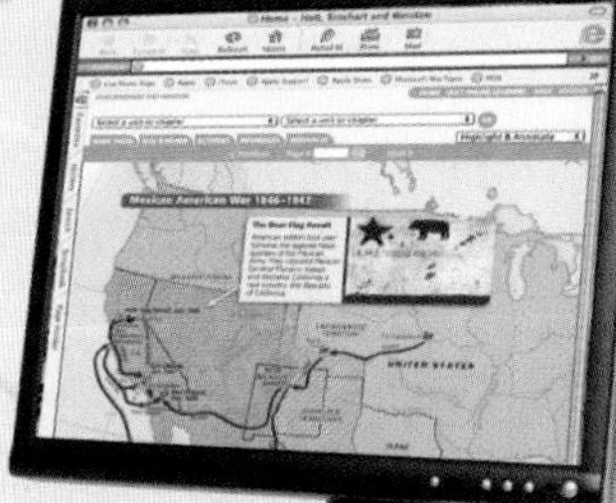

Mastering the Standards: Differentiating Instruction

Reaching Standards	Basic-level activities designed for all students encountering new material
Standards Proficiency	Intermediate-level activities designed for average students
Exceeding Standards	Challenging activities designed for honors and gifted-and-talented students
Standard English Mastery	Activities designed to improve standard English usage

Frequently Asked Questions

INSTRUCTIONAL PLANNING AND SUPPORT

Where do I find planning aids, pacing guides, lesson plans, and other teaching aids?

Annotated Teacher's Edition:
- Chapter planning guides
- Standards-based instruction and strategies
- Differentiated instruction for universal access
- Point-of-use reminders for integrating program resources

Power Presentations with Video CD-ROM

Universal Access Teacher Management System:
- Year and unit instructional benchmarking guides
- Reproducible lesson plans
- Assessment guides for diagnostic, progress, and summative end-of-the-year tests
- Options for differentiating instruction and intervention
- Teaching guides and answer keys for student workbooks

One-Stop Planner CD-ROM with Test Generator: Teacher Management System with Interactive Teacher's Editon:
- Calendar Planner
- Editable lesson plans
- All reproducible ancillaries in Adobe Acrobat (PDF) format
- ExamView Test Generator (English & Spanish)
- Game Tool for ExamView
- PuzzlePro
- Transparency and video previews

DIFFERENTIATING INSTRUCTION FOR UNIVERSAL ACCESS

What resources are available to ensure that Advanced Learners/GATE Students master the standards?

Teacher's Edition Activities:
- Battle Plans Activity, p. 93

Lesson Plans for Universal Access

Pre-AP Activities Guide for United States History: Analyzing Primary Sources

Primary Source Library CD-ROM for United States History

What resources are available to ensure that English Learners and Standard English Learners master the standards?

Teacher's Edition Activities:
- Vocabulary of the Declaration of Independence, p. 86

Lesson Plans for Universal Access

Chapter Resource File: Vocabulary Builder Activities

Spanish Chapter Summaries Audio CD Program

Online Chapter Summaries in Six Languages

One-Stop Planner CD-ROM:
- PuzzlePro, Spanish Version
- ExamView Test Generator, Spanish Version

What modified materials are available for Special Education?

The ***Universal Access Modified Worksheets and Tests CD-ROM*** provides editable versions of the following:

Vocabulary Flash Cards

Modified Vocabulary Builder Activities

Modified Chapter Review Activity

Modified Chapter Test

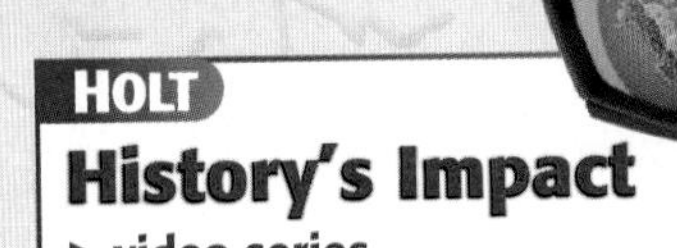

HOLT History's Impact
▶ video series
The American Revolution

What resources are available to ensure that Learners Having Difficulty master the standards?

Teacher's Edition Activities:
- Violence of Lexington and Concord, p. 80
- *Common Sense* Handbill, p. 84
- Patriot Aid, p. 95

Interactive Reader and Study Guide
Student Edition Full-Read Audio CD
Quick Facts Transparency: The American Revolution Visual Summary
Standards Review Workbook
Social Studies Skills Activity: Understanding Historical Interpretation
Interactive Skills Tutor CD-ROM

How do I intervene for students struggling to master the standards?

Interactive Reader and Study Guide
Quick Facts Transparency: The American Revolution Visual Summary
Standards Review Workbook
Social Studies Skills Activity: Understanding Historical Interpretation
Interactive Skills Tutor CD-ROM

PROFESSIONAL DEVELOPMENT

What teacher training resources are available to help me grow professionally?

- In-service and staff development as part of your Holt Social Studies product purchase
- Quick Teacher Tutorial Lesson Presentation CD-ROM
- Intensive tuition-based Teacher Development Institute
- *Teaching American History* Online 2 Module Professional Development Course
- Convenient Holt Speaker Bureau face-to-face workshop options
- PRAXIS™ Test Prep (#0089) interactive Web-based content refreshers*
- 24/7 *Ask A Professional Development Expert* at http://www.hrw.com/prodev/

* PRAXIS is a trademark of Educational Testing Service (ETS). This publication is not endorsed or approved by ETS.

Information Literacy Skills

To learn more about how History–Social Science instruction may be improved by the effective use of library media centers and information literacy skills, go to the Teacher's Resource Materials for Chapter 3 at **go.hrw.com**, keyword: SS8 MEDIA.

The following materials were developed by the Division for Public Education of the American Bar Association. These materials are part of the **Democracy and Civic Education** supplement.
- Constitution Study Guide
- Supreme Court Case Studies

Chapter Preview

Standards Focus

Standards by Section

Section 1: HSS 8.1

Section 2: HSS 8.1.2

Section 3: HSS 8.1.3

Section 4: HSS 8.1

Teacher's Edition

HSS **Analysis Skills:** CS 1, CS 3, HR 1, HR 4, HR 5, HI 1, HI 2, HI 4, HI 5

Preview Grade 8 Standards

HSS **8.2** Students analyze the political principles underlying the U.S. Constitution and compare the enumerated and implied powers of the federal government.

8.2.2 Analyze the Articles of Confederation and the Constitution and the success of each in implementing the ideals of the Declaration of Independence.

8.2.3 Evaluate the major debates that occurred during the development of the Constitution and their ultimate resolutions in such areas as shared power among institutions, divided state-federal power, slavery, the rights of individuals and states (later addressed by the addition of the Bill of Rights), and the status of American Indian nations under the commerce clause.

Focus on Speaking

The **Chapter Resource File** provides a Focus on Speaking worksheet to help students prepare, organize, and present their oral reports.

CRF: Focus on Speaking Activity: Giving an Oral Report

CHAPTER 3 1774–1783

The American Revolution

California Standards

History–Social Science

8.1 Students understand the major events preceding the founding of the nation and relate their significance to the development of American constitutional democracy.

Analysis Skills

HI 5 Students recognize that interpretations of history are subject to change.

English–Language Arts

Writing 8.2.1.a Relate a clear, coherent incident, event, or situation by using well-chosen details.

Reading 8.1.3 Use word meanings within the appropriate context.

FOCUS ON SPEAKING

Giving an Oral Report The Revolutionary War was a very exciting time in our history, a time filled with deeds of courage and daring and ending with an amazing victory for the underdog. As you read this chapter, you will learn about the great events and heroic people of that time. Then you will prepare and give an oral report on the history of the American Revolution.

UNITED STATES

1774 The First Continental Congress meets.

1775 The Revolutionary War begins with the fighting at Lexington and Concord.

1774

WORLD

74 CHAPTER 3

Introduce the Chapter

Standards Proficiency

Considering the Pros and Cons of War

HSS 8.1; HSS **Analysis Skills:** HI 1, HI 2

1. Ask students to suggest some current pros and cons of the United States going to war. (If the United States is currently at war, have students suggest pros and cons of being at war.) Write students' suggestions for the class to see.
2. If students need help, have them consider the financial and human costs of war and how war might affect relations with other nations.
3. Next, remind students of the problems between the American colonies and Great Britain in the early 1770s. Ask students to imagine that they are colonial leaders debating whether to go to war against Great Britain. Ask students to suggest some pros and cons. Have students consider the size of the colonies and their lack of a unified economy or military.
4. List students' ideas for them to see and have students copy the list. Then, as they study the chapter, have students note how accurate their predictions were. LS **Verbal/Linguistic**

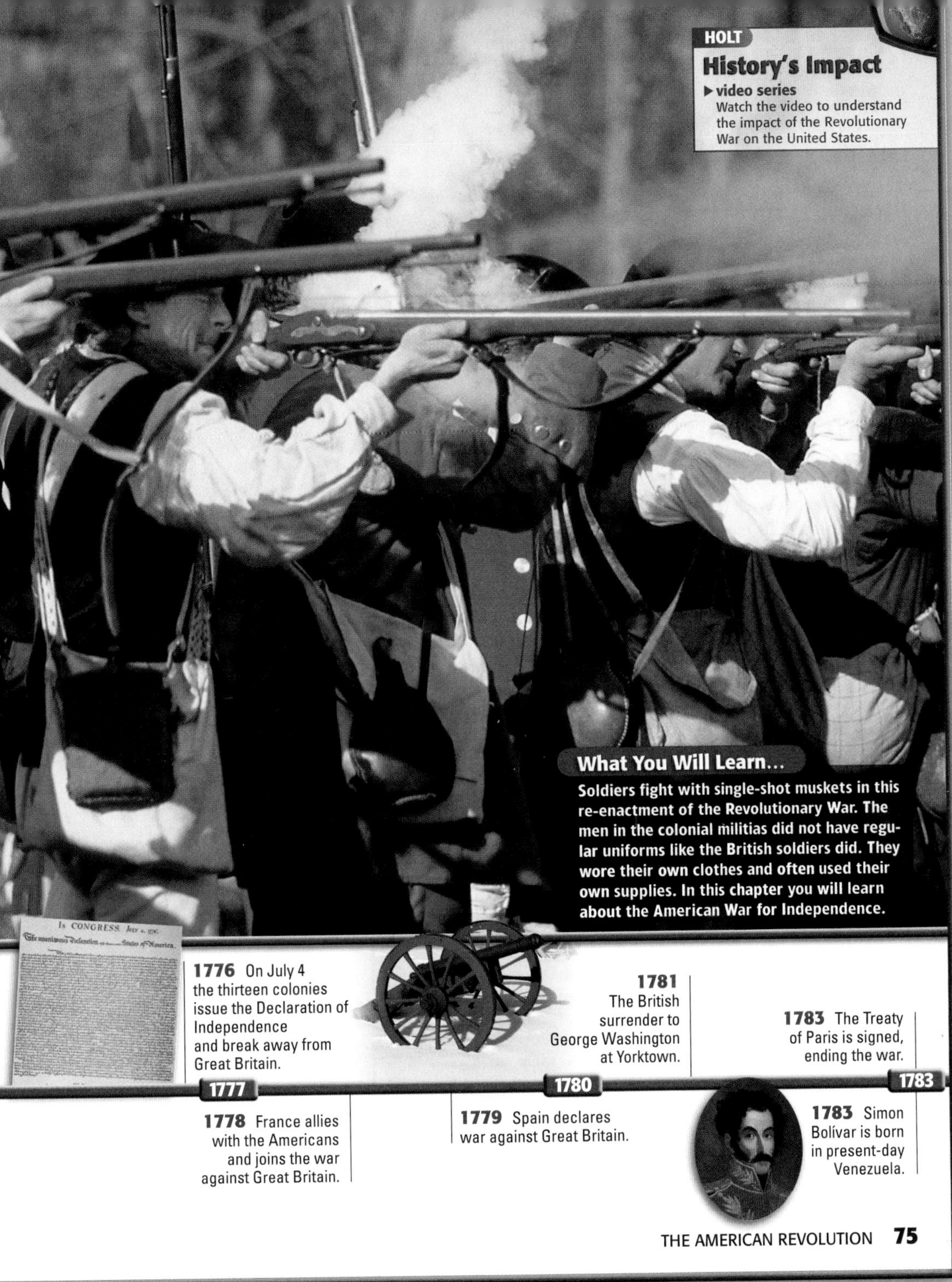

HOLT
History's Impact
▶ **video series**
Watch the video to understand the impact of the Revolutionary War on the United States.

What You Will Learn...

Soldiers fight with single-shot muskets in this re-enactment of the Revolutionary War. The men in the colonial militias did not have regular uniforms like the British soldiers did. They wore their own clothes and often used their own supplies. In this chapter you will learn about the American War for Independence.

1776 On July 4 the thirteen colonies issue the Declaration of Independence and break away from Great Britain.

1781 The British surrender to George Washington at Yorktown.

1783 The Treaty of Paris is signed, ending the war.

1777 — 1780 — 1783

1778 France allies with the Americans and joins the war against Great Britain.

1779 Spain declares war against Great Britain.

1783 Simon Bolívar is born in present-day Venezuela.

THE AMERICAN REVOLUTION **75**

Chapter Preview

HOLT
History's Impact
▶ **video series**
See the Video Teacher's Guide for strategies for using the chapter video **The American Revolution**.

Chapter Big Ideas

Section 1 The tensions between the colonies and Great Britain led to armed conflict. **HSS** 8.1

Section 2 The colonies formally declared their independence from Great Britain. **HSS** 8.1.2

Section 3 Patriot forces faced many obstacles in the war against Britain. **HSS** 8.1.3

Section 4 The war spread to the South, where the British were finally defeated. **HSS** 8.1

Explore the Picture

The Long Rifle At the time of the American Revolution, many colonists used a gun known as a long rifle or Kentucky rifle. A rifle is a type of gun with a grooved barrel. The grooves spin the ball, or bullet, as it is shot. Compared to a musket, a long rifle can shoot a ball farther and with greater accuracy. On the other hand, soldiers could fire and reload muskets faster than rifles. Rifles also lacked bayonets for use in hand-to-hand combat.

Analyzing Visuals What can you tell about the weapons and style of fighting in the Revolutionary War from this picture? *used muskets or rifles, stood in close ranks to shoot, did not always shoot from behind cover*

go.hrw.com
Online Resources
Chapter Resources:
KEYWORD: SS8 US3
Teacher Resources:
KEYWORD: SS8 TEACHER

Explore the Time Line

1. What year did the American Revolution begin, and what year did it end? *1775; 1783*
2. When did colonial leaders issue the Declaration of Independence? *1776*
3. What other countries fought against Britain during the American Revolution? *France, Spain*
4. Where and when did the British surrender to end the fighting in the war? *Yorktown, 1781*

HSS Analysis Skills: CS 1

Info to Know

French Aid in the War A turning point in the American Revolution occurred when France joined the colonies in their fight against Great Britain. The French had remained bitter over the loss of their North American holdings after the French and Indian War. As a result, they were eager to weaken Britain's control in North America. During the American Revolution, the French proved to be a valuable ally, particularly in the colonial victory at the Battle of Yorktown, which ended the war.

Reading Social Studies

Understanding Themes

Two themes are covered in the chapter—geography and politics. These two ideas played important roles in the events leading up to the independence of the United States. Ask students to predict how geography might have played a factor in the Revolutionary War. Would geography have helped or hurt the Patriots? Why? Then discuss with students the role of politics in the independence of the United States. How might political views have led the colonists to demand their freedom?

Main Ideas in Social Studies

Focus on Reading Ask students to bring in an article from a newspaper or magazine. Have each student read his or her article and then choose two paragraphs at random. Have students use the steps listed on this page to identify the main idea of each paragraph. Remind students to identify the general topic of the paragraph, highlight important facts and details related to that topic, and then determine the author's point. Have students write their answers to each step.

Reading Social Studies

by Kylene Beers

Economics | Geography | Politics | Religion | Society and Culture | Science and Technology

Focus on Themes In this chapter you will read about the events of the Revolutionary War, the war by which the United States won its independence. You will learn about some of the major battles that occurred between the American colonists and the British army and how **geography** sometimes affected their outcomes. You will also read the Declaration of Independence, one of the most important **political** documents in all of American history.

Main Ideas in Social Studies

Focus on Reading When you are reading, it is not always necessary to remember every tiny detail of the text. Instead, what you want to remember are the main ideas, the most important concepts around which the text is based.

Identifying Main Ideas Most paragraphs in history books include main ideas. Sometimes the main idea is stated clearly in a single sentence. At other times, the main idea is suggested, not stated. However, that idea still shapes the paragraph's content and the meaning of all of the facts and details in it.

Colonists known as Patriots chose to fight for independence. Loyalists—sometimes called Tories—were those who remained loyal to Great Britain. Historians estimate that 40 to 45 percent of Americans were Patriots, while 20 to 30 percent were Loyalists. The rest were neutral.

Topic: The paragraph is about Americans' loyalties during the Revolutionary War.

+

Facts and Details:
- Patriots wanted independence.
- Loyalists wanted to remain part of Great Britain.
- Some people stayed neutral.

Main Idea: Americans' loyalties were divided as the colonies prepared for the Revolutionary War.

Steps in Identifying Main Ideas

1. Read the paragraph. Ask yourself, "What is this paragraph mostly about, or its topic?"
2. List the important facts and details that relate to that topic.
3. Ask yourself, "What seems to be the most important point the writer is making about the topic?" Or ask, "If the writer could say only one thing about this paragraph, what would it be?" This is the **main idea** of the paragraph.

Additional reading support can be found in the Interactive Reader and Study Guide

Reading and Skills Resources

Reading Support
- Interactive Reader and Study Guide
- Student Edition on Audio CD
- Spanish Chapter Summaries Audio CD Program

Social Studies Skills Support
- Interactive Skills Tutor CD-ROM

Vocabulary Support
- **CRF:** Vocabulary Builder Activities
- **CRF:** Chapter Review Activity
- Universal Access Modified Worksheets and Tests CD-ROM:
  - Vocabulary Flash Cards
  - Vocabulary Builder Activity
  - Chapter Review Activity
- OSP Holt PuzzlePro

Standards Focus

ELA Reading 8.2.0

ELA Reading 8.2.0 Read and understand grade-level-appropriate material.

You Try It!

The following passage is from the chapter you are about to read. Read it and then answer the questions below.

Americans and the War Effort

During the war more than 230,000 soldiers served in the Continental Army. The typical soldier was young, often under the legal age of 16. Most had little money, no property, and few opportunities in life. The army offered low pay, often rotten food, hard work, cold, heat, poor clothing and shelter, harsh discipline, and a high chance of becoming a casualty. Yet for some young men and boys, it represented change and excitement.

Finding and keeping dedicated soldiers throughout the long, hard war would be a constant chore. In time, the Continental Congress required states to supply soldiers. Men who could afford it often paid others, such as slaves or apprentices, to fight in their places.

From Chapter 3, p. 90

After you have read the passage, answer the following questions.

1. The main idea of the second paragraph is stated in a sentence. Which sentence expresses the main idea?
2. What is the first paragraph about? What facts and details are included in the paragraph? Based on your answers to these questions, what is the main idea of the first paragraph?

As you read Chapter 3, identify the main ideas of the paragraphs you are reading.

Key Terms and People

Chapter 3

Section 1
First Continental Congress *(p. 78)*
minutemen *(p. 79)*
Redcoats *(p. 80)*
Second Continental Congress *(p. 80)*
Continental Army *(p. 80)*
George Washington *(p. 80)*
Battle of Bunker Hill *(p. 81)*

Section 2
Common Sense (p. 83)
Thomas Paine *(p. 83)*
Thomas Jefferson *(p. 84)*
Declaration of Independence *(p. 84)*
Patriots *(p. 84)*
Loyalists *(p. 84)*

Section 3
mercenaries *(p. 92)*
Battle of Trenton *(p. 93)*
Battle of Saratoga *(p. 94)*
Marquis de Lafayette *(p. 95)*
Bernardo de Gálvez *(p. 95)*
John Paul Jones *(p. 97)*
George Rogers Clark *(p. 97)*

Section 4
Francis Marion *(p. 99)*
Comte de Rochambeau *(p. 100)*
Battle of Yorktown *(p. 100)*
Treaty of Paris of 1783 *(p. 101)*

Academic Vocabulary

Success in school is related to knowing academic vocabulary—the words that are frequently used in school assignments and discussions. In this chapter, you will learn the following academic words:

reaction *(p. 79)*
strategy *(p. 94)*

Reading Social Studies

Key Terms and People

Preteach the key terms and people for this chapter by reviewing each term with the class. Then instruct students to define or identify each term or person in the list at left. Have students select ten terms from the list and create a word search using those terms. Have students write the description of each term or person as a clue. When students have finished their word search, have them exchange puzzles with a partner. Then have each student complete a word search by circling the key terms and people identified by the clues.
LS Verbal/Linguistic, Visual/Spatial

Focus on Reading

See the **Focus on Reading** questions in this chapter for more practice on this reading social studies skill.

Reading Social Studies Assessment

See the **Standards Review** at the end of this chapter for student assessment questions related to this reading skill.

Teaching Tip

Point out to students that writing a main idea statement is not the same thing as summarizing a paragraph. Help students learn how to find the main idea by asking them to identify what point the author is trying to make in a paragraph. Point out to students that not all details in a paragraph may relate to the main idea. Occasionally other facts and details are used in order to add interest. Remind students to look only for details that relate to the general topic of the paragraph or passage.

Answers

You Try It! 1. *the first sentence;* **2.** *topic—soldiers in the Continental Army; details—230,000 soldiers, soldiers were young, had little money, army pay was low, work was hard; possible main idea—The life of a soldier in the Continental Army was difficult, but exciting.*

Preteach

Bellringer

If YOU were there . . . Use the **Daily Bellringer Transparency** to help students answer the question.

 Daily Bellringer Transparency, Section 1

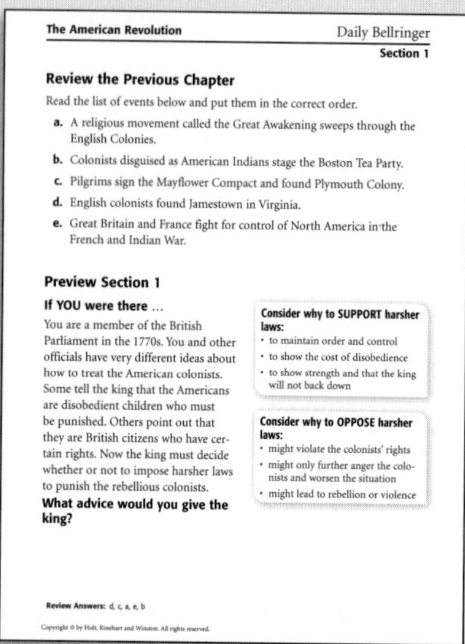

The American Revolution Daily Bellringer

Section 1

Review the Previous Chapter

Read the list of events below and put them in the correct order.

a. A religious movement called the Great Awakening sweeps through the English Colonies.
b. Colonists disguised as American Indians stage the Boston Tea Party.
c. Pilgrims sign the Mayflower Compact and found Plymouth Colony.
d. English colonists found Jamestown in Virginia.
e. Great Britain and France fight for control of North America in the French and Indian War.

Preview Section 1

If YOU were there ...

You are a member of the British Parliament in the 1770s. You and other officials have very different ideas about how to treat the American colonists. Some tell the king that the Americans are disobedient children who must be punished. Others point out that they are British citizens who have certain rights. Now the king must decide whether or not to impose harsher laws to punish the rebellious colonists.

What advice would you give the king?

Consider why to SUPPORT harsher laws:
- to maintain order and control
- to show the cost of disobedience
- to show strength and that the king will not back down

Consider why to OPPOSE harsher laws:
- might violate the colonists' rights
- might only further anger the colonists and worsen the situation
- might lead to rebellion or violence

Review Answers: d, c, a, e, b

Academic Vocabulary

Review with students the high-use academic term in this section.

reaction response (p. 79)

CRF: Vocabulary Builder Activity, Section 1

Standards Focus

HSS 8.1

Means: Students understand the major events that led up to the founding of the United States, such as the American Revolution.

Matters: The American Revolution resulted in the formation of the United States as an independent nation.

SECTION 1

The Revolution Begins

What You Will Learn...

Main Ideas

1. The First Continental Congress demanded certain rights from Great Britain.
2. Armed conflict between British soldiers and colonists broke out with the "shot heard 'round the world."
3. The Second Continental Congress created the Continental Army to fight the British.

The Big Idea

The tensions between the colonies and Great Britain led to armed conflict.

Key Terms and People

First Continental Congress, *p. 78*
minutemen, *p. 79*
Redcoats, *p. 80*
Second Continental Congress, *p. 80*
Continental Army, *p. 80*
George Washington, *p. 80*
Battle of Bunker Hill, *p. 81*

HSS 8.1. Students understand the major events preceding the founding of the nation and relate their significance to the development of American constitutional democracy.

If YOU were there...

You are a member of the British Parliament in the 1770s. You and other officials have very different ideas about how to treat the American colonists. Some tell the king that the Americans are disobedient children who must be punished. Others point out that they are British citizens who have certain rights. Now the king must decide whether or not to impose harsher laws to punish the rebellious colonists.

What advice would you give the king?

BUILDING BACKGROUND Taxes and harsh new laws led some colonists to protest against the British. In some places, the protests turned violent. The British government, however, refused to listen to the colonists, ignoring their demands for more rights. That set the stage for war.

First Continental Congress

The closing of the port of Boston was the final insult that led all of the colonies except Georgia to send delegates to the **First Continental Congress** —a gathering of delegates from throughout the colonies. At Carpenters' Hall in Philadelphia, they remained locked in weeks of tense debates. Virginia delegate Patrick Henry and other radicals believed that violence was unavoidable. Delegates from Pennsylvania and New York had strict orders to seek peace.

At this historic crossroads, the delegates compromised. They halted all trade with Britain and alerted the colonial militias to prepare for war. Meanwhile, they drafted a Declaration of Rights, a list of 10 resolutions that included the right to "life, liberty, and property."

King George refused to consider the Declaration of Rights. Instead, British colonial leaders ordered their troops to prepare to seize the colonial militias' weapons.

Teach the Big Idea: Master the Standards

Standards Proficiency

The Revolution Begins HSS 8.1; HSS Analysis Skills: CS 1, HI 1, HI 2

1. **Teach** Ask students the Main Idea questions to teach this section.
2. **Apply** Create a two-column chart for the students to see. Label the columns *British Actions* and *American Reactions*. Have students copy the chart and list the British actions and the resulting American reactions that led to the outbreak of the American Revolution. **LS Verbal/Linguistic, Visual/Spatial**
3. **Review** As you review the section, have students share information from their charts. Use the information to complete the master chart you created.
4. **Practice/Homework** Have students choose one of the American reactions and either write a letter to the editor or create a political cartoon in support of the action. **LS Verbal/Linguistic**

Alternative Assessment Handbook, Rubrics 7: Charts; 27: Political Cartoons; and 43: Writing to Persuade

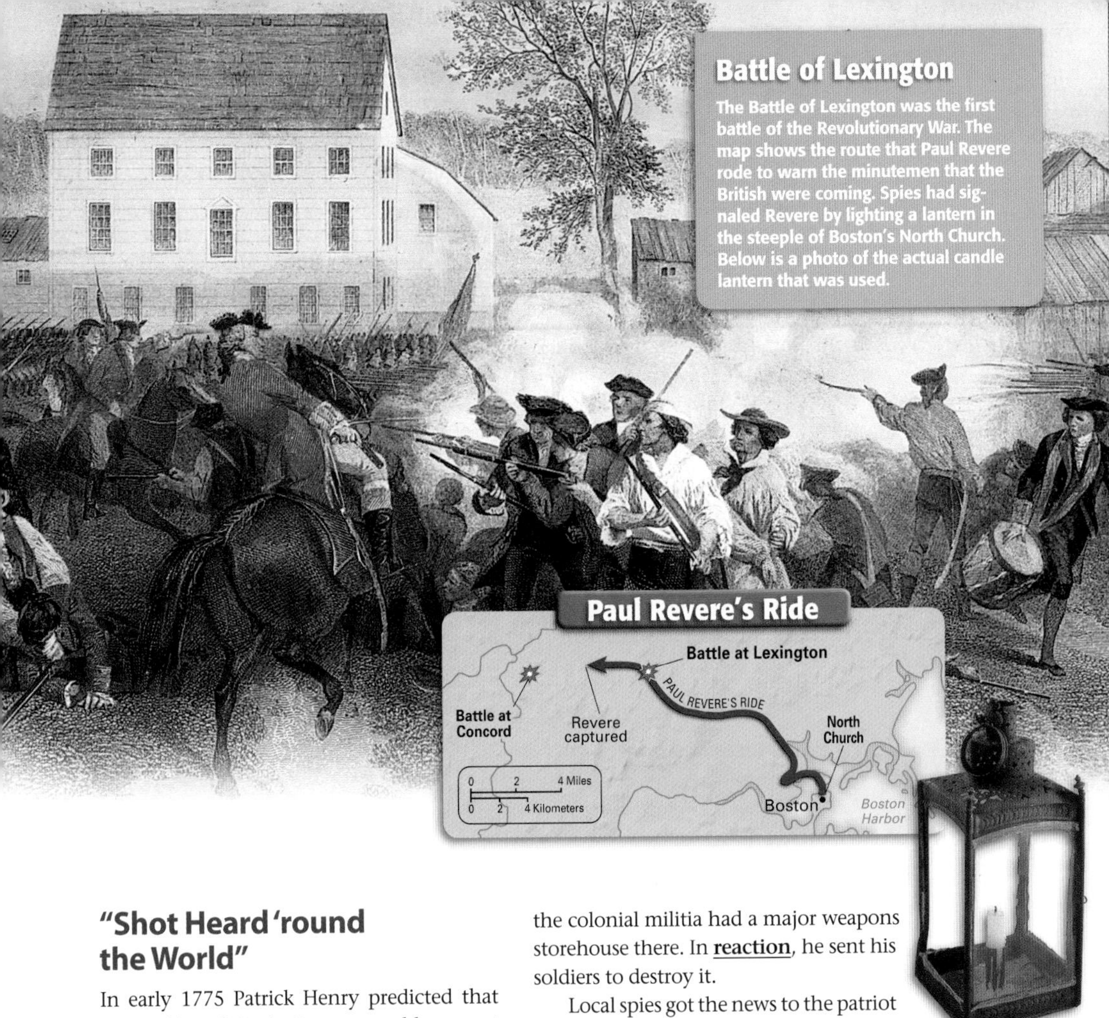

Battle of Lexington

The Battle of Lexington was the first battle of the Revolutionary War. The map shows the route that Paul Revere rode to warn the minutemen that the British were coming. Spies had signaled Revere by lighting a lantern in the steeple of Boston's North Church. Below is a photo of the actual candle lantern that was used.

"Shot Heard 'round the World"

In early 1775 Patrick Henry predicted that news of hostilities in Boston would come at any moment. Addressing the hesitation of some of his fellow Virginia legislators, Henry uttered these famous words:

> "Gentlemen may cry, Peace, Peace—but there is no peace. The war is actually begun!... I know not what course others may take; but as for me, give me liberty or give me death!"
>
> —Patrick Henry, quoted in *Eyewitnesses and Others*

One month later, on the night of April 18, a force of 700 British soldiers headed for Concord, a town about 20 miles west of Boston. British general Thomas Gage had heard that the colonial militia had a major weapons storehouse there. In reaction, he sent his soldiers to destroy it.

Local spies got the news to the patriot group, the Sons of Liberty. On a prearranged signal, Paul Revere, William Dawes, and Samuel Prescott set off on horseback to sound the alert that the British were coming.

Across the countryside, drums and church bells called to duty the **minutemen** —members of the civilian volunteer militia. At dawn the British troops arrived at the town of Lexington, near Concord, where 70 armed minutemen awaited the British advance.

"Don't fire unless fired upon," the captain yelled to his minutemen. "But if they mean to have a war, let it begin here!"

ACADEMIC VOCABULARY
reaction response

Critical Thinking: Identifying Points of View

Standards Proficiency

Interview with Patrick Henry

HSS 8.1; HSS **Analysis Skills:** HR 1, HR 4, HR 5, HI 1

1. Discuss with students Patrick Henry's role in the First Continental Congress and his predictions of violence in Boston.
2. Ask a volunteer to read aloud the quote from Patrick Henry on this page. Have students discuss the quote. Why does Henry think the colonies are already at war? Ask students if they agree with his view. What does he mean by "give me liberty or give me death"?
3. Next, ask students to imagine that they are news reporters interviewing Patrick Henry. Have students work in pairs to write three to five questions to ask Henry about the events in this section. Each pair should then write the answers they think Henry would have given, based on the text.
4. Have volunteers act out their mock interviews. LS **Interpersonal, Verbal/Linguistic**

Alternative Assessment Handbook, Rubric 37: Writing Assignments

CRF: Primary Source Activity: Patrick Henry: The Voice of Freedom

Direct Teach

Main Idea

1 First Continental Congress

The First Continental Congress demanded certain rights from Great Britain.

Describe How did Britain react to the Declaration of Rights? *King George III refused to consider them; British colonial leaders ordered the seizure of the militias' weapons.*

Draw Conclusions Why did the First Continental Congress alert the colonial militias to prepare for war? *possible answers—to be prepared in case efforts to resolve problems with Great Britain failed; because relations with Great Britain were deteriorating*

CRF: Primary Source Activity: Patrick Henry: The Voice of Freedom

HSS 8.1; HSS **Analysis Skills:** HI 1

Main Idea

2 "Shot Heard 'round the World"

Armed conflict between British soldiers and colonists broke out with the "shot heard 'round the world."

Explain Why did a British force march on Concord? *had orders to destroy or confiscate weapons the colonial militia was storing there*

Summarize How did the colonists react to the British advance? *They spread the word and used drums and church bells to call minutemen to prepare to meet the British soldiers.*

CRF: History and Geography Activity: Early Battles Around Boston

HSS 8.1; HSS **Analysis Skills:** HI 1

Direct Teach

Main Idea

❷ "Shot Heard 'round the World"

Armed conflict between British soldiers and colonists broke out with the "shot heard 'round the world."

Identify Cause and Effect How did the minutemen respond to the battle at Lexington? *attacked the British force as it retreated to Boston*

Evaluate In your opinion, which side won the fighting at Lexington and Concord, and why? *possible answer—minutemen, because they suffered fewer overall casualties*

Map Transparency: British Retreat from Boston

HSS 8.1; HSS **Analysis Skills:** HI 1

Did you know . . .

After the battles at Lexington and Concord, some 10,000 colonial civilians moved out of Boston as the town became a base for British troops. By July 1775, some 13,500 British troops occupied the city.

Answers

Interpreting Maps 1. *control of Boston meant control of the harbor*
2. *by ship, because the red dashed line shows they went by sea*

Reading Check *a shot that rang out as British troops arrived at Lexington; made colonists angrier with Britain and encouraged them to fight*

Suddenly, a shot rang out. To this day, no one knows who fired this "shot heard 'round the world."

The battle ended in minutes with only a few shots fired. When the musket smoke cleared, 8 minutemen lay dead, and 10 were wounded. The British, with only one man wounded, marched on to Concord. They destroyed the weapons they found.

As the British retreated to Boston, the roads swarmed with minutemen, firing from behind every tree, fence, and building. The British **Redcoats**, soldiers wearing red uniforms, made an easy target. By the end of the day more than 250 British soldiers were dead, wounded, or missing. The minutemen counted fewer than 100 casualties.

READING CHECK **Identifying Cause and Effect** What led to the fighting at Lexington and Concord, and how did it affect the colonies' conflict with Great Britain?

Second Continental Congress

In May 1775, delegates from 12 colonies met in Philadelphia for the **Second Continental Congress**. This second gathering of delegates from the colonies was still far from unified. Some called for a war, others for peace. Once again, they compromised. The Congress did not break away from Britain, but it declared the Massachusetts militia to be the **Continental Army**. This military force would carry out the fight against Britain. Congress named a Virginian, **George Washington**, to command the army.

As Washington prepared for war, the Congress pursued peace. On July 5 the delegates signed the Olive Branch Petition, asking the king to restore harmony between Britain and the colonies. King George refused to read it and looked for new ways to punish the colonies.

British Retreat from Boston

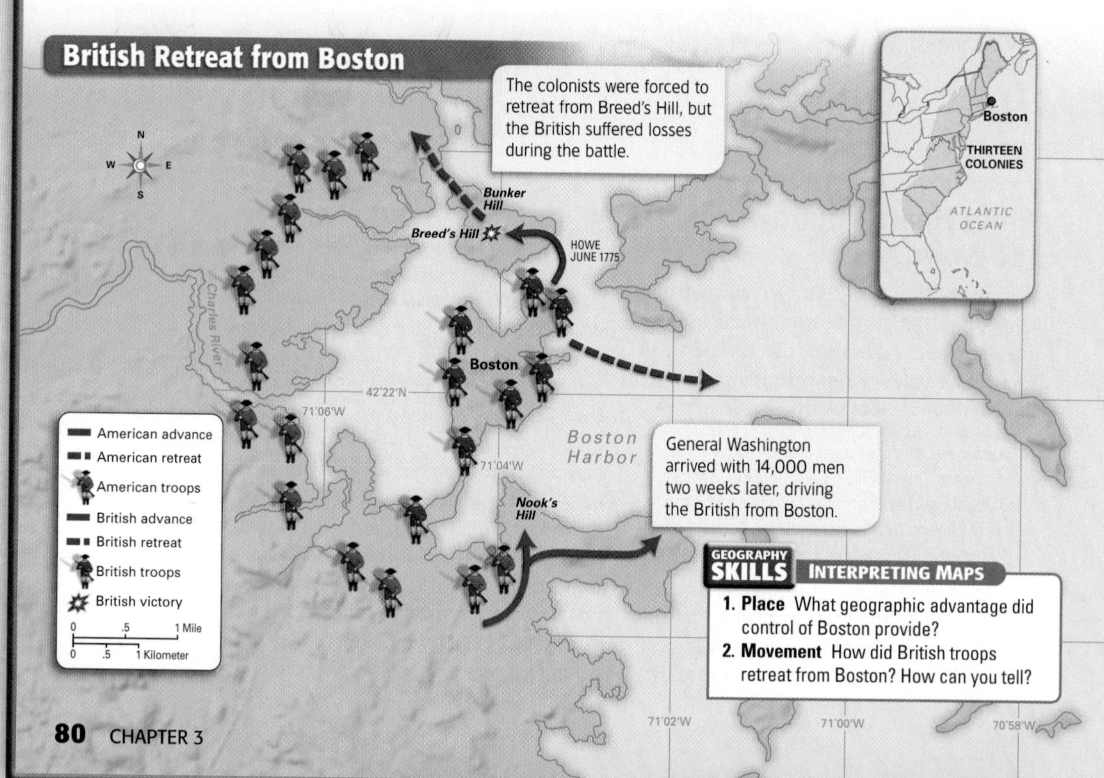

GEOGRAPHY SKILLS **INTERPRETING MAPS**

1. **Place** What geographic advantage did control of Boston provide?
2. **Movement** How did British troops retreat from Boston? How can you tell?

Differentiating Instruction for Universal Access

Learners Having Difficulty — Reaching Standards

1. Copy the graphic organizer for students to see. Omit the blue sample answers.
2. Have students copy the concept web and complete it by entering key people, dates, and events associated with Lexington and Concord.
3. Then discuss how the outbreak of fighting affected colonial relations with Great Britain.

LS **Visual/Spatial**

HSS 8.1; HSS **Analysis Skills:** CS 1, HI 1

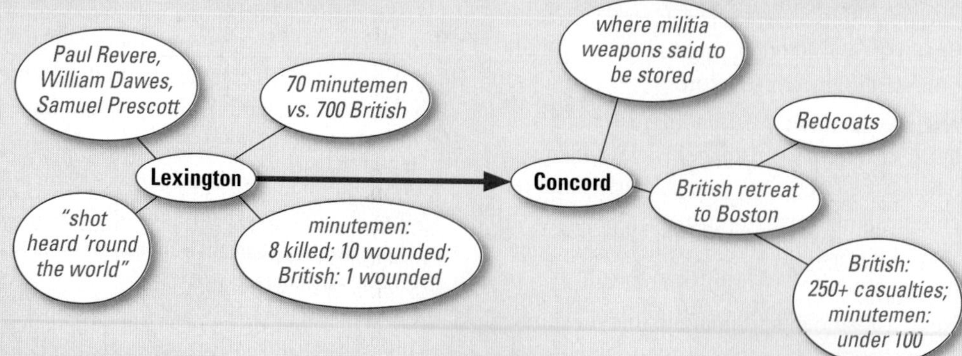

Battle of Bunker Hill

While Congress discussed peace, Massachusetts went on the offensive. Desperate for supplies, leaders in Boston authorized Benedict Arnold to raise a force of 400 men to attack the British at Fort Ticonderoga. On May 10, 1775, during an early morning storm, the Patriots quickly took the fort and its large supply of weapons.

Meanwhile, the poorly supplied minutemen kept the British pinned down inside the city of Boston. As the British were making plans to break the colonial siege south of Boston, they awoke on June 17 to a stunning sight. The colonial forces had quietly dug in at Breed's Hill, a point overlooking northern Boston. The Redcoats would have to cross Boston Harbor in boats and fight their way up the hill.

As the British force of 2,400 advanced, the 1,600 Americans waited. Low on gunpowder, the commander ordered his troops not to fire "until you see the whites of their eyes."

Finally, the colonists rained down their fire on the attackers. Climbing the exposed hillside with their heavy packs, the Redcoats were cut down. Twice they retreated. Stepping over the dead and wounded along the way, they marched back up the hill for a third try.

The colonists were now out of ammunition. As the British rushed toward them, Patriots threw rocks. They swung their empty guns like clubs. They fought with their bare hands. At last, the Americans had to retreat.

For the British, it was a tragic victory. They suffered more than 1,000 casualties, about double the American losses. This battle, called the **Battle of Bunker Hill,** proved the colonists could take on the British.

British Retreat from Boston

Two weeks later, on July 3, General George Washington arrived to take command of the Continental Army of about 14,000 men. After months of preparation, in March 1776, Washington used the Fort Ticonderoga cannons to fire on the British from Nook's Hill overlooking Boston.

British guns could not reach the top of the hill. On March 7, General William Howe retreated from Boston. The birthplace of the rebellion was back in colonial hands.

READING CHECK **Identifying Cause and Effect** How did geography influence the early battles around Boston?

SUMMARY AND PREVIEW The colonists could not avoid war with Great Britain. In the next section you will read about the Declaration of Independence.

Section 1 Assessment

go.hrw.com
Online Quiz
KEYWORD: SS8 HP3

Reviewing Ideas, Terms, and People HSS 8.1

1. a. **Identify** What was the **First Continental Congress?**
   b. **Make Inferences** Why did the First Continental Congress send the Declaration of Rights to the king?
   c. **Elaborate** Why do you think King George III refused to consider the colonists' Declaration of Rights?
2. a. **Identify** Who warned the colonists of the British advance toward Concord?
   b. **Analyze** Why did the British army march on Lexington and Concord?
   c. **Elaborate** What do you think is meant by the expression the "shot heard 'round the world"?
3. a. **Describe** What was the purpose of the **Second Continental Congress**?
   b. **Draw Conclusions** How was the **Continental Army** able to drive British forces out of Boston?
   c. **Evaluate** How would you evaluate the performance of the Continental Army in the early battles of the war? Explain your answer.

Critical Thinking

4. **Summarizing** Copy the graphic organizer below. Use it to summarize the actions and results of the First and Second Continental Congresses.

Continental Congress	Actions Taken	Results
First		
Second		

FOCUS ON SPEAKING 

5. **Thinking about the Beginning** You'll have about five minutes for your report and only a minute or two to talk about the beginning of the war. What are the one or two most important things you want to say about the beginning?

Direct Teach

Main Idea

❸ Second Continental Congress

The Second Continental Congress created the Continental Army to fight the British.

Identify Who was appointed leader of the Continental Army? *George Washington*

Make Judgments Do you think the Second Continental Congress was wise in having Washington prepare for war as it sought peace? Explain your answer. *possible answer—Yes, the colonists needed to be prepared in case Britain attacked or did not accept the Olive Branch Petition.*

HSS 8.1; HSS **Analysis Skills:** HI 1

Review & Assess

Close

Have students review the section by discussing whether they think war was inevitable or could have been avoided if the colonists had acted differently.

Review

Online Quiz, Section 1

Assess

SE Section 1 Assessment

PASS: Section 1 Quiz

Alternative Assessment Handbook

Reteach/Classroom Intervention

California Standards Review Workbook

Interactive Reader and Study Guide, Section 1

Interactive Skills Tutor CD-ROM

Section 1 Assessment Answers

1. a. meeting of colonial delegates to determine what to do about the crisis in Boston
   b. to tell him the rights the colonies wanted
   c. possible answer—angry and did not think the colonists had a right to protest
2. a. Paul Revere, William Dawes, Samuel Prescott
   b. to destroy militia weapons stored in Concord
   c. possible answer—The first shot of the American Revolution had a large impact on the world.
3. a. created a Continental Army for defense, while pursuing peace with Great Britain
   b. placed cannons on Nook's Hill overlooking Boston; exposed British were forced to retreat
   c. possible answer—did well for its size and experience, and drove the British from Boston
4. First: actions—halted trade with Britain, prepared militias for war, Declaration of Rights; results—British acted to seize the militias' weapons; Second: actions—formed Continental Army, sent Olive Branch Petition; results—fighting continued
5. possible answers—Despite colonial attempts at peace, fighting broke out in the colonies.

Answers

Reading Check *Hills near Boston enabled the Continental Army to take the high ground, which gave them an advantage over the British in battle and helped them retake Boston.*

Biography

Reading Focus Question

Have students discuss the introductory question. Ask them to consider not only the benefits of leadership but also the challenges and disadvantages, such as being attacked in the press. Tell students to keep their answers in mind as they read the biography.

Info to Know

Washington's Early Life George Washington spent most of his early childhood on a farm near Fredericksburg, Virginia. He received irregular schooling, first with a local church leader and later with a schoolmaster. His main education came not from books but from hands-on training in outdoor occupations. He mastered tobacco growing and raising livestock, and early in his teens became familiar with surveying.

Linking to Today

Washington's Legacy George Washington may have lived more than 200 years ago, but his legacy remains apparent. He appears on both the U.S. quarter and $1 bill. He is enshrined at the Washington Monument in Washington D.C. His image is carved in the national memorial at Mount Rushmore, South Dakota, along with those of Thomas Jefferson, Abraham Lincoln, and Theodore Roosevelt. In addition, numerous places, naval ships, and public schools have been named in Washington's honor.

BIOGRAPHY

George Washington

What would you do if you were asked to lead a new country?

When did he live? 1732–1799

Where did he live? George Washington was a true American, born in the Virginia colony. As president, he lived in New York City and Philadelphia, the nation's first two capitals. When he retired, he returned to his plantation at Mount Vernon.

What did he do? Although Washington was a wealthy farmer, he spent most of his life in the military and in politics. Leading the colonial forces to victory in the Revolutionary War, he then helped shape the new government of the United States. On April 30, 1789, he was sworn in as the first president of the United States.

Why is he so important? George Washington inspired Americans and helped to unite them. One of his great accomplishments as president was to keep the peace with Britain and France. Upon leaving the presidency, he urged Americans to avoid becoming divided.

Drawing Conclusions How might Washington's leadership in the Revolutionary War have prepared him for his role as president?

KEY EVENTS

- **1775** Serves in Second Continental Congress; selected commander of the Continental Army
- **1789** Inaugurated as president
- **1793** Begins second term as president
- **1796** Publishes his Farewell Address and retires to his plantation at Mount Vernon
- **1799** Dies at Mount Vernon; his will frees his slaves

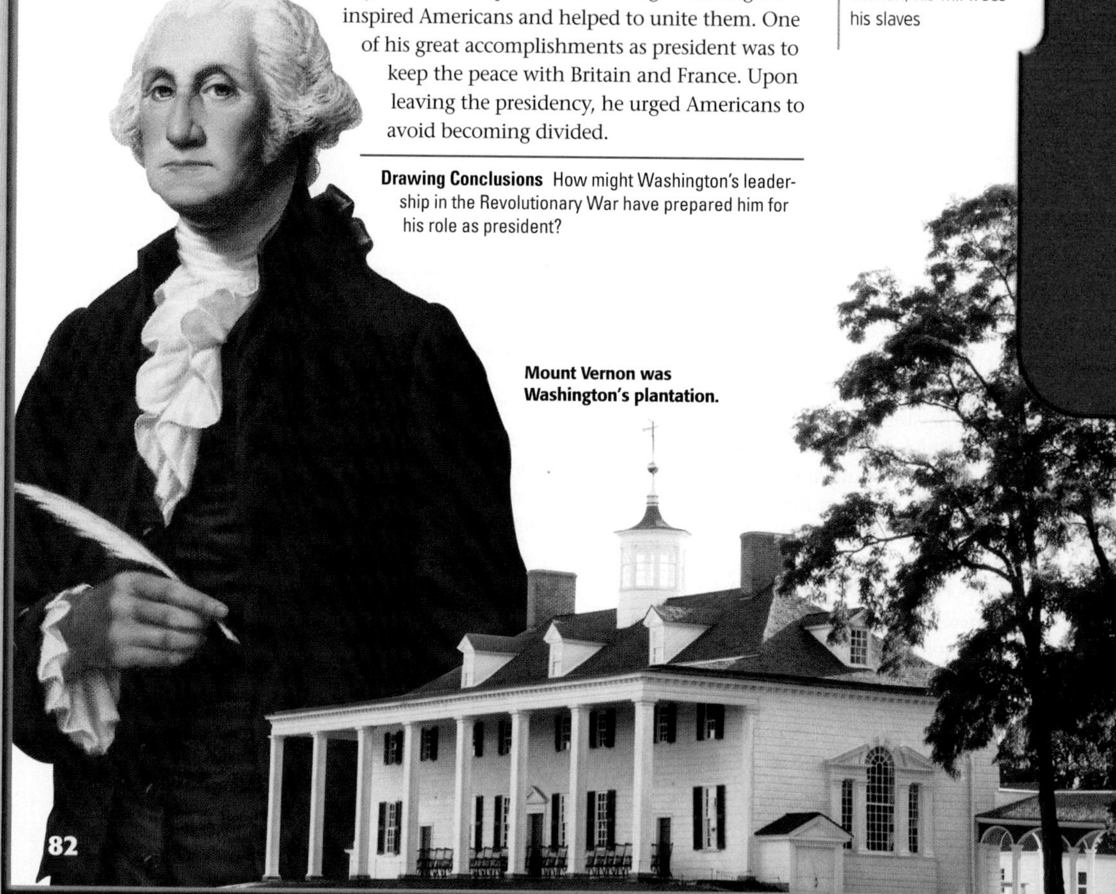

Mount Vernon was Washington's plantation.

82

Collaborative Learning

Standards Proficiency

Washington Time Capsule

HSS 8.1; HSS **Analysis Skills:** HI 1

1. Present the following scenario: A caretaker at Mount Vernon has discovered a time capsule that George Washington buried on the grounds. Inside were 10 items and a letter from Washington. In the letter, he explains that the items symbolize the major achievements and events in his life. What are the 10 items in the time capsule?
2. Organize students into small groups. Tell each group to list the major achievements and events in Washington's life. Students should then select 10 items to represent these achievements and events. Last, each group should write Washington's letter, listing the 10 items and explaining why he included each of them.
3. Have each group share some of the items it listed with the class. Then lead students in a brief discussion of Washington's significance.

Alternative Assessment Handbook, Rubric 14: Group Activity

Answers

Drawing Conclusions *He gained experience directing others, managing resources, dealing with crises and challenges, overcoming obstacles, making decisions, and working with a diverse group of people under trying circumstances.*

Declaring Independence

If YOU were there...

You live on a farm in New York in 1776. The conflicts with the British have torn your family apart. Your father is loyal to King George and wants to remain British. But your mother is a fierce Patriot, and your brother wants to join the Continental Army. Your father and others who feel the same way are moving to British-held Canada. Now you must decide what you will do.

Would you decide to go to Canada or support the Patriots?

BUILDING BACKGROUND The outbreak of war took some colonists by surprise. Many American colonists, like the farmer above, did not favor independence from Britain. Gradually, though, the idea of independence became more popular.

Paine's *Common Sense*

"[T]here is something very absurd in supposing a continent to be perpetually [forever] governed by an island." This argument against British rule over America appeared in ***Common Sense***, a 47-page pamphlet published in January 1776 that urged separation from Great Britain. *Common Sense* was published anonymously—that is, without the author's name. The author, **Thomas Paine**, argued that citizens, not kings and queens, should make laws. At a time when monarchs ruled much of the world, this was a bold idea.

News of the work spread throughout the colonies, eventually selling some 500,000 copies. Paine reached a wide audience by writing as a common person speaking to common people. *Common Sense* changed the way many colonists viewed their king. It made a strong case for economic freedom and for the right to military self-defense. It cried out against tyranny—that is, the abuse of government power. Thomas Paine's words rang out in his time, and they have echoed throughout American history.

READING CHECK **Supporting a Point of View** Would you have agreed with Thomas Paine? Explain your answer.

SECTION 2

What You Will Learn...

Main Ideas

1. Thomas Paine's *Common Sense* led many colonists to support independence.
2. Colonists had differing reactions to the Declaration of Independence.

The Big Idea

The colonies formally declared their independence from Great Britain.

Key Terms and People

Common Sense, *p. 83*
Thomas Paine, *p. 83*
Thomas Jefferson, *p. 84*
Declaration of Independence, *p. 84*
Patriots, *p. 84*
Loyalists, *p. 84*

HSS 8.1.2 Analyze the philosophy of government expressed in the Declaration of Independence, with an emphasis on government as a means of securing individual rights (e.g., key phrases such as "all men are created equal, that they are endowed by their Creator with certain unalienable Rights").

Preteach

Bellringer

If YOU were there . . . Use the **Daily Bellringer Transparency** to help students answer the question.

Daily Bellringer Transparency, Section 2

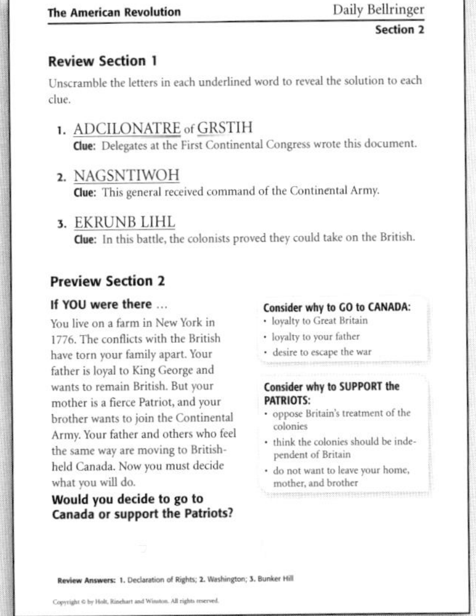

The American Revolution — Daily Bellringer, Section 2

Review Section 1

Unscramble the letters in each underlined word to reveal the solution to each clue.

1. ADCILONATRE of GRSTIH
   Clue: Delegates at the First Continental Congress wrote this document.
2. NAGSNTIWOH
   Clue: This general received command of the Continental Army.
3. EKRUNB LIHL
   Clue: In this battle, the colonists proved they could take on the British.

Preview Section 2

If YOU were there ...

You live on a farm in New York in 1776. The conflicts with the British have torn your family apart. Your father is loyal to King George and wants to remain British. But your mother is a fierce Patriot, and your brother wants to join the Continental Army. Your father and others who feel the same way are moving to British-held Canada. Now you must decide what you will do.

Would you decide to go to Canada or support the Patriots?

Consider why to GO to CANADA:
- loyalty to Great Britain
- loyalty to your father
- desire to escape the war

Consider why to SUPPORT the PATRIOTS:
- oppose Britain's treatment of the colonies
- think the colonies should be independent of Britain
- do not want to leave your home, mother, and brother

Review Answers: 1. Declaration of Rights; 2. Washington; 3. Bunker Hill

Building Vocabulary

Preteach or review the following terms:

anonymously without giving a name (p. 83)

Enlightenment movement during the 1700s that emphasized the use of reason and logic to improve society (p. 84)

ideals guiding standards or principles (p. 85)

social contract agreement between the people and the government (p. 84)

tyranny abuse of government power (p. 83)

unalienable impossible to take away (p. 84)

CRF: Vocabulary Builder Activity, Section 2

Teach the Big Idea: Master the Standards

Standards Proficiency

Declaring Independence HSS 8.1.2; HSS Analysis Skills: CS 1, HI 1

Materials: heavy paper or poster board, colored markers

1. **Teach** Ask students the Main Idea questions to teach this section.
2. **Apply** Have students create their own versions of the Declaration of Independence. Give each student heavy paper and colored markers. Instead of the text of the Declaration, have students write the main ideas stated in the document. Encourage groups to illustrate the ideas. **LS Verbal/Linguistic, Visual/Spatial**
3. **Review** As you review the section, ask for volunteers to explain the main ideas and ideals expressed in the Declaration.
4. **Practice/Homework** Have each student create a political cartoon that illustrates some of the reactions to the Declaration of Independence and its failure to recognize the rights of women and enslaved African Americans. **LS Visual/Spatial**

Alternative Assessment Handbook, Rubrics 27: Political Cartoons; and 37: Writing Assignments

Standards Focus

HSS 8.1.2

Means: Analyze the view of government stated in the Declaration of Independence, with a focus on individual rights such as equality and liberty.

Matters: America's government is based on the ideas expressed in the Declaration, such as freedom and individual rights.

Direct Teach

Main Idea

❶ Paine's *Common Sense*

Thomas Paine's *Common Sense* led many colonists to support independence.

Explain What arguments did Thomas Paine present in *Common Sense? Citizens should make the laws; colonies should be independent.*

Find Main Ideas What was the significance of *Common Sense? changed the way many colonists viewed the king and the colonies' right to rebel and declare independence*

HSS 8.1; HSS **Analysis Skills:** HI 1, HI 2

Info to Know

Reactions to the Declaration of Independence The language of the Declaration of Independence received both criticism and praise throughout the colonies. Some colonial newspapers pointed out the irony of such statements as "all men are created equal" in a slave-holding nation. One newspaper in South Carolina noted that as a clergyman read the Declaration of Independence aloud, a slave held a parasol over the clergyman's head and fanned his face.

go.hrw.com
Online Resources
KEYWORD: SS8 US3
ACTIVITY: Patriots vs. Loyalists Essay

Signing the Declaration of Independence

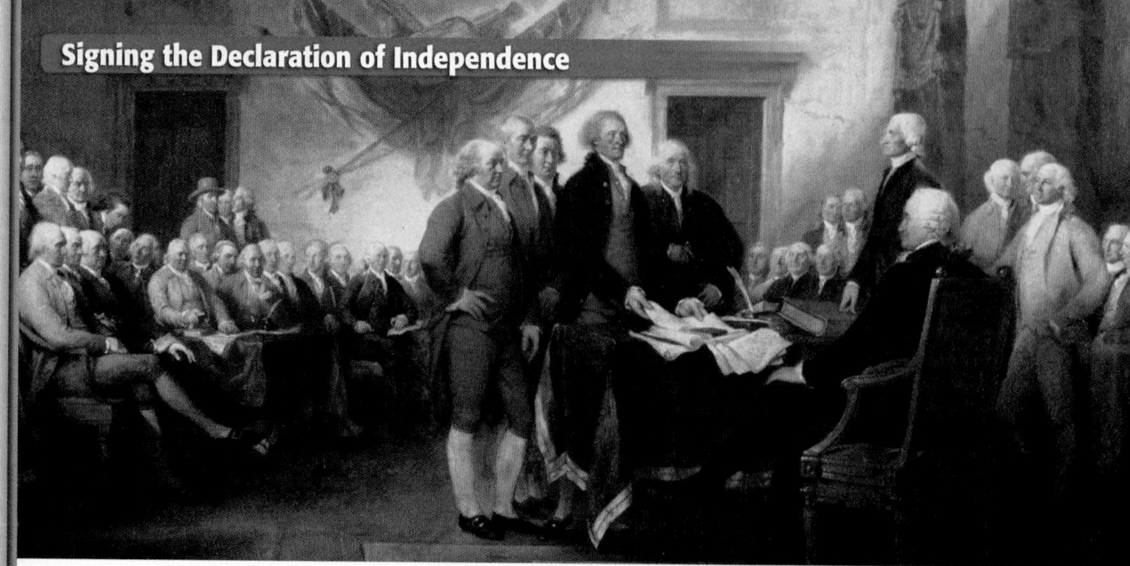

Independence for Colonies

Many colonial leaders agreed with Paine. They thought that the colonies should be free. In June 1776 the Second Continental Congress created a committee to write a document declaring the colonies' independence.

A New Philosophy of Government

THE IMPACT TODAY The Continental Congress voted for independence on July 2. However, because the Declaration was not approved until July 4, the fourth is celebrated today as Independence Day.

The committee members were John Adams, Benjamin Franklin, **Thomas Jefferson**, Robert R. Livingston, and Roger Sherman. Jefferson was the document's main author.

The **Declaration of Independence** formally announced the colonies' break from Great Britain. In doing so, it expressed three main ideas. The first idea Jefferson argued was that all men possess unalienable rights. He stated that these basic rights include "life, liberty, and the pursuit of happiness."

Jefferson's next argument was that King George III had violated the colonists' rights by passing unfair laws and interfering with colonial governments. Jefferson accused the king of taxing colonists without their consent and he felt that the large British army in the colonies violated colonists' rights.

Third, Jefferson argued that the colonies had the right to break from Britain. He was influenced by the Enlightenment idea of the social contract, which states that governments and rulers must protect the rights of citizens. In exchange, the people agree to be governed. Jefferson said that because King George III had broken the social contract, the colonists should no longer obey him.

On July 4, 1776, the Continental Congress approved the Declaration of Independence. This act broke all ties to the British Crown. The United States of America was born.

Choosing Sides

Colonists known as **Patriots** chose to fight for independence. **Loyalists** —sometimes called Tories—were those who remained loyal to Great Britain. Historians estimate that 40 to 45 percent of Americans were Patriots, while 20 to 30 percent were Loyalists. The rest were neutral.

Once the Declaration was signed, Loyalists and Patriots became opponents. More than 50,000 Loyalists fled during the Revolution. The war tore apart families. Even the great Patriot Benjamin Franklin had a Loyalist son.

Collaborative Learning

Reaching Standards

Common Sense Handbill

HSS 8.1.2; HSS **Analysis Skills:** HR 5, HI 1

1. Discuss with students how Thomas Paine's *Common Sense* influenced many colonists to support independence from Great Britain.
2. Organize students into pairs and ask them to imagine that they are colonists who were influenced by *Common Sense*. Have each pair create a handbill advertising *Common Sense* and supporting Thomas Paine's ideas. Suggest students address the following ideas: breaking away from Great Britain, the unfairness of the system of monarchy, and the idea that the people and not rulers should make the laws.
3. After students have finished, have them discuss if Paine's ideas have influenced them. **LS Verbal/Linguistic, Visual/Linguistic**

Alternative Assessment Handbook, Rubrics 2: Advertisements; and 14: Group Activity

Answers

Reading Check (p. 83) *possible answers—yes, because the king had abused his power, and citizens should have the right to self-rule; no, because the monarchy was a good system even if the current monarch was abusing the people's rights*

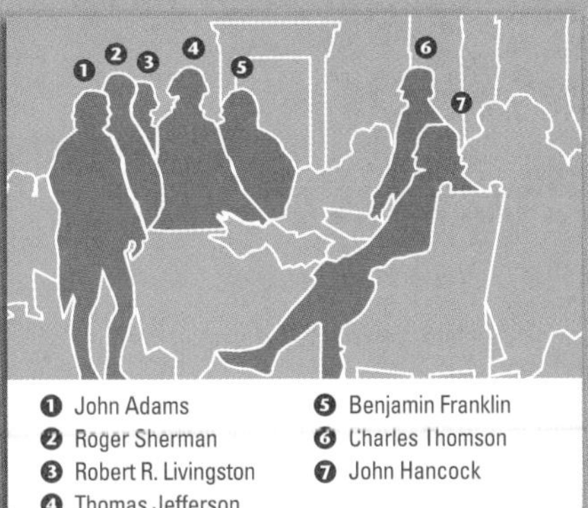

The Declaration of Independence was adopted on July 4, 1776. This painting shows 47 of the 56 signers of the document. The man sitting on the right is John Hancock, who was the president of the Second Continental Congress. He is accepting the Declaration from the committee that wrote it.

How realistic do you think this painting is?

Other Reactions to the Declaration

Today we can see that the Declaration ignored many colonists. At least one delegate's wife, Abigail Adams, tried to influence her husband to include women in the Declaration. Although many women were Patriots, the Declaration did not address their rights.

Nor did the Declaration recognize the rights of enslaved African Americans. The Revolution raised questions about whether slavery should exist in a land that valued liberty. Some Patriot writers had compared living under British rule to living as slaves. The difference between the ideals of liberty and the practice of slavery was a subject of great disagreement among Americans.

In July 1776 slavery was legal in all of the colonies. By the 1780s the New England colonies were taking steps to end slavery. Even so, the conflict over slavery continued long after the Revolutionary War had ended.

READING CHECK **Finding Main Ideas** What groups were unrepresented in the Declaration of Independence?

SUMMARY AND PREVIEW In 1776 the colonists declared their independence. The Declaration of Independence has inspired Americans throughout history with its message of freedom and equality. In order to maintain their freedom, however, colonists would have to battle the British army and win a war. In the next section you will learn about some of the battles that took place early during the Revolutionary War. Early in the war, it seemed as if the British would defeat the colonists.

Section 2 Assessment

go.hrw.com **Online Quiz** KEYWORD: SS8 HP3

Reviewing Ideas, Terms, and People HSS 8.1.2

1. **a. Identify** Who was **Thomas Paine**?
   b. Make Inferences Why do you think Thomas Paine originally published **Common Sense** anonymously?
   c. Elaborate Do you think that most colonists would have supported independence from Britain without Thomas Paine's publication of *Common Sense*? Explain your answer.
2. **a. Identify** What two sides emerged in response to the **Declaration of Independence**? What did each side favor?
   b. Explain What arguments did the authors of the Declaration of Independence give for declaring the colonies free from British control?
   c. Predict How might some groups use the Declaration of Independence in the future to gain rights?

Critical Thinking

3. **Summarizing** Copy the web below. Use it to identify the main ideas in the Declaration of Independence.

FOCUS ON SPEAKING

4. **Gathering Ideas about the Declaration of Independence** Imagine you were living at the time of the American Revolution. What was new and surprising about the colonists' actions? In one or two minutes, what is the most important thing you can say about the colonies' declaring independence?

Direct Teach

Main Idea

2 Independence for Colonies

Colonists had differing reactions to the Declaration of Independence.

Recall What was the significance of the Declaration of Independence? *It formally broke all ties between the colonies and Great Britain and created the United States of America.*

Summarize What were the three main arguments in the Declaration? *See the answer to Question 2b below.*

CRF: Biography Activity: John Hancock

HSS 8.1; HSS **Analysis Skills:** HR 5, HI 1

Review & Assess

Close

Have students discuss whether the colonists were justified in declaring independence.

Review

go.hrw.com Online Quiz, Section 2

Assess

SE Section 2 Assessment

PASS: Section 2 Quiz

Alternative Assessment Handbook

Reteach/Classroom Intervention

California Standards Review Workbook

Interactive Reader and Study Guide, Section 2

Interactive Skills Tutor CD-ROM

Section 2 Assessment Answers

1. **a.** author of *Common Sense,* a pamphlet that persuaded many colonists to favor independence
   b. possible answers—fear of punishment; to avoid the spotlight
   c. possible answers—Yes, England was being unfair; No, it had a significant impact on public opinion.
2. **a.** Patriots—chose to fight for independence; Loyalists—remained loyal to Great Britain
   b. All men possess the unalienable rights of "life, liberty, and the pursuit of happiness"; the king had violated colonists' rights by passing unfair laws; the king had broken the social contract with the colonists, so they had the right to break from Britain.
   c. by citing the ideals of equality and liberty stated in the document as support for rights
3. See the answer to Question 2b.
4. possible answer—In a bold move for the time, colonial leaders spoke out against the rule of monarchy, stated that the British government had denied their rights, and issued the Declaration of Independence to break from Britain and form the new nation of the United States of America.

Answers

Signing the Declaration of Independence *The event may have looked something like this representation, but this image was most likely not entirely accurate.*

Reading Check *women and enslaved African Americans*

Historical Documents

Primary Source

Reading Like a Historian

Declaration of Independence

To help students practice reading the Declaration of Independence like historians, ask them the following questions:

- Who wrote and signed the document? What do you know about these people?
- What basic ideas about people and government did the authors and signers hold? Did the people for whom the Declaration was being written hold the same views?
- Why did the authors write the document? What did they hope to achieve?

Activity The Case for Independence Discuss with students the way in which Jefferson and the other authors logically build a case for the right of the colonies to declare independence. Have students, working as a class or in small groups, create graphic organizers that show the logical progression of points in the case for independence.

LS Logical/Mathematical

HSS 8.1.2; **HSS Analysis Skills:** HR 4, HR 5, HI 1

Exploring the Document

Top: *The Declaration shows that it is possible for people to change the government in power when it no longer reflects the people's will.*

Bottom: *Students might point to words such as* absolute despotism, repeated injuries and usurpations, tyranny, refused, forbidden, *and* obstructed *and mention that these words convey a sense of injustice that Jefferson and the other members of the Continental Congress thought the colonists had suffered at the hands of Great Britain.*

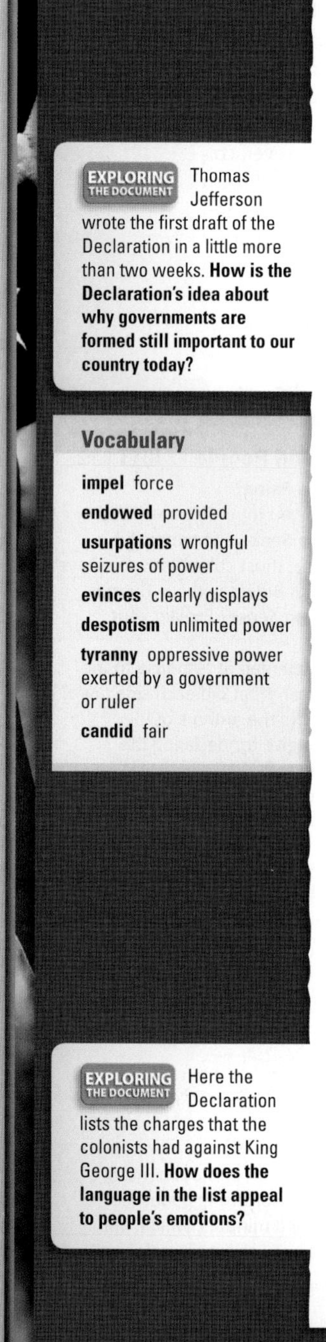

EXPLORING THE DOCUMENT Thomas Jefferson wrote the first draft of the Declaration in a little more than two weeks. **How is the Declaration's idea about why governments are formed still important to our country today?**

Vocabulary

impel force

endowed provided

usurpations wrongful seizures of power

evinces clearly displays

despotism unlimited power

tyranny oppressive power exerted by a government or ruler

candid fair

EXPLORING THE DOCUMENT Here the Declaration lists the charges that the colonists had against King George III. **How does the language in the list appeal to people's emotions?**

The Declaration of Independence

In Congress, July 4, 1776

The unanimous Declaration of the thirteen united States of America,

When in the Course of human events, it becomes necessary for one people to dissolve the political bands which have connected them with another, and to assume among the Powers of the earth, the separate and equal station to which the Laws of Nature and of Nature's God entitle them, a decent respect to the opinions of mankind requires that they should declare the causes which **impel** them to the separation.

We hold these truths to be self-evident, that all men are created equal, that they are **endowed** by their Creator with certain unalienable Rights, that among these are Life, Liberty, and the pursuit of Happiness. That to secure these rights, Governments are instituted among Men, deriving their just powers from the consent of the governed, That whenever any Form of Government becomes destructive of these ends, it is the Right of the People to alter or to abolish it, and to institute new Government, laying its foundation on such principles and organizing its powers in such form, as to them shall seem most likely to effect their Safety and Happiness. Prudence, indeed, will dictate that Governments long established should not be changed for light and transient causes; and accordingly all experience hath shown, that mankind are more disposed to suffer, while evils are sufferable, than to right themselves by abolishing the forms to which they are accustomed. But when a long train of abuses and **usurpations**, pursuing invariably the same Object **evinces** a design to reduce them under absolute **Despotism**, it is their right, it is their duty, to throw off such Government, and to provide new Guards for their future security.—Such has been the patient sufferance of these Colonies; and such is now the necessity which constrains them to alter their former Systems of Government. The history of the present King of Great Britain is a history of repeated injuries and usurpations, all having in direct object the establishment of an absolute **Tyranny** over these States. To prove this, let Facts be submitted to a **candid** world.

He has refused his Assent to Laws, the most wholesome and necessary for the public good.

He has forbidden his Governors to pass Laws of immediate and pressing importance, unless suspended in their operation till his Assent should be obtained; and when so suspended, he has utterly neglected to attend to them.

Differentiating Instruction for Universal Access

English-Language Learners

Standards Proficiency | Standard English Mastery

Materials: translations of the Declaration of Independence in students' native languages (optional)

1. Help students with the difficult vocabulary and phrasing in the Declaration of Independence by writing short, simple summaries of each paragraph or portion of the document.
2. Once students understand the meaning of a portion of the text, help them work through the actual wording. Have students list any words they do not understand. As students work, circulate and help students define the words they listed. If possible, pair English learners with English speakers to complete the activity.
3. **Extend** Provide translations of the Declaration of Independence in students' native languages. Have students use the translations to help them understand the English version.

LS Verbal/Linguistic

HSS 8.1.2

Alternative Assessment Handbook, Rubrics 1: Acquiring Information

He has refused to pass other Laws for the accommodation of large districts of people, unless those people would **relinquish** the right of Representation in the Legislature, a right **inestimable** to them and **formidable** to tyrants only.

He has called together legislative bodies at places unusual, uncomfortable, and distant from the depository of their Public Records, for the sole purpose of fatiguing them into compliance with his measures.

He has dissolved Representative Houses repeatedly, for opposing with manly firmness his invasions on the rights of the people.

He has refused for a long time, after such dissolutions, to cause others to be elected; whereby the Legislative Powers, incapable of **Annihilation**, have returned to the People at large for their exercise; the State remaining in the mean time exposed to all the dangers of invasion from without, and **convulsions** within.

He has endeavored to prevent the population of these States; for that purpose obstructing the Laws of **Naturalization of Foreigners**; refusing to pass others to encourage their migration hither, and raising the conditions of new **Appropriations of Lands**.

He has obstructed the Administration of Justice, by refusing his Assent to Laws for establishing Judiciary Powers.

He has made Judges dependent on his Will alone, for the **tenure** of their offices, and the amount and payment of their salaries.

He has erected **a multitude of** New Offices, and sent hither swarms of Officers to harass our people, and eat out their substance.

He has kept among us, in times of peace, Standing Armies without the Consent of our legislature.

He has affected to render the Military independent of and superior to the Civil Power.

He has combined with others to subject us to a jurisdiction foreign to our constitution, and unacknowledged by our laws; giving his Assent to their Acts of pretended legislation:

For **quartering** large bodies of armed troops among us:

For protecting them, by a mock Trial, from Punishment for any Murders which they should commit on the Inhabitants of these States:

For cutting off our Trade with all parts of the world:

For imposing taxes on us without our Consent:

For depriving us in many cases, of the benefits of Trial by Jury:

Vocabulary

relinquish release, yield
inestimable priceless
formidable causing dread
annihilation destruction
convulsions violent disturbances
naturalization of foreigners the process by which foreign-born persons become citizens
appropriations of lands setting aside land for settlement
tenure term
a multitude of many
quartering lodging, housing

Colonists had been angry over British tax policies since just after the French and Indian War. **Why were the colonists protesting British tax policies?**

Historical Documents

Info to Know

Signing the Declaration On July 1, 1776, three days before the Declaration of Independence was signed, just nine of the colonies firmly supported independence. Because a vote was to be taken on July 2, supporters of independence spent the day trying to convince opposing delegates of the need for self government. One supporter, Richard Henry Lee, finally swayed South Carolina delegate Edward Rutledge, who agreed to vote for independence if the delegates from Pennsylvania and Delaware did so as well.

The following morning was spent waiting for Delaware delegate Caesar Rodney, who had been home caring for his sick wife. Rodney finally arrived, covered with mud after a frantic ride over rain-soaked roads. He cast his vote in favor of independence, and the delegates of South Carolina and Pennsylvania followed suit.

Exploring the Document

They were angry that they were being taxed without representation.

Historical Documents

Info to Know

Celebrating Independence Day In a letter, John Adams declared that July 2, the day the Continental Congress voted for independence, should be celebrated with "poems and parade, with shows, games, sports, guns, bells, bonfires, and illuminations." However, the nation celebrates Independence Day on July 4, the day the Continental Congress approved the final draft of the Declaration. Most members did not sign the document until August 2.

The Declaration and American Soldiers After the Declaration of Independence was passed by the Continental Congress, the members requested copies be made for the commanders of the troops fighting the Revolutionary War. Official word of the Declaration of Independence reached General George Washington in New York on July 9, 1776. He then ordered that all troops be gathered for a reading of the document in order to help boost their morale.

Exploring the Document

Tyrant *means a ruler who abuses his or her right to rule by treating subjects unfairly and harshly.*

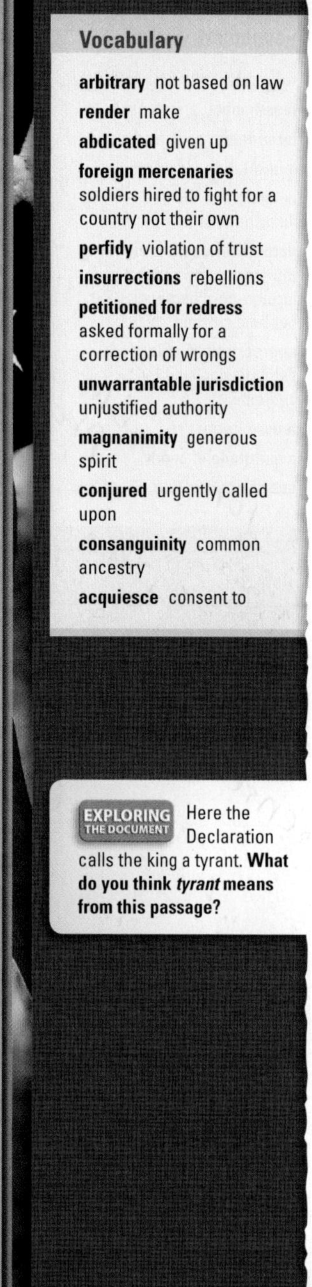

Vocabulary

arbitrary not based on law
render make
abdicated given up
foreign mercenaries soldiers hired to fight for a country not their own
perfidy violation of trust
insurrections rebellions
petitioned for redress asked formally for a correction of wrongs
unwarrantable jurisdiction unjustified authority
magnanimity generous spirit
conjured urgently called upon
consanguinity common ancestry
acquiesce consent to

EXPLORING THE DOCUMENT Here the Declaration calls the king a tyrant. **What do you think *tyrant* means from this passage?**

For transporting us beyond Seas to be tried for pretended offences:

For abolishing the free System of English Laws in a neighboring Province, establishing therein an **Arbitrary** government, and enlarging its Boundaries so as to **render** it at once an example and fit instrument for introducing the same absolute rule into these Colonies:

For taking away our Charters, abolishing our most valuable Laws, and altering fundamentally the Forms of our Governments:

For suspending our own Legislature, and declaring themselves invested with Power to legislate for us in all cases whatsoever.

He has **abdicated** Government here, by declaring us out of his Protection and waging War against us.

He has plundered our seas, ravaged our Coasts, burnt our towns, and destroyed the lives of our people.

He is at this time transporting large armies of **foreign mercenaries** to complete the works of death, desolation and tyranny, already begun with circumstances of Cruelty & **perfidy** scarcely paralleled in the most barbarous ages, and totally unworthy the Head of a civilized nation.

He has constrained our fellow Citizens taken Captive on the high Seas to bear Arms against their Country, to become the executioners of their friends and Brethren, or to fall themselves by their Hands.

He has excited domestic **insurrections** amongst us, and has endeavored to bring on the inhabitants of our frontiers, the merciless Indian Savages, whose known rule of warfare, is an undistinguished destruction of all ages, sexes and conditions.

In every stage of these Oppressions We have **Petitioned for Redress** in the most humble terms: Our repeated Petitions have been answered only by repeated injury. A Prince, whose character is thus marked by every act which may define a Tyrant, is unfit to be the ruler of a free People.

Nor have We been wanting in attention to our British brethren. We have warned them from time to time of attempts by their legislature to extend an **unwarrantable jurisdiction** over us. We have reminded them of the circumstances of our emigration and settlement here. We have appealed to their native justice and **magnanimity**, and we have **conjured** them by the ties of our common kindred to disavow these usurpations, which, would inevitably interrupt our connections and correspondence. They too have been deaf to the voice of justice and of **consanguinity**. We must, therefore, **acquiesce** in the necessity, which denounces our Separation, and hold them, as we hold the rest of mankind, Enemies in War, in Peace Friends.

Collaborative Learning

Standards Proficiency

Celebrating the Declaration of Independence HSS 8.1.2

Prep Required

1. Have students conduct research to find out some of the ways in which their community celebrates Independence Day. Have students share their findings. Then ask volunteers to share some of their family traditions for the holiday.
2. Next, have students discuss ways to celebrate not only independence but also the ideals expressed in the Declaration of Independence. Have students work as a class to list activities.
3. Have the class prepare to hold a celebration of the ideals in the Declaration of Independence. Have students choose activities and decorations and work in committees to prepare them.
4. Have students hold their Declaration of Independence celebration. LS **Interpersonal, Kinesthetic, Verbal/Linguistic**

Alternative Assessment Handbook, Rubrics 14: Group Activity; and 30: Research

We, therefore, the Representatives of the united States of America, in General Congress, Assembled, appealing to the Supreme Judge of the world for the **rectitude** of our intentions, do, in the Name, and by Authority of the good People of these Colonies, solemnly publish and declare, That these United Colonies are, and of Right ought to be Free and Independent States; that they are Absolved from all Allegiance to the British Crown, and that all political connection between them and the State of Great Britain, is and ought to be totally dissolved; and that as Free and Independent States, they have full Power to levy War, conclude Peace, contract Alliances, establish Commerce, and to do all other Acts and Things which Independent States may of right do. And for the support of this Declaration, with a firm reliance on the Protection of Divine Providence, we mutually pledge to each other our Lives, our Fortunes and our sacred Honor.

John Hancock
Button Gwinnett
Lyman Hall
George Walton
William Hooper
Joseph Hewes
John Penn
Edward Rutledge
Thomas Heyward, Jr.
Thomas Lynch, Jr.
Arthur Middleton
Samuel Chase
William Paca
Thomas Stone
Charles Carroll of Carrollton
George Wythe
Richard Henry Lee
Thomas Jefferson

Benjamin Harrison
Thomas Nelson, Jr.
Francis Lightfoot Lee
Carter Braxton
Robert Morris
Benjamin Rush
Benjamin Franklin
John Morton
George Clymer
James Smith
George Taylor
James Wilson
George Ross
Caesar Rodney
George Read
Thomas McKean
William Floyd
Philip Livingston
Francis Lewis

Lewis Morris
Richard Stockton
John Witherspoon
Francis Hopkinson
John Hart
Abraham Clark
Josiah Bartlett
William Whipple
Samuel Adams
John Adams
Robert Treat Paine
Elbridge Gerry
Stephen Hopkins
William Ellery
Roger Sherman
Samuel Huntington
William Williams
Oliver Wolcott
Matthew Thornton

Vocabulary

rectitude rightness

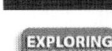

EXPLORING THE DOCUMENT Here is where the document declares the independence of the colonies. **Whose authority does the Congress use to declare independence?**

EXPLORING THE DOCUMENT The Congress adopted the final draft of the Declaration of Independence on July 4, 1776. A formal copy, written on parchment paper, was signed on August 2, 1776.

EXPLORING THE DOCUMENT The following is part of a passage that the Congress removed from Jefferson's original draft: "He has waged cruel war against human nature itself, violating its most sacred rights of life and liberty in the persons of a distant people who never offended him, captivating and carrying them into slavery in another hemisphere, or to incur miserable death in their transportation thither." **Why do you think the Congress deleted this passage?**

Historical Documents

Info to Know

The Signers The 56 signers of the Declaration of Independence shared many characteristics. Almost all were Protestant white males who were fairly wealthy. In addition, 48 of the signers were born in America.

Did you know . . .

As president of the Second Continental Congress, John Hancock was the first delegate to sign the Declaration of Independence. He signed his name largely and it stands out from the other names. According to legend, Hancock wanted to make certain that King George III would see his name. As a result, the name *John Hancock* has become a slang expression for a person's signature.

CRF: Biography Activity: John Hancock

Exploring the Document

Top: *"by Authority of the good People of these colonies"*

Bottom: *possible answers—Slavery was controversial, and many colonies—particularly those in the South—did not wish to abolish it; delegates from pro-slavery colonies would likely not have agreed to sign the Declaration if the passage had remained.*

Preteach

Bellringer

If YOU were there . . . Use the **Daily Bellringer Transparency** to help students answer the question.

 Daily Bellringer Transparency, Section 3

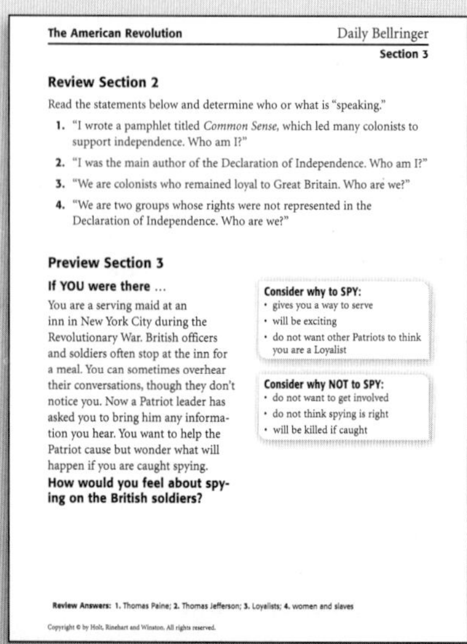

The American Revolution Daily Bellringer
Section 3

Review Section 2

Read the statements below and determine who or what is "speaking."

1. "I wrote a pamphlet titled *Common Sense*, which led many colonists to support independence. Who am I?"
2. "I was the main author of the Declaration of Independence. Who am I?"
3. "We are colonists who remained loyal to Great Britain. Who are we?"
4. "We are two groups whose rights were not represented in the Declaration of Independence. Who are we?"

Preview Section 3

If YOU were there ...

You are a serving maid at an inn in New York City during the Revolutionary War. British officers and soldiers often stop at the inn for a meal. You can sometimes overhear their conversations, though they don't notice you. Now a Patriot leader has asked you to bring him any information you hear. You want to help the Patriot cause but wonder what will happen if you are caught spying.

How would you feel about spying on the British soldiers?

Consider why to SPY:
- gives you a way to serve
- will be exciting
- do not want other Patriots to think you are a Loyalist

Consider why NOT to SPY:
- do not want to get involved
- do not think spying is right
- will be killed if caught

Review Answers: 1. Thomas Paine; 2. Thomas Jefferson; 3. Loyalists; 4. women and slaves

Academic Vocabulary

Review with students the high-use academic term in this section.

strategy a plan for fighting a battle or war (p. 94)

CRF: Vocabulary Builder Activity, Section 3

Standards Focus

HSS 8.1.3

Means: Analyze the effect of the American Revolution on other nations, with a focus on France.

Matters: Other nations supported America's efforts for independence and helped in the fight against Great Britain. Today, events in the United States—in times of peace and war—continue to affect relations with other nations.

SECTION 3

Patriots Gain New Hope

What You Will Learn...

Main Ideas

1. Many Americans contributed to the war effort.
2. Despite early defeats by Britain, the Patriots claimed some victories.
3. Saratoga was a turning point in the war.
4. The winter at Valley Forge tested the strength of Patriot forces.
5. The war continued at sea and in the West.

The Big Idea

Patriot forces faced many obstacles in the war against Britain.

Key Terms and People

mercenaries, *p. 92*
Battle of Trenton, *p. 93*
Battle of Saratoga, *p. 94*
Marquis de Lafayette, *p. 95*
Bernardo de Gálvez, *p. 95*
John Paul Jones, *p. 97*
George Rogers Clark, *p. 97*

HSS 8.1.3 Analyze how the American Revolution affected other nations, especially France.

If YOU were there...

You are a serving maid at an inn in New York City during the Revolutionary War. British officers and soldiers often stop at the inn for a meal. You can sometimes overhear their conversations, though they don't notice you. Now a Patriot leader has asked you to bring him any information you hear. You want to help the Patriot cause but wonder what will happen if you are caught spying.

How would you feel about spying on the British soldiers?

BUILDING BACKGROUND Colonists from many different backgrounds worked for the Patriot cause. Although men did most of the actual fighting, women like the maid above also made important contributions. Women and those too old to fight also kept farms and shops running, providing food and supplies. In spite of the colonists' efforts, winning the war was a great challenge.

Americans and the War Effort

During the war more than 230,000 soldiers served in the Continental Army. The typical soldier was young, often under the legal age of 16. Most had little money, no property, and few opportunities in life. The army offered low pay, often rotten food, hard work, cold, heat, poor clothing and shelter, harsh discipline, and a high chance of becoming a casualty. Yet for some young men and boys, it represented change and excitement.

Finding and keeping dedicated soldiers throughout the long, hard war would be a constant chore. In time, the Continental Congress required states to supply soldiers. Men who could afford it often paid others, such as slaves or apprentices, to fight in their places.

One question facing George Washington was whether to recruit African Americans. Many white southerners opposed the idea, and at first Washington banned African Americans from serving. When the British promised freedom to any slave who fought on their side,

Teach the Big Idea: Master the Standards

Standards Proficiency

Patriots Gain New Hope HSS 8.1.3; HSS **Analysis Skills:** CS 1, HI 1, HI 2

1. **Teach** Ask students the Main Idea questions to teach this section.
2. **Apply** Create a two-column chart for students to see. Label the columns *Major Battles* and *Challenges*. Have students copy the chart and complete it by listing and describing the major battles in this section. Then have students describe the challenges the Patriots faced at various stages. **LS Verbal/Linguistic, Visual/Spatial**
3. **Review** As you review the section, have students share information from their charts.
4. **Practice/Homework** Ask students to imagine that they are a Patriot soldier at one of the battles listed in their charts. Have them write a letter home describing their impression of the battle. **LS Intrapersonal, Verbal/Linguistic**

Alternative Assessment Handbook, Rubrics 7: Charts; and 25: Personal Letters

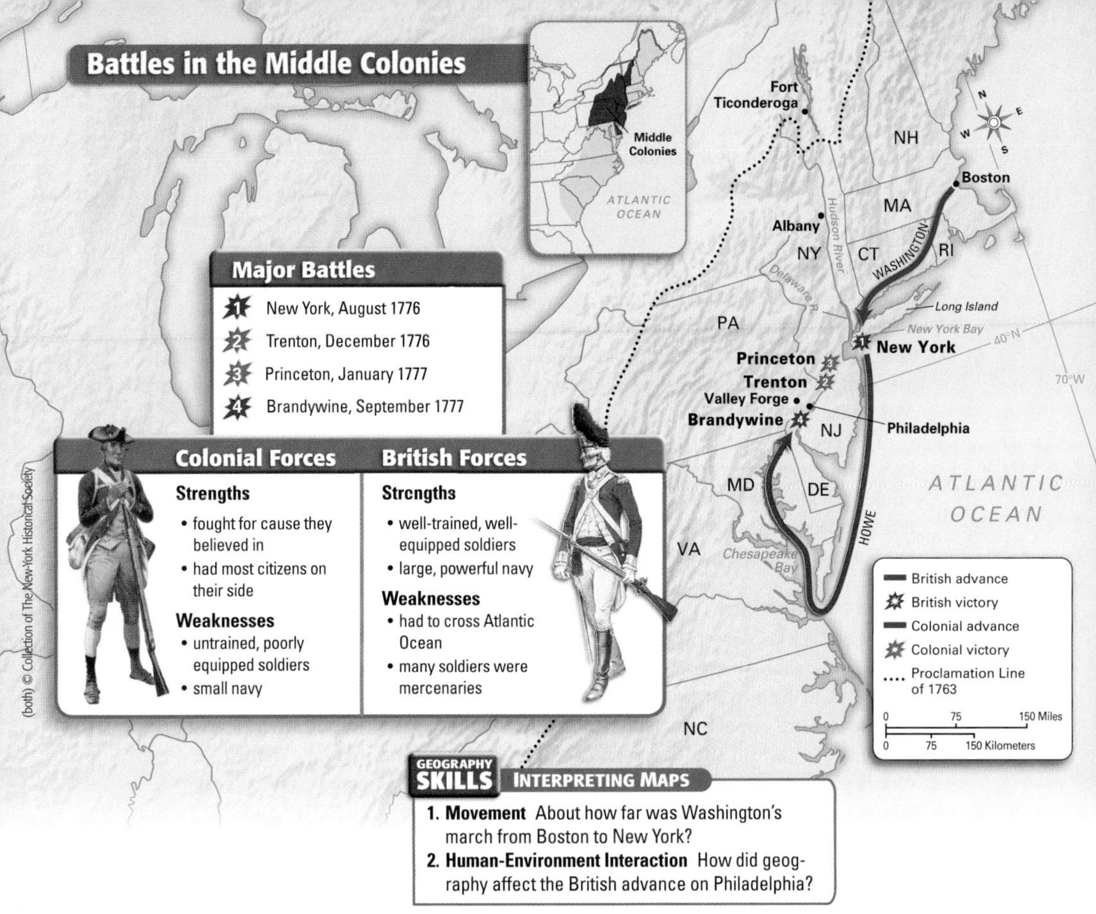

GEOGRAPHY SKILLS INTERPRETING MAPS

1. **Movement** About how far was Washington's march from Boston to New York?
2. **Human-Environment Interaction** How did geography affect the British advance on Philadelphia?

however, thousands signed on. In response, the Continental Army began allowing free African Americans to serve.

Native Americans fought on both sides during the war. Indians who had been pushed off their lands by colonial settlers aided the British. Mohawk leader Thayendanegea (thah-yuhn-dah-ne-GAY-uh) persuaded many Iroquois to support the British. The Patriots had to work hard just to keep other American Indians neutral.

While men served as soldiers, many Patriot women ran farms and businesses. Others helped the army by raising money for supplies or making clothing. Women served as messengers, nurses, and spies. A few disguised themselves as men to fight in the war.

Perhaps the most famous woman to serve in the war was Mary Ludwig Hays. She earned the nickname Molly Pitcher by bringing water to the troops. When her husband was wounded in a 1778 battle, she took his place loading cannons. Another woman, Deborah Sampson, dressed as a man and fought in several battles.

READING CHECK **Summarizing** How did various groups of colonists contribute to the war effort?

THE IMPACT TODAY

Women are still banned from ground combat, but in Operation Iraqi Freedom women operated warships and flew combat jets and helicopters for the first time in a major air-ground conflict.

Direct Teach

Main Idea

1 Americans and the War Effort

Many Americans contributed to the war effort.

Explain Why did the Continental Army begin allowing free African Americans to serve? *to counter Britain's promise of freedom to any slave who joined the British*

Summarize In what ways did women help the Patriot cause? *ran farms and businesses; raised money and made clothing for army; served as messengers, nurses, and spies*

Make Judgments In your opinion, should wealthy Patriots have been allowed to pay substitutes to fight in their place? *Answers will vary but should indicate an understanding of the economy and society of the time.*

CRF: Biography Activity: Phillis Wheatley

Map Transparency: Battles in the Middle Colonies

HSS Analysis Skills: HI 1

Interpreting Charts

Colonial and British Forces

Evaluating Who do you think had the advantage at the start of the war—the British or the Patriot forces? *possible answers—the British, because they were well-trained and well-equipped; the Americans, because they were fighting in their own land for a cause in which they believed*

Critical Thinking: Finding Main Ideas

Standards Proficiency

Patriot Recruitment Posters

HSS Analysis Skills: HI 1

Materials: construction paper or small poster board, colored markers and pens

1. Have students create Patriot recruitment posters to encourage enlistment in the Continental Army.
2. Students' posters should explain the benefits of enlisting, the advantages the Patriots have, and why the war is being fought. Encourage students to include one or more illustrations to enhance their posters.
3. As an option, have students create a Patriot recruitment poster directed at a specific group, such as free African Americans, Native Americans, or women. The poster should reflect the issues the group faced during the war and the ways in which the group contributed to the Patriot cause.
4. Ask volunteers to share their posters with the class. **LS Visual/Spatial**

Alternative Assessment Handbook, Rubric 28: Posters

Answers

Interpreting Maps 1. *about 200 miles;* 2. *To get close to Philadelphia, the British had to travel far south by sea and then go north over land.*

Reading Check *Young, white men enlisted; some free African Americans and Native Americans joined the Patriots; women helped raise money and make clothes, and some served as messengers, nurses, and spies.*

Direct Teach

Main Idea

❷ Early Defeats

Despite early defeats by Britain, the Patriots claimed some victories.

Recall What early defeats did the Patriots experience? *Canada—defeated at Quebec; New York—British slowly drove the Patriots out of New York and into New Jersey.*

Draw Conclusions Why do you think the Patriots were defeated in New York? *possible answers—They were outnumbered; British soldiers were better trained and equipped.*

Make Judgments Do you think the Patriots should have invaded British Canada? Why or why not? *possible answers—Yes, a victory there would have been worth the risk; no, the Patriots did not have enough men and supplies to risk on such an endeavor.*

CRF: Biography Activity: Haym Salomon

HSS 8.1.3; **HSS Analysis Skills:** HI 1

Checking for Understanding

True or False Answer each statement *T* if it is true or *F* if it is false. If false, explain why.

1. Hessians fought for the British because they were loyal to Britain. *F, The Hessians were mercenaries who fought for money, not loyalty.*
2. Howe's British force was much better equipped than Washington's Patriot force. *T*
3. General George Washington's successful defense against the Hessian attack at Trenton was an important Patriot victory. *F, Washington launched the attack at Trenton.*

Early Defeats

The War for Independence did not explode with "the shot heard 'round the world." Instead, it gathered steam throughout 1776, becoming more intense and deadly.

Defeat in Canada

Some Patriots thought British-controlled Canada should be the "14th colony." At Quebec, General Richard Montgomery joined forces with General Benedict Arnold. Yet neither army had cannons with which to bring down Quebec's high walls.

The generals decided to take a chance. They would wait for a snowstorm, hoping it would provide cover for a bold advance. The attack failed, and Montgomery was killed. The Patriots' hopes of taking Canada faded.

Defeat in New York

New York City became the first major battleground. General Washington had moved his troops to New York, expecting the British arrival. Sure enough, in late June 1776, a large fleet of British ships approached New York Bay. Led by General William Howe, the British force pushed the Continental Army off of Long Island.

Howe's 32,000 soldiers were much better equipped than Washington's 23,000 men, most of whom were militia. The Patriot general had to use all of his leadership skills just to save his army.

In a series of battles, Howe pounded the Continental Army, forcing it to retreat farther and farther. The Redcoats captured many Patriots as well as valuable supplies. After several months of fighting, the British pushed Washington across the Hudson River into New Jersey. Howe's revenge for his defeat at Boston was complete.

During the New York campaigns, a young Connecticut officer named Nathan Hale went behind British lines to get secret information. Seized by the British with documents hidden in the soles of his shoes, Hale was ordered to be hanged. Before his execution, he is said to have declared, "I regret that I have but one life to lose for my country."

Crossing the Delaware

George Washington and his troops crossed the partially frozen Delaware River on the night of December 25, 1776. This daring act led to a key Patriot victory at the Battle of Trenton. German American artist Emanuel Leutze created this famous painting of the event in 1851. *Washington Crossing the Delaware* now hangs in the Metropolitan Museum of Art in New York City.

What feelings do you think Leutze wanted to inspire with this painting?

Victory in New Jersey

In November 1776 the tattered Continental Army was on the run, retreating through New Jersey. Washington's remaining 6,000 men were tired and discouraged. The one-year contract for many of them would end on December 31. Who would re-enlist in this losing army, and who would volunteer to replace the soldiers who left? Washington's army—the hope of the Revolution—was in danger of simply vanishing.

Thinking that the rebellion would end soon, Howe left New Jersey in the hands of soldiers from the German state of Hesse. The Hessians were **mercenaries** — foreign soldiers who fight not out of loyalty, but for pay.

On December 7 Washington retreated across the Delaware River into Pennsylvania. Even with 2,000 fresh militiamen from Pennsylvania, the Patriots were near the end. "These are the times that try men's souls," wrote Thomas Paine in the first of a series of pamphlets called *The American Crisis*, which he began in late 1776.

Critical Thinking: Analyzing/Evaluating Information

Standards Proficiency

Analyzing Patriot Battle Strategies

HSS Analysis Skills: HI 1, HI 2

1. Organize students into small groups and have each group brainstorm different strategies that an army might use to defeat a more powerful opponent. After a brief amount of time, have each group share some of its ideas with the class.
2. Draw a chart with two columns and five rows. Label the columns *Main Strategy* and *Evaluation*. Label the rows *Quebec, New York, Trenton, Princeton,* and *Saratoga*.
3. Have each group copy the chart and describe the Patriots' main strategy at each battle. Then have the groups analyze and write an evaluation of each strategy. Was it the best strategy to use in that situation? Why or why not? Have each group share some of its evaluations with the class. **LS Interpersonal, Verbal/Linguistic**

Alternative Assessment Handbook, Rubrics 7: Charts; and 16: Judging Information

Answers

Crossing the Delaware *possible answer—feelings of patriotism, courage, and pride*

Without a victory, Washington would lose his army. He decided to take a big chance and go on the **offensive**. The Americans would attack the Hessians at Trenton, New Jersey.

On Christmas night, 1776, with a winter storm lashing about them, Washington and 2,400 soldiers silently rowed across the ice-clogged Delaware River. As morning broke, the men, short on supplies and many with no shoes, marched through the snow to reach the enemy camp.

The Hessians, having celebrated the holiday the night before, were fast asleep when the Patriots sprang upon them. American soldiers took more than 900 prisoners. This battle, called the **Battle of Trenton,** was an important Patriot victory.

British general Charles Cornwallis rushed to stop Washington as he marched northeast to Princeton. On the night of January 2, 1777, the Patriots left their campfires burning, then slipped into the darkness and circled behind the British troops. In the morning, Washington attacked. A local resident witnessed it:

> "The battle was plainly seen from our door ... and the guns went off so quick and many together that they could not be numbered ... Almost as soon as the firing was over, our house was filled and surrounded with General Washington's men."
>
> —Anonymous, quoted in *Voices of 1776* by Richard Wheeler

FOCUS ON READING

You might not know what *offensive* means in this context. The sentence after the word explains that here it means "attacking."

As Washington watched the Redcoats flee Princeton, he cheered, "It is a fine fox chase, my boys!" Now, new soldiers joined the chase. Others re-enlisted. The army—and the Revolution—was saved.

READING CHECK **Summarizing** Explain General Washington's strategy at the Battle of Trenton.

Direct Teach

Main Idea

❷ Early Defeats

Despite early defeats by Britain, the Patriots claimed some victories.

Identify Who were the Hessians? *mercenaries from the German state of Hesse who fought for the British*

Contrast How did the Patriot's actions at the Battle of Trenton differ from their actions at New York? *Patriots were on the defensive in New York, but on the offensive at Trenton.*

Evaluate Why do you think more Americans joined the Patriot efforts after the Battle of Trenton? *possible answers—They were inspired by the Patriot victory; they felt America had a chance against the British.*

CRF: Literature Activity: *The Crisis, No. 1,* by Thomas Paine

HSS 8.1.3; **HSS** **Analysis Skills:** HI 1

Analyzing Visuals

Crossing the Delaware

1. Why do you think this scene was so popular? *possible answer—The scene made Americans feel patriotic and proud because of its show of American heroism and endurance.*
2. What color scheme did Leutze use in his painting? Why do you think he chose this scheme? *red, white, and blue; symbolizes the United States; arouses feelings of patriotism*

Differentiating Instruction for Universal Access

Advanced Learners/GATE — Exceeding Standards

Materials: butcher paper, art supplies, colored pens

1. Organize students into small groups and assign each group one of the following battles: Trenton, Princeton, or Saratoga.
2. Instruct each group to draw a map illustrating what the Patriot battle plans might have looked like. Have students refer to their texts for help. Maps should include a legend identifying troop movements and Patriot and British forces.
3. Next, have each group write a paragraph explaining one of the following: the outcome and significance of the battle; an analysis of the Patriot strategies at the battle; and, for the Battle of Saratoga, why the battle was a turning point in the war. **LS** **Verbal/Linguistic, Visual/Spatial**

HSS 8.1.3; **HSS** **Analysis Skills:** CS 3

Alternative Assessment Handbook, Rubrics 20: Map Creation; and 42: Writing to Inform

Answers

Reading Check *He went on the offensive and launched a surprise attack against the Hessians on Christmas Day, when they were still asleep from celebrating the holiday the night before.*

Direct Teach

Main Idea

❸ Turning Point at Saratoga

Saratoga was a turning point in the war.

Describe What was the British strategy for cutting off New England? *British general John Burgoyne's army would move south from Canada, take Fort Ticonderoga, and go on to Albany. General Howe's army would sail up the Hudson River from New York City to meet Burgoyne's army.*

Analyze What essential element of this strategy proved to be a weakness? *It required perfect timing in a day when communication was limited.*

Evaluate What role did chance play in the Patriot victory at Saratoga? *British general Howe chose not to follow the plan, which left Burgoyne's army outnumbered and alone.*

Map Transparency: Battle of Saratoga

HSS 8.1.3; HSS **Analysis Skills:** HI 1, HI 2, HI 4

Biography

Benedict Arnold (1741–1801) Until 1779, Benedict Arnold served the Patriots with distinction and honor, participating in the attack on Quebec and leading troops in the Battle of Saratoga. In 1778, General George Washington made Arnold the commander of Philadelphia. There, however, Arnold held secret meetings with the British, in which he made plans to surrender West Point to them. When Arnold's plan was discovered, he escaped on a British ship and later fled to Britain. Despite his service to their country, even the British looked down on Arnold as a traitor. Ever since, the name *Benedict Arnold* has been a synonym for traitor.

Turning Point at Saratoga

The two quick defeats stung the British. In the spring of 1777, they wanted a victory.

British General John Burgoyne came up with a plan to push through New York, capture the Hudson River valley, and cut off New England from the other colonies. The strategy required perfect timing.

ACADEMIC VOCABULARY
strategy a plan for fighting a battle or war

According to the plan, Burgoyne's army would invade from Canada, recapture Fort Ticonderoga, and sweep south to Albany. General Howe, in New York City, would sail up the Hudson River to meet him, strangling New England.

Indeed, Burgoyne took Ticonderoga in early July and then headed toward Albany. Here the timing went wrong for the British. Unknown to Burgoyne, Howe had his own plans. He left New York, sailed up the Chesapeake Bay, and captured the colonial capital of Philadelphia. Delegates to the Continental Congress were forced to flee.

Meanwhile, Burgoyne's wagons and cannons became bogged down in thick forests. The Patriots had chopped down large trees and dammed rivers to create obstacles. All along the route, militiamen swarmed out of nowhere to attack the Redcoats. As Burgoyne neared Saratoga, New York, he found himself alone and outnumbered.

When fighting broke out near Saratoga, the Americans scored a major victory. Patriot General Horatio Gates crushed the British attempts to advance. Benedict Arnold then led a bold charge that forced the British to retreat. Burgoyne found himself surrounded. On October 17, 1777, he surrendered his entire army to General Gates.

The **Battle of Saratoga** in New York was the greatest victory yet for the American forces. Morale soared. Patriot James Thacher wrote, "This event will make one of the most brilliant pages of American history."

Battle of Saratoga

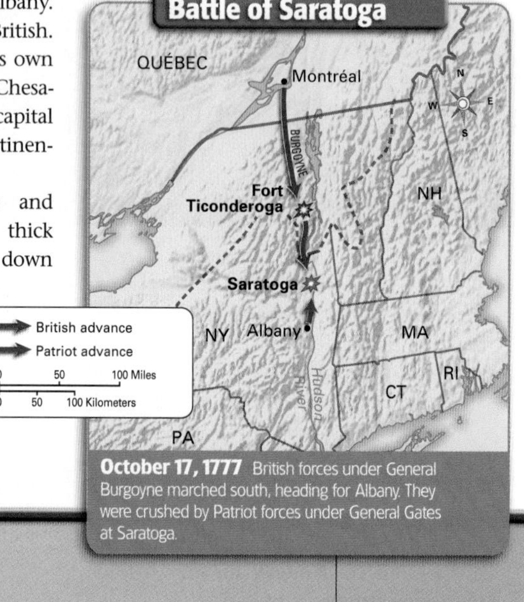

October 17, 1777 British forces under General Burgoyne marched south, heading for Albany. They were crushed by Patriot forces under General Gates at Saratoga.

Time Line
The Patriots Gain Ground

1776

December 27, 1776 Patriots win the Battle of Trenton.

1777

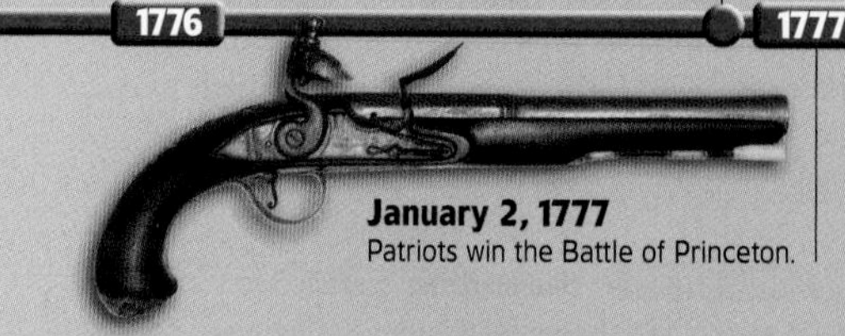

January 2, 1777 Patriots win the Battle of Princeton.

July 27, 1777 Marquis de Lafayette arrives in Philadelphia to offer his assistance to the Patriot cause.

Critical Thinking: Identifying Cause and Effect

Standards Proficiency

Battle of Saratoga

HSS 8.1.3; HSS **Analysis Skills:** CS 1, HI 1, HI 2

1. Discuss the major events leading to the Patriot victory at the Battle of Saratoga.
2. Have students create a cause-and-effect chart illustrating how the Battle of Saratoga became a turning point in the war. Remind students to include information on how the victory at Saratoga affected the Patriots and U.S. relations with foreign nations, such as France and Spain.
3. Next, ask students to annotate their charts with notes identifying ways that foreign aid changed the course of the Revolutionary War.
4. Ask for volunteers to share information from their charts. Create a correct master chart for students to see. LS **Verbal/Linguistic, Visual/Spatial**

Alternative Assessment Handbook, Rubrics 6: Cause and Effect; and 7: Charts

The victory at Saratoga gave the Patriots something they had been desperately seeking: foreign help. It came from Britain's powerful enemies, France and Spain. Britain's old ally, Holland, also joined the fight on the side of the Patriots.

Help from France

Benjamin Franklin, a skilled diplomat, had gone to France in 1776 to work out details for an alliance. The Battle of Saratoga finally persuaded the French that the Americans could win the war. In May 1778 the Continental Congress ratified a treaty of support with France.

A Frenchman and a Prussian

"The welfare of America is closely bound up with the welfare of mankind," declared a young French nobleman, the **Marquis de Lafayette**. Inspired by the ideas of the Revolution, Lafayette came to America in the summer of 1777. He volunteered to serve in the Continental Army without pay. Although he spoke little English, had not seen battle, and was not yet 20 years old, Lafayette received the high post of major general.

Though wounded in his first battle outside Philadelphia, Lafayette went on to become a skilled military officer. In addition to his military service, he contributed $200,000 of his own money to support the Revolution and helped persuade France to send more aid to the Americans.

In February 1778 another European officer came to serve heroically under Washington. Baron Friedrich von Steuben came with a lifetime of military experience from his home country of Prussia (in modern-day Germany). Congress quickly put him to work training the Continental Army.

Von Steuben led with a combination of respect and fear. Although he could not speak the language of his men, he memorized English commands in order to teach them basic military skills. Von Steuben's drills worked. He turned the Continental Army into a tough fighting force.

Spain Supports the Patriots

Spain, also a bitter enemy of Britain, joined the war in 1779. **Bernardo de Gálvez**, the governor of Spanish Louisiana, became a key ally to the Patriots. Gálvez gathered a small army of Spanish soldiers, French Americans, colonists, and Indians. Together, they made their way east from Louisiana. Gálvez seized British posts all the way to Pensacola, Florida.

READING CHECK **Summarizing** Why was the Battle of Saratoga a turning point in the war?

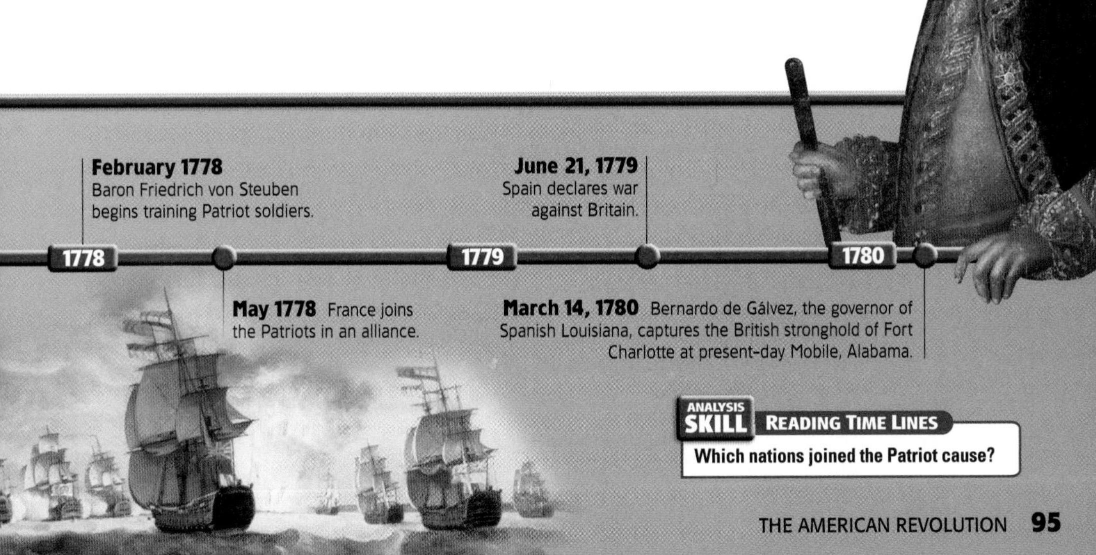

February 1778 Baron Friedrich von Steuben begins training Patriot soldiers.
June 21, 1779 Spain declares war against Britain.
1778
1779
1780
May 1778 France joins the Patriots in an alliance.
March 14, 1780 Bernardo de Gálvez, the governor of Spanish Louisiana, captures the British stronghold of Fort Charlotte at present-day Mobile, Alabama.

ANALYSIS SKILL **READING TIME LINES**

Which nations joined the Patriot cause?

Direct Teach

Main Idea

3 Turning Point at Saratoga

Saratoga was a turning point in the war.

Explain Why did the Marquis de Lafayette join the Continental Army? *He was inspired by the ideals of the American Revolution.*

Identify Cause and Effect How did the Battle of Saratoga lead to French aid for the Patriots? *The Patriot victory at the battle convinced French leaders that Americans could win the war and made the French willing to provide aid.*

Activity Have students prepare a brief speech that Benjamin Franklin might have used to persuade the French government to help the Americans. **LS Verbal/Linguistic**

- Alternative Assessment Handbook, Rubric 43: Writing to Persuade
- **CRF:** Biography Activity: Bernardo de Gálvez

HSS 8.1.3; **HSS Analysis Skills:** HI 1, HI 2

Reading Time Lines

The Patriots Gain Ground

1. How long after the Marquis de Lafayette offered his services to the Patriots did France ally with them? *about nine months*
2. What important British stronghold did Bernardo de Gálvez capture, and when? *Fort Charlotte at present-day Mobile, Alabama; March 14, 1780*

HSS 8.1.3; **HSS Analysis Skills:** CS 1

Differentiating Instruction for Universal Access

Learners Having Difficulty

Reaching Standards

1. To help students understand how foreign nations and individuals aided the Patriots, copy the chart for students to see. Omit the blue answers.
2. Have students copy and complete the chart. Review the answers as a class. **LS Visual/Spatial**

HSS 8.1.3; **HSS Analysis Skills:** HI 1

Alternative Assessment Handbook, Rubric 13: Graphic Organizers

Nation/Individual	Contribution
France and Spain	*provided military supplies, soldiers*
Marquis de Lafayette	*served in Continental Army; gave money; persuaded France to send more aid*
Bernardo de Gálvez	*led a force that seized British posts from Louisiana to Florida*
Baron Friedrich von Steuben	*taught military skills to Continental Army*

Answers

Reading Time Lines *France, Spain*

Reading Check *General Burgoyne surrendered his entire army, which was a much-needed victory and helped raise morale for the Patriots.*

Direct Teach

Main Idea

4 Winter at Valley Forge

The winter at Valley Forge tested the strength of Patriot forces.

Identify What was Valley Forge? *the Patriots' winter camp, located about 20 miles north of Philadelphia*

Draw Conclusions Why do you think that soldiers remained at Valley Forge despite the harsh conditions? *possible answers—out of patriotism, duty, honor, respect for Washington, belief in Patriot cause*

Contrast How did the Patriots' situation at Valley Forge that winter contrast with that of the British at Philadelphia? *While the Patriots endured harsh conditions, the British soldiers lived a life of luxury in Philadelphia and enjoyed social events.*

CRF: Primary Source Activity: Benjamin Rush's Letter to George Washington on the Care of the Wounded

HSS 8.1.3; **HSS Analysis Skills:** HI 1

Primary Source

Valley Forge

Activity **Standard English Mastery**

Vocabulary Building Have students list each word in the excerpt with which they are unfamiliar. Next, have students share their lists. Make a class list and help students to define each word. Then have each student write a one- to two-sentence summary of the meaning of the passage. Remind students to use standard English. Last, ask for volunteers to share their summaries. Write them down for students to see. Critique each example. Point out any errors in grammar or the use of standard English.

HSS Analysis Skills: HR 4

Answers

Analyzing Primary Sources *because conditions were so harsh and desperate, yet the soldiers still showed readiness and contentment*

Reading Check *harsh winter weather; lack of supplies, adequate shelter, clothing, and food; illness*

Primary Source

JOURNAL ENTRY

Valley Forge

A surgeon at Valley Forge, Albigence Waldo kept a journal of what he saw during the winter of 1777–78.

"The Army which has been surprisingly healthy hitherto, now begins to grow sickly from the continued fatigues they have suffered this Campaign. Yet they still show a spirit of Alacrity [cheerful readiness] and Contentment not to be expected from so young Troops. I am Sick—discontented—and out of humour. Poor food—hard lodging—Cold Weather—fatigue—Nasty Cloaths [clothes]—nasty Cookery . . . smoke and Cold—hunger and filthyness—A pox on my bad luck."

—Albigence Waldo, quoted in *Eyewitnesses and Others*

ANALYSIS SKILL **ANALYZING PRIMARY SOURCES**

Why did Waldo seem surprised by the soldiers' attitude?

Winter at Valley Forge

The entry of France and Spain into the war came at a crucial moment. The Continental Army was running very low on supplies. In December 1777, Washington settled his 12,000 men at Valley Forge, about 20 miles north of Philadelphia. There they suffered shortages of food and clothing.

To this day, the name of Valley Forge brings to mind suffering—and courage. Yet no battles took place at this encampment. There was only one enemy: the brutal winter of 1777–78.

Washington's men lacked even the most basic protections against shin-deep snows. Over and over the general sent letters, pleading for supplies. None came.

> "To see men without clothes . . . without blankets to lie upon, without shoes . . . without a house or hut to cover them until those could be built, and submitting without a murmur, is a proof of patience and obedience which, in my opinion, can scarcely be paralleled [matched]."
>
> —George Washington, quoted in *George Washington: A Collection*

As winter roared in, soldiers quickly built crude shelters that offered little protection against the weather. Some soldiers had no shirts. Others had marched the shoes off their feet. At their guard posts, they stood on their hats to keep their feet from touching the freezing ground. One soldier wrote that getting food was the "business that usually employed us."

During that terrible winter, some 2,000 soldiers died of disease and malnutrition. Amazingly, the survivors not only stayed—they drilled and marched to the orders of Baron von Steuben, becoming better soldiers.

While the soldiers suffered through the winter at Valley Forge, the British lived a life of luxury in Philadelphia. Most of the Patriots had fled the city, leaving only Loyalists and British soldiers. Together they enjoyed the city's houses, taverns, and theaters, and held parties and balls.

READING CHECK **Finding Main Ideas**
What challenges did the Continental Army face at Valley Forge?

Collaborative Learning

Standards Proficiency

Valley Forge Skits **HSS Analysis Skills:** HR 5, HI 1, HI 2

1. Organize students into small groups. Have each group create and write a script for a short skit involving three or four soldiers at Valley Forge.
2. Tell students to set the skit in the late spring of 1778 and to have soldiers discuss the hardships they faced over the winter, how they viewed the hardships, why they remained despite them, their opinions of General Washington, and how circumstances have changed in recent weeks.
3. Have the groups assign each member a role to ensure that all group members participate in the activity. Roles might include director, actor, writer, copy editor, cue-card prompter, and so on.
4. Have each group perform its skit for the class.

LS Interpersonal, Kinesthetic, Verbal/Linguistic

Alternative Assessment Handbook, Rubrics 14: Group Activity; and 33: Skits and Reader's Theater

War at Sea and in the West

Americans fought at sea and on the western frontier. Each area posed tough challenges.

War at Sea

The Continental Navy and the marines were established in late 1775. The tiny fleet was no match for the huge British navy. So instead of fighting large battles, the Patriots attacked and sunk hundreds of individual British ships.

When war broke out, **John Paul Jones** quickly gained fame as a brave and clever sailor. In Jones's most famous victory, his ship, the *Bonhomme Richard,* suffered heavy damage. The British captain called out to Jones, "Has your ship struck [surrendered]?" He replied, "I have not yet begun to fight!" The battle continued for more than two hours. Finally, the British surrendered.

War in the West

Only in his mid-20s, **George Rogers Clark** had spent years exploring and mapping the western frontier. Now he traveled the frontier gathering soldiers from small towns.

In June 1778 Clark and 175 soldiers crossed southern Illinois to capture the British trading village of Kaskaskia. Clark then organized meetings with Indian leaders, persuading some of them to remain neutral.

During this period, the British captured the town of Vincennes on the Wabash River. Clark's forces retook the town at the Battle of Vincennes in February 1779. Clark never managed to capture Fort Detroit, Britain's major frontier base. But his efforts helped contain the British in the West.

READING CHECK **Finding Main Ideas** How did Jones and Clark help the Patriots' war effort?

SUMMARY AND PREVIEW The Patriots faced hardships as the war continued. In the next section you will see how they gained hope.

Section 3 Assessment

go.hrw.com
Online Quiz
KEYWORD: SS8 HP3

Reviewing Ideas, Terms, and People HSS 8.1.3

1. **a. Identify** What groups helped in the Patriot war effort? How did each group contribute?
   b. Analyze Why was it difficult to find and keep soldiers in the Continental Army?
2. **a. Describe** What early defeats did the Patriots face?
   b. Elaborate Do you think it was a mistake for the British to use **mercenaries** to help them fight the war? Why or why not?
3. **a. Describe** How did the **Battle of Saratoga** help the Patriots?
   b. Elaborate Why do you think foreign nations supported the colonists rather than Great Britain?
4. **a. Describe** What difficulties did the Patriots face at Valley Forge?
   b. Predict How might the winter at Valley Forge affect the Patriots' war effort?
5. **a. Identify** Who was **John Paul Jones**?
   b. Summarize How did the Patriots overcome challenges at sea and in the West?

Critical Thinking

6. **Drawing Conclusions** Copy the chart below. Use it to identify the problems first faced by the Patriots in the North, at sea, and out West. Then identify Patriot successes in these areas.

Region	Patriot Problems	Patriot Successes

FOCUS ON SPEAKING

7. **Thinking about the Dark Hours** Why was this period of the war so difficult for the Patriots? How did they struggle through? What are the one or two points that are the most important about this period of the war?

Direct Teach

Main Idea

5 War at Sea and in the West

The war continued at sea and in the West.

Identify Cause and Effect How did the size of the Continental Navy affect its strategy against the British navy? *The Patriot navy was much smaller, so Patriot leaders chose to attack individual British ships instead of fighting large naval battles.*

Draw Inferences How do you think George Rogers Clark persuaded some Indian leaders to remain neutral? *possible answers—by promising them incentives if they remained neutral; by stressing that the Patriots were winning the war*

HSS 8.1.3; HSS **Analysis Skills:** HI 1, HI 2

Review & Assess

Close

Have students review the obstacles Patriots faced during the American Revolution, and how they were able to overcome them.

Review

Online Quiz, Section 3

Assess

SE Section 3 Assessment

PASS: Section Quiz 3

Alternative Assessment Handbook

Reteach/Classroom Intervention

California Standards Review Workbook

Interactive Reader and Study Guide, Section 3

Interactive Skills Tutor CD-ROM

Section 3 Assessment Answers

1. **a.** young, white men—served and fought; some free African Americans, Native Americans—served in army; women—raised money, made clothes, served as nurses, messengers, spies
   b. because of low pay, bad conditions, risk of life
2. **a.** defeated at Quebec, Canada and in New York
   b. possible answer—yes, not as dedicated
3. **a.** morale boost for Patriots; led to foreign aid
   b. They were enemies of Great Britain.
4. **a.** harsh weather; illness; lack of supplies
   b. possible answer—may have made soldiers fight harder to make their suffering worthwhile
5. **a.** Patriot naval officer
   b. by fighting small battles; getting Indian support
6. North—problems: British were better trained and had more troops; successes: victories at Trenton, Princeton, Saratoga; Sea—problem: small navy; successes: sunk hundreds of British ships; West—problem: British control; successes: victory at Vincennes
7. See the answers to Questions 1b, 2a, 4a, and 6.

Answers

Reading Check *Jones—led naval battles against the British; Clark—helped contain the British in the West; helped some Indian leaders remain neutral*

Preteach

Bellringer

If YOU were there . . . Use the **Daily Bellringer Transparency** to help students answer the question.

Daily Bellringer Transparency, Section 4

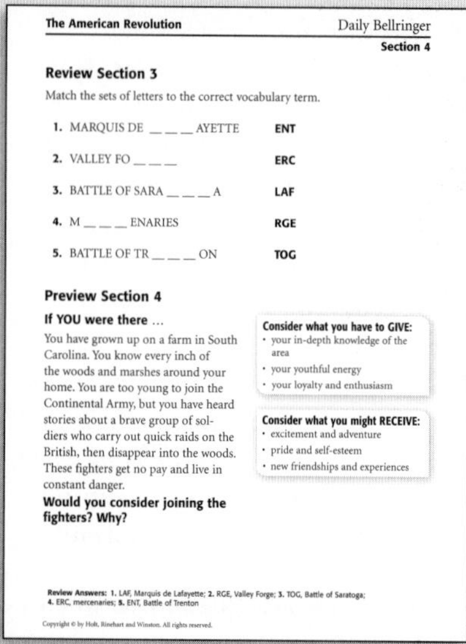

The American Revolution Daily Bellringer

Section 4

Review Section 3

Match the sets of letters to the correct vocabulary term.

1. MARQUIS DE ___ ___ ___ AYETTE — **ENT**
2. VALLEY FO ___ ___ ___ — **ERC**
3. BATTLE OF SARA ___ ___ ___ A — **LAF**
4. M ___ ___ ___ ENARIES — **RGE**
5. BATTLE OF TR ___ ___ ___ ON — **TOG**

Preview Section 4

If YOU were there ...

You have grown up on a farm in South Carolina. You know every inch of the woods and marshes around your home. You are too young to join the Continental Army, but you have heard stories about a brave group of soldiers who carry out quick raids on the British, then disappear into the woods. These fighters get no pay and live in constant danger.

Would you consider joining the fighters? Why?

Consider what you have to GIVE:
- your in-depth knowledge of the area
- your youthful energy
- your loyalty and enthusiasm

Consider what you might RECEIVE:
- excitement and adventure
- pride and self-esteem
- new friendships and experiences

Review Answers: 1. LAF, Marquis de Lafayette; **2.** RGE, Valley Forge; **3.** TOG, Battle of Saratoga; **4.** ERC, mercenaries; **5.** ENT, Battle of Trenton

Building Vocabulary

Preteach or review the following terms:

brigade military unit (p. 99)

devastation severe or widespread damage (p. 99)

guerrilla warfare swift hit-and-run attacks (p. 99)

negotiations talks held to reach an agreement or compromise (p. 101)

pitted set against (p. 98)

CRF: Vocabulary Builder Activity, Section 4

Standards Focus

HSS 8.1

Means: Students understand the major events that led up to the founding of the United States, such as the American Revolution.

Matters: The American Revolution resulted in the formation of the United States as an independent nation.

SECTION 4 Independence!

What You Will Learn...

Main Ideas

1. Patriot forces faced many problems in the war in the South.
2. The American Patriots finally defeated the British at the Battle of Yorktown.
3. The British and the Americans officially ended the war with the Treaty of Paris of 1783.

The Big Idea

The war spread to the South, where the British were finally defeated.

Key Terms and People

Francis Marion, *p. 99*
Comte de Rochambeau, *p. 100*
Battle of Yorktown, *p. 100*
Treaty of Paris of 1783, *p. 101*

HSS 8.1 Students understand the major events preceding the founding of the nation and relate their significance to the development of American constitutional democracy.

If YOU were there...

You have grown up on a farm in South Carolina. You know every inch of the woods and marshes around your home. You are too young to join the Continental Army, but you have heard stories about a brave group of soldiers who carry out quick raids on the British, then disappear into the woods. These fighters get no pay and live in constant danger.

Would you consider joining the fighters? Why?

BUILDING BACKGROUND As the war moved to the South, American forces encountered new problems. They suffered several major defeats. But American resistance in the South was strong. Backwoods fighters confused and frustrated the British army. Eventually, with help from its allies, American persistence won out.

War in the South

The war across the ocean was not going the way the British government in London had planned. The northern colonies, with their ragged, scrappy fighters, proved to be tough to tame. So the British switched strategies and set their sights on the South.

The British hoped to find support from the large Loyalist populations living in Georgia, the Carolinas, and Virginia. They also planned to free slaves and put guns in their hands as they moved across the South. Under the leadership of a new commander, General Henry Clinton, the new strategy paid off—for a while.

Brutal Fighting

The southern war was particularly brutal. Much more than in the North, this phase of the war pitted Americans—Patriots versus Loyalists—against one another in direct combat. The British also destroyed crops, farm animals, and other property as they marched through the South. One British officer, Banastre Tarleton, sowed

Teach the Big Idea: Master the Standards

Standards Proficiency

Independence! HSS 8.1; HSS Analysis Skills: CS 1, HI 1

1. **Teach** Ask students the Main Idea questions to teach this section.
2. **Apply** Ask students to identify the main events in this section. List the responses for the class to see. Next, have each student write a newspaper headline for each event. **LS Verbal/Linguistic**
3. **Review** As you review the section's main ideas, ask for volunteers to share some of their headlines with the class. List them for students to see. Then help students develop a list of details that might appear in articles accompanying the headlines.
4. **Practice/Homework** Have each student select a headline and write a brief newspaper article to go with it. **LS Verbal/Linguistic**

Alternative Assessment Handbook, Rubric 37: Writing Assignments

Swamp Fox

Francis Marion, the "Swamp Fox," leads his soldiers down a river in South Carolina. Marion built a hideout on one of the river's islands. From there, he would lead lightning-fast raids against British communication and supply lines.

Which figure do you think is Francis Marion? Why?

fear throughout the South by refusing to take prisoners and killing soldiers who tried to surrender.

Georgia, the last colony to join the Revolution, was the first to fall to the British. A force of 3,500 Redcoats easily took Savannah in 1778 and soon put in place a new colonial government.

Britain's next major target was Charleston, South Carolina. In early 1780 General Clinton landed a force of 14,000 troops around the port city. With a minimal cost of about 250 casualties, the British scored one of their biggest victories of the war. The Patriots surrendered Charleston in May, handing over four ships and some 5,400 prisoners.

A Failed Attack

In August 1780, Patriot forces led by Horatio Gates tried to drive the British out of Camden, South Carolina. The attack was poorly planned, however. Gates had only half as many soldiers as he had planned for, and most were tired and hungry. In the heat of battle, many panicked and ran. The Patriot attack quickly fell apart. Of some 4,000 American troops, only about 700 escaped.

General Nathanael Greene arrived to reorganize the army. As he rode through the southern countryside, he was discouraged by the devastation. "I have never witnessed such scenes," he later wrote.

Guerrilla Warfare

The southern Patriots switched to swift hit-and-run attacks known as guerrilla warfare. No Patriot was better at this style of fighting than **Francis Marion**. He organized Marion's Brigade, a group of guerrilla soldiers.

Marion's Brigade used surprise attacks to disrupt British communication and supply lines. Despite their great efforts, the British could not catch Marion and his men. One frustrated general claimed, "As for this . . . old fox, the devil himself could not catch him." From that point on, Marion was known as the Swamp Fox.

READING CHECK **Sequencing** List the events of the war in the South in chronological order.

Direct Teach

Main Idea

1 War in the South

Patriot forces faced many problems in the war in the South.

Explain Why did the British decide to switch strategies and focus the war in the South? *large Loyalist populations in Georgia, the Carolinas, and Virginia; planned to free slaves and have them fight*

Summarize How did guerilla colonial fighters help the Continental Army? *by surprising the British with swift hit-and-run attacks to interfere with communication and supply lines*

Draw Conclusions How would you describe the main British strategies in the South? *use Loyalist support, take and hold important southern cities; employ slaves as fighters; use harsh tactics to destroy Patriot supplies and morale*

CRF: Primary Source Activity: General Nathanael Greene Writes to His Wife

HSS 8.1; HSS **Analysis Skills:** HI 1

Info to Know

Native Americans and the War The Revolutionary War was costly to many Native Americans. Some Indian homelands, such as those of the Iroquois and Cherokee, suffered devastation and invasion by both armies. The war also divided some Indian groups and confederacies. For example, the Oneidas and Tuscaroras supported the Patriots. As a result, they were cut off from the rest of the Iroquois League, which supported the British.

Collaborative Learning

Standards **Proficiency**

War in the South Progress Reports

HSS 8.1; HSS **Analysis Skills:** HR 5, HI 1, HI 2

1. Organize students into four groups. Ask two groups to imagine that they are military leaders stationed in the South during the latter part of the war—one with the Continental Army and the other with the British Army. Ask the other two groups to imagine that they are military leaders stationed near Yorktown in 1781—one with the Continental Army and one with the British Army.
2. Have each group create a report on the progress of the war effort in its area. Encourage students to identify, describe, and explain factors that both hurt or benefited their efforts in the region. Have groups assign members roles to ensure that all students participate.
3. Ask a representative from each group to present the group's progress report to the class. Then have students discuss the events that led to the war's end. **LS Interpersonal, Verbal/Linguistic**

Alternative Assessment Handbook, Rubrics 14: Group Activity; and 42: Writing to Inform

Answers

Swamp Fox *The man in front on the horse who is looking forward; appears to be leading because of his position on the boat, his mount on horseback, his uniform, and his bearing.*

Reading Check *1778: British take Savannah, Georgia; 1780: British take Charleston, South Carolina; Patriots fail to retake Camden, South Carolina*

Direct Teach

Main Idea

❷ Battle of Yorktown

The American Patriots finally defeated the British at the Battle of Yorktown.

Recall Why did the British army move to Yorktown, Virginia? *because of harassment from the Continental Army; to maintain communications with the British naval fleet*

Find Main Ideas How did Washington and the Patriots defeat the British at Yorktown? *With the aid of the French army and navy, they surrounded and outnumbered Cornwallis, which forced him to surrender.*

Evaluate Do you think the Patriots could have won the Revolutionary War without the help of the French? *possible answers—yes, because they would have continued to fight and eventually worn down the British; no, because they lacked the troops and supplies needed to win the war.*

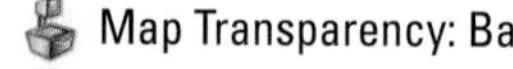

Map Transparency: Battle of Yorktown

HSS 8.1; HSS **Analysis Skills:** HI 1

go.hrw.com

Online Resources

KEYWORD: SS8 US3
ACTIVITY: Revolutionary Battle Site Tourist Brochure

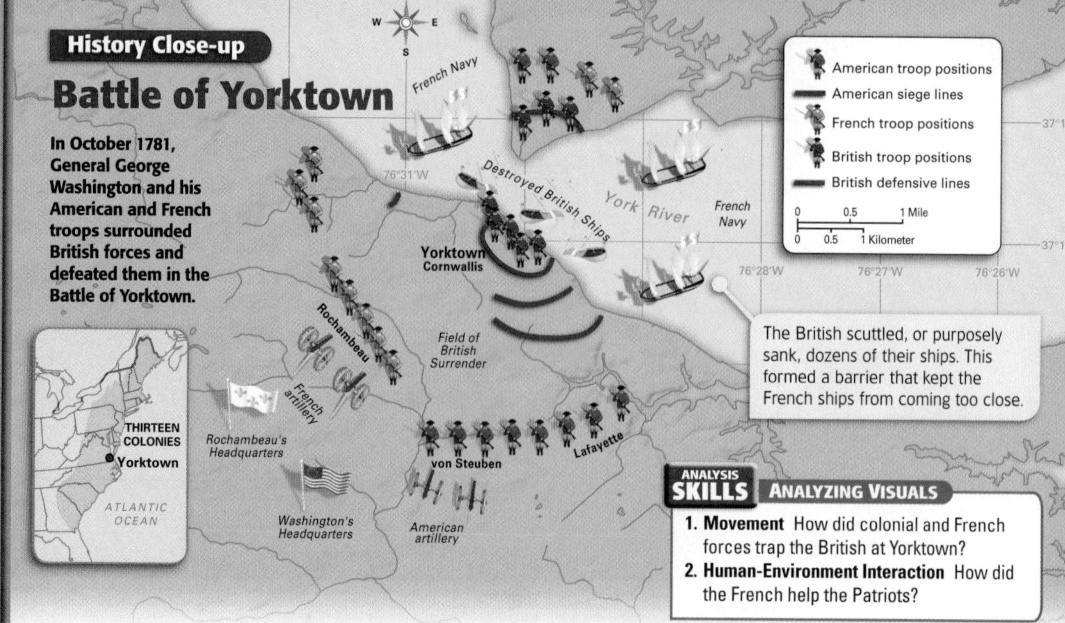

History Close-up

Battle of Yorktown

In October 1781, General George Washington and his American and French troops surrounded British forces and defeated them in the Battle of Yorktown.

The British scuttled, or purposely sank, dozens of their ships. This formed a barrier that kept the French ships from coming too close.

ANALYSIS SKILLS **ANALYZING VISUALS**

1. **Movement** How did colonial and French forces trap the British at Yorktown?
2. **Human-Environment Interaction** How did the French help the Patriots?

Battle of Yorktown

In early 1781 the war was going badly for the Patriots. They were low on money to pay soldiers and buy supplies. The help of their foreign allies had not ended the war as quickly as they had hoped. The British held most of the South, plus Philadelphia and New York City. American morale took another blow when Benedict Arnold, one of America's most gifted officers, turned traitor.

Regrouped under Nathanael Greene, the Continental Army began harassing British general Charles Cornwallis in the Carolinas. Hoping to stay in communication with the British naval fleet, Cornwallis moved his force of 7,200 men to Yorktown, Virginia. It was a fatal mistake.

General Washington, in New York, saw a chance to trap Cornwallis at Yorktown. He ordered Lafayette to block Cornwallis's escape by land. Then he combined his 2,500 troops with 4,000 French troops commanded by the **Comte de Rochambeau** (raw-shahn-BOH). Washington led the French-American force on a swift march to Virginia to cut off the other escape routes. The Patriots surrounded Cornwallis with some 16,000 soldiers. Meanwhile, a French naval fleet seized control of the Chesapeake Bay, preventing British ships from rescuing Cornwallis's stranded army.

The siege began. For weeks, the fighting steadily wore down the British defenses. In early October, Washington prepared for a major attack on the weakened British troops.

Facing near-certain defeat, on October 19, 1781, Cornwallis sent a drummer and a soldier with a white flag of surrender to Washington's camp. The Patriots took some 8,000 British prisoners—the largest British army in America.

The **Battle of Yorktown**, was the last major battle of the American Revolution. Prime Minister Lord North received word of the Yorktown surrender in November. In shock he declared, "It is all over!"

READING CHECK **Drawing Conclusions** Why did the victory at Yorktown end the war?

Critical Thinking: Finding Main Ideas

Standards Proficiency

Revolutionary War Magazine

HSS 8.1; HSS **Analysis Skills:** CS 1, HI 1

1. Review with students the major events and people from this chapter.
2. Have each student prepare a table of contents for a historical magazine about the American Revolution. Instruct students to select key people and events from the chapter to be the subjects of feature articles, spotlights, charts, and maps. Then ask students to create titles for the different articles and describe each article's content.
3. Display students' tables of contents around the classroom and have students view each other's work. **LS Verbal/Linguistic**
4. **Extend** Have students work in groups to create different sections of a historical magazine about the Revolutionary War. **LS Interpersonal, Verbal/Linguistic**

Alternative Assessment Handbook, Rubrics 14: Group Activity; and 19: Magazines

Answers

Interpreting Maps **1.** *by surrounding them on land and by cutting off British ships from being able to rescue the British army;* **2.** *by providing leadership, troops, and ships; by preventing the British from being able to retreat by sea*

Reading Check *British general Cornwallis surrendered his army, the largest British army in America, to the Patriots at the Battle of Yorktown.*

The Treaty of Paris

After Yorktown, only a few small battles took place. Lacking the money to pay for a new army, Great Britain entered into peace talks with America. Benjamin Franklin had an influential role in the negotiations.

Delegates took more than two years to come to a peace agreement. In the **Treaty of Paris of 1783**, Great Britain recognized the independence of the United States. The treaty also set America's borders. A separate treaty between Britain and Spain returned Florida to the Spanish. British leaders also accepted American rights to settle and trade west of the original thirteen colonies.

At the war's end, Patriot soldiers returned to their homes and families. The courage of soldiers and civilians had made America's victory possible. As they returned home, George Washington thanked his troops for their devotion. "I . . . wish that your latter days be as prosperous as your former ones have been glorious."

READING CHECK **Summarizing** Explain how the War for Independence finally came to an end.

North America after the Treaty of Paris of 1783

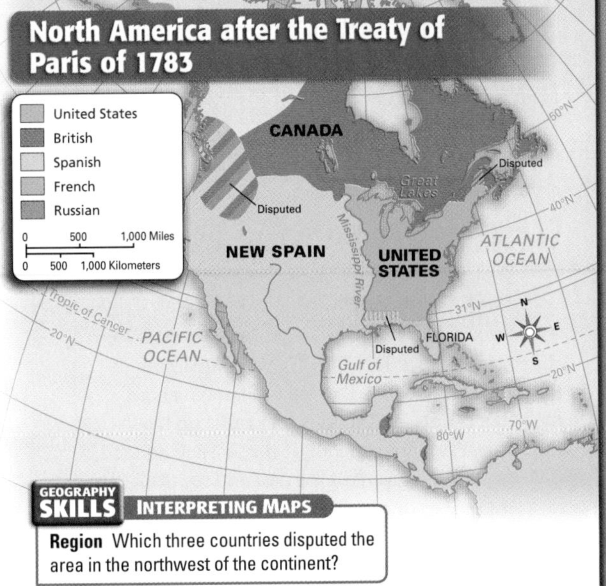

GEOGRAPHY SKILLS **INTERPRETING MAPS**

Region Which three countries disputed the area in the northwest of the continent?

SUMMARY AND PREVIEW The Americans gained their independence in 1783. In the next chapter you will learn about how they formed their first government.

Section 4 Assessment

go.hrw.com
Online Quiz
KEYWORD: SS8 HP3

Reviewing Ideas, Terms, and People HSS 8.1

1. a. **Describe** What problems did the Patriots experience in the war in the South?
   b. **Analyze** What advantages did the southern Patriots have over the British in the South?
2. a. **Describe** What was the Patriots' strategy for defeating the British at Yorktown?
   b. **Elaborate** Why do you think General Cornwallis decided to surrender at the **Battle of Yorktown**?
3. a. **Identify** Who helped to negotiate the peace treaty for the Patriots?
   b. **Predict** How might relations between Great Britain and their former colonies be affected by the war?

Critical Thinking

4. **Sequencing** Copy the graphic organizer below. Use it to list the major events that led to the end of the Revolutionary War.

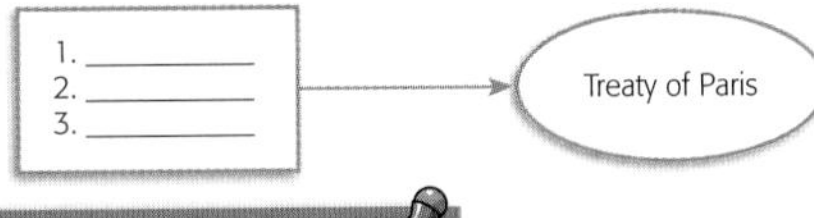

FOCUS ON SPEAKING

5. **Taking Notes on the Revolution's Ending** After reading this section, you'll have a picture of the whole war. In your talk, what do you want to say about how the war ended? Were there any moments that were especially trying for the colonists?

Section 4 Assessment Answers

1. a. brutal fighting and devastation, Patriots and Loyalists pitted against each other, several cities under British control; betrayal of Benedict Arnold
   b. knew the land, used guerrilla warfare
2. a. to use the aid of the French army and navy to surround and outnumber the British and cut off their support and retreat by sea
   b. He was surrounded and facing defeat.
3. a. Benjamin Franklin
   b. probably would worsen relations
4. (1) Cornwallis moved into Yorktown; (2) Patriot and French troops blocked the British by land and sea; (3) Cornwallis surrendered his army, the largest in the colonies, and Great Britain entered into peace talks with America.
5. possible answers: end of war—Battle of Yorktown was significant; Treaty of Paris of 1783 recognized American independence and set the nation's borders; exciting—Marion's Brigade's surprise raids; Battle of Yorktown

Direct Teach

Main Idea

3 The Treaty of Paris

The British and the Americans officially ended the war with the Treaty of Paris of 1783.

Define What was the Treaty of Paris? *peace agreement between Great Britain and the United States ending the war*

Summarize What were the terms of the treaty? *recognized U.S. independence; set U.S. borders; granted American rights to settle and trade west of the original thirteen colonies*

- Political Cartoons Activities for United States History, Cartoon 3: American Independence
- Map Transparency: North America after the Treaty of Paris of 1783
- HSS 8.1; HSS **Analysis Skills:** HI 1

Review & Assess

Close

Have students discuss the following question: *How is the American Revolution relevant today?*

Review

Online Quiz, Section 4

Assess

SE Section 4 Assessment

- PASS: Section 4 Quiz
- Alternative Assessment Handbook

Reteach/Classroom Intervention

- California Standards Review Workbook
- Interactive Reader and Study Guide, Section 4
- Interactive Skills Tutor CD-ROM

Answers

Interpreting Maps *Great Britain, Russia, and Spain*

Reading Check *Great Britain could no longer afford to continue fighting, so it entered into peace talks with the Patriots.*

Social Studies Skills

Understanding Historical Interpretation

Activity Chart for "Practice the Skill" To support the "Practice the Skill" activity, draw a two-column chart for the class to see. Label the columns *Economic Interpretation* and *Political Interpretation.* Have students copy the chart and use it to answer Question 1. Ask for volunteers to share their answers. Use the answers to create a master version of the chart. Then give students time to answer Question 2. Again, ask for volunteers to share their answers with the class. Encourage student discussion and feedback. Remind students to provide reasons to support their positions. **LS Verbal/Linguistic**

Alternative Assessment Handbook, Rubric 16: Judging Information

HSS Analysis Skills: HI 5

Social Studies Skills

Analysis | Critical Thinking | Participation | Study

HSS HI5 Students recognize that interpretations of history are subject to change as new information is uncovered.

Understanding Historical Interpretation

Define the Skill

Historical interpretations are ways of explaining the past. They are based on what is known about the people, ideas, and actions that make up history. Two historians can look at the same set of facts about a person or event of the past and see things in different ways. Their explanations of the person or event, and the conclusions they reach, can be very different. The ability to recognize, understand, and evaluate historical interpretations is a valuable skill in the study of history.

Learn the Skill

When people study the past, they decide which facts are the most important in explaining why something happened. One person may believe certain facts to be important, while other people may believe other facts are more important. Therefore, their explanation of the topic, and the conclusions they draw about it, may not be the same. In addition, if new facts are uncovered about the topic, still more interpretations of it may result.

Asking the following questions will help you to understand and evaluate historical interpretations.

1. What is the main idea in the way the topic is explained? What conclusions are reached? Be aware that these may not be directly stated but only hinted at in the information provided.
2. On what facts has the writer or speaker relied? Do these facts seem to support his or her explanation and conclusions?
3. Is there important information about the topic that the writer or speaker has dismissed or ignored? If so, you should suspect the interpretation may be inaccurate and deliberately slanted to prove a particular point of view.

Just because interpretations differ, one is not necessarily "right" and others "wrong." As long as a person considers all the evidence, and draws conclusions based on a fair evaluation of that evidence, his or her interpretation is probably acceptable.

Remember, however, that trained historians let the facts *lead* them to conclusions. People who *start* with a conclusion, select only facts that support it, and ignore opposing evidence produce interpretations that have little value for understanding history.

Practice the Skill

Two widely accepted interpretations exist of the causes of the American Revolution. One holds that the Revolution was a struggle by freedom-loving Americans to be free from harsh British rule. In this view the colonists were used to self-government and resisted British efforts to take rights they claimed. The other interpretation is that a clash of economic interests caused the Revolution. In this view, it resulted from a struggle between British and colonial merchants over control of America's economy.

Review Sections 4 and 5 of Chapter 2 and Sections 1 and 2 of Chapter 3. Then answer the following questions.

1. What facts in the textbook support the economic interpretation of the Revolution? What evidence supports the political interpretation?
2. Which interpretation seems more convincing? Explain why.

Social Studies Skills Activity: Understanding Historical Interpretation

Interpretation of the Battle of Saratoga

HSS Analysis Skills: HI 5 **Standards Proficiency**

1. Have students review the material in Section 3 under the heading "Turning Point at Saratoga." This passage describes the Battle of Saratoga as "the greatest victory yet for the American forces." This conclusion is based on expert historical interpretation.
2. Review with students the Revolutionary battles up to and including the Battle of Saratoga. Then have students discuss whether they agree with the historical interpretation that the Battle of Saratoga was the greatest American victory up to that point.
3. Have each student write one to two paragraphs either supporting or refuting this historical interpretation. Students who disagree should indicate which battle they think was "the greatest victory yet." Remind students to provide reasons to support their positions. **LS Verbal/Linguistic**

Alternative Assessment Handbook, Rubric 43: Writing to Persuade

Answers

Practice the Skill 1. *economic—one of England's main reasons for founding the colonies was to earn money from trade; British attempts to tax the colonists and crack down on smuggling led to colonial protests, unrest, and eventually violence; political—amount of colonial self-government; reactions to limits on colonial self-government; ideals expressed in the Declaration of Independence;* **2.** *Answers will vary, but students should base their answers on the interpretations they listed in the previous answer.*

CHAPTER 3 # Standards Review

Visual Summary

Use the visual summary below to help you review the main ideas of the chapter.

QUICK FACTS

Speeches and protests ignited revolutionary feelings.

Patriots fought Loyalists in the Revolutionary War.

The American colonies gained independence and became the United States.

Reviewing Vocabulary, Terms, and People

1. What were American colonists who remained loyal to Great Britain called?

a. Whigs
b. Loyalists
c. Royalists
d. Democrats

2. What was the name of the battle in which the Patriots finally defeated the British?

a. Battle of Saratoga
b. Battle of New Jersey
c. Battle of Yorktown
d. Battle of Valley Forge

3. What was the name for the colonial military force created to fight the British?

a. mercenaries
b. Redcoats
c. Hessians
d. Continental Army

4. Who was the French nobleman who helped the Patriots fight the British?

a. Bernardo de Gálvez
b. Marquis de Lafayette
c. Baron von Steuben
d. Lord Dunmore

Comprehension and Critical Thinking

SECTION 1 *(Pages 78–81)* HSS 8.1

5. a. Recall What actions did the First and Second Continental Congresses take?

b. Analyze How did the events at Lexington and Concord change the conflict between Great Britain and the colonies?

c. Elaborate Why do you think that control of Boston early in the Revolutionary War was important?

SECTION 2 *(Pages 83–85)* HSS 8.1.2

6. a. Identify Why is July 4, 1776, a significant date?

b. Draw Conclusions What effect did *Common Sense* have on colonial attitudes toward Great Britain?

c. Predict How might the Declaration of Independence lead to questions over the issue of slavery?

Answers

Visual Summary

Review and Inquiry Have students provide five to seven supporting details for each panel in the visual summary to explain the main events that led to the independence of the United States.

Quick Facts Transparency: The American Revolution Visual Summary

Reviewing Vocabulary, Terms, and People

1. b
2. c
3. d
4. b

Comprehension and Critical Thinking

5. a. First—halted all trade with Britain, had colonial militias prepare for war, drafted Declaration of Rights; Second—created Continental Army, appointed George Washington to command the army, sent Olive Branch Petition to Britain

b. The conflict became violent, and the colonists readied for war.

c. possible answer—Boston was a major colonial city and port.

Review and Assessment Resources

Review and Reinforce

SE Standards Review
CRF: Chapter Review Activity
California Standards Review Workbook
Quick Facts Transparency: The American Revolution Visual Summary
Spanish Chapter Summary Audio CD Program
Online Chapter Summaries in Six Languages
OSP Holt PuzzlePro, GameTool for ExamView
Quiz Game CD-ROM

Assess

SE Standards Assessment
PASS: Chapter Test, Forms A and B
Alternative Assessment Handbook
OSP ExamView Test Generator, Chapter Test
Universal Access Modified Worksheets and Tests CD-ROM: Chapter Test
Holt Online Assessment Program (in the Premier Online Edition)

Reteach/Intervene

Interactive Reader and Study Guide
Universal Access Teacher Management System: Lesson Plans for Universal Access
Universal Access Modified Worksheets and Tests CD-ROM
Interactive Skills Tutor CD-ROM

go.hrw.com
Online Resources
Chapter Resources:
KEYWORD: SS8 US3

Answers

6. a. date on which the Continental Congress approved the Declaration of Independence, which broke all ties to Great Britain
   b. changed the way many colonists viewed the king and independence from Britain
   c. because it states that "all men are created equal" and have unalienable rights, but at the time many colonists were slave holders
7. a. defeats in Canada, New York
   b. with victories at the Battles of Trenton and Saratoga
   c. possible answers: No—Foreign aid provided training, money, and military help at sea and on land; Yes—the tide had already begun to turn in favor of the Patriots, who would have worn down the British eventually.
8. a. knew there was a large Loyalist population in Georgia, the Carolinas, and Virginia; planned to free enslaved Africans and have them fight
   b. possible answer—because of debates over borders, the roles of France and Spain, and whether Americans could settle and trade west of the original thirteen colonies
   c. possible answers—victory at Yorktown, because the Patriots captured Britain's largest army in America; French aid, because it enabled the Patriots to surround the British army at Yorktown

Social Studies Skills

9. a
10. possible answer—The Continental Navy was a match against the British in one-on-one battles and chose not to fight in larger battles for strategic reasons.

Reviewing Themes

11. rights to life, liberty, and the pursuit of happiness
12. Forts were small and spread far apart, so troops had to travel long distances.

SECTION 3 *(Pages 90–97)* **HSS 8.1.3**

7. **a. Describe** What difficulties did the Patriots experience in the early years of the war?
   b. Analyze How did the Patriots turn the tide of war?
   c. Elaborate Do you think the Patriots could have succeeded in the war without foreign help? Explain.

SECTION 4 *(Pages 98–101)* **HSS 8.1**

8. **a. Recall** Why did the British think they might find support in the South?
   b. Make Inferences Why might it have taken more than two years for the British and the Americans to agree to the terms of the Treaty of Paris?
   c. Evaluate In your opinion, what was the most important reason for the Patriots' defeat of the British?

Social Studies Skills

Understanding Historical Interpretation *Use the Social Studies Skills taught in this chapter to answer the questions about the reading selection below.*

> The Continental Navy and the marines were established in late 1775. The tiny fleet was no match for the huge British navy. So instead of fighting large battles, the Patriots attacked and sunk hundreds of individual British ships. (p. 97)

9. Which statement from the passage is an interpretation of historical facts?
   a. The tiny fleet was no match for the huge British navy.
   b. The Patriots attacked and sunk hundreds of individual British ships.
   c. The Continental Navy and the marines were established in late 1775.
10. What might be a different interpretation of the facts?

Reviewing Themes

11. **Politics** What are three important rights listed in the Declaration of Independence?
12. **Geography** What role did geography play in the fighting that took place in the West?

Reading Skills

Understanding Words through Context Clues *Use the Reading Skills taught in this chapter to answer the question about the reading selection below.*

> Indians who had been pushed off their lands by colonial settlers aided the British. Mohawk leader Thayendanegea persuaded many Iroquois to support the British. The Patriots had to work hard just to keep other American Indians neutral. (p. 91)

13. Using context clues from the passage above, what is a possible definition of the word *neutral*?
   a. supporting the British
   b. not choosing sides
   c. settling on Indian lands
   d. leading Mohawks

Using the Internet

14. **Activity: Researching** The Battle of Saratoga showed the world that the Patriots were capable of defeating the British. Benjamin Franklin's fame as a scientist and diplomat gave him the chance to use this victory to convince France to aid the Americans. Enter the activity keyword and explain how these factors led to a Patriot victory and how the American Revolution affected France.

FOCUS ON SPEAKING

15. **Preparing Your Oral Report** Review your notes and be sure you've identified one or two important ideas, events, or people for each period of the war. Now, start to prepare your oral report by writing a one-sentence introduction to your talk. Then write a sentence or two about each period of the war. Write a concluding sentence that makes a quick connection between the Revolutionary War and our lives today. Practice your talk until you can give it with only a glance or two at your notes.

Reading Skills

13. b

Using the Internet

14. Go to the HRW Web site and enter the keyword shown to access a rubric for this activity.

KEYWORD: SS8 TEACHER

Focus on Speaking

15. **Rubric** Students' oral reports should:
   - include an introduction, two sentences on each period of the war, and a conclusion.
   - discuss the war in chronological order.
   - provide vivid descriptions to engage the audience.
   - use standard English and proper grammar.

CRF: Focus on Speaking: Giving an Oral Report

Standards Assessment

DIRECTIONS: Read each question and write the letter of the best response.

1

> "These are the times that try men's souls. The summer soldier and the sunshine patriot will, in this crisis, shrink from the service of his country, but he that stands it now, deserves the love and thanks of man and woman. Tyranny . . . is not easily conquered, yet we have this consolation with us, that the harder the conflict, the more glorious the triumph."
>
> —Thomas Paine, *The Crisis*, 1776

What point is Paine trying to make in this passage?

A that although war is glorious, many people are unwilling to take part in it

B that the price of independence may be too high for what will be gained by obtaining it

C that most colonists do not understand what sacrifices some are making for their freedom

D that despite the difficulties, the colonists' cause is worthy and they should not give up

2 What action would a Loyalist have been *least* likely to take during the Revolution?

A flee the colonies for England

B support the Olive Branch Petition

C oppose the Declaration of Independence

D join the Continental Army

3 Which of the following events took place *last?*

A The Declaration of Independence was issued.

B The Second Continental Congress met.

C The battles at Lexington and Concord occurred.

D The Battle of Bunker Hill took place.

4 Why was the Patriots' victory at the Battle of Saratoga so important to the American cause?

A It allowed the Declaration of Independence to be issued.

B It forced the British army to retreat from Boston.

C It convinced France to aid the colonies in their fight.

D It caused the British government to give up the war.

5 The most brutal and destructive fighting of the war probably occurred

A in the southern colonies.

B at Valley Forge.

C in New England.

D at Lexington and Concord.

Connecting with Past Learnings

6 The Declaration of Independence's claim that people have a right to "life, liberty, and the pursuit of happiness" shows the influence of what earlier European Enlightenment thinker?

A Luther

B Locke

C Montesquieu

D Ignatius of Loyola

7 Which other great revolution that you learned about in Grade 7 did the colonists' successful fight for independence inspire?

A the Russian Revolution

B the Glorious Revolution

C the French Revolution

D the Scientific Revolution

Answers

1. D

Break Down the Question Suggest that students go through the reading phrase by phrase and interpret each one in turn. Then have them review the reading to get its full meaning. Here, focus on the phrases "but he that stands it now, deserves the love and thanks of man and woman" and "the harder the conflict, the more glorious the triumph."

2. D

Break Down the Question This question asks what a Loyalist would likely *not* have done. Tell students to start by eliminating any actions that Loyalists likely would have taken, which leaves only answer D.

3. A

Break Down the Question This question requires students to sequence a series of events. Suggest that students first order the events they are certain about and then try to fill in the other events.

4. C

Break Down the Question This question requires students to identify cause and effect. Tell students in such cases to think about what they know about the event in question and what happened after or as a result of the event.

5. A

Break Down the Question Suggest that students first eliminate any choices where fighting did not occur (Valley Forge) and then recall what they know about the remaining options.

6. B

Break Down the Question This question requires students to recall information covered in Grade 7.

7. C

Break Down the Question This question requires students to recall information covered in Grade 7.

Intervention Resources

Reproducible

- Interactive Reader and Study Guide
- Universal Access Teacher Management System: Lesson Plans for Universal Access

Technology

- Quick Facts Transparency: The American Revolution Visual Summary
- Universal Access Modified Worksheets and Tests CD-ROM
- Interactive Skills Tutor CD-ROM

Tips for Test Taking

Study the Directions Read the following to students: To follow directions correctly you have to know what the directions are. Read all test directions as if they contain the key to lifetime happiness and several years' of allowance. Then read them again. Next, study the answer sheet. How is it laid out? How are the answer choices arranged—vertically, horizontally? Be very sure you know exactly what to do and how to do it before you make your first mark.

Standards Review

Have students review the following standards in their workbooks.

- California Standards Review Workbook: HSS 8.1.2, 8.1.3

Preteach

Bellringer

Motivate Ask students to name some of the people they have read about in this unit. Then ask them which of these people's lives would make the most interesting stories. Lead students to discuss what makes a narrative interesting. Tell students they will write a biographical narrative in this workshop.

Direct Teach

Adding Details

Move Beyond Plot Remind students that just telling what happened does not make events come alive. In addition to describing an event, students should tell what the subject thought and felt about what happened. Tell students they want to help their readers experience the events through the subject's eyes.

Using Transitions

Link It Up Model the use of transitions for students. Choose a series of events from the unit. Next, write the events for students to see. Then ask students to help you link each event with an appropriate transition word. When all events are linked, erase the transitions and challenge students to think of a new set of appropriate transition words.

Standards Focus

ELA Writing 8.1.1, 8.1.6, 8.2.1

Writing Workshop

A Biographical Narrative

Assignment

Write a biographical narrative about a person who lived in the early Americas before or during the colonial period.

You have been listening to and telling narratives all your life. A biographical narrative, a form of historical writing, is a true story about an event or brief period in a person's life.

TIP **Asking Questions** Try using the *5W-How?* questions (*Who? What? When? Where? Why? How?*) to help you think of descriptive details. Ask questions such as, **Who** was this person? **What** was he or she doing? Exactly **where** and **when** did the event occur? **How** did the person or other people react to the event?

1. Prewrite

Getting Started

- Think of all the people you read about in this unit. Which ones interested you most?
- What particular events and situations in these people's lives seem most exciting or significant?

Pick one of these events or situations as the subject of your narrative.

Creating an Interesting Narrative

Make your narrative lively and interesting by including

- **Physical descriptions** of people, places, and things, using details that appeal to the five senses (sight, hearing, touch, smell, taste)
- **Specific actions** that relate directly to the story you are telling
- **Dialogue** between the people involved or direct **quotations**
- **Background information** about the place, customs, and setting
- **All relevant details and information** needed to relate the events of the story and how they affected the person (and perhaps history)

Organize the events in your narrative in chronological order, the order in which they occurred.

ELA Writing 8.2.1 Write biographies, autobiographies, short stories, or narratives.

2. Write

You can use this framework to help you draft your narrative.

A Writer's Framework

Introduction	Body	Conclusion
■ Grab your reader's attention with a striking detail or bit of dialogue. ■ Introduce the historical person and setting, using specific details. ■ Set the scene by telling how the event or situation began.	■ Present actions and details in the order in which they occurred. ■ Connect actions with transition words like *first, then, next,* and *finally.* ■ Provide specific details to make the person and the situation come alive.	■ Wrap up the action of the narrative. ■ Tell how the person was affected by what happened. ■ Explain how the event or situation was important in the person's life and how it affected history.

106 UNIT 1

Differentiating Instruction for Universal Access

Advanced Learners/GATE — Exceeding Standards

1. Challenge students to present their narrative as a historian might by incorporating primary and secondary source quotes.
2. Instruct students to provide a footnote giving the citation, or source, for each quotation. Last, students should create a bibliography of their sources to go with their biographical narrative. LS **Verbal/Linguistic**

ELA Writing 8.2.1

English-Language Learners — Standards Proficiency

1. Write the sequence words listed in the Tip on the next page for students to see.
2. Have students write each sequence word on a note card and then write the equivalent in their primary language on the card's back.
3. Pair students and have them use the cards to quiz each other. LS **Interpersonal, Verbal/Linguistic**

ELA Writing 8.1.6

3. Evaluate and Revise

Evaluating

Read through your completed draft to make sure your narrative is complete, coherent, and clear. Then look for ways to improve it.

Evaluation Questions for a Biographical Narrative

- Does your introduction grab the reader's attention? Do you introduce the historical person and tell how the event or situation began?
- Do you include details to make the person, place, and event seem real?
- Are the actions in the story in the order they occurred?
- Have you included all of the actions and details a reader would need to understand what happened?
- Does the conclusion tell how the event or situation affected the person and history?

TIP **Showing Sequence** A clear sense of the sequence of events is important in any narrative. Here is a list of words that show those relationships.

after	next
before	now
finally	soon
first	still
(second, etc.)	then
last	when
later	while

Revising

When you revise your narrative, you may need to add transition words. Transition words help you link ideas between sentences and paragraphs. Notice the words in bold in the following sentences.

> **After** Cabeza de Vaca and the other adventurers left the beach and started inland, they separated into different groups. **Later,** Cabeza de Vaca heard that many of the others had died. **Still,** he never lost faith that he would reach his fellow Spaniards in Mexico.

4. Proofread and Publish

Proofreading

Throughout your narrative, you used transition words to link events. Make sure that you have spelled the words correctly and have not confused them with other words. For example, be sure to use two *l*'s in *finally* and not to mistake the transition word *then* for the comparative word *than*.

Publishing

One good way to share your biographical narrative is to exchange it with one or more classmates who have written about the same person you have. After reading each other's narratives, you can compare and contrast them. How are your stories similar? How do they differ?

5. Practice and Apply

Use the steps and strategies outlined in this workshop to write your biographical narrative.

Reteach

Acting Workshop

Play It Out Encourage students who are having trouble adding thoughts and feelings to their narratives to form small groups and act out each narrative as a play. Then have the student playing the subject describe his or her thoughts and feelings while the other students take notes.

Teaching Tip

Person and Tense

Remind students to use the third person and the past tense throughout their biographical narratives. When students proofread their papers, suggest that they circle all pronouns and underline all verbs to make sure they match.

Practice & Apply

Rubric

Students' biographical narratives should

- start with a striking detail or interesting bit of dialogue.
- clearly identify the subject and the historical setting.
- present actions and details in the order in which they occurred.
- correctly and effectively use transitions to link events.
- provide vivid details and dialogue to bring the person and the story alive.
- wrap up the story and explain how the situation affected the subject.
- use correct grammar, punctuation, spelling, and capitalization.

Special Education Students

Reaching Standards

1. Have special education students draw the person and events they have selected as the subject of their biographical narratives.
2. Have a classroom aide or fellow student listen and take notes while the student describes what is happening in the picture.
3. Then have the aide or fellow student use the notes to guide the special education student in writing his or her biographical narrative.
4. If the student gets stuck, direct the aide or fellow student to prompt him or her by asking questions about the picture. Questions might include: Who are the people in the picture? What are they doing? Why are they doing these things? What happened next? How do you think the person felt during these events? What sights and sounds did the person see and hear during the events? **LS Visual/Spatial**

ELA Writing 8.1.1, 8.2.1

Unit Preview

Introduce the Unit

Share the information in the chapter overviews with students.

Chapter 4 American colonists formed state and federal governments based on English laws, Enlightenment ideas, and American models of government. The federal government established by the Articles of Confederation lacked the power to rule effectively, however. To remedy this problem, American leaders wrote a new constitution that created a stronger central government. Eventually, the required nine states ratified the U.S. Constitution.

Chapter 5 The framers of the U.S. Constitution developed a federal system, dividing power between the federal and state governments. A system of checks and balances divides federal power among the legislative, executive, and judicial branches of government. To address concerns about individual rights, the first Congress added 10 amendments, known as the Bill of Rights, to the Constitution. In addition to these rights, all U.S. citizens have certain responsibilities to society.

Chapter 6 With the Constitution ratified, U.S. leaders set about creating a new federal government. These leaders faced numerous challenges, including how to pay off the national debt, how to respond to foreign threats, and how to *(continued on p. 109)*

Standards Focus

For a list of the overarching standards covered in this unit, see the first page of each chapter.

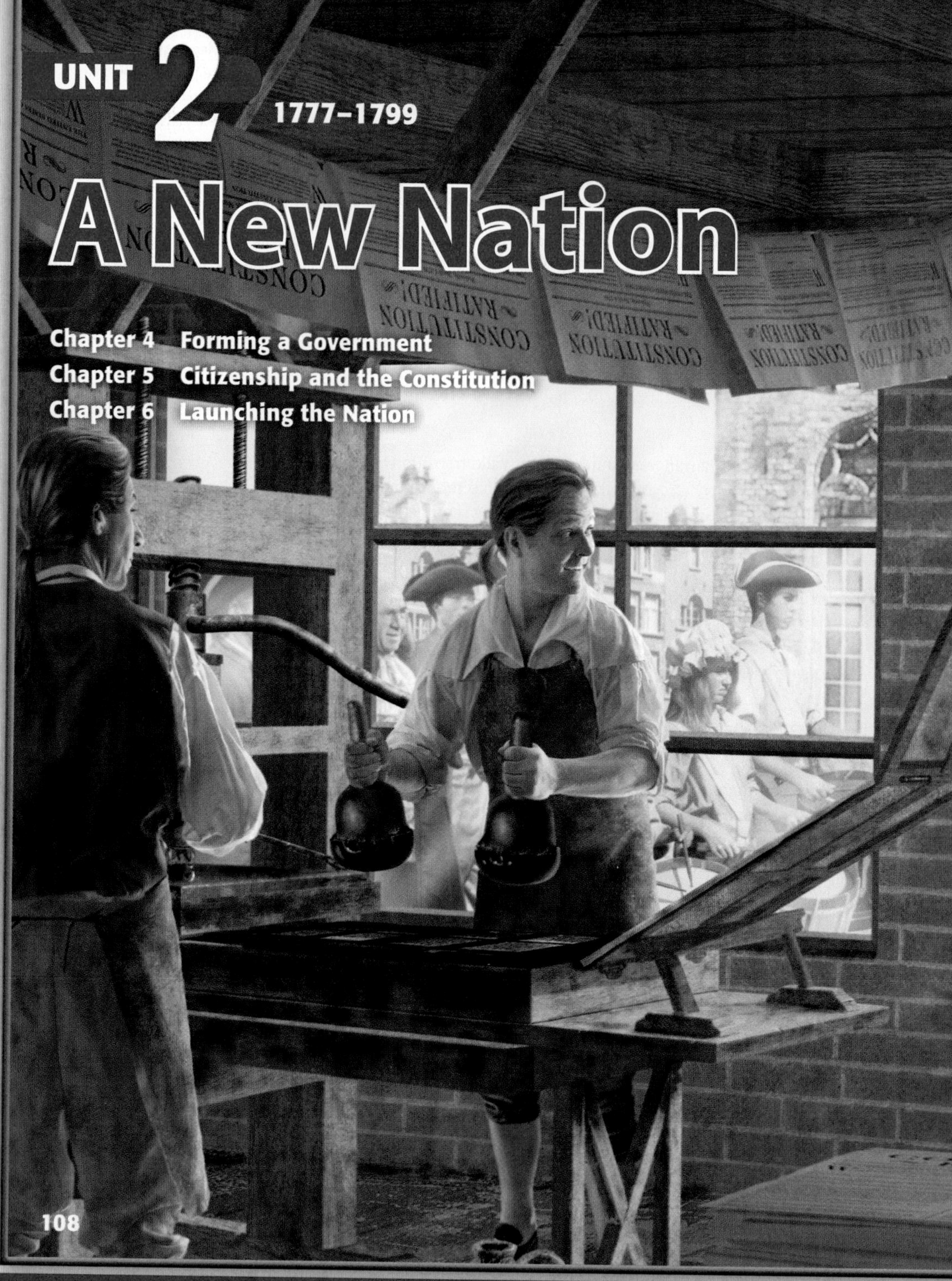

Unit Resources

Planning

- Universal Access Teacher Management System: Unit Instructional Benchmarking Guides
- One-Stop Planner CD-ROM with Test Generator: Holt Calendar Planner
- Power Presentations with Video CD-ROM
- A Teacher's Guide to Religion in the Public Schools

Standards Mastery

- Standards Review Workbook
- At Home: A Guide to Standards Mastery for United States History

Differentiating Instruction

- Universal Access Teacher Management System: Lesson Plans for Universal Access
- Pre-AP Activities Guide for United States History
- Universal Access Modified Worksheets and Tests CD-ROM

Enrichment

- **CRF 6:** Economics and History: The National Debt
- **CRF 6:** Interdisciplinary Projects: Planning the New Capital: Drama Script; Student Almanac
- Civic Participation
- Primary Source Library CD-ROM

Assessment

- Progress Assessment Support System: Benchmark Test
- OSP ExamView Test Generator: Benchmark Test
- go.hrw.com Holt Online Assessment Program (in the Premier Online Edition)
- Alternative Assessment Handbook

The **Universal Access Teacher Management System** provides a planning and instructional benchmarking guide for this unit.

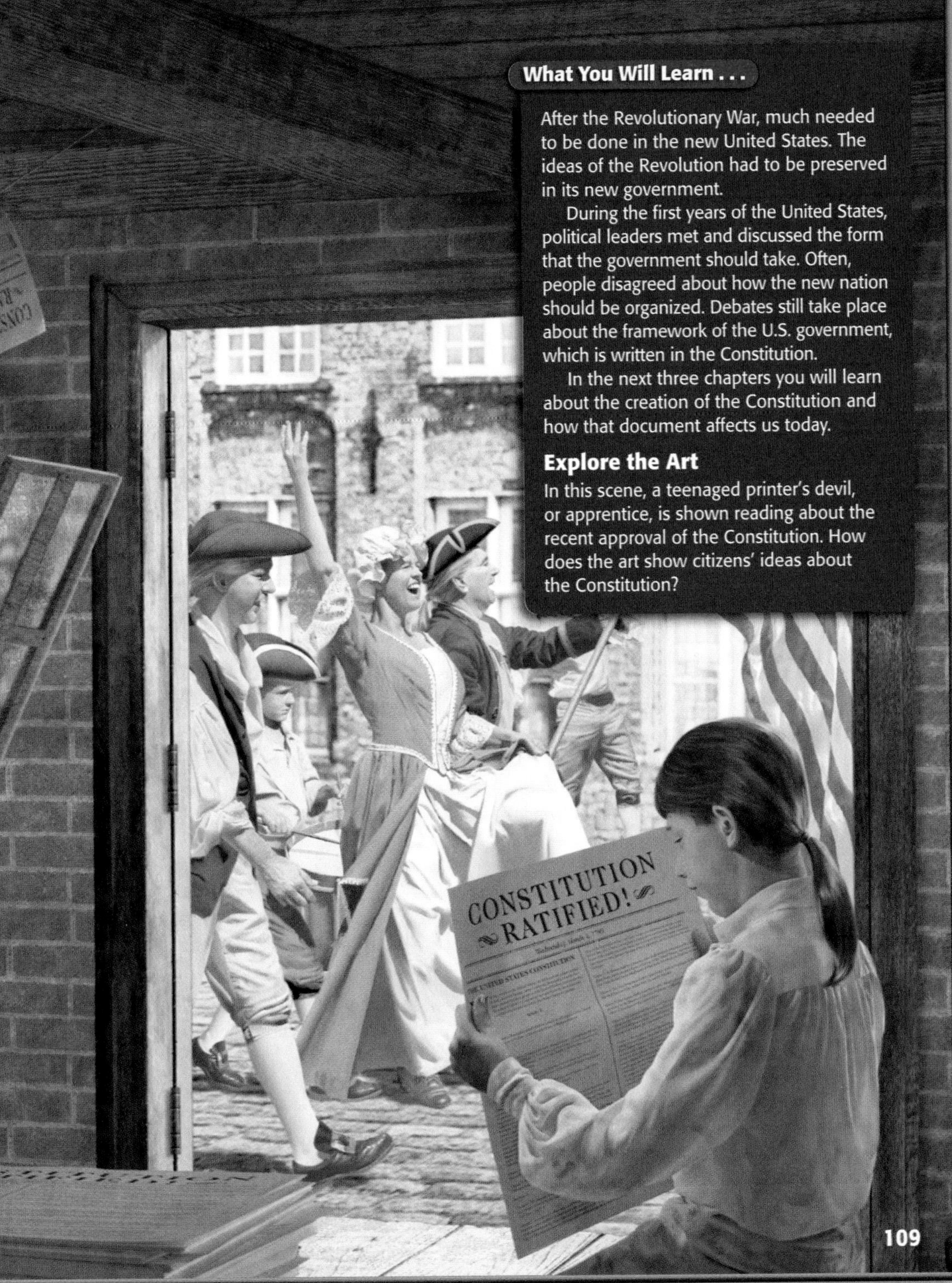

What You Will Learn . . .

After the Revolutionary War, much needed to be done in the new United States. The ideas of the Revolution had to be preserved in its new government.

During the first years of the United States, political leaders met and discussed the form that the government should take. Often, people disagreed about how the new nation should be organized. Debates still take place about the framework of the U.S. government, which is written in the Constitution.

In the next three chapters you will learn about the creation of the Constitution and how that document affects us today.

Explore the Art

In this scene, a teenaged printer's devil, or apprentice, is shown reading about the recent approval of the Constitution. How does the art show citizens' ideas about the Constitution?

Unit Preview

Unit Overview *continued*

resolve domestic conflicts. President George Washington and his administration set many precedents. Not all Americans agreed on the best course of government, however. As a result, political parties developed, although Washington warned against them.

Connect to the Unit

Activity Solving Challenges Facing New Governments Ask students to brainstorm a list of challenges that any new government might face. Have students rank the answers they suggested in order of importance. Organize students into groups and give each group one of the problems that the class decided was among the most important. Have each group come up with three solutions a government might use to meet this challenge. At the end of the unit, have students compare their solutions to the actions U.S. leaders took. **LS Interpersonal, Logical/Mathematical**

Explore the Art

Ratification celebrations for the U.S. Constitution were particularly festive in Baltimore, Maryland. After the state ratified the Constitution, the city of Baltimore held a large parade and picnic. The centerpiece of the parade was a 15-foot ship named *Federalist,* which represented the ship of state.

Today the nation celebrates the U.S. Constitution on September 17, known as Constitution Day.

About the Illustration

This illustration is an artist's conception based on available sources. However, historians are uncertain exactly what this scene looked like.

Democracy and Civic Education

Standards Proficiency

Responsibility: Civic Virtue

Research Required

Background Explain to students that part of citizenship is civic virtue, or working to promote the common good. Students can help to promote the common good in a number of ways, such as being informed citizens, promoting issues they feel strongly about, or doing volunteer work or community service.

1. Have students discuss what they think is meant by the term *common good.*
2. Lead a discussion about the ways that students can help promote the common good.
3. Then have students work as a class to create brochures or pamphlets that explain the need for civic virtue and list area volunteer and community-service opportunities for students. Have the class create and set up an information booth in their school to hand out the information to other students. **LS Interpersonal, Verbal/Linguistic**

Alternative Assessment Handbook, Rubrics 14: Group Activity; and 37: Writing Assignments

Civic Participation

Answers

Explore the Art *The parade, people's expressions, and the newspaper coverage indicate that many Americans considered the ratification of the Constitution to be a wonderful event to be celebrated and reported.*

Chapter 4 Planning Guide

Forming a Government

Chapter Overview	Reproducible Resources	Technology Resources
CHAPTER 4 **pp. 110–139** **Overview:** **In this chapter, you will learn about the founding fathers and their role in the formation of the U.S. government.** See p. 110 for the California History–Social Science standards covered in this chapter.	**Universal Access Teacher Management System:*** • Universal Access Instructional Benchmarking Guides • Lesson Plans for Universal Access **Interactive Reader and Study Guide:*** Chapter Graphic Organizer **Chapter Resource File*** • Focus on Writing Activity: A Newspaper Editorial • Social Studies Skills Activity: Determine Different Points of View • Chapter Review Activity	**One-Stop Planner CD-ROM:** Calendar Planner **Student Edition Full-Read Audio CD-ROM** **Universal Access Modified Worksheets and Tests CD-ROM** **Interactive Skills Tutor CD-ROM** **Power Presentation With Video CD-ROM** **History's Impact: United States History Video Program (VHS/DVD):** Forming a Government*
Section 1: **The Articles of Confederation** **The Big Idea:** The Articles of Confederation provided a framework for a national government. 8.3.2, 8.9.3	**Universal Access Teacher Management System:*** Section 1 Lesson Plan **Interactive Reader and Study Guide:*** Section 1 Summary **Chapter Resource File*** • Vocabulary Builder, Section 1 • History and Geography Activity: The Northwest Territory • Primary Source Activity: Iroquois Great Law of Peace	**Daily Bellringer Transparency:** Section 1* **Map Transparency:** The Land Ordinances of 1785 and 1787*
Section 2: **The New Nation Faces Challenges** **The Big Idea:** Problems faced by the young nation made it clear that a new constitution was needed. 8.2.2, 8.3.5	**Universal Access Teacher Management System:*** Section 2 Lesson Plan **Interactive Reader and Study Guide:*** Section 2 Summary **Chapter Resource File*** • Vocabulary Builder, Section 2	**Daily Bellringer Transparency:** Section 2* **Map Transparency:** The United States Faces Trade Barriers* **Quick Facts Transparency:** Weaknesses of the Articles*
Section 3: **Creating the Constitution** **The Big Idea:** A new constitution provided a framework for a stronger national government. 8.2.3	**Universal Access Teacher Management System:*** Section 3 Lesson Plan **Interactive Reader and Study Guide:*** Section 3 Summary **Chapter Resource File*** • Vocabulary Builder, Section 3 • Biography Activity: Signers of the Constitution • Primary Source Activity: Benjamin Franklin	**Daily Bellringer Transparency:** Section 3* **Quick Facts Transparency:** The Great Compromise* **Quick Facts Transparency:** The Constitution Strengthens the National Government* go.hrw.com **Internet Activity:** Biographies of Constitutional Convention Leaders
Section 4: **Ratifying the Constitution** **The Big Idea:** Americans carried on a vigorous debate before ratifying the Constitution. 8.2.7	**Universal Access Teacher Management System:*** Section 4 Lesson Plan **Interactive Reader and Study Guide:*** Section 4 Summary **Chapter Resource File*** • Vocabulary Builder, Section 4 • Biography Activity: George Mason • Biography Activity: Mercy Otis Warren • History and Geography Activity: Ratifying the Constitution • Literature Activity: *Federalist Paper* "No. 15" **Political Cartoons Activities for United States History,** Cartoon 4: Ratifying the Constitution*	**Daily Bellringer Transparency:** Section 4* **Quick Facts Transparency:** Federalists v. Antifederalists* go.hrw.com **Internet Activity:** Hamilton and Madison Articles

SE Student Edition | Print Resource | Audio CD | Video
TE Teacher's Edition | Transparency | CD-ROM | DVD
go.hrw.com | CA Standards Mastery | LS Learning Styles
OSP One-Stop Planner CD-ROM | * also on One-Stop Planner CD

Review, Assessment, Intervention

- **Standards Review Workbook***
- **Quick Facts Transparency:** Forming a Government Visual Summary*
- **Online Chapter Summaries in Six Languages**
- **Progress Assessment Support System (PASS):** Chapter Test*
- **Universal Access Modified Worksheets and Tests CD-ROM:** Modified Chapter Test
- **One-Stop Planner CD-ROM:** ExamView Test Generator (English/Spanish)
- **Alternative Assessment Handbook**

- **PASS:** Section 1 Quiz*
- **Online Quiz:** Section 1
- **Alternative Assessment Handbook**

- **PASS:** Section 2 Quiz*
- **Online Quiz:** Section 2
- **Alternative Assessment Handbook**

- **PASS:** Section 3 Quiz*
- **Online Quiz:** Section 3
- **Alternative Assessment Handbook**

- **PASS:** Section 4 Quiz*
- **Online Quiz:** Section 4
- **Alternative Assessment Handbook**

California Resources for Standards Mastery

INSTRUCTIONAL PLANNING AND SUPPORT

- Universal Access Teacher Management System*
- One-Stop Planner CD-ROM with Test Generator: Teacher Management System with Interactive Teacher's Edition

STANDARDS MASTERY

- Standards Review Workbook*
- At Home: A Guide to Standards Mastery for United States History

Holt Online Learning

To enhance learning, Internet activities are available for Biographies of Constitutional Convention Leaders and Hamilton and Madison Articles.

KEYWORD: SS8 TEACHER

- Teacher Support Page
- Content Updates
- Rubrics and Writing Models
- Teaching Tips for the Multimedia Classroom

KEYWORD: SS8 US4

- Current Events
- Document-Based Questions
- Holt Grapher
- Holt Online Atlas
- Holt Researcher
- Interactive Multimedia Activities
- Internet Activities
- Online Chapter Summaries in Six Languages
- Online Section Quizzes
- American History Maps and Charts

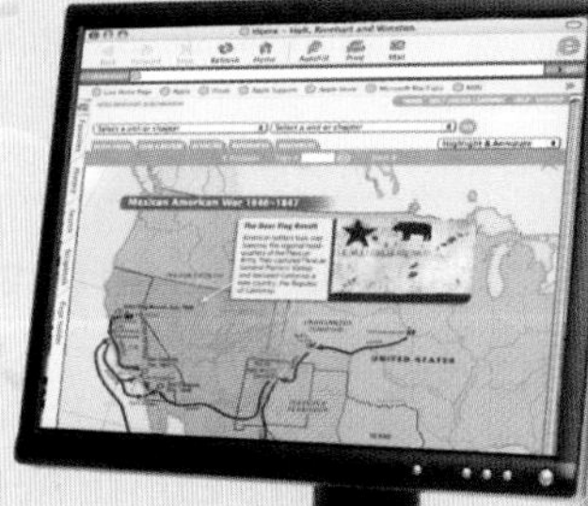

HOLT PREMIER ONLINE STUDENT EDITION

Complete online support for interactivity, assessment, and reporting

- Interactive Maps and Notebook
- Standardized Test Prep
- Homework Practice and Research Activities Online

Mastering the Standards: Differentiating Instruction

Reaching Standards	Basic-level activities designed for all students encountering new material
Standards Proficiency	Intermediate-level activities designed for average students
Exceeding Standards	Challenging activities designed for honors and gifted-and-talented students
Standard English Mastery	Activities designed to improve standard English usage

Frequently Asked Questions

INSTRUCTIONAL PLANNING AND SUPPORT

Where do I find planning aids, pacing guides, lesson plans, and other teaching aids?

Annotated Teacher's Edition:
- Chapter planning guides
- Standards-based instruction and strategies
- Differentiated instruction for universal access
- Point-of-use reminders for integrating program resources

Power Presentations with Video CD-ROM

Universal Access Teacher Management System:
- Year and unit instructional benchmarking guides
- Reproducible lesson plans
- Assessment guides for diagnostic, progress, and summative end-of-the-year tests
- Options for differentiating instruction and intervention
- Teaching guides and answer keys for student workbooks

One-Stop Planner CD-ROM with Test Generator: Teacher Management System with Interactive Teacher's Editon:
- Calendar Planner
- Editable lesson plans
- All reproducible ancillaries in Adobe Acrobat (PDF) format
- ExamView Test Generator (English & Spanish)
- Game Tool for ExamView
- PuzzlePro
- Transparency and video previews

DIFFERENTIATING INSTRUCTION FOR UNIVERSAL ACCESS

What resources are available to ensure that Advanced Learners/GATE Students master the standards?

Teacher's Edition Activities:
- Documents and Ideas, p.115
- Recipe for Government, p. 128
- Federalists v. Antifederalists, p. 133

Lesson Plans for Universal Access

Primary Source Library CD-ROM for United States History

What resources are available to ensure that English Learners and Standard English Learners master the standards?

Teacher's Edition Activities:
- International Relations Dialogues, p. 121
- Creating the Constitution, p.125
- Visualizing Balanced Government, p. 128

Lesson Plans for Universal Access

Chapter Resource File: Vocabulary Builder Activities

Spanish Chapter Summaries Audio CD Program

Online Chapter Summaries in Six Languages

One-Stop Planner CD-ROM:
- PuzzlePro, Spanish Version
- ExamView Test Generator, Spanish Version

What modified materials are available for Special Education?

The ***Universal Access Modified Worksheets and Tests CD-ROM*** provides editable versions of the following:

Vocabulary Flash Cards

Modified Vocabulary Builder Activities

Modified Chapter Review Activity

Modified Chapter Test

HOLT
History's Impact
▶ video series
Forming a Government

What resources are available to ensure that Learners Having Difficulty master the standards?

Teacher's Edition Activities:
- Writing Headlines, p. 122
- Constitutional Convention, p. 126
- Accomplishments of Benjamin Franklin, p. 131

Interactive Reader and Study Guide

Student Edition Full-Read Audio CD

Quick Facts Transparency: Forming a Government Visual Summary

Standards Review Workbook

Social Studies Skills Activity: Determine Different Points of View

Interactive Skills Tutor CD-ROM

How do I intervene for students struggling to master the standards?

Interactive Reader and Study Guide

Quick Facts Transparency: Forming a Government Visual Summary

Standards Review Workbook

Social Studies Skills Activity: Determine Different Points of View

Interactive Skills Tutor CD-ROM

PROFESSIONAL DEVELOPMENT

What teacher training resources are available to help me grow professionally?

- In-service and staff development as part of your Holt Social Studies product purchase
- Quick Teacher Tutorial Lesson Presentation CD-ROM
- Intensive tuition-based Teacher Development Institute
- *Teaching American History* Online 2 Module Professional Development Course
- Convenient Holt Speaker Bureau face-to-face workshop options
- PRAXIS™ Test Prep (#0089) interactive Web-based content refreshers*
- 24/7 *Ask A Professional Development Expert* at http://www.hrw.com/prodev/

* PRAXIS is a trademark of Educational Testing Service (ETS). This publication is not endorsed or approved by ETS.

Information Literacy Skills

To learn more about how History–Social Science instruction may be improved by the effective use of library media centers and information literacy skills, go to the Teacher's Resource Materials for Chapter 4 at **go.hrw.com**, keyword: SS8 MEDIA.

The following materials were developed by the Division for Public Education of the American Bar Association. These materials are part of the **Democracy and Civic Education** supplement.
- Constitution Study Guide
- Supreme Court Case Studies

Chapter Preview

Standards Focus

Standards by Section

Section 1: HSS 8.3.2, 8.9.3

Section 2: HSS 8.2.2, 8.3.5

Section 3: HSS 8.2

Section 4: HSS 8.2.7

Teacher's Edition

HSS **Analysis Skills:** CS 1, CS 2, HR 5, HI 1, HI 2, HI 3, HI 6

ELA Writing 8.2.4.a; Reading 8.2

Preview Grade 11 Standards

HSS **11.1** Students analyze the significant events in the founding of the nation and its attempts to realize the philosophy of government described in the Declaration of Independence.

11.1.1 Describe the Enlightenment and the rise of democratic ideas as the context in which the nation was founded.

11.1.2 Analyze the ideological origins of the American Revolution, the Founding Fathers' philosophy of divinely bestowed inalienable natural rights, the debates on the drafting and ratification of the Constitution, and the addition of the Bill of Rights.

Focus on Writing

The **Chapter Resource File** provides a Focus on Writing worksheet to help students organize and write their newspaper editorials.

CRF: Focus on Writing Activity: A Newspaper Editorial

CHAPTER 4 1777–1791

Forming a Government

California Standards

History–Social Science

8.2 Students analyze the political principles underlying the U.S. Constitution and compare the enumerated and implied powers of the federal government.

8.3 Students understand the foundation of the American political system and the ways in which citizens participate in it.

8.9 Students analyze the early and steady attempts to abolish slavery and to realize the ideals of the Declaration of Independence.

Analysis Skills

CS 1 Students explain how major events are related to one another in time.

HI 2 Students understand and distinguish cause, effect, sequence, and correlation in historical events.

HR 5 Students detect different historical points of view.

English–Language Arts

Writing 8.2.4.a Write persuasive compositions that include a well-defined thesis.

Reading 8.2.0 Students read and understand grade-level appropriate material.

FOCUS ON WRITING

A Newspaper Editorial It is 1788 and you're writing an editorial for a local newspaper. You want to convince your readers that the new Constitution will be much better than the old Articles of Confederation. In this chapter you'll find the information you need to support your opinion.

UNITED STATES

1777 The Continental Congress approves the Articles of Confederation on November 15.

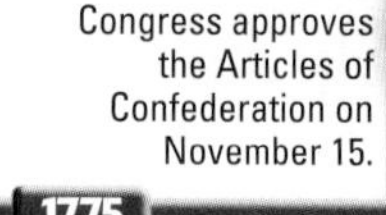

1775

WORLD

1778 The United States and France become allies.

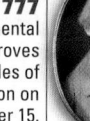

Introduce the Chapter

Standards Proficiency

Focus on Forming a New Government

HSS 8.2, 8.3; HSS **Analysis Skills:** HI 1

1. Explain to students that once the Revolutionary War began and the Declaration of Independence was signed, it was left to Americans to decide how to form a new government. Then ask students what kind of government they might want to form if they had just gained independence from a monarchy.
2. Explain to students that they are going to learn about the form of government that the Americans formed after the Revolutionary War. Have students predict some of the issues that arose as the new government was being established. Write students' predictions for them to see and save the list.
3. Have students make a copy of the predictions. Tell them to note how accurate or inaccurate each of their predictions was as they read the chapter. LS **Logical/Mathematical**

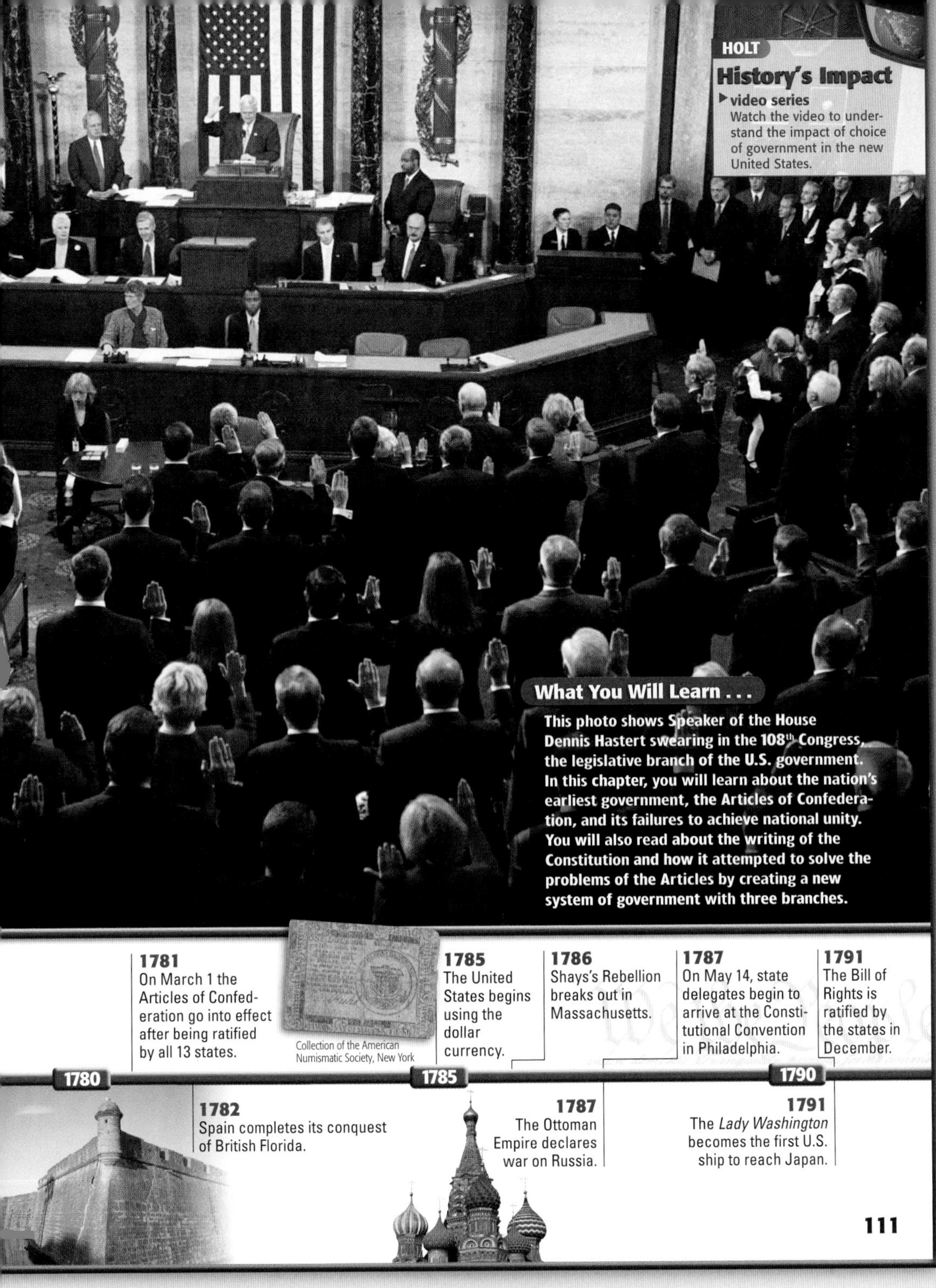

HOLT
History's Impact
▶ video series
Watch the video to understand the impact of choice of government in the new United States.
What You Will Learn . . .
This photo shows Speaker of the House Dennis Hastert swearing in the 108th Congress, the legislative branch of the U.S. government. In this chapter, you will learn about the nation's earliest government, the Articles of Confederation, and its failures to achieve national unity. You will also read about the writing of the Constitution and how it attempted to solve the problems of the Articles by creating a new system of government with three branches.
1781
On March 1 the Articles of Confederation go into effect after being ratified by all 13 states.
Collection of the American Numismatic Society, New York
1785
The United States begins using the dollar currency.
1786
Shays's Rebellion breaks out in Massachusetts.
1787
On May 14, state delegates begin to arrive at the Constitutional Convention in Philadelphia.
1791
The Bill of Rights is ratified by the states in December.
1780
1785
1790
1782
Spain completes its conquest of British Florida.
1787
The Ottoman Empire declares war on Russia.
1791
The *Lady Washington* becomes the first U.S. ship to reach Japan.
111

• Chapter Preview •

HOLT

History's Impact

▶ **video series**
See the Video Teacher's Guide for strategies for using the chapter video **Forming a Government**.

Chapter Big Ideas

Section 1 The Articles of Confederation provided a framework for a national government. **HSS** 8.3.2, 8.9.3

Section 2 Problems faced by the young nation made it clear that a new constitution was needed. **HSS** 8.2.2, 8.3.5

Section 3 A new constitution provided a framework for a stronger national government. **HSS** 8.2

Section 4 Americans carried on a vigorous debate before ratifying the Constitution. **HSS** 8.2.7

Explore the Picture

Congress in Session Every year on January 3, unless otherwise specified, members of Congress take their places in the Capitol Building in Washington, D.C., for the start of a new session. Members gather to fulfill their constitutional responsibility of making the nation's laws. Congress decides issues such as how large the U.S. armed forces will be and whether federal taxes will increase. Each session, lawmakers make decisions that affect not only national and world affairs but also your life, school, and community.

Analyzing Visuals Why might the Speaker of the House formally swear in members at the start of a new session of Congress? *to emphasize the seriousness of representatives' responsibility to make the nation's laws*

Explore the Time Line

1. How many years after the Continental Congress approved the Articles of Confederation were they ratified by all 13 states? *a little under 4 years*
2. When did the United States begin using the dollar currency? *1785*
3. What happened the same year that the Bill of Rights was ratified? *The* Lady Washington *became the first U.S. ship to reach Japan.*

HSS Analysis Skills: CS 1

Connect to Economics

United States Currency The U.S. Constitution gives Congress sole power to coin money and regulate its value. Congress established the dollar as the basic unit of money and created a national mint in Philadelphia. In 1794 Philadelphia minted the first U.S. silver dollar. It featured a liberty head on the front and an eagle on the back. The mint also produced $10 gold coins called eagles.

go.hrw.com
Online Resources
Chapter Resources:
KEYWORD: SS8 US4
Teacher Resources:
KEYWORD: SS8 TEACHER

Reading Social Studies

Understanding Themes

Ask students what might have been some areas of concern for the United States following the Revolutionary War. Help students to see that an immediate concern of U.S. leaders was the creation of a new government. Ask students how they might go about choosing a government to rule a nation. What might be some important powers of that new government? What might happen if the people do not fully support the new government? Point out to students that American society and culture was greatly affected by the new government of the United States. Remind students to focus on the key themes of politics, and society and culture as they read this chapter.

Chronological Order

Focus on Reading Ask each student to write one or two paragraphs that detail a typical school day. Have students write their descriptions in chronological order, from the time they wake up in the morning until they go to sleep. Ask students to exchange descriptions with a partner. Have each student circle words or phrases that signal chronological order. Then have students use those words to create a sequence chain that tracks the events of a typical day for that person.

Reading Social Studies

by Kylene Beers

Economics | Geography | **Politics** | Religion | **Society and Culture** | Science and Technology

Focus on Themes Visualize a row of dominoes, lined up one after the other. Push over the first one, and—one after the other—all eventually fall. In this way, the events in this chapter are like dominoes that cause each other to occur. These events, one after another, finally led to the formation of a new government and a new **society**. If you read closely, you will see that **political** disagreements started the entire process.

Chronological Order

Focus on Reading Like falling dominoes, historical events can create huge chains of results, often stretching over many years. To understand history and events, therefore, we often need to see how they are related in time.

Understanding Chronological Order The word **chronological** means "related to time." Events discussed in this history book are discussed in **sequence**, in the order in which they happened. To understand history better, you can use a sequence chain to take notes about events in the order they happened.

Sequence Chain

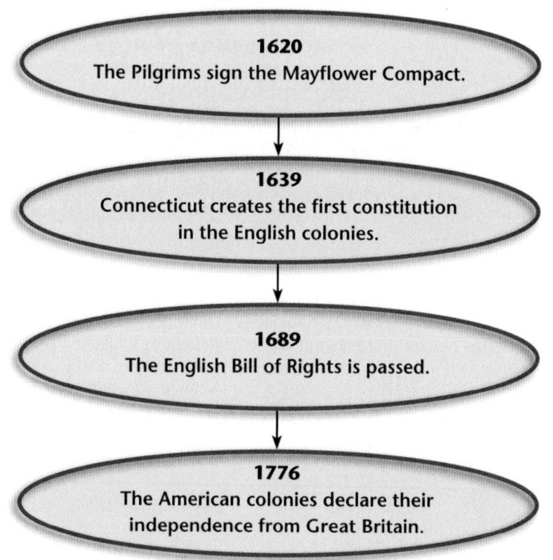

1620
The Pilgrims sign the Mayflower Compact.
1639
Connecticut creates the first constitution in the English colonies.
1689
The English Bill of Rights is passed.
1776
The American colonies declare their independence from Great Britain.

Tip: Writers sometimes signal chronological order, or sequence, by using words or phrases like these:

first, before, then, later, soon, after, before long, next, eventually, finally

Additional reading support can be found in the

Reading and Skills Resources

Reading Support

- Interactive Reader and Study Guide
- Student Edition on Audio CD
- Spanish Chapter Summaries Audio CD Program

Social Studies Skills Support

- Interactive Skills Tutor CD-ROM

Vocabulary Support

- **CRF:** Vocabulary Builder Activities
- **CRF:** Chapter Review Activity
- Universal Access Modified Worksheets and Tests CD-ROM:
  - Vocabulary Flash Cards
  - Vocabulary Builder Activity
  - Chapter Review Activity
- **OSP** Holt PuzzlePro

Standards Focus

HSS Analysis Skills: HI 2
ELA Reading 8.2.0

ELA **Analysis HI 2** Understand and distinguish sequence.
HSS **Reading 8.2.0** Students read and understand grade-level appropriate material.

You Try It!

Read the following passage and answer the questions that follow.

Farmers Rebel

From Chapter 4, p. 123

In August 1786, farmers in three western counties began a revolt. Bands of angry citizens closed down courts in western Massachusetts. Their reasoning was simple—with the courts shut down, no one's property could be taken. In September, a poor farmer and Revolutionary War Veteran, Daniel Shays, led hundreds of men in a forced shutdown of the Supreme Court in Springfield, Massachusetts. The state government ordered the farmers to stop the revolt under threat of capture and death. These threats only made Shays and his followers more determined. The uprising of farmers to protest high taxes and heavy debt became known as Shays's Rebellion.

Shay's forces were defeated by state troops in January 1787. By February many of the rebels were in prison. During their trial, 14 leaders were sentenced to death. However, the state soon freed most of the rebels, including Shays.

After you have read the passage, answer the following questions.

1. Which happened first—citizens closing courts in western Massachusetts or Shays shutting down the Supreme Court? How can you tell?
2. What happened after Shays's forces were defeated by state troops?
3. Draw a sequence chain that shows the effects of Shays' Rebellion in the order they occurred.

Before you read Chapter 4, look for clues that signal the order in which events occurred.

Key Terms and People

Chapter 4

Section 1
Magna Carta *(p. 114)*
English Bill of Rights *(p. 114)*
constitution *(p. 115)*
Virginia Statute for Religious Freedom *(p. 115)*
suffrage *(p. 115)*
Articles of Confederation *(p. 116)*
ratification *(p. 116)*
Land Ordinance of 1785 *(p. 117)*
Northwest Ordinance of 1787 *(p. 117)*
Northwest Territory *(p. 117)*

Section 2
tariffs *(p. 121)*
interstate commerce *(p. 122)*
depression *(p. 123)*
Daniel Shays *(p. 123)*
Shays's Rebellion *(p. 123)*

Section 3
Constitutional Convention *(p. 126)*
James Madison *(p. 126)*
Virginia Plan *(p. 126)*
New Jersey Plan *(p. 127)*
Great Compromise *(p. 127)*
Three-Fifths Compromise *(p. 128)*
popular sovereignty *(p. 129)*
federalism *(p. 129)*
legislative branch *(p. 129)*
executive branch *(p. 129)*
judicial branch *(p. 129)*
checks and balances *(p. 129)*

Section 4
Antifederalists *(p. 132)*
George Mason *(p. 132)*
Federalists *(p. 132)*
Federalist Papers *(p. 133)*
amendments *(p. 135)*
Bill of Rights *(p. 135)*

Academic Vocabulary

In this chapter, you will learn the following academic word:

advocate *(p. 133)*

Reading Social Studies

Key Terms and People

To help students identify and study the key terms and people, have students create a Key-Term FoldNote. Have students fold a sheet of paper in half vertically. Then have students cut along every third or fourth line from the right edge of the paper to the center fold. Students will write the term or person on the outside of each tab. As students learn each key term, have them write a description or definition on the inside. Encourage students to study these people and terms regularly.
LS Verbal/Linguistic, Kinesthetic

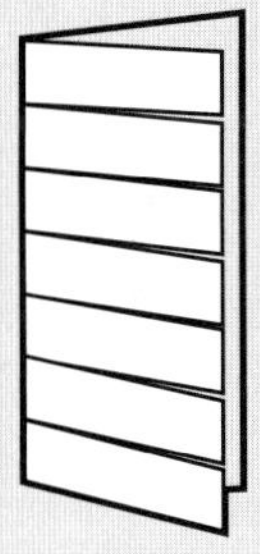

Focus on Reading

See the **Focus on Reading** questions in this chapter for more practice on this reading social studies skill.

Reading Social Studies Assessment

See the **Standards Review** at the end of this chapter for student assessment questions related to this reading skill.

Teaching Tip

Time lines are excellent tools for showing chronological order. Time lines can be created for all sorts of situations. Students could create a time line of their own lives by noting their date of birth, when certain major events occurred, such as starting school or moving to a new home. Students could also create a time line showing the history and development of their community or city. Students can even create a time line to keep track during the year of important events in U.S. history.

Answers

You Try It! 1. *citizens closed down the courts; because the passage uses dates to show order;* **2.** *the rebels were imprisoned and its leaders were sentenced to death;* **3.** *Sequence chain—Shays's forces were defeated; rebels were imprisoned and leaders sentenced to death; most rebels were freed.*

Preteach

Bellringer

If YOU were there . . . Use the **Daily Bellringer Transparency** to help students answer the question.

Daily Bellringer Transparency, Section 1

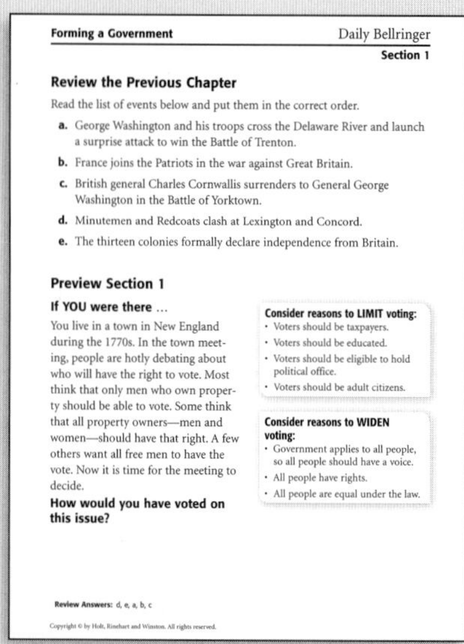
Forming a Government — Daily Bellringer — **Section 1**

Review the Previous Chapter

Read the list of events below and put them in the correct order.

a. George Washington and his troops cross the Delaware River and launch a surprise attack to win the Battle of Trenton.
b. France joins the Patriots in the war against Great Britain.
c. British general Charles Cornwallis surrenders to General George Washington in the Battle of Yorktown.
d. Minutemen and Redcoats clash at Lexington and Concord.
e. The thirteen colonies formally declare independence from Britain.

Preview Section 1

If YOU were there ...

You live in a town in New England during the 1770s. In the town meeting, people are hotly debating about who will have the right to vote. Most think that only men who own property should be able to vote. Some think that all property owners—men and women—should have that right. A few others want all free men to have the vote. Now it is time for the meeting to decide.

How would you have voted on this issue?

Consider reasons to LIMIT voting:
- Voters should be taxpayers.
- Voters should be educated.
- Voters should be eligible to hold political office.
- Voters should be adult citizens.

Consider reasons to WIDEN voting:
- Government applies to all people, so all people should have a voice.
- All people have rights.
- All people are equal under the law.

Review Answers: d, e, a, b, c

Building Vocabulary

Preteach or review the following terms:

controversial subject to debate (p. 117)

ordinance official law or rule (p. 117)

CRF: Vocabulary Builder Activity, Section 1

Standards Focus

HSS 8.3.2

Means: Explain how the Land Ordinance of 1785 and the Northwest Ordinance of 1787 created a system for selling western public lands and forming new states.

Matters: The ordinances shaped the political geography of what is now the Midwest, and many townships created under them still exist today.

HSS 8.9.3

Means: Describe how the Northwest Ordinance promoted education and banned slavery in the Northwest Territory.

Matters: The Northwest Ordinance set the standard for protecting citizens' rights in future territories and states.

SECTION 1

The Articles of Confederation

What You Will Learn . . .

Main Ideas

1. The American people examined many ideas about government.
2. The Articles of Confederation laid the base for the first national government of the United States.
3. The Confederation Congress established the Northwest Territory.

The Big Idea

The Articles of Confederation provided a framework for a national government.

Key Terms and People

HSS 8.3.2 Explain how the ordinances of 1785 and 1787 privatized national resources and transferred federally owned lands into private holding, townships, and states.

HSS 8.9.3 Describe the significance of the Northwest Ordinance in education and in the banning of slavery in new states north of the Ohio River.

If YOU were there...

You live in a town in New England during the 1770s. In the town meeting, people are hotly debating about who will have the right to vote. Most think that only men who own property should be able to vote. Some think that all property owners—men and women—should have that right. A few others want all free men to have the vote. Now it is time for the meeting to decide.

How would you have voted on this issue?

BUILDING BACKGROUND At the time of the Revolution, each of the 13 states had its own government. The rights of citizens varied from state to state. In their town meetings, people often argued about exactly what those rights ought to be. Solving such issues was one step in moving toward a national government.

Ideas about Government

The American colonies had taken a bold step in declaring their independence from Great Britain in July 1776. Their next political goal was to form a new government. To do so, the American people drew from a wide range of political ideas.

English Laws and the Enlightenment

One source of inspiration was English law. England had limited the power of its kings and queens in two documents. These were Magna Carta and the English Bill of Rights. **Magna Carta**, a document signed by King John in 1215, made the king subject to law. The **English Bill of Rights**, passed in 1689, declared the supremacy of Parliament. It kept the king or queen from passing new taxes or changing laws without Parliament's consent. As a result, the people's representatives had a strong voice in England's government.

Americans were also influenced by Enlightenment—a philosophical movement that emphasized the use of reason to examine old

Teach the Big Idea: Master the Standards

Standards Proficiency

The Articles of Confederation

HSS 8.3.2, 8.9.3; HSS **Analysis Skills:** CS 1, HI 1

1. **Teach** Ask students the Main Idea questions to teach this section.
2. **Apply** Organize students into groups of three. Assign each group one of the following topics: *Ideas about Government, Articles of Confederation,* or *Northwest Territory.* Ask students to imagine that it is the late 1700s. Have each group member create a flyer informing the American public about the group's assigned topic. **LS Verbal/Linguistic, Visual/Spatial**
3. **Review** Regroup students so that each new group includes members who worked on each topic. Have each student explain his or her flyer to the other group members.
4. **Practice/Homework** Have each student write a letter to the editor either for or against the Articles of Confederation. Students should provide support for their positions. **LS Verbal/Linguistic**

Alternative Assessment Handbook, Rubrics 14: Group Activity; and 17: Letters to Editors ideas and traditions. Philosopher John Locke believed that a social contract existed between political rulers and the people they ruled. Baron de Montesquieu argued that the only way people could achieve liberty was through the separation of governmental powers.

American Models of Government

Americans had their own models of self-government to follow, like town meetings, the Virginia House of Burgesses, and the Mayflower Compact. In 1639 the people of Connecticut drew up the English colonies' first written **constitution**. A constitution is a set of basic principles and laws that states the powers and duties of the government. In addition, the Declaration of Independence clearly set forth the beliefs on which Americans thought government should be based.

State Constitutions

To keep individual leaders from gaining too much power, the new state constitutions created limited governments, or governments in which all leaders have to obey the laws. Most state constitutions had rules to protect the rights of citizens. Some banned slavery. Some protected the rights of those accused of a crime. Thomas Jefferson's ideas about religious freedom were included in the **Virginia Statute for Religious Freedom**. This document declared that no person could be forced to attend a particular church or be required to pay for a church with tax money.

Right to Vote

Under British rule, only free, white men that owned land could vote. Many states' constitutions expanded **suffrage**, or the right to vote, by allowing any white man who paid taxes to vote. In every state, however, only landowners could hold public office. Some states originally allowed women and free African Americans to vote, but these rights were soon taken away. Suffrage would not be restored to these groups for decades to come.

READING CHECK **Comparing** What two principles were common to state constitutions written during the Revolutionary War?

Women's Suffrage

New Jersey allowed women to vote when it first joined the United States. This right was taken away by 1807.

Why do you think women were not allowed to vote in the early United States?

Direct Teach

Main Idea

❶ Ideas about Government

The American people examined many ideas about government.

Recall What documents did Americans look to when creating a new government? *Magna Carta, English Bill of Rights, Mayflower Compact, Fundamental Orders of Connecticut, Declaration of Independence, state constitutions, Virginia Statute of Religious Freedom*

Analyze Describe three key ideas from these documents that influenced U.S. government. *possible answers—rule of law, people hold the power, limited government, constitutional protection of rights, separation of powers, representative government, separation of church and state*

Make Generalizations In what ways was suffrage expanded and limited in state constitutions? *Constitutions in general expanded voting rights for white men, while limiting suffrage for African Americans and women.*

CRF: Primary Source Activity: Iroquois Great Law of Peace

HSS Analysis Skills: HI 1, HI 2

Linking to Today

Separation of Church and State Public debate over religious freedom and the separation of church and state continues today. Current examples include school prayer, the presence of religious organizations in public schools, and the words to the Pledge of Allegiance.

Differentiating Instruction for Universal Access

Advanced Learners/GATE

Exceeding Standards

1. Organize the class into three groups. Have students discuss within their groups which ideas and documents shaped American beliefs about government.
2. Next, have each group decide which document had the greatest influence and was the most important in the development of American representative government.
3. Each group should build a debate around that premise by developing arguments showing the merits and influence of the document as well as arguments showing the flaws and weaknesses of the document.
4. Have each group perform its debate for the class. **LS Interpersonal, Verbal/Linguistic**

HSS Analysis Skills: HI 1, HI 2, HI 3

Alternative Assessment Handbook, Rubric 10: Debates

Answers

Women's Suffrage *possible answer—At the time, many people thought women's place was in the home and that women did not have the ability to vote intelligently.*

Reading Check *the people hold the power of government, limited government*

Direct Teach

Main Idea

2 Articles of Confederation

The Articles of Confederation laid the base for the first national government of the United States.

Recall What was the ratification process for the Articles of Confederation? *It was sent to the state legislatures for official approval.*

Draw Conclusions Why do you think that the Committee of Thirteen did not provide for a president in the Articles of Confederation? *possible answer—feared a president might become as powerful as a monarch*

Contrast Under the Articles of Confederation, how did the power of the national government compare to that of the state governments? *possible answer—The state governments held most of the power, even being able to refuse requests from Congress.*

HSS Analysis Skills: HI 1

Info to Know

The Limits of the Articles of Confederation Under the Articles of Confederation, the states did not always respond to the requests of Congress. The legislative body did not even meet on a regular basis. Members also did not attend every meeting. A great deal of effort was required to get enough members gathered to ratify the Treaty of Paris, which ended the American Revolution.

Answers

Interpreting Maps **1.** *Illinois, Indiana, Michigan, Ohio, Wisconsin* **2.** *36 sections*

Reading Check *The states had the right to refuse requests from Congress; there was not a president or a national court system.*

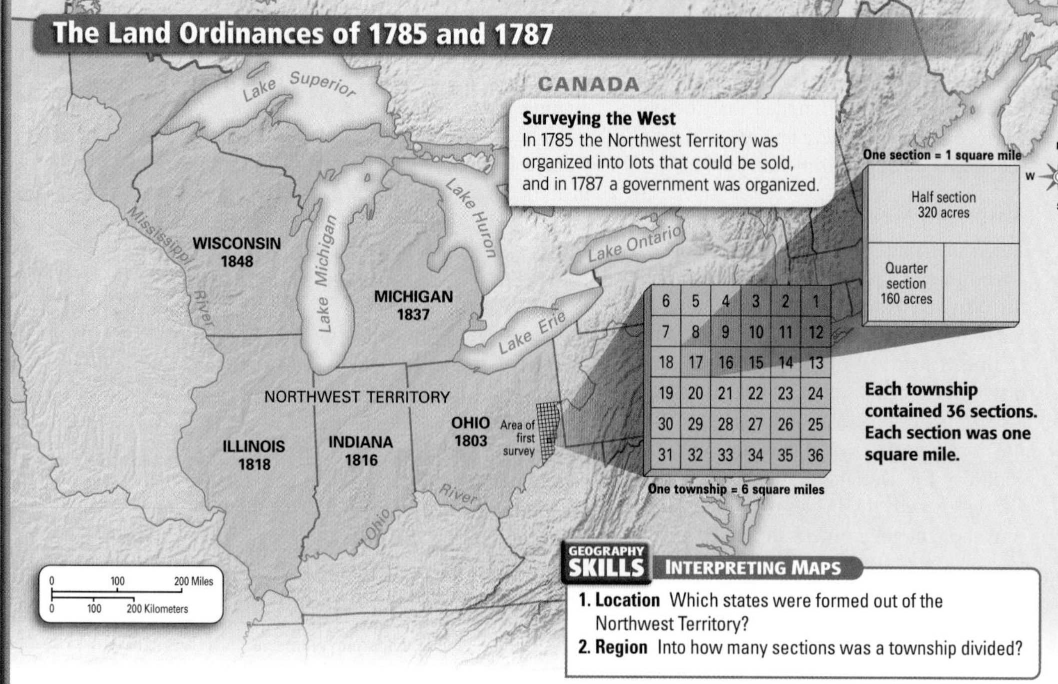

GEOGRAPHY SKILLS INTERPRETING MAPS

1. **Location** Which states were formed out of the Northwest Territory?
2. **Region** Into how many sections was a township divided?

Articles of Confederation

The Second Continental Congress was organized to create a national government. The Continental Congress appointed a Committee of Thirteen, with one member from each colony. This group was assigned to discuss and draft the Articles of Confederation, the new national constitution.

Under the **Articles of Confederation**, Congress would become the national government, but it would have limited powers in order to protect the liberties of the people. Each state had one vote in the Congress. Congress could settle conflicts among the states, make coins, borrow money, and make treaties with other countries and with Native Americans. Congress could also ask the states for money and soldiers. However, states had the power to refuse these requests. In addition, the government did not have a president or a national court system.

The Second Continental Congress passed the Articles of Confederation on November 15, 1777. Then it sent the Articles to each state legislature for **ratification**, or official approval, before the new national government could take effect.

Conflicts over claims to western lands slowed the process, but by 1779 every state except Maryland had ratified the Articles. Maryland's leaders refused to ratify until other states gave up their western land claims. Thomas Jefferson assured Maryland that western lands would be made into new states, rather than increasing territory for existing states. Satisfied with this condition, in March 1781 Maryland ratified the Articles. This put the first national government of the United States into effect.

READING CHECK **Summarizing** What were two weaknesses in the new national government?

Collaborative Learning

Standards Proficiency

Forming a Government

HSS Analysis Skills: HI 1

1. Organize students into groups. Tell each group to create a set of rules for the school. The rules must apply fairly to everyone and promote student rights. In addition, each group member must agree to the set of rules.
2. When the groups have finished, write each group's rules for students to see. Then have the class work to create one set of three to five rules. Each class member must approve all the rules.
3. Have students discuss the difficulties they encountered during the exercise. Then have them compare their experience to that of creating the Articles of Confederation. What issues and challenges did the Committee of Thirteen face? **LS Interpersonal, Verbal/Linguistic**
4. **Extend** Have each student draw a large picture of a parchment document and in it outline the powers of Congress and the states under the Articles of Confederation. **LS Verbal/Linguistic**

Alternative Assessment Handbook, Rubrics 11: Discussions; and 42: Writing to Inform

Northwest Territory

Congress had to decide what to do with the western lands now under its control and how to raise money to pay debts. It tried to solve both problems by selling the western lands. Congress passed the **Land Ordinance of 1785**, which set up a system for surveying and dividing western lands. The land was split into townships, which were 36 square miles divided into 36 lots of 640 acres each. One lot was reserved for a public school, and four lots were given to veterans. The remaining lots were sold to the public.

To form a political system for the region, Congress passed the **Northwest Ordinance of 1787**. The ordinance established the **Northwest Territory**, which included areas that are now in Illinois, Indiana, Michigan, Ohio, Minnesota, and Wisconsin. The Northwest Ordinance created a system for bringing new states into the Union. Congress agreed that the Northwest Territory would be divided into several smaller territories with a governor appointed by Congress. When the population of a territory reached 60,000, its settlers could draft their own constitution and ask to join the Union.

In addition, the law protected civil liberties and required that public education be provided. Finally, the ordinance stated that "there shall be neither slavery nor involuntary servitude [forced labor] in the . . . territory." This last condition banned slavery in the Territory and set the standard for future territories. However, slavery would continue to be a controversial issue.

THE IMPACT TODAY

Townships remained the unit of local government after the Northwest Territory was divided into states. Many of these townships still exist today.

READING CHECK **Analyzing Information** How did the Northwest Ordinance of 1787 affect the United States?

SUMMARY AND PREVIEW The Northwest Ordinance settled the future of the Northwest Territory. In the next section you will read about other challenges the new government faced.

Section 1 Assessment

go.hrw.com
Online Quiz
KEYWORD: SS8 HP4

Reviewing Ideas, Terms, and People HSS 8.3.2, 8.9.3

1. a. **Identify** What documents influenced ideas about government in the United States?
   b. **Draw Conclusions** What impact did the **Virginia Statute for Religious Freedom** have on the U.S. government?
2. a. **Identify** What was the **Articles of Confederation**?
   b. **Summarize** What powers were granted to Congress by the Articles of Confederation?
   c. **Predict** What are some possible problems that might result from the lack of a national court system?
3. a. **Describe** How were public lands in the West divided by the **Land Ordinance of 1785**?
   b. **Evaluate** In your opinion, what was the most important element of the **Northwest Ordinance of 1787**? Why?

Critical Thinking

4. **Categorizing** Copy the chart below. Use it to identify the strengths and weaknesses of the government created by the Articles of Confederation.

Articles of Confederation

Strengths	Weaknesses

FOCUS ON WRITING

5. **Thinking about the Articles of Confederation** Make a list of powers the Articles of Confederation gave the national government. Which ones seem strong? Can you think of any important powers that are missing?

Section 1 Assessment Answers

1. **a.** Magna Carta, English Bill of Rights, Mayflower Compact, Fundamental Orders of Connecticut, Declaration of Independence, state constitutions, Virginia Statute of Religious Freedom
   b. established precedent of freedom of religion
2. **a.** national constitution for first U.S. government
   b. Congress could settle conflicts between the states, make coins, borrow money, make treaties with other nations, and ask states for money and soldiers.
   c. possible answers—state courts might interpret laws differently; no federal system of appeal
3. **a.** into townships of 36 square miles divided into 36 lots of 640 acres each; four lots reserved for veterans and one for a public school
   b. established territorial representation and public education; prohibited slavery
4. strengths—limited government, Congress could settle conflicts, mint coins, borrow money, negotiate treaties; weaknesses—states could refuse requests from Congress; no president or national court system
5. Answers will vary but should reflect an understanding of the Articles of Confederation.

Direct Teach

Main Idea

❸ Northwest Territory

The Confederation Congress established the Northwest Territory.

Recall What was the purpose of the Land Ordinance of 1785? *to set up a system for surveying and dividing western public lands*

Summarize What important rights did the Northwest Ordinance of 1787 provide? *civil liberties, public education; freedom from slavery*

- **CRF:** History and Geography Activity: The Northwest Territory
- Map Transparency: The Land Ordinances of 1785 and 1787
- HSS 8.3.2, 8.9.3; HSS **Analysis Skills:** HI 1

Review & Assess

Close

Have students summarize some of the early actions of the new nation of the United States.

Review

- Online Quiz, Section 1

Assess

- SE Section 1 Assessment
- PASS: Section 1 Quiz
- Alternative Assessment Handbook

Reteach/Classroom Intervention

- California Standards Review Workbook
- Interactive Reader and Study Guide, Section 1
- Interactive Skills Tutor CD-ROM

Answers

Reading Check *created a way to incorporate new states, ban slavery, protect civil liberties, and provide public education in the Northwest Territory*

History and Geography

Activity Ship of State Graphic Organizer Draw a simple sailing ship for students to see. Have each student make a large copy of the ship and name it the *US Constitution: The Ship of State*. Then have students label different parts of the ship with the six items listed here that influenced the U.S. Constitution. Each student should write a phrase or sentence explaining the significance of each idea. In addition, encourage students to select parts of the ship that they think represent the idea in some way. Have volunteers share their work with the class. **LS Verbal/Linguistic, Visual/Spatial**

HSS 8.2.1, 8.2.5; **HSS Analysis Skills:** HI 1

Linking to Today

Parliament Today Parliament, the lawmaking body of Great Britain, is bicameral. That is, it consists of two parts, or houses. Parliament is made up of the House of Lords, appointed by the monarch, and the House of Commons, elected by the people. This system enables each house to check and improve the work of the other house. Today, however, the House of Lords holds little power. The House of Commons is now the only real lawmaking body in Britain. It has complete control of all money bills and most other public legislation.

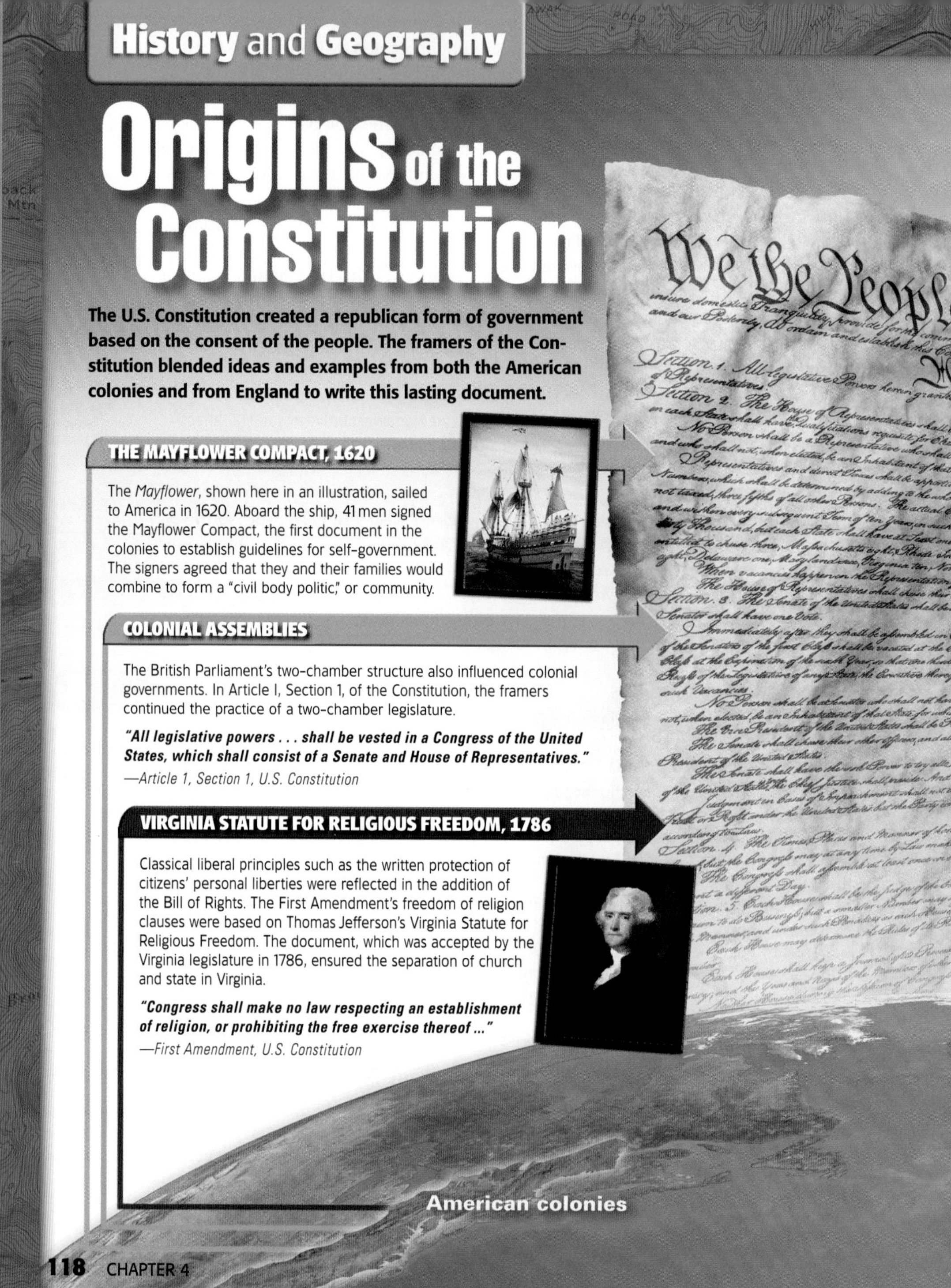

History and Geography

Origins of the Constitution

The U.S. Constitution created a republican form of government based on the consent of the people. The framers of the Constitution blended ideas and examples from both the American colonies and from England to write this lasting document.

THE MAYFLOWER COMPACT, 1620

The *Mayflower*, shown here in an illustration, sailed to America in 1620. Aboard the ship, 41 men signed the Mayflower Compact, the first document in the colonies to establish guidelines for self-government. The signers agreed that they and their families would combine to form a "civil body politic," or community.

COLONIAL ASSEMBLIES

The British Parliament's two-chamber structure also influenced colonial governments. In Article I, Section 1, of the Constitution, the framers continued the practice of a two-chamber legislature.

"All legislative powers . . . shall be vested in a Congress of the United States, which shall consist of a Senate and House of Representatives."

—Article 1, Section 1, U.S. Constitution

VIRGINIA STATUTE FOR RELIGIOUS FREEDOM, 1786

Classical liberal principles such as the written protection of citizens' personal liberties were reflected in the addition of the Bill of Rights. The First Amendment's freedom of religion clauses were based on Thomas Jefferson's Virginia Statute for Religious Freedom. The document, which was accepted by the Virginia legislature in 1786, ensured the separation of church and state in Virginia.

"Congress shall make no law respecting an establishment of religion, or prohibiting the free exercise thereof ..."

—First Amendment, U.S. Constitution

Differentiating Instruction for Universal Access

Learners Having Difficulty

Reaching Standards | Research Required

Materials: blank note cards

1. Organize the class into six groups. Assign each group one of the influences listed above.
2. Have each group use this feature as well as the text in the previous chapter to prepare flash cards that explain the significance of the group's assigned topic and how it influenced the U.S. Constitution.
3. Have volunteers from each group present some of the group's cards to the class. Correct any student misconceptions or errors.
4. Reorganize students into groups that contain one member from each of the previous groups. In these new groups, have each member in turn use his or her flash cards to quiz the other members. **LS Interpersonal, Verbal/Linguistic**

HSS 8.2.1, 8.2.5; **HSS Analysis Skills:** HI 1

Alternative Assessment Handbook, Rubric 14: Group Activity

Standards Focus

HSS 8.2 Students analyze the political principles underlying the U.S. Constitution and compare the enumerated and implied powers of the federal government.

8.2.1 Discuss the significance of the Magna Carta, the English Bill of Rights, and the Mayflower Compact.

8.2.5 Understand the significance of Jefferson's Statute for Religious Freedom as a forerunner of the First Amendment and the origins, purpose, and differing views of the founding fathers on the issue of the separation of church and state.

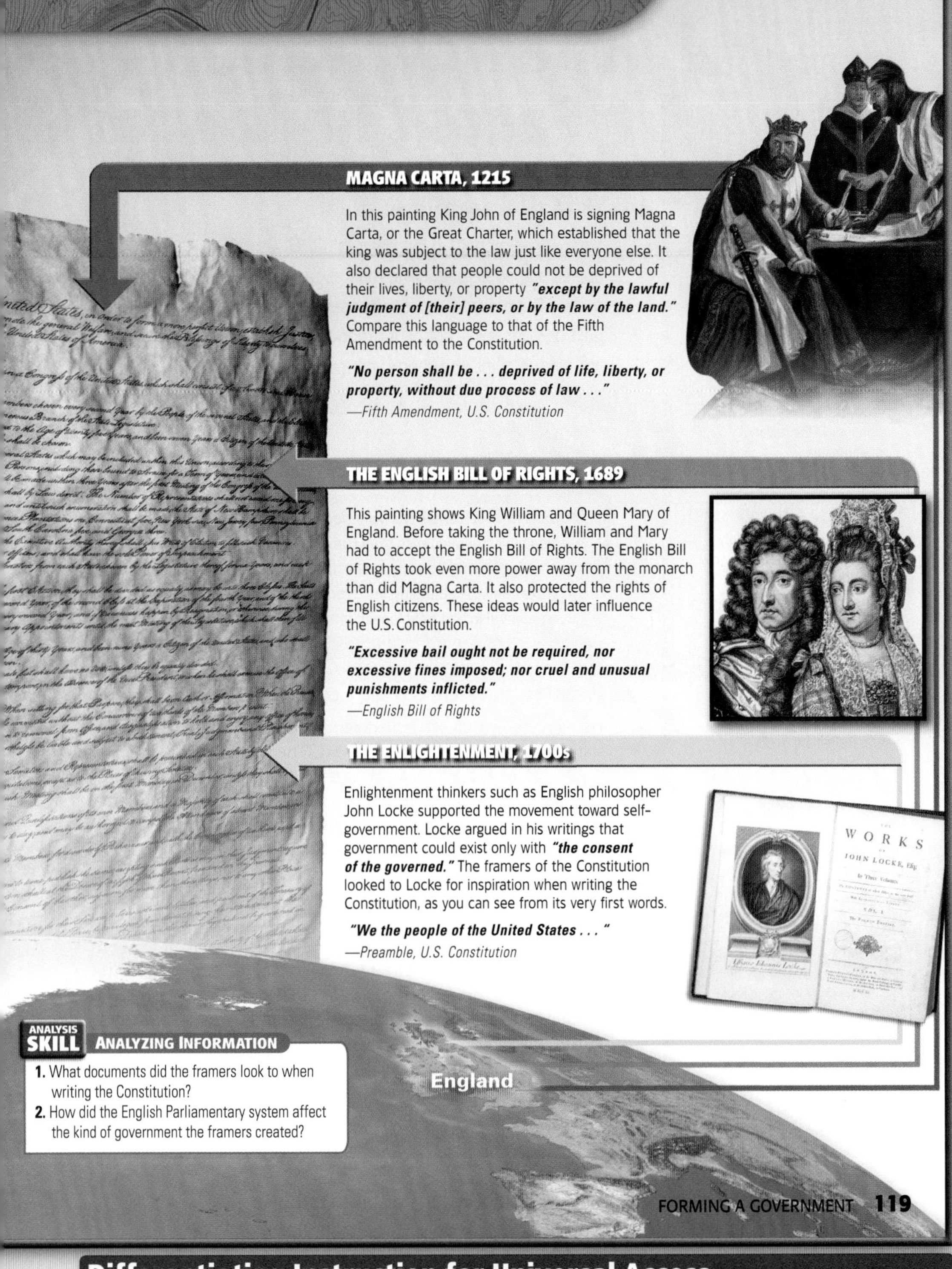

MAGNA CARTA, 1215

In this painting King John of England is signing Magna Carta, or the Great Charter, which established that the king was subject to the law just like everyone else. It also declared that people could not be deprived of their lives, liberty, or property ***"except by the lawful judgment of [their] peers, or by the law of the land."*** Compare this language to that of the Fifth Amendment to the Constitution.

"No person shall be . . . deprived of life, liberty, or property, without due process of law . . ."
—Fifth Amendment, U.S. Constitution

THE ENGLISH BILL OF RIGHTS, 1689

This painting shows King William and Queen Mary of England. Before taking the throne, William and Mary had to accept the English Bill of Rights. The English Bill of Rights took even more power away from the monarch than did Magna Carta. It also protected the rights of English citizens. These ideas would later influence the U.S. Constitution.

"Excessive bail ought not be required, nor excessive fines imposed; nor cruel and unusual punishments inflicted."
—English Bill of Rights

THE ENLIGHTENMENT, 1700s

Enlightenment thinkers such as English philosopher John Locke supported the movement toward self-government. Locke argued in his writings that government could exist only with ***"the consent of the governed."*** The framers of the Constitution looked to Locke for inspiration when writing the Constitution, as you can see from its very first words.

"We the people of the United States . . . "
—Preamble, U.S. Constitution

ANALYSIS SKILL ANALYZING INFORMATION

1. What documents did the framers look to when writing the Constitution?
2. How did the English Parliamentary system affect the kind of government the framers created?

History and Geography

World Events

Magna Carta Although Magna Carta became a cornerstone of constitutional government and rule by law, its original purpose was to limit the king's powers and protect the nobles' feudal rights. It included such concepts as church freedom, trial by jury, freedom from taxation without cause and consent, and due process of law. The document's final article empowered English barons to take up arms against the king if he violated its conditions.

Connect to Government

The British Constitution The British Constitution is not a single document. Instead, it consists partly of several great documents. Among them are Magna Carta, the Petition of Rights, the Habeas Corpus Act, the English Bill of Rights, and the Act of Settlement. It also includes acts of Parliament, which can be changed by later Parliaments. Some features of the British government have never even been written down but are based largely on tradition.

Did You Know?

The College of William and Mary was the second university established in the colonies. Chartered in 1693 and named after King William III and Queen Mary II, it is located in Williamsburg, Virginia.

Differentiating Instruction for Universal Access

Advanced Learners/GATE

Exceeding Standards | Research Required

Materials: colored markers and pencils

1. Have students discuss the ideas listed above that influenced the U.S. Constitution.
2. Ask students to imagine that they have just opened a new restaurant called Constitutional Cuisine. Have each student create a menu for the restaurant. The menu should list the ideas above as dishes and provide a description of each dish that explains the idea's significance. Encourage students to be creative in their names and descriptions.
3. Students should base the price of each dish on that idea's importance to the Constitution.
4. In addition, students might organize the dishes into categories based on ideas such as rule of law, limited government, consent of the governed, separation of powers, and individual rights. **LS Verbal/Linguistic**

HSS 8.2.1, 8.2.5; **HSS Analysis Skills:** HI 1

Alternative Assessment Handbook, Rubric 37: Writing Assignments

Answers

Analyzing Information 1. *Mayflower Compact, Virginia Statute for Religious Freedom, Magna Carta, English Bill of Rights;* **2.** *The framers used the same two-chamber structure for Congress that the British Parliament used.*

Preteach

Bellringer

If YOU were there . . . Use the **Daily Bellringer Transparency** to help students answer the question.

Daily Bellringer Transparency, Section 2

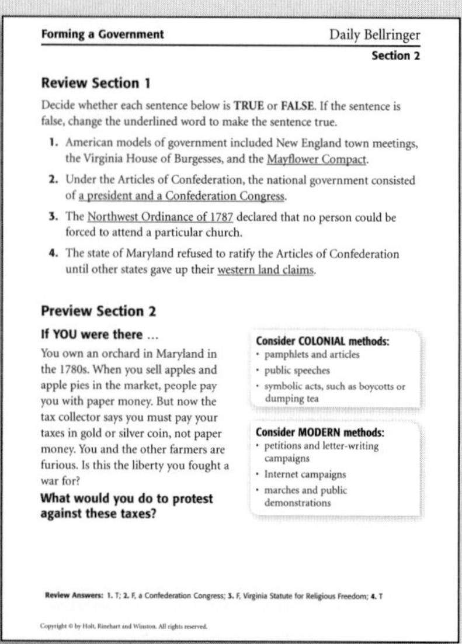

Forming a Government Daily Bellringer
Section 2

Review Section 1

Decide whether each sentence below is **TRUE** or **FALSE**. If the sentence is false, change the underlined word to make the sentence true.

1. American models of government included New England town meetings, the Virginia House of Burgesses, and the Mayflower Compact.
2. Under the Articles of Confederation, the national government consisted of a president and a Confederation Congress.
3. The Northwest Ordinance of 1787 declared that no person could be forced to attend a particular church.
4. The state of Maryland refused to ratify the Articles of Confederation until other states gave up their western land claims.

Preview Section 2

If YOU were there ...

You own an orchard in Maryland in the 1780s. When you sell apples and apple pies in the market, people pay you with paper money. But now the tax collector says you must pay your taxes in gold or silver coin, not paper money. You and the other farmers are furious. Is this the liberty you fought a war for?

What would you do to protest against these taxes?

Consider COLONIAL methods:
- pamphlets and articles
- public speeches
- symbolic acts, such as boycotts or dumping tea

Consider MODERN methods:
- petitions and letter-writing campaigns
- Internet campaigns
- marches and public demonstrations

Review Answers: **1.** T; **2.** F, a Confederation Congress; **3.** F, Virginia Statute for Religious Freedom; **4.** T

Building Vocabulary

Preteach or review the following terms:

creditors people who lend money (p. 123)

debtors people who owe money (p. 123)

inflation a rise in prices combined with the reduced value of money (p. 122)

CRF: Vocabulary Builder Activity, Section 2

Standards Focus

HSS 8.2.2

Means: Analyze the success of the Articles of Confederation in applying the ideals of the Declaration of Independence.

Matters: Americans today continue to evaluate government based on how well it applies the ideals of the Declaration.

HSS 8.3.5

Means: Understand the significance of Shays's Rebellion and explain how the national government responded to it.

Matters: Shays's Rebellion led to calls for stronger central government and, ultimately, the creation of the U.S. Constitution we have today.

SECTION 2

The New Nation Faces Challenges

What You Will Learn . . .

Main Ideas

1. The United States had difficulties with other nations.
2. Internal economic problems plagued the new nation.
3. Shays's Rebellion pointed out weaknesses in the Articles of Confederation.
4. Many Americans called for changes in the national government.

The Big Idea

Problems faced by the young nation made it clear that a new constitution was needed.

Key Terms and People

tariffs, *p. 121*
interstate commerce, *p. 122*
depression, *p. 123*
Daniel Shays, *p. 123*
Shays's Rebellion, *p. 123*

HSS 8.2.2 Analyze the Articles of Confederation and the Constitution and the success of each in implementing the ideals of the Declaration of Independence.

8.3.5 Know the significance of domestic resistance movements and ways in which the central government responded to such movements (e.g., Shays's Rebellion, the Whiskey Rebellion).

If YOU were there...

You own an orchard in Maryland in the 1780s. When you sell apples and apple pies in the market, people pay you with paper money. But now the tax collector says you must pay your taxes in gold or silver coins, not paper money. You and the other farmers are furious. Is this the liberty you fought a war for?

What would you do to protest against these taxes?

BUILDING BACKGROUND Americans surprised the world by winning their independence from Great Britain. But the 13 new states were far from being a strong nation. Internal problems, especially with taxes and the economy, led to protests and rebellion. The government also had trouble with foreign trade and treaties.

Relations with Other Countries

Under the Articles of Confederation, Congress could not force states to provide soldiers for an army. The Continental Army had disbanded, or dissolved, soon after the signing of the Treaty of Paris of 1783. Without an army, the national government found it difficult to protect its citizens against foreign threats.

Trouble with Britain

It was also difficult to enforce international treaties such as the Treaty of Paris of 1783. The United States found it especially hard to force the British to turn over "with all convenient speed" their forts on the American side of the Great Lakes. The United States wanted to gain control of these forts because they protected valuable land and fur-trade routes. Still, Britain was slow to withdraw from the area. A British official warned against the United States trying to seize the forts by force. He said that any attempt to do so would be opposed by the thousands of British soldiers who had settled in Canada after the Revolution "who are ready to fly to arms at a moment's warning."

Teach the Big Idea: Master the Standards

Standards Proficiency

The New Nation Faces Challenges

HSS 8.2.2, 8.3.5; HSS **Analysis Skills:** HI 1, HI 2

1. **Teach** Ask the Main Idea questions to teach this section.
2. **Apply** Ask students to imagine that Alexander Hamilton and James Madison have asked each of them to create a large notice to appear in U.S. newspapers announcing the Constitutional Convention. The notice should explain the weaknesses of the Articles of Confederation, the many problems that resulted, and why a Constitutional Convention is needed. The notice should also give the convention's time and place and urge all states to send delegates. **LS Verbal/Linguistic**
3. **Review** As you review the section, have volunteers share their notices with the class.
4. **Practice/Homework** Have each student create a protest sign addressing one problem with the Articles of Confederation. **LS Verbal/Linguistic**

Alternative Assessment Handbook, Rubrics 28: Posters; and 42: Writing to Inform

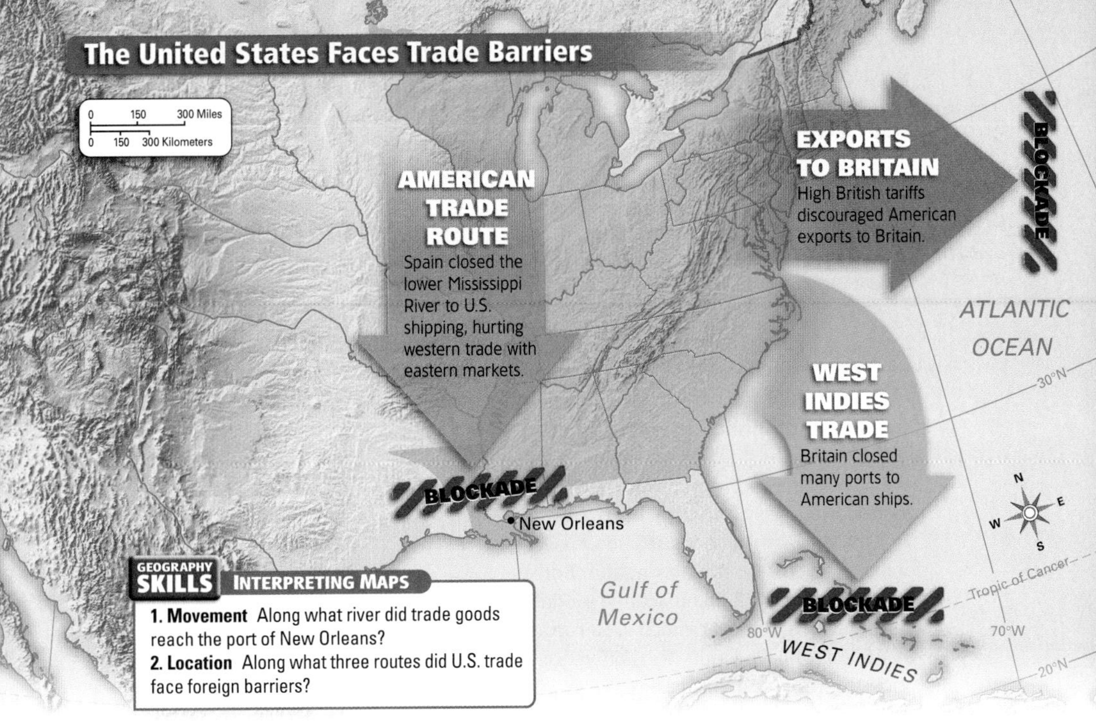

GEOGRAPHY SKILLS INTERPRETING MAPS

1. **Movement** Along what river did trade goods reach the port of New Orleans?
2. **Location** Along what three routes did U.S. trade face foreign barriers?

Trade with Britain

The United States also faced problems trading with Great Britain. After the signing of the Treaty of Paris, Britain closed many of its ports to American ships. Before the Revolutionary War, colonial ships had traded a great deal with the British West Indies and stopped there on their way to other destinations. This travel and trading stopped after 1783.

In addition, Britain forced American merchants to pay high **tariffs**—taxes on imports or exports. The tariffs applied to goods such as rice, tobacco, tar, and oil that were grown or mined in the United States and then sold in Britain. Merchants had to raise prices to cover the tariffs. Ultimately, the costs would be passed on to customers, who had to pay higher prices for the goods. The economic condition of the country was getting worse by the day.

Trade with Spain

In 1784 Spanish officials closed the lower Mississippi River to U.S. shipping. Western farmers and merchants were furious because they used the Mississippi to send goods to eastern and foreign markets. Congress tried to work out an agreement with Spain, but the plan did not receive a majority vote in Congress. The plan could not be passed. As a result, Spain broke off the negotiations.

Many state leaders began to criticize the national government. Rhode Island's representatives wrote, "Our federal government is but a name; a mere shadow without substance [power]." Critics believed that Spain might have continued to negotiate if the United States had possessed a strong military. These leaders believed that the national government needed to be more powerful.

Direct Teach

Main Idea

1 Relations with Other Countries

The United States had difficulties with other nations.

Recall What problems did the United States have with Great Britain? *Britain refused to turn over its forts as the Treaty of Paris required and closed many ports to Americans ships, which hurt the U.S. economy.*

Identify Cause and Effect How did the weaknesses of the Articles of Confederation affect U.S. relations with other nations? *The United States appeared weak because it had no army to enforce treaties or to give it a position of power in negotiations.*

Map Transparency: The United States Faces Trade Barriers

HSS 8.2.2; HSS **Analysis Skills:** HI 1, HI 2

Linking to Today

World Trade Organization International trade has changed a great deal since the 1780s. Today countries are working to make trade easier. In 1993, for example, the United States and 116 other nations expanded an earlier trade agreement to form the World Trade Organization (WTO). Members of the WTO, which went into effect in January 1995, agreed to cut tariffs and eliminate manufacturing quotas.

Critical Thinking: Solving Problems

Standards Proficiency

International Relations Dialogues

Standard English Mastery

1. Pair students. Assign one student in each pair to be an American official and the other student to be either a British or Spanish official.
2. Have each pair write a dialogue about the problems occurring between their two countries. Students' dialogues should address how each nation views the other, why problems are occurring, and suggestions for possible solutions.
3. Have each pair write a script for its dialogue. Remind students to use standard English and correct grammar, punctuation, and spelling.
4. Have volunteer pairs present their dialogues to the class. During each presentation, correct any factual errors or problems with students' standard English.
5. Conclude by having the class discuss how weaknesses in the Articles of Confederation led to international problems.

LS **Interpersonal, Verbal/Linguistic**

HSS 8.2.2; HSS **Analysis Skills:** HR 5, HI 1

Alternative Assessment Handbook, Rubric 37: Writing Assignments

Answers

Interpreting Maps 1. *Mississippi River;* **2.** *route to New Orleans; export route to Britain; route to British West Indies*

Direct Teach

Main Idea

1 Relations with Other Countries

The United States had difficulties with other nations.

Identify Cause and Effect How did closed trade markets affect the U.S. economy? *Exports fell, imports from Britain rose, and British merchants could undersell American merchants, which further hurt the economy.*

HSS 8.2.2; HSS **Analysis Skills:** HI 1, HI 2

Main Idea

2 Economic Problems

Internal economic problems plagued the new nation.

Recall What domestic economic problems did the states experience? *problems with interstate commerce, war debts, and a weak economy*

Analyze How did inflation hurt the economy? *decreased trade and business, which contributed to a depression*

HSS 8.2.2; HSS **Analysis Skills:** HI 1, HI 2

Info to Know

Trade with China In 1785 the ship *Empress of China* returned to New York from China. The ship's owners had traded more than 40 tons of ginseng for tea and other Chinese products. Many Americans hoped that this success at opening trade with China would mean the United States would not have to rely so much on trade with Great Britain.

Impact of Closed Markets

The closing of markets in the British West Indies seriously affected the U.S. economy. James Madison of Virginia wrote about the crisis.

> "The Revolution has robbed us of our trade with the West Indies . . . without opening any other channels to compensate [make up for] it. In every point of view, indeed, the trade of this country is in a deplorable [terrible] condition."
>
> —James Madison, quoted in *Independence on Trial* by Frederick W. Marks III

Farmers could no longer export their goods to the British West Indies. They also had to hire British ships to carry their goods to British markets, which was very expensive. American exports dropped while British goods flowed freely into the United States.

This unequal trade caused serious economic problems for the new nation. British merchants could sell manufactured products in the United States at much lower prices than locally made goods. This difference in prices hurt American businesses.

The Confederation Congress could not correct the problem because it did not have the authority either to pass tariffs or to order the states to pass tariffs. The states could offer little help. If one state passed a tariff, the British could simply sell their goods in another state. Most states did not cooperate in trade matters. Instead, states worked only to increase their own trade rather than working to improve the trade situation for the whole country.

In 1785 the situation led a British magazine to call the new nation the Dis-United States. As a result of the trade problems with Britain, American merchants began looking for other markets such as China, France, and the Netherlands. Despite such attempts, Britain remained the most important trading partner of the United States.

READING CHECK **Analyzing** Why was the Confederation Congress unable to solve America's economic problems?

Economic Problems

In addition to international trade issues, other challenges soon appeared. Trade problems among the states, war debts, and a weak economy plagued the states.

Trade among States

Because the Confederation Congress had no power to regulate **interstate commerce** —trade between two or more states—states followed their own trade interests. As a result, trade laws differed from state to state. This situation made trade difficult for merchants whose businesses crossed state lines.

Inflation

After the Revolutionary War, most states had a hard time paying off war debts and struggled to collect overdue taxes. To ease this hardship, some states began printing large amounts of paper money. The result was inflation. This money had

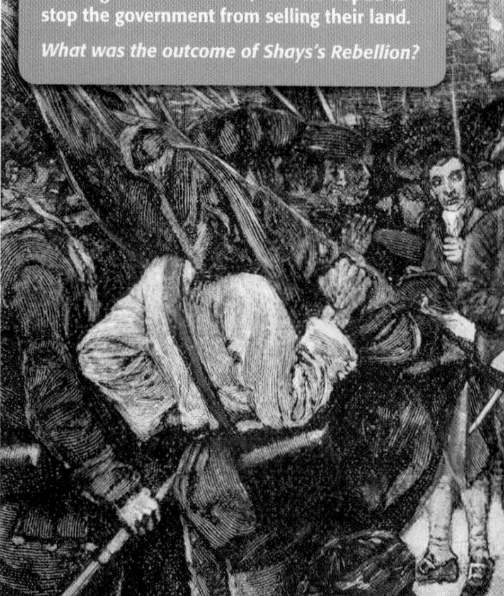

A Farmer Leads a Revolt

Daniel Shays, at the top of the steps, stands firm in the face of demands that he leave the courthouse in Springfield, Massachusetts. By shutting down the courts, farmers hoped to stop the government from selling their land.

What was the outcome of Shays's Rebellion?

Differentiating Instruction for Universal Access

Learners Having Difficulty — Reaching Standards

Materials: poster board, glue or tape

1. Organize the class into small, mixed-level groups. Ask students to imagine that they are newspaper publishers who must determine the headlines for the next issue of their papers.
2. Have each group write a headline and several subheadlines for each of the following topics: problems with Great Britain and Spain; problems associated with tariffs; economic problems that arose under the Articles of Confederation; and the consequences of Shays's Rebellion.
3. Then have each group arrange its headline and subheadlines on a poster board in the way they would appear in a newspaper.

LS Interpersonal, Verbal/Linguistic

HSS 8.2.2, 8.3.5; HSS **Analysis Skills:** HI 1

Alternative Assessment Handbook, Rubrics 14: Group Activity; and 37: Writing Assignments

Answers

A Farmer Leads a Revolt *The state militia defeated the rebellion and arrested many of those involved, who were later freed. The rebellion convinced many Americans that the Articles of Confederation were too weak.*

Reading Check *The Confederation Congress did not have the authority to pass tariffs or to order the states to do so.*

little or no real value, because states did not have gold or silver to back it up. Inflation occurs when there are increased prices for goods and services combined with the reduced value of money. Congress had no power to stop states from issuing more paper money and thus stop inflation.

Weak Economy

In Rhode Island the state legislature printed large amounts of paper money worth very little. This made debtors—people who owe money—quite happy. They could pay back their debts with paper money worth less than the coins they had borrowed. However, creditors—people who lend money—were upset. Hundreds of creditors fled Rhode Island to avoid being paid back with worthless money.

The loss of trade with Britain combined with inflation created a **depression**. A depression is a period of low economic activity combined with a rise in unemployment.

READING CHECK **Summarizing** What economic problems did the new nation face?

Shays's Rebellion

Each state handled its economic problems differently. Massachusetts refused to print worthless paper money. It tried to pay its war debts by collecting taxes on land.

Heavy Debts for Farmers

Massachusetts's tax policy hit farmers hard. As landowners, they had to pay the new taxes. However, farmers had trouble paying their debts. The courts began forcing them to sell their property. Some farmers had to serve terms in debtors' prison; others had to sell their labor.

Many government leaders in the state did not care about the problems of poor farmers, however. In some cases, farmers actually owed these leaders money.

Farmers Rebel

In August 1786, farmers in three western counties began a revolt. Bands of angry citizens closed down courts in western Massachusetts. Their reasoning was simple—with the courts shut down, no one's property could be taken. In September a poor farmer and Revolutionary War veteran, **Daniel Shays**, led hundreds of men in a forced shutdown of the Supreme Court in Springfield, Massachusetts. The state government ordered the farmers to stop the revolt under threat of capture and death. These threats only made Shays and his followers more determined. The uprising of farmers to protest high taxes and heavy debt became known as **Shays's Rebellion**.

Shays's Defeat

Shays's forces were defeated by state troops in January 1787. By February many of the rebels were in prison. During their trials, 14 leaders were sentenced to death. However, the state soon freed most of the rebels, including Shays. State officials knew that many citizens of the state agreed with the rebels and their cause.

READING CHECK **Finding Main Ideas** What led to Shays's Rebellion?

Direct Teach

Main Idea

❸ Shays's Rebellion

Shays's Rebellion pointed out weaknesses in the Articles of Confederation.

Recall What was Shays's Rebellion, and why was it significant? *uprising of Massachusetts farmers in 1786; convinced many that the Articles of Confederation were too weak*

Identify Points of View Why do you think Daniel Shays and the other rebels took the actions that they did? *pushed to the breaking point; felt they had nothing to lose*

Make Judgments Do you think the actions of Daniel Shays and the other rebels were justified? Explain your answer. *possible answers—Yes, they were fighting to save their farms; no, they had a right to protest taxes but not in the way that they did.*

HSS 8.2.2, 8.3.5; HSS **Analysis Skills:** HR 5, HI 1, HI 2

Primary Source

Two Views of Shays's Rebellion

Shays's Rebellion greatly upset many American leaders. George Washington exclaimed, "I am mortified [embarrassed] beyond expression." Washington feared that the United States must look "ridiculous in the eyes of all Europe." Not everyone saw the rebellion this way, though. Thomas Jefferson, serving as ambassador to France, responded to the event differently. "A little rebellion, now and then, is a good thing," he said. "The tree of liberty must be refreshed from time to time with the blood of patriots and tyrants."

Critical Thinking: Identifying Points of View

Standards Proficiency

HSS 8.2.2; HSS **Analysis Skills:** HR 5, HI 1, HI 2, HI 6

1. Assign each student one of the following roles: western merchant who sends items back East, eastern farmer who exports goods to British markets, North Carolina tobacco planter, Rhode Island creditor, or Massachusetts farmer.
2. Have each student write one or more journal entries about the economic problems that he or she faces. Have students refer to the text and to the United States Faces Trade Barriers map.
3. Encourage students to propose solutions to the economic problems they face.
4. **Extend** Have students think about possible solutions to the economic problems caused by the weakness of the Articles of Confederation. Then have each student write a petition to the Confederation Congress asking for specific changes to the Articles and explaining how the changes would improve the economy.

LS Logical/Mathematical, Verbal/Linguistic

Alternative Assessment Handbook, Rubrics 15: Journals; and 35: Solving Problems

Answers

Reading Check (left) *trade problems among the states, war debts, weak economy*

Reading Check (right) *growing anger among Massachusetts farmers over the state's economic policies, which led to rising debts and the risk of losing their farms, having to serve time in debtors' prison, or having to sell their labor*

• Direct Teach •

Main Idea

❹ Calls for Change

Many Americans called for changes in the national government.

Describe How did some states address the problems of the weak national government? *Some states sent delegates to the Annapolis Convention; some delegates called for a Constitutional Convention.*

Evaluate Why do you think some states chose not to send delegates to the Annapolis Convention? *possible answers—fear of losing state power; experienced fewer problems*

Quick Facts Transparency: Weaknesses of the Articles of Confederation

HSS 8.2.2; HSS **Analysis Skills:** HI 1, HI 2

• Review & Assess •

Close

Have students review the strengths and weaknesses of the Articles of Confederation.

Review

Online Quiz, Section 2

Assess

SE Section 2 Assessment

PASS: Section 2 Quiz

Alternative Assessment Handbook

Reteach/Classroom Intervention

California Standards Review Workbook

Interactive Reader and Study Guide, Section 2

Interactive Skills Tutor CD-ROM

Answers

Reading Check *because the weaknesses of the Articles of Confederation caused problems with foreign nations, international trade issues, domestic economic problems, and Shays's Rebellion*

Calls for Change

In the end, Shays's Rebellion showed the weakness of the Confederation government. It led some Americans to admit that the Articles of Confederation had failed to protect the ideals of liberty set forth in the Declaration of Independence.

Weaknesses of the Articles of Confederation — QUICK FACTS

- Most power held by states
- One branch of government
- Legislative branch has few powers
- No executive branch
- No judicial system
- No system of checks and balances

When Massachusetts had asked the national government to help put down Shays's Rebellion, Congress could offer little help. More Americans began calling for a stronger central government. They wanted leaders who would be able to protect the nation in times of crisis.

Earlier in 1786 the Virginia legislature had called for a national conference. It wanted to talk about economic problems and ways to change the Articles of Confederation. The meeting took place in Annapolis, Maryland, in September 1786.

Nine states decided to send delegates to the Annapolis Convention but some of their delegates were late and missed the meeting. Connecticut, Georgia, Maryland, and South Carolina did not respond to the request at all and sent no delegates.

Because of the poor attendance, the participants, including James Madison and Alexander Hamilton, called on all 13 states to send delegates to a Constitutional Convention in Philadelphia in May 1787. They planned to revise the Articles of Confederation to better meet the needs of the nation.

READING CHECK **Finding Main Ideas** Why did some people believe the national government needed to change?

SUMMARY AND PREVIEW Many Americans believed that Shays's Rebellion was final proof that the national government needed to be changed. In the next section you will read about the Constitutional Convention.

Section 2 Assessment

go.hrw.com **Online Quiz** KEYWORD: SS8 HP4

Reviewing Ideas, Terms, and People HSS 8.2.2, 8.3.5

1. a. **Summarize** What problems did the United States experience with Spain and Great Britain?
   b. **Predict** What are some possible results of the growing problems between the United States and Great Britain? Why?
2. a. **Describe** What difficulties were involved with **interstate commerce**?
   b. **Analyze** What was the cause of inflation in the new nation, and how could it have been prevented?
3. a. **Explain** How did Massachusetts's tax policy affect farmers?
   b. **Evaluate** Defend the actions of **Daniel Shays** and the other rebels.
4. a. **Recall** Why did Madison and Hamilton call for a Constitutional Convention?
   b. **Analyze** How did Shay's Rebellion lead to a call for change in the United States?

Critical Thinking

5. **Categorizing** Copy the graphic organizer below. Use it to identify the domestic and international problems that arose under the Articles of Confederation.

Domestic Problems	International Problems

FOCUS ON WRITING

6. **Identifying Problems** In this section you learned about several problems of the young United States. Were any of those problems made worse by the powers that the Articles of Confederation did or did not give the national government?

Section 2 Assessment Answers

1. a. Great Britain—refused to hand over forts, closed ports to U.S. ships, set high tariffs; Spain—closed Mississippi to U.S. shipping
   b. possible answer—could go to war because of problems stated in previous answer
2. a. Lack of regulation and lack of cooperation between states made trade difficult for some merchants.
   b. Some states began printing large amounts of paper money; little could be done.
3. a. Heavy taxes forced farmers to sell their land or else go into debt and risk imprisonment.
   b. Answers should show an understanding of the rebels' anger over high taxes.
4. a. weaknesses in Articles of Confederation, poor attendance at Annapolis Convention
   b. convinced many Americans that the Articles of Confederation were too weak
5. Domestic—no power to regulate interstate commerce, could not help states keep order, could not stop inflation; International—could not pass tariffs, enforce treaties
6. See answer to Question 5.

Creating the Constitution

SECTION 3

If YOU were there...

You are a merchant in Connecticut in 1787. You have been a member of your state legislature for several years. This spring, the legislature is choosing delegates to a convention to revise the Articles of Confederation. Delegates will meet in Philadelphia. It means leaving your business in others' hands for most of the summer. Still, you hope to be chosen.

Why would you want to go to the Constitutional Convention?

BUILDING BACKGROUND It didn't take long for people to realize that the Articles of Confederation had many weaknesses. By the mid-1780s most political leaders agreed that changes were needed. To make those changes, they called on people with experience in government.

Constitutional Convention

In February 1787 the Confederation Congress invited each state to send delegates to a convention in Philadelphia. The goal of the meeting was to improve the Articles of Confederation.

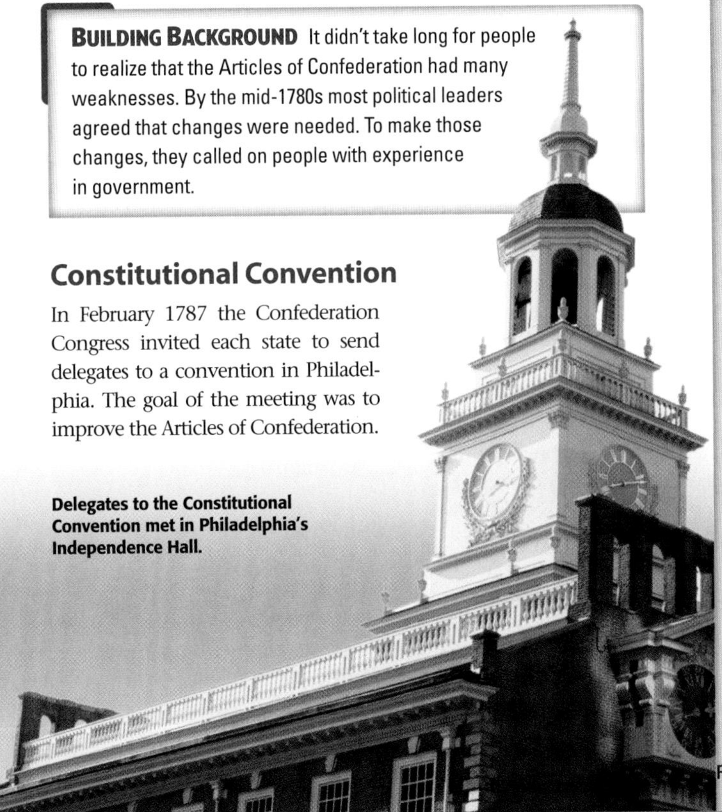

Delegates to the Constitutional Convention met in Philadelphia's Independence Hall.

What You Will Learn . . .

Main Ideas

1. The Constitutional Convention met to improve the government of the United States.
2. The issue of representation led to the Great Compromise.
3. Regional debate over slavery led to the Three-Fifths Compromise.
4. The U.S. Constitution created federalism and a balance of power.

The Big Idea

A new constitution provided a framework for a stronger national government.

Key Terms and People

Constitutional Convention, *p. 126*
James Madison, *p. 126*
Virginia Plan, *p. 126*
New Jersey Plan, *p. 127*
Great Compromise, *p. 127*
Three-Fifths Compromise, *p. 128*
popular sovereignty, *p. 129*
federalism, *p. 129*
legislative branch, *p. 129*
executive branch, *p. 129*
judicial branch, *p. 129*
checks and balances, *p. 129*

HSS 8.2 Students analyze the political principles underlying the U.S. Constitution and compare the enumerated and implied powers of the federal government.

Preteach

Bellringer

If YOU were there . . . Use the **Daily Bellringer Transparency** to help students answer the question.

Daily Bellringer Transparency, Section 3

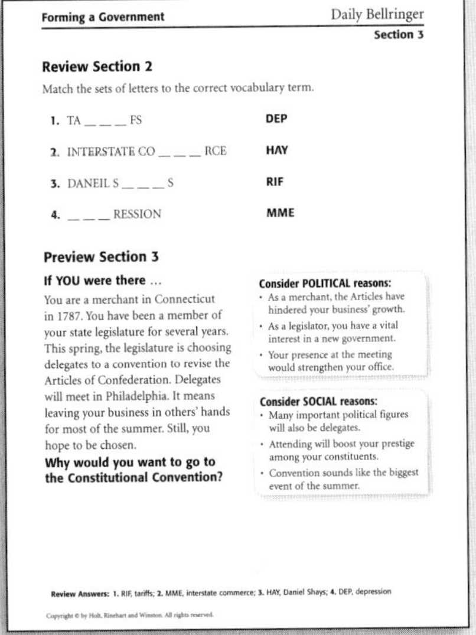

Forming a Government — Daily Bellringer, **Section 3**

Review Section 2

Match the sets of letters to the correct vocabulary term.

1. TA _ _ _ FS	**DEP**
2. INTERSTATE CO _ _ _ RCE	**HAY**
3. DANEIL S _ _ _ S	**RIF**
4. _ _ _ RESSION	**MME**

Preview Section 3

If YOU were there ...

You are a merchant in Connecticut in 1787. You have been a member of your state legislature for several years. This spring, the legislature is choosing delegates to a convention to revise the Articles of Confederation. Delegates will meet in Philadelphia. It means leaving your business in others' hands for most of the summer. Still, you hope to be chosen.

Why would you want to go to the Constitutional Convention?

Consider POLITICAL reasons:
- As a merchant, the Articles have hindered your business' growth.
- As a legislator, you have a vital interest in a new government.
- Your presence at the meeting would strengthen your office.

Consider SOCIAL reasons:
- Many important political figures will also be delegates.
- Attending will boost your prestige among your constituents.
- Convention sounds like the biggest event of the summer.

Review Answers: **1.** RIF, tariffs; **2.** MME, interstate commerce; **3.** HAY, Daniel Shays; **4.** DEP, depression

Building Vocabulary

Preteach or review the following terms:

bicameral made up of two houses (p. 127)
federal national (p. 129)
sovereignty supreme power (p. 126)
unicameral made up of one house (p. 127)

CRF: Vocabulary Builder Activity, Section 3

Teach the Big Idea: Master the Standards

Standards Proficiency

Creating the Constitution HSS 8.2

Standard English Mastery

1. **Teach** Ask students the Main Idea questions to teach this section.
2. **Apply** Have students, working either individually or with a partner, create glossaries for a handbook on the Constitutional Convention. Students' glossaries should include descriptions of key individuals, major proposals and plans, significant compromises, and legal and political terms discussed in the section. Tell students to use standard English when writing their glossaries.
3. **Review** Have students share their glossaries. Correct any errors as well as students' use of standard English. **LS Verbal/Linguistic**
4. **Practice/Homework** Have students make flow charts showing the key plans, debates, and issues that led to the Great Compromise and Three-Fifths Compromise.

Alternative Assessment Handbook, Rubrics 13: Graphic Organizer; and 42: Writing to Inform

Standards Focus

HSS 8.2

Means: Analyze the political ideals that form the basis of the U.S. Constitution and compare the different types of powers of the federal government.

Matters: The U.S. Constitution and the ideals it expresses continues to serve as the basis of the U.S. government.

Direct Teach

Main Idea

❶ Constitutional Convention

The Constitutional Convention met to improve the government of the United States.

Identify Who were some key delegates to the convention, and who served as its president? *Benjamin Franklin, James Madison, George Washington (president)*

Analyze How might the Constitution have been different if African Americans, Native Americans, and women had been able to attend the convention? *possible answer—Issues such as slavery and suffrage might have been addressed differently.*

CRF: Biography Activity: Signers of the Constitution

CRF: Primary Source Activity: Benjamin Franklin Addresses the Constitutional Convention

HSS 8.2; HSS **Analysis Skills:** HI 1, HI 2

Info to Know

A Well Prepared Man James Madison began preparing for the Constitutional Convention in the fall of 1786 by reading works of political history, classical republicanism, and modern political theory. With Thomas Jefferson's help, Madison had acquired a small library of the social and economic philosophies of the Enlightenment, including the 37-volume set of Denis Diderot's *Encyclopédie*.

go.hrw.com
Online Resources
KEYWORD: SS8 US4
ACTIVITY: Biographies of Constitutional Convention Leaders

Signing of the Constitution

Roger Sherman · James Madison · James Wilson

Meeting in Philadelphia

The **Constitutional Convention** was held in May 1787 in Philadelphia's Independence Hall to improve the Articles of Confederation. However, delegates would leave with an entirely new U.S. Constitution.

Most delegates were well educated, and many had served in state legislatures or Congress. Benjamin Franklin and **James Madison** were there. Revolutionary War hero George Washington was elected president of the Convention.

Several important voices were absent. John Adams and Thomas Jefferson could not attend. Patrick Henry chose not to attend because he did not want a stronger central government. Women, African Americans, and Native Americans did not take part because they did not yet have the rights of citizens.

READING CHECK **Summarizing** What was the purpose of the Constitutional Convention?

Great Compromise

Several issues divided the delegates to the Constitutional Convention. Some members wanted only small changes to the Articles of Confederation, while others wanted to rewrite the Articles completely.

Those delegates who wanted major changes to the Articles had different goals. For example, small and large states had different ideas about representation, economic concerns such as tariffs, and slavery. In addition, delegates disagreed over how strong to make the national government.

Virginia Plan

After the delegates had met for four days, Edmund Randolph of Virginia presented the **Virginia Plan**. He proposed a new federal constitution that would give sovereignty, or supreme power, to the central government. The legislature would be

Differentiating Instruction for Universal Access

Learners Having Difficulty

Reaching Standards

Materials: paper, art supplies, invitations (optional)

1. Have students identify the purpose of the Constitutional Convention *(to discuss ways to improve the Articles of Confederation).*
2. Then ask students to identify some characteristics that delegates would need for the convention to succeed *(government experience, education, knowledge of Enlightenment thinkers, charisma, diplomacy, patience, good listening and speaking skills).* List students' ideas for the class to see.
3. Ask students to imagine that they are creating invitations for the convention. Have each student write a persuasive invitation to send to proposed delegates. (Provide models of invitations, if possible.) The invitations should include the convention's date and location, notable individuals who will attend, and why attendance is vital. LS **Verbal/Linguistic**

Alternative Assessment Handbook, Rubric 43: Writing to Persuade

HSS 8.2; HSS **Analysis Skills:** HI 1

Answers

Reading Check *to discuss ways to improve the Articles of Confederation*

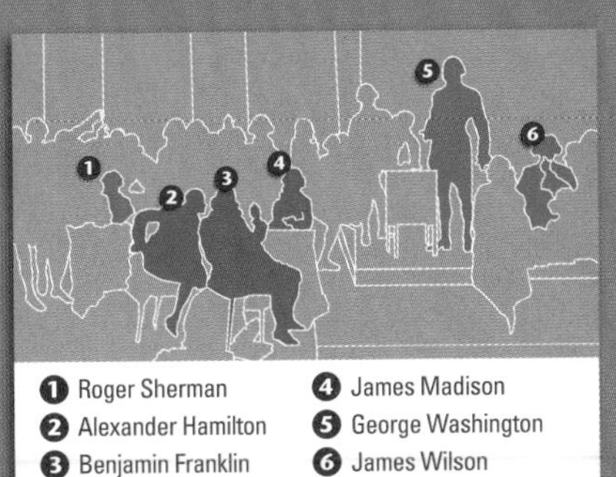

This painting shows the signing of the Constitution on September 17, 1787. James Madison, number 4 on the diagram, became known as the "Father of the Constitution" for his ideas about government and his ability to lead the delegates to agreement. ***Which person did the artist choose to make the focus of this painting? Why do you think that is?***

bicameral—made up of two houses, or groups of representatives—and chosen on the basis of state populations. Larger states would thus have more representatives than would smaller states. Delegates from the smaller states believed that it would give too much power to the larger states.

New Jersey Plan

The smaller states came up with a plan to stop the larger states from getting too much power. New Jersey delegate William Paterson presented the small-state or **New Jersey Plan**, which called for a unicameral, or one-house, legislature. The plan gave each state an equal number of votes, thus an equal voice, in the federal government. The plan gave the federal government the power to tax citizens in all states, and it allowed the government to regulate commerce.

Compromise is Reached

After a month of debate, the delegates were unable to agree on how states should be represented. The convention reached a deadlock.

Finally, Roger Sherman of Connecticut proposed a compromise plan. The legislative branch would have two houses. Each state, regardless of its size, would have two representatives in the Senate, or upper house. This would give each state an equal voice, pleasing the smaller states. In the House of Representatives, or lower house, the number of representatives for each state would be determined by the state's population. This pleased the larger states. The agreement to create a two-house legislature became known as the **Great Compromise**. James Wilson, a great speaker, saw his dream of a strong national government come true.

THE IMPACT TODAY

All U.S. states but one modeled their legislative branches on the federal one, with a House of Representatives and a Senate. Nebraska has a unicameral legislature.

READING CHECK **Contrasting** How did the Virginia Plan and New Jersey Plan differ?

QUICK FACTS

Virginia Plan
- Gave more power to national government
- Bicameral legislature
- Number in both houses based on population

Great Compromise
- Bicameral legislature
- Number of representatives based on state populations in lower house
- Number of representatives equal from each state in upper house

New Jersey Plan
- Gave more power to state governments
- Unicameral legislature
- Number of representatives equal from each state

Direct Teach

Main Idea

2 Great Compromise

The issue of representation led to the Great Compromise.

Recall What were some issues that divided delegates at the Constitutional Convention? *how much to change the Articles and differing ideas about representation, how strong to make the government, economic concerns such as tariffs, and issues such as slavery*

Summarize How did the Great Compromise combine elements of the Virginia and New Jersey Plans? *bicameral legislature, representation in lower house based on population (Virginia Plan); representation in upper house equal (New Jersey Plan)*

Evaluate Do you think the Great Compromise shared power equally between large and small states? *Answers will vary but should reflect an understanding of the compromise.*

Quick Facts Transparency: Great Compromise

HSS 8.2.3; HSS **Analysis Skills:** HI 1

Info to Know

A "Heated" Debate Can you imagine sitting in a hot room wearing a heavy suit and stockings? How about doing so in the middle of summer? That's what the framers of the Constitution did. The weather in Philadelphia during the Constitutional Convention was very hot and humid. Moreover, the delegates kept the windows closed to keep out flies and to prevent passersby from listening.

Critical Thinking: Finding Main Ideas

Standards Proficiency

Constitutional Convention Notes

HSS 8.2.3, 8.2.4; HSS **Analysis Skills:** HI 1

Background The delegates to the Constitutional Convention did not allow any outsiders, such as journalists, inside. As a result, historians rely on the careful notes that delegate James Madison took to know what took place during the convention.

1. Ask students to imagine that they are official note takers at the Constitutional Convention.
2. Have students go through the section and make three lists—one list of the main topics of debate, one list of the key decisions made, and one list of the key delegates and their contributions.
3. Have students share the information from their lists. Create master lists for the class to see.
4. **Extend** Ask students to imagine that they have shared their lists with a journalist. Have each student write an article about one aspect of the Convention, such as who attended or one of the major topics of debate. Remind students to address the journalistic questions of "who, what, when, where, and why." LS **Verbal/Linguistic**

Alternative Assessment Handbook, Rubric 37: Writing Assignment

Answers

Signing of the Constitution *Washington, because he served as the president of the convention and later as the first U.S. president*

Reading Check *Virginia Plan—central government sovereign; bicameral legislature based on population; New Jersey Plan—unicameral legislature with equal representation per state; federal government could tax the states and regulate commerce*

Direct Teach

Main Idea

❸ Three-Fifths Compromise

Regional debate over slavery led to the Three-Fifths Compromise.

Explain How did regional differences and the issue of slavery divide the Constitutional Convention? *Southern delegates wanted slaves to be counted as part of state populations, which would give southern states more power; Northerners disagreed, because northern states had fewer slaves.*

Analyze How did the Three-Fifths Compromise resolve the debate? *Delegates agreed to count each slave as three-fifths of a person when determining representation.*

Draw Conclusions Why did the delegates agree to allow the international slave trade to continue for another 20 years? *to appease southern delegates and to give southern economies, which were dependent on the international slave trade, time to adjust to its end*

HSS 8.2; HSS **Analysis Skills:** CS 1, HR 5, HI 1

Primary Source

Reading Like a Historian

Compromise and the Slave Trade

To help students read the excerpts like historians, ask the following questions:

- What states and regions of the country do Rutledge and Morris represent?
- What regional concerns and biases may have influenced each man's point of view?
- In what context was each statement made? What issues or concerns was each man addressing?

Answers

Analyzing Primary Sources *Rutledge is pro-slavery, and Morris is anti-slavery.*

Reading Check *Delegates agreed to end the international slave trade in 20 years rather than immediately.*

Primary Source

POINTS OF VIEW

Compromise and the Slave Trade

The issue of slavery highlighted the growing division between the North and the South. Gouverneur Morris of New York spoke with much emotion against the Three-Fifths Compromise. Also, the idea of banning the foreign slave trade prompted southerners such as John Rutledge of South Carolina to defend the practice.

"If the Convention thinks that North Carolina, South Carolina, and Georgia will ever agree to the plan [to prohibit slave trade], unless their right to import slaves be untouched, the expectation is vain [useless]."

—John Rutledge,
quoted in *The Atlantic Monthly,* February 1891, by Frank Gaylord Cook

"The admission of slaves into the Representation ... comes to this: that the inhabitant of [a state] who goes to the coast of Africa and ... tears away his fellow creatures from their dearest connections and damns them to the most cruel bondage [slavery], shall have more votes in a Government [established] for protection of the rights of mankind."

—Gouverneur Morris,
quoted in *Founding the Republic,* edited by John J. Patrick

ANALYSIS SKILL — ANALYZING PRIMARY SOURCES

Finding Main Ideas How did these two views of slavery differ?

Three-Fifths Compromise

The debate over representation also involved regional differences. Southern delegates wanted enslaved Africans to be counted as part of their state populations. This way they would have more representatives, and more power, in Congress. Northerners disagreed. They wanted the number of slaves to determine taxes but not representation.

To resolve this problem, some delegates thought of a compromise. They wanted to count three-fifths of the slaves in each state as part of that state's population to decide how many representatives a state would have. After much debate, the delegates voted to accept the proposal, called the **Three-Fifths Compromise**. Under this agreement each slave would be counted as three-fifths of a person when determining representation.

Another major issue was the foreign slave trade. Some of the delegates believed slavery was wrong and wanted the federal government to ban the slave trade. Others said that the southern states' economies needed the slave trade. Many southern delegates said they would leave the Union if the Constitution immediately ended the slave trade.

Worried delegates reached another compromise, agreeing to end the slave trade in 20 years. The delegates omitted, or left out, the words *slavery* and *slave* in the Constitution. They referred instead to "free Persons" and "all other Persons." Oliver Ellsworth summed up the view of many delegates. He said, "The morality or wisdom of slavery . . . are considerations belonging to the states themselves."

READING CHECK **Summarizing** What compromise was reached over the issue of the slave trade?

Differentiating Instruction for Universal Access

Advanced Learners/GATE — Exceeding Standards

Recipe for Government Have students write a recipe for creating the U.S. government. Tell them that the framers of the Constitution chose political ideas from many sources (the ingredients) to draft the Constitution. Then they decided how to balance these ideas (the measurements) and put them into practice (the directions). LS **Verbal/Linguistic**

HSS 8.2; HSS **Analysis Skills:** HI 1

Alternative Assessment Handbook, Rubric 39: Writing to Create

English-Language Learners — Standards Proficiency

Visualizing Balanced Government Have each student create a political cartoon or visual diagram illustrating how the U.S. government is balanced under the U.S. Constitution. Students might focus on one aspect, such as federalism or checks and balances, or on the topic in general. LS **Visual/Spatial**

HSS 8.2; HSS **Analysis Skills:** HI 1

Alternative Assessment Handbook, Rubrics 3: Artwork; and 27: Political Cartoons

The Living Constitution

Most Convention delegates wanted a strong national government. At the same time, they hoped to protect **popular sovereignty**, the idea that political authority belongs to the people. Americans had boldly declared this idea in the Declaration of Independence.

Federalist Government

The delegates also wanted to balance the power of the national government with the powers of the states. Therefore, the delegates created **federalism**. Federalism is the sharing of power between a central government and the states that make up a country.

Under the Constitution, each state must obey the authority of the federal, or national, government. States have control over government functions not specifically assigned to the federal government. This includes control of local government, education, the chartering of corporations, and the supervision of religious bodies. States also have the power to create and oversee civil and criminal law. States, however, must protect the welfare of their citizens.

Checks and Balances

The Constitution also balances the power among three branches, each responsible for separate tasks. The first is the **legislative branch**, or Congress. Congress is responsible for proposing and passing laws. It is made up of two houses, as created in the Great Compromise. The Senate has two members from each state. In the House of Representatives each state is represented according to its population.

The second branch, the **executive branch**, includes the president and the departments that help run the government. The executive branch makes sure the law is carried out. The third branch is the **judicial branch**. The judicial branch is made up of all the national courts. This branch is responsible for interpreting laws, punishing criminals, and settling disputes between states.

The framers of the Constitution created a system of **checks and balances**, which keeps any branch of government from becoming too powerful. For example, Congress has the power to pass bills into law. The president has the power to veto, or reject, laws that Congress passes. However, Congress can override the president's veto with a two-thirds

LINKING TO TODAY

Legislative Branch

When it first met in 1789, the U.S. House of Representatives had just 65 members. As the nation's population grew, more members were added. Today, the number has been set at 435, to prevent the size of the House from growing unmanageable. Though the numbers of women and minorities in Congress are still unrepresentative of the population as a whole, Congress has become more diverse. Linda and Loretta Sanchez, pictured here, are the first sisters to serve in Congress at the same time.

ANALYSIS SKILL ANALYZING INFORMATION

How is the change in makeup of the legislative branch shown through Linda and Loretta Sanchez?

Direct Teach

Main Idea

4 The Living Constitution

The U.S. Constitution created federalism and a balance of power.

Define What is popular sovereignty? *the idea that political authority belongs to the people*

Identify What is the main responsibility of each branch of government? *legislative—proposing and passing laws; executive—making sure laws are carried out; judicial—interpreting laws*

Analyze How did the framers put into practice the idea of popular sovereignty expressed in the Declaration of Independence? *established a system of federalism, in which government power is shared between the states and the federal government and in which states are required to protect the welfare of citizens*

Quick Facts Transparency: The Constitution Strengthens the National Government

HSS 8.2; HSS **Analysis Skills:** HI 1

Did you know . . .

The word *slavery* did not appear in the U.S. Constitution until the Thirteenth Amendment abolished the practice in 1865. In its sections protecting slavery, the Constitution used indirect wording. For example, the provision that allowed slaveholders the right to pursue runaway slaves read, "No Person held to Service or Labour in one State . . . escaping into another, shall be discharged from such Service or Labour."

Collaborative Learning

Standards Proficiency

Constitutional Convention Web Site

HSS 8.2; HSS **Analysis Skills:** HI 1

1. Organize the class into groups. Have each group design the home page of a Web site on the Constitutional Convention. Groups can create their designs on poster board or on a computer.
2. Groups' home pages should include a title, general information about the site, and a list of links to supporting pages within the Web site. These pages might provide highlights of the convention, information about key topics or debates, biographies of delegates, primary sources, links to related Web sites, and so on.
3. Groups should assign members roles to ensure that all students participate.
4. Have each group present its design to the class.
LS Interpersonal, Verbal/Linguistic, Visual/Spatial

Alternative Assessment Handbook, Rubric 14: Group Activity

Answers

Linking to Today *The two sisters are Hispanic women, representing the diversity that has become part of the legislative branch in recent times.*

Direct Teach

Info to Know

Hamilton on Government In the midst of the debates at the Constitutional Convention, Alexander Hamilton gave one of the longest speeches of the proceedings. He was a strong supporter of the British government and urged delegates to create one like it. He suggested that the presidency be a lifetime job and even offered his own plan for the government—one modeled on Britain's. The rest of the delegates appear to have politely listened to Hamilton's suggestions and then ignored them and returned to the discussion at hand.

Review & Assess

Close

Have students summarize how the U.S. Constitution resolved the weaknesses in the Articles of Confederation.

Review

go.hrw.com Online Quiz, Section 3

Assess

SE Section 3 Assessment

PASS: Section 3 Quiz

Alternative Assessment Handbook

Reteach/Classroom Intervention

California Standards Review Workbook

Interactive Reader and Study Guide, Section 3

Interactive Skills Tutor CD-ROM

Answers

Reading Check *The system of checks and balances keeps any one branch of government from becoming too powerful.*

The Constitution Strengthens the National Government

QUICK FACTS

Strengths of the Constitution	Weaknesses of the Articles of Confederation
✔ most power held by national government	• most power held by states
✔ three branches of government	• one branch of government
✔ legislative branch has many powers	• legislative branch has few powers
✔ executive branch led by president	• no executive branch
✔ judicial branch to review the laws	• no judicial system
✔ firm system of checks and balances	• no system of checks and balances

majority vote. The Supreme Court has the power to review laws passed by Congress and strike down any law that violates the Constitution by declaring it *unconstitutional*.

The final draft of the Constitution was completed in September 1787. Only 3 of the 42 delegates who remained refused to sign. The signed Constitution was sent first to Congress and then to the states for ratification. The delegates knew that the Constitution was not a perfect document but they believed they had protected the ideas of republicanism.

READING CHECK **Summarizing** Explain how the system of checks and balances works in the United States.

SUMMARY AND PREVIEW The Constitution balanced power among three branches of the federal government but was only written after many compromises. In the next section you will read about Antifederalist and Federalist views of the Constitution, and the struggle to get it approved by the States.

Section 3 Assessment

go.hrw.com Online Quiz KEYWORD: SS8 HP4

Reviewing Ideas, Terms, and People HSS 8.2

1. a. **Recall** Why did the Confederation Congress call for a **Constitutional Convention**?
   b. **Elaborate** Why do you think it was important that most delegates had served in state legislatures?
2. a. **Identify** What was the **Great Compromise**?
   b. **Draw Conclusions** How did state issues lead to debate over structure of the central government?
3. a **Explain** What was the debate between North and South over counting slave populations?
   b. **Contrast** How did delegates' views differ on the issue of the foreign slave trade?
4. a. **Recall** Why did the framers of the Constitution create a system of **checks and balances**?
   b. **Evaluate** Did the Constitution resolve the weaknesses in the Articles of Confederation? Explain your answer.

Critical Thinking

5. **Analyzing** Copy the chart shown. Use it to identify the problems that led to the Great Compromise and the Three-Fifths Compromise, what conflicting ideas were proposed, and the eventual solution that created a compromise.

	Great Compromise	Three-Fifths Compromise
Problem		
Conflicting Ideas		
Solution		

FOCUS ON WRITING

6. **Thinking about the Constitution** Look back through what you've just read and make a list of important features of the Constitution. Be sure to note important compromises.

Section 3 Assessment Answers

1. a. to improve the Articles of Confederation
   b. needed government experience
2. a. resolved opposing views in the Virginia and New Jersey Plans on how to allot state representation
   b. possible answer—Concerns over state representation led to a bicameral legislature with an upper house based on equal state votes and a lower house based on state population.
3. a. Southern delegates wanted slaves to be counted as part of state populations; Northerners disagreed.
   b. along South-North regional lines
4. a. to limit each branch's power
   b. See Quick Facts chart above.
5. Great Compromise—See the answers to Questions 2a and 2b; Three-fifths Compromise—resolved opposing southern and northern views on how to count slaves when determining state representation by counting each slave as three-fifths of a person
6. Students should describe the key issues, debates, and solutions in this section.

BIOGRAPHY

Benjamin Franklin

How did one man accomplish so much?

When did he live? 1706–1790

Where did he live? Benjamin Franklin was born in Boston but ran away to Philadelphia at age 17 and made it his home. He also crossed the Atlantic Ocean eight times and visited 10 countries.

What did he do? What *didn't* he do! He was a printer, publisher, creator of the first circulating library, the first president of the University of Pennsylvania, inventor, scientist, philosopher, musician, economist, and the first U.S. Postmaster General. In politics he was a leading revolutionary, signer of the Declaration of Independence, head of an antislavery organization, delegate to the Constitutional Convention, and diplomat.

Why is he important? Benjamin Franklin, son of a candlemaker, became a celebrity in his own time, both in America and in Europe. Few people have mastered so many fields of knowledge and accomplished so much. He invented many useful objects, from bifocal glasses to the lightning rod. One of the oldest founding fathers, Franklin inspired younger revolutionaries such as Thomas Jefferson. Franklin believed strongly that people should volunteer and be in public service.

Finding Main Ideas How did Benjamin Franklin's life reflect his belief in public service?

KEY EVENTS

1729 Becomes owner and publisher of the *Pennsylvania Gazette*

1732–1758 Publishes *Poor Richard: An Almanack*

1752 Performs famous experiment using a kite to show that electricity exists in storm clouds

1775 Submits the Articles of Confederation

1779 Appointed minister to France

1782 Helps negotiate the Treaty of Paris with Britain

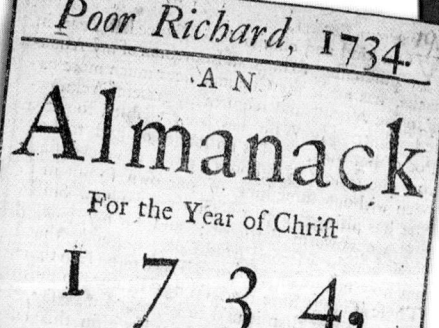

Poor Richard, 1734.
AN
Almanack
For the Year of Chrift
1734,
Being the fecond after LEAP...

Critical Thinking: Categorizing

Reaching Standards

Accomplishments of Benjamin Franklin

HSS 8.2.4; HSS **Analysis Skills:** HI 1

1. Create a chart titled *Accomplishments of Benjamin Franklin.* Ask students to identify Franklin's many accomplishments, based on the biography and time line above. List students' answers for the class to see.
2. Then help students create categories by which to organize Franklin's accomplishments. Categories might include Government Service, Inventions, Community Service, and so on. Add the category labels to your chart.
3. Have students copy the chart and complete it by listing each of Franklin's accomplishments in the correct category.
4. Review the answers as a class. Then summarize for students Franklin's significance in American history.

Alternative Assessment Handbook, Rubric 7: Charts

Biography

Reading Focus Question

Read aloud the introductory question to students. Next, have students read the information under "What did he do?" to see how much Franklin accomplished. Ask students if they can think of any people today who are as accomplished as Franklin was. Then ask students how they think Franklin was able to accomplish so much.

Linking to Today

Daylight Savings Benjamin Franklin is well known for his many inventions that made life better for people. In addition, Franklin also invented daylight savings time. In an essay written in 1784, he first suggested the practice of advancing clocks forward in the summer. During World War I many nations adopted this system to conserve fuel. Today many nations, including the United States, continue the practice of daylight savings time each spring.

Did you know . . .

During the Constitutional Convention, Ben Franklin had an aisle seat. According to some accounts, he enjoyed occasionally tripping delegates as they walked by.

Primary Sources

Poor Richard: An Almanack Benjamin Franklin published *Poor Richard: An Almanack* over a period of many decades. Write the following sayings for students to see.

- "He that lies down with dogs, shall rise up with fleas."
- "Great talkers, little doers."
- "Haste makes waste."

Ask students to choose one of the sayings, rewrite it in their own words, and then explain its meaning.

Answers

Finding Main Ideas *Most of his accomplishments and actions benefited others, from his service in government to his many inventions to his support of education and social causes.*

Preteach

Bellringer

If YOU were there . . . Use the **Daily Bellringer Transparency** to help students answer the question.

 Daily Bellringer Transparency, Section 4

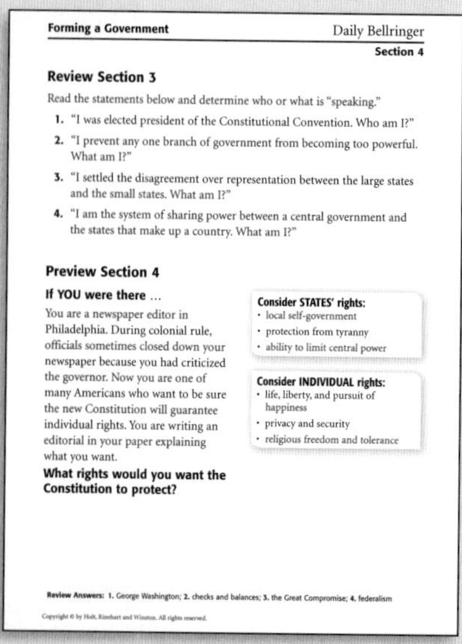

Forming a Government — Daily Bellringer

Section 4

Review Section 3

Read the statements below and determine who or what is "speaking."

1. "I was elected president of the Constitutional Convention. Who am I?"
2. "I prevent any one branch of government from becoming too powerful. What am I?"
3. "I settled the disagreement over representation between the large states and the small states. What am I?"
4. "I am the system of sharing power between a central government and the states that make up a country. What am I?"

Preview Section 4

If YOU were there ...

You are a newspaper editor in Philadelphia. During colonial rule, officials sometimes closed down your newspaper because you had criticized the governor. Now you are one of many Americans who want to be sure the new Constitution will guarantee individual rights. You are writing an editorial in your paper explaining what you want.

What rights would you want the Constitution to protect?

Consider STATES' rights:
- local self-government
- protection from tyranny
- ability to limit central power

Consider INDIVIDUAL rights:
- life, liberty, and pursuit of happiness
- privacy and security
- religious freedom and tolerance

Review Answers: 1. George Washington; 2. checks and balances; 3. the Great Compromise; 4. federalism

Academic Vocabulary

Review with students the high-use academic term in this section.

advocate to plead in favor of (p. 133)

CRF: Vocabulary Builder Activity, Section 4

SECTION 4 Ratifying the Constitution

What You Will Learn . . .

Main Ideas

1. Federalists and Antifederalists engaged in debate over the new Constitution.
2. The *Federalist Papers* played an important role in the fight for ratification of the Constitution.
3. Ten amendments were added to the Constitution to provide a Bill of Rights to protect citizens.

The Big Idea

Americans carried on a vigorous debate before ratifying the Constitution.

Key Terms and People

Antifederalists, *p. 132*
George Mason, *p. 132*
Federalists, *p. 132*
Federalist Papers, p. 133
amendments, *p. 135*
Bill of Rights, *p. 135*

8.2.7 Describe the principles of federalism, dual sovereignty, separation of powers, checks and balances, the nature and purpose of majority rule, and the ways in which the American idea of constitutionalism preserves individual rights.

If YOU were there...

You are a newspaper editor in Philadelphia. During colonial rule, officials sometimes closed down your newspaper because you had criticized the governor. Now you are one of many Americans who want to be sure the new Constitution will guarantee individual rights. You are writing an editorial in your paper explaining what you want.

What rights would you want the Constitution to protect?

BUILDING BACKGROUND The new Constitution did not make everyone happy. Even its framers knew they had not made a perfect document. Many people still did not want a strong national government. They were afraid it would become as tyrannical as the British government had been. Before approving the Constitution, they wanted to be sure that their rights would be protected.

Federalists and Antifederalists

When the Constitution was made public, a huge debate began among many Americans. **Antifederalists**—people who opposed the Constitution—thought that the Constitutional Convention should not have created a new government. Others thought the Constitution gave too much power to the central government. For some Antifederalists, the main problem was that the Constitution did not have a section that guaranteed individual rights. Delegate **George Mason** became an Antifederalist for this reason.

Many Antifederalists were small farmers and debtors. However, some were wealthy. Some Revolutionary War heroes were also strong Antifederalists, including Richard Henry Lee, Samuel Adams, and Patrick Henry. Antifederalists were challenged by many Americans who believed that the United States needed a stronger central government.

Federalists, supporters of the Constitution, included James Madison, George Washington, Benjamin Franklin, Alexander Hamilton, and John Jay. Most Federalists believed that the

Teach the Big Idea: Master the Standards

Standards Proficiency

Ratifying the Constitution 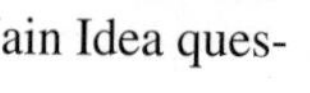 HSS 8.2.7; HSS Analysis Skills: CS 1, CS 2, HI 1

1. **Teach** Ask students the Main Idea questions to teach this section.
2. **Apply** Have each student create a flow chart for the ratification of the Constitution. Tell students to use the following as the first and last entries.
   - **September 17, 1787:** The Constitutional Convention approves the Constitution.
   - **December 1791:** States ratify the Bill of Rights.
3. **Review** As you review the section, have students share information in their flow charts. **LS Visual/Spatial**
4. **Practice/Homework** Have each student write a newspaper article about one of the events in his or her flow chart. **LS Verbal/Linguistic**

Alternative Assessment Handbook, Rubrics 13: Graphic Organizers; and 37: Writing Assignment

Standards Focus

HSS 8.2.7

Means: Describe the basic ideals in the Constitution. Focus on federalism, separation of powers, checks and balances, popular sovereignty, and individual rights.

Matters: These ideals have formed the foundation of American government for more than 200 years.

QUICK FACTS
Federalists v. Antifederalists
Alexander Hamilton
Federalist
• Supported the Constitution as an excellent plan for government
• Defended his views in the *Federalist Papers*
George Mason
Antifederalist
• Opposed the Constitution
• Believed the Constitution needed a section guaranteeing individual rights

Constitution offered a good balance of power. They thought it was a careful compromise between various political views. Many Federalists were wealthy planters, farmers, and lawyers. However, many others were poor workers and craftspeople. Merchants also supported the Constitution.

Federalists and Antifederalists debated whether the new Constitution should be approved by the state legislatures. They made speeches and printed pamphlets **advocating** their views. The Federalists had to convince people a change in the structure of government was needed. To do this, they had to overcome people's fears that the Constitution would make the government too powerful.

READING CHECK **Comparing and Contrasting** Explain the similarities and differences between the Antifederalists and the Federalists.

Federalist Papers

One of the most important defenses of the Constitution appeared in a series of essays that became known as the ***Federalist Papers***. These essays supporting the Constitution were written anonymously under the name Publius. They were actually written by Hamilton, Madison, and Jay.

The authors of the *Federalist Papers* tried to reassure Americans that the new federal government would not overpower the states. In *Federalist Paper* No. 10, Madison argued that the diversity of the United States would prevent any single group from dominating the government.

The *Federalist Papers* were widely reprinted in newspapers around the country as the debate over the Constitution continued. Finally, they were collected and published in book form in 1788.

FOCUS ON READING
Take notes on the chronological order of this section. Which was written first, the *Federalist Papers* or the Bill of Rights?

ACADEMIC VOCABULARY
advocate to plead in favor of

Direct Teach

Main Idea

1 Federalists and Antifederalists

Federalists and Antifederalists engaged in debate over the new Constitution.

Describe What were the Federalists' main arguments in favor of the Constitution? *that the Constitution offered a good balance of power and was a careful compromise between various political views*

Analyze What were the Antifederalists' main fears regarding the Constitution? *that it would create a government as tyrannical as that of Britain's and fail to protect Americans' individual rights*

CRF: Biography Activity: George Mason

Quick Facts Transparency: Federalists v. Antifederalists

HSS 8.2.4; HSS **Analysis Skills:** HR 5, HI 1

Federalists v. Antifederalists

Activity Have students write a short statement expressing what they think Hamilton and Mason might have said to each other regarding the debate over ratification of the U.S. Constitution.

HSS 8.2.4; HSS **Analysis Skills:** HR 5

go.hrw.com
Online Resources
KEYWORD: SS8 US4
ACTIVITY: Hamilton and Madison Articles

Differentiating Instruction for Universal Access

Advanced Learners/GATE

Exceeding Standards

1. Organize the class into two groups: one group representing the views of the Federalists, and the other group representing the views of the Antifederalists.
2. Have each student make a list of points that support his or her group's assigned position. Ask students to share their lists of points as two students write the lists for the class to see. Correct any student errors or misconceptions.
3. Have each student write a short persuasive essay explaining his or her position and urging other Americans to adopt it. Encourage students to create at least one visual aid, such as a chart or a graph, to support their essays.
4. Ask for volunteers to read their essays to the class. LS **Verbal/Linguistic, Visual/Spatial**

Alternative Assessment Handbook, Rubric 43: Writing to Persuade

HSS 8.2.4; HSS **Analysis Skills:** HR 5

Answers

Focus on Reading *the* Federalist Papers

Reading Check *similarities—Many were farmers; most wanted to see the Articles revised in some way; differences—Federalists supported the Constitution and a stronger central government, tended to be wealthier; Antifederalists opposed the Constitution for various reasons; tended to be less affluent.*

Direct Teach

Main Idea

❷ Federalist Papers

The *Federalist Papers* played an important role in the fight for ratification of the Constitution.

Identify Who were the main authors of the *Federalist Papers*? *Alexander Hamilton, James Madison, John Jay*

Identify Points of View What fears did the *Federalist Papers* address? *that the federal government would overpower the states; that one group would dominate the government*

- Political Cartoons Activities for United States History, Cartoon 4: Ratifying the Constitution
- **CRF:** History and Geography Activity: Ratifying the Constitution
- **CRF:** Literature Activity: *Federalist Paper* "No. 15"

HSS 8.2.7; **HSS Analysis Skills:** HR 5, HI 1

Teaching Tip

Reading Historical Documents To help students read difficult historical documents, tell students to scan the material and note any terms or phrases they do not understand. Help students define these terms and phrases. Then have students read the document carefully for its meaning.

Answers

Analyzing Primary Sources *Madison thinks that federalism forms a happy combination, where the great interests belong to the national government, and the local interests belong to the state governments.*

Reading Check *Virginia had the largest population in the nation, and New York was an important center for business and trade; political leaders needed the two states' support to maintain national unity and support for the Constitution.*

Primary Source

HISTORIC DOCUMENT

Federalist Paper No. 10

In November 1787, Number 10 in the series called the Federalist Papers *was written in support of the Constitution. In it, James Madison describes the way federalism will overcome disagreements within society.*

"A landed interest, a manufacturing interest, a mercantile [trading] interest, a moneyed interest, with many lesser interests, grow up of necessity in civilized nations, and divide them into different classes, actuated [moved] by different sentiments and views. The regulation of these various and interfering interests [opinions] forms the principal task of modern legislation, and involves the spirit of party and faction [group] in the necessary and ordinary operations of the government . . .

The federal Constitution forms a happy combination . . . the great . . . interests being referred to the national [legislature]; the local and particular to the state legislatures . . . The influence of factious leaders may kindle [start] a flame within their particular states, but will be unable to spread a general conflagration [large fire] through the other states."

—James Madison, quoted in *Living American Documents*, edited by Isidore Starr, et al.

Madison believes that lawmakers are responsible for regulating the many competing concerns that make up society.

The federal government will handle issues affecting the nation as a whole; state and local governments will handle those concerning local issues.

ANALYSIS SKILL **ANALYZING PRIMARY SOURCES**

Why does Madison think federalism will prevent disagreement?

The Constitution needed only 9 states to pass it. However, to establish and preserve national unity, each state needed to ratify it. Every state except Rhode Island held special state conventions that gave citizens the chance to discuss and vote on the Constitution.

Paul Revere served on a committee supporting ratification. He wrote of the Constitution, "The proposed . . . government, is well calculated [planned] to secure the liberties, protect the property, and guard the rights of the citizens of America."

Antifederalists also spoke out in state conventions. In New York, one citizen said, "It appears that the government will fall into the hands of the few and the great."

On December 7, 1787, Delaware became the first state to ratify the Constitution. Throughout the rest of 1787 and the first half of 1788, eight other states approved it. The Constitution went into effect in June 1788 after New Hampshire became the ninth state to ratify it.

Political leaders across America knew the new government needed the support of Virginia and New York, where debate still raged. Virginia had the largest population in the nation. New York was an important center for business and trade.

Finally, Madison and other Virginia Federalists convinced Virginia to ratify it in mid-1788. In New York, Jay and Hamilton said that New York City would break away and join the new government. New York State ratified the Constitution in July. Rhode Island was the last state to ratify it in May 1790.

READING CHECK **Drawing Conclusions** Why were Virginia and New York important to the ratification of the Constitution?

Collaborative Learning

Standards Proficiency

Commemorative Stamps

HSS 8.2.4, 8.2.7; **HSS Analysis Skills:** HI 1

Materials: art supplies

1. Explain to students that the U.S. Post Office occasionally issues special stamps to commemorate an individual or event. Organize students into groups and have each group design and create a series of commemorative stamps celebrating the Constitution and the Bill of Rights.
2. Encourage students to design stamps that represent the following: the Constitutional Convention, the debate over ratification, the *Federalist Papers*, inclusion of a Bill of Rights, and the celebration over ratification.
3. Groups should assign members specific roles or topics to ensure that all students participate.
4. Display the groups' stamps around the classroom. **LS Interpersonal, Visual/Spatial**

- Alternative Assessment Handbook, Rubrics 3: Artwork; and 14: Group Activity

Bill of Rights

Several states ratified the Constitution only after they were promised that a bill protecting individual rights would be added to it. Many Antifederalists did not think that the Constitution would protect personal freedoms.

Some Federalists said that the nation did not need a federal bill of rights because the Constitution itself was a bill of rights. It was, they argued, written to protect the liberty of all U.S. citizens.

James Madison wanted to make a bill of rights one of the new government's first priorities. In Congress's first session, Madison encouraged the legislators to put together a bill of rights. The rights would then be added to the Constitution as **amendments**, or official changes. In Article V of the Constitution, the founders had provided a way to change the document when necessary in order to reflect the will of the people. The process requires that proposed amendments must be approved by a two-thirds majority of both houses of Congress and then ratified by three-fourths of the states before taking effect.

Legislators took ideas from the state ratifying conventions, the Virginia Declaration of Rights, the English Bill of Rights, and the Declaration of Independence to make sure that the abuses listed in the Declaration of Independence would be illegal under the new government. In September 1789 Congress proposed 12 amendments and sent them to the states for ratification. By December 1791 the states had ratified the **Bill of Rights**—10 of the proposed amendments intended to protect citizens' rights.

These 10 amendments set a clear example of how to amend the Constitution to fit the needs of a changing nation. The flexibility of the U.S. Constitution has allowed it to survive for more than 200 years.

THE IMPACT TODAY
In 1789, Madison suggested an amendment limiting Congress's power over its own salary. This amendment was not passed until 1992.

READING CHECK **Summarizing** Why is being able to amend the Constitution important?

SUMMARY AND PREVIEW Early disagreements over individual rights resulted in the Bill of Rights. In the next chapter you will learn about the structure of the Constitution.

Section 4 Assessment

go.hrw.com
Online Quiz
KEYWORD: SS8 HP4

Reviewing Ideas, Terms, and People HSS 8.2.7

1. a. **Identify** Who were the **Federalists** and the **Antifederalists**?
   b. **Draw Conclusions** What was the main argument of the Antifederalists against the Constitution?
2. a. **Recall** When did the Constitution go into effect?
   b. **Draw Conclusions** Why was it important that all 13 states ratify the Constitution?
   c. **Elaborate** Do you think that the ***Federalist Papers*** played an essential role in the ratification of the Constitution? Explain your answer.
3. a. **Recall** Why did Congress add the **Bill of Rights**?
   b. **Explain** From where did legislators' ideas for the Bill of Rights come?

Critical Thinking

4. **Contrasting** Copy the chart at right and use it to identify the differing arguments for and against the Constitution.

Federalist Views		Antifederalist Views
	vs.	

FOCUS ON WRITING

5. **Organizing Your Evidence** In this section you learned how the Bill of Rights was an important addition to the Constitution. You now have all your evidence about the difference between the Articles of Confederation and the Constitution. Choose two or three of the most important points and prepare to defend the Constitution, just like Alexander Hamilton and James Madison did in the *Federalist Papers*.

Section 4 Assessment Answers

1. a. Federalists—supported the Constitution and a stronger national government; Antifederalists—opposed the Constitution
   b. gave too much power to the central government; did not contain a bill of rights
2. a. June 1788
   b. because of concerns that national unity would be weak if some states did not ratify it
   c. Answers will vary, but students should show an understanding of the arguments the *Federalist Papers* used.
3. a. because several states refused to ratify the Constitution unless one was added
   b. state ratifying conventions, Virginia Declaration of Rights, English Bill of Rights, Declaration of Independence
4. Federalist—good balance of power, careful compromise between political views, liberties and rights protected; Antifederalist—central government too strong, rights not protected
5. Students should add Federalist arguments presented in the section to their defenses.

Direct Teach

Main Idea

❸ Bill of Rights

Ten amendments were added to the Constitution to provide a Bill of Rights to protect citizens.

Identify What did the Bill of Rights protect? *citizens' individual rights*

Summarize How are amendments added to the Constitution? *Proposed amendments must be approved by a two-thirds majority of both houses of Congress and then ratified by three-fourths of the states before taking effect.*

CRF: Biography Activity: Mercy Otis Warren

HSS 8.2.7; HSS **Analysis Skills:** HI 1

Review & Assess

Close

Have students discuss why the U.S. Constitution is considered to be a living document.

Review

Online Quiz, Section 4

Assess

SE Section 4 Assessment

PASS: Section 4 Quiz

Alternative Assessment Handbook

Reteach/Classroom Intervention

California Standards Review Workbook

Interactive Reader and Study Guide, Section 4

Interactive Skills Tutor CD-ROM

Answers

Reading Check *Amendments give political leaders the opportunity to change the Constitution as the nation and Americans' needs change.*

Social Studies Skills

Determine Different Points of View

Activity Analyzing Points of View Ask students to imagine that they attended a basketball game at which their school team lost by a wide margin to a rival school's team. How might their points of view of the game differ from those of the winning team's fans? How might the players' points of view differ from those of the fans, even on the same team? Have students discuss the answers and the factors that might influence each point of view. Then have each student consider a viewpoint that he or she holds about school. Have students free-write for 10 minutes about what factors might shape their points of view. Ask for volunteers to share their answers with the class.

LS Verbal/Linguistic

- Alternative Assessment Handbook, Rubrics 11: Discussions; and 37: Writing Assignments
- Interactive Skills Tutor CD-ROM, Lesson 18: Identify Point of View and Frame of Reference

HSS Analysis Skills: HR 5

Social Studies Skills

Analysis | Critical Thinking | Participation | Study

HR5 Students detect the different historical points of view on historical events.

Determine Different Points of View

Define the Skill

A *point of view* is a person's outlook or attitude. It is the way that he or she looks at a topic or thing. Each person's point of view is shaped by his or her background. Because people's backgrounds are different, their points of view are too. Since a person's point of view shapes his or her opinions, knowing that point of view helps you understand and evaluate those opinions. Being able to detect differences in point of view is important to understanding differences in people's opinions and actions in history.

Learn the Skill

When you encounter someone's beliefs, opinions, or actions in your study of history, use the following guidelines to determine his or her point of view.

1. Look for information about the person's background.
2. Ask yourself what factors in the person's background might have influenced his or her opinion or action concerning the topic or event.
3. Be aware that sometimes the person's opinion or actions themselves will provide clues to his or her point of view.

Benjamin Lincoln led the troops that put down Shays's Rebellion in Massachusetts. He was also a state politician and a general during the Revolution. Lincoln offered this explanation of Shays's uprising.

> "Among [the main causes] I rank the ease with which … credit was obtained … in the time of [the Revolution] …. The moment the day arrived when all discovered that things were fast returning [to normal], … and that the indolent [lazy persons] and improvident [unwise persons] would soon experience the evils of their idleness and sloth, many startled [panicked] … and … complained … of the weight of public taxes … and at the cruelty of … creditors [those to whom money is owed] to call for their just dues [rightful payment]… The disaffected [unhappy people] … attempted … to stop the courts of law, and to suspend the operations of government. This they hoped to do until … an end should thereby be put to public and private debts."

Lincoln's background as a general, state official, and leader against the rebels likely gave him a negative point of view on the revolt. His reference to the rebels as lazy and unwise also provides clues to his attitude. You should weigh such factors when evaluating the accuracy of his statement.

Practice the Skill

The following statement about Shays's Rebellion came from a Massachusetts farmer. Read it and apply the guidelines to answer the questions.

> "I have labored hard … all my days. I have been … obliged to do more than my part in the [Revolution], been loaded with … rates [taxes], … have been … [abused] by sheriffs … and [debt] collectors … I have lost a great deal … [T]he great men are going to get all we have, and I think it is time for us to … put a stop to it."

1. From what point of view is this person commenting on the revolt? What is his opinion of it?
2. How does his view of himself differ from Lincoln's view of people like him?
3. Is this view of the revolt likely to be more accurate than Lincoln's view? Why or why not?

Social Studies Skills Activity: Determine Different Points of View

Federalists Versus Antifederalists

HSS Analysis Skills: HR 5 — Standards Proficiency

1. Have students review the material in Section 4 under "Federalists and Antifederalists."
2. Then have each student create a chart contrasting the points of view of the Federalists and Antifederalists. The chart should also list the factors that might have influenced each group's viewpoint.
3. Have students share their answers as you create a master chart. Then have students discuss the factors that contributed to each group's point of view. **LS Verbal/Linguistic, Visual/Spatial**
4. **Extend** Have each student write a short speech that James Madison might have given to explain his point of view on the Bill of Rights. Have volunteers deliver their speeches to the class. **LS Verbal/Linguistic**

- Alternative Assessment Handbook, Rubrics 7: Charts; and 37: Writing Assignments

Answers

Practice the Skill 1. *from the point of view of a farmer who is struggling to pay debts; supports the revolt;* **2.** *sees himself as hard working, deserving of reward for his part in the Revolution, and abused by officials and used by "great men";* **3.** *The two views are probably equally biased. Together they provide a more complete picture of the perspectives and issues involved in the rebellion.*

CHAPTER 4 # Standards Review

Visual Summary

Use the visual summary below to help you review the main ideas of the chapter.

QUICK FACTS
The Articles of Confederation
• first government of United States
• weak union of states
• weaknesses led to Shays's Rebellion
The Constitution
• framework of today's government
• strengthened national government
• three branches
• checks and balances
Bill of Rights
• first 10 amendments
• ensures basic rights

Reviewing Vocabulary, Terms, and People

Match the numbered person or term with the correct lettered definition.

1. Bill of Rights
2. checks and balances
3. constitution
4. Constitutional Convention
5. *Federalist Papers*
6. inflation
7. Northwest Territory
8. William Paterson
9. tariffs
10. Three-Fifths Compromise

a. agreement that stated that each slave would be counted as three-fifths of a person when determining representation
b. delegate to the Constitutional Convention who proposed the New Jersey Plan
c. increased prices for goods and services combined with the reduced value of money
d. area including present-day Illinois, Indiana, Michigan, Ohio, Wisconsin, and part of Minnesota
e. meetings held in Philadelphia at which delegates from the states attempted to improve the existing government
f. series of essays in support of the Constitution
g. set of basic principles that determines the powers and duties of a government
h. system that prevents any branch of government from becoming too powerful
i. taxes on imports or exports
j. the first 10 amendments to the Constitution

Answers

Visual Summary

Review and Inquiry Have students examine the visual summary.

Quick Facts Transparency: Forming a Government Visual Summary

Reviewing Vocabulary, Terms and People

1. j
2. h
3. g
4. e
5. f
6. c
7. d
8. b
9. i
10. a

Comprehension and Critical Thinking

11. a. could settle conflicts among the states, make coins, borrow money, make treaties with other countries and with Native Americans, and ask the states for money and soldiers

b. passed the Land Ordinance of 1785, which helped systemize the division of territory; passed the Northwest Ordinance of 1787, which established the Northwest Territory

c. Answers will vary, but students should show an understanding of the documents and institutions that influenced the development of the nation.

Review and Assessment Resources

Review and Reinforce

SE Standards Review
CRF: Chapter Review Activity
California Standards Review Workbook
Quick Facts Transparency: Forming a Government Visual Summary
Spanish Chapter Summaries Audio CD Program
Online Chapter Summaries in Six Languages
OSP Holt PuzzlePro; GameTool for ExamView
Quiz Game CD-ROM

Assess

SE Standards Assessment
PASS: Chapter Test, Forms A and B
Alternative Assessment Handbook
OSP ExamView Test Generator, Chapter Test
Universal Access Modified Worksheets and Tests CD-ROM: Chapter Test
Holt Online Assessment Program (in the Premier Online Edition)

Reteach/Intervene

Interactive Reader and Study Guide
Universal Access Teacher Management System: Lesson Plans for Universal Access
Universal Access Modified Worksheets and Tests CD-ROM
Interactive Skills Tutor CD-ROM

go.hrw.com
Online Resources
Chapter Resources:
KEYWORD: SS8 US4

Answers

12. a. a revolt by farmers in response to Massachusetts's tax policy

b. Answers may include that foreign nations viewed the United States as weak because its national government had few powers and the nation experienced economic problems.

c. Answers will vary, but students should be familiar with the various trade, economic, domestic, and international problems the nation faced.

13. a. established a system of federalism, created a powerful bicameral legislature, created an executive branch led by a president, created a judicial branch headed by a Supreme Court, balanced power among these three branches, created a system of checks and balances

b. Great Compromise—satisfied small states by creating an upper house with equal state representation, satisfied large states by creating a lower house with representation based on population; Three-Fifths Compromise—satisfied northern and southern states by counting each slave as three-fifths of a person to determine state representation

c. Answers will vary, but students should be aware of the unresolved issues in the Constitution, such as slavery and the lack of a bill of rights.

14. a. to protect individual rights

b. thought it should not have been created, that it gave too much power to the central government, that it needed a bill of rights

c. Answers will vary but should reflect an understanding of each group's views.

Reviewing Themes

15. problems enforcing treaties with foreign nations, limited political authority over the states

16. Political disagreements over state representation, the powers of the national government, how the government should be separated, and slavery led to compromises.

Comprehension and Critical Thinking

SECTION 1 *(Pages 114–117)* **HSS 8.3.2, 8.9.3**

11. a. Describe What powers did the Articles of Confederation give the national government?

b. Summarize What did the Confederation Congress do to strengthen the United States?

c. Evaluate Which document or institution do you think had the greatest influence on the development of the United States? Why?

SECTION 2 *(Pages 120–124)* **HSS 8.2.2, 8.3.5**

12. a. Recall What was Shays's Rebellion?

b. Draw Conclusions What was the general attitude of foreign nations toward the new government of the United States? Why?

c. Evaluate Of the problems experienced by the Confederation Congress, which do you think was the most harmful? Why?

SECTION 3 *(Pages 125–130)* **HSS 8.2**

13. a. Describe In what ways did the Constitution strengthen the central government?

b. Explain How did the two compromises reached during the Constitutional Convention satisfy competing groups?

c. Elaborate In your opinion were there any weaknesses in the Constitution? Explain your answer.

SECTION 4 *(Pages 132–135)* **HSS 8.2.7**

14. a. Recall Why was the Bill of Rights added to the Constitution?

b. Draw Conclusions Why were some Americans opposed to the Constitution?

c. Evaluate Would you have supported the Federalists or the Antifederalists? Explain your answer.

Reviewing Themes

15. Politics What political problems resulted from a weak central government under the Articles of Confederation?

16. Politics How did political disagreements lead to important compromises in the creation of the Constitution?

Reading Skills

Understanding Chronological Order *Use the Reading Skills taught in this chapter to answer the question below.*

17. Organize the following events chronologically according to the chapter.

a. *Federalist Papers* is published.

b. Constitution is ratified.

c. Articles of Confederation is ratified.

d. Shays's Rebellion occurs.

e. Constitutional Convention meets in Philadelphia.

Social Studies Skills

Determine Different Points of View *Use the Social Studies Skills taught in this chapter to answer the question below.*

18. List three differences between the Virginia Plan and the New Jersey Plan.

FOCUS ON WRITING

19. Writing Your Editorial You should start your editorial with a strong statement of your opinion about the Constitution. Then write two sentences about each of your main points of support—a weakness of the Articles of Confederation and/or a strength of the Constitution. End your editorial with a call to action: Ask the delegates to the Constitutional Convention to ratify the Constitution. Remember that you are trying to convince people to make a very important decision for our country—be persuasive.

138 CHAPTER 4

Reading Skills

17. c, d, e, a, b

Social Studies Skills

18. Virginia Plan—proposed by Edmund Randolph, bicameral legislature based on population, larger states had a greater voice in the federal government; New Jersey Plan—proposed by William Paterson, unicameral legislature with equal representation per state, states had an equal voice in the federal government

Focus on Writing

19. Rubric Students' editorials should:

- strongly and clearly express the opinion
- include at least two pieces of evidence to support the opinion
- end with a call to action
- be persuasive
- use correct grammar, punctuation, spelling, and capitalization.

Standards Assessment

DIRECTIONS: Read each question and write the letter of the best response.

1

> "The powers delegated by the proposed Constitution to the federal government are few and defined. Those which are to remain in the State governments are numerous and . . . will extend to all objects which . . . concern the lives, liberties, and properties of the people . . . The operations of the federal government will be most extensive and important in times of war and danger; those of the State governments in times of peace and security."
>
> —James Madison, *Federalist Paper* No. 45

What point was Madison making about the system of government created by the proposed Constitution?

A The states will continue to be in charge of day-to-day government of the people.
B The federal government's main function will be to keep peace among the states.
C The state governments will have greater power than the new federal government.
D The most important governing powers will be held by the new federal government.

2 Which term would *best* describe the newly independent nation in the 1780s?

A strong
B united
C troubled
D confident

3 Under the Articles of Confederation, the greatest amount of power was in the hands of the

A Congress.
B American people.
C national government.
D states.

4 The structure of the U.S. Congress was created at the Constitutional Convention by the

A Virginia Plan.
B Great Compromise.
C New Jersey Plan.
D Three-Fifths Compromise.

5 The nation's most widespread problems under the Articles of Confederation involved

A trade.
B suffrage.
C slavery.
D rebellion.

Connecting with Past Learning

6 The Articles of Confederation created a system of government *most* like that of

A the Ottoman Empire.
B feudal Europe.
C West African kingdoms.
D the Tang dynasty in China.

7 In Grade 7 you learned about Enlightenment ideas of government. What European's contributions to society were *most* like those of James Madison?

A Johannes Kepler
B Johannes Gutenberg
C Leonardo da Vinci
D Baron de Montesquieu

Answers

1. A
Break Down the Question: This questions requires students to interpret information and find the main idea. Suggest that students focus on the phrases, "Those which are to remain in the State governments . . . concern the lives, liberties, and properties of the people," and "those of the States governments in times of peace and security."

2. C
Break Down the Question: This question requires students to synthesize information in Section 1. Have students think about what they know about the nation under the Articles of Confederation.

3. D
Break Down the Question: This question requires students to recall factual information. Students should use a process of elimination to answer the question.

4. B
Break Down the Question: This question requires students to recall factual information. Students should use a process of elimination to answer the question.

5. A
Break Down the Question: This question requires students to evaluate information. Tell students to consider the types of problems the United States experienced and what most of these problems had in common.

6. A
Break Down the Question: This question connects to information covered in Grade 7.

7. D
Break Down the Question: This question connects to information covered in Grade 7.

Intervention Resources

Reproducible

- Interactive Reader and Study Guide
- Universal Access Teacher Management System: Lesson Plans for Universal Access

Technology

- Quick Facts Transparency: Forming a Government Visual Summary
- Universal Access Modified Worksheets and Tests CD-ROM
- Interactive Skills Tutor CD-ROM

Tips for Test Taking

Take It All In When students first start a test, encourage them to briefly preview the test to get a mental map of their tasks:

- Know how many questions they have to complete.
- Know where to stop.
- Set time checkpoints.
- Do the easy sections first; easy questions can be worth just as many points as hard ones.

Standards Review

Have students review the following standards in their workbooks.

- California Standards Review Workbook: HSS 8.2.2, 8.2.7, 8.3.2, 8.9.3

Chapter 5 Planning Guide

Citizenship and the Constitution

Chapter Overview	Reproducible Resources	Technology Resources
CHAPTER 5 **pp. 140–191** **Overview: In this chapter, students will learn about the Constitution, the Bill of Rights, and what it means to be a U.S. citizen.** 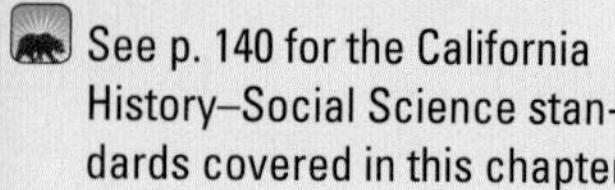 See p. 140 for the California History–Social Science standards covered in this chapter.	 **Universal Access Teacher Management System:*** • Universal Access Instructional Benchmarking Guides • Lesson Plans for Universal Access  **Interactive Reader and Study Guide:*** Chapter Graphic Organizer  **Chapter Resource File*** • Focus on Writing Activity: A Pamphlet • Social Studies Skills Activity: Determining the Context of Statements • Chapter Review Activity  **Pre-AP Activities for United States History:*** Note Taking	**One-Stop Planner CD-ROM:** Calendar Planner **Student Edition Full-Read Audio CD-ROM** **Universal Access Modified Worksheets and Tests CD-ROM** **Interactive Skills Tutor CD-ROM** **Primary Source Library CD-ROM for United States History** **Power Presentation with Video CD-ROM** **History's Impact: United States History Video Program (VHS/DVD):** Citizenship and the Constitution*
Section 1: **Understanding the Constitution** **The Big Idea:** The U.S. Constitution balances the powers of the federal government among the legislative, executive, and judicial branches. 8.2.6	 **Universal Access Teacher Management System:*** Section 1 Lesson Plan 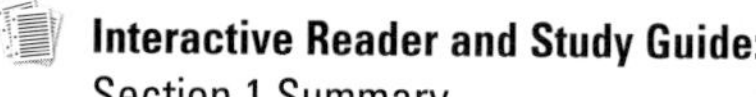 **Interactive Reader and Study Guide:*** Section 1 Summary  **Chapter Resource File*** • Vocabulary Builder, Section 1 • Biography Activity: John Jay • Biography Activity: Sandra Day O' Conner • History and Geography Activity: House Membership, 1990–2000 • Primary Source Activity: Thomas Paine	 **Daily Bellringer Transparency:** Section 1* **Quick Facts Transparency:** Separation of Powers* **Quick Facts Transparency:** Checks and Balances* **Internet Activity:** Supreme Court Case Summary
 **Section 2:** **The Bill of Rights** **The Big Idea:** The Bill of Rights was added to the Constitution to define clearly the rights and freedoms of citizens. 8.2.6, 8.3.7	**Universal Access Teacher Management System:*** Section 2 Lesson Plan **Interactive Reader and Study Guide:*** Section 2 Summary **Chapter Resource File*** • Vocabulary Builder, Section 2 • Primary Source Activity: Hortensius **Political Cartoons Activities for United States History,** Cartoon 6: The Bill of Rights: "Liberty v. Order*	**Daily Bellringer Transparency:** Section 2*
Section 3: **Rights and Responsibilities of Citizenship** **The Big Idea:** American citizenship involves great privileges and serious responsibilities. 8.3.6	**Universal Access Teacher Management System:*** Section 3 Lesson Plan **Interactive Reader and Study Guide:*** Section 3 Summary **Chapter Resource File*** • Vocabulary Builder, Section 3 • Literature Activity: *The Free Citizen* • Primary Source Activity: What It Means to Be An American: Two Views **Political Cartoons Activities for United States History,** Cartoon 5: Duties of Citizenship*	**Daily Bellringer Transparency:** Section 3*  **Internet Activity:** Tracking U.S. Immigration

MASTERING THE CALIFORNIA STANDARDS

SE Student Edition | Print Resource | Audio CD |  Video

TE Teacher's Edition | Transparency |  CD-ROM | DVD

go.hrw.com | CA Standards Mastery | LS Learning Styles

OSP One-Stop Planner CD-ROM | * also on One-Stop Planner CD

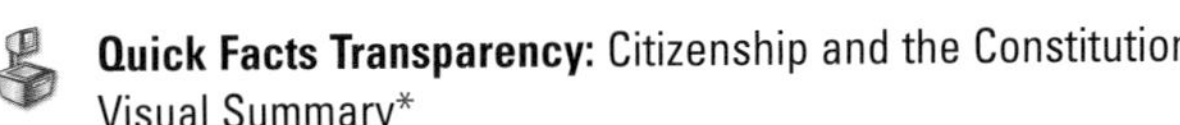

Review, Assessment, Intervention

- **Standards Review Workbook***
- **Quick Facts Transparency:** Citizenship and the Constitution Visual Summary*
- **Spanish Chapter Summaries Audio CD Program**
- **Online Chapter Summaries in Six Languages**
- **Quiz Game CD-ROM**
- **Progress Assessment Support System (PASS):** Chapter Test*
- **Universal Access Modified Worksheets and Tests CD-ROM:** Modified Chapter Test
- **One-Stop Planner CD-ROM:** ExamView Test Generator (English/Spanish)
- **Alternative Assessment Handbook**

- **PASS:** Section 1 Quiz*
- **Online Quiz:** Section 1
- **Alternative Assessment Handbook**

- **PASS:** Section 2 Quiz*
- **Online Quiz:** Section 2
- **Alternative Assessment Handbook**

- **PASS:** Section 3 Quiz*
- **Online Quiz:** Section 3
- **Alternative Assessment Handbook**

California Resources for Standards Mastery

INSTRUCTIONAL PLANNING AND SUPPORT

- **Universal Access Teacher Management System***
- **One-Stop Planner CD-ROM with Test Generator: Teacher Management System with Interactive Teacher's Edition**

STANDARDS MASTERY

- **Standards Review Workbook***
- **At Home: A Guide to Standards Mastery for United States History**

go.hrw.com Holt Online Learning

To enhance learning, Internet activities are available for a Supreme Court Case Summary and Tracking U.S. Immigration.

KEYWORD: SS8 TEACHER

- **Teacher Support Page**
- **Content Updates**
- **Rubrics and Writing Models**
- **Teaching Tips for the Multimedia Classroom**

KEYWORD: SS8 US5

- **Current Events**
- **Document-Based Questions**
- **Holt Grapher**
- **Holt Online Atlas**
- **Holt Researcher**
- **Interactive Multimedia Activities**
- **Internet Activities**
- **Online Chapter Summaries in Six Languages**
- **Online Section Quizzes**
- **American History Maps and Charts**

HOLT PREMIER ONLINE STUDENT EDITION

Complete online support for interactivity, assessment, and reporting

- **Interactive Maps and Notebook**
- **Standardized Test Prep**
- **Homework Practice and Research Activities Online**

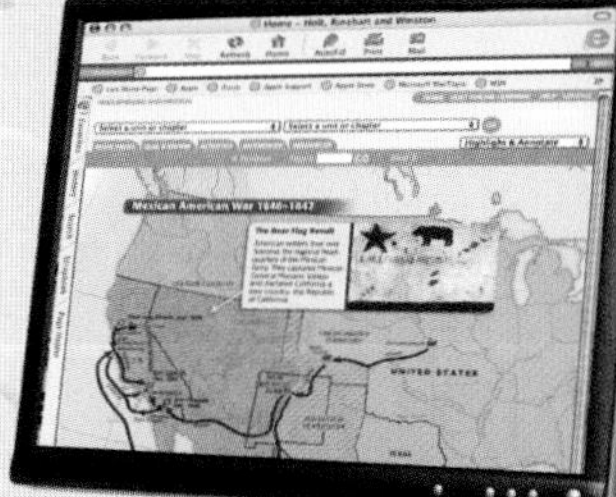

Mastering the Standards: Differentiating Instruction

Reaching Standards	Basic-level activities designed for all students encountering new material
Standards Proficiency	Intermediate-level activities designed for average students
Exceeding Standards	Challenging activities designed for honors and gifted-and-talented students
Standard English Mastery	Activities designed to improve standard English usage

Frequently Asked Questions

INSTRUCTIONAL PLANNING AND SUPPORT

Where do I find planning aids, pacing guides, lesson plans, and other teaching aids?

Annotated Teacher's Edition:
- Chapter planning guides
- Standards-based instruction and strategies
- Differentiated instruction for universal access
- Point-of-use reminders for integrating program resources

Power Presentations with Video CD-ROM

Universal Access Teacher Management System:
- Year and unit instructional benchmarking guides
- Reproducible lesson plans
- Assessment guides for diagnostic, progress, and summative end-of-the-year tests
- Options for differentiating instruction and intervention
- Teaching guides and answer keys for student workbooks

One-Stop Planner CD-ROM with Test Generator: Teacher Management System with Interactive Teacher's Editon:
- Calendar Planner
- Editable lesson plans
- All reproducible ancillaries (PDF)
- ExamView Test Generator (English & Spanish)
- Game Tool for ExamView
- PuzzlePro
- Transparency and video previews

DIFFERENTIATING INSTRUCTION FOR UNIVERSAL ACCESS

What resources are available to ensure that Advanced Learners/GATE Students master the standards?

Teacher's Edition Activities:
- Analyzing Federalism Skits, p. 145
- Ninth Amendment, p. 182
- Becoming a U.S. Citizen Poems, p. 185

Lesson Plans for Universal Access

Pre-AP Activities Guide for United States History: Note Taking

Primary Source Library CD-ROM for United States History

What resources are available to ensure that English Learners and Standard English Learners master the standards?

Teacher's Edition Activities:
- Illustrated Bill of Rights, p. 182

Lesson Plans for Universal Access

Chapter Resource File: Vocabulary Builder Activities

Spanish Chapter Summaries Audio CD Program

Online Chapter Summaries in Six Languages

One-Stop Planner CD-ROM:
- PuzzlePro, Spanish Version
- ExamView Test Generator, Spanish Version

What modified materials are available for Special Education?

Teacher's Edition Activities:
- First Amendment Activity, p. 179

The ***Universal Access Modified Worksheets and Tests CD-ROM*** provides editable versions of the following:

Vocabulary Flash Cards

Modified Vocabulary Builder Activities

Modified Chapter Review Activity

Modified Chapter Test

HOLT
History's Impact
▶ video series
Citizenship and the Constitution

What resources are available to ensure that Learners Having Difficulty master the standards?

Teacher's Edition Activities:
- Separation of Powers Trifold, p. 146

Interactive Reader and Study Guide

Student Edition Full-Read Audio CD

Quick Facts Transparency: Citizenship and the Constitution Visual Summary

Standards Review Workbook

Social Studies Skills Activity: Determine the Context of Statements

Interactive Skills Tutor CD-ROM

How do I intervene for students struggling to master the standards?

Interactive Reader and Study Guide

Quick Facts Transparency: Citizenship and the Constitution Visual Summary

Standards Review Workbook

Social Studies Skills Activity: Determine the Context of Statements

Interactive Skills Tutor CD-ROM

PROFESSIONAL DEVELOPMENT

What teacher training resources are available to help me grow professionally?

- In-service and staff development as part of your Holt Social Studies product purchase
- Quick Teacher Tutorial Lesson Presentation CD-ROM
- Intensive tuition-based Teacher Development Institute
- *Teaching American History* Online 2 Module Professional Development Course
- Convenient Holt Speaker Bureau face-to-face workshop options
- PRAXIS™ Test Prep (#0089) interactive Web-based content refreshers*
- 24/7 *Ask A Professional Development Expert* at http://www.hrw.com/prodev/

* PRAXIS is a trademark of Educational Testing Service (ETS). This publication is not endorsed or approved by ETS.

Information Literacy Skills

To learn more about how History–Social Science instruction may be improved by the effective use of library media centers and information literacy skills, go to the Teacher's Resource Materials for Chapter 5 at **go.hrw.com**, keyword: SS8 MEDIA.

The following materials were developed by the Division for Public Education of the American Bar Association. These materials are part of the **Democracy and Civic Education** supplement.
- Constitution Study Guide
- Supreme Court Case Studies

MASTERING THE CALIFORNIA STANDARDS

• Chapter Preview •

Standards Focus

Standards by Section
Section 1: HSS 8.2.6
Section 2: HSS 8.2.6, 8.3.7
Section 3: HSS 8.3.6

Teacher's Edition
HSS **Analysis Skills:** CS 1, HR 4, HR 5, HI 1, HI 2
ELA Writing: 2.5.a, Reading 8.2.4

Preview Grade 11 Standards
HSS **11.1** Students analyze the significant events in the founding of the nation and its attempts to realize the philosophy of government described in the Declaration of Independence.
11.1.2 Analyze the ideological origins of the American Revolution, the Founding Fathers' philosophy of divinely bestowed unalienable natural rights, the debates on the drafting and ratification of the Constitution, and the addition of the Bill of Rights.

Focus on Writing
The **Chapter Resource File** provides a Focus on Writing worksheet to help students organize and write their pamphlets.

CRF: Focus on Writing Activity: A Pamphlet

CHAPTER 5 1787–PRESENT

Citizenship and the Constitution

California Standards

History–Social Science

8.2 Students analyze the political principles underlying the U.S. Constitution and compare the enumerated and implied powers of the federal government.

8.3 Students understand the foundation of the American political system and the ways in which citizens participate in it.

Analysis Skills

HR 5 Determining the content of statements

English–Language Arts

Writing 2.5.a Present information purposefully and succinctly and meet the needs of the intended audience.

Reading 8.2.4 Compare the original text to a summary to determine whether the summary accurately captures the main ideas, includes critical details, and conveys the underlying meaning.

FOCUS ON WRITING

A Pamphlet Everyone in the United States benefits from our Constitution. However, many people don't know the Constitution as well as they should. In this chapter you will read about the Constitution and the rights and responsibilities it grants to citizens. Then you'll create a four-page pamphlet to share this information with your fellow citizens.

UNITED STATES

1788 The Constitution goes into effect after New Hampshire becomes the ninth state to ratify it.

1787 — 1800

1791 The Bill of Rights becomes part of the Constitution on December 15.

140 CHAPTER 5

Introduce the Chapter

Standards **Proficiency**

Focus on Citizenship HSS 8.3

1. Ask students to discuss the concept of citizenship and what it means to them.
2. Ask students if they can identify any rights and responsibilities associated with American citizenship.
3. To help students get started, write some rights and responsibilities for the class to see. Rights might include freedom of speech, freedom of religion, freedom of assembly, and the right to trial by jury. Responsibilities might include obeying laws and authority figures, paying taxes, and serving on juries.
4. Explain to students that in this chapter they will learn about two important documents—the United States Constitution and the Bill of Rights. Point out that these documents outline many of the rights and responsibilities of American citizens and affect students' lives on a daily basis. LS **Verbal/Linguistic**

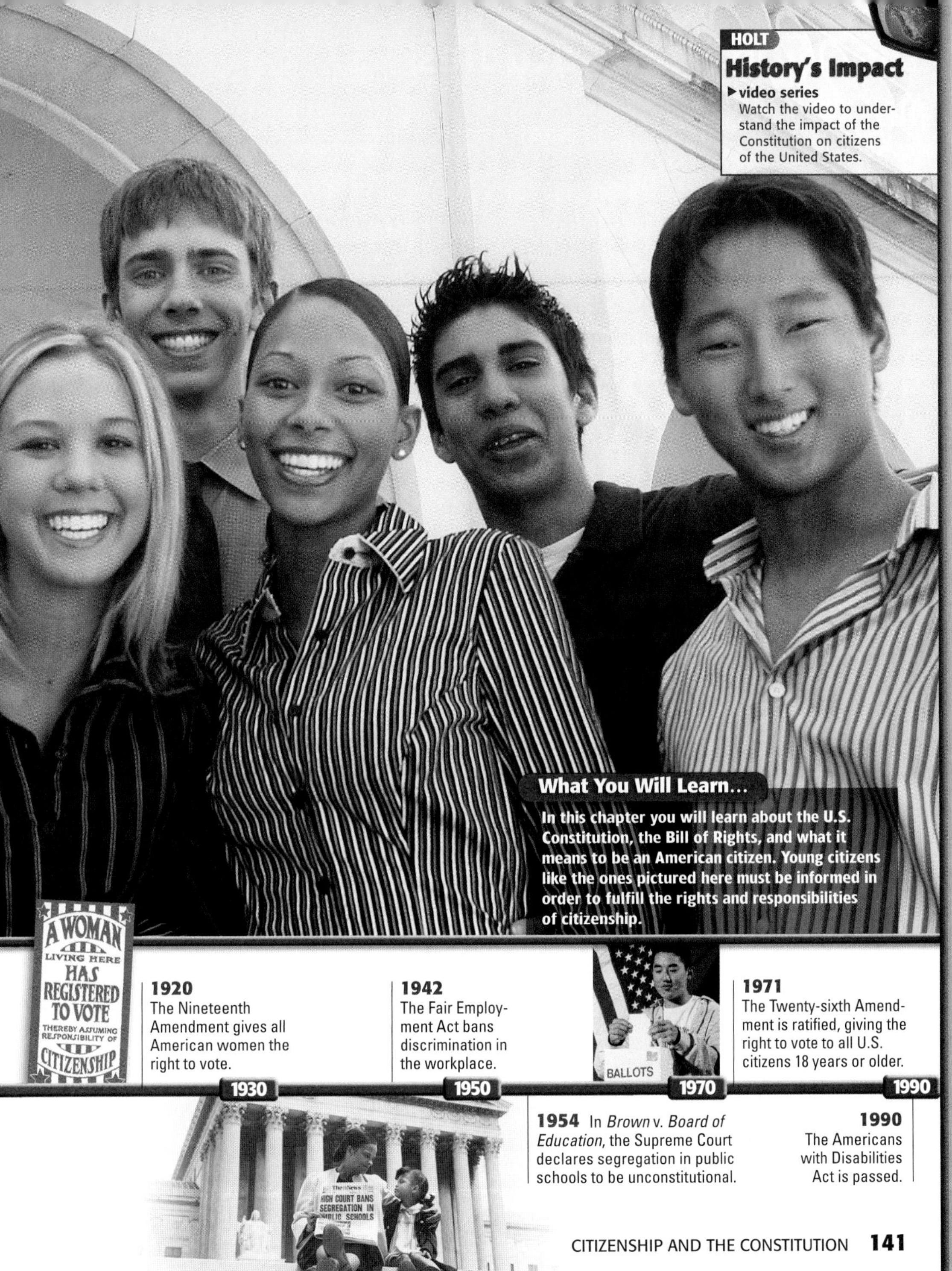

HOLT
History's Impact
▶ video series
Watch the video to understand the impact of the Constitution on citizens of the United States.

What You Will Learn...

In this chapter you will learn about the U.S. Constitution, the Bill of Rights, and what it means to be an American citizen. Young citizens like the ones pictured here must be informed in order to fulfill the rights and responsibilities of citizenship.

1920 The Nineteenth Amendment gives all American women the right to vote.

1942 The Fair Employment Act bans discrimination in the workplace.

1971 The Twenty-sixth Amendment is ratified, giving the right to vote to all U.S. citizens 18 years or older.

1930 — 1950 — 1970 — 1990

1954 In *Brown* v. *Board of Education*, the Supreme Court declares segregation in public schools to be unconstitutional.

1990 The Americans with Disabilities Act is passed.

• Chapter Preview •

HOLT
History's Impact
▶ **video series**
See the Video Teacher's Guide for strategies for using the chapter video **Citizenship and the Constitution.**

Chapter Big Ideas

Section 1 The U.S. Constitution balances the powers of the federal government among the legislative, executive, and judicial branches. **HSS** 8.2.6

Section 2 The Bill of Rights was added to the Constitution to define clearly the rights and freedoms of citizens. **HSS** 8.2.6, 8.3.7

Section 3 American citizenship involves great privileges and serious responsibilities. **HSS** 8.3.6

Explore the Picture

Becoming a U.S. Citizen The process by which foreign citizens become U.S. citizens is called naturalization. Congress established the requirements for naturalization in the Immigration and Nationality Act (INA). Among these requirements are the ability to read, write, and speak English; knowledge and understanding of U.S. history and government; belief in the principles of the U.S. Constitution; and good moral character.

Analyzing Visuals How do you think the young people in the photo feel about becoming old enough to enjoy the full rights and responsibilities of American citizenship? *possible answer—proud, happy, and excited*

Explore the Time Line

1. What year did the U.S. Constitution go into effect? *1788*
2. What became part of the U.S. Constitution on December 15, 1791? *the Bill of Rights*
3. How and when did the Nineteenth Amendment change voting rights? *1920; gave women the right to vote*
4. How and when did the Twenty-sixth Amendment change voting rights? *1971; gave all U.S. citizens 18 years or older the right to vote*

HSS Analysis Skills: CS 1

Info to Know

Freedom of Speech Seven years after the Bill of Rights was added to the Constitution, the U.S. Congress passed the Sedition Act of 1798. This act seemed to restrict freedom of speech by making it a crime for a person to say or write anything "false, scandalous and malicious against the government." The U.S. Supreme Court upheld the law's constitutionality, however. Ten people were imprisoned under this law.

go.hrw.com
Online Resources
Chapter Resources:
KEYWORD: SS8 US5
Teacher Resources:
KEYWORD: SS8 TEACHER

Reading Social Studies

Understanding Themes

Introduce the key theme of this chapter—politics—to the class by asking them to briefly explain what they know about our political system in the United States. Write students' ideas for the class to see. Help students to see which ideas are correct and which are incorrect. Have students create a collage that reflects the political ideas that were instituted by the U.S. Constitution.

Summarizing Historical Texts

Focus on Reading Organize the class into pairs. Then assign each pair of students a different amendment from the U.S. Constitution. Have groups use the steps explained at right to create a summary of their amendment. You might want to assign another amendment to groups that finish early. After students have finished, have each group present its summary to the class. Encourage students to write down the key points in each summary.

Standards Focus

ELA Reading 8.2.4

Reading Social Studies

Economics | Geography | **Politics** | Religion | Society and Culture | Science and Technology

Focus on Themes In this chapter, you will read about the three branches of government, the Bill of Rights, and the duties and responsibilities of a United States citizen. As you read about each of these topics, you will see the American **political system** at work—not only in the Bill of Rights, but through the responsibilities U.S. citizens have as they vote for leaders and work to help their communities and nation.

Summarizing Historical Texts

Focus on Reading History books are full of information. Sometimes the sheer amount of information they contain can make processing what you read difficult. In those cases, in may be helpful to stop for a moment and summarize what you've read.

Additional reading support can be found in the Interactive Reader and Study Guide

Writing a Summary A summary is a short restatement of the most important ideas in a text. The example below shows three steps used in writing a summary. First underline important details. Then write a short summary of each paragraph. Finally, combine these paragraph summaries into a short summary of the whole passage.

The Constitution

Article II, Section 1

1. The executive Power shall be vested in a President of the United States of America. He shall hold his Office during the Term of four Years, and, together with the Vice President, chosen for the same Term, be elected, as follows:

2. Each State shall appoint, in such Manner as the Legislature thereof may direct, a Number of Electors, equal to the whole Number of Senators and Representatives to which the State may be entitled in the Congress; but no Senator or Representative, or Person holding an Office of Trust or Profit under the United States, shall be appointed an Elector.

Summary of Paragraph 1
The executive branch is headed by a president and vice president, each elected for four-year terms.

Summary of Paragraph 2
The electors who choose the president and vice president are appointed. Each state has the same number of electors as it has members of Congress.

Combined Summary
The president and vice president who run the executive branch are elected every four years by state-appointed electors.

Reading and Skills Resources

Reading Support

- Interactive Reader and Study Guide
- Student Edition on Audio CD
- Spanish Chapter Summaries Audio CD Program

Social Studies Skills Support

- Interactive Skills Tutor CD-ROM

Vocabulary Support

- **CRF:** Vocabulary Builder Activities
- **CRF:** Chapter Review Activity
- Universal Access Modified Worksheets and Tests CD-ROM:
  - Vocabulary Flash Cards
  - Vocabulary Builder Activity
  - Chapter Review Activity

OSP Holt PuzzlePro

ELA Reading 8.2.4 Compare the original text to a summary.

You Try It!

The following passage is from the U.S. Constitution. As you read it, decide which facts you would include in a summary of the passage.

The Constitution

Article I, Section 2

1. The House of Representatives shall be composed of Members chosen every second Year by the People of the several States, and the Electors in each State shall have the Qualifications requisite for Electors of the most numerous branch of the State Legislature.

2. No person shall be a Representative who shall not have attained to the Age of twenty five years, and been seven Years a Citizen of the United States, and who shall not, when elected, be an Inhabitant of the State in which he shall be chosen.

After you read the passage, answer the following questions.

1. Which of the following statements best summarizes the first paragraph of this passage?

a. Congress has a House of Representatives.

b. Members of the House of Representatives are elected every two years by state electors.

2. Using the steps described on the previous page, write a summary of the second paragraph of this passage.

3. Combine the summary statement you chose in Question 1 with the summary statement you wrote in Question 2 to create a single summary of this entire passage.

As you read Chapter 5, think about what details you would include in a summary of each paragraph.

Key Terms and People

Chapter 5

Section 1
federal system *(p. 144)*
impeach *(p. 146)*
veto *(p. 146)*
executive orders *(p. 147)*
pardons *(p. 147)*
Thurgood Marshall *(p. 148)*
Sandra Day O'Connor *(p. 148)*

Section 2
James Madison *(p. 178)*
majority rule *(p. 178)*
petition *(p. 179)*
search warrant *(p. 180)*
due process *(p. 180)*
indict *(p. 180)*
double jeopardy *(p. 180)*
eminent domain *(p. 180)*

Section 3
naturalized citizens *(p. 184)*
deport *(p. 184)*
draft *(p. 185)*
political action committees *(p. 186)*
interest groups *(p. 186)*

Academic Vocabulary

Success in school is related to knowing academic vocabulary—the words that are frequently used in school as-signments and discus-sions. In this chapter, you will learn the following academic words:

distinct *(p. 145)*
influence *(p. 186)*

Teaching Tip

Summarizing may be a difficult concept for students to grasp. Students may think that every fact is an important detail. Remind students that not every fact is important when writing a summary. One way to help students keep to the important details is to have them identify the main idea of each paragraph in a few words. Then instruct students to identify only those details that support that main idea. Model this strategy for students by summarizing a paragraph or two as a class.

Reading Social Studies

Key Terms and People

Read the terms and people to students. Then ask students to choose five to eight terms with which they are unfamiliar. Have students define the terms they selected. Then have each student create a crossword puzzle using the definitions he or she wrote as clues. If time permits, have students exchange their puzzles with a partner and complete the other person's crossword. Then have students check their answers. **LS Verbal/Linguistic, Visual/Spatial**

Focus on Reading

See the **Focus on Reading** questions in this chapter for more practice on this reading social studies skill.

Reading Social Studies Assessment

See the **Standards Review** at the end of this chapter for student assessment questions related to this reading skill.

Answers

You Try It! 1. *b;* **2.** *possible answer—Members of the House of Representatives must meet certain age and residency requirements.* **3.** *Members of the House of Representatives are elected every two years and must meet certain age and residency requirements.*

Preteach

Bellringer

If YOU were there . . . Use the **Daily Bellringer Transparency** to help students answer the question.

Daily Bellringer Transparency, Section 1

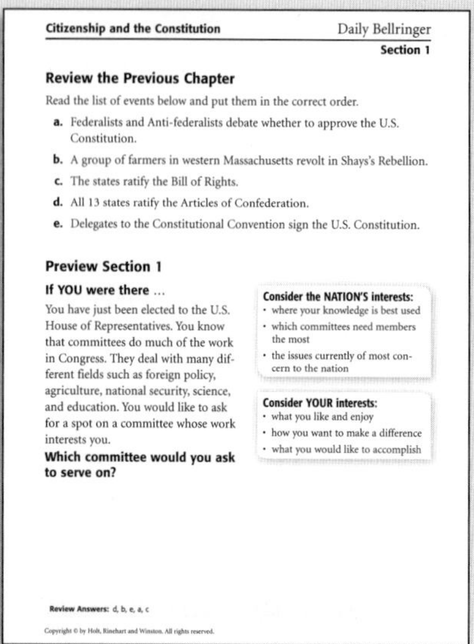

Citizenship and the Constitution — Daily Bellringer

Section 1

Review the Previous Chapter

Read the list of events below and put them in the correct order.

- **a.** Federalists and Anti-federalists debate whether to approve the U.S. Constitution.
- **b.** A group of farmers in western Massachusetts revolt in Shays's Rebellion.
- **c.** The states ratify the Bill of Rights.
- **d.** All 13 states ratify the Articles of Confederation.
- **e.** Delegates to the Constitutional Convention sign the U.S. Constitution.

Preview Section 1

If YOU were there ...

You have just been elected to the U.S. House of Representatives. You know that committees do much of the work in Congress. They deal with many different fields such as foreign policy, agriculture, national security, science, and education. You would like to ask for a spot on a committee whose work interests you.

Which committee would you ask to serve on?

Consider the NATION'S interests:
- where your knowledge is best used
- which committees need members the most
- the issues currently of most concern to the nation

Consider YOUR interests:
- what you like and enjoy
- how you want to make a difference
- what you would like to accomplish

Review Answers: d, b, e, a, c

Academic Vocabulary

Review with students the high-use academic term in this section.

distinct separate (p. 145)

Building Vocabulary

Preteach or review the following term:

apportionment system that keeps total House membership at 435 members (p. 145)

CRF: Vocabulary Builder Activity, Section 1

Standards Focus

HSS 8.2.6

Means: Describe how the Constitution divides power between the federal and state governments and among the three branches of the federal government.

Matters: The Constitution provides the foundation of the U.S. government and protects against political tyranny.

SECTION 1

Understanding the Constitution

What You Will Learn...

Main Ideas

1. The framers of the Constitution devised the federal system.
2. The legislative branch makes the nation's laws.
3. The executive branch enforces the nation's laws.
4. The judicial branch determines whether or not laws are constitutional.

The Big Idea

The U.S. Constitution balances the powers of the federal government among the legislative, executive, and judicial branches.

Key Terms and People

federal system, *p. 144*
impeach, *p. 146*
veto, *p. 146*
executive orders, *p. 147*
pardons, *p. 147*
Thurgood Marshall, *p. 148*
Sandra Day O'Connor, *p. 148*

HSS 8.2.6 Enumerate the powers of government set forth in the Constitution and the fundamental liberties ensured by the Bill of Rights.

If YOU were there...

You have just been elected to the U.S. House of Representatives. You know that committees do much of the work in Congress. They deal with many different fields such as foreign policy, agriculture, national security, science, and education. You would like to ask for a spot on a committee whose work interests you.

Which committee would you ask to serve on?

BUILDING BACKGROUND When the framers of the Constitution met in Philadelphia in 1787, they created a national government with three branches that balance one another's powers.

The Federal System

The framers of the Constitution wanted to create a government powerful enough to protect the rights of citizens and defend the country against its enemies. To do so, they set up a **federal system** of government, a system that divided powers between the states and the federal government.

The framers used the federal system, also known as federalism, to structure the Constitution. The Constitution assigns certain powers to the national government. These are called delegated powers. Among them are the rights to coin money and to regulate trade. Reserved powers are those kept by the states. These powers include creating local governments and holding elections. Concurrent powers are those shared by the federal and state governments. They include taxing, borrowing money, and enforcing laws.

Sometimes, Congress has had to stretch its delegated powers to deal with new or unexpected issues. A clause in the Constitution states that Congress may "make all Laws which shall be necessary and proper" for carrying out its duties. This clause, called the elastic clause—because it can be stretched (like elastic)—provides flexibility for the government.

READING CHECK **Summarizing** How is power divided between the federal and state governments?

Teach the Big Idea: Master the Standards

Standards Proficiency

Understanding the Constitution

HSS 8.2.6; HSS **Analysis Skills:** HI 1

1. **Teach** Ask students the Main Idea questions to teach this section.
2. **Apply** Have students scan the section and the Quick Facts diagrams. Tell students to close their books. List the three branches of government for students to see. Then call out a power of one of the branches. Have students determine to which branch the power belongs. Continue until students have assigned all the powers. LS **Visual/Spatial**
3. **Review** As you review the section's main ideas, have students summarize how the Constitution divides government power.
4. **Practice/Homework** Have each student create a mobile illustrating the division of power between the federal government and state governments and among the three branches of the federal government. LS **Visual/Spatial**

Alternative Assessment Handbook, Rubrics 3: Artwork; and 7: Charts

Separation of Powers QUICK FACTS

U.S. Constitution

Legislative Branch (Congress)	Executive Branch (President)	Judicial Branch (Supreme Court)
• Writes the laws • Confirms presidential appointments • Approves treaties • Grants money • Declares war	• Proposes laws • Administers the laws • Commands armed forces • Appoints ambassadors and other officials • Conducts foreign policy • Makes treaties	• Interprets the Constitution and other laws • Reviews lower-court decisions

Legislative Branch

The federal government has three branches, each with distinct responsibilities and powers. This separation balances the branches and keeps any one of them from growing too powerful. The first branch of government is the legislative branch, or Congress. It makes the nation's laws. Article I of the Constitution divides Congress into the House of Representatives and the Senate.

With 435 members, the House of Representatives is the larger congressional house. The U.S. Census, a population count made every 10 years, determines how many members represent each state. A system called apportionment keeps total membership at 435. If one state gains a member, another state loses one. Members must be at least 25 years old, live in the state where they were elected, and have been U.S. citizens for seven years. They serve two-year terms.

The Senate has two members, or senators, per state. Senators represent the interests of the whole state, not just a district. They must be at least 30 years old, have been U.S. citizens for nine years, and live in the state they represent. They serve six-year terms. The senior senator of a state is the one who has served the longer of the two. Members of Congress can serve an unlimited number of terms.

The political party with more members in each house is the majority party. The one with fewer members is the minority party. The leader of the House of Representatives, or Speaker of the House, is elected by House members from the majority party.

The U.S. vice president serves as president of the Senate. He takes no part in Senate debates but can vote to break ties. If he is absent, the president pro tempore (pro tem for short) leads the Senate. There is no law for how the Senate must choose this position, but it traditionally goes to the majority party's senator who has served the longest.

Congress begins sessions, or meetings, each year in the first week of January. Both houses do most of their work in committees. Each committee studies certain types of bills, or suggested laws. For example, all bills about taxes begin in the House Ways and Means Committee.

ACADEMIC VOCABULARY
distinct separate

READING CHECK **Comparing and Contrasting** What are the similarities in requirements for members of the House of Representatives and the Senate? What are the differences?

Direct Teach

Main Idea

1 The Federal System

The framers of the Constitution devised the federal system

Define What is federalism? *a government system that divides powers between the states and the federal government*

Contrast How do delegated, reserved, and concurrent powers differs? *delegated—powers granted to the federal government; reserved—powers kept by the states; concurrent—powers shared by state and federal governments*

CRF: Biography Activity: Daniel K. Inouye

HSS 8.2.6; HSS **Analysis Skills:** HI 1

Main Idea

2 Legislative Branch

The legislative branch makes the nation's laws.

Recall Which article of the Constitution defines the legislative branch? *Article I*

Draw Conclusions Why do you think the legislature performs most of its work in committees? *Legislators cannot study every bill, and committees enable legislators to share the work among groups.*

CRF: History and Geography Activity: House Membership, 1990–2000

Quick Facts Transparency: Separation of Powers

HSS 8.2.6; HSS **Analysis Skills:** HI 1

Collaborative Learning

Exceeding Standards

Analyzing Federalism Skits HSS 8.2.6; HSS **Analysis Skills:** HI 1

1. Explain that one reason the framers of the Constitution delegated some powers to the federal government—rather than reserving them for state governments—was to avoid difficult situations between the states.
2. Organize the class into five small groups. Assign each group one of the following delegated powers: the coining of money, regulating interstate and international trade, providing for national defense, declaring war, and conducting diplomacy.
3. Have each group create a skit highlighting the confusion that might occur if state governments held the delegated power. Each member of the group should participate in the skit in some way.
4. Have each group present its skit. Then lead a class discussion about the importance of the division of powers in the Constitution.
   LS Interpersonal, Kinesthetic

Alternative Assessment Handbook, Rubric 33: Skits and Reader's Theater

Answers

Reading Check (left page) *some powers are delegated to the federal government, some reserved to state governments, and others are shared*

Reading Check *similarities—must live in the state they represent and where elected; differences—Representatives must be at least 25 years old and have been U.S. citizens for seven years; senators must be at least 30 and have been U.S. citizens for nine years.*

Direct Teach

Main Idea

❸ Executive Branch

The executive branch enforces the nation's laws.

Describe What are the requirements to serve as president? *native-born U.S. citizen at least 35 years old and a U.S. resident for at least 14 years*

Analyze How does the system of checks and balances make it difficult for Congress to pass a law that the president opposes? *Congress must achieve a two-third majority vote to override a presidential veto.*

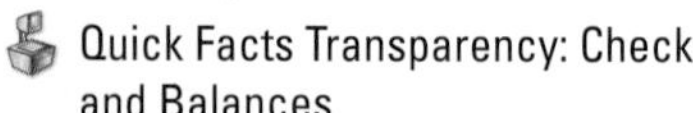
Quick Facts Transparency: Checks and Balances

HSS 8.2.6; HSS **Analysis Skills:** HI 1

Connect to Government

Exercising the Veto The president's ability to veto legislation is an important check on Congress's power. Between 1789 and 1990, presidents vetoed 2,492 bills, with 2,433 of these vetoes taking place after 1865. Congress overrode these vetoes only 103 times.

Info to Know

The Nixon Pardon Perhaps the most famous pardon in presidential history took place on September 8, 1974, when President Gerald R. Ford pardoned Richard Nixon, the former president. Nixon had resigned from office after being accused of involvement in illegal actions while president. Ford explained that he granted the pardon because prosecuting a former president would be too disturbing for the nation.

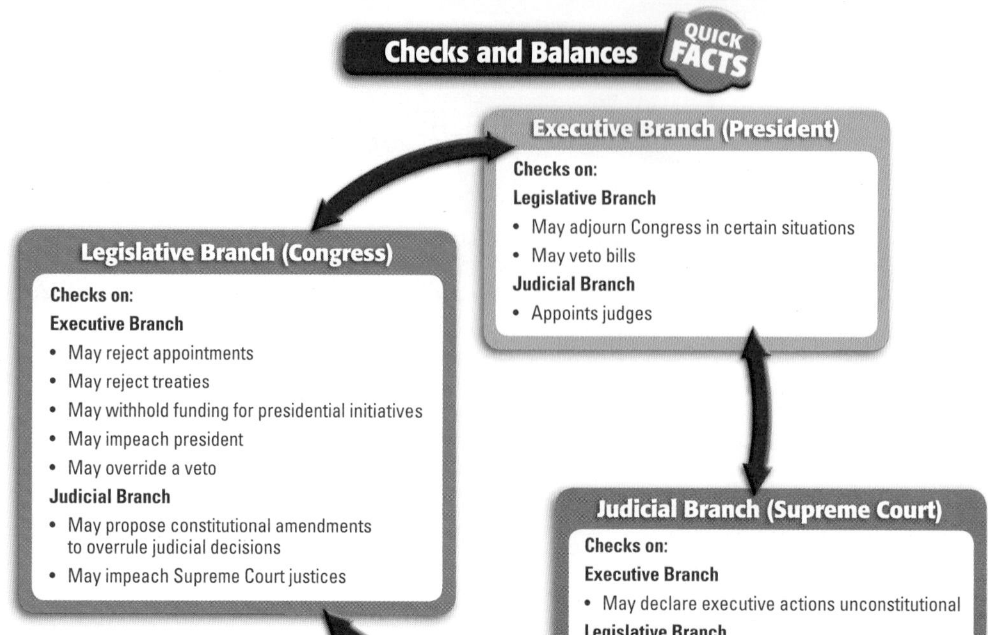

Checks and Balances
QUICK FACTS
Executive Branch (President)
Checks on:
Legislative Branch
• May adjourn Congress in certain situations
• May veto bills
Judicial Branch
• Appoints judges
Legislative Branch (Congress)
Checks on:
Executive Branch
• May reject appointments
• May reject treaties
• May withhold funding for presidential initiatives
• May impeach president
• May override a veto
Judicial Branch
• May propose constitutional amendments to overrule judicial decisions
• May impeach Supreme Court justices
Judicial Branch (Supreme Court)
Checks on:
Executive Branch
• May declare executive actions unconstitutional
Legislative Branch
• May declare laws unconstitutional

Executive Branch

Article II of the Constitution lists the powers of the executive branch. This branch enforces the laws passed by Congress.

President and Vice President

As head of the executive branch, the president is the most powerful elected leader in the United States. To qualify for the presidency or vice presidency, one must be a native-born U.S. citizen at least 35 years old. The president must also have been a U.S. resident for 14 years.

Americans elect a president and vice president every four years. Franklin D. Roosevelt, who won four times, was the only president to serve more than two terms. Now, the Twenty-second Amendment limits presidents to two terms. If a president dies, resigns, or is removed from office, the vice president becomes president for the rest of the term.

The House of Representatives can **impeach**, or vote to bring charges of serious crimes against, a president. Impeachment cases are tried in the Senate. If a president is found guilty, Congress can remove him from office. In 1868 Andrew Johnson was the first president to be impeached. President Bill Clinton was impeached in 1998. However, the Senate found each man not guilty.

Working with Congress

The president and Congress are often on different sides of an issue. However, they must still work together.

Congress passes laws. The president, however, can ask Congress to pass or reject bills. The president also can **veto**, or cancel, laws Congress has passed. Congress can try to override, or undo, the veto. However, this is difficult since it takes a two-thirds

Critical Thinking: Comparing and Contrasting

Reaching Standards

Separation of Powers Trifold

HSS 8.2.6; HSS **Analysis Skills:** HI 1

Materials: white construction paper or small poster board

1. Have students fold large pieces of paper into three equal, horizontal sections to create trifolds.
2. Have students label the sections *Legislative Branch, Executive Branch,* and *Judicial Branch.*
3. Ask volunteers to use the Separation of Powers Quick Facts diagram and the text to identify the powers and duties of each branch.

In addition, ask students to identify some government positions in each branch (such as representative, senator, president, and justice) and some requirements and duties of those positions. As volunteers provide information, have students fill in their trifolds.

LS Verbal/Linguistic, Visual/Spatial

Alternative Assessment Handbook, Rubric 7: Charts

Quick Facts Transparency: Separation of Powers

majority vote. To carry out laws affecting the Constitution, treaties, and statutes, the president issues **executive orders**. These commands have the power of law. The president also may grant **pardons**, or freedom from punishment, to persons convicted of federal crimes or facing criminal charges.

The president also commands the armed forces. In emergencies, the president can call on U.S. troops. Only Congress, however, can declare war. Other executive duties include conducting foreign relations and creating treaties. Executive departments do most of the executive branch work. As of 2004 there were 15 such departments. The president chooses department heads, who are called secretaries, and the Senate approves them. The heads make up the cabinet, which advises the president.

READING CHECK **Drawing Conclusions** What is the president's most important power?

Judicial Branch

The third branch of government, the judicial branch, is made up of a system of federal courts headed by the U.S. Supreme Court. The Constitution created the Supreme Court, but the Judiciary Act of 1789 created the system of lower district and circuit courts.

Article III generally outlines the courts' duties. Federal courts can strike down a state or federal law if the court finds a law unconstitutional. Congress can then try to revise the law to make it constitutional.

District Courts

The president makes appointments to federal courts. In an effort to keep federal judges free of party influence, the judges are given life appointments. The lower federal courts are divided according to cases over which they have jurisdiction, or authority. Each state has at least one of the 94 district courts.

THE IMPACT TODAY

In 2002 the new Department of Homeland Security was given cabinet-level status to protect against terrorism.

SUPREME COURT DECISIONS

Background of the Court

The rest of the Supreme Court Decisions you see in this book will highlight important cases of the Court. But in this first one, we'll discuss the history of the Court.

The first Supreme Court met in 1790 at the Royal Exchange in New York City. The ground floor of this building was an open-air market. When the national government moved to Philadelphia, the Court met in basement rooms in Independence Hall. Once in Washington, the Court heard cases in the Capitol building until the present Supreme Court building was completed in 1932.

Circuit Riding

Today the Supreme Court holds court only in Washington, D.C. In the past, however, the justices had to travel through assigned circuits, hearing cases together with a district judge in a practice known as riding circuit.

The justices complained bitterly about the inconvenience of travel, which was often over unpaved roads and in bad weather. This system was not just inconvenient to the justices, however. Some people worried about the fairness of a system that required justices who had heard cases at trial to rule on them again on appeal. Other people, however, thought that the practice helped keep the justices in touch with the needs and feelings of the average citizen. Eventually, circuit riding interfered so much with the increased amount of business of the Supreme Court that Congress passed a law ending the practice in the late 1800s.

Path to the Supreme Court

When a case is decided by a state or federal court, the losing side may have a chance to appeal the decision to a higher court. Under the federal system, this higher court is called the court of appeals. A person who loses in that court may then appeal to the Supreme Court to review the case. But the Supreme Court does not have to accept all appeals. It usually chooses to hear only cases in which there is an important legal principle to be decided or if two federal courts of appeals disagree on how an issue should be decided.

ANALYSIS SKILL **ANALYZING INFORMATION**

1. What are two reasons why the practice of circuit riding ended?
2. Why do you think the Supreme Court does not hear every case that is appealed to it?

Direct Teach

Main Idea

4 Judicial Branch

The judicial branch determines whether or not laws are constitutional.

Explain Why are federal judges appointed for life? *to keep them free of party influence*

Analyze What check does the judicial branch have over the legislative branch? *It can declare a law to be unconstitutional.*

CRF: Biography Activities: John Jay; Sandra Day O'Connor

HSS 8.2.6

Did you know . . .

In the nation's early years, the U.S. Supreme Court met in the basement of the Capitol Building. During one year, while the Capitol was under construction, the Court even met in a tavern. The Supreme Court did not gain its own building until 1935.

go.hrw.com
Online Resources
KEYWORD: SS8 US5
ACTIVITY: Supreme Court Case Summaries

Critical Thinking: Finding Main Ideas

Standards Proficiency

Promoting American Government

Materials: poster board, art supplies

1. Ask students to imagine that they have been selected to describe the U.S. government to citizens of another country.
2. Have students, working either individually or in small groups, create posters or presentations illustrating how the U.S. Constitution divides power between the federal and state governments and among the three branches of the federal government. In addition, students should illustrate how checks and balances provide a check on abuses of power. **LS Verbal/Linguistic, Visual/Spatial**
3. **Extend** Have each student write a speech describing how the United States benefits from its system of government and encouraging other nations to adopt the same form of government. **LS Verbal/Linguistic**

HSS 8.2.6; HSS **Analysis Skills:** HI 1

Answers

Supreme Court Decisions **1.** *The travel was inconvenient and interfered with the Supreme Court's increased work load.* **2.** *The Court usually hears only those cases in which an important legal principle is to be decided or where two federal courts of appeals disagree.*

Reading Check *possible answers—enforcing the laws, issuing executive orders, vetoing legislation, commanding the armed forces*

Direct Teach

Biography

Sandra Day O'Connor (b. 1930) Supreme Court justice Sandra Day O'Connor has achieved several firsts in her career. By 1965 she was the first female assistant attorney general in Arizona. In the Arizona Senate, she held the position of majority leader for two years—the first woman to hold such a position in the nation. When President Ronald Reagan appointed O'Connor to the Supreme Court, she was yet again the first woman to hold the position.

CRF: Biography Activity: Sandra Day O'Connor

Review & Assess

Close

Have students discuss whether the three branches of government share power equally and, if not, which branch has the most power and why.

Review

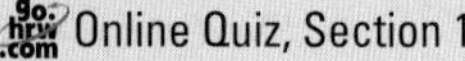
Online Quiz, Section 1

Assess

SE Section 1 Assessment

PASS: Section 1 Quiz

Alternative Assessment Handbook

Reteach/Classroom Intervention

California Standards Review Workbook

Interactive Reader and Study Guide, Section 1

Interactive Skills Tutor CD-ROM

Courts of Appeals

FOCUS ON READING Jot down a short summary of the appeals process after reading this paragraph.

If someone convicted of a crime believes the trial was unfair, he or she may take the case to the court of appeals. There are 13 courts of appeals. Each has a panel of judges to decide if cases heard in the lower courts were tried appropriately. If the judges uphold, or accept, the original decision, the original outcome stands. Otherwise, the case may be retried in the lower court.

Supreme Court

Supreme Court rulings can have dramatic effects on the nation, as in *Bush* v. *Gore*, which decided the outcome of the 2000 presidential election.

After a case is decided by the court of appeals, the losing side may appeal the decision to the Supreme Court. Thousands of cases go to the Supreme Court yearly in the hope of a hearing, but the Court has time to hear only about 100. Generally, the cases heard involve important constitutional or public-interest issues. If the Court declines to hear a case, the court of appeals decision is final.

Nine justices sit on the Supreme Court. The chief justice of the United States leads the Court. Unlike the president and members of Congress, there are no specific constitutional requirements to become a justice.

In recent decades, the Supreme Court has become more diverse. In 1967 **Thurgood Marshall** became the first African American justice. **Sandra Day O'Connor** became the first female Court justice after her 1981 appointment by President Ronald Reagan.

READING CHECK **Summarizing** Describe the structure and responsibilities of the judicial branch.

SUMMARY AND PREVIEW In this section you learned about the balance between the different branches of the federal government. In the next section you will learn about the Bill of Rights.

Section 1 Assessment

go.hrw.com
Online Quiz
KEYWORD: SS8 HP5

Reviewing Ideas, Terms, and People HSS 8.2.6

1. **a. Describe** What type of government did the Constitution establish for the United States?
   b. Contrast What is the difference between delegated, reserved, and concurrent powers?
2. **a. Recall** What role does the vice president serve in the legislative branch?
   b. Compare and Contrast In what ways are the Senate and the House of Representatives similar and different?
   c. Elaborate Why do you think the requirements for serving in the Senate are stricter than those for serving in the House of Representatives?
3. **a. Describe** What powers are granted to the president?
   b. Make Generalizations Why is it important that the president and Congress work together?
   c. Evaluate What do you think is the most important power granted to the president? Why?
4. **a. Explain** What is the main power of the judicial branch?
   b. Evaluate Which branch of government do you feel is most important? Explain your answer.

Critical Thinking

5. **Categorizing** Copy the web diagram below. Use it to identify the separation of powers that exists between the branches of the federal government.

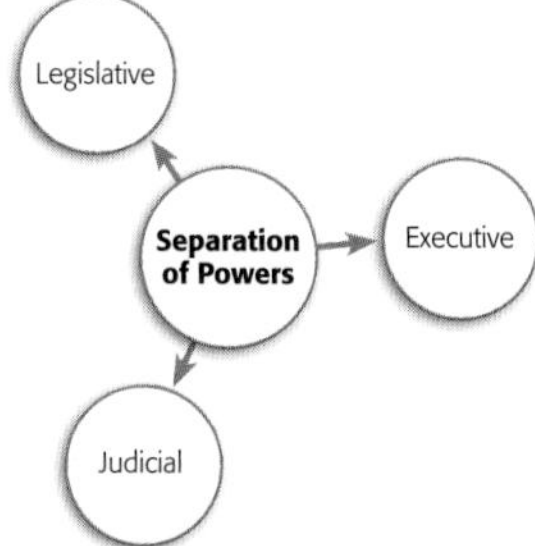

FOCUS ON WRITING

6. **Gathering Information about the Constitution** Look back through what you've just read about the Constitution. Make a list of four or five of the most important features of the Constitution. You'll put that list on the second page of your pamphlet.

Section 1 Assessment Answers

1. **a.** federal system
   b. delegated—powers granted to federal government; reserved—powers kept by states; concurrent—shared powers
2. **a.** serves as president of Senate; can break ties
   b. similar—legislative branch, make laws, meet at same time; different—requirements, size, length of terms, who they represent, leaders
   c. possible answer—because senators serve longer terms, represent a larger area, and are fewer in number than Representatives
3. **a.** powers to propose, enforce, and veto laws; command armed forces; appoint ambassadors; conduct foreign policy; make treaties; issue executive orders; grant pardons
   b. to keep the country running smoothly
   c. See answer to Question 3a.
4. **a.** to interpret the U.S. Constitution
   b. Students should support their opinions.
5. See the Quick Facts diagram on p. 145.
6. Students might mention federalism, separation of powers, and checks and balances.

Answers

Focus on Reading *A person convicted of a crime may take the case to the courts of appeal, which decides if the lower court heard the case appropriately and, if not, the lower court might retry the case.*

Reading Check *federal court system headed by the Supreme Court and including district courts and courts of appeal; interpret the Constitution; review decisions of lower courts*

BIOGRAPHY

James Madison

What would you do to create a brand-new government?

When did he live? 1751–1836

Where did he live? Like several of the founding fathers, James Madison was a Virginian. He grew up in the town of Montpelier, and he kept a home there for his whole life.

What did he do? Through the persuasive power of his writing, Madison helped create the foundations of the U.S. government.

Why is he important? Madison is known as the Father of the Constitution. A brilliant thinker, he provided many of the basic ideas in the Constitution. He argued tirelessly for a strong national government, for separate branches of government, and for rights such as freedom of religion. He then rallied support for adoption of the Constitution and the Bill of Rights. In 1809 Madison became the fourth president of the United States. As president, he led the country through another war with Britain, the War of 1812. He and his wife, Dolley, were forced to flee Washington temporarily when the British invaded the capital and set fire to the White House.

Summarizing Why is Madison known as the Father of the Constitution?

KEY EVENTS

1780
Madison serves in the Continental Congress.

1787
Madison keeps a written record of the Constitutional Convention.

1787–1788
Madison helps write the *Federalist Papers*, urging support for the Constitution.

1801–1809
Madison serves as secretary of state under President Thomas Jefferson.

1809–1817
Madison serves two terms as president.

James Madison was an important force in the writing of the Constitution.

Biography

Reading Focus Question

Have students discuss the introductory question. Ask them to consider the actions the founding fathers took to create a new government for the United States. What did the founding fathers think the purpose of government was? *(such as, to serve the people and to promote the common good)* What did they create to serve as the foundation of the government? *(U.S. Constitution)* Tell students to consider Madison's role in creating the U.S. government as they read his biography.

Info to Know

Madison: Supporter for Independence James Madison was an early supporter of colonial independence from Great Britain. While a student at the College of New Jersey (now Princeton University), he participated in demonstrations against British control of the colonies. He was later elected to Virginia's 1776 Revolutionary convention.

Madison: Father of the Constitution During Madison's lifetime, people began calling him the Father of the Constitution. He disliked the nickname, though, and thought it inappropriate. The Constitution was not "the off-spring of a single brain," he explained, but rather "the work of many heads and many hands."

Critical Thinking: Summarizing

Standards Proficiency

Tribute to Madison HSS 8.3 ; HSS Analysis Skills: HI 1

1. Ask students to imagine that they are hosting a tribute to James Madison in his later years.
2. Have each student write a short speech to introduce Madison before he speaks to the audience. The speech should summarize Madison's many accomplishments and explain his significance in the formation of the U.S. government.
3. Ask volunteers to present their Madison introductions to the class. **LS Verbal/Linguistic**
4. **Extend** Have students create the design for a plaque to award to Madison at the tribute. The plaque should focus on Madison's contributions to the writing of the Constitution and as a U.S. president. **LS Verbal/Linguistic, Visual/Spatial**

Alternative Assessment Handbook, Rubrics 3: Artwork; and 37: Writing Assignments

Answers

Summarizing *He provided many of the basic ideas in the Constitution and rallied support for its adoption.*

Historical Documents

Info to Know

The Preamble Although short, the Preamble was hotly debated in the state ratifying conventions. The delegates objected to the Preamble's opening phrase "We the People," because they had been appointed by the states, rather than elected by the people. Patrick Henry challenged this phrase during the ratifying process in Virginia, saying "The people gave them [the delegates to the Constitutional Convention] no power to use their name. That they exceeded their power is perfectly clear."

Interpret What do you think the three opening words of the Preamble to the Constitution mean? *Students might suggest that the words are stating that the American people have the power to create a Constitution and to establish a government.*

CRF: Primary Source Activity: Thomas Paine, *The Rights of Man*

Teaching Tip

Reading Roman Numerals Some students may have trouble reading the Roman numerals that appear in the Constitution. Before starting the document, spend a few minutes going over the Roman numeral system with the class. If possible, provide students with a chart defining Roman numerals through 30.

The Constitution of the United States

Preamble

The short and dignified preamble explains the goals of the new government under the Constitution.

We the People of the United States, in Order to form a more perfect Union, establish Justice, insure domestic Tranquility, provide for the common defense, promote the general Welfare, and secure the Blessings of Liberty to ourselves and our Posterity, do ordain and establish this Constitution for the United States of America.

Note: The parts of the Constitution that have been lined through are no longer in force or no longer apply because of later amendments. The titles of the sections and articles are added for easier reference.

Standards Focus

HSS 8.2.2, 8.2.3, 8.2.6, 8.2.7

Article I The Legislature

Section 1. Congress

All legislative Powers herein granted shall be vested in a Congress of the United States, which shall consist of a Senate and House of Representatives.

Section 2. The House of Representatives

1. Elections The House of Representatives shall be composed of Members chosen every second Year by the People of the several States, and the Electors in each State shall have the Qualifications requisite for Electors of the most numerous Branch of the State Legislature.

2. Qualifications No Person shall be a Representative who shall not have attained to the Age of twenty five Years, and been seven Years a Citizen of the United States, and who shall not, when elected, be an Inhabitant of that State in which he shall be chosen.

3. Number of Representatives Representatives and direct Taxes shall be apportioned among the several States which may be included within this Union, according to their respective Numbers~~, which shall be determined by adding to the whole Number of free Persons, including~~ ~~**those bound to Service**~~[1] ~~for a Term of Years, and excluding Indians not taxed, three fifths of~~ ~~**all other Persons**~~.[2] The actual **Enumeration**[3] shall be made within three Years after the first Meeting of the Congress of the United States, and within every subsequent Term of ten Years, in such Manner as they shall by Law direct. The Number of Representatives shall not exceed one for every thirty Thousand, but each State shall have at Least one Representative~~; and until such enumeration shall be made, the State of New Hampshire shall be entitled to choose three, Massachoosetts eight, Rhode-Island and Providence Plantations one, Connecticut five, New-York six, New Jersey four, Pennsylvania eight, Delaware one, Maryland six, Virginia ten, North Carolina five, South Carolina five, and Georgia three.~~

4. Vacancies When vacancies happen in the Representation from any State, the Executive Authority thereof shall issue Writs of Election to fill such Vacancies.

5. Officers and Impeachment The House of Representatives shall choose their Speaker and other Officers; and shall have the sole Power of impeachment.

Legislative Branch

Article I explains how the legislative branch, called Congress, is organized. The chief purpose of the legislative branch is to make laws. Congress is made up of the Senate and the House of Representatives.

The House of Representatives

The number of members each state has in the House is based on the population of the individual state. In 1929 Congress permanently fixed the size of the House at 435 members.

Vocabulary

[1] **those bound to Service** indentured servants

[2] **all other Persons** slaves

[3] **Enumeration** census or official population count

Historical Documents

Main Idea

Recall What two groups make up Congress? *the House of Representatives and the Senate*

Identify What information about the House of Representatives is outlined in Article I, Section 2 of the Constitution? *elections, qualifications, number of representatives, vacancies, officers, and impeachment*

Summarize What powers are granted to the House of Representatives? *to make laws, to choose the Speaker of the House and other officers, and to impeach*

HSS 8.2.2, 8.2.6

Connect to Civics: Justice

The House as a Court The House of Representatives helps make the nation's laws. Sometimes, however, the House becomes a court of law. This situation may occur if a high-ranking federal official disobeys the law. The Constitution gives the House the authority to bring charges against the individual. If the House does so, the Senate conducts the trial.

Did you know . . .

The Union passed the first income tax during the Civil War to pay for maintaining the army.

Historical Documents

Main Idea

Recall How many senators are elected from each state? *two*

Summarize What privileges are outlined in Article I, Section 6? *Senators and representatives are paid for their services out of the U.S. Treasury, and they have a number of other privileges, including immunity from arrest except in cases of treason, felony, and breach of peace.*

 Quick Facts Transparency: Federal Office Terms and Requirements

 8.2.6

Connect to Civics: Responsibility

The Seventeenth Amendment Senators are no longer "chosen by the Legislature thereof," but rather are elected by the people of their state. The Seventeenth Amendment made this change to the Constitution. Before voting, all citizens have the responsibility to learn about the candidates, such as senators and other officials.

Exploring the Document

allows one branch of government to exert power over another branch of government

Section 3. The Senate

1. Number of Senators The Senate of the United States shall be composed of two Senators from each State, ~~chosen by the Legislature thereof,~~ for six Years; and each Senator shall have one Vote.

2. Classifying Terms Immediately after they shall be assembled in Consequence of the first Election, they shall be divided as equally as may be into three Classes. The Seats of the Senators of the first Class shall be vacated at the Expiration of the second Year, of the second Class at the Expiration of the fourth Year, and of the third Class at the Expiration of the sixth Year, so that one third may be chosen every second Year; ~~and if Vacancies happen by Resignation, or otherwise, during the Recess of the Legislature of any State, the Executive thereof may make temporary Appointments until the next Meeting of the Legislature, which shall then fill such Vacancies.~~

3. Qualifications No Person shall be a Senator who shall not have attained to the Age of thirty Years, and been nine Years a Citizen of the United States, and who shall not, when elected, be an Inhabitant of that State for which he shall be chosen.

4. Role of Vice-President The Vice President of the United States shall be President of the Senate, but shall have no Vote, unless they be equally divided.

The Vice President

The only duty that the Constitution assigns to the vice president is to preside over meetings of the Senate. Modern presidents have usually given their vice presidents more responsibilities.

5. Officers The Senate shall choose their other Officers, and also a President **pro tempore**,[4] in the Absence of the Vice President, or when he shall exercise the Office of President of the United States.

6. Impeachment Trials The Senate shall have the sole Power to try all **Impeachments**.[5] When sitting for that Purpose, they shall be on Oath or Affirmation. When the President of the United States is tried, the Chief Justice shall preside: And no Person shall be convicted without the Concurrence of two thirds of the Members present.

 If the House of Representatives charges a government official with wrongdoing, the Senate acts as a court to decide if the official is guilty.
How does the power of impeachment represent part of the system of checks and balances?

7. Punishment for Impeachment Judgment in Cases of Impeachment shall not extend further than to removal from Office, and disqualification to hold and enjoy any Office of honor, Trust or Profit under the United States: but the Party convicted shall nevertheless be liable and subject to Indictment, Trial, Judgment and Punishment, according to Law.

Vocabulary

[4] **pro tempore** temporarily

[5] **Impeachments** official accusations of federal wrongdoing

Federal Office Terms and Requirements QUICK FACTS

Position	Term	Minimum Age	Residency	Citizenship
President	4 years	35	14 years in the U.S.	natural-born
Vice President	4 years	35	14 years in the U.S.	natural-born
Supreme Court Justice	unlimited	none	none	none
Senator	6 years	30	state in which elected	9 years
Representative	2 years	25	state in which elected	7 years

152 CHAPTER 5

Section 4. Congressional Elections

1. Regulations The Times, Places and Manner of holding Elections for Senators and Representatives, shall be prescribed in each State by the Legislature thereof; but the Congress may at any time by Law make or alter such Regulations, except as to the Places of choosing Senators.

2. Sessions ~~The Congress shall assemble at least once in every Year, and such Meeting shall be on the first Monday in December, unless they shall by Law appoint a different Day.~~

Section 5. Rules/Procedures

1. Quorum Each House shall be the Judge of the Elections, Returns and Qualifications of its own Members, and a Majority of each shall constitute a **Quorum**[6] to do Business; but a smaller Number may **adjourn**[7] from day to day, and may be authorized to compel the Attendance of absent Members, in such Manner, and under such Penalties as each House may provide.

2. Rules and Conduct Each House may determine the Rules of its Proceedings, punish its Members for disorderly Behaviour, and, with the Concurrence of two thirds, expel a Member.

3. Records Each House shall keep a Journal of its Proceedings, and from time to time publish the same, excepting such Parts as may in their Judgment require Secrecy; and the Yeas and Nays of the Members of either House on any question shall, at the Desire of one fifth of those Present, be entered on the Journal.

4. Adjournment Neither House, during the Session of Congress, shall, without the Consent of the other, adjourn for more than three days, nor to any other Place than that in which the two Houses shall be sitting.

Section 6. Payment

1. Salary The Senators and Representatives shall receive a Compensation for their Services, to be ascertained by Law, and paid out of the Treasury of the United States. They shall in all Cases, except Treason, Felony and Breach of the Peace, be privileged from Arrest during their Attendance at the Session of their respective Houses, and in going to and returning from the same; and for any Speech or Debate in either House, they shall not be questioned in any other Place.

2. Restrictions No Senator or Representative shall, during the Time for which he was elected, be appointed to any civil Office under the Authority of the United States, which shall have been created, or the **Emoluments**[8] whereof shall have been increased during such time; and no Person holding any Office under the United States, shall be a Member of either House during his **Continuance**[9] in Office.

Vocabulary

[6] **Quorum** the minimum number of people needed to conduct business

[7] **adjourn** to stop indefinitely

[8] **Emoluments** salary

[9] **Continuance** term

Historical Documents

Info to Know

Senate Firsts Since the Senate's first session in New York City on March 4, 1789, a number of other firsts have taken place in the U.S. Senate.

- September 30, 1788—first two senators elected: Robert Morris and William Maclay, both from Pennsylvania
- November 1816—first former senator to be elected president: James Monroe
- February 1870—first African American to take the oath as U.S. Senator: Hiram R. Revels
- November 1922—first female senator appointed: Rebecca Felton
- January 2001—first presidential First Lady to be elected senator: Hillary Rodham Clinton

Connect to Science and Technology

Availability of Information For many years, the best way for the public to learn about congressional proceedings was to consult the *Congressional Record*, a bulky set of printed volumes. With the increased availability of the Internet, tracking a congressperson's votes has become much easier. The Library of Congress publishes a Web site that covers many aspects of the government. In addition, independent organizations, such as Project Vote Smart, provide links to track congressional votes.

go.hrw.com

Online Resources

KEYWORD: SS8 US5
ACTIVITY: Library of Congress: Checking on Your Legislators

CITIZENSHIP AND THE CONSTITUTION 153

Historical Documents

Main Idea

Describe What bills may a president veto? *any bills passed by both houses and presented to him for approval*

Explain What is required to override a presidential veto? *two-thirds majority vote of Congress*

Analyze Why do you think a larger legislative majority is required to override a presidential veto than to pass a bill? *to balance power between the executive and legislative branches*

Activity **Political Cartoon** Ask students to find out what is meant by a "pocket veto." Then have them create a political cartoon to illustrate the purpose of this legislative maneuver and how it works. **LS Visual/Spatial**

HSS 8.2.2, 8.2.6

Info to Know

The Line-Item Veto In 1996 Congress passed the line-item veto, which gave the president the power to cancel specific items in spending bills. Supporters of the law hoped that it would help stop wasteful spending by allowing the president to prevent spending that he or she considered unnecessary. However, almost immediately a group of lawmakers challenged the line-item veto on constitutional grounds. In June 1998 the Supreme Court struck down the line-item veto and confirmed a lower court's ruling that it was unconstitutional.

Exploring the Document

top *Officials who are elected more frequently will be held more accountable for raising taxes.*

bottom *to provide the legislative branch with a check on the executive branch; to prevent the president from having too much power*

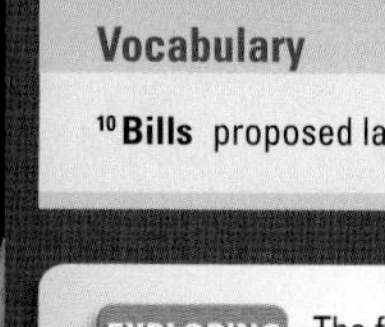

Vocabulary

[10]**Bills** proposed laws

EXPLORING THE DOCUMENT The framers felt that because members of the House are elected every two years, representatives would listen to the public and seek its approval before passing taxes. **How does Section 7 address the colonial demand of "no taxation without representation"?**

EXPLORING THE DOCUMENT The veto power of the president is one of the important checks and balances in the Constitution. **Why do you think the framers included the ability of Congress to override a veto?**

Section 7. How a Bill Becomes a Law

1. Tax Bills All **Bills**[10] for raising Revenue shall originate in the House of Representatives; but the Senate may propose or concur with Amendments as on other Bills.

2. Lawmaking Every Bill which shall have passed the House of Representatives and the Senate, shall, before it become a Law, be presented to the President of the United States: If he approve he shall sign it, but if not he shall return it, with his Objections to that House in which it shall have originated, who shall enter the Objections at large on their Journal, and proceed to reconsider it. If after such Reconsideration two thirds of that House shall agree to pass the Bill, it shall be sent, together with the Objections, to the other House, by which it shall likewise be reconsidered, and if approved by two thirds of that House, it shall become a Law. But in all such Cases the Votes of both Houses shall be determined by yeas and Nays, and the Names of the Persons voting for and against the Bill shall be entered on the Journal of each House respectively. If any Bill shall not be returned by the President within ten Days (Sundays excepted) after it shall have been presented to him, the Same shall be a Law, in like Manner as if he had signed it, unless the Congress by their Adjournment prevent its Return, in which Case it shall not be a Law.

3. Role of the President Every Order, Resolution, or Vote to which the Concurrence of the Senate and House of Representatives may be necessary (except on a question of Adjournment) shall be presented to the President of the United States; and before the Same shall take Effect, shall be approved by him, or being disapproved by him, shall be repassed by two thirds of the Senate and House of Representatives, according to the Rules and Limitations prescribed in the Case of a Bill.

How a Bill Becomes a Law

1. A member of the House or the Senate introduces a bill and refers it to a committee.
2. The House or Senate Committee may approve, rewrite, or kill the bill.

3. The House or the Senate debates and votes on its version of the bill.
4. House and Senate conference committee members work out the differences between the two versions.
5. Both houses of Congress pass the revised bill.

Section 8.

Powers Granted to Congress

1. Taxation The Congress shall have Power To lay and collect Taxes, **Duties**,[11] **Imposts**[12] and **Excises**,[13] to pay the Debts and provide for the common Defense and general Welfare of the United States; but all Duties, Imposts and Excises shall be uniform throughout the United States;

2. Credit To borrow Money on the credit of the United States;

3. Commerce To regulate Commerce with foreign Nations, and among the several States, and with the Indian Tribes;

4. Naturalization and Bankruptcy To establish an uniform **Rule of Naturalization**,[14] and uniform Laws on the subject of Bankruptcies throughout the United States;

5. Money To coin Money, regulate the Value thereof, and of foreign Coin, and fix the Standard of Weights and Measures;

6. Counterfeiting To provide for the Punishment of counterfeiting the **Securities**[15] and current Coin of the United States;

7. Post Office To establish Post Offices and post Roads;

8. Patents and Copyrights To promote the Progress of Science and useful Arts, by securing for limited Times to Authors and Inventors the exclusive Right to their respective Writings and Discoveries;

9. Courts To constitute Tribunals inferior to the supreme Court;

10. International Law To define and punish Piracies and Felonies committed on the high Seas, and Offences against the Law of Nations;

LINKING TO TODAY

Native Americans and the Commerce Clause

The commerce clause gives Congress the power to "regulate Commerce with . . . the Indian Tribes." The clause has been interpreted to mean that the states cannot tax or interfere with businesses on Indian reservations, but that the federal government can. It also allows American Indian nations to develop their own governments and laws. These laws, however, can be challenged in federal court. Although reservation land usually belongs to the government of the Indian group, it is administered by the U.S. government.

Drawing Conclusions How would you describe the status of American Indian nations under the commerce clause?

Vocabulary

[11] **Duties** tariffs

[12] **Imposts** taxes

[13] **Excises** internal taxes on the manufacture, sale, or consumption of a commodity

[14] **Rule of Naturalization** a law by which a foreign-born person becomes a citizen

[15] **Securities** bonds

6 The president signs or vetoes the bill.

7 Two-thirds majority vote of Congress is needed to approve a vetoed bill. Bill becomes a law.

ANALYSIS SKILL ANALYZING INFORMATION

Why do you think the framers created this complex system for adopting laws?

Historical Documents

Info to Know

The First Postal Service Before the Constitution was ratified, Congress had established a postal service under the Articles of Confederation. Benjamin Franklin served as the postmaster general. The postal service expanded rapidly, with revenue increasing from $37,935 in 1790 to $1,707,000 by 1829. By the early 1800s, the government considered the post office so important that the postmaster general was made into a cabinet member. This distinction ended in 1971, however. Today the postmaster general is no longer part of the cabinet.

Answers

Linking to Today *individual states or smaller nations under the umbrella of the U.S. government*

Analyzing Information *to make certain the laws passed represent the will of the people and the good of the nation*

Historical Documents

Main Idea

Describe What do Clauses 11–16 ensure and regulate? *control of the military*

Summarize What Congressional powers are explained in Clause 17? *Congress has the power to make laws for the District of Columbia, the nation's capital. Congress also has the power to regulate use of other property belonging to the national government, such as forts and arsenals.*

Make Inferences Why do you think the framers of the Constitution included a clause prohibiting titles of nobility? *Students might respond that the framers wanted to make sure that no class system or aristocracy would exist in the United States as it did in Great Britain.*

HSS 8.2.2, 8.2.3, 8.2.6

Connect to Civics: Authority

Activity Ask students to conduct research on the minimum wage law or on the creation of military academies as examples of when the elastic clause was used to meet the changing needs of American society. Then have each student write a letter to the framers of the Constitution. In their letters, students should use their research to explain how future government officials have used the elastic clause and their authority responsibly.

Vocabulary

[16] **Letters of Marque and Reprisal** documents issued by governments allowing merchant ships to arm themselves and attack ships of an enemy nation

11. War To declare War, grant **Letters of Marque and Reprisal,**[16] and make Rules concerning Captures on Land and Water;

12. Army To raise and support Armies, but no Appropriation of Money to that Use shall be for a longer Term than two Years;

13. Navy To provide and maintain a Navy;

14. Regulation of the Military To make Rules for the Government and Regulation of the land and naval Forces;

15. Militia To provide for calling forth the Militia to execute the Laws of the Union, suppress Insurrections and repel Invasions;

16. Regulation of the Militia To provide for organizing, arming, and disciplining, the Militia, and for governing such Part of them as may be employed in the Service of the United States, reserving to the States respectively, the Appointment of the Officers, and the Authority of training the Militia according to the discipline prescribed by Congress;

17. District of Columbia To exercise exclusive Legislation in all Cases whatsoever, over such District (not exceeding ten Miles square) as may, by Cession of particular States, and the Acceptance of Congress, become the Seat of the Government of the United States, and to exercise like Authority over all Places purchased by the Consent of the Legislature of the State in which the Same shall be, for the Erection of Forts, Magazines, Arsenals, dock-Yards, and other needful Buildings;—And

The Elastic Clause

The framers of the Constitution wanted a national government that was strong enough to be effective. This section lists the powers given to Congress. The last portion of Section 8 contains the so-called elastic clause.

18. Necessary and Proper Clause To make all Laws which shall be necessary and proper for carrying into Execution the foregoing Powers, and all other Powers vested by this Constitution in the Government of the United States, or in any Department or Officer thereof.

The Elastic Clause
The elastic clause has been stretched (like elastic) to allow Congress to meet changing circumstances.

Section 9. Powers Denied Congress

1. Slave Trade ~~The Migration or Importation of such Persons as any of the States now existing shall think proper to admit, shall not be prohibited by the Congress prior to the Year one thousand eight hundred and eight, but a Tax or duty may be imposed on such Importation, not exceeding ten dollars for each Person.~~

2. Habeas Corpus The Privilege of the **Writ of Habeas Corpus**[17] shall not be suspended, unless when in Cases of Rebellion or Invasion the public Safety may require it.

3. Illegal Punishment No **Bill of Attainder**[18] or **ex post facto Law**[19] shall be passed.

4. Direct Taxes No **Capitation**,[20] or other direct, Tax shall be laid, unless in Proportion to the Census or enumeration herein before directed to be taken.

5. Export Taxes No Tax or Duty shall be laid on Articles exported from any State.

6. No Favorites No Preference shall be given by any Regulation of Commerce or Revenue to the Ports of one State over those of another; nor shall Vessels bound to, or from, one State, be obliged to enter, clear, or pay Duties in another.

7. Public Money No Money shall be drawn from the Treasury, but in Consequence of Appropriations made by Law; and a regular Statement and Account of the Receipts and Expenditures of all public Money shall be published from time to time.

8. Titles of Nobility No Title of Nobility shall be granted by the United States: And no Person holding any Office of Profit or Trust under them, shall, without the Consent of the Congress, accept of any present, Emolument, Office, or Title, of any kind whatever, from any King, Prince, or foreign State.

Section 10. Powers Denied the States

1. Restrictions No State shall enter into any Treaty, Alliance, or Confederation; grant Letters of Marque and Reprisal; coin Money; emit Bills of Credit; make any Thing but gold and silver Coin a Tender in Payment of Debts; pass any Bill of Attainder, ex post facto Law, or Law impairing the Obligation of Contracts, or grant any Title of Nobility.

2. Import and Export Taxes No State shall, without the Consent of the Congress, lay any Imposts or Duties on Imports or Exports, except what may be absolutely necessary for executing it's inspection Laws: and the net Produce of all Duties and Imposts, laid by any State on Imports or Exports, shall be for the Use of the Treasury of the United States; and all such Laws shall be subject to the Revision and Control of the Congress.

3. Peacetime and War Restraints No State shall, without the Consent of Congress, lay any Duty of Tonnage, keep Troops, or Ships of War in time of Peace, enter into any Agreement or Compact with another State, or with a foreign Power, or engage in War, unless actually invaded, or in such imminent Danger as will not admit of delay.

EXPLORING THE DOCUMENT Although Congress has implied powers, there are also limits to its powers. Section 9 lists powers that are denied to the federal government. Several of the clauses protect the people of the United States from unjust treatment. **In what ways does the Constitution limit the powers of the federal government?**

Vocabulary

[17] **Writ of Habeas Corpus** a court order that requires the government to bring a prisoner to court and explain why he or she is being held

[18] **Bill of Attainder** a law declaring that a person is guilty of a particular crime

[19] **ex post facto Law** a law that is made effective prior to the date that it was passed and therefore punishes people for acts that were not illegal at the time

[20] **Capitation** a direct uniform tax imposed on each head, or person

Historical Documents

Info to Know

Writ of Habeas Corpus The term *habeas corpus* derives from Medieval Latin and means "you shall have the body." This protection against unlawful imprisonment is the only civil liberty that the framers included in the original text of the Constitution. All other basic rights and liberties guaranteed to American citizens are outlined in the Bill of Rights.

Exploring the Document

The government cannot suspend the writ of habeas corpus or pass bills of attainder or ex post facto laws.

Historical Documents

Main Idea

Identify Which branch of the government is outlined in Article II? *the executive branch*

Make Inferences Why might many of the delegates to the Constitutional Convention have opposed a one-person executive? *Students might suggest that the delegates feared that they might create another monarchy, as in Great Britain.*

Summarize How are the president and vice president elected? *They are chosen by the electoral college—electors chosen by the states according to rules established by the legislatures.*

Map Transparency: The Electoral College

HSS 8.2.2, 8.2.6

Info to Know

The U.S. President Initially, the writers of the Constitution agreed that the president would be chosen by the national legislature for a single, seven-year term. Many delegates opposed a strong executive branch. However, when the Constitution was turned over to the Committee on Style, Gouverneur Morris, who wanted a stronger executive, reworded the article outlining the role of the president. He shortened the length of the president's term, allowed the president to run for more than one term, and altered the method by which the president would be elected. These changes passed with little debate. For one, the delegates were ready to go home. For another, many members thought that George Washington would be the first president and believed that he would not abuse the power of the executive branch.

Executive Branch

The president is the chief of the executive branch. It is the job of the president to enforce the laws. The framers wanted the president's and vice president's terms of office and manner of selection to be different from those of members of Congress. They decided on four-year terms, but they had a difficult time agreeing on how to select the president and vice president. The framers finally set up an electoral system, which varies greatly from our electoral process today.

Presidential Elections

In 1845 Congress set the Tuesday following the first Monday in November of every fourth year as the general election date for selecting presidential electors.

Article II The Executive

Section 1. The Presidency

1. Terms of Office The executive Power shall be vested in a President of the United States of America. He shall hold his Office during the Term of four Years, and, together with the Vice President, chosen for the same Term, be elected, as follows:

2. Electoral College Each State shall appoint, in such Manner as the Legislature thereof may direct, a Number of Electors, equal to the whole Number of Senators and Representatives to which the State may be entitled in the Congress: but no Senator or Representative, or Person holding an Office of Trust or Profit under the United States, shall be appointed an Elector.

3. Former Method of Electing President ~~The Electors shall meet in their respective States, and vote by Ballot for two Persons, of whom one at least shall not be an Inhabitant of the same State with themselves. And they shall make a List of all the Persons voted for, and of the Number of Votes for each; which List they shall sign and certify, and transmit sealed to the Seat of the Government of the United States, directed to the President of the Senate. The President of the Senate shall, in the Presence of the Senate and House of Representatives, open all the Certificates, and the Votes shall~~

The Electoral College

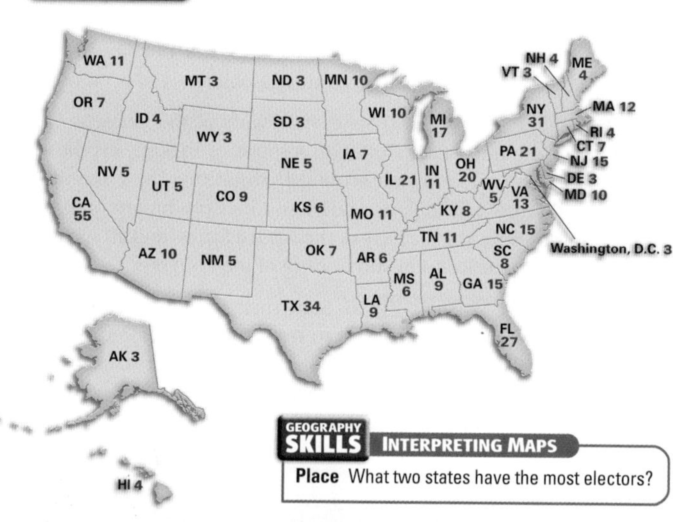

GEOGRAPHY SKILLS **INTERPRETING MAPS**

Place What two states have the most electors?

Answers

Interpreting Maps *California (55) and Texas (34)*

~~then be counted. The Person having the greatest Number of Votes shall be the President, if such Number be a Majority of the whole Number of Electors appointed; and if there be more than one who have such Majority, and have an equal Number of Votes, then the House of Representatives shall immediately choose by Ballot one of them for President; and if no Person have a Majority, then from the five highest on the List the said House shall in like Manner choose the President. But in choosing the President, the Votes shall be taken by States, the Representation from each State having one Vote; A quorum for this purpose shall consist of a Member or Members from two thirds of the States, and a Majority of all the States shall be necessary to a Choice. In every Case, after the Choice of the President, the Person having the greatest Number of Votes of the Electors shall be the Vice President. But if there should remain two or more who have equal Votes, the Senate shall choose from them by Ballot the Vice President.~~

4. Election Day The Congress may determine the Time of choosing the Electors, and the Day on which they shall give their Votes; which Day shall be the same throughout the United States.

5. Qualifications No Person except a natural born Citizen~~, or a Citizen of the United States, at the time of the Adoption of this Constitution~~, shall be eligible to the Office of President; neither shall any Person be eligible to that Office who shall not have attained to the Age of thirty five Years, and been fourteen Years a Resident within the United States.

6. Succession In Case of the Removal of the President from Office, or of his Death, Resignation, or Inability to discharge the Powers and Duties of the said Office, the Same shall devolve on the Vice President, and the Congress may by Law provide for the Case of Removal, Death, Resignation or Inability, both of the President and Vice President, declaring what Officer shall then act as President, and such Officer shall act accordingly, until the Disability be removed, or a President shall be elected.

7. Salary The President shall, at stated Times, receive for his Services, a Compensation, which shall neither be increased nor diminished during the Period for which he shall have been elected, and he shall not receive within that Period any other Emolument from the United States, or any of them.

8. Oath of Office Before he enter on the Execution of his Office, he shall take the following Oath or Affirmation:—"I do solemnly swear (or affirm) that I will faithfully execute the Office of President of the United States, and will to the best of my Ability, preserve, protect and defend the Constitution of the United States."

EXPLORING THE DOCUMENT The youngest elected president was John F. Kennedy; he was 43 years old when he was inaugurated. (Theodore Roosevelt was 42 when he assumed office after the assassination of McKinley.) **What is the minimum required age for the office of president?**

Presidential Salary

In 1999 Congress voted to set future presidents' salaries at $400,000 per year. The president also receives an annual expense account. The president must pay taxes only on the salary.

Historical Documents

Info to Know

Presidential Qualifications Political concerns of the time determined many of the qualifications for the presidency included in the U.S. Constitution. For example, during the Constitutional Convention, a rumor spread that the delegates intended to invite a foreign king to rule the country. To squelch this rumor, the delegates included a constitutional provision requiring the president to be a natural-born citizen. In addition, the delegates added a 14-year residency requirement for the president to disqualify any Loyalists who had left during the American Revolution and then returned to the United States.

Exploring the Document

35 years old

Historical Documents

Did you know . . .

The term *first lady* became common after the Civil War. Before that time, presidents' wives were referred to as Mrs. President or presidentress. Although first ladies are not mentioned in the Constitution, almost all presidents—even unmarried ones—have found someone to fill that role. For example, Dolley Madison served as first lady for widower Thomas Jefferson, before assuming that role for her own husband. Recent first ladies have done more than serve as their husbands' hostesses, however. Some first ladies—such as Eleanor Roosevelt, Betty Ford, Rosalynn Carter, and Hillary Rodham Clinton—have had highly visible roles.

go.hrw.com
Online Resources
KEYWORD: SS8 US5
ACTIVITY: First Ladies Biographies

Commander in Chief

Today the president is in charge of the army, navy, air force, marines, and coast guard. Only Congress, however, can decide if the United States will declare war.

Appointments

Most of the president's appointments to office must be approved by the Senate.

Vocabulary

[21] **Reprieves** delays of punishment

[22] **Pardons** releases from the legal penalties associated with a crime

The State of the Union

Every year the president presents to Congress a State of the Union message. In this message, the president introduces and explains a legislative plan for the coming year.

Section 2. Powers of Presidency

1. Military Powers The President shall be Commander in Chief of the Army and Navy of the United States, and of the Militia of the several States, when called into the actual Service of the United States; he may require the Opinion, in writing, of the principal Officer in each of the executive Departments, upon any Subject relating to the Duties of their respective Offices, and he shall have Power to grant **Reprieves**[21] and **Pardons**[22] for Offences against the United States, except in Cases of Impeachment.

2. Treaties and Appointments He shall have Power, by and with the Advice and Consent of the Senate, to make Treaties, provided two thirds of the Senators present concur; and he shall nominate, and by and with the Advice and Consent of the Senate, shall appoint Ambassadors, other public Ministers and Consuls, Judges of the supreme Court, and all other Officers of the United States, whose Appointments are not herein otherwise provided for, and which shall be established by Law: but the Congress may by Law vest the Appointment of such inferior Officers, as they think proper, in the President alone, in the Courts of Law, or in the Heads of Departments.

3. Vacancies The President shall have Power to fill up all Vacancies that may happen during the Recess of the Senate, by granting Commissions which shall expire at the End of their next Session.

Section 3. Presidential Duties

He shall from time to time give to the Congress Information of the State of the Union, and recommend to their Consideration such Measures as he shall judge necessary and expedient; he may, on extraordinary Occasions, convene both Houses, or either of them, and in Case of Disagreement between them, with Respect to the Time of Adjournment, he may adjourn them to such Time as he shall think proper; he shall receive Ambassadors and other public Ministers; he shall take Care that the Laws be faithfully executed, and shall Commission all the Officers of the United States.

Section 4. Impeachment

The President, Vice President and all civil Officers of the United States, shall be removed from Office on Impeachment for, and Conviction of, Treason, Bribery, or other high Crimes and Misdemeanors.

Article III The Judiciary

Section 1. Federal Courts and Judges

The judicial Power of the United States shall be vested in one supreme Court, and in such inferior Courts as the Congress may from time to time ordain and establish. The Judges, both of the supreme and inferior Courts, shall hold their Offices during good Behavior, and shall, at stated Times, receive for their Services a Compensation, which shall not be diminished during their Continuance in Office.

Section 2. Authority of the Courts

1. General Authority The judicial Power shall extend to all Cases, in Law and Equity, arising under this Constitution, the Laws of the United States, and Treaties made, or which shall be made, under their Authority;—to all Cases affecting Ambassadors, other public Ministers and Consuls;—to all Cases of admiralty and maritime Jurisdiction;—to Controversies to which the United States shall be a Party;—to Controversies between two or more States ~~—between a State and Citizens of another State;~~ —between Citizens of different States;—between Citizens of the same State claiming Lands under Grants of different States~~, and between a State, or the Citizens thereof, and foreign States, Citizens or Subjects.~~

2. Supreme Authority In all Cases affecting Ambassadors, other public Ministers and Consuls, and those in which a State shall be Party, the supreme Court shall have original Jurisdiction. In all the other Cases before mentioned, the supreme Court shall have appellate Jurisdiction, both as to Law and Fact, with such Exceptions, and under such Regulations as the Congress shall make.

Federal Judicial System
QUICK FACTS
Supreme Court
Reviews cases appealed from lower federal courts and highest state courts
Courts of Appeals
Review appeals from district courts
District Courts
Hold trials

Judicial Branch

The Articles of Confederation did not set up a federal court system. One of the first points that the framers of the Constitution agreed upon was to set up a national judiciary. In the Judiciary Act of 1789, Congress provided for the establishment of lower courts, such as district courts, circuit courts of appeals, and various other federal courts. The judicial system provides a check on the legislative branch: it can declare a law unconstitutional.

Historical Documents

Main Idea

Identify What courts does the Constitution include in the judiciary? *Supreme Court and lower federal courts established by Congress*

Explain What power does Article III give to the third branch of government? *the power to interpret the laws of the United States*

Quick Facts Transparency: Federal Judicial System

HSS 8.2.2, 8.2.6

Biography

John Marshall (1755–1835) The U.S. Supreme Court was considered a fairly unimportant institution in its early years. When John Marshall was appointed chief justice in 1801, the Supreme Court did not even have its own building. As chief justice, Marshall established the Supreme Court as the final interpreter of the Constitution and made the Court into an important check on the president and Congress.

Historical Documents

Main Idea

Identify What is the primary subject of Article IV? *relations among states*

Explain What rights are citizens entitled to if they move to or visit another state? *the same privileges and immunities of citizens of that state*

Quick Facts Transparency: Federalism

HSS 8.2.2, 8.2.3, 8.2.6, 8.2.7

Exploring the Document

allows the people rather than the federal government to determine the laws of each state

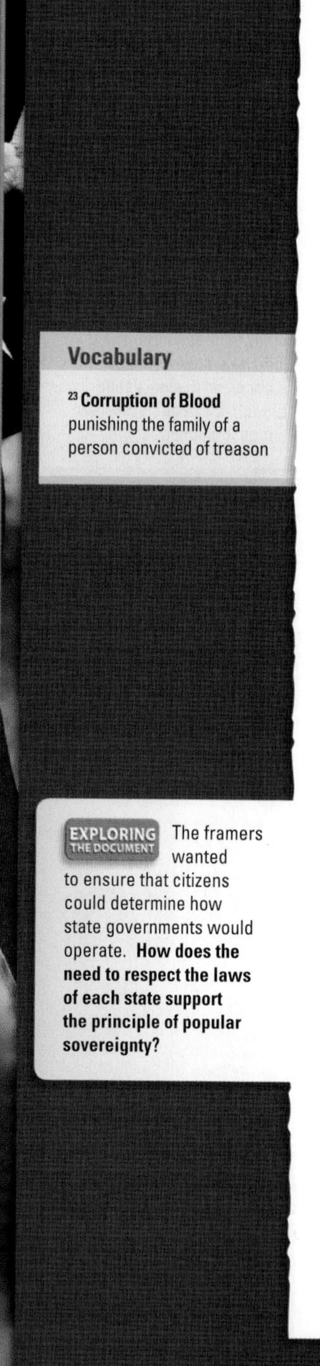

Vocabulary

[23] **Corruption of Blood** punishing the family of a person convicted of treason

EXPLORING THE DOCUMENT The framers wanted to ensure that citizens could determine how state governments would operate. **How does the need to respect the laws of each state support the principle of popular sovereignty?**

3. Trial by Jury The Trial of all Crimes, except in Cases of Impeachment, shall be by Jury; and such Trial shall be held in the State where the said Crimes shall have been committed; but when not committed within any State, the Trial shall be at such Place or Places as the Congress may by Law have directed.

Section 3. Treason

1. Definition Treason against the United States, shall consist only in levying War against them, or in adhering to their Enemies, giving them Aid and Comfort. No Person shall be convicted of Treason unless on the Testimony of two Witnesses to the same overt Act, or on Confession in open Court.

2. Punishment The Congress shall have Power to declare the Punishment of Treason, but no Attainder of Treason shall work **Corruption of Blood**,[23] or Forfeiture except during the Life of the Person attainted.

Article IV Relations among States

Section 1. State Acts and Records

Full Faith and Credit shall be given in each State to the public Acts, Records, and judicial Proceedings of every other State. And the Congress may by general Laws prescribe the Manner in which such Acts, Records and Proceedings shall be proved, and the Effect thereof.

Section 2. Rights of Citizens

1. Citizenship The Citizens of each State shall be entitled to all Privileges and Immunities of Citizens in the several States.

2. Extradition A Person charged in any State with Treason, Felony, or other Crime, who shall flee from Justice, and be found in another State, shall on Demand of the executive Authority of the State from which he fled, be delivered up, to be removed to the State having Jurisdiction of the Crime.

3. Fugitive Slaves ~~No Person held to Service or Labour in one State, under the Laws thereof, escaping into another, shall, in Consequence of any Law or Regulation therein, be discharged from such Service or Labour, but shall be delivered up on Claim of the Party to whom such Service or Labour may be due.~~

162 CHAPTER 5

Federalism 

National
Declare war
Maintain armed forces
Regulate interstate and foreign trade
Admit new states
Establish post offices
Set standard weights and measures
Coin money
Establish foreign policy
Make all laws necessary and proper for carrying out delegated powers
Shared
Maintain law and order
Levy taxes
Borrow money
Charter banks
Establish courts
Provide for public welfare
State
Establish and maintain schools
Establish local governments
Regulate business within the state
Make marriage laws
Provide for public safety
Assume other powers not delegated to the national government or prohibited to the states

ANALYSIS SKILL ANALYZING INFORMATION

Why does the power to declare war belong only to the national government?

Section 3. New States

1. Admission New States may be admitted by the Congress into this Union; but no new State shall be formed or erected within the Jurisdiction of any other State; nor any State be formed by the Junction of two or more States, or Parts of States, without the Consent of the Legislatures of the States concerned as well as of the Congress.

2. Congressional Authority The Congress shall have Power to dispose of and make all needful Rules and Regulations respecting the Territory or other Property belonging to the United States; and nothing in this Constitution shall be so construed as to Prejudice any Claims of the United States, or of any particular State.

Section 4. Guarantees to the States

The United States shall guarantee to every State in this Union a Republican Form of Government, and shall protect each of them against Invasion; and on Application of the Legislature, or of the Executive (when the Legislature cannot be convened), against domestic Violence.

The States

States must honor the laws, records, and court decisions of other states. A person cannot escape a legal obligation by moving from one state to another.

In a republic, voters elect representatives to act in their best interest. **How does Article IV protect the practice of republicanism in the United States?**

Historical Documents

Linking to Today

Admission of New States Although the framers of the Constitution wanted to allow new states to be admitted, many also wanted to preserve the power of the original states. One delegate suggested that the new states' total number of House representatives should never exceed the original states' total number of representatives.

Draw Conclusions If this suggestion had become part of the Constitution, how might it have affected the current U.S. government? *States along the Atlantic coast would have a disproportionate amount of political power.*

Exploring the Document

guarantees that every state will have a representative government

Answers

Analyzing Information *to prevent states from declaring war on one another or on a foreign nation*

Historical Documents

Linking to Today

Amendments to the Constitution Of the thousands of proposals for amendments to the Constitution, only 33 have obtained the required two-thirds vote in Congress. One historic amendment, the Equal Rights Amendment, was first proposed in 1923, but is still not part of the U.S. Constitution.

Activity Researching the ERA Organize the class into small groups to conduct research on the Equal Rights Amendment. Assign each group one of the following research topics: the text of the Equal Rights Amendment (ERA); Alice Paul, the author of the ERA; the history of the ERA; the current political status of the amendment; and arguments for and against making the ERA part of the Constitution. Have each group present its findings to the class.
LS Interpersonal, Verbal/Linguistic

Exploring the Document

See the chart, Amending the U.S. Constitution, at right; possible answer—changes in American society or culture

EXPLORING THE DOCUMENT America's founders may not have realized how long the Constitution would last, but they did set up a system for changing or adding to it. They did not want to make it easy to change the Constitution. **By what methods may the Constitution be amended? Under what sorts of circumstances do you think an amendment might be necessary?**

National Supremacy

One of the biggest problems facing the delegates to the Constitutional Convention was the question of what would happen if a state law and a federal law conflicted. Which law would be followed? Who would decide? The second clause of Article VI answers those questions. When a federal law and a state law disagree, the federal law overrides the state law. The Constitution and other federal laws are the "supreme Law of the Land." This clause is often called the supremacy clause.

Article V Amending the Constitution

The Congress, whenever two thirds of both Houses shall deem it necessary, shall propose Amendments to this Constitution, or, on the Application of the Legislatures of two thirds of the several States, shall call a Convention for proposing Amendments, which, in either Case, shall be valid to all Intents and Purposes, as Part of this Constitution, when ratified by the Legislatures of three fourths of the several States, or by Conventions in three fourths thereof, as the one or the other Mode of Ratification may be proposed by the Congress; Provided that ~~no Amendment which may be made prior to the Year One thousand eight hundred and eight shall in any Manner affect the first and fourth Clauses in the Ninth Section of the first Article; and that no State, without its Consent, shall be deprived of its equal Suffrage in the Senate.~~

Article VI Supremacy of National Government

All Debts contracted and Engagements entered into, before the Adoption of this Constitution, shall be as valid against the United States under this Constitution, as under the Confederation.

This Constitution, and the Laws of the United States which shall be made in Pursuance thereof; and all Treaties made, or which shall be made, under the Authority of the United States, shall be the supreme Law of the Land; and the Judges in every State shall be bound thereby, any Thing in the Constitution or Laws of any State to the Contrary notwithstanding.

The Senators and Representatives before mentioned, and the Members of the several State Legislatures, and all executive and judicial Officers, both of the United States and of the several States, shall be bound by Oath or Affirmation, to support this Constitution; but no religious Test shall ever be required as a Qualification to any Office or public Trust under the United States.

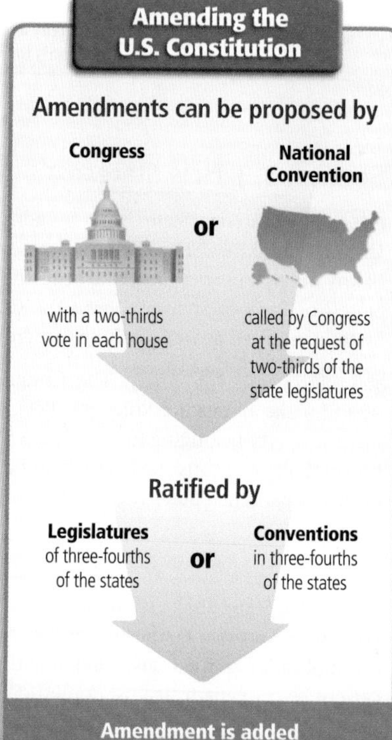

Amending the U.S. Constitution
Amendments can be proposed by
Congress
with a two-thirds vote in each house
or
National Convention
called by Congress at the request of two-thirds of the state legislatures
Ratified by
Legislatures of three-fourths of the states
or
Conventions in three-fourths of the states
Amendment is added to the Constitution.

Article VII Ratification

The Ratification of the Conventions of nine States, shall be sufficient for the Establishment of this Constitution between the States so ratifying the Same.

Done in Convention by the Unanimous Consent of the States present the Seventeenth Day of September in the Year of our Lord one thousand seven hundred and Eighty seven and of the Independence of the United States of America the Twelfth In witness whereof We have hereunto subscribed our Names,

George Washington—
President and deputy from Virginia

Delaware
George Read
Gunning Bedford Jr.
John Dickinson
Richard Bassett
Jacob Broom

Maryland
James McHenry
Daniel of St. Thomas Jenifer
Daniel Carroll

Virginia
John Blair
James Madison Jr.

North Carolina
William Blount
Richard Dobbs Spaight
Hugh Williamson

South Carolina
John Rutledge
Charles Cotesworth Pinckney
Charles Pinckney
Pierce Butler

Georgia
William Few
Abraham Baldwin

New Hampshire
John Langdon
Nicholas Gilman

Massachusetts
Nathaniel Gorham
Rufus King

Connecticut
William Samuel Johnson
Roger Sherman

New York
Alexander Hamilton

New Jersey
William Livingston
David Brearley
William Paterson
Jonathan Dayton

Pennsylvania
Benjamin Franklin
Thomas Mifflin
Robert Morris
George Clymer
Thomas FitzSimons
Jared Ingersoll
James Wilson
Gouverneur Morris

Attest:
William Jackson, Secretary

Ratification
The Articles of Confederation called for all 13 states to approve any revision to the Articles. The Constitution required that 9 out of the 13 states would be needed to ratify the Constitution. The first state to ratify was Delaware, on December 7, 1787. Almost two-and-a-half years later, on May 29, 1790, Rhode Island became the last state to ratify the Constitution.

Historical Documents

Info to Know

Signers of the Constitution At 27 years old, Jonathan Dayton was the youngest person to sign the Constitution. At 81, Benjamin Franklin was the oldest. Franklin's signature was particularly important. As one of the most renowned men in America, he lent respectability to the new document.

History Humor

Franklin's Epitaph Benjamin Franklin, well-known for his many expressions of wit and wisdom, composed his own tongue-in-cheek epitaph at the age of 22: "The body of Benjamin Franklin, Printer (like the cover of an old book, its contents torn out and stripped of its lettering and gilding), lies here, food for worms; but the work shall not be lost, for it will (as he believed) appear once more in a new and more elegant edition, revised and corrected by the Author."

Historical Documents

Main Idea

Recall What are the first 10 amendments to the Constitution called? *Bill of Rights*

Summarize What fundamental liberties are guaranteed by the First Amendment in the Bill of Rights? *freedom of religion, freedom of speech, freedom of the press, freedom of assembly*

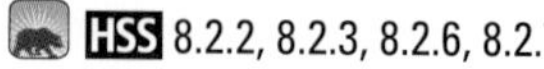

HSS 8.2.2, 8.2.3, 8.2.6, 8.2.7

World Events

Jefferson in Paris At the time of the Constitutional Convention, Thomas Jefferson was in Paris as part of a diplomatic mission to France. Jefferson became increasingly convinced of the evils of monarchy as he saw the violations of civil liberties that the French people had to tolerate. For example, the king could issue a *lettre du cachet*, which could order someone exiled or imprisoned without recourse. In addition, the aristocracy could destroy land without having to pay the owner for the damage. In his letters to delegates to the Constitutional Convention, Jefferson strongly urged the inclusion of a bill of rights.

Exploring the Document

possible answer—It is a right on which the United States was founded.

Constitutional Amendments

Note: The first 10 amendments to the Constitution were ratified on December 15, 1791, and form what is known as the Bill of Rights.

Amendments 1–10. The Bill of Rights

Amendment I

Congress shall make no law respecting an establishment of religion, or prohibiting the free exercise thereof; or abridging the freedom of speech, or of the press; or the right of the people peaceably to assemble, and to petition the Government for a redress of grievances.

Amendment II

A well regulated Militia, being necessary to the security of a free State, the right of the people to keep and bear Arms, shall not be infringed.

Amendment III

No Soldier shall, in time of peace be **quartered**[24] in any house, without the consent of the Owner, nor in time of war, but in a manner to be prescribed by law.

Amendment IV

The right of the people to be secure in their persons, houses, papers, and effects, against unreasonable searches and seizures, shall not be violated, and no **Warrants**[25] shall issue, but upon probable cause, supported by Oath or affirmation, and particularly describing the place to be searched, and the persons or things to be seized.

Amendment V

No person shall be held to answer for a capital, or otherwise **infamous**[26] crime, unless on a presentment or **indictment**[27] of a Grand Jury, except in

Bill of Rights

One of the conditions set by several states for ratifying the Constitution was the inclusion of a bill of rights. Many people feared that a stronger central government might take away basic rights of the people that had been guaranteed in state constitutions.

EXPLORING THE DOCUMENT The First Amendment forbids Congress from making any "law respecting an establishment of religion" or restraining the freedom to practice religion as one chooses. **Why is freedom of religion an important right?**

Rights of the Accused

The Fifth, Sixth, and Seventh Amendments describe the procedures that courts must follow when trying people accused of crimes.

Vocabulary

[24] **quartered** housed

[25] **Warrants** written orders authorizing a person to make an arrest, a seizure, or a search

[26] **infamous** disgraceful

[27] **indictment** the act of charging with a crime

Fundamental Liberties

Freedom of Religion

Freedom of Speech

cases arising in the land or naval forces, or in the Militia, when in actual service in time of War or public danger; nor shall any person be subject for the same offence to be twice put in jeopardy of life or limb; nor shall be compelled in any criminal case to be a witness against himself, nor be deprived of life, liberty, or property, without due process of law; nor shall private property be taken for public use, without just compensation.

Amendment VI

In all criminal prosecutions, the accused shall enjoy the right to a speedy and public trial, by an impartial jury of the State and district wherein the crime shall have been committed, which district shall have been previously **ascertained**[28] by law, and to be informed of the nature and cause of the accusation; to be confronted with the witnesses against him; to have compulsory process for obtaining witnesses in his favor, and to have the Assistance of Counsel for his defence.

Amendment VII

In suits at common law, where the value in controversy shall exceed twenty dollars, the right of trial by jury shall be preserved, and no fact tried by a jury, shall be otherwise reexamined in any Court of the United States, than according to the rules of the common law.

Amendment VIII

Excessive bail shall not be required, nor excessive fines imposed, nor cruel and unusual punishments inflicted.

Amendment IX

The enumeration in the Constitution, of certain rights, shall not be construed to deny or disparage others retained by the people.

Amendment X

The powers not delegated to the United States by the Constitution, nor prohibited by it to the States, are reserved to the States respectively, or to the people.

Trials

The Sixth Amendment makes several guarantees, including a prompt trial and a trial by a jury chosen from the state and district in which the crime was committed.

Vocabulary

[28] **ascertained** found out

EXPLORING THE DOCUMENT The Ninth and Tenth Amendments were added because not every right of the people or of the states could be listed in the Constitution. **How do the Ninth and Tenth Amendments limit the power of the federal government?**

Freedom of the Press

Freedom of Assembly

Freedom to Petition the Government

ANALYSIS SKILL ANALYZING INFORMATION

Which amendment guarantees these fundamental freedoms?

Historical Documents

Linking to Today

Speedy and Public Trial

Activity Explain to students that some trials attract heavy media attention when celebrities are involved or when the crime is particularly sensational. Ask students to bring to class newspaper and magazine articles about highly publicized criminal cases. Have students use the articles to discuss the concepts of the right to a speedy and public trial by an impartial jury. Ask students to discuss how long certain cases may have been in the news. Then have students describe situations in which impartiality might be difficult to guarantee in highly publicized criminal cases.

Exploring the Document

They extend rights to the people and to the states.

Answers

Analyzing Information

First Amendment

Historical Documents

Main Idea

Explain What does the Eleventh Amendment confirm? *No federal court may try a case in which a state is being sued by a citizen of another state or of a foreign country.*

Summarize How did the Twelfth Amendment change the electoral college? *It changed the procedure for choosing a president. The presidential electors would vote for president and vice president on separate ballots.*

Identify Cause and Effect Which three amendments do you think were a consequence of the Civil War? *Thirteenth, Fourteenth, and Fifteenth Amendments*

HSS 8.2.2, 8.2.6

Reading Time Lines

Amendments to the U.S. Constitution

Activity Have each student select one amendment on the time line that is of particular interest to him or her. Ask students to conduct research on the amendment's passage and place the amendment in a matrix of events, people, time, and place. Have students use the information to create a collage of words and images that evokes the era in which the amendment was added to the Constitution. **LS Verbal/Linguistic, Visual/Spatial**

HSS 8.2.6; **HSS Analysis Skills:** HI 1

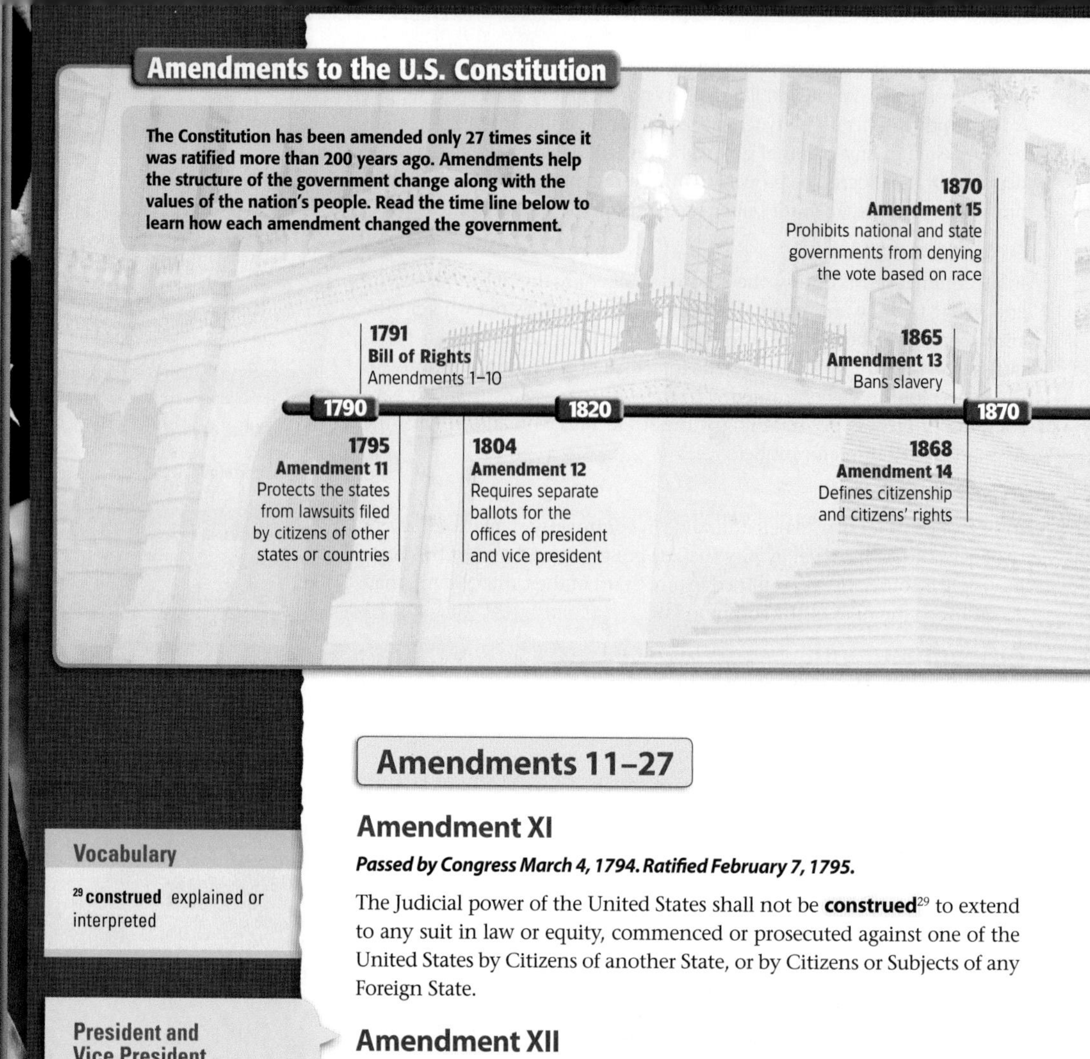

Amendments to the U.S. Constitution
The Constitution has been amended only 27 times since it was ratified more than 200 years ago. Amendments help the structure of the government change along with the values of the nation's people. Read the time line below to learn how each amendment changed the government.
1790
1820
1870
1791 Bill of Rights Amendments 1–10
1795 Amendment 11 Protects the states from lawsuits filed by citizens of other states or countries
1804 Amendment 12 Requires separate ballots for the offices of president and vice president
1865 Amendment 13 Bans slavery
1868 Amendment 14 Defines citizenship and citizens' rights
1870 Amendment 15 Prohibits national and state governments from denying the vote based on race

Amendments 11–27

Amendment XI

Passed by Congress March 4, 1794. Ratified February 7, 1795.

The Judicial power of the United States shall not be **construed**[29] to extend to any suit in law or equity, commenced or prosecuted against one of the United States by Citizens of another State, or by Citizens or Subjects of any Foreign State.

Vocabulary

[29] **construed** explained or interpreted

Amendment XII

Passed by Congress December 9, 1803. Ratified June 15, 1804.

The Electors shall meet in their respective states and vote by ballot for President and Vice-President, one of whom, at least, shall not be an inhabitant of the same state with themselves; they shall name in their ballots the person voted for as President, and in distinct ballots the person voted for as Vice-President, and they shall make distinct lists of all persons voted for as President, and of all persons voted for as Vice-President, and of the number of votes for each, which lists they shall sign and certify, and transmit sealed to the seat of the government of the United States, directed to the President of the Senate;—the President of the Senate shall, in the presence of the

President and Vice President

The Twelfth Amendment changed the election procedure for president and vice president.

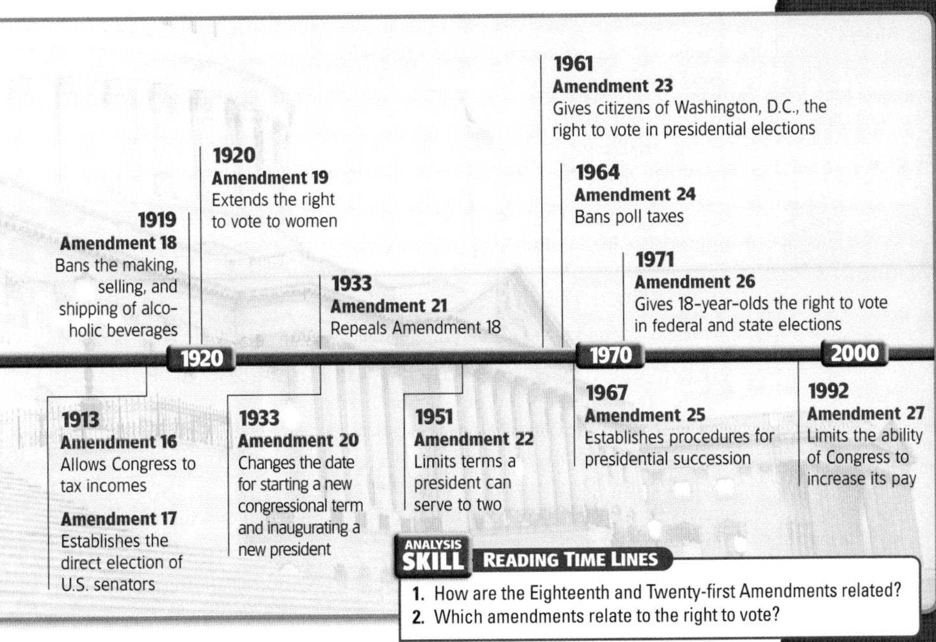
1913
Amendment 16
Allows Congress to tax incomes
Amendment 17
Establishes the direct election of U.S. senators
1919
Amendment 18
Bans the making, selling, and shipping of alcoholic beverages
1920
Amendment 19
Extends the right to vote to women
1920
1933
Amendment 20
Changes the date for starting a new congressional term and inaugurating a new president
1933
Amendment 21
Repeals Amendment 18
1951
Amendment 22
Limits terms a president can serve to two
1961
Amendment 23
Gives citizens of Washington, D.C., the right to vote in presidential elections
1964
Amendment 24
Bans poll taxes
1967
Amendment 25
Establishes procedures for presidential succession
1970
1971
Amendment 26
Gives 18-year-olds the right to vote in federal and state elections
1992
Amendment 27
Limits the ability of Congress to increase its pay
2000

ANALYSIS SKILL READING TIME LINES

1. How are the Eighteenth and Twenty-first Amendments related?
2. Which amendments relate to the right to vote?

Senate and House of Representatives, open all the certificates and the votes shall then be counted;—The person having the greatest number of votes for President, shall be the President, if such number be a majority of the whole number of Electors appointed; and if no person have such majority, then from the persons having the highest numbers not exceeding three on the list of those voted for as President, the House of Representatives shall choose immediately, by ballot, the President. But in choosing the President, the votes shall be taken by states, the representation from each state having one vote; a quorum for this purpose shall consist of a member or members from two-thirds of the states, and a majority of all the states shall be necessary to a choice. ~~And if the House of Representatives shall not choose a President whenever the right of choice shall devolve upon them, before the fourth day of March next following, then the Vice-President shall act as President, as in case of the death or other constitutional disability of the President.~~—The person having the greatest number of votes as Vice-President, shall be the Vice-President, if such number be a majority of the whole number of Electors appointed, and if no person have a majority, then from the two highest numbers on the list, the Senate shall choose the Vice-President; a quorum for the purpose shall consist of two-thirds of the whole number of Senators, and a majority of the whole number shall be necessary to a choice. But no person constitutionally ineligible to the office of President shall be eligible to that of Vice-President of the United States.

Historical Documents

Info to Know

Postwar Amendments Three amendments—the Thirteenth, Fourteenth, and Fifteenth—were meant initially to respond to changes demanded by the northern victory in the Civil War. When the Fourteenth Amendment was passed, many southerners interpreted it as punishing the South by extending civil rights to African Americans. Scholars have argued that the Fourteenth Amendment remains the most important addition to the Constitution since the Bill of Rights because of its inclusion of due process and equal protection clauses.

Evaluate Why do you think that scholars consider the Fourteenth Amendment so important? *Students might suggest that it redefined citizenship and guaranteed African Americans civil rights. It also made the Bill of Rights apply to state law.*

Answers

Reading Time Lines 1. *Eighteenth Amendment established the ban on alcohol (Prohibition); the Twenty-first Amendment repealed Prohibition.*
2. *Fifteenth, Nineteenth, Twenty-third, Twenty-fourth and Twenty-sixth Amendments*

Historical Documents

Linking to Today

Civil Liberties Throughout the 1900s, the U.S. Supreme Court extended the coverage of the civil liberties provided in the Bill of Rights. In earlier times, justices had ruled that the Bill of Rights did not override state laws. Although the Fourteenth Amendment stated that the states could not deprive citizens of their constitutional rights, few justices changed their opinions. In the mid-1900s, Justice Hugo Black began to reinterpret the Fourteenth Amendment. He believed that the guarantees in the Bill of Rights were absolute. The Civil Rights Act, passed in 1964, was the most far-reaching civil rights bill in the nation's history. This act forbids discrimination in public accommodations.

Activity Collaborative Learning Have students bring to class newspaper articles related to the exercise of civil liberties. Using these articles as discussion prompts, have students describe what they think are proper and improper limitations of civil liberties.

Abolishing Slavery

Although some slaves had been freed during the Civil War, slavery was not abolished until the Thirteenth Amendment took effect.

Protecting the Rights of Citizens

In 1833 the Supreme Court ruled that the Bill of Rights limited the federal government but not the state governments. This ruling was interpreted to mean that states were able to keep African Americans from becoming state citizens and keep the Bill of Rights from protecting them. The Fourteenth Amendment defines citizenship and prevents states from interfering in the rights of citizens of the United States.

Vocabulary

[30] **involuntary servitude** being forced to work against one's will

Amendment XIII

Passed by Congress January 31, 1865. Ratified December 6, 1865.

1. Slavery Banned Neither slavery nor **involuntary servitude,**[30] except as a punishment for crime whereof the party shall have been duly convicted, shall exist within the United States, or any place subject to their jurisdiction.

2. Enforcement Congress shall have power to enforce this article by appropriate legislation.

Amendment XIV

Passed by Congress June 13, 1866. Ratified July 9, 1868.

1. Citizenship Defined All persons born or naturalized in the United States, and subject to the jurisdiction thereof, are citizens of the United States and of the State wherein they reside. No State shall make or enforce any law which shall abridge the privileges or immunities of citizens of the United States; nor shall any State deprive any person of life, liberty, or property, without due process of law; nor deny to any person within its jurisdiction the equal protection of the laws.

2. Voting Rights Representatives shall be apportioned among the several States according to their respective numbers, counting the whole number of persons in each State, ~~excluding Indians not taxed~~. But when the right to vote at any election for the choice of electors for President and Vice-President of the United States, Representatives in Congress, the Executive and Judicial officers of a State, or the members of the Legislature thereof, is denied to any of the ~~male~~ inhabitants of such State, ~~being twenty-one years of age~~, and citizens of the United States, or in any way abridged, except for participation in rebellion, or other crime, the basis of representation therein shall be reduced in the proportion which the number of such ~~male~~ citizens shall bear to the whole number of ~~male~~ citizens ~~twenty-one years of age~~ in such State.

3. Rebels Banned from Government No person shall be a Senator or Representative in Congress, or elector of President and Vice-President, or hold any office, civil or military, under the United States, or under any State, who, having previously taken an oath, as a member of Congress, or as an officer of the United States, or as a member of any State legislature, or as an executive or judicial officer of any State, to support the Constitution of the United States, shall have engaged in insurrection or rebellion against the same, or given aid or comfort to the enemies thereof. But Congress may by a vote of two-thirds of each House, remove such disability.

4. Payment of Debts The validity of the public debt of the United States, authorized by law, including debts incurred for payment of pensions and

170 CHAPTER 5

The Reconstruction Amendments

The Thirteenth, Fourteenth, and Fifteenth Amendments are often called the Reconstruction Amendments. This is because they arose during Reconstruction, the period of American history following the Civil War. The country was reconstructing itself after that terrible conflict. A key aspect of Reconstruction was extending the rights of citizenship to former slaves.

The Thirteenth Amendment banned slavery. The Fourteenth Amendment required states to respect the freedoms listed in the Bill of Rights, thus preventing states from denying rights to African Americans. The Fifteenth Amendment gave African American men the right to vote.

African Americans participate in an election.

ANALYSIS SKILL ANALYZING INFORMATION

Why was the Thirteenth Amendment needed?

bounties for services in suppressing insurrection or rebellion, shall not be questioned. But neither the United States nor any State shall assume or pay any debt or obligation incurred in aid of insurrection or rebellion against the United States, ~~or any claim for the loss or emancipation of any slave~~; but all such debts, obligations and claims shall be held illegal and void.

5. Enforcement The Congress shall have the power to enforce, by appropriate legislation, the provisions of this article.

Amendment XV

Passed by Congress February 26, 1869. Ratified February 3, 1870.

1. Voting Rights The right of citizens of the United States to vote shall not be denied or abridged by the United States or by any State on account of race, color, or previous condition of servitude.

2. Enforcement The Congress shall have the power to enforce this article by appropriate legislation.

Historical Documents

Main Idea

Analyze Why is the guarantee of the right to vote important in a democracy? *To have equal representation under the law, all people need to have the right to vote.*

Evaluate What might the significance of the passage of the Fifteenth Amendment have been to future suffrage and civil rights movements? *It established the right of citizens to vote—regardless "of race, color, or previous condition of servitude."*

Activity Amendments Storyboard Have students create a three-panel storyboard that illustrates the significance of the Thirteenth, Fourteenth, and Fifteenth Amendments.

HSS 8.2.2, 8.2.3, 8.2.6, 8.2.7

Info to Know

African American Vote The passage of the Fourteenth and Fifteenth Amendments dramatically increased African Americans' political participation. Strikes broke out among African American workers throughout the South. The workers staged sit-ins on segregated carriages in Richmond, Virginia. When police tried to stop the protests, angry crowds formed, demanding, "Let's have our rights." Almost every institution of African American life worked to mobilize black voters and to educate new voters. So many African American laborers attended the Republican state convention in Virginia that Richmond's tobacco factories had to close.

Answers

Analyzing Information *to abolish slavery*

Historical Documents

Main Idea

Explain What did the Eighteenth Amendment ban? *the making, sale, and transport of alcohol*

Make Inferences Why do you think the Eighteenth Amendment was repealed? *Students might suggest its impracticality and enormous unpopularity.*

Elaborate What factors do you think contributed to the passage of the Nineteenth Amendment? *Students might suggest the strong leadership and determination of women as well as organized, grassroots suffrage campaigns throughout the country.*

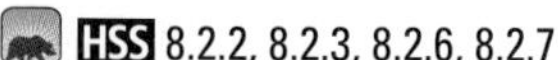
HSS 8.2.2, 8.2.3, 8.2.6, 8.2.7

Info to Know

Effects of Prohibition The Eighteenth Amendment may have banned the manufacture, sale and transportation of liquor, but it also created an underground culture of bootlegging, smuggling, and organized crime. Speakeasies—illegal bars that sold alcoholic beverages—sprang up in large cities. These bars devised elaborate gadgets to hide the illegal evidence in case of police raids. New York City alone had over 30,000 speakeasies, twice the city's number of bars before Prohibition.

Exploring the Document

the principle of direct representation

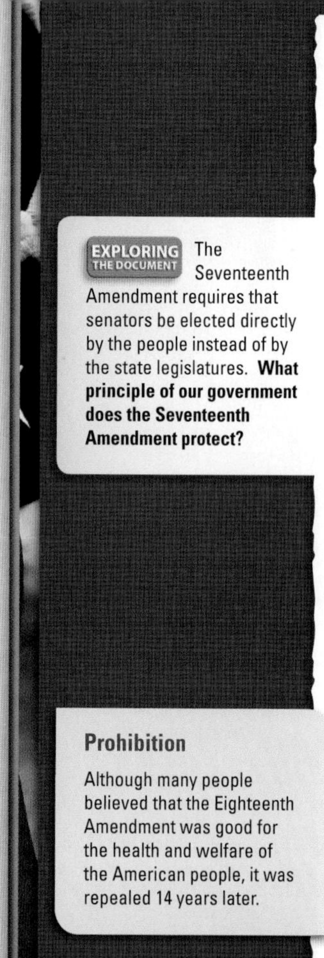

EXPLORING THE DOCUMENT The Seventeenth Amendment requires that senators be elected directly by the people instead of by the state legislatures. **What principle of our government does the Seventeenth Amendment protect?**

Prohibition

Although many people believed that the Eighteenth Amendment was good for the health and welfare of the American people, it was repealed 14 years later.

Amendment XVI

Passed by Congress July 2, 1909. Ratified February 3, 1913.

The Congress shall have power to lay and collect taxes on incomes, from whatever source derived, without apportionment among the several States, and without regard to any census or enumeration.

Amendment XVII

Passed by Congress May 13, 1912. Ratified April 8, 1913.

1. Senators Elected by Citizens The Senate of the United States shall be composed of two Senators from each State, elected by the people thereof, for six years; and each Senator shall have one vote. The electors in each State shall have the qualifications requisite for electors of the most numerous branch of the State legislatures.

2. Vacancies When vacancies happen in the representation of any State in the Senate, the executive authority of such State shall issue writs of election to fill such vacancies: *Provided*, That the legislature of any State may empower the executive thereof to make temporary appointments until the people fill the vacancies by election as the legislature may direct.

3. Future Elections ~~This amendment shall not be so construed as to affect the election or term of any Senator chosen before it becomes valid as part of the Constitution.~~

Amendment XVIII

Passed by Congress December 18, 1917. Ratified January 16, 1919. Repealed by Amendment XXI.

1. Liquor Banned ~~After one year from the ratification of this article the manufacture, sale, or transportation of intoxicating liquors within, the importation thereof into, or the exportation thereof from the United States and all territory subject to the jurisdiction thereof for beverage purposes is hereby prohibited.~~

2. Enforcement ~~The Congress and the several States shall have concurrent power to enforce this article by appropriate legislation.~~

3. Ratification ~~This article shall be inoperative unless it shall have been ratified as an amendment to the Constitution by the legislatures of the several States, as provided in the Constitution, within seven years from the date of the submission hereof to the States by the Congress.~~

172 CHAPTER 5

Women Fight for the Vote

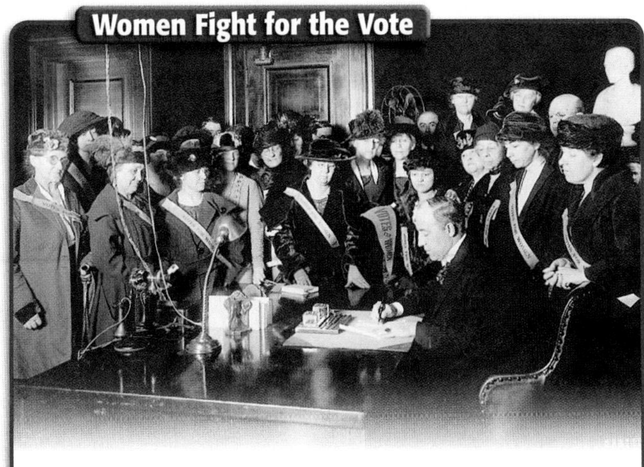

To become part of the Constitution, a proposed amendment must be ratified by three-fourths of the states. Here, suffragists witness Kentucky governor Edwin P. Morrow signing the Nineteenth Amendment in January 1920. By June of that year, enough states had ratified the amendment to make it part of the Constitution. American women, after generations of struggle, had finally won the right to vote.

ANALYSIS SKILL ANALYZING INFORMATION

What right did the Nineteenth Amendment grant?

Amendment XIX

Passed by Congress June 4, 1919. Ratified August 18, 1920.

1. Voting Rights The right of citizens of the United States to vote shall not be denied or abridged by the United States or by any State on account of sex.

2. Enforcement Congress shall have power to enforce this article by appropriate legislation.

Amendment XX

Passed by Congress March 2, 1932. Ratified January 23, 1933.

1. Presidential Terms The terms of the President and the Vice President shall end at noon on the 20th day of January, and the terms of Senators and Representatives at noon on the 3d day of January, of the years in which such terms would have ended if this article had not been ratified; and the terms of their successors shall then begin.

Women's Suffrage

Abigail Adams and others were disappointed that the Declaration of Independence and the Constitution did not specifically include women. It took many years and much campaigning before suffrage for women was finally achieved.

Historical Documents

Biography

Elizabeth Cady Stanton The efforts of Elizabeth Cady Stanton, a tireless crusader for women's rights, contributed to the passage of the Nineteenth Amendment in 1920. At her urging, in 1878 Senator Aaron A. Sargent of California introduced a women's suffrage amendment to the Constitution. This amendment was introduced and defeated repeatedly throughout Stanton's lifetime. She died in 1902, eighteen years before the passage of the amendment for which she had worked so hard.

Primary Source

Abigail Adams, "Remember the Ladies" In 1776, Abigail Adams wrote a letter to John Adams, in which she describes women's determination to be heard and represented. "In the new code of laws which I suppose it will be necessary for you to make I desire you would remember the ladies, and be more generous and favorable to them than your ancestors. Do not put such unlimited power into the hands of the husbands. Remember all men would be tyrants if they could. If particular care and attention is not paid to the ladies we are determined to foment a rebellion, and will not hold ourselves bound by any laws in which we have no voice, or representation."

Answers

Analyzing Information *granted women the right to vote*

Historical Documents

Biography

George W. Norris (1861–1944) During his long congressional career, George W. Norris not only created and worked to pass the Twentieth Amendment but also worked for the introduction of presidential primaries and for the direct election of senators. Though a Republican, Norris rarely voted along party lines. In defense of his independence, he claimed he "would rather be right than regular."

Connect to the Arts and Humanities

Inaugural Poems At the 1961 inauguration of John F. Kennedy, Robert Frost recited his poem "The Gift Outright." To honor Kennedy, Bill Clinton revived the tradition at his 1993 inauguration, during which Maya Angelou read her poem "On the Pulse of Morning."

Activity Interpreting and Reciting Poetry Have students use the library or Internet sources to locate poems read at presidential inaugurations. Ask for volunteers to read the poems aloud. Discuss what these poems convey or evoke about the significance of the moment and the promise of a new presidency.

Taking Office

In the original Constitution, a newly elected president and Congress did not take office until March 4, which was four months after the November election. The officials who were leaving office were called lame ducks because they had little influence during those four months. The Twentieth Amendment changed the date that the new president and Congress take office. Members of Congress now take office during the first week of January, and the president takes office on January 20.

2. Meeting of Congress The Congress shall assemble at least once in every year, and such meeting shall begin at noon on the 3d day of January, unless they shall by law appoint a different day.

3. Succession of Vice President If, at the time fixed for the beginning of the term of the President, the President elect shall have died, the Vice President elect shall become President. If a President shall not have been chosen before the time fixed for the beginning of his term, or if the President elect shall have failed to qualify, then the Vice President elect shall act as President until a President shall have qualified; and the Congress may by law provide for the case wherein neither a President elect nor a Vice President shall have qualified, declaring who shall then act as President, or the manner in which one who is to act shall be selected, and such person shall act accordingly until a President or Vice President shall have qualified.

4. Succession by Vote of Congress The Congress may by law provide for the case of the death of any of the persons from whom the House of Representatives may choose a President whenever the right of choice shall have devolved upon them, and for the case of the death of any of the persons from whom the Senate may choose a Vice President whenever the right of choice shall have devolved upon them.

5. Ratification ~~Sections 1 and 2 shall take effect on the 15th day of October following the ratification of this article.~~

6. Ratification ~~This article shall be inoperative unless it shall have been ratified as an amendment to the Constitution by the legislatures of three-fourths of the several States within seven years from the date of its submission.~~

Amendment XXI

Passed by Congress February 20, 1933. Ratified December 5, 1933.

1. 18th Amendment Repealed The eighteenth article of amendment to the Constitution of the United States is hereby repealed.

2. Liquor Allowed by Law The transportation or importation into any State, Territory, or Possession of the United States for delivery or use therein of intoxicating liquors, in violation of the laws thereof, is hereby prohibited.

3. Ratification ~~This article shall be inoperative unless it shall have been ratified as an amendment to the Constitution by conventions in the several States, as provided in the Constitution, within seven years from the date of the submission hereof to the States by the Congress.~~

Amendment XXII

Passed by Congress March 21, 1947. Ratified February 27, 1951.

1. Term Limits No person shall be elected to the office of the President more than twice, and no person who has held the office of President, or acted as President, for more than two years of a term to which some other person was elected President shall be elected to the office of President more than once. ~~But this Article shall not apply to any person holding the office of President when this Article was proposed by Congress, and shall not prevent any person who may be holding the office of President, or acting as President, during the term within which this Article becomes operative from holding the office of President or acting as President during the remainder of such term.~~

2. Ratification ~~This article shall be inoperative unless it shall have been ratified as an amendment to the Constitution by the legislatures of three-fourths of the several States within seven years from the date of its submission to the States by the Congress.~~

EXPLORING THE DOCUMENT From the time of President George Washington's administration, it was a custom for presidents to serve no more than two terms in office. Franklin D. Roosevelt, however, was elected to four terms. The Twenty-second Amendment restricted presidents to no more than two terms in office. **Why do you think citizens chose to limit the power of the president in this way?**

After Franklin D. Roosevelt was elected to four consecutive terms, limits were placed on the number of terms a president could serve.

Amendment XXIII

Passed by Congress June 16, 1960. Ratified March 29, 1961.

1. District of Columbia Represented The District constituting the seat of Government of the United States shall appoint in such manner as Congress may direct:

A number of electors of President and Vice President equal to the whole number of Senators and Representatives in Congress to which the District would be entitled if it were a State, but in no event more than the least populous State; they shall be in addition to those appointed by the States, but they shall be considered, for the purposes of the election of President and Vice President, to be electors appointed by a State; and they shall meet in the District and perform such duties as provided by the twelfth article of amendment.

2. Enforcement The Congress shall have power to enforce this article by appropriate legislation.

Voting Rights

Until the ratification of the Twenty-third Amendment, the people of Washington, D.C., could not vote in presidential elections.

Historical Documents

Main Idea

Recall What did the Twenty-first Amendment repeal? *prohibition*

Describe What right did the Twenty-third Amendment grant to the people of Washington, D.C.? *right to vote*

Analyze Why were citizens of Washington, D.C., not allowed to vote for president and vice president before the Twenty-third Amendment was adopted? *The District of Columbia is not a state, and the Constitution provided that only states should choose presidential electors.*

HSS 8.2.2, 8.2.3, 8.2.6, 8.2.7

Exploring the Document

possible answer—Citizens did not want any one president to gain too much power.

CITIZENSHIP AND THE CONSTITUTION 175

Historical Documents

Info to Know

Poll Taxes Congress started trying to eliminate poll taxes in 1939. These taxes had been instituted in some southern states after Reconstruction and were still in effect in five of those states in 1964. The poll tax was often explicitly adopted to discriminate against African American voters. For example, when a poll tax was passed in Virginia in 1902, one representative said, "Discrimination! Why, that is precisely what we propose."

Twenty-sixth Amendment As of 1970, four states had established a minimum voting age lower than 21. That year, Congress passed a law allowing citizens 18 and older to vote in federal elections. The U.S. Supreme Court found the law constitutional but noted that Congress did not have the power to set the voting age in state elections. To remedy any conflicts between federal and state voting standards, Congress passed the Twenty-sixth Amendment, which established 18 as the minimum voting age in all elections in the United States. The amendment was quickly ratified.

Poll Tax Amendment

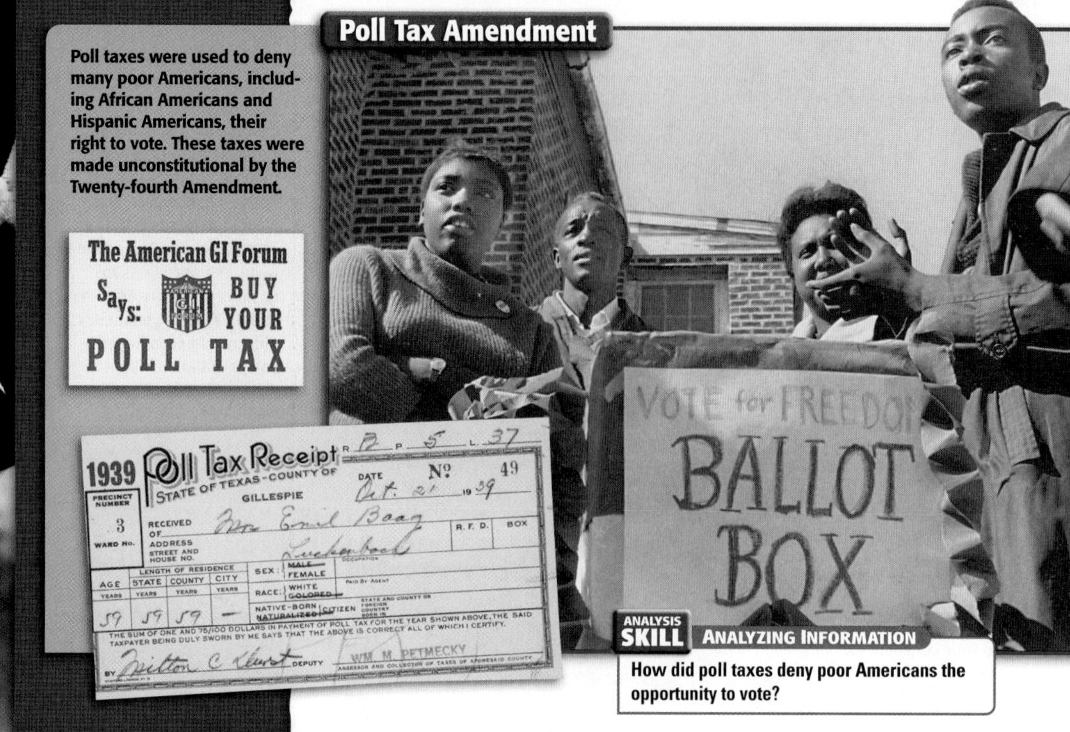

Poll taxes were used to deny many poor Americans, including African Americans and Hispanic Americans, their right to vote. These taxes were made unconstitutional by the Twenty-fourth Amendment.

ANALYSIS SKILL ANALYZING INFORMATION

How did poll taxes deny poor Americans the opportunity to vote?

Amendment XXIV

Passed by Congress August 27, 1962. Ratified January 23, 1964.

1. Voting Rights The right of citizens of the United States to vote in any primary or other election for President or Vice President, for electors for President or Vice President, or for Senator or Representative in Congress, shall not be denied or abridged by the United States or any State by reason of failure to pay poll tax or other tax.

2. Enforcement The Congress shall have power to enforce this article by appropriate legislation.

Presidential Disability

The illness of President Eisenhower in the 1950s and the assassination of President Kennedy in 1963 were the events behind the Twenty-fifth Amendment. The Constitution did not provide a clear-cut method for a vice president to take over for a disabled president or upon the death of a president. This amendment provides for filling the office of the vice president if a vacancy occurs, and it provides a way for the vice president—or someone else in the line of succession—to take over if the president is unable to perform the duties of that office.

Amendment XXV

Passed by Congress July 6, 1965. Ratified February 10, 1967.

1. Sucession of Vice President In case of the removal of the President from office or of his death or resignation, the Vice President shall become President.

2. Vacancy of Vice President Whenever there is a vacancy in the office of the Vice President, the President shall nominate a Vice President who shall take office upon confirmation by a majority vote of both Houses of Congress.

Answers

Analyzing Information *by requiring people to pay a tax to vote, which many poor people could not afford*

3. Written Declaratrion Whenever the President transmits to the President pro tempore of the Senate and the Speaker of the House of Representatives his written declaration that he is unable to discharge the powers and duties of his office, and until he transmits to them a written declaration to the contrary, such powers and duties shall be discharged by the Vice President as Acting President.

4. Removing the President Whenever the Vice President and a majority of either the principal officers of the executive departments or of such other body as Congress may by law provide, transmit to the President pro tempore of the Senate and the Speaker of the House of Representatives their written declaration that the President is unable to discharge the powers and duties of his office, the Vice President shall immediately assume the powers and duties of the office as Acting President.

Thereafter, when the President transmits to the President pro tempore of the Senate and the Speaker of the House of Representatives his written declaration that no inability exists, he shall resume the powers and duties of his office unless the Vice President and a majority of either the principal officers of the executive department or of such other body as Congress may by law provide, transmit within four days to the President pro tempore of the Senate and the Speaker of the House of Representatives their written declaration that the President is unable to discharge the powers and duties of his office. Thereupon Congress shall decide the issue, assembling within forty-eight hours for that purpose if not in session. If the Congress, within twenty-one days after receipt of the latter written declaration, or, if Congress is not in session, within twenty-one days after Congress is required to assemble, determines by two-thirds vote of both Houses that the President is unable to discharge the powers and duties of his office, the Vice President shall continue to discharge the same as Acting President; otherwise, the President shall resume the powers and duties of his office.

Amendment XXVI

Passed by Congress March 23, 1971. Ratified July 1, 1971.

1. Voting Rights The right of citizens of the United States, who are eighteen years of age or older, to vote shall not be denied or abridged by the United States or by any State on account of age.

2. Enforcement The Congress shall have power to enforce this article by appropriate legislation.

Expanded Suffrage

The Voting Rights Act of 1970 tried to set the voting age at 18. However, the Supreme Court ruled that the act set the voting age for national elections only, not for state or local elections. The Twenty-sixth Amendment gave 18-year-old citizens the right to vote in all elections.

Amendment XXVII

Originally proposed September 25, 1789. Ratified May 7, 1992.

No law, varying the compensation for the services of the Senators and Representatives, shall take effect, until an election of representatives shall have intervened.

Historical Documents

Info to Know

Congressional Pay Raises Ironically, one of the latest constitutional amendments to pass was proposed by one of the Constitution's framers, James Madison. Although amendments that have been proposed in recent decades have included a deadline for passage, Madison never included one for what became the Twenty-seventh Amendment. The amendment states that congressional pay raises cannot take effect until a new Congress meets. Madison had suggested the amendment in 1789, along with the other amendments that eventually formed the Bill of Rights. However, just six states ratified the amendment—out of the 11 needed to pass it at the time—and it was largely forgotten. Then in the 1980s, an aide to a Texas legislator began a crusade to get the amendment passed. After more than 200 years, Michigan became the required 38th state to approve the Twenty-seventh Amendment.

Preteach

Bellringer

If YOU were there . . . Use the **Daily Bellringer Transparency** to help students answer the question.

Daily Bellringer Transparency, Section 2

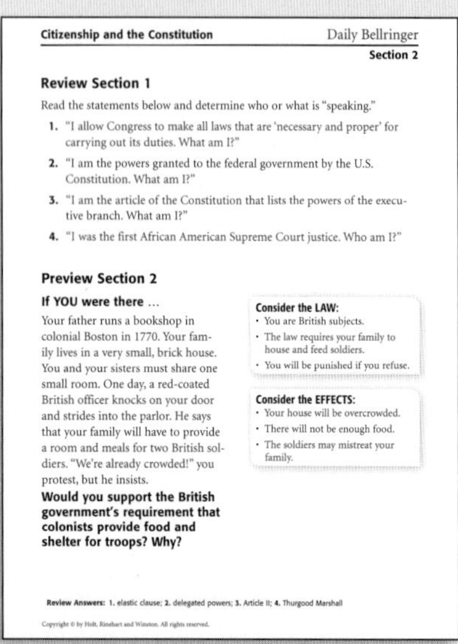

Citizenship and the Constitution — Daily Bellringer **Section 2**

Review Section 1

Read the statements below and determine who or what is "speaking."

1. "I allow Congress to make all laws that are 'necessary and proper' for carrying out its duties. What am I?"
2. "I am the powers granted to the federal government by the U.S. Constitution. What am I?"
3. "I am the article of the Constitution that lists the powers of the executive branch. What am I?"
4. "I was the first African American Supreme Court justice. Who am I?"

Preview Section 2

If YOU were there ...

Your father runs a bookshop in colonial Boston in 1770. Your family lives in a very small, brick house. You and your sisters must share one small room. One day, a red-coated British officer knocks on your door and strides into the parlor. He says that your family will have to provide a room and meals for two British soldiers. "We're already crowded!" you protest, but he insists.

Would you support the British government's requirement that colonists provide food and shelter for troops? Why?

Consider the LAW:
- You are British subjects.
- The law requires your family to house and feed soldiers.
- You will be punished if you refuse.

Consider the EFFECTS:
- Your house will be overcrowded.
- There will not be enough food.
- The soldiers may mistreat your family.

Review Answers: 1. elastic clause; 2. delegated powers; 3. Article II; 4. Thurgood Marshall

Building Vocabulary

Preteach or review the following terms:

ascertained found out (p. 181)

assembly holding meetings or demonstrating (p. 178)

infringed taken away (p. 180)

prescribed authorized (p. 180)

quartered housed (p. 180)

warrants written orders authorizing a person to make an arrest, a seizure, or a search (p. 180)

CRF: Vocabulary Builder Activity, Section 2

SECTION 2

The Bill of Rights

What You Will Learn...

Main Ideas

1. The First Amendment guarantees basic freedoms to individuals.
2. Other amendments focus on protecting citizens from certain abuses.
3. The rights of the accused are an important part of the Bill of Rights.
4. The rights of states and citizens are protected by the Bill of Rights.

The Big Idea

The Bill of Rights was added to the Constitution to define clearly the rights and freedoms of citizens.

Key Terms and People

James Madison, *p. 178*
majority rule, *p. 178*
petition, *p. 179*
search warrant, *p. 180*
due process, *p. 180*
indict, *p. 180*
double jeopardy, *p. 180*
eminent domain, *p. 180*

HSS 8.2.6 Enumerate the powers of government set forth in the Constitution and the fundamental liberties ensured by the Bill of Rights.

8.3.7 Understand the functions and responsibilities of a free press.

If YOU were there...

Your father runs a bookshop in colonial Boston in 1770. Your family lives in a very small, brick house. You and your sisters must share one small room. One day, a red-coated British officer knocks on your door and strides into the parlor. He says that your family will have to provide a room and meals for two British soldiers. "We're already crowded!" you protest, but he insists.

Would you support the British government's requirement that colonists provide food and shelter for troops? Why?

BUILDING BACKGROUND People in the American colonies resented the British soldiers stationed in their towns. They objected to sudden searches and to soldiers being housed in private homes. They disliked censorship of their newspapers. When the Constitution was written, Americans remembered those wrongs. They insisted on adding a bill of rights to the document.

First Amendment

Federalist **James Madison** promised that a bill of rights would be added to the Constitution. This promise allowed the Constitution to pass. In 1789 Madison began writing down a huge list of proposed amendments. He then presented a shorter list to the House of Representatives. Of those, the House approved 12. The states ratified 10, which took effect December 15, 1791. Those 10 amendments, called the Bill of Rights, protect U.S. citizens' individual liberties.

The protection of individual liberties is important in a representative democracy. Without safeguards, people's rights would not always be protected because of **majority rule.** This is the idea that the greatest number of people in society can make policies for everyone. While this means that most people agree on what the law should be, it also means that smaller groups might lose their rights. The Bill of Rights ensures that the rights of all citizens are protected.

The ideas spelled out in the First Amendment form the most basic rights of all U.S. citizens. These rights include freedom of religion,

Teach the Big Idea: Master the Standards

Standards Proficiency

The Bill of Rights HSS 8.2.6, 8.3.7; HSS Analysis Skills: HI 1

Prep Required

Materials: slips of paper listing either a specific right found in the Bill of Rights or a number from 1 to 10

1. **Teach** Ask students the Main Idea questions to teach this section.
2. **Apply** Discuss with students the meaning and importance of each amendment in the Bill of Rights. Make a chart of the information for students to see. **LS Verbal/Linguistic**
3. **Review** Hand each student one of the prepared slips of paper. Have students circulate to match specific rights to the correct amendment number. **LS Interpersonal, Kinesthetic**
4. **Practice/Homework** Have students draw political cartoons illustrating what could happen without the protections provided by the Bill of Rights. **LS Visual/Spatial**

Alternative Assessment Handbook, Rubrics 7: Charts; and 27: Political Cartoons

Standards Focus

HSS 8.2.6

Means: Identify and describe the basic rights and freedoms guaranteed by the Bill of Rights.

Matters: The Bill of Rights protects Americans' rights and freedoms.

HSS 8.3.7

Means: Understand the purpose and duties of a free press.

Matters: Because of a free press, Americans may openly exchange information and ideas.

freedom of the press, freedom of speech, freedom of assembly, and the right to petition.

In the spirit of Thomas Jefferson's Virginia Statute for Religious Freedom, the First Amendment begins, "Congress shall make no law respecting an establishment of religion, or prohibiting the free exercise thereof." In other words, the government cannot support or interfere with the practice of a religion. This amendment keeps the government from favoring one religion over any other or establishing an official religion.

The First Amendment also guarantees freedom of speech and of the press. This means that Americans have the right to express their own ideas and views. They also have the right to hear the ideas and views of others. Former senator Margaret Chase Smith discussed why these freedoms are important. "The key to security," she once said, "is public information."

Freedom of speech does not mean that people can say anything they want to, however. The Constitution does not protect slander—false statements meant to damage someone's reputation. Libel, or intentionally writing a lie that harms another person, is not protected, either. The Supreme Court has also ruled that speech that endangers public safety is not protected. For example, Justice Oliver Wendell Holmes declared in 1919 that falsely shouting "Fire" in a crowded theater is not protected as free speech.

Americans also have freedom of assembly, or of holding meetings. Any group may gather to discuss issues or conduct business. If people gather peacefully and do not engage in illegal activities, the government cannot interfere. The right to **petition**, or make a request of the government, is another right of the American people. Any American can present a petition to a government official. This right lets Americans show dissatisfaction with a law. They can also suggest new laws.

THE IMPACT TODAY
Free-speech protection has also been applied to "symbolic" speech—non-verbal communication that expresses an idea, such as wearing a protest button.

READING CHECK **Summarizing** What rights does the First Amendment guarantee to Americans?

Amendment I
Congress shall make no law respecting an establishment of religion, or prohibiting the free exercise thereof; or abridging the freedom of speech, or of the press; or the right of the people peaceably to assemble, and to petition the Government for a redress of grievances.

Workers use the right of assembly to protest a proposed budget in New York City.

Direct Teach

Main Idea

❶ First Amendment

The First Amendment guarantees basic freedoms to individuals.

Identify Why is the Bill of Rights' protection of individual liberties important? *to safeguard the rights of all Americans, not just the majority*

Analyze How does the First Amendment separate church and state? *It keeps the government from supporting or interfering with the practice of a religion or from favoring one religion over another.*

Elaborate Why is the freedom of assembly important? *possible answer—Groups should be able to hold peaceful public demonstrations to present their views.*

- **CRF:** Primary Source Activity: Hortensius, "An Essay on the Liberty of the Press"
- **CRF:** Political Cartoons Activities for United States History, Cartoon 6: Bill of Rights: "Liberty vs. Order"

HSS 8.2.6, 8.3.7

Analyzing Visuals

Amendment I

Have students examine the photograph at left of a rally to protest a proposed budget in New York City. Ask students to identify the First Amendment freedoms that these people are demonstrating. *freedoms of speech and assembly*

Differentiating Instruction for Universal Access

Special Education Students
Reaching Standards

1. Discuss with students the basic rights that the First Amendment protects.
2. Copy the table for students to see. Omit the blue answers in parentheses. Have students match each freedom on the left with the correct example on the right.
3. Help the class come up with additional examples for each freedom. LS **Verbal/Linguistic, Visual/Spatial**

HSS 8.2.6, 8.3.7

First Amendment Freedoms	Examples
1. Freedom of Speech *(b)*	a. The nation may not have an official religion.
2. Freedom of the Press *(d)*	b. People may voice their opinions.
3. Freedom of Religion *(a)*	c. Americans may present petitions to the government.
4. Freedom of Assembly *(e)*	d. The government cannot tell newspapers what to print.
5. Freedom of Petition *(c)*	e. People can hold meetings.

Answers

Reading Check *freedom of religion, freedom of the press, freedom of speech, freedom of assembly, and the right to petition*

Direct Teach

Main Idea

❷ Protecting Citizens

Other amendments focus on protecting citizens from certain abuses.

Identify What basic right does the Second Amendment protect? *the right to bear arms*

Analyze How does a search warrant protect Americans and their property? *It prevents authorities from searching someone's home or property without permission.*

HSS 8.2.6; HSS **Analysis Skills:** HI 1

Linking to Today

The National Guard Over time, the National Guard's federal mission has broadened. After the terrorist attacks of September 11, 2001, state and federal governments called upon the National Guard to provide security at home and assist the nation's military in combating terrorism abroad.

Info to Know

Quartering Troops In 1689, Parliament passed an act that protected British citizens from having to house or quarter troops in their homes. The British law did not apply to the colonies in America, though. During the French and Indian War (1754–63), colonists discovered that they had no legal protection against the British practice of quartering troops.

Amendment II
A well regulated Militia, being necessary to the security of a free State, the right of the people to keep and bear Arms, shall not be infringed.

Amendment III
No Soldier shall, in time of peace be quartered in any house, without the consent of the Owner, nor in time of war, but in a manner to be prescribed by law.

Amendment IV
The right of the people to be secure in their persons, houses, papers, and effects, against unreasonable searches and seizures, shall not be violated, and no Warrants shall issue, but upon probable cause, supported by Oath or affirmation, and particularly describing the place to be searched, and the persons or things to be seized.

Protecting Citizens

The Second, Third, and Fourth Amendments relate to colonial disputes with Britain and reflect many of the ideals outlined in the Declaration of Independence. The Second Amendment deals with state militias and the right to bear arms. Colonial militias played a big role in the Revolutionary War. The framers of the Constitution thought that the states needed their militias for emergencies. Today the National Guard has largely replaced organized state militias.

Supporters of gun-control laws have generally argued that the Second Amendment was intended to protect the collective right of states to maintain well-regulated militia units. Opponents hold that the amendment was meant to protect an individual's right of self-defense. The meaning of the amendment continues to be debated.

The Third Amendment prevents the military from forcing citizens to house soldiers. Before the Revolution, the British pressured colonists to shelter and feed British soldiers. British leaders also forced colonists to submit to having their property searched for illegal goods. Anger over such actions led to the Fourth Amendment rule against "unreasonable searches and seizures." Before a citizen's property can be searched, authorities must now get a **search warrant**. This order gives authorities permission to search someone's property. A judge issues this order only when it seems likely that a search might uncover evidence relating to a crime. In emergencies, however, police can make an emergency search. This may preserve evidence needed to prove possible illegal activity.

READING CHECK **Finding Main Ideas** Why were the Third and Fourth Amendments matters of great importance to Americans when the Bill of Rights was written?

Rights of the Accused

The Fifth, Sixth, Seventh, and Eighth Amendments provide guidelines for protecting the rights of the accused. According to the Fifth Amendment, the government cannot punish anyone without **due process** of law. This means that the law must be fairly applied. A grand jury decides if there is enough evidence to **indict** (en-DYT), or formally accuse, a person. Without an indictment, the court cannot try anyone for a serious crime. The Fifth Amendment also protects people from having to testify at their own criminal trial. To keep from testifying, a person need only "take the Fifth." In addition, anyone found not guilty in a criminal trial cannot face **double jeopardy**. In other words, he or she cannot be tried again for the same crime.

The final clause of the Fifth Amendment states that no one can have property taken without due process of law. There is one exception: the government's power of **eminent domain**. This is the power to take personal property to benefit the public. One example would be taking private land to build a public road. However, the government must pay the owners a fair price for the property. If the property was gained illegally, then the owners are not paid.

Collaborative Learning

Standards Proficiency

Class Bill of Rights HSS 8.2.6

1. Organize the class into groups. Have each group develop a list of 10 rights they would like to include in a "Class Bill of Rights." Tell students that the document must clearly protect students' rights while focusing on creating an effective classroom.
2. After all groups have completed their lists, ask a representative from each group to present that group's ideas to the class.
3. Make a list of the ideas for students to see. Have students discuss the ideas that appear on several lists. What concerns do they reflect? Then have students compare their lists with the Bill of Rights.
4. Have students vote to determine which 10 rights to include in their official "Class Bill of Rights." Post the list in the classroom. LS **Interpersonal, Verbal/Linguistic**

Alternative Assessment Handbook, Rubric 14: Group Activity

Answers

Reading Check *They related to disputes that American colonists had with Great Britain over quartering troops and forced search and seizure.*

The Sixth Amendment protects the rights of a person who has been indicted. It guarantees that person a speedy public trial. Public trials ensure that laws are being followed by allowing the public to witness the proceedings. Accused people have the right to know the charges against them and can hear and question witnesses testifying against them. Accused people have the right to an attorney. If they cannot pay for legal service, the government must provide it. Sometimes accused persons refuse their Sixth Amendment rights. For example, some defendants refuse the services of an attorney, while others choose to have a trial in front of a judge alone instead of before a jury. In many cases, defendants can forgo trial and agree to a plea bargain. This means that a defendant pleads guilty to a lesser charge and avoids risking conviction for a crime with a greater sentence.

The Seventh Amendment states that juries can decide civil cases. It is possible to harm another person without committing a crime. In such cases, the injured party may sue, or seek justice, in a civil court. Civil cases usually involve disputes over money or property. For example, someone might bring a civil suit against a person who refuses to repay a debt.

Amendment V

No person shall be held to answer for a capital, or otherwise infamous crime, unless on a presentment or indictment of a Grand Jury, except in cases arising in the land or naval forces, or in the Militia, when in actual service in time of War or public danger; nor shall any person be subject for the same offence to be twice put in jeopardy of life or limb; nor shall be compelled in any criminal case to be a witness against himself, nor be deprived of life, liberty, or property, without due process of law; nor shall private property be taken for public use, without just compensation.

Amendment VI

In all criminal prosecutions, the accused shall enjoy the right to a speedy and public trial, by an impartial jury of the State and district wherein the crime shall have been committed, which district shall have been previously ascertained by law, and to be informed of the nature and cause of the accusation; to be confronted with the witnesses against him; to have compulsory process for obtaining witnesses in his favor, and to have the Assistance of Counsel for his defence.

Amendment VII

In suits at common law, where the value in controversy shall exceed twenty dollars, the right of trial by jury shall be preserved, and no fact tried by a jury, shall be otherwise reexamined in any Court of the United States, than according to the rules of the common law.

A judge and jury listen to a witness in a courtroom in Orange County, California.

Direct Teach

Main Idea

❸ Rights of the Accused

The rights of the accused are an important part of the Bill of Rights.

Define What does due process of law ensure? *that the law is fairly applied*

Summarize How does the Sixth Amendment protect Americans in a court of law? *guarantees a speedy public trial, the right to know the charges against them, the right to question witnesses, and the right to an attorney*

Make Judgments Do you think the government should have the power of eminent domain? *possible answers—Yes, otherwise it might be impossible to complete public building projects, and people are paid fair value; no, the government should not be able to take people's property against their will.*

HSS 8.2.6

Info to Know

Double Jeopardy While the Fifth Amendment prohibits double jeopardy, in some circumstances an individual can be tried twice on the same evidence. By using federal civil rights laws, officials have prosecuted individuals found not guilty in criminal court cases. Because the second trials are civil trials, they do not violate double jeopardy. Prosecutors used this strategy in 1994 to try and convict a man accused of murdering civil rights workers in Mississippi in 1964.

Cross-Discipline Activity: Civics

Standards Proficiency

Justice: The Rights of the Accused Advertisements HSS 8.2.6

Materials: art supplies (optional)

1. Ask students what the Fifth, Sixth, Seventh, and Eighth Amendments have in common. *(They all focus on protecting the rights of the accused.)*
2. Organize the class into small groups. Have each group create an advertisement for a law firm that specializes in protecting and defending the rights of the accused. Ads should provide scenarios in which the rights of the accused have been violated. Ads may be for print, radio, television, or the Internet.
3. Ask group representatives to present the ads to the class. Have students identify the amendment(s) that protect against each situation in each ad. **LS Interpersonal, Verbal/Linguistic**

Alternative Assessment Handbook, Rubric 2: Advertisements

Direct Teach

Main Idea

❸ Rights of the Accused

The rights of the accused are an important part of the Bill of Rights.

Recall What is the purpose of bail? *It allows people to avoid staying in jail during a trial.*

Make Inferences Why do you think the Bill of Rights provides for bail? *because defendants have not yet been proven guilty*

Make Generalizations In what ways has the Supreme Court influenced the way states carry out the death penalty? *The Court ruled that although execution itself is not cruel and unusual, some methods of carrying out the death penalty are either cruel and unusual or unfair.*

MISCONCEPTION ALERT

Free Education? Children and young adults who attend public schools do not pay for their education. However, that does not mean that their education is free. American citizens, whether they have children in the public school system or not, share the responsibility of funding public education in their state through the payment of different kinds of taxes, such as state or property taxes.

A Right to Bail

The Eighth Amendment allows for bail. Bail is a set amount of money that defendants promise to pay the court if they fail to appear in court at the proper time.

By posting, or paying, bail, a defendant can avoid staying in jail before and during a trial. If a defendant does not show up in court for trial, the court demands the bail money be paid and issues a warrant for arrest.

The Eighth Amendment keeps courts from setting unfairly high bail. However, in cases of very serious crimes, a judge may refuse to set bail altogether. This can be the case, for example, if the court regards a defendant as being potentially dangerous to the public by being left free. A judge can also deny bail if he or she thinks the defendant will not show up for trial. In such cases the defendant must remain in jail through the trial.

Amendment VIII
Excessive bail shall not be required, nor excessive fines imposed, nor cruel and unusual punishments inflicted.

"Cruel and Unusual Punishments"

The Eighth Amendment also bans "cruel and unusual punishments" against a person convicted of a crime. For many years, Americans have debated the question of what exactly constitutes cruel and unusual punishment. The debate has often centered on the issue of capital punishment. In 1972 the Supreme Court ruled that the way in which most states carried out the death penalty was cruel and unusual. The Court also found that the ways in which many states sentenced people to death were unfair. However, a few years later, the Court ruled that not all executions were in themselves cruel and unusual.

Most states still allow the death penalty. Those that do must follow the Supreme Court's rules. To do so, many states have changed the ways in which they carry out the death penalty.

READING CHECK **Summarizing** What is the purpose of the Eighth Amendment?

Rights of States and Citizens

The final two amendments in the Bill of Rights give a general protection for other rights not addressed by the first eight amendments. These amendments also reserve some governmental powers for the states and the people.

Ninth Amendment

The Ninth Amendment says that the rights listed in the Constitution are not the only rights that citizens have. This amendment has allowed the courts and Congress to decide other basic rights of citizens.

The Constitution does not address the question of education. However, most Americans believe that it is a basic and essential right. This seems especially true in view of the fact that American citizens must be able to vote for the people who represent them in government. "Education is not just another

Amendment IX
The enumeration in the Constitution, of certain rights, shall not be construed to deny or disparage others retained by the people.

Amendment X
The powers not delegated to the United States by the Constitution, nor prohibited by it to the States, are reserved to the States respectively, or to the people.

Differentiating Instruction for Universal Access

Advanced Learners/GATE — Exceeding Standards

Ninth Amendment Have students discuss the rights they think should be included under the Ninth Amendment. List the ideas for students to see. Have the class discuss and vote on which rights to include. Discuss why the framers of the Constitution included the Ninth Amendment.
LS Interpersonal, Verbal/Linguistic

 HSS 8.2.6

Alternative Assessment Handbook, Rubric 11: Discussions

English-Language Learners — Standards Proficiency

Illustrated Bill of Rights Go through each amendment in the Bill of Rights with students. Define unfamiliar terms as needed. Then have students work as a class or in small groups to create an illustrated Bill of Rights. Students should provide at least one illustration and a short caption for each amendment. Display students' work in the classroom. **LS Interpersonal, Visual/Spatial**

HSS 8.2.6

Alternative Assessment Handbook, Rubric 3: Artwork

Answers

Reading Check *allows for bail, prevents courts from setting unfairly high bail, and bans "cruel and unusual punishment"*

consumer item. It is the bedrock [foundation] of our democracy," explained educational leader Mary Hatwood Futrell. Today state governments offer free education from elementary to high school—to all citizens.

Tenth Amendment

The Tenth Amendment recognizes that the states and the people have additional powers. These powers are any ones that the Constitution does not specifically give to Congress—the delegated powers. The Tenth Amendment makes it clear that any powers not either delegated to the federal government or prohibited to the states belong to the states and the people. Thus, the last amendment in the Bill of Rights protects citizens' rights. It helps to keep the balance of power between the federal and state governments.

READING CHECK **Summarizing** How does the Tenth Amendment protect the rights of citizens?

SUMMARY AND PREVIEW In this section you learned about the Bill of Rights. In the next section you will learn about the responsibilities of citizenship.

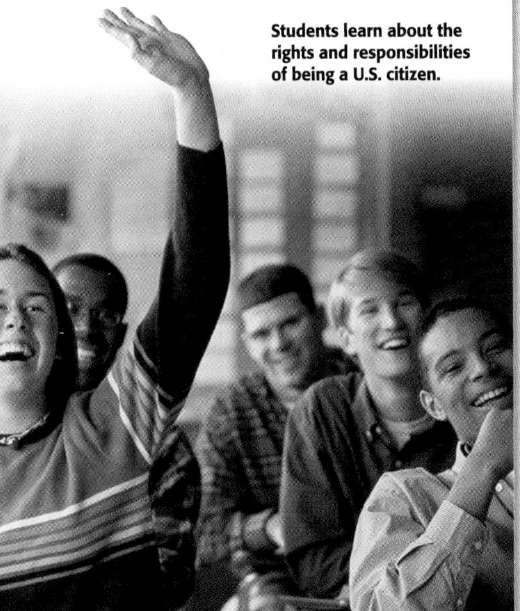
Students learn about the rights and responsibilities of being a U.S. citizen.

Section 2 Assessment

go.hrw.com
Online Quiz
KEYWORD: SS8 HP5

Reviewing Ideas, Terms, and People HSS 8.2.6, 8.3.7

1. a. **Identify** What basic rights are protected by the First Amendment?
   b. **Explain** What does the right to **petition** the government mean?
   c. **Elaborate** Why is freedom of the press an important right?
2. a. **Describe** How are citizens protected under the Third and Fourth Amendments?
   b. **Draw Conclusions** In what ways did British actions before the Revolution lead to the Second, Third, and Fourth Amendments?
3. a. **Identify** What protections does the Eighth Amendment provide for people accused of crimes?
   b. **Elaborate** Why is it important that the Bill of Rights protects people accused of crimes?
4. a. **Recall** What is the purpose of the final two amendments in the Bill of Rights?
   b. **Analyze** How does the Tenth Amendment balance power between national and state governments?

Critical Thinking

5. **Summarizing** Copy the chart below. Use it to summarize the rights guaranteed to citizens by each amendment in the Bill of Rights.

Amendment	Right
1	
2	
3	
4	
5	
6	
7	
8	
9	
10	

FOCUS ON WRITING

6. **Gathering Information about the Bill of Rights** What freedoms are guaranteed by the Bill of Rights? Make a list of the most important freedoms. You'll list those freedoms on the third page of your pamphlet.

Direct Teach

Main Idea

4 Rights of States and Citizens

The rights of states and citizens are protected by the Bill of Rights.

Identify What is the purpose of the Ninth Amendment? *It allows the courts and Congress to decide other basic rights of citizens.*

Analyze Why do most Americans believe that education is a basic and essential right? *because a representative democracy requires an educated public that can vote wisely for leaders to represent them*

 HSS 8.2.6

Review & Assess

Close

Briefly review the Bill of Rights. Have students discuss which rights they think are most important and have them explain their reasoning.

Review

Online Quiz, Section 2

Assess

SE Section 2 Assessment

PASS: Section 2 Quiz

Alternative Assessment Handbook

Reteach/Classroom Intervention

California Standards Review Workbook

Interactive Reader and Study Guide, Section 2

Interactive Skills Tutor CD-ROM

Section 2 Assessment Answers

1. a. freedom of religion, speech, press, assembly, and right to petition
   b. People may make requests of the government or suggest laws.
   c. Americans may use the media to criticize the government or policies without fear.
2. a. Third—protects citizens from housing soldiers; Fourth—protects citizens from unreasonable search and seizure
   b. They address colonial complaints against the seizure of arms, quartering troops, and forced searches and seizures.
3. a. allows for bail, prevents courts from setting unfairly high bail, bans "cruel and unusual punishment"
   b. Those accused of crimes may not be guilty.
4. a. protect citizens' rights and balance power between federal and state governments
   b. gives the states all powers not prohibited to them or delegated to federal government
5. See the amendments in the section.
6. Students might list freedoms such as those provided in the First Amendment.

Answers

Reading Check *recognizes that any powers not specifically delegated to the federal government or prohibited to the states belong to the states and to the people, which balances power between state and federal governments*

Preteach

Bellringer

If YOU were there . . . Use the **Daily Bellringer Transparency** to help students answer the question.

Daily Bellringer Transparency, Section 3

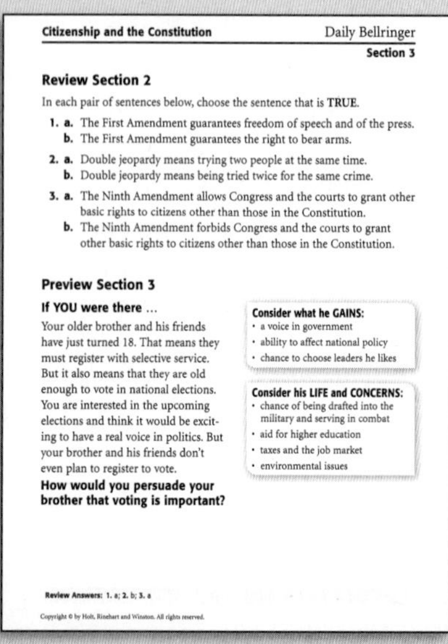

Citizenship and the Constitution — Daily Bellringer **Section 3**

Review Section 2

In each pair of sentences below, choose the sentence that is **TRUE**.

1. a. The First Amendment guarantees freedom of speech and of the press.
   b. The First Amendment guarantees the right to bear arms.
2. a. Double jeopardy means trying two people at the same time.
   b. Double jeopardy means being tried twice for the same crime.
3. a. The Ninth Amendment allows Congress and the courts to grant other basic rights to citizens other than those in the Constitution.
   b. The Ninth Amendment forbids Congress and the courts to grant other basic rights to citizens other than those in the Constitution.

Preview Section 3

If YOU were there ...

Your older brother and his friends have just turned 18. That means they must register with selective service. But it also means that they are old enough to vote in national elections. You are interested in the upcoming elections and think it would be exciting to have a real voice in politics. But your brother and his friends don't even plan to register to vote.

How would you persuade your brother that voting is important?

Consider what he GAINS:
- a voice in government
- ability to affect national policy
- chance to choose leaders he likes

Consider his LIFE and CONCERNS:
- chance of being drafted into the military and serving in combat
- aid for higher education
- taxes and the job market
- environmental issues

Review Answers: 1. a; 2. b; 3. a

Academic Vocabulary

Review with students the high-use academic term in this section.

influence change or have an effect on (p. 186)

CRF: Vocabulary Builder Activity, Section 3

go.hrw.com

Online Resources

KEYWORD: SS8 US5
ACTIVITY: Tracking U.S. Immigration

Standards Focus

HSS 8.3.6

Means: Describe the many ways the Constitution provides for citizens to participate in and influence government.

Matters: Citizens must take an active role in government for a democracy to work.

SECTION 3

Rights and Responsibilities of Citizenship

What You Will Learn...

Main Ideas

1. Citizenship in the United States is determined in several ways.
2. Citizens are expected to fulfill a number of important duties.
3. Active citizen involvement in government and the community is encouraged.

The Big Idea

American citizenship involves great privileges and serious responsibilities.

Key Terms

naturalized citizens, *p. 184*
deport, *p. 184*
draft, *p. 185*
political action committees, *p. 186*
interest groups, *p. 186*

HSS 8.3.6 Describe the basic law-making process and how the Constitution provides numerous opportunities for citizens to participate in the political process and to monitor and influence government (e.g., function of elections, political parties, interest groups).

If YOU were there...

Your older brother and his friends have just turned 18. That means they must register with selective service. But it also means that they are old enough to vote in national elections. You are interested in the upcoming elections and think it would be exciting to have a real voice in politics. But your brother and his friends don't even plan to register to vote.

How would you persuade your brother that voting is important?

BUILDING BACKGROUND Whether you are born an American citizen or become one later, citizenship brings many rights and privileges. But it also brings duties and responsibilities. Voting is both a right and a responsibility.

Gaining U.S. Citizenship

People become U.S. citizens in several ways. First, anyone born in the United States or a territory it controls is a citizen. People born in a foreign country are U.S. citizens if at least one parent is a U.S. citizen. Foreign-born people whose parents are not citizens must move to the United States to become **naturalized citizens**. Once in the United States, they go through a long process before applying for citizenship. If they succeed, they become naturalized citizens, giving them most of the rights and responsibilities of other citizens.

In the United States, legal immigrants have many of the rights and responsibilities of citizens but cannot vote or hold public office. The U.S. government can **deport**, or return to the country of origin, immigrants who break the law.

Legal immigrants over age 18 may request naturalization after living in the United States for five years. All legal immigrants have to

Teach the Big Idea: Master the Standards

Standards Proficiency

Rights and Responsibilities of Citizenship

HSS 8.3.6; HSS **Analysis Skills:** HI 1

1. **Teach** Ask students the Main Idea questions to teach this section.
2. **Apply** Ask students to imagine that they work for the immigration department. Have each student create a two-page Citizenship Guide. The guide should provide information on how to become a naturalized citizen, the duties of citizenship, participating in the political process, and serving the community. **LS Verbal/Linguistic**
3. **Review** As you review the section, have students identify and explain the duties and responsibilities of citizenship.
4. **Practice/Homework** Have each student create a collage illustrating the rights and responsibilities of citizenship. Collages might include drawings, quotations, newspaper and magazine clippings, photographs, cloth, stickers, and so on. **LS Visual/Spatial**

Alternative Assessment Handbook, Rubrics 8: Collages; and 37: Writing Assignments support themselves financially. If not, someone must assume financial responsibility for them. Immigrants must be law-abiding and support the U.S. Constitution. They must demonstrate understanding of written and spoken English. They also must show basic knowledge of U.S. history and government.

When this is done, candidates go before a naturalization court and take an oath of allegiance to the United States. They then get certificates of naturalization.

Only two differences between naturalized and native-born citizens exist. Naturalized citizens can lose their citizenship, and they cannot become president or vice president. Many famous Americans have been naturalized citizens, including scientist Albert Einstein and former secretary of state Madeleine Albright.

READING CHECK **Drawing Conclusions** Why does U.S. law have such demanding requirements for people to become naturalized citizens?

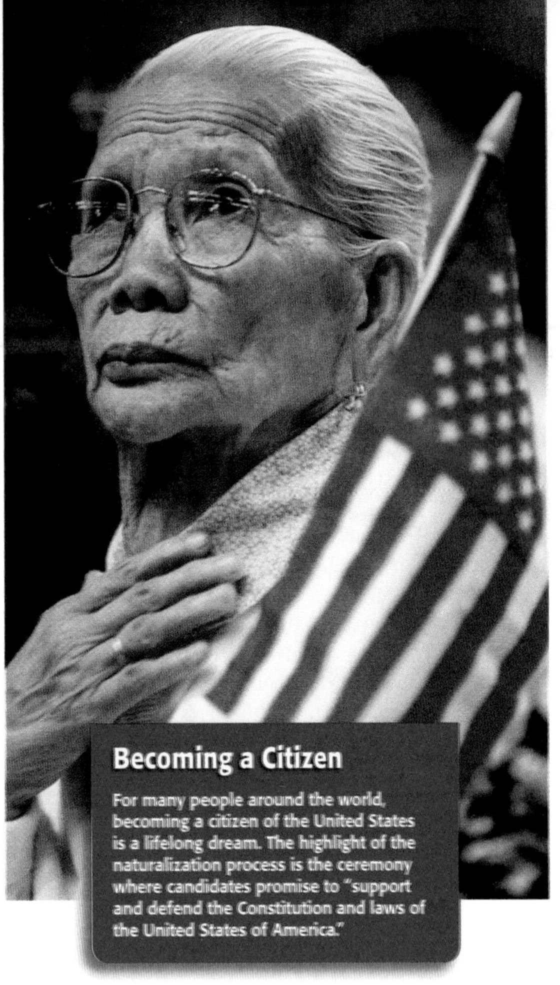

Becoming a Citizen

For many people around the world, becoming a citizen of the United States is a lifelong dream. The highlight of the naturalization process is the ceremony where candidates promise to "support and defend the Constitution and laws of the United States of America."

Duties of Citizenship

For a representative democracy to work, Americans need to fulfill their civic duties. "The stakes…are too high for government to be a spectator sport," former Texas congresswoman Barbara Jordan once said.

Citizens elect officials to make laws for them. In turn, citizens must obey those laws and respect the authorities who enforce them. Obeying laws includes knowing what they are and staying informed about changes. Ignorance of a law will not prevent a person from being punished for breaking it.

Another duty is paying taxes for services such as public roads, police, and public schools. People pay sales taxes, property taxes, and tariffs. Many Americans also pay a tax on their income to the federal, and sometimes state, government.

Citizens have the duty to defend the nation. Men 18 years or older must register with selective service. In the event of a **draft**, or required military service, those able to fight are already registered. Although women do not register, many serve in the armed forces.

Americans have the right to a trial by jury under the Sixth Amendment. To protect this right, citizens should be willing to serve on a jury when they are called. Otherwise, fulfilling each person's Sixth Amendment rights would be difficult.

READING CHECK **Making Inferences** Why does citizenship carry with it certain responsibilities?

Direct Teach

Main Idea

❶ Gaining U.S. Citizenship

Citizenship in the United States is determined in several ways.

Describe What requirements must legal immigrants meet to become naturalized citizens? *over age 18, lived in the United States for at least five years, financially supported, law-abiding, support the Constitution, show an understanding of written and spoken English, show basic knowledge of U.S. history*

Contrast What are the differences between naturalized and native-born U.S. citizens? *Naturalized citizens can lose their citizenship and cannot become president or vice president.*

CRF: Primary Source Activity: What It Means to Be an American: Two Views

HSS 8.3.6

Main Idea

❷ Duties of Citizenship

Citizens are expected to fulfill a number of important duties.

Define In your own words, define good citizenship. *Answers will vary, but students should address some of the duties of citizenship.*

Make Generalizations How are paying taxes and being a good citizen connected? *Taxes support government and pay for services that benefit citizens.*

Political Cartoons Activities for United States History, Cartoon 5: Duties of Citizenship

HSS 8.3.6

Cross-Discipline Activity: English–Language Arts

Exceeding Standards

Becoming a U.S. Citizen: "I Am a New Citizen" Poems HSS 8.3.6

1. Ask students to imagine that they, like the woman in the above photograph, have just been sworn in as U.S. citizens.
2. Have each student write a poem titled "I Am a New Citizen" that describes their emotions during the ceremony and explains why they had always dreamed of becoming a citizen of the United States.
3. Encourage students to use sensory details and figurative language, such as metaphors and similes, to express the meaning and significance of the experience.
4. Ask for volunteers to read their poems aloud to the class. **LS Verbal/Linguistic**

Alternative Assessment Handbook, Rubric 26: Poems and Songs

Answers

Reading Check (top) *to make sure people understand the rights and responsibilities of being a U.S. citizen*

Reading Check (bottom) *For a democracy to work, citizens must share in the duties required.*

Direct Teach

Main Idea

3 Citizens and Government

Active citizen involvement in government and the community is encouraged.

Describe What steps can citizens take to vote intelligently? *study information about the issues and candidates from a variety of sources*

Analyze What do you think are some positive and negative issues related to political action committees and interest groups? *positive—can help raise public and political interest in important issues; negative—can bog down the political process as groups compete to promote their issues; money raised can be used to influence politicians*

CRF: Literature Activity: *The Free Citizen,* by Theodore Roosevelt

HSS 8.3.6

Connect to Civics: Responsibility

Voter Participation Political scientists compiled information regarding voter participation in several nations during the 1980s and discovered that the United States ranked among the lowest in voter turnout. In a survey of 20 democracies, the United States ranked 19th in voter participation.

 **Get Out the Vote Speech** Have students write a speech in which they encourage Americans to cast their votes in an upcoming election.
LS Verbal/Linguistic

Responsibilities of Citizens

For representative democracy to work, citizens must do their part. Each activity pictured here serves an important role in the community.

Jury Duty

Military Service

Citizens and Government

Taking part in the elections process by voting may be a citizen's most vital duty. Through free elections, U.S. citizens choose who will lead their government.

Function of Elections

It is essential for citizens to learn as much as they can about the issues and candidates before voting. Information is available from many sources: the Internet, newspapers, television, and other media. However, voters should also be aware that some material may be propaganda or material that is biased deliberately to help or harm a cause.

In addition to voting, many Americans choose to campaign for candidates or issues. Anyone can help campaign, even if he or she is not eligible to vote. Many people also help campaigns by giving money directly or through **political action committees** (PACs), groups that collect money for candidates who support certain issues.

Influencing Government

Academic Vocabulary
influence change or have an effect on

Even after an election, people can influence officials. Political participation is part of our nation's identity and tradition. When colonists protested British rule in the 1700s, they formed committees and presented their views to political leaders.

As the new American nation grew, so did political participation. French diplomat Alexis de Tocqueville visited the United States in 1831 to study American democracy. He was amazed at the large number of political groups Americans participated in. He wrote about them:

> "What political power could ever carry on the vast multitude [large number] of lesser undertakings which the American citizens perform every day, with the assistance of the principle of association [joining a group]? Nothing, in my opinion, is more deserving of our attention than the intellectual and moral associations of America."
>
> —Alexis de Tocqueville, *Democracy in America*

U.S. citizens sometimes work with **interest groups**. These groups of people share a common interest that motivates them to take political action. Interest groups organize speeches and rallies to support their cause. However, citizens need not join a group to influence government. They can write letters to leaders of government or attend city council meetings. Active political participation is an important duty for U.S. citizens and immigrants alike.

Helping the Community

Commitment to others moves many Americans to volunteer in community service groups. Some small communities rely on volunteers for services such as fire protection and law enforcement.

Other volunteer groups help government-sponsored agencies. For example, Citizens on

Collaborative Learning

Standards Proficiency

Helping the Community HSS 8.3.6; HSS Analysis Skills: HI 1

1. Guide students in a short discussion about how volunteer groups help your local community. Ask for students to share some of their volunteer experiences.
2. Ask students to identify some specific problems or needs in the local community that would benefit from volunteer efforts.
3. Organize the class into groups of five or six. Have each group select one of the problems or needs identified in the discussion.
4. Have group members work together to develop a volunteer project to help address the local problem or need. Each group should also develop a plan for carrying out its project.
LS Interpersonal, Verbal/Linguistic

ANALYSIS SKILL ANALYZING VISUALS

Which responsibilities can you fulfill now, without waiting until you turn 18 years old?

Patrol and Neighborhood Watch groups ask volunteers to walk their neighborhoods and tell police if they observe possible criminal activity in the area. The American Red Cross helps citizens in times of natural disasters or other emergencies. The Boy Scouts and Girl Scouts plan many projects such as planting trees to improve the environment. Even simple acts such as picking up trash in parks or serving food in shelters help a community.

READING CHECK **Summarizing** In what ways do volunteer groups benefit the community?

SUMMARY AND PREVIEW In this section you learned about citizens' duties toward their nation and their communities. In the next chapter you will learn about the first government formed under the Constitution.

Section 3 Assessment

go.hrw.com **Online Quiz** KEYWORD: SS8 HP5

Reviewing Ideas, Terms, and People HSS 8.3.6

1. a. **Identify** What are the different ways in which a person can become a U.S. citizen?
   b. **Make Inferences** Why do you think the law requires an immigrant to live in the United States at least five years before he or she can apply to become a **naturalized citizen**?
2. a. **Describe** What are three duties expected of U.S. citizens?
   b. **Evaluate** In your opinion, which duty expected of citizens is the most important? Why?
3. a. **Identify** In what ways can citizens participate in the election process?
   b. **Draw Conclusions** Why is it important that citizens participate in the political process?

Critical Thinking

4. **Analyzing** Copy the graphic organizer on the right. Use it to analyze the different ways that a person can become a U.S. citizen and the responsibilities that all citizens share.

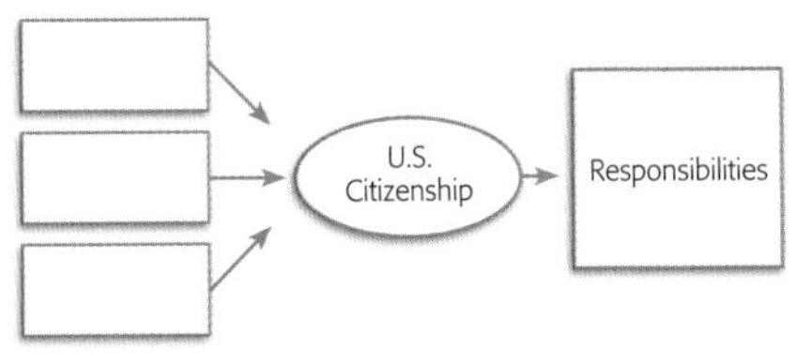

FOCUS ON WRITING

5. **Thinking about Citizenship** The last page of your pamphlet will have two parts—one part on requirements for citizenship and one part on the responsibilities of citizens. Look back through this section and make two lists, one on requirements and one on responsibilities.

Section 3 Assessment Answers

1. **a.** born in the United States or a U.S. territory, have at least one parent who is a citizen, or become a naturalized citizen
   b. to make sure people understand and fully accept the rights and responsibilities of being a U.S. citizen
2. **a.** possible answers—pay taxes, obey laws, register for military draft, serve on juries, vote
   b. Answers will vary but should reflect an understanding of the duties of citizenship, as listed in previous answer.
3. **a.** vote, campaign for candidates, work with interest groups
   b. possible answer—To work effectively, a representative democracy needs an informed and politically active citizenry.
4. become a citizen—see answer to Question 1a; responsibilities—see answer to Question 2a.
5. Students should note the information in the answers to Questions 1a and 2a.

Review & Assess

Close

Have students summarize in their own words what it means to be an American citizen. Students should address both the rights and responsibilities of citizenship.

Review

go.hrw.com Online Quiz, Section 3

Assess

SE Section 3 Assessment

PASS: Section 3 Quiz

Alternative Assessment Handbook

Reteach/Classroom Intervention

California Standards Review Workbook

Interactive Reader and Study Guide, Section 3

Interactive Skills Tutor CD-ROM

Answers

Analyzing Visuals *community service, obeying the law*

Reading Check *by providing community services such as fire protection, beautification, and help to those in need*

Social Studies Skills

Determining the Context of Statements

Activity Historical Context Chart
To extend the "Practice the Skill" activity, create a chart with four rows. Have students help you complete the chart by providing responses for each of the four points listed under "Learn the Skill." Then have students consider how well Henry's statement reflects the values, attitudes, and practices of Americans today. Encourage discussion and feedback. **LS Verbal/Linguistic, Visual/Spatial**

Alternative Assessment Handbook, Rubrics 7: Charts; and 11: Discussions

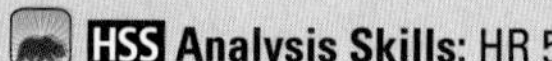

HSS Analysis Skills: HR 5

Social Studies Skills

Analysis | Critical Thinking | Participation | Study

HR5 Students determine the context in which historical statements were made.

Determining the Context of Statements

Define the Skill

A *context* is the circumstances under which something happens. *Historical context* includes values, beliefs, conditions, and practices that were common in the past. At times, some of these were quite different from what they are today. To truly understand a historical statement or event, you have to take its context into account. It is not right to judge what people in history did or said based on present-day values alone. To be fair, you must also consider the historical context of the statement or event.

Learn the Skill

To better understand something a historical figure said or wrote, use the following guidelines to determine the context of the statement.

1. Identify the speaker or writer, the date, and the topic and main idea of the statement.
2. Determine the speaker's or writer's attitude and point of view about the topic.
3. Review what you know about beliefs, conditions, or practices related to the topic that were common at the time. Find out more about the times in which the statement was made if you need to.
4. Decide how well the statement reflects the values, attitudes, and practices of people living at that time. Then, determine how well it reflects values, attitudes, and practices related to the topic today.

Applying these guidelines will give you a better understanding of statements made by the Constitution's framers. You read in Chapter 5 that the Constitution created a representative democracy. However, the original Constitution gave most Americans little voice in choosing their leaders. Only the House of Representatives was elected by the voters. Alexander Hamilton, one of Constitutional Convention's leaders, told the delegates:

> "The people are turbulent and changing; they seldom judge or determine right. Give therefore to the first [upper] class a distinct, permanent share in government. They will check the unsteadiness of the second [the masses]."

By modern standards, Hamilton's remark is undemocratic. But think about the times in which it was made. Shays's Rebellion had recently occurred. In addition, in those days most Americans had little or no education. Many could not even read or write. When its historical context is considered, the statement seems less harsh and extreme.

Practice the Skill

Read the following statement made by Patrick Henry in 1788. Then answer the questions to determine its context and better understand it.

> "The Constitution is said to have beautiful features, but . . . they appear to me horribly frightful. . . . Your dearest rights may be sacrificed by what may be a small minority . . . [that] . . . may continue forever unchangeably this government, although horribly defective."

1. What was Henry's opinion of the Constitution?
2. How might Americans' recent experience in the Revolution have caused him to feel that way?

Social Studies Skills Activity: Determining the Context of Statements

Alexis de Tocqueville Statement

HSS Analysis Skills: HR 5 — Standards Proficiency

1. Have students review the statement by Alexis de Tocqueville, located under the heading "Citizens and Government" in Section 3. Ask for a volunteer to read the quote aloud to the class. Discuss the statement's meaning.
2. Then have students use the steps listed under "Learn the Skill" to determine the context of the statement. Have students consider the following questions:
   - Why might de Tocqueville have been so impressed by this aspect of American life? *Perhaps people were not so involved in political groups in France at the time.*
   - Do you think someone touring America today would have this same impression? *Answers will vary, but students should exhibit an understanding of how times have changed and how these changes will affect peoples' impressions.* **LS Verbal/Linguistic**

Alternative Assessment Handbook, Rubric 11: Discussions

Answers

Practice the Skill **1.** *He disliked it and thought it would enable a minority to rule the majority and deny people their rights.* **2.** *Americans had recently fought to win their freedom from a monarchy they considered abusive. Many Americans at the time feared a strong central government and thought it would trample on people's rights.*

CHAPTER 5 Standards Review

Visual Summary

Use the visual summary below to help you review the main ideas of the chapter.

QUICK FACTS
The U.S. Constitution sets up a federal system of government, with powers divided between the federal government and state governments.
The powers of government are divided among three branches: the legislative, executive, and judicial branches.
A system of checks and balances prevents any one branch from becoming too powerful.
The Bill of Rights guarantees important rights and freedoms for American citizens.
Along with rights, citizens have duties: to obey laws, pay taxes, register for the draft, sit on juries, perform community service, and vote.
GOVERNMENT
CONSTITUTION
RIGHTS

Reviewing Vocabulary, Terms, and People

1. Who promised to add a bill of rights to the U.S. Constitution?
   a. Benjamin Franklin **c.** Alexander Hamilton
   b. Thomas Jefferson **d.** James Madison
2. What is the term for a person born in another country who becomes a citizen of the United States?
   a. immigrant **c.** naturalized citizen
   b. partial citizen **d.** separatist
3. What are powers granted to the states called?
   a. reserved powers **c.** stately powers
   b. concurrent powers **d.** delegated powers
4. What is the permission to look for evidence of a crime in a particular location called?
   a. petition **c.** indictment
   b. impeachment **d.** search warrant
5. What is the type of government that is run by officials elected by the people?
   a. direct democracy **c.** constitutional monarchy
   b. limited democracy **d.** representative democracy

Answers

Visual Summary

Review and Inquiry Have students examine the visual summary. Ask them why a tree is a good representation of the chapter content. *(A tree grows, as did our nation; it's strong; branches represent branches of government.)* Why is the tree trunk labeled Constitution? *(The Constitution forms the government's foundation, as a trunk forms the core of a tree.)*

Quick Facts Transparency: Citizenship and the Constitution Visual Summary

Reviewing Vocabulary, Terms, and People

1. d
2. c
3. a
4. d
5. d

Comprehension and Critical Thinking

6. **a.** legislative—make laws; executive—execute and administer laws; judicial—try cases and interpret the Constitution
   b. See the Quick Facts chart on p. 146.
   c. Answers will vary, but students should exhibit an understanding of the powers of each branch of government.

Review and Assessment Resources

Review and Reinforce

- **SE** Standards Review
- **CRF:** Chapter Review Activity
- California Standards Review Workbook
- Quick Facts Transparency: Citizenship and the Constitution Visual Summary
- Spanish Chapter Summaries Audio CD Program
- Online Chapter Summaries in Six Languages
- **OSP** Holt PuzzlePro; GameTool for ExamView
- Quiz Game CD-ROM

Assess

- **SE** Standards Assessment
- PASS: Chapter Test, Forms A and B
- Alternative Assessment Handbook
- **OSP** ExamView Test Generator, Chapter Test
- Universal Access Modified Worksheets and Tests CD-ROM: Chapter Test
- Holt Online Assessment Program (in the Premier Online Edition)

Reteach/Intervene

- Interactive Reader and Study Guide
- Universal Access Teacher Management System: Lesson Plans for Universal Access
- Universal Access Modified Worksheets and Tests CD-ROM
- Interactive Skills Tutor CD-ROM

go.hrw.com
Online Resources
Chapter Resources:
KEYWORD: SS8 US5

Answers

7. **a.** first 10 amendments to the Constitution; to protect citizens rights and freedoms against majority rule
   b. guarantees citizens' basic freedoms and prevents the government from taking certain actions such as quartering troops and using "unreasonable searches and seizures"; recognizes that states and citizens have all powers not delegated to the federal government or prohibited to the states
   c. Answers will vary, but students should exhibit an understanding of each amendment of the Bill of Rights.
8. **a.** born in United States or in a U.S. territory, at least one parent is a U.S. citizen, or become a naturalized citizen
   b. through voting, campaigning for candidates, political action committees, interest groups, writing letters to government representatives
   c. possible answer—The government would cease to function well, if at all, if citizens stopped performing duties such as voting and paying taxes.

Reading Skills

9. a

Reviewing Themes

10. possible answers—federalism, checks and balances, separation of powers, presidential powers, Bill of Rights
11. Answers will vary, but students should show an understanding that U.S. representative democracy requires that Americans vote intelligently, stay politically informed, and express their political opinions.

Social Studies Skills

12. d
13. possible answers—Yes, Americans continue to form and attend groups to sway political opinion and promote issues; no, intellectual and moral groups are not as fashionable or powerful now as they were in the 1830s.

Focus on Writing

14. **Rubric** Students' pamphlets should:
    - provide one page each on the Constitution, the Bill of Rights, and citizenship
    - have engaging titles
    - include a final summary of the importance of the Constitution and citizenship
    - use correct grammar, punctuation, spelling, and capitalization.

CRF: Focus on Writing: A Pamphlet

Comprehension and Critical Thinking

SECTION 1 *(Pages 144–148)* **HSS 8.2.6**

6. **a. Describe** Name each branch of government and explain the duties of each.
   b. Analyze What checks and balances exist between the branches of government?
   c. Evaluate Do you think the three branches of government share their power equally? Explain your answer.

SECTION 2 *(Pages 178–183)* **HSS 8.2.6, 8.3.7**

7. **a. Identify** What is the Bill of Rights, and why was it added to the Constitution?
   b. Analyze In what ways does the Bill of Rights protect individuals from the power of government?
   c. Elaborate Which of the amendments in the Bill of Rights do you think is the most important? Why?

SECTION 3 *(Pages 184–187)* **HSS 8.3.6**

8. **a. Describe** What are the ways in which a person can gain U.S. citizenship?
   b. Analyze How are citizens able to influence their government?
   c. Predict What might result if individuals failed to fulfill their duties as citizens?

Reading Skills

Understanding Summarizing *Use the Reading Skills taught in this chapter to answer the question about the reading selection below.*

> Freedom of speech does not mean that people can say anything they want to, however. The Constitution does not protect slander—false statements meant to damage someone's reputation. Libel, or intentionally writing a lie that harms another person, is not protected, either. *(p. 179)*

9. Which of the following is a good summary of the selection?
   a. Freedom of speech does not protect everything.
   b. Slander is a false statement meant to damage someone's reputation.

Reviewing Themes

10. **Politics** What important ideas has the U.S. Constitution contributed to government?
11. **Politics** Why is active political participation an important responsibility for people in the United States?

Social Studies Skills

Determining the Context of Statements *Use the Social Studies Skills taught in this chapter to answer the questions about the quotation below.*

> "What political power could ever carry on the vast multitude [large number] of lesser undertakings which the American citizens perform every day, with the assistance of the principle of association [joining a group]? Nothing, in my opinion, is more deserving of our attention than the intellectual and moral associations of America."
>
> —Alexis de Tocqueville, *Democracy in America*

12. De Tocqueville wrote this about his trip to the United States in 1831. What is his main idea?
    a. Governments can fill every need of citizens.
    b. American organizations cannot accomplish much.
    c. American organizations get too much attention.
    d. American organizations fill important needs of citizens that government cannot.
13. Do you think that de Tocqueville's statement accurately describes modern America? Why or why not?

FOCUS ON WRITING

14. **Creating a Pamphlet** You have gathered information about the Constitution, Bill of Rights, and citizenship. Use that information to create your pamphlet. On the first page, write a title and a phrase that will get your audience's attetion. On each of the following pages, you can use this format: (1) a heading and sentence at the top of the page identifying the topic of the page, and (2) the list of the most important points for that topic. Remember that page 2 is on the Constitution, page 3 is on the Bill of Rights, and page 4 is on citizenship.

Standards Assessment

DIRECTIONS: Read each question and write the letter of the best response.

1

> "What a president says and thinks is not worth five cents unless he has the people and Congress behind him. Without Congress, I'm just a six-feet-four Texan. With Congress, I'm President of the United States in the fullest sense."
>
> — President Lyndon Johnson

What point about government was President Johnson making in this remark?

- **A** The president should be directly elected by the people.
- **B** Congress should not have any ability to control the president.
- **C** The president needs the support of Congress to be effective.
- **D** Congress and the president should share some powers.

2 Which of the following rights is *not* protected in the Bill of Rights?

- **A** the right to bear arms
- **B** the right to public education
- **C** the right to jury trials
- **D** the right to free speech

3 The right of every American to be a member of a political party is an example of

- **A** the principle of dual sovereignty.
- **B** the First Amendment right to freedom of assembly.
- **C** the principle of majority rule.
- **D** the Fifth Amendment right to due process of law.

4 Which of the following is *not* a duty of citizenship?

- **A** becoming informed about important issues
- **B** volunteering to work with a community-service group
- **C** serving on a jury
- **D** speaking English

5 The right to freedom of the press would *not* protect a newspaper that

- **A** knowingly spread harmful lies about someone.
- **B** criticized an elected government official.
- **C** deliberately encouraged people to peacefully protest a law.
- **D** opposed the government in time of war.

Connecting with Past Learning

6 One of the principles built into the Constitution is that there should be checks on the power of government leaders. This idea is based on what earlier statement or document that you learned about in Grade 7?

- **A** Ninety-five Theses
- **B** Declaration of the Rights of Man
- **C** Four Noble Truths
- **D** Magna Carta

7 The legal rights and protections contained in the Bill of Rights are based on rights earlier granted to people in

- **A** France.
- **B** England.
- **C** China.
- **D** Japan.

Answers

1. C
Break Down the Question: This question requires students to interpret and summarize information. Remind students to interpret each phrase in turn and to look for key words and phrases that explain the meaning. Focus on the phrases, "unless he has the people behind him," and "With Congress, I'm President . . . in the fullest sense."

2. B
Break Down the Question: Remind students to watch for italicized words in questions that affect the meaning, such as *not* here. In questions like this, tell students to eliminate all the options that they know *are* in the Bill of Rights to narrow their choices.

3. B
Break Down the Question: This question requires students to make generalizations. Refer students who have trouble to the material in Section 2 titled "First Amendment."

4. B
Break Down the Question: This question requires students to evaluate information. See the note for Question 2 above.

5. A
Break Down the Question: This question requires students to recall factual information. See the note for Question 2 above.

6. D
Break Down the Question: This question connects to information covered in Grade 7.

7. B
Break Down the Question: This question connects to information covered in Grade 7.

Intervention Resources

Reproducible

- Interactive Reader and Study Guide
- Universal Access Teacher Management System: Lesson Plans for Universal Access

Technology

- Quick Facts Transparency: Citizenship and the Constitution Visual Summary
- Universal Access Modified Worksheets and Tests CD-ROM
- Interactive Skills Tutor CD-ROM

Tips for Test Taking

Negative Do Not Fit Tell students to watch for negative words in questions such as *never, unless, not,* and *except.* When a question contains one of these negative words, students should look for the answer that does not fit with the other answers. Have students practice this tip on Questions 2, 4, and 5 above.

Standards Review

Have students review the following standards in their workbooks.

- California Standards Review Workbook: HSS 8.2.3, 8.2.4, 8.2.5, 8.2.6, 8.3.6, 8.3.7

Chapter 6 Planning Guide

Launching the Nation

Chapter Overview	Reproducible Resources	Technology Resources
CHAPTER 6 **pp. 192–217** **Overview: In this chapter, students will learn how the nation's leaders organized their new government by paying off the national debt, dealing with foreign and domestic conflicts, and forming political parties.** See p. 192 for the California History–Social Science standards covered in this chapter.	**Universal Access Teacher Management System:*** • Universal Access Instructional Benchmarking Guides • Lesson Plans for Universal Access **Interactive Reader and Study Guide:*** Chapter Graphic Organizer **Chapter Resource File*** • Focus on Writing Activity: A Nobel Nomination • Social Studies Skills Activity: Making Group Decisions • Chapter Review Activity **Pre-AP Activities Guide for United States History:*** Identifying Main Ideas and Supporting Details	**One-Stop Planner CD-ROM:** Calendar Planner **Student Edition Full-Read Audio CD-ROM** **Universal Access Modified Worksheets and Tests CD-ROM** **Interactive Skills Tutor CD-ROM** **Primary Source Library CD-ROM for United States History** **Power Presentations with Video CD-ROM** **History's Impact: United States History Video Program (VHS/DVD):** Launching the Nation*
Section 1: **Washington Leads the New Nation** **The Big Idea:** President Washington and members of Congress established a new national government. 8.1	**Universal Access Teacher Management System:*** Section 1 Lesson Plan **Interactive Reader and Study Guide:*** Section 1 Summary **Chapter Resource File*** • Vocabulary Builder, Section 1 • Biography Activity: Alexander Hamilton • Biography Activity: Martha Washington • Literature Activity: "Rip Van Winkle"	**Daily Bellringer Transparency:** Section 1*
Section 2: **Hamilton and National Finances** **The Big Idea:** Treasury Secretary Alexander Hamilton developed a financial plan for the national government. 8.3.4	**Universal Access Teacher Management System:*** Section 2 Lesson Plan **Interactive Reader and Study Guide:*** Section 2 Summary **Chapter Resource File*** • Vocabulary Builder, Section 2 • Economics and History Activity: The National Debt • History and Geography Activity: The Nation's Capital • Interdisciplinary Projects: Planning the New Capital Drama Skit; Student Almanac • Primary Source Activity: Jefferson and Hamilton	**Daily Bellringer Transparency:** Section 2* **Quick Facts Transparency:** Hamilton's Economic Plan* go.hrw.com **Internet Activity:** Washington D.C.: Then and Now
Section 3: **Challenges for the New Nation** **The Big Idea:** The United States faced significant foreign and domestic challenges under Washington. 8.3.5, 8.4.2	**Universal Access Teacher Management System:*** Section 3 Lesson Plan **Interactive Reader and Study Guide:*** Section 3 Summary **Chapter Resource File*** • Vocabulary Builder, Section 3 • Primary Source Activity: President George Washington's Farewell Address **Political Cartoons Activities for United States History,** Cartoon 7: The French Revolution*	**Daily Bellringer Transparency:** Section 3* **Map Transparency:** Pinckney's Treaty* **Map Transparency:** Fighting in the Northwest Territory* go.hrw.com **Internet Activity:** French Revolution Chart
Section 4: **John Adams's Presidency** **The Big Idea:** The development of political parties in the United States contributed to differing ideas about the role of the federal government. 8.3.4	**Universal Access Teacher Management System:*** Section 4 Lesson Plan **Interactive Reader and Study Guide:*** Section 4 Summary **Chapter Resource File*** • Vocabulary Builder, Section 4 • Biography Activity: Abigail Adams	**Daily Bellringer Transparency:** Section 4* **Map Transparency:** The First Political Parties*

SE Student Edition  Print Resource Audio CD Video

TE Teacher's Edition Transparency CD-ROM DVD

go.hrw.com CA Standards Mastery LS Learning Styles

OSP One-Stop Planner CD-ROM * also on One-Stop Planner CD

Review, Assessment, Intervention

- **Standards Review Workbook***
- **Quick Facts Transparency:** Launching the Nation Visual Summary*
- **Spanish Chapter Summaries Audio CD Program**
- **Online Chapter Summaries in Six Languages**
- **Quiz Game CD-ROM**
- **Progress Assessment Support System (PASS):** Chapter Test*
- **Universal Access Modified Worksheets and Tests CD-ROM:** Modified Chapter Test
- **One-Stop Planner CD-ROM:** ExamView Test Generator (English/Spanish)

- **PASS:** Section 1 Quiz*
- **Online Quiz:** Section 1
- **Alternative Assessment Handbook**

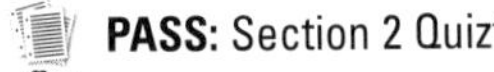

- **PASS:** Section 2 Quiz*
- **Online Quiz:** Section 2
- **Alternative Assessment Handbook**

- **PASS:** Section 3 Quiz*
- **Online Quiz:** Section 3
- **Alternative Assessment Handbook**

- **PASS:** Section 4 Quiz*
- **Online Quiz:** Section 4
- **Alternative Assessment Handbook**

California Resources for Standards Mastery

INSTRUCTIONAL PLANNING AND SUPPORT

- **Universal Access Teacher Management System***
- **One-Stop Planner CD-ROM with Test Generator: Teacher Management System with Interactive Teacher's Edition**

STANDARDS MASTERY

- **Standards Review Workbook***
- **At Home: A Guide to Standards Mastery for United States History**

Holt Online Learning

To enhance learning, Internet activities are available for Washington D.C.: Then and Now and a French Revolution Chart.

KEYWORD: SS8 TEACHER

- **Teacher Support Page**
- **Content Updates**
- **Rubrics and Writing Models**
- **Teaching Tips for the Multimedia Classroom**

KEYWORD: SS8 US6

- **Current Events**
- **Document-Based Questions**
- **Holt Grapher**
- **Holt Online Atlas**
- **Holt Researcher**
- **Interactive Multimedia Activities**
- **Internet Activities**
- **Online Chapter Summaries in Six Languages**
- **Online Section Quizzes**
- **American History Maps and Charts**

HOLT PREMIER ONLINE STUDENT EDITION

Complete online support for interactivity, assessment, and reporting

- **Interactive Maps and Notebook**
- **Standardized Test Prep**
- **Homework Practice and Research Activities Online**

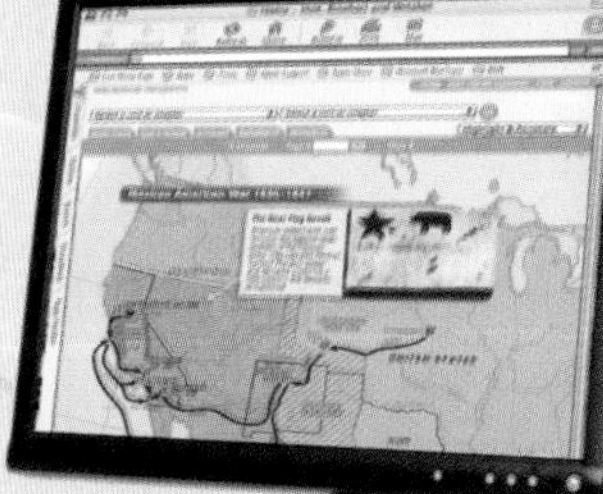

Mastering the Standards: Differentiating Instruction

Reaching Standards	Basic-level activities designed for all students encountering new material
Standards Proficiency	Intermediate-level activities designed for average students
Exceeding Standards	Challenging activities designed for honors and gifted-and-talented students
Standard English Mastery	Activities designed to improve standard English usage

Frequently Asked Questions

INSTRUCTIONAL PLANNING AND SUPPORT

Where do I find planning aids, pacing guides, lesson plans, and other teaching aids?

Annotated Teacher's Edition:
- Chapter planning guides
- Standards-based instruction and strategies
- Differentiated instruction for universal access
- Point-of-use reminders for integrating program resources

Power Presentations with Video CD-ROM

Universal Access Teacher Management System:
- Year and unit instructional benchmarking guides
- Reproducible lesson plans
- Assessment guides for diagnostic, progress, and summative end-of-the-year tests
- Options for differentiating instruction and intervention
- Teaching guides and answer keys for student workbooks

One-Stop Planner CD-ROM with Test Generator: Teacher Management System with Interactive Teacher's Editon:
- Calendar Planner
- Editable lesson plans
- All reproducible ancillaries in Adobe Acrobat (PDF) format
- ExamView Test Generator (English & Spanish)
- Game Tool for ExamView
- PuzzlePro
- Transparency and video previews

DIFFERENTIATING INSTRUCTION FOR UNIVERSAL ACCESS

What resources are available to ensure that Advanced Learners/GATE Students master the standards?

Teacher's Edition Activities:
- Résumé for Washington Activity, p. 197
- Presidential Farewell Address, p. 210
- XYZ Records Activity, p. 213

Lesson Plans for Universal Access

Pre-AP Activities Guide for United States History: Identifying Main Ideas and Supporting Details

Primary Source Library CD-ROM for United States History

What resources are available to ensure that English Learners and Standard English Learners master the standards?

Teacher's Edition Activities:
- Time Line Activity, p. 208

Lesson Plans for Universal Access

Chapter Resource File: Vocabulary Builder Activities

Spanish Chapter Summaries Audio CD Program

Online Chapter Summaries in Six Languages

One-Stop Planner CD-ROM:
- PuzzlePro, Spanish Version
- ExamView Test Generator, Spanish Version

What modified materials are available for Special Education?

The ***Universal Access Modified Worksheets and Tests CD-ROM*** provides editable versions of the following:

Vocabulary Flash Cards

Modified Vocabulary Builder Activities

Modified Chapter Review Activity

Modified Chapter Test

HOLT History's Impact
▶ video series
Launching the Nation

What resources are available to ensure that Learners Having Difficulty master the standards?

Teacher's Edition Activities:
- Hamilton's Economic Plan Activity, p. 201
- Domestic Conflicts Activity, p. 209

Interactive Reader and Study Guide
Student Edition Full-Read Audio CD
Quick Facts Transparency: Launching the Nation Visual Summary
Standards Review Workbook
Social Studies Skills Activity: Making Group Decisions
Interactive Skills Tutor CD-ROM

How do I intervene for students struggling to master the standards?

Interactive Reader and Study Guide
Quick Facts Transparency: Launching the Nation Visual Summary
Standards Review Workbook
Social Studies Skills Activity: Making Group Decisions
Interactive Skills Tutor CD-ROM

PROFESSIONAL DEVELOPMENT

What teacher training resources are available to help me grow professionally?

- In-service and staff development as part of your Holt Social Studies product purchase
- Quick Teacher Tutorial Lesson Presentation CD-ROM
- Intensive tuition-based Teacher Development Institute
- *Teaching American History* Online 2 Module Professional Development Course
- Convenient Holt Speaker Bureau face-to-face workshop options
- PRAXIS™ Test Prep (#0089) interactive Web-based content refreshers*
- 24/7 *Ask A Professional Development Expert* at http://www.hrw.com/prodev/

* PRAXIS is a trademark of Educational Testing Service (ETS). This publication is not endorsed or approved by ETS.

Information Literacy Skills

To learn more about how History–Social Science instruction may be improved by the effective use of library media centers and information literacy skills, go to the Teacher's Resource Materials for Chapter 6 at **go.hrw.com**, keyword: SS8 MEDIA.

The following materials were developed by the Division for Public Education of the American Bar Association. These materials are part of the **Democracy and Civic Education** supplement.

- Constitution Study Guide
- Supreme Court Case Studies

Chapter Preview

Standards Focus

Standards by Section
Section 1: HSS 8.1
Section 2: HSS 8.3.4
Section 3: HSS 8.3.5, 8.4.2
Section 4: HSS 8.3.4

Teacher's Edition
HSS **Analysis Skills:** CS 1, CS 2, CS 3, HR 1, HR 4, HR 5, HI 1, HI 2, HI 3
ELA Writing 2.4.a

Preview Grade 8 Standards
HSS **8.5** Students analyze U.S. foreign policy in the early Republic.
8.5.3 Outline the major treaties with American Indian nations during the administrations of the first four presidents and the varying outcomes of those treaties.
8.12 Students analyze the transformation of the American economy and the changing social and political conditions in the United States in response to the Industrial Revolution.
8.12.1 Trace patterns of agricultural and industrial development as they relate to climate, use of natural resources, markets, and trade and locate such development on a map.
8.12.3 Explain how states and the federal government encouraged business expansion through tariffs, banking, land grants, and subsidies.

Focus on Writing
The **Chapter Resource File** provides a Focus on Writing worksheet to help students write their Nobel nomination.

CRF: Focus on Writing Activity: A Nobel Nomination

CHAPTER 6 1789–1800

Launching the Nation

California Standards

History–Social Science
8.1 Students understand the major events preceding the founding of the nation and relate their significance to the development of American constitutional democracy.

8.3 Students understand the foundation of the American political system and the ways in which citizens participate in it.

8.4 Students analyze the aspirations and ideals of the people of the new nation.

8.5 Students analyze U.S. foreign policy in the early republic.

English–Language Arts
Writing 2.4.a Write persuasive compositions that provide details, reasons, and examples.

FOCUS ON WRITING
A Nobel Nomination Every year a few people are nominated for a Nobel Prize for their work to improve the world. In this chapter you will read about four great Americans—Washington, Hamilton, Jefferson, and Adams. Then you'll choose one of these great leaders and write a Nobel Prize nomination for him.

UNITED STATES
1789 George Washington becomes the first president.
1785
1789 The French Revolution begins.
WORLD

Introduce the Chapter

Standards Proficiency

Organizing the New Government HSS 8.3, 8.4; HSS **Analysis Skills:** HI 1

1. Remind students that the U.S. Constitution created a new system of government for the United States. However, the work was not yet done. The nation's leaders still needed to establish and organize this new government.
2. Write the following question for students to see: *What might your first actions be as part of the nation's new government?* Give students a few minutes to predict some of the new government's first actions. Write students' predictions for the class to see.
3. Then ask students what they think some of the challenges facing the nation's new government might be. Make a list of students' predictions.
4. Tell students to determine the accuracy of their predictions as they read the chapter. LS **Verbal/Linguistic**

Alternative Assessment Handbook, Rubric 11: Discussions

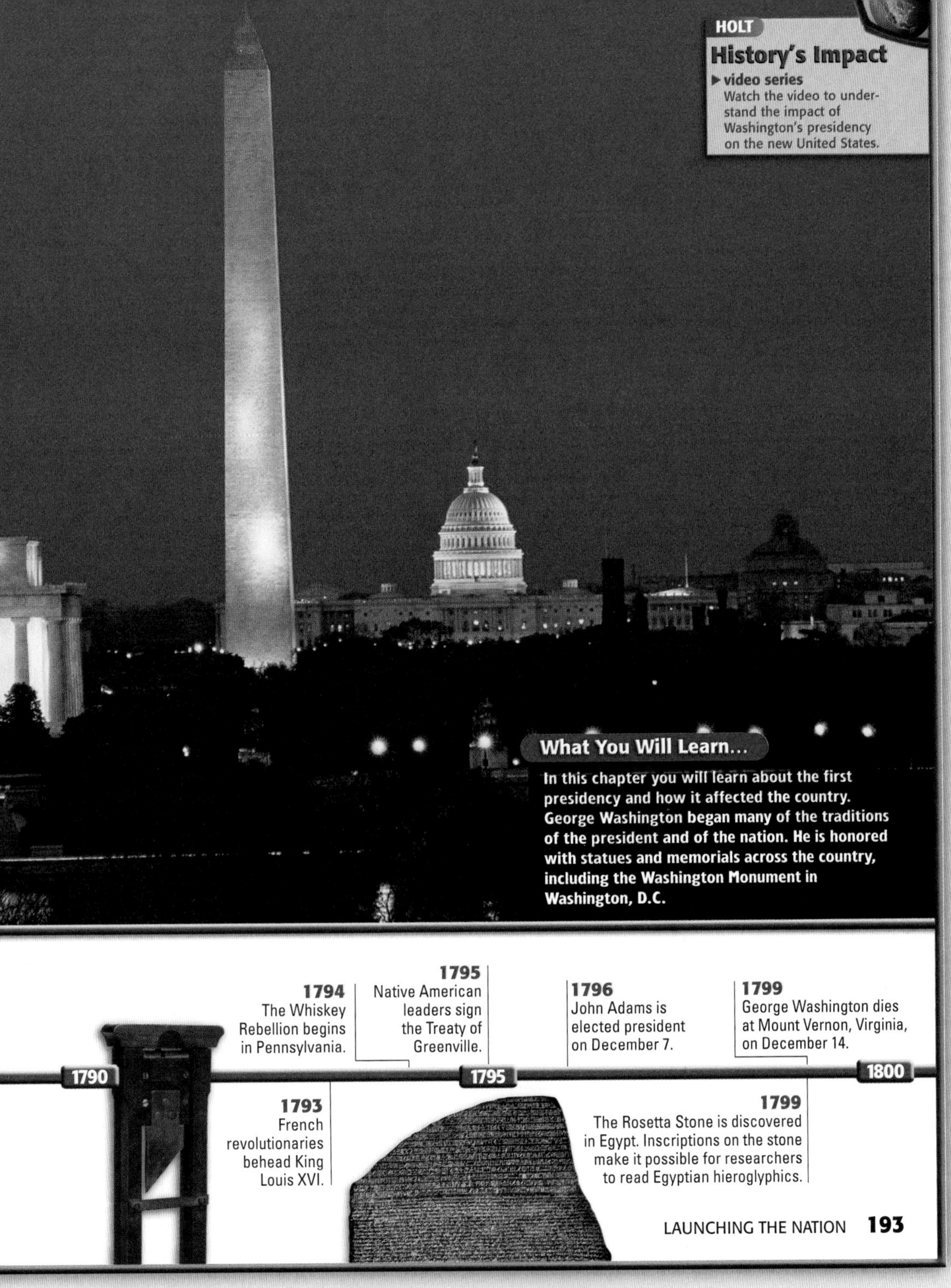

HOLT
History's Impact
▶ video series
Watch the video to understand the impact of Washington's presidency on the new United States.
What You Will Learn...
In this chapter you will learn about the first presidency and how it affected the country. George Washington began many of the traditions of the president and of the nation. He is honored with statues and memorials across the country, including the Washington Monument in Washington, D.C.
1790
1794 The Whiskey Rebellion begins in Pennsylvania.
1795 Native American leaders sign the Treaty of Greenville.
1795
1796 John Adams is elected president on December 7.
1799 George Washington dies at Mount Vernon, Virginia, on December 14.
1800
1793 French revolutionaries behead King Louis XVI.
1799 The Rosetta Stone is discovered in Egypt. Inscriptions on the stone make it possible for researchers to read Egyptian hieroglyphics.
LAUNCHING THE NATION 193

Explore the Time Line

1. When did Washington become the first U.S. president? *1789*
2. What other event began that same year? *French Revolution*
3. What did Native American leaders sign in 1795? *Treaty of Greenville*
4. Who was elected as the second president of the United States in 1796? *John Adams*

HSS Analysis Skills: CS 1

Connect to the Arts and Humanities

The Nation's Capital During Washington's presidency, the nation's capital was moved to a site along the Potomac River. This site became the city of Washington, D.C. French engineer Pierre Charles L'Enfant designed the layout of the new capital. L'Enfant envisioned a city with fountains, gardens, and public parks and a system of boulevards radiating out from the city center. Today, Washington, D.C. is a cultural center as well as the seat of the nation's government.

Chapter Preview

HOLT

History's Impact

▶ **video series**
See the Video Teacher's Guide for strategies for using the chapter video **Launching the Nation.**

Chapter Big Ideas

Section 1 President Washington and members of Congress established a new national government. **HSS** 8.1

Section 2 Treasury secretary Alexander Hamilton developed a financial plan for the national government. **HSS** 8.3.4

Section 3 The United States faced significant foreign and domestic challenges under Washington. **HSS** 8.3.5, 8.4.2

Section 4 The development of political parties in the United States contributed to differing ideas about the role of the federal government. **HSS** 8.3.4

Explore the Picture

The Washington Monument Of the many statues and monuments dedicated to George Washington, the Washington Monument is perhaps the most famous. The monument was designed by architect Robert Mills, who also designed the U.S. Treasury Building and the Patent Office. Construction began in 1848, but was halted for various reasons in the mid-1850s. Building finally resumed in 1880, and the monument was officially opened to the public in 1888. Built of granite covered with marble, the monument rises more than 555 feet and is topped by an aluminum pyramid. It remains the world's tallest masonry structure.

Analyzing Visuals The Washington Monument symbolizes Washington and his leadership. What adjectives might describe the monument? *possible answers—impressive, towering, influential, powerful, dignified, elegant*

go.hrw.com
Online Resources

Chapter Resources:
KEYWORD: SS8 US6
Teacher Resources:
KEYWORD: SS8 TEACHER

Reading Social Studies

Understanding Themes

Introduce students to the two main themes of this chapter—politics and economics—by asking students to make a list of different items that might need to be addressed by the new government created by the U.S. Constitution. Remind students that the previous government was weak at the national level. Point out to students that although the Constitution formed the new government, many political and economic decisions still had to be made by the new government.

Inferences about History

Focus on Reading Have students write two inferences about daily life, current events in the news, or pop culture. Tell them to make one of the inferences an educated guess and the other one a weak guess. After several minutes, have students hand in their inferences. Read several inferences aloud and allow students to guess which inferences are based on an educated guess and which are not. Discuss with the class what makes a good inference, noting the importance of reliable facts and sound judgment.

Reading Social Studies

by Kylene Beers

Economics | Geography | Politics | Religion | Society and Culture | Science and Technology

Focus on Themes This chapter, titled "Launching a Nation," describes how the early leaders established this nation's **political** and **economic** systems. You will read about Washington's presidency, Hamilton's plan for financial security for the nation, the establishment of two parties to elect the president, and Jefferson's struggles with both Washington and Hamilton. Throughout the chapter, you will see that disagreement often defined these early days.

Inferences about History

Focus on Reading What's the difference between a good guess and a weak guess? A good guess is an *educated* guess. In other words, the guess is based on some knowledge or information. That's what an **inference** is, an educated guess.

Making Inferences About What You Read To make an inference, combine information from your reading with what you already know, and make an educated guess about what it all means. Once you have made several inferences, you may be able to draw a conclusion that ties them all together.

Question What kind of person was Alexander Hamilton?

Inside the Text
- Hamilton ran a company when he was just a teenager.
- He had a career as a lawyer.
- He became the Secretary of the Treasury under Washington.

Outside the Text
- Running a company takes intelligence and cleverness.
- Becoming a lawyer takes dedication.
- Washington probably wanted someone clever and capable.

Inference Alexander Hamilton was an intelligent, clever, and dedicated man.

Steps for Making Inferences
1. Ask a question.
2. Note information "Inside the Text."
3. Note information "Outside the Text."
4. **Use both sets of information to make an educated guess, or inference.**

Additional reading support can be found in the Interactive Reader and Study Guide

Reading and Skills Resources

Reading Support
- Interactive Reader and Study Guide
- Student Edition on Audio CD
- Spanish Chapter Summaries Audio CD Program

Social Studies Skills Support
- Interactive Skills Tutor CD-ROM

Vocabulary Support
- **CRF:** Vocabulary Builder Activities
- **CRF:** Chapter Review Activity
- Universal Access Modified Worksheets and Tests CD-ROM:
  - Vocabulary Flash Cards
  - Vocabulary Builder Activity
  - Chapter Review Activity
- OSP Holt PuzzlePro

Standards Focus

ELA Reading 8.2.0

ELA **Reading 8.2.0** Read and understand grade-level-appropriate material.

You Try It!

Read the following passage and answer the questions that follow.

Economic Differences

From Chapter 6, p. 202–203

Hamilton wanted new forms of economic growth. He wanted to promote manufacturing and business. He even suggested that the government award a prize to companies that made excellent products.

In addition, Hamilton wanted to pass higher tariffs. Known as protective tariffs, these taxes would raise the prices of foreign products. Hamilton hoped this would cause Americans to buy U.S. goods. As a result, American manufacturing would be protected from foreign competition.

Jefferson worried about depending too much on business and manufacturing. He believed that farmers were the most independent voters . . . Jefferson wanted to help farmers by keeping the costs of the goods they bought low. Lower tariffs would help keep prices low.

After you read the passage, answer the following questions.

1. Which two questions can be answered directly from the text above and which one requires that you make an inference?
   - **a.** Who wanted higher tariffs, Hamilton or Jefferson?
   - **b.** Why do you think Hamilton and Jefferson had different views on the importance of manufacturing?
   - **c.** Which man wanted to help the farmers?
2. To answer question b, it might help to know that Hamilton lived in New York City and Jefferson was from the more rural area of Virginia. Use that information and information in the passage to explain why one man valued manufacturing more than the other.

Key Terms and People

Chapter 6

Section 1
electoral college *(p. 196)*
Martha Washington *(p. 196)*
precedent *(p. 197)*
Judiciary Act of 1789 *(p. 198)*

Section 2
Alexander Hamilton *(p. 200)*
national debt *(p. 200)*
bonds *(p. 201)*
speculators *(p. 201)*
Thomas Jefferson *(p. 201)*
loose construction *(p. 204)*
strict construction *(p. 204)*
Bank of the United States *(p. 204)*

Section 3
French Revolution *(p. 205)*
Neutrality Proclamation *(p. 206)*
privateers *(p. 206)*
Jay's Treaty *(p. 207)*
Pinckney's Treaty *(p. 207)*
Little Turtle *(p. 208)*
Battle of Fallen Timbers *(p. 209)*
Treaty of Greenville *(p. 209)*
Whiskey Rebellion *(p. 209)*

Section 4
political parties *(p. 212)*
Federalist Party *(p. 212)*
Democratic-Republican Party *(p. 212)*
XYZ affair *(p. 214)*
Alien and Sedition Acts *(p. 215)*
Kentucky and Virginia Resolutions *(p. 215)*

Academic Vocabulary

In this chapter, you will learn the following academic words:

agreement *(p. 199)*
neutral *(p. 206)*

As you read Chapter 6, remember that you need to combine what you already know with the information in the chapter to make inferences.

Reading Social Studies

Key Terms and People

Introduce the key terms and people for this chapter by having students define or describe each term or person. Then have students write a paragraph in which they use at least seven key terms or people. Remind students to use each term correctly. **LS Verbal/Linguistic**

Focus on Reading

See the **Focus on Reading** questions in this chapter for more practice on this reading social studies skill.

Reading Social Studies Assessment

See the **Standards Review** at the end of this chapter for student assessment questions related to this reading skill.

Teaching Tip

To help students learn how to make inferences, have students create a T-chart. Ask students to label one column of the chart *Inside the Text,* and the other column *Outside the Text.* Then have students pay attention to the details in the passage above to complete the first column, and use their own outside knowledge on the subject to complete the second column. Students should then use the information in each column to make an inference.

Answers

You Try It! 1. *answered directly—a and c; inference—b;* **2.** *Because Hamilton was from an urban area that relied on manufacturing, he supported laws that favored manufacturing. Jefferson on the other hand did not feel strongly about manufacturing because he was from a region that relied economically on farming.*

Preteach

Bellringer

If YOU were there . . . Use the **Daily Bellringer Transparency** to help students answer the question.

 Daily Bellringer Transparency, Section 1

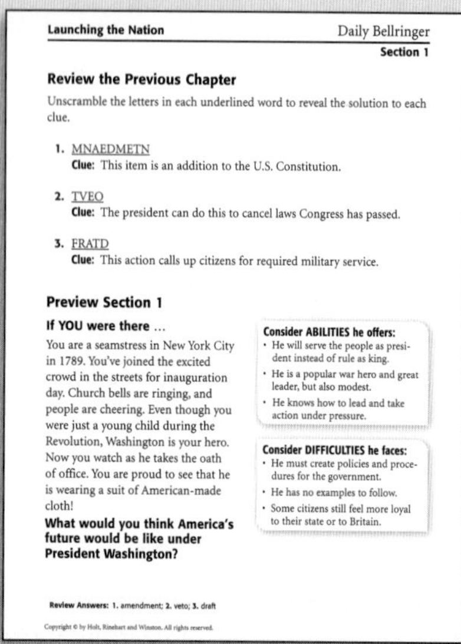

Launching the Nation Daily Bellringer

Section 1

Review the Previous Chapter

Unscramble the letters in each underlined word to reveal the solution to each clue.

1. MNAEDMETN
   Clue: This item is an addition to the U.S. Constitution.
2. TVEO
   Clue: The president can do this to cancel laws Congress has passed.
3. FRATD
   Clue: This action calls up citizens for required military service.

Preview Section 1

If YOU were there ...

You are a seamstress in New York City in 1789. You've joined the excited crowd in the streets for inauguration day. Church bells are ringing, and people are cheering. Even though you were just a young child during the Revolution, Washington is your hero. Now you watch as he takes the oath of office. You are proud to see that he is wearing a suit of American-made cloth!

What would you think America's future would be like under President Washington?

Consider ABILITIES he offers:
- He will serve the people as president instead of rule as king.
- He is a popular war hero and great leader, but also modest.
- He knows how to lead and take action under pressure.

Consider DIFFICULTIES he faces:
- He must create policies and procedures for the government.
- He has no examples to follow.
- Some citizens still feel more loyal to their state or to Britain.

Review Answers: 1. amendment; 2. veto; 3. draft

Academic Vocabulary

Review with students the high-use academic term in this section.

agreement a decision reached by two or more people or groups (p. 199)

CRF: Vocabulary Builder Activity, Section 1

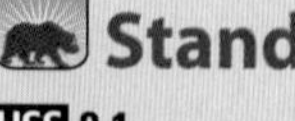

Standards Focus

HSS 8.1

Means: Students understand the significance of the major events of George Washington's presidency.

Matters: The national government established several practices during Washington's presidency that continue to shape government today.

SECTION 1

Washington Leads a New Nation

What You Will Learn...

Main Ideas

1. In 1789 George Washington became the first president of the United States.
2. Congress and the president organized the executive and judicial branches of government.
3. Americans had high expectations of their new government.

The Big Idea

President Washington and members of Congress established a new national government.

Key Terms and People

George Washington, *p. 196*
electoral college, *p. 196*
Martha Washington, *p. 196*
precedent, *p. 197*
Judiciary Act of 1789, *p. 198*

HSS 8.1 Students understand the major events preceding the founding of the nation and relate their significance to the development of American constitutional democracy.

If YOU were there...

You are a seamstress in New York City in 1789. You've joined the excited crowd in the streets for inauguration day. Church bells are ringing, and people are cheering. Even though you were just a young child during the Revolution, Washington is your hero. Now you watch as he takes the oath of office. You are proud to see that he is wearing a suit of American-made cloth.

What would you think America's future would be like under President Washington?

BUILDING BACKGROUND George Washington was more than just a popular war hero. People naturally looked to him as a national leader. He had taken part in the Continental Congresses and in creating the Constitution. He helped establish and strengthen the new national government.

The First President

Americans believed in **George Washington**. They saw him as an honest leader and a hero of the Revolution. Many believed he should be the first U.S. president. Washington had been looking forward to retirement and a quiet life on his Virginia farm. When he hesitated at becoming a candidate for the presidency, his friends convinced him to run. Fellow politician Gouverneur Morris told him, "Should the idea prevail [win] that you would not accept the presidency, it should prove fatal . . . to the new government." Morris concluded confidently, "Of all men, you are the best fitted to fill that office."

In January 1789 each of the 11 states that had passed the Constitution sent electors to choose the first president. These delegates formed a group called the **electoral college**—a body of electors who represent the people's vote in choosing the president. The electoral college selected Washington unanimously, and John Adams became his vice president.

Washington's wife, First Lady **Martha Washington**, entertained guests and attended social events with her husband. She described the

Teach the Big Idea: Master the Standards

Standards Proficiency

Washington Leads a New Nation

HSS 8.1; HSS **Analysis Skills:** HI 1

Materials: blank note cards

1. **Teach** Ask students the Main Idea questions to teach this section.
2. **Apply** Give each student three note cards. Have students write one of the section's blue heads on each card. On the back of the first two cards, have students record the actions that Washington and Congress took and the precedents they set to organize the national government. On the back of the third card, have students record Americans' expectations for the new government. LS **Verbal/Linguistic**
3. **Review** As you review, have students share the information on their note cards.
4. **Practice/Homework** Have each student take on the role of an American in 1790, and write a journal entry describing his or her emotions about Washington's election.

Alternative Assessment Handbook, Rubrics 1: Acquiring Information; and 15: Journals scene to her niece: "I have not had one half-hour to myself since the day of my arrival." She ran the presidential household with style.

Other women, such as author Judith Sargent Murray, believed that women needed to play a greater role in the new nation than Martha Washington did. Murray, Abigail Adams, and others believed in Republican Motherhood, the idea that women played an important role in teaching their children to be good citizens.

Some promoters of Republican Motherhood did not expect women to participate in politics or business. Other people, however, hoped that Republican Motherhood would lead to greater opportunities for women. They hoped more women would receive an education. Only a few families were willing to provide much education for their daughters, and adult women rarely had the time or money to get an education later in life. Most women in the early republic faced long days managing their households and working hard inside or outside the home to support their families.

READING CHECK **Analyzing** Why was Washington selected to be president?

Organizing the Government

Hard work also lay ahead for members of the new government. The new federal government had to create policies and procedures that would determine the future of the country. As President Washington noted in a letter to James Madison, "The first of everything in our situation will serve to establish a precedent." A **precedent** is an action or decision that later serves as an example.

Congress created departments in the executive branch for different areas of national policy. Washington met with the department heads, or cabinet members, who advised him. For two of his most important cabinet positions, Washington chose carefully. He picked Alexander Hamilton as secretary of the treasury and Thomas Jefferson as secretary of state. Henry Knox served as secretary of war, and Samuel Osgood was chosen as postmaster general. Hamilton was a gifted economic planner, and Jefferson had served as ambassador to France. Knox had helped Washington run the Continental Army, and Osgood had government experience.

❶ Henry Knox, secretary of war
❷ Thomas Jefferson, secretary of state
❸ Edmund Randolph, attorney general
❹ Alexander Hamilton, secretary of the treasury
❺ George Washington, president

The First Cabinet

Washington's cabinet members kept him informed on political matters and debated important issues with one another. Each of the men chosen had experience that made him a wise choice to advise the nation's first president. By 1792 cabinet meetings were a common practice.

ANALYSIS SKILL **ANALYZING VISUALS**

How do you think a modern cabinet meeting might look different from the one shown here?

Direct Teach

Main Idea

❶ The First President

In 1789 George Washington became the first president of the United States.

Describe By what process was George Washington elected president? *The 11 states that had passed the Constitution selected electors, who unanimously voted for Washington.*

Analyze How might the idea of Republican Motherhood have influenced women in the new nation? *possible answer—encouraged them to take a greater interest in politics, education, and social concerns*

CRF: Biography Activity: Martha Washington

HSS 8.1; **HSS** **Analysis Skills:** HI 1

Main Idea

❷ Organizing the Government

Congress and the president organized the executive and judicial branches of government.

Describe How did cabinet members and the president interact? *Cabinet members advised the president.*

Make Inferences Why do you think Washington chose Jefferson and Hamilton for important cabinet positions? *They were experienced government leaders and had participated in the Constitutional Convention.*

CRF: Biography Activity: Alexander Hamilton

HSS 8.4.4; **HSS** **Analysis Skills:** HI 1

Differentiating Instruction for Universal Access

Advanced Learners/GATE **Exceeding Standards**

Materials: photocopies of a model résumé

1. Tell students that a résumé is a record of a person's qualifications and experience, which a person submits to apply for a job. Instruct students to create a résumé for George Washington as if he were applying for the job of U.S. president.
2. Provide students with photocopies of a proper résumé to use as a model.
3. Students' résumés should provide information about Washington's leadership experience and communicate why he would be good for the job of president.
4. Conclude by discussing with the class why Americans elected Washington as their first president. **LS** **Verbal/Linguistic**

Alternative Assessment Handbook, Rubric 31: Résumés

HSS 8.1; **HSS** **Analysis Skills:** HI 1

Answers

Analyzing Visuals *possible answers—Style of dress, setting, and equipment would be more modern; Secret Service would be present.*

Reading Check *Americans saw him as an honest leader and a hero of the Revolution, and many believed he should be the first president.*

Direct Teach

Main Idea

2 Organizing the Government

Congress and the president organized the executive and judicial branches of government.

Explain What was the purpose of the Judiciary Act of 1789? *set up three levels of federal courts and defined their powers and relationships to the state courts*

Summarize How were federal judges selected? *The president nominated them, and Congress either approved or rejected candidates.*

HSS 8.1; HSS **Analysis Skills:** HI 1

Info to Know

A Rough Start When George Washington became president, there was no White House to live in. Instead, the president and First Lady Martha Washington lived in a house on 3 Cherry Street in New York City. Although nicknamed the Palace, the house was not tremendously glamorous. For example, the ceilings were so low that one woman's hat caught fire when she brushed against the chandelier.

Today we know that presidents have cabinet meetings with their top advisers. This practice started during Washington's presidency and were common by 1792.

To set up the federal court system and the courts' location, Congress passed the **Judiciary Act of 1789**. This act created three levels of federal courts and defined their powers and relationship to the state courts. It set up federal district courts and circuit courts of appeals. The president nominated candidates for federal judgeships. Those candidates then had to be approved or rejected by the Senate. Washington wrote about the importance of these duties:

> "I have always been persuaded that the stability and success of the national government ... would depend in a considerable degree on the interpretation and execution of its laws. In my opinion, therefore, it is important that the judiciary system should not only be independent in its operations, but as perfect as possible in its formation."
>
> —George Washington, quoted in *The Real George Washington*, edited by Parry et al.

The basic parts of the federal government were now in place. Leaders began to face the challenges of the new nation. Hard work lay ahead.

READING CHECK **Finding Main Ideas** What two important precedents were established for the federal government?

Americans' Expectations of Government

Most Americans had high expectations for their government. They wanted improved trade, free from too many restrictions. But they also expected the government to protect them and to keep the economy stable. However, the idea of belonging to one united nation was new to them.

In 1790 the United States was home to almost 4 million people. Most Americans lived in the countryside and worked on farms. Farmers wanted fair tax laws and the right to settle western lands. They did not want the government to interfere with their daily lives.

Other Americans worked in towns as craftspeople, laborers, or merchants. These people looked to the government to help their businesses. Most merchants wanted simpler trade laws established. Manufacturers wanted laws to protect them from foreign competitors.

Critical Thinking: Identifying Points of View

Standards Proficiency

Letters to President Washington

HSS 8.1; HSS **Analysis Skills:** HR 5, HI 1

1. Have students discuss the expectations that Americans had for their new national government. Remind students of the problems that Americans had been facing under the Articles of Confederation.
2. Divide the class in half. Assign one half the role of American farmers in 1790. Assign the other half the role of merchants or manufacturers in New York City in 1790.
3. Have each student write a letter to President Washington from the point of view of his or her assigned role. In their letters, students should congratulate Washington on his election and share their hopes and concerns for the new national government.
4. Ask for volunteers to read their letters aloud. Conclude by having students compare and contrast America in 1790 with America today. **LS Verbal/Linguistic**

Alternative Assessment Handbook, Rubric 41: Writing to Express

Answers

Reading Check *established executive departments and cabinet; established the federal court system by passing the Judiciary Act of 1789*

Some Americans lived in growing cities like New York, shown above. However, the new republic was overwhelmingly rural. Most Americans lived and worked on farms.

Why might rural Americans and urban Americans want different things from their new government?

Most cities were small. Only New York City and Philadelphia had populations larger than 25,000. New York City was the first capital of the United States, and it represented the spirit of the new nation. Although badly damaged during the Revolution, the city had already begun to recover. Citizens got rid of many signs of British rule.

New York City had a bustling economy. International trade and business became more active. A French visitor to New York City noted the city's energy.

> "Everything in the city is in motion; everywhere the shops resound [ring out] with the noise of workers . . . one sees vessels arriving from every part of the world."
>
> —A French visitor to New York, quoted in *New York in the American Revolution* by Wilbur Abbott

Academic Vocabulary

agreement a decision reached by two or more people or groups

In 1792 some 24 stockbrokers signed an **agreement** under a buttonwood tree on Wall Street. This agreement was the foundation for what later became the New York Stock Exchange. It cemented Wall Street's image as the economic hub of the United States.

The Impact Today

Today the New York Stock Exchange is the largest market for securities, or stocks, in the world.

By 1790 the city's population had topped 33,000 and was growing rapidly. To many officials, this vibrant city reflected the potential future of the new nation. It was thus a fitting place for the capital.

Reading Check **Analyzing** Why was New York City chosen as the first capital of the United States?

Summary and Preview Americans, led by President George Washington, set up their new government. In the next section you will read about Alexander Hamilton's economic plan.

Section 1 Assessment

go.hrw.com **Online Quiz** KEYWORD: SS8 HP6

Reviewing Ideas, Terms, and People HSS 8.1

1. a. **Describe** What role did the electoral college play in **George Washington's** election to the presidency?
   b. **Summarize** What were some of **Martha Washington's** duties as First Lady?
2. a. **Describe** What **precedent** did President Washington and Congress establish regarding the executive branch?
   b. **Explain** What was the purpose of the **Judiciary Act of 1789**?
   c. **Evaluate** What do you think was the most important element of the Judiciary Act of 1789? Why?
3. a. **Recall** What city served as the first capital of the United States? Why?
   b. **Draw Conclusions** What expectations did most Americans have of their government?

Critical Thinking

4. **Generalizing** Copy the graphic organizer below. Use it to identify the expectations that farmers and merchants had of the new U.S. government.

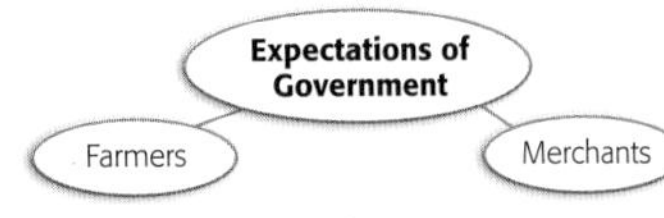

Focus on Writing

5. **Thinking about Washington's Contributions** In this section you learned some things about George Washington as president. Jot down one or two things you could use to support his nomination for a Nobel Prize.

Direct Teach

Main Idea

3 Americans' Expectations of Government

Americans had high expectations of their new government.

Identify What did farmers want from the new national government? *fair tax laws; the right to settle western lands; no interference from the government*

Summarize What was daily life like in early national America? *Most people lived in rural areas and farmed; some lived and worked in towns; most cities were small, but the nation did have a few large cities, such as New York City.*

HSS 8.1; HSS **Analysis Skills:** HI 1

Review & Assess

Close

Have students discuss if they would have liked to have been the first U.S. president.

Review

Online Quiz Section 1

Assess

SE Section 1 Assessment

PASS: Section 1 Quiz

Alternative Assessment Handbook

Reteach/Classroom Intervention

California Standards Review Workbook

Interactive Reader and Study Guide, Section 1

Interactive Skills Tutor CD-ROM

Section 1 Assessment Answers

1. **a.** represented the people's vote; voted to elect George Washington as the first president
   b. entertained guests, attended social events with her husband, ran presidential household
2. **a.** created executive departments, the heads of which served as a cabinet to the president
   b. created three levels of federal courts, defined their powers and relationships to state courts
   c. possible answers—creation of courts of appeals, because Americans could appeal rulings; creation of federal district courts, because provided justice across the country
3. **a.** New York City; was one of the largest U.S. cities and a center of economic activity
   b. wanted improved trade free from too many restrictions, protection, and a stable economy
4. Farmers—fair tax laws, right to settle western lands, no government interference; Merchants—help with their businesses, simple trade laws, protection from foreign competition
5. possible answers—first U.S. president; set many precedents, established practice of cabinet meetings

Answers

A Rural Nation *They had different interests. To farmers, land was important; to business owners, laws to help their businesses grow were important.*

Reading Check *It was one of the largest cities; it was a center of economic activity.*

Preteach

Bellringer

If YOU were there . . . Use the **Daily Bellringer Transparency** to help students answer the question.

Daily Bellringer Transparency, Section 2

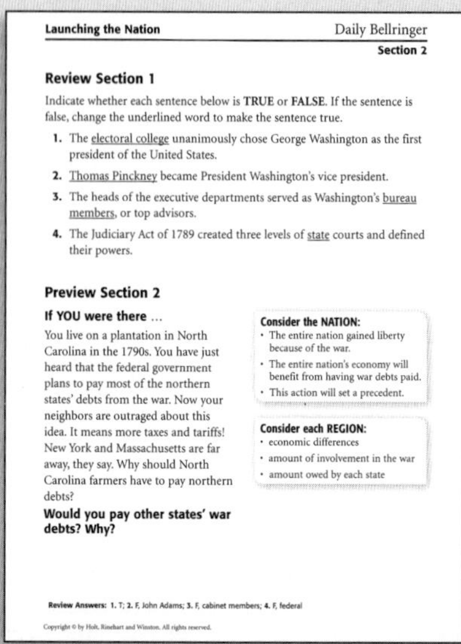

Launching the Nation — Daily Bellringer

Section 2

Review Section 1

Indicate whether each sentence below is **TRUE** or **FALSE**. If the sentence is false, change the underlined word to make the sentence true.

1. The electoral college unanimously chose George Washington as the first president of the United States.
2. Thomas Pinckney became President Washington's vice president.
3. The heads of the executive departments served as Washington's bureau members, or top advisors.
4. The Judiciary Act of 1789 created three levels of state courts and defined their powers.

Preview Section 2

If YOU were there ...

You live on a plantation in North Carolina in the 1790s. You have just heard that the federal government plans to pay most of the northern states' debts from the war. Now your neighbors are outraged about this idea. It means more taxes and tariffs! New York and Massachusetts are far away, they say. Why should North Carolina farmers have to pay northern debts?

Would you pay other states' war debts? Why?

Consider the NATION:
- The entire nation gained liberty because of the war.
- The entire nation's economy will benefit from having war debts paid.
- This action will set a precedent.

Consider each REGION:
- economic differences
- amount of involvement in the war
- amount owed by each state

Review Answers: 1. T; 2. F, John Adams; 3. F, cabinet members; 4. F, federal

Building Vocabulary

Preteach or review the following terms:

mint a place to make coins (p. 203)

monopoly sole or exclusive control (p. 203)

tariff an extra charge on goods (p. 203)

CRF: Vocabulary Builder Activity, Section 2

Standards Focus

HSS 8.3.4

Means: Understand how the political views of Thomas Jefferson and Alexander Hamilton differed and how these differences led to the development of two political parties.

Matters: Politics in the United States remains divided between two main political parties.

SECTION 2

Hamilton and National Finances

What You Will Learn...

Main Ideas

1. Hamilton tackled the problem of settling national and state debt.
2. Thomas Jefferson opposed Hamilton's views on government and the economy.
3. Hamilton created a national bank to strengthen the U.S. economy.

The Big Idea

Treasury secretary Alexander Hamilton developed a financial plan for the national government.

Key Terms and People

Alexander Hamilton, *p. 200*
national debt, *p. 200*
bonds, *p. 200*
speculators, *p. 201*
Thomas Jefferson, *p. 201*
loose construction, *p. 204*
strict construction, *p. 204*
Bank of the United States, *p. 204*

HSS 8.3.4 Understand how the conflicts between Thomas Jefferson and Alexander Hamilton resulted in the emergence of two political parties (e.g., view of foreign policy, Alien and Sedition Acts, economic policy, National Bank, funding and assumption of the Revolutionary debt).

If YOU were there...

You live on a plantation in North Carolina in the 1790s. You have just heard that the federal government plans to pay most of the northern states' debts from the war. Now your neighbors are outraged about this idea. It means more taxes and tariffs! New York and Massachusetts are far away, they say. Why should North Carolina farmers have to pay northern debts?

Would you pay other states' war debts? Why?

BUILDING BACKGROUND Some of the new nation's biggest problems were economic. The national and state governments had run up huge debts during the war. But the proposed solutions to these problems revealed differences in regional viewpoints. Southern planters and northern businesspeople had very different views of how the national economy should develop.

Settling the Debt

Alexander Hamilton seemed born with a head for economics. While still in his teens, he helped run a shipping company in his native British West Indies. Family friends then sent him to the American colonies for an education. Hamilton eventually married into a wealthy New York family and began practicing law. He served as Washington's aide and as a delegate to four Continental Congresses.

National Debt

As secretary of the treasury, Hamilton's biggest challenge was paying off the **national debt**—money owed by the United States—from the Revolutionary War. The United States owed about $11.7 million to foreign countries and about $40.4 million to U.S. citizens. During the war the government raised money with bonds. **Bonds** are certificates of debt that carry a promise to buy back the bonds at a higher price. But the government could not afford to keep this promise. Bondholders who needed money sold

Teach the Big Idea: Master the Standards

Standards Proficiency

Hamilton and National Finances

HSS 8.3.4; HSS Analysis Skills: CS 1, HR 1, HR 5, HI 1

1. **Teach** Ask students the Main Idea questions to teach this section.
2. **Apply** Have students, working either individually or in pairs, use the blue and red headings in this section to create an outline of the information. Tell students to write at least two supporting details under each heading. Encourage students to write their supporting details in sentence form. **LS Verbal/Linguistic**
3. **Review** Have students share information from their outlines with the class. Create a master outline for the class to see and use it to correct any student errors.
4. **Practice/Homework** Have each student use the information in his or her outline to create a five-question quiz about the section content. **LS Verbal/Linguistic**

Alternative Assessment Handbook, Rubric 37: Writing Assignments

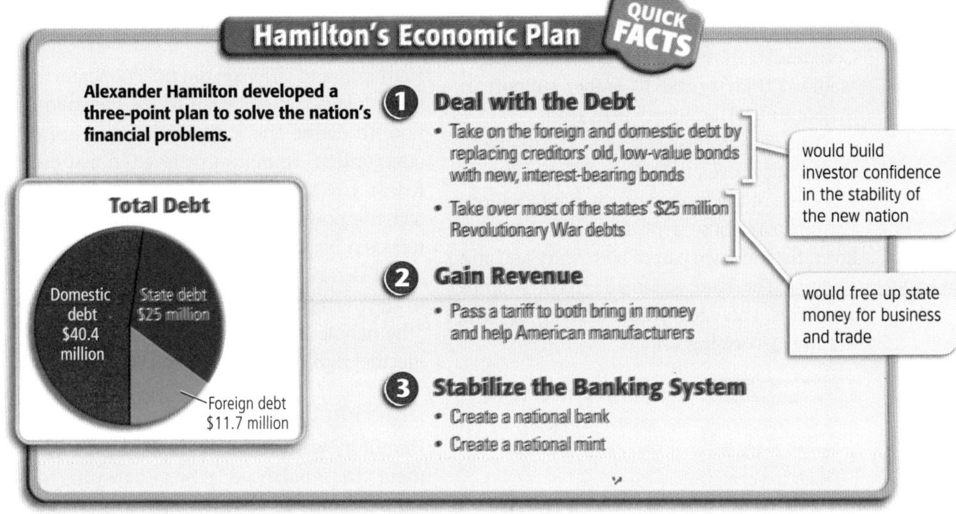

their bonds for less than the original value to **speculators**, or people who buy items at low prices in the hope that the value will rise and they can sell the items for a profit.

Hamilton's Economic Plan
QUICK FACTS
Alexander Hamilton developed a three-point plan to solve the nation's financial problems.
Total Debt
Domestic debt $40.4 million
State debt $25 million
Foreign debt $11.7 million
1 Deal with the Debt
• Take on the foreign and domestic debt by replacing creditors' old, low-value bonds with new, interest-bearing bonds
• Take over most of the states' $25 million Revolutionary War debts
would build investor confidence in the stability of the new nation
would free up state money for business and trade
2 Gain Revenue
• Pass a tariff to both bring in money and help American manufacturers
3 Stabilize the Banking System
• Create a national bank
• Create a national mint

Hamilton wanted to pay the foreign debt immediately and gradually repay the total value of all bonds. The second part of his plan caused disagreements because paying full value would allow speculators to make a profit. Hamilton thought this was fair. He said, "He [the speculator] paid what the commodity [bond] was worth . . . and took the risks."

Thomas Jefferson disagreed. He thought the idea cheated bondholders who had sold their bonds at low prices. Jefferson wrote, "Immense sums were thus filched [stolen] from the poor and ignorant." But more politicians agreed with Hamilton. In 1790 the government exchanged old bonds for new, more reliable ones that were guaranteed.

States' Debts

The states owed $25 million for Revolutionary War expenses. Hamilton wanted the federal government to pay for $21.5 million of this debt. Hamilton believed that this action would help the federal government. He thought that paying the states' debts would help the national economy. Debtor states would not have to spend so much on repayment and would have money to develop business and trade. Increased business and trade would put more money back into the national economy.

The South, however, did not want to help the federal government pay the debts of other states. States such as Virginia and North Carolina did not have many war debts. They thought Hamilton's idea was unfair. Patrick Henry said he did not believe that the Constitution gave Congress the power to pay state debts. Hamilton knew that he needed the help of southern representatives to get his plan approved.

Moving the Capital

Hamilton also knew that he had something to bargain with. Southern officials wanted to change the location of the nation's capital. Many southerners thought that having the capital in New York gave the northern states too much influence over national policy. Hamilton, Jefferson, and James Madison met in June 1790. Hamilton

Direct Teach

Main Idea

1 Settling the Debt

Hamilton tackled the problem of settling national and state debt.

Explain What economic problem did the young nation face, and how did Alexander Hamilton propose to solve it? *high national debt; pay the foreign debt immediately; gradually pay back the full value of bonds*

Identify Points of View Why did Jefferson oppose paying the full value of bonds? *would reward speculators and cheat the original bondholders who sold at low prices*

Make Judgments Do you think Hamilton's plan for the federal government to take over state war debts was fair to southern states? *possible answers—yes, all the states benefited from the Revolutionary War and should help pay for it; no, southern states had few war debts and should not pay.*

- **CRF:** Economics and History Activity: The National Debt
- **CRF:** History and Geography Activity: The Nation's Capital
- **CRF:** Interdisciplinary Projects: Planning the Nation's Capital Drama Skit; Student Almanac
- Quick Facts Transparency: Hamilton's Economic Plan
- **HSS** 8.3.4; **HSS Analysis Skills:** HR 5, HI 1

Info to Know

The Confusing National Debt When he accepted the position of treasury secretary, Alexander Hamilton faced a large and confusing national debt with several different creditors. The debt included IOUs written by the quartermaster, the officer in charge of army supplies; winning tickets from lotteries that the government had held to raise money and could not repay; and certificates that soldiers had received when the government had been unable to pay them for their military service. It was Hamilton's task to sort through this paperwork in an attempt to reduce the national debt.

Differentiating Instruction for Universal Access

Learners Having Difficulty

Reaching Standards

1. Have students examine the above Quick Facts: Hamilton's Economic Plan. Go over the various elements of Hamilton's economic plan as a class.
2. To help students better understand the nation's economic problems and Hamilton's financial plan, compare them to aspects of an individual's personal finances, such as credit card debt, IOUs, balancing a checkbook, checking and savings accounts, and so on.
3. Have students go through the Quick Facts chart and explain Hamilton's economic plan in their own words point by point.
LS Verbal/Linguistic, Visual/Spatial

- **HSS** 8.3.4; **HSS Analysis Skills:** CS 3, HI 1
- Alternative Assessment Handbook, Rubric 11: Discussions
- **CRF:** Economics and History Activity: The National Debt
- Quick Facts Transparency: Hamilton's Economic Plan

Direct Teach

Main Idea

❷ Jefferson Opposes Hamilton

Thomas Jefferson opposed Hamilton's views on government and the economy.

Recall What did Hamilton think a strong central government should do? *balance power between the masses and the wealthy*

Contrast How did Jefferson's and Hamilton's views on how to promote economic growth differ? *Hamilton—promote manufacturing and business and pass higher tariffs; Jefferson—promote agriculture and keep tariffs low*

Develop Defend either Hamilton's or Jefferson's view of democracy. *Answers should reflect an understanding of each point of view.*

CRF: Primary Source Activity: Jefferson and Hamilton Disagree about Government

HSS 8.3.4; HSS **Analysis Skills:** HI 1

Info to Know

Sectional Tensions The debate over Hamilton's economic plans revealed tensions between northern and southern states. Most speculators lived in the North. In the South, Virginians in particular hated Hamilton's programs. Virginia senator George Mason expressed his dismay, saying that Hamilton has "done us more injury than Great Britain."

go.hrw.com
Online Resources
KEYWORD: SS8 US6
ACTIVITY: Washington D.C.: Then and Now

Answers

Biography *He was free, highly educated, and had a paying job.*

Reading Check *Southerners thought the plan was unfair because southern states had few war debts; Hamilton agreed to get the national capital moved farther south.*

promised to convince northern members of Congress to move the capital. Jefferson and Madison then agreed to gather support in the South for Hamilton's debt plan.

The compromise worked. The national capital was moved to Philadelphia in 1791 for 10 years. For the capital's permanent location, Washington chose a place on the Potomac River that included part of both Maryland and Virginia. The land was made up of swamps and farms. This site would eventually become the city of Washington, D.C.

THE IMPACT TODAY Washington, D.C., and the surrounding areas are home to more than 7 million people today. The city is not only the nation's capital but also a major tourist attraction.

READING CHECK **Identifying Points of View** How did southerners feel about the federal government paying state war debts, and how did Hamilton change their minds?

BIOGRAPHY

Benjamin Banneker (1731–1806)

Benjamin Banneker was born to a free African American family in rural Maryland. He attended a Quaker school but was largely self-educated. He was a skilled mathematician and scientist. His mathematical skills prompted Thomas Jefferson to give him a job surveying the land for the new national capital.

Draw Conclusions How was Benjamin Banneker's life different from most African Americans' of the time?

Jefferson Opposes Hamilton

Hamilton and Jefferson did not cooperate for long. Instead, they began to disagree about how to define the authority of the central government. Hamilton believed in a strong federal government. Jefferson wanted to protect the powers of the states. Their conflict reflected basic differences in their opinions about democracy. Hamilton had little faith in the average individual. He once said that "the people . . . seldom judge or determine [decide] right."

Differing Views

Hamilton wanted a strong central government that balanced power between the "mass of the people" and wealthier citizens. He believed that his approach would protect everyone's liberties while keeping the people from having too much power.

Jefferson disagreed strongly with Hamilton's views of the average citizen's ability to make decisions for the country. He admitted that "the people can not be all, and always, well informed." However, Jefferson believed that it was the right of the people to rule the country.

Economic Differences

Hamilton and Jefferson also fought over how the country's economy should grow. Hamilton wanted new forms of economic growth. He wanted to promote manufacturing and business. He even suggested that the

U.S. Capitol in Washington, D.C.

Critical Thinking: Contrasting

Standards Proficiency

Hamilton vs. Jefferson

HSS 8.3.4; HSS **Analysis Skills:** HR 5, HI 1

1. Lead students in a discussion contrasting Hamilton's and Jefferson's views.
2. Copy the graphic organizer for students to see. Omit the blue answers. Have each student copy the organizer and complete it by listing Hamilton's arguments for and Jefferson's arguments against Hamilton's economic plan. **LS Verbal/Linguistic, Visual/Spatial**

Alternative Assessment Handbook, Rubric 13: Graphic Organizers

Hamilton	Jefferson
pay full value of bonds	
• *builds investor confidence; speculators took the risks, so fair*	• *rewards speculators; cheats bondholders who sold bonds at low prices*
pass higher tariffs	
• *protects American manufacturing from foreign competition*	• *hurts farmers by raising costs of imports*
create a national bank	
• *"necessary and proper"; gives central government a place to deposit money*	• *elastic clause refers to necessity, not convenience*

Primary Source

POINT OF VIEW

Role of a Citizen

Alexander Hamilton thought that the average citizen had no interest in public affairs.

"We must take man as we find him, and if we expect him to serve the public, [we] must interest his passions in doing so. A reliance on pure patriotism has been the source of many of our errors."

—**Alexander Hamilton,** quoted in *Odd Destiny: The Life of Alexander Hamilton* by Marie B. Hecht

Thomas Jefferson believed that each citizen could work to better society.

"It is my principle that the will of the Majority should always prevail [win] . . . Above all things I hope the education of the common people will be attended to; [I am] convinced that on their good sense we may rely with the most security for the preservation of a due degree of liberty."

—**Thomas Jefferson,** from *Thomas Jefferson: A Biography in His Own Words*

ANALYSIS SKILL **ANALYZING POINTS OF VIEW**

How did the views of Hamilton and Jefferson differ?

government award a prize to companies that made excellent products.

In addition, Hamilton wanted to pass higher tariffs. Known as protective tariffs, these taxes would raise the prices of foreign products. Hamilton hoped this would cause Americans to buy U.S. goods. As a result, American manufacturing would be protected from foreign competition.

Jefferson worried about depending too much on business and manufacturing. He believed that farmers were the most independent voters. They did not depend on other people's work to make a living.

Jefferson wrote, "Our governments will remain virtuous [pure] for many centuries; as long as they are chiefly agricultural." Jefferson wanted to help farmers by keeping the costs of the goods they bought low. Lower tariffs would help keep prices low.

READING CHECK **Summarizing** What were the main differences between Hamilton and Jefferson concerning the power of the nation's government?

National Debate

Hamilton's and Jefferson's differences became more and more public in early 1791. The two men had very different opinions about how the government should approach its economic problems.

Hamilton's Plan for a National Bank

Hamilton wanted to start a national bank where the government could safely deposit its money. The bank would also make loans to the government and businesses. Hamilton also thought that the United States should build a national mint, a place to make coins. Then the country could begin issuing its own money.

THE IMPACT TODAY The U.S. Mint was established in 1792 and now produces between 11 billion and 20 billion coins each year.

Hamilton knew that people who wanted to protect states' rights might have a strong reaction to the idea of a national bank, so he suggested limiting it to a 20-year charter. After that time Congress could decide whether to extend the charter. Hamilton also asked each state to start its own bank so the national bank would not have a monopoly.

Direct Teach

Main Idea

❸ National Debate

Hamilton created a national bank to strengthen the U.S. economy.

Identify What was the function of the Bank of the United States? *to provide a safe place for the federal government's money; to make loans to the government and businesses; to stabilize the economy*

Summarize How did Hamilton's plan for a national bank address states' rights? *proposed limiting the bank's charter to 20 years; encouraged states to start their own banks to prevent a monopoly*

Evaluate Do you agree with loose construction or strict construction of the Constitution? *Answers will vary but should reflect an understanding of each term.*

HSS 8.3.4; HSS **Analysis Skills:** HR 5, HI 1

Connect to Economics

Tariffs Nations usually establish tariffs for two reasons—to provide a source of income for the government and to promote the development of domestic industries by raising the price of imports. Economic planners hope that making foreign goods more expensive will lead people to buy goods made in their own country.

Cooperative Learning

Standards **Proficiency**

Strict and Loose Construction

HSS 8.3.4; HSS **Analysis Skills:** HR 5, HI 1

1. Write the definitions of loose construction and strict construction for students to see. Ask students if they can think of examples of loose and strict construction at the school or in their community.
2. Organize the class into pairs. Have one partner from each pair create a brief description of his or her interpretation of loose construction. Have the other partner create a description of his or her interpretation of strict construction.
3. Then have each pair write one to two paragraphs explaining how loose and strict construction affected debates over Hamilton's financial plan. LS **Interpersonal, Verbal/Linguistic**

Alternative Assessment Handbook, Rubrics 9: Comparing and Contrasting; and 37: Writing Assignments

Answers

Analyzing Points of View *Hamilton thought the average citizen was not interested in public affairs; Jefferson thought that educated citizens would act to preserve liberty.*

Reading Check *Hamilton—wanted a strong central government; did not trust the judgment of the masses; Jefferson—wanted to protect the power of the states; believed in the average citizen's ability to make good decisions for the nation*

Direct Teach

Linking to Today

The Federal Reserve The Federal Reserve, commonly called the "Fed," serves as the nation's central bank today. The national government created the Federal Reserve system in 1913 to stabilize the nation's monetary and banking systems. The Fed supervises member banks, holds cash reserves, and moves money into or out of circulation. The Fed is organized into two levels—national and district. At the national level, a 7-member Board of Governors makes the key decisions. At the district level, 12 Federal Reserve banks serve different regions of the nation.

Review & Assess

Close

Have students discuss Hamilton's and Jefferson's differing views of democracy. Which view do students think most Americans hold today?

Review

Online Quiz, Section 2

Assess

SE Section 2 Assessment

PASS: Section 2 Quiz

Alternative Assessment Handbook

Reteach/Classroom Intervention

California Standards Review Workbook

Interactive Reader and Study Guide, Section 2

Interactive Skills Tutor CD-ROM

Answer

Reading Check *They thought a national bank would strengthen and stabilize the nation's economy.*

Jefferson's Opposes the Bank

Both Jefferson and Madison believed that Hamilton's plans for the economy gave too much power to the federal government. They also thought the U.S. Constitution did not give Congress the power to create a bank. But Hamilton quoted the elastic clause, which states that Congress can "make all laws which shall be necessary and proper" to govern the nation.

Hamilton declared that the clause allowed the government to create a national bank. Hamilton believed in loose construction of the Constitution. **Loose construction** means that the federal government can take reasonable actions that the Constitution does not specifically forbid.

Jefferson thought that the elastic clause should be used only in special cases. He wrote to President Washington, "The Constitution allows only the means which are 'necessary,' not those which are merely 'convenient.'" Jefferson believed in strict construction of the Constitution. People who favor **strict construction** think that the federal government should do only what the Constitution specifically says it can do.

President Washington and Congress agreed with Hamilton. They hoped a bank would offer stability for the U.S. economy. In February 1791 Congress enacted the charter for the **Bank of the United States**—the country's first national bank. The bank played an important role in making the U.S. economy more stable.

READING CHECK **Drawing Conclusions** Why did Congress and the president agree to create a national bank?

SUMMARY AND PREVIEW Washington and Hamilton developed plans for paying the national debt. In the next section you will read about the U.S. neutrality policy.

Section 2 Assessment

go.hrw.com Online Quiz KEYWORD: SS8 HP6

Reviewing Ideas, Terms, and People HSS 8.3.4

1. a. **Describe** What economic problems did the new government face?
   b. **Summarize** What compromise did **Alexander Hamilton, Thomas Jefferson**, and James Madison reach regarding repayment of state debts?
2. a. **Identify** What disagreement did Jefferson and Hamilton have over the central government?
   b. **Draw Conclusions** Hamilton was a New Yorker, while Jefferson was from Virginia. How do you think that affected their views on the economy?
   c. **Elaborate** Do you agree with Hamilton or Jefferson regarding the average citizen's ability to make decisions for the country? Explain your answer.
3. a. **Recall** Why did Jefferson oppose the creation of the **Bank of the United States**?
   b. **Contrast** What is the difference between **loose construction** and **strict construction** of the Constitution?
   c. **Elaborate** Defend Alexander Hamilton's stance in favor of the creation of a national bank.

Critical Thinking

4. **Contrasting** Copy the chart below. Use it to contrast the ideas of Hamilton and Jefferson on the topics listed.

	Hamilton	Jefferson
Bonds		
Democracy		
Economy		
Tariffs		
National Bank		
Constitution		

FOCUS ON WRITING

5. **Gathering Information about Hamilton and Jefferson** Both Hamilton and Jefferson were strong leaders who helped shape the government of the young United States. What could you say about either of them to support a nomination for a Nobel Prize?

Section 2 Assessment Answers

1. a. high national debt from Revolutionary War
   b. support for Hamilton's plan for state debts in exchange for national capital farther south
2. a. Jefferson—protect states' powers; Hamilton—strong central government
   b. Hamilton favored manufacturing and trade, more common in the North; Jefferson favored farming, important to the southern economy.
   c. Answers should reflect an understanding of each man's viewpoint.
3. a. thought it gave the federal government too much power and that it was unconstitutional
   b. loose—federal government can take necessary actions not prohibited; strict—can do only what Constitution says
   c. possible answers—safe place to deposit federal money; will stabilize the economy
4. Hamilton—full value; strong central government; manufacturing and business; higher tariffs; for; loose construction; Jefferson—full price cheats bondholders; right of the people to rule; farming; lower tariffs; against; strict construction
5. possible answer—served in Cabinet positions

Challenges for the New Nation

SECTION 3

If YOU were there...

You are the captain of an American merchant ship in the 1790s. Your ship has just picked up cargo in the French West Indies. You are headed back to your home port of Philadelphia. Suddenly, a British warship pulls alongside your ship. Marines swarm aboard. They order you into the nearest harbor and seize your goods.

How would this incident affect your views of Great Britain?

BUILDING BACKGROUND As the new nation tried to get organized, it faced economic problems and internal divisions. Even more difficult challenges came from conflicts in Europe. The United States could not avoid being caught up in fighting between France and Great Britain.

Remaining Neutral

Tensions between France and Britain began to build after the French people rebelled against their king. On July 14, 1789, citizens of Paris attacked and captured the Bastille, a hated fortress and prison that stood as a mighty symbol of royal power.

The storming of the Bastille was one of the first acts of the **French Revolution** —a rebellion of French people against their king in 1789. The French people overthrew their king and created a republican government.

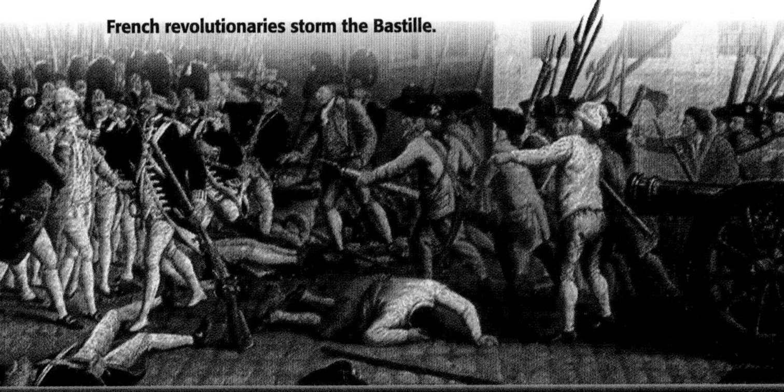
French revolutionaries storm the Bastille.

What You Will Learn...

Main Ideas

1. The United States tried to remain neutral regarding events in Europe.
2. The United States and Native Americans came into conflict in the Northwest Territory.
3. The Whiskey Rebellion tested Washington's administration.
4. In his Farewell Address, Washington advised the nation.

The Big Idea

The United States faced significant foreign and domestic challenges under Washington.

Key Terms and People

French Revolution, *p. 205*
Neutrality Proclamation, *p. 206*
privateers, *p. 206*
Jay's Treaty, *p. 207*
Pinckney's Treaty, *p. 207*
Little Turtle, *p. 208*
Battle of Fallen Timbers, *p. 209*
Treaty of Greenville, *p. 209*
Whiskey Rebellion, *p. 209*

HSS 8.3.5 Know the significance of domestic resistance movements and ways in which the central government responded to such movements (e.g., Shays's Rebellion, the Whiskey Rebellion).

8.4.2 Explain the policy significance of famous speeches (e.g., Washington's Farewell Address, Jefferson's 1801 Inaugural Address, John Q. Adams's Fourth of July 1821 Address).

Preteach

Bellringer

If YOU were there . . . Use the **Daily Bellringer Transparency** to help students answer the question.

Daily Bellringer Transparency, Section 3

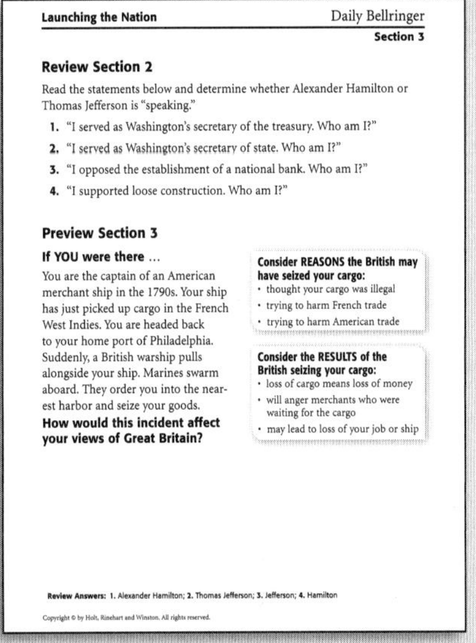
Launching the Nation — Daily Bellringer
Section 3

Review Section 2

Read the statements below and determine whether Alexander Hamilton or Thomas Jefferson is "speaking."

1. "I served as Washington's secretary of the treasury. Who am I?"
2. "I served as Washington's secretary of state. Who am I?"
3. "I opposed the establishment of a national bank. Who am I?"
4. "I supported loose construction. Who am I?"

Preview Section 3

If YOU were there ...

You are the captain of an American merchant ship in the 1790s. Your ship has just picked up cargo in the French West Indies. You are headed back to your home port of Philadelphia. Suddenly, a British warship pulls alongside your ship. Marines swarm aboard. They order you into the nearest harbor and seize your goods.

How would this incident affect your views of Great Britain?

Consider REASONS the British may have seized your cargo:
- thought your cargo was illegal
- trying to harm French trade
- trying to harm American trade

Consider the RESULTS of the British seizing your cargo:
- loss of cargo means loss of money
- will anger merchants who were waiting for the cargo
- may lead to loss of your job or ship

Review Answers: **1.** Alexander Hamilton; **2.** Thomas Jefferson; **3.** Jefferson; **4.** Hamilton

Academic Vocabulary

Review with students the high-use academic term in this section.

neutral unbiased, not favoring either side in a conflict (p. 206)

CRF: Vocabulary Builder Activity, Section 3

Teach the Big Idea: Master the Standards

Standards Proficiency

Challenges for the New Nation

HSS 8.3.5, 8.4.2; HSS **Analysis Skills:** CS 1, HI 1

1. **Teach** Ask students the Main Idea questions to teach this section.
2. **Apply** Create a three-column chart for students to see. Title the chart *Washington's Presidency* and label the columns *Foreign Relations, Domestic Conflicts,* and *Farewell Address*. Have students copy the chart and complete it by identifying and describing the main events and/or issues in each category. **LS Verbal/Linguistic, Visual/Spatial**
3. **Review** As you review the section, have students share the information in their charts.
4. **Practice/Homework** Have each student create a menu for a new restaurant celebrating Washington's presidency. Students should choose names for the restaurant and dishes that reflect the major events in his presidency. **LS Verbal/Linguistic**

Alternative Assessment Handbook, Rubrics 7: Charts; and 37: Writing Assignments

Standards Focus

HSS 8.3.5

Means: Describe the causes of the Whiskey Rebellion and explain how the government responded to the rebellion.

Matters: The Whiskey Rebellion proved the authority of the federal government to pass taxes and to put down domestic rebellions.

HSS 8.4.2

Means: Describe the key points of Washington's Farewell Address and explain its significance in American history.

Matters: Washington's Farewell Address had a major influence on U.S. politics and foreign relations.

Direct Teach

Main Idea

1 Remaining Neutral

The United States tried to remain neutral regarding events in Europe.

Recall What significant American event helped inspire the French Revolution? *American Revolution*

Identify Cause and Effect How did Washington respond to conflicts between France and Great Britain? *issued the Neutrality Proclamation, stating that the United States would not take sides in European conflicts*

Elaborate How did Edmond Genet and American privateers threaten U.S. neutrality? *Their actions could have led Great Britain to attack the United States and draw it into war.*

Political Cartoons Activities for United States History, Cartoon 7: The French Revolution

HSS 8.4.1, 8.5.2; HSS **Analysis Skills:** CS 1, HI 1, HI 2

World Events

American Influence In August 1789, French revolutionaries issued the Declaration of the Rights of Man and of the Citizen, a document modeled after the Declaration of Independence. The Marquis de Lafayette—a Frenchman who had fought in the Revolutionary War alongside Washington—helped write this document. Lafayette sent the key to the Bastille to President Washington, saying, "It is a tribute which I owe to you, as a son to my adoptive father, as an aide-de-camp to my General, as a Missionary of Liberty to its Patriarch."

go.hrw.com
Online Resources
KEYWORD: SS8 US6
ACTIVITY: French Revolution Chart

Answers

Focus on Reading *The French revolted against their monarchy and put in place a republican government based on democratic principles.*

FOCUS ON READING
What can you tell about France before 1793 using this paragraph and what you already know about democracies?

Many French citizens had been inspired to take action by the American Revolution. Many Americans, in turn, supported the French Revolution. They thought that France was creating the same kind of democracy as the United States.

Some Americans worried about the French Revolution's violent riots and attacks on traditional authority. Revolutionaries shocked many Americans by beheading King Louis XVI in January 1793 and Queen Marie-Antoinette later that year.

A few years after the French Revolution started, France and Great Britain went to war. Some Americans supported the French, while others backed the British. Some wanted to remain **neutral**.

ACADEMIC VOCABULARY
neutral unbiased, not favoring either side in a conflict

The Neutrality Proclamation

The debate divided Congress and Washington's cabinet. Washington presented his opinion to Congress on April 22, 1793:

> "The duty and interest of the United States require that they should with sincerity and good faith adopt and pursue a conduct friendly and impartial [unbiased] towards the belligerent [fighting] powers."
>
> —George Washington, quoted in *The Real George Washington* by Parry et al.

This **Neutrality Proclamation** stated that the United States would not take sides with any European countries that were at war. Washington believed his plan was the safest for the long run, but not everyone agreed.

Some members of Congress criticized Washington's ideas. James Madison believed that the president had gone beyond his authority. He questioned Washington's right to issue the proclamation without the approval of Congress.

The French Question

France's new representative to the United States, Edmond Genet (zhuh-NAY), asked American sailors to help France fight England by commanding **privateers**. Privateers were private ships hired by a country to attack its enemies. Washington told Genet that using American privateers violated U.S. neutrality. Jefferson wanted the French revolutionaries to succeed, but even he agreed that allowing France to use American privateers against England was a bad idea.

Jefferson was still upset by U.S. policy toward France. He believed that the United States should back France because France had supported the United States during the Revolutionary War. Hamilton, on the other hand, was pro-British. He hoped to strengthen trading ties with Britain—the most powerful trading nation in the world at the time. Jefferson thought that Hamilton had too much influence on the president's foreign policy and that Hamilton consequently interfered with Jefferson's role as secretary of state. Jefferson decided to resign from Washington's cabinet in 1793.

Time Line

The Struggle for Neutrality

1789

April 1789 George Washington becomes president.

July 1789 French citizens storm the Bastille.

October 1790 British-backed Little Turtle defeats U.S. forces under General Josiah Harmar.

1793

April 1793 President Washington issues the Neutrality Proclamation.

November 1794 Jay's Treaty sparks protest throughout the United States.

206

Critical Thinking: Finding Main Ideas

Standards Proficiency

Neutrality Proclamation Press Release

HSS 8.4.1, 8.5.2; HSS **Analysis Skills:** HI 1, HI 2

Materials: current White House press release (optional)

1. Ask students to imagine that they are press secretaries to President Washington. Have each student create a press release announcing the Neutrality Proclamation. If possible, provide a sample press release as a model.
2. The press release should summarize the contents of the proclamation and explain Washington's reasons for making it.
3. Ask for a volunteer to role play the press secretary and to read aloud his or her press release to the class. Have other students play the role of reporters and ask questions.
4. Conclude by having students evaluate Washington's decision to have the nation remain neutral and whether they agree with it. Students should provide support for their points of view. LS **Verbal/Linguistic**

Alternative Assessment Handbook, Rubric 42: Writing to Inform

Jay's Treaty

There were other threats to U.S. neutrality. In late 1793 the British seized ships carrying food to the French West Indies. Hundreds of the ships were neutral American merchant ships. Also, British officers were helping Native Americans fight settlers.

Washington wanted to prevent another war with the British. He sent Chief Justice John Jay to London to work out a compromise. The British knew the United States lacked a strong navy and that U.S. businesses relied heavily on British trade. However, the British did not want to fight another war in America.

In November 1794 the two sides signed Jay's Treaty. **Jay's Treaty** settled the disputes that had arisen between the United States and Great Britain in the early 1790s. The British would pay damages on seized American ships and abandon their forts on the northwestern frontier. The United States agreed to pay debts it owed the British.

The treaty was unpopular and sparked violent protests. Citizens and congressional leaders thought the treaty hurt trade and did not punish Britain enough for some of its actions. Southerners were especially angry that the treaty did not ask Britain to repay them for slaves that Britain had set free during the Revolutionary War. Washington did not like the treaty but believed it was the most that could be done. At his urging the Senate approved the treaty.

Pinckney's Treaty

American businesses faced problems as well. The Spanish disputed the border between the United States and Florida. Spain closed the port of New Orleans to U.S. trade in 1784. This hurt the American economy because all goods moving down the Mississippi to places in the East or overseas had to pass through New Orleans.

Washington asked Ambassador Thomas Pinckney to meet with Spanish officials to discuss the problem. He asked the Spaniards to reopen New Orleans to U.S. trade. Pinckney also asked for the right of deposit in New Orleans. This right would allow American boats to transfer goods in New Orleans without paying cargo fees.

Spanish minister Manuel de Godoy (goh-THOY) tried to delay reaching an agreement, hoping Pinckney would become desperate and sign a treaty that favored the Spanish. He was worried that the United States and Great Britain might join against Spain after signing Jay's Treaty. Pinckney was patient, however, and his patience was rewarded.

In October 1795, Godoy agreed to **Pinckney's Treaty**, which settled the border and trade disputes with Spain. Under the treaty Spain agreed to recognize the U.S. southern boundary as 31°N latitude. Spain's government also reopened the port at

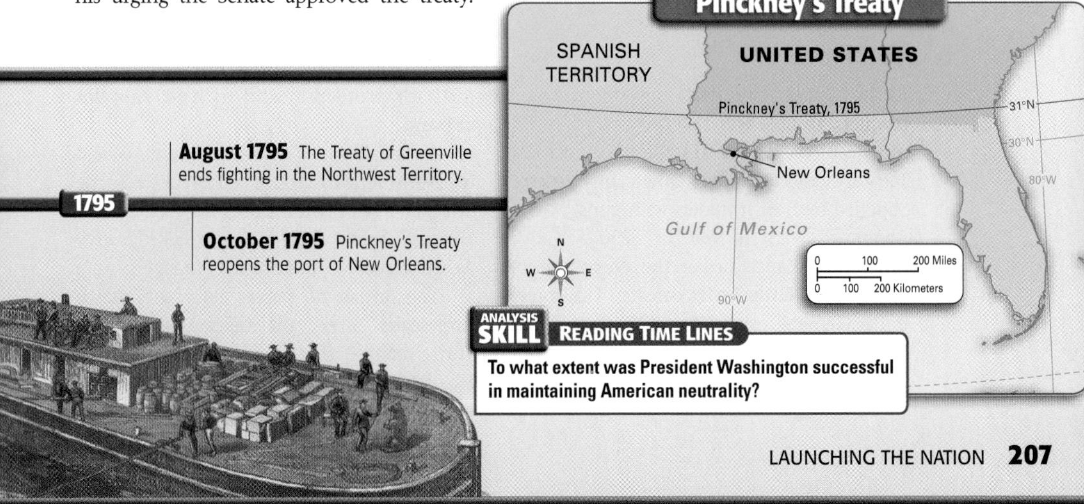

ANALYSIS SKILL **READING TIME LINES**

To what extent was President Washington successful in maintaining American neutrality?

Direct Teach

Main Idea

❶ Remaining Neutral

The United States tried to remain neutral regarding events in Europe.

Recall What conflicts with the British prompted Jay's Treaty? *The British were seizing neutral American merchant ships and helping Native Americans fight settlers.*

Identify Points of View Why did some Americans protest Jay's Treaty? *thought it hurt trade and failed to make the British stop kidnapping American sailors or pay for slaves the British freed during the Revolutionary War*

Evaluate How was Thomas Pinckney effective in dealing with the Spanish? *He was patient, and Spain agreed to his terms—recognized the U.S. southern boundary; gave American ships access to the port at New Orleans and the right of deposit.*

Map Transparency: Pinckney's Treaty

HSS 8.4.1, 8.5.2; HSS **Analysis Skills:** HR 5, HI 1

Did you know . . .

Thomas Jefferson objected to the use of the word *neutrality* in President Washington's Neutrality Proclamation. Jefferson argued that using the word *neutrality* would lead Great Britain to continue practices on the high seas that Americans opposed. Washington agreed and removed the word. Thus, the word *neutrality* never actually appears in the Neutrality Proclamation.

Critical Thinking: Identifying Cause and Effect

Standards Proficiency

Two Treaties Chart

HSS 8.4.1, 8.5.2; HSS **Analysis Skills:** CS 1, HI 1, HI 2

1. Divide the class. Have one half of the class create cause-and-effect charts for Jay's Treaty. Have the other half of the class create cause-and-effect charts for Pinckney's Treaty.
2. Each student should draw a box in the middle of a piece of paper and write the name of his or her assigned treaty in the box. Above the box, students should identify and describe the events that led to the treaty. Below the box, students should explain the terms of the treaty and its results.
3. Then pair students who worked on different charts. Have students explain their charts to their partners. Encourage students to provide peer feedback on the accuracy of their partners' charts.
4. Review the information in students' charts as a class. LS **Interpersonal, Visual/Spatial**

Alternative Assessment Handbook, Rubrics 6: Cause and Effect; and 7: Charts

Answers

Reading Time Lines *successful except for conflicts with Native Americans; avoided conflicts with Spain through Pinckney's Treaty*

Direct Teach

Main Idea

❷ Conflict in the Northwest Territory

The United States and Native Americans came into conflict in the Northwest Territory.

Recall Why did Native Americans in the northwest go to war in the early 1790s, and who led them? *because Americans continued to settle the Northwest Territory; Miami chief Little Turtle*

Identify Cause and Effect What were the results of the Battle of Fallen Timbers? *U.S. victory broke the strength of Indian forces in the region; led to Treaty of Greenville, under which Native Americans gave up much of their land for $20,000 and a guarantee of their safety*

Interpret What did Little Turtle mean when he said "The trail has been long and bloody; it has no end"? *He knew that the U.S. Army would not stop fighting his people and that settlers would not stop coming.*

Map Transparency: Fighting in the Northwest Territory

HSS 8.5.3; **HSS Analysis Skills:** HR 4, HR 5, HI 1, HI 2

Interpreting Maps

Fighting in the Northwest Territory

Place What victories did Native Americans achieve against U.S. forces in the early 1790s? *Harmar's Battle, St. Clair's Battle*

Map Transparency: Fighting in the Northwest Territory

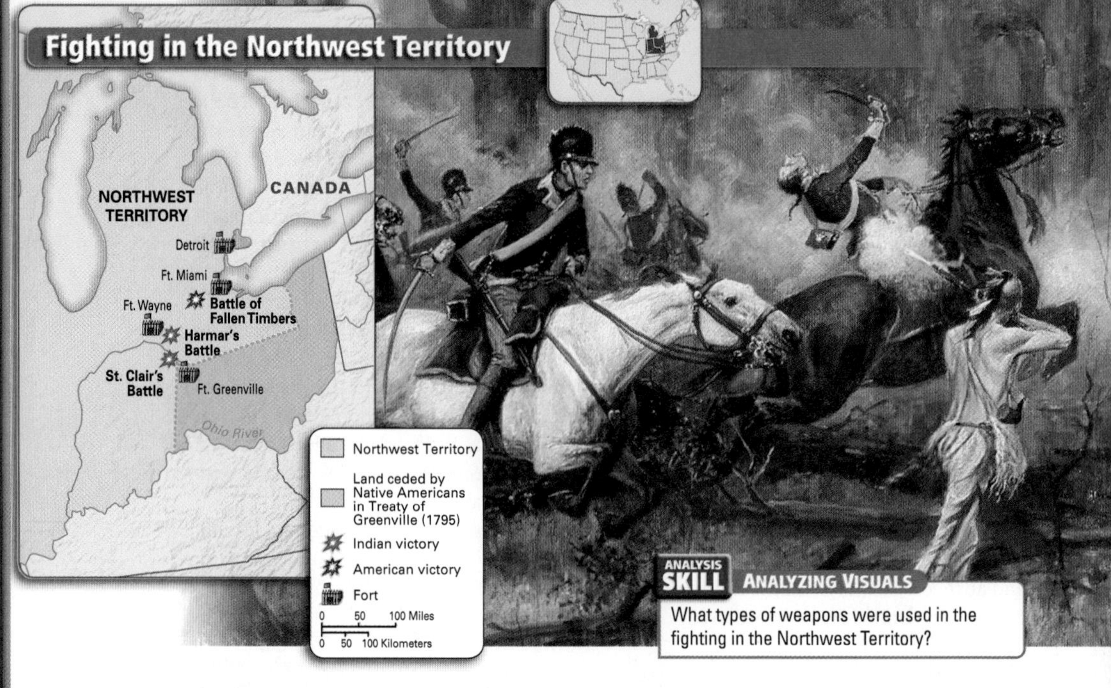

ANALYSIS SKILL ANALYZING VISUALS

What types of weapons were used in the fighting in the Northwest Territory?

New Orleans to American ships and gave them the right of deposit. Because it opened the frontier to more expansion, Washington and most other Americans believed that Pinckney's Treaty was a successful compromise.

READING CHECK **Summarizing** Why did President Washington want the United States to remain neutral?

Conflict in the Northwest Territory

As the United States dealt with international conflicts, trouble was also brewing at home. Americans continued to settle the Northwest Territory despite Native Americans' protests. Supplied by British traders with guns, Native Americans went to war. In 1790 a Native American alliance under the command of Miami chief **Little Turtle** defeated U.S. forces under General Josiah Harmar. Then in 1791, Native Americans defeated General Arthur St. Clair's troops.

General Wayne Takes Command

In 1792 President Washington gave command of the army in the West to General Anthony Wayne. Wayne's task was to bring troops to the frontier to fight against the Indians. In 1793 General Wayne arrived in Ohio. Many of his men were ill from smallpox and influenza, so they were unable to fight well.

Wayne's troops moved north and built Fort Greenville, where they remained during the winter. They built additional forts for protection and to have supplies at hand.

As the summer of 1794 neared, several Native American groups led by Little Turtle attacked a supply train near the fort. Wayne and his men responded. They attacked Native American towns and burned crops.

The British no longer aided the Native Americans after this defeat, and Little Turtle realized that they were outmatched. He urged his people to seek peace.

Differentiating Instruction for Universal Access

English-Language Learners **Standards Proficiency**

1. Organize the class into small groups and have each group create a time line of the conflicts that took place with Native Americans in the Northwest Territory in the early 1790s.
2. Time lines should include at least six key dates and entries for events from 1790 to 1795. Encourage the groups to provide annotations and illustrations to enhance their time lines.
3. Display the groups' time lines in the classroom. Use them to lead a class review of the cause-and-effect relationships among the events.
LS Interpersonal, Visual/Spatial

Alternative Assessment Handbook, Rubrics 14: Group Activity; and 36: Time Lines

HSS 8.5.3; **HSS Analysis Skills:** CS 1, CS 2, HI 1, HI 2

Answers

Analyzing Visuals *swords or sabers, shotguns or rifles*

Reading Check *thought neutrality was the safest and most reasonable plan for the long run*

"The trail has been long and bloody; it has no end. The [whites] . . . are many. They are like the leaves of the trees. When the frost comes they fall and are blown away. But when the sunshine comes again they come back more plentiful than ever before."

—Little Turtle, quoted in *The Ohio Frontier* by Douglas Hurt

The End of Conflict

On August 20, 1794, Native Americans fought Wayne's troops in the **Battle of Fallen Timbers** and were defeated. The battle was named for an area where many trees had been destroyed by a tornado. Wayne's forces burned Indians' villages and fields. The strength of Indian forces in the region was broken.

The frontier war soon ended. In August 1795, Native American leaders signed the **Treaty of Greenville**, which gave the United States claim to most Indian lands in the Northwest Territory. The treaty also guaranteed the safety of citizens there. In exchange, Native Americans received $20,000 worth of goods and an acknowledgment of their claim to the lands they still held.

READING CHECK **Finding Main Ideas** What conflicts did the United States face in the late 1700s?

The Whiskey Rebellion

Other conflicts occurred on the frontier. Congress passed a tax on American-made whiskey in March 1791. The tax was part of Hamilton's plan to raise money to help pay the federal debt. He was also testing the power of the federal government to control the states' actions.

Reaction in the West

People in areas such as western Pennsylvania were bitter about the tax. They were already angry with the federal government, which they believed did not protect settlers from Native American attacks and did not allow settlers enough opportunities for trade. The farmers' corn crops were often made into whiskey, which was easier to transport than the corn. Because cash was rare, whiskey became like money in their region. The farmers believed that the tax was aimed specifically at them.

Farmers who produced small amounts of whiskey for trade argued that they could not afford the tax. They believed they should be able to keep the money they had made from a product they created themselves. Protests in 1792 led President Washington to issue a proclamation saying that people had to obey the law.

Westerners also disliked the fact that cases about the law were to be tried in a district court. These courts were usually far away from the people they affected and were a great inconvenience to them.

Whiskey Rebellion Is Crushed

The complaints of western Pennsylvanians were at first expressed peacefully. But by 1794 fighting had broken out. In what became known as the **Whiskey Rebellion**, farmers lashed out against the tax on whiskey. Protesters refused to pay the tax. They even tarred and feathered tax collectors. Some called themselves the new Sons of Liberty.

Incidents of violence spread to other states. President Washington feared that the rebels threatened the federal government's authority. He believed he needed to make people understand that the Constitution gave Congress the right to pass and enforce the tax.

Washington declared that he could "no longer remain a passive [inactive] spectator" in the event. He personally led the army in military action against the rebellion—the first and only time an American president has done so. The army of about 13,000 men approached western Pennsylvania in November 1794. By this time most of the rebels had fled. The Whiskey Rebellion ended without a battle.

READING CHECK **Supporting a Point of View** Defend the viewpoint of the Pennsylvania farmers who did not want to pay the whiskey tax.

Direct Teach

Main Idea

3 The Whiskey Rebellion

The Whiskey Rebellion tested Washington's administration.

Recall Why did Congress pass a tax on American-made whisky? *to raise money to pay off the federal debt; to test the power of the federal government to control states' actions*

Summarize What occurred during the Whiskey Rebellion? *Western Pennsylvania farmers' protests against the whiskey tax turned violent; Washington led forces against the rebels, who mostly fled.*

Evaluate What was the significance of the Whiskey Rebellion? *helped emphasize the authority of the federal government to pass taxes and to put down domestic rebellions*

HSS 8.3.5; HSS **Analysis Skills:** HI 1, HI 2

Answers

Reading Check (left) *They faced a border dispute with Spanish-controlled Florida and conflicts with Native Americans in the Northwest.*

Reading Check (right) *possible answers—They had made the whiskey and should have been able to keep the profits from its sale; they could not afford the tax and had to travel long distances to plead their case.*

Differentiating Instruction for Universal Access

Learners Having Difficulty — Reaching Standards

1. To help students explain the domestic conflicts the United States faced in the late 1700s, draw the graphic organizer for students to see. Omit the blue sample answers.
2. Have students copy the organizer and complete it by listing the key people, events, and issues in each conflict. **LS Visual/Spatial**

Alternative Assessment Handbook, Rubric 13: Graphic Organizers

HSS 8.3.5; HSS **Analysis Skills:** HI 1

Domestic Conflicts, Late 1700s

Northwest Territory	Whiskey Rebellion
• *Native Americans went to war over American settlement in the region.* • *Miami chief Little Turtle* • *General Anthony Wayne* • *Battle of Fallen Timbers* • *U.S. victory broke Indian strength in region.* • *Treaty of Greenville*	• *Congress passed a whiskey tax.* • *Western Pennsylvania farmers protested tax.* • *Fighting broke out.* • *President Washington led army against the rebellion; rebels fled.* • *showed authority of the federal government*

Direct Teach

Primary Source

Washington's Farewell Address

Activity A Farewell Address Have students discuss if they think Washington's advice on political parties and foreign nations is applicable today. Then ask students to imagine that they are the current president of the United States. What advice would they give the nation if they were retiring today? Have each student make a bulleted list of topics that he or she would address.
LS Verbal/Linguistic

Alternative Assessment Handbook, Rubric 11: Discussions

Connect to Science and Technology

Getting the Word Out President Washington sent the draft of his Farewell Address to the publisher of the Philadelphia newspaper *American Daily Advertiser*. The *Advertiser* printed the address, and other newspapers soon picked it up. In this way, Americans slowly learned about the president's Farewell Address. Today, modern communications devices enable Americans to hear or read presidential messages immediately instead of waiting weeks or months.

Primary Source

HISTORICAL DOCUMENT

Washington's Farewell Address

On September 19,1796, President George Washington's Farewell Address first appeared in a Philadelphia newspaper. In it, Washington wrote about the nation's economy, political parties, and foreign policy.

While, then, every part of our country . . . feels an immediate and particular interest in union, all the parts combined cannot fail to find in the united mass . . . greater strength, greater resource, proportionally greater security from external danger, [and] a less frequent interruption of their peace by foreign nations; . . .

I have already **intimated**[1] to you the danger of [political] parties in the state, with particular reference to the founding of them on geographical **discriminations**[2]. Let me now take a more **comprehensive**[3] view, and warn you in the most solemn manner against the **baneful**[4] effects of the spirit of party, generally.

If, in the opinion of the people, the distribution or **modification**[5] of the constitutional powers be in any particular wrong, let it be corrected by an amendment . . .

Promote, then, as an object of primary importance, institutions for the general **diffusion**[6] of knowledge . . . As the structure of a government gives force to public opinion, it is essential that public opinion should be enlightened . . .

[Avoid] likewise the accumulation of debt, . . . not ungenerously throwing upon **posterity**[7] the burden, which we ourselves ought to bear . . .

Observe good faith and justice towards all nations; **cultivate**[8] peace and harmony with all . . .

The great rule of conduct for us, in regard to foreign nations, is . . . to have with them as little political connection as possible.

It is our true policy to steer clear of permanent alliances with any portion of the foreign world . . . There can be no greater error than to expect, or **calculate**[9] upon real favors from nation to nation. It is an illusion, which experience must cure, which a just pride ought to discard.

The duty of holding a neutral conduct may be inferred . . . from the obligation which justice and humanity impose on every nation . . . to maintain **inviolate**[10] the relations of peace and **amity**[11] towards other nations.

Washington lists the benefits of uniting the states under one government.

In this phrase, Washington emphasizes his warning against the dangers of political parties.

Washington points out the need for education.

This is Washington's advice to the new nation about foreign policy.

[1] **intimated**: told
[2] **discriminations**: differences
[3] **comprehensive**: complete
[4] **baneful**: destructive
[5] **modification**: change
[6] **diffusion**: spreading
[7] **posterity**: future generations
[8] **cultivate**: seek
[9] **calculate**: plan
[10] **inviolate**: unchanging
[11] **amity**: friendship

ANALYSIS SKILL ANALYZING PRIMARY SOURCES

1. What events happened before Washington left office that might have led to his warning against political parties?
2. Why did Washington suggest neutrality as a foreign policy?

Critical Thinking: Comparing Primary Sources

Exceeding Standards

Presidential Farewell Addresses

Research Required

1. Have students conduct research to find a farewell address from a recent U.S. president. Tell students to read the address and note the key points.
2. Next, have students complete **Primary Source Activity: President George Washington's Farewell Address, in the Chapter Resource File.**
3. Then have each student write an essay comparing the recent Farewell Address to Washington's. The essay should compare tone, major points, and issues. Encourage students to include quotes from each document to support the points in their essays.
4. Ask for volunteers to read their essays to the class. **LS Verbal/Linguistic**

Alternative Assessment Handbook, Rubric 42: Writing to Inform

CRF: Primary Source Activity: President George Washington's Farewell Address

HSS 8.4.2; **HSS Analysis Skills:** CS 1, HR 4, HI 1, HI 3

Answers

Analyzing Primary Sources

1. *disagreements between Jefferson and Hamilton; Jefferson's resignation*
2. *thought that alliances with other nations were illusions; that alliances could draw the nation into war*

Washington Says Farewell

In 1796 Washington decided not to run for a third presidential term. He wrote that he was "tired of public life" and "devoutly [strongly] wished for retirement." He also wanted to remind Americans that the people were the country's true leaders.

With the help of Alexander Hamilton and James Madison, Washington wrote his Farewell Address. In it he spoke about what he believed were the greatest dangers to the American republic. Among these were the dangers of foreign ties and political conflicts at home. Washington warned against forming permanent ties with other countries because choosing sides could draw the United States into war.

He also worried about growing political conflicts within the nation. Washington believed that disagreements between political groups weakened government. Political unity, he said, was a key to national success. Washington left office warning the nation to work out its differences and protect its independence. Washington also warned against too much public debt. He thought the government should try not to borrow money. He wanted future generations to be protected from debt.

He concluded his speech by looking forward to his retirement and praising his country. "I anticipate . . . the sweet enjoyment . . . of good laws under a free government, the ever favorite object of my heart."

READING CHECK **Finding Main Ideas** What issues did Washington believe were most dangerous to the future of the new nation?

SUMMARY AND PREVIEW Americans responded to foreign and domestic conflict during Washington's presidency. In the next section you will read about the formation of political parties in the United States and the presidency of John Adams.

Section 3 Assessment

go.hrw.com **Online Quiz** KEYWORD: SS8 HP6

Reviewing Ideas, Terms, and People HSS 8.3.5, 8.4.2

1. a. **Describe** What did Washington's **Neutrality Proclamation** state?
   b. **Compare and Contrast** In what ways were **Jay's Treaty** and **Pinckney's Treaty** similar and different?
2. a. **Identify** Who were the leaders of American Indian and U.S. forces in the conflict in the Northwest Territory?
   b. **Predict** What are some possible consequences of the **Treaty of Greenville** for American Indians in the Northwest Territory?
3. a. **Recall** Why did Congress tax American-made whiskey?
   b. **Explain** How did the tax lead to the **Whiskey Rebellion**?
   c. **Elaborate** Why do you think that President Washington personally led the army against westerners in the Whiskey Rebellion?
4. a. **Describe** What warnings did Washington give the nation in his Farewell Address?
   b. **Draw Conclusions** Why did Washington not run for a third term as president?

Critical Thinking

5. **Categorizing** Copy the graphic organizer below and use it to identify the causes and effects of conflict in the Northwest Territory.

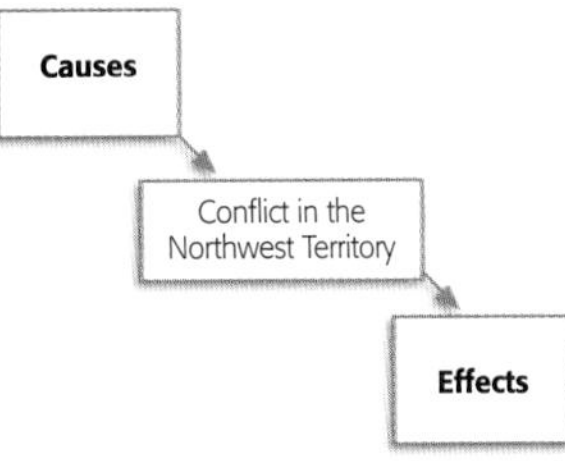

FOCUS ON WRITING

6. **Thinking about Washington, Hamilton, and Jefferson** In this section you read about the activities of these three men during a difficult time for our country. What did you learn that you could add to a Nobel Prize nomination for any of these leaders?

Section 3 Assessment Answers

1. a. The United States would not take sides in any European conflicts.
   b. similar—compromises that settled disputes with foreign nations; different—Americans were more satisfied with Pinckney's Treaty.
2. a. Little Turtle; U.S. generals Josiah Harmar, Arthur St. Clair, Anthony Wayne
   b. possible answer—Native Americans there would continue to lose land to settlers.
3. a. to raise money to help pay the national debt
   b. Farmers in western Pennsylvania were angry about the tax; peaceful protests turned violent.
   c. show his support for federal authority to tax
4. a. warned the nation about the dangers of foreign ties, political divisions, public debt
   b. tired of public life and ready for retirement
5. Causes—Americans continued to settle Northwest Territory, British supplied Native Americans with guns, Little Turtle led Native Americans into war; Effects—broke Indian power in region; led to Treaty of Greenville
6. Students should create additional entries for Washington, Hamilton, and Jefferson.

Direct Teach

Main Idea

4 Washington Says Farewell

In his Farewell Address, Washington advised the nation.

Explain Why did Washington warn against growing political conflicts within the nation? *thought they weakened government and that political unity was key to national success*

Drawing Conclusions Why do you think Washington's Farewell Address is considered a significant historical document? *possible answer—Because he was the nation's first president; it was the first presidential Farewell Address.*

CRF: Primary Source Activity: President George Washington's Farewell Address

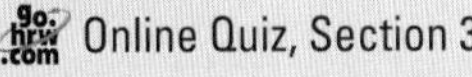
HSS 8.4.2; HSS **Analysis Skills:** HI 1

Review & Assess

Close

Have students review Washington's recommendations for the nation in his Farewell Address and then predict how well they were followed.

Review

Online Quiz, Section 3

Assess

SE Section 3 Assessment

PASS: Section 3 Quiz

Alternative Assessment Handbook

Reteach/Classroom Intervention

California Standards Review Workbook

Interactive Reader and Study Guide, Section 3

Interactive Skills Tutor CD-ROM

Answers

Reading Check *foreign ties, political conflicts, and public debt*

Preteach

Bellringer

If YOU were there . . . Use the **Daily Bellringer Transparency** to help students answer the question.

 Daily Bellringer Transparency, Section 4

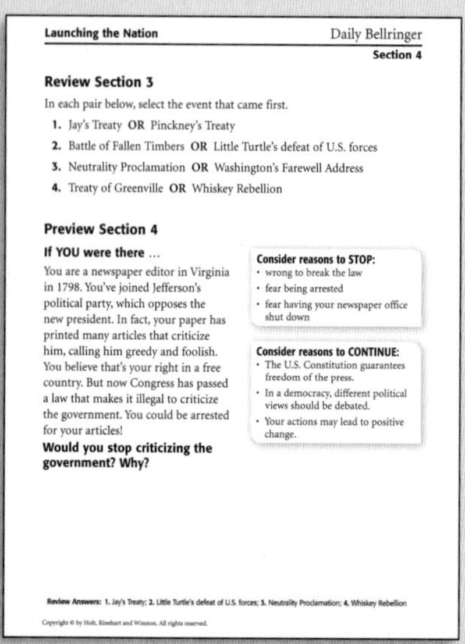

Launching the Nation — Daily Bellringer — Section 4

Review Section 3

In each pair below, select the event that came first.

1. Jay's Treaty **OR** Pinckney's Treaty
2. Battle of Fallen Timbers **OR** Little Turtle's defeat of U.S. forces
3. Neutrality Proclamation **OR** Washington's Farewell Address
4. Treaty of Greenville **OR** Whiskey Rebellion

Preview Section 4

If YOU were there ...

You are a newspaper editor in Virginia in 1798. You've joined Jefferson's political party, which opposes the new president. In fact, your paper has printed many articles that criticize him, calling him greedy and foolish. You believe that's your right in a free country. But now Congress has passed a law that makes it illegal to criticize the government. You could be arrested for your articles!

Would you stop criticizing the government? Why?

Consider reasons to STOP:
- wrong to break the law
- fear being arrested
- fear having your newspaper office shut down

Consider reasons to CONTINUE:
- The U.S. Constitution guarantees freedom of the press.
- In a democracy, different political views should be debated.
- Your actions may lead to positive change.

Review Answers: 1. Jay's Treaty; 2. Little Turtle's defeat of U.S. forces; 3. Neutrality Proclamation; 4. Whiskey Rebellion

Building Vocabulary

Preteach or review the following terms:

dignity seriousness, impressiveness (p. 213)

resolution formal decision (p. 215)

rivalry competition (p. 212)

tribute payment by one ruler or state to another (p. 214)

CRF: Vocabulary Builder Activity, Section 4

Standards Focus

HSS 8.3.4

Means: Understand how the views of Thomas Jefferson and Alexander Hamilton on issues such as the Alien and Sedition Acts led to the development of two political parties.

Matters: Political parties continue to have a strong influence on U.S. politics today.

SECTION 4

John Adams's Presidency

What You Will Learn...

Main Ideas

1. The rise of political parties created competition in the election of 1796.
2. The XYZ affair caused problems for President John Adams.
3. Controversy broke out over the Alien and Sedition Acts.

The Big Idea

The development of political parties in the United States contributed to differing ideas about the role of the federal government.

Key Terms

political parties, *p. 212*
Federalist Party, *p. 212*
Democratic-Republican Party, *p. 212*
XYZ affair, *p. 214*
Alien and Sedition Acts, *p. 215*
Kentucky and Virginia Resolutions, *p. 215*

HSS 8.3.4 Understand how the conflicts between Thomas Jefferson and Alexander Hamilton resulted in the emergence of two political parties (e.g., view of foreign policy, Alien and Sedition Acts, economic policy, National Bank, funding and assumption of the Revolutionary debt).

If YOU were there...

You are a newspaper editor in Virginia in 1798. You've joined Jefferson's political party, which opposes the new president. In fact, your paper has printed many articles that criticize him, calling him greedy and foolish. You believe that's your right in a free country. But now Congress has passed a law that makes it illegal to criticize the government. You could be arrested for your articles!

Would you stop criticizing the government? Why?

BUILDING BACKGROUND People within the new United States had differing viewpoints on many issues. Personal rivalries among political leaders also created divisions in the new nation. Trying to limit dissent in the country, the federal government passed several unpopular laws.

The Election of 1796

The election of 1796 began a new era in U.S. politics. For the first time, more than one candidate ran for president. **Political parties**, groups that help elect people and shape policies, had begun to form during Washington's presidency. Despite Washington's warnings about political parties, the rivalry between two parties dominated the 1796 election.

Alexander Hamilton helped found the **Federalist Party**, which wanted a strong federal government and supported industry and trade. The Federalists chose John Adams and Thomas Pinckney as candidates. Adams knew he was not well liked in the South or the West, but he hoped people would support him after they thought about his years of loyal public service.

Thomas Jefferson and James Madison founded the **Democratic-Republican Party**. Its members, called Republicans, wanted to limit the federal government's power. (This party is not related to today's Republican Party.) They chose Thomas Jefferson and Aaron Burr as their candidates.

Teach the Big Idea: Master the Standards

Standards Proficiency

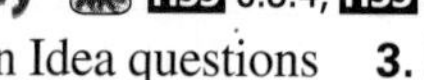

John Adams's Presidency HSS 8.3.4; HSS Analysis Skills: CS 1, HR 5, HI 1, HI 2

1. **Teach** Ask students the Main Idea questions to teach this section.
2. **Apply** Have each student draw a box on a piece of paper and label the box *Presidency of John Adams*. Students should then connect the box to three, large empty boxes below it. In each box, tell students to describe an event in this section that divided Federalists and Republicans. Tell students to use the section headings as clues.
   LS Visual/Spatial
3. **Review** As you review the section, have students share the information they listed.
4. **Practice/Homework** Have each student create two bumper stickers, one expressing the view of the Federalist Party and one expressing the view of the Democratic-Republican Party on a major event or issue in this section. **LS Verbal/Linguistic**

Alternative Assessment Handbook, Rubrics 13: Graphic Organizers; and 34: Slogans and Banners

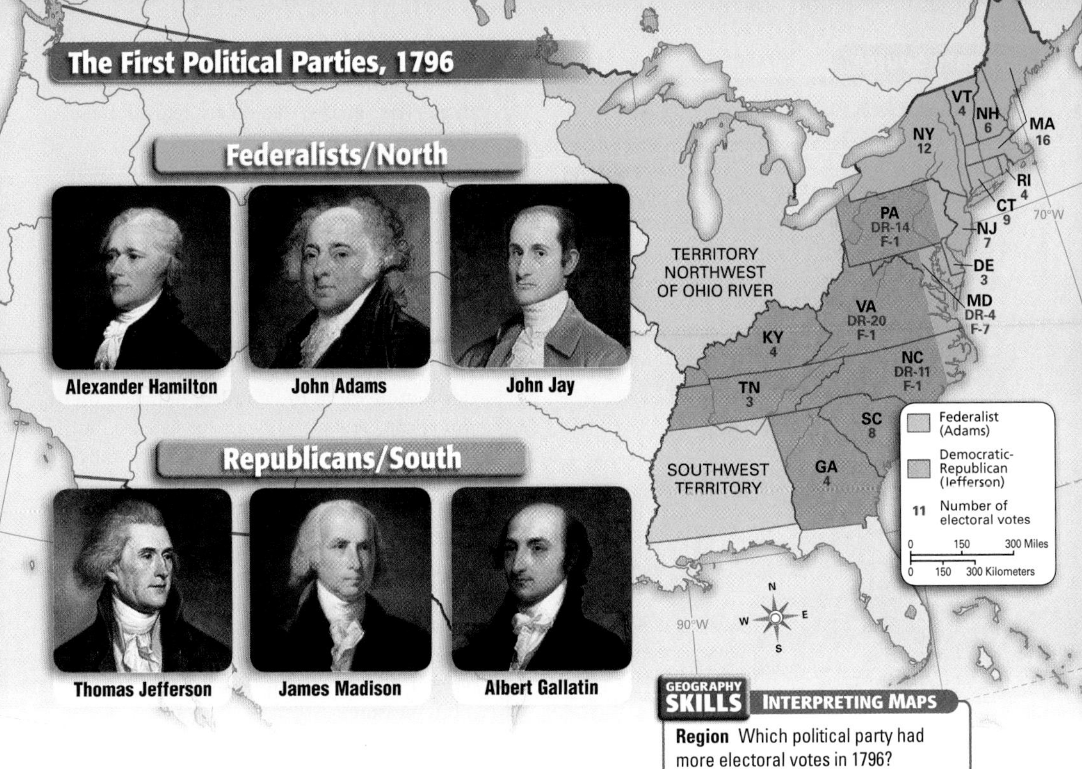

GEOGRAPHY SKILLS INTERPRETING MAPS

Region Which political party had more electoral votes in 1796?

Party differences were based partly on where and how people lived. Businesspeople in the cities tended to support the Federalists. Farmers in more isolated areas generally favored the Democratic-Republicans. Both sides attacked each other. Republicans called Adams a royalist—an insult to a man so involved in the Revolution. The Federalists accused the Republicans of favoring the French.

In the end, Adams defeated Jefferson. At the time, the person who came in second in a presidential election became vice president. So, after months of campaigning against one another, Adams and Jefferson took office together.

READING CHECK **Finding Main Ideas** How did the election of 1796 change the nature of politics in the United States?

President Adams and the XYZ Affair

John Adams had the challenging task of following Washington as president. The people had adored Washington. Adams would have to work hard to win the people's trust.

A New President

At first glance, John Adams did not appear well suited for the presidency. Although Adams had been a leading Patriot during the American Revolution and had later served as a foreign diplomat, he lacked Washington's dignity, and most people saw him as a cold and distant person. Still, many people—even his opponents—respected Adams. They recognized his hard work, honesty, and intelligence.

Direct Teach

Main Idea

1 The Election of 1796

The rise of political parties created competition in the election of 1796.

Recall Why was the election of 1796 different from the previous election? *Political parties began to form and, as a result, more than one candidate ran for president.*

Make Generalizations What role did geography play in the two political parties? *Federalists—cities, North; Republicans—farms, more isolated areas, South and West*

Map Transparency: The First Political Parties

HSS 8.3.4; HSS **Analysis Skills:** CS 1, HI 1, HI 2

Biography

John Adams (1735–1826) Adams was well prepared for the presidency. In addition to serving as Washington's vice president, Adams had served in the Massachusetts state legislatures and attended the First Continental Congress. In 1779 he had been elected to the Massachusetts Constitutional Convention, where he wrote the first draft of the state constitution.

CRF: Biography Activity: Abigail Adams

Differentiating Instruction for Universal Access

Advanced Learners/GATE — Exceeding Standards

1. Discuss the significance of the XYZ affair with the class. Then ask students to imagine that they are official record keepers for Congress and are taking notes on the congressional debates about the XYZ affair.
2. Have students write out the "official" record of the debates, including a time line of the actual events of the XYZ affair.
3. Students should include Americans' reaction to the affair as well as reasons for and against declaring war on France.
4. Ask volunteers to present their work to the class. LS **Verbal/Linguistic**

Alternative Assessment Handbook, Rubric 36: Time Lines

HSS 8.3.4; HSS **Analysis Skills:** CS 1, CS 2, HR 5, HI 1

Answers

Interpreting Maps *Federalist Party*

Reading Check *It saw the rise of political parties and more than one candidate for president for the first time.*

Direct Teach

Main Idea

❷ President Adams and the XYZ Affair

The XYZ affair caused problems for President John Adams.

Explain Why was following Washington a challenge for President Adams? *Americans adored Washington but saw Adams as less dignified and somewhat cold.*

Recall What did Adams hope to accomplish by sending diplomats to France? *improve French relations*

Summarize How did Adams react to the XYZ affair? *informed Congress, asked it to expand the navy and create a peacetime army in case of war, and worked to reopen peace talks with France*

Make Judgments Do you think Adams should have pushed for war? Why or why not? *Answers will vary but should reflect an understanding of the reasons for and against war at the time.*

CRF: Biography Activity: Abigail Adams

HSS 8.3.4; HSS **Analysis Skills:** HI 1

Checking for Understanding

True or False Answer each statement *T* if it is True or *F* if it is false. If false, explain why.

1. In the presidential election of 1796, political parties played a role for the first time. *T*
2. The XYZ affair almost led to war between France and the United States. *T*
3. The Democratic-Republican Party strongly supported the Alien and Sedition Acts. *F, the Federalists supported the acts.*

Answers

Interpreting Political Cartoons *the woman is being robbed*

Reading Check *Americans, angry about the French request for a bribe (tribute), were willing to fund the military to fight the French.*

Primary Source

POLITICAL CARTOON

After the XYZ affair, French ships continued to attack American merchant ships. In this cartoon, the United States is represented by the woman. The men, symbolizing the French, are taking valuables from her. The people in the distance are other European nations.

Why do you think this man is encouraging the woman to look away?

These people aren't helping the woman. What do you think the cartoon is suggesting by this?

ANALYSIS SKILL **INTERPRETING POLITICAL CARTOONS**

How does the cartoon show that America is being preyed upon by the French?

The United States and France

One of Adams's first goals as president was to improve the relationship between the United States and France. You may remember that the French had once tried to hire American privateers to help them fight Great Britain, a practice Washington frowned upon. Adams sent U.S. diplomats to Paris to smooth over the conflict and to negotiate a treaty to protect U.S. shipping.

When the diplomats arrived in France, they learned that French foreign minister Talleyrand would not speak with them. Instead, they had a strange and secret visit from three French agents. Shockingly, the agents said that Talleyrand would discuss a treaty only in exchange for a $250,000 bribe. The French government also wanted a loan of $12 million. The amazed diplomats refused these demands.

In March 1798 President Adams told Congress that the peace-seeking mission had failed. He described the French terms, substituting the letters X, Y, and Z for the names of the French agents. Upon hearing the disgraceful news, Federalists in Congress called for war with France.

The **XYZ affair**, as the French demand for a bribe came to be called, outraged the American public. "Millions for defense, but not one cent for tribute!" became the rallying cry of the American people.

Preparations for War

Fearing war, Adams asked Congress to expand the navy to a fleet of more than 30 ships. He thought war with France might be unavoidable. He also decided the United States should keep a peacetime army. Congress approved both measures.

Although Adams had asked Congress for military support, he did not want to go to war with France. He was worried about its cost. So he did not ask Congress to declare war. Instead, he tried to reopen peace talks with France.

Peace Efforts

Adams's decision not to declare war stunned Federalists. Despite intense pressure from members of his own party, Adams refused to change his mind.

American and French ships, however, began fighting each other in the Caribbean. Adams sent a representative to France to engage in talks to try to end the fighting. The United States and France eventually signed a treaty. Adams then forced two members of his cabinet to resign for trying to block his peace efforts.

READING CHECK **Identifying Points of View** What did Americans mean when they said "Millions for defense, but not one cent for tribute"?

Collaborative Learning

Standards Proficiency

Talk-Radio History

HSS 8.3.4; HSS **Analysis Skills:** HI 1

1. Have students use a talk-radio format to hold a panel discussion on John Adams's presidency. Organize the class into three groups and assign each group one of the following topics: (a) the XYZ affair; (b) the Alien and Sedition Acts; and (c) the Virginia and Kentucky Resolutions.
2. Select two students in each group to sit on a panel and answer questions from "callers." The other students will serve as callers. All group members should help prepare questions and answers about the group's assigned topic.
3. Have each group conduct its talk-radio show for the class. Students should "call in" to the talk-radio show and ask questions. Panel members should respond. Then give students in other groups a chance to ask questions.

LS Interpersonal, Verbal/Linguistic

Alternative Assessment Handbook, Rubric 14: Group Activity

The Alien and Sedition Acts

Many Democratic-Republicans continued to sympathize with France. Federalists, angered by their stand, called them "democrats, mob-ocrats, and all other kinds of rats."

In 1798, the Federalist-controlled Congress passed four laws known together as the **Alien and Sedition Acts**. These laws were said to protect the United States, but the Federalists intended them to crush opposition to war. The most controversial was the Sedition Act, which forbade anyone from publishing or voicing criticism of the federal government. In effect, this cancelled basic protections of freedom of speech and freedom of the press.

The two main Democratic-Republican leaders, Thomas Jefferson and James Madison, viewed these acts as a misuse of the government's power. Attacking the problem at the state level, they wrote resolutions passed by the Kentucky legislature in 1798 and in Virginia in 1799. Known as the **Kentucky and Virginia Resolutions**, these documents argued that the Alien and Sedition Acts were unconstitutional. They stated that the federal government could not pass these acts because they interfered with state government. Madison and Jefferson pressured Congress to repeal the Alien and Sedition Acts. Congress did not, although it allowed the acts to expire within a few years.

The Kentucky and Virginia Resolutions did not have the force of national law, but they supported the idea that states could challenge the federal government. This idea would grow to have a tremendous impact on American history later in the 1800s.

READING CHECK **Analyzing** How did the Kentucky and Virginia Resolutions support the rights of states?

SUMMARY AND PREVIEW Political parties formed to reflect different viewpoints. In the next chapter you will read about Thomas Jefferson's presidency.

Section 4 Assessment

go.hrw.com
Online Quiz
KEYWORD: SS8 HP6

Reviewing Ideas, Terms, and People HSS 8.3.4

1. **a. Recall** What two **political parties** emerged before the election of 1796? Who were the founders of each party?
   b. Analyze What effect did political parties have on the election of 1796?
   c. Elaborate Do you think it was difficult for Adams and Jefferson to serve together as president and vice president? Explain your answer.
2. **a. Recall** What was one of Adams's first goals as president?
   b. Make Inferences Why were Federalists shocked by Adams's decision to resume peace talks with the French?
3. **a. Identify** What did the **Alien and Sedition Acts** state?
   b. Explain What idea regarding states' rights did the **Kentucky and Virginia Resolutions** support?
   c. Elaborate Would you have supported the Alien and Sedition Acts? Explain your answer.

Critical Thinking

4. **Contrasting** Copy the chart below. Use it to identify the differences between the two political parties that emerged in the late 1700s.

Federalist Party	Democratic-Republican Party

FOCUS ON WRITING

5. **Gathering Information about John Adams** Take some notes about John Adams's contributions that would support his nomination for the Nobel Prize. Then begin to compare and contrast all four leaders you have studied in this chapter. Which one will you nominate?

Section 4 Assessment Answers

1. **a.** Federalist Party, Hamilton; Democratic-Republican Party, Jefferson and Madison
   b. resulted in more than one candidate running for president for the first time
   c. possible answers—yes, the bitter campaign would have made it difficult for them to get along; no, they were professionals and would have worked together for the good of the nation
2. **a.** to improve U.S. relations with France
   b. They had expected him to call for war.
3. **a.** forbade anyone from publishing or voicing criticism of the federal government
   b. States could challenge the federal government.
   c. possible answers—yes, kept the nation unified; no, violated free speech
4. Federalist—strong federal government, supported industry and trade, urban business-people, supported war with France and Alien and Sedition Acts; Democratic-Republican—limit federal government's power, farmers, sympathized with France
5. possible answer—kept the nation out of war despite conflicts

Direct Teach

Main Idea

❸ The Alien and Sedition Acts

Controversy broke out over the Alien and Sedition Acts.

Identify Why did the Federalist-controlled Congress pass the Alien and Sedition Acts? *to crush opposition to war against France; to keep Republicans from criticizing the government*

Elaborate How do you think Americans today would react to the Alien and Sedition Acts? *Answers will vary but should reflect an understanding of the acts and how they limited freedoms of sppech and of the press.*

HSS 8.3.4; HSS **Analysis Skills:** HI 1

Review & Assess

Close

Have students discuss how the development of two political parties shaped John Adams's presidency.

Review

Online Quiz, Section 4

Assess

SE Section 4 Assessment

PASS: Section 4 Quiz

Alternative Assessment Handbook

Reteach/Classroom Intervention

California Standards Review Workbook

Interactive Reader and Study Guide, Section 4

Interactive Skills Tutor CD-ROM

Answers

Reading Check *They supported the idea that states could challenge the federal government.*

Social Studies Skills

Making Group Decisions

Activity Planning a School Improvement Project Ask students to imagine that they are on a committee to improve the appearance of the school. Organize students into small- to medium-sized groups. Have each group decide on a project for improving the school's appearance and a method for raising money to fund the project. Each group should appoint a member to take notes and record ideas. Remind the groups to give each member a chance to speak and to participate. Groups should also discuss how they will determine a final decision, such as by voting or by group consensus. Let the groups know in advance exactly how much time they have. When the time is up, have each group share its decisions with the class. Then have students apply the questions under "Practice the Skill" to the activity and discuss the answers. **LS Interpersonal**

Alternative Assessment Handbook, Rubric 14: Group Activity

Social Studies Skills

Analysis | Critical Thinking | **Participation** | Study

HSS Participation Skill Develop group interaction skills.

Making Group Decisions

Define the Skill

Democracy is one of the most valued principles of American society. It is based on the idea that the members of society, or representatives they choose, make the decisions that affect society. Decision-making would be much more efficient if just one person decided what to do and how to do it. However, that method is not at all democratic.

Making decisions as a group is a complicated and difficult skill. However, it is an important one at all levels of society—from governing the nation to making group decisions at school, in the community, and with your friends. At every level, the skill is based on the ability of the group's members to interact in effective and cooperative ways.

Learn the Skill

Think about the job the first Congress faced after the Constitution was ratified. The nation was still millions of dollars in debt from the Revolutionary War. Congress had to find a way to pay these debts as well as raise money to run the government.

Leaders like Jefferson and Hamilton had ideas about how to accomplish these goals. However, neither man could act alone. In a democracy the group—in this case Congress—must make the decisions and take the actions.

This task was complicated by the fact that Jefferson and Hamilton disagreed on what to do. Each man's supporters in Congress pushed his point of view. Fortunately, its members were able to overcome their differences, compromise on goals and actions, and accept group decisions they might not have agreed with personally. Had they not possessed this ability and skill, the nation's early years might have been even more difficult than they were.

Like that first Congress, being part of an effective group requires that you behave in certain ways.

1. **Be an active member.** Take part in setting the group's goals and in making its decisions. Participate in planning and taking group action.
2. **Take a position.** State your views and work to persuade other members to accept them. However, also be open to negotiating and compromising to settle differences within the group.
3. **Be willing to take charge if leadership is needed.** But also be willing to follow the leadership of other members.

Practice the Skill

Suppose that you are a member of the first Congress. With a group of classmates, you must decide what and who should be taxed to raise the money the government needs. Remember that you are an elected official. If you do something to upset the people, you could lose your job. When your group has finished, answer the following questions.

1. Did your group have a plan for completing its task? Did it discuss what taxes to pass? Compared to other members, how much did you take part in those activities?
2. How well did your group work together? What role did you play in that? Was it a positive contribution or a negative one? Explain.
3. Was your group able to make a decision? If not, why? If so, was compromise involved? Do you support the decision? Explain why or why not.

Social Studies Skills Activity: Making Group Decisions

Addressing Relations with France

Standards Proficiency

1. Organize students into small groups. Have the groups review the material under the heading "The French Question" in Section 3.
2. Ask students to imagine that they are members of President Washington's Cabinet. Their task is to recommend solutions for dealing with the situation with French representative Edmond Genet and his recruitment of American privateers.
3. Remind students that they want to make France respect U.S. neutrality but not provoke a war with France.
4. Have each group come up with one to two courses of action. Remind the groups to give each member a chance to participate.
5. Have each group share its solutions with the class. Then have each group discuss its decision-making process. **LS Interpersonal**

Alternative Assessment Handbook, Rubric 14: Group Activity

Answers

Practice the Skill *Answers will vary, but students should indicate an understanding of the roles and obligations of group members in making decisions. Students should answer each question and adequately describe and evaluate the decision-making process in their groups. Students should also exhibit an understanding of compromise and negotiation.*

CHAPTER 6

Standards Review

Visual Summary

Use the visual summary below to help you review the main ideas of the chapter.

Reviewing Vocabulary, Terms, and People

Complete each sentence by filling in the blank with the correct term or person.

1. The ______________ established the structure of the federal court system and its relationship to state courts.
2. Federalists angered many Republicans when they passed the ______________ to protect the United States from traitors.
3. As president, Washington was able to establish several __________, or decisions that serve as examples for later action.
4. Farmers in western Pennsylvania protested taxes in the ____________.
5. The ______________ was created in order to strengthen the U.S. economy.

Comprehension and Critical Thinking

SECTION 1 *(Pages 196–199)* **HSS** 8.1

6. a. **Recall** What precedents did President Washington and Congress establish for the executive and judicial branches?

   b. **Draw Conclusions** Why did Americans select George Washington as their first president?

   c. **Evaluate** Do you think the newly established government met the expectations of its citizens? Why or why not?

SECTION 2 *(Pages 200–204)* **HSS** 8.3.4

7. a. **Identify** What changes did Alexander Hamilton make to the national economy?

   b. **Contrast** In what ways did Hamilton and Jefferson disagree on the economy?

   c. **Evaluate** Which of Hamilton's economic plans do you think was the most important to the new nation? Why?

Answers

Visual Summary

Review and Inquiry Have volunteers create a cluster diagram of the information in the visual summary for the class to see. Then ask students what the visual summary communicates that a cluster diagram cannot. *Students should focus on the visual elements: image of Washington implies his dignity, strength, and influence in leading the country; the sail implies progress; the waves imply danger.*

Quick Facts Transparency: Launching the Nation Visual Summary

Reviewing Vocabulary, Terms, and People

1. Judiciary Act of 1789
2. Alien and Sedition Acts
3. precedents
4. Whiskey Rebellion
5. Bank of the United States

Comprehension and Critical Thinking

6. a. departments and cabinet in the executive branch; Judiciary Act of 1789 to create three levels of federal courts

   b. thought he was honest, patriotic, and a good leader

   c. possible answers—Yes, the citizens re-elected Washington so their expectations must have been met; no, the new government had too many problems.

Review and Assessment Resources

Review and Reinforce

- **SE** Standards Review
- **CRF:** Chapter Review Activity
- California Standards Review Workbook
- Quick Facts Transparency: Launching the Nation Visual Summary
- Spanish Chapter Summaries Audio CD Program
- Online Chapter Summaries in Six Languages
- **OSP** Holt PuzzlePro; GameTool for ExamView
- Quiz Game CD-ROM

Assess

- **SE** Standards Assessment
- PASS: Chapter Test, Forms A and B
- Alternative Assessment Handbook
- **OSP** ExamView Test Generator, Chapter Test
- Universal Access Modified Worksheets and Tests CD-ROM: Chapter Test
- Holt Online Assessment Program (in the Premier Online Edition)

Reteach/Intervene

- Interactive Reader and Study Guide
- Universal Access Teacher Management System: Lesson Plans for Universal Access
- Universal Access Modified Worksheets and Tests CD-ROM
- Interactive Skills Tutor CD-ROM

go.hrw.com
Online Resources
Chapter Resources:
KEYWORD: SS8 US6

Answers

7. a. had the federal government repay bonds at full value and take on much of the states' war debts, increased tariffs, proposed a national bank and national mint
b. Hamilton—focused on business and manufacturing, wanted higher tariffs and a national bank; Jefferson—focused on farmers, wanted lower tariffs; opposed a national bank
c. possible answers—raising tariffs, protected American manufacturing; National Bank—stabilized the economy
8. a. remaining neutral, conflicts with Britain on the high seas and on the frontier, conflict with Spain over access to New Orleans, conflicts with Native Americans in the northwest, Whiskey Rebellion
b. thought neutrality was the safest and most reasonable plan
c. possible answer—successful, nation overcame several challenges and avoided war with Britain
9. a. Rivalry between the parties dominated the election and resulted in more than one candidate running for president for the first time.
b. Some Americans supported the acts, while other Americans strongly opposed them, saying they were unconstitutional.
c. possible answers—The two parties would continue to oppose each other and not work together; Congress would be divided; leaders would focus on party goals and not the common good.

Reviewing Themes

10. national debt, including money owed to foreign nations, money owed on Revolutionary War bonds, and states' war debts; Hamilton developed a plan to pay the foreign debt immediately, gradually repay the full value of bonds, raise tariffs to increase revenue, take on much of the states' war debts, and create a national bank and mint.
11. Politics become more divisive and sectionalized, but at the same time offered Americans more of a choice in candidates and views.

SECTION 3 *(Pages 205–211)* **HSS** 8.3.5, 8.4.2

8. a. **Describe** What challenges did the nation face during Washington's presidency?
b. **Make Inferences** Why did Washington believe that it was important for the United States to remain neutral in foreign conflicts?
c. **Evaluate** Rate the success of Washington's presidency. Explain the reasons for your rating.

SECTION 4 *(Pages 212–215)* **HSS** 8.3.4

9. a. **Describe** What role did political parties play in the election of 1796?
b. **Analyze** How did the Alien and Sedition Acts create division among some Americans?
c. **Predict** How might the political attacks between the Federalist and Democratic-Republican parties lead to problems in the future?

Reviewing Themes

10. **Economics** What economic problems troubled the nation at the beginning of Washington's presidency? How were they solved?
11. **Politics** How did the creation of political parties change politics in the United States?

Using the Internet

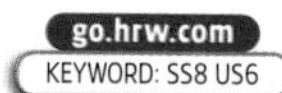

12. **Activity: Creating a Poster** In 1798 war with France seemed on the horizon. The Federalist-controlled Congress passed a law that made it a crime to criticize the government in print. In 1971 war raged in Vietnam and the president used a court order to stop publication of information critical of the government's actions in Vietnam. What do these events have in common? Enter the activity keyword. Then research the Alien and Sedition Acts and the Pentagon Papers case during the Vietnam War. Create a poster to display your information and to illustrate the connection between a free press and a democratic society.

Reading Skills

Understanding Assumptions by Inferring *Use the Reading Skills taught in this chapter to answer the question about the reading selection below.*

> Party differences were based partly on where and how people lived. Businesspeople in the cities tended to support the Federalists. Farmers in more isolated areas generally favored the Democratic-Republicans. *(p. 213)*

13. Which of the following statements can be inferred from the section?
a. Farmers wanted a large federal government.
b. Urban Americans were usually Republicans.
c. Merchants supported John Adams.
d. People in the cities had different concerns than did the rural population.

Social Studies Skills

Making Group Decisions *Use the Social Studies Skills taught in this chapter to answer the questions below.*

Get together with a group of three or four students and discuss the Alien and Sedition Acts. Answer the following questions individually and as a group.

14. Do you think that limits were needed on Americans' speeches and printed articles at the time?
15. What other ideas might Congress have considered to solve the problem of disagreement?

Focus on Writing

16. **Writing a Nobel Nomination** Now that you've chosen your nominee for the Nobel Prize, you can start to write your nomination. Begin with a sentence that identifies the person you are nominating. Then give at least three reasons for your nomination. Each reason should include a specific achievement or contribution of this person. End your nomination with a sentence that sums up your reasons for nominating this person for the Nobel Prize. Be persuasive. You need to convince the Nobel Prize committee that this person deserves the prize more than anyone else in the world!

Using the Internet

12. Go to the HRW Web site and enter the keyword shown to access a rubric for this activity.

KEYWORD: SS8 US6

Reading Skills

13. d

Social Studies Skills

14. Answers will vary but students should present their views within the context of the period.
15. possible answers—suggested compromises to address some of each party's concerns; found ways to resolve the issues that were dividing the nation

Focus on Writing

16. **Rubric** Students' Nobel nominations should:
- clearly identify the person being nominated
- provide at least three specific reasons for the nomination
- be persuasive
- use correct grammar, punctuation, spelling, and capitalization.

CRF: Focus on Writing: A Nobel Nomination

Standards Assessment

DIRECTIONS: Read each question and write the letter of the best response.

1

- Increase the federal government's power so it can provide strong leadership.
- Allow the federal government to pay the states' Revolutionary War debts.
- Encourage the growth of American manufacturing and business.
- Create a national bank that could make loans to the government and to business.

Which early leader would have been most *opposed* to such ideas?

A John Adams
B Alexander Hamilton
C Thomas Jefferson
D George Washington

2 In the 1790s, most Americans

A lived in the countryside and worked on family farms.
B lived in small towns and worked as laborers or craftspeople.
C lived in cities and worked as laborers, craftspeople, or merchants.
D lived west of the Appalachian Mountains or wanted to move West.

3 In his Farewell Address in 1796, President Washington advised Americans of

A the nation's need for a national bank.
B his fear of a British invasion to end American independence.
C his wish that the office of president be given more power.
D the dangers of ties with foreign nations.

4 President Washington demonstrated the government's power under the new Constitution to enforce federal law in the way he handled the

A Whiskey Rebellion.
B Alien and Sedition Acts.
C XYZ affair.
D Judiciary Act of 1789.

5 The two-party system that exists in American politics today first arose during the election of which president?

A George Washington
B John Adams
C Thomas Jefferson
D James Madison

Connecting with Past Learning

6 The war between Great Britain and France that raged during the presidencies of Washinton and Adams was one of many conflicts between those two nations. Earlier wars between them included

A the War of the Roses.
B the Glorious Revolution.
C the Hundred Years' War.
D the Crusades.

7 In Grade 7 you learned about Martin Luther's protest of the way in which the Catholic Church raised money. Which event in the United States was also a protest against methods of raising money?

A the XYZ affair
B Washington's Farewell Address
C the Judiciary Act of 1789
D the Whiskey Rebellion

Answers

1. C
Break Down the Question This question requires students to synthesize information. Remind students to look for words in questions that might ask for the opposite of something, such as the word *opposed* here. Tell students first to try to identify the leader who did support these views *(Hamilton)* and then try to identify who most opposed that person *(Jefferson)*.

2. A
Break Down the Question This question requires students to recall factual information. Have students consider where most Americans lived at the time.

3. D
Break Down the Question Tell students who are unsure about the answer to try to think of Washington's various actions in office, such as the Neutrality Proclamation. Students should then look for the option that best aligns with those actions.

4. A
Break Down the Question Tell students first to eliminate any events that did not take place during Washington's administration (B and C). Then have students consider what they know about the remaining two choices.

5. B
Break Down the Question Tell students to consider what they know about Washington's election. *(It was unanimous.)* Students should then eliminate Jefferson and Madison because students have not yet studied their administrations.

6. C
Break Down the Question This question connects to information covered in Grade 7.

7. D
Break Down the Question This question connects to information covered in Grade 7.

Intervention Resources

Reproducible

- Interactive Reader and Study Guide
- Universal Access Teacher Management System: Lesson Plans for Universal Access

Technology

- Quick Facts Transparency: Launching the Nation Visual Summary
- Universal Access Modified Worksheets and Tests CD-ROM
- Interactive Skills Tutor CD-ROM

Tips for Test Taking

Jot It Down Quickly Read the following to students: You might have made a special effort to memorize some information for a test. If you are worried you will forget, use this strategy. As soon as the testing period begins, jot the information down on the back of your test or on a piece of scratch paper. You can then stop worrying about forgetting and focus on the test.

Standards Review

Have students review the following standards in their workbooks.

- California Standards Review Workbook: HSS 8.3.3, 8.3.4, 8.3.5

Preteach

Bellringer

Motivate Ask volunteers to explain a political process, such as the division of power in Congress. Next, discuss as a class why clear explanations of political processes are important. Lead students to conclude that explanations are important because political participation and awareness is essential in a democracy. Tell students that in this workshop they will write a paper explaining a political process.

Direct Teach

Considering Audience

Adjusting Readability Tell students that when they write something, they should consider whether their audience will understand it. One way to increase comprehension is to adjust readability. Explain that three main factors contribute to a text's readability: difficulty of vocabulary, sentence length, and paragraph length. Select a paragraph from the textbook and have students work as a class to rewrite it at a lower readability level. Help students simplify vocabulary, shorten sentences, and, if appropriate, break up the paragraph. Then have students practice the skill independently on a second paragraph. Remind students to make certain the new version makes sense, is grammatically and factually correct, and includes all the main points in the original.

Writing Workshop

Explaining a Political Process

Assignment

Write a paper explaining how the federal system balances power among the legislative, executive, and judicial branches of government.

How do you register to vote? What is the difference between a civil court and a federal court? When we want to know about a process or system of our government, we often turn to written explanations.

TIP Using a Graphic Organizer A chart like the following can help you organize the body of your explanation.

Legislative	Executive	Judicial

ELA Writing 8.2.6 Write technical documents.

1. Prewrite

Considering Purpose and Audience

In this assignment, you will be writing for an audience of middle school students. You'll need to

- identify questions they might have about the process or system
- identify factors or details that might confuse them

As you plan your paper, keep your audience in mind.

Collecting and Organizing the Information

The big idea, or thesis, of your explanation will be that the federal system balances the power among the three branches of government. To collect information about each branch and its powers, you can use a chart like the one on the left. Be sure to note the relationships among the parts. Also, note the important characteristics of each part. When you have completed the chart, you will have the basic organization of your paper.

2. Write

You can use this framework to help you write your first draft.

A Writer's Framework

Introduction
- State the big idea of your paper.
- Explain briefly why this topic is important to the reader.

Body
- Identify the important characteristics of each part of the process or system.
- Explain any relationships between or among the parts.
- Define terms your readers might not know.
- Where appropriate, include graphics to illustrate your explanation.

Conclusion
- Restate your big idea in different words.
- Summarize your main points.

Differentiating Instruction for Universal Access

Learners Having Difficulty

Reaching Standards

1. As students gather information, have them list any terms they do not understand.
2. Tell students to look up each of the terms in a thesaurus to find more familiar synonyms.
3. Then have students replace the difficult terms with the synonyms they found and reread the information. **LS Verbal/Linguistic**

ELA Reading 8.1.1

Special Education Students

Reaching Standards

1. Have a group of three students role play the three branches of government.
2. Have the student playing the legislative branch write a bill/law on two pieces of paper and give them to the other two students. Each of these students should then explain what his or her branch will do with the bill/law. **LS Interpersonal, Kinesthetic**

ELA Reading 8.2.0

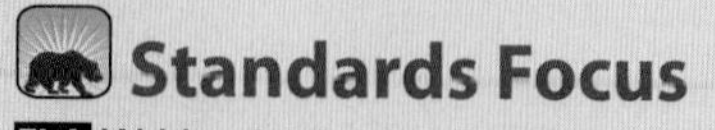

ELA Writing 8.1.4, 8.2.6; Reading 8.1.1, 8.2.0

3. Evaluate and Revise

Evaluating

Clear, straightforward language is important when explaining how things work. Use the following questions to discover ways to improve your paper.

Evaluation Questions for an Explanation of a Process or System

- Does your big-idea statement accurately reflect your explanation of the process or system?
- Do you discuss each part of the process or system in logical order?
- Do you include details and information to explain each part of the process or system?
- If you used bulleted or numbered lists, are the items parallel—that is, do they have the same grammatical forms or structures?
- Does your conclusion restate your big idea and explain the importance of your topic?

TIP **Using Bulleted Lists** The items in a bulleted list should be in the **same** grammatical forms or structures.

Not the same:

Duties of the legislative branch include

- interpret laws
- overseeing lower courts

The same:

Duties of the legislative branch include

- interpreting laws
- overseeing lower courts

Revising

Sometimes a complex explanation sounds even more complex when you try to explain it in a paragraph. In those cases, a bulleted list of facts or examples may make it easier for your readers to understand the information you are presenting. As you revise your paper, consider whether you have any information you should put in a bulleted list.

4. Proofread and Publish

Proofreading

If you use special formatting in your paper, it is important to make sure that it is consistent. Here are some things to check:

- If you have used boldface or italic type, have you always used it in the same way—for important information, for a heading, for a technical term?
- If you have used a list of items, have you consistently used numbers or bullets?

Publishing

Since you are writing this paper for students, you might find a student in the sixth or seventh grade to read it. Find out whether your explanation seems clear and interesting.

5. Practice and Apply

Use the steps and strategies outlined in this workshop to write your explanation of a process or system.

Reteach

Using Graphics

Making a Flow Chart To help students having trouble understanding the relationships among the branches of government, make a flow chart illustrating the relationships. Use labeled arrows to explain the different relationships among the three branches. Then, for each arrow, have students write a few sentences explaining the relationship represented by that arrow.

Teaching Tip

Avoiding Passive Voice Tell students that they should not use passive voice when writing explanations. Have students exchange papers and circle any passive verbs. Then have students rewrite their papers to eliminate the passive verbs.

Practice & Apply

Rubric

Students' explanations of the federal system should

- begin with a clear statement of the big idea.
- accurately and clearly explain how political power is balanced among the three branches of government.
- indicate an understanding of the system of checks and balances.
- define key terms related to the federal system.
- use a clear and logical organization.
- be written at a middle school level.
- include graphics as visual aids.
- end with a summary and a restatement of the big idea.
- use correct grammar, punctuation, spelling, and capitalization.

Advanced Learners/GATE **Exceeding Standards**

1. Challenge advanced learners to incorporate excerpts from the U.S. Constitution into their papers to support and enhance their explanations of how the federal system balances power among the three branches of government.
2. Alternatively, have advanced students extend their papers by explaining how the separation of powers benefits the American people and promotes the public good. Encourage students to conduct outside research to expand upon the information covered in their papers.
LS Verbal/Linguistic

ELA Writing 8.2.6

Unit Preview

Introduce the Unit

Share the information in the chapter overviews with students.

Chapter 7 Thomas Jefferson's presidency was marked by expansion and conflict. The nation almost doubled in size, and exploration led to new knowledge of the West.

Chapter 8 James Monroe's presidency was known as the Era of Good Feelings. This period was a time of relative peace, economic growth, and increasing nationalism. The United States asserted itself in foreign affairs, and American culture developed a national identity. At the same time, disputes over slavery began to divide the nation.

Chapter 9 The expansion of political rights and the election of Andrew Jackson signaled the growing power of the American people. Jackson's presidency was marked by political conflicts, growing sectional differences, economic problems, and the removal of Native Americans from the Southeast.

Chapter 10 In the 1830s, settlers in Texas rebelled against Mexican rule and gained independence. Meanwhile, other settlers braved difficult trails to reach Oregon and California. In 1846, conflicts with Mexico led to war. A U.S. victory resulted in a large gain in territory, including California, where gold was soon discovered.

Standards Focus

For a list of the overarching standards covered in this unit, see the first page of each chapter.

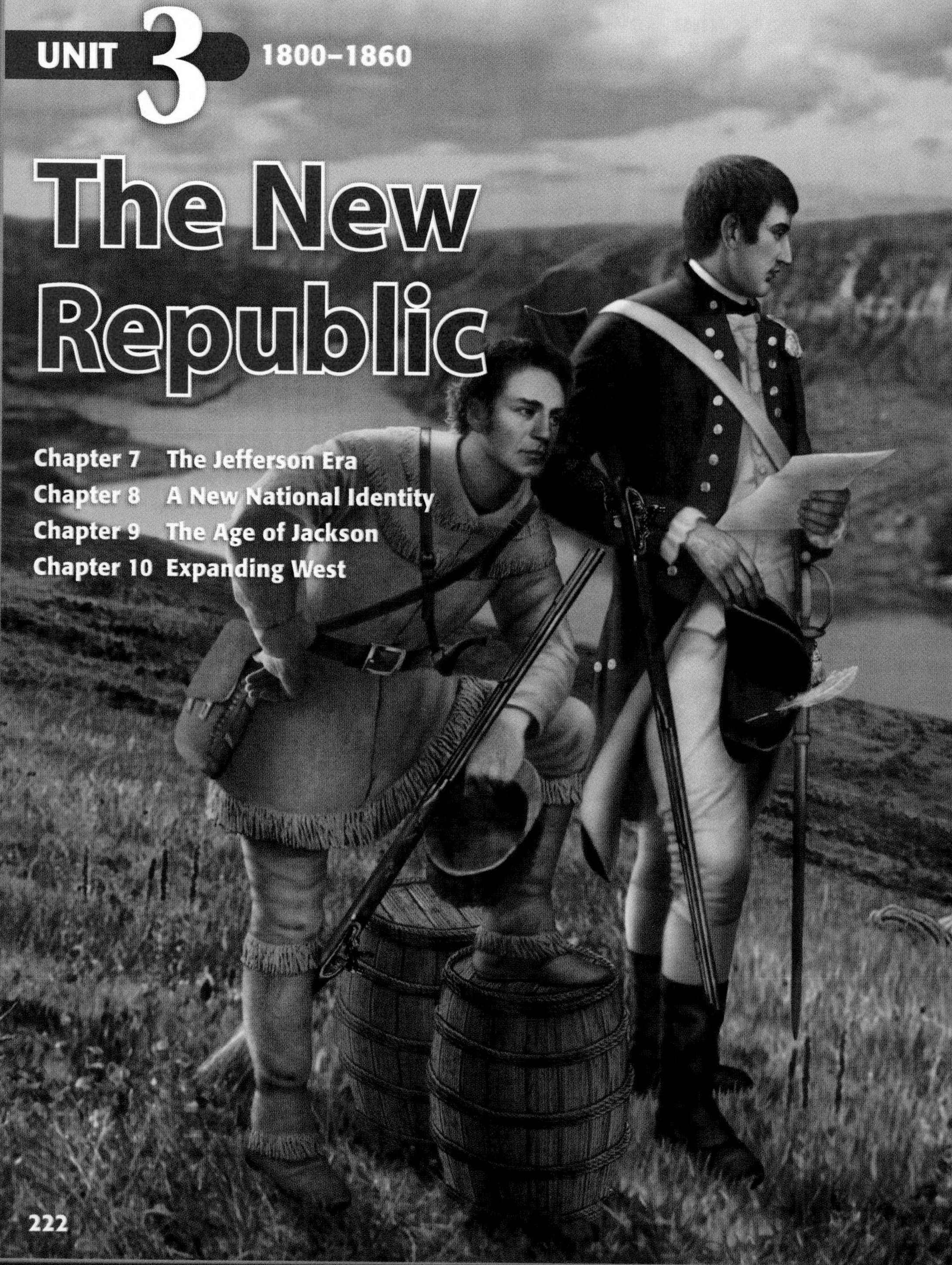

Unit Resources

Planning

- Universal Access Teacher Management System: Unit Instructional Benchmarking Guides
- One-Stop Planner CD-ROM with Test Generator: Holt Calendar Planner
- Power Presentations with Video CD-ROM
- A Teacher's Guide to Religion in the Public Schools

Standards Mastery

- Standards Review Workbook
- At Home: A Guide to Standards Mastery for United States History

Differentiating Instruction

- Universal Access Teacher Management System: Lesson Plans for Universal Access
- Pre-AP Activities Guide for United States History
- Universal Access Modified Worksheets and Tests CD-ROM

Enrichment

- **CRF 7:** Economics and History: Embargoes—Economic Diplomacy
- **CRF 9:** Economics and History: The Panic of 1837
- **CRF 10:** Interdisciplinary Project: Share the Westward Adventure Skit
- Civic Participation
- Primary Source Library CD-ROM

Assessment

- Progress Assessment Support System: Benchmark Test
- OSP ExamView Test Generator: Benchmark Test
- Holt Online Assessment Program (in the Premier Online Edition)
- Alternative Assessment Handbook

The **Universal Access Teacher Management System** provides a planning and instructional benchmarking guide for this unit.

What You Will Learn...

By the time the country had experienced two presidential terms, people had begun to think of themselves as Americans. A new sense of pride and unity influenced all areas of American society, from politics to art, from economics to religion. Settlers began moving deeper into the continent and the Untied States began to grow. In the next four chapters, you will learn about the first expansion of the young nation.

Explore the Art

In this picture, Lewis and Clark are shown asking advice from Sacagawea, a teenaged Shoshone Indian who helped them on their exploration of the continent. How does this picture show the challenges facing the explorers?

223

Unit Preview

Connect to the Unit

Activity **A Time Collage** Briefly discuss with students what the idea of national identity means. Begin by having students describe what it means to be an American. Explain to students that during the early 1800s people were just beginning to develop a sense of what it meant to be an American.

Tell students that during this unit they are going to create a linear time collage. Hang a large strip of butcher paper on the wall of the classroom. Divide the paper into seven sections and label them from 1800 to 1860. After each chapter, have students place images that apply to the topics in that chapter in the appropriate places on the time line. At the end of the unit, have students discuss how the images reflect a sense of American identity.
LS Interpersonal, Visual/Spatial

Explore the Art

Have students examine the painting at left. Ask students to predict how the three individuals—Lewis, Clark, and Sacagawea—might have played a role in building the new nation. Then ask students to discuss how the painting expresses the optimism of the young nation.

About the Illustration

This illustration is an artist's conception based on available sources. However, historians are uncertain exactly what this scene looked like.

Democracy and Civic Education

Standards Proficiency

Responsibility: Participating in the Political Process

Research Required

Background Explain that democracy expanded in the mid-1800s. More Americans gained the right to vote and the ways in which citizens could participate in the political process expanded.

1. Discuss with students why it is important in a republic to have an informed citizenry that actively participates in the political process. Then discuss with students the ways in which they can participate in politics.
2. Have students choose an issue facing their school or community. During the study of this unit, have students work as a class to gather information about the issue.
3. Then help students decide upon a course of action for addressing the issue. Students might write to a local or state official, organize a community awareness campaign, or form an organization to address the issue.
LS Interpersonal, Verbal/Linguistic

Alternative Assessment Handbook, Rubrics 14: Group Activity; and 30: Research

Civic Participation

Answers

Explore the Art *illustrates the rugged landscape over which they will have to travel and the limited transportation available*

Chapter 7 Planning Guide

The Jefferson Era

Chapter Overview	Reproducible Resources	Technology Resources
CHAPTER 7 **pp. 224–255** **Overview: In this chapter, students will study the presidency of Thomas Jefferson, the Louisiana Purchase, the War of 1812, and other challenges the nation faced as it grew.** See p. 224 for the California History–Social Science standards covered in this chapter.	**Universal Access Teacher Management System:*** • Universal Access Instructional Benchmarking Guides • Lesson Plans for Universal Access **Interactive Reader and Study Guide:*** Chapter Graphic Organizer **Chapter Resource File*** • Focus on Writing Activity: Letter of Recommendation • Social Studies Skills Activity: Working in Groups to Solve Issues • Chapter Review Activity **Pre-AP Activities Guide for United States History:*** Analyzing Thesis Statements	**One-Stop Planner CD-ROM:** Calendar Planner **Student Edition Full-Read Audio CD-ROM** **Universal Access Modified Worksheets and Tests CD-ROM** **Interactive Skills Tutor CD-ROM** **Primary Source Library CD-ROM for United States History** **Power Presentations with Video CD-ROM** **History's Impact: United States History Video Program (VHS/DVD):** The Jefferson Era*
Section 1: **Jefferson Becomes President** **The Big Idea:** Thomas Jefferson's election began a new era in American government. 8.4.1, 8.4.2	**Universal Access Teacher Management System:*** Section 1 Lesson Plan **Interactive Reader and Study Guide:*** Section 1 Summary **Chapter Resource File*** • Vocabulary Builder, Section 1 • Biography Activity: Aaron Burr • Primary Source Activity: Jefferson's 1801 Inaugural Address **U.S. Supreme Court Case Studies:** *Marbury* v. *Madison* (1803)	**Daily Bellringer Transparency:** Section 1* **Quick Facts Transparency:** The Election of 1800* **Internet Activity:** Thomas Jefferson and Politics Essay
Section 2: **The Louisiana Purchase** **The Big Idea:** Under President Jefferson's leadership, the United States added the Louisiana Territory. 8.4.1, 8.8.2	**Universal Access Teacher Management System:*** Section 2 Lesson Plan **Interactive Reader and Study Guide:*** Section 2 Summary **Chapter Resource File*** • Vocabulary Builder, Section 2 • Biography Activity: Sacagawea • History and Geography Activity: Pike Explores the Southwest **Political Cartoons Activities for United States History,** Cartoon 9: The Louisiana Purchase*	**Daily Bellringer Transparency:** Section 2* **Map Transparency:** The Louisiana Purchase and Western Expeditions*
Section 3: **The Coming of War** **The Big Idea:** Challenges at home and abroad led the United States to declare war on Great Britain. 8.5.1	**Universal Access Teacher Management System:*** Section 3 Lesson Plan **Interactive Reader and Study Guide:*** Section 3 Summary **Chapter Resource File*** • Vocabulary Builder, Section 3 • Biography Activity: Tecumseh • Economics and History Activity: Embargoes • Literature Activity: *A Warrior's Speech* • Primary Source Activity: A Shawnee Leader Seeks Allies **Political Cartoons Activities for United States History,** Cartoon 8: Party Politics in the Jefferson Era*	**Daily Bellringer Transparency:** Section 3*
Section 4: **The War of 1812** **The Big Idea:** Great Britain and the United States went to battle in the War of 1812. 8.5.1	**Universal Access Teacher Management System:*** Section 4 Lesson Plan **Interactive Reader and Study Guide:*** Section 4 Summary **Chapter Resource File*** • Vocabulary Builder, Section 4 • Biography Activity: Dolley Madison	**Daily Bellringer Transparency:** Section 4* **Map Transparency:** The War of 1812* **Quick Facts Transparency:** Analyzing the War of 1812* **Internet Activity:** "The Star-Spangled Banner" Poster

SE Student Edition  Print Resource Audio CD  Video

TE Teacher's Edition  Transparency CD-ROM  DVD

go.hrw.com CA Standards Mastery LS Learning Styles

OSP One-Stop Planner CD-ROM * also on One-Stop Planner CD

Review, Assessment, Intervention

- **Standards Review Workbook***
- **Quick Facts Transparency:** The Jefferson Era Visual Summary*
- **Spanish Chapter Summaries Audio CD Program**
-  **Online Chapter Summaries in Six Languages**
- **Quiz Game CD-ROM**
- **Progress Assessment Support System (PASS):** Chapter Test*
- **Universal Access Modified Worksheets and Tests CD-ROM:** Modified Chapter Test
- **One-Stop Planner CD-ROM:** ExamView Test Generator (English/Spanish)

- **PASS:** Section 1 Quiz*
-  **Online Quiz:** Section 1
-  **Alternative Assessment Handbook**

-  **PASS:** Section 2 Quiz*
-  **Online Quiz:** Section 2
-  **Alternative Assessment Handbook**

-  **PASS:** Section 3 Quiz*
-  **Online Quiz:** Section 3
-  **Alternative Assessment Handbook**

-  **PASS:** Section 4 Quiz*
-  **Online Quiz:** Section 4
-  **Alternative Assessment Handbook**

California Resources for Standards Mastery

INSTRUCTIONAL PLANNING AND SUPPORT

- **Universal Access Teacher Management System***

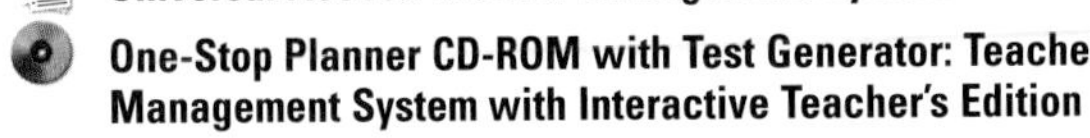

- **One-Stop Planner CD-ROM with Test Generator: Teacher Management System with Interactive Teacher's Edition**

STANDARDS MASTERY

-  **Standards Review Workbook***
- **At Home: A Guide to Standards Mastery for United States History**

go.hrw.com Holt Online Learning

To enhance learning, Internet activities are available for a Thomas Jefferson and Politics Essay and "The Star-Spangled Banner" Poster.

KEYWORD: SS8 TEACHER

- **Teacher Support Page**
- **Content Updates**
- **Rubrics and Writing Models**
- **Teaching Tips for the Multimedia Classroom**

KEYWORD: SS8 US7

- **Current Events**
- **Document-Based Questions**
- **Holt Grapher**
- **Holt Online Atlas**
- **Holt Researcher**
- **Interactive Multimedia Activities**
- **Internet Activities**
- **Online Chapter Summaries in Six Languages**
- **Online Section Quizzes**
- **American History Maps and Charts**

HOLT PREMIER ONLINE STUDENT EDITION

Complete online support for interactivity, assessment, and reporting

- **Interactive Maps and Notebook**
- **Standardized Test Prep**
- **Homework Practice and Research Activities Online**

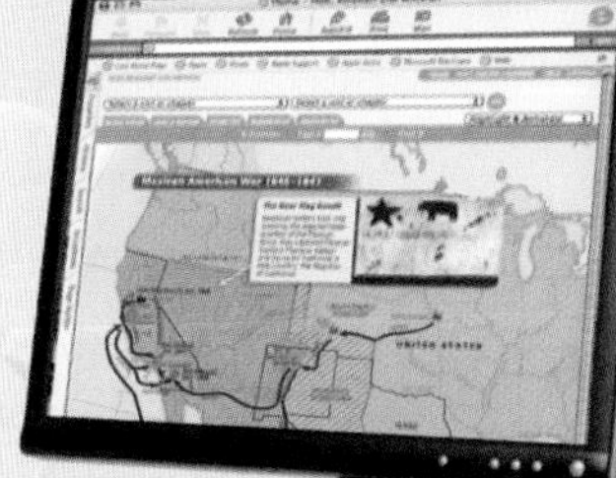

Mastering the Standards: Differentiating Instruction

Reaching Standards	Basic-level activities designed for all students encountering new material
Standards Proficiency	Intermediate-level activities designed for average students
Exceeding Standards	Challenging activities designed for honors and gifted-and-talented students
Standard English Mastery	Activities designed to improve standard English usage

Frequently Asked Questions

INSTRUCTIONAL PLANNING AND SUPPORT

Where do I find planning aids, pacing guides, lesson plans, and other teaching aids?

Annotated Teacher's Edition:
- Chapter planning guides
- Standards-based instruction and strategies
- Differentiated instruction for universal access
- Point-of-use reminders for integrating program resources

Power Presentations with Video CD-ROM

Universal Access Teacher Management System:
- Year and unit instructional benchmarking guides
- Reproducible lesson plans
- Assessment guides for diagnostic, progress, and summative end-of-the-year tests
- Options for differentiating instruction and intervention
- Teaching guides and answer keys for student workbooks

One-Stop Planner CD-ROM with Test Generator: Teacher Management System with Interactive Teacher's Editon:
- Calendar Planner
- Editable lesson plans
- All reproducible ancillaries in Adobe Acrobat (PDF) format
- ExamView Test Generator (English & Spanish)
- Game Tool for ExamView
- PuzzlePro
- Transparency and video previews

DIFFERENTIATING INSTRUCTION FOR UNIVERSAL ACCESS

What resources are available to ensure that Advanced Learners/GATE Students master the standards?

Teacher's Edition Activities:
- Thomas Jefferson Report Card, p. 230
- "The Star-Spangled Banner," p. 248

Lesson Plans for Universal Access

Pre-AP Activities Guide for United States History: Analyzing Thesis Statements

Primary Source Library CD-ROM for United States History

What resources are available to ensure that English Learners and Standard English Learners master the standards?

Teacher's Edition Activities:
- Election of 1800 Activity, p. 229

Lesson Plans for Universal Access

Chapter Resource File: Vocabulary Builder Activities

Spanish Chapter Summaries Audio CD Program

Online Chapter Summaries in Six Languages

One-Stop Planner CD-ROM:
- PuzzlePro, Spanish Version
- ExamView Test Generator, Spanish Version

What modified materials are available for Special Education?

The ***Universal Access Modified Worksheets and Tests CD-ROM*** provides editable versions of the following:

Vocabulary Flash Cards

Modified Vocabulary Builder Activities

Modified Chapter Review Activity

Modified Chapter Test

MASTERING THE CALIFORNIA STANDARDS

What resources are available to ensure that Learners Having Difficulty master the standards?

Teacher's Edition Activities:
- *Marbury* v. *Madison* Graphic Organizer, p. 231
- Louisiana Purchase Time Line Activity, p. 236
- The Journey West, p. 237
- Embargo Act of 1807 Activity, p. 242

Interactive Reader and Study Guide

Student Edition Full-Read Audio CD

Quick Facts Transparency: The Jefferson Era

Standards Review Workbook

Social Studies Skills Activity: Working in Groups to Solve Issues

Interactive Skills Tutor CD-ROM

How do I intervene for students struggling to master the standards?

Interactive Reader and Study Guide

Quick Facts Transparency: The Jefferson Era

Standards Review Workbook

Social Studies Skills Activity: Working in Groups to Solve Issues

Interactive Skills Tutor CD-ROM

PROFESSIONAL DEVELOPMENT

What teacher training resources are available to help me grow professionally?

- In-service and staff development as part of your Holt Social Studies product purchase
- Quick Teacher Tutorial Lesson Presentation CD-ROM
- Intensive tuition-based Teacher Development Institute
- *Teaching American History* Online 2 Module Professional Development Course
- Convenient Holt Speaker Bureau face-to-face workshop options
- PRAXIS™ Test Prep (#0089) interactive Web-based content refreshers*
- 24/7 *Ask A Professional Development Expert* at http://www.hrw.com/prodev/

* PRAXIS is a trademark of Educational Testing Service (ETS). This publication is not endorsed or approved by ETS.

Information Literacy Skills

To learn more about how History–Social Science instruction may be improved by the effective use of library media centers and information literacy skills, go to the Teacher's Resource Materials for Chapter 7 at **go.hrw.com**, keyword: SS8 MEDIA.

The following materials were developed by the Division for Public Education of the American Bar Association. These materials are part of the **Democracy and Civic Education** supplement.
- Constitution Study Guide
- Supreme Court Case Studies

• Chapter Preview •

Standards Focus

Standards by Section
Section 1: HSS 8.4.1, 8.4.2
Section 2: HSS 8.4.1, 8.8.2
Section 3: HSS 8.5.1
Section 4: HSS 8.5.1

Teacher's Edition
HSS **Analysis Skills:** CS 1, CS 2, CS 3, HR 4, HR 5, HI 1, HI 2, HI 4

Preview Grade 8 Standards
HSS **8.5** Students analyze U.S. foreign policy in the early Republic.
8.5.2 Know the changing boundaries of the United States and describe the relationships the country had with its neighbors (current Mexico and Canada) and Europe, including the influence of the Monroe Doctrine, and how those relationships influenced westward expansion and the Mexican-American War.
8.8 Students analyze the divergent paths of the American people in the West from 1800 to the mid-1800s and the challenges they faced.
8.8.1 Discuss the election of Andrew Jackson as president in 1828, the importance of Jacksonian democracy, and his actions as president (e.g., the spoils system, veto of the National Bank, policy of Indian removal, opposition to the Supreme Court).

Focus on Writing
The **Chapter Resource File** provides a Focus on Writing worksheet to help students organize and write their letters of recommendation.

CRF: Focus on Writing Activity: A Letter of Recommendation

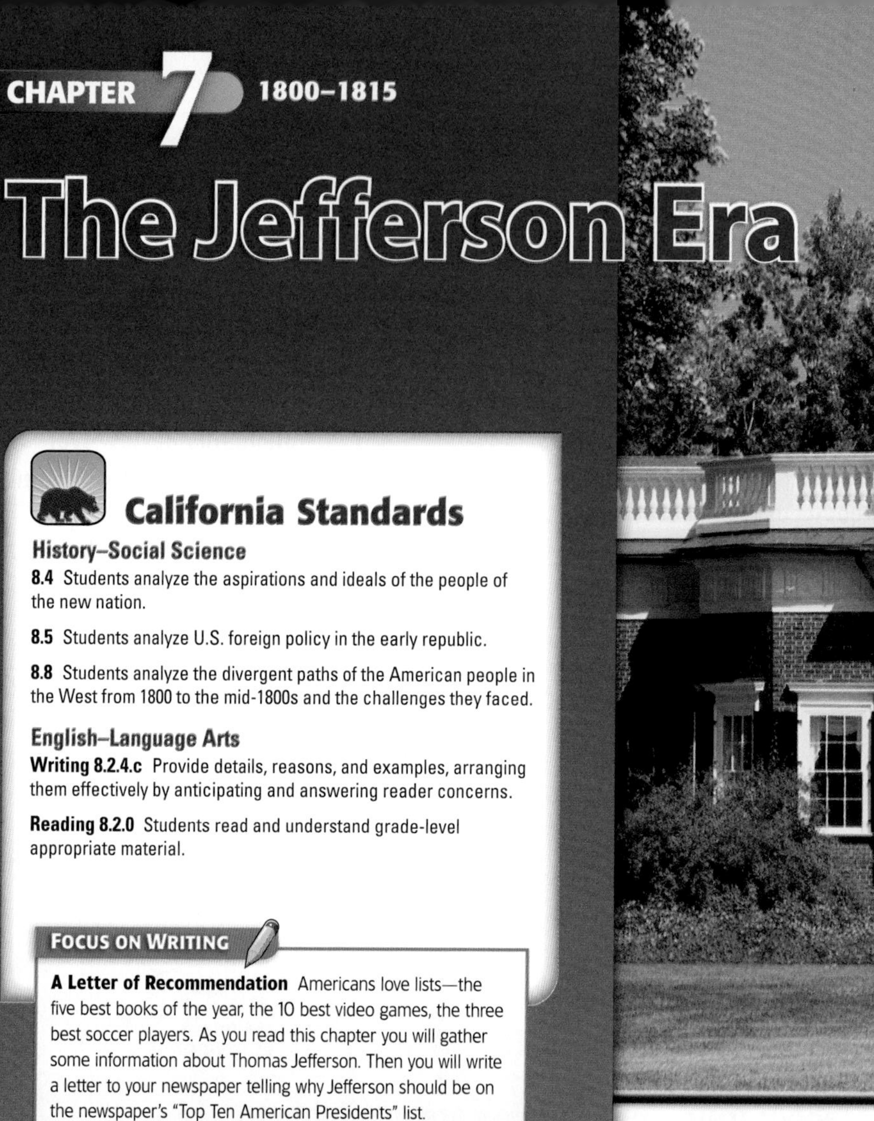

CHAPTER 7 1800–1815

The Jefferson Era

California Standards

History–Social Science

8.4 Students analyze the aspirations and ideals of the people of the new nation.

8.5 Students analyze U.S. foreign policy in the early republic.

8.8 Students analyze the divergent paths of the American people in the West from 1800 to the mid-1800s and the challenges they faced.

English–Language Arts

Writing 8.2.4.c Provide details, reasons, and examples, arranging them effectively by anticipating and answering reader concerns.

Reading 8.2.0 Students read and understand grade-level appropriate material.

FOCUS ON WRITING

A Letter of Recommendation Americans love lists—the five best books of the year, the 10 best video games, the three best soccer players. As you read this chapter you will gather some information about Thomas Jefferson. Then you will write a letter to your newspaper telling why Jefferson should be on the newspaper's "Top Ten American Presidents" list.

UNITED STATES

1801 Thomas Jefferson takes office.

1803 U.S. Senate approves the Louisiana Purchase.

1800

WORLD

1802 An army of former slaves led by Toussaint-Louverture defeats a French army in Haiti.

Introduce the Chapter

Standards Proficiency

Focus on the Jefferson Administration

HSS 8.4, 8.5; HSS **Analysis Skills:** HI 1

1. Explain to students that the presidential election of 1800 was very close. Have students use what they learned in the last chapter to predict what some of the main issues in the election might have been. (*Students might suggest the extent of the federal government's power, the Bank of the United States, relations with France, and the Alien and Sedition Acts.*)
2. Next, have students preview the chapter by reading the section titles and the blue headings and by looking at the images.
3. Then ask students if they can tell from this quick preview what some of the important events of the Jefferson era were. List students' responses for the class to see.
4. Conclude by having students discuss which of the events they listed would have been most significant to the development of the United States. Tell students to keep the discussion in mind as they study the chapter.

LS **Verbal/Linguistic, Visual/Spatial**

HOLT

History's Impact

▶ **video series**
Watch the video to understand the impact of Jefferson's presidency on the growth of America.

What You Will Learn...

In this chapter you will learn about the presidency of Thomas Jefferson. A man of many talents, Jefferson looked back to classical architecture to design his Virginia home, Monticello.

1804 Lewis and Clark begin their westward journey.

1807 Congress passes the Embargo Act.

1812 Congress declares war against Great Britain.

1815 The Battle of New Orleans is fought.

1805 — 1810 — 1815

1807 The slave trade is abolished in the British Empire.

1814 Kurozumi Munetada founds an influential Shinto religious sect that stresses patriotism in Japan.

THE JEFFERSON ERA **225**

• Chapter Preview •

HOLT

History's Impact

▶ **video series**
See the Video Teacher's Guide for strategies for using the chapter video **The Jefferson Era**.

Chapter Big Ideas

Section 1 Thomas Jefferson's election began a new era in American government. **HSS** 8.4.1, 8.4.2

Section 2 Under President Jefferson's leadership, the United States added the Louisiana Territory. **HSS** 8.4.1, 8.8.2

Section 3 Challenges at home and abroad led the United States to declare war on Great Britain. **HSS** 8.5.1

Section 4 Great Britain and the United States went to battle in the War of 1812. **HSS** 8.5.1

Explore the Picture

Monticello Thomas Jefferson designed and built Monticello, his plantation home near Charlottesville, Virginia. Inside, the house provided a library for Jefferson's large collection of books as well as space for his many inventions. Outside, the grounds featured gardens where Jefferson experimented with growing new types of plants, flowers, and vegetables.

Analyzing Visuals The portion of Monticello covered by the white dome is called the Dome Room. How might Jefferson have used this room? *possible answers—for weather or astronomical observations; for observing his plantation*

go.hrw.com

Online Resources

Chapter Resources:
KEYWORD: SS8 US7

Teacher Resources:
KEYWORD: SS8 TEACHER

Explore the Time Line

1. Who led a slave rebellion in Haiti in 1802 that defeated a French army? *Toussaint-Louverture*
2. When did the British Empire abolish the slave trade? *1807*
3. Whom did the United States go to war against during this period, and when did the war begin? *Great Britain; 1812*
4. Which event do you think led to the expansion of the United States? *U.S. Senate's approval of the Louisiana Purchase in 1803.*

HSS Analysis Skills: CS 1

Info to Know

Jefferson Thomas Jefferson had a good-humored nature. A brilliant conversationalist, he could talk just as easily about chemistry or horse racing as politics or philosophy. He loved architecture, art, and geography. He not only knew French, Greek, Italian, Latin, and Spanish but also studied some 40 Native American languages. At the same time, Jefferson struggled with a deep sense of loneliness. The death of his wife, Martha Wayles Skelton, and of five of his six children caused him untold grief.

Reading Social Studies

Understanding Themes

Two themes—geography and politics—are the focus of this chapter. Students will learn about the Louisiana Purchase and the expedition of Lewis and Clark. Help students understand the challenges that the geography of the West presented to the exploration of these lands. As students read the chapter, help them see the relationship between geography and politics during this time in American history.

Public Documents in History

Focus on Reading Have students consider the types of public documents that they have already seen or studied. The Declaration of Independence and the U.S. Constitution are two examples that students should know. They may also be familiar with state laws concerning driving or voter information bulletins that are published before an election. Point out to students that these are all examples of public documents. Guide students in a discussion of the language used in public documents. Ask students why public documents might be of use to historians.

Reading Social Studies

Economics | **Geography** | **Politics** | Religion | Society and Culture | Science and Technology

Focus on Themes In this chapter you will learn about Thomas Jefferson's presidency. You will read what happened when Jefferson's first run to be president ended in a tie. After that, you will learn about his decision to buy Louisiana from the French, see how he encouraged the exploration of the West, and discover why, during his second term, America found herself at war with Great Britain. You will see how America's expanding **geography** and **politics** were intertwined.

Public Documents in History

Focus on Reading Historians use many types of documents to learn about the past. These documents can often be divided into two types—private and public. Private documents are those written for a person's own use, such as letters, journals, or notebooks. Public documents, on the other hand, are available for everyone to read and examine. They include such things as laws, tax codes, and treaties.

Graphic organizers are available in the

Studying Public Documents Studying public documents from the past can tell us a great deal about politics and society of the time. However, public documents can often be confusing or difficult to understand. When you read such a document, you may want to use a list of questions like the one below to be sure you understand what you're reading.

You can often figure out the topic of a public document from the title and introduction.

Public documents often use unfamiliar words or use familiar words in unfamiliar ways. For example, the document on the next page uses the word *augmented.* Do you know what the word means in this context? If not, you should look it up.

Many public documents deal with several issues and will therefore have several main ideas.

Question Sheet for Public Documents

1. What is the topic of the document?
2. Do I understand what I'm reading?
3. Is there any vocabulary in the document that I do not understand?
4. What parts of the document should I re-read?
5. What are the main ideas and details of the document?
6. What have I learned from reading this document?

Reading and Skills Resources

Reading Support

- Interactive Reader and Study Guide
- Student Edition on Audio CD
- Spanish Chapter Summaries Audio CD Program

Social Studies Skills Support

- Interactive Skills Tutor CD-ROM

Vocabulary Support

- **CRF:** Vocabulary Builder Activities
- **CRF:** Chapter Review Activity
- Universal Access Modified Worksheets and Tests CD-ROM:
  - Vocabulary Flash Cards
  - Vocabulary Builder Activity
  - Chapter Review Activity
- **OSP** Holt PuzzlePro

Standards Focus

ELA Reading 8.2.6

ELA **Reading 8.2.6** Use information from a variety of consumer and public documents to explain a situation or solve a problem.

You Try It!

The passage below was taken from a Post Office notice from 1815. Read the passage and then answer the questions that follow.

Rates of Postage

Postmasters will take notice, that by an act of Congress, passed on the 23d instant, the several rates of postage are augmented fifty per cent; and that after the first of February next, the Rates of Postage for single Letters will be,

For any distance not exceeding 40 miles, 12 cents

Over 40 miles and not exceeding 90 miles, 15 cents

Over 90 miles and not exceeding 150 miles, 18 1/2 cents

Over 150 miles and not exceeding 300 miles, 25 1/2 cents

Over 300 miles and not exceeding 500 miles, 30 cents

Over 500 miles, 37 1/2 cents

Double letters, or those composed of two pieces of paper, double those rates.

Triple letters, or those composed of three pieces of paper, triple those rates.

Packets, or letters composed of four or more pieces of paper, and weighing one ounce or more, avoirdupois, are to be rated equal to one single letter for each quarter ounce.

After reading the document above, answer the following questions.

1. What is this document about?
2. What was the main idea or ideas of this document? What supporting details were included?
3. Look at the word *packets* in the last paragraph of the document. The word is not used here in the same way we usually use *packets* today. What does the word mean in this case? How can you tell?
4. Are there any other words in this passage with which you are unfamiliar? How might not knowing those words hinder your understanding of the passage?

Key Terms and People

Chapter 7

Section 1
John Adams *(p. 228)*
Thomas Jefferson *(p. 228)*
John Marshall *(p. 232)*
Marbury v. *Madison (p. 232)*
judicial review *(p. 232)*

Section 2
Louisiana Purchase *(p. 236)*
Meriwether Lewis *(p. 237)*
William Clark *(p. 237)*
Lewis and Clark expedition *(p. 237)*
Sacagawea *(p. 238)*
Zebulon Pike *(p. 238)*

Section 3
USS *Constitution (p. 240)*
impressment *(p. 241)*
embargo *(p. 241)*
Embargo Act *(p. 241)*
Non-Intercourse Act *(p. 242)*
Tecumseh *(p. 242)*
Battle of Tippecanoe *(p. 244)*
War Hawks *(p. 244)*
James Madison *(p. 245)*

Section 4
Oliver Hazard Perry *(p. 247)*
Battle of Lake Erie *(p. 247)*
Andrew Jackson *(p. 248)*
Treaty of Fort Jackson *(p. 248)*
Battle of New Orleans *(p. 248)*
Hartford Convention *(p. 249)*
Treaty of Ghent *(p. 249)*

Academic Vocabulary

In this chapter you will learn the following academic words:

functions *(p. 231)*
consequences *(p. 249)*

As you read Chapter 7, look for passages from other public documents. What can these documents teach you about the past?

Reading Social Studies

Key Terms and People

Preteach the key terms and people for this chapter by hosting a vocabulary game for students. Write the key terms and people for students to see. Then organize the class into teams. Read aloud definitions or descriptions, and have teams take turns guessing which term identifies the description. If one team guesses incorrectly, allow the next team an opportunity to guess the answer. Assign points for each correct answer. You might want to have students keep a list of correct descriptions for each term. **LS Interpersonal, Verbal/Linguistic**

Focus on Reading

See the **Focus on Reading** questions in this chapter for more practice on this reading social studies skill.

Reading Social Studies Assessment

See the **Standards Review** at the end of this chapter for student assessment questions related to this reading skill.

Teaching Tip

Students will often be called upon to interpret public documents. Point out to students that they should use the same techniques to analyze a public document as they do with any type of document. Have students practice reading public documents by showing them some examples, such as laws, deeds, and government proclamations. Libraries and the Internet are good places to find public documents. Encourage students to use these documents in their research.

Answers

You Try It! 1. *postage rates;* **2.** *main idea—Congress has raised postage rate; details—postage rates depend on the distance a letter will travel, letters with more than one piece of paper cost more to send, packets over one ounce are charged by the quarter ounce;* **3.** *large envelopes; they hold more than four pieces of paper and weigh more than one ounce.* **4.** *possible answers—augmented, avoirdupois; it might lead to a misinterpretation of the document.*

Preteach

Bellringer

If YOU were there . . . Use the **Daily Bellringer Transparency** to help students answer the question.

 Daily Bellringer Transparency, Section 1

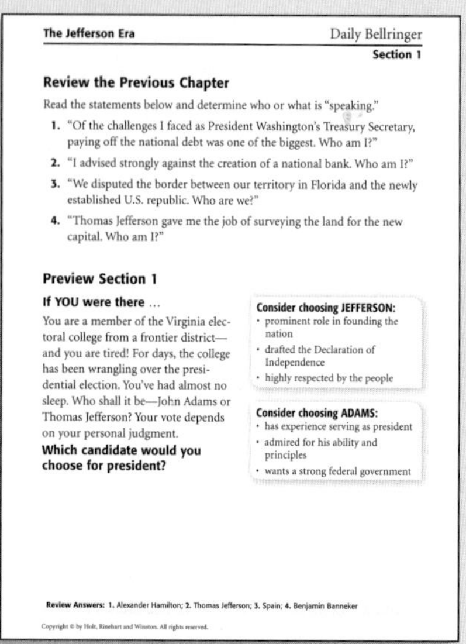

The Jefferson Era — Daily Bellringer

Section 1

Review the Previous Chapter

Read the statements below and determine who or what is "speaking."

1. "Of the challenges I faced as President Washington's Treasury Secretary, paying off the national debt was one of the biggest. Who am I?"
2. "I advised strongly against the creation of a national bank. Who am I?"
3. "We disputed the border between our territory in Florida and the newly established U.S. republic. Who are we?"
4. "Thomas Jefferson gave me the job of surveying the land for the new capital. Who am I?"

Preview Section 1

If YOU were there ...

You are a member of the Virginia electoral college from a frontier district—and you are tired! For days, the college has been wrangling over the presidential election. You've had almost no sleep. Who shall it be—John Adams or Thomas Jefferson? Your vote depends on your personal judgment.

Which candidate would you choose for president?

Consider choosing JEFFERSON:
- prominent role in founding the nation
- drafted the Declaration of Independence
- highly respected by the people

Consider choosing ADAMS:
- has experience serving as president
- admired for his ability and principles
- wants a strong federal government

Review Answers: **1.** Alexander Hamilton; **2.** Thomas Jefferson; **3.** Spain; **4.** Benjamin Banneker

Academic Vocabulary

Review with students the high-use academic term in this section.

functions uses or purposes (p. 231)

CRF: Vocabulary Builder Activity, Section 1

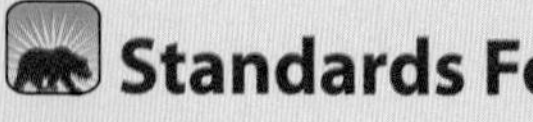

Standards Focus

HSS 8.4.1

Means: Describe the political differences between the Federalists and the Democratic-Republicans during Jefferson's presidency.

Matters: Political parties continue to shape politics and to hold differing views about the role of government.

HSS 8.4.2

Means: Explain the importance of Thomas Jefferson's 1801 inaugural address.

Matters: Famous political speeches, such as Jefferson's inaugural address, have shaped American views of government and politics.

SECTION 1

Jefferson Becomes President

What You Will Learn...

Main Ideas

1. The election of 1800 marked the first peaceful transition in power from one political party to another.
2. President Jefferson's beliefs about the federal government were reflected in his policies.
3. *Marbury* v. *Madison* increased the power of the judicial branch of government.

The Big Idea

Thomas Jefferson's election began a new era in American government.

Key Terms and People

John Adams, *p. 228*
Thomas Jefferson, *p. 228*
John Marshall, *p. 232*
Marbury v. *Madison*, *p. 232*
judicial review, *p. 232*

HSS 8.4.1 Describe the country's physical landscapes, political divisions, and territorial expansion during the terms of the first four presidents.

8.4.2 Explain the policy significance of famous speeches (e.g., Washington's Farewell Address, Jefferson's 1801 Inaugural Address, John Q. Adams's Fourth of July 1821 Address).

If YOU were there...

You are a member of the Virginia electoral college from a frontier district—and you are tired! For days, the college has been wrangling over the presidential election. You've had almost no sleep. Who shall it be—Aaron Burr or Thomas Jefferson? Your vote depends on your personal judgment.

Which candidate would you choose for president?

BUILDING BACKGROUND John Adams had not been a popular president, but many still admired his ability and high principles. Both he and Thomas Jefferson had played major roles in winning independence and shaping the new government. Now, political differences sharply divided the two men and their supporters. In the election of 1800, voters were also divided.

The Election of 1800

In the presidential election of 1800, Federalists **John Adams** and Charles C. Pinckney ran against Democratic-Republicans **Thomas Jefferson** and Aaron Burr. Each party believed that the American republic's survival depended upon the success of their candidates. With so much at stake, the election was hotly contested.

Unlike today, candidates did not travel around giving speeches. Instead, the candidates' supporters made their arguments in letters and newspaper editorials. Adams's supporters claimed that Jefferson was a pro-French radical. Put Jefferson in office, they warned, and the violence and chaos of the French Revolution would surely follow. Plus, Federalists argued, Jefferson's interest in science and philosophy proved that he wanted to destroy organized religion.

Democratic-Republican newspapers responded that Adams wanted to crown himself king. What else, they asked, could be the purpose of the Alien and Sedition Acts? Republicans also hinted that Adams would use the newly created permanent army to limit Americans' rights.

Teach the Big Idea: Master the Standards

Standards Proficiency

Jefferson Becomes President HSS 8.4.1, 8.4.2; HSS Analysis Skills: CS 1, HI 1

1. **Teach** Ask students the Main Idea questions to teach this section.
2. **Apply** Have students list the section's key people, events, and issues. Write the list for students to see. Then ask students to imagine that they are news reporters. Have each student write a headline for each main event and issue. Model the activity by doing the first headline for students. **LS Verbal/Linguistic**
3. **Review** As you review the section, have students share their related headlines with the class.
4. **Practice/Homework** Select one headline and have each student write an article or draw a political cartoon to accompany the headline. **LS Verbal/Linguistic, Visual/Spatial**

Alternative Assessment Handbook, Rubrics 27: Political Cartoons; and 42: Writing to Inform

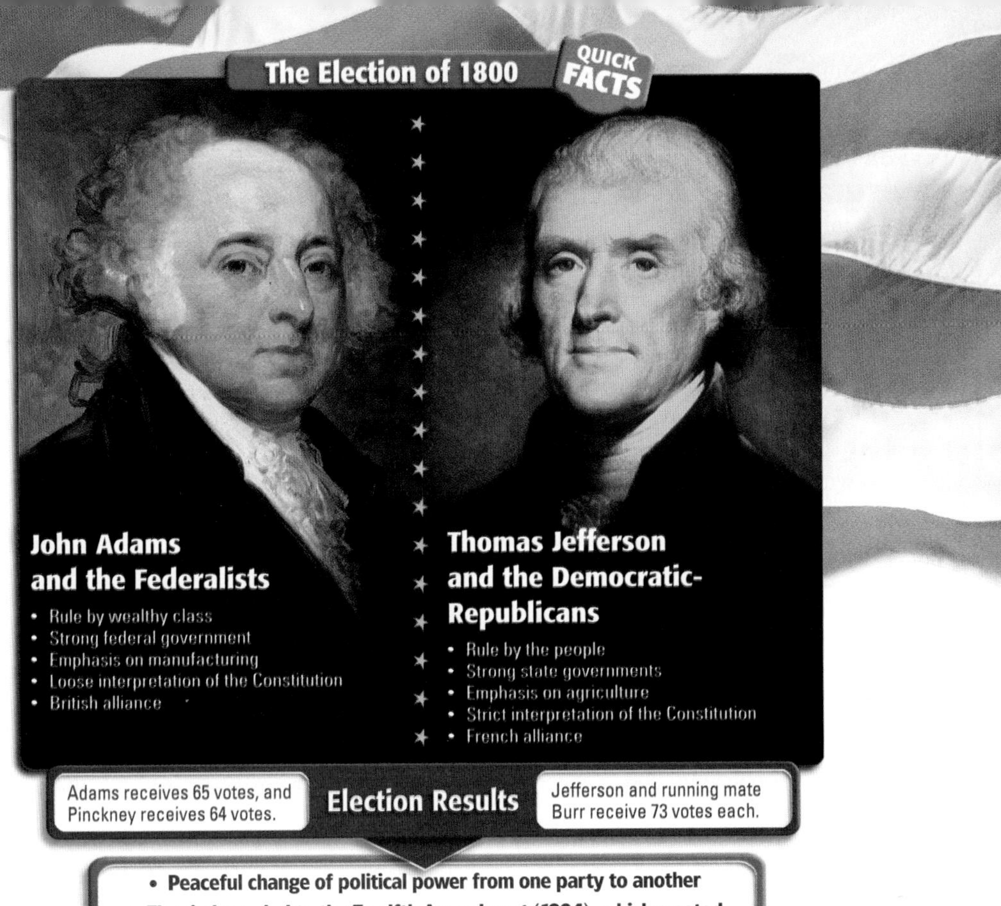
The Election of 1800
QUICK FACTS
John Adams and the Federalists
• Rule by wealthy class
• Strong federal government
• Emphasis on manufacturing
• Loose interpretation of the Constitution
• British alliance
Thomas Jefferson and the Democratic-Republicans
• Rule by the people
• Strong state governments
• Emphasis on agriculture
• Strict interpretation of the Constitution
• French alliance
Adams receives 65 votes, and Pinckney receives 64 votes.
Election Results
Jefferson and running mate Burr receive 73 votes each.
• Peaceful change of political power from one party to another
• The tied race led to the Twelfth Amendment (1804), which created a separate ballot for president and vice president.

When the election results came in, Jefferson and Burr had won 73 electoral votes each to 65 for Adams and 64 for Pinckney. The Democratic-Republicans had won the election, but the tie between Jefferson and Burr caused a problem. Under the Constitution at that time, the two candidates with the most votes became president and vice president. The decision went to the House of Representatives as called for in the Constitution.

The House, like the electoral college, also deadlocked. Days went by as vote after vote was called, each ending in ties. Exhausted lawmakers put their heads on their desks and slept between votes. Some napped on the floor.

Jefferson finally won on the thirty-sixth vote. The election marked the first time that one party had replaced another in power in the United States.

The problems with the voting system led Congress to propose the Twelfth Amendment. This amendment created a separate ballot for president and vice president.

READING CHECK **Analyzing Information** What was significant about Jefferson's victory?

Direct Teach

Main Idea

❶ The Election of 1800

The election of 1800 marked the first peaceful transition in power from one political party to another.

Identify Who were the candidates in the election, and what party did each represent? *See chart at left.*

Contrast How did the two parties' positions in the election differ? *See chart at left.*

Identify Cause and Effect Why did the election lead to the Twelfth Amendment? *because Jefferson and Burr tied; showed the need to have separate tickets for president and vice president*

Activity **Campaign Slogans** Have each student create a campaign slogan for each political party in the election of 1800.

- Alternative Assessment Handbook, Rubric 34: Slogans and Banners
- **CRF:** Biography Activity: Aaron Burr
- Quick Facts Transparency: The Election of 1800
- **HSS** 8.4.1; **HSS Analysis Skills:** HI 1, HI 2

QUICK FACTS Election of 1800

Summarize Have students find the Twelfth Amendment to the U.S. Constitution in their textbooks and rewrite it in their own words.

HSS Analysis Skills: HR 4

go.hrw.com Online Resources

KEYWORD: SS8 US7
ACTIVITY: Thomas Jefferson and Politics Essay

Differentiating Instruction for Universal Access

English-Language Learners Standards Proficiency

1. Help students go through the Quick Facts chart above. Define any words or terms with which students are unfamiliar.
2. Then have each student create a large copy of the chart and add symbols or drawings to represent each party characteristic and election result. Model the activity to help students get started. Draw a hammer to show Federalists' emphasis on manufacturing and a sheaf of wheat to show Democratic-Republicans' emphasis on agriculture.
3. As students work, check that each one accurately understands the chart.
4. Have volunteers share some of the symbols they created with the class. **LS Visual/Spatial**

- Alternative Assessment Handbook, Rubrics 3: Artwork; and 7: Charts
- Quick Facts Transparency: The Election of 1800
- **HSS** 8.4.1; **HSS Analysis Skills:** CS 1, HI 1, HI 2

Answers

Reading Check *The election was the first time that one party had replaced another in power in the United States.*

Direct Teach

Main Idea

❷ Jefferson's Policies

President Jefferson's beliefs about the federal government were reflected in his policies.

Recall In his 1801 inaugural address, what political ideas does Jefferson express? *support for the will of the majority, limited government, and protection of civil liberties*

Analyze How did Jefferson and Congress put these Democratic-Republican ideas into practice? *will of the majority—did away with unpopular taxes; limited government—cut military funds and size, kept government small; civil liberties—let Alien and Sedition Acts expire*

Make Generalizations In what ways did Jefferson try to make his inauguration a reflection of Democratic-Republican ideals? *walked to the Capitol rather than ride in a carriage or on horseback; stressed need for limited government and protection of civil liberties in his inaugural address*

CRF: Primary Source Activity: Jefferson's 1801 Inaugural Address

HSS 8.4.1, 8.4.2; **HSS Analysis Skills:** HI 1, HI 2

Primary Source

Jefferson's Inaugural Address

Draw Conclusions Based on his phrase "shall not take from the mouth of labor the bread it has earned," what do you think was Jefferson's position on taxation? Explain your answer. *He did not support taxing the money that people earned from their work.*

HSS 8.4.2; **HSS Analysis Skills:** HR 4

Answers

Analyzing Primary Sources *"frugal Government," "free to regulate their own pursuits of industry and improvement"*

Primary Source

SPEECH

Jefferson's Inaugural Address

On March 4, 1801, Thomas Jefferson gave his first inaugural address. In the following excerpt, Jefferson describes his thoughts on the nation's future.

"Let us, then, fellow citizens, unite with one heart and one mind . . . [E]very difference of opinion is not a difference of principle. We have called by different names brethren[1] of the same principle. We are all republicans; we are all federalists."

By using phrases like these, Jefferson tries to reassure his political opponents.

"Still one thing more, fellow citizens, a wise and frugal[2] Government, which shall restrain men from injuring one another, shall leave them otherwise free to regulate their own pursuits of industry and improvement, and shall not take from the mouth of labor the bread it has earned. This is the sum of good government . . ."

Here Jefferson states his opinion of what is essential to good government.

This phrase shows Jefferson's determination to keep government small.

1. **brethren**: brothers 2. **frugal**: thrifty

ANALYSIS SKILL **ANALYZING PRIMARY SOURCES**

What words and phrases indicate Jefferson's support for a small national government?

Jefferson's Policies

When Jefferson took office, he brought with him a style and political ideas different from those of Adams and Washington. Jefferson was less formal than his predecessors, and he wanted to limit the powers of government.

Jefferson Is Inaugurated

Americans looked forward with excitement to Jefferson's first speech as president. People from across the nation gathered in the new capital, Washington, D.C., to hear him. Curious travelers looked with pride at the partially completed Capitol building and at the executive mansion (not yet called the White House). The two buildings dominated the surrounding homes and forests.

THE IMPACT TODAY

A monument to Thomas Jefferson was completed in 1943 and is one of the most frequently visited sites in Washington, D.C.

Small businesses dotted the landscape. At one of these, a modest boardinghouse, the president-elect was putting the finishing touches on his speech. On the morning of March 4, 1801, he left the boardinghouse and walked to the Capitol. The leader of a republic, Jefferson believed, should not ride in fancy carriages.

Jefferson read his speech in a quiet voice. He wanted to make it clear that he supported the will of the majority. He also stressed the need for a limited government and the protection of civil liberties.

From these humble surroundings in which Jefferson delivered his speech, Washington eventually grew into a large and impressive city. Over the years, the Capitol and the executive mansion were joined by other state buildings and monuments. Jefferson, who had long dreamed of a new national capital that would be independent of the interests of any one state, was pleased to be a part of this process of building a federal city.

Jefferson in Office

President Jefferson faced the task of putting his republican ideas into practice. One of his first actions was to select the members of his cabinet. His choices included James Madison as secretary of state and Albert Gallatin as secretary of the treasury.

Jefferson would also benefit from the Democratic-Republican Party's newly won control of both houses of Congress. At Jefferson's urging, Congress allowed the hated Alien and Sedition Acts to expire. Jefferson

Critical Thinking: Evaluating Information

Exceeding Standards

Thomas Jefferson Report Card

HSS 8.4.1, 8.4.2; **HSS Analysis Skills:** HR 4, HI 1

1. Discuss with students Jefferson's main actions in office. As you do, list for students the Democratic-Republican ideas Jefferson supported and the Federalist ideas he kept.
2. Next, have students explain how Jefferson's actions in office reflected the Democratic-Republican views that he expressed in his 1801 inaugural address.
3. Have each student use the information in this section to create a report card for Jefferson's first presidential administration.
4. Students' report cards should list Jefferson's main goals, as expressed in his inaugural address, and then provide a grade for each goal based on Jefferson's actions in office. Students should also explain each grade. **LS Verbal/Linguistic**

Alternative Assessment Handbook, Rubric 16: Judging Information

CRF: Primary Source Activity: Jefferson's 1801 Inaugural Address lowered military spending and reduced the size of the army. The navy was cut to seven active ships. Jefferson and Gallatin hoped that saving this money would allow the government to repay the national debt. Jefferson also asked Gallatin to find ways to get rid of domestic taxes, like the tax on whiskey. The Democratic-Republican-led Congress passed the laws needed to carry out these policies.

The entire national government in 1801 consisted only of several hundred people. Jefferson preferred to keep it that way. He believed that the primary **functions** of the federal government were to protect the nation from foreign threats, deliver the mail, and collect customs duties.

Jefferson did recognize that some of the Federalist policies—such as the creation of the Bank of the United States—should be kept. Although Jefferson had battled Hamilton over the Bank, as president he agreed to leave it in place.

READING CHECK **Summarizing** What policy changes did Democratic-Republicans introduce, and which Federalist policies did Jefferson keep?

Marbury v. *Madison*

Although Republicans controlled the presidency and Congress, Federalists dominated the federal judiciary. In an effort to continue their control over the judiciary, Federalist legislators passed the Judiciary Act of 1801 shortly before their terms of office ended. This act created 16 new federal judgeships that President Adams filled with Federalists before leaving office. The Republican press called these people midnight judges, arguing that Adams had packed the judiciary with Federalists the night before he left office.

Some of these appointments were made so late that the documents that authorized them had not been delivered by the time Adams left office. This led to controversy once Jefferson took office. William Marbury, named as a justice of the peace by President Adams, did not receive his documents before Adams left office. When Jefferson took office, Marbury demanded the documents. On Jefferson's advice, however, the new secretary of state, James Madison, refused to deliver them. Jefferson argued that the appointment of the midnight judges was not valid.

ACADEMIC VOCABULARY
functions uses or purposes

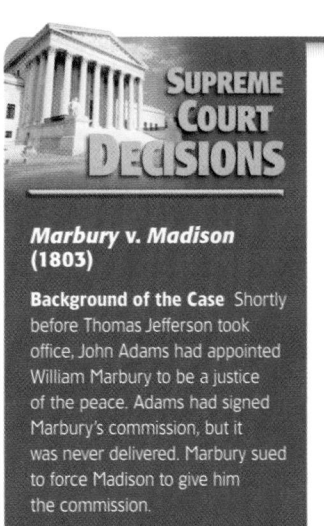

SUPREME COURT DECISIONS

Marbury v. Madison (1803)

Background of the Case Shortly before Thomas Jefferson took office, John Adams had appointed William Marbury to be a justice of the peace. Adams had signed Marbury's commission, but it was never delivered. Marbury sued to force Madison to give him the commission.

The Court's Ruling
The Court ruled that the law Marbury based his claim on was unconstitutional.

The Court's Reasoning
The Judiciary Act of 1789 gave the Supreme Court the authority to hear a wide variety of cases, including those like Marbury's. But the Supreme Court ruled that Congress did not have the power to make such a law. Why? Because the Constitution limits the types of cases the Supreme Court can hear. Thus, the law was in conflict with the Constitution and had to be struck down.

Why It Matters
Marbury v. *Madison* was important for several reasons. It confirmed the Supreme Court's power to declare acts of Congress unconstitutional. By doing so, it established the Court as the final authority on the Constitution. This helped make the judicial branch of government equal to the other two branches. Chief Justice John Marshall and later federal judges would use this power of judicial review as a check on the legislative and executive branches.

ANALYSIS SKILL **ANALYZING INFORMATION**

1. What do you think it means to be the final authority on the Constitution?
2. How did *Marbury* v. *Madison* affect the Constitution's system of checks and balances?

Direct Teach

Main Idea

❸ *Marbury* v. *Madison*

Marbury v. *Madison* increased the power of the judicial branch of government.

Identify What was the Judiciary Act of 1801? *created 16 new federal judgeships that President Adams filled the night before he left office; thus the label "midnight judges"*

Explain Why did Federalist members of Congress pass the act? *to retain control of the judiciary because Democratic-Republicans had gained control of the executive and legislative branches*

Identify Cause and Effect What happened as a result of James Madison's refusal to deliver William Marbury's appointment papers? *Marbury brought suit and asked the Supreme Court to order Madison to deliver the papers under the Judiciary Act of 1789.*

U.S. Supreme Court Case Studies: *Marbury* v. *Madison* (1803)

HSS 8.4.1; HSS **Analysis Skills:** HI 1, HI 2

Did you know . . .

The outgoing secretary of state who failed to deliver William Marbury's appointment papers was none other than John Marshall. Marshall was chief justice when the Supreme Court heard the case of *Marbury* v. *Madison*.

Critical Thinking: Finding Main Ideas

Reaching Standards

Marbury v. *Madison* Graphic Organizer HSS 8.4.1; HSS **Analysis Skills:** HI 1

1. To help students understand the significance of *Marbury* v. *Madison*, copy the graphic organizer for students to see. Omit the blue answers.
2. Have students copy the graphic organizer and complete it by identifying the significance of the case. LS **Visual/Spatial**

Alternative Assessment Handbook, Rubric 13: Graphic Organizers

U.S. Supreme Court Case Studies: *Marbury* v. *Madison* (1803)

Marbury v. Madison

Legislative Branch | **Judicial Branch** | **Executive Branch**

Judicial Branch
- *established Supreme Court's power of judicial review—power to declare acts of Congress unconstitutional*
- *made the Supreme Court the final authority on the U.S. Constitution*
- *strengthened power of the judicial branch in relation to other two branches*

Answers

Supreme Court Decisions **1.** *Once a decision is made, there is no higher court to overturn it.* **2.** *provided the judicial branch with a check on the other two branches, which made it equal to the other two branches*

Reading Check *Democratic-Republican policies introduced—reduced the size of the military, allowed the Alien and Sedition Acts to expire, eliminated domestic taxes such as the whiskey tax; Federalist policy kept—kept Bank of the United States*

Direct Teach

Main Idea

3 *Marbury* v. *Madison*

Marbury v. *Madison* increased the power of the judicial branch of government.

Summarize Explain the Supreme Court's ruling in *Marbury* v. *Madison*. *The Court ruled that it did not have the authority to hear cases such as Marbury's and, thus, that the law upon which the case was based was unconstitutional.*

Analyze How does the power of judicial review strengthen the role of the judicial branch? *gives it a check on the other branches of government*

CRF: Biography Activity: John Marshall

HSS 8.4.1; **HSS Analysis Skills:** HI 1

Review & Assess

Close

Have students work as a class to write a summary of Jefferson's first term in office as president.

Review

go.hrw.com Online Quiz, Section 1

Assess

SE Section 1 Assessment

PASS: Section 1 Quiz

Alternative Assessment Handbook

Reteach/Classroom Intervention

California Standards Review Workbook

Interactive Reader and Study Guide, Section 1

Interactive Skills Tutor CD-ROM

Answers

Reading Check *established the U.S. Supreme Court's power of judicial review, which strengthened the judicial branch's power in relation to the other two branches of government*

Marbury brought suit, asking the Supreme Court to order Madison to deliver the appointment papers. Marbury claimed that the Judiciary Act of 1789 gave the Supreme Court the power to do so.

John Marshall, a Federalist appointed by John Adams, was the chief justice of the United States. Chief Justice Marshall and President Jefferson disagreed about many political issues. When Marshall agreed to hear Marbury's case, Jefferson protested, saying that the Federalists "have retired into the judiciary as a stronghold." Marshall wrote the Court's opinion in ***Marbury* v. *Madison***, a case that helped establish the Supreme Court's power to check the power of the other branches of government. The Constitution, Chief Justice Marshall noted, gave the Supreme Court authority to hear only certain types of cases. A request like Marbury's was not one of them. The law that Marbury's case depended upon was, therefore, unconstitutional.

John Marshall served as chief justice of the United States for 34 years.

In denying Marbury's request in this way, the Court avoided a direct confrontation with Jefferson's administration. But more importantly, it established the Court's power of **judicial review**, the power to declare an act of Congress unconstitutional. Marshall and later federal judges would use this power of judicial review to make the judiciary a much stronger part of the national government.

READING CHECK **Analyzing Information** Why was *Marbury* v. *Madison* an important ruling?

SUMMARY AND PREVIEW A peaceful transfer of power took place in Washington after the election of 1800. In the next section you will read about the Louisiana Purchase.

Section 1 Assessment

go.hrw.com **Online Quiz** KEYWORD: SS8 HP7

Reviewing Ideas, Terms, and People HSS 8.4.1, 8.4.2

1. a. **Identify** What were the political parties and who were their candidates in the election of 1800?
   b. **Analyze** Why was the election of 1800 significant?
2. a. **Describe** What ideas for government did **Thomas Jefferson** stress in his inaugural address?
   b. **Compare and Contrast** What similarities and differences did Jefferson's Republican government have with the previous Federalist one?
   c. **Elaborate** Defend Jefferson's preference for keeping the national government small.
3. a. **Identify** Who was **John Marshall**?
   b. **Draw Conclusions** Why is the power of **judicial review** important?
   c. **Predict** How might the ***Marbury* v. *Madison*** ruling affect future actions by Congress?

Critical Thinking

4. **Categorizing** Copy the chart below. Use it to show how President Jefferson continued some Federalist policies while introducing Republican policies.

Jefferson as President

Federalist Policies	Republican Policies

FOCUS ON WRITING

5. **Gathering Ideas about a Person's Accomplishments** Look back through what you have just read to see what you have learned about Jefferson's decisions in office. Make a list of the traits you think each decision shows in Jefferson.

Section 1 Assessment Answers

1. a. Federalists—John Adams, Charles C. Pinckney; Republicans—Thomas Jefferson, Aaron Burr
   b. first peaceful transfer of power from one U.S. political party to another
2. a. the will of the majority, limited government, and the protection of civil liberties
   b. similarities—national bank, small federal government; differences—Jefferson cut military spending and taxes, let Alien and Sedition Acts expire.
   c. Jefferson believed that limiting government would protect civil liberties.
3. a. Chief justice of the United States who wrote the opinion in *Marbury* v. *Madison*
   b. It gave the Supreme Court the power to declare an act of Congress unconstitutional, which strengthened the judicial branch's power.
   c. Congress would be more aware of whether proposed laws are constitutional.
4. Federalist—kept Bank of the United States; Republican—cut military spending and taxes, let Alien and Sedition Acts expire
5. Students might list characteristics such as intelligence, humility, leadership, and so on.

BIOGRAPHY

Thomas Jefferson

How would you inspire people to seek freedom?

When did he live? He was born on April 13, 1743. He died on July 4, 1826, within hours of the death of President John Adams, his rival and friend. The date was also the fiftieth anniversary of the Declaration of Independence.

Where did he live? He was born in Albemarle County, Virginia, where he inherited a large estate from his father. At age 26 he began building his elegant lifetime home, Monticello, which he designed himself. He spent much of his life away from home, in Philadelphia; Washington, D.C.; and Europe. Yet he always longed to return to his peaceful home.

What did he do? Jefferson wanted only three of his accomplishments listed on his tomb: author of the Declaration of American Independence, author of the Virginia Statute for Religious Freedom, and Father of the University of Virginia. What did he *not* mention? Governor of Virginia, lawyer, revolutionary leader, writer, philosopher, inventor, architect, plant scientist, book collector, musician, astronomer, ambassador, secretary of state—and, of course, president of the United States.

Why is he important? Jefferson's powerful words in the Declaration of Independence have inspired people throughout the world to seek freedom, equality, and self-rule. His most celebrated achievement as president (1801–1809) was the purchase of the Louisiana Territory from France. The Louisiana Purchase of 1803 nearly doubled the size of the United States. Jefferson then sponsored the Lewis and Clark expedition to explore this new territory.

Evaluating Why has Thomas Jefferson been a hero to generations of Americans?

Thomas Jefferson wrote the Declaration of Independence and later served as president of the United States.

KEY EVENTS

- **1767** Begins practicing law in Virginia
- **1769–1776** Serves in Virginia House of Burgesses
- **1776** Drafts the first version of the Declaration of Independence
- **1789** Appointed secretary of state by George Washington
- **1801** Inaugurated as president
- **1803** Authorizes the purchase of Louisiana from France
- **1809** Retires to Monticello

Biography

Reading Focus Question

Have students discuss the introductory question. Ask them to consider the actions that the American colonists took to seek freedom as well as actions people take today. Tell students to keep their answers in mind as they read the biography.

Info to Know

Jefferson: The Renaissance Man Thomas Jefferson was a man of many talents. He was knowledgeable in architecture, agriculture, law, philosophy, and science. He wrote, however, that science was his "supreme delight." Jefferson enjoyed observing and recording nature and corresponded with scientists around the world. He also enjoyed putting his knowledge to practical use. His inventions range from an improved plow design, to a two-faced clock, to a device that attached to his hand and made copies of whatever he wrote.

Jefferson: The Bibliophile Jefferson's passion for science was matched by his passion for books. He preferred the classics and could read in seven languages. In 1815 his personal library totaled more than 6,500 volumes. His library later became the basis of what is now the Library of Congress.

Jefferson: The Real Man Although multitalented, Jefferson lacked some qualities expected of leaders. He was not a good public speaker. He was shy, spoke quietly, and often mumbled.

Critical Thinking: Analyzing Information

Standards Proficiency

Analyzing Jefferson's Epitaph HSS 8.4; HSS **Analysis Skills:** HI 1

1. Ask students to discuss why Jefferson chose to list only three of his many accomplishments on his tomb. Have students review some of the accomplishments he left out (listed above under "What did he do?").
2. Explain to students that Jefferson wanted his tomb to list the ways in which he gave to the American people, not his achievements.
3. Have students, working either individually or in small groups, write their own epitaphs for Thomas Jefferson. Tell students their epitaphs should list what they think are Jefferson's most important contributions and accomplishments.

Alternative Assessment Handbook, Rubric 14: Group Activity; and 37: Writing Assignments

Answers

Evaluating *because his words and actions have inspired people throughout the world to seek freedom, equality, and self-rule*

Preteach

Bellringer

If YOU were there . . . Use the **Daily Bellringer Transparency** to help students answer the question.

Daily Bellringer Transparency, Section 2

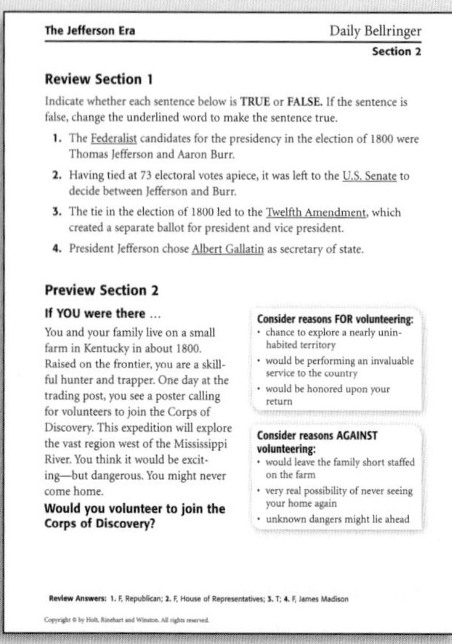

The Jefferson Era Daily Bellringer

Section 2

Review Section 1

Indicate whether each sentence below is **TRUE** or **FALSE.** If the sentence is false, change the underlined word to make the sentence true.

1. The Federalist candidates for the presidency in the election of 1800 were Thomas Jefferson and Aaron Burr.
2. Having tied at 73 electoral votes apiece, it was left to the U.S. Senate to decide between Jefferson and Burr.
3. The tie in the election of 1800 led to the Twelfth Amendment, which created a separate ballot for president and vice president.
4. President Jefferson chose Albert Gallatin as secretary of state.

Preview Section 2

If YOU were there ...

You and your family live on a small farm in Kentucky in about 1800. Raised on the frontier, you are a skillful hunter and trapper. One day at the trading post, you see a poster calling for volunteers to join the Corps of Discovery. This expedition will explore the vast region west of the Mississippi River. You think it would be exciting—but dangerous. You might never come home.

Would you volunteer to join the Corps of Discovery?

Consider reasons FOR volunteering:
- chance to explore a nearly uninhabited territory
- would be performing an invaluable service to the country
- would be honored upon your return

Consider reasons AGAINST volunteering:
- would leave the family short staffed on the farm
- very real possibility of never seeing your home again
- unknown dangers might lie ahead

Review Answers: 1. F, Republican; 2. F, House of Representatives; 3. T; 4. F, James Madison

Building Vocabulary

Preteach or review the following terms:

strict constructionist one who thinks the federal government may do only what the U.S. Constitution specifically says it may do (p. 236)

surveying mapping out (p. 237)

CRF: Vocabulary Builder Activity, Section 2

Standards Focus

HSS 8.4.1

Means: Describe how the purchase of the Louisiana Territory increased the country's size during Jefferson's presidency.

Matters: Many current states were formed out of the Louisiana Territory.

HSS 8.8.2

Means: Explain why Americans chose to explore and settle the West and describe the challenges explorers faced.

Matters: The region of the West is now home to many Americans and contains some major population centers.

SECTION 2

The Louisiana Purchase

What You Will Learn...

Main Ideas

1. As American settlers moved West, control of the Mississippi River became more important to the United States.
2. The Louisiana Purchase almost doubled the size of the United States.
3. Expeditions led by Lewis, Clark, and Pike increased Americans' understanding of the West.

The Big Idea

Under President Jefferson's leadership, the United States added the Louisiana Territory.

Key Terms and People

Louisiana Purchase, *p. 236*
Meriwether Lewis, *p. 237*
William Clark, *p. 237*
Lewis and Clark expedition, *p. 237*
Sacagawea, *p. 238*
Zebulon Pike, *p. 238*

HSS 8.4.1 Describe the country's physical landscapes, political divisions, and territorial expansion during the terms of the first four presidents.

8.8.2 Describe the purpose, challenges, and economic incentives associated with westward expansion, including the concept of Manifest Destiny (e.g., the Lewis and Clark expedition, accounts of the removal of Indians, the Cherokees' "Trail of Tears," settlement of the Great Plains) and the territorial acquisitions that spanned numerous decades.

If YOU were there...

You and your family live on a small farm in Kentucky in about 1800. Raised on the frontier, you are a skillful hunter and trapper. One day at the trading post, you see a poster calling for volunteers to join the Corps of Discovery. This expedition will explore the vast region west of the Mississippi River. You think it would be exciting—but dangerous. You might never come home.

Would you volunteer to join the Corps of Discovery?

BUILDING BACKGROUND As the 1800s began, the United States was expanding steadily westward. More lands were opened, and settlers moved in to occupy them. Americans were also curious about the vast lands that lay farther West. Adventurous explorers organized expeditions to find out more about those lands.

Americans Settlers Move West

By the early 1800s, thousands of Americans settled in the area between the Appalachians and the Mississippi River. As the region's population grew, Kentucky, Tennessee, and Ohio were admitted to the Union. Settlers in these states depended upon the Mississippi and Ohio rivers to move their products to eastern markets.

New Orleans, located at the mouth of the Mississippi, was a very important port. Its busy docks were filled with settlers' farm products and valuable furs bought from American Indians. Many of these cargoes were then sent to Europe. At the same time, manufactured goods passed through the port on their way upriver. As American dependence on the river grew, Jefferson began to worry that a foreign power might shut down access to New Orleans.

> "There is on the globe one single spot, the possessor of which is our natural and habitual enemy. It is New Orleans, through which the produce of three-eighths of our territory must pass to market."
>
> —Thomas Jefferson, quoted in *Annals of America, Volume 4, 1797–1820*

Teach the Big Idea: Master the Standards

Standards Proficiency

The Louisiana Purchase HSS 8.4.1, 8.8.2; HSS Analysis Skills: CS 1, CS 2, HI 1, HI 2

1. **Teach** Ask students the Main Idea questions to teach this section.
2. **Apply** Have each student create a time line of key events related to the Louisiana Purchase. **LS Visual/Spatial**
3. **Review** Review students' time lines as a class. Have students discuss the ways in which the United States benefited from the purchase of Louisiana.
4. **Practice/Homework** Have each student create a Louisiana Purchase fact sheet. The fact sheet should include information such as a summary of how and why the purchase took place, the date and cost, the size and location of the Louisiana Territory, and so on. **LS Verbal/Linguistic**

Alternative Assessment Handbook, Rubrics 36: Time Lines; and 42: Writing to Inform

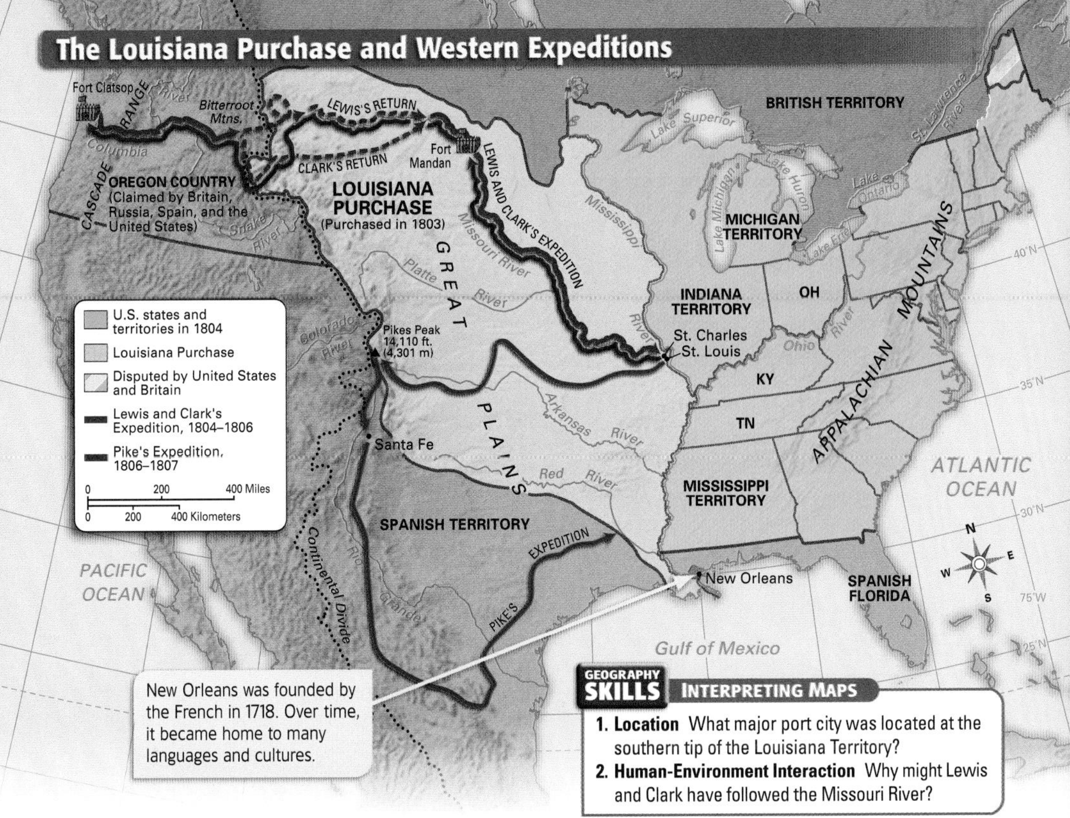

GEOGRAPHY SKILLS INTERPRETING MAPS

1. **Location** What major port city was located at the southern tip of the Louisiana Territory?
2. **Human-Environment Interaction** Why might Lewis and Clark have followed the Missouri River?

Spain controlled both New Orleans and Louisiana. This region stretched west from the mighty Mississippi River to the great Rocky Mountains. Although Spain owned Louisiana, Spanish officials found it impossible to keep Americans out of the territory. "You can't put doors on open country," the foreign minister said in despair.

Years of effort failed to improve Spain's position. Under a secret treaty, Spain agreed to trade Louisiana to France, passing the problem on to someone else. One Spanish officer expressed his relief. "I can hardly wait to leave them [the Americans] behind me," he said.

READING CHECK **Analyzing Information** Why was New Orleans important to settlers in the western regions of the United States?

Louisiana

In 1802, just before handing over Louisiana to France, Spain closed New Orleans to American shipping. Angry farmers worried about what this would do to the economy. President Jefferson asked the U.S. ambassador to France, Robert R. Livingston, to try to buy New Orleans. Jefferson sent James Monroe to help Livingston.

Napoléon and Louisiana

France was led by Napoléon (nuh-POH-lee-uhn), a powerful ruler who had conquered most of Europe. He dreamed of rebuilding France's empire in North America.

Napoléon's strategy was to use the French colony of Haiti, in the Caribbean, as a supply

Direct Teach

Main Idea

1 American Settlers Move West

As American settlers moved West, control of the Mississippi River became more important to the United States.

Describe What had occurred west of the Appalachians by the early 1800s? *Thousands of Americans had settled in the area, and new states were admitted to the Union.*

Identify Which two nations controlled Louisiana and New Orleans at this time? *Spain, then France*

Summarize Why did Americans depend on the Mississippi River and access to New Orleans? *to move products to and from eastern markets*

HSS 8.8.2; HSS **Analysis Skills:** CS 1, HI 1

Interpreting Maps

The Louisiana Purchase and Western Expeditions

Region What river formed the eastern boundary of Louisiana? *Mississippi River*

Location From which city did both the Lewis and Clark and the Pike expeditions begin? *St. Louis*

Map Transparency: The Louisiana Purchase and Western Expeditions

HSS 8.4.1; HSS **Analysis Skills:** CS 3, HI 1

Collaborative Learning

Standards Proficiency

Louisiana Purchase Skits

HSS 8.4.1; HSS **Analysis Skills:** CS 1, HI 1

1. Have students work as a class to list five to six key events related to the Louisiana Purchase. Briefly discuss each event with students. (For a list of key events, see the time line in the Differentiating Instruction for Universal Access activity on the next page.)
2. Organize students into small groups and assign each group one of the key events. Have each group create a short skit or dialogue about its assigned event. Each group should write a script that includes a cast of characters. Have groups assign members roles or tasks to ensure that each student participates.
3. In the correct order, groups should re-enact before the class each of the key events of the Louisiana Purchase. LS **Interpersonal, Kinesthetic**

Alternative Assessment Handbook, Rubric 33: Skits and Reader's Theater

Answers

Interpreting Maps 1. *New Orleans;* 2. *provided a natural path; traveled by boat; hoped it would empty into the Pacific Ocean*

Reading Check *It provided a major port for international and domestic trade.*

Direct Teach

Main Idea

❷ Louisiana

The Louisiana Purchase almost doubled the size of the United States.

Explain Why did Jefferson want to buy New Orleans from France? *Before handing over Louisiana to France, Spain had closed New Orleans to American shipping, which hurt American farmers.*

Sequence What chain of events led to the Louisiana Purchase? *See the time line in the Differentiating Instruction activity below.*

Analyze What role did chance play in the Louisiana Purchase? *Students should describe the various setbacks that led France to sell Louisiana.*

Political Cartoons Activities for United States History, Cartoon 9: The Louisiana Purchase

Map Transparency: The Louisiana Purchase and Western Expeditions

HSS 8.4.1, 8.8.2; HSS **Analysis Skills:** CS 1, HI 1, HI 2, HI 4

base. From there he could send troops to Louisiana. However, enslaved Africans had revolted and freed themselves from French rule. Napoléon sent troops to try to regain control of the island, but they were defeated in 1802. This defeat ended his hopes of rebuilding a North American empire.

Jefferson Buys Louisiana

The American ambassador got a surprising offer during his negotiations with French foreign minister Charles Talleyrand. When the Americans tried to buy New Orleans, Talleyrand offered to sell all of Louisiana.

With his hopes for a North American empire dashed, Napoléon had turned his attention back to Europe. France was at war with Great Britain, and Napoléon needed money for military supplies. He also hoped that a larger United States would challenge British power.

Livingston and Monroe knew a bargain when they saw one. They quickly accepted the French offer to sell Louisiana for $15 million.

The news pleased Jefferson. But as a strict constructionist, he was troubled. The Constitution did not mention the purchase of foreign lands. He also did not like spending large amounts of public money. Nevertheless, Jefferson agreed to the purchase in the belief that doing so was best for the country.

On October 20, 1803, the Senate approved the agreement of the **Louisiana Purchase**, which roughly doubled the size of the United States. With the $15 million in the French treasury, Napoléon boasted, "I have given England a rival who, sooner or later, will humble her pride."

READING CHECK **Making Inferences** Why was the Louisiana Purchase important to the future of the United States?

The Journey West

The time line and photographs you see here show some of the key events and places of the Lewis and Clark expedition. Read the journal entries to get an idea of what the explorers faced.

A large keelboat and two smaller boats were needed to get the supply-heavy expedition moving west.

Small boats helped the travelers move supplies across the Great Plains.

May 14, 1804 The expedition begins near St. Louis.

August 3, 1804 The first official council between representatives of the United States and Plains Indians is held.

October 1804 – April 1805 The expedition establishes Fort Mandan to spend the winter. There, the explorers meet a French fur trader and his wife, Sacagawea.

April 7, 1805 We are about to penetrate a country at least 2,000 miles in width, on which the foot of civilized man had never trodden (walked upon).
—Meriwether Lewis

Answers

Reading Check *It roughly doubled the size of the United States, which would benefit future western settlement and economic growth.*

Differentiating Instruction for Universal Access

Learners Having Difficulty — Reaching Standards

1. To help students understand the sequence of events that led to the Louisiana Purchase, copy the time line for students to see. Omit the blue answers.
2. Have students copy the time line. Then help students complete it as you discuss each event. LS **Visual/Spatial**

HSS 8.4.1, 8.8.2; HSS **Analysis Skills:** CS 1, CS 2, HI 1, HI 2

LOUISIANA PURCHASE

1800 → **Spain trades Louisiana to France.**

1802 →
- **Spain** *closes New Orleans to the United States.*
- **Jefferson instructs** *Livingston and Monroe to try to buy New Orleans from France.*
- **France** *offers to sell all of Louisiana because of setbacks in Haiti and a war against Great Britain.*

1803 → **The United States buys** *Louisiana for $15 million.*

→ **The Louisiana Purchase roughly doubles** *the size of the United States.*

Explorers Head West

Americans knew little about western Native Americans or the land they lived on. President Jefferson wanted to learn more about the people and land of the West. He also wanted to see if there was a river route that could be taken to the Pacific Ocean.

Lewis and Clark Expedition

In 1803 the president asked Congress to fund an expedition to explore the West. To lead it, he chose former army captain **Meriwether Lewis**. Lewis then chose his friend Lieutenant **William Clark** to be the co-leader of the expedition.

To prepare for the journey, Lewis spent weeks studying with experts about plants, surveying, and other subjects. This knowledge would allow him to take careful notes on what he saw. With Clark, Lewis carefully selected about 50 skilled frontiersmen to join the Corps of Discovery, as they called their group.

In May 1804 the **Lewis and Clark expedition** began its long journey to explore the Louisiana Purchase. The Corps of Discovery traveled up the Missouri River to the village of St. Charles. Once past this village the men would receive no more letters, fresh supplies, or reinforcements.

Lewis and Clark used the Missouri River as their highway through the unknown lands. As they moved upstream, a lookout on the boats kept a sharp eye out for sandbars and for tree stumps hidden underwater. When darkness fell, the weary explorers would pull their boats ashore. They cooked, wrote in their journals, and slept. Swarms of gnats, flies, and mosquitoes often interrupted their sleep.

The expedition relied on 24 horses to cross the Rocky Mountains.

The explorers paddled down the Columbia River toward the Pacific in five canoes.

August 12, 1805 Lewis climbs the first ridge to the Continental Divide.

September 1805 The expedition nearly starves. Local peoples help the explorers.

November 7, 1805 The expedition reaches a bay of the Pacific Ocean.

August 23, 1805 The hills or mountains were not like those I had seen, but like the side of a tree straight up.
–William Clark

ANALYSIS SKILL READING TIME LINES

On what date did the explorers reach the western most point of their journey?

Direct Teach

Main Idea

❸ Explorers Head West

Expeditions led by Lewis, Clark, and Pike increased Americans' understanding of the West.

Recall What were the members of the Lewis and Clark expedition called? *the Corps of Discovery*

Summarize What were some challenges the expedition faced? *traveling through a mostly uncharted area, no ability to receive new supplies, transportation difficulties, insects, fear of hostile attack*

Make Inferences What characteristics and skills do you think members of the expedition needed? *possible answers—courage; endurance; ability to hunt, track, survey, and make maps as well as scientific notes and drawings*

HSS 8.4.1, 8.8.2; HSS **Analysis Skills:** HI 1

Info to Know

The Corps of Discovery The Corps of Discovery represented a variety of backgrounds and nationalities. The varied group included French-Canadian fur traders, an African American named York, and a Shoshone woman named Sacagawea. The group even included a Newfoundland dog, Seaman.

Linking to Today

The Lewis and Clark Trail The National Park System has designated the Lewis and Clark trail as a National Historic Trail. Today the trail crosses 11 states.

Critical Thinking: Analyzing Visuals

Reaching Standards

The Journey West

HSS 8.4.1, 8.8.2; HSS **Analysis Skills:** CS 1, CS 3, HI 1

1. Have students examine the diagram titled "The Journey West" above.
2. Have students examine the photos. Ask students to describe the types of terrain the explorers crossed *(Great Plains and mountain ranges)*.
3. Ask students to identify the forms of transportation used *(keelboats, small boats, horses, canoes)*.
4. Ask volunteers to read aloud the time line entries. At the proper times in the sequence, have volunteers also read aloud the journal excerpts.
5. Then have students discuss what theme runs through the journal entries *(theme of new and awe-inspiring encounters)*. LS **Verbal/Linguistic, Visual/Spatial**

Alternative Assessment Handbook, Rubric 11: Discussions

Answers

Reading Time Lines
November 7, 1805

Direct Teach

Main Idea

❸ Explorers Head West

Expeditions led by Lewis, Clark, and Pike increased Americans' understanding of the West.

Identify Who was Sacagawea? *She was a Shoshone woman who helped the Lewis and Clark expedition along with her husband, a French fur trader.*

Summarize What did the Lewis and Clark expedition achieve? *learned about western lands and paths, made contact with many Native American groups, collected data about western plants and animals*

Identify Points of View How do you think Native Americans viewed the Lewis and Clark expedition? *possible answer—with a mix of curiosity, interest, uncertainty, fear*

CRF: Biography Activity: Sacagawea

HSS 8.8.2; HSS **Analysis Skills:** HR 5, HI 1

Checking for Understanding

True or False Answer each statement *T* if it is true and *F* if it is false. If false, explain why.

1. The Nez Percé provided food for the Lewis and Clark expedition. *T*
2. Lewis and Clark succeeded in finding a river route across the West to the Pacific Ocean. *F; They did not find a river route.*
3. Zebulon Pike's report of his expedition offered many Americans their first description of the Pacific Northwest. *F; the Southwest*

HSS 8.8.2

Answers

Analyzing Primary Sources *its lush grass and huge herds of buffalo, elk, and antelope*

Primary Source

JOURNAL ENTRY

September 17, 1804, Great Plains

While traveling across the Great Plains, Meriwether Lewis marveled at the richness of the land.

"The shortness . . . of grass gave the plain the appearance throughout its whole extent of beautiful bowling-green in fine order . . . this scenery, already rich, pleasing, and beautiful was still farther heightened by immense herds of Buffaloe, deer Elk and Antelopes which we saw in every direction feeding on the hills and plains. I do not think I exaggerate when I estimate the number of Buffalo which could be compre[hend]ed at one view to amount to 3000."

—Meriwether Lewis, quoted in *Original Journals of the Lewis and Clark Expedition*, edited by Reuben Bold Theraites

ANALYSIS SKILL ANALYZING PRIMARY SOURCES

What did Lewis find so impressive about the Great Plains?

Insects were not the only cause of sleeplessness for the Corps of Discovery. As weeks passed without seeing any Native Americans, the explorers wondered what their first encounter would be like.

Contact with Native Americans

During the summer of 1804 the Corps of Discovery had pushed more than 600 miles upriver without seeing any Native Americans. But when the men spotted huge buffalo herds in the distance, they guessed that Indian groups would be nearby. Many Indian groups depended on the buffalo for food, clothing, and tools.

Lewis used interpreters to talk to the leaders of each of the peoples they met. He told them that the United States now owned the land on which the Native Americans lived. Yet the explorers relied on the goodwill of the people they met. **Sacagawea** (sak-uh-juh-WEE-uh), a Shoshone from the Rocky Mountains, accompanied the group with her husband, a French fur trader who lived with the Mandan Indians and served as a guide and interpreter. Sacagawea helped the expedition by naming plants and by gathering edible fruits and vegetables for the group. At one point, the group met with Sacagawea's brother, who provided horses and a guide to lead the expedition across the mountains.

After crossing the Rocky Mountains, Lewis and Clark followed the Columbia River. Along the way they met the powerful Nez Percé. Like the Shoshone, the Nez Percé provided the expedition with food. At last, in November 1805, Lewis and Clark reached the Pacific Ocean. The explorers stayed in the Pacific Northwest during the rough winter. In March 1806 Lewis and Clark set out on the long trip home.

Lewis and Clark had not found a river route across the West to the Pacific Ocean. But they had learned much about western lands and paths across the Rockies. The explorers also established contact with many Native American groups and collected much valuable information about western plants and animals.

Pike's Exploration

In 1806 a young army officer named **Zebulon Pike** was sent on another mission to the West. He was ordered to find the starting point of the Red River. This was important because the United States considered the Red River to be a part of the Louisiana Territory's western border with New Spain.

Heading into the Rocky Mountains, in present-day Colorado, Pike tried to reach the summit of the mountain now known as Pike's Peak. In 1807 he traveled into Spanish-held lands until Spanish cavalry arrested him. They suspected Pike of being a spy. When he was finally released, he returned to the United States and reported on his trip. Despite his imprisonment, he praised the opportunities for doing business with the Spanish in the Southwest. Pike's

Collaborative Learning

Standards Proficiency

Expedition Murals

HSS 8.8.2; HSS **Analysis Skills:** CS 1, CS 3, HI 1

Materials: butcher paper, art supplies

1. Organize the class into two groups and assign one group the Lewis and Clark expedition and the other group Pike's exploration.
2. Have each group create a mural of its assigned expedition. The mural should illustrate the goal of the expedition, the route traveled, geographic landmarks spotted, Native American groups encountered, and other significant achievements.
3. Each group should also write a paragraph identifying and explaining the images in its mural. Before students start, have each group submit a small drawing of its mural for approval.
4. Display the murals in the classroom and have each group explain its mural to the class.

LS Interpersonal, Visual/Spatial

Alternative Assessment Handbook, Rubrics 3: Artwork; and 14: Group Activity

LINKING TO TODAY

The Louisiana Purchase

Lewis and Clark would be surprised to see what has become of the lands they explored. The lands of the Louisiana Purchase are rich with natural resources and support enormous agricultural production.

Natural Resources oil, natural gas, coal, gemstones, copper, iron ore, lead, zinc, silver, limestone, sulphur, diamonds, helium

Major Agricultural and Livestock Production rice, cattle, chicken, hogs, corn, wheat, sugarcane, cotton, dairy products, hay

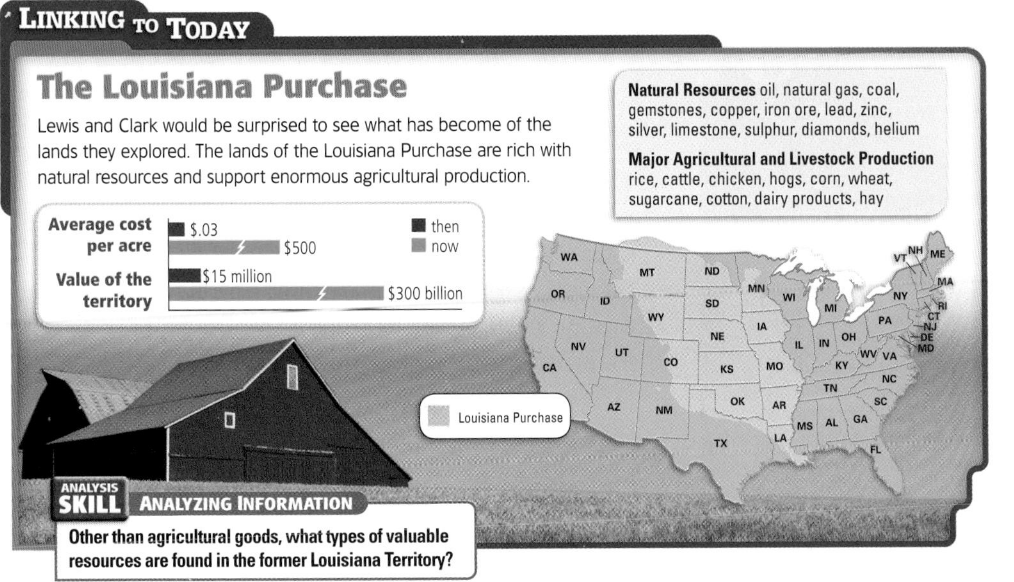

ANALYSIS SKILL **ANALYZING INFORMATION**

Other than agricultural goods, what types of valuable resources are found in the former Louisiana Territory?

report offered many Americans their first description of the Southwest.

READING CHECK **Supporting a Point of View** What would you do if you were Pike and found yourself in Spanish territory?

SUMMARY AND PREVIEW The Louisiana Purchase nearly doubled the size of the United States. In the next section you will learn about increasing tensions between the United States and Great Britain.

Section 2 Assessment

go.hrw.com **Online Quiz** KEYWORD: SS8 HP7

Reviewing Ideas, Terms, and People HSS 8.4.1, 8.8.2

1. a. **Identify** What new states were added to the Union by the early 1800s?
   b. **Explain** Why were New Orleans and the Mississippi River important to setters in the West?
2. a. **Recall** What two reasons did Napoléon have for selling Louisiana to the United States?
   b. **Summarize** Why was the **Louisiana Purchase** important to the United States?
   c. **Predict** What are some possible results of expansion into the Louisiana Purchase?
3. a. **Describe** What areas did the Lewis and Clark expedition and the Pike expedition explore?
   b. **Draw Conclusions** Why were **Meriwether Lewis** and **William Clark** chosen to lead the exploration of the Louisiana Purchase?

Critical Thinking

4. **Sequencing** Copy the graphic organizer below. Use it to show what events led to the Louisiana Purchase and what steps the United States took to learn about the Louisiana Territory afterward.

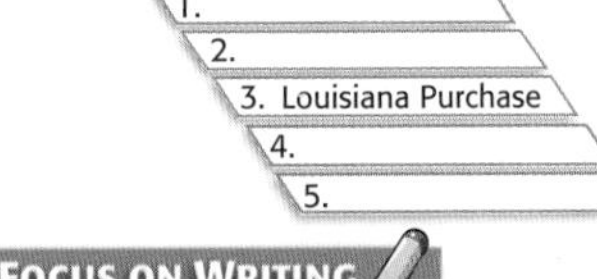

FOCUS ON WRITING

5. **Gathering Information about a Person's Actions** Make a list of Jefferson's actions–the ones that would put him on that top-ten list. Add any new character traits you have discovered.

Section 2 Assessment Answers

1. a. Kentucky, Tennessee, and Ohio
   b. Settlers used the river and the port at New Orleans to transport products to and from markets.
2. a. needed money for a war against Britain; hoped that a larger United States would challenge Britain's power in North America
   b. It roughly doubled the size of the nation.
   c. possible answers—addition of new states; conflict with Native Americans; westward settlement; U.S. population growth
3. a. present-day western United States
   b. Lewis—Jefferson's assistant, former army captain, outdoorsman; Clark—served with Lewis in the military, drew maps, could lead
4. (1) Spain gave Louisiana to France; (2) France suffered setbacks in Haiti and went to war against Britain; Napoleon, in need of money, offered to sell Louisiana to the United States; (4) United States roughly doubles in size; (5) Expeditions sent westward.
5. Actions might include the Louisiana Purchase and the Lewis and Clark expedition.

Direct Teach

Main Idea

3 Explorers Head West

Expeditions led by Lewis, Clark, and Pike increased Americans' understanding of the West.

Recall What was the purpose of Pike's expedition? *to find the origin of the Red River, which the United States claimed formed Louisiana's western border with New Spain*

Describe Where did Pike go, and what famous landmark did he see? *to the Southwest, Spanish-held lands, Pike's Peak*

CRF: History and Geography Activity: Pike Explores the Southwest

HSS 8.8.2; HSS **Analysis Skills:** HI 1

Review & Assess

Close

Have students discuss the ways in which the United States benefited from the Louisiana Purchase.

Review

Online Quiz, Section 2

Assess

SE Section 2 Assessment

PASS: Section 2 Quiz

Alternative Assessment Handbook

Reteach/Classroom Intervention

California Standards Review Workbook

Interactive Reader and Study Guide, Section 2

Interactive Skills Tutor CD-ROM

Answers

Linking to Today *oil, natural gas, coal, gemstones, copper, iron ore, lead, zinc, silver, limestone, sulphur, diamonds, helium*

Reading Check *possible answers—consider the opportunities, weigh the benefits and costs of staying, try to establish friendly ties, try to trade, leave*

Preteach

Bellringer

If YOU were there . . . Use the **Daily Bellringer Transparency** to help students answer the question.

Daily Bellringer Transparency, Section 3

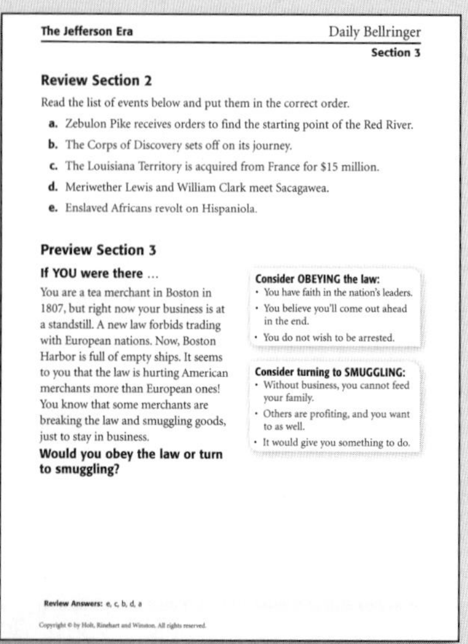

The Jefferson Era Daily Bellringer **Section 3**

Review Section 2

Read the list of events below and put them in the correct order.

- **a.** Zebulon Pike receives orders to find the starting point of the Red River.
- **b.** The Corps of Discovery sets off on its journey.
- **c.** The Louisiana Territory is acquired from France for $15 million.
- **d.** Meriwether Lewis and William Clark meet Sacagawea.
- **e.** Enslaved Africans revolt on Hispaniola.

Preview Section 3

If YOU were there ...

You are a tea merchant in Boston in 1807, but right now your business is at a standstill. A new law forbids trading with European nations. Now, Boston Harbor is full of empty ships. It seems to you that the law is hurting American merchants more than European ones! You know that some merchants are breaking the law and smuggling goods, just to stay in business.

Would you obey the law or turn to smuggling?

Consider OBEYING the law:
- You have faith in the nation's leaders.
- You believe you'll come out ahead in the end.
- You do not wish to be arrested.

Consider turning to SMUGGLING:
- Without business, you cannot feed your family.
- Others are profiting, and you want to as well.
- It would give you something to do.

Review Answers: e, c, b, d, a

Building Vocabulary

Preteach or review the following terms:

brazen bold and without shame (p. 241)

neutrality not taking part or supporting either side in a war (p. 241)

Northwest Territory lands including present-day Illinois, Indiana, Michigan, Ohio, Wisconsin, and part of Minnesota (p. 242)

petitions formal written requests (p. 242)

repeal cancellation (p. 242)

CRF: Vocabulary Builder Activity, Section 3

Standards Focus

HSS 8.5.1

Means: Discuss the events that led to the outbreak of the War of 1812.

Matters: The War of 1812 was the first major conflict the United States faced after declaring independence from Great Britain.

SECTION 3

The Coming of War

What You Will Learn...

Main Ideas

1. Violations of U.S. neutrality led Congress to enact a ban on trade.
2. Native Americans, Great Britain, and the United States came into conflict in the West.
3. The War Hawks led a growing call for war with Great Britain.

The Big Idea

Challenges at home and abroad led the United States to declare war on Great Britain.

Key Terms and People

USS *Constitution*, *p. 240*
impressment, *p. 241*
embargo, *p. 241*
Embargo Act, *p. 241*
Non-Intercourse Act, *p. 242*
Tecumseh, *p. 242*
Battle of Tippecanoe, *p. 244*
War Hawks, *p. 244*
James Madison, *p. 245*

HSS 8.5.1 Understand the political and economic causes and consequences of the War of 1812 and know the major battles, leaders, and events that led to a final peace.

If YOU were there...

You are a tea merchant in Boston in 1807, but right now your business is at a standstill. A new law forbids trading with European nations. Now, Boston Harbor is full of empty ships. It seems to you that the law is hurting American merchants more than European ones! You know that some merchants are breaking the law and smuggling goods, just to stay in business.

Would you obey the law or turn to smuggling?

BUILDING BACKGROUND The United States tried to stay neutral in the conflicts between France and Great Britain, but it was impossible to avoid getting involved. French and British ships interfered with American trade across the Atlantic. The British also caused trouble along the western frontier. Many Americans began to urge war with Great Britain.

Violations of Neutrality

During the late 1700s and early 1800s, American merchant ships fanned out across the oceans. The overseas trade, while profitable, was also risky. Ships had to travel vast distances, often through violent storms. Merchant ships sailing in the Mediterranean risked capture by pirates from the Barbary States of North Africa, who would steal cargo and hold ships' crews for ransom. Attacks continued until the United States sent the **USS *Constitution***, a large warship, and other ships to end them.

The Barbary pirates were a serious problem, but an even larger threat soon loomed. When Great Britain and France went to war in 1803, each country wanted to stop the United States from supplying goods to the other. Each government passed laws designed to prevent American merchants from trading with the other. In addition, the British and French navies captured many American merchant ships searching for war supplies.

The real trouble, however, started when Britain began stopping and searching American ships for sailors who had run away from the British navy, forcing the sailors to return to British ships.

Teach the Big Idea: Master the Standards

Standards Proficiency

The Coming of War

HSS 8.5.1; HSS **Analysis Skills:** CS 1, CS 2, HI 1, HI 2

1. **Teach** Ask students the Main Idea questions to teach this section.
2. **Apply** Have each student use the section and the time line in it to create his or her own drawing of the Road to the War of 1812. Students should draw a winding road and alongside it provide annotations and illustrations depicting the main events and issues covered in this section.
   LS Verbal/Linguistic, Visual/Spatial
3. **Review** Have students use their drawings to review the causes of the War of 1812.
4. **Practice/Homework** Have each student create a recruitment poster urging Americans to enlist in the fight against the British. Students should include at least two reasons for the war. **LS Verbal/Linguistic, Visual/Spatial**

Alternative Assessment Handbook, Rubrics 28: Posters; and 36: Time Lines

The USS *Constitution*

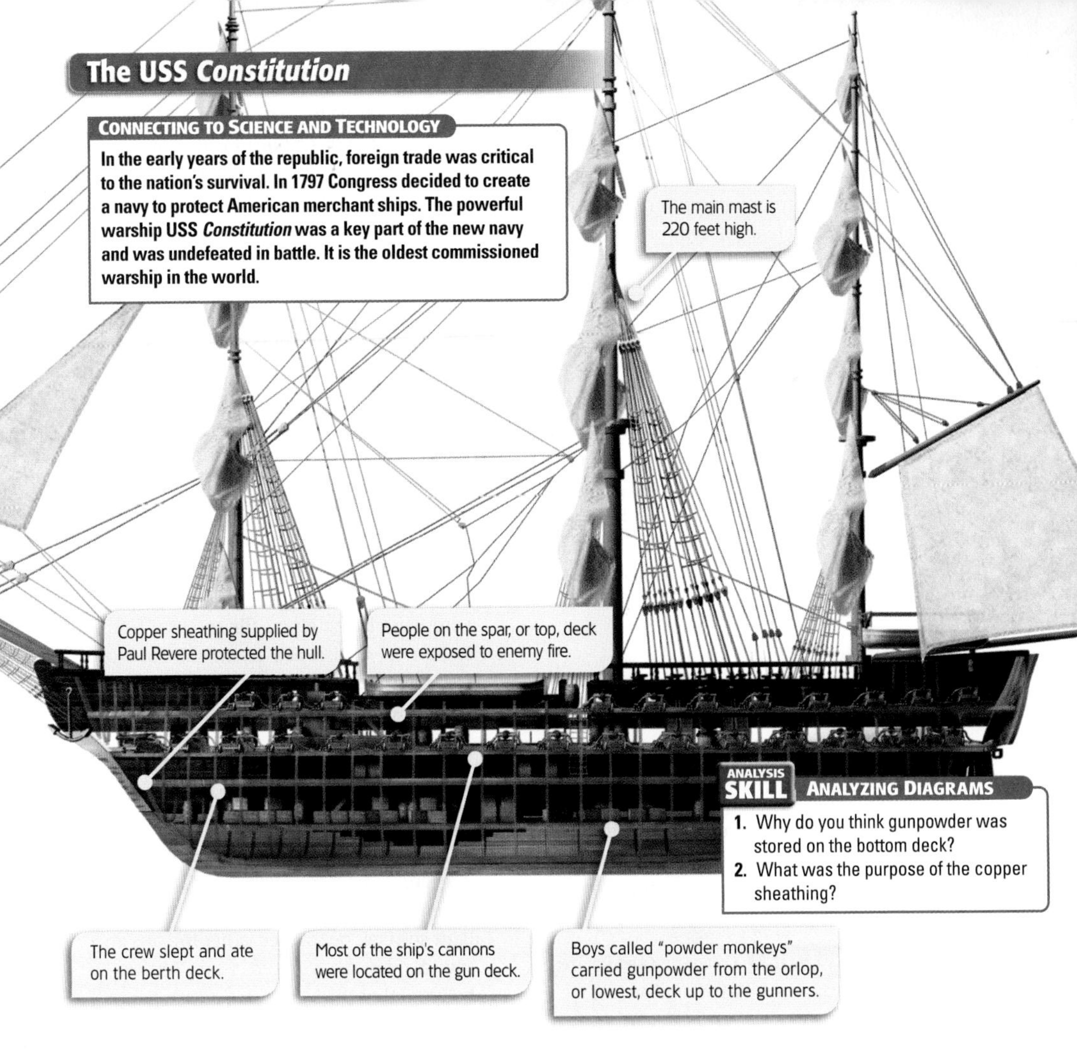

CONNECTING TO SCIENCE AND TECHNOLOGY
In the early years of the republic, foreign trade was critical to the nation's survival. In 1797 Congress decided to create a navy to protect American merchant ships. The powerful warship USS *Constitution* was a key part of the new navy and was undefeated in battle. It is the oldest commissioned warship in the world.
The main mast is 220 feet high.
Copper sheathing supplied by Paul Revere protected the hull.
People on the spar, or top, deck were exposed to enemy fire.
The crew slept and ate on the berth deck.
Most of the ship's cannons were located on the gun deck.
Boys called "powder monkeys" carried gunpowder from the orlop, or lowest, deck up to the gunners.

ANALYSIS SKILL ANALYZING DIAGRAMS

1. Why do you think gunpowder was stored on the bottom deck?
2. What was the purpose of the copper sheathing?

Sometimes U.S. citizens were captured by accident. This **impressment**, or the practice of forcing people to serve in the army or navy, continued despite American protests.

Soon Britain was even targeting American navy ships. In June 1807, for example, the British ship *Leopard* stopped the U.S. Navy ship *Chesapeake* and tried to remove sailors. When the captain of the *Chesapeake* refused, the British took the sailors by force. The brazen attack on the *Chesapeake* stunned Americans.

The Embargo Act

Great Britain's violations of U.S. neutrality sparked intense debate in America about how to respond. Some people wanted to go to war. Others favored an **embargo**, or the banning of trade, against Britain.

Jefferson, who had easily won re-election in 1804, supported an embargo. At his urging, in late 1807 Congress passed the **Embargo Act**. The law essentially banned trade with all foreign countries. American ships could not sail to foreign ports. American ports were also

Direct Teach

Main Idea

1 Violations of Neutrality

Violations of U.S. neutrality led Congress to enact a ban on trade.

Recall What dangers did American ships face on the high seas? *storms; pirates; British and French search and seizure; British impressment*

Analyze How did Great Britain's actions on the high seas affect its relationship with the United States? *Americans were stunned by British impressment; some wanted to go to war; the Embargo Act was passed.*

Political Cartoons Activities for United States History, Cartoon 8: Party Politics in the Jefferson Era

CRF: Economics and History Activity: Embargoes—Economic Diplomacy

HSS 8.5.1; HSS **Analysis Skills:** HI 1

Connect to Science and Technology

Old Ironsides The USS *Constitution* is a medium-sized ship known as a frigate. It is 204 feet in length and has thick wooden planking and a heavily reinforced frame. Despite its heavy frame, the *Constitution* was a fast warship. In battle, it required a crew of 450 and carried more than 50 cannons, more than many ships its size. The *Constitution*'s toughness in battle earned it the nickname Old Ironsides. Today the ship is a popular tourist attraction docked in Boston Harbor.

Critical Thinking: Identifying Points of View

Standards Proficiency

Letters about the Embargo Act

HSS 8.5.1; HSS **Analysis Skills:** HR 5, HI 1, HI 2

1. Ask students to imagine that they are American merchants and that Congress has just passed the Embargo Act.
2. Have each student write a petition asking President Jefferson for a repeal of the Embargo Act. Students should indicate in their petitions why they want the Embargo Act repealed.
3. Ask volunteers to read their petitions to the class. Close with a discussion of the causes and effects of the Embargo Act and how Americans viewed it. LS **Verbal/Linguistic**
4. **Extend** Have each student write a letter from President Jefferson in response to the petition. The letter should explain why Jefferson supports the Embargo Act and try to convince the merchant to do likewise. LS **Verbal/Linguistic**

Alternative Assessment Handbook, Rubric 17: Letters to Editors; and 37: Writing Assignments

Answers

Analyzing Diagrams 1. *possible answers—so it was not exposed to enemy fire, to keep it dry;* **2.** *to protect the ship's hull*

Direct Teach

Main Idea

1 Violations of Neutrality

Violations of U.S. neutrality led Congress to enact a ban on trade.

Recall Why did Congress pass the Embargo Act? *to punish Britain and France and to protect American merchant ships from capture*

Identify Cause and Effect How did the Embargo Act affect Jefferson's popularity? *damaged it and helped revive the Federalist Party*

Evaluate How successful was the Embargo Act? *not very—had little effect on Britain and France; financially hurt American merchants*

Political Cartoons Activities for United States History, Cartoon: 8: Party Politics in the Jefferson Era

CRF: Economics and History Activity: Embargoes—Economic Diplomacy

HSS 8.5.1; HSS **Analysis Skills:** HI 1, HI 2

Reading Time Lines

America's Road to War

Activity News Bulletins Have students transform each entry on the time line into a "live" news bulletin, such as students might see on TV or hear on the radio. Ask volunteers to deliver their news bulletins to the class.

HSS 8.5.1; HSS **Analysis Skills:** CS 1, HI 1

Answers

Reading Check *similar—banned foreign trade, hurt the American economy; different—The Non-Intercourse Act banned American trade only with Britain and France and their colonies.*

closed to British ships. Congress hoped that the embargo would punish Britain and France and protect American merchant ships from capture.

The effect of the law was devastating to American merchants. Without foreign trade, they lost enormous amounts of money. Northern states that relied heavily on trade were especially hard hit by the embargo. Congressman Josiah Quincy of Massachusetts, in a speech before Congress, described the situation. "All the business of the nation is in disorder. All the nation's industry is at a standstill," he said.

The embargo damaged Jefferson's popularity and strengthened the Federalist Party. Angry merchants sent Jefferson hundreds of petitions demanding the repeal of the Embargo Act. One New Englander said the embargo was like "cutting one's throat to stop the nosebleed." Even worse, the embargo had little effect on Britain and France.

Non-Intercourse Act

In 1809 Congress tried to revive the nation's trade by replacing the unpopular act with the **Non-Intercourse Act**. This new law banned trade only with Britain, France, and their colonies. It also stated that the United States would resume trading with the first side that stopped violating U.S. neutrality. In time, however, the law was no more successful than the Embargo Act.

READING CHECK **Comparing and Contrasting** In what ways were the Embargo Act and the Non-Intercourse Act similar and different?

Conflict in the West

Disagreements between Great Britain and the United States went beyond the neutrality issue. In the West, the British and Native Americans again clashed with American settlers over land.

The Conflict over Land

In the early 1800s, Native Americans in the old Northwest Territory continued to lose land as thousands of settlers poured into the region. The United States had gained this land in the Treaty of Greenville, but Indian leaders who had not agreed to the treaty protested the settlers' arrival. Frustrated Indian groups considered what to do. In the meantime, Britain saw an opportunity to slow America's westward growth. British agents from Canada began to arm Native Americans who were living along the western frontier. Rumors of British activity in the old Northwest Territory quickly spread, filling American settlers with fear and anger.

Tecumseh Resists U.S. Settlers

Soon an Indian leader emerged who seemed more than capable of halting the American settlers. **Tecumseh** (tuh-KUHM-suh), a Shawnee chief, had watched angrily as Native Americans were pushed off their land. A brilliant speaker, he warned other Indians about the dangers they faced from settlers. He believed that the Native Americans had to do what white Americans had done: unite.

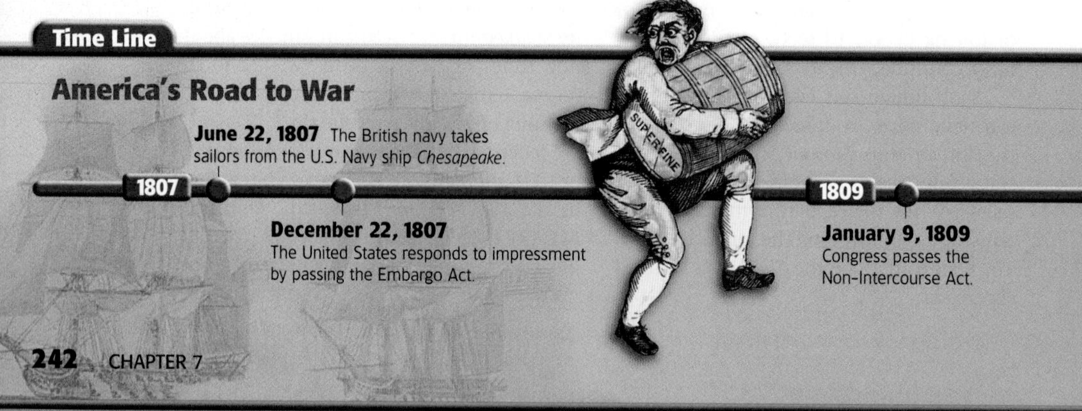

Time Line
America's Road to War
June 22, 1807 The British navy takes sailors from the U.S. Navy ship *Chesapeake*.
1807
December 22, 1807 The United States responds to impressment by passing the Embargo Act.
SUPERFINE
1809
January 9, 1809 Congress passes the Non-Intercourse Act.

Differentiating Instruction for Universal Access

Learners Having Difficulty

Reaching Standards

1. To help students understand the effects of the Embargo Act of 1807, copy the graphic organizer for students to see. Omit the blue answers.
2. Have students copy the graphic organizer by providing the information requested.
3. Review the answers as a class. **LS Visual/Spatial**

Alternative Assessment Handbook, Rubric 13: Graphic Organizers

HSS 8.5.1; HSS **Analysis Skills:** HI 1, HI 2

Embargo Act of 1807
- **What it did:** *essentially banned trade with all foreign countries*
- **Why it was passed:** *to punish Britain and France; to protect American merchant ships from capture*

Political Effects
hurt Jefferson's popularity; revived the Federalist Party

Economic Effects
was devastating to American merchants

Primary Source

POLITICAL CARTOON

The unpopularity of the Embargo Act prompted political cartoonists to show visually how the act was hurting American trade.

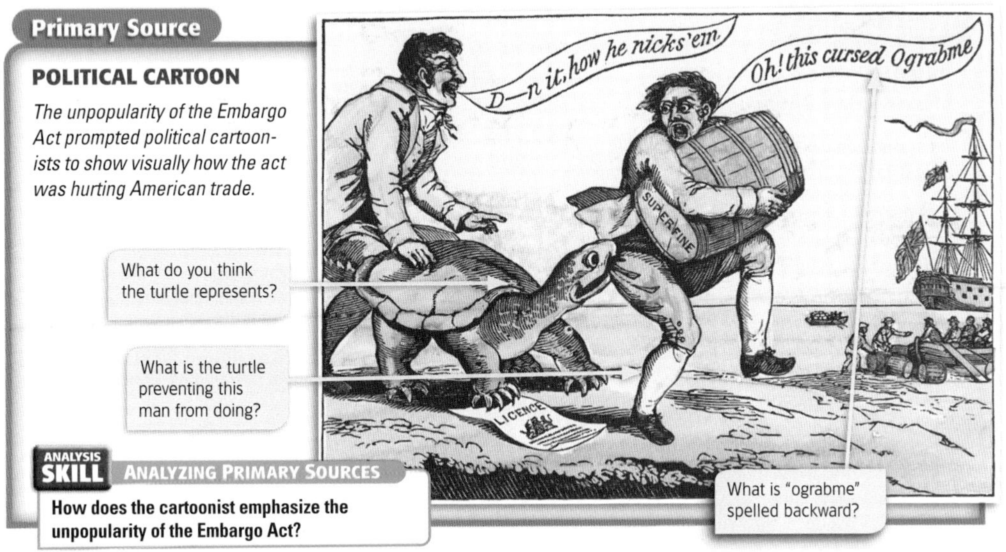

D—n it, how he nicks 'em
Oh! this cursed Ograbme
SUPERFINE
LICENCE

What do you think the turtle represents?

What is the turtle preventing this man from doing?

What is "ograbme" spelled backward?

ANALYSIS SKILL ANALYZING PRIMARY SOURCES

How does the cartoonist emphasize the unpopularity of the Embargo Act?

Tecumseh hoped to unite the Native Americans of the northwestern frontier, the South, and the eastern Mississippi Valley. He was helped by his brother, a religious leader called the Prophet. They founded a village called Prophetstown for their followers near the Wabash and Tippecanoe rivers.

The Battle of Tippecanoe

The governor of the Indiana Territory, William Henry Harrison, watched Tecumseh's activities with alarm. Harrison called him "one of those uncommon geniuses which spring up occasionally to . . . overturn the established order." The governor was convinced that Tecumseh had British backing. If true, Tecumseh could be a serious threat to American power in the West.

In 1810 Tecumseh met face to face with Harrison. The governor urged him to follow the Treaty of Greenville that had been signed in 1795. Tecumseh replied, "The white people have no right to take the land from the Indians, because the Indians had it first." No single chief, he insisted, could sell land belonging to all American Indians who used it. In response, Harrison warned Tecumseh not to resist the power of the United States.

June 18, 1812
The United States declares war against Britain.

November 4, 1811
When the twelfth Congress convenes, Kentucky representative Henry Clay leads the call for war against Britain.

ANALYSIS SKILL READING TIME LINES

What events led to war against Great Britain?

Direct Teach

Main Idea

❷ Conflict in the West

Native Americans, Great Britain, and the United States came into conflict in the West.

Identify Who was Tecumseh, and what did he want to accomplish? *Shawnee chief and influential Native American leader; wanted to unite Native Americans against U.S. settlers pushing them off their lands*

Explain Why did Great Britain want to help Native Americans along the western frontier? *hoped to slow the westward growth of the United States*

Identify Points of View How did William Henry Harrison view Tecumseh? *possible answer—with respect for his intelligence and abilities and with fear for the threat he felt Tecumseh posed*

CRF: Biography Activity: Tecumseh

HSS 8.5.1; **HSS Analysis Skills:** HR 5, HI 1

Connect to Economics

U.S. Exports From 1807 to 1809, the total value of all U.S. exports dropped from $108 million to $22 million. During the same period, the total value of U.S. exports to Great Britain dropped from $23 million to $3 million.

Draw Conclusions What does this data say about the trade relationship between Great Britain and the United States? *The United States was dependent on trade with Britain, which made up a significant portion of total U.S. trade before the Embargo Act.*

Critical Thinking: Finding Main Ideas

Standards Proficiency

Frontier Interviews

HSS 8.5.1; **HSS Analysis Skills:** HR 5, HI 1

1. Ask students to imagine that they are roving reporters assigned to the old Northwest Territory in the early 1800s.
2. Have each student write a series of short interviews with Tecumseh, a British agent, and Governor William Henry Harrison. In their interviews, students should ask the individuals to explain their goals, current activities, and future plans.
3. Then have each student combine his or her interviews into a newspaper article on the frontier situation.
4. Ask volunteers to read their articles aloud to the class. Then lead a class discussion on the effects of the Battle of Tippecanoe on Native Americans and on U.S.-British relations.

Alternative Assessment Handbook, Rubric 37: Writing Assignments

Answers

Analyzing Primary Sources *by showing Americans trying to load goods illegally onto a British ship as a turtle holds them back and one man curses the embargo in frustration*

Reading Time Lines *British impressment, such as the* Chesapeake *incident; Embargo Act; Non-Intercourse Act; calls for war*

• Direct Teach •

Main Idea

❸ Call for War

The War Hawks led a growing call for war with Great Britain.

Identify Who were the War Hawks? *several young members of Congress who took the lead in calling for war*

Contrast Describe the views of the opposing sides in the war debate. *War Hawks—stop British influence among frontier Indians, invade Canada, end British trade restrictions; opponents to war—renew friendly business ties with Britain, foolish to fight Britain's larger and better equipped military*

Evaluate What did the United States risk by declaring war against Britain in 1812? *human and economic losses; being defeated; losing independence*

CRF: Literature Activity: *A Warrior's Speech* by Chief Tecumseh

CRF: Primary Source Activity: A Shawnee Leader Seeks Allies

HSS 8.5.1; HSS **Analysis Skills:** HR 5, HI 1

Primary Source

Views of War

Activity Ask volunteers to read each excerpt aloud. Have students discuss each man's point of view. Then have students suggest how they think each man would have responded to the other's statement. **LS Verbal/Linguistic**

HSS 8.5.1; HSS **Analysis Skills:** HR 4, HR 5, HI 1

Primary Source

POINTS OF VIEW

Views of War

Tecumseh urged Native Americans to unite to oppose what he called the "evil" of white settlement.

"The only way to stop this evil is for all the red men to unite in claiming a common and equal right to the land, as it was at first, and should be yet. Before, the land never was divided, but belonged to all, for the use of each person. No group had a right to sell, not even to each other, much less to strangers who want all and will not do with less."

—**Tecumseh**

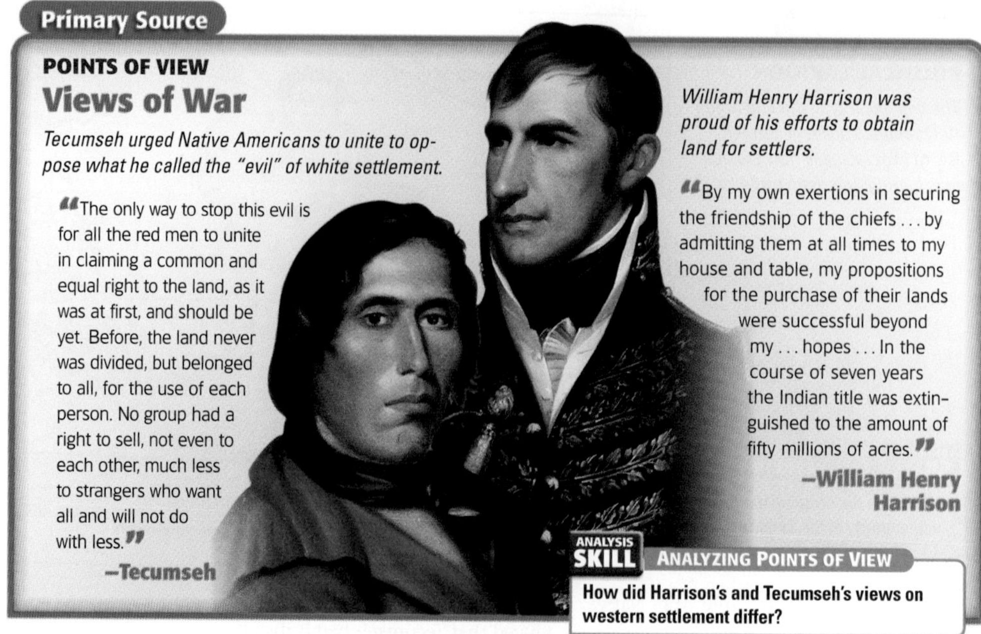

William Henry Harrison was proud of his efforts to obtain land for settlers.

"By my own exertions in securing the friendship of the chiefs . . . by admitting them at all times to my house and table, my propositions for the purchase of their lands were successful beyond my . . . hopes . . . In the course of seven years the Indian title was extinguished to the amount of fifty millions of acres."

—**William Henry Harrison**

ANALYSIS SKILL ANALYZING POINTS OF VIEW

How did Harrison's and Tecumseh's views on western settlement differ?

Tecumseh traveled south to ask the Creek nation to join his forces. In his absence, Harrison attacked. Harrison raised an army and marched his troops close to Prophetstown. Fighting broke out when the Prophet ordered an attack on Harrison's camp on November 7, 1811.

The Indians broke through army lines, but Harrison maintained a "calm, cool, and collected" manner, according to one observer. During the all-day battle, Harrison's soldiers forced the Indian warriors to retreat and then destroyed Tecumseh's village. Said Chief Shabbona, "With the smoke of that town and loss of that battle, I lost all hope." Although Tecumseh was safe, U.S. forces defeated Tecumseh and his followers in the **Battle of Tippecanoe**. The defeat destroyed Tecumseh's dream of a great Indian confederation. He fled to Canada.

FOCUS ON READING

What words did Calhoun use that had strong emotions tied to them for Americans? (See "The War Hawks" section.)

READING CHECK **Finding Main Ideas**

Why were U.S. officials worried about Tecumseh's actions?

Call for War

The evidence of British support for Tecumseh further inflamed Americans. A Democratic-Republican newspaper declared, "The war on the Wabash [River] is purely BRITISH." Many Americans felt that Britain had encouraged Tecumseh to attack settlers in the West.

The War Hawks

Several young members of Congress—called **War Hawks** by their opponents—took the lead in calling for war against Britain. These legislators, most of whom were from the South and West, were led by Henry Clay of Kentucky, John C. Calhoun of South Carolina, and Felix Grundy of Tennessee. They saw war as the only answer to British insults. "If we submit," Calhoun warned, "the independence of this nation is lost." Calls for war grew. Leaders wanted to put a stop to British influence among Native Americans. They also wanted to invade

Collaborative Learning

Standards Proficiency

War Rally

HSS 8.5.1; HSS **Analysis Skills:** HR 5, HI 1

Materials: poster board, art supplies

1. Ask students to imagine that they are going to a war rally in Washington in 1812. Organize the class into four groups and assign each group to be War Hawks, New England Federalists, others opposed to war, or journalists.
2. Have the first three groups prepare speeches, signs, and banners supporting their positions. Have the journalists write questions to ask each group. In addition, assign some students specific people to portray, such as Henry Clay.
3. Assign students in each group specific tasks to perform based on their ability levels and learning styles.
4. Hold the class rally. You might want to reserve a large space, such as the school's gym, for the activity.

Alternative Assessment Handbook, Rubric 14: Group Activity

Answers

Analyzing Points of View *Tecumseh thought the land belonged to Native Americans and that white settlement was evil; Harrison wanted the land for U.S. settlers.*

Focus on Reading *"independence . . . is lost"*

Reading Check *Tecumseh was trying to unite all Native Americans in the northwestern frontier, the South, and the eastern Mississippi Valley against settlers and the expansion of settlement.*

Canada and gain more land for settlement. Others were angered by British trade restrictions that hurt southern planters and western farmers. War Hawks gave emotional speeches urging Americans to stand up to Great Britain.

The Opposition

The strongest opponents of the War Hawks were New England Federalists. British trade restrictions and impressment had hurt New England's economy. People there wanted to renew friendly business ties with Britain instead of fighting another war.

Other politicians argued that war with Great Britain would be foolish. They feared that the United States was not yet ready to fight powerful Britain. America's army and navy were small and poorly equipped compared to Britain's military. In addition, Americans could produce only a fraction of the military supplies Britain could. Senator Obadiah German of New York pleaded with the War Hawks to be patient: "Prior to any declaration of war . . . my plan would be, and my first wish is, to prepare for it—to put the country in complete armor."

Declaring War

Republican **James Madison** was elected president in 1808. He faced the difficulty of continuing an unpopular trade war begun by Jefferson. He also felt growing pressure from the War Hawks. By 1812 he decided that Congress must vote on war. Speaking to Congress, Madison blasted Great Britain's conduct. He asked Congress to decide how the nation should respond.

When Congress voted a few days later, the War Hawks won. For the first time in the nation's brief history, Congress had declared war. Months later, Americans elected Madison to a second term. He would serve as commander in chief during the War of 1812.

READING CHECK **Summarizing** Why did the United States declare war in 1812?

SUMMARY AND PREVIEW Conflicts on the frontier and with Great Britain dominated U.S. foreign policy under Jefferson and Madison. In the next section you will read about the War of 1812.

Section 3 Assessment

go.hrw.com
Online Quiz
KEYWORD: SS8 HP7

Reviewing Ideas, Terms, and People HSS 8.5.1

1. **a. Describe** In what ways did the war between France and Britain cause problems for the United States?
   b. Make Inferences What were the reasons for the failure of the **Embargo Act**?
   c. Elaborate Why do you think embargoes against Britain and France failed?
2. **a. Describe** What was **Tecumseh's** goal?
   b. Explain What role did Great Britain play in the conflict between the United States and American Indians on the western frontier?
3. **a. Identify** Who were the **War Hawks**? Why did they support war with Britain?
   b. Elaborate Would you have supported going to war against Great Britain? Explain your answer.

Critical Thinking

4. **Identifying Cause and Effect** Copy the graphic organizer below. Use it to identify the causes of the War of 1812.

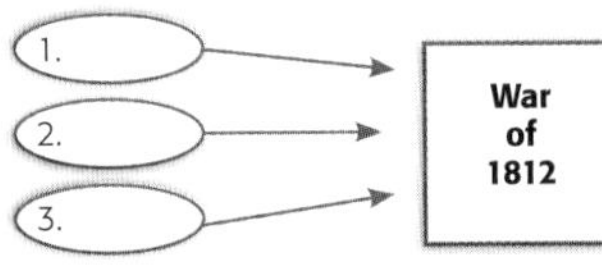

FOCUS ON WRITING

5. **Taking Notes** Take notes about any of Jefferson's actions and character traits you can identify during the buildup to war with Britain. Save this information for the top-ten list you will create at the end of the chapter.

Direct Teach

Info to Know

Madison Becomes President In 1808, Thomas Jefferson declined to run for a third term as president. Instead, he supported his secretary of state, James Madison, as the Democratic-Republican candidate. Although criticism of the Embargo Act had hurt the Republicans, Madison easily won over Federalist candidate Charles C. Pinckney. Madison went on to serve two terms as the nation's fourth president.

Review & Assess

Close

Have students review in order the series of events that led to the U.S. declaration of war against Great Britain, starting with the war between Britain and France.

Review

Online Quiz, Section 3

Assess

SE Section 3 Assessment

PASS: Section 3 Quiz

Alternative Assessment Handbook

Reteach/Classroom Intervention

California Standards Review Workbook

Interactive Reader and Study Guide, Section 3

Interactive Skills Tutor CD-ROM

Section 3 Assessment Answers

1. **a.** Both nations began stopping and searching American ships.
   b. ineffective, hurt American economy
   c. possible answer—Britain and France were able to trade elsewhere.
2. **a.** to unite Native Americans and stop the spread of American settlement
   b. Britain supplied military aid to Indians.
3. **a.** Congress members who called for war; wanted to stop British influence among frontier Indians, invade Canada, and end trade restrictions
   b. Answers will vary, but students should exhibit an understanding of the causes that led the United States to declare war.
4. (1) Great Britain's impressment and violations of U.S. neutrality; (2) Britain's military aid to frontier Native Americans; (3) calls for war
5. Students should take notes on Jefferson's foreign relations policies and problems.

Answers

Reading Check *British impressment of American sailors, British influence of American Indians on the frontier; unpopular trade war not working; growing pressure from War Hawks*

Preteach

Bellringer

If YOU were there . . . Use the **Daily Bellringer Transparency** to help students answer the question.

Daily Bellringer Transparency, Section 4

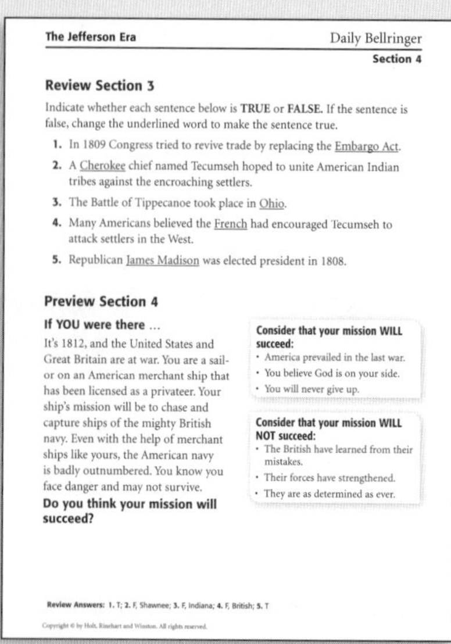

The Jefferson Era Daily Bellringer

Section 4

Review Section 3

Indicate whether each sentence below is **TRUE** or **FALSE.** If the sentence is false, change the underlined word to make the sentence true.

1. In 1809 Congress tried to revive trade by replacing the Embargo Act.
2. A Cherokee chief named Tecumseh hoped to unite American Indian tribes against the encroaching settlers.
3. The Battle of Tippecanoe took place in Ohio.
4. Many Americans believed the French had encouraged Tecumseh to attack settlers in the West.
5. Republican James Madison was elected president in 1808.

Preview Section 4

If YOU were there ...

It's 1812, and the United States and Great Britain are at war. You are a sailor on an American merchant ship that has been licensed as a privateer. Your ship's mission will be to chase and capture ships of the mighty British navy. Even with the help of merchant ships like yours, the American navy is badly outnumbered. You know you face danger and may not survive.

Do you think your mission will succeed?

Consider that your mission WILL succeed:
- America prevailed in the last war.
- You believe God is on your side.
- You will never give up.

Consider that your mission WILL NOT succeed:
- The British have learned from their mistakes.
- Their forces have strengthened.
- They are as determined as ever.

Review Answers: **1.** T; **2.** F, Shawnee; **3.** F, Indiana; **4.** F, British; **5.** T

Academic Vocabulary

Review with students the high-use academic term in this section.

consequences the effects of a particular event or events (p. 249)

CRF: Vocabulary Builder Activity, Section 4

Standards Focus

HSS 8.5.1

Means: Understand the key battles, leaders, and events of the War of 1812, and describe the results of the war.

Matters: The War of 1812 was the first major conflict the United States faced after declaring independence from Britain.

SECTION 4

The War of 1812

What You Will Learn...

Main Ideas

1. American forces held their own against the British in the early battles of the war.
2. U.S. forces stopped British offensives in the East and South.
3. The effects of the war included prosperity and national pride.

The Big Idea

Great Britain and the United States went to battle in the War of 1812.

Key Terms and People

Oliver Hazard Perry, *p. 247*
Battle of Lake Erie, *p. 247*
Andrew Jackson, *p. 248*
Treaty of Fort Jackson, *p. 248*
Battle of New Orleans, *p. 248*
Hartford Convention, *p. 249*
Treaty of Ghent, *p. 249*

HSS 8.5.1 Understand the political and economic causes and consequences of the War of 1812 and know the major battles, leaders, and events that led to a final peace.

If YOU were there...

It's 1812, and the United States and Great Britain are at war. You are a sailor on an American merchant ship that has been licensed as a privateer. Your ship's mission will be to chase and capture ships of the mighty British navy. Even with the help of merchant ships like yours, the American navy is badly outnumbered. You know you face danger and may not survive.

Do you think your mission will succeed?

BUILDING BACKGROUND Anger against Great Britain's actions finally provoked the United States into the War of 1812. Britain's great navy gave it a clear advantage at sea, but the war was also fought on several other fronts. Victories in major battles along the frontier gave Americans a new sense of unity.

Early Battles

In the summer of 1812 the United States found itself in a war with one of the world's most powerful nations. Despite the claims by the War Hawks, the War of 1812 would not be a quick and easy fight.

War at Sea

When the war began, the British navy had hundreds of ships. In contrast, the U.S. Navy had fewer than 20 ships. None of them was as powerful as the greatest British warships.

Most of the British navy's ships, however, were scattered around the globe. Although small, the U.S. Navy had well-trained sailors and powerful new warships such as the USS *Constitution*. American vessels defeated British ships several times in one-on-one duels. Such victories embarrassed the British and raised American morale. Eventually, the British ships blockaded America's seaports.

Battles Along the Canadian Border

American leaders hoped to follow up victories at sea with an overland invasion of Canada. Three attacks were planned—from Detroit, from Niagara Falls, and from up the Hudson River valley toward Montreal.

Teach the Big Idea: Master the Standards

Standards Proficiency

The War of 1812  HSS 8.5.1; HSS Analysis Skills: CS 1, HI 1, HI 2

1. **Teach** Ask students the Main Idea questions to teach this section.
2. **Apply** Have each student divide a sheet of paper into six window panes and label the panes *War at Sea, Battles Along the Canadian Border, The Creek War, British Attacks in the East, The Battle of New Orleans,* and *Effects of the War*. (The titles match headings in the section.) Tell students to use words, phrases, headlines, and drawings to record the key ideas, events, and people for each topic. **LS Verbal/Linguistic, Visual/Spatial**
3. **Review** Have students share some of their entries from each window pane.
4. **Practice/Homework** Have each student create a commemorative stamp depicting a significant event of the war. **LS Visual/Spatial**

Alternative Assessment Handbook, Rubric 3: Artwork

GEOGRAPHY SKILLS INTERPRETING MAPS

1. **Location** According to the map, what major southern port was affected by the British blockade?
2. **Region** Which battles took place in the Great Lakes region?

The attack from Detroit failed in August 1812 when British soldiers and Indians led by Tecumseh captured Fort Detroit. The other two American attacks failed when state militia troops refused to cross the Canadian border, arguing that they did not have to fight in a foreign country.

In 1813 the United States went on the attack again. A key goal was to break Britain's control of Lake Erie. The navy gave the task to Commodore **Oliver Hazard Perry**. After building a small fleet, Perry sailed out to meet the British on September 10, beginning the **Battle of Lake Erie**. The battle ended when the British surrendered. Perry sent a message to General William Henry Harrison: "We have met the enemy and they are ours." Perry's victory forced the British to withdraw, giving the U.S. Army new hope.

With American control of Lake Erie established, General Harrison marched his army into Canada. At the Battle of the Thames River in October 1813, he defeated a combined force of British troops and Native Americans. Harrison's victory ended British power in the Northwest. Tecumseh's death

Direct Teach

Main Idea

1 Early Battles

American forces held their own against the British in the early battles of the war.

Describe What were the U.S. Navy's strengths and weaknesses early in the war? *strengths—powerful new warships, well-trained sailors, British navy scattered; weaknesses—smaller and weaker than British navy*

Summarize Trace the early battles along the Canadian border. *After a failed invasion of Canada, the United States won the Battle of Lake Erie, forcing the British off the lake, and the Battle of the Thames River, ending British power in the Northwest.*

Draw Conclusions Why do you think many of the war's early battles took place along the Canadian border? *Canada was British territory.*

Map Transparency: The War of 1812

HSS 8.5.1; HSS **Analysis Skills:** HI 1

Interpreting Maps

The War of 1812

Drawing Conclusions Why do you think the British attacked New Orleans? *to try to gain control of the city's port and the Mississippi River*

Map Transparency: The War of 1812

HSS 8.5.1; HSS **Analysis Skills:** CS 3

Collaborative Learning

Standards Proficiency

War of 1812 Trading Cards

HSS 8.5.1; HSS **Analysis Skills:** HI 1

Prep Required

Materials: blank index cards, art supplies

1. Organize students into small groups. Have the members of each group discuss and list the main events, people, and issues of the War of 1812.
2. Have each group rank the list by order of significance. Give each group 10 index cards. Have the groups create trading cards for the 10 most significant people, events, battles, and issues of the war. On the front of each card, students should provide a name and an image for a person or event. On the back of each card, students should provide facts about the person or event on the front of the card.
3. Have each group share its cards with the class. Lead a class discussion of the activity. Which events and people did all the groups include? Which did only one group include?

LS Interpersonal, Verbal/Linguistic

Alternative Assessment Handbook, Rubric 14: Group Activity

Answers

Interpreting Maps 1. *New Orleans;* **2.** *Battles of Fort Detroit, Lake Erie, and Thames*

Direct Teach

Main Idea

❷ Great Britain on the Offensive

U.S. forces stopped British offensives in the East and South.

Summarize How did the war progress in the East? *The British took Washington, D.C., but U.S. forces at Fort McHenry stopped the British invasion of Baltimore, and the British retreated.*

Analyze What was unusual about the Battle of New Orleans? *took place after the war had ended*

CRF: Biography Activity: Dolley Madison

HSS 8.5.1; **HSS Analysis Skills:** CS 1, HI 1

Info to Know

"The Star-Spangled Banner" A young American named Francis Scott Key watched anxiously as British forces shelled Fort McHenry. As night fell, he wondered whether the American flag would still be flying over the fort in the morning. Early the next day, through the mist and smoke, Key saw with joy that the flag still flew. The British attack had failed. To celebrate, he wrote "The Star-Spangled Banner." It became the national anthem in 1931.

go.hrw.com

Online Resources

KEYWORD: SS8 US7
ACTIVITY: "The Star-Spangled Banner" Poster

during the fighting also dealt a blow to the British alliance with Native Americans in the region.

The Creek War

Meanwhile, war with American Indians erupted in the South. Creek Indians, angry at American settlers for pushing into their lands, took up arms in 1813. A large force attacked Fort Mims on the Alabama River, destroying the fort and killing close to 250 of its defenders. In response, the commander of the Tennessee militia, **Andrew Jackson**, gathered about 2,000 volunteers to move against the Creek nation.

In the spring of 1814 Jackson attacked the Creek along the Tallapoosa River in Alabama. Jackson's troops won this battle, the Battle of Horseshoe Bend. The **Treaty of Fort Jackson**, signed late in 1814, ended the Creek War and forced the Creek to give up millions of acres of their land.

THE IMPACT TODAY

Inspired by the Americans' strength at Fort McHenry, Francis Scott Key wrote the national anthem, "The Star-Spangled Banner."

READING CHECK **Comparing** What advantages did Great Britain and the United States have at the start of the war?

First Lady Saves Washington's Portrait

Dolley Madison refused to leave Washington, D.C., until a famous portrait of the first president was saved from the executive mansion.

Great Britain on the Offensive

Despite U.S. success on the western and southern frontiers, the situation in the East grew worse. After defeating France in April 1814, the British sent more troops to America.

British Attacks in the East

Now reinforced, the British attacked Washington, D.C. President Madison was forced to flee when the British broke through U.S. defenses. The British set fire to the White House, the Capitol, and other government buildings.

The British sailed on to Baltimore, Maryland, which was guarded by Fort McHenry. They shelled the fort for 25 hours. The Americans refused to surrender Fort McHenry. The British chose to retreat instead of continuing to fight.

The Battle of New Orleans

After the attack on Washington, the British moved against New Orleans. British commanders hoped to capture the city and thus take control of the Mississippi River.

Andrew Jackson commanded the U.S. forces around New Orleans. His troops were a mix of regular soldiers, including two battalions of free African Americans, a group of Choctaw Indians, state militia, and pirates led by Jean Lafitte.

The battle began on the morning of January 8, 1815. Some 5,300 British troops attacked Jackson's force of about 4,500. The British began marching toward the U.S. defenses, but they were caught on an open field. The British were cut down with frightening speed. More than 2,000 British soldiers were killed or wounded. The Americans, for their part, had suffered about 70 casualties. The **Battle of New Orleans** made Andrew Jackson a hero and was the last major conflict of the War of 1812.

READING CHECK **Finding Main Ideas** What happened at the Battle of New Orleans?

Cross-Discipline Activity: Music

Exceeding Standards

"The Star-Spangled Banner" **HSS** 8.5.1; **HSS Analysis Skills:** HI 1

Prep Required

Materials: Lyrics and a recording of "The Star-Spangled Banner"

1. Play for students a recording of "The Star-Spangled Banner." Have students share what they feel when they hear the national anthem.
2. Provide students with the song's lyrics. Instruct students to write new lyrics to the tune of "The Star-Spangled Banner" that describe another significant battle or event of the War of 1812. Alternatively, have students compile a series of images depicting key events of the war and create a slide show that could be accompanied by "The Star-Spangled Banner."
3. Close by having students discuss how "The Star-Spangled Banner" exemplifies the mood of Americans following the War of 1812.

LS Auditory/Musical, Verbal/Linguistic

Alternative Assessment Handbook, Rubrics 26: Poems and Songs; and 29: Presentations

Answers

Reading Check (left) *Great Britain—most powerful nation in the world, hundreds of warships; U.S.—defeated some British warships in one-on-one battles, war on home territory*

Reading Check (right) *major American victory; Andrew Jackson became a hero.*

Analyzing the War of 1812 — QUICK FACTS

Causes of the War
- Impressment of American sailors
- Interference with American shipping
- British military aid to Native Americans

Effects of the War
- Increased sense of national pride
- American manufacturing boosted
- Native American resistance weakened

Effects of the War

Before the battle of New Orleans, a group of New England Federalists gathered secretly at Hartford, Connecticut. At the **Hartford Convention**, Federalists agreed to oppose the war and send delegates to meet with Congress. Before the delegates reached Washington, however, news arrived that the war had ended. Some critics now laughed at the Federalists, and the party lost much of its political power.

Slow communications at the time meant that neither the Federalists nor Jackson knew about the **Treaty of Ghent**. The treaty, which had been signed in Belgium on December 24, 1814, ended the War of 1812.

Though each nation returned the territory it had conquered, the fighting did have several consequences. The War of 1812 produced intense feelings of patriotism among many Americans for having stood up to the mighty British. The war also broke the power of many Native American groups. Finally, a lack of goods caused by the interruption in trade boosted American manufacturing.

ACADEMIC VOCABULARY
consequences the effects of a particular event or events

READING CHECK **Analyzing Information** What were the main effects of the War of 1812?

SUMMARY AND PREVIEW The War of 1812 convinced Americans that the young nation would survive. In the next chapter you will see how the United States continued to grow.

Section 4 Assessment

go.hrw.com **Online Quiz** KEYWORD: SS8 HP7

Reviewing Ideas, Terms, and People HSS 8.5.1

1. **a. Identify** What losses did American forces face in the early battles of the War of 1812? What victories did they win?
   b. Make Generalizations What role did American Indians play in the war?
2. **a. Describe** What attacks did the British lead against American forces?
   b. Evaluate What do you think were the two most important battles of the war? Why?
3. **a. Identify** What was the purpose of the **Hartford Convention**?
   b. Draw Conclusions How did the United States benefit from the War of 1812?

Critical Thinking

4. **Comparing and Contrasting** Copy the chart below. Use it to compare and contrast the significant details of the major military battles during the War of 1812.

Battle	Details (Winner, Location, Importance)

FOCUS ON WRITING

5. **Organizing Your Ideas** Reorder the items on your lists from least important to most important.

Direct Teach

Main Idea

3 Effects of the War

The effects of the war included prosperity and national pride.

Describe What were the terms of the Treaty of Ghent? *ended the war, returned all conquered territory, left other issues to future negotiations*

Evaluate Do you think the War of 1812 was a success from the American point of view? Explain. *possible answers—yes, for the reasons listed in Quick Facts chart at left; no, because the war did not resolve issues of British impressment*

Quick Facts Transparency: Analyzing the War of 1812

HSS 8.5.1; HSS **Analysis Skills:** HI 1

Review & Assess

Close

Have students discuss how the course of history might have been different had Great Britain won the War of 1812.

Review

Online Quiz, Section 4

Assess

SE Section 4 Assessment

PASS: Section 4 Quiz

Alternative Assessment Handbook

Reteach/Classroom Intervention

California Standards Review Workbook

Interactive Reader and Study Guide, Section 4

Interactive Skills Tutor CD-ROM

Section 4 Assessment Answers

1. **a.** losses—Fort Detroit, failed invasions of Canada; victories—Battles of Lake Erie, Thames River, Horseshoe Bend
   b. often sided with British; Creek War
2. **a.** attacks at Washington, D.C., Fort McHenry and Baltimore, and New Orleans
   b. possible answer—Fort McHenry, Americans stopped the British invasion; Lake Erie, Americans regained control of Lake Erie
3. **a.** to organize Federalist opposition to the war
   b. increased national pride; boosted manufacturing
4. Fort Detroit—British, Detroit, Britain gained control of Lake Erie; Lake Erie—U.S., Lake Erie, Americans regained control of Lake Erie; Thames River—U.S., Thames River, broke British and Native American Indian in the Northwest; Washington D.C.—Britain, Washington D.C., Britain took the capitol; Fort McHenry—U.S., Baltimore, Americans stopped British invasion; New Orleans—U.S., New Orleans, last major conflict
5. Students should reorder and rank their lists.

Answers

Reading Check *increased feelings of patriotism among Americans; broke power of many Native American groups; boosted American manufacturing*

History and Geography

Activity **Illustrating the Growing America** Ask students if they have ever heard the United States referred to as a young country. Point out that the United States is about 230 years old, a comparatively young nation by historical standards. Ask students to think of the United States as a developing child. In its first years, it was like an infant—13 states born along the Atlantic coast. Over time, the child began to have growth spurts—growing larger and more self-sufficient with each addition of territory. Have each student create a political cartoon or drawing that illustrates this idea of the expansion of the United States up to 1820. Have volunteers explain their cartoons or drawings to the class. **LS Visual/Spatial**

HSS 8.8.2; HSS **Analysis Skills:** CS 3

Info to Know

Population Boom The U.S. population more than doubled between 1790 and 1820, increasing from about 3.9 million to 10.1 million. The number of Americans in the West grew particularly fast during this period. In 1790 about 4 percent of the U.S. population lived west of the Appalachians. By 1820 this figure had grown significantly.

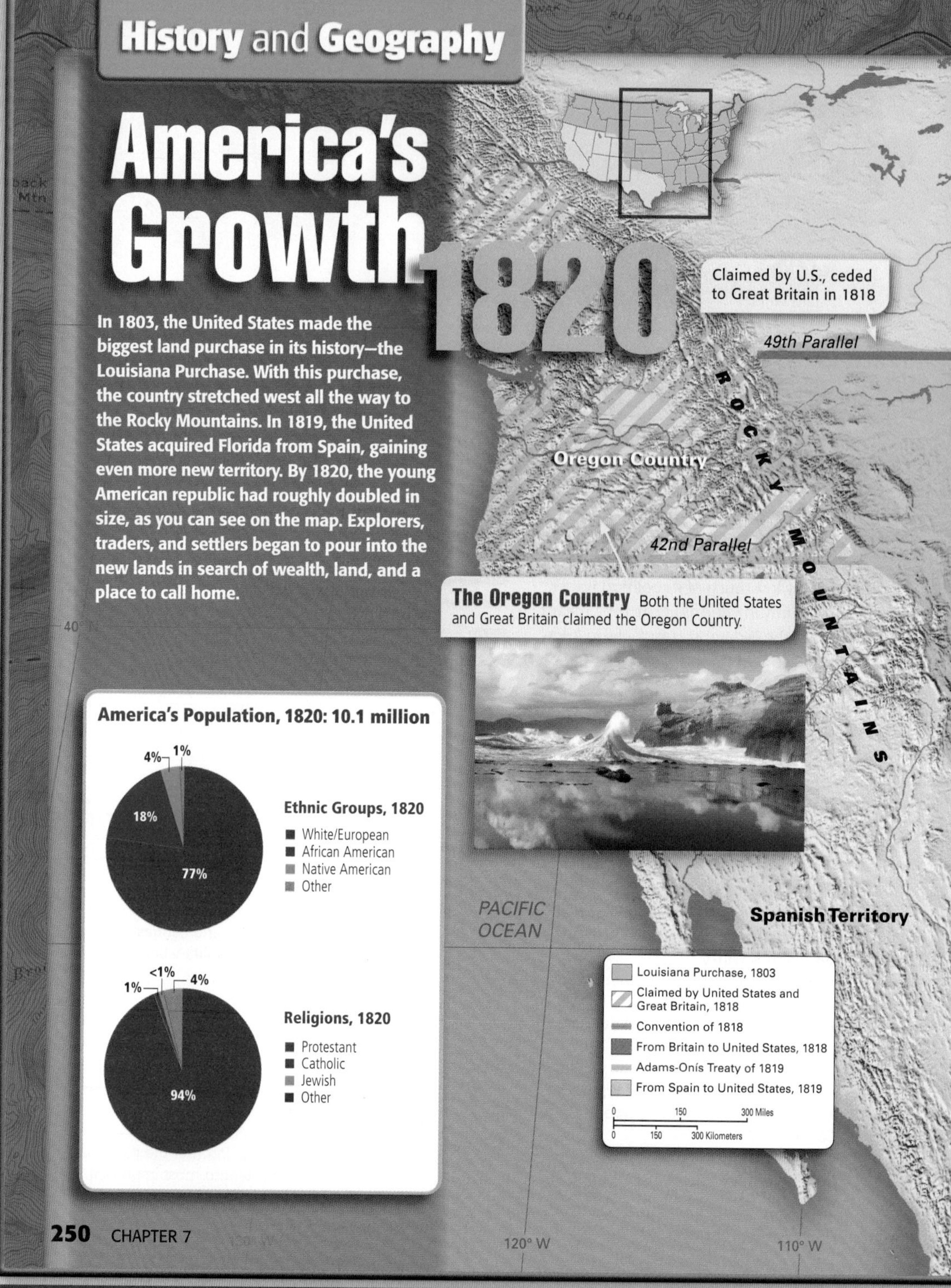

History and Geography
America's Growth 1820
In 1803, the United States made the biggest land purchase in its history—the Louisiana Purchase. With this purchase, the country stretched west all the way to the Rocky Mountains. In 1819, the United States acquired Florida from Spain, gaining even more new territory. By 1820, the young American republic had roughly doubled in size, as you can see on the map. Explorers, traders, and settlers began to pour into the new lands in search of wealth, land, and a place to call home.
Claimed by U.S., ceded to Great Britain in 1818
49th Parallel
ROCKY MOUNTAINS
Oregon Country
42nd Parallel
The Oregon Country Both the United States and Great Britain claimed the Oregon Country.
America's Population, 1820: 10.1 million
Ethnic Groups, 1820
White/European
African American
Native American
Other
77%
18%
4%
1%
Religions, 1820
Protestant
Catholic
Jewish
Other
94%
4%
1%
<1%
PACIFIC OCEAN
Spanish Territory
Louisiana Purchase, 1803
Claimed by United States and Great Britain, 1818
Convention of 1818
From Britain to United States, 1818
Adams-Onís Treaty of 1819
From Spain to United States, 1819
0 150 300 Miles
0 150 300 Kilometers
120° W
110° W
250 CHAPTER 7

Critical Thinking: Summarizing

Standards Proficiency

The Nation in 1820

HSS 8.8.2; HSS **Analysis Skills:** CS 3

1. Have volunteers read aloud the introduction and captions above. Then have students discuss the information in the feature.
2. Ask students to write a description of the United States in 1820 for someone who has never been there. Students should answer some or all of the following questions in their descriptions: What states and territories make up the United States? What major physical features does the United States include? What bodies of water form natural boundaries for the United States? What other nations have claims to lands near the United States? What is the distance from the northernmost point to the southernmost point of the United States? What is the distance from the easternmost point to the westernmost point?
3. Have volunteers present their descriptions to the class. **LS Verbal/Linguistic**

Alternative Assessment Handbook, Rubric 40: Writing to Describe

Standards Focus

HSS 8.8 Students analyze the divergent paths of the American people in the West from 1800 to the mid-1800s and the challenges they faced.

8.8.2 Describe the purpose, challenges, and economic incentives associated with westward expansion, including the concept of Manifest Destiny (e.g., the Lewis and Clark Expedition, accounts of the removal of Indians, the Cherokees' "Trail of Tears," settlement of the Great Plains) and the territorial acquisitions that spanned numerous decades.

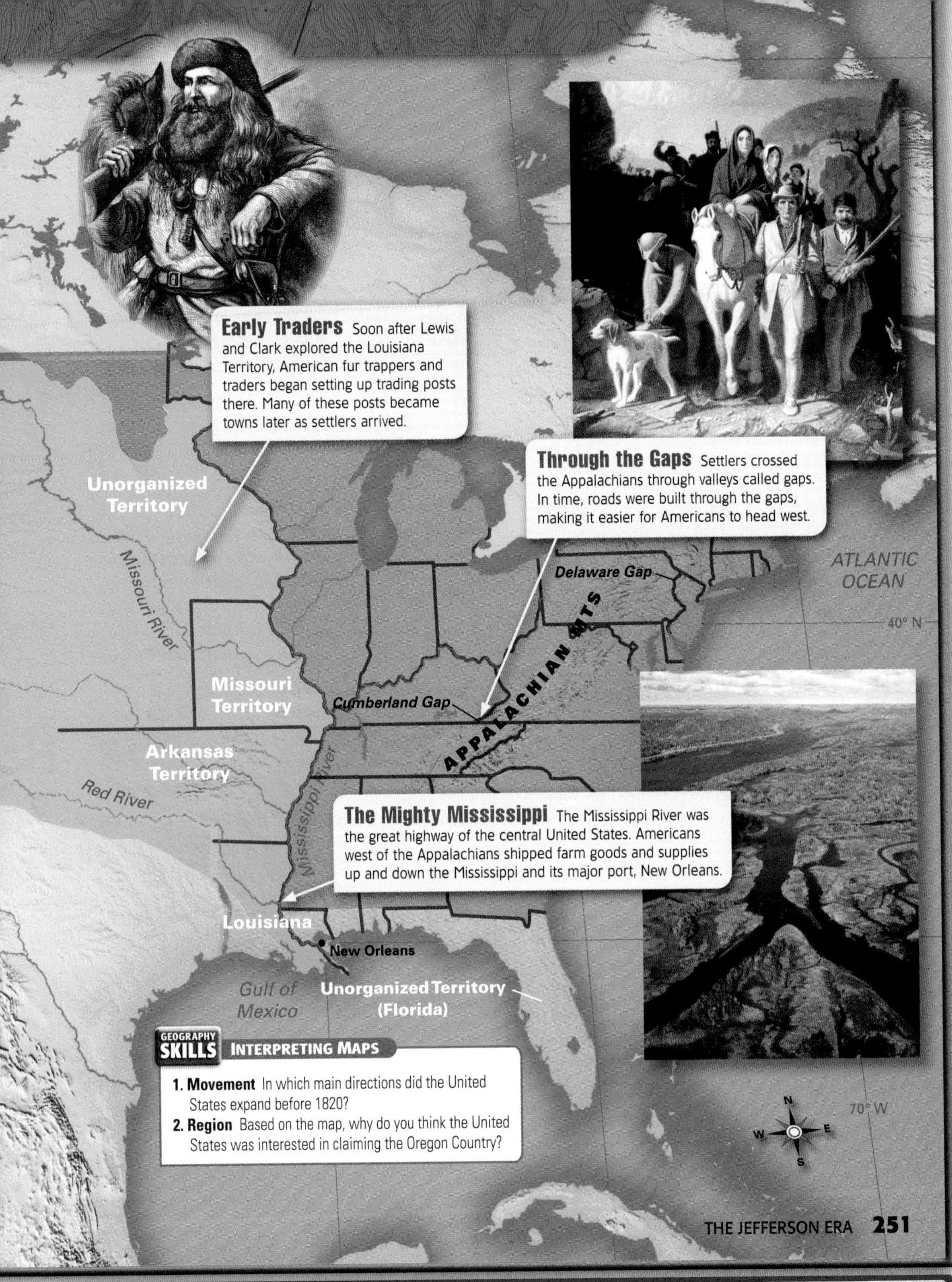

Early Traders Soon after Lewis and Clark explored the Louisiana Territory, American fur trappers and traders began setting up trading posts there. Many of these posts became towns later as settlers arrived.
Through the Gaps Settlers crossed the Appalachians through valleys called gaps. In time, roads were built through the gaps, making it easier for Americans to head west.
The Mighty Mississippi The Mississippi River was the great highway of the central United States. Americans west of the Appalachians shipped farm goods and supplies up and down the Mississippi and its major port, New Orleans.
Unorganized Territory
Missouri River
Missouri Territory
Arkansas Territory
Red River
Mississippi River
Cumberland Gap
APPALACHIAN MTS
Delaware Gap
ATLANTIC OCEAN
40° N
Louisiana
New Orleans
Gulf of Mexico
Unorganized Territory (Florida)
70° W
N
S
E
W

GEOGRAPHY SKILLS INTERPRETING MAPS

1. **Movement** In which main directions did the United States expand before 1820?
2. **Region** Based on the map, why do you think the United States was interested in claiming the Oregon Country?

History and Geography

Connect to Geography

Cumberland Gap The Cumberland Gap provided a route west for many American settlers. This gap is located near the point where the states of Kentucky, Virginia, and Tennessee now meet. Daniel Boone, who led pioneers west, blazed the Wilderness Trail through the Cumberland Gap. The main migration of settlers through the Cumberland Gap occurred between 1775 and 1810. During this period, between 200,000 and 300,000 people passed through the gap heading west. The Cumberland Gap National Historical Park now preserves part of the valley.

Connect to Math

Calculating Growth In 1790 the United States and its territories totaled 888,811 square miles. The Louisiana Purchase of 1803 added an additional 827,192 square miles of land. After the 1819 treaty negotiations with Spain, the United States gained Florida, which added another 58,560 square miles. In addition, the United States received other territories totaling 13,443 square miles.

Activity Have students determine the size of the United States at the end of 1803 and 1819. *(1803–1,716,003 square miles; 1819—1,788,006 square miles)* Then have students determine the percentage of the 1819 total that came from the Louisiana Purchase and from land acquired from Spain *(Louisiana Purchase—46.3 percent; from Spain—4 percent).*

Critical Thinking: Summarizing

Standards Proficiency

Research Required

Daniel Boone Biography

Materials: *The Adventures of Colonel Daniel Boone* (optional)

1. Explain to students that Daniel Boone is one of our nation's most legendary frontiersmen and is best known for his exploration of Kentucky.
2. Have each student conduct research on Daniel Boone's life, contributions, and achievements.
3. Have students use their research to write biographical sketches of Boone, with a focus on his contributions to westward expansion and settlement.
4. **Extend** Have students locate and read part or all of *The Adventures of Colonel Daniel Boone.* Students should summarize what they read in a paragraph or short essay.
LS Verbal/Linguistic

HSS 8.8.2; HSS **Analysis Skills:** HR 4, HI 1, HI 2

Alternative Assessment Handbook, Rubrics 4: Biographies; and 37: Writing Assignments

Answers

Interpreting Maps 1. *mainly northwest and west; some south;* **2.** *possible answer—continued the United States westward to the Pacific Ocean and provided additional ports*

Social Studies Skills

Working in Groups to Solve Issues

Activity Discussing the Banning of Cell Phones on Campus Ask students to imagine that they are members of the student council. The school board wants to ban the use of cell phones on campus. The student council opposes this action. Organize students into groups and assign half the members each position. Have students role play a discussion between the student council and the school board. Group members should try to find one solution to the issue and be prepared to compromise and negotiate if needed. Remind students to respect and listen to differing views and to give each member a chance to participate. Groups should select one member on each side to take notes. Each group should then write down its final solution. After students have completed the activity, have each group share its solution with the class and describe the decision-making process. Students should discuss any problems the group had and how well the group was able to compromise and listen to opposing views. **LS Interpersonal**

Alternative Assessment Handbook, Rubric 14: Group Activity

Answers

Practice the Skill 1. *This refusal might lead to antagonism between members and further prevent any ability to compromise. In addition, one cannot fully present one's position without understanding others' points of view.* **2.** *because a compromise gives all members something they want, instead of only certain members getting their way; leads to more group support for the final decision*

Social Studies Skills

Analysis | Critical Thinking | **Participation** | Study

HSS Participation Skills Develop personal skills.

Working in Groups to Solve Issues

Define the Skill

You already know that the decision-making process is more difficult in a group than it is if just one person makes the decisions. However, group decision-making becomes an even greater challenge when controversial issues are involved.

Group members must have additional skills for the group to function effectively when conflict exists within it. These include respect for differing views, the arts of persuasion and negotiation, and an ability to compromise. A group may not be able to find solutions to controversial problems unless its members have these skills.

Learn the Skill

Some of the biggest challenges Congress faced in the early 1800s were related to the war between Great Britain and France. Some Americans supported the British, while others favored the French. Both countries hoped for American help. When the United States would not take sides, they each began interfering with U.S. ships on the open seas.

As you read in this chapter, Congress tried to solve this problem by passing the Embargo Act. That solution was controversial, however. The northern states were hard hit by the law's ban on overseas trade. Their representatives in Congress demanded a less extreme action. The result was the Non-Intercourse Act. This law was a compromise between members who wanted to lift the trade ban and those who wanted to continue it. Congress was able to solve this problem because its members were able to work around their differences.

The skills Congress needed to reach its solution are valuable ones for any group that must make decisions involving controversial issues. They include the following attitudes and behaviors.

1. **Willingness to take a position.** If an issue is controversial, it is likely that group members will have differing opinions about it. You have a right to state your views and try to persuade others that you are correct.
2. **Willingness to listen to differing views.** Every other member has the same right you do. You have a duty to listen to their views, even if you do not agree. Disrespect for those whose views differ from yours makes it more difficult for the group to reach a solution.
3. **Willingness to debate.** Debate is a form of "healthy" argument because it defends and attacks ideas instead of the people who hold them. Debating the group's differences of opinion is an important step in reaching a solution.
4. **Willingness to negotiate and compromise.** If debate does not produce agreement, a compromise may be needed. Often it is better to have a solution that members may not like, but can accept, than to have no agreement at all.

Practice the Skill

Check your understanding of the skill by answering the following questions.

1. Why would refusing to listen to other members make group decision-making more difficult?
2. Why is compromise often a better solution than forcing a decision on members who disagree?

Social Studies Skills Activity: Working in Groups to Solve Issues

Posters about How to Work in Groups

Standards Proficiency

1. Ask students to imagine that they are members of a student government council. The council's discussions often lead to disagreements and arguments that seem to go nowhere and rarely result in decisions.
2. Have each student create a poster to display at council meetings. The poster should provide advice for working in groups to solve issues. Students' posters should address and elaborate upon each of the four points listed under "Learn the Skill." In addition, students' posters should explain the importance of being able to work in groups to solve issues.
3. Have volunteers share their work with the class. Select the best student posters to display in public areas of the school. **LS Verbal/Linguistic, Visual/Spatial**

Alternative Assessment Handbook, Rubric 28: Posters

CHAPTER 7

Standards Review

Visual Summary

Use the visual summary below to help you review the main ideas of the chapter.

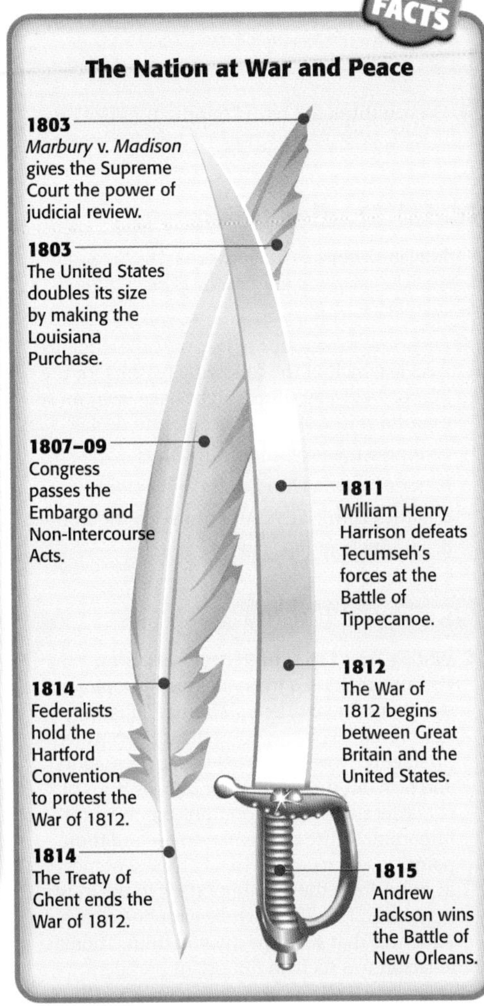

QUICK FACTS
The Nation at War and Peace
1803
Marbury v. Madison gives the Supreme Court the power of judicial review.
1803
The United States doubles its size by making the Louisiana Purchase.
1807–09
Congress passes the Embargo and Non-Intercourse Acts.
1811
William Henry Harrison defeats Tecumseh's forces at the Battle of Tippecanoe.
1812
The War of 1812 begins between Great Britain and the United States.
1814
Federalists hold the Hartford Convention to protest the War of 1812.
1814
The Treaty of Ghent ends the War of 1812.
1815
Andrew Jackson wins the Battle of New Orleans.

Reviewing Vocabulary, Terms, and People

Complete each sentence by filling in the blank with the correct term or person.

1. The War of 1812 ended soon after the U.S. victory over the British at the ______________.
2. After winning the election of 1800, __________ became the third president of the United States.
3. The power of the Supreme Court to declare acts of Congress unconstitutional is known as ______________.
4. After U.S. neutrality was violated, the United States issued an __________ against trade with foreign nations.
5. In 1803 Congress approved the _________ , which added former French territory in the West to the United States.

Comprehension and Critical Thinking

SECTION 1 *(Pages 228–232)* **HSS 8.4.1, 8.4.2**

6. **a. Recall** What were the key issues in the election of 1800?

   b. Analyze In what ways did *Marbury* v. *Madison* affect the power of the judicial branch?

   c. Evaluate Which of Jefferson's new policies do you think was most important? Why?

SECTION 2 *(Pages 234–239)* **HSS 8.4.1, 8.8.2**

7. **a. Describe** What was the purpose of the Lewis and Clark expedition?

   b. Draw Conclusions What are three ways in which the United States benefited from the Louisiana Purchase.

   c. Evaluate Do you think that Napoléon made a wise decision when he sold Louisiana to the United States? Explain your answer.

Answers

Visual Summary

Review and Inquiry Have students examine the visual summary. Ask students to create flash cards for the events. Students should put the date on one side and the event on the other. Have students find five other significant dates and events to make additional flash cards. Students can quiz each other using the flash cards.

Quick Facts Transparency: The Jefferson Era Visual Summary

Reviewing Vocabulary, Terms, and People

1. Battle of Fort McHenry
2. Thomas Jefferson
3. judicial review
4. embargo
5. Louisiana Purchase

Comprehension and Critical Thinking

6. **a.** size of the national government; relations with France, civil liberties
   b. increased the power of the judicial branch in relation to the other two branches
   c. Answers will vary, but students should identify one of Jefferson's new policies and provide reasons to support the choice.

Review and Assessment Resources

Review and Reinforce

SE Standards Review

CRF: Chapter Review Activity

California Standards Review Workbook

Quick Facts Transparency: The Jefferson Era Visual Summary

Spanish Chapter Summaries Audio CD Program

Online Chapter Summaries in Six Languages

OSP Holt PuzzlePro; GameTool for ExamView

Quiz Game CD-ROM

Assess

SE Standards Assessment

PASS: Chapter Test, Forms A and B

Alternative Assessment Handbook

OSP ExamView Test Generator, Chapter Test

Universal Access Modified Worksheets and Tests CD-ROM: Chapter Test

Holt Online Assessment Program (in the Premier Online Edition)

Reteach/Intervene

Interactive Reader and Study Guide

Universal Access Teacher Management System: Lesson Plans for Universal Access

Universal Access Modified Worksheets and Tests CD-ROM

Interactive Skills Tutor CD-ROM

go.hrw.com
Online Resources
Chapter Resources:
KEYWORD: SS8 US7

Answers

7. **a.** to learn more about the people and land of the west; to see if there was a river route to the Pacific Ocean
   b. gained a large increase in territory, new resources, land for farming and livestock, and control of New Orleans
   c. possible answers—yes, he needed to focus on Europe; no, New Orleans was a major port city, and Louisiana held potential resources.
8. **a.** War Hawks
   b. for—British impressment and violation of neutrality, British influence over frontier Indians, trade restrictions ineffective and hurting the economy; against—should renew friendly ties with Britain, cannot compete against Britain's powerful military
   c. possible answer—Britain and France could trade elsewhere.
9. **a.** led troops to victory against the Creek at Battle of Horseshoe Bend and against the British at Battle of New Orleans
   b. Washington, D.C. was the capitol, and New Orleans was a major port.
   c. might be seen as more of a military power; might convince others that the American experiment in democracy will survive

Reviewing Themes

10. Great Plains, Rocky Mountains, Pacific coastal region
11. The Federalist Party lost much of its political power.

Using the Internet

12. Go to the HRW Web site and enter the keyword shown to access

KEYWORD: SS8 TEACHER

SECTION 3 *(Pages 240–245)* HSS 8.5.1

8. **a. Identify** What group led the call for war with Great Britain?
   b. Contrast What arguments were given in favor of war with Great Britain? What arguments were given against war with Britain?
   c. Elaborate In your opinion, why were the Embargo Act and the Non-Intercourse Act unsuccessful?

SECTION 4 *(Pages 246–249)* HSS 8.5.1

9. **a. Identify** What role did Andrew Jackson play in the War of 1812?
   b. Make Inferences Why did the British want to capture the cities of Washington and New Orleans?
   c. Predict In what ways might the U.S. victory over Great Britain in the war affect the status of the United States in the world?

Reviewing Themes

10. **Geography** Through what geographic regions did the Lewis and Clark expedition travel?
11. **Politics** What impact did the Hartford Convention have on American politics?

Using the Internet

12. **Activity: Journal Entry** Prior to Lewis and Clark's expedition, some thought that woolly mammoths, unicorns, and seven-foot-tall beavers lived in the uncharted West. The Corps of Discovery set off to find out the truth about this uncharted land. They also wanted to search for a Northwest Passage that would speed commerce and bring wealth to the young nation. Enter the activity keyword. Research the Web sites and take the point of view of one of the explorers. Write a series of journal entries outlining the thoughts, feelings, discoveries, and events surrounding the journey. Include drawings of what you might have seen in the West in your journal entries.

Reading Skills

Understanding How Propaganda Creates Bias
Use the Reading Skills taught in this chapter to answer the question about the reading selection below.

The Republican press called these people midnight judges, arguing that Adams had packed the judiciary with Federalists the night before he left office. *(p. 231)*

13. Do you think the term "midnight judges" is biased? Why or why not?

Social Studies Skills

Working in Groups to Solve Issues *Use the Social Studies Skills taught in this chapter to answer the questions below.*

14. Organize into groups of two or three students. Decide which of the following reasons for the War of 1812 you think might have been most important in Congress's decision to declare war.
   a. impressment of American sailors
   b. trade barriers with Britain and France
   c. battles with Native Americans on the frontier
   d. gaining land in Canada

FOCUS ON WRITING

15. **Writing Your Letter of Recommendation** You already have a main idea and an opinion statement for your letter: Thomas Jefferson deserves to be on the list of the top-ten American presidents. Now, look at all your information and pick out three or four points—actions or character traits—that you think are the most important. Write a sentence on each of those points to add to your letter. Put the sentences in order, from the least important to the most important. Finally, conclude with one or two sentences that sum up why you think Thomas Jefferson was such an important president.

Reading Skills

13. Answers will vary, but students should support their answers and demonstrate an understanding of bias.

Social Studies Skills

14. Group members should work together to select an answer and to supply reasons to support it.

Focus on Writing

15. **Rubric** Students' letters of recommendation should:
   - include at least three supporting points.
   - present the points from least to most important.
   - end with a summary.
   - use correct grammar, punctuation, spelling, and capitalization.

CRF: Focus on Writing: A Letter of Recommendation

Standards Assessment

DIRECTIONS: Read each question and write the letter of the best response.

1

> "Though the will of the majority is in all cases to prevail, that will, to be rightful, must be reasonable . . . [T]he minority possess their equal rights, which equal laws must protect . . . Let us then, fellow citizens, unite with one heart and one mind . . . We have been called by different names brethren of the same principle. We are all republicans; we are all federalists."
>
> —President Thomas Jefferson, Inaugural Address, 1801

What did Jefferson mean in making this statement?

A that the Federalists should not run a candidate in 1804
B that citizens should support the nation despite their political differences
C that the Republicans should not be punished for their views
D that all Americans should join a political party

2 The Supreme Court's decision in the 1803 case *Marbury* v. *Madison* is an example of

A checks and balances.
B reserved powers.
C delegated powers.
D dual sovereignty.

3 What goal of President Jefferson led to the Louisiana Purchase?

A to learn more about the lands and peoples east of the Mississippi River
B to increase the president's constitutional powers in the area of foreign affairs
C to help end the war between Great Britain and France
D to allow Americans to ship goods overseas through the port of New Orleans

4 The least important reason the United States went to war with Britain in 1812 was

A the hope of acquiring part of Canada.
B to stop British influence among Indian groups on the frontier.
C to protect the rights of U.S. ships on the high seas.
D a desire to help the French.

5 Most of the fighting in the War of 1812 took place

A in Europe.
B in Canada.
C in the United States.
D at sea.

Connecting with Past Learning

6 Meriwether Lewis and William Clark have the most in common with

A Marco Polo.
B Genghis Khan.
C Hernán Cortés.
D Francis Bacon.

7 In Grade 7 you learned about Ferdinand Magellan. His accomplishments in world history were most like those of which American in the early 1800s?

A Andrew Jackson
B Tecumseh
C Zebulon Pike
D Oliver Hazard Perry

Answers

1. B
Break Down the Question Point out to students that the phrase "Let us then" indicates that Jefferson is about to make his main point—"unite with one heart and one mind." He then ends by restating the idea of unity: "We are all republicans; we are all federalists."

2. A
Break Down the Question This question asks students to recall the meaning of checks and balances. Help students having trouble to make the connection between judicial review and checks and balances.

3. D
Break Down the Question Point out to students that the word *led* in the question means that they need to identify a cause. Tell students that in such cases they should think about what happened before the event.

4. A
Break Down the Question Point out to students the word *least* in the question. This word indicates that they are to choose the least important cause of the war. Students should first eliminate any options that are not causes (D) and then rank the remaining options.

5. C
Break Down the Question Suggest that students first eliminate any places where fighting did not occur (in Europe) and then recall what they know about the remaining options.

6. C
Break Down the Question This question requires students to recall information covered in Grade 7.

7. C
Break Down the Question This question requires students to recall information covered in Grade 7.

Intervention Resources

Reproducible

- Interactive Reader and Study Guide
- Universal Access Teacher Management System: Lesson Plans for Universal Access

Technology

- Quick Facts Transparency: The Jefferson Era Visual Summary
- Universal Access Modified Worksheets and Tests CD-ROM
- Interactive Skills Tutor CD-ROM

Tips for Test Taking

Anticipate the Answers Read the following to students: Before you read the answer choices, answer the question yourself. Then read the choices. If the answer you gave is among the choices listed, it is probably correct!

Standards Review

Have students review the following standards in their workbooks.

- California Standards Review Workbook: HSS 8.4.1, 8.5.1, 8.5.3

Chapter 8 Planning Guide

A New National Identity

Chapter Overview	Reproducible Resources	Technology Resources
CHAPTER 8 **pp. 256–279** **Overview:** **In this chapter, students will analyze the development of both American foreign policy and culture.**  See p. 256 for the California History–Social Science standards covered in this chapter.	**Universal Access Teacher Management System:*** • Universal Access Instructional Benchmarking Guides • Lesson Plans for Universal Access 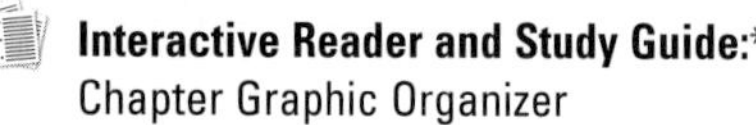 **Interactive Reader and Study Guide:*** Chapter Graphic Organizer  **Chapter Resource File*** • Focus on Writing Activity: Character Sketch • Social Studies Skills Activity: Identifying Central Issues • Chapter Review Activity	**One-Stop Planner CD-ROM:** Calendar Planner **Student Edition Full-Read Audio CD-ROM** **Universal Access Modified Worksheets and Tests CD-ROM** **Primary Source Library CD-ROM for United States History** **Power Presentations with Video CD-ROM** **History's Impact: United States History Video Program (VHS/DVD):** A New National Identity* **A Teacher's Guide to Religion in the Public Schools***
Section 1: **American Foreign Policy** **The Big Idea:** The United States peacefully settled disputes with foreign powers. 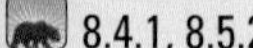 8.4.1, 8.5.2	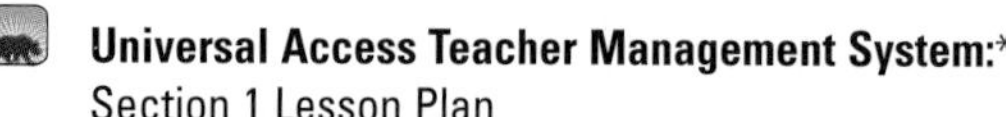 **Universal Access Teacher Management System:*** Section 1 Lesson Plan 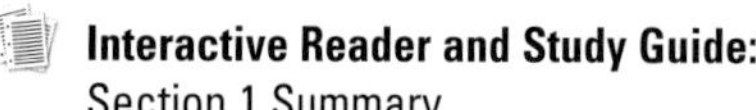 **Interactive Reader and Study Guide:*** Section 1 Summary  **Chapter Resource File*** • Vocabulary Builder, Section 1 • Primary Source Activity: Alexis de Tocqueville's Democracy in America • Primary Source Activity: John Quincy Adams's Fourth of July 1821 Address 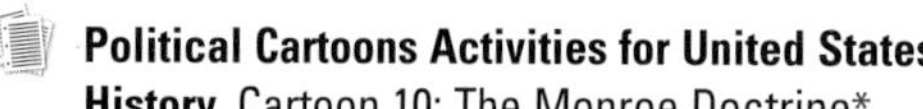 **Political Cartoons Activities for United States History,** Cartoon 10: The Monroe Doctrine*	 **Daily Bellringer Transparency:** Section 1* **Map Transparency:** U.S. Boundary Changes, 1818–1819*
Section 2: **Nationalism and Sectionalism** **The Big Idea:** A rising sense of national unity allowed regional differences to be set aside and national interests to be served.  8.4.1, 8.6.2	 **Universal Access Teacher Management System:*** Section 2 Lesson Plan **Interactive Reader and Study Guide:*** Section 2 Summary  **Chapter Resource File*** • Vocabulary Builder, Section 2 • History and Geography Activity: The National Road	**Daily Bellringer Transparency:** Section 2* **Map Transparency:** U.S. Roads and Canals, 1850* **Map Transparency:** The Missouri Compromise, 1820* **Internet Activity:** Erie Canal and National Road Map or Brochure
Section 3: **American Culture** **The Big Idea:** As the United States grew, developments in many cultural areas contributed to the creation of a new American identity. 8.4.4	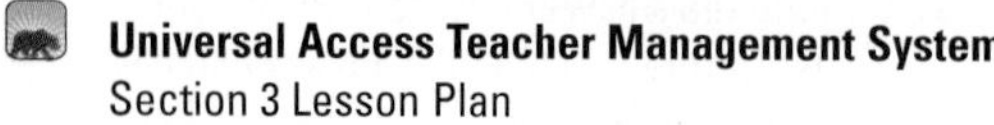 **Universal Access Teacher Management System:*** Section 3 Lesson Plan **Interactive Reader and Study Guide:*** Section 3 Summary  **Chapter Resource File*** • Vocabulary Builder, Section 3 • Biography Activities: Thomas Cole; Catherine Maria Sedgwick; Noah Webster • Literature Activity: *The Prairie,* by James Fenimore Cooper	 **Daily Bellringer Transparency:** Section 3* **Internet Activity:** American Culture Display

MASTERING THE CALIFORNIA STANDARDS

SE Student Edition  Print Resource  Audio CD  Video

TE Teacher's Edition 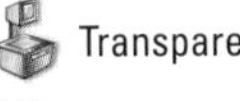 Transparency  CD-ROM  DVD

go.hrw.com CA Standards Mastery Learning Styles

OSP One-Stop Planner CD-ROM * also on One-Stop Planner CD

Review, Assessment, Intervention

Standards Review Workbook*

Quick Facts Transparency: A New National Identity Visual Summary*

Spanish Chapter Summaries Audio CD Program

Online Chapter Summaries in Six Languages

Progress Assessment Support System (PASS): Chapter Test*

Universal Access Modified Worksheets and Tests CD-ROM: Modified Chapter Test

One-Stop Planner CD-ROM: ExamView Test Generator (English/Spanish)

Alternative Assessment Handbook

PASS: Section 1 Quiz*

Online Quiz: Section 1

Alternative Assessment Handbook

PASS: Section 2 Quiz*

Online Quiz: Section 2

Alternative Assessment Handbook

PASS: Section 3 Quiz*

Online Quiz: Section 3

Alternative Assessment Handbook

California Resources for Standards Mastery

INSTRUCTIONAL PLANNING AND SUPPORT

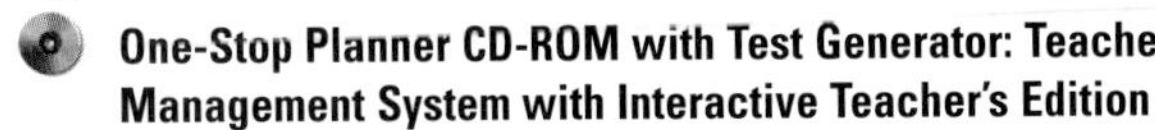
Universal Access Teacher Management System*

One-Stop Planner CD-ROM with Test Generator: Teacher Management System with Interactive Teacher's Edition

STANDARDS MASTERY

Standards Review Workbook*

At Home: A Guide to Standards Mastery for United States History

Holt Online Learning

To enhance learning, Internet activities are available for an Erie Canal and National Road Map or Brochure and an American Culture Display.

KEYWORD: SS8 TEACHER

- **Teacher Support Page**
- **Content Updates**
- **Rubrics and Writing Models**
- **Teaching Tips for the Multimedia Classroom**

KEYWORD: SS8 US8

- **Current Events**
- **Document-Based Questions**
- **Holt Grapher**
- **Holt Online Atlas**
- **Holt Researcher**
- **Interactive Multimedia Activities**
- **Internet Activities**
- **Online Chapter Summaries in Six Languages**
- **Online Section Quizzes**
- **American History Maps and Charts**

HOLT PREMIER ONLINE STUDENT EDITION

Complete online support for interactivity, assessment, and reporting

- **Interactive Maps and Notebook**
- **Standardized Test Prep**
- **Homework Practice and Research Activities Online**

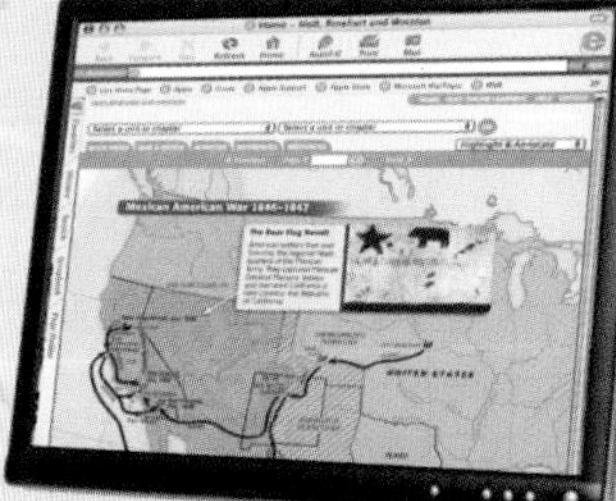

Mastering the Standards: Differentiating Instruction

Reaching Standards	Basic-level activities designed for all students encountering new material
Standards Proficiency	Intermediate-level activities designed for average students
Exceeding Standards	Challenging activities designed for honors and gifted-and-talented students
Standard English Mastery	Activities designed to improve standard English usage

Frequently Asked Questions

INSTRUCTIONAL PLANNING AND SUPPORT

Where do I find planning aids, pacing guides, lesson plans, and other teaching aids?

Annotated Teacher's Edition:
- Chapter planning guides
- Standards-based instruction and strategies
- Differentiated instruction for universal access
- Point-of-use reminders for integrating program resources

Power Presentations with Video CD-ROM

Universal Access Teacher Management System:
- Year and unit instructional benchmarking guides
- Reproducible lesson plans
- Assessment guides for diagnostic, progress, and summative end-of-the-year tests
- Options for differentiating instruction and intervention
- Teaching guides and answer keys for student workbooks

One-Stop Planner CD-ROM with Test Generator: Teacher Management System with Interactive Teacher's Editon:
- Calendar Planner
- Editable lesson plans
- All reproducible ancillaries in Adobe Acrobat (PDF) format
- ExamView Test Generator (English & Spanish)
- Game Tool for ExamView
- PuzzlePro
- Transparency and video previews

DIFFERENTIATING INSTRUCTION FOR UNIVERSAL ACCESS

What resources are available to ensure that Advanced Learners/GATE Students master the standards?

Teacher's Edition Activities:
- Landscape Art and Poetry, p. 272
- Writing Historical Fiction, p. 274

Lesson Plans for Universal Access

Primary Source Library CD-ROM for United States History

What resources are available to ensure that English Learners and Standard English Learners master the standards?

Teacher's Edition Activities:
- Then and Now Poster, p. 265

Lesson Plans for Universal Access

Chapter Resource File: Vocabulary Builder Activities

Spanish Chapter Summaries Audio CD Program

Online Chapter Summaries in Six Languages

One-Stop Planner CD-ROM:
- PuzzlePro, Spanish Version
- ExamView Test Generator, Spanish Version

What modified materials are available for Special Education?

The ***Universal Access Modified Worksheets and Tests CD-ROM*** provides editable versions of the following:

Vocabulary Flash Cards

Modified Vocabulary Builder Activities

Modified Chapter Review Activity

Modified Chapter Test

What resources are available to ensure that Learners Having Difficulty master the standards?

Teacher's Edition Activities:
- American Writers of the Early 1800s, p. 271
- Group Interpretation, p. 274

Interactive Reader and Study Guide

Student Edition Full-Read Audio CD

Quick Facts Transparency: A New National Identity Visual Summary

Standards Review Workbook

Social Studies Skills Activity: Identifying Central Issues

Interactive Skills Tutor CD-ROM

How do I intervene for students struggling to master the standards?

Interactive Reader and Study Guide

Quick Facts Transparency: A New National Identity Visual Summary

Standards Review Workbook

Social Studies Skills Activity: Identifying Central Issues

Interactive Skills Tutor CD-ROM

PROFESSIONAL DEVELOPMENT

What teacher training resources are available to help me grow professionally?

- In-service and staff development as part of your Holt Social Studies product purchase
- Quick Teacher Tutorial Lesson Presentation CD-ROM
- Intensive tuition-based Teacher Development Institute
- *Teaching American History* Online 2 Module Professional Development Course
- Convenient Holt Speaker Bureau face-to-face workshop options
- PRAXIS™ Test Prep (#0089) interactive Web-based content refreshers*
- 24/7 *Ask A Professional Development Expert* at http://www.hrw.com/prodev/

* PRAXIS is a trademark of Educational Testing Service (ETS). This publication is not endorsed or approved by ETS.

Information Literacy Skills

To learn more about how History–Social Science instruction may be improved by the effective use of library media centers and information literacy skills, go to the Teacher's Resource Materials for Chapter 8 at **go.hrw.com**, keyword: SS8 MEDIA.

The following materials were developed by the Division for Public Education of the American Bar Association. These materials are part of the **Democracy and Civic Education** supplement.
- Constitution Study Guide
- Supreme Court Case Studies

Chapter Preview

Standards Focus

Standards by Section
Section 1: HSS 8.4.1, 8.5.2
Section 2: HSS 8.4.1, 8.6.2
Section 3: HSS 8.4.4

Teacher's Edition
HSS **Analysis Skills:** CS 1, CS 3, HR 1, HR 3, HR 5, HI 1, HI 2, HI 3, HI 6
ELA Writing 8.1.1, Reading 8.2.0

Preview Grade 8 Standards
HSS **8.6** Students analyze the divergent paths of the American people from 1800 to the mid-1800s and the challenges they faced, with emphasis on the Northeast.
8.6.1 Discuss the influence of industrialization and technological developments on the region, including human modification of the landscape and how physical geography shaped human actions (e.g., growth of cities, deforestation, farming, mineral extraction).
8.6.5 Trace the development of the American education system from its earliest roots, including the roles of religious and private schools and Horace Mann's campaign for free public education and its assimilating role in American culture.

Focus on Writing
The **Chapter Resource File** provides a Focus on Writing worksheet to help students organize and write their character sketches.
CRF: Focus on Writing Activity: A Character Sketch

CHAPTER 8 1812–1830

A New National Identity

California Standards

History–Social Science
8.4 Students analyze the aspirations and ideals of the people of the new nation.
8.5 Students analyze U.S. foreign policy in the early Republic.
8.6 Students analyze the divergent paths of the American people from 1800 to the mid-1800s and the challenges they faced, with emphasis on the Northeast.

Analysis Skills
HI 1 Students explain the central issues and problems from the past.

English–Language Arts
Writing 8.1.1 Create compositions that establish a controlling impression.
Reading 8.2.0 Students read and understand grade-level appropriate material.

FOCUS ON WRITING
A Character Sketch Nations, like people, have characters. For example, a nation might be described as peaceful or aggressive, prosperous or struggling. In this chapter you'll read about the United States as a new nation with a new identity, or character. Then you'll write a paragraph describing that character.

UNITED STATES

1816 James Monroe is elected president.

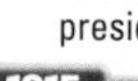
1815

WORLD
1815 Napoléon returns to power in France but is defeated at the Battle of Waterloo.

Introduce the Chapter

Standards Proficiency

The Character of a Country HSS 8.4

1. Ask students to think about the character of the early United States as they have learned from their studies. Have students imagine the country as a person. How would they describe this person—young, feisty, aggressive, soft-spoken, opinionated? Write their descriptions for students to see and save the list.
2. Explain to students that they are going to learn how the United States began to be considered a major power in the North American continent. They will learn about the beginnings of U.S. foreign policy and the continued growth of the nation as it began to struggle internally with issues of slavery.
3. Have students copy the list of descriptions. At the chapter's close, discuss with students how the nation has matured. Ask students what additional qualities they would add to their list describing the nation.
LS **Logical/Mathematical**

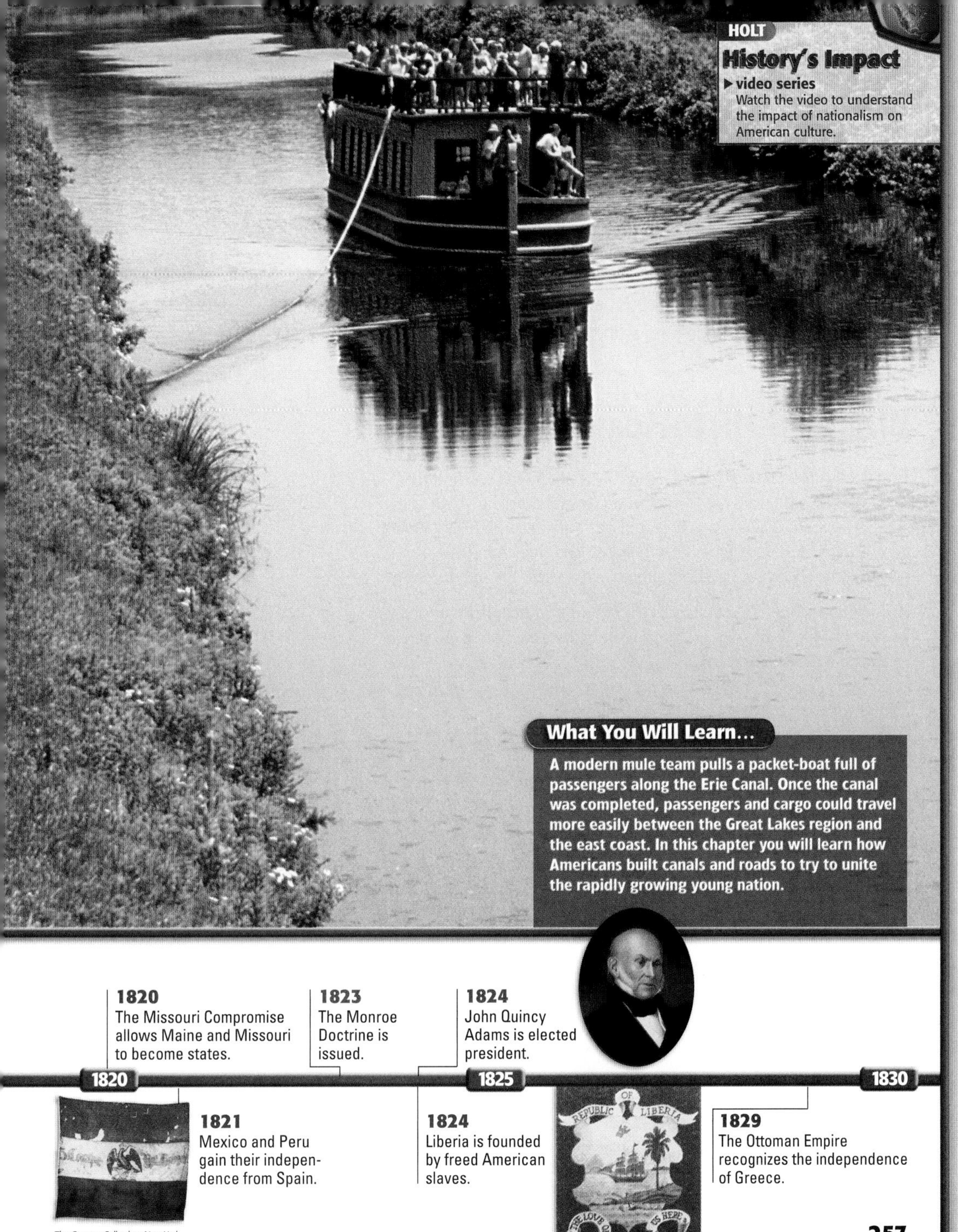

HOLT
History's Impact
▶ video series
Watch the video to understand the impact of nationalism on American culture.

What You Will Learn...

A modern mule team pulls a packet-boat full of passengers along the Erie Canal. Once the canal was completed, passengers and cargo could travel more easily between the Great Lakes region and the east coast. In this chapter you will learn how Americans built canals and roads to try to unite the rapidly growing young nation.

1820 The Missouri Compromise allows Maine and Missouri to become states.

1821 Mexico and Peru gain their independence from Spain.

The Granger Collection, New York

1823 The Monroe Doctrine is issued.

1824 John Quincy Adams is elected president.

1824 Liberia is founded by freed American slaves.

1829 The Ottoman Empire recognizes the independence of Greece.

1820 — 1825 — 1830

257

• Chapter Preview •

HOLT
History's Impact
▶ **video series**
See the Video Teacher's Guide for strategies for using the chapter video **A New National Identity**

Chapter Big Ideas

Section 1 The United States peacefully settled disputes with foreign powers. **HSS** 8.4.1, 8.5.2

Section 2 A rising sense of national unity allowed some regional differences to be set aside and national interests to be served. **HSS** 8.4.1, 8.6.2

Section 3 As the United States grew, developments in many cultural areas contributed to the creation of a new American identity. **HSS** 8.4.4

Explore the Picture

The Erie Canal The Erie Canal was one of the largest projects in a boom period for canal building in the early 1800s. Canal transportation was cheaper and easier than overland transportation, but building canals was also very expensive.

Analyzing Visuals What can you tell from the photo about transporting goods by canal? *possible answers—transport larger quantities than by horse; many boats can use the same waterway; a more direct route than by land*

go.hrw.com
Online Resources
Chapter Resources:
KEYWORD: SS8 US8
Teacher Resources:
KEYWORD: SS8 TEACHER

Explore the Time Line

1. In what year did James Monroe become president of the United States? *1816*
2. What two major U.S. events happened during Monroe's presidency? *the Missouri Compromise, the Monroe Doctrine*
3. When did Mexico and Peru gain their independence from Spain? *1821*
4. Which country was founded by freed American slaves? When? *Liberia; 1824*

HSS Analysis Skills: CS 1

Info to Know

Transportation Americans' experiences during the War of 1812 contributed to a push for better transportation following the war. When the British blockaded the U.S. coastline, American merchants and farmers were forced to rely on overland transportation to get goods to market. They found that the roads were terrible. A four-horse team pulling a wagon full of goods took 75 days to make the journey from Worcester, Massachusetts, to Charleston, South Carolina!

Reading Social Studies

Understanding Themes

Introduce the key themes of this chapter—politics and culture—by asking students to read the Focus on Themes section on this page. Have students pay attention to the specific issues that affected politics and society and culture in the United States. Preview for students the important political and cultural events mentioned in this chapter, such as the Missouri Compromise and the rise of Hudson River School. Then have each student draw a picture that represents one event and its related theme.

Bias and Historical Events

Focus on Reading Point out to students that letters to the editor and political cartoons commonly display bias. Provide students with a copy of a recent letter to the editor or political cartoon from a local newspaper. Have each student follow the steps listed on this page to analyze the document for bias. You many even want to provide an example of an unbiased letter so that students can compare the two. Discuss with students why recognizing bias might be important in evaluating sources for research.

Reading Social Studies

by Kylene Beers

Economics | Geography | **Politics** | Religion | **Society and Culture** | Science and Technology

Focus on Themes This chapter is titled "A New National Identity" because it explains how the United States government established relations with European powers and how Americans developed a strong sense of national pride even as they struggled with important state issues. You will learn about the Monroe Doctrine, the Missouri Compromise, the Cumberland Road project, and the rise of music, literature, and public schools—events that changed the country's **culture** and **politics**.

Bias and Historical Events

Focus on Reading As you read this chapter, you will find that some people supported the idea of using federal dollars to create new and better roads. Others, however, did not think federal dollars should be used that way. People who can only see one side of an issue or situation may become biased, or prejudiced against the opposite view.

Graphic organizers are available in the

Recognizing Bias To understand the events and people in history, you have to be able to recognize a speaker or writer's bias. Here are some steps you can take to do that.

"The wickedest road, I do think, the hard-heartedest road, that ever wheel rumbled upon."
Frances Anne (Kemble) Butler, Journal

1. The word *wickedest* is full of emotion.
2. A British actress, perhaps she didn't like the United States.
3. This information is based on her personal experience and she is recording it in her own personal journal.
4. Most of this statement is opinion. Where are the facts about the actual condition of the road?

Steps to Recognize Bias

1. **Look at the words and images.** Are they emotionally charged? Do they present only one side or one point of view?
2. **Look at the writer.** What's the writer's back-ground and what does that tell you about the writer's point of view?
3. **Look at the writer's sources.** Where does the writer get his or her information? Does the writer rely on sources who only support one point of view?
4. **Look at the information.** How much is fact and how much is opinion? Remember, facts can be proven. Opinions are personal beliefs—they can easily be biased.

Reading and Skills Resources

Reading Support

- Interactive Reader and Study Guide
- Student Edition on Audio CD
- Spanish Chapter Summaries Audio CD Program

Social Studies Skills Support

- Interactive Skills Tutor CD-ROM

Vocabulary Support

- **CRF:** Vocabulary Builder Activities
- **CRF:** Chapter Review Activity
- Universal Access Modified Worksheets and Tests CD-ROM:
  - Vocabulary Flash Cards
  - Vocabulary Builder Activity
  - Chapter Review Activity
- OSP Holt PuzzlePro

Standards Focus

ELA Reading 8.2.0

ELA Reading 8.2.0 Students read and understand grade-level appropriate material.

You Try It!

The following passage is from the chapter you are getting ready to read. As you read the passage, think about living during the early to mid-1800s when there were no public schools.

Architecture and Education

From Chapter 8, p. 273

Americans also embraced educational progress. Several early American political leaders expressed a belief that democracy would only succeed in a country of educated and enlightened people. But there was no general agreement on who should provide that education.

Eventually, the idea of a state-funded public school gathered support. In 1837 Massachusetts lawmakers created a state board of education. Other states followed this example and the number of public schools slowly grew.

After you read the passage, answer the following questions.

1. You are the editor of your town's newspaper in the year 1835. You think schools should be financed by the state government rather than the federal government. You decide to write an editorial to express your opinion. Which of the phrases below would reveal your personal bias to your readers? Why? What words in each statement create bias?

- **a.** Overbearing federal government
- **b.** Protecting state interests
- **c.** Powerful federal government
- **d.** Concerned state citizens

2. If you were going to write the editorial described in question 1, how could you avoid biased statements? How do you think this might affect people's reactions to your writing?

Key Terms and People

Chapter 8

Section 1
Rush-Bagot Agreement *(p. 260)*
Convention of 1818 *(p. 260)*
James Monroe *(p. 261)*
Adams-Onís Treaty *(p. 261)*
Simon Bolívar *(p. 262)*
Monroe Doctrine *(p. 262)*

Section 2
nationalism *(p. 264)*
Henry Clay *(p. 264)*
American System *(p. 264)*
Cumberland Road *(p. 265)*
Erie Canal *(p. 265)*
Era of Good Feelings *(p. 265)*
sectionalism *(p. 266)*
Missouri Compromise *(p. 267)*
John Quincy Adams *(p. 267)*

Section 3
Washington Irving *(p. 270)*
James Fenimore Cooper *(p. 271)*
Hudson River school *(p. 272)*
Thomas Cole *(p. 272)*
George Caleb Bingham *(p. 272)*

Academic Vocabulary

Success in school is related to knowing academic vocabulary—the words that are frequently used in school assignments and discussions. In this chapter, you will learn the following academic words:

circumstances *(p. 262)*
incentive *(p. 265)*

As you read Chapter 8, study the primary source documents carefully. Do you see any examples of bias?

Reading Social Studies

Key Terms and People

Preteach the key terms and people from this chapter by having students create a three-panel flip chart FoldNote like the one below. Have students fold a piece of paper in half from top to bottom. Then have them fold the paper into thirds from side to side. Have students cut along each of the vertical fold lines to the fold in the middle of the paper. Have students label the flaps *Section 1*, *2*, and *3*, then have them write the key terms or people for that section on the outside of the flap. On the inside of the chart, have students define or describe each term.
Encourage students to review these terms and people regularly.
LS Verbal/Linguistic

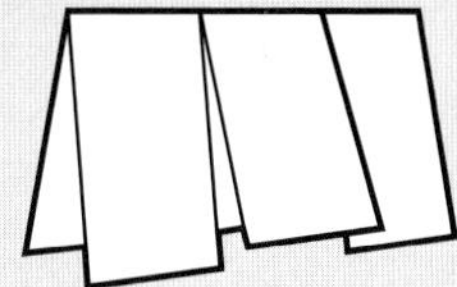

Focus on Reading

See the **Focus on Reading** questions in this chapter for more practice on this reading social studies skill.

Reading Social Studies Assessment

See the **Standards Review** at the end of this chapter for student assessment questions related to this reading skill.

Teaching Tip

Point out to students that oftentimes bias is used in order to persuade readers to the author's point of view. Remind students to look for words that express emotion, the writer's background, and statements that express opinion rather than fact.

Answers

You Try It! 1. *a; because it slants people's opinion away from federal government; words that create bias—overbearing, protecting, powerful, and concerned;* **2.** *Student editorials should explain the negative results of federal control of public education.*

Preteach

Bellringer

If YOU were there . . . Use the **Daily Bellringer Transparency** to help students answer the questions.

Daily Bellringer Transparency, Section 1

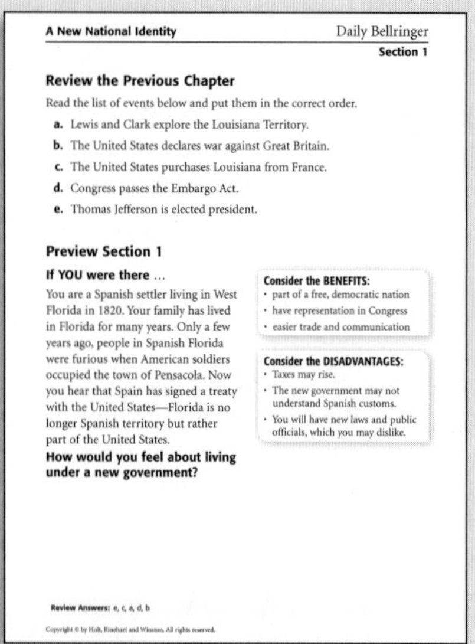

A New National Identity Daily Bellringer
Section 1

Review the Previous Chapter

Read the list of events below and put them in the correct order.

a. Lewis and Clark explore the Louisiana Territory.
b. The United States declares war against Great Britain.
c. The United States purchases Louisiana from France.
d. Congress passes the Embargo Act.
e. Thomas Jefferson is elected president.

Preview Section 1

If YOU were there ...

You are a Spanish settler living in West Florida in 1820. Your family has lived in Florida for many years. Only a few years ago, people in Spanish Florida were furious when American soldiers occupied the town of Pensacola. Now you hear that Spain has signed a treaty with the United States—Florida is no longer Spanish territory but rather part of the United States.

How would you feel about living under a new government?

Consider the BENEFITS:
- part of a free, democratic nation
- have representation in Congress
- easier trade and communication

Consider the DISADVANTAGES:
- Taxes may rise.
- The new government may not understand Spanish customs.
- You will have new laws and public officials, which you may dislike.

Review Answers: e, c, a, d, b

Academic Vocabulary

Review with students the high-use academic term in this section.

circumstances surrounding situation (p. 262)

CRF: Vocabulary Builder Activity, Section 1

Standards Focus

HSS 8.4.1
Means: Describe how the borders of the United States expanded during the early 1800s.
Matters: Today many Americans live in the territory that the United States gained during this period.

HSS 8.5.2
Means: Analyze U.S. foreign policy in the early and mid-1800s.
Matters: The Monroe Doctrine continues to shape the relationship between European nations, the United States, and Latin America.

SECTION 1

American Foreign Policy

What You Will Learn...

Main Ideas

1. The United States and Great Britain settled their disputes over boundaries and control of waterways.
2. The United States gained Florida in an agreement with Spain.
3. With the Monroe Doctrine, the United States strengthened its relationship with Latin America.

The Big Idea

The United States peacefully settled disputes with foreign powers.

Key Terms and People

Rush-Bagot Agreement, *p. 260*
Convention of 1818, *p. 260*
James Monroe, *p. 261*
Adams-Onís Treaty, *p. 261*
Simon Bolívar, *p. 262*
Monroe Doctrine, *p. 262*

HSS 8.4.1 Describe the country's physical landscapes, political divisions, and territorial expansion during the terms of the first four presidents.

8.5.2 Know the changing boundaries of the United States and describe the relationships the country had with its neighbors (current Mexico and Canada) and Europe, including the influence of the Monroe Doctrine, and how those relationships influenced westward expansion and the Mexican-American War.

If YOU were there...

You are a Spanish settler living in West Florida in 1820. Your family has lived in Florida for many years. Only a few years ago, people in Spanish Florida were furious when American soldiers occupied the town of Pensacola. Now you hear that Spain has signed a treaty with the United States—Florida is no longer Spanish territory but rather part of the United States.

How would you feel about living under a new government?

BUILDING BACKGROUND The War of 1812 left the United States stronger and more self-confident. The new nation had remained strong against a great European power. The United States then turned to diplomacy as a way to settle international issues.

Settling Disputes with Great Britain

The Treaty of Ghent ended the War of 1812, yet there were issues left unresolved. The United States and British Canada both wanted to keep their navies and fishing rights on the Great Lakes. In the spring of 1817, the two sides compromised with the **Rush-Bagot Agreement**, which limited naval power on the Great Lakes for both the United States and British Canada.

Another treaty with Britain gave the United States fishing rights off parts of the Newfoundland and Labrador coasts. This treaty, known as the **Convention of 1818**, also set the border between the United States and Canada at 49°N latitude as far west as the Rocky Mountains. Interest in the valuable fur trade in the Oregon Country was another issue resolved by this treaty. Both countries agreed to occupy the Pacific Northwest together, an agreement that would be tested in the years to come.

READING CHECK **Summarizing** What were the main disputes between the United States and Britain?

260 CHAPTER 8

Teach the Big Idea: Master the Standards

Standards Proficiency

American Foreign Policy

HSS 8.4.1, 8.5.2; HSS **Analysis Skills:** CS 1, HI 2, HI 6

1. **Teach** Ask students the Main Idea questions to teach this section.
2. **Apply** Explain to students that foreign policy develops as nations try to solve international problems. Create a chart with two columns and four rows for students to see. Label the columns *Dispute and How Resolved*, and *U.S. Benefits or Costs*. Label the rows *Britain, Spain,* and *Latin America*. Have each student copy and complete the chart. **LS Visual/Spatial**
3. **Review** As you review the section's main ideas, have students help you complete a master copy of the chart.
4. **Practice/Homework** Have students read, listen to, or view the daily news and take notes on current international disputes. Then have students discuss some of the disputes they listed and how countries might try to resolve them. **LS Logical/Mathematical**

Alternative Assessment Handbook, Rubric 7: Charts

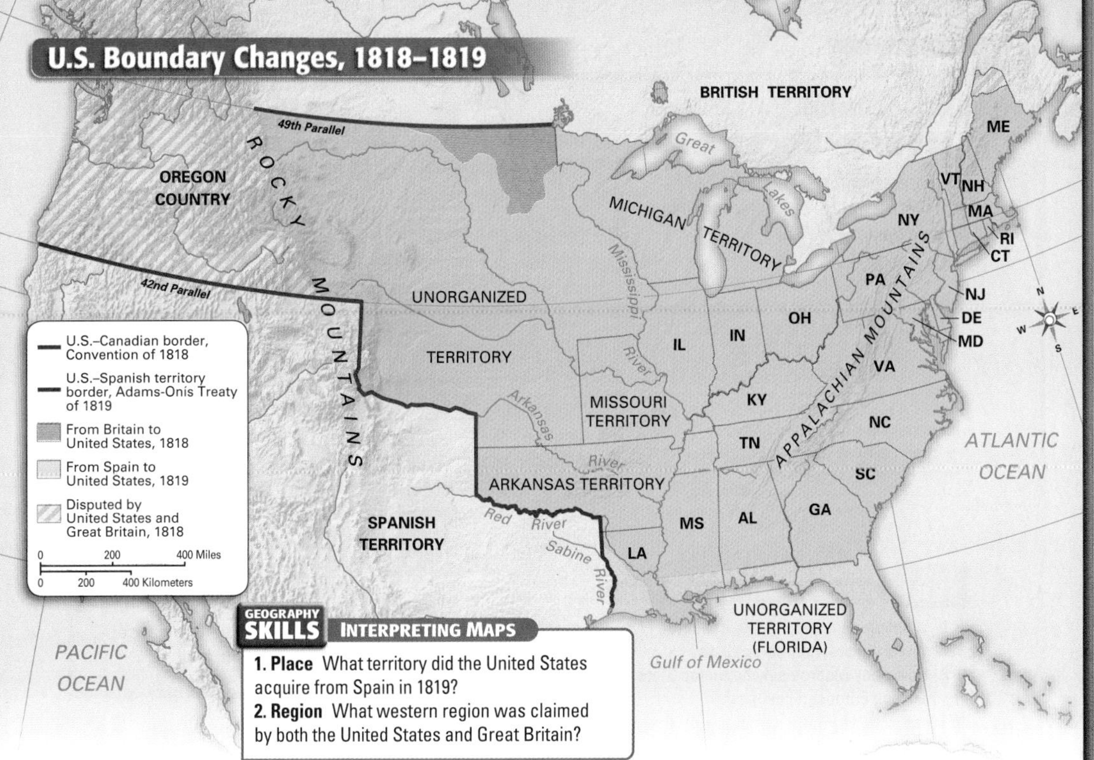

GEOGRAPHY SKILLS **INTERPRETING MAPS**

1. **Place** What territory did the United States acquire from Spain in 1819?
2. **Region** What western region was claimed by both the United States and Great Britain?

United States Gains Florida

The United States also had a dispute over its southern border with Spanish Florida. In 1818 Secretary of State John Quincy Adams, son of John and Abigail Adams, held talks with Spanish diplomat Luis de Onís about letting Americans settle in Florida. Meanwhile, President **James Monroe**, elected in 1816, had sent U.S. troops to secure the U.S.–Florida border. General Andrew Jackson led these soldiers.

At the same time, conflicts arose between the United States and the Seminole Indians of Florida. The Seminole often helped runaway slaves and sometimes raided U.S. settlements. In April 1818 Jackson's troops invaded Florida to capture Seminole raiders. This act began the First Seminole War. During the war Jackson took over most of Spain's important military posts. Then he overthrew the governor of Florida. He carried out these acts against Spain without receiving direct orders from President Monroe. Jackson's actions upset Spanish leaders. Most Americans, however, supported Jackson.

Jackson's presence in Florida convinced Spanish leaders to negotiate. In 1819 the two countries signed the **Adams-Onís Treaty**, which settled all border disputes between Spain and the United States. Under this treaty, Spain gave East Florida to the United States. In return, the United States gave up its claims to what is now Texas. U.S. leaders also agreed to pay up to $5 million of U.S. citizens' claims against Spain.

THE IMPACT TODAY

Florida was admitted as a U.S. state in 1845 and is now home to about 16 million people.

READING CHECK **Summarizing** How were the disagreements between the United States and Spanish Florida settled?

Direct Teach

Main Idea

❶ Settling Disputes with Great Britain

The United States and Great Britain settled their disputes over boundaries and control of waterways.

Identify Which agreement limited naval power on the Great Lakes? *Rush-Bagot Agreement of 1817*

Elaborate Why do you think the United States and Britain agreed to share the Pacific Northwest? *possible answer—The fur trade was too valuable for either country to give up the region.*

- Map Transparency: U.S. Boundary Changes, 1818–1819
- **CRF:** Primary Source Activity: Alexis de Tocqueville's Democracy in America
- **HSS** 8.5.2; **HSS Analysis Skills:** HI 1, HI 2

Main Idea

❷ United States Gains Florida

The United States gained Florida in an agreement with Spain.

Identify What country controlled Florida in 1818? *Spain*

Elaborate Why do you think most Americans supported Jackson's actions in Florida? *resented Seminole Indians helping runaway slaves and raiding settlements; wanted to expand U.S. territory*

- **HSS** 8.5.2; **HSS Analysis Skills:** HI 1, HI 2

Cross-Discipline Activity: Civics

Standards Proficiency

Resolving a Problem through Compromise HSS 8.5.2

1. Write the following definition of compromise for students to see:

   compromise an agreement in which each side gives up some demands

2. Work with students to come up with several school-related scenarios that could be solved through compromise.
3. Organize students into small groups and assign each group a scenario. Have each group state the issue or dispute and develop a solution that requires compromise. Each group should create a written description of its problem and solution.
4. Conclude with a group discussion on the importance of compromise as a political tool. Ask students to explain how compromise was used to solve disputes between the United States and other countries. **LS Interpersonal, Logical/Mathematical**

- Alternative Assessment Handbook, Rubric 35: Solving Problems

Answers

Interpreting Maps 1. *Florida, part of Louisiana;* **2.** *Oregon Country*

Reading Check (left page) *Naval and fishing rights on the Great Lakes, location of U.S. Canadian border, Northwest fur trade*

Reading Check *The Adams-Onís Treaty gave Florida to the United States in exchange for claims to Texas.*

Direct Teach

Main Idea

3 Monroe Doctrine

With the Monroe Doctrine, the United States strengthened its relationship with Latin America.

Identify Cause and Effect What events in Latin America led to the Monroe Doctrine? *struggles for independence in Latin America*

Draw Conclusions Why do you think the United States chose not to issue a joint statement with Great Britain to keep European influence out of Latin America? *did not want British influence in the area, either; United States and Britain were competing for trade in the Americas.*

Make Judgments Do you think the Monroe Doctrine was a good or bad idea for U.S. foreign policy? *possible answers: good—made the United States strong in the eyes of world; bad—may have hurt the nation's relationships with European countries*

- **CRF:** Primary Source Activity: John Quincy Adams's Fourth of July 1821 Address
- Political Cartoons Activities for United States History: Cartoon 10: The Monroe Doctrine

HSS 8.5.2; HSS **Analysis Skills:** HI 1, HI 2

Primary Source

The Monroe Doctrine

The Monroe Doctrine became an important U.S. policy statement. Later presidents invoked the Monroe Doctrine to build the Panama Canal and to confront the Soviet Union over missiles it had built in Cuba.

Answers

Analyzing Primary Sources

1. *European interference in Latin America would be seen as hostile to the United States.* **2.** *The United States would not interfere with existing colonies.*

Primary Source

HISTORIC DOCUMENT

The Monroe Doctrine

President James Monroe established the foundation for U.S. foreign policy in Latin America in the Monroe Doctrine of 1823.

The occasion has been judged proper for asserting . . . that the American continents . . . are henceforth not to be considered as subjects for future colonization by any European powers . . .

The political system of the allied powers is essentially different . . . from that of America. We . . . declare that we should consider any attempt on their part to extend their system to any portion of this hemisphere as dangerous to our peace and safety . . .

In this phrase, Monroe warns European nations against trying to influence events in the Western Hemisphere.

With the existing colonies . . . we have not interfered and shall not interfere. But with the governments who have declared their independence and maintained it, and whose independence we have . . . acknowledged, we could not view any interposition[1] for the purpose of oppressing them . . . by any European power in any other light than as the manifestation[2] of an unfriendly disposition[3] toward the United States.

Monroe notes here the difference between existing colonies and newly independent countries.

[1] **interposition:** interference
[2] **manifestation:** evidence
[3] **disposition:** attitude

ANALYSIS SKILL ANALYZING PRIMARY SOURCES

1. What warning did President Monroe give to European powers in the Monroe Doctrine?
2. How does Monroe say the United States will treat existing European colonies?

Monroe Doctrine

ACADEMIC VOCABULARY
circumstances surrounding situation

Meanwhile, Spain had other problems. By the early 1820s most of the Spanish colonies in the Americas had declared independence. Revolutionary fighter **Simon Bolívar**, called the Liberator, led many of these struggles for independence. The political circumstances surrounding the revolutions reminded most American leaders of the American Revolution. As a result, they supported these struggles.

After Mexico broke free from Spain in 1821, President Monroe grew worried. He feared that rival European powers might try to take control of newly independent Latin American countries. He was also concerned about Russia's interest in the northwest coast of North America.

Secretary of State Adams shared President Monroe's concerns. In a speech before Congress, Adams said that the United States had always been friendly with European powers, and that the country did not want to be involved in wars with European countries. He implied that he supported the newly independent countries, but said the United States would not fight their battles.

Great Britain was also interested in restraining the influence of other European nations in the Americas. This was because Britain had formed close trading ties with most of the independent Latin American countries. Britain wanted to issue a joint statement with the United States to warn the rest of Europe not to interfere in Latin America.

Instead, Secretary of State Adams and President Monroe decided to put together a document protecting American interests. The **Monroe Doctrine**, was an exclusive statement of American policy warning European powers not to interfere with the Americas.

Critical Thinking: Identifying Points of View

Standards Proficiency

Monroe Doctrine News Articles

HSS 8.5.2; HSS **Analysis Skills:** HR 5, HI 1, HI 2

1. Have students write a newspaper article about the Monroe Doctrine.
2. Students should choose whether they would like to be a reporter for a U.S. newspaper or a reporter from a country in Europe.
3. Encourage students to come up with a headline and a political cartoon, illustration, or other visual aid to accompany their newspaper articles.
4. Ask volunteers to share their articles with the class. Encourage feedback.
5. Conclude by leading a class discussion on the various points of view that Americans and others had toward the Monroe Doctrine.
   LS Verbal/Linguistic, Visual/Spatial

Alternative Assessment Handbook, Rubric 23: Newspapers

The doctrine was issued by the president on December 2, 1823, during his annual message to Congress.

The Monroe Doctrine had four basic points.

1. The United States would not interfere in the affairs of European nations.
2. The United States would recognize, and not interfere with, colonies that already existed in North and South America.
3. The Western Hemisphere was to be off-limits to future colonization by any foreign power.
4. The U.S. government would consider any European power's attempt to colonize or interfere with any nation in the Western Hemisphere to be a hostile act.

Some Europeans strongly criticized the Monroe Doctrine, but few European countries challenged it. The doctrine has remained important to U.S. foreign policy. The United States has continued to consider Latin America within its sphere of influence—the area a nation claims some control over. At times, it has intervened in Latin American affairs when its own interests, such as national security, were at risk.

READING CHECK **Analyzing** What effect did the revolutions in Latin America have on U.S. foreign policy?

SUMMARY AND PREVIEW In this section you learned that U.S. foreign policy was characterized by both compromise and strong leadership in the years following the War of 1812. In the next section you will learn about the rising sense of national pride that developed as the United States grew and expanded.

Section 1 Assessment

go.hrw.com
Online Quiz
KEYWORD: SS8 HP8

Reviewing Ideas, Terms, and People HSS 8.4.1, 8.5.2

1. a. **Identify** What issues were settled between the United States and Great Britain in 1817 and 1818?
   b. **Make Inferences** Why would the United States and Britain agree to occupy the Pacific Northwest together?
2. a. **Recall** What problems existed between Spain and the United States?
   b. **Analyze** Why was the **Adams-Onís Treaty** important?
   c. **Evaluate** Do you think that Andrew Jackson was right to act without orders? Explain your answer.
3. a. **Describe** What did the **Monroe Doctrine** state?
   b. **Contrast** How did the Monroe Doctrine differ from Adams's Fourth of July Address?
   c. **Elaborate** What do you think the newly independent Latin American countries thought of the Monroe Doctrine?

Critical Thinking

4. **Identifying Cause and Effect** Copy the chart below. Use it to identify the foreign policy issues the United States had to deal with between 1817–1823 and the result of each.

Dispute	Year	Result

FOCUS ON WRITING

5. **Determining Relationships** One of the main ways you can tell about someone's character is by how he or she treats others . As you read this section, start a list of words and phrases that describe how the United States acted in relationships with other nations. For example, lists might include words and phrases like "willing to compromise" and "firm."

Section 1 Assessment Answers

1. a. naval and fishing rights, U.S.-Canadian border dispute, Northwest fur trade
   b. interest in the fur trade, keep Russian out
2. a. disputes over Texas and Spanish Florida
   b. settled border disputes with Spain
   c. possible answers: no—military leaders should not attack other countries without orders; yes—it forced Spain to negotiate.
3. a. Europe should stay out of Western Hemisphere; U.S. will not interfere in European affairs.
   b. Adams said the United States would not fight the battles of Latin American countries; Monroe Doctrine threatened force against European intervention.
   c. possible answers: good—kept Europeans from interfering; bad—gave the United States control over Latin America
4. sample answer: rights to waterways of the Great Lakes; 1817; Rush-Bagot Agreement limited both sides' naval power on Great Lakes
5. possible answers—forceful, strong, rude, protective, possessive, diplomatic

Direct Teach

Info to Know

Politics and the Monroe Doctrine The Monroe Doctrine played a role in the presidential ambitions of John Quincy Adams, who hoped to succeed Monroe in the White House. Adams knew that many Americans were suspicious of him because he desired close relations with Great Britain. When the British wanted to issue a joint declaration opposing European influence in the Americas, Adams persuaded Monroe to issue the doctrine without British involvement. Americans approved of this decision, and Adams avoided being attacked as pro-British in the 1824 election.

go.hrw.com
Online Resources
KEYWORD: SS8 US8
ACTIVITY: Revolutions in Latin America

Review & Assess

Close

Have students work individually to write a brief summary of the major agreements and doctrines discussed in this section.

Review

Online Quiz, Section 1

Assess

SE Section 1 Assessment

PASS: Section 1 Quiz

Alternative Assessment Handbook

Reteach-Classroom Intervention

California Standards Review Workbook

Interactive Reader and Study Guide, Section 1

Interactive Skills Tutor CD-ROM

Answers

Reading Check *The United States wanted to keep European influence out of newly independent countries; created Monroe Doctrine, warning European nations not to interfere in the Western Hemisphere.*

Preteach

Bellringer

If YOU were there . . . Use the **Daily Bellringer Transparency** to help students answer the questions.

Daily Bellringer Transparency, Section 2

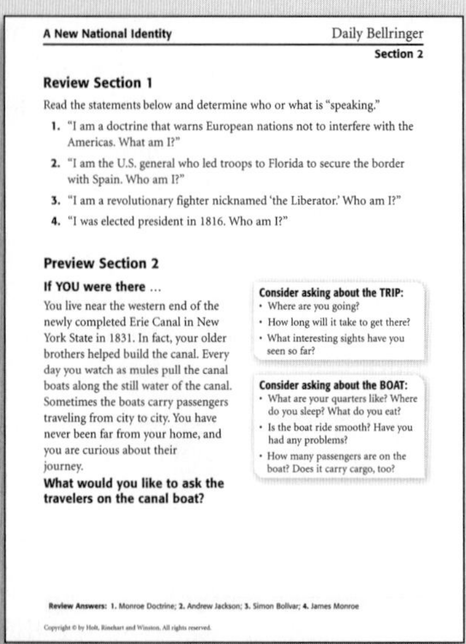
A New National Identity Daily Bellringer

Section 2

Review Section 1

Read the statements below and determine who or what is "speaking."

1. "I am a doctrine that warns European nations not to interfere with the Americas. What am I?"
2. "I am the U.S. general who led troops to Florida to secure the border with Spain. Who am I?"
3. "I am a revolutionary fighter nicknamed 'the Liberator.' Who am I?"
4. "I was elected president in 1816. Who am I?"

Preview Section 2

If YOU were there ...

You live near the western end of the newly completed Erie Canal in New York State in 1831. In fact, your older brothers helped build the canal. Every day you watch as mules pull the canal boats along the still water of the canal. Sometimes the boats carry passengers traveling from city to city. You have never been far from your home, and you are curious about their journey.

What would you like to ask the travelers on the canal boat?

Consider asking about the TRIP:
- Where are you going?
- How long will it take to get there?
- What interesting sights have you seen so far?

Consider asking about the BOAT:
- What are your quarters like? Where do you sleep? What do you eat?
- Is the boat ride smooth? Have you had any problems?
- How many passengers are on the boat? Does it carry cargo, too?

Review Answers: **1.** Monroe Doctrine; **2.** Andrew Jackson; **3.** Simon Bolívar; **4.** James Monroe

Academic Vocabulary

Review with students the high-use academic term in this section.

incentive something that leads people to follow a certain course of action (p. 265)

CRF: Vocabulary Builder Activity, Section 2

Standards Focus

HSS 8.4.1
Means: Describe the nation's physical and political divisions and how the nation expanded during the early 1800s.
Matters: National interest take precedence over regional differences.

HSS 8.6.2
Means: Explain how roads and canals united the nation.
Matters: A strong transportation system continues to unite the United States today.

SECTION 2

Nationalism and Sectionalism

What You Will Learn...

Main Ideas

1. Growing nationalism led to improvements in the nation's transportation systems.
2. The Missouri Compromise settled an important regional conflict.
3. The outcome of the election of 1824 led to controversy.

The Big Idea

A rising sense of national unity allowed some regional differences to be set aside and national interests to be served.

Key Terms and People

nationalism, *p. 264*
Henry Clay, *p. 264*
American System, *p. 264*
Cumberland Road, *p. 265*
Erie Canal, *p. 265*
Era of Good Feelings, *p. 265*
sectionalism, *p. 266*
Missouri Compromise, *p. 267*
John Quincy Adams, *p. 267*

HSS 8.4.1 Describe the country's physical landscapes, political divisions, and territorial expansion during the terms of the first four presidents.

8.6.2 Outline the physical obstacles to and the economic and political factors involved in building a network of roads, canals, and railroads (e.g., Henry Clay's American System).

If YOU were there...

You live near the western end of the newly completed Erie Canal in New York State in 1831. In fact, your older brothers helped build the canal. Every day you watch as mules pull the canal boats along the still water of the canal. Sometimes the boats carry passengers traveling from city to city. You have never been far from your home, and you are curious about their journey.

What would you like to ask the travelers on the canal boat?

BUILDING BACKGROUND Peace, prosperity, and a growing country gave Americans a sense of national unity. In practical terms, building roads and canals also helped unify the nation. They made travel easier, linking people from different regions of the country. Nevertheless, some regional conflicts continued.

Growing Nationalism

Pleased by successful negotiations with foreign powers, Americans enjoyed a rising sense of nationalism. **Nationalism** is feelings of pride and loyalty to a nation. This new national unity found a strong supporter in U.S. Representative **Henry Clay** from Kentucky.

Clay believed that a strong national economy would promote national feeling and reduce regional conflicts. He developed a plan that came to be known as the **American System**—a series of measures intended to make the United States economically self-sufficient. To build the economy, he pushed for a national bank that would provide a single currency, making interstate trade easier. Clay wanted the money from a protective tariff to be used to improve roads and canals. These internal improvements would unite the country.

Some members of Congress believed that the Constitution did not permit the federal government to spend money on internal improvements. Clay argued that the possible gains for the country justified federal action.

Teach the Big Idea: Master the Standards

Standards Proficiency

Nationalism and Sectionalism

HSS 8.4.1, 8.6.2; HSS **Analysis Skills:** CS 1, HR 1, HI 1

1. **Teach** Ask students the Main Idea questions to teach this chapter.
2. **Apply** Organize students into three groups. Assign each group a main idea from the section. Have each group create a 10-question quiz on its topic as well as a separate answer key. Have groups exchange quizzes, complete the ones they receive, and then return the completed quizzes to their authors for grading. **LS Interpersonal, Verbal/Linguistic**
3. **Review** As you review the section, have the groups share questions and answers from their quizzes.
4. **Practice/Homework** Have each student select one quiz question to explore in a paragraph. Students should address the questions who, what, where, when, why, and how, as applicable, in their paragraphs. **LS Verbal/Linguistic**

Alternative Assessment Handbook, Rubrics 1: Acquiring Information; and 37: Writing Assignments

Roads and Canals

In the early 1800s most roads in the United States were made of dirt, making travel difficult. British actress Frances Kemble described one New York road she had struggled along during a visit in the 1830s.

> "The wickedest road, I do think, the cruellest, hard-heartedest road, that ever [a] wheel rumbled upon."
>
> —Frances Anne (Kemble) Butler, *Journal*

To improve the nation's roads, Congress agreed with Clay and invested in road building. The **Cumberland Road** was the first road built by the federal government. It ran from Cumberland, Maryland, to Wheeling, a town on the Ohio River in present-day West Virginia. Construction began in 1815. Workers had to cut a 66-foot-wide band, sometimes through forest, to make way for the road. Then they had to use shovels and pickaxes to dig a 12- to 18-inch roadbed, which they filled with crushed stone. All of the work had to be done without the benefit of today's bulldozers and steamrollers.

By 1818 the road reached Wheeling. By 1833 the National Road, as the expansion was called, stretched to Columbus, Ohio. By 1850 it reached all the way to Illinois.

Meanwhile, Americans tried to make water transportation easier by building canals. One of the largest projects was the **Erie Canal**, which ran from Albany to Buffalo, New York.

Construction of the canal began in 1817 and was completed in 1825. Using shovels, British, German, and Irish immigrants dug the entire canal by hand. The canal cost millions of dollars, but it proved to be worth the expense. The Erie Canal allowed goods and people to move between towns on Lake Erie and New York City and the east coast. Its success served as an incentive for a canal-building boom across the country.

ACADEMIC VOCABULARY
incentive something that leads people to follow a certain course of action

Era of Good Feelings

From 1815 to 1825 the United States enjoyed the **Era of Good Feelings**, an era of peace, pride, and progress. The phrase was coined

U.S. Roads and Canals, 1850

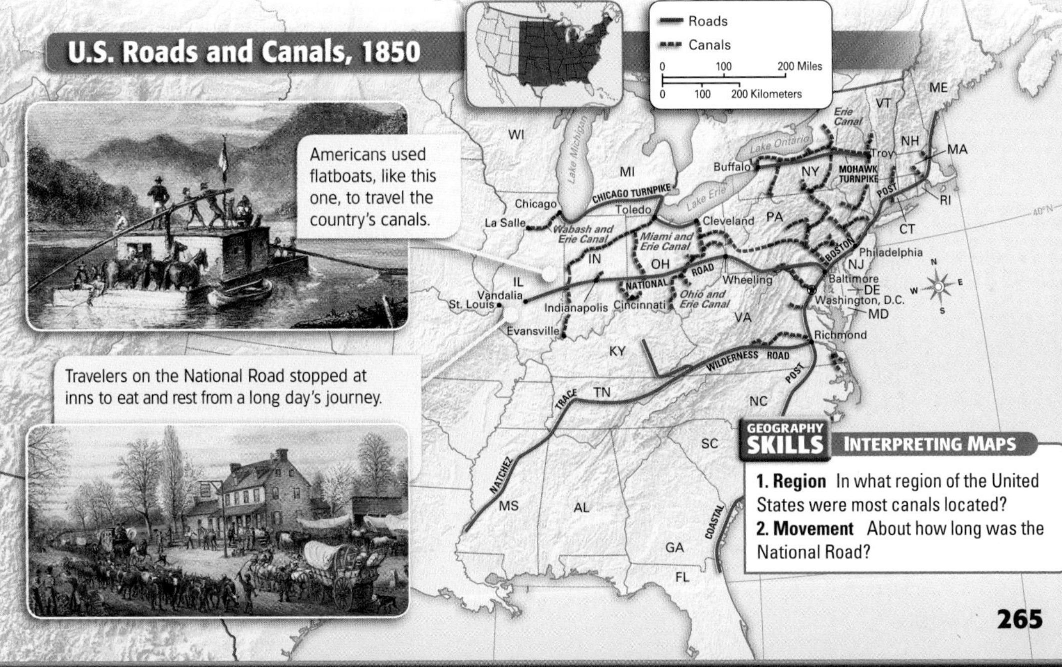

GEOGRAPHY SKILLS INTERPRETING MAPS

1. **Region** In what region of the United States were most canals located?
2. **Movement** About how long was the National Road?

Differentiating Instruction for Universal Access

English-Language Learners

Standards Proficiency | Prep Required

Materials: art supplies, poster board

1. Find and bring to class examples of items that promote school spirit, such as trophies; school colors; and buttons, folders, or notebooks that feature the school mascot.
2. Explain that nations also have symbols that promote national unity, such as flags, anthems, symbolic figures, slogans, and so on.
3. Ask students what symbols might have represented growing nationalism in the early 1800s. *(Students might suggest the American flag, a map of the growing country, or an image of the Erie Canal.)*
4. Have students create a Then-and-Now poster that provides a symbol for nationalism in the early 1800s and one for nationalism today.
LS Visual/Spatial

Alternative Assessment Handbook, Rubric 28: Posters

HSS Analysis Skills: HI 1

Direct Teach

Main Idea

1 Growing Nationalism

Growing nationalism led to improvements in the nation's transportation systems.

Define What is nationalism? *feelings of pride and loyalty to a nation*

Recall What was the purpose of the American System? *to make the nation economically self-sufficient*

Evaluate How does nationalism benefit from roads and canals? *Linking goods and people helps create a unified nation and culture.*

CRF: History and Geography Activity: The National Road

Map Transparency: U.S. Roads and Canals, 1850

HSS 8.6.2; **HSS Analysis Skills:** HI 2

Checking for Understanding

True or False Answer each statement *T* if it is true or *F* if it is false. If false, explain why.

1. The Cumberland Road was a dirt road. *F; crushed stone*
2. The Erie Canal connected Lake Erie to the East coast. *T*
3. The Era of Good Feelings was an era of peace, pride, and progress. *T*

HSS 8.6.2

go.hrw.com
Online Resources
KEYWORD: SS8 US8
ACTIVITY: Erie Canal and National Road Map or Brochure

Answers

Interpreting Maps 1. *the Northeast* 2. *about 600 miles*

Direct Teach

Main Idea

❷ Missouri Compromise

The Missouri Compromise settled an important regional conflict.

Explain What problem did Missouri's request for statehood cause? *threatened to upset the balance of power between the free states and the slave states in the Senate*

Analyze How did the Missouri Compromise satisfy both the North and the South? *kept the number of free states and slave states equal and maintained the balance of power*

Make Judgments If you were a senator in 1819, would you have voted for or against the Missouri Compromise? Why? *possible answers: against—to prevent the spread of slavery; for—to preserve the peace between the states*

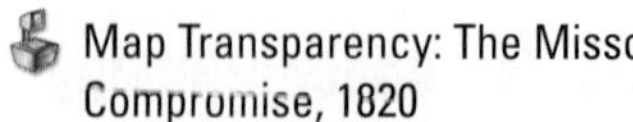
Map Transparency: The Missouri Compromise, 1820

HSS 8.9.5; HSS **Analysis Skills:** HI 1, HI 2

History Humor

What are the three rules of diplomacy?

1. Compromise
2. Compromise
3. Compromise

The Missouri Compromise, 1820

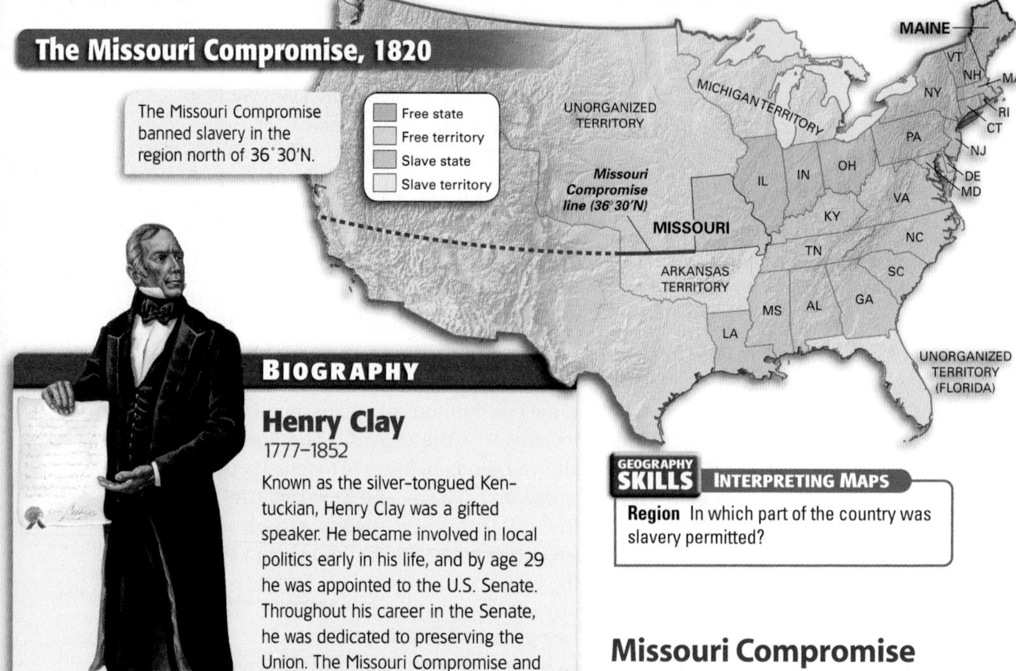

GEOGRAPHY SKILLS INTERPRETING MAPS

Region In which part of the country was slavery permitted?

BIOGRAPHY

Henry Clay

1777–1852

Known as the silver-tongued Kentuckian, Henry Clay was a gifted speaker. He became involved in local politics early in his life, and by age 29 he was appointed to the U.S. Senate. Throughout his career in the Senate, he was dedicated to preserving the Union. The Missouri Compromise and a later agreement, the Compromise of 1850, helped to ease sectional tensions, at least temporarily.

Analyzing Why did Henry Clay work for compromises between regions?

by a Boston editor in 1817 during James Monroe's visit to New England early in his presidency.

The emphasis on national unity was strengthened by two Supreme Court case decisions that reinforced the power of the federal government. In the 1819 case *McCulloch* v. *Maryland*, the Court asserted the implied powers of Congress in allowing for the creation of a national bank. In the 1824 case *Gibbons* v. *Ogden*, the Court said that the states could not interfere with the power of Congress to regulate interstate commerce.

READING CHECK **Drawing Inferences** How did new roads and canals affect the economy?

Missouri Compromise

Even during the Era of Good Feelings, disagreements between the different regions—known as **sectionalism**—threatened the Union. One such disagreement arose in 1819 when Congress considered Missouri's application to enter the Union as a slave state. At the time, the Union had 11 free states and 11 slave states. Adding a new slave state would have tipped the balance in the Senate in favor of the South.

To protect the power of the free states, the House passed a special amendment. It declared that the United States would accept Missouri as a slave state, but importing enslaved Africans into Missouri would be illegal. The amendment also set free the children of Missouri slaves. Southern politicians angrily opposed this plan.

North Carolina senator Nathaniel Macon wanted to continue adding slave states. "Why depart from the good old way, which has kept us in quiet, peace, and harmony?" he asked. Eventually, the Senate rejected the amendment. Missouri was still not a state.

Critical Thinking: Identifying Points of View

Standards Proficiency

The Missouri Compromise

HSS 8.9.5; HSS **Analysis Skills:** CS 3, HR 5, HI 1

1. Write the following for students to see: **North—100 South—76**
2. Explain to students that these numbers show the North/South split in the House of Representatives at the time of the Missouri Compromise. While all 76 southern representatives voted to allow Missouri to enter the Union as a slave state, only 14 northerners voted for the measure.
3. Ask students how many votes were needed for a House majority *(88)* and how many the measure received *(90)*.
4. Have each student draw a copy of the map shown above. Then have students annotate the map by listing the political, economic, and social points of view in the free states and the slave states that were dividing the nation and which the Missouri Compromise addressed.
5. Ask volunteers to share the information they listed. **LS Visual/Spatial**

Alternative Assessment Handbook, Rubrics 11: Discussions; and 20: Map Creation

Answers

Interpreting Maps *South*

Biography *wanted to preserve the Union*

Reading Check *easier to transport goods across the nation*

Henry Clay convinced Congress to agree to the **Missouri Compromise**, which settled the conflict that had arisen from Missouri's application for statehood. This compromise had three main conditions:

1. Missouri would enter the Union as a slave state.
2. Maine would join the Union as a free state, keeping the number of slave and free states equal.
3. Slavery would be prohibited in any new territories or states formed north of 36°30' latitude—Missouri's southern border.

Congress passed the Missouri Compromise in 1820. Despite the success of the compromise, there were still strong disagreements between the North and South over the expansion of slavery.

READING CHECK **Drawing Conclusions** Why did Henry Clay propose the Missouri Compromise to resolve the issue of Missouri statehood?

The Election of 1824

Soon, a presidential election also brought controversy. Andrew Jackson won the most popular votes in 1824. However, he did not have enough electoral votes to win office. Under the Constitution, the House of Representatives had to choose the winner. When the House chose **John Quincy Adams** as president, Jackson's supporters claimed that Adams had made a **corrupt bargain** with Henry Clay. These accusations grew after Adams chose Clay to be secretary of state. The controversy weakened Adams's support.

FOCUS ON READING
How is the term **corrupt bargain** an example of semantic slanting?

READING CHECK **Drawing Inferences** Why did Adams have weak support during his presidency?

SUMMARY AND PREVIEW Strong nationalistic feeling contributed to the development of America's politics and economy. In the next section you will read about the development of a new national culture.

Section 2 Assessment

go.hrw.com
Online Quiz
KEYWORD: SS8 HP8

Reviewing Ideas, Terms, and People HSS 8.4.1, 8.6.2

1. a. **Describe** What was the **Era of Good Feelings?**
   b. **Analyze** Explain the impact the *McCulloch* v. *Maryland* and *Gibbons* v. *Ogden* decisions had on the federal government.
   c. **Predict** How would transportation improvements eventually aid the economy of the United States?
2. a. **Recall** What role did **Henry Clay** play in the debate over Missouri's statehood?
   b. **Explain** What problem did Missouri's request for statehood cause?
   c. **Elaborate** Was the **Missouri Compromise** a good solution to the debate between free states and slave states? Explain your answer.
3. a. **Identify** Who were the candidates in the presidential election of 1824? How was the winner determined?
   b. **Draw Conclusions** Why did **John Quincy Adams** lose popular support following the election of 1824?

Critical Thinking

4. **Identifying Cause and Effect** Copy the web diagram below. Use it to describe how the feeling of nationalism in the Era of Good Feelings affected the growth and development of the United States.

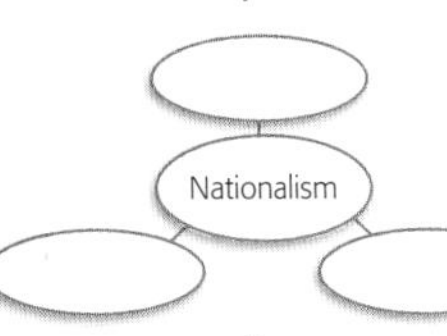

FOCUS ON WRITING

5. **Judging Self-Esteem** Another way you can tell about people's characters is by how they view themselves. Are they self-confident? Do they make healthy choices? As you read this section, think of the United States as a person and jot down notes about the view the United States had of itself. Is the new nation pleased with itself? Does it feel confident or confused?

Section 2 Assessment Answers

1. a. from 1815 to 1825, an era of peace, pride, and progress in the United States
   b. reinforced the power of the federal government
   c. made movement of goods cheaper, easier
2. a. proposed the Missouri Compromise
   b. threatened to upset Senate balance of power between free states and slave states
   c. possible answer: no—only put aside the problem, did not solve it
3. a. Andrew Jackson, John Quincy Adams; no electoral winner, so House chose winner
   b. popular vote went to Jackson; suspicion of corrupt bargain with Clay
4. possible answers: circle one—peace: successful international negotiations; circle two—economy: American System helps national economy; circle three—roads and canals: bring people together
5. possible answers—Nation sees itself as confident with strong opinions, willing to work hard and take risks, proud of progress but recognizes flaws.

Direct Teach

Main Idea

❸ The Election of 1824

The outcome of the election of 1824 led to controversy.

Identify Who won the popular vote in 1824, and who became president? *Andrew Jackson; John Quincy Adams*

Make Inferences What evidence did Jackson's supporters have to support their claim that Adams made a corrupt bargain with Henry Clay? *Adams chose Clay to be secretary of state, which might appear to be reward for Clay's support in the House vote.*

HSS **Analysis Skills:** HI 1, HI 2

Review & Assess

Close

Have students summarize the factors that affected nationalism and sectionalism during the Monroe administration.

Review

Online Quiz, Section 2

Assess

SE Section 2 Assessment
PASS: Section 2 Quiz
Alternative Assessment Handbook

Reteach-Classroom Intervention

California Standards Review Workbook
Interactive Reader and Study Guide, Section 2
Interactive Skills Tutor CD-ROM

Answers

Focus on Reading *negative labeling led people to feel the election was unfair and view Adams in a bad light*

Reading Check (left) *to preserve the Union*

Reading Check (right) *did not win the popular vote; controversial appointment of Henry Clay as secretary of state*

History and Geography

Activity Erie Canal Grand Opening Flier Lead a discussion on the Erie Canal. Have each student create a flyer advertising the opening of the canal that provides information about why canal transportation is better than other available options. Students should consider both people traveling west as well as those shipping goods.
LS Verbal/Linguistic, Visual/Spatial

HSS 8.6.1; **HSS Analysis Skills:** CS 3

Connect to Geography

The Canal Route The Erie Canal was built through the Mohawk Valley, a natural pass through the Appalachian Mountains in eastern New York. Colonists had learned this route from Native Americans. This location was chosen because no locks or aqueducts would be needed for some 80 miles.

Teaching Tip

Relate to the Familiar
Relate the height of the Erie Canal to objects with which students are familiar. Tell students to use 10 feet as the average height of a one-story building. Have students use this figure to estimate how many stories a building would need to be to equal the rise of the Erie Canal. *(60 stories)*

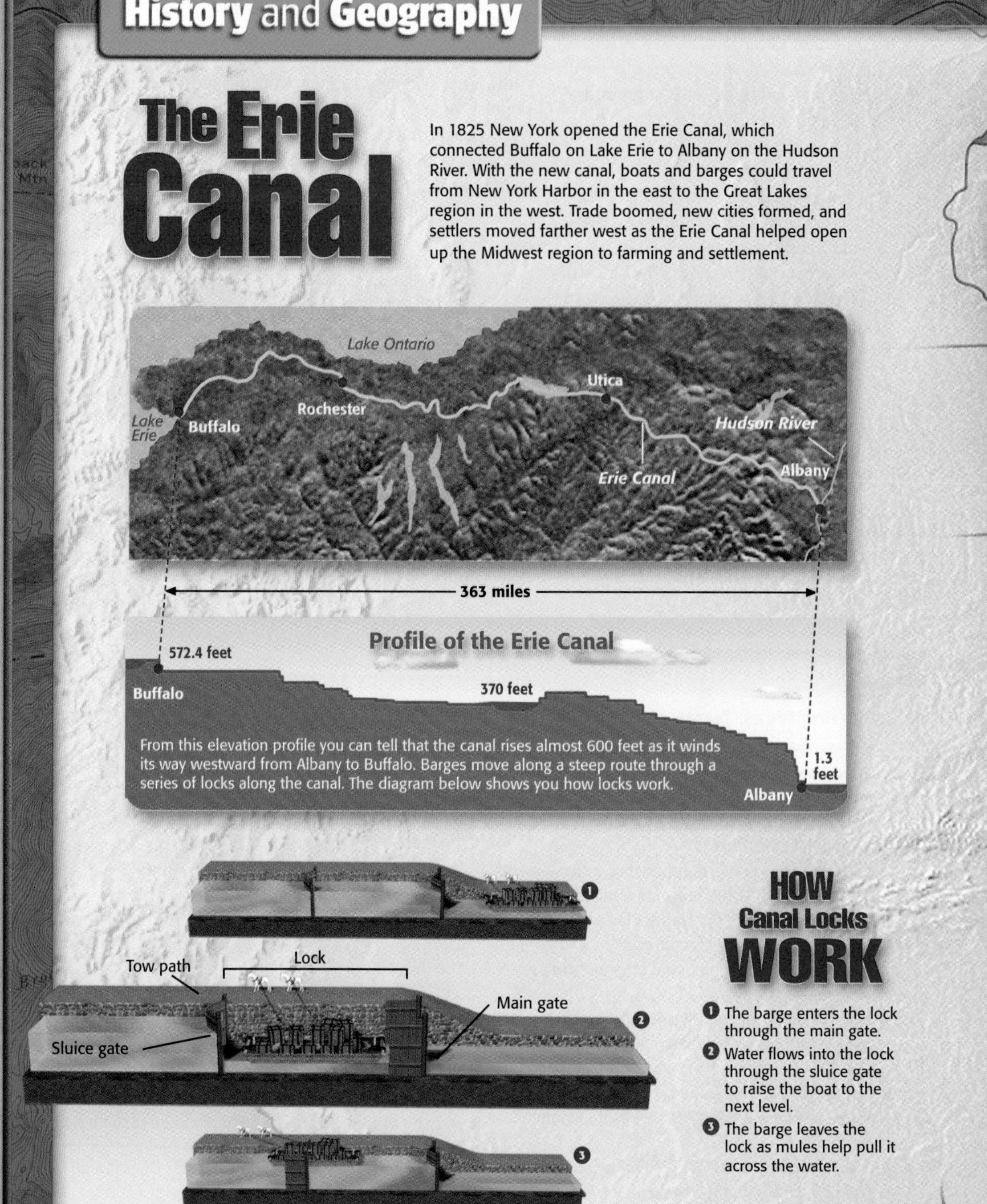

History and Geography
The Erie Canal
In 1825 New York opened the Erie Canal, which connected Buffalo on Lake Erie to Albany on the Hudson River. With the new canal, boats and barges could travel from New York Harbor in the east to the Great Lakes region in the west. Trade boomed, new cities formed, and settlers moved farther west as the Erie Canal helped open up the Midwest region to farming and settlement.
Lake Ontario
Lake Erie
Buffalo
Rochester
Utica
Hudson River
Erie Canal
Albany
363 miles
Profile of the Erie Canal
572.4 feet
Buffalo
370 feet
1.3 feet
Albany
From this elevation profile you can tell that the canal rises almost 600 feet as it winds its way westward from Albany to Buffalo. Barges move along a steep route through a series of locks along the canal. The diagram below shows you how locks work.
HOW Canal Locks WORK
Tow path
Lock
Main gate
Sluice gate
1 The barge enters the lock through the main gate.
2 Water flows into the lock through the sluice gate to raise the boat to the next level.
3 The barge leaves the lock as mules help pull it across the water.
268 CHAPTER 8

Critical Thinking: Comparing and Contrasting

Standards Proficiency

Modern Canals **HSS** 8.6.1; **HSS Analysis Skills:** CS 3, HI 1, HI 2

Research Required

1. Have each student conduct research on a canal in use today, such as the Panama Canal, the Suez Canal, the New York Canal System, the Sault Sainte Marie canals, the Intracoastal Waterway, or the Illinois Waterway.
2. Have each student create a chart comparing and contrasting the modern canal to the Erie Canal. Assign students specific points of comparison (such as the information listed in the Erie Canal Fast Facts on the next page) and have students provide the same information for each canal. Then have students write a summary explaining the significance of each canal.
3. Have volunteers share their charts with the class. **LS Verbal/Linguistic, Visual/Spatial**

Alternative Assessment Handbook, Rubrics 7, Charts; 9: Comparing and Contrasting; and 30: Research

Standards Focus

HSS 8.6 Students analyze the divergent paths of the American people from 1800 to the mid-1800s and the challenges they faced, with emphasis on the Northeast.
8.6.1 Discuss the influence of industrialization and technological developments on the region, including human modification of the landscape and how physical geography shaped human actions (e.g., growth of cities, deforestation, farming, mineral extraction).

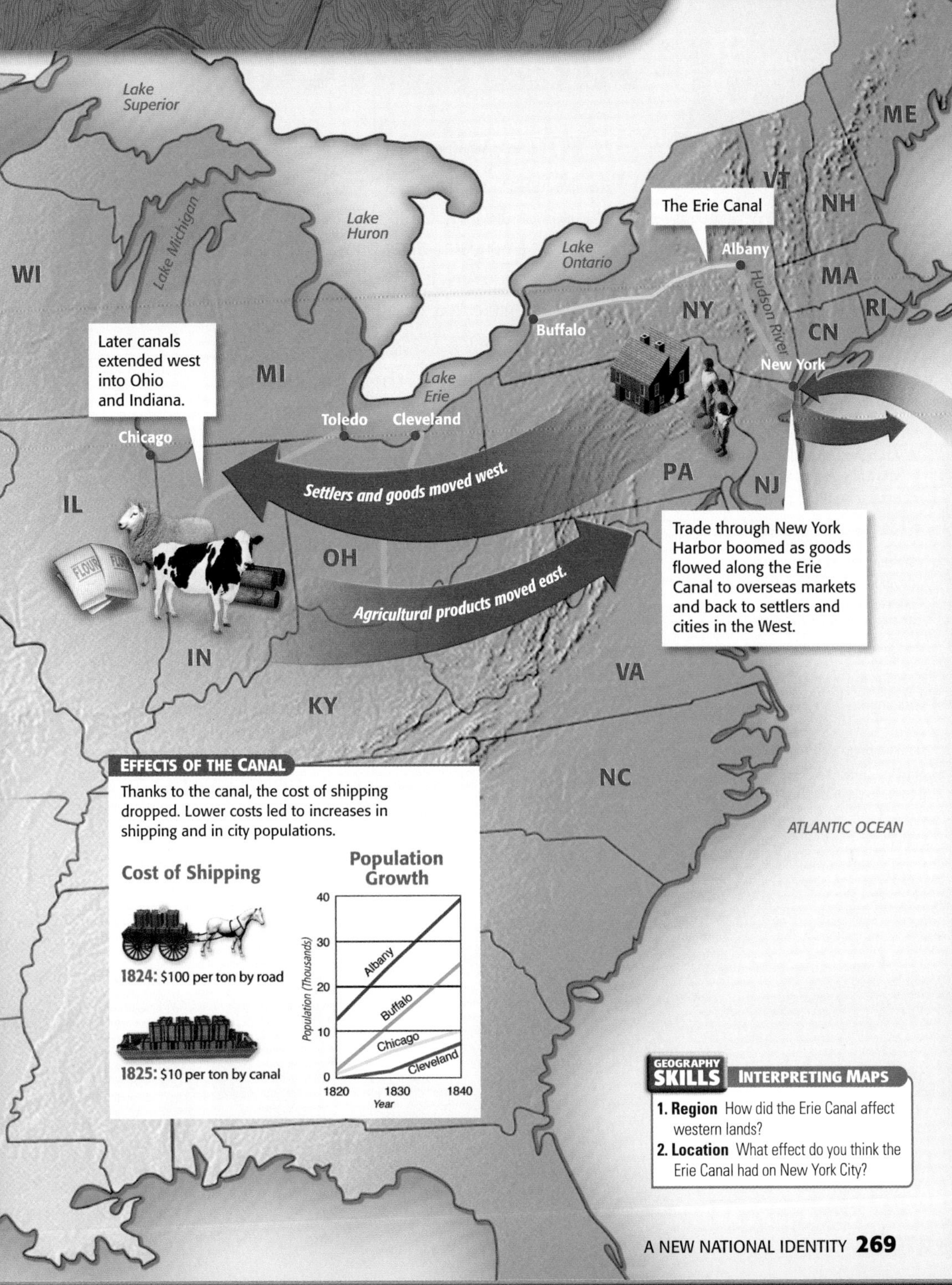

Lake Superior
Lake Michigan
Lake Huron
Lake Ontario
Lake Erie
WI
MI
IL
IN
OH
KY
PA
NY
VT
NH
ME
MA
RI
CN
NJ
VA
NC
Hudson River
ATLANTIC OCEAN
The Erie Canal
Albany
Buffalo
New York
Toledo
Cleveland
Chicago
FLOUR
Later canals extended west into Ohio and Indiana.
Settlers and goods moved west.
Agricultural products moved east.
Trade through New York Harbor boomed as goods flowed along the Erie Canal to overseas markets and back to settlers and cities in the West.
EFFECTS OF THE CANAL
Thanks to the canal, the cost of shipping dropped. Lower costs led to increases in shipping and in city populations.
Cost of Shipping
1824: $100 per ton by road
1825: $10 per ton by canal
Population Growth
Population (Thousands)
40
30
20
10
0
1820
1830
1840
Year
Albany
Buffalo
Chicago
Cleveland
GEOGRAPHY SKILLS
INTERPRETING MAPS
1. Region How did the Erie Canal affect western lands?
2. Location What effect do you think the Erie Canal had on New York City?

History and Geography

Info to Know

Erie Canal Fast Facts
opened: October 25, 1825
cost: about $7 million
endpoints: Buffalo and Albany, New York
length: 363 miles (584 km)
width: 40 feet (12 m)
towpath width: 14 feet
depth: 4 feet (1.2 m)
total number of locks: 83
total number of aqueducts: 18
nicknames: "Clinton's Folly," "Clinton's Big Ditch"

Linking to Today

Erie Canal Today Many of the Erie Canal's original 83 locks are still in use today, although the locks' sizes have been changed to accommodate larger vessels. People also use the canal towpaths for recreation, such as walking, bicycling, and even cross-country skiing.

Did you know . . .

When work began on the Erie Canal, the United States did not have a single school of engineering.

Connect to Economics

A Sound Investment Profits from the Erie Canal paid for the cost of the project within nine years of the canal's opening. The canal soon made New York the busiest port in the United States.

Did You Know . . .

New York Governor DeWitt Clinton was a major supporter of the Erie Canal project. Clinton's image was featured on the U.S. $1,000 bill, printed between 1869 and 1880.

Cross-Discipline Activity: Music

Exceeding Standards

Erie Canal Song

HSS 8.6.1; HSS **Analysis Skills:** CS 3

Prep Required

Materials: lyrics and recording of the song "The Erie Canal," by Thomas S. Allen, 1905

1. Distribute to students copies of the lyrics for the song "The Erie Canal." Next, play a recording of the song. Have students discuss the song's meaning and why the Erie Canal was chosen as a topic for a popular song.
2. Organize students into small groups and have each group write new lyrics to the tune of "The Erie Canal" that describe the effects and significance of the canal as described above.
3. Have each group perform its new version of "The Erie Canal" for the class.

LS Auditory/Musical, Interpersonal

Alternative Assessment Handbook, Rubrics 14: Group Activity; and 26: Poems and Songs

Answers

Interpreting Maps 1. *It enabled trade goods to be shipped farther west, so trade boomed, new cities formed and others grew, and settlers moved farther west.* **2.** *possible answer—greatly increased the amount of goods traded through New York City and helped the city grow and prosper*

Preteach

Bellringer

If YOU were there . . . Use the Daily Bellringer Transparency to help students answer the question.

 Daily Bellringer Transparency, Section 3

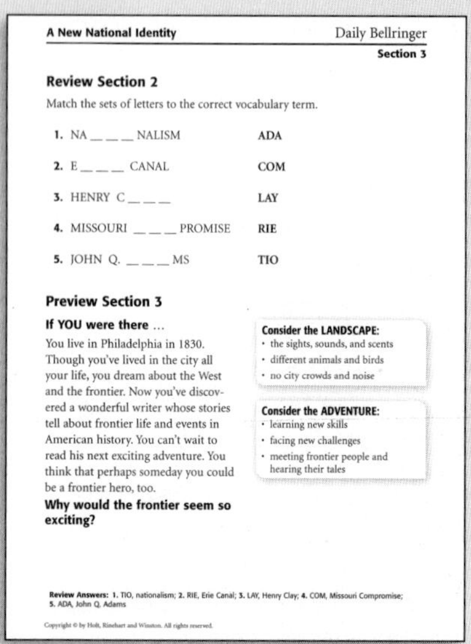

A New National Identity — Daily Bellringer, **Section 3**

Review Section 2

Match the sets of letters to the correct vocabulary term.

1. NA __ __ __ NALISM	ADA
2. E __ __ __ CANAL	COM
3. HENRY C __ __ __	LAY
4. MISSOURI __ __ __ PROMISE	RIE
5. JOHN Q. __ __ __ MS	TIO

Preview Section 3

If YOU were there ...

You live in Philadelphia in 1830. Though you've lived in the city all your life, you dream about the West and the frontier. Now you've discovered a wonderful writer whose stories tell about frontier life and events in American history. You can't wait to read his next exciting adventure. You think that perhaps someday you could be a frontier hero, too.

Why would the frontier seem so exciting?

Consider the LANDSCAPE:
- the sights, sounds, and scents
- different animals and birds
- no city crowds and noise

Consider the ADVENTURE:
- learning new skills
- facing new challenges
- meeting frontier people and hearing their tales

Review Answers: **1.** TIO, nationalism; **2.** RIE, Erie Canal; **3.** LAY, Henry Clay; **4.** COM, Missouri Compromise; **5.** ADA, John Q. Adams

Building Vocabulary

Preteach or review the following terms:

revival renewed faith (p. 272)

satire writing that uses ridicule (p. 271)

CRF: Vocabulary Builder Activity, Section 3

go.hrw.com

Online Resources

KEYWORD: SS8 US8
ACTIVITY: American Culture Display

Standards Focus

HSS 8.4.4

Means: Discuss the early development of America's unique cultural identity.

Matters: U.S. culture became separate from that of Great Britain and Europe.

SECTION 3

American Culture

What You Will Learn...

Main Ideas

1. American writers created a new style of literature.
2. A new style of art showcased the beauty of America and its people.
3. American ideals influenced other aspects of culture, including religion and music.
4. Architecture and education were affected by cultural ideals.

The Big Idea

As the United States grew, developments in many cultural areas contributed to the creation of a new American identity.

Key Terms and People

Washington Irving, *p. 270*
James Fenimore Cooper, *p. 271*
Hudson River school, *p. 272*
Thomas Cole, *p. 272*
George Caleb Bingham, *p. 272*

HSS 8.4.4 Discuss daily life, including traditions in art, music, and literature, of early national America (e.g., through writings by Washington Irving, James Fenimore Cooper).

If YOU were there...

You live in Philadelphia in 1830. Though you've lived in the city all your life, you dream about the West and the frontier. Now you've discovered a wonderful writer whose stories tell about frontier life and events in American history. You can't wait to read his next exciting adventure. You think that perhaps someday you could be a frontier hero, too.

Why would the frontier seem so exciting?

BUILDING BACKGROUND Until the early 1800s, Americans took most of their cultural ideas from Great Britain and Europe. But as American politics and the economy developed, so too did a new national culture. Writers and artists were inspired by American history and the American landscape.

American Writers

Like many people the world over, Americans expressed their thoughts and feelings in literature and art and sought spiritual comfort in religion and music. Developments in education and architecture also reflected the growing national identity.

One of the first American writers to gain international fame was **Washington Irving**. Born in 1783, he was named after George Washington. Irving's works often told about American

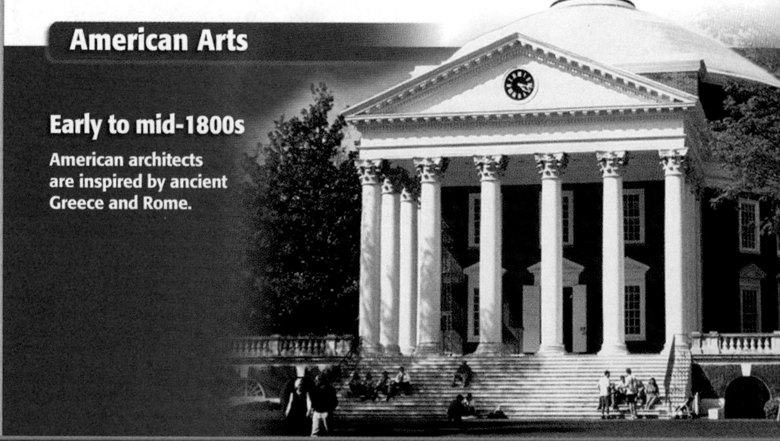

American Arts

Early to mid-1800s

American architects are inspired by ancient Greece and Rome.

Teach the Big Idea: Master the Standards

Standards Proficiency

American Culture

HSS 8.4.4; HSS **Analysis Skills:** CS 2, HI 1, HI 3

Materials: blank note cards

1. **Teach** Ask students the Main Idea questions to teach this section.
2. **Apply** Have each student create flash cards for two to three of the key people or ideas covered in the text under each of the blue headings. On the front of each card, students should label a person or idea. On the back of each card, students should provide a bulleted list of details and a one-sentence summary of how the person or idea contributed to a developing American identity. **LS Verbal/Linguistic**
3. **Review** Have students share information from their flash cards.
4. **Practice/Homework** Have students use their flash cards to create annotated time lines for the section. **LS Visual/Spatial**

Alternative Assessment Handbook, Rubric 36: Time Lines

history. Through a humorous form of writing called satire, Irving warned that Americans should learn from the past and be cautious about the future.

Irving shared this idea in one of his best-known short stories, "Rip Van Winkle." This story describes a man who falls asleep during the time of the American Revolution. He wakes up 20 years later to a society he does not recognize. Irving published this and another well-known tale, "The Legend of Sleepy Hollow," in an 1819–20 collection.

In some of his most popular works, Irving combined European influences with American settings and characters. His work served as a bridge between European literary traditions and a new type of writer who focused on authentically American characters and society.

Perhaps the best known of these new writers was **James Fenimore Cooper**. Cooper was born to a wealthy New Jersey family in 1789. Stories about the West and the Native Americans who lived on the frontier fascinated him. These subjects became the focus of his best-known works.

Cooper's first book was not very successful, but his next novel, *The Spy*, was a huge success. Published in 1821, it was an adventure story set during the American Revolution. It appealed to American readers' patriotism and desire for an exciting, action-filled story.

In 1823 Cooper published *The Pioneers*, the first of five novels featuring the heroic character Natty Bumppo. Cooper's novels told of settling the western frontier and included historical events. For example, his novel *The Last of the Mohicans* takes place during the French and Indian War. By placing fictional characters in a real historical setting, Cooper popularized a type of writing called historical fiction.

Some critics said that Cooper's characters were not interesting. They particularly criticized the women in his stories; one writer labeled them "flat as a prairie." Other authors of historical fiction, such as Catharine Maria Sedgwick, wrote about interesting heroines. Sedgwick's characters were inspired by the people of the Berkshire Hills region of Massachusetts, where she lived. Her works include *A New-England Tale* and *Hope Leslie*.

READING CHECK **Analyzing** How did American writers such as Irving and Cooper help create a new cultural identity in the United States?

A New Style of Art

The writings of Irving and Cooper inspired painters. These artists began to paint landscapes that showed the history of America and the beauty of the land. Earlier American painters had mainly painted portraits. By the

1827
John Audubon begins publishing *The Birds of America*, which is highly admired in England.

Direct Teach

Main Idea

1 American Writers

American writers created a new style of literature.

Identify What historical events did Cooper use as settings in his novels? *American Revolution, French and Indian War*

Contrast How are Cooper's works different than Sedgwick's? *Sedgwick's characters are more interesting than Cooper's; Cooper set stories on frontier, Sedgwick's in New England.*

Elaborate Why do you think Irving used his stories to caution Americans about the future? *wanted the new country to live up to its potential*

- **CRF:** Biography Activities: Catherine Maria Sedgwick; Noah Webster
- **CRF:** Literature Activity: *The Prairie*, by James Fenimore Cooper
- **HSS** 8.4.4; **HSS** **Analysis Skills:** HI 1

Info to Know

Catharine Maria Sedgwick Although she came from a wealthy family, Sedgwick's novels often criticized the wealthy and powerful. Her work reflected the more democratic values of her era. In *Hope Leslie*, for example, Sedgwick criticized the treatment that Native Americans had received from American settlers.

Differentiating Instruction for Universal Access

Learners Having Difficulty — Reaching Standards

1. Draw the graphic organizer for students to see. Omit the blue, italicized answers.
2. Have each student copy the graphic organizer and complete it by identifying significant writers of the early 1800s and describing what they wrote about. **LS Verbal/Linguistic, Visual/Spatial**

 **HSS** 8.4.4

Alternative Assessment Handbook: Rubric 13: Graphic Organizers

Favorite American Writers of the Early 1800s

Writers	Subjects
Washington Irving, James Fenimore Cooper, Catharine Maria Sedgwick	*American Revolution, settlement, and the landscape*

Universal Access Resources
See page 255c for additional resources for differentiating instruction for universal access.

Answers

Reading Check *The characters and settings in their novels created a new vision of Americans, both at home and abroad.*

Direct Teach

Main Idea

2 A New Style of Art

A new style of art showcased the beauty of America and its people.

Recall Who was one of the founders of the Hudson River school? *Thomas Cole*

Summarize How had the style of American painting changed by the 1840s? *More artists were combining scenes of American landscapes with scenes from daily life.*

CRF: Biography Activity: Thomas Cole

HSS 8.4.4; HSS **Analysis Skills:** HI 1

Main Idea

3 Religion and Music

American ideals influenced other aspects of culture, including religion and music.

Explain What was the purpose of revival meetings? *reawakening religious faith*

Evaluate Why was a song about the Battle of New Orleans a good campaign song for Andrew Jackson? *Jackson had led American forces to a convincing victory over a larger British force at the battle.*

HSS 8.4.4; HSS Analysis Skills: HI 1

1830s the Hudson River school had emerged. The artists of the **Hudson River school** created paintings that reflected national pride and an appreciation of the American landscape. They took their name from the subject of many of their paintings—the Hudson River valley.

Landscape painter **Thomas Cole** was a founder of the Hudson River school. He had moved to the United States from Britain in 1819. He soon recognized the unique qualities of the American landscape. As his work gained fame, he encouraged other American artists to show the beauty of nature. "To walk with nature as a poet is the necessary condition of a perfect artist," Cole once said.

By the 1840s the style of American painting was changing. More artists were trying to combine images of the American landscape with scenes from people's daily lives. An important example of this style is *Fur Traders Descending the Missouri* by **George Caleb Bingham**. This painting shows the rugged, lonely lives of traders in the West.

READING CHECK **Finding Main Ideas** How did the style of American art change to reflect the American way of life in the early 1800s?

Religion and Music

Through the early and mid-1800s, several waves of religious revivalism swept the United States. During periods of revivalism, meetings were held for the purpose of reawakening religious faith. These meetings sometimes lasted for days and included large sing-alongs.

At many revival meetings people sang songs called spirituals. Spirituals are a type of folk hymn found in both white and African American folk-music traditions. This type of song developed from the practice of calling out text from the Bible. A leader would call out the text one line at a time, and the congregation would sing the words using a familiar tune. Each singer added his or her own style to the tune. The congregation of singers sang freely as inspiration led them.

While spirituals reflected the religious nature of some Americans, popular folk music of the period reflected the unique views of the growing nation in a different way. One of the most popular songs of the era was "Hunters of Kentucky," which celebrated the Battle of New Orleans. It became an anthem for the spirit of nationalism in the United States and was used successfully in Andrew Jackson's campaign for the presidency in 1828.

READING CHECK **Summarizing** How did music reflect American interests in the early and mid-1800s?

Architecture and Education

American creativity extended to the way in which people designed buildings. Before the American Revolution, most architects followed the style used in Great Britain. After the

American Arts (continued)

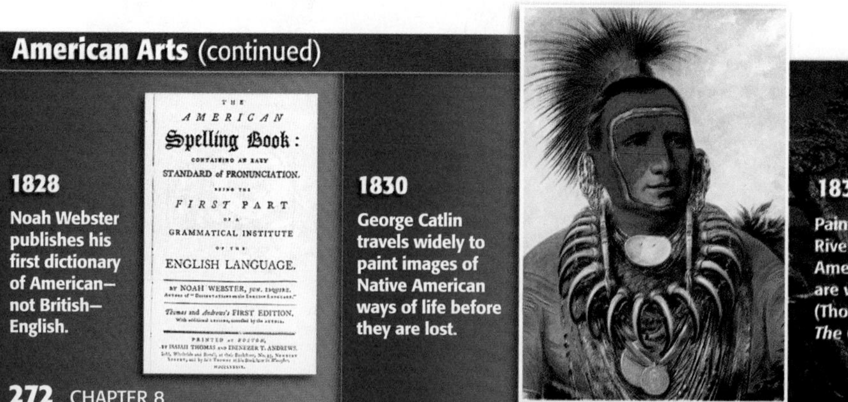

THE
AMERICAN
Spelling Book:
STANDARD of PRONUNCIATION.
FIRST PART
GRAMMATICAL INSTITUTE
ENGLISH LANGUAGE.

1828 Noah Webster publishes his first dictionary of American—not British—English.

1830 George Catlin travels widely to paint images of Native American ways of life before they are lost.

1836 Painters of the Hudson River school prove American landscapes are worthy of art. (Thomas Cole's *The Oxbow*, 1836)

Critical Thinking: Identifying Points of View

Exceeding Standards

Landscape Art and Poetry

HSS 8.4.4; HSS **Analysis Skills:** HI 1

1. Write the words *wild grandeur* for students to see. Ask students what they think the phrase means. Define *grandeur* if needed.
2. Explain that nature poet William Bryant admired painter Thomas Cole's "scenes of wild grandeur peculiar to our country." Write the quote for students to see. Ask students, based on the quotation and the paintings in this section, what qualities Bryant and Cole admired in America *(ruggedness, wild spaces, untamed nature).*
3. Discuss with students how the American landscape has changed and how modern Americans view nature.
4. Have each student either write a poem or create a drawing or painting that conveys the student's feelings about American wilderness and nature.
5. Ask volunteers to present their works to the class. LS **Verbal/Linguistic, Visual/Spatial**

Alternative Assessment Handbook: Rubrics 3: Artwork; and 41: Writing to Express

Answers

Reading Check (left) *movement away from portraiture toward landscape painting, reflected Americans' new nationalism and pride in their country*

Reading Check (right) *spirituals—reflected emphasis on religion and revivalism; folk music—reflected spirit of nationalism*

Revolution, leaders such as Thomas Jefferson called for Americans to model their architecture after the styles used in ancient Greece and Rome. Many Americans admired the ancient civilization of Greece and the Roman Republic because they contained some of the same democratic and republican ideals as the new American nation did.

As time went by, more architects followed Jefferson's ideas. Growing American cities soon had distinctive new buildings designed in the Greek and Roman styles. These buildings were usually made of marble or other stone and featured large, stately columns.

Americans also embraced educational progress. Several early American political leaders expressed a belief that democracy would only succeed in a country of educated and enlightened people. But there was no general agreement on who should provide that education.

Eventually, the idea of a state-funded public school gathered support. In 1837 Massachusetts lawmakers created a state board of education. Other states followed this example, and the number of public schools slowly grew.

READING CHECK **Identifying Points of View** Why did some Americans call for new architectural styles and more education after the American Revolution?

ANALYSIS SKILL **ANALYZING INFORMATION**

How do these artistic developments show Americans' increasing sense of identity?

SUMMARY AND PREVIEW As the United States grew, so did a unique national identity. In Chapter 9 you will read about the changing face of American democracy.

Section 3 Assessment

go.hrw.com **Online Quiz** KEYWORD: SS8 HP8

Reviewing Ideas, Terms, and People HSS 8.4.4

1. a. **Describe** What topics interested American writers in the early 1800s?
   b. **Draw Conclusions** Why is **Washington Irving** considered an important American writer?
2. a. **Identify** What influence did **Thomas Cole** have on American painters?
   b. **Describe** How did American painting styles change from the early period to the mid-1800s?
3. a. **Describe** What effect did religious revivalism have on American music?
   b. **Elaborate** Why do you think folk songs like "Hunters of Kentucky" were popular?
4. a. **Identify** On what historical examples did many American architects model their buildings?
   b. **Predict** What might be some possible results of the growing interest in education in the United States?

Critical Thinking

5. **Categorizing** Copy the graphic organizer below and use it to identify the shared characteristics of the new American cultural identity that emerged in the early and mid-1800s.

Writers	
Painters	
Music	
Architecture	
Religion	

FOCUS ON WRITING

6. **Identifying Values** You can tell much about someone's values by what that person makes. For instance, you could guess that a person who creates a collage of personal mementos for a friend's birthday is creative and values personal relationships. As you read this section, make note of what the United States created and what it valued.

Direct Teach

Main Idea

4 Architecture and Education

Architecture and education were affected by cultural ideals.

Identify What are some features of the Greek and Roman architectural styles? *use of marble or other stone and large, stately columns*

Predict What issues do you think arose when people first proposed public education? *race, income, gender*

HSS 8.4.4; HSS **Analysis Skills:** HI 1

Review & Assess

Close

Have students summarize the many ways in which literature, art, and architecture combined to create a sense of national identity.

Review

Online Quiz Section 3

Assess

SE Section 3 Assessment

PASS: Section 3 Quiz

Alternative Assessment Handbook

Reteach-Classroom Intervention

California Standards Review Workbook

Interactive Reader and Study Guide, Section 3

Interactive Skills Tutor CD-ROM

Section 3 Assessment Answers

1. a. American history, the frontier
   b. bridge between European traditions and the new American style
2. a. founder of the Hudson River school; encouraged artists to concentrate on the beauty of nature
   b. from portraits, to landscapes, to landscape with scenes from daily life
3. a. led to the development of the spiritual form
   b. celebrated national pride
4. a. to show the link between American democracy and the ideals of Greece and Rome
   b. more colleges, equal rights movements
5. writers—American characteristics/settings; painters—pride in American landscape; music—faith, national pride; architecture—imitated Greece/Rome; religion—revivalism, renewed faith
6. possible answers—historical fiction, landscape art, spiritual and nationalist music, Roman and Greek architecture; valued self, religion, classical ideals

Answers

Analyzing Information *Americans were looking at their own wildlife, language, people, and landscapes for inspiration.*

Reading Check *wanted architecture similar to Greece and Rome, which provided the models for the U.S. political system; thought education was good for democracy*

Literature in History

The Last of the Mohicans

As You Read As students read, have them take notes on descriptive words and phrases they find that might describe Natty Bumppo, such as *sunburnt and long-faded complexion.* Then have students draw a picture or write a summary of Bumppo's characteristics based on the words they listed. Discuss with students why Bumppo's image appealed to American readers of the period.

Meet the Writer

James Fenimore Cooper Cooper's action-packed stories illustrated two distinct ways of life. He portrayed Native American life as free and respectful of nature. On the other hand, many Europeans in his stories were rule-driven and disrespectful of the environment. Cooper's works also showed concern for individual freedoms and property rights.

Did You Know . . .

Cooper's *Leather-Stocking Tales* follow Natty Bumppo from a young man to old age. In the order of the hero's life, they are: *The Deerslayer* (1841), *The Last of the Mohicans* (1826), *The Pathfinder* (1840), *The Pioneers* (1823), and *The Prairie* (1827).

Literature in History

Literature of the American Frontier

from *The Last of the Mohicans*

by James Fenimore Cooper (1789–1851)

About the Reading The Last of the Mohicans *is one of five novels known as the* Leatherstocking Tales. *These novels follow the life and adventures of American pioneer Natty Bumppo (also known as Leatherstocking, Hawkeye, and the Deerslayer). Bumppo is the perfect woodsman: resourceful, honest, kind to both his friends and his enemies, but always a loner at heart.*

AS YOU READ **Try to imagine what Natty Bumppo looks like.**

On that day, two men were lingering on the banks of a small but rapid stream . . . While one of these loiterers showed the red skin and wild accoutrements of a native of the woods, the other exhibited, through the mask of his rude and nearly savage equipments, the brighter though sunburnt and long-faded complexion of one who might claim descent from a European parentage. ❶

The frame of the white man, judging by such parts as were not concealed by his clothes, was like that of one who had known hardships and exertion from his earliest youth. His person, though muscular, was rather attenuated than full; but every nerve and muscle appeared strung and indurated by unremitted exposure and toil. He wore a hunting shirt of forest green, fringed with faded yellow, and a summer cap of skins which had been shorn of their fur. He also bore a knife in a girdle of wampum, ❷ like that which confined the scanty garments of the Indian, but no tomahawk. His moccasins were ornamented after the . . . fashion of the natives, while the only part of his underdress which appeared below the hunting frock was a pair of buckskin leggings that laced at the sides, and which were gartered above the knees with the sinews of a deer. A pouch and horn completed his personal accoutrements, though a rifle of great length, which the theory of the more ingenious whites had taught them was the most dangerous of all firearms, leaned against a neighboring sapling.

GUIDED READING

WORD HELP

accoutrements dress and gear
rude crude, rough
attenuated made thin
indurated hardened
unremitted ongoing
gartered fastened
ingenious clever

❶ ***What do you learn about Natty Bumppo in the first paragraph?***

❷ A "girdle of wampum" is a belt strung with beads. Wampum were used by Native Americans for both money and decoration.

Make a list of the items Bumppo wears and carries. What does each item suggest about him?

HSS 8.4.4 Discuss daily life, including traditions in art, music, and literature, of early national America (e.g., through writings by Washington Irving, James Fenimore Cooper).

ELA Reading 8.3.7 Analyze a work of literature, showing how it reflects heritage.

Differentiating Instruction for Universal Access

Learners Having Difficulty — Reaching Standards

Group Interpretation Organize the class into small groups and assign each group one of the selections to interpret in the students' own words. One member of each group should record the group's descriptions and organize them into a coherent summary. Have a volunteer from each group read the summary aloud. Discuss the differences in each group's interpretation.
LS Interpersonal, Verbal/Linguistic

HSS 8.4.4; HSS **Analysis Skills:** HR 3; ELA Reading 8.2.4, Writing 8.2.2

Advanced Learners/GATE — Exceeding Standards

Writing Historical Fiction Ask students to imagine that they are historical fiction writers like Cooper. Have students use a historical event in this chapter as the basis for a short story with fictional characters. Have students either briefly describe their story ideas or write their stories. Ask for volunteers to share their ideas or stories. Then discuss how historical fiction is a useful tool in studying history. **LS Verbal/Linguistic**

HSS 8.4.4; ELA Writing 8.2.2

Answers

Guided Reading 1. *has at least one Native American friend; likes spending time in nature; is of European descent;* **2.** *green hunting shirt (he hunts); cap of skins (he traps); a knife, a rifle, and a pouch and horn (he is resourceful and can protect himself); a girdle of wampums and moccasins (he trades or interacts with Native Americans); buckskin leggings (he travels through rough terrain)*

from *The Legend of Sleepy Hollow*

by Washington Irving (1783–1859)

About the Reading *"The Legend of Sleepy Hollow" has been called one of the first American short stories. Even though it is based on an old German folktale, its setting, a small village in the Hudson River valley, is American through and through. Irving's knack for capturing the look and the feel of the region made the story instantly popular—as did the tale's eerie central character, a horseman without a head.*

AS YOU READ **Try to picture both the ghost and the setting.**

The dominant spirit, however, that haunts this enchanted region, and seems to be commander in chief of all the powers of the air, is the apparition of a figure on horseback without a head. It is said by some to be the ghost of a Hessian trooper, ❶ whose head had been carried away by a cannon ball, in some nameless battle during the revolutionary war, and who is ever and anon seen by the country folk, hurrying along in the gloom of night, as if on the wings of the wind. His haunts are not confined to the valley, but extend at times to the adjacent roads, and especially to the vicinity of a church at no great distance. Indeed, certain of the most authentic historians of those parts, who have been careful in collecting and collating the floating facts concerning this spectre, allege, that the body of the trooper having been buried in the church yard, the ghost rides forth to the scene of battle in nightly quest of his head, ❷ and that the rushing speed with which he sometimes passes along the hollow, like a midnight blast, is owing to his being belated, and in a hurry to get back to the church yard before day break.

Such is the general purport of this legendary superstition, which has furnished materials for many a wild story in that region of shadows; and the spectre is known, at all the country firesides, by the name of The Headless Horseman of Sleepy Hollow. ❸

GUIDED READING

WORD HELP

dominant prevailing; ruling
apparition a ghostlike form that appears suddenly
collating comparing
spectre ghost
allege to firmly state
purport sense; gist

❶ A Hessian trooper is a German mercenary soldier from the American Revolution.

How and when is the horseman said to have died?

❷ ***Why does the horseman ride forth each night?***

❸ ***What is happening "at all the country firesides"? What does this suggest about how early Americans entertained themselves?***

CONNECTING LITERATURE TO HISTORY

1. **Drawing Inferences** The writing of the period reflects a new national culture and identity. What do these passages suggest about the thoughts, feelings, or lives of early Americans?
2. **Making Predictions** *The Last of the Mohicans* takes place during the French and Indian War. Whose side do you think Natty Bumppo would most likely take—that of the French and Indians, that of the English, or neither? Explain.
3. **Drawing Conclusions** Both of these stories were very popular in their time. Why do you think these stories were so popular? What is it about the stories that makes them entertaining?

Literature in History

The Legend of Sleepy Hollow

As You Read As students read, have them copy down words from the excerpt that set a spooky atmosphere, such as *spirit, haunts,* and *enchanted.* Inform students that legends and superstitions feed on common fears or traditional beliefs. Ask students for examples of superstitions they know. Then lead a discussion on why superstitions helped make *The Legend of Sleepy Hollow* so popular.

Meet the Writer

Washington Irving During his lifetime, Irving was also a lawyer, businessman, and a U.S. diplomat to England and Spain. His true passion was writing, however. He devoted himself entirely to writing in 1817. Unfavorable reviews of his *Tales of a Traveller* (1824) led him to give up writing fiction, though. He instead wrote histories and biographies until his death. His grave, fittingly, is in the Sleepy Hollow Cemetery and is now a national historic landmark.

Critical Thinking: Evaluating Information

Standards Proficiency

Literary Biographical Posters

Research Required

1. Have students use the library or the Internet to conduct research on Cooper, Irving, or another writer covered in this chapter.
2. Students should write three to four questions about the selected author that they would like to answer through their research. Students should then use the questions to guide their research.
3. Have each student use the information to create a poster that shows an image of the writer, gives a short biographical description, and provides a listing of the writer's most well-known works. **LS Verbal/Linguistic**

Alternative Assessment Handbook, Rubric 28: Posters; and 30: Research

HSS 8.4.4; **HSS Analysis Skills:** HR 1, HI 1

Answers

Guided Reading **1.** *A cannon ball knocked off his head during the Revolutionary War;* **2.** *to look for his head;* **3.** *People tell stories about the headless horseman; Early Americans shared stories around their campfires as a means of entertainment.*

Connecting Literature to History
1. *possible answer—*Mohicans *suggests that Americans viewed the frontier and those who lived there as wild and untamed.* Sleepy Hollow *suggests that Americans loved to hear and to tell imaginative stories with a basis in history;* **2.** *possible answer—French and Indian side, because he seems to have a strong relationship with the Native Americans;* **3.** *possible answers—popular because early Americans could see themselves in the stories, helped shape their national image; entertaining because stories showed the exciting and sometimes mysterious side of the New World*

Social Studies Skills

Identifying Central Issues

Activity Central Issues in the Community Write the following statement for students to see: *The school district's budget will be cut $300,000 next year.* Tell students this statement is hypothetical. Ask students to identify the most important questions and concerns that people might have in response to this news. Responses might include the following: What will the schools have to cut to lower their budgets—such as teachers, textbooks, art classes, and so on? Will classes be bigger? Will extracurricular activities be cut? Will free lunches be cut? After a brief period of discussion, ask students to identify what all these concerns have in common. Lead students to realize that the central issue involved is how will budget cuts affect educational quality and school life. To extend the activity, have students practice the skill on an article from their school or local newspaper. **LS Logical/Mathematical**

Alternative Assessment Handbook, Rubric 11: Discussions

Interactive Skills Tutor CD-ROM: Lesson 12: Identify Issues and Problems

HSS Analysis Skills: HI 1

Social Studies Skills

Analysis | Critical Thinking | Participation | Study

HI1 Students explain the central issues of the past.

Identifying Central Issues

Define the Skill

The reasons for historical events are often complex and difficult to determine. An accurate understanding of them requires the ability to identify the central issues involved. A *central issue* is the main topic of concern in a discussion or dispute. In history, these issues are usually matters of public debate or concern. They generally involve political, social, moral, economic, or territorial matters.

Being able to identify central issues lets you go beyond what the participants in an event said and gain a more accurate understanding of it. The skill also useful for understanding issues today, and for the evaluating statements of those involved.

Learn the Skill

In this chapter you learned about dispute that arose over Missouri's admission to the Union. Yet that was not what this controversy was really about. Recognizing the central issue in this dispute helps you understand why each side fought so hard over just one state.

Use the following steps to identify central issues when you read about historical events.

1. Identify the main subject of the information.
2. Determine the nature and purpose of what you are reading. Is it a primary source or a secondary one? Why has the information been provided?
3. Find the strongest or most forceful phrases or statements in the material. These are often clues to the issues or ideas the speaker or writer thinks most central or important.
4. Determine how the information might be connected to the major events or controversies that were concerning the nation at the time.

Practice the Skill

Soon after the Missouri Compromise passed, Secretary of State John Quincy Adams wrote:

> "The impression produced upon my mind by the progress of this discussion [the dispute over Missouri] is that the bargain between freedom and slavery contained in the Constitution . . . is morally and politically vicious, . . . cruel and oppressive. . . . I have favored this Missouri Compromise, believing it to be all that can be effected [accomplished] under the present Constitution, and from an extreme unwillingness to put the Union at hazard [risk]. But perhaps it would have been a . . . bolder course to have persisted in the restriction upon Missouri till it should have terminated [ended] in a convention of the states to . . . amend the Constitution. This would have produced a new Union of thirteen or fourteen states unpolluted with slavery. . . . If the Union must be dissolved, slavery is precisely the question upon which it ought to break. For the present, however, this contest [issue] is laid to sleep."

Apply the steps to identifying central issues to analyze Adams's statement and answer the following questions

1. About what subject was Adams writing? What was his reason for making these remarks?
2. What did Adams believe was the most important issue in the dispute? What strong language does he use to indicate this?
3. What evidence suggests Adams did not think the breakup of the Union the central issue?

Answers

Practice the Skill 1. *Missouri Compromise; to discuss why he supported the Missouri Compromise and to explain his views on the issues involved;* **2.** *the issue of slavery; "that the bargain between freedom and slavery contained in the Constitution . . . is morally and politically vicious, . . . cruel and oppressive. . . ." and "if the Union must be dissolved, slavery is precisely the question upon which it ought to break."* **3.** *his comment about what might have been a bolder course of action, which might have produced a new Union of fewer states in which slavery was banned*

Social Studies Skills Activity: Identifying Central Issues

Guided and Independent Practice

HSS Analysis Skills: HI 1 **Standards Proficiency**

1. Have volunteers read aloud the Section 1 text titled "United States Gains Florida."
2. Have students work as a class to go through the four steps listed under "Learn the Skill" to identify the central issues in this text. *(In this text, the central issues were the disagreements between the United States and Spain over American settlement and actions in Florida.)*
3. Then assign students the text in Section 1 titled "Monroe Doctrine." Have students work independently to identify the central foreign policy issue dealt with by the doctrine. Discuss the answer as a class. *(President Monroe wanted to prevent European nations from gaining control of newly independent Latin American countries, protect American interests, and avoid wars with Europe.)* **LS Verbal/Linguistic**

Alternative Assessment Handbook, Rubric 1: Acquiring Information

CHAPTER 8

Standards Review

Visual Summary

Use the visual summary below to help you review the main ideas of the chapter.

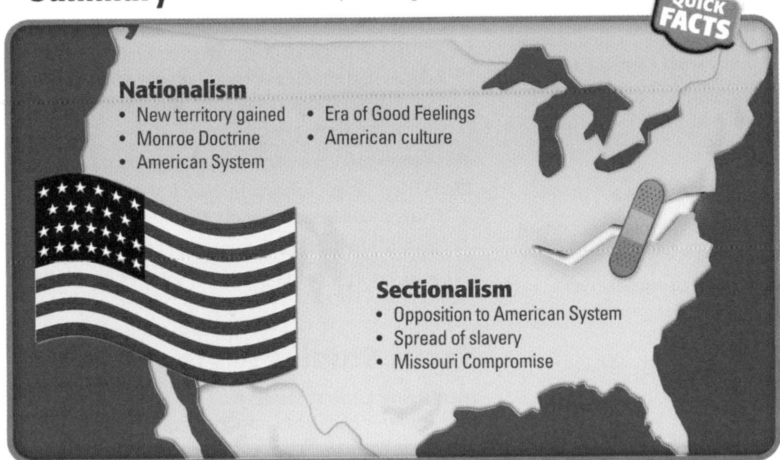

Reviewing Vocabulary, Terms, and People

Match the word in the left column with the correct definition in the right column.

1. American System
2. George Caleb Bingham
3. Simon Bolívar
4. Henry Clay
5. Erie Canal
6. Hudson River school
7. James Monroe
8. Monroe Doctrine
9. nationalism
10. Rush-Bagot Agreement

a. an agreement that limited naval power on the Great Lakes for both the United States and British Canada

b. American artist known for his focus on the American landscape and people

c. sense of pride and devotion to a nation

d. a group of American artists in the mid-1800s who focused on the American landscape

e. a leader of independence movements in Latin America, known as the Liberator

f. the plan to raise tariffs in order to finance internal improvements such as roads and canals

g. president who promoted the acquisition of Florida, closer ties to Latin America, and presided during the Era of Good Feelings

h. project that connected the Hudson River to Lake Erie and improved trade and transportation

i. representative from Kentucky who promoted improvements in transportation and the Missouri Compromise

j. U.S. declaration that any attempt by a foreign nation to establish colonies in the Americas would be viewed as a hostile act

Answers

Visual Summary

Review and Inquiry Have students use the Visual Summary to review the chapter's key terms and ideas. Be sure students understand the symbolism of both the flag and the bandage in the image.

Quick Facts Transparency: A New National Identity Visual Summary

Reviewing Vocabulary, Terms, and People

1. f
2. b
3. e
4. i
5. h
6. d
7. g
8. j
9. c
10. a

Review and Assessment Resources

Review and Reinforce

SE Standards Review

CRF: Chapter Review Activity

California Standards Review Workbook

Quick Facts Transparency: A New National Identity Visual Summary

Spanish Chapter Summaries Audio CD Program

Online Chapter Summaries in Six Languages

OSP Holt PuzzlePro; GameTool for ExamView

Quiz Game CD-ROM

Assess

SE Standards Assessment

PASS: Chapter Test, Forms A and B

Alternative Assessment Handbook

OSP ExamView Test Generator, Chapter Test

Universal Access Modified Worksheets and Tests CD-ROM: Chapter Test

Holt Online Assessment Program (in the Premier Online Edition)

Reteach/Intervene

Interactive Reader and Study Guide

Universal Access Teacher Management System: Lesson Plans for Universal Access

Universal Access Modified Worksheets and Tests CD-ROM

Interactive Skills Tutor CD-ROM

go.hrw.com
Online Resources
Chapter Resources:
KEYWORD: SS8 US8

Answers

Comprehension and Critical Thinking

11. a. (1) United States would not interfere in European affairs or wars; (2) United States would recognize existing colonies in Americas; (3) Americas were off limits to future colonization; (4) United States would treat interference in Latin American countries as a threat and respond accordingly.
b. agreed to Rush-Bagot Agreement, which limited naval power on the Great Lakes, set the boundary at the 49th parallel, and shared the fur trade in the Northwest
c. possible answer: Monroe Doctrine—established the United States as the main power in the Western Hemisphere

12. a. territories gained; roads and canals built
b. northern and southern members of Congress disagreed about whether to admit Missouri to the Union as a slave state; agreed to the Missouri Compromise, which brought in Missouri as a slave state and Maine as a free state.
c. possible answer—might have weakened national unity and faith in democracy

13. a. Spirituals reflected the emphasis on religion; folk music reflected an interest in American heroes.
b. American artists and writers wanted cultural independence and a separate identity from Europe.
c. possible answer: art—prefer landscapes to portraits

Reviewing Themes

14. Success made Americans proud of their country and its leadership.

15. desire to show the country's uniqueness, rising nationalism, and improvements in education

Using the Internet

16. Go to the HRW Web site and enter the keyword shown to access a rubric for this activity.

KEYWORD: SS8 US8

Comprehension and Critical Thinking

SECTION 1 *(Pages 260–263)* **HSS 8.4.1, 8.5.2**

11. a. Identify What were the four main points of the Monroe Doctrine?
b. Draw Conclusions How did the United States compromise in its disputes with British Canada?
c. Evaluate Which of the issues that the United States faced with foreign nations do you think was most important? Why?

SECTION 2 *(Pages 264–267)* **HSS 8.4.1, 8.6.2**

12. a. Recall What developments helped strengthen national unity in this period?
b. Analyze How was the disagreement over Missouri's statehood an example of sectionalism? How was the disagreement resolved?
c. Predict What effect might the election of 1824 have on national unity? Why?

SECTION 3 *(Pages 270–273)* **HSS 8.4.4**

13. a. Describe How did popular music show the interests of Americans in the early 1800s?
b. Make Inferences Why do you think new American styles of art and literature emerged?
c. Elaborate Which element of American culture of the early 1800s do you find most appealing? Why?

Reviewing Themes

14. Politics How did the relations of the United States with foreign nations lead to a rise in nationalism?

15. Society and Culture What led to the creation of a uniquely American culture?

Using the Internet

16. Activity: Researching In this chapter, you learned about the development of a new, creative spirit in American arts. Artists created works that featured American scenes and characters. Enter the activity keyword and research the development of American culture in art and literature. Then create a visual display.

Reading Skills

Understanding Semantic Slanting *Use the Reading Skills taught in this chapter to answer the question about the reading selection below.*

> When the House chose John Quincy Adams as president, Jackson's supporters claimed that Adams had made a corrupt bargain with Henry Clay. These accusations grew after Adams chose Clay to be secretary of state. *(p. 267)*

17. Which of the following used a slanted definition, according to the above selection?
a. Andrew Jackson
b. supporters of Jackson
c. Henry Clay
d. John Quincy Adams

Social Studies Skills

Identifying Central Issues *Use the Social Studies Skills taught in this chapter to answer the question about the reading selection below.*

> [Henry Clay] developed a plan that came to be known as the American System—a series of measures intended to make the United States economically self-sufficient. To build the economy, he pushed for a national bank that would provide a single currency, making interstate trade easier. Clay wanted the money from a protective tariff to be used to improve roads and canals. *(p. 264)*

18. Which of the following is the central issue addressed by the American System?
a. economic unity
b. protective tariff
c. national bank
d. improving roads and canals

FOCUS ON WRITING

19. Writing a Character Sketch Write a paragraph describing your overall impression of the nation's character. Write one sentence describing each of these aspects of the United States: its relationships with others, its feelings about itself, and its values.

Reading Skills

17. b

Social Studies Skills

18. a

Focus on Writing

19. Rubric Students' character sketches should:
- start with an overall impression of the nation.
- describe the nation's relationships with others, feelings about itself, and values.
- use proper grammar, punctuation, spelling, and capitalization.

CRF: Focus on Writing Activity: A Character Sketch

Standards Assessment

DIRECTIONS: Read each question and write the letter of the best response.

1 Use the map to answer the following question.

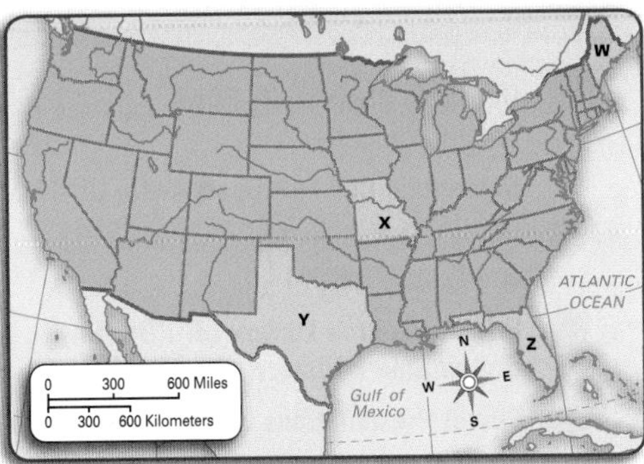

The present-day state that became part of the United States in the Adams-Onís Treaty of 1819 is shown on the map by the letter

A W.
B X.
C Y.
D Z.

2 The principle that European nations could establish no more colonies in North and South America was set forth in the

A Missouri Compromise.
B Rush-Bagot Agreement.
C Monroe Doctrine.
D Convention of 1818.

3 The Missouri Compromise had a significant effect on the United States because it

A established the present border with Canada.
B prohibited slavery north of Missouri's southern border.
C led to the expansion of roads and canals.
D settled conflicts between Native Americans in the West and the federal government.

4 Greek- and Roman-style architecture became common in the United States in the early 1800s because of

A the popularity of President George Washington, who liked the building style.
B Americans' admiration for the ideals of Greek democracy and republicanism.
C the nation's desire to build as strong a military as the Greeks and Romans had.
D Americans' great feeling of nationalism after the War of 1812.

5 Which painting would have been typical of an artist of the Hudson River school in the 1830s and 1840s?

A a portrait of a famous American
B a Native American hunting game
C a portrait of an ancient Greek or Roman lawmaker
D a scene showing America's natural beauty

Connecting with Past Learning

6 Which person that you learned about in Grade 7 made a contribution to his or her society similar to James Fenimore Cooper's contribution to American society?

A Constantine
B Lady Murasaki Shikibu
C Mansa Musa
D Confucius

Answers

1. D
Break Down the Question Students need to recall information and recognize Florida on a map. Refer students who miss the question to the material "United States Gains Florida" and the map "U.S. Boundary Changes, 1818–1819" in Section 1.

2. C
Break Down the Question This question requires students to recall factual information. Students should use a process of elimination to answer the question. Refer students who miss the question to the material "Monroe Doctrine" in Section 1.

3. C
Break Down the Question This question requires students to recall cause and effect. Refer students who miss the question to the material "Missouri Compromise" in Section 2.

4. B
Break Down the Question Although A, C, and D may *seem* correct to students who do not recall the material completely, these distracters are incorrect. Refer students who miss the question to the material "Architecture and Education" in Section 3.

5. D
Break Down the Question This question requires students to recall factual information. Refer students who miss the question to the material "A New Style of Art" in Section 3.

6. B
Break Down the Question This question requires students to recall information covered in grade 7.

Intervention Resources

Reproducible

- Interactive Reader and Study Guide
- Universal Access Teacher Management System: Lesson Plans for Universal Access

Technology

- Quick Facts Transparency: A New National Identity Visual Summary
- Universal Access Modified Worksheets and Tests CD-ROM
- Interactive Skills Tutor CD-ROM

Tips for Test Taking

How Much Do I Write? If an open-ended question contains one of the following terms, then students will probably need to write several sentences to provide a complete answer.

- defend
- describe
- explain
- justify
- why
- write

Remind students that they can also provide drawings or sketches to enhance what they write.

Standards Review

Have students review the following standards in their workbooks.

California Standards Review Workbook: HSS 8.4.2, 8.4.4, 8.6.2

Chapter 9 Planning Guide

The Age of Jackson

Chapter Overview	Reproducible Resources	Technology Resources
CHAPTER 9 **pp. 280–303** **Overview: In this chapter, students will study the presidency of Andrew Jackson, the increased conflict between the northern and southern states that marked his administration, and Jackson's policies toward Native Americans.** See p. 280 for the California History–Social Science standards covered in this chapter.	**Universal Access Teacher Management System:*** • Universal Access Instructional Benchmarking Guides • Lesson Plans for Universal Access **Interactive Reader and Study Guide:*** Chapter Graphic Organizer **Chapter Resource File*** • Focus on Writing Activity: An Interview • Social Studies Skills Activity: Solving Problems • Chapter Review Activity	**One-Stop Planner CD-ROM:** Calendar Planner **Student Edition Full-Read Audio CD-ROM** **Universal Access Modified Worksheets and Tests CD-ROM** **Primary Source Library CD-ROM for United States History** **Power Presentations with Video CD-ROM** **History's Impact: United States History Video Program (VHS/DVD):** The Age of Jackson*
Section 1: **Jacksonian Democracy** **The Big Idea:** The expansion of voting rights and the election of Andrew Jackson signaled the growing power of the American people. 8.8.1	**Universal Access Teacher Management System:*** Section 1 Lesson Plan **Interactive Reader and Study Guide:*** Section 1 Summary **Chapter Resource File*** • Vocabulary Builder, Section 1	**Daily Bellringer Transparency:** Section 1*
Section 2: **Jackson's Administration** **The Big Idea:** Andrew Jackson's presidency was marked by political conflicts. 8.10.1, 8.10.3	**Universal Access Teacher Management System:*** Section 2 Lesson Plan **Interactive Reader and Study Guide:*** Section 2 Summary **Chapter Resource File*** • Vocabulary Builder, Section 2 • Biography Activity: John C. Calhoun • Biography Activity: Daniel Webster • Economics and History Activity: The Panic of 1837 • Primary Source Activity: President Jackson's Proclamation Regarding Nullification • Primary Source Activity: The Bank War of 1832 **Political Cartoons Activities for United States History,** Cartoon 11: Jackson and the Bank* **U.S. Supreme Court Case Studies:** *McCulloch* v. *Maryland**	**Daily Bellringer Transparency:** Section 2* **Quick Facts Transparency:** Regions of the United States, Early 1800s* go.hrw.com **Internet Activity:** Calhoun and Webster Debate Nullification
Section 3: **Indian Removal** **The Big Idea:** President Jackson supported a policy of Indian removal. HSS 8.8.1	**Universal Access Teacher Management System:*** Section 3 Lesson Plan **Interactive Reader and Study Guide:*** Section 3 Summary **Chapter Resource File*** • Vocabulary Builder, Section 3 • Biography Activities: Black Hawk; Sequoya • History and Geography Activity: The Seminole Wars • Literature Activity: *Surrender Speech* by Chief Black Hawk **U.S. Supreme Court Case Studies:** *Worchester* v. *Georgia* (1832)*	**Daily Bellringer Transparency:** Section 3* **Map Transparency:** Second Seminole War* go.hrw.com **Internet Activity:** Indian Removal

SE Student Edition  Print Resource  Audio CD Video

TE Teacher's Edition  Transparency  CD-ROM DVD

go.hrw.com CA Standards Mastery **LS** Learning Styles

OSP One-Stop Planner CD-ROM * also on One-Stop Planner CD

Review, Assessment, Intervention

- **Standards Review Workbook***
-  **Quick Facts Transparency:** The Age of Jackson Visual Summary*
- **Spanish Chapter Summaries Audio CD Program**
- **Online Chapter Summaries in Six Languages**
- **Quiz Game CD-ROM**
- **Progress Assessment Support System (PASS):** Chapter Test*
- **Universal Access Modified Worksheets and Tests CD-ROM:** Modified Chapter Test
- **One-Stop Planner CD-ROM:** ExamView Test Generator (English/Spanish)

- **PASS:** Section 1 Quiz*
-  **Online Quiz:** Section 1
-  **Alternative Assessment Handbook**

-  **PASS:** Section 2 Quiz*
-  **Online Quiz:** Section 2
- **Alternative Assessment Handbook**

-  **PASS:** Section 3 Quiz*
-  **Online Quiz:** Section 3
- **Alternative Assessment Handbook**

California Resources for Standards Mastery

INSTRUCTIONAL PLANNING AND SUPPORT

- **Universal Access Teacher Management System***
- **One-Stop Planner CD-ROM with Test Generator: Teacher Management System with Interactive Teacher's Edition** 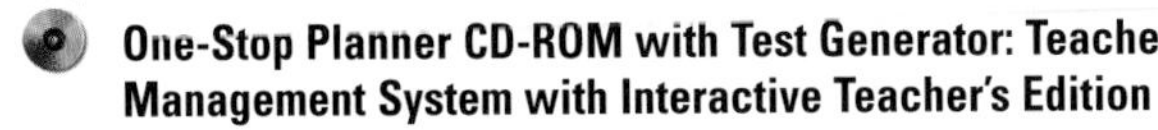

STANDARDS MASTERY

-  **Standards Review Workbook***
- **At Home: A Guide to Standards Mastery for United States History**

Holt Online Learning

To enhance learning, Internet activities are available for Calhoun and Webster Debate Nullification and Indian Removal.

KEYWORD: SS8 TEACHER

- **Teacher Support Page**
- **Content Updates**
- **Rubrics and Writing Models**
- **Teaching Tips for the Multimedia Classroom**

KEYWORD: SS8 US9

- **Current Events**
- **Document-Based Questions**
- **Holt Grapher**
- **Holt Online Atlas**
- **Holt Researcher**
- **Interactive Multimedia Activities**
- **Internet Activities**
- **Online Chapter Summaries in Six Languages**
- **Online Section Quizzes**
- **American History Maps and Charts**

HOLT PREMIER ONLINE STUDENT EDITION

Complete online support for interactivity, assessment, and reporting

- **Interactive Maps and Notebook**
- **Standardized Test Prep**
- **Homework Practice and Research Activities Online**

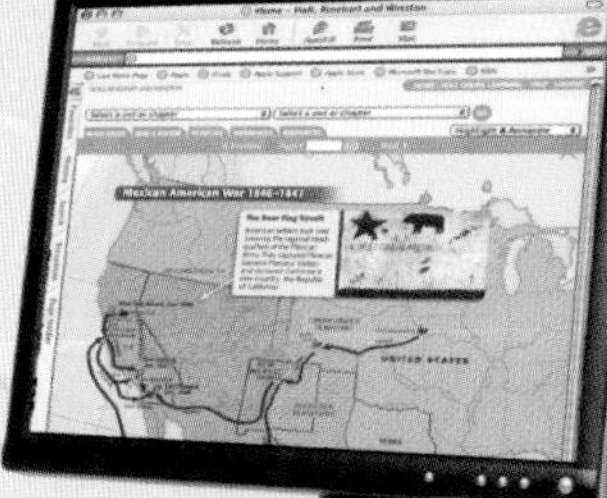

Mastering the Standards: Differentiating Instruction

Reaching Standards	Basic-level activities designed for all students encountering new material
Standards Proficiency	Intermediate-level activities designed for average students
Exceeding Standards	Challenging activities designed for honors and gifted-and-talented students
Standard English Mastery	Activities designed to improve standard English usage

Frequently Asked Questions

INSTRUCTIONAL PLANNING AND SUPPORT

Where do I find planning aids, pacing guides, lesson plans, and other teaching aids?

Annotated Teacher's Edition:
- Chapter planning guides
- Standards-based instruction and strategies
- Differentiated instruction for universal access
- Point-of-use reminders for integrating program resources

Power Presentations with Video CD-ROM

Universal Access Teacher Management System:
- Year and unit instructional benchmarking guides
- Reproducible lesson plans
- Assessment guides for diagnostic, progress, and summative end-of-the-year tests
- Options for differentiating instruction and intervention
- Teaching guides and answer keys for student workbooks

One-Stop Planner CD-ROM with Test Generator: Teacher Management System with Interactive Teacher's Editon:
- Calendar Planner
- Editable lesson plans
- All reproducible ancillaries in Adobe Acrobat (PDF) format
- ExamView Test Generator (English & Spanish)
- Game Tool for ExamView
- PuzzlePro
- Transparency and video previews

DIFFERENTIATING INSTRUCTION FOR UNIVERSAL ACCESS

What resources are available to ensure that Advanced Learners/GATE Students master the standards?

Teacher's Edition Activities:
- Election of 1828 Political Advertisements, p. 285
- Jackson's Memoirs, p. 291
- Speech Opposing Indian Removal Act, p. 295

Lesson Plans for Universal Access

Primary Source Library CD-ROM for United States History

What resources are available to ensure that English Learners and Standard English Learners master the standards?

Teacher's Edition Activities:

Lesson Plans for Universal Access

Chapter Resource File: Vocabulary Builder Activities

Spanish Chapter Summaries Audio CD Program

Online Chapter Summaries in Six Languages

One-Stop Planner CD-ROM:
- PuzzlePro, Spanish Version
- ExamView Test Generator, Spanish Version

What modified materials are available for Special Education?

The ***Universal Access Modified Worksheets and Tests CD-ROM*** provides editable versions of the following:

Vocabulary Flash Cards

Modified Vocabulary Builder Activities

Modified Chapter Review Activity

Modified Chapter Test

HOLT **History's Impact**
▶ video series
The Age of Jackson

What resources are available to ensure that Learners Having Difficulty master the standards?

Teacher's Edition Activities:
- Regional Views on Issues, p. 289

Interactive Reader and Study Guide

Student Edition Full-Read Audio CD

Quick Facts Transparency: The Age of Jackson Visual Summary

Standards Review Workbook

Social Studies Skills Activity: Solving Problems

Interactive Skills Tutor CD-ROM

How do I intervene for students struggling to master the standards?

Interactive Reader and Study Guide

Quick Facts Transparency: The Age of Jackson Visual Summary

California Standards Review Workbook

Social Studies Skills Activity: Solving Problems

Interactive Skills Tutor CD-ROM

PROFESSIONAL DEVELOPMENT

What teacher training resources are available to help me grow professionally?

- In-service and staff development as part of your Holt Social Studies product purchase
- Quick Teacher Tutorial Lesson Presentation CD-ROM
- Intensive tuition-based Teacher Development Institute
- *Teaching American History* Online 2 Module Professional Development Course
- Convenient Holt Speaker Bureau face-to-face workshop options
- PRAXIS™ Test Prep (#0089) interactive Web-based content refreshers*
- 24/7 *Ask A Professional Development Expert* at http://www.hrw.com/prodev/

* PRAXIS is a trademark of Educational Testing Service (ETS). This publication is not endorsed or approved by ETS.

Information Literacy Skills

To learn more about how History–Social Science instruction may be improved by the effective use of library media centers and information literacy skills, go to the Teacher's Resource Materials for Chapter 9 at **go.hrw.com**, keyword: SS8 MEDIA.

The following materials were developed by the Division for Public Education of the American Bar Association. These materials are part of the **Democracy and Civic Education** supplement.
- Constitution Study Guide
- Supreme Court Case Studies

Chapter Preview

Standards Focus

Standards by Section
Section 1: HSS 8.8.1
Section 2: HSS 8.4.3, 8.10.1, 8.10.3
Section 3: HSS 8.8.1

Teacher's Edition
HSS **Analysis Skills:** CS 1, CS 3, HR 4, HR 5, HI 1, HI 2, HI 3, HI 5, HI 6
ELA Listening and Speaking 1.1.2, 2.24; Writing 8.2.5.a; Reading 8.2.0

Preview Grade 8 Standards
HSS **8.8** Students analyze the divergent paths of the American people in the West from 1800 to the mid-1800s and the challenges they faced.
8.8.2 Describe the purpose, challenges, and economic incentives associated with westward expansion, including the concept of Manifest Destiny (e.g., the Lewis and Clark expedition, accounts of the removal of Indians, the Cherokees' "Trail of Tears," settlement of the Great Plains), and the territorial acquisitions that spanned numerous decades.

Focus on Writing

The **Chapter Resource File** provides a Focus on Writing worksheet to help students organize and write their interviews.

CRF: Focus on Writing Activity: An Interview

CHAPTER 9 1828–1840

The Age of Jackson

California Standards

History–Social Science

8.4 Students analyze the aspirations and ideals of the people of the new nation.

8.8 Students analyze the divergent paths of the American people in the West from 1800 to the mid-1800s and the challenges they faced.

8.10 Students analyze the multiple causes, key events, and complex consequences of the Civil War.

English–Language Arts

Writing 8.2.5.a Present information purposefully and succinctly and meet the needs of the intended audience.

Reading 8.2.0 Students read and understand grade-level appropriate material.

FOCUS ON WRITING

An Interview You are a reporter for a large city newspaper in the year 1837. Andrew Jackson has just left office, and you have been given the assignment of interviewing him about his presidency and his role in American politics. As you read this chapter, you will write interview questions for your interview with Jackson.

UNITED STATES

1828
Andrew Jackson is elected president.

Sequoya finishes a written language for the Cherokee.

1830

WORLD

1829
Louis Braille publishes a reading system for the blind.

Introduce the Chapter

Standards Proficiency

A Controversial Character HSS 8.8.1

1. Tell students that they are going to learn about the presidency of Andrew Jackson, a strong man who often found himself in disagreements with others on national issues.
2. Ask students to scan the chapter and examine the section titles, major headings, photographs, maps, and charts. Have students identify some of the controversial actions taken by Jackson. Make a list of students' responses for the class to see.
3. Explain to students that previewing a text can help them familiarize themselves with what they are about to read and make it easier to learn. Have students copy the list of topics they suggested and then jot down anything they learned about them based on their preview of the chapter. Next, have students write any questions they have about the text.
4. Tell students to add information to their lists and to answer their questions as they read the chapter. LS **Verbal/Linguistic, Visual/Spatial**

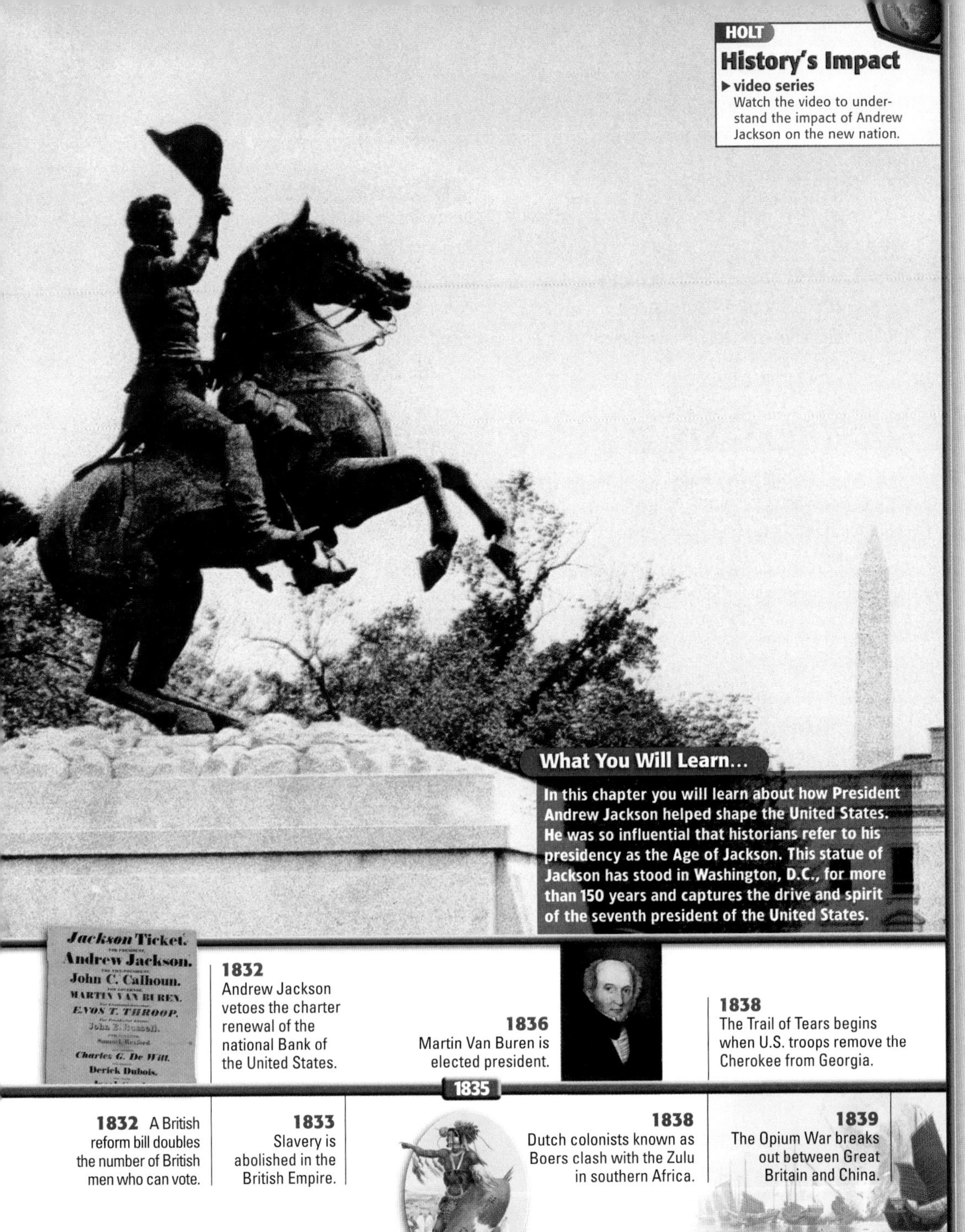

HOLT
History's Impact
▶ video series
Watch the video to understand the impact of Andrew Jackson on the new nation.
What You Will Learn...
In this chapter you will learn about how President Andrew Jackson helped shape the United States. He was so influential that historians refer to his presidency as the Age of Jackson. This statue of Jackson has stood in Washington, D.C., for more than 150 years and captures the drive and spirit of the seventh president of the United States.
Jackson Ticket.
Andrew Jackson.
John C. Calhoun.
1832 Andrew Jackson vetoes the charter renewal of the national Bank of the United States.
1836 Martin Van Buren is elected president.
1838 The Trail of Tears begins when U.S. troops remove the Cherokee from Georgia.
1835
1832 A British reform bill doubles the number of British men who can vote.
1833 Slavery is abolished in the British Empire.
1838 Dutch colonists known as Boers clash with the Zulu in southern Africa.
1839 The Opium War breaks out between Great Britain and China.
281

• Chapter Preview •

HOLT

History's Impact

▶ **video series**

See the Video Teacher's Guide for strategies for using the chapter video **The Age of Jackson**.

Chapter Big Ideas

Section 1 The expansion of voting rights and the election of Andrew Jackson signaled the growing power of the American people. **HSS** 8.8.1

Section 2 Andrew Jackson's presidency was marked by political conflicts. **HSS** 8.4.3, 8.10.1, 8.10.3

Section 3 President Jackson supported a policy of Indian removal. **HSS** 8.8.1

Explore the Picture

Statue of Andrew Jackson The statue of Andrew Jackson pictured at left stands in the center of Lafayette Park in Washington, D.C. The statue honors Jackson's leadership in the Battle of New Orleans during the War of 1812. Cast by sculptor Clark Mills, the statue was made from a bronze cannon captured during Jackson's last campaign against the Spanish in Florida. As the first equestrian statue in the United States, it is remarkable for its perfect balance, with the center of gravity based in the horse's hind feet.

Analyzing Visuals What details in the statue symbolize Jackson's drive and spirit? *possible answers—the way in which he is tipping his hat in salute; his upright mount on the rearing horse, which suggests strength and determination*

Explore the Time Line

1. In what year was Andrew Jackson elected president? *1828*
2. What did Andrew Jackson veto in 1832? *charter of the Bank of the United States*
3. What is the Trail of Tears, and when did it begin? *U.S. troops' removal of Cherokee from Georgia, which began in 1838*
4. What major contribution did Sequoya make, and when? *developed a written language for the Cherokee in 1828*

HSS Analysis Skills: CS 1

Info to Know

Jackson's Veto Power Andrew Jackson referred to the Second Bank of the United States as the "monster bank" and viewed it as a pawn of the rich and powerful in the eastern states. Jackson's 1832 veto of the charter of the Bank was only one among many vetoes he made in his quest to be a president for the poor rather than the rich.

go.hrw.com

Online Resources

Chapter Resources:
KEYWORD: SS8 US9

Teacher Resources:
KEYWORD: SS8 TEACHER

Reading Social Studies

Understanding Themes

Introduce the main themes from this chapter—economics and politics—by asking students to explain how politics and economics might be intertwined. Help students to see that political decisions are sometimes based on economic factors. For example Northerners felt that tariffs would benefit manufacturing, therefore the federal government passed the so-called Tariff of Abominations. Ask students to think of situations in which political decisions might have an effect on economic conditions.

Drawing Conclusions about the Past

Focus on Reading Have students practice the skill of drawing conclusions. Ask students to bring in a newspaper or magazine article on a subject of interest to them. Then have each student read his or her article and select one or two paragraphs over which to make inferences. Have students write down several facts from their articles. Then have students write down two or three inferences based on those facts. Lastly, have students draw sound conclusions from their facts and inferences. Ask students to exchange papers and analyze their partner's conclusions.

Reading Social Studies

by Kylene Beers

Economics | Geography | Politics | Religion | Society and Culture | Science and Technology

Focus on Themes In this chapter you will read about the events that shaped the United States from 1828-1838. You will see how **political** and **economic** decisions were intertwined. For instance, you will read about the tensions between southern and northern states over tariff regulations. You will also read about the forced relocation of many Native Americans to the West. Understanding how economic issues led to political decisions will help you understand this time.

Drawing Conclusions about the Past

Focus on Reading Writers don't always tell you everything you need to know about a subject. Sometimes you need to think critically about what they have said and see what it all adds up to.

Drawing Conclusions Earlier in this book you learned how to make inferences. Sometimes when you read, you will need to make several inferences and put them together. The result is a **conclusion**, an informed judgment that you make by combining information.

Additional reading support can be found in the Interactive Reader and Study Guide

Election of 1828

The 1828 campaign focused a great deal on the candidates' personalities. Jackson's campaigners described him as a war hero. They said he had been born poor and rose to success through his own hard work.

Adams was a Harvard graduate whose father had been the second U.S. president. Jackson's supporters described Adams as being out of touch with everyday people . . . When the ballots were counted, Jackson had defeated Adams, winning a record number of popular votes. *(pp. 285–286)*

Inference: Jackson shared many qualities with American voters.

\+

Inference: Adams enjoyed many privileges that most Americans did not.

\+

Inference: Jackson easily won the election by a huge majority.

Conclusion: In 1828, Americans chose a president to whom they could relate.

Reading and Skills Resources

Reading Support

- Interactive Reader and Study Guide
- Student Edition on Audio CD
- Spanish Chapter Summaries Audio CD Program

Social Studies Skills Support

- Interactive Skills Tutor CD-ROM

Vocabulary Support

- **CRF:** Vocabulary Builder Activities
- **CRF:** Chapter Review Activity
- Universal Access Modified Worksheets and Tests CD-ROM:
  - Vocabulary Flash Cards
  - Vocabulary Builder Activity
  - Chapter Review Activity
- OSP Holt PuzzlePro

Standards Focus

ELA Reading 8.2.0

ELA Reading 8.2.0 Students read and understand grade-level appropriate material.

You Try It!

The following passage is from the chapter you are getting ready to read. As you read the passage, look for the facts of the situation.

The Election of 1834

In 1834 a new political party formed to oppose Jackson. Its members called themselves Whigs, after an English political party that opposed the monarchy to make the point that Jackson was using his power like a king. The Whig Party favored the idea of a weak president and a strong Congress. Unable to agree on a presidential candidate, the Whigs nominated four men to run against Vice President Martin Van Buren. With strong backing from Jackson, Van Buren won the election.

From Chapter 9, p. 292

After you read the passage, answer the following questions.

1. From this passage, what can you infer about President Jackson's popularity with the Whig Party?
2. The Whigs could not choose a single presidential candidate, so they nominated four men. Based on what you know about elections from your studies and your past experiences, how do you think this affected the votes each man received?
3. Jackson's backing helped Van Buren win the presidency. From this, what can you infer about Jackson's popularity with the American people as a whole?
4. Using the inferences you made answering questions 1 through 3, draw a conclusion about why Van Buren won the election of 1834.

Key Terms and People

Chapter 9

Section 1

nominating conventions *(p. 285)*
Jacksonian Democracy *(p. 285)*
Democratic Party *(p. 285)*
John C. Calhoun *(p. 285)*
spoils system *(p. 286)*
Martin Van Buren *(p. 286)*
Kitchen Cabinet *(p. 286)*

Section 2

Tariff of Abominations *(p. 289)*
states' rights doctrine *(p. 290)*
nullification crisis *(p. 290)*
Daniel Webster *(p. 291)*
McCulloch v. *Maryland* *(p. 292)*
Whig Party *(p. 292)*
Panic of 1837 *(p. 293)*
William Henry Harrison *(p. 293)*

Section 3

Indian Removal Act *(p. 294)*
Indian Territory *(p. 294)*
Bureau of Indian Affairs *(p. 294)*
Sequoya *(p. 295)*
Worcester v. *Georgia* *(p. 296)*
Trail of Tears *(p. 296)*
Black Hawk *(p. 297)*
Osceola *(p. 297)*

Academic Vocabulary

Success in school is related to knowing academic vocabulary—the words that are frequently used in school assignments and discussions. In this chapter, you will learn the following academic words:

criteria *(p. 290)*
contemporary *(p. 295)*

As you read Chapter 9, use your personal background knowledge and experience to draw conclusions about what you are reading.

Reading Social Studies

Key Terms and People

Preteach the key terms and people from this chapter to the class. Then have each student write a sentence for each key term. Remind students to use each term correctly. Have students rewrite their sentences, leaving blanks where the key term or person belongs. Have students exchange papers with a partner and complete the fill-in-the-blank activity.
LS Verbal/Linguistic

Focus on Reading

See the **Focus on Reading** questions in this chapter for more practice on this reading social studies skill.

Reading Social Studies Assessment

See the **Standards Review** at the end of this chapter for student assessment questions related to this reading skill.

Teaching Tip

Remind students that there will be times when they have to draw conclusions to fill in small gaps in the text. Tell students to look carefully at the labels of questions in the textbook. When they see a label that reads *Draw Conclusions,* students should use facts from the text and their own knowledge of similar situations to draw a logical conclusion. Help students practice this skill by asking them questions that require them to draw on their own knowledge.

Answers

You Try It! 1. *Jackson was very unpopular with the Whigs because they felt he had too much power.* **2.** *It lowered the number of votes each man received.* **3.** *Jackson remained very popular and the people supported the candidate that he endorsed.* **4.** *Van Buren won the election of 1834 because the Whig Party disliked Jackson, they had too many candidates in the election, and the people supported Jackson's choice for president.*

Preteach

Bellringer

If YOU were there . . . Use the **Daily Bellringer Transparency** to help students answer the question.

Daily Bellringer Transparency, Section 1

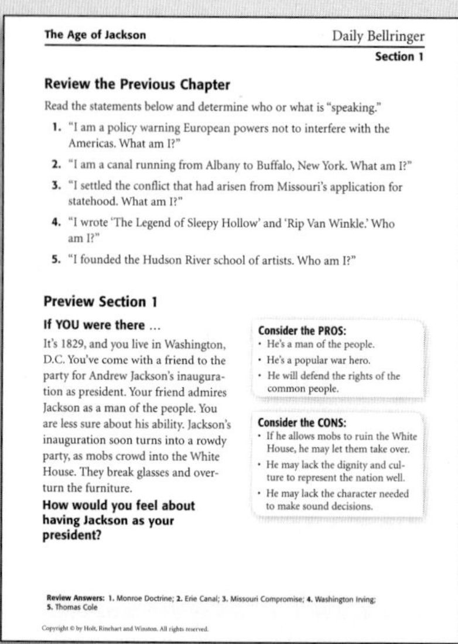

The Age of Jackson Daily Bellringer
Section 1

Review the Previous Chapter

Read the statements below and determine who or what is "speaking."

1. "I am a policy warning European powers not to interfere with the Americas. What am I?"
2. "I am a canal running from Albany to Buffalo, New York. What am I?"
3. "I settled the conflict that had arisen from Missouri's application for statehood. What am I?"
4. "I wrote 'The Legend of Sleepy Hollow' and 'Rip Van Winkle.' Who am I?"
5. "I founded the Hudson River school of artists. Who am I?"

Preview Section 1

If YOU were there ...

It's 1829, and you live in Washington, D.C. You've come with a friend to the party for Andrew Jackson's inauguration as president. Your friend admires Jackson as a man of the people. You are less sure about his ability. Jackson's inauguration soon turns into a rowdy party, as mobs crowd into the White House. They break glasses and overturn the furniture.

How would you feel about having Jackson as your president?

Consider the PROS:
- He's a man of the people.
- He's a popular war hero.
- He will defend the rights of the common people.

Consider the CONS:
- If he allows mobs to ruin the White House, he may let them take over.
- He may lack the dignity and culture to represent the nation well.
- He may lack the character needed to make sound decisions.

Review Answers: **1.** Monroe Doctrine; **2.** Erie Canal; **3.** Missouri Compromise; **4.** Washington Irving; **5.** Thomas Cole

Building Vocabulary

Preteach or review the following terms:

cabinet presidential advisors (p. 286)

inauguration a formal ceremony to place someone in office (p. 286)

spoils as used here, valued goods (p. 286)

CRF: Vocabulary Builder Activity, Section 1

Standards Focus

HSS 8.8.1

Means: Explain the importance of Jacksonian Democracy, describe the election of 1828, and explain Jackson's use of the spoils system.

Matters: The expansion of democracy that occurred in the 1820s and 1830s led to the increased political participation and power that Americans enjoy today.

SECTION 1

Jacksonian Democracy

What You Will Learn...

Main Ideas

1. Democracy expanded in the 1820s as more Americans held the right to vote.
2. Jackson's victory in the election of 1828 marked a change in American politics.

The Big Idea

The expansion of voting rights and the election of Andrew Jackson signaled the growing power of the American people.

Key Terms and People

nominating conventions, *p. 285*
Jacksonian Democracy, *p. 285*
Democratic Party, *p. 285*
John C. Calhoun, *p. 285*
spoils system, *p. 286*
Martin Van Buren, *p. 286*
Kitchen Cabinet, *p. 286*

HSS 8.8.1 Discuss the election of Andrew Jackson as president in 1828, the importance of Jacksonian democracy, and his actions as president (e.g., the spoils system, veto of the National Bank, policy of Indian removal, opposition to the Supreme Court).

If YOU were there...

It's 1829, and you live in Washington, D.C. You've come with a friend to the party for Andrew Jackson's inauguration as president. Your friend admires Jackson as a man of the people. You are less sure about his ability. Jackson's inauguration soon turns into a rowdy party, as mobs crowd into the White House. They break glasses and overturn the furniture.

How would you feel about having Jackson as your president?

BUILDING BACKGROUND In the early years of the United States, the right to vote belonged mainly to a few—free white men who owned property. As the country grew, more men were given the right to vote. This expansion of democracy led to the election of Andrew Jackson, a war hero. But not everyone approved of Jackson.

Expansion of Democracy

America in the early 1800s was changing fast. In the North, workshops run by the craftspeople who owned them were being replaced by large-scale factories owned by businesspeople and staffed by hired workers. In the South, small family farms began to give way to large cotton plantations, owned by wealthy white people and worked by enslaved African Americans. Wealth seemed to be concentrating into fewer hands. Many ordinary Americans felt left behind.

These same people also began to believe they were losing power in their government. In the late 1700s some Americans thought that government was best managed by a small group of wealthy, property-owning men. Government policies seemed targeted to help build the power of these people. The result was a growing belief that the wealthy were tightening their grip on power in the United States.

Hoping for change, small farmers, frontier settlers, and slaveholders rallied behind reform-minded Andrew Jackson, the popular hero of the War of 1812 and presidential candidate in the 1824 election. They believed Jackson would defend the rights of the common

Teach the Big Idea: Master the Standards

Standards Proficiency

Jacksonian Democracy HSS 8.8.1; HSS Analysis Skills: HI 1

1. **Teach** Ask students the Main Idea questions to teach this section.
2. **Apply** Pair students and have each pair use the term *Jacksonian Democracy* to create an acrostic. For each letter in *Jacksonian Democracy*, students should find a key term, figure, event, or issue from the section that includes that letter. Students should then write the terms horizontally so that the letters in *Jacksonian Democracy* align vertically.
   LS Interpersonal, Verbal/Linguistic
3. **Review** To review the section, have students share terms from their acrostics.
4. **Practice/Homework** Have students imagine they have just attended a Jackson inauguration party. Have each student write a journal entry about the election, the party, and the expansion of democracy.
   LS Intrapersonal, Verbal/Linguistic
   Alternative Assessment Handbook, Rubric 15: Journals

LINKING TO TODAY

Democracy in Action

Democracy spread in the early 1800s as more people became active in politics. Many of these people lived in the new western states. In these mostly rural areas, a political rally could be as simple as neighboring farmers meeting to talk about the issues of the day, as the farmers in the painting on the right are doing.

During the early 1800s democracy and demonstrations blossomed in the United States. The demonstrators of today owe much to the Americans of Andrew Jackson's time. Today, political rallies are a familiar sight in communities all over the country.

ANALYSIS SKILL ANALYZING INFORMATION

How are the people in both pictures practicing democracy?

people and the slave states. And they had been bitterly disappointed in the way Jackson had lost the 1824 election because of the decision in the House of Representatives.

During the time of Jackson's popularity, a number of democratic reforms were made. Many states changed their qualifications for voters. They lowered or even eliminated the requirement that men own a certain amount of property in order to vote or hold office. Political parties began holding public **nominating conventions**, where party members choose the party's candidates. Previously, candidates were selected by party leaders. This period of expanding democracy in the 1820s and 1830s later became known as **Jacksonian democracy**.

READING CHECK **Finding Main Ideas** How did voting rights change in the early 1800s?

Election of 1828

Jackson supporters were determined that their candidate would win the 1828 election. The **Democratic Party** arose from these supporters of Jackson. Many people who backed President Adams began calling themselves National Republicans.

The 1828 presidential contest was a rematch of the 1824 election. Once again, John Quincy Adams faced Andrew Jackson. Jackson chose Senator **John C. Calhoun** as his vice presidential running mate.

The Campaign

The 1828 campaign focused a great deal on the candidates' personalities. Jackson's campaigners described him as a war hero who had been born poor and rose to success through his own hard work.

THE IMPACT TODAY

Just as they did in the 1820s, presidential campaigns today frequently focus on personal image—strong versus weak or government-insider versus newcomer, for example.

Direct Teach

Main Idea

1 Expansion of Democracy

Democracy expanded in the 1820s as more Americans held the right to vote.

Explain How did the change in the method of selecting electors expand democracy? *The people instead of state legislatures were allowed to nominate electors.*

Analyze Why do historians call the expansion of voting rights during this period Jacksonian Democracy? *because Andrew Jackson was a popular politician who supported majority rule and benefited from the expansion of democracy*

Evaluate Why do you think Jackson was a popular presidential candidate? *was a popular war hero, his supporters thought he would defend the rights of common people*

HSS 8.8.1; HSS **Analysis Skills:** HI 1

Info to Know

Jacksonian Democracy In the early 1900s, historians argued that Andrew Jackson's election signaled the triumph of the common people over social elites. More recently, historians have argued that Jackson's supporters actually hoped to increase their own economic standing and to become more like the elites. Historians still agree, though, that the changes in politics in the 1820s and 1830s marked a turning point in U.S. political history.

Collaborative Learning

Exceeding Standards

Election of 1828 Political Advertisements

Prep Required | Research Required

Materials: video or DVD camera, tapes, and player

1. Organize the class into large groups and assign each group either Andrew Jackson or John Quincy Adams. Have each group create a 30-second political advertisement in support of its candidate for the 1828 election.
2. Instruct the groups to assign each member a specific role, such as director, researcher, designer, writer, editor, actor, props person, or cameraperson.
3. Have each group write, act, and record its political ad. Then show the ads to the class.
4. Conclude by leading a class discussion about how the expansion in democracy in the 1820s and the 1828 campaign led to a new pattern in American political participation and power.

LS Interpersonal, Kinesthetic

Alternative Assessment Handbook, Rubrics 2: Advertisements; and 14: Group Activity

HSS 8.8.1; HSS **Analysis Skills:** HI 1, HI 3

Answers

Linking to Today *They are exercising their rights to assemble and freely discuss and express ideas.*

Reading Check *Many states expanded voting rights to include more white men; allowed the people to nominate their electors.*

Direct Teach

Main Idea

❷ Election of 1828

Jackson's victory in the election of 1828 marked a change in American politics.

Identify Who were the candidates in the election of 1828, and what party did each represent? *John Quincy Adams, National Republican party; Andrew Jackson, Democratic Party*

Draw Conclusions Why did Jackson's supporters view his victory as a win for the common people? *because most of his supporters were farmers and settlers, as opposed to members of the eastern elite*

Make Judgments What is your opinion of the spoils system? *possible answers: approve—an appropriate reward for hard work; disapprove—could lead to corruption*

HSS 8.8.1; HSS **Analysis Skills:** HI 1, HI 2

Primary Source

LETTER

People's President

Washington resident Margaret Bayard Smith was surprised by the chaos surrounding Jackson's inauguration.

"What a scene did we witness! . . . a rabble, a mob, of boys, . . . women, children, scrambling, fighting, romping . . . Cut glass and china to the amount of several thousand dollars had been broken. . . . But it was the people's day, and the people's President, and the people would rule."

—Margaret Bayard Smith, quoted in *Eyewitness to America*, edited by David Colbert

ANALYSIS SKILL ANALYZING PRIMARY SOURCES

How does the author view the people that support Jackson?

Adams was a Harvard graduate whose father had been the second U.S. president. Jackson's supporters described Adams as being out of touch with everyday people. Even a fan of Adams agreed that he was "as cold as a lump of ice." In turn, Adams's supporters said Jackson was hot tempered, crude, and ill-equipped to be president of the United States. When the ballots were counted, Jackson had defeated Adams, winning a record number of popular votes.

Jackson's Inauguration

Jackson's supporters saw his victory as a win for the common people. A crowd cheered outside the Capitol as he took his oath of office. The massive crowd followed Jackson to a huge party on the White House lawn. The few police officers on hand had difficulty controlling the partygoers.

As president, Jackson rewarded some of his supporters with government jobs. This **spoils system**—the practice of giving government jobs to political backers—comes from the saying "to the victor belong the spoils [valued goods] of the enemy."

Secretary of State **Martin Van Buren** was one of Jackson's strongest allies in his official cabinet. President Jackson also relied a great deal on his **Kitchen Cabinet**, an informal group of trusted advisers who sometimes met in the White House kitchen.

READING CHECK **Analyzing** How might the spoils system cause disputes?

SUMMARY AND PREVIEW The expansion of democracy swept Andrew Jackson into office. In the next section you will read about the increasing regional tensions that occurred during Jackson's presidency.

Section 1 Assessment

go.hrw.com
Online Quiz
KEYWORD: SS8 HP9

Reviewing Ideas, Terms, and People HSS 8.8.1, 8.10.1, 8.10.3

1. **a. Recall** What changes did the new western states make that allowed more people to vote?
   b. Draw Conclusions How did **nominating conventions** allow the people more say in politics?
   c. Predict How might changes to the voting process brought about by **Jacksonian Democracy** affect politics in the future?
2. **a. Recall** What two new political parties faced off in the election of 1828? Which candidate did each party support?
   b. Make Inferences Why did **Andrew Jackson** have more popular support than did Adams?
   c. Evaluate Do you think the spoils system was an acceptable practice? Explain your answer.

Critical Thinking

3. **Sequencing** Copy the graphic organizer below. Use it to identify the events leading up to Jackson's victory in the election of 1828.

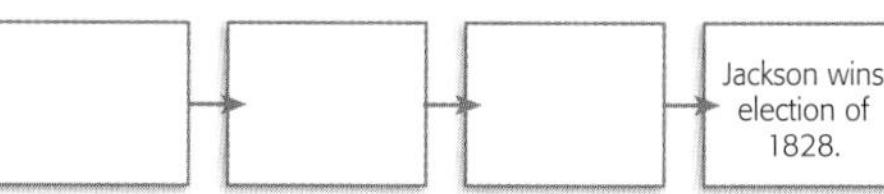
Jackson wins election of 1828.

FOCUS ON WRITING

4. **Noting Significance** As you read this section, note things that made Jackson's political campaign and election significant in the history of American politics.

Review & Assess

Close

Have students summarize Jacksonian Democracy.

Review

Online Quiz, Section 1

Assess

SE Section 1 Assessment

PASS: Section 1 Quiz

Alternative Assessment Handbook

Reteach/Classroom Intervention

California Standards Review Workbook

Interactive Reader and Study Guide, Section 1

Interactive Skills Tutor CD-ROM

Answers

Analyzing Primary Sources *as "a rabble, a mob"*

Reading Check *People who were not rewarded might cause discord.*

Section 1 Assessment Answers

1. **a.** loosened voting requirements to let more white men vote; gave the people the right to nominate their electors
   b. by giving people more of a say in deciding a political party's candidates
   c. possible answer—expansion in voting might lead to elected officials who represent a broader range of the common people's views
2. **a.** Democrats—Andrew Jackson; National Republicans—John Quincy Adams
   b. Jackson was a popular war hero and seen as a self-made man; Adams was seen as elite and out of touch with everyday people.
   c. possible answers—yes, just reward for hard work; no, could lead to corruption
3. Students' charts might include the following: expansion of voting rights; involvement of people in nominating conventions; formation of Democratic Party
4. Students should note how the expansion of voting rights and political involvement and the election of Jackson signaled the growing political power of the American people.

Andrew Jackson

If you were president, how would **you** use your powers?

When did he live? 1767–1845

Where did he live? Jackson was born in Waxhaw, a region along the border of the North and South Carolina colonies. In 1788 he moved to Nashville, Tennessee, which was still a part of North Carolina. There he built a mansion called the Hermitage. He lived in Washington as president, then retired to the Hermitage, where he died.

What did he do? Jackson had no formal education, but he taught himself law and became a successful lawyer. He became Tennessee's first representative to the U.S. Congress and also served in the Senate. Jackson became a national hero when his forces defeated the Creek and Seminole Indians. He went on to battle the British in the Battle of New Orleans during the War of 1812. Jackson was elected as the nation's seventh president in 1828 and served until 1837.

Why is he so important? Jackson's belief in a strong presidency made him both loved and hated. He vetoed as many bills as the six previous presidents together. Jackson also believed in a strong Union. When South Carolina tried to nullify, or reject, a federal tariff, he threatened to send troops into the state to force it to obey.

Identifying Cause and Effect Why did Jackson gain loyal friends and fierce enemies?

KEY EVENTS

1796–1797
Served in the U.S. House of Representatives

1797–1798
Served in the U.S. Senate

1798–1804
Served on the Tennessee Supreme Court

1821
Governor of Florida Territory

1823–1825
Served in the U.S. Senate

1829–1837
Served as president of the United States

1832
Vetoed rechartering the Second Bank of the United States. Threatened to send troops to South Carolina when it tried to nullify a federal tariff

Jackson received a scar from a British officer as a boy.

Biography

Reading Focus Question

To help students discuss the introductory question, remind them of the president's powers, such as issuing proclamations and vetoing legislation. Then instruct students as they read the biography to note the ways in which Jackson used his powers as president.

Info to Know

"Old Hickory" Jackson's belief in a strong presidency paralleled his own strong will. He received the nickname "Old Hickory" during the War of 1812, because of his reputation for being as tough as the hard wood of a hickory tree. During the war, Jackson received orders to move his troops to Mississippi. When he arrived, he was told to disband the troops. Instead, Jackson marched his troops back to Tennessee. He walked the entire way, because he had given his horse to a wounded soldier.

Jackson's Legacy In his own day, Jackson was extremely popular. Since his death, however, scholars have debated his legacy. On one hand, Jackson helped broaden democracy by pushing for the expansion of voting rights for white men. On the other hand, he did little to increase equality for other groups and violated Native Americans' treaty rights and legal claims. Perhaps most controversial is Jackson's interpretation of the balance of powers. Jackson insisted that Congress consult him before considering legislation. He also rejected the principle that the Supreme Court was the final interpreter of the laws.

Critical Thinking: Evaluating Information

Standards Proficiency

Overheard Dinner Conversation

HSS 8.8.1; HSS **Analysis Skills:** HR 5, HI 1

1. Ask students to imagine that they are attending a dinner in honor of Andrew Jackson and his contributions to the nation. At the next table, two people are arguing the merits of Jackson's legacy. Impressed by the points they are making, students decide to jot them down.
2. Have students create notes of the imaginary discussion at the next table. The discussion should address Jackson's presidency as well as his other actions in service to the nation. One person in the discussion should argue in favor of Jackson's greatness; the other should argue against it.
3. **Extend** Have students express and defend their own points of view of Jackson and his presidency.

Alternative Assessment Handbook, Rubrics 16: Judging Information; and 37: Writing Assignments

Answers

Identifying Cause and Effect *because of his belief in a strong presidency and because of his actions as president, such as his opposition to the Bank of the United States and the forced removal of the Cherokee*

Preteach

Bellringer

If YOU were there . . . Use the **Daily Bellringer Transparency** to help students answer the question.

Daily Bellringer Transparency, Section 2

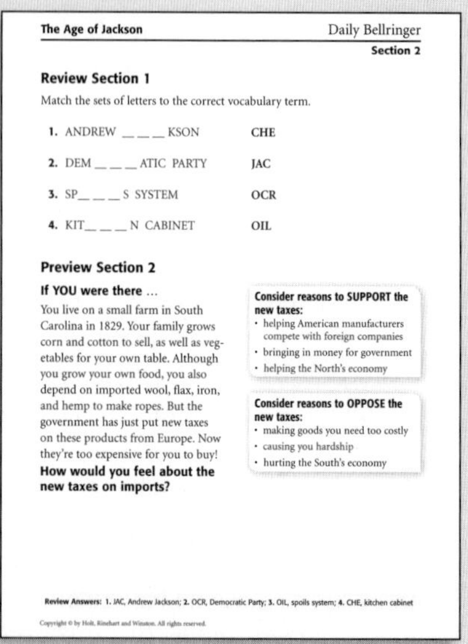

The Age of Jackson — Daily Bellringer **Section 2**

Review Section 1

Match the sets of letters to the correct vocabulary term.

1. ANDREW _ _ _ KSON	CHE
2. DEM _ _ _ ATIC PARTY	JAC
3. SP_ _ _ S SYSTEM	OCR
4. KIT_ _ _ N CABINET	OIL

Preview Section 2

If YOU were there ...

You live on a small farm in South Carolina in 1829. Your family grows corn and cotton to sell, as well as vegetables for your own table. Although you grow your own food, you also depend on imported wool, flax, iron, and hemp to make ropes. But the government has just put new taxes on these products from Europe. Now they're too expensive for you to buy!

How would you feel about the new taxes on imports?

Consider reasons to SUPPORT the new taxes:
- helping American manufacturers compete with foreign companies
- bringing in money for government
- helping the North's economy

Consider reasons to OPPOSE the new taxes:
- making goods you need too costly
- causing you hardship
- hurting the South's economy

Review Answers: 1. JAC, Andrew Jackson; 2. OCR, Democratic Party; 3. OIL, spoils system; 4. CHE, kitchen cabinet

Academic Vocabulary

Review with students the high-use academic term in this section.

criteria basic requirements (p. 290)

CRF: Vocabulary Builder Activity, Section 2

Standards Focus

HSS 8.4.3

Means: Analyze the rise of capitalism in the United States and the economic problems and conflicts that arose.

Matters: Capitalism continues to shape the U.S. economy today.

HSS 8.10.1

Means: Explain the conflict between state and federal authority during Jackson's presidency, and how Daniel Webster and John C. Calhoun viewed this conflict.

Matters: Growing conflicts over state versus federal authority would eventually divide the nation in the Civil War.

HSS 8.10.3

Means: Identify the constitutional issues involved in the Nullification Crisis.

Matters: The conflict marked the first time South Carolina threatened to leave the nation. The second instance would result in civil war.

SECTION 2 Jackson's Administration

What You Will Learn...

Main Ideas

1. Regional differences grew during Jackson's presidency.
2. The rights of the states were debated amid arguments about a national tariff.
3. Jackson's attack on the Bank sparked controversy.
4. Jackson's policies led to the Panic of 1837.

The Big Idea

Andrew Jackson's presidency was marked by political conflicts.

Key Terms and People

Tariff of Abominations, *p. 289*
states' rights doctrine, *p. 290*
nullification crisis, *p. 290*
Daniel Webster, *p. 290*
McCulloch v. *Maryland*, *p. 292*
Whig Party, *p. 292*
Panic of 1837, *p. 293*
William Henry Harrison, *p. 293*

HSS 8.4.3 Analyze the rise of capitalism and the economic problems and conflicts that accompanied it (e.g. Jackson's opposition to the National Bank; early decisions of the U.S. Supreme Court that reinforced the sanctity of contracts and a capitalist economic system of law.

8.10.1 Compare the conflicting interpretations of state and federal authority as emphasized in the speeches and writings of statesmen such as Daniel Webster and John C. Calhoun.

8.10.3 Identify the constitutional issues posed by the doctrine of nullification and secession and the earliest origins of that doctrine.

If YOU were there...

You live on a small farm in South Carolina in 1829. Your family grows corn and cotton to sell, as well as vegetables for your own table. Although you grow your own food, you also depend on imported wool, flax, iron, and hemp to make ropes. But the government has just put new taxes on these products from Europe. Now they're too expensive for you to buy!

How would you feel about the new taxes on imports?

BUILDING BACKGROUND Even though Americans had a new feeling of national unity, different sections of the country still had very different interests. The industrial North competed with the agricultural South and the western frontier. As Congress favored one section over another, political differences also grew.

Sectional Differences Increase

Regional differences had a major effect on Andrew Jackson's presidency. Americans' views of Jackson's policies were based on where they lived and the economy of those regions.

Three Regions Emerge

There were three main U.S. regions in the early 1800s. The North, first of all, had an economy based on trade and on manufacturing. Northerners supported tariffs because tariffs helped them compete with British factories. Northerners also opposed the federal government's sale of public land at cheap prices. Cheap land encouraged potential laborers to move from northern factory towns to the West.

The second region was the South. Its economy was based on farming. Southern farmers raised all types of crops, but the most popular were the cash crops of cotton and tobacco. Southerners sold a large portion of their crops to foreign nations.

Teach the Big Idea: Master the Standards

Standards **Proficiency**

Jackson's Administration HSS 8.4.3, 8.10.1, 8.10.3; HSS **Analysis Skills:** HI 1, HI 2

1. **Teach** Ask students the Main Idea questions to teach this section.
2. **Apply** For each of the section key terms and people, have students write a sentence explaining how that term or person relates to the sectional and/or political conflicts that took place during Jackson's presidency. Then have each student create a flowchart that links all the key terms and people. LS **Verbal/Linguistic, Visual/Spatial**
3. **Review** As you review the section's main ideas, have volunteers share the information they listed about each key term or person.
4. **Practice/Homework** Have each student select one of the key terms or people and write a news article about that event, issue, or person. LS **Verbal/Linguistic**

Alternative Assessment Handbook, Rubrics 7: Charts; and 42: Writing to Inform

Regions of the United States, Early 1800s

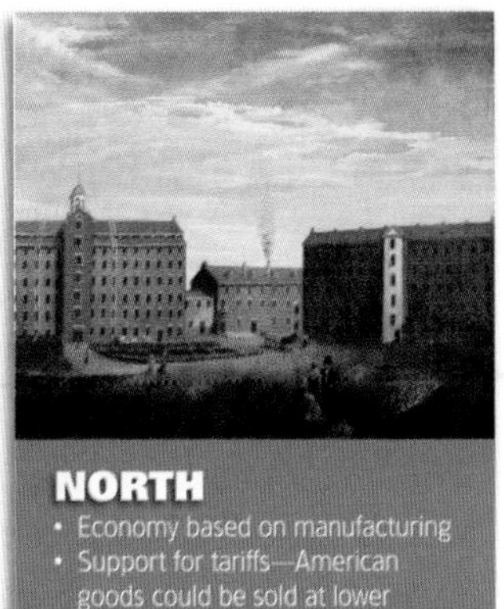

NORTH
- Economy based on manufacturing
- Support for tariffs—American goods could be sold at lower prices than could British goods

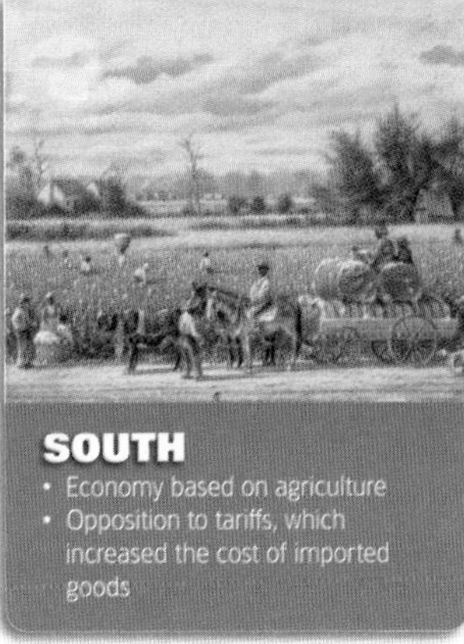

SOUTH
- Economy based on agriculture
- Opposition to tariffs, which increased the cost of imported goods

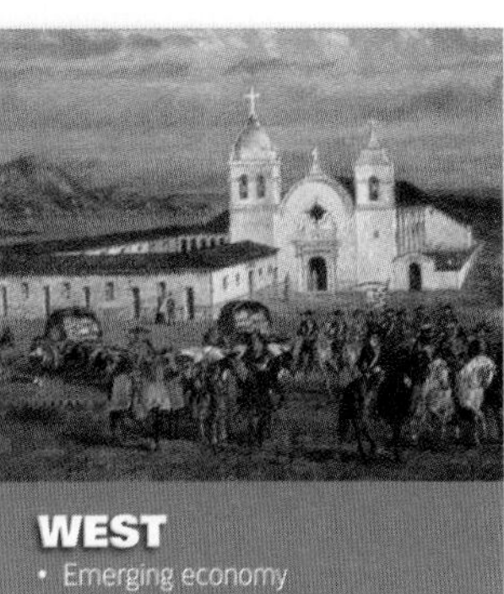

WEST
- Emerging economy
- Support for internal improvements and the sale of public lands

Southerners imported their manufactured goods. Tariffs made imported goods more expensive for southern farmers. In addition, high tariffs angered some of the South's European trading partners. These trading partners would likely raise their own tariffs in retaliation. To avoid this situation, southerners called for low tariffs.

Southerners also relied on enslaved African Americans to work the plantations. The issue of slavery would become increasingly controversial between the North and South.

In the third region, the West, the frontier economy was just emerging. Settlers supported policies that boosted their farming economy and encouraged further settlement. Western farmers grew a wide variety of crops. Their biggest priority was cheap land and internal improvements such as better roads and water transportation.

Tariff of Abominations

Tariffs became one of the first issues that President Jackson faced. In 1827, the year before Jackson's election, northern manufacturers began to demand a tariff on imported woolen goods. Northerners wanted the tariff to protect their industries from foreign competition, especially from Great Britain.

British companies were driving American ones out of business because they could manufacture goods more cheaply than American businesses could. The tariff northerners wanted, however, was so high that importing wool would be impossible. Southerners opposed the tariff, claiming it would hurt their economy.

Before Andrew Jackson took office, Congress placed a high tariff on imports, causing angry southerners to call it the **Tariff of Abominations**. (An abomination is a hateful thing.) Southern voters were outraged.

President John Quincy Adams signed the tariff legislation, even though he did not fully support it. In early U.S. history, presidents tended to reserve veto power for legislation that they believed violated the Constitution. Signing the tariff bill meant Adams would surely be defeated in his re-election bid. The new tariff added fuel to the growing sectional differences plaguing the young nation.

READING CHECK **Summarizing** Describe the sectional economic differences in the United States during the early 1800s.

Direct Teach

Main Idea

1 Sectional Differences Increase

Regional differences grew during Jackson's presidency.

Recall During Jackson's presidency, what was the main factor in determining whether people supported or opposed political policies? *the region where people lived*

Contrast Why were northerners and southerners at odds over tariffs? *because their economies differed; higher tariffs helped the industrial North but hurt the agricultural South*

Quick Facts Transparency: Regions of the United States, Early 1800s

HSS Analysis Skills: HR 5, HI 1

Connect to Economics

Southerners and the Tariff Some southerners based opposition to tariffs on the "forty-bale" theory. According to this theory, a 40 percent tariff on imports made from cotton, such as clothing, would raise prices by 40 percent. This increase, in theory, would then reduce the purchase of cotton goods by 40 percent. As a result, manufacturers' demand for southern cotton would drop by 40 percent. Southerners argued that they then would lose the profit on 40 out of every 100 bales of cotton. Although the forty-bale theory was not sophisticated, it appealed to many southerners.

Analyze What are some possible weaknesses of the forty-bale theory? *possible answer—assumes that consumers will buy less when prices rise, which is not always the case with necessities, such as clothing*

HSS Analysis Skills: HI 6

Differentiating Instruction for Universal Access

Learners Having Difficulty — Reaching Standards

Materials: blank outline maps of the United States; colored pencils or markers

1. Give each student a blank outline map of the United States. Have students mark the nation's political borders in 1820. (Refer students to the map in the feature "History and Geography, America's Growth: 1820.")
2. Instruct students to draw caption boxes pointing roughly to the areas of the North, the South, and the West. Have students enter the information in the Quick Facts on this page into the appropriate boxes on their maps.
3. Then write three or four political issues of the period for students to see, such as tariffs, manufacturing, the sale of public lands, and internal improvements. Help students understand the views of each region toward each issue. **LS Verbal/Linguistic, Visual/Spatial**

HSS Analysis Skills: CS 3, HR 5, HI 1

Answers

Reading Check *See the Quick Facts at the top of the page for a summary.*

Direct Teach

Main Idea

❷ States' Rights Debate

The rights of the states were debated amid arguments about a national tariff.

Explain How did southerners use the states' rights doctrine to support the idea of nullification? *stated that states had the greater power and, thus, had the right to reject any federal law with which they disagreed*

Identify Points of View How did Webster and Jackson view the nullification crisis? *both opposed nullification; Webster—thought national unity was more important that states' rights; Jackson—threatened to use federal troops to enforce federal laws*

- **CRF:** Biography Activities: John C. Calhoun; Daniel Webster
- **CRF:** Primary Source Activity: President Jackson's Proclamation Regarding Nullification
- **HSS** 8.10.1, 8.10.3; **HSS Analysis Skills:** HR 5, HI 1

go.hrw.com
Online Resources
KEYWORD: SS8 US9
ACTIVITY: Calhoun and Webster Debate Nullification

Answers

Focus on Reading *that the debate further increased sectional tensions that would continue to divide the nation*

States' Rights Debate

When Andrew Jackson took office in 1829, he was forced to respond to the growing conflict over tariffs. At the core of the dispute was the question of an individual state's right to disregard a law that had been passed by the U.S. Congress.

Nullification Crisis

ACADEMIC VOCABULARY
criteria basic requirements

Early in his political career, Vice President John C. Calhoun had supported the criteria needed for a strong central government. But in 1828 when Congress passed the Tariff of Abominations, Calhoun joined his fellow southerners in protest. Economic depression and previous tariffs had severely damaged the economy of his home state, South Carolina. It was only beginning to recover in 1828. Some leaders in the state even spoke of leaving the Union over the issue of tariffs.

FOCUS ON READING
What conclusions can you draw about the importance of the states' rights debate after reading this section?

In response to the tariff, Calhoun drafted the *South Carolina Exposition and Protest.* It stated that Congress should not favor one state or region over another. Calhoun also used the Protest to advance the **states' rights doctrine.** He argued that, because the states had formed the national government, state power should be greater than federal power. He believed states had the right to nullify, or reject, any federal law they judged to be unconstitutional.

Calhoun's theory was controversial, and it drew some fierce challengers. Many of them were from the northern states that had benefited from increased tariffs. These opponents believed that the American people, not the individual states, made up the Union. Conflict between the supporters and the opponents of nullification deepened. The dispute became known as the **nullification crisis.**

Although he chose not to put his name on his *Exposition and Protest,* Calhoun did resign from the vice presidency. Martin Van Buren replaced him as vice president when Jackson was re-elected to a second term. John C. Calhoun is the only vice president in our history to resign his office.

The Hayne-Webster Debate

The debate about states' rights began early in our nation's history. Thomas Jefferson and James Madison supported the states' power to disagree with the federal government in the Virginia and Kentucky Resolutions of 1798–99. Some of the delegates at the Hartford Convention supported states' rights. But Calhoun's theory went further. He believed that states could judge whether a law was or was not constitutional. This position put the power of the Supreme Court in question.

The issue of nullification was intensely debated on the floor of the Senate in 1830. Robert Y. Hayne, senator from South Carolina, defended states' rights. He argued that nullification gave states a way to lawfully protest against federal legislation. **Daniel Webster** of Massachusetts argued that the United States was one nation, not a pact among independent states. He believed that the welfare of the nation should override that of individual states.

Jackson Responds

Although deeply opposed to nullification, Jackson was also concerned about economic problems in the southern states. In 1832 Jackson urged Congress to pass another tariff that lowered the previous rate. South Carolina thought the slight change was inadequate. The state legislature took a monumental step; it decided to test the doctrine of states' rights.

South Carolina's first action was to pass the Nullification Act. It declared that the 1828 and 1832 tariffs were "null, void...[and not] binding upon this State, its officers or citizens." South Carolina threatened to withdraw from the Union if federal troops were used to collect duties. The legislature also voted to form its own army. Jackson was enraged.

The president sternly condemned nullification. Jackson declared that he would enforce the law in South Carolina. At his request, Congress passed the Force Bill

Critical Thinking: Finding Main Ideas

Standards Proficiency

Nullification Crisis Graphic Organizer

HSS 8.10.1, 8.10.3; **HSS Analysis Skills:** HI 1

1. To help students understand the issues involved in the Nullification Crisis, draw the graphic organizer for students to see. Omit the blue, italicized answers.
2. Have each student copy the organizer and complete it by explaining the key figures, events, and issues on each side.
LS Verbal/Linguistic, Visual/Spatial

Alternative Assessment Handbook, Rubric 13: Graphic Organizers

States' Rights
- **Southern opinion of tariffs:** *abominable*
- **States' Rights:** *state power should be greater than federal power*
- **Nullification:** *States' have the right to nullify federal laws with which they disagree.*
- **John C. Calhoun:** *major proponent*

Nullification Crisis

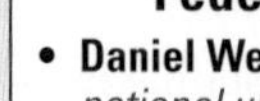

Federal Authority
- **Daniel Webster:** *promoted national unity over states' rights*
- **President Jackson:** *opposed nullification*
- **Actions/Results:** *Jackson wanted to send troops to enforce tariffs; Congress and South Carolina compromised to lower tariffs gradually.*

approving use of the army if necessary. In light of Jackson's determined position, no other state chose to support South Carolina.

Early in 1833, Henry Clay of Kentucky had proposed a compromise that would lower the tariff little by little over several years.

As Jackson's intentions became clear, both the U.S. Congress and South Carolina moved quickly to approve the compromise. The Congress would decrease the tariff, and South Carolina's leaders would enforce the law.

Despite the compromise, neither side changed its beliefs about states' rights. The argument would continue for years, ending in the huge conflict known as the Civil War.

READING CHECK **Summarizing** What led to the nullification crisis, and why was it important?

Jackson Attacks the Bank

President Jackson upheld federal authority in the nullification crisis. He did not, however, always support greater federal power. For example, he opposed the Second Bank of the United States, founded by Congress in 1816.

The Second Bank of the United States was given a 20-year charter. This charter gave it the power to act exclusively as the federal government's financial agent. The Bank held federal deposits, made transfers of federal funds between states, and dealt with any payments or receipts involving the federal government. It also issued bank notes, or paper currency. Some 80 percent of the Bank was privately owned, but its operations were supervised by Congress and the president.

Many states, particularly in the South, had opposed the Bank. Small farmers believed that the Bank only helped wealthy businesspeople. Jackson also questioned the legality of the Bank. He believed it was an unconstitutional extension of the power of Congress. The states, he thought, should have the power to control the banking system.

Some states decided to take action. Maryland tried to pass a tax that would limit the

Primary Source

POINTS OF VIEW

States' Rights vs. the Union

The framers of the Constitution created a document that was remarkable in its scope. But a few issues were unresolved. One of the most controversial was the matter of states' rights versus the authority of the federal government. Daniel Webster insisted that the interests of the Union should prevail. John C. Calhoun believed that the powers of the states were greater.

"While the Union lasts we have high, exciting, gratifying prospects spread out before us, for us and our children. God grant that in my day . . . my eyes shall be turned to behold the gorgeous ensign of the republic . . . bearing for its motto . . . Liberty and Union, now and forever one and inseparable."

—**Daniel Webster**

from the Hayne-Webster debate, 1830

"If there be no protective power in the reserved rights of the states, they must in the end be forced to rebel . . ."

—**John C. Calhoun**

from a letter to Virgil Maxcy, September 11, 1830

ANALYSIS SKILL ANALYZING PRIMARY SOURCES

Finding Main Ideas How did the views of Calhoun and Webster differ?

Direct Teach

Main Idea

❸ Jackson Attacks the Bank

Jackson's attack of the bank sparked controversy.

Describe How did the state of Maryland try to take action against the Second Bank of the United States? *It passed a tax to limit the operations of the Bank's state branch, and took the branch cashier, James McCulloch, to court when he refused to pay the tax.*

Identify Cause and Effect What occurred as a result of this action? *The case went to the U.S. Supreme Court, which ruled in* McCulloch v. Maryland *that the Bank was constitutional.*

Evaluate Were Jackson's actions to weaken the Bank's power effective? *His actions weakened the bank's power and helped western expansion but also led to inflation, which hurt the economy.*

- Political Cartoons Activities for United States History, Cartoon 11: Jackson and the Bank
- **CRF:** Primary Source Activity: The Bank War of 1832—Two Views
- U.S. Supreme Court Case Studies: *McCulloch* v. *Maryland*
- **HSS** 8.1.1, 8.10.1; **HSS Analysis Skills:** HI 1, HI 2, HI 6

Differentiating Instruction for Universal Access

Advanced Learners/GATE **Exceeding Standards**

1. Have each student write an outline of a chapter that might have appeared in Jackson's memoirs. The chapter should address Jackson's thoughts about the U.S. Supreme Court case *McCulloch* v. *Maryland* and the Second Bank of the United States, his actions to defeat the Bank, and how his actions affected the U.S. economy.
2. Pair students and have partners exchange outlines. Each student should then evaluate his or her partner's outline from the point of view of Jackson's publisher. Students should consider the clarity and order of the material and its publication value. Then have students revise their outlines based on the reviews.

LS Interpersonal, Verbal/Linguistic

HSS 8.4.3, 8.10.3; **HSS Analysis Skills:** HR 5, HI 1

Alternative Assessment Handbook, Rubric 42: Writing to Inform

Answers

Analyzing Primary Sources *Webster strongly supported federal power, whereas Calhoun supported the rights of the states.*

Reading Check *Southern states asserted their power to nullify tariffs, which most Southerners opposed; it demonstrated the nation's growing sectionalism and division over the issue of federal versus state power.*

Direct Teach

Main Idea

4 Panic of 1837

Jackson's policies led to the Panic of 1837.

Define What was the Whig Party? *political party formed by a group of Jackson's opponents*

Explain What helped Van Buren win the election in 1836? *strong support from Jackson; division of Whig support among four candidates*

Analyze What role did the economy play in the presidential election of 1840? *The Panic of 1837 decreased support for the incumbent Van Buren, which helped Whig candidate William Henry Harrison win the election.*

CRF: Economics and History Activity: The Panic of 1837

HSS Analysis Skills: HI 1, HI 2

Teaching Tip

Modernize the Symbol
The symbol of the hydra in the political cartoon at right may be unfamiliar to students. To help students understand the cartoon better, ask them to suggest images that political cartoonists today might use to portray either a difficult political problem for a president to solve or a president who is in a conflict with several political opponents.

Answers

Analyzing Primary Sources *It shows that many politicians opposed Jackson's policies*

Reading Check *Small farmers, particularly in the South, thought the Bank benefited only wealthy businesspeople; Jackson questioned the Bank's legality.*

Primary Source

POLITICAL CARTOON

Jackson against the Bank

Andrew Jackson's fight with the Bank was the subject of many political cartoons, like this one.

In this scene, Jackson is shown fighting a hydra that represents the national bank. The hydra is a mythological monster whose heads grow back when cut off. The heads of the hydra are portraits of politicians who opposed Jackson's policies.

Nicholas Biddle is at the center of the hydra. Why?

Andrew Jackson fights the hydra with a cane labeled "veto."

Why do you think the cartoonist chose this monster to represent the Bank?

ANALYSIS SKILL ANALYZING PRIMARY SOURCES

How does this image show the difficulty Jackson had politically?

Bank's operations. James McCulloch, cashier of the Bank's branch in Maryland, refused to pay this tax. The state took him to court, and the resulting case went all the way to the U.S. Supreme Court. In ***McCulloch v. Maryland***, the Court ruled that the national bank was constitutional.

Nicholas Biddle, the Bank's director, decided to push for a bill to renew the Bank's charter in 1832. Jackson campaigned strongly for the bill's defeat. "I will kill it," he promised. True to his word, Jackson vetoed the legislation when Congress sent it to him.

Congress could not get the two-thirds majority needed to override Jackson's veto. Jackson also weakened the Bank's power by moving most of its funds to state banks. In many cases, these banks used the funds to offer easy credit terms to people buying land. While this practice helped expansion in the West, it also led to inflation.

In the summer of 1836 Jackson tried to slow this inflation. He ordered Americans to use only gold or silver—instead of paper bank notes—to buy government-owned land. This policy did not help the national economy as Jackson had hoped. Jackson did improve the economy by lowering the national debt. However, his policies opened the door for approaching economic troubles.

READING CHECK **Analyzing** Why did critics of the Second Bank of the United States oppose it?

Panic of 1837

Jackson was still very popular with voters in 1836. Jackson chose not to run in 1836, and the Democrats nominated Vice President Martin Van Buren.

In 1834 a new political party formed to oppose Jackson. Its members called themselves Whigs, after an English political party that opposed the monarchy, to make the point that Jackson was using his power like a king. The **Whig Party** favored the idea of a weak president and a strong Congress. Unable to agree on a presidential candidate, the Whigs nominated four men to run against Vice President Martin Van Buren. With strong backing from Jackson, Van Buren won the election.

Critical Thinking: Identifying Cause and Effect

Standards Proficiency

1840 Whig Campaign Flyer

HSS Analysis Skills: HR 5, HI 1, HI 2

Materials: paper, colored markers, current political campaign flyer (optional)

1. Have each student create a campaign flyer supporting Whig candidate William Henry Harrison in the election of 1840.
2. Students' fliers should address the Panic of 1837, public views of Van Buren's presidency, and Harrison's background and character versus that of Van Buren. If possible, provide students with a copy of a current political campaign advertisement to use as a model.
3. Ask for volunteers to explain their fliers to the class. Use the activity to launch a guided discussion of the causes and effects of the Panic of 1837 and the outcome of the election of 1840. **LS Intrapersonal, Visual/Spatial**

Alternative Assessment Handbook, Rubric 37: Writing Assignments

Supreme Court and Capitalism

CONNECT TO ECONOMICS

During the early 1800s, the Supreme Court made several rulings that helped define federal power over contracts and commerce. These rulings reinforced capitalism as the ruling economic system in the United States.

What effect did the Supreme Court have on economic development?

1810	1819		1824
Fletcher* v. *Peck State legislatures could not pass laws violating existing contracts.	***Dartmouth College* v. *Woodward*** State legislatures could not pass laws to change the charters of institutions or businesses.	***McCulloch* v. *Maryland*** States do not have right to tax federal institutions	***Gibbons* v. *Ogden*** Only federal government has the right to regulate interstate and foreign commerce

Shortly after Van Buren took office, the country experienced the **Panic of 1837**, a severe economic depression. Jackson's banking policies and his unsuccessful plan to curb inflation contributed to the panic. But people blamed Van Buren.

In 1840 the Whigs united against the weakened Van Buren to stand behind one candidate, **William Henry Harrison**, an army general. Harrison won in an electoral landslide. The Whigs had achieved their goal of winning the presidency.

READING CHECK **Identifying Cause and Effect** What contributed to the Panic of 1837, and how did it affect the 1840 election?

SUMMARY AND PREVIEW The states' rights debate dominated much of Jackson's presidency. In the next section you will learn about the removal of American Indians from the southeastern United States.

Section 2 Assessment

go.hrw.com
Online Quiz
KEYWORD: SS8 HP9

Reviewing Ideas, Terms, and People HSS 8.10.1, 8.10.3

1. a. **Recall** On what were the economies of the northern, southern, and western states based?
   b. **Predict** How might the sectional issues involved in the dispute over the **Tariff of Abominations** lead to future problems between North and South?
2. a. **Describe** What roles did **Daniel Webster** and John C. Calhoun play in the **nullification crisis**?
   b. **Summarize** What idea did supporters of the **states' rights doctrine** promote?
3. a. **Describe** What problems resulted from weakening the Bank?
   b. **Draw Conclusions** Why did Jackson veto the bill to renew the Second Bank of the United States?
4. a. **Recall** What caused the **Panic of 1837**?
   b. **Summarize** How did the **Whig Party** win the election of 1840?
   c. **Elaborate** Why do you think Jackson chose not to run for the presidency in 1836? Do you think he made the right decision? Why?

Critical Thinking

5. **Summarizing** Copy the graphic organizer below on your own sheet of paper. Use it to identify the problems that the nation faced during Jackson's presidency.

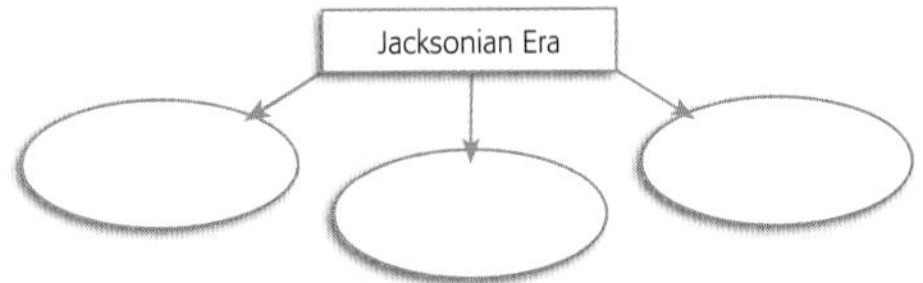

FOCUS ON WRITING

6. **Identifying Important Conflicts** Stories about conflict sell newspapers. As you read this section, list important conflicts that occurred during Jackson's presidency and note the role Jackson played in creating or resolving the conflicts.

Direct Teach

Interpreting Charts

Supreme Court and Capitalism

Compare What do all four of these cases have in common? *issues of federal versus state authority*

Review & Assess

Close

Have students summarize how political and economic policies during Jackson's presidency contributed to sectional divisions in the nation.

Review

Online Quiz, Section 2

Assess

SE Section 2 Assessment

PASS: Section 2 Quiz

Alternative Assessment Handbook

Reteach/Classroom Intervention

California Standards Review Workbook

Interactive Reader and Study Guide, Section 2

Interactive Skills Tutor CD-ROM

Section 2 Assessment Answers

1. a. North—trade and manufacturing, South—agriculture, West—farming and settlement
   b. possible answer—might have contributed to increased sectional divisions in Congress
2. a. Calhoun supported nullification and states' rights; Webster opposed nullification and supported national unity over states' rights.
   b. state power should be greater than federal
3. a. Smaller banks began offering easy credit terms for buying land, which led to inflation.
   b. did not think the bank was constitutional
4. a. Jackson's banking policies; inflation
   b. united behind one candidate, Harrison, and emphasized his war record, log-cabin roots
   c. Students should note that Jackson's actions had angered many.
5. Sectional Differences—people divided over political policies by region; Nullification Crisis—states' rights versus federal authority over tariffs; National Bank—Jackson opposed Bank, led to economic problems
6. Notes should address conflicts listed above.

Answers

Connect to Economics *helped define federal power over contracts and commerce; reinforced capitalism*

Reading Check *cause—Jackson's banking policies and unsuccessful plan to curb inflation; effect—Whig Party candidate, William Henry Harrison, won the election of 1840*

Preteach

Bellringer

If YOU were there . . . Use the **Daily Bellringer Transparency** to help students answer the question.

Daily Bellringer Transparency, Section 3

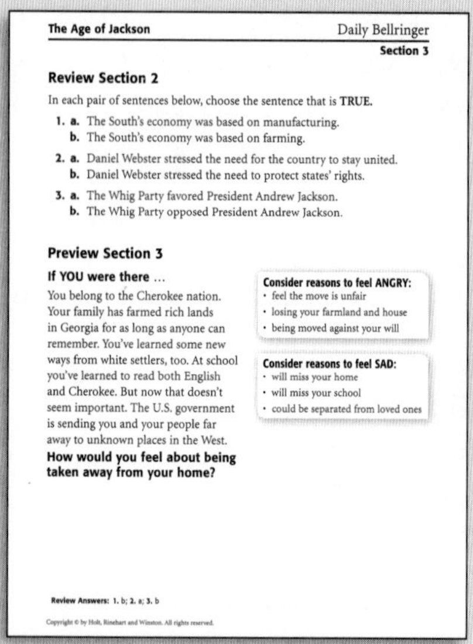

The Age of Jackson — Daily Bellringer **Section 3**

Review Section 2

In each pair of sentences below, choose the sentence that is **TRUE.**

1. **a.** The South's economy was based on manufacturing.
   b. The South's economy was based on farming.
2. **a.** Daniel Webster stressed the need for the country to stay united.
   b. Daniel Webster stressed the need to protect states' rights.
3. **a.** The Whig Party favored President Andrew Jackson.
   b. The Whig Party opposed President Andrew Jackson.

Preview Section 3

If YOU were there ...

You belong to the Cherokee nation. Your family has farmed rich lands in Georgia for as long as anyone can remember. You've learned some new ways from white settlers, too. At school you've learned to read both English and Cherokee. But now that doesn't seem important. The U.S. government is sending you and your people far away to unknown places in the West.

How would you feel about being taken away from your home?

Consider reasons to feel ANGRY:
- feel the move is unfair
- losing your farmland and house
- being moved against your will

Consider reasons to feel SAD:
- will miss your home
- will miss your school
- could be separated from loved ones

Review Answers: 1. b; 2. a; 3. b

Academic Vocabulary

Review with students the high-use academic term in this section.

contemporary existing at the same time (p. 295)

CRF: Vocabulary Builder Activity, Section 3

Standards Focus

HSS 8.8.1

Means: Explain Jackson's policy of Indian removal and how it opposed the U.S. Supreme Court.

Matters: Jackson's policy of Indian removal had lasting and devastating effects on Native Americans in the Southeast.

SECTION 3

Indian Removal

What You Will Learn...

Main Ideas

1. The Indian Removal Act authorized the relocation of Native Americans to the West.
2. Cherokee resistance to removal led to disagreement between Jackson and the Supreme Court.
3. Other Native Americans resisted removal with force.

The Big Idea

President Jackson supported a policy of Indian removal.

Key Terms and People

Indian Removal Act, *p. 294*
Indian Territory, *p. 294*
Bureau of Indian Affairs, *p. 294*
Sequoya, *p. 295*
Worcester v. *Georgia*, *p. 296*
Trail of Tears, *p. 296*
Black Hawk, *p. 297*
Osceola, *p. 297*

HSS 8.8.1 Discuss the election of Andrew Jackson as president in 1828, the importance of Jacksonian democracy, and his actions as president (e.g., the spoils system, veto of the National Bank, policy of Indian removal, opposition to the Supreme Court).

If YOU were there...

You belong to the Cherokee nation. Your family has farmed rich lands in Georgia for as long as anyone can remember. You've learned some new ways from white settlers, too. At school you've learned to read both English and Cherokee. But now that doesn't seem important. The U.S. government is sending you and your people far away to unknown places in the West.

How would you feel about being taken away from your home?

BUILDING BACKGROUND President Andrew Jackson had become famous as an Indian fighter. He had no sympathy with Native Americans' claim to the lands where they had always lived. With public support, he reversed the government's pledge to respect Indian land claims. The result was the brutal removal of the southeastern peoples to empty lands in the West.

Indian Removal Act

Native Americans had long lived in settlements stretching from Georgia to Mississippi. However, President Jackson and other political leaders wanted to open this land to settlement by American farmers. Under pressure from Jackson, Congress passed the **Indian Removal Act** in 1830, authorizing the removal of Native American who lived east of the Mississippi River to lands in the West.

Congress then established **Indian Territory**—U.S. land in what is now Oklahoma where Native Americans were moved to. Some supporters of this plan, like John C. Calhoun, argued that removal to Indian Territory would protect Indians from further conflicts with American settlers. "One of the greatest evils to which they are subject is that incessant [constant] pressure of our population," he noted. "To guard against this evil . . . there ought to be the strongest . . . assurance that the country given [to] them should be theirs." To manage Indian removal to western lands, Congress approved the creation of a new government agency, the **Bureau of Indian Affairs**.

Teach the Big Idea: Master the Standards

Standards Proficiency

Indian Removal

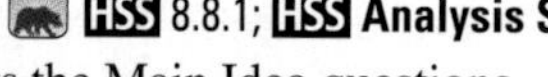

HSS 8.8.1; HSS **Analysis Skills:** CS 1, HR 5, HI 1, HI 2

1. **Teach** Ask students the Main Idea questions to teach this section.
2. **Apply** Organize students into small groups. Assign each group one of the following: (1) Choctaw, Creek, and Chickasaw; (2) Cherokee; (3) Fox, Sauk, and Seminole. Have each group create a storyboard that uses images and captions to narrate how the policy of Indian removal affected its assigned Native American group(s). **LS Interpersonal, Visual/Spatial**
3. **Review** As you review the section, have each group explain its storyboard to the class.
4. **Practice/Homework** Have each student write a poem from the point of view of a Native American in response to the U.S. government's policy of Indian removal during this period. **LS Verbal/Linguistic**

Alternative Assessment Handbook, Rubrics 26: Poems and Songs; and 29: Presentations

Indian Removal

During the Trail of Tears, thousands of Cherokee died from disease, starvation, and harsh weather. They were forced to walk hundreds of miles to their new land in the West. Other Native Americans were also moved, with similar results.

What can you see in this painting that indicates this was a difficult journey?

The Choctaw were the first Indians sent to Indian Territory. The Mississippi legislature abolished the Choctaw government and then forced the Choctaw leaders to sign the Treaty of Dancing Rabbit Creek. This treaty gave more than 7.5 million acres of their land to the state. The Choctaw moved to Indian Territory during a disastrous winter trip. Federal officials in charge of the move did not provide enough food or supplies to the Choctaw, most of whom were on foot. About one-fourth of the Choctaw died of cold, disease, or starvation.

News of the Choctaw's hardships caused other Indians to resist removal. When the Creek resisted in 1836, federal troops moved in and captured some 14,500 of them. They led the Creek, many in chains, to Indian Territory. One Creek woman remembered the trip being filled with "the awful silence that showed the heartaches and sorrow at being taken from the homes and even separation from loved ones." The Chickasaw, who lived in upper Mississippi, negotiated a treaty for better supplies on their trip to Indian Territory. Nevertheless, many Chickasaw lives were also lost during removal.

READING CHECK **Finding Main Ideas** What major changes did President Jackson make to U.S. policy regarding Native Americans?

Cherokee Resistance

Many Cherokee had believed that they could prevent conflicts and avoid removal by adopting the **contemporary** culture of white people. In the early 1800s they invited missionaries to set up schools where Cherokee children learned how to read and write in English. The Cherokee developed their own government modeled after the U.S. Constitution with an election system, a bicameral council, and a court system. All of these were headed by a principal chief.

ACADEMIC VOCABULARY
contemporary existing at the same time

A Cherokee named **Sequoya** used 86 characters to represent Cherokee syllables to create a writing system for their own complex language. In 1828 the Cherokee began publishing a newspaper printed in both English and Cherokee.

The adoption of white culture did not protect the Cherokee. After gold was discovered on their land in Georgia, their treaty rights

Direct Teach

Main Idea

❶ Indian Removal Act

The Indian Removal Act authorized the relocation of Native Americans to the West.

Explain Why did government officials want to relocate Native Americans in the Southeast to lands in the West? *to open the Indians' land to white settlers*

Identify Points of View Based on their actions, how do you think Native Americans viewed the Indian Removal Act? *possible answers—with outrage, fear, helplessness, desire to fight the act*

Predict How might the Southeast be different today if Native Americans had successfully resisted removal? *possible answer—Native Americans might form a larger percentage of the region's population, hold more positions of leadership, and have had a greater influence on the region.*

HSS 8.8.1; HSS **Analysis Skills:** HR 5, HI 1

go.hrw.com
Online Resources
KEYWORD: SS8 US9
ACTIVITY: Indian Removal

Critical Thinking: Supporting a Point of View

Exceeding Standards

Speech Opposing Indian Removal Act

HSS 8.8.1; HSS **Analysis Skills:** HR 5, HI 1, HI 2

1. Ask students to imagine that they were members of Congress during the debate over the passage of the Indian Removal Act. Have each student write and deliver a speech that a Congress member opposed to the act might have given.
2. Students' speeches should address the purpose of the act, the terms of the act, and the potential effects of the act for both Native Americans and white settlers.
3. Remind students to provide support for their points of view and to address possible arguments against their positions.
4. Have each student deliver his or her speech to the class. Conclude by having students discuss the short-and long-term effects of the Indian Removal Act. LS **Logical/Mathematical, Verbal/Linguistic**

Alternative Assessment Handbook, Rubric 24: Oral Presentations

Answers

Indian Removal *The way the people are bundled up to stay warm indicates cold weather; The expressions on people's faces and the amount of property they are moving suggests a long, hard journey.*

Reading Check *authorized the removal of Native Americans who lived east of the Mississippi River to lands to the west in Indian Territory*

Direct Teach

Main Idea

❷ Cherokee Resistance

Cherokee resistance to removal led to disagreement between Jackson and the Supreme Court.

Explain Why did the adoption of white culture not protect the Cherokee from removal? *because gold was discovered on their land*

Summarize What steps did the Cherokee take to try to resist removal, and what was the result? *They sued the state, and their case went to the Supreme Court, which ruled in their favor; the state of Georgia ignored the ruling and removed them anyway; during the Trail of Tears, many Cherokee died.*

CRF: Biography Activity: Sequoya

U.S. Supreme Court Case Studies: *Worchester* v. *Georgia* (1832)

HSS 8.8.1; **HSS Analysis Skills:** HR 5, HI 1, HI 2

Connect to Government

Worcester* v. *Georgia The status of Indian nations in the courts remained undefined until the Supreme Court case *Worcester* v. *Georgia*. In his decision, Chief Justice John Marshall wrote that the "acts of Georgia are repugnant to the Constitution . . . [and] in direct hostility with treaties [that] . . . solemnly pledge the faith of the United States to restrain their citizens from trespassing on [Cherokee land]."

were ignored. Georgia leaders began preparing for the Cherokee's removal. When they refused to move, the Georgia militia began attacking Cherokee towns. In response, the Cherokee sued the state. They said that they were an independent nation and claimed that the government of Georgia had no legal power over their lands.

In 1832 the Supreme Court, under the leadership of Chief Justice John Marshall, agreed. In ***Worcester* v. *Georgia*** the Court ruled that the Cherokee nation was a distinct community in which the laws of Georgia had no force. The Court also stated that only the federal government, not the states, had authority over Native Americans.

THE IMPACT TODAY

Today more than 60,000 Cherokee or Cherokee descendants live in present-day Oklahoma.

Georgia, however, ignored the Court's ruling, and President Jackson took no action to make Georgia follow the ruling. "John Marshall has made his decision; now let him enforce it," Jackson supposedly said. By not enforcing the Court's decision, Jackson violated his presidential oath to uphold the laws of the land. However, most members of Congress and American citizens did not protest the ways Jackson removed Native Americans.

In the spring of 1838, U.S. troops began to remove all Cherokee to Indian Territory. A few were able to escape and hide in the mountains of North Carolina. After the Cherokee were removed, Georgia took their businesses, farms, and property.

The Cherokee's 800-mile forced march became known as the **Trail of Tears**. During the march, the Cherokee suffered from disease, hunger, and harsh weather. Almost one-fourth of the 18,000 Cherokee died on the march.

READING CHECK **Finding Main Ideas** What was the *Worcester* v. *Georgia* ruling, and what was Jackson's response?

Primary Source

PERSONAL ACCOUNTS

Trail of Tears

The Cherokee knew that they would be forced to march West, but they did not know that so many of their people would die on the way. Here are two accounts of the Trail of Tears, one written before it started and one written after, both by Cherokee who made the trip.

March 10, 1838
Beloved Martha, I have delayed writing to you so long. . . . If we Cherokees are to be driven to the west by the cruel hand of oppression to seek a new home in the west, it will be impossible. . . . It is thus all our rights are invaded."

—Letter from Jenny, a Cherokee girl, just before her removal

"Long time we travel on way to new land. People feel bad when they leave Old Nation. Women cry and make sad wails, Children cry and many men cry . . . but they say nothing and just put heads down and keep on go towards West. Many days pass and people die very much."

—Recollections of a survivor of the Trail of Tears

ANALYSIS SKILL **ANALYZING POINTS OF VIEW**

1. What is different about the concerns of the Cherokee before and after the Trail of Tears?
2. How do you think the survivors of the Trail of Tears felt when they reached their new homeland?

Cross-Discipline Activity: Art

Indian Removal Memorial

HSS 8.8.1; **HSS Analysis Skills:** HR 5, HI 1

Materials: art supplies; images of memorials, such as Vietnam Veterans Memorial (optional)

1. Have students describe the main actions and events that led to the removal of Native American groups in the Southeast.
2. Then have students, working either individually or in small groups, design memorials for the many Native Americans in the Southeast who died either resisting removal or being forcibly removed. Give students choices for their memorials, such as a statue, a plaque, or a marker to set along the route of the Trail of Tears. Each student or group should write a paragraph explaining the memorial.
3. Display the memorials in the classroom. **LS Verbal/Linguistic, Visual/Spatial**

Alternative Assessment Handbook, Rubric 3: Artwork

Answers

Analyzing Points of View
1. *before—author is concerned about rights, tone is angry; after—author concerned about the tragedy of the Trail of Tears.* **2.** *possible answers—exhausted, sad, angry, relieved*

Reading Check *The Supreme Court ruled that the laws of Georgia did not apply to the Cherokee nation; Jackson did not take any action to enforce the Court's ruling.*

Other Native Americans Resist

Other Native Americans decided to fight U.S. troops to avoid removal. Chief **Black Hawk**, a leader of Fox and Sauk Indians, decided to fight rather than leave Illinois. By 1832, however, the Sauk forces were running out of food and supplies, and by 1850 they had been forced to leave.

In Florida, Seminole leaders were forced to sign a removal treaty that their followers decided to ignore. A leader named **Osceola** called upon his followers to resist with force, and the Second Seminole War began. Osceola was captured and soon died in prison. His followers, however, continued to fight. Some 4,000 Seminole were removed and hundreds of others killed. Eventually, U.S. officials decided to give up the fight. Small groups of Seminole had resisted removal, and their descendants live in Florida today.

READING CHECK **Evaluating** How effective was Native American resistance to removal?

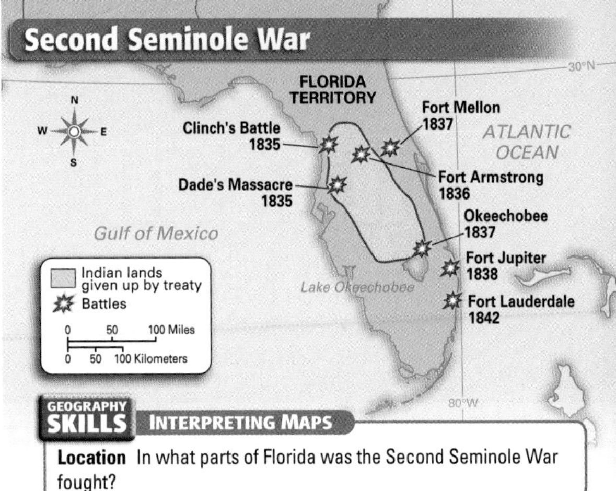

GEOGRAPHY SKILLS INTERPRETING MAPS

Location In what parts of Florida was the Second Seminole War fought?

SUMMARY AND PREVIEW President Jackson supported the removal of thousands of Native Americans from their traditional lands to the federal territory in the West. In the next chapter you will learn about the westward growth of the nation as farmers, ranchers, and other settlers moved West.

Section 3 Assessment

go.hrw.com **Online Quiz** KEYWORD: SS8 HP9

Reviewing Ideas, Terms, and People HSS 8.8.1

1. a. **Identify** What Native American groups were affected by the **Indian Removal Act**? Where were they relocated?
   b. **Explain** Why did government officials want to relocate Native Americans to the West?
   c. **Predict** What are some possible effects that the Indian Removal Act might have on Native Americans already living in the West?
2. a. **Identify** What was the **Trail of Tears**?
   b. **Analyze** Why did the state of Georgia want to relocate the Cherokee, and what did the Cherokee do in response?
   c. **Elaborate** What do you think of President Jackson's refusal to enforce the ***Worcester* v. *Georgia*** ruling?
3. a. **Describe** What led to the Second Seminole War?
   b. **Compare and Contrast** How were the Seminole and the Sauk resistance efforts similar and different?

Critical Thinking

4. **Comparing and Contrasting** Copy the chart below. Use it to identify Native American groups removed during this period and their responses to removal.

Native American Group	Response to Removal

FOCUS ON WRITING

5. **Understanding Causes and Effects** As you read, identify the causes and effects of the Jackson administration's policy of Indian relocation.

Direct Teach

Main Idea

3 Other Native Americans Resist

Other Native Americans resisted removal with force.

Identify and Compare Who were Chief Black Hawk and Osceola, and what did they have in common? *Black Hawk—leader of Fox and Sauk Indians; Osceola—Seminole leader; both called on followers to resist removal with force*

- **CRF:** Biography Activity: Black Hawk
- **CRF:** History and Geography Activity: The Seminole Wars
- **CRF:** Literature Activity: *Surrender Speech* by Chief Black Hawk
- Map Transparency: Second Seminole War

HSS 8.8.1; HSS **Analysis Skills:** HI 1

Review & Assess

Close

Have students summarize the effects of Jackson's Indian removal policy.

Review

Online Quiz, Section 3

Assess

SE Section 3 Assessment

- PASS: Section 3 Quiz
- Alternative Assessment Handbook

Reteach/Classroom Intervention

- California Standards Review Workbook
- Interactive Reader and Study Guide, Section 3
- Interactive Skills Tutor CD-ROM

Section 3 Assessment Answers

1. **a.** Choctaw, Creek, Chickasaw, Cherokee, Fox, Sauk, Seminole; Indian Territory
   b. to open up more lands for settlement
   c. possible answer—conflict with newcomers, competition for resources
2. **a.** 800-mile forced march of the Cherokee from their lands in Georgia to Indian Territory, during which many Cherokee died
   b. why—gold had been found on their lands; Cherokee response—sued state of Georgia
   c. possible answers—His decision was unfair and possibly unconstitutional
3. **a.** When Seminole leaders were forced to sign a removal treaty, other Seminole fought.
   b. similar—both resisted; different—Sauk were removed, many of the Seminole resisted
4. Choctaw and Chickasaw—sent to Indian Territory; Cherokee—adopted white culture then sued state, sent to Indian Territory; Sauk—fought, removed; Seminole—fought, ultimately successful in resistance
5. Students should indicate that the Indian removal policy led to the removal and death of many Native Americans in the Southeast.

Answers

Interpreting Maps *East coast and north central*

Reading Check *Overall, not effective, although some Native Americans successfully resisted removal.*

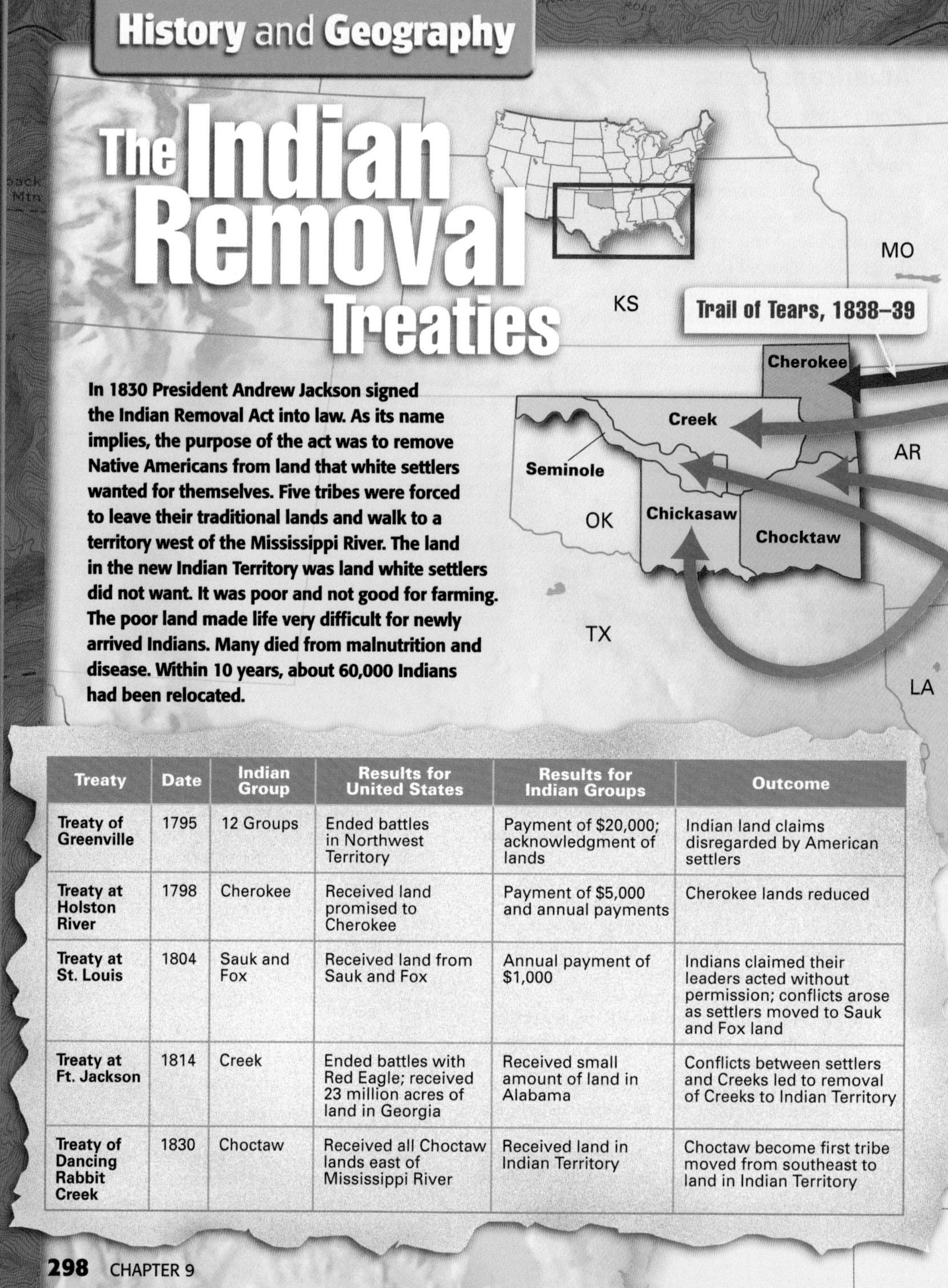

In 1830 President Andrew Jackson signed the Indian Removal Act into law. As its name implies, the purpose of the act was to remove Native Americans from land that white settlers wanted for themselves. Five tribes were forced to leave their traditional lands and walk to a territory west of the Mississippi River. The land in the new Indian Territory was land white settlers did not want. It was poor and not good for farming. The poor land made life very difficult for newly arrived Indians. Many died from malnutrition and disease. Within 10 years, about 60,000 Indians had been relocated.

Treaty	Date	Indian Group	Results for United States	Results for Indian Groups	Outcome
Treaty of Greenville	1795	12 Groups	Ended battles in Northwest Territory	Payment of $20,000; acknowledgment of lands	Indian land claims disregarded by American settlers
Treaty at Holston River	1798	Cherokee	Received land promised to Cherokee	Payment of $5,000 and annual payments	Cherokee lands reduced
Treaty at St. Louis	1804	Sauk and Fox	Received land from Sauk and Fox	Annual payment of $1,000	Indians claimed their leaders acted without permission; conflicts arose as settlers moved to Sauk and Fox land
Treaty at Ft. Jackson	1814	Creek	Ended battles with Red Eagle; received 23 million acres of land in Georgia	Received small amount of land in Alabama	Conflicts between settlers and Creeks led to removal of Creeks to Indian Territory
Treaty of Dancing Rabbit Creek	1830	Choctaw	Received all Choctaw lands east of Mississippi River	Received land in Indian Territory	Choctaw become first tribe moved from southeast to land in Indian Territory

298 CHAPTER 9

History and Geography

Activity Analyzing Trends and Patterns Read aloud to students the information in the feature and then lead a discussion about Indian removal and its effects. Next, have students examine the table and the map and look for trends and patterns in U.S.–Native American relations. Have volunteers identify trends and patterns. *(trends—Over time the U.S. government offered Native Americans a decreasing amount of money and then land in exchange for Indian land in treaties. The land offered amounted to removal. patterns—pattern of conflict, treaties, and removal)* To extend the activity, have each student write a short essay summarizing trends and patterns in Indian Removal Treaties and the effects of the treaties.
LS Verbal/Linguistic

HSS 8.8.1, 8.8.2; **HSS Analysis Skills:** CS 3, HI 2, HI 3

Standards Focus

HSS 8.8 Students analyze the divergent paths of the American people in the West from 1800 to the mid-1800s and the challenges they faced.

8.8.1 Discuss the election of Andrew Jackson as president in 1828, the importance of Jacksonian democracy, and his actions as president (e.g., the spoils system, veto of the National Bank, policy of Indian removal, opposition to the Supreme Court).

8.8.2 Describe the purpose, challenges, and economic incentives associated with westward expansion, including the concept of Manifest Destiny (e.g., the Lewis and Clark expedition, accounts of the removal of Indians, the Cherokees' "Trail of Tears," settlement of the Great Plains) and the territorial acquisitions that spanned numerous decades.

Critical Thinking: Analyzing Information

Standards Proficiency

Effects of Indian Removal

HSS 8.8.1, 8.8.2; **HSS Analysis Skills:** HI 1, HI 2, HI 3

Materials: 18" × 12" sheets of light-colored construction paper

1. Organize students into groups of three. Have each group select one sign maker. The other two members will serve as writers.
2. Distribute one sheet of construction paper to each group. Have the sign maker fold the paper to make two sections that are 9" × 12" and then open the sheet. Instruct students to write Indian Relocation across the top of the page and label the two columns *Effects on Native Americans' Lives* and *Effects on Settlers' Lives.*
3. Instruct the groups to discuss the ways that lives were changed by Indian removal and treaties and have writers record the group's observations in the appropriate columns.
4. Have group volunteers share some of their observations with the class. **LS Interpersonal, Verbal/Linguistic**

Alternative Assessment Handbook, Rubrics 7: Charts; and 14: Group Activity

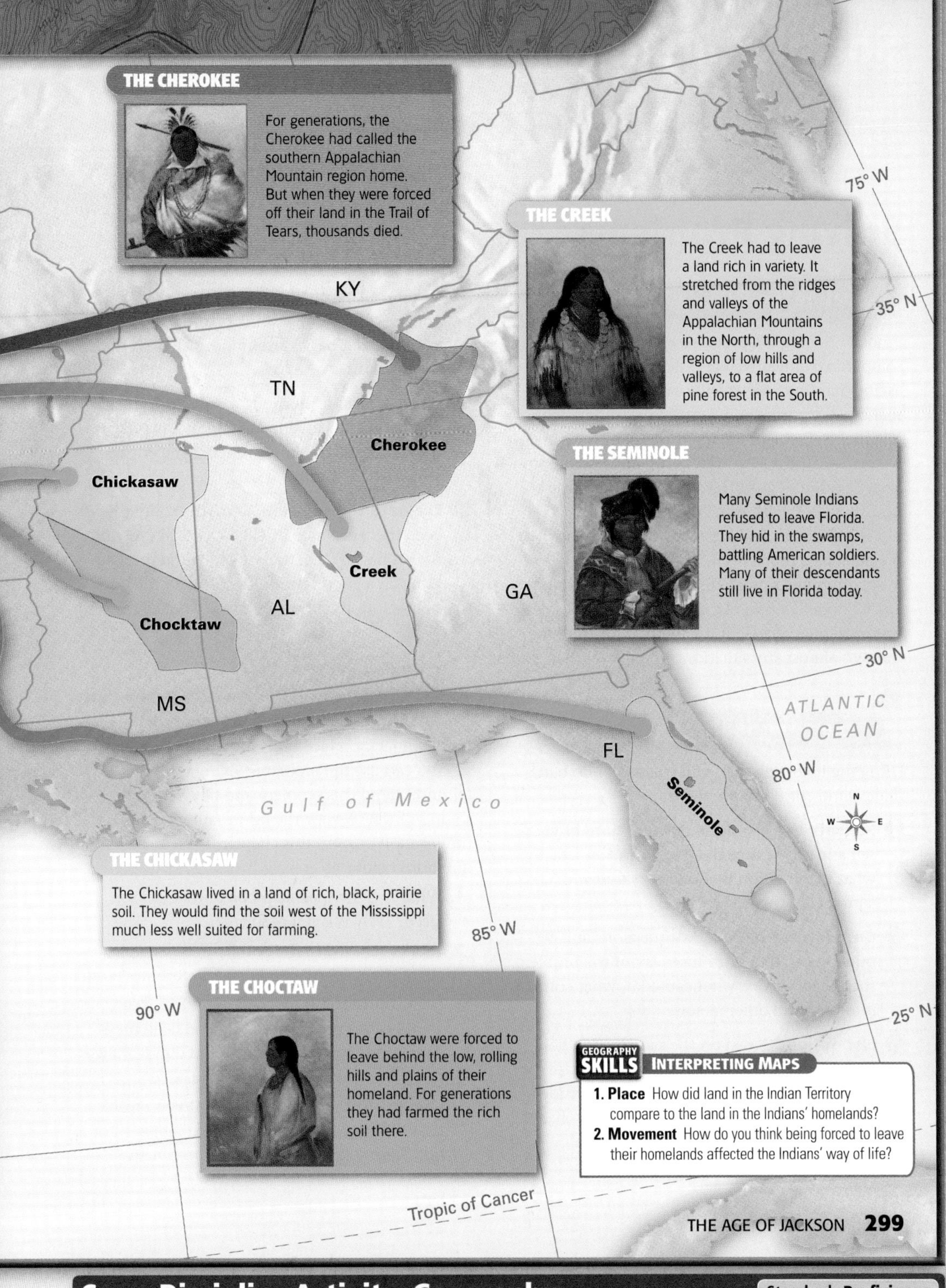

THE CHEROKEE
For generations, the Cherokee had called the southern Appalachian Mountain region home. But when they were forced off their land in the Trail of Tears, thousands died.
THE CREEK
The Creek had to leave a land rich in variety. It stretched from the ridges and valleys of the Appalachian Mountains in the North, through a region of low hills and valleys, to a flat area of pine forest in the South.
THE SEMINOLE
Many Seminole Indians refused to leave Florida. They hid in the swamps, battling American soldiers. Many of their descendants still live in Florida today.
THE CHICKASAW
The Chickasaw lived in a land of rich, black, prairie soil. They would find the soil west of the Mississippi much less well suited for farming.
THE CHOCTAW
The Choctaw were forced to leave behind the low, rolling hills and plains of their homeland. For generations they had farmed the rich soil there.
KY
TN
AL
GA
MS
FL
Chickasaw
Cherokee
Creek
Chocktaw
Seminole
75° W
35° N
30° N
80° W
85° W
90° W
25° N
ATLANTIC OCEAN
Gulf of Mexico
Tropic of Cancer
N
E
S
W

GEOGRAPHY SKILLS INTERPRETING MAPS

1. **Place** How did land in the Indian Territory compare to the land in the Indians' homelands?
2. **Movement** How do you think being forced to leave their homelands affected the Indians' way of life?

History and Geography

Linking to Today

Native American Populations A little less than half of the 2 million Native Americans in the United States today live on or near the nation's more than 250 Indian reservations. Each year the Native American population continues to grow. Of the total number of Native Americans, the majority live west of the Mississippi River, particularly in Arizona, California, Oklahoma, New Mexico, and South Dakota.

Info to Know

Native American Literacy While in the Cherokee Regiment of the U.S. Army, in the early 1800s, Sequoya recognized the need for Native American literacy. Many Native Americans were unable to read military orders, send letters home, record events, or even read the treaties they signed. The creation of Talking Leaves, the Cherokee written language, had begun.

Linking to Today

The Cherokee Historians estimate that when Europeans arrived in North America, about 22,000 Cherokee lived in the present-day southeastern United States. Today the largest concentrations of Cherokee are the Eastern Band in North Carolina and the Cherokee Nation of Oklahoma. The federal government also recognizes one other Cherokee group, the United Bank of Keetoowahs, in Oklahoma. More than 50 other groups that are not recognized by the federal government also claim Cherokee heritage.

Cross-Discipline Activity: Geography

Standards Proficiency

Comparing and Contrasting Regions

Research Required

1. Organize students into five groups and assign each group one of the Native American groups labeled on the map.
2. Have each group conduct research on the climate and physical geography of the assigned group's traditional homelands as well as the climate and physical geography of the area to which the group was relocated.
3. Instruct each group to create a large table comparing and contrasting the two regions. Encourage students to include images or photographs of the regions to enhance their tables. Groups should then write a summary of the differences between the two regions.
4. Have each group present its work to the class.
5. Have students discuss how geographic differences contributed to the hardships Native Americans faced when forced to relocate.

LS Interpersonal, Verbal/Linguistic

HSS 8.8.1, 8.8.2; **HSS Analysis Skills:** CS 3, HI 1, HI 2

Alternative Assessment Handbook, Rubrics 7: Charts; 14: Group Activity; and 30: Research

Answers

Interpreting Maps 1. *The land in Indian Territory was poor and not good for farming, whereas many of the relocated Indians came from areas with fertile soils, plains, and rolling hills.*
2. *possible answer—They had to adjust to a new climate and learn how to hunt differently, grow food differently, and rely on different materials for their homes and clothing.*

Social Studies Skills

Solving Problems

Activity Problem-Solving Role Play Organize students into groups to practice their problem-solving skills. Assign each group a current or hypothetical issue or problem within the school or community. Then have each group address this issue by writing an outline incorporating the steps included on this page. Groups should begin by identifying the problem and should conclude by suggesting a solution. Have a volunteer from each group present his or her group's outline to the class. Encourage other students to evaluate each group's solution. **LS Interpersonal, Logical/Mathematical**

Alternative Assessment Handbook, Rubric 35: Solving Problems

Interactive Skills Tutor CD-ROM: Lessons 12: Identify Issues and Problems; and 16: Identify Possible Solutions and Predict Consequences

Answers

Practice the Skill 1. *The South Carolina legislature passed a resolution nullifying the tariffs of 1828 and 1832 and threatened to secede if the federal government used force to try to collect the duties. This situation posed a problem because it threatened federal authority and the Union.* **2.** *passage of the 1832 tariff; passage of the 1828 tariffs and the states' rights doctrine;* **3.** *Answers will vary, but students should provide logical advantages and disadvantages for each proposed solution.* **4.** *Answers will vary, but students should exhibit an understanding of the advantages and disadvantages of using troops and provide reasons to support why another solution, if offered, would have been better.*

Social Studies Skills

Analysis | Critical Thinking | Participation | Study

HSS Participation Skill Develop personal skills.

Solving Problems

Define the Skill

Problem solving is a process for finding workable solutions to difficult situations. The process involves asking questions, identifying and evaluating information, comparing and contrasting, and making judgments. Problem solving is useful in studying history because it helps you better understand problems a person or group faced at a point in time and how they dealt with those difficulties.

The ability to understand and evaluate how people solved problems in the past also can help in solving similar problems today. The skill can be applied to many other kinds of difficulties besides historical ones as well. It is a method for thinking through almost any situation.

Learn the Skill

Using the following steps will enable you to better understand and solve problems.

1. **Identify the problem.** Ask questions of yourself and others to make sure you know exactly what the situation is and understand why it is a problem.
2. **Gather information.** Ask questions and do other research to learn more about the problem, such as its history, what caused it, what contributes to it, and other factors.
3. **List options.** Based on the information you have gathered, identify possible options for solving the problem that you might consider. Be aware that your final solution will probably be better and easier to reach if you have as many options as possible to consider.
4. **Evaluate the options.** Weigh each option you are considering. Think of and list the advantages it has as a solution, as well as its potential disadvantages.
5. **Choose and implement a solution.** After comparing the advantages and disadvantages of each possible solution, choose the one that seems best and apply it.
6. **Evaluate the solution.** Once the solution has been tried, evaluate its effectiveness in solving the problem. This step will tell you if the solution was a good one, or if another of the possible solutions should be tried instead.

Practice the Skill

One of the most challenging situations that President Jackson faced was the nullification crisis. You can use the problem-solving skills to better understand this problem and to evaluate his solution for it. Review the information about the nullification crisis in this chapter. Then answer the questions below.

1. What was the specific problem that Jackson faced? Why was it a problem?
2. What event led to the problem? What earlier circumstances and conditions contributed to it?
3. List possible solutions to the problem that you would have considered if you had been president, along with advantages and disadvantages.
4. Jackson threatened to send troops to South Carolina to enforce federal law. Do you think his solution was the best one? Explain why, or if not, what solution would have been better.

Social Studies Skills Activity: Solving Problems

Alternate Solutions to Indian Removal

Standards Proficiency

1. Have students review the text in Section 3 under the headings "Indian Removal Act" and "Cherokee Resistance."
2. Organize students into groups and ask the groups to imagine that they are members of the U.S. Congress at that time. Have each group consider a solution to the problem of American settlers wanting to move into Native American lands that does not require forcing Native Americans to move and that respects their right to their lands.
3. Each group should create a flow chart showing its responses for each of the steps listed under "Learn the Skill."
4. Have a representative from each group present his or her group's flow chart to the class. Have students evaluate each group's proposed solution and discuss possible advantages and disadvantages. **LS Interpersonal, Logical/Mathematical**

Alternative Assessment Handbook, Rubrics 14: Group Activity; and 35: Solving Problems

CHAPTER 9

Standards Review

Visual Summary

Use the visual summary below to help you review the main ideas of the chapter.

QUICK FACTS
SLAM!
Jackson's Policies Shut the Door on Key Issues
Second Bank of the United States Jackson vetoed the legislation to renew the Bank's charter and removed federal funds from the Bank.
Indian Removal Jackson pressured Congress to pass a law to move Native Americans out of the Southeast and into Indian Territory.
Nullification Crisis Jackson threatened to send federal troops into South Carolina to enforce federal law.

Reviewing Vocabulary, Terms, and People

Complete each sentence by filling in the blank with the correct term or person.

1. In the Supreme Court case of ______________, the Court ruled that the federal government, not the states, had authority over the Cherokee.
2. President Jackson's group of advisers was known as the ____________ because of where its members met in the White House.
3. ____________ served as Andrew Jackson's vice president until he resigned due to the dispute over nullification.
4. The ____________ supported the power of the states over the federal government.
5. The practice of rewarding supporters with positions in government is known as the _______.

Comprehension and Critical Thinking

SECTION 1 *(Pages 284–286)* **HSS 8.8.1**

6. a. **Identify** What changes took place in the early 1800s that broadened democracy in the United States?
   b. **Analyze** How was Jackson's victory in the election of 1828 a reflection of a change in American politics?
   c. **Evaluate** Do you think the changes brought about by Jacksonian Democracy went far enough in expanding democracy? Why or why not?

SECTION 2 *(Pages 288–293)* **HSS 8.10.1, 8.10.3**

7. a. **Describe** What conflicts troubled the Jackson administration?

Answers

Visual Summary

Review and Inquiry Ask students how the images in the Visual Summary relate to the chapter content. For instance, what is the significance of the door slammed shut? Could any of Jackson's policies be represented by an open door? Which ones? What other symbols could be used to represent some of the policies of the Jackson administration?

Quick Facts Transparency: The Age of Jackson Visual Summary

Reviewing Vocabulary, Terms, and People

1. *Worcester* v. *Georgia*
2. kitchen cabinet
3. John C. Calhoun
4. states' rights doctrine
5. spoils system

Comprehension and Critical Thinking

6. a. Many states expanded voting rights to enable more white men to vote; some states allowed voters to nominate their electors; political parties began holding nominating conventions.
   b. More people had the vote, and Jackson and Calhoun received a record number of popular votes.
   c. Students should note that voting rights expanded but still excluded groups such as African Americans, Native Americans, and women.

Review and Assessment Resources

Review and Reinforce

- SE Standards Review
- **CRF:** Chapter Review Activity
- California Standards Review Workbook
- Quick Facts Transparency: The Age of Jackson Visual Summary
- Spanish Chapter Summaries Audio CD Program
- Online Chapter Summaries in Six Languages
- OSP Holt PuzzlePro; GameTool for ExamView
- Quiz Game CD-ROM

Assess

- SE Standards Assessment
- PASS: Chapter Test, Forms A and B
- Alternative Assessment Handbook
- OSP ExamView Test Generator, Chapter Test
- Universal Access Modified Worksheets and Tests CD-ROM: Chapter Test
- Holt Online Assessment Program (in the Premier Online Edition)

Reteach/Intervene

- Interactive Reader and Study Guide
- Universal Access Teacher Management System: Lesson Plans for Universal Access
- Universal Access Modified Worksheets and Tests CD-ROM
- Interactive Skills Tutor CD-ROM

go.hrw.com
Online Resources
Chapter Resources:
KEYWORD: SS8 US9

Answers

7. **a.** Tariff of Abominations, Nullification Crisis, issues connected to the Second Bank of the United States, inflation
b. led to Jackson's veto, inflation of the economy, and angered members of Congress
c. possible answer—might lead to increasing sectional divisions in the nation that could possibly threaten the unity of the nation

8. **a.** Cherokee who created a writing system for the Cherokee language
b. Cherokee—adopted white culture, appealed to the U.S. courts; Seminole—fought
c. possible answers—Yes, he did not personally agree with the decision; no, Jackson failed to fulfill his duties as president and to respect the power of the judiciary.

Reviewing Themes

9. Whig Party; favored a weak president

10. desire for land and wealth—Farmers wanted land, and gold was discovered on Cherokee land.

Social Studies Skills

11. a

Reading Skills

12. a

---

b. Draw Conclusions What were the results of the conflict over the Second Bank of the United States?

c. Predict How might sectional differences and the debate over states' rights lead to future problems for the United States?

SECTION 3 *(Pages 294–297)* **HSS 8.8.1**

8. **a. Identify** Who was Sequoya? What important contribution did he make?
b. Contrast In what different ways did the Cherokee and the Seminole attempt to resist removal to Indian Territory?
c. Elaborate Do you agree with Jackson's refusal to enforce the *Worcester* v. *Georgia* ruling? Why or why not?

Reviewing Themes

9. **Politics** What new political party rose in opposition to President Andrew Jackson? What was the party's attitude toward the power of the president?

10. **Economics** What economic factors influenced the policy of Indian removal?

Social Studies Skills

Solving Problems *Use the Social Studies Skills taught in this chapter to answer the question about the reading selection below.*

> Northerners wanted the tariff to protect their industries from foreign competition, especially from Great Britain. British companies were driving smaller American companies out of business by selling factory goods more cheaply than Americans could afford to make them . . . Southerners opposed the tariff, claiming it would hurt their economy. *(p. 289)*

11. Which of the following might be a reasonable solution to the problem discussed above?
a. passing a low tariff
b. passing a high tariff only in the South
c. Britain passing a tariff
d. selling northern and British goods for a higher price

Reading Skills

Drawing Conclusions *Use the Reading Skills taught in this chapter to answer the question about the reading selection below.*

> Native Americans had long lived in settlements stretching from Georgia to Mississippi. However, President Jackson and other political leaders wanted to open this land to settlement by American farmers. *(p. 294)*

12. Which statement below can you conclude from the passage above?
a. Farmers moved onto the Native Americans' land after they were removed.
b. Native Americans wanted to move from their lands.
c. Native Americans resisted removal.
d. Government officials had to use force to remove Native Americans from their land.

Using the Internet

13. **Activity: Writing a newspaper** Enter the activity keyword and research Jackson's presidency. Then create a party newspaper, using the template provided, that supports or criticizes his policies. Use evidence to support your articles either in favor or against his policies. Write from the point of view of a supporter or from the point of view of a political enemy.

FOCUS ON WRITING

14. **Writing Interview Questions** Review the notes you have taken about Jackson's political significance, the conflicts he was involved in, and the causes and effects of his policies toward Indians. Then, based on your notes, begin writing questions for your interview with Jackson. What will the readers of your newspaper want to learn more about? Write at least 10 interview questions that your readers will want to know the answer to.

Using the Internet

13. Go to the HRW Web site and enter the keyword shown to access a rubric for this activity.

KEYWORD: SS8 US9

Focus on Writing

14. **Rubric** Students' interview questions should:
- require more than a yes or no answer.
- address Jackson's campaign and election, the conflicts he was involved in, and the causes and effects of his Indian policies.
- use correct grammar, punctuation, spelling, and capitalizations.

CRF: Focus on Writing Activity: An Interview

Standards Assessment

DIRECTIONS: Read each question and write the letter of the best response.

1

> "The people have preserved . . . their . . . Constitution, for forty years, and have seen their happiness, prosperity, and renown grow with its growth, and strengthen with its strength. . . . I have not coolly weighed the chances of preserving liberty when the bonds that unite us together shall be broken . . . [Let us not have] 'Liberty first and Union afterwards,' but . . . that other sentiment, dear to every true American heart,—Liberty and Union, now and forever, one and inseparable!"
>
> –Daniel Webster

From the content of this passage, one could conclude that the writer would have been opposed to

A a protective tariff.
B nationalism.
C nullification.
D internal improvements.

2 **The position the speaker took in this 1830 speech is *most* like that of which other American leader of the time?**

A Andrew Jackson
B John C. Calhoun
C William Henry Harrison
D John Tyler

3 **The era surrounding the presidency of Andrew Jackson is *best* known for an expansion in**

A freedom of speech.
B religious toleration.
C states' rights.
D voting rights.

4 **Which of the following was *least important* to the South's economy in the 1830s?**

A small farming
B manufacturing
C plantation agriculture
D trade

5 **What action did the Cherokee take to resist their removal from Georgia and North Carolina to the West?**

A sued the state of Georgia in the courts
B destroyed neighbors' farms and businesses
C went to war against the U.S. government
D staged a protest called the Trail of Tears

Connecting with Past Learning

6 **The debate between John C. Calhoun and Daniel Webster over states' rights was *most like* the debate between**

A the Patriots and the Loyalists.
B the Antifederalists and the Federalists.
C England and France during the French and Indian War.
D the large states and the small states during the Constitutional Convention.

7 **Which person would have been *most likely* to have supported the ideals of Jacksonian Democracy if he had been alive at the time?**

A Charlemagne
B Prince Shotoku of Japan
C John Locke
D Mansa Musa

Answers

1. C
Break Down the Question: To help students identify the overall meaning of a passage, tell them to look for key repeated words or phrases. Here, point out the repetition of the idea of unity expressed through the words *unity, Union,* and *one and inseparable*. Then tell students to identify which answer is most *opposed* to unity or Union?

2. A
Break Down the Question: This question requires students to identify the speaker's position in the speech and then compare it to the positions of other figures in the chapter. Refer students who have trouble to the text titled "States' Rights Debate" in Section 2.

3. D
Break Down the Question: If students have a hard time choosing between options *C* and *D*, point out that the question asks for the issue for which the era is *best* known.

4. B
Break Down the Question: Remind students to pay attention to italicized words. Here, the phrase *least important* means that more than one answer may be partially correct.

5. A
Break Down the Question: This question requires students to recall factual information. Refer students who have trouble to the text titled "Cherokee Resistance" in Section 3.

6. B
Break Down the Question: This question connects to information covered in Chapter 4.

7. C
Break Down the Question: This question connects to information covered in Grade 7.

Intervention Resources

Reproducible

- Interactive Reader and Study Guide
- Universal Access Teacher Management System: Lesson Plans for Universal Access

Technology

- Quick Facts Transparency: The Age of Jackson Visual Summary
- Universal Access Modified Worksheets and Tests CD-ROM
- Interactive Skills Tutor CD-ROM

Tips for Test Taking

Significant Details Students will often be asked to recall details from a reading passage. Tell students in such situations to read the question before they read the passage. Then, as they read the passage, students should underline key details. Remind students that the correct answer will not always precisely match the wording of the passage, however.

Standards Review

Have students review the following standards in their workbooks.

- California Standards Review Workbook: HSS 8.4.3, 8.8.1

Chapter 10 Planning Guide

Expanding West

Chapter Overview	Reproducible Resources	Technology Resources
CHAPTER 10 **pp. 304–337** **Overview: In this chapter, students will examine the movement of Americans to the West and the expansion of U.S. influence in Texas and California.** See p. 304 for the California History–Social Science standards covered in this chapter.	**Universal Access Teacher Management System:*** • Universal Access Instructional Benchmarking Guides • Lesson Plans for Universal Access **Interactive Reader and Study Guide:*** Chapter Graphic Organizer **Chapter Resource File*** • Focus on Writing Activity: Outline for a Documentary Film • Social Studies Skills Activity: Interpreting Maps: Expansion • Chapter Review Activity **Pre-AP Activities Guide for United States History:*** Document-Based Questions	**One-Stop Planner CD-ROM:** Calendar Planner **Student Edition Full-Read Audio CD-ROM** **Universal Access Modified Worksheets and Tests CD-ROM** **Interactive Skills Tutor CD-ROM** **Primary Source Library CD-ROM for United States History** **Power Presentations with Video CD-ROM** **History's Impact: United States History Video Series (VHS/DVD):** Expanding West* **A Teacher's Guide to Religion in the Public Schools***
Section 1: **Trails to the West** **The Big Idea:** The American West attracted a variety of settlers. 8.8.2	**Universal Access Teacher Management System:*** Section 1 Lesson Plan **Interactive Reader and Study Guide:*** Section 1 Summary **Chapter Resource File*** • Vocabulary Builder, Section 1 • Biography Activity: James P. Beckwourth	**Daily Bellringer Transparency:** Section 1* **Map Transparency:** Trails Leading West*
Section 2: **The Texas Revolution** **The Big Idea:** In 1836, Texas gained its independence from Mexico. 8.8.5, 8.8.6	**Universal Access Teacher Management System:*** Section 2 Lesson Plan **Interactive Reader and Study Guide:*** Section 2 Summary **Chapter Resource File*** • Vocabulary Builder, Section 2 • Biography Activity: Lorenzo de Zavala • Interdisciplinary Project: Westward Adventure	**Daily Bellringer Transparency:** Section 2* **Quick Facts Transparency:** Gone to Texas* **Map Transparency:** The Texas Revolution* go.hrw.com **Internet Activity:** Texas Revolution Ballad
Section 3: **The Mexican-American War** **The Big Idea:** The ideals of manifest destiny and the outcome of the Mexican American War led to U.S. expansion to the Pacific Ocean. 8.8.6	**Universal Access Teacher Management System:*** Section 3 Lesson Plan **Interactive Reader and Study Guide:*** Section 3 Summary **Chapter Resource File*** • Vocabulary Builder, Section 3 • History and Geography Activity: Spanish Missions • Primary Source Activities: A Mexican Views the War; From the Journal of Junípero Serra **Political Cartoons Activities for United States History,** Cartoon 12: James Polk and Foreign Policy*	**Daily Bellringer Transparency:** Section 3* **Map Transparency:** Mexican-American War, 1846–1847* go.hrw.com **Internet Activity:** Spanish Missions Model
Section 4: **The California Gold Rush** **The Big Idea:** The California gold rush changed the future of the West. 8.8.3, 8.8.5, 8.9.4	**Universal Access Teacher Management System:*** Section 4 Lesson Plan **Interactive Reader and Study Guide:*** Section 4 Summary **Chapter Resource File*** • Vocabulary Builder, Section 3 • Biography Activity: Bridget "Biddy" Mason • Biography Activity: Levi Strauss • Literature Activity: *New Orleans to San Francisco in '49* by Tabetha F. Bingham • Primary Source Activity: Family Letters **Political Cartoons Activities for United States History,** Cartoon 13: The California Gold Rush*	**Daily Bellringer Transparency:** Section 4*

SE Student Edition  Print Resource  Audio CD Video

TE Teacher's Edition  Transparency CD-ROM DVD

 go.hrw.com CA Standards Mastery **LS** Learning Styles

OSP One-Stop Planner CD-ROM * also on One-Stop Planner CD

Review, Assessment, Intervention

- **Standards Review Workbook***
- **Quick Facts Transparency:** Expanding West Visual Summary*
- **Spanish Chapter Summaries Audio CD Program**
- **Online Chapter Summaries in Six Languages**
- **Quiz Game CD-ROM**
- **Progress Assessment Support System (PASS):** Chapter Test*
- **Universal Access Modified Worksheets and Tests CD-ROM:** Modified Chapter Test
- **One-Stop Planner CD-ROM:** ExamView Test Generator (English/Spanish)
- **Alternative Assessment Handbook**
- **Holt Online Assessment Program (HOAP),** in the Holt Premier Online Student Edition

---

- **PASS:** Section 1 Quiz*
- **Online Quiz:** Section 1
- **Alternative Assessment Handbook**

- **PASS:** Section 2 Quiz*
- **Online Quiz:** Section 2
- **Alternative Assessment Handbook**

- **PASS:** Section 3 Quiz*
- **Online Quiz:** Section 3
- **Alternative Assessment Handbook**

- **PASS:** Section 4 Quiz*
- **Online Quiz:** Section 4
- **Alternative Assessment Handbook**

California Resources for Standards Mastery

INSTRUCTIONAL PLANNING AND SUPPORT

- **Universal Access Teacher Management System***
- **One-Stop Planner CD-ROM with Test Generator: Teacher Management System with Interactive Teacher's Edition**

STANDARDS MASTERY

- **Standards Review Workbook***
- **At Home: A Guide to Standards Mastery for United States History**

go.hrw.com Holt Online Learning

To enhance learning, Internet activities are available for a Texas Revolution Ballad and a Spanish Missions Model.

KEYWORD: SS8 TEACHER

- **Teacher Support Page**
- **Content Updates**
- **Rubrics and Writing Models**
- **Teaching Tips for the Multimedia Classroom**

KEYWORD: SS8 US10

- **Current Events**
- **Document-Based Questions**
- **Holt Grapher**
- **Holt Online Atlas**
- **Holt Researcher**
- **Interactive Multimedia Activities**
- **Internet Activities**
- **Online Chapter Summaries in Six Languages**
- **Online Section Quizzes**
- **American History Maps and Charts**

HOLT PREMIER ONLINE STUDENT EDITION

Complete online support for interactivity, assessment, and reporting

- **Interactive Maps and Notebook**
- **Standardized Test Prep**
- **Homework Practice and Research Activities Online**

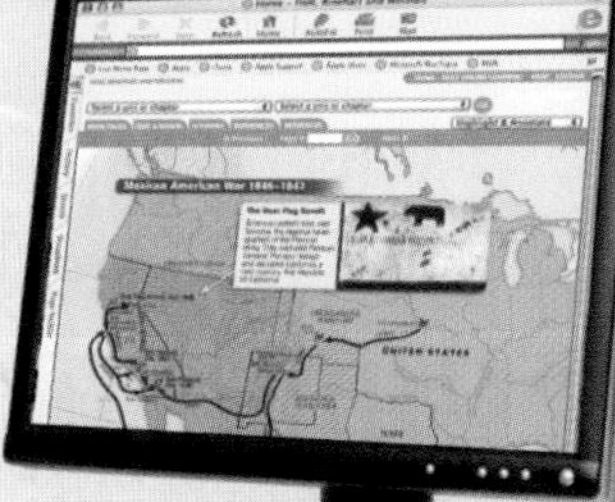

Mastering the Standards: Differentiating Instruction

Reaching Standards	Basic-level activities designed for all students encountering new material
Standards Proficiency	Intermediate-level activities designed for average students
Exceeding Standards	Challenging activities designed for honors and gifted-and-talented students
Standard English Mastery	Activities designed to improve standard English usage

Frequently Asked Questions

INSTRUCTIONAL PLANNING AND SUPPORT

Where do I find planning aids, pacing guides, lesson plans, and other teaching aids?

Annotated Teacher's Edition:
- Chapter planning guides
- Standards-based instruction and strategies
- Differentiated instruction for universal access
- Point-of-use reminders for integrating program resources

Power Presentations with Video CD-ROM

Universal Access Teacher Management System:
- Year and unit instructional benchmarking guides
- Reproducible lesson plans
- Assessment guides for diagnostic, progress, and summative end-of-the-year tests
- Options for differentiating instruction and intervention
- Teaching guides and answer keys for student workbooks

One-Stop Planner CD-ROM with Test Generator:
- Calendar Planner
- Editable lesson plans
- All reproducible ancillaries in Adobe Acrobat (PDF) format
- ExamView Test Generator (English & Spanish)
- Game Tool for ExamView
- PuzzlePro
- Transparency and video previews

DIFFERENTIATING INSTRUCTION FOR UNIVERSAL ACCESS

What resources are available to ensure that Advanced Learners/GATE Students master the standards?

Teacher's Edition Activities:
- Western Trails Scrapbook, p. 310
- Talking about California, p. 319
- Songs for the Road to War, p. 320
- Gold Rush Newspaper, p. 329

Lesson Plans for Universal Access

Primary Source Library CD-ROM for United States History

What resources are available to ensure that English Learners and Standard English Learners master the standards?

Teacher's Edition Activities:
- California Life Collage, p. 318

Lesson Plans for Universal Access

Chapter Resource File: Vocabulary Builder Activities

Spanish Chapter Summaries Audio CD Program

Online Chapter Summaries in Six Languages

One-Stop Planner CD-ROM:
- PuzzlePro, Spanish Version
- ExamView Test Generator, Spanish Version

What modified materials are available for Special Education?

Teacher's Edition Activities:
- Compare and Contrast Chart, p. 318

The ***Universal Access Modified Worksheets and Tests CD-ROM*** provides editable versions of the following:

Vocabulary Flash Cards

Modified Vocabulary Builder Activities

Modified Chapter Review Activity

Modified Chapter Test

What resources are available to ensure that Learners Having Difficulty master the standards?

Teacher's Edition Activities:

- Mexican-American War Time Line, p. 322
- California Fever Ad, p. 328

Interactive Reader and Study Guide

Student Edition Full-Read Audio CD

Quick Facts Transparency: Expanding West Visual Summary

Standards Review Workbook

Social Studies Skills Activity: Interpreting Maps: Expansion

Interactive Skills Tutor CD-ROM

How do I intervene for students struggling to master the standards?

Interactive Reader and Study Guide

Quick Facts Transparency: Expanding West Visual Summary

Standards Review Workbook

Social Studies Skills Activity: Interpreting Maps: Expansion

Interactive Skills Tutor CD-ROM

PROFESSIONAL DEVELOPMENT

What teacher training resources are available to help me grow professionally?

- In-service and staff development as part of your Holt Social Studies product purchase
- Quick Teacher Tutorial Lesson Presentation CD-ROM
- Intensive tuition-based Teacher Development Institute
- *Teaching American History* Online 2 Module Professional Development Course
- Convenient Holt Speaker Bureau face-to-face workshop options
- PRAXIS™ Test Prep (#0089) interactive Web-based content refreshers*
- 24/7 *Ask A Professional Development Expert* at http://www.hrw.com/prodev/

* PRAXIS is a trademark of Educational Testing Service (ETS). This publication is not endorsed or approved by ETS.

Information Literacy Skills

To learn more about how History–Social Science instruction may be improved by the effective use of library media centers and information literacy skills, go to the Teacher's Resource Materials for Chapter 10 at **go.hrw.com**, keyword: SS8 MEDIA.

The following materials were developed by the Division for Public Education of the American Bar Association. These materials are part of the **Democracy and Civic Education** supplement.

- Constitution Study Guide
- Supreme Court Case Studies

• Chapter Preview •

Standards Focus

Standards by Section

Section 1: HSS 8.8.2
Section 2: HSS 8.8.5, 8.8.6
Section 3: HSS 8.8.6
Section 4: HSS 8.8.3, 8.8.5, 8.9.4

Teacher's Edition

HSS **Analysis Skills:** CS 1, CS 2, CS 3, HR 1, HR 4, HR 5, HI 1, HI 2, HI 4

Preview Grade 8 Standards

HSS **8.12** Students analyze the transformation of the American economy and the changing social and political conditions in the United States in response to the Industrial Revolution.
8.12.1 Trace patterns of agricultural and industrial development as they relate to climate, use of natural resources, markets, and trade and locate such development on a map.
8.12.2 Identify the reasons for the development of federal Indian policy and the wars with American Indians and their relationship to agricultural development and industrialization.
8.12.8 Identify the characteristics and impact of Grangerism and Populism.

Focus on Writing

The **Chapter Resource File** provides a Focus on Writing worksheet to help students create the outlines for their documentary films.

CRF: Focus on Writing Activity: Outline for a Documentary Film

CHAPTER 10 1800–1855

Expanding West

California Standards

History–Social Science

8.8 Students analyze the divergent paths of the American people in the West from 1800 to the mid-1800s and the challenges they faced.

8.9 Students analyze the early and steady attempts to abolish slavery and to realize the ideals of the Declaration of Independence.

Analysis Skills

CS 3 Students use a variety of maps and documents to identify physical and cultural features of neighborhoods, cities, states, and countries.

English–Language Arts

Writing 8.2.1.c Employ narrative and descriptive strategies.

Reading 8.2.0 Students read and understand grade-level appropriate material.

FOCUS ON WRITING

Outline for a Documentary Film Many documentary films have been made about the history of the United States, but there is always room for one more. In this chapter you will read about the westward expansion of the United States, a period filled with excitement and challenge. Then you will create an outline for a documentary film to be used in middle-school history classes.

UNITED STATES

1811 John Jacob Astor founds the fur-trading post Astoria on the Columbia River.

1810

WORLD

Introduce the Chapter

Standards Proficiency

Focus on Westward Expansion

HSS 8.8; HSS **Analysis Skills:** HR 5, HI 1, HI 2

1. Ask students why people in the eastern United States might have wanted to move West during the mid-1800s. What factors were pulling or pushing Americans to go West? Write the labels *Push Factors* and *Pull Factors* for students to see. Have students predict what some of these factors were. Write students' responses under the applicable headings and save the list.
2. Next, have students discuss what challenges settlers might have faced while traveling West and then while building new settlements.
3. Then have students identify the groups who already lived in the West where Americans were going. Ask students to predict how Native Americans and Mexican settlers in the West might have viewed the newly arriving U.S. settlers.
4. Explain to students that they are going to learn about the westward expansion of the United States during the mid-1800s. Tell students that the idea of westward expansion would become an important part of American culture. LS **Verbal/Linguistic**

HOLT
History's Impact
▶ video series
Watch the video to understand the impact of conflict on settlement in the West.

What You Will Learn...

In this chapter you will learn about how the United States expanded west. The country acquired vast amounts of territory in a short time. Lured by land and gold, hundreds of thousands of Americans followed trails west in search of a better life. However, many Californio families, like the one pictured here, had already lived in California for generations.

1820

1821 Mexico wins its independence from Spain.

1827 The United States and Great Britain agree to continue joint occupation of Oregon Country.

1830

1838 Californios revolt unsuccessfully against the Mexican government.

1840

1842 China gives Great Britain control of the island of Hong Kong.

1846 The United States declares war against Mexico.

1848 Gold is discovered in California on January 24.

1850

1854 Commodore Matthew Perry negotiates a trade treaty with Japan.

EXPANDING WEST **305**

• Chapter Preview •

HOLT
History's Impact
▶ **video series**
See the Video Teacher's Guide for strategies for using the chapter video **Expanding West**.

Chapter Big Ideas

Section 1 The American West attracted a variety of settlers. **HSS** 8.8.2

Section 2 In 1836, Texas gained its independence from Mexico. **HSS** 8.8.5, 8.8.6

Section 3 The United States expanded to the Pacific Ocean due to manifest destiny and the Mexican-American War. **HSS** 8.8.6

Section 4 The California gold rush changed the future of the West. **HSS** 8.8.3, 8.8.5, 8.9.4

Explore the Picture

The Lugo Family Spanish and Mexican families, such as the Lugo family pictured at left, had been living in the West for generations when U.S. settlers began coming to the region. The Lugo family were major landowners in Spanish California. The family's clothing reflects the region's Spanish heritage.

Analyzing Visuals How many generations can you identify in the photograph? *Answers will vary, but the photo shows around four generations of the family.*

go.hrw.com
Online Resources
Teacher Resources:
KEYWORD: SS8 US10
Teacher Resources:
KEYWORD: SS8 TEACHER

Explore the Time Line

1. When did the United States declare war against Mexico? *1846*
2. With what nation did the United States agree to joint occupation of Oregon Country in 1827? *Great Britain*
3. How long after John Jacob Astor founded the fur-trading post Astoria was gold discovered in California? *37 years*
4. Based on the time line, what are some major themes in this chapter? *geography (expansion), politics (war, conflict, and foreign relations)*

HSS Analysis Skills: CS 1

Info to Know

The West and the American Character
American movement West affected not only the physical size of the United States but also American culture. According to historian Frederick Jackson Turner, Americans are proud of their frontier history and the qualities it took to survive and thrive in the harsh conditions of the West. These qualities included individualism, self-reliance, mobility, and optimism. To this day, Americans celebrate these qualities as part of the national character.

Reading Social Studies

Understanding Themes

Introduce this chapter to students by telling them that the chapter deals with westward expansion. Ask students to suggest ways in which geography might have affected the settlement of the West. Have students examine a map to help them formulate their answers. Then ask students to predict what economic issues might have led to or resulted from westward expansion. Have each student create an illustration that shows how the two themes of economics and geography might have affected the settlement of the West.

Vocabulary in Context

Focus on Reading Choose a paragraph or two that contain words with which students are likely to be unfamiliar. Write the unfamiliar words for the class to see. Have students read the entire paragraph looking for clues as to the meaning of each word. Then have students write out their definitions of the terms. When students are finished, have them look the words up in a dictionary and write down the definition given there. Ask students if their definition came close to the one in the dictionary. What clues did they use to arrive at their definition?

Reading Social Studies

by Kylene Beers

Economics | Geography | Politics | Religion | Society and Culture | Science and Technology

Focus on Themes In this chapter, you will read about the American people as they continued their westward expansion. You will read about the famous Oregon and Santa Fe trails, Texas's fight for independence from Mexico, and Mexico's war with the United States. Finally, you will read about the California Gold Rush that brought thousands of people west. As you read each section, you will see how **economic** issues affected the growth of different **geographic** areas.

Vocabulary in Context

Focus on Reading In Chapter 3 you learned how writers sometimes give you clues to a word's meaning in the same or a nearby sentence. Those clues are usually definitions, restatements in different words, or comparisons or contrasts. But what do you do if you don't know the word and the writer doesn't think to give you a direct clue?

Additional reading support can be found in the

Using Broader Context Clues If the writer doesn't give you one of those direct clues, you have to try to figure out the meaning of the word for yourself.

1. Read the whole paragraph and look for information that will help you figure out the meaning.
2. Look up the word in the dictionary to be sure of its meaning.

Notice how a student used information from the whole paragraph to learn the meaning of two unknown words.

> In 1844, the Whigs passed up Tyler and chose Senator Henry Clay of Kentucky as their presidential candidate. At first opposing *annexation*, Clay changed his mind due to pressure from southern voters. The Democratic Party chose former Tennessee governor James K. Polk to oppose Clay. Both candidates strongly favored *acquiring* Texas and Oregon, but Polk was perceived as the *expansionist* candidate. *(p. 317)*

I'm not sure about *annexation*. The southerners convinced Clay to be for it. Maybe if I read some more.

Oh, both presidential candidates favored acquiring Texas and Oregon. Maybe *annexation* means almost the same thing as *acquiring*. I'll check the dictionary.

The dictionary definition is "to add or attach." That's close. Now what about *expansionist*? I know one meaning of *expand* is similar to *add*. An *expansionist* was probably someone who wanted to add to or expand the country.

Reading and Skills Resources

Reading Support

- Interactive Reader and Study Guide
- Student Edition on Audio CD
- Spanish Chapter Summaries Audio CD Program

Social Studies Skills Support

- Interactive Skills Tutor CD-ROM

Vocabulary Support

- **CRF:** Vocabulary Builder Activities
- **CRF:** Chapter Review Activity
- Universal Access Modified Worksheets and Tests CD-ROM:
  - Vocabulary Flash Cards
  - Vocabulary Builder Activity
  - Chapter Review Activity
- OSP Holt PuzzlePro

Standards Focus

ELA Reading 8.1.3

ELA Reading 8.1.3 Use word meanings within the appropriate context.

You Try It!

The following passage is from the chapter you are about to read. Read the passage and then answer the questions.

American Settlement in the Mexican Cession

From Chapter 10, p. 323

The war ended after Scott took Mexico City. Under the Treaty of Guadalupe Hidalgo, signed in February 1848, Mexico turned over much of its northern territory to the United States. Known as the Mexican Cession, this land included the present-day states of California, Nevada, and Utah . . .

In exchange for this vast territory, the United States agreed to pay Mexico $15 million. In addition, the United States agreed to assume claims of more than $3 million held by American citizens against the Mexican government.

Refer to the passages to answer the following questions.

1. Do you know what the word *cession* means? What clues in the first paragraph can help you figure out what the word might mean? Use those clues to write a definition of cession.
2. Look *cession* up in a dictionary. How does your definition compare to the dictionary definition?
3. In your experience, what does the word *assume* usually mean? Do you think that meaning is the one used in the second paragraph? If not, what do you think *assume* means in this case?
4. Look *assume* up in a dictionary. Does one of its meanings match the one you came up with?

As you read Chapter 10, use context clues to figure out the meanings of unfamiliar words. Check yourself by looking the words up in a dictionary.

Key Terms and People

Chapter 10

Section 1
John Jacob Astor *(p. 308)*
mountain men *(p. 308)*
Oregon Trail *(p. 309)*
Santa Fe Trail *(p. 310)*
Mormons *(p. 310)*
Brigham Young *(p. 311)*

Section 2
Father Miguel Hidalgo y Costilla *(p. 312)*
empresarios (p. 312)
Stephen F. Austin *(p. 313)*
Antonio López de Santa Anna *(p. 313)*
Alamo *(p. 314)*
Battle of San Jacinto *(p. 314)*

Section 3
manifest destiny *(p. 316)*
James K. Polk *(p. 317)*
Californios *(p. 319)*
Bear Flag Revolt *(p. 320)*
Treaty of Guadalupe Hidalgo *(p. 323)*
Gadsden Purchase *(p. 323)*

Section 4
John Sutter *(p. 327)*
Donner party *(p. 327)*
forty-niners *(p. 327)*
prospect *(p. 328)*
placer mines *(p. 328)*

Academic Vocabulary

Success in school is related to knowing academic vocabulary—the words that are frequently used in school assignments and discussions. In this chapter, you will learn the following academic words:

explicit *(p. 313)*
elements *(p. 319)*

Reading Social Studies

Key Terms and People

To preview the key terms and people from this chapter, have the class create an illustrated children's book about the West. Each page in the book will be dedicated to a separate term or person and will define or identify that word, as well as include an illustration. Assign each student a term or person from the list at left. Have students look up the importance of their term. Then have students create a page for the children's book. Combine all the pages together to complete the book.
LS Visual/Spatial, Verbal/Linguistic

Focus on Reading

See the **Focus on Reading** questions in this chapter for more practice on this reading social studies skill.

Reading Social Studies Assessment

See the **Standards Review** at the end of this chapter for student assessment questions related to this reading skill.

Teaching Tip

Many times primary sources contain words with which students will be unfamiliar. In these instances, remind students to first attempt to figure out the meaning of the word based on the content of the whole paragraph. Encourage students to use a dictionary to define words about which they are unsure. Help students practice defining words based on context by asking them to read primary source documents on a regular basis.

Answers

You Try It! 1. *clues*—Mexico turned over much of its northern territory, this land included; *possible definition—a cession is an area of land that one country gives to another;* **2.** *dictionary definition— the act of yielding property to another;* **3.** *to guess or suppose; no; to take over;* **4.** *yes; to take on or adopt*

Preteach

Bellringer

If YOU were there . . . Use the **Daily Bellringer Transparency** to help students answer the question.

 Daily Bellringer Transparency, Section 1

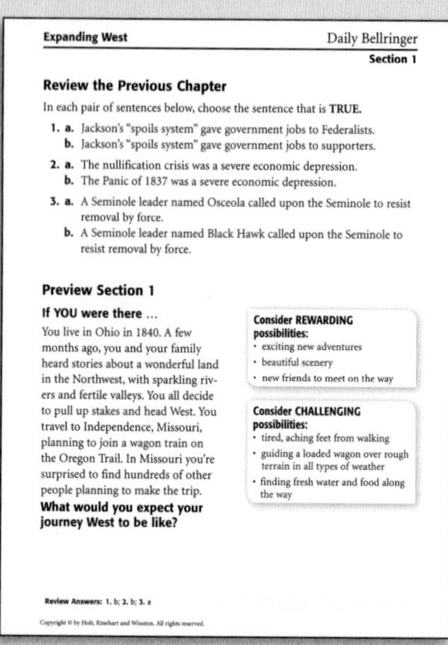

Expanding West — Daily Bellringer — **Section 1**

Review the Previous Chapter

In each pair of sentences below, choose the sentence that is **TRUE.**

1. a. Jackson's "spoils system" gave government jobs to Federalists.
   b. Jackson's "spoils system" gave government jobs to supporters.
2. a. The nullification crisis was a severe economic depression.
   b. The Panic of 1837 was a severe economic depression.
3. a. A Seminole leader named Osceola called upon the Seminole to resist removal by force.
   b. A Seminole leader named Black Hawk called upon the Seminole to resist removal by force.

Preview Section 1

If YOU were there ...

You live in Ohio in 1840. A few months ago, you and your family heard stories about a wonderful land in the Northwest, with sparkling rivers and fertile valleys. You all decide to pull up stakes and head West. You travel to Independence, Missouri, planning to join a wagon train on the Oregon Trail. In Missouri you're surprised to find hundreds of other people planning to make the trip.

What would you expect your journey West to be like?

Consider REWARDING possibilities:
- exciting new adventures
- beautiful scenery
- new friends to meet on the way

Consider CHALLENGING possibilities:
- tired, aching feet from walking
- guiding a loaded wagon over rough terrain in all types of weather
- finding fresh water and food along the way

Review Answers: 1. b; 2. b; 3. a

Building Vocabulary

Preteach or review the following terms:

Oregon Country early to mid-1800s name for the Pacific Northwest (p. 309)

persecuted to be treated unfairly or cruelly because of religious beliefs, race, ethnicity, or gender (p. 311)

CRF: Vocabulary Builder Activity, Section 1

SECTION 1

Trails to the West

What You Will Learn...

Main Ideas

1. During the early 1800s, Americans moved west of the Rocky Mountains to settle and trade.
2. The Mormons traveled west in search of religious freedom.

The Big Idea

The American West attracted a variety of settlers.

Key Terms and People

John Jacob Astor, *p. 308*
mountain men, *p. 308*
Oregon Trail, *p. 309*
Santa Fe Trail, *p. 311*
Mormons, *p. 311*
Brigham Young, *p. 311*

HSS 8.8.2 Describe the purpose, challenges, and economic incentives associated with westward expansion, including the concepts of Manifest Destiny (e.g., the Lewis and Clark expedition, accounts of the removal of Indians, the Cherokees' "Trail of Tears," settlement of the Great Plains) and the territorial acquisitions that spanned numerous decades.

If YOU were there...

You live in Ohio in 1840. A few months ago, you and your family heard stories about a wonderful land in the Northwest, with sparkling rivers and fertile valleys. You all decide to pull up stakes and head West. You travel to Independence, Missouri, planning to join a wagon train on the Oregon Trail. In Missouri, you're surprised to find hundreds of other people planning to make the trip.

What would you expect your journey West to be like?

BUILDING BACKGROUND Many Americans in the Jacksonian Era were restless, curious, and eager to be on the move. The American West drew a variety of settlers. Some looked for wealth and adventure. Others, like this family on its way to the Northwest, dreamed of rich farmland and new homes.

Americans Move West

In the early 1800s, Americans pushed steadily westward, moving even beyond the territory of the United States. They traveled by canoe and flatboat, on horseback, and by wagon train. Some even walked much of the way.

The rush to the West occurred, in part, because of a hat. The "high hat," made of water-repellent beaver fur, was popular in the United States and Europe. While acquiring fur for the hats, French, British, and American companies gradually killed off the beaver population in the East. Companies moved west in search of more beavers. Most of the first non-Native Americans who traveled to the Rocky Mountains and the Pacific Northwest were fur traders and trappers.

American merchant **John Jacob Astor** created one of the largest fur businesses, the American Fur Company. His company bought skins from western fur traders and trappers who became known as **mountain men**. These adventurers were some of the first easterners to explore and map the Rocky Mountains and lands west of them. Mountain men lived lonely and often dangerous lives. They trapped animals on their own, far from towns and settlements. Mountain men such as Jedediah Smith, Manuel Lisa, Jim Bridger, and Jim

Teach the Big Idea: Master the Standards

Standards Proficiency

Trails to the West HSS 8.8.2; HSS Analysis Skills: HI 1

1. **Teach** Ask students the Main Idea questions to teach this section.
2. **Apply** Create a four-column chart for students to see. Title the chart *Americans Move West* and label the columns *Why, How, Where,* and *When*. Have students use the information in the section to complete the chart. Students should list the reasons why Americans went West, the ways in which they traveled, the trails they took, and when they went. **LS Verbal/Linguistic**
3. **Review** To review the section's main ideas, have students help you complete a master copy of the chart.
4. **Practice/Homework** Have each student create an advertisement for a wagon train heading West. The ad should persuade people to join the wagon train and provide information about the trip. **LS Verbal/Linguistic, Visual/Spatial**

Alternative Assessment Handbook, Rubrics 2: Advertisements; and 7: Charts

Standards Focus

HSS 8.8.2

Means: Describe the reasons for westward expansion, including economic and territorial reasons, and the challenges settlers faced as they went West.

Matters: Americans who moved West helped shape the region, which is now part of the United States.

Trails Leading West

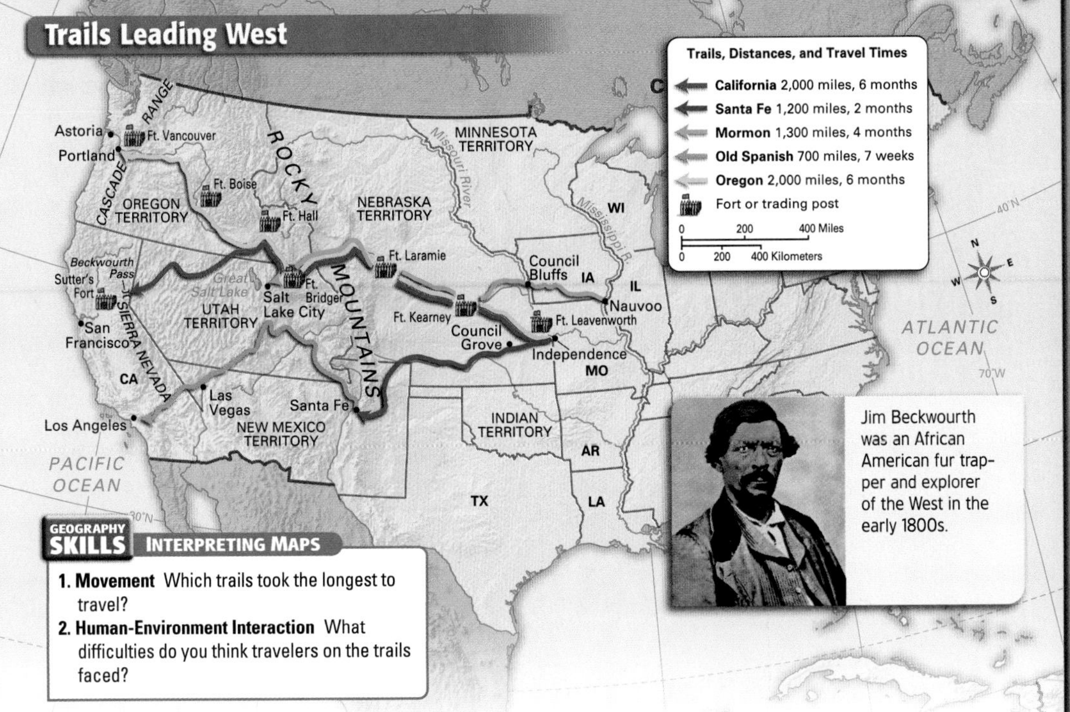

Jim Beckwourth was an African American fur trapper and explorer of the West in the early 1800s.

GEOGRAPHY SKILLS INTERPRETING MAPS

1. **Movement** Which trails took the longest to travel?
2. **Human-Environment Interaction** What difficulties do you think travelers on the trails faced?

Beckwourth survived many hardships during their search for wealth and adventure. To survive on the frontier, mountain men adopted Native American customs and clothing. In addition, they often married Native American women. The Indian wives of trappers often worked hard to contribute to their success.

Pioneer William Ashley saw that frequently bringing furs out of the Rocky Mountains was expensive. He asked his traders to stay in the mountains and meet once a year to trade and socialize. This practice helped make the fur trade more profitable. The yearly meeting was known as the rendezvous. At the rendezvous, mountain men and Native American trappers sold their fur to fur-company agents. It was thus important to bring as many furs as possible. One trapper described the people at a typical rendezvous in 1837. He saw Americans, Canadian French, some Europeans, and "Indians, of nearly every tribe in the Rocky Mountains."

The rendezvous was filled with celebrating and storytelling. At the same time, the meeting was also about conducting business. Western artist Alfred Jacob Miller described how trade was begun in the rendezvous camp.

> "The Fur Company's great tent is raised; the Indians erect their picturesque [beautiful] white lodges; the accumulated [collected] furs of the hunting season are brought forth and the Company's tent is a . . . busy place."
>
> —Alfred Jacob Miller, quoted in *The Fur Trade of the American West*, by David J. Wishart

In 1811, John Jacob Astor founded a fur-trading post called Astoria at the mouth of the Columbia River. Astoria was one of the first American settlements in what became known as Oregon Country. American Indians occupied the region, which was rich in forests, rivers, and wildlife. However, Britain, Russia, Spain, and the United States all claimed the land. The United States based its claim on

Direct Teach

Main Idea

1 Americans Move West

During the early 1800s, Americans moved west of the Rocky Mountains to settle and trade.

Recall What trade first drew Americans to the West? *fur trade*

Find Main Ideas Why did settlers go to Oregon Country? *rich resources, mild climate, Panic of 1837*

Make Judgments Would you have taken a wagon trail West in the 1840s? Use the text to explain your answer. *Students' answers should show an understanding of the challenges of going West by wagon train.*

CRF: Biography Activity: James Beckwourth

Map Transparency: Trails Leading West

HSS 8.8.2; HSS **Analysis Skills:** HI 1

Interpreting Maps

Trails Leading West

The U.S. Army set up forts along western trails to protect settlers.

Locate What forts are located along the Oregon Trail? *Forts Leavenworth, Kearney, Laramie, Hall, Boise, Vancouver*

Answers

Interpreting Maps 1. *California and Oregon trails—about six months;* **2.** *attacks from Native Americans, hunger, harsh weather, difficult terrain*

Differentiating Instruction for Universal Access

Learners Having Difficulty

Reaching Standards

1. To help students understand why and how Americans moved West during the 1840s, draw the graphic organizer here for students to see. Omit the blue, italicized answers.
2. Have students copy and complete the graphic organizer. Then review the answers as a class. LS **Visual/Spatial**

HSS 8.8.2; HSS **Analysis Skills:** HI 1

Reasons Went West: *rich resources, land, mild climate*

California/Oregon Trails: *MO or IA to Oregon Country or CA; about 2,000 miles long*

Santa Fe Trail: *Independence, MO, to Santa Fe, Mexico; used mainly as a trade route*

Challenges: *shortages of food, supplies, and water; rough weather; geographic barriers*

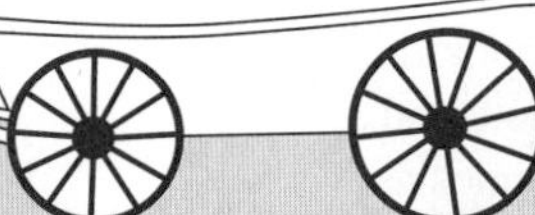

Direct Teach

Main Idea

❷ Mormons Travel West

The Mormons traveled west in search of religious freedom.

Identify Who established the Church of Jesus Christ of Latter-day Saints? *Joseph Smith*

Make Generalizations Why did the Mormon settlement in Utah succeed? *It was well-planned, with broad roads and surrounding farms, and Mormon leaders maintained discipline and order.*

HSS 8.8.2; HSS **Analysis Skills:** HI 1

Did you know. . .

European demand for hats made from beaver pelts fueled the fur trade in America. The soft fur was removed from the skin, fashioned into felt, and molded into hats. Gentlemen wore beaver hats to be fashionable, and some armies made them part of their uniforms. At the height of the fad, an estimated 100,000 beavers a year were trapped and killed for hats.

Info to Know

The California Trail An average day on the California Trail usually began at 4 A.M. After organizing livestock and yoking the oxen to the wagons, settlers began the day's journey. Travel ended at nightfall, when settlers circled their wagons. Although Native American attacks were rare, the trip was unpleasant and dangerous. In 1849 some 1,500 people died on the California Trail.

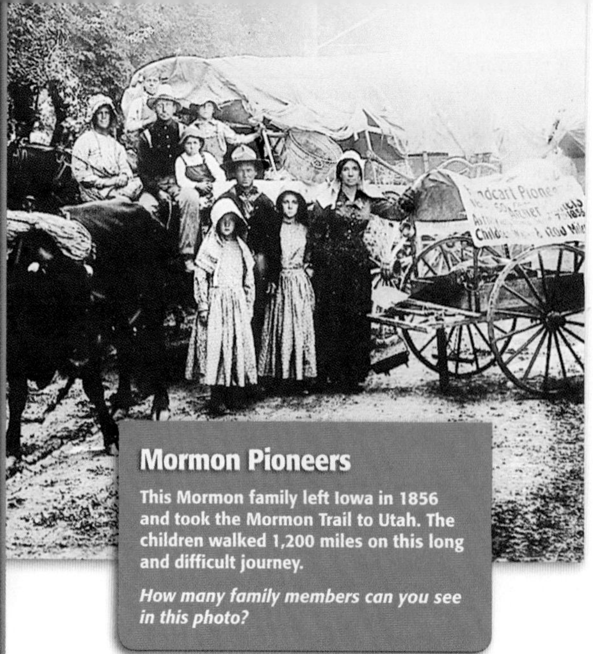

Mormon Pioneers

This Mormon family left Iowa in 1856 and took the Mormon Trail to Utah. The children walked 1,200 miles on this long and difficult journey.

How many family members can you see in this photo?

the exploration of merchant captain Robert Gray, who had reached the mouth of the Columbia River in 1792.

Recognizing the huge economic value of the Pacific Northwest, the United States made treaties in which Spain and Russia gave up their claims to various areas. The United States also signed treaties with Britain allowing both countries to occupy Oregon Country, the Columbia River, and its surrounding lands.

By the 1840s, the era of American fur trading in the Pacific Northwest was drawing to a close. The demand for beaver furs had fallen because fashions changed. Too much trapping had also greatly reduced the number of beavers. Some mountain men gave up their work and moved back east. Their daring stories, however, along with the treaties made by the U.S. government, inspired other Americans to move West. Lured by rich resources and a mild climate, easterners poured into Oregon Country in the 1840s. These new settlers soon replaced the mountain men on the frontier.

The Oregon Trail

Many settlers moving to Oregon Country and other western areas followed the 2,000-mile-long **Oregon Trail**, which stretched from places such as Independence, Missouri, or Council Bluffs, Iowa, west into Oregon Country. The trail followed the Platte and Sweetwater Rivers over the Plains. After it crossed the Rocky Mountains, the trail forked. The northern branch led to the Willamette Valley in Oregon. The other branch went to California and became known as the California Trail.

Traveling the trail challenged the strength and determination of pioneer families. The journey usually began after the rainy season ended in late spring and lasted about six months. The cost, about $600 for a family of four, was high at a time when a typical worker usually made about $1.50 per day. Young families made up most groups of settlers. They gathered in wagon trains for the trip. There could be as few as 10 wagons or as many as several dozen in a wagon train.

The wagons were pulled by oxen, mules, or horses. Pioneers often walked to save their animals' strength. They kept up a tiring pace, traveling from dawn until dusk. Settler Jesse Applegate recalled the advice he received from an experienced Oregon pioneer: "Travel, *travel*, TRAVEL . . . Nothing is good that causes a moment's delay."

Some pioneers brought small herds of cattle with them on the trail. They faced severe hardships, including shortages of food, supplies, and water. Rough weather and geographic barriers, such as rivers and mountains, sometimes forced large numbers of pioneers to abandon their wagons. In the early days of the Oregon Trail, many Native Americans helped the pioneers, acting as guides and messengers. They also traded goods for food. Although newspapers reported Native American "massacres" of pioneers, few settlers died during Indian attacks.

The settlers who arrived safely in Oregon and California found generally healthy

Collaborative Learning

Exceeding Standards

Western Trails Scrapbook

HSS 8.8.2; HSS **Analysis Skills:** HR 1, HR 4 — Research Required

1. Organize students into groups. Have each group use the library or other resources to locate letters, diaries, journals, and images about life on the Oregon, California, and Santa Fe trails.
2. Have group members list recurring themes, problems, attitudes, and moods found in the entries as well as factors that varied along the trails.
3. Have each group create a scrapbook that combines primary source accounts and images to illustrate recurring themes as well as unique aspects of life on the western trails. Groups might want to assign a topic or focus to each page or spread of their scrapbook.
4. Display the scrapbooks in the classroom and give students time to view them.

LS Interpersonal, Verbal/Linguistic, Visual/Spatial

Alternative Assessment Handbook, Rubrics 30: Research; and 32: Scrapbooks

Answers

Mormon Pioneers *nine*

and pleasant climates. By 1845 some 5,000 settlers occupied the Willamette Valley.

The Santa Fe Trail

The **Santa Fe Trail** was another important path west. It led from Independence, Missouri, to Santa Fe, New Mexico. It followed an ancient trading route first used by Native Americans. American traders loaded their wagon trains with cloth and other manufactured goods to exchange for horses, mules, and silver from Mexican traders in Santa Fe.

The long trip across blazing deserts and rough mountains was dangerous. But the lure of high profits encouraged traders to take to the trail. One trader reported a 2,000 percent profit on his cargo. The U.S. government helped protect traders by sending troops to ensure that Native Americans were not a threat.

READING CHECK **Contrasting** How were the Oregon and Santa Fe trails different?

Mormons Travel West

One large group of settlers traveled to the West in search of religious freedom. In 1830 a young man named Joseph Smith founded the Church of Jesus Christ of Latter-day Saints in western New York. The members of Joseph Smith's church became known as **Mormons**. Smith told his followers that he had found and translated a set of golden tablets containing religious teachings. The writings were called the *Book of Mormon*.

Church membership grew rapidly. However, certain beliefs and practices caused Mormons to be persecuted. For example, beginning in the 1850s some Mormon men practiced polygamy—a practice in which one man is married to several women at the same time. This practice was outlawed by the church in 1890.

In the early 1830s Smith and his growing number of converts left New York. They formed new communities, first in Ohio, then in Missouri, and finally in Illinois. All three communities eventually failed, and an anti-Mormon mob murdered Smith in 1844. Following Smith's murder, **Brigham Young** became head of the Mormon Church. Young chose what is now Utah as the group's new home, and thousands of Mormons took the Mormon Trail to the area near the Great Salt Lake, where they prospered. By 1860 there were about 40,000 Mormons in Utah.

READING CHECK **Finding Main Ideas** Why did Mormons move West?

SUMMARY AND PREVIEW Some of the first Americans to move West were fur traders and trappers. Settlers soon followed. In the next section you will learn about the Texas Revolution.

Section 1 Assessment

Reviewing Ideas, Terms, and People HSS 8.8.2

1. **a. Identify** What was the **Oregon Trail**?
   b. Elaborate Would you have chosen to leave your home to travel West? Why?
2. **a. Identify** Who are the **Mormons**?
   b. Summarize What difficulties led Mormons to move to Utah?

Critical Thinking

3. **Categorizing** Copy the chart below. Identify different trails to the West, describe the people who traveled along each trail, and explain their motives for traveling west.

Trails	Travelers	Motives

FOCUS ON WRITING

4. **Describing Trails West** As you read this section, note important topics that you might want to cover in your documentary film. In addition, write down ideas about how you might present information about each topic. For example, will you use a narrator to tell the life story of Joseph Smith, or will you have actors present it dramatically?

• Review & Assess •

Close

Have students revisit and discuss the predictions they made in the Chapter Introduction activity. How accurate were students' predictions?

Review

Online Quiz, Section 1

Assess

SE Section 1 Assessment

PASS: Section 1 Quiz

Alternative Assessment Handbook

Reteach/Classroom Intervention

California Standards Review Workbook

Interactive Reader and Study Guide, Section 1

Interactive Skills Tutor CD-ROM

Section 1 Assessment Answers

1. **a.** a trail that led more than 2,000 miles West across the Rocky Mountains to Oregon Country; one of the main routes of western settlement
   b. Answers will vary but should reflect an understanding of the difficulties of traveling west, such as shortages of food and water, rough weather, and geographic barriers.
2. **a.** members of the Church of Jesus Christ of Latter-day Saints, founded by Joseph Smith
   b. religious persecution and failed communities elsewhere
3. Oregon/California Trail—Americans who wanted to settle in Oregon Country because of its rich resources and mild climate; Santa Fe Trail—American traders who hoped to profit from trading goods with Mexicans in Santa Fe, Mexico; Mormon Trail—Mormons who wanted to escape persecution and build a new community in Utah
4. Students should take notes on topics related to the fur trade in the Northwest and to the Oregon, Santa Fe, and Mormon trails.

Answers

Reading Check (left) *Oregon Trail—longer and more expensive to travel, used by settlers moving West; Santa Fe Trail—shorter, used as a trade route*

Reading Check (right) *to build a community and escape religious persecution*

Preteach

Bellringer

If YOU were there . . . Use the **Daily Bellringer Transparency** to help students answer the question.

 Daily Bellringer Transparency, Section 2

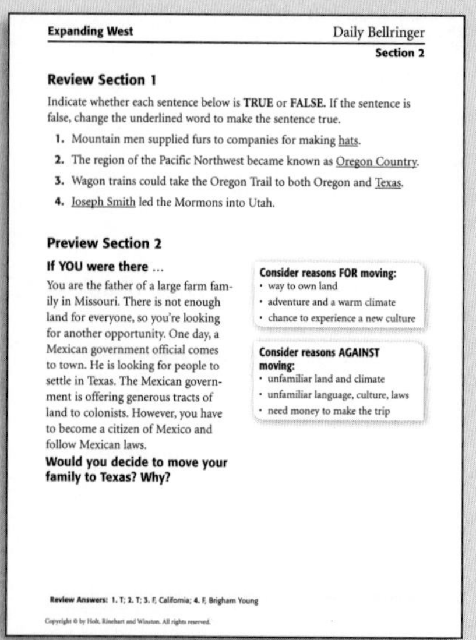

Expanding West Daily Bellringer

Section 2

Review Section 1

Indicate whether each sentence below is **TRUE** or **FALSE.** If the sentence is false, change the underlined word to make the sentence true.

1. Mountain men supplied furs to companies for making hats.
2. The region of the Pacific Northwest became known as Oregon Country.
3. Wagon trains could take the Oregon Trail to both Oregon and Texas.
4. Joseph Smith led the Mormons into Utah.

Preview Section 2

If YOU were there ...

You are the father of a large farm family in Missouri. There is not enough land for everyone, so you're looking for another opportunity. One day, a Mexican government official comes to town. He is looking for people to settle in Texas. The Mexican government is offering generous tracts of land to colonists. However, you have to become a citizen of Mexico and follow Mexican laws.

Would you decide to move your family to Texas? Why?

Consider reasons FOR moving:
- way to own land
- adventure and a warm climate
- chance to experience a new culture

Consider reasons AGAINST moving:
- unfamiliar land and climate
- unfamiliar language, culture, laws
- need money to make the trip

Review Answers: 1. T; 2. T; 3. F, California; 4. F, Brigham Young

Academic Vocabulary

Review with students the high-use academic term in this section.

explicitly fully revealed without vagueness (p. 313)

CRF: Vocabulary Builder Activity, Section 2

Standards Focus

HSS 8.8.5

Means: Discuss Mexican settlements, particularly in Texas, as well as Mexican cultural traditions, attitudes toward slavery, and systems for granting land to settlers.

Matters: Mexican settlement and culture have strongly influenced the American Southwest.

HSS 8.8.6

Means: Describe the main events of the Texas War for Independence and explain its short- and long-term effects on Americans' lives, including the lives of Mexican Americans today.

Matters: The war had a significant and far-reaching effect on life in the American Southwest.

SECTION 2

The Texas Revolution

What You Will Learn...

Main Ideas

1. Many American settlers moved to Texas after Mexico achieved independence from Spain.
2. Texans revolted against Mexican rule and established an independent nation.

The Big Idea

In 1836, Texas gained its independence from Mexico.

Key Terms and People

Father Miguel Hidalgo y Costilla, *p. 312*
empresarios, *p. 312*
Stephen F. Austin, *p. 313*
Antonio López de Santa Anna, *p. 313*
Alamo, *p. 314*
Battle of San Jacinto, *p. 314*

HSS 8.8.5 Discuss Mexican settlements and their locations, cultural traditions, attitudes toward slavery, land-grant system, and economics.

8.8.6 Describe the Texas War for Independence and the Mexican-American War, including territorial settlements, the aftermath of the wars, and the effects the wars had on the lives of Americans, including Mexican Americans today.

If YOU were there...

You are the father of a large farm family in Missouri. There is not enough land for everyone, so you're looking for another opportunity. One day, a Mexican government official comes to town. He is looking for people to settle in Texas. The Mexican government is offering generous tracts of land to colonists. However, you have to become a citizen of Mexico and follow Mexican laws.

Would you decide to move your family to Texas? Why?

BUILDING BACKGROUND Spain controlled a vast amount of territory in what would later become the American Southwest. The Spanish built missions and forts in Texas to establish control of that region. But the settlements were far apart, and conflicts with Native Americans discouraged Spanish settlers from moving to Texas. When Mexico became an independent republic, it actively looked for more settlers.

American Settlers Move to Texas

Mexico had a long, unprotected border that stretched from Texas to California. Mexico's Spanish rulers worried constantly about attacks from neighbors. They also were concerned about threats from within Mexico.

Their fears were justified. Mexicans moved to overthrow Spanish rule in the early 1800s. In September 1810 **Father Miguel Hidalgo y Costilla,** a Mexican priest, led a rebellion of about 80,000 poor Indians and mestizos, or people of Indian and Spanish ancestry. They hoped that if Mexico became independent from the Spanish monarchy, their lives would improve.

Hidalgo's revolt failed, but the rebellion he started grew. In 1821 Mexico became independent. In 1824 it adopted a republican constitution that declared rights for all Mexicans. The new Mexican government hired **empresarios**, or agents, to bring settlers to Texas. They paid the agents in land.

Teach the Big Idea: Master the Standards

Standards Proficiency

The Texas Revolution HSS 8.8.5, 8.8.6; HSS Analysis Skills: CS 1, CS 2, HI 1

1. **Teach** Ask students the Main Idea questions to teach this section.
2. **Apply** Discuss the main events in this section related to Mexican independence from Spain, the Texas War for Independence, and the aftermath of these events. Then have students create annotated time lines covering these events. Students' time lines should provide brief captions explaining the significance of each entry. **LS Visual/Spatial**
3. **Review** As you review the section's main ideas, have students check their time lines to see if they accurately traced the main events in the section.
4. **Practice/Homework** Have students copy their time lines onto a larger piece of paper and then add drawings to illustrate at least four of the events on their time lines. **LS Visual/Spatial**

Alternative Assessment Handbook, Rubrics 3: Artwork; and 36: Time Lines

Settling Texas

Stephen F. Austin, shown at left, and other settlers were empresarios—they received land from the Mexican government for the purpose of bringing settlers to Texas. Their holdings were guaranteed with a contract like the one below.

Why do you think the Mexican government wanted to attract settlers to Texas?

In 1822 one young agent, **Stephen F. Austin**, started a colony on the lower Colorado River. The first 300 families became known as the Old Three Hundred. Austin's successful colony attracted other agents, and American settlers flocked to the region.

In exchange for free land, settlers had to obey Mexican laws. But some settlers often explicitly ignored these laws. For example, despite the ban on slavery, many brought slaves. Concerned that it was losing control to the growing American population, Mexico responded. In 1830, it banned further settlement by Americans. Angry about the new law, many Texans began to think of gaining independence from Mexico.

Meanwhile, Mexico had come under the rule of General **Antonio López de Santa Anna**. He soon suspended Mexico's republican constitution and turned his attention to the growing unrest in Texas.

READING CHECK **Finding Main Ideas** Why did settlers move to Texas?

Texans Revolt against Mexico

In October 1835 the Mexican army tried to remove a cannon from the town of Gonzales, Texas. Rebels stood next to the cannon. Their flag read, "Come and take it." In the following battle, the rebels won. The Texas Revolution, also known as the Texas War for Independence, had begun.

ACADEMIC VOCABULARY
explicit fully revealed without vagueness

Texas Independence

On March 2, 1836, Texans declared their independence from Mexico. The new Republic of Texas was born. Both the declaration and the constitution that shortly followed were modeled after the U.S. documents. The Texas constitution, however, made slavery legal.

Delegates to the new Texas government chose politician David Burnet as president and Lorenzo de Zavala as vice president. Another revolutionary, Sam Houston, was named to head the Texas army. Austin went to the United States to seek money and troops.

Direct Teach

Main Idea

1 American Settlers Move to Texas

Many American settlers moved to Texas after Mexico achieved independence from Spain.

Identify When did Mexico achieve independence from Spain? *1821*

Analyze Why is Stephen F. Austin an important figure in Texas history? *In 1822 he started a colony of American settlers in Mexican Texas, which thrived and attracted more American settlers to Texas.*

Make Judgments Do you agree with the decision of Mexican officials to ban further American settlement in Texas in 1830? *Answers will vary but should reflect an understanding that Mexico banned U.S. settlement because American settlers were not following Mexican laws, and Mexico was concerned about losing control.*

CRF: Interdisciplinary Project: Share the Westward Adventure

HSS 8.8.5; HSS **Analysis Skills:** HI 1, HI 2

go.hrw.com
Online Resources
KEYWORD: SS8 US10
ACTIVITY:
Texas Revolution Ballad

Critical Thinking: Finding Main Ideas

Standards Proficiency

Texas Issues Broadsides

HSS 8.8.5, 8.8.6; HSS **Analysis Skills:** HR 5, HI 1, HI 2

Materials: poster board, art supplies

1. Discuss with students the reasons why Mexico opened Texas up to American settlement, why American settlers went to Texas, why tensions developed between Texas settlers and the Mexican government, and the main events that led to the Texas War for Independence.
2. Organize the class into three groups and assign each group one of the following broadsides: one promoting American settlement in Texas, one urging the Mexican government to close Texas to American settlement, and one urging Texas settlers to declare independence from Mexico. Have each student create the broadside assigned to his or her part of the class.
3. Have volunteers from each group share their broadsides with the class.
   LS Verbal/Linguistic, Visual/Spatial

Alternative Assessment Handbook, Rubric 28: Posters

Answers

Settling Texas *possible answers—to settle the land; to protect northern Mexico from attack*

Reading Check *lure of the promise of free land*

Direct Teach

Main Idea

❷ Texans Revolt against Mexico

Texans revolted against Mexican rule and established an independent nation.

Recall When did Texas declare independence from Mexico? *March 2, 1836*

Evaluate How did Santa Anna's decision to execute the Texas prisoners at Goliad hurt the Mexican war effort? *The prisoners' deaths rallied the Texas forces and motivated them to avenge the deaths.*

Draw Conclusions Why do you think most Texans hoped the United States would annex Texas? *possible answer—Many Texans had originally lived in the United States and still saw themselves as part of that nation.*

CRF: Biography Activity: Lorenzo de Zavala

Map Transparency: The Texas Revolution

HSS 8.8.6; **HSS Analysis Skills:** CS 1, HI 1, HI 2

Biography

Juan Seguín (1806–1890) Born in San Antonio, Texas, in 1806, Juan Seguín became a well-known Tejano politician. Seguín led a troop of Tejano cavalry in the Texas victory at San Jacinto. After the Texas Revolution, he served in the Texas Senate and later as mayor of San Antonio. In 1842, however, he moved his family to Mexico because of rising tensions between Anglos and Tejanos in Texas.

Battle at the Alamo

Focus on Reading Use this section to summarize the events of the battle at the Alamo.

The Texans' actions angered Santa Anna. He began assembling a force of thousands to stop the rebellion.

A hastily created army of Texas volunteers had been clashing with Mexican troops for months. Under Colonel Jim Travis, a small force took the town of San Antonio. It then occupied the **Alamo**, an abandoned mission near San Antonio that became an important battle site in the Texas Revolution. Volunteers from the United States, including frontiersman Davy Crockett and Colonel Jim Bowie, joined the Alamo's defense.

The rebels, numbering fewer than 200, hoped to stall the huge Mexican force while a larger Texas army assembled. For almost two weeks, from February 23 to March 6, 1836, the Texans held out. Travis managed to get a message to other Texans through enemy lines:

> "I call on you in the name of Liberty, of patriotism, and everything dear to the American character, to come to our aid with all dispatch [speed] ... VICTORY OR DEATH."
>
> —William Travis, from a letter written at the Alamo, 1836

Before dawn on March 6, the Mexican army attacked. Despite heavy losses, the army overcame the Texans. All the defenders of the Alamo were killed, though some civilians survived. Following a later battle, at Goliad, Santa Anna ordered the execution of 350 prisoners who had surrendered. Texans were enraged by the massacres.

Battle of San Jacinto

Santa Anna now chased the untrained forces of Sam Houston. Outnumbered, the Texans fled east. Finally, they reorganized at the San Jacinto River, near Galveston Bay. There, the Texans took a stand.

Santa Anna was confident of victory, but he was careless in choosing the site for his camp. On the afternoon of April 21, 1836, while Mexican troops were resting, Houston's forces swarmed the camp, shouting, "Remember the Alamo! Remember Goliad!"

The fighting ended swiftly. Santa Anna's army was destroyed. In the **Battle of San Jacinto**, the Texans captured Santa Anna and forced him to sign a treaty giving Texas its independence.

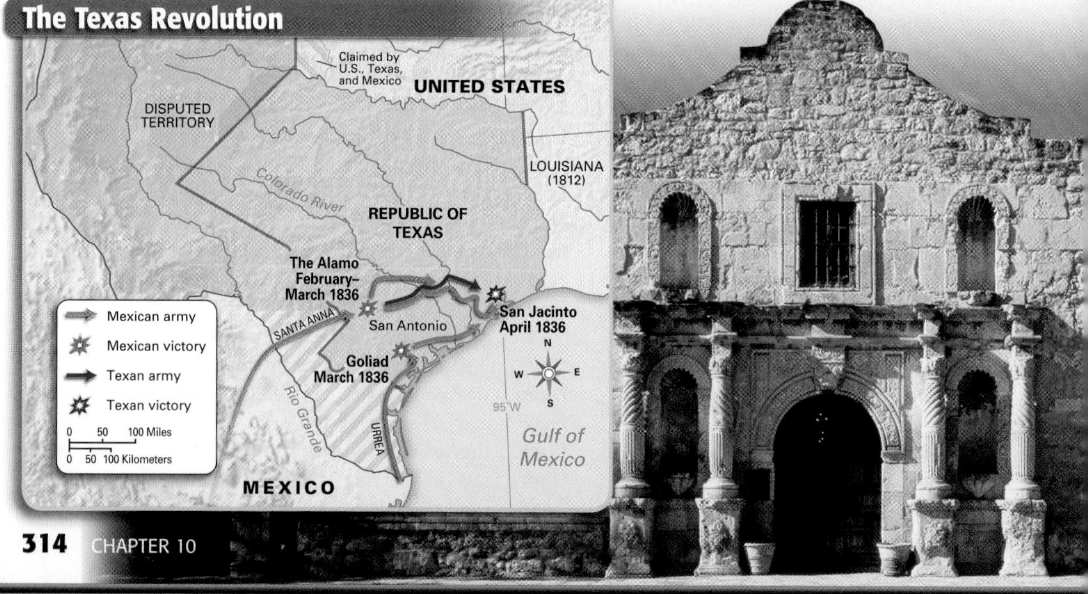

314 CHAPTER 10

Critical Thinking: Comparing and Contrasting

Standards Proficiency

Rebellions Comparison Chart

HSS 8.8.6; **HSS Analysis Skills:** CS 1, HI 1

1. Create a chart with four rows and two columns for students to see. Title the chart *Rebellions* and label each row as follows: *Reasons for Rebellion, Major Figures, Major Battles,* and *Main Effects of the Rebellion.* Label the columns *Mexico* and *Texas.*
2. Have students work either independently or as a class to complete the chart. If time allows, have students conduct research to find additional information beyond that provided in the textbook.
3. Discuss with students the similarities and differences between the Mexican rebellion for independence from Spain and the Texas rebellion for independence from Mexico. **LS Visual/Spatial**
4. **Extend** Have students create a similar chart comparing and contrasting the Texas and American revolutions. **LS Visual/Spatial**

Alternative Assessment Handbook, Rubric 7: Charts

An Independent Nation

Sam Houston was the hero of the new independent nation of Texas. The republic created a new town named Houston and made it the capital. Voters elected Sam Houston as president. Stephen F. Austin became secretary of state.

To increase the population, Texas offered land grants. American settlers came from nearby southern states, often bringing slaves with them to help grow and harvest cotton.

Most Texans hoped that the United States would annex, or take control of, Texas, making it a state. The U.S. Congress also wanted to annex Texas. But President Andrew Jackson refused. He was concerned that admitting Texas as a slave state would upset the fragile balance of free and slave states. The president also did not want to have a war with Mexico over Texas.

Finally, Jackson did recognize Texas as an independent nation. France did so in 1839. Britain, which wanted to halt U.S. expansion, recognized Texas in 1840.

The Mexican government, however, did not recognize Santa Anna's forced handover of Texas. In 1837 the republic organized the Texas Rangers to guard its long frontier from Mexican and Native American attacks. Finally, in 1844 Texas and Mexico signed a peace treaty.

READING CHECK **Finding Main Ideas** What issues did the new nation of Texas face?

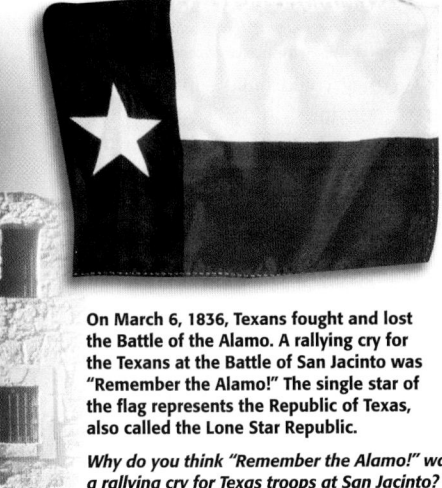

On March 6, 1836, Texans fought and lost the Battle of the Alamo. A rallying cry for the Texans at the Battle of San Jacinto was "Remember the Alamo!" The single star of the flag represents the Republic of Texas, also called the Lone Star Republic.

Why do you think "Remember the Alamo!" was a rallying cry for Texas troops at San Jacinto?

SUMMARY AND PREVIEW American settlers in Texas challenged the Mexican government and won their independence. In the next section you will learn about the war between Mexico and the United States.

Section 2 Assessment

Reviewing Ideas, Terms, and People HSS 8.8.5, 8.8.6

1. **a. Identify** What role did **Stephen F. Austin** play in the settlement of Texas?
   b. Make Inferences Why did Mexican officials want to bring more settlers to Texas?
   c. Evaluate Do you think Mexico's requirements for foreign immigrants were reasonable or unreasonable? Explain.
2. **a. Describe** What were the important battles in the War for Texas Independence? Why was each important?
   b. Make Inferences Why did Texas offer land grants to settlers?
   c. Predict What problems might the Republic of Texas face?

Critical Thinking

3. **Sequencing** Copy the time line below. Use it to list important events of the Texas Revolution.

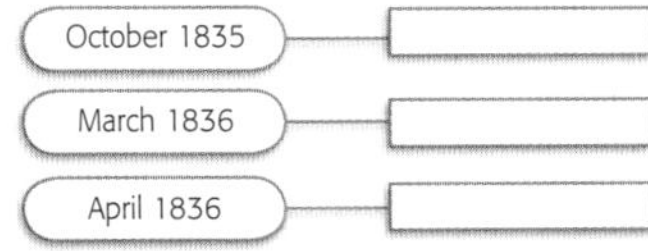

FOCUS ON WRITING

4. **Explaining the Texas Revolution** As you read this section, make note of the most important players and events in the story of how Texas gained independence from Mexico. Consider also how you will present information about these people and events to your film's audience. What words, images, and sounds will make the story of the revolution come alive for them?

Direct Teach

Linking to Today

Texas Today Texas is the second largest state in the nation. As of 2000, Texas was home to nearly 21 million people. Almost one-third of Texans are Hispanic or Latino. That's more than 6 million people!

Review & Assess

Close

Have students discuss if they think Texas independence from Mexico was inevitable. Remind students to provide reasons to support their points of view.

Review

Online Quiz, Section 2

Assess

SE Section 2 Assessment

PASS: Section 2 Quiz

Alternative Assessment Handbook

Reteach/Classroom Intervention

California Standards Review Workbook

Interactive Reader and Study Guide, Section 2

Interactive Skills Tutor CD-ROM

Section 2 Assessment Answers

1. **a.** started a colony on the lower Colorado River
   b. Few Mexicans lived in Texas, and the Mexican government wanted to attract more settlers to protect and control the region better.
   c. possible answers: yes—because Mexico controlled the region and had the right to demand settlers follow its laws; no—because the Mexican government had no right to tell settlers what religion to practice
2. **a.** Gonzales—began the revolution; Alamo—inspired Texans to resist; San Jacinto—Santa Anna was defeated
   b. increase population; control the region
   c. possible answers—economic problems, such as issuing currency, defending borders, establishing and enforcing laws, and diplomatic relations with other nations
3. October 1835—Battle at Gonzales; March 1836—declaration of independence from Mexico, formation of Republic of Texas; Battle of the Alamo; April 1836—Battle of San Jacinto
4. Images and sounds might include the Gonzales cannon, the Alamo, and rallying cries such as "Remember the Alamo! Remember Goliad!"

Answers

The Texas Revolution *Texas troops wanted to avenge and honor the memory of those who sacrificed their lives defending the Alamo.*

Reading Check *U.S. annexation, foreign recognition, conflicts with Mexico and Native Americans*

Preteach

Bellringer

If YOU were there . . . Use the **Daily Bellringer Transparency** to help students answer the question.

Daily Bellringer Transparency, Section 3

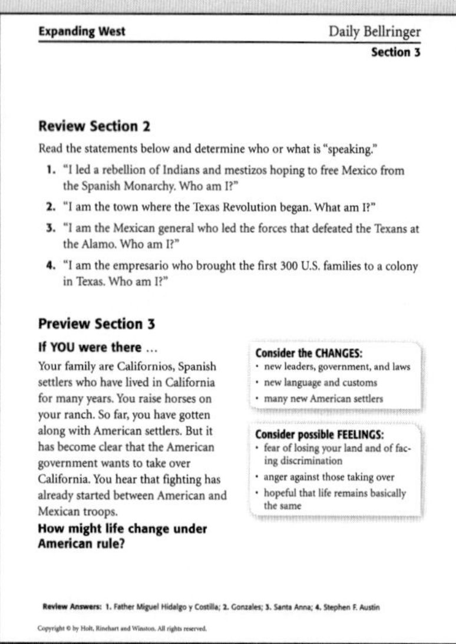

Expanding West — Daily Bellringer — Section 3

Review Section 2

Read the statements below and determine who or what is "speaking."

1. "I led a rebellion of Indians and mestizos hoping to free Mexico from the Spanish Monarchy. Who am I?"
2. "I am the town where the Texas Revolution began. What am I?"
3. "I am the Mexican general who led the forces that defeated the Texans at the Alamo. Who am I?"
4. "I am the empresario who brought the first 300 U.S. families to a colony in Texas. Who am I?"

Preview Section 3

If YOU were there ...

Your family are Californios, Spanish settlers who have lived in California for many years. You raise horses on your ranch. So far, you have gotten along with American settlers. But it has become clear that the American government wants to take over California. You hear that fighting has already started between American and Mexican troops.

How might life change under American rule?

Consider the CHANGES:
- new leaders, government, and laws
- new language and customs
- many new American settlers

Consider possible FEELINGS:
- fear of losing your land and of facing discrimination
- anger against those taking over
- hopeful that life remains basically the same

Review Answers: 1. Father Miguel Hidalgo y Costilla; 2. Gonzales; 3. Santa Anna; 4. Stephen F. Austin

Academic Vocabulary

Review with students the high-use academic term in this section.

element the basic parts of an individual's surroundings (p. 319)

CRF: Vocabulary Builder Activity, Section 3

Standards Focus

HSS 8.8.6

Means: Describe the main events of the Mexican-American War and explain how it affected Americans' lives, including the lives of Mexican Americans today.

Matters: The Mexican-American War had a significant and far-reaching effect on life in the American Southwest.

SECTION 3

The Mexican-American War

What You Will Learn...

Main Ideas

1. Many Americans believed that the nation had a manifest destiny to claim new lands in the West.
2. As a result of the Mexican-American War, the United States added territory in the Southwest.
3. American settlement in the Mexican Cession produced conflict and a blending of cultures.

The Big Idea

The ideals of manifest destiny and the outcome of the Mexican-American War led to U. S. expansion to the Pacific Ocean.

Key Terms and People

manifest destiny, *p. 316*
James K. Polk, *p. 317*
vaqueros, *p. 319*
Californios, *p. 319*
Bear Flag Revolt, *p. 320*
Treaty of Guadalupe Hidalgo, *p. 323*
Gadsden Purchase, *p. 323*

HSS 8.8.6 Describe the Texas War for Independence and the Mexican-American War, including territorial settlements, the aftermath of the wars, and the effects the wars had on the lives of Americans, including Mexican Americans today.

If YOU were there...

Your family are Californios, Spanish settlers who have lived in California for many years. You raise horses on your ranch. So far, you have gotten along with American settlers. But it has become clear that the American government wants to take over California. You hear that fighting has already started between American and Mexican troops.

How might life change under American rule?

BUILDING BACKGROUND Mexican independence set the stage for conflict and change in the West and Southwest. At the same time, American settlers continued to move westward, settling in the Mexican territories of Texas and California. American ambitions led to clashes with Mexico and the people who already lived in Mexico's territories.

Manifest Destiny

"We have it in our power to start the world over again."

—Thomas Paine, from his pamphlet *Common Sense*

Americans had always believed they could build a new, better society founded on democratic principles. In 1839 writer John O'Sullivan noted, "We are the nation of human progress, and who will, what can, set limits to our onward march?"

Actually, there was one limit: land. By the 1840s the United States had a booming economy and population. Barely 70 years old, the nation already needed more room for farms, ranches, businesses, and ever-growing families. Americans looked West to what they saw as a vast wilderness, ready to be taken.

Some people believed it was America's **manifest destiny**, or obvious fate, to settle land all the way to the Pacific Ocean in order to spread democracy. O'Sullivan coined the term in 1845. He wrote that it was America's "manifest destiny to overspread and to possess the whole continent which Providence [God] has given us for the development of the great experiment of liberty . . . "

Teach the Big Idea: Master the Standards

Standards Proficiency

The Mexican-American War

HSS 8.8.6; HSS **Analysis Skills:** CS 1, HI 1

1. **Teach** Ask students the Main Idea questions to teach this section.
2. **Apply** Have students work as a class to help you list the main events and issues in this section. Then have students write a news headline for each event or issue. **LS Verbal/Linguistic**
3. **Review** As you review the section's main ideas, have students share their headlines. Encourage feedback and discussion of headlines.
4. **Practice/Homework** Have each student select one of their headlines—or assign students a headline or topic—and create a political cartoon to go with it. Students should provide short captions explaining their political cartoons. Have volunteers share their cartoons with the class. **LS Visual/Spatial**

Alternative Assessment Handbook, Rubrics 27: Political Cartoons; and 42: Writing to Inform

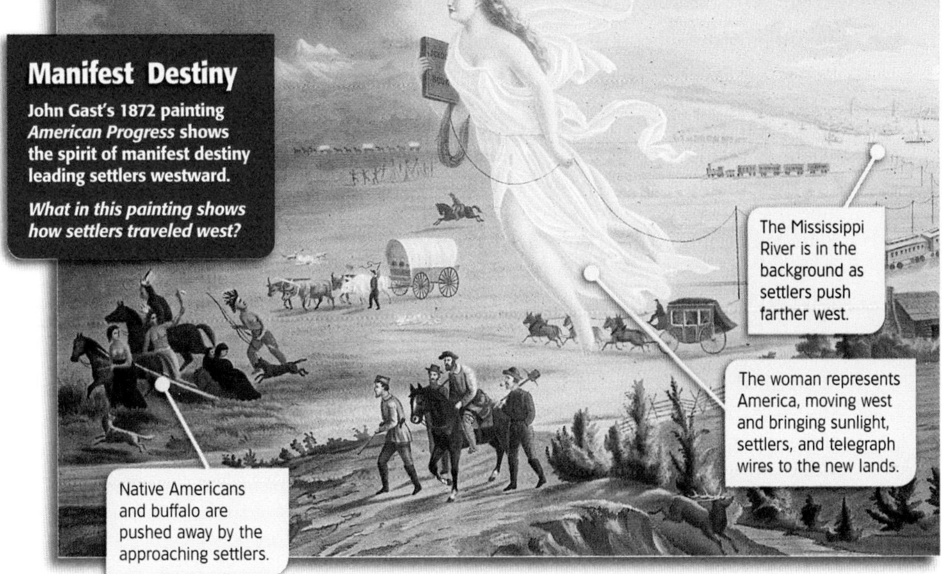

The Mississippi River is in the background as settlers push farther west.
The woman represents America, moving west and bringing sunlight, settlers, and telegraph wires to the new lands.
Native Americans and buffalo are pushed away by the approaching settlers.

Manifest Destiny

John Gast's 1872 painting *American Progress* shows the spirit of manifest destiny leading settlers westward.

What in this painting shows how settlers traveled west?

In the 1840s and 1850s, manifest destiny was tied up with the slavery issue. If America expanded, would slavery be allowed in the new territories? Several presidents became involved in the difficult issue. Among them was President John Tyler. A pro-slavery Whig, Tyler wanted to increase the power of the southern slave states by annexing Texas. His fellow Whigs disagreed.

In 1844, the Whig Party passed up Tyler and chose Senator Henry Clay of Kentucky as its presidential candidate. At first opposing annexation, Clay changed his mind due to pressure from southern politicians. The Democratic Party chose former Tennessee governor **James K. Polk** to oppose Clay. Both candidates strongly favored acquiring Texas and Oregon.

Southerners feared the loss of Texas, a possible new slave state. Others worried that Texas might become an ally of Britain. These concerns helped Polk narrowly defeat Clay.

Acquiring New Territory

President Polk quickly set out to fulfill his campaign promise to annex Oregon and Texas. By the 1820s, Russia and Spain had given up their claims to Oregon Country. Britain and the United States had agreed to occupy the territory together.

As more Americans settled there, they began to ask that Oregon become part of the United States. Polk wanted to protect these settlers' interests. Some politicians noted that Oregon Country would provide a Pacific port for the growing U.S. trade with China.

Meanwhile, Britain and the United States disagreed over how to draw the United States–Canadian border. American expansionists cried, "Fifty-four forty or fight!" This slogan referred to 54°40' north latitude, the line to which Americans wanted their northern territory to extend.

Neither side really wanted a war, though. In 1846 Great Britain and the United States signed a treaty that gave the United States all Oregon land south of the forty-ninth parallel. This treaty drew the border that still exists today. Oregon became an organized U.S. territory in February 1848.

Texas came next. By March 1845, Congress had approved annexation and

Direct Teach

Main Idea

❶ Manifest Destiny

Many Americans believed that the nation had a manifest destiny to claim new lands in the West.

Identify Who won the presidential election in 1844, and why? *James K. Polk, because many voters supported expansion and he was perceived as the expansionist candidate*

Explain What did "Fifty-four forty or fight!" mean? *slogan used by American expansionists who wanted the U.S.-Canadian border at that parallel*

Identify Points of View How do you think people of other cultures and nations viewed the idea of manifest destiny? *possible answer—Some may have viewed it as an arrogant position, whereas others with similar views might have supported the idea.*

Political Cartoons Activities for United States History, Cartoon 12: James Polk and Foreign Policy

HSS 8.8.2; HSS **Analysis Skills:** HR 5, HI 1

Critical Thinking: Identifying Points of View

Standards Proficiency

Illustrating Manifest Destiny

HSS 8.8.2; HSS **Analysis Skills:** HR 5, HI 1

1. Write the two John O' Sullivan quotations (found on the previous page) for students to see. Have students paraphrase the quotations in modern English.
2. Have students discuss the quotations and the idea of manifest destiny. Students should consider the various reasons that Americans supported and opposed manifest destiny.
3. Then have each student create a political cartoon or drawing that captures the idea of manifest destiny in the United States in the 1840s. Display the cartoons or drawings for students to view.
4. Close with a class discussion about how the idea of manifest destiny led Americans to expand the borders of the United States. LS **Visual/Spatial**

Alternative Assessment Handbook, Rubrics 3: Artwork; and 27: Political Cartoons

Answers

Manifest Destiny *on foot, on horseback, in trains, wagons, and stagecoaches*

Direct Teach

Main Idea

1 Manifest Destiny

Many Americans believed that the nation had a manifest destiny to claim new lands in the West.

Sequence List in order the events leading to U.S. acquisition of Texas and Oregon. *March 1845: U.S. Congress approves Texas annexation; June 1845: Texas Congress approves annexation; 1846: treaty with Britain establishes U.S.-Canadian border; 1848: Oregon a U.S. territory*

Recall What served as the focus of everyday life in California during Spanish rule? *the missions*

Summarize What happened to the missions after Mexico gained independence from Spain? *Mexico ended the mission system, and the mission lands went to the wealthiest Californios, who created vast ranchos.*

Compare How was life for California Indians similar under Spain and Mexico? *Either willingly or by force, Indians adopted Spanish and Mexican ways of life and performed much of the hard labor.*

CRF: History and Geography Activity: Spanish Missions in California

CRF: Primary Source Activity: From the Journal of Junipero Serra

HSS 8.8.5; HSS **Analysis Skills:** HI 1

go.hrw.com
Online Resources
KEYWORD: SS8 US10
ACTIVITY:
Spanish Missions Model

needed only the support of the Republic of Texas. Americans continued to pour into Texas. Texas politicians hoped that joining the United States would help solve the republic's financial and military problems. The Texas Congress approved annexation in June 1845. Texas became part of the United States in December. This action angered the Mexican government, which considered Texas to be a "stolen province."

California under Mexico

Although the annexation of Texas angered Mexico, it still had settlements in other areas of the present-day Southwest to govern. New Mexico was the oldest settled area, with its capital at Santa Fe. Mexico also controlled present-day Arizona, Nevada, and California.

During early Spanish rule, the mission system had dominated much of the present-day Southwest. Over time, it had become less important there, especially in New Mexico, where settlers lived in small villages. In California, however, missions remained the focus of everyday life. Missions under later Spanish rule carried out huge farming and ranching operations using the labor of Native Americans. Some of the Indians came willingly to the missions. Others were brought by force. Usually, they were not allowed to leave the mission once they had arrived. They had to adopt the clothing, food, and religion of the Spanish priests.

Missions often sold their goods to local pueblos, or towns, that arose near the missions and presidios. One wealthy California settler, Mariano Guadalupe Vallejo, remembered the early days.

> "We were the pioneers of the Pacific coast, building towns and missions while General [George] Washington was carrying on the war of the Revolution."
>
> —Mariano Guadalupe Vallejo, quoted in *Eyewitnesses and Others*

After winning independence from Spain in 1821, Mexico began to change old Spanish

History Close-up

Ranch Life

Spanish and Mexican *vaqueros*, or cowboys, were expert horseriders. They used their horses to herd cattle on the ranches of the Spanish Southwest.

Vaqueros were known for their specially designed hats.
Leather chaps protected riders from dust and scrapes.
Saddles like these were highly prized by *vaqueros*.

ANALYSIS SKILL ANALYZING VISUALS

What features of the *vaqueros'* life are shown in this painting?

Differentiating Instruction for Universal Access

English-Language Learners

Prep Required
Standards Proficiency

Materials: magazines, poster board, art supplies

California Life Collage Organize students into small groups. Have each group create a collage, in which one half of the collage shows images related to life in California under Spanish rule and the other half depicts life in California under Mexican rule. LS **Visual/Spatial**

HSS 8.8.5; HSS **Analysis Skills:** CS 1, HI 1

Alternative Assessment Handbook, Rubric 8: Collages

Special Education Students

Reaching Standards

Compare-and-Contrast Chart Create a chart with two columns and two rows for students to see. Title the chart *California under Spain and Mexico.* Label the columns *Similarities* and *Differences* and the rows *Spanish Rule* and *Mexican Rule.* Have students work in pairs to complete the chart. Then discuss the answers as a class. LS **Visual/Spatial**

HSS 8.8.5; HSS **Analysis Skills:** CS 1, HI 1

Alternative Assessment Handbook, Rubric 7: Charts

Answers

Analyzing Visuals *activities, clothing, tools of their trade, environment*

policies toward California and Texas. In 1833, for example, Mexico ended the mission system in California. Mission lands were broken up, and huge grants were given to some of the wealthiest California settlers, including Vallejo. They created vast ranchos, or ranches, with tens of thousands of acres of land. ***Vaqueros***, or cowboys, managed the large herds of cattle and sheep. Cowhides were so valuable that they were called "California banknotes." Hides were traded for household items and luxury goods with ship captains from the eastern United States. Some settlers also made wine and grew citrus fruits.

Although they had been freed from the missions, for most California Indians the elements of life changed very little. They continued to herd animals and do much of the hard physical labor on ranches and farms. Some, however, ran away into the wilderness or to the nearby towns of San Diego and Los Angeles.

The Californios

Because of the great distance between California and the center of Mexico's government, by the early 1820s California had only around 3,200 colonists. These colonists, called **Californios**, felt little connection to their faraway government.

Californios developed a lasting reputation for hospitality and skilled horse riding. In *Two Years Before the Mast*, American novelist Richard Henry Dana Jr. wrote about his encounters with Californio culture. He described, for example, what happened after a Californio served a feast to Dana and a friend.

> "We took out some money and asked him how much we were to pay. He shook his head and crossed himself, saying that it was charity—that the Lord gave it to us."
>
> —Richard Henry Dana Jr. from *Two Years Before the Mast*

In addition to traders and travelers, a small number of settlers also arrived from the United States. They were called Anglos by the Californios. Although there were few Anglo settlers in California, their calls for independence increased tensions between Mexico and the United States.

BIOGRAPHY

Mariano Guadalupe Vallejo
1808–1890

Mariano Guadalupe Vallejo was born to an influential Californio family in Monterey. He joined the Mexican army shortly after Mexico's independence from Spain. He was soon put in charge of Mexico's efforts to increase settlement in northern California. Vallejo eventually became the richest man in California, owning enormous amounts of land and livestock. He welcomed American rule of California, believing it would result in self-government for Californios. Vallejo served at the state constitutional convention as well as in the first state senate.

Analyzing Why did Vallejo encourage American rule of California?

READING CHECK **Drawing Inferences** How did manifest destiny affect Spanish and Mexican rule in California?

ACADEMIC VOCABULARY
elements the basic parts of an individual's surroundings

Mexican-American War

Diplomatic relations between Mexico and the United States became increasingly strained. U.S. involvement in California and Texas contributed to this tension.

Conflict Breaks Out

Mexico had long insisted that its northern border lay along the Nueces River. The United States said the border was farther south, along the Rio Grande. In June 1845 President Polk ordered General Zachary Taylor to lead an army into the disputed region.

Polk sent diplomat John Slidell to Mexico City to try to settle the border dispute. Slidell

Direct Teach

Did you know. . .

The city of Los Angeles, California, started as a Spanish mission—the Mission San Gabriel Arcángel, built in 1771. Ten years later, a town was founded nearby along what is now the Los Angeles River. By 1835, nearly 1,250 people lived in Los Angeles.

Info to Know

Blending of Cultures in New Mexico In Spanish New Mexico, the Pueblo Indians greatly influenced the Spanish colonists. The Pueblo introduced the Spanish to southwestern foods such as beans and corn. The Spanish also began building with adobe, as the Pueblo did. In turn, the Spanish changed many aspects of Pueblo life by introducing new tools and new foods, such as peaches, to the region.

Spanish Missions and Native American Beliefs The Christian view of existence and afterlife often differed from Native Americans' beliefs. For example, many American Indians found it hard to accept the idea that immortality was a reward for a lifetime of good deeds. They believed that rewards were given in this life, and the afterlife was simply an idealized version of the known world. To overcome such resistance, Spanish missionaries sometimes modified Christian beliefs and rituals to adapt them to Native American cultures.

Advanced Learners/GATE **Exceeding Standards**

1. Organize students into pairs and have each pair write a dialogue between a Californio and a newly arrived Anglo settler in the early 1840s.
2. The Californio should explain what his or her life is like and how life has changed in California since Mexico gained independence from Spain. The Anglo settler should explain in turn why he or she has chosen to come to California.
3. Students' dialogues should address issues of manifest destiny, differences between Californios and Anglos, and life in California under both Spanish and Mexican rule.
4. Have volunteer pairs perform their dialogues for the class. **LS Interpersonal, Verbal/Linguistic**

HSS 8.8.2, 8.8.5; **HSS Analysis Skills:** HI 1

Alternative Assessment Handbook, Rubric 37: Writing Assignments

Answers

Biography *He hoped American rule would lead to more self-government for Californios.*

Reading Check *Anglos began settling in California, where they called for independence, which created tension between Mexico and the United States.*

Direct Teach

Main Idea

❷ Mexican-American War

As a result of the Mexican-American War, the United States added territory in the Southwest.

Recall Why did the United States declare war against Mexico? *disagreement over the U.S.-Mexico border; Mexican attack on U.S. soldiers stationed in disputed area*

Summarize Briefly describe the Bear Flag Revolt. *In 1846 a small group of American settlers seized Sonoma and declared California an independent nation, but U.S. forces soon arrived and claimed the region.*

Make Generalizations What did the American public think of the war with Mexico? *Many Americans supported the war, and many men signed up to fight, but many Whigs and abolitionists opposed the war.*

Map Transparency: Mexican-American War, 1846–1847

HSS 8.8.6; HSS **Analysis Skills:** CS 1, HR 5, HI 1, HI 2

Info to Know

Opposition to the War Henry David Thoreau, a writer and philosopher, opposed the Mexican-American War. He spent a night in jail rather than pay taxes that might support the war effort. Thoreau described his views on peaceful resistance to the government in an essay titled "Civil Disobedience." His ideas later inspired the civil rights leader Martin Luther King Jr.

came with an offer to buy New Mexico and California for $30 million. Mexican officials refused to speak to him.

In March 1846, General Taylor led his troops to the Rio Grande. He camped across from Mexican forces stationed near the town of Matamoros, Mexico. In April, the Mexican commander told Taylor to withdraw from Mexican territory. Taylor refused. The two sides clashed, and several U.S. soldiers were killed.

President Polk delivered the news to Congress.

> "Mexico has passed the boundary of the United States, has invaded our territory, and shed American blood upon the American soil ... The two nations are now at war."
>
> —James K. Polk, from his address to Congress, May 11, 1846

Polk's war message was persuasive. Two days later, Congress declared war on Mexico.

War Begins

At the beginning of the war with Mexico, the U.S. Army had better weapons and equipment. Yet it was greatly outnumbered and poorly prepared. The government put out a call for 50,000 volunteers. About 200,000 responded. Many were young men who thought the war would be a grand adventure in a foreign land.

On the home front, many Americans supported the war. However, many Whigs thought the war was unjustified and avoidable. Northern abolitionists also opposed the conflict. They feared the spread of slavery into southwestern lands.

While Americans debated the war, fighting proceeded. General Taylor's soldiers won battles south of the Nueces River. Taylor then crossed the Rio Grande and occupied Matamoros, Mexico. While Taylor waited for more men, Polk ordered General Stephen Kearny to attack New Mexico. On August 18, 1846, Kearny took Santa Fe, the capital city, without a fight. He claimed the entire province of New Mexico for the United States and marched west to California, where another conflict with Mexico was already under way.

The Bear Flag Revolt

In 1846, only about 500 Americans lived in the huge province of California, in contrast to about 12,000 Californios. Yet, in the spirit of manifest destiny, a small group of American settlers seized the town of Sonoma, north of San Francisco, on June 14. Hostilities began between the two sides when the Americans took some horses that were intended for the Mexican militia. In what became known as the **Bear Flag Revolt**, the Americans declared California to be an independent nation. Above the town, the rebels hoisted a hastily made flag of a grizzly bear facing a red star. Californios laughed at the roughly-made bear, thinking it "looked more like a pig than a bear."

John C. Frémont, a U.S. Army captain, was leading a mapping expedition across the Sierra Nevadas when he heard of the possible war with Mexico. Frémont went to Sonoma and quickly joined the American settlers in their revolt against the Californios. Because war had already broken out between the United States and Mexico, Frémont's actions were seen as beneficial to the American cause in the region. His stated goal, however, was Californian independence, not to annex California to the United States. During the revolt, several important Californios were taken prisoner, including Mariano Vallejo. Vallejo and his brother were held at an Anglo settlement for two months without any formal charges being brought against them. Long after his release, Vallejo wrote a history of California that included an account of his time as a bear flag prisoner.

But the bear flag was quick to fall. In July, U.S. naval forces came ashore in California and raised the stars and stripes. Kearny's army arrived from the East. The towns of San Diego, Los Angeles, and San Francisco fell rapidly. In August, U.S. Navy Commodore Robert Stockton claimed California for the United States. Some Californios continued to resist until early 1847, when they surrendered.

Collaborative Learning

Exceeding Standards

Songs for the Road to War HSS 8.8.6; HSS **Analysis Skills:** CS 1, HI 1, HI 2

1. Write the following events for students to see:
   - U.S. annexation of Texas
   - U.S.-Mexico border disputes
   - conflicts between Mexican and U.S. troops
   - declaration of war against Mexico by the U.S. Congress
2. Organize students into small groups. Ask the groups to imagine that they are songwriters at the time of the Mexican-American War. They have been hired to write a song describing the events leading to the war. The song should either increase patriotism or serve as an anthem for those opposing the war.
3. Select and play a tune for students to use or have each group choose an existing tune they like. Students should write catchy lyrics to go with the tune.
4. Have each group sing its song to the class.
   LS Auditory/Musical, Interpersonal

Alternative Assessment Handbook, Rubric 26: Poems and Songs

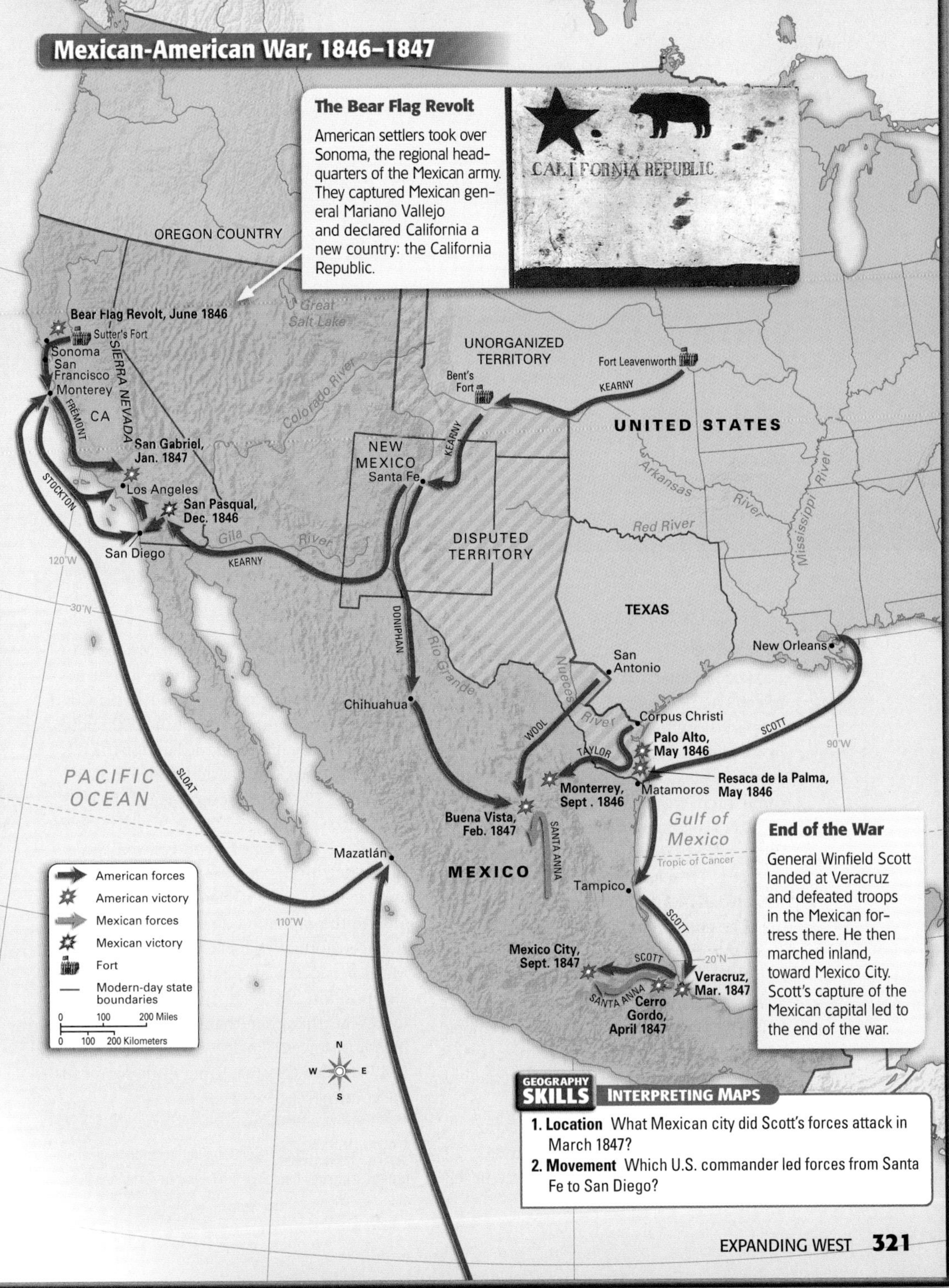

Direct Teach

Interpreting Maps

Mexican-American War 1846–1847

Within months of the war's start, U.S. forces had captured all the major cities and towns along the coast of California and controlled much of the territory north of Mexico City.

Locate Where did most of the fighting in the war take place? *in disputed parts of Texas and in Mexico along the Gulf Coast, inland, and in California*

Map Transparency: Mexican-American War 1846–1847

HSS 8.8.6; HSS **Analysis Skills:** CS 3

Connect to Journalism

A War of Many Firsts The Mexican-American War was the first U.S. war fought mainly on foreign soil. It was also the first time that many newspapers sent reporters to cover a U.S. conflict. Reporters used horses to send news articles back to their papers in the East. The war was also one of the first to be photographed.

Did you know . . .

The standard U.S. Army uniform in the war was sky blue, but many soldiers disliked the color. As a result, some regiments created their own uniforms, complete with frills such as feathers, fringe, and silk. One Indiana soldier whose uniform was dark blue with silver lace said, "Let 'em go to . . . with their sky blue. I'll be blowed if they make a Regular out of me."

Critical Thinking: Analyzing Information

Standards Proficiency

Reporting the War

HSS 8.8.6; HSS **Analysis Skills:** CS 1, HI 1, HI 2

1. Ask students to imagine that they are newspaper reporters covering the Mexican-American War. Have each student write an article about one of the major events or battles shown on the map above as if they were present.
2. The article should include a headline, date, byline, and a clear and chronological account of events. Articles should also address the questions "who, when, where, what, and how."
3. Tell students that newspapers of the time often sensationalized stories to sell more papers. Encourage students to use this same approach when writing their headlines and articles. Students might also include on-the-spot "interviews."
4. Ask volunteers to read their articles aloud to the class. LS **Verbal/Linguistic**

Alternative Assessment Handbook, Rubrics 23: Newspapers; and 42: Writing to Inform

Answers

Interpreting Maps 1. *Veracruz;* **2.** *General Stephen Kearny*

Direct Teach

Main Idea

❷ Mexican-American War

As a result of the Mexican-American War, the United States added territory in the Southwest.

Identify Who led the U.S. forces to victory at the Battle of Buena Vista? *U.S. general Zachary Taylor*

Analyze Why do you think General Scott attacked Veracruz before Mexico City? *Veracruz was located on the coast, it was the strongest fortress in Mexico, and its defeat was needed to break Mexican resistance.*

Make Judgments Do you agree with President Polk's decision to replace Taylor with Scott? Explain. *Answers will vary, but students should exhibit an understanding of why Polk replaced Taylor and of the accomplishments of both Taylor and Scott.*

CRF: Primary Source Activity: A Mexican Views the War

HSS 8.8.6; HSS **Analysis Skills:** CS 1, HI 1, HI 2

Answers

Reading Check *Santa Fe, Aug. 18, 1846; Buena Vista, Feb. 1847; Veracruz, Mar. 29, 1847; Cerro Gordo, April 1847; Mexico City, Sept.14, 1847*

American soldier

War's End

In Mexico General Taylor finally got the reinforcements he needed. He drove his forces deep into enemy lands. Santa Anna, thrown from office after losing Texas, returned to power in Mexico in September 1846. Quickly, he came after Taylor.

The two armies clashed at Buena Vista in February 1847. After a close battle with heavy casualties on both sides, the Mexican Army retreated. The next morning, the cry went up: "The enemy has fled! The field is ours!"

Taylor's success made him a war hero back home. The general's popularity troubled President Polk, and when Taylor's progress stalled, Polk gave the command to General Winfield Scott. A beloved leader, he was known by his troops as "Old Fuss and Feathers" because of his strict military discipline.

Scott sailed to the port of Veracruz, the strongest fortress in Mexico. On March 29, after an 88-hour artillery attack, Veracruz fell. Scott moved on to the final goal, Mexico City, the capital. Taking a route similar to one followed by Spanish conquistador Hernán Cortés in 1519, the Americans pushed 200 or so miles inland. Santa Anna tried to stop the U.S. forces at Cerro Gordo in mid-April, but failed. By August 1847, U.S. troops were at the edge of Mexico City.

After a truce failed, Scott ordered a massive attack on Mexico City. Mexican soldiers and civilians fought fierce battles in and around the capital. At a military school atop the steep, fortified hill of Chapultepec, young Mexican cadets bravely defended their hopeless position. At least one soldier jumped to his death rather than surrender to the invading forces. Finally, on September 14, 1847, Mexico City fell. Santa Anna soon fled the country.

READING CHECK **Sequencing** In chronological order, list the key battles of the Mexican-American War.

Critical Thinking: Sequencing

Reaching Standards

Mexican-American War Time Line

HSS 8.8.6; HSS **Analysis Skills:** CS 1, CS 2, HI 1, HI 2

1. To help students understand the sequence of events in the Mexican War, copy the graphic organizer here for students to see. Omit the blue, italicized answers.
2. Have students copy the time line and complete it by describing the key events of the war. Review the answers as a class.
   LS Visual/Spatial

Alternative Assessment Handbook, Rubric 36: Time Lines

- **March 1846** — *U.S. and Mexican troops clash.*
- **August 1846** — *California is controlled by American forces.*
- **August 1846** — *U.S. troops under Kearny take Santa Fe, New Mexico*
- **February 1847** — *Santa Anna and Taylor battle at Buena Vista.*
- **September 1847** — *U.S. troops under Scott capture Mexico City.*

Battle of Buena Vista

After the two-day Battle of Buena Vista, the American army gained control of northern Mexico. At the beginning of the battle, Mexican forces outnumbered the Americans. But the Mexicans suffered more than twice as many casualties.

Why was the Battle of Buena Vista a turning point in the Mexican-American War?

Mexican soldier

American Settlement in the Mexican Cession

The war ended after Scott took Mexico City. In February 1848, the United States and Mexico signed the **Treaty of Guadalupe Hidalgo**, which officially ended the war and forced Mexico to turn over much of its northern territory to the United States. Known as the Mexican Cession, this land included the present-day states of California, Nevada, and Utah. In addition, it included most of Arizona and New Mexico and parts of Colorado and Wyoming. The United States also won the area claimed by Texas north of the Rio Grande. The Mexican Cession totaled more than 500,000 square miles and increased the size of the United States by almost 25 percent.

Agreements and Payments

In exchange for this vast territory, the United States agreed to pay Mexico $15 million. In addition, the United States assumed claims of more than $3 million held by American citizens against the Mexican government. The treaty also addressed the status of Mexicans in the Mexican Cession. The treaty provided that they would be "protected in the free enjoyment of their liberty and property, and secured in the free exercise of their religion." The Senate passed the treaty in March 1848.

After the war with Mexico, some Americans wanted to guarantee that any southern railroad to California would be built completely on American soil. James Gadsden, U.S. minister to Mexico, negotiated an important agreement with Mexico in December 1853. Under the terms of the **Gadsden Purchase**, the U.S. government paid Mexico $10 million. In exchange, the United States received the southern parts of what are now Arizona and New Mexico. With this purchase, the existing boundary with Mexico was finally fixed.

Surge of American Settlers

After the Mexican-American War, a flood of Americans moved to the Southwest. American newcomers struggled against longtime residents to control the land and other valuable resources, such as water and minerals. Most Mexicans, Mexican Americans, and Native Americans faced legal, economic, and social discrimination. As a result, they found it difficult to protect their rights.

The Treaty of Guadalupe Hidalgo promised to protect Mexican American residents' property rights. Yet differences between Mexican and U.S. land laws led to great confusion. The U.S. government often made Mexican American landowners go to court to prove that they had titles to their land. Landowners had to pay their own travel costs as well as those of witnesses and interpreters. They also had to pay attorneys' and interpreters' fees. These legal battles often bankrupted landowners. New settlers also tended to ignore Mexican legal concepts, such as community property or community water rights.

Direct Teach

Main Idea

❸ American Settlement in the Mexican Cession

American settlement in the Mexican Cession produced conflict and a blending of cultures.

Find Main Ideas What treaty resolved the war, and what did each side gain under the treaty? *Treaty of Guadalupe Hidalgo; United States—Mexican Cession; Mexico—$15 million and release from American claims of more than $3 million*

Contrast For Mexicans, how did life under American rule differ from that promised in the Treaty of Guadalupe Hidalgo? *The treaty promised that Mexicans' liberties and property would be secured, but in reality Mexicans and Mexican Americans faced discrimination and loss of land.*

HSS 8.8.6; HSS **Analysis Skills:** HI 1, HI 2

Biography

Zachary Taylor (1784–1850) Taylor's troops called him "Old Rough and Ready" because of his casual dress. Taylor rarely wore a uniform or signs of his rank. One officer claimed, "He looks more like an old farmer going to market . . . than anything."

Although sidelined by President Polk, Taylor was too popular to stay down. The next year he won the presidential election. However, after a little over a year in office, he died of cholera.

Collaborative Learning

Standards Proficiency

Treaty of Guadalupe Hidalgo

HSS 8.8.6; HSS **Analysis Skills:** CS 1, HI 1

Materials: art supplies, butcher paper/poster board

1. Review the terms of the Treaty of Guadalupe Hidalgo and its short- and long-term effects.
2. Organize students into small groups. Tell half the groups that they oppose the treaty and the other half that they support it.
3. Ask the groups to imagine that they are attending a panel discussion on the treaty. Have each group create the following set of documents: (a) a map showing land acquisitions under the treaty, (b) a summary of the treaty's provisions, and (c) a position statement expressing the group's viewpoint on the treaty.
4. Each group should select a spokesperson to represent the group in a panel discussion on the treaty. LS **Interpersonal, Verbal/Linguistic**

Alternative Assessment Handbook, Rubrics 20: Map Creation; and 37: Writing Assignments

Answers

Battle of Buena Vista *The American victory in the battle gave U.S. forces control of northern Mexico.*

Direct Teach

Main Idea

❸ American Settlement in the Mexican Cession

American settlement in the Mexican Cession produced conflict and a blending of cultures.

Analyze Why did conflicts occur between the different groups living in the American Southwest? *because of a desire to control valuable resources; different laws and views regarding property and water rights, lack of respect for Native American lands and holy places*

Summarize How did different cultures shape one another in the American Southwest? *use of English and Spanish; mix of heritage of place-names; celebration of Mexican and American holidays; cultural sharing of skills, knowledge, traditions*

Make Judgments Do you agree with Brigham Young's view of water use and water rights? Why or why not? *Answers will vary, but students should exhibit an understanding of the importance of water rights and access in the dry climate of the West.*

HSS 8.8.6; **HSS Analysis Skills:** HR 5, HI 1

Linking to Today

Mexican Americans Today

Region Outside of the Southwest, what regions of the United States have large percentages of Mexican Americans? *Southeast, particularly Florida and North Carolina; Great Lakes region*

HSS Analysis Skills: CS 3

LINKING TO TODAY

Mexican Americans Today

Today Mexican Americans are about 8 percent of the U.S. population. More than 20 million Mexican Americans live in all 50 states. Many who live in the West are descended from people who lived there long before the region became part of the United States.

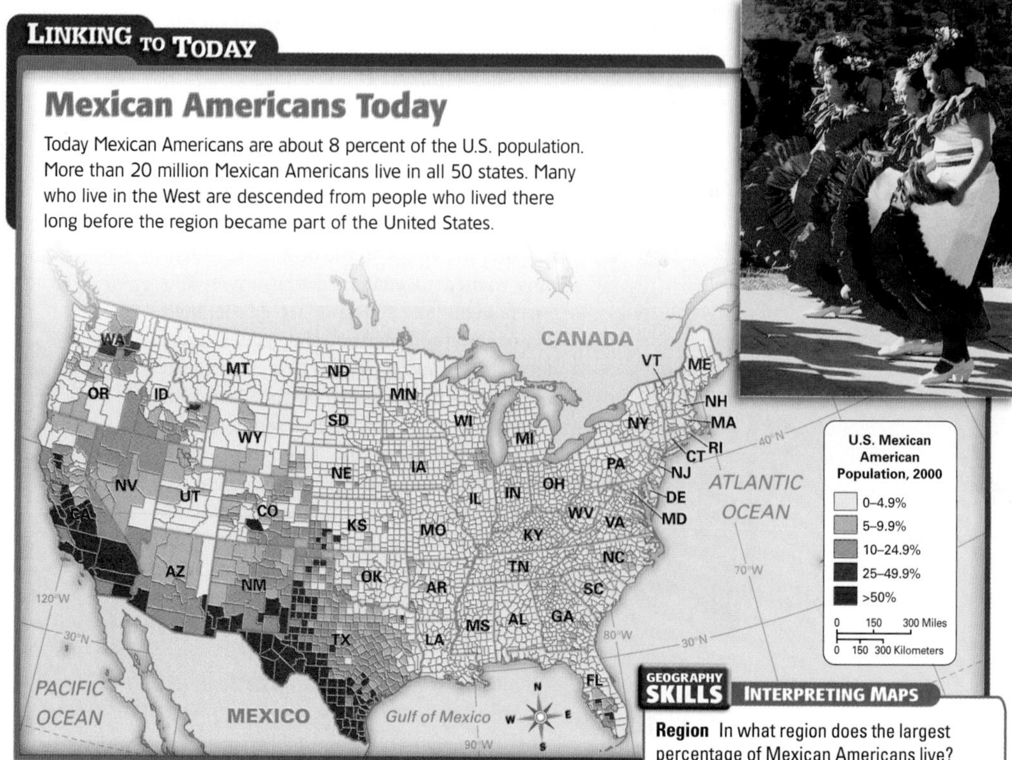

GEOGRAPHY SKILLS INTERPRETING MAPS

Region In what region does the largest percentage of Mexican Americans live?

THE IMPACT TODAY

Mexican holidays like Cinco de Mayo and Día de los Muertos are still popular holidays in the Southwest.

White settlers also battled with American Indians over property rights. In some areas, for example, new white settlers soon outnumbered southwestern Native Americans. The Anglo settlers often tried to take control of valuable water resources and grazing lands. In addition, settlers rarely respected Indian holy places. Native American peoples such as the Navajo and the Apache tried to protect their land and livestock from the settlers. Indians and settlers alike attacked one another to protect their interests.

Cultural Encounters

Despite conflicts, different cultures shaped one another in the Southwest. In settlements with large Mexican populations, laws were often printed in both English and Spanish. Names of places—such as San Antonio, San Diego, and Santa Barbara—show Hispanic heritage. Other place-names, such as Taos and Tesuque, are derived from Native American words. Communities throughout the Southwest regularly celebrated both Mexican and American holidays.

Mexican and Native American knowledge and traditions also shaped many local economies. Mexican Americans taught Anglo settlers about mining in the mountains. Many ranching communities were first started by Mexican settlers. In addition, Mexican Americans introduced new types of saddles and other equipment to American ranchers. Adobe, developed by the Anasazi Indians, was adopted from the Pueblo people by the Spanish. It is still commonly

Cross-Discipline Activity: Geography

Standards Proficiency

Water Rights **HSS** 8.8.6; **HSS Analysis Skills:** CS 1, HR 1, HI 1

Research Required

1. Have students use the library and other resources to conduct research on water-rights laws in one or more states in the Southwest today.
2. If students have difficulty, suggest they investigate water issues related to California, the Colorado River, or the Rio Grande.
3. Tell students to write three questions to guide and focus their research. Then have students take notes on the information they find.
4. Give students several options for presenting their information, such as creating a computer or multimedia presentation, a triptych, or a report.
5. Have volunteers present quick summaries of what they learned to the class.

LS Verbal/Linguistic, Visual/Spatial

Alternative Assessment Handbook, Rubrics 22: Multimedia Presentations; 29: Presentations; and 30: Research

Answers

Interpreting Maps *Southwest, particularly the region of the U.S.-Mexican border*

used by American residents in New Mexico, Arizona, and California.

Trade also changed the Southwest. For example, the Navajo created handwoven woolen blankets to sell to Americans. Americans in turn brought manufactured goods and money to the Southwest. Due to exchanges like these, the economies of many Mexican American and Native American communities in the Southwest began to change.

Water Rights

In the East water-use laws commonly required owners whose land bordered streams or rivers to maintain a free flow of water. These restrictions generally prevented landowners from constructing dams because doing so would infringe upon the water rights of neighbors downstream.

In the typically dry climate of the West, large-scale agriculture was not possible without irrigation. Dams and canals were required to direct scarce water to fields. This need conflicted with the accepted eastern tradition of equal access to water.

Brigham Young established a strict code regulating water rights for the Mormon community. In any dispute over water use, the good of the community would outweigh the interests of individuals. Young's approach stood as an example for modern water laws throughout the West.

READING CHECK **Summarizing** What were some of the early important agreements between the United States and Mexico, and why were they significant?

SUMMARY AND PREVIEW America's westward expansion continued rapidly after the Mexican-American War. In the next section you will learn about the California gold rush.

Section 3 Assessment

go.hrw.com
Online Quiz
KEYWORD: SS8 HP10

Reviewing Ideas, Terms, and People HSS 8.8.6

1. **a. Define** What was **manifest destiny**?
   b. Make Inferences Why was westward expansion such an important issue in the election of 1844?
   c. Evaluate Do you think California benefited from Mexican independence? Why or why not?
2. **a. Recall** Why did the United States declare war on Mexico?
   b. Summarize What was General Winfield Scott's strategy for winning the war with Mexico?
   c. Elaborate Would you have sided with those who opposed the war with Mexico or with those who supported it? Why?
3. **a. Describe** What conflicts did American settlers, Native Americans, and Mexican Americans in the Mexican Cession experience?
   b. Draw Conclusions Why were water rights so important in the American Southwest?
   c. Evaluate In your opinion, what was the most important effect of the annexation of the Mexican Cession?

Critical Thinking

4 **Identifying Cause and Effect** Copy the graphic organizer below onto your own sheet of paper. Use it to identify the causes and effects of the Mexican-American War.

FOCUS ON WRITING

5. **Explaining the Mexican-American War** How will you convey ideas, such as manifest destiny, in a film? How will you explain to your audience the Mexican-American War's role in expansion of the United States? Consider these questions as you read this section.

Section 3 Assessment Answers

1. **a.** belief that U.S. territory should extend to the Pacific Ocean
   b. because of the related slavery issues and because both candidates supported expansion
   c. Possible answers—yes, gained statehood; no, led to discrimination against many Californios and Native Americans
2. **a.** border disputes; Mexican attack on U.S. forces in disputed territory; Polk's call for war
   b. to take the Mexican capital, Mexico City
   c. Answers will vary but should reflect an understanding of Americans' different views about the war.
3. **a.** conflicts over control of land and water
   b. because of the West's generally dry climate
   c. Answers will vary but should reflect an understanding of the effects, listed in next answer.
4. causes—see answer to Question 2a; effects—expansion of United States, cultural blending and conflicts among groups in the Southwest
5. Students should consider various aspects of U.S. western expansion.

Direct Teach

Linking to Today

Water Usage in the West In 1902 the federal government created the Bureau of Reclamation. The Bureau built dams, reservoirs, and canals to bring additional water to dry western regions. Today the Bureau manages all the water in 17 states west of the Mississippi River.

Review & Assess

Close

Ask students to review how the idea of manifest destiny led to the Mexican-American War and affected life in what is now the American Southwest.

Review

go.hrw.com Online Quiz, Section 3

Assess

SE Section 3 Assessment

PASS: Section 3 Quiz

Alternative Assessment Handbook

Reteach/Classroom Intervention

California Standards Review Workbook

Interactive Reader and Study Guide, Section 3

Interactive Skills Tutor CD-ROM

Answers

Reading Check *Treaty of Guadalupe Hidalgo; Gadsden Purchase; greatly increased the size of the United States; set the current border between Mexico and the United States; affected life of Mexican and Native Americans living in what is now the American Southwest*

Preteach

Bellringer

If YOU were there . . . Use the **Daily Bellringer Transparency** to help students answer the question.

Daily Bellringer Transparency, Section 4

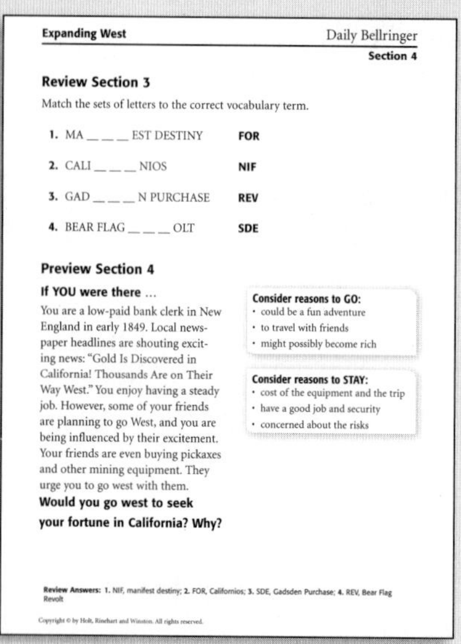
Expanding West — Daily Bellringer, Section 4

Review Section 3

Match the sets of letters to the correct vocabulary term.

1. MA _ _ _ EST DESTINY — **FOR**
2. CALI _ _ _ NIOS — **NIF**
3. GAD _ _ _ N PURCHASE — **REV**
4. BEAR FLAG _ _ _ OLT — **SDE**

Preview Section 4

If YOU were there ...

You are a low-paid bank clerk in New England in early 1849. Local newspaper headlines are shouting exciting news: "Gold Is Discovered in California! Thousands Are on Their Way West." You enjoy having a steady job. However, some of your friends are planning to go West, and you are being influenced by their excitement. Your friends are even buying pickaxes and other mining equipment. They urge you to go west with them.

Would you go west to seek your fortune in California? Why?

Consider reasons to GO:
- could be a fun adventure
- to travel with friends
- might possibly become rich

Consider reasons to STAY:
- cost of the equipment and the trip
- have a good job and security
- concerned about the risks

Review Answers: 1. NIF, manifest destiny; 2. FOR, Californios; 3. SDE, Gadsden Purchase; 4. REV, Bear Flag Revolt

Building Vocabulary

Preteach or review the following terms:

famine severe food shortage (p. 330)

hospitality kind, friendly treatment of visitors (p. 327)

nugget as used here, a lump of metal in its natural state (p. 327)

CRF: Vocabulary Builder Activity, Section 4

Standards Focus

HSS 8.8.3

Means: Describe life for women in the West, particularly in California during and after the California gold rush.

Matters: The status that western women gained influenced later rights for women.

HSS 8.8.5

Means: Discuss the location, culture, and economy of Mexican settlement in California.

Matters: Mexican settlement strongly influenced life in the Southwest.

HSS 8.9.4

Means: Discuss how the issue of slavery affected U.S. expansion in the West.

Matters: Slavery was a key issue in the debate over statehood for California.

SECTION 4

The California Gold Rush

What You Will Learn...

Main Ideas

1. The discovery of gold brought settlers to California.
2. The gold rush had a lasting impact on California's population and economy.

The Big Idea

The California gold rush changed the future of the West.

Key Terms and People

John Sutter, *p. 327*
Donner party, *p. 327*
forty-niners, *p. 327*
prospect, *p. 328*
placer miners, *p. 328*

HSS 8.8.3 Describe the role of pioneer women and the new status that western women achieved (e.g., Laura Ingalls Wilder, Annie Bidwell; slave women gaining freedom in the West; Wyoming granting suffrage to women in 1869).

8.8.5 Discuss Mexican settlements and their locations, cultural traditions, attitudes toward slavery, land-grant system, and economics.

8.9.4 Discuss the importance of the slavery issue as raised by the annexation of Texas and California's admission to the union as a free state under the Compromise of 1850.

If YOU were there...

You are a low-paid bank clerk in New England in early 1849. Local newspaper headlines are shouting exciting news: "Gold Is Discovered in California! Thousands Are on Their Way West." You enjoy having a steady job. However, some of your friends are planning to go West, and you are being influenced by their excitement. Your friends are even buying pickaxes and other mining equipment. They urge you to go West with them.

Would you go west to seek your fortune in California? Why?

BUILDING BACKGROUND At the end of the Mexican-American War, the United States gained control of Mexican territories in the West, including all of the present-day state of California. American settlements in California increased slowly at first. Then, the discovery of gold brought quick population growth and an economic boom.

Discovery of Gold Brings Settlers

In the 1830s and 1840s, Americans who wanted to move to California started up the Oregon Trail. At the Snake River in present-day Idaho, the trail split. People bound for California took the southern route, which became known as the California Trail. This path ran through the Sierra Nevada mountain range. American emigrants and traders on the California Trail tried to cross these mountains before the season's first snows.

Although many Americans traveled along the California Trail, few actually settled in California. American merchants were usually more interested in trading goods made in factories than in establishing settlements. They traded for gold and silver coins, hides, and tallow (animal fat used to make soap and candles) from Mexico. California became a meeting ground for traders from Mexico and the United States.

Before the Mexican-American War, California's population consisted mostly of Mexicans and Native Americans. When Mexico

326 CHAPTER 10

Teach the Big Idea: Master the Standards

Standards Proficiency

The California Gold Rush

HSS 8.8.3, 8.8.5, 8.9.4; HSS **Analysis Skills:** HI 1, HI 2

1. **Teach** Ask students the Main Idea questions to teach this section.
2. **Apply** Ask students to imagine that gold has just been discovered on the grounds of their school. Have students predict some short- and long-term consequences of the find. Write the predictions for students to see. Then have students compare and contrast their predictions to the effects of the California gold rush. LS **Verbal/Linguistic**
3. **Review** To review the section's main ideas, have students explain the causes and effects of the California gold rush.
4. **Practice/Homework** Have each student write one to three paragraphs summarizing the historical significance of the California gold rush. LS **Verbal/Linguistic**

Alternative Assessment Handbook, Rubrics 11: Discussions; and 42: Writing to Inform controlled California, Mexican officials did not want many Americans to settle there. However, in 1839 they did give Swiss immigrant **John Sutter** permission to start a colony. Sutter's Fort, located near the Sacramento River, soon became a popular rest stop for many American emigrants. These new arrivals praised Sutter's hospitality and helpfulness. By the mid-1840s some Anglo Californians were publishing newspaper advertisements and guidebooks encouraging other settlers to move West.

The **Donner party** was a group of western travelers who went to California but were stranded in the Sierra Nevada Mountains during winter. The party began its journey West in the spring of 1846. Trying to find a shortcut, the group left the main trail and got lost. When the Donner party reached the Sierra Nevada Mountains, they became trapped by heavy snows. They were stuck and had almost no food.

A rescue party found the starving and freezing group in February 1847. Of the original 87 travelers, 42 had died.

Gold in California

In January 1848, Sutter sent a carpenter named James Marshall to build a sawmill beside a nearby river. While working near Sutter's Mill, Marshall glanced at the ground. "I reached my hand down and picked it up; it made my heart thump, for I was certain it was gold."

Sutter and Marshall agreed to keep the discovery a secret. However, when they examined the work site the next day, they met a Spanish-speaking Native American worker holding a nugget and shouting, "Oro [gold]! Oro! Oro!"

Sutter's workers soon quit to search for gold. Stories of the discovery rapidly spread across the country. President Polk added to the national excitement by confirming the California gold strike in his farewell message to Congress in December 1848. In 1849 about 80,000 gold-seekers came to California, hoping to strike it rich. These gold-seeking migrants to California were called **forty-niners**. As one Iowa woman who

"Gold Fever"

"Gold fever" brought 80,000 people, like this miner, to California in 1849 alone. One California newspaper captured the excitement: "The whole country, from San Francisco to Los Angeles, and from the sea shore to the base of the Sierra Nevadas, resounds with the cry of 'gold, GOLD, GOLD!' while the field is left half planted, the house half built, and everything neglected but the manufacture of shovels and pickaxes." Below is a piece of jewelry made from nuggets found in California.

Why was everything neglected except for "the manufacture of shovels and pickaxes"?

Direct Teach

Main Idea

1 Discovery of Gold Brings Settlers

The discovery of gold brought settlers to California.

Identify Who made up the majority of travelers on the California Trail before the gold rush? *American merchants trading manufactured goods to Mexican merchants for gold, silver, hides, and tallow*

Sequence What sequence of events led to the California gold rush? *John Sutter began building a sawmill. His carpenter, James Marshall, discovered gold while working. Word of the discovery soon spread.*

Elaborate Why was the United States lucky in the timing of the California gold rush? *If gold had been found a few years earlier, California would have still been Mexican land.*

HSS 8.8.5; HSS **Analysis Skills:** CS 1, HI 1, HI 4

Biography

John Sutter (1803–1880) You might think that John Sutter became wealthy from the discovery of gold. Just the opposite occurred, though. As word of the gold discovery spread, Sutter's workers left him, and gold seekers overran his land. What's more, Sutter had received his land from the Mexican government and was unable to defend his title in the U.S. courts. By 1852—just four years after the discovery of gold—he was bankrupt.

Collaborative Learning

Standards Proficiency

Gold Rush Guide

HSS 8.8.2; HSS **Analysis Skills:** HI 1

Prep Required

Materials: heavy white paper, art supplies

1. Organize students into small groups and ask group members to imagine that they are heading to California during the gold rush.
2. Have group members brainstorm and list items they might need for the long trip West as well as supplies they might need once they arrive out West.
3. After a set period, have each group share some of the items it listed with the class.
4. Then give each group two sheets of heavy white paper and have students fold and staple the sheets to make a four-page booklet.
5. Have each group create a Gold Rush Guide for forty-niners. The guide should include ways to get to California, supplies to obtain, and tips for success. LS **Interpersonal, Verbal/Linguistic**

Alternate Assessment Handbook, Rubrics 14: Group Activity; and 37: Writing Assignment

Answers

"Gold Fever" *The lure of instant wealth mining gold led people to rush off, forgetting everything else except the tools needed for mining—shovels and pickaxes.*

Direct Teach

Main Idea

1 Discovery of Gold Brings Settlers

The discovery of gold brought settlers to California.

Define Who was able to "stake a claim"? *the first person on a site*

Analyze Why was the lack of a court system a problem in the early days of the gold rush? *In the case of competing claims, no court system was available to decide the claim, and violence sometimes erupted.*

Make Inferences What effects do you think gold mining had on the California environment? *possible answer—Gold mining harmed the environment because of the need to move large amounts of earth and dig tunnels.*

CRF: Literature Activity: *New Orleans to San Francisco in '49*

Political Cartoons Activities for United States History, Cartoon 13: The California Gold Rush

HSS Analysis Skills: HI 1

Info to Know

The Daily Drudgery of Mining Few of the thousands of prospectors who flocked to California realized how difficult mining would be. Panning for gold was the simplest mining technique but also the most labor-intensive. First, a miner dug a load of dirt to fill the pan. The miner then submerged the pan in water and shook it until any gold deposits settled on the bottom. Most gold miners worked 50 pans during a 10-hour day. One forty-niner said that prospecting combined "the various arts of canal-digging, ditching, laying stone walls, ploughing, and hoeing potatoes."

Staking a Claim

left to find gold recalled, "At that time the 'gold fever' was contagious, and few, old or young, escaped the malady [sickness]." Nearly 80 percent of the forty-niners were Americans, while the rest came from all over the world.

Most forty-niners braved long and often dangerous journeys to reach California. Many easterners and Europeans arrived via sea routes. Midwestern gold-seekers usually traveled West in wagon trains. Most forty-niners first arrived in San Francisco. This port town became a convenient trade center and stopping point for travelers. As a result, its population increased from around 800 in March 1848 to more than 25,000 by 1850.

Staking a Claim

Few of the forty-niners had any previous gold-mining experience. The work was difficult and time-consuming. The forty-niners would **prospect**, or search for gold, along the banks of streams or in shallow surface mines. The early forty-niners worked an area that ran for 70 miles along rivers in northern California.

The first person to arrive at a site would "stake a claim." Early miners frequently banded together to prospect for gold. The miners agreed that each would keep a share of whatever gold was discovered. When one group abandoned a claim, more recent arrivals often took it over, hoping for success. Sometimes, two or more groups arrived in an area at the same time. In the early gold-rush days, before courts were established, this competition often led to conflict. Occasionally, violent disputes arose over competing claims.

Mining methods varied according to the location. The most popular method, placer (PLA-suhr) mining, and was done along rivers and streams. **Placer miners** used pans or other devices to wash gold nuggets out of loose rock and gravel. To reach gold deposits buried in

Differentiating Instruction for Universal Access

Learners Having Difficulty

Reaching Standards

1. Ask students to imagine that it is 1849 and a wagon train firm has hired them to create an advertisement urging people to go to California.
2. Copy the graphic organizer here for students to see. Omit the blue, italicized answers.
3. Have students copy the organizer and complete it by listing the reasons people went to California in 1849. **LS Visual/Spatial**

HSS Analysis Skills: HI 1

Catch the Fever!
HEAD TO CALIFORNIA!!!!
IT OFFERS ALL THE FOLLOWING:
- *Get rich mining for gold.*
- *Open your own business in a booming mining town.*
- *Work in farming or ranching.*

COME TO CALIFORNIA TODAY!!

Miners came to California from around the world to make their fortune. In the photo on the left, Anglo and Chinese miners work together in Auburn Ravine in 1852. Above, a woman joins men to look for gold. Fewer women than men moved west to search for gold, but the ones that did often found greater social and economic opportunity than they had in the east.

Why might people leave their homes and travel long distances in search of gold?

the hills, miners had to dig shafts and tunnels. These tasks were usually pursued by mining companies, rather than by individuals.

In 1853 California's yearly gold production peaked at more than $60 million. Individual success stories inspired many miners. One lucky man found two and a half pounds of gold after only 15 minutes of work. Two African American miners found a rich gold deposit that became known as Negro Hill in honor of their discovery. The vast majority of miners, however, did not become rich. Forty-niner Alonzo Delano commented that the "lean, meager [thin], worn-out and woebegone [sorrowful] miner...might daily be seen at almost every point in the upper mines."

Life in the Mining Camps

Mining camps sprang up wherever enough people gathered to look for gold. These camps had colorful names, such as Hangtown or Poker Flat.

Miners in the camps came from many cultures and backgrounds. Most miners were young, unmarried men in search of adventure. Only around 5 percent of gold-rush immigrants were women or children. The hardworking women generally made good money by cooking meals, washing clothes, and operating boardinghouses. One such woman, Catherine Haun, recalled her first home in California.

> "We were glad to settle down and go housekeeping in a shed that was built in a day of lumber purchased with the first fee ... For neighbors, we had a real live saloon. I never have received more respectful attention than I did from these neighbors."
>
> —Catherine Haun, quoted in *Ordinary Americans*, edited by Linda R. Monk

Haun's husband was a lawyer. He concluded that he could make more money practicing law than he could panning for gold. He was one of many people who made a good living supplying miners with food, clothing, equipment, and other services. Miners paid high prices for basic necessities because the large amounts of gold in circulation caused severe inflation in California. A loaf of bread, for example, might cost 5 cents in the East, but it would sell for 50 to 75 cents in San Francisco. Eggs sometimes sold for $1 a piece.

Some settlers took full advantage of these conditions for free enterprise. Biddy Mason and her family, for instance, had arrived in California as slaves. A Georgia slaveholder had brought them during the gold-rush years. Mason quickly discovered that most Californians opposed slavery, particularly in the gold mines. She and her family gained their freedom and moved to the small village of Los Angeles. There she saved money until she could purchase some land. Over time, Mason's property increased in value from $250 to $200,000. She became one of the wealthiest landowners in California, a community leader, and a well-known supporter of charities.

Direct Teach

Main Idea

❶ Discovery of Gold Brings Settlers

The discovery of gold brought settlers to California.

Recall What types of work did people do in mining camps? *Many people prospected; others supplied goods to miners or ran businesses that catered to miners.*

Analyze What percentage of gold rush immigrants were women, and what opportunities did the gold rush provide them? *around 5 percent; they could make money running businesses that catered to miners.*

Draw Conclusions How did attitudes toward slavery in California benefit Biddy Mason? *She and her family, after gaining their freedom from slavery, were able to become wealthy landowners in Los Angeles because most Californians opposed slavery.*

CRF: Biography Activity: Biddy Mason

CRF: Primary Source Activity: Family Letters During the California Gold Rush

HSS 8.8.3, 8.8.5; **HSS Analysis Skills:** HR 5, HI 1, HI 2

Did you know . . .

In today's dollars, the $60 million of gold produced in 1853 would be worth around $1.4 billion.

Advanced Learners/GATE **Exceeding Standards**

1. Organize the class into small groups, and have each group refer to the information in this section to prepare a newspaper for a Gold Rush mining town.
2. Groups should include stories about miners and their successes and failures, about life in the mining town, and about some of the problems mining towns experienced.
3. In addition, encourage students to include visuals as well as advertisements and classified ads for jobs, goods, and services in the town.
4. Each group should assign members specific project roles such as editor, copy editor, writer, illustrator, and graphic designer.
5. Display the groups' newspapers in the classroom for students to view. **LS Interpersonal, Verbal/Linguistic**

HSS 8.8.3; **HSS Analysis Skills:** HI 1, HI 2

Alternative Assessment Handbook, Rubric 23: Newspapers

Answers

Staking a Claim *Many foreigners were escaping problems in their home countries, while women found greater economic and social opportunities.*

Direct Teach

Main Idea

1 Discovery of Gold Brings Settlers

The discovery of gold brought settlers to California.

Explain Why did many Chinese immigrants go to California during the gold rush? *lure of gold and to escape economic hardship and famine in southeastern China*

Summarize What challenges did immigrant miners face in California? *lack of welcome by Americans, monthly tax, discrimination, violence, limited legal redress*

Draw Conclusions Why do you think the courts favored Americans over immigrants? *possible answer—because judges thought immigrants shouldn't take away opportunities from Americans*

CRF: Biography Activity: Levi Strauss

HSS Analysis Skills: HI 1, HI 2

World Events

China and the Gold Rush In the mid-1800s China was in political and economic chaos. A tiny minority of wealthy people owned much of the land, while the vast majority of people were peasants who owned little. Such conditions encouraged hundreds of thousands of Chinese to seek their fortunes in the American West between 1850 and 1882.

Westward Movement in the United States

Causes

- Americans believe in the idea of manifest destiny.
- The United States acquires vast new lands in the West.
- Pathfinders open trails to new territories.
- Gold is discovered in California.

Effects

- Native Americans are forced off lands.
- Americans travel west to settle new areas.
- The United States stretches to the Pacific Ocean.
- California experiences a population boom.

Immigrants to California

Today California is the nation's most populous state.

The lure of gold in California attracted miners from around the world. Many were from countries that had seen few immigrants to the United States in the past. They were drawn to California by the lure of wealth. For example, famine and economic hardship in southeastern China caused many Chinese men to leave China for America. Most hoped to find great wealth, and then return home to China. These immigrants were known in Chinese as *gam saan haak*, or "travelers to Gold Mountain." Between 1849 and 1853 about 24,000 Chinese men moved to California. "From far and near we came and were pleased," wrote merchant Lai Chun-chuen in 1855.

Chinese immigrants soon discovered that many Americans did not welcome them, however. In 1852, California placed a high monthly tax on all foreign miners. Chinese miners had no choice but to pay this tax if they wanted to prospect for gold in California. Some Chinese workers were the targets of violent attacks. If the Chinese miners dared to protest the attacks, the legal system favored Americans over immigrants.

Despite such treatment, many Chinese immigrants still worked in the gold mines. Some looked for other jobs. Others opened their own businesses. A newspaper reported Chinese working as "ploughmen, laundrymen, place miners, woolen spinners and weavers, domestic servants, cigar makers, [and] shoemakers."

In 1849 alone, about 20,000 immigrants arrived in California not only from China but also from Europe, Mexico, and South America. Like most American gold-seekers, these new arrivals intended to return home after they had made their fortunes. However, many decided to stay. Some began businesses. For example, Levi Strauss, a German immigrant, earned a fortune by making tough denim pants for miners.

READING CHECK **Categorizing** What types of people came to California during the gold rush?

Impact on California

During the Spanish and Mexican periods of settlement, California's population grew slowly. The arrival of the forty-niners changed this dramatically.

Population Boom

California's population explosion made it eligible for statehood only two years after being acquired by the United States. In 1850 California became the 31st state.

However, fast population growth had negative consequences for many Californios and California Native Americans. One early observer of the gold rush described why.

> "The Yankee regarded every man but [his own kind] as an interloper [trespasser], who had no right to come to California and pick up the gold of 'free and enlightened citizens.'"
>
> —W. Kelly, quoted in *The Other Californians*, by Robert F. Heizer and Alan F. Almquist

Critical Thinking: Identifying Points of View

Standards Proficiency

Chinese Immigrant Letters

HSS Analysis Skills: HR 5, HI 1

1. Discuss with students the experiences of Chinese immigrants who came to California during the gold rush.
2. Have students use the information to write a series of letters from a male Chinese immigrant to family and friends back in China. The letters should provide detailed descriptions of prospecting, life in mining towns, and other experiences. In addition, letters should either encourage the immigrant's family or friends to make the trip or discourage them from coming. Students should consider why Chinese immigrants came to California and the challenges they faced.
3. Have volunteers read some of their letters to the class. Encourage feedback and discussion. **LS Verbal/Linguistic**

Alternative Assessment Handbook, Rubric 40: Writing to Describe

Answers

Reading Check *U.S. easterners and midwesterners, including enslaved African Americans, and immigrants from China, Europe, Mexico, and South America*

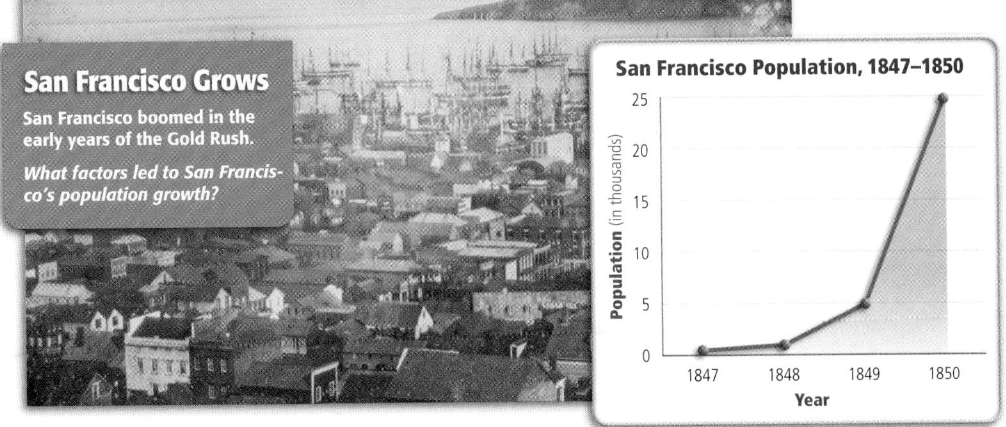

San Francisco Grows

San Francisco boomed in the early years of the Gold Rush.

What factors led to San Francisco's population growth?

Economic Growth

In addition to rapid population growth, a flood of new businesses and industries transformed California's economy. Gold mining remained an important part of the state's early economy. But Californians soon discovered other ways to make a living. Farming and ranching, for example, became industries for those willing to do the necessary hard labor.

California faced an obstacle to growth, though. The state was isolated from the rest of the country. It was difficult to bring in and ship out goods. The answer to the isolation problem was to bring the railroad all the way to California. Californians would have to wait almost 20 years for that. Completion of the transcontinental railroad in 1869 at last gave Californians the means to grow a stronger economy.

READING CHECK **Analyzing Information** What political effect resulted from California's rapid population growth?

SUMMARY AND PREVIEW Americans moved West to create new lives and seize new opportunities. In the next chapter you will learn about the Industrial Revolution in America.

Section 4 Assessment

go.hrw.com
Online Quiz
KEYWORD: SS8 HP10

Reviewing Ideas, Terms, and People

HSS 8.8.3, 8.8.5, 8.9.4

1. a. **Recall** Why was Sutter's Mill important?
   b. **Summarize** What types of people participated in the California gold rush, and how did they take part in it?
   c. **Elaborate** What are some possible problems caused by the arrival of so many new settlers to California?
2. a. **Describe** How did some people hope to solve the problem of California's isolation from the rest of the country?
   b. **Draw Inferences** What effect did California's rapid population growth have on Californios and Native Americans?
   c. **Evaluate** Overall, do you think that the gold rush had a positive or negative effect on California? Explain.

Critical Thinking

3. **Evaluating** Copy the web diagram below. Use it to show how the discovery of gold changed California.

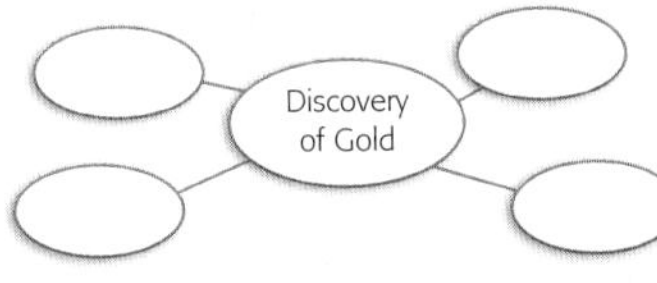

FOCUS ON WRITING

4. **Describing the California Gold Rush** As you read this section, take note of significant events and effects of the gold rush. Consider also how your film can convey the excitement of that time in American history.

Section 4 Assessment Answers

1. a. popular rest stop for many American emigrants and the site near where gold was discovered in 1848, which began the gold rush
   b. male and some female Americans; immigrants from China, Europe, Mexico, South America; mined, provided goods and services
   c. possible answers—fighting over claims, discrimination, economic hardship
2. a. by building a railroad connecting California with the rest of the United States
   b. faced discrimination, poor treatment
   c. possible answers—positive, it led to statehood; negative, it led to discrimination for many
3. possible answers—population boom; increased diversity of population through immigration; statehood; economic transformation and growth; discrimination of Californios and Native Americans
4. Students should consider the events and effects of the gold rush.

Direct Teach

Main Idea

❷ Impact on California

The gold rush had a lasting impact on California's population and economy.

Recall When did California become a state? *1850, only two years after being acquired by the United States*

Identify Points of View How do you think Californios and Native Americans viewed the gold rush and the population boom that resulted? *possible answer—not positively, because they faced discrimination from Americans who viewed them as trespassers not entitled to gold*

Quick Facts Transparency: Westward Movement in the United States

HSS Analysis Skills: CS 1, HR 5, HI 1, HI 2

Review & Assess

Close

Have students summarize how the gold rush affected life in California.

Review

Online Quiz, Section 4

Assess

SE Section 4 Assessment

PASS: Section 4 Quiz

Alternative Assessment Handbook

Reteach/Classroom Intervention

California Standards Review Workbook

Interactive Reader and Study Guide, Section 4

Interactive Skills Tutor CD-ROM

Answers

San Francisco Grows *gold rush and influx of forty-niners and others looking for gold or to open businesses serving miners*

Reading Check *It became the thirty-first state only two years after being acquired by the United States.*

History and Geography

Activity America's Growth Time Line Have students examine the feature and describe how the nation expanded between 1820 and 1853. Then have each student create a large time line that shows how the United States expanded during that time. Instruct students to divide their time lines into five-year periods. Students should also write a short description for each entry.

Then ask students to discuss how they think people already living in California and Oregon felt as thousands more people poured into the areas during the 1840s and 1850s. Conclude by having students identify and discuss the costs and benefits of U.S. westward expansion during this period.
LS Verbal/Linguistic, Visual/Spatial

HSS 8.8.2; HSS **Analysis Skills:** CS 1, CS 2, CS 3, HI 1, HI 2, HI 6

Linking to Today

California Today During the 1840s California's population was comprised of only a few thousand people. Now, almost 34 million people live in California, the third largest state in land area. The "Golden State," as it is officially nicknamed, also has an enormous economy. If California were an independent country, it would have one of the ten strongest economies in the world.

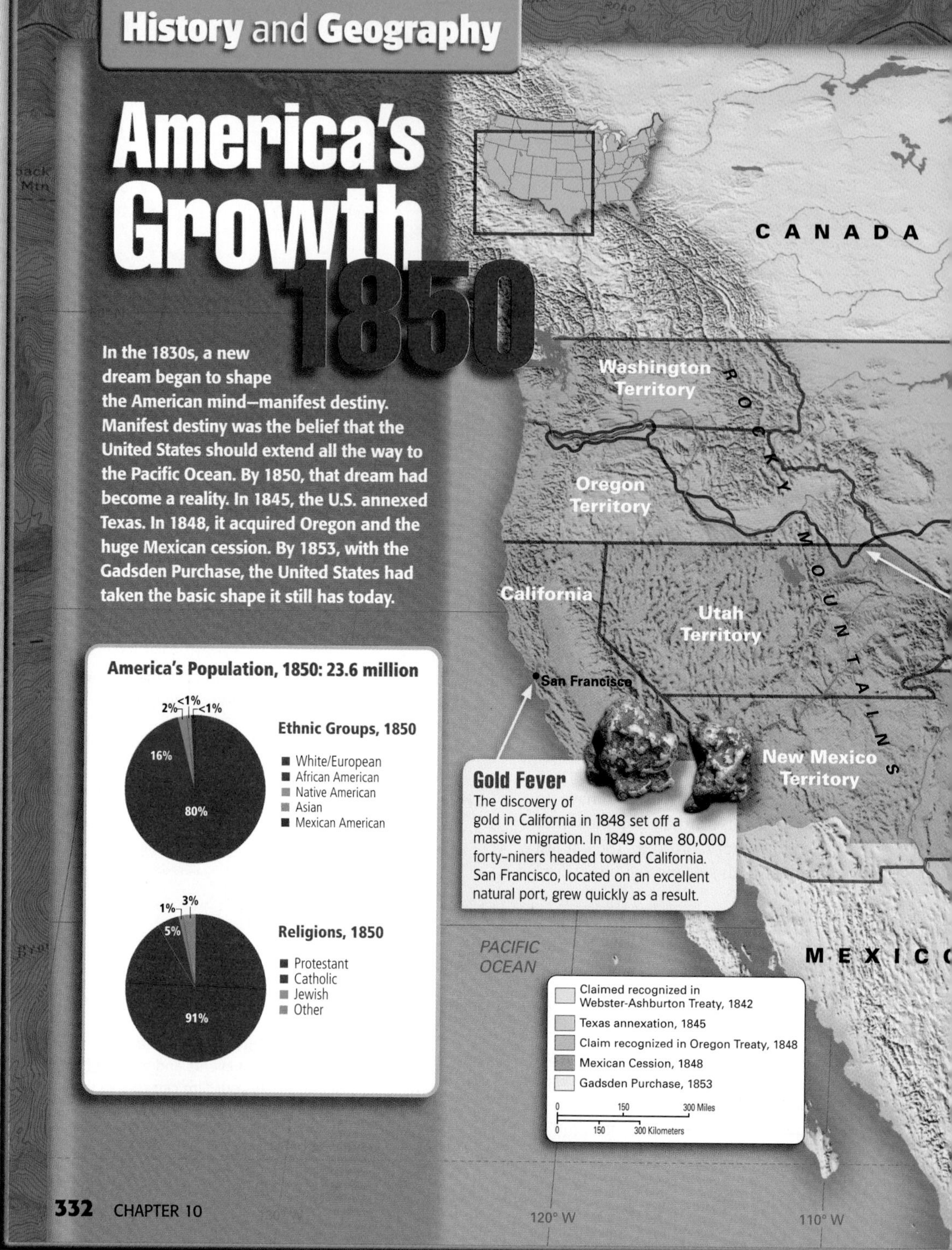

History and Geography
America's Growth 1850
In the 1830s, a new dream began to shape the American mind—manifest destiny. Manifest destiny was the belief that the United States should extend all the way to the Pacific Ocean. By 1850, that dream had become a reality. In 1845, the U.S. annexed Texas. In 1848, it acquired Oregon and the huge Mexican cession. By 1853, with the Gadsden Purchase, the United States had taken the basic shape it still has today.
America's Population, 1850: 23.6 million
Ethnic Groups, 1850
White/European
African American
Native American
Asian
Mexican American
80%
16%
2%
<1%
<1%
Religions, 1850
Protestant
Catholic
Jewish
Other
91%
5%
1%
3%
CANADA
Washington Territory
Oregon Territory
California
Utah Territory
San Francisco
New Mexico Territory
ROCKY MOUNTAINS
MEXICO
PACIFIC OCEAN
Gold Fever
The discovery of gold in California in 1848 set off a massive migration. In 1849 some 80,000 forty-niners headed toward California. San Francisco, located on an excellent natural port, grew quickly as a result.
Claimed recognized in Webster-Ashburton Treaty, 1842
Texas annexation, 1845
Claim recognized in Oregon Treaty, 1848
Mexican Cession, 1848
Gadsden Purchase, 1853
0 150 300 Miles
0 150 300 Kilometers
120° W
110° W
332 CHAPTER 10

Social Studies Skills: Interpreting Maps

Standards Proficiency

The West: Then and Now

HSS 8.8.2; HSS **Analysis Skills:** CS 3, HI 1

1. Display a current map of the United States for students to see. Cover up the western region of the map. Ask students to discuss ways in which the United States might be different had these western states not become part of the Union. *possible answers—Other nations would control the area, the U.S. population would be much smaller, and the nation would lose the area's resources.*
2. Then ask students to compare the map above to the current U.S. map (now uncovered). Ask students to identify the states eventually created from the land that the United States gained between 1842 and 1853.
3. Conclude by reviewing the significant historical events (e.g., the Texas War for Independence and the Mexican-American War) that had a major effect on the boundaries of the United States. **LS Visual/Spatial**

Alternative Assessment Handbook, Rubric 21: Map Reading

Standards Focus

HSS 8.8 Students analyze the divergent paths of the American people in the West from 1800 to the mid-1800s and the challenges they faced.

8.8.2 Describe the purpose, challenges, and economic incentives associated with westward expansion, including the concepts of Manifest Destiny (e.g. the Lewis and Clark expedition, accounts of the removal of Indians, the Cherokees' "Trail of Tears," settlement of the Great Plains) and the territorial acquisitions that spanned numerous decades.

Water Rights Water was critical in the dry West. Bitter disputes arose over who had the water rights to streams. Gold Rush miners developed a simple system: whoever used the water first owned the rights to it. In other parts of the West, the community as a whole had a right to use the water source.
Manifest Destiny With the belief that the United States was destined to spread across the continent, called manifest destiny, settlers headed West to tame new lands. Supporters of manifest destiny believed it was God's will that the United States should expand and spread democracy across North America.
GREAT PLAINS
Oregon Trail
Missouri River
Mississippi River
Unorganized Territory
Indian Territory
The Rocky Mountains The Rocky Mountains were a gigantic obstacle to settlers on their way West. Pathfinders like Lt. John C. Frémont traveled widely in the region, making maps and noting possible trails. The South Pass, through which the Oregon Trail ran, was one of the few easy ways through the great chain of mountains.
ATLANTIC OCEAN
Claimed by Texas
Texas
Gulf of Mexico
30°
N
W
E
S
70° W
Tropic of Cancer
90° W

GEOGRAPHY SKILLS INTERPRETING MAPS

1. **Movement** Why did San Francisco grow so rapidly?
2. **Human-Environment Interaction** Why was water so important in the West?

History and Geography

MISCONCEPTION ALERT

A Salty River? A desalination plant—or a facility that takes the salt out of water—has been built near the Colorado River in Arizona. But wait, isn't the water in the Colorado River fresh water? Yes and no. Farmers spray water from the river onto fields for irrigation. Because the desert soil contains so much salt, the runoff water is salty. The desalination plant purifies the runoff water so it can be sent back into the Colorado River and reused.

Info to Know

The Mexican Cession The territory granted to the United States by the Mexican Cession had long belonged to Spain and then Mexico. By 1850, however, the Hispanic population in the region was outnumbered by settlers from the United States.

Connect to Geography

Hispanics in the Southwest According to the 2000 census, about 19.7 million Hispanic or Latino Americans lived in Arizona, California, New Mexico, and Texas. This figure is more than half the total Hispanic population of the entire United States. Nearly 3.7 million Asian Americans and some 2.25 million African Americans also lived in California, making it the most diverse state in the nation.

Cross-Discipline Activity: Math

Exceeding Standards

Graphing Hispanic Populations

HSS 8.8.2; HSS **Analysis Skills:** CS 3

1. Have students use information from the U.S. Census Bureau to obtain data about the current Hispanic population in each of the states in the Southwest.
2. Have each student use the data to create a bar graph showing the percentage of each state's population that is Hispanic. Then have each student create a circle graph that shows the percentage of the nation's total Hispanic population that lives in each of the states of the Southwest. Remind students to provide a title, a legend, and a caption for each graph.
3. Ask volunteers to share their graphs with the class. LS **Visual/Spatial**

Alternative Assessment Handbook, Rubrics 7: Charts; and 30: Research

Answers

Interpreting Maps 1. *The city was located on an excellent natural port for arriving ships and during the Gold Rush thousands of people went there.* **2.** *The West is arid, and water is needed for people, crops, and livestock.*

Social Studies Skills

Interpreting Maps: Expansion

Activity Expansion Maps Scavenger Hunt Have students go on an expansion map scavenger hunt. Give students a set amount of time to find three examples of expansion maps in their textbooks. Have students mark the pages of each map. Award the first student to find three maps a prize of some kind. Have the winning student identify the pages on which the maps are located. Then guide students in interpreting each of the three maps. Conclude by having each student write a few sentences describing in his or her own words what an expansion map is. **LS Visual/Spatial**

- Alternative Assessment Handbook, Rubric 21: Map Reading
- Interactive Skills Tutor CD-ROM, Lesson 6: Interpret Maps, Graphs, Charts, Visuals, and Political Cartoons

HSS Analysis Skills: CS 3

Social Studies Skills

Analysis | Critical Thinking | Participation | Study

CS3 Students use a variety of maps and documents to identify physical and cultural features.

Interpreting Maps: Expansion

Define the Skill

Maps show features on Earth's surface. These can be physical features, such as mountains and rivers, or human features, such as roads and settlements. Historical maps show an area as it was in the past. Some show how a nation's boundaries changed over time. Interpreting maps can answer questions about history as well as geography.

Learn the Skill

Follow these steps to gain information from a map.

1. Read the title to determine what the map is about and the time period it covers.
2. Study the legend or key to understand what the colors or symbols on the map mean. Note the map scale, which is used to measure distances.
3. Note the map's other features. Maps often contain labels and other information in addition to what is explained in the legend or key.

Practice the Skill

Interpret the map below to answer the following questions about the expansion of the United States.

1. The addition of which territory almost doubled the size of the United States.
2. What was the smallest expansion of U.S. borders, and when did it take place?
3. According to the map, when did California become part of the United States?
4. What choice of overland routes did a traveler have for getting to California?
5. What physical obstacles does the map show such a traveler would face?

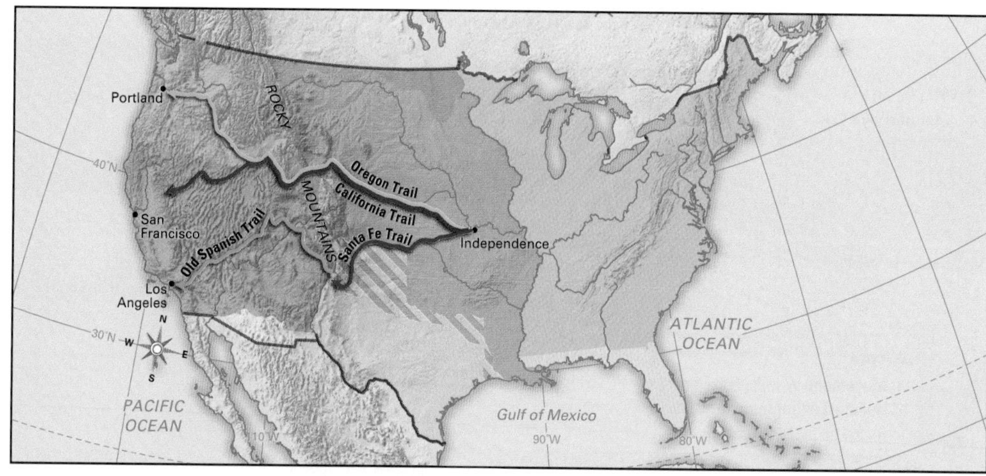

Social Studies Skills Activity: Interpreting Maps: Expansion

Interpreting Expansion Maps

HSS Analysis Skills: CS 3

Standards Proficiency

1. Display a modern political map of the United States for students to see. (One is available in the Atlas in the back of the textbook.)
2. Have students compare the map to the one shown above. Ask students to identify the states that are now located in each of the areas of expansion labeled on the map above. Use the activity to make certain students understand how to read the expansion map.
3. Then have each student write a paragraph describing the information in the map above. Tell students to be as thorough as possible.
4. Next, ask for a volunteer to read his or her description to the class. Then ask students which is easier to understand, the written description or the map. Use the question to help students understand the use of expansion maps in the study of history. **LS Visual/Spatial**

- Alternative Assessment Handbook, Rubrics 21: Map Reading

Answers

Practice the Skill **1.** *Louisiana Territory;* **2.** *Gadsden Purchase in 1853;* **3.** *1848;* **4.** *California Trail, Old Spanish Trail;* **5.** *Rocky Mountains*

CHAPTER 10 # Standards Review

Visual Summary

Use the visual summary below to help you review the main ideas of the chapter.

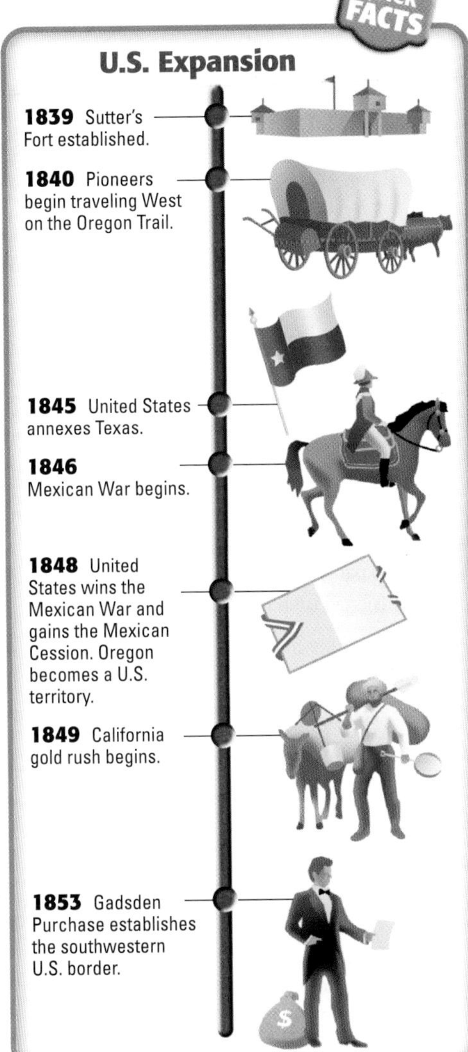
QUICK FACTS
U.S. Expansion
1839 Sutter's Fort established.
1840 Pioneers begin traveling West on the Oregon Trail.
1845 United States annexes Texas.
1846 Mexican War begins.
1848 United States wins the Mexican War and gains the Mexican Cession. Oregon becomes a U.S. territory.
1849 California gold rush begins.
1853 Gadsden Purchase establishes the southwestern U.S. border.

Reviewing Vocabulary, Terms, and People

Identify the correct term or person from the chapter that best fits each of the following descriptions.

1. Mexican priest who led a rebellion for independence from Spain
2. Spanish colonists in California
3. A group of pioneers who were stranded in the Sierra Nevada Mountains and struggled to survive the winter
4. Agents hired by the Mexican government to attract settlers to Texas
5. The belief that the United States was meant to expand across the continent to the Pacific Ocean
6. Members of the Church of Jesus Christ of Latter-day Saints
7. Fur traders and trappers who lived west of the Rocky Mountains and in the Pacific Northwest
8. Mexican ruler who fought to keep Texas from gaining independence
9. Swiss immigrant who received permission from Mexico to start a colony in California
10. Western trail from Missouri to New Mexico that was an important route for trade between American and Mexican merchants

Comprehension and Critical Thinking

SECTION 1 *(Pages 308–311)* **HSS 8.8.2**

11. a. **Identify** What different groups of people traveled West?

b. **Draw Conclusions** Why did Brigham Young move the Mormon community to Utah?

c. **Predict** What are some possible problems that might result from American settlement in the West?

Answers

Visual Summary

Review and Inquiry Have students use the visual summary to explain the causes and effects of the events from the time line.

Quick Facts Transparency: Expanding West Visual Summary

Reviewing Terms and People

1. Father Miguel Hidalgo y Costilla
2. Californios
3. Donner party
4. empresarios
5. manifest destiny
6. Mormons
7. mountain men
8. Antonio López de Santa Anna
9. John Sutter
10. Santa Fe Trail

Comprehension and Critical Thinking

11. a. merchants, traders, settlers, Mormons

b. in search of religious freedom after other communities failed

c. conflict with Native Americans and other existing settlers, issues related to slavery and statehood

Review and Assessment Resources

Review and Reinforce

SE Standards Review

CRF: Chapter Review Activity

California Standards Review Workbook

Quick Facts Transparency: Expanding West Visual Summary

Spanish Chapter Summaries Audio CD Program

Online Chapter Summaries in Six Languages

OSP Holt PuzzlePro; GameTool for ExamView

Quiz Game CD-ROM

Assess

SE Standards Assessment

PASS: Chapter Test, Forms A and B

Alternative Assessment Handbook

OSP ExamView Test Generator, Chapter Test

Universal Access Modified Worksheets and Tests CD-ROM: Chapter Test

Holt Online Assessment Program (in the Premier Online Edition)

Reteach/Intervene

Interactive Reader and Study Guide

Universal Access Teacher Management System: Lesson Plans for Universal Access

Universal Access Modified Worsheets and Tests CD-ROM

Interactive Skills Tutor CD-ROM

go.hrw.com
Online Resources
Chapter Resources:
KEYWORD: SS8 US10

Answers

12. a. Austin—empresario who founded an American colony in Mexican Texas; Santa Anna—leader of Mexico, who led forces against the Texans in the Texas War for Independence

b. anger over some Mexican actions, such as banning of further American settlement and the importation of slaves; Santa Anna's suspension of Mexico's republican constitution

c. in both, the people in a colonial region fought against their mother country for protection of what they saw as their rights and liberties

13. a. concerns over the spread of slavery, balance of power between slave and free states

b. Mining, ranching, saddles, and adobe are examples of Mexican and Native American influence on American settlers.

c. problems related to governing and protecting such a large area

14. a. Both provided goods and services to miners, some opened and ran their own businesses; some immigrants mined.

b. possible answers—difficult to support and care for a family while prospecting; had few attachments to prevent them from going to California

c. continued population and economic growth, continued discrimination against Hispanics and Native Americans

SECTION 2 *(Pages 312–315)* **HSS 8.8.5, 8.8.6**

12. a. Identify Who were Stephen F. Austin and Antonio López de Santa Anna?

b. Draw Conclusions Why did settlers in Texas rebel against Mexican rule?

c. Elaborate In what ways was the Texas struggle for independence similar to that of the United States?

SECTION 3 *(Pages 316–325)* **HSS 8.8.6**

13. a. Recall Why were some Americans opposed to the annexation of new territories?

b. Draw Conclusions What economic and cultural influences did Native Americans and Mexican Americans have on American settlers in the Mexican Cession?

c. Predict What are some possible problems the acquisition of so much territory might cause the United States?

SECTION 4 *(Pages 326–331)* **HSS 8.8.3, 8.8.5, 8.9.4**

14. a. Identify What roles did women and immigrants play in the California gold rush?

b. Make Inferences Why were most gold-rush settlers young, unmarried men?

c. Predict What long-term effects might the gold rush have on California's future?

Reviewing Themes

15. Economics What role did economics play in the desire of Americans to go West?

16. Geography What were the main trails to the West, and what areas did they pass through?

Reading Skills

Summarizing *Use the Reading Skills taught in this chapter to answer the question about the reading selection below.*

> The war ended after Scott took Mexico City. In February 1848, the United States and Mexico signed the Treaty of Guadalupe Hidalgo, which officially ended the war and forced Mexico to turn over much of its northern territory to the United States. *(p. 323)*

17. Summarize the selection at the bottom of column one in one sentence.

Social Studies Skills

Interpreting Maps: Expansion *Use the Social Studies Skills taught in this chapter to answer the question about the map below.*

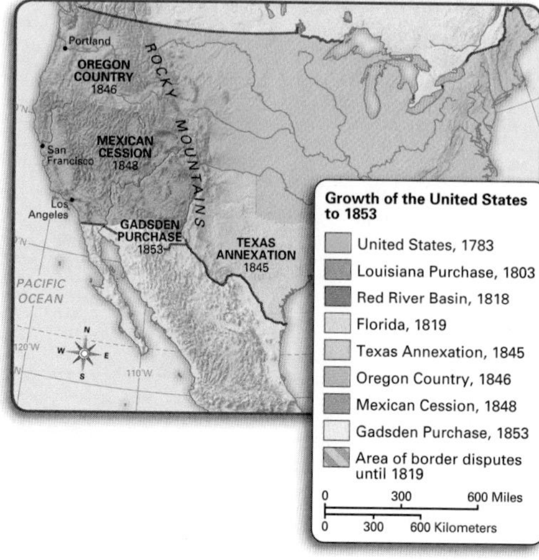

18. According to the map, what was the largest single expansion of the United States?

a. Louisiana Purchase **c.** Mexican Cession

b. Gadsden Purchase **d.** Spanish Cession

Focus on Writing

19. Writing an Outline for a Documentary Film Look back through all your notes, and choose one topic from this chapter that you think would make a good 10-minute documentary. Your outline should be organized by scene (no more than 3 scenes), in chronological order. For each scene, give the following information: main idea of scene, costumes and images to be used, audio to be used, and length of scene. As you plan, remember that the audience will be students your own age.

Reviewing Themes

15. possible answer—Many Americans went West in hopes of improving their lives economically.

16. See the map on p. 309.

Reading Skills

17. possible answer—Under the Treaty of Guadalupe Hidalgo, Mexico turned over much of its northern territory to the United States.

Social Studies Skills

18. a

Focus on Writing

19. Rubric Students' outlines for documentary films should:

- clearly introduce the main idea
- include images
- include narration that explains the images
- be informative and appealing

CRF: Focus on Writing: Outline for a Documentary Film

Standards Assessment

DIRECTIONS: Read each question and write the letter of the best response. Use the map below to answer question 1.

1

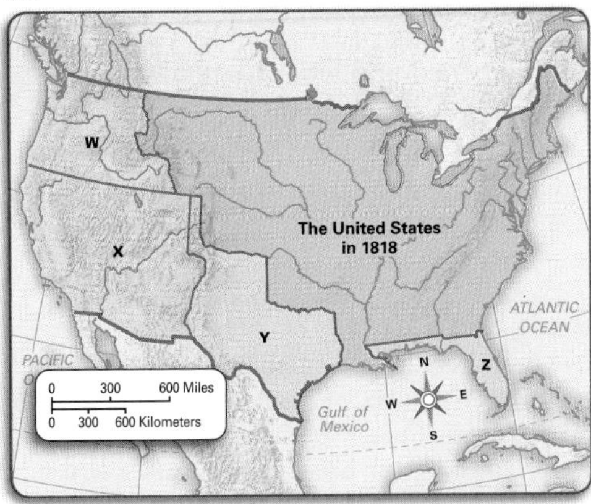

The part of the present-day United States that was once claimed by Britain, Spain, and Russia is shown on the map by the letter

A W.

B X.

C Y.

D Z.

2 In general, what position did Californios take toward the Mexican War?

A They supported the war because they wanted independence from Mexico.

B They supported the war because they wanted to become U.S. citizens.

C They opposed the war because they feared it might bring an end to slavery.

D They opposed the war because they did not want to lose control of California.

3 What was the *main* reason John Jacob Astor founded Astoria at the mouth of the Columbia River in 1811?

A Plenty of freshwater and saltwater fish were available for residents to eat.

B The soil there was rich and good for farming.

C Trappers could use the river to bring furs from the mountains to trade.

D The location offered easy protection from attacks by Native Americans or the French.

4 The *main* attraction of Texas for many Americans in the 1820s and 1830s was the

A freedom to practice the Catholic faith.

B availability of cheap or free land.

C desire to become citizens of Mexico.

D Mexican rebellion against Spain.

5 Which of the following was *not* due to the Mexican-American War?

A Mexican foods and festivals became more important to American culture.

B Prosperity of Mexican landowners in the Southwest increased under U.S. rule.

C Mexican Americans introduced new ideas and equipment to the United States.

D The size of the United States increased by about 25 percent.

Connecting with Past Learnings

6 In a previous chapter you learned that Puritans traveled to the Americas in search of religious freedom. Which group had similar motives for its migration to the West?

A Californios

B empresarios

C mountain men

D Mormons

7 In Grade 7 you learned of explorers who raced to find wealth during the Age of Exploration. Which group below was most similar to these explorers?

A the Donner party

B forty-niners

C Mexican Americans

D Calilfornios

Answers

1. A

Break Down the Question Students need to note the lines indicating the border of each lettered region.

2. D

Break Down the Question Point out that the italicized phrase *In general* means that more than one answer may be correct and that students must choose the one that provides the best answer.

3. C

Break Down the Question Point out the italicized word *main* and explain to students that they need to identify the most *important* reason that Astor founded Astoria.

4. B

Break Down the Question This question requires students to recall factual information. Refer students who miss the question to the material "American Settlers Move to Texas" in Section 2.

5. B

Break Down the Question Point out to students that the word *not* means that they need to identify which of the answers was not true.

6. D

Break Down the Question This question requires students to recall information covered in Chapter 2.

7. B

Break Down the Question This question requires students to recall information covered in Grade 7.

Intervention Resources

Reproducible

- Interactive Reader and Study Guide
- Universal Access Teacher Management System: Lesson Plans for Universal Access

Technology

- Quick Facts Transparency: Expanding West Visual Summary
- Universal Access Modified Worksheets and Tests CD-ROM
- Interactive Skills Tutor CD-ROM

Tips for Test Taking

In Your Own Words Sometimes the wording of a question might be a bit different than the language you are used to using. Read the question and then restate it in your own words to make sure you understand what is being asked.

Standards Review

Have students review the following standards in their workbooks.

- California Standards Review Workbook: 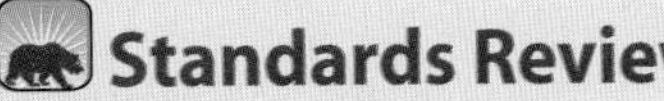 HSS 8.4.3, 8.8.1, 8.10.1, 8.10.3

Preteach

Bellringer

Motivate Write the following for students to see: "Lissa was excited when she received her first driver's license." Ask students to brainstorm causes and effects of the event. Then have students consider the effects they listed as causes and list further effects. Help students build a cause-and-effect chain. Explain that in this workshop students will write a paper explaining causes or effects of a historical event.

SE Social Studies Skills 19: Short- and Long-term Causal Patterns

CRF 19: Social Studies Skills Activity: Short- and Long-term Causal Patterns

Interactive Skills Tutor CD-ROM, Lesson 7: Identify Cause and Effect

Direct Teach

Determining Causes

Get Your Reasons Straight Remind students that not all the details they will read about as they study the War of 1812 will be causes or effects. Have students double-check the causes or effects they identified by asking one of the following questions:

- **Causes:** How did this action or situation contribute to the war?
- **Effects:** How did the war lead to this event or situation?

Organizing

How Important Is It? Explain to students that they have two choices when organizing information by importance—from least to most important, and from most to least important. Suggest that students who are organizing by order of importance make two outlines, one using each option. Then have students choose the option that works best.

Standards Focus

HSS Analysis Skills: HI 2

ELA Writing 8.2.0, 8.2.3.d; Reading 8.1.3

Assignment

Write a paper explaining the causes or the effects of the War of 1812.

Cause and Effect in History

Historians try to make sense of an event by considering why the event happened and what resulted from it. Exploring causes and effects can provide a deeper understanding of historical events and how they are connected to one another.

1. Prewrite

Identifying Causes and Effects

A **cause** is an action or a situation that makes something else happen. What happens is called an **effect**. For example, if you stay up too late watching TV (cause), you might find yourself nodding off in class (effect). Often an event or situation will have several causes as well as several effects. In those cases, we may look at the order in which the causes or effects occurred, or we may look at their relative importance.

Researching and Organizing

For this paper, you will write about the causes or the effects of the event —the War of 1812. Gather information from the chapter in this textbook, an encyclopedia, or another source recommended by your teacher.

- Look for two or three reasons (causes) why the War of 1812 (the event or situation) occurred.
- At the same time, consider the war as a cause. Look for two or three effects of the war.

Then choose whether to write about the causes or the effects.

TIP Using a Graphic Organizer Use a graphic organizer like this to organize your research.

Cause 1
↓
Cause 2
↓
Event or Situation
↓
Effect
↓
Effect

ELA Writing 8.2.0 Students write narrative, expository, persuasive, and descriptive essays of at least 500 to 700 words.

2. Write

You can use this framework to help you write your first draft.

A Writer's Framework

Introduction	Body	Conclusion
■ Begin with a quote or interesting fact about the event. ■ Identify the event you will discuss. [The War of 1812] ■ Identify whether you will be discussing the causes or the effects.	■ Present the causes or effects in chronological (time) order or order of importance. ■ Explain each cause or effect in its own paragraph, providing support with facts and examples.	■ Summarize your ideas about the causes or the effects of the event [the war].

Differentiating Instruction for Universal Access

English-Language Learners

Standards Proficiency | Standard English Mastery

1. Students may not be familiar with the transitional cause-and-effect words and phrases listed in the second Tip on the next page.
2. List the words and phrases and help students define each one. Then have the class use each word or phrase in a sentence.
3. Some students may be confused by the way that placement of transitions within a sentence can vary in English. Some appear before the ideas to which they connect, and some after. Illustrate this point by having students identify the idea to which each cause-and-effect transition connects.
4. Last, have students scan the text on the War of 1812 and look for cause-and-effect transitions. Help students identify the ideas to which each one connects. **LS Verbal/Linguistic**

ELA Reading 8.1.3

3. Evaluate and Revise

Evaluating

Drawing clear, logical connections is the key to writing about causes and effects. Use these questions to evaluate and revise your paper.

Evaluation Questions for an Explanation of Causes or Effects

- Does the introduction begin with an interesting quotation or fact?
- Does the introduction identify the event [the war] and the causes or events to be discussed?
- Is each cause or effect explained in its own paragraph?
- Do facts and examples help to explain each cause or effect and connect it to the event [the war]?
- Are the causes or effects organized clearly—by chronological order or order of importance?
- Does the conclusion summarize the causes or effects and their importance?

TIP Recognizing False Cause-and-Effect In planning your essay, be careful to avoid false cause-and-effect relationships. The fact that one thing happened before or after another doesn't mean one caused the other. For example, the fact that James Madison was elected in 1808, just four years before the War of 1812, does not mean his election caused the War of 1812.

Revising

Make sure the connections between the war and its causes or effects are clear by sharing your paper with a classmate. If your classmate is confused, add background information. If he or she disagrees with your conclusions, add evidence or rethink your reasoning.

TIP Using Transitions Here are some transitional words and phrases that show cause or effect relationships: *because, as a result, therefore, for, since, so, consequently, for this reason*

4. Proofread and Publish

Proofreading

Some transitional words and phrases need to be set off from the sentence with commas. Here are two examples:

- The Louisiana Territory was a huge region of land. *As a result*, the size of the United States almost doubled when the land was purchased.
- Jefferson wanted to know more about the land he had purchased. *Therefore*, he asked Congress to fund an expedition.

Check your paper to see if you need to add commas after or around any transitional words or phrases.

Publishing

Get together with a classmate and share causes and/or effects. Compare your lists to see whether you have identified different causes or effects. Share your findings with your class.

5. Practice and Apply

Use the steps and strategies outlined in this workshop to write your explanation of the causes or effects of the War of 1812.

Reteach

Check Organization

Sort It Out Have students trade papers. In the margin next to each paragraph have students write a word or a phrase identifying the cause or effect discussed. Have them write "divide paragraph" next to any paragraph with more than one cause or effect. Have them write "combine paragraphs" next to any paragraphs that discuss the same cause or effect and then draw an arrow linking the two paragraphs to combine.

Teaching Tip

Stay on Topic Remind students that each paragraph must have a topic sentence. In most cases, it should be the first sentence of the paragraph. Check students' papers as they write and point out any paragraphs without topic sentences.

Practice & Apply

Rubric

Students' explanations of causes or effects should

- begin with an interesting quote or fact about the War of 1812.
- clearly identify the topic.
- accurately explain the causes or effects of the War of 1812.
- provide a paragraph and support for each cause or effect.
- follow either chronological order or order of importance.
- end with a summary.
- use correct grammar, punctuation, spelling, and capitalization.

Advanced Learners/GATE

Exceeding Standards

1. Have students prepare their papers as if they are making a presentation to Congress either during or after the War of 1812.
2. Students writing a paper on the war's causes should present an analysis of the causes and recommend ways that war might have been avoided. Students writing a paper on the war's effects should provide solutions for addressing the negative effects. LS **Verbal/Linguistic**

ELA Writing 8.2.0

Learners Having Difficulty

Reaching Standards

1. If students have trouble identifying cause and effect, have them practice the skill on an easier selection. Choose an applicable selection from a fifth or sixth grade history text.
2. Have students work in pairs to create a cause-and-effect chart for the selection. Tell students to look for the cause-and-effect transitions listed above to help them. Correct any student errors. LS **Logical/Mathematical**

ELA Writing 8.2.3.d

Unit Preview

Introduce the Unit

Share the information in the chapter overviews with students.

Chapter 11 During the early 1800s the Industrial Revolution dramatically changed the way in which goods were made. Americans' lives changed as well as many people began working in factories. These changes were coupled with dramatic changes in transportation and technology.

Chapter 12 The invention of the cotton gin created a new cash crop for the South—cotton. This crop soon dominated the southern economy. Cotton production depended heavily on slave labor. Enslaved Africans were forced to perform hard labor and suffered terrible conditions. Nonetheless, slaves developed a rich culture and a deep religious sense.

Chapter 13 In the first part of the 1800s, Americans looked for more intense meaning in their lives through deeper religious commitment, philosophy, and Romantic art and literature. Waves of immigrants led to rapid growth of cities and a rise in urban problems. Meanwhile, a number of Americans began working to reform society and to end slavery.

(continued on p. 341)

Standards Focus

For a list of the overarching standards covered in this unit, see the first page of each chapter.

UNIT 4 1790–1860

The Nation Expands

340

Unit Resources

Planning

- Universal Access Teacher Management System: Unit Instructional Benchmarking Guides
- One-Stop Planner CD-ROM with Test Generator: Holt Calendar Planner
- Power Presentations with Video CD-ROM
- A Teacher's Guide to Religion in the Public Schools

Standards Mastery

- Standards Review Workbook
- At Home: A Guide to Standards Mastery for United States History

Differentiating Instruction

- Universal Access Teacher Management System: Lesson Plans for Universal Access
- Pre-AP Activities Guide for United States History
- Universal Access Modified Worksheets and Tests CD-ROM

Enrichment

- **CRF 11:** Interdisciplinary Project: Using Measurements
- **CRF 14:** Economics and History: Economic Rivalry
- Civic Participation
- Primary Source Library CD-ROM

Assessment

- Progress Assessment Support System: Benchmark Test
- OSP ExamView Test Generator: Benchmark Test
- Holt Online Assessment Program (in the Premier Online Edition)
- Alternative Assessment Handbook

The **Universal Access Teacher Management System** provides a planning and instructional benchmarking guide for this unit.

What You Will Learn...

The United States continued to grow in size and wealth, experiencing a new revolution of technology and business as did other parts of the world. During the earliest phases of expansion, regions of the United States developed differently from each other. Citizens differed in their ideas of progress, government, and religion. For the success of the nation, they tried to compromise on their disagreements. In the next four chapters, you will learn about two regions in the United States, and how they were alike and different.

Explore the Art

In this picture, fifteen-year-old Maria Weems escapes slavery disguised as a Washington, D.C., coach driver. What does this scene suggest about the dangers of escaping slavery?

341

Unit Preview

Unit Overview *continued*

Chapter 14 In the mid-1800s tensions between the North and the South heightened over slavery. In 1860, Abraham Lincoln became president without winning a single southern state. As a result, several southern states left the Union.

Connect to the Unit

Activity Focus on Regional Differences Ask students to discuss the differences between regions of the United States today. How is the East Coast different from the West Coast? How is the Midwest different from the Southwest? After a brief discussion, point out that differences between the North and the South led to growing tensions during the first part of the 1800s.

Create a Venn diagram for students to see and label the circles *North* and *South*. Have students use what they have learned so far to predict what some of the similarities and differences might be.
LS Verbal/Linguistic, Visual/Spatial

Explore the Art

Maria Weems was an actual teenager who fled the Virginia plantation where she was enslaved. Disguised as a boy, she acted as a coachman for a white doctor, who helped slaves escape. Weems traveled with the doctor and took care of his carriage and horses as they made the long, dangerous journey to the North. Like all fugitive slaves, Weens was considered a felon and pursued by slave catchers. She successfully gained her freedom, however.

About the Illustration

This illustration is an artist's conception based on available sources. However, historians are uncertain exactly what this scene looked like.

Democracy and Civic Education

Standards Proficiency

Justice: Opposing Unjust Laws

Research Required

Background Explain that in the 1830s, some Americans began taking more organized action to try to achieve abolition, or a complete end to slavery. These Americans considered the laws that allowed for slavery to be unjust.

1. Have students discuss what citizens should do when they think a law is unjust. What makes a law unjust? What actions can citizens take to try to change unjust laws? How can citizens work to promote justice in their local communities?
2. Organize students into groups. Have each group conduct research on actions citizens can take to oppose unjust laws.
3. Then have each group use its research to create a storyboard for a televised public service announcement to educate Americans on what they can do to oppose unjust laws.
LS Interpersonal, Verbal/Linguistic, Visual/Spatial

Alternative Assessment Handbook, Rubrics 14: Group Activity; and 29: Presentations

Civic Participation

Answers

Explore the Art *that it was dangerous enough that enslaved Africans had to wear disguises and travel at night in hopes of avoiding capture and gaining freedom*

Chapter 11 Planning Guide

The North

Chapter Overview	Reproducible Resources	Technology Resources
CHAPTER 11 **pp. 342–371** **Overview: In this chapter, students will analyze the economic, cultural, physical, and social effects of technological improvements on the Northern states.** See p. 342 for the California History–Social Science standards covered in this chapter.	**Universal Access Teacher Management System:*** • Universal Access Instructional Benchmarking Guides • Lesson Plans for Universal Access **Interactive Reader and Study Guide:*** Chapter Graphic Organizer **Chapter Resource File*** • Focus on Writing Activity: Newspaper Advertisement • Social Studies Skills Activity: Personal Convictions and Bias • Chapter Review Activity	**One-Stop Planner CD-ROM:** Calendar Planner **Student Edition Full-Read Audio CD-ROM** **Universal Access Modified Worksheets and Tests CD-ROM** **Power Presentations with Video CD-ROM** **History's Impact: United States History Video Program (VHS/DVD):** The North*
Section 1: **The Industrial Revolution in America** **The Big Idea:** The Industrial Revolution transformed the way goods were produced in the United States. 8.6.1	**Universal Access Teacher Management System:*** Section 1 Lesson Plan **Interactive Reader and Study Guide:*** Section 1 Summary **Chapter Resource File*** • Vocabulary Builder, Section 1 • Biography Activity: Samuel Slater	**Daily Bellringer Transparency:** Section 1* go.hrw.com **Internet Activity:** Samuel Slater Plaque
Section 2: **Changes in Working Life** **The Big Idea:** The introduction of factories changed working life for many Americans. 8.6.1	**Universal Access Teacher Management System:*** Section 2 Lesson Plan **Interactive Reader and Study Guide:*** Section 2 Summary **Chapter Resource File*** • Vocabulary Builder, Section 2 • Biography Activity: Sarah Bagley	**Daily Bellringer Transparency:** Section 2* go.hrw.com **Internet Activity:** Lowell Girls Scrapbook
Section 3: **The Transportation Revolution** **The Big Idea:** New forms of transportation improved business, travel, and communication in the United States. 8.6.1	**Universal Access Teacher Management System:*** Section 3 Lesson Plan **Interactive Reader and Study Guide:*** Section 3 Summary **Chapter Resource File*** • Vocabulary Builder, Section 3 • History and Geography Activity: The Transportation Revolution • Literature Activity: Mark Twain Pilots a Steamboat **Political Cartoons Activities for United States History,** Cartoon 14: Fears of the Railroad*	**Daily Bellringer Transparency:** Section 3* **Map Transparency:** Transportation Routes, 1850*
Section 4: **More Technological Advances** **The Big Idea:** Advances in technology led to new inventions that continued to change daily life and work. 8.6.1	**Universal Access Teacher Management System:*** Section 4 Lesson Plan **Interactive Reader and Study Guide:*** Section 4 Summary **Chapter Resource File*** • Vocabulary Builder, Section 4 • Biography Activity: John Deere • Interdisciplinary Project: Using Measurements	**Daily Bellringer Transparency:** Section 4*

MASTERING THE CALIFORNIA STANDARDS

SE Student Edition | Print Resource | Audio CD | Video
TE Teacher's Edition | Transparency | CD-ROM | DVD
go.hrw.com | CA Standards Mastery | LS Learning Styles
OSP One-Stop Planner CD-ROM | * also on One-Stop Planner CD

Review, Assessment, Intervention

- **Standards Review Workbook***
- **Quick Facts Transparency:** The North Visual Summary*
- **Spanish Chapter Summaries Audio CD Program**
- **Progress Assessment Support System (PASS):** Chapter Test*
- **Universal Access Modified Worksheets and Tests CD-ROM:** Modified Chapter Test
- **One-Stop Planner CD-ROM:** ExamView Test Generator (English/Spanish)

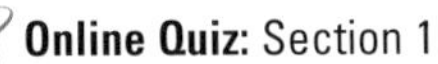

- **PASS:** Section 1 Quiz*
- **Online Quiz:** Section 1
- **Alternative Assessment Handbook**

- **PASS:** Section 2 Quiz*
- **Online Quiz:** Section 2
- **Alternative Assessment Handbook**

- **PASS:** Section 3 Quiz*
- **Online Quiz:** Section 3
- **Alternative Assessment Handbook**

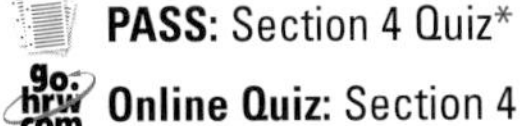

- **PASS:** Section 4 Quiz*
- **Online Quiz:** Section 4
- **Alternative Assessment Handbook**

California Resources for Standards Mastery

INSTRUCTIONAL PLANNING AND SUPPORT

- **Universal Access Teacher Management System***
- **One-Stop Planner CD-ROM with Test Generator: Teacher Management System with Interactive Teacher's Edition**

STANDARDS MASTERY

- **Standards Review Workbook***
- **At Home: A Guide to Standards Mastery for United States History**

go.hrw.com Holt Online Learning

To enhance learning, Internet activities are available for a Samuel Slater Plaque and a Lowell Girls Scrapbook.

KEYWORD: SS8 TEACHER

- **Teacher Support Page**
- **Content Updates**
- **Rubrics and Writing Models**
- **Teaching Tips for the Multimedia Classroom**

KEYWORD: SS8 US11

- **Current Events**
- **Document-Based Questions**
- **Holt Grapher**
- **Holt Online Atlas**
- **Holt Researcher**
- **Interactive Multimedia Activities**
- **Internet Activities**
- **Online Chapter Summaries in Six Languages**
- **Online Section Quizzes**
- **American History Maps and Charts**

HOLT PREMIER ONLINE STUDENT EDITION

Complete online support for interactivity, assessment, and reporting

- **Interactive Maps and Notebook**
- **Standardized Test Prep**
- **Homework Practice and Research Activities Online**

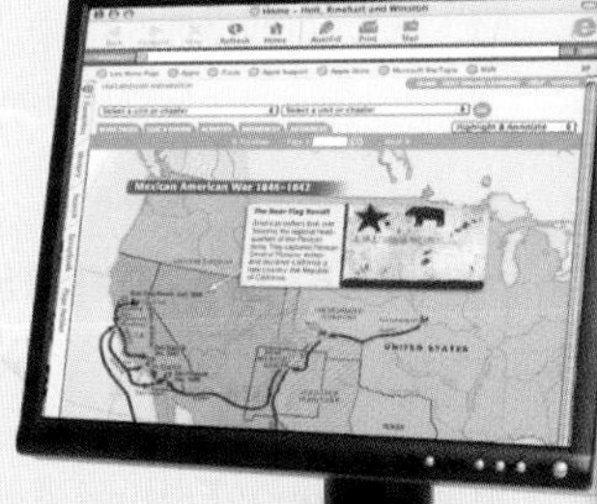

Mastering the Standards: Differentiating Instruction

Reaching Standards	Basic-level activities designed for all students encountering new material
Standards Proficiency	Intermediate-level activities designed for average students
Exceeding Standards	Challenging activities designed for honors and gifted-and-talented students
Standard English Mastery	Activities designed to improve standard English usage

Frequently Asked Questions

INSTRUCTIONAL PLANNING AND SUPPORT

Where do I find planning aids, pacing guides, lesson plans, and other teaching aids?

Annotated Teacher's Edition:
- Chapter planning guides
- Standards-based instruction and strategies
- Differentiated instruction for universal access
- Point-of-use reminders for integrating program resources

Power Presentations with Video CD-ROM

Universal Access Teacher Management System:
- Year and unit instructional benchmarking guides
- Reproducible lesson plans
- Assessment guides for diagnostic, progress, and summative end-of-the-year tests
- Options for differentiating instruction and intervention
- Teaching guides and answer keys for student workbooks

One-Stop Planner CD-ROM with Test Generator: Teacher Management System with Interactive Teacher's Editon:
- Calendar Planner
- Editable lesson plans
- All reproducible ancillaries in Adobe Acrobat (PDF) format
- ExamView Test Generator (English & Spanish)
- Game Tool for ExamView
- PuzzlePro
- Transparency and video previews

DIFFERENTIATING INSTRUCTION FOR UNIVERSAL ACCESS

What resources are available to ensure that Advanced Learners/GATE Students master the standards?

Teacher's Edition Activities:
- Analyzing Changes in Manufacturing, p. 349
- A *Lowell Offering* Excerpt, p. 354
- Bagley Speech, p. 356
- Baltimore and Ohio Railroad, p. 361

Lesson Plans for Universal Access

Primary Source Library CD-ROM for United States History

What resources are available to ensure that English Learners and Standard English Learners master the standards?

Teacher's Edition Activities:
- Industrial Revolution Headlines, p. 347
- Steamboat Headlines, p. 359

Lesson Plans for Universal Access

Chapter Resource File: Vocabulary Builder Activities

Spanish Chapter Summaries Audio CD Program

Online Chapter Summaries in Six Languages

One-Stop Planner CD-ROM:
- PuzzlePro, Spanish Version
- ExamView Test Generator, Spanish Version

What modified materials are available for Special Education?

The ***Universal Access Modified Worksheets and Tests CD-ROM*** provides editable versions of the following:

Vocabulary Flash Cards

Modified Vocabulary Builder Activities

Modified Chapter Review Activity

Modified Chapter Test

What resources are available to ensure that Learners Having Difficulty master the standards?

Teacher's Edition Activities:
- Innovations Activity, p. 348
- Transportation Revolution Drawing, p. 360
- Invention Paper, p. 365

Interactive Reader and Study Guide

Student Edition Full-Read Audio CD

Quick Facts Transparency: The North Visual Summary

Standards Review Workbook

Social Studies Skills Activity: Personal Convictions and Bias

Interactive Skills Tutor CD-ROM

How do I intervene for students struggling to master the standards?

Interactive Reader and Study Guide

Quick Facts Transparency: The North Visual Summary

Standards Review Workbook

Social Studies Skills Activity: Personal Convictions and Bias

Interactive Skills Tutor CD-ROM

PROFESSIONAL DEVELOPMENT

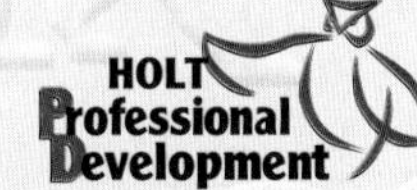

What teacher training resources are available to help me grow professionally?

- In-service and staff development as part of your Holt Social Studies product purchase
- Quick Teacher Tutorial Lesson Presentation CD-ROM
- Intensive tuition-based Teacher Development Institute
- *Teaching American History* Online 2 Module Professional Development Course
- Convenient Holt Speaker Bureau face-to-face workshop options
- PRAXIS™ Test Prep (#0089) interactive Web-based content refreshers*
- 24/7 *Ask A Professional Development Expert* at http://www.hrw.com/prodev/

* PRAXIS is a trademark of Educational Testing Service (ETS). This publication is not endorsed or approved by ETS.

Information Literacy Skills

To learn more about how History–Social Science instruction may be improved by the effective use of library media centers and information literacy skills, go to the Teacher's Resource Materials for Chapter 11 at **go.hrw.com**, keyword: SS8 MEDIA.

The following materials were developed by the Division for Public Education of the American Bar Association. These materials are part of the **Democracy and Civic Education** supplement.
- Constitution Study Guide
- Supreme Court Case Studies

MASTERING THE CALIFORNIA STANDARDS

Chapter Preview

Standards Focus

Standards by Section
Section 1: HSS 8.6.1
Section 2: HSS 8.6.1
Section 3: HSS 8.6.1
Section 4: HSS 8.6.1

Teacher's Edition
HSS **Analysis Skills:** CS 1, HR 1, HR 4, HR 5, HI 1, HI 2, HI 3, HI 6
ELA Writing 8.2.4.b; Reading 8.2.0

Preview Grade 8 Standards
HSS **8.12** Students analyze the transformation of the American economy and the changing social and political conditions in the United States in response to the Industrial Revolution.
8.12.1 Trace patterns of agricultural and industrial development as they relate to climate, use of natural resources, markets, and trade and locate such development on a map.
8.12.3 Explain how states and the federal government encouraged business expansion through tariffs, banking, land grants, and subsidies.
8.12.5 Examine the location and effects of urbanization, renewed immigration, and industrialization (e.g., the effects on social fabric of cities, wealth and economic opportunity, the conservation movement).
8.12.6 Discuss child labor, working conditions, and laissez-faire policies toward big business and examine the labor movement, including its leaders (e.g., Samuel Gompers), its demand for collective bargaining, and its strikes and protests over labor conditions.

Focus on Writing

The **Chapter Resource File** provides a Focus on Writing worksheet to help students organize and write their newspaper advertisements.

CRF: Focus on Writing Activity: Newspaper Advertisement

CHAPTER 11 1790–1860

The North

California Standards

History–Social Sciences
8.6 Students analyze the divergent paths of the American people from 1800 to the mid-1800s and the challenges they faced, with emphasis on the Northeast.

Analysis Skills
HI 1 Students explain the central issues and problems from the past.

HI 2 Students understand and distinguish cause, effect, sequence, and correlation in historical events.

English–Language Arts
Writing 8.2.4.b Present detailed evidence, examples, and reasoning to support arguments.

Reading 8.2.0 Students read and understand grade-level appropriate material.

FOCUS ON WRITING

Newspaper Advertisement The Industrial Revolution was a time when a great many new inventions were introduced. You work for an advertising agency, and your job is to design an advertisement for one of the inventions mentioned in this chapter. As you read, take notes on the inventions, their inventors, and how they changed life in the United States. Then choose one invention and design a newspaper advertisement to persuade readers to buy or use the invention.

UNITED STATES

1807 Robert Fulton's *Clermont* becomes the first commercially successful steamboat.

1790

WORLD

1790 The first steam-powered mill opens in Great Britain.

342 CHAPTER 11

Introduce the Chapter

Standards Proficiency

Farm Versus Factory HSS 8.6.1

1. Organize the students into two groups: those who work on farms and those who work in factories. You might want to show students pictures of modern-day farms and factories to get them thinking about daily activities, how hard they might have to work, where they would live, and how life differs in rural and urban areas.
2. Start a classroom discussion by asking students to complete these sentences: (a) "Working on a farm is better than working in a factory because . . . ," and (b) "Working in a factory is better than working on a farm because . . ."
3. List responses for students to see. Tell students to keep these responses in mind as they read the chapter and learn about how the Industrial Revolution changed life for Americans at home and at work.
LS Verbal/Linguistic

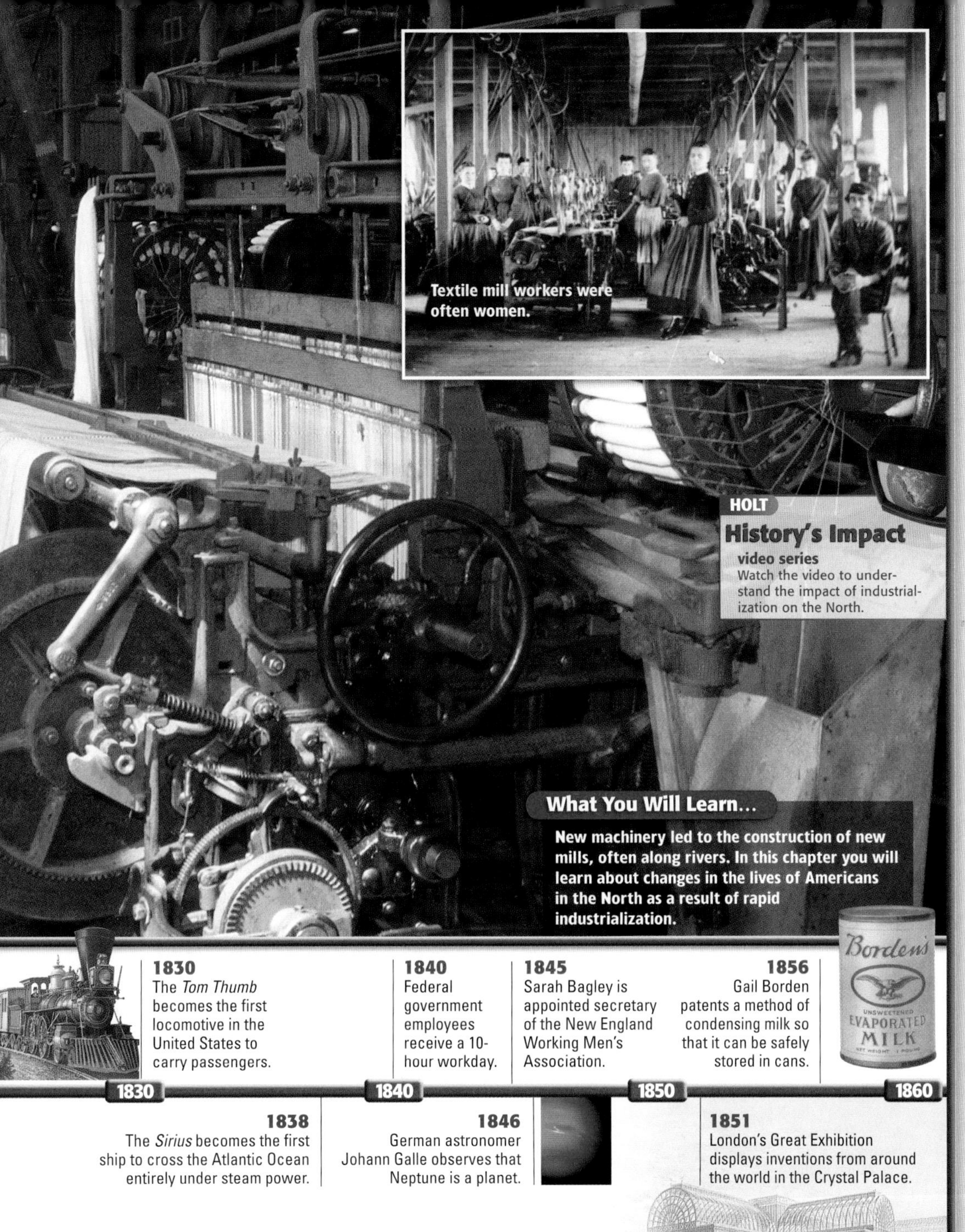
Textile mill workers were often women.

HOLT
History's Impact
video series
Watch the video to understand the impact of industrialization on the North.

What You Will Learn...
New machinery led to the construction of new mills, often along rivers. In this chapter you will learn about changes in the lives of Americans in the North as a result of rapid industrialization.

1830 The *Tom Thumb* becomes the first locomotive in the United States to carry passengers.

1838 The *Sirius* becomes the first ship to cross the Atlantic Ocean entirely under steam power.

1840 Federal government employees receive a 10-hour workday.

1845 Sarah Bagley is appointed secretary of the New England Working Men's Association.

1846 German astronomer Johann Galle observes that Neptune is a planet.

1851 London's Great Exhibition displays inventions from around the world in the Crystal Palace.

1856 Gail Borden patents a method of condensing milk so that it can be safely stored in cans.

1830 1840 1850 1860

THE NORTH **343**

• Chapter Preview •

HOLT

History's Impact

▶ **video series**

See the Video Teacher's Guide for strategies for using the chapter video **The North**.

Chapter Big Ideas

Section 1 The Industrial Revolution transformed the way goods were produced in the United States. **HSS** 8.6.1

Section 2 The introduction of factories changed working life for many Americans. **HSS** 8.6.1

Section 3 New forms of transportation improved business, travel, and communication in the United States. **HSS** 8.6.1

Section 4 Advances in technology led to new inventions that continued to change daily life and work. **HSS** 8.6.1

Explore the Picture

Water-Powered Mills Textile mills built in the early 1800s relied on water for power. Flowing rivers or waterfalls turned waterwheels that powered the mill machinery inside. With developments in steam-powered machinery, factories began to shift to steam power. As a result, factories were no longer necessarily built along rivers and streams. Today, however, old mills can still be found along many streams and rivers, particularly in the Northeast.

Analyzing Visuals How do you think a textile mill, like the one shown in the picture, might change a town? Students might suggest that it provided employment for many but also affected the environment.

Explore the Time Line

1. When did the first steam-powered mill open in Great Britain? *1790*
2. How long after the first commercially successful steamboat in the United States was the nation's first passenger locomotive? *23 years*
3. How and when did working conditions change for government employees during this period? *Employees received a 10-hour workday in 1840.*

HSS Analysis Skills: CS 1

Info to Know

The *Sirius* Two ships competed to be the first to cross the Atlantic Ocean under steam power. The *Sirius* left England a few days before the *Great Western*, but arrived in New York just a few hours before her competitor. The *Sirius* actually ran out of coal near the end of the race. The captain refused to hoist the sails and instead fed cabin doors, a spare mast, and even furniture into the furnace.

go.hrw.com
Online Resources
Chapter Resources:
KEYWORD: SS8 US11
Teacher Resources:
KEYWORD: SS8 TEACHER

Reading Social Studies

Understanding Themes

Introduce this chapter by asking students how goods were produced in the United States prior to the 1800s. Point out to students that goods were made by hand before the Industrial Revolution introduced machines and factories to manufacturing. Ask students what types of technology would have been necessary to do this. Then ask students what sort of economic effects this faster method of producing goods might have had. Remind students to pay attention to the two themes of the chapter—science and technology, and economics.

Causes and Effects in History

Focus on Reading Point out to students that causes and effects can be seen in everyday life, not just in historical events. Ask students to think of events in their lives or in their community that have a clear cause-and-effect sequence. Have each student create a cause and effect chain that has at least four links. Then have students cut their chain into separate events so that each event is on a separate piece of paper. Have students exchange papers with a partner. Then have each student try to piece together the events in the cause and effect chain. Ask students to go over the proper sequence with their partners.

Reading Social Studies

by Kylene Beers

Economics | Geography | Politics | Religion | Society and Culture | Science and Technology

Focus on Themes As you read this chapter, you will learn about how increased **science and technology** brought about what is called the Industrial Revolution. As a result of the Industrial Revolution, you will see how American **economic** patterns changed. Next, you will read about how family life changed as more and more people went to work in factories. Finally, you will see how new methods of transportation changed where people lived and how new inventions affected daily life and work.

Causes and Effects in History

Focus on Reading Have you heard the saying, "We have to understand the past to avoid repeating it."? That is one reason we look for causes and effects in history.

Cause and Effect Chains You might say that all of history is one long chain of causes and effects. It may help you to understand the course of history better if you draw out such a chain as you read.

> Since the 1790s, wars between European powers had interfered with U.S. trade. American customers were no longer able to get all the manufactured goods they were used to buying from British and European manufacturers . . . Americans began to buy the items they needed from American manufacturers instead of from foreign suppliers. As profits for American factories grew, manufacturers began to spend more money expanding their factories . . .
>
> At the same time, many Americans began to realize that the United States had been relying too heavily on foreign goods. *(p. 351)*

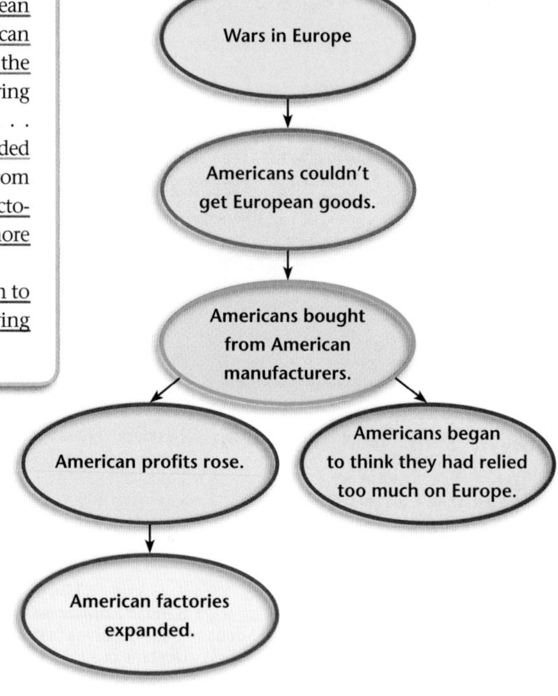

Additional reading support can be found in the Interactive Reader and Study Guide

Reading and Skills Resources

Reading Support

- Interactive Reader and Study Guide
- Student Edition on Audio CD
- Spanish Chapter Summaries Audio CD Program

Social Studies Skills Support

- Interactive Skills Tutor CD-ROM

Vocabulary Support

- **CRF:** Vocabulary Builder Activities
- **CRF:** Chapter Review Activity
- Universal Access Modified Worksheets and Tests CD-ROM:
  - Vocabulary Flash Cards
  - Vocabulary Builder Activity
  - Chapter Review Activity
- OSP Holt PuzzlePro

Standards Focus

HSS Analysis Skills: HI 2

ELA Reading 8.2.0

ELA **Analysis HI 2** Understand and distinguish cause and effect.
HSS **Reading 8.2.0** Students read and understand grade-level appropriate material.

You Try It!

The following passage is from the chapter you about to read. As you read each paragraph, ask yourself what is the cause and what is the effect of what is being discussed.

Workers Organize

From Chapter 11, p. 356

Factories continued to spread in the 1800s. Craftspeople, who made goods by hand, felt threatened. Factories quickly produced low-priced goods. To compete with factories, shop owners had to hire more workers and pay them less . . .

The wages of factory workers also went down as people competed for jobs. A wave of immigration in the 1840s brought people from other, poorer countries. They were willing to work for low pay. More immigrants came to the Northeast, where the mills were located, than to the South. Competition for jobs also came from people unemployed during the Panic of 1837.

After you have read the passage, answer the following questions.

1. What cause is being discussed in the first paragraph? What were its effects?
2. Draw a cause and effect chain that shows the events described in the first paragraph.
3. What main effect is discussed in the second paragraph? How many causes are given for it?
4. Draw a cause and effect chain that shows the events described in the second paragraph.

As you read Chapter 11, look for words that signal causes or effects. Picture these causes and effects as the links in a cause and effect chain.

Key Terms and People

Chapter 11

Section 1
Industrial Revolution *(p. 347)*
textiles *(p. 347)*
Richard Arkwright *(p. 347)*
Samuel Slater *(p. 348)*
technology *(p. 349)*
Eli Whitney *(p. 349)*
interchangeable parts *(p. 349)*
mass production *(p. 349)*

Section 2
Rhode Island system *(p. 353)*
Francis Cabot Lowell *(p. 354)*
Lowell system *(p. 354)*
trade unions *(p. 356)*
strikes *(p. 356)*
Sarah G. Bagley *(p. 357)*

Section 3
Transportation Revolution *(p. 358)*
Robert Fulton *(p. 359)*
Clermont (p. 359)
Gibbons v. *Ogden (p. 359)*
Peter Cooper *(p. 360)*

Section 4
Samuel F. B. Morse *(p. 364)*
telegraph *(p. 364)*
Morse code *(p. 365)*
John Deere *(p. 366)*
Cyrus McCormick *(p. 366)*
Isaac Singer *(p. 367)*

Academic Vocabulary

Success in school is related to knowing academic vocabulary—the words that are frequently used in school assignments and discussions. In this chapter, you will learn the following academic words:

efficient *(p. 347)*
concrete *(p. 357)*

Reading Social Studies

Key Terms and People

Read the list aloud so that students will know how to pronounce each term or name. Then organize the students into pairs and assign each pair a person or term from the list. Have each pair identify the importance of the person or term. Then have each group draw a picture that represents the significance of that term or person. Have each student present the term, description or definition, and illustration to the class. Encourage students to take notes on the presentations. **LS Verbal/Linguistic, Visual/Spatial, Interpersonal**

Focus on Reading

See the **Focus on Reading** questions in this chapter for more practice on this reading social studies skill.

Reading Social Studies Assessment

See the **Standards Review** at the end of this chapter for student assessment questions related to this reading skill.

Teaching Tip

Students may occasionally have difficulty identifying causes and effects as they read. Point out to students that causes and effects are often signaled by certain words. Ask students what words might signal causes and effects. Help them see that words like *as, since, because,* and *motivated by* all indicate causes. Some words that signal effect are: *led to, resulted in, as a result, began to, therefore,* and *then.*

Answers

You Try It! 1. *cause—factories continued to spread; effects—craftspeople felt threatened, shop owners had to compete with factories by hiring more workers, workers were paid less;* **2.** *Factories spread; craftspeople felt threatened; more workers were hired; each shop worker was paid less;* **3.** *effect—wages went down; three causes—a wave of immigration, immigrants willing to work for lower wages, and competition for jobs due to unemployment;* **4.** *causes— immigration and unemployment; effects—wages went down, immigrants willing to work for low pay, immigrants move to northeast.*

Preteach

Bellringer

If YOU were there . . . Use the **Daily Bellringer Transparency** to help students answer the question.

Daily Bellringer Transparency, Section 1

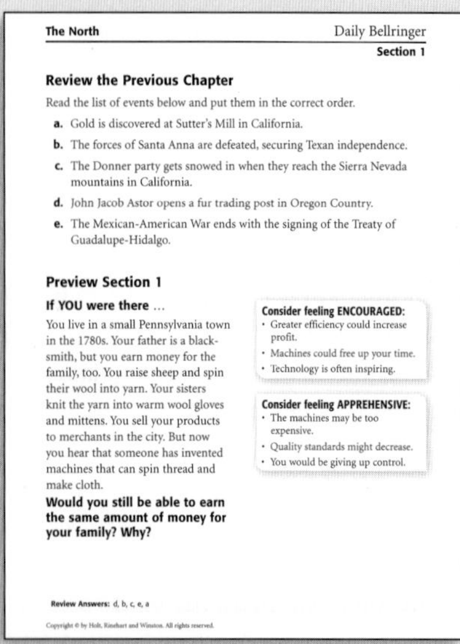

The North | Daily Bellringer
Section 1

Review the Previous Chapter

Read the list of events below and put them in the correct order.

a. Gold is discovered at Sutter's Mill in California.

b. The forces of Santa Anna are defeated, securing Texan independence.

c. The Donner party gets snowed in when they reach the Sierra Nevada mountains in California.

d. John Jacob Astor opens a fur trading post in Oregon Country.

e. The Mexican-American War ends with the signing of the Treaty of Guadalupe-Hidalgo.

Preview Section 1

If YOU were there ...

You live in a small Pennsylvania town in the 1780s. Your father is a blacksmith, but you earn money for the family, too. You raise sheep and spin their wool into yarn. Your sisters knit the yarn into warm wool gloves and mittens. You sell your products to merchants in the city. But now you hear that someone has invented machines that can spin thread and make cloth.

Would you still be able to earn the same amount of money for your family? Why?

Consider feeling ENCOURAGED:
- Greater efficiency could increase profit.
- Machines could free up your time.
- Technology is often inspiring.

Consider feeling APPREHENSIVE:
- The machines may be too expensive.
- Quality standards might decrease.
- You would be giving up control.

Review Answers: d, b, c, e, a

Academic Vocabulary

Review with students the high-use academic term in this section.

efficient productive and not wasteful (p. 347)

CRF: Vocabulary Builder Activity, Section 1

Standards Focus

HSS 8.6.1

Means: Discuss the growth of industrialization in the Northeast and its effects on the region.

Matters: The Industrial Revolution changed both the way goods were made and the lives of workers.

SECTION 1

The Industrial Revolution in America

What You Will Learn...

Main Ideas

1. The invention of new machines in Great Britain led to the beginning of the Industrial Revolution.
2. The development of new machines and processes brought the Industrial Revolution to the United States.
3. Despite a slow start in manufacturing, the United States made rapid improvements during the War of 1812.

The Big Idea

The Industrial Revolution transformed the way goods were produced in the United States.

Key Terms and People

Industrial Revolution, *p. 347*
textiles, *p. 347*
Richard Arkwright, *p. 347*
Samuel Slater, *p. 348*
technology, *p. 349*
Eli Whitney, *p. 349*
interchangeable parts, *p. 349*
mass production, *p. 349*

HSS 8.6.1 Discuss the influence of industrialization and technological developments on the region, including human modification of the landscape and how physical geography shaped human actions (e.g., growth of cities, deforestation, farming, mineral extraction).

If YOU were there...

You live in a small Pennsylvania town in the 1780s. Your father is a blacksmith, but you earn money for the family, too. You raise sheep and spin their wool into yarn. Your sisters knit the yarn into warm wool gloves and mittens. You sell your products to merchants in the city. But now you hear that someone has invented machines that can spin thread and make cloth.

Would you still be able to earn the same amount of money for your family? Why?

BUILDING BACKGROUND In the early 1700s making goods depended on the hard work of humans and animals. It had been that way for hundreds of years. Then new technology brought a change so radical that it is called a revolution. It began in Great Britain and soon spread to the United States.

Beginning of the Industrial Revolution

At the beginning of the 1700s, the majority of people in Europe and the United States were farmers. They made most of what they needed by hand. For example, female family members usually made clothing. First, they used a spinning wheel to spin raw materials, such as cotton or wool, into thread. Then they used a hand loom to weave the thread into cloth.

Some families produced extra cloth to sell to merchants, who sold it for a profit. In towns, a few skilled workers made goods by hand in their own shops. These workers included blacksmiths, carpenters, and shoemakers. Their ways of life had stayed the same for generations.

A Need for Change

By the mid-1700s, however, changes in Great Britain led to a greater demand for manufactured goods. As agriculture and roads

Teach the Big Idea: Master the Standards

Standards Proficiency

The Industrial Revolution in America

HSS 8.6.1; HSS **Analysis Skills:** HI 1, HI 2, HI 3

1. **Teach** Ask students the Main Idea questions to teach this section.
2. **Apply** Create a flow chart by writing the section's main ideas in large, vertically stacked boxes. Have students copy the flow chart and complete it by entering supporting details about the main ideas into the boxes. **LS Visual/Spatial**
3. **Review** As you review the section, have students share the information in their flow charts and discuss the cause-and-effect connections among events. Ask students to explain how the section's main ideas relate.
4. **Practice/Homework** Have students create poster-sized, illustrated versions of their flow charts. **LS Visual/Spatial**

Alternative Assessment Handbook, Rubrics 13: Graphic Organizers; and 28: Posters

Textile Mill and Water Frame
SCIENCE AND TECHNOLOGY
A water frame adapts the power of flowing water into energy that moves wheels and gears through a system of belts. These wheels and gears then move parts of machines such as looms and spinning wheels.
5 After the thread was spun, it moved to the loom to be woven into cloth. Workers called spoolers watched the looms and made sure that the spools of thread were kept straight.
4 Then the raw cotton was spun into thread on a spinning frame.
3 A machine for cleaning the raw cotton was the first step.
1 Flowing water from a river turned the waterwheel. The giant wheel turned smaller gears connected to belts. 2 These belts moved parts of the machinery in the mill.
5
4
3
2
1

ANALYSIS SKILL **ANALYZING VISUALS**

What provided the power for the machines in the mill?

improved, cities and populations grew. Overseas trade also expanded. Traditional manufacturing methods did not produce enough goods to meet everyone's needs.

People began creating ways to use machines to make things more efficient. These changes led to the **Industrial Revolution**, a period of rapid growth in using machines for manufacturing and production that began in the mid-1700s.

Textile Industry

The first important breakthrough of the Industrial Revolution took place in how **textiles**, or cloth items, were made. Before the Industrial Revolution, spinning thread took much more time than making cloth. Several workers were needed to spin enough thread to supply a single weaver.

In 1769 Englishman **Richard Arkwright** invented a large spinning machine called a water frame. The water frame could produce dozens of cotton threads at the same time. It lowered the cost of cotton cloth and increased the speed of textile production.

The water frame used flowing water as its source of power. Merchants began to build large textile mills, or factories, near rivers and streams. The mills were filled with spinning machines. Merchants began hiring people to work in the mills.

Additional improvements also speeded up the spinning process. Britain soon had the world's most productive textile manufacturing industry.

ACADEMIC VOCABULARY

efficient productive and not wasteful

READING CHECK **Drawing Conclusions**
How did machines speed up textile manufacturing?

Direct Teach

Main Idea

1 Beginning of the Industrial Revolution

The invention of new machines in Great Britain led to the beginning of the Industrial Revolution.

Describe Describe labor in Europe in the beginning of the 1700s. *Most people were farmers and made most of the goods they needed in their homes by hand. Some people sold extra items to merchants, who then sold the goods for a profit. Some skilled workers produced goods in their own shops for sale.*

Identify Cause and Effect What was the result of increased demand for manufactured goods in Great Britain? *Traditional manufacturing methods could not meet the demand, so people began to develop machines to make things more efficiently.*

Evaluate What might be some costs and benefits of faster textile production as a result of new machines? *costs—some skilled laborers would be out of work, work would be done in factories instead of at home; benefits—lower textile prices and increased supply*

HSS 8.6.1; HSS **Analysis Skills:** HI 1, HI 2, HI 6

Info to Know

Factory Work In the early 1700s, most cotton thread and cloth was made in people's homes. As a result, workers had much independence and could work at their own pace. This situation changed as factories were built. Many women and children joined the workforce. In addition, many skilled weavers were forced to work for the same pay as unskilled factory workers.

Differentiating Instruction for Universal Access

English-Language Learners

Standards Proficiency | Standard English Mastery

1. Lead a discussion on the beginning of the Industrial Revolution. Have students develop four key points about the topic. Write the points for students to see.
2. Ask students to write four newspaper headlines based on the points. Have volunteers present their headlines to the class.
3. Then have students select one of the four headlines and write a five-sentence article to go with it. Circulate to help students with their grammar and use of standard English. LS **Verbal/Linguistic**

HSS 8.6.1; HSS **Analysis Skills:** HI 1, HI 2

Alternative Assessment Handbook, Rubric 42: Writing to Inform

Universal Access Resources

See p. 341c of the Chapter Planner for additional resources for differentiating instruction for universal access.

Answers

Analyzing Visuals *flowing water from a river*

Reading Check *The water frame could produce dozens of cotton threads at the same time, whereas before people could produce only one thread at a time.*

Direct Teach

Main Idea

❷ New Machines and Processes

The development of new machines and processes brought the Industrial Revolution to the United States.

Recall Who was Samuel Slater, and how did he contribute to the textile industry in the United States? *skilled British mechanic who brought the knowledge of British textile machines to the United States, which led to the development of American textile mills*

Analyze Why were most American mills located in New England? *The region had many rivers and streams to power the mills, and the region's merchants were willing to invest.*

CRF: Biography Activity: Samuel Slater

HSS 8.6.1; HSS Analysis Skills: HI 1, HI 2

Info to Know

Opposition to Mills Not all Americans welcomed industrial innovations from Great Britain. Some Americans thought the import of British industry threatened American self-sufficiency. Others argued that mill owners violated people's water rights by building dams. In one case, some people sabotaged the dam that fed a Slater mill.

Analyzing Visuals

Elements of Mass Production

Mass production often requires financial resources beyond the means of an individual owner. Have students discuss how mass production may have led to corporate ownership of the large manufacturing firms of today.

go.hrw.com

Online Resources

KEYWORD: SS8 US 11
ACTIVITY: Samuel Slater Plaque

Answers

Connect to Economics
interchangeable parts, machine tools, division of labor

New Machines and Processes

New machines encouraged the rise of new processes in business and manufacturing. As the machines used to make products became more efficient, the processes involved changed dramatically.

Slater and His Secrets

The new textile machines allowed Great Britain to produce cloth faster and cheaper than other countries could. To protect British industry, the British Parliament had made it illegal for skilled mechanics or machine plans to leave the country. Disguised as a farmer, **Samuel Slater**, a skilled British mechanic, immigrated to the United States after carefully memorizing the designs of textile mill machines. Soon after arriving, he sent a letter to Moses Brown, who owned a textile business in New England. Slater claimed he could improve the way textiles were manufactured in the United States.

Brown had one of his workers test Slater's knowledge of machinery. Slater passed. Brown's son, Smith Brown, and son-in-law, William Almy, formed a partnership with Slater. In 1793 they opened their first mill in Pawtucket, Rhode Island. The production of cotton thread by American machines had begun. Slater ran the mill and the machinery. He was confident that his new machines would work well.

> "If I do not make as good yarn as they do in England, I will have nothing for my services, but will throw the whole of what I have attempted over the bridge."
>
> —Samuel Slater, quoted in *The Ingenious Yankees*, by Joseph and Francis Gies

Slater's machines worked, and the Pawtucket mill became a success. Slater's wife also invented a new cotton thread for sewing. In 1798 Slater formed his own company to build a mill. By the time he died in 1835, he owned all or part of 13 textile mills.

Other Americans began building textile mills. Most were located in the Northeast. In New England in particular, merchants had the money to invest in new mills. More importantly, this region had many rivers and streams that provided a reliable supply of power. Fewer mills were built in the South, partly because investors in the South concentrated on expanding agriculture. There, agriculture was seen as an easier way to make money.

Elements of Mass Production

CONNECT TO ECONOMICS

Mass-production techniques allow manufacturers to efficiently create more goods for the marketplace. Mass production requires the use of interchangeable parts, machine tools, and the division of labor.

What are the three elements of mass production?

Interchangeable Parts

Eli Whitney developed the idea of using interchangeable parts. Interchangeable, or identical, parts are needed so each part does not have to be custom-made by hand.

Yale University Art Gallery, Trumbull Collection

Machine Tools

Machine tools like this one make parts that are identical and therefore interchangeable.

Differentiating Instruction for Universal Access

Learners Having Difficulty

Reaching Standards

1. Draw the following graphic organizer for students to see. Omit the blue answers.
2. Have each student copy the organizer and complete it by describing the innovations of Slater and Whitney and the effects of those innovations. LS **Visual/Spatial**

HSS 8.6.1; HSS **Analysis Skills:** HI 1, HI 2

Alternative Assessment Handbook, Rubric 13: Graphic Organizers

Samuel Slater **Innovation:** *machine production of cotton thread in mills*	→	**Effects** • *spread of textile mills, many in New England* • *increased productivity of American textiles*
Eli Whitney **Innovation:** *idea of interchangeable parts*	→	**Effects** • *easy to assemble and replace parts* • *mass production*

A Manufacturing Breakthrough

Despite these great changes, most manufacturing was still done by hand. In the late 1790s the U.S. government worried about a possible war with France, so it wanted more muskets for the army. Skilled workers made the parts for each weapon by hand. No two parts were exactly alike, and carefully fitting all the pieces together took much time and skill. As a result, American gun makers could not produce the muskets quickly enough to satisfy the government's demand. Factories needed better **technology**, the tools used to produce items or to do work.

In 1798 inventor **Eli Whitney** tried to address some of these problems. Whitney gave officials a proposal for mass-producing guns for the U.S. government using water-powered machinery. Whitney explained the benefits of his ideas.

> "I am persuaded that machinery moved by water [and] adapted to this business would greatly reduce the labor and facilitate [ease] the manufacture of this article."
>
> —Eli Whitney, quoted in *Technology in America*, edited by Carroll W. Pursell

Whitney also came up with the idea of using **interchangeable parts**—parts of a machine that are identical. Using interchangeable parts made machines easier to assemble and broken parts easier to replace. Whitney promised to build 10,000 muskets in two years. The federal government gave him money to build his factory, and in 1801 Whitney was called to Washington, D.C., to give a demonstration.

Whitney stood before President John Adams and his secetary of war. He had an assortment of parts for 10 guns. He then randomly chose parts and quickly assembled them into muskets. To the audience's amazement, he repeated the process several times.

Whitney's Influence

Whitney had proven that American inventors could improve upon the new British technology. Machines that produced matching parts soon became standard in industry. Interchangeable parts sped up **mass production**, the efficient production of large numbers of identical goods.

READING CHECK **Summarizing** How did Eli Whitney influence American manufacturing?

Division of Labor
Mass production uses a division of labor in which the work is divided among several people, each doing a specific task, like the worker shown here.

Mass-Produced Goods
The end result are goods that have been mass-produced. Eli Whitney used mass-production techniques to manufacture firearms.

Direct Teach

Main Idea

❷ New Machines and Processes

The development of new machines and processes brought the Industrial Revolution to the United States.

Identify Who was Eli Whitney? *American inventor who created the idea of interchangeable parts, which helped lead to mass production*

Analyze What was the advantage of water-powered machinery? *unlimited source of power; reduced labor needs and increased productivity*

Find Main Ideas What new manufacturing pattern emerged as a result of Whitney's idea of using interchangeable parts? *mass production*

Identify Cause and Effect How did the idea of interchangeable parts lead to mass production? *instead of producing parts by hand, machines produced many identical parts, which led to mass production*

HSS 8.6.1; HSS **Analysis Skills:** HI 1, HI 2, HI 3

Connect to Economics

Workers and Mass Production With mass production came a new problem for factory owners—how to motivate workers to attend to their machines. Factory work involved considerable boredom, monotony, and stress. Some British factory owners tried to create a new work discipline by trying to control workers' private and work lives. To achieve this goal, business owners built company towns. In these towns, factory owners owned and controlled all the stores and housing.

Critical Thinking: Comparing and Contrasting

Exceeding Standards

Analyzing Changes in Manufacturing

HSS 8.6.1; HSS **Analysis Skills:** CS 1, HI 1, HI 2, HI 3

1. Ask students to imagine that they are on a government investigative commission examining the state of American manufacturing in the early 1800s.
2. Have each student write a short report describing the state of manufacturing before industrialization and how the innovations of Samuel Slater and Eli Whitney have changed manufacturing processes in the United States and have affected the environment. In addition, students should address the slow growth of manufacturing and suggest some actions to improve it.
3. Have volunteers read their reports to the class. Encourage student feedback and discussion.

LS **Verbal/Linguistic**

Alternative Assessment Handbook, Rubrics 9: Comparing and Contrasting; and 42: Writing to Inform

Answers

Reading Check *He came up with the idea of interchangeable parts and proposed producing guns using water-powered machinery.*

Direct Teach

Main Idea

3 Slow Start in Manufacturing

Despite a slow start in manufacturing, the United States made rapid improvements during the War of 1812.

Explain According to Albert Gallatin, why were so few factories being built in the United States? *attractiveness of farming, abundance of cheap land, high price of labor, lack of capital to invest in factories*

Identify Cause and Effect How did the War of 1812 affect American manufacturing? *The war prevented the import of many foreign goods, which led Americans to buy American-made goods, which in turn led to increased manufacturing.*

Make Inferences Do you think all Americans supported higher tariffs? *possible answer—People who bought foreign goods, such as farmers, likely would have opposed higher tariffs.*

HSS 8.6.1; HSS **Analysis Skills:** CS 1, HI 1, HI 2

Linking to Today

Modern Manufacturing

Activity Have students find articles, with pictures if possible, about manufacturing in the United States today. Post students' articles on a class bulletin board. Then review a few of the articles each day during the study of this chapter.
LS Verbal/Linguistic

Answers

Linking to Today *Complex products made of multiple parts can be assembled quickly.*

LINKING TO TODAY

Modern Manufacturing

The word *manufacture* comes from Latin words that mean "to make by hand." Yet in modern manufacturing, machines—not human hands—do most of the work.

A key feature of modern manufacturing is the assembly line. An assembly line is a long conveyer belt. As the product moves along the belt, or "down the line," workers assemble it. Often, the workers use machines to help them. On a growing number of assembly lines, there are no workers at all: the product is assembled by computer-controlled robots.

Although a far cry from Eli Whitney's factory, modern factories use the same elements of mass production that Whitney did more than 200 years ago.

ANALYSIS SKILL **ANALYZING INFORMATION**

How do interchangeable parts help the modern assembly line work?

Slow Start in Manufacturing

Despite the hard work of people such as Samuel Slater and Eli Whitney, manufacturing in the United States grew slowly. In 1810 Secretary of the Treasury Albert Gallatin suggested some reasons why there were so few factories in the United States.

> "[The reasons include] . . . the superior attractions of agricultural pursuits [farming], . . . the abundance of land compared with the population, the high price of labor, and the want [lack] of sufficient capital [investment]."
>
> —Albert Gallatin, quoted in *Who Built America*, edited by Bruce C. Levine et al.

Gallatin and others believed that few people would choose to work in a factory if they could own their own farm instead. In Great Britain, on the other hand, land was more scarce and more expensive than in the United States. As a result, fewer people were able to own farms. British factory workers generally were willing to work for lower wages than factory workers in the United States were.

Because British manufacturers had plenty of factory workers with technical skills, they could produce large amounts of goods less expensively than most American businesses could. Consequently, they could charge lower prices for the goods. Lower British prices made it difficult for many American manufacturers to compete with British companies. This situation in turn discouraged American investors from spending the money needed to build new factories and machinery. As a result, only a few industries had found a place in the American economy. These included cotton goods, flour milling, weapons, and iron production.

Critical Thinking: Analyzing Information

Standards Proficiency

Factory Owner Letter Requesting a Loan

HSS 8.6.1; HSS **Analysis Skills:** HI 1, HI 2, HI 3

1. Ask students to imagine that they are American manufacturers in 1814 seeking bank loans to expand their factories.
2. Have each student write a letter to convince a bank to give him or her a loan.
3. In their letters, students should address the benefits of mass production, the need to promote American manufacturing, the goods they are producing at their factories, and the factories' profit potential.
4. Have volunteers read their letters to the class.
LS Logical/Mathematical, Verbal/Linguistic

Alternative Assessment Handbook, Rubric 43: Writing to Persuade

These circumstances began to change around the time of the War of 1812. Since the 1790s, wars between European powers had interfered with U.S. trade. American customers were no longer able to get all the manufactured goods they were used to buying from British and European manufacturers. Then, during the War of 1812, British ships blockaded eastern seaports, preventing foreign ships from delivering goods. Americans began to buy the items they needed from American manufacturers instead of from foreign suppliers. As profits for American factories grew, manufacturers began to spend more money expanding their factories. State banks and private investors began to lend money to manufacturers for their businesses.

At the same time, many Americans began to realize that the United States had been relying too heavily on foreign goods. If the United States could not meet its own needs, it might be weak and open to attack. Former president Thomas Jefferson, who had once opposed manufacturing, changed his mind. He, too, realized that the United States was too dependent on imports.

> "To be independent for the comforts of life we must fabricate [make] them ourselves. We must now place the manufacturer by the side of the agriculturalist [farmer]."
>
> —Thomas Jefferson, from *The Writings of Thomas Jefferson*, edited by P. L. Ford

In February 1815, New Yorkers celebrated the end of the War of 1812 and the return of free trade. The streets were decorated and filled with merchants whose ships were loaded with goods. "With Peace and Commerce, America Prospers," declared one display. Eager businesspeople prepared to lead the United States into a period of industrial growth. They urged northern politicians to pass higher tariffs on foreign goods to protect American companies.

READING CHECK **Analyzing** How did the War of 1812 aid the growth of American manufacturing?

American dependence on some foreign goods, such as oil, is still being debated today.

SUMMARY AND PREVIEW The Industrial Revolution started with the textile industry in England but soon spread to the United States. In the next section you will learn about how the spread of factories changed the working lives of many Americans.

Section 1 Assessment

go.hrw.com
Online Quiz
KEYWORD: SS8 HP11

Reviewing Ideas, Terms, and People HSS 8.6.1

1. a. **Identify** What was the first industry to begin to use machines to manufacture goods?
   b. **Predict** In what ways might life for workers change as a result of the **Industrial Revolution**?
2. a. **Recall** In what part of the United States were most mills located? Why?
   b. **Draw Conclusions** How did the ideas of **Samuel Slater** and **Eli Whitney** affect manufacturing in the United States?
   c. **Evaluate** Whose contributions do you think were more important—Slater's textile machines or Whitney's **interchangeable parts**? Why?
3. a. **Identify** What event encouraged the growth of American manufacturing? Why?
   b. **Contrast** Why was manufacturing in Great Britain in the early years more successful than that in the United States?

Critical Thinking

4. **Drawing Conclusions** Copy the chart below. Use it to identify contributions that led to the growth of manufacturing in the United States and what effect each contribution had.

Contribution	Effect on Manufacturing

FOCUS ON WRITING

5. **Noting Inventions** In your notebook, create a three-column chart. In the first column, list any inventions mentioned in this section. In the second column, identify the inventor. In the third column, describe the invention and its benefits.

Review & Assess

Close

Briefly review the ways in which the Industrial Revolution came to the United States.

Review

go.hrw.com Online Quiz, Section 1

Assess

SE Section 1 Assessment

PASS: Section 1 Quiz

Alternative Assessment Handbook

Reteach/Classroom Intervention

California Standards Review Workbook

Interactive Reader and Study Guide, Section 1

Interactive Skills Tutor CD-ROM

Section 1 Assessment Answers

1. a. textile industry
   b. move from working on farms or in homes to working in factories; loss of work for some skilled laborers; poorer working conditions
2. a. Northeast; had many rivers and streams to provide a reliable supply of water power
   b. led to spread of mills, the growth of the American textile industry, mass production, and the cheaper manufacture of goods
   c. Answers will vary but should reflect an understanding of each man's contributions.
3. a. War of 1812; with the loss of many foreign imports, Americans bought more American goods, which increased manufacturing
   b. Britain had less available, cheap land; and thus more workers and lower wages.
4. Arkwright's water frame—lowered costs, increased speed, led to textile mills; Slater's export of British textile machine designs—led to American textile mills; Whitney's interchangeable parts—led to mass production; War of 1812; see answer to 3a.
5. See the previous answer.

Answers

Reading Check *The war prevented the import of many foreign goods, which led Americans to buy American-made goods, which in turn led to increased manufacturing.*

Preteach

Bellringer

If YOU were there . . . Use the **Daily Bellringer Transparency** to help students answer the question.

 Daily Bellringer Transparency, Section 2

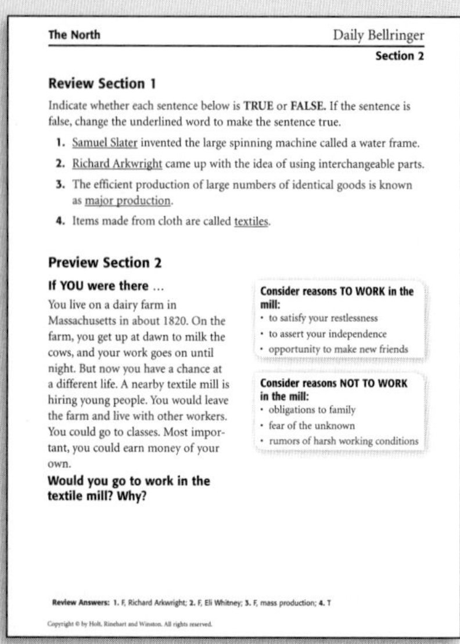

The North Daily Bellringer

Section 2

Review Section 1

Indicate whether each sentence below is **TRUE** or **FALSE.** If the sentence is false, change the underlined word to make the sentence true.

1. Samuel Slater invented the large spinning machine called a water frame.
2. Richard Arkwright came up with the idea of using interchangeable parts.
3. The efficient production of large numbers of identical goods is known as major production.
4. Items made from cloth are called textiles.

Preview Section 2

If YOU were there ...

You live on a dairy farm in Massachusetts in about 1820. On the farm, you get up at dawn to milk the cows, and your work goes on until night. But now you have a chance at a different life. A nearby textile mill is hiring young people. You would leave the farm and live with other workers. You could go to classes. Most important, you could earn money of your own.

Would you go to work in the textile mill? Why?

Consider reasons TO WORK in the mill:
- to satisfy your restlessness
- to assert your independence
- opportunity to make new friends

Consider reasons NOT TO WORK in the mill:
- obligations to family
- fear of the unknown
- rumors of harsh working conditions

Review Answers: **1.** F, Richard Arkwright; **2.** F, Eli Whitney; **3.** F, mass production; **4.** T

Academic Vocabulary

Review with students the high-use academic term in this section.

concrete specific, real (p. 357)

CRF: Vocabulary Builder Activity, Section 2

Standards Focus

HSS 8.6.1

Means: Discuss how the Industrial Revolution changed the way people in the Northeast worked.

Matters: Many people work today according to patterns established during the Industrial Revolution.

SECTION 2

Changes in Working Life

What You Will Learn...

Main Ideas

1. The spread of mills in the Northeast changed workers' lives.
2. The Lowell System revolutionized the textile industry in the Northeast.
3. Workers organized to reform working conditions.

The Big Idea

The introduction of factories changed working life for many Americans.

Key Terms and People

Rhode Island system, *p. 353*
Francis Cabot Lowell, *p. 354*
Lowell system, *p. 354*
trade unions, *p. 356*
strikes, *p. 356*
Sarah G. Bagley, *p. 357*

HSS 8.6.1 Discuss the influence of industrialization and technological developments on the region, including human modification of the landscape and how physical geography shaped human actions (e.g., growth of cities, deforestation, farming, mineral extraction).

If YOU were there...

You live on a dairy farm in Massachusetts in about 1820. On the farm, you get up at dawn to milk the cows, and your work goes on until night. But now you have a chance at a different life. A nearby textile mill is hiring young people. You would leave the farm and live with other workers. You could go to classes. Most important, you could earn money of your own.

Would you go to work in the textile mill? Why?

BUILDING BACKGROUND As factories and mills were established, the way people worked changed drastically. One dramatic change was the opportunity that factory work gave to young women. For young women in farm families, it was almost the only chance they had to earn their own money and a measure of independence.

Mills Change Workers' Lives

Workers no longer needed the specific skills of craftspeople to run the machines of the new mills. The lives of workers changed along with their jobs. Resistance to these changes sometimes sparked protests.

Many mill owners in the United States could not find enough people to work in factories because other jobs were available. At first, Samuel Slater and his two partners used apprentices—young men who worked for several years to learn the trade. However, they often were given only simple work. For example, their jobs included feeding cotton into the machines and cleaning the mill equipment. They grew tired of this work and frequently left. Apprentice James Horton, for example, ran away from Slater's mill. "Mr. Slater . . . keep me always at one thing . . . ," Horton complained. "I might have stayed there until this time and never knew nothing."

Eventually, Slater began to hire entire families who moved to Pawtucket to work in the mills. This practice allowed Slater to fill his labor needs at a low cost. Children as well as adults worked in the mills.

Teach the Big Idea: Master the Standards

Standards Proficiency

Changes in Working Life 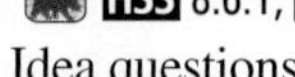 HSS 8.6.1; HSS Analysis Skills: HR 5, HI 1, HI 2, HI 3

1. **Teach** Ask students the Main Idea questions to teach this section.
2. **Apply** Ask students to imagine that they are factory workers who also write for a workers' magazine. Have each student write an article titled "Factory Life" describing how factories have changed workers' lives in the Northeast. Students should address the effects of factories on farm families and craftspeople, the type of factory systems that developed, the advantages and disadvantages of mill work, and the role of labor unions.
3. **Review** Ask volunteers to read their articles aloud. Discuss them to review the section.
4. **Practice/Homework** Have each student create a political cartoon for the magazine that contrasts the reality of mill work with the image owners promoted. **LS Visual/Spatial**

Alternative Assessment Handbook, Rubrics 27: Political Cartoons; and 42: Writing to Inform

Primary Source

NEWSPAPER ADVERTISEMENT

Family Wanted

This advertisement appeared in a Mendon, Rhode Island, newspaper in 1823. In it, a company requests that families come to work at a factory. The practice of hiring entire families was common at the time, especially in Britain. In America, it became known as the Rhode Island system.

The advertisement requests more than one family.

Why do you think Blackstone wants large families?

FAMILIES WANTED.

THREE or four Families of large size, and good characters, may find employment at Blackstone Manufactory.

STEPHEN TRIPP,

Agent Blackstone Manufacturing Co.

Mendon, Nov. 27. tf.

ANALYSIS SKILL ANALYZING PRIMARY SOURCES

Drawing Conclusions Do you think advertisements like this one had the effect the companies wanted?

On most farms children worked to help their families. Therefore, few people complained about the hiring of children to work in factories. H. Humphrey, an author of books on raising children, told parents that children needed to be useful. Humphrey wrote, "If he [a child] will not study, put him on to a farm, or send him into the shop, or in some other way provide regular employment for him." The machines made many tasks in the mill simple enough for children to do. Mill owners profited because they paid children low wages. Adults usually earned as much in a day as most children did in a week.

To attract families to his mill, Slater built housing for the workers. He also provided them with a company store where they could buy necessities. In addition, he started the practice of paying workers with credit at the company store. Instead of paying the full price for an item all at once, small payments could be made over a period of time. This practice allowed Slater to reinvest his money in his business.

Slater's strategy of hiring families and dividing factory work into simple tasks became known as the **Rhode Island system**. Mill owners throughout the Northeast copied Slater's methods. Owners advertised with "Men with growing families wanted." They also sent recruiters to poor communities to find new workers. For many people, the chance to work in a factory was a welcome opportunity to earn money and to learn a new skill.

One of the earliest of the mill towns, Sla-tersville, was named after Samuel Slater. The town was built by Slater and his brother John. It included two houses for workers and their families, the owner's house, the company store, and the Slatersville Mill. The mill was the largest and most modern industrial building of its time.

The mills employed not only the textile workers who operated the machinery but also machine part makers and dam builders. Although the company store sold food and necessary items to workers, mill towns supported the same variety of businesses any other town needed to thrive. These included tailors and dressmakers, butchers, and other small workshops.

READING CHECK **Summarizing** What problem did Slater have in his mills, and how did he solve it?

Direct Teach

Main Idea

1 Mills Change Workers' Lives

The spread of mills in the Northeast changed workers' lives.

Recall What was the Rhode Island system, and why did Samuel Slater decide to adopt it? *what—practice of hiring families and dividing factory work into simple tasks; why—because apprentices grew tired of the work and often left, and families provided several workers at low cost*

Identify Cause and Effect What were some effects of Slater's use of the Rhode Island system? *Other mill owners began using the system; mill towns developed to provide mill families with a place to live and shop.*

Compare In what ways was a mill town similar to other small towns in the United States at the time? *Mill towns provided a variety of businesses, just as in other towns.*

HSS 8.6.1; HSS **Analysis Skills:** HI 1, HI 2, HI 3

Primary Source

Family Wanted

Draw Conclusions Why does the advertisement request large families? *The larger the family, the more low-paid workers a factory owner gained, because factory owners paid children less.*

Critical Thinking: Finding Main Ideas

Standards Proficiency

Slater's Mill Want Ad HSS 8.6.1; HSS Analysis Skills: HR 5, HI 1, HI 2

1. Have each student create an advertisement seeking employees for Slater's mills. Students should address the following questions in their advertisements:
   - What types of workers does Slater want to attract?
   - What segments of society might want to work in a mill?
   - What incentives might appeal to and attract possible employees?
   - Why would a person want to work in one of Slater's mills as opposed to another mill?
2. Have volunteers share their advertisements with the class.
3. Then lead a discussion on working conditions in mills during this period. LS **Verbal/Linguistic**

Alternative Assessment Handbook, Rubric 2: Advertisements

Answers

Analyzing Primary Sources *possible answer—yes, because people were looking for work and farm families were used to their children working.*

Reading Check *He had trouble finding enough people to work in his mills. He began hiring entire families to work at low wages and divided factory work into simple tasks; also built housing for workers and provided a company store.*

Direct Teach

Main Idea

1 The Lowell System

The Lowell system revolutionized the textile industry in the Northeast.

Recall What system did Francis Cabot Lowell use in his mills, and who did he hire under this system? *Lowell system; young, unmarried women from local farms*

Explain Why did young women want to work in the Lowell mills? *ability to make own money; higher wages than they could earn elsewhere*

Summarize What were working and living conditions like for Lowell girls? *worked hard for 12 to 14 hours a day; bells provided a rigid schedule, lived in clean boardinghouses, encouraged to use free time to take classes and form clubs*

Predict How do you think mill workers felt as owners kept increasing the size and speed of their machines? *possible answers—angry at having to work harder, tired from overwork, wanted higher wages*

HSS 8.6.1; **HSS Analysis Skills:** HI 1, HI 2, HI 3

Info to Know

Working Women In addition to the mills, women in the Northeast had other opportunities for work in the early 1800s. One historical study found that the jobs available to women depended upon their race and ethnicity. Native-born women in New England could find clerical and sales jobs. Immigrant women often found semiskilled factory work. Newer immigrant women and free African American women were largely limited to domestic service.

go.hrw.com
Online Resources
KEYWORD: SS8 US11
ACTIVITY: Lowell Girls Scrapbook

The Lowell System

Not all mill owners followed this system. **Francis Cabot Lowell**, a businessman from New England, developed a very different approach. His ideas completely changed the textile industry in the Northeast.

The **Lowell system** was based on water-powered textile mills that employed young, unmarried women from local farms. The system included a loom that could both spin thread and weave cloth in the same mill. Lowell constructed boardinghouses for the women. Boardinghouse residents were given a room and meals along with their jobs.

With financial support from investors of the Boston Manufacturing Company, Lowell's first textile mill opened in Waltham, Massachusetts, in 1814. "From the first starting of the first power loom there was not . . . doubt about the success," wrote one investor. In 1822, the company built a larger mill in a Massachusetts town later named Lowell. Visitors to Lowell were amazed by the clean factories and neatly kept boardinghouses as well as the new machinery.

The young millworkers soon became known as Lowell girls. The mills paid them between $2 and $4 each week. The workers paid $1.25 for room and board. These wages were much better than those women could earn per week in other available jobs, such as domestic work.

Many young women came to Lowell from across New England. They wanted the chance to earn money instead of working on the family farm. "I must of course have something of my own before many more years have passed over my head," wrote one young woman. The typical Lowell girl worked at the mills for about four years.

Unlike other factory workers, the Lowell girls were encouraged to use their free time to take classes and form women's clubs. They even wrote their own magazine, the *Lowell Offering*. Lucy Larcom, who started working at Lowell at age 11, later praised her fellow workers.

No record exists today of the name of this girl, who worked in a mill around 1850. Judging from the photograph, if she were in school today, she would probably be in the seventh or eighth grade. Although hard to see in this photograph, her hands and arms are scratched and swollen—telltale signs of the hard labor required of young girls who worked up to 14 hours per day.

Time Table of the Lowell Mills

Morning Bells	
First bell	4:30 AM
Second bell	5:30 AM
Third bell	6:20 AM
Dinner (Lunch) Bells	
Ring out	12:00 PM
Ring in	12:35 PM
Evening Bells	
Ring out	6:30 PM
Except on Saturday Evenings	

—*The Table of the Lowell Mills, October 21, 1851*

Social Studies Skills: Assessing the Credibility of Primary Sources

A *Lowell Offering* Excerpt

HSS 8.6.1; **HSS Analysis Skills:** HR 4, HR 5 **Exceeding Standards**

Background Some people criticized the *Lowell Offering* for providing an unrealistic view of mill life. For example, one cover made the mill look more like a garden than a factory. In 1845 Harriet Farley, the editor, defended the magazine.

1. Read aloud the following: "We have never published anything which our own experience had convinced us was unfair. But, if in our sketches, there is too much light, and too little shade, let our excuse be . . . We have not thought it necessary to state . . . that our life was a toilsome one—for we supposed that would be universally understood."
2. Have students discuss how Farley defends the magazine's image of mill life and whether her argument is valid. What factors might have influenced her viewpoint? Why might the editors have chosen to ignore the harsh realities of mill life? **LS Verbal/Linguistic**

Alternative Assessment Handbook: Rubric 16: Judging Information

History Close-up
Life of a Mill Girl
Girls had to keep their hair pulled back so it did not get caught in the machines, resulting in serious injury—or death.
Windows were rarely opened, to prevent air from blowing the threads. The result is a hot, stuffy room.
The air is dirty and causes breathing problems. One visitor remarked, "The atmosphere . . . is charged with cotton filaments and dust, which . . . are very injurious to the lungs."
This girl is straightening threads as they enter the power loom, a job that cut her hands.
Girls must shout to be heard above the noise of the power looms. Visitors to the mill routinely referred to the sound of the machines as "deafening."
ANALYSIS SKILL ANALYZING VISUALS
Judging from the photograph on page 354, what might be the condition of the girl's hands in this illustration? Why?

Direct Teach

History Close-up

Life of a Mill Girl

Activity Lowell Girl Journal Entry Ask students to imagine that they have found an old journal written by a Lowell girl. Have students use the information in the images and captions at left to write one journal entry describing a day in the life of a Lowell girl.
LS Intrapersonal, Verbal/Linguistic

Alternative Assessment Handbook, Rubric 15: Journals

Biography

Lucy Larcom (1826–1893) Lucy Larcom provides an example of one Lowell girl's life. Larcom was 1 of 10 children, several of whom worked in the Lowell mills. The Larcom family moved to Lowell, Massachusetts, after the father died. Together, Lucy and her sisters Abigail, Emeline, and Lydia earned almost $230 in factory wages in 1836. Besides supporting their mother and family, two of the Larcom sisters became accomplished writers. Emeline played a central role in founding *Operatives' Magazine*, a literary journal. Lucy became a noted poet and editor, and the author of *A New England Girlhood*.

Did You Know . . .

The minor league baseball team in Lowell, Massachusetts is named the Lowell Spinners in honor of the region's history of textile mills.

Collaborative Learning

Standards Proficiency

Lowell Offering Magazine

HSS 8.6.1; HSS **Analysis Skills:** HR 5, HI 1

Materials: heavy white paper, art supplies

1. Organize students into small groups. Ask the groups to imagine that they are contributors to the *Lowell Offering* magazine.
2. Have each group fold and staple together two pieces of paper to create a "magazine." Students should design a cover for the magazine and fill the inside pages with articles and other items related to life and working conditions in the Lowell mills. In addition to articles, students might include artwork, poetry, an advice column, stories, editorials, club listings, schedules and menus, and so on. Groups might also create a slogan or mill song to print on the inside or back cover.
3. If time allows, have students conduct research on the Lowell girls to enhance the contents of their magazines. **LS Verbal/Linguistic**

Alternative Assessment Handbook, Rubrics 14: Group Activity; and 19: Magazines

Answers

Analyzing Visuals *scratched and swollen; Straightening threads as they entered the power loom would have cut her hands.*

Direct Teach

Main Idea

3 Workers Organize

Workers organized to reform working conditions.

Explain What had happened to the wages of craftspeople and factory workers by the 1840s? *craftspeople—to compete with factories, shop owners hired more workers and paid them less; factory workers—wages went down as competition for jobs increased*

Make Inferences Why did employers think that union workers prevented them from competing? *Employers thought they would have to pay union workers higher wages, which would make it harder for them to sell finished goods at lower prices than their competitors.*

HSS 8.6.1; HSS **Analysis Skills:** HR 5, HI 1, HI 2

Checking for Understanding

True or False Answer each statement *T* if it is true or *F* if it is false. If false, explain why.

1. Samuel Slater's system of hiring families and dividing factory work into simple tasks became known as the Lowell system. *F; Rhode Island system*
2. Many young women did not want to work in the mills because they could earn more working at home. *F; Many did want to work in the mills because they could earn more than at other jobs.*
3. Trade unions worked to improve pay and working conditions. *T*

Answers

Analyzing Primary Sources *Bagley viewed it as similar to slavery.*

Reading Check *Lowell system—employed young, unmarried women from local farms; Rhode Island system employed entire families*

Primary Source

MAGAZINE ARTICLE

Sarah G. Bagley and Workers' Rights

Lowell girl Sarah G. Bagley wrote magazine articles and made speeches about working in the mills. She organized workers to help change conditions.

Bagley believes that most mill girls would leave their jobs if they could.

"Is anyone such a fool as to suppose that out of six thousand factory girls in Lowell, sixty would be there if they could help it? Whenever I raise the point that it is immoral to shut us up in a close room twelve hours a day in the most monotonous and tedious of employment I am told that we have come to the mills voluntarily and we can leave when we will. Voluntarily! . . . the whip which brings us to Lowell is necessity. We must have money; a father's debts are to be paid, an aged mother to be supported, a brother's ambition to be aided and so the factories are supplied. Is this to act from free will?. . . Is this freedom? To my mind it is slavery."

Bagley says that mill girls work to help their family members.

—Sarah G. Bagley, quoted in *The Belles of New England: The Women of the Textile Mills and the Families Whose Wealth They Wove,* by William Moran

ANALYSIS SKILL ANALYZING PRIMARY SOURCES

How did Bagley view the idea that workers must endure poor conditions?

"I regard it as one of the privileges [advantages] of my youth that I . . . [grew] up among those active, interesting girls, whose lives . . . had principle [ideals] and purpose distinctly their own."

—Lucy Larcom, from *A New England Girlhood*

Mill life was hard, however. The workday was between 12 and 14 hours long, and daily life was carefully controlled. Ringing bells ordered workers to breakfast or lunch. Employees had to work harder and faster to keep up with new equipment. Cotton dust also began to cause health problems, such as chronic cough, for workers.

THE IMPACT TODAY

In the 1950s, labor union membership reached its peak; about 40 percent of the workforce belonged to unions. Today only about 14 percent of the working population belongs to a labor union.

READING CHECK **Contrasting** How was the Lowell system different from the Rhode Island system?

Workers Organize

Factories continued to spread in the 1800s. Craftspeople, who made goods by hand, felt threatened. Factories quickly produced low-priced goods. To compete with factories, shop owners had to hire more workers and pay them less. Shoemaker William Frazier complained about the situation in the mid-1840s. "We have to sit on our seats from twelve to sixteen hours per day, to earn one dollar."

The wages of factory workers also went down as people competed for jobs. A wave of immigration in the 1840s brought people from other, poorer countries. They were willing to work for low pay. More immigrants came to the Northeast, where the mills were located, than to the South. Competition for jobs also came from people unemployed during the financial Panic of 1837. For example, about 50,000 workers in New York City alone had lost their jobs.

The Beginning of Trade Unions

Facing low wages and the fear of losing their jobs, skilled workers formed **trade unions**, groups that tried to improve pay and working conditions. Eventually, unskilled factory workers also formed trade unions. Most employers did not want to hire union workers. Employers believed that the higher cost of union employees prevented competition with other manufacturers.

Sometimes labor unions staged protests called **strikes**. Workers on strike refuse to work until employers meet their demands. Most early strikes were not successful, however. Courts and police usually supported companies, not striking union members.

Differentiating Instruction for Universal Access

Advanced Learners/GATE Exceeding Standards

1. Ask students to imagine that they work for the New England Working Men's Association. Have each student write a speech for Sarah G. Bagley to raise money for the association's efforts to improve working conditions in the mills.
2. Students' speeches should summarize the following issues: working conditions, increased competition for jobs, decreasing wages, the 10-hour workday, child labor, and union organization.
3. Have volunteers present their speeches to the class. Conclude by having students describe how Bagley and others contributed to the early labor-union movement. LS **Verbal/Linguistic**

HSS 8.6.1; HSS **Analysis Skills:** HR 5, HI 1

Alternative Assessment Handbook, Rubric 43: Writing to Persuade

Labor Reform Efforts

A strong voice in the union movement was that of millworker **Sarah G. Bagley**. She founded the Lowell Female Labor Reform Association in 1844 and publicized the struggles of factory laborers. The association's two main goals were to influence an investigation of working conditions by the Massachusetts state legislature and to obtain a 10-hour workday. Members of the association passed out pamphlets and circulated petitions.

President Martin Van Buren had granted a 10-hour workday in 1840 for many federal employees. Bagley wanted this rule to apply to employees of private businesses. These men and women often worked 12 to 14 hours per day, six days per week.

Many working men and women supported the 10-hour-workday campaign, despite the opposition of business owners. In 1845 Sarah Bagley was elected vice president of the New England Working Men's Association. She was the first woman to hold such a high-ranking position in the American labor movement.

Over time, the unions achieved some concrete legal victories. Connecticut, Maine, New Hampshire, Ohio, Pennsylvania, and a few other states passed 10-hour-workday laws.

ACADEMIC VOCABULARY
concrete specific, real

For factory workers in other states, long hours remained common. One witness described how children were "summoned by the factory bell before daylight" and worked until eight o'clock at night "with nothing but [a] recess of forty-five minutes to get their dinner." Union supporters continued to fight for work reforms such as an end to child labor in factories during the 1800s.

READING CHECK **Finding Main Ideas** Why did workers form unions, and what were the main goals of union reformers?

SUMMARY AND PREVIEW With the growth of factories, workers faced new opportunities and challenges. In the next section you will learn about how the Transportation Revolution brought changes to commerce and the daily lives of Americans.

Section 2 Assessment

go.hrw.com
Online Quiz
KEYWORD: SS8 HP11

Reviewing Ideas, Terms, and People HSS 8.6.1

1. a. **Identify** What problems did many mill owners have in finding workers?
   b. **Analyze** How did Samuel Slater's **Rhode Island system** change employment practices in mills?
2. a. **Describe** What was life like for mill workers in the **Lowell system**?
   b. **Make Inferences** Why would young women have wanted to go to work in the Lowell mills?
3. a. **Recall** Why did workers form **trade unions**?
   b. **Predict** What are some possible problems that might arise between factory owners and trade unions?

Critical Thinking

4. **Drawing Conclusions** Copy the graphic organizer shown. Use it to identify the ways in which each leader affected the lives of workers.

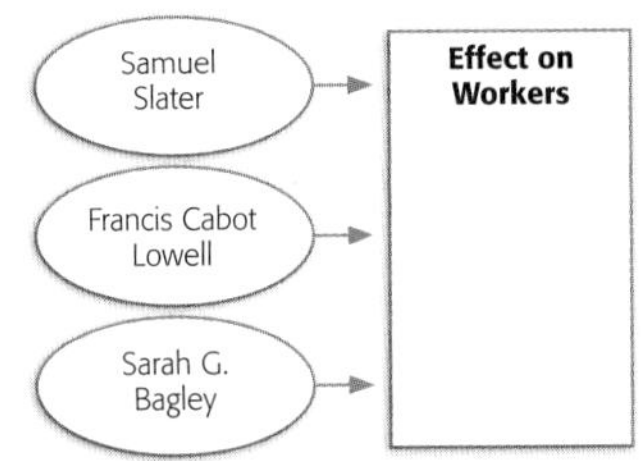

FOCUS ON WRITING

5. **Examining Working Conditions** This section tells about mill life and conditions for workers. In the chart you started for the first section, list the two labor systems used by mills, the person who developed each, and the benefits of each system.

Direct Teach

Main Idea

3 Workers Organize

Workers organized to reform working conditions.

Identify Who was Sarah G. Bagley, and why was she important? *a key player in the labor union movement; first woman to hold a high position in labor movement, played a leading role in reforming working conditions*

Summarize How did labor unions improve working conditions in the mid-1800s? *some states passed 10-hour workday laws*

CRF: Biography Activity: Sarah Bagley

HSS 8.6.1; HSS **Analysis Skills:** HI 1, HI 2

Review & Assess

Close

Have students summarize how life for workers in the Northeast changed during the early and mid-1800s.

Review

Online Quiz, Section 2

Assess

SE Section 2 Assessment

PASS: Section 2 Quiz

Alternative Assessment Handbook

Reteach/Classroom Intervention

California Standards Review Workbook

Interactive Reader and Study Guide, Section 2

Interactive Skills Tutor CD-ROM

Section 2 Assessment Answers

1. a. difficulty finding and keeping enough workers willing to do simple work all day
   b. Entire families, including children, began working in the mills; mill towns developed.
2. a. Workers, mostly young women, worked hard for 12 to 14 hours per day, lived in boardinghouses, and were encouraged to use their free time to take classes and form clubs.
   b. wanted the chance to earn money; preferable to life on a farm or as a servant; could earn more than in other jobs
3. a. concerns about low wages, job competition, and working conditions
   b. Strikes could lead to conflict and possible violence as owners tried to end them.
4. Slater—hired entire families to work in mills, divided work into simple tasks; Lowell—hired young women to work in mills, encouraged education and women's clubs; Bagley—worked for labor reform; founded the Lowell Female Labor Reform Association
5. Students should describe Slater's Rhode Island system and Lowell's Lowell system.

Answers

Reading Check *Workers formed unions in an attempt to increase wages and improve working conditions. The main goals of unions were to improve working conditions and wages and to obtain a 10-hour workday.*

Preteach

Bellringer

If YOU were there . . . Use the **Daily Bellringer Transparency** to help students answer the question.

Daily Bellringer Transparency, Section 3

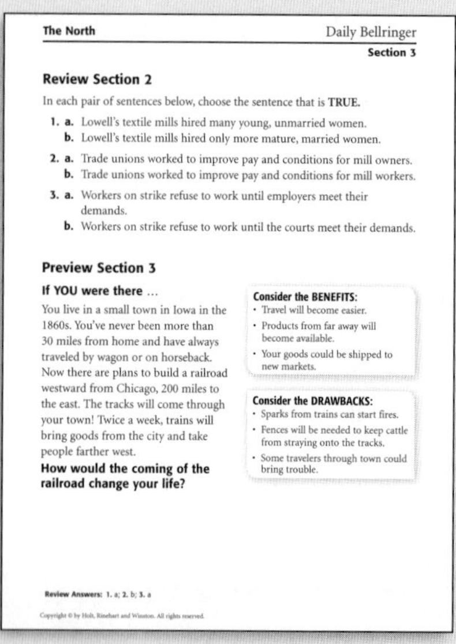
The North — Daily Bellringer — Section 3

Review Section 2

In each pair of sentences below, choose the sentence that is **TRUE.**

1. a. Lowell's textile mills hired many young, unmarried women.
   b. Lowell's textile mills hired only more mature, married women.
2. a. Trade unions worked to improve pay and conditions for mill owners.
   b. Trade unions worked to improve pay and conditions for mill workers.
3. a. Workers on strike refuse to work until employers meet their demands.
   b. Workers on strike refuse to work until the courts meet their demands.

Preview Section 3

If YOU were there ...

You live in a small town in Iowa in the 1860s. You've never been more than 30 miles from home and have always traveled by wagon or on horseback. Now there are plans to build a railroad westward from Chicago, 200 miles to the east. The tracks will come through your town! Twice a week, trains will bring goods from the city and take people farther west.

How would the coming of the railroad change your life?

Consider the BENEFITS:
- Travel will become easier.
- Products from far away will become available.
- Your goods could be shipped to new markets.

Consider the DRAWBACKS:
- Sparks from trains can start fires.
- Fences will be needed to keep cattle from straying onto the tracks.
- Some travelers through town could bring trouble.

Review Answers: 1. a; 2. b; 3. a

Building Vocabulary

Preteach or review the following terms:

deposits concentrations of minerals lying in an underground pocket (p. 363)

monopolistic when one company controls an industry or market (p. 359)

CRF: Vocabulary Builder Activity, Section 3

Standards Focus

HSS 8.6.1

Means: Discuss how advances in travel changed life in the United States, including the American economy and landscape.

Matters: The Transportation Revolution ushered in the modern age of business and travel and had long-lasting effects on the environment.

SECTION 3

The Transportation Revolution

What You Will Learn...

Main Ideas

1. The Transportation Revolution affected trade and daily life.
2. The steamboat was one of the first developments of the Transportation Revolution.
3. Railroads were a vital part of the Transportation Revolution.
4. The Transportation Revolution brought many changes to American life and industry.

The Big Idea

New forms of transportation improved business, travel, and communication in the United States.

Key Terms and People

HSS 8.6.1 Discuss the influence of industrialization and technological developments on the region, including human modification of the landscape and how physical geography shaped human actions (e.g., growth of cities, deforestation, farming, mineral extraction).

If YOU were there...

You live in a small town in Iowa in the 1860s. You've never been more than 30 miles from home and have always traveled by wagon or on horseback. Now there are plans to build a railroad westward from Chicago, 200 miles to the east. The tracks will come through your town! Twice a week, trains will bring goods from the city and take people farther west.

How would the coming of the railroad change your life?

BUILDING BACKGROUND The Industrial Revolution changed how goods were made. It brought great changes in the ways that many Americans lived. But changes in technology led to major changes in other areas of life, too. Changes in transportation would bring remote parts of America closer together.

Trade and Daily Life

During the 1800s the United States experienced a **Transportation Revolution** —a period of rapid growth in the speed and convenience of travel because of new methods of transportation. The Transportation Revolution created a boom in business across the country, particularly by reducing shipping time and costs. As one foreign observer declared in 1835, "The Americans . . . have joined the Hudson to the Mississippi, and made the Atlantic Ocean communicate with the Gulf of Mexico."

These improvements were made possible largely by the invention of two new forms of transportation: the steamboat and steam-powered trains. They enabled goods, people, and information to travel rapidly and efficiently across the United States.

READING CHECK **Finding Main Ideas** What benefits did the Transportation Revolution bring to trade and daily life?

Teach the Big Idea: Master the Standards

Standards Proficiency

The Transportation Revolution

HSS 8.6.1; HSS **Analysis Skills:** HI 1

1. **Teach** Ask students the Main Idea questions to teach this section.
2. **Apply** Have each student write the Big Idea, listed above, in the middle of a piece of paper. Above the Big Idea, have students draw a box and label it *Causes*. Below the Big Idea, have students draw a box and label it *Effects*. Have students list the factors that led to new forms of transportation and identify what those new forms were. Then have students describe the effects of the Transportation Revolution. LS **Visual/Spatial**
3. **Review** Have the class review the causes and effects of the Transportation Revolution.
4. **Practice/Homework** Have each student write a paragraph summarizing the significance of the Transportation Revolution. LS **Verbal/Linguistic**

Alternative Assessment Handbook, Rubrics 13: Graphic Organizers; and 37: Writing Assignments

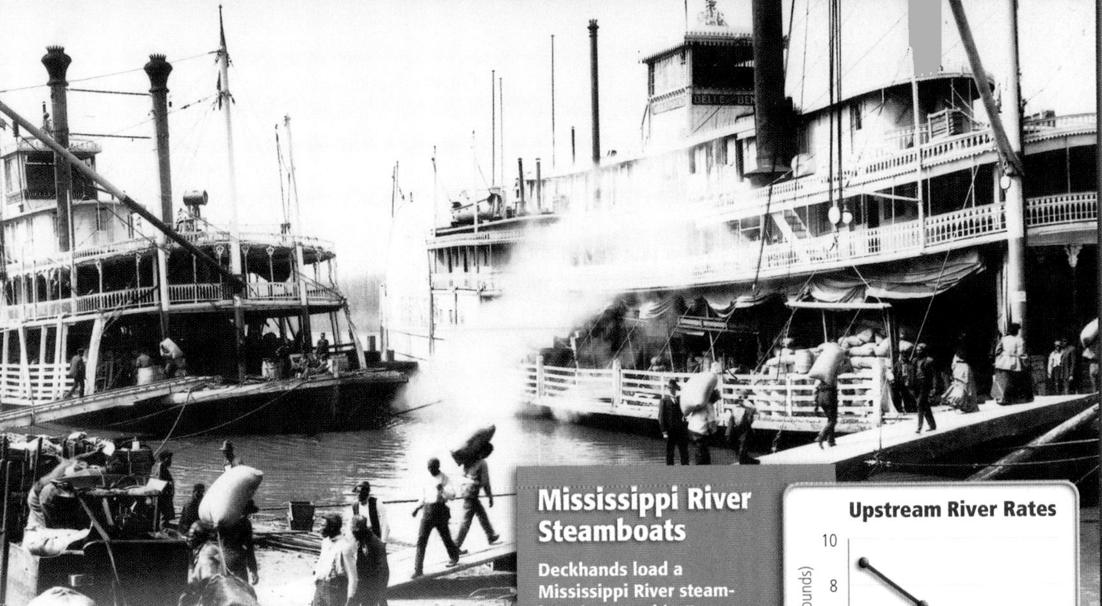

Mississippi River Steamboats

Deckhands load a Mississippi River steamboat in Memphis, Tennessee. By the mid-1800s, hundreds of steamboats traveled up and down American rivers. Steamboats enabled Americans to ship more goods farther, faster, and for less money than ever before.

Upstream River Rates

Steamboats

American and European inventors had developed steam-powered boats in the late 1700s. However, they were not in wide use until the early 1800s.

Steamboat Era

In 1803 American **Robert Fulton** tested his first steamboat design in France. Several years later, he tested the first full-sized commercial steamboat, called the ***Clermont***, in the United States. On August 9, 1807, the *Clermont* traveled against the current up the Hudson River without trouble. Demand for steamboat ferry service soon arose.

The steamboat was well suited for river travel. It could move upriver and did not rely on wind power. Steamboats increased trade and profits because goods could be moved quickly and thus more cheaply. More than 500 steamboats were in use in the United States by 1840. By the 1850s, steamboats were also being used to carry people and goods across the Atlantic Ocean.

Gibbons v. *Ogden*

Increased steamboat shipping led to conflict over waterway rights. In 1819 Aaron Ogden sued Thomas Gibbons for operating steamboats in New York waters that Ogden said he owned. Gibbons did not have a license to operate in New York, but argued that his federal license gave him the right to use New York waterways.

In the case of ***Gibbons* v. *Ogden***, which reached the Supreme Court in 1824, the Court reinforced the federal government's authority to regulatee trade between the states by ending monopolistic control over waterways in several states. The ruling freed up waters to even greater trade and shipping.

READING CHECK **Summarizing** Explain the effects of the *Gibbons* v. *Ogden* ruling.

Direct Teach

Main Idea

❶ Trade and Daily Life

The Transportation Revolution affected trade and daily life.

Define What was the Transportation Revolution? *a period of rapid growth in the speed and convenience of travel because of new forms of transportation*

Identify What two new modes of transportation largely contributed to the Transportation Revolution? *steamboats; steam-powered trains*

HSS 8.6.1; HSS **Analysis Skills:** CS 1, HI 1

Main Idea

❷ Steamboats

The steamboat was one of the first developments of the Transportation Revolution.

Recall Who was Robert Fulton? *American steamboat designer who produced the first full-sized commercial steamboat, the* Clermont

Explain Why were steamboats well suited for river travel? *could travel upriver; did not rely on wind power*

Make Inferences Why do you think Ogden did not want Gibbons to operate a steamboat service in New York? *because Ogden had a monopoly; he wanted to keep all the business and profits for himself*

CRF: Literature Activity: Mark Twain Pilots a Steamboat

Supreme Court Case Studies: *Gibbons* v. *Ogden* (1824)

HSS 8.6.1; HSS Analysis Skills: HI 1

Differentiating Instruction for Universal Access

English-Language Learners

Reaching Standards

1. Have students examine the image on this page. Ask them to explain what the various people in the image are doing. Next, have students examine the way the people are dressed. What two categories of people can students identify based on dress? *(passengers and workers loading cargo)* Based on these groups, what services did steamboats provide? *(passenger and freight services)*
2. Guide students in a discussion about the development of the steamboat and how it affected trade and daily life.
3. Then have each student write at least three newspaper headlines about steamboat development and its effects.
4. Have volunteers present their headlines to the class. LS **Verbal/Linguistic, Visual/Spatial**

HSS 8.6.1; HSS **Analysis Skills:** HI 1, HI 2

Alternative Assessment Handbook, Rubric 42: Writing to Inform

Answers

Reading Check (previous page) *connected people and improved communication across the nation by making travel faster and more convenient; reduced shipping time and costs, which led to a boom in business across the nation*

Reading Check *reinforced the federal government's authority over the states*

Direct Teach

Main Idea

3 American Railroads

Railroads were a vital part of the Transportation Revolution.

Identify Where and when were steam-powered trains first developed? *in Great Britain in the early 1800s*

Analyze What was the significance of the 1830 race involving the *Tom Thumb* locomotive? *Although the locomotive lost, the race showed the power and speed of even a small locomotive and helped lead to railroad fever in the United States.*

Summarize In what ways did railroads affect daily life? *reduced travel time, linked many major cities, helped tie communities together, sped up communication and the pace of life*

Make Inferences Why do you think railroad companies became some of the nation's most powerful businesses? *possible answers—controlled passenger and freight transportation; profited from the growth of trade*

Political Cartoons Activities for United States History, Cartoon 14: Fears of the Railroad

HSS 8.6.1; HSS **Analysis Skills:** CS 1, HI 1, HI 2

Analyzing Visuals

The Steam Train

Activity Riding in a Steam Engine Ask students to imagine that it is the mid-1800s and they are riding on a steam locomotive for the first time. The engineer invites them to join him in the engine car. Have students describe what it is like there based on the images and information at right. *(Students might suggest that it is loud, hot, steamy, and rough travel but exciting.)*

American Railroads

What the steamboat did for water travel, the train did for overland travel. Steam-powered trains had first been developed in Great Britain in the early 1800s. However, they did not become popular in the United States until the 1830s. In 1830 **Peter Cooper** built a small but powerful locomotive called the *Tom Thumb*. He raced the locomotive against a horse-drawn railcar. Eyewitness John Latrobe later described the race, in which *Tom Thumb* had a slow start and fell behind. Latrobe wrote, "The pace increased, the passengers shouted, the engine gained on the horse . . . then the engine passes the horse, and a great hurrah hailed the victory." Unfortunately for Cooper, victory was spoiled when *Tom Thumb* broke down and lost the race near the end.

Despite the defeat, the contest showed the power and speed of even a small locomotive. Railroad fever soon spread. By 1840 railroad companies had laid about 2,800 miles of track—more than existed in all of Europe. French economist Michel Chevalier described Americans as having "a perfect passion for railroads."

As more railroads were built, engineers and mechanics overcame many tough challenges. Most British railroads, for example, ran on straight tracks across flat ground. In the United States, however, many railroads had to run up and down steep mountains, around tight curves, and over swift rivers. Railroad companies also built the tracks quickly and often with the least expensive materials available. As time went on, engineers and mechanics built heavier, faster, and more powerful steam locomotives.

By 1860 about 30,000 miles of railroad linked almost every major city in the eastern United States. As a result, the economy surged forward. For example, American locomotives hauled more freight than those in any other country. The railroad companies quickly became some of the most powerful businesses in the nation. As the railroad sys-

The Steam Train

SCIENCE AND TECHNOLOGY

Boiling water produces steam, which pushes pistons back and forth in a steam engine. These pistons are connected to rods that rotate the wheels of the locomotive.

Why does the train have a firebox?

1 As steam follows the path of the white arrows in to the cylinder, the pressure pushes the piston in the direction of the large blue arrow. Connecting rods turn the wheel half a turn.

2 When the small valve rod moves, the other valve is blocked, pushing steam into the other side of the cylinder. The pressure moves the piston in the direction of the large blue arrow and the wheel completes a turn.

Piston

Differentiating Instruction for Universal Access

Learners Having Difficulty — Reaching Standards

Materials: art supplies

1. Lead a discussion on the innovations of the Transportation Revolution and the effects of those innovations on the economy and daily life in the United States.
2. Have each student create a drawing illustrating innovations of the Transportation Revolution.
3. Then have each student write a caption for his or her drawing explaining how transportation innovations changed life in the United States. **LS Visual/Spatial**

HSS 8.6.1; HSS **Analysis Skills:** HI 1, HI 2

Alternative Assessment Handbook, Rubric 3: Artwork

Answers

Science and Technology *to heat the water in order to produce steam, which powers the train's pistons* tem grew, manufacturers and farmers were able to send their goods to distant markets.

In addition to their tremendous economic impact, the railroads made a powerful impression on the senses of passengers and observers. Trains were the fastest form of transportation most people had ever experienced. While wagons often traveled less than 2 miles per hour, locomotives averaged about 20 miles per hour. Writer George Templeton Strong of New York City described the thrill of a steam train passing by in the night:

> "Whizzing and rattling and panting, with its fiery furnace gleaming in front, its chimney vomiting fiery smoke above, and its long train of cars rushing along behind like the body and tail of a gigantic dragon— . . . and all darting forward at the rate of twenty miles an hour. Whew!"
>
> —George Templeton Strong, quoted in *The Market Revolution* by Charles Sellers

Riding on the early trains was often an adventure, but it could also be quite dangerous. Engineers trying to stay on time sometimes traveled too fast. English citizen Charles Richard Weld was on a railroad car that flew off the tracks. To his amazement, the other passengers did not complain about the accident. Instead, they praised the engineer for trying to keep on schedule!

Passengers accepted such risks because the railroads reduced travel time dramatically. Railroads also helped tie communities together. In 1847 Senator Daniel Webster spoke for many people in the United States when he declared that the railroad "towers above all other inventions of this or the preceding age."

READING CHECK **Drawing Inferences** In what ways did railroads affect the economy of the United States?

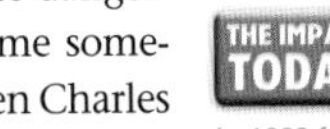

THE IMPACT TODAY

In 1883 four standard time zones were introduced in the United States to help railroads offer uniform train schedules. Today travelers might cross one or more time zones in a single airplane flight.

Direct Teach

Biography

Peter Cooper (1791–1883) With little formal education, Peter Cooper became one of the foremost inventors and manufacturers of the American Industrial Revolution. His contributions to the railroad were matched by his success in business, including iron manufacturing. Skilled at a number of trades, Cooper invented several new products, including a type of washing machine and a waterpower device for canal barges. In addition, Cooper promoted social reforms such as paid police forces and firefighters and improved public sanitation. In 1859 he founded a school providing free courses in science, engineering, and art. In his later years he said, "I have endeavored to remember that the object of life is to do good."

Connect to Science and Technology

Steam Power Before the Industrial Revolution began, people used natural sources of energy to do work. These sources included animals, waterpower, and wind power. Steam power provided a new source of energy. The first steam engines were built in the early 1700s in Europe. In the 1800s American Oliver Evans helped develop a smaller and more powerful steam engine. This engine was ideal for steamboats running on the Mississippi River or trains racing across the American countryside. Engineers continued to use and improve steam engines throughout the 1800s.

Analyze How do you think steam engines changed the way people lived and worked? *possible answer—Steam engines enabled people to live and work in a wider variety of locations.*

Critical Thinking: Acquiring Information

Exceeding Standards

Baltimore and Ohio Railroad

Research Required

1. Have students work in groups to conduct research on the Baltimore and Ohio Railroad, the first steam-operated railway in the United States to provide both freight and passenger service.
2. Organize students into small groups to investigate different aspects of the railroad. Topics for research might include locomotives and cars, routes of tracks, formation of the company, history of the company's growth, and leaders of the company. Each group should write one or more questions to guide its research.
3. Have each group create a display combining articles, captions, drawings, diagrams, and maps about its topic.
4. Display students' work in the classroom.
   LS Interpersonal, Verbal/Linguistic

Alternative Assessment Handbook, Rubrics 29: Presentations; and 30: Research

HSS 8.6.1; **HSS Analysis Skills:** CS 1, HR 1, HI 1

Answers

Reading Check *reduced shipping times and costs, which led to a surge in the economy and the rapid growth of powerful railroad companies*

Direct Teach

Main Idea

4 Transportation Revolution Brings Changes

The Transportation Revolution brought many changes to American life and industry.

Recall How did the railroads affect settlement patterns in the United States? *Towns and cities along rail lines grew, while those not near railroads suffered; some cities developed into transportation hubs.*

Identify Cause and Effect How did the coal industry change the landscape? *New coal mining towns developed, and coal mines created deep gashes in the earth.*

Analyze How were the railroad and steel industries interrelated? *Railroads transported steel to build factories and machines; steel was used to make the rails for trains.*

CRF: History and Geography Activity: The Transportation Revolution

Map Transparency: Transportation Routes, 1850

HSS 8.6.1; **HSS Analysis Skills:** CS 1, HI 1, HI 2

Info to Know

The Railroad in the Midwest In 1850, Illinois was still a frontier state, with 8 of its 10 cities located on Lake Michigan or along the Mississippi or Illinois rivers. Railroads brought a population explosion to formerly small Illinois towns. Between 1850 and 1855, Cairo, Illinois, grew from 300 to 1,300 inhabitants; Vandalia, Illinois, grew from 360 to 1,000; and Freeport, Illinois, grew from 1,400 to 5,000 residents.

Transportation Routes, 1850

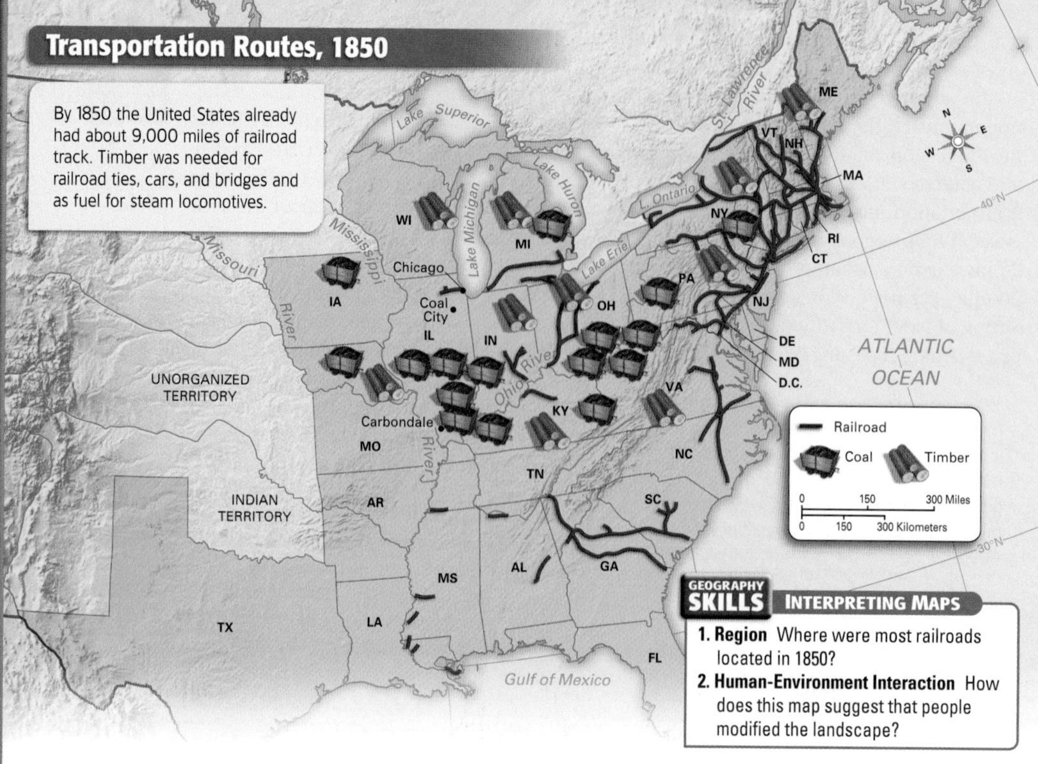

By 1850 the United States already had about 9,000 miles of railroad track. Timber was needed for railroad ties, cars, and bridges and as fuel for steam locomotives.

GEOGRAPHY SKILLS INTERPRETING MAPS

1. **Region** Where were most railroads located in 1850?
2. **Human-Environment Interaction** How does this map suggest that people modified the landscape?

Transportation Revolution Brings Changes

The Transportation Revolution brought many changes to America. Steamboats and railroads made getting goods to distant markets much easier and less costly. People in all areas of the nation now had access to products made and grown far away. More than ever before, there was a national economy. The wealth, however, was centered in the North.

Railroads contributed to the expansion of the borders of the nation and guided population growth. Towns sprang up at railroad junctions. Those towns that did not have railroads nearby suffered. Cities grew as trains brought new residents and raw materials for industry and construction. The growing prosperity of the nation, especially in the North, encouraged Americans to take pride in their country.

A New Fuel

The Transportation Revolution also increased the use of certain natural resources that had not been important until then. Throughout the early Transportation Revolution, wood was the primary source of fuel for trains and steamboats, as well as for cooking, light, and heat. As faster locomotives were built, coal replaced wood as the main source of power. A half ton of coal produces as much energy as two tons of wood but at half the cost. Coal also became popular for heating homes. Railroads transported the coal from mines to towns and cities.

As the demand for coal increased, a coal-mining industry developed in many states, including Pennsylvania, western Virginia, and Illinois. Coal mining changed the landscape in a number of ways. New towns, such as Coal City and Carbondale in Illinois,

Critical Thinking: Analyzing Information

Standards Proficiency

Railroads, Coal, and Steel Diagram

HSS 8.6.1; **HSS Analysis Skills:** CS 1, HI 1, HI 2

1. Guide students in a discussion of the relationships among wood, coal, iron, steel, and the railroad industry.
2. Have students refer to their texts to understand how and why coal replaced timber as a fuel source, and why steel replaced iron. Make a class list of the uses of coal and steel.
3. Then have each student create a diagram showing the relationship among the railroad industry and the coal and steel industries.
4. Have volunteers explain their diagrams with the class. Correct any student errors. **LS Visual/Spatial**

Alternative Assessment Handbook, Rubric 7: Charts

Answers

Interpreting Maps 1. *in the northeast;* 2. *Americans laid tracks and built tunnels and bridges for railroads, cut down trees and cleared forests for timber, and dug mines in the earth for coal.*

sprang up in places where coal deposits existed. Miners made deep gashes in the earth removing the coal.

Later, in the 1870s, the demand for coal increased as the demand for steel grew. Steel is made through a smelting process—heating iron ore to very high temperatures. Coal was used to fire the furnaces. Steel, which is much stronger than iron, was increasingly used to build factories and the machines they produced. Steel was also used to make the rails that trains ride on.

The growing market for steel helped fuel the need for more railroads. Railroads transported steel to places where new factories were being built. Railroads also brought new steel farming tools and machines to farmers in the Midwest. Using the new equipment, farmers produced more crops. Railroads then transported their harvests to markets.

Effects of Railroads

The railroads played a role in the growth of other businesses as well. The logging industry expanded as people in the growing towns and cities needed wood for houses and furniture. As newspaper publishing increased, demand for paper grew. Lumber items became the primary product of New England. Settlers spreading out across the Midwest cut down trees and plowed up prairies to make farmland. Deforestation, or cutting down and removing trees, took place on a large scale.

Railroads also caused cities to grow. Some cities became transportation hubs. Chicago was one such city. Its location on Lake Michigan made it an ideal transportation hub, linking the Midwest to the East and South.

READING CHECK **Analyzing Information** What role did railroads play in the growth of the coal industry?

SUMMARY AND PREVIEW The Transportation Revolution changed the way business was done. In the next section you will learn about more technological advances.

FOCUS ON READING
What causes and effects do you see in this section?

Section 3 Assessment

go.hrw.com
Online Quiz
KEYWORD: SS8 HP11

Reviewing Ideas, Terms, and People HSS 8.6.1

1. a. **Identify** What forms of transportation were improved or invented at this time?
   b. **Explain** What effect did the **Transportation Revolution** have on the United States?
2. a. **Describe** What were the benefits of steamboat travel?
   b. **Analyze** What effect did the ruling in the ***Gibbons* v. *Ogden*** case have on federal government?
3. a. **Describe** What event showed the power and speed of locomotives?
   b. **Draw Conclusions** How did railroads affect trade and business in the United States?
   c. **Elaborate** Why do you think Americans were fascinated by railroads?
4. a. **Describe** What physical obstacles did railroad construction in the United States face?
   b. **Analyze** What effects did the Transportation Revolution have on the U.S. economy?
   c. **Elaborate** Do you think the Transportation Revolution played a role in deforestation? Explain.

Critical Thinking

5. **Sequencing** Copy the time line on your own paper. Use it to list the key events that led to the emergence of the steamboat and the locomotive in the United States.

Emergence of the Steamboat and Locomotive

Late 1700s	1807	1824	1830	1840	1860

FOCUS ON WRITING

6. **Describing Travel Inventions** Add the steamboat and locomotive to your list. Note the individuals involved in their development as well as how these new methods of travel changed life for people in the United States.

Review & Assess

Close

Briefly review the ways in which the Transportation Revolution changed American trade, industry, and life.

Review

go.hrw.com Online Quiz, Section 3

Assess

SE Section 3 Assessment

PASS: Section 3 Quiz

Alternative Assessment Handbook

Reteach/Classroom Intervention

California Standards Review Workbook

Interactive Reader and Study Guide, Section 3

Interactive Skills Tutor CD-ROM

Section 3 Assessment Answers

1. a. steamboats, steam-powered trains
   b. made travel faster, more convenient; reduced shipping time and costs
2. a. could go upriver; did not need wind power
   b. reinforced its authority over the states
3. a. 1830 race that pitted the locomotive Tom Thumb against a horse-drawn railcar
   b. economy grew, became easier and faster to get goods to distant markets, railroad companies became powerful businesses
   c. possible answer—At the time, locomotives were the fastest, most powerful machines.
4. a. steep mountains, uneven land, swift rivers
   b. created a national economy; led to new industries and the growth of other industries
   c. yes, wood for tracks and growing cities
5. Late 1700s—steamboat invented; 1807—*Clermont*; 1824—*Gibbons* v. *Ogden*; 1830—*Tom Thumb* race; 1840—more than 500 steamboats in use and about 2,800 miles of railroad track; 1860—30,000 miles of railroad links many major cities in the East
6. Students should identify the key people and effects of the Transportation Revolution.

Answers

Focus on Reading *changes in environment because of logging and mining; rising demand for coal as a result of rising demand for steel; rising demand for steel because of new factories, machines, and rails; rising demand for railroads to transport steel and harvests; rising demand for wood as a result of growing towns and newspaper publishing; deforestation as a result of rising demand for wood; city growth as a result of access to railroads*

Reading Check *As faster trains were built, coal replaced wood as the main source of power.*

Preteach

Bellringer

If YOU were there . . . Use the **Daily Bellringer Transparency** to help students answer the question.

 Daily Bellringer Transparency, Section 4

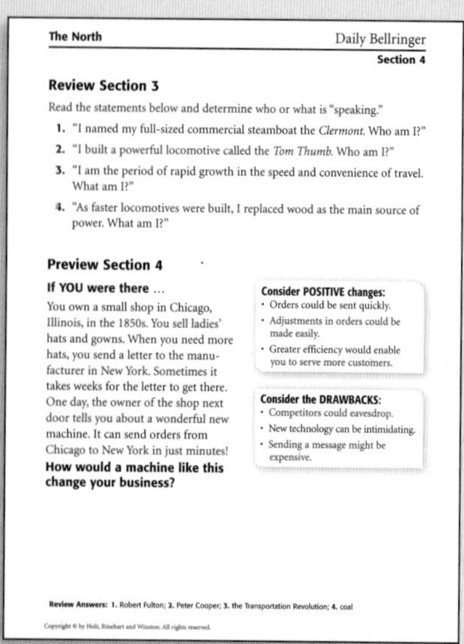

The North — Daily Bellringer
Section 4

Review Section 3

Read the statements below and determine who or what is "speaking."

1. "I named my full-sized commercial steamboat the *Clermont*. Who am I?"
2. "I built a powerful locomotive called the *Tom Thumb*. Who am I?"
3. "I am the period of rapid growth in the speed and convenience of travel. What am I?"
4. "As faster locomotives were built, I replaced wood as the main source of power. What am I?"

Preview Section 4

If YOU were there ...

You own a small shop in Chicago, Illinois, in the 1850s. You sell ladies' hats and gowns. When you need more hats, you send a letter to the manufacturer in New York. Sometimes it takes weeks for the letter to get there. One day, the owner of the shop next door tells you about a wonderful new machine. It can send orders from Chicago to New York in just minutes!

How would a machine like this change your business?

Consider POSITIVE changes:
- Orders could be sent quickly.
- Adjustments in orders could be made easily.
- Greater efficiency would enable you to serve more customers.

Consider the DRAWBACKS:
- Competitors could eavesdrop.
- New technology can be intimidating.
- Sending a message might be expensive.

Review Answers: 1. Robert Fulton; 2. Peter Cooper; 3. the Transportation Revolution; 4. coal

Building Vocabulary

Preteach or review the following terms:

magnetism force of attraction for iron exerted by magnets or by electrical charges or currents (p. 364)

reaper harvesting machine (p. 366)

transcontinental crossing the continent (p. 365)

CRF: Vocabulary Builder Activity, Section 4

Standards Focus

HSS 8.6.1

Means: Discuss how new inventions changed the way that Americans lived, worked, and communicated.

Matters: Advances in technology improved life for many people, as they continue to do today.

SECTION 4

More Technological Advances

What You Will Learn...

Main Ideas

1. The telegraph made swift communication possible from coast to coast.
2. With the shift to steam power, businesses built new factories closer to cities and transportation centers.
3. Improved farm equipment and other labor-saving devices made life easier for many Americans.
4. New inventions changed lives in American homes.

The Big Idea

Advances in technology led to new inventions that continued to change daily life and work.

Key Terms and People

Samuel F. B. Morse, *p. 364*
telegraph, *p. 364*
Morse code, *p. 365*
John Deere, *p. 366*
Cyrus McCormick, *p. 366*
Isaac Singer, *p. 367*

HSS 8.6.1 Discuss the influence of industrialization and technological developments on the region, including human modification of the landscape and how physical geography shaped human actions (e.g., growth of cities, deforestation, farming, mineral extraction).

If YOU were there...

You own a small shop in Chicago, Illinois, in the 1850s. You sell ladies' hats and gowns. When you need more hats, you send a letter to the manufacturer in New York. Sometimes it takes weeks for the letter to get there. One day, the owner of the shop next door tells you about a wonderful new machine. It can send orders from Chicago to New York in just minutes!

How would a machine like this change your business?

BUILDING BACKGROUND The Industrial and Transportation revolutions had far-reaching effects on Americans' lives. They led to still more innovations in technology. Some of the new machines and devices speeded up processes for business owners. Others made life easier for people at home.

Telegraph Speeds Communication

In 1832 **Samuel F. B. Morse** perfected the **telegraph** —a device that could send information over wires across great distances. To develop the telegraph, Morse studied electricity and magnetism.

Time Line

American Inventions

1798 Eli Whitney proposed the idea of mass producing guns. Machines like this one made it possible for workers to make interchangeable parts efficiently.

1831 Cyrus McCormick invents the mechanical reaper. Harvesting grain becomes eight times more efficient.

Teach the Big Idea: Master the Standards

Standards Proficiency

More Technological Advances

HSS 8.6.1; HSS **Analysis Skills:** HI 1, HI 2, HI 3

1. **Teach** Ask students the Main Idea questions to teach this section.
2. **Apply** Ask students to imagine that they are writers for an 1800s magazine called "New Technology Today." Have each student write an article describing the new inventions covered in this section and explaining how they are improving life for Americans at home and at work. **LS Verbal/Linguistic**
3. **Review** To review, have volunteers read their articles aloud. Correct any student errors or misconceptions.
4. **Practice/Homework** Have each student, working for the same magazine, write a fictional interview with one of the key people in this section. **LS Verbal/Linguistic**

Alternative Assessment Handbook, Rubric 42: Writing to Inform

Morse put the work of other scientists together in a practical machine.

The telegraph sent pulses, or surges, of electric current through a wire. The telegraph operator tapped a bar, called a telegraph key, that controlled the length of each pulse. At the other end of the wire, these pulses were changed into clicking sounds. A short click was called a dot. A long click was called a dash. Morse's partner, Alfred Lewis Vail, developed a system known as **Morse code**—different combinations of dots and dashes that represent each letter of the alphabet. For example, *dot dot dot, dash dash dash, dot dot dot* is the distress signal called SOS. Skilled telegraph operators could send and receive many words per minute.

Several years passed before Morse was able to connect two locations with telegraph wires. Despite that achievement, people doubted his machine. Some people did not think that he was reading messages sent from miles away. They claimed that he was making lucky guesses.

Morse's break came during the 1844 Democratic National Convention in Baltimore, Maryland. A telegraph wired news of the presidential candidate's nomination to politicians in Washington. The waiting politicians responded, "Three cheers for the telegraph!" Telegraphs were soon sending and receiving information for businesses, the government, newspapers, and private citizens.

BIOGRAPHY

Samuel F. B. Morse
(1791–1872)

Like steamboat creator Robert Fulton, Samuel F. B. Morse began his career as a painter rather than as an inventor. In 1832 Morse was a widower struggling to raise his three children alone. He became interested in the idea of sending messages electrically. Morse hoped he could invent a device that would earn him enough money to support his family. Eventually, earnings from the telegraph made Morse extremely wealthy.

Drawing Conclusions What motivated Morse to invent the telegraph?

The telegraph grew with the railroad. Telegraph companies strung their wires on poles along railroads across the country. They established telegraph offices in many train stations. Thousands of miles of telegraph line were added every year in the 1850s. The first transcontinental line was finished in 1861. By the time he died in 1872, Morse was famous across the United States.

READING CHECK **Identifying Cause and Effect** What event led to the widespread use of the telegraph, and what effect did the telegraph have on cross-country communications?

1832 Samuel F. B. Morse invents the telegraph. Long-distance communication becomes almost instantaneous.

1837 John Deere invents the steel plow. The tough prairie sod can be cut and the thick soil ploughed without having to constantly clean the plow.

Direct Teach

Main Idea

❶ Telegraph Speeds Communication

The telegraph made swift communication possible from coast to coast.

Describe Who invented the telegraph, and what is it? *Samuel F. B. Morse; a device that sends electric pulses through a wire to another location*

Explain How does Morse code work? *A system of dots and dashes or long and short clicks is used to represent the different letters in the alphabet.*

Evaluate What significant event occurred in 1861, and how do you think it changed the nation? *what—completion of the first transcontinental telegraph wire; effects—sped communication, made the nation seem more united, increased business productivity as a result of faster communication*

HSS 8.6.1; HSS **Analysis Skills:** HI 1, HI 2

Linking to Today

Telegraphs: Hello and Goodbye

By 1866, telegraph cables had been run across the Atlantic Ocean. Cable technology of the 1870s enabled multiple uses along a single line. After Thomas Edison patented the telephone in 1876, telegraph and telephone messages shared the same lines. Despite fears that the telephone would replace the telegraph, the technology flourished for many years. Today, modern communication such as e-mail has made the telegraph obsolete.

Activity **New Technology Poster** Have each student create a poster showing a communication device that they predict might replace the cell phone or e-mail.

Differentiating Instruction for Universal Access

Learners Having Difficulty
Reaching Standards | Prep Required

1. Give each student a sheet of paper with the name of an invention described in this section written on it.
2. Have students write brief notes or draw pictures on the reverse side of the paper to describe the invention's purpose, facts about its creation, details about how it influenced society, or its advantages over earlier devices.
3. Have volunteers read or show the clues on the back of their papers and have the rest of the class try to identify the invention.
4. Have students share and keep their papers as study aids. LS **Verbal/Linguistic, Visual/Spatial**

HSS 8.6.1; HSS **Analysis Skills:** HI 1, HI 2, HI 3

Alternative Assessment Handbook, Rubric 1: Acquiring Information

Answers

Biography *wanted to earn enough money to support his family, was interested in the idea of sending messages electronically*

Reading Check *event—Democratic National Convention of 1844; effect—news and information could travel quickly over long distances*

Direct Teach

Main Idea

❷ Steam Power and New Factories

With the shift to steam power, businesses built new factories closer to cities and transportation centers.

Recall What began to replace water power in factories? *steam power*

Identify Cause and Effect How did the use of steam power change where factories were located? *Factories no longer had to be located on streams or waterfalls, so owners began to build factories near cities for better access to workers and markets.*

HSS 8.6.1; HSS **Analysis Skills:** HI 1, HI 2, HI 3

Main Idea

❸ Improved Farm Equipment

Improved farm equipment and other labor-saving devices made life easier for many Americans.

Recall What problem was John Deere trying to solve with his steel plow? *existing iron plows were not strong enough to plow thick soil*

Identify Cause and Effect How did Cyrus McCormick's mechanical reaper change agriculture? *enabled farmers to harvest huge fields*

CRF: Biography Activity: John Deere

HSS 8.6.1; HSS **Analysis Skills:** HI 1, HI 2

Steam Power and New Factories

At the start of the Industrial Revolution, most factories ran on waterpower. In time, however, factory owners began using steam power. This shift brought major changes to the nation's industries. Water-powered factories had to be built near streams or waterfalls. In contrast, steam power allowed business owners to build factories almost anywhere. Yet the Northeast was still home to most of the nation's industry. By 1860 New England alone had as many factories as the entire South did.

Some companies decided to build their factories closer to cities and transportation centers. This provided easier access to workers, allowing businesses to lower wages. Being closer to cities also reduced shipping costs. Cities soon became the center of industrial growth. People from rural areas as well as foreign countries flocked to the cities for factory jobs.

Factory workers improved the designs of many kinds of machines. Mechanics invented tools that could cut and shape metal, stone, and wood with great precision. By the 1840s this new machinery was able to produce interchangeable parts. Within a short period of time, the growing machine-tool industry was even making customized equipment.

READING CHECK **Finding Main Ideas** What changes resulted from the shift to steam power?

Improved Farm Equipment

During the 1830s, technology began transforming the farm as well as the factory. In 1837 blacksmith **John Deere** saw that friends in Illinois had difficulty plowing thick soil with iron plows. He thought a steel blade might work better. His design for a steel plow was a success. By 1846 Deere was selling 1,000 plows per year.

In 1831 **Cyrus McCormick** developed a new harvesting machine, the mechanical reaper, which quickly and efficiently cut down wheat. He began mass producing his reapers in a Chicago factory. McCormick used new methods to encourage sales. His company advertised, gave demonstrations, and provided a repair and spare parts department. He also let customers buy on credit.

The combination of Deere's plow and McCormick's reaper allowed Midwestern farmers to plant and harvest huge crop fields. By 1860, U.S. farmers were producing more than 170 million bushels of wheat and more than 800 million bushels of corn per year.

READING CHECK **Summarizing** What marketing methods did McCormick use to help sell his farm equipment?

American Inventions (continued)

1849 Walter Hunt invents the safety pin.

W. Hunt.
Pin.
No. 6281. Patented Apr. 10. 1849.
Fig. 1. Fig. 2.

UNITED STATES PATENT OFFICE.

WALTER HUNT, OF NEW YORK, N. Y., ASSIGNOR TO WM. RICHARDSON AND JNO. RICHARDSON.

DRESS-PIN.

Specification of Letters Patent No. 6,281, dated April 10, 1849.

To all whom it may concern:
Be it known that I, WALTER HUNT, of the city, county, and State of New York, have invented a new and useful Improvement in the Make or Form of Dress-Pins, of which ...

... to the bar C, (see Figs. 6, 7 and 8,) which combined with the advantages of the spring and catch, renders it equally ornamental, and at the same time more secure and durable than any other plan of a clasp pin, heretofore in use, there being no joint to break or ... get loose as in other plans.

1851 Isaac Singer improves the sewing machine. The production and repair of clothing becomes much easier.

Collaborative Learning

Standards Proficiency

New Technology Jingles HSS 8.6.1; HSS **Analysis Skills:** HI 1, HI 2

Materials: recordings of product jingles (optional)

1. Organize students into small groups. Assign each group one of the inventions or advances in technology mentioned in this section.
2. Have each group write a jingle promoting either the sale of the item or its use (such as the use of the telegraph service).
3. If possible, play recordings of some product jingles for students before they start working. Allow the groups to select existing tunes to use for their jingles.
4. Have each group practice its jingle and then perform it for the class. LS **Interpersonal, Verbal/Linguistic**

Alternative Assessment Handbook, Rubrics 2: Advertisements; and 26: Poems and Songs

Answers

Reading Check (left) *Factories were built closer to cities, which led to lower wages and shipping costs, made cities industrial centers, drew immigrants and rural people, and led to urban growth.*

Reading Check (right) *advertisements, demonstrations, provided repair and spare parts departments, offered credit*

Changing Life at Home

Many inventions of the Industrial Revolution simply made life easier. When Alexis de Tocqueville of France visited the United States in the early 1830s, he identified what he called a very American quality.

> "[Americans want] to be always making life more comfortable and convenient, to avoid trouble, and to satisfy the smallest wants [desires] without effort and almost without cost."
>
> —Alexis de Tocqueville, from *Democracy in America*

The sewing machine was one of these conveniences. Elias Howe, a factory apprentice in Lowell, Massachusetts, first invented it. **Isaac Singer** then made improvements to Howe's design. Like McCormick, Singer allowed customers to buy his machines on credit and provided service. By 1860 Singer's company was the world's largest maker of sewing machines.

Other advances improved on everyday items. In the 1830s, iceboxes cooled by large blocks of ice became available. Iceboxes stored fresh food safely for longer periods. Iron cookstoves began replacing cooking fires and stone hearths.

Companies also began to mass produce earlier inventions. This allowed many families to buy household items, such as clocks, that they could not afford in the past. For example, a clock that cost $50 in 1800 was selling for only $1.50 by the 1850s. Additional useful items created during this period include matches introduced in the 1830s, and the safety pin, invented in 1849. All of these inventions helped make life at home more convenient for an increasing number of Americans.

THE IMPACT TODAY New inventions, such as cell phones, laptop computers, and microwave ovens, continue to make life easier and more convenient for people today.

READING CHECK **Analyzing** How did labor-saving inventions affect daily life?

SUMMARY AND PREVIEW New machines and inventions changed the way Americans lived and did business in the early 1800s. In the next section you will learn how agricultural changes affected the South.

1859 Manufactured goods become more valuable than agricultural goods in the country's economy for the first time. The United States is becoming a modern industrial nation.

ANALYSIS SKILL READING TIME LINES

Which two inventions improved American agriculture?

Section 4 Assessment

go.hrw.com Online Quiz KEYWORD: SS8 HP11

Reviewing Ideas, Terms, and People HSS 8.6.1

1. a. **Describe** How did the **telegraph** work?
   b. **Predict** What impact might the telegraph have on the future of the United States?
2. a. **Describe** How did waterpowered factories differ from steam-powered factories?
   b. **Explain** How did the shift to steam power lead to the growth of cities?
3. a. **Identify** What contributions did **Cyrus McCormick** and **John Deere** make to farming?
   b. **Analyze** What effect did new inventions have on agriculture in the United States?
4. a. **Identify** What inventions improved life at home?
   b. **Evaluate** Which invention do you think had the greatest effect on the daily lives of Americans? Why?

Critical Thinking

5. **Identifying Cause and Effect** Copy the diagram below. Use it to show the effects that new advances had on the United States.

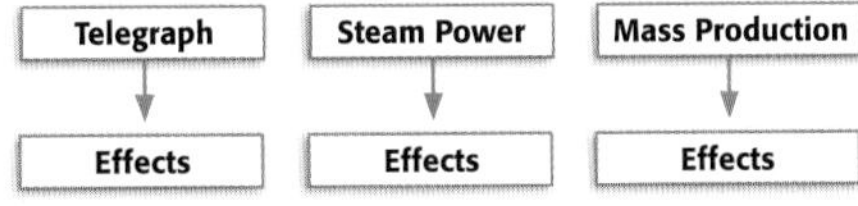

FOCUS ON WRITING

6. **Describing Technological Advances** Add notes about the inventions mentioned in this section to your chart. Think about which invention you will use for your newspaper advertisement.

Direct Teach

Main Idea

❹ Changing Life at Home

New inventions changed lives in American homes.

Explain What other new inventions improved daily life for Americans? *sewing machine, icebox, iron cookstove, matches, safety pin*

Evaluate Do you think de Tocqueville's opinion of Americans is still true today? Why or why not? *possible answer—Yes, because Americans continue to create devices to improve life.*

CRF: Interdisciplinary Project: Using Measurements

HSS 8.6.1; HSS **Analysis Skills:** HR 4, HI 1, HI 2

Review & Assess

Close

Briefly review the ways in which new technology and inventions changed American life and business.

Review

go.hrw.com Online Quiz, Section 4

Assess

SE Section 4 Assessment

PASS: Section 4 Quiz

Alternative Assessment Handbook

Reteach/Classroom Intervention

California Standards Review Workbook

Interactive Reader and Study Guide, Section 4

Interactive Skills Tutor CD-ROM

Section 4 Assessment Answers

1. **a.** sent pulses of current through a wire, pulses were changed into clicking sounds. A code assigned letters to different clicks.
   b. more unified nation, business growth
2. **a.** Water-powered factories had to be located near running water; steam-powered factories could be built almost anywhere.
   b. Factories were built closer to cities, which drew immigrants and people from rural areas.
3. **a.** McCormick—mechanical reaper; Deere—steel plow
   b. larger harvests, ability to farm more land
4. **a.** sewing machine, icebox, iron cookstove, matches, safety pin
   b. Answers will vary but should reflect an knowledge of the effects of new inventions.
5. Telegraph—Information could travel quickly over long distances; Steam Power—factories moved, people moved to cities, cities grew; Mass Production—more families were able to buy useful household items, such as clocks
6. Students should describe the inventions.

Answers

Reading Time Lines *steel plow, mechanical reaper*

Reading Check *People could do things faster and more easily and conveniently, had more time for leisure.*

Social Studies Skills

Personal Conviction and Bias

Activity Bias in the News

Materials: copies of newspaper front and editorial pages

1. Pass out photocopies of the editorial page and the front page from a local newspaper. Have students contrast the articles that appear on each page. Guide students in determining that the front-page news coverage is mainly objective reporting of facts. The editorial page likely contains many opinionated items.
2. Next, have students examine the editorials and letters to the editor. Ask students to identify any biases the writers might hold. How are these biases shaping the writers' viewpoints and opinions? See if students can find examples of stereotyping or prejudice.
3. Then assign students one editorial or letter to the editor. Have each students create a three-column chart listing the verifiable statements, or facts; the unverifiable statements, or opinions; and any examples of bias. Review students' charts as a class.

LS Verbal/Linguistic

Alternative Assessment Handbook, Rubric 7: Charts

Interactive Skills Tutor CD-ROM, Lesson 20: Evaluate Sources of Information for Authenticity, Reliability, and Bias

Social Studies Skills

Analysis | Critical Thinking | **Participation** | Study

HSS Participation Develop social and political participation skills.

Personal Conviction and Bias

Define the Skill

Everyone has *convictions,* or firmly-held beliefs. However, when we let our beliefs automatically slant or shape our point of view on topics, we may be showing bias. *Bias* is a fixed idea or opinion about someone or something. Some bias is based on a set of ideas about a group to which the person or thing belongs. This type of bias is called a *stereotype.* If the group is defined by race, religion, age, gender, or similar characteristics, the bias is known as *prejudice.*

Bias, stereotypes, and prejudice are not always negative in nature. They include favorable opinions too. For example, the belief a student is good at math because that person is male is a bias that shows both stereotyping and prejudice.

We should always be on guard for the presence of personal bias. Eliminating stereotyping and prejudice is particularly important. However, even "good" biases can slant how we view, judge, and communicate information. Honest and accurate communication requires that the information and ideas we express be as free of bias as possible.

Learn the Skill

Not all beliefs are biases, even if those beliefs are strongly held. Biases are beliefs that have little or no evidence to support them. The more unreasonable a person's view is in light of facts and evidence, the more likely it is that the belief is a bias.

Another characteristic of bias is the person's reluctance to question his or her belief if it is challenged by evidence. Sometimes people stubbornly cling to views that overwhelming evidence proves wrong. This is why bias is defined as a "fixed" idea or opinion. One of the most damaging effects of bias, and a good reason for trying to avoid it, is that it can prevent us from learning new things.

The following precautions can help you to reduce the amount of bias you hold and express.

1. When discussing a topic, keep in mind beliefs and experiences in your own background that might affect how you feel about the topic.
2. Try to not mix statements of fact with statements of opinion. Clearly separate and indicate what you *know* to be true from what you *believe* to be true.
3. Avoid using emotional, positive, or negative words when communicating factual information.

Practice the Skill

In 1834 Tennessee congressman Davy Crockett visited the textile mills at Lowell, Massachusetts. Read his account of the "Lowell girls" who worked in the factory and complete the activity below.

> "Here are thousands [of young women], useful to others, ...with the prospect before them of future comfort and respectability ...There are more than five thousand females employed in Lowell; and when you come to see the amount of labour performed by them, in superintending [operating] the different machinery, you will be astonished."

Suppose that you were a "Lowell girl" who has just read this account of Crockett's visit. Write a letter to the editor of the *Lowell Offering* reacting to the biases and stereotypes about women that Crockett shows in his account.

Social Studies Skills Activity: Personal Conviction and Bias

Identifying Bias in Primary Sources

Standards Proficiency

1. Have students review "Primary Source: Sarah G. Bagley and Workers' Rights" in Section 2 of this chapter.
2. Write the following questions for students to see. Have students work in pairs or in small groups to answer the questions.
   - What beliefs and experiences in Bagley's background might have shaped her views?
   - What opinions does she present?
   - What emotional or negative language does she use?
   - What biases and stereotypes does the passage reveal?
3. Discuss students' answers as a class. If time allows, have students compare and contrast the biases of Crockett to those of Bagley.

LS Interpersonal, Verbal/Linguistic

Alternative Assessment Handbook, Rubric 16: Judging Information

Answers

Practice the Skill *Answers will vary, but students should note that Crockett assumes that the work the women are doing makes them useful and will help ensure their respectability. He also thinks everyone will be astonished to see the amount and type of work the women are doing.*

CHAPTER 11

Standards Review

Visual Summary

Use the visual summary below to help you review the main ideas of the chapter.

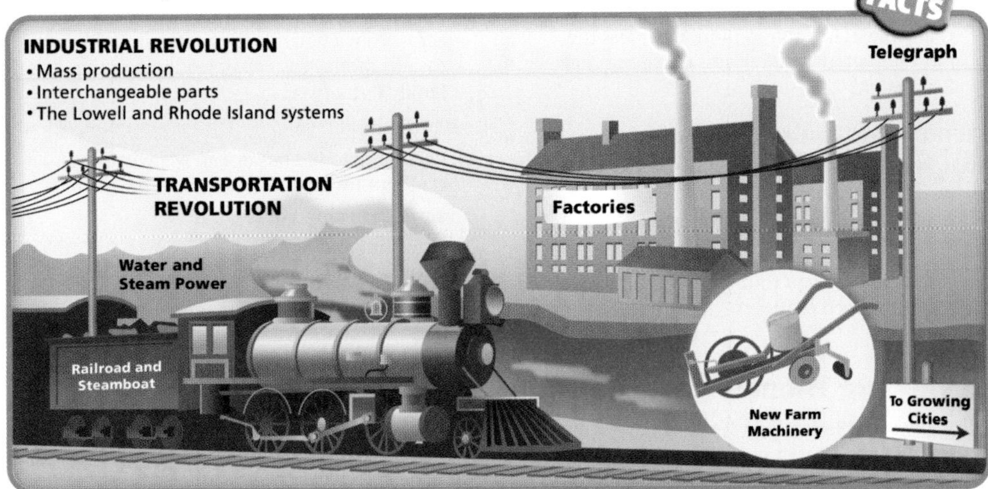

Reviewing Vocabulary, Terms, and People

Complete each sentence below by filling in the blank with the correct term or person from the chapter.

1. The system of ____________ was developed to represent letters of the alphabet when sending telegraph messages.
2. The first American woman to hold a high-ranking position in the labor movement was ______________________________.
3. The ___________ was a period of rapid growth in the use of machines and manufacturing.
4. The first locomotive in the United States was built by ______________________________.
5. Workers would sometimes go on _________ to force factory owners to meet their demands for better pay and working conditions.
6. The ___________ industry, which produced cloth items, was the first to use machines for manufacturing.

Comprehension and Critical Thinking

SECTION 1 *(Pages 346–351)* **HSS 8.6.1**

7. **a. Identify** What ideas did Eli Whitney want to apply to the manufacture of guns?
   b. Analyze How did the War of 1812 lead to a boom in manufacturing in the United States?
   c. Elaborate Why do you think the Industrial Revolution began in Great Britain rather than in the United States?

SECTION 2 *(Pages 352–357)* **HSS 8.6.1**

8. **a. Describe** What was mill life like?
   b. Draw Conclusions How did the Rhode Island system and the Lowell system change the lives of American workers?
   c. Evaluate Were reformers such as Sarah G. Bagley effective in improving labor conditions? Why?

Answers

Visual Summary

Review and Inquiry Each of the inventions shown in the picture can be seen as in some way contributing to the growth of cities. Have students list the key events and people connected to each invention shown. Then have each student write a paragraph describing how the visual summary illustrates the overall effects of the Industrial Revolution.

Quick Facts Transparency: The North Visual Summary

Reviewing Vocabulary, Terms, and People

1. Morse code
2. Sarah G. Bagley
3. Industrial Revolution
4. Peter Cooper
5. strike
6. textile

Comprehension and Critical Thinking

7. **a.** interchangeable parts and the use of machines powered by water
   b. The War of 1812 stopped the export of many foreign goods, which led Americans to buy American goods, which in turn increased manufacturing.
   c. possible answer—Great Britain had more trouble meeting the demand for goods, which led to the development of machines to improve efficiency.

Review and Assessment Resources

Review and Reinforce

- SE Standards Review
- CRF: Chapter Review Activity
- California Standards Review Workbook
- Quick Facts Transparency: The North Visual Summary
- Spanish Chapter Summaries Audio CD Program
- Online Chapter Summaries in Six Languages
- OSP Holt PuzzlePro; GameTool for ExamView
- Quiz Game CD-ROM

Assess

- SE Standards Assessment
- PASS: Chapter Test, Forms A and B
- Alternative Assessment Handbook
- OSP ExamView Test Generator, Chapter Test
- Universal Access Modified Worksheets and Tests CD-ROM: Chapter Test
- Holt Online Assessment Program (in the Premier Online Edition)

Reteach/Intervene

- Interactive Reader and Study Guide
- Universal Access Teacher Management System: Lesson Plans for Universal Access
- Universal Access Modified Worksheets and Tests CD-ROM
- Interactive Skills Tutor CD-ROM

go.hrw.com
Online Resources
Chapter Resources:
KEYWORD: SS8 US11

Answers

8. a. monotonous work for long hours; sometimes dangerous
b. Many people, including women and children, moved to towns or cities and began working in factories instead of on farms or at home.
c. possible answers—Yes, several states passed 10-hour workday laws; no, success was limited because the courts and police supported the owners.
9. a. business and trade grew; improved travel for people
b. possible answers—They had a successful business that the country depended upon, owned lots of land, and were a huge employer.
c. Students' answers will vary, but should reflect an understanding of the ways in which the Transportation Revolution changed the economy and life in the United States.
10. a. shifted to using steam power, which enabled factories to be built almost anywhere
b. People could communicate quickly over long distances.
c. Answers will vary, but students should consider working conditions in factories and how factories affected the local environment, such as through increased pollution.

Reviewing Themes

11. Students might mention the water frame, the steam engine, the steamboat, the railroad, the telegraph, the mechanical reaper, the sewing machine, the icebox, or even matches or safety pins. Students should provide reasons to support their selections.
12. The Industrial Revolution created a boom in business and led to economic growth and expansion. With advances in manufacturing, agriculture, transportation, and communication, farms and businesses were able to produce more goods faster and at lower prices, and trade increased.

SECTION 3 *(Pages 358–363)* **HSS 8.6.1**

9. **a. Describe** How were Americans affected by the introduction of steamboats?
b. Make Inferences How did railroad companies become some of the most powerful businesses in the country?
c. Elaborate In your opinion, what was the most important result of the Transportation Revolution?

SECTION 4 *(Pages 364–367)* **HSS 8.6.1**

10. **a. Recall** What important change took place in how factories were powered?
b. Draw Conclusions How did the telegraph affect communication in the United States?
c. Evaluate Do you think moving factories close to cities helped or hurt working life? Explain.

Reviewing Themes

11. **Science and Technology** Rank what you think are the three most important inventions of the Industrial Revolution. Explain your choices.
12. **Economics** What was the overall effect of the Industrial Revolution on the U.S. economy?

Using the Internet

13. **Activity: Advertisement** The Industrial Revolution changed the way goods were produced. New inventions created easier, faster, or completely new ways of doing things. Enter the activity keyword and research inventions made between 1790 and 1860. Then create an advertisement for one of the inventions that might have appeared in a magazine during that time in history.

Reading Skills

Understanding Cause and Effect Structure *Use the Reading Skills taught in this chapter to answer the question about the reading selection below.*

> Many young women came to Lowell from across New England. They wanted the chance to earn money instead of working on the family farm. *(p. 354)*

14. According to the passage above, what was a cause for moving to Lowell?
a. working long hours
b. earning money
c. meeting people
d. working on a farm

Social Studies Skills

Personal Conviction and Bias *Use the Social Studies Skills taught in this chapter to answer the question about the reading selection below.*

> "Is anyone such a fool as to suppose that out of six thousand factory girls in Lowell, sixty would be there if they could help it?"
> —Sarah G. Bagley, quoted in *The Belles of New England* by William Moran

15. Do you think that Bagley's opposition to the Lowell system was unfairly biased? Why or why not?

FOCUS ON WRITING

16. **Writing Your Newspaper Advertisement** Look over your chart, and choose one invention for your advertisement. Then answer these questions to help you plan your advertisement: Who is your audience? Who will buy this invention? How will the invention benefit this audience? What words or phrases will best persuade this audience? Once you have answered these questions, design your advertisement. To draw readers' attention to your ad, include an illustration, a catchy heading, and a few lines of text.

Using the Internet

13. Go to the HRW Web site and enter the keyword shown to access a rubric for this activity.

KEYWORD: SS8 TEACHER

Reading Skills

14. b

Social Studies Skills

15. Answers will vary, but students should exhibit an understanding of bias and provide examples from the reading selection to support their positions.

Focus on Writing

16. **Rubric** Students' newspaper advertisements should
- briefly describe the invention
- explain the benefits of the invention and who can use it
- be persuasive
- include an illustration and catchy heading that grabs readers' attention

CRF: Focus on Writing: Newspaper Advertisement

Standards Assessment

DIRECTIONS: Read each question and write the letter of the best response.

1

> "The little money I could earn—one dollar a week, besides the price of my board—was needed in the family, and I must return [from home] to the mill . . . I began to reflect on life rather seriously for a girl of twelve or thirteen. What was I here for? What would I make of myself? . . . We did not forget that we were working girls . . . clearing away a few weeds from the overgrown track of independent labor for other women . . . [so that] no real odium [disrespect] could be attached to any honest toil that any self-respecting woman might undertake."
>
> —from *A New England Girlhood* by Lucy Larcom (1824–1893)

From the content of this passage, you can determine that the writer was commenting about

A the mass-production system.
B the Lowell system.
C the Rhode Island system.
D the trade union system.

2 The first machines of the Industrial Revolution were powered by

A electricity.
B water.
C animals.
D coal.

3 The earliest important evidence of the Industrial Revolution in America was found in

A the way cotton was processed for market.
B the production of tobacco products.
C the manufacture of cloth and thread.
D the construction of the first steam railroads.

4 The Transportation Revolution of the mid-1800s had all of the following effects *except*

A reducing the time and cost of shipping products.
B helping to create a boom in business and agriculture across the nation.
C making travel upstream on rivers faster and easier.
D limiting the federal government's ability to control trade among states.

5 What change in technology allowed business owners to sell their goods in markets across the country?

A the Lowell system
B the growth of railroads
C the invention of the telegraph
D the Arkwright system

Connecting with Past Learning

6 Which inventor's contribution that you learned about in Grade 7 changed the world in much the same way that Samuel F. B. Morse's invention changed it during the Industrial Revolution?

A Marco Polo
B Archimedes
C Johannes Gutenberg
D Sir Isaac Newton

7 The economic growth and change that the Industrial and Transportation revolutions brought to America were *most* like earlier economic changes that occurred in

A Japan.
B India.
C Africa.
D England and Holland.

Answers

1. B
Break Down the Question: Point out to students that the source and author of a reading selection often provides a clue to what the selection is about. For example, the name of the source and the author here reveal that the speaker was a New England girl, and thus likely a Lowell girl.

2. B
Break Down the Question: This question requires students to place events in their correct sequence. Point out that the question focuses on the Industrial Revolution, which eliminates options A and C.

3. C
Break Down the Question: This question requires students to recall factual information. Refer students who have trouble to Section 1.

4. D
Break Down the Question: This question requires students to identify cause and effect. Remind students that the word *except* means they should choose the answer that is *not* an effect of the Industrial Revolution.

5. B
Break Down the Question: This question requires students to identify cause and effect. Refer students who have trouble to Section 3.

6. C
Break Down the Question: This question connects to information covered in Grade 7.

7. D
Break Down the Question: This question connects to information covered in Grade 7.

Intervention Resources

Reproducible

- Interactive Reader and Study Guide
- Universal Access Teacher Management System: Lesson Plans for Universal Access

Technology

- Quick Facts Transparency: The North Visual Summary
- Universal Access Modified Worksheets and Tests CD-ROM
- Interactive Skills Tutor CD-ROM

Tips for Test Taking

Go With Your Gut When taking tests, a person's first impulse about an answer is many times correct. Tell students to consider carefully before changing their answers to multiple choice or true-false questions. If students do decide to change an answer, they should do so because they are confident about the change.

Standards Review

Have students review the following standards in their workbooks.

- California Standards Review Workbook: HSS 8.6.1

Chapter 12 Planning Guide

The South

Chapter Overview	Reproducible Resources	Technology Resources
CHAPTER 12 pp. 372–395 **Overview: In this chapter, students will study the development of the South's social structure during the early 1800s.** See p. 372 for the California History–Social Science standards covered in this chapter.	**Universal Access Teacher Management System:*** • Universal Access Instructional Benchmarking Guides • Lesson Plans for Universal Access **Interactive Reader and Study Guide:*** Chapter Graphic Organizer **Chapter Resource File*** • Focus on Writing Activity: Biographical Sketch • Social Studies Skills Activity: Interpreting Graphs • Chapter Review Activity	**One-Stop Planner CD-ROM:** Calendar Planner **Student Edition Full-Read Audio CD-ROM** **Universal Access Modified Worksheets and Tests CD-ROM** **Interactive Skills Tutor CD-ROM** **Primary Source Library CD-ROM for United States History** **Power Presentation with Video CD-ROM** **History's Impact: United States History Video Program (VHS/DVD):** The South* **A Teacher's Guide to Religion in the Public Schools***
Section 1: **Growth of the Cotton Industry** **The Big Idea:** The invention of the cotton gin made the South a one-crop economy and increased the need for slave labor. 8.7.1, 8.7.2	**Universal Access Teacher Management System:*** Section 1 Lesson Plan **Interactive Reader and Study Guide:*** Section 1 Summary **Chapter Resource File*** • Vocabulary Builder, Section 1 • Biography Activity: Eli Whitney • History and Geography Activity: Cotton in the South	**Daily Bellringer Transparency:** Section 1* **Map Transparency:** The Cotton Kingdom* go.hrw.com **Internet Activity:** Tredegar Iron Works Report
Section 2: **Free Southern Society** **The Big Idea:** Southern society centered around agriculture 8.7.3, 8.7.4, 8.9.6	**Universal Access Teacher Management System:*** Section 2 Lesson Plan **Interactive Reader and Study Guide:*** Section 2 Summary **Chapter Resource File*** • Vocabulary Builder, Section 2 • Biography Activity: Mary Boykin Chesnut • Literature Activity: *Plantation Life Before Emancipation,* by R. Q. Mallard, D. D. • Primary Source Activity: Frances Anne Kemble, *Journal of a Residence on a Georgian Plantation*	**Daily Bellringer Transparency:** Section 2*
Section 3: **The Slave System** **The Big Idea:** The slave system in the South produced harsh living conditions and occasional rebellions. 8.7.2	**Universal Access Teacher Management System:*** Section 3 Lesson Plan **Interactive Reader and Study Guide:*** Section 3 Summary **Chapter Resource File*** • Vocabulary Builder, Section 3 • Biography Activity: Nat Turner • Biography Activity: Denmark Vesey • Primary Source Activity: The Denmark Vesey Conspiracy • Primary Source Activity: Jacob Stroyer, *My Life in the South*	**Daily Bellringer Transparency:** Section 3* **Map Transparency:** Nat Turner's Rebellion* go.hrw.com **Internet Activity:** Slave Cabin Drawings

MASTERING THE CALIFORNIA STANDARDS

SE Student Edition  Print Resource Audio CD Video

TE Teacher's Edition  Transparency  CD-ROM DVD

go.hrw.com go.hrw.com CA Standards Mastery LS Learning Styles

OSP One-Stop Planner CD-ROM * also on One-Stop Planner CD

Review, Assessment, Intervention

- **Standards Review Workbook***
- **Quick Facts Transparency:** The South Visual Summary*
- **Spanish Chapter Summaries Audio CD Program**
- **Online Chapter Summaries in Six Languages**
- **Quiz Game CD-ROM**
- **Progress Assessment Support System (PASS):** Chapter Test*
- **Universal Access Modified Worksheets and Tests CD-ROM:** Modified Chapter Test
- **One-Stop Planner CD-ROM:** ExamView Test Generator (English/Spanish)
- **Alternative Assessment Handbook**
- **Holt Online Assessment Program (HOAP),** in the Holt Premier Online Student Edition

---

- **PASS:** Section 1 Quiz*
- **Online Quiz:** Section 1
- **Alternative Assessment Handbook**

- **PASS:** Section 2 Quiz*
- **Online Quiz:** Section 2
- **Alternative Assessment Handbook**

- **PASS:** Section 3 Quiz*
- **Online Quiz:** Section 3
- **Alternative Assessment Handbook**

California Resources for Standards Mastery

INSTRUCTIONAL PLANNING AND SUPPORT

- **Universal Access Teacher Management System***
- **One-Stop Planner CD-ROM with Test Generator: Teacher Management System with Interactive Teacher's Edition**

STANDARDS MASTERY

- **Standards Review Workbook***
- **At Home: A Guide to Standards Mastery for United States History**

go.hrw.com Holt Online Learning

To enhance learning, Internet activities are available for a Tredegar Iron Works Report and Slave Cabin Drawings.

KEYWORD: SS8 TEACHER

- **Teacher Support Page**
- **Content Updates**
- **Rubrics and Writing Models**
- **Teaching Tips for the Multimedia Classroom**

KEYWORD: SS8 US12

- **Current Events**
- **Document-Based Questions**
- **Holt Grapher**
- **Holt Online Atlas**
- **Holt Researcher**
- **Interactive Multimedia Activities**
- **Internet Activities**
- **Online Chapter Summaries in Six Languages**
- **Online Section Quizzes**
- **American History Maps and Charts**

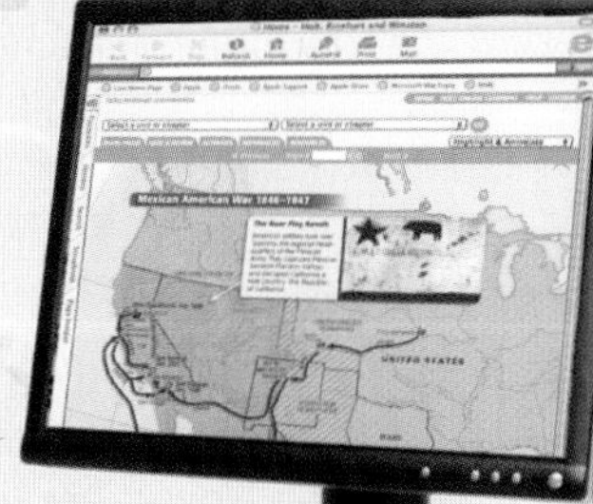

HOLT PREMIER ONLINE STUDENT EDITION

Complete online support for interactivity, assessment, and reporting

- **Interactive Maps and Notebook**
- **Standardized Test Prep**
- **Homework Practice and Research Activities Online**

Mastering the Standards: Differentiating Instruction

Reaching Standards	Basic-level activities designed for all students encountering new material
Standards Proficiency	Intermediate-level activities designed for average students
Exceeding Standards	Challenging activities designed for honors and gifted-and-talented students
Standard English Mastery	Activities designed to improve standard English usage

Frequently Asked Questions

INSTRUCTIONAL PLANNING AND SUPPORT

Where do I find planning aids, pacing guides, lesson plans, and other teaching aids?

Annotated Teacher's Edition:
- Chapter planning guides
- Standards-based instruction and strategies
- Differentiated instruction for universal access
- Point-of-use reminders for integrating program resources

Power Presentations with Video CD-ROM

Universal Access Teacher Management System:
- Year and unit instructional benchmarking guides
- Reproducible lesson plans
- Assessment guides for diagnostic, progress, and summative end-of-the-year tests
- Options for differentiating instruction and intervention
- Teaching guides and answer keys for student workbooks

One-Stop Planner CD-ROM with Test Generator: Teacher Management System with Interactive Teacher's Editon:
- Calendar Planner
- Editable lesson plans
- All reproducible ancillaries in Adobe Acrobat (PDF) format
- ExamView Test Generator (English & Spanish)
- Game Tool for ExamView
- PuzzlePro
- Transparency and video previews

DIFFERENTIATING INSTRUCTION FOR UNIVERSAL ACCESS

What resources are available to ensure that Advanced Learners/GATE Students master the standards?

Teacher's Edition Activities:
- Dependence on Cotton Editorial, p. 380
- Slavery: An Oral History, p. 388
- Nat Turner Dialogue, p. 390

Lesson Plans for Universal Access

Primary Source Library CD-ROM for United States History

What resources are available to ensure that English Learners and Standard English Learners master the standards?

Teacher's Edition Activities:
- Challenging the Slavery System, p. 390

Lesson Plans for Universal Access

Chapter Resource File: Vocabulary Builder Activities

Spanish Chapter Summaries Audio CD Program

Online Chapter Summaries in Six Languages

One-Stop Planner CD-ROM:
- PuzzlePro, Spanish Version
- ExamView Test Generator, Spanish Version

What modified materials are available for Special Education?

The *Universal Access Modified Worksheets and Tests CD-ROM* provides editable versions of the following:

Vocabulary Flash Cards

Modified Vocabulary Builder Activities

Modified Chapter Review Activity

Modified Chapter Test

What resources are available to ensure that Learners Having Difficulty master the standards?

Teacher's Edition Activities:
- Cotton Boom Analysis, p. 378
- Life in the Urban South, p. 384
- Slave Category Identification, p. 387

Interactive Reader and Study Guide

Student Edition Full-Read Audio CD

Quick Facts Transparency: The South Visual Summary

Standards Review Workbook

Social Studies Skills Activity: Interpreting Graphs

Interactive Skills Tutor CD-ROM

How do I intervene for students struggling to master the standards?

Interactive Reader and Study Guide

Quick Facts Transparency: The South Visual Summary

Standards Review Workbook

Social Studies Skills Activity: Interpreting Graphs

Interactive Skills Tutor CD-ROM

PROFESSIONAL DEVELOPMENT

What teacher training resources are available to help me grow professionally?

- In-service and staff development as part of your Holt Social Studies product purchase
- Quick Teacher Tutorial Lesson Presentation CD-ROM
- Intensive tuition-based Teacher Development Institute
- *Teaching American History* Online 2 Module Professional Development Course
- Convenient Holt Speaker Bureau face-to-face workshop options
- PRAXIS™ Test Prep (#0089) interactive Web-based content refreshers*
- 24/7 *Ask A Professional Development Expert* at http://www.hrw.com/prodev/

* PRAXIS is a trademark of Educational Testing Service (ETS). This publication is not endorsed or approved by ETS.

Information Literacy Skills

To learn more about how History–Social Science instruction may be improved by the effective use of library media centers and information literacy skills, go to the Teacher's Resource Materials for Chapter 12 at **go.hrw.com**, keyword: SS8 MEDIA.

The following materials were developed by the Division for Public Education of the American Bar Association. These materials are part of the **Democracy and Civic Education** supplement.
- Constitution Study Guide
- Supreme Court Case Studies

MASTERING THE CALIFORNIA STANDARDS

• Chapter Preview •

Standards Focus

Standards by Section
Section 1: HSS 8.7.1, 8.7.2
Section 2: HSS 8.7.3, 8.7.4, 8.9.6
Section 3: HSS 8.7.2

Teacher's Edition
HSS **Analysis Skills:** CS 1, HR 4, HR 5, HI 1, HI 2, HI 3, HI 6
ELA Writing 8.2.1.c; Reading 8.2.2

Preview Grade 8 Standards
HSS **8.10** Students analyze the multiple causes, key events, and complex consequences of the Civil War.
8.10.2 Trace the boundaries constituting the North and the South, the geographical differences between the two regions, and the differences between agrarians and industrialists.

Focus on Writing

The **Chapter Resource File** provides a Focus on Writing worksheet to help students organize and write their biographical sketches.

CRF: Focus on Writing Activity: Biographical Sketch

CHAPTER 12 1790–1860

The South

California Standards

History–Social Science

8.7 Students analyze the divergent paths of the American people in the South from 1800 to the mid-1800s and the challenges they faced.

8.9 Students analyze the early and steady attempts to abolish slavery and to realize the ideals of the Declaration of Independence.

English–Language Arts

Writing 8.2.1.c Employ narrative and descriptive strategies.

Reading 8.2.2 Analyze text that uses proposition and support patterns.

FOCUS ON WRITING

Biographical Sketch In this chapter you will learn about life in the South during the first half of the nineteenth century. Read the chapter, and then write a two-paragraph biographical sketch about a day in the life of a person living on a large cotton farm in the South. You might choose to write about a wealthy male landowner, his wife, or an enslaved man or woman working on the farm. As you read, think about what life would have been like for the different people who lived and worked on the farm. Take notes about farm life in your notebook.

UNITED STATES

1793 Eli Whitney invents the cotton gin.

1800

1794 France ends slavery in its colonies.

WORLD

Introduce the Chapter

Standards Proficiency

Impact of Technology HSS 8.7; HSS Analysis Skills: HI 1, HI 2, HI 3

1. Tell students that in this chapter they will learn how a single invention revived the economy the South.
2. Have students think of new technology and inventions that they have seen in their lifetimes *(e.g., cell phone, DVD, GPS).* Write the answers for students to see.
3. Then ask students how life has changed because of each new piece of technology or invention. What impact has there been on jobs, communication, and leisure, for example? Are there health or safety issues related to the new invention or technology? Can students predict other changes that might occur in their lifetimes? LS **Verbal/Linguistic**

HOLT
History's Impact
▶ video series
Watch the video to understand the impact of regional economies on national culture.

What You Will Learn...

These enslaved people were photographed on a South Carolina plantation in the year 1861. The issue of slavery would have a serious and dramatic impact on the history of the entire United States. In this chapter you will learn how the South developed an agricultural economy, and how that economy was dependent on the labor of enslaved people.

1808 A congressional ban on importing slaves into the United States takes effect.

1831 Nat Turner's Rebellion leads to fears of further slave revolts in the South.

1848 Joseph R. Anderson becomes the owner of the Tredegar Iron Works, the South's only large iron factory.

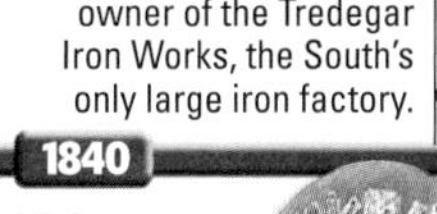

1820 — 1840 — 1860

1807 Parliament bans the slave trade in the British Empire.

1835 Alexis de Tocqueville publishes *Democracy in America.*

1837 Victoria is crowned queen of Great Britain.

1858 A treaty at Tianjin, China, gives Hong Kong to the United Kingdom.

• Chapter Preview •

HOLT
History's Impact
▶ **video series**
See the Video Teacher's Guide for strategies for using the chapter video **The South**.

Chapter Big Ideas

Section 1 The invention of the cotton gin made the South a one-crop economy and increased the need for slave labor. HSS 8.7.1, 8.7.2

Section 2 Southern society centered around agriculture. HSS 8.7.3, 8.7.4, 8.9.6

Section 3 The slave system in the South produced harsh living conditions and occasional rebellions. HSS 8.7.2

Explore the Picture

Life on a Southern Plantation

From sunrise to sunset, enslaved Africans' lives were controlled. A ringing bell or blowing horn called workers to the fields before dawn. On cotton plantations, June was a particularly hard month because the fields had to be broken up by hand with tools. Under the glare of the hot sun, each adult slave was expected to break up a half acre of ground per day.

Analyzing Visuals What evidence can you see in the photo that life for enslaved Africans on a southern plantation was harsh? *possible answer—The people shown have no shoes; they carry hand tools; they are not smiling.*

go.hrw.com
Online Resources
Chapter Resources:
KEYWORD: SS8 US12
Teacher Resources:
KEYWORD: SS8 TEACHER

Explore the Time Line

1. What did Eli Whitney invent in 1793? *the cotton gin*
2. In what year did the U.S. Congress ban the import of slaves into the country? *1808*
3. Which two countries limited aspects of slavery and the slave trade prior to the 1808 U.S. ban? *France and Great Britain*
4. What effect did Nat Turner's Rebellion in 1831 have? *fears of further slave revolts in the South*

HSS **Analysis Skills:** CS 1

Info to Know

Congressional Ban on Importing Slaves Even though the United States banned the importation of enslaved Africans in 1808, the ban did not undermine or end slavery. Planters in need of labor in Georgia and South Carolina hurried to beat the ban by importing tens of thousands of enslaved Africans before the ban took effect. The illegal smuggling of slaves continued, and the slave population increased as children—the next generation of slaves—were born into slavery.

Reading Social Studies

Understanding Themes

Two themes, economics and culture, are presented in this chapter about the South. Ask students to recall ways in which the economy of the South was different than that of the rest of the United States. Remind students that the South depended economically on agriculture. Then ask students to predict how the society and culture of the South might have been affected by this reliance on agriculture. Ask students to write down their predictions and to see which ones are correct as they read the chapter.

Online Research

Focus on Reading Organize the class into small groups. Have students in each group discuss their Internet use and Web sites that they find useful for conducting research. Ask groups to list what they find most valuable about those sites, such as quality of information, layout, and ease of use. Remind students that not all Web sites contain verifiable information. Ask students to list how they determine the quality of information when they are using the Internet. Have each group report its opinions to the class. Discuss the qualities of a Web site that are most important to consider when conducting research.

Reading Social Studies

by Kylene Beers

Economics | Geography | Politics | Religion | Society and Culture | Science and Technology

Focus on Themes This chapter takes you into the heart of the South from 1800 through he mid-1800s. As you read, you will discover that the South depended on cotton as its **economic** backbone, especially after the invention of the cotton gin. You will also read about the slave system in the South during this time and about the harsh living conditions slaves endured. As you will see, the South was home to a variety of **societies and cultures**.

Online Research

Focus on Reading Researching history topics on the Web can give you access to valuable information. However, just because the information is on the Web doesn't mean it is automatically valuable!

Additional reading support can be found in the Interactive Reader and Study Guide

Evaluating Web Sites Before you use information you find online, you need to evaluate the site it comes from. The checklist below can help you determine if the site is worth your time.

Evaluating Web Sites

Site: ____________ **URL:** ____________ **Date of access:** ____________

Rate each item on this 1–3 scale. Then add up the total score.

	No	Some	Yes
I. Authority			
a. Authors are clearly identified by name.	1	2	3
b. Contact information is provided for authors.	1	2	3
c. Author's qualifications are clearly stated.	1	2	3
d. Site has been updated recently.	1	2	3
II. Content			
a. Site's information is useful to your project.	1	2	3
b. Information is clear and well-organized.	1	2	3
c. Information appears to be at the right level.	1	2	3
d. Links to additional important information are provided.	1	2	3
e. Information can be verified in other sources.	1	2	3
f. Graphics are helpful, not just decorative.	1	2	3
III. Design and Technical Elements			
a. Pages are readable and easy to navigate.	1	2	3
b. Links to other sites work.	1	2	3

Total Score ____________

36–28 = very good site **28–20 = average site** **below 20 = poor site**

Reading and Skills Resources

Reading Support
- Interactive Reader and Study Guide
- Student Edition on Audio CD
- Spanish Chapter Summaries Audio CD Program

Social Studies Skills Support
- Interactive Skills Tutor CD-ROM

Vocabulary Support
- **CRF:** Vocabulary Builder Activities
- **CRF:** Chapter Review Activity
- Universal Access Modified Worksheets and Tests CD-ROM:
  - Vocabulary Flash Cards
  - Vocabulary Builder Activity
  - Chapter Review Activity

OSP Holt PuzzlePro

Standards Focus
ELA Reading 8.2.0

ELA **Reading 8.2.0** Read and understand grade-level-appropriate material.

You Try It!

The passage below is from the chapter you are about to read.

Cotton Becomes Profitable

Cotton had been grown in the New World for centuries, but it had not been a very profitable crop. Before cotton could be spun into thread for weaving into cloth, the seeds had to be removed from the cotton fibers.

Long-staple cotton, also called black-seed cotton, was fairly easy to process. Workers could pick the seeds from the cotton with relative ease. But long-staple cotton grew well in only a few places in the South. More common was short-staple cotton, also known as green-seed cotton. Removing the seeds from this cotton was difficult and time consuming. A worker could spend an entire day picking the seeds from the single pound of cotton.

From Chapter 12, p. 376

After you read the passage, complete the following activity.

Suppose that after reading this passage you decide to do some research on cotton growing. You use a search engine that directs you to a site. At that site, you find the information described below. Using the evaluation criteria listed on the previous page, decide if this is a site you would recommend to others.

a. The authors of the site are listed as "Bob and Mack, good friends who enjoy working together."

b. The site was last updated on "the last time we got together."

c. The title of the site is "Cotton Pickin'." There are few headings.

d. This ten-page site includes nine pages about the authors' childhood on a cotton farm. No illustrations are included.

e. Pages are very long; but, they load quickly as there are no graphics. There is one link to a site selling cotton clothing.

Key Terms and People

Chapter 12

Section 1
cotton gin *(p. 377)*
planters *(p. 378)*
cotton belt *(p. 379)*
factors *(p. 379)*
Tredegar Iron Works *(p. 379)*

Section 2
yeomen *(p. 384)*

Section 3
folktales *(p. 389)*
spirituals *(p. 389)*
Nat Turner *(p. 390)*
Nat Turner's Rebellion *(p. 390)*

Academic Vocabulary

Success in school is related to knowing academic vocabulary—the words that are frequently used in school assignments and discussions. In this chapter, you will learn the following academic words:

primary *(p. 380)*
aspect *(p. 388)*

As you read Chapter 12, think about what topics would be interesting to research on the Web. If you do some research on the Web, remember to use the evaluation list to analyze the Web site.

Reading Social Studies

Key Terms and People

Preteach the key terms and people from this chapter by asking students what they think each term means or who each person was. Ask the class to identify the terms or people about which they know the least. Write the list of terms for the class to see. Have each student define or identify the terms or people. Then have each student draw an illustration to represent each term or person.
LS Verbal/Linguistic, Visual/Spatial

Focus on Reading

See the **Focus on Reading** questions in this chapter for more practice on this reading social studies skill.

Reading Social Studies Assessment

See the **Standards Review** at the end of this chapter for student assessment questions related to this reading skill.

Teaching Tip

Remind students of the importance of citing their sources correctly. Stress to students that as they evaluate a Web site, they should write down important information about that site. Among the items students should include in their documentation are the author or authors of a Web site, the exact URL, or address, of the site, the date they accessed the Web site, the date the site was last revised, and the name of the Web site.

Answers

You Try It! *Students should conclude that they would not want to recommend this site to others. Students should note that, among other things, the Web site was not written by qualified authors, nor does it provide useful information about growing cotton.*

Preteach

Bellringer

If YOU were there . . . Use the **Daily Bellringer Transparency** to help students answer the question.

 Daily Bellringer Transparency, Section 1

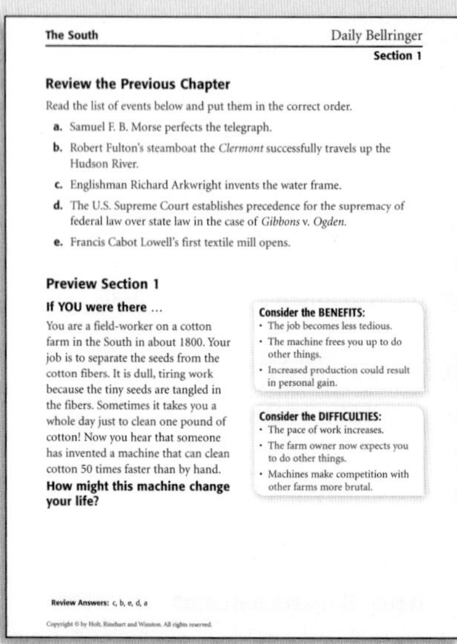

The South — Daily Bellringer — **Section 1**

Review the Previous Chapter

Read the list of events below and put them in the correct order.

- **a.** Samuel F. B. Morse perfects the telegraph.
- **b.** Robert Fulton's steamboat the *Clermont* successfully travels up the Hudson River.
- **c.** Englishman Richard Arkwright invents the water frame.
- **d.** The U.S. Supreme Court establishes precedence for the supremacy of federal law over state law in the case of *Gibbons* v. *Ogden*.
- **e.** Francis Cabot Lowell's first textile mill opens.

Preview Section 1

If YOU were there ...

You are a field-worker on a cotton farm in the South in about 1800. Your job is to separate the seeds from the cotton fibers. It is dull, tiring work because the tiny seeds are tangled in the fibers. Sometimes it takes you a whole day just to clean one pound of cotton! Now you hear that someone has invented a machine that can clean cotton 50 times faster than by hand.

How might this machine change your life?

Consider the BENEFITS:
- The job becomes less tedious.
- The machine frees you up to do other things.
- Increased production could result in personal gain.

Consider the DIFFICULTIES:
- The pace of work increases.
- The farm owner now expects you to do other things.
- Machines make competition with other farms more brutal.

Review Answers: c, b, e, d, a

Academic Vocabulary

Review with students the high-use academic term in this section.

primary main, most important (p. 380)

CRF: Vocabulary Builder Activity, Section 1

Standards Focus

HSS 8.7.1

Means: Describe how a farm-based economy developed in the South. Identify the cotton-producing states in the South. Discuss why cotton and the cotton gin were important in the South.

Matters: The cotton culture shaped life in the South for decades to come.

HSS 8.7.2

Means: Explain how the system of slavery began, how it developed, and ways different groups tried to end or continue it.

Matters: Slavery had a deep effect on thousands of enslaved Africans and their descendents.

SECTION 1

Growth of the Cotton Industry

What You Will Learn...

Main Ideas

1. The invention of the cotton gin revived the economy of the South.
2. The cotton gin created a cotton boom in which farmers grew little else.
3. Some people encouraged southerners to focus on other crops and industries.

The Big Idea

The invention of the cotton gin made the South a one-crop economy and increased the need for slave labor.

Key Terms and People

cotton gin, *p. 377*
planters, *p. 378*
cotton belt, *p. 379*
factors, *p. 379*
Tredegar Iron Works, *p. 381*

HSS 8.7.1 Describe the development of the agrarian economy in the South, identify the locations of the cotton-producing states, and discuss the significance of cotton and the cotton gin.

8.7.2 Trace the origins and development of slavery; its effects on black Americans and on the region's political, social, religious, economic, and cultural development; and identify the stategies that were tried to both overturn and preserve it (e.g., through the writings and historical documents on Nat Turner, Denmark Vesey).

If YOU were there...

You are a field-worker on a cotton farm in the South in about 1800. Your job is to separate the seeds from the cotton fibers. It is dull, tiring work because the tiny seeds are tangled in the fibers. Sometimes it takes you a whole day just to clean one pound of cotton! Now you hear that someone has invented a machine that can clean cotton 50 times faster than by hand.

How might this machine change your life?

BUILDING BACKGROUND Sectional differences had always existed between different regions of the United States. The revolutionary changes in industry and transportation deepened the differences between North and South. The South remained mainly agricultural. New technology helped the region become the Cotton Kingdom.

Reviving the South's Economy

Before the American Revolution, three crops dominated southern agriculture—tobacco, rice, and indigo. These crops, produced mostly by enslaved African Americans, played a central role in the southern economy and culture.

After the American Revolution, however, prices for tobacco, rice, and indigo dropped. When crop prices fell, the demand for and the price of slaves also went down. In an effort to protect their incomes, many farmers tried, with little success, to grow other crops that needed less labor. Soon, however, cotton would transform the southern economy and greatly increase the demand for slave labor.

Cotton Becomes Profitable

Cotton had been grown in the New World for centuries, but it had not been a very profitable crop. Before cotton could be spun into thread for weaving into cloth, the seeds had to be removed from the cotton fibers.

Teach the Big Idea: Master the Standards

Standards Proficiency

Growth of the Cotton Industry

HSS 8.7.1; HSS **Analysis Skills:** HI 1, HI 2

1. **Teach** Ask students the Main Idea questions to teach this section.
2. **Apply** Help students understand the significance of the cotton gin to southern agriculture and the South's economy. Have students use information in the section to write a brief encyclopedia entry about the cotton gin. In their entries, have students answer the questions who, what, when, where, how, and why. **LS Verbal/Linguistic**
3. **Review** As you review the section, invite volunteers to read aloud portions of their encyclopedia entries.
4. **Practice/Homework** Ask students to imagine they are southern farm workers who spent all day removing seeds from just one pound of cotton. Have them write journal entries reacting to news of the invention of the cotton gin. **LS Verbal/Linguistic**

Alternative Assessment Handbook, Rubric 15: Journals

Cotton Gin

SCIENCE AND TECHNOLOGY

Eli Whitney's cotton gin enabled workers to easily remove seeds from cotton fibers. The result was a dramatic increase in cotton production in the South.

How did the cotton gin remove seeds from cotton fibers?

1. The operator turned the crank.
2. The crank turned a roller with teeth that stripped the seeds away from the cotton fiber.
3. Brushes on a second roller lifted the seedless cotton off the teeth of the first cylinder and dropped it out of the machine.
4. A belt connected the rollers so that they would both turn when the crank was turned.

Long-staple cotton, also called black-seed cotton, was fairly easy to process. Workers could pick the seeds from the cotton with relative ease. But long-staple cotton grew well in only a few places in the South. More common was short-staple cotton, which was also known as green-seed cotton. Removing the seeds from this cotton was difficult and time consuming. A worker could spend an entire day picking the seeds from a single pound of short-staple cotton.

By the early 1790s the demand for American cotton began increasing rapidly. For instance, in Great Britain, new textile factories needed raw cotton that could be used for making cloth, and American cotton producers could not keep up with the high demand for their cotton. These producers of cotton needed a machine that could remove the seeds from the cotton more rapidly.

Eli Whitney's Cotton Gin

Northerner Eli Whitney finally patented such a machine in 1793. The year before, Whitney had visited a Georgia plantation owned by Catherine Greene where workers were using a machine to remove seeds from long-staple cotton. This machine did not work well on short-staple cotton, and Greene asked Whitney if he could improve it. By the next spring, Whitney had perfected his design for the **cotton gin**, a machine that removes seeds from short-staple cotton. ("Gin" is short for engine.) The cotton gin used a hand-cranked cylinder with wire teeth to pull cotton fibers from the seeds.

Whitney hoped to keep the design of the gin a secret, but the machine was so useful that his patent was often ignored by other manufacturers. Whitney described how his invention would improve the cotton business.

THE IMPACT TODAY

The same patent law that protected Whitney's invention of the the cotton gin protects the rights of inventors today.

Direct Teach

Main Idea

1 Reviving the South's Economy

The invention of the cotton gin revived the economy of the South.

Explain Why was there less demand for slave labor after the American Revolution? *Crop prices had fallen; landowners cut production or switched to crops that required less labor.*

Summarize What problem did the cotton gin solve? *the difficult and time-consuming process of removing seeds from short-staple cotton*

Predict What effect do you think the cotton gin had on the demand for slave labor? Why? *Demand increased because the cotton gin led to increased cotton farming.*

CRF: Biography Activity: Eli Whitney

HSS 8.7.1; HSS **Analysis Skills:** HI 1, HI 2

Did you know . . .

How did Eli Whitney get the idea for his cotton gin? One legend claims a farm cat inspired Whitney. As the story goes, Whitney saw a farm cat try to claw at chickens. The cat waited patiently for the chickens to come near the fence. When they did, the cat quickly shot its paw through the fence, but was only able to pluck the chickens' feathers with its claws.

Collaborative Learning

Standards **Proficiency**

Cotton Gin Marketing Campaign

HSS 8.7. 1; HSS **Analysis Skills:** HI 1

1. Ask students to consider different ways they have seen one consumer good, such as a car, advertised. Explain that when a product is introduced to consumers, often a marketing campaign—made up of several different components in different media—is created.
2. Organize the class into small groups to develop a class marketing campaign to promote Eli Whitney's cotton gin. Assign each group one of the following products to create: logo and slogan, brochure, poster, and newspaper print advertisement. Encourage students to make each part of the campaign reflect how the cotton gin works and its benefits to buyers.
3. Have each group present its part of the marketing campaign and display the final products in the classroom. LS **Interpersonal, Verbal/Linguistic, Visual/Spatial**

Alternative Assessment Handbook, Rubrics 14: Group Activity; and 29: Presentations

Answers

Science and Technology *A hand-cranked roller with wire teeth pulled cotton fibers away from the seeds.*

Direct Teach

Main Idea

❷ The Cotton Boom

The cotton gin created a cotton boom in which farmers grew little else.

Recall How did the cotton gin affect cotton production in the South? *made cotton so profitable that many southern farmers began growing cotton, and cotton production spread and increased rapidly*

Identify Cause and Effect Increased cotton production led to an economic boom in the South. What were the effects of this economic boom on the region? *attracted new settlers, built up wealth among wealthy white southerners, firmly embedded slavery in the South*

CRF: History and Geography Activity: Cotton in the South

Map Transparency: The Cotton Kingdom

HSS 8.7.1 **HSS Analysis Skills:** HI 2

Interpreting Maps

The Cotton Kingdom

Before and After Which states (or future states) produced cotton before 1820? *Virginia, North Carolina, South Carolina, Georgia, Alabama, Tennessee, Mississippi, Louisiana* Which grew cotton after 1820? *Missouri, Arkansas, Texas, Florida, Oklahoma (Indian Territory)*

Map Transparency: The Cotton Kingdom

Info to Know

Cotton Gin Patent After perfecting the cotton gin, Eli Whitney was given the sole right to make the machine in 1794. But other people were easily able to make cotton gins, and began doing so. Whitney sued planters for violating his rights, but he gained next to nothing from his legal battles.

Answers

Interpreting Charts 1. *the South;* 2. *2.1 million bales*

Reading Check *made processing cotton easier and quicker; increased production of cotton as a cash crop; led to an economic boom*

"One man will clean ten times as much cotton as he can in any other way before known and also clean it much better than in the usual mode [method]. This machine may be turned by water or with a horse, with the greatest ease, and one man and a horse will do more than fifty men with the old machines."

—Eli Whitney, quoted in *Eli Whitney and the Birth of American Technology* by Constance McLaughlin Green

Whitney's gin revolutionized the cotton industry. **Planters**—large-scale farmers who held more than 20 slaves—built cotton gins that could process tons of cotton much faster than hand processing. A healthy crop almost guaranteed financial success because of high demand from the textile industry.

READING CHECK **Drawing Conclusions** What effects did the cotton gin have on the southern economy?

The Cotton Boom

Whitney's invention of the cotton gin made cotton so profitable that southern farmers abandoned other crops in favor of growing cotton. The removal of Native Americans opened up more land for cotton farmers in the Southeast. Meanwhile, the development of new types of cotton plants helped spread cotton production throughout the South as far west as Texas.

Production increased rapidly—from about 2 million pounds in 1791 to roughly a billion pounds by 1860. As early as 1840, the United States was producing more than half of the cotton grown in the entire world. The economic boom attracted new settlers, built up wealth among wealthy white southerners, and firmly put in place the institution of slavery in the South.

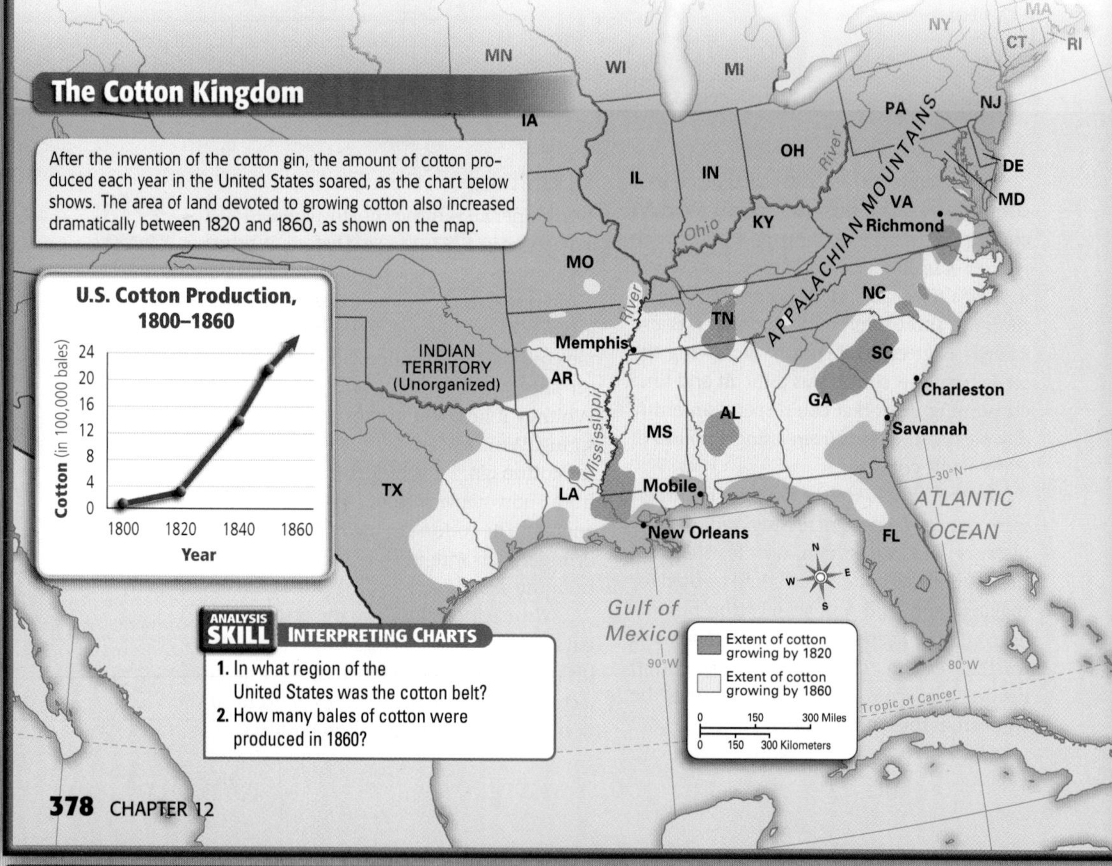

ANALYSIS SKILL **INTERPRETING CHARTS**

1. In what region of the United States was the cotton belt?
2. How many bales of cotton were produced in 1860?

Differentiating Instruction for Universal Access

Learners Having Difficulty

Reaching Standards

1. Review with students the positive and negative effects of the cotton boom.
2. Draw the chart on the right for students to see. Omit the blue, italicized answers.
3. Have students copy the chart and complete it by listing the positive and negative effects of the cotton boom on the South's economy.
LS Visual/Spatial

HSS 8.7.1, 8.7.2; **HSS Analysis Skills:** HI 1, HI 2

Effects of Cotton Boom

Positive	Negative
• *Growth of economy* • *Build-up of wealth* • *The South became a major player in world trade.* • *Development of cotton trade* • *Growth of cotton-related industries*	• *increased reliance on one crop—cotton* • *firmly embedded the institution of slavery in the South* • *increased internal slave trade*

Cotton Belt

Cotton had many advantages as a cash crop. It cost little to market. Unlike food staples, harvested cotton could be stored for a long time. Because cotton was lighter than other staple crops, it also cost less to transport long distances.

Farmers eager to profit from growing cotton headed west to find land. Farmers also began to apply scientific methods to improve crop production. Cotton had one disadvantage as a crop—it rapidly used up the nutrients in the soil. After a few years, cotton could make the land useless for growing anything. Some agricultural scientists recommended crop rotation—changing the crop grown on a particular plot of land every few years. Different crops needed different nutrients, so crop rotation would keep the land fertile longer. Other agricultural scientists began to study soil chemistry, in an effort to keep the land rich and productive.

As the cotton belt grew, farmers continued trying to improve the crop. Agricultural scientists worked at crossbreeding short-staple cotton with other varieties. As a result, new, stronger types of cotton were soon growing throughout the cotton belt. This led to expansion of the cotton industry through the 1860s.

The cotton boom involved much more than growing and harvesting cotton. Harvested cotton had to be ginned, pressed into bales, and then shipped to market or to warehouses. Special agents helped do everything from marketing cotton to customers to insuring crops against loss or damage. Factories were built to produce items needed by cotton farmers, such as ropes to bale cotton.

Growing and harvesting cotton required many field hands. Rather than pay wages to free workers, planters began to use more slave labor. Congress had made bringing slaves into the United States illegal in 1808. However, the growing demand for slaves led to an increase in the slave trade within the United States.

Cotton Trade

In an 1858 speech before the U.S. Senate, South Carolina politician James Henry Hammond declared, "Cotton is King!" Without cotton, Hammond claimed, the world economy would fail. He believed that southern cotton was one of the most valuable resources in the world. Southern cotton was used to make cloth in England and the North. Many southerners shared Hammond's viewpoints about cotton. Southerner David Christy declared, "King cotton is a profound [learned] statesman, and knows what measures will best sustain [protect] his throne."

The cotton boom made the South a major player in world trade. Great Britain became the South's most valued foreign trading partner. Southerners also sold tons of cotton to the growing textile industry in the northeastern United States. This increased trade led to the growth of major port cities in the South, including Charleston, South Carolina; Savannah, Georgia; and New Orleans, Louisiana.

THE IMPACT TODAY

The Port of New Orleans remains a major seaport. It handles about 85 million tons of cargo annually.

In these cities, crop brokers called **factors** managed the cotton trade. Farmers sold their cotton to merchants, who then made deals with the factors. Merchants and factors also arranged loans for farmers who needed to buy supplies. They often advised farmers on how to invest profits. Once farmers got their cotton to the port cities factors arranged for transportation aboard trading ships.

However, shipping cotton by land to port cities was very difficult in the South. The few major road projects at the time were limited to the Southeast. Most southern farmers had to ship their goods on the region's rivers. On the Ohio and Mississippi rivers, flatboats and steamboats carried cotton and other products to port. Eventually, hundreds of steamboats traveled up and down the mighty Mississippi River each day.

READING CHECK **Identifying Cause and Effect** What effect did the cotton boom have on the slave trade within the United States?

Direct Teach

Main Idea

2 The Cotton Boom

The cotton gin created a cotton boom in which farmers grew little else.

Describe What were the advantages of cotton as a crop? *cost little to market, could be stored for a long time, cost less to transport, highly profitable*

Identify Cause and Effect What were the effects of the growing demand for labor? *an increase in the use of slave labor and of the slave trade within the United States*

Summarize What role did the region's rivers play in the cotton trade? *used to transport cotton in flatboats and steamboats to port cities*

Activity **Flowchart** Have students create a flowchart of developments in the South's economy after the invention of the cotton gin. **LS Verbal/Linguistic**

HSS 8.7.1, 8.7.2; HSS **Analysis Skills:** HI 2

Linking to Today

Cotton Products Raw cotton is still sold to the textile industry and made into cotton goods today. Have students brainstorm a list of as many cotton products as possible that they use regularly. *(clothes, cotton balls, bed sheets and blankets, towels)*

Critical Thinking: Analyzing Information

Standards Proficiency

Costs and Benefits of Cotton

HSS 8.7.1, 8.7.2; HSS **Analysis Skills:** HI 1, HI 6

1. Give students the following scenario: After the invention of the cotton gin, a southern planter is trying to decide whether to switch to growing cotton. The planter decides to create a costs-benefits chart to help make the decision.
2. Have each student create a costs-benefits chart that such a planter might have made. The chart should list the benefits and costs of making the switch to cotton. Remind students to consider the negative effects the cotton boom had on enslaved Africans in the South.
3. Ask volunteers to share information from their charts as you create a master chart. **LS Verbal/Linguistic**

Alternative Assessment Handbook, Rubric 7: Charts

Answers

Reading Check *increased the slave trade between the states*

Direct Teach

Main Idea

❸ Other Crops and Industries

Some people encouraged southerners to focus on other crops and industries.

Recall What were some other important crops in the South? *corn, rice, sweet potatoes, wheat, sugarcane, tobacco, hemp, and flax*

Explain Why were most southern factories built to serve the needs of farmers? *The South's economy centered on agriculture.*

Analyze Why did some people encourage southerners to try a variety of crops and investments? *reliance on one crop was risky; wanted to modernize and promote industry; to keep the soil healthy*

HSS 8.7.1; HSS **Analytical Skills:** HI 1

Analyzing Visuals

The South's Cotton Economy Have students examine the image at right to answer the following:

- Where was most cotton processed? *in the South*
- Where were most of the textile mills to which sailing ships carried cotton? *northeastern United States, Great Britain*

Connect to Geography

Tobacco and the South Farmers found that healthy tobacco plants needed nutrient-rich soils. Tobacco so badly bleached the land of nutrients that after just three years, the soil required 20 years of rest before it was useable for farming again. Before farmers learned to rotate crops, they instead rotated fields, planting tobacco on fresh land until the soil's nutrients were exhausted.

The South's Cotton Economy

Eli Whitney's cotton gin began the cotton boom. Soon, the Cotton Kingdom stretched across the South. For the cotton planters to succeed, they had to get their cotton to market.

Enslaved African Americans did most of the planting, harvesting, and processing of cotton.

Cotton was shipped on river steamboats to major ports such as Charleston.

From southern ports, sailing ships carried the cotton to distant textile mills.

Other Crops and Industries

Some leaders worried that the South was depending too much on cotton. They wanted southerners to try a variety of cash crops and investments.

Academic Vocabulary
primary main, most important

Food and Cash Crops

One such crop was corn, the primary southern food crop. By the late 1830s the top three corn-growing states in the nation were all in the South. The South's other successful food crops included rice, sweet potatoes, wheat, and sugarcane.

Production of tobacco, the South's first major cash crop, was very time consuming because tobacco leaves had to be cured, or dried, before they could be shipped to market. In 1839 a slave discovered a way to improve the drying process by using heat from burning charcoal. This new, faster curing process increased tobacco production.

Partly as a result of the cotton boom, hemp and flax also became major cash crops. Their fibers were used to make rope and sackcloth. Farmers used the rope and sackcloth to bundle cotton into bales.

Industry

Many of the first factories in the South were built to serve farmers' needs by processing crops such as sugarcane. In 1803 the nation's first steam-powered sawmill was built in Donaldsonville, Louisiana. This new technology enabled lumber companies to cut, sort, and clean wood quickly.

By the 1840s, entrepreneurs in Georgia began investing in cotton mills. In 1840, there were 14 cotton mills; by the mid-1850s, there were more than 50. A few mill owners followed the model established by Francis Cabot Lowell. However, most built small-scale factories on the falls of a river for water power. A few steam-powered mills were built in towns without enough water power.

Southerners such as Hinton Rowan Helper encouraged industrial growth in the South.

> "We should . . . keep pace with the progress of the age. We must expand our energies, and acquire habits of enterprise and industry; we should rouse ourselves from the couch of lassitude [laziness] and inure [set] our minds to thought and our bodies to action."
>
> — Hinton Rowan Helper, *The Impending Crisis of the South: How to Meet It*

Critical Thinking: Identifying Points of View

Exceeding Standards

Dependence on Cotton Editorial

HSS 8.7.1, 8.7.2; HSS **Analysis Skills:** HI 1, HI 2

1. Ask students to imagine themselves as one of the southern leaders who worried about overreliance on cotton. Have each student write an editorial to support his or her position.
2. Editorials should include a position statement, present at least two strong reasons to support the position, and provide evidence (such as examples or statistics) to support each reason.
3. Remind students that some of the readers of their editorials will have different points of view on the issue. Students should try to address these people's concerns and convince them to change their positions.
4. Ask for volunteers to read their editorials aloud. LS **Verbal/Linguistic**

Alternative Assessment Handbook, Rubric 43: Writing to Persuade

A large amount of cotton was sold to textile mills in the northeastern United States.

Textile mills in Great Britain were the largest foreign buyers of southern cotton.

ANALYSIS SKILL **DRAWING CONCLUSIONS**

Why do you think cotton was so important to the South's economy?

Joseph R. Anderson followed Helper's advice. In 1848 he became the owner of the **Tredegar Iron Works** in Richmond, Virginia—one of the most productive iron works in the nation. It was the only factory to produce bridge materials, cannons, steam engines, and other products.

FOCUS ON READING What kind of Web site would you look for to learn more about the Tredegar Iron Works?

Industry, however, remained a small part of the southern economy. Southern industry faced stiff competition from the North and from England, both of which could produce many goods more cheaply. And as long as agricultural profits remained high, southern investors preferred to invest in land.

READING CHECK **Making Inferences** Why were there fewer industries in the South?

SUMMARY AND PREVIEW You have read about how southern farmers worked to improve farming methods. In the next section you will read about the structure of southern society.

Section 1 Assessment

go.hrw.com **Online Quiz** KEYWORD: SS8 HP12

Reviewing Ideas, Terms, and People

HSS 8.7.1, 8.7.2

1. a. **Describe** How did the **cotton gin** make processing cotton easier?
   b. **Draw Conclusions** Why had slavery been on the decline before the invention of the cotton gin? How did slavery change as a result of the cotton gin?
2. a. **Identify** What areas made up the **cotton belt**?
   b. **Evaluate** Do you think the South should have paid more attention to its industrial growth? Why?
3. a. **Describe** What other crops and industries were encouraged in the South?
   b. **Make Inferences** Why were some southern leaders worried about the South's reliance on cotton?

Critical Thinking

4. **Identifying Cause and Effect** Copy the graphic organizer below. Use it to show events that led to the cotton boom and to list the effects of increased cotton production on slavery and the southern economy.

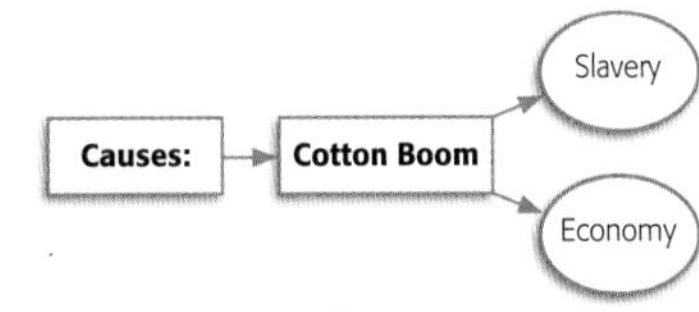

FOCUS ON WRITING

5. **Noting Life on the Cotton Farm** In your notebook, note how Whitney's gin changed life on the farm. Also note other details about cotton farming you could include in your sketch.

Direct Teach

Connect to Economics

Reliance on Cotton Have students think about some of the problems that might occur for an economy dependent on one crop. *Bad weather, labor shortages, or plague could ruin the crop and lead to a downturn in the economy.*

go.hrw.com **Online Resources**
KEYWORD: SS8 US12
ACTIVITY: Tredegar Iron Works Report

Review & Assess

Close

Have students describe the South's economy before and after the development of the cotton gin.

Review

Online Quiz, Section 1

Assess

SE Section 1 Assessment

PASS: Section 1 Quiz

Alternative Assessment Handbook

Reteach/Classroom Intervention

California Standards Review Workbook

Interactive Reader and Study Guide, Section 1

Interactive Skills Tutor CD-ROM

Section 1 Assessment Answers

1. **a.** much faster way to remove seeds from cotton fibers than by hand
   b. Crop prices had fallen and the demand for farm workers had declined; cotton gin led to an increase in the production of cotton, which created more demand for slave labor.
2. **a.** land stretching from Virginia to Texas
   b. possible answer—Yes, it was dangerous for the South's economy to be totally dependent on agriculture and one crop.
3. **a.** corn, rice, sweet potatoes, wheat, sugarcane, mills, iron works
   b. reliance on one crop was risky
4. Causes—invention of the cotton gin, cotton's many advantages as a cash crop; Slavery—increased demand for slave labor, increase in slave trade in the United States; Economy—build-up of wealth, dependence on cotton
5. possible answers—more growing and harvesting of cotton; more slave labor; trade became important part of southern economy; South reliant on one crop; little investment in industry

Answers

Drawing Conclusions *because cotton was highly profitable and was in high demand*

Focus on Reading *Internet search engines; encyclopedia sites; Richmond, Virginia historical society sites*

Reading Check *People thought cash crops were a better investment than industry.*

Preteach

Bellringer

If YOU were there . . . Use the **Daily Bellringer Transparency** to help students answer the question.

Daily Bellringer Transparency, Section 2

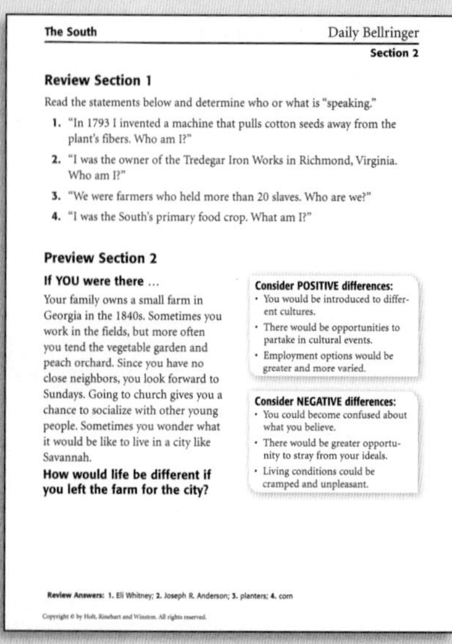
The South — Daily Bellringer — Section 2

Review Section 1

Read the statements below and determine who or what is "speaking."

1. "In 1793 I invented a machine that pulls cotton seeds away from the plant's fibers. Who am I?"
2. "I was the owner of the Tredegar Iron Works in Richmond, Virginia. Who am I?"
3. "We were farmers who held more than 20 slaves. Who are we?"
4. "I was the South's primary food crop. What am I?"

Preview Section 2

If YOU were there ...

Your family owns a small farm in Georgia in the 1840s. Sometimes you work in the fields, but more often you tend the vegetable garden and peach orchard. Since you have no close neighbors, you look forward to Sundays. Going to church gives you a chance to socialize with other young people. Sometimes you wonder what it would be like to live in a city like Savannah.

How would life be different if you left the farm for the city?

Consider POSITIVE differences:
- You would be introduced to different cultures.
- There would be opportunities to partake in cultural events.
- Employment options would be greater and more varied.

Consider NEGATIVE differences:
- You could become confused about what you believe.
- There would be greater opportunity to stray from your ideals.
- Living conditions could be cramped and unpleasant.

Review Answers: 1. Eli Whitney; 2. Joseph R. Anderson; 3. planters; 4. corn

Building Vocabulary

Preteach or review the following terms:

descendant a person related to an individual in the past (p. 385)

discrimination unfair treatment of a person or group (p. 385)

CRF: Vocabulary Builder Activity, Section 2

Standards Focus

HSS 8.7.3
Means: Describe characteristics of life in white Southern society.
Matters: Different social classes in southern society helped fuel the Civil War.

HSS 8.7.4
Means: Identify how the lives of free blacks were different in the North and in the South.
Matters: African Americans continue to fight discrimination in parts of the South.

HSS 8.9.6
Means: Describe what laws limited the opportunities for free African Americans.
Matters: Free African Americans faced many challenges in the South.

SECTION 2

Southern Society

What You Will Learn...

Main Ideas

1. Southern society and culture consisted of four main groups.
2. Free African Americans in the South faced a great deal of discrimination.

The Big Idea

Southern society centered around agriculture.

Key Term

yeomen, *p. 384*

HSS 8.7.3 Examine the characteristics of white Southern society and how the physical environment influenced events and conditions prior to the Civil War.

8.7.4 Compare the lives of and opportunities for free blacks in the North with those of free blacks in the South.

8.9.6 Describe the lives of free blacks and the laws that limited their freedom and economic opportunities.

If YOU were there...

Your family owns a small farm in Georgia in the 1840s. Sometimes you work in the fields, but more often you tend the vegetable garden and peach orchard. Since you have no close neighbors, you look forward to Sundays. Going to church gives you a chance to socialize with other young people. Sometimes you wonder what it would be like to live in a city like Savannah.

How would life be different if you left the farm for the city?

BUILDING BACKGROUND Although the South had some industry, agriculture was the heart of the southern economy. Cotton was king. As a result, wealthy plantation families were the most prominent social class in southern society. Small farmers, however, made up the largest part of the population.

Southern Society and Culture

Popular fiction often made it seem that all white southerners had many slaves and lived on large plantations. Many fiction writers wrote about wealthy southern families who had frequent, grand parties. The ideal image of the South included hospitality and well-treated slaves on beautiful plantations that almost ran themselves.

This romantic view was far from the reality. During the first half of the 1800s, only about one-third of white southern families had slaves. Fewer families had plantations. Despite their small numbers, these planters had a powerful influence over the South. Many served as political leaders. They led a society made up of many different kinds of people, including yeomen farmers, poor whites, slaves, and free African Americans. Each of these segments of society contributed to the economic success of the South.

Teach the Big Idea: Master the Standards

Standards Proficiency

Southern Society

HSS 8.7.3, 8.7.4, 8.9.6; HSS **Analysis Skills:** HI 1

1. **Teach** Ask students the Main Idea questions to teach this section.
2. **Apply** Ask students to fold a piece of paper into four quarters. Label each quarter with one of the following social groups in free southern society: *planters, yeomen, poor whites,* and *free African Americans.* Have students use the information in this section to fill in each section of their papers. **LS Verbal/Linguistic**
3. **Review** To review the section's main ideas, have students help you complete a master copy of the chart.
4. **Practice/Homework** Have each student write a one-sentence summary for each part of the chart. Then have students combine their sentences to create a one-paragraph summary of the chart. **LS Verbal/Linguistic**

Alternative Assessment Handbook, Rubric 7: Charts

Planters

As the wealthiest members of southern society, planters also greatly influenced the economy. Some showed off their wealth by living in beautiful mansions. Many others chose to live more simply. A visitor described wealthy planter Alexander Stephens's estate as "an old wooden house" surrounded by weeds. Some planters saved all of their money to buy more land and slaves.

Male planters were primarily concerned with raising crops and supervising slave laborers. They left the running of the plantation household to their wives. The planter's wife oversaw the raising of the children and supervised the work of all slaves within the household. Slave women typically cooked, cleaned, and helped care for the planter's children. Wives also took on the important social duties of the family. For example, many southern leaders discussed political issues at the dances and dinners hosted by their wives.

Planters often arranged their children's marriages based on business interests. Lucy Breckinridge, the daughter of a wealthy Virginia planter, was married by arrangement in 1865. Three years earlier, she had described in her journal how she dreaded the very thought of marriage. "A woman's life after she is married, unless there is an immense amount of love, is nothing but suffering and hard work." How Breckinridge's life in her own arranged marriage would have turned out cannot be known. She died of typhoid fever just months after her wedding.

History Close-up

A Southern Plantation

A typical plantation had fields as well as many buildings where different work was done. This picture shows some of the more important buildings that were a part of the plantation system.

Slave Cabins
Slaves lived crowded together in small cabins. Cabins are crude, wooden structures with dirt floors.
Fields
Barn
Warehouse
Smokehouse
Cotton-Ginning Shed
This sizable plantation had several large cotton gins. The vital machines were housed in a shed to protect them from the weather.
Overseer's House
Plantation House
The planter and his family lived in the plantation house. The planter's wife was in charge of running the household.
Stable
Fields

ANALYSIS SKILL ANALYZING VISUALS

How can you tell that the owner of this plantation was wealthy?

Direct Teach

Main Idea

1 Southern Society and Culture

Southern society and culture consisted of four main groups.

Recall About how many white southern families had slaves in the first half of the 1800s? *one-third*

Contrast How did the social status of planters and yeomen differ? *Planters had more power and wealth than yeomen.*

Evaluate Why might some wealthy planters prefer to live simply? *possible answers—did not enjoy society life; preferred to use money to buy more land or slaves*

- **CRF:** Biography Activity: Mary Boykin Chesnut
- **CRF:** Literature Activity: Plantation Life before Emancipation
- **CRF:** Primary Source Activity: Frances Anne Kemble, *Journal of a Residence on a Georgian Plantation*

HSS 8.7.3; **HSS Analysis Skills:** HI 2

History Close-up
A Southern Plantation

Antebellum (Latin for "before the war") refers to the style of plantation houses such as the one shown here. This Classical Revival style was popular in the South in the 30 years prior to the Civil War. Features include a symmetrical design, pillars, gabled roofs, wrap-around balconies, and evenly spaced windows.

Collaborative Learning

Standards Proficiency

The Southern News

HSS 8.7.3; **HSS Analysis Skills:** HI 1

1. Organize the class into small groups. Have each group create the front page of a southern newspaper, including a masthead, headlines, articles, advertisements, and illustrations.
2. Encourage students to direct their newspapers towards a target audience of one of the four main groups in southern society in the first half of the 1800s.
3. Have each group present its front page to the class. Then discuss with students the topics and issues of importance to southern society.

LS Interpersonal, Verbal/Linguistic

Alternative Assessment Handbook, Rubrics 14: Group Activity; and 23: Newspapers

Answers

Analyzing Visuals *plantation house is huge, beautiful mansion; has large stable, two cotton gin sheds, many slave cabins*

Direct Teach

Main Idea

1 Southern Society and Culture

Southern society and culture consisted of four main groups.

Recall How big was the typical yeoman farm? *100 acres*

Summarize How was religion an important part of southern society? *Most white southerners shared similar religious beliefs; neighbors often visited only at church events; slaveholders used religion to defend slavery.*

HSS 8.7.3, 8.9.6; HSS **Analysis Skills:** HI 1

Info to Know

Free African Americans in the South Free African Americans in the South were more likely to live in cities than in rural areas. By 1860, free African Americans outnumbered slaves 10 to 1 in Baltimore and 5 to 1 in Washington. On the eve of the Civil War, New Orleans was home to 10,000 free African Americans. In the cities, the discrimination that free African Americans faced could be harsh. For example, an 1832 Baltimore law stated that free African Americans were subject to the same treatment and punishment as enslaved Africans.

Free African Americans in the South

In 1860 about 1 out of 50 African Americans in the South was free. Many worked in skilled trades, like this barber in Richmond, Virginia. In Charleston, South Carolina, a system of badges was set up to distinguish between free African Americans and slaves.

How would the work of the free African American in this picture be different from that of slaves in the South?

Yeomen and Poor Whites

Most white southerners were **yeomen**, owners of small farms. Yeomen owned few slaves or none at all. The typical farm averaged 100 acres. Yeomen took great pride in their work. In 1849 a young Georgia man wrote, "I desire above all things to be a 'Farmer.' It is the most honest, upright, and sure way of securing all the comforts of life."

Yeoman families, including women and children, typically worked long days at a variety of tasks. Some yeomen held a few slaves, but worked along side them.

The poorest of white southerners lived on land that could not grow cash crops. They survived by hunting, fishing, raising small gardens, and doing odd jobs for money.

Religion and Society

Most white southerners shared similar religious beliefs. Because of the long distances between farms, families often saw their neighbors only at church events, such as revivals or socials. Rural women often played volunteer roles in their churches. Wealthy white southerners thought that their religion justified their position in society and the institution of slavery. They argued that God created some people, like themselves, to rule others. This belief opposed many northern Christians' belief that God was against slavery.

Urban Life

Many of the largest and most important cities in the South were strung along the Atlantic coast and had begun as shipping centers. Although fewer in number, the southern cities were similar to northern cities. City governments built public water systems and provided well-maintained streets. Public education was available in some places. Wealthy residents occasionally gave large sums of money to charities, such as orphanages and public libraries. Southern urban leaders wanted their cities to appear as modern as possible.

As on plantations, slaves did much of the work in southern cities. Slaves worked as domestic servants, in mills, in shipyards, and at skilled jobs. Many business leaders held slaves or hired them from nearby plantations.

READING CHECK **Summarizing** What different groups made up southern society?

Differentiating Instruction for Universal Access

Learners Having Difficulty — Reaching Standards

1. Draw the graphic organizer for students to see. Omit the blue, italicized answers.
2. Have each student copy the graphic organizer and complete it by identifying as many details as possible that describe southern city life.
3. Have students use their organizers to make a general statement about life in the urban South. LS **Visual/Spatial**

HSS 8.7.3; HSS **Analysis Skills:** HI 1

Alternative Assessment Handbook, Rubric 13: Graphic Organizers

Life in the Urban South

Public Services	Role of Slavery
• *Water systems* • *Well-maintained streets* • *Some public education*	• *Manual labor* • *Domestic servants* • *Hired from nearby plantations*

Answers

Free African Americans in the South *has a skilled job; earns a wage*

Reading Check *wealthy planters, yeomen, poor whites, enslaved Africans, and free African Americans*

Free African Americans and Discrimination

Although the vast majority of African Americans in the South were enslaved, more than 250,000 free African Americans lived in the region by 1860. Some were descendants of slaves who were freed after the American Revolution. Others were descendants of refugees from Toussaint L'Ouverture's Haitian Revolution in the late 1790s. Still others were former slaves who had run away, been freed by their slaveholder, or earned enough money to buy their freedom.

Free African Americans lived in both rural and urban areas. Most lived in the countryside and worked as paid laborers on plantations or farms. Free African Americans in cities often worked a variety of jobs, mostly as skilled artisans. Some, like barber William Johnson of Natchez, Mississippi, became quite successful in their businesses. Some free African Americans, especially those in the cities, formed social and economic ties with one another. Churches often served as the center of their social lives.

Free African Americans faced constant discrimination from white southerners. Many governments passed laws limiting the rights of free African Americans. Most free African Americans could not vote, travel freely, or hold certain jobs. In some places, free African Americans had to have a white person represent them in any business transaction. In others, laws restricted where they were allowed to live or conduct business.

Many white southerners argued that free African Americans did not have the ability to take care of themselves, and they used this belief to justify the institution of slavery. "The status of slavery is the only one for which the African is adapted," wrote one white Mississippian. To many white southerners, the very existence of free African Americans threatened the institution of slavery.

READING CHECK **Finding Main Ideas** What challenges did free African Americans face in the South?

SUMMARY AND PREVIEW Southern society was led by rich planters but included other groups as well. In the next section you will read about life under slavery.

Section 2 Assessment

go.hrw.com
Online Quiz
KEYWORD: SS8 HP12

Reviewing Ideas, Terms, and People

HSS 8.7.3, 8.7.4, 8.9.6

1. a. **Identify** What was the largest social group in the South? How did its members make a living?
   b. **Compare** In what ways were southern cities similar to northern cities?
   c. **Elaborate** Which southern social class do you think had the most difficult life? Why?
2. a. **Describe** What jobs were available to free African Americans in the South?
   b. **Analyze** Why did many white southerners fear free African Americans?
   c. **Elaborate** Why do you think that discrimination against free African Americans was harsher in the South than in the North?

Critical Thinking

3. **Comparing and Contrasting** Copy the Venn diagram below. Add to it lines which you will fill in to identify ways in which planters' and yeomen's lives were similar and different.

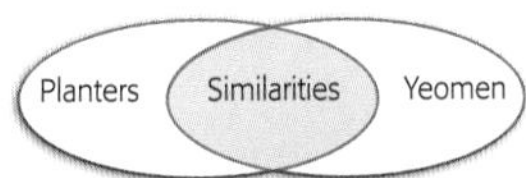

FOCUS ON WRITING

4. **Describing the Life of Cotton Farmers** In your notebook, describe the different roles played by male planters and their wives. What challenges would female planters have faced? When would the planters have had a chance to socialize?

Section 2 Assessment Answers

1. a. yeomen; owned and operated small farms
   b. both provided public services, such as water systems, streets, education
   c. possible answer—enslaved Africans; no rights and long days of hard, physical labor
2. a. (cities) skilled artisans or craftspeople, (rural) plantation or farm workers
   b. feared that they would start rebellions and viewed them as a threat to slavery
   c. Some southerners feared the influence free African Americans might have on slaves.
3. Planters—large plantations, wealthy, more than 20 slaves, political and economic influence; Yeomen—small farms, owned few or no slaves, worked long days; Similarities—white, depended on agriculture for their livelihood
4. Planters supervised growing of crops; wives ran plantation household. Answers will vary, but female planters might have faced challenges such as social pressure and a lack of legal rights. Planters socialized at dances and dinners organized by wives and at church functions.

Direct Teach

Main Idea

2 Free African Americans and Discrimination

Free African Americans in the South faced a great deal of discrimination.

Recall What were the main types of jobs that free African Americans held in the South? *worked as paid laborers on plantations or farms, worked as skilled artisans in cities*

Summarize How had free African Americans often gained their freedom? *ancestors were freed after American Revolution, were descendants of refugees from the Haitian Revolution, bought their freedom*

HSS 8.7.4, 8.9.6; HSS **Analysis Skills:** HI 1

Review & Assess

Close

Summarize the five main groups that made up southern society and describe the role of each group in the South's agricultural economy.

Review

Online Quiz, Section 2

Assess

SE Section 2 Assessment

PASS: Section 2 Quiz

Alternative Assessment Handbook

Reteach/Classroom Intervention

California Standards Review Workbook

Interactive Reader and Study Guide, Section 2

Interactive Skills Tutor CD-ROM

Answers

Reading Check *discrimination and harsh laws that limited where they could live, what work they could do, and with whom they could meet*

Preteach

Bellringer

If YOU were there . . . Use the **Daily Bellringer Transparency** to help students answer the question.

Daily Bellringer Transparency, Section 3

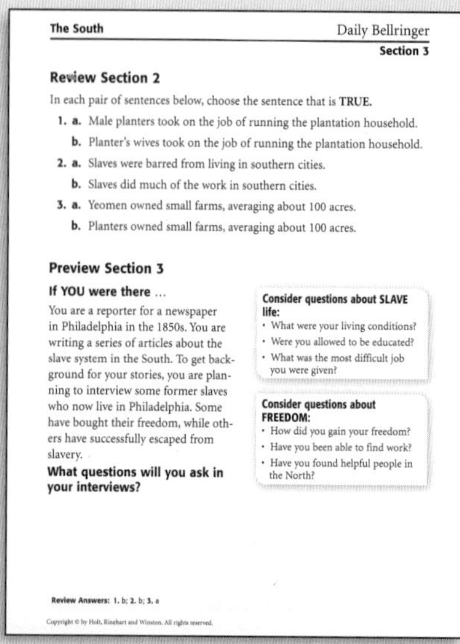

The South — Daily Bellringer — Section 3

Review Section 2

In each pair of sentences below, choose the sentence that is **TRUE.**

1. a. Male planters took on the job of running the plantation household.
   b. Planter's wives took on the job of running the plantation household.
2. a. Slaves were barred from living in southern cities.
   b. Slaves did much of the work in southern cities.
3. a. Yeomen owned small farms, averaging about 100 acres.
   b. Planters owned small farms, averaging about 100 acres.

Preview Section 3

If YOU were there ...

You are a reporter for a newspaper in Philadelphia in the 1850s. You are writing a series of articles about the slave system in the South. To get background for your stories, you are planning to interview some former slaves who now live in Philadelphia. Some have bought their freedom, while others have successfully escaped from slavery.

What questions will you ask in your interviews?

Consider questions about SLAVE life:
- What were your living conditions?
- Were you allowed to be educated?
- What was the most difficult job you were given?

Consider questions about FREEDOM:
- How did you gain your freedom?
- Have you been able to find work?
- Have you found helpful people in the North?

Review Answers: 1. b; 2. b; 3. a

Academic Vocabulary

Review with students the high-use academic term in this section.

aspect part (p. 388)

CRF: Vocabulary Builder, Section 3

Standards Focus

HSS 8.7.2

Means: Describe the effects of slavery on enslaved Africans, their descendants, and the South. Identify ways different groups tried to end or continue the system of slavery.

Matters: Enslaved Africans tried to challenge and rebel against the slave system, just as slaveholders tried to preserve it.

SECTION 3

The Slave System

What You Will Learn...

Main Ideas

1. Slaves worked at a variety of jobs on plantations.
2. Life under slavery was difficult and dehumanizing.
3. Slave culture centered around family, community, and religion.
4. Slave uprisings led to stricter slave codes in many states.

The Big Idea

The slave system in the South produced harsh living conditions and occasional rebellions.

Key Terms and People

folktales, *p. 389*
spirituals, *p. 389*
Nat Turner, *p. 390*
Nat Turner's Rebellion, *p. 390*

HSS 8.7.2 Trace the origins and development of slavery; its effects on black Americans and on the region's political, social, religious, economic, and cultural development; and identify the stategies that were tried to both overturn and preserve it (e.g., through the writings and historical documents on Nat Turner, Denmark Vesey).

If YOU were there...

You are a reporter for a newspaper in Philadelphia in the 1850s. You are writing a series of articles about the slave system in the South. To get background for your stories, you are planning to interview some former slaves who now live in Philadelphia. Some have bought their freedom, while others have successfully escaped from slavery.

What questions will you ask in your interviews?

BUILDING BACKGROUND While most white southern families were not slaveholders, the southern economy depended on the work of slaves. This was true not only on large plantations but also on smaller farms and in the cities. Few chances existed for enslaved African Americans to escape their hard lives.

Slaves and Work

Most enslaved African Americans lived in rural areas where they worked on farms and plantations. Enslaved people on small farms usually did a variety of jobs. On large plantations, most slaves were assigned to specific jobs, and most worked in the fields. Most slaveholders demanded that slaves work as much as possible. Supervisors known as drivers, who were sometimes slaves themselves, made sure that slaves followed orders and carried out punishments.

Working in the Field

Most plantation owners used the gang-labor system. In this system, all field hands worked on the same task at the same time. They usually worked from sunup to sundown. Former slave Harry McMillan had worked on a plantation in South Carolina. He recalled that the field hands usually did not even get a break to eat lunch. "You had to get your victuals [food] standing at your hoe," he remembered.

Men, women, and even children older than about 10 usually did the same tasks. Sickness and poor weather rarely stopped the work. "The times I hated most was picking cotton when the frost was on the bolls [seed pods]," recalled former Louisiana slave Mary Reynolds. "My hands git sore and crack open and bleed."

Teach the Big Idea: Master the Standards

Standards Proficiency

The Slave System HSS 8.7.2; HSS Analysis Skills: HI 1

1. **Teach** Ask students the Main Idea questions to teach this section.
2. **Apply** Write the Big Idea for students to see. Below it, write the following headings from the section: *Slaves and Work, Life Under Slavery, Slave Culture,* and *Slave Uprisings.*
3. **Review** As you review the section, have volunteers share important points from the text that support the Big Idea. Write the information under the appropriate headings.
4. **Practice/Homework** Ask students to imagine that they are northerners visiting the South. Have each student write a letter home describing his or her observations about the slave system. LS **Verbal/Linguistic, Visual/Spatial**

Alternative Assessment Handbook, Rubrics 7: Charts; and 25: Personal Letters

Working in the Planter's Home

Some slaves worked as butlers, cooks, or nurses in the planter's home. These slaves often had better food, clothing, and shelter than field hands did, but they often worked longer hours. They had to serve the planter's family 24 hours a day.

Working at Skilled Jobs

On larger plantations, some enslaved African Americans worked at skilled jobs, such as blacksmithing or carpentry. Sometimes planters let these slaves sell their services to other people. Often planters collected a portion of what was earned but allowed slaves to keep the rest. In this way, some skilled slaves earned enough money to buy their freedom from their slaveholders. For example, William Ellison earned his freedom in South Carolina by working for wages as a cotton gin maker. For years, he worked late at night and on Sundays. He bought his freedom with the money he earned. Eventually, he was also able to buy the freedom of his wife and daughter.

READING CHECK **Summarizing** What were some types of work done by enslaved people on plantations?

Life Under Slavery

Generally, slaveholders viewed slaves as property, not as people. Slaveholders bought and sold slaves to make a profit. The most common method of sale was at an auction. The auction itself determined whether families would be kept together or separated. Sometimes a buyer wanted a slave to fill a specific job, such as heavy laborer, carpenter, or blacksmith. The buyer might be willing to pay for the slave who could do the work, but not for that slave's family. Families would then be separated with little hope of ever getting back together.

Slave traders sometimes even kidnapped free African Americans and then sold them into slavery. For example, Solomon Northup, a free African American, was kidnapped in Washington, D.C. He spent 12 years as a slave until he finally proved his identity and gained his release.

Living Conditions

Enslaved people often endured poor living conditions. Planters housed them in dirt-floor cabins with few furnishings and often leaky roofs. The clothing given to them was usually simple and made of cheap, coarse fabric. Some slaves tried to brighten up their

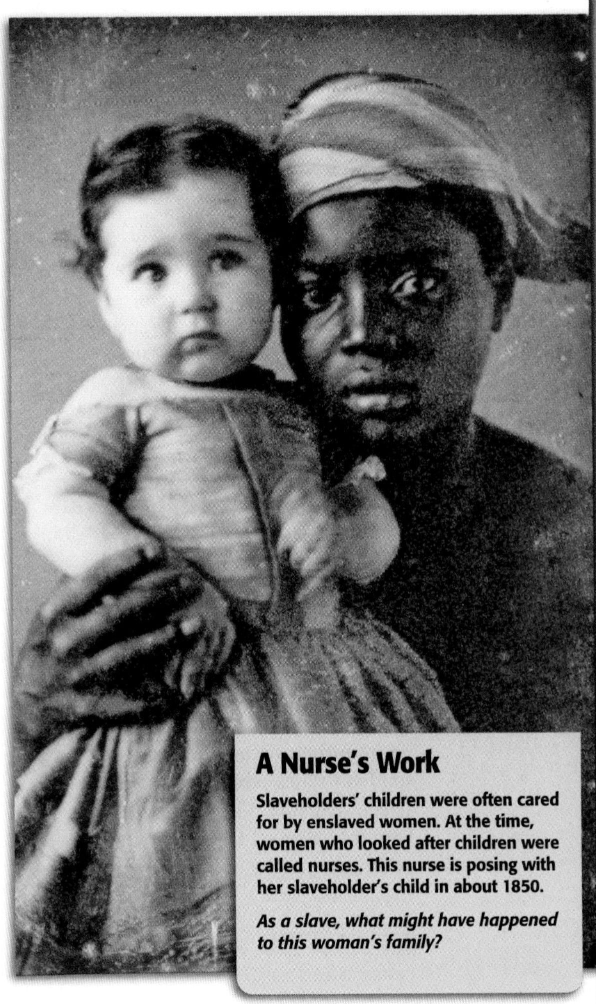

A Nurse's Work

Slaveholders' children were often cared for by enslaved women. At the time, women who looked after children were called nurses. This nurse is posing with her slaveholder's child in about 1850.

As a slave, what might have happened to this woman's family?

Direct Teach

Main Idea

1 Slaves and Work

Slaves worked at a variety of jobs on plantations.

Describe What was work in the fields like for enslaved Africans? *In all weather, adults and children older than about 10 worked from sunup to sundown often at the same tasks.*

Contrast How was life different for slaves working in the planter's home? *better food, clothing, and shelter; longer hours*

Analyze How were some skilled slaves able to buy their freedom? *saved money from selling their services to other people*

HSS 8.7.2; HSS **Analysis Skills:** HI 1, HI 2

Main Idea

2 Life Under Slavery

Life under slavery was difficult and dehumanizing.

Describe How did slaveholders generally view slaves? *as their property*

Elaborate Why did separated slave families have little hope of getting back together? *lived far apart with little chance of gaining freedom*

CRF: Primary Source Activity: Jacob Stroyer, *My Life in the South*

HSS 8.7.2; HSS **Analysis Skills:** HI 1

Linking to Today

African Craft of Ironwork Enslaved Africans brought with them from Africa the ancient craft of ironmaking. In sections of Charleston and New Orleans, you can still see elaborate wrought-iron balconies, gates, and lamp brackets created by black ironsmiths in the 1700s and 1800s.

Differentiating Instruction for Universal Access

Learners Having Difficulty

Reaching Standards

1. Create a three-column chart for students to see. Write the boldfaced headings below at the top of each column. Read aloud the italicized answers in random order and have students write them down.
   - **Agricultural Slaves:** *gang-labor; worked sunup to sundown; worked when sick; worked in poor weather*
   - **Slaves in the Home:** *butlers, cooks, nurses; better food, clothing, shelter; 24 hours a day*
   - **Skilled Slaves:** *blacksmiths, carpenters; might sell services to others; might save enough money to buy freedom*
2. Have students copy the chart and complete it by placing each answer under the appropriate heading. Then review the answers as a class. **LS Verbal/Linguistic**

HSS 8.7.2; HSS **Analysis Skills:** HI 1

Alternative Assessment Handbook, Rubric 7: Charts

Answers

A Nurse's Work *possible answer—separated at a slave auction*

Reading Check *field workers, butlers, cooks, nurses, blacksmiths, carpenters*

Direct Teach

Main Idea

❷ Life Under Slavery

Life under slavery was difficult and dehumanizing.

Recall How did planters encourage obedience? *more food or better living conditions; harsh punishments*

Draw Conclusions What effects do you think states' strict slave codes had on enslaved Africans' lives? *possible answer—kept slaves isolated, illiterate, and powerless*

HSS 8.7.2; HSS **Analysis Skills:** HI 1

Connect to Science

Health of Slaves Poor diet, exhaustion, unsanitary living conditions, and exposure to the outdoor elements made slaves vulnerable to many health problems and diseases, including blindness, rickets, scurvy, leprosy, tuberculosis, and pneumonia. Outbreaks of cholera and yellow fever frequently occurred as well. Poor diet and health contributed to a low life expectancy for enslaved Africans. For example, in Louisiana in 1850, an enslaved man could expect to live only 29 years, an enslaved woman only 34 years.

go.hrw.com
Online Resources
KEYWORD: SS8 US12
ACTIVITY: Slave Cabin Drawings

clothing by sewing on designs from discarded scraps of material. In this way, they expressed their individuality and personalized the clothing assigned to them by the planters.

Likewise, many slaves did what they could to improve their small food rations. Some planters allowed slaves to keep their own gardens for vegetables, and chickens for eggs. Other slaves were able to add a little variety to their diet by fishing or picking wild berries.

Punishment and Slave Codes

Some planters offered more food or better living conditions to encourage slaves' obedience. However, most slaveholders used punishment instead. Some would punish one slave in front of others as a warning to them all. Harry McMillan recalled some of the punishments he had witnessed.

> "The punishments were whipping, putting you in the stocks [wooden frames to lock people in] and making you wear irons and a chain at work. Then they had a collar to put round your neck with two horns, like cows' horns, so that you could not lie down ... Sometimes they dug a hole like a well with a door on top. This they called a dungeon keeping you in it two or three weeks or a month, or sometimes till you died in there."
>
> —Harry McMillan, quoted in *Major Problems in the History of the American South, Volume I*, edited by Paul D. Escott and David R. Goldfield

Academic Vocabulary
aspect part

To further control slaves' actions, many states passed strict laws called slave codes. Some laws prohibited slaves from traveling far from their homes. Literacy laws in most southern states prohibited the education of slaves. Alabama, Virginia, and Georgia had laws that allowed the fining and whipping of anyone caught teaching enslaved people to read and write.

Reading Check **Summarizing** How did slaveholders control slaves?

A Slave's Daily Life

Typical Daily schedule:

3:00 a.m.	*Out of bed, tend animals*
6:00 a.m.	*Prayers*
7:00 a.m.	*Start work*
12:00 p.m.	*Lunch*
1:00 p.m.	*Return to work*
7:00 p.m.	*Dinner*
8:00 p.m.	*Return to work*
11:00 p.m.	*Lights out*

Slave Culture

Many enslaved Africans found comfort in their community and culture. They made time for social activity, even after exhausting workdays, in order to relieve the hardship of their lives.

Family and Community

Family was the most important **aspect** of slave communities, and slaves feared separation more than they feared punishment. Josiah Henson never forgot the day that he and his family were auctioned. His mother begged the slaveholder who bought her to buy Josiah, too. The slaveholder refused, and Henson's entire family was separated. "I must have been then between five or six years old," he recalled years later. "I seem to see and hear my poor weeping mother now."

Critical Thinking: Analyzing Primary Sources

Exceeding Standards

Slavery: An Oral History

HSS 8.7.2; HSS **Analysis Skills:** HR 4, HR 5 — Research Required

Background: Explain to students that during the 1930s, more than 2,300 first-person narratives of former slaves were recorded and collected in *Born in Slavery: Slave Narratives from the Federal Writers' Project, 1936–1938.* This seventeen-volume collection is available online through the Library of Congress.

1. Ask students to conduct research on the oral histories of former slaves recorded in the slave narratives from the Federal Writers' Project.
2. Ask each student to identify one primary source that he or she finds particularly descriptive or moving in its portrayal of the slavery experience.
3. Have students take turns reading aloud their selections and invite them to share their responses. LS **Verbal/Linguistic**

Alternative Assessment Handbook, Rubric 30: Research

Answers

Reading Check *harsh punishments and strict slave codes*

The lives of slaves revolved around the work that was required of them. For many, this meant doing the backbreaking work of harvesting and loading tons of cotton. Most slaves found hope and a short escape from their daily misery in Sunday church services. Others sought to escape permanently and ran away, hoping to reach the freedom of the North. A failed escape attempt, however, could result in a cruel whipping—or worse.

What different aspects of slavery are shown in these pictures?

Hauling the Whole Week's Pickings by William Henry Brown, The Historic New Orleans Collection

Enslaved parents kept their heritage alive by passing down family histories as well as African customs and traditions. They also told **folktales**, or stories with a moral, to teach lessons about how to survive under slavery. Folktales often included a clever animal character called a trickster. The trickster—which often represented slaves—defeated a stronger animal by outwitting it. Folktales reassured slaves that they could survive by outsmarting more powerful slaveholders.

Religion

Religion also played an important part in slave culture. By the early 1800s many slaves were Christians. They came to see themselves, like the slaves in the Old Testament, as God's chosen people, much like the Hebrew slaves in ancient Egypt who had faith that they would someday live in freedom.

Some slaves sang **spirituals**, emotional Christian songs that blended African and European music, to express their religious beliefs. For example, "The Heavenly Road" reflected slaves' belief in their equality in the eyes of God.

> "Come, my brother, if you never did pray,
> I hope you pray tonight;
> For I really believe I am a child of God
> As I walk on the heavenly road."
>
> —Anonymous, quoted in *Afro-American Religious History*, edited by Milton C. Sernett

Slaves blended aspects of traditional African religions with those of Christianity. They worshipped in secret, out of sight of slaveholders. Some historians have called slave religion the invisible institution.

THE IMPACT TODAY

The musical influence of these inspirational slave songs can be heard today in gospel music.

Cross-Discipline Activity: Music

Standards Proficiency

Spirituals HSS 8.7.2; HSS Analysis Skills: HI 1

Prep Required

Materials: recordings and lyrics of spirituals

1. Play several recordings of spirituals to acquaint students with the music's tones and rhythms. Distribute lyrics for students to read and study.
2. Pair students. Try to match students who enjoy music with those who enjoy creative writing. Have each pair write its own spiritual. Students might set their lyrics to an existing tune.
3. Invite pairs to perform their songs, to record and play them for the class, or to display their lyrics and musical arrangements in the classroom. LS **Auditory/Musical, Interpersonal**

Alternative Assessment Handbook, Rubrics 26: Poems and Songs

Direct Teach

Main Idea

❸ Slave Culture

Slave culture centered around family, community, and religion.

Recall What did slaves fear more than physical punishment? *separation from their families*

Explain How did enslaved parents work to ensure that their children never forgot their heritage? *passed down family histories, customs, traditions*

Elaborate Why did enslaved Africans worship in secret? *possible answer—Slaveholders would not approve of mixing traditional African religions with Christianity or the focus on equality in God's eyes.*

HSS 8.7.2; HSS **Analysis Skills:** HI 1

Analyzing Visuals

A Slave's Daily Life

The collage *Hauling the Whole Week's Pickings* is one of several that artist William Henry Brown created in 1842. Brown created the collages while in Mississippi on a visit to a cotton plantation owned by the Vick family. The collages, which Brown made for the Vick family's children, portray the everyday lives of slaves on the plantation.

Analyzing Primary Sources If you kept to the Daily Schedule shown, how much sleep would you get a night? *4 hours*

Info to Know

Followers of Islam Enslaved Africans from Muslim areas of West Africa brought their religion to North America. On plantations along the coasts of Georgia and South Carolina, many slaves practiced Muslim traditions.

Answers

A Slave's Daily Life *work on the plantation and a religious service*

Direct Teach

Main Idea

4 Slave Uprisings

Slave uprisings led to stricter slave codes in many states.

Identify What was the most violent U.S. slave revolt? When did it occur? *Nat Turner's Rebellion; August 1831*

Elaborate How do you think slaves responded to stronger slave codes? *possible answer—increased desire to run away or revolt*

- **CRF:** Biography Activities: Nat Turner; Denmark Vesey
- **CRF:** Primary Source Activity: The Denmark Vesey Conspiracy
- Map Transparency: Nat Turner's Rebellion

HSS 8.7.2; HSS **Analysis Skills:** HI 1, HI 2

Nat Turner's Rebellion

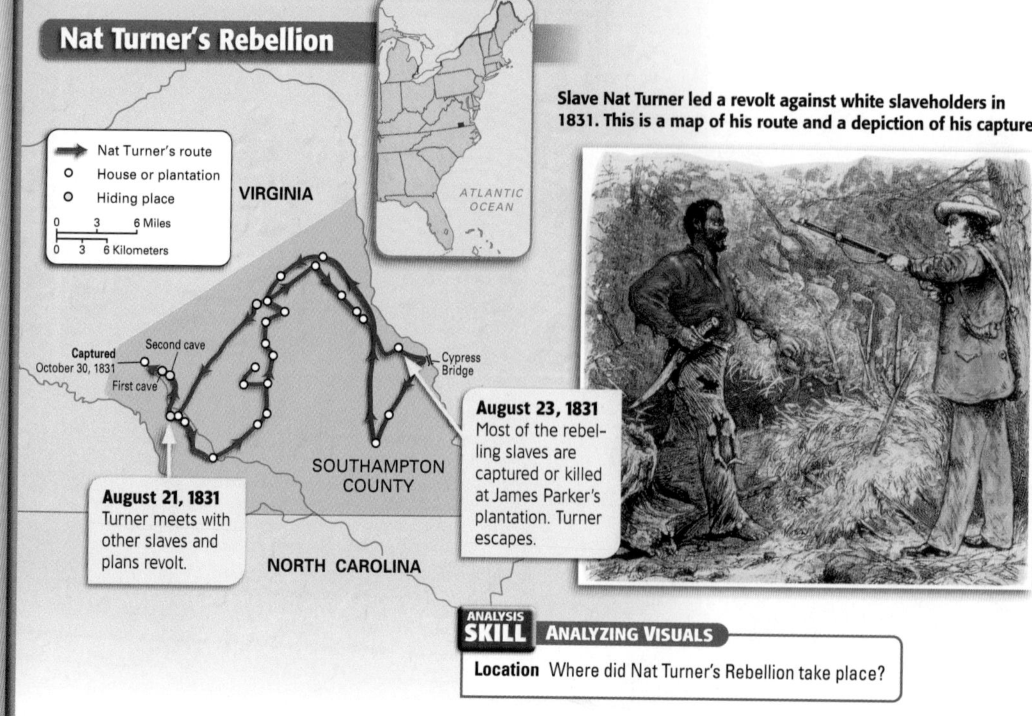

Slave Nat Turner led a revolt against white slaveholders in 1831. This is a map of his route and a depiction of his capture.

ANALYSIS SKILL ANALYZING VISUALS

Location Where did Nat Turner's Rebellion take place?

Seeds of Rebellion

Maintaining their own religious beliefs and practices was only one way in which enslaved people resisted slaveholders' attempts to control them completely. In small ways, slaves rebelled against the system daily. Sometimes they worked slower to protest long hours in the fields. Other times they ran away for a few days to avoid an angry slaveholder. Some slaves tried to escape permanently, but most left only for short periods, often to go and visit relatives.

Gaining freedom by escaping to the North was hard. If discovered, slaves were captured and sent back to their slaveholders, where they faced certain punishment or death. However, thousands of enslaved people succeeded in escaping.

READING CHECK **Summarizing** How did slaves' religious beliefs affect their attitudes toward slavery?

Slave Uprisings

Although violent slave revolts were relatively rare, white southerners lived in fear of them. Two planned rebellions were stopped before they began. Gabriel Prosser planned a rebellion near Richmond, Virginia, in 1800. Denmark Vesey planned one in Charleston, South Carolina, in 1822. Authorities executed most of those involved in planning these rebellions. Though Vesey was executed as the leader of the Charleston conspiracy, several accounts written after his death by antislavery writers claimed he was a hero.

The most violent slave revolt in the United States occurred in 1831 and is known as **Nat Turner's Rebellion.** Nat Turner, a slave from Southampton County, Virginia, believed that God had told him to end slavery. On an August night in 1831, Turner led a group of slaves in a plan to kill all of the slaveholders and their families in the county. First, they

Answers

Analyzing Visuals *Southampton County, Virginia*

Reading Check *helped them believe that one day they would be free; helped them endure slavery; helped them see themselves as equal*

Differentiating Instruction for Universal Access

English-Language Learners — Standards Proficiency

1. Copy the graphic organizer for students to see. Omit the blue, italicized answers.
2. Have each student copy the graphic organizer and complete it by listing the ways in which enslaved Africans challenged the slavery system.
3. Review the answers then lead a discussion about why these tactics failed to end the system of slavery. LS **Visual/Spatial**

HSS 8.7.2; HSS **Analysis Skills:** HI 1

Challenging the Slavery System: *working slower*; *running away*; *violent revolts*

Advanced Learners/GATE — Exceeding Standards

Nat Turner Dialogue Have students write an imagined dialogue between Nat Turner and a fellow enslaved African. In the dialogue, Turner should persuade his fellow worker to join his rebellion. LS **Verbal/Linguistic**

- Alternative Assessment Handbook, Rubric 43: Writing to Persuade

HSS 8.7.2; HSS **Analysis Skills:** HI 1

attacked the family that held Turner as a slave. Soon they had killed about 60 white people in the community.

More than 100 innocent slaves who were not part of Turner's group were killed in an attempt to stop the rebellion. Turner himself led authorities on a chase around the countryside for six weeks. He hid in caves and in the woods before he was caught and brought to trial. Before his trial, Turner made a confession. He expressed his belief that the revolt was justified and worth his death: "I am willing to suffer the fate that awaits me." He was executed on November 11, 1831. After the rebellion, many states strengthened their slave codes. The new codes placed stricter control on the slave population. Despite the resistance of enslaved people, slavery continued to spread.

READING CHECK **Finding Main Ideas**
What was Nat Turner's Rebellion, and what happened as a result?

SUMMARY AND PREVIEW Several groups of African Americans attempted to end slavery by rebellion. All of the attempts failed. In the next chapter you will read about efforts to reform American society.

Primary Source

LETTER

Nat Turner's Rebellion

In 1831 a white southerner who had escaped the rebellion wrote a letter describing the mood of the area where Nat Turner had killed slaveholders.

"The oldest inhabitants of our county have never experienced such a distressing [terrible] time, as we have had since Sunday night last. The [slaves], about fifteen miles from this place, have massacred from 50 to 75 women and children, and some 8 or 10 men. Every house, room and corner in this place is full of women and children, driven from home, who had to take to the woods, until they could get to this place. We are worn out with fatigue [tiredness]."

—*Richmond Enquirer*, quoted in *The Southampton Slave Revolt of 1831* by Henry I. Tragle

The author believes no one in the county has been through a worse event.

The author says that many people went into hiding when the rebellion began.

ANALYSIS SKILL **ANALYZING PRIMARY SOURCES**
What emotions do you think the author of this letter was feeling?

Section 3 Assessment

go.hrw.com
Online Quiz
KEYWORD: SS8 HP12

Reviewing Ideas, Terms, and People

HSS 8.7.2

1. a. **Identify** What different types of work were done by slaves on plantations?
   b. **Elaborate** Do you think that skilled slaves had advantages over other slaves? Why or why not?
2. a. **Describe** What were living conditions like for most slaves?
   b. **Summarize** In what different ways did slaveholders encourage obedience from their slaves?
3. a. **Recall** What was the purpose of **folktales**?
   b. **Explain** How did slaves try to maintain a sense of community?
4. a. **Describe** What was the outcome of **Nat Turner's Rebellion**?
   b. **Elaborate** What do you think were some reasons why slaves rebelled?

Critical Thinking

5. **Evaluating** Copy the graphic organizer below. Then add information to describe life under slavery.

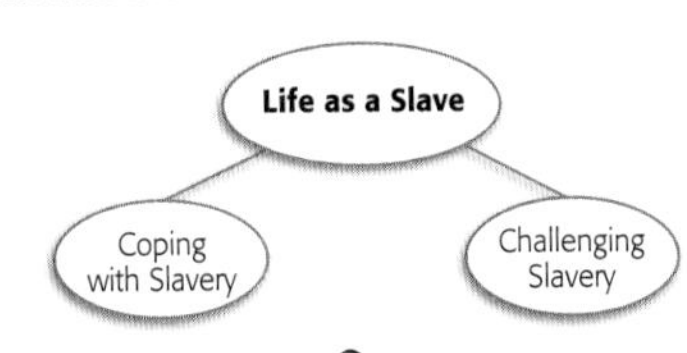

FOCUS ON WRITING

6. **Describing the Life of Slaves** Add notes about the life of slaves to your notebook. What would it have been like to be a slave? How would it have felt to have been separated from your family?

Direct Teach

Primary Source

Reading Like a Historian

Nat Turner's Rebellion Help students practice reading the document like historians. Ask:

- Who wrote this letter, and why?
- Where was this letter published?
- How is the author's account of the incident different from what you have read in this section? Why do you think the two accounts differ?

HSS 8.7.2; HSS **Analysis Skills:** HR 4

Review & Assess

Close

Have students describe in their own words the daily lives of slaves and how they responded to slavery.

Review

Online Quiz, Section 3

Assess

SE Section 3 Assessment

PASS: Section 3 Quiz

Alternative Assessment Handbook

Reteach/Classroom Intervention

California Standards Review Workbook

Interactive Reader and Study Guide, Section 3

Interactive Skills Tutor CD-ROM

Section 3 Assessment Answers

1. a. agricultural, domestic, and skilled
   b. possible answer—yes, skilled work possibly more interesting, could have chance to buy freedom
2. a. severe work schedules and working conditions; harsh punishments; poor clothing, food, and shelter
   b. more food or improved working conditions, punishment, slave codes
3. a. to teach how to survive under slavery
   b. through religion and folktales
4. a. About 60 white people and more than 100 innocent slaves killed; Turner executed; many states strengthened slave codes
   b. hardship, injustice, lack of freedom
5. Coping with Slavery—community, folktales, religion; Challenging Slavery— work slower, try to escape, rebellion
6. possible answers: life as a slave—hard work, strict punishment, discrimination, religious faith and folktales help to cope; separated from family—anger and sadness, community becomes like family

Answers

Analyzing Primary Sources *fear, horror, exhaustion*

Reading Check *1831 slave rebellion in which 60 white people were killed; revolt failed; Turner was executed; states adopted stricter slave codes*

Social Studies Skills

Interpreting Graphs

Activity **Graphs in the Media**

Materials: copies of various graphs from magazines and newspapers

Before class, find at least one example of a bar graph, a line graph, and a circle graph in magazines or newspapers. Display each graph in turn for the class to see. Have students identify each type of graph. Then ask students to describe the information shown in the graph legend. Have students identify what each color in the graph represents. Next, ask students to identify the labels in the graph and use them to explain what information the graph is showing. To test students' understanding, ask one to two questions about each graph that require students to interpret the information in the graph and to identify relationships or trends shown.

LS Visual/Spatial

Alternative Assessment Handbook, Rubric 7: Charts

Interactive Skills Tutor CD-ROM, Lesson 6: Interpret Maps, Graphs, Charts, Visuals, and Political Cartoons

Social Studies Skills

Analysis | Critical Thinking | Participation | **Study**

Interpreting Graphs

Define the Skill

Graphs are drawings that classify and display data in a clear, visual format. There are three basic types of graphs. *Line graphs* and *bar graphs* plot changes in quantities over time. Bar graphs are also used to compare quantities within a category at a particular time. *Circle graphs,* also called *pie graphs,* have a similar use. The circle represents the whole of something, and the slices show what proportion of the whole is made by each part.

Being able to interpret graphs accurately lets you see and understand relationships more easily than in tables or in written explanations. This is especially true if the information is detailed or the relationships are complicated.

Learn the Skill

The following guidelines will help you interpret data that is presented as a graph.

1. Read the title to identify the subject and purpose of the graph. Note the kind of graph, remembering what each type is designed to indicate. Also note how the graph's subject relates to any printed material that accompanies it
2. Study the graph's parts. Place close attention to the labels that define each axis. Note the units of measure. Identify the categories used. If there are different colors on bars or lines in the graph, determine what those differences mean.
3. Analyze the data in the graph. Note any increases or decreases in quantities. Look for trends, changes, and other relationships in the data.
4. Apply the information in the graph. Use the results of your analysis to draw conclusions. Ask yourself what generalizations can be made about the trends, changes, or relationships shown in the graph.

Practice the Skill

The graph below is a double-line graph. It shows both changes and relationships over time. This type of graph allows you to see how changes in one thing compare with changes in something else. Apply the guidelines to interpret the graph and answer the questions that follow.

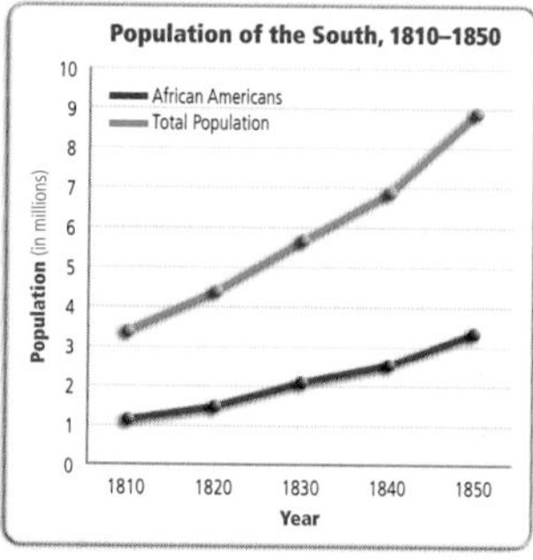

1. What is shown on each axis of this graph? What are the units of measure on each axis?
2. What do each of the lines represent?
3. What was the total population of the South in 1810? in 1850? By how much did the African American population grow during that period?
4. Was the white population or the black population growing faster? Explain how you know.

Social Studies Skills Activity: Interpreting Graphs

Graph Quiz

Standards Proficiency

1. Have students examine the graph "U.S. Cotton Production, 1800–1860" on p. 378. Have each student create a three-question quiz about the graph. Assign students the type of quiz to create, such as multiple choice, short answer, or true-false.
2. Have each student create a separate answer key for his or her quiz.
3. Then have students exchange quizzes with partners. Students should answer the quizzes they receive and return them to their authors for grading.
4. Then have each student write a few sentences summarizing the information shown in the graph. Ask for volunteers to read their summaries to the class. **LS Interpersonal, Verbal/Linguistic**

Alternative Assessment Handbook, Rubrics 7: Charts; and 37: Writing Assignments

Answers

Practice the Skill 1. *vertical axis—Population (in millions), in units of one million; horizontal axis—year, in ten-year increments;* **2.** *blue—African American population in the South, 1810–1850; green—total population in the South, 1810–1850;* **3.** *1810—about 3.25 million; 1850—about 8.9 million; almost 2 million;* **4.** *white population, calculated by subtracting growth of African American population from growth of total population*

CHAPTER 12

Standards Review

Visual Summary

Use the visual summary below to help you review the main ideas of the chapter.

QUICK FACTS

Southern Society Planters were at the top of southern society.
Cotton Economy In addition to cotton, southern farmers grew other cash crops and staple crops.
Slavery The strength of the southern economy depended on slave labor.

Reviewing Vocabulary, Terms, and People

Match the definition on the left with the correct term on the right.

1. A region of cotton-producing areas that stretched from South Carolina to Texas
2. Emotional songs that mixed African and European music and expressed religious beliefs
3. Owners of small farms who made up the largest social class in the South
4. Crop brokers who often managed the cotton trade in the South
5. Wealthy farmers and plantation owners

a. cotton belt
b. factors
c. planters
d. spirituals
e. yeomen

Comprehension and Critical Thinking

SECTION 1 *(Pages 376–381)* **HSS 8.7.1, 8.7.2**

6. **a. Describe** How did the cotton gin lead to a cotton boom in the South?
   b. Analyze What were the positive and negative results of the cotton boom?
   c. Evaluate Do you think that the South suffered as a result of its reliance on cotton? Why or why not?

SECTION 2 *(Pages 382–385)* **HSS 8.7.3, 8.7.4, 8.9.6**

7. **a. Describe** What three groups made up white southern society?
   b. Compare and Contrast In what ways were the lives of free African Americans and white southerners similar and different?
   c. Predict What might have been the attitude of yeomen and poor white southerners toward slavery? Why?

Answers

Visual Summary

Review and Inquiry Ask students how the images in the Visual Summary relate to the chapter content. Have students describe what important ideas in the chapter are not part of the visual.

Quick Facts Transparency: The South Visual Summary

Reviewing Vocabulary, Terms, and People

1. a
2. d
3. e
4. b
5. c

Comprehension and Critical Thinking

6. **a.** made cotton easier to process, more cotton was planted
   b. positive—created wealth, boosted southern economy; negative—increased demand for slaves, led to an economy that was overly dependent on cotton
   c. possible answer—yes, had nothing else to depend upon during times when cotton prices fell

Review and Assessment Resources

Review and Reinforce

- **SE** Chapter Standards Review
- **CRF:** Chapter Review Activity
- California Standards Review Workbook
- Quick Facts Transparency: The South Visual Summary
- Spanish Chapter Summaries Audio CD Program
- Online Chapter Summary in Six Languages
- **OSP** Holt PuzzlePro; GameTool for ExamView
- Quiz Game CD-ROM

Assess

- **SE** Standards Assessment
- PASS: Chapter Test, Forms A and B
- Alternative Assessment Handbook
- **OSP** ExamView Test Generator, Chapter Test
- Universal Access Modified Worksheets and Tests CD-ROM: Chapter Test
- Holt Online Assessment Program (in the Premier Online Edition)

Reteach/Intervene

- Interactive Reader and Study Guide
- Universal Access Teacher Management System: Lesson Plans for Universal Access
- Universal Access Modified Worksheets and Tests CD-ROM
- Interactive Skills Tutor CD-ROM

go.hrw.com
Online Resources
Chapter Resources:
KEYWORD: SS8 US12

Answers

7. a. planters, yeomen, and poor white southerners
b. similar—both had a degree of freedom; different—African Americans suffered harsh discrimination and legal restrictions.
c. possible answers—might have felt no connection to slavery since they generally did not own slaves; might have liked it because the slaves did most of the difficult physical labor and menial tasks

8. a. work slower, run away, revolts
b. By passing down their family heritage, telling stories, and holding onto their religious beliefs, slaves could find meaning in their lives despite the arduous conditions under which they lived. Religion helped slaves hope for freedom, even if it meant waiting for the next life.
c. possible answers—greater control of slaves; more widespread encouragement of slavery; harsher life for enslaved Africans

Reviewing Themes

9. Planters grew wealthy, some yeomen were able to own their own land, slaves worked even harder under harsh conditions.
10. The southern economy grew, wealth built up among wealthy white southerners, the South became a major player in the world trade of cotton, a cotton trade developed, and cotton-related industries grew.
11. The cotton gin led to an increase in slavery and production of cotton. Scientific agriculture helped farmers diversify their crops and not exhaust the land.

Using the Internet

12. Go to the HRW Web site and enter the keyword shown to access a rubric for this activity.

KEYWORD: SS8 TEACHER

SECTION 3 *(Pages 386–391)* **HSS 8.7.2**

8. **a. Identify** What are some small ways in which slaves tried to challenge the slave system?
b. Make Inferences How did religion and family help slaves cope with their lives?
c. Predict What could be some possible results of stronger strengthening of slave codes in the South?

Reviewing Themes

9. **Society and Culture** How were the different social classes in the South affected by the cotton boom?
10. **Economics** How did the cotton boom affect the economy of the South?
11. **Technology and Innovation** What effects did the cotton gin and scientific agriculture have on life in the South?

Using the Internet

12. **Activity: Writing Diary Entries** Enslaved African Americans faced harsh working and living conditions. Many tried to escape the slave system. Enter the activity keyword and research the attempts by enslaved African Americans to reach the North and the people who assisted them. Imagine you were trying to help slaves travel to freedom. Write four entries into a diary. In each entry, describe your experiences. Include thumbnail maps to trace their trip.

Reading Skills

Evaluating Web-Based Information *Use the Reading Skills taught in this chapter to answer the question below.*

13. Which of the following would be the best Web site to find information about life in the South before the Civil War?

Social Studies Skills

Interpreting Graphs *Use the Social Studies Skills taught in this chapter to answer the questions about the graph below.*

14. What span of time saw the largest increase in cotton production?
a. 1800 to 1820
b. 1820 to 1840
c. 1840 to 1860
d. after 1860
15. About what year did cotton production reach 1.2 million bales per year?
a. 1800
b. 1820
c. 1840
d. 1860

FOCUS ON WRITING

16. **Writing Your Biographical Sketch** Look over your notes about life on a cotton farm. Then choose an imaginary person to write about. Think about what life would have been like for this person. What might he or she have looked like? How might he or she have spoken? What might a typical day have been like? Once you have answered these questions, write two paragraphs about a day in the life of this person.

Reading Skills

13. b

Social Studies Skills

14. b
15. c

Focus on Writing

16. **Rubric** Students' biographical sketches should
- identify the imaginary person and his or her social class
- describe what the person does and how he or she looks
- accurately describe a typical day in the life of a person from the selected social class
- use precise nouns and adjectives
- provide two paragraphs

CRF: Focus on Writing Activity: Biographical Sketch

Standards Assessment

DIRECTIONS: Read each question and write the letter of the best response.

1

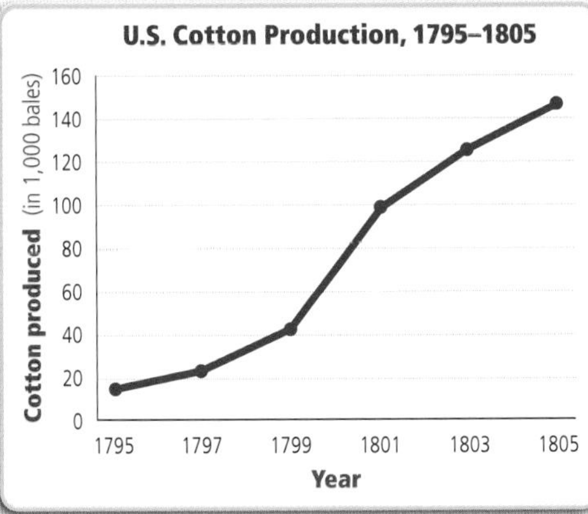

The *main* reason for the changes shown in the graph was

A the invention and use of the cotton gin.
B a decline in the number of slaves.
C the end of the international slave trade.
D a switch from food crops to cash crops.

2 All of the following helped enslaved African Americans to endure and survive slavery *except*

A religion.
B slave codes.
C spirituals.
D folktales.

3 Because some southerners feared farmers had become too reliant on cotton, they encouraged farmers to

A stop using the cotton gin.
B try growing a variety of cash crops.
C demand higher tariffs.
D introduce cotton and slavery to the West.

4 Which statement accurately describes southern society in the mid-1800s?

A Very few white southerners owned slaves.
B Few white southerners owned the land they farmed.
C All African Americans in the South were held in slavery.
D Most white southerners were small farmers.

5 Free African Americans in the South in the early and mid-1800s

A had the same rights and freedoms as white southerners.
B had few rights and freedoms.
C usually had escaped from slavery.
D did not exist as a class of people.

Connecting with Past Learning

6 In Grade 7 you learned about the manors that developed in Europe during feudalism. Who in the South in the 1800s would have been most like the head of a manor in the Middle Ages?

A a factor
B a yeoman farmer
C a planter
D a slaveholder

7 In 73 BC a gladiator named Spartacus led a slave revolt against Rome. His action can be compared to that of which American in the mid-1800s?

A Alexander Stephens
B Eli Whitney
C Nat Turner
D Frederick Douglass

Answers

1. A
Break Down the Question Students need to note the upward trend of cotton production and recall that the invention of the cotton gin in 1793 was responsible for the cotton boom.

2. B
Break Down the Question Point out to students that the italicized word *except* means that they need to identify which of the answers is the exception.

3. B
Break Down the Question This question requires students to recall factual information. Refer students who miss this question to the material "Other Crops and Industries" in Section 1.

4. D
Break Down the Question By using the process of elimination, students who correctly recall information in the material "Southern Society and Culture" in Section 2 will realize that only *D* can be the correct answer.

5. B
Break Down the Question Refer students who miss the question to the material "Free African Americans and Discrimination" in Section 3.

6. C
Break Down the Question This question requires students to recall information covered in Grade 7.

7. C
Break Down the Question This question requires students to recall information covered in Grade 7.

Intervention Resources

Reproducible

- Interactive Reader and Study Guide
- Universal Access Teacher Management System: Lesson Plans for Universal Access

Technology

- Quick Facts Transparency: The South Visual Summary
- Universal Access Modified Worksheets and Tests CD-ROM
- Interactive Skills Tutor CD-ROM

Tips for Test Taking

Master the Question #2 To help students answer questions testing reading comprehension, have them do the following:

- First, read the selection.
- Next, master the questions.
- Then reread the selection. The answers will be clearer with a second reading.

Remind students that tests are not meant to trick them but to test their knowledge and ability to think clearly.

Standards Review

Have students review the following standards in their workbooks.

- California Standards Review Workbook: HSS 8.7.1, 8.7.2, 8.7.3, 8.7.4

Chapter 13 Planning Guide

New Movements in America

MASTERING THE CALIFORNIA STANDARDS

Chapter Overview	Reproducible Resources	Technology Resources
CHAPTER 13 **pp. 396–433** **Overview:** **In this chapter, students will learn about the changing American society of the early 1800s.** See p. 396 for the California History–Social Science standards covered in this chapter.	**Universal Access Teacher Management System:*** • Universal Access Instructional Benchmarking Guides • Lesson Plans for Universal Access **Interactive Reader and Study Guide:*** Chapter Graphic Organizer **Chapter Resource File*** • Focus on Writing Activity: Persuasive Letter • Social Studies Skills Activity: Accepting Social Responsibility • Chapter Review Activity	**One-Stop Planner CD-ROM:** Calendar Planner **Student Edition Full-Read Audio CD-ROM** **Power Presentations with Video CD-ROM** **History's Impact: United States History Video Program (VHS/DVD):** New Movements in America* **A Teacher's Guide to Religion in the Public Schools***
Section 1: **Immigrants and Urban Challenges** **The Big Idea:** The population of the United States grew rapidly in the early 1800s with the arrival of millions of immigrants. 8.6.1, 8.6.3	**Universal Access Teacher Management System:*** Section 1 Lesson Plan **Interactive Reader and Study Guide:*** Section 1 Summary **Chapter Resource File*** • Vocabulary Builder, Section 1	**Daily Bellringer Transparency:** Section 1* **Quick Facts Transparency:** Push-Pull Factors of Immigration*
Section 2: **American Arts** **The Big Idea:** New movements in art and literature influenced many Americans in the early 1800s. 8.6.7	**Universal Access Teacher Management System:*** Section 2 Lesson Plan **Interactive Reader and Study Guide:*** Section 2 Summary **Chapter Resource File*** • Vocabulary Builder, Section 2 • Literature Activity: *Jack and Jill*	**Daily Bellringer Transparency:** Section 2* go.hrw.com **Internet Activity:** Who's Who of Transcendentalism
Section 3: **Reforming Society** **The Big Idea:** Reform movements in the early 1800s affected religion, education, and society. 8.6.4, 8.6.5	**Universal Access Teacher Management System:*** Section 3 Lesson Plan **Interactive Reader and Study Guide:*** Section 3 Summary **Chapter Resource File*** • Vocabulary Builder, Section 3 • Biography Activities: Dorothea Dix; Charles Finney; Mary Lyon and Emma Willard **Political Cartoons Activities for United States History,** Cartoon 15: Temperance Reform*	**Daily Bellringer Transparency:** Section 3 go.hrw.com **Internet Activity:** Education Reformers Interview
Section 4: **The Movement to End Slavery** **The Big Idea:** In the mid-1800s debate over slavery increased as abolitionists organized to challenge slavery in the United States. 8.9.1	**Universal Access Teacher Management System:*** Section 4 Lesson Plan **Interactive Reader and Study Guide:*** Section 4 Summary **Chapter Resource File*** • Vocabulary Builder, Section 4 • Biography Activity: Abolitionists • History and Geography Activity: The Underground Railroad • Primary Source Activity: David Walker • Primary Source Activity: Frederick Douglass	**Daily Bellringer Transparency:** Section 4* **Map Transparency:** The Underground Railroad*
Section 5: **Women's Rights** **The Big Idea:** Reformers sought to improve women's rights in American society. 8.6.6	**Universal Access Teacher Management System:*** Section 5 Lesson Plan **Interactive Reader and Study Guide:*** Section 5 Summary **Chapter Resource File*** • Vocabulary Builder, Section 5 • Biography Activity: Suffragettes • Primary Source Activity: Letter to Lucretia Mott	**Daily Bellringer Transparency:** Section 5*

SE Student Edition | Print Resource | Audio CD | Video

TE Teacher's Edition | Transparency | CD-ROM | DVD

go.hrw.com | CA Standards Mastery | **LS** Learning Styles

OSP One-Stop Planner CD-ROM | * also on One-Stop Planner CD

Review, Assessment, Intervention

 **Standards Review Workbook***

Quick Facts Transparency: New Movements in America Visual Summary*

 **Spanish Chapter Summaries Audio CD Program**

 **Progress Assessment Support System (PASS):** Chapter Test*

 **Universal Access Modified Worksheets and Tests CD-ROM:** Modified Chapter Test

One-Stop Planner CD-ROM: ExamView Test Generator (English/Spanish)

 **PASS:** Section 1 Quiz*

 **Online Quiz:** Section 1

 **Alternative Assessment Handbook**

 **PASS:** Section 2 Quiz*

Online Quiz: Section 2

 **Alternative Assessment Handbook**

 **PASS:** Section 3 Quiz*

 **Online Quiz:** Section 3

 **Alternative Assessment Handbook**

 **PASS:** Section 4 Quiz*

 **Online Quiz:** Section 4

 **Alternative Assessment Handbook**

 **PASS:** Section 5 Quiz*

 **Online Quiz:** Section 5

 **Alternative Assessment Handbook**

California Resources for Standards Mastery

INSTRUCTIONAL PLANNING AND SUPPORT

 **Universal Access Teacher Management System***

One-Stop Planner CD-ROM with Test Generator: Teacher Management System with Interactive Teacher's Edition

STANDARDS MASTERY

 **Standards Review Workbook***

At Home: A Guide to Standards Mastery for United States History

go.hrw.com Holt Online Learning

To enhance learning, Internet activities are available for a Who's Who of Transcendentalism and an Education Reformers Interview.

KEYWORD: SS8 TEACHER

- **Teacher Support Page**
- **Content Updates**
- **Rubrics and Writing Models**
- **Teaching Tips for the Multimedia Classroom**

KEYWORD: SS8 US13

- **Current Events**
- **Document-Based Questions**
- **Holt Grapher**
- **Holt Online Atlas**
- **Holt Researcher**
- **Interactive Multimedia Activities**
- **Internet Activities**
- **Online Chapter Summaries in Six Languages**
- **Online Section Quizzes**
- **American History Maps and Charts**

HOLT PREMIER ONLINE STUDENT EDITION

Complete online support for interactivity, assessment, and reporting

- **Interactive Maps and Notebook**
- **Standardized Test Prep**
- **Homework Practice and Research Activities Online**

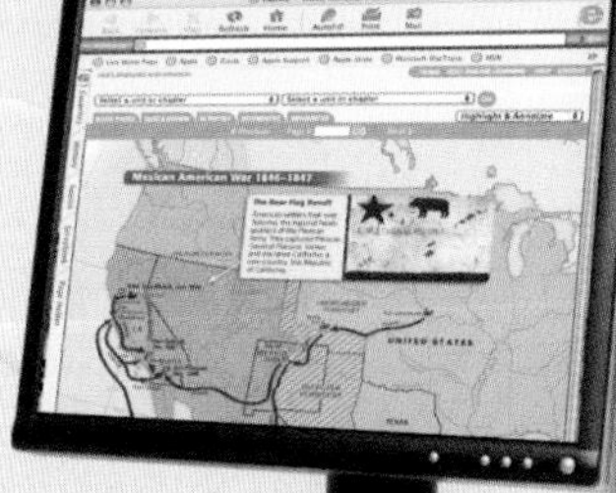

Mastering the Standards: Differentiating Instruction

Reaching Standards	Basic-level activities designed for all students encountering new material
Standards Proficiency	Intermediate-level activities designed for average students
Exceeding Standards	Challenging activities designed for honors and gifted-and-talented students
Standard English Mastery	Activities designed to improve standard English usage

Frequently Asked Questions

INSTRUCTIONAL PLANNING AND SUPPORT

Where do I find planning aids, pacing guides, lesson plans, and other teaching aids?

Annotated Teacher's Edition:
- Chapter planning guides
- Standards-based instruction and strategies
- Differentiated instruction for universal access
- Point-of-use reminders for integrating program resources

Power Presentations with Video CD-ROM

Universal Access Teacher Management System:
- Year and unit instructional benchmarking guides
- Reproducible lesson plans
- Assessment guides for diagnostic, progress, and summative end-of-the-year tests
- Options for differentiating instruction and intervention
- Teaching guides and answer keys for student workbooks

One-Stop Planner CD-ROM with Test Generator: Teacher Management System with Interactive Teacher's Editon:
- Calendar Planner
- Editable lesson plans
- All reproducible ancillaries in Adobe Acrobat (PDF) format
- ExamView Test Generator (English & Spanish)
- Game Tool for ExamView
- PuzzlePro
- Transparency and video previews

DIFFERENTIATING INSTRUCTION FOR UNIVERSAL ACCESS

What resources are available to ensure that Advanced Learners/GATE Students master the standards?

Teacher's Edition Activities:
- Mid-1850s Classified Newspaper, p. 402
- Addressing the Opposition, p. 425

Lesson Plans for Universal Access

Primary Source Library CD-ROM for United States History

What resources are available to ensure that English Learners and Standard English Learners master the standards?

Teacher's Edition Activities:
- Immigration Activity, p. 401
- Abolitionist Movement Activity, p. 417

Lesson Plans for Universal Access

Chapter Resource File: Vocabulary Builder Activities

Spanish Chapter Summaries Audio CD Program

Online Chapter Summaries in Six Languages

One-Stop Planner CD-ROM:
- PuzzlePro, Spanish Version
- ExamView Test Generator, Spanish Version

What modified materials are available for Special Education?

The ***Universal Access Modified Worksheets and Tests CD-ROM*** provides editable versions of the following:

Vocabulary Flash Cards

Modified Vocabulary Builder Activities

Modified Chapter Review Activity

Modified Chapter Test

What resources are available to ensure that Learners Having Difficulty master the standards?

Teacher's Edition Activities:
- City Growth Activity, p. 403
- American Romantic Movement, p. 406
- Commendation Awards, p. 414
- "Who Am I?" Game, p. 418
- Abolitionist Movement Activity, p. 424
- Women's Rights Collage, p. 427

Interactive Reader and Study Guide

Student Edition Full-Read Audio CD

Quick Facts Transparency: New Movements in America Visual Summary

Standards Review Workbook

Social Studies Skills Activity: Accepting Social Responsibility

Interactive Skills Tutor CD-ROM

How do I intervene for students struggling to master the standards?

Interactive Reader and Study Guide

Quick Facts Transparency: New Movements in America Visual Summary

Standards Review Workbook

Social Studies Skills Activity: Accepting Social Responsibility

Interactive Skills Tutor CD-ROM

PROFESSIONAL DEVELOPMENT

What teacher training resources are available to help me grow professionally?

- In-service and staff development as part of your Holt Social Studies product purchase
- Quick Teacher Tutorial Lesson Presentation CD-ROM
- Intensive tuition-based Teacher Development Institute
- *Teaching American History* Online 2 Module Professional Development Course
- Convenient Holt Speaker Bureau face-to-face workshop options
- PRAXIS™ Test Prep (#0089) interactive Web-based content refreshers*
- 24/7 *Ask A Professional Development Expert* at http://www.hrw.com/prodev/

* PRAXIS is a trademark of Educational Testing Service (ETS). This publication is not endorsed or approved by ETS.

Information Literacy Skills

To learn more about how History–Social Science instruction may be improved by the effective use of library media centers and information literacy skills, go to the Teacher's Resource Materials for Chapter 13 at **go.hrw.com**, keyword: SS8 MEDIA.

The following materials were developed by the Division for Public Education of the American Bar Association. These materials are part of the **Democracy and Civic Education** supplement.
- Constitution Study Guide
- Supreme Court Case Studies

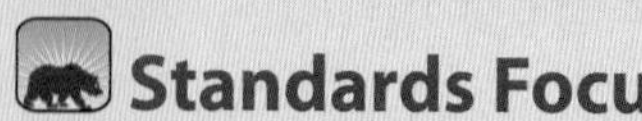

Chapter Preview

Standards Focus

Standards by Section
Section 1: HSS 8.6.1, 8.6.3
Section 2: HSS 8.6.7
Section 3: HSS 8.6.4, 8.6.5
Section 4: HSS 8.9.1
Section 5: HSS 8.6.6

Teacher's Edition
HSS **Analysis Skills:** CS 1, CS 2, CS 3, HR 1, HR 4, HR 5, HI 1, HI 2, HI 3
ELA Writing 8.2.4, Reading 8.2.6

Preview Grade 8 Standards
HSS **8.12** Students analyze the transformation of the American economy and the changing social and political conditions in the United States in response to the Industrial Revolution.
8.12.1 Trace patterns of agricultural and industrial development as they relate to climate, use of natural resources, markets, and trade and locate such development on a map.
8.12.5 Examine the location and effects of urbanization, renewed immigration, and industrialization (e.g., the effects on social fabric of cities, wealth and economic opportunity, the conservation movement)
8.12.7 Identify the new sources of large-scale immigration and the contributions of immigrants to the building of cities and the economy; explain the ways in which new social and economic patterns encouraged assimilation of newcomers into the mainstream amidst growing cultural diversity; and discuss the new wave of nativism.

Focus on Writing
The **Chapter Resource File** provides a Focus on Writing worksheet to help students organize and write their persuasive letters.

CRF: Focus on Writing Activity: Persuasive Letter

CHAPTER 13 1815–1850

New Movements in America

California Standards

History–Social Science
8.6 Students analyze the divergent paths of the American people from 1800 to the mid-1800s and the challenges they faced, with emphasis on the Northeast.

8.9 Students analyze the early and steady attempts to abolish slavery and to realize the ideals of the Declaration of Independence.

English–Language Arts
Writing 8.2.4 Write persuasive compositions.

Reading 8.2.6 Use information from a variety of consumer, workplace, and public documents.

FOCUS ON WRITING

Persuasive Letter Your local newspaper is running a competition for students to answer the question, "What event or movement in history had the greatest impact on life in the United States?" This chapter tells about many important events and movements in the United States. As you read, take notes on each. Then decide which you believe has most affected life for people in the United States. Write a letter to the newspaper arguing your position.

UNITED STATES

1817 Thomas Gallaudet founds a school for people who have hearing impairments.

1820

WORLD

1824 British laws making trade unions illegal are repealed.

Introduce the Chapter

Standards Proficiency

Focus on Activism

HSS **Analysis Skills:** HI 1, HI 3

1. Explain to students that Americans have developed a strong tradition of identifying social problems and creating groups and strategies to solve those problems.
2. Lead a guided discussion about activism in the United States today. Ask students to identify some activist organizations, such as Mothers Against Drunk Driving (MADD) or Habitat for Humanity. What methods do these groups use to effect change and promote their cause? What other social problems or issues exist today? What actions might students take?
3. Explain that activism, or reform, became a major trend in the United States in the early and mid-1800s. As students read the chapter, ask them to compare the issues reformers addressed in the 1800s to those activists address today. LS **Verbal/Linguistic**

Alternative Assessment Handbook, Rubric 11: Discussions

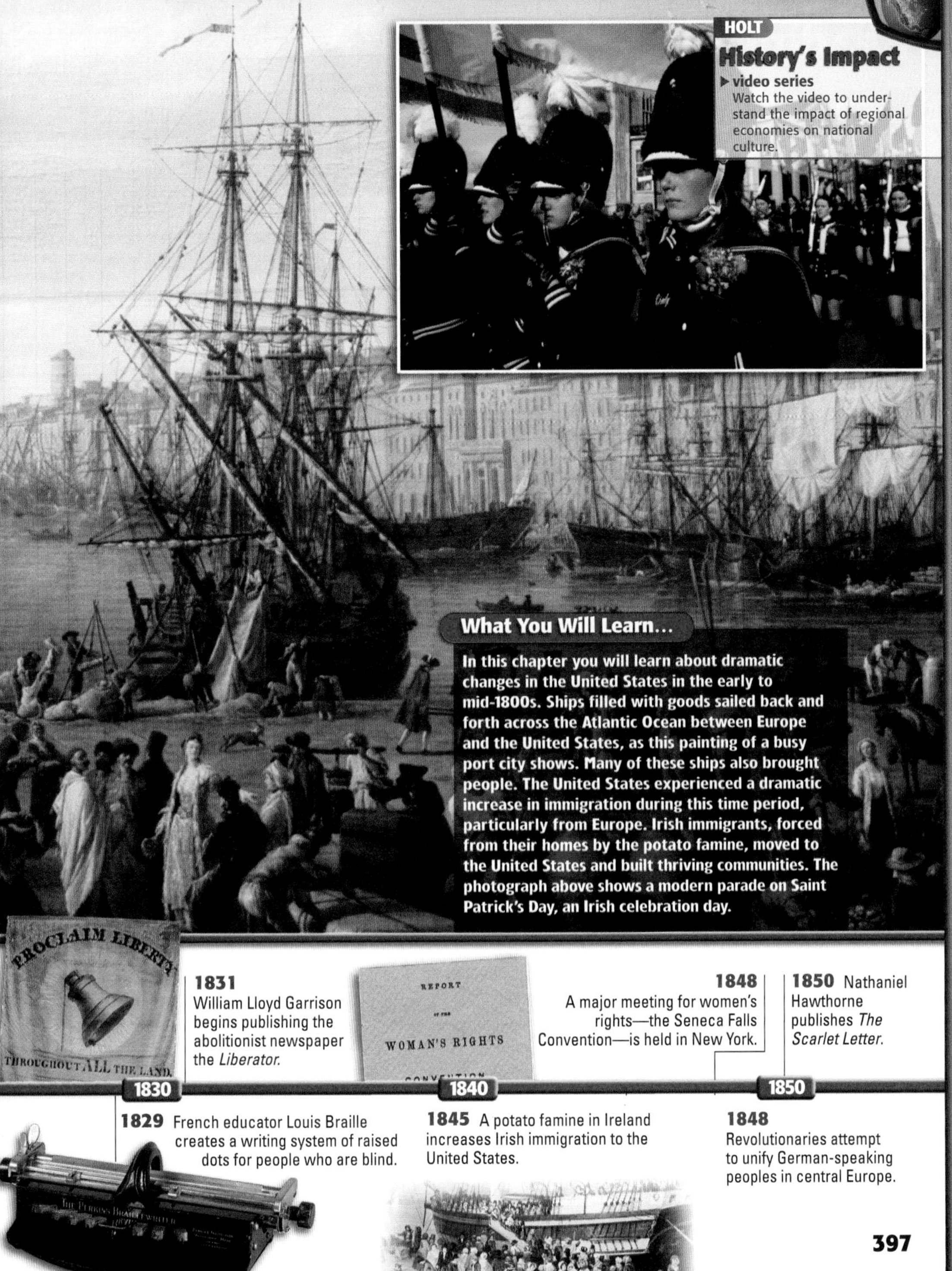

HOLT

History's Impact

▶ **video series**

Watch the video to understand the impact of regional economies on national culture.

What You Will Learn...

In this chapter you will learn about dramatic changes in the United States in the early to mid-1800s. Ships filled with goods sailed back and forth across the Atlantic Ocean between Europe and the United States, as this painting of a busy port city shows. Many of these ships also brought people. The United States experienced a dramatic increase in immigration during this time period, particularly from Europe. Irish immigrants, forced from their homes by the potato famine, moved to the United States and built thriving communities. The photograph above shows a modern parade on Saint Patrick's Day, an Irish celebration day.

1829 French educator Louis Braille creates a writing system of raised dots for people who are blind.

1830

1831 William Lloyd Garrison begins publishing the abolitionist newspaper the *Liberator.*

1840

1845 A potato famine in Ireland increases Irish immigration to the United States.

1848 A major meeting for women's rights—the Seneca Falls Convention—is held in New York.

1848 Revolutionaries attempt to unify German-speaking peoples in central Europe.

1850

1850 Nathaniel Hawthorne publishes *The Scarlet Letter.*

397

• Chapter Preview •

HOLT

History's Impact

▶ **video series**

See the Video Teacher's Guide for strategies for using the chapter video **New Movements in America**.

Chapter Big Ideas

Section 1 The population of the United States grew rapidly in the early 1800s with the arrival of millions of immigrants. **HSS** 8.6.1, 8.6.3

Section 2 New movements in art and literature influenced many Americans in the early 1800s. **HSS** 8.6.7

Section 3 Reform movements in the early 1800s affected religion, education, and society. **HSS** 8.6.4, 8.6.5

Section 4 In the mid-1800s, debate over slavery increased as abolitionists organized to challenge slavery in the United States. **HSS** 8.9.1

Section 5 Reformers sought to improve women's rights in American society. **HSS** 8.6.6

Explore the Picture

Growing Immigration Between 1840 and 1860, more than 4 million immigrants came to the United States to begin new lives. The largest groups came from Ireland and Germany. Many of these immigrants entered the United States at New York Harbor. Beginning in 1855, immigrants passed through a central processing center on arrival. There, officials took down immigrants' names and provided information to try to help new immigrants.

Analyzing Visuals Based on the image, what might be some initial hardships that immigrants faced? *moving their belongings, finding their way around in a large, strange city*

Explore the Time Line

1. Who founded a school for the hearing impaired, and when? *Thomas Gallaudet, 1817*
2. In what year was a major meeting for women's rights held, and what was it called? *1848; Seneca Falls Convention*
3. What event caused an increase in Irish immigration to the United States? *potato famine in 1845*

HSS Analysis Skills: CS 1

Info to Know

Braille Writing System The Braille system of writing for the blind consists of one to six dots arranged in 63 different combinations. Over time, additional versions of Braille have been developed for math, scientific writing, and computers. More recently, the use of Braille has begun decreasing with developments in computer-voice technology.

go.hrw.com

Online Resources

Chapter Resources:
KEYWORD: SS8 US13

Teacher Resources:
KEYWORD: SS8 TEACHER

Reading Social Studies

Understanding Themes

Introduce the main themes of this chapter to the class. Discuss with students several movements that affected society and culture in the United States at this time, such as abolition, immigration, and the Second Great Awakening. Ask students how some of these issues might have been affected by the religious beliefs of some Americans. Help students to understand what effects religion and society and culture had on these new movements in America.

Information and Propaganda

Focus on Reading Locate examples of each type of propaganda discussed on this page. Share those examples with the class. Then ask students to identify each type of propaganda and what information they used to determine that. Ask students to locate their own examples of propaganda by looking at magazines, Web sites, and other resources. Encourage students to share their examples with the class.

Reading Social Studies

by Kylene Beers

Economics | Geography | Politics | **Religion** | **Society and Culture** | Science and Technology

Focus on Themes The mid-1800s was a time of change in America. **Society and culture** changed for several reasons: thousands of immigrants arrived in America; women began to work hard for equal rights; and the North and South debated more and more over the slavery issue. **Religious** beliefs helped shape people's views toward abolition—the move to end slavery—and women's suffrage—the move to give women the right to vote. This chapter discusses all these issues.

Information and Propaganda

Focus on Reading Where do you get information about historical events and people? One source is this textbook and others like it. You can expect the authors of your textbook to do their best to present the facts objectively and fairly. But some sources of historical information may have a totally different purpose in mind. For example, ads in political campaigns may contain information, but their main purpose is to persuade people to act or think in a certain way.

Graphic organizers are available in the

Recognizing Propaganda Techniques Propaganda is created to change people's opinions or get them to act in a certain way. Learn to recognize propaganda techniques, and you will be able to separate propaganda from the facts.

"People who don't support public education are greedy monsters who don't care about children!" → **Name Calling** Using loaded words, words that create strong positive or negative emotions, to make someone else's ideas seem inappropriate or wrong.

"People all around the country are opening free public schools. It's obviously the right thing to do." → **Bandwagon** Encouraging people to do something because "everyone else is doing it."

"If we provide free education for all children, everyone will be able to get jobs. Poverty and unemployment will disappear." → **Oversimplification** Making a complex situation seem simple, a complex problem seem easy to solve.

Reading and Skills Resources

Reading Support

- Interactive Reader and Study Guide
- Student Edition on Audio CD
- Spanish Chapter Summaries Audio CD Program

Social Studies Skills Support

- Interactive Skills Tutor CD-ROM

Vocabulary Support

- **CRF:** Vocabulary Builder Activities
- **CRF:** Chapter Review Activity
- Universal Access Modified Worksheets and Tests CD-ROM:
  - Vocabulary Flash Cards
  - Vocabulary Builder Activity
  - Chapter Review Activity
- OSP Holt PuzzlePro

Standards Focus

ELA Reading 8.2.0

ELA Reading 8.2.0 Read and understand grade-level-appropriate materials.

You Try It!

The flyer below was published in the year 1837. Read it and then answer the questions that follow.

Flyer from 1837

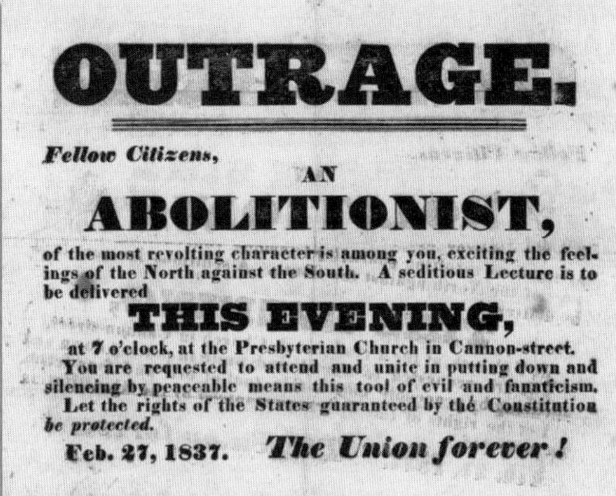
OUTRAGE.

Fellow Citizens,

AN

ABOLITIONIST,

of the most revolting character is among you, exciting the feelings of the North against the South. A seditious Lecture is to be delivered

THIS EVENING,

at 7 o'clock, at the Presbyterian Church in Cannon-street. You are requested to attend and unite in putting down and silencing by peaceable means this tool of evil and fanaticism. Let the rights of the States guaranteed by the Constitution be protected.

Feb. 27, 1837. The Union forever!

After studying the flyer, answer the following questions.

1. What is the purpose of this flyer?
2. Who do you think distributed this flyer?
3. Do you think this flyer is an example of propaganda? Why or why not? If you think it is propaganda, what kind is it?
4. If you were the subject of this flyer, how would you feel? How might you respond to it?

As you read Chapter 13, look carefully at all the primary sources. Do any of them include examples of propaganda?

Key Terms and People

Chapter 13

Section 1
nativists *(p. 402)*
Know-Nothing Party *(p. 402)*
middle class *(p. 402)*
tenements *(p. 404)*

Section 2
transcendentalism *(p. 405)*
Ralph Waldo Emerson *(p. 405)*
Margaret Fuller *(p. 405)*
Henry David Thoreau *(p. 405)*
utopian communities *(p. 406)*
Nathaniel Hawthorne *(p. 406)*
Edgar Allan Poe *(p. 407)*
Emily Dickinson *(p. 407)*
Henry Wadsworth Longfellow *(p. 407)*
Walt Whitman *(p. 407)*

Section 3
Second Great Awakening *(p. 410)*
Charles Grandison Finney *(p. 410)*
Lyman Beecher *(p. 410)*
temperance movement *(p. 411)*
Dorothea Dix *(p. 412)*
common-school movement *(p. 412)*
Horace Mann *(p. 412)*
Catharine Beecher *(p. 413)*
Thomas Gallaudet *(p. 413)*

Section 4
abolition *(p. 416)*
William Lloyd Garrison *(p. 417)*
American Anti-Slavery Society *(p. 417)*
Angelina and Sarah Grimké *(p. 417)*
Frederick Douglass *(p. 418)*
Sojourner Truth *(p. 418)*
Underground Railroad *(p. 418)*
Harriet Tubman *(p. 420)*

Section 5
Elizabeth Cady Stanton *(p. 426)*
Lucretia Mott *(p. 426)*
Seneca Falls Convention *(p. 426)*
Declaration of Sentiments *(p. 426)*
Lucy Stone *(p. 427)*
Susan B. Anthony *(p. 427)*

Academic Vocabulary

implicit *(p. 402)*
abstract *(p. 406)*

Reading Social Studies

Key Terms and People

Have students look over the list of key terms and people. Review with students each term that relates to a social, cultural, or reform movement *(nativism, transcendentalism, temperance, common-school movement, abolition, women's rights)*. Then have students preview the chapter and write a sentence about each movement and why it was important. You might wish to have students use related key terms in the same sentence. Ask for volunteers to share these sentences with the class.

Focus on Reading

See the **Focus on Reading** questions in this chapter for more practice on this reading social studies skill.

Reading Social Studies Assessment

See the **Standards Review** at the end of this chapter for student assessment questions related to this reading skill.

Teaching Tip

Students may come across propaganda from time to time when doing research on the Internet. Ask students to carefully evaluate the Web sites they come across. Remind students of the important questions to ask to evaluate a Web site, which they learned in the previous chapter. Point out to students that occasionally they may visit a site that uses the propaganda techniques mentioned here. Ask students how propaganda Web sites might affect the validity of their research.

Answers

You Try It! 1. *possible answers—to inform supporters of slavery that an abolitionist would be delivering a lecture in their community; to encourage supporters of slavery to stop the meeting;* **2.** *possible answers—a slave holder or opponent of abolition;* **3.** *yes, because it uses name calling to make abolition seem wrong;* **4.** *Students' answers will vary, but should indicate that the flyer is trying to appeal to people's emotions.*

Preteach

Bellringer

If YOU were there . . . Use the **Daily Bellringer Transparency** to help students answer the question.

Daily Bellringer Transparency, Section 1

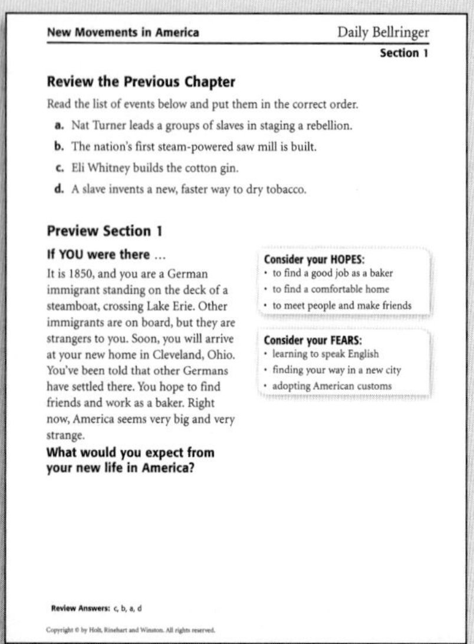

New Movements in America — Daily Bellringer — **Section 1**

Review the Previous Chapter

Read the list of events below and put them in the correct order.

a. Nat Turner leads a groups of slaves in staging a rebellion.
b. The nation's first steam-powered saw mill is built.
c. Eli Whitney builds the cotton gin.
d. A slave invents a new, faster way to dry tobacco.

Preview Section 1

If YOU were there ...

It is 1850, and you are a German immigrant standing on the deck of a steamboat, crossing Lake Erie. Other immigrants are on board, but they are strangers to you. Soon, you will arrive at your new home in Cleveland, Ohio. You've been told that other Germans have settled there. You hope to find friends and work as a baker. Right now, America seems very big and very strange.

What would you expect from your new life in America?

Consider your HOPES:
- to find a good job as a baker
- to find a comfortable home
- to meet people and make friends

Consider your FEARS:
- learning to speak English
- finding your way in a new city
- adopting American customs

Review Answers: c, b, a, d

Academic Vocabulary

Review with students the high-use academic term in this section:

implicit understood though not clearly put into words (p. 402)

Building Vocabulary

Preteach or review the following terms:

epidemics rapid spread of disease (p. 404)

rural in the country (p. 401)

CRF: Vocabulary Builder Activity, Section 1

Standards Focus

HSS 8.6.1

Means: Discuss how the Industrialization and Transportation Revolutions contributed to the growth of cities in the mid-1800s.

Matters: American cities continue to experience periods of rapid growth and to face challenges as a result of this growth.

HSS 8.6.3

Means: Explain why immigration to the United States rose during the mid-1800s, and how this immigration affected city growth.

Matters: Today many cities in the Northeast and Midwest still reflect the heritage of the many immigrants who settled in those regions in the mid-1800s.

SECTION 1

Immigrants and Urban Challenges

What You Will Learn...

Main Ideas

1. Millions of immigrants, mostly German and Irish, arrived in the United States despite anti-immigrant movements.
2. Industrialization led to the growth of cities.
3. American cities experienced urban problems due to rapid growth.

The Big Idea

The population of the United States grew rapidly in the early 1800s with the arrival of millions of immigrants.

Key Terms

nativists, *p. 402*
Know-Nothing Party, *p. 402*
middle class, *p. 402*
tenements, *p. 404*

HSS 8.6.1 Discuss the influence of industrialization and technological developments on the region, including human modification of the landscape and how physical geography shaped human actions (e.g., growth of cities, deforestation, farming, mineral extraction).

8.6.3 List the reasons for the wave of immigration from Northern Europe to the United States and describe the growth in the number, size, and spatial arrangements of cities (e.g., Irish immigrants and the Great Irish Famine).

If YOU were there...

It is 1850, and you are a German immigrant standing on the deck of a steamboat, crossing Lake Erie. Other immigrants are on board, but they are strangers to you. Soon, you will arrive at your new home in Cleveland, Ohio. You've been told that other Germans have settled there. You hope to find friends and work as a baker. Right now, America seems very big and very strange.

What would you expect from your new life in America?

BUILDING BACKGROUND The revolutions in industry, transportation, and technology were not the only major changes in the United States in the mid-1800s. Millions of immigrants, mostly from Europe, swelled the population. Some settled in the rich farmland of the Midwest, while others moved to cities.

Millions of Immigrants Arrive

In the mid-1800s, large numbers of immigrants crossed the Atlantic Ocean to begin new lives in the United States. More than 4 million of them settled in the United States between 1840 and 1860, most from Europe. More than 3 million of these immigrants arrived from Ireland and Germany. Many of them were fleeing economic or political troubles in their native countries.

Fleeing the Irish Potato Famine

Most immigrants from the British Isles during that period were Irish. In the mid-1840s, potato blight, a disease that causes rot in potatoes, left many families in Ireland with little food. More than a million Irish people died of starvation and disease. Even more fled to the United States.

Most Irish immigrants were very poor. Many settled in cities in Massachusetts, New Jersey, New York, and Pennsylvania. They worked at unskilled jobs in the cities or on building canals and

Teach the Big Idea: Master the Standards

Standards Proficiency

Immigrants and Urban Challenges

HSS 8.6.1, 8.6.3; HSS **Analysis Skills:** CS 1, HR 1, HI 1, HI 2

1. **Teach** Ask students the Main Idea questions to teach this section.
2. **Apply** Discuss how and why immigration to the United States increased during the mid-1800s. Then have each student create a list of questions that he or she would like to have asked an immigrant of that time period. As students read the section, have them answer as many of their questions as possible. **LS Verbal/Linguistic**
3. **Review** Have students share their questions and answers as well as some of their unanswered questions.
4. **Practice/Homework** Have each student create a five-question quiz, with answer key, for the section. Encourage students to address the causes and effects of immigration. **LS Verbal/Linguistic**

Alternative Assessment Handbook, Rubrics 6: Cause and Effect; and 37: Writing Assignments

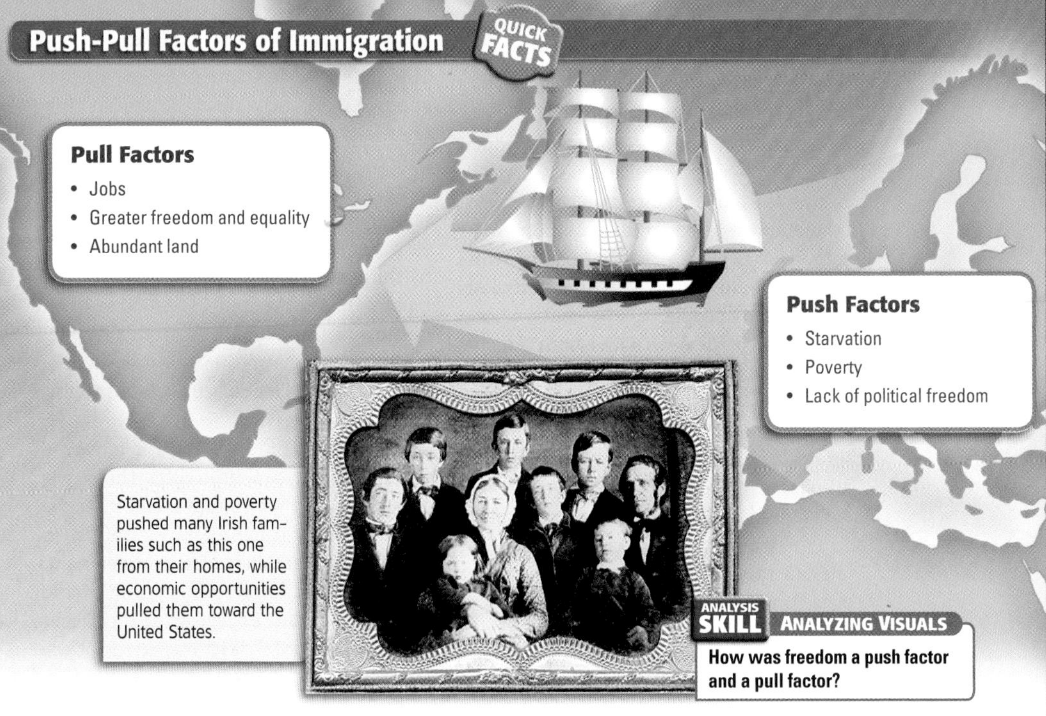

Starvation and poverty pushed many Irish families such as this one from their homes, while economic opportunities pulled them toward the United States.

ANALYSIS SKILL ANALYZING VISUALS

How was freedom a push factor and a pull factor?

railroads. Irish women often worked as domestic servants for wealthy families, laboring 16 or more hours per day. In 1849 a Boston health committee reported that low wages forced most Irish immigrants to live in poor housing.

Still, many immigrants enjoyed a new feeling of equality. Patrick Dunny wrote home to his family about this situation.

> "People that cuts a great dash [style] at home ... think it strange [in the United States] for the humble class of people to get as much respect as themselves."
>
> —Patrick Dunny, quoted in *Who Built America?* by Bruce Levine et al.

A Failed German Revolution

Many Germans also came to the United States during this time. In 1848 some Germans had staged a revolution against harsh rule. Some educated Germans fled to the United States to escape persecution caused by their political activities. Most German immigrants, however, were working class, and they came for economic reasons. The United States seemed to offer both greater economic opportunity and more freedom from government control. While most Irish immigrants were Catholics, German immigrant groups included Catholics, Jews, and Protestants.

German immigrants were more likely than the Irish to become farmers and live in rural areas. They moved to midwestern states where more land was available. Unlike the Irish, a high percentage of German immigrants arrived in the United States with money. Despite their funds and skills, German immigrants often were forced to take low-paying jobs. Many German immigrants worked as tailors, seamstresses, bricklayers,

THE IMPACT TODAY

Many immigrants still come to the United States today. More than 16.4 million entered the United States between 1980 and 2000.

Direct Teach

Main Idea

1 Millions of Immigrants Arrive

Millions of immigrants, mostly German and Irish, arrived in the United States despite anti-immigrant movements.

Recall What two groups formed the majority of immigrants to the United States during the mid-1800s? *Irish and German immigrants*

Contrast How did Irish and German immigrants tend to differ? *Irish—came to escape potato famine, starvation, disease; most poor and Catholic; most settled in cities and worked at unskilled jobs; Germans—came to escape political persecution or to pursue economic opportunity; Catholics, Lutherans, and Jews; more likely to settle in Midwest and farm; many had some money*

Quick Facts Transparency: Push-Pull Factors of Immigration

HSS 8.6.3; HSS **Analysis Skills:** HI 1

Info to Know

German Aid Societies New immigrants faced many dangers in the United States, including scam artists, dangerous jobs, and poor housing. As a result, societies formed to help newcomers adjust to and prosper in their new country. One such group was the German Society of the City of New York. This group worked for the passage of state and federal laws to protect immigrants and achieved success despite heavy opposition. The German Society still exists today.

Differentiating Instruction for Universal Access

English-Language Learners

Standards Proficiency **Standard English Mastery**

1. Have students examine the Quick Facts above. Discuss with students the reasons that many immigrants—particularly Irish and German immigrants—came to the United Sates in the mid-1800s.
2. Ask students to imagine that they are either Irish or German immigrants traveling to the United States in the mid-1800s. Have students, working individually or in small groups, create a series of drawings illustrating the reasons they left their homeland, their experiences on the ship, and what they hope to find in the United States.
3. Then work with students to help them write short captions for their drawings using standard English. **LS Visual/Spatial**

HSS 8.6.3; HSS **Analysis Skills:** CS 3, HI 1, HI 2

Alternative Assessment Handbook, Rubric 3: Artwork

Quick Facts Transparency: Push-Pull Factors of Immigration

Answers

Analyzing Visuals *push—left because of lack of political freedom; pull—drawn by greater U.S. freedom* servants, clerks, cabinetmakers, bakers, and food merchants.

Anti-Immigration Movements

Industrialization and the waves of people from Europe greatly changed the American labor force. While many immigrants went to the Midwest to get farmland, other immigrants filled the need for cheap labor in towns and cities. Industrial jobs in the Northeast attracted many people.

Yet a great deal of native-born Americans feared losing their jobs to immigrants who might work for lower wages. Some felt **implicitly** threatened by the new immigrants' cultures and religions. For example, before Catholic immigrants arrived, most Americans were Protestants. Conflicts between Catholics and Protestants in Europe caused American Protestants to mistrust Catholic immigrants. Those Americans and others who opposed immigration were called **nativists**.

ACADEMIC VOCABULARY
implicit understood though not clearly put into words

In the 1840s and 1850s some nativists became politically active. An 1844 election flyer gave Americans this warning.

FOCUS ON READING
Look carefully at the quotation to the right from an election flyer. Does it include any examples of propaganda?

> "Look at the . . . thieves and vagabonds [tramps] roaming our streets . . . monopolizing [taking] the business which properly belongs to our own native and true-born citizens."
>
> —Election flyer, quoted in *Who Built America?* by Bruce Levine et al.

In 1849 nativists founded a political organization, the **Know-Nothing Party**, that supported measures making it difficult for foreigners to become citizens or hold office. Its members wanted to keep Catholics and immigrants out of public office. They also wanted to require immigrants to live in the United States for 21 years before becoming citizens. Know-Nothing politicians had some success getting elected during the 1850s. Later, disagreements over the issue of slavery caused the party to fall apart.

READING CHECK **Understanding Cause and Effect** Why did the Know-Nothing Party try to limit the rights of immigrants?

Rapid Growth of Cities

The Industrial Revolution led to the creation of many new jobs in American cities. These city jobs drew immigrants from many nations as well as migrants from rural parts of the United States. The Transportation Revolution helped connect cities and made it easier for people to move to them. As a result of these two trends, American cities grew rapidly during the mid-1800s. Cities in the northeastern and Middle Atlantic states grew the most. By the mid-1800s, three-quarters of the country's manufacturing jobs were in these areas.

The rise of industry and the growth of cities changed American life. Those who owned their own businesses or worked in skilled jobs benefited most from those changes. The families of these merchants, manufacturers, professionals, and master craftspeople made up a growing social class. This new **middle class** was a social and economic level between the wealthy and the poor. Those in this new middle class built large, dignified homes that demonstrated their place in society.

In the growing cities, people found entertainment and an enriched cultural life. Many living in these cities enjoyed visiting places such as libraries and clubs, or attending concerts or lectures. In the mid-1800s people also attended urban theaters. Favorite pastimes, such as bowling and playing cards, also provided recreation for urban residents.

Cities during this time were compact and crowded. Many people lived close enough to their jobs that they could walk to work. Wagons carried goods down streets paved with stones, making a noisy, busy scene. One observer noted that the professionals in New York City always had a "hurried walk."

READING CHECK **Summarizing** How did the Industrial Revolution affect life in American cities?

Direct Teach

Main Idea

❶ Millions of Immigrants Arrive

Millions of immigrants, mostly German and Irish, arrived in the United States despite anti-immigrant movements.

Summarize How did immigration change the American labor force in the mid-1800s? *Many immigrants went to the Midwest to farm; others filled the need for cheap labor in towns and cities, especially in the Northeast.*

Identify Cause and Effect How did anti-Catholicism contribute to the creation of the Know-Nothing Party? *Nativists formed the Know-Nothing Party in part to keep Catholics out of public office.*

HSS 8.6.3; HSS **Analysis Skills:** HI 1, HI 2

Main Idea

❷ Rapid Growth of Cities

Industrialization led to the growth of cities.

Recall In which regions did U.S. cities grow the most during the mid-1800s? Why? *Northeast and mid-Atlantic states; contained three quarters of the country's manufacturing jobs*

Categorize What types of jobs did the new middle class hold? *skilled workers such as master craftspeople and business owners such as merchants, manufacturers, and professionals*

HSS 8.6.1; HSS **Analysis Skills:** HI 1

Answers

Focus on Reading *yes, presents a highly biased view of immigrants*

Reading Check (left) *felt threatened by immigrants' different cultures and worried that they might lose jobs to immigrants who would work for lower wages*

Reading Check (right) *Improvements in transportation and the rise of new jobs in industry led many people to move to urban areas.*

Collaborative Learning

Exceeding Standards

Mid-1850s Classified Newspaper

HSS 8.6.3; HSS **Analysis Skills:** HI 1, HI 2

Materials: poster board, art supplies, word processing software (optional)

1. Organize students into small groups. Ask them to imagine that they work at a classified weekly in New York City in the mid-1800s.
2. Have each group create a classified-ad page that includes ads for jobs directed at immigrants, ads for farmland for sale in the Midwest, notices for meetings of immigrant aid societies, and notices for meetings of nativist groups and the Know-Nothing Party.
3. Groups can write their ads and then arrange them on poster board, or students might use computers to create their classified ad pages. Display students' work around the classroom.
LS Interpersonal, Verbal/Linguistic

Alternative Assessment Handbook, Rubrics 14: Group Activity; and 23: Newspapers

History Close-up
New York City, mid-1800s
In the mid-1800s, cities such as New York City lured thousands of people in search of jobs and a better life. Many city dwellers found life difficult in the crowded urban conditions.
Many city residents, particularly immigrants, lived in crowded, unsafe conditions.
Many immigrants and other poor city dwellers worked long hours in factories at dangerous jobs.
Women—and frequently children—labored all day in small rooms making clothing to be sold to the wealthy.
City streets were crowded with people buying, selling, and transporting goods.
The first floor of the building served many purposes—living quarters, kitchen, and work space. Here, garments were finished for sale.
PICKLES 1c
ANALYSIS SKILL ANALYZING VISUALS
How is this scene similar to one you might see in a large American city today? How is it different?
403

Direct Teach

History Close-up

New York City, mid-1800s

Have students examine the image and then ask them the following:

- What types of work are visible in the image? *dressmaking, market trade, hauling goods*
- What were dwellings like for many city residents? *crowded, limited furnishings, drab and unsanitary*
- Based on the image, what might be some problems that people experienced in cities in the mid-1800s? *possible answers—crowding, dirty streets from horses, poor housing and working conditions, disease as a result of crowding*

Activity Step into the Picture Ask students to imagine that they are one of the people in the image. Have them write a letter from that person's perspective to a friend who lives elsewhere describing an average day in New York City. **LS Verbal/Linguistic, Visual/Spatial**

Alternative Assessment Handbook, Rubric 40: Writing to Describe

HSS 8.6.1, 8.6.3; **HSS Analysis Skills:** HI 1, HI 2

Info to Know

Nativism Turns Violent In some cases, nativism in the mid-1800s turned violent, particularly in eastern U.S. cities. For example, in 1834 a mob burned down the Ursuline Convent outside Boston, Massachusetts. In 1844 a protest by a nativist group led to a riot in Philadelphia, Pennsylvania. Similar riots and attacks on Catholic churches occurred elsewhere.

Differentiating Instruction for Universal Access

Learners Having Difficulty

Reaching Standards

1. Discuss with students the reasons for the rapid growth of U.S. cities and the problems that developed as a result of this growth.
2. Draw the graphic organizer onto the chalkboard. Omit the blue, italicized answers.
3. Have each student copy and complete the organizer. **LS Visual/Spatial**

HSS 8.6.1, 8.6.3; **HSS Analysis Skills:** HI 1, HI 2

Alternative Assessment Handbook, Rubric 13: Graphic Organizers

Growth of U.S. Cities

Reasons for Growth	Problems of Growth
• increased immigration from Europe • *Transportation Revolution connected cities.* • *Industrial Revolution created new jobs.* • *People moved to cities seeking work.*	• overcrowding • *poor, unsafe, dirty housing conditions* • *lack of public services* • *poor sanitation* • *diseases and epidemics* • *no permanent police force or firefighters*

Answers

Analyzing Visuals *similar—crowded street with people going about their work, open-air marketplace where people are buying and selling goods, people living and working in close quarters, factories; different—horses and buggies, technology, clothing*

Direct Teach

Main Idea

❸ Urban Problems

American cities experienced urban problems due to rapid growth.

Recall What urban problems developed as a result of rapid growth of cities in the mid-1800s? *overcrowding, poor and unsafe housing, lack of public services, unhealthy conditions, disease and epidemics, crime, fire danger, no permanent police force or fire protection*

Make Judgments Despite urban problems, do you think immigrants preferred life in America to that in their home countries? Why? *possible answer—yes, because life in America was still better than the conditions they left behind*

 HSS 8.6.1; HSS **Analysis Skills:** HI 1

Review & Assess

Close

Have students review the causes and effects of increased U.S. immigration in the mid-1800s.

Review

 Online Quiz, Section 1

Assess

SE Section 1 Assessment

PASS: Section 1 Quiz

Alternative Assessment Handbook

Reteach/Classroom Intervention

California Standards Review Workbook

Interactive Reader and Study Guide, Section 1

Interactive Skills Tutor CD-ROM

Answers

Reading Check *Cities did not have the necessary plans, public services, or regulations to deal with the rapid growth that was occurring.*

Urban Problems

American cities in the mid-1800s faced many challenges due to rapid growth. Because public and private transportation was limited, city residents had to live near their workplaces. In addition, there was a lack of safe housing. Many city dwellers, particularly immigrants, could afford to live only in **tenements**—poorly designed apartment buildings that housed large numbers of people. These structures were often dirty, overcrowded, and unsafe.

Public services were also poor. The majority of cities did not have clean water, public health regulations, or healthful ways to get rid of garbage and human waste. Under these conditions, diseases spread easily, and epidemics were common. In 1832 and 1849, for example, New York City suffered cholera epidemics that killed thousands.

City life held other dangers. As urban areas grew, they became centers of criminal activity. Most cities—including New York, Boston, and Philadelphia—had no permanent or organized force to fight crime. Instead, they relied on volunteer night watches, which offered little protection.

Fire was another constant and serious danger in crowded cities. There was little organized fire protection. Most cities were served by volunteer fire companies. Firefighters used hand pumps and buckets to put out fires. In addition, there were not enough sanitation workers and road maintenance crews. These shortages and flaws caused health and safety problems for many city residents.

READING CHECK **Analyzing** Why did so many American cities have problems in the mid-1800s?

SUMMARY AND PREVIEW Immigrants expected a better life in America, but not all Americans welcomed newcomers. The rapid growth of cities caused many problems. In the next section you will read about how America developed its own style of art and literature.

Section 1 Assessment

go.hrw.com **Online Quiz** KEYWORD: SS8 HP13

Reviewing Ideas, Terms, and People HSS 8.6.1, 8.6.3

1. **a. Identify** Who were the **nativists**?
   b. Compare and Contrast In what ways were Irish and German immigrants to the United States similar and different?
   c. Predict How might the rise of anti-immigrant groups lead to problems in the United States?
2. **a. Describe** What led to the growth of cities?
   b. Analyze How did the rise of industrialization and the growth of cities change American society?
3. **a. Describe** What were **tenements**?
   b. Summarize What problems affected American cities in the mid-1800s?
   c. Evaluate What do you think was the biggest problem facing cities in the United States? Why?

Critical Thinking

4. **Identifying Cause and Effect** Copy the graphic organizer like the one shown onto your own sheet of paper. Use it to identify the causes and effects of immigration and urban growth.

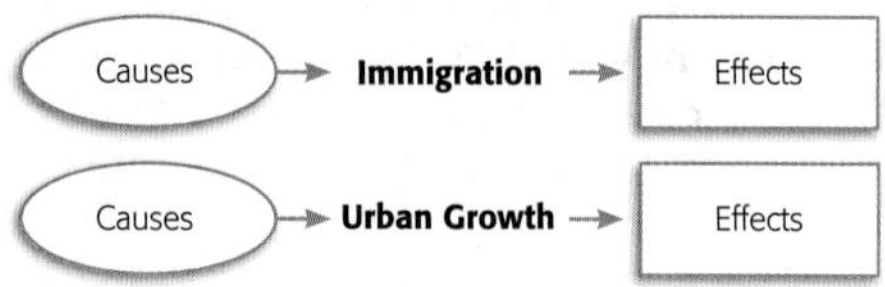

FOCUS ON WRITING

5. **Identifying Important Events** In your notebook, create a two-column chart. In the first column, list events described in this section. In the second column, write a description of each event and a note about how it changed life in the United States.

Section 1 Assessment Answers

1. **a.** Americans who opposed immigration
   b. similar—sought economic opportunity, forced to take low-paying jobs; different—reasons for coming, religions, economic status, where settled, jobs they held
   c. could lead to violence against immigrants
2. **a.** Better transportation and the Industrial Revolution led people to move to cities.
   b. A new social class, the middle class, developed; urban problems increased.
3. **a.** poorly designed apartment buildings that housed large numbers of people
   b. overcrowding, unsafe housing, lack of public services, epidemics, crime, fire danger
   c. Students should discuss one of the problems listed in the previous answer.
4. immigration—causes: economic, political issues; effects: rapid population and city growth, anti-immigration movements; urban growth—causes: industrialization, immigration; effects: more urban problems
5. Students should list events related to the causes and effects of increased immigration.

American Arts

SECTION 2

If YOU were there...

You are a teacher living in Massachusetts in the 1840s. Some of your neighbors have started an experimental community. They want to live more simply than present-day society allows. They hope to have time to write and think, while still sharing the work. Some people will teach, others will raise food. You think this might be an interesting place to live.

What would you ask the leaders of the community?

BUILDING BACKGROUND Great changes were taking place in American culture. The early 1800s brought a revolution in American thought. Artists, writers, and philosophers pursued their ideals and developed truly American styles.

Transcendentalists

Some New England writers and philosophers found spiritual wisdom in **transcendentalism**, the belief that people could transcend, or rise above, material things in life. Transcendentalists also believed that people should depend on themselves and their own insights, rather than on outside authorities. Important transcendentalists included **Ralph Waldo Emerson**, **Margaret Fuller**, and **Henry David Thoreau**.

Walden Pond, where Thoreau lived for two years

What You Will Learn...

Main Ideas

1. Transcendentalists and utopian communities withdrew from American society.
2. American Romantic painters and writers made important contributions to art and literature.

The Big Idea

New movements in art and literature influenced many Americans in the early 1800s.

Key Terms and People

transcendentalism, *p. 405*
Ralph Waldo Emerson, *p. 405*
Margaret Fuller, *p. 405*
Henry David Thoreau, *p. 405*
utopian communities, *p. 406*
Nathaniel Hawthorne, *p. 406*
Edgar Allan Poe, *p. 407*
Emily Dickinson, *p. 407*
Henry Wadsworth Longfellow, *p. 407*
Walt Whitman, *p. 407*

HSS 8.6.7 Identify common themes in American art as well as transcendentalism and individualism (e.g., writings about and by Ralph Waldo Emerson, Henry David Thoreau, Herman Melville, Louisa May Alcott, Nathaniel Hawthorne, Henry Wadsworth Longfellow).

Teach the Big Idea: Master the Standards

Standards Proficiency

American Arts HSS 8.6.7; HSS Analysis Skills: HI 1

1. **Teach** Ask students the Main Idea questions to teach this section.
2. **Apply** Have students write each of the blue headings in the section on a piece of paper. Tell students to leave space below each heading. Have students read the material under each heading and create an outline for the content under that heading.
LS Verbal/Linguistic
3. **Review** To review the section, have volunteers share with the class the information they provided in their outlines.
4. **Practice/Homework** Have each student write an imaginary interview with one of the key figures covered in the section. The interview should include at least five questions and answers. **LS Verbal/Linguistic**

Alternative Assessment Handbook, Rubric 37: Writing Assignments

Preteach

Bellringer

If YOU were there . . . Use the **Daily Bellringer Transparency** to help students answer the question.

Daily Bellringer Transparency, Section 2

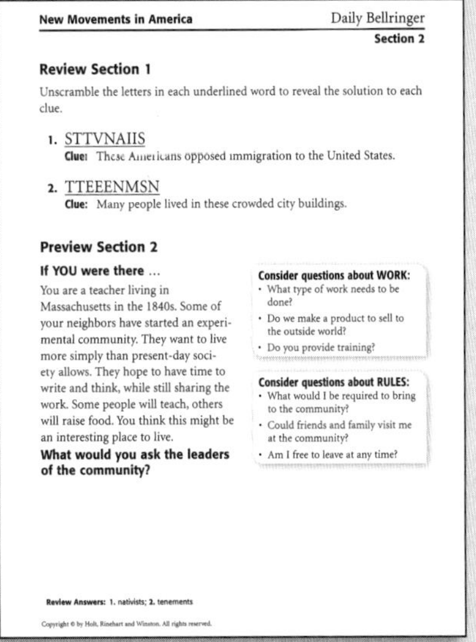

New Movements in America — Daily Bellringer **Section 2**

Review Section 1

Unscramble the letters in each underlined word to reveal the solution to each clue.

1. STTVNAIIS
Clue: These Americans opposed immigration to the United States.
2. TTEEENMSN
Clue: Many people lived in these crowded city buildings.

Preview Section 2

If YOU were there ...

You are a teacher living in Massachusetts in the 1840s. Some of your neighbors have started an experimental community. They want to live more simply than present-day society allows. They hope to have time to write and think, while still sharing the work. Some people will teach, others will raise food. You think this might be an interesting place to live.

What would you ask the leaders of the community?

Consider questions about WORK:
- What type of work needs to be done?
- Do we make a product to sell to the outside world?
- Do you provide training?

Consider questions about RULES:
- What would I be required to bring to the community?
- Could friends and family visit me at the community?
- Am I free to leave at any time?

Review Answers: 1. nativists; 2. tenements

Academic Vocabulary

Review with students the high-use academic term in this section:

abstract expressing a quality or idea without reference to an actual thing (p. 406)

Building Vocabulary

Preteach or review the following terms:

insights personal perceptions of the nature of people or things (p. 405)

self-reliance dependence on self to accomplish things and make decisions (p. 406)

transcend rise above (p. 405)

CRF: Vocabulary Builder Activity, Section 2

Standards Focus

HSS 8.6.7

Means: Identify common themes in American culture, including transcendentalism and individualism. Identify the significant works of Emerson, Thoreau, Melville, Alcott, Hawthorne, and Longfellow.

Matters: American culture of the mid-1800s helped to shape people's lives, thoughts, and actions. Many of these works of art and literature are now considered classics.

Direct Teach

Main Idea

1 Transcendentalists

Transcendentalists and utopian communities withdrew from American society.

Define In your own words, explain transcendentalism. *possible answer—belief that people should rise above material things, depend on themselves and their own insights, and live simply in tune with nature*

Identify Who were some key transcendentalists? *Ralph Waldo Emerson, Margaret Fuller, Henry David Thoreau*

Make Judgments Do you think utopian communities are possible? Why or why not? *possible answers—yes, if people agree to work for the good of the group; no, because inherent human weaknesses will cause all attempts to fail*

HSS 8.6.7; HSS **Analysis Skills:** HI 1

Biography

Emily Dickinson (1830–1886) Emily Dickinson did not achieve fame during her lifetime. Of the more than 1,775 poems that she wrote, only 10 were published while she was alive. Not until 1955—nearly 80 years after her death—were all of her poems collected and published.

go.hrw.com
Online Resources
KEYWORD: SS8 US13
ACTIVITY:
Who's Who of Transcendentalism

Art of the Romantic Movement

Asher Durand's *The First Harvest in the Wilderness*

Emerson was a popular writer and thinker who argued that Americans should disregard institutions and follow their own beliefs. "What I must do is all that concerns me, not what the people think," he wrote in an essay called "Self-Reliance." Fuller edited the famous transcendentalist publication *The Dial*. Thoreau advised self-reliance and simple living away from society in natural settings. He wrote his book *Walden* after living for two years at Walden Pond.

Some transcendentalists formed a community at Brook Farm, Massachusetts, in the 1840s. It was one of many experiments with **utopian communities**, groups of people who tried to form a perfect society. People in utopian communities pursued **abstract** spirituality and cooperative lifestyles. However, few communities lasted for long. In most, members did not work together well.

ACADEMIC VOCABULARY
abstract expressing a quality or idea without reference to an actual thing

READING CHECK **Drawing Inferences** Why did most utopian communities last for only a short time?

American Romanticism

Ideas about the simple life and nature also inspired painters and writers in the early and mid-1800s. Some joined the Romantic movement that had begun in Europe. Romanticism involved a great interest in nature, an emphasis on individual expression, and a rejection of many established rules. These painters and writers felt that each person brings a unique view to the world. They believed in using emotion to guide their creative output. Some Romantic artists, like Thomas Cole, painted the American landscape. Their works celebrated the beauty and wonder of nature in the United States. Their images contrasted with the huge cities and corruption of nature that many Americans saw as typical of Europe.

Many female writers, like Ann Sophia Stephens, wrote historical fiction that was popular in the mid-1800s. New England writer **Nathaniel Hawthorne** wrote *The Scarlet Letter* during that period. One of the greatest classics of Romantic literature, it explored Puritan

Differentiating Instruction for Universal Access

Learners Having Difficulty — Reaching Standards

1. Draw the graphic organizer for students to see. Omit the blue, italicized answers.
2. Have each student copy the organizer and complete it by listing the main influences of the key people and ideas related to the American Romantic movement.
LS Visual/Spatial

HSS 8.6.7; HSS **Analysis Skills:** HI 1

Alternative Assessment Handbook, Rubric 13: Graphic Organizers

American Romantic Movement
↓
Ideas
simple life, nature, emotion, individualism, democracy and American history
↓
Artists and Writers
artists: Thomas Cole (Hudson River school); writers: Stephens, Hawthorne, Melville, Poe, Dickinson, Longfellow, Whitman

Answers

Reading Check *because members did not work together well enough for the groups to survive*

CONNECT TO THE ARTS

Artists of the Hudson River school celebrated nature in their dramatic paintings. Their work was made popular by their leader, Thomas Cole. Other important painters of the Hudson River school were Frederick Church and Asher Durand.

What words would you use to describe this painting?

❶ The light in the painting has a delicate, glowing quality. Hudson River school painters pioneered this technique.

❷ The human presence in this scene is dwarfed by nature but is in harmony with it.

life in the 1600s. Hawthorne's friend Herman Melville, a writer and former sailor, wrote novels about the sea, such as *Moby-Dick* and *Billy Budd*. Many people believe that *Moby-Dick* is one of the finest American novels ever written.

American Romantic authors also wrote a great deal of poetry. The poet **Edgar Allan Poe**, also a short story writer, became famous for a haunting poem called "The Raven." Other gifted American poets included **Emily Dickinson**, **Henry Wadsworth Longfellow**, and **Walt Whitman**. Most of Dickinson's short, thoughtful poems were not published until after her death. Longfellow, the best-known poet of the mid-1800s, wrote popular story-poems, like *The Song of Hiawatha*. Whitman praised American individualism and democracy in his simple, unrhymed poetry. In his poetry collection *Leaves of Grass,* he wrote, "The United States themselves are essentially the greatest poem."

READING CHECK **Summarizing** Who were some American Romantic authors, and why were they important?

SUMMARY AND PREVIEW American Romantic artists and authors were inspired by ideas about the simple life, nature, and spirituality. In the next section you will learn about ideas that changed American society.

Section 2 Assessment

go.hrw.com
Online Quiz
KEYWORD: SS8 HP13

Reviewing Ideas, Terms, and People HSS 8.6.7

1. a. **Identify** What were the main teachings of **transcendentalism**?
   b. **Summarize** What **utopian community** was established in the United States, and what was its goal?
   c. **Elaborate** Do you agree with transcendentalists that Americans put too much emphasis on institutions and traditions? Explain your answer.
2. a. **Recall** Who were some important American authors and poets at this time?
   b. **Explain** What ideas did artists in the Romantic movement express?
   c. **Evaluate** Do you think the Romantic movement was important to American culture? Explain.

Critical Thinking

3. **Comparing and Contrasting** Copy the graphic organizer below. Use it to identify the similarities and differences between transcendentalism and the Romantic movement in art and literature.

Transcendentalism | Similarities | Romanticism

FOCUS ON WRITING

4. **Describing Artistic Movements** Two artistic movements are described in this section, transcendentalism and romanticism. Write these two movements in the first column of your chart. Then in the second column, write a brief description of each and explain how writings from each either described or influenced life in the United States.

Direct Teach

Main Idea

❷ American Romanticism

American Romantic painters and writers made important contributions to art and literature.

Define What was the Romantic movement? *movement that began in Europe, drew on individual emotion and perspective, celebration of nature and simple life*

Summarize Describe Walt Whitman's poetry. *praised American individualism and democracy; simple; unrhymed*

CRF: Literature Activity: *Jack and Jill,* by Louisa May Alcott

HSS 8.6.7, HSS **Analysis Skills:** HI 1

Review & Assess

Close

Have students summarize new movements in art and literature.

Review

Online Quiz, Section 2

Assess

SE Section 2 Assessment

PASS: Section 2 Quiz

Alternative Assessment Handbook

Reteach/Classroom Intervention

California Standards Review Workbook

Interactive Reader and Study Guide, Section 2

Interactive Skills Tutor CD-ROM

Section 2 Assessment Answers

1. **a.** the belief that people could transcend, or rise above, material things in life
   b. Brook Farm; tried to form a perfect society
   c. possible answers—Yes, America needed to focus on the individual ruggedness and natural wilderness that made it great; no, these institutions and traditions worked.
2. **a.** Ann Sophia Stephens, Nathaniel Hawthorne, Herman Melville, Edgar Allan Poe, Emily Dickinson, Henry Wadsworth Longfellow, and Walt Whitman
   b. beauty and wonder of nature, emotion, individualism, democracy and history
   c. possible answers—Yes, the movement helped America develop an independent culture; no, the movement just copied Europe.
3. similar—focus on nature and simple life, individualism, personal insight; different—transcendentalism: philosophy; Romantics: focused more on emotion and American history
4. Students should address the ideas of each movement, described in the previous answer.

Answers

Connect to the Arts *possible answers—calm, open, beautiful, wild, panoramic, majestic*

Reading Check *See Answer 2a at left; wrote clearly American literature.*

Literature in History

"The Midnight Ride of Paul Revere"

As You Read Before students read the poem, have them each write a few sentences describing what they think a hero is. Next, as students read the poem, have them list the ways in which Longfellow describes Revere as a hero. Then ask students to discuss how their descriptions of a hero compare to Longfellow's.

Connect to Literature

The Fireside Poets Henry Wadsworth Longfellow was among a group of Boston poets known as the Fireside Poets. In addition to Longfellow, the group included Oliver Wendell Holmes, James Russell Lowell, and John Greenleaf Whittier. They were called Fireside Poets because people often read their poems aloud at the fireside as family entertainment.

Meet the Writer

Henry Wadsworth Longfellow (1807–1882) A prolific poet as well as a translator of many languages, Longfellow was the most popular American poet of his time. For many Americans, he became the symbolic figure of the Poet: wise, graybearded, and living in a world of romance. His most popular poems include *The Song of Hiawatha* (1855) and *The Courtship of Miles Standish* (1858).

Literature of the Young Nation: Romanticism and Realism

from "The Midnight Ride of Paul Revere"

by Henry Wadsworth Longfellow (1807–1882)

About the Reading *"The Midnight Ride of Paul Revere" was published in a book called* Tales of a Wayside Inn. *The book is a collection of poems that tell well-known stories from history and mythology. By including the story of Paul Revere with other famous stories, Longfellow helped increase the importance of Paul Revere's ride.*

As You Read **Notice how Longfellow describes Revere as a hero.**

Listen my children and you shall hear
Of the midnight ride of Paul Revere,
On the eighteenth of April, in Seventy-five;
Hardly a man is now alive
Who remembers that famous day and year. ❶

He said to his friend, "If the British march
By land or sea from the town to-night,
Hang a lantern aloft in the belfry arch
Of the North Church tower as a signal light,—
One if by land, and two if by sea;
And I on the opposite shore will be,
Ready to ride and spread the alarm
Through every . . . village and farm,
For the country folk to be up and to arm." ❷

. . . .

Meanwhile, his friend, through alley and street
Wanders and watches with eager ears,
Till in the silence around him he hears
The muster of men at the barrack door,
The sound of arms, and the tramp of feet,
And the measured tread of the grenadiers,
Marching down to their boats on the shore. ❸

Guided Reading

Word Help

belfry bell tower
muster gathering
barrack building where soldiers meet
grenadiers a soldier that throws grenades

❶ When the poem was written, there were still a few people alive who had lived during the Revolution.

❷ Longfellow uses poetic language to make Revere's story more dramatic.

❸ The sounds of the night are described to help the reader feel the excitement.

HSS 8.6.7 Identify common themes in American art as well as transcendentalism and individualism (e.g., writings about and by Ralph Waldo Emerson, Henry David Thoreau, Herman Melville, Louisa May Alcott, Nathaniel Hawthorne, Henry Wadsworth Longfellow).

Differentiating Instruction for Universal Access

Special Education Students — Reaching Standards

Materials: blank paper, colored pens or pencils, old magazines and newspapers

1. Read "The Midnight Ride of Paul Revere" aloud to the class. Discuss the meaning of the passage with students. If necessary, review the historical background. Then help students list the key events that occur in the passage.
2. Have each student create a piece of artwork that illustrates the passage. Students might choose to create a drawing, a comic strip, or a collage.
3. Instruct students to incorporate several of the key events from the passage into their artwork. In addition, each student should write a caption describing his or her artwork.
4. Display students' artwork in the classroom. **LS Visual/Spatial**

HSS 8.6.7

Alternative Assessment Handbook, Rubric 3: Artwork

from *Little Women*

by Louisa May Alcott (1832–1888)

About the Reading Little Women *is a novel about four sisters living in a small New England town before the Civil War. Still popular with young people today,* Little Women *describes a family much like the one Louisa May Alcott grew up in. Alcott based the main character, Jo March, on herself. Like Alcott, Jo was different from most women of her time. She was outspoken, eager for adventure, and in conflict with the role her society expected her to play.*

AS YOU READ **Try to understand how Jo is different from Aunt March.**

Jo happened to suit Aunt March, who was lame and needed an active person to wait upon her. The childless old lady had offered to adopt one of the girls when the troubles came, and was much offended because her offer was declined . . .

The old lady wouldn't speak to them for a time, but happening to meet Jo at a friend's, . . . she proposed to take her for a companion.❶ This did not suit Jo at all, but she accepted the place since nothing better appeared, and to everyone's surprise, got on remarkably well with her irascible relative . . .

I suspect that the real attraction was a large library of fine books, which was left to dust and spiders since Uncle March died . . . The dim, dusty room, with the busts staring down from the tall bookcases, the cozy chairs, the globes, and, best of all, the wilderness of books, in which she could wander where she liked, made the library a region of bliss to her . . . ❷

Jo's ambition was to do something very splendid. What it was she had no idea, as yet, but left it for time to tell her, and, meanwhile, found her greatest affliction in the fact that she couldn't read, run, and ride as much as she liked.❸ A quick temper, sharp tongue, and restless spirit were always getting her into scrapes, and her life was a series of ups and downs, which were both comic and pathetic. But the training she received at Aunt March's was just what she needed, and the thought that she was doing something to support herself made her happy in spite of the perpetual "Josy-phine!"

GUIDED READING

WORD HELP

lame disabled
irascible angry
bliss happiness
ambition hope for the future
affliction problem
pathetic very sad
perpetual constant

❶ ***Some women kept companions to help entertain them and perform small chores. Why might Jo not want to be a companion?***

❷ ***How does Jo differ from ideas about women in the 1880s?***

❸ ***What might Jo be able to do for work in the 1800s?***

CONNECTING LITERATURE TO HISTORY

1. **Drawing Conclusions** Henry Wadsworth Longfellow was the most popular American poet of his time. How does his version of Paul Revere's ride increase the importance of the story?
2. **Comparing and Contrasting** The lives of women in the 1800s were very different from the lives of women today. How does this excerpt of *Little Women* show some similarities and differences between now and then?

Literature in History

Little Women

As You Read Tell students as they read the passage to list adjectives and phrases that describe Jo and Aunt March. Ask volunteers to share some of the items they listed. Then have students use the lists to contrast Jo and Aunt March.

Meet the Writer

Louisa May Alcott (1832–1888)

The daughter of an impractical Massachusetts philosopher, Louisa May Alcott had to work hard from childhood to support her mother and three sisters. She tried sewing, teaching in country schools, working as a domestic, and serving as a Civil War nurse before finding fame as a writer. The success of *Little Women* enabled Alcott to write in her journal, "Paid up all the debts . . . !"

Cross-Discipline Activity: Literature

Standards Proficiency

Character Analysis Chart HSS 8.6.7

1. Have students read the passage from *Little Women.* Then have each student create a three-column chart and label the columns *Jo, Interactions,* and *Aunt March.*
2. In the middle column, have students list each interaction between Jo and Aunt March in the passage, including inferred interactions. In the other columns, have students describe what each interaction reveals about each character.
3. Ask volunteers to share the information they listed in their charts. Have students discuss each character and how Alcott reveals their personalities.
4. Then have students discuss how the two women's characters and interactions reflect aspects of American society in the mid-1800s.
LS Verbal/Linguistic

Alternative Assessment Handbook, Rubrics 7: Charts; and 11: Discussions

Answers

Guided Reading 1. *possible answer—She is active and the job will prevent her from running, riding, and reading as much as she would like.*
2. *Jo is outspoken, active, and ambitious at a time when women were expected to be focused on domestic concerns.*
3. *possible answers—seamstress, mill worker, writer, teacher, reformer, companion, domestic*

Connecting Literature to History
1. *Longfellow's version presents Paul Revere as the lone, heroic rider who spread the news of the approaching British.*
2. *reveals that women's personalities may be much the same but that opportunities for women in the 1800s were more limited*

Preteach

Bellringer

If YOU were there . . . Use the **Daily Bellringer Transparency** to help students answer the question.

 Daily Bellringer Transparency, Section 3

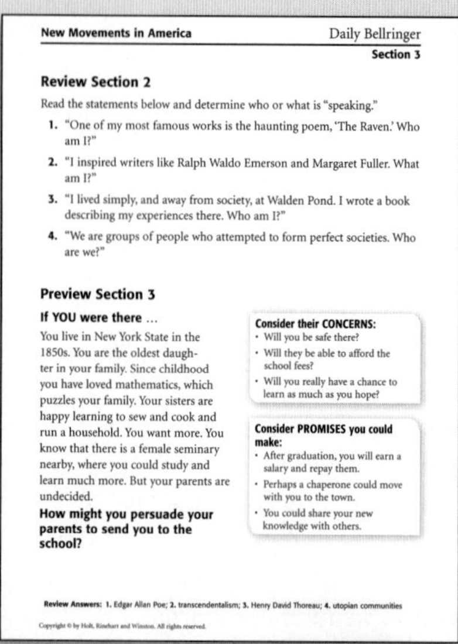
New Movements in America — Daily Bellringer
Section 3

Review Section 2

Read the statements below and determine who or what is "speaking."

1. "One of my most famous works is the haunting poem, 'The Raven.' Who am I?"
2. "I inspired writers like Ralph Waldo Emerson and Margaret Fuller. What am I?"
3. "I lived simply, and away from society, at Walden Pond. I wrote a book describing my experiences there. Who am I?"
4. "We are groups of people who attempted to form perfect societies. Who are we?"

Preview Section 3

If YOU were there ...

You live in New York State in the 1850s. You are the oldest daughter in your family. Since childhood you have loved mathematics, which puzzles your family. Your sisters are happy learning to sew and cook and run a household. You want more. You know that there is a female seminary nearby, where you could study and learn much more. But your parents are undecided.

How might you persuade your parents to send you to the school?

Consider their CONCERNS:
- Will you be safe there?
- Will they be able to afford the school fees?
- Will you really have a chance to learn as much as you hope?

Consider PROMISES you could make:
- After graduation, you will earn a salary and repay them.
- Perhaps a chaperone could move with you to the town.
- You could share your new knowledge with others.

Review Answers: 1. Edgar Allan Poe; 2. transcendentalism; 3. Henry David Thoreau; 4. utopian communities

Building Vocabulary

Preteach or review the following terms:

conversion moving to faith or belief (p. 410)

offenders people who break a law (p. 412)

revivals emotional religious meetings (p. 410)

segregated separate (p. 414)

temperance avoidance of alcohol (p. 411)

CRF: Vocabulary Builder Activity, Section 3

Standards Focus

HSS 8.6.4

Means: Explain how free African Americans in the North founded churches and schools to improve equality and their opportunities.
Matters: Many black churches and colleges founded during this period still exist today.

HSS 8.6.5

Means: Describe how Horace Mann's efforts led to improved public education and greater opportunities for Americans.
Matters: Mann's efforts increased educational opportunities for many segments of American society and helped shape the American public education system of today.

SECTION 3

Reforming Society

What You Will Learn...

Main Ideas

1. The Second Great Awakening sparked interest in religion.
2. Social reformers began to speak out about temperance and prison reform.
3. Improvements in education reform affected many segments of the population.
4. Northern African American communities became involved in reform efforts.

The Big Idea

Reform movements in the early 1800s affected religion, education, and society.

Key Terms and People

Second Great Awakening, *p. 410*
Charles Grandison Finney, *p. 410*
Lyman Beecher, *p. 410*
temperance movement, *p. 411*
Dorothea Dix, *p. 412*
common-school movement, *p. 412*
Horace Mann, *p. 412*
Catharine Beecher, *p. 413*
Thomas Gallaudet, *p. 413*

HSS 8.6.4 Study the lives of black Americans who gained freedom in the North and founded schools and churches to advance their rights and communities.

8.6.5 Trace the development of the American education system from its earliest roots, including the roles of religious and private schools and Horace Mann's campaign for free public education and its assimilating role in American culture.

If YOU were there...

You live in New York State in the 1850s. You are the oldest daughter in your family. Since childhood you have loved mathematics, which puzzles your family. Your sisters are happy learning to sew and cook and run a household. You want more. You know that there is a female seminary nearby, where you could study and learn much more. But your parents are undecided.

How might you persuade your parents to send you to the school?

BUILDING BACKGROUND Along with changes in American culture, changes were also taking place in American society. A religious revival swept the country. Reform-minded men and women tried to improve all aspects of society, from schools to taverns. Reforms in education opened up new opportunities for young women.

Second Great Awakening

During the 1790s and early 1800s, some Americans took part in a Christian renewal movement called the **Second Great Awakening**. It swept through towns across upstate New York and through the frontier regions of Kentucky, Ohio, Tennessee, and South Carolina. By the 1820s and 1830s, this new interest in religion had spread to New England and the South.

Charles Grandison Finney was one of the most important leaders of the Second Great Awakening. After experiencing a dramatic religious conversion in 1821, Finney left his career as a lawyer and began preaching. He challenged some traditional Protestant beliefs, telling congregations that each individual was responsible for his or her own salvation. He also believed that sin was avoidable. Finney held revivals, emotional prayer meetings that lasted for days. Many people converted to Christianity during these revivals. Finney told new converts to prove their faith by doing good deeds.

Finney's style of preaching and his ideas angered some traditional ministers, like Boston's **Lyman Beecher**. Beecher wanted to prevent Finney from holding revivals in his city. "You mean to

Teach the Big Idea: Master the Standards

Standards Proficiency

Reforming Society HSS 8.6.4, 8.6.5; HSS Analysis Skills: HI 1, HI 2

1. **Teach** Ask students the Main Idea questions to teach this section
2. **Apply** Create a four-column chart for students to see. Title the chart *Reforming Society* and label the columns *Why, Who, What,* and *When*. Have each student copy the chart and use the information in the section to complete it. Students should list why reform was needed, key reformers, the reform efforts they made, and when these reforms occurred. **LS Verbal/Linguistic, Visual/Spatial**
3. **Review** To review, have students help you complete a master copy of the chart.
4. **Practice/Homework** Ask students to conduct research on one reformer in the section who interests them. Each student should find one fact about the reformer to share with the class. **LS Verbal/Linguistic**

Alternative Assessment Handbook, Rubrics 7: Charts; and 30: Research carry a streak of fire to Boston. If you attempt it, as the Lord liveth, I'll meet you . . . and fight every inch of the way." Despite the opposition of Beecher and other traditional ministers, Finney's appeal remained powerful. Also, the First Amendment guarantee of freedom of religion prevented the government from passing laws banning the new religious practices. Ministers were therefore free to spread their message of faith and salvation to whomever wished to listen.

Due to the efforts of Finney and his followers, church membership across the country grew a great deal during the Second Great Awakening. Many new church members were women and African Americans. The African Methodist Episcopal Church spread across the Middle Atlantic states. Although the movement had begun in the Northeast and on the frontier, the Second Great Awakening renewed some people's religious faith throughout America.

READING CHECK **Drawing Conclusions** What impact did the Second Great Awakening have on religion in America?

Social Reformers Speak Out

Renewed religious faith often led to involvement in movements to reform society. Urban growth had caused problems that reformers wanted to fix. Members of the growing middle class, especially women, often led the efforts. Many of the women did not work outside the home and hired servants to care for their households. This gave them time to work in reform groups. Social reformers tackled alcohol abuse, prison and education reform, and slavery.

Temperance Movement

Many social reformers worked to prevent alcohol abuse. They believed that Americans drank too much. In the 1830s, on average, an American consumed seven gallons of alcohol per year. Countless Americans thought that alcohol abuse caused social problems, such as family violence, poverty, and criminal behavior.

Americans' worries about the effects of alcohol led to the growth of a **temperance movement**. This reform effort urged people to use self-discipline to stop drinking hard liquor.

Reform Movements

Reform movements in America included religious meetings called revivals, where preachers urged huge crowds of people to seek salvation. The temperance movement, an effort to convince people to avoid drinking alcohol, promoted posters like the one shown here. *How might the scenes in this poster encourage people to stop drinking?*

411

Direct Teach

Main Idea

❶ Second Great Awakening

The Second Great Awakening sparked interest in religion.

Identify What areas of the United States were affected by the Second Great Awakening? *upstate New York, frontier regions of Kentucky, Ohio, Tennessee, South Carolina, New England, and the South*

Evaluate Why do you think many people were drawn to Finney's preaching? *possible answer—He was a charismatic preacher, willing to challenge traditional beliefs.*

CRF: Biography Activity: Charles Finney

HSS 8.6.4; HSS **Analysis Skills:** HI 1

Main Idea

❷ Social Reformers Speak Out

Social reformers began to speak out about temperance and prison reform.

Explain How did the Second Great Awakening contribute to social reform? *Renewed religious faith led people to want to improve society.*

Analyze What social problems did people think were caused by alcohol abuse, and what movement formed to address these problems? *family violence, poverty, and criminal behavior; temperance movement*

Political Cartoons Activities for United States History, Cartoon 15: Temperance Reform

Critical Thinking: Finding Main Ideas

Standards Proficiency

Second Great Awakening Magazine Cover

HSS 8.6.4; HSS **Analysis Skills:** HI 1, HI 2, HI 3

Materials: art supplies, heavy-stock paper

1. Lead a discussion on the Second Great Awakening and its effects on society.
2. Then ask students to imagine that they work at an early 1800s magazine that covers trends in society. Have students, working either individually or in small groups, create a cover for an edition of the magazine on the Second Great Awakening.
3. The cover should provide the name of the magazine, titles and tag lines for articles in the magazine, and one or more images. The article titles and tag lines should cover all aspects of the Second Great Awakening as well as some other issues of the day.
4. Display the covers around the classroom. **LS Verbal/Linguistic, Visual/Spatial**

Alternative Assessment Handbook, Rubric 19: Magazines

Answers

Reform Movements *by showing how temperance promotes a strong, happy family life*

Reading Check *Church membership increased, particularly among women and African Americans, and some people's religious faith increased across the nation.*

Reformers asked people to limit themselves to beer and wine in small amounts. Groups like the American Temperance Society and the American Temperance Union helped to spread this message. Minister Lyman Beecher spoke widely about the evils of alcohol. He claimed that people who drank alcohol were "neglecting the education of their families—and corrupting their morals."

Prison Reform

Another target of reform was the prison system. **Dorothea Dix** was a middle-class reformer who visited prisons throughout Massachusetts beginning in 1841. Dix reported that mentally ill people frequently were jailed with criminals. They were sometimes left in dark cells without clothes or heat and were chained to the walls and beaten. Dix spoke of what she saw to the state legislature.

THE IMPACT TODAY

McGuffey's Readers were among the first "graded" textbooks. Organizing classes by grades was a new idea that is standard practice today.

In response, the Massachusetts government built facilities for the mentally ill. Dix's work had a nationwide effect. Eventually, more than 100 state hospitals were built to give mentally ill people professional care.

Prisons also held runaway children and orphans. Some had survived only by begging or stealing, and they got the same punishment as adult criminals. Boston mayor Josiah Quincy asked that young offenders receive different punishments than adults. In the 1820s, several state and local governments founded reform schools for children who had been housed in prisons. There, children lived under strict rules and learned useful skills.

Some reformers also tried to end the overcrowding and cruel conditions in prisons. Their efforts led to the creation of houses of correction. These institutions did not use punishment alone to change behavior. They also offered prisoners education.

READING CHECK **Summarizing** How did reformers change the punishment of criminals?

Improvements in Education

Another challenge facing America in the early 1800s was poor public education. Most American families believed that some schooling was useful. However, many children worked in factories or on farms to help support their families. If children could read the Bible, write, and do simple math, that was often considered to be enough.

Education in the Early 1800s

The availability of education varied widely. New England had the most schools, while the South and West had the fewest. Few teachers were trained. Schoolhouses were small, and students of all ages and levels worked in one room.

McGuffey's Readers were the most popular textbooks. William Holmes McGuffey, an educator and minister, put selections from British and American literature in them as well as reading lessons and instruction in moral and social values.

Social background and wealth affected the quality of education. Rich families sent children to private schools or hired tutors. However, poor children had only public schools. Girls could go to school, but parents usually thought that girls needed little education and kept them home. Therefore, few girls learned to read.

Common-School Movement

Reformers thought that education made children responsible citizens. People in the **common-school movement** wanted all children taught in a common place, regardless of background. **Horace Mann** was a leader of this movement.

In 1837 Mann became Massachusetts's first secretary of education. He convinced the state to double its school budget and raise teachers' salaries. He lengthened the school year and began the first school for teacher training. Mann's success set a standard for education reform throughout the country.

Direct Teach

Main Idea

❷ Social Reformers Speak Out

Social reformers began to speak out about temperance and prison reform.

Identify How did Dorothea Dix contribute to the improvement of American society? *Dix pushed for better conditions and facilities for the mentally ill, which led to the creation of many state hospitals.*

Draw Conclusions How were reform schools an improvement over prisons? *Children were not treated as adult offenders and learned useful skills.*

Activity **Civics: Responsibility** Have students write short essays in response to the following question: *Do you think individuals can still make a difference in society, such as Dorothea Dix and Josiah Quincy did?* Ask volunteers to read their essays aloud to the class. **LS Verbal/Linguistic**

Alternative Assessment Handbook, Rubric 37: Writing Assignment

CRF: Biography Activity: Dorothea Dix

HSS Analysis Skills: HI 1, HI 2

Connect to Science and Technology

Access to Textbooks Technological developments in the early 1800s also helped improved education. New printing techniques made producing textbooks less expensive. Textbooks became more widely distributed, and more students had access to them.

Critical Thinking: Solving Problems

Standards Proficiency

Prisoners' Bill of Rights **HSS Analysis Skills:** HI 1

1. Describe the conditions in prisons during the early 1800s. Then organize students into small groups and ask the groups to imagine that they are members of an organization involved in prison reform in the early 1800s.
2. Have each group's members discuss what they hope to achieve through reform. Students should consider living conditions in prisons, who should be placed in prisons, the privileges prisoners should be allowed, and how to deal with juvenile offenders.
3. Have each group provide its suggestions for reform in the form of a prisoners' bill of rights.
4. Write some of the suggested reforms for the class to see. Then have students compare their ideas to the actual reform efforts made in the early 1800s. **LS Verbal/Linguistic**

Alternative Assessment Handbook, Rubrics 14: Group Activity; and 37: Writing Assignment

Answers

Reading Check *worked to reform prisons by building state hospitals for the mentally ill, providing reform schools for young offenders, and creating houses of correction for adult offenders*

Women's Education

Education reform created greater opportunities for women. **Catharine Beecher** started an all-female academy in Hartford, Connecticut. The first college-level educational institution available to women was the Troy Female Seminary, opened by Emma Willard in 1821. Several other women's colleges opened during the 1830s, including Mount Holyoke College. Mary Lyon began Mount Holyoke in 1837 as a place for women to develop skills to be of service to society.

Teaching People with Special Needs

Efforts to improve education also helped people with special needs. In 1831 Samuel Gridley Howe opened the Perkins School for the Blind in Massachusetts. Howe traveled widely, talking about teaching people with visual impairment. **Thomas Gallaudet** improved the education and lives of people with hearing impairments. He founded the first free American school for hearing-impaired people in 1817.

READING CHECK **Summarizing** What were Horace Mann's achievements?

BIOGRAPHY

Horace Mann

1796–1859

Born in Franklin, Massachusetts, Mann had little schooling, but he educated himself well enough at the local library to get into Brown University and attend law school. Despite a busy law practice, he served in the Massachusetts legislature for 10 years. He was also an outspoken advocate for public education. In 1837 the state created the post of secretary of education for him. His achievements in that office made him famous. He later served in the U.S. House of Representatives and as president of Antioch College in Ohio. His influence on education is reflected by the fact that many American schools are named for him.

Analyzing Information How do you think Mann's own education influenced his desire for public schools?

Primary Source

SPEECH

Horace Mann to the Board of Education

In a speech to the newly created Massachusetts Board of Education, Horace Mann, the board's first secretary, described the purpose of the public school system.

"[T]here should be a free district school, sufficiently safe, and sufficiently good, for all of the children... where they may be well instructed in the rudiments [basics] of knowledge, formed to propriety of demeanor [good behavior], and imbued [filled] with the principles of duty... It is on this common platform, that a general acquaintanceship [friendship] should be formed between the children of the same neighborhood. It is here, that the affinities [qualities] of a common nature should unite them together."

—Horace Mann, quoted in *The Republic and the School*, edited by Lawrence A. Cremin

Mann believed all students should receive free education.

Neighborhood children should attend school together to form a common bond.

ANALYSIS SKILL **ANALYZING PRIMARY SOURCES**

Besides knowledge, what purpose did Mann believe the public schools had?

Direct Teach

Main Idea

❸ Improvements in Education

Improvements in education reform affected many segments of the population.

Recall What factors affected access to education in the early 1800s? *social background and wealth*

Summarize How did Horace Mann work to reform education? *He led the common-school movement, which called for all children to be taught in a common place and worked to improve educational funding, training, and pay for teachers.*

Analyze Why do you think reformers wanted all children taught in a common school? *So that all students would receive the same educational experience.*

Identify Cause and Effect How did reform efforts improve access to education? *Efforts led to academies and colleges for women and schools for the blind and hearing-impaired.*

CRF: Biography Activity: Mary Lyon and Emma Willard

HSS 8.6.5; **HSS Analysis Skills:** HR 5, HI 1, HI 2

go.hrw.com

Online Resources

KEYWORD: SS8 US13
ACTIVITY: Education Reformers Interview

Collaborative Learning

Standards Proficiency

Education in Early 1800s America

HSS 8.6.4, 8.6.5; **HSS Analysis Skills:** CS 2, HI 1

Materials: butcher paper, colored markers, art supplies

1. Organize students into small groups. Have each group create an annotated time line of educational reform from 1800 to 1860.
2. The groups' time lines should cover the significant people, events, and ideas connected with the common-school movement and the expansion of educational opportunities for African Americans, women, and people with special needs.
3. Each group should provide a title for its time line and a brief caption summarizing each time line entry. Encourage students to illustrate their time lines with drawings or photographs.

LS Interpersonal, Visual/Spatial

Alternative Assessment Handbook, Rubrics 14: Group Activity; and 36: Time Lines

Answers

Biography *He did not receive much schooling, but had a desire to be educated, which may have given him a desire to help other people who felt the same way.*

Analyzing Primary Sources *to provide a safe environment, teach good behavior and morals, and to form neighborhood bonds among children*

Reading Check *set a national standard for education reform; leader of common-school movement; first Massachusetts Secretary of Education; convinced state to increase school budget and teachers' salaries, lengthen school year; began first school for teacher training*

Direct Teach

Main Idea

4 African American Communities

Northern African American communities became involved in reform efforts.

Describe How did Quakers in Philadelphia influence opportunities for African Americans? *Quakers believed in equality and supported education for African Americans.*

Contrast How did educational opportunities for African Americans differ across the nation? *Free African Americans in the North and Midwest had some chances to attend school, but in the South laws barred most enslaved Africans from getting an education.*

Draw Conclusions How might attending college have improved African Americans' opportunities? *possible answer—They could get better jobs and learn the skills to serve as community leaders.*

HSS 8.6.4, 8.6.5; **HSS Analysis Skills:** HI 1, HI 2

Connect to Civics: Justice

School Segregation More than 100 years before the Supreme Court case *Brown* v. *the Board of Education of Topeka* (1954), another court case addressed segregation in America's schools. In 1848, Benjamin Roberts, an African American printer, sued the Boston School Committee for making his five-year-old daughter Sarah attend an all-black school. Charles Sumner and black attorney Robert Morris provided the defense in the case, but without success. In 1850 the Massachusetts Supreme Judicial Court ruled in *Sarah C. Roberts* v. *The City of Boston* that segregated schools were constitutional. The case served as a precedent, or standard, in later cases involving racial segregation, including *Plessy* v. *Ferguson* (1896).

New Opportunities

African American Communities

Free African Americans usually lived in segregated, or separate, communities in the North. Most of them lived in cities such as New York, Boston, and Philadelphia. Community leaders were often influenced by the Second Great Awakening and its spirit of reform.

Founded by former slave Richard Allen, the Free African Religious Society became a model for other groups that pressed for racial equality and the education of blacks. In 1816, Allen became the first bishop of the African Methodist Episcopal Church, or AME Church. This church broke away from white Methodist churches after African Americans were treated poorly in some white congregations.

Other influential African Americans of the time, such as Alexander Crummel, pushed for the creation of schools for black Americans. The New York African Free School in New York City educated hundreds of children, many of whom became brilliant scholars and important African American leaders. Philadelphia also had a long history of educating African Americans. This was largely because Philadelphia was a center of Quaker influence, and the Quakers believed strongly in equality. The city ran seven schools for African American students by the year 1800. In 1820 Boston followed Philadelphia's lead and opened a separate elementary school for African American children. The city began allowing them to attend school with whites in 1855.

African Americans rarely attended college because few colleges would accept them. In 1835 Oberlin College became the first to do so. Harvard University soon admitted African Americans, too. African American colleges were founded beginning in the 1840s. In 1842 the Institute for Colored Youth opened in Philadelphia. Avery College, also in Pennsylvania, was founded in 1849.

Differentiating Instruction for Universal Access

Learners Having Difficulty

Reaching Standards | Prep Required

Materials: art supplies, sample certificates of commendation or awards (optional)

1. If available, show students sample certificates of commendation or awards. Explain that such items are often given to people in appreciation for their efforts or contributions.
2. Ask students to select one of the reformers mentioned in this section and to create a certificate of commendation for that person. The commendation should include the person's name, a description of the reform or problem he or she is associated with, and a summary of the person's efforts or contributions.
3. Then hold a mock award ceremony at which volunteers read aloud their certificates of commendation. **LS Verbal/Linguistic**

HSS 8.6.4, 8.6.5; **HSS Analysis Skills:** HI 1

Alternative Assessment Handbook, Rubric 37: Writing Assignment

This photograph (left) of the 1855 class at Oberlin College shows the slow integration of African Americans into previously white colleges. Some churches also became more integrated, and preachers like the one pictured above began calling for equality between races.

Why might preachers have been particularly influential in calls for more integration?

While free African Americans had some opportunities to attend school in the North and Midwest, few had this chance in the South. Laws in the South barred most enslaved people from getting any education, even at the primary school level. While some slaves learned to read on their own, they almost always did so in secret. Slaveholders were fearful that education and knowledge in general might encourage a spirit of revolt among enslaved African Americans.

READING CHECK **Drawing Conclusions** Why was it difficult for African Americans to get an education in the South in the early 1800s?

SUMMARY AND PREVIEW The efforts of reformers led to improvements in many aspects of American life in the early to mid-1800s. In the next section you will learn about reform-minded people who opposed the practice of slavery.

Section 3 Assessment

go.hrw.com **Online Quiz** KEYWORD: SS8 HP13

Reviewing Ideas, Terms, and People HSS 8.6.4, 8.6.5

1. **a. Identify** What was the **Second Great Awakening**, and who was one of its leaders?
   b. Summarize What effects did the Second Great Awakening have on religion in the United States?
2. **a. Identify** What role did **Dorothea Dix** play in social reforms of the early 1800s?
   b. Summarize What different reforms helped improve the U.S. prison system?
   c. Elaborate How might the Second Great Awakening have led to the growth of social reform movements?
3. **a. Identify** What was the **common-school movement**, and who was one of its leaders?
   b. Analyze Why did reformers set out to improve education in the United States?
   c. Evaluate Do you think **Horace Mann's** ideas for educational reform were good ones? Explain.
4. **a. Recall** In what cities were the first public schools for African Americans located?
   b. Draw Conclusions How did free African Americans benefit from educational reforms?

Critical Thinking

5. **Categorizing** Copy the chart below onto your own sheet of paper. Use it to identify reform leaders and the accomplishments of each movement.

Movement	Leaders	Accomplishments
Prison and Mental Health Reform		
Temperance		
Education		

FOCUS ON WRITING

6. **Choosing Important Events** This section covers the reform of social issues such as religion, prisons, and education. Write the reforms described in your chart. Write a note about the reform and about the important people involved in it. Think about how each one influenced life in the United States.

Section 3 Assessment Answers

1. **a.** Christian renewal movement; Charles Grandison Finney
   b. Church membership grew, and religious faith was renewed nationwide.
2. **a.** Dix pushed for facilities for the mentally ill.
   b. reform schools, houses of correction
   c. Renewed religious faith led people to want to help others and improve society.
3. **a.** movement to educate all children in a common place; Horace Mann
   b. poor, limited public education
   c. possible answer—yes, because they increased access to and funding for education
4. **a.** New York, Philadelphia, and Boston
   b. More African Americans had the chance to attend public schools and colleges.
5. Prison/Mental Health—Dix, Quincy; state hospitals, reform schools; Temperance—Beecher; alcohol abuse; Education—Mann, common-school; Beecher, all-female academy; Howe and Gallaudet, special needs; Crummel, African Americans
6. See previous answer.

Direct Teach

Biography

Harriet Jacobs (1813–1897) Harriet Jacobs was born into slavery and orphaned at a young age. She learned to read from her first mistress. After Jacobs escaped slavery and fled North, she wrote *Incidents in the Life of a Slave Girl.* Jacobs' emotionally charged account was a fierce indictment of slavery. On the title page, Jacobs writes, "Northerners know nothing at all about Slavery. They think it is perpetual bondage only. They have no conception of the depth of *degradation* involved in that word, *Slavery;* if they had, they would never cease their efforts until so horrible a system was overthrown." Jacobs' narrative was rediscovered during the civil rights movement of the 1960s. Many experts considered the account to be a work of fiction until scholars authenticated it in 1981.

Review & Assess

Close

Have students review the major reform movements and leading reformers covered in this section.

Review

Online Quiz, Section 3

Assess

SE Section 3 Assessment

PASS: Section 3 Quiz

Alternative Assessment Handbook

Reteach/Classroom Intervention

California Standards Review Workbook

Interactive Reader and Study Guide, Section 3

Interactive Skills Tutor CD-ROM

Answers

New Opportunities *because they were community leaders, and many people heard them speak*

Reading Check *Southern laws barred educating most enslaved people because slaveholders feared education would lead to slave revolts.*

Preteach

Bellringer

If YOU were there . . . Use the **Daily Bellringer Transparency** to help students answer the question.

Daily Bellringer Transparency, Section 4

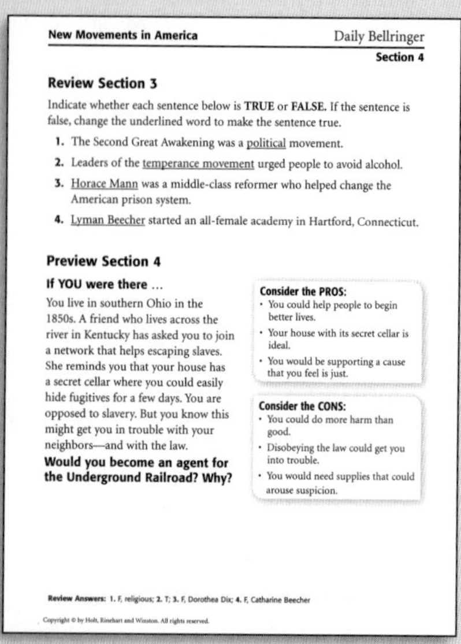

New Movements in America — Daily Bellringer — **Section 4**

Review Section 3

Indicate whether each sentence below is **TRUE** or **FALSE.** If the sentence is false, change the underlined word to make the sentence true.

1. The Second Great Awakening was a political movement.
2. Leaders of the temperance movement urged people to avoid alcohol.
3. Horace Mann was a middle-class reformer who helped change the American prison system.
4. Lyman Beecher started an all-female academy in Hartford, Connecticut.

Preview Section 4

If YOU were there ...

You live in southern Ohio in the 1850s. A friend who lives across the river in Kentucky has asked you to join a network that helps escaping slaves. She reminds you that your house has a secret cellar where you could easily hide fugitives for a few days. You are opposed to slavery. But you know this might get you in trouble with your neighbors—and with the law.

Would you become an agent for the Underground Railroad? Why?

Consider the PROS:
- You could help people to begin better lives.
- Your house with its secret cellar is ideal.
- You would be supporting a cause that you feel is just.

Consider the CONS:
- You could do more harm than good.
- Disobeying the law could get you into trouble.
- You would need supplies that could arouse suspicion.

Review Answers: 1. F, religious; 2. T; 3. F, Dorothea Dix; 4. F, Catharine Beecher

Building Vocabulary

Preteach or review the following terms:

emancipation freedom from slavery (p. 417)

narrative a story or account (p. 418)

obstructed blocked or hindered (p. 420)

CRF: Vocabulary Builder Activity, Section 4

Standards Focus

HSS 8.9.1

Means: Describe the movement to end slavery and identify its leaders.

Matters: The efforts of abolitionists helped lead to the end of slavery in the United States. Today, individual Americans continue to take action to end human rights abuses.

SECTION 4

The Movement to End Slavery

What You Will Learn...

Main Ideas

1. Americans from a variety of backgrounds actively opposed slavery.
2. Abolitionists organized the Underground Railroad to help enslaved Africans escape.
3. Despite efforts of abolitionists, many Americans remained opposed to ending slavery.

The Big Idea

In the mid-1800s, debate over slavery increased as abolitionists organized to challenge slavery in the United States.

Key Terms and People

abolition, *p. 416*
William Lloyd Garrison, *p. 417*
American Anti-Slavery Society, *p. 417*
Angelina and Sarah Grimké, *p. 417*
Frederick Douglass, *p. 418*
Sojourner Truth, *p. 418*
Underground Railroad, *p. 418*
Harriet Tubman, *p. 420*

8.9.1 Describe the leaders of the movement (e.g., John Quincy Adams and his proposed constitutional amendment, John Brown and the armed resistance, Harriet Tubman and the Underground Railroad, Benjamin Franklin, Theodore Weld, William Lloyd Garrison, Frederick Douglass.)

If YOU were there...

You live in southern Ohio in the 1850s. A friend who lives across the river in Kentucky has asked you to join a network that helps escaping slaves. She reminds you that your house has a secret cellar where you could easily hide fugitives for a few days. You are opposed to slavery. But you know this might get you in trouble with your neighbors—and with the law.

Would you become an agent for the Underground Railroad? Why?

BUILDING BACKGROUND The early 1800s brought many movements for social reform in the United States. Perhaps the most important and far-reaching was the movement for the abolition of slavery. While reformers worked to end slavery, many also took risks to help slaves to escape.

Americans Oppose Slavery

Some Americans had opposed slavery since before the country was founded. Benjamin Franklin was the president of the first antislavery society in America, the Pennsylvania Society for Promoting the Abolition of Slavery. In the 1830s, Americans took more organized action supporting **abolition**, or a complete end to slavery.

Differences among Abolitionists

Abolitionists came from many different backgrounds and opposed slavery for various reasons. The Quakers were among the first groups to challenge slavery on religious grounds. Other religious leaders gave speeches and published pamphlets that moved many Americans to support abolition. In one of these, abolitionist Theodore Weld wrote that "everyman knows that slavery is a curse." Other abolitionists referred to the Declaration of Independence. They reminded people that the American Revolution had been fought in the name of liberty.

Teach the Big Idea: Master the Standards

Standards Proficiency

The Movement to End Slavery HSS 8.9.1; HSS Analysis Skills: HR 5, HI 1

1. **Teach** Ask students the Main Idea questions to teach this section.
2. **Apply** Have each student, working individually or in pairs, write a summary of each part of the section, indicated by the blue headings. **LS Verbal/Linguistic**
3. **Review** As you review the section, have volunteers share their summaries. Write them for the class to see and ask students to provide supporting details for each one.
4. **Practice/Homework** Ask students to imagine that they belong to an antislavery society. Have them create fliers announcing the group's next meeting, at which Harriet Tubman will be speaking. The fliers should explain the group's goals, why Americans should support abolition, and what Tubman will be talking about. **LS Verbal/Linguistic**

Alternative Assessment Handbook, Rubric 37: Writing Assignments

Antislavery reformers did not always agree on the details, however. They differed over how much equality they thought African Americans should have. Some believed that African Americans should receive the same treatment as white Americans. In contrast, other abolitionists were against full political and social equality.

Some abolitionists wanted to send freed African Americans to Africa to start new colonies. They thought that this would prevent conflicts between the races in the United States. In 1817 a minister named Robert Finley started the American Colonization Society, an organization dedicated to establishing colonies of freed slaves in Africa. Five years later, the society founded the colony of Liberia on the west coast of Africa. About 12,000 African Americans eventually settled in Liberia. However, many abolitionists who once favored colonization later opposed it. Some African Americans also opposed it. David Walker was one such person. In his 1829 essay, *Appeal to the Colored Citizens of the World*, Walker explained his opposition to colonization.

> "The greatest riches in all America have arisen from our blood and tears: and they [whites] will drive us from our property and homes, which we have earned with our blood."
>
> —David Walker, quoted in *From Slavery to Freedom* by John Hope Franklin and Alfred A. Moss Jr.

"Where there is a
human being,
I see God-given rights . . ."
—William Lloyd Garrison

Spreading the Abolitionist Message

Abolitionists found many ways to further their cause. Some went on speaking tours or wrote pamphlets and newspaper articles. John Greenleaf Whittier wrote abolitionist poetry and literature. **William Lloyd Garrison** published an abolitionist newspaper, the *Liberator*, beginning in 1831. In 1833 Garrison also helped found the **American Anti-Slavery Society**. Its members wanted immediate emancipation and racial equality for African Americans. Garrison later became its president.

Both the *Liberator* and the Anti-Slavery Society relied on support from free African Americans. Society members spread antislavery literature and petitioned Congress to end federal support of slavery. In 1840 the American Anti-Slavery Society split. One group wanted immediate freedom for enslaved African Americans and a bigger role for women. The others wanted gradual emancipation and for women to play only minor roles in the movement.

Angelina and Sarah Grimké, two white southern women, were antislavery activists of the 1830s. They came from a South Carolina slaveholding family but disagreed with their parents' support of slavery. Angelina Grimké tried to recruit other white southern women in a pamphlet called *Appeal to the Christian Women of the South* in 1836.

> "I know you do not make the laws, but . . . if you really suppose you can do nothing to overthrow slavery you are greatly mistaken . . . Try to persuade your husband, father, brothers, and sons that slavery is a crime against God and man."
>
> —Angelina Grimké, quoted in *The Grimké Sisters from South Carolina*, edited by Gerda Lerner

This essay was very popular in the North. In 1839 the Grimké sisters wrote *American Slavery As It Is*. The book was one of the most important antislavery works of its time.

Direct Teach

Main Idea

❶ Americans Oppose Slavery

Americans from a variety of backgrounds actively opposed slavery.

Recall What were some reasons that abolitionists opposed slavery? *for religious reasons, was morally wrong, because it went against the right to liberty for which the American Revolution had been fought*

Contrast How did some abolitionists differ in their views toward African Americans? *differed over how much equality they thought African Americans should have and whether to support colonization*

Draw Conclusions How did Angelina Grimké believe women could help bring an end to slavery? *by persuading the men in their lives that slavery was wrong*

CRF: Biography Activity: Abolitionists

CRF: Primary Source Activity: David Walker, "An Appeal to the Colored Citizens of the World"

HSS 8.9.1; **HSS Analysis Skills:** HR 4, HR 5, HI 1

World Events

British Abolitionists Many American abolitionists looked to Great Britain for examples of how to oppose slavery. The British abolitionist movement began in the 1780s, and achieved success in 1807 when Britain outlawed the slave trade. In 1834 a law abolishing slavery throughout the British Empire went into effect. British antislavery efforts did not stop, however. In 1840 the British and Foreign Anti-Slavery Society held the Worlds's Anti-Slavery Convention in London. Convention members asked the British government to pressure other countries to end slavery. In the mid-1800s, British warships began stopping slave ships and freeing any enslaved Africans they found.

Differentiating Instruction for Universal Access

English-Language Learners

Standards Proficiency

1. Copy the graphic organizer for students to see. Omit the blue, italicized answers.
2. Have each student copy the organizer and complete it by listing the leaders and main methods of the abolitionist movement.
3. Then have students discuss what methods reformers and activists might use today.

LS Visual/Spatial

HSS 8.9.1; **HSS Analysis Skills:** HI 1

Abolitionist Movement
movement to end slavery completely

Leaders	Methods
• *Frederick Douglass* • *William Lloyd Garrison* • *Angelina and Sarah Grimké* • *Sojourner Truth* • *Harriet Tubman* • *and others*	• *lectures, speeches* • *pamphlets* • *newspapers, articles* • *antislavery societies* • *nonfiction books, plays, poetry, novels* • *petitions to Congress*

Direct Teach

Main Idea

1 Americans Oppose Slavery

Americans from a variety of backgrounds actively opposed slavery.

Identify Who were some leading abolitionists? *Theodore Weld, David Walker, William Lloyd Garrison, Robert Finley, Angelina and Sarah Grimké, Frederick Douglass, Sojourner Truth, Harriet Jacobs, William Wells Brown, (discussed later, John Quincy Adams and Harriet Tubman)*

Interpret In the quotation on this page, what does Frederick Douglass mean when he says the Fourth of July is not his? *possible answer—that the freedom enjoyed and celebrated by some Americans was not available to enslaved African Americans or even fully to free African Americans*

Elaborate How did the words of former enslaved Africans, such as Frederick Douglass, serve as powerful weapons in the abolitionist movement? *provided firsthand accounts of the cruel and harsh reality of slavery*

HSS 8.9.1; HSS **Analysis Skills:** HR 4, HR 5, HI 1

Connect to Science

The North Star Fugitive slaves traveling by night often used the North Star to determine their route, because this star marks the general location of the North Pole.

Make Inferences Why do you think Frederick Douglass named his newspaper *North Star? possible answer—to refer to his own escape from slavery; to express that he hoped the paper would guide people in their quest to end slavery*

African American Abolitionists

Many former slaves were active in the antislavery cause. **Frederick Douglass** escaped from slavery when he was 20 and went on to become one of the most important African American leaders of the 1800s. Douglass secretly learned to read and write as a boy, despite a law against it. His public-speaking skills impressed members of the Anti-Slavery Society. In 1841 they asked him to give regular lectures.

At a Fourth of July celebration in 1852, he captured the audience's attention with his powerful voice.

> "The blessings in which you, this day, rejoice, are not enjoyed in common ... This Fourth of July is *yours*, not *mine*. You may rejoice, I must mourn."
>
> —Frederick Douglass, quoted in *From Slavery to Freedom* by John Hope Franklin and Alfred A. Moss Jr.

In addition to his many speaking tours in the United States and Europe, Douglass published a newspaper called the *North Star* and wrote several autobiographies. His autobiographies were intended to show the injustices of slavery.

Another former slave, **Sojourner Truth**, also contributed to the abolitionist cause. She claimed God had called her to travel through the United States and preach the truth about slavery and women's rights. With her deep voice and quick wit, Truth became legendary in the antislavery movement for her fiery and dramatic speeches.

Other African Americans wrote narratives about their experiences as slaves to expose the cruelties that many slaves faced. In 1861, Harriet Jacobs published *Incidents in the Life of a Slave Girl*, one of the few slave narratives by a woman. William Wells Brown wrote an antislavery play as well as a personal narrative in the form of a novel called *Clotel*.

READING CHECK **Finding Main Ideas** In what ways did African Americans participate in the abolition movement?

The Underground Railroad

By the 1830s, a loosely organized group had begun helping slaves escape from the South. Free African Americans, former slaves, and a few white abolitionists worked together. They created what became known as the **Underground Railroad**. The organization was not an actual railroad but was a network of people who arranged transportation and hiding places for fugitives, or escaped slaves.

Fugitives would travel along routes that led them to northern states or sometimes into Canada. At no time did the Railroad have a central leadership. No one person, or group of people, was ever officially in charge. Despite the lack of any real structure, the Underground Railroad managed to achieve dramatic results.

Often wearing disguises, fugitives moved along the "railroad" at night, led by people known as conductors. Many times, the fugitives had no other guideposts but the stars. They stopped to rest during the day at "stations," often barns, attics, or other places on property owned by abolitionists known as station masters. The station masters hid and fed the fugitives.

Harriet Tubman was a courageous conductor on the Underground Railroad.

Collaborative Learning

Reaching Standards

"Who Am I?" Game HSS 8.9.1; HSS **Analysis Skills:** HI 1

Materials: small box from which students can draw slips of paper

1. Assign each student one of the individuals mentioned in the section. Have each student use the information in the text to write a description of the individual's contributions to the fight against slavery—without mentioning the individual's name.
2. Have students place their descriptions in a box. Then ask volunteers to pick descriptions from the box and read them aloud to the class.
3. Have other students try to identify the individuals described. Students should not answer their own descriptions.
   LS Verbal/Linguistic

Alternative Assessment Handbook, Rubric 40: Writing to Describe

Answers

Reading Check *gave public lectures and wrote narratives, plays, and novels describing their experiences and the harsh reality of slavery*

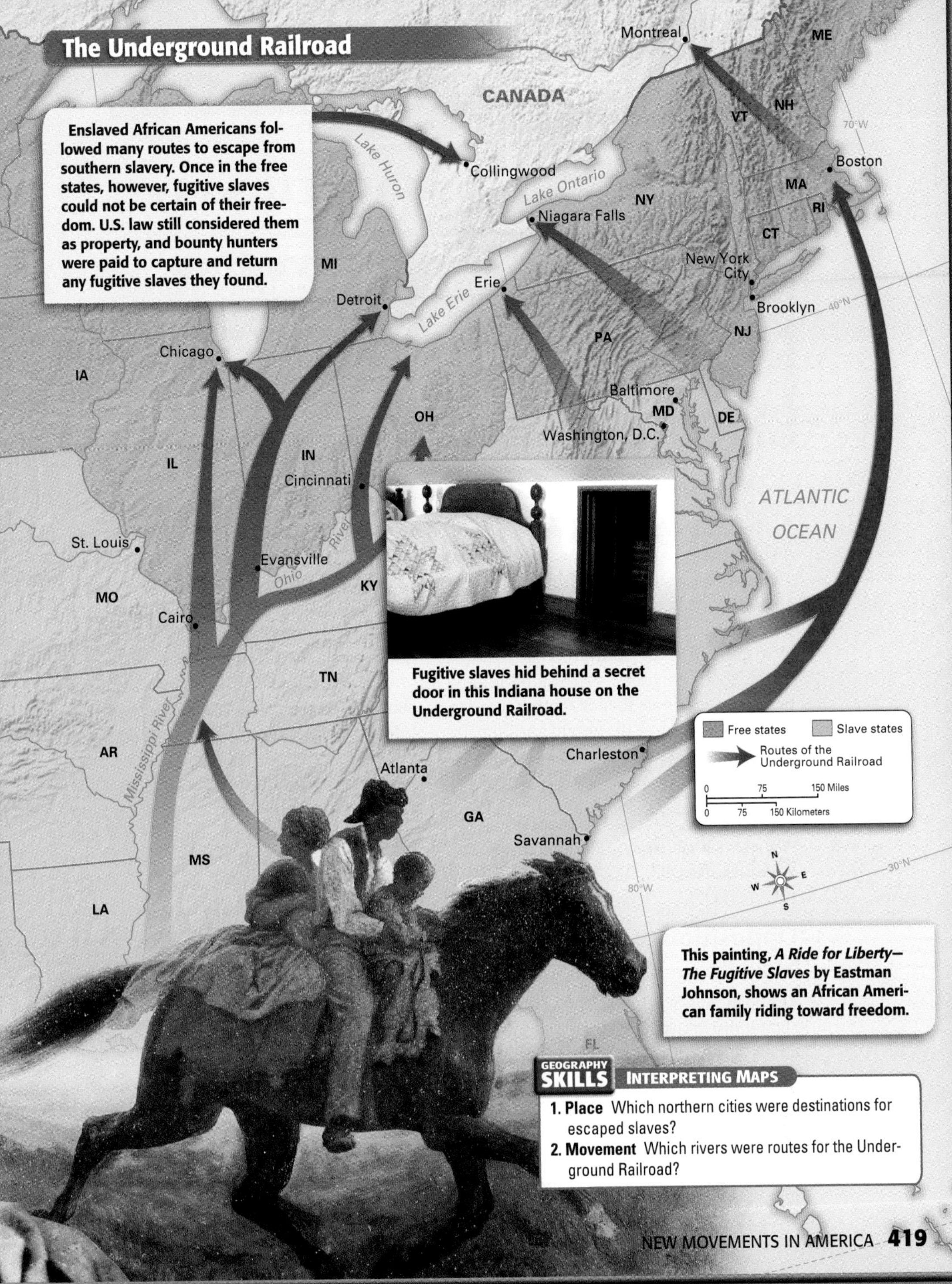

Fugitive slaves hid behind a secret door in this Indiana house on the Underground Railroad.

This painting, *A Ride for Liberty—The Fugitive Slaves* by Eastman Johnson, shows an African American family riding toward freedom.

GEOGRAPHY SKILLS INTERPRETING MAPS

1. **Place** Which northern cities were destinations for escaped slaves?
2. **Movement** Which rivers were routes for the Underground Railroad?

Direct Teach

Main Idea

❷ The Underground Railroad

Abolitionists organized the Underground Railroad to help enslaved Africans escape.

Recall What was the Underground Railroad, and who was its most famous conductor? *a network of people who arranged transportation and hiding places for fugitives, or escaped slaves; Harriet Tubman*

Analyze How might the lack of a central leadership have benefited the Underground Railroad? *possible answer—might make it harder to find and stop the people in the network*

- **CRF:** History and Geography Activity: The Underground Railroad
- **CRF:** Primary Source Activity: Frederick Douglass, "What the Black Man Wants"
- Map Transparency: The Underground Railroad

HSS 8.9.1; **HSS Analysis Skills:** HI 1

Info to Know

Levi Coffin House The room shown at left is in the Levi Coffin house, in Newport, Indiana. This house was one of the most successful Underground Railroad stations. The house's owners, Levi and Catharine Coffin, were devout Quakers. They helped nearly 2,000 fugitives reach freedom.

Critical Thinking: Making Inferences

Standards Proficiency

Underground Railroad Account

HSS 8.9.1; **HSS Analysis Skills:** CS 3, HR 5, HI 1, HI 2

1. Have students examine the above map. Ask volunteers to describe some of the main routes of fugitives on the Underground Railroad. Ask: Where were fugitives going? What geographic obstacles did they face on the way? What other risks and difficulties did fugitives and those helping them face?
2. Then ask students to imagine that they are conductors on the Underground Railroad. A fugitive they are guiding to freedom does not know how to write and has asked them to take down his or her thoughts and feelings about the experience.
3. Have each student write a series of three to five short entries describing the fugitive's experiences and his or her feelings about the freedom and new life awaiting.
LS Intrapersonal, Verbal/Linguistic

- Alternative Assessment Handbook, Rubric 41: Writing to Express
- Map Transparency: The Underground Railroad

Answers

Interpreting Maps **1.** *Montreal and Collingwood, Canada; Boston, MA; Niagara Falls, NY; Erie, PA; Detroit, MI; Chicago, IL;* **2.** *Mississippi and Ohio rivers*

Direct Teach

Main Idea

❸ Opposition to Ending Slavery

Despite efforts of abolitionists, many Americans remained opposed to ending slavery.

Explain What was the purpose of the gag rule in Congress? *to prevent members of Congress from discussing the many anti-slavery petitions they received*

Make Inferences How did John Quincy Adams contribute to the abolitionist movement? *He was able to get the gag rule overturned.*

Identify Cause and Effect What effect did Nat Turner's Rebellion have on southern attitudes about slavery? *Open talk about slavery ended for fear of future slave revolts.*

HSS 8.9.1; **HSS Analysis Skills:** CS 1, HI 1, HI 2

Did you know . . .

Most fugitives traveled by foot or in wagons with hidden compartments, but some used other means of escape. In 1849, Henry "Box" Brown escaped slavery by shipping himself in a box from Richmond, Virginia, to an antislavery office in Philadelphia, Pennsylvania. After some 27 hours in a 3-by-2-foot crate, Brown gained his freedom.

Primary Source

HANDBILL

Anti-Abolitionist Rally

Members of an anti-abolitionist group used this flyer to call people together in order to disrupt a meeting of abolitionists in 1837.

OUTRAGE.

Fellow Citizens,

AN

ABOLITIONIST,

of the most revolting character is among you, exciting the feelings of the North against the South. A seditious Lecture is to be delivered

THIS EVENING,

at 7 o'clock, at the Presbyterian Church in Cannon-street.

You are requested to attend and unite in putting down and silencing by peaceable means this tool of evil and fanaticism.

Let the rights of the States guaranteed by the Constitution be protected.

Feb. 27, 1837. *The Union forever!*

Seditious means "guilty of rebelling against lawful authority."

The group believes abolition violates the Constitution.

ANALYSIS SKILL ANALYZING PRIMARY SOURCES

What emotional language does this handbill use to get its message across?

The most famous and daring conductor on the Underground Railroad was **Harriet Tubman**. When Tubman escaped slavery in 1849, she left behind her family. She swore that she would return and lead her whole family to freedom in the North. Tubman returned to the South 19 times, successfully leading her family and more than 300 other slaves to freedom. At one time the reward for Tubman's capture reportedly climbed to $40,000, a huge amount of money at that time.

READING CHECK **Drawing Inferences** Why were the operations of the Underground Railroad kept secret?

Opposition to Ending Slavery

Although the North was the center of the abolitionist movement, many white northerners agreed with the South and supported slavery. Others disliked slavery but opposed equality for African Americans.

Newspaper editors and politicians warned that freed slaves would move north and take jobs from white workers. Some workers feared losing jobs to newly freed African Americans, whom they believed would accept lower wages. Abolitionist leaders were threatened with violence as some northerners joined mobs. Such a mob killed abolitionist Elijah Lovejoy in 1837 in Alton, Illinois.

The federal government also obstructed abolitionists. Between 1836 and 1844, the U.S. House of Representatives used what was called a gag rule. Congress had received thousands of antislavery petitions. Yet the gag rule forbade members of Congress from discussing them. This rule violated the First Amendment right of citizens to petition the government. But southern members of Congress did not want to debate slavery. Many northern Congressmembers preferred to avoid the issue.

Eventually, representative and former president John Quincy Adams was able to get the gag rule overturned. His resolution to enact a constitutional amendment halting the expansion of slavery never passed, however.

Many white southerners saw slavery as vital to the South's economy and culture. They also felt that outsiders should not

Critical Thinking: Identifying Points of View

Standards Proficiency

Report on Opposition to Abolition

HSS 8.9.1; **HSS Analysis Skills:** HR 5, HI 1

1. Ask students to imagine that they are members of an antislavery society. The head of the society wants to know more about the views of people who oppose abolition and the students have been selected to gather the information and report back.
2. Have each student create a large graphic or chart that identifies and explains both the views of northerners who oppose abolition and the views of southerners toward abolitionists and slavery.
3. In addition, each student should suggest ways that the antislavery society can address some of these views in its fight to end slavery.
4. Ask for volunteers to present their "reports" to the class. **LS Visual/Spatial**

Alternative Assessment Handbook, Rubrics 7: Charts; and 13: Graphic Organizers

Answers

Analyzing Primary Sources *language charged with fear and anger—"Outrage," "revolting character," "seditious Lecture," and "tool of evil and fanaticism"*

Reading Check *to make it difficult for fugitives, conductors, and station masters to be followed or captured*

Sojourner Truth was a former slave who became a leading abolitionist.

interfere with their way of life. After Nat Turner's Rebellion in 1831, when Turner led some slaves to kill slaveholders, open talk about slavery diappeared in the South. It became dangerous to voice antislavery sentiments in southern states. Abolitionists like the Grimké sisters left rather than air unpopular views to hostile neighbors. Racism, fear, and economic dependence on slavery made emancipation all but impossible in the South.

READING CHECK **Drawing Conclusions** Why did many northern workers oppose the abolition movement?

SUMMARY AND PREVIEW The issue of slavery grew more controversial in the United States during the first half of the nineteenth century. In the next section you will learn about women's rights.

Section 4 Assessment

go.hrw.com
Online Quiz
KEYWORD: SS8 HP13

Reviewing Ideas, Terms, and People HSS 8.9.1

1. a. **Identify** What contributions did **William Lloyd Garrison** make to the abolition movement?
   b. **Draw Conclusions** In what ways did contributions from African Americans aid the struggle for abolition?
   c. **Elaborate** What do you think about the American Colonization Society's plan to return free African Americans to Liberia?
2. a. **Describe** How did the **Underground Railroad** work?
   b. **Explain** Why did **Harriet Tubman** first become involved with the Underground Railroad?
   c. **Evaluate** Do you think the Underground Railroad was a success? Why or why not?
3. a. **Describe** What action did Congress take to block abolitionists?
   b. **Analyze** Why did some Americans oppose equality for African Americans?
   c. **Predict** How might the debate over slavery lead to conflict in the future?

Critical Thinking

4. **Analyzing** Copy the chart below. Use it to identify the different abolitionist movements that existed, members of each movement, and the methods used by each group to oppose slavery.

Movement	Members	Methods

FOCUS ON WRITING

5. **Describing Abolition** Add notes about the abolitionist movement and its leaders to your chart. Be sure to note how abolitionists influenced life in the United States. What were they fighting for? Who opposed them, and why?

Direct Teach

Linking to Today

Human Rights Just as abolitionists fought to end slavery during the 1800s, social activists today continue to fight human rights abuses. Modern-day activists use many of the same techniques that antislavery activists did. Methods include speaking tours, petition drives, and letter-writing campaigns. The Internet also provides a powerful tool for today's activists.

Review & Assess

Close

Have students predict and discuss how the abolitionist movement might have contributed to future conflicts.

Review

Online Quiz, Section 4

Assess

SE Section 4 Assessment

PASS: Section 4 Quiz

Alternative Assessment Handbook

Reteach/Classroom Intervention

California Standards Review Workbook

Interactive Reader and Study Guide, Section 4

Interactive Skills Tutor CD-ROM

Section 4 Assessment Answers

1. **a.** published an antislavery newspaper; helped found American Anti-Slavery Society
   b. helped show horrors of slavery
   c. Answers will vary but should reflect an understanding of the plan.
2. **a.** Traveling at night and resting at stations during the day, conductors led fugitives north.
   b. After she escaped slavery she vowed to return and bring her family to freedom.
   c. possible answer—yes, helped many fugitives gain freedom
3. **a.** gag rule to ban talk of antislavery petitions
   b. held racist attitudes; feared losing jobs; saw slavery as vital to South's economy
   c. possible answer—by increasing divisions between groups or regions of the country
4. American Anti-Slavery Society—William Lloyd Garrison, publications and petitions; American Colonization Society—Robert Finley, send free African Americans to Africa; Underground Railroad—Harriet Tubman, help enslaved Africans escape to freedom
5. See the information in the previous answer.

Answers

Reading Check *feared that they would lose their jobs because they believed that newly freed slaves would work for lower wages*

Biography

Reading Focus Question

Have students discuss the introductory question. Ask them to consider actions they would take today as well as those they might have taken in the mid-1800s to help enslaved people. Have students list their ideas. Then as students read the biography have them compare their ideas to the actions Douglass took to help enslaved Africans.

CRF: Primary Source Activity: Frederick Douglass, "What the Black Man Wants"

Info to Know

Douglass and his Thirst for Knowledge While living with the shipbuilder Hugh Auld, Douglass began learning to read and write after he asked Auld's wife, Lucretia, to teach him. When an excited Lucretia told her husband about the progress Douglass had made, Auld told his wife to stop teaching Douglass because it was against the law. Auld also feared that Douglass might revolt against his enslavement and gain his freedom. Douglass's thirst for knowledge was so great, however, that he found ways to continue learning. At one point, he used bread crumbs to pay for lessons. After Douglass escaped to freedom, he retained a lifelong passion for reading and writing.

Did you know . . .

In 1877, Douglass traveled to Maryland, where he visited his former slaveholder, Thomas Auld, who had beaten and starved him years before. During their meeting, Auld apologized to Douglass, and the two parted on good terms.

BIOGRAPHY

Frederick Douglass

As a freed slave, how would you help people still enslaved?

When did he live? 1817–1895

Where did he live? Frederick Douglass was born in rural Maryland. At age six he was sent to live in Baltimore, and at age 20 he escaped to New York City. For most of his life, Douglass lived in Rochester, New York, making his home into a stop along the Underground Railroad. He travelled often, giving powerful antislavery speeches to audiences throughout the North and in Europe.

What did he do? After hearing the abolitionist William Lloyd Garrison speak in 1841, Douglass began his own speaking tours about his experiences as a slave. In mid-life he wrote an autobiography and started an abolitionist newspaper called the *North Star*. During the Civil War, Douglass persuaded black soldiers to fight for the North.

Why is he important? Douglass was the most famous African American in the 1800s. His personal stories and elegant speaking style helped the abolitionist movement to grow. His words remain an inspiration to this day.

Drawing Conclusions What made Frederick Douglass's speeches and writings so powerful?

KEY EVENTS

- **1817** Born a slave in Maryland
- **1837** Escapes slavery disguised as a sailor
- **1841** Begins his career as a speaker on abolition
- **1845** Writes *Narrative of the Life of Frederick Douglass*, his first autobiography
- **1847** Publishes first issue of the *North Star*
- **1863** Meets President Lincoln and becomes an adviser
- **1889** Named American consul general to Haiti
- **1895** Dies in Washington, D.C.

Frederick Douglass began publishing the *North Star*, an abolitionist newspaper, in 1847.

THE NORTH STAR.

Collaborative Learning

Standards Proficiency

Legacy of Frederick Douglass Mural

HSS 8.9.1; HSS **Analysis Skills:** CS 1, HI 1

Materials: butcher paper, art supplies

1. Have students list Frederick Douglass's many contributions. Write the list for students to see. Use the list to lead a discussion on Douglass's significance in his time and the lasting effects of his actions on society.
2. Then have students, working as a class or in small groups, create a mural about Frederick Douglass to display in the school. The mural should use text and images to highlight Douglass's actions and contributions in the fight against slavery. If time allows, have students conduct research to find quotations from Douglass to add to the mural. Display the completed mural in the school.

LS Interpersonal, Visual/Spatial

Alternative Assessment Handbook, Rubrics 3: Artwork; and 14: Group Activity

Answers

Drawing Conclusions *He had experienced slavery firsthand and was a powerful and charismatic speaker.*

Women's Rights

SECTION 5

If YOU were there...

You are a schoolteacher in New York State in 1848. Although you earn a small salary, you still live at home. Your father does not believe that unmarried women should live alone or look after their own money. One day in a shop, you see a poster about a public meeting to discuss women's rights. You know your father will be angry if you go to the meeting. But you are very curious.

Would you attend the meeting? Why?

BUILDING BACKGROUND Women were active in the movements to reform prisons and schools. They fought for temperance and worked for abolition. But with all their work for social change, women still lacked many rights and opportunities of their own. Throughout the 1800s, the women's rights movement gradually became stronger and more organized.

What You Will Learn...

Main Ideas

1. Influenced by the abolition movement, many women struggled to gain equal rights for themselves.
2. Calls for women's rights met opposition from men and women.
3. The Seneca Falls Convention launched the first organized women's rights movement in the United States.

The Big Idea

Reformers sought to improve women's rights in American society.

Key Terms and People

Elizabeth Cady Stanton, *p. 426*
Lucretia Mott, *p. 426*
Seneca Falls Convention, *p. 426*
Declaration of Sentiments, *p. 426*
Lucy Stone, *p. 427*
Susan B. Anthony, *p. 427*

HSS 8.6.6 Examine the women's suffrage movement (e.g., biographies, writings, and speeches of Elizabeth Cady Stanton, Margaret Fuller, Lucretia Mott, Susan B. Anthony).

Women's Struggle for Equal Rights

Fighting for the rights of African Americans led many female abolitionists to fight for women's rights. In the mid-1800s, these women found that they had to defend their right to speak in public, particularly when a woman addressed both men and women. For example, members of the press, the clergy, and even some male abolitionists criticized the Grimké sisters. These critics thought that the sisters should not give public speeches. They did not want women to leave their traditional female roles. The Grimkés protested that women had a moral duty to lead the antislavery movement.

Early Writings for Women's Rights

In 1838 Sarah Grimké published a pamphlet arguing for equal rights for women. She titled it *Letters on the Equality of the Sexes and the Condition of Women.*

> "I ask no favors for my sex . . . All I ask our brethren [brothers] is that they will take their feet from off our necks, and permit us to stand upright on that ground which God designed us to occupy."
>
> —Sarah Grimké, quoted in *The Grimké Sisters from South Carolina,* edited by Gerda Lerner

Preteach

Bellringer

If YOU were there . . . Use the **Daily Bellringer Transparency** to help students answer the question.

Daily Bellringer Transparency, Section 5

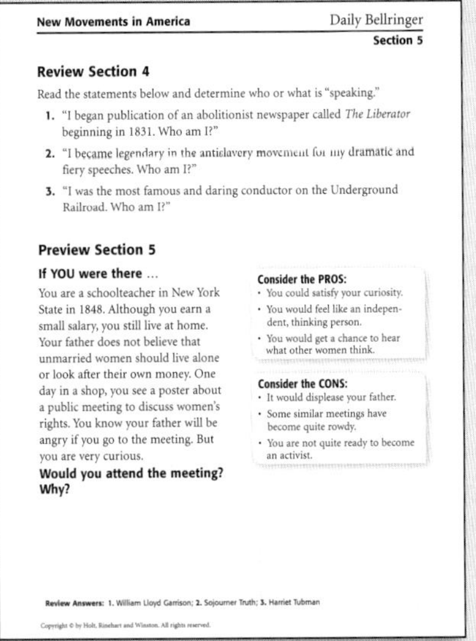

New Movements in America — Daily Bellringer **Section 5**

Review Section 4

Read the statements below and determine who or what is "speaking."

1. "I began publication of an abolitionist newspaper called *The Liberator* beginning in 1831. Who am I?"
2. "I became legendary in the antislavery movement for my dramatic and fiery speeches. Who am I?"
3. "I was the most famous and daring conductor on the Underground Railroad. Who am I?"

Preview Section 5

If YOU were there ...

You are a schoolteacher in New York State in 1848. Although you earn a small salary, you still live at home. Your father does not believe that unmarried women should live alone or look after their own money. One day in a shop, you see a poster about a public meeting to discuss women's rights. You know your father will be angry if you go to the meeting. But you are very curious.

Would you attend the meeting? Why?

Consider the PROS:
- You could satisfy your curiosity.
- You would feel like an independent, thinking person.
- You would get a chance to hear what other women think.

Consider the CONS:
- It would displease your father.
- Some similar meetings have become quite rowdy.
- You are not quite ready to become an activist.

Review Answers: 1. William Lloyd Garrison; 2. Sojourner Truth; 3. Harriet Tubman

Building Vocabulary

Preteach or review the following terms:

sojourner a traveler (p. 424)

suffrage right to vote (p. 425)

CRF: Vocabulary Builder Activity, Section 5

Teach the Big Idea: Master the Standards

Standards Proficiency

Women's Rights HSS 8.6.6; HSS Analysis Skills: CS 1, CS 2, HR 5, HI 1, HI 2

1. **Teach** Ask students the Main Idea questions to teach this section.
2. **Apply** Have each student create a time line of the key events in the early women's rights movement. Above the time line, have students list the goals and leaders of the movement. Below the time line, have students list the opposition to the movement.
   LS Verbal/Linguistic, Visual/Spatial
3. **Review** Have volunteers share information from their time lines and lists. Create master versions for the class to see.
4. **Practice/Homework** Organize students into small groups and have each group write lyrics to an existing tune to create a Women's Rights Anthem for the Seneca Falls Convention. **LS Auditory/Musical, Interpersonal**

Alternative Assessment Handbook, Rubrics 26: Poems and Songs; and 36: Time Lines

Standards Focus

HSS 8.6.6

Means: Describe the women's suffrage movement and identify its key leaders.

Matters: The efforts of the women's suffrage movement helped pave the way for American women to gain the vote and the rights they enjoy today.

Direct Teach

Main Idea

❶ Women's Struggle for Equal Rights

Influenced by the abolition movement, many women struggled to gain equal rights for themselves.

Identify Who were some leaders in the early struggle for women's rights? *Sarah and Angelina Grimké, Margaret Fuller, Sojourner Truth*

Analyze How did the Grimké sisters' actions regarding marriage reflect their views on women's rights? *Both women disliked traditional views of marriage. Sarah chose not to marry because she thought it made her more of a slave than a wife. Angelina's marriage vows did not include the word* obey, *and her husband gave up his legal right to control her property.*

Draw Conclusions In the quotation, what message does Sojourner Truth express? *possible answer—that women are more capable than men give them credit for*

HSS 8.6.6; HSS **Analysis Skills:** HR 4, HR 5, HI 1

Linking to Today

Activity Changing Attitudes Toward Women During this section, discuss with students the ways in which attitudes toward women have changed—and continue to change—in American society. Remind students to keep these changes in mind in particular as they study opposition to women's rights.

Sarah Grimké also argued for equal educational opportunities. She pointed out laws that negatively affected women. In addition, she demanded equal pay for equal work.

Sarah Grimké never married. She explained that the laws of the day gave a husband complete control of his wife's property. Therefore, she feared that by marrying, she would become more like a slave than a wife. Her sister, Angelina, did marry, but she refused to promise to obey her husband during their marriage ceremony. She married Theodore Weld, an abolitionist. Weld agreed to give up his legal right to control her property after they married. For the Grimkés, the abolitionist principles and women's rights principles were identical.

In 1845 the famous transcendentalist Margaret Fuller published *Woman in the Nineteenth Century.* This book used well-known sayings to explain the role of women in American society. Fuller used democratic and transcendentalist principles to stress the importance of individualism to all people, especially women. The book influenced many leaders of the women's rights movement.

Sojourner Truth

Sojourner Truth was another powerful supporter of both abolition and women's rights. She had been born into slavery in about 1797. Her birth name was Isabella Baumfree. She took the name Sojourner Truth because she felt that her mission was to be a sojourner, or traveler, and spread the truth. Though she never learned to read or write, she impressed many well-educated people. One person who thought highly of her was the author Harriet Beecher Stowe. Stowe said that she had never spoken "with anyone who had more . . . personal presence than this woman." Truth stood six feet tall and was a confident speaker.

In 1851 Truth gave a speech that is often quoted to this day.

> "That man over here says that women need to be helped into carriages and lifted over ditches, and to have the best place everywhere. Nobody ever helps me into carriages or over mud puddles, or gives me any best place ... Look at me! I have ploughed and planted and ... no man could head [outwork] me. And ain't I a woman?"
>
> —Sojourner Truth, quoted in *A History of Women in America* by Carol Hymowitz and Michaele Weissman

Truth, the Grimké sisters, and other supporters of the women's movement were determined to be heard.

READING CHECK **Drawing Inferences** Why would reformers link the issues of abolition and women's rights?

Time Line

Women's Voting Rights

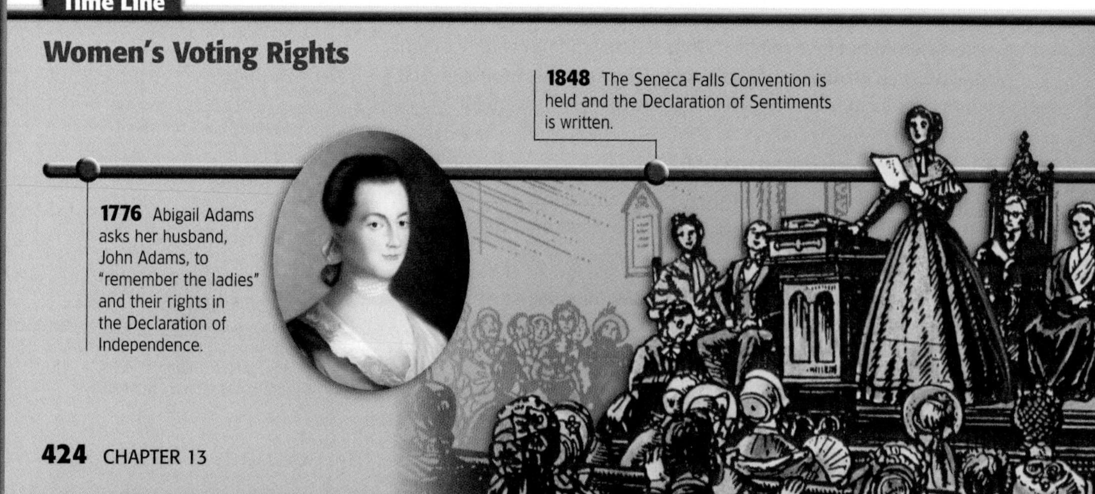

1776 Abigail Adams asks her husband, John Adams, to "remember the ladies" and their rights in the Declaration of Independence.

1848 The Seneca Falls Convention is held and the Declaration of Sentiments is written.

Differentiating Instruction for Universal Access

Learners Having Difficulty — Reaching Standards

1. Draw the graphic organizer for students to see. Omit the blue, italicized answers.
2. Have each student copy the chart and complete it by explaining how the abolitionist movement influenced the women's rights movement. **LS Visual/Spatial**

HSS 8.6.6; HSS **Analysis Skills:** HI 1, HI 2

Alternative Assessment Handbook, Rubric 13: Graphic Organizers

Abolitionist Movement

Female abolitionists found they often had to defend their right to speak in public, particularly when addressing men; Fighting for others' rights led women to want to fight for their own.

Women's Rights Movement

Answers

Reading Check *Female abolitionists discovered that they often had to defend their right to speak in public, and fighting for others' rights led women to want to fight for their own.*

Opposing the Call for Women's Rights

Publications about women's rights first appeared in the United States shortly after the American Revolution. However, women's concerns did not become a national issue with strong opposition for many more years.

The Movement Grows

The change took place when women took a more active and leading role in reform and abolition. Other social changes also led to the rise of the women's movement. Women took advantage of better educational opportunities in the early 1800s. Their efforts on behalf of reform groups helped them learn how to organize more effectively and to work together.

Another benefit of reform-group work was that some men began to fight for women's rights. Many activists, both men and women, found it unacceptable that women were not allowed to vote or sit on juries. They were also upset that married women in many states had little or no control over their own property.

Opposition to Women's Rights

Like the abolitionist movement, the struggle for women's rights faced opposition. Many people did not agree with some of the goals of the women's rights movement. Some women believed that they did not need new rights. They said that women were not unequal to men, only different. Some critics believed that women should not try to work in public for social changes. Women were welcome to work for social change, but only from within their homes. "Let her not look away from her own little family circle for the means of producing moral and social reforms," wrote T. S. Arthur. His advice appeared in a popular women's magazine called *The Lady at Home*.

Some people also thought that women lacked the physical or mental strength to survive without men's protection. They believed that a woman should go from the protection of her father's home to that of her husband's. They also thought that women could not cope with the outside world; therefore, a husband should control his wife's property. Despite opposition, women continued to pursue their goal of greater rights.

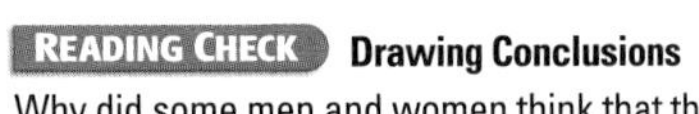

Drawing Conclusions Why did some men and women think that the women's rights movement was misguided?

1872 Susan B. Anthony is arrested while trying to vote in New York.

1890 Wyoming's new state constitution includes women's suffrage.

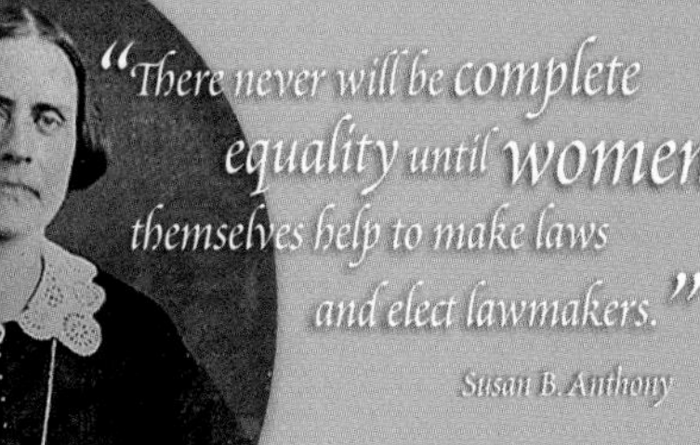

"There never will be complete equality until women themselves help to make laws and elect lawmakers."
Susan B. Anthony

1911 The National Association Opposed to Woman Suffrage is formed.

1920 On August 26, the Nineteenth Amendment is declared ratified by Congress, giving women the right to vote.

ANALYSIS SKILL READING TIME LINES

Women in Wyoming could vote how many years before women in the rest of the country could?

Direct Teach

Main Idea

❷ Opposing the Call for Women's Rights

Calls for women's rights met opposition from men and women.

Recall What social changes led women to become more interested in women's rights? *women's growing involvement in reform and abolition, improved educational opportunities for women, and the knowledge women gained from reform work about how to work together and organize more effectively*

Identify Points of View Why did some women oppose the call for women's rights? *did not believe they needed new rights, thought they were equal to men and just had different roles, and thought women should focus on their families*

HSS 8.6.6; HSS **Analysis Skills:** HR 5, HI 1, HI 2

Info to Know

Dress Reform Female reformers also fought for what most women today consider a personal right—freedom of dress. During the mid-1800s, women were expected to wear long skirts that weighed about 20 pounds and corsets that put extreme pressure on the abdominal area. These corsets often broke ribs and damaged internal organs. Some women's rights activists began wearing bloomers—baggy pants worn under a short skirt. People would follow these women and jeer, however. As a result, many women's rights activists stopped wearing them because they distracted people from the more important demand for women's suffrage.

Critical Thinking: Identifying Points of View

Exceeding Standards

Addressing the Opposition

HSS 8.6.6; HSS **Analysis Skills:** HR 5, HI 1

1. Review with students the reasons some Americans opposed the women's rights movement.
2. Ask students to imagine that they are supporters of the women's rights movement in the mid-1800s. Have each student write an editorial responding to the criticisms of the women's rights movement.
3. Students' editorials should address each of the reasons Americans opposed the movement. Remind students to provide reasons to support their positions and to back up their reasons with facts and examples.
4. Have volunteers read their essays to the class. LS **Verbal/Linguistic**

Alternative Assessment Handbook, Rubric 43: Writing to Persuade

Answers

Reading Time Lines *30 years*

Reading Check *thought that women were equal to men and just had different roles, women should not work for change in public, women's responsibilities were in the home, women lacked the physical and mental strength to survive, women could not cope with the outside world*

Direct Teach

Main Idea

❸ Seneca Falls Convention

The Seneca Falls Convention launched the first organized women's rights movement in the United States.

Recall Why did Elizabeth Cady Stanton and Lucretia Mott decide to hold the Seneca Falls Convention? *because they were not allowed to participate in the World's Anti-Slavery Convention in 1840 and made to sit behind a curtain*

Summarize Why was the Seneca Falls Convention important? *It brought together many reformers and was the first public meeting on women's rights in the United States.*

CRF: Biography Activity: Suffragettes

CRF: Primary Source Activity: Elizabeth Cady Stanton, Letter to Lucretia Mott, 1876

HSS 8.6.6; HSS **Analysis Skills:** HI 1, HI 2

Primary Source

Reading Like a Historian

Declaration of Sentiments Help students practice reading the document like historians. Ask:

- What political views of the period shaped the document?
- What did the authors hope to gain by writing the document?
- How did patterning the document after the Declaration of Independence give it more power?

Answers

Analyzing Primary Sources *because it stated the inalienable rights people should have, but it failed to extend those rights to women*

Primary Source

HISTORIC DOCUMENT

Declaration of Sentiments

At the 1848 Seneca Falls Convention, 100 people signed the Declaration of Sentiments, a document declaring the rights of women. The wording of the document purposely echoed the Declaration of Independence.

We hold these truths to be self-evident: that all men and women are created equal; that they are endowed by their Creator with certain inalienable[1] rights; that among these are life, liberty, and the pursuit of happiness; that to secure these rights governments are instituted, deriving their just powers from the consent of the governed. Whenever any form of government becomes destructive of these ends, it is the right of those who suffer from it to refuse allegiance[2] to it, and to insist upon the institution of a new government, laying its foundation on such principles, and organizing its powers in such form, as to them shall seem most likely to effect their safety and happiness.

The authors use the same words that are in the Declaration of Independence, but include women.

Here the women demand that they become a part of government.

1. **inalienable** not able to be taken away 2. **allegiance** loyalty

ANALYSIS SKILL ANALYZING PRIMARY SOURCES

Why would women want to use the Declaration of Independence as a source for their own declaration?

Seneca Falls Convention

In 1840 **Elizabeth Cady Stanton** attended the World's Anti-Slavery Convention in London, England, while on her honeymoon. She discovered that, unlike her husband, she was not allowed to participate. All women in attendance had to sit behind a curtain in a separate gallery of the convention hall. William Lloyd Garrison, who had helped found the American Anti-Slavery Society, sat with them in protest.

The treatment of women abolitionists at the convention angered Stanton and her new friend, **Lucretia Mott**. Apparently, even many abolitionists did not think that women were equal to men. Stanton and Mott wanted to change this, so they planned to "form a society to advance the rights of women." Eight years passed before Stanton and Mott finally announced the **Seneca Falls Convention**, the first public meeting about women's rights held in the United States. It opened on July 19, 1848, in Seneca Falls, New York.

Declaration of Sentiments

The convention organizers wrote a **Declaration of Sentiments**. This document detailed beliefs about social injustice toward women. They used the Declaration of Independence as the basis for the language for their Declaration of Sentiments. The authors included 18 charges against men—the same number that had been charged against King George III. The Declaration of Sentiments was signed by some 100 people.

About 240 people attended the Seneca Falls Convention, including men such as abolitionist Frederick Douglass. Many other reformers who also worked in the temperance and abolitionist movements were present. Several women who participated in the convention worked in nearby factories. One of them, 19-year-old Charlotte Woodward, signed the Declaration of Sentiments. She worked long hours in a factory, making gloves. Her wages were very low, and she could not even keep her earnings. She had to turn her wages over to her father.

Collaborative Learning

Standards Proficiency

Seneca Falls Convention Promotional Piece

HSS 8.6.6; HSS **Analysis Skills:** HR 5, HI 1

Materials: art supplies

1. Organize students into small groups. Have half the groups create promotional pieces to encourage attendance at the Seneca Falls Convention. Have the other half of the groups create similar items discouraging attendance. Promotional items might include fliers, posters, and buttons. To modernize the activity, have students create radio and television spots instead.
2. Students should focus on the purpose of the convention and what the people holding it hoped to achieve. Remind students to use messages that would appeal to Americans in the mid-1800s.
3. Have each group present its work to the class.

LS Interpersonal, Verbal/Linguistic

Alternative Assessment Handbook, Rubrics 14: Group Activity; and 29: Presentations

Women's Rights Leaders

After the convention, the struggle continued. Women's rights activists battled many difficulties and much opposition. Still, they kept working to obtain greater equality for women. Among the many women working for women's rights, three became important leaders: Lucy Stone, Susan B. Anthony, and Elizabeth Cady Stanton. Each brought different strengths to the fight for women's rights.

Lucy Stone was a well-known spokesperson for the Anti-Slavery Society. In the early years of the women's rights movement, Stone became known as a gifted speaker. Elizabeth Cady Stanton called her "the first who really stirred the nation's heart on the subject of women's wrongs."

Susan B. Anthony brought strong organizational skills to the women's rights movement. She did much to turn the fight for women's rights into a political movement. Anthony argued that women and men should receive equal pay for equal work. She also believed that women should be allowed to enter traditionally male professions, such as religion and law. Anthony was especially concerned with laws that affected women's control of money and property.

Anthony led a campaign to change laws regarding the property rights of women. She wrote in her diary that no woman could ever be free without "a purse of her own." After forming a network to cover the entire state of New York, she collected more than 6,000 signatures to petition for a new property-rights law. In 1860, due largely to the efforts of Anthony, New York finally gave married women ownership of their wages and property. Other states in the Northeast and Midwest soon created similar laws.

THE IMPACT TODAY

As of the year 2000, women earned about 75 percent as much as men in the United States did.

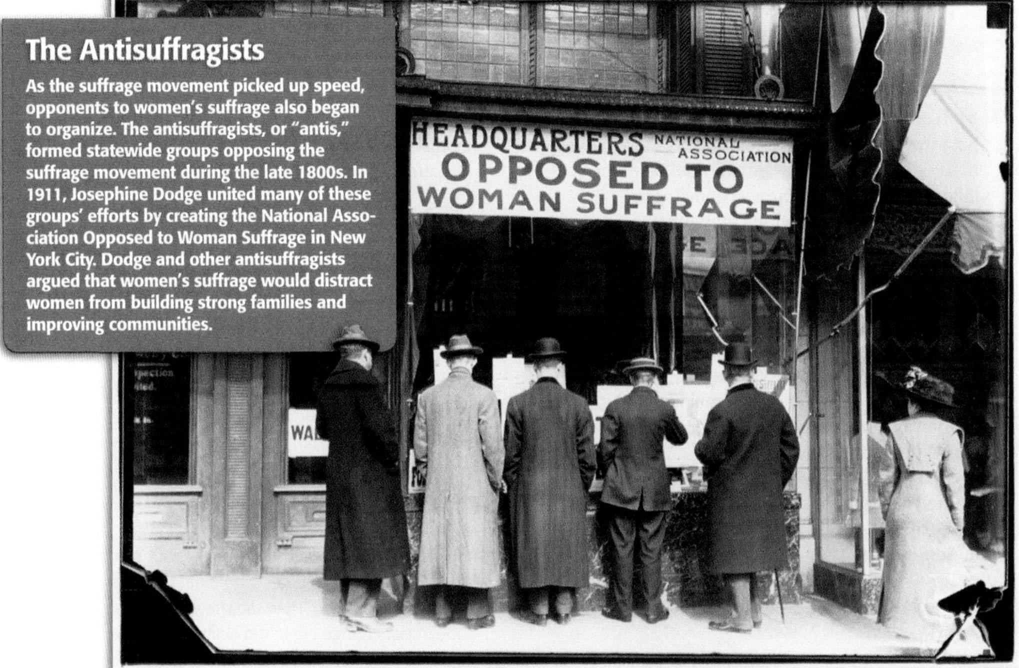

The Antisuffragists

As the suffrage movement picked up speed, opponents to women's suffrage also began to organize. The antisuffragists, or "antis," formed statewide groups opposing the suffrage movement during the late 1800s. In 1911, Josephine Dodge united many of these groups' efforts by creating the National Association Opposed to Woman Suffrage in New York City. Dodge and other antisuffragists argued that women's suffrage would distract women from building strong families and improving communities.

Direct Teach

Main Idea

❸ Seneca Falls Convention

The Seneca Falls Convention launched the first organized women's rights movement in the United States.

Identify Who became the three main leaders of the women's rights movement? *Lucy Stone, Susan B. Anthony, Elizabeth Cady Stanton*

Make Judgments What do you think was the most important issue of the women's rights movement? Why? *possible answer—the right to vote, because the ability to protect one's rights is seriously limited without a political voice*

HSS 8.6.6; HSS **Analysis Skills:** HI 1,

Teaching Tip

Using Mnemonics

Students may struggle to learn the names of the many leaders of the different reform movements covered in this chapter. To help students, have them use a mnemonic. Tell students to list the leaders of each movement. Then, for each movement, have students write a sentence in which each word begins with the first letter of a leader's name. The sentence should have some connection to the goals of the movement. Have volunteers share their sentences with the class.

Critical Thinking: Comparing and Contrasting

Reaching Standards

Women's Rights Collage

HSS 8.6.6; HSS **Analysis Skills:** HI 1, HI 3

Materials: magazines, newspapers, paper, glue

1. Review with students the limited opportunities and rights that women in the mid-1800s had in the categories of education, politics, and employment.
2. Have students, working individually or in small groups, create collages illustrating the gains women have made in each of the above categories. Students should write short captions explaining their collages.
3. Display the collages in the classroom.

LS **Visual/Spatial**

Alternative Assessment Handbook, Rubric 8: Collages

Direct Teach

Linking to Today

Women's Rights National Historical Park The National Park Service has designated certain areas and homes in Seneca Falls, New York, as the Women's Rights National Historical Park. The park includes the building where the Seneca Falls Convention took place and the home of Elizabeth Cady Stanton.

Review & Assess

Close

Have students review the early women's rights movement, including the significant leaders and events.

Review

Online Quiz, Section 5

Assess

SE Section 5 Assessment

PASS: Section 5 Quiz

Alternative Assessment Handbook

Reteach/Classroom Intervention

California Standards Review Workbook

Interactive Reader and Study Guide, Section 5

Interactive Skills Tutor CD-ROM

Elizabeth Cady Stanton wrote many of the documents and speeches of the movement, which were often delivered by Anthony. Stanton was a founder and important leader of the National Woman Suffrage Association. This organization was considered one of the more radical groups because of its position that abolition was not a more important cause than women's rights.

Not every battle was won. Other major reforms, such as women's right to vote, were not achieved at this time. Still, more women than ever before became actively involved in women's rights issues. This increased activity was one of the movement's greatest accomplishments.

READING CHECK **Identifying Points of View** What did Susan B. Anthony mean when she said that no woman could be free without "a purse of her own"?

Lucy Stone worked for equal rights for women and African Americans.

SUMMARY AND PREVIEW Women's rights became a major issue in the mid-1800s, as women began to demand a greater degree of equality. In the next chapter you will read about western expansion.

Section 5 Assessment

go.hrw.com
Online Quiz
KEYWORD: SS8 HP13

Reviewing Ideas, Terms, and People HSS 8.6.6

1. **a. Identify** What role did Sojourner Truth play in both the abolition and women's rights movements?
   b. Analyze How did the abolition movement influence women to demand equal rights?
2. **a. Identify** What limitations on women's rights did many activists find unacceptable?
   b. Summarize Why did many Americans oppose equal rights for women?
   c. Elaborate What arguments might you use to counter the arguments of men and women who opposed equal rights for women?
3. **a. Recall** Who were the three main leaders of the women's rights movement, and how did they each contribute to the movement?
   b. Draw Conclusions Why might working-class women like Charlotte Woodward have supported the **Seneca Falls Convention** and the **Declaration of Sentiments**?
   c. Evaluate Do you agree with **Susan B. Anthony** that women should receive equal pay for equal work? Explain your answer.

Critical Thinking

4. **Sequencing** Copy the graphic organizer onto your own sheet of paper. Use it to identify some of the important events in the women's rights movement.

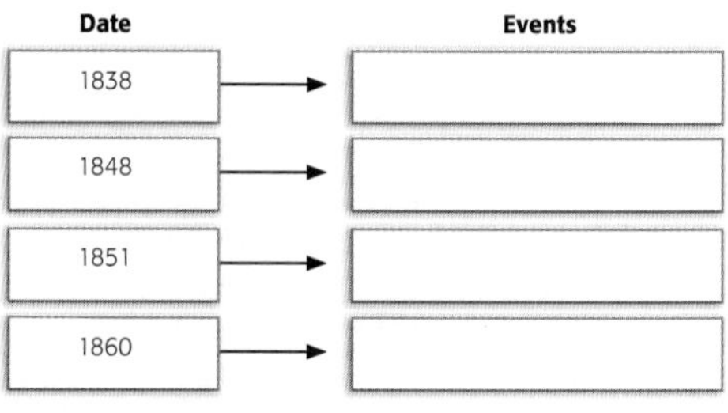

FOCUS ON WRITING

5. **Describing Women's Suffrage** Add notes about the women's suffrage movement to your chart. Note important leaders and describe what they were fighting for. Ask yourself, "How did the women's suffrage movement change life in the United States?"

Section 5 Assessment Answers

1. **a.** as a public speaker and supporter
   b. Female abolitionists found they were denied some rights.
2. **a.** lacked the right to vote, married women lost control of money and property, limited educational opportunities, pay inequalities
   b. thought women and men were equal just different; women should focus on the home; women lacked the physical and mental strength to cope with some things
   c. Answers will vary, but arguments should address the issues in the previous answer.
3. **a.** Lucy Stone—spokesperson; Susan B. Anthony—strong organizer; Elizabeth Cady Stanton—wrote documents and speeches
   b. wanted control of her own money
   c. possible answers—Yes, women and men are equal and should be paid the same; no, men need to earn more to support families.
4. 1838—Sarah Grimké pamphlet; 1848—Seneca Falls Convention; 1851—Sojourner Truth speech; 1860—New York gives married women control of wages, property
5. See Answers 3a and 4 above.

Answers

Reading Check *Anthony meant that without any financial independence or economic power, women would never have true political or social equality.*

BIOGRAPHY

Elizabeth Cady Stanton

What steps would you take to bring about nationwide change?

When did she live? 1815–1902

Where did she live? Elizabeth Cady Stanton was born in Johnstown, New York. She married a prominent abolitionist and settled in Seneca Falls, New York, where she had seven children. Later in life she traveled widely, giving lectures and speeches across the country.

What did she do? Stanton and fellow activist Lucretia Mott organized the nation's first women's rights convention, at Seneca Falls in 1848. She and Susan B. Anthony founded the National Woman Suffrage Association in 1869. For nearly six decades, she spoke and wrote passionately about women's rights.

Why is she important? Stanton helped author the Declaration of Sentiments, which demanded equal rights for women, including the right to vote. A brilliant speaker and debater, Stanton spoke out against laws that kept married women from owning property, earning wages, and keeping custody of their children.

Finding Main Ideas What problems did Stanton try to correct? What problems did she face in accomplishing her goals?

KEY EVENTS

- **1815** Born in Johnstown, New York
- **1840** Meets Lucretia Mott at the World's Anti-Slavery Convention, where they are barred from participating
- **1848** Helps organize the first national meeting of women's suffrage reformers at Seneca Falls, New York
- **1851** Meets Susan B. Anthony, with whom she will later lead the National Woman Suffrage Association
- **1895** Publishes the Woman's Bible
- **1902** Dies in New York City

Elizabeth Cady Stanton helped author the Declaration of Sentiments at the Seneca Falls Convention.

A WOMAN'S DECLARATION OF INDEPENDENCE 1848

Resolutions

Biography

Reading Focus Question

Have students discuss the introductory question before reading the biography. Ask students what actions they might take to effect change and what issues they might address. Then instruct students as they read the biography to note the actions Stanton took to bring about nationwide change, even though she lacked many legal and political rights.

CRF: Biography Activity: Suffragettes

CRF: Primary Source Activity: Elizabeth Cady Stanton, Letter to Lucretia Mott, 1876

Info to Know

Stanton's Education As a young girl, Stanton went to a coed school, but she later wrote that she was "the only girl in the higher classes of mathematics and the languages." Because she was female, she was not allowed to attend college. Stanton had studied law with her father, a judge, but as a woman, she was not allowed to practice law.

A Strong Woman Stanton never shied away from controversy. She urged reforms in divorce laws and in women's styles of dress. Her support of women's suffrage went against the beliefs of many of her fellow reformers. Still, Stanton did not bend. Seventeen years after her death, her goal of suffrage for women became a reality.

Critical Thinking: Finding Main Ideas

Standards Proficiency

Persuasive Letter about Stanton

HSS 8.6.6; HSS **Analysis Skills:** HI 1

1. Ask students to imagine the following scenario: The school library has displayed posters of several famous Americans. None of the posters is of a woman, however.
2. Have each student write a letter to the school librarian asking him or her to display a poster of Elizabeth Cady Stanton in the library.
3. Students' letters should explain why Stanton should be included by listing her significant achievements and contributions in gaining rights for women. LS **Verbal/Linguistic**
4. **Extend** Have each student create a sketch of the Stanton poster to display in the library. The poster should highlight Stanton's legacy. LS **Visual/Spatial**

Alternative Assessment Handbook, Rubrics 28: Posters; and 43: Writing to Persuade

Answers

Finding Main Ideas *problems tried to correct—ending slavery; gaining equal rights for women; changing laws that prevented women from owning property, earning wages, and keeping custody of their children; problems faced—opposition of those who opposed women's rights*

Social Studies Skills

Accepting Social Responsibility

Activity Getting Involved Lead students in a discussion about the need for all members of society to behave in socially responsible ways. Ask students to identify the socially responsible behaviors mentioned in the lesson *(obligation to not do anything that harms society; duty to participate in society by exercising the rights and responsibilities of membership, such as keeping informed about issues; and supporting change to benefit society).* Write the list for students to see.

Then have students discuss ways in which they can get involved to bring about change to benefit society. Help students consider means of protest as well as other means. Then give students 15 minutes to free-write about why Americans should get involved and take action to improve society. Have volunteers read their responses to the class. Encourage discussion and feedback.

LS Verbal/Linguistic

Alternative Assessment Handbook, Rubric 37: Writing Assignments

Answers

Practice the Skill 1. *possible answer—yes, because slavery is morally wrong, corrupts a society that supports it, and harms all members of society who are enslaved;* **2.** *possible answers—yes, because I want to act on my beliefs; no, because I am afraid I will put the rest of my family at harm;* **3.** *possible answers—yes, I would be willing to help, but I am not willing to break the law; no, I believe that the law is wrong and that my actions will not hurt anyone but rather help people.* **4.** *possible answer—yes, because I would be acting to help others in society, and my actions might help bring about changes that will improve society.*

Social Studies Skills

Analysis | Critical Thinking | **Participation** | Study

HSS Participation Skill Develop social and political participation skills.

Accepting Social Responsibility

Define the Skill

A *society* is an organized group of people who share a common set of activities, traditions, and goals. You are part of many societies—your school, community, and nation are just three. Every society's strength depends on the support and contributions of its members. *Social responsibility* is the obligation that every person has to the societies in which he or she is a member.

Learn the Skill

As a part of your school, community, and nation, you have obligations to the people around you. The most obvious is to do nothing to harm your society. You also have a duty to be part of it. At the very least, this means exercising the rights and responsibilities of membership. These include being informed about issues in your society.

Another level of social responsibility is support of change to benefit society. This level of involvement goes beyond being informed about issues to trying to do something about them. If you take this important step, here are some points to consider.

1. Few efforts to change society have everyone's support. Some people will want things to stay the same. They may treat you badly if you work for change. You must be prepared for this possibility if you decide to take action.
2. Sometimes efforts to improve things involve opposing laws or rules that need to be changed. No matter how just your cause is, if you break law or rules, you must be willing to accept the consequences of your behavior.
3. Remember that violence is *never* an acceptable method for change. People who use force in seeking change are not behaving in a socially responsible manner, even if their cause is good.

This chapter was filled with the stories of socially responsible people. Many of them devoted their lives to changing society for the better. Some did so at great personal risk. Boston abolitionist William Lloyd Garrison barely escaped with his life from a local mob that tried to lynch him because of his views.

Garrison and the other reformers you read about demonstrated the highest level of social responsibility. They saw an issue they believed to be a problem in society, and they worked tirelessly to change it and make society better.

Practice the Skill

Review the "If you were there" scene on page 416. Imagine yourself as that Ohioan. You believe slavery to be wrong. However, you also respect the law, and it is illegal to help an escaped slave. In addition, you know that most of your neighbors do not feel as you do about slavery. They might harm you or your property if you take this stand against it.

1. Would agreeing to your friend's request help benefit society? Explain why or why not.
2. Are you willing to risk the anger of your neighbors? Why or why not?
3. Is the idea of breaking the law or possibly going to jail a factor in your decision? Explain.
4. Would agreeing to your friend's request be a socially responsible thing to do? Explain why or why not?

Social Studies Skills Activity: Accepting Social Responsibility

Posters Promoting Social Responsibility

Standards Proficiency

Materials: art supplies, colored markers, poster board

1. Have students create posters urging their fellow students to get involved in change to benefit society. Students might focus the theme of their posters on a specific type of involvement or cause, or instead focus on social action and involvement in general.
2. Students' posters should include a slogan and one or more images. Students might also include additional text to explain the meaning of their message. Remind students that when creating posters one or two large, emotionally charged images often are more powerful than many smaller images.
3. Display students' posters in public areas of the school. **LS Visual/Spatial**

Alternative Assessment Handbook, Rubric 28: Posters

CHAPTER 13 Standards Review

Visual Summary

Use the visual summary below to help you review the main ideas of the chapter.

Reviewing Vocabulary, Terms, and People

1. Which of the following authors wrote about Puritan life in *The Scarlet Letter*?

a. Emily Dickinson **c.** Thomas Gallaudet
b. Herman Melville **d.** Nathaniel Hawthorne

2. Which document expressed the complaints of supporters of women's rights?

a. Declaration of the Rights of Women **c.** Letters on Women's Rights
b. Declaration of Sentiments **d.** Seneca Falls Convention

3. As leader of the common-school movement, who worked to improve free public education?

a. Walt Whitman **c.** Lyman Beecher
b. Horace Mann **d.** Sojourner Truth

Comprehension and Critical Thinking

SECTION 1 *(Pages 400–404)* **HSS 8.6.1, 8.6.3**

4. a. Identify What political party was founded by nativists, and what policies did it support?

b. Analyze What factors caused U.S. cities to grow so fast?

c. Evaluate Do you think that the benefits of city life outweighed its drawbacks? Explain.

SECTION 2 *(Pages 405–407)* **HSS 8.6.7**

5. a. Describe Who were some important transcendentalists, and what ideas did they promote?

b. Compare and Contrast In what ways were transcendentalists and Romantics similar and different?

c. Elaborate Which movement appeals to you more—American transcendentalism or Romanticism? Why?

Answers

Visual Summary

Review and Inquiry Have students list key events and people for each sign. Then have students write a brief paragraph describing how the visual summary captures the spirit of the reform movements of the 1800s.

Quick Facts Transparency: New Movements in America Visual Summary

Reviewing Vocabulary, Terms, and People

1. d

2. b

3. b

Comprehension and Critical Thinking

4. a. Know-Nothing Party, policies to keep Catholics and immigrants out of public office

b. Transportation improvements and new jobs created by the Industrial Revolution led many people to move to urban areas.

c. Students' answers will vary but should describe the benefits and drawbacks of living in a city.

5. a. Emerson, Fuller, Thoreau; belief that people could rise above material things, should be self-reliant, and live simply in tune with nature

b. similar—focus on nature and simple life, individualism, personal insight; different—transcendentalism: a philosophy; Romantics: focused more on emotion and history

c. Answers should show an understanding of both movements.

Review and Assessment Resources

Review and Reinforce

- SE Standards Review
- **CRF:** Chapter Review Activity
- California Standards Review Workbook
- Quick Facts Transparency: New Movements in America Visual Summary
- Spanish Chapter Summaries Audio CD Program
- Online Chapter Summaries in Six Languages
- OSP Holt PuzzlePro; GameTool for ExamView
- Quiz Game CD-ROM

Assess

- SE Standards Assessment
- PASS: Chapter Test, Forms A and B
- Alternative Assessment Handbook
- OSP Examview Test Generator, Chapter Test
- Universal Access Modified Worksheets and Tests CD-ROM: Chapter Test
- Holt Online Assessment Program (in the Premier Online Edition)

Reteach/Intervene

- Interactive Reader and Study Guide
- Universal Access Teacher Management System: Lesson Plans for Universal Access
- Universal Access Modified Worksheets and Tests CD-ROM
- Interactive Skills Tutor CD-ROM

go.hrw.com
Online Resources
Chapter Resources:
KEYWORD: SS8 US13

Answers

6. a. alcohol abuse, prison reform, and education reform
b. Reformers believed that education made children responsible citizens.
c. Answers will vary but should demonstrate an understanding of the reform movements of the period and their effects.

7. a. religious reasons, thought slavery was morally wrong, thought slavery went against the right to liberty for which the American Revolution had been fought
b. northerners—feared that freed African Americans would work for lower wages and take away jobs; southerners—thought slavery was vital to the Southern economy
c. Answers will vary but should reflect an understanding of the methods used, such as speeches, publications, literature, antislavery societies, and petitions to Congress.

8. a. women's involvement in the abolitionist movement and the discrimination they faced; improved educational opportunities for women, and the knowledge women gained from reform work
b. possible answer—They wanted control over their wages.
c. Answers will vary but should reflect that the movement had achieved some success but that women still could not vote.

Using the Internet

9. Go to the HRW Web site and enter the keyword shown to access a rubric for this activity.

KEYWORD: SS8 TEACHER

Reading Skills

10. d

SECTION 3 *(Pages 410–415)* **HSS 8.6.4, 8.6.5**

6. **a. Identify** What important reform movements became popular in the early 1800s?
b. Analyze Why did education become an important topic for reformers in the 1800s?
c. Evaluate Which reform movement do you think had the greatest effect on the United States? Why?

SECTION 4 *(Pages 416–421)* **HSS 8.9.1**

7. **a. Recall** What are the different reasons why people supported abolition?
b. Make Inferences How did northerners and southerners differ in their opposition to abolition?
c. Evaluate Which of the methods used by abolitionists to oppose slavery do you think was most successful? Why?

SECTION 5 *(Pages 423–428)* **HSS 8.6.6**

8. **a. Recall** What led many women to question their place in American society?
b. Make Inferences Why did female factory workers like Charlotte Woodward support the women's rights movement?
c. Evaluate By 1860 do you think the women's movement had been successful? Explain your answer.

Using the Internet

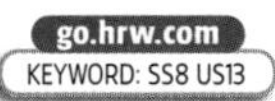

9. **Activity: Creating Visuals** The *Liberator* and *North Star* were two newspapers that encouraged the end of slavery. Enter the activity keyword and research the influence of abolitionist newspapers, such as those written by William Lloyd Garrison and Frederick Douglass. Then create a visual display that illustrates how each newspaper represented the abolitionist point of view.

Reading Skills

Understanding Propaganda *Use the Reading Skills taught in this chapter to answer the question below.*

10. Which of the following is NOT an example of propaganda?
a. a flyer protesting new tax laws
b. an ad about a political candidate
c. a radio announcement sponsored by an interest group
d. a list of camping rules from a park

Reviewing Themes

11. **Society and Culture** What social and cultural changes took place from 1800 to the mid-1800s?
12. **Religion** What role did religion play in the reform movement that took place in the early 1800s?

Social Studies Skills

Accepting Social Responsibility *Use the Social Studies Skills taught in this chapter to fill in the chart below.*

13.

Action	Is it socially responsible?	Why or why not?
Removing litter from a park		
Voting		
Reading a political magazine		
Running a red light		

FOCUS ON WRITING

14. **Writing Your Persuasive Letter** You've described a number of important events and political, religious, and artistic movements in your notebook. Now, it's time to choose the one you consider most important. Think about how it changed life for people in the United States. Then write a two-paragraph persuasive letter to the newspaper, arguing for the event or movement you chose. In the first paragraph, identify the event or movement you chose as well as a thesis explaining why it is important. In the second paragraph, include details about the event or movement that support your thesis. Close with one or two sentences that sum up your points.

Reviewing Themes

11. Immigration increased; cities grew rapidly, and urban problems developed; transcendentalists and American Romantics enriched the culture; Second Great Awakening increased church membership and religious faith; reformers worked to improve education, care for the mentally ill, prisons, and women's rights and to fight alcohol abuse and slavery.

12. The Second Great Awakening spurred the development of reform, and more women became involved in reform movements because of their moral and religious beliefs.

Social Studies Skills

13. Students should note that the first three are socially responsible and that the last is not and explain why.

Focus on Writing

14. **Rubric** Students' letters should:
- provide a thesis explaining why the event or movement chosen is the most important
- provide details that support the thesis
- end with a summary
- include a salutation and a closing

CRF: Focus on Writing Activity: Persuasive Letter

Standards Assessment

DIRECTIONS: Read each question and write the letter of the best response.

1

> "It is demonstrably the right and duty of woman, equally with man, to promote every righteous cause, by every righteous means; and especially in regard to the great subjects of morals and religion, it is . . . her right to participate with her brother in teaching them, both in private and in public, by writing and by speaking . . . and in any assemblies proper to be held."

The content of this passage suggests that it is *most likely* from

- **A** the Declaration of Sentiments of the Seneca Falls Convention.
- **B** a sermon of the Second Great Awakening.
- **C** Ralph Waldo Emerson's transcendentalist essay "Self-Reliance."
- **D** the platform of the Know-Nothing Party.

2 A potato blight in Europe brought a large number of immigrants to the United States who were

- **A** Jewish.
- **B** German.
- **C** Irish.
- **D** Protestant.

3 All of these American writers of the mid-1800s are famous poets *except*

- **A** Henry David Thoreau.
- **B** Edgar Allan Poe.
- **C** Walt Whitman.
- **D** Emily Dickinson.

4 The most famous leader of the Underground Railroad was

- **A** Frederick Douglass.
- **B** Harriet Tubman.
- **C** William Lloyd Garrison.
- **D** Harriet Beecher Stowe.

5 Which of these statements about the education of African Americans in the mid-1800s is *not* true?

- **A** Educational opportunities generally were greater in the North than in the South.
- **B** African American students often went to separate schools from white students.
- **C** Opportunities for college were rare until black colleges were founded in the 1840s.
- **D** Southern African Americans benefited from the educational reforms of Horace Mann.

Connecting with Past Learning

6 In Grade 7 you learned that political unrest resulting from the Reformation caused some Europeans to flee in the 1600s. Later political unrest brought which group of immigrants to the United States in the mid-1800s?

- **A** Chinese
- **B** Irish
- **C** Germans
- **D** Russians

7 The Declaration of Sentiments can *best* be compared to which earlier document in American history?

- **A** the Mayflower Compact
- **B** the Declaration of Independence
- **C** the Constitution of the United States
- **D** the Monroe Doctrine

Answers

1. A

Break Down the Question: Remind students to look for clues to meaning in a passage, such as the many references to women in the passage here.

2. C

Break Down the Question: This question requires students to recall factual information. Refer students who have trouble to the text titled "Fleeing the Irish Potato Famine" in Section 1.

3. A

Break Down the Question: This question requires students to recall factual information. Point out that the word *except* means students should select the person who was *not* a poet.

4. B

Break Down the Question: This question requires students to recall factual information. Refer students who have trouble to the text titled "The Underground Railroad" in Section 4.

5. D

Break Down the Question: Remind students to choose the answer that is not true. Refer students who have trouble to the text titled "African American Communities" in Section 3.

6. C

Break Down the Question: This question connects to information covered in Grade 7.

7. B

Break Down the Question: This question connects to information covered in Chapter 3.

Intervention Resources

Reproducible

- Interactive Reader and Study Guide
- Universal Access Teacher Management System: Lesson Plans for Universal Access

Technology

- Quick Facts Transparency: New Movements in America Visual Summary
- Universal Access Modified Worksheets and Tests CD-ROM
- Interactive Skills Tutor CD-ROM

Tips for Test Taking

Spot Those Numbers Have students ever said, "I got off by one number and spent most of my time fixing my answer sheet"? To help students avoid this problem, tell them to do the following:

- Each time you answer a question, match the number of the question to the numbered space on the answer sheet.
- If you skip a question, leave the answer space blank.
- Keep a list of the questions you have skipped, but not on your answer sheet. You do not want to erase any more than necessary.

Standards Review

Have students review the following standards in their workbooks.

- California Standards Review Workbook: HSS 8.6.1, 8.6.3, 8.6.4, 8.6.5, 8.6.6, 8.6.7, 8.7.2, 8.9.2, 8.9.6

Chapter 14 Planning Guide

A Divided Nation

Chapter Overview	Reproducible Resources	Technology Resources
CHAPTER 14 **pp. 434–463** **Overview: In this chapter, students will study the events leading up to the Civil War.** See p. 434 for the California History–Social Science standards covered in this chapter.	**Universal Access Teacher Management System:*** • Universal Access Instructional Benchmarking Guides • Lesson Plans for Universal Access **Interactive Reader and Study Guide:*** Chapter Graphic Organizer **Chapter Resource File*** • Focus on Writing Activity: An Autobiographical Sketch • Social Studies Skills Activity: Assessing Primary and Secondary Sources • Chapter Review Activity **Pre-AP Activities Guide for United States History:** *Making Generalizations	**One-Stop Planner CD-ROM:** Calendar Planner **Student Edition Full-Read Audio CD-ROM** **Universal Access Modified Worksheets and Tests CD-ROM** **Interactive Skills Tutor CD-ROM** **Primary Source Library CD-ROM for United States History** **Power Presentations with Video CD-ROM** **History's Impact: United States History Video Program (VHS/DVD):** A Divided Nation*
Section 1: **The Debate Over Slavery** **The Big Idea:** Antislavery literature and the annexation of new lands intensified the debate over slavery. 8.9.4, 8.10.1	**Universal Access Teacher Management System:*** Section 1 Lesson Plan **Interactive Reader and Study Guide:*** Section 1 Summary **Chapter Resource File*** • Vocabulary Builder, Section 1 • Biography Activity: Sojourner Truth • Economics and History Activity: Economic Rivalry • History and Geography Activity: Free and Slave States • Primary Source Activity: Wiliam P. Newman **Political Cartoons Activities for United States History, Cartoon 16:** Antislavery Poster*	**Daily Bellringer Transparency:** Section 1* **Quick Facts Transparency:** Upsetting the Balance* go.hrw.com **Internet Activity:** Slave Narratives
Section 2: **Trouble in Kansas** **The Big Idea:** The Kansas-Nebraska Act heightened tensions in the conflict over slavery. 8.9.5, 8.10.2	**Universal Access Teacher Management System:*** Section 2 Lesson Plan **Interactive Reader and Study Guide:*** Section 2 Summary **Chapter Resource File*** • Vocabulary Builder, Section 2 • Biography Activity: Stephen Douglas • Primary Source Activity: Charles Sumner	**Daily Bellringer Transparency:** Section 2* **Map Transparency:** From Compromise to Conflict*
Section 3: **Political Divisions** **The Big Idea:** The split over the issue of slavery intensified due to political division and judicial decisions. 8.10.4	**Universal Access Teacher Management System:*** Section 3 Lesson Plan **Interactive Reader and Study Guide:*** Section 3 Summary **Chapter Resource File*** • Vocabulary Builder, Section 3 • Biography Activity: Dred Scott • Literature Activity: Chicago Speech of 1858 **U.S. Supreme Court Case Studies:** *Dred Scott* v. *Sanford* (1857)	**Daily Bellringer Transparency:** Section 3* **Quick Facts Transparency:** A Growing Conflict* go.hrw.com **Internet Activity:** Lincoln-Douglas Debates Graphic Organizer
Section 4: **The Nation Divides** **The Big Idea:** The United States broke apart due to the growing conflict over slavery. 8.9.1, 8.10.3	**Universal Access Teacher Management System:*** Section 4 Lesson Plan **Interactive Reader and Study Guide:*** Section 4 Summary **Chapter Resource File*** • Vocabulary Builder, Section 4 • Biography Activity: Jefferson Davis • Primary Source Activity: John Brown	**Daily Bellringer Transparency:** Section 4* **Map Transparency:** The Election of 1860*

SE Student Edition  Print Resource  Audio CD Video

TE Teacher's Edition  Transparency  CD-ROM  DVD

go.hrw.com CA Standards Mastery Learning Styles

OSP One-Stop Planner CD-ROM * also on One-Stop Planner CD

Review, Assessment, Intervention

 **Standards Review Workbook***

 **Quick Facts Transparency:** A Divided Nation Visual Summary*

 **Spanish Chapter Summaries Audio CD Program**

 **Online Chapter Summaries in Six Languages**

 **Progress Assessment Support System (PASS):** Chapter Test*

 **Universal Access Modified Worksheets and Test CD-ROM:** Modified Chapter Test

 **One-Stop Planner CD-ROM:** ExamView Test Generator (English/Spanish)

 **Holt Online Assessment Program (HOAP),** in the Holt Premier Online Student Edition

 **PASS:** Section 1 Quiz*

 **Online Quiz:** Section 1

Alternative Assessment Handbook

 **PASS:** Section 2 Quiz*

 **Online Quiz:** Section 2

Alternative Assessment Handbook

 **PASS:** Section 3 Quiz*

 **Online Quiz:** Section 3

Alternative Assessment Handbook

 **PASS:** Section 4 Quiz*

 **Online Quiz:** Section 4

Alternative Assessment Handbook

California Resources for Standards Mastery

INSTRUCTIONAL PLANNING AND SUPPORT

 **Universal Access Teacher Management System***

 **One-Stop Planner CD-ROM with Test Generator: Teacher Management System with Interactive Teacher's Edition**

STANDARDS MASTERY

 **Standards Review Workbook***

 **At Home: A Guide to Standards Mastery for United States History**

Holt Online Learning

To enhance learning, Internet activities are available for Slave Narratives and a Lincoln-Douglas Debates Graphic Organizer.

KEYWORD: SS8 TEACHER

- **Teacher Support Page**
- **Content Updates**
- **Rubrics and Writing Models**
- **Teaching Tips for the Multimedia Classroom**

KEYWORD: SS8 US14

- **Current Events**
- **Document-Based Questions**
- **Holt Grapher**
- **Holt Online Atlas**
- **Holt Researcher**
- **Interactive Multimedia Activities**
- **Internet Activities**
- **Online Chapter Summaries in Six Languages**
- **Online Section Quizzes**
- **American History Maps and Charts**

HOLT PREMIER ONLINE STUDENT EDITION

Complete online support for interactivity, assessment, and reporting

- **Interactive Maps and Notebook**
- **Standardized Test Prep**
- **Homework Practice and Research Activities Online**

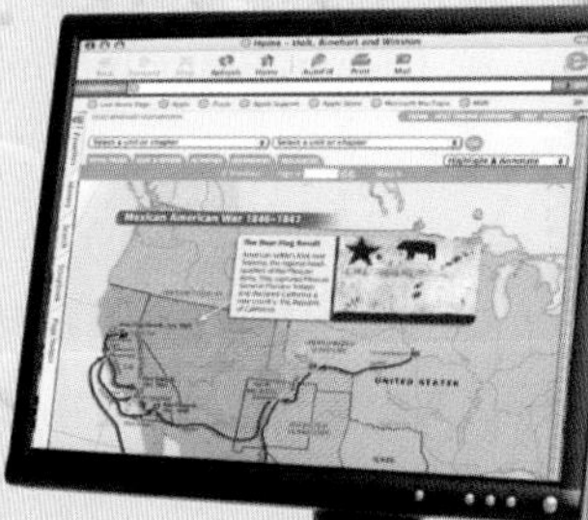

Mastering the Standards: Differentiating Instruction

Reaching Standards	Basic-level activities designed for all students encountering new material
Standards Proficiency	Intermediate-level activities designed for average students
Exceeding Standards	Challenging activities designed for honors and gifted-and-talented students
Standard English Mastery	Activities designed to improve standard English usage

Frequently Asked Questions

INSTRUCTIONAL PLANNING AND SUPPORT

Where do I find planning aids, pacing guides, lesson plans, and other teaching aids?

Annotated Teacher's Edition:
- Chapter planning guides
- Standards-based instruction and strategies
- Differentiated instruction for universal access
- Point-of-use reminders for integrating program resources

Power Presentations with Video CD-ROM

Universal Access Teacher Management System:
- Year and unit instructional benchmarking guides
- Reproducible lesson plans
- Assessment guides for diagnostic, progress, and summative end-of-the-year tests
- Options for differentiating instruction and intervention
- Teaching guides and answer keys for student workbooks

One-Stop Planner CD-ROM with Test Generator: Teacher Management System with Interactive Teacher's Editon:
- Calendar Planner
- Editable lesson plans
- All reproducible ancillaries in Adobe Acrobat (PDF) format
- ExamView Test Generator (English & Spanish)
- Game Tool for ExamView
- PuzzlePro
- Transparency and video previews

DIFFERENTIATING INSTRUCTION FOR UNIVERSAL ACCESS

What resources are available to ensure that Advanced Learners/GATE Students master the standards?

Teacher's Edition Activities:
- Congressional Committee Activity, p. 447
- Interview with Dred Scott, p. 452

Lesson Plans for Universal Access

Pre-AP Activities Guide for United States History: Making Generalizations

Primary Source Library CD-ROM for United States History

What resources are available to ensure that English Learners and Standard English Learners master the standards?

Teacher's Edition Activities:
- Political Divisions Letters, p. 450
- Vocabulary Activity, p. 456

Lesson Plans for Universal Access

Chapter Resource File: Vocabulary Builder Activities

Spanish Chapter Summaries Audio CD Program

Online Chapter Summaries in Six Languages

One-Stop Planner CD-ROM:
- PuzzlePro, Spanish Version
- ExamView Test Generator, Spanish Version

What modified materials are available for Special Education?

The ***Universal Access Modified Worksheets and Tests CD-ROM*** provides editable versions of the following:

Vocabulary Flash Cards

Modified Vocabulary Builder Activities

Modified Chapter Review Activity

Modified Chapter Test

What resources are available to ensure that Learners Having Difficulty master the standards?

Teacher's Edition Activities:
- Key Terms Activity, p. 440
- Kansas-Nebraska Act, p. 446
- Political Party Changes, p. 451

Interactive Reader and Study Guide

Student Edition Full-Read Audio CD

Quick Facts Transparency: A Divided Nation Visual Summary

Standards Review Workbook

Social Studies Skills Activity: Assessing Primary and Secondary Sources

Interactive Skills Tutor CD-ROM

How do I intervene for students struggling to master the standards?

Interactive Reader and Study Guide

Quick Facts Transparency: A Divided Nation Visual Summary

Standards Review Workbook

Social Studies Skills Activity: Assessing Primary and Secondary Sources

Interactive Skills Tutor CD-ROM

PROFESSIONAL DEVELOPMENT

What teacher training resources are available to help me grow professionally?

- In-service and staff development as part of your Holt Social Studies product purchase
- Quick Teacher Tutorial Lesson Presentation CD-ROM
- Intensive tuition-based Teacher Development Institute
- *Teaching American History* Online 2 Module Professional Development Course
- Convenient Holt Speaker Bureau face-to-face workshop options
- PRAXIS™ Test Prep (#0089) interactive Web-based content refreshers*
- 24/7 *Ask A Professional Development Expert* at http://www.hrw.com/prodev/

* PRAXIS is a trademark of Educational Testing Service (ETS). This publication is not endorsed or approved by ETS.

Information Literacy Skills

To learn more about how History–Social Science instruction may be improved by the effective use of library media centers and information literacy skills, go to the Teacher's Resource Materials for Chapter 14 at **go.hrw.com**, keyword: SS8 MEDIA.

The following materials were developed by the Division for Public Education of the American Bar Association. These materials are part of the **Democracy and Civic Education** supplement.
- Constitution Study Guide
- Supreme Court Case Studies

Chapter Preview

Standards Focus

Standards by Section

Section 1: HSS 8.9.4, 8.10.1

Section 2: HSS 8.9.5, 8.10.2

Section 3: HSS 8.10.4

Section 4: HSS 8.9.1, 8.10.3

Teacher's Edition

HSS **Analysis Skills:** CS 1, CS 2, HR 3, HR 4, HR 5, HI 1, HI 2

ELA Writing 8.2.1; Reading 8.2.0

Preview Grade 8 and 11 Standards

HSS **8.10** Students analyze the multiple causes, key events, and complex consequences of the Civil War.

8.10.8 Explain how the war affected combatants, civilians, the physical environment, and future warfare.

8.11 Students analyze the character and lasting consequences of Reconstruction.

11.10 Students analyze the development of federal civil rights and voting rights.

Focus on Writing

The **Chapter Resource File** provides a Focus on Writing worksheet to help students organize and write their autobiographical sketches.

CRF: Focus on Writing Activity: Writing an Autobiographical Sketch

CHAPTER 14 1848–1860

A Divided Nation

California Standards

History–Social Science

8.9 Students analyze the early and steady attempts to abolish slavery and to realize the ideals of the Declaration of Independence.

8.10 Students analyze the multiple causes, key events, and complex consequences of the Civil War.

Analysis Skills

HR 3 Students distinguish relevant from irrelevant information.

HR 4 Students assess the credibility of primary and secondary sources.

English–Language Arts

Writing 8.2.1 Write biographies, autobiographies, short stories, or narratives.

Reading 8.2.0 Students read and understand grade-level appropriate materials.

FOCUS ON WRITING

Writing an Autobiographical Sketch When you read about history, it can be difficult to imagine how the events you read about affected ordinary people. In this chapter you will read about slavery in the United States. Then you will write an autobiography of a fictional character, telling how these events affected him or her. Your fictional character can live in any part of the United States. He or she might be an enslaved African, a southern plantation owner, a northern abolitionist, or a settler in one of the new territories. Your classmates are your audience.

UNITED STATES

1848 The Free-Soil Party is formed on August 9.

1848

WORLD

1848 Revolutionary movements sweep across Europe.

434 CHAPTER 14

Introduce the Chapter

Standards Proficiency

Resolving Differences and Compromise

1. Ask students to imagine an issue that might divide their school. For example, suppose one group wants to eliminate the lunch break so that students can go home earlier. A second group wants to keep the lunch break and current school hours. Have students consider the pros and cons of each side.
2. Next, focus students' attention on how they might resolve such a dispute. Would they compromise? Would they vote and make all students abide by the majority decision? Have students explore several resolution options.
3. Then have students consider the pros and cons of each choice. For example, what might be positive and negative results of compromising?
4. Explain to students that they are going to learn about how the issue of slavery increasingly divided the nation, sometimes with violent results, and how the nation's leaders tried to resolve the problem. LS **Verbal/Linguistic**

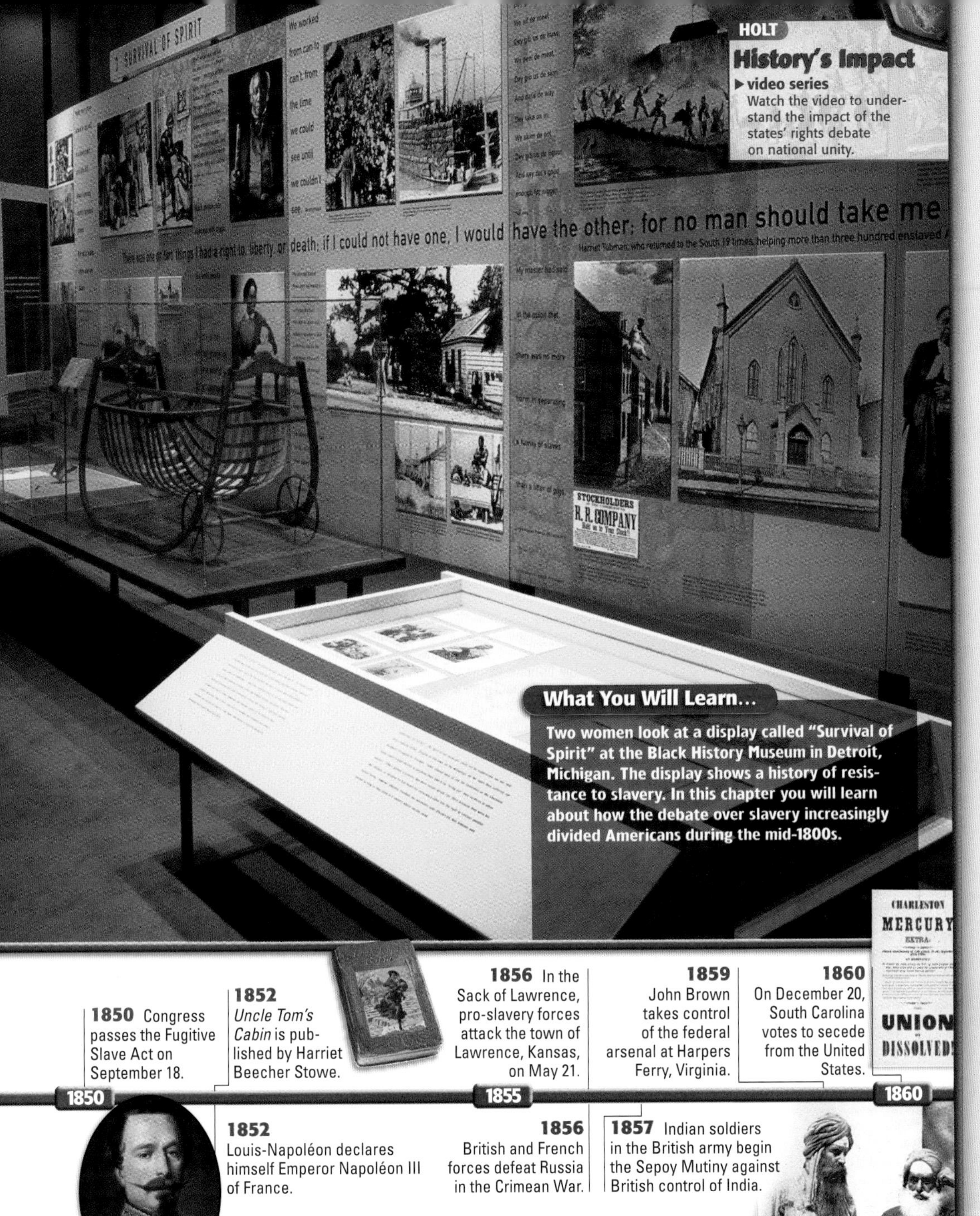

HOLT

History's Impact

▶ **video series**
Watch the video to understand the impact of the states' rights debate on national unity.

What You Will Learn...

Two women look at a display called "Survival of Spirit" at the Black History Museum in Detroit, Michigan. The display shows a history of resistance to slavery. In this chapter you will learn about how the debate over slavery increasingly divided Americans during the mid-1800s.

1850 Congress passes the Fugitive Slave Act on September 18.

1852 *Uncle Tom's Cabin* is published by Harriet Beecher Stowe.

1856 In the Sack of Lawrence, pro-slavery forces attack the town of Lawrence, Kansas, on May 21.

1859 John Brown takes control of the federal arsenal at Harpers Ferry, Virginia.

1860 On December 20, South Carolina votes to secede from the United States.

1850 — 1855 — 1860

1852 Louis-Napoléon declares himself Emperor Napoléon III of France.

1856 British and French forces defeat Russia in the Crimean War.

1857 Indian soldiers in the British army begin the Sepoy Mutiny against British control of India.

• Chapter Preview •

HOLT

History's Impact

▶ **video series**
See the Video Teacher's Guide for strategies for using the chapter video **A Divided Nation**.

Chapter Big Ideas

Section 1 Antislavery literature and the annexation of new lands intensified the debate over slavery. **HSS** 8.9.4, 8.10.1

Section 2 The Kansas-Nebraska Act heightened tensions in the conflict over slavery. **HSS** 8.9.5, 8.10.2

Section 3 The split over the issue of slavery intensified due to political division and judicial decisions. **HSS** 8.10.4

Section 4 The United States broke apart due to the growing conflict over slavery. **HSS** 8.9.1, 8.10.3

Explore the Picture

Survival of Spirit The Charles H. Wright Museum of African American History in Detroit, Michigan, is the world's largest African American history museum. Dr. Charles Wright, the museum's founder, started the museum to enrich the spirits of African Americans by giving them a sense of where they came from.

Analyzing Visuals Why do you think the exhibit shown in the photograph is called Survival of Spirit? *possible answer—because the exhibit highlights how African Americans endured, fought, escaped, and overcame slavery*

go.hrw.com

Online Resources

Chapter Resources:
KEYWORD: SS8 US14
Teacher Resources:
KEYWORD: SS8 TEACHER

Explore the Time Line

1. When did John Brown attack the federal arsenal at Harpers Ferry, Virginia? *1859*
2. What happened in South Carolina the year after the incident at Harpers Ferry? *South Carolina seceded from the United States.*
3. Slave narratives and books, such as Harriet Beecher Stowe's *Uncle Tom's Cabin,* helped people in the United States and Europe learn about the harsh realities of slavery. When was *Uncle Tom's Cabin* published? *1852*

HSS Analysis Skills: CS 1

Info to Know

Shifts in U.S. Political Parties Increasingly divided over slavery, Americans saw the rise and fall of political parties during the mid-1800s. The Free-Soil Party formed in 1848 to support free labor and to oppose the spread of slavery. By 1854 the party was gone, as was the Whig Party. That same year, some members of both parties joined with some abolitionists and Democrats to form the Republican Party. In 1860 this party would nominate an Illinois politician named Abraham Lincoln for president.

Reading Social Studies

Understanding Themes

Remind students about the debate that existed in the United States over the issue of slavery. Ask students how that debate might have had political ramifications for the United States. Ask students to predict some of those effects. Then ask students how the society and culture of the United States might have been affected by this growing division over slavery, and the resulting political effects. Help students to understand that the issue of slavery was the subject of much controversy.

Facts, Opinions, and the Past

Focus on Reading Bring in copies of the local newspaper or pages from different types of magazines. Organize the class into small groups and give each group different pages. Ask each group to find examples of facts and opinions in the pages it was given. Remind students that even in reputable newspapers or magazines, authors express opinions. Have each group present the facts and the opinions it found. Review these as a class and evaluate them.

Reading Social Studies

by Kylene Beers

Economics | Geography | **Politics** | Religion | **Society and Culture** | Science and Technology

Focus on Themes This chapter describes the growing tension between the North and the South over the slavery issue. You will read what happened as more states were admitted to the Union and people argued if they should be slave states or not. You will read about events that widened the division between the North and South so that the South finally chose to secede from the Union. Throughout the chapter you will see that **cultural** differences influenced **political** decisions.

Facts, Opinions, and the Past

Focus on Reading When you are trying to learn about history, would you rather read facts or the author's opinion? You would prefer facts, of course. Separating facts from opinions about historical events helps you know what really happened.

Additional reading support can be found in the Interactive Reader and Study Guide

Identifying Facts and Opinions Something is a **fact** if there is a way to prove it or disprove it. For example, research can prove or disprove the following statement: "Abraham Lincoln belonged to the Republican Party." But research can't prove the following statement because it is just an **opinion**, or someone's belief: "Lincoln was the greatest president in American history."

Use the process below to decide whether a statement is fact or opinion.

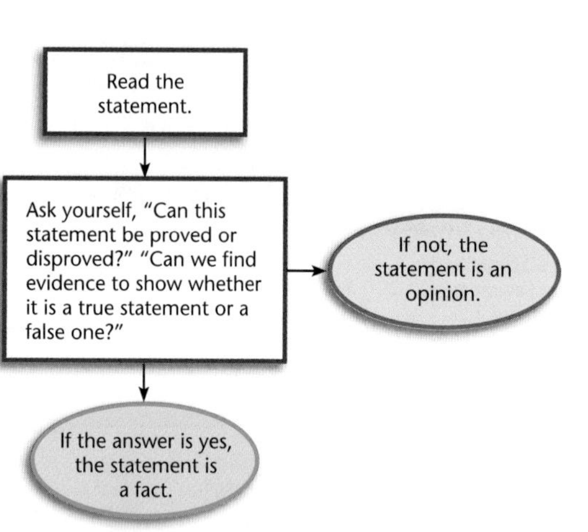

Read the statement.
Ask yourself, "Can this statement be proved or disproved?" "Can we find evidence to show whether it is a true statement or a false one?"
If not, the statement is an opinion.
If the answer is yes, the statement is a fact.

Reading and Skills Resources

Reading Support

- Interactive Reader and Study Guide
- Student Edition on Audio CD
- Spanish Chapter Summaries Audio CD Program

Social Studies Skills Support

- Interactive Skills Tutor CD-ROM

Vocabulary Support

- **CRF:** Vocabulary Builder Activities
- **CRF:** Chapter Review Activity
- Universal Access Modified Worksheets and Tests CD-ROM:
  - Vocabulary Flash Cards
  - Vocabulary Builder Activity
  - Chapter Review Activity

OSP Holt PuzzlePro

Standards Focus

HSS **Analysis Skills:** HR 2
HSS Reading 8.2.0

ELA **Reading 8.2.0** Read and understand grade-level-appropriate material.

HSS **Analysis HR 2** Distinguish fact from opinion.

You Try It!

The following passage tells about the debates that Abraham Lincoln had with Stephen Douglas. All the statements in this passage are facts. What makes them facts and not opinions?

The Lincoln-Douglas Debates

In 1858 Illinois Republicans nominated Abraham Lincoln for the U.S. Senate. His opponent was Democrat Stephen Douglas, who had represented Illinois in the Senate since 1847. Lincoln challenged Douglas in what became the historic Lincoln-Douglas debates.

In each debate, Lincoln stressed that the central issue of the campaign was the spread of slavery in the West. He said that the Democrats were trying to spread slavery across the nation.

Lincoln talked about the *Dred Scott* decision. He said that African Americans were "entitled to all the natural rights" listed in the Declaration of Independence, specifically mentioning "the right to life, liberty, and the pursuit of happiness."

From Chapter 14, pp. 452–453

Identify each of the following as a fact or an opinion and then explain your choice.

1. Lincoln accused the Democrats of trying to spread slavery across the nation.
2. The Lincoln-Douglas debates were the most important debates in the history of the nation.
3. Stephen Douglas was a U.S. Senator from Illinois.
4. Abraham Lincoln ran against Douglas in the 1858 Senate election.
5. Most Americans believed that the *Dred Scott* decision was a good one.
6. Lincoln was the best debater people from Illinois had ever heard.

Key Terms and People

Chapter 14

Academic Vocabulary

In this chapter, you will learn the following academic words:

As you read Chapter 14, look closely at quotes from historical figures. Are these quotes showing you facts or opinions?

Reading Social Studies

Key Terms and People

Preteach the key terms and people from this chapter by reviewing each term or person with the class. Then have each student create a set of flashcards using the key terms and people. Have students write the term or name on one side of the card and the definition or description of that term on the other side. Encourage students to use their flashcards regularly to study these people and terms. **LS Verbal/Linguistic, Kinesthetic**

Focus on Reading

See the **Focus on Reading** questions in this chapter for more practice on this reading social studies skill.

Reading Social Studies Assessment

See the **Standards Review** at the end of this chapter for student assessment questions related to this reading skill.

Teaching Tip

Remind students of the sources they should use when checking facts. These include reliable sources such as encyclopedias, almanacs, dictionaries, public documents, and scientific journals. Remind students that even when they use verifiable sources, they should be able to find the same information in more than one source. Finally, remind students to evaluate sources from the Internet carefully.

Answers

You Try It! **1.** *fact; it is supported by information in the passage;* **2.** *opinion; this cannot be proved;* **3.** *fact; this is supported by the passage;* **4.** *fact; this is stated in the passage;* **5.** *opinion; this cannot be verified or proved;* **6.** *opinion; there is no evidence to prove this*

Preteach

Bellringer

If YOU were there . . . Use the **Daily Bellringer Transparency** to help students answer the question.

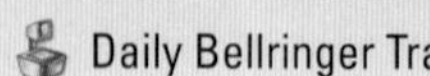
Daily Bellringer Transparency, Section 1

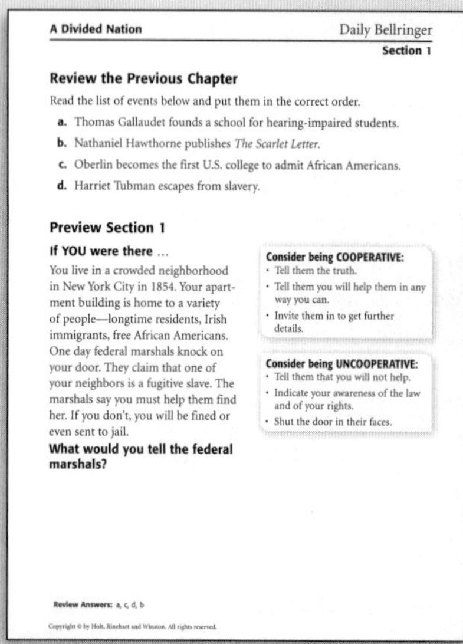

A Divided Nation — Daily Bellringer, **Section 1**

Review the Previous Chapter

Read the list of events below and put them in the correct order.

a. Thomas Gallaudet founds a school for hearing-impaired students.
b. Nathaniel Hawthorne publishes *The Scarlet Letter.*
c. Oberlin becomes the first U.S. college to admit African Americans.
d. Harriet Tubman escapes from slavery.

Preview Section 1

If YOU were there ...

You live in a crowded neighborhood in New York City in 1854. Your apartment building is home to a variety of people—longtime residents, Irish immigrants, free African Americans. One day federal marshals knock on your door. They claim that one of your neighbors is a fugitive slave. The marshals say you must help them find her. If you don't, you will be fined or even sent to jail.

What would you tell the federal marshals?

Consider being COOPERATIVE:
- Tell them the truth.
- Tell them you will help them in any way you can.
- Invite them in to get further details.

Consider being UNCOOPERATIVE:
- Tell them that you will not help.
- Indicate your awareness of the law and of your rights.
- Shut the door in their faces.

Review Answers: a, c, d, b

Building Vocabulary

Preteach or review the following terms:

abolitionists people working to end slavery (p. 442)

proviso a condition, as part of an agreement (p. 438)

secession formally withdrawing (p. 440)

sovereignty supreme authority (p. 438)

CRF: Vocabulary Builder Activity, Section 1

Standards Focus

HSS 8.9.4

Means: Discuss the significance of slavery in the admission of new states and territories, with a focus on California.

Matters: Growing tensions between free and slave states divided the nation.

HSS 8.10.1

Means: Contrast the views of Daniel Webster and John C. Calhoun toward state and federal authority, with a focus on the Compromise of 1850.

Matters: Disagreements over state versus federal authority continue to divide politicians today.

SECTION 1

The Debate over Slavery

What You Will Learn...

Main Ideas

1. The addition of new land in the West renewed disputes over the expansion of slavery.
2. The Compromise of 1850 tried to solve the disputes over slavery.
3. The Fugitive Slave Act caused more controversy.
4. Abolitionists used antislavery literature to promote opposition.

The Big Idea

Antislavery literature and the annexation of new lands intensified the debate over slavery.

Key Terms and People

popular sovereignty, *p. 438*
Wilmot Proviso, *p. 438*
sectionalism, *p. 439*
Free-Soil Party, *p. 439*
Compromise of 1850, *p. 441*
Fugitive Slave Act, *p. 441*
Anthony Burns, *p. 442*
Uncle Tom's Cabin, p. 443
Harriet Beecher Stowe, *p. 443*

HSS 8.9.4 Discuss the importance of the slavery issue as raised by the annexation of Texas and California's admission to the union as a free state under the Compromise of 1850.

HSS 8.10.1 Compare the conflicting interpretations of state and federal authority as emphasized in the speeches and writings of statesmen such as Daniel Webster and John C. Calhoun.

If YOU were there...

You live in a crowded neighborhood in New York City in 1854. Your apartment building is home to a variety of people—longtime residents, Irish immigrants, free African Americans. One day federal marshals knock on your door. They claim that one of your neighbors is a fugitive slave. The marshals say you must help them find her. If you don't, you will be fined or even sent to jail.

What would you tell the federal marshals?

BUILDING BACKGROUND Some reform movements of the 1800s drew stubborn and often violent opposition. This was especially true of the abolitionist movement. Pro-slavery supporters fought for laws to protect slavery and extend the slave system. These laws were a threat to African Americans in the North.

New Land Renews Slavery Disputes

The United States added more than 500,000 square miles of land as a result of winning the Mexican-American War in 1848. The additional land caused bitter debate about slavery. The Missouri Compromise of 1820 had divided the Louisiana Purchase into either free or slave regions. It prohibited slavery north of latitude 36°30′ but let Missouri become a slave state. In the 1840s President James K. Polk wanted to extend the 36°30′ line to the West coast, dividing the Mexican Cession into two parts—one free and one enslaved. Some leaders, including Senator Lewis Cass of Michigan, encouraged **popular sovereignty**, the idea that political power belongs to the people, who should decide on banning or allowing slavery.

Regional Differences about Slavery

Some northerners wanted to outlaw slavery in all parts of the Mexican Cession. During the war, Representative David Wilmot offered the **Wilmot Proviso**, a document stating that "neither slavery nor involuntary servitude shall ever exist in any part of [the] territory."

Teach the Big Idea: Master the Standards

Standards Proficiency

The Debate over Slavery

HSS 8.9.4, 8.10.1; HSS **Analysis Skills:** HI 1, HI 2

1. **Teach** Ask students the Main Idea questions to teach this section.
2. **Apply** Draw a two-column chart and label the columns *Cause* and *Effect*. Have students copy the chart and complete it by listing the major cause-and-effect relationships between events in the section. Model the activity for students by listing the following: *cause—gain of Mexican Cession; effect—renewed bitter debate over slavery.*
   LS Verbal/Linguistic
3. **Review** As you review the section's main ideas, have students share the cause-and-effect relationships they listed.
4. **Practice/Homework** Have each student create either a letter to the editor or a political cartoon opposing the Fugitive Slave Act.
   LS Verbal/Linguistic, Visual/Spatial

Alternative Assessment Handbook, Rubrics 7: Charts; 27: Political Cartoons; and 37: Writing Assignments

Upsetting the Balance QUICK FACTS

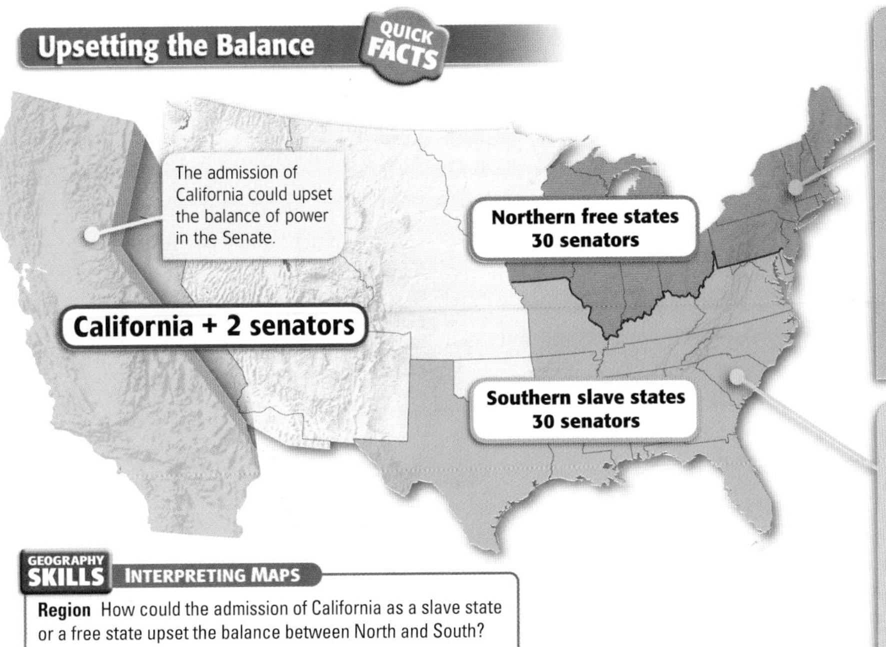

Free States
Connecticut
Illinois
Indiana
Iowa
Maine
Massachusetts
Michigan
New Hampshire
New Jersey
New York
Ohio
Pennsylvania
Rhode Island
Vermont
Wisconsin

Slave States
Alabama
Arkansas
Delaware
Florida
Georgia
Kentucky
Louisiana
Maryland
Mississippi
Missouri
North Carolina
South Carolina
Tennessee
Texas
Virginia

GEOGRAPHY SKILLS INTERPRETING MAPS

Region How could the admission of California as a slave state or a free state upset the balance between North and South?

The northern-controlled House passed the document, but in the Senate, the South had more power. The Wilmot Proviso did not pass. Before this time, politicians had usually supported the ideas of their political parties. However, the Wilmot Proviso spurred a debate that showed growing **sectionalism**, or favoring the interests of one section or region over the interests of the entire country.

To attract voters, the Democrats and the Whigs did not take a clear position on slavery in the presidential campaign of 1848. In response, antislavery northerners formed a new party, the **Free-Soil Party**, which supported the Wilmot Proviso. They worried that slave labor would mean fewer jobs for white workers. Party members chose former president Martin Van Buren as their candidate. The new party won 10 percent of the popular vote, drawing away votes from Democrat Lewis Cass. Whig candidate Zachary Taylor won a narrow victory.

The California Question

The California gold rush caused such rapid population growth that California applied to join the Union as a state instead of as a territory. But would California enter the Union as a free state or a slave state?

Most Californians opposed slavery, which had been illegal when the state was part of Mexico. Also, many forty-niners had come from free states. But if California became a free state, the balance between free and slave states would change, favoring the free states.

In the South, an imbalance was unacceptable. "We are about permanently to destroy the balance of power between the sections," said Senator Jefferson Davis of Mississippi. He and many other southerners did not want California to enter the Union as a free state.

READING CHECK **Drawing Inferences** Why did sectionalism in the United States increase in the late 1840s?

THE IMPACT TODAY

Small parties still affect presidential elections in a similar way today.

Direct Teach

Main Idea

1 New Land Renews Slavery Disputes

The addition of new land in the West renewed disputes over the expansion of slavery.

Identify What was the Wilmot Proviso? *legislation to ban slavery in the Mexican Cession*

Contrast How did the Wilmot Proviso differ from popular sovereignty? *Wilmot Proviso—see above answer; popular sovereignty—proposed to let the people of each new territory decide whether to ban or allow slavery*

Evaluate Why did southerners not want to upset the balance of power by letting California enter the Union as a free state? *Southerners feared that if they were outnumbered in Congress, they would not be able to stop legislation that they opposed, such as legislation to ban or limit slavery.*

- **CRF:** Economics and History Activity: Economic Rivalry
- **CRF:** History and Geography Activity: Free and Slave States
- Quick Facts Transparency: Upsetting the Balance

HSS 8.9.4; HSS **Analysis Skills:** HI 1, HI 2

Critical Thinking: Contrasting

Standards Proficiency

Slavery Dispute Flyers HSS 8.9.4, 8.9.5; HSS **Analysis Skills:** HR 5, HI 1

Materials: paper, colored pencils and markers

1. Ask students to explain the difference between the Wilmot Proviso and popular sovereignty. Write the answer for students to see. Then ask students to identify the groups who supported each position. Have students consider different groups, such as abolitionists and slaveholders, as well as different regions of the country.
2. Pair students and have each pair create two flyers, one in favor of the Wilmot Proviso and the other in favor of popular sovereignty. The flyers should explain the proposed plan to residents in new territories and persuade them to support the plan.
3. Ask for volunteers to share their flyers with the class. LS **Interpersonal, Verbal/Linguistic**

Alternative Assessment Handbook, Rubric 43: Writing to Persuade

Answers

Interpreting Maps *because the nation had an equal number of free and slave states and, thus, senators*

Reading Check *because of the Mexican Cession and Californians' request for statehood, which renewed the sectionally based dispute over the expansion of slavery into new lands*

Direct Teach

Main Idea

❷ Compromise of 1850

The Compromise of 1850 tried to solve the disputes over slavery.

Recall What were the five key points of Henry Clay's Compromise of 1850? *See the list at right.*

Summarize In their response to the Compromise of 1850, what views did senators Seward, Calhoun, and Webster represent? *Seward—antislavery view: opposed compromise because wanted California admitted without qualifications; Calhoun—southern view: opposed compromise because did not want balance of power upset; Webster—supported compromise as a way to preserve the Union*

Predict Do you think the Compromise of 1850 settled the question of slavery in the United States? Why or why not? *possible answer—no, because the issue would continue to arise as new territories requested statehood, the nation remained sectionally divided, and enslaved African Americans and abolitionists would continue to fight the injustice of slavery*

HSS 8.9.4, 8.10.1; **HSS Analysis Skills:** HR 5, HI 1, HI 2

Primary Source

Reading Like a Historian

Comparing Documents Help students practice reading the documents like historians. Ask:

- What major issues do the two passages address?
- How do the two passages differ in tone?
- What assumptions does each speaker make?

HSS 8.9.4, 8.10.1; **HSS Analysis Skills:** HR 4, HI 1

Answers

Analyzing Primary Sources *He thought secession would lead to war and wanted to preserve the Union.*

Compromise of 1850

Senator Henry Clay of Kentucky had helped to settle the Missouri crisis of 1819–20 and the nullification crisis of 1832–33 by proposing compromises. He now had another plan to help the nation maintain peace. His ideas were designed to give both sides things that they wanted:

1. California would enter the Union as a free state.
2. The rest of the Mexican Cession would be federal land. In this territory, popular sovereignty would decide on slavery.
3. Texas would give up land east of the upper Rio Grande. In return, the government would pay Texas's debts from when it was an independent republic.
4. The slave trade—but not slavery—would end in the nation's capital.
5. A more effective fugitive slave law would be passed.

Clay's plan drew attack, especially regarding California. Senator William Seward of New York defended antislavery views and wanted California admitted "directly, without conditions, without qualifications, and without compromise." However, Senator John C. Calhoun of South Carolina argued that letting California enter as a free state would destroy the nation's balance. He warned people of issues that would later start the Civil War. Calhoun asked that the slave states be allowed "to separate and part in peace."

Primary Source

SPEECH

The Seventh of March Speech

On March 7, 1850, Daniel Webster spoke on the floor of the Senate in favor of the Compromise of 1850.

I hear with distress and anguish the word "secession." Secession! Peaceable secession! Sir, your eyes and mine are never destined to see the miracle. The dismemberment [taking apart] of this vast country without convulsion! The breaking up of the fountains of the great deep without ruffing the surface! Who is so foolish, I beg every body's pardon, as to expect to see any such thing? . . . There can be no such thing as peaceable secession.

—quoted in *Daniel Webster: The Completest Man*, edited by Kenneth Shewmaker

Webster is upset by talk of secession.

Webster is saying that just as it is impossible to move water in the ocean without making waves, it is impossible for states to peacefully secede.

ANALYSIS SKILL **ANALYZING PRIMARY SOURCES**

Why did Webster support the Compromise of 1850?

Henry Clay introduced the Compromise of 1850 on the Senate floor.

Daniel Webster spoke eloquently in support of the compromise.

Differentiating Instruction for Universal Access

Learners Having Difficulty

Reaching Standards | Standard English Mastery

1. List the section's Key Terms and People for students to see. Help students define them.
2. Next, ask students to write eight sentences that summarize the section and use all the key terms and people. Students should write two sentences for each subsection, indicated by the blue headings.
3. Ask students who have trouble putting thoughts into words to summarize each part of the section aloud. Then help students get their ideas on paper.
4. As a class, students should share their sentences for each subsection. Write them for students to see. Correct any errors and improve students' use of standard English. Have the students help you work on the sentences until you have a model summary of the section. **LS Verbal/Linguistic**

HSS 8.9.4, 8.10.1; **HSS Analysis Skills:** HI 1

Alternative Assessment Handbook, Rubric 37: Writing Assignments

In contrast, Senator Daniel Webster of Massachusetts favored Clay's plan:

> "I wish to speak today, not as a Massachusetts man, nor as a Northern man, but as an American . . . I speak today for the preservation of the Union. Hear me for my cause."
>
> —Daniel Webster, quoted in *Battle Cry of Freedom* by James M. McPherson

Webster criticized northern abolitionists and southerners who talked of secession.

A compromise was enacted that year and seemed to settle most disputes between free and slave states. It achieved the majority of Clay's proposals. With the **Compromise of 1850**, California was able to enter the Union as a free state. The rest of the Mexican Cession was divided into two territories—Utah and New Mexico—where the question of whether to allow slavery would be decided by popular sovereignty.

Texas agreed to give up its land claims in New Mexico in exchange for financial aid from the federal government. The compromise outlawed the slave trade in the District of Columbia and established a new fugitive slave law.

READING CHECK **Analyzing** How was Texas affected by the Compromise of 1850?

Fugitive Slave Act

The newly passed **Fugitive Slave Act** made it a crime to help runaway slaves and allowed officials to arrest those slaves in free areas. Slaveholders were permitted to take suspected fugitives to U.S. commissioners, who decided their fate.

Details of the Fugitive Slave Act

Slaveholders could use testimony from white witnesses, but enslaved African Americans accused of being fugitives could not testify. Nor could people who hid or helped a runaway slave—they faced six months in jail and a $1,000 fine. Commissioners who rejected a slaveholder's claim earned $5 while those who returned suspected fugitives to slaveholders earned $10. Clearly, the commissioners benefited from helping slaveholders.

Reactions to the Fugitive Slave Act

Enforcement of the Fugitive Slave Act began immediately. In September 1850—the same month the law was passed—federal marshals arrested African American James Hamlet. They returned him to a slaveholder in

John C. Calhoun was weak and near death. He had his speech in support of slavery read to the Senate for him.

Primary Source

SPEECH

Southern View of the Compromise of 1850

John C. Calhoun from South Carolina wrote a speech saying that the proposed compromise did not go far enough to satisfy the South.

> "I have, senators, believed from the first that the agitation of the subject of slavery would, if not prevented by some timely and effective measure, end in disunion . . . The South asks for justice, simple justice, and less she ought not to take. She has no compromise to offer but the Constitution, and no concession or surrender to make."

Agitation means "unrest."

Calhoun believes the South's position is supported by the Constitution.

ANALYSIS SKILL **ANALYZING PRIMARY SOURCES**

Why did Calhoun urge southern senators to vote against the compromise?

Direct Teach

Main Idea

❸ Fugitive Slave Act

The Fugitive Slave Act caused more controversy.

Define What was the purpose of the Fugitive Slave Act? *made it a crime to help runaway slaves and allowed officials to arrest those slaves in free areas*

Summarize How was the Fugitive Slave Act biased in favor of slaveholders? *prevented fugitive slaves and those who helped them from testifying, used monetary rewards to encourage commissioners to decide in favor of slaveholders*

Draw Conclusions Why do you think that of 343 fugitive slave cases, fugitive slaves were declared free only 11 times? *Students should mention the bias of the law, such as restrictions on who could testify.*

CRF: Primary Source Activity: William P. Newman, A Response to the Fugitive Slave Act

HSS 8.9.4; HSS **Analysis Skills:** HI 1, HI 2

Info to Know

Approving the Compromise Henry Clay was unable to get his compromise approved as a whole. On the advice of fellow legislator Stephen Douglas, Clay divided the bill into separate parts. The plan worked. Each of the separate measures passed, usually by votes that revealed sectional biases.

Critical Thinking: Identifying Points of View

Standards Proficiency

Debate over Slavery Chart

HSS 8.9.4; HSS **Analysis Skills:** HR 5, HI 1

Materials: construction paper or poster board

1. As students read the section, have them make a list of the key leaders connected to the slavery issue. Lists should include David Wilmot, Lewis Cass, Jefferson Davis, Henry Clay, Daniel Webster, and John C. Calhoun.
2. Then ask each student to create a large chart of the leaders on construction paper or poster board. For each leader, students should provide a short caption identifying the person and his view on the slavery issue. To illustrate each person's views students might also include short quotes where available. Tell students to group the leaders according to the leaders' views.
3. Have students share the information they listed to help you create a large master chart. Display the master chart in the classroom and add to it during the study of the chapter.

LS Verbal/Linguistic, Visual/Spatial

Alternative Assessment Handbook, Rubric 7: Charts

Answers

Analyzing Primary Sources *Calhoun thought the proposed compromise did not satisfy the South and provide justice.*

Reading Check *Texas gave up land claims in New Mexico in exchange for financial help from the government.*

Direct Teach

Connect to Literature

Slave Narratives Frederick Douglass's autobiography is only one of a number of slave narratives. One historian has estimated that more than 6,000 such narratives exist. The earliest known narrative—the story of Adam, the "servant of John Saffin, Esquire"—was published in 1703. Douglass's work, however, is probably the best known.

Checking for Understanding

Select the best answer for each of the following.

1. The debate over California's admission as a free state revealed increased
   a. popular sovereignty.
   b. *sectionalism.*
   c. slavery.
   d. unity.
2. What did Henry Clay propose to solve the debate over California?
   a. *Compromise of 1850*
   b. Free-Soil Party
   c. popular sovereignty
   d. Wilmot Proviso
3. Why did many northerners dislike the Fugitive Slave Act?
   a. too soft on the North
   b. ineffective
   c. *unfair*
   d. too hard on the South

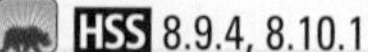 HSS 8.9.4, 8.10.1; HSS **Analysis Skills:** HR 5, HI 1

go.hrw.com
Online Resources
KEYWORD: SS8 US14
ACTIVITY: Slave Narratives

Primary Source

PHOTOGRAPH

A Fugitive Slave Convention

The Fugitive Slave Act enraged abolitionists. To protest the new law, they held many meetings to publicly denounce it. One such meeting was held in 1850 in the small town of Cazenovia in central New York, a center for abolitionist activity. About 2,000 people—including many former slaves—attended the convention. They listened to speeches, made plans, and raised their voices for freedom. This photo was a point of pride for the delegates, but it also was used by opponents of the movement as a symbol of the poor morals of abolitionists: Not only were whites allowed to mix with African Americans, women and men were allowed to mix as well. This angered many people.

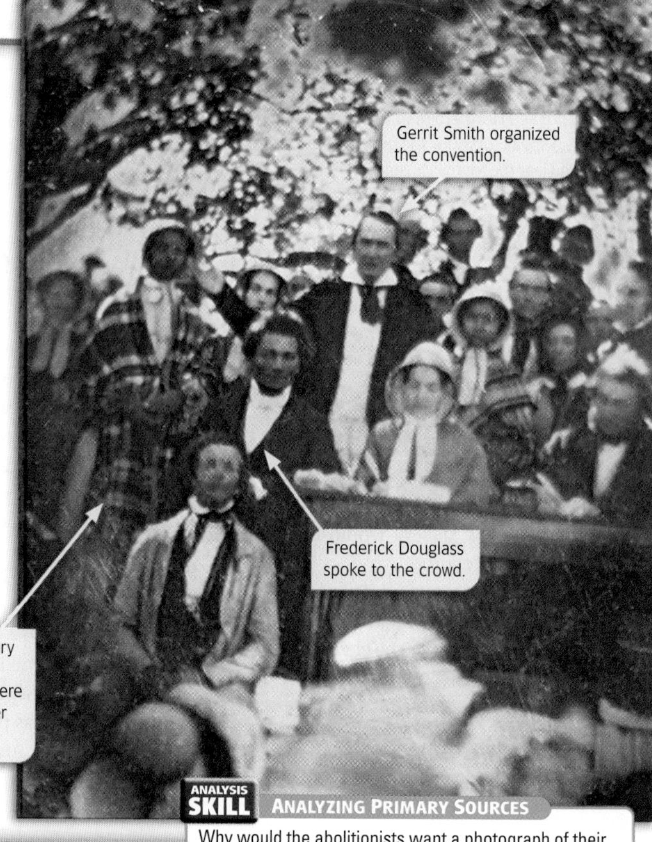

Gerrit Smith organized the convention.

Frederick Douglass spoke to the crowd.

The Edmonson sisters, Mary (left) and Emily, tried to escape from slavery but were captured. Abolitionists later purchased their freedom.

ANALYSIS SKILL ANALYZING PRIMARY SOURCES

Why would the abolitionists want a photograph of their convention?

Maryland, although he had lived in New York City for three years.

Thousands of northern African Americans fled to Canada in fear. In the 10 years after Congress passed the Fugitive Slave Act, some 343 fugitive slave cases were reviewed. The accused fugitives were declared free in only 11 cases.

The Fugitive Slave Act upset northerners, who were uncomfortable with the commissioners' power. Northerners disliked the idea of a trial without a jury. They also disapproved of commissioners' higher fees for returning slaves. Most were horrified that some free African Americans had been captured and sent to the South.

Most northerners opposed to the Act peacefully resisted, but violence did erupt. In 1854 **Anthony Burns**, a Virginia fugitive slave, was arrested in Boston. Abolitionists used force while trying to rescue him from jail, killing a deputy marshal. A federal ship was ordered to return Burns to Virginia after his trial. Many people in the North, particularly in Massachusetts, were outraged. The event persuaded many to join the abolitionist cause.

READING CHECK **Drawing Conclusions** What concerns did northerners have about the Fugitive Slave Act?

Cross-Discipline Activity: Literature

Standards Proficiency

Harriet Beecher Stowe Book Signing

HSS 8.9.4; HSS **Analysis Skills:** HR 5, HI 1

Materials: *Uncle Tom's Cabin* (optional)

1. Ask students to imagine that they belong to an abolitionist group sponsoring an event at which Harriet Beecher Stowe will be signing copies of *Uncle Tom's Cabin*. Have each student create a newspaper piece promoting the event.
2. The promotional piece should briefly describe who Harriet Beecher Stowe is, explain what *Uncle Tom's Cabin* is about, and promote the sale of the book. At the same time, the piece should subtly promote the views of Stowe and other abolitionists regarding slavery and the Fugitive Slave Act.
3. If possible, provide copies of *Uncle Tom's Cabin* and have students select excerpts from the book to include in their promotional pieces. LS **Verbal/Linguistic**

Alternative Assessment Handbook, Rubrics 2: Advertisements; and 43: Writing to Persuade

Answers

Analyzing Primary Sources *possible answers—a symbol of pride; showed support for their cause*

Reading Check *Northerners worried that accused fugitives were not granted due process and that commissioners would be biased because of differences in fees.*

Antislavery Literature

Abolitionists in the North used the stories of fugitive slaves like James Hamlet and Anthony Burns to gain sympathy for their cause. Slave narratives also educated people about their hardships.

Fiction also informed people about the evils of slavery. ***Uncle Tom's Cabin***, the antislavery novel written by **Harriet Beecher Stowe**, spoke out powerfully against slavery. Stowe, the daughter of Connecticut minister Lyman Beecher, moved to Ohio when she was 21. There she met fugitive slaves and learned about the cruelties of slavery. The Fugitive Slave Act greatly angered Stowe. She decided to write a book that would educate northerners about the realities of slavery.

Uncle Tom's Cabin was published in 1852. The main character, a kindly enslaved African American named Tom, is taken from his wife and sold "down the river" in Louisiana. Tom becomes the slave of cruel Simon Legree. In a rage, Legree has Tom beaten to death.

The novel electrified the nation and sparked outrage in the South. Louisa McCord, a famous southern writer, questioned the "foul imagination which could invent such scenes."

Within a decade, more than 2 million copies of *Uncle Tom's Cabin* had been sold in the United States. The book's popularity caused one northerner to remark that Stowe and her book had created "two millions of abolitionists." Stowe later wrote *A Key to Uncle Tom's Cabin* to answer those who had criticized her book.

The impact of Stowe's book is suggested by her reported meeting with Abraham Lincoln in 1862, a year after the start of the Civil War. Lincoln supposedly said to Stowe that she was "the little lady who made this big war." Her book is still widely read today as a source of information about the harsh realities of slavery.

READING CHECK **Identifying Cause and Effect** Why did abolitionists use antislavery literature to promote their cause, and what effect did it have on the slavery debate?

SUMMARY AND PREVIEW The United States experienced increasing disagreement over the issue of slavery. The Compromise of 1850 and the Fugitive Slave Act tried to address these disagreements with legislation. In the next section you will read about another disputed law concerning slavery, the Kansas-Nebraska Act, and the violence it sparked.

Section 1 Assessment

go.hrw.com
Online Quiz
KEYWORD: SS8 HP14

Reviewing Ideas, Terms, and People HSS 8.9.4, 8.10.1

1. **a. Describe** What ideas did the **Free-Soil Party** promote?
   b. Predict What are some possible results of the growing sectional debate over slavery?
2. **a. Describe** What were the major points of the **Compromise of 1850**?
   b. Contrast What differing opinions emerged toward Henry Clay's proposed compromise?
3. **a. Identify** What were the effects of the **Fugitive Slave Act**?
   b. Draw Conclusions Why did some Americans believe the Fugitive Slave Act was unfair?
4. **a. Identify** What are three examples of antislavery literature?
   b. Elaborate Do you think literature was an effective tool against slavery? Why or why not?

Critical Thinking

5. **Evaluating** Copy the web diagram below onto a sheet of your own paper. Use it to explain how the Compromise of 1850, the Fugitive Slave Act, and antislavery literature affected the debate over slavery.

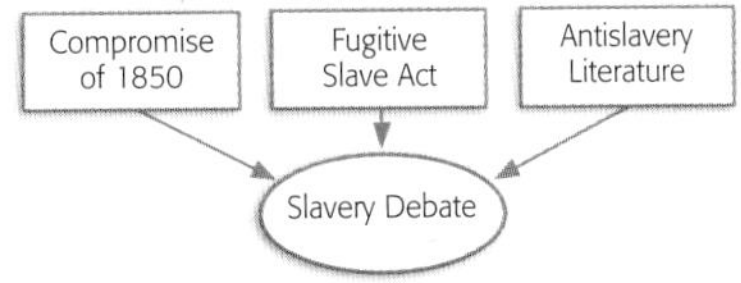

FOCUS ON WRITING

6. **Taking Notes on the Debate over Slavery** Make some notes on the Wilmot Proviso, the Free-Soil Party, the Compromise of 1850, and the Fugitive Slave Act. Decide how your character feels about each of these. How do the Compromise of 1850 and the Fugitive Slave Act affect your character?

Direct Teach

Main Idea

4 Antislavery Literature

Abolitionists used antislavery literature to promote opposition.

Identify What important antislavery novel was published in 1852, and who was its author? Uncle Tom's Cabin, *by Harriet Beecher Stowe*

Identify Cause and Effect What effect did *Uncle Tom's Cabin* have? *electrified the nation, sparked outrage in the South, and increased abolitionist support*

- **CRF:** Biography Activity: Sojourner Truth
- Political Cartoons Activities for United States History, Cartoon 16: Antislavery Poster
- HSS 8.9.4; HSS **Analysis Skills:** HI 1, HI 2

Review & Assess

Close

Have students summarize the ways in which the nation tried to deal with increasing tensions and sectionalism over the issue of slavery.

Review

go.hrw.com Online Quiz, Section 1

Assess

SE Section 1 Assessment

- PASS: Section 1 Quiz
- Alternative Assessment Handbook

Reteach/Classroom Intervention

- California Standards Review Workbook
- Interactive Reader and Study Guide, Section 1
- Interactive Skills Tutor CD-ROM

Section 1 Assessment Answers

1. **a.** supported the Wilmot Proviso
   b. possible answers—continued conflicts in Congress; secession of slave states; civil war
2. **a.** See the list on p. 440.
   b. Calhoun—against, destroys balance of power between free and slave states; slave states should leave the Union; Webster—for, preserves the Union
3. **a.** upset many northerners; many fugitive slaves returned; some violent opposition
   b. restrictions on who could testify, trial without a jury, biased fee structure
4. **a.** slave narratives, Uncle Tom's Cabin, A Key to Uncle Tom's Cabin
   b. possible answers—yes, helped people realize the cruelty of slavery; no, read only by those who opposed slavery
5. Compromise of 1850—sparked debate between leaders and increased sectionalism; Fugitive Slave Act—upset many northerners and angered abolitionists; Antislavery Literature—educated and persuaded people
6. Students should show an understanding of Americans' different views toward slavery.

Answers

Reading Check *helped educate people about the hardships of enslaved African Americans; increased sympathy and support for the abolitionist movement*

Literature in History

Uncle Tom's Cabin

As You Read As students read, have them list words and phrases that appeal to their emotions. Next, ask volunteers to share some of the words and phrases they listed. What feelings and sentiments does each one provoke? Why? Have students discuss the sentiments that Stowe hoped to evoke in her readers and why. Close by having students discuss how Stowe's ability to provoke certain feelings contributed to her novel's lasting influence.

Meet the Writer

Harriet Beecher Stowe (1811–1896) Born in Litchfield, Connecticut, Stowe was the seventh of nine children. Her father was a prominent Presbyterian minister, and her strong religious upbringing and faith shaped her life. After marrying, Stowe began writing stories and essays to supplement her husband's small income. The success of *Uncle Tom's Cabin* made her an instant celebrity. Her later novels include *Minister's Wooing* (1859), *The Pearl of Orr's Island* (1862), and *Oldtown Folks* (1869). She was elected to the National Women's Hall of Fame in 1910.

Antislavery Literature

from Uncle Tom's Cabin

by Harriet Beecher Stowe (1811–1896)

About the Reading *Published nine years before the outbreak of the Civil War,* Uncle Tom's Cabin *focused the nation's attention on the cruelties of slavery. In the following section, Stowe describes how a slave named Eliza is trying to escape to save her son from being sold.*

AS YOU READ **Look for details that appeal to your feelings.**

It is impossible to conceive of a human creature more wholly desolate and forlorn than Eliza when she turned her footsteps from Uncle Tom's cabin . . .

The boundaries of the farm, the grove, the wood lot passed by her dizzily as she walked on; and still she went, leaving one familiar object after another, slacking not, pausing not, till reddening daylight found her many a long mile from all traces of any familiar objects upon the open highway. ❶

She had often been, with her mistress, to visit some connections in the little town of T—, not far from the Ohio River, and knew the road well. ❷ To go thither, to escape across the Ohio River, were the first hurried outlines of her plan of escape; beyond that she could only hope in God . . .

GUIDED READING

WORD HELP

conceive imagine
desolate alone
forlorn unhappy
slacking slowing down
thither there
constrained forced
composedly calmly

❶ ***What detail tells you how long Eliza has walked up to this point?***

❷ ***Why do you think she chooses that escape route?***

ELA **Reading 8.3** Students read and respond to historically or culturally significant works of literature that reflect and enhance their studies of history and social science.

CONNECTING LITERATURE TO HISTORY

1. **Slaves had no legal rights. They were considered to be property, not human beings.** How do the actions and dialogue in this passage contradict these ideas about slaves?
2. **Frederick Douglass, Sojourner Truth, and other former slaves wrote narratives about their experiences. Yet these true stories did not have as much impact as Stowe's novel.** Why do you think this fictional story about slavery had more impact than true slave narratives?

Cross-Discipline Activity: Literature

Standards Proficiency

Uncle Tom's Cabin Book Jacket

HSS 8.9.4; HSS **Analysis Skills:** HI 1

Materials: sample book jacket or book jacket template, heavy white paper, colored markers

1. Have each student create a book jacket for *Uncle Tom's Cabin*. Provide either a model book jacket or a book jacket template for students to use.
2. Students should fold a piece of paper to create front and back covers, a spine, and end flaps.
3. On the front cover, students should provide the title and author of the novel, a promotional tag line, and a strong image. On the end flaps, students should provide a brief summary of the book, followed by a brief biography of the author. On the spine, students should list the title and author. On the back cover, students should provide comments about the book's influence. **LS Verbal/Linguistic, Visual/Spatial**

Alternative Assessment Handbook, Rubrics 3: Artwork; and 42: Writing to Inform

Answers

Guided Reading **1.** *mentions of having gone many a mile, of leaving familiar sights behind, of the day ending;* **2.** *because she has been there once before so she is slightly familiar with it*

Connecting Literature to History
1. *The passage shows that slaves have feelings for others and themselves, just like all human beings.* **2.** *Fiction can be made more dramatic and interesting than real-life accounts.*

Trouble in Kansas

SECTION 2

If YOU were there...

You live on a New England farm in 1855. You often think about moving West. But the last few harvests have been bad, and you can't afford it. Now the Emigrant Aid Society offers to help you get to Kansas. To bring in antislavery voters like you, they'll give you a wagon, livestock, and farm machines. Still, you know that Kansas might be dangerous.

Would you decide to risk settling in Kansas?

BUILDING BACKGROUND The argument over the extension of slavery grew stronger and more bitter. It dominated American politics in the mid-1800s. Laws that tried to find compromises ended by causing more violence. The bloodiest battleground of this period was in Kansas.

Election of 1852

Four leading candidates for the Democratic presidential nomination emerged in 1852. It became clear that none of them would win a majority of votes. Frustrated delegates at the Democratic National Convention turned to **Franklin Pierce**, a little-known politician from New Hampshire. Pierce promised to honor the Compromise

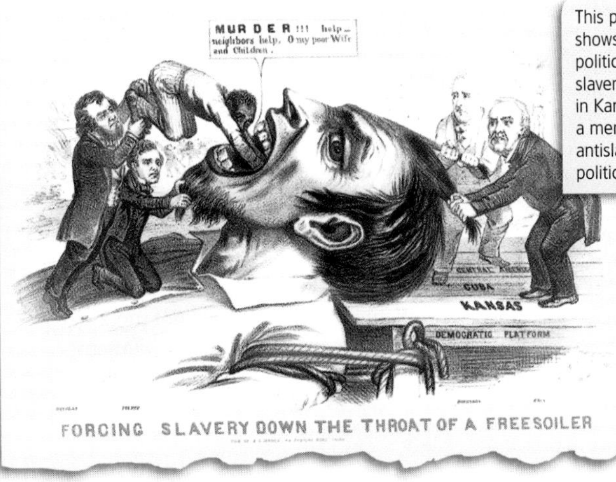

MURDER!!! help— neighbors help. O my poor Wife and Children.
CUBA
KANSAS
DEMOCRATIC PLATFORM
FORCING SLAVERY DOWN THE THROAT OF A FREESOILER

This political cartoon shows pro-slavery politicians forcing slavery on a settler in Kansas who is a member of the antislavery Free-Soil political party.

What You Will Learn...

Main Ideas

1. The debate over the expansion of slavery influenced the election of 1852.
2. The Kansas-Nebraska Act allowed voters to allow or prohibit slavery.
3. Pro-slavery and antislavery groups clashed violently in what became known as "Bleeding Kansas."

The Big Idea

The Kansas-Nebraska Act heightened tensions in the conflict over slavery.

Key Terms and People

Franklin Pierce, *p. 445*
Stephen Douglas, *p. 446*
Kansas-Nebraska Act, *p. 447*
Pottawatomie Massacre, *p. 449*
Charles Sumner, *p. 449*
Preston Brooks, *p. 449*

HSS 8.9.5 Analyze the significance of the States' Rights Doctrine, the Missouri Compromise (1820), the Wilmot Proviso (1846), the Compromise of 1850, Henry Clay's role in the Missouri Compromise and the Compromise of 1850, the Kansas-Nebraska Act (1854), the *Dred Scott* v. *Sandford* decision (1857), and the Lincoln-Douglas debates (1858).

HSS 8.10.2 Trace the boundaries constituting the North and the South, the geographical differences between the two regions, and the differences between agrarians and industrialists.

Preteach

Bellringer

If YOU were there . . . Use the **Daily Bellringer Transparency** to help students answer the question.

Daily Bellringer Transparency, Section 2

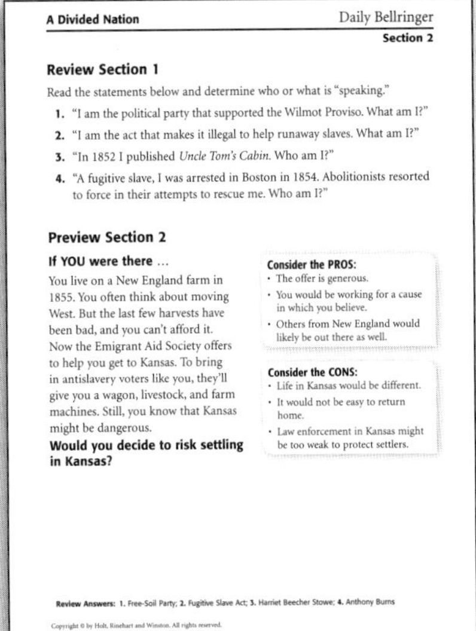

A Divided Nation — Daily Bellringer, Section 2

Review Section 1

Read the statements below and determine who or what is "speaking."

1. "I am the political party that supported the Wilmot Proviso. What am I?"
2. "I am the act that makes it illegal to help runaway slaves. What am I?"
3. "In 1852 I published *Uncle Tom's Cabin*. Who am I?"
4. "A fugitive slave, I was arrested in Boston in 1854. Abolitionists resorted to force in their attempts to rescue me. Who am I?"

Preview Section 2

If YOU were there ...

You live on a New England farm in 1855. You often think about moving West. But the last few harvests have been bad, and you can't afford it. Now the Emigrant Aid Society offers to help you get to Kansas. To bring in antislavery voters like you, they'll give you a wagon, livestock, and farm machines. Still, you know that Kansas might be dangerous.

Would you decide to risk settling in Kansas?

Consider the PROS:
- The offer is generous.
- You would be working for a cause in which you believe.
- Others from New England would likely be out there as well.

Consider the CONS:
- Life in Kansas would be different.
- It would not be easy to return home.
- Law enforcement in Kansas might be too weak to protect settlers.

Review Answers: 1. Free-Soil Party; 2. Fugitive Slave Act; 3. Harriet Beecher Stowe; 4. Anthony Burns

Academic Vocabulary

Review with students the high-use academic term in this section.

implications things that are inferred or deduced (p. 447)

CRF: Vocabulary Builder Activity, Section 2

Teach the Big Idea: Master the Standards

Standards Proficiency

Trouble in Kansas

HSS 8.9.5, 8.10.2; **HSS Analysis Skills:** CS 1, HR 5, HI 1, HI 2

1. **Teach** Ask students the Main Idea questions to teach this section.
2. **Apply** Have each student list the section's blue and red headings on a piece of paper and leave room below each heading. Then instruct students to make short entries under each heading that detail the significant people, places, and events that contributed to violence in Kansas and in the Senate. **LS Verbal/Linguistic**
3. **Review** As you review the section's main ideas, have students share their notes on the issues and events that led to violence.
4. **Practice/Homework** Have each student write a one-paragraph radio news report for each of the blue headings in the section. Have volunteers present their reports to the class.

Alternative Assessment Handbook, Rubrics 37: Writing Assignments; and 42: Writing to Inform

Standards Focus

HSS 8.9.5

Means: Analyze the significance of the Kansas-Nebraska Act of 1854.

Matters: The Kansas-Nebraska Act further inflamed the sectional tensions over slavery.

HSS 8.10.2

Means: Describe how differences between the North and the South contributed to violence in Kansas and increased sectional tensions.

Matters: Differences between the regions of the North and the South contributed to tensions over slavery.

Direct Teach

Main Idea

1 Election of 1852

The debate over the expansion of slavery influenced the election of 1852.

Explain Whom did the Democrats choose as their presidential candidate in 1852, and why? *Franklin Pierce; because none of the other nominees could win a majority of votes, and southerners trusted Pierce on the issue of slavery because he promised to honor the Compromise of 1850 and enforce the Fugitive Slave Act*

Analyze How did the Whigs' decision to nominate Winfield Scott as their candidate in 1852 backfire? *Scott's limited support of the Compromise of 1850 led southern voters to distrust him, and he lost.*

Map Transparency: From Compromise to Conflict

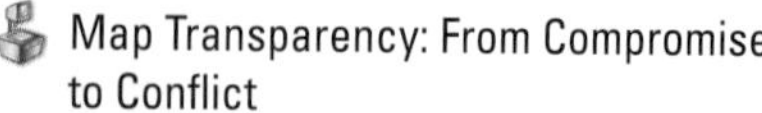

HSS 8.9.5; HSS **Analysis Skills:** HI 1, HI 2

Answers

Focus on Reading *Everything is a fact except for the following phrase, which is an opinion—"this had been a good strategy."*

Reading Check *The debate over the expansion of slavery was the main issue, and Pierce's support of the Compromise of 1850 and Fugitive Slave Act helped him win the election.*

From Compromise to Conflict

The Missouri Compromise, 1820
Under the Missouri Compromise of 1820, there are an equal number of free states (orange) and slave states (green).

Free state
Free territory
Slave state
Slave territory

The Compromise of 1850
The Compromise of 1850 allowed for one more free state than slave state, but also passed a strict fugitive slave law.

of 1850 and the Fugitive Slave Act. Therefore, southerners trusted Pierce on the issue of slavery.

FOCUS ON READING
What facts and what opinions are mentioned in this paragraph?

The opposing Whigs also held their convention in 1852. In other presidential elections, they had nominated well-known former generals such as William Henry Harrison and Zachary Taylor. This had been a good strategy, as both men had won. The Whigs decided to choose another war hero. They passed over the current president, Millard Fillmore, because they believed that his strict enforcement of the Fugitive Slave Act would cost votes. Instead, they chose Winfield Scott, a Mexican War hero. Southerners did not trust Scott, however, because he had not fully supported the Compromise of 1850.

Pierce won the election of 1852 by a large margin. Many Whigs viewed the election as a painful defeat, not just for their candidate, but for their party.

READING CHECK **Drawing Conclusions** What issues determined the outcome of the presidential election of 1852?

The Kansas-Nebraska Act

In his inaugural address, President Pierce expressed his hope that the slavery issue had been put to rest "and that no sectional . . . excitement may again threaten the durability [stability] of our institutions." Less than a year later, however, a proposal to build a railroad to the West coast helped revive the slavery controversy and opened a new period of sectional conflict.

Douglas and the Railroad

Ever since entering Congress in the mid-1840s, **Stephen Douglas** had supported the idea of building a railroad to the Pacific Ocean. Douglas favored a line running from Chicago. The first step toward building such a railroad would be organizing what remained of the Louisiana Purchase into a federal territory. The Missouri Compromise required that this land be free territory and eventually free states.

Southerners in Congress did not support Douglas's plan, recommending a southern route for the railroad. Their preferred line

Differentiating Instruction for Universal Access

Learners Having Difficulty — Reaching Standards

1. Draw the graphic organizer for students to see. Omit the blue, italicized answers.
2. Have each student copy the graphic organizer and complete it by describing the Kansas-Nebraska Act and the events that resulted. LS **Visual/Spatial**

HSS 8.9.5; HSS **Analysis Skills:** HI 1, HI 2

Alternative Assessment Handbook, Rubric 13: Graphic Organizers

Kansas-Nebraska Act
- **When passed:** *1854*
- **What it did:** *divided rest of Louisiana Purchase into Kansas and Nebraska territories*
- **How it dealt with slavery:** *removed Missouri Compromise's limit on slavery north of 36°30′ latitude; let residents vote whether to allow slavery*

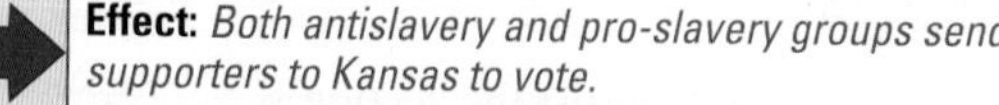

Effect: *Both antislavery and pro-slavery groups send supporters to Kansas to vote.*

Effect: *With help from Missouri voters, pro-slavery forces gain control of legislature. Antislavery forces form own legislature in response.*

Effect: *Pro-slavery forces try to arrest antislavery government, leading to the Sack of Lawrence and one death.*

Effect: *Abolitionist John Brown leads Pottawatomie Massacre, in which five pro-slavery men are killed.*

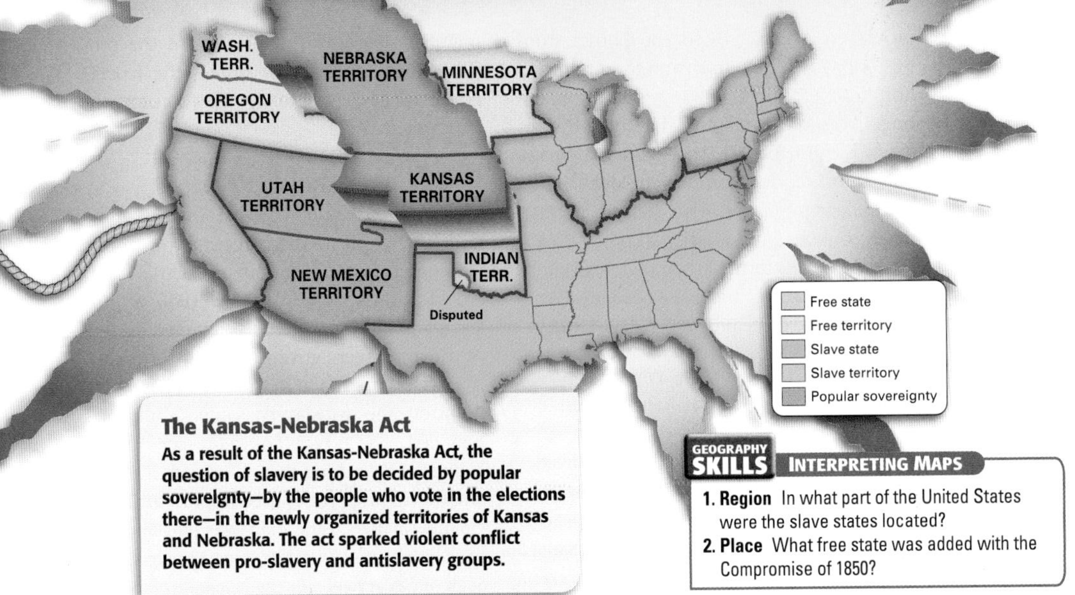

The Kansas-Nebraska Act

As a result of the Kansas-Nebraska Act, the question of slavery is to be decided by popular soverelgnty—by the people who vote in the elections there—in the newly organized territories of Kansas and Nebraska. The act sparked violent conflict between pro-slavery and antislavery groups.

GEOGRAPHY SKILLS **INTERPRETING MAPS**

1. **Region** In what part of the United States were the slave states located?
2. **Place** What free state was added with the Compromise of 1850?

ran from New Orleans, across Texas and New Mexico Territory, to southern California. Determined to have the railroad start in Chicago, Douglas asked a few key southern senators to support his plan. They agreed to do so if the new territory west of Missouri was opened to slavery.

Two New Territories

In January 1854, Douglas introduced what became the **Kansas-Nebraska Act**, a plan that would divide the remainder of the Louisiana Purchase into two territories—Kansas and Nebraska—and allow the people in each territory to decide on the question of slavery. The act would eliminate the Missouri Compromise's restriction on slavery north of the 36° 30′ line.

Antislavery northerners were outraged by the implications. Some believed the proposal was part of a terrible plot to turn free territory into a "dreary region . . . inhabited by masters and slaves." All across the North, citizens attended protest meetings and sent anti-Nebraska petitions to Congress.

Even so, with strong southern support—and with Douglas and President Pierce pressuring their fellow Democrats to vote for it—the measure passed both houses of Congress and was signed into law on May 30, 1854. Lost amid all the controversy over the territorial bill was Douglas's proposed railroad to the Pacific Ocean. Congress would not approve the construction of such a railroad until 1862.

Kansas Divided

Antislavery and pro-slavery groups rushed their supporters to Kansas. One of the people who spoke out strongly against slavery in Kansas was Senator Seward.

> "Gentlemen of the Slave States ... I accept [your challenge] in ... the cause of freedom. We will engage in competition for ... Kansas, and God give the victory to the side which is stronger in numbers as it is in right."
>
> —William Henry Seward, quoted in *The Impending Crisis, 1848–1861* by David M. Potter

Elections for the Kansas territorial legislature were held in March 1855. Almost 5,000

ACADEMIC VOCABULARY
implications things that are inferred or deduced

• Direct Teach •

Main Idea

❷ The Kansas-Nebraska Act

The Kansas-Nebraska Act allowed voters to allow or prohibit slavery.

Describe What were the main points of the Kansas-Nebraska Act? *divided the new territory into Kansas and Nebraska territories; popular sovereignty to decide slavery; Missouri Compromise slavery restriction removed*

Identify Cause and Effect What were some immediate results of the act? *Both antislavery and pro-slavery forces rushed supporters to Kansas to vote against or for slavery; led to formation of two governments.*

Predict What problems do you think might result from having two territorial legislatures? *confusion over laws, lawlessness, lack of central authority, possibly violence*

CRF: Biography Activity: Stephen Douglas

HSS 8.9.5, 8.10.2; **HSS Analysis Skills:** CS 1, HI 1, HI 2

Connect to Geography

Meanwhile, in Nebraska Unlike in Kansas, slavery did not become an issue in Nebraska because of the territory's location. The region was too far north to support the type of agriculture that relied on slave labor.

Advanced Learners/GATE **Exceeding Standards**

1. Organize students into small groups. Ask the groups to imagine that they are congressional committees formed after the Sack of Lawrence and the Pottawatomie Massacre. Their task is to discover how the slavery issue led to the outbreak of violence in Kansas.
2. Have each group prepare a report on the topic. The report should (a) describe the events that occurred in Kansas; (b) recommend what steps, if any, could have been taken to avoid the violence; and (c) recommend which Kansas legislature the U.S. government should support, if either.
3. Organize a mock congressional hearing at which the groups present their reports.

LS Logical/Mathematical, Verbal/Linguistic

HSS 8.9.5, 8.10.2; **HSS Analysis Skills:** HI 1, HI 2

Alternative Assessment Handbook, Rubrics 14: Group Activity; and 42: Writing to Inform

Answers

Interpreting Maps **1.** *the South* **2.** *California*

Direct Teach

Main Idea

3 Bleeding Kansas

Pro-slavery and antislavery groups clashed violently in what became known as "Bleeding Kansas."

Describe What was the situation in Kansas in early 1856? *two opposing governments and an angry and armed populace*

Summarize What occurred during the Sack of Lawrence? *A pro-slavery posse came to arrest leaders of the antislavery government and, not finding them, took out their anger by burning and looting the city.*

Identify Cause and Effect How did the Sack of Lawrence lead to further violence? *It angered abolitionist John Brown, who led an attack that became known as the Pottawatomie Massacre, during which he and his men killed five pro-slavery men.*

Evaluate Why do you think the situation in Kansas led to violence in the Senate chambers? *The violence and the slavery issue so inflamed people that they lost control of themselves.*

CRF: Primary Source Activity: Charles Sumner on the Crime against Kansas

HSS 8.9.5; HSS **Analysis Skills:** CS 1, HR 5, HI 1, HI 2

pro-slavery voters crossed the border from Missouri, voted in Kansas, and then returned home. As a result, the new legislature had a huge pro-slavery majority. The members of the legislature passed strict laws that made it a crime to question slaveholders' rights and said that those who helped fugitive slaves could be put to death. In protest, antislavery Kansans formed their own legislature 25 miles away in Topeka. President Pierce only recognized the pro-slavery legislature.

READING CHECK **Analyzing** Why did northerners dislike the Kansas-Nebraska Act?

Bleeding Kansas

By early 1856 Kansas had two opposing governments, and the population was angry. Settlers had moved to Kansas to homestead in peace, but the controversy over slavery began to affect everyone.

In April 1856, a congressional committee arrived in Kansas to decide which government was legitimate. Although committee members declared the election of the pro-slavery legislature to be unfair, the federal government did not follow their recommendations.

Attack on Lawrence

The new pro-slavery settlers owned guns, and antislavery settlers received weapons shipments from friends in the East. Then, violence broke out. In May 1856 a pro-slavery grand jury in Kansas charged leaders of the antislavery government with treason. About 800 men rode to the city of Lawrence to arrest the antislavery leaders, but they had fled. The posse took its anger out on Lawrence by setting fires, looting buildings, and destroying presses used to print antislavery newspapers. One man was killed in the pro-slavery attack that became known as the Sack of Lawrence.

John Brown's Response

Abolitionist John Brown was from New England, but he and some of his sons had moved to Kansas in 1855. The Sack of Lawrence made him determined to "fight fire with fire" and to "strike terror in the hearts of the pro-slavery people." On the night of May 24, 1856, along Pottawatomie Creek, Brown and his men killed five pro-slavery men in Kansas in what became known as

"Bleeding Kansas"

Abolitionists and pro-slavery forces clashed in Kansas, killing many people. Shown here is a group of abolitionists who took the law into their own hands to free one of their group from prison.

Why might these men have fought against slavery?

John Noy was imprisoned for his abolitionist activities but was freed by other abolitionists

Collaborative Learning

Standards Proficiency

The Nightly News from Kansas

HSS 8.9.5, 8.10.2; HSS **Analysis Skills:** CS 1, HR 5, HI 1, HI 2

1. Organize students into five groups and have each group create a TV newscast about one of the following: Kansas-Nebraska Act, formation of two Kansas governments, Sack of Lawrence, Pottawatomie Massacre, or the caning of Charles Sumner.
2. Each group should assign members roles, such as anchors, on-the-spot reporters, interviewees, writers, and so on. The TV report should provide coverage of the assigned event as well as interviews with key figures and others. Encourage the groups to include visual aids in their reports.
3. Have each group perform its newscast for the class. After each newscast, point out any missing information or inaccuracies.

LS Interpersonal, Kinesthetic

Alternative Assessment Handbook, Rubrics 14: Group Activity; and 33: Skits and Reader's Theater

Answers

"Bleeding Kansas" *felt it was unfair, cruel, unjust, and immoral*

Reading Check *It eliminated the Missouri Compromise's restriction on slavery north of 36°30′.*

the **Pottawatomie Massacre**. Brown and his men dragged the pro-slavery men out of their cabins and killed them with swords. The abolitionist band managed to escape capture. Brown declared that his actions had been ordered by God.

Kansas collapsed into civil war, and about 200 people were killed. The events in "Bleeding Kansas" became national front-page stories. In September 1856, a new territorial governor arrived and began to restore order.

The cartoon above shows Preston Brooks beating Charles Sumner with his cane. Sumner's only protection is a quill pen symbolically representing the law.

Brooks Attacks Sumner

Congress also reacted to the violence of the Sack of Lawrence. Senator **Charles Sumner** of Massachusetts criticized pro-slavery people in Kansas and personally insulted Andrew Pickens Butler, a pro-slavery senator from South Carolina. Representative **Preston Brooks**, a relative of Butler's, responded strongly. On May 22, 1856, Brooks used a walking cane to beat Sumner unconscious in the Senate chambers.

Dozens of southerners sent Brooks new canes, but northerners were outraged and called the attacker "Bully Brooks". Brooks only had to pay a $300 fine to the federal court. It took Sumner three years before he was well enough to return to his Senate duties.

READING CHECK **Summarizing** What were some of the results of the intense division in Kansas?

SUMMARY AND PREVIEW The Kansas-Nebraska Act produced a national uproar. In the next section you will read about divisions in political parties.

Section 2 Assessment

go.hrw.com
Online Quiz
KEYWORD: SS8 HP14

Reviewing Ideas, Terms, and People HSS 8.9.5, 8.10.2

1. a. **Identify** What issues influenced the outcome of the election of 1852?
   b. **Draw Conclusions** Why did northern and southern Democrats support **Franklin Pierce**?
2. a. **Recall** What did the **Kansas-Nebraska Act** do?
   b. **Explain** Why did antislavery and pro-slavery groups encourage people to move to Kansas?
   c. **Evaluate** Would you have supported or opposed the Kansas-Nebraska Act? Why?
3. a. **Describe** What was the **Pottawatomie Massacre**?
   b. **Analyze** How did **Charles Sumner**'s views on "Bleeding Kansas" create conflict?
   c. **Elaborate** Do you think **Preston Brooks**'s punishment was reasonable? Why or why not?

Critical Thinking

4. **Sequencing** Copy the graphic organizer at the top of the right column onto your own sheet of paper. Use it to show events that led to violence in Kansas.

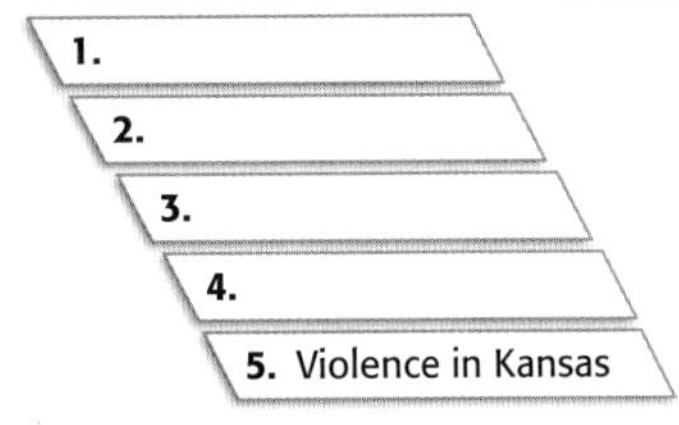

FOCUS ON WRITING

5. **Taking Notes on the Trouble in Kansas** Make some notes on the election of 1852, the Kansas-Nebraska Act, and the events in Kansas. Decide how your character feels about each of these. How do these events affect your character?

Section 2 Assessment Answers

1. a. Fugitive Slave Act, Compromise of 1850
   b. He promised to honor the Compromise of 1850 and the Fugitive Slave Act.
2. a. created two new territories, in which popular sovereignty would decide the slavery issue; eliminated the Missouri Compromise's restriction on slavery north of 36°30′ latitude
   b. to try to make Kansas a free or slave state
   c. possible answers—yes, gave the people the power; no, allowed the expansion of slavery
3. a. 1856 incident in which John Brown led a group that killed five pro-slavery men
   b. His criticisms of pro-slavery Kansans and of a pro-slavery senator led a legislator to cane him senseless in the Senate chambers.
   c. possible answer—unreasonable, because Sumner could not work for three years
4. (1) election of Democrat Franklin Pierce as president; (2) Kansas-Nebraska Act; (3) rush of antislavery and pro-slavery activists to Kansas; (4) Kansas divided, with two opposing governments and angry, armed populace
5. Students should address each of the major events in this section.

Direct Teach

Info to Know

John Brown's Northern Support People on both sides of the slavery issue supported the use of violence. For example, many antislavery northerners considered John Brown a hero. In 1857 several wealthy Bostonians agreed to provide Brown with financial support so that he could organize a small army in the event that violence in Kansas continued. Businessperson John Carter Brown stated that he was glad there were "some Northern men true to the great cause of freedom," and he gave $100 to support Brown's cause.

Review & Assess

Close

Have students compare and contrast northern and southern views of the Kansas-Nebraska Act and then summarize the events that followed its passage.

Review

Online Quiz, Section 2

Assess

SE Section 2 Assessment

PASS: Section 2 Quiz

Alternative Assessment Handbook

Reteach/Classroom Intervention

California Standards Review Workbook

Interactive Reader and Study Guide, Section 2

Interactive Skills Tutor CD-ROM

Answers

Reading Check *Two opposing governments formed, Kansans became angry, and violence broke out in Kansas and in Congress.*

Preteach

Bellringer

If YOU were there . . . Use the **Daily Bellringer Transparency** to help students answer the question.

 Daily Bellringer Transparency, Section 3

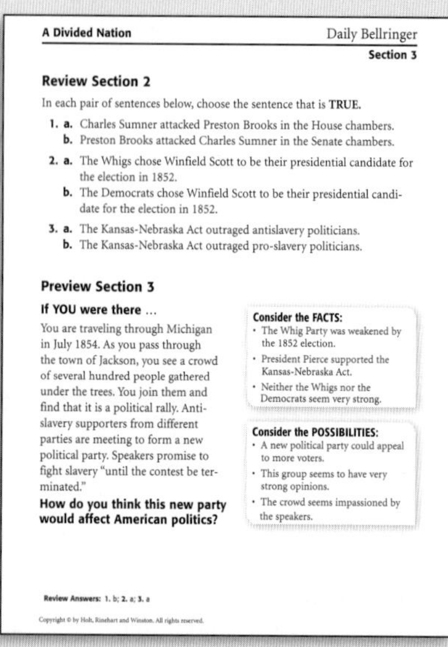

A Divided Nation — Daily Bellringer **Section 3**

Review Section 2

In each pair of sentences below, choose the sentence that is **TRUE.**

1. **a.** Charles Sumner attacked Preston Brooks in the House chambers.
   b. Preston Brooks attacked Charles Sumner in the Senate chambers.
2. **a.** The Whigs chose Winfield Scott to be their presidential candidate for the election in 1852.
   b. The Democrats chose Winfield Scott to be their presidential candidate for the election in 1852.
3. **a.** The Kansas-Nebraska Act outraged antislavery politicians.
   b. The Kansas-Nebraska Act outraged pro-slavery politicians.

Preview Section 3

If YOU were there ...

You are traveling through Michigan in July 1854. As you pass through the town of Jackson, you see a crowd of several hundred people gathered under the trees. You join them and find that it is a political rally. Antislavery supporters from different parties are meeting to form a new political party. Speakers promise to fight slavery "until the contest be terminated."

How do you think this new party would affect American politics?

Consider the FACTS:
- The Whig Party was weakened by the 1852 election.
- President Pierce supported the Kansas-Nebraska Act.
- Neither the Whigs nor the Democrats seem very strong.

Consider the POSSIBILITIES:
- A new political party could appeal to more voters.
- This group seems to have very strong opinions.
- The crowd seems impassioned by the speakers.

Review Answers: 1. b; 2. a; 3. a

Academic Vocabulary

Review with students the high-use academic term in this section.

complex difficult, not simple (p. 451)

CRF: Vocabulary Builder Activity, Section 3

Standards Focus

HSS 8.10.4

Means: Describe the importance of Abraham Lincoln's "House Divided" speech.

Matters: Lincoln stated that he believed the nation would survive but only if it ceased to be divided. Today the nation is strong and unified, having survived the test of the Civil War.

SECTION 3

Political Divisions

What You Will Learn...

Main Ideas

1. Political parties in the United States underwent change due to the movement to expand slavery.
2. The *Dred Scott* decision created further division over the issue of slavery.
3. The Lincoln-Douglas debates brought much attention to the conflict over slavery.

The Big Idea

The split over the issue of slavery intensified due to political division and judicial decisions.

Key Terms and People

Republican Party, *p. 450*
James Buchanan, *p. 450*
John C. Frémont, *p. 451*
Dred Scott, *p. 451*
Roger B. Taney, *p. 452*
Abraham Lincoln, *p. 452*
Lincoln-Douglas debates, *p. 453*
Freeport Doctrine, *p. 454*

HSS 8.10.4 Discuss Abraham Lincoln's presidency and his significant writings and speeches and their relationship to the Declaration of Independence, such as his "House Divided" speech (1858), Gettysburg Address (1863), Emancipation Proclamation (1863), and inaugural addresses (1861 and 1865).

If YOU were there...

You are traveling through Michigan in July 1854. As you pass through the town of Jackson, you see a crowd of several hundred people gathered under the trees. You join them and find that it is a political rally. Antislavery supporters from different parties are meeting to form a new political party. Speakers promise to fight slavery "until the contest be terminated."

How do you think this new party will affect American politics?

BUILDING BACKGROUND The slavery question continued to divide the country and lead to violence. The issue not only dominated American politics in the mid-1800s but also brought changes in the makeup of American political parties.

Political Parties Undergo Change

Democrat Stephen Douglas had predicted that the Kansas-Nebraska Act would "raise a . . . storm." He was right. The Kansas-Nebraska Act brought the slavery issue back into the national spotlight. Some Whigs, Democrats, Free-Soilers, and abolitionists joined in 1854 to form the **Republican Party**, a political party united against the spread of slavery in the West.

Democrats were in trouble. Those who supported the Kansas-Nebraska Act were not re-elected. The Whig Party also fell apart when northern and southern Whigs refused to work together. A senator from Connecticut complained, "The Whig Party has been killed off . . . by that miserable Nebraska business." Some Whigs and Democrats joined the American Party, also known as the Know-Nothing Party. At the party's convention, delegates argued over slavery, then chose former president Millard Fillmore as their candidate for the election of 1856.

The Democrats knew they could not choose a strong supporter of the Kansas-Nebraska Act, such as President Pierce or Senator Douglas. They nominated **James Buchanan** of Pennsylvania. Buchanan had a great deal of political experience as Polk's secretary of state. Most

Teach the Big Idea: Master the Standards

Standards Proficiency

Political Divisions

HSS 8.10.4; HSS **Analysis Skills:** HR 5, HI 1

Standard English Mastery

1. **Teach** Ask students the Main Idea questions to teach this section.
2. **Apply** Ask students to imagine that they are abolitionists in the 1850s. Have each student write three short letters to a fellow abolitionist in Great Britain. The letters should describe the changes in U.S. political parties, the *Dred Scott* decision, and the Lincoln-Douglas debates. Tell students to describe the events and to identify various groups' views of them. LS **Verbal/Linguistic**
3. **Review** As you review the section's main ideas, have volunteers read their letters aloud. Correct errors to improve students' use of standard English.
4. **Practice/Homework** Have each student write a fourth letter predicting how these events might affect the nation's future.

Alternative Assessment Handbook, Rubrics 25: Personal Letters; and 41: Writing to Express importantly, he had been in Great Britain as ambassador during the Kansas-Nebraska Act dispute and had not been involved in the debate.

At their first nominating convention, the Republicans chose explorer **John C. Frémont** as their candidate. He had little political experience, but he stood against the spread of slavery. The public saw Republicans as a single-issue party. They had almost no supporters outside of the free states.

On election day, Buchanan won 14 of the 15 slave states and became the new president. Frémont won 11 of the 16 free states. Fillmore won only one state—Maryland. Buchanan had won the election.

READING CHECK **Summarizing** What were the major political parties in the election of 1856, and who was the candidate for each party?

Dred Scott Decision

Just two days after Buchanan became president, the Supreme Court issued a historic ruling about slavery. News of the decision threw the country back into crisis. The Court reviewed and decided the complex case involving an enslaved man named **Dred Scott**.

ACADEMIC VOCABULARY
complex difficult, not simple

Dred Scott Sues for Freedom

Dred Scott was the slave of Dr. John Emerson, an army surgeon who lived in St. Louis, Missouri. In the 1830s, Emerson had taken Scott on tours of duty in Illinois and the Wisconsin Territory. After they returned to Missouri, the doctor died, and Scott became the slave of Emerson's widow. In 1846 Scott sued for his freedom in the Missouri state courts, arguing that he had become free when he lived in free territory. Though a lower court ruled in

SUPREME COURT DECISIONS

Dred Scott v. Sandford (1857)

Background of the Case Born a slave in Virginia, Dred Scott moved with his slaveholder to the free state of Illinois and then to the Wisconsin Territory. After returning to the South, Scott sued for his freedom. He claimed that because he had lived in a state that banned slavery, he was no longer a slave.

The Court's Ruling
The Court ruled that African Americans, whether free or slave, were not considered citizens of the United States, and therefore had no right to sue in federal court. It also decided that the Missouri Compromise was unconstitutional.

The Court's Reasoning
Chief Justice Roger B. Taney wrote in the majority opinion that the Court did not believe that African Americans were included in the Constitution's definition of citizens and that they "had no rights which the white man was bound to respect." Addressing a side issue in the case, the opinion also stated that Congress could not outlaw slavery in the territories. This struck down the Missouri Compromise, which had made slavery illegal in territories north of the 36°30′ dividing line.

Why It Matters
The *Dred Scott* case was seen as a setback to abolitionist ideas against slavery. It reduced the status of free African Americans and upheld the view of slaves as property without rights or protection under the Constitution. It also took from Congress the power to ban slavery in its territories, which would aid the spread of slavery in new states. Because of its pro-slavery decision, the reputation of the Court suffered greatly in parts of the North.

ANALYSIS SKILL **ANALYZING INFORMATION**

1. Why do you think the Court ruled that African Americans had no access to federal courts?
2. How did this case affect abolitionist efforts?

Direct Teach

Main Idea

1 Political Parties Undergo Change

Political parties in the United States underwent change due to the movement to expand slavery.

Identify Members of which groups united to form the new Republican Party? *Whigs, Democrats, Free-Soilers, abolitionists*

Elaborate Who won the election of 1856, and what advantages did he have over the other candidates? *James Buchanan of Pennsylvania; He was experienced in politics and was overseas during the heat of the Kansas-Nebraska Act debate, so he was not connected to one side or the other in people's minds.*

HSS 8.9.5; HSS **Analysis Skills:** HI 1, HI 2

Answers

Analyzing Information 1. *because the Court did not believe that African Americans, free or enslaved, were included in the Constitution's definition of citizens;* **2.** *was a setback to abolitionist efforts, particularly in stopping the expansion of slavery*

Reading Check *Republicans, John C. Frémont; Democrats, James Buchanan; Know-Nothing Party, Millard Fillmore*

Differentiating Instruction for Universal Access

Learners Having Difficulty — Reaching Standards

1. Explain to students that the Kansas-Nebraska Act caused changes in the makeup of U.S. political parties.
2. Draw the graphic organizer for students to see. Omit the blue, italicized answers. Have students copy the graphic organizer and complete it by listing changes that occurred in U.S. political parties as a result of the Kansas-Nebraska Act. **LS Visual/Spatial**

HSS 8.9.5; HSS **Analysis Skills:** HI 1, HI 2

Alternative Assessment Handbook, Rubric 13: Graphic Organizers

Kansas-Nebraska Act

Republican Party	Democratic Party	Whig Party	Know-Nothing Party
Some members of the Whig, Democratic, and Free-Soil parties formed this party to oppose the spread of slavery.	*Most of those who voted for the act suffered politically; Buchanan, who had no connection to the act, was nominated in 1856.*	*Party fell apart when it became divided between northern and southern Whigs.*	*Some Whigs and Democrats joined this secretive party, which nominated former president Fillmore in 1856.*

Direct Teach

Main Idea

❷ *Dred Scott* Decision

The *Dred Scott* decision created further division over the issue of slavery.

Recall Who was Dred Scott, and why did he sue? *an enslaved man who sued for his freedom after his slaveholder died*

Summarize Why was the *Dred Scott* decision significant? *It increased sectional tensions, overturned the Missouri Compromise, increased the chance of the spread of slavery, and declared that African Americans were not citizens.*

Develop Briefly defend Dred Scott's right to freedom. *possible answers—All people born in the United States should be citizens; human beings have a right to freedom, and slavery is wrong; he had lived on free soil, and his slaveholder was dead.*

- **CRF:** Biography Activity: Dred Scott
- U.S. Supreme Court Case Studies: *Dred Scott* v. *Sanford* (1857)
- Quick Facts Transparency: A Growing Conflict
- HSS 8.9.5; HSS **Analysis Skills:** HI 1

Biography

Dred Scott (c. 1795–1858) Following the Supreme Court ruling in his case, Scott and his family were bought by Henry Blow, who freed them. Scott worked as a hotel porter in St. Louis until his death in 1858.

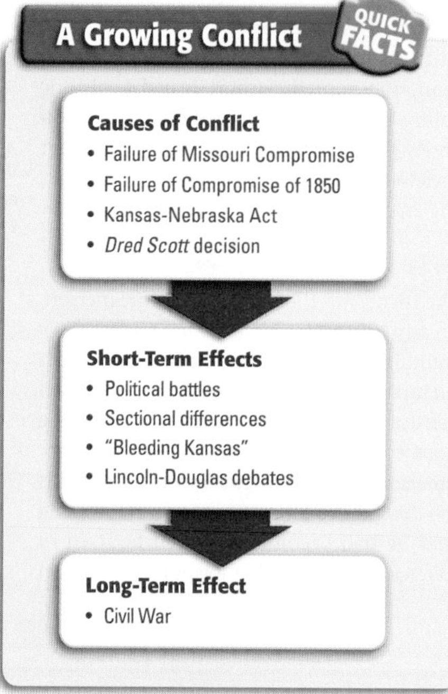

his favor, the Missouri Supreme Court overturned this ruling.

Scott's case reached the U.S. Supreme Court 11 years later, in 1857. The justices—a majority of whom were from the South—had three key issues before them. First, the Court had to rule on whether Scott was a citizen. Only citizens could sue in federal court. Second, the Court had to decide if his time living on free soil made him free. Third, the Court had to determine the constitutionality of prohibiting slavery in parts of the Louisiana Purchase.

The Supreme Court's Ruling

Chief Justice **Roger B. Taney** (TAW-nee), himself from a slaveholding family in Maryland, wrote the majority opinion in the *Dred Scott* decision in March 1857. First, he addressed the issue of Dred Scott's citizenship. Taney said the nation's founders believed that African Americans "had no rights which a white man was bound to respect." He therefore concluded that all African Americans, whether slave or free, were not citizens under the U.S. Constitution. Thus, Dred Scott did not have the right to file suit in federal court.

Taney also ruled on the other issues before the Court. As to whether Scott's residence on free soil made him free, Taney flatly said it did not. Because Scott had returned to the slave state of Missouri, the chief justice said, "his *status*, as free or slave, depended on the laws of Missouri."

Finally, Taney declared the Missouri Compromise restriction on slavery north of 36°30′ to be unconstitutional. He pointed out that the Fifth Amendment said no one could "be deprived of life, liberty, or property without due process of law." Because slaves were considered property, Congress could not prohibit someone from taking slaves into a federal territory. Under this ruling, Congress had no right to ban slavery in any federal territory.

Most white southerners cheered this decision. It "covers every question regarding slavery and settles it in favor of the South," reported a Georgia newspaper. Another newspaper, the New Orleans *Picayune*, assured its readers that the ruling put "the whole basis of the . . . Republican organization under the ban of law."

The ruling stunned many northerners. The Republicans were particularly upset because their platform in 1856 had argued that Congress held the right to ban slavery in the federal territories. Now the nation's highest court had ruled that Congress did not have this right.

Indeed, some northerners feared that the spread of slavery would not stop with the federal territories. Illinois lawyer **Abraham Lincoln** warned that a future Court ruling, or what he called "the next *Dred Scott* decision," would prohibit states from banning slavery.

Critical Thinking: Drawing Conclusions

Exceeding Standards

Interview with Dred Scott HSS 8.9.5; HSS Analysis Skills: HR 5, HI 1

1. Ask students to imagine that they are abolitionist reporters covering Dred Scott's case. They have been granted an exclusive interview with Dred Scott following the Supreme Court's ruling in the case.
2. Have each student use the information in the text to write a fictional interview with Scott. Students should ask Scott why he sued for his freedom, how the Supreme Court ruled on his case, and what his reaction to the decision was. Students should write both their questions and Scott's answers.
3. Have volunteers share their interviews with the class. LS **Verbal/Linguistic**
4. **Extend** Have students use the Declaration of Independence and the Fifth Amendment as a basis for a defense of Scott's freedom. LS **Logical/Mathematical, Verbal/Linguistic**

- Alternative Assessment Handbook, Rubrics 11: Discussions; and 37: Writing Assignments

Primary Source

SPEECH

A House Divided

In 1858 Abraham Lincoln gave a passionate speech to Illinois Republicans about the dangers of the disagreement over slavery. Some considered it a call for war.

"In my opinion, it [disagreement over slavery] will not cease [stop], until a crisis shall have been reached and passed. "A house divided against itself cannot stand." I believe this government cannot endure permanently half slave and half free. I do not expect the Union to be dissolved—I do not expect the house to fall—but I do expect it will cease to be divided."

This line is a paraphrase of a line in the Bible.

Lincoln expresses confidence that the Union will survive.

—Abraham Lincoln,
quoted in *Abraham Lincoln: Speeches and Writings 1832–1858* edited by Don E. Fehrenbacher

ANALYSIS SKILL ANALYZING PRIMARY SOURCES

What do you think Lincoln meant by "crisis"?

"We shall *lie down* pleasantly dreaming that the people of *Missouri* are on the verge of [close to] making their state *free;* and we shall *awake* to the *reality,* instead, that the 90 Supreme Court has made *Illinois* a *slave state.*"

—Abraham Lincoln, quoted in *The Collected Works of Abraham Lincoln*, edited by Roy P. Basler

READING CHECK **Summarizing** What were the major rulings of the *Dred Scott* decision?

Lincoln-Douglas Debates

In 1858 Illinois Republicans nominated Abraham Lincoln for the U.S. Senate. His opponent was Democrat Stephen Douglas, who had represented Illinois in the Senate since 1847. Lincoln challenged Douglas in what became the historic **Lincoln-Douglas debates.**

In each debate, Lincoln stressed that the central issue of the campaign was the spread of slavery in the West. He said that the Democrats were trying to spread slavery across the nation.

Lincoln talked about the *Dred Scott* decision. He said that African Americans were "entitled to all the natural rights" listed in the Declaration of Independence, specifically mentioning "the right to life, liberty, and the pursuit of happiness." However, Lincoln believed that African Americans were not necessarily the social or political equals of whites. Hoping to cost Lincoln votes, Douglas charged that Lincoln "thinks that the Negro is his brother . . ."

Douglas also criticized Lincoln for saying that the nation could not remain "half slave and half free." Douglas said that the statement revealed a Republican desire to make every state a free state. This, he warned, would only lead to "a dissolution [destruction] of the Union" and "warfare between the North and the South."

At the second debate, in the northern Illinois town of Freeport, Illinois, Lincoln pressed Douglas on the apparent contradiction between the Democrats' belief in popu-

THE IMPACT TODAY

Today political debates are televised and can be seen around the world.

Direct Teach

Main Idea

❸ Lincoln-Douglas Debates

The Lincoln-Douglas debates brought much attention to the conflict over slavery.

Recall What was Lincoln's response to the *Dred Scott* decision? *He said African Americans were "entitled to all the natural rights" listed in the Declaration of Independence, such as the "right to life, liberty, and the pursuit of happiness."*

Contrast How did Douglas oppose Lincoln's views on slavery and African Americans? *Douglas tried to shock voters by saying Lincoln thought African Americans were his brothers and wanted to make all states free.*

Elaborate Why do you think the Republican Party challenged Douglas's run for the Senate? *possible answer—thought his strong support of the Kansas-Nebraska Act might have weakened his chances for re-election*

CRF: Biography Activity: Stephen Douglas

CRF: Literature Activity: Chicago Speech of 1858 by Stephen Douglas

HSS 8.9.5; **HSS** **Analysis Skills:** HR 5, HI 1

Primary Source

A House Divided

Activity **Political Cartoon** Have each student create a political cartoon to illustrate Lincoln's main point in the "House Divided" speech. Students should use the line "A house divided against itself cannot stand" as the caption for their cartoons. **LS** **Visual/Spatial**

Critical Thinking: Comparing and Contrasting

Standards Proficiency

Contrasting Lincoln and Douglas

HSS 8.9.5; **HSS** **Analysis Skills:** HR 5, HI 1

1. Have each student write two paragraphs, one on Stephen Douglas and one on Abraham Lincoln. The paragraphs should examine how each man contributed to the political debate over slavery during this period.
2. Tell students to include information about the candidates' positions on slavery, popular sovereignty, state control versus federal control in the territories, and the *Dred Scott* decision. In addition, students should indicate which party supported each man in the Senate race of 1858.
3. Then have each student write a third paragraph comparing and contrasting the viewpoints of Douglas and Lincoln on the slavery issue.
4. Ask volunteers to read their paragraphs aloud to the class. **LS** **Verbal/Linguistic**

Alternative Assessment Handbook, Rubric 42: Writing to Inform

Answers

Analyzing Primary Sources *possible answers—secession; war*

Reading Check *Scott was not a citizen and could not sue in federal court; Scott's residence on free soil did not make him free; the Missouri Compromise's ban on slavery north of 36°30′ was unconstitutional.*

Direct Teach

Info to Know

The Lincoln-Douglas Debates The fact that Lincoln lost the Illinois race for U.S. Senate to Douglas did not necessarily indicate that his views were not popular with Illinois voters. At that time, state legislatures, and not the people, elected senators. Although Republicans held some seats in the Illinois legislature, Democrats had done well in the 1856 elections and were able to ensure that Douglas won the Senate seat.

go.hrw.com
Online Resources
KEYWORD: SS8 US14
ACTIVITY: Lincoln-Douglas Debates Graphic Organizer

Review & Assess

Close

Discuss the ways that the political parties chose to deal with the issue of slavery. Include views on popular sovereignty as well as state versus federal control in the territories.

Review

Online Quiz, Section 3

Assess

SE Section 3 Assessment
PASS: Section 3 Quiz
Alternative Assessment Handbook

Reteach/Classroom Intervention

California Standards Review Workbook
Interactive Reader and Study Guide, Section 3
Interactive Skills Tutor CD-ROM

Lincoln-Douglas Debates

Lincoln ran for the U.S. Senate in Illinois against Douglas in 1858. The two men debated seven times at various locations around the state. Lincoln lost the election but gained national recognition.

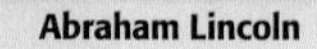
Abraham Lincoln

Stephen Douglas

lar sovereignty and the *Dred Scott* decision. Lincoln asked Douglas to explain how, if Congress could not ban slavery from a federal territory, Congress could allow the citizens of that territory to ban it.

Douglas responded that it did not matter what the Supreme Court decided about slavery. He argued that "the people have the lawful means to introduce it or exclude it as they please, for the reason that slavery cannot exist a day or an hour anywhere, unless it is supported by local police regulations."

This notion that the police would enforce the voters' decision if it contradicted the Supreme Court's decision in the Dred Scott case became known as the **Freeport Doctrine.**

The Freeport Doctrine put the slavery question back in the hands of American citizens. It helped Douglas win the Senate seat. Lincoln, while not victorious, made a strong important leader of the Republican Party.

READING CHECK **Drawing Inferences** Why did Abraham Lincoln make slavery's expansion the central issue of the Lincoln-Douglas debates?

SUMMARY AND PREVIEW The *Dred Scott* decision and the Lincoln-Douglas debates dealt with the conflict over slavery in the western territories. In the next section you will read about how the conflict broke apart the Union.

Section 3 Assessment

go.hrw.com
Online Quiz
KEYWORD: SS8 HP14

Reviewing Ideas, Terms, and People HSS 8.10.4

1. **a. Identify** What was the major issue of the newly formed **Republican Party**?
   b. Draw Conclusions How did the Kansas-Nebraska Act affect political parties?
   c. Elaborate Why do you think **James Buchanan** won the election of 1856?
2. **a. Identify** Who was **Roger B. Taney**, and why was he important?
   b. Draw Conclusions How did the ***Dred Scott* decision** affect the Missouri Compromise and the expansion of slavery?
   c. Predict What problems might result from the Supreme Court's ruling in the *Dred Scott* case?
3. **a. Recall** What was the major issue of the **Lincoln-Douglas debates**?
   b. Make Inferences Despite his loss in the election, how did Lincoln become the leader of the Republican Party?

Critical Thinking

4. **Summarizing** Copy the graphic organizer below onto your own paper. Use it to identify the issues involved in the *Dred Scott* case and the Supreme Court's rulings.

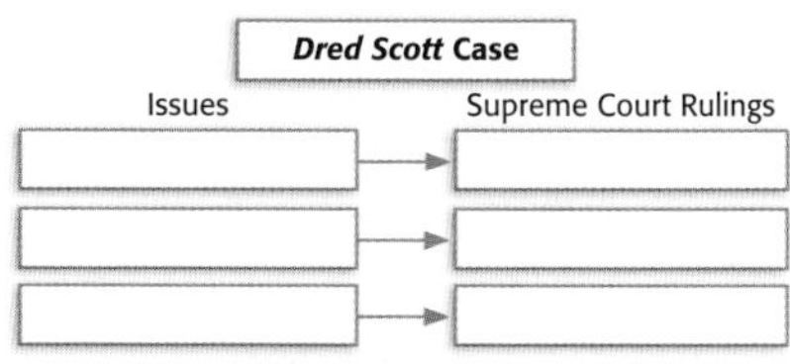

FOCUS ON WRITING

5. **Taking Notes on the Political Divisions** Make some notes on the Republican Party, the *Dred Scott* decision, and the Lincoln-Douglas debates. Decide how your character feels about each of these. How do these events affect your character?

Section 3 Assessment Answers

1. **a.** opposition to the spread of slavery
   b. led some to form the Republican Party; hurt northern Democrats who voted for the act; divided and then led to the end of the Whig Party; led some to join the Know-Nothing Party
   c. He had political experience but was not involved in the Kansas-Nebraska Act.
2. **a.** chief justice of the United States who wrote the majority opinion in the Dred Scott case
   b. overturned the Missouri Compromise, which opened all the territories to slavery
   c. more sectional tensions and conflict
3. **a.** spread of slavery in the West
   b. His strong showing in the debate gained him national prominence.
4. Issue: Was Scott a U.S. citizen? Ruling: no; Issue: Had Scott's time living in a free state made him a free man? Ruling: no; Issue: Was it constitutional to prohibit slavery in parts of the Louisiana Purchase? Ruling: no
5. Students should describe how the *Dred Scott* decision and the discussions in the Lincoln-Douglas debates would affect their characters.

Answers

Reading Check *He wanted to show Douglas's role in the Kansas-Nebraska Act and emphasize the Democrats' support of the spread of slavery*

The Nation Divides

SECTION 4

If YOU were there...

You work for the weekly newspaper in Harpers Ferry, Virginia. You strongly oppose slavery, but you think the question ought to be resolved by laws, not bloodshed. Now your paper has sent you to interview the famous abolitionist John Brown in prison. His raids in "Bleeding Kansas" killed several people. Now he is in jail for attacking a federal arsenal and taking weapons.

What questions would you ask John Brown?

BUILDING BACKGROUND Unpopular compromises and court decisions deepened the divisions between pro-slavery and antislavery advocates. The Lincoln-Douglas debates attracted more attention to the issue. As the disagreements grew, violence increased, though many Americans hoped to avoid it. But it was too late to keep the nation unified.

Raid on Harpers Ferry

In 1858 John Brown tried to start an uprising. He wanted to attack the federal arsenal in Virginia and seize weapons there. He planned to arm local slaves. Brown expected to kill or take hostage white southerners who stood in his way. He urged abolitionists to give him money so that he could support a small army. But after nearly two years, Brown's army had only about 20 men.

On the night of October 16, 1859, **John Brown's raid** began when he and his men took over the arsenal in Harpers Ferry, Virginia, in hopes of starting a slave rebellion. He sent several of his men into the countryside to get slaves to join him. However, enslaved African Americans did not come to Harpers Ferry, fearing punishment if they took part. Instead, local white southerners attacked Brown. Eight of his men and three local men were killed. Brown and some followers retreated to a firehouse.

Federal troops arrived in Harpers Ferry the following night. The next morning, Colonel Robert E. Lee ordered a squad of marines to storm the firehouse. In a matter of seconds, the marines killed two more of Brown's men and captured the rest—including Brown.

What You Will Learn...

Main Ideas

1. John Brown's raid on Harpers Ferry intensified the disagreement between free states and slave states.
2. The outcome of the election of 1860 divided the United States.
3. The dispute over slavery led the South to secede.

The Big Idea

The United States broke apart due to the growing conflict over slavery.

Key Terms and People

John Brown's raid, *p. 455*
John C. Breckinridge, *p. 457*
Constitutional Union Party, *p. 457*
John Bell, *p. 457*
secession, *p. 458*
Confederate States of America, *p. 458*
Jefferson Davis, *p. 458*
John J. Crittenden, *p. 459*

HSS 8.9.1 Describe the leaders of the movement (e.g., John Quincy Adams and his proposed constitutional amendment, John Brown and the armed resistance, Harriet Tubman and the Underground Railroad, Benjamin Franklin, Theodore Weld, William Lloyd Garrison, Frederick Douglass).

8.10.3 Identify the constitutional issues posed by the doctrine of nullification and secession and the earliest origins of that doctrine.

Teach the Big Idea: Master the Standards

Standards Proficiency

The Nation Divides HSS 8.9.1, 8.10.3; HSS Analysis Skills: HR 5, HI 1

Materials: poster board, art supplies

1. **Teach** Ask students the Main Idea questions to teach this section.
2. **Apply** Number students from one to three. Have each of the "ones" create a poster to recruit supporters for John Brown's army. Ask each of the "twos" to create a campaign poster for the election of 1860 and assign each student a specific candidate to support. Have each of the "threes" create a poster to urge the southern states to secede. **LS Verbal/Linguistic, Visual/Spatial**
3. **Review** As you review the section's main ideas, have volunteers explain their posters.
4. **Practice/Homework** Have each student write a paragraph addressing the issue of slavery and the election of President Lincoln from either a northern or a southern point of view.

Alternative Assessment Handbook, Rubrics 28: Posters; and 41: Writing to Express

Preteach

Bellringer

If YOU were there . . . Use the **Daily Bellringer Transparency** to help students answer the question.

Daily Bellringer Transparency, Section 4

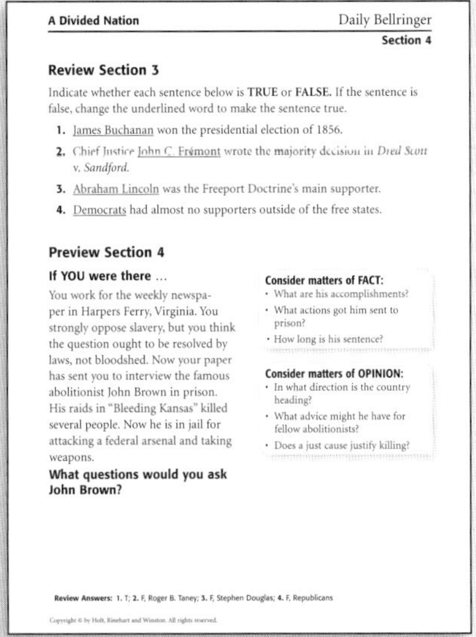

A Divided Nation — Daily Bellringer, **Section 4**

Review Section 3

Indicate whether each sentence below is **TRUE** or **FALSE.** If the sentence is false, change the underlined word to make the sentence true.

1. James Buchanan won the presidential election of 1856.
2. Chief Justice John C. Frémont wrote the majority decision in *Dred Scott v. Sandford.*
3. Abraham Lincoln was the Freeport Doctrine's main supporter.
4. Democrats had almost no supporters outside of the free states.

Preview Section 4

If YOU were there ...

You work for the weekly newspaper in Harpers Ferry, Virginia. You strongly oppose slavery, but you think the question ought to be resolved by laws, not bloodshed. Now your paper has sent you to interview the famous abolitionist John Brown in prison. His raids in "Bleeding Kansas" killed several people. Now he is in jail for attacking a federal arsenal and taking weapons.

What questions would you ask John Brown?

Consider matters of FACT:
- What are his accomplishments?
- What actions got him sent to prison?
- How long is his sentence?

Consider matters of OPINION:
- In what direction is the country heading?
- What advice might he have for fellow abolitionists?
- Does a just cause justify killing?

Review Answers: **1.** T; **2.** F, Roger B. Taney; **3.** F, Stephen Douglas; **4.** F, Republicans

Building Vocabulary

Preteach or review the following terms:

arsenal storehouse of weapons (p. 455)

conspiracy a plan among people to commit a crime (p. 456)

moderate not extreme, in the middle (p. 457)

treason betraying one's country by waging war against it or by aiding its enemies (p. 456)

CRF: Vocabulary Builder Activity, Section 4

Standards Focus

HSS 8.9.1

Means: Describe the role of John Brown in the movement to abolish slavery.
Matters: John Brown forced the issue of slavery by trying to provoke a slave rebellion.

HSS 8.10.3

Means: Discuss the beginnings of secession and its relation to the U.S. Constitution.
Matters: When pro-slavery states began to secede from the Union, the stage was set for the Civil War.

Direct Teach

Main Idea

❶ Raid on Harpers Ferry

John Brown's raid on Harpers Ferry intensified the disagreement between free states and slave states.

Describe What was the result of John Brown's raid on Harpers Ferry? *Some of Brown's men were killed, some local white southerners were killed, and Brown and some of his men were captured. Brown was hanged. Many southerners felt scared and began talking about leaving the Union.*

Compare and Contrast How were Lincoln's views similar to and different from John Brown's? *similar—Lincoln agreed with Brown that slavery was wrong; different—Lincoln opposed the use of violence and treason.*

CRF: Primary Source Activity: John Brown, Address to the Court

HSS 8.9.1; HSS **Analysis Skills:** HR 5, HI 1

Primary Source

Reading Like a Historian

John Brown's Last Speech Help students practice reading the selection like historians. Ask:

- When did John Brown deliver this speech?
- What is his purpose?
- What personal biases shaped Brown's defense of his actions?

HSS 8.9.1; HSS **Analysis Skills:** HR 4

Primary Source

SPEECH

John Brown's Last Speech

At his trial, after being pronounced guilty, John Brown spoke in his own defense about his plan to free slaves.

"I intended certainly to have made a clean thing of that matter [freeing slaves] . . . I never did intend murder or treason, or the destruction of property, or to excite or incite the slaves to rebellion, or to make insurrection [revolt] . . . Had I interfered in the manner which I admit . . . in behalf of the rich, the powerful, the intelligent, the so-called great . . . it would have been all right, and every man in this Court would have deemed it an act worthy of reward rather than punishment . . . I believe that to have interfered as I have done . . . in behalf of His despised poor, is no wrong, but right."

—John Brown,
quoted in *The Life, Trial and Execution of Captain John Brown*

Brown says he never meant to start a rebellion.

By *His*, Brown means God's.

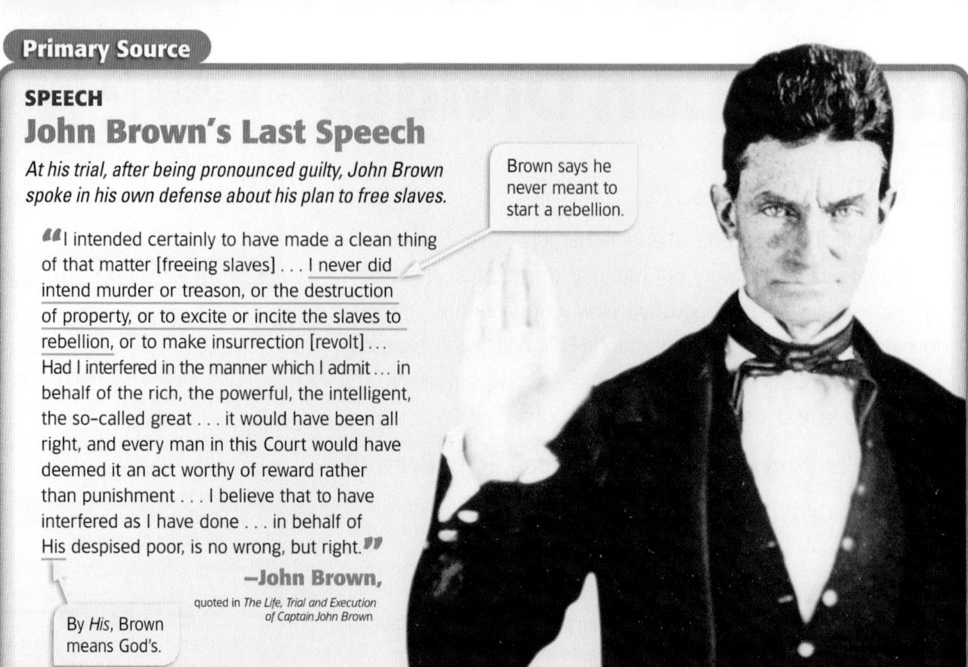

ANALYSIS SKILL **ANALYZING PRIMARY SOURCES**

How does Brown contrast his ideas with the Court's ideas?

Brown was quickly convicted of treason, murder, and conspiracy. Some of his men received death sentences. John A. Copeland, a fugitive slave, defended his actions. "If I am dying for freedom, I could not die for a better cause." Convinced that he also would be sentenced to death, Brown delivered a memorable speech.

"Now, if it is deemed [thought] necessary that I should forfeit [give up] my life for the furtherance of the ends of justice, and mingle [mix] my blood . . . with the blood of millions in this slave country whose rights are disregarded by wicked, cruel, and unjust enactments, I say, let it be done."

—John Brown, quoted in *John Brown, 1800–1859* by Oswald Garrison Villard

As expected, the judge ordered Brown to be hanged. The sentence was carried out one month later on December 2, 1859.

Many northerners mourned John Brown's death, but some abolitionists criticized his extreme actions. Abraham Lincoln said Brown "agreed with us in thinking slavery wrong." However, Lincoln continued, "That cannot excuse violence, bloodshed, and treason."

Most southern whites—both slaveholders and non-slaveholders—felt threatened by the actions of John Brown. They worried that a "John Brown the Second" might attack. One South Carolina newspaper voiced these fears: "We are convinced the safety of the South lies only outside the present Union." Another newspaper stated that "the sooner we get out of the Union, the better."

READING CHECK **Drawing Conclusions** Why did John Brown's raid lead some southerners to talk about leaving the Union?

Answers

Analyzing Primary Sources *Whereas the court ruled that John Brown should be punished, he stated that his actions were right.*

Reading Check *Southerners worried that other opponents of slavery would attack them or incite slave rebellions and that leaving the Union was the only way to protect their safety.*

Differentiating Instruction for Universal Access

English-Language Learners

Standards Proficiency | Standard English Mastery

1. Write the following terms for the class to see:
   - **arm**
   - **arsenal**
   - **conspiracy**
   - **ferry**
   - **marines**
   - **mourned**
   - **raid**
   - **squad**
   - **treason**
   - **uprising**
2. Work with students as a class to locate each term and define it as used in the text.
3. Then have students work in pairs or small groups to create a sequential flowchart listing the events connected to John Brown's raid.
4. Have students share the events they listed with the class. List events for students to see. Then help students use the list to write a summary of John Brown's raid. Model for students the use of standard English and correct grammar. LS **Verbal/Linguistic**

HSS 8.9.1, 8.10.3; HSS **Analysis Skills:** CS 1, CS 2, HI 1, HI 2

Alternative Assessment Handbook, Rubrics 36: Time Lines; and 37: Writing Assignments

Election of 1860

In this climate of distrust, Americans prepared for another presidential election in 1860. The northern and southern Democrats could not agree on a candidate. Northern Democrats chose Senator Stephen Douglas. Southern Democrats backed the current vice president, **John C. Breckinridge** of Kentucky, who supported slavery in the territories.

Meanwhile, a new political party emerged. The **Constitutional Union Party** recognized "no political principles other than the Constitution of the country, the Union of the states, and the enforcement of the laws." Members of this new party met in Baltimore, Maryland, and selected **John Bell** of Tennessee as their candidate. Bell was a slaveholder, but he had opposed the Kansas-Nebraska Act in 1854.

Senator William Seward of New York was the Republican's leading candidate at the start of their convention. But it turned out that Lincoln appealed to more party members. A moderate who was against the spread of slavery, Lincoln promised not to abolish slavery where it already existed.

Douglas, Breckinridge, and Bell each knew he might not win the election. They hoped to win enough electoral votes to prevent Lincoln from winning in the electoral college. But with a unified Republican Party behind him, Lincoln won. Although he received the highest number of votes, he won only about 40 percent of the overall popular vote.

Lincoln won 180 of 183 electoral votes in free states. Douglas had the second-highest number of popular votes, but he won only one state. He earned just 12 electoral votes. Breckinridge and Bell split electoral votes in other slave states.

The election results angered southerners. Lincoln did not campaign in their region and did not carry any southern states, but he became the next president. The election signaled that the South was losing its national political power.

READING CHECK **Analyzing** Why was Lincoln viewed by many as a moderate candidate during his campaign for the presidency?

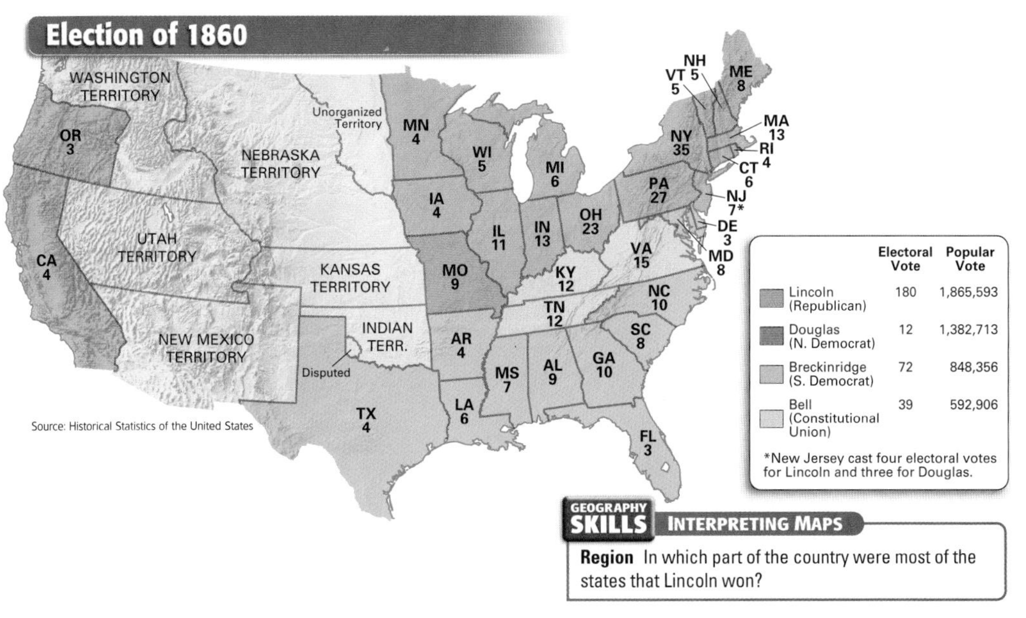

Direct Teach

Main Idea

❷ Election of 1860

The outcome of the election of 1860 divided the United States.

Identify Who were the candidates in the election of 1860, and which political party did each represent? *Stephen Douglas, northern Democrats; John Breckinridge, southern Democrats; Abraham Lincoln, Republicans; John Bell, Constitutional Union Party*

Analyze Why did the South feel it was losing power after the election of 1860? *Lincoln had won the election without carrying a single southern state.*

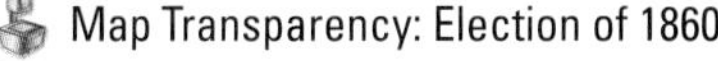

Map Transparency: Election of 1860

HSS 8.10.3; HSS **Analysis Skills:** HR 5, HI 1

Info to Know

Constitutional Union Party The Constitutional Union Party claimed that because platforms "have had the effect to mislead and deceive the people, and at the same time to widen the political divisions of the country," it would release only a brief platform. In fact, party members hoped to unify the country by rising above the slavery dispute. This strategy was popular in the Upper South. Party candidate John Bell won the states of Kentucky, Tennessee, and Virginia. However, after the outbreak of the Civil War, the party fell apart.

Critical Thinking: Identifying Points of View

Standards Proficiency

Election of 1860 Newspaper Articles

HSS 8.10.3; HSS **Analysis Skills:** HR 5, HI 1, HI 2

1. Organize students into groups of six and assign each group member one of the following newspapers: northern abolitionist paper, northern Republican paper, northern Democratic paper, southern Democratic paper, or Constitutional Union Party paper.
2. Ask students to imagine that they are reporters for their assigned papers. Have each student write a headline and a one-paragraph article about the results of the election of 1860.
3. Ask volunteers to read their headlines and articles aloud to the class. Then have students compare and contrast how people in different regions of the country and different groups viewed the election of 1860.
LS Verbal/Linguistic

Alternative Assessment Handbook, Rubric 37: Writing Assignments

Answers

Interpreting Maps *the Northeast*

Reading Check *He opposed the spread of slavery but promised not to abolish it where it already existed.*

Direct Teach

Main Idea

❸ The South Secedes

The dispute over slavery led the South to secede.

Explain How did the southern states respond to the election of 1860, and why? *Several seceded, starting with South Carolina, and formed the Confederate States of America. They believed their economy and way of life were at stake and that slavery was threatened.*

Analyze Why did southerners who supported secession believe the action was constitutional? *The states had voluntarily joined the Union, so they should be free to leave.*

CRF: Biography Activity: Jefferson Davis

HSS 8.10.3; **HSS Analysis Skills:** HR 5, HI 1

Did you know . . .

On January 9, 1861, the mayor of New York City, Democrat Fernando Wood, proposed to the city council that the city join the southern states in seceding. Wood wanted to form a new city made up of Manhattan, Staten Island, and Long Island. The proposal did not pass.

The South Secedes

Lincoln insisted that he would not change slavery in the South. However, he said that slavery could not expand and thus would eventually die out completely. That idea angered many southerners.

Southerners' Reactions

People in the South believed their economy and way of life would be destroyed without slave labor. They reacted immediately. Within a week of Lincoln's election, South Carolina's legislature called for a special convention. The delegates considered **secession**, or formally withdrawing from the Union. South Carolina elected to dissolve "the union now subsisting [existing] between South Carolina and other States." Southern secessionists believed that they had a right to leave the Union. They pointed out that each of the original states had voluntarily joined the Union by holding a special convention that had ratified the Constitution. Surely, they reasoned, states could leave the Union by the same process.

Critics of secession thought this argument was ridiculous. President Buchanan said the Union was not "a mere voluntary association of States, to be dissolved at pleasure by any one of the contracting parties." President-elect Abraham Lincoln agreed, saying, "No State, upon its own mere motion, can lawfully get out of the Union." Lincoln added, "They can only do so against [the] law, and by revolution."

The Confederate States of America

Mississippi, Florida, Alabama, Georgia, Louisiana, and Texas also seceded to form the **Confederate States of America**, also called the Confederacy. Its new constitution guaranteed citizens the right to own slaves.

Delegates from seceded states elected **Jefferson Davis** of Mississippi as president of the Confederacy. Davis had hoped to be the commanding general of Mississippi's troops. He responded to the news of his election with reluctance.

While the South Carolina representatives were meeting to discuss secession, Congress

Jefferson Davis takes the oath of office for president of the Confederate States of America.

Rebel Government

This photograph is of the first inauguration of Jefferson Davis as the president of the Confederate States of America. A former U.S. secretary of war, Davis was elected president of the confederacy in 1861.

How does this photo show the state of the southern government?

Collaborative Learning

Standards Proficiency

Issue of Secession

HSS 8.10.3; **HSS Analysis Skills:** HR 5, HI 1, HI 2

1. Organize students into groups and ask them to imagine that they are members of the South Carolina secession convention.
2. Have each group draft a formal letter to President Lincoln informing him that South Carolina is officially seceding from the Union. The letter should list and explain the events and other causes that led to the decision.
3. Have group representatives read the letters to the class. Then have students discuss—first in their groups and then as a class—whether states have the right to secede and, if so, under what circumstances. **LS Verbal/Linguistic**

Alternative Assessment Handbook, Rubrics 11: Discussions; and 37: Writing Assignments

Answers

Rebel Government *depicts it as having broken away from the Union and having chosen its own president*

examined a plan to save the Union. Senator **John J. Crittenden** of Kentucky proposed a series of constitutional amendments that he believed would satisfy the South by protecting slavery. Crittenden hoped the country could avoid secession and a civil war.

Lincoln disagreed with Crittenden's plan. He believed there could be no compromise about the extension of slavery. Lincoln wrote, "The tug has to come and better now than later." A Senate committee voted on Crittenden's plan, and every Republican rejected it, as Lincoln had requested.

When the southern states seceded, the question of who owned federal property in the South arose. For instance, the forts in the harbor of Charleston, South Carolina, were federal property. However, Confederate president Davis and the Confederacy were ready to prevent the federal army from controlling the property.

Lincoln Takes Office

President Lincoln was inaugurated on March 4, 1861. In writing his inaugural address, Lincoln looked to many of the nation's founding documents. Referring to the idea that governments receive "their just powers from the consent of the governed," a line from the Declaration of Independence, Lincoln stated, "This country, with its institutions, belongs to the people who inhabit it. Whenever they grow weary of the existing Government, they can exercise their *constitutional* right of amending it or their *revolutionary* right to dismember [take apart] or overthrow it. I can not be ignorant of the fact that many worthy and patriotic citizens are desirous [wanting] of having the National Constitution amended . . ."

While he believed that U.S. citizens had the power to change their government through majority consent, he opposed the idea that southern states could leave the Union because they were unhappy with the government's position on slavery.

He announced in his inaugural address that he would keep all government property in the seceding states. However, he also tried to convince southerners that his government would not provoke a war. He hoped that, given time, southern states would return to the Union.

READING CHECK **Drawing Conclusions** Why did some southern states secede from the Union?

SUMMARY AND PREVIEW The secession of the southern states hinted at the violence to come. In the next chapter you will read about the Civil War.

Section 4 Assessment

go.hrw.com
Online Quiz
KEYWORD: SS8 HP14

Reviewing Ideas, Terms, and People HSS 8.9.1, 8.10.3

1. **a. Recall** Why did John Brown want to seize the federal arsenal at Harpers Ferry?
   b. Explain Why did some abolitionists disagree with Brown's actions?
2. **a. Identify** List the candidates in the presidential election of 1860, and what party each supported.
   b. Predict How might Abraham Lincoln's victory in the election of 1860 lead to future problems?
3. **a. Identify** What states made up the **Confederate States of America**?
   b. Explain Why did Lincoln disagree with **John J. Crittenden**'s plan to keep the Union together?
   c. Elaborate Do you believe that the southern states had the right to secede? Why or why not?

Critical Thinking

4. **Summarizing** Copy the graphic organizer below onto your own sheet of paper. Use it to identify the causes of the secession of southern states.

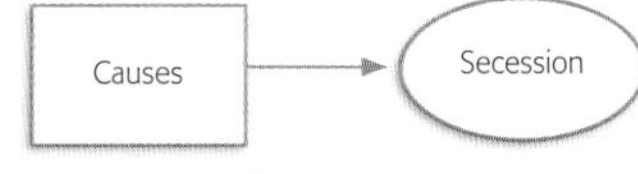

FOCUS ON WRITING

5. **Taking Notes on Secession** Make some notes on the raid on Harpers Ferry, the election of 1860, and the secession of the South. Decide how your character feels about each of these. How do these events affect your character?

Section 4 Assessment Answers

1. **a.** wanted to start and arm a slave uprising
   b. believed violence was not the answer to the slavery issue
2. **a.** Stephen Douglas, Northern Democrats; John Breckinridge, Southern Democrats; Abraham Lincoln, Republicans; John Bell, Constitutional Union Party
   b. possible answer—Southerners might feel they had lost political power and that slavery was threatened and so choose to secede.
3. **a.** South Carolina, Mississippi, Florida, Alabama, Georgia, Louisiana, Texas
   b. Lincoln believed there could be no compromise over the spread of slavery.
   c. possible answers—Yes, states have a right to leave the Union if people feel the government is denying their rights; no, secession harms the strength of the nation; if states can leave whenever people are unhappy, the federal government loses its authority.
4. Causes—fear resulting from John Brown's raid and similar events; Lincoln's election
5. Students should describe how their character feels about how these events led to secession.

Direct Teach

Main Idea

❸ The South Secedes

The dispute over slavery led the South to secede.

Describe What was the plan that John J. Crittenden proposed to preserve the Union? *a series of constitutional amendments related to slavery issues that were meant to pacify the South and thereby avoid secession*

Identify Points of View In his inaugural address, what view did Lincoln express regarding secession? *He stated that the government receives its power from the people and that Americans have the right to change the government through either constitutional amendments or revolution, but he opposed secession.*

HSS 8.10.3; HSS **Analysis Skills:** HR 5, HI 1

Review & Assess

Close

Have students review the causes of secession and then discuss whether it was inevitable.

Review

Online Quiz, Section 4

Assess

SE Section 4 Assessment

PASS: Section 4 Quiz

Alternative Assessment Handbook

Reteach/Classroom Intervention

California Standards Review Workbook

Interactive Reader and Study Guide, Section 4

Interactive Skills Tutor CD-ROM

Answers

Reading Check *They believed the election of 1860 showed that they had lost power and that Abraham Lincoln's views on slavery would lead to its end.*

Social Studies Skills

Assessing Primary and Secondary Sources

Activity Graphic Organizer Have students discuss the importance of using both primary and secondary sources in the study of history. Then have each student create a graphic organizer of his or her choosing that illustrates what primary and secondary sources are, the problems with each (such as bias), and how they combine to provide a better picture of history. **LS Verbal/Linguistic, Visual/Spatial**

- Alternative Assessment Handbook, Rubric 13: Graphic Organizers
- Interactive Skills Tutor CD-ROM, Lesson 2: Identify Primary and Secondary Sources; Lesson 17: Interpret Primary Sources

HSS Analysis Skills: HR 3

Social Studies Skills

Analysis | Critical Thinking | Participation | Study

HR3 Students distinguish relevant from irrelevant information.

Assessing Primary and Secondary Sources

Define the Skill

All historical information comes from primary and secondary sources. *Primary sources* are documents written by someone who witnessed or took part in an event. They include diaries, letters, autobiographies, and newspaper reports. *Secondary sources* are accounts of events written after the events have occurred by someone who did not witness or take part in them. They retell, interpret, and summarize information from primary sources History books and biographies are examples of secondary sources.

Historical sources often disagree. One writer's version of an event may be different from another writer's version. You must assess the reliability of a primary or secondary source in order to weigh its value to you as a source of accurate information.

Learn the Skill

Use these guidelines to analyze and evaluate primary and secondary sources.

1. Identify the nature of the material. Is it a first-hand, eye-witness account or is it based on information provided by others?
2. Evaluate the author. If the material is a secondary source, what qualifications does the author have to interpret the sources from which it came? If the material is a primary source, what was the author's connection to the event he or she is writing about?
3. Determine the audience. Was the source meant to be seen by the public? Was it meant for a friend, or for the writer alone? The intended audience can influence a source's content.
4. Determine the purpose. Even authors of primary sources can have reasons to distort the truth to suit their own purposes. Look for evidence of emotion, exaggeration, opinion, or bias that may have influenced the account.
5. Look for documentation. Look for other information or evidence that supports the source's account. Compare sources whenever possible.

Practice the Skill

The passage below concerns the attack on Lawrence, Kansas, that you read about in this chapter. The passage contains both a primary and a secondary source. The secondary account was written by John A. Garraty, a well-known historian. Review the information on page 448, analyze the passage, and answer the questions that follow.

"Sheriff Jones, at the head of an army of Missourians. marched into Lawrence. In broad daylight they threw the printing presses of two newspapers into a river. They burned down the Free State Hotel and other buildings. Antislavery Kansans seethed with rage. One eyewitness described the attack."

Sheriff Jones, after looking at the flames rising from the hotel and saying that it was 'the happiest day of his life,' dismissed the troops and they began their lawless destruction."

1. Did the author of the primary source likely support the attackers or the people of Lawrence? What clues in the passage suggest this?
2. For whom was the primary source likely written?
3. Which source is more reliable for information about this incident? Explain why.

Social Studies Skills Activity: Assessing Primary and Secondary Sources

Evaluating Sources

HSS Analysis Skills: HR 3 — **Standards Proficiency**

1. Have students review the text in Section 2 under the heading "Brooks Attacks Sumner." Ask students to closely examine the image. Lead students through the five steps under "Learn the Skill" to evaluate the image.
2. Then have students examine the textbook coverage of the event. Again, lead students through the five steps under "Learn the Skill" to evaluate this source.
3. Then have students discuss why the two sources combine to provide a more complete account of the event than any one alone. **LS Verbal/Linguistic, Visual Spatial**

- Alternative Assessment Handbook, Rubric 11: Discussions

Answers

Practice the Skill 1. *people of Lawrence; phrase "lawless destruction";* **2.** *possible answers—not enough information provided to tell;* **3.** *secondary source, because historians try to report events objectively, while eyewitness accounts usually present a view shaped by their personal opinions and biases*

CHAPTER 14

Standards Review

Visual Summary

Use the visual summary below to help you review the main ideas of the chapter.

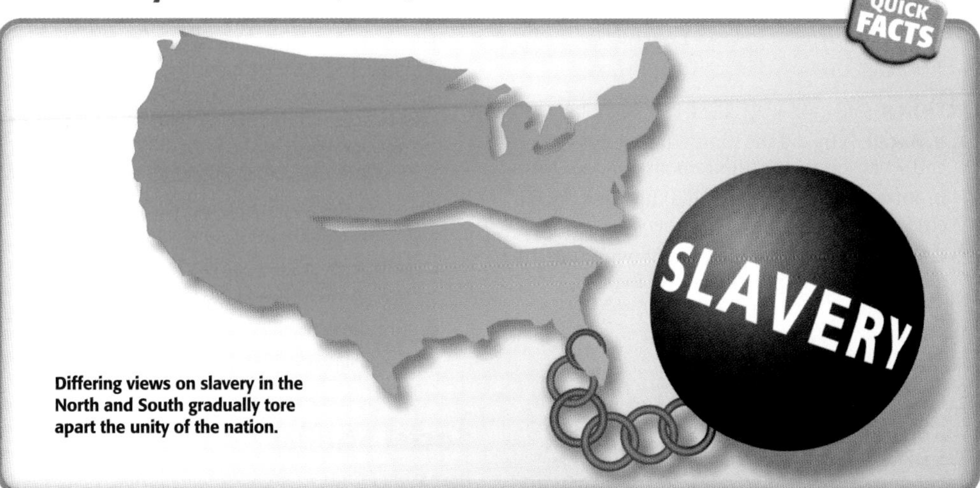

Differing views on slavery in the North and South gradually tore apart the unity of the nation.

Reviewing Vocabulary, Terms, and People

Identify the correct term or person from the chapter that best fits each of the following descriptions.

1. belief that voters should be given the right to decide if slavery would be permitted or banned
2. chief justice of the Supreme Court who wrote the majority opinion for the *Dred Scott* decision
3. Democratic candidate for president in 1852 who promised to enforce the Compromise of 1850 and the Fugitive Slave Act
4. a fugitive slave whose arrest led to violence between government officials and abolitionists
5. Republican candidate for the presidency in 1856 who opposed the spread of slavery in the West
6. slave who sued for freedom, claiming that by living in free territory, he had earned his freedom
7. Stephen Douglas's claim that states and territories should determine the issue of slavery through popular sovereignty

Comprehension and Critical Thinking

SECTION 1 *(Pages 438–443)* **HSS 8.9.4, 8.10.1**

8. **a. Describe** How did literature aid the antislavery movement?

   b. Draw Conclusions How did the issue of slavery promote sectionalism?

   c. Evaluate Do you think the Compromise of 1850 was a good solution? Explain your answer.

SECTION 2 *(Pages 445–449)* **HSS 8.9.5, 8.10.2**

9. **a. Identify** Who were the candidates in the presidential election of 1852, and what issues did each support?

   b. Analyze How did the Kansas-Nebraska Act lead to growing hostility between pro-slavery and antislavery supporters?

   c. Elaborate Why do you think "Bleeding Kansas" produced intense controversy between many Americans?

Answers

Visual Summary

Review and Inquiry The ball and chain (marked "Slavery") attached to the lower half of the United States seems to be pulling the country apart. Have students write a paragraph about how the slavery issue gradually divided the nation until it broke apart in secession. Students should include how geographic and economic differences between the North and the South contributed to sectionalism.

Quick Facts Transparency: A Divided Nation Visual Summary

Reviewing Vocabulary, Terms, and People

1. popular sovereignty
2. Roger B. Taney
3. Franklin Pierce
4. Anthony Burns
5. John C. Frémont
6. Dred Scott
7. Freeport Doctrine

Comprehension and Critical Thinking

8. **a.** educated people about the hardships of slavery and gained sympathy for abolitionism

   b. Because the South's economy was dependent on slave labor and the North's was not, the regions became divided over the slavery issue, which encouraged leaders to promote sectional interests.

Review and Assessment Resources

Review and Reinforce

- **SE** Standards Review
- **CRF:** Chapter Review Activity
- California Standards Review Workbook
- Quick Facts Transparency: A Divided Nation Visual Summary
- Spanish Chapter Summaries Audio CD Program
- Online Chapter Summaries in Six Languages
- **OSP** Holt PuzzlePro; GameTool for ExamView
- Quiz Game CD-ROM

Assess

- **SE** Standards Assessment
- PASS: Chapter Test, Forms A and B
- Alternative Assessment Handbook
- **OSP** ExamView Test Generator, Chapter Test
- Universal Access Modified Worksheets and Tests CD-ROM: Chapter Test
- Holt Online Assessment Program (in the Premier Online Edition)

Reteach/Intervene

- Interactive Reader and Study Guide
- Universal Access Teacher Management System: Lesson Plans for Universal Access
- Universal Access Modified Worksheets and Tests CD-ROM
- Interactive Skills Tutor CD-ROM

go.hrw.com
Online Resources
Chapter Resources:
KEYWORD: SS8 US14

Answers

c. possible answers—Yes, it prevented secession for the moment and appeased both the North and the South; no, it only postponed the resolution of the slavery issue.

9. a. Franklin Pierce—promised to honor the Compromise of 1850 and the Fugitive Slave Act; Winfield Scott—limited support of the Compromise of 1850

b. It removed the Missouri Compromise's restriction on slavery in the Kansas and Nebraska territories and let popular sovereignty decide the slavery issue.

c. because of the violence and tensions over the issue of slavery

10. a. a slave who sued for his freedom; the case declared that African Americans were not citizens and ruled that the Missouri Compromise was unconstitutional

b. The issue led to the formation of new parties and to the end of some existing parties.

c. hoped his support for the Kansas-Nebraska Act had weakened his chance for re-election

11. a. They feared more attacks like John Brown's raid, were angry over the election of 1860, and felt their economy and way of life were threatened. Lincoln tried to convince southern states to return.

b. because Lincoln had won without carrying one southern state

c. possible answers—Yes, he was fighting for justice and to free people from bondage; no, violence is never right.

Reviewing Themes

12. changed the makeup of political parties and created new ones aligned with sectional pro-slavery and antislavery views

13. electrified the nation, sparked outrage in the South, increased sectional tensions and support for abolitionism

SECTION 3 *(Pages 450–454)* **HSS 8.10.4**

10. a. Identify Who was Dred Scott, and why was his case important?

b. Analyze How were political parties affected by the debate over slavery?

c. Elaborate Why do you think Republicans challenged Stephen Douglas's run for the Senate?

SECTION 4 *(Pages 455–459)* **HSS 8.9.1, 8.10.3**

11. a. Recall Why did the southern states secede, and what was the North's response?

b. Draw Conclusions Why did the results of the election of 1860 anger southerners?

c. Evaluate Do you think John Brown was right to use violence to protest slavery? Explain.

Reviewing Themes

12. Politics How did sectionalism affect American politics?

13. Society and Culture What effect did Harriet Beecher Stowe's book *Uncle Tom's Cabin* have on the debate over slavery?

Using the Internet

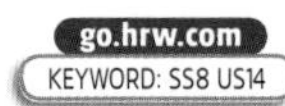

14. Activity: Creating a Newspaper Harriet Beecher Stowe's novel and John Brown's raids were two important events that created more debate over slavery and heightened tension between sides. Enter the activity keyword and learn more about antislavery actions. Then create a newspaper with which to display your research. Remember to write from the point of view of someone from the mid-1800s.

Reading Skills

Understanding Fact and Opinion *Use the Reading Skills taught in this chapter to answer the question about the reading selection below.*

> In 1858 John Brown tried to start an uprising. He wanted to attack the federal arsenal in Virginia and seize weapons there. He planned to arm local slaves. Brown expected to kill or take hostage white southerners who stood in his way. *(p. 455)*

15. Based on the reading above, which of the following statements is an opinion?

a. John Brown's raid was in 1858.

b. John Brown hated all slaveholders.

c. John Brown's raid took place in Virginia.

d. Local slaves helped John Brown.

Social Studies Skills

Assessing Primary and Secondary Sources *Use the Social Studies Skills taught in this chapter to answer the question below.*

16. Which of the following is *not* an example of a primary source used in this chapter?

a. *A People's History of the United States* by Howard Zinn

b. The Seventh of March speech by Daniel Webster

c. A House Divided speech by Abraham Lincoln

d. John Brown's last speech

FOCUS ON WRITING

17. Writing Your Autobiography Review your notes. Then write your autobiography, being sure to mention each of the events from your notes. Tell how your character heard about each event, what he or she was doing at the time, how he or she felt about the event, and how it affected him or her. What are your character's hopes and fears for the future?

Using the Internet

14. Go to the HRW Web site and enter the keyword shown to access a rubric for this activity.

KEYWORD: SS8 US14

Reading Skills

15. b

Social Studies Skills

16. a

Focus on Writing

17. Rubric Students' autobiographies should:

- explain how each of the chapter's key events affected the character
- describe how the character learned and felt about each key event
- describe the character's hopes and fears for the future

CRF: Focus on Writing Activity: Writing an Autobiographical Sketch

Standards Assessment

DIRECTIONS: Read each question and write the letter of the best response. Use the map below to answer question 1.

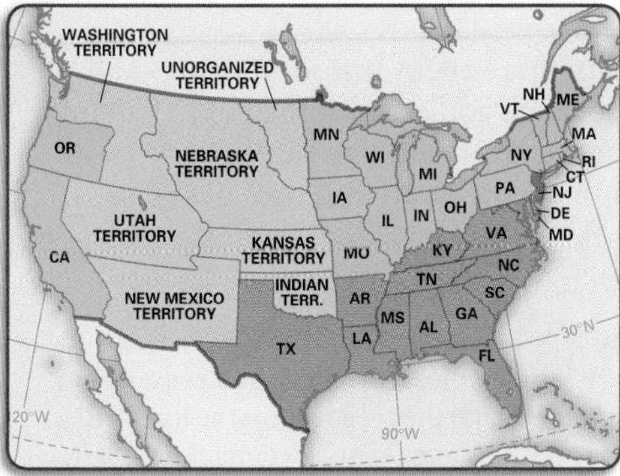

From the information in this map, you can conclude that it shows

- **A** the provisions of the Compromise of 1850.
- **B** the results of the election of 1860.
- **C** the formation of the Confederacy.
- **D** the results of the *Dred Scott* decision.

2 Which leader was responsible for settling the dispute over the expansion of slavery that arose after the Mexican War?

- **A** David Wilmot
- **B** Henry Clay
- **C** Abraham Lincoln
- **D** Jefferson Davis

3 California's admission as a free state after the Mexican War aroused controversy because

- **A** many Californians already held slaves.
- **B** it would upset the balance between free states and slave states.
- **C** Mexico still claimed that California was part of Mexico's territory.
- **D** most Californians wanted independence.

4 Widespread violence erupted in Kansas over slavery in the mid-1850s *mainly* due to

- **A** the practice of popular sovereignty.
- **B** the Pottawatomie Massacre.
- **C** the Missouri Compromise.
- **D** the threat of secession.

5 The Kansas-Nebraska Act of 1854 directly or indirectly led to all of the following *except*

- **A** the rise of the Republican Party.
- **B** the collapse of the Whig Party.
- **C** Abraham Lincoln's election as president.
- **D** The Missouri Compromise.

Connecting with Past Learning

6 The Compromise of 1850 temporarily settled differences between the North and South over the spread of slavery. Earlier in Grade 8 you learned about another compromise over slavery that took place

- **A** during the American Revolution.
- **B** at the Constitutional Convention.
- **C** during the War of 1812.
- **D** in the Treaty of Paris of 1783.

7 Several southern states seceded after Lincoln's election as president in 1860. What earlier event also threatened the nation by greatly angering the South?

- **A** ratification of the Constitution in 1789
- **B** Henry Clay's proposal of the American System after the War of 1812
- **C** Andrew Jackson's defeat in the presidential election of 1824
- **D** passage of a protective tariff in 1828

Answers

1. A

Break Down the Question: Option B is not correct because the map does not include numbers of state electors. Option D does not make sense for a map, and Option C is incorrect because the map does not identify the seceding states.

2. B

Break Down the Question: This question requires students to recall factual information. Refer students who have trouble to the text titled "Compromise of 1850" in Section 1.

3. B

Break Down the Question: Explain that a question sometimes provides clues to its answer. For example, point out the phrase "admission as a free state" in this question.

4 A

Break Down the Question: This question requires students to identify cause and effect. Explain that Option B is incorrect because it is an example of the violence, not a cause. Option D is an effect of the violence.

5. D

Break Down the Question: This question also requires students to identify cause and effect. Point out that the word *except* means students should select the answer that was *not* an effect.

6. B

Break Down the Question: This question connects to information covered in Chapter 4.

7. D

Break Down the Question: This question connects to information covered in Chapter 9.

Intervention Resources

Reproducible

- Interactive Reader and Study Guide
- Universal Access Teacher Management System: Lesson Plans for Universal Access

Technology

- Quick Facts Transparency: A Divided Nation Visual Summary
- Universal Access Modified Worksheets and Tests CD-ROM
- Interactive Skills Tutor CD-ROM

Tips for Test Taking

Rely on 50/50 When students have no idea what an answer is, tell them to do the following to make an educated guess:

- Read every choice carefully.
- Eliminate the least likely choice, then the next, and so on until one answer is left.
- Watch out for distracters—choices that are true but either too broad, too narrow, or not relevant.
- If more than one choice seems correct, see if "All of the above" is an option. If none of the choices seems correct, look for "None of the above."

Standards Review

Have students review the following standards in their workbooks.

- California Standards Review Workbook: **HSS** 8.9.1, 8.9.4, 8.9.5, 8.10.1, 8.10.2, 8.10.3

Preteach

Bellringer

Motivate Write the words *cat* and *dog* for students to see. Ask students how the two animals are similar. Then ask students how they are different. Explain that comparing (showing how things are similar) and contrasting (showing how things are different) is one way to learn about events and people in history. Tell students that they will write a paper comparing and contrasting a historical topic.

Interactive Skills Tutor CD-ROM, Lesson 1: Compare and Contrast

Direct Teach

Writing a Thesis

Make a Point After students have selected the topic of their paper and made lists of similarities and differences, have them examine the lists. Were the two groups or events they compared mainly alike or mainly different? Did certain similarities or differences stand out as significant or influential? Have students write one sentence in answer to each question. Tell students to use the sentences as a starting point for selecting and writing a thesis.

Organizing

Once Around the Block Students who use the block style to organize their papers should check that they address the same points in the same order for each topic. Have students use a different color of ink to underline each point they made about the first topic. Then have students use the same colors to underline the points they made about the second topic. The colors and order should match.

Comparing People and Events

Assignment
Write a paper comparing and contrasting one of the following: (1) America before and after the Industrial Revolution, (2) the lives of free blacks in the North with the lives of free blacks in the South.

One way to learn more about historical figures and events is to compare and contrast them. By studying how the figures or events are alike and different, you can begin to see each one more clearly.

1. Prewrite

Getting Started

"How are they alike?" "How are they different?" Jot down answers to these questions as you research the presidents or the Industrial Revolution. Group your answers into points of comparison. For example, points of comparison for the lives of free blacks might be work, education, etc. Points of comparison for the Industrial Revolution might be factories or farming.

TIP Using Graphic Organizers Venn diagrams help you focus on similarities and differences. Write details the subjects have in common in the overlapping area. Write details that make each subject different in the sections that do not overlap.

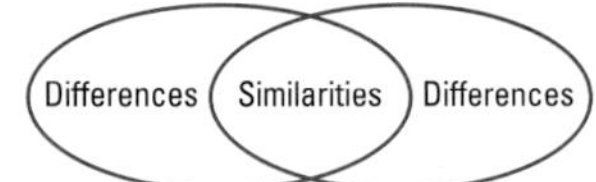

Organizing Your Information

There are two ways to organize a compare-and-contrast paper.

- **Block Style** Say everything you have to say about one subject. Then say everything you have to say about the second subject. Discuss the points of comparison in the same order for each subject.
- **Point-by-Point Style** Discuss the points of comparison one at a time. Explain how the subjects are alike and different on one point of comparison, then another, and so on. Discuss the subjects in the same order for each point of comparison.

ELA Writing 8.1.1 Create compositions that establish a controlling impression, have a coherent thesis, and end with a clear and well-supported conclusion.

2. Write

You can use this framework with your notes to help you write your first draft.

A Writer's Framework

Introduction	Body	Conclusion
■ Identify the two subjects and give background information to help readers understand your comparisons. ■ State your big idea, or main purpose, in comparing and contrasting them.	■ Use block or point-by-point organization. ■ Use three points of comparison. ■ Support your points with specific historical facts, details, and examples.	■ Restate your big idea. ■ Summarize the points you made. ■ Expand on your big idea, perhaps by relating it to later historical events or other historical figures.

Differentiating Instruction for Universal Access

Special Education Students — Reaching Standards

1. Have special education students work in small groups to create Venn diagrams before writing.
2. Have an aide read a short part of the relevant portion of the textbook aloud. Then have the students add the information to their diagrams. Have the aide continue to read the text aloud, stopping frequently to allow students to add to their Venn diagrams. **LS Visual/Spatial**

ELA Writing 8.2.3d

English-Language Learners — Standards Proficiency, Standard English Mastery

1. Have English learners write the drafts for their papers in their primary language.
2. Students should then refer back to these drafts as they write their final papers in English.
3. Before students write in English, review the rules for forming comparative and superlative adjectives and adverbs. Provide guided practice as needed. **LS Verbal/Linguistic**

ELA Writing 8.1.1

Standards Focus

ELA Writing 8.1.1, 8.2.3.d

3. Evaluate and Revise

Evaluating

Use these questions to discover ways to improve your paper.

Evaluation Questions for a Comparison/Contrast Paper

- Do you introduce both subjects in the first paragraph?
- Do you provide relevant background information in a clear and concise manner?
- Do you state your big idea in the introduction?
- Do you include three points of comparison between the subjects?
- Do you use either the block style or point-by-point style to organize your points of comparison?
- Do you support your points of comparison with appropriate historical facts, details, and examples?
- Do you restate your big idea and summarize your points?

TIP Making Meaning Clear

One way to make relationships between ideas clear is to repeat key or similar words and phrases in your writing. For example, you can use similar wording when comparing two historical figures on the same point of comparison.

EXAMPLE

Samuel Slater filled his labor needs by hiring entire families to work in the mills. Frances Lowell filled his labor needs by hiring young, unmarried women to work in the mills.

Revising

As you reread your paper, look for sentences that start with *There was* or *There were*. Sentences beginning with *There was/There were* tend to be weak: The verbs *was* and *were* do not convey any action.

Weak

There was a decline in southern agriculture after the American Revolution.

Stronger

Southern agriculture declined after the American Revolution.

4. Proofread and Publish

Proofreading

In a research report, you may be referring to the titles of your sources of information. Check to see whether you have punctuated any titles according to these guidelines.

- Underling (if you are writing) or italics (if you are using a computer) for books, movies, TV programs, Internet sites, and magazines or newspapers
- Quotation marks for magazine articles, newspaper articles, chapters in a book

Publishing

Share your paper with one or more classmates. After reading each other's papers, you can compare and contrast them.

5. Practice and Apply

Use the steps and strategies outlined in this workshop to write your paper comparing and contrasting two people or events.

Reteach

Providing Support

Back It Up Remind students that describing the similarities and differences for each group or period is not enough. Students must also support their descriptions with facts and examples. Have students circle each claim or point they make about each group or period in their papers. Then have students underline the support for each claim or point. If they have not provided support, have them ask themselves, "How do I know this point?" Then have students provide an answer in their papers.

Teaching Tip

Sentence Variety Tell students that comparison-contrast papers can become monotonous because they are highly structured. Explain that the papers will be more enjoyable to read if students vary their sentence structures, such as the way they start sentences. Help students rework, combine, or break sentences as needed to increase variety.

Practice & Apply

Rubric

Students' comparison-contrast papers should

- present a clear statement of the big idea, or main purpose.
- provide historical background to place the topic in context.
- use either block or point-by-point organization.
- provide three points of comparison and support for each one.
- end with a summary and a restatement of the big idea.
- use correct grammar, punctuation, spelling, and capitalization.

Learners Having Difficulty

Reaching Standards

1. For students who have trouble getting words on paper, write the outline at right for them to see. Explain that the outline shows the question(s) they should answer in each part of their comparison-contrast papers.
2. Have students copy the outline and leave plenty of room to add information below each part. Then have students complete the outline by answering the questions. Encourage students to use complete sentences.

I. **Introduction:** What two things are you comparing and contrasting? What do you want to show by comparing and contrasting them?

II. **Body Paragraphs:** What is one way the two things are alike or different? How do you know? What is a second way? How do you know? What is a third way? How do you know?

III. **Conclusion:** Briefly, what have you stated in your paper? **LS Verbal/Linguistic**

ELA Writing 8.1.1

Unit Preview

Introduce the Unit

Share the information in the chapter overviews with students.

Chapter 15 Soon after Lincoln's inauguration, South Carolina opened fire on Fort Sumter, which began the Civil War. Initially, the South won several major battles. The North then turned the tide of the war with victories in both the West and the East. In April 1865 the Confederates surrendered, and the North won the war. The war resulted in terrible death and destruction but also led to the long-sought freedom of enslaved Africans.

Chapter 16 After the suffering and bloodshed of the Civil War, the nation worked to rebuild. This period of time is called Reconstruction. The United States faced two major challenges—to reunite the country and to define the rights of African Americans. In 1865 the Thirteenth Amendment ended slavery in the United States. Additional amendments extended citizenship and other rights to African Americans. In time, however, politicians who opposed Reconstruction gained power. Southern states began passing laws limiting African Americans' civil rights. Many former slaves continued to work on plantations, now for low wages. Meanwhile, the South worked to develop an industrial base.

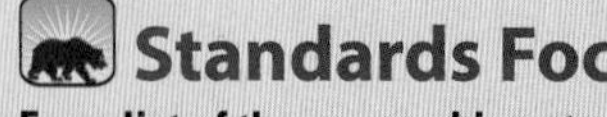

For a list of the overarching standards covered in this unit, see the first page of each chapter.

UNIT 5 1861–1877

The Nation Breaks Apart

466

Unit Resources

Planning

- Universal Access Teacher Management System: Unit Instructional Benchmarking Guides
- One-Stop Planner CD-ROM with Test Generator: Holt Calendar Planner
- Power Presentations with Video CD-ROM
- A Teacher's Guide to Religion in the Public Schools

Standards Mastery

- Standards Review Workbook
- At Home: A Guide to Standards Mastery for United States History

Differentiating Instruction

- Universal Access Teacher Management System: Lesson Plans for Universal Access
- Pre-AP Activities Guide for United States History
- Universal Access Modified Worksheets and Tests CD-ROM

Enrichment

- **CRF 15:** Interdisciplinary Project: The Ironclads: The *Monitor* and the *Virginia*
- **CRF 16:** Economics and History: The Devastation of War
- Civic Participation
- Primary Source Library CD-ROM

Assessment

- Progress Assessment Support System: Benchmark Test
- OSP ExamView Test Generator: Benchmark Test
- Holt Online Assessment Program (in the Premier Online Edition)
- Alternative Assessment Handbook

The **Universal Access Teacher Management System** provides a planning and instructional benchmarking guide for this unit.

What You Will Learn...

As compromise after compromise had failed, war between the states became unavoidable. The American Civil War tested the strength of the bond between the states. During the Civil War, Americans fought each other on battlefields and in government. Ideas about slavery and sovereignty led many soldiers to fight. Eventually, the nation was reunited, but deep scars remained. In the next two chapters you will learn about the war and its aftermath, when rebuilding the South became a priority.

Explore the Art

This illustration shows Union and Confederate troops at the Battle of Shiloh, which took place in Tennessee in April 1862. *What aspects of the Civil War does this picture show?*

467

Unit Preview

Connect to the Unit

Activity Analyzing the Costs and Benefits of War Create a cause-and-effect chart for students to see. Ask students to consider warfare in general and to discuss some of the causes of war. Write students' ideas in the chart. Next, ask students to discuss some of the effects of war. Challenge students to consider both positive and negative effects. Add students' responses to the chart. Then have students discuss the costs and benefits of warfare. When do students think war is justified? In what situations do they think the benefits of war outweigh the costs?

Save the cause-and-effect chart. At the end of the unit, have students review the chart and then create a second chart listing the causes and effects of the Civil War, including long-term effects. Conclude by having students examine the costs and benefits of the Civil War and Reconstruction.

LS Logical/Mathematical, Visual/Spatial

Explore the Art

Both the North and the South tried to keep underage boys out of their armies. Many boys lied about their ages to join, however, such as 15-year-old Elisha Stockwell pictured at left. Stockwell's father would not let him enlist. So Elisha told his parents he was going to a dance. Instead, he joined the Union army. During the Battle of Shiloh, Stockwell was wounded. He survived the war, but many young soldiers did not.

About the Illustration

This illustration is an artist's conception based on available sources. However, historians are uncertain exactly what this scene looked like.

Democracy and Civic Education

Standards Proficiency

Justice: Equal Protection of the Laws

Research Required

Background Explain to students that the Fourteenth Amendment (1868) ensures the equal protection of the laws. This protection guarantees that no person or group will be treated differently under the law from any other person or group in a similar situation unless a just and good reason exists for doing so.

1. Have students work in small groups to conduct research on how effective the equal protection clause has been over time. How have various groups used the clause to extend civil rights and to fight segregation, particularly during the 1950s and 1960s?
2. Have each group use its research to create a brochure for immigrants to inform them about their right to equal protection of the laws. The brochure should explain the concept and provide examples of how it has been used.

LS Interpersonal, Verbal/Linguistic

Alternative Assessment Handbook, Rubrics 14: Group Activity; and 37: Writing Assignment

Civic Participation

Answers

Explore the Art *possible answers—type of weaponry, equipment, and uniforms; methods of warfare and fighting; the death and destruction of the war; the age range of soldiers fighting in the war*

Chapter 15 Planning Guide

The Civil War

Chapter Overview	Reproducible Resources	Technology Resources
CHAPTER 15 pp. 466–507 **Overview:** **In this chapter, students will analyze the events of the Civil War along with the effect these events had on the lives of Americans.** See p. 466 for the California History–Social Science standards covered in this chapter.	**Universal Access Teacher Management System:*** • Universal Access Instructional Benchmarking Guides • Lesson Plans for Universal Access **Interactive Reader and Study Guide:*** Chapter Graphic Organizer **Chapter Resource File*** • Focus on Writing Activity: A Newspaper Article • Social Studies Skills Activity: Interpreting Political Cartoons • Chapter Review Activity **Pre-AP Activities Guide for United States History:*** Supporting Arguments	**One-Stop Planner CD-ROM:** Calendar Planner **Student Edition Full-Read Audio CD-ROM** **Universal Access Modified Worksheets and Tests CD-ROM** **Interactive Skills Tutor CD-ROM** **Primary Source Library CD-ROM for United States History** **Power Presentations with Video CD-ROM** **History's Impact: United States History Video Program (VHS/DVD):** The Civil War*
Section 1: **The War Begins** **The Big Idea:** Civil War broke out between the North and the South in 1861. 8.10.3, 8.10.4, 8.10.6, 8.10.7	**Universal Access Teacher Management System:*** Section 1 Lesson Plan **Interactive Reader and Study Guide:*** Section 1 Summary **Chapter Resource File*** • Vocabulary Builder, Section 1 • History and Geography Activity: Choosing Sides **Political Cartoons Activities for United States History,** Cartoon 17: The Folly of Secession*	**Daily Bellringer Transparency:** Section 1* **Map Transparency:** Charleston, South Carolina Area Forts* **Quick Facts Transparency:** North Versus South*
Section 2: **The War in the East** **The Big Idea:** Confederate and Union forces faced off in Virginia and at sea. 8.10.5, 8.10.6	**Universal Access Teacher Management System:*** Section 2 Lesson Plan **Interactive Reader and Study Guide:*** Section 2 Summary **Chapter Resource File*** • Vocabulary Builder, Section 2 • Biography Activity: Thomas "Stonewall" Jackson • Interdisciplinary Project: The Ironclads	**Daily Bellringer Transparency:** Section 2* **Map Transparency:** Battles in the East* **Map Transparency:** Union Blockade*
Section 3: **The War in the West** **The Big Idea:** Fighting in the Civil War spread to the western United States. 8.10.5, 8.10.6	**Universal Access Teacher Management System:*** Section 3 Lesson Plan **Interactive Reader and Study Guide:*** Section 3 Summary **Chapter Resource File*** • Vocabulary Builder, Section 3 • Primary Source Activity: The Battle of Shiloh	**Daily Bellringer Transparency:** Section 3* **Map Transparency:** The War in the West*
Section 4: **Daily Life During War** **The Big Idea:** The lives of many Americans were affected by the Civil War. 8.10.4, 8.10.5, 8.10.7	**Universal Access Teacher Management System:*** Section 4 Lesson Plan **Interactive Reader and Study Guide:*** Section 4 Summary **Chapter Resource File*** • Vocabulary Builder, Section 4 • Biography Activities: Clara Barton; William Carney • Primary Source Activity: *Andersonville Diary* • Primary Source Activity: Civil War Diary	**Daily Bellringer Transparency:** Section 4* **Map Transparency:** Emancipation Proclamation* go.hrw.com **Internet Activity:** Civil War Authors
Section 5: **The Tide of War Turns** **The Big Idea:** Union victories in 1863, 1864, and 1865 brought the Civil War to an end. 8.10.6, 8.10.7	**Universal Access Teacher Management System:*** Section 5 Lesson Plan **Interactive Reader and Study Guide:*** Section 5 Summary **Chapter Resource File*** • Vocabulary Builder, Section 5 • Biography Activity: William Tecumseh Sherman	**Daily Bellringer Transparency:** Section 5* **Map Transparency:** Pickett's Charge* **Map Transparency:** Final Campaigns* **Quick Facts Transparency:** Causes and Effects of The Civil War* go.hrw.com **Internet Activity:** 3-D Model of Gettysburg and Other Battles

SE Student Edition  Print Resource Audio CD  Video

TE Teacher's Edition  Transparency  CD-ROM  DVD

go.hrw.com CA Standards Mastery **LS** Learning Styles

OSP One-Stop Planner CD-ROM * also on One-Stop Planner CD

Review, Assessment, Intervention

 **Standards Review Workbook***

Quick Facts Transparency: The Civil War Visual Summary*

Spanish Chapter Summaries Audio CD Program

 **Online Chapter Summaries in Six Languages**

Progress Assessment Support System (PASS): Chapter Test*

 **Universal Access Modified Worksheets and Tests CD-ROM:** Modified Chapter Test

 **One-Stop Planner CD-ROM:** ExamView Test Generator (English/Spanish)

 **Holt Online Assessment Program (HOAP),** in the Holt Premier Online Student Edition

 **PASS:** Section 1 Quiz*

 **Online Quiz:** Section 1

Alternative Assessment Handbook

 **PASS:** Section 2 Quiz*

Online Quiz: Section 2

 **Alternative Assessment Handbook**

 **PASS:** Section 3 Quiz*

 **Online Quiz:** Section 3

 **Alternative Assessment Handbook**

 **PASS:** Section 4 Quiz*

 **Online Quiz:** Section 4

 **Alternative Assessment Handbook**

 **PASS:** Section 5 Quiz*

 **Online Quiz:** Section 5

 **Alternative Assessment Handbook**

California Resources for Standards Mastery

INSTRUCTIONAL PLANNING AND SUPPORT

 **Universal Access Teacher Management System***

 **One-Stop Planner CD-ROM with Test Generator: Teacher Management System with Interactive Teacher's Edition**

STANDARDS MASTERY

 **Standards Review Workbook***

At Home: A Guide to Standards Mastery for United States History

go.hrw.com Holt Online Learning

To enhance learning, Internet activities are available for Civil War Authors and a 3-D Model of Gettysburg and Other Battles.

KEYWORD: SS8 TEACHER

- **Teacher Support Page**
- **Content Updates**
- **Rubrics and Writing Models**
- **Teaching Tips for the Multimedia Classroom**

KEYWORD: SS8 US15

- **Current Events**
- **Document-Based Questions**
- **Holt Grapher**
- **Holt Online Atlas**
- **Holt Researcher**
- **Interactive Multimedia Activities**
- **Internet Activities**
- **Online Chapter Summaries in Six Languages**
- **Online Section Quizzes**
- **American History Maps and Charts**

HOLT PREMIER ONLINE STUDENT EDITION

Complete online support for interactivity, assessment, and reporting

- **Interactive Maps and Notebook**
- **Standardized Test Prep**
- **Homework Practice and Research Activities Online**

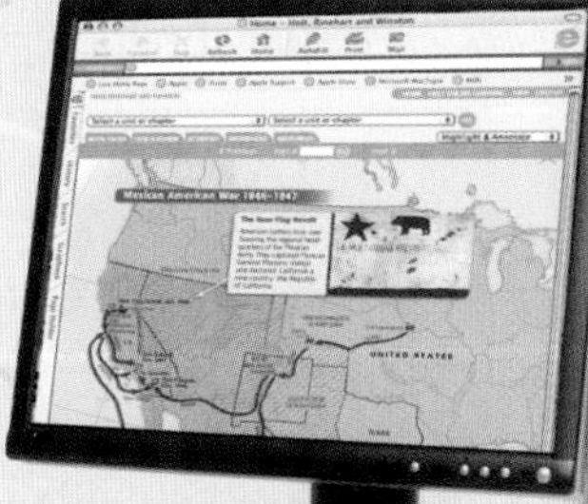

Mastering the Standards: Differentiating Instruction

Reaching Standards	Basic-level activities designed for all students encountering new material
Standards Proficiency	Intermediate-level activities designed for average students
Exceeding Standards	Challenging activities designed for honors and gifted-and-talented students
Standard English Mastery	Activities designed to improve standard English usage

Frequently Asked Questions

INSTRUCTIONAL PLANNING AND SUPPORT

Where do I find planning aids, pacing guides, lesson plans, and other teaching aids?

Annotated Teacher's Edition:
- Chapter planning guides
- Standards-based instruction and strategies
- Differentiated instruction for universal access
- Point-of-use reminders for integrating program resources

Power Presentations with Video CD-ROM

Universal Access Teacher Management System:
- Year and unit instructional benchmarking guides
- Reproducible lesson plans
- Assessment guides for diagnostic, progress, and summative end-of-the-year tests
- Options for differentiating instruction and intervention
- Teaching guides and answer keys for student workbooks

One-Stop Planner CD-ROM with Test Generator: Teacher Management System with Interactive Teacher's Editon:
- Calendar Planner
- Editable lesson plans
- All reproducible ancillaries in Adobe Acrobat (PDF) format
- ExamView Test Generator (English & Spanish)
- Game Tool for ExamView
- PuzzlePro
- Transparency and video previews

DIFFERENTIATING INSTRUCTION FOR UNIVERSAL ACCESS

What resources are available to ensure that Advanced Learners/GATE Students master the standards?

Teacher's Edition Activities:
- Researching the Civil War, p. 475
- Civil War Battle Songs, p. 481
- Military Draft Debate, p. 494

Lesson Plans for Universal Access

Pre-AP Activities Guide for United States History: Supporting Arguments

Primary Source Library CD-ROM for United States History

What resources are available to ensure that English Learners and Standard English Learners master the standards?

Teacher's Edition Activities:
- Storyboard/Cartoon Strip, p. 482

Lesson Plans for Universal Access

Chapter Resource File: Vocabulary Builder Activities

Spanish Chapter Summaries Audio CD Program

Online Chapter Summaries in Six Languages

One-Stop Planner CD-ROM:
- PuzzlePro, Spanish Version
- ExamView Test Generator, Spanish Version

What modified materials are available for Special Education?

The ***Universal Access Modified Worksheets and Tests CD-ROM*** provides editable versions of the following:

Vocabulary Flash Cards

Modified Vocabulary Builder Activities

Modified Chapter Review Activity

Modified Chapter Test

What resources are available to ensure that Learners Having Difficulty master the standards?

Teacher's Edition Activities:

- Civil War Battles, p. 479
- African American Union Soldiers, p. 492

Interactive Reader and Study Guide

Student Edition Full-Read Audio CD

Quick Facts Transparency: The Civil War Visual Summary

Standards Review Workbook

Social Studies Skills Activity: Interpreting Political Cartoons

Interactive Skills Tutor CD-ROM

How do I intervene for students struggling to master the standards?

Interactive Reader and Study Guide

Quick Facts Transparency: The Civil War Visual Summary

Standards Review Workbook

Social Studies Skills Activity: Interpreting Political Cartoons

Interactive Skills Tutor CD-ROM

PROFESSIONAL DEVELOPMENT

What teacher training resources are available to help me grow professionally?

- In-service and staff development as part of your Holt Social Studies product purchase
- Quick Teacher Tutorial Lesson Presentation CD-ROM
- Intensive tuition-based Teacher Development Institute
- *Teaching American History* Online 2 Module Professional Development Course
- Convenient Holt Speaker Bureau face-to-face workshop options
- PRAXIS™ Test Prep (#0089) interactive Web-based content refreshers*
- 24/7 *Ask A Professional Development Expert* at http://www.hrw.com/prodev/

* PRAXIS is a trademark of Educational Testing Service (ETS). This publication is not endorsed or approved by ETS.

Information Literacy Skills

To learn more about how History–Social Science instruction may be improved by the effective use of library media centers and information literacy skills, go to the Teacher's Resource Materials for Chapter 15 at **go.hrw.com**, keyword: SS8 MEDIA.

The following materials were developed by the Division for Public Education of the American Bar Association. These materials are part of the **Democracy and Civic Education** supplement.

- Constitution Study Guide
- Supreme Court Case Studies

Chapter Preview

Standards Focus

Standards by Section

Section 1: HSS 8.10.3, 8.10.4, 8.10.6, 8.10.7
Section 2: HSS 8.10.5, 8.10.6
Section 3: HSS 8.10.5, 8.10.6
Section 4: HSS 8.10.4, 8.10.5, 8.10.7
Section 5: HSS 8.10.6, 8.10.7

Teacher's Edition

HSS **Analysis Skills:** CS 1, CS 2, CS 3, HR 4, HR 5, HI 1, HI 2, HI 3, HI 4
ELA Writing 8.2.0

Preview Grade 8 Standards

HSS **8.11** Students analyze the character and lasting consequences of Reconstruction.
8.11.1 List the original aims of Reconstruction and describe its effects on the political and social structures of different regions.

Focus on Writing

The **Chapter Resource File** provides a Focus on Writing worksheet to help students organize and write their newspaper articles.

CRF: Focus on Writing Activity: Writing a Newspaper Article

CHAPTER 15 1861–1865

The Civil War

California Standards

History–Social Science

8.10 Students analyze the multiple causes, key events, and complex consequences of the Civil War.

Analysis Skills

HR 4 Students assess the credibility of primary and secondary sources.

English–Language Arts

Writing 8.2.0 Students write narratives, expository, persuasive, and descriptive essays.

FOCUS ON WRITING

Writing a Newspaper Article For most of this nation's history, newspapers have been an important way for citizens to learn about what is happening in the United States. In this chapter you will read about the main events of the Civil War. Then you will choose one of these events and write a newspaper article about it.

UNITED STATES

1861 Confederate guns open fire on Fort Sumter on April 12. Confederates win the first battle of the Civil War on July 21 at Bull Run in Virginia.

1861

WORLD

1861 Great Britain and France decide to buy cotton from Egypt instead of from the Confederacy.

Introduce the Chapter

Standards Proficiency

Focus on the Effects of War HSS 8.10; HSS Analysis Skills: HI 2

1. Ask students to imagine that the people in part of their state have risen up against the U.S. government, which they claim is abusing its power and denying their rights. Tell students to imagine that some of their friends and even members of their family have decided to fight with the rebels.
2. Have students discuss the results of such a situation. How would they feel if they had to fight against family members and friends in battle? What would it be like if battles were taking place in their local community? What would be some of the effects on the people and local environment?
3. Explain to students that the Civil War divided Americans and resulted in extreme death and destruction across large parts of the nation. Tell students as they study the chapter to note how the war affected soldiers, civilians, and the environment. LS **Verbal/Linguistic**

HOLT

History's Impact

▶ **video series**
Watch the video to understand the impact of the Civil War.

What You Will Learn...

In this chapter you will learn how the resources of the North enabled it to defeat the South in the Civil War. Among those who marched off to war were these drummer boys of the Union army.

1862 The *Monitor* fights the *Virginia* on March 9.

1863 The Emancipation Proclamation is issued on January 1.

1865 General Robert E. Lee surrenders to General Ulysses S. Grant on April 9.

1862 — 1863 — 1864 — 1865

1862 An imperial decree expels foreigners from Japan.

1864 With the support of French troops, Archduke Maximilian of Austria becomes emperor of Mexico.

1864 The Taiping Rebellion in China ends after the capture of Nanjing in July.

• Chapter Preview •

HOLT

History's Impact

▶ **video series**
See the Video Teacher's Guide for strategies for using the chapter video **The Civil War**.

Chapter Big Ideas

Section 1 Civil War broke out between the North and the South in 1861. **HSS** 8.10.3, 8.10.4, 8.10.6, 8.10.7

Section 2 Confederate and Union forces faced off in Virginia and at sea. **HSS** 8.10.5, 8.10.6

Section 3 Fighting in the Civil War spread to the western United States. **HSS** 8.10.5, 8.10.6

Section 4 The lives of many Americans were affected by the Civil War. **HSS** 8.10.4, 8.10.5, 8.10.7

Section 5 Union victories in 1863, 1864, and 1865 brought the Civil War to an end. **HSS** 8.10.6, 8.10.7

Explore the Picture

Young Soldiers Thousands of boys and teenagers fought in the Civil War. Many boys who joined the army served as drummers, such as the ones shown in the picture at left. The beat of the drum was an important way to communicate orders to soldiers. As a result, drummers often found themselves in the target of enemy fire.

Analyzing Visuals What do the expressions on the drummers' faces suggest about what they might be feeling and thinking? *possible answers—They seem to look determined and focused on their work ahead. Some look like they might be nervous or afraid.*

Explore the Time Line

1. When was the first battle of the Civil War, and where did it occur? *July 21, 1861; at Bull Run in Virginia*
2. In what year did a sea battle take place between the *Monitor* and the *Virginia*? *1862*
3. When was the Emancipation Proclamation issued? *January 1, 1863*
4. How long was the Civil War? *about four years*

HSS Analysis Skills: CS 1

Info to Know

Response to the Fall of Fort Sumter The Confederate attack on Fort Sumter in April 1861 began the Civil War. News of the attack spread quickly by telegraph throughout the North and the South. In the North, people were stunned by the news. In Boston, sorrowful bells tolled all day. In much of the South, people rushed into the streets to celebrate. The secretary of war for the Confederacy proclaimed that the Confederate flag would "float over the dome of the old Capitol in Washington" by May.

go.hrw.com

Online Resources

Chapter Resources:
KEYWORD: SS8 US15

Teacher Resources:
KEYWORD: SS8 TEACHER

Reading Social Studies

Understanding Themes

Two themes—politics and society and culture—are presented in this chapter. Ask students to think about some of the effects that a civil war might have on a nation. Guide students in a discussion of the challenges that individuals and governments might face. Tell students that as they study this chapter, they will learn about the problems Americans faced during the Civil War, and how they worked to overcome those social and political problems.

Supporting Facts and Details

Focus on Reading Explain to students that writers are more effective when they provide credible statements that explain or prove their points. To illustrate this to students, ask each student to write a short paragraph explaining what they know about their local government. Ask students to evaluate their paragraphs. Ask them what is missing that could make their writing more effective. Help students to see that by adding anecdotes, facts and statistics, quotes, and examples, their paragraph would be more interesting and informative.

Reading Social Studies

Economics | Geography | **Politics** | Religion | **Society and Culture** | Science and Technology

Focus on Themes As you read this chapter about the Civil War, you will see that this was a time in our history dominated by two major concerns: **politics** and **society and culture**. You will not only read about the political decisions made during this war, but will see how the war affected all of American society. You will read about the causes and the key events during the war and the many consequences of this war. This chapter tells of one of the most important events in our history.

Supporting Facts and Details

Focus on Reading Main ideas and big ideas are just that, ideas. How do we know what those ideas really mean?

Additional reading support can be found in the

Understanding Ideas and Their Support A main idea or big idea may be a kind of summary statement, or it may be a statement of the author's opinion. Either way, a good reader looks to see what support—facts and various kinds of details—the writer provides. If the writer doesn't provide good support, the ideas may not be trustworthy.

Notice how the passage below uses facts and details to support the main idea.

Civil War armies fought in the ancient battlefield formation that produced massive casualties. Endless rows of troops fired directly at one another, with cannonballs landing amid them. When the order was given, soldiers would attach bayonets to their guns and rush toward their enemy. Men died to gain every inch of ground.

Despite the huge battlefield losses, the biggest killer in the Civil War was not the fighting. It was diseases such as typhoid, pneumonia, and tuberculosis. Nearly twice as many soldiers died of illnesses as died in combat.

From Chapter 15, pp. 495–496

The main idea is stated first.

These sentences provide details about the challenges soldiers faced.

The writer concludes with some facts as support.

Writers support propositions with . . .

1. **Facts and statistics**—Facts are statements that can be proved. Statistics are facts in number form.
2. **Examples**—specific instances that illustrate the facts
3. **Anecdotes**—brief stories that help explain the facts
4. **Definitions**—explain unusual terms or words
5. **Comments from the experts or eyewitnesses**—help support the reasons

Reading and Skills Resources

Reading Support

- Interactive Reader and Study Guide
- Student Edition on Audio CD
- Spanish Chapter Summaries Audio CD Program

Social Studies Skills Support

- Interactive Skills Tutor CD-ROM

Vocabulary Support

- **CRF:** Vocabulary Builder Activities
- **CRF:** Chapter Review Activity
- Universal Access Modified Worksheets and Tests CD-ROM:
  - Vocabulary Flash Cards
  - Vocabulary Builder Activity
  - Chapter Review Activity
- OSP Holt PuzzlePro

Standards Focus

ELA Reading 8.2.2

ELA Reading 8.2.2 Analyze text that uses proposition and support patterns.

You Try It!

The following passage is from the chapter you are about to read. As you read it, look for the writer's main idea and support.

> In February 1862, Grant let an assault force into Tennessee. With help from navy gunboats, Grant's Army of Tennessee took two outposts on key rivers in the west. On February 6, he captured Fort Henry on the Tennessee River. Several days later he took Fort Donelson on the Cumberland River.
>
> Fort Donelson's commander asked for the terms of surrender. Grant replied, "No terms except and unconditional and immediate surrender can be accepted." The fort surrendered. The North gave a new name to Grant's initials: "Unconditional Surrender" Grant.
>
> *From Chapter 15, p. 484*

After you read the passage, answer the following questions.

1. Which sentence best states the writer's main idea?
   - **A.** The fort surrendered.
   - **B.** In February 1862, Grant led an assault force into Tennessee.
   - **C.** Fort Donelson's commander asked for the terms of surrender.
2. Which method of support is not used to support the main idea?
   - **A.** Facts
   - **B.** Comments from experts or eyewitnesses
   - **C.** Anecdotes
3. Which sentence in this passage provides a comment from an expert or eyewitness?

As you read Chapter 15, pay attention to the details that the writers have chosen to support their main ideas.

Key Terms and People

Chapter 15

Section 1
Fort Sumter *(p. 472)*
border states *(p. 474)*
Winfield Scott *(p. 475)*
cotton diplomacy *(p. 475)*

Section 2
Thomas "Stonewall" Jackson *(p. 478)*
First Battle of Bull Run *(p. 479)*
George B. McClellan *(p. 480)*
Robert E. Lee *(p. 480)*
Seven Days' Battle *(p. 480)*
Second Battle of Bull Run *(p. 480)*
Battle of Antietam *(p. 481)*
ironclads *(p. 482)*

Section 3
Ulysses S. Grant *(p. 484)*
Battle of Shiloh *(p. 485)*
David Farragut *(p. 485)*
Siege of Vicksburg *(p. 486)*

Section 4
emancipation *(p. 491)*
Emancipation Proclamation *(p. 491)*
contrabands *(p. 493)*
54th Massachusetts Infantry *(p. 493)*
Copperheads *(p. 494)*
habeas corpus *(p. 494)*
Clara Barton *(p. 496)*

Section 5
George G. Meade *(p. 498)*
Battle of Gettysburg *(p. 498)*
George Pickett *(p. 499)*
Pickett's Charge *(p. 499)*
Gettysburg Address *(p. 500)*
Wilderness Campaign *(p. 500)*
William Tecumseh Sherman *(p. 501)*
total war *(p. 502)*
Appomattox Courthouse *(p. 502)*

Academic Vocabulary

In this chapter, you will learn the following academic words:

innovation *(p. 482)*
execute *(p. 500)*

Reading Social Studies

Key Terms and People

Assign each student a key term or person from the list at left. Have students define or identify their assigned term or name, then have students explain the importance of that term during the Civil War. Ask students to imagine that they are creating a series of bumper stickers with historical themes. Have each student create a slogan for a bumper sticker that relates the importance of the term or person they were assigned. Remind students to keep their slogan short, interesting, and to the point. One example might be, "Ironclads—Try as you might, you can't sink 'em!"
LS Verbal/Linguistic, Visual/Spatial

Focus on Reading

See the **Focus on Reading** questions in this chapter for more practice on this reading social studies skill.

Reading Social Studies Assessment

See the **Standards Review** at the end of this chapter for student assessment questions related to this reading skill.

Teaching Tip

To help reinforce the importance of supporting details, select a paragraph or two from the textbook. Then rewrite each paragraph, omitting facts, examples, anecdotes, and quotes. Have students read what little of the paragraph remains. Then ask students what types of information they might add to the paragraph to provide support for the main idea.

Answers

You Try It! 1. *b;* **2.** *c;* **3.** *second sentence in second paragraph; "Grant replied, 'No terms except an unconditional and immediate surrender can be accepted.'"*

Preteach

Bellringer

If YOU were there . . . Use the **Daily Bellringer Transparency** to help students answer the question.

Daily Bellringer Transparency, Section 1

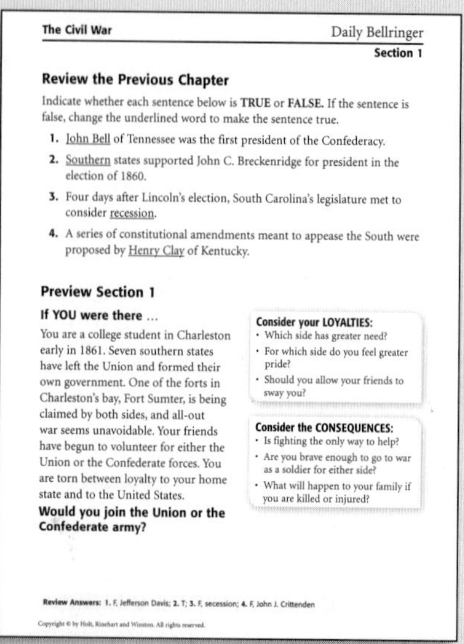

The Civil War — Daily Bellringer — Section 1

Review the Previous Chapter

Indicate whether each sentence below is **TRUE** or **FALSE.** If the sentence is false, change the underlined word to make the sentence true.

1. John Bell of Tennessee was the first president of the Confederacy.
2. Southern states supported John C. Breckenridge for president in the election of 1860.
3. Four days after Lincoln's election, South Carolina's legislature met to consider recession.
4. A series of constitutional amendments meant to appease the South were proposed by Henry Clay of Kentucky.

Preview Section 1

If YOU were there ...

You are a college student in Charleston early in 1861. Seven southern states have left the Union and formed their own government. One of the forts in Charleston's bay, Fort Sumter, is being claimed by both sides, and all-out war seems unavoidable. Your friends have begun to volunteer for either the Union or the Confederate forces. You are torn between loyalty to your home state and to the United States.

Would you join the Union or the Confederate army?

Consider your LOYALTIES:
- Which side has greater need?
- For which side do you feel greater pride?
- Should you allow your friends to sway you?

Consider the CONSEQUENCES:
- Is fighting the only way to help?
- Are you brave enough to go to war as a soldier for either side?
- What will happen to your family if you are killed or injured?

Review Answers: 1. F, Jefferson Davis; 2. T; 3. F, secession; 4. F, John J. Crittenden

Building Vocabulary

Preteach or review the following terms:

mint place to make coins (p. 472)

secede to separate from the Union (p. 472)

CRF: Vocabulary Builder Activity, Section 1

Standards Focus

HSS 8.10.3

Means: Describe the constitutional issues connected with secession.

Matters: President Abraham Lincoln's refusal to recognize the right of secession helped lead to the outbreak of the Civil War.

HSS 8.10.4

Means: Discuss the major events of Abraham Lincoln's presidency.

Matters: President Lincoln's ideas still remain influential.

HSS 8.10.6

Means: Describe the major events and battles of the start of the Civil War.

Matters: Studying past wars enables people to understand warfare better.

HSS 8.10.7

Means: Explain how the war affected the lives of soldiers and civilians as well as the environment and future warfare.

Matters: The Civil War caused death and destruction but led to the end of slavery.

SECTION 1

The War Begins

What You Will Learn...

Main Ideas

1. Following the outbreak of war at Fort Sumter, Americans chose sides.
2. The Union and the Confederacy prepared for war.

The Big Idea

Civil war broke out between the North and the South in 1861.

Key Terms and People

Fort Sumter, *p. 473*
border states, *p. 474*
Winfield Scott, *p. 475*
cotton diplomacy, *p. 475*

HSS 8.10.3 Identify the constitutional issues posed by the doctrine of nullification and secession and the earliest origins of that doctrine.

8.10.4 Discuss Abraham Lincoln's presidency and his significant writings and speeches and their relationship to the Declaration of Independence, such as his "House Divided" speech (1858), Gettysburg Address (1863), Emancipation Proclamation (1863), and inaugural addresses (1861 and 1865).

8.10.6 Describe critical developments and events in the war, including the major battles, geographical advantages and obstacles, technological advances, and General Lee's surrender at Appomattox.

8.10.7 Explain how the war affected combatants, civilians, the physical environment, and future warfare.

If YOU were there...

You are a college student in Charleston in early 1861. Seven southern states have left the Union and formed their own government. One of the forts in Charleston's bay, Fort Sumter, is being claimed by both sides, and all-out war seems unavoidable. Your friends have begun to volunteer for either the Union or the Confederate forces. You are torn between loyalty to your home state and to the United States.

Would you join the Union or the Confederate army?

BUILDING BACKGROUND The divisions within the United States reached a breaking point with the election of Abraham Lincoln in 1860. Several southern states angrily left the Union to form a new confederation. In border states such as Virginia and Kentucky, people were divided. The question now was whether the United States could survive as a disunified country.

Americans Choose Sides

Abraham Lincoln became president on the eve of a four-year national nightmare. Furious at Lincoln's election and fearing a federal invasion, seven southern states had seceded. The new commander in chief tried desperately to save the Union.

In his inaugural address, Lincoln promised not to end slavery where it existed. The federal government "will not assail [attack] you. You can have no conflict without being yourselves the aggressors," he said, trying to calm southerners' fears. However, Lincoln also stated his intention to preserve the Union. He refused to recognize secession, declaring the Union to be "unbroken."

In fact, after decades of painful compromises, the Union was badly broken. From the lower South, a battle cry was arising, born out of fear, rage—and excitement. Confederate officials began seizing branches of the federal mint, arsenals, and military outposts. In the highly charged atmosphere, it would take only a spark to unleash the heat of war.

Teach the Big Idea: Master the Standards

Standards Proficiency

The War Begins

HSS 8.10.3, 8.10.4, 8.10.6, 8.10.7; HSS **Analysis Skills:** HR 5, HI 1, HI 2

1. **Teach** Ask students the Main Idea questions to teach this section.
2. **Apply** Discuss with students the crisis Lincoln faced upon becoming president, including his views on secession. Then discuss how the attack on Fort Sumter triggered the outbreak of the Civil War. Draw a jagged circle for students to see and label it *Fort Sumter*. Below the circle, draw three large boxes and label them *Americans Choose Sides, The North Versus the South,* and *Preparing for War.* **LS Visual/Spatial**
3. **Review** Have students help you complete each box by listing main ideas for that topic. Have students copy the completed chart.
4. **Practice/Homework** Have each student write a journal entry from the point of view of someone in the North or the South expressing his or her views on the outbreak of war. **LS Verbal/Linguistic**

Alternative Assessment Handbook, Rubrics 7: Charts; and 15: Journals

In 1861, that spark occurred at **Fort Sumter**, a federal outpost in Charleston, South Carolina, that was attacked by Confederate troops, beginning the Civil War. Determined to seize the fortress—which controlled the entrance to Charleston harbor—the Confederates ringed the harbor with heavy guns. Instead of surrendering the fort, Lincoln decided to send in ships to provide badly needed supplies to defend the fort. Confederate officials demanded that the federal troops evacuate. The fort's commander, Major Robert Anderson, refused.

Before sunrise on April 12, 1861, Confederate guns opened fire on Fort Sumter. A witness wrote that the first shots brought "every soldier in the harbor to his feet, and every man, woman, and child in the city of Charleston from their beds." The Civil War had begun.

The fort, although massive, stood little chance. Its heavy guns faced the Atlantic Ocean, not the shore. After 34 hours of cannon blasts, Fort Sumter surrendered. "The last ray of hope for preserving the Union has expired at the assault upon Fort Sumter . . ." Lincoln wrote.

Reaction to Lincoln's Call

The fall of Fort Sumter stunned the North. Lincoln declared the South to be in a state of rebellion and asked state governors for 75,000 militiamen to put down the rebellion. States now had to choose: Would they secede, or would they stay in the Union? Democratic Senator Stephen Douglas, speaking in support of Lincoln's call for troops, declared, "There can be no neutrals in this war, *only patriots—or traitors.*"

Charleston, South Carolina, Area Forts

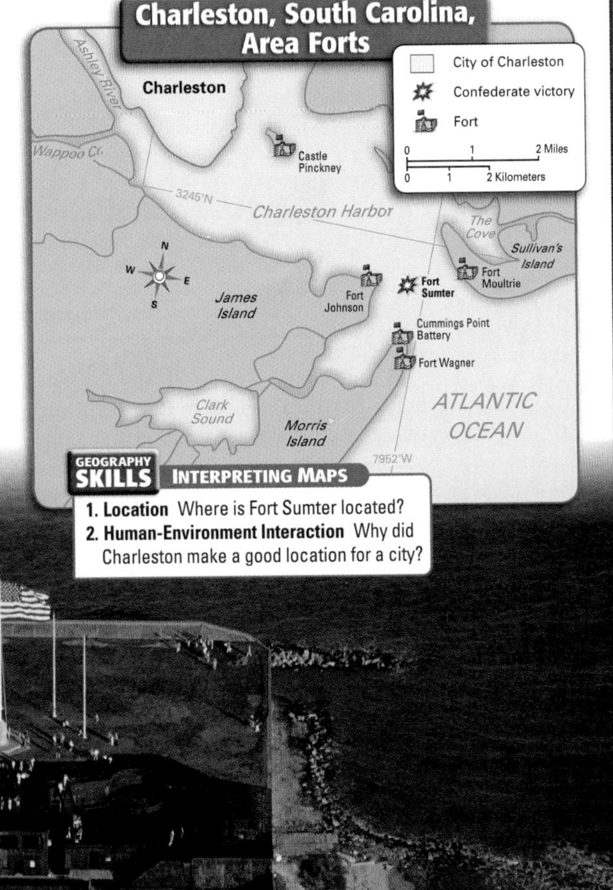

GEOGRAPHY SKILLS INTERPRETING MAPS

1. **Location** Where is Fort Sumter located?
2. **Human-Environment Interaction** Why did Charleston make a good location for a city?

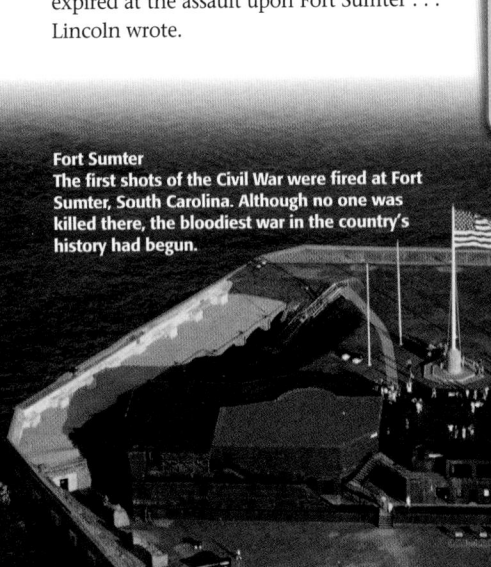

Fort Sumter
The first shots of the Civil War were fired at Fort Sumter, South Carolina. Although no one was killed there, the bloodiest war in the country's history had begun.

Direct Teach

Main Idea

1 Americans Choose Sides

Following the outbreak of war at Fort Sumter, Americans chose sides.

Recall What event led to the start of the Civil War, and when did it occur? *Confederate attack on Fort Sumter on April 12, 1861*

Draw Conclusions How did the issue of secession contribute to the attack on Fort Sumter? *possible answer—Because South Carolina had seceded, its leaders believed they had the right to take Fort Sumter, which they considered to no longer be in federally controlled territory.*

Evaluate Do you think war could have been avoided? Why or why not? *possible answers—Yes, Lincoln had stated in his Inaugural Address that he would respect southerners' concerns; no, war was inevitable once southern states seceded.*

Political Cartoons Activities for United States History, Cartoon 17: The Folly of Secession

Map Transparency: Charleston, South Carolina, Area Forts

HSS 8.10.3, 8.10.4, 8.10.6; **HSS Analysis Skills:** CS 1, HR 4, HI 1, HI 2

Info to Know

Meanwhile, in Florida While events were unfolding at Fort Sumter, a similar situation was taking place at Fort Pickens near Pensacola, Florida. The Union forces at the fort were running low on supplies, and the Confederates were preparing to attack. Then news arrived of the fighting at Fort Sumter. The Confederates withdrew from the area to focus their efforts elsewhere.

Collaborative Learning

Standards Proficiency

Front Page News: Fort Sumter

HSS 8.10.6; **HSS Analysis Skills:** HR 5, HI 1, HI 2

1. Organize the class into small groups and have each group create the front page of a newspaper covering the attack on Fort Sumter. Half of the groups should create their pages from the point of view of a southern newspaper. The other half of the groups should create pages for a northern newspaper.
2. Each group should create a masthead, two articles with headlines, an editorial, and a political cartoon explaining what happened and why the event was significant.
3. To ensure that all students participate, have groups assign each member specific tasks. Students might use poster board or computer software to produce their news pages.
4. Have each group present its front page to the class. **LS Interpersonal, Verbal/Linguistic, Visual/Spatial**

Alternative Assessment Handbook, Rubric 23: Newspapers

Answers

Interpreting Maps 1. *at the entrance to Charleston Harbor in South Carolina;* **2.** *possible answer—It had a large harbor.*

Direct Teach

Main Idea

1 Americans Choose Sides

Following the outbreak of war at Fort Sumter, Americans chose sides.

Explain Why were the border states significant? *Kentucky and Missouri controlled parts of important rivers; Maryland separated Washington, D.C. from the rest of the North.*

Summarize Describe the strategies of the North and the South. *North—destroy the South's economy by blockading southern ports, gain control of the Mississippi River to divide the South; capture Richmond, the Confederate capital; South—fight until the North is worn down; capture Washington, D.C.; win foreign allies through cotton diplomacy*

Identify Points of View How did the war affect family loyalties and friendships on each side? *deeply divided families and friends as people chose different sides*

- **CRF:** History and Geography Activity: Choosing Sides
- Quick Facts Transparency: North Versus South
- HSS 8.10.6, 8.10.7; HSS **Analysis Skills:** HR 5, HI 1, HI 2

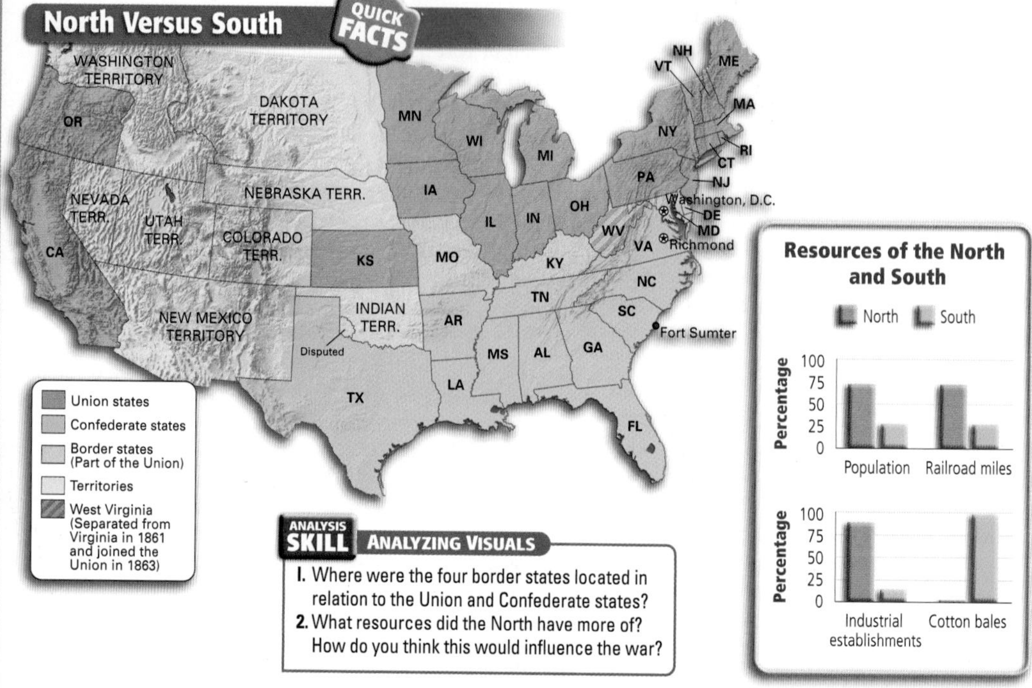

ANALYSIS SKILL ANALYZING VISUALS

1. Where were the four border states located in relation to the Union and Confederate states?
2. What resources did the North have more of? How do you think this would influence the war?

Pennsylvania, New Jersey, and the states north of them rallied to the president's call. The crucial slave states of the Upper South—North Carolina, Tennessee, Virginia, and Arkansas—seceded. They provided soldiers and supplies to the South. Mary Boykin Chesnut, whose husband became a Confederate congressman, wrote in her diary during this time:

> "I did not know that one could live in such days of excitement…Everybody tells you half of something, and then rushes off…to hear the last news."

Wedged between the North and the South were the key **border states** of Delaware, Kentucky, Maryland, and Missouri—slave states that did not join the Confederacy. Kentucky and Missouri controlled parts of important rivers. Maryland separated the Union capital, Washington, D.C., from the North.

People in the border states were deeply divided on the war. The president's own wife, Mary Todd Lincoln, had four brothers from Kentucky who fought for the Confederacy. Lincoln sent federal troops into the border states to help keep them in the Union. He also sent soldiers into western Virginia, where Union loyalties were strong. West Virginia set up its own state government in 1863.

The North Versus the South

Numbers tell an important story about the Civil War. Consider the North's advantages. It could draw soldiers and workers from a population of 22 million, compared with the South's 5.5 million. One of its greatest advantages was its network of roads, canals, and railroads. Some 22,000 miles of railroad track could move soldiers and supplies throughout the North. The South had only about 9,000 miles of track.

Finally, the Union had money. It had a more developed economy, banking system, and currency. The South had to start printing its own Confederate dollars. Some states

Critical Thinking: Evaluating Information

Standards Proficiency

The North Versus the South

HSS 8.10.6; HSS **Analysis Skills:** HI 1, HI 2

1. Organize the class into small groups. Assign the North to half the groups and the South to the other half. Ask students to imagine that they are military advisers for their side at the start of the Civil War.
2. Each group should prepare a report for its president that analyzes the strengths and weaknesses of the other side at the start of the war. Students should address both available resources and military strategies. Encourage students to incorporate maps, charts, and graphs as visual aids. Students might use presentation software as well.
3. Have volunteer groups share their reports with the class. Conclude with a discussion about the strengths and weaknesses of each side at the start of the war. LS **Interpersonal, Logical/Mathematical**

- Alternative Assessment Handbook, Rubrics 29: Presentations; and 42: Writing to Inform

Answers

Analyzing Visuals **1.** *between the Union and Confederate states;* **2.** *population, railroad miles, industrial establishments; give the North an advantage over the South* printed their own money, too. This led to financial chaos.

The Confederacy had advantages as well. With its strong military tradition, the South put many brilliant officers into battle. Southern farms provided food for its armies. The South's best advantage, however, was strategic. It needed only to defend itself until the North grew tired of fighting. Southern soldiers fought mostly on their home soil, while the North had to occupy large areas of enemy territory.

Taking advantage of the Union's strengths, General **Winfield Scott** developed a two-part strategy: (1) destroy the South's economy with a naval blockade of southern ports; (2) gain control of the Mississippi River to divide the South. Other leaders urged an attack on Richmond, Virginia, the Confederate capital.

The South hoped to wear down the North and to capture Washington, D.C. Confederate president Jefferson Davis also tried to win foreign allies through **cotton diplomacy**. This was the idea that Great Britain would support the Confederacy because it needed the South's raw cotton to supply its booming textile industry. Cotton diplomacy did not work as the South had hoped. Britain had large supplies of cotton, and it got more from India and Egypt.

READING CHECK **Comparing** What advantages did the North and South have leading up to the war?

Preparing for War

The North and the South now rushed to war. Neither side was prepared for it.

Volunteer Armies

Volunteer militias had sparked the revolution that created the United States. Now they would battle for its future. At the start of the war, the Union army had only 16,000 soldiers. Within months that number had swelled to a half million. Southern men rose

Union and Confederate Soldiers

Early in the war, uniforms differed greatly, especially in the Confederate army. Uniforms became simpler and more standard as the war dragged on.

The soldiers carried food, extra ammunition, and other items in their haversacks.
Each soldier was armed with a bayonet, a knife that can be attached to the barrel of a rifle. The bayonets were stored in scabbards on their belts.
Confederate Soldier
Both soldiers were also armed with single-shot, muzzle-loading rifles.
Union Soldier

ANALYSIS SKILL ANALYZING VISUALS

How are the Union and Confederate uniforms and equipment similar and different?

Direct Teach

Main Idea

❷ Preparing for War

The Union and the Confederacy prepared for war.

Recall How many troops did the Union have at the war's start? *16,000*

Identify Points of View For what reasons were many southerners fighting, and how did southerners view the North's preparation for war? *to defend their land and ways of life; as preparation to invade*

HSS 8.10.6, 8.10.7; HSS **Analysis Skills:** HR 5, HI 1

Info to Know

The Blue and the Gray Towns formed volunteer militia units, which then combined to form regiments. As a result, the variety of uniforms within regiments varied greatly, from elaborate homemade uniforms to uniforms dating back to the Revolutionary War. Soldiers soon learned the importance of consistent uniforms, however, particularly regarding color. For example, at the Battle of Bull Run, Confederate soldiers learned this lesson when their blue uniforms created confusion about which side they were on.

Differentiating Instruction for Universal Access

Advanced Learners-GATE

Exceeding Standards | Research Required

Materials: poster board, markers, crayons

1. Organize the class into five groups.
2. Assign each group one of the following topics to research, focusing on the start of the Civil War: strategies, volunteers and training, military medicine, home front preparations, and the U.S. Sanitary Commission. Students should look for primary and secondary sources to bring alive the call to arms.
3. Have each group use its findings to create a poster or triptych that shows how soldiers or civilians prepared for war.
4. Display students' work in the class.

LS **Interpersonal, Verbal/Linguistic**

HSS 8.10.6, 8.10.7; HSS **Analysis Skills:** HR 4, HI 1

Alternative Assessment Handbook, Rubrics 28: Posters; 29: Presentations; and 30: Research

Answers

Analyzing Visuals *similar equipment and weapons; uniforms different colors and styles*

Reading Check *North—larger population; network of roads, canals, and railroads; more money; South—military tradition and brilliant officers; farms to provide food for its armies; fighting on home soil so needed only to defend itself until the North tired of fighting*

Direct Teach

Main Idea

❷ Preparing for War

The Union and the Confederacy prepared for war.

Describe In what ways did civilians support the troops? *raised money, provided aid, and served as nurses*

Explain What was the purpose of the U.S. Sanitary Commission? *to send bandages, medicines, and food to Union army camps and hospitals*

Summarize What problems did both armies face at the start of the war? *shortages of supplies and inexperienced volunteers who needed to be trained in basic combat*

HSS 8.10.6, 8.10.7; **HSS Analysis Skills:** HI 1

Review & Assess

Close

Have students discuss how Americans on each side viewed the Civil War at its start and how these views probably changed over time.

Review

Online Quiz, Section 1

Assess

SE Section 1 Assessment

PASS: Section 1 Quiz

Alternative Assessment Handbook

Reteach/Classroom Intervention

California Standards Review Workbook

Interactive Reader and Study Guide, Section 1

Interactive Skills Tutor CD-ROM

Answers

Reading Check *soldiers—volunteered, trained to learn combat basics; civilians—raised money, provided aid, served as nurses*

up to defend their land and their ways of life. Virginian Thomas Webber came to fight "against the invading foe [enemy] who now pollute the sacred soil of my beloved native state." When Union soldiers asked one captured rebel why he was fighting, he replied, "I'm fighting because you're down here."

Helping the Troops

Civilians on both sides helped those in uniform. They raised money, provided aid for soldiers and their families, and ran emergency hospitals. In the Union, tens of thousands of volunteers worked with the U.S. Sanitary Commission to send bandages, medicines, and food to Union army camps and hospitals. Some 3,000 women served as nurses in the Union army.

Training the Soldiers

Both the Union and Confederate armies faced shortages of clothing, food, and even rifles. Most troops lacked standard uniforms and simply wore their own clothes. Eventually, each side chose a color for their uniforms. The Union chose blue. The Confederates wore gray.

The problem with volunteers was that many of them had no idea how to fight. Schoolteachers, farmers, and laborers all had to learn the combat basics of marching, shooting, and using bayonets.

In a letter to a friend, a Union soldier described life in the training camp.

> "We have been wading through mud knee deep all winter ... For the last two weeks we have been drilled almost to death. Squad drill from 6 to 7 A.M. Company drill from 9 to 11 A.M. Batallion Drill from 2 to 4 1/2 P.M. Dress Parade from 5 to 5 1/2 P.M. and non-commissioned officers' school from 7 to 8 in the evening. If we don't soon become a well drilled Regiment, we ought to."
>
> —David R. P. Shoemaker, 1862

With visions of glory and action, many young soldiers were eager to fight. They would not have to wait long.

READING CHECK **Summarizing** How did soldiers and civilians prepare for war?

SUMMARY AND PREVIEW As citizens chose sides in the Civil War, civilians became involved in the war effort. In the next section you will learn about some early battles in the war.

Section 1 Assessment

go.hrw.com **Online Quiz** KEYWORD: SS8 HP15

Reviewing Ideas, Terms, and People **HSS** 8.10.3, 8.10.4, 8.10.6, 8.10.7

1. a. **Identify** What event triggered the war between the Union and the Confederacy?
   b. **Contrast** How did the Union's strategy differ from that of the Confederacy?
   c. **Evaluate** Which side do you believe was best prepared for war? Explain your answer.
2. a. **Describe** How did women take part in the war?
   b. **Summarize** In what ways were the armies of the North and South unprepared for war?
   c. **Elaborate** Why did men volunteer to fight in the war?

Critical Thinking

3. **Summarizing** Copy the chart below. Use it to identify the strengths and weaknesses of the North and South at the start of the war.

	Union	Confederacy
Strengths		
Weaknesses		

FOCUS ON WRITING

4. **Taking Notes on the War's Beginning** As you read this section, take notes on the crisis at Fort Sumter and on the recruiting and training of the armies. Be sure to answer the following questions: Who? Where? When? Why? and How?

Section 1 Assessment Answers

1. a. Confederate attack on Fort Sumter
   b. North—blockade southern ports to destroy the South's economy, control the Mississippi River to divide the South; South—fight until the North was worn down, win foreign allies through cotton diplomacy
   c. Answers should reflect an understanding of each side's strengths and weaknesses.
2. a. raised money, served in the U.S. Sanitary Commission, served as nurses
   b. shortages of supplies, inexperienced troops who needed training in basic combat
   c. for glory and action, out of loyalty and patriotism; in the South, to defend their land and ways of life
3. Strengths—Union: larger population, better transportation network, stronger economy; Confederacy: military tradition, strategic advantage of fighting on home soil; Weaknesses—Union: fighting in enemy territory; Confederacy: lack of developed economy and banking system
4. Students' notes should be categorized to address each of the questions listed.

BIOGRAPHY

Abraham Lincoln

What would you do to save the struggling Union?

When did he live? 1809–1865

Where did he live? Abraham Lincoln was born in a log cabin to a poor family in Kentucky. Growing up in Kentucky and Illinois, Lincoln went to school for less than a year. He taught himself law and settled in Springfield, where he practiced law and politics. As president he lived in Washington, D.C. There, at age 56, his life was cut short by an assassin, John Wilkes Booth.

What did he do? The issue of slavery defined Lincoln's political career. He was not an abolitionist, but he strongly opposed extending slavery into the territories. In a series of famous debates against Senator Stephen Douglas of Illinois, Lincoln championed his views on slavery and made a brilliant defense of democracy and the Union. As president, Lincoln led the nation through the Civil War.

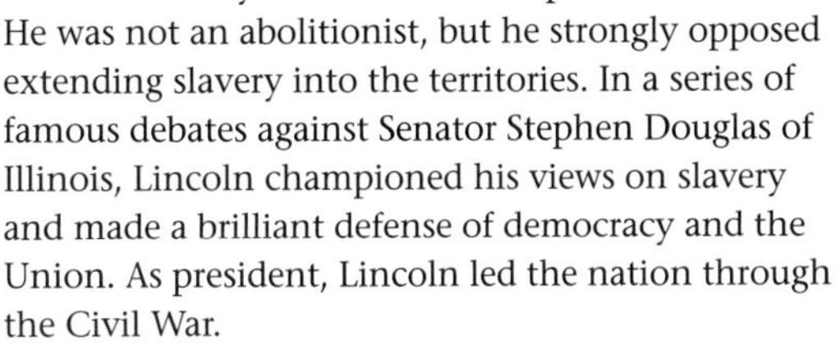

Why is he important? Lincoln is one of the great symbols of American democracy. "A house divided against itself cannot stand," he declared in a debate with Douglas. In 1863 Lincoln issued the Emancipation Proclamation. His address to commemorate the bloody battlefield at Gettysburg is widely considered to be one of the best political speeches in American history.

Summarizing Why is Lincoln such an important figure in American history?

Abraham Lincoln led the United States during the Civil War.

KEY EVENTS

- **1834** Elected to the Illinois legislature
- **1842** Marries Mary Todd
- **1858** Holds series of famous debates with U.S. Senator Stephen Douglas
- **1860** Elected president on November 6
- **1863** Issues the Emancipation Proclamation on January 1
- **1863** Gives the Gettysburg Address on November 19
- **1865** Gives second inaugural address on March 4
- **1865** Shot on April 14; dies the next day

Critical Thinking: Summarizing

Standards Proficiency

Abraham Lincoln Acrostic HSS 8.10.4; HSS Analysis Skills: HI 1

1. Have students discuss Lincoln's achievements and his importance in American history.
2. Ask students to suggest words and short phrases that describe Lincoln, his accomplishments, and his legacy. Create a list for students to see.
3. Then have students create an acrostic out of Lincoln's name. First, write *Abraham Lincoln* vertically in all capital letters. Second, model the activity by selecting a word from the list that includes an *A* (or use *Gettysburg Address*). Write the word vertically so that it uses the *A* in *Abraham.*
4. Then have students work individually or in mixed-ability pairs to complete the acrostic.
5. Have volunteers share some of their answers with the class. LS **Verbal/Linguistic**

Alternative Assessment Handbook, Rubric 13: Graphic Organizers

Biography

Reading Focus Question

Have students discuss the introductory question before reading the biography. Remind students of the crisis that Abraham Lincoln faced when he took office as president. Ask students how they might have acted in his place to preserve the Union. Encourage discussion. Then have students note as they read the biography the ways in which Lincoln supported the preservation of the Union during his lifetime.

MISCONCEPTION ALERT

Gettysburg Address Despite what is commonly stated, Abraham Lincoln did not hastily write the Gettysburg Address during the train trip to the battlefield. Two copies of the speech exist, the earliest of which was written on White House stationery and the other on lined paper. Most scholars believe the stationery version to be the one that Lincoln read from at Gettysburg. However, based on actual accounts of the speech, small differences exist between this written copy and Lincoln's actual speech. As a result, some scholars believe that the version of the speech that Lincoln actually used is now lost, because Lincoln usually did not vary much from his written speeches.

Info to Know

Lincoln and Booth Abraham Lincoln and John Wilkes Booth had crossed paths several times before the fatal assassination. Lincoln had previously attended a production of a play at Ford's Theatre in which Booth was one of the stars. At Lincoln's second inauguration, Booth was an invited guest and can even be seen in several photos of the event.

Answers

Summarizing *He symbolized American democracy and the vision of a unified nation, and he acted to preserve those ideals.*

Preteach

Bellringer

If YOU were there . . . Use the **Daily Bellringer Transparency** to help students answer the question.

Daily Bellringer Transparency, Section 2

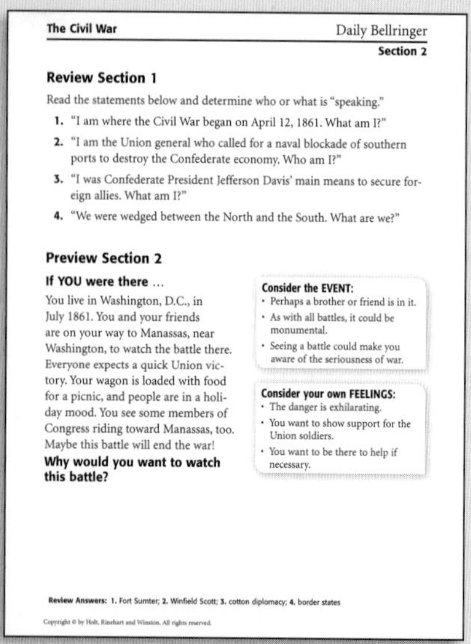
The Civil War — Daily Bellringer, **Section 2**

Review Section 1

Read the statements below and determine who or what is "speaking."

1. "I am where the Civil War began on April 12, 1861. What am I?"
2. "I am the Union general who called for a naval blockade of southern ports to destroy the Confederate economy. Who am I?"
3. "I was Confederate President Jefferson Davis' main means to secure foreign allies. What am I?"
4. "We were wedged between the North and the South. What are we?"

Preview Section 2

If YOU were there ...

You live in Washington, D.C., in July 1861. You and your friends are on your way to Manassas, near Washington, to watch the battle there. Everyone expects a quick Union victory. Your wagon is loaded with food for a picnic, and people are in a holiday mood. You see some members of Congress riding toward Manassas, too. Maybe this battle will end the war!

Why would you want to watch this battle?

Consider the EVENT:
- Perhaps a brother or friend is in it.
- As with all battles, it could be monumental.
- Seeing a battle could make you aware of the seriousness of war.

Consider your own FEELINGS:
- The danger is exhilarating.
- You want to show support for the Union soldiers.
- You want to be there to help if necessary.

Review Answers: **1.** Fort Sumter; **2.** Winfield Scott; **3.** cotton diplomacy; **4.** border states

Academic Vocabulary

Review with students the high-use academic term in this section.

innovation a new idea or way of doing something (p. 482)

Building Vocabulary

Preteach or review the following terms:

casualties people who are killed, wounded, captured, or missing in a military conflict (p. 480)

peninsula land mass surrounded on three sides by water (p. 479)

CRF: Vocabulary Builder Activity, Section 2

Standards Focus

HSS 8.10.5

Means: Identify the leaders in the North and the South, and describe the views of leaders and soldiers on both sides during the Civil War.

Matters: Studying the lives and views of the people who fought the Civil War helps us better understand the war's events and its outcome.

HSS 8.10.6

Means: Describe the major battles in the East during the early part of the Civil War and how geography and technology affected the battles.

Matters: Studying past wars enables people to understand warfare better.

SECTION 2

The War in the East

What You Will Learn...

Main Ideas

1. Union and Confederate forces fought for control of the war in Virginia.
2. The Battle of Antietam gave the North a slight advantage.
3. The Confederacy attempted to break the Union naval blockade.

The Big Idea

Confederate and Union forces faced off in Virginia and at sea.

Key Terms and People

Thomas "Stonewall" Jackson, *p. 479*
First Battle of Bull Run, *p. 479*
George B. McClellan, *p. 479*
Robert E. Lee, *p. 479*
Seven Days' Battles, *p. 480*
Second Battle of Bull Run, *p. 480*
Battle of Antietam, *p. 481*
ironclads, *p. 482*

HSS 8.10.5 Study the views and lives of leaders (e.g., Ulysses S. Grant, Jefferson Davis, Robert E. Lee) and soldiers on both sides of the war, including those of black soldiers and regiments.

8.10.6 Describe critical developments and events in the war, including the major battles, geographical advantages and obstacles, technological advances, and General Lee's surrender at Appomattox.

If YOU were there...

You live in Washington, D.C., in July 1861. You and your friends are on your way to Manassas, near Washington, to watch the battle there. Everyone expects a quick Union victory. Your wagon is loaded with food for a picnic, and people are in a holiday mood. You see some members of Congress riding toward Manassas, too. Maybe this battle will end the war!

Why would you want to watch this battle?

BUILDING BACKGROUND The shots fired at Fort Sumter made the war a reality. Neither the North nor the South was really prepared. Each side had some advantages—more industry and railroads in the North, a military tradition in the South. The war in the East centered in the region around the two capitals: Washington, D.C., and Richmond, Virginia.

War in Virginia

The troops that met in the first major battle of the Civil War found that it was no picnic. In July 1861, Lincoln ordered General Irvin McDowell to lead his 35,000-man army from the Union capital, Washington, to the Confederate capital, Richmond. The soldiers were barely trained. McDowell complained that they "stopped every moment to pick blackberries or get water; they would not keep in the ranks." The first day's march covered only five miles.

Bull Run/Manassas

McDowell's army was headed to Manassas, Virginia, an important railroad junction. If McDowell could seize Manassas, he would control the best route to the Confederate capital. Some 22,000 Confederate troops under the command of General Pierre G. T. Beauregard were waiting for McDowell and his troops along a creek called Bull Run. For two days, Union troops tried to find a way around the Confederates. During that time, Beauregard requested assistance, and

Teach the Big Idea: Master the Standards

Standards Proficiency

The War in the East

HSS 8.10.5, 8.10.6; HSS **Analysis Skills:** HI 1, HI 2

1. **Teach** Ask students the Main Idea questions to teach this section.
2. **Apply** As students read this section, have them make lists of the key people and battles discussed. Have students write two facts about each person, two details about each battle, and one detail about each battle's outcome and significance or consequence.
3. **Review** As you review the section's main ideas, have volunteers share the information they listed about each person or battle.
4. **Practice/Homework** Ask students to imagine that they are southern or northern journalists covering the early battles of the Civil War. Have each student choose one battle and write an eyewitness account of it. Ask volunteers to read their accounts to the class. **LS Verbal/Linguistic**

Alternative Assessment Handbook, Rubric 40: Writing to Describe

General Joseph E. Johnston headed toward Manassas with another 10,000 Confederate troops. By July 21, 1861, they had all arrived.

That morning, Union troops managed to cross the creek and drive back the left side of the Confederate line. Yet one unit held firmly in place.

"There is Jackson standing like a stone wall!" cried one southern officer. "Rally behind the Virginians!" At that moment, General **Thomas "Stonewall" Jackson** earned his famous nickname.

A steady stream of Virginia volunteers arrived to counter the attack. The Confederates surged forward, letting out their terrifying "rebel yell." One eyewitness described the awful scene.

> "There is smoke, dust, wild talking, shouting; hissings, howlings, explosions. It is a new, strange, unanticipated experience to the soldiers of both armies, far different from what they thought it would be."
>
> —Charles Coffin, quoted in *Voices of the Civil War* by Richard Wheeler

The battle raged through the day, with rebel soldiers still arriving. Finally, the weary Union troops gave out. They tried to make an orderly retreat back across the creek, but the roads were clogged with the fancy carriages of panicked spectators. The Union army scattered in the chaos.

The Confederates lacked the strength to push north and capture Washington, D.C. But clearly, the rebels had won the day. The **First Battle of Bull Run** was the first major battle of the Civil War, and the Confederates' victory. The battle is also known as the first Battle of Manassas. It shattered the North's hopes of winning the war quickly.

More Battles in Virginia

The shock at Bull Run persuaded Lincoln of the need for a better trained army. He put his hopes in General **George B. McClellan**. The general assembled a highly disciplined force of 100,000 soldiers called the Army of the Potomac. The careful McClellan spent months training. Lincoln grew impatient. Against his better judgment, Lincoln finally agreed to McClellan's plan of attack on Richmond. Instead of marching south for a direct assault, McClellan slowly brought his force through the peninsula between the James and York rivers. More time slipped away.

In June 1862, with McClellan's force poised outside Richmond, the Confederate army in Virginia came under the command of General **Robert E. Lee**. A graduate of the U.S. Military Academy at West Point, Lee had served in the Mexican War and had led federal troops at Harpers Ferry. Lee was willing to take risks and make unpredictable moves to throw Union forces off balance.

During the summer of 1862, Lee strengthened his positions. On June 26, he attacked,

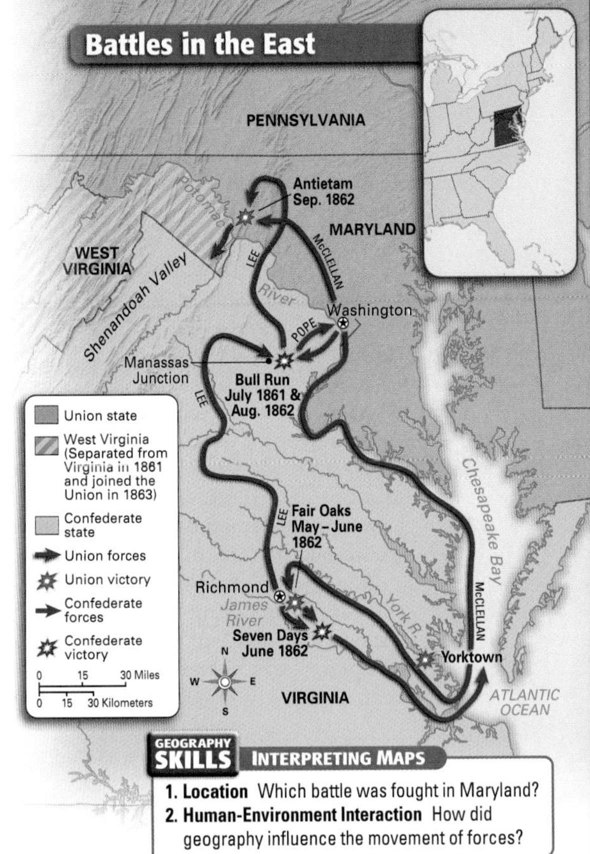

GEOGRAPHY SKILLS INTERPRETING MAPS

1. **Location** Which battle was fought in Maryland?
2. **Human-Environment Interaction** How did geography influence the movement of forces?

THE IMPACT TODAY

Many Americans continue to be fascinated by the Civil War. Some history buffs regularly stage re-enactments of famous battles, complete with uniforms, guns, and bayonets.

Direct Teach

Main Idea

1 War in Virginia

Union and Confederate forces fought for control of the war in Virginia.

Identify What was the first major battle of the Civil War, and which side won? *First Battle of Bull Run, Confederate victory*

Identify Points of View Union general McDowell complained that the soldiers stopped to pick berries and would not keep in the ranks. Based on this observation, what can you conclude about the attitudes of Union soldiers early in the war? *They did not take the war or the battle seriously and thought the North would quickly defeat the South.*

CRF: Biography Activity: Thomas "Stonewall" Jackson

Map Transparency: Battles in the East

HSS 8.10.5, 8.10.6; **HSS Analysis Skills:** CS 1, HR 5, HI 1

Did you know . . .

Some early editions of northern newspapers incorrectly announced a Union victory at Bull Run. Later editions corrected the error.

Answers

Interpreting Maps 1. *Antietam;* **2.** *Forces often moved along rivers.*

Differentiating Instruction for Universal Access

Learners Having Difficulty

Reaching Standards **HSS** 8.10.6; **HSS Analysis Skills:** HI 1, HI 2

1. Copy the graphic organizer for students to see. Omit the blue, italicized answers.
2. Have each student copy the organizer onto paper and use the text on the above pages to complete it. Review the answers as a class.
3. Encourage students to create a similar chart for each major battle in the chapter. For some battles, students will want to add boxes for key leaders, casualties, and other important information. **LS Visual/Spatial**

Alternative Assessment Handbook, Rubric 13: Graphic Organizers

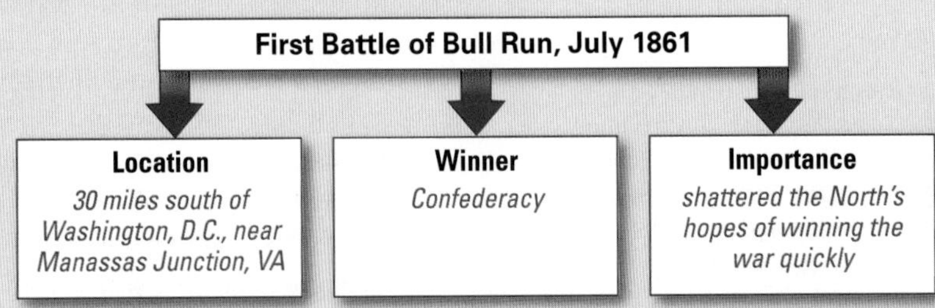

Direct Teach

Main Idea

❶ War in Virginia

Union and Confederate forces fought for control of the war in Virginia.

Recall Who became the leader of the main Union army, and what was this army called? *General George B. McClellan; Army of the Potomac*

Identify Who became the new leader of the Confederate Army, and what skills did he bring to the job? *Robert E. Lee, experienced soldier, skilled strategist, risk-taker*

Summarize Describe the Seven Days' Battles and the outcome. *series of battles in the summer of 1862 between McClellan's and Lee's forces in Virginia; Confederate victory; Lee protected Richmond and forced McClellan to retreat.*

Elaborate How did Lee defeat General Pope's Union forces at the Second Battle of Bull Run? *Lee split his forces and attacked Pope's army from two sides.*

HSS 8.10.5, 8.10.6; HSS **Analysis Skills:** CS 1, HI 1

Info to Know

McClellan Union general George B. McClellan's strengths included his abilities to organize and plan. After the first defeat at Bull Run, he helped restore order and morale to the Army of the Potomac. McClellan's unwillingness to take action against the Confederate army led to criticism, however. Leaders in Washington began to accuse him of not wanting to fight or of being pro-South. One 1862 political cartoon showed Lincoln having to carry McClellan to get him to Richmond.

launching a series of clashes known as the **Seven Days' Battles** that forced the Union army to retreat from near Richmond. Confederate General D. H. Hill described one failed attack. "It was not war—it was murder," he said. Lee saved Richmond and forced McClellan to retreat.

A frustrated Lincoln ordered General John Pope to march directly on Richmond from Washington. Pope told his soldiers, "Let us look before us and not behind. Success and glory are in the advance."

Jackson wanted to defeat Pope's army before it could join up with McClellan's larger Army of the Potomac. Jackson's troops met Pope's Union forces on the battlefield in August in 1862. The three-day battle became known as the **Second Battle of Bull Run,** or the Second Battle of Manassas.

The first day's fighting was savage. Captain George Fairfield of the 7th Wisconsin regiment later recalled, "What a slaughter! No one appeared to know the object of the fight, and there we stood for one hour, the men falling all around." The fighting ended in a stalemate.

On the second day, Pope found Jackson's troops along an unfinished railroad grade. Pope hurled his men against the Confederates. But the attacks were pushed back with heavy casualties on both sides.

On the third day, the Confederates crushed the Union army's assault and forced it to retreat in defeat. The Confederates had won a major victory, and General Robert E. Lee decided it was time to take the war to the North.

READING CHECK **Sequencing** List in order the events that forced Union troops out of Virginia.

Battle of Antietam

Confederate leaders hoped to follow up Lee's successes in Virginia with a major victory on northern soil. On September 4, 1862, some 40,000 Confederate soldiers began crossing into Maryland. Once General Robert E. Lee

Eyewitness at Antietam

James Hope was a professional artist who joined the Union army. Too sick to fight at Antietam, Hope was reassigned to work as a scout and a mapmaker. He sketched scenes from the battle as it happened and later used his sketches to make paintings like this one.

Collaborative Learning

Standards Proficiency

Early Battles Illustrated Articles

HSS 8.10.6; HSS **Analysis Skills:** CS 3, HI 1, HI 2

1. Organize the class into eight groups. Assign each group one of the four key battles in this section—First Battle of Bull Run, Seven Days' Battles, Second Battle of Bull Run, or the Battle of Antietam. Two groups will have each battle. Have one of the groups adopt the perspective of a northern newspaper and the other adopt that of a southern newspaper.
2. Have each group create a newspaper article, with a headline, about the significance of its assigned battle. In addition, students should provide a map or illustration showing the location of the battle and troop movements. Encourage groups to use computer software to lay out their articles and visuals.
3. Display students' illustrated articles around the classroom. LS **Interpersonal, Verbal/Linguistic, Visual/Spatial**

Alternative Assessment Handbook, Rubrics 14: Group Activity; and 29: Presentations

Answers

Reading Check *Lee led a series of attacks known as the Seven Day's Battles, which forced the Army of the Potomac to retreat; Lincoln then ordered General John Pope to march on Richmond; Lee and Jackson surprised Pope's Union force by attacking from both sides at the Second Battle of Bull Run, which pushed most of the Union forces out of Virginia.*

arrived in the town of Frederick, he issued a Proclamation to the People of Maryland, urging them to join the Confederates. However, his words would not be enough to convince Marylanders to abandon the Union. Union soldiers, however, found a copy of Lee's battle plan, which had been left at an abandoned Confederate camp. General McClellan learned that Lee had divided his army in order to attack Harpers Ferry. McClellan planned a counterattack.

The two armies met along Antietam Creek in Maryland on September 17, 1862. The battle lasted for hours. By the end of the day, the Union had suffered more than 12,000 casualties. The Confederates endured more than 13,000 casualties. Union officer A. H. Nickerson later recalled, "It seemed that everybody near me was killed." The **Battle of Antietam,** also known as the Battle of Sharpsburg, was the bloodiest single-day battle of the Civil War—and of U.S. history. More soldiers were killed and wounded at the Battle of Antietam than the deaths of all Americans in the American Revolution, War of 1812, and Mexican-American War combined. Antietam also was an important victory for the Union. Lee had lost many of his troops, and his northward advance had been stopped.

READING CHECK **Analyzing** Why was the Battle of Antietam significant?

BIOGRAPHY

Robert E. Lee
(1807–1870)

Robert E. Lee was born into a wealthy Virginia family in 1807. Lee fought in the Mexican-American War, helping to capture Veracruz. When the Civil War began, President Lincoln asked Lee to lead the Union army. Lee declined and resigned from the U.S. Army to become a general in the Confederate army.

Drawing Conclusions How did Lee's choice reflect the division of the states?

Mathew Brady was a photographer who worked to document the Civil War on film. This photo of dead Confederate soldiers at Antietam was taken by a photographer from Brady's studio.

ANALYSIS SKILL **ANALYZING VISUALS**

How do you think photographs like this one affected the civilians who saw them?

Direct Teach

Main Idea

❷ Battle of Antietam

The Battle of Antietam gave the North a slight advantage.

Explain How did Confederate leaders hope to follow up Lee's successes in Virginia? *with a major victory on northern soil*

Recall Who was the leader on each side in the Battle of Antietam, and which side won? *McClellan, Union; Lee, Confederates; Union victory*

Analyze What part did error and chance play in the Union victory at Antietam? *A copy of Lee's battle plan was left at a Confederate camp, and by chance Union soldiers found it, enabling McClellan to attack when Lee's forces were divided.*

HSS 8.10.6; HSS **Analysis Skills:** HI 1, HI 4

Connect to Science and Technology

Photographing the Civil War In 1862, Mathew Brady shocked New Yorkers when he showed photographs of the aftermath of Antietam. Brady and other photographers followed the Union army to record events with their cameras. The early cameras were bulky and could only be used to take pictures of still objects. As a result, the photographs of the Civil War were mostly portraits of soldiers and scenes of camp life. Brady's pictures of battlefields were taken only after the fighting had stopped.

Cross-Discipline Activity: Music

Exceeding Standards

Civil War Battle Songs

HSS 8.10.6; HSS **Analysis Skills:** HI 1, HI 2

Prep Required

Materials: lyrics, sheet music, or recordings of Civil War songs (optional)

1. If possible, play some examples of Civil War songs for students or provide lyrics or sheet music of some popular Civil War songs.
2. Divide the class in half. Assign half the class the South and the other half the North. Have each student write the lyrics to a song celebrating its side's victory in a battle covered in this section. The song should describe some of the major events and people of the battle as well as its significance. Tell students to make their songs rousing and patriotic. Students can use an existing tune or create their own tune for their songs.
3. Have volunteers present or perform their songs. LS **Auditory/Musical, Verbal/Linguistic**

Alternative Assessment Handbook, Rubric 26: Poems and Songs

Answers

Biography *As a Virginian, Lee chose to remain loyal to his home state, which had seceded from the Union, instead of to the nation.*

Analyzing Visuals *possible answer—caused horror and sadness; emphasized the deadly toll the war was taking*

Reading Check *Union forces stopped Lee's advance into the North, and Lee lost many of his troops.*

Direct Teach

Main Idea

3 Breaking the Union's Blockade

The Confederacy attempted to break the Union naval blockade.

Recall Which side held the naval advantage in the war, and why? *Union; had most of the U.S. Navy's small fleet, many experienced naval officers, and enough industry to build more ships*

Make Inferences Why might control of the seas benefit a power at war? *provide the ability to ship goods and supplies to troops and to prevent enemies from receiving supplies*

Elaborate How did the ironclads signal a revolution in naval warfare? *They introduced new materials and features—such as heavy iron armor and revolving gun towers—that were major advances over wooden ships powered by wind and sails.*

- **CRF:** Interdisciplinary Project: The Ironclads: The *Monitor* and the *Virginia*
- Map Transparency: Union Blockade
- **HSS** 8.10.6; **HSS Analysis Skills:** HI 1, HI 2, HI 3

Primary Source

Anaconda Plan

Have students examine the images in the political cartoon. Ask them to describe how the cartoonist uses the images to present a negative view of the South. *He shows enslaved Africans being mistreated or shot and Union supporters being hanged.*

Primary Source

POLITICAL CARTOON

Anaconda Plan

This cartoon shows visually the North's plan to cut off supplies to the South through naval blockades, a strategy called the Anaconda Plan.

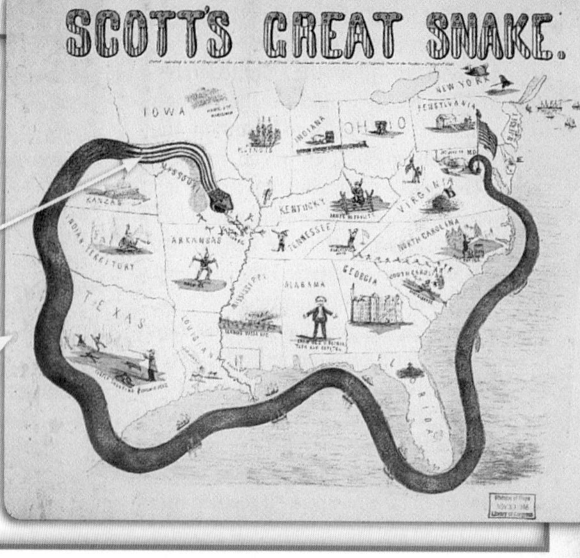

Why is the snake's head red, white, and blue?

How does the cartoonist show what the snake represents?

ANALYSIS SKILL ANALYZING PRIMARY SOURCES

Why do you think the plan was called the Anaconda Plan?

Breaking the Union's Blockade

While the two armies fought for control of the land, the Union navy controlled the sea. The North had most of the U.S. Navy's small fleet, and many experienced naval officers had remained loyal to the Union. The North also had enough industry to build more ships.

The Union's Naval Strategy

ACADEMIC VOCABULARY
innovation a new idea or way of doing something

The Union navy quickly mobilized to set up a blockade of southern ports. The blockade largely prevented the South from selling or receiving goods, and it seriously damaged the southern economy.

The blockade was hard to maintain because the Union navy had to patrol thousands of miles of coastline from Virginia to Texas. The South used small, fast ships to outrun the larger Union warships. Most of these blockade runners traveled to the Bahamas or Nassau to buy supplies for the Confederacy. These ships, however, could not make up for the South's loss of trade. The Union blockade reduced the number of ships entering southern ports from 6,000 to 800 per year.

Clash of the Ironclads

Hoping to take away the Union's advantage at sea, the Confederacy turned to a new type of warship—**ironclads**, or ships heavily armored with iron. The Confederates had captured a Union steamship, the *Merrimack*, and turned it into an ironclad, renamed the *Virginia*. One Union sailor described the **innovation** as "a huge half-submerged crocodile." In early March 1862, the ironclad sailed into Hampton Roads, Virginia, an important waterway guarded by Union ships. Before nightfall, the *Virginia* easily sank two of the Union's wooden warships, while it received minor damage. A Baltimore reporter predicted doom the next day.

> "There appeared no reason why the iron monster might not clear [Hampton] Roads of our fleet, [and] destroy all the stores [supplies] and warehouses on the beach."
>
> —quoted in *The Rebellion Record, Vol. 4*

Differentiating Instruction for Universal Access

English-Language Learners

Standards Proficiency | Research Optional

Materials: pictures of ironclads (optional)

1. Pair students and have each pair create a storyboard or historical cartoon strip that illustrates the sequence of events in the clash of the ironclads the *Monitor* and the *Virginia*.
2. Have students use the information in the section to list the sequence of events for their storyboards or cartoon strips. In addition, encourage students to conduct research on the way the ironclads looked to make the illustrations more realistic.
3. Students should provide captions for each panel in their storyboards or cartoon strips.
4. Display students' storyboards or cartoon strips in the classroom. **LS Interpersonal, Visual/Spatial**

- **HSS** 8.10.6; **HSS Analysis Skills:** CS 1, HI 1, HI 2
- Alternative Assessment Handbook, Rubrics 3: Artwork; and 29: Presentations

Answers

Analyzing Primary Sources

Anacondas are constricting, water-loving snakes. Like an anaconda, the strategy was water-based and constrictive. The blockade was meant to snake along the South's coast, squeeze the South's economy, and thereby strike at the South's heart.

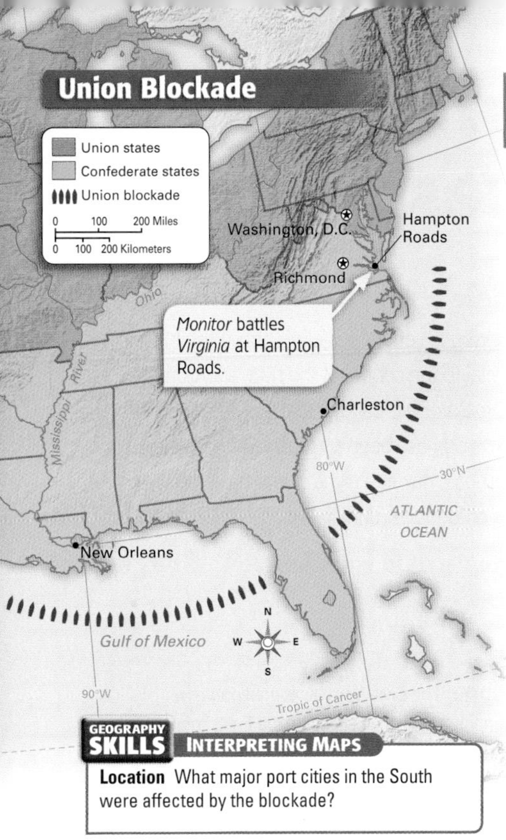

GEOGRAPHY SKILLS INTERPRETING MAPS

Location What major port cities in the South were affected by the blockade?

The Union navy had already built its own ironclad, the *Monitor*, designed by Swedish-born engineer John Ericsson. Ericsson's ship had unusual new features, such as a revolving gun tower. One Confederate soldier called the *Monitor* "a tin can on a shingle!" Although small, the *Monitor* carried powerful guns and had thick plating.

When the *Virginia* returned to Hampton Roads later that month, the *Monitor* was waiting. After several hours of fighting, neither ship was seriously damaged, but the *Monitor* forced the *Virginia* to withdraw. This success saved the Union fleet and continued the blockade. The clash of the ironclads also signaled a revolution in naval warfare. The days of wooden warships powered by wind and sails were drawing to a close.

THE IMPACT TODAY

The *Monitor* sank in North Carolina in the winter of 1862. The shipwreck was located by scientists in 1973, and efforts to save it for further study continue today.

READING CHECK **Evaluating** How effective was the Union blockade?

SUMMARY AND PREVIEW The early battles of the Civil War were centered in the East. In the next section you will read about battles in the West.

Section 2 Assessment

go.hrw.com **Online Quiz** KEYWORD: SS8 HP15

Reviewing Ideas, Terms, and People HSS 8.10.5, 8.10.6

1. **a. Identify** List the early battles in the East and the outcome of each battle.
   b. Elaborate Why do you think the Union lost the **First Battle of Bull Run?**
2. **a. Describe** What costly mistake did the Confederacy make before the **Battle of Antietam?**
   b. Analyze What was the outcome of the **Battle of Antietam,** and what effect did it have on both the North and the South?
   c. Elaborate Why do you think General **George B. McClellan** did not finish off General **Robert E. Lee's** troops when he had the chance?
3. **a. Describe** What was the Union's strategy in the war at sea?
   b. Draw Conclusions Why were **ironclads** more successful than older, wooden ships?

Critical Thinking

4. **Analyzing** Copy the chart below onto your own sheet of paper. Use it to identify the major battles that took place at the beginning of the war and to explain why each was significant.

Battle	Winner	Significance

FOCUS ON WRITING

5. **Taking Notes on the War in the East** As you read this section, take notes on the First Battle of Bull Run, the Seven Days' Battles, the Second Battle of Bull Run, and the Battle of Antietam. Be sure to answer the following questions: Who? Where? When? Why? and How?

Direct Teach

Connect to Economics

Blockade Runners The blockade-running business was quite profitable for those willing to risk being targets of northern ships. For example, salt, which sold for $6.50 a ton in the Bahamas, sold for $1,700 a ton in the South. Coffee, which sold for $249 in the Bahamas, brought $5,500 in the South. A successful blockade captain could earn $5,000 on one run, while a captain in the merchant service would only earn about $150 for equivalent work.

Review & Assess

Close

Have students discuss which side they think was winning the war at this point. Encourage students to identify specific battles and outcomes to support their positions.

Review

Online Quiz, Section 2

Assess

SE Section 2 Assessment

PASS: Section 2 Quiz

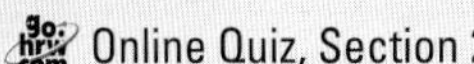Alternative Assessment Handbook

Reteach/Classroom Intervention

California Standards Review Workbook

Interactive Reader and Study Guide, Section 2

Interactive Skills Tutor CD-ROM

Section 2 Assessment Answers

1. **a.** See the answer to Question 4.
   b. Union soldiers were untrained and did not take the battle seriously.
2. **a.** left behind a copy of Lee's battle plan
   b. tremendous losses on both sides; stopped the Confederates' northward advance
   c. possible answers—He was overly cautious; his own forces had suffered terrible losses and may not have been able to press the attack.
3. **a.** to blockade southern ports and thereby squeeze the South's trade and economy
   b. protected with iron plating; more powerful features, such as revolving gun towers
4. First Battle of Bull Run—Confederacy, shattered Union hopes of a quick war; Seven Day's Battles—Confederacy, forced a Union retreat; Second Battle of Bull Run—Confederacy, pushed most Union forces out of Virginia; Antietam—Union, stopped Confederates' northward advance
5. Students should provide information similar to that in the previous answer as well as key dates, locations, and leaders for each battle.

Answers

Interpreting Maps *Charleston, South Carolina; New Orleans, Louisiana*

Reading Check *Although hard to maintain, the blockade effectively limited southern trade and seriously damaged the southern economy.*

Preteach

Bellringer

If YOU were there . . . Use the **Daily Bellringer Transparency** to help students answer the question.

Daily Bellringer Transparency, Section 3

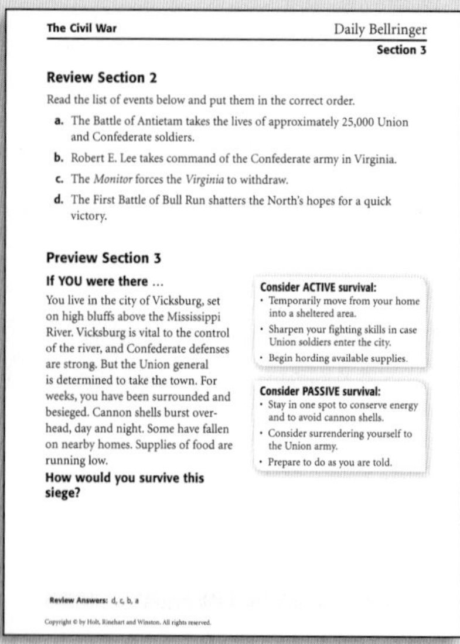

The Civil War — Daily Bellringer, Section 3

Review Section 2

Read the list of events below and put them in the correct order.

a. The Battle of Antietam takes the lives of approximately 25,000 Union and Confederate soldiers.
b. Robert E. Lee takes command of the Confederate army in Virginia.
c. The *Monitor* forces the *Virginia* to withdraw.
d. The First Battle of Bull Run shatters the North's hopes for a quick victory.

Preview Section 3

If YOU were there ...

You live in the city of Vicksburg, set on high bluffs above the Mississippi River. Vicksburg is vital to the control of the river, and Confederate defenses are strong. But the Union general is determined to take the town. For weeks, you have been surrounded and besieged. Cannon shells burst overhead, day and night. Some have fallen on nearby homes. Supplies of food are running low.

How would you survive this siege?

Consider ACTIVE survival:
- Temporarily move from your home into a sheltered area.
- Sharpen your fighting skills in case Union soldiers enter the city.
- Begin hording available supplies.

Consider PASSIVE survival:
- Stay in one spot to conserve energy and to avoid cannon shells.
- Consider surrendering yourself to the Union army.
- Prepare to do as you are told.

Review Answers: d, c, b, a

Building Vocabulary

Preteach or review the following terms:

campaign series of related military operations in a war (p. 484)

maneuvers strategic movement of troops, ships, or firepower (p. 484)

CRF: Vocabulary Builder Activity, Section 3

Standards Focus

HSS 8.10.5

Means: Identify the key leaders in the war in the West, and describe the views of leaders and soldiers on both sides during the Civil War.
Matters: Studying the lives and views of the people who fought the Civil War helps us better understand the war's events and its outcome.

HSS 8.10.6

Means: Describe the major battles in the West during the Civil War and how geography and technology affected the battles.
Matters: Studying past wars enables people to understand warfare better.

SECTION 3

The War in the West

What You Will Learn...

Main Ideas

1. Union strategy in the West centered on control of the Mississippi River.
2. Confederate and Union troops struggled for dominance in the Far West.

The Big Idea

Fighting in the Civil War spread to the western United States.

Key Terms and People

Ulysses S. Grant, *p. 484*
Battle of Shiloh, *p. 485*
David Farragut, *p. 485*
Siege of Vicksburg, *p. 486*

HSS 8.10.5 Study the views and lives of leaders (e.g., Ulysses S. Grant, Jefferson Davis, Robert E. Lee) and soldiers on both sides of the war, including those of black soldiers and regiments.

8.10.6 Describe critical developments and events in the war, including the major battles, geographical advantages and obstacles, technological advances, and General Lee's surrender at Appomattox.

If YOU were there...

You live in the city of Vicksburg, set on high bluffs above the Mississippi River. Vicksburg is vital to the control of the river, and Confederate defenses are strong. But the Union general is determined to take the town. For weeks, you have been surrounded and besieged. Cannon shells burst overhead, day and night. Some have fallen on nearby homes. Supplies of food are running low.

How would you survive this siege?

BUILDING BACKGROUND The Civil War was fought on many fronts, all across the continent and even at sea. In the East, fighting was at first concentrated in Virginia. In the West, cities and forts along the Mississippi River were the main target of Union forces. Northern control of the river would cut off the western states of the Confederacy.

Union Strategy in the West

While Lincoln fumed over the cautious, hesitant General McClellan, he had no such problems with **Ulysses S. Grant**. Bold and restless, Grant grew impatient when he was asked to lead defensive maneuvers. He wanted to be on the attack. As a commander of forces in the Union's western campaign, he would get his wish.

The western campaign focused on taking control of the Mississippi River. This strategy would cut off the eastern part of the Confederacy from sources of food production in Arkansas, Louisiana, and Texas. From bases on the Mississippi, the Union army could attack southern communication and transportation networks.

In February 1862, Grant led an assault force into Tennessee. With help from navy gunboats, Grant's Army of Tennessee took two outposts on key rivers in the west. On February 6, he captured Fort Henry on the Tennessee River. Several days later he took Fort Donelson on the Cumberland River.

Fort Donelson's commander asked for the terms of surrender. Grant replied, "No terms except an unconditional and immediate

Teach the Big Idea: Master the Standards

Standards Proficiency

The War in the West

HSS 8.10.5, 8.10.6; HSS **Analysis Skills:** CS 1, HR 1, HI 1, HI 2

1. **Teach** Ask students the Main Idea questions to teach this section.
2. **Apply** Have each student list the section's Key Terms and People. Under each name, have students write the following questions: *Why is this person significant? What did this person accomplish? When? Where?* Under each event, have students write the following questions: *Why is this event significant? When and where did this event occur? What happened during this event?* As students read the section, have them write the answer to each question. **LS Verbal/Linguistic**
3. **Review** As you review the section, have volunteers share their answers.
4. **Practice/Homework** Have each student create a five-question quiz for the section as well as an answer key. Have students exchange quizzes, complete them, and then return them for grading. **LS Verbal/Linguistic**

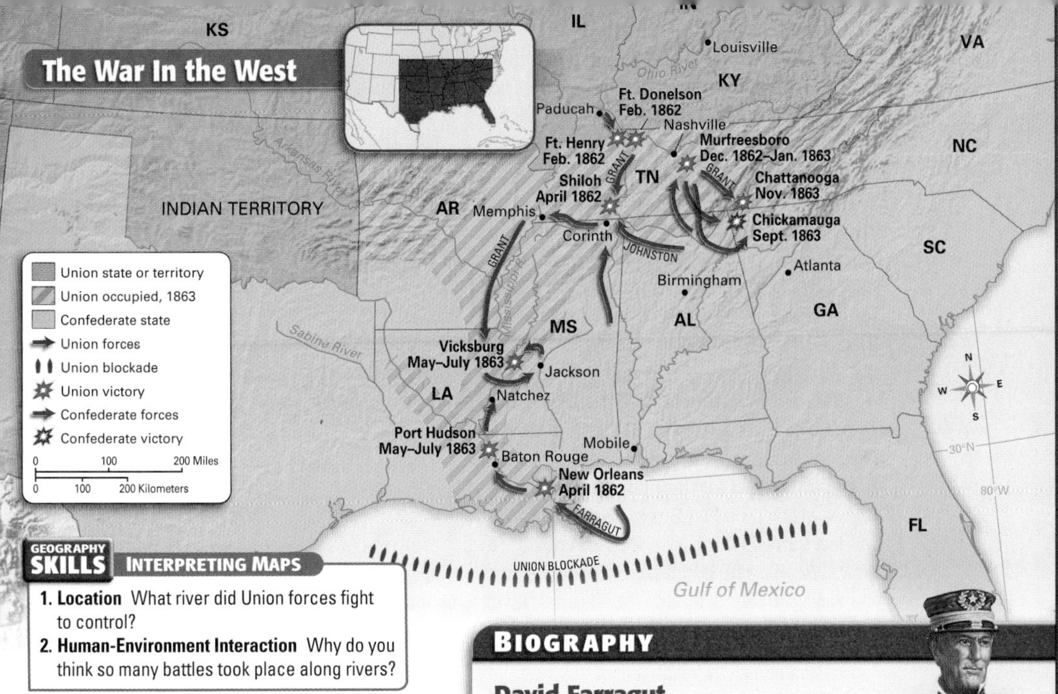

GEOGRAPHY SKILLS INTERPRETING MAPS

1. **Location** What river did Union forces fight to control?
2. **Human-Environment Interaction** Why do you think so many battles took place along rivers?

surrender can be accepted." The fort surrendered. The North gave a new name to Grant's initials: "Unconditional Surrender" Grant.

Advancing south in Tennessee, General Grant paused near Shiloh Church to await the arrival of the Army of Ohio. Grant knew that the large rebel army of General A. S. Johnston was nearby in Corinth, Mississippi, but he did not expect an attack. Instead of setting up defenses, he worked on drilling his new recruits.

In the early morning of April 6, 1862, the rebels sprang on Grant's sleepy camp. This began the **Battle of Shiloh**, in which the Union army gained greater control of the Mississippi River valley.

During the bloody two-day battle, each side gained and lost ground. Johnston was killed on the first day. The arrival of the Ohio force helped Grant regain territory and push the enemy back into Mississippi. The armies finally gave out, each with about 10,000 casualties. Both sides claimed victory, but, in fact, the victor was Grant.

BIOGRAPHY

David Farragut

(1801–1870)

David Farragut was born in Tennessee to a Spanish father and an American mother. At age seven Farragut was adopted by a family friend who agreed to train the young boy for the navy. Farragut received his first navy position—midshipman at large—at age nine and commanded his first vessel at 12. He spent the rest of his life in the U.S. Navy. Although he lived in the South, when the Civil War broke out, he decided to move his family to the North. Farragut led key attacks on the southern ports of Vicksburg and New Orleans. In 1866 he was named the first admiral of the U.S. navy.

Drawing Inferences How did Farragut help the war effort of the North?

Control of the Mississippi River

As Grant battled his way down the Mississippi, the Union navy prepared to blast its way upriver to meet him. The first obstacle was the port of New Orleans, the largest city in the Confederacy and the gateway to the Mississippi River.

Direct Teach

Main Idea

1 Union Strategy in the West

Union strategy in the West centered on control of the Mississippi River.

Explain What was the focus of the Union's western campaign? *to gain control of the Mississippi River and thereby cut off the eastern part of the South from western food production*

Analyze Why was Grant considered the victor at the Battle of Shiloh? *regained territory, pushed the Confederates back into Mississippi, gained greater control of Mississippi Valley*

CRF: Primary Source Activity: The Battle of Shiloh, April 1862

Map Transparency: The War in the West

HSS 8.10.5, 8.10.6; **HSS Analysis Skills:** CS 1, HI 1, HI 2

Teaching Tip

Sequencing Events

Some students may have difficulty understanding the correct order of battles covered in different sections. For example, students might incorrectly think the Battle of Antietam took place before that of Shiloh because they studied Antietam first. To help students keep events in order, create a class time line of chapter events.

Critical Thinking: Summarizing

Standards Proficiency

Interviews with Grant and Farragut

1. Discuss with students the main events of the war in the West. Then ask students to imagine that they are roving correspondents for a newspaper during the Civil War. Vicksburg has just surrendered, and their editor has assigned them to interview either Ulysses S. Grant or Admiral David Farragut.
2. Pair students and assign each pair either Grant or Farragut. Have each pair write at least 10 questions and answers for the interview. Questions should address the goals of the campaign in the West, the fighting in which the assigned leader has been involved, the significance of this action, and the leader's views on the progress of the war in the West.
3. Have volunteer pairs act out their interviews. **LS Interpersonal, Verbal/Linguistic**

HSS 8.10.5, 8.10.6; **HSS Analysis Skills:** CS 1, HR 1, HR 5, HI 1, HI 2

Alternative Assessment Handbook, Rubric 37: Writing Assignments

Answers

Interpreting Maps 1. *Mississippi River;* **2.** *possible answers—both armies were vying for control of one major river, the Mississippi; both armies often traveled along rivers.*

Biography *As a strong naval commander, Farragut was able to lead the Union navy to key victories in major Confederate ports.*

Direct Teach

Main Idea

1 Union Strategy in the West

Union strategy in the West centered on control of the Mississippi River.

Explain How was Admiral Farragut able to capture New Orleans? *Unable to destroy the two forts protecting the city, he camouflaged his fleet and led a daring and successful pre-dawn dash past the forts, after which he easily took New Orleans.*

Identify Cause and Effect Why did Grant decide to starve Vicksburg into surrender? *The city's strategic geographic location on a high cliff above the Mississippi River made invasion all but impossible, and Farragut's cannons could not reach the city.*

HSS 8.10.6; HSS **Analysis Skills:** CS 1, HI 1, HI 2

Info to Know

The War in Indian Territory The Civil War divided Native Americans in Indian Territory. The Choctaw, Chickasaw, Cherokee, Creek, and Seminole nations split, with some supporting the Confederacy and others the Union. Some 10,000 Native Americans served with the Confederates during the war. By the war's end in 1865, an estimated 6,000 to 10,000 Native Americans had died as a result of the fighting.

With 18 ships and 700 men, Admiral **David Farragut** approached the two forts that guarded the entrance to New Orleans from the Gulf of Mexico. Unable to destroy the forts, Farragut decided to race past them.

The risky operation would take place at night. Farragut had his wooden ships wrapped in heavy chains to protect them like ironclads. Sailors slapped Mississippi mud on the ships' hulls to make them hard to see. Trees were tied to the masts to make the ships look like the forested shore.

Before dawn on April 24, 1862, the warships made their daring dash. The Confederates fired at Farragut's ships from the shore and from gunboats. They launched burning rafts, one of which scorched Farragut's own ship. But his fleet slipped by the twin forts and made it to New Orleans. The city fell on April 29.

Farragut sailed up the Mississippi River, taking Baton Rouge, Louisiana, and Natchez, Mississippi. He then approached the city of Vicksburg, Mississippi.

The Siege of Vicksburg

Vicksburg's geography made invasion all but impossible. Perched on 200-foot-high cliffs above the Mississippi River, the city could rain down firepower on enemy ships or on soldiers trying to scale the cliffs. Deep gorges surrounded the city, turning back land assaults. Nevertheless, Farragut ordered Vicksburg to surrender.

> "Mississippians don't know, and refuse to learn, how to surrender . . . If Commodore Farragut . . . can teach them, let [him] come and try."
>
> —Colonel James L. Autry, military commander of Vicksburg

Farragut's guns had trouble reaching the city above. It was up to General Grant. His solution was to starve the city into surrender.

General Grant's troops began the **Siege of Vicksburg** in mid-May, 1863, cutting off the city and shelling it repeatedly. As food ran out, residents and soldiers survived by eating horses, dogs, and rats. "We are utterly cut off from the world, surrounded by a circle of fire," wrote one woman. "People do noth-

Primary Source

SPEECH

Response to Farragut

The mayor of New Orleans considered the surrender of the city to the Union navy:

> "We yield to physical force alone and maintain allegiance to the Confederate States; beyond this, a due respect for our dignity, our rights and the flag of our country does not, I think, permit us to go."
>
> **–Mayor John T. Monroe,** quoted in *Confederate Military History, Vol. 10*

ANALYSIS SKILL **ANALYZING PRIMARY SOURCES**

How does Monroe's statement reveal his attitude about surrender?

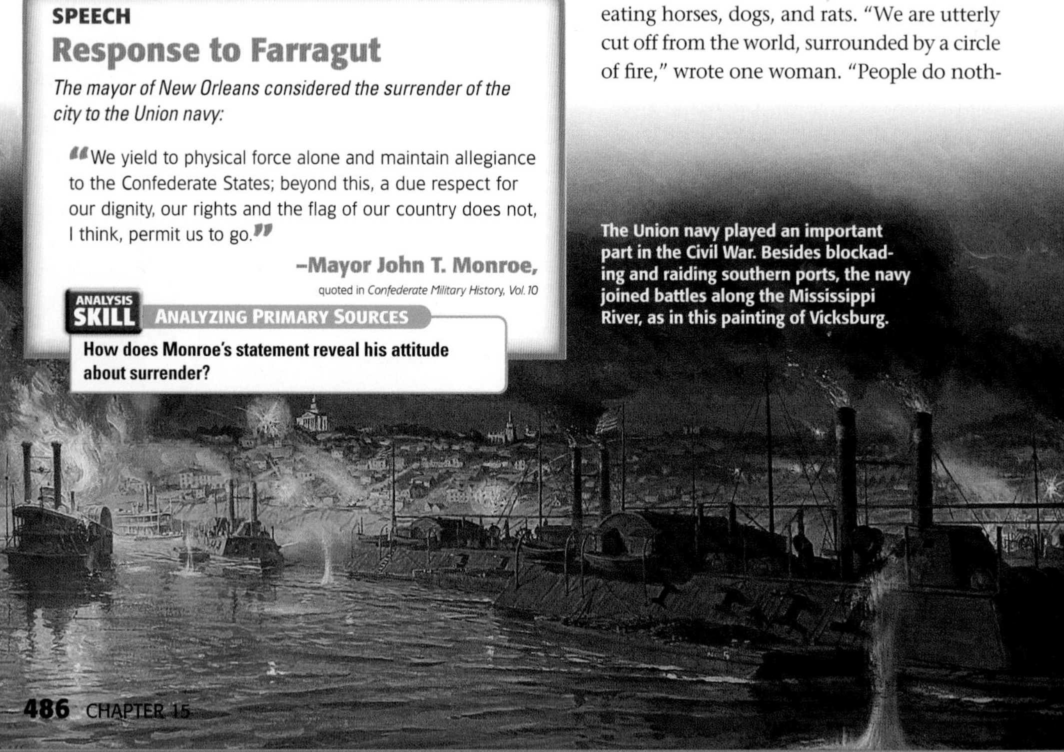

The Union navy played an important part in the Civil War. Besides blockading and raiding southern ports, the navy joined battles along the Mississippi River, as in this painting of Vicksburg.

Critical Thinking: Identifying Points of View

Standards Proficiency

Letter from Vicksburg

HSS 8.10.6; HSS **Analysis Skills:** HR 5, HI 1, HI 2

1. Review with students the events of the Siege of Vicksburg. Then have students examine the History and Geography feature "Vicksburg" that follows this section.
2. Ask students to imagine that they are either Confederate soldiers or civilians in Vicksburg during the Union siege of the city. Have each student write a letter to an imaginary friend or family member living elsewhere in the South telling them about the experience.
3. Students' letters should describe the siege, such as the constant shelling and the lack of food and supplies, their feelings about it, whether they think the city should surrender, and what the consequences of surrendering might be.
4. Have volunteers read their letters to the class. **LS Verbal/Linguistic**

Alternative Assessment Handbook, Rubric 25: Personal Letters

Answers

Analyzing Primary Sources *shows that although he is surrendering he remains loyal to the South*

ing but eat what they can get, sleep when they can, and dodge the shells."

The Confederate soldiers were also sick and hungry. In late June a group of soldiers sent their commander a warning.

> "The army is now ripe for mutiny [rebellion], unless it can be fed. If you can't feed us, you'd better surrender us, horrible as the idea is."
>
> —Confederate soldiers at Vicksburg to General John C. Pemberton, 1863

On July 4, Pemberton surrendered. Grant immediately sent food to the soldiers and civilians. He later claimed that "the fate of the Confederacy was sealed when Vicksburg fell."

READING CHECK **Summarizing** How did the Union gain control of the Mississippi River?

Struggle for the Far West

Early on in the war, the Union halted several attempts by Confederate armies to control lands west of the Mississippi. In August 1861, a Union detachment from Colorado turned back a Confederate force at Glorieta Pass. Union volunteers also defeated rebel forces at Arizona's Pichaco Pass.

Confederate attempts to take the border state of Missouri also collapsed. Failing to seize the federal arsenal at St. Louis mid-1861, the rebels fell back to Pea Ridge in northwestern Arkansas. There, in March 1862, they attacked again, aided by some 800 Cherokee. The Indians hoped the Confederates would give them greater freedom. In addition, slavery was legal in Indian Territory, and some Native Americans who were slaveholders supported the Confederacy. Despite being outnumbered, Union forces won the Battle of Pea Ridge. The Union defense of Missouri held.

Pro-Confederate forces remained active in the region throughout the war. They attacked Union forts and raided towns in Missouri and Kansas, forcing Union commanders to keep valuable troops stationed in the area.

READING CHECK **Analyzing** What was the importance of the fighting in the Far West?

SUMMARY AND PREVIEW The North and the South continued their struggle with battles in the West. A number of key battles took place in the Western theatre, and several important Union leaders emerged from these battles. One, Ulysses S. Grant would soon become even more important to the Union army. In the next section you will learn about the lives of civilians, enslaved Africans, and soldiers during the war.

Section 3 Assessment

go.hrw.com
Online Quiz
KEYWORD: SS8 HP15

Reviewing Ideas, Terms, and People HSS 8.10.5, 8.10.6

1. **a. Identify** What role did **Ulysses S. Grant** play in the war in the West?
   b. Explain Why was the **Battle of Shiloh** important?
   c. Elaborate Do you think President Lincoln would have approved of Grant's actions in the West? Why or why not?
2. **a. Describe** How did the Union take New Orleans, and why was it an important victory?
   b. Draw Conclusions How were civilians affected by the **Siege of Vicksburg?**
   c. Predict What might be some possible results of the Union victory at Vicksburg?
3. **a. Recall** Where did fighting take place in the Far West?
   b. Analyze Why did Native Americans join Confederate forces in the West?

Critical Thinking

4. **Identifing Cause and Effect** Copy the graphic organizer below onto your own sheet of paper. Use it to identify the causes and effects of the battles listed.

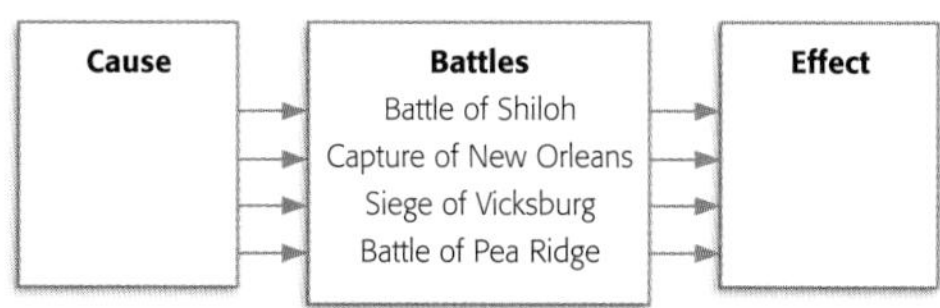

FOCUS ON WRITING

5. **Taking Notes on the War in the West** As you read this section, take notes on the fight for the Mississippi River and the Siege of Vicksburg. Be sure to answer the following questions: Who? Where? When? Why? and How?

Section 3 Assessment Answers

1. **a.** commander of Union forces in the West
   b. See answer to Question 4.
   c. possible answer—yes, Grant fought, won.
2. **a.** naval night operation from the Gulf of Mexico; gained control of lower Mississippi
   b. suffered bombardment and starvation
   c. Responses should show that the victory gave the Union control of the Mississippi.
3. **a.** New Mexico, Arizona, Missouri, Kansas
   b. They hoped the Confederates would give them more freedom; some held slaves.
4. Shiloh—Rebel surprise attack on Grant's base; increased Union control of Mississippi Valley; New Orleans—Farragut's dash past forts; Union advanced into southern territory; Vicksburg—Vicksburg's location; Union controlled Mississippi River; Pea Ridge—rebels' failure to seize federal arsenal at St. Louis; Union kept control of Missouri.
5. Students should cover Grant and Farragut and the applicable battles listed in the previous answer.

Direct Teach

Main Idea

❷ Struggle for the Far West

Confederate and Union troops struggled for dominance in the Far West.

Describe What early actions did Confederate forces take to control lands west of the Mississippi River? *They invaded New Mexico at Glorieta Pass, Arizona at Pichaco Pass, and Missouri at St. Louis.*

Identify Points of View Why did some Cherokee fight for the South? *They hoped the Confederates would give them greater freedom, and some Cherokee were slaveholders.*

HSS 8.10.6; HSS **Analysis Skills:** HI 1

Review & Assess

Close

Have students summarize the war in the Far West.

Review

Online Quiz, Section 3

Assess

SE Section 3 Assessment

PASS: Section 3 Quiz

Alternative Assessment Handbook

Reteach/Classroom Intervention

California Standards Review Workbook

Interactive Reader and Study Guide, Section 3

Interactive Skills Tutor CD-ROM

Answers

Reading Check (top) *A naval Union force took New Orleans and other cities as it moved up the river; Grant moved down the river and took Vicksburg.*

Reading Check (bottom) *The Union stopped Confederate attempts to control the area.*

History and Geography

Activity Vicksburg Strategy Headlines Have students read the feature. Ask a volunteer to explain why Lincoln thought Vicksburg was such an important Union target. Next, have students trace the stages in the Vicksburg strategy. For each stage, ask students to identify the geographic factors that affected Grant's decisions and actions at that point. Then have students write at least one newspaper headline for each stage numbered on the map at right. Ask volunteers to read their headlines to the class. **LS Verbal/Linguistic, Visual/Spatial**

HSS 8.10.7; HSS **Analysis Skills:** CS 3, HI 1, HI 2

Info to Know

Grant's Supply Strategy Instead of waiting for supply wagons, Union general Ulysses S. Grant had his troops live off the land. The soldiers combed the southern countryside taking horses, oxen, farm wagons, and even carriages from area farms and plantations. Grant knew from earlier campaigns that the farms in Mississippi had plenty of food as well, and his troops raided for cattle, pigs, and other goods.

History and Geography

The Vicksburg Strategy

"Vicksburg is the key!" President Abraham Lincoln declared. "The war can never be brought to a close until that key is in our pocket." Vicksburg was so important because of its location on the Mississippi River, a vital trade route and supply line. Union ships couldn't get past the Confederate guns mounted on the high bluffs of Vicksburg. Capturing Vicksburg would give the Union control the Mississippi, stealing a vital supply line and splitting the Confederacy in two. The task fell to General Ulysses S. Grant.

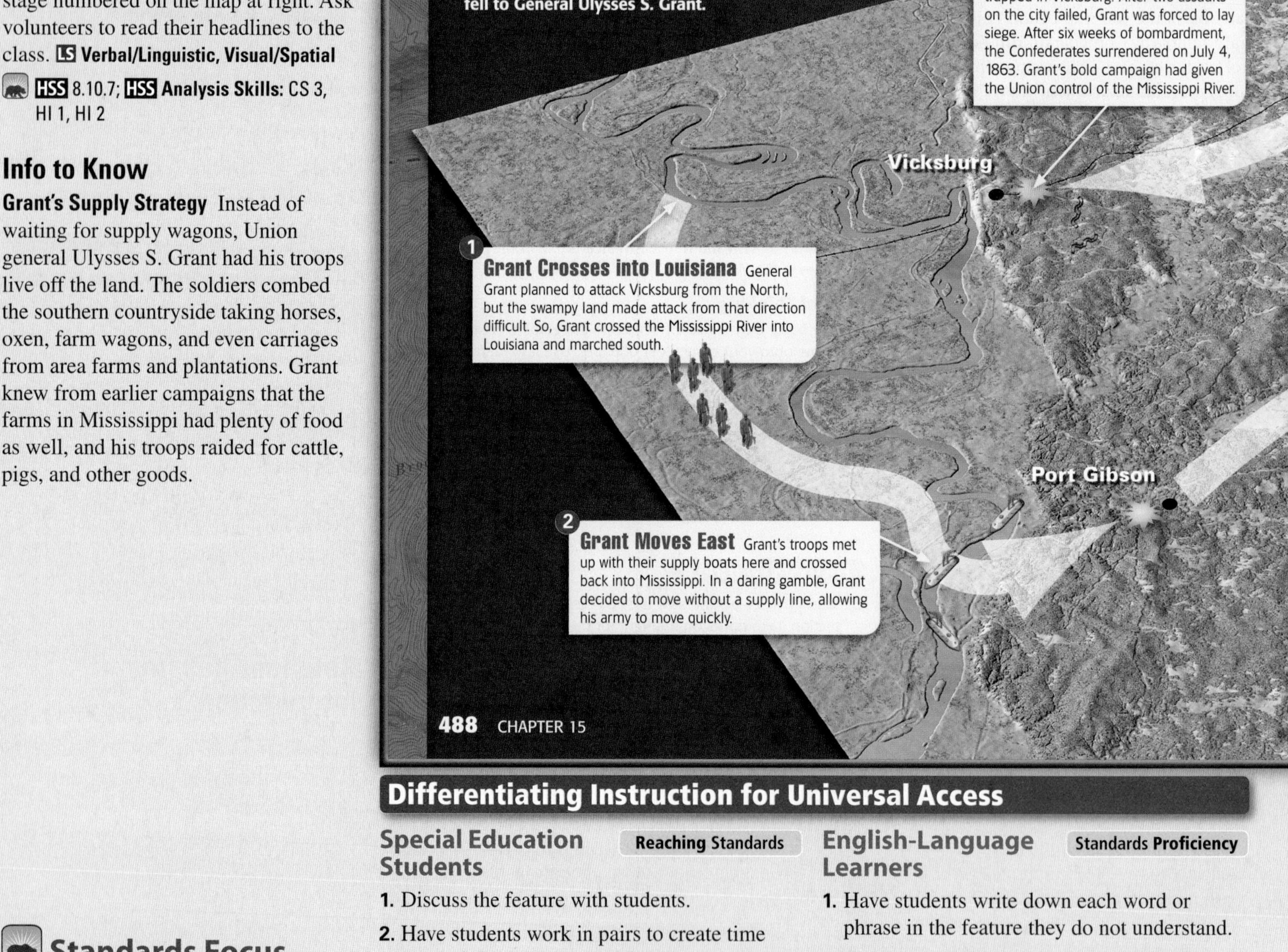

Vicksburg
Port Gibson
1 Grant Crosses into Louisiana General Grant planned to attack Vicksburg from the North, but the swampy land made attack from that direction difficult. So, Grant crossed the Mississippi River into Louisiana and marched south.
2 Grant Moves East Grant's troops met up with their supply boats here and crossed back into Mississippi. In a daring gamble, Grant decided to move without a supply line, allowing his army to move quickly.
4 The Siege of Vicksburg Grant now had 30,000 Confederate troops trapped in Vicksburg. After two assaults on the city failed, Grant was forced to lay siege. After six weeks of bombardment, the Confederates surrendered on July 4, 1863. Grant's bold campaign had given the Union control of the Mississippi River.

Differentiating Instruction for Universal Access

Special Education Students — Reaching Standards

1. Discuss the feature with students.
2. Have students work in pairs to create time lines of the events in the Vicksburg campaign shown above. Students should note one detail about each event. **LS Visual/Spatial**

HSS 8.10.7; HSS **Analysis Skills:** CS 1, CS 2, HI 1

Alternative Assessment Handbook, Rubric 36: Time Lines

English-Language Learners — Standards Proficiency

1. Have students write down each word or phrase in the feature they do not understand.
2. Organize students into mixed-ability pairs. Have partners look up the definitions of the words on their lists. Then have partners quiz each other on the words' meanings. **LS Interpersonal, Verbal/Linguistic**

HSS 8.10.7

Standards Focus

HSS 8.10 Students analyze the multiple causes, key events, and complex consequences of the Civil War.

8.10.7 Describe critical developments and events in the war, including the major battles, geographical advantages and obstacles, technological advances, and General Lee's surrender at Appomattox.

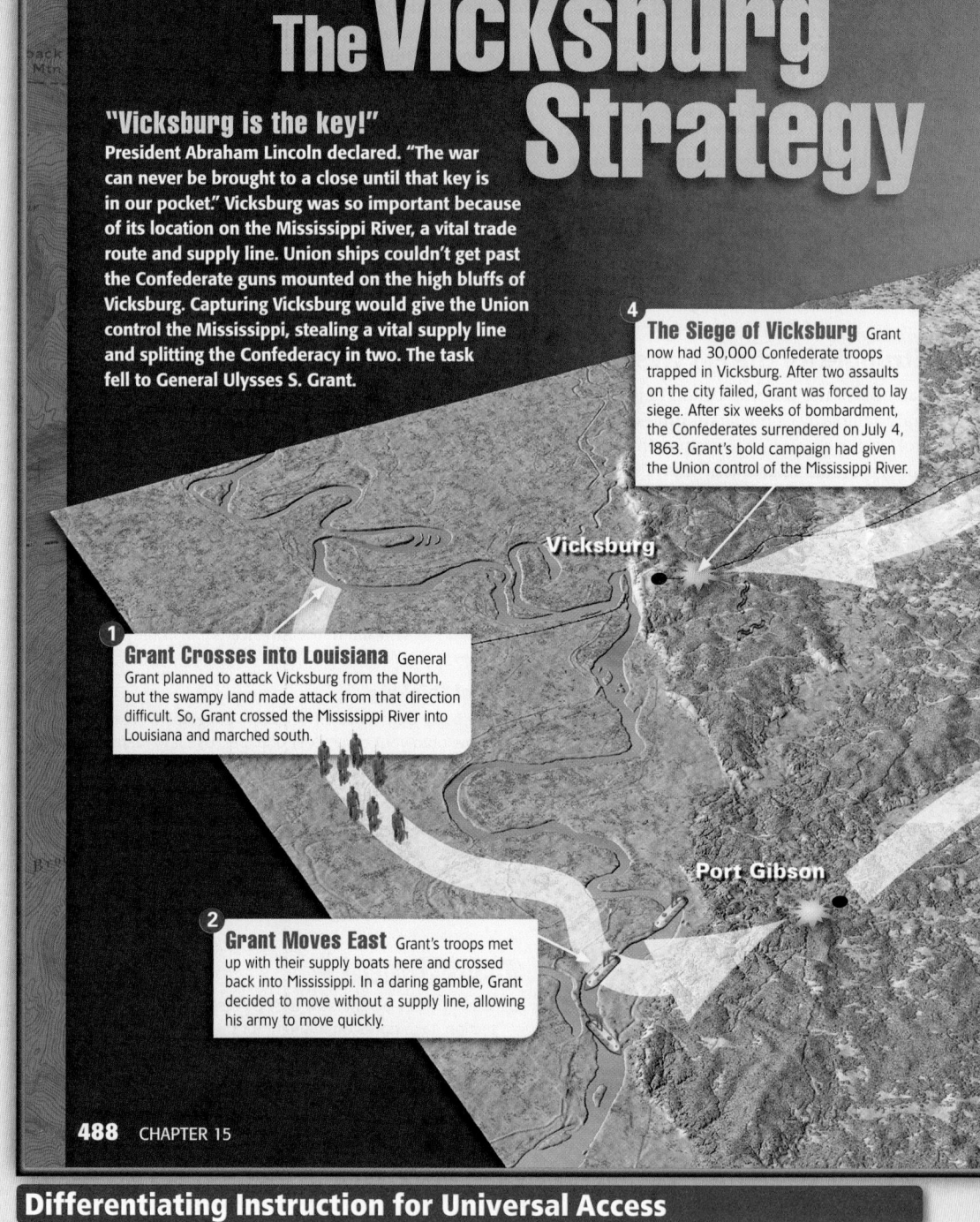

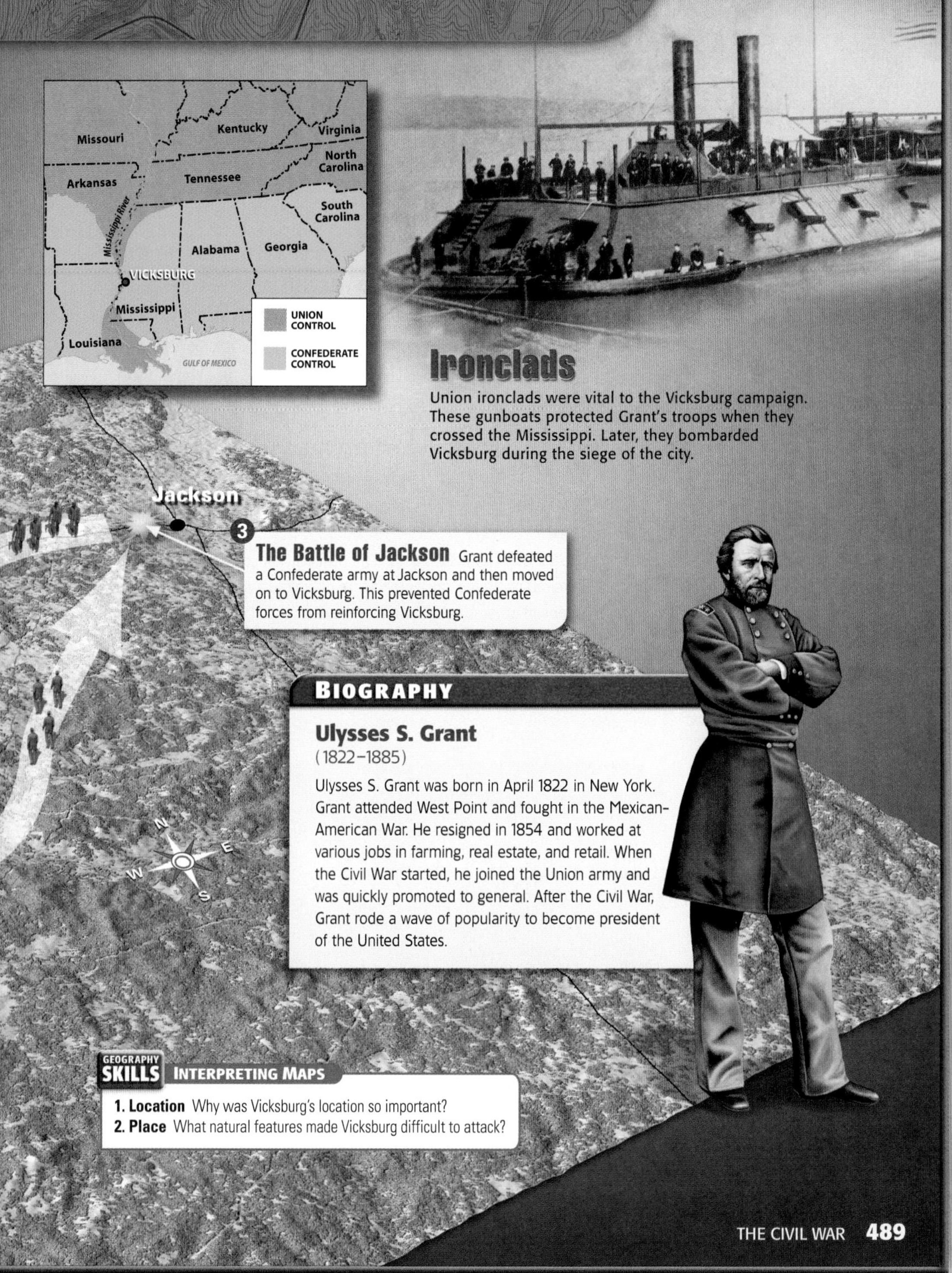

Ironclads

Union ironclads were vital to the Vicksburg campaign. These gunboats protected Grant's troops when they crossed the Mississippi. Later, they bombarded Vicksburg during the siege of the city.

The Battle of Jackson Grant defeated a Confederate army at Jackson and then moved on to Vicksburg. This prevented Confederate forces from reinforcing Vicksburg.

BIOGRAPHY

Ulysses S. Grant
(1822–1885)

Ulysses S. Grant was born in April 1822 in New York. Grant attended West Point and fought in the Mexican-American War. He resigned in 1854 and worked at various jobs in farming, real estate, and retail. When the Civil War started, he joined the Union army and was quickly promoted to general. After the Civil War, Grant rode a wave of popularity to become president of the United States.

GEOGRAPHY SKILLS INTERPRETING MAPS

1. **Location** Why was Vicksburg's location so important?
2. **Place** What natural features made Vicksburg difficult to attack?

History and Geography

Info to Know

Vicksburg Cave Homes The city of Vicksburg was built on a hill. During the Siege of Vicksburg, the city's residents burrowed a system of more than 500 caves in the side of the hill in which to take cover from the Union artillery attacks. Caves for a single family usually had one or two chambers. Some large caves could hold as many as 200 people. People furnished their caves with carpets, furniture, cook stoves, and mirrors. They also built shelves into the walls to hold candles and other belongings.

Info to Know

Terms of Surrender Although General Grant originally demanded an unconditional surrender from the Confederates at Vicksburg, his final terms were more lenient. Grant decided it would be too costly and time-consuming to take the Confederate prisoners to Union prison camps. Instead, he allowed most of the defeated soldiers to surrender their weapons and leave as prisoners on parole.

Did you know . . .

The Confederate surrender ended the Siege of Vicksburg on July 4, 1863. As a result, the city's residents did not celebrate Independence Day for more than 80 years.

Critical Thinking: Analyzing Primary Sources

Standards Proficiency

The Mighty Mississippi

HSS 8.10.7; HSS **Analysis Skills:** HR 4, HI 2

Background After the fall of Vicksburg, President Abraham Lincoln summed up the event's significance: "The father of waters rolls unvexed to the sea."

1. Write the above quotation from Lincoln for student to see. Discuss the expression "the father of waters" with students so that they understand that Lincoln was talking about the Mississippi River.
2. Organize the class into small groups. Have each group discuss this quotation and the importance of the Mississippi River to both the North and the South during the Civil War.
3. Then have each student write a brief essay explaining the quotation and the significance of the Siege of Vicksburg to the Civil War.

Alternative Assessment Handbook, Rubrics 14: Group Activity; and 37: Writing Assignments

Answers

Interpreting Maps 1. *Capturing Vicksburg would give the Union control of the Mississippi River, which would cut off a vital supply line for the South and cut the Confederacy in two.* **2.** *It was located on high bluffs directly above the Mississippi and the land to the north was swampy, which made attack from that approach difficult.*

Preteach

Bellringer

If YOU were there . . . Use the **Daily Bellringer Transparency** to help students answer the question.

 Daily Bellringer Transparency, Section 4

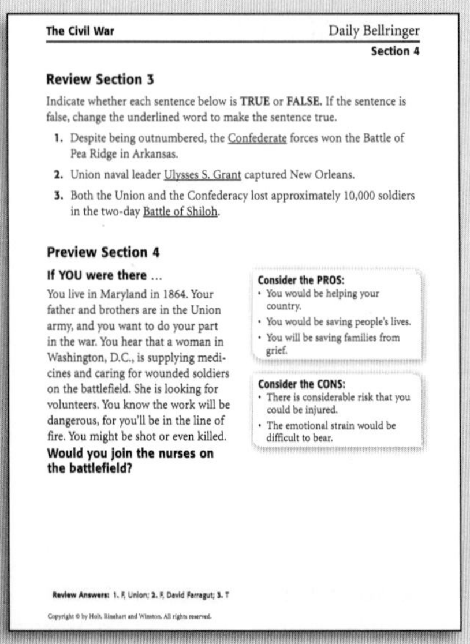

The Civil War Daily Bellringer

Section 4

Review Section 3

Indicate whether each sentence below is **TRUE** or **FALSE.** If the sentence is false, change the underlined word to make the sentence true.

1. Despite being outnumbered, the Confederate forces won the Battle of Pea Ridge in Arkansas.
2. Union naval leader Ulysses S. Grant captured New Orleans.
3. Both the Union and the Confederacy lost approximately 10,000 soldiers in the two-day Battle of Shiloh.

Preview Section 4

If YOU were there ...

You live in Maryland in 1864. Your father and brothers are in the Union army, and you want to do your part in the war. You hear that a woman in Washington, D.C., is supplying medicines and caring for wounded soldiers on the battlefield. She is looking for volunteers. You know the work will be dangerous, for you'll be in the line of fire. You might be shot or even killed.

Would you join the nurses on the battlefield?

Consider the PROS:
- You would be helping your country.
- You would be saving people's lives.
- You will be saving families from grief.

Consider the CONS:
- There is considerable risk that you could be injured.
- The emotional strain would be difficult to bear.

Review Answers: 1. F, Union; 2. F, David Farragut; 3. T

Building Vocabulary

Preteach or review the following term:

abolitionist supporter of the movement to end slavery (p. 491)

CRF: Vocabulary Builder Activity, Section 4

 Standards Focus

HSS 8.10.4

Means: Discuss the major events, issues, documents, and speeches of Abraham Lincoln's presidency.

Matters: Today, Lincoln is considered one of the greatest American presidents, and his ideas remain influential.

HSS 8.10.5

Means: Identify the leaders in the North and the South, and describe the views of leaders and soldiers on both sides during the war.

Matters: Studying the lives and views of the people who fought the Civil War helps us better understand the war's events and its outcome.

HSS 8.10.7

Means: Explain how the war affected the lives of soldiers and civilians as well as the environment and future warfare.

Matters: The Civil War caused much death and destruction but also led to the end of slavery.

SECTION 4

Daily Life during the War

What You Will Learn...

Main Ideas

1. The Emancipation Proclamation freed slaves in Confederate states.
2. African Americans participated in the war in a variety of ways.
3. President Lincoln faced opposition to the war.
4. Life was difficult for soldiers and civilians alike.

The Big Idea

The lives of many Americans were affected by the Civil War.

Key Terms and People

emancipation, *p. 491*
Emancipation Proclamation, *p. 491*
contrabands, *p. 493*
54th Massachusetts Infantry, *p. 493*
Copperheads, *p. 494*
habeas corpus, *p. 494*
Clara Barton, *p. 496*

HSS 8.10.4 Discuss Abraham Lincoln's presidency and his significant writings and speeches and their relationship to the Declaration of Independence, such as his "House Divided" speech (1858), Gettysburg Address (1863), Emancipation Proclamation (1863), and inaugural addresses (1861 and 1865).

8.10.5 Study the views and lives of leaders (e.g., Ulysses S. Grant, Jefferson Davis, Robert E. Lee) and soldiers on both sides of the war, including those of black soldiers and regiments.

8.10.7 Explain how the war affected combatants, civilians, the physical environment, and future warfare.

If YOU were there...

You live in Maryland in 1864. Your father and brothers are in the Union army, and you want to do your part in the war. You hear that a woman in Washington, D.C., is supplying medicines and caring for wounded soldiers on the battlefield. She is looking for volunteers. You know the work will be dangerous, for you'll be in the line of fire. You might be shot or even killed.

Would you join the nurses on the battlefield?

BUILDING BACKGROUND The Civil War touched almost all Americans. Some 3 million men fought in the two armies. Thousands of other men and women worked behind the lines, providing food, supplies, medical care, and other necessary services. Civilians could not escape the effects of war, as the fighting destroyed farms, homes, and cities.

Emancipation Proclamation

Teach the Big Idea: Master the Standards

Standards Proficiency

Daily Life during the War HSS 8.10.4, 8.10.5, 8.10.7; HSS Analysis Skills: CS 1, HI 1, HI 2, HI 3

Materials: paper, stapler

1. **Teach** Ask students the Main Idea questions to teach this section.
2. **Apply** Have each student take four sheets of paper and fold and staple them to create an eight-page booklet. On each left-hand page, have students write one of the section's blue headings. Below the heading, students should list the key people, events, and issues in that part of the text. Students should use the right-hand page to provide drawings, phrases, and charts that relate to the information on the left-hand page. **LS Verbal/Linguistic, Visual/Spatial**
3. **Review** As you review the section, have volunteers share the information they listed.
4. **Practice/Homework** Have students write a short summary for each part of their booklets. **LS Verbal/Linguistic**

Alternative Assessment Handbook, Rubrics 3: Artwork; and 37: Writing Assignments

Emancipation Proclamation

At the heart of the nation's bloody struggle were millions of enslaved African Americans. Abolitionists urged President Lincoln to free them.

"You know I dislike slavery," Lincoln had written to a friend in 1855. In an 1858 speech, he declared, "There is no reason in the world why the negro is not entitled to all the natural rights numerated in the Declaration of Independence—the right to life, liberty, and the pursuit of happiness." Yet as president, Lincoln found **emancipation,** or the freeing of slaves, to be a difficult issue. He did not believe he had the constitutional power. He also worried about the effects of emancipation.

Lincoln Issues the Proclamation

Northerners had a range of opinions about abolishing slavery.

- The Democratic Party, which included many laborers, opposed emancipation. Laborers feared that freed slaves would come north and take their jobs at lower wages.
- Abolitionists argued that the war was pointless if it did not win freedom for African Americans. They warned that the Union would remain divided until the problem was resolved.
- Some in Lincoln's government predicted that emancipation would anger voters, causing Republicans to be defeated in the 1862 midterm elections. Lincoln worried about losing support for the war.
- Others, including Secretary of War Edwin Stanton, agreed with Lincoln's reasoning. The use of slave labor was helping the Confederacy make war. Therefore, as commander in chief, the president could free the slaves in all rebellious states. Freed African Americans could then be recruited into the Union army.

For several weeks in 1862, Lincoln worked intensely, thinking, writing, and rewriting. He finally wrote the **Emancipation Proclamation**, the order to free the Confederate slaves. The proclamation declared that:

> "...all persons held as slaves within any State or designated part of a State the people whereof shall then be in rebellion against the United States shall be then, thenceforward, and forever free."
>
> —Emancipation Proclamation, 1862

The painting at left shows Lincoln and his cabinet after the signing of the Emancipation Proclamation. Above is a photo of former slaves that were freed by the proclamation.

How do you think the Emancipation Proclamation would affect the Civil War?

Emancipation Proclamation

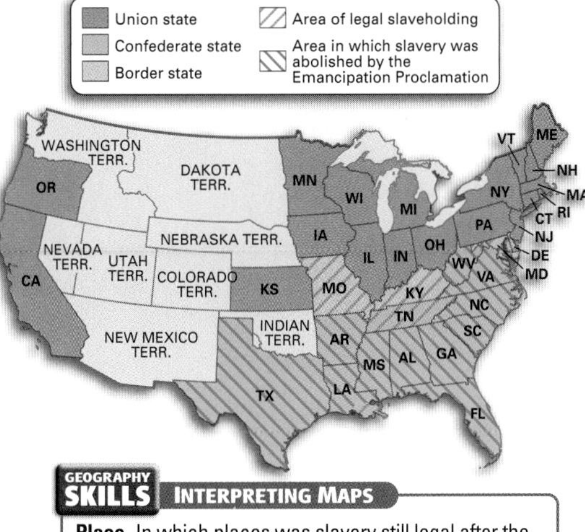

GEOGRAPHY SKILLS INTERPRETING MAPS

Place In which places was slavery still legal after the Emancipation Proclamation?

Direct Teach

Main Idea

1 Emancipation Proclamation

The Emancipation Proclamation freed slaves in Confederate states.

Identify What issue lay at the heart of the Civil War? *slavery and the millions of African Americans living in bondage*

Identify Points of View Why did some northerners oppose abolishing slavery? *feared that freed slaves would work for lower wages and take jobs; feared that emancipation would weaken support for the war*

Evaluate How did Lincoln address the difficult issue of emancipation, and why did he make this choice? *He issued a military proclamation freeing all enslaved Africans in rebellious states. He did not believe he had the constitutional power to end slavery but as commander-in-chief he believed he could take action to stop slave labor from being used to help the southern war effort.*

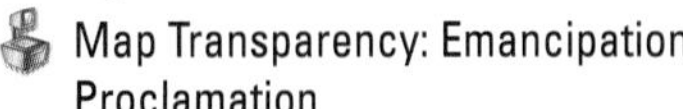
Map Transparency: Emancipation Proclamation

HSS 8.10.4, 8.10.5, 8.10.7; HSS **Analysis Skills:** HR 5, HI 1, HI 3

Info to Know

Support for Lincoln After the Emancipation Proclamation was issued, an African American congregation in Baltimore raised about $580 to buy Lincoln a Bible. The cover had a picture of Lincoln breaking off the chains of a slave working in a cotton field.

Critical Thinking: Identifying Points of View

Standards Proficiency

Emancipation Proclamation

HSS 8.10.4, 8.10.7; HSS **Analysis Skills:** HR 4, HI 3

1. Have students read the Emancipation Proclamation (provided in the back of the textbook) as a class and summarize its main points. Guide the class in a discussion of the importance of the proclamation and its impact on the North and the South.
2. Ask students to identify how different groups in the North reacted to the proclamation. Encourage students to elaborate on why some northerners might have opposed it.
3. Then ask students to imagine that they lived during the time of the Civil War and Lincoln has just issued the Emancipation Proclamation. Have each student write a letter to Lincoln expressing support for the proclamation and explaining how he or she thinks it will affect the war. Have volunteers read their letters to the class. LS **Verbal/Linguistic**

Alternative Assessment Handbook, Rubric 41: Writing to Express

Answers

Interpreting Maps *Missouri, Kentucky, Maryland, Delaware, Tennessee, and the southern tip of Louisiana*

Emancipation Proclamation *possible answer—might hurt the South's ability to wage war as slaves escape to Union camps; might help the northern war effort as freed slaves join the Union ranks*

Direct Teach

Main Idea

1 Emancipation Proclamation

The Emancipation Proclamation freed slaves in Confederate states.

Identify Points of View Why did some abolitionists criticize the Emancipation Proclamation? *because it did not end slavery completely or free all slaves*

Make Judgments Do you think Lincoln should have expanded the Emancipation Proclamation to free all slaves? Why or why not? *possible answers—no, because he might have lost political support and the border states might have left the Union, thereby risking the war and any chance for helping slaves; yes, because slavery is morally wrong*

Activity Celebrating Emancipation Have each student create a poem from the point of view of a freed slave celebrating the Emancipation Proclamation.

Alternative Assessment Handbook, Rubric 26: Poems and Songs

HSS 8.10.4, 8.10.5, 8.10.7; **HSS Analysis Skills:** HR 5, HI 1, HI 3

World Events

European Reactions to Emancipation

The Emancipation Proclamation drew the attention of many Europeans. Some workers from Manchester, England, wrote to President Lincoln, "We joyfully honor you . . . [for] your belief in the words of your great founders: 'All men are created free and equal.'"

Answers

Reading Check *possible answers—Abolitionists supported it, although some thought it did not go far enough; some laborers feared they would lose their jobs to freed slaves who might work for less.*

New Soldiers

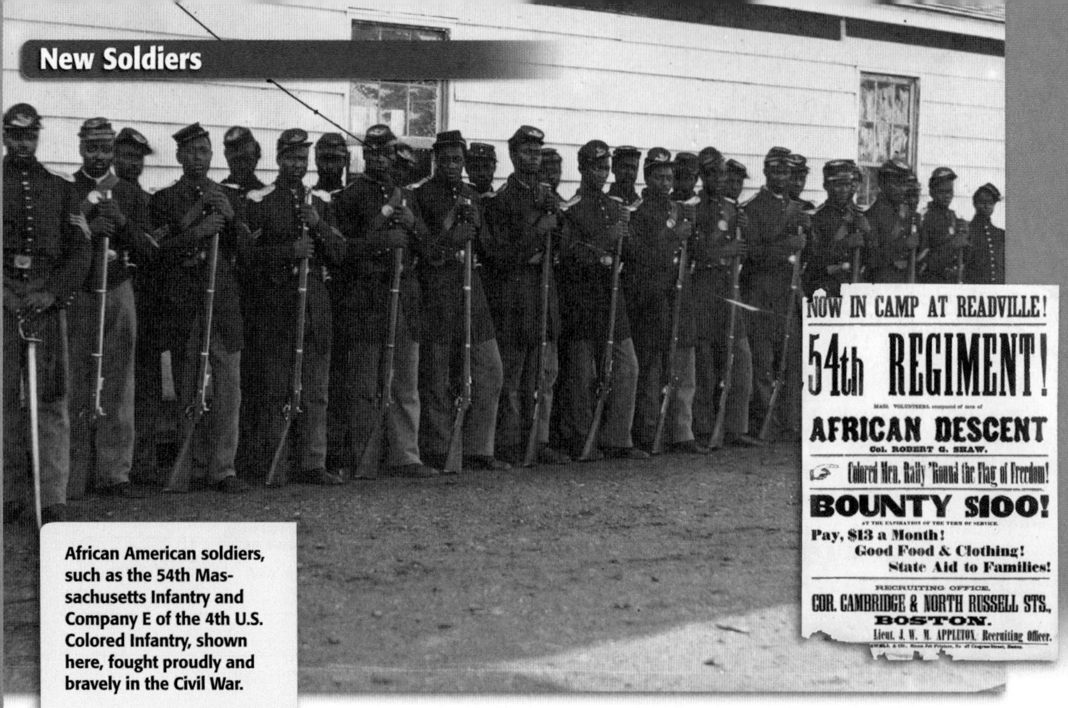

NOW IN CAMP AT READVILLE!
54th REGIMENT!
AFRICAN DESCENT
Col. ROBERT G. SHAW.
Colored Men, Rally 'Round the Flag of Freedom!
BOUNTY $100!
Pay, $13 a Month!
Good Food & Clothing!
State Aid to Families!
RECRUITING OFFICE,
COR. CAMBRIDGE & NORTH RUSSELL STS.,
BOSTON.

African American soldiers, such as the 54th Massachusetts Infantry and Company E of the 4th U.S. Colored Infantry, shown here, fought proudly and bravely in the Civil War.

The Emancipation Proclamation was a military order that freed slaves only in areas controlled by the Confederacy. In fact, the proclamation had little immediate effect. It was impossible for the federal government to enforce the proclamation in the areas where it actually applied—the states in rebellion that were not under federal control. The proclamation did not stop slavery in the border states, where the federal government would have had the power to enforce it. The words written in the Emancipation Proclamation were powerful, but the impact of the document was more symbolic than real.

Lincoln wanted to be in a strong position in the war before announcing his plan. The Battle of Antietam gave him the victory he needed. He issued the Emancipation Proclamation on September 22, 1862. The proclamation went into effect on January 1, 1863.

Reaction to the Proclamation

New Year's Eve, December 31, 1862: In "night watch" meetings at many African American churches, worshippers prayed, sang, and gave thanks. When the clocks struck midnight, millions were free. Abolitionists rejoiced. Frederick Douglass called January 1, 1863, "the great day which is to determine the destiny not only of the American Republic, but that of the American Continent."

William Lloyd Garrison was quick to note, however, that "slavery, as a system" continued to exist in the loyal slave states. Yet where slavery remained, the proclamation encouraged many enslaved Africans to escape when the Union troops came near. They flocked to the Union camps and followed them for protection. The loss of slaves crippled the South's ability to wage war.

READING CHECK **Finding Main Ideas** How did northerners view the Emancipation Proclamation?

Differentiating Instruction for Universal Access

Learners Having Difficulty — Reaching Standards

1. Review the information about African American soldiers in this section. Then draw the chart for students to see. Omit the blue, italicized answers.
2. Have each student copy the chart and complete it by listing reasons why African Americans joined the Union and some of the hardships they faced. **LS Visual/Spatial**

African American Union Soldiers	
Reasons Joined	**Hardships Faced**
• *freedom* • *citizenship* • *honor* • *respect* • *pay*	• *if captured, often killed or sold into slavery* • *received less pay than white soldiers* • *no guarantee of gaining the rights of citizenship*

HSS 8.10.4, 8.10.5, 8.10.7; **HSS Analysis Skills:** HI 1

Alternative Assessment Handbook, Rubric 7: Charts

Primary Source

LETTER

June 23, 1863

Joseph E. Williams, an African American soldier and recruiter from Pennsylvania, wrote this letter describing why African Americans fought for the Union.

"We are now determined to hold every step which has been offered to us as citizens of the United States for our elevation [benefit], which represent justice, the purity, the truth, and aspiration [hope] of heaven. We must learn deeply to realize the duty, the moral and political necessity for the benefit of our race...Every consideration of honor, of interest, and of duty to God and man, requires that we should be true to our trust."

—quoted in *A Grand Army of Black Men*, edited by Edwin S. Redkey

ANALYSIS SKILL ANALYZING PRIMARY SOURCES

Why did Williams think being soldiers was so important for African Americans?

African Americans Participate in the War

As the war casualties climbed, the Union needed even more troops. African Americans were ready to volunteer. Not all white northerners were ready to accept them, but eventually they had to. Frederick Douglass believed that military service would help African Americans gain rights.

"Once let the black man get upon his person the brass letters, U.S.; ... and a musket on his shoulder and bullets in his pocket, and there is no power on earth which can deny that he has earned the right to citizenship."

—Frederick Douglass

Congress began allowing the army to sign up African American volunteers as laborers in July 1862. The War Department also gave **contrabands,** or escaped slaves, the right to join the Union army in South Carolina. Free African Americans in Louisiana and Kansas also formed their own units in the Union army. By the spring of 1863, African American army units were proving themselves in combat. They took part in a Union attack on Port Hudson, Louisiana, in May.

One unit stood out above the others. The **54th Massachusetts Infantry** consisted mostly of free African Americans. In July 1863 this regiment led a heroic charge on South Carolina's Fort Wagner. The 54th took heavy fire and suffered huge casualties in the failed operation. About half the regiment was killed, wounded, or captured. Edward L. Pierce, a correspondent for the *New York Tribune,* wrote, "The Fifty-fourth did well and nobly…They moved up as gallantly as any troops could, and with their enthusiasm they deserved a better fate." The bravery of the 54th regiment made it the most celebrated African American unit of the war.

About 180,000 African Americans served with the Union army. They received $10 a month, while white soldiers got $13. They were usually led by white officers, some from abolitionist families.

African Americans faced special horrors on the battlefield. Confederates often killed their black captives or sold them into slavery. In the 1864 election, Lincoln suggested rewarding African American soldiers by giving them the right to vote.

READING CHECK **Analyzing Information** How did African Americans support the Union?

Direct Teach

Main Idea

❷ African Americans Participate in the War

African Americans participated in the war in a variety of ways.

Identify Why did the 54th Massachusetts Infantry become the most celebrated African American unit of the Civil War? *The unit, consisting mostly of free African Americans, led a heroic charge on South Carolina's Fort Wagner and suffered heavy losses.*

Interpret How did Frederick Douglass believe that military service would help African Americans? *He believed that by serving in the military African Americans would earn the right to citizenship.*

CRF: Biography Activity: William Carney

HSS 8.10.5, 8.10.7; **HSS** **Analysis Skills:** HR 4, HR 5, HI 1

Info to Know

African American Soldiers In July 1862, African Americans were officially allowed to join the Union army. Many men responded to the call. Although African Americans made up only 2 percent of the North's population, they made up nearly 10 percent of the Union army by the war's end.

Cross-Discipline Activity: Civics

Standards Proficiency

Responsibility: Military Service

HSS 8.10.5; **HSS** **Analysis Skills:** HR 4, HR 5

1. Discuss with students the above quotation by Frederick Douglass. Have students explain what Douglass is expressing in the statement.
2. Ask students why Douglass thought military service would prove that African Americans had earned the right to citizenship *(possible answer—because military service is a sign of good citizenship)*. Ask students if they agree with Douglass.
3. Then have students examine the primary source letter above. Have students compare and contrast the views of Douglass and Williams on military service. Help students understand that both men saw the rights and responsibilities of citizenship as connected.
4. Conclude by having students discuss why African Americans fought for the Union, and why military service is an important duty of citizenship.

Alternative Assessment Handbook, Rubric 11: Discussions

Answers

Analyzing Primary Sources *He saw military service as a moral and political duty in response to the freedom African Americans had received and the gains they had made toward citizenship.*

Reading Check *served as soldiers and fought bravely for the Union*

Direct Teach

Main Idea

3 Growing Opposition

President Lincoln faced opposition to the war.

Define What is a military draft? *forced military service*

Identify Points of View Why did the Copperheads oppose the war? *They sympathized with the South, opposed abolition, and believed the war was unnecessary and that too many Americans were being killed.*

Analyze Why did some people call the Civil War "a rich man's war and a poor man's fight"? *While rich men bought their way out of military service, poor men were being drafted to fight the war.*

Activity Northern Draft Political Cartoons Have students draw two political cartoons, one supporting and one opposing the northern draft.

Alternative Assessment Handbook, Rubric 27: Political Cartoons

HSS 8.10.5, 8.10.7; HSS **Analysis Skills:** HR 5, HI 1

Info to Know

Civil War Armies The Union and Confederate armies followed similar paths when it came to filling their ranks. Both started with short enlistment terms that were lengthened to three years or the duration of the war. Both armies eventually had difficulties filling their quotas with volunteers and had to resort to drafting men. When Union army volunteers re-enlisted after their three-year terms, they received a 30-day leave, transportation home, and a $400 bonus.

Growing Opposition

The deepening shadows in Lincoln's face reflected the huge responsibilities he carried. Besides running the war, he had to deal with growing tensions in the North.

Copperheads

As the months rolled on and the number of dead continued to increase, a group of northern Democrats began speaking out against the war. Led by U.S. Representative Clement L. Vallandigham of Ohio, they called themselves Peace Democrats. Their enemies called them Copperheads, comparing them to a poisonous snake. The name stuck.

Many **Copperheads** were midwesterners that sympathized with the South and opposed abolition. They believed the war was not necessary and called for its end. Vallandigham asked what the war had gained, and then said, "Let the dead at Fredericksburg and Vicksburg answer."

Lincoln saw the Copperheads as a threat to the war effort. To silence them, he suspended the right of habeas corpus. **Habeas corpus** is a constitutional protection against unlawful imprisonment. Ignoring this protection, Union officials jailed their enemies, including some Copperheads, without evidence or trial. Lincoln's action greatly angered Democrats and some Republicans.

Northern Draft

In March 1863, war critics erupted again when Congress approved a draft, or forced military service. For $300, men were allowed to buy their way out of military service. For an unskilled laborer, however, that was nearly a year's wages. Critics of the draft called the Civil War a "rich man's war and a poor man's fight."

In July 1863, riots broke out when African Americans were brought into New York City to replace striking Irish dock workers. The city happened to be holding a war draft at the same time. The two events enraged rioters, who attacked African Americans and draft offices. More than 100 people died.

In this tense situation, the northern Democrats nominated former General George McClellan for president in 1864. They called

Infantry Family

While wealthy civilians could avoid military service, poorer men were drafted to serve in the Union army. This member of the 31st Pennsylvania Infantry brought his family along with him. His wife probably helped the soldier with many daily chores such as cooking and laundry.

Why would soldiers bring their families to live with them in camp?

Differentiating Instruction for Universal Access

Advanced Learners/GATE — Exceeding Standards

1. Explain that the U.S. Constitution gives Congress the power to raise and support armies but does not mention conscription or a military draft. During the Civil War, both the North and the South resorted to using drafts.
2. Organize students into two groups. Have one group support a military draft, and have the other group oppose it. Have students work independently to jot down their ideas and arguments. Then give the groups time to prepare defenses and arguments supporting their assigned positions. If time allows, have students conduct research on the topic.
3. Hold a debate between the two sides and serve as the moderator. Afterward, discuss the reasons for the drafts in the Civil War.

LS **Interpersonal, Logical/Mathematical**

HSS 8.10.5, 8.10.7; HSS **Analysis Skills:** HR 5

Alternative Assessment Handbook, Rubric 10: Debates

Answers

Infantry Family *possible answers—to prepare food, mend clothes, make life easier for the soldiers and their families* for an immediate end to the war. Lincoln defeated McClellan in the popular vote, winning by about 400,000 votes out of 4 million cast. The electoral vote was not even close. Lincoln won 212 to 21.

READING CHECK **Identifying Cause and Effect** Who opposed the war, and how did Lincoln respond to the conflict?

Difficult Lives of Soldiers

Young, fresh recruits in both armies were generally eager to fight. Experienced troops, however, knew better.

On the Battlefield

Civil War armies fought in the ancient battlefield formation that produced massive casualties. Endless rows of troops fired directly at one another, with cannonballs landing amid them. When the order was given, soldiers would attach bayonets to their guns and rush toward their enemy. Men died to gain every inch of ground.

Doctors and nurses in the field saved many lives. Yet they had no medicines to stop infections that developed after soldiers were wounded. Many soldiers endured the horror of having infected legs and arms amputated without painkillers. Infections from minor injuries caused many deaths.

Despite the huge battlefield losses, the biggest killer in the Civil War was not the fighting. It was diseases such as typhoid, pneumonia, and tuberculosis. Nearly twice as many soldiers died of illnesses as died in combat.

Prisoners of War

Military prisoners on both sides lived in unimaginable misery. In prison camps, such as Andersonville, Georgia, and Elmira, New York, soldiers were packed into camps designed to hold only a fraction of their number. Soldiers had little shelter, food, or clothing. Starvation and disease killed thousands of prisoners.

LINKING TO TODAY

Battlefield Communications

The drummer was an essential member of every Civil War unit. Drummers served army commanders by drumming specific beats that directed troop movements during battle. Different beats were used to order troops to prepare to attack, to fire, to cease fire, and to signal a truce. Drummers had to stay near their commanders to hear orders. This meant that the drummers—some as young as nine years old—often saw deadly combat conditions.

The Civil War gave birth to the Signal Corps, the army unit devoted to communications. Today battlefield communications are primarily electronic. Radio, e-mail, facsimile, and telephone messages, often relayed by satellites, enable orders and other information to be transmitted nearly instantaneously all over the globe.

Union Signal Corps

Modern battlefield communications

ANALYSIS SKILL **ANALYZING INFORMATION**

Why is communication so important on the battlefield?

Direct Teach

Main Idea

4 Difficult Lives of Soldiers

Life was difficult for soldiers and civilians alike.

Explain Why was the Civil War death toll so high? *firing at close range, bayoneting, lack of medicine and medical treatment*

Make Generalizations How did life for women, the elderly, and children change during the war? *They had to take over work, such as farm work and factory jobs, formerly done by men who were fighting.*

CRF: Primary Source Activity: John L. Ranson, *Andersonville Diary*

HSS 8.10.7; HSS **Analysis Skills:** HI 1

Biography

Johnny Clem One of the most famous Civil War drummers was Johnny Clem. At the age of nine, Clem ran away from his home in Ohio to join the Union army. Clem went from drummer boy to soldier during the Battle of Shiloh. After his drum was shattered, young Clem picked up a gun and began firing. Within two years, he was promoted to sergeant to become the youngest noncommissioned officer in the Union army. After the Civil War, Clem attended West Point and made the military his career.

go.hrw.com
Online Resources
KEYWORD: SS8 US15
ACTIVITY: Civil War Authors

Critical Thinking: Finding Main Ideas

Standards **Proficiency**

Civil War Letters

HSS 8.10.7; HSS **Analysis Skills:** HI 1

1. Review with students the experiences of soldiers and civilians in the Civil War and the ways in which civilians aided the war effort.
2. Then have each student write a series of letters between an imaginary Civil War soldier and his wife or sister back on the home front.
3. Students' letters should describe the different experiences of soldiers and civilians, the hardships each faced, and some of the ways in which women supported the war effort. Encourage students to make their letters expressive and descriptive while remaining true to the history.
4. Have volunteers read some of their letters to the class. LS **Verbal/Linguistic**

Alternative Assessment Handbook, Rubric 25: Personal Letters

Answers

Analyzing Information *enables leaders to control troop movements*

Reading Check *Copperheads; Lincoln suspended the right of habeas corpus, which enabled Union officials to jail their enemies without evidence or trial.*

Direct Teach

Main Idea

4 Difficult Lives of Soldiers

Life was difficult for soldiers and civilians alike.

Identify Who was Clara Barton? *"Angel of the battlefield" who worked at field hospitals. Her work formed the basis for the future American Red Cross.*

Identify Cause and Effect How did the Civil War affect the North's economy? *The lack of workers caused wages to rise, and the northern economy boomed as production and prices soared.*

CRF: Biography Activity: Clara Barton

CRF: Primary Source Activity: Civil War Era Diary

HSS 8.10.7; **HSS Analysis Skills:** HI 1, HI 2

Review & Assess

Close

Have students describe in their own words life during the Civil War.

Review

Online Quiz, Section 4

Assess

SE Section 4 Assessment

PASS: Section 4 Quiz

Alternative Assessment Handbook

Reteach/Classroom Intervention

California Standards Review Workbook

Interactive Reader and Study Guide, Section 4

Interactive Skills Tutor CD-ROM

Life as a Civilian

The war effort involved all levels of society. Women as well as people too young or too old for military service worked in factories and on farms. Economy in the North boomed as production and prices soared. The lack of workers caused wages to rise by 43 percent between 1860 and 1865.

THE IMPACT TODAY

The American Red Cross today supplies victims of natural disasters with relief aid.

Women were the backbone of civilian life. On the farms, women and children performed the daily chores usually done by men. One visitor to Iowa in 1862 reported that he "met more women . . . at work in the fields than men." Southern women also managed farms and plantations.

One woman brought strength and comfort to countless wounded Union soldiers. Volunteer **Clara Barton** organized the collection of medicine and supplies for delivery to the battlefield. At the field hospitals, the "angel of the battlefield" soothed the wounded and dying and assisted doctors as bullets flew around her. Barton's work formed the basis for the future American Red Cross.

Clara Barton founded the American Red Cross.

In the South, Sally Louisa Tompkins established a small hospital in Richmond, Virginia. By the end of the war, it had grown into a major army hospital. Jefferson Davis recognized her value to the war effort by making her a captain in the Confederate army.

READING CHECK **Analyzing** How did women help the war effort on both sides?

SUMMARY AND PREVIEW Many lives were changed by the war. In the next section you will learn about the end of the war.

Section 4 Assessment

go.hrw.com **Online Quiz** KEYWORD: SS8 HP15

Reviewing Ideas, Terms, and People HSS 8.10.4, 8.10.5, 8.10.7

1. **a. Recall** Why did some Americans want to end slavery?
   b. Contrast How did reactions to the **Emancipation Proclamation** differ?
   c. Elaborate Do you think that the **emancipation** of slaves should have extended to the border states? Explain your answer.
2. **a. Recall** Why did some northerners want to recruit African Americans into the Union army?
   b. Contrast In what ways did African American soldiers face more difficulties than white soldiers did?
3. **a. Identify** Who were **Copperheads**, and why did they oppose the war?
   b. Evaluate Should President Lincoln have suspended the right to **habeas corpus**? Why?
4. **a. Describe** What were conditions like in military camps?
   b. Draw Conclusions How did the war change life on the home front?

Critical Thinking

5. **Categorizing** Copy the chart below onto your own sheet of paper. Use it to identify the ways in which people in the North and the South contributed to the war effort.

People	Contributions
Women and Children	
African Americans	
Soldiers	

FOCUS ON WRITING

6. **Taking Notes on Life During the War** As you read this section, take notes on Lincoln's emancipation of the slaves, African American soldiers, and women who provided medical care for soldiers. Be sure to answer the following questions: Who? Where? When? Why? and How?

Section 4 Assessment Answers

1. **a.** possible answers—all deserve natural rights; Union would be divided until ended
   b. Democrats opposed it; some abolitionists thought should end all slavery; African Americans rejoiced; many slaves escaped
   c. possible answers—yes, slavery is wrong; no, border states might have left the Union and cost the North the war
2. **a.** The Union needed more troops.
   b. often killed or sold into slavery when captured; paid less than white soldiers
3. **a.** northern Democrats who opposed the war; sympathized with South, opposed abolition
   b. possible answers—yes, the war effort was threatened; no, violated people's rights
4. **a.** unsanitary, with many illnesses; deadly
   b. All levels of society took on farm and factory work; North's economy boomed.
5. Women and Children—provided medical care and support, worked on farms and in factories; African Americans and Soldiers—fought
6. Notes should include key people and issues.

Answers

Reading Check *Women worked in factories and on farms, cared for wounded soldiers, organized collections of medicine and supplies, worked in field hospitals, and established hospitals.*

The Tide of War Turns

SECTION 5

If YOU were there...

You live in southern Pennsylvania in 1863, near a battlefield where thousands died. Now people have come from miles around to dedicate a cemetery here. You are near the front of the crowd. The first speaker impresses everyone with two hours of dramatic words and gestures. Then President Lincoln speaks—just a few minutes of simple words. Many people are disappointed.

Why do you think the president's speech was so short?

BUILDING BACKGROUND Many people, especially in the North, had expected a quick victory, but the war dragged on for years. The balance of victories seemed to seesaw between North and South, and both sides suffered terrible casualties. The last Confederate push into the North ended at Gettysburg in one of the bloodiest battles of the war.

What You Will Learn...

Main Ideas

1. The Battle of Gettysburg in 1863 was a major turning point in the war.
2. During 1864, Union campaigns in the East and South dealt crippling blows to the Confederacy.
3. Union troops forced the South to surrender in 1865, ending the Civil War.

The Big Idea

Union victories in 1863, 1864, and 1865 brought the Civil War to an end.

Key Terms and People

George G. Meade, *p. 498*
Battle of Gettysburg, *p. 498*
George Pickett, *p. 499*
Pickett's Charge, *p. 499*
Gettysburg Address, *p. 500*
Wilderness Campaign, *p. 500*
William Tecumseh Sherman, *p. 501*
total war, *p. 502*
Appomattox Courthouse, *p. 502*

HSS 8.10.6 Describe critical developments and events in the war, including the major battles, geographical advantages and obstacles, technological advances, and General Lee's surrender at Appomattox.

8.10.7 Explain how the war affected combatants, civilians, the physical environment, and future warfare.

Three Days at Gettysburg

Gettysburg was the largest and bloodiest battle of the Civil War. In three days, more than 51,000 soldiers were killed, wounded, captured, or went missing. It was an important victory for the Union, and it stopped Lee's plan of invading the North.

Artillery played a key role in the Battle of Gettysburg on July 1, 1863.

Day One: July 1, 1863

Preteach

Bellringer

If YOU were there . . . Use the **Daily Bellringer Transparency** to help students answer the question.

 Daily Bellringer Transparency, Section 5

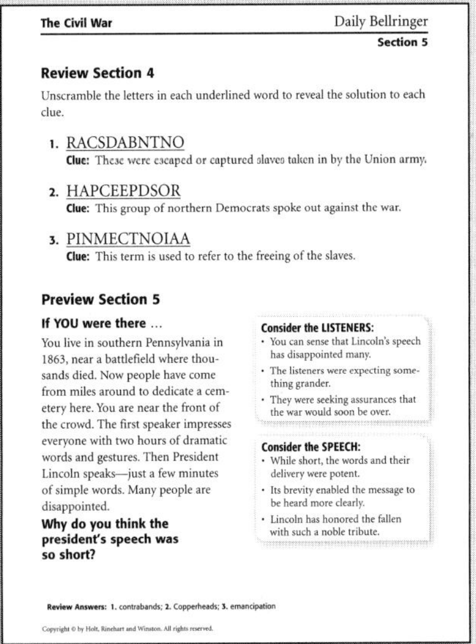

The Civil War | Daily Bellringer | Section 5

Review Section 4

Unscramble the letters in each underlined word to reveal the solution to each clue.

1. RACSDABNTNO
   Clue: These were escaped or captured slaves taken in by the Union army.
2. HAPCEEPDSOR
   Clue: This group of northern Democrats spoke out against the war.
3. PINMECTNOIAA
   Clue: This term is used to refer to the freeing of the slaves.

Preview Section 5

If YOU were there ...

You live in southern Pennsylvania in 1863, near a battlefield where thousands died. Now people have come from miles around to dedicate a cemetery here. You are near the front of the crowd. The first speaker impresses everyone with two hours of dramatic words and gestures. Then President Lincoln speaks—just a few minutes of simple words. Many people are disappointed.

Why do you think the president's speech was so short?

Consider the LISTENERS:
- You can sense that Lincoln's speech has disappointed many.
- The listeners were expecting something grander.
- They were seeking assurances that the war would soon be over.

Consider the SPEECH:
- While short, the words and their delivery were potent.
- Its brevity enabled the message to be heard more clearly.
- Lincoln has honored the fallen with such a noble tribute.

Review Answers: 1. contrabands; **2.** Copperheads; **3.** emancipation

Academic Vocabulary

Review with students the high-use academic term in this section.

execute to perform, carry out (p. 500)

CRF: Vocabulary Builder Activity, Section 5

Teach the Big Idea: Master the Standards

Standards **Proficiency**

The Tide of War Turns HSS 8.10.6, 8.10.7; HSS **Analysis Skills:** CS 1, CS 2, HR 5, HI 1, HI 2

1. **Teach** Ask students the Main Idea questions to teach this section.
2. **Apply** Discuss the events that led to the end of the war. Then have each student create a visual diagram titled *The Road to Surrender*. The diagram should use one or more images to show the key events from the Battle of Gettysburg on that led to Lee's surrender at Appomattox Courthouse. Students should incorporate dates. **LS Visual/Spatial**
3. **Review** As you review the section, have volunteers share their visual diagrams.
4. **Practice/Homework** Have each student write a newspaper editorial about Lee's surrender at Appomattox Courthouse. Students should decide whether to write the editorial from the perspective of a northerner or a southerner. **LS Verbal/Linguistic**

Alternative Assessment Handbook, Rubrics 3: Artwork; and 41: Writing to Express

Standards Focus

HSS 8.10.6

Means: Describe the major battles of the last part of the Civil War, and General Robert E. Lee's surrender at Appomattox Courthouse.
Matters: Studying past wars enables people to understand warfare better.

HSS 8.10.7

Means: Explain how the war affected the lives of soldiers and civilians as well as the environment and future warfare.
Matters: The Civil War caused much death and destruction but also led to the end of slavery.

Direct Teach

Main Idea

1 Battle of Gettysburg

The Battle of Gettysburg in 1863 was a major turning point in the war.

Explain Why did Lee again launch attacks within Union territory? *He hoped that a victory on northern soil would break the North's will to fight and convince other nations to recognize the Confederacy.*

Recall When did the Battle of Gettysburg begin, and what event triggered the start of the battle? *July 1, 1863; A Confederate raiding party ran into Union general George G. Meade's cavalry near the small town of Gettysburg, Pennsylvania.*

Evaluate Who had the best military position at the start of the battle, and why was the position a good one? *the Union troops, who had dug in atop Cemetery Ridge and Culp's Hill; provided strong defensive positions*

HSS 8.10.6, 8.10.7; HSS **Analysis Skills:** CS 1, HI 1, HI 2

Linking to Today

Reunion at Gettysburg Fifty years after the decisive Battle of Gettysburg, Civil War veterans from both the North and the South returned to the battleground for a three-day reunion. Thousands of tourists came as well. According to one attendee, the high point of the gathering was a re-enactment of Pickett's Charge.

go.hrw.com
Online Resources
KEYWORD: SS8 US15
ACTIVITY: 3-D Model of Gettysburg and Other Battles

Battle of Gettysburg

In December 1862 Confederate forces under the command of General Robert E. Lee triumphed at Fredericksburg, Virginia. The Confederates were outnumbered, yet they defeated a Union army led by General Ambrose Burnside.

Confederates on the Move

In the spring of 1863, Lee split his forces and caught the Union army off guard near the town of Chancellorsville. They defeated a larger Union force again, but with heavy casualities. While riding at the front lines, Lee's trusted general, Stonewall Jackson, was accidentally shot by his own troops. Jackson died a few days later.

General Lee launched more attacks within Union territory. As before, his goal was to break the North's will to fight. He also hoped that a victory would convince other nations to recognize the Confederacy.

First Day

In early June 1863, Lee cut across northern Maryland into southern Pennsylvania. His forces gathered west of a small town called Gettysburg. Lee was unaware that Union soldiers were encamped closer to town. He had been suffering from lack of enemy information for three days because his cavalry chief "Jeb" Stuart was not performing his duties. Stuart and his cavalry had gone off on their own raiding party, disobeying Lee's orders.

Another Confederate raiding party went to Gettysburg for boots and other supplies. There, Lee's troops ran right into Union general **George G. Meade**'s cavalry, triggering the **Battle of Gettysburg,** a key battle that finally turned the tide against the Confederates. The battle began on July 1, 1863, when the Confederate raiding party and the Union forces began exchanging fire. The larger Confederate forces began to push the Union troops back.

In the heat of battle, Union forces looked for the best defensive position. They dug in on top of two hills south of town—Cemetery Ridge and Culp's Hill. The Confederate raiding party camped at Seminary Ridge, which ran parallel to the Union forces. The Union troops, however, had the better position. Both camps called for their main forces to reinforce them and prepare for combat the next day.

Three Days at Gettysburg (continued)

Day Two: July 2, 1863, 10 a.m.

Union soldiers desperately defended Little Round Top from a fierce Confederate charge.

498 CHAPTER 15

Collaborative Learning

Standards Proficiency

Battle of Gettysburg Storyboards

HSS 8.10.6, 8.10.7; HSS **Analysis Skills:** CS 1, CS 3, HI 1, HI 2

1. Have students work in pairs or in small groups to create storyboards that depict through illustrations and an easy-to-understand narrative the main events in the Battle of Gettysburg. Students should break down the storyboards into three main parts to represent each day of the battle.
2. Partners or group members might work together to create the illustrations and narrative or divide up the work. Storyboards might include maps, chart, and photographs as well as illustrations.
3. Display students' storyboards around the classroom. Then have students discuss the importance of geography in the Union's victory in the Battle of Gettysburg.

LS Interpersonal, Visual/Spatial

Alternative Assessment Handbook, Rubrics 3: Artwork; and 14: Group Activity

Second Day

On July 2, Lee ordered an attack on the left side of the Union line. Lee knew that he could win the battle if his troops captured Little Round Top from the Union forces. From this hill, Lee's troops could easily fire down on the line of Union forces. Union forces and Confederate troops fought viciously for control of Little Round Top. The Union, however, held off the Confederates.

Pickett's Charge

On the third day of battle, Lee planned to rush the center of the Union line. This task fell to three divisions of Confederate soldiers. General **George Pickett** commanded the largest unit. In late afternoon, nearly 15,000 men took part in **Pickett's Charge**—a failed Confederate attack up Cemetery Ridge. Fewer than half of the soldiers reached the top.

Lee ordered Pickett to organize his division for a possible counterattack. "General Lee, I have no division now," Pickett replied.

On the fourth day Lee held his position but began planning to retreat to Virginia. In all, nearly 75,000 Confederate soldiers and 90,000 Union troops had fought during the Battle of Gettysburg.

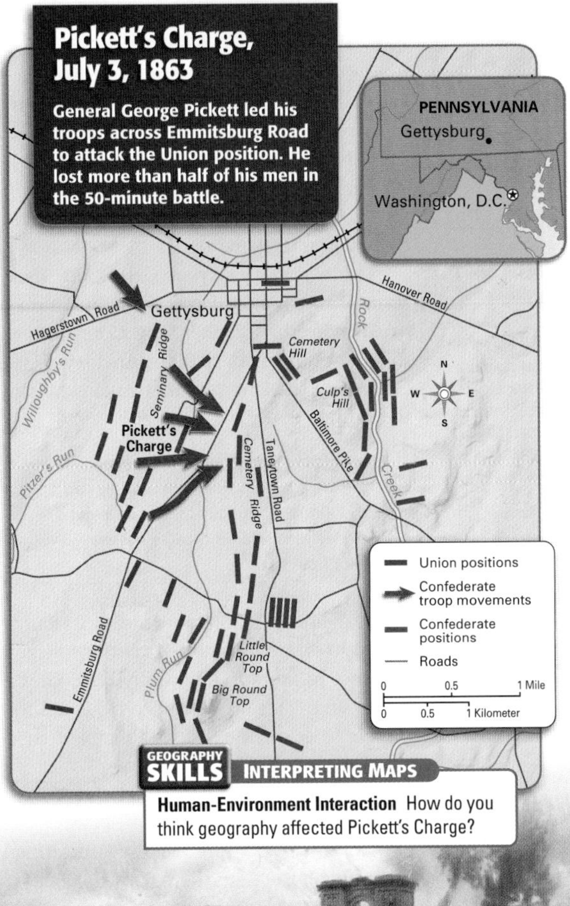

GEOGRAPHY SKILLS INTERPRETING MAPS

Human-Environment Interaction How do you think geography affected Pickett's Charge?

Pickett's Charge

Pickett's Charge proved a disaster for the Confederate attackers. Fewer than half of them survived.

Day Three: July 3, 1863, 3 p.m.

Direct Teach

Main Idea

❶ Battle of Gettysburg

The Battle of Gettysburg in 1863 was a major turning point in the war.

Describe Describe Pickett's Charge and its significance. *Some 15,000 Confederates, led by General George Pickett, charged the center of the Union line up Cemetery Ridge. More than half died, contributing to Lee's decision to retreat.*

Make Inferences Why do you think Lee ordered an attack on the center of the Union line? *possible answers—hoped to break the middle of the Union line so as to divide it; thought the Union line was weak at that point*

Map Transparency: Pickett's Charge, July 3, 1863

HSS 8.10.6, 8.10.7; **HSS Analysis Skills:** HI 1, HI 2

Info to Know

Desertion in the Civil War In 1863, both Union and Confederate forces were experiencing high numbers of deserters. In response, President Lincoln offered amnesty (a government pardon) to all Union deserters who returned to duty. Jefferson Davis, the president of the Confederacy, soon did the same. The Confederate army experienced higher rates of desertion than the Union army, however. By the end of 1864, nearly half of all Confederate soldiers had left the ranks.

Critical Thinking: Sequencing

Standards **Proficiency**

Later Civil War Time Line

HSS 8.10.6; **HSS Analysis Skills:** CS 1, CS 2, HI 1, HI 2

1. Write the events shown at right *in random order* for students to see. Omit the blue, italicized dates.
2. Have each student create a time line that places the events in their proper sequence, provides the date of each event, and provides a short annotation explaining the importance of each event. **LS Visual/Spatial**

Alternative Assessment Handbook, Rubric 36: Time Lines

July 3, 1863:	Battle of Gettysburg; Union capture of Vicksburg
May–June 1864:	Wilderness Campaign
Sept. 2, 1864:	Atlanta falls to Sherman's Union army.
Dec. 10, 1864:	Sherman's army invades Savannah, GA.
April 2, 1865:	Grant forces Lee's army to retreat from Richmond, VA.
April 9, 1865:	Lee surrenders to Grant at Appomattox Courthouse.

Answers

Interpreting Maps *Confederate soldiers had to charge uphill, which put them in a weaker position than the Union soldiers on top of the hill.*

Direct Teach

Main Idea

1 Battle of Gettysburg

The Battle of Gettysburg in 1863 was a major turning point in the war.

Recall At what event did Lincoln deliver the Gettysburg Address? *at the dedication of the Gettysburg battlefield cemetery*

Elaborate In the Gettysburg Address, how did Lincoln express the reasons for which the war was being fought? *He referenced the ideals of liberty, equality, democracy, and unity.*

Draw Conclusions Why do you think the short Gettysburg Address is one of the most famous speeches in American History? *because of the important ideals expressed and the power and emotion of the language*

HSS 8.10.4, 8.10.6, 8.10.7; HSS **Analysis Skills:** HR 4, HI 1

Connect to Science and Technology

Photos of the Gettysburg Address?

No photographs captured President Abraham Lincoln's image as he delivered the Gettysburg Address. The speech lasted only about two minutes—much shorter than the average speech of the era—and the photographer was still setting up his camera when Lincoln finished the speech and sat down. One historian has pointed out that Lincoln spoke so briefly that the photographer probably did not even have time to get his camera's shutter open.

Aftermath of Gettysburg

Gettysburg was a turning point in the war. Lee's troops would never again launch an attack in the North. The Union victory at Gettysburg also took place on the same day as Grant's capture of Vicksburg, Mississippi. These victories made northerners believe that the war could be won.

Focus on Reading
The first sentence of the paragraph to the right is a proposition. The rest of this paragraph supports the idea.

The Union victory at Gettysburg had come at a high price. Union casualties numbered more than 23,000. The Confederacy suffered more than 28,000 casualties. One Gettysburg resident saw the battlefield after the fighting ended.

> "As we ... looked down into the chasms ... we beheld the dead lying there just as they had fallen during the struggle ... It was an awful spectacle! Dead soldiers, bloated horses, shattered cannon."
>
> —Tillie Pierce, 1863

In addition, the Union win at Gettysburg helped to end the South's search for foreign influence in the war. After Gettysburg, Great Britain and France refused to provide aid to the Confederacy. The South's attempt at cotton diplomacy failed.

The Gettysburg Address

On November 19, 1863, at the dedicating ceremony of the Gettysburg battlefield cemetery, President Lincoln gave a speech called the **Gettysburg Address**, in which he praised the bravery of Union soldiers and renewed his commitment to winning the Civil War. This short but moving speech is one of the most famous in American history. In one of its frequently quoted lines, Lincoln referenced the Declaration of Independence and its ideals of liberty, equality, and democracy. He reminded listeners that the war was being fought for those reasons.

Academic Vocabulary
execute to perform, carry out

Lincoln rededicated himself to winning the war and preserving the Union. A difficult road still lay ahead.

Reading Check **Analyzing** Why was Gettysburg a turning point?

Union Campaigns Cripple the Confederacy

Lincoln had been impressed with General Grant's successes in capturing Vicksburg. He transferred Grant to the East and gave him command of the Union army. In early 1864, Grant forced Lee to fight a series of battles in Virginia that stretched Confederate soldiers and supplies to their limits.

Wilderness Campaign in the East

From May through June, the armies fought in northern and central Virginia. Union troops launched the **Wilderness Campaign**—a series of battles designed to capture the Confederate capital at Richmond, Virginia. The first battle took place in early May, in woods about 50 miles outside of Richmond. Grant then ordered General Meade to Spotsylvania, where the fighting raged for 10 days.

Over the next month, Union soldiers moved the Confederate troops back toward Richmond. However, Grant experienced his worst defeat at the Battle of Cold Harbor in early June, just 10 miles northeast of Richmond. In only a few hours the Union army suffered 7,000 casualties. The battle delayed Grant's plans to take the Confederate capital.

Union forces had suffered twice as many casualties as the Confederates had, yet Grant continued his strategy. He knew he would be getting additional soldiers, and Lee could not. Grant slowly but surely advanced his troops through Virginia. He told another officer, "I propose to fight it out on this line if it takes all summer."

After Cold Harbor, General Grant moved south of Richmond. He had hoped to take control of the key railroad junction at Petersburg, Virginia. Lee's army, however, formed a solid defense, and Grant could not execute his attack. Grant was winning the war, but he still had not captured Richmond. Facing re-election, Lincoln was especially discouraged by this failure.

Critical Thinking: Analyzing Primary Sources

Standards Proficiency

The Gettysburg Address

HSS 8.10.4, 8.10.6, 8.10.7; HSS **Analysis Skills:** HR 4, HI 1

1. Have students read the Gettysburg Address as a class. The speech is located in the textbook's Historical Documents section.
2. Work through the speech a few sentences at a time to help students understand the language. Have students paraphrase the speech in modern language as you go.
3. Ask students to discuss the reasons for which Lincoln stated the war was being fought—such as the ideals of liberty, equality, and democracy—and why these reasons still resonate so powerfully with Americans.
4. Then ask students to imagine that they are newspaper reporters covering the dedication of the Gettysburg battlefield cemetery. Have each student write an article describing Lincoln's speech and its significance. Students should include excerpts from the speech in their articles. LS **Verbal/Linguistic**

Alternative Assessment Handbook, Rubric 42: Writing to Inform

Answers

Reading Check *weakened the South; was the last Confederate attack on Union soil; ended the South's hopes of gaining foreign support and allies*

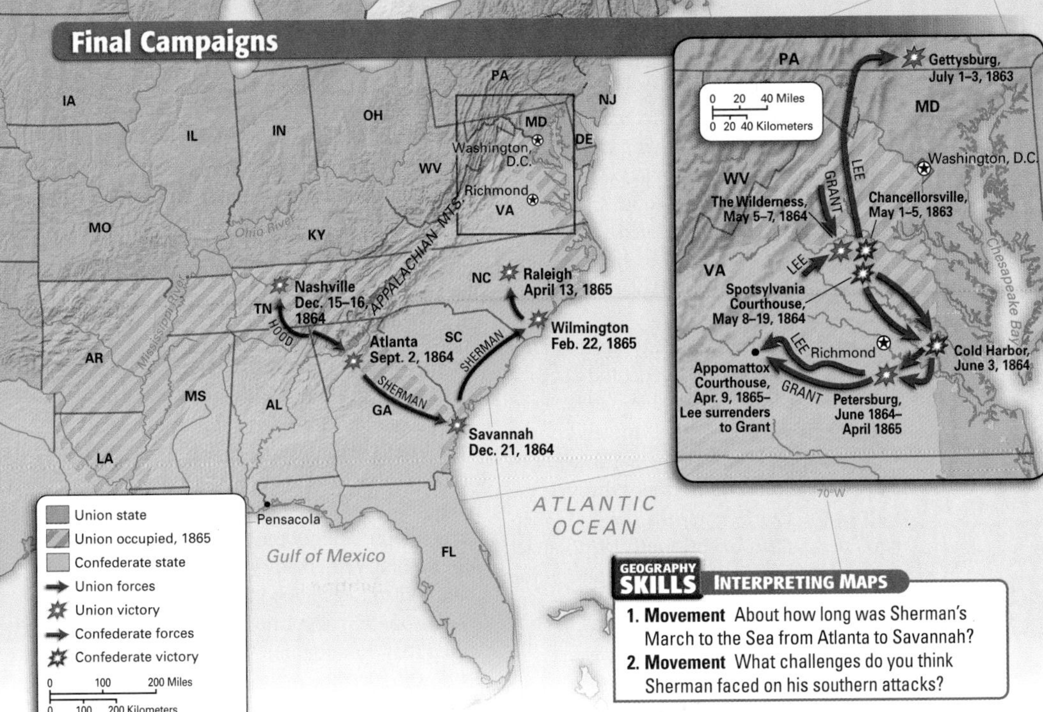

GEOGRAPHY SKILLS INTERPRETING MAPS

1. **Movement** About how long was Sherman's March to the Sea from Atlanta to Savannah?
2. **Movement** What challenges do you think Sherman faced on his southern attacks?

Sherman Strikes the South

Lincoln needed a victory for the Union army to help him win re-election in 1864. The bold campaign of General **William Tecumseh Sherman** provided this key victory. Sherman carried out the Union plan to destroy southern railroads and industries.

In the spring of 1864, Sherman marched south from Tennessee with 100,000 troops. His goal was to take Atlanta, Georgia, and knock out an important railroad link. From May through August, Sherman's army moved steadily through the Appalachian Mountains toward Atlanta. Several times, Sherman avoided defenses set up by Confederate general Joseph Johnston.

In July, Sherman was within sight of Atlanta. Confederate president Jefferson Davis gave General John Hood command of Confederate forces in the region. Hood repeatedly attacked Sherman in a final attempt to save Atlanta, but the Union troops proved stronger. The Confederate troops retreated as Sherman held Atlanta under siege.

Atlanta fell to Sherman's troops on September 2, 1864. Much of the city was destroyed by artillery and fire. Sherman ordered the residents who still remained to leave. Responding to his critics, Sherman later wrote, "War is war, and not popularity-seeking." The loss of Atlanta cost the South an important railroad link and its center of industry.

Many people in the North had been upset with the length of the war. However, the capture of Atlanta showed that progress was being made in defeating the South. This success helped to convince Union voters to re-elect Lincoln in a landslide.

Sherman did not wait long to begin his next campaign. His goal was the port city of Savannah, Georgia. In mid-November 1864,

Direct Teach

Main Idea

2 Union Campaigns Cripple the Confederacy

During 1864, Union campaigns in the East and South dealt crippling blows to the Confederacy.

Identify What two important Union leaders led campaigns in the East in 1864? *Generals Ulysses S. Grant and William Tecumseh Sherman*

Recall What was the Wilderness Campaign? *series of battles the Union army launched in northern and central Virginia from May through June 1864*

Analyze Why was Grant's Wilderness Campaign successful despite the high casualty toll? *The campaign also took a huge toll on Lee's army, which could not get reinforcements, and the Union army closed in on Richmond.*

CRF: Biography Activity: William Tecumseh Sherman

Map Transparency: Final Campaigns

HSS 8.10.6; **HSS Analysis Skills:** HI 1

Teaching Tip

Visualizing the Union's Progress Have students contrast the amount of Union-occupied territory in the map at left to that in "The War in the West" map in Section 3. Have students discuss what they can conclude based on the difference.

Critical Thinking: Finding Main Ideas

Standards Proficiency

Final Battles Web Site

HSS 8.10.6; **HSS Analysis Skills:** CS 1, HI 1

Research Required

1. Have students use library, Internet, and other resources to conduct research on the battles covered in this section.
2. Have students, working either individually or in small groups, use the research to develop the design for a Web site that shows how the Civil War progressed after Gettysburg.
3. The Web site's home page, or main page, should provide a general overview of the final push that led to Union victory. In addition, the home page should include links to pages providing in-depth coverage of specific battles, individuals, and other key events.
4. Students should incorporate maps, charts, photographs, and other visuals in their Web sites. **LS Interpersonal, Verbal/Linguistic**

Alternative Assessment Handbook: Rubric 29: Presentations; and 30: Research

Answers

Interpreting Maps 1. *about 200 miles;* **2.** *fighting in enemy territory; long distances to march; maintaining supplies*

Direct Teach

Main Idea

❸ The South Surrenders

Union troops forced the South to surrender in 1865, ending the Civil War.

Describe How did Grant cut off Lee's escape to North Carolina? *He surrounded Lee's army just west of Richmond.*

Summarize What was the condition of Lee's Confederate troops at this point? *They were tired and hungry and lacked weapons and supplies.*

Recall When and where did Lee surrender to Grant? *Appomattox Courthouse, April 9, 1865*

Analyze What do the terms of the surrender reveal about Grant's character and his feelings for Lee? *The terms reveal Grant's fairness and civility as well as his tremendous respect for Lee and his soldiers.*

Quick Facts Transparency: Causes and Effects of the Civil War

HSS 8.10.6, 8.10.7; HSS **Analysis Skills:** HR 5, HI 1, HI 2

MISCONCEPTION ALERT

Appomattox Courthouse Make certain that students understand that Appomattox Courthouse is not the name of a courthouse but of the town where Lee and Grant met to discuss the terms of surrender. The two men met to discuss the surrender at the McLean home, not a courthouse.

Sherman left Atlanta with a force of about 60,000 men. He said he would "make Georgia howl!"

During his March to the Sea, Sherman practiced **total war**—destroying civilian and economic resources. Sherman believed that total war would ruin the South's economy and its ability to fight. He ordered his troops to destroy railways, bridges, crops, livestock, and other resources. They burned plantations and freed slaves.

Sherman's army reached Savannah on December 10, 1864. They left behind a path of destruction 60 miles wide. Sherman believed that this march would speed the end of the war. He wanted to break the South's will to fight by marching Union troops through the heart of the Confederacy. In the end, Sherman's destruction of the South led to anger and resentment toward the people of the North that would last for generations.

READING CHECK **Drawing Conclusions** How did Sherman hope to help the Union with his total-war strategy?

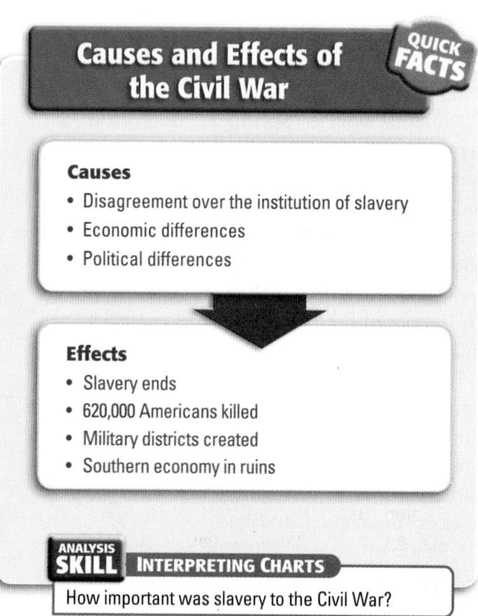

Causes and Effects of the Civil War
QUICK FACTS
Causes
• Disagreement over the institution of slavery
• Economic differences
• Political differences
Effects
• Slavery ends
• 620,000 Americans killed
• Military districts created
• Southern economy in ruins

ANALYSIS SKILL **INTERPRETING CHARTS**

How important was slavery to the Civil War?

The South Surrenders

In early April, Sherman closed in on the last Confederate defenders in North Carolina. At the same time, Grant finally broke through the Confederate defenses at Petersburg. On April 2, Lee was forced to retreat from Richmond.

Fighting Ends

By the second week of April 1865, Grant had surrounded Lee's army and demanded the soldiers' surrender. Lee hoped to join other Confederates in fighting in North Carolina, but Grant cut off his escape just west of Richmond. Lee tried some last minute attacks but could not break the Union line. Lee's forces were running low on supplies. General James Longstreet told about the condition of Confederate troops. "Many weary soldiers were picked up . . . some with, many without, arms [weapons],—all asking for food."

Trapped by the Union army, Lee recognized that the situation was hopeless. "There is nothing left for me to do but go and see General Grant," Lee said, "and I would rather die a thousand deaths."

On April 9, 1865, the Union and Confederate leaders met at a home in the small town of **Appomattox Courthouse** where Lee surrendered to Grant, thus ending the Civil War.

During the meeting, Grant assured Lee that his troops would be fed and allowed to keep their horses, and they would not be tried for treason. Then Lee signed the surrender documents. The long, bloody war had finally ended. Grant later wrote that he found the scene at Appomattox Courthouse more tragic than joyful.

> "I felt . . . sad and depressed at the downfall of a foe [enemy] who had fought so long and valiantly [bravely], and had suffered so much for a cause, though that cause was, I believe, one of the worst for which a people ever fought."
>
> —Ulysses S. Grant

Critical Thinking: Analyzing and Predicting

Standards Proficiency

Letter about Lee's Surrender

HSS 8.10.6, 8.10.7; HSS **Analysis Skills:** HI 1, HI 2

1. Discuss with students the events leading up to Lee's surrender and what it meant for the future of the Union. Have students consider how the war had affected the people, economies, property, and land on both sides. Then have students predict how the surrender will affect the nation.
2. Ask students to imagine that they were one of the soldiers who witnessed Lee's surrender at Appomattox Courthouse. Have each student adopt the point of view of either a southern or northern soldier and write a letter to a friend or family member about the surrender. Students' letters should describe the events that led to the surrender as well as the surrender itself and then speculate about the effects of the surrender.
3. Ask for volunteers to read their letters to the class. LS **Verbal/Linguistic**

Alternative Assessment Handbook, Rubric 25: Personal Letters

Answers

Interpreting Charts *It was an integral and central issue.*

Reading Check *He hoped to ruin the South's economy and its ability to fight.*

Surrender at Appomattox

Union general Grant rose to shake hands with Confederate general Lee after the surrender. Grant allowed Lee to keep his sword and Lee's men to keep their horses.

Why was it important for Grant and Lee to shake hands? Why or why not?

As General Lee returned to his troops, General Grant stopped Union forces from cheering their victory. "The war is over," Grant said with relief. "The rebels are our countrymen again."

The Effects of the War

The Civil War had deep and long-lasting effects. Almost 620,000 Americans lost their lives during the four years of fighting.

The defeat of the South ended slavery there. The majority of former slaves, however, had no homes or jobs. The southern economy was in ruins.

A tremendous amount of hostility remained, even after the fighting had ceased. The war was over, but the question remained: How could the United States be united once more?

READING CHECK **Predicting** What problems might the Union face following the Civil War?

SUMMARY AND PREVIEW After four long years of battles, the Civil War ended with General Lee's surrender at Appomattox Courthouse. In the next chapter you will read about the consequences of the war in the South.

Section 5 Assessment

go.hrw.com **Online Quiz** KEYWORD: SS8 HP15

Reviewing Ideas, Terms, and People HSS 8.10.6, 8.10.7

1. a. **Identify** What was the **Gettysburg Address**?
   b. **Analyze** Why was geography important to the outcome of the **Battle of Gettysburg**?
   c. **Predict** How might the war have been different if Confederate forces had won the Battle of Gettysburg?
2. a. **Recall** What was the purpose of the **Wilderness Campaign**?
   b. **Draw Conclusions** In what way was the capture of Atlanta an important victory for President Lincoln?
3. a. **Identify** What events led to Lee's surrender at **Appomattox Courthouse**?
   b. **Summarize** What problems did the South face at the end of the war?

Critical Thinking

4. **Sequencing** Copy the graphic organizer onto your own sheet of paper. Use it to fill in and explain the events that led to the end of the Civil War.

July 1–3, 1863
May–June, 1864
September 2, 1864
December 10, 1864
April 2, 1865
April 9, 1865

FOCUS ON WRITING

5. **Taking Notes on the End of the War** As you read this section, take notes on the Battle of Gettysburg, the Wilderness Campaign, the fall of Atlanta, and the South's surrender. Be sure to answer the following questions: Who? Where? When? Why? and How?

Direct Teach

Checking for Understanding

True or False Answer each statement *T* if it is true or *F* if it is false. If false, explain why.

1. The Wilderness Campaign was a major turning point in the Civil War. *F; Battle of Gettysburg*
2. In his inaugural address, Lincoln reminded Americans of the ideals for which the war was being fought. *F; Gettysburg Address*
3. General William Tecumseh Sherman practiced total war during his March to the Sea. *T*

HSS 8.10.4, 8.10.6, 8.10.7; HSS **Analysis Skills:** HI 1, HI 2

Review & Assess

Close

Review with students the major battles that led to the South's defeat, beginning with Gettysburg and ending with Lee's surrender.

Review

Online Quiz, Section 5

Assess

SE Section 5 Assessment

PASS: Section 5 Quiz

Alternative Assessment Handbook

Reteach/Classroom Intervention

California Standards Review Workbook

Interactive Reader and Study Guide, Section 5

Interactive Skills Tutor CD-ROM

Section 5 Assessment Answers

1. **a.** short but moving speech that Lincoln gave at the dedication of the Gettysburg battlefield cemetery; famous in American history
   b. Hills provided Union forces with strong defensive positions that helped them win.
   c. possible answers—France and Great Britain might have aided the Confederacy, the South might have gone on to win the war.
2. **a.** to stretch Lee's forces; to reach Richmond
   b. showed that progress was being made in defeating the South, which helped convince Union voters to re-elect Lincoln as president
3. **a.** Wilderness Campaign; break in Confederate defenses at Petersburg; Lee's army forced to retreat from Richmond and then surrounded
   b. possible answers—an uncertain future, a ruined economy, enormous task of rebuilding
4. Battle of Gettysburg; Wilderness Campaign; Sherman's army takes Atlanta; Sherman's army reaches Savannah; Lee forced to retreat from Richmond; Lee surrenders to Grant
5. Students should mention the key battles and the roles of Grant, Sherman, and Lee.

Answers

Surrender at Appomattox *to show respect and a desire for the Union to be restored*

Reading Check *possible answers—helping the South recover from the devastation and destruction of the war; bringing the South back into the Union; overcoming remaining animosity between northerners and southerners*

Social Studies Skills

Interpreting Political Cartoons

Activity Interpreting Current Political Cartoons

Materials: photocopies of current political cartoons

Make photocopies of several political cartoons from a local newspaper. Organize students into small groups and give each group one of the political cartoons to interpret. If possible, make enough photocopies so that each group member has one. Have each group go through the steps listed under "Learn the Skill" to analyze and interpret its cartoon. One member should record the group's interpretations. Then display each political cartoon for the entire class to see. As you display each cartoon, have the group that analyzed that cartoon share its interpretation with the class. **LS Interpersonal, Visual/Spatial**

- Alternative Assessment Handbook, Rubrics 14: Group Activity; and 27: Political Cartoons
- Interactive Skills Tutor CD-ROM, Lesson 6: Interpret Maps, Graphs, Charts, Visuals, and Political Cartoons
- **HSS Analysis Skills:** HR 4

Social Studies Skills

Analysis | Critical Thinking | Participation | Study

HSS HR4 Students access the credibility of primary and secondary sources.

Interpreting Political Cartoons

Define the Skill

Political cartoons are drawings that express views on important issues. They have been used throughout history to influence public opinion. The ability to interpret political cartoons will help you understand issues and people's attitudes about them.

Learn the Skill

Political cartoons use both words and images to convey their message. They often contain caricatures or symbolism. A caricature is a drawing that exaggerates the features of a person or object. Symbolism is the use of one thing to represent something else. Cartoonists use these techniques to help make their point clear. They also use titles, labels, and captions to get their message across.

Use these steps to interpret political cartoons.

1. Read any title, labels, and caption to identify the cartoon's general topic.
2. Identify the people and objects. Determine if they are exaggerated and, if so, why. Identify any symbols and analyze their meaning.
3. Draw conclusions about the message the cartoonist is trying to convey.

The following cartoon was published in the North in 1863. The cartoonist has used symbols to make his point. Lady Liberty, representing the Union, is being threatened by the Copperheads.. The cartoonist has expressed his opinion of these people by drawing them as the poisonous snake for which they were named. This cartoon clearly supports the Union's continuing to fight the war.

Practice the Skill

Apply the guidelines to interpret this cartoon and answer the questions that follow.

1. What do the tree and the man in it symbolize?
2. What policy or action of President Lincoln is this cartoon supporting?

Social Studies Skills Activity: Interpreting Political Cartoons

Views of Secession

HSS Analysis Skills: HR 4

Standards Proficiency

Materials: Political Cartoons Activities for United States History, Cartoon 17: The Folly of Secession

1. Give each student a copy of **Political Cartoons Activities for United States History, Cartoon 17: The Folly of Secession.**
2. Have students work as a class to go through the steps listed above under "Learn the Skill" to analyze the political cartoon.
3. Then have each student work independently to complete the political cartoon worksheet. **LS Visual/Spatial**
4. **Extend** Have each student create a political cartoon about secession from the southern point of view. Have volunteers show and explain their political cartoons to the class. **LS Visual/Spatial**

- Alternative Assessment Handbook, Rubric 27: Political Cartoons

Answers

Practice the Skill 1. *the Confederacy and the institution of slavery;* **2.** *his decision to attack the institution of slavery to cripple the Confederate war effort*

CHAPTER 15

Standards Review

Visual Summary

Use the visual summary below to help you review the main ideas of the chapter.

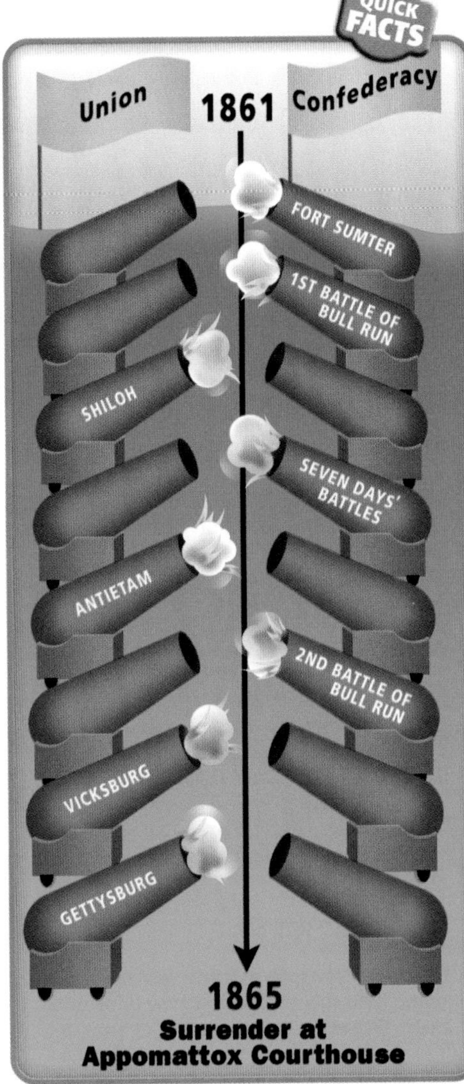

Reviewing Vocabulary, Terms, and People

Match the numbered definitions with the correct terms from the list below.

a. contrabands
b. cotton diplomacy
c. Second Battle of Bull Run
d. Siege of Vicksburg
e. Thomas "Stonewall" Jackson

1. Attack by Union general Ulysses S. Grant that gave the North control of the Mississippi River
2. Confederate general who held off Union attacks and helped the South win the First Battle of Bull Run
3. Important Confederate victory in which General Robert E. Lee defeated Union troops and pushed into Union territory for the first time
4. Southern strategy of using cotton exports to gain Britain's support in the Civil War
5. Term given to escaped slaves from the South

Comprehension and Critical Thinking

SECTION 1 *(Pages 472–476)* **HSS 8.10.3, 8.10.4, 8.10.6, 8.10.7**

6. **a. Identify** When and where did fighting in the U.S. Civil War begin?
   b. Analyze How did civilians help the war effort in both the North and the South?
   c. Elaborate Why do you think the border states chose to remain in the Union despite their support of slavery?

SECTION 2 *(Pages 478–483)* **HSS 8.10.5, 8.10.6**

7. **a. Identify** What was the first major battle of the war? What was the outcome of the battle?
   b. Analyze What was the Union army hoping to accomplish when it marched into Virginia at the start of the war?
   c. Evaluate Was the Union's naval blockade of the South successful? Why or why not?

Answers

Visual Summary

Review and Inquiry Have students identify one to two key facts related to each event shown.

Quick Facts Transparency: The Civil War Visual Summary

Reviewing Vocabulary, Terms, and People

1. d
2. e
3. c
4. b
5. a

Comprehension and Critical Thinking

6. **a.** April 12, 1861, at Fort Sumter in South Carolina
   b. raised money, provided aid, served as nurses
   c. possible answers—loyalty to the Union, opposition to secession, did not depend as heavily on slavery as states in the Upper and Lower South
7. **a.** First Battle of Bull Run, Confederate victory and shattered the North's hopes of winning the war quickly
   b. defeat the South and quickly end the war
   c. Yes, the blockade effectively limited southern trade and seriously damaged the southern economy.

Review and Assessment Resources

Review and Reinforce

- SE Standards Review
- **CRF:** Chapter Review Activity
- California Standards Review Workbook
- Quick Facts Transparency: The Civil War Visual Summary
- Spanish Chapter Summaries Audio CD Program
- Online Chapter Summaries in Six Languages
- OSP Holt PuzzlePro; Game Tool for ExamView
- Quiz Game CD-ROM

Assess

- SE Standards Assessment
- PASS: Chapter Test, Forms A and B
- Alternative Assessment Handbook
- OSP ExamView Test Generator, Chapter Test
- Universal Access Modified Worksheets and Tests CD-ROM: Chapter Test
- Holt Online Assessment Program (in the Premier Online Edition)

Reteach/Intervene

- Interactive Reader and Study Guide
- Universal Access Teacher Management System: Lesson Plans for Universal Access
- Universal Access Modified Worksheets and Tests CD-ROM
- Interactive Skills Tutor CD-ROM

go.hrw.com
Online Resources
Chapter Resources:
KEYWORD: SS8 US15

SECTION 3 *(Pages 484–487)* **HSS 8.10.5, 8.10.6**

8. **a. Identify** Which side did the Cherokee support in the fighting at Pea Ridge? Why?

   b. Draw Conclusions What progress did Union leaders make in the war in the West?

   c. Evaluate Which victory in the West was most valuable to the Union? Why?

SECTION 4 *(Pages 490–496)* **HSS 8.10.4, 8.10.5, 8.10.7**

9. **a. Describe** What responsibilities did women take on during the war?

   b. Analyze What opposition to the war did President Lincoln face, and how did he deal with that opposition?

   c. Predict What might be some possible problems that the newly freed slaves in the South might face?

SECTION 5 *(Pages 497–503)* **HSS 8.10.6, 8.10.7**

10. **a. Recall** When and where did the war finally end?

    b. Compare and Contrast How were the efforts of Generals Grant and Sherman at the end of the war similar and different?

    c. Elaborate What do you think led to the South's defeat in the Civil War? Explain.

Social Studies Skills

Interpreting Political Cartoons *Use the Social Studies Skills taught in this chapter to answer the questions about the political cartoon below.*

11. What do you think the artist is saying about politicians with this cartoon?

Reading Skills

Understanding Propositions and Support *Use the Reading Skills taught in this chapter to answer the question about the reading selection below.*

> Lee was unaware that Union soldiers were encamped closer to town. He had been suffering from lack of enemy information for three days because his cavalry chief "Jeb" Stuart was on a "joy ride." Stuart and his cavalry had gone off on their own raiding party, disobeying Lee's orders. *(p. 498)*

12. What is the main proposition of the above reading section?

    a. "Jeb" Stuart was on a "joy ride."

    b. Stuart and his cavalry had gone off on their own.

    c. Stuart and his cavalry disobeyed Lee's orders.

    d. Lee was suffering from a lack of enemy information.

Reviewing Themes

13. **Society and Culture** What effects did the Civil War have on American society?

14. **Politics** What political difficulties did the Emancipation Proclamation cause for President Lincoln?

Using the Internet

15. **Activity: Writing a Poem** Soldiers in the Civil War came from all walks of life. Despite the hope for glory and adventure, many encountered dangerous and uncomfortable conditions. Enter the activity keyword to learn more about Civil War soldiers. After viewing photographs and reading letters, write a poem describing the life of a soldier. Your poem should reflect on the soldier's emotions and experiences.

FOCUS ON WRITING

16. **Write Your Newspaper Article** Review your notes. Then choose the subject you think would make the best newspaper article. Write an attention-grabbing headline. Then write your article, giving as many facts as possible.

Answers

8. **a.** Many supported the South because they hoped the Confederacy would give them greater freedom and because some Native Americans were slaveholders.

   b. gained control of the Mississippi River, which divided the South; held Union territory in the Far West

   c. possible answers—victory at Vicksburg, because its fall gave the Union control of the entire Mississippi Valley; victory at New Orleans, because it opened the way for the Union to gain control of the Mississippi River

9. **a.** worked on farms and in factories; provided medical support and aid, established and worked at hospitals

   b. Copperheads opposed the war; Lincoln suspended the right of habeas corpus.

   c. possible answers—lack of basic necessities, such as housing, clothing, food; lack of work; risk of capture

10. **a.** April 9, 1865; Appomattox Courthouse, Virginia

    b. similar—waged campaigns to wear down the Confederate forces; different—Sherman waged total war and captured major southern cities; Grant pressed Lee's army.

    c. possible answer—Their smaller population and limited manufacturing led to their being outnumbered in battle and resulted in serious shortages.

Social Studies Skills

11. that they are threatening the Union's survival and war effort

Reading Skills

12. d

Reviewing Themes

13. possible answers—resulted in many deaths and much destruction of property and land, led to freedom for enslaved Africans, led to new roles for women, improved northern economy, destroyed southern economy, created lingering anger and resentment in the South

14. If he emancipated all the slaves, he risked going against the Constitution and losing political support in the strategic border states; if he emancipated only some of the slaves, he risked angering some abolitionists.

Using the Internet

15. Go to the HRW Web site and enter the keyword shown to access a rubric for this activity.

    KEYWORD: SS8 TEACHER

Focus on Writing

16. **Rubric** Students' newspaper articles should
    - have an attention-grabbing headline.
    - describe one of the events in the chapter.
    - answer the questions Who? Where? When? Why? and How?
    - included as many facts as possible about the selected event.
    - use proper grammar, punctuation, spelling, and capitalization.

CRF: Focus on Writing Activity: Writing a Newspaper Article

Standards Assessment

DIRECTIONS: Read each question and write the letter of the best response. Use the map below to answer question 1.

1

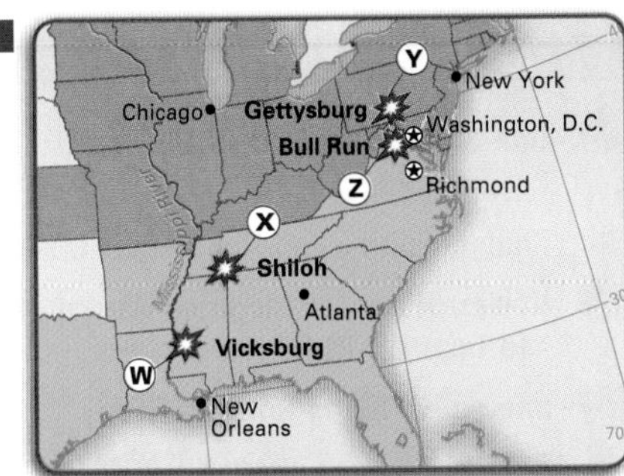

The place where two major battles of the Civil War were fought is indicated on the map by what letter?

A W

B X

C Y

D Z

2 The Battle of Gettysburg was an important battle of the Civil War because

A it was an overwhelming Confederate victory.

B the Union army's advance on the Confederate capital was stopped.

C it ended Lee's hopes of advancing into northern territory.

D it enabled the Union to control the Mississippi River.

3 Overall command of Confederate forces in Virginia during most of the Civil War was held by

A Jefferson Davis.

B William Tecumseh Sherman.

C Thomas "Stonewall" Jackson.

D Robert E. Lee.

4 Which of Lincoln's speeches and writings reflected the statement of the Declaration of Independence that "all men are created equal"?

A the Emancipation Proclamation

B the first inaugural address (1861)

C the second inaugural address (1865)

D the Gettysburg Address

5 The tactics that Sherman used against Confederate armies in the South were based on what strategy?

A cutting off troops from their officers

B a naval blockade of southern ports

C destroying the South's resources and economy

D hit-and-run attacks on major southern cities

Connecting with Past Learning

6 In this chapter you learned about how civil war can divide a country and bring about change. Which struggle that you learned about in Grade 6 was similar in this way?

A 1642 defeat of King Charles of England by Oliver Cromwell

B the Inquisition

C the Opium War

D the Hundred Years' War

7 In the War of 1812 the British navy blockaded American seaports in the hope that the U.S. economy would suffer and the United States would surrender. Which Civil War strategy was similar?

A General Winfield Scott's plan to destroy the southern economy

B General William Tecumseh Sherman's March to the Sea

C General Ulysses S. Grant's capture of Vicksburg

D Admiral David Farragut's defeat of New Orleans

Answers

1. D

Break Down the Question This question requires students to interpret the map and then recall factual information. Have students first try to identify the location where two battles were fought and then find the location on the map.

2. C

Break Down the Question This question requires students to identify cause and effect. Refer students who miss the question to Section 5.

3. D

Break Down the Question This question requires students to recall factual information. Suggest that students first eliminate all non-Confederate leaders (B) to narrow their choices.

4 D

Break Down the Question This question requires students to recall the main points expressed in the Gettysburg Address. Refer students who have trouble to the text in Section 5 titled "The Gettysburg Address."

5. C

Break Down the Question This question requires students to identify the main idea. Refer students who have trouble to the text in Section 5 titled "Sherman Strikes the South."

6. D

Break Down the Question This question connects to information covered in Grade 6.

7. A

Break Down the Question This question connects to information covered in Chapter 7.

Intervention Resources

Reproducible

- Interactive Reader and Study Guide
- Universal Access Teacher Management System: Lesson Plans for Universal Access

Technology

- Quick Facts Transparency: The Civil War Visual Summary
- Universal Access Modified Worksheets and Tests CD-ROM
- Interactive Skills Tutor CD-ROM

Tips for Test Taking

Try, Try, Try Read the following to students: Keep at it. Don't give up. This sounds obvious, so why say it? You might be surprised by how many students do give up. Remember, the last question is worth just as much as the first question, and the questions do not get harder as you go. If the question you just finished was really hard, an easier one is probably coming up soon. Take a deep breath and keep on slogging. Give it your all, all the way to the end.

Standards Review

Have students review the following standards in their workbooks.

- California Standards Review Workbook: HSS 8.10.3, 8.10.4, 8.10.5, 8.10.6

Chapter 16 Planning Guide

Reconstruction

MASTERING THE CALIFORNIA STANDARDS

Chapter Overview	Reproducible Resources	Technology Resources
CHAPTER 16 **pp. 508–35** **Overview: In this chapter, students will learn about the challenges that faced the nation after the Civil War and the efforts made to meet those challenges.** 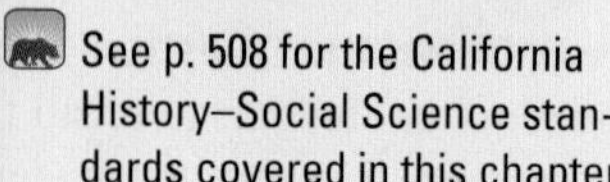 See p. 508 for the California History–Social Science standards covered in this chapter.	**Universal Access Teacher Management System:*** • Universal Access Instructional Benchmarking Guides • Lesson Plans for Universal Access **Interactive Reader and Study Guide:*** Chapter Graphic Organizer **Chapter Resource File*** • Focus on Writing Activity: Job History • Social Studies Skills Activity: Chance, Oversight, and Error in History • Chapter Review Activity 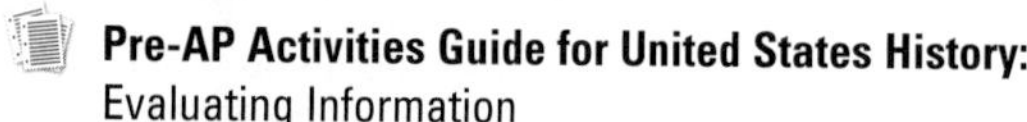 **Pre-AP Activities Guide for United States History:*** Evaluating Information	**One-Stop Planner CD-ROM:** Calendar Planner **Student Edition Full-Read Audio CD-ROM** **Universal Access Modified Worksheets and Tests CD-ROM** **Interactive Skills Tutor CD-ROM** **Primary Source Library CD-ROM for United States History** **Power Presentations with Video CD-ROM**  **History's Impact: United States History Video Program (VHS/DVD):** Reconstruction*
Section 1: **Rebuilding the South** **The Big Idea:** The nation faced many problems in rebuilding the Union.  8.10.7, 8.11.1, 8.11.3, 8.11.5	 **Universal Access Teacher Management System:*** Section 1 Lesson Plan **Interactive Reader and Study Guide:*** Section 1 Summary 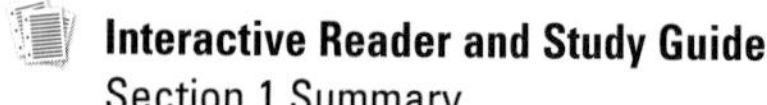 **Chapter Resource File*** • Vocabulary Builder, Section 1  • Biography Activity: Andrew Johnson • Economics and History Activity: The Devastation of War **Political Cartoons Activities for United States History,** Cartoon 18: Lincoln Repairing the Union*	**Daily Bellringer Transparency:** Section 1* **Internet Activity:** Population Chart
Section 2: **The Fight over Reconstruction** **The Big Idea:** The return to power of the pre-war southern leadership led Republicans in Congress to take control of Reconstruction. 8.11.3, 8.11.5	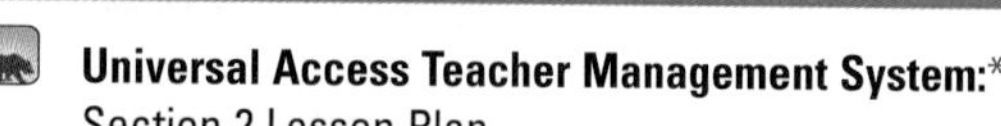 **Universal Access Teacher Management System:*** Section 2 Lesson Plan **Interactive Reader and Study Guide:*** Section 2 Summary 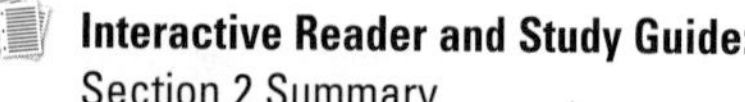 **Chapter Resource File*** • Vocabulary Builder, Section 2 • Biography Activity: Thaddeus Stevens • History and Geography Activity: The Reconstruction Acts	 **Daily Bellringer Transparency:** Section 2* **Map Transparency:** Reconstruction Military Districts*  **Quick Facts Transparency:** The Reconstruction Amendments* **Internet Activity:** Writing Editorials for a Newspaper
Section 3: **Reconstruction In the South**  **The Big Idea:** As Reconstruction ended, African Americans faced new hurdles and the South attempted to rebuild. 8.11.1, 8.11.3, 8.11.4	 **Universal Access Teacher Management System:*** Section 3 Lesson Plan **Interactive Reader and Study Guide:*** Section 3 Summary  **Chapter Resource File*** • Vocabulary Builder, Section 3  • Biography Activity: Blanche K. Bruce • Literature Activity: The Jim Crow Laws • Primary Source Activities: *Plessy* v. *Ferguson*; Reconstruction and the Ku Klux Klan  **U.S. Supreme Court Case Studies**  • *Civil Rights Cases* (1883) • *Plessy* v. *Ferguson* (1896)	 **Daily Bellringer Transparency:** Section 3* **Map Transparency:** African American Representation in the South, 1870*  **Quick Facts Transparency:** Hopes Raised and Denied*

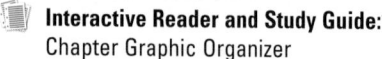

SE Student Edition | Print Resource | Audio CD | Video
TE Teacher's Edition | Transparency | CD-ROM | DVD
go.hrw.com | CA Standards Mastery | **LS** Learning Styles
OSP One-Stop Planner CD-ROM | *also on One-Stop Planner CD

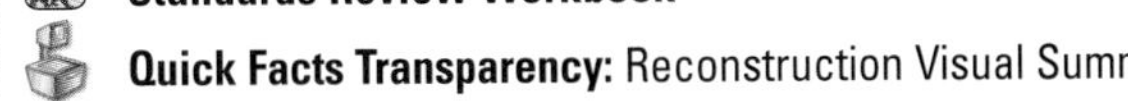

Review, Assessment, Intervention

- **Standards Review Workbook***
- **Quick Facts Transparency:** Reconstruction Visual Summary*
- **Spanish Chapter Summaries Audio CD Program**
- **Online Chapter Summaries in Six Languages**
- **Progress Assessment Support System (PASS):** Chapter Test*
- **Universal Access Modified Worksheets and Tests CD-ROM:** Modified Chapter Test
- **One-Stop Planner CD-ROM:** ExamView Test Generator (English/Spanish)
- **Holt Online Assessment Program (HOAP),** in the Holt Premier Online Student Edition

- **PASS:** Section 1 Quiz*
- **Online Quiz:** Section 1
- **Alternative Assessment Handbook**

- **PASS:** Section 2 Quiz*
- **Online Quiz:** Section 2
- **Alternative Assessment Handbook**

- **PASS:** Section 3 Quiz*
- **Online Quiz:** Section 3
- **Alternative Assessment Handbook**

California Resources for Standards Mastery

INSTRUCTIONAL PLANNING AND SUPPORT

- **Universal Access Teacher Management System***
- **One-Stop Planner CD-ROM with Test Generator: Teacher Management System with Interactive Teacher's Edition**

STANDARDS MASTERY

- **Standards Review Workbook***
- **At Home: A Guide to Standards Mastery for United States History**

Holt Online Learning

To enhance learning, Internet activities are available for a Population Chart and Writing Editorials for a Newspaper.

KEYWORD: SS8 TEACHER

- **Teacher Support Page**
- **Content Updates**
- **Rubrics and Writing Models**
- **Teaching Tips for the Multimedia Classroom**

KEYWORD: SS8 US16

- **Current Events**
- **Document-Based Questions**
- **Holt Grapher**
- **Holt Online Atlas**
- **Holt Researcher**
- **Interactive Multimedia Activities**
- **Internet Activities**
- **Online Chapter Summaries in Six Languages**
- **Online Section Quizzes**
- **American History Maps and Charts**

HOLT PREMIER ONLINE STUDENT EDITION

Complete online support for interactivity, assessment, and reporting

- **Interactive Maps and Notebook**
- **Standardized Test Prep**
- **Homework Practice and Research Activities Online**

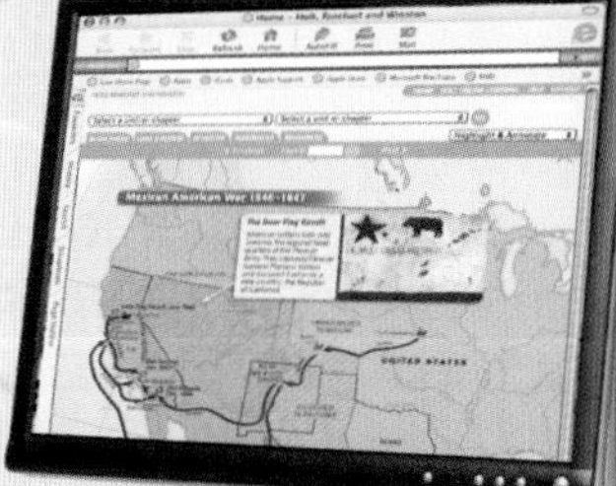

Mastering the Standards: Differentiating Instruction

Reaching Standards	Basic-level activities designed for all students encountering new material
Standards Proficiency	Intermediate-level activities designed for average students
Exceeding Standards	Challenging activities designed for honors and gifted-and-talented students
Standard English Mastery	Activities designed to improve standard English usage

Frequently Asked Questions

INSTRUCTIONAL PLANNING AND SUPPORT

Where do I find planning aids, pacing guides, lesson plans, and other teaching aids?

Annotated Teacher's Edition:
- Chapter planning guides
- Standards-based instruction and strategies
- Differentiated instruction for universal access
- Point-of-use reminders for integrating program resources

Power Presentations with Video CD-ROM

Universal Access Teacher Management System:
- Year and unit instructional benchmarking guides
- Reproducible lesson plans
- Assessment guides for diagnostic, progress, and summative end-of-the-year tests
- Options for differentiating instruction and intervention
- Teaching guides and answer keys for student workbooks

One-Stop Planner CD-ROM with Test Generator: Teacher Management System with Interactive Teacher's Editon:
- Calendar Planner
- Editable lesson plans
- All reproducible ancillaries in Adobe Acrobat (PDF) format
- ExamView Test Generator (English & Spanish)
- Game Tool for ExamView
- PuzzlePro
- Transparency and video previews

DIFFERENTIATING INSTRUCTION FOR UNIVERSAL ACCESS

What resources are available to ensure that Advanced Learners/GATE Students master the standards?

Teacher's Edition Activities:
- Lincoln Speech Analysis, p. 513
- Reconstruction Debate, p. 527
- Reconstruction Essay, p. 530

Lesson Plans for Universal Access

Pre-AP Activities Guide for United States History: Evaluating Information

Primary Source Library CD-ROM for United States History

What resources are available to ensure that English Learners and Standard English Learners master the standards?

Teacher's Edition Activities:
- Acrostic Activity, p. 519
- Political Cartoon Activity, p. 529

Lesson Plans for Universal Access

Chapter Resource File: Vocabulary Builder Activities

Spanish Chapter Summaries Audio CD Program

Online Chapter Summaries in Six Languages

One-Stop Planner CD-ROM:
- PuzzlePro, Spanish Version
- ExamView Test Generator, Spanish Version

What modified materials are available for Special Education?

Teacher's Edition Activities:
- Reconstruction T-chart, p. 513

The ***Universal Access Modified Worksheets and Tests CD-ROM*** provides editable versions of the following:

Vocabulary Flash Cards

Modified Vocabulary Builder Activities

Modified Chapter Review Activity

Modified Chapter Test

What resources are available to ensure that Learners Having Difficulty master the standards?

Teacher's Edition Activities:
- Making Political Slogans, p. 525
- Cause-and-Effect Graphic Organizer, p. 526
- Letter Activity, p. 529

Interactive Reader and Study Guide

Student Edition Full-Read Audio CD

Quick Facts Transparency: Reconstruction Visual Summary

Standards Review Workbook

Social Studies Skills Activity: Chance, Oversight, and Error in History

Interactive Skills Tutor CD-ROM

How do I intervene for students struggling to master the standards?

Interactive Reader and Study Guide

Quick Facts Transparency: Reconstruction Visual Summary

Standards Review Workbook

Social Studies Skills Activity: Chance, Oversight, and Error in History

Interactive Skills Tutor CD-ROM

PROFESSIONAL DEVELOPMENT

What teacher training resources are available to help me grow professionally?

- In-service and staff development as part of your Holt Social Studies product purchase
- Quick Teacher Tutorial Lesson Presentation CD-ROM
- Intensive tuition-based Teacher Development Institute
- *Teaching American History* Online 2 Module Professional Development Course
- Convenient Holt Speaker Bureau face-to-face workshop options
- PRAXIS™ Test Prep (#0089) interactive Web-based content refreshers*
- 24/7 *Ask A Professional Development Expert* at http://www.hrw.com/prodev/

* PRAXIS is a trademark of Educational Testing Service (ETS). This publication is not endorsed or approved by ETS.

Information Literacy Skills

To learn more about how History–Social Science instruction may be improved by the effective use of library media centers and information literacy skills, go to the Teacher's Resource Materials for Chapter 16 at **go.hrw.com**, keyword: SS8 MEDIA.

The following materials were developed by the Division for Public Education of the American Bar Association. These materials are part of the **Democracy and Civic Education** supplement.
- Constitution Study Guide
- Supreme Court Case Studies

Chapter Preview

Standards Focus

Standards by Section
Section 1: HSS 8.10.7, 8.11.1, 8.11.3, 8.11.5
Section 2: HSS 8.11.3, 8.11.5
Section 3: HSS 8.11.1, 8.11.3, 8.11.4

Teacher's Edition
HSS **Analysis Skills:** CS 1, CS 2, HR 1, HR 4, HR 5, HI 1, HI 2, HI 3, HI 4
ELA Writing 8.2.3, 8.2.5; Reading 8.2.0

Preview Grade 11 Standards
HSS **11.10** Students analyze the development of federal civil rights and voting rights.
11.10.1 Explain how demands of African Americans helped produce a stimulus for civil rights, including President Roosevelt's ban on racial discrimination in defense industries in 1941 and how African Americans' service in World War II produced a stimulus for President Truman's decision to end segregation in the armed forces in 1948.
11.10.2 Examine and analyze the key events, policies, and court cases in the evolution of civil rights, including *Dred Scott* v. *Sandford*, *Plessy* v. *Ferguson*, *Brown* v. *Board of Education*, *Regents of the University of California* v. *Bakke*, and California Proposition 209.

Focus on Writing

The **Chapter Resource File** provides a Focus on Writing worksheet to help students organize and write their job histories.

CRF: Focus on Writing Activity: Job History

CHAPTER 16 1865–1877

Reconstruction

California Standards

History–Social Science

8.10 Students analyze the multiple causes, key events, and complex consequences of the Civil War.

8.11 Students analyze the character and lasting consequences of Reconstruction.

Analysis Skills

HR 3 Students distinguish relevant from irrelevant information.

HI 4 Students recognize the role of chance, oversight, and error in history.

English–Language Arts

Writing 8.2.5 Write documents related to career development.

Reading 8.2.0 Students read and understand grade-level apporpriate material.

FOCUS ON WRITING

Job History When the Civil War ended, it was time to rebuild. People were ready to get back to work. But life had changed for many people and would continue to change. As you read this chapter, think about jobs people may have had during Reconstruction.

UNITED STATES

1865 Abraham Lincoln is assassinated.

1865

WORLD

1865 Black Jamaicans rebel against the wealthy planter class.

Introduce the Chapter

Standards Proficiency

Focus on Rebuilding HSS 8.10

1. Have students imagine that their town or city has been devastated by a natural disaster. For example, traffic signals do not work, hospitals and schools are closed, grocery stores have been stripped of food, and power and water plants have been destroyed.
2. Ask students to list, in order of importance, what the town should focus on rebuilding or replacing first. Ask for volunteers to share their lists with the class.
3. Explain to students that they will be learning about the efforts to rebuild and reunite the United States following the Civil War. Inform students that not only were cities and farmland destroyed but the nation had to be put back together. Ask students to use their prior knowledge to predict what social, economic, and political issues might cause the North and South to disagree over priorities in rebuilding the nation. LS **Verbal/Linguistic**

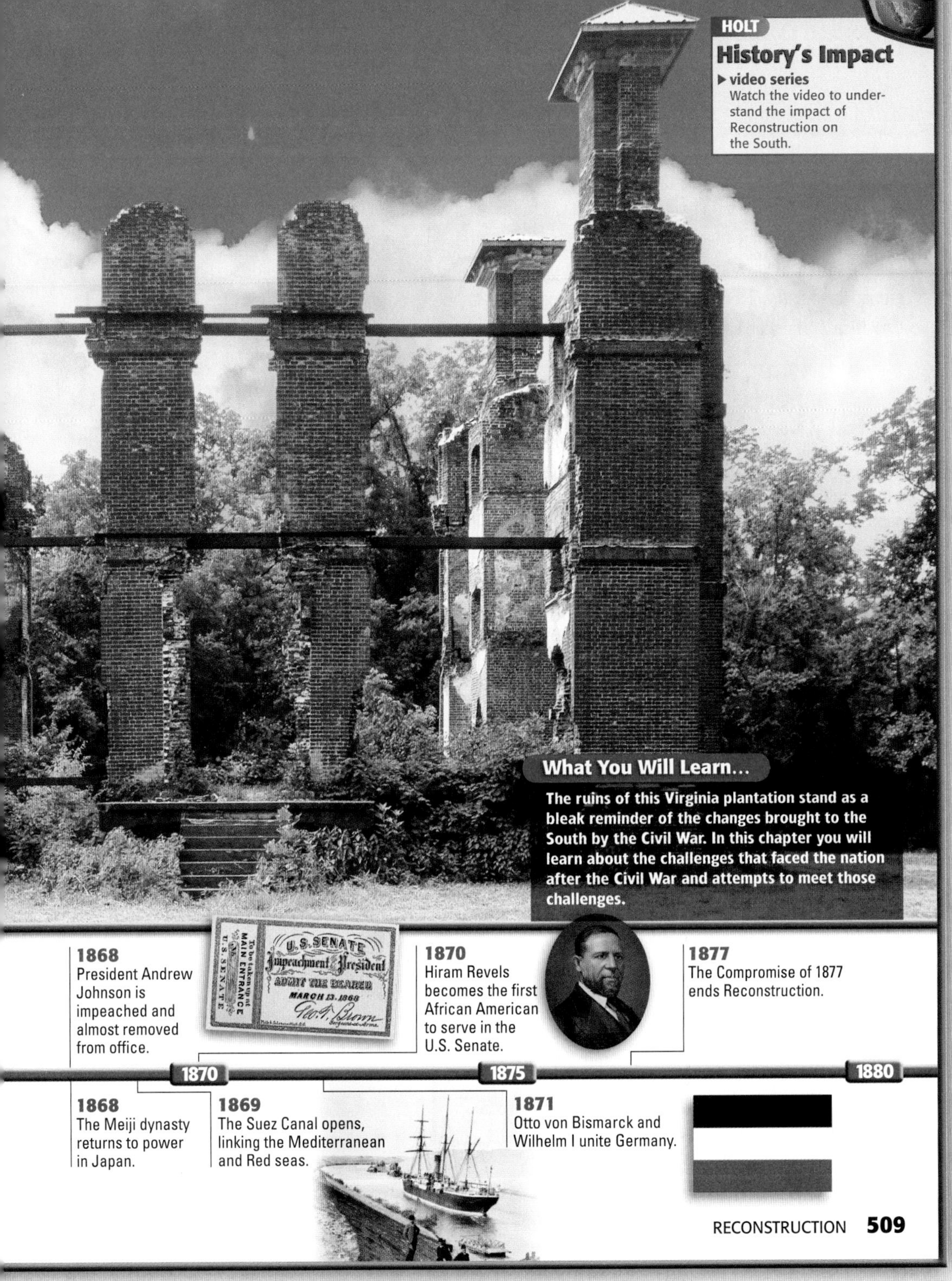
HOLT

History's Impact

▶ **video series**
Watch the video to understand the impact of Reconstruction on the South.

What You Will Learn...

The ruins of this Virginia plantation stand as a bleak reminder of the changes brought to the South by the Civil War. In this chapter you will learn about the challenges that faced the nation after the Civil War and attempts to meet those challenges.

1868 President Andrew Johnson is impeached and almost removed from office.

1870 Hiram Revels becomes the first African American to serve in the U.S. Senate.

1877 The Compromise of 1877 ends Reconstruction.

1870 · 1875 · 1880

1868 The Meiji dynasty returns to power in Japan.

1869 The Suez Canal opens, linking the Mediterranean and Red seas.

1871 Otto von Bismarck and Wilhelm I unite Germany.

RECONSTRUCTION **509**

• Chapter Preview •

HOLT

History's Impact

▶ **video series**
See the Video Teacher's Guide for strategies for using the chapter video **Reconstruction.**

Chapter Big Ideas

Section 1 The nation faced many problems in rebuilding the Union. **HSS** 8.10.7, 8.11.1, 8.11.3, 8.11.5

Section 2 The return to power of the pre-war southern leadership led Republicans in Congress to take control of Reconstruction. **HSS** 8.11.3, 8.11.5

Section 3 As Reconstruction ended, African Americans faced new hurdles and the South attempted to rebuild. **HSS** 8.11.1, 8.11.3, 8.11.4

Explore the Picture

Aftermath of War There are many ruins of plantations across the South today. Many plantations were damaged during the fighting that took place during the Civil War. Others were abandoned by their owners, who could no longer afford to run their plantations. The ruin reflected by this image shows the great challenges that faced the nation as it attempted to rebuild in the aftermath of the Civil War.

Analyzing Visuals How might the sight of abandoned or damaged plantations have affected people after the Civil War? *Wealthy southerners might have been angered or saddened by such sights. Former slaves might have felt justice had been served and seen the ruins as a symbol of the end of slavery.*

Explore the Time Line

1. In what year was President Abraham Lincoln assassinated? *1865*
2. What event occurred in Jamaica in the same year that Abraham Lincoln was assassinated? *Black Jamaicans rebelled against the planters.*
3. How many years passed between the assassination of Abraham Lincoln and the end of Reconstruction? *12 years*
4. Which president was impeached in 1868? *Andrew Johnson*

HSS Analysis Skills: CS 1

World Events

Connecting Two Seas In 1869 the Suez Canal opened, connecting the Mediterranean and Red seas. This artificial channel is just over 100 miles in length. Because the levels of both seas are relatively equal, the builders did not need to construct locks to raise or lower ships. The creation of the Suez Canal reduced the voyage from Europe to the Indian Ocean by about 5,000 miles. By 1945 the number of annual shipments through the canal peaked at 984,000. In recent years, however, traffic has dropped, as more cargo is sent by other means.

go.hrw.com

Online Resources

Chapter Resources:
KEYWORD: SS8 US16

Teacher Resources:
KEYWORD: SS8 TEACHER

Reading Social Studies

Understanding Themes

Point out to students that during Reconstruction, many political changes took place in an effort to mend the damage done by war and to grant rights to the newly-freed slaves. Ask students what political changes might have been necessary and how each change would have affected both the North and the South. What social and cultural changes might have taken place during Reconstruction? What different groups might have been affected by these changes? Help students understand the importance of these two themes.

Analyzing Historical Information

Focus on Reading Read students an article from a current, popular magazine or a short article from the local newspaper. Have students take notes as you read. Tell them to record only the relevant information from your reading. When finished, have several volunteers read their notes. Compile a list of the relevant information for all to see. Then guide students in a discussion of what was important, and what was not. Tell students that when they analyze historical information, they are using this same skill, figuring out what is important or relevant, and what is not.

Reading Social Studies

by Kylene Beers

Economics | Geography | **Politics** | Religion | **Society and Culture** | Science and Technology

Focus on Themes In this chapter, you will read about the time immediately after the Civil War. You will see how the government tried to help the South rebuild itself and will learn about how life changed for African Americans after slavery was declared illegal. You will read about the **political** conflicts that emerged as southern leadership worked to gain control of Reconstruction efforts. Throughout the chapter, you will read how the **culture** of the South changed after the War.

Analyzing Historical Information

Focus on Reading History books are full of information. As you read, you are confronted with names, dates, places, terms, and descriptions on every page. You don't want to have to deal with anything unimportant or untrue.

Identifying Relevant and Essential Information Information in a history book should be relevant to the topic you're studying. It should also be essential to understanding that topic and verifiable. Anything else distracts from the material you are studying.

The first passage below includes several pieces of irrelevant and nonessential information. In the second, this information has been removed. Note how much easier the revised passage is to comprehend.

First Passage

President Abraham Lincoln, who was very tall, wanted to reunite the nation as quickly and painlessly as possible. He had proposed a plan for readmitting the southern states even before the war ended, which happened on a Sunday. Called the Ten Percent Plan, it offered southerners amnesty, or official pardon for all illegal acts supporting the rebellion. Today a group called Amnesty International works to protect the rights of prisoners. Lincoln's plan certainly would have worked if it would have been implemented.

Lincoln's appearance and the day on which the war ended are not essential facts.

Amnesty International is not relevant to this topic.

There is no way to prove the accuracy of the last sentence.

Revised Passage

President Abraham Lincoln wanted to reunite the nation as quickly and painlessly as possible. He had proposed a plan for readmitting the southern states even before the war ended. Called the Ten Percent Plan, it offered southerners amnesty, or official pardon for all illegal acts supporting the rebellion.

From Chapter 16, p. 513

Additional reading support can be found in the

Reading and Skills Resources

Reading Support

- Interactive Reader and Study Guide
- Student Edition on Audio CD
- Spanish Chapter Summaries Audio CD Program

Social Studies Skills Support

- Interactive Skills Tutor CD-ROM

Vocabulary Support

- **CRF:** Vocabulary Builder Activities
- **CRF:** Chapter Review Activity
- Universal Access Modified Worksheets and Tests CD-ROM:
  - Vocabulary Flash Cards
  - Vocabulary Builder Activity
  - Chapter Review Activity
- OSP Holt PuzzlePro

Standards Focus

HSS Analysis Skills: HI 3

ELA Reading: 8.2.0

ELA **Analysis HI 3** Distinguish relevant, essential, and verifiable information.
HSS **Reading 8.2.0** Students read and understand grade-level-appropriate material.

You Try It!

The following passage is adapted from the chapter you are about to read. As you read, look for irrelevant, nonessential, or unverifiable information.

The Freedman's Bureau

In 1865 Congress established the Freedmen's Bureau, an agency providing relief for freed people and certain poor people in the South. The Bureau had a difficult job. It may have been one of the most difficult jobs ever. At its high point, about 900 agents served the entire South. All 900 people could fit into one hotel ballroom today. Bureau commissioner Oliver O. Howard eventually decided to use the Bureau's limited budget to distribute food to the poor and to provide education and legal help for freedpeople. One common food in the south at that time was salted meat. The Bureau also helped African American war veterans. Today the Department of Veterans' Affairs assists American war veterans.

From Chapter 16, p. 530

After you read the passage, answer the following questions.

1. Which sentence in this passage is unverifiable and should be cut?
2. Find two sentences in this passage that are irrelevant to the discussion of the Freedmen's Bureau. What makes those sentences irrelevant?
3. Look at the last sentence of the passage. Do you think this sentence is essential to the discussion? Why or why not?

As you read Chapter 16, ask yourself what makes the information you are reading essential to a study of Reconstruction.

Key Terms and People

Chapter 16

Section 1
Reconstruction *(p. 512)*
Ten Percent Plan *(p. 513)*
Thirteenth Amendment *(p. 514)*
Freedmen's Bureau *(p. 516)*
Andrew Johnson *(p. 517)*

Section 2
Black Codes *(p. 518)*
Radical Republicans *(p. 519)*
Civil Rights Act of 1866 *(p. 520)*
Fourteenth Amendment *(p. 521)*
Reconstruction Acts *(p. 521)*
impeachment *(p. 522)*
Fifteenth Amendment *(p. 523)*

Section 3
Hiram Revels *(p. 525)*
Ku Klux Klan *(p. 526)*
Compromise of 1877 *(p. 527)*
poll tax *(p. 528)*
segregation *(p. 528)*
Jim Crow laws *(p. 528)*
Plessy v. *Ferguson* *(p. 529)*
sharecropping *(p. 529)*

Academic Vocabulary

Success in school is related to knowing academic vocabulary—the words that are frequently used in school assignments an discussions. In this chapter, you will learn the following academic words:

procedure *(p. 513)*
principle *(p. 520)*

Reading Social Studies

Key Terms and People

Introduce the key terms and people from this chapter by reviewing with the class each term and its description. Check to see that students understand the meaning of each term. Then have each student write three multiple-choice questions over terms or people from the list. Have students exchange questions with a partner and answer the questions. Have each pair review the correct answers together. **LS Verbal/Linguistic, Interpersonal**

Focus on Reading

See the **Focus on Reading** questions in this chapter for more practice on this reading social studies skill.

Reading Social Studies Assessment

See the **Standards Review** at the end of this chapter for student assessment questions related to this reading skill.

Teaching Tip

Remind students that when there are quotes included in the text, it is important to read them and understand what the author is saying. Quotes may not necessarily include essential information; they may be reinforcing material that has already been discussed in the text. Sometimes, however, quotes by a well-known individual whose statements and beliefs were influential can be essential in analyzing historical information.

Answers

You Try It! 1. It may have been one of the most difficult jobs ever **2.** All 900 people could fit into one hotel ballroom today; One common food in the South at that time was salted meat; Today the Department of Veterans' Affairs assists American war veterans. *They do not pertain to the Freedmen's Bureau.*
3. *not essential; the paragraph is about the Freedmen's Bureau, not about current affairs*

Preteach

Bellringer

If YOU were there . . . Use the **Daily Bellringer Transparency** to help students answer the question.

Daily Bellringer Transparency, Section 1

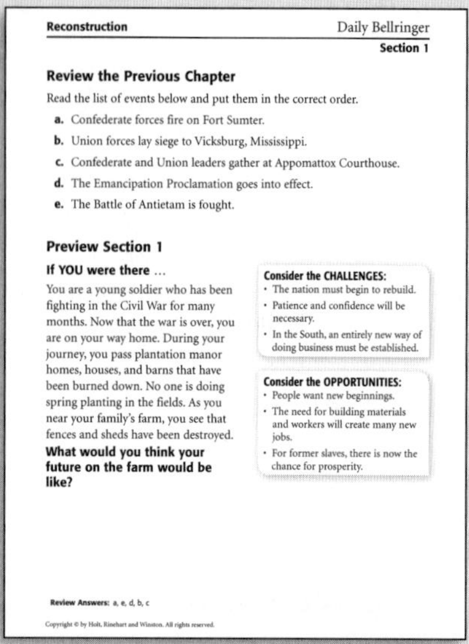
Reconstruction — Daily Bellringer
Section 1

Review the Previous Chapter

Read the list of events below and put them in the correct order.

- **a.** Confederate forces fire on Fort Sumter.
- **b.** Union forces lay siege to Vicksburg, Mississippi.
- **c.** Confederate and Union leaders gather at Appomattox Courthouse.
- **d.** The Emancipation Proclamation goes into effect.
- **e.** The Battle of Antietam is fought.

Preview Section 1

If YOU were there ...

You are a young soldier who has been fighting in the Civil War for many months. Now that the war is over, you are on your way home. During your journey, you pass plantation manor homes, houses, and barns that have been burned down. No one is doing spring planting in the fields. As you near your family's farm, you see that fences and sheds have been destroyed.

What would you think your future on the farm would be like?

Consider the CHALLENGES:
- The nation must begin to rebuild.
- Patience and confidence will be necessary.
- In the South, an entirely new way of doing business must be established.

Consider the OPPORTUNITIES:
- People want new beginnings.
- The need for building materials and workers will create many new jobs.
- For former slaves, there is now the chance for prosperity.

Review Answers: a, e, d, b, c

Academic Vocabulary

Review with students the high-use academic term in this section.

procedure a series of steps taken to accomplish a task (p. 513)

CRF: Vocabulary Builder Activity, Section 1

Standards Focus

HSS 8.10.7
Means: Discuss the effects of the Civil War on soldiers, civilians, and the environment as well as on future wars.
Matters: The Civil War had a huge effect on the United States.

8.11.1
Means: List the original goals of Reconstruction and its effects on government and society in the United States.
Matters: Reconstruction continued to divide the North and the South.

8.11.3
Means: Explain the freedoms of and restrictions on African Americans after the Civil War.
Matters: Reconstruction policies initially helped freedpeople, but restrictions on their rights soon became common.
(continued on p. 513)

SECTION 1

Rebuilding the South

What You Will Learn...

Main Ideas

1. President Lincoln and Congress differed in their views as Reconstruction began.
2. The end of the Civil War meant freedom for African Americans in the South.
3. President Johnson's plan began the process of Reconstruction.

The Big Idea

The nation faced many problems in rebuilding the Union.

Key Terms and People

Reconstruction, *p. 512*
Ten Percent Plan, *p. 513*
Thirteenth Amendment, *p. 514*
Freedmen's Bureau, *p. 516*
Andrew Johnson, *p. 517*

HSS 8.10.7 Explain how the war affected combatants, civilians, the physical environment, and future warfare.

8.11.1 List the original aims of Reconstruction and describe its effects on the political and social structures of different regions.

8.11.3 Understand the effects of the Freedmen's Bureau and the restrictions placed on the rights and opportunities of freedmen, including racial segregation and "Jim Crow" laws.

8.11.5 Understand the Thirteenth, Fourteenth, and Fifteenth Amendments to the Constitution and analyze their connection to Reconstruction.

If YOU were there...

You are a young soldier who has been fighting in the Civil War for many months. Now that the war is over, you are on your way home. During your journey, you pass plantation manor homes, houses, and barns that have been burned down. No one is doing spring planting in the fields. As you near your family's farm, you see that fences and sheds have been destroyed.

What would you think your future on the farm would be like?

BUILDING BACKGROUND When the Civil War ended, much of the South lay in ruins. Like the young soldier above, many people returned to destroyed homes and farms. Harvests of corn, cotton, rice, and other crops fell far below normal. Many farm animals had been killed or were roaming free. These were some of the challenges in restoring the nation.

Reconstruction Begins

After the Civil War ended in 1865, the U.S. government faced the problem of dealing with the defeated southern states. The nation dealt with the challenges of **Reconstruction**, the process of readmitting the former Confederate states to the Union. It lasted from 1865 to 1877.

Teach the Big Idea: Master the Standards

Standards Proficiency

Rebuilding the South HSS 8.10.7, 8.11.1, 8.11.3, 8.11.5; HSS Analysis Skills: HR 1, HI 1, HI 2

1. **Teach** Ask students the Main Idea questions to teach this section.
2. **Apply** Have each student examine the main ideas for this section. Then have students create as many questions for each main idea as they can. For example, for the first main idea, students might ask why President Lincoln and Congress differed in their views about Reconstruction. **LS Verbal/Linguistic**
3. **Review** Have students review the section and provide answers for each of the questions they created.
4. **Practice/Homework** Have students use their questions and answers to write a one-page summary about the effect that rebuilding the South had on American society. **LS Verbal/Linguistic**

Alternative Assessment Handbook, Rubric 1: Acquiring Information

Damaged South

Tired southern soldiers returned home to find that the world they had known before the war was gone. Cities, towns, and farms had been ruined. Because of high food prices and widespread crop failures, many southerners faced starvation. The Confederate money held by most southerners was now worthless. Banks failed, and merchants had gone bankrupt because people could not pay their debts.

Former Confederate general Braxton Bragg was one of many southerners who faced economic hardship. He found that "*all, all* was lost, except my debts." In South Carolina, Mary Boykin Chesnut wrote in her diary about the isolation she experienced after the war. "We are shut in here. . . . All RR's [railroads] destroyed—bridges gone. We are cut off from the world."

Lincoln's Plan

President Abraham Lincoln wanted to reunite the nation as quickly and painlessly as possible. He had proposed a plan for readmitting the southern states even before the war ended. Called the **Ten Percent Plan**, it offered southerners amnesty, or official pardon, for all illegal acts supporting the rebellion. To receive amnesty, southerners had to do two things. They had to swear an oath of loyalty to the United States. They also had to agree that slavery was illegal. Once 10 percent of voters in a state made these pledges, they could form a new government. The state then could be readmitted to the Union.

Louisiana quickly elected a new state legislature under the Ten Percent Plan. Other southern states that had been occupied by Union troops soon followed Louisiana back into the United States.

Wade-Davis Bill

Some politicians argued that Congress, not the president, should control the southern states' return to the Union. They believed that Congress had the power to admit new states. Also, many Republican members of Congress thought the Ten Percent Plan did not go far enough. A senator from Michigan expressed their views.

> "The people of the North are not such fools as to ... turn around and say to the traitors, 'all you have to do [to return] is ... take an oath that henceforth you will be true to the Government.'"
>
> –Senator Jacob Howard, quoted in *Reconstruction: America's Unfinished Revolution, 1863–1877,* by Eric Foner

Two Republicans—Senator Benjamin Wade and Representative Henry Davis—had an alternative to Lincoln's plan. Under the procedure of the Wade-Davis bill, a state had to meet two conditions before it could rejoin the Union. First, it had to ban slavery. Second, a majority of adult males in the state had to take the loyalty oath.

ACADEMIC VOCABULARY
procedure a series of steps taken to accomplish a task

War destroyed Richmond, Virginia, once the proud capital of the Confederacy.

Direct Teach

Main Idea

1 Reconstruction Begins

President Lincoln and Congress differed in their views as Reconstruction began.

Describe What problems did the South face following the Civil War? *cities, towns, and farms destroyed; high food prices; crops destroyed; Confederate money worthless; failed banks; merchants bankrupt*

Evaluate Which plan would you have supported, the Ten Percent Plan or the Wade-Davis Bill? Why? *possible answers: Ten Percent—It would reunite the nation faster and not be too harsh on the South; Wade-Davis—it would be stricter on the South.*

- **CRF:** Economics and History Activity: The Devastation of War
- Political Cartoons Activities for United States History, Cartoon 18: Lincoln Repairing the Union

HSS 8.10.7, 8.11.1; HSS **Analysis Skills:** CS 1, HI 1

Did you know . . .

Louisiana was the first Confederate state to meet the requirements of Lincoln's Ten Percent Plan. Occupied by Union military forces during the Civil War, the state held a convention in 1864 and drafted a new constitution outlawing slavery. Despite the state's having met the president's requirements for readmission to the Union, Congress refused to allow Louisiana representatives to take their seats in Washington.

Differentiating Instruction for Universal Access

Advanced Learners/GATE

Exceeding Standards | Research Required

1. Have students locate and read a copy of Abraham Lincoln's second inaugural address.
2. Have each student write a short summary of the speech, including a short explanation of Lincoln's views on Reconstruction.
3. Discuss with students their interpretations of Lincoln's ideas. LS **Verbal/Linguistic**

HSS 8.11.1; HSS **Analysis Skills:** HR 5

Special Education Students

Reaching Standards

1. To help students answer the guided reading question, draw a T-chart for students to see. Label one side of the chart *Ten Percent Plan,* and the other *Wade-Davis Bill.* Have each student copy and complete the chart.
2. Review with students the characteristics of each plan for Reconstruction. LS **Verbal/Linguistic**

HSS 8.11.1; HSS **Analysis Skills:** HI 1

Standards Focus *continued*

HSS 8.11.5

Means: Understand the purpose of the Thirteenth, Fourteenth, and Fifteenth amendments.

Matters: Three important Reconstruction amendments changed life for African Americans.

Direct Teach

Primary Source

Reading Like a Historian

Help students practice reading the documents like historians. Ask:

- Who placed the advertisement? Why? *Saml. [Samuel] Dove; looking for family members who were separated and sold to different slaveholders.*
- Why might the people on the boat be leaving Richmond? *possible answers—The city has been damaged in the war; African Americans are leaving the South now that they are free.*

HSS 8.11; HSS **Analysis Skills:** HR 4, HR 5

Info to Know

Pocket Veto The U.S. Congress approved the Wade-Davis Bill just before adjourning in 1864. The end of the congressional session made it possible for President Lincoln to use a pocket veto to kill the measure. Usually, if a president does not sign a bill within 10 days while Congress is in session, the bill automatically becomes a law. However, if Congress is adjourned, a bill dies if the president does not sign it. A pocket veto cannot be overturned by a congressional vote.

Testing New Freedoms

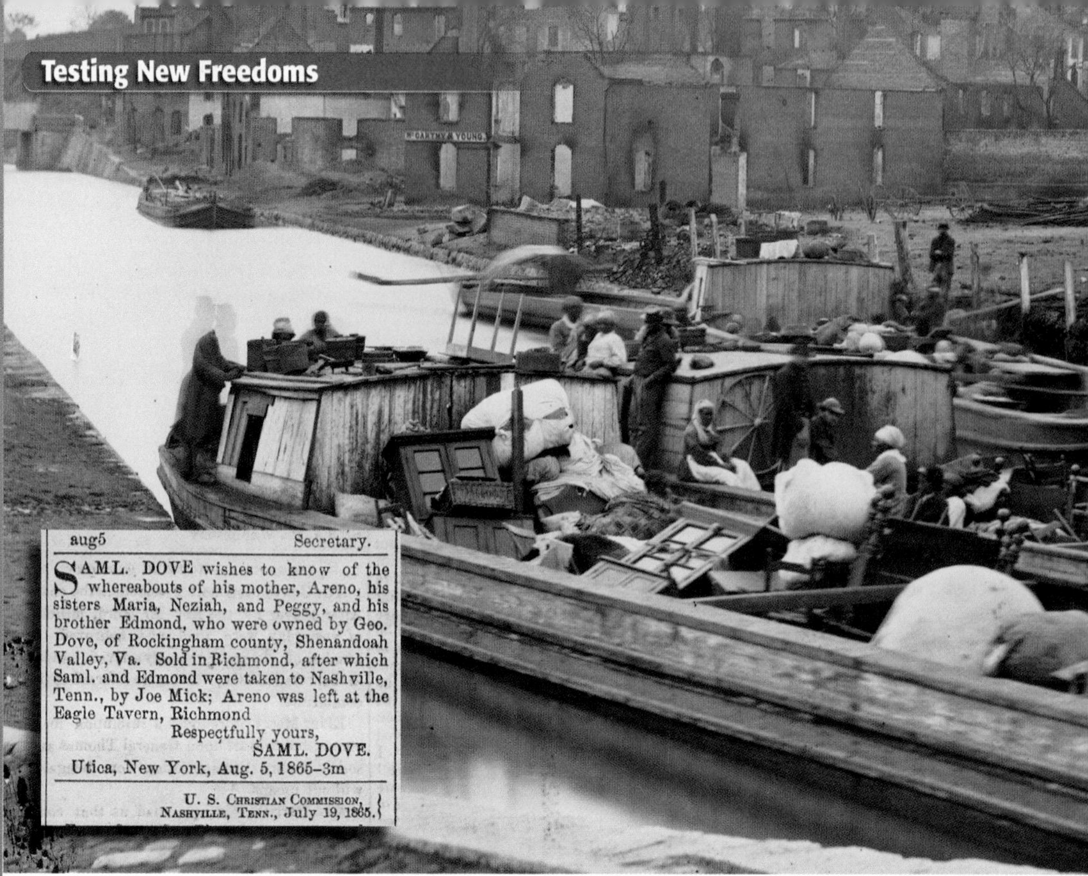

aug5 Secretary.

SAML. DOVE wishes to know of the whereabouts of his mother, Areno, his sisters Maria, Neziah, and Peggy, and his brother Edmond, who were owned by Geo. Dove, of Rockingham county, Shenandoah Valley, Va. Sold in Richmond, after which Saml. and Edmond were taken to Nashville, Tenn., by Joe Mick; Areno was left at the Eagle Tavern, Richmond

Respectfully yours,
SAML. DOVE.
Utica, New York, Aug. 5, 1865–3m

U. S. Christian Commission,
Nashville, Tenn., July 19, 1865.

Under the Wade-Davis bill, only southerners who swore that they had never supported the Confederacy could vote or hold office. In general, the bill was much stricter than the Ten Percent Plan. Its provisions would make it harder for southern states to rejoin the Union quickly.

President Lincoln therefore refused to sign the bill into law. He thought that few southern states would agree to meet its requirements. He believed that his plan would help restore order more quickly.

READING CHECK **Contrasting** How was the Ten Percent Plan different from the Wade-Davis Bill?

Freedom for African Americans

One thing Republicans agreed on was abolishing slavery. The Emancipation Proclamation had freed slaves only in areas that had not been occupied by Union forces, not in the border states. Many people feared that the federal courts might someday declare it unconstitutional.

Slavery Ends

On January 31, 1865, at President Lincoln's urging, Congress proposed the **Thirteenth Amendment**. This amendment made slavery illegal throughout the United States.

Collaborative Learning

Standards Proficiency

Congressional Committees

HSS 8.11.1; HSS **Analysis Skills:** HI 1

1. Review with students the Reconstruction plans of Congress and President Lincoln. Ask students why Congress might have opposed the Ten Percent Plan and what Lincoln disliked about the Wade-Davis Bill.
2. Organize students into small groups. Ask them to imagine that they are members of Congress in 1864. Have them work in committees to write a plan that they think Lincoln would have accepted for readmitting the states. Encourage students to consider what rules they would set to ensure that ex-Confederates would support the Union and end slavery. Remind students to use standard grammar, spelling, sentence structure, and punctuation in their plans.
3. Ask groups to present their plans to the class. After all groups have presented their proposals, lead a class discussion of the pros and cons of each plan. LS **Interpersonal, Verbal/Linguistic**

Alternative Assessment Handbook, Rubrics 14: Group Activity; and 24: Oral Presentations

Answers

Reading Check *Ten Percent Plan—Ten percent of all voters in Confederate states had to pledge loyalty to the Union and accept slavery as illegal; Wade-Davis Bill—A majority of voters in Confederate states had to pledge loyalty to the Union, and only southerners who had never supported the Confederacy could vote or hold office.*

The freedpeople at left have packed their household belongings and are leaving Richmond. Many people traveled in search of relatives. Others placed newspaper advertisements looking for long-lost relatives. For other freedpeople, like the couple above, freedom brought the right to marry.

In what ways did former slaves react to freedom?

The amendment was ratified and took effect on December 18, 1865. When abolitionist William Lloyd Garrison heard the news, he declared that his work was now finished. He called for the American Anti-Slavery Society to break up. Not all abolitionists agreed that their work was done, however. Frederick Douglass insisted that "slavery is not abolished until the black man has the ballot [vote]."

Freedom brought important changes to newly freed slaves. Many couples held ceremonies to legalize marriages that had not been recognized under slavery. Many freedpeople searched for relatives who had been sold away from their families years earlier. Others placed newspaper ads seeking information about their children. Many women began to work at home instead of in the fields. Still others adopted children of dead relatives to keep families together. Church members established voluntary associations and mutual-aid societies to help those in need.

Now that they could travel without a pass, many freedpeople moved from mostly white counties to places with more African Americans. Other freedpeople traveled simply to test their new freedom of movement. A South Carolina woman explained this need. "I must go, if I stay here I'll never know I'm free."

For most former slaves, freedom to travel was just the first step on a long road toward equal rights and new ways of life. Adults took new last names and began to insist on being called Mr. or Mrs. as a sign of respect, rather than by their first names or by nicknames. Freedpeople began to demand the same economic and political rights as white citizens. Henry Adams, a former slave, argued that "if I cannot do like a white man I am not free."

Forty Acres to Farm?

Many former slaves wanted their own land to farm. Near the end of the Civil War, Union general William Tecumseh Sherman had issued an order to break up plantations in coastal South Carolina and Georgia. He wanted to divide the land into 40-acre plots and give them to former slaves as compensation for their forced labor before the war.

Many white planters refused to surrender their land. Some freedpeople pointed out that it was only fair that they receive some of this land because their labor had made the plantations prosper. In the end, the U.S. government returned the land to its original owners. At this time, many freedpeople were unsure about where they would live, what kind of work they would do, and what rights they had. Many freedoms that were theirs by law were difficult to enforce.

Direct Teach

Main Idea

❷ Freedom for African Americans

The end of the Civil War meant freedom for African Americans in the South.

Identify Which amendment abolished slavery? *the Thirteenth*

Explain After the Civil War, why did some African Americans feel they were not free? *They could not vote and did not have the same economic and political rights as white men did.*

Draw Inferences Why might some newly freed slaves choose to remain in the South? *possible answers—It was familiar; they had family there.*

HSS 8.11.1; HSS **Analysis Skills:** CS 1, HI 1

go.hrw.com
Online Resources
KEYWORD: SS8 US16
ACTIVITY: Population Chart

MISCONCEPTION ALERT

Resettlement Some students might assume that African Americans flocked to the North after gaining their freedom. Point out to students that in fact most freedpeople remained in the South. Many moved to southern cities and towns where African American schools and churches created a sense of community. Other freedpeople chose to remain near the plantations they had known all their lives.

Critical Thinking: Summarizing

Standards **Proficiency**

Creating a Documentary Film

HSS 8.11.1; HSS **Analysis Skills:** CS 1, HI 1, HI 2

1. Review with students the effect that freedom had on many African Americans. Discuss the various changes that occurred, as well as the effect those changes had on the lives of former slaves.
2. Ask students to imagine that they are documentary filmmakers living during the period of Reconstruction. Their assignment is to create a documentary about the changes African Americans experienced after the ratification of the Thirteenth Amendment.
3. Have students create storyboards for their documentaries. Remind students to consider whom they would interview for the film, what scenes they would like to show, and what changes they might focus on.
4. Once the storyboards are complete, have each student write an introduction and conclusion for his or her film. LS **Verbal/Linguistic, Visual/Spatial**

Alternative Assessment Handbook, Rubric 41: Writing to Express

Answers

Testing New Freedoms *pursued new opportunities, married, looked for long-lost relatives, traveled*

Direct Teach

Main Idea

❷ Freedom for African Americans

The end of the Civil War meant freedom for African Americans in the South.

Recall What were the goals of the Freedmen's Bureau? *to distribute food to poor people, provide education and legal help for freedpeople, and assist African American war veterans*

Describe Who taught at the schools for African Americans? *mostly women who were committed to helping freedpeople*

Make Inferences How did education for African Americans benefit both black and white southerners? *possible answers—created access to better education, provided more educated workers*

HSS 8.11.3 HSS **Analysis Skills:** HI 1, HI 2

Linking to Today

Howard University Howard University was named for Oliver O. Howard, the head of the Freedmen's Bureau. The university opened in May 1867 in response to the move to provide more educational opportunities for freedpeople. The original goal of the school was "training for preachers and teachers." From the beginning, Howard University was open to men and women of all races. Today Howard University has expanded to include schools of law, dentistry, medicine, education, social work, business, and more.

Freedmen's Bureau

In 1865 Congress established the **Freedmen's Bureau**, an agency providing relief for freedpeople and certain poor people in the South. The Bureau had a difficult job. At its high point, about 900 agents served the entire South. Bureau commissioner Oliver O. Howard eventually decided to use the Bureau's limited budget to distribute food to the poor and to provide education and legal help for freedpeople. The Bureau also helped African American war veterans.

The Freedmen's Bureau played an important role in establishing more schools in the South. Laws against educating slaves meant that most freedpeople had never learned to read or write. Before the war ended, however, northern groups, such as the American Missionary Association, began providing books and teachers to African Americans. The teachers were mostly women who were committed to helping freedpeople. One teacher said of her students, "I never before saw children so eager to learn. . . . It is wonderful how [they] . . . can have so great a desire for knowledge, and such a capacity for attaining [reaching] it."

After the war, some freedpeople organized their own education efforts. For example, Freedmen's Bureau agents found that some African Americans had opened schools in abandoned buildings. Many white southerners continued to believe that African Americans should not be educated. Despite opposition, by 1869 more than 150,000 African American students were attending more than 3,000 schools. The Freedmen's Bureau also helped establish several universities for African Americans, including Howard and Fisk universities.

Students quickly filled the new classrooms. Working adults attended classes in the evening. African Americans hoped that education would help them to understand and protect their rights and to enable them to find better jobs. Both black and white southerners benefited from the effort to provide greater access to education in the South.

READING CHECK **Analyzing** How did the Freedmen's Bureau help reform education in the South?

Helping the Freedpeople

Congress created the Freedmen's Bureau to help freedpeople and poor southerners recover from the Civil War. The Bureau assisted people by:

- **providing supplies and medical services**
- **establishing schools**
- **supervising contracts between freedpeople and employers**
- **taking care of lands abandoned or captured during the war**

What role did the Freedmen's Bureau play during Reconstruction?

Critical Thinking: Supporting a Point of View

Standards Proficiency

Writing a Proposal HSS 8.11.3; HSS **Analysis Skills:** HI 1

1. Review with students the goals and accomplishments of the Freedmen's Bureau. Then ask students to imagine that they are serving on a committee working to promote the contributions of the Freedmen's Bureau.
2. Organize students into pairs. Ask each pair to select some method of honoring and promoting the accomplishments of the Freedmen's Bureau. Examples might include a commemorative postage stamp, a statue or historical marker, or even a national holiday. Have students develop the specifics for their plans.
3. Have each pair of students write a proposal that explains why the Freedmen's Bureau deserves an honor and what the memorial would be like. Encourage students to create an image of the memorial, if applicable.
4. Have volunteers share their proposals with the class. LS **Interpersonal, Visual/Spatial**

Alternative Assessment Handbook, Rubric 43: Writing to Persuade

Answers

Helping the Freedpeople *See the bulleted list above the question.*

Reading Check *It helped establish schools and several colleges in the South.*

President Johnson's Reconstruction Plan

While the Freedmen's Bureau was helping African Americans, the issue of how the South would politically rejoin the Union remained unresolved. Soon, however, a tragic event ended Lincoln's dream of peacefully reuniting the country.

A New President

On the evening of April 14, 1865, President Lincoln and his wife attended a play at Ford's Theater in Washington, D.C. During the play, John Wilkes Booth, a southerner who opposed Lincoln's policies, sneaked into the president's theater box and shot him. Lincoln was rushed to a boardinghouse across the street, where he died at about 7:30 the next morning. Vice President **Andrew Johnson** was sworn into office quickly. Reconstruction had now become his responsibility. He would have to win the trust of a nation shocked at their leader's death.

Johnson's plan for bringing southern states back into the Union was similar to Lincoln's plan. However, he decided that wealthy southerners and former Confederate officials would need a presidential pardon to receive amnesty. Johnson shocked Radical Republicans by eventually pardoning more than 7,000 people by 1866.

New State Governments

Johnson was a Democrat whom Republicans had put on the ticket in 1864 to appeal to the border states. A former slaveholder, he was a stubborn man who would soon face a hostile Congress.

Johnson offered a mild program for setting up new southern state governments. First, he appointed a temporary governor for each state. Then he required that the states revise their constitutions. Next, voters elected state and federal representatives. The new state government had to declare that secession was illegal. It also had to ratify the Thirteenth Amendment and refuse to pay Confederate debts.

By the end of 1865, all the southern states except Texas had created new governments. Johnson approved them all and declared that the United States was restored. Newly elected representatives came to Washington from each reconstructed southern state. However, Republicans complained that many new representatives had been leaders of the Confederacy. Congress therefore refused to readmit the southern states into the Union. Clearly, the nation was still divided.

READING CHECK **Summarizing** What was President Johnson's plan for Reconstruction?

SUMMARY AND PREVIEW In this section you learned about early plans for Reconstruction. In the next section, you will learn that disagreements about Reconstruction became so serious that the president was almost removed from office.

Section 1 Assessment

go.hrw.com
Online Quiz
KEYWORD: SS8 HP16

Reviewing Ideas, Terms, and People HSS 8.10.7, 8.11.1, 8.11.3, 8.11.5

1. a. **Identify** What does **Reconstruction** mean?
   b. **Summarize** What was President Lincoln's plan for Reconstruction?
2. a. **Recall** What is the **Thirteenth Amendment**?
   b. **Elaborate** In your opinion, what was the most important accomplishment of the **Freedmen's Bureau**? Explain.
3. a. **Recall** Why was President Lincoln killed?
   b. **Analyze** Why did some Americans oppose President Johnson's Reconstruction plan?

Critical Thinking

4. **Explaining** Copy the chart below and use it to explain the federal government's solutions for solving the problems presented by Reconstruction.

Problems	Solutions

FOCUS ON WRITING

5. **Considering Historical Context** Many people planned to continue doing what they had done before the war. Others planned to start a new life. How do you think events and conditions you just read about might have affected their plans?

Section 1 Assessment Answers

1. a. the process of reuniting and rebuilding the nation after the Civil War
   b. offer amnesty if people swore loyalty to the U.S. and agreed that slavery was illegal; a state could be readmitted once 10 percent of the state's voters had done this
2. a. a constitutional amendment that made slavery illegal in the United States
   b. possible answer—creating more educational opportunities in the South; creating a better educated workforce.
3. a. Booth opposed Lincoln's policies.
   b. New representatives from the South had been Confederate leaders.
4. Problems—readmission of southern states, freeing slaves, helping rebuild; Solutions—Ten Percent Plan, Wade-Davis Bill, and Johnson's plan, ratifying the Thirteenth Amendment, creation of Freedmen's Bureau
5. Aftermath of war made it impossible for some to resume former life; others gained new opportunities.

Direct Teach

Main Idea

3 President Johnson's Reconstruction Plan

President Johnson's plan began the process of Reconstruction.

Explain After President Johnson approved the new governments of the southern states, Republicans complained. Why? *complained that many of the new southern representatives had been Confederate leaders and that Johnson's plan was too lenient on the South*

CRF: Biography Activity: Andrew Johnson

HSS 8.11.1; HSS **Analysis Skills:** HI 1

Review & Assess

Close

Have students write a short paragraph that summarizes the section.

Review

Online Quiz, Section 1

Assess

SE Section 1 Assessment

PASS: Section 1 Quiz

Alternative Assessment Handbook

Reteach/Classroom Intervention

California Standards Review Workbook

Interactive Reader and Study Guide, Section 1

Interactive Skills Tutor CD-ROM

Answers

Reading Check *Johnson wanted southern states to revise their constitutions, elect new representatives, declare secession illegal, and ratify the Thirteenth Amendment.*

Preteach

Bellringer

If YOU were there . . . Use the **Daily Bellringer Transparency** to help students answer the question.

 Daily Bellringer Transparency, Section 2

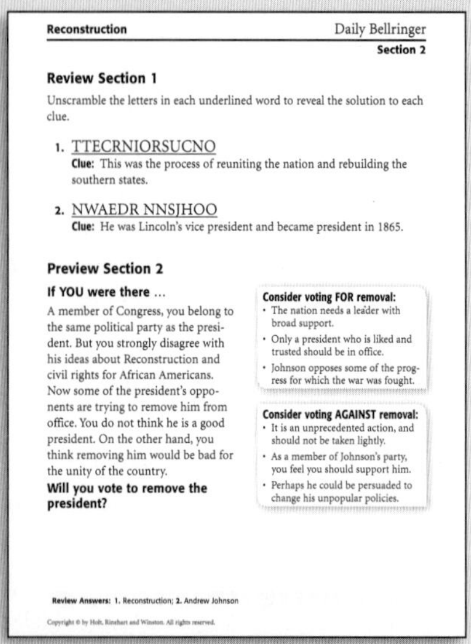

Reconstruction — Daily Bellringer Section 2

Review Section 1

Unscramble the letters in each underlined word to reveal the solution to each clue.

1. TTECRNIORSUCNO
   Clue: This was the process of reuniting the nation and rebuilding the southern states.
2. NWAEDR NNSJHOO
   Clue: He was Lincoln's vice president and became president in 1865.

Preview Section 2

If YOU were there ...

A member of Congress, you belong to the same political party as the president. But you strongly disagree with his ideas about Reconstruction and civil rights for African Americans. Now some of the president's opponents are trying to remove him from office. You do not think he is a good president. On the other hand, you think removing him would be bad for the unity of the country.

Will you vote to remove the president?

Consider voting FOR removal:
- The nation needs a leader with broad support.
- Only a president who is liked and trusted should be in office.
- Johnson opposes some of the progress for which the war was fought.

Consider voting AGAINST removal:
- It is an unprecedented action, and should not be taken lightly.
- As a member of Johnson's party, you feel you should support him.
- Perhaps he could be persuaded to change his unpopular policies.

Review Answers: 1. Reconstruction; 2. Andrew Johnson

Academic Vocabulary

Review with students the high-use academic term in this section.

principle basic belief, rule, or law (p. 520)

Building Vocabulary

Preteach or review the following term:

moderate one who holds views that are not extreme or excessive (p. 519)

CRF: Vocabulary Builder Activity, Section 2

Standards Focus

HSS 8.11.3

Means: Explain the freedoms of and restrictions on African Americans after the Civil War.

Matters: Reconstruction policies initially helped freedmen, but restrictions on their rights soon became common.

HSS 8.11.5

Means: Understand the purpose of the Thirteenth, Fourteenth, and Fifteenth Amendments.

Matters: Three important Reconstruction amendments changed life for African Americans.

SECTION 2

The Fight over Reconstruction

What You Will Learn...

Main Ideas

1. Black Codes led to opposition to President Johnson's plan for Reconstruction.
2. The Fourteenth Amendment ensured citizenship for African Americans.
3. Radical Republicans in Congress took charge of Reconstruction.
4. The Fifteenth Amendment gave African Americans the right to vote.

The Big Idea

The return to power of the pre-war southern leadership led Republicans in Congress to take control of Reconstruction.

Key Terms and People

HSS 8.11.3 Understand the effects of the Freedmen's Bureau and the restrictions placed on the rights and opportunities of freedmen, including racial segregation and "Jim Crow" laws.

8.11.5 Understand the Thirteenth, Fourteenth, and Fifteenth Amendments to the Constitution and analyze their connection to Reconstruction.

If YOU were there...

A member of Congress, you belong to the same political party as the president. But you strongly disagree with his ideas about Reconstruction and civil rights for African Americans. Now some of the president's opponents are trying to remove him from office. You do not think he is a good president. On the other hand, you think removing him would be bad for the unity of the country.

Will you vote to remove the president?

BUILDING BACKGROUND Americans were bitterly divided about what should happen in the South during Reconstruction. They disagreed about ending racial inequality and guaranteeing civil rights for African Americans. These conflicts split political parties. They led to showdowns between Congress and the president. Political fights even threatened the president's job.

Opposition to President Johnson

In 1866 Congress continued to debate the rules for restoring the Union. Meanwhile, new state legislatures approved by President Johnson had already begun passing laws to deny African Americans' civil rights. "This is a white man's government, and intended for white men only," declared Governor Benjamin F. Perry of South Carolina.

Black Codes

Soon, every southern state passed **Black Codes**, or laws that greatly limited the freedom of African Americans. They required African Americans to sign work contracts, creating working conditions similar to those under slavery. In most southern states, any African Americans who could not prove they were employed could be arrested. Their punishment might be one year of work without pay. African Americans were also prevented from owning guns. In addition, they were not allowed to rent property except in cities.

The Black Codes alarmed many Americans. As one Civil War veteran asked, "If you call this freedom, what do you call slavery?"

Teach the Big Idea: Master the Standards

Standards Proficiency

The Fight over Reconstruction

HSS 8.11.3, 8.11.5; HSS **Analysis Skills:** HI 1

1. **Teach** Ask students the Main Idea questions to teach this section.
2. **Apply** Draw a four-column chart for students to see. Label the columns *Opposition to President Johnson, Fourteenth Amendment, Congress Takes Control,* and *Fifteenth Amendment.* Have each student make a copy of the chart and complete it by listing the section's main ideas and events in the appropriate column. LS **Verbal/Linguistic**
3. **Review** To review the section's main ideas, have students help you complete the master copy of the chart.
4. **Practice/Homework** For each column in the chart, have students write one to three sentences summarizing the information they identified. LS **Verbal/Linguistic**

Alternative Assessment Handbook, Rubric 7: Charts

African Americans organized to oppose the codes. One group sent a petition to officials in South Carolina.

> "We simply ask . . . that the same laws which govern *white men* shall govern *black men* . . . that, in short, we be dealt with as others are—in equity [equality] and justice."
>
> —Petition from an African American convention held in South Carolina, quoted in *There Is a River: The Black Struggle for Freedom in America* by Vincent Harding

Radical Republicans

The Black Codes angered many Republicans who felt the South was returning to its old ways. Most Republicans were moderates who wanted the South to have loyal state governments. They also believed that African Americans should have rights as citizens. They hoped that the national government would not have to force the South to follow federal laws.

Radical Republicans on the other hand, took a harsher stance. They wanted the federal government to force change in the South. Like the moderates, they thought the Black Codes were cruel and unjust. The radicals, however, wanted the federal government to be much more involved in Reconstruction. They feared that too many southern leaders remained loyal to the former Confederacy and would not enforce the new laws. Thaddeus Stevens

Primary Source

POLITICAL CARTOON

Supporting Radical Republican Ideas

Republicans were outraged to see former Confederates return to power as leaders of the Democratic Party. This 1868 political cartoon shows former Confederates Raphael Semmes and Nathan Bedford Forrest. Semmes was a Confederate admiral who had captured 62 Union merchant ships during the Civil War. Forrest was a cavalry officer known for brutality who later founded the Ku Klux Klan.

LEADERS OF THE DEMOCRATIC PARTY.

THE PIRATE SEMMES.

THE BUTCHER FORREST.

How do the actions of the people in these illustrations support the artist's point of view?

How do events in the background of these illustrations support the artist's point of view?

ANALYSIS SKILL ANALYZING PRIMARY SOURCES

Why do you think that the men are shown in their Confederate uniforms?

Direct Teach

Main Idea

❶ Opposition to President Johnson

Black Codes led to opposition to President Johnson's plan for Reconstruction.

Describe In what ways did Black Codes limit the freedom of African Americans? *by requiring them to sign work contracts and to have a job or be subject to arrest, and by forbidding the ownership of guns and the rental of property in cities*

Explain What were Radical Republicans' goals for Reconstruction? *They wanted the federal government to be much more involved and the South to change much more before returning to the Union.*

HSS 8.11.3; HSS **Analysis Skills:** HI 1, HI 2

Primary Source

Reading Like a Historian

Supporting Radical Republican Ideas Help students practice reading the political cartoon like historians. Ask:

- What is the point of view expressed in the political cartoon?
- Does the cartoon appear to be objective about the subject matter? What indicates that?

Differentiating Instruction for Universal Access

English-Language Learners Standards Proficiency

1. Organize students into mixed-ability pairs. Have each pair review the information on opposition to President Johnson's Reconstruction plan.
2. Explain to students that an acrostic is a type of poem in which the first letter from each line spells out a word. Have students create an acrostic for one of the key terms or people discussed under this heading. Each acrostic should reflect the views or concepts associated with the key term or person. You may want to model an example for the class by using a person or idea from the previous section for your acrostic.
3. As students work on their acrostics, they might require assistance thinking of words to fit in their poem. Help students or refer them to a thesaurus. LS **Verbal/Linguistic**

HSS 8.11.3; HSS **Analysis Skills:** HI 1

Alternative Assessment Handbook, Rubric 26: Poems and Songs

Answers

Analyzing Primary Sources *possible answers—to show that they are still Confederates at heart; to show that the Confederacy condoned their actions.*

Direct Teach

Main Idea

❷ Fourteenth Amendment

The Fourteenth Amendment ensured citizenship for African Americans.

Recall What was the purpose of the proposed Freedmen's Bureau Bill, and why did Johnson veto it? *It was supposed to give the Freedmen's Bureau more powers; he did not want Congress to pass any laws until southern states were represented.*

Explain Why was the Civil Rights Act of 1866 created? *When Johnson vetoed the Freedmen's Bureau Bill, Congress countered by passing the Civil Rights Act of 1866.*

Generalize What rights did the Fourteenth Amendment protect? *defined citizens and guaranteed citizens equal protection*

- **CRF:** Biography Activity: Thaddeus Stevens
- Map Transparency: Reconstruction Military Districts
- HSS 8.11.3, 8.11.5; HSS **Analysis Skills:** HI 1

go.hrw.com
Online Resources
KEYWORD: SS8 US16
ACTIVITY: Writing Editorials for a Newspaper

Answers

Identifying Points of View *Johnson felt that the military government would cause the South to resent the federal government, but Stevens believed that the federal government should control the South.*

Reading Check *similar—Both wanted loyalty to the Union and rights for African Americans; different—Moderates wanted little federal involvement, but radicals wanted more rights for African Americans and more federal involvement.*

520

Primary Source

POINTS OF VIEW
Johnson vs. Stevens

President Andrew Johnson argued that the South should not be placed under military control.

"Military governments . . . established for an indefinite period, would have divided the people into the vanquishers and the vanquished, and would have envenomed [made poisonous] hatred rather than have restored affection."
—Andrew Johnson

Thaddeus Stevens believed that Congress had the power to treat the South as conquered territory.

"The future condition of the conquered power depends on the will of the conqueror. They must come in as new states or remain as conquered provinces. Congress . . . is the only power that can act in the matter."
—Thaddeus Stevens

ANALYSIS SKILL **IDENTIFYING POINTS OF VIEW**
How did Johnson's and Stevens's views on the South differ?

of Pennsylvania and Charles Sumner of Massachusetts were the leaders of the Radical Republicans.

A harsh critic of President Johnson, Stevens was known for his honesty and sharp tongue. He wanted economic and political justice for both African Americans and poor white southerners. Sumner had been a strong opponent of slavery before the Civil War. He continued to argue tirelessly for African Americans' civil rights, including the right to vote and the right to fair laws.

Both Stevens and Sumner believed that President Johnson's Reconstruction plan was a failure. Although the Radicals did not control Congress, they began to gain support among moderates when President Johnson ignored criticism of the Black Codes. Stevens believed the federal government could not allow racial inequality to survive.

READING CHECK **Comparing and Contrasting** How were Radical Republicans and moderate Republicans similar and different?

ACADEMIC VOCABULARY
principle basic belief, rule, or law

Fourteenth Amendment

Urged on by the Radicals in 1866, Congress proposed a new bill. It would give the Freedmen's Bureau more powers. The law would allow the Freedmen's Bureau to use military courts to try people accused of violating African Americans' rights. The bill's supporters hoped that these courts would be fairer than local courts in the South.

Johnson versus Congress

To the surprise of many in Congress, Johnson vetoed the Freedmen's Bureau Bill. He insisted that Congress could not pass any new laws until the southern states were represented in Congress. Johnson also argued that the Freedmen's Bureau was unconstitutional.

Republicans responded with the **Civil Rights Act of 1866**. This act provided African Americans with the same legal rights as white Americans. President Johnson once again used his veto power. He argued that the act gave too much power to the federal government. He also rejected the principle of equal

Collaborative Learning

Standards Proficiency

Breaking News on the Fourteenth Amendment

Research Required

1. Organize students into groups. Students will research, write, and enact a newscast featuring the lead story of the day, "Fourteenth Amendment Is Ratified." Have students use the library, Internet, or other resources to gather information.
2. Have each group create a news skit summarizing events leading up to the ratification of the amendment. Remind groups to provide information regarding the provisions of the Fourteenth Amendment as well as voting information from Congress and from some of the states.
3. Encourage students to act out dialogue between anchors or have students cut to a reporter standing by "on the scene."
4. Have each group perform its broadcast.
LS Interpersonal, Verbal/Linguistic

- Alternative Assessment Handbook, Rubrics 14: Group Activity; and 33: Skits and Reader's Theater
- HSS 8.11.3, 8.11.5; HSS **Analysis Skills:** HI 1

rights for African Americans. Congress, however, overrode Johnson's veto.

Many Republicans worried about what would happen when the southern states were readmitted. Fearing that the Civil Rights Act might be overturned, the Republicans proposed the **Fourteenth Amendment** in the summer of 1866. The Fourteenth Amendment included the following provisions.

1. It defined all people born or naturalized within the United States, except Native Americans, as citizens.
2. It guaranteed citizens the equal protection of the laws.
3. It said that states could not "deprive any person of life, liberty, or property, without due process of law."
4. It banned many former Confederate officials from holding state or federal offices.
5. It made state laws subject to federal court review.
6. It gave Congress the power to pass any laws needed to enforce it.

1866 Elections

President Johnson and most Democrats opposed the Fourteenth Amendment. As a result, civil rights for African Americans became a key issue in the 1866 congressional elections. To help the Democrats, Johnson traveled around the country defending his Reconstruction plan. Johnson's speaking tour was a disaster. It did little to win votes for the Democratic Party. Johnson even got into arguments with people in the audiences of some of his speaking engagements.

Two major riots in the South also hurt Johnson's campaign. On May 1, 1866, a dispute in Memphis, Tennessee, took place between local police and black Union soldiers. The dispute turned into a three-day wave of violence against African Americans. About three months later, another riot took place during a political demonstration in New Orleans. During that dispute, 34 African Americans and three white Republicans were killed.

READING CHECK **Summarizing** What issue did the Fourteenth Amendment address, and how did it affect the congressional elections of 1866?

Congress Takes Control of Reconstruction

The 1866 elections gave the Republican Party a commanding two-thirds majority in both the House and the Senate. This majority gave the Republicans the power to override any presidential veto. In addition, the Republicans became united as the moderates joined with the Radicals. Together, they called for a new form of Reconstruction.

Reconstruction Acts

In March 1867, Congress passed the first of several **Reconstruction Acts**. These laws divided the South into five districts. A U.S. military commander controlled each district.

Reconstruction Military Districts

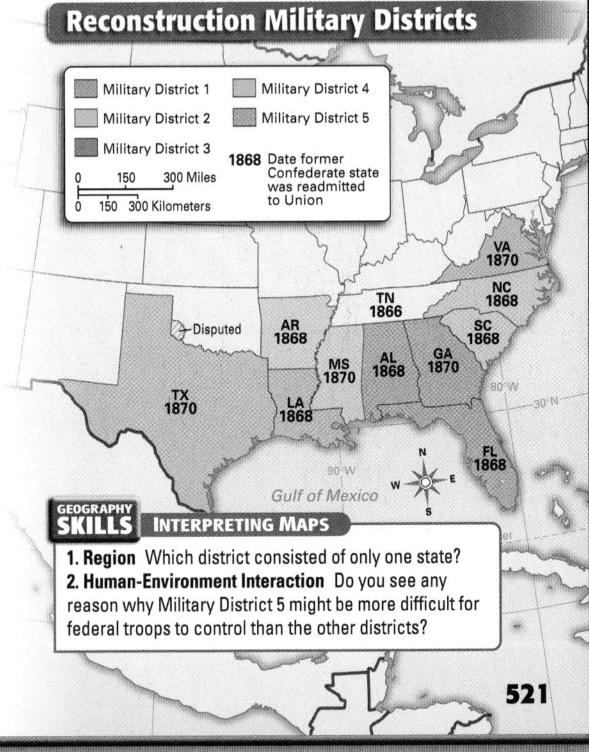

GEOGRAPHY SKILLS **INTERPRETING MAPS**

1. **Region** Which district consisted of only one state?
2. **Human-Environment Interaction** Do you see any reason why Military District 5 might be more difficult for federal troops to control than the other districts?

Direct Teach

Did you know . . .

President Johnson often got into arguments with audience members during his speaking tour in 1866. During one of his speeches, someone in the audience cried out, "Hang Jeff Davis!" Johnson replied angrily, "Why not Thad Stevens?"

Info to Know

Southern Riots One of the worst riots during the campaign of 1866 took place in Memphis, Tennessee, in May 1866. The riot began when African American veterans protested the arrest of an African American carriage driver after he was involved in a collision with a white driver. Three days of racial violence followed, resulting in the deaths of 48 people and the burning and looting of countless buildings in South Memphis.

Interpreting Maps

Reconstruction Military Districts

Location Which military district was the last to be readmitted to the Union? *District 1, Virginia*

Place What southern state was readmitted without having been made part of a military district? *Tennessee*

Map Transparency: Reconstruction Military Districts

Critical Thinking: Summarizing

Standards Proficiency

Covering the Elections of 1866

HSS 8.11.3; HSS **Analysis Skills:** HI 1, HI 2

1. Review the events under the heading 1866 Elections. Discuss with students the key issue of the elections as well as President Johnson's speaking tour and the riots that broke out during this period.
2. Ask each student to select one of the events discussed. Have each student write a newspaper article about the event from the perspective of a reporter at the time.
3. Remind students that their newspaper articles must explain the "who, what, when, where, why, and how" surrounding the event. Articles should also include an attention-grabbing headline, a byline, and a dateline.
4. Ask volunteers to share their newspaper articles with the class. LS **Verbal/Linguistic**

Alternative Assessment Handbook, Rubric 23: Newspapers

Answers

Interpreting Maps **1.** *District 1, Virginia;* **2.** *larger, farther away from Washington, D.C.*

Reading Check *equal protection under the law for all citizens; led to civil rights becoming the key issue in the 1866 elections and to violence over the dispute*

Direct Teach

Main Idea

3 Congress Takes Control of Reconstruction

Radical Republicans in Congress took charge of Reconstruction.

Describe How were states to be readmitted under the Reconstruction Acts? *States had to write a new constitution supporting the Fourteenth Amendment and give African American men the right to vote.*

Identify Cause and Effect What led Congress to call for the impeachment of President Johnson, and what was the result of the impeachment trial? *Johnson removed a cabinet official, which Congress had to approve; Johnson was not convicted.*

Recall Who won the election of 1868? *Ulysses S. Grant*

CRF: History and Geography Activity: The Reconstruction Acts

Quick Facts Transparency: The Reconstruction Amendments

HSS 8.11.5; HSS **Analysis Skills:** CS 1, HI 1, HI 2

MISCONCEPTION ALERT

Impeachment People often misunderstand the meaning of the word *impeachment.* The term does not mean "removal from office." It means only that a public official has been charged with improper conduct of some sort.

Did you know . . .

In the history of the United States, two presidents have faced impeachment proceedings—Andrew Johnson in 1868 and Bill Clinton in 1998. Both presidents were acquitted of the charges.

The military would remain in control of the South until the southern states rejoined the Union. To be readmitted, a state had to write a new state constitution supporting the Fourteenth Amendment. Finally, the state had to give African American men the right to vote.

Thaddeus Stevens was one of the new Reconstruction Acts' most enthusiastic supporters. He spoke in Congress to defend the acts.

"Have not loyal blacks quite as good a right to choose rulers and make laws as rebel whites? Every man, no matter what his race or color . . . has an equal right to justice, honesty, and fair play with every other man; and the law should secure him those rights."

–Thaddeus Stevens, quoted in *Sources of the American Republic,* edited by Marvin Meyers et al.

The Reconstruction Amendments QUICK FACTS

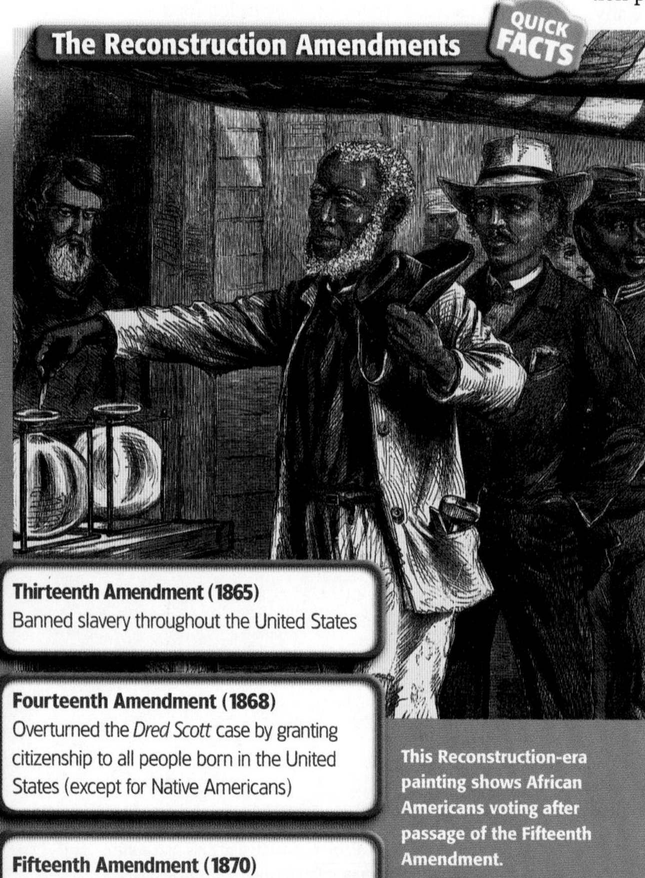

Thirteenth Amendment (1865)
Banned slavery throughout the United States

Fourteenth Amendment (1868)
Overturned the *Dred Scott* case by granting citizenship to all people born in the United States (except for Native Americans)

Fifteenth Amendment (1870)
Gave African American men the right to vote

This Reconstruction-era painting shows African Americans voting after passage of the Fifteenth Amendment.

What right did the Fifteenth Amendment protect?

President on Trial

President Johnson strongly disagreed with Stevens. He argued that African Americans did not deserve the same treatment as white people. The Reconstruction Acts, he said, used "powers not granted to the federal government or any one of its branches." Knowing that Johnson did not support its Reconstruction policies, Congress passed a law limiting his power. This law prevented the president from removing cabinet officials without Senate approval. Johnson quickly broke the law by firing Edwin Stanton, the secretary of war.

For the first time in United States history, the House of Representatives responded by voting to impeach the president. **Impeachment** is the process used by a legislative body to bring charges of wrongdoing against a public official. The next step, under Article I of the Constitution, was a trial in the Senate. A two-thirds majority was required to find Johnson guilty and remove him from office.

Although Johnson was unpopular with Republicans, some of them believed he was being judged unfairly. Others did not trust the president pro tempore of the Senate, Benjamin Wade. He would become president if Johnson were removed from office. By a single vote, Senate Republicans failed to convict Johnson. Even so, the trial broke his power as president.

Election of 1868

Johnson did not run for another term in 1868. Instead, the Demo-

Collaborative Learning

Exceeding Standards

Conducting an Impeachment Trial HSS 8.11

Research Required

1. As a class, conduct a mock impeachment trial for President Andrew Johnson.
2. Organize the class into four groups. Assign one group to act as impeachment managers for the House of Representatives and to present the case against the president. Have the second group prepare a defense of the president. Assign a third group to prepare and ask questions of witnesses. The fourth group will listen to testimony and vote on the charges presented.
3. Have each group use the library, Internet, or other resources to gather information about the impeachment proceedings against Andrew Johnson. Then have the class stage the mock trial.
4. After the trial, discuss with students what happened during each aspect of the actual case and how it affected Reconstruction.

LS Interpersonal, Verbal/Linguistic

Alternative Assessment Handbook, Rubric 10: Debates

Answers

The Reconstruction Amendments *the right of African American men to vote* crats chose former New York governor Horatio Seymour as their presidential candidate. The Republicans chose Ulysses S. Grant. As a war hero, Grant appealed to many northern voters. He had no political experience but supported the congressional Reconstruction plan. He ran under the slogan "Let Us Have Peace."

Shortly after Grant was nominated, Congress readmitted seven southern states—Alabama, Arkansas, Florida, Georgia, Louisiana, North Carolina, and South Carolina. (Tennessee had already been readmitted in 1866.) Under the terms of readmission, these seven states approved the Fourteenth Amendment. They also agreed to let African American men vote. However, white southerners used violence to try to keep African Americans away from the polls.

Despite such tactics, hundreds of thousands of African Americans voted for Grant and the "party of Lincoln." The *New Orleans Tribune* reported that many former slaves "see clearly enough that the Republican party [is] their political life boat." African American votes helped Grant to win a narrow victory.

READING CHECK **Analyzing** To what voters did Grant appeal in the presidential election of 1868?

Fifteenth Amendment

After Grant's victory, Congressional Republicans wanted to protect their Reconstruction plan. They worried that the southern states might try to keep black voters from the polls in future elections. Also, some Radical Republicans argued that it was not fair that many northern states still had laws preventing African Americans from voting. After all, every southern state was required to grant suffrage to African American men.

In 1869 Congress proposed the **Fifteenth Amendment**, which gave African American men the right to vote. Abolitionist William Lloyd Garrison praised "this wonderful, quiet, sudden transformation of four millions of human beings from . . . the auction block to the ballot-box." The amendment went into effect in 1870. It was one of the last important Reconstruction laws passed at the federal level.

The Fifteenth Amendment did not please every reformer, however. Many women were angry because the amendment did not also grant them the right to vote.

THE IMPACT TODAY

Today the Voting Rights Act of 1965 enforces and expands the voting protections of the Fifteenth Amendment.

READING CHECK **Finding Main Ideas** How did Radical Republicans take control of Reconstruction?

SUMMARY AND PREVIEW In this section you learned that Congress took control of Reconstruction away from President Johnson and took steps to protect the rights of African Americans. In the next section you will learn about increasing opposition to Reconstruction.

Section 2 Assessment

go.hrw.com
Online Quiz
KEYWORD: SS8 HP16

Reviewing Ideas, Terms, and People

HSS 8.11.3, 8.11.5

1. a. **Describe** What were **Black Codes**?
   b. **Make Inferences** Why did Republicans think Johnson's Reconstruction plan was a failure?
2. a. **Recall** What was the **Civil Rights Act of 1866**?
   b. **Summarize** Why was the **Fourteenth Amendment** important?
3. a. **Recall** Why was President Johnson impeached?
   b. **Evaluate** Which element of the **Reconstruction Acts** do you believe was most important? Why?
4. a. **Recall** What does the **Fifteenth Amendment** state?
   b. **Elaborate** Do you think that women should have been included in the Fifteenth Amendment? Explain.

Critical Thinking

5. **Analyzing** Copy the chart below. Use it to identify the main provisions of the fourteenth Amendment and their effects.

Provisions	Effects

FOCUS ON WRITING

6. **Recognizing Cause-and-Effect Relationships** As you have read in this section, social and political unrest continued long after the war ended. How could this unrest cause people to leave their jobs? What new jobs might they find?

Direct Teach

Main Idea

4 Fifteenth Amendment

The Fifteenth Amendment gave African Americans the right to vote.

Identify When did the Fifteenth Amendment go into effect? *1870*

Make Predictions What effect might the Fifteenth Amendment have on women in the United States? *possible answers—They might be angry that they did not gain the right to vote; they might demand voting rights.*

Activity **Illustrated Amendments** Have students create a drawing for each of the three Reconstruction amendments. LS **Visual/Spatial**

HSS 8.11.5; HSS **Analysis Skills:** CS 1, HI 1

Review & Assess

Close

Discuss with the class how Congress changed Reconstruction.

Review

Online Quiz, Section 2

Assess

SE Section 2 Assessment

PASS: Section 2 Quiz

Alternative Assessment Handbook

Reteach/Classroom Intervention

California Standards Review Workbook

Interactive Reader and Study Guide, Section 2

Interactive Skills Tutor CD-ROM

Section 2 Assessment Answers

1. **a.** laws that limited rights and opportunities for African Americans
   b. It allowed Black Codes and returned Confederate leaders to power.
2. **a.** It provided African Americans the same rights as white Americans.
   b. See the numbered list on p. 521.
3. **a.** He removed a cabinet official without the approval of Congress.
   b. possible answer—gave African Americans the right to vote; because that allowed them a say in government
4. **a.** It gave African American citizens the right to vote in all states.
   b. Answers will vary, but students should provide a rationale for their answers.
5. Provisions—see list on p. 521; effects—former slaves granted citizenship, protected from restrictions of Black Codes, removed Confederate leaders from power in the South, and gave Congress more control over enforcing these laws.
6. possible answer—Riots might cause people to flee jobs in the South.

Answers

Reading Check (left) *northern voters and African Americans;* **(right)** *The 1866 elections gave them a majority in both houses of Congress; they overrode presidential vetoes and took power from Johnson.*

Preteach

Bellringer

If YOU were there . . . Use the **Daily Bellringer Transparency** to help students answer the question.

 Daily Bellringer Transparency, Section 3

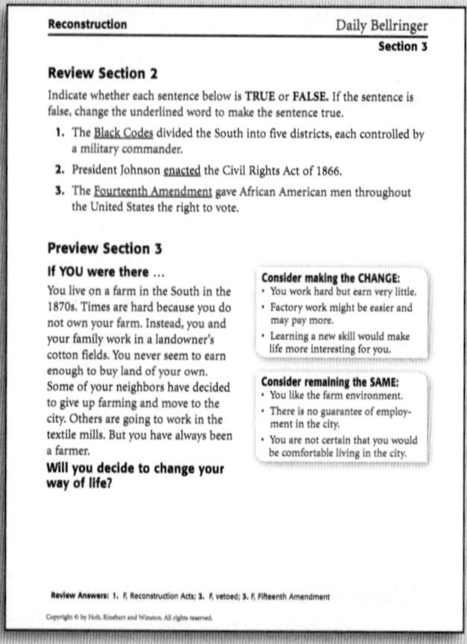

Reconstruction — Daily Bellringer — Section 3

Review Section 2

Indicate whether each sentence below is TRUE or FALSE. If the sentence is false, change the underlined word to make the sentence true.

1. The Black Codes divided the South into five districts, each controlled by a military commander.
2. President Johnson enacted the Civil Rights Act of 1866.
3. The Fourteenth Amendment gave African American men throughout the United States the right to vote.

Preview Section 3

If YOU were there ...

You live on a farm in the South in the 1870s. Times are hard because you do not own your farm. Instead, you and your family work in a landowner's cotton fields. You never seem to earn enough to buy land of your own. Some of your neighbors have decided to give up farming and move to the city. Others are going to work in the textile mills. But you have always been a farmer.

Will you decide to change your way of life?

Consider making the CHANGE:
- You work hard but earn very little.
- Factory work might be easier and may pay more.
- Learning a new skill would make life more interesting for you.

Consider remaining the SAME:
- You like the farm environment.
- There is no guarantee of employment in the city.
- You are not certain that you would be comfortable living in the city.

Review Answers: 1. F, Reconstruction Acts; 2. F, vetoed; 3. F, Fifteenth Amendment

Building Vocabulary

Preteach or review the following term:

carpetbaggers northerners who moved to the South during Reconstruction (p. 524)

CRF: Vocabulary Builder Activity, Section 3

Standards Focus

HSS 8.11.1
Means: List the original goals of Reconstruction and its effects on government and society in the United States.
Matters: Reconstruction continued to divide the North and the South.

HSS 8.11.3
Means: Explain the freedoms of and restrictions on African Americans after the Civil War.
Matters: Reconstruction policies initially helped freedpeople, but restrictions on their rights soon became common.

HSS 8.11.4
Means: Explain the origins of the Ku Klux Klan and its effects on the South.
Matters: The Ku Klux Klan used violence and terror to maintain segregation.

SECTION 3

Reconstruction in the South

What You Will Learn...

Main Ideas

1. Reconstruction governments helped reform the South.
2. The Ku Klux Klan was organized as African Americans moved into positions of power.
3. As Reconstruction ended, the rights of African Americans were restricted.
4. Southern business leaders relied on industry to rebuild the South.

The Big Idea

As Reconstruction ended, African Americans faced new hurdles and the South attempted to rebuild.

Key Terms and People

Hiram Revels, *p. 525*
Ku Klux Klan, *p. 526*
Compromise of 1877, *p. 527*
poll tax, *p. 528*
segregation, *p. 528*
Jim Crow laws, *p. 528*
Plessy v. *Ferguson*, *p. 529*
sharecropping, *p. 529*

HSS 8.11.1 List the original aims of Reconstruction and describe its effects on the political and social structures of different regions.

8.11.3 Understand the effects of the Freedmen's Bureau and the restrictions placed on the rights and opportunities of freedmen, including racial segregation and "Jim Crow" laws.

8.11.4 Trace the rise of the Ku Klux Klan and describe the Klan's effects.

If YOU were there...

You live on a farm in the South in the 1870s. Times are hard because you do not own your farm. Instead, you and your family work in a landowner's cotton fields. You never seem to earn enough to buy land of your own. Some of your neighbors have decided to give up farming and move to the city. Others are going to work in the textile mills. But you have always been a farmer.

Will you decide to change your way of life?

BUILDING BACKGROUND Reconstruction affected politics and economics in the South. Republican and Democratic politicians fought over policies and programs. New state governments began reforms, but later leaders ended many of them. Some parts of the southern economy improved. However, many farmers, like the family above, went through hard times.

Reconstruction Governments

After Grant became president in 1869, the Republicans seemed stronger than ever. They controlled most southern governments, partly because of the support of African American voters. However, most of the Republican officeholders were unpopular with white southerners.

Carpetbaggers and Scalawags

Some of these office-holders were northern-born Republicans who had moved South after the war. Many white southerners called them carpetbaggers. Supposedly, they had rushed South carrying all their possessions in bags made from carpeting. Many southerners resented these northerners, accusing them—often unfairly—of trying to profit from Reconstruction.

Southern Democrats cared even less for white southern Republicans. They referred to them as scalawags, or greedy rascals. Democrats believed that these southerners had betrayed the South by

Teach the Big Idea: Master the Standards

Standards Proficiency

Reconstruction in the South

HSS 8.11.1, 8.11.3, 8.11.4; HSS **Analysis Skills:** HI 1

1. **Teach** Ask students the Main Idea questions to teach this section.
2. **Apply** Help students list the main people, events, and issues in the section. Then ask students to imagine that they are news reporters. Have each student write one news headline for each of the section's main events and issues. Model the activity for students by doing the first headline as a class. **LS Verbal/Linguistic**
3. **Review** As you review the section's main ideas, have students share their related headlines with the class.
4. **Practice/Homework** Select one headline and have each student write a news article or draw a political cartoon to accompany the headline. **LS Verbal/Linguistic, Visual/Spatial**

Alternative Assessment Handbook, Rubrics 27: Political Cartoons; and 42: Writing to Inform

African American Representation in the South, 1870

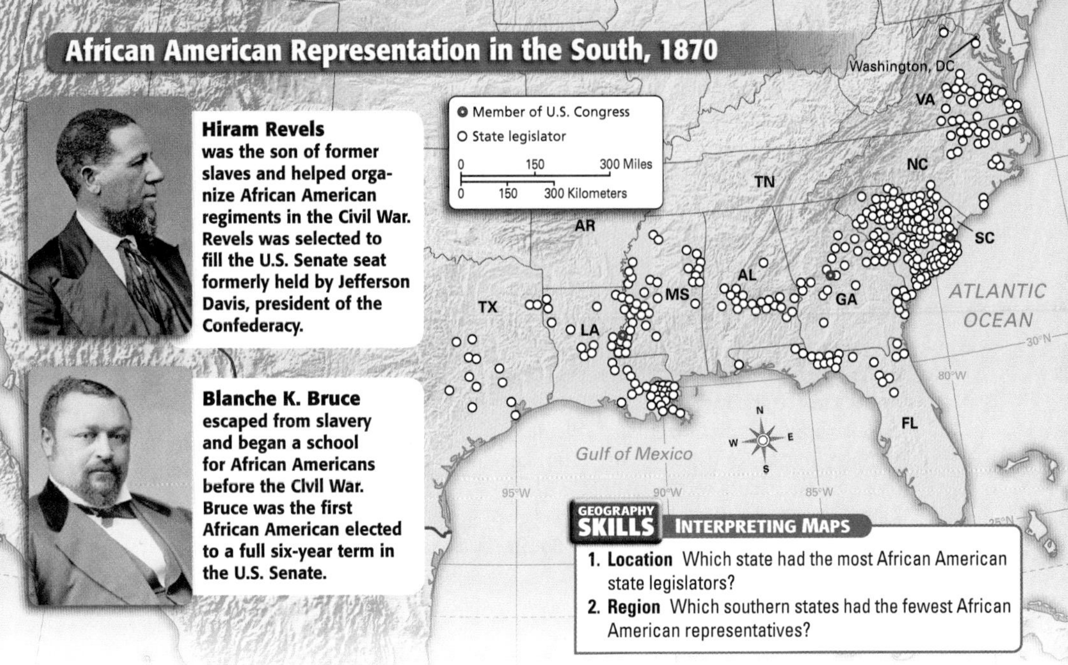

Hiram Revels was the son of former slaves and helped organize African American regiments in the Civil War. Revels was selected to fill the U.S. Senate seat formerly held by Jefferson Davis, president of the Confederacy.

Blanche K. Bruce escaped from slavery and began a school for African Americans before the Civil War. Bruce was the first African American elected to a full six-year term in the U.S. Senate.

GEOGRAPHY SKILLS INTERPRETING MAPS

1. **Location** Which state had the most African American state legislators?
2. **Region** Which southern states had the fewest African American representatives?

voting for the Republican Party. Many southern Republicans were small farmers who had supported the Union during the war. Others, like Mississippi governor James Alcorn, were former members of the Whig Party. They preferred to become Republicans rather than join the Democrats.

African American Leaders

African Americans were the largest group of southern Republican voters. During Reconstruction, more than 600 African Americans won election to state legislatures. Some 16 of these politicians were elected to Congress. Other African Americans held local offices in counties throughout the South.

African American politicians came from many backgrounds. **Hiram Revels** was born free in North Carolina and went to college in Illinois. He became a Methodist minister and served as a chaplain in the Union army. In 1870 Revels became the first African American in the U.S. Senate. He took over the seat previously held by Confederate president Jefferson Davis. Unlike Revels, Blanche K. Bruce grew up in slavery in Virginia. Bruce became an important Republican in Mississippi and served one term as a U.S. senator.

State Governments Change Direction

Reconstruction governments provided money for many new programs and organizations in the South. They helped to establish some of the first state-funded public school systems in the South. They also built new hospitals, prisons, and orphanages and passed laws prohibiting discrimination against African Americans.

FOCUS ON READING
How does the heading of this section tell you about what you will learn?

Southern states under Republican control spent large amounts of money. They aided the construction of railroads, bridges, and public buildings. These improvements were intended to help the southern economy recover from the war. To get the money for these projects, the Reconstruction governments raised taxes and issued bonds.

READING CHECK **Summarizing** What reforms did Reconstruction state governments carry out?

Direct Teach

Main Idea

1 Reconstruction Governments

Reconstruction governments helped reform the South.

Contrast How were scalawags and carpetbaggers different? *Scalawags were southerners who supported Reconstruction governments, whereas carpetbaggers were northerners who moved to the South.*

Summarize How did African Americans participate in government during Reconstruction? *voted, served as representatives in state legislatures and in Congress, and held local offices*

Make Inferences Why did southern Reconstruction governments focus on building railroads and bridges? *They wanted to improve the transportation and economy of the South to rebuild after the war*

- **CRF:** Biography Activity: Blanche K. Bruce
- Map Transparency: African American Representation in the South, 1870
- **HSS** 8.11.1; **HSS Analysis Skills:** HI 1

Did you know . . .

One well-known northerner who moved to the South during Reconstruction was novelist Harriet Beecher Stowe. In the 1860s Stowe and her family purchased a winter home near Jacksonville, Florida. She spent much of her time there helping to establish schools for African Americans and improving the lives of freedpeople.

Critical Thinking: Summarizing

Reaching Standards

Making Political Slogans **HSS** 8.11.1; **HSS Analysis Skills:** HI 1, HI 2

1. Review with students the new Reconstruction governments created in the South. Have students discuss the policies of many southern governments.
2. Ask students to imagine that they are Republican officials in the South. Have each student create two or three political banners with slogans that describe reforms enacted by Republican governments. Remind students that political banners should help promote the accomplishments of their party.
3. Have students illustrate their banners. Display students banners around the classroom.
LS Verbal/Linguistic, Visual/Spatial

- Alternative Assessment Handbook, Rubric 34: Slogans and Banners

Answers

Interpreting Maps **1.** *South Carolina;* **2.** *Tennessee, Arkansas, Texas, Florida*

Focus on Reading *The heading tells you the main idea of the section.*

Reading Check *established public schools; built hospitals, prisons, and orphanages; passed laws prohibiting discrimination; aided the construction of railroads, bridges, and public buildings*

Direct Teach

Main Idea

❷ Ku Klux Klan

The Ku Klux Klan was organized as African Americans moved into positions of power.

Explain Why did resistance to Reconstruction increase? *Some southerners claimed the new governments were corrupt, illegal, and unjust; disapproved of African American officeholders; and disliked having federal troops in their states.*

Summarize How did the federal government address the activities of the Ku Klux Klan? *Congress passed laws that made it a federal crime to interfere with elections or to deny citizens equal protection under the law.*

CRF: Primary Source Activity: Reconstruction and the Ku Klux Klan

HSS 8.11.4; HSS **Analysis Skills:** HI 1, CS 2

Info to Know

Stopping the Klan As violence against African Americans mounted, many Americans demanded that the government take action. Congress responded to this call in 1870 and 1871 by passing legislation designed to stop violence and discrimination against African Americans. Known as the Enforcement Acts, these laws were designed to enforce the Fifteenth Amendment and to stop the Ku Klux Klan. The Enforcement Acts authorized President Grant to send federal troops to restore order. In 1871 nine counties in South Carolina were placed under martial law after an outbreak of Klan violence. Due to the Enforcement Acts, hundreds of Klan members were tried and imprisoned, leading to the Klan's decline.

Ku Klux Klan

As more African Americans took office, resistance to Reconstruction increased among white southerners. Democrats claimed that the Reconstruction governments were corrupt, illegal, and unjust. They also disliked having federal soldiers stationed in their states. Many white southerners disapproved of African American officeholders. One Democrat noted, "'A white man's government' [is] the most popular rallying cry we have." In 1866 a group of white southerners in Tennessee created the **Ku Klux Klan**. This secret society opposed civil rights, particularly suffrage, for African Americans. The Klan used violence and terror against African Americans. The group's membership grew rapidly as it spread throughout the South. Klan members wore robes and disguises to hide their identities. They attacked—and even murdered—African Americans, white Republican voters, and public officials, usually at night.

Local governments did little to stop the violence. Many officials feared the Klan or were sympathetic to its activities. In 1870 and 1871 the federal government took action. Congress passed laws that made it a federal crime to interfere with elections or to deny citizens equal protection under the law.

Within a few years, the Klan was no longer an organized threat. But groups of whites continued to assault African Americans and Republicans throughout the 1870s.

READING CHECK **Drawing Conclusions** Why did southerners join the Ku Klux Klan?

The Ku Klux Klan

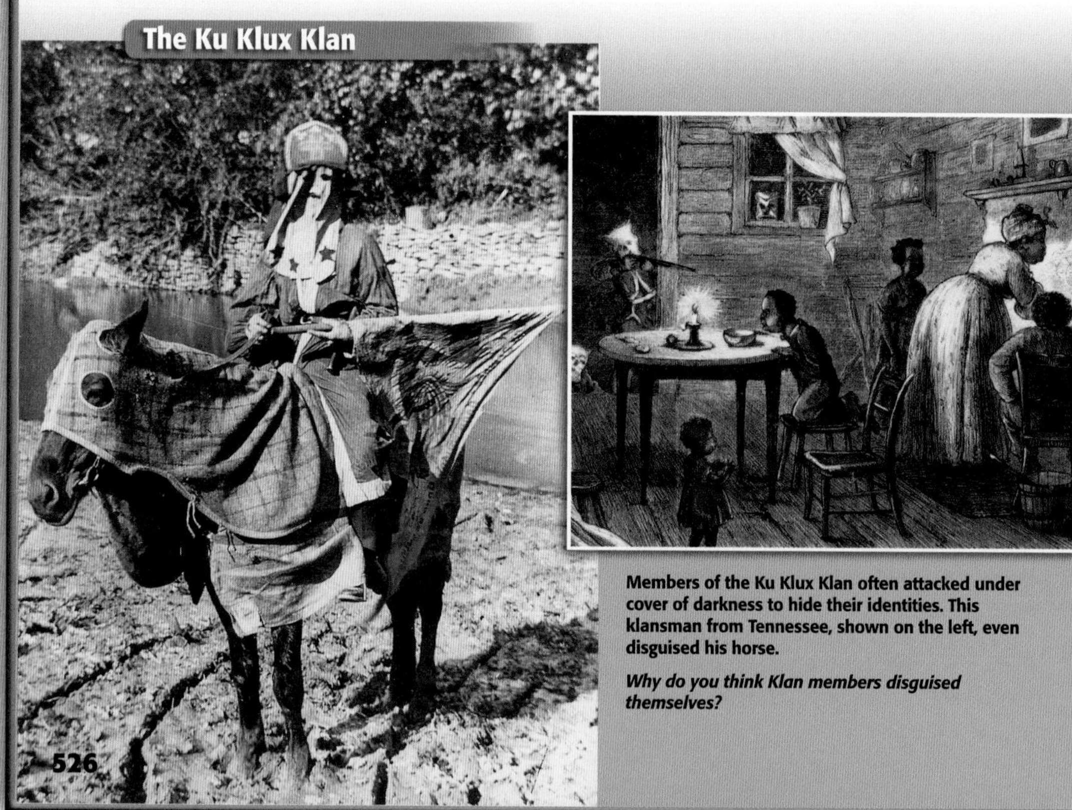

Members of the Ku Klux Klan often attacked under cover of darkness to hide their identities. This klansman from Tennessee, shown on the left, even disguised his horse.

Why do you think Klan members disguised themselves?

Critical Thinking: Identifying Cause and Effect

Reaching Standards

Cause-and-Effect Graphic Organizer

HSS 8.11.4; HSS **Analysis Skills:** HI 1, HI 2

1. Discuss with students the details of the rise of the Ku Klux Klan and the effects the Klan had on the South during Reconstruction.
2. To help students understand the causes and effects of the rise of the Ku Klux Klan, draw the graphic organizer for students to see. Omit the blue, italicized answers.
3. Have students copy the graphic organizer and complete it by identifying the causes and effects of the rise of the Klan.

LS **Verbal/Linguistic, Visual/Spatial**

Rise of the Ku Klux Klan

Causes	Effects
• *opposition to African American leaders* • *unhappy with federal troops in South* • *dislike of Reconstruction governments*	• *violence against African Americans and white Republicans* • *Local leaders do little to stop them.* • *Federal government stops them.*

Answers

The Ku Klux Klan *because their actions were illegal*

Reading Check *They were unhappy with changes introduced by Reconstruction governments.*

526

Reconstruction Ends

The violence of the Ku Klux Klan was not the only challenge to Reconstruction. Republicans slowly lost control of southern state governments to the Democratic Party. The General Amnesty Act of 1872 allowed former Confederates, except those who had held high ranks, to serve in public office. Many of these former Confederates, most of whom were Democrats, were soon elected to southern governments.

The Republican Party also began losing its power in the North. Although President Grant was re-elected in 1872, financial and political scandals in his administration upset voters. In his first term, a gold-buying scheme in which Grant's cousin took a leading role led to a brief crisis on the stock market called Black Friday. During his second term, his personal secretary was involved in the Whiskey Ring scandal, in which whiskey distillers and public officials worked together to steal liquor taxes from the federal government. Furthermore, people blamed Republican policies for the Panic of 1873.

Panic of 1873

This severe economic downturn began in September 1873 when Jay Cooke and Company, a major investor in railroads and the largest financier of the Union's Civil War effort, declared bankruptcy. The company had lied about the value of land along the side of the Northern Pacific Railroad that it owned and was trying to sell. When the truth leaked out, the company failed.

The failure of such an important business sent panic through the stock market, and investors began selling shares of stock more rapidly than people wanted to buy them. Companies had to buy their shares back from the investors. Soon, 89 of the nations 364 railroads had failed as well. The failure of almost 18,000 other businesses followed within two years, leaving the nation in an economic crisis. By 1876 unemployment had risen to 14 percent, with an estimated 2 million people out of work. The high unemployment rate set off numerous strikes and protests around the nation, many involving railroad workers. In 1874 the Democrats gained control of the House of Representatives. Northerners were becoming less concerned about southern racism and more concerned about their financial well-being.

Election of 1876

Republicans could tell that northern support for Reconstruction was fading. Voters' attention was shifting to economic problems. In 1874 the Republican Party lost control of the House of Representatives to the Democrats. The Republicans in Congress managed to pass one last civil rights law. The Civil Rights Act of 1875 guaranteed African Americans equal rights in public places, such as theaters and public transportation. But as Americans became increasingly worried about economic problems and government corruption, the Republican Party began to abandon Reconstruction.

Republicans selected Ohio governor Rutherford B. Hayes as their 1876 presidential candidate. He believed in ending federal support of the Reconstruction governments. The Democrats nominated New York governor Samuel J. Tilden. During the election, Democrats in the South again used violence at the polls to keep Republican voters away.

The election between Hayes and Tilden was close. Tilden appeared to have won. Republicans challenged the electoral votes in Oregon and three southern states. A special commission of members of Congress and Supreme Court justices was appointed to settle the issue.

The commission narrowly decided to give all the disputed votes to Hayes. Hayes thus won the presidency by one electoral vote. In the **Compromise of 1877**, the Democrats agreed to accept Hayes's victory. In return, they wanted all remaining federal troops removed from the South. They also asked for funding for internal improvements in the South and

Direct Teach

Main Idea

❸ Reconstruction Ends

As Reconstruction ended, the rights of African Americans were restricted.

Explain How was the United States affected by the Panic of 1873? *People blamed Republicans for the panic, almost 18,000 businesses declared bankruptcy, and unemployment rose, leading to protests.*

Analyze What issues caused the Republican Party to abandon Reconstruction? *Americans became increasingly worried about economic problems and corruption, and Republicans lost control of the House of Representatives.*

HSS 8.11.1; HSS **Analysis Skills:** CS 1, HI 1

Info to Know

Disputed Election The election of 1876 was the subject of much debate and investigation. The popular election, held in November 1876, favored Samuel J. Tilden by 250,000 votes over Rutherford B. Hayes. Election results in Florida, Louisiana, South Carolina, and Oregon, however, were disputed. After investigation by an electoral commission, Hayes was declared the winner of the election in March 1877—almost four months after the election.

Differentiating Instruction for Universal Access

Advanced Learners/GATE **Exceeding Standards**

1. Have students use their textbooks or class notes to determine the main factors that led to the end of Reconstruction. Then ask students to decide which factor they believe was the most important in ending Reconstruction.
2. Have students prepare to debate the factor they feel was most important. Remind students to support their stance with specific details and to be prepared to counter opposing arguments.
3. Have several different students engage in a debate over the issue. Moderate the debate. When students have finished the debate, ask all students to vote on which factor they believe was the most important in leading to the end of Reconstruction. LS **Interpersonal, Verbal/Linguistic**

HSS 8.11.1; HSS **Analysis Skills:** HI 1, HI 2

Alternative Assessment Handbook, Rubric 10: Debates

Direct Teach

Main Idea

❸ Reconstruction Ends

As Reconstruction ended, the rights of African Americans were restricted.

Identify Who were the Redeemers? *Democrats who brought their party back in control of southern state governments*

Analyze In what ways were African American men restricted from voting? *Being forced to pay a poll tax or pass a literacy test denied voting rights because many African American men had not been to school or did not have the extra money for the tax.*

Evaluate How did segregation become the key issue in the *Plessy* v. *Ferguson* case? *because Plessy, an African American, refused to leave a restricted whites-only part of a train*

- **CRF:** Primary Source Activity: *Plessy* v. *Ferguson*
- **CRF:** Literature, Activity: The Jim Crow Laws
- U.S. Supreme Court Case Studies: *Plessy* v. *Ferguson* (1896)

HSS 8.11.3; **HSS Analysis Skills:** HI 1

Did you know . . .

The *Plessy* v. *Ferguson* decision stood for 58 years. In 1954 the Supreme Court reversed the *Plessy* v. *Ferguson* decision with the landmark case *Brown* v. *Board of Education*. In that decision the Supreme Court ruled that segregation in public education was a denial of equal protection of the law.

Answers

Analyzing Information **1.** *The Court stated that the Thirteenth Amendment did not apply and that the Fourteenth Amendment protected against only political barriers, not social ones.* **2.** *It legalized segregation by saying "separate but equal" facilities were acceptable.*

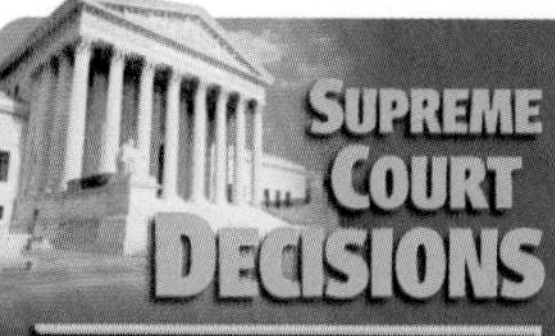

Supreme Court Decisions

***Plessy* v. *Ferguson* (1896)**

Background of the Case In 1892, Homer Plessy took a seat in the "whites only" car of a train in Louisiana. He was arrested, put on trial, and convicted of violating Louisiana's segregation law. Plessy argued that the Louisiana law violated the Thirteenth Amendment and denied him the equal protection of the law as guaranteed.

The Court's Ruling

The Court ruled that the Louisiana "separate-but-equal" law was constitutional.

The Court's Reasoning

The Court stated that the Thirteenth and Fourteenth Amendments did not apply. The Court decided that the case had nothing to do with the abolition of slavery mentioned in the Thirteenth Amendment. The justices also ruled that the Fourteenth Amendment was not designed to eliminate social barriers to equality between the races, only political barriers.

Justice John Marshall Harlan disagreed with the Court's ruling. In a dissenting opinion, he wrote that "in respect of civil rights, all citizens are equal before the law."

Why It Matters

Plessy was important because it approved the idea of separate but equal facilities for people based on race. The doctrine of separate but equal led to segregation in trains, buses, schools, restaurants, and many other social institutions.

The separate-but-equal doctrine led to unequal treatment of minority groups for decades. It was finally struck down by another Supreme Court ruling, *Brown* v. *Board of Education*, in 1954.

ANALYSIS SKILL — ANALYZING INFORMATION

1. **Why did the Court reject Plessy's arguments?**
2. **Why was *Plessy* v. *Ferguson* an important Supreme Court case?**

the appointment of a southern Democrat to the president's cabinet. Shortly after he took office in 1877, President Hayes removed the last of the federal troops from the South.

Redeemers

Gradually, Democrats regained control of state governments in the South. In each state, they moved quickly to get rid of the Reconstruction reforms.

Democrats who brought their party back to power in the South were called Redeemers. They came from a variety of backgrounds. For instance, U.S. senator John T. Morgan of Alabama was a former general in the Confederate army. Newspaper editor Henry Grady of Georgia was interested in promoting southern industry.

Redeemers wanted to reduce the size of state government and limit the rights of African Americans. They lowered state budgets and got rid of a variety of social programs. The Redeemers cut property taxes and reduced public funding for schools. They also succeeded in limiting African Americans' civil rights.

African Americans' Rights Restricted

Redeemers set up the poll tax in an effort to deny the vote to African Americans. The **poll tax** was a special tax people had to pay before they could vote.

Some states also targeted African American voters by requiring them to pass a literacy test. A so-called grandfather clause written into law affected men whose fathers or grandfathers could vote before 1867. In those cases, a voter did not have to pay a poll tax or pass a literacy test. As a result, almost every white man could escape the voting restrictions.

Redeemer governments also introduced legal **segregation**, the forced separation of whites and African Americans in public places. **Jim Crow laws**—laws that enforced segregation—became common in southern states in the 1880s.

African Americans challenged Jim Crow laws in court. In 1883, however, the U.S. Supreme Court ruled that the Civil Rights Act of 1875 was unconstitutional. The Court

Cross-Discipline Activity: Government

Exceeding Standards

Supreme Court Decisions

HSS 8.11.3; **HSS Analysis Skills:** HI 2, HI 3 — Research Required

1. Review with students the details of the *Plessy* v. *Ferguson* ruling. Then discuss with the class the 1954 Supreme Court ruling *Brown* v. *Board of Education*, which reversed the *Plessy* decision.
2. Organize the class into small groups. Have each group use the library, the Internet, or other resources to conduct research on both Supreme Court rulings.
3. Have each group create a poster that compares and contrasts the two Supreme Court decisions, including the effect of each on African Americans and other minorities. Ask students to make their posters visually appealing. Then have each group write a short paragraph that draws conclusions about why the Supreme Court reversed its earlier conclusion.

Alternative Assessment Handbook, Rubrics 28: Posters; and 37: Writing Assignments also ruled that the Fourteenth Amendment applied only to the actions of state governments. This ruling allowed private individuals and businesses to practice segregation.

Plessy v. *Ferguson*

In 1896, the U.S. Supreme Court returned to the issue of segregation. When Homer Plessy, an African American, refused to leave the whites-only Louisiana train car he was riding on, he was arrested and accused of breaking a state law requiring separate cars for blacks and whites. Plessy sued the railroad company and lost. His lawyers argued that the law violated his right to equal treatment under the Fourteenth Amendment. He then appealed to the U.S. Supreme Court. The Supreme Court ruled against Plessy in ***Plessy* v. *Ferguson***. Segregation was allowed, said the Court, if "separate-but-equal" facilities were provided. Among the justices, only John Marshall Harlan disagreed with the Court's decision. He explained his disagreement in a dissenting opinion:

> "In the eye of the law, there is in the country no superior, dominant [controlling], ruling class of citizens.... Our constitution is color-blind, and neither knows nor tolerates classes among citizens. In respect of civil rights, all citizens are equal before the law."

Despite Harlan's view, segregation became widespread across the country. African Americans were forced to use separate public schools, libraries, and parks. When they existed, these facilities were usually of poorer quality than those created for whites. In practice, these so-called separate but equal facilities were separate and unequal.

Farming in the South

Few African Americans in the South could afford to buy or even rent farms. Moving West also was costly. Many African Americans therefore remained on plantations. Others tried to make a living in the cities.

African Americans who stayed on plantations often became part of a system known as **sharecropping**, or sharing the crop. Landowners provided the land, tools, and supplies, and sharecroppers provided the labor. At harvest time, the sharecropper usually had to give most of the crop to the landowner. Whatever remained belonged to the sharecropper. Many sharecroppers hoped to save enough money from selling their share of the crops to one day be able to buy a farm. Unfortunately, only a few ever achieved this dream.

Instead, most sharecroppers lived in a cycle of debt. When they needed food, clothing, or supplies, most families had to buy goods on credit because they had little cash.

Hopes Raised and Denied

Slavery	Freedom	Rights Denied
• No rights • Forced labor • No freedom of movement without permission • Family members sold away from one another • No representation in government	• Slavery banned • Free to work for wages • Could move and live anywhere • Many families reunited • Could serve in political office	• Sharecropping system put in place • Ability to vote and hold office restricted • White leadership regained control of southern state governments

Direct Teach

Main Idea

3 African Americans' Rights Restricted

As Reconstruction ended, the rights of African Americans were restricted.

Analyze Why did many African Americans stay on plantations? *too costly to buy or rent farms or to move west*

Predict Why would the cycle of debt continue for sharecroppers? *There would be continuing problems with weather, poor harvests, and low crop prices, making it nearly impossible for sharecroppers to escape debt.*

Quick Facts Transparency: Hopes Raised and Denied

HSS 8.11.3; HSS **Analysis Skills:** HI 1, HI 2

Linking to Today

African American Civil Rights

When Reconstruction ended, African Americans lost many of the rights they had gained. Over time, however, African Americans have fought to regain access to all the rights of citizenship. By the 1960s, the push for greater civil rights for African Americans had become a true social movement in America. African Americans were joined in these efforts by Americans from all walks of life. Their efforts changed people's attitudes and led to greater civil rights for African Americans as well as other minorities.

Differentiating Instruction for Universal Access

Learners Having Difficulty — Reaching Standards

1. Ask students to explain how poll taxes, Jim Crow laws, and the *Plessy* v. *Ferguson* decision affected African Americans. Write student comments for everyone to see.
2. Have each student write a one-page letter to a northern newspaper from the perspective of a southern African American. The letter should describe how the person's life has changed since the end of Reconstruction.
3. Ask volunteers to read their letters to the class. LS **Verbal/Linguistic**

HSS 8.11.3; HSS **Analysis Skills:** HI 1, HI 2

Alternative Assessment Handbook, Rubric 17: Letters to Editors

English-Language Learners — Standards **Proficiency**

1. Ask students to explain how poll taxes, Jim Crow laws, and the *Plessy* v. *Ferguson* decision affected African Americans. Write student comments for everyone to see.
2. Have students create a political cartoon that expresses the point of view of a southern African American. Explain to students that political cartoons often try to draw attention to a problem or issue by using satire.
3. Ask volunteers to share their cartoons with the class. LS **Visual/Spatial**

HSS 8.11.3; HSS **Analysis Skills:** HI 1, HI 2

Alternative Assessment Handbook, Rubric 27: Political Cartoons

Direct Teach

Main Idea

4 Rebuilding Southern Industry

Southern business leaders relied on industry to rebuild the South.

Identify What was the most successful industrial development in the South after Reconstruction? *textile production*

Summarize What were the benefits and drawbacks of mill work? *benefits—Entire families were employed, women were valued workers, and it was an alternative to farming; drawbacks—tedious work and long hours, asthma, brown-lung disease, injuries, death, few advancement opportunities for women*

HSS 8.11.1; HSS **Analysis Skills:** HI 1

Info to Know

Railroads Another way the South modernized its economy was by building railroads. From 1877 to 1900, the South built railroad lines at a faster rate than did the nation as a whole. Railroad building had an immediate effect on the southern economy. Landowners profited by selling lumber to railroad companies, who could use it as railroad ties. Farm families also made money by selling chickens, eggs, meat, and other farm products to railroad workers. Once the railroads were complete, southern towns and cities were connected to the rest of the nation.

The New South

When sharecroppers sold their crops, they hoped to be able to pay off these debts. However, bad weather, poor harvests, or low crop prices often made this dream impossible.

Sharecroppers usually grew cotton, one of the South's most important cash crops. When too many farmers planted cotton, however, the supply became excessive. As a result, the price per bale of cotton dropped. Many farmers understood the drawbacks of planting cotton. However, farmers felt pressure from banks and others to keep raising cotton. A southern farmer explained why so many sharecroppers depended on cotton:

> "Cotton is the thing to get credit on in this country....You can always sell cotton ... [Y]ou load up your wagon with wheat or corn ...and I doubt some days whether you could sell it."
>
> –Farmer quoted in *The Promise of the New South,* by Edward L. Ayers

READING CHECK **Finding Main Ideas** How were African Americans' rights restricted?

Rebuilding Southern Industry

The southern economy suffered through cycles of good and bad years as cotton prices went up and down. Some business leaders hoped industry would strengthen the southern economy and create a New South.

Southern Industry

Henry Grady, an Atlanta newspaper editor, was a leader of the New South movement. "The new South presents . . . a diversified [varied] industry that meets the complex needs of this complex age," he wrote. Grady and his supporters felt that with its cheap and abundant labor, the South could build factories and provide a workforce for them.

The most successful industrial development in the South involved textile production. Businesspeople built textile mills in many small towns to produce cotton fabric. Many people from rural areas came to work in the mills, but African Americans were not allowed to work in most of them.

Differentiating Instruction for Universal Access

Advanced Learners/GATE — Exceeding Standards

1. Write the following statement for students to see: *The effects of Reconstruction were revolutionary.* Discuss with students the meaning of the word *revolutionary.*
2. Ask students whether they agree with the statement. Then have students write one-page papers explaining their views and supporting their positions.
3. Remind students that to support their points of view, they need to consider political, social, and economic effects of Reconstruction.
4. Encourage students to support their conclusion with specific examples, quotations, or comparisons. LS **Verbal/Linguistic**

HSS 8.11.1, 8.11.3, 8.11.4; HSS **Analysis Skills:** HI 1

Alternative Assessment Handbook, Rubric 37: Writing Assignments

Answers

Reading Check *legally segregated from white Americans, forced to pay poll taxes, and discriminated against*

"The New South...is stirred with the breath of a new life."

—Henry Grady

Atlanta rebuilt quickly after the war, becoming a leading railroad and industrial center. Newspaper editor Henry Grady gave stirring speeches about the need for industry in the South. He became one of the best-known spokesmen of the "New South."

Why might Grady point to Atlanta as a model for economic change?

Southern Mill Life

Work in the cotton mills appealed to farm families who had trouble making ends meet. As one mill worker explained, "It was a necessity to move and get a job, rather than depend on the farm." Recruiters sent out by the mills promised good wages and steady work.

Entire families often worked in the same cotton mill. Mills employed large numbers of women and children. Many children started working at about the age of 12. Some children started working at an even earlier age. Women did most of the spinning and were valued workers. However, few women had the opportunity to advance within the company.

Many mill workers were proud of the skills they used, but they did not enjoy their work. One unhappy worker described it as "the same thing over and over again. . . . The more you do, the more they want done." Workers often labored 12 hours a day, six days a week. Cotton dust and lint filled the air, causing asthma and an illness known as brown-lung disease. Fast-moving machinery caused injuries and even deaths. Despite the long hours and dangerous working conditions, wages remained low. However, mill work did offer an alternative to farming.

READING CHECK **Finding Main Ideas** What did southern business leaders hope industry would do?

SUMMARY AND PREVIEW In this section you learned about the end of Reconstruction. In the next chapter you will learn about America's continued westward expansion.

Section 3 Assessment

go.hrw.com
Online Quiz
KEYWORD: SS8 HP16

Reviewing Ideas, Terms, and People

HSS 8.11.1, 8.11.3, 8.11.4

1. a. **Identify** Who were some prominent African American leaders during Reconstruction?
   b. **Evaluate** What do you think was the most important change made by Reconstruction state governments? Explain your answer.
2. a. **Recall** Why didn't some local governments stop the **Ku Klux Klan**?
   b. **Draw Conclusions** How did the Ku Klux Klan's use of terror interfere with elections in the South?
3. a. **Recall** How did Reconstruction come to an end?
   b. **Explain** What was the relationship between **Jim Crow laws** and **segregation**?
4. a. **Identify** Who was **Henry Grady**, and why was he important?
   b. **Predict** What are some possible results of the rise of the "New South"?

Critical Thinking

5. **Comparing** Copy the chart below. Use it to compare the rights of African Americans before and after Reconstruction.

Before	After

WRITING JOURNAL

6. **Relating Historical Change to Individual Choice** Despite the difficulties of Reconstruction, the Freedmen's Bureau and plans to bring industry to the "New South" did create new jobs. What might have led people to leave their jobs for new ones?

Direct Teach

Checking for Understanding

True or False Answer each statement *T* if it is true or *F* if it is false. If the statement is false, explain why.

1. Reconstruction was led by Democrats in Congress. *F; led by Republicans*
2. Several competing plans were proposed for Reconstruction. *T*
3. African Americans earned the right to vote in the Thirteenth Amendment. *F; the Fifteenth Amendment*

Review & Assess

Close

Ask students to write a short description of life in the South after the end of Reconstruction.

Review

Online Quiz, Section 3

Assess

SE Section 3 Assessment

PASS: Section 3 Quiz

Alternative Assessment Handbook

Reteach/Classroom Intervention

California Standards Review Workbook

Interactive Reader and Study Guide, Section 3

Interactive Skills Tutor CD-ROM

Section 3 Assessment Answers

1. **a.** Hiram Revels and Blanche K. Bruce
   b. possible answers: education—It led to a better-educated workforce; transportation—it improved the economy.
2. **a.** They were either afraid of or sympathized with them.
   b. They attacked voters and public officials, preventing some people from voting.
3. **a.** Republicans began to abandon Reconstruction due to other problems, and the disputed election of 1876 led to a compromise officially ending Reconstruction.
   b. Jim Crow laws were segregation laws.
4. **a.** a leader of the New South movement
   b. possible answer—Discrimination against African Americans might continue.
5. Before—voted, moved and lived anywhere, participated in politics; After—limited voting rights, limited work opportunities, sharecropping, little or no political participation
6. mill jobs, desire to escape sharecropping

Answers

The New South *It rebuilt quickly, becoming a railroad and industrial center in the South.*

Reading Check *strengthen the southern economy and create a New South*

Social Studies Skills

Chance, Oversight, and Error in History

Activity **Make it Personal** Ask students if they think differently about chance, oversight, and error after learning about the critical ways in which they can shape history. After a brief discussion, ask volunteers to share examples of when chance, oversight, or error shaped events in their lives. Then challenge students to identify examples in which chance, oversight, or error have shaped recent national or world events. Correct students' interpretations where necessary. Use the discussion to make certain that students understand the difference among error, chance, and oversight and how they can affect historical events. **LS Intrapersonal, Verbal/Linguistic**

Alternative Assessment Handbook, Rubric 11: Discussions

HSS Analysis Skills: HI 4

Social Studies Skills

Analysis | Critical Thinking | Participation | Study

HSS HI4 Students recognize the role of chance, oversight, and error in history.

Chance, Oversight, and Error in History

Understand the Skill

Sometimes, history can seem very routine. One event leads to others which, in turn, lead to still others. You learn to look for cause-and-effect relationships among events. You learn how point of view and bias can influence decisions and actions. These approaches to the study of history imply that the events of the past are orderly and predictable.

In fact, many of the events of the past *are* orderly and predictable! They may seem even more so since they're over and done with, and we know how things turned out. Yet, predictable patterns of behavior *do* exist throughout history. Recognizing them is one of the great values and rewards of studying the past. As the philosopher George Santayana once famously said, Those who cannot remember the past are condemned to repeat it."

At its most basic level, however, history is people, and people are "human." They make mistakes. Unexpected things happen to them, both good things and bad. This is the unpredictable element of history. The current phrase "stuff happens" is just as true of the past as it is today. Mistakes, oversights, and just plain "dumb luck" have shaped the course of history—and have helped to make the study of it so exciting!

Learn the Skill

California merchant John Sutter decided to build a sawmill along the nearby American River in 1848. He planned to sell the lumber it produced to settlers who were moving into the area. Sutter put James W. Marshall to work building the mill. To install the large water wheel that would power the saw, Marshall first had to deepen the river bed next to the mill. During his digging, he noticed some shiny bits of yellow metal in the water. The result of this accidental find was the California Gold Rush, which sent thousands of Americans to California, and speeded settlement of the West.

In 1863 the army of Confederate General Robert E. Lee invaded Maryland. The Civil War had been going well for the South. Lee hoped a southern victory on Union soil would convince the British to aid the South in the war. However, a Confederate officer forgot his cigars as his unit left its camp in the Maryland countryside. Wrapped around the cigars was a copy of Lee's battle plans. When a Union soldier came upon the abandoned camp, he spotted the cigars. This chance discovery enabled the Union army to defeat Lee at the Battle of Antietam. The Union victory helped keep the British out of the war. More importantly, it allowed President Lincoln to issue the Emancipation Proclamation and begin the process of ending slavery in the United States.

Practice and Apply the Skill

In April 1865 President Lincoln was assassinated while attending the theater in Washington, D.C. Bodyguard John Parker was stationed outside the door of the President's box. However, Parker left his post to find a seat from which he could watch the play. This allowed the killer to enter the box and shoot the unprotected President.

Write an essay about how this chance event altered the course of history. How might Reconstruction, North–South relations, and African Americans' struggle for equality have be different had Lincoln lived?

Answers

Practice and Apply the Skill *Essays will vary, but students may speculate that Reconstruction might have been less bitter had Lincoln lived. His strength, experience, and popularity—particularly as compared to that of Andrew Johnson—might have kept the Radical Republicans from gaining control over Reconstruction. This change might have resulted in a Reconstruction plan that stressed unity and forgiveness more and, thus, might have resulted in less bitterness and resentment on the part of the South toward the North.*

Social Studies Skills Activity: Chance, Oversight, and Error in History

Analyzing Previous Chapters **HSS Analysis Skills:** HI 4

Standards Proficiency

1. Organize students into small groups and assign each group a chapter that they have studied recently.
2. Have each group scan the chapter and look for events where chance, oversight, or error played a role in influencing the course of history.
3. Each group should make a list of the instances it finds and write a brief explanation of the way in which chance, oversight, or error shaped history in that instance.
4. Have each group share its findings with the class. Correct students' interpretations where necessary. Then conclude by having students predict how the course of history might have changed if some of the instances they mentioned had turned out differently. **LS Interpersonal, Verbal/Linguistic**

Alternative Assessment Handbook, Rubric 14: Group Activity

CHAPTER 16

Standards Review

Visual Summary

Use the visual summary below to help you review the main ideas of the chapter.

QUICK FACTS

Reform During Reconstruction, the Freedmen's Bureau opened schools for former slaves and performed other services to help the poorest southerners.

Dispute Differing ideas about how to govern the South led to conflicts between African Americans and white southerners, as well as between Republicans and Democrats.

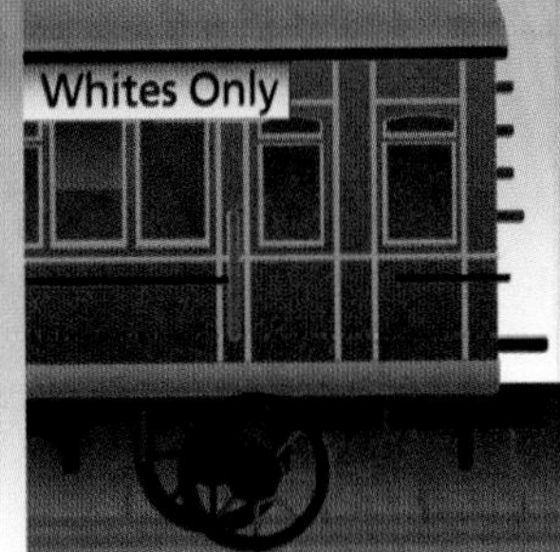

Division After the Compromise of 1877 ended Reconstruction, segregation laws were enacted by southern governments and upheld by the U.S. Supreme Court.

Reviewing Vocabulary, Terms, and People

Complete each sentence by filling in the blank with the correct term or person from the chapter.

1. _______________ were laws that allowed racial segregation in public places.
2. The Radical Republicans were led by _______, a member of Congress from Pennsylvania.
3. The period from 1865 to 1877 that focused on reuniting the nation is known as _______.
4. Following the Civil War, many African Americans in the South made a living by participating in the _________ system.
5. After opposing Congress, Andrew Johnson became the first president to face _____ proceedings.
6. The _____ Amendment made slavery in the United States illegal.
7. In 1870, _______ became the first African American to serve in the U.S. Senate.

Comprehension and Critical Thinking

SECTION 1 *(Pages 512–517)* **HSS 8.10.7, 8.11.1, 8.11.3, 8.11.5**

8. a. **Describe** How did the lives of African Americans change after the Civil War?

   b. **Compare and Contrast** How was President Johnson's Reconstruction plan similar and different from President Lincoln's Ten Percent Plan?

   c. **Evaluate** Which of the three Reconstruction plans that were originally proposed do you think would have been the most successful? Why?

SECTION 2 *(Pages 518–523)* **HSS 8.11.3, 8.11.5**

9. a. **Identify** Who were the Radical Republicans, and how did they change Reconstruction?

   b. **Analyze** How did the debate over the Fourteenth Amendment affect the election of 1866?

   c. **Elaborate** Do you think Congress was right to impeach President Andrew Johnson? Explain.

Answers

Visual Summary

Review and Inquiry Have students use the visual summary to explain the results of Reconstruction.

Quick Facts Transparency: Reconstruction Visual Summary

Reviewing Vocabulary, Terms, and People

1. Jim Crow laws
2. Thaddeus Stevens
3. Reconstruction
4. sharecropping
5. impeachment
6. Thirteenth
7. Hiram Revels

Comprehension and Critical Thinking

8. a. They were able to move about freely, legalize marriages, and search for missing relatives.

   b. similar—granted amnesty, recognized that slavery is illegal; different—Johnson's plan required a temporary governor, declaration that secession was illegal, and refusal to pay Confederate debts; Lincoln's plan required an oath of loyalty from at least 10 percent of the voters in a state.

   c. Answers will vary, but students should indicate why the plan they chose would have been more successful than the others.

Review and Assessment Resources

Review and Reinforce

- SE Standards Review
- **CRF:** Chapter Review Activity
- California Standards Review Workbook
- Quick Facts Transparency: Reconstruction Visual Summary
- Spanish Chapter Summaries Audio CD Program
- Online Chapter Summaries in Six Languages
- OSP Holt PuzzlePro; GameTool for ExamView
- Quiz Game CD-ROM

Assess

- SE Standards Assessment
- PASS: Chapter Test, Forms A and B
- Alternative Assessment Handbook
- OSP ExamView Test Generator, Chapter Test
- Universal Access Modified Worksheets and Tests CD-ROM: Chapter Test
- Holt Online Assessment Program (in the Premier Online Edition)

Reteach/Intervene

- Interactive Reader and Study Guide
- Universal Access Teacher Management System: Lesson Plans for Universal Access
- Universal Access Modified Worksheets and Tests CD-ROM
- Interactive Skills Tutor CD-ROM

go.hrw.com
Online Resources
Chapter Resources:
KEYWORD: SS8 US16

Answers

9. a. Republicans who wanted the federal government to be much more involved in Reconstruction; they took control of Reconstruction away from President Johnson
   b. Debate over civil rights for African Americans became the key issue of the election of 1866 and even led to riots.
   c. possible answers: yes—He defied the law by firing Edwin Stanton without their approval; no—Congress did not have the power to limit the president.
10. a. They tried to help the South recover from the war by establishing public schools, hospitals, and prisons; passing laws prohibiting discrimination against African Americans; and aiding the construction of railroads, bridges, and public buildings.
    b. They worked to limit the rights of African Americans, reduce the size of state governments, eliminate social programs, and prevent African Americans from voting.
    c. Answers will vary, but students should support their answers with specific examples.

Reviewing Themes

11. The key political struggle was between Republicans, who supported rights for African Americans and strict guidelines for readmitting southern states, and Democrats, who favored leniency toward southern states and limited freedoms for African Americans.
12. The rights of African Americans were severely limited by poll taxes, Jim Crow laws, and the separate-but-equal doctrine. Many southerners were negatively affected by the sharecropping system and poor working conditions in mills.

SECTION 3 *(Pages 524–531)* **HSS 8.11.1, 8.11.3, 8.11.4**

10. **a. Describe** What reforms did Reconstruction governments in the South support?
    b. Draw Conclusions In what ways did southern governments attempt to reverse the accomplishments of Reconstruction?
    c. Evaluate Do you think the South was successful or unsuccessful in its rebuilding efforts? Explain your answer.

Reviewing Themes

11. **Politics** Explain the political struggles that took place during Reconstruction.
12. **Society and Culture** How were the lives of ordinary southerners affected in the years after Reconstruction?

Using the Internet

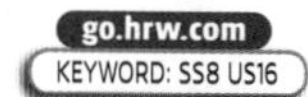

13. **Activity: Drawing conclusions** A challenge for anyone trying to understand Reconstruction is drawing conclusions from primary and secondary sources from the time period. This activity will help you see how complex this can be. Enter the activity keyword, and then rate the credibility of the sources provided. Make sure you explain whether the source is a primary or secondary source, whether or not you think the source is credible, and the reasons for your thoughts.

Reading Skills

Reading for Essential and Relevant Information *Use the Reading Skills taught in this chapter to answer the question about the reading selection below.*

> Radical Republicans wanted the South to change much more than it already had before it could return to the Union. Like the moderates, they thought the Black Codes were cruel and unjust. The radicals, however, wanted the federal government to be much more involved in Reconstruction. *(p. 519)*

14. Which of the following is relevant information for the passage above?
    a. Thaddeus Stevens was a Radical Republican.
    b. Andrew Johnson was a Democrat.
    c. Radical Republicans wanted the federal government to make major changes in the South.
    d. Radical Republicans were eventually removed from power.

Social Studies Skills

Chance, Oversight, and Error in History *Use the Social Studies Skills taught in this chapter to answer the question about the reading selection below.*

> Johnson's speaking tour was a disaster. It did little to win votes for the Democratic Party. He even got into arguments with people in the audience. *(p. 521)*

15. Which of the following is an example of chance, oversight, or error that affected history?
    a. Johnson got into arguments with audiences.
    b. The tour was a disaster.
    c. The tour didn't win votes.
    d. Johnson spoke for the Democratic Party.

FOCUS ON WRITING

16. **Writing A Job History** Review your notes about the changing job scene during Reconstruction. Put yourself in the shoes of a person living then. It could be anyone—a returning soldier, a shopkeeper, a schoolteacher, or a politician. What jobs would that person seek? Why would he or she leave one job for another?

    Write a brief job history for that person during Reconstruction. Include at least four jobs. Make each job description 2 to 4 sentences long. End each one with a sentence or two about why the person left that job. Add one sentence explaining why they took the next job. Be sure to include specific historical details.

Using the Internet

13. Go to the HRW Web site and enter the keyword shown to access a rubric for this activity.

KEYWORD: SS8 TEACHER

Reading Skills

14. c

Social Studies Skills

15. d

Focus on Writing

16. **Rubric** Students' job histories should:
    - include at least four job descriptions.
    - end each description with an explanation of why the person left.
    - explain why the person took each job.
    - include specific historical details.

Standards Assessment

DIRECTIONS: Read each question and write the letter of the best response. Use the map below to answer question 1.

1

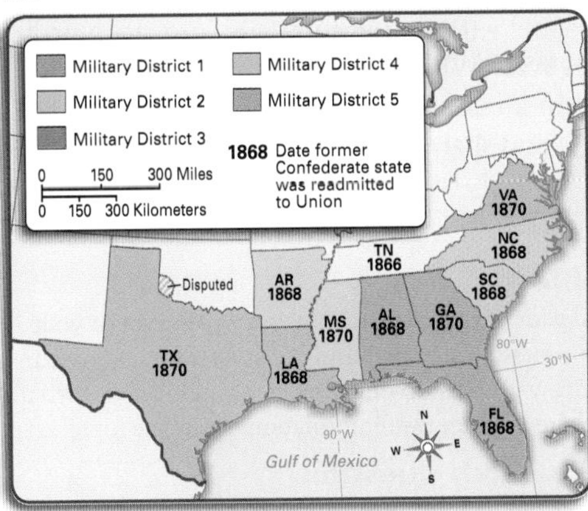

Which military district contained the largest number of states?

A Military District 2
B Military District 3
C Military District 4
D Military District 5

2 What can you infer from the map information?

A South Carolina was difficult to reconstruct.
B The largest number of troops was in Military District 1.
C Military District 5 was the last district to end Reconstruction.
D Tennessee was readmitted to the Union before the other southern states.

3 The quickest approach to reuniting the nation was proposed by the

A Ten Percent Plan.
B Wade-Davis Bill.
C Civil Rights Act of 1866.
D Compromise of 1877.

4 What development convinced Republicans in Congress to take control of Reconstruction from the president?

A President Abraham Lincoln was assassinated by a southern sympathizer.
B President Andrew Johnson vetoed the Wade-Davis bill.
C Southern states began passing Black Codes to deprive African Americans of their freedoms.
D White southern women refused to support the Fifteenth Amendment.

5 All of the following limited opportunities for African Americans in the South after Reconstruction ended *except*

A sharecropping.
B the Redeemers.
C Jim Crow laws.
D carpetbaggers.

Connecting with Past Learning

6 During Reconstruction, southerners were ruled by a small number of outsiders known as carpetbaggers. This situation is *most* similar to the period of

A Mongol rule over China
B Roman control over Italy
C Chinese control of Japan
D Aztec rule over the Olmec

7 In Grade 7 you learned about Bartolomé de Las Casas's effort to improve conditions for Native Americans. This was *most* similar to which group's efforts during Reconstruction?

A Redeemers
B Radical Republicans
C Democrats
D sharecroppers

Answers

1. B
Break Down the Question: Students should note that District 3 has three states, more than any other district.

2. D
Break Down the Question: Point out to students that answer choices A, B, and C cannot be inferred from the map, but D can.

3. A
Break Down the Question: This question requires students to recall factual information from Section 1.

4. C
Break Down the Question: This question requires students to recall factual information from Section 2.

5. D
Break Down the Question: Remind students that the word *except* in the question means that they should identify the answer choice that is *not* true.

6. A
Break Down the Question: This question requires students to recall information covered in Grade 7.

7. B
Break Down the Question: Point out to students that Radical Republicans were most likely to try to improve conditions during Reconstruction.

Intervention Resources

Reproducible

- Interactive Reader and Study Guide
- Universal Access Teacher Management System: Universal Access Lesson Plans

Technology

- Quick Facts Transparency: Reconstruction Visual Summary
- Universal Access Modified Worksheets and Tests CD-ROM
- Interactive Skills Tutor CD-ROM

Tips for Test Taking

Find the Main Idea Tell students that the main goal of a reading comprehension section is to test their understanding of a reading passage. Have students keep these suggestions in mind when they read a selection on a test:

- Read the passage once to get a general overview of the topic.
- If you don't understand the passage at first, keep reading. Try to find the main idea.
- Then read the questions so that you know what to look for when you reread the passage.

Standards Review

Have students review the following standards in their workbooks.

- California Standards Review Workbook: HSS 8.10.4, 8.10.7, 8.11.1, 8.11.3, 8.11.4, 8.11.5

Preteach

Bellringer

Motivate Ask students to think about topics related to the Civil War that interested them. What Civil War topics would students like to know more about? What questions do students have about these topics? Write the questions for students to see. Then tell students that in this workshop they will answer a similar question by conducting research and writing an informative report.

Direct Teach

Finding Historical Information

Ask an Expert Another source students might consult is an expert on their topic. Students might arrange an interview with an expert or attend a presentation that he or she is giving. If students plan to interview a person, they should write out several questions in advance and leave space after each question for taking notes. If students wish to record an interview, remind them to ask the person's permission in advance.

ELA Writing 8.2.3.c

Taking Notes

Keep It Relevant Tell students that when they are not sure whether to take notes on a piece of information, they should ask themselves, "Does this information help answer my research question?" If the answer is yes, they should include the information in their notes. If the answer is no, they should not.

Standards Focus

HSS Analysis Skills: HR 4
ELA Writing 8.1.6, 8.2.3, 8.2.3.a, 8.2.3.b, 8.2.3.c, 8.2.3.d

Assignment

Collect information and write an informative report on a topic related to the Civil War.

A Social Studies Report

All research begins with a question. Why did the North win the Civil War? Why did Abraham Lincoln choose Ulysses S. Grant? In a research report, you find answers to questions like these and share what you learn with your reader.

TIP **Narrowing the Task** The key to a successful research report is picking a topic that is broad enough that you can find information, but narrow enough that you can cover it in detail. To narrow a subject, focus on one aspect of the larger subject. Then think about whether that one aspect can be broken down into smaller parts. Here's an example of how to narrow a topic:
Too Broad: Civil War Leaders
Less Broad: Civil War Generals
Narrower: Robert E. Lee's Role in the Civil War

1. Prewrite

Choosing a Subject

Since you will spend a lot of time researching and writing about your topic, pick one that interests you. First, think of several topics related to the Civil War. Narrow your list to one topic by thinking about what interests you and where you can find information about the topic.

Developing a Research Question

A guiding question related to your topic will help focus your research. For example, here is a research question for the topic "Robert E. Lee's Role in the Civil War": *How did Lee's decision to turn down the leadership of the Union Army affect the Civil War?* The answer to this question becomes the thesis, or the big idea of your report.

Finding Historical Information

Use at least three sources of historical information besides your textbook. Good sources include

- books, maps, magazines, newspapers
- television programs, movies, Internet sites, CD-ROMs

For each source, write down the kinds of information shown below. When taking notes, put a circled number next to each source.

Encyclopedia article
① "Title of Article." Name of Encyclopedia. Edition or year published.
Book
② Author. Title. City of Publication: Publisher, Year published.
Magazine or newspaper article
③ Author. "Title of Article." Publication name Date: page number(s)
Internet site
④ Author (if known). "Document title." Web Site. Date of electronic publication. Date information was accessed <url>

ELA **Writing 8.2.3** Write research reports.

Differentiating Instruction for Universal Access

Learners Having Difficulty — Reaching Standards

1. When doing research, students need to learn to evaluate each source quickly to determine its usefulness. As guided practice, write the list of fictional sources at right for students to see. Have students identify which of the sources they think would be most helpful for an informative report on Ulysses S. Grant.
2. Have students use the following scale to rate each source: 4 = extremely useful; 3 = useful; 2 = might be useful; 1 = not useful.

- *Ulysses S. Grant: A Biography* (book)
- *The Life and Times of Lincoln* (book)
- "Grant's Military Campaigns" (historical journal article)
- "Interactive History of the Civil War" (university Web site)
- "My General Grant Page" (personal Web site)

LS Verbal/Linguistic

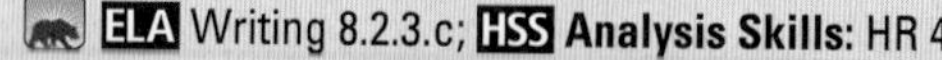
ELA Writing 8.2.3.c; HSS **Analysis Skills:** HR 4

536 UNIT 5

Taking Notes

As you read the source material, take thorough notes on facts, statistics, comparisons, and quotations. Take special care to spell names correctly and to record dates and facts accurately. If you use a direct quotation from a source, copy it word for word and enclose it in quotation marks. Along with each note, include the number of its source and its page number.

Organizing Your Ideas and Information

Informative research reports are usually organized in one of these ways:

- Chronological order (the order that events occurred)
- Order of importance
- Causes (actions or situations that make something else happen) and effects (what happened as a result of something else)

Use one of these orders to organize your notes in an outline. Here is a partial outline for a paper on Robert E. Lee.

The Thesis/Big Idea: Robert E. Lee's decision to decline the leadership of the Union Army had serious consequences for the path of the Civil War.

I. Lee's Military Expertise
  A. Achievements at the U.S. Military Academy
  B. Achievements during the Mexican War
II. Lee's Personality and Character
  A. Intelligence and strength
  B. Honesty and fairness
  C. Daring and courage
III. Lee's Military Victories
  A. Battle of Fredericksburg
  B. Battle of Chancellorsville

TIP Seeing Different Viewpoints Consult a variety of sources, including those with different points of view on the topic. Reading sources with different opinions will give you a more complete picture of your subject. For example, reading articles about Robert E. Lee written by a southern writer as well as a northern writer may give you a more balanced view of Lee.

TIP Recording Others Ideas You will be taking three types of notes.
Paraphrases Restatements of all the ideas in your own words.
Summaries Brief restatements of only the most important parts.
Direct quotations The writer's exact words inside quotation marks.

2. Write

You can use this framework to help you write your first draft.

A Writer's Framework

Introduction	Body	Conclusion
■ Start with a quote or an interesting historical detail to grab your reader's attention. ■ State the main idea of your report. ■ Provide any historical background readers need to understand your main idea.	■ Present your information under at least three main ideas, using logical order. ■ Write at least one paragraph for each of these main ideas. ■ Add supporting details, facts, or examples to each paragraph.	■ Restate your main idea, using slightly different words. ■ Include a general comment about your topic. ■ You might comment on how the historical information in your report relates to later historical events.

Direct Teach

Writing Introductions

First Things Last Tell students that they will probably be able to write a stronger introduction after they have drafted the body of the paper. Have students begin by writing their thesis statement. They should then start a new paragraph to begin the body of the report. After they have drafted the body, have students reread the report and then write the introduction. Have students ask themselves the following questions before they write the introduction:

- How can I grab my readers' attention?
- How can I set the scene for what I am about to discuss in the rest of my report?
- How can I make my readers want to read more?

Writing the Body

The Right Fit Explain to students that if they are having trouble making their reports flow, they may need to reconsider the kind of organization they chose. Tell students to scan their papers for transitions and other words that determine the logical relationship of the information. For instance, words such as *because, therefore,* and *so* indicate a cause-and-effect relationship. Words such as *first, next, then,* and *after* indicate a chronological relationship. Words such as *primarily, main,* and *major* indicate a relationship based on importance. Students should make sure they are using the organization that best matches what they are trying to say. If not, students should create a new outline with a different organization and then use the outline to revise their drafts.

Advanced Learners/GATE — Exceeding Standards

1. Challenge students to choose a research topic about which there is some disagreement or controversy. Students should then address in their reports the complexity of their topics, the reasons for controversy, and the discrepancies in the available information.
2. Check students' topics to make sure you approve before students begin their research. **LS Verbal/Linguistic**

ELA Writing 8.2.3.a

Special Education Students — Reaching Standards

1. Assign all special education students one topic.
2. Have an aide take the students as a group to the library to assist with research. The aide should instruct students in the use of card catalogs, computer catalogs, and library media centers.
3. The aide should then help the students select and find sources. **LS Verbal/Linguistic**

ELA Writing 8.2.3.b

Direct Teach

Studying a Model

Identify Organization Lead a class discussion to identify the type of organization used in the model research paper. Write the three types of organization for students to see. Have students consider each type of organization in turn.

- **Chronological order:** Point out that although the first body paragraph describes Lee's education and the last discusses his actions during the war, the middle body paragraph discusses his personality, which does not fit a chronological scheme.
- **Cause and effect:** Point out that while the thesis states a cause and effect (Lee's decision strengthened the South and likely lengthened the war), the supporting points are not related by cause and effect.
- **Order of importance:** Students should conclude that the model is organized by order of importance.

Then discuss whether the most important main ideas are provided first or last *(last, because Lee's actual performance in the field is the strongest evidence).*

Technology Tip

Using Technology to Provide Visual Aids Students may want to include maps, charts, diagrams, or illustrations in their papers. Explain that many word-processing programs include drawing tools or provide ways to import graphics from other computer programs. Encourage students who want to include visual aids to find out more about the graphic tools available.

ELA Writing 8.2.3.d

Studying a Model

Here is a model of a research report. Study it to see how one student developed a paper. The first and the concluding paragraphs are shown in full. The paragraphs in the body of the paper are summarized.

INTRODUCTORY PARAGRAPH

Attention grabber

Statement of thesis

"I cannot raise my hand against my birthplace, my home, my children." With these words, Robert E. Lee changed the course of the Civil War. Abraham Lincoln had turned to Lee as his first choice for commander of the Union Army. However, Lee turned Lincoln down, choosing instead to side with his home state of Virginia and take command of the Confederate Army. Lee's decision to turn Lincoln down weakened the North and strengthened the Confederates, turning what might have been an easy victory for the North into a long, costly war.

BODY PARAGRAPHS

In the first part of the body, the student points out that Lee graduated from the U.S. Military Academy at West Point, served in the Mexican War, and was a member of the Union Army. She goes on to explain that he would have been a strong leader for the North, and his absence made the North weaker.

In the middle of the report, the writer discusses Lee's personality and character. She includes information about the strength of character he showed while in the military academy and while leading the Confederate Army. She discusses and gives examples of his intelligence, his daring, his courage, and his honesty.

In the last part of the body of the report, the student provides examples of Lee leading the outnumbered Confederate Army to a series of victories. The student provides details of the battles of Fredericksburg and Chancellorsville and explains how a lesser general than Lee may have lost both battles.

CONCLUDING PARAGRAPH

Summary of main points

Restatement of big idea

Lee's brilliant and resourceful leadership bedeviled a series of Union generals. He won battles that most generals would have lost. If Lee had used these skills to lead the larger and more powerful Union Army, the Civil War might have ended in months instead of years.

Cross-Discipline Activity: Math

Standards Proficiency

Research Guided Practice

ELA Writing 8.2.3.b; HSS **Analysis Skills:** HR 4

1. Send students to the library on an information scavenger hunt. Tell them their task is to find out how much the Civil War cost in lives and money. The monetary cost might include both the costs of maintaining the armies and the property losses suffered by civilians. The first student to find the information from a credible source wins.
2. Ask students to use their textbooks to calculate how many months, weeks, and days the Civil War lasted.
3. As a class, divide the monetary and human costs of the war by its length to determine the costs per month, week, and day. Explain to students that the actual costs were not incurred evenly throughout the period, so the numbers produced by the class are averages, not actual figures.
4. Use the findings to discuss the effects of war on soldiers, civilians, property, economies, and the environment. LS **Logical/Mathematical, Verbal/Linguistic**

3. Evaluate and Revise

Evaluating and Revising Your Draft

Evaluate your first draft by carefully reading it twice. Ask the questions below to decide which parts of your first draft should be revised.

Evaluation Questions for an Informative Report

- Does the introduction attract the readers' interest and state the big idea/thesis of your report?
- Does the body of your report have at least three paragraphs that develop your big idea? Is the main idea in each paragraph clearly stated?
- Have you included enough information to support each of your main ideas? Are all facts, details, and examples accurate? Are all of them clearly related to the main ideas they support?
- Is the report clearly organized? Does it use chronological order, order of importance, or cause and effect?
- Does the conclusion restate the big idea of your report? Does it end with a general comment about the importance or significance of your topic?
- Have you included at least three sources in your bibliography? Have you included all the sources you used and not any you did not use?

TIP **Organizing Your Time** By creating a schedule and following it, you can avoid that panicky moment when the due date is near and you haven't even started your research. To create your schedule and manage your time, include these six steps.

1 Develop a question and research your topic (10% of your total time).
2 Research and take notes (25%).
3 Write your main idea statement and create an outline (15%).
4 Write a first draft (25%).
5 Evaluate and revise your first draft (15%).
6 Proofread and publish your report (10%).

4. Proofread and Publish

Proofreading

To improve your report before sharing it, check the following:

- The spelling and capitalization of all proper names for people, places, things, and events.
- Punctuation marks around any direct quotation.
- Your list of sources (Works Cited or Bibliography) against a guide to writing research papers. Make sure you follow the examples in the guide when punctuating and capitalizing your source listings.

Publishing

Choose one or more of these ideas to publish your report.

- Share your report with your classmates by turning it into an informative speech.
- Submit your report to an online discussion group that focuses on the Civil War and ask for feedback.
- With your classmates, create a magazine that includes reports on several different topics or post the reports on your school Web site.

5. Practice and Apply

Use the steps and strategies outlined in this workshop to research and write an informative report on the Civil War.

Reteach

Proofreading

Shift into Reverse

Standard English Mastery Tell students that one reason it is difficult for people to proofread their own work is that they are too familiar with it. Since they know what they meant to say, it can be difficult for them to realize when their words do not convey their ideas. One way to counteract this familiarity is to proofread backwards. First, have students start at the end of the paper and look at each word in reverse order to make sure every word is used and spelled correctly. Then have students start at the end of the paper and read each sentence in reverse order to make sure every sentence is grammatically correct and written in standard English.

Practice & Apply

Integrating Facts, Details, and Examples

Go with the Flow Some students may become bogged down in details. Direct these students to write a first draft without worrying about including specific facts, details, or examples. Next, instruct students to put a letter next to each fact, detail, or example in their notes. Then have students write each letter next to the paragraph in their drafts where they want to insert the information.

Rubric

Students' reports should

- start with an interesting quote or historical detail.
- provide a clear thesis statement.
- present at least three main points about the chosen topic.
- provide at least one paragraph for each main point.
- provide supporting details, facts, and examples for each main point.
- end with a summary and a general comment about the topic.
- use correct grammar, punctuation, spelling, and capitalization.

Collaborative Learning

Standards Proficiency

Peer Editing ELA Writing 8.1.6

Standard English Mastery

1. Divide students into groups of four.
2. One student will pretend to be an author submitting his or her work to a scholarly journal. The other three students will pretend to be the editorial board of the journal. The first board member will examine the report to see if it meets the journal's standards for grammar, usage, and mechanics. The second board member will determine whether the content of the report is coherent and interesting enough to publish. The third board member will decide whether the report meets professional standards for factual accuracy based on the provided documentation and Bibliography or Works Cited.
3. The report will be "accepted" only if all board members agree that it meets the journal's standards. Have students trade roles until all four reports have been reviewed.

LS Interpersonal, Verbal/Linguistic

Unit Preview

Introduce the Unit

Share the information in the chapter overviews with students.

Chapter 17 Continued westward expansion brought economic change and conflict. Mining, ranching, and railroads changed the economy of the West. Offers of free land encouraged farmers to settle in the Great Plains. At the same time, more conflicts broke out between white settlers and Native Americans.

Chapter 18 The Second Industrial Revolution led to new sources of power and to advances in transportation and communications. New forms of business organization also emerged, and more workers joined labor unions. In the late 1800s, a new wave of immigration led some cities to experience dramatic growth.

Chapter 19 In the late 1800s, reformers addressed the problems caused by rapid urban growth and industrial advances. These efforts resulted in new laws and regulations. Meanwhile, labor unions sought to improve working conditions, women fought for and won the right to vote, and African Americans and other groups sought civil rights. *(continued on p. 541)*

Standards Focus

For a list of the overarching standards covered in this unit, see the first page of each chapter.

UNIT 6 1850–1929

A Growing America

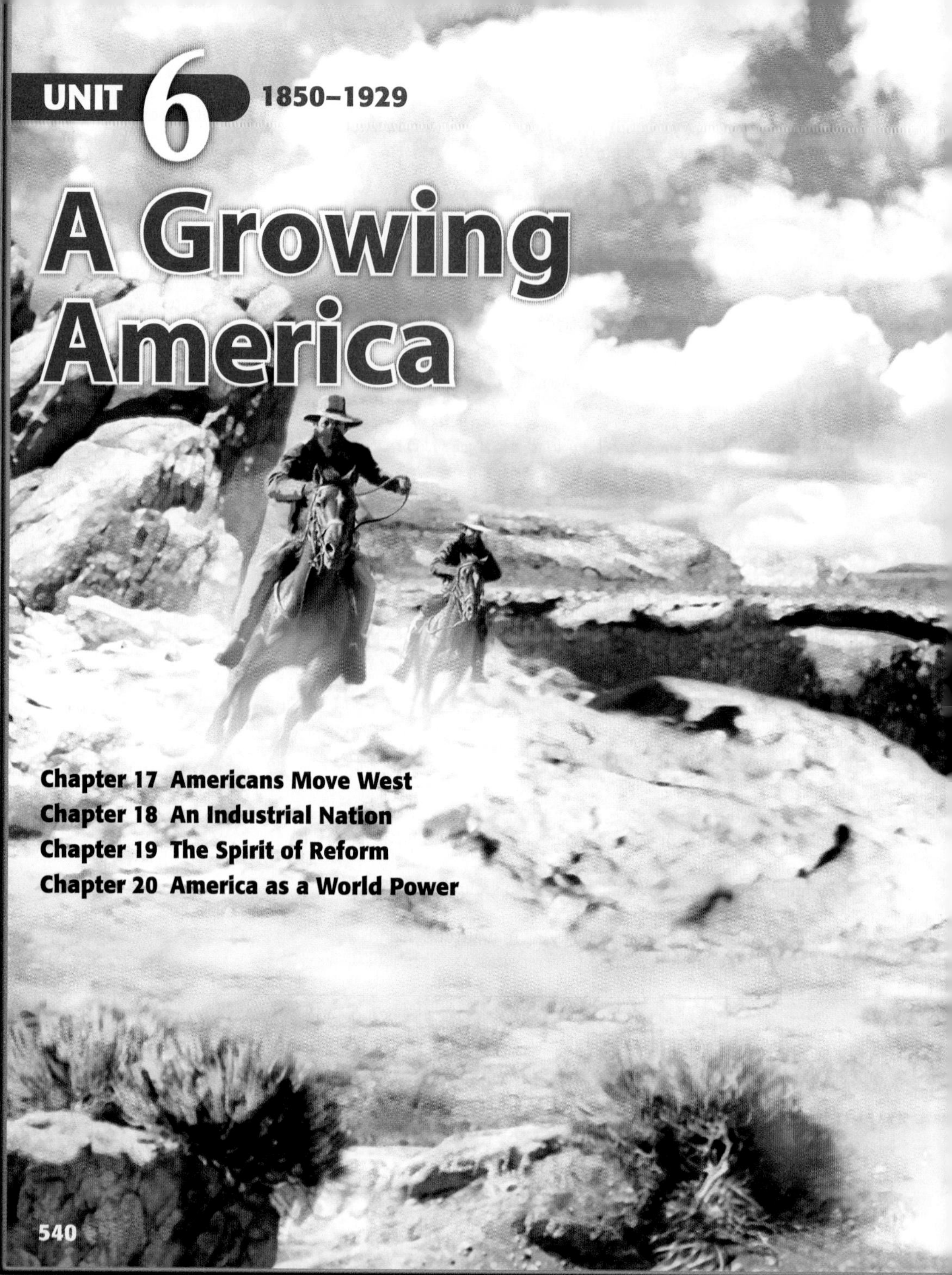

Unit Resources

Planning

- Universal Access Teacher Management System: Unit Instructional Benchmarking Guides
- One-Stop Planner CD-ROM with Test Generator: Holt Calendar Planner
- Power Presentations with Video CD-ROM
- A Teacher's Guide to Religion in the Public Schools

Standards Mastery

- Standards Review Workbook
- At Home: A Guide to Standards Mastery for United States History

Differentiating Instruction

- Universal Access Teacher Management System: Lesson Plans for Universal Access
- Pre-AP Activities Guide for United States History
- Universal Access Modified Worksheets and Tests CD-ROM

Enrichment

- **CRF 18:** Economics and History: Monopolies and Trusts
- **CRF 18:** Interdisciplinary Project: Technology Time Line
- Civic Participation
- Primary Source Library CD-ROM

Assessment

- Progress Assessment Support System: Benchmark Test
- OSP ExamView Test Generator: Benchmark Test
- Holt Online Assessment Program (in the Premier Online Edition)
- Alternative Assessment Handbook

The **Universal Access Teacher Management System** provides a planning and instructional benchmarking guide for this unit.

What You Will Learn...

After the American Civil War, the United States began a process of building a new economy and political structure. Events in the rest of the world began affecting the nation more noticeably.

During this period of expansion, the U.S. population spread across the continent. New immigrants and new technology began to change life in many parts of the country, especially in cities. Eventually, America would gain power over possessions on the other side of the globe. In the last four chapters, you will learn about changes in the United States that helped the country increase its size, wealth, and power.

Explore the Art

In this picture, a teenage Buffalo Bill Cody flees from bandits on his Pony Express route. How does this picture show the importance of communication in the expansion of the United States?

Unit Preview

Unit Overview *continued*

Chapter 20 In the late 1800s the United States began to acquire overseas territories and to increase trade with Asian countries. Victory in the Spanish-American War gave the United States more territories and further influence abroad. The United States also became more involved with Latin America.

Connect to the Unit

Activity Visual Chapter Preview Have students write down each of the chapter titles on a sheet of paper. Share the information in the chapter overviews with the class. Then have students scan the headings, images, maps, and charts in each chapter in this unit. Have students use the visual preview to write five questions that they have about each chapter. At the end of the unit, discuss students' questions and answers. **LS Verbal/Linguistic, Visual/Spatial**

Explore the Art

William "Buffalo Bill" Cody went to work for a wagon freight company as a mounted messenger at age 11. He was 14 when he began delivering U.S. mail for the Pony Express. Cody was one of many teens who rode for the Pony Express, which advertised for "skinny, expert riders willing to risk death daily." Cody went on to become a buffalo hunter, U.S. Army scout, Indian fighter, and later the host of his own Wild West show.

About the Illustration

This illustration is an artist's conception based on available sources. However, historians are uncertain exactly what this scene looked like.

Democracy and Civic Education

Standards Proficiency

Authority: Local Government and Public Policy

Research Required

Background Explain to students that reformers in the late 1800s and early 1900s expanded voting power and democracy at state and local levels. Reforms included direct primaries, recalls, initiatives, referendums, the direct election of senators, and new forms of city governments.

1. Organize students into small groups and have each group conduct research to learn about the local government.
2. Each group should create a display or software presentation showing the structure of the local government. In addition, students should indicate how public policy is formed at the local level and ways in which citizens can shape local public policy.
3. **Extend** Have a local government official speak to the class. Students should prepare questions to ask the speaker in advance. **LS Interpersonal, Verbal/Linguistic**

Alternative Assessment Handbook, Rubrics 29: Presentations; and 30: Research

Civic Participation

Answers

Explore the Art *possible answer— The dangerous conditions under which the mail is being delivered indicates the importance of mail delivery and the difficulties people faced to communicate.*

Chapter 17 Planning Guide

Americans Move West

Chapter Overview	Reproducible Resources	Technology Resources
CHAPTER 17 pp. 542–569 **Overview:** In this chapter, students will analyze the increased migration of Americans westward across the continent, along with the conflicts this migration caused. See p. 542 for the California History–Social Science standards covered in this chapter.	**Universal Access Teacher Management System:*** • Universal Access Instructional Benchmarking Guides • Lesson Plans for Universal Access **Interactive Reader and Study Guide:*** Chapter Graphic Organizer **Chapter Resource File*** • Focus on Writing Activity: A Letter • Social Studies Skills Activity: Migration Maps • Chapter Review Activity	**One-Stop Planner CD-ROM:** Calendar Planner **Student Edition Full-Read Audio CD-ROM** **Universal Access Modified Worksheets and Tests CD-ROM** **Interactive Skills Tutor CD-ROM** **Primary Source Library CD-ROM for United States History** **Power Presentations with Video CD-ROM** **History's Impact: United States History Video Program (VHS/DVD):** Americans Move West*
Section 1: **Miners, Ranchers, and Railroads** **The Big Idea:** As more settlers moved West, mining, ranching, and railroads soon transformed the western landscape. 8.8.2	**Universal Access Teacher Management System:*** Section 1 Lesson Plan **Interactive Reader and Study Guide:*** Section 1 Summary **Chapter Resource File*** • Vocabulary Builder, Section 1 • Biography Activity: Nat Love • Literature Activity: *A Letter From a Pony Express Rider* by Lucius Lodosky Hickock • Primary Source Activity: E. C. Abbott's Memoirs of Cowhands and Cattle Drives **Political Cartoons Activities for United States History,** Cartoon 19: Transcontinental Railroad*	**Daily Bellringer Transparency:** Section 1* **Map Transparency:** Reasons for Westward Expansion* **Map Transparency:** Routes West* **Quick Facts Transparency:** Effects of the Transcontinental Railroad* go.hrw.com **Internet Activity:** Myths and Realities of the West Display
Section 2: **Wars for the West** **The Big Idea:** Native Americans and the U.S. government came into conflict over land in the West. 8.12.2	**Universal Access Teacher Management System:*** Section 2 Lesson Plan **Interactive Reader and Study Guide:*** Section 2 Summary **Chapter Resource File*** • Vocabulary Builder, Section 2 • Biography Activity: George Armstrong Custer • Biography Activity: Sarah Winnemucca • History and Geography Activity: Conflicts with the Indians • Primary Source Activity: Battle of the Little Bighorn	**Daily Bellringer Transparency:** Section 2* **Map Transparency:** Native American Land Loss in the West, 1850–90* go.hrw.com **Internet Activity:** Geronimo Diary
Section 3: **Farming and Populism** **The Big Idea:** Settlers on the Great Plains created new communities and unique political groups. 8.8.2, 8.12.8	**Universal Access Teacher Management System:*** Section 3 Lesson Plan **Interactive Reader and Study Guide:*** Section 3 Summary **Chapter Resource File*** • Vocabulary Builder, Section 3 • Biography Activity: Laura Ingalls Wilder **Political Cartoons Activities for United States History,** Cartoon 20: Farmers Face Hard Times*	**Daily Bellringer Transparency:** Section 3*

MASTERING THE CALIFORNIA STANDARDS

SE Student Edition | Print Resource | Audio CD | Video

TE Teacher's Edition | Transparency | CD-ROM | DVD

go.hrw.com | CA Standards Mastery | **LS** Learning Styles

OSP One-Stop Planner CD-ROM | * also on One-Stop Planner CD

Review, Assessment, Intervention

- **Standards Review Workbook***
- **Quick Facts Transparency:** Americans Move West Visual Summary*
- **Spanish Chapter Summaries Audio CD Program**
- **Online Chapter Summaries in Six Languages**
- **Progress Assessment Support System (PASS):** Chapter Test*
- **Universal Access Modified Worksheets and Tests CD-ROM:** Modified Chapter Test
- **One-Stop Planner CD-ROM:** ExamView Test Generator (English/Spanish)

- **PASS:** Section 1 Quiz*
- **Online Quiz:** Section 1
- **Alternative Assessment Handbook**

- **PASS:** Section 2 Quiz*
- **Online Quiz:** Section 2
- **Alternative Assessment Handbook**

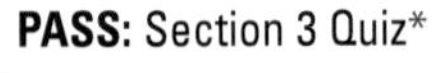

- **PASS:** Section 3 Quiz*
- **Online Quiz:** Section 3
- **Alternative Assessment Handbook**

California Resources for Standards Mastery

INSTRUCTIONAL PLANNING AND SUPPORT

- **Universal Access Teacher Management System***
- **One-Stop Planner CD-ROM with Test Generator: Teacher Management System with Interactive Teacher's Edition**

STANDARDS MASTERY

- **Standards Review Workbook***
- **At Home: A Guide to Standards Mastery for United States History**

Holt Online Learning

To enhance learning, Internet activities are available for a Myths and Realities of the West Display and a Geronimo Diary.

KEYWORD: SS8 TEACHER

- **Teacher Support Page**
- **Content Updates**
- **Rubrics and Writing Models**
- **Teaching Tips for the Multimedia Classroom**

KEYWORD: SS8 US17

- **Current Events**
- **Document-Based Questions**
- **Holt Grapher**
- **Holt Online Atlas**
- **Holt Researcher**
- **Interactive Multimedia Activities**
- **Internet Activities**
- **Online Chapter Summaries in Six Languages**
- **Online Section Quizzes**
- **American History Maps and Charts**

HOLT PREMIER ONLINE STUDENT EDITION

Complete online support for interactivity, assessment, and reporting

- **Interactive Maps and Notebook**
- **Standardized Test Prep**
- **Homework Practice and Research Activities Online**

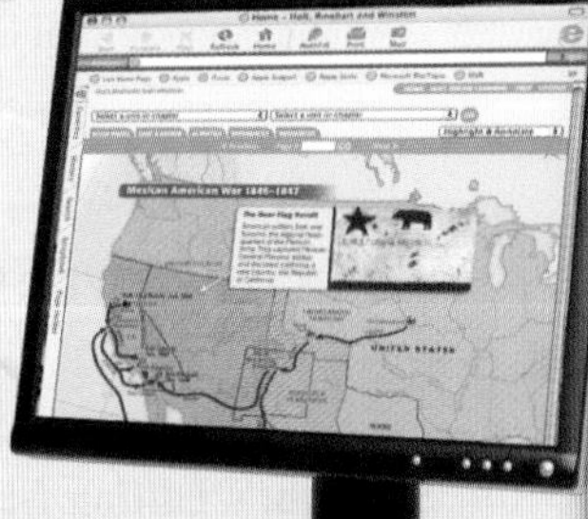

Mastering the Standards: Differentiating Instruction

Reaching Standards	Basic-level activities designed for all students encountering new material
Standards Proficiency	Intermediate-level activities designed for average students
Exceeding Standards	Challenging activities designed for honors and gifted-and-talented students
Standard English Mastery	Activities designed to improve standard English usage

Frequently Asked Questions

INSTRUCTIONAL PLANNING AND SUPPORT

Where do I find planning aids, pacing guides, lesson plans, and other teaching aids?

Annotated Teacher's Edition:
- Chapter planning guides
- Standards-based instruction and strategies
- Differentiated instruction for universal access
- Point-of-use reminders for integrating program resources

Power Presentations with Video CD-ROM

Universal Access Teacher Management System:
- Year and unit instructional benchmarking guides
- Reproducible lesson plans
- Assessment guides for diagnostic, progress, and summative end-of-the-year tests
- Options for differentiating instruction and intervention
- Teaching guides and answer keys for student workbooks

One-Stop Planner CD-ROM with Test Generator: Teacher Management System with Interactive Teacher's Editon:
- Calendar Planner
- Editable lesson plans
- All reproducible ancillaries in Adobe Acrobat (PDF) format
- ExamView Test Generator (English & Spanish)
- Game Tool for ExamView
- PuzzlePro
- Transparency and video previews

DIFFERENTIATING INSTRUCTION FOR UNIVERSAL ACCESS

What resources are available to ensure that Advanced Learners/GATE Students master the standards?

Teacher's Edition Activities:
- Mining Mock Trial, p. 547
- Modern Reservations, p. 555
- 1896 Presidential Debate, p. 564

Lesson Plans for Universal Access

Primary Source Library CD-ROM for United States History

What resources are available to ensure that English Learners and Standard English Learners master the standards?

Teacher's Edition Activities:
- Boomtown Map, p. 548

Lesson Plans for Universal Access

Chapter Resource File: Vocabulary Builder Activities

Spanish Chapter Summaries Audio CD Program

Online Chapter Summaries in Six Languages

One-Stop Planner CD-ROM:
- PuzzlePro, Spanish Version
- ExamView Test Generator, Spanish Version

What modified materials are available for Special Education?

The ***Universal Access Modified Worksheets and Tests CD-ROM*** provides editable versions of the following:

Vocabulary Flash Cards

Modified Vocabulary Builder Activities

Modified Chapter Review Activity

Modified Chapter Test

What resources are available to ensure that Learners Having Difficulty master the standards?

Teacher's Edition Activities:
- Cattle Kingdom Comic Books, p. 549
- Conditions in the West, p. 550
- Plains Indian Museum Exhibit, p. 554
- In-depth Oral Reports, p. 556
- Groups of the Great Plains, p. 561
- Daily Life on the Plains Mural, p. 562

Interactive Reader and Study Guide

Student Edition Full-Read Audio CD

Quick Facts Transparency: Americans Move West Visual Summary

Standards Review Workbook

Social Studies Skills Activity: Migration Maps

Interactive Skills Tutor CD-ROM

How do I intervene for students struggling to master the standards?

Interactive Reader and Study Guide

Quick Facts Transparency: Americans Move West Visual Summary

Standards Review Workbook

Social Studies Skills Activity: Migration Maps

Interactive Skills Tutor CD-ROM

PROFESSIONAL DEVELOPMENT

What teacher training resources are available to help me grow professionally?

- In-service and staff development as part of your Holt Social Studies product purchase
- Quick Teacher Tutorial Lesson Presentation CD-ROM
- Intensive tuition-based Teacher Development Institute
- *Teaching American History* Online 2 Module Professional Development Course
- Convenient Holt Speaker Bureau face-to-face workshop options
- PRAXIS™ Test Prep (#0089) interactive Web-based content refreshers*
- 24/7 *Ask A Professional Development Expert* at http://www.hrw.com/prodev/

* PRAXIS is a trademark of Educational Testing Service (ETS). This publication is not endorsed or approved by ETS.

Information Literacy Skills

To learn more about how History–Social Science instruction may be improved by the effective use of library media centers and information literacy skills, go to the Teacher's Resource Materials for Chapter 17 at **go.hrw.com**, keyword: SS8 MEDIA.

The following materials were developed by the Division for Public Education of the American Bar Association. These materials are part of the **Democracy and Civic Education** supplement.
- Constitution Study Guide
- Supreme Court Case Studies

MASTERING THE CALIFORNIA STANDARDS

Chapter Preview

Standards Focus

Standards by Section
Section 1: HSS 8.8.2
Section 2: HSS 8.12.2
Section 3: HSS 8.8.2, 8.12.8

Teacher's Edition
HSS **Analysis Skills:** CS 1, CS 2, CS 3, HR 1, HR 5, HI 1, HI 2
ELA Writing 8.2.5, Reading 8.2.0

Preview Grade 11 Standards
HSS **11.2** Students analyze the relationship among the rise of industrialization, large-scale rural to urban migration and massive immigration from Southern and Eastern Europe.
11.2.2 Describe the changing landscape, including the growth of cities linked by industry and trade, and the development of cities divided according to race, ethnicity, and class.

Focus on Writing

The **Chapter Resource File** provides a Focus on Writing worksheet to help students organize and write a letter.

CRF: Focus on Writing Activity: Writing a Letter

CHAPTER 17 1850–1890

Americans Move West

California Standards

History–Social Science

8.8 Students analyze the divergent paths of the American people in the West from 1800 to the mid-1800s and the challenges they faced.

8.12 Students analyze the transformation of the American economy and the changing social and political conditions in the United States in response to the Industrial Revolution.

Analysis Skills

CS 3 Students use a variety of maps and documents to identify physical and cultural features of neighborhoods, cities, states, and countries.

English–Language Arts

Writing 8.2.1 Write biographies, autobiographies, short stories, or narratives.

Reading 8.2.0 Students read and understand grade-level appropriate material.

FOCUS ON WRITING

Writing a Letter Before telephones and e-mail, one way to communicate with people far away was by letter. In this chapter, you will read about the settlement of the West by European Americans. Suppose you were an Irish immigrant working on a railroad that crossed the Great Plains. What might you have seen or experienced? After you read the chapter, you will write a letter to your sister in Ireland telling her about your experiences.

UNITED STATES

1860 The Pony Express begins delivering mail between East and West.

1850 — 1860

WORLD

1855 Paris holds a World's Fair.

Introduce the Chapter

Standards Proficiency

Moving Out West

1. Tell students that in this chapter they will learn that the United States population grew rapidly in the mid-1800s. Farmers, miners, and ranchers settled throughout the West.
2. Ask students to consider what kind of work they would choose to do in the West—farming, mining, or ranching. Then have students explain their choices.
3. Ask students to imagine the working conditions of each vocation, and what challenges each might involve.
4. Remind students that in many cases, farms, mines, and ranches developed in areas already occupied by Native Americans. What cultural conflict might result as American businesses and settlers came into contact with Native Americans? LS **Interpersonal, Verbal/Linguistic**

HOLT
History's Impact
▶ video series
Watch the video to understand the impact of technological improvements on the West.
What You Will Learn...
In this chapter you will learn about how the great American West changed in the late 1800s. Settlers poured into the region and built mines, ranches, farms, and railroads. In this photo, modern pioneers re-create a wagon journey from the 1800s.
10 MILES OF TRACK, LAID IN ONE DAY. APRIL 28TH 1869
1869 The first transcontinental railroad is completed.
1874 Gold is discovered in the Black Hills of the Dakotas.
1879 Thousands of African Americans migrate from the South to Kansas.
1890 The Massacre at Wounded Knee occurs.
1870
1880
1890
1864 French scientist Louis Pasteur invents the purification process of pasteurization.
ORIENT-EXPRESS
1883 The Orient Express railway makes its first run from Paris to Istanbul.
1888 Brazil abolishes slavery.
AMERICANS MOVE WEST 543

Chapter Preview

HOLT
History's Impact
▶ **video series**
See the Video Teacher's Guide for strategies for using the chapter video **Americans Move West**.

Chapter Big Ideas

Section 1 As more settlers moved West, mining, ranching, and railroads soon transformed the western landscape. HSS 8.8.2

Section 2 Native Americans and the U.S. government came into conflict over land in the West. HSS 8.12.2

Section 3 Settlers on the Great Plains created new communities and unique political groups. HSS 8.8.2, 8.12.8

Explore the Picture

Wagon Trains Wagon trains of up to 100 wagons were a frequent mode of transportation westward into the American frontier. At a distance their white canvas tops so resembled the sails of ships that the wagons were nicknamed prairie schooners. Groups would assemble in the early spring, hire guides, assign roles, buy supplies, and wait for favorable weather before beginning their months-long journeys.

Analyzing Visuals What kinds of obstacles and dangers might a wagon train like this one expect to face? *possible answers—harsh weather, rough terrain, crossing mountains and rivers, sick or injured horses, attacks by Native Americans*

go.hrw.com
Online Resources
Chapter Resources:
KEYWORD: SS8 US17
Teacher Resources:
KEYWORD: SS8 TEACHER

Explore the Time Line

1. In what year was gold discovered in the Dakotas? *1874*
2. What mail delivery system between East and West began in 1860? *the Pony Express*
3. In what year was the transcontinental railroad finished? *1869*
4. How long after the transcontinental railroad was completed did the Orient Express make its first run? *14 years*

HSS **Analysis Skills:** CS 1

Info to Know

The Orient Express On October 4, 1883, the Orient Express, the first European transcontinental railroad, took its initial trip from Paris to present-day Istanbul. Since no railcar had ever been built with such luxury in mind, the line became a favorite among Europe's social elite and royalty. The Orient Express ran continually from 1883 to 1977 (with two service suspensions for World Wars I and II), when it closed following a long period of declining passenger volume. The line was reopened in 1982 and still runs today, though along shortened lines.

Reading Social Studies

Understanding Themes

Ask students to share what they know about the settlement of the West. Then ask students how the geography of the West played a role in where people settled and how they earned a living. Ask students to discuss what technological advancements allowed settlers to live in the West. Point out to students that geography and technology are the two main themes of this chapter.

Questioning

Focus on Reading Distribute copies of a newspaper article to the class and call on students to read the article aloud. Then select a paragraph at random from the article and ask students to re-read just that paragraph. Have students apply the questions *who*, *what*, *when*, *where*, *why*, *how*, and *what if*, to the paragraph. Have students write their answers on their own sheet of paper. After students have finished, review the paragraph with the class. Ask volunteers to share their answers, and how they reached the answer, with the class. Discuss with students the benefits of using questions to analyze a text.

Reading Social Studies

by Kylene Beers

Economics | Geography | Politics | Religion | Society and Culture | Science and Technology

Focus on Themes In this chapter you will follow the development of the United States from the mid-1800s through the 1890s. You will learn that California was admitted to the Union in 1850. You will find out about the struggles that people faced as the movement West continued and people settled the Great Plains. You will learn about the **technological** advancements made during this time as well as the difficult **geographical** obstacles miners and ranchers faced in the West.

Questioning

Focus on Reading When newspaper reporters want to get to the heart of a story, they ask certain questions: who, what, when, where, why, and how. When you are reading a history book, you can use the same questions to get to the heart of what happened in the past.

Additional reading support can be found in the

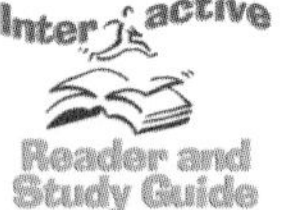

Hypothetical Questions You can also use questions to dig deeper than what is in the text. You can ask hypothetical, or what if, questions. These questions ask what might have happened had events occurred differently. Sometimes asking such questions can help history come alive.

In 1862 Congress passed two important land acts that helped open the West to settlers. The Homestead Act gave government-owned land to small farmers. Any adult who was a U.S. citizen or planned to become one could receive 160 acres of land. In exchange, homesteaders promised to live on the land for five years. The Morrill Act granted more than 17 million acres of federal land to the states. *(p. 560)*

Who? Congress

What? encouraged new settlement

Where? the West

When? 1862

How? Congress gave land to anyone who agreed to settle on it for five years.

Why? Perhaps Congress feared what would happen to Western lands if they remained unsettled.

What if? If Congress had not passed these laws, people might not have moved West. The U.S. might not have grown as quickly as it did.

Reading and Skills Resources

Reading Support

- Interactive Reader and Study Guide
- Student Edition on Audio CD
- Spanish Chapter Summaries Audio CD Program

Social Studies Skills Support

- Interactive Skills Tutor CD-ROM

Vocabulary Support

- **CRF:** Vocabulary Builder Activities
- **CRF:** Chapter Review Activity
- Universal Access Modified Worksheets and Tests CD-ROM:
  - Vocabulary Flash Cards
  - Vocabulary Builder Activity
  - Chapter Review Activity
- OSP Holt PuzzlePro

Standards Focus

HSS **Analysis Skills:** HR 1
ELA Reading 8.2.0

ELA **Analysis HR 1** Frame questions that can be answered by historical study and research.
HSS **Reading 8.2.0** Students read and understand grade-level-appropriate material.

You Try It!

Read the following passage and then answer the questions below.

Building Communities

Women were an important force in the settling of the frontier. They joined in the hard work of farming and ranching and helped build communities out of the widely spaced farms and small towns. Their role in founding communities facilitated a strong voice in public affairs. Wyoming women, for example, were granted suffrage in the new state's constitution, which was approved in 1869. Annie Bidwell, one of the founders of Chico, California, used her influence to support a variety of moral and social causes such as women's suffrage and temperance.

From Chapter 17, p. 549

Answer these questions based on the passage you just read.

1. Who is this passage about?
2. What did they do?
3. When did they do this?
4. How do you think they accomplished it?
5. Why do you think they were able to accomplish so much?
6. How can knowing this information help you understand the past?
7. What if women in the West had been given more rights? Fewer rights? How might the West have been different?

As you read Chapter 17, ask questions like who, what, when, where, why, how, and what if to help you analyze what you are reading.

Key Terms and People

Chapter 17

Section 1

frontier *(p. 546)*
Comstock Lode *(p. 547)*
boomtowns *(p. 548)*
Cattle Kingdom *(p. 549)*
vaqueros *(p. 549)*
cattle drive *(p. 549)*
Chisholm Trail *(p. 549)*
Pony Express *(p. 550)*
transcontinental railroad *(p. 550)*

Section 2

Treaty of Fort Laramie *(p. 554)*
reservations *(p. 555)*
Crazy Horse *(p. 555)*
Treaty of Medicine Lodge *(p. 555)*
George Armstrong Custer *(p. 556)*
Sitting Bull *(p. 556)*
Battle of the Little Bighorn *(p. 556)*
Massacre at Wounded Knee *(p. 557)*
Long Walk *(p. 557)*
Ghost Dance *(p. 558)*
Sarah Winnemucca *(p. 558)*
Dawes General Allotment Act *(p. 558)*

Section 3

Homestead Act *(p. 560)*
Morrill Act *(p. 560)*
Exodusters *(p. 561)*
sodbusters *(p. 561)*
dry farming *(p. 561)*
Annie Bidwell *(p. 561)*
National Grange *(p. 563)*
deflation *(p. 564)*
William Jennings Bryan *(p. 564)*
Populist Party *(p. 564)*

Academic Vocabulary

In this chapter, you will learn the following academic words:

establish *(p. 548)*
facilitate *(p. 561)*

Reading Social Studies

Key Terms and People

Introduce the key terms and people from this chapter by briefly reviewing each term and person with the class. Instruct students to look in the chapter for more information on each term. Then have students write a statement for each term or person that provides a description of the item, and then asks, "Who am I?" For example, "I am a reformer who called for improvements for Native Americans. Who am I?" Collect the statements from students and read some of them to the class.
LS Verbal/Linguistic

Focus on Reading

See the **Focus on Reading** questions in this chapter for more practice on this reading social studies skill.

Reading Social Studies Assessment

See the **Standards Review** at the end of this chapter for student assessment questions related to this reading skill.

Teaching Tip

Explain to students that journalists use many of these questions when they are writing news articles. This is a simple, easy-to-remember way to include important information and significant details about any event. Read a lead paragraph from the front page of a daily newspaper to the class, and ask students to try to identify which of questions the journalist included in his or her story. Ask students to identify which question journalists would rarely use. Why might they not use that question?

Answers

You Try It! 1. *women on the western frontier;* **2.** *farmed and ranched, helped build communities, and supported moral and social causes;* **3.** *in the mid to late 1800s;* **4.** *possible answer—through hard work and dedication;* **5.** *They were adventurous, hard working, and independent.* **6.** *possible answer—it helps us understand the role of women in the West.* **7.** *possible answers: more rights—they might have played a larger role in government; fewer rights—women would not have been as important a force in the West.*

Preteach

Bellringer

If YOU were there . . . Use the **Daily Bellringer Transparency** to help students answer the question.

 Daily Bellringer Transparency, Section 1

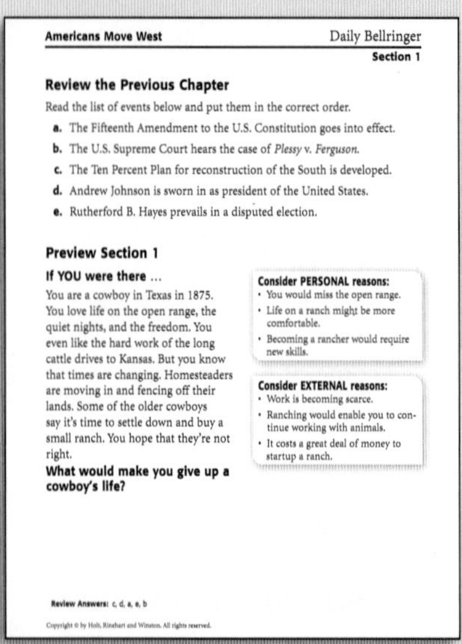

Americans Move West — Daily Bellringer — **Section 1**

Review the Previous Chapter

Read the list of events below and put them in the correct order.

a. The Fifteenth Amendment to the U.S. Constitution goes into effect.
b. The U.S. Supreme Court hears the case of *Plessy* v. *Ferguson*.
c. The Ten Percent Plan for reconstruction of the South is developed.
d. Andrew Johnson is sworn in as president of the United States.
e. Rutherford B. Hayes prevails in a disputed election.

Preview Section 1

If YOU were there ...

You are a cowboy in Texas in 1875. You love life on the open range, the quiet nights, and the freedom. You even like the hard work of the long cattle drives to Kansas. But you know that times are changing. Homesteaders are moving in and fencing off their lands. Some of the older cowboys say it's time to settle down and buy a small ranch. You hope that they're not right.

What would make you give up a cowboy's life?

Consider PERSONAL reasons:
- You would miss the open range.
- Life on a ranch might be more comfortable.
- Becoming a rancher would require new skills.

Consider EXTERNAL reasons:
- Work is becoming scarce.
- Ranching would enable you to continue working with animals.
- It costs a great deal of money to startup a ranch.

Review Answers: c, d, a, e, b

Academic Vocabulary

Review with students the high-use academic term in this section.

establish to set up or create (p. 548)

CRF: Vocabulary Builder Activity, Section 1

Standards Focus

HSS 8.8.2

Means: Describe how and why the United States expanded west.

Matters: Mining, ranching, and railroads drew many to the West and led to conflict with Native Americans.

SECTION 1

Miners, Ranchers, and Railroads

What You Will Learn...

Main Ideas

1. A mining boom brought growth to the West.
2. The demand for cattle created a short-lived Cattle Kingdom on the Great Plains.
3. East and West were connected by the transcontinental railroad.

The Big Idea

As more settlers moved West, mining, ranching, and railroads soon transformed the western landscape.

Key Terms

frontier, *p. 546*
Comstock Lode, *p. 547*
boomtowns, *p. 548*
Cattle Kingdom, *p. 549*
cattle drive, *p. 549*
Chisholm Trail, *p. 549*
Pony Express, *p. 550*
transcontinental railroad, *p. 550*

HSS 8.8.2 Describe the purpose, challenges, and economic incentives associated with westward expansion, including the concept of Manifest Destiny (e.g., the Lewis and Clark expedition, accounts of the removal of Indians, the Cherokees' "Trail of Tears," settlement of the Great Plains) and the territorial acquisitions that spanned numerous decades.

If YOU were there...

You are a cowboy in Texas in 1875. You love life on the open range, the quiet nights, and the freedom. You even like the hard work of the long cattle drives to Kansas. But you know that times are changing. Homesteaders are moving in and fencing off their lands. Some of the older cowboys say it's time to settle down and buy a small ranch. You hope that they're not right.

What would make you give up a cowboy's life?

BUILDING BACKGROUND In the years following the Civil War, the U.S. population grew rapidly. Settlements in the West increased. More discoveries of gold and silver attracted adventurers, while the open range drew others. Thousands of former Civil War soldiers also joined the move West.

Mining Boom Brings Growth

During the years surrounding the War, most Americans had thought of the Great Plains and other western lands as the Great American Desert. In the years following the Civil War, Americans witnessed the rapid growth of the U.S. population and the spread of settlements throughout the West. With the admission of the state of California to the Union in 1850, the western boundary of the American **frontier**—an undeveloped area—had reached the Pacific Ocean.

The frontier changed dramatically as more and more people moved westward. Settlers built homes, fenced off land, and laid out ranches and farms. Miners, ranchers, and farmers remade the landscape of the West as they adapted to their new surroundings. The geography of the West was further changed by the development and expansion of a large and successful railroad industry that moved the West's natural resources to eastern markets. Gold and silver were the most valuable natural resources, and mining companies used the growing railroad network to bring these precious metals to the East.

Teach the Big Idea: Master the Standards

Standards Proficiency

Miners, Ranchers, and Railroads

HSS 8.8.2; HSS **Analysis Skills:** HI 1

1. **Teach** Ask students the Main Idea questions to teach this section.
2. **Apply** Organize the class into small groups. Ask each group to create a poster to advertise one of the following jobs: miner, rancher, railroad worker. Instruct students to list or draw things that might influence a person from the eastern United States or from another country to move west to work in this position. Ask volunteers to present their posters to the class and display posters for the class to see. **LS Visual/Spatial**
3. **Review** To review the section's main ideas, have students refer back to their posters and discuss the challenges related to these fields.
4. **Practice/Homework** Have each student write a persuasive letter of application for one of the three jobs. **LS Verbal/Linguistic**

Alternative Assessment Handbook, Rubrics 28: Posters; and 43: Writing to Persuade

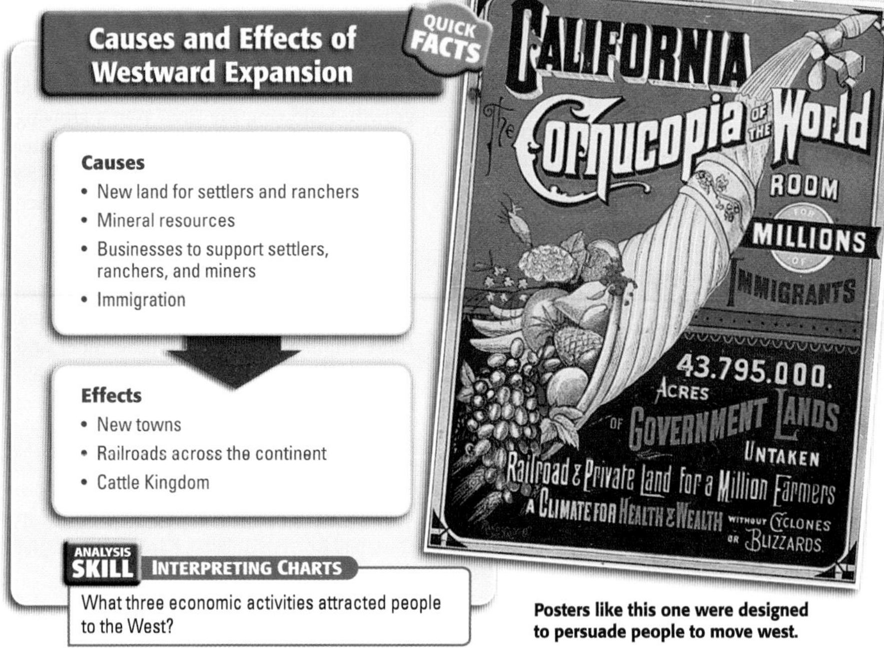

ANALYSIS SKILL INTERPRETING CHARTS

What three economic activities attracted people to the West?

Posters like this one were designed to persuade people to move west.

Big Business

Most of the precious metals were located in western Nevada. In 1859 miner Henry Comstock discovered a huge deposit of gold and silver in Nevada that became called the **Comstock Lode**. The deposit was incredibly rich and deep. In just the first year after its discovery, the Comstock Lode lured thousands of California miners to Nevada. Over the next 20 years, the Comstock Lode produced more than $500 million worth of gold and silver.

Expensive equipment was needed to remove the silver and gold that were trapped within quartz rock. Larger mining companies bought up land claims from miners who could not afford this machinery. As a result, mining became a big business in the West.

As companies dug bigger and deeper mines, the work became more dangerous. Miners had to use unsafe equipment, such as elevator platforms without protective walls. They worked in dark tunnels and breathed hot, stuffy air. They suffered from lung disease caused by dusty air. Miners often were injured or killed by poorly planned explosions or by cave-ins. Fire was also a great danger. Mining was therefore one of the most dangerous jobs in the country. In the West, worries about safety and pay led miners to form several unions in the 1860s.

Settlers

People from all over the world came to work in the western mines. Some miners came from the eastern United States. Others emigrated from Europe, Central and South America, and Asia. Many Mexican immigrants and Mexican Americans were experienced miners. They were skilled in assaying, or testing, the contents of valuable ore. One newspaper reporter wrote, "Here were congregated the most varied elements of humanity . . . belonging to almost every nationality and every status of life."

Collaborative Learning

Exceeding Standards

Mining Mock Trial

HSS 8.8.2; HSS **Analysis Skills:** HI 1, HI 2

1. Discuss with students the challenges faced by miners in the West and how big businesses changed mining. Tell students that they will create and participate in a mock trial in which a group of miners are suing one of the big mining companies over hazardous working conditions.
2. Organize the class into five small groups. Assign each group one of the following roles: the defense, the plaintiff, the judge, witnesses, and a jury. Have each group prepare for their role in the mock trial by writing questions they might ask during the trial.
3. Have students stage the mock trial. Have the judge group moderate the trial and ensure that the groups follow proper courtroom procedures.
4. After all the testimony has been heard, have the jury decide whether the miners have a legitimate claim. LS **Interpersonal, Kinesthetic**

Alternative Assessment Handbook, Rubrics 14: Group Activity; and 33: Skits and Reader's Theater

Direct Teach

Main Idea

1 Mining Boom Brings Growth

A mining boom brought growth to the West.

Identify Who was Henry Comstock? *miner who found a rich and deep deposit of gold and silver in Nevada in 1859*

Summarize What made mining dangerous? *unsafe equipment, poor conditions inside the mine, dusty air, cave-ins, fire*

Make Judgments Why do you think people from other countries came to America to work the mines? *possible answers—needed jobs; thought they could get rich by mining; to escape poor conditions in their old countries*

Quick Facts Transparency: Causes and Effects of Westward Expansion

HSS 8.8.2; HSS **Analysis Skills:** HI 1

Info to Know

Mining Unions In 1864 the Miners' Protective Association (MPA), in response to the harsh working conditions associated with mining the Comstock Lode, organized the first miner's strike. The demands of the MPA—increased wages, improved working conditions, and shorter hours—spread throughout the mining industry. In 1893 the labor movement expanded to the city of Butte, Montana. There, the Western Federation of Miners (WFM) organized other labor groups in the hope of preventing the U.S. military from intervening in labor disputes. By 1903 the WFM had more than 50,000 members.

Answers

Interpreting Charts *ranching, mining, farming*

Direct Teach

Main Idea

1 Mining Boom Brings Growth

A mining boom brought growth to the West.

Define What is a boomtown? *a community created by the mining industry to support the workers*

Summarize How did women help support the boomtown economy? *washing, cooking, making clothes, chopping wood, raising families, teaching, and newspaper writing*

Draw Conclusions Why do you think boomtowns often disappeared after the local mine closed? *possible answer—The whole economy centered around the mine, so when the mine left, the economy faltered.*

CRF: Biography Activity: Nat Love

CRF: Primary Source Activity: E. C. Abbott's Memoirs of Cowhands and Cattle Drives

HSS 8.8.2, HSS **Analysis Skills:** HI 1, HI 2

go.hrw.com

Online Resources

KEYWORD: SS8 US17
ACTIVITY: Myths and Realities of the West Display

New Towns

Mining booms also produced **boomtowns**, communities that grew suddenly when a mine opened. They disappeared just as quickly when the mine closed. Most boomtowns had general stores, saloons, and boardinghouses.

Few women or families lived in boomtowns. "I was never so lonely and homesick in all my life," wrote one young woman. Women washed, cooked, made clothes, and chopped wood. They also raised families, established schools, and wrote for newspapers. Their work helped turn some mining camps into successful, permanent towns.

ACADEMIC VOCABULARY
establish to set up or create

READING CHECK **Summarizing** What risks did miners face?

The Cattle Kingdom

The cattle industry was another area of rapid growth. Following the Civil War, a growing economy and population created a greater demand for beef in the East. Cattle worth $3 to $6 each in Texas could be sold for $38 each in Kansas. In New York, they could be sold for $80 each. The most popular breed of cattle was the longhorn. The Longhorn spread quickly throughout western Texas. Because these animals needed very little water and could survive harsh weather, they were well-suited to the dry, desert-like environment of western Texas. But how could Texas ranchers move the longhorns to eastern markets?

In 1867 businessman Joseph McCoy discovered a solution. He built pens for cattle in the small town of Abilene, Kansas. The Kansas

Myth and Reality in the Wild West

No episode in American history has given rise to as many myths as the Wild West. Writers of dime novels, popular in the East, helped created the myths in the years after the Civil War. Even today, popular books, television shows, and movies continue to portray the West in ways that are more myth than reality.

Myth: The cowboy was a free-spirited individual.
Reality: Most cowboys were employees. Many joined labor unions and even went on strike.

Myth: Western cowtowns were wild places where cowboys had gunfights, and there was little law and order.
Reality: Most were orderly cities with active law enforcement. Showdowns rarely, if ever, occurred.

Myth: Almost all cowboys were Anglo Americans.
Reality: About 25 percent of cowboys were African Americans, and 12 percent were Hispanic.

Differentiating Instruction for Universal Access

English-Language Learners
Standards Proficiency

Materials: art supplies

1. Reread with students the description of a boomtown, and discuss what some of these towns may have been like.
2. Ask students to draw a map of the layout of a boomtown as they imagine it would look. Ask them to name their boomtown, to describe the kind of people who lived there, and to point out the mines on which the town depended.
3. Ask for volunteers to present their maps to the class and to describe some of the people and places they included.
4. Display students' maps for the class to see. **LS Visual/Spatial**

HSS 8.8.2; HSS **Analysis Skills:** CS 3, HI 1

Alternative Assessment Handbook, Rubric 20: Map Creation

Answers

Reading Check *injury or death from unsafe machinery, explosions, fires, cave-ins, lung disease from poor air quality*

Pacific Railroad line went through Abilene. As a result, cattle could be shipped by rail from there. Soon, countless Texas ranchers were making the trip north to Abilene to sell their herds of cattle.

Around the same time, cattle ranching began to expand onto the Great Plains. The Great Plains from Texas to Canada, where many ranchers raised cattle in the late 1800s, became known as the **Cattle Kingdom**. Ranchers grazed huge herds on public land called the open range. The land had once been occupied by Plains Indians and buffalo herds.

Importance of Cowboys

The workers who took care of the ranchers' cattle were known as cowhands or cowboys. They borrowed many techniques and tools from vaqueros (bah-KER-ohs), Mexican ranch hands who cared for cattle and horses. From vaqueros came the western saddle and the lariat—a rope used for lassoing cattle. The cowboys also borrowed the vaqueros' broad felt hat. However, they changed it into the familiar high-peaked cowboy hat.

One of the cowboy's most important and dangerous duties was the **cattle drive**. On these long journeys, cowboys herded cattle to the market or to the northern Plains for grazing. The trips usually lasted several months and covered hundreds of miles. The **Chisholm Trail**, which ran from San Antonio, Texas, to the cattle town of Abilene, Kansas, was one of the earliest and most popular routes for cattle drives. It was blazed, or marked, by Texas cowboy Jesse Chisholm in the late 1860s.

At times, rowdy cowboys made life in cattle towns rough and violent. There were rarely shoot-outs in the street, but there was often disorderly behavior. Law officials such as Wyatt Earp became famous for keeping the peace in cattle towns.

Marshal Wyatt Earp

Deadwood, South Dakota

End of the Open Range

As the cattle business boomed, ranchers faced more competition for use of the open range. Farmers began to buy range land on the Great Plains where cattle had once grazed. Small ranchers also began competing with large ranchers for land. Then in 1874, the invention of barbed wire allowed westerners to fence off large amounts of land cheaply. The competition between farmers, large ranchers, and small ranchers increased. This competition led to range wars, or fights for access to land.

Focus on Reading
Ask yourself questions about the information in this paragraph to help you understand the competition between farmers and ranchers.

Making matters worse, in 1885 and 1886, disaster struck the Cattle Kingdom. The huge cattle herds on the Plains had eaten most of the prairie grass. Unusually severe winters in both years made the ranching situation even worse. Thousands of cattle died, and many ranchers were ruined financially. The Cattle Kingdom had come to an end.

READING CHECK **Drawing Conclusions**
Why did the Cattle Kingdom come to an end?

Direct Teach

Main Idea

❷ The Cattle Kingdom

The demand for cattle created a short-lived Cattle Kingdom on the Great Plains.

Define What was the open range? *public land, once occupied by Plains Indians and buffalo herds, used by ranchers for their cattle*

Summarize Why were longhorns a popular breed in western Texas? *could withstand harsh weather, needed little water*

Draw Conclusions What important conditions made the development of the Cattle Kingdom possible? *expanded economy and population created demand for beef, breeding of Texas Longhorn, railroad, and removal of Plains Indians, buffalo*

HSS 8.8.2; HSS **Analysis Skills:** CS 1, HI 1, HI 2

Info to Know

Vaqueros In addition to acquiring herding techniques and protective clothing from the vaqueros, American cowboys adopted much of the vaqueros' ranching vocabulary. For example, the word *lariat* comes from the Spanish *la reate*, *stampede* from *stampida*, and *lasso* from *lazo*.

Did you know . . .

With the cattle boom, the diet of the American public changed dramatically. People began to consider beef as a healthy alternative to pork. The cattle boom became a significant source of income for hundreds of cattle ranchers, and serving beef at the dinner table became a symbol of wealth and the "good life" for many Americans.

Collaborative Learning

Reaching Standards

Cattle Kingdom Comic Books

HSS 8.8.2; HSS **Analysis Skills:** CS 1, HI 1, HI 2

Materials: art supplies

1. Review with students the causes of the rise of the Cattle Kingdom and reasons for its eventual decline.
2. Organize the class into several small groups. Have each group create a comic book that highlights the major events and changes that took place in the cattle industry during the mid-1800s.
3. Comic books should depict these significant details: the breeding of Texas longhorn cattle, the building of holding pens for cattle along railroad lines, the range wars, and the end of the open range.
4. Encourage students to share their comic books with the class. LS **Visual/Spatial, Verbal/Linguistic**

Alternative Assessment Handbook, Rubrics 3: Artwork; and 14: Group Activity

Answers

Focus on Reading *possible questions—Who settled on the open range? Why was there competition?*

Reading Check *range wars, cattle had eaten most of Plains' prairie grass, severe winters in 1885 and 1886*

Direct Teach

Main Idea

❸ The Transcontinental Railroad

East and West were connected by the transcontinental railroad.

Define What was the Pony Express? *a system of messengers on horseback that carried mail between relay stations on a 2,000-mile route*

Explain Why did the federal government support the transcontinental railroad? *to encourage westward expansion of economy and population*

Summarize What were some geographic challenges railroad companies faced? *crossing mountain ranges, snowstorms, harsh weather, and getting food and supplies to workers in remote regions*

- **CRF:** Literature Activity: *A Letter from a Pony Express Rider,* by Lucius Lodosky Hickok
- Political Cartoons Activities for United States History Cartoon 19: Transcontinental Railroad
- Map Transparency: Routes West

HSS 8.8.2; **HSS Analysis Skills:** HI 1, HI 2

Connect to Geography

Standard Time Zones By the 1880s increased communication and travel between the East and the West necessitated the introduction of a standard time system. In 1883 at a Chicago meeting of railroad owners, William F. Allen proposed a new system of four equal time zones to replace the previous system of telling time based on the position of the sun. Although the new system was adopted almost immediately, it was not formally recognized until Congress passed the Standard Time Zone Act of 1918.

Answers

Interpreting Maps *Sacramento*

The Transcontinental Railroad

As more Americans began moving West, the need to send goods and information between the East and West increased. Americans searched for ways to improve communication and travel across the country.

In 1860 a system of messengers on horseback called the **Pony Express** began to carry messages west. The messengers carried mail between relay stations on a route about 2,000 miles long. However, telegraph lines, which sent messages faster, quickly put the Pony Express out of business.

Some Americans wanted to build a **transcontinental railroad**—a railroad that would cross the continent and connect the East to the West. The federal government, therefore, passed the Pacific Railway Acts in 1862 and in 1864. These acts gave railroad companies loans and large land grants that could be sold to pay for construction costs. Congress had granted more than 131 million acres of public land to railroad companies. In exchange, the government asked the railroads to carry U.S. mail and troops at a lower cost. Many railroad companies were inspired to begin laying miles of tracks.

Great Race

Two companies, the Central Pacific and the Union Pacific, led the race to complete the transcontinental railroad. In February 1863, the Central Pacific began building east from Sacramento, California. At the end of the year, the Union Pacific started building west from Omaha, Nebraska.

The Union Pacific hired thousands of railroad workers, particularly Irish immigrants. Chinese immigrants made up some 85 percent of the Central Pacific workforce. The railroad's part-owner Leland Stanford praised them, but he paid them less than other laborers. Chinese crews also were given the most dangerous tasks and had to work longer hours than other railroad laborers. They took the job, however, because the $30 a month

Routes West

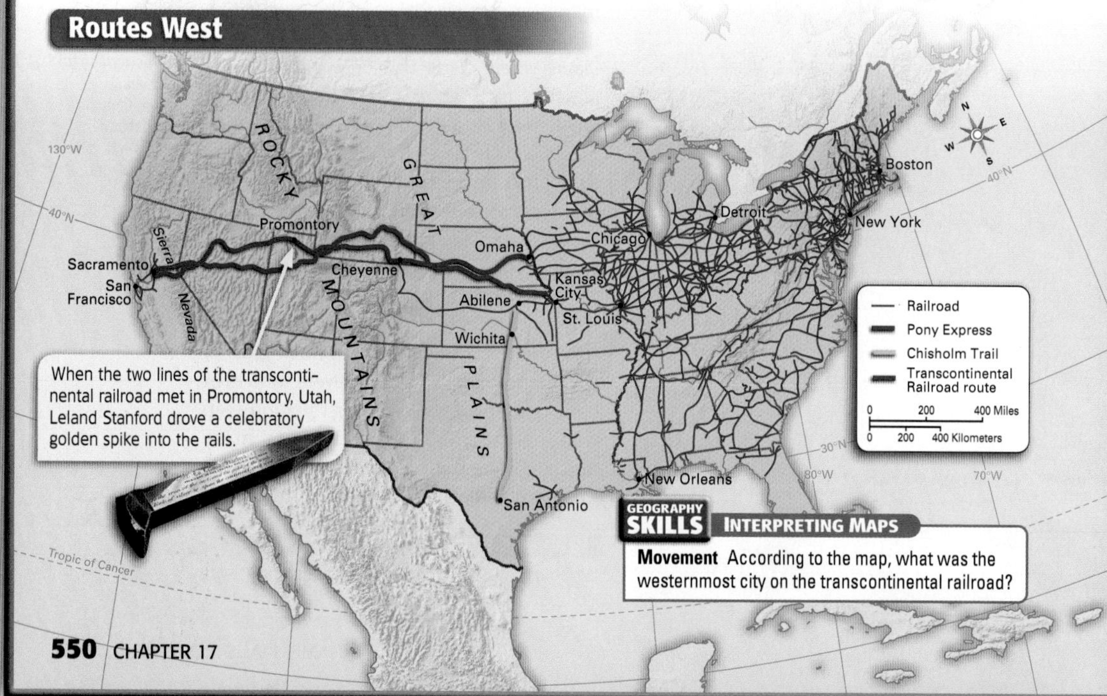

When the two lines of the transcontinental railroad met in Promontory, Utah, Leland Stanford drove a celebratory golden spike into the rails.

GEOGRAPHY SKILLS INTERPRETING MAPS

Movement According to the map, what was the westernmost city on the transcontinental railroad?

Differentiating Instruction for Universal Access

Learners Having Difficulty

Reaching Standards

1. To help students compare and contrast the conditions that miners, cowboys, and rail workers faced, copy the graphic organizer for the class to see. Omit the blue answers.
2. Have students copy and complete the organizer. Review the answers as a class. **LS Visual/Spatial**

- Alternative Assessment Handbook, Rubric 13: Graphic Organizers

HSS 8.8.2; **HSS Analysis Skills:** HI 1

Miners	Cowboys	Rail Workers
• unbearable heat • poor air that often lacked oxygen • cave-ins • fires • unsafe equipment	*• long journeys covering hundreds of miles • violence and disorderly behavior by other cowboys • harsh terrain and rough weather*	*• harsh terrain • rough weather • lack of food and supplies • long hours*

that the Central Pacific paid was as much as 10 times what they could earn in China.

Railroad companies faced many geographic challenges. For example, Central Pacific workers struggled to cross the Sierra Nevada mountain range in California. Breaking apart its rock formations required setting carefully controlled explosions using large amounts of blasting powder and the explosive nitroglycerin. And in the winter of 1866, snowdrifts more than 60 feet high trapped and killed dozens of workers.

Meanwhile, Union Pacific workers faced harsh weather on the Great Plains. In addition, the company pressured them to work at a rapid pace—at times laying 250 miles of track in six months. Faced with great geographic obstacles, the Central Pacific took four years to lay the first 115 miles of track.

For both railroad companies, providing food and supplies for workers was vital. This job became more difficult in remote areas. The railroad companies consequently often relied on local resources. Professional hunters, such as William "Buffalo Bill" Cody, shot thousands of buffalo to feed Union Pacific workers.

Golden Spike

Congress required the two completed rail lines to connect at Promontory, Utah. On May 10, 1869, a golden spike was used to connect the railroad tie joining the two tracks. Alexander Toponce witnessed the event.

> "Governor Stanford, president of the Central Pacific, took the sledge [hammer], and the first time he struck he missed the spike and hit the rail. What a howl went up! Irish, Chinese, Mexicans, and everybody yelled with delight. 'He missed it'... Then Stanford tried it again and tapped the spike."
>
> —Alexander Toponce, quoted in *A Treasury of Railroad Folklore,* edited by B. A. Botkin and Alvin F. Harlo

The railroad companies were not finished, though. Following completion of the transcontinental railroad, companies continued building railroads until the West was crisscrossed with rail lines.

The Central Pacific and Union Pacific connected their tracks at Promontory, Utah, in 1869, completing the transcontinental railroad.

Direct Teach

World Events

The Railroads of India As the United States was completing the world's first transcontinental railroad, Great Britain was building a huge railroad system in India to transport goods to and from remote regions. Between 1859 and 1869, Indian workers laid more than 5,000 miles of track. Workers had to build 81 bridges and 38 tunnels just to get through one mountain range. By 1900 the Indian rail network was the second largest in Asia after Russia's. The railroad carried mail, freight, and passengers.

Did you know . . .

In 1863 the Union Pacific Railroad laid its tracks through the city of Omaha, Nebraska, causing the population to soar from 1,833 in 1860 to 102,555 by 1900.

Checking for Understanding

True or False Answer each statement *T* if it is true or F if it is false. If it is false, explain why.

1. The Pony Express benefited from telegraph lines. *F; Telegraph lines put the Pony Express out of business.*
2. The transcontinental railroad was built largely by Irish and Chinese immigrants. *T*
3. The Central Pacific and Union Pacific railroads met in Promontory, Utah. *T*

 HSS 8.8.2

Critical Thinking: Evaluating Information

Standards Proficiency

Railroad Ad Campaign HSS 8.8.2; HSS Analysis Skills: HI 1

1. Ask students to imagine that they work for an advertising agency in the late 1800s. A railroad company has just hired them to create a campaign to increase the public's awareness of the railroad's influence on the settlement and economic development of the West.
2. Have each student design a magazine advertisement that features text and illustrations to promote the railroad. Advertisements should stress details such as the speed of travel, improvements in communication, and the growth of western businesses.
3. Display the students' advertisements in the classroom and give students time to view them. LS **Verbal/Linguistic, Visual/Spatial**

Alternative Assessment Handbook, Rubric 2: Advertisements

Direct Teach

Main Idea

❸ The Transcontinental Railroad

East and West were connected by the transcontinental railroad.

Identify What goods were shipped east via the railroad? *wood, metals, meat, and grain*

Analyze How many more miles of railroad tracks were there in 1890 than in 1865? *about 164,000*

Quick Facts Transparency: Effects of the Transcontinental Railroad

HSS 8.8.2; HSS **Analysis Skills:** HI 2

Review & Assess

Close

Have students summarize the impact that mining, the cattle boom, and the transcontinental railroads had on the western United States.

Review

go.hrw.com Online Quiz, Section 1

Assess

SE Section 1 Assessment

PASS: Section 1 Quiz

Alternative Assessment Handbook

Reteach/Classroom Intervention

California Standards Review Workbook

Interactive Reader and Study Guide, Section 1

Interactive Skills Tutor CD-ROM

QUICK FACTS

Effects of the Transcontinental Railroad

- **Increased settlement of the West**
- **Increased business activity and east-west trade**
- **Helped make the railroad industry one of the most powerful in the country**

Results of the Railroad

The transcontinental railroad increased both economic growth and the population in the West. Railroad companies provided better transportation for people and goods. They also sold land to settlers, which encouraged people to move West.

THE IMPACT TODAY
Today's businesses ship goods across the country using railroads, the interstate highway system, and airplanes.

New railroads helped businesses. Western timber companies, miners, ranchers, and farmers shipped wood, metals, meat, and grain east by railroad. In exchange, eastern businesses shipped manufactured goods to the West.

Railroad companies encouraged people to put their money into the railroad business, which they did—sometimes unwisely. Railroad speculation and the collapse of railroad owner Jay Cooke's banking firm helped start the Panic of 1873. By the 1880s, many small western railroads were deeply in debt. Despite such setbacks, Americans remained interested in railroad investments. In 1865 only about 35,000 miles of railroad track existed. By 1890 there were about 199,000 miles in operation. Railroads had become one of the biggest industries in the United States.

READING CHECK **Finding Main Ideas** How did the railroad affect the development of the West?

SUMMARY AND PREVIEW In this section you learned that the mining of gold and silver, the cattle boom, the transcontinental railroad, and the opportunity for land and work increased settlement of the West. In the next section you will learn about how this settlement led to conflicts with Native Americans.

Section 1 Assessment

go.hrw.com **Online Quiz** KEYWORD: SS8 HP17

Reviewing Ideas, Terms, and People HSS 8.8.2

1. **a. Recall** Why did Americans move West in the years following the Civil-War?
   b. Draw Conclusions What effect did the discovery of the **Comstock Lode** have on the West?
   c. Evaluate Do you think women were important to the success of mining towns? Why or why not?
2. **a. Recall** What led to the cattle boom in the West?
   b. Analyze Why was there competition between ranchers and farmers to settle in the Great Plains?
   c. Evaluate What played the biggest role in ending the **Cattle Kingdom**? Why?
3. **a. Recall** When and where did the Union Pacific and Central Pacific lines meet?
   b. Make Generalizations How do you think the **transcontinental railroad** improved people's lives?

Critical Thinking

4. **Comparing** Copy the graphic organizer below onto your own sheet of paper. Use it to compare how mining and railroads led to the settlement and development of the West.

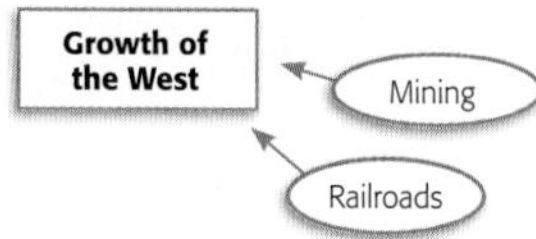

FOCUS ON WRITING

5. **Taking Notes on Mining, Ranching, and the Railroads** As you read this section, take notes on how mining, ranching, and railroads changed the West. How might a railroad worker feel about these changes?

Section 1 Assessment Answers

1. **a.** to settle land, get riches from gold or silver, and east was becoming overpopulated
   b. drew settlers out West with the idea of striking it rich
   c. possible answer—yes, raised families, taught at schools, and established towns
2. **a.** population growth led to increased demand for beef; development of longhorn breed
   b. ranchers wanted open range for grazing; farmers fenced land for crops
   c. possible answer—Overgrazing left no more food for the cattle to eat.
3. **a.** in Promontory Utah, in 1869
   b. easier, quicker travel, shipping led to growth of towns
4. mining—big business, employed many, boomtowns; railroads—improved communication and transportation, encouraged settlement, improved economy by ease of shipping
5. possible answer—Mining, ranching, and railroads turned the West from frontier into a home for settlers; railroad workers might feel overwhelmed by laying tracks across entire West.

Answers

Reading Check *The Railroad increased economic growth and the population by transporting people and goods, shortening travel times, encouraging settlement by selling land, and helping businesses.*

Wars for the West

SECTION 2

If YOU were there...

You are a member of the Sioux nation, living in Dakota Territory in 1875. These lands are sacred to your people, and the U.S. government has promised them to you. But now gold has been found here, and the government has ordered you to give up your land. Some Sioux leaders want to fight. Others say that it is of no use, that the soldiers will win.

Would you fight to keep your lands?

BUILDING BACKGROUND Miners, ranchers, and farmers all moved West in the years after the Civil War. The arrival of settlers and the U.S. army to the Great Plains meant the end of the way of life of the Indians who lived there. The coming of the railroad began this destruction, with the killing of thousands of buffalo. Treaties were made but did not protect Indian lands from settlers.

Settlers Encounter the Plains Indians

As miners and settlers began crossing the Great Plains in the mid-1800s, they pressured the federal government for more access to western lands. To protect these travelers, U.S. officials sent agents to negotiate treaties with the Plains Indians.

The Plains Indians lived in the Great Plains, which stretch north into Canada and south into Texas. Indian groups such as the Apache and the Comanche lived in and around Texas and

The Plains Indians depended on two animals—the horse and the buffalo.

What You Will Learn...

Main Ideas

1. As settlers moved to the Great Plains, they encountered the Plains Indians.
2. The U.S. Army and Native Americans fought in the northern plains, the Southwest, and the Far West.
3. Despite efforts to reform U.S. policy toward Native Americans, conflict continued.

The Big Idea

Native Americans and the U.S. government came into conflict over land in the West.

Key Terms and People

Treaty of Fort Laramie, *p. 554*
reservations, *p. 555*
Crazy Horse, *p. 555*
Treaty of Medicine Lodge, *p. 555*
buffalo soldiers, *p. 556*
George Armstrong Custer, *p. 556*
Sitting Bull, *p. 556*
Battle of the Little Bighorn, *p. 556*
Massacre at Wounded Knee, *p. 557*
Long Walk, *p. 557*
Geronimo, *p. 557*
Ghost Dance, *p. 558*
Sarah Winnemucca, *p. 558*
Dawes General Allotment Act, *p. 558*

HSS 8.12.2 Identify the reasons for the development of federal Indian policy and the wars with American Indians and their relationship to agricultural development and industrialization.

Teach the Big Idea: Master the Standards

Standards Proficiency

Wars for the West HSS 8.12.2; HSS Analysis Skills: CS 3, HI 1

1. **Teach** Ask students the Main Idea questions to teach this section.
2. **Apply** Draw a chart listing the following geographical areas: *Great Plains, Southwest, Far West.* Organize the class into groups, assigning at least one group to each area. Have groups identify ways in which Native Americans in their assigned area came into conflict with the U.S. government. **LS Verbal/Linguistic**
3. **Review** To review the section's main ideas, have volunteers from each group share their findings. Write their responses on the master chart for students to see.
4. **Practice/Homework** Have each student write a journal entry from the point of view of a Native American facing U.S. westward expansion. **LS Verbal/Linguistic**

Alternative Assessment Handbook, Rubrics 7: Charts; and 15: Journals

Preteach

Bellringer

If YOU were there . . . Use the **Daily Bellringer Transparency** to help students answer the question.

Daily Bellringer Transparency, Section 2

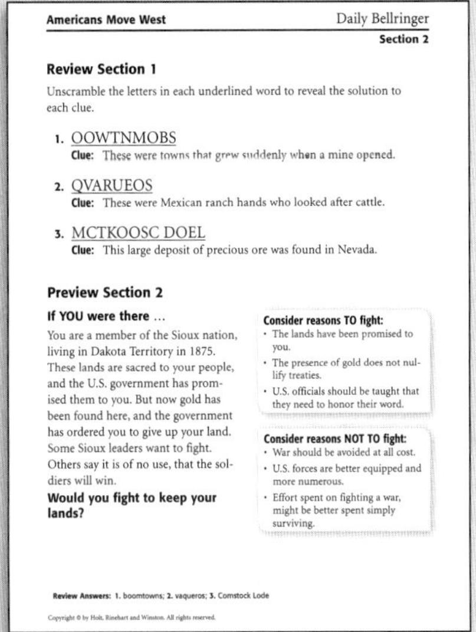

Americans Move West Daily Bellringer **Section 2**

Review Section 1

Unscramble the letters in each underlined word to reveal the solution to each clue.

1. OOWTNMOBS
   Clue: These were towns that grew suddenly when a mine opened.
2. QVARUEOS
   Clue: These were Mexican ranch hands who looked after cattle.
3. MCTKOOSC DOEL
   Clue: This large deposit of precious ore was found in Nevada.

Preview Section 2

If YOU were there ...

You are a member of the Sioux nation, living in Dakota Territory in 1875. These lands are sacred to your people, and the U.S. government has promised them to you. But now gold has been found here, and the government has ordered you to give up your land. Some Sioux leaders want to fight. Others say it is of no use, that the soldiers will win.

Would you fight to keep your lands?

Consider reasons TO fight:
- The lands have been promised to you.
- The presence of gold does not nullify treaties.
- U.S. officials should be taught that they need to honor their word.

Consider reasons NOT TO fight:
- War should be avoided at all cost.
- U.S. forces are better equipped and more numerous.
- Effort spent on fighting a war, might be better spent simply surviving.

Review Answers: 1. boomtowns; 2. vaqueros; 3. Comstock Lode

Building Vocabulary

Preteach or review the following terms:

ambush to launch a surprise attack (p. 555)

negotiate to reach an agreement (p. 553)

CRF: Vocabulary Builder Activity, Section 2

Standards Focus

HSS 8.12.2

Means: Explain why the United States government developed policies regarding American Indians, and why they engaged in wars with Native Americans.

Matters: With westward expansion, the economic interests of the United States prevailed over the interests of Native Americans.

Direct Teach

Main Idea

❶ Settlers Encounter the Plains Indians

As settlers moved to the Great Plains, they encountered the Plains Indians.

Recall How did plains Indians use buffalo? *for food, shelter, clothing, utensils, and tools*

Contrast What was different about the ways settlers, miners, and Native Americans used the land? *Settlers were farming and ranching, miners were looking for gold, Native Americans were hunting.*

Activity Uses of Buffalo Ask students to imagine that they are teaching young Plains Indian children how to use buffalo. Have them write a description of the many uses of buffalo. **LS Verbal/Linguistic**

Alternative Assessment Handbook, Rubric 42: Writing to Inform

Map Transparency: Native American Land Loss in the West, 1850–1890

HSS 8.12.2; **HSS Analysis Skills:** HI 1, HI 2

Did you know . . .

Just how did the Comanche get their name? The Spanish were the first to use the name *Comanche,* but according to anthropologist Marvin K. Opler, the term actually came from the Ute word *Komantcia,* which means "anyone who wants to fight me all the time." To the Spanish, *Komantcia* sounded like *Comanche.*

what is now Oklahoma. The Cheyenne and the Arapaho lived in different regions across the central Plains. The Pawnee lived in parts of Nebraska. To the north were the Sioux. These groups spoke many different languages. However, they used a common sign language to communicate and they shared a similar lifestyle.

Hunting Buffalo

For survival, Plains Indians depended on two animals—the horse and the buffalo. The Spanish brought horses to America in the 1500s. Plains Indians learned to ride horses, and hunters used them to follow buffalo herds year-round. While on horseback, most Plains Indian hunters used a short bow and arrows to shoot buffalo from close range.

Plains Indians used buffalo for food, shelter, clothing, utensils, and tools. Women dried buffalo meat to make jerky. They made tepees and clothing from buffalo hides, and cups and tools from buffalo horns. As one Sioux explained, "When our people killed a buffalo, all of the animal was utilized [used] in some manner; nothing was wasted." The Plains Indians prospered. By 1850, some 75,000 Native Americans lived on the Plains.

Struggle to Keep Land

Miners and settlers were also increasing in numbers—and they wanted Indians' land. The U.S. government tried to avoid disputes by negotiating the **Treaty of Fort Laramie,** the first major treaty between the U.S. government and Plains Indians. Two years later, several southern Plains nations signed a treaty at Fort Atkinson in Nebraska. These treaties recognized Indian claims to most of the Great Plains. They also allowed the United States to build forts and roads and to travel across Indian homelands. The U.S. government promised to pay for any damages to Indian lands.

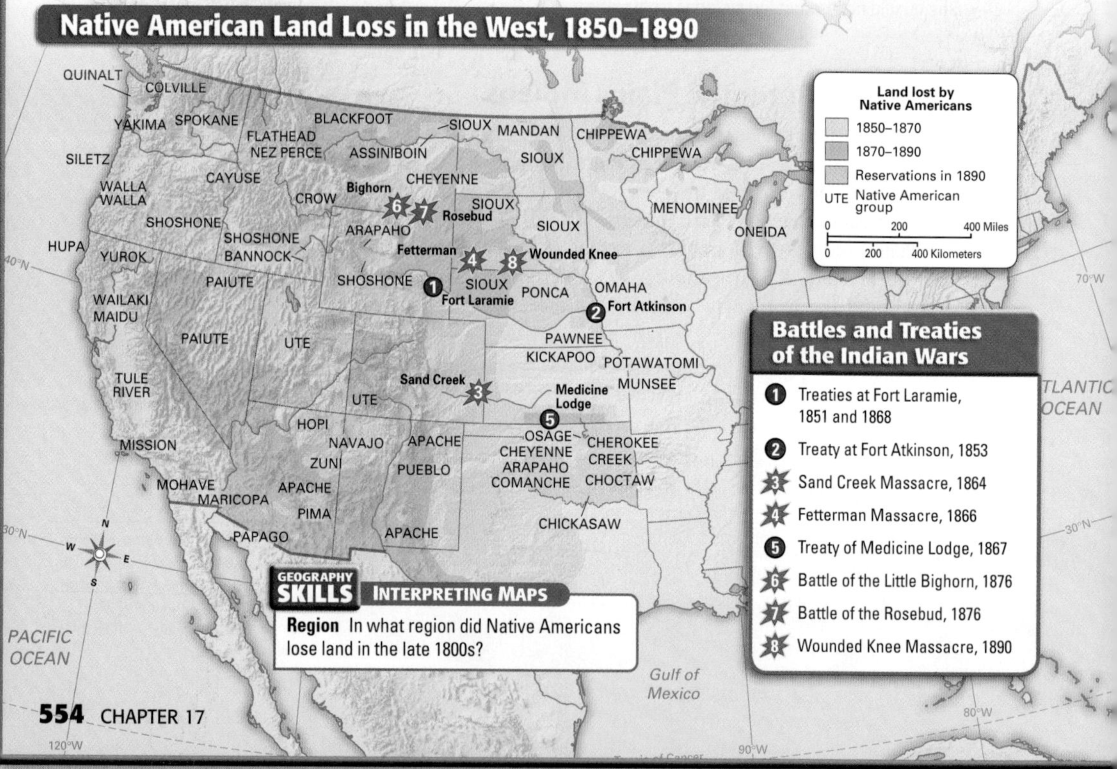

Collaborative Learning

Reaching Standards

Plains Indian Museum Exhibit

HSS 8.12.2; **HSS Analysis Skills:** HI 1

1. Review with students the importance of the horse and buffalo to the Plains Indians.
2. Organize the class into two groups. Ask each group to create a museum exhibit that depicts the animals used by the Plains Indians, the ways that the animals were used, and why the animals were important.
3. Ask students to provide both text and visual displays or models in their exhibits.
4. Display student exhibits for the class to see and lead a discussion on how the lifestyle of the Plains Indians was different from that of American settlers. **LS Visual/Spatial, Verbal/Linguistic**

Alternative Assessment Handbook, Rubrics 3: Artwork, and 14: Group Activity

Answers

Interpreting Maps *Southwest, Great Plains*

LINKING TO TODAY

Tribal Councils

Native Americans have long held tribal councils to make decisions on behalf of the group. Today this tradition of Native American government continues. There are more than 500 tribal governments in the United States. Tribal governments provide a wide range of services, including law enforcement, health care, and education. Here, a member of the Blackfoot Tribal Council addresses the Montana state legislature.

ANALYSIS SKILL ANALYZING INFORMATION

What types of services do tribal governments provide?

The treaties did not keep the peace for long. In 1858 the discovery of gold in what is now Colorado brought thousands of miners to the West. They soon clashed with the Cheyenne and the Arapaho. In 1861 the U.S. government negotiated new treaties with Plains Indians. These treaties created **reservations**, areas of federal land set aside for Native Americans. The government expected Indians to stay on the reservations, which made hunting buffalo almost impossible.

Pioneers and miners continued to cross the Great Plains. Many miners used the Bozeman Trail. To protect them, the U.S. Army built forts along the trail, which ran through favored Sioux hunting grounds. The Sioux responded with war. In late 1866, **Crazy Horse** and a group of Sioux ambushed and killed 81 cavalry troops.

In 1868, under the Second Treaty of Fort Laramie, the government agreed to close the Bozeman Trail, abandon the forts, and provide reservation land to the Sioux.

The U.S. government also negotiated for southern Plains Indians to move off their land. In the 1867 **Treaty of Medicine Lodge**, most southern Plains Indians agreed to live on reservations. However, many Indians did not want to give up their hunting grounds. Fighting soon broke out between the Comanche and Texans. The U.S. Army and the Texas Rangers were unable to defeat the Comanche, so they cut off the Comanche's access to food and water. In 1875, the last of the Comanche war leaders surrendered.

READING CHECK **Summarizing** What was the federal policy toward the Plains Indians in the 1860s and 1870s?

Direct Teach

Main Idea

1 Settlers Encounter the Plains Indians

As settlers moved to the Great Plains, they encountered the Plains Indians.

Define What is a reservation? *an area of federal land set aside for Native Americans*

Analyze Why did the United States negotiate treaties with the Plains Indians? *to avoid land disputes*

Elaborate Why were Plains Indians unwilling to stay on reservations? *needed access to hunt buffalo, culture depended on buffalo hunting to survive*

HSS 8.12.2; HSS **Analysis Skills:** HI 1, HI 2

Linking to Today

National Museum of the American Indian In the fall of 2004, the National Museum of the American Indian, part of the Smithsonian Institution, opened in Washington, D.C. to share and honor the vibrant cultures of Native Americans from North, Central, and South America. The remarks made by the museum's director, a Southern Cheyenne, reflect its importance:

> "As a museum, it celebrates . . . the truly great accomplishments of Native peoples of the Americas long before others came. It also insists that Native communities and cultures are very much alive, if often challenged by hard circumstances."
>
> —W. Richard West, Jr.

Draw Conclusions What do you think are some challenges that Native Americans face today? *possible answers—loss of lands, economic problems, discrimination, modernization vs. tradition*

Differentiating Instruction for Universal Access

Advanced Learners/GATE

Exceeding Standards | Research Required

1. Ask students to use the library or the Internet to research modern reservations.
2. Questions students should answer include: where are the reservations located, what name do the people call themselves, what is their view of their people's history, and what challenges does reservation life pose today. Have students include information on how modern Native Americans make their living on reservations today.
3. Ask for volunteers to present their findings to the class. LS **Verbal/Linguistic**

HSS 8.12.2; HSS **Analysis Skills:** HR 1, HI 1, HI 2

Alternative Assessment Handbook, Rubric 30: Research

Answers

Analyzing Information *law enforcement, health care, education*

Reading Check *move Plains Indians off their lands and onto reservations*

Direct Teach

Main Idea

❷ Fighting on the Plains

The U.S. Army and Native Americans fought in the northern plains, the Southwest, and the Far West.

Identify Which U.S. and Sioux leaders battled at the Little Bighorn? *U.S.—George Armstrong Custer; Sioux—Crazy Horse, Sitting Bull*

Draw Conclusions Why did the U.S. government want the Sioux to sell back their reservation? *to access gold discovered in the Black Hills*

Analyze Why did the Sioux eventually surrender? *lost their two most important leaders, Crazy Horse and Sitting Bull*

- **CRF:** Biography Activity: George Armstrong Custer
- **CRF:** History and Geography Activity: Conflicts with the Indians
- **CRF:** Primary Source Activity: The Battle of the Little Bighorn

HSS 8.12.2; HSS **Analysis Skills:** HI 1, HI 2

Connect to Arts and the Humanities

Battle of the Little Bighorn The Battle of the Little Bighorn, depicted in the painting on this page, is one of the most commonly depicted images in Western art. As with much of the art that depicts life in the old West, the paintings of the battle are more romantic than they are historically accurate. They portray George Armstrong Custer and his troops fighting the American Indians in the face of defeat.

Answers

Two Views of a Historic Battle *painting—Sioux outnumber and surround U.S. soldiers, Custer central focus; drawing—all combatants on horseback, dead soldiers are maimed*

The Native Americans are shown surrounding a small force of U.S. soldiers.
General Custer is shown standing among his men as he fires.

Two Views of a Historic Battle

CONNECT TO THE ARTS

Art historians have identified about 1,000 paintings of the Battle of the Little Bighorn. The painting on the this page was painted in 1899. The painting on the next page is one of the many colored-pencil drawings of the battle done by Red Horse, who participated in the fight. He drew them five years after the battle.

How do these paintings show the influences of different cultures?

Fighting on the Plains

In the northern Plains, Southwest, and Far West, Native Americans continued to resist being moved to and confined on reservations. The U.S. government sent troops, including African American cavalry, who the Indians called **buffalo soldiers**, into the area to force the Indians to leave.

Battles on the Northern Plains

As fighting on the southern Plains came to an end, new trouble started in the north. In 1874, Lieutenant Colonel **George Armstrong Custer's** soldiers discovered gold in the Black Hills of the Dakotas. **Sitting Bull**, a leader of the Lakota Sioux, protested U.S. demands for the land.

> "What treaty that the whites have kept has the red man broken? Not one. What treaty that the white man ever made with us have they kept? Not one."
>
> —Sitting Bull, quoted in *Touch the Earth* by T. C. McLuhan

Other Sioux leaders listened to Sitting Bull and refused to give up land. Fighting soon broke out between the army and the Sioux.

On June 25, 1876, Custer's scouts found a Sioux camp along the Little Bighorn River in Montana Territory. Leading 264 of his soldiers, Custer raced ahead without waiting for any supporting forces. In the **Battle of the Little Bighorn**, Sioux forces led by Crazy Horse and Sitting Bull surrounded and defeated Custer and his troops. Newspapers called the battle "Custer's Last Stand" because his entire command was killed. It was the worst defeat the U.S. Army suffered in the West. The Battle of the Little Bighorn was also the Sioux's last major victory.

In 1881, Sitting Bull and a few followers returned from Canada where they had moved. They had run out of food during the hard winter. He joined the Sioux on Standing Rock Reservation in Dakota Territory.

Collaborative Learning

Reaching Standards

In-depth Oral Reports

HSS 8.12.2; HSS **Analysis Skills:** HR 1, HI 1, HI 2 — Research Required

1. Discuss with students three of the major incidents between the U.S. government and Native Americans: the Battle of the Little Bighorn, the Long Walk, and the Massacre at Wounded Knee.
2. Organize the class into three groups and have each group use the library or the Internet to conduct in-depth research on one of the incidents listed. Students should locate information about the participants of their assigned event, causes, and results of the event.
3. Have each group prepare an oral presentation of their findings, including visual aids, as needed. Each group should delegate research, illustrations, and presentation tasks.
4. Have each group present its findings to the class. LS **Interpersonal, Verbal/Linguistic**

Alternative Assessment Handbook, Rubrics 14: Group Activity; 24: Oral Presentations; and 30: Research

These are wounded men.
The U.S. Army is shown on horseback in this painting.

Almost a decade later, in 1890, while following orders to arrest Sitting Bull, reservation police killed him. Many Sioux left the reservations in protest. Later that year, the U.S. Army shot and killed about 150 Sioux near Wounded Knee Creek in South Dakota. This **Massacre at Wounded Knee** was the last major incident on the Great Plains.

Southwest

The Navajo lived in what became Arizona and New Mexico. In 1863 the Navajo refused to settle on a reservation. In response, U.S. troops made raids on the Navajo's fields, homes, and livestock.

When the Navajo ran out of food and shelter, they started surrendering to the U.S. army. In 1864, the army led Navajo captives on the **Long Walk**. On this 300-mile march the Navajo were forced to walk across the desert to a reservation in Bosque Redondo, New Mexico. Along the way, countless Navajo died.

Far West

The United States had promised to let the peaceful Nez Percé keep their land in Oregon. Within a few years, however, the government ordered the Nez Percé to a reservation in what is now Idaho. Before leaving, a few angry Nez Percé killed some local settlers and tried to escape to Canada. Near the border, U.S. troops overtook them and sent them to a reservation in what is now Oklahoma.

Final Battles

By the 1880s, most Native Americans had stopped fighting. The Apache of the Southwest, however, continued to battle the U.S. army. A Chiricahua Apache named **Geronimo** and his small band of raiders avoided capture for many years. In September 1886, Geronimo surrendered, ending the Apache armed resistance.

READING CHECK **Contrasting** How did the Apache resistance differ from that of the Navajo?

Direct Teach

Main Idea

❷ Fighting on the Plains

The U.S. Army and Native Americans fought in the northern plains, the Southwest, and the Far West.

Define What was the Long Walk? *300-mile march in which the U.S. army led Navajo captives across desert to New Mexico reservation*

Draw Conclusions Why did the Navajo surrender to the United States? *Because U.S. troops raided their homes and animals, the Navajo ran out of food and shelter.*

HSS 8.12.2; HSS **Analysis Skills:** HI 1, HI 2

Biography

Geronimo (1829–1909) Many Apache found it difficult to get along with Geronimo. He had grown bitter after Mexican soldiers killed his mother, wife, and children. Despite this bitterness, other Apache admired Geronimo for his ability to handle difficult situations.

Geronimo led his own band of troops. He was captured several times, but usually managed to escape. After his final surrender in 1886, Geronimo was sentenced to perform hard labor as a prisoner of war in a Florida work camp. In 1894, he was sent to Fort Sill, Oklahoma, where he died in 1909. Geronimo is one of the few Native American leaders during the wars for the West to have died of natural causes. His courage and determination to remain free made him a legend.

Critical Thinking: Summarizing

Standards Proficiency

Descriptions of Conflicts HSS 8.12.2; HSS **Analysis Skills:** HI 1, HI 2

1. Review with students the conflicts that took place between Native Americans and the U.S. government in the mid-1800s.
2. Have each student select a conflict from this period. Ask students to imagine that they were observers of the event or battle they selected. Then have each student write a letter to a family member explaining what led up to the conflict and describing the event itself. Remind students to use descriptive language in their letters.
3. Then have students create an illustration of the event that they could include with their letters.
4. Encourage volunteers to read their letters aloud to the class. LS **Verbal/Linguistic**

Alternative Assessment Handbook, Rubrics 25: Personal Letters; and 40: Writing to Describe

go.hrw.com
Online Resources
KEYWORD: SS8 US17
ACTIVITY: Geronimo Diary

Answers

Reading Check *Navajo were starved into surrender; Apache offered armed resistance for years*

• Direct Teach •

Main Idea

❸ Conflict Continues

Despite efforts to reform U.S. policy toward Native Americans, conflict continued.

Identify What was the Ghost Dance? *a religious movement that predicted the return of the buffalo herds and the disappearance of white settlers*

Evaluate Why do you think some reformers wanted Native Americans to adopt the ways of white people? *possible answer—foresaw Plains Indians' dependency on buffalo hunt would eventually come to an end*

CRF: Biography Activity: Sarah Winnemucca

 **HSS** 8.12.2; **HSS Analysis Skills:** HI I, HI 2

• Review & Assess •

Close

Have students draw a series of illustrations that summarize the section and relate to the big idea and main ideas.

Review

go.hrw.com Online Quiz, Section 2

Assess

SE Section 2 Assessment

PASS: Section 2 Quiz

Alternative Assessment Handbook

Reteach/Classroom Intervention

California Standards Review Workbook

Interactive Reader and Study Guide, Section 2

Interactive Skills Tutor CD-ROM

Conflict Continues

By the 1870s, many Native Americans lived on reservations, where land was usually not useful for farming or buffalo hunting. Many Indians were starving.

A Paiute Indian named Wovoka began a religious movement, the **Ghost Dance**, that predicted the arrival of paradise for Native Americans. In this paradise, the buffalo herds would return and the settlers would disappear.

U.S. officials did not understand the meaning of the Ghost Dance. They feared it would lead to rebellion, so they tried to end the movement, which had spread to other groups, including the Sioux. After the massacre in 1890 at Wounded Knee, the Ghost Dance movement gradually died out.

In the late 1870s, a Paiute Indian named **Sarah Winnemucca** called for reform. She gave lectures on problems of the reservation system. Writer Helen Hunt Jackson published a book that pushed for reform of U.S. Indian policy in 1881.

Sarah Winnemucca spoke out for the fair treatment of her people.

Some reformers believed that Native Americans should adopt the ways of white people. The **Dawes General Allotment Act** of 1887 tried to lessen traditional influences on Indian society by making land ownership private rather than shared. The act also promised—but failed to deliver—U.S. citizenship to Native Americans. After breaking up reservation land, the government sold the acreage remaining. The Act took about two-thirds of Indian land.

READING CHECK **Evaluating** How did reformers try to influence Native Americans' lives?

SUMMARY AND PREVIEW In this section you read about conflict in the settlement of the West. In the next section you will learn more about Great Plains settlers.

Section 2 Assessment

go.hrw.com **Online Quiz** KEYWORD: SS8 HP17

Reviewing Ideas, Terms, and People HSS 8.12.2

1. **a. Describe** What animals did Plains Indians depend on, and how did they use those animals?
   b. Analyze How did U.S. policy toward the Plains Indians change in the late 1850s?
   c. Elaborate Would you have agreed to move to a **reservation**? Why or why not?
2. **a. Describe** What events led to the **Battle of the Little Bighorn**?
   b. Elaborate Why do you think most Indian groups eventually stopped resisting the United States?
3. **a. Describe** How did the **Dawes General Allotment Act** affect American Indians?
   b. Predict What effect do you think the **Massacre at Wounded Knee** would have on relations between Plains Indians and the United States?

Critical Thinking

4. **Identifying Cause and Effect** Copy the chart below. Use it to list the causes and effects of conflicts between the United States and Native Americans on the Great Plains.

Causes	Conflicts	Effects

FOCUS ON WRITING

5. **Taking Notes on the Wars for the West** As you read this section, take notes on the wars between the U.S. government and the Plains Indians. How might a railroad worker have experienced these conflicts?

Section 2 Assessment Answers

1. **a.** buffalo—for food, clothing, shelter; horse—to hunt buffalo
   b. New treaties placed Native Americans on reservations.
   c. possible answer—no, because the U.S. actions were unfair and illegal
2. **a.** gold found on Black Hills reservation; Lakota Sioux refused to give up land; Custer attacked without support and was massacred
   b. possible answer—not enough weapons, soldiers, food, or shelter to continue
3. **a.** It led to greater loss of Native American land.
   b. possible answer—distrust, fear
4. causes—U.S. interest in mining on Native American land, crossing and settling land; conflicts—Crazy Horse ambush, Battle of Little Bighorn, Navajo Long Walk; effects—treaties, violent conflict, wars, Native Americans forced onto reservations
5. Students' notes will vary; a railroad worker may have only seen conflict from afar.

Answers

Reading Check *religious movements, lectures, books, attempts to adopt ways of white people*

BIOGRAPHY

Chief Joseph

What would you do to protect your home and your ways of life?

When did he live? 1840–1904

Where did he live? Chief Joseph lived in the Wallowa Valley, the Nez Percé homeland, in present-day Oregon.

What did he do? Chief Joseph led his people in an effort to hold on to the Nez Percé homeland and to avoid war with the United States. For years, Joseph and a band of Nez Percé refused to move as white settlers moved into the valley. Finally, after being threatened with attack, Joseph gave in. An army led by General Oliver Otis Howard eventually chased the Nez Percé across Idaho, Wyoming, and Montana. They were sent to a reservation in modern-day Oklahoma, where many died.

Why is he so important? Chief Joseph's surrender speech earned him a place in American history. The band of 700 people, including only 200 warriors, made a courageous three-month, 1,400-mile trek, hoping to cross into Canada for protection. Exhausted, hungry, and freezing, Joseph's people collapsed just short of the Canadian border. In later years, the chief spoke about what had happened.

Cause and Effect What brought suffering to Chief Joseph and his people?

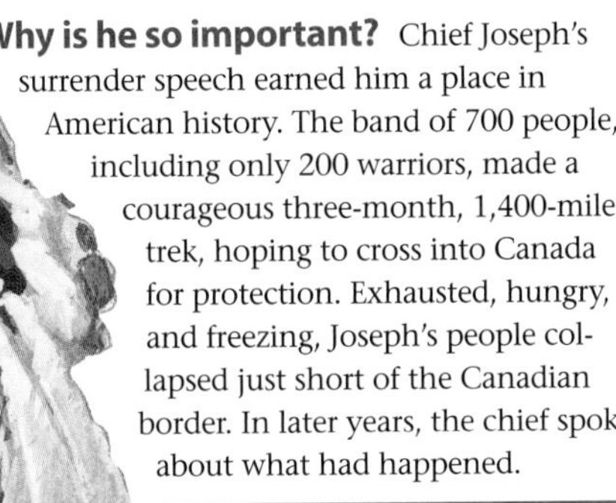

Chief Joseph of the Nez Percé nation tried to protect his people from the advancement of white settlers.

Speech

"I am tired of fighting. Our chiefs are killed ... The old men are all dead ... It is cold, and we have no blankets. The little children are freezing to death. My people, some of them, have run away to the hills, and have no blankets, no food. No one knows where they are—perhaps freezing to death. I want to have time to look for my children, and see how many of them I can find. Maybe I shall find them among the dead. Hear me, my chiefs! I am tired. My heart is sick and sad. From where the sun now stands I will fight no more forever."

—Chief Joseph of the Nez Percé, surrender speech, October 5, 1877

Biography

Reading Focus Question

Have students discuss the introductory question before reading the biography. Ask students to consider what options are available to Americans today to protect their homes and ways of life (security systems, police, laws). Then ask students what options they think were available to Chief Joseph and the Nez Percé in the 1870s.

Info to Know

His Father's Last Words In 1871, when Chief Joseph's father was dying, he urged his son, "You must stop your ears whenever you are asked to sign a treaty selling your home . . . This country holds your father's body. Never sell the bones of your father and mother."

Chief Joseph's Return In 1899, Chief Joseph visited Wallowa Valley for the first time since his departure in 1877. Instead of the untamed open range he remembered, Joseph saw fence lines, irrigation ditches, and cultivated fields. Joseph pleaded with local landowners to sell some of their land to his people, but they refused. On a second trip to Wallowa Valley in 1900, Joseph was taken by a government official to see his father's grave. As they traveled over acres of farmland, Joseph began to worry that the grave had been destroyed. He found that the grave had been ransacked and a local dentist had displayed Joseph's father's skull in his office.

Critical Thinking: Identifying Points of View

Standards Proficiency

Memorializing Chief Joseph

HSS 8.12.2; HSS **Analysis Skills;** HI 1 HI 2

Background For centuries, most Native Americans relied on spoken language for diplomacy, decision making, and the preservation of their history and culture. As a result, Native Americans developed a strong oral tradition.

1. Have students prepare a class memorial service for Chief Joseph that incorporates the oral tradition of Native Americans.
2. Students should create short oral eulogies that praise the life of Chief Joseph. Eulogies might express the point of view of different people from Chief Joseph's life (such as members of the Nez Percé, his family, U.S. soldiers, or army leaders) or the student's point of view.
3. Have students hold a class memorial for Chief Joseph at which they present their oral eulogies. LS **Auditory/Musical, Intrapersonal, Verbal/Linguistic**

Alternative Assessment Handbook, Rubric 24: Oral Presentations

Answers

Cause and Effect *They were exhausted, hungry, and freezing from the long journey to Canada to seek protection.*

Preteach

Bellringer

If YOU were there . . . Use the **Daily Bellringer Transparency** to help students answer the question.

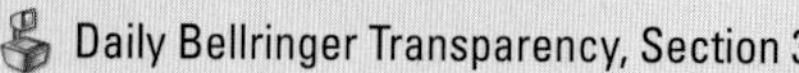
Daily Bellringer Transparency, Section 3

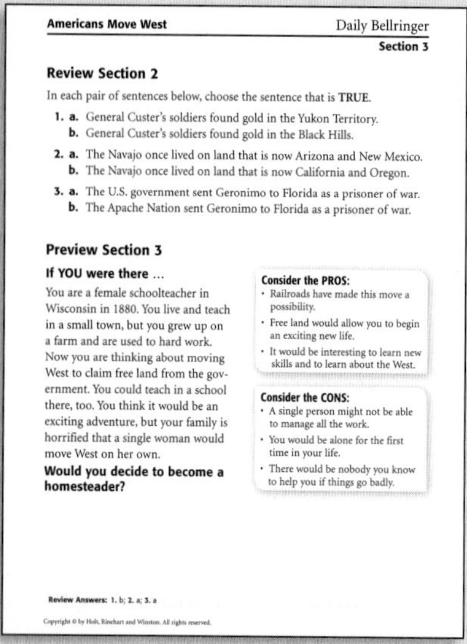

Americans Move West — Daily Bellringer — **Section 3**

Review Section 2

In each pair of sentences below, choose the sentence that is **TRUE**.

1. **a.** General Custer's soldiers found gold in the Yukon Territory.
   b. General Custer's soldiers found gold in the Black Hills.
2. **a.** The Navajo once lived on land that is now Arizona and New Mexico.
   b. The Navajo once lived on land that is now California and Oregon.
3. **a.** The U.S. government sent Geronimo to Florida as a prisoner of war.
   b. The Apache Nation sent Geronimo to Florida as a prisoner of war.

Preview Section 3

If YOU were there ...

You are a female schoolteacher in Wisconsin in 1880. You live and teach in a small town, but you grew up on a farm and are used to hard work. Now you are thinking about moving West to claim free land from the government. You could teach in a school there, too. You think it would be an exciting adventure, but your family is horrified that a single woman would move West on her own.

Would you decide to become a homesteader?

Consider the PROS:
- Railroads have made this move a possibility.
- Free land would allow you to begin an exciting new life.
- It would be interesting to learn new skills and to learn about the West.

Consider the CONS:
- A single person might not be able to manage all the work.
- You would be alone for the first time in your life.
- There would be nobody you know to help you if things go badly.

Review Answers: 1. b; 2. a; 3. a

Academic Vocabulary

Review with students the high-use academic term in this section.

facilitate to bring about (p. 562)

CRF: Vocabulary Builder Activity, Section 3

Standards Focus

HSS 8.8.2

Means: Describe how and why the United States expanded west.

Matters: Mining, ranching, and railroads drew many people to the West and led to conflict with Native Americans.

HSS 8.12.8

Means: Describe the National Grange and Populism and discuss their importance in U.S. History.

Matters: Political movements helped farmers in the West, who faced economic challenges.

SECTION 3

Farming and Populism

What You Will Learn...

Main Ideas

1. Many Americans started new lives on the Great Plains.
2. Economic challenges led to the creation of farmers' political groups.
3. By the 1890s, the western frontier had come to an end.

The Big Idea

Settlers on the Great Plains created new communities and unique political groups.

Key Terms and People

Homestead Act, *p. 560*
Morrill Act, *p. 560*
Exodusters, *p. 561*
sodbusters, *p. 561*
dry farming, *p. 561*
Annie Bidwell, *p. 562*
National Grange, *p. 563*
deflation, *p. 564*
William Jennings Bryan, *p. 564*
Populist Party, *p. 564*

HSS 8.8.2 Describe the purpose, challenges, and economic incentives associated with westward expansion, including the concept of Manifest Destiny (e.g., the Lewis and Clark expedition, accounts of the removal of Indians, the Cherokees' "Trail of Tears," settlement of the Great Plains) and the territorial acquisitions that spanned numerous decades.

8.12.8 Identify the characteristics and impact of Grangerism and Populism.

If YOU were there...

You are a female schoolteacher in Wisconsin in 1880. You live and teach in a small town, but you grew up on a farm and are used to hard work. Now you are thinking about moving West to claim free land from the government. You could teach in a school there, too. You think it would be an exciting adventure, but your family is horrified that a single woman would move West on her own.

Would you decide to become a homesteader?

BUILDING BACKGROUND By the 1870s and 1880s, the Great Plains had been 'tamed'and made more welcoming to settlers. The end of the open cattle range was coming, and the Indian wars were nearly over. The government moved to encourage permanent settlements in the West by offering land to homesteaders.

New Lives on the Plains

In 1862 Congress passed two important land grant acts that helped open the West to settlers. The **Homestead Act** gave government-owned land to small farmers. Any adult who was a U.S. citizen or planned to become one could receive 160 acres of land. In exchange, homesteaders promised to live on the land for five years. The **Morrill Act** granted more than 17 million acres of federal land to the states. The act required each state to sell this land and use the money to build colleges to teach agriculture and engineering.

Settling the Plains

People from all over the country moved West. Many farming families moved from areas where farmland was becoming scarce or expensive, such as New England. Many single women moved West. The Homestead Act granted land to unmarried women, which was unusual for the time.

The promise of land and a life free of discrimination also drew a large group of African Americans West. In 1879, some

Teach the Big Idea: Master the Standards

Standards Proficiency

Farming and Populism HSS 8.8.2, 8.12.8; HSS Analysis Skills: HI 1, HI 2

1. **Teach** Ask students the Main Idea questions to teach this section.
2. **Apply** Create a chart, titled *Farmers on the Great Plains,* with three columns headed *Reasons for Moving, Challenges of Farming,* and *Political Challenges,* for students to see. Have students identify facts for each topic. **LS Verbal/Linguistic**
3. **Review** As you review the section, have students help you fill in the master chart with the appropriate information.
4. **Practice/Homework** Ask students to create a poster to encourage individuals and families to move west. **LS Verbal/Linguistic, Visual/Spatial**

Alternative Assessment Handbook, Rubrics 7: Charts; and 28: Posters

20,000 to 40,000 southern African Americans moved to Kansas. Known as **Exodusters**, these southerners made a mass exodus, or departure from the South. A number of black communities soon developed.

Western homesteads also were attractive to immigrants. Norwegian, Swedish, Danish, German, and Czech immigrants formed many small communities on the Great Plains.

Farming the Plains

Plains farmers had many unique challenges. The seasons were extreme. Weather could be extreme. Also, the root-filled sod, or dirt, beneath the Plains grass was very tough. The hard work of breaking up the sod earned Plains farmers the nickname **sodbusters**.

In the 1890s, western Plains farmers began **dry farming**, a new method of farming that shifted the focus away from water-dependent crops such as corn. Instead, farmers grew more hardy crops like red wheat. In addition, by the 1880s, mechanical farming was becoming common. By using machinery, farmers could work much more quickly on large fields with fewer workers. Farmers shipped their harvest east by train. From there, crops were shipped overseas. The Great Plains soon became known as the breadbasket of the world.

Primary Source

LETTER

Letter from the Plains, 1863

In a letter to her family in Norway, immigrant Gro Svendsen describes her new life as a farmer on the plains of Iowa.

> "I remember I used to wonder when I heard that it would be impossible to keep the milk here as we did at home. Now I have learned that it is indeed impossible because of the heat here in the summertime . . . It's difficult, too, to preserve the butter. One must pour brine [salt water] over it or salt it.
>
> The thunderstorms are so violent that one might think it was the end of the world . . . Quite often the lightning strikes down both cattle and people, damages property, and splinters sturdy oak trees into many pieces."

—quoted in *Sources in American History*

ANALYSIS SKILL ANALYZING PRIMARY SOURCES

What might be some of the differences between Norway and Svendsen's new home in Iowa?

Pioneers like this family often lived in houses made of sod because there were few trees for lumber on the Plains.

Direct Teach

Main Idea

1 New Lives on the Plains

Many Americans started new lives on the Great Plains.

Recall How did the Homestead Act and the Morrill Act provide open up the West? *land grants to small farmers; land for states to sell to build colleges*

Summarize What were some of the challenges of farming on the Plains? *extreme weather, tough sod*

Make Inferences Why did the Plains farmers give up on crops such as corn? *not enough water on Plains*

HSS 8.8.2; **HSS Analysis Skills:** HI 1, HI 2

Primary Source

Reading Like a Historian

Letter from the Plains, 1863 Help students practice reading the document like historians. Ask the following:

- Who wrote this letter, and to whom?
- Does she write only the facts, or does she express her feelings and opinions, too?

Info to Know

Blizzards on the Plains Winter weather was said to be particularly harrowing on the Great Plains. Blizzard winds carried fine ice particles through the air with such force that no animal or person could stand to be exposed to the wind for very long. When these storms hit, settlers placed ropes along the perimeters of their houses to serve as guides to keep them from getting lost and freezing to death in the blinding snow and extreme cold.

Differentiating Instructions for Universal Access

Learners Having Difficulty

Reaching Standards

1. To help students identify the groups that settled the Great Plains and why they moved there, copy the graphic organizer for students to see. Omit the blue, italicized answers.
2. Have students copy and complete the organizer. Then review the answers as a class. **LS Verbal/Linguistic, Visual/Spatial**

Groups	Reasons for Moving
• *Exodusters* • *Norwegian, Swedish, Danish, German, and Czech Immigrants* • *New England farmers* • *Single women*	• *equal rights* • *more economic opportunity* • *land grants* • *inexpensive land*

Alternative Assessment Handbook, Rubric 13: Graphic Organizers

HSS 8.8.2; **HSS Analysis Skills:** HI 2

Answers

Analyzing Primary Sources *summer heat, violent thunder storms*

Direct Teach

Main Idea

1 New Lives on the Plains

Many Americans started new lives on the Great Plains.

Identify Who was Annie Bidwell? *community founder who supported a variety of moral and social causes*

Evaluate How did the formation of communities help the settlers? *helped one another in times of need, formed churches and schools*

CRF: Biography Activity: Laura Ingalls Wilder

HSS 8.8.2; HSS **Analysis Skills:** HI 1, HI 2

Main Idea

2 Farmers' Political Groups

Economic challenges led to the creation of farmers' political groups.

Finding Main Ideas Why did farm incomes fall? *Overproduction led to falling crop prices.*

Identify What is the National Grange? *a social and educational organization for farmers*

Judgments Do you think the government should have regulated railroad rates to help farmers? *possible answers: yes—the government should help make rates fair; no—the government should not interfere with businesses.*

HSS 8.12.8; HSS **Analysis Skills:** HI 2

Did you know . . .

In 1874 a locust plague hit the Great Plains, blocking out the sun. The pests devoured not only crops but the wool off live sheep and the clothes off people's backs!

Answers

Reading Check *alike—farming was important, established schools and churches; different—extreme weather, different crops, difficult conditions*

Building Communities

Women were an important force in the settling of the frontier. They joined in the hard work of farming and ranching and helped build communities out of the widely spaced farms and small towns. Their role in founding communities facilitated a strong voice in public affairs. Wyoming women, for example, were granted the vote in the new state's constitution, which was approved in 1869. **Annie Bidwell**, one of the founders of Chico, California, used her influence to support a variety of moral and social causes such as women's suffrage and temperance.

ACADEMIC VOCABULARY
facilitate to bring about

Many early settlers found life on their remote farms to be extremely difficult. Farmers formed communities so that they could assist one another in times of need. One of the first things that many pioneer communities did was establish a local church and school.

Children helped with many chores around the farms. Author Laura Ingalls Wilder was one of four children in a pioneer family. Wilder's books about settlers' lives on the prairie are still popular today.

READING CHECK **Comparing and Contrasting** How were settlers' lives alike and different from their lives in the East?

Farmers' Political Groups

From 1860 to 1900, the U.S. population more than doubled. To feed this growing population, the number of farms tripled. With modern machines, farmers in 1900 could harvest a bushel of wheat almost 20 times faster than they could in 1830.

Farm Incomes Fall

The combination of more farms and greater productivity, however, led to overproduction. Overproduction resulted in lower prices for crops. As their incomes decreased, many farmers found it difficult to pay bills. Farmers who could not make their mortgage payments lost their farms and homes. Many of these homeless farmers became tenant farmers who worked land owned by others. By 1880, one-fourth of all farms were rented by tenants, and the number continued to grow.

The National Grange

Many farmers blamed businesspeople—wholesalers, brokers, grain buyers, and especially railroad owners—for making money at their expense. As economic conditions worsened, farmers began to follow the example of other workers. They formed associations to protect and help their interests.

Time Line
Farming and the Rise of Populism
1862 President Lincoln signs the bill that authorizes the transcontinental railroad.
1867 The National Grange is founded.
1879 Exodusters move to Kansas.
562

Collaborative Learning

Reaching Standards

Daily Life on the Plains Mural

HSS 8.8.2; HSS **Analysis Skills:** CS 3, HR 1, HI 1

Materials: art supplies, poster boards

1. Organize students into small groups and review with them the information in "Farming on the Plains."
2. Have groups work together to create a mural depicting a day in the life of a settler and how settlers adapted to their environment.
3. Display students' murals in the classroom and ask each group to explain the activities it has depicted in their murals. LS **Visual/Spatial**

Alternative Assessment Handbook, Rubrics 3: Artwork; and 14: Group Activity

One such organization was founded by Oliver Hudson Kelley, who toured the South in 1866 for the U.S. Department of Agriculture. Kelley saw firsthand how the country's farmers suffered. Afterward, Kelley and several government clerks formed the National Grange of the Patrons of Husbandry in 1867. The **National Grange** was a social and educational organization for farmers. (*Grange* is an old word for granary.) Local chapters were quickly founded, and membership grew rapidly.

The Grange campaigned for political candidates who supported farmers' goals. The organization also called for laws that regulated rates charged by railroads. The U.S. Supreme Court ruled in 1877 that the government could regulate railroads because they affected the public interest. In 1886, the Court said that the federal government could only regulate companies doing business across state lines. Rate regulation for railroad lines within states fell to the state governments.

In February 1887 Congress passed the Interstate Commerce Act, providing national regulations over trade between states and creating the Interstate Commerce Commission to ensure fair railroad rates. However, the commission lacked power to enforce its regulations.

Agricultural Supply and Demand

CONNECTING TO ECONOMICS

Supply **is the amount of a good that is available. Demand is the amount of a good that people want to buy. When supply exceeds demand, prices fall.**

What happened to the price of wheat as the supply increased?

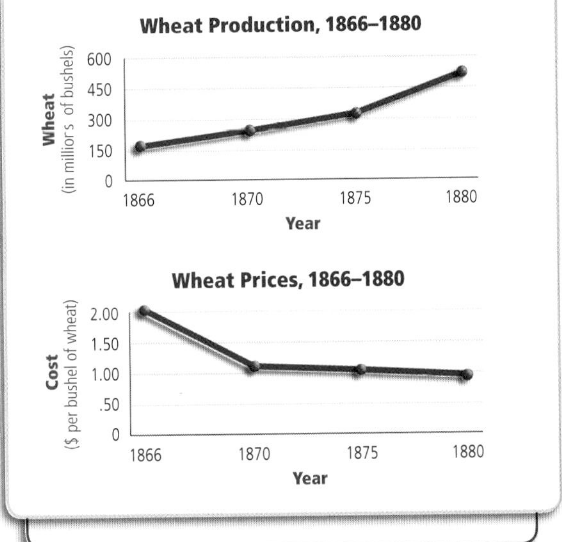

1887 The Interstate Commerce Commission is formed to regulate railroad prices.

1892 The national Populist Party is formed.

1896 The Populist Party backs William Jennings Bryan as the Democratic presidential candidate.

ANALYSIS SKILL **READING TIME LINES**

How many years after the authorization of the transcontinental railroad was the Interstate Commerce Commission created?

Direct Teach

Linking to Today

National Grange The National Grange, the nation's oldest national agricultural organization, is still in existence today and has approximately 300,000 members nationwide. Instead of focusing mainly on agriculture, the organization now aids persons in rural communities. Some of the issues that the organization deals with today are rural highways and infrastructure, rural schools, regional dairy compacts, and the preservation of farmland.

Draw Conclusions Why do you think that the organization still exists? *possible answer—Farmers and people living in rural areas need representatives who understand their unique needs and concerns*

Reading Time Lines

Farming and the Rise of Populism Have students examine the time line to answer the following questions.

- What problem does the cartoon portray? *difficulties between farmers and railroads*
- How many years after the founding of the National Grange was the Populist Party formed? *25 years*

Critical Thinking: Finding Main Ideas

Standards Proficiency

Letters to Congress

HSS 8.12.8; HSS **Analysis Skills:** HI 1

1. Ask students to imagine that they are Plains farmers living during the late 1800s.
2. Review with students some of the economic and political challenges farmers faced during this period.
3. Next, ask students to imagine that they have been asked to lead a local group of farmers campaigning for political and economic change. Have each student write a letter to Congress listing the group's goals that they would like politicians to address.
4. Ask for volunteers to read some of their goals to the class. LS **Intrapersonal, Verbal/Linguistic**

Alternative Assessment Handbook, Rubric 43: Writing to Persuade

Answers

Agricultural Supply and Demand *the cost of wheat went down sharply, then leveled off*

Reading Time Lines *25 years*

Direct Teach

Main Idea

❷ Farmers' Political Groups

Economic challenges led to the creation of farmers' political groups.

Identify What were the Farmers' Alliances? *political organizations formed by farmers to elect candidates that would help them*

Summarize What were the Populist Party's main issues? *government ownership of railroads, telegraph and telephone systems; free silver coinage; eight-hour work day; limits on immigration*

Make Judgments What did the 1896 election results say about Americans' view on the free silver debate? *possible answers—most opposed to it; not a big enough issue for majority to choose Bryan*

HSS 8.8.2, 8.12.8; **HSS Analysis Skills:** HI 1, HI 2

Connect to Economics

Inflation Supporters of the Free Silver Movement, including many Plains farmers, were essentially demanding inflationary money. When the supply of circulating currency rises beyond the needs of trade, the oversupply of currency leads to a general increase in the price of goods and services. Inflation can stimulate businesses and help wages rise, but the increase in wages often does not make up for the increase in the prices.

Free Silver Debate

Money issues also caused problems for farmers. Many farmers hoped that help would come from new laws affecting the money supply.

Since 1873 the United States had been on the gold standard, meaning that all paper money had to be backed by gold in the treasury. As a result, the money supply grow more slowly than the nation's population and led to **deflation**—a decrease in the money supply and overall lower prices. One solution was to allow the unlimited coining of silver and to back paper currency with silver. This was the position of those in the Free Silver movement.

During the late 1870s, there was a great deal of support for the Free Silver Movement. Many farmers began backing political candidates who favored free silver coinage. One such candidate was **William Jennings Bryan** of Nebraska.

The two major political parties, however, largely ignored the money issue. After the election of 1888, the Republican-controlled Congress passed the Sherman Silver Purchase act. The Act increased the amount of silver purchased for coinage. However, this did not help farmers as much as they had hoped.

Populist Party

To have greater power, many farmers organized to elect candidates that would help them. These political organizations became known as the Farmers' Alliances.

In the 1890 elections the Alliances were a strong political force. State and local wins raised farmers' political hopes. At a conference in Cincinnati, Ohio, in 1891, Alliance leaders met with labor and reform groups. Then, at a convention in St. Louis in February 1892, the Alliances formed a new national political party.

The new party was called the **Populist Party**, and it called for the government to own railroads and telephone and telegraph systems. It also favored the "free and unlimited coinage of silver." To gain the votes of workers, the Populists backed an eight-hour workday and limits on immigration.

The concerns of the Populists were soon put in the national spotlight. During the Panic of 1893, the U.S. economy experienced a crisis that some critics blamed on the shortage of gold. The failure of several major railroad companies also contributed to the economic problems.

The Panic of 1893 led more people to back the Populist call for economic reform. In 1896 the Republicans nominated William McKinley for president. McKinley was firmly against free coinage of silver. The Democrats nominated William Jennings Bryan, who favored free coinage.

The Populists had to decide between running their own candidate, and thus splitting the silver vote, or supporting Bryan. They decided to support Bryan. The Republicans had a well-financed campaign, and they won the election. McKinley's victory in 1896 marked the end of both the Populist Party and the Farmers' Alliances.

READING CHECK **Summarizing** Why did farmers, laborers, and reformers join to form the Populist Party?

BIOGRAPHY

William Jennings Bryan

1860–1925

William Jennings Bryan was born in Illinois but moved to Nebraska when he finished law school. He was elected Nebraska's first Democratic congress member in 1890. Through his political campaigns and work as a newspaper editor, he became one of the best-known supporters of Populist ideas. After a dramatic speech at the 1896 Democratic National Convention, Bryan was nominated for the presidency. He was the youngest presidential candidate up to that time. Although he lost the election, he continued to be an influential speaker.

Making Inferences Why was Bryan's support of Populist ideas important?

564

Collaborative Learning

Exceeding Standards

1896 Presidential Debate HSS 8.12.8; **HSS Analysis Skills:** HR 1, HR 5 — Research Required

1. Organize the class into two groups to form a debate. Have one group represent the supporters of William Jennings Bryan and the other represent supporters of William McKinley.
2. Have students divide and delegate responsibilities so that some students conduct research, others write speeches, and some prepare debate points and rules for debate. Each group will nominate one person to act as the presidential candidate, then stage a mock presidential debate.
3. At the end of the debate, have students vote for one of the candidates. Discuss with students the reasons their election results were the same as or different from the historical results. **LS Interpersonal, Visual/Spatial**

Alternative Assessment Handbook, Rubrics 10: Debate; and 30: Research

Answers

Biography *His speech supporting Populist ideas earned him a presidential nomination.*

Reading Check *hoped to gain power and make changes to benefit common interests*

Guthrie, Oklahoma

Oklahoma Land Rush

- The Rush began at noon on April 22, 1889.
- Some witnesses said they could feel the ground shake as 50,000 people raced to claim land.
- Single women and widows could claim land on an equal basis with men.
- Many settlers were dismayed to find some people had claimed land before the rush legally began. These people were called sooners.

End of the Frontier

By 1870 only small portions of the Great Plains remained unsettled. For most of the next two decades, this land remained open range.

In March 1889, government officials announced that homesteaders could file claims on land in what is now the state of Oklahoma. This land had belonged to Creek and Seminole Indians. Within a month, about 50,000 people rushed to Oklahoma to stake their claims.

In all, settlers claimed more than 11 million acres of former Indian land in the famous Oklahoma land rush. This huge wave of pioneers was the last chapter of the westward movement. By the early 1890s, the frontier had ceased to exist in the United States.

READING CHECK **Finding Main Ideas** What event signaled the closing of the frontier?

SUMMARY AND PREVIEW In this section you read about the challenges settlers faced. In the next chapter you will read about the growth of America's industrial power and how that growth affected American lives.

Section 3 Assessment

go.hrw.com
Online Quiz
KEYWORD: SS8 HP17

Reviewing Ideas, Terms, and People HSS 8.8.2, 8.12.8

1. a. **Describe** What groups settled in the Great Plains?
   b. **Explain** How did the U.S. government make lands available to western settlers?
   c. **Elaborate** Would you have chosen to settle on the frontier? Why or why not?
2. a. **Recall** What was the goal of the **National Grange**?
   b. **Make Inferences** Why did the **Populist Party** want the government to own railroads and telegraph and telephone systems?
   c. **Evaluate** Do you think farmers were successful in bringing about economic and political change? Explain.
3. a. **Recall** What was the Oklahoma land rush?
   b. **Explain** Why did the frontier cease to exist in the United States?

Critical Thinking

4. **Comparing and Contrasting** Copy the diagram onto your own sheet of paper. Use it to show the similarities and differences among the National Grange, the Farmers' Alliances, and the Populist Party.

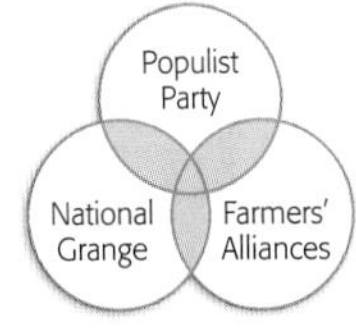

FOCUS ON WRITING

5. **Taking Notes on Farming the Great Plains** As you read this section, take notes on the growth of farming on the Great Plains. How did farmers interact with the railroads? What changes might have been apparent to a railroad worker?

Direct Teach

Main Idea

3 End of the Frontier

By the 1890s, the western frontier had come to an end.

Recall To whom did the land claimed by homesteaders in the Oklahoma land rush previously belong? *Creek and Seminole Indians*

Evaluate Why do you think so many people rushed to Oklahoma to claim land? *possible answer—It was one of the last remaining places in the United States open for settlement.*

HSS 8.8.2, 8.12.8; HSS **Analysis Skills:** HI 1, HI 2

Review & Assess

Close

Have students summarize the opportunities and the challenges of farming the Great Plains.

Review

Online Quiz, Section 3

Assess

SE Section 3 Assessment

PASS: Section 3 Quiz

Alternative Assessment Handbook

Reteach/Classroom Intervention

California Standards Review Workbook

Interactive Reader and Study Guide, Section 3

Interactive Skills Tutor CD-ROM

Section 3 Assessment Answers

1. a. farming families, single women, Exodusters, immigrants
   b. Homestead and Morrill Acts
   c. possible answers—no, too dangerous, risky; yes, good opportunities
2. a. social and educational organization for farmers
   b. to help control prices
   c. possible answer—yes, Interstate Commerce Act ensured fair rates
3. a. 50,000 people rushed to Oklahoma to stake claims on newly-opened territory
   b. Americans had settled all frontier land and what was left of the open range.
4. National Grange—campaigned for pro-farmer politicians, called to regulate railroads; Populist Party—wanted government ownership of railroad, telephone, telegraph to regulate rates; Farmers' alliances—local political organizations
5. Farmers may have used the railroads to ship goods or lost land to the railroad. Railroad workers may have seen more people come west and settle.

Answers

Reading Check *Oklahoma land rush*

Social Studies Skills

Comparing Migration Maps

Activity Timed Comparison Give students a set amount of time and have them use it to list as many differences between the 1850 and 1890 maps as possible. When the time is up, ask for volunteers to share some of the differences they listed. Correct students' interpretations as needed. List the differences for students to see and discuss them. Then have each student write a few sentences summarizing U.S. migration and settlement from 1850 to 1890. Ask for volunteers to read their summaries to the class. **LS Visual/Spatial**

- Alternative Assessment Handbook, Rubrics 21: Map Reading; and 37: Writing Assignments
- Interactive Skills Tutor CD-ROM, Lesson 6: Interpret Maps, Graphs, Charts, Visuals, and Political Cartoons

Social Studies Skills

Analysis | Critical Thinking | Participation | **Study**

Comparing Migration Maps

Define the Skill

One of the best ways of using geography to learn history is by comparing maps. This skill allows you to see changes over time. It also helps you see relationships between one factor, such as population growth, and another factor, such as transportation routes or economic activities in an area.

Learn the Skill

Follow these steps to compare information on maps.

1. Apply basic map skills by reading the title and studying the legend and symbols for each map.
2. Note the date of each map and the area it covers. Maps compared for changes over time should include the same areas. Those used to look for relationships should have similar dates.
3. Note similarities or differences. Closely examine and compare each map's patterns and symbols.
4. Apply critical thinking skills. Make generalizations and draw conclusions about the relationships you find.

Practice the Skill

Use the maps below to answer the following questions.

1. What present-day state was unsettled by Americans in 1850 and almost completely settled in 1890?
2. Which other two present-day states show the most settlement by Americans from 1850–1890?
3. Why do you think the West coast was settled before the interior of the United States?
4. According to the maps, how might rivers have shaped the settlement of the West?

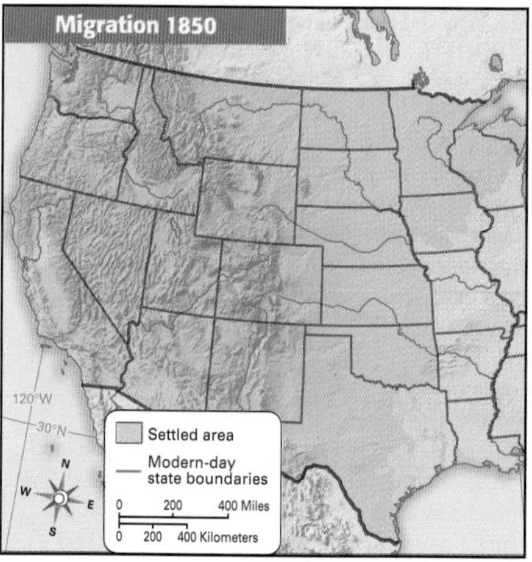

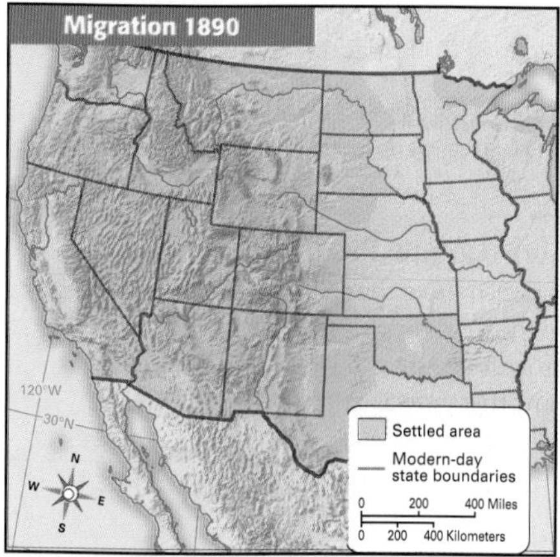

Social Studies Skills Activity: Comparing Migration Maps

Map Comparison Quiz

Standards Proficiency

1. To extend the "Practice the Skill" activity, have each student create a five-question quiz about the two maps above. At least two questions in the quiz should require a comparison of the two maps to answer. Assign students the type of quiz to create, such as multiple choice, short answer, or true-false. In addition, each student should create a separate answer key for his or her quiz.
2. Review and correct students' quizzes and answers keys.
3. Then have students exchange quizzes with partners. Students should answer the quizzes they receive and return them to their authors for grading. **LS Interpersonal, Visual/Spatial**

- Alternative Assessment Handbook, Rubrics 21: Map Reading; and 37: Writing Assignments

Answers

Practice the Skill 1. *Kansas;* 2. *California and either Nebraska or Colorado;* 3. *People arrived on the coast by ship and settled there first. The Rocky Mountains and the aridness of the Great Plains then slowed migration and settlement inland.* 4. *The maps show that people settled along or near rivers.*

CHAPTER 17 Standards Review

Visual Summary

Use the visual summary below to help you review the main ideas of the chapter.

QUICK FACTS

The American West

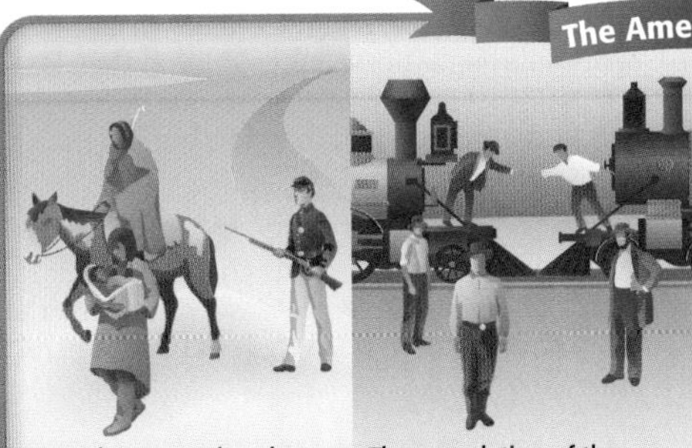

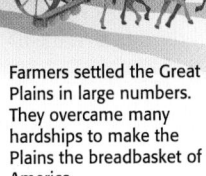

As settlers moved to the West, they came into conflict with American Indians. The U.S. government defeated Indian resistance and moved many tribes to reservations.

The completion of the transcontinental railroad in 1869 opened the West to more settlement. Gold and silver strikes also drew people hoping to get rich.

The railroads helped make the rise of the Cattle Kingdom possible. Cowboys drove huge herds of cattle from ranches to railway stations to be shipped to the East.

Farmers settled the Great Plains in large numbers. They overcame many hardships to make the Plains the breadbasket of America.

Reviewing Vocabulary, Terms, and People

1. Who was the leader of the 7th Cavalry in the Battle of the Little Bighorn?
   a. Cyrus McCormick
   b. Leland Stanford
   c. William Jennings Bryan
   d. George Armstrong Custer
2. What act gave millions of acres of federal lands to the states, which were to sell them and use those funds to build agricultural and engineering colleges?
   a. Morrill Act
   b. Sherman Act
   c. Pacific Railway Act
   d. Interstate Commerce Act
3. Which frontier woman was instrumental in supporting reform efforts in the West?
   a. Sarah Winnemucca
   b. Laura Ingalls Wilder
   c. Annie Bidwell
   d. Lucretia Mott

Comprehension and Critical Thinking

SECTION 1 *(Pages 546–552)* **HSS 8.8.2**

6. **a. Recall** Why were many Americans eager to move to the western frontier?
   b. Analyze How did railroads and ranching change the landscape of the West?
   c. Elaborate In your opinion, which made the greatest changes to the West—mining, ranching, or railroads? Explain your answer.

SECTION 2 *(Pages 553–558)* **HSS 8.12.2**

7. **a. Describe** What was life like for the Plains Indians before and after the arrival of large numbers of American settlers?
   b. Draw Conclusions Why did the spread of the Ghost Dance movement cause concern for U.S. officials?
   c. Elaborate What do you think about the reservation system established by the United States?

Answers

Visual Summary

Review and Inquiry Have students study the visual summary. Ask them to write a descriptive paragraph of each group represented.

Quick Facts Transparency: Americans Move West Visual Summary

Reviewing Vocabulary, Terms, and People

1. d

2. a

3. c

Comprehension and Critical Thinking

4. a. to make money as miners, farmers, or cattle ranchers

b. open plains were fenced, grass was eaten by cattle, railroad tracks were built over much of the land and new towns were built.

c. possible answer—railroads; brought many new settlers and new economic opportunities to the West

5. a. before—had their own land, could hunt and live traditionally; after—struggled, lost their land, killed or forced onto reservations where it was hard to find enough food

b. The movement promoted the idea of a paradise where settlers disappeared, so U.S. officials may have seen this as a threat of rebellion or violence against them.

c. Answers will vary, but students should show an understanding of the reservation system.

Review and Assessment Resources

Review and Reinforce

- **SE** Standards Review
- **CRF:** Chapter Review Activity
- California Standards Review Workbook
- Quick Facts Transparency: Americans Move West Visual Summary
- Spanish Chapter Summaries Audio CD Program
- Online Chapter Summaries in Six Languages
- **OSP** Holt PuzzlePro; Game Tool for ExamView
- Quiz Game CD-ROM

Assess

- **SE** Standards Assessment
- PASS: Chapter Test, Forms A and B
- Alternative Assessment Handbook
- **OSP** ExamView Test Generator, Chapter Test
- Universal Access Modified Worksheets and Tests CD-ROM: Chapter Test
- Holt Online Assessment Program (in the Premier Online Edition)

Reteach/Intervene

- Interactive Reader and Study Guide
- Universal Access Teacher Management System: Lesson Plans for Universal Access
- Universal Access Modified Worksheets and Tests CD-ROM
- Interactive Skills Tutor CD-ROM

go.hrw.com
Online Resources
Chapter Resources:
KEYWORD: SS8 US17

Answers

6. **a.** National Grange, Farmers' Alliances, and the Populist Party; They were formed to protect farmers' interests.
   b. Women raised families, ran businesses, taught schools, helped establish towns, influenced moral and social causes.
   c. possible answers—overuse of natural resources, no more room for expansion, eventual overcrowding, and lack of available land

Reviewing Themes

7. mountain ranges, harsh weather, and having to work in remote areas that were hard to get food and supplies to
8. Mechanical farm equipment made it easier to farm the dry, hard soil of the Plains. Machinery allowed farmers to work more quickly on large fields with fewer workers.

Using the Internet

9. Go to the HRW Web site and enter the keyword shown to access a rubric for this activity.

KEYWORD: SS8 US17

SECTION 3 *(Pages 560–565)* **HSS 8.8.2, 8.12.8**

8. **a. Identify** What political organizations did western farmers create? Why did farmers create these organizations?
   b. Analyze How did women participate in the settling of the American frontier?
   c. Predict How might the end of the frontier in the United States affect the nation?

Reviewing Themes

9. **Geography** What geographic obstacles did miners, ranchers, and railroad workers face in the West?
10. **Science and Technology** What types of technology did farmers on the Great Plains use, and how did it benefit them?

Using the Internet

11. **Activity: Creating a Presentation** Our view of the settlement of the west is heavily influenced by popular culture. Writers, painters, and illustrators provided a steady flow of words and images that sensationalized life in the American West. Later, film makers and television producers also contributed to the myth of the *Wild West.* "When legend becomes fact," said one actor in the classic western movie *The Man Who Shot Liberty Valance,* "print the legend." How does legend affect our view of this part of our history? Enter the activity keyword. Analyze the myths and realities of the West and the ways in which they shaped our view of that time period. Then create a visual display or PowerPoint presentation to present your research.

Reading Skills

Understanding Through Questioning *Use the Reading Skills taught in this chapter to answer the question about the reading selection below.*

> For survival, Plains Indians depended on two animals—the horse and the buffalo. The Spanish brought horses to America in the 1500s. Plains Indians learned to ride horses, and hunters used them to follow buffalo herds year-round. *(p. 554)*

12. Write two or three questions you have about the information in the passage above. Remember to use the five W's—Who? What? When? Where? and Why?

Social Studies Skills

Comparing Migration Maps *Use the Social Studies Skills taught in this chapter to answer the questions about the map below.*

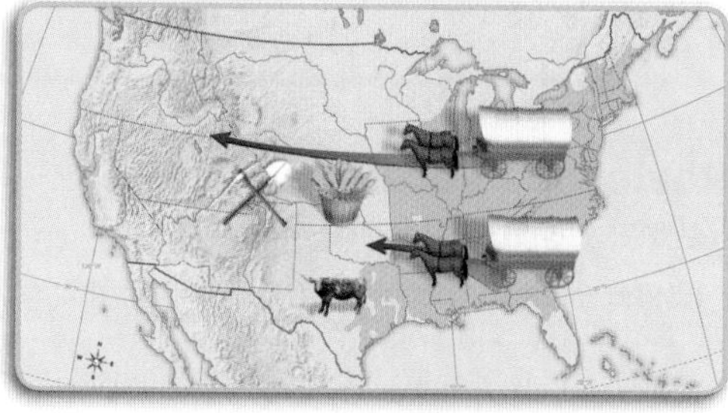

13. According to the map above, for what reasons did settlers migrate to the West?
    a. for mining, ranching, and farming
    b. for jobs in manufacturing
    c. for the homes in the major cities there
    d. for the fishing industry

FOCUS ON WRITING

14. **Writing Your Letter** Review your notes. Then write a letter to your sister back in Ireland about your experiences on the Great Plains. Describe all the changes you have seen. Use colorful language and precise details to make your sister feel as though she were there.

Reading Skills

10. Possible answers might include: What animals did the Plains Indians depend on for survival? How did the Plains Indians acquire those animals?

Social Studies Skills

11. a

Focus on Writing

12. **Rubric** Students' letters should:
    - express the point of view of an Irish immigrant.
    - clearly indicate the main idea.
    - include three or four main points about life on the Great Plains.
    - end with a conclusion that summarized the main point.

CRF: Focus on Writing: Writing a Letter

Standards Assessment

DIRECTIONS: Read each question and write the letter of the best response.

1

- Government ownership of railroads
- Free and unlimited coinage of silver
- An eight-hour day for industrial workers
- Strict limits on foreign immigration
- Election of officials who will help farmers

Which of the following intended to accomplish the changes listed above in American society?

A the Morrill Act
B the Populist Party
C the National Grange
D the Homestead Act

2 The goal of many reformers who wanted to help Native Americans in the late 1800s was to

A get Indians to adopt the ways of white people.
B return to Indians all the land that had been taken from them.
C relocate all the nations to create an American Indian state in Oklahoma.
D negotiate treaties to bring peace to the frontier.

3 What played the *most* important part in the growth of the West's population and economy between 1865 and 1900?

A the mining industry
B the Cattle Kingdom
C the Populist Party
D the railroad

4 In general, the policy of the United States government toward Native Americans in the West was to

A send the army to track them down, engage them in battle, and kill them.
B move them onto reservations and open their homelands to white settlers.
C kill all the buffalo so that they could not continue their traditional way of life.
D drive them into Canada or Mexico to be dealt with by that country's government.

5 The biggest problem facing western farmers in the late 1800s was

A a scarcity of good, cheap land to farm.
B their lack of organization to achieve change.
C overproduction and low crop prices.
D the threat of attacks by Native Americans.

Connecting with Past Learning

6 In Grade 7 you learned about the relationship of serfs to the land during the feudal period in Europe. Which group in the United States in the late 1800s had a relationship to the land that was similar to the serfs' relationship?

A reservation Indians
B Exodusters
C dry farmers
D vaqueros

7 The living conditions that reservation Indians faced in the late 1800s were most like those faced in earlier times by

A small farmers in the South.
B Loyalists during the Revolution.
C Irish immigrants in the North.
D African American slaves.

Answers

1. B
Break Down the Question Students need to recall the platform for the Populist Party and recognize that the distracter answers are too limited.

2. A
Break Down the Question Students must remember who the reformers were and what their goals were.

3. B
Break Down the Question Point out that the word *most* means that more than one answer may be correct and that students must choose the one that provides the best answer.

4. B
Break Down the Question Point out that the phrase *in general* means that more than one answer may be correct and that students must choose the one that provides the best answer.

5. C
Break Down the Question The word *biggest* indicates that more than one answer may be correct, but students must choose the answer that was the biggest problem during the indicated time.

6. A
Break Down the Question Students should recall that medieval serfs, like reservation Indians were bound to the land they worked.

7. D
Break Down the Question Students should recall that like African American slaves, reservation Indians were denied equal rights and the freedom to live where they wanted.

Intervention Resources

Reproducible

- Interactive Reader and Study Guide
- Universal Access Teacher Management System: Lesson Plans for Universal Access

Technology

- Quick Facts Transparency: Americans Move West Visual Summary
- Universal Access Modified Worksheets and Tests CD-ROM
- Interactive Skills Tutor CD-ROM

Tips for Test Taking

Search for Skips and Smudges Read the following tip to students. To avoid losing points on machine-graded tests, make sure you

- did not skip any answers,
- provided only one answer per question,
- made your marks dark enough, and
- kept all marks neatly within the lines.

Then erase all smudges and stray pencil marks on your answer sheet. Cleanly erase those places where you changed your mind. Check everything. You are the only person who can!

Standards Review

Have students review the following standards in their workbooks.

California Standards Review Workbook: HSS 8.8.2, 8.12.2, 8.12.8

Chapter 18 Planning Guide

An Industrial Nation

MASTERING THE CALIFORNIA STANDARDS

Chapter Overview	Reproducible Resources	Technology Resources
CHAPTER 18 **pp. 570–601** **Overview: In this chapter, students will learn about how the United States became an industrial power in the late 1800s.** See p. 570 for the California History–Social Science standards covered in this chapter.	**Universal Access Teacher Management System:*** • Universal Access Instructional Benchmarking Guides • Lesson Plans for Universal Access **Interactive Reader and Study Guide:*** Chapter Graphic Organizer **Chapter Resource File*** • Focus on Writing Activity: A Memo • Social Studies Skills Activity: Analyzing Cost and Benefits • Chapter Review Activity **Pre-AP Activities Guide for United States History:*** Writing Thesis Statements	**One-Stop Planner CD-ROM:** Calendar Planner **Student Edition Full-Read Audio CD-ROM** **Universal Access Modified Worksheets and Tests CD-ROM** **Primary Source Library CD-ROM for United States History** **Power Presentations with Video CD-ROM** **History's Impact: United States History Video Program (VHS/DVD):** An Industrial Nation*
Section 1: **The Second Industrial Revolution** **The Big Idea:** The Second Industrial Revolution led to new sources of power and advances in transportation and communication. 8.12.1, 8.12.9	**Universal Access Teacher Management System:*** Section 1 Lesson Plan **Interactive Reader and Study Guide:*** Section 1 Summary **Chapter Resource File*** • Vocabulary Builder, Section 1 • Biography Activity: Inventors • Biography Activity: Orville and Wilbur Wright • Interdisciplinary Project: Technology Time Line	**Daily Bellringer Transparency:** Section 1* **Quick Facts Transparency:** Factors Affecting Industrial Growth*
Section 2: **Big Business** **The Big Idea:** The growth of big business in the late 1800s led to the creation of monopolies. 8.12.3, 8.12.4, 8.12.6	**Universal Access Teacher Management System:*** Section 2 Lesson Plan **Interactive Reader and Study Guide:*** Section 2 Summary **Chapter Resource File*** • Vocabulary Builder, Section 2 • Biography Activity: Leland Stanford • Economics and History Activity: Monopolies and Trusts	**Daily Bellringer Transparency:** Section 2*
Section 3: **Industrial Workers** **The Big Idea:** Changes in the workplace led to a rise in labor unions and workers' strikes. 8.12.6	**Universal Access Teacher Management System:*** Section 3 Lesson Plan **Interactive Reader and Study Guide:*** Section 3 Summary **Chapter Resource File*** • Vocabulary Builder, Section 3 • Biography Activity: Mother Jones • History and Geography Activity: Pullman's Company Town • Primary Source Activity: Samuel Gompers	**Daily Bellringer Transparency:** Section 3* **Map Transparency:** Major Labor Strikes, Late 1800s* go.hrw.com **Internet Activity:** Steelworkers go.hrw.com **Internet Activity:** Mary Harris Jones
Section 4: **A New Wave of Immigration** **The Big Idea:** A new wave of immigration in the late 1800s brought large numbers of immigrants to the United States. 8.12.5, 8.12.7	**Universal Access Teacher Management System:*** Section 4 Lesson Plan **Interactive Reader and Study Guide:*** Section 4 Summary **Chapter Resource File*** • Vocabulary Builder, Section 4 • Literature Activity: Poetry from Angel Island **U.S. Supreme Court Case Studies:** *Yick Wo* v. *Hopkins* (1886)	**Daily Bellringer Transparency:** Section 4*
Section 5: **City Life** **The Big Idea:** Cities in the United States experienced dramatic expansion in the late 1800s. 8.12.5	**Universal Access Teacher Management System:*** Section 5 Lesson Plan **Interactive Reader and Study Guide:*** Section 5 Summary **Chapter Resource File*** • Vocabulary Builder, Section 5 • Primary Source Activity: *McGuffey's Reader* **Political Cartoons Activities Guide for United States History,** Cartoon 21: Urban Life and Tenements*	**Daily Bellringer Transparency:** Section 5*

SE Student Edition  Print Resource  Audio CD Video

TE Teacher's Edition  Transparency  CD-ROM DVD

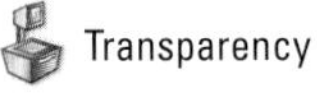 go.hrw.com  CA Standards Mastery Learning Styles

OSP One-Stop Planner CD-ROM * also on One-Stop Planner CD

Review, Assessment, Intervention

 **Standards Review Workbook***

 **Quick Facts Transparency:** An Industrial Nation Visual Summary*

Spanish Chapter Summaries Audio CD Program

  **Online Chapter Summaries in Six Languages**

 **Progress Assessment Support System (PASS):** Chapter Test*

Universal Access Modified Worksheets and Tests CD-ROM: Modified Chapter Test

 **One-Stop Planner CD-ROM:** ExamView Test Generator (English/Spanish)

PASS: Section 1 Quiz*

 **Online Quiz:** Section 1

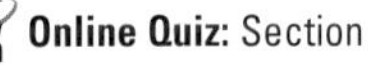 **Alternative Assessment Handbook**

 **PASS:** Section 2 Quiz*

Online Quiz: Section 2

 **Alternative Assessment Handbook**

 **PASS:** Section 3 Quiz*

Online Quiz: Section 3

 **Alternative Assessment Handbook**

 **PASS:** Section 4 Quiz*

Online Quiz: Section 4

Alternative Assessment Handbook

 **PASS:** Section 5 Quiz*

Online Quiz: Section 5

 **Alternative Assessment Handbook**

California Resources for Standards Mastery

INSTRUCTIONAL PLANNING AND SUPPORT

Universal Access Teacher Management System*

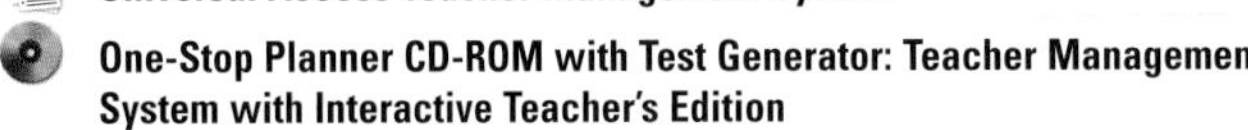

One-Stop Planner CD-ROM with Test Generator: Teacher Management System with Interactive Teacher's Edition

STANDARDS MASTERY

Standards Review Workbook*

At Home: A Guide to Standards Mastery for United States History

Holt Online Learning

To enhance learning, Internet activities are available for Steelworkers and Mary Harris Jones.

KEYWORD: SS8 TEACHER

- Teacher Support Page
- Content Updates
- Rubrics and Writing Models
- Teaching Tips for the Multimedia Classroom

KEYWORD: SS8 US18

- Current Events
- Document-Based Questions
- Holt Grapher
- Holt Online Atlas
- Holt Researcher
- Interactive Multimedia Activities
- Internet Activities
- Online Chapter Summaries in Six Languages
- Online Section Quizzes
- American History Maps and Charts

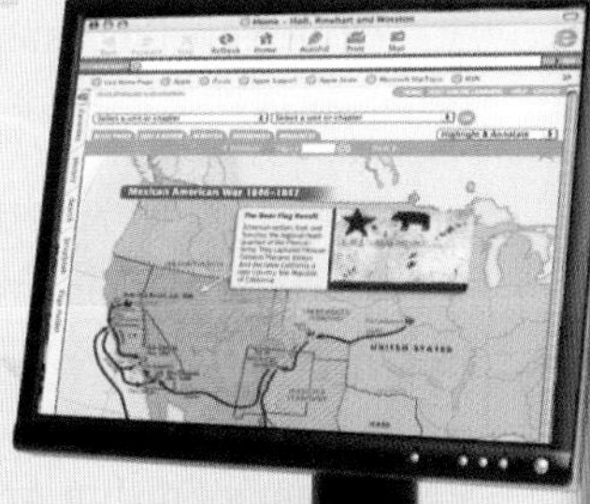

HOLT PREMIER ONLINE STUDENT EDITION

Complete online support for interactivity, assessment, and reporting

- Interactive Maps and Notebook
- Standardized Test Prep
- Homework Practice and Research Activities Online

Mastering the Standards: Differentiating Instruction

Reaching Standards	Basic-level activities designed for all students encountering new material
Standards Proficiency	Intermediate-level activities designed for average students
Exceeding Standards	Challenging activities designed for honors and gifted-and-talented students
Standard English Mastery	Activities designed to improve standard English usage

Frequently Asked Questions

INSTRUCTIONAL PLANNING AND SUPPORT

Where do I find planning aids, pacing guides, lesson plans, and other teaching aids?

Annotated Teacher's Edition:
- Chapter planning guides
- Standards-based instruction and strategies
- Differentiated instruction for universal access
- Point-of-use reminders for integrating program resources

Power Presentations with Video CD-ROM

Universal Access Teacher Management System:
- Year and unit instructional benchmarking guides
- Reproducible lesson plans
- Assessment guides for diagnostic, progress, and summative end-of-the-year tests
- Options for differentiating instruction and intervention
- Teaching guides and answer keys for student workbooks

One-Stop Planner CD-ROM with Test Generator: Teacher Management System with Interactive Teacher's Editon:
- Calendar Planner
- Editable lesson plans
- All reproducible ancillaries in Adobe Acrobat (PDF) format
- ExamView Test Generator (English & Spanish)
- Game Tool for ExamView
- PuzzlePro
- Transparency and video previews

DIFFERENTIATING INSTRUCTION FOR UNIVERSAL ACCESS

What resources are available to ensure that Advanced Learners/GATE Students master the standards?

Teacher's Edition Activities:
- Studying the Stock Market, p. 580
- Labor Strikes, p. 586
- The New Colossus, p. 589

Lesson Plans for Universal Access

Pre-AP Activities Guide for United States History: Writing Thesis Statements

Primary Source Library CD-ROM for United States History

What resources are available to ensure that English Learners and Standard English Learners master the standards?

Teacher's Edition Activities:
- Newspaper Article, p. 577
- Statue of Liberty Poem, p. 589

Lesson Plans for Universal Access

Chapter Resource File: Vocabulary Builder Activities

Spanish Chapter Summaries Audio CD Program

Online Chapter Summaries in Six Languages

One-Stop Planner CD-ROM:
- PuzzlePro, Spanish Version
- ExamView Test Generator, Spanish Version

What modified materials are available for Special Education?

The ***Universal Access Modified Worksheets and Tests CD-ROM*** provides editable versions of the following:

Vocabulary Flash Cards

Modified Vocabulary Builder Activities

Modified Chapter Review Activity

Modified Chapter Test

What resources are available to ensure that Learners Having Difficulty master the standards?

Teacher's Edition Activities:
- Cause and Effect Posters, p. 575
- Industrial Workers, p. 584
- City Life, p. 594
- Urban Developments, p. 595

Interactive Reader and Study Guide

Student Edition Full-Read Audio CD

Quick Facts Transparency: An Industrial Nation Visual Summary

Standards Review Workbook

Social Studies Skills Activity: Analyzing Costs and Benefits

Interactive Skills Tutor CD-ROM

How do I intervene for students struggling to master the standards?

Interactive Reader and Study Guide

Quick Facts Transparency: An Industrial Nation Visual Summary

Standards Review Workbook

Social Studies Skills Activity: Analyzing Costs and Benefits

Interactive Skills Tutor CD-ROM

PROFESSIONAL DEVELOPMENT

What teacher training resources are available to help me grow professionally?

- In-service and staff development as part of your Holt Social Studies product purchase
- Quick Teacher Tutorial Lesson Presentation CD-ROM
- Intensive tuition-based Teacher Development Institute
- *Teaching American History* Online 2 Module Professional Development Course
- Convenient Holt Speaker Bureau face-to-face workshop options
- PRAXIS™ Test Prep (#0089) interactive Web-based content refreshers*
- 24/7 *Ask A Professional Development Expert* at http://www.hrw.com/prodev/

* PRAXIS is a trademark of Educational Testing Service (ETS). This publication is not endorsed or approved by ETS.

Information Literacy Skills

To learn more about how History–Social Science instruction may be improved by the effective use of library media centers and information literacy skills, go to the Teacher's Resource Materials for Chapter 18 at **go.hrw.com**, keyword: SS8 MEDIA.

The following materials were developed by the Division for Public Education of the American Bar Association. These materials are part of the **Democracy and Civic Education** supplement.
- Constitution Study Guide
- Supreme Court Case Studies

Chapter Preview

Standards Focus

Standards by Section

Section 1: HSS 8.12.1, 8.12.9
Section 2: HSS 8.12.4, 8.12.6
Section 3: HSS 8.12.6
Section 4: HSS 8.12.7
Section 5: HSS 8.12.5

Teacher's Edition

HSS **Analysis Skills:** CS 1, CS 2, CS 3, HR 1, HR 5, HI 1, HI 2, HI 3, HI 6
ELA Writing 8.2.0, Reading 8.2.0

Preview Grade 11 Standards

HSS **11.2** Students analyze the relationship among the rise of industrialization, large-scale rural-to-urban migration, and massive immigration from Southern and Eastern Europe.

11.2.1 Know the effects of industrialization on living and working conditions, including the portrayal of working conditions and food safety in Upton Sinclair's *The Jungle.*

11.2.2 Describe the changing landscape, including the growth of cities linked by industry and trade, and the development of cities divided according to race, ethnicity, and class.

Focus on Writing

The **Chapter Resource File** provides a Focus on Writing worksheet to help students organize and create their memos.

CRF: Focus on Writing Activity: A Memo

CHAPTER 18 1876–1900

An Industrial Nation

California Standards

History–Social Science

8.12 Students analyze the transformation of the American economy and the changing social and political conditions in the United States in response to the Industrial Revolution.

Analysis Skills

HI 6 Students interpret basic indications of economic performance.

English–Language Arts

Writing 8.2.0 Write documents related to career development.

Reading 8.2.0 Students read and understand grade-level appropriate materials.

FOCUS ON WRITING

A Memo You are a writer at a television network, and you have an idea for a TV drama series set in the late 1800s. Draft a memo to your boss telling her about your story idea. As you read this chapter, gather information about the people, places, and events of this time period. Then write your memo. Tell about the basic plot, the cast of characters, and the setting of your series.

UNITED STATES

1879 Thomas Edison invents the first lightbulb.

1870

WORLD

1876 German engineer Nikolaus A. Otto perfects a gasoline-powered engine.

Introduce the Chapter

Standards Proficiency

Focus on Industry and Technology

1. Discuss with students how industrialization has changed life in the United States. Explain that before goods were mass produced, they were made by hand.
2. Have students create a chart with two columns. In the first column, have them list technological innovations we may take for granted, such as electricity, the telephone, etc. In the second column, have students explain how these technologies, and the way they are produced, have affected American society. For instance, e-mail and cell phones have improved communication.
3. Discuss the list with the class, then review some of the changes brought on by industrialization and increased immigration in the late 1800s. Ask students to identify why an immigrant may have wanted to come to the United States in the late 1800s, and what might attract an immigrant to the United States today.

LS **Verbal/Linguistic**

HOLT
History's Impact
▶ video series
Watch the video to understand the impact of industrialization on the United States.
What You Will Learn...
In this chapter you will learn about how the United States became an industrial power in the late 1800s. A new wave of immigrants provided the labor, and the combination of industry and immigration led to increased urbanization of the country. Cities like San Francisco, shown here, began to take the shape that they still have today. In fact, much of what we know as modern America developed during this important period.
1880
1883 The island volcano of Krakatau in the Pacific Ocean erupts in one of the world's greatest natural disasters.
1886 The American Federation of Labor is formed on December 8.
1889 The Eiffel Tower is built in Paris.
1890
1890 Congress passes the Sherman Antitrust Act.
1892 On June 29 the Homestead strike begins. Carnegie Steel Company refuses to negotiate with the union.
1900
1898 French scientists Pierre and Marie Curie discover radium.
571

• Chapter Preview •

HOLT

History's Impact

▶ **video series**
See the Video Teacher's Guide for strategies for using the chapter video **An Industrial Nation**.

Chapter Big Ideas

Section 1 The Second Industrial Revolution led to new sources of power and advances in transportation and communication. **HSS** 8.12.1, 8.12.9

Section 2 The growth of big business in the late 1800s led to the creation of monopolies. **HSS** 8.12.4, 8.12.6

Section 3 Changes in the workplace led to a rise in labor unions and workers' strikes. **HSS** 8.12.6

Section 4 A new wave of immigration in the late 1800s brought large numbers of immigrants to the United States. **HSS** 8.12.7

Section 5 Cities in the United States experienced dramatic expansion in the late 1800s. **HSS** 8.12.5

Explore the Picture

San Francisco In the late 1800s inventions and improvements made urban life much easier. This photo of Market Street in San Francisco, California, shows many elements of urban life at the turn-of-the-century. From cable cars to department stores and skyscrapers, San Francisco epitomized an industrialized, urban center.

Analyzing Visuals Have students examine the image and identify at least three modern inventions shown in the picture. *Answers may include tall buildings, a department store, electric trolleys, and streetlights.*

Explore the Time Line

1. How many years passed from the formation of the American Federation of Labor to the Homestead Strike? *about 5 years*
2. In what year did Pierre and Marie Curie discover radium? *1898*
3. Which two inventions listed on the time line would have a major impact on the development of city life? *gasoline-powered engines and the electric light bulb*
4. What two inventions took place in the 1870s? *the invention of a gasoline-powered engine and the invention of the first lightbulb*

HSS Analysis Skills: CS 1

Info to Know

The Eiffel Tower The Eiffel Tower was built in honor of the 100th anniversary of the French Revolution. To prepare for the International Exhibition of Paris of 1889, a competition was held to design a monument for the event. Bridge designer and engineer Gustave Eiffel's plan was the winning design for the Exhibition. The structure took 300 steel workers and about two years to build. Until 1930, it was the world's tallest man-made structure, standing at over 1,050 feet.

go.hrw.com

Online Resources

Chapter Resources:
KEYWORD: SS8 US18
Teacher Resources:
KEYWORD: SS8 TEACHER

Reading Social Studies

Understanding Themes

Tell students that they will be learning about the economic and social changes that resulted from the Second Industrial Revolution and the rise of powerful corporations. Ask students to predict what types of inventions and new ideas might have resulted from this period. Point out to students that the light bulb, the telephone, automobiles, and the use of petroleum all originated at this time. Then ask students to discuss what effects inventions like these might have had on the economy and on society during the Second Industrial Revolution.

Organization of Facts and Information

Focus on Reading Organize the class into four groups. Ask each group to imagine that they are preparing a weather report for a television news station. Assign each group one of the four patterns of organization listed on this page. Then, have each group write and deliver a report on some aspect of the weather for its newscast. In their presentations, students must also create a graphic organizer that matches the pattern they were assigned. The graphic organizer should contain the information they are presenting. When the groups have finished their presentations, use the graphic organizers to review the patterns of organization.

Standards Focus

ELA Reading 8.2.0

Reading Social Studies

by Kylene Beers

Economics | Geography | Politics | Religion | Society and Culture | Science and Technology

Focus on Themes In this chapter, you will read about the advancements in transportation and communication made during what is called the Second Industrial Revolution. You will learn about the rise of powerful corporations. You will also read about the immigrants who arrived in the late 1800s and will see what happened to the cities as these immigrants moved in record numbers into urban areas. Throughout the chapter, you will see how **society** was affected by the changing **economy**.

Organization of Facts and Information

Focus on Reading How are clothes organized in a department store? How are files arranged in a file cabinet? Clear organization helps us find the product we need, and it also helps us find facts and information.

Additional reading support can be found in the Interactive Reader and Study Guide

Understanding Structural Patterns Writers use structural patterns to organize information in sentences or paragraphs. What's a structural pattern? It's simply a way of organizing information. Learning to recognize those patterns will make it easier for you to read and understand social studies texts.

Patterns of Organization

Pattern	Clue Words	Graphic Organizer
Cause-effect shows how one thing leads to another	as a result, therefore, because, therefore, this led to	Cause → Effect, Effect → Effect
Chronological Order shows the sequence of events or actions.	after, before, first, then, not long after, finally	First → Next → Last
Comparison-contrast points our similarities and/or differences.	although, but, however, on the other hand, similarly, also	Differences / Similarities
Listing presents information in categories such as size, location or importance.	also, most important, for example, in fact	Category • Fact • Fact • Fact

To use text structure to improve your understanding, follow these steps:

1. Look for the main idea of the passage you are reading.
2. Then look for clues that signal a specific pattern.
3. Look for other important ideas and think about how the ideas connect. Is there any obvious pattern?
4. Use a graphic organizer to map the relationships among the facts and details.

Reading and Skills Resources

Reading Support

- Interactive Reader and Study Guide
- Student Edition on Audio CD
- Spanish Chapter Summaries Audio CD Program

Social Studies Skills Support

- Interactive Skills Tutor CD-ROM

Vocabulary Support

- **CRF:** Vocabulary Builder Activities
- **CRF:** Chapter Review Activity
- Universal Access Modified Worksheets and Tests CD-ROM:
  - Vocabulary Flash Cards
  - Vocabulary Builder Activity
  - Chapter Review Activity

OSP Holt PuzzlePro

ELA Reading 8.2.0 Describe and connect essential ideas, arguments, and perspectives of text using knowledge of text structure, organization, and purpose.

You Try It!

The following passages are from the chapter you are about to read. As you read each set of sentences, ask yourself what structural pattern the writer used to organize the information.

Recognizing Structural Patterns

(A) "Great advances in communications technologies took place in the late 1800s. By 1861, telegraph wires connected the East and West coasts. Five years later, a cable on the floor of the Atlantic Ocean connected the United States and Great Britain." *(p. 577)*

(B) "Many business leaders justified these corrupt practices through their belief in social Darwinism . . . Other business leaders, however, claimed that the rich had a duty to aid the poor." *(p. 581)*

(C) "During the late 1800s, several factors led to a decline in the quality of working conditions. Machines run by unskilled workers were eliminating the jobs of many skilled craftspeople. These low-paid workers could be replaced easily." *(p. 584)*

After you read the passages, answer the questions below:

1. Reread passage A. What structural pattern did the writer use to organize this information? How can you tell?
2. Reread passage B. What structural pattern did the writer use to organize this information? How can you tell? Why do you think the writer chose this pattern?
3. Reread passage C. What structural pattern did the writer use to organize this information? How can you tell? Why do you think the writer chose this pattern?

As you read Chapter 18, think about the organization of the ideas. Ask yourself why the writer chose to organize the information in this way.

Key Terms and People

Chapter 18

Section 1
Second Industrial Revolution *(p. 575)*
Bessemer process *(p. 575)*
Thomas Alva Edison *(p. 576)*
patents *(p. 576)*
Alexander Graham Bell *(p. 577)*
Wilbur and Orville Wright *(p. 578)*

Section 2
corporations *(p. 579)*
Andrew Carnegie *(p. 580)*
vertical integration *(p. 580)*
John D. Rockefeller *(p. 580)*
horizontal integration *(p. 581)*
trust *(p. 581)*
Leland Stanford *(p. 581)*
social Darwinism *(p. 581)*
Sherman Antitrust Act *(p. 582)*

Section 3
Frederick W. Taylor *(p. 584)*
Knights of Labor *(p. 585)*
Terence W. Powderly *(p. 585)*
Samuel Gompers *(p. 586)*
American Federation of Labor *(p. 585)*
collective bargaining *(p. 586)*
Mary Harris Jones *(p. 586)*
Haymarket Riot *(p. 586)*
Homestead Strike *(p. 587)*
Pullman Strike *(p. 587)*

Section 4
old immigrants *(p. 588)*
new immigrants *(p. 588)*
steerage *(p. 588)*
benevolent societies *(p. 591)*
Chinese Exclusion Act *(p. 593)*
Immigration Restriction League *(p. 593)*

Section 5
mass transit *(p. 595)*
suburbs *(p. 595)*
mass culture *(p. 595)*
department stores *(p. 596)*
settlement houses *(p. 597)*
Hull House *(p. 597)*
Jane Addams *(p. 597)*

Academic Vocabulary

In this chapter, you will learn the following academic words:
implement *(p. 577)*
acquire *(p. 593)*

Reading Social Studies

Key Terms and People

Preteach the key terms and people in this chapter by having students create a Four-Corner FoldNote. Tell students to label the four sides *People*, *Events*, *Things*, and *Ideas*. As you read each word, have students repeat it after you. Then have students write that word on the correct section of the FoldNote. Discuss any terms that students do not recognize.

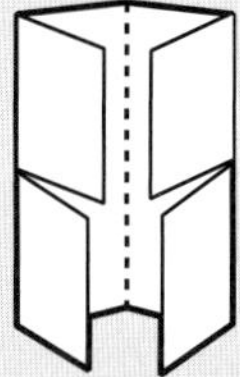

Focus on Reading

See the **Focus on Reading** questions in this chapter for more practice on this reading social studies skill.

Reading Social Studies Assessment

See the **Standards Review** at the end of this chapter for student assessment questions related to this reading skill.

Teaching Tip

Understanding the structural patterns of texts not only helps writers who are organizing text, but it also helps students to understand what they are reading. Stress the importance of learning this skill as a way for students to better understand not only textbooks, but any material they read. Remind students that before they write an essay or prepare a presentation for class, they should take time to think about the organizational pattern that works best for the information they are trying to present.

Answers

You Try It! 1. *chronological; the writer lists dates and time periods in chronological order.* **2.** *comparison-contrast; it describes one view, and then presents an opposing view.* **3.** *words like* therefore *and* as a result*; causes—machines replaced jobs, low-paid workers needed little training; effects—workers could be replaced easily, workers worried about complaining about their jobs.*

Preteach

Bellringer

If YOU were there . . . Use the **Daily Bellringer Transparency** to help students answer the question.

 Daily Bellringer Transparency, Section 1

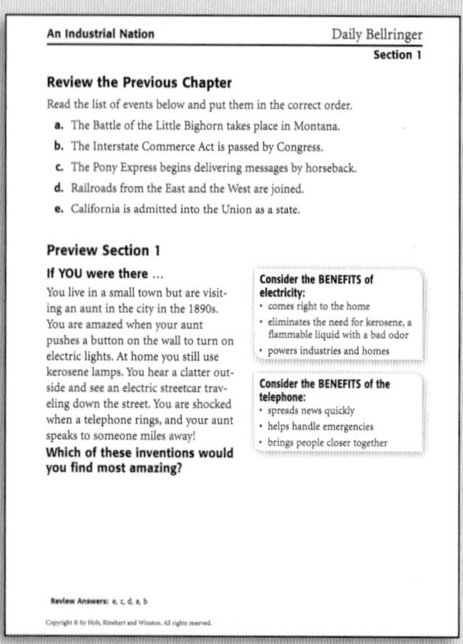

An Industrial Nation Daily Bellringer

Section 1

Review the Previous Chapter

Read the list of events below and put them in the correct order.

a. The Battle of the Little Bighorn takes place in Montana.
b. The Interstate Commerce Act is passed by Congress.
c. The Pony Express begins delivering messages by horseback.
d. Railroads from the East and the West are joined.
e. California is admitted into the Union as a state.

Preview Section 1

If YOU were there ...

You live in a small town but are visiting an aunt in the city in the 1890s. You are amazed when your aunt pushes a button on the wall to turn on electric lights. At home you still use kerosene lamps. You hear a clatter outside and see an electric streetcar traveling down the street. You are shocked when a telephone rings, and your aunt speaks to someone miles away!

Which of these inventions would you find most amazing?

Consider the BENEFITS of electricity:
- comes right to the home
- eliminates the need for kerosene, a flammable liquid with a bad odor
- powers industries and homes

Consider the BENEFITS of the telephone:
- spreads news quickly
- helps handle emergencies
- brings people closer together

Review Answers: e, c, d, a, b

Academic Vocabulary

Review with students the high-use academic term in this section.

implement to put in place (p. 577)

CRF: Vocabulary Builder Activity, Section 1

Standards Focus

HSS 8.12.1

Means: Understand the development of agriculture and industry in terms of climate, natural resources, markets, and trade and locate geographic areas where these developments took place.

Matters: Patterns of agricultural and industrial development changed as a result of industrialization.

8.12.9

Means: Identify important inventors and understand how their inventions affected daily life.

Matters: Inventions from the Second Industrial Revolution have shaped today's world in many ways.

SECTION 1

The Second Industrial Revolution

What You Will Learn...

Main Ideas

1. Breakthroughs in steel processing led to a boom in railroad construction.
2. Advances in the use of oil and electricity improved communications and transportation.
3. A rush of inventions changed the lives of Americans.

The Big Idea

The Second Industrial Revolution led to new sources of power and advances in transportation and communication.

Key Terms and People

Second Industrial Revolution, *p. 575*
Bessemer process, *p. 575*
Thomas Edison, *p. 576*
patents, *p. 576*
Alexander Graham Bell, *p. 577*
Henry Ford, *p. 577*
Wilbur and Orville Wright, *p. 578*

HSS 8.12.1 Trace patterns of agricultural and industrial development as they relate to climate, use of natural resources, markets, and trade and locate such development on a map.

8.12.9 Name the significant inventors and their inventions and identify how they improved the quality of life (e.g., Thomas Edison, Alexander Graham Bell, Orville and Wilbur Wright).

If YOU were there...

You live in a small town but are visiting an aunt in the city in the 1890s. You are amazed when your aunt pushes a button on the wall to turn on electric lights. At home you still use kerosene lamps. You hear a clatter outside and see an electric streetcar traveling down the street. You are shocked when a telephone rings, and your aunt speaks to someone miles away!

Which of these inventions would you find most amazing?

BUILDING BACKGROUND The first Industrial Revolution in America began in the early 1800s. It changed the way products were made, from handwork to machines. It moved the workplace from cottages to factories. Later, it brought advances in transportation and communication. The Second Industrial Revolution built on these changes, introducing new technology and new sources of power.

Teach the Big Idea: Master the Standards

Standards Proficiency

The Second Industrial Revolution

HSS 8.12.1, 8.12.9; HSS **Analysis Skills:** CS 3

1. **Teach** Ask students the Main Idea questions to teach this section.
2. **Apply** Give students a blank outline map of the United States. As they read this section, have students use their maps to locate and identify the places discussed in the section. Students should also create a key or legend identifying the reason the place is important. For example, oil was first pumped in Titusville, Pennsylvania, and Thomas Edison's research was done in Menlo Park, New Jersey. LS **Visual/Spatial**
3. **Review** Have students work in groups to share and compare their maps.
4. **Practice/Homework** Have students select an event from their maps that they feel had a great effect on daily life. Have them write essays explaining and defending their choices. LS **Verbal/Linguistic**

Alternative Assessment Handbook, Rubrics 20: Map Creation; and 37: Writing Assignments

Breakthroughs in Steel Processing

Technological advances were important to the **Second Industrial Revolution**, a period of rapid growth in U.S. manufacturing in the late 1800s. By the mid-1890s, the United States had become the world's industrial leader.

The Steel Industry

Some of the most important advances in technology happened in the steel industry. Steel is iron that has been made stronger by heat and the addition of other metals. In the mid-1850s Henry Bessemer invented the **Bessemer process**, a way to manufacture steel quickly and cheaply by blasting hot air through melted iron to quickly remove impurities. Before, turning several tons of iron ore into steel took a day or more. The Bessemer process took only 10 to 20 minutes.

The Bessemer process helped increase steel production. U.S. mills had produced 77,000 tons of steel in 1870. By 1879 production had risen to more than 1 million tons in one year.

Riding the Rails

As steel dropped in price, so did the cost of building railroads. Companies built thousands of miles of new steel track. The design of elegant passenger and sleeping cars improved passenger service. Manufacturers and farmers sent products to market faster than ever by rail. Cities where major rail lines crossed, such as Chicago, grew rapidly. Railroads also increased western growth by offering free tickets to settlers. Rail travel made the journey west faster and safer. Finally, as rail travel and shipping increased, railroads and related industries began employing more people.

QUICK FACTS

Factors Affecting Industrial Growth

- Greater ability to use natural resources
- A growing population
- Transportation advances
- Rising immigration
- Inventions and innovations
- Increasing business investment
- Government policies assisting business, such as protective tariffs

READING CHECK **Identifying Cause and Effect** How did steel processing change in the 1850s, and how did this affect the United States?

Homestead Steel Mill

Steel mills like this one in Homestead, Pennsylvania, were the center of the new steel industry that led to advancements in rail travel. Workers used the Bessemer process to make steel more quickly.

How do you think mills like this one affected the surrounding area?

575

Critical Thinking: Identifying Cause and Effect

Reaching Standards

Cause and Effect Posters

HSS 8.12.1; HSS **Analysis Skills:** HI 1, HI 2

1. Review with students the information about breakthroughs in steel processing. Ask students to identify the important breakthrough and the results it had.
2. Write the following for students to see: *U.S. steel production increases.* Then have students identify the causes of the rise in steel production, as well as its effects.
3. Have each student create a cause and effect poster that illustrates the causes of the rise in U.S. steel production and the effects of this rise. Remind students that there may be more than one result. Encourage students to make their posters visually appealing.
4. Ask volunteers to share their posters with the class. **LS Visual/Spatial**

Alternative Assessment Handbook, Rubrics 6: Cause and Effect; and 28: Posters

Direct Teach

Main Idea

1 Breakthroughs in Steel Processing

Breakthroughs in steel processing led to a boom in railroad construction.

Describe How did the Bessemer process change the steel industry? *It made changing iron ore into steel much faster than before, which led to an increase in steel production.*

Analyze How did the Bessemer process affect industry in the United States? *It helped increase steel production, which caused steel prices to drop, led to more railroads, and increased shipping.*

Quick Facts Transparency, Factors Affecting Industrial Growth

HSS 8.12.1; HSS **Analysis Skills:** CS 1, HI 1

Connect to Science

The Bessemer Process Two men—American William Kelly and Englishman Henry Bessemer—simultaneously developed ideas for improving steel manufacturing. Kelly and Bessemer both discovered that forcing air into molten iron would generate intense heat. Oxygen from this blast of air would react with impurities in the iron, making it possible to remove the impurities as slag, and creating a higher-quality steel. Bessemer actually built the converter that made possible the process bearing his name. The Bessemer process was first used in the United States in November 1864, in a factory in Wyandotte, Michigan.

Answers

Homestead Steel Mill *possible answers—it provided jobs, created pollution*

Reading Check *The Bessemer process made the production of steel faster and cheaper and increased steel production in the United States, which in turn benefited other industries.*

Direct Teach

Main Idea

❷ Use of Oil and Electricity

Advances in the use of oil and electricity improved communications and transportation.

Recall What were some of the uses of kerosene? *cooking, heating, and lighting*

Analyze What problem did Thomas Edison face regarding the use of electricity, and how did he solve it? *Few homes or businesses could get electricity; he built a power plant and supplied electricity to large cities.*

Draw Conclusions What effect did competition have on the use of electricity? *Westinghouse and Edison competed to build power systems, which led to the rapid spread of electricity in the United States.*

CRF: Biography Activity: Inventors

HSS 8.12.1; HSS **Analysis Skills:** HI 1, HI 2

Info to Know

History of Patents Patents have been around in various forms since the Renaissance. The framers of the U.S. Constitution provided for patents to protect the rights of inventors. Article 1, Section 8, grants Congress the power "to promote the Progress of Science and useful Arts by securing for limited Times to Authors and Inventors the exclusive Right to their respective Writings and Discoveries." The first patent in the United States was granted in 1790 to an inventor who had developed a better way of making potash, a substance used for making soap and other items.

Time Line
The Spirit of Innovation
1854 Henry Bessemer patents a method for making cast steel.
1850
1860
1852 Elisha Otis invents the elevator safety brake, making elevators safe for people.
SAFE FOR ONLY 25 MEN AT ONE TIME. DO NOT WALK CLOSE TOGETHER NOR RUN, JUMP OR TROT. BREAK STEP!
1869 John Roebling begins work on the Brooklyn Bridge.
© Collection of the New York Historical Society

Use of Oil and Electricity

The Second Industrial Revolution was characterized by dramatic developments in the use and distribution of oil and electricity. These power sources fueled other changes.

Oil as a Power Source

An important technological breakthrough in the late 1800s was the use of petroleum, or oil, as a power source. People had known about oil for many years but had discovered few ways to use it. However, in the 1850s, chemists invented a way to convert crude, or unprocessed, oil into a fuel called kerosene. Kerosene could be used for cooking, heating, and lighting. Suddenly there was a demand for oil.

Focus on Reading
How does this paragraph show the cause and effect structure?

As demand grew, people began searching for a reliable source for oil. In 1859 Edwin L. Drake proved that it was possible to pump crude oil from the ground. Soon, wildcatters, or oil prospectors, drilled for oil in Ohio, Pennsylvania, and West Virginia. Oil became a big business as these states began producing millions of barrels per year. Oil companies built refineries to turn the crude oil into finished products like kerosene. One oil company supervisor referred to oil workers as "men who are supplying light for the world."

Electricity Spreads

In addition to kerosene, electricity became a critical source of light and power during the Second Industrial Revolution. The possible uses of electricity interested inventors like **Thomas Edison**. His research center in Menlo Park, New Jersey, was called an invention factory. Edison explained his practical approach to science.

> "I do not regard myself as a pure scientist, as so many persons have insisted that I am. I do not search for the laws of nature ... for the purpose of learning truth. I am only a professional inventor ... with the object [goal] of inventing that which will have commercial utility [use]."
>
> —Thomas Edison, quoted in *American Made*, by Harold C. Livesay

Edison eventually held more than 1,000 **patents**, exclusive rights to make or sell inventions. Patents allowed inventors to protect their inventions from being manufactured by others.

In 1878 Edison announced that he would soon invent a practical electric light. By the end of 1879 Edison and his team of inventors had created the electric lightbulb. The public was excited. However, Edison had a problem. At the time, few homes or businesses could get electricity. Edison therefore built a power plant that began supplying electricity to dozens of New York City buildings in

Cross-Discipline Activity: Science

Standards Proficiency

Inventions Science Fair

HSS 8.12.9; HSS **Analysis Skills:** HR 1, HI 2

Research Required

1. Review with students the advances that took place in the late 1800s as a result of the Second Industrial Revolution. Discuss with students advancements that have had a major effect on their world, such as electricity.
2. Tell students that they will research one of the inventions discussed in this section and create a science fair exhibit that explains how the invention or process works. Assign students to small groups and have each group research an invention.
3. Have students use their research to create a poster that explains how the idea or process works, what it is used for, and what effect it has had on the world.
4. Conduct a class science fair and have each group present their exhibit to the class.

LS Visual/Spatial, Verbal/Linguistic, Interpersonal

Alternative Assessment Handbook, Rubrics 28: Posters; and 29: Presentations

Answers

Focus on Reading *It starts with the words* As demand grew, *which are common cause and effect signal words.*

1872 Elijah McCoy receives the patent for his device that oiled machine engines.

1876 Alexander Graham Bell invents the telephone.

1879 Thomas Edison creates a durable electric lightbulb.

1887 Harriet Strong receives a patent for her advances in dam and reservoir construction.

1893 Frank and Charles Duryea successfully test their first gasoline-powered automobile.

September 1882. The *New York Times* reported that with electric lighting in the newspaper offices, "it seemed almost like writing by daylight. However, Edison's equipment could not send electricity over long distances. As a result, his power company, Edison Electric, provided electricity mainly to central cities.

In the late 1880s, George Westinghouse built a power system that could send electricity across many miles. As Edison and Westinghouse competed, the use of electricity spread rapidly in the nation's cities. After a while, electricity soon lit homes and businesses and powered city factories. Electricity also was used to power streetcars in cities across the nation.

READING CHECK **Drawing Conclusions** Why did people begin to pump oil from the ground?

Rush of Inventions

In the late 1800s, inventors focused on finding solutions to practical problems. Communication and transportation took the lead.

Advances in Communication

Great advances in communication technologies took place in the late 1800s. By 1861, telegraph wires connected the East and West coasts. Five years later, a telegraph cable on the floor of the Atlantic Ocean connected the United States and Great Britain.

However, the telegraph carried only written messages and was difficult for untrained people to use. These problems were solved in March 1876, when inventor **Alexander Graham Bell** patented the telephone. Bell was a Scottish-born speech teacher who studied the science of sound. He called the telephone a "talking telegraph."

Telephone companies raced to lay thousands of miles of phone lines. By 1880 there were about 55,000 telephones in the United States, and by 1900 there were almost 1.5 million.

THE IMPACT TODAY

AT&T Corporation is a direct descendant of Bell's original company. AT&T pioneered the use of telephone cables across the oceans, satellite communications, and a radar system for the U.S. Defense Department.

Automobiles and Planes

In 1876 a German engineer invented an engine powered by gasoline, another fuel made from oil. In 1893 Charles and J. Frank Duryea used a gasoline engine to build the first practical motorcar in the United States. By the early 1900s, thousands of cars were being built in the United States.

At first, only the wealthy could buy these early cars. **Henry Ford** introduced the Model T in 1908. Ford was the first to **implement** the moving assembly line in manufacturing, a process that greatly reduced the cost of building a product, thus making cars more affordable.

ACADEMIC VOCABULARY
implement to put in place

Direct Teach

Main Idea

3 Rush of Inventions

A rush of inventions changed the lives of Americans.

Recall What advances were made in communication and transportation? *the telegraph connected the United States and Britain, the telephone was invented, automobiles were invented and became more affordable, and the first piloted flight in a gas-powered airplane was made.*

Analyze How did telephones improve communication? *They allowed people to communicate by voice over long distances.*

Making Inferences How do you think telephones and automobiles changed the lives of people who used them? *They made life easier because people could communicate over long-distances and travel from place to place quickly.*

CRF: Biography Activity: Orville and Wilbur Wright

CRF: Interdisciplinary Project: Technology Time Line

HSS 8.12.1; **HSS Analysis Skills:** HI 1, HI 2

Info to Know

Telephone Companies At first, the telephone was considered so unusual that Western Union called it a toy and refused to buy the rights from Alexander Graham Bell. However, the potential of the telephone quickly became apparent, and many companies tried to start their own phone services. In 1879 the Bell Telephone Company successfully sued Western Union after it started the American Speaking Telephone Company. Bell himself faced 587 lawsuits contesting his exclusive patent on the telephone. Bell won every case, including 13 that went all the way to the Supreme Court.

Answers

Reading Check *People began to search for a more reliable source for oil, and Edwin L. Drake proved it was possible to pump crude oil from the ground*

Differentiating Instruction for Universal Access

English-Language Learners

Standards Proficiency **Standard English Mastery**

1. Organize students into mixed-ability pairs. Then have each pair review the information on the advances in the use of oil and electricity.
2. Ask each pair to select two events that played a role in the use of oil and electricity. Then have each pair work together to write a newspaper headline for that event. Remind students that newspaper headlines should catch the readers' attention and give some information about the event. Encourage students to look at actual newspaper headlines before writing their own.
3. Ask students to read their headlines to the class. Then have each pair of students select one of their headlines and write the entire newspaper article. Remind students to write their articles using standard English.

LS Verbal/Linguistic, Interpersonal

HSS 8.12.9; **HSS Analysis Skills:** HI 1, HI 2

Alternative Assessment Handbook, Rubric 23: Newspapers

Direct Teach

Teaching Tip

To help students remember the inventors and inventions discussed in this section, have them create jingles in which they include the name of each inventor and invention. Suggest that students use a familiar melody as the basis of their jingle. Ask volunteers to share their jingles with the class. Then have the class vote on their favorite jingle.

Review & Assess

Close

Review with students the major inventions and processes discussed in the section.

Review

Online Quiz, Section 1

Assess

SE Section 1 Assessment

PASS: Section 1 Quiz

Alternative Assessment Handbook

Reteach/Classroom Intervention

California Standards Review Workbook

Interactive Reader and Study Guide, Section 1

Interactive Skills Tutor CD-ROM

Time Line

The Spirit of Innovation

1893 George Ferris displays the first Ferris Wheel at the World's Columbian Exposition in Chicago.

1900

1903 Orville Wright makes the first flight in a motorized airplane.

ANALYSIS SKILL **READING TIME LINES**

When was the telephone invented?

New engine technology helped make another breakthrough in transportation possible—air flight. Brothers **Wilbur and Orville Wright** built a lightweight airplane that used a small, gas-powered engine. In Kitty Hawk, North Carolina, Orville Wright made the first piloted flight in a gas-powered plane on December 17, 1903. This invention would change the way that many Americans traveled in the future and would increase the demand for oil production.

READING CHECK **Comparing** What new inventions excited the public in the 1800s, and how were they used?

SUMMARY AND PREVIEW The Second Industrial Revolution led to advances in energy sources, communication, and transportation. In the next section you will learn about the growth of big business.

Section 1 Assessment

go.hrw.com Online Quiz KEYWORD: SS8 HP18

Reviewing Ideas, Terms, and People HSS 8.12.1, 8.12.9

1. a. **Describe** What was the **Bessemer process**?
 b. **Summarize** How did improvements to railroads affect the economy and transportation in the United States?
 c. **Elaborate** What do you think was the most important effect of the Bessemer process? Why?
2. a. **Identify** What is kerosene, and for what could it be used?
 b. **Explain** What problem did **Thomas Edison** face regarding the use of electricity, and how did he solve it?
3. a. **Recall** What contribution did **Wilbur** and **Orville Wright** make to transportation?
 b. **Draw Conclusions** How did **Alexander Graham Bell's** invention improve life in the United States?
 c. **Elaborate** Why do you think there was a rush of inventions in the late 1800s?

Critical Thinking

4. **Analyzing** Copy the chart below and use it to identify important inventors of the Second Industrial Revolution, their contributions, and why each was important.

Person	Work	Importance

FOCUS ON WRITING

5. **Taking Notes about Inventors** In your notebook, write a list of the inventors and their inventions mentioned in this section. How might you include them in your TV series?

Section 1 Assessment Answers

1. a. a process of making steel quickly and cheaply by blasting air through melted iron
 b. It led to faster transportation and travel and more employment.
 c. possible answer—Steel production increased, causing steel prices to drop and lowering the cost of building railroads.
2. a. a fuel made from petroleum; cooking, heating, and home lighting.
 b. Few locations could receive electricity; he built a power plant to supply electricity to New York City buildings.
3. a. They built a gas-powered airplane.
 b. It allowed for faster communication.
 c. possible answer—People were inspired by other inventions.
4. Edison—electric lighting, inexpensive form of lighting; Wright Brothers—gas-powered airplane, improved transportation; Bell— telephone, improved communication; Bessemer—Bessemer process, improved steel production
5. Responses might include Alexander Graham Bell, who invented the telephone, or Orville and Wilbur Wright, who made the first piloted flight.

Answers

Reading Time Lines *1876*

Reading Check *airplanes for flying; electricity for power; telegraphs and telephones for communicating; automobiles for transportation*

Big Business

SECTION 2

If YOU were there...

It is 1895, and your town is home to a large corporation. The company's founder and owner, a wealthy man, lives in a mansion on a hill. He is a fair employer but not especially generous. Many townspeople work in his factory. You and other town leaders feel that he should contribute more to local charities and community organizations.

How could this business leader help the town more?

BUILDING BACKGROUND Advanced technology along with the use of oil and electric power helped American businesses grow. Soon the shape of the American economy changed. Some companies grew so large that they began to dominate entire industries.

Dominance of Big Business

In the late 1800s many entrepreneurs formed their businesses as **corporations**, or businesses that sell portions of ownership called stock shares. The leaders of these corporations were some of the most widely respected members of American society in the late 1800s. Political leaders praised prosperous businesspeople as examples of American hard work, talent, and success.

New sales techniques like those taught by John H. Patterson helped change business practices.

What You Will Learn...

Main Ideas

1. The rise of corporations and powerful business leaders led to the dominance of big business in the United States.
2. People and the government began to question the methods of big business.

The Big Idea

The growth of big business in the late 1800s led to the creation of monopolies.

Key Terms and People

corporations, *p. 579*
Andrew Carnegie, *p. 580*
vertical integration, *p. 580*
John D. Rockefeller, *p. 580*
horizontal integration, *p. 581*
trust, *p. 581*
Leland Stanford, *p. 581*
social Darwinism, *p. 581*
monopoly, *p. 582*
Sherman Antitrust Act, *p. 582*

HSS 8.12.4 Discuss entrepreneurs, industrialists, and bankers in politics, commerce, and industry (e.g., Andrew Carnegie, John D. Rockefeller, Leland Stanford).

8.12.6 Discuss child labor, working conditions, and laissez-faire policies toward big business and examine the labor movement, including its leaders (e.g., Samuel Gompers), its demand for collective bargaining, and its strikes and protests over labor conditions.

Preteach

Bellringer

If YOU were there . . . Use the **Daily Bellringer Transparency** to help students answer the question.

Daily Bellringer Transparency, Section 2

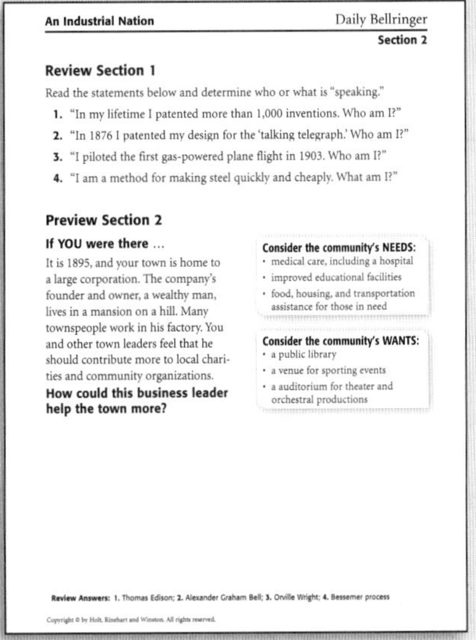

An Industrial Nation — Daily Bellringer, Section 2

Review Section 1

Read the statements below and determine who or what is "speaking."

1. "In my lifetime I patented more than 1,000 inventions. Who am I?"
2. "In 1876 I patented my design for the 'talking telegraph.' Who am I?"
3. "I piloted the first gas-powered plane flight in 1903. Who am I?"
4. "I am a method for making steel quickly and cheaply. What am I?"

Preview Section 2

If YOU were there ...

It is 1895, and your town is home to a large corporation. The company's founder and owner, a wealthy man, lives in a mansion on a hill. Many townspeople work in his factory. You and other town leaders feel that he should contribute more to local charities and community organizations.

How could this business leader help the town more?

Consider the community's NEEDS:
- medical care, including a hospital
- improved educational facilities
- food, housing, and transportation assistance for those in need

Consider the community's WANTS:
- a public library
- a venue for sporting events
- a auditorium for theater and orchestral productions

Review Answers: 1. Thomas Edison; 2. Alexander Graham Bell; 3. Orville Wright; 4. Bessemer process

Academic Vocabulary

Review with students the high-use academic term in this section:

acquire to get (p. 580)

CRF: Vocabulary Builder Activity, Section 2

Teach the Big Idea: Master the Standards

Standards Proficiency

Big Business HSS 8.12.4, 8.12.6; HSS Analysis Skills: CS 1, HI 1

1. **Teach** Ask students the Main Idea questions to teach this section.
2. **Apply** Have students create an outline of this section. Ask students to use the same headings and subheadings as used in the section. Then have students identify three or four specific details to support each heading or subheading. Remind students to include bolded terms or people in their outlines. **LS Verbal/Linguistic**
3. **Review** Organize the class into small groups. Have students in each group compare and contrast their outlines as a review of the section.
4. **Practice/Homework** Have students use their outlines to write a one-page summary of the section. Remind students to write the summary in their own words. **LS Verbal/Linguistic**

Alternative Assessment Handbook, Rubric 37: Writing Assignments

Standards Focus

HSS 8.12.4

Means: Explain the role important businesspeople played in shaping government, trade, and industry.

Matters: Individuals played a major role in the development of U.S. business and industry and in shaping government policies toward businesses.

8.12.6

Means: Examine working conditions, child labor, the labor movement and its strategies, and government policies toward big business.

Matters: The growth of big business led to new movements and policies to protect workers and businesses.

Direct Teach

Main Idea

1 Dominance of Big Business

The rise of corporations and powerful business leaders led to the dominance of big businesses in the United States.

Describe What role do stockholders play in corporations? *Individuals purchase stock in return for a percentage of profits, but do not run its day-to-day business.*

Explain Why are corporations advantageous for stockholders? *They can only lose the money they have invested and they are free to sell stock to whomever they want.*

Elaborate Why do you think Andrew Carnegie was one of the most admired businesspeople of his time? *possible answer—due to his great success in the steel industry and vertical integration*

HSS 8.12.4; HSS **Analysis Skills:** HI 1

Info to Know

New York Stock Exchange One of the world's largest stock markets, the New York Stock Exchange (NYSE) was founded in New York City in 1792. A meeting of some 24 New York stockbrokers under a buttonwood tree on Wall Street led to the Buttonwood Agreement, which established the Exchange. The first listed company was the Bank of New York. Today, the NYSE lists stocks for some 2,800 companies.

Corporations Generate Wealth

Successful corporations reward not only the people who found them but also investors who hold stock. Stockholders in a corporation typically get a percentage of profits based on the amount of stock they own. Although stockholders actually own the corporation, they do not run its day-to-day business. Instead, they elect a board of directors that chooses the corporation's main leaders, such as the president.

Corporations provided several important advantages over earlier business forms. Stockholders in a corporation are not responsible for business debts. If a corporation fails financially, the stockholders lose only the money that they invested. Stockholders are also usually free to sell their stock to whomever they want, whenever they want. As a result, corporations encouraged more investment in businesses. By 1900 more than 100 million shares per year were being traded on the New York Stock Exchange.

ACADEMIC VOCABULARY
acquire to get

Business Leaders

Countless business leaders became wealthy, powerful, and famous because of the business boom. **Andrew Carnegie** was one of the most admired businesspeople of the time. Born in Scotland, Carnegie came to the United States as a poor immigrant. As a teenager he took a job with a railroad company and quickly worked his way up to the position of railroad superintendent.

In 1873, he focused his efforts on steelmaking. Carnegie expanded his business by buying out competitors when steel prices were low. By 1901 Carnegie's mills were producing more steel than all of Great Britain's mills combined. Carnegie's businesses succeeded largely through **vertical integration**, or ownership of businesses involved in each step of a manufacturing process. For example, to lower production costs, Carnegie **acquired** the iron ore mines, coalfields, and railroads needed to supply and support his steel mills.

John D. Rockefeller was also successful in consolidating, or combining, businesses. By age 21, while a partner in a wholesale business, he decided to start an oil-refining company. In only 10 years his Standard Oil Company was the country's largest oil refiner. Like Carnegie, Rockefeller used vertical

The Rise of Investing

Investors purchased stock in corporations in record numbers in the late 1800s. They received stock certificates, like the one shown here, to document their part ownership in corporations. Corporations used the money raised by selling stocks to expand. Standard Oil Company financed the building of this refinery in Richmond, California, by selling stock.

Why did investors buy stock?

Cross-Discipline Activity: Economics

Exceeding Standards

Studying the Stock Market

HSS 8.12.4; HSS **Analysis Skills:** HR 1, HI 2 — Research Required

1. Review with students the advantages of corporations and the way in which corporations function. Tell students that stock is traded in several major stock markets, including the New York Stock Exchange and the NASDAQ in the United States.
2. Have each student choose a company that was in existence during the late 1800s and track the stock of that company. Companies might include U.S. Steel, Western Union, or Ford Motor Company. Discuss the symbols used by corporations and how to find symbols for companies they will track.
3. Have students track the value of stock for the companies they selected for a set period of time. Then have students create a line graph that depicts changes in value over this period.
4. Have students display their line graph for the class to see. **LS Visual/Spatial, Verbal/Linguistic**

Alternative Assessment Handbook, Rubric 1: Acquiring Information

Answers

The Rise of Investing *They wanted to share in the profits of the corporation.*

Primary Source

POLITICAL CARTOON

Antitrust

The wealth and size of trusts such as Standard Oil made many Americans fear the influence of business leaders over government.

What do you think the smokestacks on the Capitol building represent?

What does the position of the White House suggest?

© Collection of the New York Historical Society

ANALYSIS SKILL ANALYZING PRIMARY SOURCES

How does the cartoonist show Rockefeller's power?

integration. For example, the company controlled most of the pipelines it used.

Rockefeller's company also developed **horizontal integration**, or owning all businesses in a certain field. By 1880 his companies controlled about 90 percent of the oil refining business in the United States. He also formed a **trust**, a legal arrangement grouping together a number of companies under a single board of directors. To earn more money, trusts often tried to get rid of competition and to control production.

Leland Stanford was another important business leader of the late 1800s. He made a fortune selling equipment to miners. While governor of California, he became one of the founders of the state's Central Pacific railroad. Stanford also founded Stanford University.

Late in life, Stanford argued that industries should be owned and managed cooperatively by workers. He believed this would be the fulfillment of democracy.

READING CHECK **Comparing and Contrasting** Why did Andrew Carnegie use vertical integration?

Questioning the Methods of Big Business

By the late 1800s, people and the government were becoming uncomfortable with child labor, low wages, and poor working conditions. They began to view big business as a problem.

Social Darwinism

Many business leaders justified their business methods through their belief in **social Darwinism**, a view of society based on scientist Charles Darwin's theory of natural selection. Social Darwinists thought that Darwin's "survival of the fittest" theory decided which human beings would succeed in business and in life in general.

Other business leaders, however, believed that the rich had a duty to aid the poor. These leaders tried to help the less fortunate through philanthropy, or giving money to charities. Carnegie, Rockefeller, Stanford, and other business leaders gave away large sums. Carnegie gave away more than $350 million to charities, about $60 million of which went to

Direct Teach

Main Idea

❷ Questioning the Methods of Big Business

People and the government began to question the methods of big business.

Define What is social Darwinism? *the view that Darwin's "survival of the fittest" theory determines who would succeed in business and in life*

Make Inferences Why did some business leaders give money to charity? *They felt that the rich had a duty to aid the poor.*

CRF: Biography Activity: Leland Stanford

HSS 8.12.4; HSS **Analysis Skills:** CS 1, HI 1

Info to Know

Big Business and Philanthropy
American industrialists were well-known for their philanthropy to important causes. John D. Rockefeller, head of Standard Oil, established foundations for medical research and education. Steel magnate Andrew Carnegie gave generously to universities, public libraries, and cultural institutions, including the well-known Carnegie Hall theater in New York City. California's Stanford University was founded by a grant from railroad tycoon Leland Stanford in honor of his son, and only child, who died of typhoid fever.

Critical Thinking: Supporting a Point of View

Standards **Proficiency**

Big Business Panel Discussion

HSS 8.12.6; HSS **Analysis Skills:** HR 1, HI 1

1. Review the meaning of social Darwinism and how it was interpreted and viewed during the Second Industrial Revolution. Ask students what problems might have caused people to question the practices of big business. How did business leaders respond to the criticism?
2. Organize the class into three groups, one representing business leaders, one representing workers, and one representing government. Tell the students that they will stage a panel discussion about the methods of big business. Ask each group to write a short opening statement that explains their stance on the methods of big business. Then have students write questions to ask during the discussion.
3. On the day of the panel discussion, select several students to serve as moderators and on the panel. Have the other students serve as audience members who ask questions of the panel. LS **Verbal/Linguistic, Interpersonal**

Alternative Assessment Handbook, Rubric 10: Debates

Answers

Analyzing Primary Sources *by making him much larger and putting the White House in his hands*

Reading Check *to increase control and profits and lower production costs*

Direct Teach

Main Idea

❷ Questioning the Methods of Big Business

People and the government began to question the methods of big business.

Explain Why did critics oppose the practices of big business? *They believed big business used unfair practices like driving smaller competitors out of business and creating monopolies.*

Evaluate Was the Sherman Antitrust Act successful in curbing the power of wealthy trusts? Why? *No, because it did not legally define a trust and was too difficult to enforce.*

CRF: Economics and History Activity: Monopolies and Trusts

HSS 8.12.6; **HSS Analysis Skills:** HI 1, HI 2

Review & Assess

Close

Have students write a short summary of this section as a review.

Review

Online Quiz, Section 2

Assess

SE Section 2 Assessment

PASS: Section 2 Quiz

Alternative Assessment Handbook

Reteach/Classroom Intervention

California Standards Review Workbook

Interactive Reader and Study Guide, Section 2

Interactive Skills Tutor CD-ROM

Answers

Reading Check *Voters were concerned about the political power of trusts and wanted the government to control monopolies and trusts.*

fund public libraries to expand access to books. By the late 1800s, various charities had received millions of dollars from philanthropists.

The Antitrust Movement

Critics of big business said that many business leaders earned their fortunes through unfair business practices. These criticisms grew stronger in the 1880s as corporations became more powerful. Large corporations often used their size and strength to drive smaller competitors out of business. Carnegie and Rockefeller, for example, pressured railroads to charge their companies lower shipping rates. Powerful trusts also arranged to sell goods and services below market value. Smaller competitors went out of business trying to match those prices. Then the trusts raised prices again.

Some people became concerned when a trust gained a **monopoly**, or total ownership of a product or service. Critics argued that monopolies reduced necessary competition. Competition, they believed, kept prices low and the quality of goods and services high.

Some Americans also worried about the political power of wealthy trusts. Union leader John W. Hayes called trusts "the common enemy of society." Many citizens and small businesses wanted the government to help control monopolies and trusts. People who favored trusts responded that trusts were more efficient and gave the consumer dependable products or services.

Many members of Congress favored big business. However, elected officials could not ignore the concerns of voters. In July 1890 Congress passed the **Sherman Antitrust Act**, a law that made it illegal to create monopolies or trusts that restrained trade. It stated that any "attempt to monopolize . . . any part of the trade or commerce among the several States" was a crime. However, the act did not clearly define a trust in legal terms. The antitrust laws were therefore difficult to enforce. Corporations and trusts kept growing in size and power.

READING CHECK **Analyzing** How did concerns about trusts lead to the Sherman Antitrust Act?

SUMMARY AND PREVIEW In the late 1800s some corporations became monopolies that dominated industries such as oil. In the next section you will learn about how industrial workers organized to improve working conditions.

Section 2 Assessment

go.hrw.com
Online Quiz
KEYWORD: SS8 HP18

Reviewing Ideas, Terms, and People HSS 8.12.3, 8.12.4, 8.12.6

1. a. **Identify** What are **horizontal** and **vertical integration**?
   b. **Explain** What are the benefits of investing in **corporations**?
   c. **Evaluate** What do you think about the business methods of **Carnegie, Rockefeller,** and **Stanford**?
2. a. **Describe** What is **social Darwinism**?
   b. **Summarize** What concerns did critics of big business have regarding **trusts**?
   c. **Evaluate** Was the **Sherman Antitrust Act** successful? Why or why not?

Critical Thinking

3. **Contrasting** Copy the graphic organizer shown at right. Use it to contrast the views of business leaders who favored monopolies with those of Americans who opposed monopolies.

Business Leaders' Views	vs.	Views of People Against Monopolies

FOCUS ON WRITING

4. **Describing Business Leaders** Add the business leaders described in this section to your notes. Think about what role they might play in your drama series.

Section 2 Assessment Answers

1. **a.** horizontal—owning all businesses in a certain field; vertical—ownership of businesses involved in each step of manufacturing
   b. Stockholders receive a share of profits, and are not responsible for business debts.
   c. Answers should show an understanding of the impact made by each business leader.
2. **a.** a view of society based on Charles Darwin's theory of natural selection; the fittest would succeed in business and in life in general.
   b. they used unfair business practices to drive competitors out of the marketplace
   c. not successful; it did not clearly define a trust and was difficult to enforce
3. business leaders—use vertical and horizontal integration to dominate business, create trusts to get rid of competition, social Darwinism; people against monopolies—big businesses were causing problems, forcing smaller companies out of business, and creating monopolies
4. Responses might include Rockefeller and Carnegie, and how each used vertical and horizontal integration to expand their business.

BIOGRAPHY

Andrew Carnegie, John D. Rockefeller, and Leland Stanford

How would you go about building an industry?

Andrew Carnegie (1835–1919) Born in Scotland, Carnegie rose to become a multibillionaire in the steel industry. He brought new technologies to his steel mills and made them extremely efficient. In 1901 he sold Carnegie Steel Company for $250 billion, making him the richest man in the world.

John D. Rockefeller (1839–1937) Rockefeller got his start in the oil business in Cleveland, Ohio. Rockefeller's Standard Oil Company quickly bought out its competitors throughout the United States. To better control oil production and delivery, Rockefeller also bought railroad rights, terminals, and pipelines.

Leland Stanford (1825–1893) Leland Stanford was born to a New York farming family that sent him to excellent private schools. After practicing law in Wisconsin, he made his career in California. Stanford was instrumental in building the western section of the transcontinental railroad. He then plunged into politics, serving one term as governor. His political connections helped him obtain huge state land grants and other benefits for his railroad companies. As president of Central Pacific and Southern Pacific, he oversaw the laying of thousands of miles of track throughout the West.

Why are they so important? Carnegie, Rockefeller, and Stanford helped make America the world's greatest industrial power by the end of the 1800s. They built giant industries that made goods cheaply by keeping workers' wages low. They also engaged in ruthless business practices to defeat their competition and create monopolies. The Sherman Anti-Trust Act was passed in reaction to the Standard Oil monopoly. Later in life, all three men became philanthropists, people devoted to charity work. Rockefeller's philanthropies gave out $500 million in his lifetime. Carnegie spent $350 million, funding educational grants, concert halls, and nearly 3,000 public libraries. Stanford founded Stanford University in 1884.

Finding Main Ideas
Why are these three men important figures in U.S. History?

Biography

Reading Focus Question

Ask students to consider how they might go about building a multibillion dollar industry. Have students consider what it would take to build an industry. Examples might include investors, political connections, and ambition. Ask students how people might feel about a businessperson who is able to build an industry from the ground up.

Info to Know

Standard Oil Trust In the late 1800s and early 1900s John D. Rockefeller's oil trust controlled virtually all oil production, processing, and transportation in the United States. In 1892 the Ohio Supreme Court forced Rockefeller to dissolve the trust, although it continued to operate until 1911 when the trust was finally forced to break apart. Today, former Standard Oil companies still remain, but as independent companies, among them are ExxonMobil, Chevron, and Amoco.

Did you know . . .

Andrew Carnegie's first job was as a bobbin boy at a cotton factory in Pennsylvania, where he made about $1.20 a week. Fifty-two years later, at the age of 64, Carnegie sold his Carnegie Steel Company for $480 million.

Critical Thinking: Summarizing

Standards Proficiency

Writing Eulogies

HSS 8.12.4; HSS **Analysis Skills:** HI 1, HI 3

1. Review with students the biographies of John D. Rockefeller, Andrew Carnegie, and Leland Stanford.
2. Ask each student to imagine that he or she has been selected to give the eulogy at the funeral of one of these famous American business leaders. Ask students to select which man they will eulogize.
3. Remind students that family members, trusted friends, and advisors will be in attendance. Ask students to consider what they will say in a eulogy. Then have each student write a one-page eulogy evaluating the life and achievements of the person selected.
4. Ask volunteers to deliver their eulogy to the class. LS **Verbal/Linguistic**

Alternative Assessment Handbook, Rubric 37: Writing Assignments

Answers

Finding Main Ideas *They each built companies that made millions of dollars, introduced new business practices or technologies, and made many charitable contributions.*

Preteach

Bellringer

If YOU were there . . . Use the **Daily Bellringer Transparency** to help students answer the question.

Daily Bellringer Transparency, Section 3

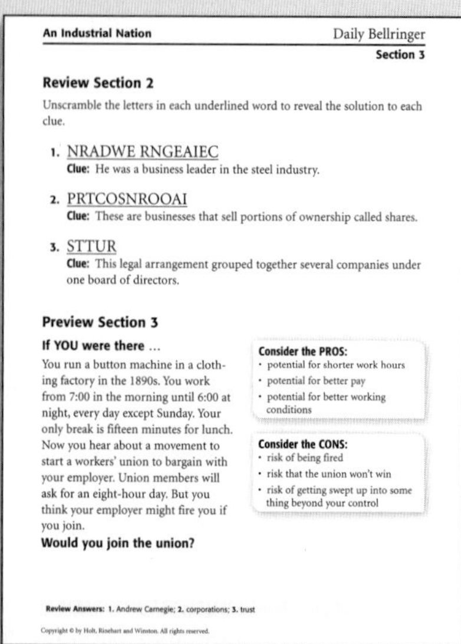

An Industrial Nation Daily Bellringer

Section 3

Review Section 2

Unscramble the letters in each underlined word to reveal the solution to each clue.

1. NRADWE RNGEAIEC
   Clue: He was a business leader in the steel industry.
2. PRTCOSNROOAI
   Clue: These are businesses that sell portions of ownership called shares.
3. STTUR
   Clue: This legal arrangement grouped together several companies under one board of directors.

Preview Section 3

If YOU were there ...

You run a button machine in a clothing factory in the 1890s. You work from 7:00 in the morning until 6:00 at night, every day except Sunday. Your only break is fifteen minutes for lunch. Now you hear about a movement to start a workers' union to bargain with your employer. Union members will ask for an eight-hour day. But you think your employer might fire you if you join.

Would you join the union?

Consider the PROS:
- potential for shorter work hours
- potential for better pay
- potential for better working conditions

Consider the CONS:
- risk of being fired
- risk that the union won't win
- risk of getting swept up into some thing beyond your control

Review Answers: 1. Andrew Carnegie; **2.** corporations; **3.** trust

Building Vocabulary

Preteach or review the following terms:

conspiracy an agreement among two or more people to perform an illegal act (p. 587)

specialization the act of concentrating on a specific activity (p. 584)

strike a temporary stoppage of work by employees (p. 586)

CRF: Vocabulary Builder Activity, Section 3

Standards Focus

HSS 8.12.6

Means: Examine working conditions, child labor, the labor movement and its strategies, and government policies toward big business.

Matters: The growth of big business led to new movements and policies to protect workers and businesses.

SECTION 3 Industrial Workers

What You Will Learn...

Main Ideas

1. The desire to maximize profits and become more efficient led to poor working conditions.
2. Workers began to organize and demand improvements in working conditions and pay.
3. Labor strikes often turned violent and failed to accomplish their goals.

The Big Idea

Changes in the workplace led to a rise in labor unions and workers' strikes.

Key Terms and People

Frederick W. Taylor, *p. 584*
Knights of Labor, *p. 585*
Terence V. Powderly, *p. 585*
Samuel Gompers, *p. 585*
American Federation of Labor, *p. 585*
collective bargaining, *p. 586*
Mary Harris Jones, *p. 586*
Haymarket Riot, *p. 586*
Homestead Strike, *p. 587*
Pullman Strike, *p. 587*

HSS 8.12.6 Discuss child labor, working conditions, and laissez-faire policies toward big business and examine the labor movement, including its leaders (e.g., Samuel Gompers), its demand for collective bargaining, and its strikes and protests over labor conditions.

If YOU were there...

You run a button machine in a clothing factory in the 1890s. You work from 7:00 in the morning until 6:00 at night, every day except Sunday. Your only break is 15 minutes for lunch. Now you hear about a movement to start a workers' union to bargain with your employer. Union members will ask for an eight-hour workday. But you think your employer might fire you if you join.

Would you join the union?

BUILDING BACKGROUND The rise of corporations and the establishment of monopolies gave big business a great deal of power. An antitrust movement arose to try to limit the power of trusts. Workers themselves began to organize and take action against bad working conditions and other problems.

Maximizing Profits and Efficiency

During the late 1800s, several factors led to a decline in the quality of working conditions. Machines run by unskilled workers were eliminating the jobs of many skilled craftspeople. These low-paid workers could be replaced easily. Factories began to focus on specialization, or workers repeating a single step again and again. Specialization brought costs down and caused production to rise. But it also made workers tired, bored, and more likely to be injured. Specialization allowed for Henry Ford's idea of a moving assembly line to speed production. Ford's use of the moving assembly line allowed automobiles to be made more quickly and cheaply. Automobiles soon became available to a wider segment of the population than ever before.

In 1909 **Frederick W. Taylor**, an efficiency engineer, published a popular book called *The Principles of Scientific Management.* He encouraged managers to view workers as interchangeable parts of the production process. In factories, managers influenced by Taylor paid less attention to working conditions. Injuries increased, and as conditions grew worse, workers looked for ways to bring about change.

READING CHECK **Identifying Cause and Effect** Why did companies begin to use scientific management, and how did it affect workers?

Teach the Big Idea: Master the Standards

Reaching Standards

Industrial Workers HSS 8.12.6; HSS Analysis Skills: HI 1, HR 5

1. **Teach** Ask students the Main Idea questions to teach this section.
2. **Apply** Organize the class into two groups. Assign one group to represent labor unions and workers and the other to represent the management of a large company. Ask students to imagine that their company has been operating on a ten-hour workday for many years, which has been highly profitable. Now, the labor union wants to cut the workers' hours to eight per day. Ask each group to develop points in support of their position, then stage a mock debate to argue for their cause. **LS Interpersonal**
3. **Review** As you review the section, ask students to discuss labor and management views of labor issues.
4. **Practice/Homework** Ask each student to list the pros and cons of labor unions. **LS Verbal/Linguistic**

Alternative Assessment Handbook, Rubrics 10: Debates; and 37: Writing Assignments

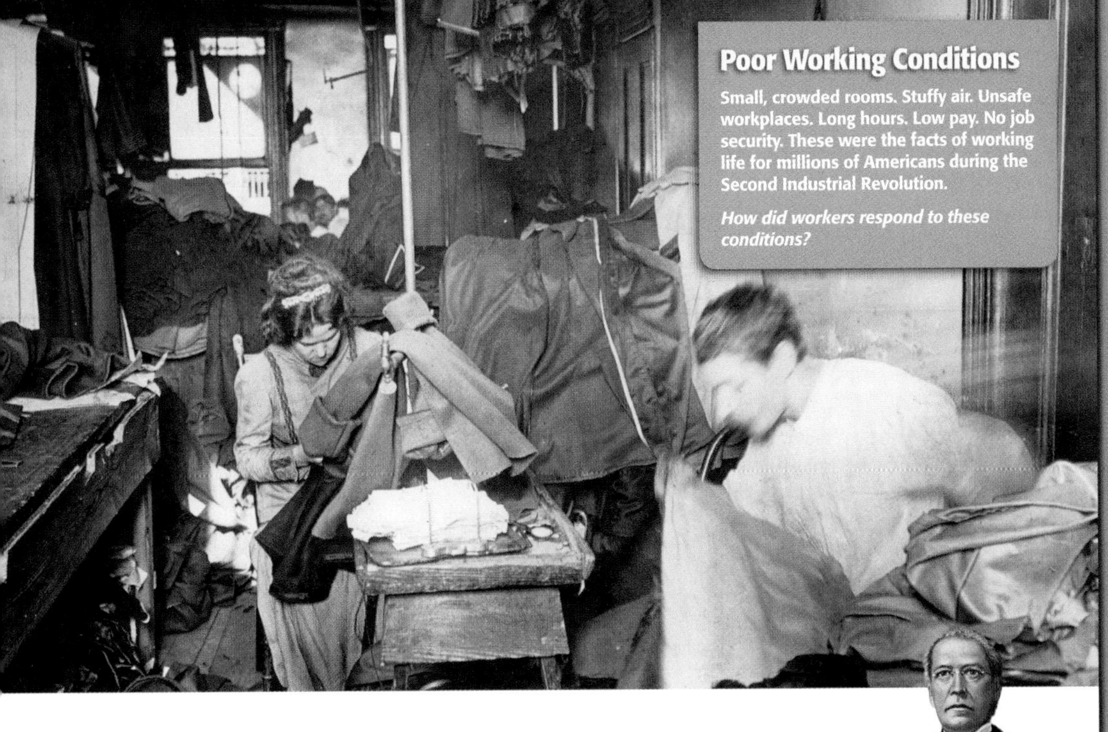

Poor Working Conditions

Small, crowded rooms. Stuffy air. Unsafe workplaces. Long hours. Low pay. No job security. These were the facts of working life for millions of Americans during the Second Industrial Revolution.

How did workers respond to these conditions?

Workers Organize

Workers formed labor unions to get better wages and working conditions for all workers in a factory or industry. The first national labor union, the **Knights of Labor**, was founded in the 1870s. It pushed for an eight-hour workday, equal pay for equal work, and an end to child labor. Union members also wanted the government to regulate trusts. Unlike most unions at the time, the Knights included both skilled and unskilled workers. The Knights of Labor was originally organized much like a secret society. In 1879, **Terence V. Powderly** became leader of the Knights. He ended all secrecy, creating the first truly national labor union in the United States.

Another early labor union was the **American Federation of Labor (AFL)**, led by **Samuel Gompers**. Unlike the Knights, the **American Federation of Labor (AFL)** organized individual national unions, such as the mineworkers' and steelworkers' unions. The

BIOGRAPHY

Samuel Gompers

1850–1924

Samuel Gompers was born in London. He came to the United States with his parents in 1863 at age 13. He worked as a cigar maker and joined a local union, eventually becoming its president. The Cigarmakers Union was reorganized and later joined the American Federation of Labor. Gompers became the AFL's first president and remained so, except for the year 1895, until his death. He campaigned for basic trade-union rights, such as the right to picket and to organize boycotts and strikes. His efforts on behalf of workers helped organized labor to gain respect.

Summarizing How did Samuel Gompers help the labor-union movement?

Direct Teach

Main Idea

1 Maximizing Profits and Efficiency

The desire to maximize profits and become more efficient led to poor working conditions.

Recall Why did factories focus on specialization? *It brought down costs and increased production.*

Explain How did machines lead to a decrease in jobs? *Skilled craftspeople were no longer needed, and a single machine could replace several workers.*

HSS 8.12.6; HSS **Analysis Skills:** HI 1, HI 2

Main Idea

2 Workers Organize

Workers began to organize and demand improvements in working conditions and pay.

Recall What were two important labor unions in the late 1800s? *the Knights of Labor and the American Federation of Labor*

Make Inferences Why did collective bargaining give workers a greater chance of success? *because laborers worked together to convince employers to meet their demands*

CRF: Biography Activity: Mother Jones

CRF: Primary Source Activity: Samuel Gompers, Testimony before Congress

HSS 8.12.6; HSS **Analysis Skills:** HI 1

go.hrw.com
Online Resources
KEYWORD: SS8 US18
ACTIVITY: Steelworkers

Critical Thinking: Supporting a Point of View

Standards Proficiency

Expressing Workers' Views

HSS 8.12.6; HSS **Analysis Skills:** CS 1, HI 1

1. Review with students the decline in the quality of working conditions that many factories experienced in the late 1800s. Ask students to discuss what effect these poor conditions might have had on the workers. Remind students that many workers responded by organizing labor unions to represent the demands of workers.
2. Have students make a list of complaints that workers may have had about their working conditions and steps that labor unions might have taken to correct these problems.
3. Have students create speeches, songs, or poems that express these ideas. For example a song might tell of poor working conditions and encourage workers to join a union. Remind students that they must include both complaints of workers and the goals of labor unions.
4. Ask volunteers to share their speeches, songs, or poems with the class. LS **Verbal/Linguistic, Auditory/Musical**

Alternative Assessment Handbook, Rubrics 24: Oral Presentations; and 26: Poems and Songs

Answers

Reading Check (p. 584) *to help increase efficiency; working conditions grew worse, injuries increased, and workers looked for ways to bring about change*

Poor Working Conditions *formed labor unions to get better wages and working conditions*

Biography *campaigned for basic trade union rights*

Direct Teach

Main Idea

❸ Labor Strikes

Labor strikes often turned violent and failed to accomplish their goals.

Recall What were union members protesting during the Homestead Strike? *a plan to buy new machinery and cut jobs*

Analyze Did the Haymarket Riot help or hurt the labor movement? *possible answer—hurt, because it resulted in a decline in Knights of Labor membership*

Make Judgments Do you think strikes are an effective and appropriate way to handle labor disputes? Explain. *Answers will vary, but students should use examples from the text to support their answer.*

CRF: History and Geography Activity: Pullman's Company Town

Map Transparency: Major Labor Strikes, Late 1800s

HSS 8.12.6; HSS **Analysis Skills:** HI 1

go.hrw.com
Online Resources
KEYWORD: SS8 US18
ACTIVITY: Mary Harris Jones

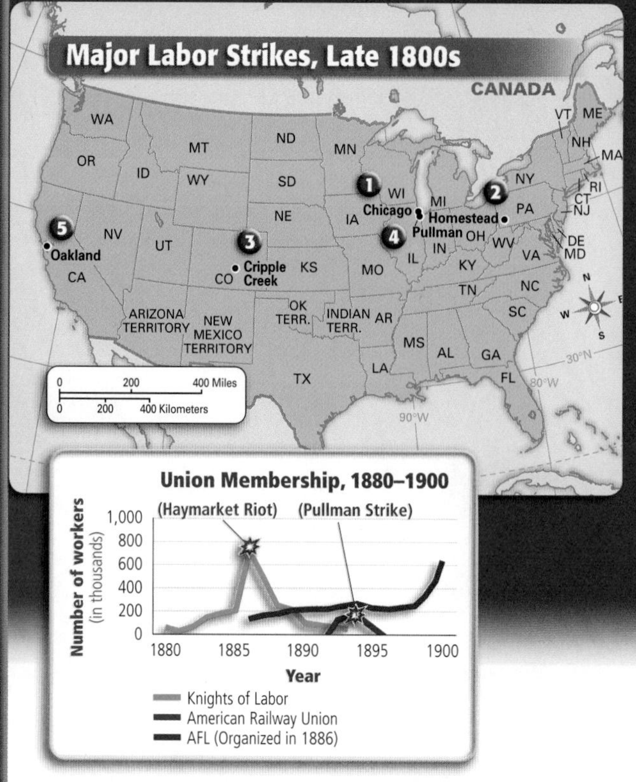

❶ **Haymarket Riot** In May 1886 the Haymarket Riot erupted between protesters and police in Chicago. It resulted in the decline of the Knights of Labor.

❷ **Homestead Strike** In 1892 a strike occurred at Carnegie Steel Company in Homestead, Pennsylvania. The resulting fight left workers and Pinkerton guards dead.

❸ **Colorado Miners' Strike** In the summer of 1893, gold miners at Cripple Creek, Colorado, went on strike for higher wages and a shorter workday.

❹ **Pullman Strike** The Pullman strike of 1894 began with workers who made the Pullman train cars. It soon spread to workers who worked on trains pulling the sleeper cars.

❺ **California Railroad Strike** In 1894 railroad workers in Oakland went on strike in the Bay Area's first major strike. Supporting Chicago Pullman workers, they halted passenger, freight, and mail trains for months.

ANALYSIS SKILL ANALYZING INFORMATION

How did conflicts between striking workers and authorities affect union membership?

AFL also limited its membership to skilled workers. This gave the union great bargaining power but left out most workers. The AFL tried to get better wages, hours, and working conditions for laborers. By 1890 the AFL's membership was larger than that of the Knights. With **collective bargaining**—all workers acted collectively, or together—workers had a much greater chance of success in negotiating with management. Most employers opposed collective bargaining. One company president said, "I shall never give in. I would rather go out of business."

THE IMPACT TODAY
In 1955 the AFL merged with the Congress of Industrial Organizations to become the AFL-CIO. Today the organization has more than 13 million members.

Many women took active roles in unions. For example, **Mary Harris Jones**, an Irish immigrant, worked for better conditions for miners. A fiery speaker, she organized strikes and helped educate workers.

READING CHECK **Contrasting** How did the Knights of Labor and the AFL differ?

Labor Strikes

By the late 1800s, other unions were gaining strength. Major workers' strikes swept the country and included miners in Colorado, steel workers in Pennsylvania, and railroad workers in Illinois and California. The first major labor strike began in 1886 in Chicago.

In May 1886, thousands of union members in Chicago went on strike because they wanted an eight-hour workday. Two strikers were killed in a fight with police. The next night, workers met at Haymarket Square to protest the killings. In what became known as the **Haymarket Riot,** someone threw a bomb that wounded many police officers and killed eight. The police fired into the crowd, killing several people and wounding 100 others.

Differentiating Instruction for Universal Access

Advanced Learners/GATE

Exceeding Standards | Research Required

1. Review with students the major labor strikes discussed above. Discuss the causes and results of these strikes.
2. Ask each student to select one of the major labor strikes from the map above and use the library, Internet, or other resources to research information about that strike. Students should identify the cause of the strike, how the strike was settled, and the results of the strike.
3. Have students write a newspaper or magazine article about the strike and its results. If possible, have students include quotations from the sources they researched.
4. Ask volunteers to read their article aloud to the class.

Alternative Assessment Handbook, Rubrics 23: Newspapers; and 30: Research

HSS 8.12.6; HSS **Analysis Skills:** HR 1, HI 1

Universal Access Resources
See page 569c for additional resources for differentiating instruction for universal access.

Answers

Analyzing Information *often resulted in decline*

Reading Check *Knights of Labor—had both skilled and unskilled workers; AFL—had skilled workers, was organized into individual unions, and was larger than the Knights of Labor*

Eight people, some of whom were not at the riot, were arrested and convicted of conspiracy. One of them had a Knights of Labor membership card. Though Knights leadership had not supported the strike, several local chapters had. Membership in the Knights fell quickly.

Sometimes, business owners succeeded in breaking up unions. In 1892, a violent strike called the **Homestead strike** took place at Andrew Carnegie's Homestead steel factory in Pennsylvania. Union members there protested a plan to buy new machinery and cut jobs. The company refused to negotiate with the union and locked workers out of the plant. The workers responded by seizing control of the plant. Gunfire erupted on July 6, when the Pinkerton detectives—hired by the company to break the union—tried to enter the plant. A fierce battle raged for 14 hours, leaving 16 people dead. The governor called out the state militia to restore order. Continuing for four more months, the union was eventually defeated.

Another major strike happened at George Pullman's Pullman Palace Car Company in the company town of Pullman, Illinois. Most of the company workers lived there, paying high rents. During the depression that began in 1893, Pullman laid off about half of the workers and cut pay for those that were left, without lowering their rents. On May 11, 1894, workers began the **Pullman strike** which stopped traffic on many railroad lines until federal courts ordered the workers to return to their jobs. President Grover Cleveland sent federal troops to Chicago to stop the strike. Such defeats seriously damaged the labor movement for years.

READING CHECK **Analyzing** What were the effects of early major strikes on workers?

SUMMARY AND PREVIEW Workers formed unions to fight for better conditions and to keep their jobs. In the next section, you will learn about a new wave of immigrants in the late 1800s.

Section 3 Assessment

go.hrw.com
Online Quiz
KEYWORD: SS8 HP18

Reviewing Ideas, Terms, and People HSS 8.12.6

1. a. **Recall** Why did conditions in factories begin to decline?
   b. **Draw Conclusions** How were workers affected by specialization and scientific management?
   c. **Evaluate** Do you think scientific management made businesses more successful? Explain.
2. a. **Identify** What role did **Mary Harris Jones** play in the labor movement?
   b. **Analyze** Why did workers demand **collective bargaining**, and why did business owners oppose it?
   c. **Elaborate** Do you think the demands made by labor unions were reasonable? Explain your answer.
3. a. **Describe** What major labor strikes took place in the late 1800s?
   b. **Evaluate** Do you think President Cleveland was right to use federal troops to end the **Pullman Strike?** Explain.

Critical Thinking

4. **Analyzing** Copy the chart below. Use it to list the major labor conflicts of the late 1800s, their causes, and their outcomes.

Date	Conflict	Causes	Outcome
May 1886			
June 1892			
May 1894			

FOCUS ON WRITING

5. **Taking Notes on the Labor Movement** Take notes about what life was like for workers during this time. How might you include the labor movement in your series?

Direct Teach

Info to Know

Labor Day Labor unions in the late 1800s organized the first Labor Day celebrations in the United States. Union leaders Peter J. McGuire and Matthew Maguire first suggested the idea of a celebration to honor American workers. The first observance of American laborers took place in September 1882 with a parade in New York City. Two years later, the Knights of Labor pushed to make the first Monday in September an annual celebration of Labor Day. Shortly after the Pullman strike in 1894, Congress officially made Labor Day a national holiday.

Review & Assess

Close

Review with students the hardships industrial workers faced, the steps they took to try to address those problems, and the consequences of their efforts.

Review

Online Quiz, Section 3

Assess

SE Section 3 Assessment

PASS: Section 3 Quiz

Alternative Assessment Handbook

Reteach/Classroom Intervention

California Standards Review Workbook

Interactive Reader and Study Guide, Section 3

Interactive Skills Tutor CD-ROM

Section 3 Assessment Answers

1. a. scientific management encouraged managers to pay less attention to working conditions
   b. specialization—workers became tired, bored, and likely to be injured; scientific management—working conditions declined
   c. possible answers—yes, they became more efficient; no, workers were unhappy
2. a. organized strikes, gave speeches, and educated workers
   b. Workers would have a better chance of success with collective bargaining, but employers did not want to give in to unions.
   c. Students' answers will vary, but should support their stance with specific details.
3. a. Haymarket Riot, Homestead Strike, and Pullman Strike
   b. Students' answers should indicate why President Cleveland used federal troops.
4. May 1886—Haymarket Riot; June 1892—Homestead Strike; May 1894—Pullman Strike; see map on p. 586 for causes and outcomes
5. Possible responses might include one of the strikes or actions by labor unions.

Answers

Reading Check *Strikes that turned violent did not benefit workers; companies received help from the government to end strikes.*

Preteach

Bellringer

If YOU were there . . . Use the **Daily Bellringer Transparency** to help students answer the question.

 Daily Bellringer Transparency, Section 4

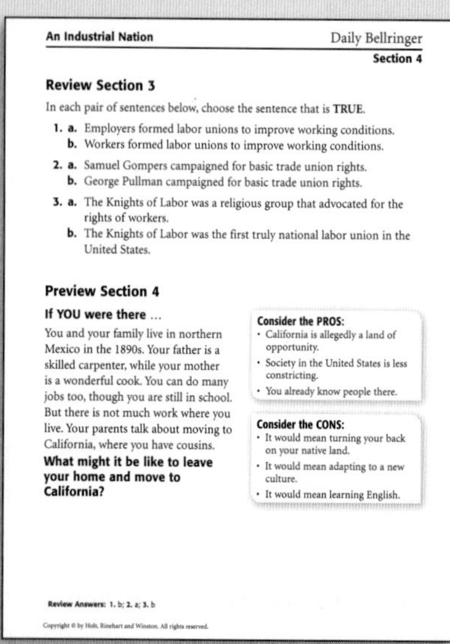

An Industrial Nation | Daily Bellringer | Section 4

Review Section 3

In each pair of sentences below, choose the sentence that is **TRUE**.

1. a. Employers formed labor unions to improve working conditions.
   b. Workers formed labor unions to improve working conditions.
2. a. Samuel Gompers campaigned for basic trade union rights.
   b. George Pullman campaigned for basic trade union rights.
3. a. The Knights of Labor was a religious group that advocated for the rights of workers.
   b. The Knights of Labor was the first truly national labor union in the United States.

Preview Section 4

If YOU were there ...

You and your family live in northern Mexico in the 1890s. Your father is a skilled carpenter, while your mother is a wonderful cook. You can do many jobs too, though you are still in school. But there is not much work where you live. Your parents talk about moving to California, where you have cousins.

What might it be like to leave your home and move to California?

Consider the PROS:
- California is allegedly a land of opportunity.
- Society in the United States is less constricting.
- You already know people there.

Consider the CONS:
- It would mean turning your back on your native land.
- It would mean adapting to a new culture.
- It would mean learning English.

Review Answers: 1. b; 2. a; 3. b

Academic Vocabulary

Review with students the high-use academic term in this section.

policy rule, course of action (p. 593)

CRF: Vocabulary Builder Activity, Section 4

Standards Focus

HSS 8.12.7

Means: Explain the new wave of immigration to the United States in the late 1800s, the contributions of these immigrants, how they were absorbed into American society, and the reaction of people opposed to immigration.

Matters: Immigration in the late 1800s helped build the nation's economy and enrich American culture.

SECTION 4

A New Wave of Immigration

What You Will Learn...

Main Ideas

1. The late 1800s brought a wave of new immigrants from southern and eastern Europe and Mexico.
2. Some Americans opposed immigration and tried to enact restrictions against it.

The Big Idea

A new wave of immigration in the late 1800s brought large numbers of immigrants to the United States.

Key Terms and People

old immigrants, *p. 588*
new immigrants, *p. 588*
steerage, *p. 588*
benevolent societies, *p. 591*
Chinese Exclusion Act, *p. 593*
Immigration Restriction League, *p. 593*

HSS 8.12.7 Identify the new sources of large-scale immigration and the contributions of immigrants to the building of cities and the economy; explain the ways in which new social and economic patterns encouraged assimilation of newcomers into the mainstream amidst growing cultural diversity; and discuss the new wave of nativism.

If YOU were there...

You and your family live in northern Mexico in the 1890s. Your father is a skilled carpenter, while your mother is a wonderful cook. You can do many jobs too, though you are still in school. But there is not much work where you live. Your parents talk about moving to California, where you have cousins.

What might it be like to leave your home and move to California?

BUILDING BACKGROUND Since its beginnings, America has attracted people from many parts of the world. They came for land, jobs, religious freedom, and the chance to start new lives. In the late 1800s, rapid economic growth created jobs and opportunities that drew new groups of immigrants.

New Immigrants

During the late 1800s, immigrants continued to come to the United States by the millions. Immigration patterns, however, began to change. Immigrants who had arrived before the 1880s were now called **old immigrants** . They were mostly from Great Britain, Germany, Ireland, and Scandinavia. Most of them were Protestants, except for the Irish and some Germans who were Catholic. Many were skilled workers who spoke English. Often the old immigrants settled in the rural areas outside cities and became farmers.

After 1880, many more immigrants came to the United States, and they came from many different places. More than 5 million came during the 1880s, as had come between 1800 and 1860. The majority of these **new immigrants**, who came during and after the 1880s, were from southern and eastern Europe. Thousands of Czechs, Greeks, Hungarians, Italians, Poles, Russians, and Slovaks came to the United States looking for new opportunities and better lives. Southern Italy sent large numbers of immigrants. Immigrant Miriam Zunser hoped "for all manner of miracles [in] a strange, wonderful land!"

Teach the Big Idea: Master the Standards

Standards Proficiency

A New Wave of Immigration

HSS 8.12.7; HSS **Analysis Skills:** CS 2, CS 3, HI 1, HI 2

1. **Teach** Ask students the Main Idea questions to teach this section.
2. **Apply** Have students work in small groups to create a scrapbook that chronicles the immigrant experience in the United States. Have each group create a scrapbook that has a page dedicated to each heading in the section. Remind students to use illustrations, letters, photographs, and captions to paint a picture of life for immigrants in the United States. **LS Visual/Spatial, Verbal/Linguistic**
3. **Review** Have groups exchange their scrapbooks and study the illustrations and captions as a review of the section.
4. **Practice/Homework** Have each student create a one-page visual summary of the section. Remind students that the summary should illustrate the big idea and main ideas of the section. **LS Visual/Spatial**

Alternative Assessment Handbook, Rubrics 3: Artwork; and 32: Scrapbooks

Many were seeking economic opportunity in the industrial boom of the late 1800s. Others were escaping political or religious persecution. Most brought new cultural practices with them. The immigrants included Eastern Orthodox Christians, Roman Catholics, and Jews.

Many immigrants were eager for the job opportunities that arose during the industrial boom of the late 1800s. Before coming to America, many had received encouraging letters from friends and relatives who had immigrated earlier. Those earlier immigrants not only sent letters to their relatives and friends back home, but often they sent money to help pay for the journey to the United States. To attract immigrants, railroad and steamship companies hired business agents who tended to paint unrealistic pictures of easy wealth and happiness in the United States.

Immigrants usually faced a difficult journey to America. Most traveled in **steerage**, an area below a ship's deck where steering mechanisms were located. In these cramped conditions, passengers often experienced seasickness and sometimes death.

New arrivals had to go to immigration processing centers run by state and local governments. In 1892 a receiving office was opened on Ellis Island in New York Harbor. Over the next 40 years, millions of immigrants came through the Ellis Island center.

In the processing centers, officials interviewed immigrants to decide whether to let them enter the country. Officials also conducted physical examinations. They did not allow those who carried an infectious disease to enter. Most immigrants were admitted. After admission, they entered the United States to find work and build new lives.

THE IMPACT TODAY

During the late 1800s and early 1900s, many Asian Indians immigrated to the United States. Some of these immigrants came from Punjab, a province in present-day India and Pakistan, and were members of the Sikh religion. Sikhs settled in California by the thousands and worked initially in the railroad and lumber industries. Today their descendants run successful farms and other businesses.

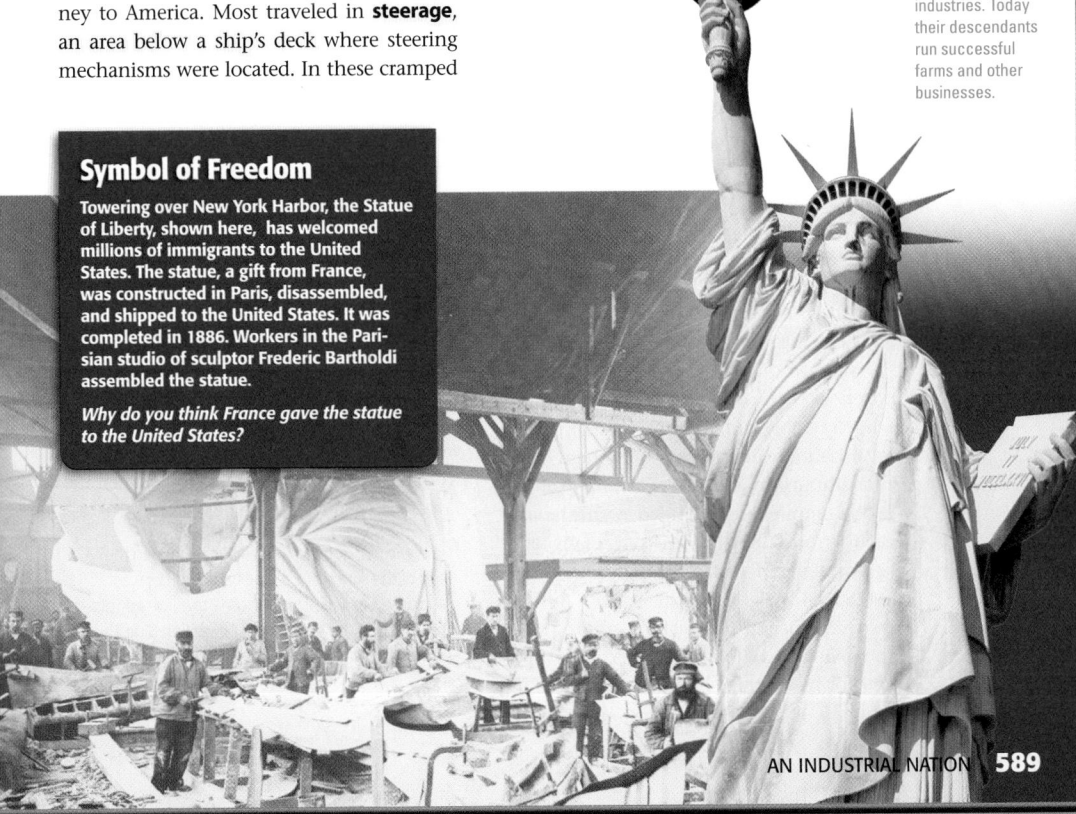

Symbol of Freedom

Towering over New York Harbor, the Statue of Liberty, shown here, has welcomed millions of immigrants to the United States. The statue, a gift from France, was constructed in Paris, disassembled, and shipped to the United States. It was completed in 1886. Workers in the Parisian studio of sculptor Frederic Bartholdi assembled the statue.

Why do you think France gave the statue to the United States?

Direct Teach

Main Idea

1 New Immigrants

The late 1800s brought a wave of new immigrants from southern and eastern Europe and Mexico.

Identify Who were the "old immigrants"? *immigrants who came to America before the 1880s from such countries as Great Britain, Germany, Ireland, and Scandinavia*

Draw Conclusions Why were processing centers like the one on Ellis Island used? *so the government could officially interview immigrants entering the United States, and perhaps refuse to admit some*

Evaluate Would you have made the difficult to journey to the United States to find new opportunities? Why or why not? *Answers should reflect students' understanding of the difficulties of traveling to the United States and the hope for a better life.*

CRF: Literature Activity: Poetry from Angel Island

HSS 8.12.7; HSS **Analysis Skills:** HI 1, HI 2

Info to Know

Angel Island Immigrants arriving on the West Coast of the United States were also required to undergo processing at an immigration center—Angel Island. Located in San Francisco Bay, Angel Island was dubbed by some the "Ellis Island of the West." The predominately Asian immigrants at Angel Island faced strict immigration laws. Entrance was often limited to those with certain skills or people who could prove their parents were born in the United States.

Differentiating Instruction for Universal Access

English-Language Learners

Reaching Standards | Prep Required

1. Locate and distribute a copy of Emma Lazarus's poem "The New Colossus."
2. Point out to students that this poem appears at the base of the Statue of Liberty. Have students work in mixed-ability pairs to read the poem. Then have pairs paraphrase the last five lines of the poem.
3. Encourage volunteers to share their work with the class. LS **Verbal/Linguistic**

HSS 8.12; HSS **Analysis Skills:** HR 3

Advanced Learners/GATE

Exceeding Standards | Research Required

1. Have students read Emma Lazarus's poem, "The New Colossus."
2. Point out that the poem takes its name from a famous ancient statue. Have students conduct research to identify the statue from which it takes its name. *(the Colossus at Rhodes)* Then have students write a poem that could have been placed at its base in ancient times. LS **Verbal/Linguistic, Intrapersonal**

HSS 8.12; HSS **Analysis Skills:** HI 1

Answers

Symbol of Freedom *possible answer—as a gift to show goodwill and strengthen the relationship between the two countries*

Direct Teach

Main Idea

❶ New Immigrants

The late 1800s brought a wave of new immigrants from southern and eastern Europe and Mexico.

Explain Why did immigrants move into neighborhoods with other people from the same country? *to be familiar with the language and culture, and to help each other adapt to life in the United States*

Summarize What are some of the ways immigrants helped preserve their old customs once they were in America? *They published newspapers in their own language, founded schools, clubs, and places of worship.*

Activity Life as an Immigrant Have students select an image from these pages and write a description from the point of view of one of the persons pictured. Students should describe why he or she chose to come to America and what life was like as an immigrant. **LS Verbal/Linguistic**

Alternative Assessment Handbook, Rubric 37: Writing Assignments

HSS 8.12.7; **HSS Analysis Skills:** CS 1, HI 1

Teaching Tip

Some students may not know the difference between **immigrate** (to come into a country) and **emigrate** (to leave one's place of residence). Explain and clarify these different meanings. Have students write sentences in which they use each term correctly.

In this photo, Japanese men and Chinese women arrive in California to begin a new life in the United States.

Augustin and Maria Lozano and their two children moved from Mexico to California. Many Mexican immigrants moved into the Southwest.

Immigrant Neighborhoods

Many immigrants moved into neighborhoods with others who came from the same country. In these neighborhoods they could hear their own language, eat familiar foods, and keep their customs.

Many immigrant groups published newspapers in their own languages and founded schools, clubs, and places of worship. These organizations helped preserve their beliefs and customs. In New York City, for example, Jewish immigrants founded a theater that gave performances in the Yiddish language.

Immigrants often opened local shops and small neighborhood banks. Business owners helped new arrivals by offering credit and giving small loans. Such aid was important for newcomers because there were few commercial banks in most immigrant neighborhoods. In 1904 Italian immigrant Amadeo Peter Giannini started the Bank of Italy in San Francisco. This bank later became the Bank of America.

Even with neighborhood support, immigrants often found city life difficult. Many immigrants lived in tenements—poorly built, overcrowded apartments. They often had to work under exhausting conditions. One young woman described the difference between her hopes and realities in the new land.

> "[I dreamed] of the golden stairs leading to the top of the American palace where father was supposed to live. [I] went 'home' to ... an ugly old tenement in the heart of the Lower East Side. There were stairs to climb but they were not golden."
>
> —Miriam Shomer Zunser, *Yesterday: A Memoir of a Russian Jewish Family*

Social Studies Skills Activity: Cost-Benefit Analysis

Standards Proficiency

Moving to America

HSS 8.12.7; **HSS Analysis Skills:** HI 1, HI 2, HI 6

1. Review with students the life many new immigrants experienced in the United States. Ask students what reasons these immigrants had for leaving their native countries. How did life compare in the United States? Write students' ideas for the class to see.
2. Have each student make a list of the costs immigrants might have faced in moving to America. Students should note financial, personal, and social costs of the move, such as discrimination or leaving friends behind.
3. Then have students make a list of the benefits that immigrants received by moving to the United States, for example higher wages.
4. Ask students to examine the costs and benefits immigrants faced. Then have students write a short paragraph in which they determine whether the benefits of moving to America outweighed the costs. Remind students to provide examples from their lists.

Alternative Assessment Handbook, Rubric 37: Writing Assignments

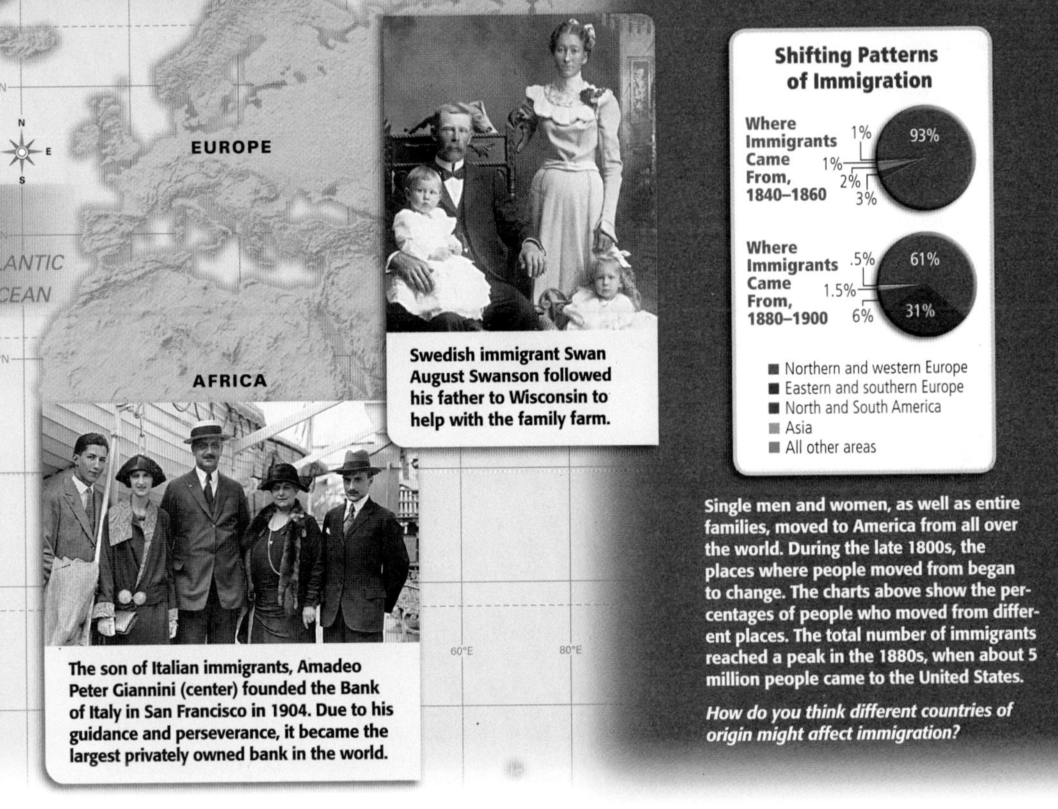

Swedish immigrant Swan August Swanson followed his father to Wisconsin to help with the family farm.

The son of Italian immigrants, Amadeo Peter Giannini (center) founded the Bank of Italy in San Francisco in 1904. Due to his guidance and perseverance, it became the largest privately owned bank in the world.

Single men and women, as well as entire families, moved to America from all over the world. During the late 1800s, the places where people moved from began to change. The charts above show the percentages of people who moved from different places. The total number of immigrants reached a peak in the 1880s, when about 5 million people came to the United States.

How do you think different countries of origin might affect immigration?

Some immigrant communities formed **benevolent societies**. These aid organizations offered immigrants help in cases of sickness, unemployment, and death. At that time, there were few national government agencies to provide such aid.

Adjusting to a New Life

Many immigrants tried to adjust to their new country. They often encouraged their children to adopt American customs. In public schools, the immigrant children learned English using McGuffey Readers, illustrated textbooks that taught basic reading and writing and emphasized basic values such as hard work and thrift. Many immigrants successfully met the challenges of living in a new country. They built strong futures for their families in the United States.

Immigrant Workers

Many new immigrants had worked on farms in their homelands. Unfortunately, few could afford to buy land in the United States. Instead, they found jobs in cities, where, by 1900, most of the country's manufacturing took place.

Having come from rural areas, few new immigrants were skilled in manufacturing or industrial work. They often had no choice but to take low-paying, unskilled jobs in garment or steel factories and construction. Long hours were common.

Not all industrial labor took place in large factories. Some immigrants worked long hours for little pay in small shops or mills located in or near working-class neighborhoods. Often associated with the

Direct Teach

Main Idea

❶ New Immigrants

The late 1800s brought a wave of new immigrants from southern and eastern Europe and Mexico.

Recall What types of jobs did many immigrants take? *unskilled jobs in garment or steel factories, working in sweatshops, some were skilled workers or opened small businesses*

Explain Where did most immigrants settle? Why? *Most settled in large cities because they could not afford to purchase land and wanted to be close to manufacturing jobs.*

Make Inferences Why did most Mexican immigrants settle in the Southwest? *It was close to their native country.*

HSS 8.12.7; HSS **Analysis Skills:** HI 1, HI 2

Linking to Today

New York's Chinatown New York City's Chinatown is the site of the largest concentration of Chinese in the western hemisphere. Within its two-square-mile boundaries live 70,000 to 150,000 people, though today there are also immigrants from many other countries living there as well. During the late 1800s, many Chinese immigrants moved to this area for the familiarity and the help other Chinese immigrants provided. Today the area attracts many visitors and offers restaurants, fruit and fish markets, and souvenir shops on its winding, crowded streets.

Collaborative Learning

Standards Proficiency

Immigrant Life

HSS 8.12.7; HSS **Analysis Skills:** HR 1, HI 1

Research Required

1. Organize the class into five groups. Have each group research the life of immigrants from one the following countries in the late 1800s and early 1900s: China, Russia, Mexico, Poland, or Italy.
2. Students should locate information about how many immigrants came from the country, reasons why people left, and what jobs immigrants from this country might have held once they arrived in the United States. Ask students to research where the immigrants usually settled, whether these groups formed immigrant neighborhoods, and where many of these neighborhoods were located.
3. Have groups use their research to create a one-act play about a family from this country who has come to the United States.
4. Have each group perform their play for the class. LS **Interpersonal, Verbal/Linguistic**

Alternative Assessment Handbook, Rubrics 30: Research; and 33: Skits and Reader's Theater

Answers

Coming to America *possible answers—It might affect where immigrants settled in the United States.*

Direct Teach

Main Idea

❷ Opposition to Immigration

Some Americans opposed immigration and tried to enact restrictions against it.

Explain Why did some labor unions oppose immigration? *They feared immigrants would take away jobs from union members.*

Summarize What were the goals of the Immigration Restriction League, and how did the group try to enact its goals? *They wanted to reduce the number of immigrants entering the country; by demanding that all immigrants know how to read and write before entering the country.*

U.S. Supreme Court Case Studies: *Yick Wo* v. *Hopkins*

HSS 8.12.7; HSS **Analysis Skills:** HI 1, HI 2

Did you know . . .

In 1897 the Immigration Restriction League convinced members of Congress to pass a bill requiring immigrants to pass a literacy test. The bill was sent to President Grover Cleveland, who vetoed the measure, calling it "illiberal, narrow, and un-American."

LINKING TO TODAY

Asian Americans Today

Today more than 12 million people in the United States are of Asian origin. They account for nearly 5 percent of the U.S. population—or about 1 in 20 Americans. Asian Americans trace their roots to various countries, including China, India, the Philippines and, like this family, Vietnam. Most Asian Americans live in the West. California has by far the largest Asian American population of any state.

ANALYSIS SKILL ANALYZING INFORMATION

Why have so many people immigrated to the United States?

clothing industry, these workplaces were called sweatshops because of long hours and hot, unhealthy working conditions.

Immigrants with appropriate skills sometimes found work in a wide range of occupations. Some immigrants worked as bakers, cooks, carpenters, masons, metalworkers, or skilled machinists. Other immigrants saved, shared, or borrowed money to open small businesses, such as barbershops, laundries, restaurants, or street vending carts. New immigrants often opened the same types of businesses in which other immigrants from the same country were already succeeding.

Mexican Immigrants

In the late 1800s large numbers of immigrants began arriving from Mexico. Many Mexicans had been displaced from their homes by the Mexican-American War.

Most Mexican immigrants settled in the Southwest, where they found work on the railroads and in construction companies, steel mills, mines, and canneries. Other Mexican immigrants worked on large commercial farms in Arizona, Texas, and California.

READING CHECK **Summarizing** How did new immigrants help themselves and others?

Opposition to Immigration

Anti-immigrant feelings grew along with the rise in immigration in the late 1800s. Some labor unions opposed immigration because their members feared immigrants

Critical Thinking: Supporting a Point of View

Standards Proficiency

Political Cartoons

HSS 8.12.7; HSS **Analysis Skills:** HI 1, HI 2

1. Review with the class the opposition that emerged to immigration in the late 1800s. Tell students that despite opposition, immigration continued, and many Americans supported immigration.
2. Ask students to brainstorm reasons why nativists failed to slow immigration. Then have each student create a political cartoon that is critical of the nativist response to immigration.
3. Remind students that political cartoons attempt to point out a problem or make a point about an issue, often using humor. Ask students to use symbols or people to represent ideas and to make their cartoon easy to understand.
4. Ask volunteers to share their political cartoons with the class. Then lead a class discussion about the main points of the cartoons and how the creators of the cartoons made their point.

Alternative Assessment Handbook, Rubric 27: Political Cartoons

Answers

Analyzing Information *possible answers—economic opportunity, freedom, escape from oppression*

Reading Check *They published newspapers and founded schools, clubs, and places of worship; opened local shops and small neighborhood banks; formed benevolent societies.*

would take jobs away. Many business leaders, however, wanted low-paid workers because they kept labor costs low.

Other Americans called nativists feared that too many new immigrants were being allowed into the country. Many nativists held racial and ethnic prejudices. Nativists thought that the new immigrants' poverty and presumed lack of education might harm American society.

Some nativists were violent toward immigrants. Others worked to pass laws stopping or limiting immigration. For example, in 1880, about 105,000 Chinese immigrants lived in the United States. Two years later, Congress passed the **Chinese Exclusion Act**, banning Chinese people from immigrating to the United States for 10 years. This law marked the first time a nationality was banned from entering the country. Although the law violated treaties with China, the Congress continued to renew the law for decades to come. In 1892, another law was passed restricting convicts, immigrants with certain diseases, and those likely to need public assistance.

To further lower the number of immigrants, nativists in Boston founded the **Immigration Restriction League** in 1894, which demanded that all immigrants know how to read and write before entering the country. Supporters hoped this policy would limit immigration from eastern and southern Europe. Despite such opposition, immigrants continued to arrive in large numbers.

ACADEMIC VOCABULARY
policy rule, course of action

READING CHECK **Analyzing** Why did nativists oppose immigration, and what steps did they take against it?

SUMMARY AND PREVIEW Immigrants helped build the nation's economy and cities, but they met some resistance. In the next section you will learn about life in urban America.

Section 4 Assessment

go.hrw.com
Online Quiz
KEYWORD: SS8 HP18

Reviewing Ideas, Terms, and People HSS 8.12.5, 8.12.7

1. a. **Identify** What was Ellis Island?
   b. **Contrast** What differences existed between the **old immigrants** and the **new immigrants**?
2. a. **Identify** What job opportunities were available to new immigrants?
   b. **Summarize** How did immigrants attempt to adapt to their new lives in the United States?
   c. **Elaborate** Why do you think many immigrants tolerated difficult living and working conditions?
3. a. **Recall** How did the **Chinese Exclusion Act** affect the Chinese American population?
   b. **Explain** Why were some American business leaders supportive of the new immigrants?
   c. **Predict** How might the growing opposition to immigration lead to problems in the United States?

Critical Thinking

4. **Drawing Conclusions** Copy the graphic organizer below onto your own sheet of paper. Use it to identify the struggles of new immigrants.

FOCUS ON WRITING

5. **Writing about Immigrants and Their Lives** Add new immigrants to the list of potential characters for your series. Take notes about what life was like for them.

Direct Teach

Did you know . . .

Opponents to immigration did have some success limiting the flow of immigrants to the United States. A law passed in 1891 banned the immigration of contract laborers, criminals, polygamists, people without a means of earning a living, and people with a contagious disease.

Review & Assess

Close

Have students discuss immigration to the United States in the late 1800s. Do they think it helped or hurt the United States?

Review

Online Quiz, Section 4

Assess

SE Section 4 Assessment
PASS: Section 4 Quiz
Alternative Assessment Handbook

Reteach/Classroom Intervention

California Standards Review Workbook
Interactive Reader and Study Guide, Section 4
Interactive Skills Tutor CD-ROM

Section 4 Assessment Answers

1. **a.** immigration processing center in New York
   b. new—from southern and eastern Europe and Mexico; old—from western Europe
2. **a.** unskilled jobs in garment or steel factories, some opened small businesses
   b. lived with immigrants from same country, kept traditions, encouraged children to adopt American customs, founded places of worship, schools, and benevolent societies
   c. possible answers—willing to tolerate difficulties to live in the US; it was an improvement over life in their native lands
3. **a.** caused the Chinese population to drop
   b. wanted many new and low paid workers
   c. possible answers—increasing polarization, social tension, possibility of violence
4. education—did not speak English, often lacked formal education; culture—different customs and religions; work—forced to take low-paying jobs; living conditions—poorly built tenements
5. Students should add immigrants to their list of characters and describe what their life was like.

Answers

Reading Check *They held prejudices against immigrants and thought the new immigrants' poverty and lack of education would hurt American society; they took part in violence against immigrants and worked to get laws passed to stop or limit immigration.*

Preteach

Bellringer

If YOU were there . . . Use the **Daily Bellringer Transparency** to help students answer the question.

 Daily Bellringer Transparency, Section 5

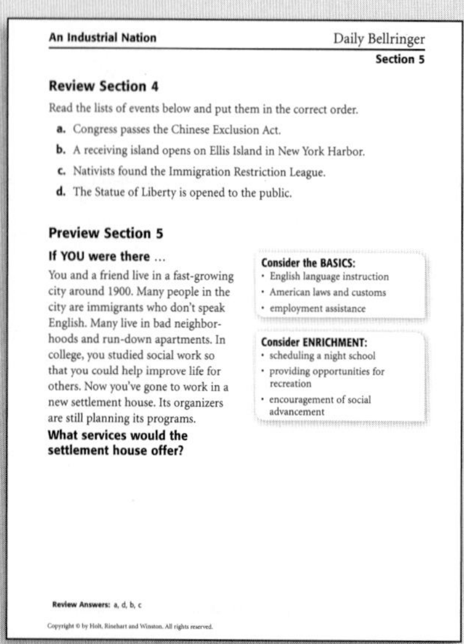

An Industrial Nation — Daily Bellringer — Section 5

Review Section 4

Read the lists of events below and put them in the correct order.

- **a.** Congress passes the Chinese Exclusion Act.
- **b.** A receiving island opens on Ellis Island in New York Harbor.
- **c.** Nativists found the Immigration Restriction League.
- **d.** The Statue of Liberty is opened to the public.

Preview Section 5

If YOU were there ...

You and a friend live in a fast-growing city around 1900. Many people in the city are immigrants who don't speak English. Many live in bad neighborhoods and run-down apartments. In college, you studied social work so that you could help improve life for others. Now you've gone to work in a new settlement house. Its organizers are still planning its programs.

What services would the settlement house offer?

Consider the BASICS:
- English language instruction
- American laws and customs
- employment assistance

Consider ENRICHMENT:
- scheduling a night school
- providing opportunities for recreation
- encouragement of social advancement

Review Answers: a, d, b, c

Building Vocabulary

Preteach or review the following term:

sanitation disposal of waste or sewage (p. 596)

CRF: Vocabulary Builder Activity, Section 5

Standards Focus

HSS 8.12.5

Means: Examine where urbanization, new immigration, and industrialization took place and identify their effects on cities and society.

Matters: Industrialization and immigration led to the rapid growth of large cities and changes in culture and society in the United States.

SECTION 5

City Life

What You Will Learn...

Main Ideas

1. New technology and ideas were developed to deal with the growth of urban areas.
2. The rapid growth of cities created a variety of urban problems.

The Big Idea

Cities in the United States experienced dramatic expansion in the late 1800s.

Key Terms and People

mass transit, *p. 595*
suburbs, *p. 595*
mass culture, *p. 595*
department stores, *p. 596*
settlement houses, *p. 597*
Hull House, *p. 597*
Jane Addams, *p. 597*

HSS 8.12.5 Examine the location and effects of urbanization, renewed immigration, and industrialization (e.g., the effects on social fabric of cities, wealth and economic opportunity, the conservation movement).

If YOU were there...

You and a friend live in a fast-growing city around 1900. Many people in the city are immigrants who don't speak English. Many live in bad neighborhoods and run-down apartments. In college, you studied social work so that you could help improve life for others. Now you've gone to work in a new settlement house. Its organizers are still planning its programs.

What services would the settlement house offer?

BUILDING BACKGROUND Industrial growth and a new wave of immigration swelled the populations of American cities in the late 1800s. City life offered excitement and new kinds of entertainment, but urban areas also had problems with overcrowding and poor living conditions.

Growth of Urban Areas

During the late 1800s, immigrants and native-born Americans moved to cities in record numbers, causing rapid urban growth. In 1850, only six U.S. cities had a population greater than 100,000. By 1900 there were more than 35 such cities.

In midwestern cities the population grew especially rapidly during these years. Chicago's population rose from 30,000 in 1850 to 1.7 million in 1900. By 1900 about 40 percent of Americans lived in urban areas.

Some city residents were businesspeople and skilled workers. But many more were poor laborers. As farm equipment replaced people in the countryside, large numbers of rural residents moved to the cities. In the 1890s African Americans from the rural South began moving to northern cities to seek jobs, as did thousands of immigrants. They hoped to escape discrimination and find better economic and educational opportunities.

New Technology

The rapid growth of cities placed a great strain on available downtown space. In the mid-1800s typical downtown city buildings were five stories tall. Larger structures had been impossible to construct,

Teach the Big Idea: Master the Standards

Reaching Standards

City Life HSS 8.12.5; HSS **Analysis Skills:** HI 1, HI 2

1. **Teach** Ask students the Main Idea questions to teach this section.
2. **Apply** Have students make a list of innovations that enabled cities to grow, such as skyscrapers and elevators, and why cities attracted people. Have students make a second list of city problems and how people attempted to address those problems. **LS Verbal/Linguistic**
3. **Review** Discuss city life with students. Then take a class poll on whether or not students would have moved to cities. Have volunteers share reasons why they would have enjoyed or disliked city life.
4. **Practice/Homework** Have students write a short essay explaining whether or not they believe the advantages of living in an American city in the late 1800s outweighed the disadvantages. **LS Verbal/Linguistic**

Alternative Assessment Handbook, Rubrics 11: Discussions; and 37: Writing Assignments

Steel-Framed Buildings

Architect Louis Sullivan helped pioneer the design of department stores with this building, built for Carson, Pirie, and Scott Co. in 1912. Sullivan also designed the Chicago Stock Exchange building and other buildings across the country. The building was designed using steel as a strong frame.

How do you think the steel industry influenced architects such as Louis Sullivan?

because building materials were either too weak or too heavy to be used in taller buildings. However, this situation changed as stronger and cheaper steel became available. Soon architects such as Louis Sullivan of Chicago began designing multistory buildings called skyscrapers. These buildings used metal frames to support their weight. They allowed developers to use limited city space more efficiently. New devices like the safety elevator, patented by Elisha Otis in 1857, helped people quickly move up and down inside skyscrapers.

As city centers became heavily populated, attempts were made to ease traffic through **mass transit**, or public transportation designed to move lots of people. By the late 1860s New York City had elevated trains running on tracks above the streets. Chicago followed in the early 1890s.

Some cities built underground railroads that were called subways. In 1897 the first subway in the United States opened in Boston. In 1904, the first line of the New York City subway system began operation. Cable cars, first used in the 1870s, became quite common. Electric trolleys also achieved popularity during the 1890s. These streetcars cheaply and quickly carried people in the cities to and from work.

Many middle-class Americans who could afford it moved to **suburbs**, residential neighborhoods outside of downtown areas. Mass transit networks, such as trolleys, subways, and commuter trains, made such moves possible. People could live in the suburbs and work in the cities.

New Ideas

The United States began to develop forms of **mass culture**, or leisure and cultural activities shared by many people. One factor contributing to mass culture was a boom in publishing. The invention of the Linotype, an automatic typesetting machine, greatly reduced the time and cost of printing. In 1850 there were fewer than 300 daily newspapers in the United States. Because of the use of Linotype machines, by 1900 there were more than 2,000 newspapers.

Direct Teach

Main Idea

1 Growth of Urban Areas

New technology and ideas were developed to deal with the growth of urban areas.

Explain Why did U.S. cities grow rapidly in the late 1800s? *rural residents moved to cities as farm equipment replaced their labor, African Americans from the South and immigrants began moving to cities to seek jobs*

Draw Conclusions Why did some people begin to move to suburbs? *to escape overcrowding and poor conditions in cities and because mass transit could now transport them to their jobs in cities*

CRF: Primary Source Activity: A Selection from McGuffey's Reader

HSS 8.12.5; HSS **Analysis Skills:** CS 1, HI 1, HI 2

Info to Know

Introduction of Skyscrapers A group of architects led by engineer William Le Baron Jenney used iron or steel girders for the frames of their innovative skyscraper designs. In 1884 these architects, called the Chicago School, finished their first triumph—the Home Insurance Company Building of Chicago. Their buildings, some of which were only eight stories high, towered above neighboring structures. Moreover, they caught on largely because of other new inventions such as elevators and electric lights.

Differentiating Instruction for Universal Access

Learners Having Difficulty

Reaching Standards

1. To help students understand the growth of cities and the new ideas and technology associated with urbanization, draw the chart for students to see. Omit the blue, italicized answers.
2. Have students copy the chart and complete it by identifying the benefits of many urban ideas and technologies. LS **Visual/Spatial, Verbal/Linguistic**

HSS 8.12.5; HSS **Analysis Skills:** HI 1, HI 2

Urban Developments	Benefits
Skyscrapers	• *enabled developers to utilize limited city space more efficiently*
Mass Transit	• *allowed people to live in suburbs and work in city* • *quick and cheap travel*
Mass Culture	• *newspapers* • *department stores* • *open public spaces*

Answers

Steel-Framed Buildings *Stronger and cheaper iron made it possible to build new kinds of buildings.*

Direct Teach

Main Idea

❷ Urban Problems

The rapid growth of cities created a variety of urban problems.

Define What is a settlement house? *a neighborhood center in a poor area*

Describe What were some of the problems experienced by people living in tenements? *overcrowding, health problems caused by lack of sanitation, little fresh air or natural light, lack of running water, safety standards were not upheld, landlords did not fix things, fire, and crime*

Draw Conclusions How do you think settlement houses benefited the poor? *possible answers—offered education, recreation, and social activities; gave the poor a place to escape bad living conditions and connect with other people*

Political Cartoons Activities for United States History, Cartoon 21: Urban Life and Tenements

HSS 8.12.5; HSS **Analysis Skills:** CS 1, HI 1

Info to Know

Mass Culture and Sports Another example of mass culture was the rise of spectator sports like baseball and basketball. In 1869 Aaron Champion organized the first professional baseball team, the Cincinnati Red Stockings. By 1890 professional baseball teams across the United States were drawing an estimated 60,000 fans daily. In Springfield, Massachusetts James Naismith invented the game of basketball in 1891. By the mid-1890s colleges had created both male and female teams. Basketball was one of the few sports during the late 1800s in which women's participation was encouraged.

Answers

Hull House *by educating them in kindergarten*

Reading Check *newspapers, department stores, world fairs, amusement parks, public parks*

Big cities often had many newspapers. Newspaper publishers such as Joseph Pulitzer and William Randolph Hearst competed for readers by using color printing. By 1900 the daily newspaper had become a powerful cultural force in people's lives.

Giant retail shops, or **department stores**, also appeared in some city centers during the late 1800s. Low prices, large quantities of products, and newspaper advertising were used to bring in customers. The public was also attracted by fancy window displays.

World fairs are another example of mass culture. At the Philadelphia Centennial Exposition in 1876 and the Chicago Exposition in 1893, millions of people came to see the latest technological inventions. The demand for public entertainment also led to the creation of amusement parks, such as New York's Coney Island. People from all walks of life were able to enjoy these parks because of inexpensive train fares and entrance tickets.

As cities grew, people became aware of the need for open public space. The large-scale landscape architect Frederick Law Olmsted became nationally famous. He designed Central Park in New York City as well as many state and national parks.

READING CHECK **Summarizing** What forms of mass culture were available in urban areas?

Urban Problems

Despite the new public parks, skyscrapers, and mass transit, many urban areas were not ready for rapid population growth in the late 1800s. Population increases in cities often led to shortages of affordable housing.

Many families lived in tiny apartments in overcrowded tenements. Journalist Jacob Riis described these conditions: "Nine lived in two rooms, one about ten feet square that served as parlor, bedroom, and eating room, the other a small hall room made into a kitchen."

Overcrowding and lack of sanitation often led to disease and health problems. Tenements frequently were packed together in areas close to factories. Rooms had few windows to let in light or fresh air. Running water and indoor plumbing were scarce. Most cities did not have laws requiring landlords to fix their tenements or to maintain safety standards.

Fire and crime were also common problems. By the late 1800s, many major cities were

Hull House

Neighborhood children attended kindergarten at Hull House in Chicago. Their parents, who were members of the working poor, were often immigrants. Children like these had few other options for education.

How did Hull House try to improve the lives of children?

Critical Thinking: Supporting a Point of View

Standards Proficiency

Writing a Petition HSS 8.12.5; HSS **Analysis Skills:** CS 1, HI 1, HI 2

1. Review with the class the difficulties of tenement life. Have students create lists of the problems that existed in tenement buildings.
2. Ask students to imagine that they live in a large city in the late 1800s. Tenement residents have decided to organize and demand improvements. Ask students to imagine that they have been elected to serve on the improvement committee.
3. Have each student draft a petition to the building's owner demanding changes. The petition should name and describe each problem in the building, its impact on the residents, and a proposed solution to the problem.
4. After students have finished their draft, have them discuss their ideas and come to consensus on a final petition.
5. Display the class petition for everyone to see. **LS Verbal/Linguistic, Interpersonal**

Alternative Assessment Handbook, Rubrics 11: Discussions; and 37: Writing Assignments hiring full-time firefighters and peace officers. Other than these improvements, the reform work of most city governments was limited by internal corruption or lack of funds.

Due to the lack of government aid in the 1800s, many private organizations stepped in to help the poor. Some individuals set up **settlement houses**, or neighborhood centers in poor areas that offered education, recreation, and social activities. Settlement houses were staffed by professionals and volunteers.

The most famous settlement house was Chicago's **Hull House**. It was founded by **Jane Addams** and Ellen Gates Starr in 1889. Addams and Starr moved into a run-down building in a poor neighborhood and turned it into Hull House. The staff focused on the needs of immigrant families and also worked for reforms, such as child labor laws and the eight-hour workday.

READING CHECK **Drawing Conclusions** What technologies improved city life?

BIOGRAPHY

Jane Addams

1860–1935

Jane Addams was born in Cedarville, Illinois. Like many upper-class women of the era, she received a college education but found few jobs open to her. In 1888, on a visit to England with classmate Ellen Gates Starr, she visited a London settlement house. On their return to the United States, Addams and Starr opened a settlement house in Chicago. They started a kindergarten and a public playground. Addams also became involved in housing safety and sanitation issues, factory inspection, and immigrants' rights. In 1931 she shared the Nobel Peace Prize for her work.

Summarizing How did Jane Addams try to improve the lives of workers?

SUMMARY AND PREVIEW In the late 1800s many people came to cities to find work, causing a variety of problems. In the next chapter you will learn about how a new spirit of political reform swept the nation.

Section 5 Assessment

go.hrw.com
Online Quiz
KEYWORD: SS8 HP18

Reviewing Ideas, Terms, and People HSS 8.12.5

1. a. **Define** What is **mass transit?** What made mass transit necessary?
   b. **Explain** Why did African Americans move to northern cities in such large numbers in the 1890s?
   c. **Evaluate** Which improvement to urban living do you think had the greatest impact on people's lives? Explain your answer.
2. a. **Describe** What were conditions like in tenements?
   b. **Summarize** What problems resulted from the rapid growth of cities?
   c. **Evaluate** Do you think efforts to improve urban problems were successful? Why or why not?

Critical Thinking

3. **Categorizing** Copy the chart below onto your own sheet of paper. Use it to identify the problems faced by growing cities in the late 1800s and responses to those problems.

Urban Problem	Response

FOCUS ON WRITING

4. **Describing Setting** A city like the ones you have read about could serve as the setting of your TV series. How could you describe the city?

Direct Teach

Did you know . . .

In 1850 the city of Chicago had a population of some 30,000 people and a police force of only nine people! In 1855 that force was increased to 90.

Linking to Today

Hull House Association The goals and work of Jane Addams live on in the form of the Jane Addams Hull House Association. The organization, which operates close to 100 programs, has maintained Jane Addam's goal of improving people's self-reliance. Some of these programs include child care, foster care, job training, and literacy.

Review & Assess

Close

Ask students to discuss the reasons for rapid urbanization and some of the problems and new technologies that resulted.

Review

go.hrw.com Online Quiz, Section 5

Assess

SE Section 5 Assessment

PASS: Section 5 Quiz

Alternative Assessment Handbook

Reteach/Classroom Intervention

California Standards Review Workbook

Interactive Reader and Study Guide, Section 5

Interactive Skills Tutor CD-ROM

Section 5 Assessment Answers

1. a. public transportation; as cities became more crowded and people moved further from city centers, it became necessary to find a way to move people quickly and cheaply.
   b. in search of jobs, better economic and educational opportunities, and to escape discrimination
   c. Answers will vary but should reflect students' knowledge of technologies and ideas that improved life during this period.
2. a. They were crowded, unsafe, and unhealthy.
   b. shortages of affordable housing, crime, overcrowding, corruption or lack of funds in city governments
   c. Answers will vary but should reflect students' knowledge of the efforts made to improve urban problems.
3. crime—development of police forces; housing problems—creation of settlement houses; fire—development of fire departments
4. Students should take notes on the setting of urban America described in this section for their drama series.

Answers

Biography *She opened a settlement house and became involved in housing safety, sanitation issues, factory inspection, and immigrants' rights.*

Reading Check *mass transit, safety elevator, Linotype*

Social Studies Skills

Analyzing Costs and Benefits

Activity Cost-Benefit Analysis in the News Find a newspaper article about a current event in which students might be interested (an election, trial, arrest, environmental concern, and so on). The event and the article's coverage of it should provide students with enough information to determine costs and benefits. Provide each student with a photocopy of the article. Create a costs-benefits chart for students to see. Model the activity by listing one cost and one benefit. Then have students complete the chart independently. Review students' answers as a class. Encourage discussion of any effects that some students see as benefits and other students see as costs.

LS Logical/Mathematical

Alternative Assessment Handbook, Rubric 7: Charts

HSS Analysis Skills: HI 6

Social Studies Skills

Analysis | Critical Thinking | Participation | Study

HSS HI 6 Students interpret basic indicators of economic performance and conduct cost-benefit analyses of economic and political issues.

Analyzing Costs and Benefits

Define the Skill

Everything you do has both costs and benefits connected to it. *Benefits* are things that you gain from something. *Costs* are what you give up to obtain benefits. For example, if you buy a video game, the benefits of your action include the game itself and the enjoyment of playing it. The most clear cost is what you pay for the game. However, there are other costs that do not involve money. One is the time you spend playing the game. This is a cost because you give up something else, such as doing your homework or watching a TV show, when you choose to play the game.

The ability to analyze costs and benefits is a valuable life skill as well as a useful tool in the study of history. Weighing an action's benefits against its costs can help you decide whether or not to take it.

Learn the Skill

Analyzing the costs and benefits of historical events will help you to better understand and evaluate them. Follow these guidelines to do a cost-benefit analysis of an action or decision in history.

1. First determine what the action or decision was trying to accomplish. This step is needed in order to determine which its effects were benefits and which were costs.
2. Then look for the positive or successful results of the action or decision. These are its benefits.
3. Consider the negative or unsuccessful effects of the action or decision. Also think about what positive things would have happened if it had *not* occurred. All these things are its costs.
4. Making a chart of the costs and benefits can be useful. By comparing the list of benefits to the list of costs you can better understand the action or decision and evaluate it.

For example, you learned in Chapter 18 that the United States attracted millions of new immigrants in the late 1800s. A cost-benefit analysis of the nation's immigration policies might produce a chart like this one.

Benefits	Costs
Immigrants provided workers needed by growing industries	Overcrowding and poor living conditions in U.S. cities
Immigrants made more money that they could have in their home countries	Low wages paid to immigrants kept the earnings of other workers down
Immigrants found more opportunity in America then in their home countries	Long hours of work under poor conditions for low pay
Immigrants built strong futures for their families	

Based on this chart, one might conclude that the nation's immigration policy was a good one.

Practice the Skill

Among the changes that occurred in the early 1900s was an increase in specialization and efficiency in the workplace. Use information from the chapter and the guidelines above to do a cost-benefit analysis of this development. Then write a paragraph explaining whether or not it was a wise one.

Social Studies Skills Activity: Analyzing Costs and Benefits

Big Business Costs-and-Benefits Chart

HSS Analysis Skills: HI 6 **Standards Proficiency**

1. Lead a brief review of Section 2, which covers the growth of big business.
2. Ask students to create costs-and-benefits charts for the growth of big business. Break down the topic and assign students either corporations, horizontal and vertical integration, trusts, or government antitrust measures.
3. Have volunteers share their answers as you complete master charts for the class to see. Then have students use the activity to analyze government policy in dealing with big business. **LS Logical/Mathematical**
4. **Extend** Have each student write a short essay analyzing government policies toward trusts based on the cost-benefit analysis.

Alternative Assessment Handbook, Rubrics 7: Charts; and 37: Writing Assignments

Answers

Practice the Skill *possible benefits—increased production, lower costs of production, greater use of machines, less need for workers' skills, greater control over workers and the workplace; possible costs—lower pay, loss of worker freedom, worsening working conditions; factors that might be listed as benefits or costs—rise of labor unions; Students' final analyses should provide a valid interpretation of the cost-benefit analysis provided.*

CHAPTER 18

Standards Review

Visual Summary

Use the visual summary below to help you review the main ideas of the chapter.

QUICK FACTS

Inventions and Big Business
- Bessemer process
- Lightbulb
- Automobile
- Growth of corporations

Immigration
- New immigrants from eastern and southern Europe
- Nativism
- Benevolent societies

Labor Movement
- Knights of Labor
- American Federation of Labor
- Haymarket Riot
- Homestead Strike

Reviewing Vocabulary, Terms, and People

Identify the descriptions below with the correct term or person from the chapter.

1. Labor organization that represented both skilled and unskilled laborers and was the first national labor union in the United States
2. Public transportation systems built to ease transportation in crowded cities
3. A way of making steel quickly and cheaply by blasting hot air through melted iron to quickly remove waste
4. Founded Hull House with Ellen Gates Starr in Chicago in 1889
5. Powerful business leader who helped to found the Central Pacific Railroad
6. Organizations created by immigrants to help each other in times of sickness, unemployment, or other troubles
7. A method of negotiating for better wages or working conditions in which all workers act together to ensure a better chance for success

Comprehension and Critical Thinking

SECTION 1 *(Pages 574–578)* **HSS 8.12.1, 8.12.9**

8. a. **Identify** What was the Second Industrial Revolution?

   b. **Draw Conclusions** Why were advances in transportation and communication important to the Second Industrial Revolution?

   c. **Elaborate** Which invention do you think had the greatest effect on people's live in the late 1800s? Explain your answer.

SECTION 2 *(Pages 579–582)* **HSS 8.12.3, 8.12.4, 8.12.6**

9. a. **Recall** What criticisms were made of business leaders and trusts?

   b. **Analyze** How did the rise of corporations and powerful business leaders lead to the growth of big business?

   c. **Evaluate** Do you think the growth of big business helped or hurt ordinary Americans? Explain your answer.

Answers

Visual Summary

Review and Inquiry Have students use the chapter visual summary to identify the effects of the Second Industrial Revolution and immigration.

Quick Facts Transparency: An Industrial Nation Visual Summary

Reviewing Vocabulary, Terms, and People

1. Knights of Labor
2. mass transit
3. Bessemer process
4. Jane Addams
5. Leland Stanford
6. benevolent societies
7. collective bargaining

Comprehension and Critical Thinking

8. **a.** a time in the late 1800s of rapid growth in U.S. manufacturing and production

   b. Advances like the telephone and automobiles and airplanes helped improve production and growth in the United States.

   c. Answers will vary, but students should indicate the effects of the invention on people's lives.

9. **a.** They earned money through unfair business practices and used their size and strength to drive smaller competitors out of business.

   b. They used practices like vertical integration and trusts to dominate entire industries, create monopolies, and drive competitors out of business.

Review and Assessment Resources

Review and Reinforce

- **SE** Standards Review
- **CRF:** Chapter Review Activity
- California Standards Review Workbook
- Quick Facts Transparency: An Industrial Nation Visual Summary
- Spanish Chapter Summaries Audio CD Program
- Online Chapter Summaries in Six Languages
- **OSP** Holt PuzzlePro; GameTool for ExamView
- Quiz Game CD-ROM

Assess

- **SE** Standards Assessment
- PASS: Chapter Test, Forms A and B
- Alternative Assessment Handbook
- **OSP** ExamView Test Generator, Chapter Test
- Universal Access Modified Worksheets and Tests CD-ROM: Chapter Test
- Holt Online Assessment Program (in the Premier Online Edition)

Reteach/Intervene

- Interactive Reader and Study Guide
- Universal Access Teacher Management System: Lesson Plans for Universal Access
- Universal Access Modified Worksheets and Tests CD-ROM
- Interactive Skills Tutor CD-ROM

go.hrw.com
Online Resources
Chapter Resources:
KEYWORD: SS8 US18

Answers

c. possible answers: helped—it led to important advances like oil and steel production and provided more jobs; hurt—it led to the creation of trusts which created higher prices and drove small competitors out of business

10. a. Scientific management led many managers to pay less attention to working conditions, machines replaced skilled workers with unskilled workers, and specialization made employees tired, bored, and more likely to be injured.

b. Labor unions represented large numbers of workers and could use collective bargaining to negotiate with business owners, while individuals had no such influence.

c. possible answer—They hurt the labor movement because many unions declined in membership as a result of labor strikes.

11. a. from southern and eastern Europe and Mexico

b. Immigrants in the late 1800s were from eastern and southern Europe, while previous immigrants had come from Great Britain, Germany, Ireland, and Scandinavia.

c. Students' answers will vary, but they should show an understanding of the difficulties faced by immigrants and reasons why immigrants came to the United States.

12. a. Rapid growth occurred as a result of the wave of immigration to the United States, and as rural residents and African Americans moved to cities in search of jobs.

b. transportation problems, housing shortages, overcrowding, lack of sanitation, and crime; addressed problems by creating mass transit systems and private aid organizations, like settlement houses, to help improve neighborhoods

c. possible answers: in cities—because there were many sources of entertainment and to be close to jobs; in suburbs—to be away from overcrowded cities

SECTION 3 *(Pages 584–587)* **HSS 8.12.6**

10. a. Recall What led to poor working conditions in factories during the Second Industrial Revolution?

b. Make Inferences Why did labor unions have a better chance of improving working conditions than laborers did on their own?

c. Evaluate Did the strikes of the 1880s and 1890s hurt or help the labor movement in the long run? Explain your answer.

SECTION 4 *(Pages 588–593)* **HSS 8.12.7**

11. a. Identify From what parts of the world did the new wave of immigrants come?

b. Analyze In what ways did immigration patterns in the United States change in the late 1800s?

c. Elaborate In your opinion, were the difficulties immigrants faced worth the benefits of life in the United States? Explain.

SECTION 5 *(Pages 594–597)* **HSS 8.12.5**

12. a. Recall Why did American cities experience such rapid growth in the late 1800s?

b. Analyze What problems did cities face as a result of rapid growth, and how were these problems solved?

c. Elaborate Would you have preferred to live in the city or in a suburb? Why?

Reviewing Themes

13. Economics How did the rise of big business affect consumers in the United States?

14. Society and Culture How did the lives of city dwellers change with the rise of mass culture?

Using the Internet

15. Activity: Creating a Time Line Technology in some sense has been part of human history since we began to write history. All tools are, in a sense, technology. In this chapter you read about new scientific discoveries that had positive and negative effects. Enter the activity keyword. Then choose one technological innovation mentioned in the chapter and trace its development to the present day. Create an illustrated time line to present your research.

Reading Skills

Understanding the Structural Patterns of Texts *Use the Reading Skills taught in this chapter to answer the question about the reading selection below.*

> New arrivals had to go to immigration processing centers run by state and local governments. In 1892 a receiving office was opened on Ellis Island in New York Harbor. Over the next 40 years, millions of immigrants came through the Ellis Island center. *(p. 589)*

16. By which structural pattern is the above passage organized?

a. enumeration

b. chronology

c. comparison and contrast

d. cause and effect

Social Studies Skills

Analyzing Cost and Benefits *Use the Social Studies Skills taught in this chapter to answer the question below.*

17. Write two costs and two benefits of the Pullman Strike from the point of view of the workers who participated.

Focus on Writing

18. Writing Your Memo Look back over your notes about the people, places, and events of the late 1800s. Decide which of these you will include in your television drama series. Then draft a one- to two-paragraph memo to your boss briefly describing the series. Remember to describe the basic plot, setting, and characters.

Reviewing Themes

13. led to monopolies and trusts, which drove competition out of business and forced prices to rise

14. more entertainment such as "window shopping," fairs, amusement parks, and public parks

Using the Internet

15. Go to the HRW Web site and enter the keyword shown to access a rubric for this activity.

KEYWORD: SS8 TEACHER

Reading Skills

16. b

Social Studies Skills

17. possible answers: costs—they could lose their jobs; benefits—higher wages, shorter working hours, improved working conditions

Focus on Writing

18. Rubric Students' memos should:

- describe series' plot, characters, and setting
- include correct spelling, punctuation, and grammar

Standards Assessment

DIRECTIONS: Read each question and write the letter of the best response. Use the map below to answer question 1.

1

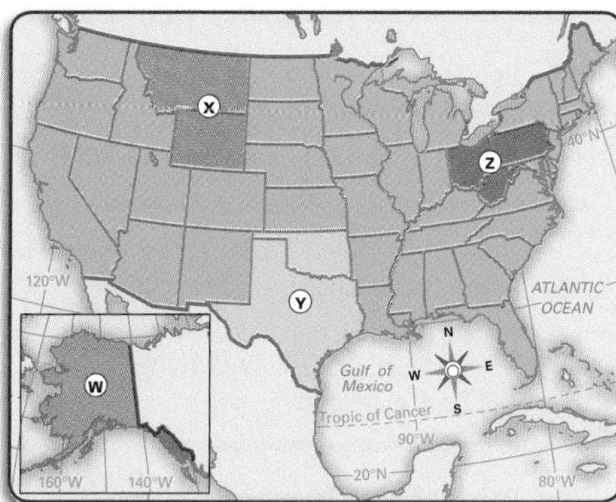

Which area on the map provided the petroleum for the oil-refining industry that arose in the United States in the mid- to late 1800s?

A the area labeled W
B the area labeled X
C the area labeled Y
D the area labeled Z

2 The person *most* responsible for making the steel industry a big business in the United States is

A John D. Rockefeller.
B Andrew Carnegie.
C Henry Bessemer.
D Leland Stanford.

3 The growth of American industry in the late 1800s was accompanied by all of the following developments *except*

A the arrival of large numbers of immigrants.
B the organization of workers into labor unions.
C declining food production from U.S. farms.
D rapid population growth in U.S. cities.

4 Which of the following is associated with providing a better life for urban immigrants in the late 1800s and early 1900s?

A the department store
B the suburb
C the tenement
D the settlement house

5 Immigrants to the United States in the late 1800s and early 1900s came *mainly* from

A southern and eastern Europe.
B Japan, China, and the rest of Asia.
C Mexico and Central America.
D northern and western Europe.

Connecting with Past Learning

6 In Grade 7 you learned about Johann Gutenberg's development of the printing press. The contribution of which American listed below was *least* like Gutenberg's?

A Samuel Gompers
B George Westinghouse
C Thomas Edison
D Alexander Graham Bell

7 The attitudes of the Immigration Restriction League in the late 1800s were *most* like those of Americans in earlier times who were part of the

A Free-Soil Party.
B Know-Nothing Party.
C abolitionist movement.
D transcendentalist movement.

Answers

1. D
Break Down the Question Students should recall from Section 1 that prospectors drilled for oil in Ohio, Pennsylvania and West Virginia.

2. B
Break Down the Question Point out to students that the question asks who made steel a big business, not who improved steel technology.

3. C
Break Down the Question Remind students that the word *except* in the question indicates that they should look for the choice that is not true.

4. D
Break Down the Question Students should recall that settlement houses worked to improve conditions in immigrant neighborhoods.

5. A
Break Down the Question This question requires students to recall factual information from Section 4.

6. A
Break Down the Question Students should recall that like Gutenberg, Westinghouse, Edison, and Bell were all inventors, whereas Gompers was involved in the labor movement.

7. B
Break Down the Question This question requires students to recall factual information from Chapter 11.

Intervention Resources

Reproducible

- Interactive Reader and Study Guide
- Universal Access Teacher Management System: Lesson Plans for Universal Access

Technology

- Quick Facts Transparency: An Industrial Nation Visual Summary
- Universal Access Modified Worksheets and Tests CD-ROM
- Interactive Skills Tutor CD-ROM

Tips for Test Taking

I'm Stuck! Read the following to students: If you come across a question that stumps you, don't get frustrated or worried. First master the question to make sure you understand what is being asked and then work through many of the strategies you have previously learned. If you are still stuck, circle the question and go on to others. Come back to the problem question later. What if you still have no idea? Practice the 50/50 strategy and then take your best educated guess.

Standards Review

Have students review the following standards in their workbooks.

- California Standards Review Workbook: HSS 8.12.1, 8.12.4, 8.12.5, 8.12.6, 8.12.7, 8.12.9

Chapter 19 Planning Guide

The Spirit of Reform

Chapter Overview	Reproducible Resources	Technology Resources
CHAPTER 19 **pp. 602–635** **Overview: In this chapter, students will analyze the Reform Movement of the late 1800s and early 1900s.** See p. 602 for the California History–Social Science standards covered in this chapter.	**Universal Access Teacher Management System:*** • Universal Access Instructional Benchmarking Guides • Lesson Plans for Universal Access **Interactive Reader and Study Guide:*** Chapter Graphic Organizer **Chapter Resource File*** • Focus on Writing Activity: Campaign Promises • Social Studies Skills Activity: Short- and Long-Term Causal Patterns • Chapter Review Activity	**One-Stop Planner CD-ROM:** Calendar Planner **Student Edition Full-Read Audio CD-ROM** **Universal Access Modified Worksheets and Tests CD-ROM** **Power Presentations with Video CD-ROM** **History's Impact: United States History Video Program (VHS/DVD):** The Spirit of Reform*
Section 1: **The Gilded Age** **The Big Idea:** Politics during the Gilded Age was plagued by corruption. 8.12.5	**Universal Access Teacher Management System:*** Section 1 Lesson Plan **Interactive Reader and Study Guide:*** Section 1 Summary **Chapter Resource File*** • Vocabulary Builder, Section 1 **Political Cartoons Activities Guide for United States History,** Cartoon 22: Tammany Hall*	**Daily Bellringer Transparency:** Section 1* **Quick Facts Transparency:** Political Machines*
Section 2: **The Progressive Movement** **The Big Idea:** From the late 1800s through the early 1900s, the progressive movement addressed problems that faced American society. 8.12.5	**Universal Access Teacher Management System:*** Section 2 Lesson Plan **Interactive Reader and Study Guide:*** Section 2 Summary **Chapter Resource File*** • Vocabulary Builder, Section 2 • Biography Activity: Nellie Bly • Literature Activity: *The Making of an American* • Primary Source Activity: Jacob Riis	**Daily Bellringer Transparency:** Section 2* **Quick Facts Transparency:** Tenement Life* **Quick Facts Transparency:** Expanding Democracy* go.hrw.com **Internet Activity:** City Planning
Section 3: **Reforming the Workplace** **The Big Idea:** In the early 1900s progressives and reformers focused on improving conditions for American workers. 8.12.6	**Universal Access Teacher Management System:*** Section 3 Lesson Plan **Interactive Reader and Study Guide:*** Section 3 Summary **Chapter Resource File*** • Vocabulary Builder, Section 3 • Primary Source Activity: Reform Efforts **U.S. Supreme Court Case Studies:** *Lochner* v. *New York* (1905)	**Daily Bellringer Transparency:** Section 3*
Section 4: **The Rights of Women and Minorities** **The Big Idea:** The progressive movement made advances for the rights of women and some other minorities. 8.12.5	**Universal Access Teacher Management System:*** Section 4 Lesson Plan **Interactive Reader and Study Guide:*** Section 4 Summary **Chapter Resource File*** • Vocabulary Builder, Section 4 • Biography Activities: Wong Kim Ark; George Washington Carver; Ida B. Wells • History and Geography Activity: Patterns of Immigration • Primary Source Activity: Washington and Du Bois	**Daily Bellringer Transparency:** Section 4*
Section 5: **The Progressive Presidents** **The Big Idea:** American presidents in the early 1900s did a great deal to promote progressive reform. 8.12.5	**Universal Access Teacher Management System:*** Section 5 Lesson Plan **Interactive Reader and Study Guide:*** Section 5 Summary **Chapter Resource File*** • Vocabulary Builder, Section 5 • Biography Activity: John Muir **Political Cartoons Activities Guide for United States History,** Cartoon 23: The Power of Trusts*	**Daily Bellringer Transparency:** Section 5* **Map Transparency:** Election of 1912 **Quick Facts Transparency:** The Progressive Amendments, 1909–1920 go.hrw.com **Internet Activity:** National Park Service

SE Student Edition  Print Resource  Audio CD Video

TE Teacher's Edition  Transparency  CD-ROM  DVD

go.hrw.com CA Standards Mastery Learning Styles

OSP One-Stop Planner CD-ROM * also on One-Stop Planner CD

Review, Assessment, Intervention

 **Standards Review Workbook***

 **Quick Facts Transparency:** The Spirit of Reform Visual Summary*

 **Spanish Chapter Summaries Audio CD Program**

 **Progress Assessment Support System (PASS):** Chapter Test*

 **Universal Access Modified Worksheets and Tests CD-ROM:** Modified Chapter Test

 **One-Stop Planner CD-ROM:** ExamView Test Generator (English/Spanish)

 **PASS:** Section 1 Quiz*

 **Online Quiz:** Section 1

 **Alternative Assessment Handbook**

 **PASS:** Section 2 Quiz*

 **Online Quiz:** Section 2

 **Alternative Assessment Handbook**

 **PASS:** Section 3 Quiz*

 **Online Quiz:** Section 3

 **Alternative Assessment Handbook**

 **PASS:** Section 4 Quiz*

 **Online Quiz:** Section 4

 **Alternative Assessment Handbook**

 **PASS:** Section 5 Quiz*

 **Online Quiz:** Section 5

 **Alternative Assessment Handbook**

California Resources for Standards Mastery

INSTRUCTIONAL PLANNING AND SUPPORT

 **Universal Access Teacher Management System***

One-Stop Planner CD-ROM with Test Generator: Teacher Management System with Interactive Teacher's Edition

STANDARDS MASTERY

 **Standards Review Workbook***

 **At Home: A Guide to Standards Mastery for United States History**

go.hrw.com Holt Online Learning

To enhance learning, Internet activities are available for City Planning and National Park Service.

KEYWORD: SS8 TEACHER

- **Teacher Support Page**
- **Content Updates**
- **Rubrics and Writing Models**
- **Teaching Tips for the Multimedia Classroom**

KEYWORD: SS8 US19

- **Current Events**
- **Document-Based Questions**
- **Holt Grapher**
- **Holt Online Atlas**
- **Holt Researcher**
- **Interactive Multimedia Activities**
- **Internet Activities**
- **Online Chapter Summaries in Six Languages**
- **Online Section Quizzes**
- **American History Maps and Charts**

HOLT PREMIER ONLINE STUDENT EDITION

Complete online support for interactivity, assessment, and reporting

- **Interactive Maps and Notebook**
- **Standardized Test Prep**
- **Homework Practice and Research Activities Online**

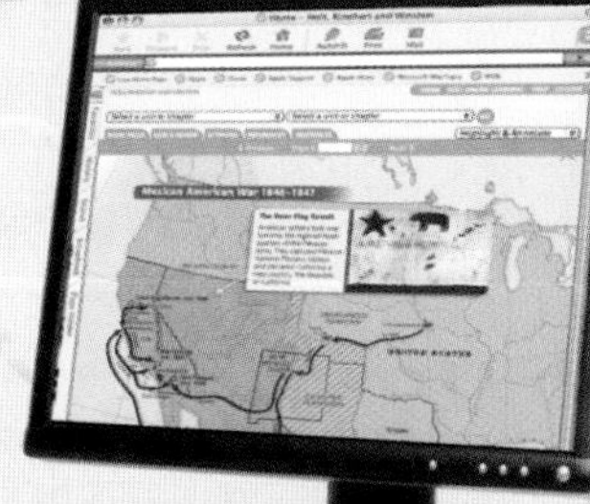

Mastering the Standards: Differentiating Instruction

Reaching Standards	Basic-level activities designed for all students encountering new material
Standards Proficiency	Intermediate-level activities designed for average students
Exceeding Standards	Challenging activities designed for honors and gifted-and-talented students
Standard English Mastery	Activities designed to improve standard English usage

Frequently Asked Questions

INSTRUCTIONAL PLANNING AND SUPPORT

Where do I find planning aids, pacing guides, lesson plans, and other teaching aids?

Annotated Teacher's Edition:
- Chapter planning guides
- Standards-based instruction and strategies
- Differentiated instruction for universal access
- Point-of-use reminders for integrating program resources

Power Presentations with Video CD-ROM

Universal Access Teacher Management System:
- Year and unit instructional benchmarking guides
- Reproducible lesson plans
- Assessment guides for diagnostic, progress, and summative end-of-the-year tests
- Options for differentiating instruction and intervention
- Teaching guides and answer keys for student workbooks

One-Stop Planner CD-ROM with Test Generator: Teacher Management System with Interactive Teacher's Editon:
- Calendar Planner
- Editable lesson plans
- All reproducible ancillaries in Adobe Acrobat (PDF) format
- ExamView Test Generator (English & Spanish)
- Game Tool for ExamView
- PuzzlePro
- Transparency and video previews

DIFFERENTIATING INSTRUCTION FOR UNIVERSAL ACCESS

What resources are available to ensure that Advanced Learners/GATE Students master the standards?

Teacher's Edition Activities:
- Documentary Film Script, p. 611
- Child Laborer Photo, p. 616
- Tenement Description, p. 620
- Women's Rights Poster, p. 623

Lesson Plans for Universal Access

Primary Source Library CD-ROM for United States History

What resources are available to ensure that English Learners and Standard English Learners master the standards?

Teacher's Edition Activities:
- Voting Reforms Poster, p. 613
- Visual Imagery Activity, p. 620

Lesson Plans for Universal Access

Chapter Resource File: Vocabulary Builder Activities

Spanish Chapter Summaries Audio CD Program

Online Chapter Summaries in Six Languages

One-Stop Planner CD-ROM:
- PuzzlePro, Spanish Version
- ExamView Test Generator, Spanish Version

What modified materials are available for Special Education?

Teacher's Edition Activities:
- Progressive Reformers, p. 612

The ***Universal Access Modified Worksheets and Tests CD-ROM*** provides editable versions of the following:

Vocabulary Flash Cards

Modified Vocabulary Builder Activities

Modified Chapter Review Activity

Modified Chapter Test

What resources are available to ensure that Learners Having Difficulty master the standards?

Teacher's Edition Activities:

- Labor Reform Time Line, p. 616
- Early Conservation Efforts, p. 628
- Roosevelt and Taft Venn Diagram, p. 629

Interactive Reader and Study Guide

Student Edition Full-Read Audio CD

Quick Facts Transparency: The Spirit of Reform Visual Summary

Standards Review Workbook

Social Studies Skills Activity: Short- and Long-Term Causal Patterns

Interactive Skills Tutor CD-ROM

How do I intervene for students struggling to master the standards?

Interactive Reader and Study Guide

Quick Facts Transparency: The Spirit of Reform Visual Summary

Standards Review Workbook

Social Studies Skills Activity: Short- and Long-Term Causal Patterns

Interactive Skills Tutor CD-ROM

PROFESSIONAL DEVELOPMENT

What teacher training resources are available to help me grow professionally?

- In-service and staff development as part of your Holt Social Studies product purchase
- Quick Teacher Tutorial Lesson Presentation CD-ROM
- Intensive tuition-based Teacher Development Institute
- *Teaching American History* Online 2 Module Professional Development Course
- Convenient Holt Speaker Bureau face-to-face workshop options
- PRAXIS™ Test Prep (#0089) interactive Web-based content refreshers*
- 24/7 *Ask A Professional Development Expert* at http://www.hrw.com/prodev/

* PRAXIS is a trademark of Educational Testing Service (ETS). This publication is not endorsed or approved by ETS.

Information Literacy Skills

To learn more about how History–Social Science instruction may be improved by the effective use of library media centers and information literacy skills, go to the Teacher's Resource Materials for Chapter 19 at **go.hrw.com**, keyword: SS8 MEDIA.

The following materials were developed by the Division for Public Education of the American Bar Association. These materials are part of the **Democracy and Civic Education** supplement.

- Constitution Study Guide
- Supreme Court Case Studies

 Chapter Preview

Standards Focus

Standards by Section

Section 1: HSS 8.12.5
Section 2: HSS 8.12.5
Section 3: HSS 8.12.6
Section 4: HSS 8.12.5
Section 5: HSS 8.12.5

Teacher's Edition

HSS **Analysis Skills:** CS 1, CS 2, HR 1, HR 3, HR 4, HR 5, HI 1, HI 2, HI 3
ELA Speaking 8.2.4, Reading 8.2.0, 8.6.3; Writing 8.2.2a

Preview Grade 11 Standards

HSS **11.2** Students analyze the relationship among the rise of industrialization, large-scale rural-to-urban migration, and massive immigration from Southern and Eastern Europe.

11.2.1 Know the effects of industrialization on living and working conditions, including the portrayal of working conditions and food safety in Upton Sinclair's *The Jungle*.

11.2.2 Describe the changing landscape, including the growth of cities linked by industry and trade, and the development of cities divided according to race, ethnicity, and class.

Focus on Speaking

The **Chapter Resource File** provides a Focus on Speaking worksheet to help students create their campaign promises.

CRF: Focus on Speaking Activity: Campaign Promises

CHAPTER 19 1865–1920

The Spirit of Reform

California Standards

History–Social Science

8.12 Students analyze the transformation of the American economy and the changing social and political conditions in the United States in response to the Industrial Revolution.

Analysis Skills

HI 2 Students understand and distinguish cause, effect, sequence, and correlation in historical events.

HR 2 Students distinguish fact from opinion in historical narratives.

English–Language Arts

Speaking 8.2.4 Deliver persuasive presentations.

Reading 8.2.0 Students read and understand grade-level appropriate material.

FOCUS ON SPEAKING

Campaign Promises In this chapter you will read about the political corruption of the Gilded Age and the reform movements that followed. Then you will create and present a list of campaign promises that you would make if you were a politician running for office in the United States in the late 1800s. Serious problems face the nation, and you must convince voters that you should be the one to tackle those problems.

UNITED STATES

1868 Ulysses S. Grant is elected president.

1865 — 1870

1871 The British Parliament legalizes labor unions.

WORLD

602 CHAPTER 19

Introduce the Chapter

Standards Proficiency

Working for Reform HSS 8.12

1. Ask students if they can recall any recent changes in school policy, or if there are current school policies they would like to see changed.
2. Ask students to discuss what they think is the best way to introduce change in the school. Are there methods that might be counterproductive, meaning that they might cause the people with the authority to make changes to be less open to change? What methods would students use to try to bring about change in their school? List the responses for students to see.
3. Tell students that in this chapter they will learn about ways in which Americans worked to improve their society in the late 1800s and early 1900s. Have students think about the methods they listed as they read through the chapter.

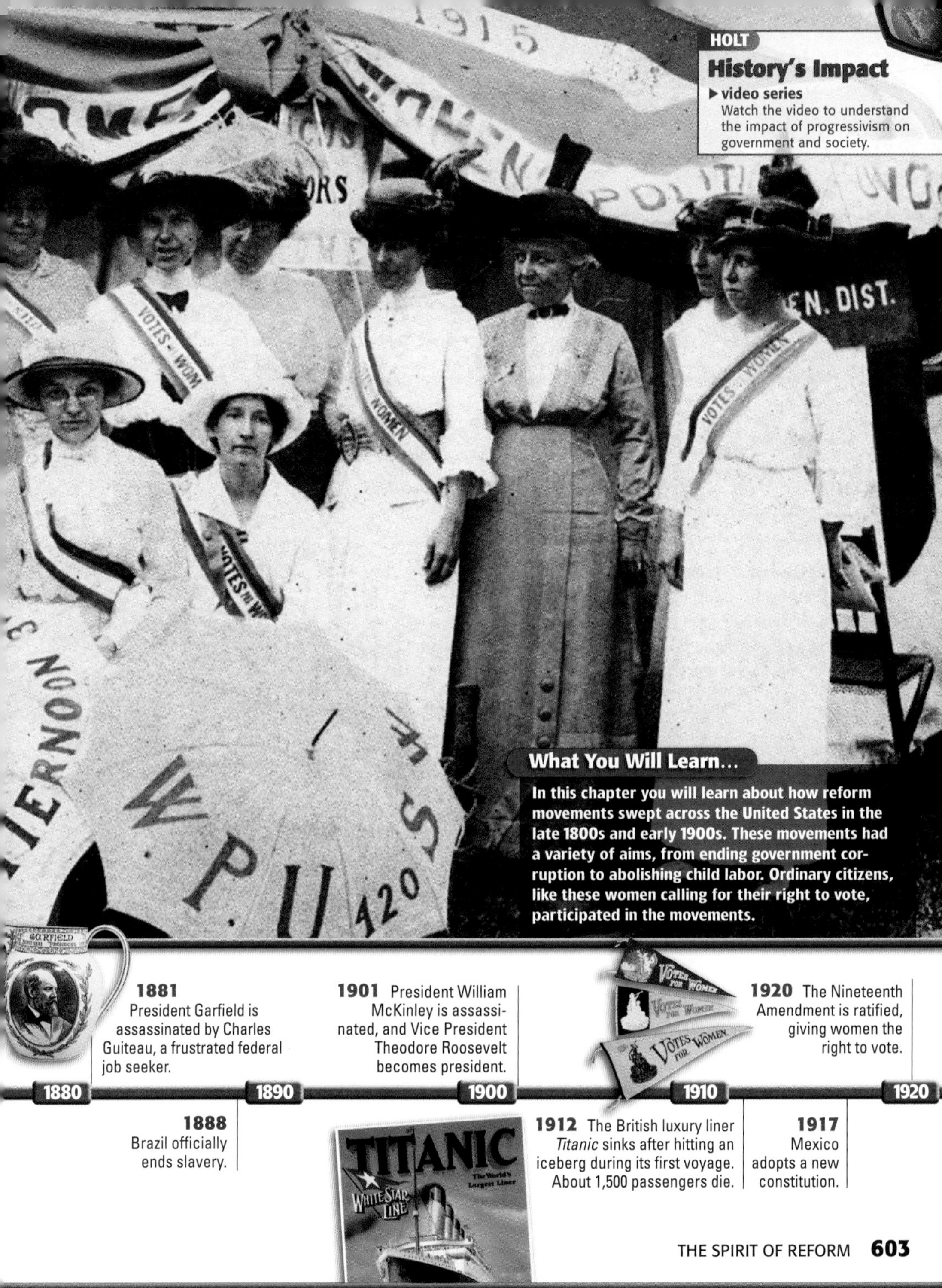

HOLT

History's Impact

▶ **video series**

Watch the video to understand the impact of progressivism on government and society.

What You Will Learn...

In this chapter you will learn about how reform movements swept across the United States in the late 1800s and early 1900s. These movements had a variety of aims, from ending government corruption to abolishing child labor. Ordinary citizens, like these women calling for their right to vote, participated in the movements.

1881 President Garfield is assassinated by Charles Guiteau, a frustrated federal job seeker.

1888 Brazil officially ends slavery.

1901 President William McKinley is assassinated, and Vice President Theodore Roosevelt becomes president.

1912 The British luxury liner *Titanic* sinks after hitting an iceberg during its first voyage. About 1,500 passengers die.

1917 Mexico adopts a new constitution.

1920 The Nineteenth Amendment is ratified, giving women the right to vote.

1880 | 1890 | 1900 | 1910 | 1920

THE SPIRIT OF REFORM **603**

• Chapter Preview •

HOLT

History's Impact

▶ **video series**

See the Video Teacher's Guide for strategies for using the chapter video **The Spirit of Reform**.

Chapter Big Ideas

Section 1 Politics during the Gilded Age was plagued by corruption. **HSS** 8.12.5

Section 2 From the late 1800s through the early 1900s, the progressive movement addressed problems that faced American society. **HSS** 8.12.5

Section 3 In the early 1900s progressives and reformers focused on improving conditions for American workers. **HSS** 8.12.6

Section 4 The progressive movement made advances for the rights of women and some other minorities. **HSS** 8.12.5

Section 5 American presidents in the early 1900s did a great deal to promote progressive reform. **HSS** 8.12.5

Explore the Picture

Women and Reform Previous generations of women had joined reform efforts because they were an acceptable way for women to influence politics and society. By the late 1800s, women were enrolling in colleges in increasing numbers. Women's career choices remained limited, however. As a result, many college-educated, middle class women joined reform efforts as a way to use their knowledge of medicine, sociology, and other subjects.

Analyzing Visuals What methods are the women in the photograph using to promote the right for women to vote? *organized publicity, banners and literature, sashes, umbrellas, holding daily teas*

Explore the Time Line

1. In what year was slavery abolished in Brazil? *1888*
2. Why and when did the Titanic sink? *hit an iceberg; 1912*
3. Who assassinated President Garfield in 1881? *Charles Guiteau*
4. What amendment gave women the right to vote in the United States? *Nineteenth Amendment*

HSS Analysis Skills: CS 1

Linking to Today

The League of Women Voters Activism to support women's voting issues continues today. The League of Women Voters is an organization that encourages women to vote and stay informed about political issues.

go.hrw.com

Online Resources

Chapter Resources:
KEYWORD: SS8 US19

Teacher Resources:
KEYWORD: SS8 TEACHER

Reading Social Studies

Understanding Themes

Introduce the two key themes of this chapter—politics and culture—by telling students that during this period there were many problems related to government corruption. Ask students to make a list of the types of corruption that might affect politics. Point out to students that corruption at this time ranged from buying votes to granting government positions to supporters. Then have students add a second column to their list. Ask students to list ways that reform efforts might have curbed corruption in politics. Ask students what other reforms were needed to improve society at this time.

Historical Fact and Historical Fiction

Focus on Reading Ask students to compare documentaries about history with historical movies they may have seen. Have students point out the differences between the two. Remind students that while the characters, particularly in the movie, may have been based on real people, many of the details may have come from the author's imagination. Ask students how they could determine what was fact and what was fiction in a film. Point out to students that they should think critically whenever they see movies based on history.

Reading Social Studies

by Kylene Beers

Economics | Geography | Politics | Religion | Society and Culture | Science and Technology

Focus on Themes In this chapter, you will read about a time called the Gilded Age, which was a time marked by corrupt **politics**. You will learn about the people who worked to reform dishonest political practices, and see that they also worked to improve other areas of society—for example, the working conditions that children and poor workers faced. Finally, you will read about several presidents of the early 1900s who supported ideas and initiatives that promoted **social** reform.

Historical Fact and Historical Fiction

Focus on Reading When you read a book like *The Summer of My German Soldier* or see a movie about the civil war, do you ever wonder how much is fiction and how much is fact?

Additional reading support can be found in the

Separating Fact from Fiction Historical fiction gives readers a chance to meet real historical people and real historical events in the framework of a made-up story. Some of what you read in historical fiction could be verified in an encyclopedia, but other parts existed only in the author's mind until he or she put it on paper. As a good reader, you should know the different between facts, which can be proved or verified, and fiction.

Notice how one reader determined which details could be verified, or proved.

> That was a <u>woman filling her pail</u> by the hydrant you just bumped against. <u>The sinks are in the hallway</u>, that all the tenants may have access—and all be poisoned alike by their summer stenches. Hear the pump squeak! It is the lullaby of tenement house babes. In summer, when <u>a thousand thirsty throats pant for a cooling drink</u> in this block, it is worked in vain. . . .
>
> From *How the Other Half Lives*, by Jacob Riis

The woman filling her pail isn't a fact I can check. He's just using her as an example of what women did.

We could probably check city records to see whether the buildings really had sinks in the hallways.

The writer is generalizing here. We probably can't prove 1000 thirsty throats. We could find out whether the city's water pumps actually went dry in the summer. That's verifiable.

Reading and Skills Resources

Reading Support

- Interactive Reader and Study Guide
- Student Edition on Audio CD
- Spanish Chapter Summaries Audio CD Program

Social Studies Skills Support

- Interactive Skills Tutor CD-ROM

Vocabulary Support

- **CRF:** Vocabulary Builder Activities
- **CRF:** Chapter Review Activity
- Universal Access Modified Worksheets and Tests CD-ROM:
  - Vocabulary Flash Cards
  - Vocabulary Builder Activity
  - Chapter Review Activity
- OSP Holt PuzzlePro

Standards Focus

HSS Analysis Skills: HR 2, HR 3

ELA **Analysis HR 2** Distinguish fact from opinion in historical narrative and stories.
ELA **Analysis HR 3** Distinguish verifiable from unverifiable information.

You Try It!

The following passage is from a literature excerpt in the chapter you are about to read. Read the passage and then answer the questions below.

> There was never the least attention paid to what was cut up for sausage; there would come back from Europe old sausage that had been rejected, and that was mouldy and white—it would be dosed with borax and glycerine, and dumped into hoppers, and made over again for home consumption. There would be meat that had tumbled out on the floor, in the dirt and sawdust, where the workers had tramped and spit uncounted billions of consumption germs. There would be meat stored in great piles in rooms and the water from leaky roofs would drip over it, and thousands of rats would race about on it.
>
> From *The Jungle,* by Upton Sinclair

After you read the passages, answer the questions below:

1. Do you think the first sentence—the one beginning with *There* and ending with *consumption*—is factual? Why? Where could you look to verify your hunches or prove those facts?
2. Look at the last sentence. Do you think it is a fact that roofs leaked on the meat that was stored in these rooms? How could you prove or disprove that fact?
3. If there are details in historical fiction that you cannot verify, does that make the historical fiction weak? Why or why not?

As you read Chapter 19, ask yourself which details could be used to create an interesting historical fiction novel.

Key Terms and People

Chapter 19

Section 1
political machines *(p. 606)*
William Marcy Tweed *(p. 607)*
Rutherford B. Hayes *(p. 607)*
James A. Garfield *(p. 607)*
Chester A. Arthur *(p. 607)*
Grover Cleveland *(p. 608)*
Benjamin Harrison *(p. 608)*
William McKinley *(p. 608)*
spoils system *(p. 608)*
Pendleton Civil Service Act *(p. 608)*

Section 2
progressives *(p. 610)*
muckrakers *(p. 610)*
John Dewey *(p. 612)*
Joseph McCormack *(p. 612)*
direct primary *(p. 613)*
Seventeenth Amendment *(p. 613)*
recall *(p. 613)*
initiative *(p. 613)*
referendum *(p. 613)*
Robert M. La Follette *(p. 614)*
Wisconsin Idea *(p. 614)*

Section 3
Florence Kelley *(p. 616)*
Triangle Shirtwaist Fire *(p. 618)*
workers' compensation laws *(p. 618)*
Lochner v. *New York* *(p. 618)*
capitalism *(p. 619)*
socialism *(p. 619)*
William "Big Bill" Haywood *(p. 619)*
Industrial Workers of the World *(p. 619)*

Section 4
Women's Christian Temperance Union *(p. 623)*
Eighteenth Amendment *(p. 623)*
National American Woman Suffrage Association *(p. 623)*
Alice Paul *(p. 624)*
National Woman's Party *(p. 624)*
Nineteenth Amendment *(p. 624)*
Booker T. Washington *(p. 624)*
Ida B. Wells *(p. 624)*
W. E. B. Du Bois *(p. 624)*
National Association for the Advancement of Colored People *(p. 625)*

Academic Vocabulary
motive (p. 612)

Reading Social Studies

Key Terms and People

Preteach the key terms and people for this chapter by hosting a vocabulary game for students. Write the terms and people for students to see. Then organize the class into teams. Read aloud definitions or descriptions, and have teams take turns guessing which term identifies the description you gave. If one team guesses incorrectly, allow the next team an opportunity to guess the answer. Assign points for each correct answer. You might want to have students keep a list of correct descriptions for each term. **LS Verbal/Linguistic, Interpersonal**

Focus on Reading

See the **Focus on Reading** questions in this chapter for more practice on this reading social studies skill.

Reading Social Studies Assessment

See the **Standards Review** at the end of this chapter for student assessment questions related to this reading skill.

Teaching Tip

Students can learn a great deal by reading historical fiction, but they need to understand that they are reading fiction. Tell students that as they read historical fiction they should ask themselves which facts are verifiable and which are fiction. You might wish to bring in a historical fiction novel and read two or three paragraphs to students, having them make a list of what they believe are verifiable facts.

Answers

You Try It! **1.** *yes, because there might be records that note if the meat was returned from Europe or witnesses who saw first-hand what happened during processing;* **2.** *could be fact; examine documents such as health and sanitation records or company notes;* **3.** *yes, because the story might not be believable*

Preteach

Bellringer

If YOU were there . . . Use the **Daily Bellringer Transparency** to help students answer the question.

 Daily Bellringer Transparency, Section 1

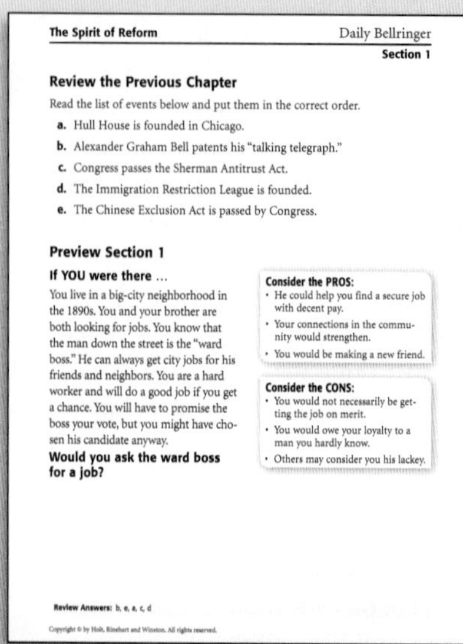

The Spirit of Reform Daily Bellringer

Section 1

Review the Previous Chapter

Read the list of events below and put them in the correct order.

a. Hull House is founded in Chicago.

b. Alexander Graham Bell patents his "talking telegraph."

c. Congress passes the Sherman Antitrust Act.

d. The Immigration Restriction League is founded.

e. The Chinese Exclusion Act is passed by Congress.

Preview Section 1

If YOU were there ...

You live in a big-city neighborhood in the 1890s. You and your brother are both looking for jobs. You know that the man down the street is the "ward boss." He can always get city jobs for his friends and neighbors. You are a hard worker and will do a good job if you get a chance. You will have to promise the boss your vote, but you might have chosen his candidate anyway.

Would you ask the ward boss for a job?

Consider the PROS:
- He could help you find a secure job with decent pay.
- Your connections in the community would strengthen.
- You would be making a new friend.

Consider the CONS:
- You would not necessarily be getting the job on merit.
- You would owe your loyalty to a man you hardly know.
- Others may consider you his lackey.

Review Answers: b, e, a, c, d

Building Vocabulary

Preteach or review the following terms:

corruption dishonest behavior (p. 606)

gilded covered with a thin layer of gold; something that seems good on the outside but in reality is not (p. 606)

CRF: Vocabulary Builder Activity, Section 1

Standards Focus

HSS 8.12.5

Means: Examine how immigration and industrialization led to inequality in wealth and to political corruption.

Matters: American society continues to address issues of economic inequality and political corruption.

SECTION 1 The Gilded Age

What You Will Learn...

Main Ideas

1. Political corruption was common during the Gilded Age.
2. Presidents during the Gilded Age confronted the issue of corruption.
3. In an effort to clean up political corruption, limits were put on the spoils system.

The Big Idea

Politics during the Gilded Age was plagued by corruption.

Key Terms and People

political machines, *p. 606*
William Marcy Tweed, *p. 607*
Rutherford B. Hayes, *p. 607*
James A. Garfield, *p. 607*
Chester A. Arthur, *p. 607*
Grover Cleveland, *p. 608*
Benjamin Harrison, *p. 608*
William McKinley, *p. 608*
spoils system, *p. 608*
Pendleton Civil Service Act, *p. 608*

HSS 8.12.5 Examine the location and effects of urbanization, renewed immigration, and industrialization (e.g., the effects on social fabric of cities, wealth and economic opportunity, the conservation movement).

If YOU were there...

You live in a big-city neighborhood in the 1890s. You and your brother are both looking for jobs. You know that the man down the street is the "ward boss." He can always get city jobs for his friends and neighbors. You are a hard worker and will do a good job if you get a chance. You will have to promise the boss your vote, but you might have chosen his candidate anyway.

Would you ask the ward boss for a job?

BUILDING BACKGROUND The late 1800s were a time of contrasts in American life. Great wealth made in business existed alongside poverty and tenement life. In politics, money led to corruption and dishonesty. The period became known as the Gilded Age. The name came from a novel by Mark Twain and Charles Dudley Warner that ridiculed political life.

Political Corruption

The last quarter of the nineteenth century in America is often called the Gilded Age. The authors Mark Twain and Charles Dudley coined this term for the era. The term highlights the inequality between wealthy business owners, who had profited from the Industrial Revolution, and workers, who often worked under terrible conditions for little pay. Many people began to believe that the government should help fix the inequality. The first step was to get rid of corruption in politics.

Political Machines

In the late 1800s city and county politics were strongly influenced by **political machines**—powerful organizations that used both legal and illegal methods to get their candidates elected to public office. For example, members of political machines at times stuffed ballot boxes with votes for their candidates. Political machines sometimes paid people for their votes or bribed vote counters. Through such actions, a political party could control local government.

Machines were run by leaders called bosses. The machine's boss frequently traded favors for votes. In exchange for votes, the

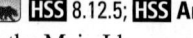

Teach the Big Idea: Master the Standards

Standards Proficiency

The Gilded Age HSS 8.12.5; HSS **Analysis Skills:** HI 1, HI 2

1. **Teach** Ask students the Main Idea questions to teach this section.
2. **Apply** Have students write a newspaper article that explains politics during the Gilded Age. Instruct them to take notes to use for their articles as they read through the section.
3. **Review** Once students have finished reading the section and have compiled their notes, have them share their ideas and notes with the class. Make sure there are no main topics missing. Be sure to emphasize the importance of political corruption during the Gilded Age.
4. **Practice/Homework** Have students write their articles and include an attention-grabbing headline. Students should also create one illustration or political cartoon they believe typifies the Gilded Age.

LS Verbal/Linguistic, Visual/Spatial

Alternative Assessment Handbook, Rubrics 3: Artwork; 27: Political Cartoons; and 42: Writing to Inform boss might offer city jobs or allow an illegal business to operate. The bosses drew much of their support from immigrants. One Boston politician explained the role of the machine boss. "There's got to be . . . somebody that any bloke [man] can come to . . . and get help."

New York City's political machine, Tammany Hall, was one of the most notorious. After winning city elections in 1888, members of Tammany Hall rewarded their supporters with about 12,000 jobs. As boss of Tammany Hall, **William Marcy Tweed** may have stolen up to $200 million from the city.

Corruption in Washington

Corruption was also common in the federal government at this time. Many people viewed the administration of Republican Ulysses S. Grant—who was elected in 1868 and re-elected in 1872—as corrupt. During Grant's second term, federal officials were jailed for taking bribes from whiskey distillers in exchange for allowing the whiskey makers to avoid paying taxes. This scandal and others caused many Americans to question the honesty of national leaders.

READING CHECK **Finding Main Ideas** How was political corruption a local and national problem during the Gilded Age?

Presidents Confront Corruption

During the 1876 presidential campaign, Democrats called for government reform. Their candidate, Samuel J. Tilden, had reformed his own party. Tilden promised to run an honest administration in Washington, D.C.

The Republican Party chose Civil War hero **Rutherford B. Hayes**, who was known for his honesty. Hayes was also a reformer who promised "thorough, radical, and complete" changes in the government. In the disputed election that followed, a special electoral committee chose Hayes over Tilden by a narrow margin.

Republicans won another close presidential victory in 1880, when their candidates, reformer **James A. Garfield** and his vice president, **Chester A. Arthur**, were elected. On July 2, 1881, Charles Guiteau, an angry and mentally unstable federal job seeker, confronted President Garfield at a Washington railroad station. He shouted, "Arthur [is] President now," and then shot Garfield twice. The president died from his wounds in September, and Vice President Arthur became president.

In the 1884 election, Republicans nominated James Blaine. Many Republican

Political Machines — QUICK FACTS

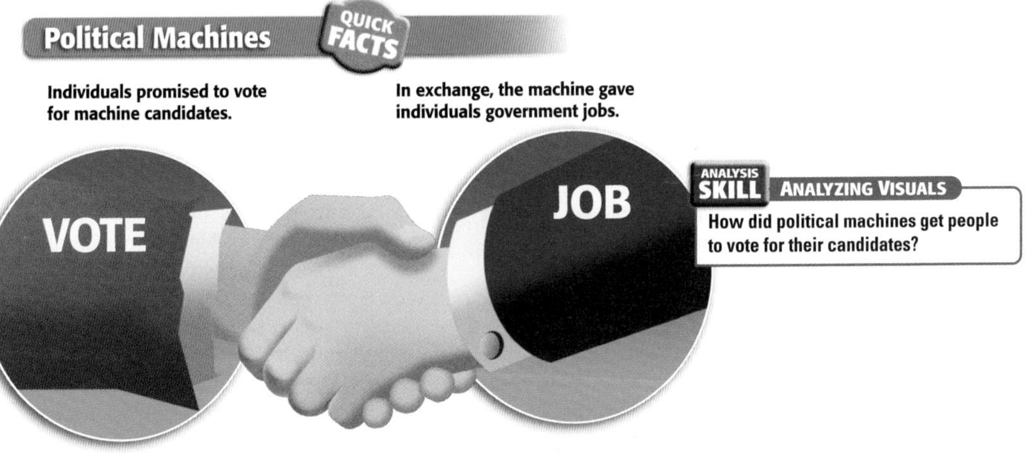

Individuals promised to vote for machine candidates.
In exchange, the machine gave individuals government jobs.
VOTE
JOB

ANALYSIS SKILL **ANALYZING VISUALS**
How did political machines get people to vote for their candidates?

Direct Teach

Main Idea

❶ Political Corruption

Political corruption was common during the Gilded Age.

Identify What were two illegal ways political machines ensured their candidates were elected? *stuffing ballot boxes, buying votes*

Summarize Why is Tammany Hall infamous? *rewarded thousands of supporters with jobs; Tweed may have stolen as much as $200 million from the city.*

Political Cartoons Activities for United States History, Cartoon 22: Tammany Hall

Quick Facts Transparency: Political Machines

HSS 8.12.5; HSS **Analysis Skills:** HI 1

Main Idea

❷ Presidents Confront Corruption

Presidents during the Gilded Age confronted the issue of corruption.

Recall What did Rutherford B. Hayes promise during his 1876 campaign? *"thorough, radical, and complete" changes in the government*

Draw Conclusions What was the major theme of many presidential elections from 1876 to 1896? *reform and elimination of corruption in government*

HSS 8.12.5; HSS **Analysis Skills:** CS 1, HI 1, HI 3

Critical Thinking: Solving Problems

Standards Proficiency

Letters to the Editor HSS 8.12.5; HSS **Analysis Skills:** HI 1, HI 2

1. Review with students the political corruption that affected local, state, and national politics during the Gilded Age.
2. Ask students to imagine that they are living during the Gilded Age in a city that suffers from a great deal of political corruption. Have students write letters to the editor of their local newspaper in which they demand that something be done to stop the political corruption.
3. Students should cite specific examples of corruption that are taking place in local politics and suggest solutions for how to curb the corruption.
4. Ask volunteers to share their letters with the class. LS **Verbal/Linguistic**

Alternative Assessment Handbook, Rubric 17: Letters to Editors

Answers

Analyzing Visuals *exchanged promises of city jobs or favors for votes*

Reading Check *political machines in the cities; bribery, scandal, and spoils system in the federal government*

Direct Teach

Main Idea

3 Efforts to Clean Up Political Corruption

In an effort to clean up political corruption, limits were put on the spoils system.

Explain What were some of the major problems caused by the spoils system? *constant change in employees, jobs given to unqualified candidates, political corruption*

Analyze How did the Pendleton Civil Service Act change government hiring practices? *It required many government job applicants to pass an exam.*

Evaluate How did the Pendleton Civil Service Act limit the spoils system? *It limited the ability of elected officials to give jobs to unqualified people on the basis of political support alone.*

HSS 8.12.5; HSS **Analysis Skills:** HI 1, HI 2

Biography

Chester A. Arthur (1829–1886) When Charles Guiteau shot President James A. Garfield, many Americans were horrified at the thought of Chester A. Arthur becoming president. These Americans viewed Arthur as a corrupt politician who opposed reform. After being shot, Garfield lived for 80 days before he died. During that time, Arthur rose in public opinion. Many Americans thought that he acted with dignity during the crisis and showed great concern for Garfield and his family. After Garfield died, Arthur participated in a national outpouring of grief.

Gilded Age Presidents

Rutherford B. Hayes
Republican
In office 1877–1881

James A. Garfield
Republican
In office 1881

Chester A. Arthur
Republican
In office 1881–1885

reformers associated Blaine with corruption. They left their party and backed the Democratic nominee, **Grover Cleveland**. Unlike Blaine, Cleveland was known for his honesty. After a campaign full of personal attacks, voters elected Cleveland as president. Cleveland involved himself in all the day-to-day details of the presidency. He worked hard to hire and fire government workers based on merit, not party loyalty.

Four years later, in 1888, Cleveland lost the election. The new president, Republican **Benjamin Harrison**, helped to control inflation and to pass the Sherman Antitrust Act, which regulated monopolies.

In 1892, having won both the popular and the electoral vote, Cleveland beat Harrison. In 1896 the next president, Republican candidate **William McKinley**, worked well enough with Congress to be re-elected in 1900. McKinley avoided scandals and helped win back public trust in the government.

THE IMPACT TODAY Tests are still required for many federal positions, including secretarial positions, air traffic control, and law enforcement.

READING CHECK **Sequencing** List the presidents between 1876 and 1900 in chronological order and state their years in office.

Efforts to Clean Up Political Corruption

Reacting to the corruption of the Gilded Age, many Americans called for changes in the civil service, or government jobs. They disliked the **spoils system**, the practice of giving jobs to supporters after a candidate wins an election. President Thomas Jefferson was the first to reward supporters with jobs. Subsequently, each time a new party took power, it replaced many current government officials. Most new employees were unqualified and untrained. By 1829 about 20 percent of officeholders were being replaced after presidential elections.

By the late 1800s government corruption was so widespread that reformers demanded that only qualified people be given government jobs. In response, President Hayes made minor reforms, such as firing a powerful member of the New York Republican political machine. President Garfield also attempted reforms before he was assassinated.

Finally, President Chester Arthur backed the **Pendleton Civil Service Act**. This law, passed in 1883, set up a merit system for awarding federal jobs. Under the Pendleton

Critical Thinking: Analyzing

Standards Proficiency

Analyzing Political Cartoons

HSS 8.12.5; HSS **Analysis Skills:** HR 4

Research Required

1. Tell students that during the Gilded Age one of the most influential political cartoonists was Thomas Nast. Nast first popularized many of the characters used in modern-day political cartoons, such as Uncle Sam.
2. Have each student complete **Political Cartoons Activities Guide for United States History, Cartoon 22: Tammany Hall.** Then have students conduct research to find another Thomas Nast political cartoon dealing with political corruption.
3. Have each student write a short analysis of the selected political cartoon. The analysis should identify the subject, the symbols used, and the message.
4. **Extend** Have students create their own political cartoons about political corruption. **LS Visual/Spatial, Verbal/Linguistic**

Alternative Assessment Handbook, Rubrics 27: Political Cartoons; and 37: Writing Assignments

Political Cartoons Activities for United States History, Cartoon 22: Tammany Hall

Answers

Reading Check *Hayes, 1877–1881; Garfield, 1881; Arthur, 1881–1885; Cleveland, 1885–1889 and 1893–1897; Harrison, 1889–1893; McKinley, 1897–1901*

Grover Cleveland
Democrat
In office 1885–1889, 1893–1897

Benjamin Harrison
Republican
In office 1889–1893

William McKinley
Republican
In office 1897–1901

Act, more than 10 percent of government job applicants had to pass an exam before they could be hired. It was a start to reforming the whole government.

READING CHECK **Analyzing Information** What factors led to civil service reform?

SUMMARY AND PREVIEW Presidents and reformers worked to end corruption in government. In the next section you will read about how progressive reformers worked to improve the problems plaguing other parts of society.

Section 1 Assessment

go.hrw.com **Online Quiz** KEYWORD: SS8 HP19

Reviewing Ideas, Terms, and People HSS 8.12.5

1. a. **Recall** What was the main goal of **political machines** during the Gilded Age?
   b. **Elaborate** Why do you think corruption became so widespread during the Gilded Age?
2. a. **Identify** Who were **James A. Garfield** and **Chester A. Arthur**?
   b. **Draw Conclusions** Why did **Rutherford B. Hayes** appeal to voters in the election of 1876?
   c. **Evaluate** Do you think that presidents during the Gilded Age effectively dealt with government corruption? Explain your answer.
3. a. **Identify** What was the **Pendleton Civil Service Act**?
   b. **Predict** Do you think the system of testing created by the Pendleton Civil Service Act would work to reduce corruption in the spoils system? Why or why not?

Critical Thinking

4. **Categorizing** Copy the graphic organizer below onto your own sheet of paper. Use it to identify examples of government corruption that existed during the Gilded Age.

FOCUS ON SPEAKING

5. **Addressing Political Corruption** How would you address the problem of political corruption during the Gilded Age? Jot down notes about campaign promises you might make to convince people that you could handle the widespread political corruption of the day.

Section 1 Assessment Answers

1. a. to get their candidates elected to office
   b. possible answer—not enough laws in place to prevent it
2. a. Garfield was elected president in 1880, but assassinated in 1881; Arthur was the vice-president who succeeded him.
   b. He was honest and supported reforms.
   c. Answers will vary, but students should note that although presidents worked to limit political corruption with some success, it still existed.
3. a. It required some federal job applicants to pass an exam before they were hired.
   b. possible answers—Yes, it would eliminate unqualified applicants; no, applicants might cheat on exams.
4. possible answers—political machines, stuffing ballot boxes, paying for votes, bribing vote counters, theft, and the spoils system
5. Responses might include putting an end to political machines and the spoils system.

Direct Teach

Checking for Understanding

True or False Answer each statement *T* if it is true or *F* if it is false. If false, explain why.

1. President Grover Cleveland continued the practice of awarding government jobs to loyal supporters. *F; He used a merit system rather than loyalty.*
2. Under President Benjamin Harrison, the Sherman Antitrust Act was passed. *T*
3. President Chester A. Arthur backed the Pendleton Civil Service Act. *T*

HSS 8.12.5

Review & Assess

Close

Have students discuss political corruption in local and federal government during the Gilded Age and how the federal government took steps to clean up corruption.

Review

Online Quiz, Section 1

Assess

SE Section 1 Assessment

PASS: Section 1 Quiz

Alternative Assessment Handbook

Reteach/Classroom Intervention

California Standards Review Workbook

Interactive Reader and Study Guide, Section 1

Interactive Skills Tutor CD-ROM

Answers

Reading Check *dissatisfaction with corruption and incompetence in government*

Preteach

Bellringer

If YOU were there . . . Use the **Daily Bellringer Transparency** to help students answer the question.

 Daily Bellringer Transparency, Section 2

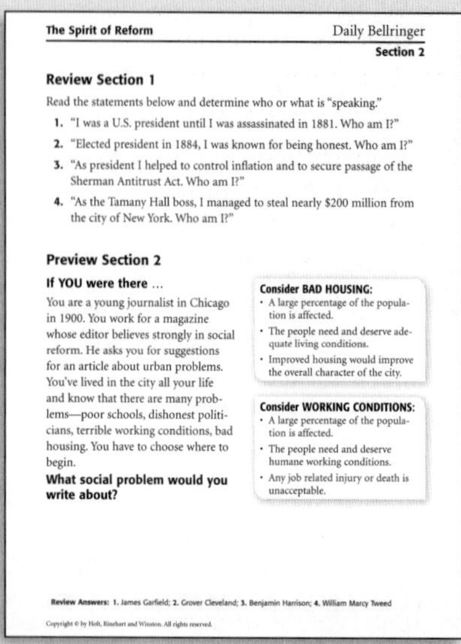

The Spirit of Reform Daily Bellringer **Section 2**

Review Section 1

Read the statements below and determine who or what is "speaking."

1. "I was a U.S. president until I was assassinated in 1881. Who am I?"
2. "Elected president in 1884, I was known for being honest. Who am I?"
3. "As president I helped to control inflation and to secure passage of the Sherman Antitrust Act. Who am I?"
4. "As the Tamany Hall boss, I managed to steal nearly $200 million from the city of New York. Who am I?"

Preview Section 2

If YOU were there ...

You are a young journalist in Chicago in 1900. You work for a magazine whose editor believes strongly in social reform. He asks you for suggestions for an article about urban problems. You've lived in the city all your life and know that there are many problems—poor schools, dishonest politicians, terrible working conditions, bad housing. You have to choose where to begin.

What social problem would you write about?

Consider BAD HOUSING:
- A large percentage of the population is affected.
- The people need and deserve adequate living conditions.
- Improved housing would improve the overall character of the city.

Consider WORKING CONDITIONS:
- A large percentage of the population is affected.
- The people need and deserve humane working conditions.
- Any job related injury or death is unacceptable.

Review Answers: **1.** James Garfield; **2.** Grover Cleveland; **3.** Benjamin Harrison; **4.** William Marcy Tweed

Academic Vocabulary

Review with students the high-use academic term in this section.

motive a reason for doing something (p. 612)

Building Vocabulary

Preteach or review the following term:

zoning a section of an area or territory established for a specific use (p. 611)

CRF: Vocabulary Builder Activity, Section 2

Standards Focus

HSS 8.12.5

Means: Examine how city growth, new immigration, and industrialization led to a reform movement in the late 1800s and early 1900s.

Matters: American society continues to benefit from the reforms of the Gilded Age.

SECTION 2

The Progressive Movement

What You Will Learn...

Main Ideas

1. Progressives pushed for urban and social reforms to improve the quality of life.
2. Progressive reformers expanded the voting power of citizens and introduced reforms in local and state governments.

The Big Idea

From the late 1800s through the early 1900s, the progressive movement addressed problems that faced American society.

Key Terms and People

progressives, *p. 610*
muckrakers, *p. 610*
John Dewey, *p. 612*
Joseph McCormack, *p. 612*
direct primary, *p. 613*
Seventeenth Amendment, *p. 613*
recall, *p. 613*
initiative, *p. 613*
referendum, *p. 613*
Robert M. La Follette, *p. 614*
Wisconsin Idea, *p. 614*

HSS 8.12.5 Examine the location and effects of urbanization, renewed immigration, and industrialization (e.g., the effects on social fabric of cities, wealth and economic opportunity, the conservation movement).

If YOU were there...

You are a young journalist in Chicago in 1900. You work for a magazine whose editor believes strongly in social reform. He asks you for suggestions for an article about urban problems. You've lived in the city all your life and know that there are many problems—poor schools, dishonest politicians, terrible working conditions, bad housing. You have to choose where to begin.

Which social problem would you write about?

BUILDING BACKGROUND The so-called Gilded Age suffered political corruption at all levels of government. Great inequalities existed between wealthy business owners and most of the labor force. Cities had severe problems, too. In reaction to these conditions, a social reform movement began that tried to improve many areas of American life.

Progressives Push for Reforms

Progressives were a group of reformers who worked to solve problems caused by the rapid industrial and urban growth of the late 1800s. These reformers fought problems such as crime, disease, and poverty by trying to eliminate their causes. Most progressives were part of the growing middle class. They fought for reforms ranging from education programs in poor neighborhoods to better working conditions.

Some journalists urged progressives to action by writing about corruption in business and politics. These journalists were soon nicknamed muckrakers because they "raked up" and exposed the muck, or filth, of society. **Muckrakers** wrote about troubling issues like child labor, racial discrimination, slum housing, and corruption in business. Lincoln Steffens exposed scandals in city politics through articles in *McClure's Magazine*. Another muckracker, Ida Tarbell, wrote a series of articles describing the unfair business practices of Standard Oil Company. Their articles angered many politicians and business leaders but helped to unite progressives.

Teach the Big Idea: Master the Standards

Standards **Proficiency**

The Progressive Movement 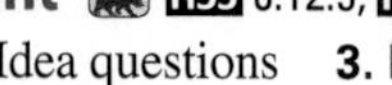 HSS 8.12.5; HSS Analysis Skills: HI 1, HI 2, HI 3

1. **Teach** Ask students the Main Idea questions to teach this section.
2. **Apply** Create a two-column chart for students to see. Title the chart *Progressive Reforms* and label the columns *Area of Reform* and *Changes Made.* Have each student copy the chart and use the information in the section to complete it.
LS Verbal/Linguistic, Visual/Spatial
3. **Review** Ask volunteers to share the information in their charts. Use the information to create a master chart for the class to see.
4. **Practice/Homework** Assign students one of the categories from the chart. Have each student write a short essay explaining why these changes needed to be made and how they improved life. **LS Verbal/Linguistic**

Alternative Assessment Handbook, Rubrics 7: Charts; and 37: Writing Assignments

Muckrakers influenced voters, causing them to question corrupt practices and to pressure politicians to call for reforms.

A major goal for progressive reformers was to help the urban poor. Many immigrants and native-born Americans had moved to U.S. cities looking for work. They often lived in crowded tenement buildings. As a result, thousands of families lived in unclean and unsafe conditions.

Lawrence Veiller was a progressive housing reformer who described the effects of tenement living on children and society.

> "A child living its early years in dark rooms, without sunlight or fresh air, does not grow up to be a normal, healthy person ... It is not of such material that strong nations are made."
>
> —Lawrence Veiller, quoted in *Readings in American History, Vol. 2*

City Planning

Progressives addressed these problems in several ways. Veiller helped to get the 1901 New York State Tenement House Act passed. This law required new buildings to have better ventilation and running water. The act became a model for housing reform in other states.

Other progressives started settlement houses similar to Jane Addams's Hull House in Chicago, usually located in poor areas where immigrants lived. They tried to improve education, housing, and sanitation.

The movement for urban reform led to new professions, such as city planning and civil engineering. City planners worked with local leaders to control urban growth. They passed zoning laws and safer building codes and opened new public parks. Civil engineers improved city transportation by paving streets and building bridges. Sanitation engineers tried to solve problems concerning pollution, waste disposal, and impure water supplies.

Death rates dropped a great deal in areas where planners and engineers addressed urban leadership, structures, and services. Gradually, progressive improvements gave American cities some of the best public services in the world.

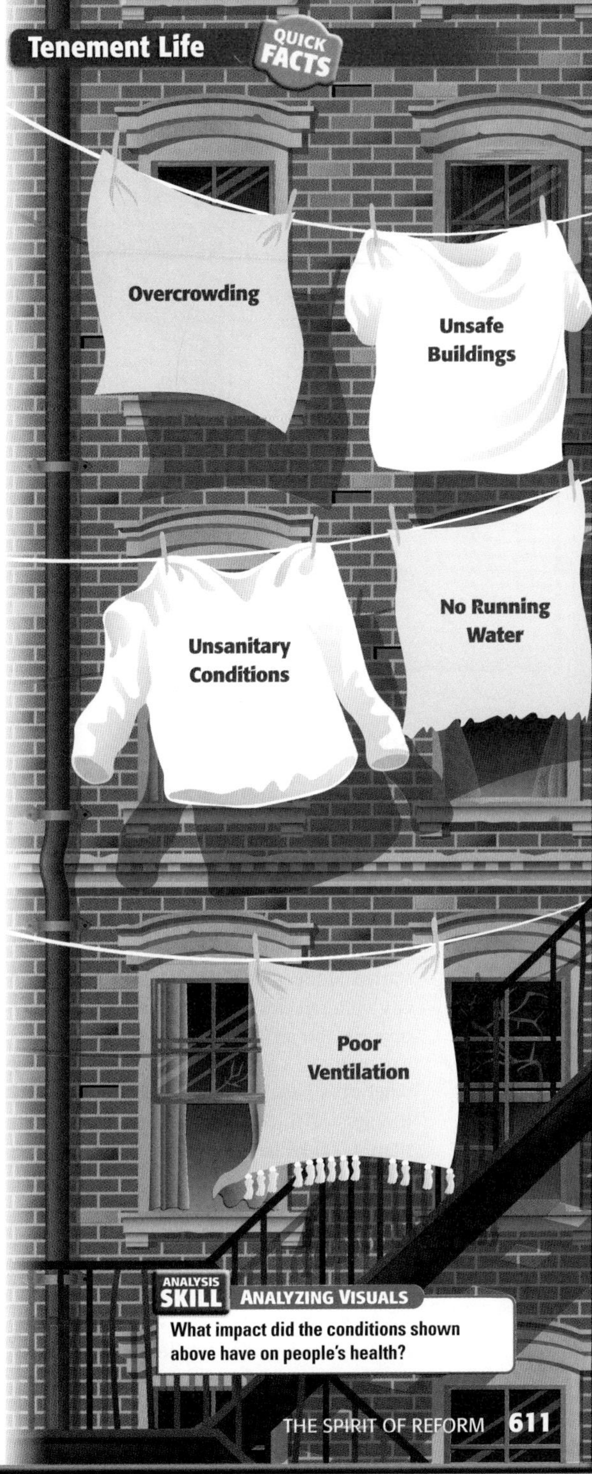

ANALYSIS SKILL ANALYZING VISUALS

What impact did the conditions shown above have on people's health?

Direct Teach

Main Idea

1 Progressives Push for Reforms

Progressives pushed for urban and social reforms to improve the quality of life.

Recall About what types of problems did muckrakers write? *issues such as poverty, crime, child labor, racial discrimination, slum housing, and corruption in business and politics*

Summarize Why were muckrakers important to the progressive movement? *They helped publicize problems, influence voters, and unite progressives.*

Identify Cause and Effect Why was city planning necessary, and what was the result of city planning? *Cities had become unsafe and overcrowded; passage of zoning laws, creation of parks, improved transportation and sanitation*

CRF: Biography Activity: Nellie Bly

Quick Facts Transparency: Tenement Life

HSS 8.12.5; **HSS Analysis Skills:** HI 1, HI 2

Biography

Ida Tarbell (1857–1944) Journalist Ida Tarbell was the daughter of an independent oil producer in Pennsylvania. When John D. Rockefeller's Standard Oil Company began swallowing up independent oil companies, Tarbell's father's company went bankrupt. In 1900 tht magazine *McClure's* assigned her to investigate Standard Oil. Tarbell published her findings in a series of 19 articles on Standard Oil's business practices, and later in a book, *The History of Standard Oil Company.*

Critical Thinking: Evaluating Information

Exceeding Standards

Documentary Film Script

HSS 8.12.5; **HSS Analysis Skills:** HI 1

1. Ask students to imagine they are modern-day screenwriters working on a documentary film about progressive reforms.
2. Have students work in pairs or in small groups to develop an outline or storyboard for the documentary. To limit the scope of the activity, assign each pair or group specific reforms to address.
3. Students' outlines or storyboards should describe or depict the film's main topics or scenes, as well as what a narrator might say.
4. **Extend** Have students locate photographs that could be used in their documentaries. **LS Verbal/Linguistic, Visual/Spatial**

Alternative Assessment Handbook, Rubric 40: Writing to Describe

go.hrw.com
Online Resources
KEYWORD: SS8 US19
ACTIVITY: City Planning

Answers

Analyzing Visuals *contributed to serious public health problems, led to spread of disease*

• Direct Teach •

Main Idea

1 Progressives Push for Reforms

Progressives pushed for urban and social reforms to improve the quality of life.

Recall How did progressive reforms affect education? *Reformers pushed for new public high schools that provided courses in job training and citizenship, and opened more than 4,000 kindergartens in the nation.*

Analyze How did John Dewey influence teaching methods? *He encouraged problem-solving skills not just the memorization of facts.*

Make Generalizations How did the American Medical Association support progressive reform? *by supporting laws to protect public health and showing how professionals could unite to improve society*

- **CRF:** Literature Activity: *The Making of an American*
- **CRF:** Primary Source Activity: Jacob Riis
- **HSS** 8.12.5 **HSS** **Analysis Skills:** HI 1, HI 2

Primary Source

Reading Like a Historian

The Other Half Help students practice reading the document like historians. Ask: What point is Jacob Riis, the photographer, trying to make? How does this photograph fit into time and place in history?

HSS 8.12.5; **HSS** **Analysis Skills:** HR 4

Primary Source

PHOTOGRAPH

The Other Half

In 1890 Jacob Riis published How the Other Half Lives. *The book was a collection of photographs of residents of New York City tenement buildings, including families and immigrants. The conditions of life that were shown in the photographs shocked many wealthier Americans. The photograph to the right was taken by Riis.*

Air and light were often cut off by the surrounding buildings.
This family of seven lived in this one room.
Furniture was placed wherever there was room.
Museum of the City of New York

ANALYSIS SKILL ANALYZING PRIMARY SOURCES

How might this photograph encourage people to become reformers?

Social Reforms

Progressive leaders also worked to reform education. Many more children began going to school in the late 1800s. States passed laws requiring children to attend school.

THE IMPACT TODAY In most states students must attend school until age 16. In recent years several states have raised or considered raising that age to 17 or 18.

Reformers pushed for new public high schools to provide courses in citizenship, health, and job training. Progressives also started kindergarten programs to help poor city children. In 1873 reformer Susan Blow opened the first American public kindergarten in St. Louis, Missouri. Kindergartens taught basic social skills to children between the ages of three and seven. By 1898 more than 4,000 kindergartens had opened in the United States.

John Dewey was an important philosopher and a key supporter of early childhood education. His motive was to help children learn problem-solving skills, not just memorize facts. This, he thought, would help them in everyday life. Dewey's teaching methods became a model for progressive education across the country.

ACADEMIC VOCABULARY **motive** a reason for doing something

Progressives also tried to improve the education of medical professionals. In the late 1800s the United States lacked well-trained and professionally organized doctors. Researchers knew the causes of diseases such as malaria, pneumonia, yellow fever, and tuberculosis. However, there were few medical organizations that could help spread this knowledge.

Under the leadership of **Joseph McCormack**, the American Medical Association (AMA) was reorganized in 1901 to bring together local medical organizations. The AMA also supported laws designed to protect public health. This group showed how progressives could unite professionals to help improve society. Other professional organizations followed.

READING CHECK **Finding Main Ideas** What urban and social reforms did progressives favor?

Answers

Analyzing Primary Sources *possible answers—It might encourage people to be sympathetic to less fortunate individuals; it might inspire them to help change conditions like these.*

Reading Check *tenement reform; settlement houses; city planning; improved sanitation, education, and professional organizations*

Differentiating Instruction for Universal Access

Special Education Students

Reaching Standards

1. Review with students the reforms made by progressives in the areas of urban poverty, tenement reform, city planning, and education. Ask students which reforms they think were most important and why.
2. Pair students and tell them to imagine that they are reformers who are going to lead a parade to celebrate the reforms progressives have accomplished. Ask each pair to create two parade banners that highlight urban and social progressive reforms.
3. Ask volunteers to describe their banners to the class. **LS Visual/Spatial, Verbal/Linguistic**

HSS 8.12.5; **HSS** **Analysis Skills:** HI 1, HI 2

Alternative Assessment Handbook, Rubric 34: Slogans and Banners

Expansion of Voting Power

Some progressives worked to change state and local governments in order to reduce the power of political machines. In many locations, reformers ended the use of ballots designed by political parties to list only one party's candidates. They replaced these corrupt ballots with government-prepared ballots listing all candidates. Under pressure from reformers, many states adopted secret ballots, giving every voter a private vote.

Reformers also hoped to expand voting power. For example, reformers favored the direct primary. The **direct primary** allows voters to choose candidates for public office directly. Previously, party leaders had selected candidates. Progressives also favored the **Seventeenth Amendment**, which allowed Americans to vote directly for U.S. senators. Before the constitutional amendment passed in 1913, state legislatures had elected senators.

Other reform measures allowed voters to take action against corrupt politicians. For example, some states and cities gave unhappy voters the right to sign a petition asking for a special vote. The purpose of that vote was to **recall**, or remove, an official before the end of his or her term. If enough voters signed the petition, the vote took place. The official could then be removed from office if there was a majority of recall votes.

In California, Oregon and the Midwest, progressives worked on reforms to give voters direct influence over new laws. A procedure called the **initiative** allowed voters to propose a new law by collecting signatures on a petition. If enough signatures could be gathered, the proposed law was voted on at the next election.

Another procedure, called the **referendum**, permitted voters to approve or reject a law that had already been proposed or passed by government. This process gave voters a chance to overrule laws they opposed.

THE IMPACT TODAY

In 2003 California voters recalled Governor Gray Davis. Arnold Schwarzenegger was elected to replace Davis as governor.

Government Reforms

In addition to working for greater voter participation, progressives attempted to change the way city governments operated. Business

Angels of Mercy

In the late 1800s, settlement houses set up visiting nurses programs. Trained nurses visited tenement houses to care for the sick, especially children. The nurses also taught tenement dwellers about the importance of sanitation in preventing the spread of disease. These compassionate women pioneered the idea of public health as we know it today.

Why would someone want to work as a visiting nurse?

Direct Teach

Main Idea

❷ Expansion of Voting Power

Progressive reformers expanded the voting power of citizens and introduced reforms in local and state governments.

Identify Which amendment gave people the right to vote directly for U.S. Senators? *Seventeenth Amendment*

Contrast How is an initiative different from a referendum? *An initiative is a procedure whereby citizens can propose a law by collecting a certain number of signatures on a petition; a referendum is a procedure where voters can approve or reject a law already proposed or passed by the government.*

Analyze How do the political reforms discussed in this section make politics more democratic? *They give citizens more direct control of the government and reduced the potential for corruption.*

HSS 8.12.5; HSS **Analysis Skills:** HI 1

Did you know . . .

In 2003, California's 37th governor, Gray Davis, became only the second governor in the United States to be recalled from office. About 55 percent of Californians voted in favor of Governor Davis's recall, largely due to concerns over his handling of a statewide energy crisis and a budget shortfall.

Differentiating Instruction for Universal Access

English-Language Learners **Standards Proficiency**

1. Organize the class into mixed-ability pairs. Assign each pair of students one of the following topics: secret ballot, Seventeenth Amendment, direct primary, recall, initiative, or referendum.
2. Have each pair use the information in the text to write a description of the assigned topic. Review the descriptions with the class to ensure that all students understand the terms and how they affect our democracy.
3. Have each student create a poster that defines the term, explains how it will help the general public, and why it is important to participate in politics.
4. When students are finished, have volunteers present their posters to the class.
LS Verbal/Linguistic, Visual/Spatial

HSS 8.12.5; HSS **Analysis Skills:** HI 1

Alternative Assessment Handbook, Rubric 28: Posters

Answers

Angels of Mercy *possible answers— to improve the community, to help people*

Direct Teach

Main Idea

❷ Expansion of Voting Power

Progressive reformers expanded the voting power of citizens and introduced reforms in local and state governments.

Define What was the Wisconsin Idea? *a program to make state government more professional and reduce the power of political machines*

Draw Conclusions Why was the Wisconsin Idea significant? *became a model of government reform for other states*

Quick Facts Transparency: Expanding Democracy

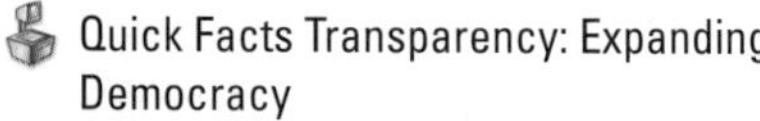

HSS 8.12.5; HSS **Analysis Skills:** HI 1, HI 2

Review & Assess

Close

Ask if students can think of present-day examples of how the reforms from this period affect society and politics today.

Review

Online Quiz, Section 2

Assess

SE Section 2 Assessment

PASS: Section 2 Quiz

Alternative Assessment Handbook

Reteach/Classroom Intervention

California Standards Review Workbook

Interactive Reader and Study Guide, Section 2

Interactive Skills Tutor CD-ROM

Answers

Reading Check *expanded voting power through direct primaries and direct election of U.S. senators; gave voters direct influence over laws through initiatives and referendums; led reforms to limit political machines*

QUICK FACTS — Expanding Democracy

Direct Primaries	Voters choose candidates.
Recall	Voters can remove an official from office.
Initiatives	Voters can propose laws by petition.
Referendum	Voters can overrule a law.
17th Amendment	Senators are elected directly by voters.

leaders and other professionals led reforms to make local governments more efficient and responsive to citizens' needs.

Some reformers wanted governments to be run like a business. Several cities changed to council-manager governments. Under this system, voters elect a city council. The council then appoints a professional manager to run the city. Other business-minded reformers supported the commission form of government, which is headed by a group of elected officials. Each official manages a major city agency, such as housing, sanitation, or transportation. The council-manager and commission forms of government were most popular in small to medium-sized cities. These cities had fewer problems than large cities did.

State governments faced some of the same problems that cities experienced. Corrupt local officials were often part of statewide political machines. In Wisconsin, Republican **Robert M. La Follette** challenged the power of the party bosses. La Follette favored the direct primary, new state commissions made up of specialists in reform issues, and tax reform. He also wanted to use professionals to address social problems.

La Follette won the governor's race in 1900. He soon began a program of reforms. Called the **Wisconsin Idea**, the program aimed to decrease the power of political machines and to make state government more professional. This idea became a model for progressive reformers in other states.

READING CHECK **Evaluating** How did progressives work to change voting procedures and city and state governments?

SUMMARY AND PREVIEW Progressives worked to reform city life and government. In the next section you will learn about reforms in working conditions.

Section 2 Assessment

go.hrw.com **Online Quiz** KEYWORD: SS8 HP19

Reviewing Ideas, Terms, and People HSS 8.12.5

1. **a. Identify** Who were **muckrakers**, and what effect did they have on reform?
   b. Explain According to **progressives**, what was the cause of poor conditions in U.S. cities?
   c. Evaluate Which urban or social reform do you think was most important? Why?
2. **a. Describe** What new ideas and practices were introduced to give voters more power?
   b. Draw Conclusions How did progressive reforms limit the power of political machines?
   c. Elaborate Why do you think **Robert M. La Follette**'s **Wisconsin Idea** was popular with voters?

Critical Thinking

3. **Categorizing** Copy the chart below. Use it to categorize the various progressive reforms that improved society, politics, and cities.

Progressive Reforms		
Social	Political	Urban

FOCUS ON SPEAKING

4. **Addressing Social Problems** Rapid industrial and urban growth during the late 1800s caused serious social problems such as poverty and disease. How would you address such problems? What campaign promises would you make to assure voters that you could make the necessary reforms?

Section 2 Assessment Answers

1. **a.** journalists who wrote about troubling issues; helped unite progressives and influence voters
   b. rapid industrial and urban growth
   c. Answers will vary, but students should exhibit an understanding of the effects of urban and social reforms of the progressives.
2. **a.** direct primary, Seventeenth Amendment, recalls, initiative, referendum
   b. made voting a more direct process, enabled voters to remove elected officials from office, protected voters with secret ballots, made local governments more professional
   c. He challenged party bosses; favored direct primaries, state commissions, tax reforms; and addressed social problems
3. Social—education reforms and professional organizations; Urban—improved tenement housing, transportation, and sanitation; Political—secret ballots, direct primary, recall, initiative, referendum, council-manager city governments, Wisconsin Idea
4. Possible responses might include promising to improve education or to give voters more power.

Reforming the Workplace

SECTION 3

If YOU were there...

You have been working in a hat factory since 1900, when you were eight years old. Now you are experienced enough to run one of the sewing machines. You don't earn as much as older workers, but your family needs every penny you bring home. Still, the long hours make you very tired. One day you hear that people are trying to stop children from doing factory work.

How would you feel about this social reform?

BUILDING BACKGROUND Urged on by muckraking journalists and public support, progressive reformers worked in many areas. One important target was the workplace. Since the Second Industrial Revolution, more and more children and adults were working long hours in terrible conditions.

Improving Conditions for Children

Progressives and other reformers began to focus their attention on working children. Low wages for unskilled workers in the late 1800s meant that many more children had to work to help support their families.

Young children did much of the factory work in the late 1800s.

What You Will Learn...

Main Ideas

1. Reformers attempted to improve conditions for child laborers.
2. Unions and reformers took steps to improve safety in the workplace and working hours.

The Big Idea

In the early 1900s progressives and reformers focused on improving conditions for American workers.

Key Terms and People

Florence Kelley, *p. 616*
Triangle Shirtwaist Fire, *p. 618*
workers' compensation laws, *p. 618*
capitalism, *p. 619*
socialism, *p. 619*
William "Big Bill" Haywood, *p. 619*
Industrial Workers of the World, *p. 619*

HSS 8.12.6 Discuss child labor, working conditions, and laissez-faire policies toward big business and examine the labor movement, including its leaders (e.g., Samuel Gompers), its demand for collective bargaining, and its strikes and protests over labor conditions.

Teach the Big Idea: Master the Standards

Standards Proficiency

Reforming the Workplace HSS 8.12.6; HSS Analysis Skills: HI 1, HI 2

1. **Teach** Ask students the Main Idea questions to teach this section.
2. **Apply** Have each student create a two-column chart and label the columns *Labor Issues* and *Reforms.* In the first column, students should list the working conditions created by industrialization. In the second column, students should list the ways in which progressives tried to address labor problems.
3. **Review** Discuss with students the strategies that were used by progressives to reform the workplace.
4. **Practice/Homework** Ask students to use the information in their charts to write a letter to an editor on the issue of child labor reform. **LS Verbal/Linguistic**

Alternative Assessment Handbook, Rubrics 7: Charts; and 17: Letters to Editors

Preteach

Bellringer

If YOU were there . . . Use the **Daily Bellringer Transparency** to help students answer the question.

Daily Bellringer Transparency, Section 3

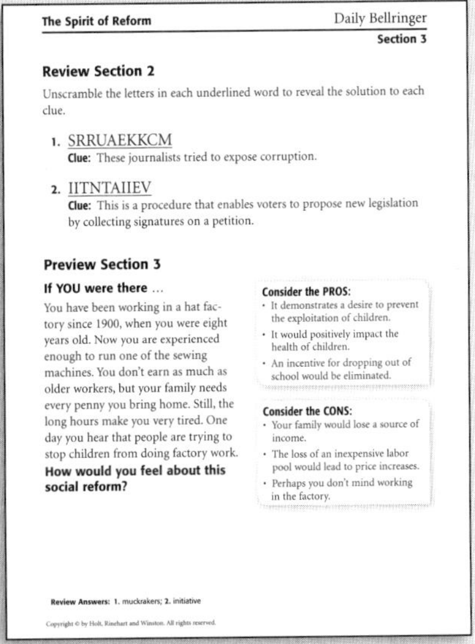

The Spirit of Reform — Daily Bellringer — Section 3

Review Section 2

Unscramble the letters in each underlined word to reveal the solution to each clue.

1. SRRUAEKKCM
   Clue: These journalists tried to expose corruption.
2. IITNTAIIEV
   Clue: This is a procedure that enables voters to propose new legislation by collecting signatures on a petition.

Preview Section 3

If YOU were there ...

You have been working in a hat factory since 1900, when you were eight years old. Now you are experienced enough to run one of the sewing machines. You don't earn as much as older workers, but your family needs every penny you bring home. Still, the long hours make you very tired. One day you hear that people are trying to stop children from doing factory work.

How would you feel about this social reform?

Consider the PROS:
- It demonstrates a desire to prevent the exploitation of children.
- It would positively impact the health of children.
- An incentive for dropping out of school would be eliminated.

Consider the CONS:
- Your family would lose a source of income.
- The loss of an inexpensive labor pool would lead to price increases.
- Perhaps you don't mind working in the factory.

Review Answers: 1. muckrakers; 2. initiative

Building Vocabulary

Preteach or review the following terms:

boarder one who pays for meals and sometimes lodging (p. 616)

compensation something given or received as payment or reparation for a loss (p. 618)

CRF: Vocabulary Builder Activity, Section 3

Standards Focus

HSS 8.12.6

Means: Examine working conditions, child labor, and the labor movement and its strategies.

Matters: The labor reforms of the progressive era laid the foundation for the protections American workers have today.

Direct Teach

Main Idea

❶ Improving Conditions for Children

Reformers attempted to improve conditions for child laborers.

Identify Who was Florence Kelly? *She was involved in Hull House and the National Consumers' League, and led the fight against child labor and lobbied for labor laws to protect women and children.*

Explain Why were children employed at factories? *They received lower wages, so they were cheaper to hire.*

Evaluate How effective were the reforms for child labor? *possible answer—somewhat effective because some laws were passed, but others were declared unconstitutional*

CRF: Primary Source Activity: Reform Efforts

HSS 8.12.6; HSS **Analysis Skills:** HI 1

Info to Know

Child Labor Activist Mary Harris Jones was known as "Mother" Jones. She crusaded for the rights of child workers as well as those of adults. In 1897 she organized children during a textile strike in Kensington, Pennsylvania. She marched on Washington with 10,000 children who worked in the mills. According to Jones, many of these children had lost fingers—and some even whole hands—in the mills. Most of the children were thin and sickly looking. They carried banners that read "We Want Time to Play."

Children at Work

Children sold newspapers or shined shoes on the streets. Girls often cooked and cleaned for boarders staying with their families. Girls also worked at home with their mothers, sewing clothes or making handcrafts.

Many children also worked outside the home in industry. In 1900 more than 1.75 million children age 15 and under worked in mines, mills, and factories. Businesses did not have to pay unskilled children high wages.

One wealthy reformer, Marie Van Vorst, posed as a poor woman to investigate child labor conditions. She saw children as young as seven years old working in a South Carolina textile mill. Some girls received as little as 40 cents per day for their work. Van Vorst described working with one young child:

> "Through the looms I catch sight of ... my landlord's little child. She is seven; so small that they have a box for her to stand on ... I can see only her fingers as they clutch at the flying spools;"
>
> —Marie Van Vorst, quoted in *A History of Women in America*, edited by Carol Hymowitz

This girl—and other children like her—provided cheap labor for manufacturers and brought home only small amounts of money to help their families to survive.

Calls for Reform

Reporters published accounts of working conditions for child laborers. Progressives and others then began to call for new reforms.

Florence Kelley, who was involved in Chicago's Hull House, led the progressive fight against child labor. She traveled throughout the United States lobbying for labor laws to protect women and children. She served as a board member of the National Consumers' League—the major lobbying group for women's and children's labor issues—and later founded the National Child Labor Committee to work for laws against child labor.

During the early 1900s, reformers finally succeeded in getting laws passed to ease the conditions of child labor. Her strategy was to "investigate, educate, legislate, and enforce." In 1912 the state of Massachusetts passed the first minimum wage law, and a commission was created to establish rates for child workers.

In 1916 and 1919 Congress passed federal child labor laws. The laws banned child-labor products from interstate commerce. The Supreme Court, however, ruled that the laws were unconstitutional. It argued that the laws went beyond the purpose for federal regulation of interstate commerce.

READING CHECK **Finding Main Ideas** How did reformers try to improve child labor conditions?

History Close-up

Working Conditions in Factories

In the early 1900s photographer Lewis Hine began to document the hardships endured by child laborers. Hine took this photograph and hundreds more like it. He labeled this one: "A typical glass works boy, night shift. Said he was 16 years old. 1 A.M. Indiana, 08/19/08." Such photographs, which company owners did not want the public to see, helped lead to the passage of child labor laws, which improved conditions for workers like this boy and those in the glass works factory illustration at right.

Differentiating Instruction for Universal Access

Learners Having Difficulty

Reaching Standards

1. As students read this section, have them create a time line showing major events like the passage of labor-reform laws and major court rulings that affected laborers in the United States.
2. Beneath the events and dates listed on the time lines, have students explain why reforms were needed and why the Supreme Court ruled the way that it did. LS **Verbal/Linguistic**

Advanced Learners/GATE

Exceeding Standards

1. Have students examine the images of child laborers in this section.
2. Then have each student select one image and write a description of the scene to convince a congressional committee to support the reform of child labor.
3. Ask volunteers to share their descriptions. LS **Verbal/Linguistic, Visual/Spatial**

HSS 8.12.6; HSS **Analysis Skills:** CS 1, CS 2, HI 1

Answers

Reading Check *lobbied and formed organizations to work for laws against child labor through minimum wage laws*

Hot air blew from the glass ovens into the working space.
Adult workers closely supervised child workers.
Workers wore no protection against the fires and machinery.
Temperatures in the ovens used to make glass were over 2,000° Fahrenheit.
Bending and lifting often left young workers tired and sore after their long day's work.
617

ANALYSIS SKILL ANALYZING VISUALS

Using the photograph and this illustration, what can you tell about the life and work of these boys?

Direct Teach

Connect to Literature

Charles Dickens Famed English novelist Charles Dickens grew up during the Industrial Revolution. As a boy he went to work in a factory to help support his family, who had fallen on hard times. His time in the factory left an impression on him, as he became an outspoken opponent of child labor. Issues relating to factory work and child labor are recurring themes in Dickens' books, such as *David Copperfield* and *Oliver Twist.*

Info to Know

Child Labor Laws After child labor laws were ruled unconstitutional, reformers looked for other ways to regulate working conditions for children. In the mid-1920s, Congress passed a constitutional amendment that would have allowed them to pass legislation regarding child labor. However, only 28 of the needed 38 states ratified the amendment. Then in 1938 Congress passed the Fair Labor Standards Act, and child labor legislation became a reality. This act set the minimum working age at 14 for nonmanufacturing jobs and at 18 for hazardous jobs.

Critical Thinking: Supporting a Point of View

Standards Proficiency

Interviews with Child Laborers

HSS 8.12.6; HSS **Analysis Skills:** HR 1, HI 1

1. Review with students the illustration above and working conditions child laborers faced.
2. Organize the class into pairs. Ask students to imagine that they live during the late 1800s and early 1900s. Ask one student in each pair to play the role of a journalist and the other to play the role of a child laborer.
3. Have the journalist in each pair write 10 interview questions, while the partner rereads the description of working conditions for children in factories.
4. Have each pair conduct an interview and write the dialogue of that interview for a magazine article. Remind students to discuss working conditions and what effect reforms might have on child laborers.
5. Ask volunteers to share their interviews with the class. **LS Interpersonal, Verbal/Linguistic**

Alternative Assessment Handbook, Rubric 37: Writing Assignments

Answers

Analyzing Visuals *possible answer—It was hard and dangerous work and a difficult life.*

Direct Teach

Main Idea

❷ Safety and Working Hours

Unions and reformers took steps to improve safety in the workplace and working hours.

Explain Why was the Triangle Shirtwaist Factory fire so tragic? *Women could not escape the fire because the factory owners had locked the doors to prevent theft of materials.*

Compare and Contrast How were *Lochner* v. *New York* and *Muller* v. *Oregon* similar and different? *similar—both concerned hours of work; different—In* Lochner, *the Court ruled that states could not restrict employers and workers from entering into labor agreements, but in* Muller, *the Court upheld laws limiting women's hours of work.*

Elaborate Why did reformers fight for workers' compensation laws? *allowed employees a measure of financial security if they suffered job-related injuries and could not work as a result*

U.S. Supreme Court Case Studies: *Lochner* vs. *New York* (1905)

HSS 8.12.6; **HSS Analysis Skills:** HI 1, HI 2

Primary Source

Reading Like a Historian

Triangle Shirtwaist Fire Help students practice reading the document like historians. Ask:

- What evidence does Ethel Monick give about working conditions in the factory?
- What effect might Ethel Monick's testimony have had on workplace safety reforms?

Primary Source

TRIAL TRANSCRIPT

Triangle Shirtwaist Fire

Ethel Monick was one of the teenaged factory workers who survived the fire at the Triangle Shirtwaist Company. In the trial that followed the disaster, she described her experience in the fire.

I seen the fire and then I seen all the girls rushing down to the place to escape. So I tried to go through the Greene Street door, and there were quick girls there and I seen I can't get out there, so I went to the elevator, and then I heard the elevator fall down, so I ran through to the Washington Place side, and I went over to the Washington Place side and there wasn't any girls there, so I ran over the doors and none was over there. So I went over to the door. I tried the door and I could not open it, so I thought I was not strong enough to open it, so I hollered girls here is a door, and they all rushed over and they tried to open it, but it was locked and they hollered "the door is locked and we can't open it!"

ANALYZING PRIMARY SOURCES

How does Ethel Monick describe her escape?

FOCUS ON READING

Read the excerpt from the trial transcript on this page. Is a first-person account of an event considered historical fact?

Safety and Working Hours

Child labor reform was only part of the progressive effort to help American workers. Many progressives also favored laws to ensure workers' safety, regulations limiting work hours, and other protections of workers' rights.

Workplace Safety

Tragic accidents in workplaces led reformers to call for laws protecting workers from unsafe conditions. In 1900 some 35,000 people were killed in industrial accidents. About 500,000 suffered injuries.

In 1911 a shocking accident took place at the Triangle Shirtwaist Company, a clothing factory that employed mostly immigrant women in New York City. As about 500 workers, mostly women and girls, prepared to leave the clothing factory one day, a fire broke out. The workers tried to escape through exit doors but found them locked. Owners had locked the factory doors to reduce theft of materials. By the time firefighters brought the fire under control, 146 workers had died. At a memorial service for the fire victims, union leader Rose Schneiderman called for action. "It is up to the working people to save themselves." The **Triangle Shirtwaist Fire** and similar accidents led to laws that improved factory safety standards.

Labor leaders and reformers also fought for **workers' compensation laws**, which would guarantee a portion of lost wages to workers injured on the job. In 1902 Maryland became the first of many states to pass a workers' compensation law. However, workplace laws were not always strictly enforced. Working conditions therefore remained poor in many places.

The Courts and Labor

Some business leaders opposed workplace regulations. They believed that the economy should operate without any government interference. State and federal courts began using the Fourteenth Amendment to support these views. The courts argued that this amendment protected businesses against laws that took their property without due process of law.

In 1897 the state of New York passed a law that limited bakers to a 10-hour workday. But a bakery owner named Joseph Lochner challenged the law. He claimed that it interfered

Collaborative Learning

Standards Proficiency

Organizing a Union

HSS 8.12.6; **HSS Analysis Skills:** HI 1

1. Review with the class the efforts taken to improve working conditions for children and workplace safety, and to limit working hours. Ask students what role labor unions played in these reform efforts.
2. Organize the class into small groups. Ask the groups to imagine that they are union leaders who want to push for progressive reforms such as working fewer hours each day, eliminating child labor, or creating stricter safety standards.
3. Have each group design a handbill to distribute to workers that identifies and explains one important reform and how it will affect workers in a particular job. In their handbills, students should ask workers to join the union and explain why it will help improve their lives.
4. Have groups present their handbills to the class. **LS Interpersonal, Verbal/Linguistic**

Alternative Assessment Handbook, Rubrics 2: Advertisements; and 14: Group Activity

Answers

Analyzing Primary Sources *as panicked, fearful, and terrifying*

Focus on Reading *It is historical fact in that it is a record of that person's view of events; however, the person's view of events might be biased or inaccurate.*

with his right to run his business. The case eventually went to the U.S. Supreme Court in 1905. In *Lochner* v. *New York* the Court ruled that states could not restrict the rights of employers and workers to enter into any type of labor agreement. The New York law was declared unconstitutional.

The Supreme Court did uphold some limits on working hours for women and children. In the 1908 *Muller* v. *Oregon* case, the Court upheld laws restricting women's work hours. The justices stated that a woman's health is of public concern. *Muller* v. *Oregon* was the first case that progressives had won using arguments based on economic, scientific, and social evidence. Such victories encouraged progressives and labor leaders to attempt more reforms.

Labor Organizations

Labor unions also tried to improve working conditions. Union membership rose from more than 800,000 in 1900 to about 5 million in 1920. Led by Samuel Gompers, the American Federation of Labor (AFL) remained one of the strongest labor unions. The AFL focused on better working conditions and pay for skilled workers. Gompers supported **capitalism**, an economic system in which private businesses run most industries, and competition determines how much goods cost.

Some union members, however, supported **socialism**—a system in which the government owns and operates a country's means of production. Socialists hoped that the government would protect workers.

In 1905 a group of socialists and union leaders founded a union that welcomed immigrants, women, African Americans, and others not welcome in the AFL. Led by **William "Big Bill" Haywood**, this socialist union was called the **Industrial Workers of the World** (IWW) and wanted to organize all workers into one large union that would overthrow capitalism. Staging strikes across the country, the IWW frightened business leaders and many other Americans. Strong opposition weakened the IWW, and by 1920 the union had almost disappeared.

READING CHECK **Analyzing** How did reforms change the workplace?

SUMMARY AND PREVIEW Reformers worried about working conditions in factories. In the next section you will learn about how women and minorities struggled for their rights.

Section 3 Assessment

go.hrw.com
Online Quiz
KEYWORD: SS8 HP19

Reviewing Ideas, Terms, and People HSS 8.12.6

1. a. **Recall** What jobs did child laborers often hold?
   b. **Explain** Why did businesses employ children in factories?
   c. **Elaborate** Why do you think reformers began to demand improvements to child labor conditions?
2. a. **Identify** What events led to the movement to improve workplace safety?
   b. **Make Inferences** Why did the **Industrial Workers of the World** union frighten some people?
   c. **Predict** What conflicts might arise between supporters of **capitalism** and **socialism**?

Critical Thinking

3. **Analyzing** Copy the graphic organizer shown at right. Use it to describe how progressives tried to reform child labor, women's labor, and workplace conditions.

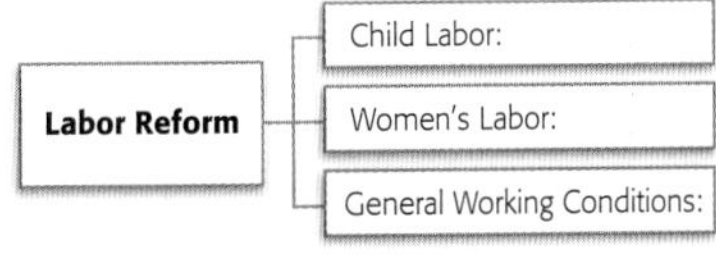

FOCUS ON SPEAKING

4. **Addressing Problems in the Workplace** How would you address problems in the workplace? Make notes on campaign promises you might make to assure voters that you would address issues of child labor and workplace safety.

Direct Teach

Info to Know

Industrial Workers of the World
Founded in 1905 in Chicago, the IWW opposed capitalism and argued that workers were fighting a bitter class struggle. The IWW vowed to organize lumber workers, migrant farm workers, miners, and textile workers to overthrow the capitalist system. Known as Wobblies, IWW members pursued their goals through boycotts, general strikes, and industrial sabotage. Their greatest hour came in 1912, when they led 10,000 workers in a successful strike against the textile mills of Lawrence, Massachusetts.

Review & Assess

Close

Have students consider how the reform movements discussed in this section led to major improvements in workplace safety and standards.

Review

Online Quiz, Section 3

Assess

SE Section 3 Assessment

PASS: Section 3 Quiz

Alternative Assessment Handbook

Reteach/Classroom Intervention

California Standards Review Workbook

Interactive Reader and Study Guide, Section 3

Interactive Skills Tutor CD-ROM

Section 3 Assessment Answers

1. **a.** sold newspapers; shined shoes; cooked and cleaned for boarders; made garments, artificial flowers, costume jewelry; worked in factories
   b. Businesses did not have to pay high wages to unskilled children.
   c. possible answer—The work was unhealthy, dangerous, and prevented children from attending school.
2. **a.** workplace injuries and tragic accidents such as the Triangle Shirtwaist Fire
   b. possible answers—They wanted to overthrow capitalism; they staged large strikes.
   c. possible answer—conflicts between unions that favor capitalism and those that favor socialism
3. Child labor—lobbying groups, minimum wage law in Massachusetts, attempts at federal laws; Women's labor—restriction of hours; General working conditions—workers' compensation laws, workplace safety
4. Students should make notes on how they would address child labor and workplace safety.

Answers

Reading Check *led to minimum wage laws and rates for child workers, improved factory safety standards, workers' compensation laws, and some limits on work hours*

Literature in History

How The Other Half Lives

As You Read Ask students to create three lists, one each for *smell, see,* and *hear*. Instruct students to write down details about Cherry Street in each list as they read the passage.

Meet the Writer

Jacob Riis Born in Denmark, Jacob Riis came to the United States in 1870 at age 21. As an immigrant, he worked at many menial and low-paying jobs and slept in substandard housing and alleyways. Eventually, he found a job as a police photographer and reporter and became a social reformer. His great passion as a writer was defending the rights of the poor and bringing attention to their plight.

Did you know . . .

By 1880, New York City had some 37,000 tenements, which were home to more than 1 million people. More than 100,000 of these residents lived in rear apartments that were unfit for human habitation.

Literature in History

Reform Literature

from *How the Other Half Lives*

by Jacob Riis (1849–1914)

About the Reading How the Other Half Lives *describes the overcrowded houses where immigrants lived in New York City. Its author, Jacob Riis, was a newspaper reporter. His nonfiction book made Americans aware of the extremes of poverty suffered by working people. Riis believed that every human being deserved a decent, safe place to live.* How the Other Half Lives *led to reforms and new laws that improved housing conditions.*

AS YOU READ **Look for details that help you see, hear, and smell Cherry Street.**

Cherry Street. Be a little careful, please! ❶ The hall is dark and you might stumble over the children pitching pennies back there. Not that it would hurt them; kicks and cuffs are their daily diet. They have little else. Here where the hall turns and dives into utter darkness is a step, and another, another. A flight of stairs. You can feel your way, if you cannot see it. Close? Yes! What would you have? All the fresh air that ever enters these stairs comes from the hall door that is forever slamming, and from the windows of dark bedrooms that in turn receive from the stairs their sole supply of the elements God meant to be free . . . That was a woman filling her pail by the hydrant you just bumped against. The sinks are in the hallway, that all the tenants may have access—and all be poisoned alike by their summer stenches. Hear the pump squeak! It is the lullaby of tenement house babes. In summer, when a thousand thirsty throats pant for a cooling drink in this block, it is worked in vain . . . ❷

The sea of a mighty population, held in galling fetters, heaves uneasily in the tenements . . . If it rise once more, no human power may avail to check it. The gap between the classes in which it surges, unseen, unsuspected by the thoughtless, is widening day by day . . . I know of but one bridge that will carry us over safe, a bridge founded upon justice and built of human hearts.

GUIDED READING

WORD HELP

cuffs punches
utter complete
close stuffy
sole only
access right to use
stenches bad smells
in vain without success
galling causing pain; irritating
fetters chains
heaves rises and falls

❶ ***The writer wants you to imagine that he is taking you on a tour of the building. Why do you think he chooses this way to describe the place?***

❷ ***Find one detail that appeals to each sense: sight, sound, smell, taste, and touch. How would you sum up, in one sentence, the place that Riis describes?***

ELA Reading 8.3.7 Analyze a work of literature, showing how it reflects the heritage, traditions, attitudes, and beliefs of its author.

Differentiating Instruction for Universal Access

English-Language Learners

Standards Proficiency — Standard English Mastery

1. Tell students that vivid imagery is language that creates word pictures and appeals to the senses.
2. Help students list and define words in the passage that appeal to the senses. Then have students illustrate a scene from the passage. **LS Visual/Spatial**

ELA Reading 8.6.3

Advanced Learners/GATE

Exceeding Standards

1. Have students use the information in the section and in this passage to write their own descriptions of tenement life.
2. Students should follow the style of Jacob Riis and create strong, vivid images. **LS Verbal/Linguistic**

Alternative Assessment Handbook, Rubric 40: Writing to Describe

ELA Writing 8.2.2a

Answers

Guided Reading **1.** *It makes the reader feel as if he or she is actually there.* **2.** *sight—dark, sound—squeak of pump, smell—summer stenches, taste—panting for a cooling drink; possible answer—It was a dark, deadly, and unhappy place to live.*

from *The Jungle*

by Upton Sinclair (1878–1968)

About the Reading The Jungle *focused the nation's attention on immigrant workers in the meatpacking industry. Upton Sinclair's novel showed bosses forcing human beings to live and work like jungle animals. He also described, in shocking detail, how meat was handled. Sinclair published his book in 1906. Later that same year, the government passed the Pure Food and Drug Act and the Meat Inspection Act. Many Americans even gave up eating meat for a while.*

AS YOU READ **Look for details that create one overwhelming effect.**

There was never the least attention paid to what was cut up for sausage; ❶ there would come back from Europe old sausage that had been rejected, and that was mouldy and white—it would be dosed with borax and glycerine, and dumped into hoppers, and made over again for home consumption. There would be meat that had tumbled out on the floor, in the dirt and sawdust, where the workers had tramped and spit uncounted billions of consumption germs. ❷ There would be meat stored in great piles in rooms and the water from leaky roofs would drip over it, and thousands of rats would race about on it. It was too dark in these storage places to see well, but a man would run his hand over these piles of meat and sweep off handfuls of the dried dung of rats. ❸ These rats were nuisances, and the packers would put poisoned bread out for them and they would die, and then rats, bread, and meat would go into the hoppers together . . . ❹ There was no place for the men to wash their hands before they ate their dinner, and so they made a practice of washing them in the water that was to be ladled into the sausage.

GUIDED READING

WORD HELP

borax white powder used in manufacturing and cleaning

glycerine sweet, sticky liquid

hoppers containers

consumption eating; tuberculosis, a lung disease that was fatal at that time

ladled added with a large spoon

❶ ***What overall effect or mood does Sinclair create?***

❷ ***Based on the details in this passage, what were the packers most concerned about?***

❸ ***Why do you think rats were considered nuisances?***

❹ ***Find details that reveal how one improvement in working conditions might have resulted in healthier sausage.***

CONNECTING LITERATURE TO HISTORY

1. **Identify Cause and Effect** Jacob Riis and Upton Sinclair were both muckraking journalists. Why do you think so much muck existed in the tenements and in the meatpacking business? Why had people ignored those terrible conditions for so long?
2. **Identify Cause and Effect** Both Riis and Sinclair believed that improving conditions for immigrants would benefit all of society. Explain how one specific change in the tenements might have a favorable effect on everyone. Then explain how one specific change in meat handling might affect everyone.
3. **Compare and Contrast** Both *How the Other Half Lives* and *The Jungle* inspired progressives to work for reform. Which work do you think had the greater effect on its readers? Use details from each passage to explain your answer.

Literature in History

The Jungle

As You Read Have students read through the passage without stopping. After they finish, tell them to note how the passage creates a continuous line of thought and how it affected them.

Meet the Writer

Upton Sinclair A prolific writer, Upton Sinclair authored more than 80 works during his lifetime. He became a well-known muckraker with the publication of *The Jungle.* Sinclair even attempted politics—he ran for governor of California in 1934.

Linking to Today

Fast Food Reporting A book called *Fast Food Nation* by Eric Schlosser was published in 2002. Like *The Jungle*, it addressed issues of concern in the food industry. Schlosser's report on the fast food industry became a bestseller and raised concerns with many Americans.

Cross-Discipline Activity: Civics

Standards Proficiency

Consumer Protection HSS 8.12.6; HSS **Analysis Skills:** HI 1, HI 2

Background After reading *The Jungle*, President Theodore Roosevelt persuaded Congress to pass the Pure Food and Drug Act of 1906. The act banned the manufacture, sale, or transportation of mislabeled or contaminated food and drugs. It was one of the first acts aimed at protecting consumers.

1. Ask students to imagine that they are speechwriters for President Roosevelt. He is planning to make a speech in favor of the Pure Food and Drug Act.
2. Have each student write a speech for Roosevelt to persuade members of Congress to vote in favor of this law.
3. Ask volunteers to present their speeches to the class. LS **Verbal/Linguistic**

Alternative Assessment Handbook, Rubric 43: Writing to Persuade

Answers

Guided Reading **1.** *one of disgust* **2.** *profit and getting meat processed cheaply and quickly* **3.** *They were on, and often in, the meat.* **4.** *possible answer—Getting rid of the rats would allow the meat to be cleaner.*

Connecting Literature to History
1. *There were no regulations to keep conditions healthy. They didn't have the political power or influence to make changes.* **2.** *possible answer—Improved sewer lines would lead to healthier living conditions; providing meatpackers a place to clean themselves would lead to clean water in the sausages.* **3.** *Students' answers will vary, but should use appropriate evidence from the passages to support their arguments.*

Preteach

Bellringer

If YOU were there . . . Use the **Daily Bellringer Transparency** to help students answer the question.

Daily Bellringer Transparency, Section 4

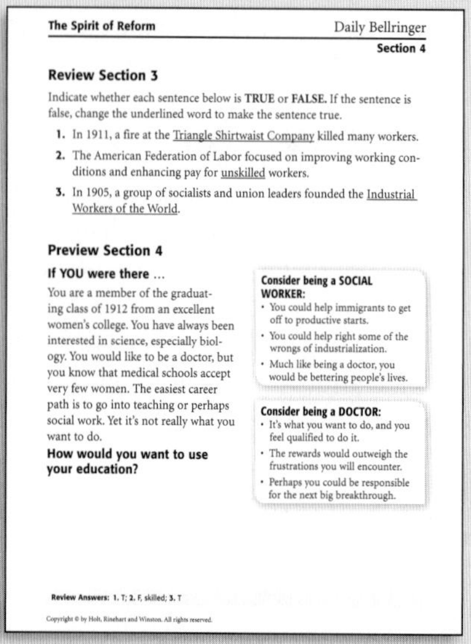

The Spirit of Reform — Daily Bellringer **Section 4**

Review Section 3

Indicate whether each sentence below is **TRUE** or **FALSE.** If the sentence is false, change the underlined word to make the sentence true.

1. In 1911, a fire at the Triangle Shirtwaist Company killed many workers.
2. The American Federation of Labor focused on improving working conditions and enhancing pay for unskilled workers.
3. In 1905, a group of socialists and union leaders founded the Industrial Workers of the World.

Preview Section 4

If YOU were there ...

You are a member of the graduating class of 1912 from an excellent women's college. You have always been interested in science, especially biology. You would like to be a doctor, but you know that medical schools accept very few women. The easiest career path is to go into teaching or perhaps social work. Yet it's not really what you want to do.

How would you want to use your education?

Consider being a SOCIAL WORKER:
- You could help immigrants to get off to productive starts.
- You could help right some of the wrongs of industrialization.
- Much like being a doctor, you would be bettering people's lives.

Consider being a DOCTOR:
- It's what you want to do, and you feel qualified to do it.
- The rewards would outweigh the frustrations you will encounter.
- Perhaps you could be responsible for the next big breakthrough.

Review Answers: 1. T; 2. F, skilled; 3. T

Building Vocabulary

Preteach or review the following terms:

discrimination prejudicial treatment of individuals (p. 624)

reservations public lands set aside for use by Native Americans (p. 625)

temperance avoidance of alcohol (p. 622)

CRF: Vocabulary Builder Activity, Section 4

Standards Focus

HSS 8.12.5

Means: Examine the effects of city growth, new immigration, and industrialization on American cities and society.

Matters: Today, activists continue to work to address urban and social problems and to fight for equal rights for women and minorities.

SECTION 4

The Rights of Women and Minorities

What You Will Learn...

Main Ideas

1. Female progressives fought for temperance and the right to vote.
2. African American reformers challenged discrimination and called for equality.
3. Progressive reform did not benefit all minorities.

The Big Idea

The progressive movement made advances for the rights of women and some other minorities.

Key Terms and People

Woman's Christian Temperance Union, *p. 623*
Eighteenth Amendment, *p. 623*
National American Woman Suffrage Association, *p. 623*
Alice Paul, *p. 624*
National Woman's Party, *p. 624*
Nineteenth Amendment, *p. 624*
Booker T. Washington, *p. 624*
Ida B. Wells, *p. 624*
W. E. B. Du Bois, *p. 624*
National Association for the Advancement of Colored People, *p. 625*

HSS 8.12.5 Examine the location and effects of urbanization, renewed immigration, and industrialization (e.g., the effects on social fabric of cities, wealth and economic opportunity, the conservation movement).

If YOU were there...

You are a member of the graduating class of 1912 from an excellent women's college. You have always been interested in science, especially biology. You would like to be a doctor, but you know that medical schools accept very few women. The easiest career path for you is to go into teaching or perhaps social work. Yet it's not really what you want to do.

How would you want to use your education?

BUILDING BACKGROUND The progressives had a wide variety of goals. Besides attacking social problems such as child labor, they tried to reform government and make it more democratic. Changes in women's education affected the movement, as college-educated women became leaders in working for reforms.

Women Fight for Temperance and Voting Rights

New educational opportunities drew more women into the progressive movement. In the late 1800s women began attending colleges like Smith and Vassar in record numbers. In 1870 only about 20 percent of college students were women. By 1910 that number had doubled. The goal of female students was "to develop as fully as may be the powers of womanhood," said Sophia Smith, founder of Smith College.

Many female graduates entered fields such as social work and teaching. They found it much harder to enter professions such as law and medicine, which were dominated by men. Denied access to such professions, women played a major role in reform movements. Women's clubs campaigned for dozens of causes, including temperance, women's suffrage, child welfare, and political reform.

Teach the Big Idea: Master the Standards

Standards Proficiency

The Rights of Women and Minorities

HSS 8.12.5; HSS **Analysis Skills:** HI 1, HI 2

1. **Teach** Ask students the Main Idea questions to teach this section.
2. **Apply** Have each student create a list of issues that women and minority groups faced during the late 1800s. Have students explain how reformers addressed or failed to address the issues and whether reform efforts solved the problem fairly and adequately.
3. **Review** Create a class list of the issues that students have listed. Discuss related reform efforts and how successful they were.
4. **Practice/Homework** Have students select two issues from their lists, one they think was successfully resolved and one they think was not. Have each student create a graphic organizer that compares and contrasts the two issues. **LS Verbal/Linguistic**

Alternative Assessment Handbook, Rubrics 9: Comparing and Contrasting; and 13: Graphic Organizers

Two causes that women's reform groups took up were temperance, or avoidance of alcohol, and women's right to vote. Since the 1840s temperance reformers had blamed alcohol for society's problems. By the 1870s more than 1,000 saloons had been forced to shut down by these reformers. One radical temperance fighter was Carry Nation. In the 1890s Nation became famous for storming into saloons with a hatchet, smashing bottles.

In 1874 reformers from many different backgrounds formed the **Woman's Christian Temperance Union** (WCTU), which fought for adoption of local and state laws restricting the sale of alcohol. Under the leadership of Frances Willard, the organization started 10,000 branches. In 1919 temperance efforts eventually led to the passage of the **Eighteenth Amendment**, banning the production, sale, and transportation of alcoholic beverages throughout the United States.

Women reformers also fought for the right to vote, or suffrage. Many people, however, opposed giving women the vote. Political bosses worried about the anti-corruption efforts of women. Some businesspeople worried that women voters would support child labor laws and minimum wage laws. Some people believed that women should only be homemakers and mothers and not politically active citizens.

Elizabeth Cady Stanton and Susan B. Anthony founded the **National American Woman Suffrage Association** (NAWSA) in 1890 to get women the vote. That same year, women gained the right to vote in Wyoming. Colorado, Idaho, and Utah followed in the 1890s.

Carrie Chapman Catt had fought successfully for women's suffrage in the West. After becoming president of the NAWSA in 1900, she mobilized more than 1 million volunteers for the movement. She argued that women should have a voice in creating laws that affected them.

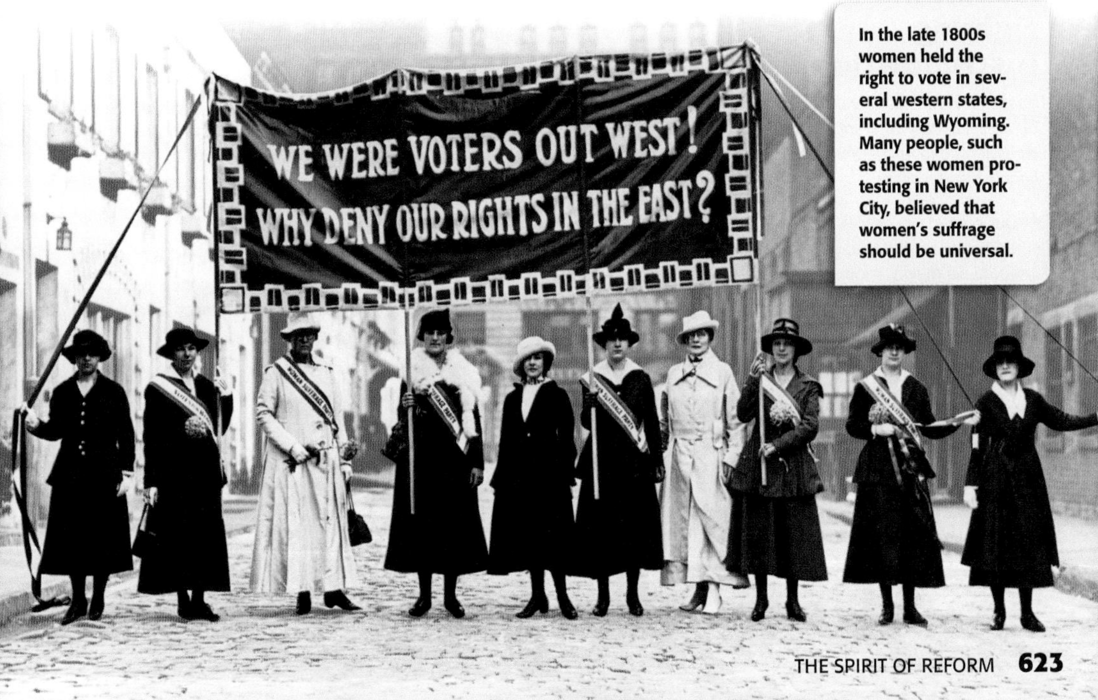

WE WERE VOTERS OUT WEST!
WHY DENY OUR RIGHTS IN THE EAST?

In the late 1800s women held the right to vote in several western states, including Wyoming. Many people, such as these women protesting in New York City, believed that women's suffrage should be universal.

Direct Teach

Main Idea

❶ Women Fight for Temperance and Voting Rights

Female progressives fought for temperance and the right to vote.

Recall What did the Eighteenth and Nineteenth Amendments accomplish? *Eighteenth Amendment banned the sale of alcohol; Nineteenth Amendment granted women the right to vote.*

Explain Why did temperance reformers oppose alcohol consumption? *believed alcohol was a major social problem that added to family poverty*

Predict What might be some of the long-term effects of giving women the right to vote? *possible answers—more democratic government, government that is more responsive to women's needs, increase in women's rights reforms*

HSS 8.12.5; **HSS Analysis Skills:** HI 1, HI 2

Linking to Today

Women and Education Today women make up approximately 57 percent of the total college population in the United States. They earn 56 percent of all the bachelor's degrees awarded. However, women still tend to major in education, humanities, and library science. Women earn only 17 percent of engineering bachelor's degrees, and only 30 percent of those receiving doctoral degrees in business are women.

Did you know . . .

In 1872, Susan B. Anthony was fined $100 for illegally voting in the United States presidential election.

Differentiating Instruction for Universal Access

Advanced Learners/GATE

Exceeding Standards | Research Required

Background The Equal Rights Amendment was first introduced to Congress in the 1920s. The amendment sought equal rights under the law, regardless of sex. In the 1970s Congress approved the amendment, but it failed to be ratified by the required majority of 38 states.

1. Pair students and have some conduct research on women's suffrage and others on the Equal Rights Amendment.
2. Have students prepare two posters—one on women's suffrage and the other on the Equal Rights Amendment. Posters should include slogans, brief biographies, and images of the key figures.
3. Then hold a class discussion about why the suffrage movement was successful, while the Equal Rights Amendment failed.

LS Verbal/Linguistic

HSS 8.12.5; **HSS Analysis Skills:** HI 1, HI 2

Alternative Assessment Handbook, Rubrics 28: Posters; and 30: Research

However, some women believed that the NAWSA did not go far enough. In 1913 **Alice Paul** founded what would become the **National Woman's Party** (NWP). The NWP was a powerful and controversial alternative to the NAWSA that used parades and public demonstrations, picketing, hunger strikes, and other means of protest to draw attention to the suffrage cause. Paul and other NWP leaders were even jailed for their actions.

Suffragists finally succeeded in gaining the vote. The **Nineteenth Amendment** was declared ratified by the U.S. Congress in 1920 and gave American women the right to vote.

READING CHECK **Analyzing** What methods did reformers use to draw attention to the temperance and women's suffrage movements?

African Americans Challenge Discrimination

White reformers often overlooked issues such as racial discrimination and segregation. Some African American leaders such as **Booker T. Washington** did not. Born into slavery, Washington became a respected educator while in his twenties. He encouraged African Americans to improve their educational and economic well-being rather than fight discrimination.

Other African Americans, such as journalist **Ida B. Wells**, spoke out against discrimination. In her Memphis newspaper called *Free Speech*, she drew attention to the lynching of African American men. Because of death threats, she was forced to move to the North, where she continued campaigning for change.

W. E. B. Du Bois also took a direct approach to fighting racial injustice. Born in Massachusetts, Du Bois was a college

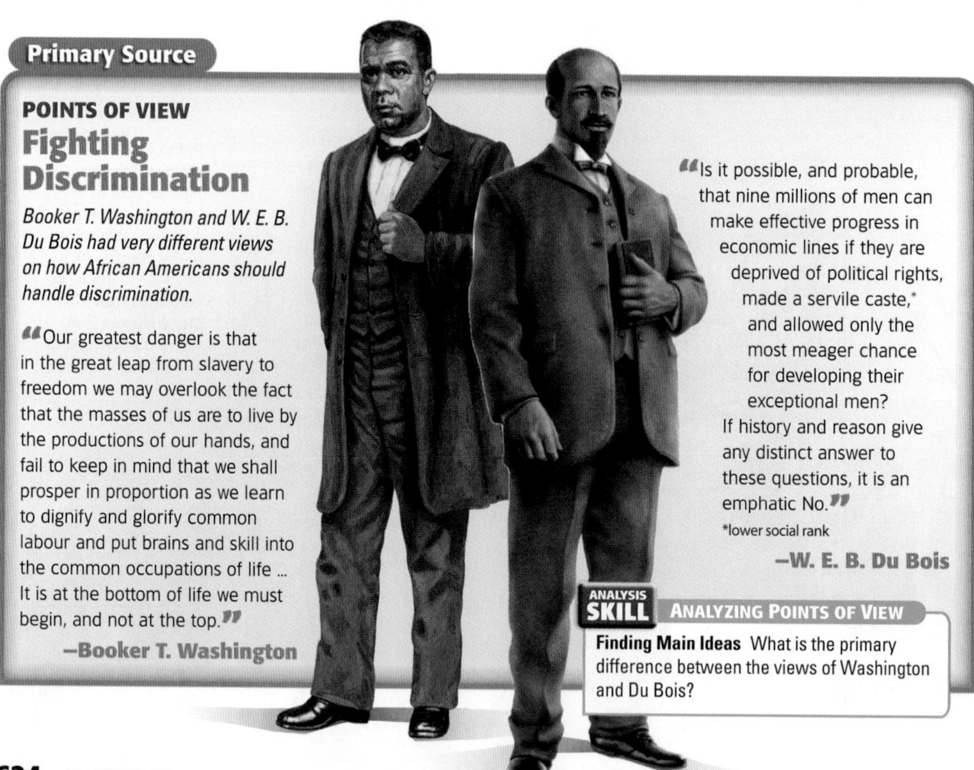

Primary Source

POINTS OF VIEW

Fighting Discrimination

Booker T. Washington and W. E. B. Du Bois had very different views on how African Americans should handle discrimination.

"Our greatest danger is that in the great leap from slavery to freedom we may overlook the fact that the masses of us are to live by the productions of our hands, and fail to keep in mind that we shall prosper in proportion as we learn to dignify and glorify common labour and put brains and skill into the common occupations of life ... It is at the bottom of life we must begin, and not at the top."

—**Booker T. Washington**

"Is it possible, and probable, that nine millions of men can make effective progress in economic lines if they are deprived of political rights, made a servile caste,* and allowed only the most meager chance for developing their exceptional men? If history and reason give any distinct answer to these questions, it is an emphatic No."

*lower social rank

—**W. E. B. Du Bois**

ANALYSIS SKILL **ANALYZING POINTS OF VIEW**

Finding Main Ideas What is the primary difference between the views of Washington and Du Bois?

Direct Teach

Main Idea

❷ African Americans Challenge Discrimination

African American reformers challenged discrimination and called for equality.

Identify Who was Ida B. Wells? *African American journalist and editor of Memphis newspaper,* Free Speech, *who spoke out against lynching of African American men*

Elaborate What strategy did Booker T. Washington suggest that African Americans follow to improve themselves? *education and work, thereby improving their position*

CRF: Biography Activities: George Washington Carver; Ida B. Wells

CRF: Primary Source Activity: Washington and Du Bois

HSS 8.12.5; **HSS** **Analysis Skills:** HI 1

Biography

W. E. B. Du Bois (1868–1963) W. E. B. Du Bois was a civil rights leader, writer, and professor of economics, history, and sociology. *The Souls of Black Folk,* published in 1903, was one of his most influential works and is still widely read today. In it, Du Bois discusses racism and states that race relations are the key problem of the 1900s. Toward the end of his life, Du Bois became so frustrated with the progress of civil rights in the United States that in 1962, he renounced his American citizenship and emigrated to Ghana.

Answers

Analyzing Points of View *Washington—African Americans should better their educational and economic well-being rather than fight discrimination. Du Bois—African Americans should use the legal system to fight discrimination.*

Reading Check *Some used radical methods, while most joined various women's rights groups and held parades and public demonstrations.*

Collaborative Learning

Standards Proficiency

African American Civil Rights

Research Required

1. Organize students into small groups. Have each group conduct research on Booker T. Washington, the Tuskegee Institute, W. E. B. Du Bois, the Niagara Movement, and the origins of the NAACP. Have each group use its research to create a short television-news segment about the fight for African Americans' civil rights during the late 1800s.
2. Segments should include interviews, information about how African American leaders tried to improve conditions, types of discrimination, the effects of *Guinn* v. *United States*, and the National Urban League. Encourage students to use charts and other visual aids to present their information.
3. After students have completed their segments, have them present their news reports to the rest of the class. **LS Interpersonal, Verbal/Linguistic**

HSS 8.12.5; **HSS** **Analysis Skills:** CS 1, HI 1, HI 2

Alternative Assessment Handbook, Rubrics 14: Group Activity; 29: Presentations; and 30: Research

Left Behind

Unfortunately, progressive reforms did not help everyone. Non-European immigrants received much less attention than their European counterparts. Immigrants from Mexico, who faced some of the worst working conditions, were largely ignored. Many Mexican immigrants, like these migrant farm workers living in California, worked from sunup to sundown for little pay. Progressive reforms did nothing to improve their situation.

Why do you think progressive reforms did not help all groups?

graduate who earned a doctorate from Harvard University. He publicized cases of racial prejudice.

In 1909 Du Bois and other reformers founded the **National Association for the Advancement of Colored People** (NAACP), an organization that called for economic and educational equality for African Americans. The NAACP attacked discrimination by using the courts. In 1915 it won the important case of *Guinn* v. *United States*, which outlawed so-called grandfather clauses. These were used in the South to keep African Americans from voting. Those clauses imposed qualifications on African American voters unless the voters' grandfathers had been allowed to vote.

Another important organization, the National Urban League, was formed in 1911. This organization aided many African Americans moving from the South by helping them to find jobs and housing.

READING CHECK **Contrasting** What was the purpose of the NAACP?

Progressive Reform Failures

The progressive movement left behind members of other minority groups. In the 1890s the Native American population in the United States had declined to fewer than 250,000, its lowest point ever. To deal with poverty among Native Americans, the Society of American Indians was started in 1911. Society members wanted Native Americans to adopt the ways of white society. They believed this might end widespread poverty.

Many Native Americans, however, wanted to preserve their traditional culture. Despite their poverty, by 1912 some 2,000 Cherokee had refused to accept nonreservation lands granted to them. Eventually, new laws let Native Americans stay on reservations.

Some immigrant groups were also ignored by white progressives. For example, many Chinese immigrants who came to the United States for gold mining and railroad jobs had hard lives. With the passage of the Chinese Exclusion Act of 1882, immigration

THE IMPACT TODAY

Today the NAACP has around 2,200 adult branches and 1,700 branches for young people.

Direct Teach

Main Idea

3 Progressive Reform Failures

Progressive reform did not benefit all minorities.

Recall When and why was the society of American Indians formed? *1911; to deal with poverty among Native Americans*

Evaluate Why do you think the Cherokee refused to follow the provisions of the Dawes Act? *would have to move to unknown territory, lose land guaranteed to them, lose their traditional culture and way of life*

CRF: History and Geography Activity: Patterns of Immigration

HSS 8.12.5; **HSS** **Analysis Skills:** HI 1, HI 2

Info to Know

The Niagara Movement In 1905 W. E. B. Du Bois and others met at Niagara Falls. The group drafted a Declaration of Principles, which protested discrimination against African Americans and asked for the support of others in ending that discrimination. The Niagara Movement, as this group was called, lasted only a few years before disbanding because of a lack of financial support.

Critical Thinking: Solving Problems

Standards Proficiency

Letters to the Editor **HSS** 8.12.5; **HSS** **Analysis Skills:** CS 1, HI 1

1. Have students reread the information in the text under the heading "Progressive Reform Failures." Have students select one of the three groups discussed in the text, either Native Americans or Chinese or Mexican immigrants.
2. Have each student create a letter to the editor of a newspaper in the early 1900s. The letter should explain issues members of this group are facing and suggest ways in which reforms might be enacted.
3. Organize the class into small groups where students can share their work. Ask each group to select one letter to share with the class. **LS Verbal/Linguistic**

Alternative Assessment Handbook, Rubric 17: Letters to Editors

Answers

Reading Check *to promote economic and educational equality for African Americans and to fight discrimination*

Left Behind *possible answer—progressive groups may not have had members from those groups, they may have been concerned with other issues.*

Direct Teach

Main Idea

❸ Progressive Reform Failures

Progressive reform did not benefit all minorities.

Recall What was the Chinese Exclusion Act of 1882? *a law that prohibited Chinese people from immigrating to the United States for 10 years*

Contrast What happened to Chinese immigration rates compared to Mexican immigration rates between 1901 and 1930, and why? *Chinese immigration slowed because of the Chinese Exclusion Act; Mexican immigration increased because of the ease in crossing the border.*

CRF: Biography Activity: Wong Kim Ark

Review & Assess

Close

Have students write a short summary of the rights that women and some minorities won during this time.

Review

Online Quiz, Section 4

Assess

SE Section 4 Assessment

PASS: Section 4 Quiz

Alternative Assessment Handbook

Reteach/Classroom Intervention

California Standards Review Workbook

Interactive Reader and Study Guide, Section 4

Interactive Skills Tutor CD-ROM

Answers

Reading Check *Progressive reform did not benefit all minorities.*

Chinese Americans built strong communities in the face of discrimination and violence. Here, Chinese children study in an American classroom.

slowed. The law prohibited Chinese people from immigrating to the United States for 10 years. Congress later extended the ban, attempting to make immigration from China permanently illegal.

Chinese immigrants also faced anti-Chinese riots in several western states and territories during the late 1800s. For protection, many Chinese Americans formed their own communities in cities such as San Francisco.

While Chinese immigration dropped, Mexican immigration rose. During this time, immigrants could move fairly easily across the U.S. borders with both Mexico and Canada. Most Mexican immigrants moved to areas that had once been part of Mexico. Mexican immigrants became a key part of the southwestern and western economies.

READING CHECK **Summarizing** What were the limitations of progressive reforms?

SUMMARY AND PREVIEW Citizens worked for progressive reforms. In the next section you will read about the progressive presidents and their goals.

Section 4 Assessment

go.hrw.com Online Quiz KEYWORD: SS8 HP19

Reviewing Ideas, Terms, and People HSS 8.12.5

1. a. **Identify** What did the **Eighteenth** and **Nineteenth Amendments** accomplish?
   b. **Summarize** How did **Alice Paul** and the **National Woman's Party** try to draw attention to the issue of women's suffrage?
2. a. **Identify** What role did **Ida B. Wells** play in reform efforts for African Americans?
   b. **Contrast** How did **Booker T. Washington** differ from other African American leaders?
   c. **Evaluate** Do you think the **National Association for the Advancement of Colored People** was successful in fighting discrimination? Explain.
3. a. **Describe** What discrimination did Chinese Americans face?
   b. **Summarize** How were some minority groups overlooked by the progressive movement?

Critical Thinking

4. **Analyzing** Copy the diagram shown. Use it to identify the progressive reforms introduced by the temperance movement, the women's suffrage movement, and by African Americans.

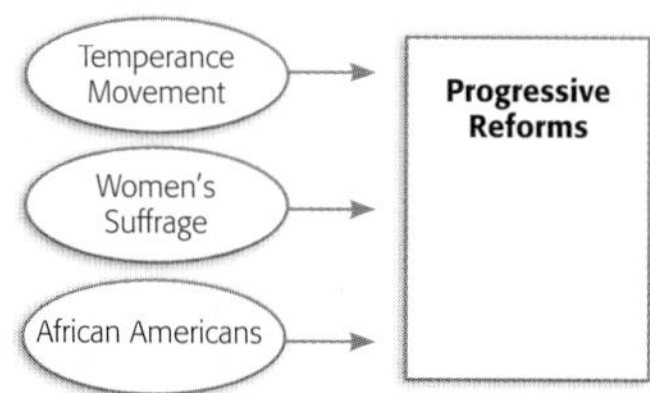

FOCUS ON SPEAKING

5. **Addressing the Rights of Women and Minorities** Consider your positions on education for women, women's suffrage, temperance, discrimination, and segregation. What promises would you make in regard to these issues? Think about how you would make your ideas acceptable to the American public. Would you be willing to compromise your ideals?

Section 4 Assessment Answers

1. a. Eighteenth—prohibition; Nineteenth—gave women the right to vote
   b. by using parades and public demonstrations
2. a. publicized lynching through her newspaper
   b. He encouraged African Americans to improve educational and economic well-being rather than fight discrimination.
   c. possible answers: yes—they won *Guinn* v. *United States*; no—they did not completely end discrimination.
3. a. faced riots and laws limiting immigration
   b. Many progressive reforms ignored minority groups such as Native Americans and Chinese and Mexican immigrants.
4. Temperance—laws to restrict sale of alcohol, Eighteenth Amendment; Women's Suffrage—women's rights organizations, Nineteenth Amendment; African Americans—opposed lynching and discrimination, outlawed grandfather clauses
5. Responses might include promising to support women's suffrage and ending discrimination.

The Progressive Presidents

SECTION 5

If YOU were there...

It is 1912 and you're voting in your first presidential election! This election is unusual—there are three major candidates. One is the popular former president Theodore Roosevelt, who is running as a third-party candidate. He thinks the Republican candidate will not make enough progressive reforms. But the Democratic candidate is a progressive reformer, too.

Who would you vote for? Why?

BUILDING BACKGROUND Political corruption was one early target of the progressive reformers. Some politicians themselves joined the progressives. They believed that government—local, state, and national—had a role in improving society and people's lives.

Roosevelt's Progressive Reforms

During a summer tour after his second inauguration in 1901, President William McKinley met a friendly crowd in Buffalo, New York. Suddenly, anarchist Leon Czolgosz stepped forward and shot the president. A little more than a week later, McKinley died. After the assassination, Vice President **Theodore Roosevelt** took office.

Roosevelt's Square Deal

Roosevelt believed the interests of businesspeople, laborers, and consumers should be balanced for the public good. He used this policy—known as the Square Deal—in the coal miners' strike in 1902. Roosevelt knew the strike might leave the country without heating fuel for the coming winter. He therefore threatened to take over the mines unless managers agreed to **arbitration**, a formal process to settle disputes, with the strikers.

> "The labor unions shall have a square deal, and the corporations shall have a square deal, and in addition all private citizens shall have a square deal."
>
> —President Theodore Roosevelt, quoted in *The Presidency of Theodore Roosevelt*, by Lewis L. Gould

The strike ended after Roosevelt's intervention.

What You Will Learn...

Main Ideas

1. Theodore Roosevelt's progressive reforms tried to balance the interests of business, consumers, and laborers.
2. William Howard Taft angered progressives with his cautious reforms.
3. Woodrow Wilson enacted banking and antitrust reforms.

The Big Idea

American presidents in the early 1900s did a great deal to promote progressive reform.

Key Terms and People

Theodore Roosevelt, *p. 627*
arbitration, *p. 627*
Pure Food and Drug Act, *p. 628*
conservation, *p. 628*
William Howard Taft, *p. 629*
Progressive Party, *p. 629*
Woodrow Wilson, *p. 629*
Sixteenth Amendment, *p. 630*
Federal Reserve Act, *p. 630*
Clayton Antitrust Act, *p. 630*
Federal Trade Commission, *p. 630*

HSS 8.12.5 Examine the location and effects of urbanization, renewed immigration, and industrialization (e.g., the effects on social fabric of cities, wealth and economic opportunity, the conservation movement).

Preteach

Bellringer

If YOU were there . . . Use the **Daily Bellringer Transparency** to help students answer the question.

Daily Bellringer Transparency, Section 5

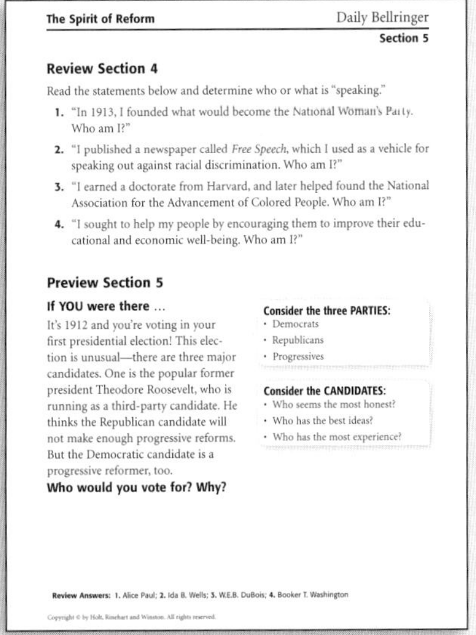

The Spirit of Reform — Daily Bellringer, Section 5

Review Section 4

Read the statements below and determine who or what is "speaking."

1. "In 1913, I founded what would become the National Woman's Party. Who am I?"
2. "I published a newspaper called *Free Speech*, which I used as a vehicle for speaking out against racial discrimination. Who am I?"
3. "I earned a doctorate from Harvard, and later helped found the National Association for the Advancement of Colored People. Who am I?"
4. "I sought to help my people by encouraging them to improve their educational and economic well-being. Who am I?"

Preview Section 5

If YOU were there ...

It's 1912 and you're voting in your first presidential election! This election is unusual—there are three major candidates. One is the popular former president Theodore Roosevelt, who is running as a third-party candidate. He thinks the Republican candidate will not make enough progressive reforms. But the Democratic candidate is a progressive reformer, too.

Who would you vote for? Why?

Consider the three PARTIES:
- Democrats
- Republicans
- Progressives

Consider the CANDIDATES:
- Who seems the most honest?
- Who has the best ideas?
- Who has the most experience?

Review Answers: 1. Alice Paul; 2. Ida B. Wells; 3. W.E.B. DuBois; 4. Booker T. Washington

Academic Vocabulary

Review with students the high-use academic term in this section.

various of many types (p. 629)

Building Vocabulary

Preteach or review the following terms:

anarchist a person who believes in a political theory that government is not necessary (p. 627)

refuge a place that provides shelter or protection (p. 628)

CRF: Vocabulary Builder Activity, Section 5

Teach the Big Idea: Master the Standards

Standards **Proficiency**

The Progressive Presidents HSS 8.12.5; HSS **Analysis Skills:** HR 1, HI 1

1. **Teach** Ask the students the Main Idea questions to teach this section.
2. **Apply** This section discusses three presidents: Theodore Roosevelt, William Taft, and Woodrow Wilson. As students read the section, have them take notes on the accomplishments and reforms of each president.
3. **Review** Write the three presidents' names for students to see. Ask volunteers to identify the reforms and accomplishments of each president. As students name a reform, discuss its impact with the class. For example, President Wilson implemented income tax in 1913. Federal income taxes are now a major source of revenue for the federal government.
4. **Practice/Homework** Have students select the president in this section they think made the biggest contribution and write a paragraph explaining why. **LS Verbal/Linguistic**

Alternative Assessment Handbook, Rubrics 11: Discussions; and 37: Writing Assignments

Standards Focus

HSS 8.12.5

Means: Examine the effects of urbanization, new immigration, and industrialization on American cities and society.

Matters: Some presidents in the early 1900s tried to institute reforms to improve people's lives.

Direct Teach

Main Idea

1 Roosevelt's Progressive Reforms

Theodore Roosevelt's progressive reforms tried to balance the interests of business, consumers, and laborers.

Explain What was the Square Deal? *Roosevelt's policy of balancing the interests of business, labor, and consumers*

Predict What might be some long-term effects of Roosevelt's protection of nature and its resources? *Land and resources might be preserved for future use and enjoyment.*

CRF: Biography Activity: John Muir

HSS 8.12.5; HSS **Analysis Skills:** HI 1, HI 2

Did you know . . .

Among the treasures of the National Park Service are California's redwood forests. Some of these beautiful trees are more than 2,000 years old and can reach a height of 300 feet. One forest, located some 15 miles north of San Francisco, is dedicated to conservationist John Muir. In 1905, California congressman William Kent and his wife purchased 295 acres of redwood forest and donated it to the U.S. federal government. In 1908 that land was preserved as the Muir Woods National Monument.

go.hrw.com
Online Resources
KEYWORD: SS8 US19
ACTIVITY: National Park System

The National Park System

In 1872 Yellowstone National Park, located mostly in Wyoming, became the first national park in the United States—and the world. Today there are 55 national parks in the country. They are managed by the National Park Service (NPS), an agency of the federal government established in 1916. The NPS also oversees national seashores, lakeshores, rivers, trails, and historic sites and monuments.

President Theodore Roosevelt and conservationist John Muir in Yosemite National Park in California

Cathedral Rocks, Yosemite National Park

Regulating Big Business

Roosevelt also made regulating big business a top goal of his first administration. Muckrakers helped build public support for more regulation. For instance, Upton Sinclair's account of the meat-processing industry in his 1906 novel, *The Jungle,* shocked the public. Roosevelt opened an investigation and later got Congress to pass a meat inspection law.

In 1906 Congress also passed the **Pure Food and Drug Act**. This law stopped the manufacture, sale, or transport of mislabeled or contaminated food and drugs sold in interstate commerce. Finally, Roosevelt persuaded Congress to regulate railroad shipping rates. The public largely supported this expansion of federal regulatory powers.

Conservation

Roosevelt strongly supported **conservation**, or protection of nature and its resources. Supporters of conservation had differing reasons for supporting the cause. Preservationists, for example, believed that nature should be preserved because of its beauty. Many preservationists, such as John Muir, wanted to protect the remaining ancient forests from logging. Other conservationists wanted to save the natural resources of the United States. For example, Chief Forester Gifford Pinchot valued forests because of the resources they provide to build "prosperous homes."

These views came into conflict in the Hetch Hetchy Valley controversy of 1913. Muir wanted the valley to remain part of Yosemite National Park, but Pinchot wanted it to become a water source for nearby San Francisco. Pinchot's victory in the controversy encouraged preservationists to found the National Park Service.

By 1870, tens of millions of acres of federal lands had been sold or given to private mining, logging, and railroad companies. Such companies opposed efforts to conserve federal land. But while Roosevelt was in office, the Forest Service gained control over nearly 150 million acres of public land. Roosevelt doubled the number of national parks, created 16 national monuments, and started 51 wildlife refuges.

READING CHECK **Summarizing** What reforms did Roosevelt support?

Differentiating Instruction for Universal Access

Learners Having Difficulty — Reaching Standards

1. Review with the class early conservation efforts in the United States. Discuss the views of preservationists and conservationists and the arguments in support of each view.
2. Have each student create a list of reasons why nature should be protected. Then have each student create a poster that illustrates various attitudes towards conservationism.
3. Encourage students to share their posters with the class.
4. **Extend** Have students conduct research on modern-day conservation efforts and then create a poster that illustrates modern ideas about conserving nature. LS **Visual/Spatial**

HSS 8.12.5; HSS **Analysis Skills:** HR 1, HI 1

Alternative Assessment Handbook, Rubric 28: Posters

Answers

Reading Check *arbitration between labor and business, business regulation, conservation, and railroad shipping rate regulation*

Taft Angers Progressives

Theodore Roosevelt hoped that his secretary of war, **William Howard Taft**, would take his place as president in 1908. Like Roosevelt, Taft opposed socialism and favored business regulation. With Roosevelt's help, Taft beat William Jennings Bryan in the election of 1908.

Taft's Administration

Despite their friendship, Roosevelt and Taft held different ideas about how a president should act. Taft thought Roosevelt had claimed more power than a president was constitutionally allowed.

Therefore, Taft chose to move more cautiously as president toward reform and regulation. This upset progressives who wanted to destroy trusts entirely. Although Taft's administration started twice as many antitrust suits as Roosevelt's had, progressives were still not satisfied.

Taft angered progressives further by signing the Payne-Aldrich Tariff of 1909. Progressives wanted reductions in tariffs to lower prices for consumers. Although the Payne-Aldrich Tariff reduced some rates, it raised others.

Taft's battle with Roosevelt's close friend and ally Gifford Pinchot also proved to be politically costly. In 1909 Pinchot accused Secretary of the Interior Richard Ballinger of hurting conservation efforts by leasing public lands to big business. Taft decided to fire Pinchot, which upset conservationists and various other progressives, including Roosevelt.

ACADEMIC VOCABULARY
various of many types

Taft transferred more land into government reserves than Roosevelt had. However, he continued to lose progressive support.

Election of 1912

Roosevelt, furious with Taft, decided to run for president again in 1912. Taft won the Republican nomination. Roosevelt and his followers then formed the **Progressive Party**, nicknamed the Bull Moose Party after Roosevelt said he was "as strong as a bull moose." The party's platform was based on Roosevelt's New Nationalism, a plan he developed in 1910 for more regulation and social welfare programs.

The Democratic Party chose **Woodrow Wilson**, the former president of Princeton University. In 1910 Wilson was elected governor of New Jersey. With his New Freedom program, Wilson called for government action against monopolies in order to allow free competition. He also wanted to lower tariffs and expand small businesses.

Election of 1912

	Electoral Vote	Popular Vote
Wilson (Democrat)	435	6,296,547
T. Roosevelt (Progressive)	88	4,118,571
Taft (Republican)	8	3,486,720

*California cast eleven electoral votes for Roosevelt and two for Wilson.

GEOGRAPHY SKILLS INTERPRETING MAPS

Region In which areas of the country did Wilson win?

Direct Teach

Main Idea

❷ Taft Angers Progressives

William Howard Taft angered progressives with his cautious reforms.

Identify What was Roosevelt's New Nationalism plan? *the basis of the Bull Moose Party platform; a plan for more regulation and social welfare programs*

Analyze Why did Roosevelt decide to run for president again in 1912, and what party did he form? *angry at Taft; Bull Moose*

Evaluate Was the anger that progressives had toward Taft justified? *Answers will vary, but students should recognize the reforms Taft instituted.*

Map Transparency: Election of 1912

HSS 8.12.5; HSS **Analysis Skills:** HI 1, HI 2

Critical Thinking: Comparing and Contrasting

Reaching Standards

Roosevelt and Taft Venn Diagram HSS 8.12.5

1. Review with students the administrations of Theodore Roosevelt and William Howard Taft. Discuss how each president dealt with progressive reforms.
2. Have each student create a Venn diagram in which they compare and contrast the attitudes of Roosevelt and Taft toward progressive reform. Remind students to identify the ways in which Roosevelt and Taft were similar and the ways in which they were different.
3. Ask volunteers to share information from their Venn diagrams as you create a master Venn diagram for the class to see.
4. Then have students write one to two paragraphs explaining which president they think did more to promote reform.
LS Verbal/Linguistic, Visual/Spatial

Alternative Assessment Handbook, Rubrics 9: Compare and Contrast; and 13: Graphic Organizers

Answers

Interpreting Maps *all regions across the nation*

Direct Teach

Main Idea

❸ Wilson's Reforms

Woodrow Wilson enacted banking and antitrust reforms.

Describe What was the Underwood Tariff Act? *law that lowered tariffs and placed an income tax on personal earnings*

Identify What amendment allowed for a federal income tax? *Sixteenth Amendment*

Summarize What is the purpose of the Federal Reserve? *to regulate the economy and money supply*

Political Cartoons Activities for United States History, Cartoon 23: The Power of Trusts

HSS 8.12.5; HSS **Analysis Skills:** HI 1

MISCONCEPTION ALERT

Explain to students that the Federal Reserve is not a bank that an average citizen can walk into or that has ATM machines. Only other banks may borrow money from the Federal Reserve system. There are 12 Federal Reserve districts. Federal Reserve banks are located in Atlanta, Boston, Chicago, Cleveland, Dallas, Kansas City, Minneapolis, New York City, Philadelphia, Richmond (VA), San Francisco, and St. Louis.

Primary Source

POLITICAL CARTOON

Wilson and Big Business

Cartoons like this one showed big business as greedy. President Wilson is the farmer, who is protecting his crop of lettuce.

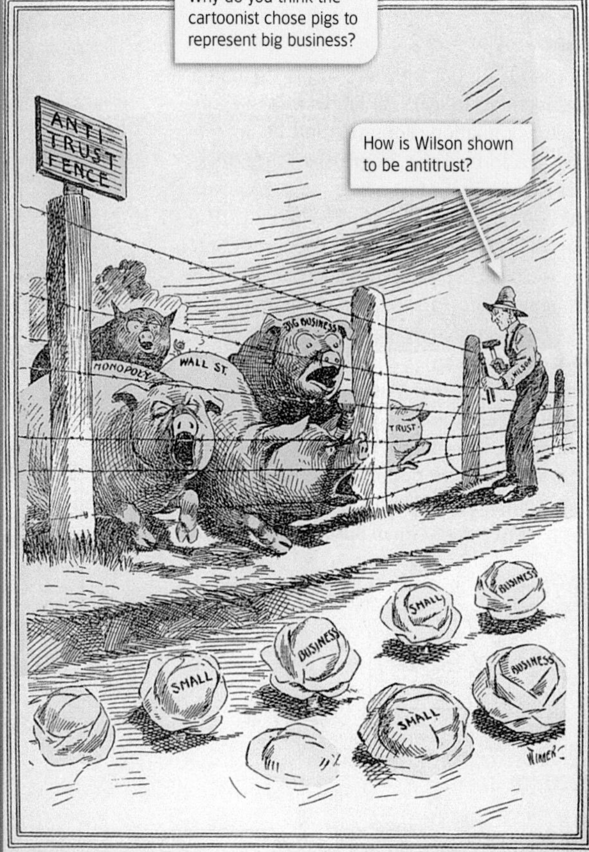

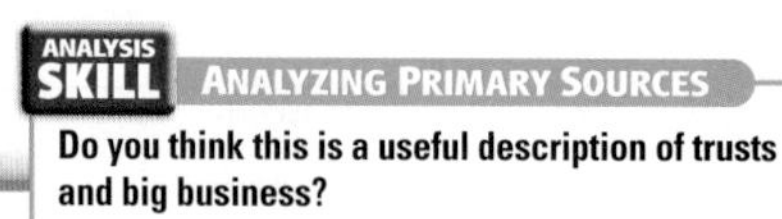

Do you think this is a useful description of trusts and big business?

Wilson, Roosevelt, Taft, and Eugene V. Debs, the Socialist Party candidate, all were reformers. They disagreed, however, on specific reforms and on how to achieve them. The split between Taft and Roosevelt divided the Republican vote. Wilson won the electoral vote by a wide margin.

READING CHECK **Analyzing** Which of Taft's actions angered Roosevelt and other progressives?

Wilson's Reforms

In his inaugural address, Wilson spoke of the terrible social conditions under which many working-class Americans lived.

> "We have been proud of our industrial achievements, but we have not hitherto [yet] stopped thoughtfully enough to count the human cost, . . . the fearful physical and spiritual cost to the men and women and children upon whom the . . . burden of it all has fallen."
>
> —Woodrow Wilson, quoted in *America Enters the World*, by Page Smith

Reform legislation was Wilson's top goal. He pushed for two measures soon after taking office: tariff revision and banking reform.

Wilson backed the Underwood Tariff Act of 1913, which lowered tariff rates. The act also introduced a version of the modern income tax on personal earnings. In February 1913, this new tax was made possible by ratification of the **Sixteenth Amendment**. This amendment allows the federal government to impose direct taxes on citizens' incomes.

President Wilson next addressed banking reform with the 1913 **Federal Reserve Act**. The act created a national banking system called the Federal Reserve to regulate the economy.

Wilson also pushed for laws to regulate big business. The **Clayton Antitrust Act** of 1914 strengthened federal laws against monopolies. The **Federal Trade Commission**, created in 1914, had the power to investigate and punish unfair trade practices.

Critical Thinking: Supporting a Point of View

Standards Proficiency

Political Cartoons

HSS 8.12.5; HSS **Analysis Skills:** CS 1, HR 5, HI 1

1. Review the political cartoon on this page with the class. Ask students to identify the message of the cartoon. Then ask students to identify and discuss the symbols the cartoonist uses.
2. Have students reread the section to locate a topic about which they could create their own political cartoons. Possible issues might include Taft's cautious attitude toward reform or Roosevelt's regulation of big business.
3. Then have each student create his or her own political cartoon. Remind students to use symbols to represent ideas or people, and to make their position on the issue clear.
4. Ask students to exchange cartoons. Then have each student write a short interpretation of the cartoon he or she examines. Students should identify the cartoon's topic, message, and symbols. **LS Visual/Spatial**

Alternative Assessment Handbook, Rubric 27: Political Cartoons

Answers

Analyzing Primary Sources *possible answer—yes, because it sheds light on the greediness of big business, which led to reform*

Reading Check *cautious attitude toward reform and regulation, inability to eliminate trusts entirely, signing of the Payne-Aldrich Tariff, removal of Gifford Pinchot*

The Progressive Amendments, 1909–1920

QUICK FACTS

Number	Description	Proposed by Congress	Ratified by States
16th	Federal income tax	1909	1913
17th	Senators elected by people rather than state legislatures	1912	1913
18th	Manufacture, sale, and transport of alcohol prohibited	1917	1919
19th	Women's suffrage	1919	1920

Preparing to run for re-election in 1916, Wilson helped pass the Keating-Owen Child Labor Act. The act limited the hours of child workers and prevented the sale across state lines of goods made with child labor. He also granted workers' compensation, or the payment of benefits to a worker injured on or made ill by the job, to federal employees. In addition, he supported the Adamson Act, which limited the workday on the nation's railroads to eight hours.

Wilson's actions helped him to win the people's support and the 1916 election. He had showed great skill and determination in guiding his reform programs through Congress.

READING CHECK **Summarizing** What major reforms were carried out under President Wilson?

SUMMARY AND PREVIEW The progressive presidents tried to change American society for the better. In the next chapter you will learn about how the United States became a world power.

Section 5 Assessment

go.hrw.com
Online Quiz
KEYWORD: SS8 HP19

Reviewing Ideas, Terms, and People HSS 8.12.5

1. a. **Describe** What progressive reforms did **Theodore Roosevelt** support?
   b. **Analyze** Why were some Americans concerned about the use of natural resources?
   c. **Evaluate** Do you think Roosevelt's reforms benefitted the nation? Why or why not?
2. a. **Identify** What was the **Progressive Party**? Why was it created?
   b. **Compare and Contrast** How were the administrations of **William Howard Taft** and Roosevelt similar and different?
   c. **Elaborate** Do you think progressives were justified in their opposition to Taft? Explain your answer.
3. a. **Recall** What was **Woodrow Wilson**'s top goal as president?
   b. **Analyze** How did Wilson reform the banking industry?
   c. **Evaluate** Which president do you think had the biggest effect on progressive reform—Roosevelt, Taft, or Wilson? Explain your choice.

Critical Thinking

4. **Comparing and Contrasting** Copy the diagram below onto your own sheet of paper. Use it to compare and contrast the reforms of the progressive presidents.

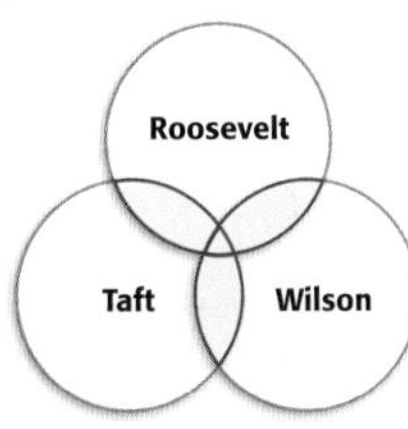

FOCUS ON SPEAKING

5. **Addressing the Ideas of Roosevelt, Taft, and Wilson** Do you agree or disagree with presidents Roosevelt, Taft, and Wilson? Take notes on any of their ideas that you would include in your campaign promises.

Section 5 Assessment Answers

1. a. mediation during strikes, trust busting, conservation
   b. wanted to preserve nature, resources
   c. possible answer—Yes, he limited the power of trusts and helped consumers.
2. a. created by Roosevelt to run against Taft because Roosevelt had lost the Republican nomination to Taft
   b. similar: trust busting, reforms; different: Taft more cautious, less popular
   c. Answers will vary but should demonstrate a knowledge of Taft's actions.
3. a. reform legislation
   b. created the Federal Reserve
   c. Answers will vary but should demonstrate a knowledge of each president's actions.
4. Roosevelt—trustbuster, mediator, conservation; Taft—trustbuster, conservation; Wilson—Underwood Tariff, Sixteenth Amendment, Federal Reserve, Clayton Antitrust Act, Keating-Owen Child Labor Act
5. Students should address the issues in the previous answer.

Direct Teach

Main Idea

3 Wilson's Reforms

Woodrow Wilson enacted banking and antitrust reforms.

Recall How did Woodrow Wilson help federal workers? *He granted them workers' compensation.*

Explain How did President Wilson protect child workers? *helped pass the Keating-Owen Child Labor Act, which limited the hours children could work*

Quick Facts Transparency: The Progressive Amendments, 1909–1920

HSS 8.12.5; HSS **Analysis Skills:** HI 1

Review & Assess

Close

Review the reforms enacted by Presidents Roosevelt, Taft, and Wilson. Discuss how these reforms continue to affect life today.

Review

Online Quiz, Section 5

Assess

SE Section 5 Assessment

PASS: Section 5 Quiz

Alternative Assessment Handbook

Reteach/Classroom Intervention

California Standards Review Workbook

Interactive Reader and Study Guide, Section 2

Interactive Skills Tutor CD-Rom

Answers

Reading Check *Underwood Tariff Act, Federal Reserve Act, Keating-Owen Child Labor Act*

Social Studies Skills

Short- and Long-Term Causal Patterns

Activity Analyzing Effects
Identify a topic or concern that students care about—for example, a local issue, an environmental issue, or a current international conflict. Write the issue for students to see and below it create a two-column chart. Label the columns *Short-Term Effects* and *Long-Term Effects*. Have the class brainstorm short-term effects first. List them in the appropriate column. If students need help, list a few examples to get them started. Then help students to consider and list possible long-term effects of the event. Conclude by having students summarize the difference between short- and long-term effects. **LS Visual/Spatial**

- Alternative Assessment Handbook, Rubric 7: Charts
- Interactive Skills Tutor CD-ROM, Lesson 7: Identify Cause and Effect

HSS Analysis Skills: HI 2

Social Studies Skills

Analysis | Critical Thinking | Participation | Study

HI2 Students understand and distinguish long- and short-term causal relations.

Short- and Long-term Causal Patterns

Define the Skill

Most historical events are the result of other events. When something happens as a result of other things that occur, it is an effect of those things. Some events in take place soon after the things that cause them. Such events are called *short-term effects*. In contrast, *long-term effects* can occur years, decades, or even hundreds of years after the events that caused them. Being able to recognize short-term and long-term cause-and-effect relationships well help you to better understand historical events.

Learn the Skill

As you learned in the Reading Social Studies for Chapter 11, "clue words" can sometimes reveal a cause-and-effect relationship between events. Often, however, such language clues may not be present. Therefore, when you study history, you should always look for other clues that might explain why an action or event occurred.

Short-term effects are usually fairly easy to identify. In historical writing they are often closely linked to the event the caused them. For example, consider this passage from Chapter 19.

> "In 1872 the *New York Sun* printed a story about corruption involving Congress. The owners of the Union Pacific Railroad had started a construction company called Crédit Mobilier. The owners gave or sold shares in Crédit Mobilier to members of Congress. In return, these Congressmen approved large federal land grants to Crédit Mobilier. Many Americans questioned the honesty of national leaders."

This passage contains no "clue words." Yet it is clear that cause-and-effect relationships exist. Congress's action in giving large amounts of land to Crédit Mobilier was caused by the payoffs its members received from the company. And an effect of this scandal was that Americans questioned their leaders' honesty.

Recognizing long-term causal relationships is often more difficult. Since long-term effects take place well after the event that caused them, they may not be discussed at the same time as their cause. This is why you should always question why an event occurred as you learn about it. For example, in 1971 Congress passed the first federal law to protect the health and safety of all workers. This law was a long-term result of efforts begun years earlier by the progressives you read about in this chapter.

Many long-term effects result from major forces running through history that make things happen. They include economics, science and technology, expansion, conflict and cooperation among people, cultural clashes and differences, and moral and religious issues. Ask yourself if one of these forces is involved in the event being studied. if so, the event may have long-term effects that you should be on the lookout for when studying later events.

Practice and Apply the Skill

Review the information in Chapter 19 and answer these questions to practice recognizing short- and long-term causal relationships.

1. All packaged food today must have its contents listed on the container. This requirement is a long-term effect of what progressive reform?
2. Write a paragraph explaining the effects of the "muckrakers" on the news media today.

Social Studies Skills Activity: Short- and Long-Term Causal Patterns

Conservation Flow Chart

HSS Analysis Skills: HI 2 — Standards **Proficiency**

1. Pair students and have each pair create a large flow chart showing some of the short- and long-term effects of President Theodore Roosevelt's support of conservation. Suggest that students use different colors to distinguish between short-term effects and long-term effects.
2. Model the activity by listing one short-term effect: *the number of national parks in the nation doubled.* Circulate as students work to help them structure their flow charts.
3. When students have finished the activity, have volunteers share some of their answers as you create a master flow chart. **LS Interpersonal, Visual/Spatial**

- Alternative Assessment Handbook, Rubrics 6: Cause and Effect; and 13: Graphic Organizers

Answers

Practice and Apply the Skill 1. *Pure Food and Drug Act of 1906;* **2.** *Answers will vary, but students should recognize the connection between Progressive muckraking and the objective investigative journalism of today.*

CHAPTER 19 Standards Review

Visual Summary

Use the visual summary below to help you review the main ideas of the chapter.

QUICK FACTS

Progressives hoped to improve society through reform. Their goals included:

- Temperance
- Women's suffrage
- Big-business regulation
- Conservation
- Tariff and banking reform

Reviewing Vocabulary, Terms, and People

Complete each sentence by filling in the blank with the correct term or person from the chapter.

1. Some Americans supported the system of ______________________, which proposed government ownership of the country's means of production.
2. Republican ______________ began a program to reform state politics in Wisconsin.
3. The ______________ granted women in the United States the right to vote.
4. Created under President Woodrow Wilson, the ______________ was established to investigate businesses accused of unfair business practices.
5. During the Gilded Age, ______________ often dominated local politics and used corruption to get their candidates elected.
6. ____________ were journalists who wrote about troubling issues like child labor, slum housing, and corruption.

Comprehension and Critical Thinking

SECTION 1 *(Pages 606–609)* **HSS 8.12.5**

7. a. **Describe** What tactics did bosses and political machines use to gain control of local governments?

   b. **Draw Conclusions** What effect did President Garfield's assassination have on reform efforts?

   c. **Evaluate** Do you think the reforms made by presidents during the Gilded Age helped cut back on government corruption? Explain.

SECTION 2 *(Pages 610–614)* **HSS 8.12.5**

8. a. **Recall** What led to the creation of the progressive movement?

   b. **Analyze** What changes did progressives make to urban life, education, and government?

   c. **Elaborate** Which progressive reform do you think had the greatest effect on Americans? Explain.

Answers

Visual Summary

Review and Inquiry Have students use the chapter visual summary to identify the progressive reforms that changed the United States.

Quick Facts Transparency: The Spirit of Reform Visual Summary

Reviewing Vocabulary, Terms, and People

1. socialism
2. Robert M. La Follette
3. Nineteenth Amendment
4. Federal Trade Commission
5. political machines
6. Muckrakers

Comprehension and Critical Thinking

7. a. They stuffed ballot boxes, paid people for their votes, bribed vote counters, traded favors for votes, offered jobs, and gained the support of immigrants to control local governments.

   b. Chester A. Arthur became president and backed the Pendleton Civil Service Act, which set up a merit system for awarding some federal jobs.

   c. possible answer—yes, because the Pendleton Civil Service Act set up a merit system to award government jobs, and presidents worked to help win back public trust

Review and Assessment Resources

Reproducible

- SE Standards Review
- CRF: Chapter Review Activity
- California Standards Review Workbook
- Quick Facts Transparency: The Spirit of Reform Visual Summary
- Spanish Chapter Summaries Audio CD Program
- Online Chapter Summaries in Six Languages
- OSP Holt PuzzlePro; GameTool for ExamView
- Quiz Game CD-ROM

Assess

- SE Standards Assessment
- PASS: Chapter Test, Forms A and B
- Alternative Assessment Handbook
- OSP ExamView Test Generator, Chapter Test
- Universal Access Modified Worksheets and Tests CD-ROM: Chapter Test
- Holt Online Assessment Program (in the Premier Online Edition)

Reteach/Intervene

- Interactive Reader and Study Guide
- Universal Access Teacher Management System: Lesson Plans for Universal Access
- Universal Access Modified Worksheets and Tests CD-ROM
- Interactive Skills Tutor CD-ROM

go.hrw.com
Online Resources
Chapter Resources:
KEYWORD: SS8 US19

Answers

8. a. Reformers wanted to solve problems caused by rapid industrial and urban growth.
b. Progressives worked to improve sanitation, transportation, and living conditions in large cities; they introduced new courses and mandatory school attendance for children, and expanded the voting power of citizens through direct primaries, the Seventeenth Amendment, referendums, recalls, and initiatives.
c. Answers should show a knowledge of the reforms mentioned in the last answer and provide reasons to support the chosen reform.
9. a. Laws were passed to create minimum wages for adult and children workers, limit the age at which children could work, improve workplace safety for factory workers, and establish workers' compensation laws for individuals injured on the job.
b. In capitalism, private businesses run most industries and competition determines how much goods cost; in socialism, governments own and operate businesses and control the cost of goods.
c. Answers will vary, but students should show an understanding of the effect of reforms on businesses.
10. a. Chinese and Mexican immigrants and Native Americans
b. instrumental in passage of Eighteenth Amendment, which banned the production, sale and transportation of alcohol, and Nineteenth Amendment, which granted women right to vote
c. Answers will vary, but students should show an understanding of Washington's ideas.
11. a. He took a cautious attitude toward reform and regulation.
b. They each attempted to regulate the power of big business.
c. Answers will vary, but students should demonstrate an understanding of progressive reforms and the effects they had on society.

SECTION 3 *(Pages 615–619)* **HSS 8.12.6**

9. a. **Identify** What reforms were made to improve working conditions, and who was affected by these reforms?
b. **Contrast** What are the differences between capitalism and socialism?
c. **Elaborate** If you were a business owner, would you have supported the progressive workplace reforms? Explain your answer.

SECTION 4 *(Pages 622–626)* **HSS 8.12.5**

10. a. **Recall** What minority groups were overlooked by progressive reform efforts?
b. **Analyze** How did women's involvement in the progressive movement lead to constitutional change?
c. **Elaborate** Do you agree with Booker T. Washington's approach to improving life for African Americans? Explain your answer.

SECTION 5 *(Pages 627–631)* **HSS 8.12.5**

11. a. **Describe** How did William Howard Taft disappoint progressives?
b. **Compare** In what ways were the reforms of presidents Roosevelt, Taft, and Wilson similar?
c. **Elaborate** Would you have supported progressive reforms? Explain your answer

Reviewing Themes

12. **Politics** What role did political machines play in local politics during the Gilded Age?
13. **Society and Culture** How were children affected by the movement for workplace reforms?

Reading Skills

Historical Fact and Historical Fiction *Use the Reading Skills taught in this chapter to answer the questions about the reading selection below.*

> The sea of a mighty population, held in galling fetters [heavy chains], heaves uneasily in the tenements . . . If it rise once more, no human power may avail to check it. *(p. 620)*
> —Jacob Riis, *How the Other Half Lives*

14. Which statement below is an example of historical fact from the selection above?
a. New York had a large population.
b. New York's population was held in fetters.
c. Nothing could stop New York's population from unrest.
d. Tenements were built to house immigrants.

Social Studies Skill

Short- and Long-term Causal Patterns *Use the Social Studies Skills taught in this chapter to answer the questions about the reading selection below.*

> Under the leadership of Joseph McCormack, the American Medical Association (AMA) was reorganized in 1901 to bring together local medical organizations. The AMA also supported laws designed to protect public health. This group showed how progressives could unite professionals to help improve society. *(p. 612)*

15. According to the passage above, what was a short-term effect of the reorganization of the AMA?
a. Laws protecting the public health were passed.
b. Doctors learned from each other.
c. National medical standards were created.
d. Joseph McCormack was elected president of the AMA.
16. After reading the rest of the chapter, what do you think might be a long-term effect of the reorganization of the AMA?

FOCUS ON SPEAKING

17. **Share Your Campaign Promises** Review your notes about possible campaign promises. Which promises will be most helpful to get you elected? Look at your promises to see whether they focus on issues important to voters. Then write a speech including your campaign promises that you can deliver to your class.

Reviewing Themes

12. They dominated local and state politics by getting their candidates elected to public office.
13. Minimum wage legislation, as well as laws to establish minimum age requirements helped improve working conditions for children.

Reading Skills

14. a

Social Studies Skills

15. a
16. possible answer—It helped improve medical treatment for individuals and to establish guidelines for drugs and treatment.

Focus on Speaking

17. **Rubric** Students' oral reports should:
- include an introduction, two sentences on each period of the war, and a conclusion.
- discuss the war in chronological order.
- provide vivid descriptions to engage the audience.
- use standard English and proper grammar.

CRF: Focus on Speaking Activity: Campaign Promises

Standards Assessment

DIRECTIONS: Read each question and write the letter of the best response.

1

Which progressive reformer would have been most interested in this photograph?

A Theodore Roosevelt
B Woodrow Wilson
C Carrie Chapman Catt
D Florence Kelley

2 One direct result of immigration and urban growth was the rise of

A political machines.
B the civil service system.
C the spoils system.
D primary elections.

3 What was the *main* idea behind the creation of the civil service system in the late 1800s?

A Government jobs should be rewarded to persons who support the party in power.
B Government workers should be required to support the elected officials who hire them.
C Government employees should be qualified to do the jobs for which they were hired.
D Government jobs should not be filled with employees who serve in those jobs for life.

4 The Nineteenth Amendment to the Constitution increased democracy in the United States by

A granting women the right to vote.
B allowing the people of each state to elect their senators.
C establishing direct primary elections.
D enabling voters to remove elected officials from office before the end of their terms.

5 Progressive reformers were *least* successful in achieving which of the following reforms?

A women's suffrage
B expanded voting rights
C improved safety standards for workers
D a ban on child labor

Connecting with Past Learning

6 Earlier in this course you learned about the reforms accomplished by educator Horace Mann. Which reformer made a similar contribution to society in the late 1800s?

A Jane Addams
B John Dewey
C Robert M. La Follette
D Alice Paul

7 In this chapter you learned about W. E. B. Du Bois's struggle to fight racial injustice. Which other American made a similar contribution to society?

A William Tecumseh Sherman
B Samuel Gompers
C Frederick Douglass
D Henry David Thoreau

Answers

1. D
Break Down the Question Remind students that Florence Kelley was involved in efforts to improve child labor working conditions.

2. A
Break Down the Question Point out that answer choices B, C, and D can be eliminated, as they were not results of urban growth.

3. C
Break Down the Question This question requires students to recall factual information from Section 1.

4. A
Break Down the Question This question requires students to recall factual information from Section 4.

5. D
Break Down the Question This question requires students to recall factual information from Section 3.

6. B
Break Down the Question This question requires students to recall factual information from Chapter 13.

7. C
Break Down the Question This question requires students to recall factual information from Chapter 13.

Intervention Resources

Reproducible

- Interactive Reader and Study Guide
- Universal Access Teacher Management System: Universal Access Lesson Plans

Technology

- Quick Facts Transparency: The Spirit of Reform Visual Summary
- Universal Access Modified Worksheets and Tests CD-ROM
- Interactive Skills Tutor CD-ROM

Tips for Test Taking

Minutes to Go If students become short on time, they should quickly scan the unanswered questions to see which might be easiest to answer. Students should then go with their instincts and, starting with the easiest questions, answer as many of the remaining questions as possible.

Standards Review

Have students review the following standards in their workbooks.

- California Standards Review Workbook: HSS 8.12.5, 8.12.6

Chapter 20 Planning Guide

America Becomes a World Power

Chapter Overview	Reproducible Resources	Technology Resources
CHAPTER 20 **pp. 636–667** **Overview: In this chapter, students will analyze the social and political events and ideas of the United States as it grew into a world power.**  See p. 636 for the California History–Social Science standards covered in this chapter.	**Universal Access Teacher Management System:*** • Universal Access Instructional Benchmarking Guides • Lesson Plans for Universal Access 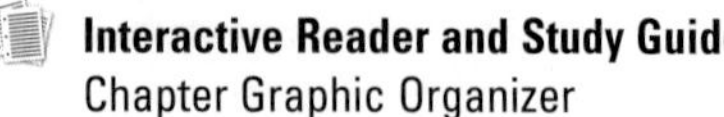 **Interactive Reader and Study Guide:*** Chapter Graphic Organizer  **Chapter Resource File*** • Focus on Writing Activity: A List of Pros and Cons and a Recommendation • Social Studies Skills Activity: Continuity and Change in History • Chapter Review Activity	**One-Stop Planner CD-ROM:** Calendar Planner **Student Edition Full-Read Audio CD-ROM** **Universal Access Modified Worksheets and Tests CD-ROM** **Primary Source Library CD-ROM for United States History** **Power Presentations with Video CD-ROM** **History's Impact: United States History Video Program (VHS/DVD):** America Becomes a World Power*
Section 1: **The United States Gains Overseas Territories** **The Big Idea:** In the last half of the 1800s, the United States joined the race for control of overseas territories.  8.12	**Universal Access Teacher Management System:*** Section 1 Lesson Plan  **Interactive Reader and Study Guide:*** Section 1 Summary  **Chapter Resource File*** • Vocabulary Builder, Section 1 • Biography Activity: Queen Liliuokalani • Biography Activity: William H. Seward • Literature Activity: *The Story of Seward's Folly* • Primary Source Activity: Japan and the West	 **Daily Bellringer Transparency:** Section 1* **Map Transparency:** U.S. Territories in the Pacific*  **Map Transparency:** Imperialism in China, 1900*
Section 2: **The Spanish-American War** **The Big Idea:** The United States expanded into new parts of the world as a result of the Spanish-American War.  8.12	**Universal Access Teacher Management System:*** Section 2 Lesson Plan 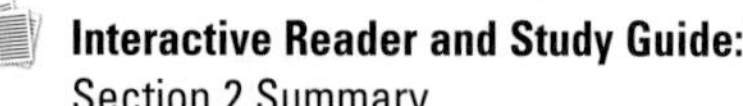 **Interactive Reader and Study Guide:*** Section 2 Summary  **Chapter Resource File*** • Vocabulary Builder, Section 2 • Primary Source Activity: The *Maine* Explosion	 **Daily Bellringer Transparency:** Section 2* **Map Transparency:** War in the Caribbean* **Map Transparency:** War in the Philippines*  **Internet Activity:** Stephen Crane War Dispatches
Section 3: **The United States and Latin America** **The Big Idea:** The United States expanded its role in Latin America in the early 1900s. 8.12.3	 **Universal Access Teacher Management System:*** Section 3 Lesson Plan **Interactive Reader and Study Guide:*** Section 3 Summary  **Chapter Resource File*** • Vocabulary Builder, Section 3 • History and Geography Activity: Territories in Latin America 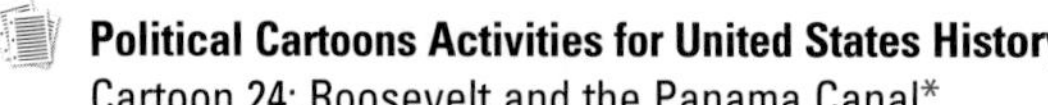 **Political Cartoons Activities for United States History,** Cartoon 24: Roosevelt and the Panama Canal*	 **Daily Bellringer Transparency:** Section 3* **Map Transparency:** The Panama Canal* **Quick Facts Transparency:** U.S. Foreign Policy*
 **Section 4:** **The United States and Mexico** **The Big Idea:** The Mexican Revolution threatened relations between the United States and Mexico.  8.12	 **Universal Access Teacher Management System:*** Section 4 Lesson Plan 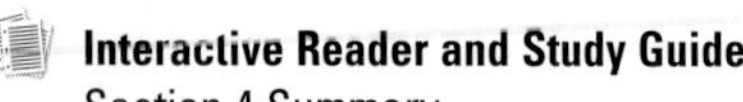 **Interactive Reader and Study Guide:*** Section 4 Summary  **Chapter Resource File*** • Vocabulary Builder, Section 4	 **Daily Bellringer Transparency:** Section 4* **Map Transparency:** United States in Latin America*  **Internet Activity:** Mexican Revolution Mural

MASTERING THE CALIFORNIA STANDARDS

SE Student Edition | Print Resource | Audio CD | Video
TE Teacher's Edition | Transparency | CD-ROM | DVD
go.hrw.com | CA Standards Mastery | **LS** Learning Styles
OSP One-Stop Planner CD-ROM | * also on One-Stop Planner CD

Review, Assessment, Intervention

- **Standards Review Workbook***
- **Quick Facts Transparency:** America Becomes a World Power Visual Summary*
- **Spanish Chapter Summaries Audio CD Program**
- **Online Chapter Summaries in Six Languages**
- **Quiz Game CD-ROM**
- **Progress Assessment Support System (PASS):** Chapter Test*
- **Universal Access Modified Worksheets and Tests CD-ROM:** Modified Chapter Test
- **One-Stop Planner CD-ROM:** ExamView Test Generator (English/Spanish)

- **PASS:** Section 1 Quiz*
- **Online Quiz:** Section 1
- **Alternative Assessment Handbook**

- **PASS:** Section 2 Quiz*
- **Online Quiz:** Section 2
- **Alternative Assessment Handbook**

- **PASS:** Section 3 Quiz*
- **Online Quiz:** Section 3
- **Alternative Assessment Handbook**

- **PASS:** Section 4 Quiz*
- **Online Quiz:** Section 4
- **Alternative Assessment Handbook**

California Resources for Standards Mastery

INSTRUCTIONAL PLANNING AND SUPPORT

- **Universal Access Teacher Management System***
- **One-Stop Planner CD-ROM with Test Generator: Teacher Management System with Interactive Teacher's Edition**

STANDARDS MASTERY

- **Standards Review Workbook***
- **At Home: A Guide to Standards Mastery for United States History**

Holt Online Learning

To enhance learning, Internet activities are available for Stephen Crane War Dispatches and a Mexican Revolution Mural.

KEYWORD: SS8 TEACHER

- **Teacher Support Page**
- **Content Updates**
- **Rubrics and Writing Models**
- **Teaching Tips for the Multimedia Classroom**

KEYWORD: SS8 US20

- **Current Events**
- **Document-Based Questions**
- **Holt Grapher**
- **Holt Online Atlas**
- **Holt Researcher**
- **Interactive Multimedia Activities**
- **Internet Activities**
- **Online Chapter Summaries in Six Languages**
- **Online Section Quizzes**
- **American History Maps and Charts**

HOLT PREMIER ONLINE STUDENT EDITION

Complete online support for interactivity, assessment, and reporting

- **Interactive Maps and Notebook**
- **Standardized Test Prep**
- **Homework Practice and Research Activities Online**

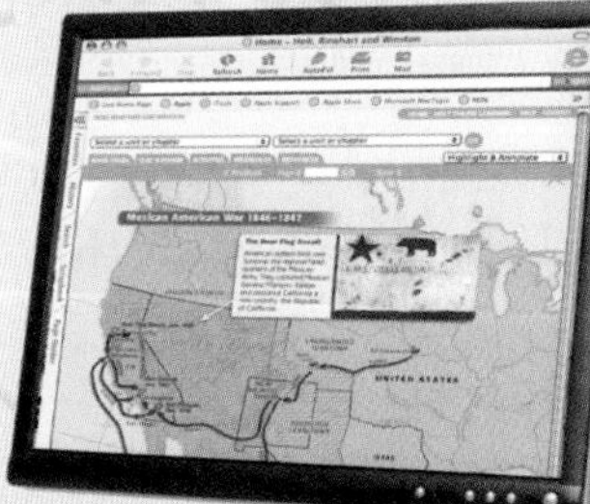

Mastering the Standards: Differentiating Instruction

Reaching Standards	Basic-level activities designed for all students encountering new material
Standards Proficiency	Intermediate-level activities designed for average students
Exceeding Standards	Challenging activities designed for honors and gifted-and-talented students
Standard English Mastery	Activities designed to improve standard English usage

Frequently Asked Questions

INSTRUCTIONAL PLANNING AND SUPPORT

Where do I find planning aids, pacing guides, lesson plans, and other teaching aids?

Annotated Teacher's Edition:
- Chapter planning guides
- Standards-based instruction and strategies
- Differentiated instruction for universal access
- Point-of-use reminders for integrating program resources

Power Presentations with Video CD-ROM

Universal Access Teacher Management System:
- Year and unit instructional benchmarking guides
- Reproducible lesson plans
- Assessment guides for diagnostic, progress, and summative end-of-the-year tests
- Options for differentiating instruction and intervention
- Teaching guides and answer keys for student workbooks

One-Stop Planner CD-ROM with Test Generator: Teacher Management System with Interactive Teacher's Editon:
- Calendar Planner
- Editable lesson plans
- All reproducible ancillaries in Adobe Acrobat (PDF) format
- ExamView Test Generator (English & Spanish)
- Game Tool for ExamView
- PuzzlePro
- Transparency and video previews

DIFFERENTIATING INSTRUCTION FOR UNIVERSAL ACCESS

What resources are available to ensure that Advanced Learners/GATE Students master the standards?

Teacher's Edition Activities:
- Isolationism vs. Imperialism, p. 641
- Panama Canal Negotiations, p. 654

Lesson Plans for Universal Access

Primary Source Library CD-ROM for United States History

What resources are available to ensure that English Learners and Standard English Learners master the standards?

Teacher's Edition Activities:
- Roosevelt Corollary, p. 656

Lesson Plans for Universal Access

Chapter Resource File: Vocabulary Builder Activities

Spanish Chapter Summaries Audio CD Program

Online Chapter Summaries in Six Languages

One-Stop Planner CD-ROM:
- PuzzlePro, Spanish Version
- ExamView Test Generator, Spanish Version

What modified materials are available for Special Education?

Teacher's Edition Activities:
- Hawaii Acquisition, p. 642

The ***Universal Access Modified Worksheets and Tests CD-ROM*** provides editable versions of the following:

Vocabulary Flash Cards

Modified Chapter Review Activity

Modified Vocabulary Builder Activities

Modified Chapter Test

HOLT
History's Impact
▶ video series
America Becomes a World Power

What resources are available to ensure that Learners Having Difficulty master the standards?

Teacher's Edition Activities:
- Spanish-American War, p. 650
- Paired Main Idea Activity, p. 660

Interactive Reader and Study Guide

Student Edition Full-Read Audio CD

Quick Facts Transparency: America Becomes a World Power Visual Summary

Standards Review Workbook

Social Studies Skills Activity: Continuity and Change in History

Interactive Skills Tutor CD-ROM

How do I intervene for students struggling to master the standards?

Interactive Reader and Study Guide

Quick Facts Transparency: America Becomes a World Power Visual Summary

Standards Review Workbook

Social Studies Skills Activity: Continuity and Change in History

Interactive Skills Tutor CD-ROM

PROFESSIONAL DEVELOPMENT

What teacher training resources are available to help me grow professionally?

- In-service and staff development as part of your Holt Social Studies product purchase
- Quick Teacher Tutorial Lesson Presentation CD-ROM
- Intensive tuition-based Teacher Development Institute
- *Teaching American History* Online 2 Module Professional Development Course
- Convenient Holt Speaker Bureau face-to-face workshop options
- PRAXIS™ Test Prep (#0089) interactive Web-based content refreshers*
- 24/7 *Ask A Professional Development Expert* at http://www.hrw.com/prodev/

* PRAXIS is a trademark of Educational Testing Service (ETS). This publication is not endorsed or approved by ETS.

Information Literacy Skills

To learn more about how History–Social Science instruction may be improved by the effective use of library media centers and information literacy skills, go to the Teacher's Resource Materials for Chapter 20 at **go.hrw.com**, keyword: SS8 MEDIA.

The following materials were developed by the Division for Public Education of the American Bar Association. These materials are part of the **Democracy and Civic Education** supplement.
- Constitution Study Guide
- Supreme Court Case Studies

Chapter Preview

Standards Focus

Standards by Section
Section 1: HSS 8.12
Section 2: HSS 8.12
Section 3: HSS 8.12.3
Section 4: HSS 8.12

Teacher's Edition
HSS **Analysis Skills:** CS 1, CS 2, HR 1, HR 4, HR 5, HI 1, HI 2, HI 3, HI 6
ELA Writing 8.2.4.b; Reading 8.2.3

Preview Grade 11 Standards
HSS **11.4** Students trace the rise of the United States to its role as a world power in the twentieth century.
11.4.2 Describe the Spanish-American War and U.S. expansion in the South Pacific.
11.4.3 Discuss America's role in the Panama Revolution and the building of the Panama Canal.
11.4.4 Explain Theodore Roosevelt's Big Stick diplomacy, William Taft's Dollar Diplomacy, and Woodrow Wilson's Moral Diplomacy, drawing on relevant speeches.

Focus on Writing
The **Chapter Resource File** provides a Focus on Writing worksheet to help students write a list of pros and cons and a recommendation.

CRF: Focus on Writing Activity: A List of Pros and Cons and a Recommendation

CHAPTER 20 1867–1910

America Becomes a World Power

California Standards

History–Social Science
8.12 Students analyze the transformation of the American economy and the changing social and political conditions in the United States in response to the Industrial Revolution.

Analysis Skills
HI 3 Students explain the sources of historical continuity and how the combination of ideas and events explains the emergence of new patterns.

English–Language Arts
Writing 8.2.4.b Present detailed evidence, examples, and reasoning to support arguments, differentiating between fact and opinion.
Reading 8.2.3 Find similarities and differences between texts in the treatment, scope, or organization of ideas.

FOCUS ON WRITING

A List of Pros and Cons and a Recommendation In the last half of the 1800s, the United States ended its policy of isolationism, or avoiding entanglement in the business of other nations. As a result, the country became more involved in international affairs. As you read this chapter, you will analyze this decision and use the results of your analysis to guide U.S. policy in the future. In order to analyze the advantages and disadvantages of an aggressive foreign policy, you will need to create a list of the pros and cons of U.S involvement with other nations in the late 1800s and early 1900s. As you create your list, note which items are facts and which are opinions—either yours or someone else's.

UNITED STATES

1867 The United States buys Alaska.

WORLD

1868 Japan begins a time of modernization known as the Meiji Restoration.

636 CHAPTER 20

Introduce the Chapter

Standards Proficiency

Becoming a World Power HSS 8.12

1. Write the following for students to see: *Alaska, Cuba, Hawaii, Midway Islands, Panama, Philippine Islands, Puerto Rico,* and *Samoa.* Ask students to locate each place on a world map. Students can use a wall map or the textbook's almanac.
2. Tell students that they are going to learn about how the United States gained territories and became a world power in the late 1800s and early 1900s.
3. Have students preview the chapter by scanning the section titles, headings, photos, and maps.
4. Then ask students to predict the methods the United Sates used to become a world power. *(acquiring territory, use of military force to open trade, war, providing aid through technology)*
5. Write students' predictions for the class to see. Tell students to evaluate their predictions as they study the chapter. LS **Verbal/Linguistic**

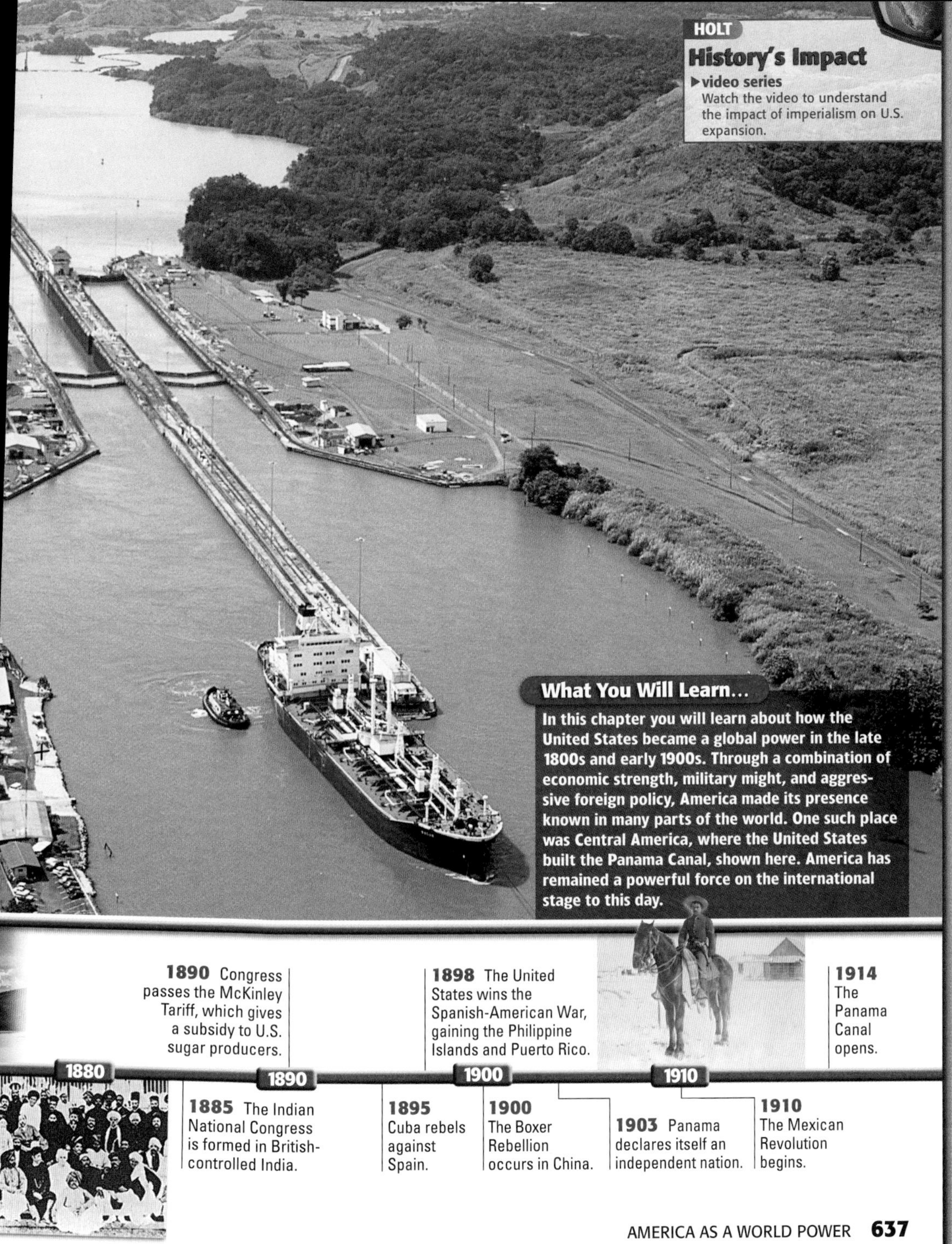

HOLT

History's Impact

▶ **video series**
Watch the video to understand the impact of imperialism on U.S. expansion.

What You Will Learn...

In this chapter you will learn about how the United States became a global power in the late 1800s and early 1900s. Through a combination of economic strength, military might, and aggressive foreign policy, America made its presence known in many parts of the world. One such place was Central America, where the United States built the Panama Canal, shown here. America has remained a powerful force on the international stage to this day.

1880 | 1890 | 1900 | 1910

1885 The Indian National Congress is formed in British-controlled India.

1890 Congress passes the McKinley Tariff, which gives a subsidy to U.S. sugar producers.

1895 Cuba rebels against Spain.

1898 The United States wins the Spanish-American War, gaining the Philippine Islands and Puerto Rico.

1900 The Boxer Rebellion occurs in China.

1903 Panama declares itself an independent nation.

1910 The Mexican Revolution begins.

1914 The Panama Canal opens.

AMERICA AS A WORLD POWER **637**

• Chapter Preview •

HOLT

History's Impact

▶ **video series**
See the Video Teacher's Guide for strategies for using the chapter video **America Becomes a World Power**.

Chapter Big Ideas

Section 1 In the last half of the 1800s, the United States joined the race for control of overseas territories. **HSS** 8.12

Section 2 The United States expanded into new parts of the world as a result of the Spanish-American War. **HSS** 8.12

Section 3 The United States expanded its role in Latin America in the early 1900s. **HSS** 8.12.3

Section 4 The Mexican Revolution threatened relations between the United States and Mexico. **HSS** 8.12

Explore the Picture

Panama Canal The Panama Canal operates 24 hours a day, 365 days a year. In fact, 13,000 to 14,000 vessels pass through the canal each year. This amount represents approximately 5 percent of the world's trade. From the visitor's center at the Panama Canal, one can see vessels moving through the canal just a few yards away.

Analyzing Visuals What changes might have occurred in shipping between 1914 and now? *larger ships, more ships, ships from many more countries*

go.hrw.com

Online Resources

Chapter Resources:
KEYWORD: SS8 US20
Teacher Resources:
KEYWORD: SS8 TEACHER

Explore the Time Line

1. What did the United Sates gain in 1898? *the Philippine Islands and Puerto Rico*
2. From 1885 to 1910 there were several rebellions. Which ones are listed on the time line? *Cuba rebels against Spain, Boxer Rebellion in China, and the Mexican Revolution*
3. How many years passed between Panama's independence and the opening of the Panama Canal? *11 years*
4. In what year did the United States acquire Alaska? *1867*

HSS Analysis Skills: CS 1

Info to Know

Indian National Congress The political party the Indian National Congress was dedicated to Indian independence from Great Britain. In its early years the Indian National Congress passed moderate resolutions in favor of independence. However, as British imperialism led to increasing poverty in India, the Indian National Congress began to call for more radical measures to oppose British rule. The Indian National Congress was instrumental in helping India gain independence from Great Britain in the 1940s.

Reading Social Studies

Understanding Themes

Introduce this chapter's key themes by asking students to predict what types of economic and political factors might have led the United States to seek a greater role in world affairs. Then ask students to consider in what ways the U.S. economy and politics might have been affected by the rise of the United States as a world power. Have students create an illustration that depicts either a cause or an effect of growing U.S. interaction in world politics and economics.

Comparing Historical Texts

Focus on Reading Share with students an event or issue over which there are differing views. An example is the debate over violence in video games. Have students examine the opposing views of the issue. Ask the class to identify who might support each issue, and what the arguments for and against might be. Have students look at the issue in terms of what the two sides have to say. Ask students how that issue might be viewed by historians in the future.

Reading Social Studies

by Kylene Beers

Economics | Geography | Politics | Religion | Society and Culture | Science and Technology

Focus on Themes In this chapter you will learn how **political** decisions and **economic** policies have affected our relationships with other countries. In particular you will read about what happened as the United States gained control of overseas territories, went to war against Spain, and expanded its interests into Latin America. As you read of these events, you will be able to compare the actions and reactions of different leaders.

Comparing Historical Texts

Focus on Reading A good way to learn what people in the past thought is to read what they wrote. However, most documents will only tell you one side of the story. By comparing writings by different people, you can learn a great deal about both sides of a historical issue or debate.

Additional reading support can be found in the

Comparing Texts When you compare historical texts, you should consider several things: who wrote the documents and what the documents were meant to achieve. To do this, you need to find the writers' main point or points.

Document 1

"We have cherished the policy of non-interference with affairs of foreign governments wisely inaugurated by Washington, keeping ourselves free from entanglement, either as allies or foes, content to leave undisturbed with them the settlement of their own domestic concerns."

–President William McKinley, First Inaugural Address, 1897

Document 2

"Therefore, Mr. President, here is a war with terrible characteristics flagrant at our very doors [in Cuba]. We have the power to bring it to an end. I believe that the whole American people would welcome steps in that direction."

–Senator Henry Cabot Lodge, Speech in Congress, 1896

Document 1	Document 2
Writer	
President William McKinley	Senator Henry Cabot Lodge
Main point	
The United States should not involve itself in the affairs of other countries.	The United States should go to war in Cuba.
Both Sides of the Issue	
Americans were torn over the war in Cuba. Some thought the United States should remain uninvolved as it always had. Others thought it was time for a change in foreign policy.	

Reading and Skills Resources

Reading Support

- Interactive Reader and Study Guide
- Student Edition on Audio CD
- Spanish Chapter Summaries Audio CD Program

Social Studies Skills Support

- Interactive Skills Tutor CD-ROM

Vocabulary Support

- **CRF:** Vocabulary Builder Activities
- **CRF:** Chapter Review Activity
- Universal Access Modified Worksheets and Tests CD-ROM:
  - Vocabulary Flash Cards
  - Vocabulary Builder Activity
  - Chapter Review Activity
- OSP Holt PuzzlePro

Standards Focus

ELA Reading 8.2.3

ELA Reading 8.2.3 Find similarities and differences between texts in the treatment, scope, or organization of ideas.

You Try It!

Read the following passages, both taken from presidential addresses to Congress. As you read, look for the main point each president makes in his address.

Foreign Policy

In treating of our foreign policy and of the attitude that this great Nation should assume in the world at large, it is absolutely necessary to consider the Army and the Navy, and the Congress, through which the thought of the Nation finds its expression, should keep ever vividly in mind the fundamental fact that it is impossible to treat our foreign policy, whether this policy takes shape in the effort to secure justice for others or justice for ourselves, save as conditioned upon the attitude we are willing to take toward our Army, and especially toward our Navy.

—President Theodore Roosevelt, Message to Congress, 1904

The diplomacy of the present administration has sought to respond to modern ideas of commercial intercourse. This policy has been characterized as substituting dollars for bullets. It is one that appeals alike to idealis-tic humanitarian sentiments, to the dictates of sound policy and strategy, and to legitimate commercial aims.

—President William Howard Taft, Message to Congress, 1912

After you read the passages, answer the following questions.

1. What was the main point Roosevelt made in his address?
2. What was the main point Taft made in his address?
3. How can a comparison of Roosevelt's and Taft's addresses to Congress help you understand the issues that shaped U.S. foreign policy in the early 1900s?

As you read Chapter 20, use the compare/contrast graphic organizer to help you note the similarities and differences of events or policies.

Key Terms and People

Chapter 20

Section 1
imperialism *(p. 640)*
isolationism *(p. 641)*
William H. Seward *(p. 641)*
subsidy *(p. 642)*
Liliuokalani *(p. 642)*
consul general *(p. 644)*
spheres of influence *(p. 644)*
John Hay *(p. 644)*
Open Door Policy *(p. 644)*
Boxer Rebellion *(p. 645)*

Section 2
Joseph Pulitzer *(p. 646)*
William Randolph Hearst *(p. 646)*
yellow journalism *(p. 646)*
Teller Amendment *(p. 647)*
Emilio Aguinaldo *(p. 648)*
Anti-Imperialist League *(p. 650)*
Platt Amendment *(p. 650)*

Section 3
Hay-Herrán Treaty *(p. 653)*
Philippe Bunau-Varilla *(p. 653)*
Hay–Bunau–Varilla Treaty *(p. 655)*
Panama Canal *(p. 655)*
Roosevelt Corollary *(p. 656)*
dollar diplomacy *(p. 657)*

Section 4
Porfirio Díaz *(p. 659)*
Francisco Madero *(p. 660)*
Mexican Revolution *(p. 660)*
Victoriano Huerta *(p. 660)*
Venustiano Carranza *(p. 661)*
Francisco "Pancho" Villa *(p. 661)*
Emiliano Zapata *(p. 661)*
ABC Powers *(p. 661)*
John J. Pershing *(p. 661)*

Academic Vocabulary

In this chapter, you will learn the following academic words:

process *(p. 644)*
role *(p. 656)*

Reading Social Studies

Key Terms and People

To help students identify and study key terms and people, have students create a Key-Term FoldNote. Have students fold a sheet of paper in half vertically. Then have students cut along every third or fourth line from the right edge of the paper to the center fold. Students will write the term or person on the outside of each tab. As students learn each key term, have them write a description or definition on the inside. Encourage students to study these people and terms regularly. **LS Verbal/Linguistic, Kinesthetic**

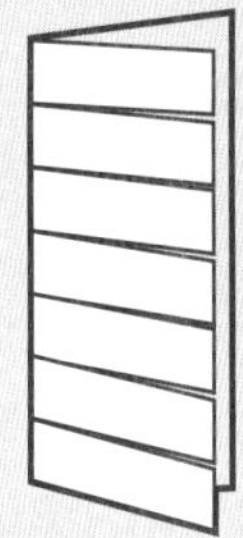

Focus on Reading

See the **Focus on Reading** questions in this chapter for more practice on this reading social studies skill.

Reading Social Studies Assessment

See the **Standards Review** at the end of this chapter for student assessment questions related to this reading skill.

Teaching Tip

Remind students that there is never just one side to an issue. Encourage students to find opposing viewpoints to all issues by researching primary source documents and public records. Explain to the class that a complete view of an event or issue includes examining all points of view.

Answers

You Try It! 1. *that American foreign policy relies on the backing of the military;* **2.** *that U.S. foreign policy should use economic incentives, not military ones;* **3.** *Students should recognize that some Americans supported using force in foreign policy, while others preferred to use economics.*

Preteach

Bellringer

If YOU were there . . . Use the **Daily Bellringer Transparency** to help students answer the question.

Daily Bellringer Transparency, Section 1

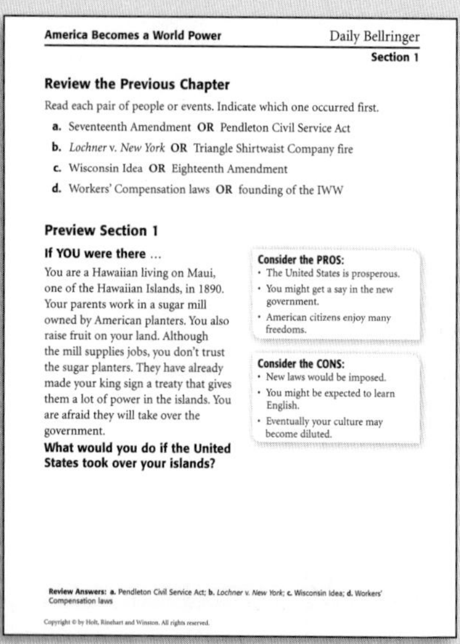

America Becomes a World Power — Daily Bellringer, **Section 1**

Review the Previous Chapter

Read each pair of people or events. Indicate which one occurred first.

a. Seventeenth Amendment **OR** Pendleton Civil Service Act

b. *Lochner* v. *New York* **OR** Triangle Shirtwaist Company fire

c. Wisconsin Idea **OR** Eighteenth Amendment

d. Workers' Compensation laws **OR** founding of the IWW

Preview Section 1

If YOU were there ...

You are a Hawaiian living on Maui, one of the Hawaiian Islands, in 1890. Your parents work in a sugar mill owned by American planters. You also raise fruit on your land. Although the mill supplies jobs, you don't trust the sugar planters. They have already made your king sign a treaty that gives them a lot of power in the islands. You are afraid they will take over the government.

What would you do if the United States took over your islands?

Consider the PROS:
- The United States is prosperous.
- You might get a say in the new government.
- American citizens enjoy many freedoms.

Consider the CONS:
- New laws would be imposed.
- You might be expected to learn English.
- Eventually your culture may become diluted.

Review Answers: a. Pendleton Civil Service Act; **b.** *Lochner* v. *New York*; **c.** Wisconsin Idea; **d.** Workers' Compensation laws

Academic Vocabulary

Review with students the following high-use academic term in this section.

process a series of steps by which a task is accomplished (p. 644)

Building Vocabulary

Preteach or review the following term:

treaty a formal agreement between two or more countries, especially in reference to terms of trade or peace (p. 642)

CRF: Vocabulary Builder Activity, Section 1

Standards Focus

HSS 8.12

Means: Examine changes in the U.S. economy, government, and society that occurred as a result of the Industrial Revolution.

Matters: Economic changes that resulted from the Industrial Revolution led the U.S. government to acquire new territories overseas.

SECTION 1

The United States Gains Overseas Territories

What You Will Learn...

Main Ideas

1. The United States ended its policy of isolationism.
2. Because of its economic importance, Hawaii became a U.S. territory.
3. The United States sought trade with Japan and China.

The Big Idea

In the last half of the 1800s, the United States joined the race for control of overseas territories.

Key Terms and People

imperialism, *p. 640*
isolationism, *p. 641*
William H. Seward, *p. 641*
subsidy, *p. 642*
Liliuokalani, *p. 642*
consul general, *p. 644*
spheres of influence, *p. 644*
John Hay, *p. 644*
Open Door Policy, *p. 644*
Boxer Rebellion, *p. 645*

HSS 8.12 Students analyze the transformation of the American economy and the changing social and political conditions in the United States in response to the Industrial Revolution.

If YOU were there...

You are a Hawaiian living on Maui, one of the Hawaiian Islands, in 1890. Your parents work in a sugar mill owned by American planters. You also raise fruit on your land. Although the mill supplies jobs, you don't trust the sugar planters. They have already made your king sign a treaty that gives them a lot of power in the islands. You are afraid they will take over the government.

What would you do if the United States took over your islands?

BUILDING BACKGROUND Until the mid-1800s, most Americans had little interest in being involved with the rest of the world diplomatically. The Civil War and Reconstruction kept their interest focused on challenges at home. In the meantime, though, European nations were busily acquiring overseas territories. The United States decided it was time to join them.

End of Isolationism

In the 1800s, powerful Western nations around the world wanted to build naval bases and protect shipping routes. This work was an aspect of **imperialism**—building an empire by founding colonies or conquering other nations. Between 1870 and 1914, Europeans extended their colonial empires. They controlled most of Africa and Southeast Asia.

Roots of Imperialism

Several forces drove this wave of European imperialism. Countries wanted sources of raw materials—such as copper, rubber, and tin—to fuel industrial growth. At the same time, businesspeople needed new markets for their manufactured goods. Many Europeans also thought colonies were a source of power and national pride.

Teach the Big Idea: Master the Standards

Standards Proficiency

The United States Gains Overseas Territories HSS 8.12; HSS Analysis Skills: CS 1, HI 1

1. **Teach** Ask students the Main Idea questions to teach this section.
2. **Apply** Have students read the section and write an outline. Have students use the same headings and subheadings as in the section. Remind students to provide at least three supporting details for each heading, and to include any key terms and people from the section in their outlines.
3. **Review** Have students quiz each other about the section as a review. Allow students to use the outlines they created to help them answer questions.
4. **Practice/Homework** Have students write a one-page summary of the section based on the outlines they have written.
   LS Verbal/Linguistic

Alternative Assessment Handbook, Rubric 37: Writing Assignments

In contrast, the United States did not build an empire until the late 1800s. Previously, American presidents had followed a limited policy of **isolationism** — avoiding involvement in the affairs of other countries. President George Washington, for example, had warned Americans "to steer clear of permanent alliances" with other countries—particularly European ones. U.S. leaders tried to follow this advice by staying out of overseas conflicts.

Not everyone favored isolationism, however. Some Americans thought the United States needed to expand to keep the country's economy strong. For example, Alfred T. Mahan, in *The Influence of Sea Power upon History,* wrote that the United States needed a strong navy. Published in 1890, Mahan's book argued that the navy could protect U.S. economic interests. Mahan also explained that a strong navy needed overseas bases and places for ships to refuel. Senator Henry Cabot Lodge repeated the call for economic expansion through naval power.

Seward's Folly

In 1867 the United States greatly expanded its territory when Secretary of State **William H. Seward** arranged the purchase of Alaska from Russia for $7.2 million. The cost was less than two cents per acre—cheaper than the four cents per acre paid for Louisiana. People thought Alaska was worthless and laughed at the purchase, calling it Seward's Folly and the "Alaskan Icebox." The purchase of Alaska added some 600,000 square miles that contained natural resources such as wildlife, minerals, and timber.

In addition, the Midway Islands in the Pacific were annexed by the United States in 1867. Midway was a good base for the U.S. Navy. The United States also wanted the island group of Samoa for similar reasons. The United States and Germany agreed to divide Samoa between them in 1899.

THE IMPACT TODAY
The United States still has hundreds of military bases in foreign countries.

READING CHECK **Analyzing** Why did U.S. leaders end isolationist policies in the late 1800s?

A Powerful Navy

During the late 1800s and early 1900s, the U.S. government began building up its naval forces in an effort to protect its commercial interests overseas. As U.S. senator Henry Cabot Lodge said, "Commerce follows the flag, and we should build up a navy strong enough to give protection to Americans in every quarter of the globe."

What did Lodge mean when he said, "commerce follows the flag"?

Direct Teach

Main Idea

1 End of Isolationism

The United States ended its policy of isolationism.

Contrast How does isolationism differ from imperialism? *isolationism—avoiding involvement in the affairs of other countries; imperialism—building an empire by founding colonies or conquering other nations*

Elaborate Why did some people call William H. Seward's acquisition of Alaska a folly? *possible answer—thought the land in Alaska was not worth the money paid for it*

- **CRF:** Biography Activity: William H. Seward
- **CRF:** LIterature Activity: *The Story of Seward's Folly*

HSS 8.12; **HSS Analysis Skills:** HI 1, HI 2

Info to Know

Mahan's Ideas Alfred Thayer Mahan saw Great Britain as the model of a country that relied on a strong navy to build a powerful trading empire. Mahan pointed out that Britain commanded sea lanes to the East through the Mediterranean and the Suez Canal and to the West through the Atlantic. Mahan hoped that the United States could develop an equally important sea route through a canal across Central America.

Critical Thinking: Evaluating Information

Exceeding Standards

Isolationism vs. Imperialism

HSS 8.12; **HSS Analysis Skills:** HI 2, HI 3 — Research Required

1. Organize the class into small groups. Assign each group one of two positions, either in support of continuing America's isolationism or in favor of imperialism and seeking territories.
2. Have each group conduct research on its side of the debate. Ask groups to brainstorm arguments that support their view as well as arguments to refute the views of opponents.
3. Ask students to imagine that their group has been asked to testify before Congress. Have each group prepare a presentation that explains why the United States should pursue a policy of isolationism or imperialism.
4. Have each group deliver its presentation to the class. When presentations are finished, guide students in a discussion about why some Americans favored expansionist policies over isolationism. **LS Interpersonal, Logical/Mathematical**

Alternative Assessment Handbook, Rubrics 24: Oral Presentations; and 43: Writing to Persuade

Answers

A Powerful Navy *U.S. expansion would keep the U.S. economy strong.*

Reading Check *to keep the economy strong, to provide bases and refueling places for the U.S. Navy; to gain raw materials and markets for industrial growth; to keep up with European countries; to provide national pride and power*

Direct Teach

Main Idea

❷ Hawaii Becomes a U.S. Territory

Because of its economic importance, Hawaii became a U.S. territory.

Analyze Why were the Hawaiian Islands such a desirable territory? *possible answers—the sugar industry and the islands' strategic location in the middle of the Pacific*

Draw Inferences How were missionaries in Hawaii involved in the eventual overthrow of the Hawaiian monarchy? *possible answers—Some missionaries became wealthy and powerful sugar planters who had economic and political ties to the U.S. government.*

CRF: Biography Activity: Queen Liliuokalani

Map Transparency: U.S. Territories in the Pacific

HSS 8.12; **HSS Analysis Skills:** CS 1, HI 1

Biography

Queen Liliuokalani (1838–1917) Queen Liliuokalani championed Hawaiian nationalism. After the revolt in 1893 that ended her short reign, she worked to reclaim her throne and pledged to regain "Hawaii for the Hawaiians." In 1895, royalists who wanted to return Liliuokalani to power rebelled against Sanford B. Dole. They were defeated, and Liliuokalani was placed under house arrest. Eventually, she abdicated the throne and pledged her loyalty to the new Republic of Hawaii. Throughout her life, Liliuokalani remained a symbol of Hawaiian pride and history.

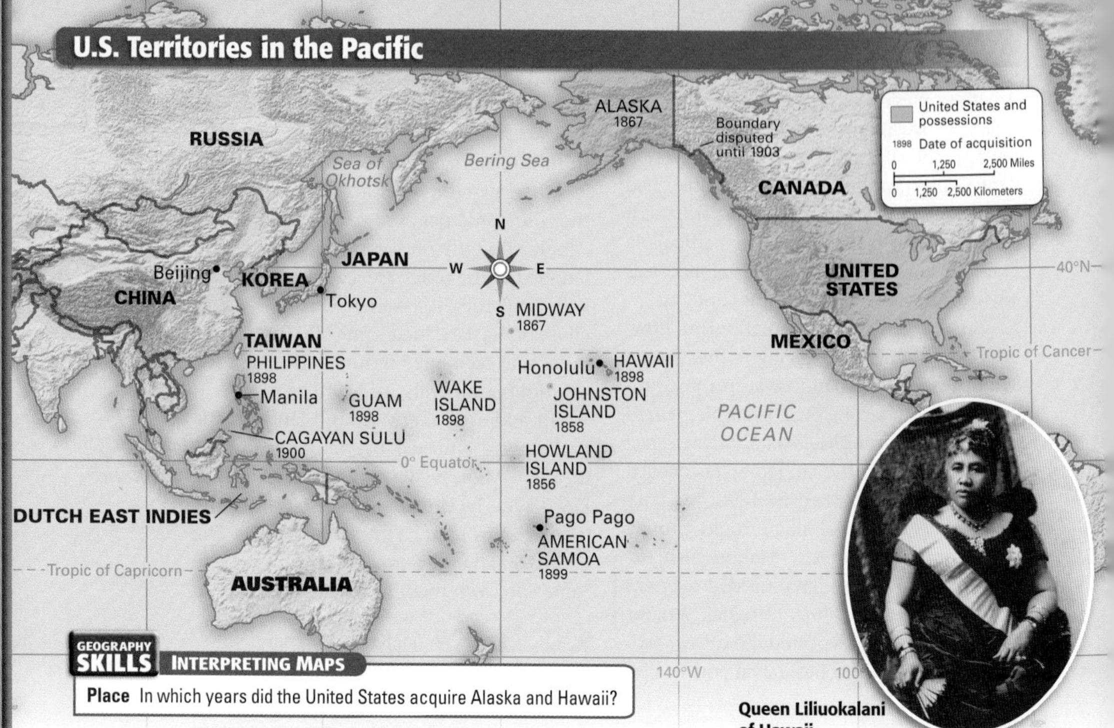

Queen Liliuokalani of Hawaii

Hawaii Becomes a U.S. Territory

Even more appealing than Samoa were the Hawaiian Islands. Hawaiians first saw Europeans when British explorer Captain James Cook arrived. Trading and whaling ships in the Pacific began stopping in Hawaii. Later, American missionaries came and attempted to convert Hawaiians to Christianity. The missionaries opened businesses and raised crops, such as sugarcane. Some missionary families became rich sugar planters.

By the 1840s, most shops and shipyards in Hawaii were owned by Americans. Sugar had become a leading export of the Hawaiian economy. An 1875 treaty allowed Hawaiian sugar to be shipped duty-free to the United States. A duty is a tax on imported items. In return, Hawaii agreed not to give territory or special privileges to any other country. The planters' power grew. In 1887 they made Hawaiian king Kalakaua (kah-LAH-KAH-ooh-ah) sign a new constitution granting more power to the planter-controlled parliament. Many Hawaiians worried that foreigners were becoming too powerful. Native Hawaiians called this new constitution the "bayonet constitution" because Kalakaua was forced to sign it at gunpoint.

Today, sugarcane is Hawaii's most valuable crop.

Hawaiian sugar planters suffered a major economic setback in 1890 when Congress passed the McKinley Tariff. This law allowed all countries to ship sugar duty-free to the United States. However, the tariff also gave U.S. sugar producers a **subsidy**, or bonus payment, of two cents per pound. Prices for Hawaiian sugar dropped, and the islands' economy collapsed.

In 1891, King Kalakaua died, and his sister **Liliuokalani** (li-lee-uh-woh-kuh-LAHN-ee) became queen. In 1893 Queen Liliuokalani proposed a new constitution that would

Differentiating Instruction for Universal Access

Special Education Students

Reaching Standards

1. Review with the class the events that led up to the United States's acquisition of Hawaii as a territory. You may want to write several of the events for students to see.
2. Have students create an illustrated time line of the events that led to the annexation of Hawaii. Ask students to use their own artwork or copies of images from library or Internet sources to illustrate their time lines.
3. Have students present their completed time lines to the class. **LS Visual/Spatial**

HSS 8.12; **HSS Analysis Skills:** CS 1, CS 2, HI 1

Alternative Assessment Handbook, Rubrics 3: Artwork; and 36: Time Lines

Universal Access Resources

See page 635c of the Chapter Planner for additional resources for differentiating instruction for universal access.

Answers

Interpreting Maps *Alaska: 1867; Hawaii: 1898*

return power to the monarchy. The planters revolted. John L. Stevens, U.S. minister to Hawaii, called 150 Marines ashore to support the revolt, and it succeeded without a battle. The planters formed a new government and appointed lawyer Sanford B. Dole as president. Acting without authority from the U.S. State Department, Stevens recognized, or formally acknowledged, the new government. He declared Hawaii to be under U.S. control on February 1, 1893. "The Hawaiian pear is now fully ripe," wrote Stevens, "and this is the golden hour for the United States to pluck it."

President Grover Cleveland disapproved of the revolt and sent a representative, James Blount, to hear both sides of the disagreement. Blount decided the Hawaiian people wanted Liliuokalani restored to power, but Dole and his revolutionary government refused to allow it. Cleveland refused to annex Hawaii but did not effectively help restore the monarchy. The islands remained an independent republic until July 7, 1898, when Congress annexed them. In 1900 Hawaii became a U.S. territory, but it did not become the fiftieth state until 1959.

READING CHECK **Summarizing** What effects did the McKinley Tariff have on Hawaii?

United States Seeks Trade with Japan and China

Economic interests also drew the United States to Japan and China. The United States wanted to open and secure trade markets in both Asian countries.

Opening Trade with Japan

By the mid-1800s, some European powers had formed strong trade ties with most East Asian countries. However, the island nation of Japan had isolated itself from the rest of the world for hundreds of years. Only the Dutch East India Company was allowed to trade at one port in Japan. Japan's leaders also banned travel to other countries.

The United States wanted to open Japan's trade market before Europeans arrived. President Millard Fillmore sent Commodore Matthew Perry to secure "friendship, commerce, a supply of coal and provisions." Perry attempted a peaceful alliance in 1853, but he was not successful. He returned to Japan in 1854 with seven warships. He gave Japanese leaders gifts and tried to show some of the benefits that Japanese-American trade would have.

Perry Arrives in Japan

U.S. ships are docked in the harbor.
What might these men have been thinking while standing in the parade?

CONNECT TO THE ARTS

This 1854 painting shows Commodore Perry landing at Yokohama, Japan. He staged a parade to disembark and meet the imperial commissioners that represented the emperor. This gathering was the first official meeting between an agent of the United States and officials from Japan.

How does this picture show American imperialism and its effects on Japan?

643

Direct Teach

Main Idea

❸ United States Seeks Trade with Japan and China

The United States sought trade with Japan and China.

Analyze How did the United States persuade Japan to open up to trade? *Commodore Matthew Perry went to Japan and used a show of military force and of the benefits of trade to persuade Japanese leaders to open trade with the United States.*

Summarize How did Japan change as a result of its trade with the United States? *began to modernize and industrialize and become a major imperial power*

Activity **News Broadcast** Have students work in groups to prepare and present news broadcasts that feature Commodore Perry's successful negotiations with Japan. **LS Verbal/Linguistic**

- Alternative Assessment Handbook, Rubric 24: Oral Presentations
- **CRF:** Primary Source Activity: Fukuzawa Yukichi on Japan and the West

HSS 8.12; **HSS** **Analysis Skills:** HI 1, HI 2

World Events

Japan's Changing Society After the commercial treaty of 1858 allowed people from the United States and several European countries to enter Japan, members of the samurai, or warrior class, made frequent attacks on westerners. However, the samurai soon realized that they could not keep foreigners out of the country. The samurai then began to push for reforms and modernization within the Japanese government.

Social Studies Skills Activity: Continuity and Change **Standards Proficiency**

Japan in the Meiji Restoration **HSS** 8.12; **HSS** **Analysis Skills:** HI 1, HI 3

1. Review with students the opening of trade with Japan. Ask students to discuss the effect that trade with the United States had on Japan.
2. Ask students to imagine that they are an aide to Commodore Matthew Perry and that he has returned to Japan in 1894, forty years since he was last there. Have students draft a letter from Commodore Perry to the president in which he discusses the changes that have taken place in Japan since his last visit. Students should also mention the things about Japan that have stayed the same over the years.
3. Remind students to use correct spelling, grammar, and punctuation in their letters.
4. Encourage volunteers to share their letters with the class. **LS Verbal/Linguistic**

- Alternative Assessment Handbook, Rubric 25: Personal Letters

Answers

Connect to the Arts *It shows the use of U.S. military power to spread U.S. economic influence into Japan.*

Reading Check *Prices for Hawaiian sugar dropped and the islands' economy collapsed.*

Direct Teach

Main Idea

❸ United States Seeks Trade with Japan and China

The United States sought trade with Japan and China.

Recall Why did the United States issue the Open Door Policy? *U.S. leaders feared they would be shut out of Chinese markets by other countries.*

Identify Who were the Boxers? *a group of Chinese nationalists who opposed foreign involvement and who were frustrated by hunger and homelessness in China*

Analyze What was the result of the Boxer Rebellion? *The Boxers were defeated by foreign military forces, China had to pay foreign nations $333 million, and the Open Door Policy remained in effect.*

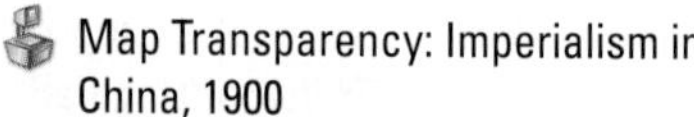
Map Transparency: Imperialism in China, 1900

HSS 8.12; HSS **Analysis Skill:** HI 1

World Events

The Boxer Rebellion The Boxers were members of a Chinese secret society known as the Fists of Righteous Harmony. Many of the people who were attracted to the Boxer movement were unemployed soldiers, Grand Canal boatmen who had lost their livelihoods after foreigners introduced railroads to China, and peasant farmers suffering from a drought that had ravaged China. In 1896, Boxers took to harassing Chinese Christians and attacking foreign missionaries, churches, railways, and mines.

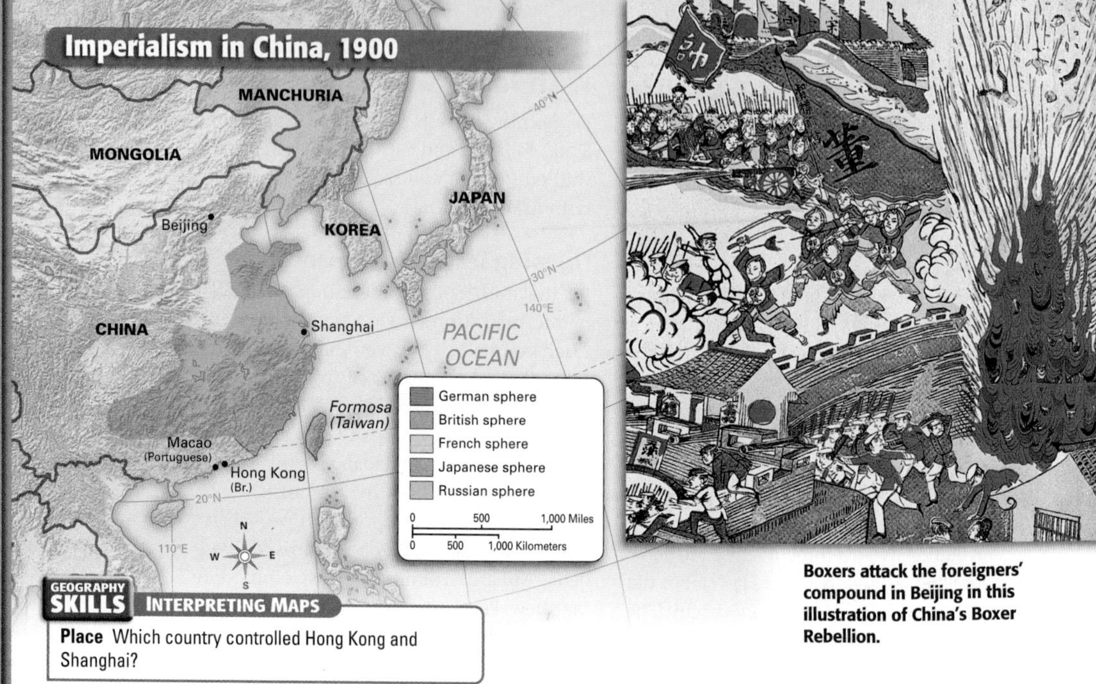

GEOGRAPHY SKILLS INTERPRETING MAPS

Place Which country controlled Hong Kong and Shanghai?

Boxers attack the foreigners' compound in Beijing in this illustration of China's Boxer Rebellion.

This effort—and the presence of American military power—persuaded Japanese leaders to sign a treaty opening trade with the United States. In 1856 Townsend Harris arrived in Japan as the first U.S. **consul general**, or chief diplomat. Despite some Japanese opposition, he negotiated a commercial treaty expanding trade in 1858.

ACADEMIC VOCABULARY
process a series of steps by which a task is accomplished.

Some Japanese leaders wanted trade with the United States. In 1868, people who favored the process of industrialization came to power in Japan, beginning a 40-year period of modernization known as the Meiji (MAY-jee) Restoration. The government also sent Japanese students to the West to study science, technology, and western government.

By the 1890s, Japan was becoming a major imperial power. In 1894–95 Japan defeated China in the Sino-Japanese War, gaining new territory and enjoying the same trade privileges in China as European countries. In 1904 the Japanese launched a sneak attack against Russian forces stationed in China. President Theodore Roosevelt helped negotiate a peace treaty to end the war a year later. The Japanese had won the respect they desired. Japan gained Korea, a lease on Port Arthur in China, and other rights. In less than 50 years, Japan had become a major world power.

Foreign Powers in China

After Japan defeated China, other countries quickly took advantage of China's weakness. These nations seized **spheres of influence**—areas where foreign nations controlled trade and natural resources. Germany, Great Britain, France, Japan, and Russia all took control of areas of China.

Fearing that the United States would be closed out of Chinese markets, Secretary of State **John Hay** took action. He sent notes to Japan and most European countries in 1899, announcing the **Open Door Policy**, the idea that all nations should have equal access to trade in China. This policy was neither accepted nor rejected by the European

Critical Thinking: Analyzing Information

Standards Proficiency

Boxer Rebellion Newspaper Articles

Research Required

1. Have students reread the information in the text about the Chinese Boxers. Then, have students use library or Internet sources to gather additional information on the Boxer Rebellion.
2. Ask students to create a series of three newspaper articles dealing with the causes of the rebellion, the events that took place, and the effects that the rebellion had on U.S.-Chinese relations.
3. Ask volunteers to share information from their articles with the class.
4. When students have completed their articles, have them work in small groups to combine their articles into a newspaper. Display the newspapers for the class to see.

LS Interpersonal, Verbal/Linguistic

Alternative Assessment Handbook, Rubric 23: Newspapers

HSS 8.12; HSS **Analysis Skills:** HI 1, HI 2

Answers

Interpreting Maps *Great Britain*

powers and Japan. Hay, however, announced that it had been accepted. However, within China, there was strong resentment of the control held by foreign nations.

In 1900, this hostility was represented by a group called the Boxers. In their language, the group was known as the Fists of Righteous Harmony. The Boxers were Chinese nationalists who were angered by foreign involvement in China. They also were frustrated by the hunger and homelessness caused by a series of natural disasters.

In June 1900, the Boxers took to the streets of Beijing, China's capital, and laid siege to the walled settlement where foreigners lived. During the revolt, called the **Boxer Rebellion**, the Chinese nationalists killed more than 200 people. The Chinese government, also upset with western influence in China, supported the Boxers.

For two months the siege continued. Military forces, including U.S. Marines, fought their way from the port of Tianjin to Beijing. The Boxers were soon defeated, and China was forced to execute 10 officials who had taken part in the rebellion and to make a $333 million cash payment to foreign governments—$25 million of which went to the United States. Secretary of State Hay then sent another Open Door note to Japan and the European nations. Hay wanted to prevent any European colonization of China that would limit U.S. influence. The Open Door Policy remained in effect long after the Boxer Rebellion.

READING CHECK **Identifying Cause and Effect** What factors led to the Boxer Rebellion in China, and what was the result?

SUMMARY AND PREVIEW The United States greatly expanded its territory and influence with acquisitions in the Pacific. In the next section you will learn about the causes and conflicts of the Spanish-American War.

Section 1 Assessment

go.hrw.com
Online Quiz
KEYWORD: SS8 HP20

Reviewing Ideas, Terms, and People HSS 8.12

1. a. **Describe** What policy had the United States followed regarding other countries?
   b. **Analyze** Why did the United States expand to Alaska and islands in the Pacific?
   c. **Evaluate** Do you think **William H. Seward**'s purchase of Alaska was a good decision? Explain.
2. a. **Recall** What became Hawaii's leading export?
   b. **Sequence** What events led to Hawaii's annexation as a U.S. territory?
   c. **Elaborate** What do you think about the planters' revolt against Queen **Liliuokalani**?
3. a. **Describe** How did United States persuade Japanese leaders to sign a trade treaty?
   b. **Contrast** How was the U.S. experience establishing trade with China different from U.S. attempts to open trade with Japan?
   c. **Evaluate** Do you think Japan made the right decision in agreeing to open trade with the United States? Explain your answer.

Critical Thinking

4. **Generalizing** Copy the chart below. Use it to identify areas or trade rights gained by the United States as well as the benefits each provided.

American Expansion

Areas or Trade Rights Gained	Benefits for United States

FOCUS ON WRITING

5. **Identifying Pros and Cons of U.S. Involvement Overseas** What did the United States gain from its involvement in these areas of the world? What were the drawbacks? As you read this section, identify pros and cons to add to your list.

Direct Teach

Did you know . . .

After the Boxer Rebellion, China was ordered to pay the United States $25 million, of which the United States returned $17 million. The Chinese used most of the money to fund the education of Chinese students in the United States.

Review & Assess

Close

Ask students to recall how the United States gained land or influence in Alaska, Hawaii, Japan, and China.

Review

go.hrw.com Online Quiz, Section 1

Assess

SE Section 1 Assessment

PASS: Section 1 Quiz

Alternative Assessment Handbook

Research/Classroom Intervention

California Standards Review Workbook

Interactive Reader and Study Guide, Section 1

Interactive Skills Tutor CD-ROM

Section 1 Assessment Answers

1. a. isolationism
   b. to keep its economy strong, to gain naval bases, and to expand its influence
   c. possible answer—Yes, it brought a wealth of fur, minerals, and timber under U.S. control.
2. a. sugar
   b. King Kalakaua forced to sign constitution giving planters more power; Queen Liliuokalani restores monarchy; planters revolt and set up republic; Hawaii annexed.
   c. Students should express a reasonable opinion about the revolt.
3. a. Perry used trade gifts and military presence.
   b. Japan treated as a trade partner; China dominated by several nations.
   c. possible answers—Yes, trade with the U.S. facilitated Japan's modernization; no, Japan gave up its traditions and isolationism.
4. Areas—Alaska, Hawaii, Japan, China; benefits—natural resources, sites for naval bases, markets for new products
5. possible answers: pros—economic power, trade partners; cons—some nations grew to dislike the United States, costly wars

Answers

Reading Check *causes—resentment toward foreign nations, anger at Chinese government, natural disasters; results—200 people killed, Boxers defeated and officials executed, China forced to pay $333 million to foreign nations.*

Preteach

Bellringer

If YOU were there . . . Use the **Daily Bellringer Transparency** to help students answer the question.

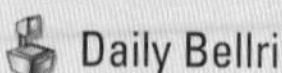 Daily Bellringer Transparency, Section 2

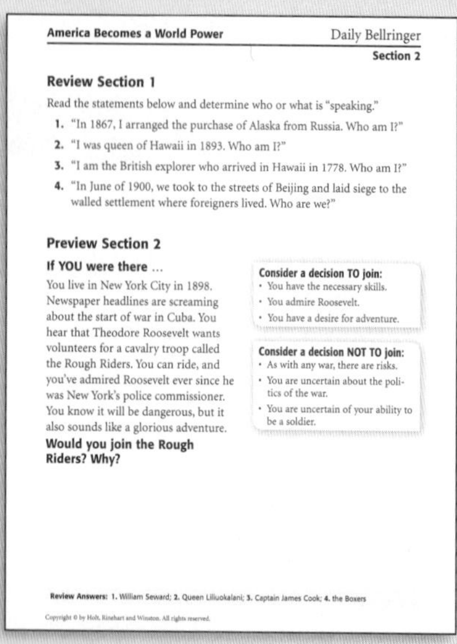

America Becomes a World Power — Daily Bellringer — **Section 2**

Review Section 1

Read the statements below and determine who or what is "speaking."

1. "In 1867, I arranged the purchase of Alaska from Russia. Who am I?"
2. "I was queen of Hawaii in 1893. Who am I?"
3. "I am the British explorer who arrived in Hawaii in 1778. Who am I?"
4. "In June of 1900, we took to the streets of Beijing and laid siege to the walled settlement where foreigners lived. Who are we?"

Preview Section 2

If YOU were there ...

You live in New York City in 1898. Newspaper headlines are screaming about the start of war in Cuba. You hear that Theodore Roosevelt wants volunteers for a cavalry troop called the Rough Riders. You can ride, and you've admired Roosevelt ever since he was New York's police commissioner. You know it will be dangerous, but it also sounds like a glorious adventure.

Would you join the Rough Riders? Why?

Consider a decision TO join:
- You have the necessary skills.
- You admire Roosevelt.
- You have a desire for adventure.

Consider a decision NOT TO join:
- As with any war, there are risks.
- You are uncertain about the politics of the war.
- You are uncertain of your ability to be a soldier.

Review Answers: **1.** William Seward; **2.** Queen Liliuokalani; **3.** Captain James Cook; **4.** the Boxers

Building Vocabulary

Preteach or review the following terms:

blockade isolation of a harbor that prevents the entrance and exit of traffic (p. 649)

casualties those injured, killed, or captured in battle (p. 649)

resolution a formal statement (p. 647)

CRF: Vocabulary Builder Activity, Section 2

Standards Focus

HSS 8.12

Means: Examine changes in the U.S. economy, government, and society that occurred as a result of the Industrial Revolution.

Matters: Economic changes that resulted from the Industrial Revolution helped the U.S. government become a world power.

SECTION 2

The Spanish-American War

What You Will Learn...

Main Ideas

1. Americans supported aiding Cuba in its struggle against Spain.
2. In 1898 the United States went to war with Spain in the Spanish-American War.
3. The United States gained territories in the Caribbean and Pacific.

The Big Idea

The United States expanded into new parts of the world as a result of the Spanish-American War.

Key Terms and People

Joseph Pulitzer, *p. 646*
William Randolph Hearst, *p. 646*
yellow journalism, *p. 646*
Teller Amendment, *p. 647*
Emilio Aguinaldo, *p. 648*
Theodore Roosevelt, *p. 648*
Anti-Imperialist League, *p. 650*
Platt Amendment, *p. 650*

HSS 8.12 Students analyze the transformation of the American economy and the changing social and political conditions in the United States in response to the Industrial Revolution.

If YOU were there...

You live in New York City in 1898. Newspaper headlines are screaming about the start of war in Cuba. You hear that Theodore Roosevelt wants volunteers for a cavalry troop called the Rough Riders. You can ride, and you've admired Roosevelt ever since he was New York's police commissioner. You know it will be dangerous, but it also sounds like a glorious adventure.

Would you join the Rough Riders? Why?

BUILDING BACKGROUND In the late 1800s, the United States became more involved in international affairs than ever before. The main focus was Asia and the Pacific region. Then in the 1890s, Americans became more interested in the island of Cuba, a Spanish colony in the Caribbean. Some Cubans had begun to revolt against the Spanish government there. Many Americans sympathized with the rebels fighting to win Cuba's independence from Spain.

Americans Support Aiding Cuba

Trying to end a rebellion, in 1897 Spain offered to grant Cubans self-government without full independence. Cuban rebels refused. This conflict was widely reported in U.S. newspapers, causing Americans to support the Cubans. The *New York World,* published by **Joseph Pulitzer**, was very critical of the Spanish, as was **William Randolph Hearst**'s *New York Journal.* In competition for readers and customers, both men printed sensational, often exaggerated news stories. This technique is called **yellow journalism**.

Despite growing support for military action, President Grover Cleveland remained opposed to U.S. involvement in Cuba. However, in 1896 William McKinley, a supporter of Cuban independence, was elected president.

READING CHECK **Analyzing** How did the American press affect public support for Cuba's independence?

Teach the Big Idea: Master the Standards

Standards Proficiency

The Spanish-American War

HSS 8.12; HSS **Analysis Skills:** CS 1, CS 2, HI 1, HI 2

1. **Teach** Ask students the Main Idea questions to teach this section.
2. **Apply** Have each student create a three-column chart. Have students title their charts *The Spanish-American War* and label the columns *Causes, Course of War,* and *Results.* Then have students reread the section to identify specific details for each column. **LS Verbal/Linguistic**
3. **Review** Have students discuss the details they included on their charts. Encourage students to add events or details they do not already have on their charts.
4. **Apply/Homework** Have each student create a time line of the Spanish-American War using the chart he or she prepared. Have students divide the time line into three sections, one for each column of their charts. Remind students to place events in chronological order. **LS Verbal/Linguistic, Visual/Spatial**

Alternative Assessment Handbook, Rubrics 6: Cause and Effect; and 36: Time Lines

War with Spain

In February 1898, Hearst published a letter written by the Spanish minister to the United States, Enrique Dupacy de Lôme. The letter said President McKinley was a weak leader. Many Americans were outraged, and the Spanish government was embarrassed.

On January 25, even before Hearst published de Lôme's letter, the United States sent the battleship USS *Maine* to Havana Harbor to protect American citizens and economic interests. Senator Mark Hanna compared this action to "waving a match in an oil well for fun." On February 15, the USS *Maine* exploded and sank with a loss of 260 men. Although the cause of the explosion was unclear, the American press immediately blamed Spain. "Remember the *Maine*!" became a rallying cry for angry Americans.

McKinley requested $50 million to prepare for war, and Congress approved the money. Spain offered to negotiate but still would not consider Cuban independence. Although Cuba was not a U.S. territory, Congress issued a resolution on April 20 that declared Cuba independent and demanded that Spain leave the island within three days. Attached to the resolution was the **Teller Amendment**, which stated that the United States had no interest in taking control of Cuba. In response to the resolution, Spain declared war on the United States. The next day, Congress passed, and McKinley signed, a declaration of war against Spain.

"Remember the *Maine*!"

Most of the men aboard the USS *Maine* were sleeping when a terrible explosion demolished the forward third of the ship at 9:40 p.m., February 15, 1898. The rest of the ship sunk quickly. Some 266 men were killed.

Who did many in the United States blame for the explosion?

Direct Teach

Main Idea

❶ Americans Support Aiding Cuba

Americans supported aiding Cuba in its struggle against Spain.

Define What is yellow journalism? *sensational, often exaggerated news stories*

Make Inferences Why did Americans support Cuba? *possible answers—Americans felt sympathy for the Cubans who wanted independence from Spain; they were swayed by yellow journalism.*

CRF: Primary Source Activity: The *Maine* Explosion

HSS 8.12; **HSS Analysis Skills:** HI 1

Info to Know

Yellow Journalism Joseph Pulitzer was the first to engage in yellow journalism, but William Randolph Hearst quickly responded and proved better at it. To sell papers and get support for U.S. military action in Cuba, Hearst hired artist and illustrator Frederic Remington to provide pictures of conditions on the island. Remington supposedly sent Hearst a telegram from Cuba that read, "Everything is quiet. There is no trouble here. There will be no war." Hearst is said to have answered, "You furnish [provide] the pictures and I'll furnish the war."

go.hrw.com
Online Resources
KEYWORD: SS8 US20
ACTIVITY: Stephen Crane War Dispatches

Critical Thinking: Identifying Bias

Standards Proficiency

Yellow Journalism

HSS 8.12; **HSS Analysis Skills:** HR 4, HR 5

1. Review with students the role that yellow journalism played in rousing public support for war with Spain.
2. Have students use material from the textbook to create sensational headlines that may have run in newspapers prior to and during the Spanish-American War. Remind students to consider the political bias of American newspapers at the time.
3. When students have finished, ask volunteers to share their headlines with the class.
4. Guide students in a general discussion of the role of the press in shaping American public opinion. Ask students how bias can affect public opinion, and how students might identify such bias in the media and elsewhere. **LS Verbal/Linguistic**

Alternative Assessment Handbook, Rubrics 11: Discussions; and 43: Writing to Persuade

Answers

Reading Check (previous page) *by printing sensational stories that led Americans to support independence for Cuba*

"Remember the Maine" *Spain*

Direct Teach

Main Idea

❷ War with Spain

In 1898 the United States went to war with Spain in the Spanish-American War.

Recall What happened to the U.S. battleship the USS *Maine*? *It exploded in Havana Harbor, and 260 American sailors were killed in the explosion.*

Locate In what two regions did the Spanish-American War take place? Why? *in the Pacific and in the Caribbean; the United States wanted to defeat Spain's Pacific fleet and free Cuba.*

Summarize What problems faced American soldiers during the Spanish-American War? *training was poor, shortages of bullets and rifles, uniforms not suited to tropical heat, disease, and poor food*

Map Transparency: War in the Philippines

Map Transparency: War in the Caribbean

HSS 8.12; HSS **Analysis Skills:** HI 1

Info to Know

Conditions in American Camps

Lieutenant Colonel Alfred A. Woodhull served as a surgeon in the U.S. Army. Woodhull observed many health problems at Camp Thomas, where more than 425 American soldiers died. The most serious danger of infection came from the pileup of garbage. Woodhull noted that some regiments attempted to burn their kitchen garbage in furnaces, but no one had taken steps to build large enough furnaces to dispose of the refuse properly. This lack of hygiene led to pollution and the spread of illness and disease.

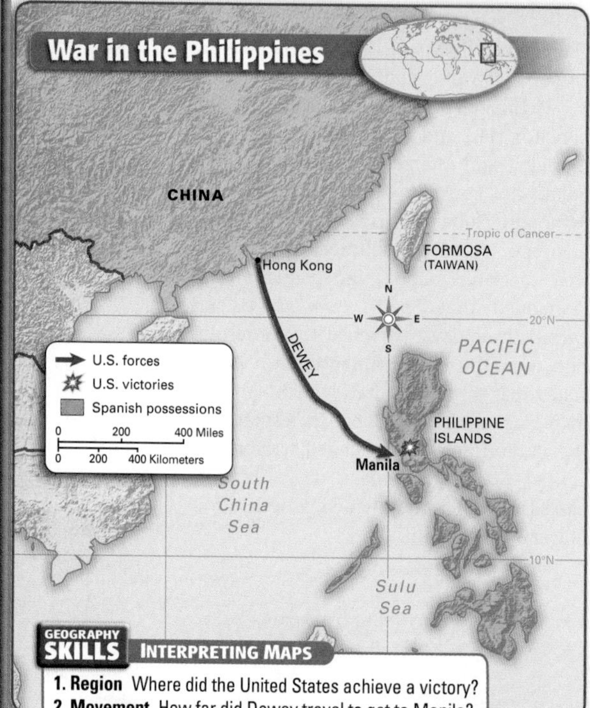

GEOGRAPHY SKILLS INTERPRETING MAPS

1. **Region** Where did the United States achieve a victory?
2. **Movement** How far did Dewey travel to get to Manila?

Fighting in the Pacific

While attention was focused on Cuba, the U.S. Navy won a quick victory nearly halfway around the world in the Pacific Ocean. Commodore George Dewey, commander of the American Asiatic squadron at Hong Kong, had been ordered to be prepared to attack the Spanish Philippines in the event of war. Dewey arrived at the Philippines with four large warships and two smaller gunboats. On May 1, ignoring reports that mines barred his way, he boldly sailed into Manila Bay and destroyed the Spanish Pacific fleet stationed there. Dewey's forces sank or captured 10 ships. The Spanish lost 381 lives, but none of Dewey's men were killed.

Dewey's victory put him in an awkward position. He had defeated the Spanish but did not have enough troops to occupy and secure the island. He decided to wait for reinforcements. Troops eventually arrived, and on August 13, one day after the war had ended, U.S. troops and Filipino rebels led by **Emilio Aguinaldo** (ahg-ee-NAHL-doh) took control of the Philippine capital, Manila.

War in the Caribbean

The U.S. Army was completely unprepared to train and supply the soldiers needed for the Spanish-American War. At the start of the war, the army had about 28,000 soldiers. Yet in the months that followed, more than 280,000 soldiers saw active duty. The army did not have enough rifles or bullets for these soldiers. It did not even have appropriate clothing for the troops, and many soldiers received warm woolen uniforms to wear in Cuba's tropical heat.

The soldiers faced hard living conditions once in Cuba. Army food was canned meat, which one general called "embalmed beef." Fewer than 2,500 U.S. soldiers died during the war. Only a small percentage of them died in battle. Many more died from yellow fever.

The most colorful group of soldiers was the Rough Riders. Second in command of this group was Lieutenant Colonel **Theodore Roosevelt**. Roosevelt had organized the Rough Riders to fight in Cuba. Volunteers included Native Americans, college athletes, cowboys, miners, and ranchers. Newspaper accounts of the Rough Riders' heroism earned the group the admiration of the American public. Four privates of the African American 10th Cavalry, who served with the Rough Riders, received the Congressional Medal of Honor.

In June U.S. ships trapped the Spanish Caribbean fleet in the harbor of Santiago de Cuba. The powerful U.S. Navy blockaded the harbor, making it safer for troops to land nearby. Landing ashore on June 22 and aided by Cuban rebels, the U.S. troops moved to capture the hills around the main Spanish forces at Santiago. At the village

Cross-Discipline Activity: English-Language Arts

Standards Proficiency

The Rough Riders HSS 8.12; HSS **Analysis Skills:** HI 1, HI 2

Research Required

Background During the Spanish-American War, American songwriters promoted the war with popular songs that celebrated the bravery of U.S. troops and the daring of U.S. victories. These patriotic songs served to shape public opinion of events in Cuba and the Philippines.

1. Review with students the role the Rough Riders played in the Spanish-American War. Then have students use the library, Internet, or other resources to research more information about the actions and heroism of the Rough Riders.
2. Have each student select a battle, person, or action that represents the bravery of the Rough Riders and then write song lyrics or a poem about the selected topic.
3. Encourage volunteers to share their song lyrics or poems with the class. Then engage the class in a discussion of why the actions of the Rough Riders gained the admiration of Americans.

LS Auditory/Musical, Verbal/Linguistic

Alternative Assessment Handbook, Rubric 26: Poems and Songs

Answers

Interpreting Maps 1. *Manila;* 2. *about 800 miles*

Fighting in Cuba

The Rough Riders became the most celebrated fighting men of the Spanish-American War. The painting to the right shows the Battle of San Juan Hill. The Rough Riders captured Kettle Hill with the 9th and 10th cavalry units, made up of African Americans.

of El Caney on July 1, 1898, some 7,000 U.S. soldiers, aided by Cuban rebels, overwhelmed about 600 Spanish defenders.

The main U.S. force then attacked and captured San Juan Hill. The Rough Riders and the 9th and 10th cavalries, made up of African Americans, captured nearby Kettle Hill. A journalist on the scene described their charge.

> "It was a miracle of self-sacrifice, a triumph of bulldog courage . . . The fire of the Spanish riflemen . . . doubled and trebled [tripled] in fierceness, the crests of the hills crackled and burst in amazed roars and rippled with waves of tiny flame. But the blue line [of United States soldiers] crept steadily up and on."
>
> —Richard Harding Davis, quoted in *The American Reader*, edited by Paul M. Angle

On July 3, 1898, the commander of the Spanish fleet decided to try breaking through the U.S. blockade. Every Spanish ship was destroyed in the battle. American forces suffered only two casualties. Santiago

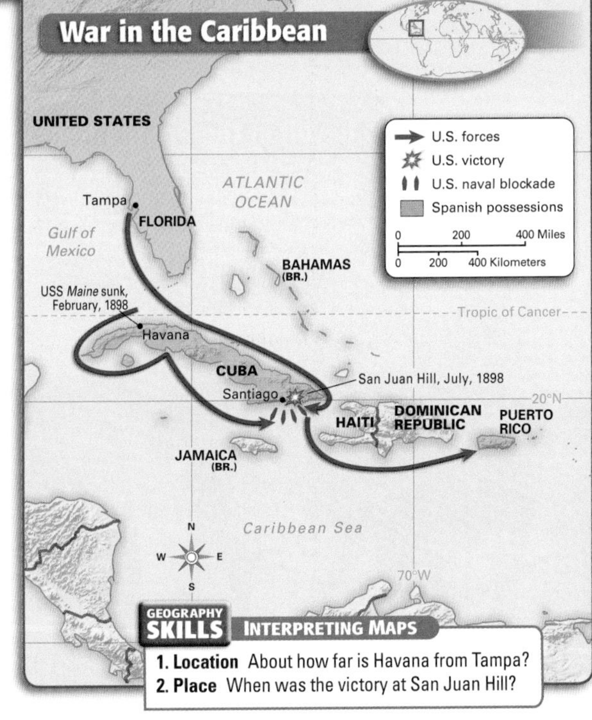

GEOGRAPHY SKILLS INTERPRETING MAPS

1. **Location** About how far is Havana from Tampa?
2. **Place** When was the victory at San Juan Hill?

Direct Teach

Connect to Science and Technology

Filming the War The Spanish-American War was the first U.S. war to be captured by moving pictures. Invented in the 1880s, motion picture cameras were used to record footage of events surrounding the conflict in Cuba. Cameramen filmed events like the burial of victims of the *Maine* explosion, military preparations for war, and the homecoming of troops. Although actual battles were not filmed, several reenactments of battles were staged and filmed in order to "satisfy the craving of the general public" for details about events of the war.

Info to Know

Buffalo Soldiers In the late 1800s the United States Army formed cavalry regiments made up of African American soldiers. These regiments were mainly stationed in the western United States and fought Native Americans. In 1898, however, these Buffalo Soldiers were sent to the Caribbean to fight in the Spanish-American War, where many were honored for their bravery in battle.

Checking for Understanding

True or False Answer each statement *T* if it is true or *F* if it is false. If false, explain why.

1. U.S. naval forces quickly defeated the Spanish Pacific fleet in the Philippines. *T*
2. Emilio Aguinaldo was the second in command of the Rough Riders. *F; Theodore Roosevelt was second in command of the Rough Riders.*
3. In the fighting in Cuba, U.S. troops were aided by Cuban rebels. *T*

HSS 8.12

Collaborative Learning

Standards Proficiency

Discussing Territories

HSS 8.12; HSS **Analysis Skills:** HI 1

1. Organize the class into small groups. Assign each group to represent one of the following Spanish territories: Cuba, the Philippines, or Puerto Rico. Tell the members of each group that they have been asked by leaders in the territory to plan for the future once the war is over.
2. Remind students to discuss how each territory plans to rule itself, and what the policy toward the United States will be. Territories can choose to seek U.S. protection, pursue statehood, or establish an independent nation.
3. Groups must decide which of these options to pursue for their particular territories. Ask students to explain why they selected the option they chose, and what steps the territory's leaders ought to take. Have groups write short position papers outlining their ideas.
4. Ask each group to give a brief presentation of its ideas to the class.

Alternative Assessment Handbook, Rubrics 14: Group Activity; and 43: Writing to Persuade

Answers

Interpreting Maps **1.** *about 400 miles;* **2.** *July 1898*

Direct Teach

Main Idea

3 United States Gains Territories

The United States gained territories in the Caribbean and Pacific.

Identify What did the Anti-Imperialist League oppose? *U.S. actions to build a colonial empire*

Analyze How did the Platt Amendment alter U.S. policy toward Cuba as stated in the Teller Amendment? *The Platt Amendment limited Cuba's right to make treaties and allowed the United States to intervene in Cuban affairs, which differed from the Teller Amendment's statement that the United States had no interest in taking control of Cuba.*

Explain Why did the U.S. annexation of the Philippines lead to conflict with Filipino rebels? *The United States decided to keep the islands rather than grant them independence, which led to a guerilla war against the United States that lasted three years.*

HSS 8.12; **HSS Analysis Skills:** HI 1

surrendered on July 17. A few days later, U.S. troops invaded Spanish-held Puerto Rico, where they met little resistance. Puerto Rico soon surrendered. Spain asked for peace and signed a cease-fire agreement on August 12, 1898.

READING CHECK **Comparing** How was fighting in the Pacific and the Caribbean similar?

United States Gains Territories

As part of this agreement, the United States established a naval base in Cuba at Guantánamo Bay. The base is still in operation today.

The peace treaty placed Cuba, Guam, Puerto Rico, and the Philippines under U.S. control. Some Americans formed the **Anti-Imperialist League**, a group that opposed the treaty and the creation of an American colonial empire. The peace treaty was approved, however, by a vote of 57 to 27 in the Senate—one vote more than the two-thirds majority needed.

Revolt in the Philippines

When the U.S. government decided to keep the Philippines, many Filipinos revolted. Here, a U.S. soldier checks the identification of some Filipino villagers during the rebellion.

Cuba

The Teller Amendment declared that the United States would not annex Cuba. However, McKinley wanted to create stability and increase U.S. economic activity, so he set up a military government there. He appointed General Leonard Wood as governor, and Wood quickly began building schools and a sanitation system.

To fight disease, Dr. Walter Reed, head of the army's Yellow Fever Commission, was sent to Cuba in 1900. He and his volunteers proved that yellow fever was transmitted by mosquitoes. Getting rid of standing water helped health officials to control the disease.

Wood also oversaw the drafting of a Cuban constitution. The document included the **Platt Amendment**, which limited Cuba's right to make treaties and allowed the United States to intervene in Cuban affairs. It also required Cuba to sell or lease land to the United States. The Cubans reluctantly accepted the amendment, and U.S. troops withdrew. The amendment remained in force until 1934, and the U.S. government stayed actively involved in Cuban affairs until the late 1950s.

The Philippines

Spain had surrendered the Philippines in return for a $20 million payment from the United States. Many Americans believed that it would be wrong to annex the islands without receiving consent from Filipinos. Other people agreed with McKinley, who said that the United States would benefit from the islands' naval and commercial value, and that annexing the islands would keep Europeans from seizing them.

Filipino rebels, however, had helped U.S. forces to capture Manila. They had expected to gain independence after the war. When the United States decided instead to keep the islands, Auginaldo's rebels started a guerrilla war against the American forces. Hundreds of thousands of Filipinos died

Differentiating Instruction for Universal Access

Learners Having Difficulty

Reaching Standards

1. To help students understand the results of the Spanish-American War, draw the chart for students to see. Omit the blue answers.
2. Have students complete the chart by identifying U.S. actions towards each former Spanish possession. Then have students identify what became of that territory.
3 Review the answers with the class.

LS Verbal/Linguistic, Visual/Spatial

HSS 8.12; **HSS Analysis Skills:** CS 1, HI 1, HI 2

Territory	U.S. Actions	Results
Cuba	*included Platt Amendment*	*U.S. had right to intervene in Cuban affairs*
Philippines	*annexed the islands; fought Filipino rebels for three years*	*U.S. gave Philippines self-rule; full independence in 1946*
Puerto Rico	*annexed as a territory*	*made a commonwealth*

Answers

Reading Check *The U.S. easily defeated Spanish fleets in both the Pacific and in Cuba; local rebels in both Cuba and the Philippines helped U.S. troops.*

before the conflict ended more than three years later, in 1902. Congress passed the Philippine Government Act that same year. It provided that an appointed governor and a two-house legislature would rule the Philippines. The lower house was to be elected. In 1946 the United States granted full independence to the Philippines.

Puerto Rico

Like Cubans and the Filipinos, Puerto Ricans had hoped for independence after the war. Instead, the U.S. government made the island a territory. On April 12, 1900, the Foraker Act established a civil government in Puerto Rico. It was headed by a governor and included a two-house legislature.

A debate over the new territories soon arose. People who lived in Puerto Rico were considered citizens of the island but not of the United States. In 1917, the Jones Act gave Puerto Ricans U.S. citizenship and made both houses of the legislature elective. However, another 30 years passed before Puerto Ricans could elect their own governor. In 1952 Puerto Rico became a commonwealth. This unique status means that the island has its own constitution and elected officials but remains in full association with the United States.

THE IMPACT TODAY

Most Puerto Ricans wish to remain a U.S. commonwealth rather than becoming an independent nation. However, statehood is a controversial issue in Puerto Rico, with slightly more people supporting remaining a commonwealth.

READING CHECK **Summarizing** What territories did the United States gain due to the war?

SUMMARY AND PREVIEW America fought a war with Spain and gained new territories. In the next section you will learn about U.S. interests in Latin America.

Section 2 Assessment

go.hrw.com
Online Quiz
KEYWORD: SS8 HP20

Reviewing Ideas, Terms, and People HSS 8.12

1. a. **Recall** What was the cause of the conflict between Cuba and Spain?
   b. **Analyze** How did **yellow journalism** affect public support for American military action in Cuba?
2. a. **Describe** What event triggered the war between the United States and Spain?
   b. **Make Inferences** Why did the U.S. Navy attack Spain's Pacific fleet?
   c. **Elaborate** Why do you think the United States was so successful in defeating Spain?
3. a. **Identify** What territories did the United States gain as a result of the war?
   b. **Analyze** Why did some Americans oppose the annexation of the Philippines?

Critical Thinking

4. **Categorizing** Copy the graphic organizer at the right. Use it to identify the arguments for and against taking control of foreign territories.

Arguments for Imperialism	vs.	Arguments against Imperialism

FOCUS ON WRITING

5. **Identifying Pros and Cons of U.S. Involvement in the Spanish-American War** As you read this section, add to your pros and cons list by identifying American losses and gains as a result of the Spanish-American War. What were the costs in human lives? What were the gains in territory? Can you identify any more abstract losses and gains? For example, what about the American ideal of the right of a people to govern themselves? Was this ideal compromised or strengthened?

Direct Teach

Main Idea

3 United States Gains Territories

The United States gained territories in the Caribbean and Pacific.

Analyze Why would the United States want to keep European nations out of the Philippines? *Students might suggest that the United States hoped to benefit from a monopoly on trade with the Philippines.*

Summarize What were the Foraker and Jones Acts? *Foraker—established a civil government in Puerto Rico with a governor and a two-house legislature; Jones—made Puerto Ricans U.S. citizens.*

HSS 8.12; HSS **Analysis Skills:** HI 1

Review & Assess

Close

Ask students to review how the United States gained land or influence in Cuba, the Philippines, Guam, and Puerto Rico.

Review

Online Quiz, Section 2

Assess

SE Section 2 Assessment

PASS: Section 2 Quiz

Alternative Assessment Handbook

Research/Classroom Intervention

California Standards Review Workbook

Interactive Reader and Study Guide, Section 2

Interactive Skills Tutor CD-ROM

Section 2 Assessment Answers

1. a. Cuba wanted independence.
   b. fueled public support for war with Spain
2. a. the explosion of the *Maine* led the U.S. to declare Cuba independent and war broke out
   b. to gain control of the Philippines; to eliminate the threat of that fleet
   c. had a stronger navy and was supported by local rebels
3. a. Cuba, Guam, Puerto Rico, the Philippines
   b. believed it was wrong to annex the Philippines without the consent of the Filipino people; opposed U.S. imperialism
4. Arguments for—increase U.S. influence, naval and commercial value of new territories, keep Europeans from seizing territories; Arguments against—cost in U.S. lives, many U.S. citizens were opposed, would anger those in territories
5. Losses—lives lost, expensive to control territories; Gains—new territories, new allies

Answers

Reading Check *Cuba had self rule, but the Platt Amendment gave U.S. permission to intervene; Guam was annexed as a territory; Puerto Rico was annexed and made a commonwealth; the Philippines was originally annexed but given self-rule and later independence.*

Preteach

Bellringer

If YOU were there . . . Use the **Daily Bellringer Transparency** to help students answer the question.

Daily Bellringer Transparency, Section 3

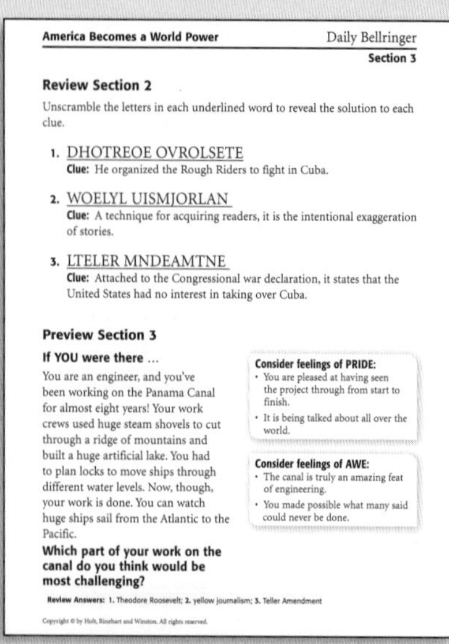
America Becomes a World Power — Daily Bellringer — **Section 3**

Review Section 2

Unscramble the letters in each underlined word to reveal the solution to each clue.

1. DHOTREOE OVROLSETE
   Clue: He organized the Rough Riders to fight in Cuba.
2. WOELYL UISMJORLAN
   Clue: A technique for acquiring readers, it is the intentional exaggeration of stories.
3. LTELER MNDEAMTNE
   Clue: Attached to the Congressional war declaration, it states that the United States had no interest in taking over Cuba.

Preview Section 3

If YOU were there ...

You are an engineer, and you've been working on the Panama Canal for almost eight years! Your work crews used huge steam shovels to cut through a ridge of mountains and built a huge artificial lake. You had to plan locks to move ships through different water levels. Now, though, your work is done. You can watch huge ships sail from the Atlantic to the Pacific.

Which part of your work on the canal do you think would be most challenging?

Consider feelings of PRIDE:
- You are pleased at having seen the project through from start to finish.
- It is being talked about all over the world.

Consider feelings of AWE:
- The canal is truly an amazing feat of engineering.
- You made possible what many said could never be done.

Review Answers: 1. Theodore Roosevelt; 2. yellow journalism; 3. Teller Amendment

Academic Vocabulary

Review with students the following high-use academic term in this section.

role assigned behavior (p. 656)

Building Vocabulary

Preteach or review the following term:

isthmus a narrow strip of land that connects two larger pieces of land (p. 653)

CRF: Vocabulary Builder Activity, Section 3

Standards Focus

HSS 8.12.3

Means: Explain how the U.S. government promoted expansion by using tariffs, loans, and subsidies.

Matters: The Unites States expanded its influence in Latin America through economic and other means.

SECTION 3

The United States and Latin America

What You Will Learn...

Main Ideas

1. The United States built the Panama Canal.
2. Theodore Roosevelt changed U.S. policy toward Latin America.
3. Presidents Taft and Wilson promoted U.S. interests in Latin America.

The Big Idea

The United States expanded its role in Latin America in the early 1900s.

Key Terms and People

Hay-Herrán Treaty, *p. 653*
Philippe Bunau-Varilla, *p. 653*
Hay–Bunau-Varilla Treaty, *p. 653*
Panama Canal, *p. 655*
Roosevelt Corollary, *p. 656*
dollar diplomacy, *p. 657*

HSS 8.12.3 Explain how states and the federal government encouraged business expansion through tariffs, banking, land grants, and subsidies.

If YOU were there...

You are an engineer, and you've been working on the Panama Canal for almost eight years! Your work crews used huge steam shovels to cut through a ridge of mountains and built a huge artificial lake. You had to plan locks to move ships through different water levels. Now, though, your work is done. You can watch huge ships sail from the Atlantic to the Pacific.

Which part of your work on the canal do you think would be most challenging?

BUILDING BACKGROUND In 1823, the Monroe Doctrine stated that Americans had a special interest in protecting Latin America from European influence. That doctrine continued to shape U.S. foreign policy toward Latin America. The United States then wanted land in Central America in order to build a canal that would link the Atlantic and Pacific.

Building the Panama Canal

In the late 1800s some U.S. leaders began exploring ways to dig a canal across the narrow neck of Central America. Such a canal would link the Atlantic and Pacific oceans and cut 8,000 miles off the voyage by ship from the West and East coasts of the United States. It would also allow the U.S. Navy to link its Atlantic and Pacific naval fleets quickly.

Teach the Big Idea: Master the Standards

Standards **Proficiency**

The United States and Latin America

HSS 8.12.3; HSS **Analysis Skills:** CS 1, CS 2, HI 1, HI 2

1. **Teach** Ask students the Main Idea questions to teach this section.
2. **Apply** Have students write the section's main headings on paper. As students finish reading each part of this section, they should create a time line of the important events, treaties, and people.
3. **Review** As you review the section's main ideas, guide students in a discussion of the relationships between the United States and its Latin American neighbors.
4. **Practice/Homework** Have students refer to the events and people on their time lines. Assign them to choose two events that they feel show a strong cause-and-effect relationship. Have students write a paragraph, illustrated with a flow chart, demonstrating the relationship between the two events.

Alternative Assessment Handbook Rubrics 6: Cause and Effect; 36: Time Lines

The Treaties

In 1850 the United States and Great Britain signed the Clayton-Bulwer Treaty, which called for them to jointly build and maintain a canal. However, that canal was never built. In 1881 a French company headed by Ferdinand de Lesseps, who had engineered the Suez Canal in Egypt, began work in Central America. By 1887, after spending nearly $300 million and losing some 20,000 lives, the company was financially ruined. Less than one-third of the planned 51-mile canal had been dug.

No one was a stronger supporter of a Central American canal than President Theodore Roosevelt. He believed naval power was important to U.S. security and strength. Earlier, Roosevelt had written, "I believe we should build the [Central American] canal at once, and, in the meantime, . . . we should build a dozen new battleships." In 1901 Secretary of State John Hay negotiated the Hay-Pauncefote Treaty with Great Britain. The British gave up interest in the canal project, and the United States agreed to open the future canal to all vessels at all times.

Hay then began negotiations with Colombia, where the Isthmus of Panama was located. Hay and the Colombian minister, Thomas Herrán, soon reached an agreement. According to the agreement, called the **Hay–Herrán Treaty**, the United States would pay $10 million plus $250,000 a year for a 99-year lease on a strip of land across the isthmus. The agreement was approved by the U.S. Senate in 1903. However, the Colombian senate rejected the plan.

Philippe Bunau-Varilla, chief engineer of the French canal company, offered an alternative. He told Hay and Roosevelt of a possible revolt he was planning in the Colombian province of Panama. He hoped that the United States would support the revolt with troops and money.

Revolution in Panama

On November 2, 1903, a U.S. warship arrived in Colón, Panama. The next day a revolt began. Colombian forces tried to stop the rebellion but could not reach Panama. Dense jungles blocked land routes, and the U.S. warship blocked sea lanes. Panama then declared itself an independent country. The United States quickly recognized the new nation on November 6.

One week later, Bunau-Varilla arrived in Washington, D.C., as the Panamanian minister to the United States. Five days later, he signed the **Hay-Bunau-Varilla Treaty**. The terms of this agreement were identical to those of the Hay-Herrán Treaty, except the canal zone was widened to 10 miles.

The massive Gatun locks, shown here under construction in 1914, raise ships 85 feet onto Gatun Lake, an inland waterway of the Panama Canal.

Direct Teach

Main Idea

❶ Building the Panama Canal

The United States built the Panama Canal.

Identify How many miles shorter would the sea voyage from the Atlantic to the Pacific Ocean be with a canal through Central America? *about 8,000 miles shorter*

Summarize What happened during the French attempt to build the Panama Canal? *The company spent $300 million, lost 20,000 lives, and went bankrupt, not even completing 1/3 of the digging required to complete the canal.*

Drawing Conclusions Why did the United States support the Panamanian revolution? *U.S. leaders saw it as the best chance to secure the route for the Panama Canal.*

Political Cartoons Activities for United States History, Cartoon 24: Roosevelt and the Panama Canal

Map Transparency: The Panama Canal

HSS 8.12.1; HSS **Analysis Skill:** HI 1

Info to Know

Nicaragua Many U.S. congress members believed that a canal should be cut through Nicaragua, but Philippe Bunau-Varilla wanted Congress to choose the Panama route instead. Then a volcano erupted on a Caribbean island, destroying a city and killing nearly 30,000 people. Bunau-Varilla sent each senator a postage stamp picturing one of Nicaragua's many volcanoes, one of which was located within 100 miles of the proposed canal. Members of Congress soon came to the decision that Panama was a better location for the canal.

Collaborative Learning

Standards Proficiency

The Panama Canal HSS 8.12.3; HSS **Analysis Skills:** HI 1, HI 6

1. Guide students in a discussion about the difficulties that the United States overcame to build the Panama Canal. Then have students create a list of the costs and benefits of building the canal.
2. Organize students in small groups to write short stories in which people such as diplomats, doctors, and engineers talk about what they did to overcome obstacles involved in building the canal and how it will benefit the entire world. Stories might mention fighting diseases, blasting and shoveling through the mountains, and negotiating agreements with foreign countries.
3. Have students share their stories of the problems and benefits of building the canal. **LS Verbal/Linguistic**

Alternative Assessment Handbook, Rubrics 14: Group Activity; and 37: Writing Assignments

Direct Teach

Info to Know

Colombia It took nearly 20 years for Colombia to forgive the United States for the way it aided the Panamanian revolt for independence. During the 1910s, oil was discovered in Colombia, and the United States hoped to gain oil concessions from the country. To regain Columbia's friendship, in 1921 the United States agreed to pay $25 million in compensation for the Panama Canal.

Connect to Geography

Panama Canal Construction of the Panama Canal lasted some 10 years. One group of workers dredged an approach channel and built a dam and locks on the Atlantic side. Another group dredged a passage from the Pacific Ocean through the Bay of Panama and constructed two smaller sets of locks. The hardest task fell to a third group, which had to blast an eight-mile-long channel through the mountainous Continental Divide. Geologic faults, heavy rains, and shifting earth caused frequent and often fatal avalanches. Finally, on October 10, 1913, President Woodrow Wilson signaled crews to dynamite the protective dike at the south end of the channel. In a dramatic finale, water from the two sides rushed together, and the world now had a "Path Between the Seas."

Map Transparency: The Panama Canal

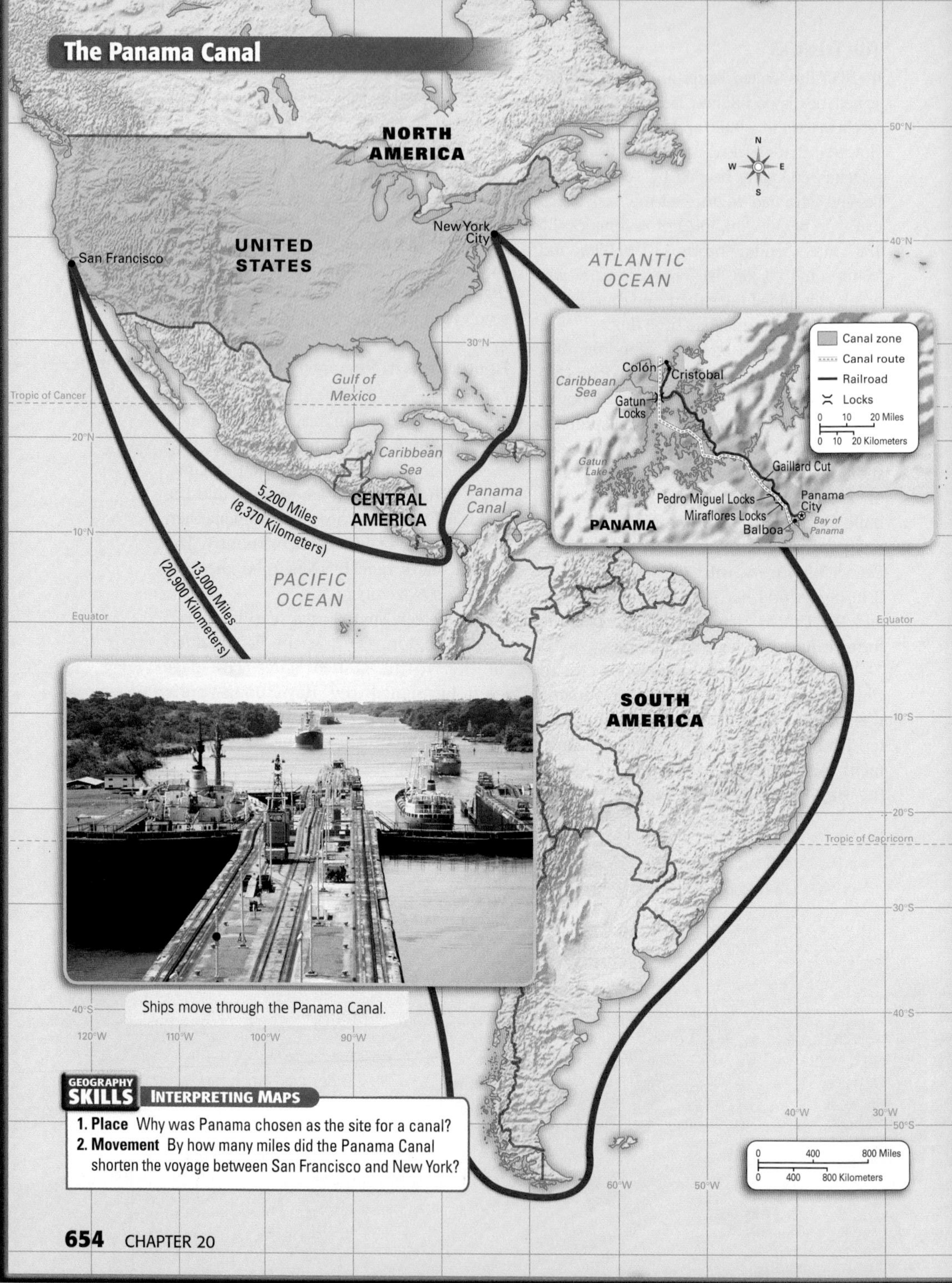

Ships move through the Panama Canal.

GEOGRAPHY SKILLS INTERPRETING MAPS

1. **Place** Why was Panama chosen as the site for a canal?
2. **Movement** By how many miles did the Panama Canal shorten the voyage between San Francisco and New York?

654 CHAPTER 20

Differentiating Instruction for Universal Access

Advanced Learners/GATE

Exceeding Standards | Research Required

1. Have students conduct outside research into the individuals involved with and the negotiations over the Panama Canal. Students should use library resources or the Internet to gather information.
2. Have students work in small groups to write a short play about the main participants in the negotiations for the Panama Canal. Characters should include Theodore Roosevelt, John Hay, Thomas Herrán, and Philippe Bunau-Varilla.
3. Each group should also have a narrator, who will add to the play by telling the "real" story behind some of the negotiations, such as the information Bunau-Varilla had about the Panamanian revolt.
4. Have each group perform its skit for the class.
LS Interpersonal, Kinesthetic

HSS 8.12.3; HSS **Analysis Skills:** HR 1, HI 1

Alternative Assessment Handbook, Rubric 33: Skits and Reader's Theater

Answers

Interpreting Maps 1. *It was the shortest distance between the Atlantic and Pacific Oceans;* **2.** *7800 miles.*

Building the Canal

Building the canal proved to be very difficult. The first obstacle to overcome was tropical disease. The canal route ran through 51 miles of jungles and swamps filled with mosquitoes, many of which carried the deadly diseases malaria and yellow fever.

Dr. William C. Gorgas, who had helped Dr. Walter Reed identify and stamp out the disease in Cuba, organized a successful effort to rid the canal route of disease-carrying mosquitoes. If Gorgas had not been successful, the canal's construction would have taken much longer. It also would have cost much more in terms of both lives and money.

Even with the reduced risk of disease, the work was very dangerous in the high mountain range of central Panama. Most of the canal had to be blasted out of solid rock. Workers used dozens of steam shovels to cut a narrow, eight-mile-long channel through the mountains. On one occasion, a bolt of lightning struck a 12-ton explosive charge, killing seven workers. Sometimes workers died when their shovels struck unexploded charges. One West Indian worker recalled, "The flesh of men flew in the air like birds every day."

Leadership was also problematic. The project went through a series of chief engineers. Finally, Colonel George W. Goethals of the Army Corps of Engineers made significant progress.

Some 6,000 lives were lost during the American construction of the **Panama Canal**, which was finally opened to traffic on August 15, 1914, linking the Atlantic and Pacific Oceans. It had taken 10 years to complete, and about 240 million cubic yards of earth had been removed. The cost was $375 million in addition to the nearly $300 million spent in the earlier failed French effort. In the end, however, the world had its "highway between the oceans."

READING CHECK **Drawing Conclusions** Why did building the canal cost so many lives?

BIOGRAPHY

Theodore Roosevelt
1858–1919

Theodore Roosevelt was born into a wealthy family from New York City. He suffered from poor health as a child but became involved in many sports as he grew older. He spent two years on his ranch in the Dakota Territory, where he served as deputy sheriff. While in the West, he became an avid hunter and conservationist. When he returned to the East, he returned to his political career as an important reformer. A strong supporter of imperialism and the Spanish-American War, he recruited a cavalry division called the Rough Riders. As President McKinley's vice president, Roosevelt became president upon McKinley's assassination.

Analyzing How might Roosevelt's time in the West have shaped his decisions as president?

Roosevelt Changes U.S. Policy

The Panama Canal allowed the United States to become more involved in Latin America. In 1823, President James Monroe had warned European nations not to interfere in the Western Hemisphere. In what became known as the Monroe Doctrine, he outlined his views. "The American continents . . . are henceforth not to be considered as subjects for future colonization by any European powers." The United States would view any such actions as a threat to its safety.

The Monroe Doctrine had become a major principle of U.S. foreign policy. When Monroe presented the doctrine, America did not have the military strength to enforce it. As the United States grew stronger, particularly after the Spanish-American War, it became less dependent upon British naval power to enforce the Doctrine.

During the late 1800s, many European investors had made loans to a number of

THE IMPACT TODAY
The Panama Canal is still an important shipping route. About 260 million tons of cargo go through the canal each year.

Direct Teach

Main Idea

❷ Roosevelt Changes U.S. Policy

Theodore Roosevelt changed U.S. policy toward Latin America.

Recall What was the Monroe Doctrine? *a major principle of U.S. foreign policy stating that the United States would not tolerate other countries interfering in the affairs of Latin America*

Explain Why did the United States become involved in Latin American affairs in the late 1800s? *Latin American nations owed debts to European nations; the U.S. became a third-party negotiator of these loans.*

CRF: History and Geography Activity: Territories in Latin America

HSS 8.12.3; HSS **Analysis Skill:** HI 1

Connect to Science

Curing Yellow Fever Remind students that during the Spanish-American War yellow fever took a large toll on American troops. Working in Cuba, Dr. Walter Reed had theorized that mosquitoes transmitted yellow fever, but proving that theory was difficult because animals were not used to test disease at that time. So Reed and other doctors in his commission let mosquitoes bite them. When some came down with yellow fever, the experiment proved Reed's point.

Critical Thinking: Comparing and Contrasting

Standards Proficiency

Roosevelt's Foreign Policy HSS 8.12.3; HSS Analysis Skills: HI 1

1. Draw a Venn diagram for students to see. Label the left circle *Before Roosevelt,* and label the right circle *During Roosevelt.* Title the diagram *U.S. Policies toward Latin America.*
2. Ask members of the class to list U.S. foreign policies that existed before Roosevelt's presidency and the ways in which foreign policy changed during his presidency. Policies that stayed the same should be listed in the middle portion of the diagram where the two circles overlap.
3. Ask students to suggest possible reasons for the changes that occurred in U.S. policy toward Latin America.
4. Have students copy the diagram and keep it as a study tool. LS **Visual/Spatial**

Alternative Assessment Handbook, Rubric 13: Graphic Organizers

Answers

Biography *He became an avid conservationist, which shaped his domestic policies.*

Reading Check *disease, natural disasters, explosives, accidents*

Direct Teach

Main Idea

❷ Roosevelt Changes U.S. Policy

Theodore Roosevelt changed U.S. policy toward Latin America.

Recall Why did Britain and Germany blockade Venezuela? *They wanted Venezuela to repay its foreign debts.*

Evaluating Why was President Roosevelt eager to expand U.S. political control in South America? *Roosevelt saw the United States as the "police officer" of the Western Hemisphere. This meant that he was willing to use U.S. military and economic force to influence and control South American nations.*

Activity **Slogans** Have students paraphrase the proverb used by Roosevelt, "Speak softly and carry a big stick," and create an original slogan that means the same thing. **LS Verbal/Linguistic**

Alternative Assessment Handbook, Rubric 34: Slogans and Banners

HSS 8.12.3; **HSS Analysis Skill:** HI 1

Latin American countries. For example, Venezuela, under the rule of dictator Cipriano Castro, fell deeply in debt to British and German investors. In 1902 Venezuela refused to repay these debts or to have the claims settled by a neutral third party.

European leaders wanted to act but were worried about the Monroe Doctrine. In 1901, however, Roosevelt had stated that the United States did "not guarantee any State against punishment if it misconducts itself." The European countries thought this meant that they could collect their debts. Great Britain and Germany sent ships to blockade Venezuela. Castro then asked Roosevelt to propose having the matter settled by a third party, which the Europeans accepted.

Academic Vocabulary
role assigned behavior

In 1904 a similar situation arose in the Caribbean country of the Dominican Republic. Again, European countries considered using force to collect debts, but the presence of European forces in the Caribbean would violate the Monroe Doctrine. Furthermore, their presence could threaten U.S. power in the region.

Roosevelt knew that U.S. officials would have to force debtor nations to repay their loans in order to keep European nations from directly intervening in Latin America. In December 1904, he created what became known as the **Roosevelt Corollary** to the Monroe Doctrine. This addition to the doctrine warned that the United States would intervene in any wrongdoing by nations in the Western Hemisphere.

This new **role** of the United States as "police officer" of the Western Hemisphere suited Roosevelt's style. In 1900 he said, "I have always been fond of the West African proverb: 'Speak softly and carry a big stick, you will go far.'"

Reading Check **Finding Main Ideas** Why did Roosevelt create the Roosevelt Corollary?

Primary Source

POLITICAL CARTOON

Roosevelt's Imperialism

Roosevelt's foreign policy is shown visually in this cartoon. Theodore Roosevelt is the giant leading a group of ships that represent debt collection. The U.S. president is patrolling the Caribbean Sea and Latin American countries, trying to enforce the payment of debts to European countries.

What do you think this stick represents?

Why are these vessels warships?

Analysis Skill **Analyzing Primary Sources**
How does the cartoonist show visually the parts of the Roosevelt Corollary?

Differentiating Instruction for Universal Access

English-Language Learners — Exceeding Standards

1. Have students list events in Latin America that led President Roosevelt to issue the Roosevelt Corollary. Guide students in a discussion of these events and ask students to decide which were the most important.
2. Have each student create a graph, table, or other visual representation of the steps that led to the Roosevelt Corollary. *(Visuals may include the opening of the Panama Canal or Latin American countries refusing to pay their debts.)*
3. Once students are finished, have volunteers share their work with the class.
4. Have students vote on which visual best illustrates the sequence of events that led to the change in U.S. involvement in Latin America under President Roosevelt. **LS Visual/Spatial**

HSS 8.12.3; **HSS Analysis Skills:** HI 1, HI 2

Alternative Assessment Handbook, Rubric 6: Cause and Effect

Answers

Analyzing Primary Sources *U.S. warships are seen ready to act in Latin America and Roosevelt is carrying a big stick to show that the U.S. would enforce payments.*

Reading Check *It clarified the policing role that the U.S. would take in Latin American affairs. It also reminded Latin American nations that they would have to repay foreign debts.*

U.S. Foreign Policy

Departing from the example set by the nation's first president, George Washington, later presidents increased U.S. involvement around the world, particularly in Latin America.

Washington's Farewell Address
The United States will not become involved in European affairs.

Monroe Doctrine
The United States will defend its interests in the Western Hemisphere and keep European powers out.

Roosevelt Corollary
The United States will police wrongdoing by nations in the Western Hemisphere.

Taft's Dollar Diplomacy
The United States will use economic means to aid its interests in Latin America.

Wilson and Democracy
The United States will promote and protect democracy in the Western Hemisphere.

Taft and Wilson Promote U.S. Interests

William Howard Taft, who became president in 1909, also acted to protect U.S. interests in Latin America. Just a few years later, in 1913, President Woodrow Wilson would take a completely different approach to securing America's stake in Latin America.

Taft's Dollar Diplomacy

Instead of Roosevelt's big-stick policy Taft used a policy known as **dollar diplomacy**—influencing governments through economic, not military, intervention. He wanted to encourage stability and keep Europeans out of Latin America by expanding American business interests there.

> "[Dollar diplomacy] has been characterized as substituting dollars for bullets. It is ... directed to the increase of American trade ... [and] the substitution of arbitration [negotiation] and reason for war in the settlement of international disputes."
>
> —William Howard Taft, quoted in *The Annals of America*

Taft therefore tried to replace European investments in Latin America with U.S. investments. For example, in June 1911 the United States agreed to assist Nicaragua. The United States would help obtain private loans from American banks to pay Nicaragua's national debt. In return, Nicaraguan leaders would allow U.S. troops in Nicaragua whenever America's leaders felt it necessary. The United States signed a similar agreement with Honduras.

Although the Senate rejected both agreements, the Taft administration followed the treaty terms anyway. In July, Nicaragua failed to repay a large loan from British investors. Secretary of State Philander Chase Knox helped to obtain a $1.5 billion loan for Nicaragua from American bankers. In exchange, the bankers gained control of the National Bank of Nicaragua and the government-owned railway. Local anger over this agreement soon led to revolt in Nicaragua. Taft chose to send U.S. Marines to protect American interests.

Focus on Reading
Compare and contrast the foreign policies of Presidents Roosevelt and Taft using the quotations by each on pages 656–657.

Direct Teach

Main Idea

❸ Taft and Wilson Promote U.S. Interests

Presidents Taft and Wilson promoted U.S. interests in Latin America.

Summarize How did Taft's dollar diplomacy differ from Theodore Roosevelt's approach toward Latin America? *Roosevelt looked to military solutions, whereas Taft wanted to expand American business interests in the region and replace European investments with U.S. investments.*

Analyze What did American bankers gain in response to their loan to Nicaragua, and why was this significant? *The National Bank of Nicaragua and the government-owned railway; meant that the United States would have significant control over the economy and transportation in Nicaragua*

Draw Conclusions Wilson sent troops to Latin America more often than any previous president. Why do you think this was so? *Wilson was interested in democracy, so he sent to troops to stabilize governments and to prevent other nations from controlling Latin American countries.*

Quick Facts Transparency: U.S. Foreign Policy

HSS 8.12.3; HSS **Analysis Skills:** HI 1, HI 2

Quick Facts: U.S. Foreign Policy

Activity Have students study the visual. Ask students to compare and contrast the main goal of each foreign policy. If time allows, ask students to bring in current media articles that discuss U.S. relations with Latin America today.

Critical Thinking: Drawing Inferences

Standards Proficiency

Presidential Policies

HSS 8.12.3; HSS **Analysis Skills:** HI 1, HI 2

Research Required

1. Assign each student to conduct research on one of the following presidents: Roosevelt, Taft, or Wilson. Students should use library or Internet sources. In addition, have each student reread the information in the text about each president.
2. When students have finished their research, have them prepare short speeches on how their assigned presidents might enforce the Monroe Doctrine in Latin America. *Speeches might mention the Roosevelt Corollary for Roosevelt, dollar diplomacy for Taft, or the promotion of democratic governments friendly to the United States for Wilson.*
3. When students have finished their speeches, guide students in a discussion about which approach might be most effective.

LS Verbal/Linguistic

Alternative Assessment Handbook, Rubrics 1: Acquiring Information; and 24: Oral Presentations

Answers

Focus on Reading *Roosevelt wanted to influence Latin American nations with force, whereas Taft wanted to use trade.*

• Review & Assess •

Close

Ask students to select five issues from the text relating to U.S. policy, and then write questions about these issues. As a class, review and then answer the questions.

Review

go.hrw.com Online Quiz, Section 3

Assess

SE Section 3 Assessment

PASS: Section 3 Quiz

Alternative Assessment Handbook

Research/Classroom Intervention

California Standards Review Workbook

Interactive Reader and Study Guide, Section 3

Interactive Skills Tutor CD-ROM

Wilson Intervenes

When President Woodrow Wilson took office in 1913, he rejected Taft's dollar diplomacy. Wilson disliked the role of big business in foreign affairs and said he would not act to support any "special group or interests." Instead, he believed the United States had a moral obligation to promote democracy in Latin America.

Wilson often opposed imperialist ideas. Yet he sent troops into Latin America more often than any other president before him. For example, the Caribbean country of Haiti had serious financial difficulties. The country also suffered a series of political revolutions. In 1915, Haitian president Guillaume Sam ordered about 160 political prisoners executed. As a result, he was overthrown and killed in another revolt.

Previously, Germany and France had briefly sent troops to Haiti to protect their interests. Wilson feared that those countries might try to take control of Haiti. To prevent this, U.S. Marines landed in Haiti on July 29, 1915, and quickly restored peace.

Similar events took place in the Dominican Republic. In 1911 the Dominican president was killed, and the government became unstable. By threatening to withhold customs revenue, Secretary of State Knox forced the Dominicans to accept a U.S.-backed government. Fearing more political unrest, in 1916 President Wilson declared martial law on the island and set up a government run by the U.S. Navy.

Many Latin Americans resented U.S. control over their governments. Some began to view U.S. involvement in the region with hostility.

READING CHECK **Finding Main Ideas** What events led Taft and Wilson to intervene in Latin America?

SUMMARY AND PREVIEW The United States and Latin America established relationships through both conflicts and agreements. In the next section you will learn about how the relationship between the United States and Mexico changed in the early 1900s.

Section 3 Assessment

go.hrw.com **Online Quiz** KEYWORD: SS8 HP20

Reviewing Ideas, Terms, and People HSS 8.12.3

1. **a. Recall** Why did the United States want to build a canal in Central America?
   b. Analyze What challenges did the builders of the **Panama Canal** face, and how did they overcome each challenge?
   c. Elaborate Defend the U.S. decision to support the revolution in Panama.
2. **a. Describe** What problem was causing conflict between European and Latin American nations?
   b. Summarize How and why did Theodore Roosevelt change U.S. policy toward Latin America?
   c. Elaborate What did Roosevelt mean by "speak softly and carry a big stick"?
3. **a. Recall** What did Woodrow Wilson believe was the United States' obligation in Latin America?
   b. Compare and Contrast In what ways were the policies of Presidents Taft and Wilson toward Latin America similar and different?

Critical Thinking

4. **Categorizing** Copy the web diagram below. Use it to identify American policy toward Latin America under Presidents Roosevelt, Taft, and Wilson.

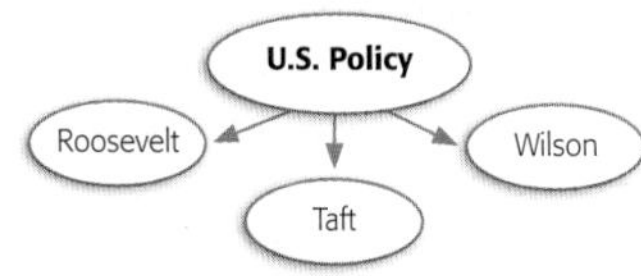

FOCUS ON WRITING

5. **Identifying Pros and Cons of U.S. Involvement in Latin America** What were the pros and cons of the construction of the Panama Canal and interventionist U.S. policies toward Latin America? Take notes for your list as you read this section.

Section 3 Assessment Answers

1. **a.** to link Atlantic and Pacific Oceans; shorten sea voyage between East and West coasts; move U.S. Navy quickly
   b. disease, mountains, leadership; rid the canal of mosquitoes, used explosives and steam shovels, appointed Goethals
   c. possible answer—helped Panama gain independence and wealth
2. **a.** debts Latin American nations owed
   b. Roosevelt Corollary; to keep European nations from intervening in Latin America
   c. use diplomacy along with military force
3. **a.** to promote democracy
   b. similar—wanted to quell unrest in Latin America that threatened U.S. interests; different—Taft used economic influence; Wilson used democracy
4. Roosevelt—Roosevelt Corollary; Taft—dollar diplomacy, Wilson—promotion of democracy; All—use of force when needed
5. pros—strengthened economy, protected U.S. interests; cons—costly in lives and money, led to Latin American resentment

Answers

Reading Check *Taft sent U.S. Marines to protect American interests in Nicaragua. Wilson sent troops into Haiti and later into the Dominican Republic to quell civil unrest.*

The United States and Mexico

SECTION 4

If YOU were there...

You are a Mexican American living in California in 1914. Ever since the Mexican Revolution in 1911, you have been worried about your parents in Mexico. They are teachers in Guadalajara, and you're not sure what their politics are. But you know that violence could happen anywhere. Now your relatives have written to you asking whether they should come to California.

What advice would you give your family?

BUILDING BACKGROUND In the late 1800s, many people from Mexico moved to the United States. Often, they joined relatives in California or the Southwest who had lived there when those territories were part of Mexico. In the early 1900s, the Mexican Revolution led many other Mexicans to think about moving to the United States.

The Mexican Revolution

Porfirio Díaz was president of Mexico from 1877 to 1880 and from 1884 to 1911, a total of 30 years. During his rule the United States

Francisco "Pancho" Villa (center) and fellow Mexican revolutionaries

What You Will Learn...

Main Ideas

1. In 1910 Mexicans revolted against their government.
2. The Mexican Revolution threatened U.S. interests economically and politically.

The Big Idea

The Mexican Revolution threatened relations between the United States and Mexico.

Key Terms and People

HSS 8.12 Students analyze the transformation of the American economy and the changing social and political conditions in the United States in response to the Industrial Revolution.

Preteach

Bellringer

If YOU were there . . . Use the **Daily Bellringer Transparency** to help students answer the question.

Daily Bellringer Transparency, Section 4

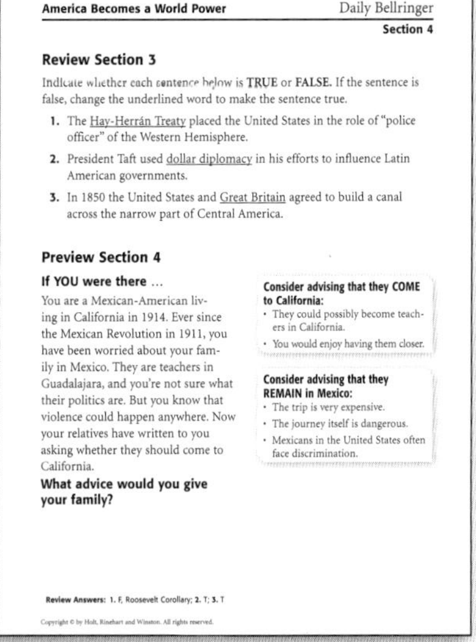

America Becomes a World Power — Daily Bellringer, **Section 4**

Review Section 3

Indicate whether each sentence below is **TRUE** or **FALSE.** If the sentence is false, change the underlined word to make the sentence true.

1. The Hay-Herrán Treaty placed the United States in the role of "police officer" of the Western Hemisphere.
2. President Taft used dollar diplomacy in his efforts to influence Latin American governments.
3. In 1850 the United States and Great Britain agreed to build a canal across the narrow part of Central America.

Preview Section 4

If YOU were there ...

You are a Mexican-American living in California in 1914. Ever since the Mexican Revolution in 1911, you have been worried about your family in Mexico. They are teachers in Guadalajara, and you're not sure what their politics are. But you know that violence could happen anywhere. Now your relatives have written to you asking whether they should come to California.

What advice would you give your family?

Consider advising that they COME to California:
- They could possibly become teachers in California.
- You would enjoy having them closer.

Consider advising that they REMAIN in Mexico:
- The trip is very expensive.
- The journey itself is dangerous.
- Mexicans in the United States often face discrimination.

Review Answers: 1. F, Roosevelt Corollary; 2. T; 3. T

Building Vocabulary

Preteach or review the following terms:

diplomatic related to negotiations between countries (p. 661)

persecution cruel or harsh treatment (p. 660)

CRF: Vocabulary Builder Activity, Section 4

Teach the Big Idea: Master the Standards

Standards Proficiency

The United States and Mexico HSS 8.12; HSS **Analysis Skills:** HR 1, CS 2

1. **Teach** Ask students the Main Idea questions to teach this section.
2. **Apply** Have students create a chart listing the Mexican leaders in this section and the years they ruled. In a second column, have students list the U.S. president in power at the time of each Mexican leader. Then have students add two details about each Mexican leader and one detail about each U.S. president and his actions toward Mexico.
3. **Review** As you review the section's main ideas, ask volunteers to share the information in their charts with the class.
4. **Practice/Homework** Have students write a one-page summary on how the Mexican Revolution threatened relations between the United States and Mexico. LS **Visual/Spatial, Verbal/Linguistic**

Alternative Assessment Handbook, Rubrics 7: Charts; and 37: Writing Assignments

Standards Focus

HSS 8.12

Means: Examine changes in the U.S. economy, government, and society that occurred as a result of the Industrial Revolution.

Matters: Economic changes that resulted from the Industrial Revolution helped the U.S. government become a world power.

Direct Teach

Main Idea

1 The Mexican Revolution

In 1910 Mexicans revolted against their government.

Recall What Mexican industries did Americans invest in? *land, manufacturing, mining, oil, and railways*

Explain Why did the Mexican Revolution cause many Mexicans to flee to the United States? *Many Mexicans fled to escape the violence.*

Drawing Conclusions Why was peace in Mexico important to the United States? *U.S. businesses had invested more than $1 billion in Mexico and wanted to maintain stability in the region to protect these interests.*

Map Transparency, United States in Latin America

HSS 8.12; HSS Analysis Skills: CS 1, HI 1

Info to Know

Mexico's Class System Porfirio Díaz had allowed his friends and associates to gain communal village lands for private use. Díaz thought this policy would improve agricultural production. However, this policy gave land ownership to very few Mexicans and divided rural Mexicans into two classes: the *hacendados*, or rich owners of estates, and *peonies*, or landless workers.

go.hrw.com
Online Resources
KEYWORD: SS8 US20
ACTIVITY: Mexican Revolution Mural

United States in Latin America

Guantánamo Bay The United States maintains a naval base on the island of Cuba.

Puerto Rico The island remains a commonwealth of the United States.

Panama Canal The United States turned the canal over to Panama but kept the right to defend it.

GEOGRAPHY SKILLS INTERPRETING MAPS

1. **Region** What parts of this region does the United States still control?
2. **Place** Which country was a U.S. protectorate for the longest period of time?

became the biggest investor in Mexico. By 1913 Americans had invested more than $1 billion in Mexican land, manufacturing, mining, oil, and railways.

Díaz ruled the Mexican people harshly. He imprisoned his opponents and rewarded his supporters. Most of Mexico's 15 million people were landless and poor. Many Mexicans found a new leader in democratic reformer **Francisco Madero**, who called for mass participation in elections and the removal of Díaz. He gained broad support and began the **Mexican Revolution** of 1910. During this uprising, Díaz was forced to resign. Because the Taft administration wanted a stable government in Mexico, it quickly recognized the Madero administration.

The revolution caused many Mexicans to flee to the United States to escape violence and find better jobs. Others wanted to avoid political persecution. These immigrants came from all levels of Mexican society. Between 1905 and 1915, more than 120,000 Mexicans immigrated to the United States.

Despite Madero's victory, the struggle for power continued in Mexico. In February 1913 General **Victoriano Huerta** took power and had Madero killed. The violence angered Woodrow Wilson, who was about to become president of the United States.

READING CHECK **Identifying Cause and Effect** What caused the Mexican Revolution, and what were its immediate effects?

Differentiating Instruction for Universal Access

Learners Having Difficulty

Reaching Standards

1. Pair students and have each pair reread this section. As they read, students should find and write down the main idea of each paragraph. Model the activity for students by doing the first paragraph.
2. Assign each pair the text under one of the section's blue headings. Have students use the main ideas they developed to write a summary of two to three sentences for each paragraph in the assigned subsection.
3. Work through the section as a class. Have volunteers share their main ideas and summaries. Correct any errors.
4. Then pair students who summarized different subsections. Have partners quiz each other on their subsections. **LS Interpersonal, Verbal/Linguistic**

HSS 8.12; HSS **Analysis Skills:** HI 1

Alternative Assessment Handbook, Rubric 42: Writing to Inform

Answers

Interpreting Maps **1.** *Puerto Rico, the U.S. Virgin Islands, and Guantánamo Bay, Cuba;* **2.** *Nicaragua*

Reading Check *the harsh rule of Porfirio Díaz and the poverty of most of Mexico's 15 million people; democratic reformer Francisco Madero gained control, Díaz was forced to resign, and many Mexicans immigrated to the United States.*

U.S. Response to the Mexican Revolution

Wilson refused to recognize the new government. As time passed, a revolt against Huerta, led by **Venustiano Carranza**, gained support. In addition, two other major revolutionaries were leading movements to overthrow Huerta. **Francisco "Pancho" Villa** led rebels in the north, and **Emiliano Zapata** led rebels in the south. Both were heroes to Mexico's poor.

The Mexican economy was weakened by the fighting. American business leaders feared they would lose investments there. Public pressure on Wilson to intervene grew. On April 20, 1914, he asked Congress to approve the use of force in Mexico.

Meanwhile, Wilson learned that a German ship carrying an arms supply was heading to the port of Veracruz, Mexico. To keep the weapons from reaching Huerta, Wilson ordered the U.S. Navy to seize Veracruz. In late April 1914, U.S. forces captured the city. Huerta broke off diplomatic ties, and the two countries came to the brink of war. Then, the **ABC Powers**—Argentina, Brazil, and Chile—offered to negotiate the dispute. Wilson accepted the proposed settlement, but Huerta and Carranza did not. In July, Huerta fled. In August, Carranza and his forces captured Mexico City and set up a new government. U.S. troops then withdrew from Veracruz.

Although Huerta was no longer in power, Villa and Zapata continued their revolts. Villa attacked Americans in Mexico. In response, Wilson sent General **John J. Pershing** and 15,000 soldiers into Mexico. Pershing's U.S. Expeditionary force chased Villa more than 300 miles but failed to capture him.

In 1917 Carranza approved a new constitution to bring order to Mexico. However, in 1920, the forces of Álvaro Obregón, a trusted aid, killed the Mexican dictator. After 1920 peace gradually returned to Mexico.

READING CHECK **Summarizing** How did Wilson respond to events in Mexico?

SUMMARY AND PREVIEW America fought a war with Spain and gained new territories. In the epilogue you will learn briefly about the history of the United States in the late 1900s and 2000s.

Section 4 Assessment

go.hrw.com
Online Quiz
KEYWORD: SS8 HP20

Reviewing Ideas, Terms, and People HSS 8.12

1. a. **Describe** Why did many Mexicans oppose the rule of **Porfirio Díaz**?
   b. **Explain** How was the United States immediately affected by the Mexican Revolution?
2. a. **Recall** What led Woodrow Wilson to send U.S. troops into Mexico in 1916?
   b. **Analyze** Why did some Americans want Wilson to intervene in the Mexican Revolution, and what actions did the United States take?
   c. **Evaluate** Should President Wilson have become involved in Mexican politics? Why or why not?

Critical Thinking

3. **Identifing Cause and Effect** Copy the graphic organizer like the one shown onto your own sheet of paper. Use it to identify causes of the Mexican Revolution and to describe its effects on Mexico and the United States.

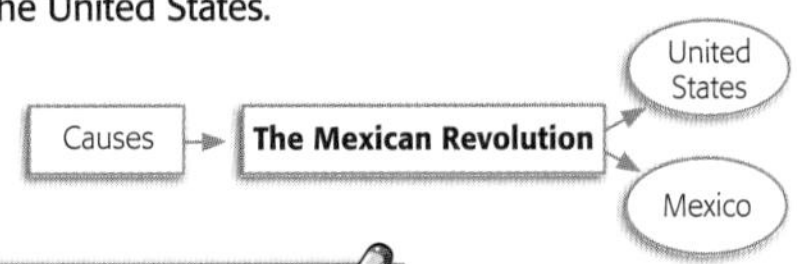

FOCUS ON WRITING

4. **Identifying Pros and Cons of U.S. Involvement in the Mexican Revolution** Add to your pros and cons list by noting the advantages and disadvantages of Wilson's decision to intervene in the Mexican Revolution. Be sure to consider the immigration of thousands of Mexicans to the United States. How might these people have contributed to the rich cultural heritage of the United States?

Direct Teach

Main Idea

❷ U.S. Response to the Mexican Revolution

The Mexican Revolution threatened U.S. interests economically and politically.

Explain Why did President Wilson refuse to recognize the Huerta government? *because Huerta had Madero killed and the violence angered Wilson*

Identify Which nations made up the ABC Powers, and how did they intervene in U.S.-Mexico relations? *Argentina, Brazil, and Chile; they offered to negotiate with the Mexican and U.S. governments to resolve the dispute between the two countries.*

HSS 8.12; HSS **Analysis Skills:** HI 1

Review & Assess

Close

Review U.S.-Mexico relations during this period.

Review

Online Quiz, Section 4

Assess

SE Section 4 Assessment

PASS: Section 4 Quiz

Alternative Assessment Handbook

Research/Classroom Intervention

California Standards Review Workbook

Interactive Reader and Study Guide, Section 4

Interactive Skills Tutor CD-ROM

Section 4 Assessment Answers

1. a. He ruled harshly.
   b. Many Mexicans immigrated to the United States.
2. a. Villa attacked Americans in Mexico.
   b. Business leaders feared losing investments in Mexico, and Villa attacked Americans in Mexico; Wilson asked Congress to approve use of force in Mexico, seized Veracruz, and sent U.S. soldiers to Mexico after Villa.
   c. Answers will vary but should exhibit an understanding of the pros and cons.
3. Causes—revolt against the harsh rule of Díaz; U.S.—Many Mexicans fled to the United States to escape persecution or violence; Wilson used military force in Mexico; Mexico—struggle for power, political instability, continued revolts
4. pros—helped bring stability to Mexico, Mexican immigrants enriched the culture of the United States; cons—almost led to war with Mexico, attacks against Americans

Answers

Reading Check *asked Congress to approve the use of force in Mexico, seized Veracruz, sent U.S. soldiers to Mexico after Villa*

History and Geography

Activity Analyzing U.S. Involvement in World Affairs Have students examine the feature and identify the ways in which it shows U.S. involvement in world events *(such as through a military presence, inventions and technology, and trade)*. Ask students how they think other countries felt about this growing U.S. involvement in world affairs. Then ask students how they think Americans viewed growing U.S. involvement in world affairs. Conclude by leading a discussion about the level of U.S. involvement in world affairs today. How has it changed or increased since 1900? What have been some of the costs and benefits of this change? **LS Verbal/Linguistic, Visual/Spatial**

HSS Analysis Skills: CS 3, HI 1, HI 6

Connect to Economics

Imperialism and Foreign Trade The desire for trade guided much of U.S. foreign policy in the early 1900s. Events such as the annexation of Hawaii, the construction of the Panama Canal, and even the Spanish-American War were all economically linked. Alfred Thayer Mahan, a well-known naval officer and author of the time, argued that foreign trade was necessary for national growth. Mahan also supported a strong merchant marine and overseas commercial outposts to help achieve this goal.

World Events

Asia Asian empires experienced dramatic changes around 1900. China, which had been the largest empire in the world, suffered a series of political crises. These led to the loss of many of its territories and eventually to the overthrow of its emperor in 1911. Meanwhile, the tiny nation of Japan was becoming the leading Asian power. Its empire expanded with military victories over China and Russia.

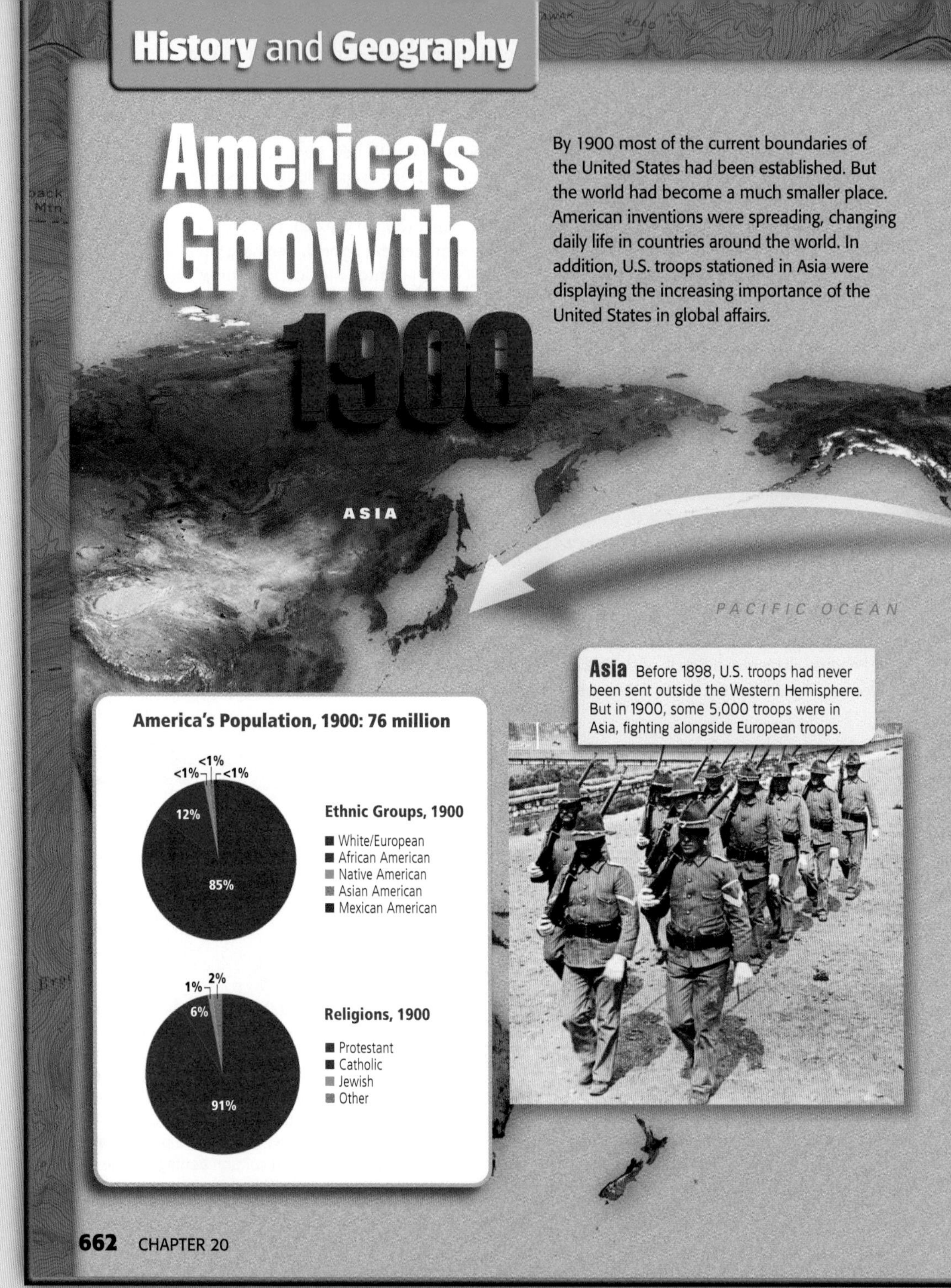

By 1900 most of the current boundaries of the United States had been established. But the world had become a much smaller place. American inventions were spreading, changing daily life in countries around the world. In addition, U.S. troops stationed in Asia were displaying the increasing importance of the United States in global affairs.

Asia Before 1898, U.S. troops had never been sent outside the Western Hemisphere. But in 1900, some 5,000 troops were in Asia, fighting alongside European troops.

662 CHAPTER 20

Critical Thinking: Sequencing

Standards Proficiency

America's Growth Time Line

HSS Analysis Skills: CS 1, CS 2, HI 1

Materials: butcher paper, colored markers

1. Have students work in small groups to create time lines that bring together the information in the textbook's America's Growth features for 1760, 1820, 1850, and 1900.
2. On the top of the time line, have students list the events in which the United States gained territory. On the bottom of the time line, have students provide the population of the United States in 1760, 1820, 1850, and 1900.
3. Have each group discuss the relationships between the nation's expansion and its population. Each group should list its conclusions.
4. Then have the groups display their time lines. Ask volunteers from each group to share some of its group's conclusions. Conclude with a summary of America's growth over time. **LS Interpersonal, Visual/Spatial**

Alternative Assessment Handbook, Rubrics 14: Group Activity; and 36: Time Lines

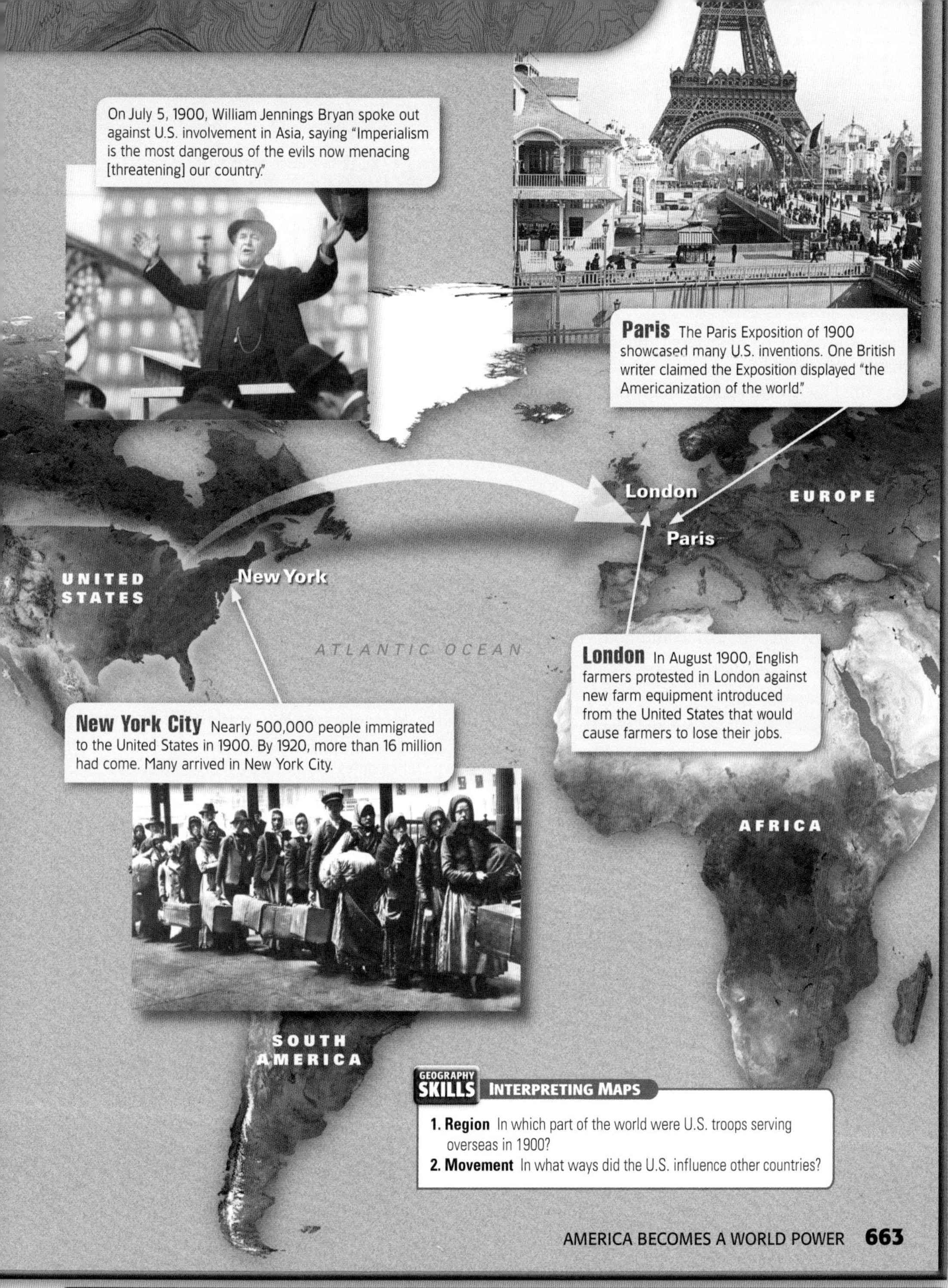

On July 5, 1900, William Jennings Bryan spoke out against U.S. involvement in Asia, saying "Imperialism is the most dangerous of the evils now menacing [threatening] our country."
Paris The Paris Exposition of 1900 showcased many U.S. inventions. One British writer claimed the Exposition displayed "the Americanization of the world."
London
EUROPE
Paris
UNITED STATES
New York
ATLANTIC OCEAN
London In August 1900, English farmers protested in London against new farm equipment introduced from the United States that would cause farmers to lose their jobs.
New York City Nearly 500,000 people immigrated to the United States in 1900. By 1920, more than 16 million had come. Many arrived in New York City.
AFRICA
SOUTH AMERICA

GEOGRAPHY SKILLS **INTERPRETING MAPS**

1. **Region** In which part of the world were U.S. troops serving overseas in 1900?
2. **Movement** In what ways did the U.S. influence other countries?

History and Geography

World Events

Paris Exposition of 1900 In 1900, Paris, France held a fair to celebrate technology and progress. The Paris Exposition of 1900 drew more than 57 million people from around the world. Exhibits showcased the marvels of the present and the future, including moving sidewalks and the world's first escalator. Well-known Americans who attended included writer and educator W.E.B. Du Bois and band leader John Philip Sousa.

Connect to Geography

Immigrant Migration As the network of railroads increased and systems of communication improved, many immigrants began settling inland rather than staying in cities on the East or West coast. This migration resulted in the presence of distinct ethnic traditions and cultures in many western cities.

Critical Thinking: Analyzing Information

Standards Proficiency

Americanization Collages

Prep Required

Materials: poster board, old magazines and newspapers, scissors, glue

1. Have students discuss the meaning of the term *Americanization*. Have them discuss the positive and negative aspects of Americanization.
2. Explain to students that the United States has a strong influence on nations around the world today, with both positive and negative effects. Have students discuss what some of these effects might be. Then have students discuss how people in other countries today might view America's influence.
3. Have students work in groups to create large collages illustrating examples of American influence around the world today. Each group should then write a caption summarizing the information in its collage.

HSS 11.2.3, 11.2.6; **HSS Analysis Skills:** HI 2

Alternative Assessment Handbook, Rubric 8: Collages

Answers

Interpreting Maps **1.** *Asia;* **2.** *through political influence, military presence, trade, technology, and inventions*

Continuity and Change in History

Activity Identifying Forces of Continuity and Change Review the major themes listed in the "Learn the Skill" section. Then have each student select either a major current event, a major recent event, or a major event they have learned about in the textbook. Have each student write a short essay explaining which of the forces of continuity and change apply to the event. Students should select at least two themes and write a short paragraph on each one. Remind students to provide reasons to support their selections. Have volunteers read their essays to the class.
LS Verbal/Linguistic

- Alternative Assessment Handbook, Rubric 37: Writing Assignments
- Interactive Skills Tutor CD-ROM, Lesson 11: Identify Changes and Continuities over Time
- **HSS Analysis Skills:** HI 3

Social Studies Skills

Analysis | Critical Thinking | Participation | Study

HRO **HI 3** Students explain the sources of historical continuity.

Continuity and Change in History

Define the Skill

A well-known saying claims that "the more things change, the more they stay the same." Nowhere does this observation apply better than to the study of history. Any look back over the past will show many changes—nations expanding or shrinking, empires rising and falling, changes in leadership, people on the move, to name just a few.

The reasons for change have not changed, however. The same general forces have driven the actions of people and nations across time. These forces are the "threads" that run through history and give it *continuity,* or connectedness. They are the "sameness" in a world of continuous change.

Learn the Skill

You can find the causes of all events of the past in one or more of these major forces or themes that connect all history.

1. **Cooperation and Conflict:** Throughout time, people and groups have worked together to achieve goals. They have also opposed others who stood in the way of their goals.
2. **Cultural Invention and Interaction:** The values and ideas expressed in peoples' art, literature, customs, and religion have enriched the world . But the spread of cultures and their contact with other cultures has produced conflict as well.
3. **Geography and Environment:** Physical environment and natural resources have shaped how people live. Efforts to gain, protect, or make good use of land and resources have been major causes of cooperation and conflict in history.
4. **Science and Technology:** *Technology,* or the development and use of tools, has helped humans across time maker better use of their environment. Science has changed their knowledge of the world, and changed their lives too.
5. **Economic Opportunity and Development:** From hunting and gathering to herding, farming, manufacturing, and trade, people have tried to make the most of their resources. The desire for a better life has also been a major reason people have moved from one place to another.
6. **The Impact of Individuals:** Political, religious, military, business, and other leaders have been a major influence in history. The actions of many ordinary people have also shaped history
7. **Nationalism and Imperialism:** *Nationalism* is the desire of a people to have their own country. *Imperialism* is the desire of a people to control other peoples. Both have existed across time.
8. **Political and Social Systems:** People have always been part of groups—families, villages, nations, religious groups, for example. The groups to which people belong shape how they relate to people around them.

Practice the Skill

Check your understanding of continuity and change in history by answering the following questions.

1. What forces of history are illustrated by the events in Chapter 20? Explain with examples.
2. How do the events in this chapter show continuity with earlier periods in U.S. history?

Answers

Practice the Skill 1. *possible answers—Conflict and Cooperation (such as the Spanish-American War), Geography and Environment (such as the acquisition of Hawaii), The Impact of Individuals (such as the actions of Roosevelt and Wilson), and Nationalism and Imperialism (such as in the Cuban revolution and in U.S. activities overseas);* **2.** *Answers will vary, but students should note that U.S. expansion of the late 1800s and early 1900s was a continuation of the general growth of the nation throughout its history.*

Social Studies Skills Activity: Continuity and Change in History

Continuity and Change Mural

HSS Analysis Skills: HI 3 — Standards Proficiency

Materials: art supplies, colored markers, butcher paper

1. Organize students into eight small groups or pairs. Assign each group or pair one of the eight themes listed in the "Learn the Skill" section above.
2. Have each group or pair use butcher paper to create a mural illustrating its theme. Students should incorporate events from the chapters they have studied in the textbook as well as modern examples. Students might include drawings, photographs, slogans, quotes, maps, and charts in their murals.
3. Display all the murals and have students try to identify which theme each one represents. Then have each group or pair explain the images in its mural to the class.

LS Interpersonal, Visual/Spatial

- Alternative Assessment Handbook, Rubric 3: Artwork

CHAPTER 20 **Standards Review**

Visual Summary

Use the visual summary below to help you review the main ideas of the chapter.

QUICK FACTS

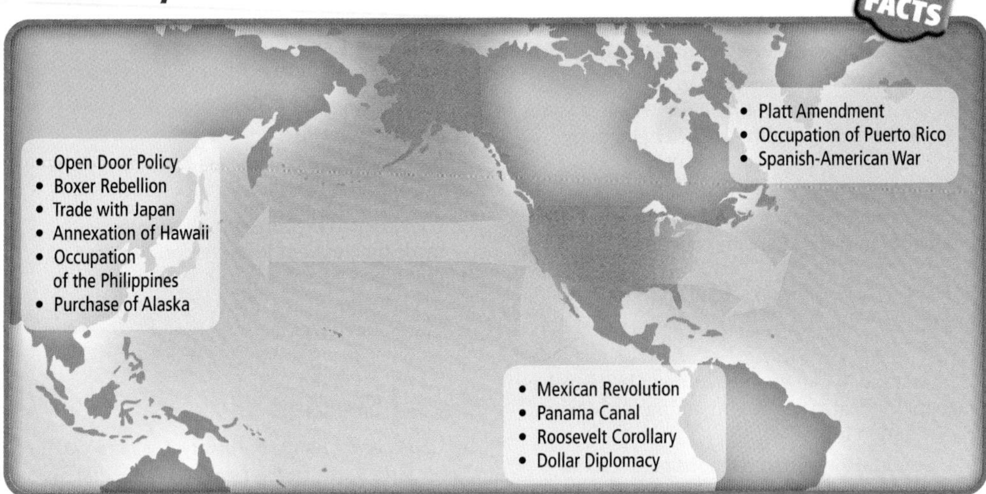

Reviewing Vocabulary, Terms, and People

1. In which of the following did the United States declare that it had no interest in annexing Cuba?
a. Roosevelt Corollary **c.** Open Door Policy
b. Hay-Herrán Treaty **d.** Teller Amendment

2. Which Hawaiian leader upset sugar planters by restoring the power of the monarchy?
a. Liliuokalani **c.** Maui
b. Meiji **d.** Kalakaua

3. Who was responsible for encouraging Panama to revolt against Colombian control?
a. Francisco Madero **c.** Emiliano Zapata
b. John Hay **d.** Philippe Bunau-Varilla

4. Who led U.S. forces into Mexico after attacks against U.S. citizens by Mexican rebels?
a. John Hay **c.** John J. Pershing
b. William H. Seward **d.** William Taft

5. What group opposed expansion of the United States into foreign territories?
a. Open Door Society **c.** Rough Riders
b. Anti-Imperialist League **d.** ABC Powers

Comprehension and Critical Thinking

SECTION 1 *(Pages 640–645)* HSS 8.12

5. a. Identify To what areas did the United States expand in the late 1800s?

b. Draw Conclusions How did the U.S. economy benefit from contacts with foreign nations and territories?

c. Elaborate Which policy would you have supported—isolationism or imperialism? Explain your answer.

SECTION 2 *(Pages 646–651)* HSS 8.12

6. a. Describe What events led to U.S. involvement in the Spanish-American War?

Answers

Visual Summary

Review and Inquiry Use the visual summary to review the expansion of U.S. power around the world.

Quick Facts Transparency: America Becomes a World Power Visual Summary

Reviewing Vocabulary, Terms, and People

1. d
2. a
3. d
4. c
5. b

Comprehension and Critical Thinking

6. a. Alaska, Hawaii, Japan, China
b. Contacts improved trade, brought raw materials to the United States, and opened new markets for the United States.
c. Answers will vary, but students should exhibit an understanding of each term and provide reasons to support their opinions.

7. a. Spain refused to grant Cuba independence, American journalists sensationalized the conflict, the USS *Maine* exploded, the U.S. Congress declared Cuba independent, Spain declared war on the United States.
b. The United States gained control of Cuba, Puerto Rico, Guam, and the Philippines.

Review and Assessment Resources

Review and Reinforce

SE Standards Review
CRF: Chapter Review Activity
California Standards Review Workbook
Quick Facts Transparency: America Becomes a World Power Visual Summary
Spanish Chapter Summaries Audio CD Program
Online Chapter Summaries in Six Languages
OSP Holt PuzzlePro; GameTool for ExamView
Quiz Game CD-ROM

Assess

SE Standards Assessment
PASS: Chapter Test, Forms A and B
Alternative Assessment Handbook
OSP ExamView Test Generator, Chapter Test
Universal Access Modified Worksheets and Tests CD-ROM: Chapter Test
Holt Online Assessment Program (in the Premier Online Edition)

Reteach/Intervene

Interactive Reader and Study Guide
Universal Access Teacher Management System: Lesson Plans for Universal Access
Universal Access Modified Worksheets and Tests CD-ROM
Interactive Skills Tutor CD-ROM

go.hrw.com
Online Resources
Chapter Resources:
KEYWORD: SS6 US20

Answers

c. possible answers—They might think the Unites States would try to gain independence for other colonies or that the United States was overly aggressive.

8. a. The United States became involved with the Panama revolution for independence, built the Panama Canal, and encouraged Latin American nations to pay their debts with the Roosevelt Corollary and with dollar diplomacy.
b. The United States expanded its role because politics in Latin America affected U.S. economic and military interests and because the United States wanted to limit direct European intervention in Latin America.
c. Answers will vary with some students supporting the increased role the United States was taking, and others stating that Latin American governments should be left to their own fate.

9. a. He ruled the Mexican people harshly; poverty and landlessness were rampant in Mexico.
b. The United States was the biggest investor in Mexico, with American investments in land, manufacturing, mining, oil, and railways.
c. possible answers—might lead to increased tensions between the two countries as instability in Mexico led American business leaders to fear the loss of investments, and violence in Mexico affected Americans in Mexico and living near the Mexican border.

b. Analyze How did the United States benefit from the Spanish-American War?

c. Predict How might foreign countries view the actions of the United States in the Spanish-American War?

SECTION 3 *(Pages 652–658)* **HSS 8.12.3**

7. **a. Identify** In what ways did the United States get involved in Latin America?
b. Draw Conclusions Why did the United States expand its role in Latin America in the early 1900s?
c. Elaborate Do you think the United States should have been as actively involved in Latin America as it was? Explain your answer.

SECTION 4 *(Pages 659–661)* **HSS 8.12**

8. **a. Recall** Why did Mexicans revolt against Porfirio Díaz?
b. Analyze What was the nature of U.S. involvement in Mexico before and during the Mexican Revolution in 1910?
c. Predict How might relations between the United States and Mexico be affected by the Mexican Revolution?

Using the Internet

9. **Activity: Creating a Poster** The Panama Canal was opened on August 15, 1914. It took 10 years to build, cost a total of more than $600 million, and took some 6,000 lives. Enter the activity keyword and research the effects of human and geographic factors on the construction of the Panama Canal. Physical factors include landforms, climate, and weather. Human factors should focus on the use of technology and reasons humans modified the environment, along with the hazards they faced. Then create a poster about the canal that highlights the most important details.

Reviewing Themes

10. **Economics** What economic reasons did the United States have for ending its policy of isolationism?

11. **Politics** How did the policy of imperialism affect American politics in the late 1800s and early 1900s?

Reading Skills

Comparing Historical Texts *Use the Reading Skills taught in this chapter to answer the question below.*

12. Look back at the foreign-policy statements made by President Roosevelt on page 656 and President Taft on page 657. What words illustrate the presidents' main points in their views of U.S. foreign policy?

Social Studies Skill

Continuity and Change in History *Use the Social Studies Skills taught in this chapter to answer the question below.*

13. Pick three of the themes listed on page 664 and explain how the building of the Panama Canal relates to them.

FOCUS ON WRITING

21. **Writing Your List of Pros and Cons** Review your notes and choose the pros and cons to include in your final list. Decide whether you want to include only facts, only opinions, or some of each. How can your analysis of history help guide U.S. foreign policy in the future? When you have finished your list, use it as the basis for a paragraph recommending either that the United States continue to involve itself in the affairs of other nations or that it pull back from such involvement.

Using the Internet

10. Go to the HRW Web site and enter the keyword shown to access a rubric for this activity.

KEYWORD: SS8 US20

Reviewing Themes

11. U.S. leaders wanted to keep the economy strong by expanding overseas to gain new markets for manufactured goods and new sources of raw materials to fuel industrial growth.

12. Imperialism shaped U.S. foreign and economic policy, with each president forming different policies to further and protect U.S. interests abroad.

Reading Skills

13. Roosevelt—left column: punishment, misconducts itself; right column: speak softly, big stick; Taft: substituting dollars for bullets, increase of American trade, settlement of international disputes

Social Studies Skills

14. The following themes apply: geography and environment, science and technology, economic opportunity and development, nationalism and imperialism.

Focus on Writing

15. **Rubric** Students' lists of pros and cons should
- accurately analyze U.S. involvement in world affairs.
- include a paragraph giving a clear recommendation for future foreign policy.
- support the recommendation with logical reasons based on the list.

Standards Assessment

DIRECTIONS: Read each question and write the letter of the best response. Use the map below to answer question 1.

1

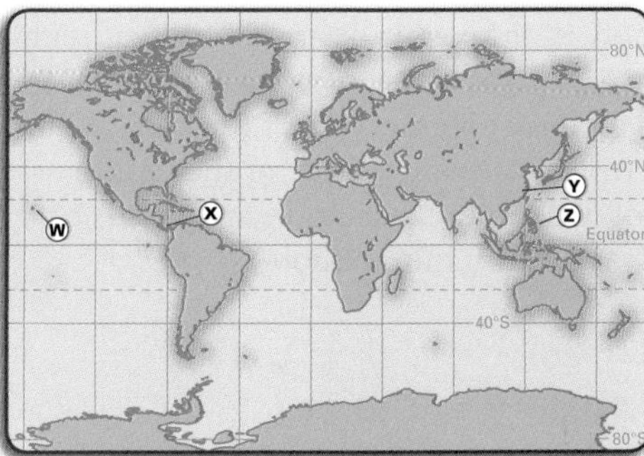

Of the places marked on the map, the only one in which the United States did not control territory in the late 1800s and early 1900s is shown by the letter

A W.
B X.
C Y.
D Z.

2 The practice of using American businesses and economic aid to influence foreign governments and achieve U.S. goals in Latin America is known as

A imperialism.
B dollar diplomacy.
C isolationism.
D the big stick.

3 During the Mexican Revolution, President Wilson sent U.S. forces to Veracruz, Mexico. Which U.S. policy did this act best express?

A Roosevelt Corollary
B Dollar Diplomacy
C Teller Amendment
D isolationism

4 Which two nations did the United States hope to trade with in the 1800s rather than annex?

A Hawaii and Japan
B Japan and China
C China and Cuba
D Cuba and Hawaii

5 What was the *main* reason President Woodrow Wilson used military force against Mexico in the early 1900s?

A He wished to protect Texas against the claims of the Mexican government.
B He opposed the harsh rule of Mexico's dictator Porfirio Díaz.
C He wanted to capture Mexican revolutionary leader Emiliano Zapata.
D He hoped to shape Mexico's government and protect American business interests.

Connecting with Past Learning

6 In this chapter you learned how the United States gained control of new territories as a result of its victory in the Spanish-American War. Which of the following that you learned about earlier in Grade 8 had a similar result for the United States?

A Civil War
B War of 1812
C Mexican War
D Revolutionary War

7 Which earlier U.S. president, like Woodrow Wilson, also became involved in a conflict in Mexico?

A John Quincy Adams
B Andrew Jackson
C William McKinley
D James K. Polk

Answers

1. C
Break Down the Question Students should recall that the United States established trade with China but did not control any territory there.

2. B
Break Down the Question This question requires students to recall factual information from Section 3.

3. A
Break Down the Question Point out to students that sending troops to Mexico would be part of the Roosevelt Corollary, which stated that the United States would use force to police Latin America.

4. B
Break Down the Question This question requires students to recall factual information from Section 1.

5. D
Break Down the Question This question requires students to identify the main idea and generalize. Tell students to consider what concerns drove all of Wilson's actions regarding Mexico.

6. C
Break Down the Question This question requires students to recall factual information from Chapter 10.

7. D
Break Down the Question This question requires students to recall factual information from Chapter 10.

Intervention Resources

Reproducible

- Interactive Reader and Study Guide
- Universal Access Teacher Management System: Universal Access Lesson Plans

Technology

- Quick Facts Transparency: America Becomes a World Power Visual Summary
- Universal Access Modified Worksheets and Tests CD-ROM
- Interactive Skills Tutor CD-ROM

Tips for Test Taking

I'm Done! Whoa! Tell students they are not finished with a test until they have checked it. First, students should look at how much time is left. Then, budgeting their time, students should review their answers for any careless mistakes, such as leaving a question blank or marking two answers for one question. Next, students should erase any stray marks. Finally, students should review the hardest questions. There is nothing to be gained from finishing first!

Standards Review

Have students review the following standards in their workbooks.

- California Standards Review Workbook: HSS 8.12.3

Preteach

Bellringer

Motivate Have students think of a time when they were successful in persuading someone to agree with something or do something (for example, in persuading their parents to let them stay up past their bedtime). Ask students how they managed to persuade the other person. What arguments did they use? What other methods of persuasion did they use? Explain that presenting logical, sound, and convincing reasons and evidence is the most effective method of persuasion—and a highly useful skill in life. Tell students that they will hone their persuasive skills in this workshop.

Direct Teach

Stating Your Opinion

Take a Stand Some students may not have a strong opinion about either topic. Suggest that these students ask themselves what might have happened if things had been different—if the United States had not gone to war with Spain or had not built the Panama Canal. Tell students to list the hypothetical consequences or effects. Next, have students list the effects of each event as it actually happened. Then have students examine the two lists and determine whether each effect is positive or negative. Which list contains more positive effects? Students should chose the position that results, in their opinion, in more positive consequences.

Standards Focus

ELA Writing 8.2.4, 8.2.4.a, 8.2.4.b, 8.2.4.c

Writing Workshop

Persuasion and History

Assignment

Write a persuasive essay either for or against one of these topics:

(1) the United States going to war with Spain in 1898

(2) the building of the Panama Canal

You have probably heard people disagree about current political events—perhaps a new law or a government leader. People also disagree about events of the past. When we disagree about historical events, those of the past or those of the present, we can use persuasive arguments to convince others to agree with our opinion.

TIP Using Order of Importance How do you know whether to start or end with your most important or most convincing reason? If you are worried about getting your readers to read your entire paper, you might try to catch their attention by starting with the most convincing reason. If you are concerned that your readers remember one point after they finish reading, you may want to place that point, or reason, at the end of your paper.

ELA **Writing 8.2.4** Write persuasive compositions.

1. Prewrite

Stating Your Opinion

Persuasion starts with an opinion or a position on a topic. Choose one of the topics in the assignment and decide on your opinion, either for or against. Write your opinion in a statement: it will be the big idea of your persuasive paper. For example, here is an opinion statement about the second topic:

The United States was right to build the Panama Canal.

Building and Organizing a Logical Argument

A strong persuasive essay includes a logical argument, sound reasoning, and proof in support of an opinion. Reasons tell *why* you have an opinion. Proof, or evidence, includes facts, examples, or expert opinions.

- **Opinion:** *The reforms implemented by the Progressives improved the lives of many Americans.*
- **Reason:** *Progressive reforms improved cities.*
- **Evidence:** *Lawrence Veiller helped pass the 1901 New York State Tenement House Act.*

Persuasive writing is usually organized by order of importance.

2. Write

Here is a framework to help you write your first draft.

A Writer's Framework

Introduction	Body	Conclusion
■ Start with an interesting opener, such as a quotation or a surprising fact. ■ Include your opinion statement, or big idea, for the paper.	■ Present one reason and its supporting evidence in each body paragraph. ■ Address your reasons by order of importance.	■ Restate your opinion in different words. ■ Summarize your reasons. ■ Make a connection to a current event.

Differentiating Instruction for Universal Access

Learners Having Difficulty
Reaching Standards

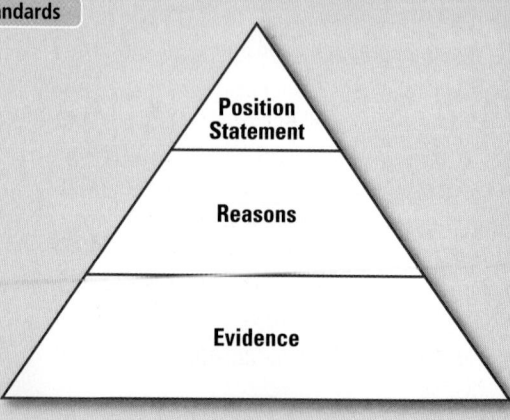

1. Some students may benefit from studying a spatial representation of the relationship among a position statement, reasons, and evidence.
2. Draw the pyramid at right for students to see. Explain how a position statement is supported by reasons, which are in turn supported by evidence. Have students copy the pyramid and use it to organize their ideas.
LS **Visual/Spatial**

ELA Writing 8.2.4.b

Position Statement

Reasons

Evidence

3. Evaluate and Revise

Evaluating

Use these questions to discover ways to improve your draft.

Evaluation Questions for a Persuasive Essay

- Does your introduction include a clear statement of your opinion on the topic?
- Do you present your reasons by order of importance in the body paragraphs?
- Do you provide at least three reasons to support your opinion?
- Do you include facts, examples, or expert opinions to support each reason?
- Do you restate your opinion in different words in your conclusion?
- Does your conclusion include a summary of the reasons that support your opinion?

TIP **Fact vs. Opinion** Knowing the difference between a fact and an opinion is important for both writers and readers of persuasive essays.

- **Facts** are statements that can be proven true or false. *The Spanish-American War began in 1898.*
- **Opinions** are statements of personal belief and cannot be proven. *Theodore Roosevelt was the greatest hero of the Spanish-American War.*

Revising

Your essay will be more forceful if you write in the active voice.

Passive voice: *Spain's Pacific fleet was destroyed by Dewey's ships.*

Active voice: *Dewey's ships destroyed Spain's Pacific fleet.*

Active voice is more forceful, and often clearer, because it makes a stronger connection between the action and the actor. However, we may use passive voice because we do not know, or do not want to say, who the actor is or was.

Example: *Spain's Pacific fleet was destroyed during the war.*

4. Proofread and Publish

Proofreading

If you are writing your paper on a computer, you should use the spell-check feature to look for spelling errors. However, the spell-check feature will not help much if you have used the wrong word. Here are some examples to look for: *their/they're, its/it's, accept/except, affect/effect, advice/advise, altar/alter, capitol/capital.* When you spot one of these words in your paper, check your dictionary to make sure you have used the correct word.

Publishing

Share your essay with a classmate who took an opinion opposed to yours. Review each other's reasons. Can one of you persuade the other?

5. Practice and Apply

Use the steps and strategies in this workshop to write a persuasive essay.

Reteach

Evaluating

Map Structure On their drafts, have students make a rectangle around their opinion statement. It should appear in the first paragraph. Then have students circle each supporting reason. The paper should provide one reason at or near the beginning of each paragraph and at least three reasons. Finally, have students underline each piece of evidence. The paper should provide at least two pieces of evidence for each reason. Students should check to make sure that each piece of evidence supports the reason that is the topic of that paragraph. Then have students draw a wavy line under any sentence containing support for a different point of view than the position stated in the paper. Students should cut any support that does not fit.

MISCONCEPTION ALERT

More is Not Always Better

Students may try to include as many reasons as possible to support their positions, including weak reasons. Explain to students that a weak reason or piece of evidence can actually damage the overall strength of an argument by tainting the rest of it. Remind students to include only strong reasons and evidence in their papers.

Practice & Apply

Rubric

Students' persuasive essays should

- provide a clear position statement.
- include at least three reasons to support the position.
- provide supporting evidence for each reason.
- provide one paragraph for each reason and its evidence.
- present the reasons in order of importance.
- end with a summary and a restatement of the position.
- use correct grammar, punctuation, spelling, and capitalization.

English-Language Learners

Standards Proficiency **Standard English Mastery**

1. Have English learners demonstrate to the class or to a small group how the passive and active voices are formed in their primary languages.
2. Then have students practice forming the active voice. Write the sentences at right for students to see. Have students change each sentence from the passive to the active voice. Help English learners to understand how to construct the active voice in English.

LS Verbal/Linguistic

- U.S. involvement in Cuba was opposed by President Cleveland.
- Sensational stories were printed by William Randolph Hearst's newspaper.
- A canal in Central America was strongly supported by President Theodore Roosevelt.
- The United States was enabled by the Panama Canal to be more involved in Latin America.

EPILOGUE

Linking Past to Present

America became a global power in the 1900s as U.S. troops fought in two world wars.

America Since 1914

The United States of America is a very different place today than it was in 1914. The nation is now bigger, more powerful, and more involved in world affairs. It has changed from a nation where most people lived in small towns to one in which most people live in cities, many with populations of more than 1 million people. The nation is also a more democratic place today—more Americans have access to the privileges and responsibilities of citizenship than at any other time in the country's history.

Despite these differences, America faces many of the same challenges that it faced in 1914. For example, Americans still debate what role the nation should play in world affairs. They debate questions about civil rights, religion, taxes, and the role of government in their lives. They worry about the health of the environment, children, and the poor, just as they did in 1914.

Americans do not always agree on these issues. But they do believe strongly in their right to debate and to disagree. The freedom to do so—in peaceful and productive ways—is an indication of the fundamental health of the nation.

America as a Global Power

In 1914 World War I began in Europe. As the war spread, many Americans believed that the United States should stay out of the conflict. By 1917, however, the United States had entered the war, and American soldiers fought and died on the battlefields of Europe.

That experience forever changed the United States. America had stepped onto the world stage with its military and industrial might. As a result, the world began to look at America differently, and the country's isolation from the rest of the world lessened.

War tore Europe apart again in the 1930s and 1940s during World War II. Again, some Americans wanted the country to stay out of the conflict, but when Japan attacked the United States at Pearl Harbor in late 1941, the United States was forced to enter the global struggle. Once again, America demonstrated that it had become a global power and achieved victory on the battlefield.

Martin Luther King, Jr., (center) helped lead the fight for civil rights in America.

The Civil Rights Era

The U.S. victory in World War II had other consequences as well. Millions of World War II veterans returned home ready to start new lives in peacetime. These veterans enrolled in college in record numbers, settled into the nation's cities and new suburbs, and started families.

Soldiers who had fought on the side of democracy abroad also fought for democracy at home. This was especially true of the nation's African American and Mexican American soldiers. Their efforts to seek greater access to the rights of citizenship helped invigorate the civil rights movement. They were joined in these efforts by Americans from all walks of life—people who believed that America worked best when the promises of freedom were open to all.

By the 1960s, the push for greater civil rights had become a true social movement in America. It was a grassroots effort on the part of ordinary Americans to change both people's attitudes and federal laws. César Chávez, for example, led the fight to win more rights for migrant workers. This movement for greater civil, educational, and political rights among racial and ethnic groups helped spur the women's rights movement of the 1960s and 1970s as well.

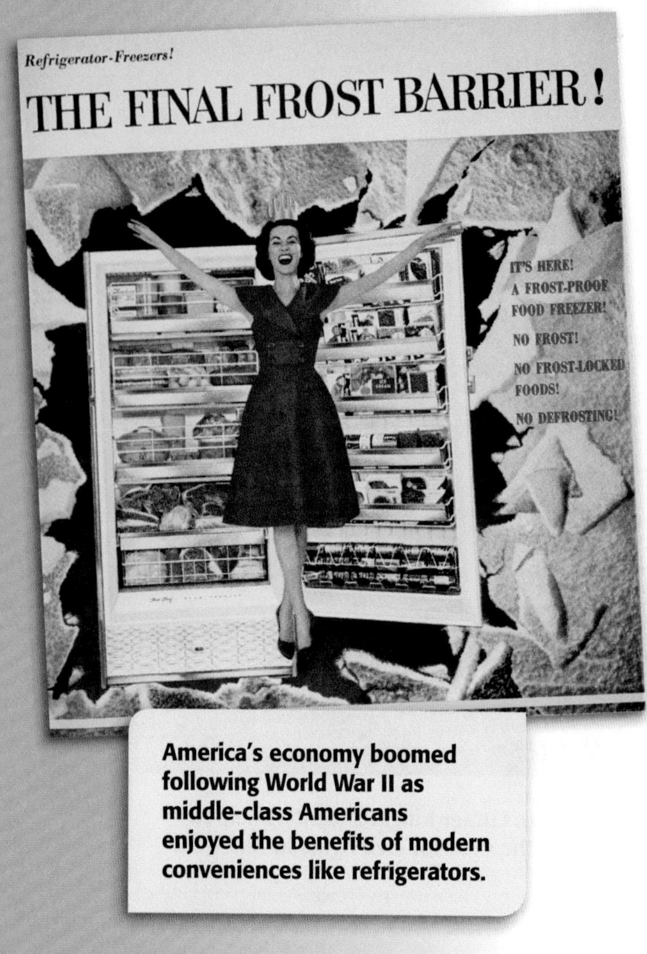

Refrigerator-Freezers!
THE FINAL FROST BARRIER!
IT'S HERE!
A FROST-PROOF
FOOD FREEZER!
NO FROST!
NO FROST-LOCKED
FOODS!
NO DEFROSTING!

America's economy boomed following World War II as middle-class Americans enjoyed the benefits of modern conveniences like refrigerators.

Economic Changes and Challenges

The U.S. economy has also changed dramatically since 1914. The Great Depression of the 1930s was a huge economic collapse that affected millions of Americans. But the U.S. economy eventually recovered, and after World War II the nation enjoyed a long period of prosperity. Many Americans joined the middle class for the first time. During the 1950s and 1960s they bought homes, televisions and appliances, and cars in record numbers.

Since the 1970s, the economy has had more ups and downs. Industrial jobs, which were once so plentiful in America, have become far less important in recent decades. Many American companies have moved their factories overseas to take advantage of lower wages in other countries. As a result, the U.S. economy is now becoming more of a service economy—one in which workers provide services (like banking or law) instead of actually making products.

A major challenge that lies ahead for America is helping all of its citizens enjoy the benefits of living in such a rich country. As the country adds more and more technical and information-based jobs, education is becoming even more critical to helping people develop successful careers.

Immigration and Democracy

Immigration has been an important feature of the United States ever since the country first began. Since 1914, this strong tradition of immigration has continued. During the 1900s, people from every corner of the world came to America to settle. These new immigrants were Buddhists, Christians, Muslims, and Sikhs. They came from Latin America, Africa, Asia, and Europe. They came in search of a brighter future, greater freedom, and a chance to start their lives over again—and they came to become Americans.

With its long history of immigration, America is one of the most ethnically diverse places in the world. Here, Sikhs celebrate their culture at a parade in New York.

Immigrants also came to the United States to enjoy the benefits of democracy. The United States was the world's first modern democracy, and many people around the world today look to America as an example of a democratic, free, and open society.

Since 1914, American democracy has grown even stronger. More people participate in the democratic process than ever before, and there is a healthy debate over the many issues the country faces now and will face in the coming years. America's citizens care greatly about these important issues and about American democracy.

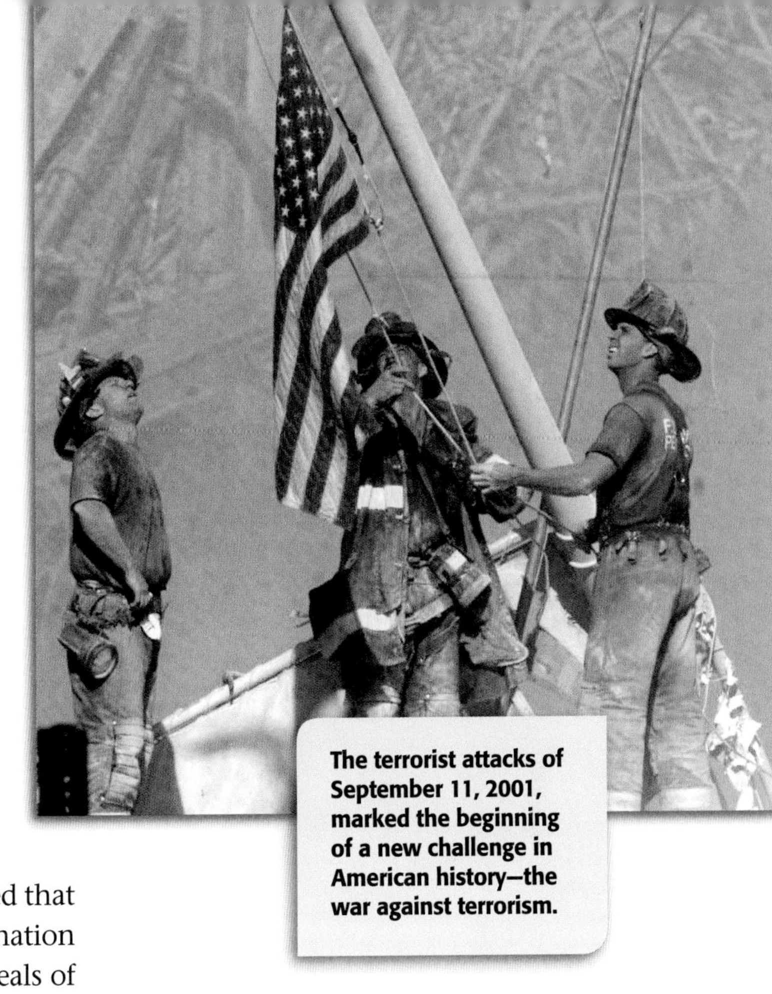

The terrorist attacks of September 11, 2001, marked the beginning of a new challenge in American history—the war against terrorism.

America Then and Now

In the years since 1914, the United States has faced many difficult challenges. The terrorist attacks of September 11, 2001 are the latest of these challenges. But the same things that made America strong before 1914 are the same things that make it strong today.

More than 200 years ago, the Founding Fathers insisted that the United States of America was an experiment—a new nation devoted to the possibility that principles of virtue and ideals of freedom could be supported by democracy, justice, and the rule of law. Today, just as then, this experiment works best when American citizens exercise their rights carefully and seriously.

America today is connected to the America of the past. It is connected through the enduring meaning of such documents as the Declaration of Independence and the U.S. Constitution. These documents are as important today as they were in the late 1700s when they were first created. In both practical and idealistic terms, they outline what America stands for, what America means, and where America is going.

Cities such as St. Louis, shown here, are part of America's past, present, and future. Once a small town known as the Gateway to the West, St. Louis has grown into a large and modern American city.

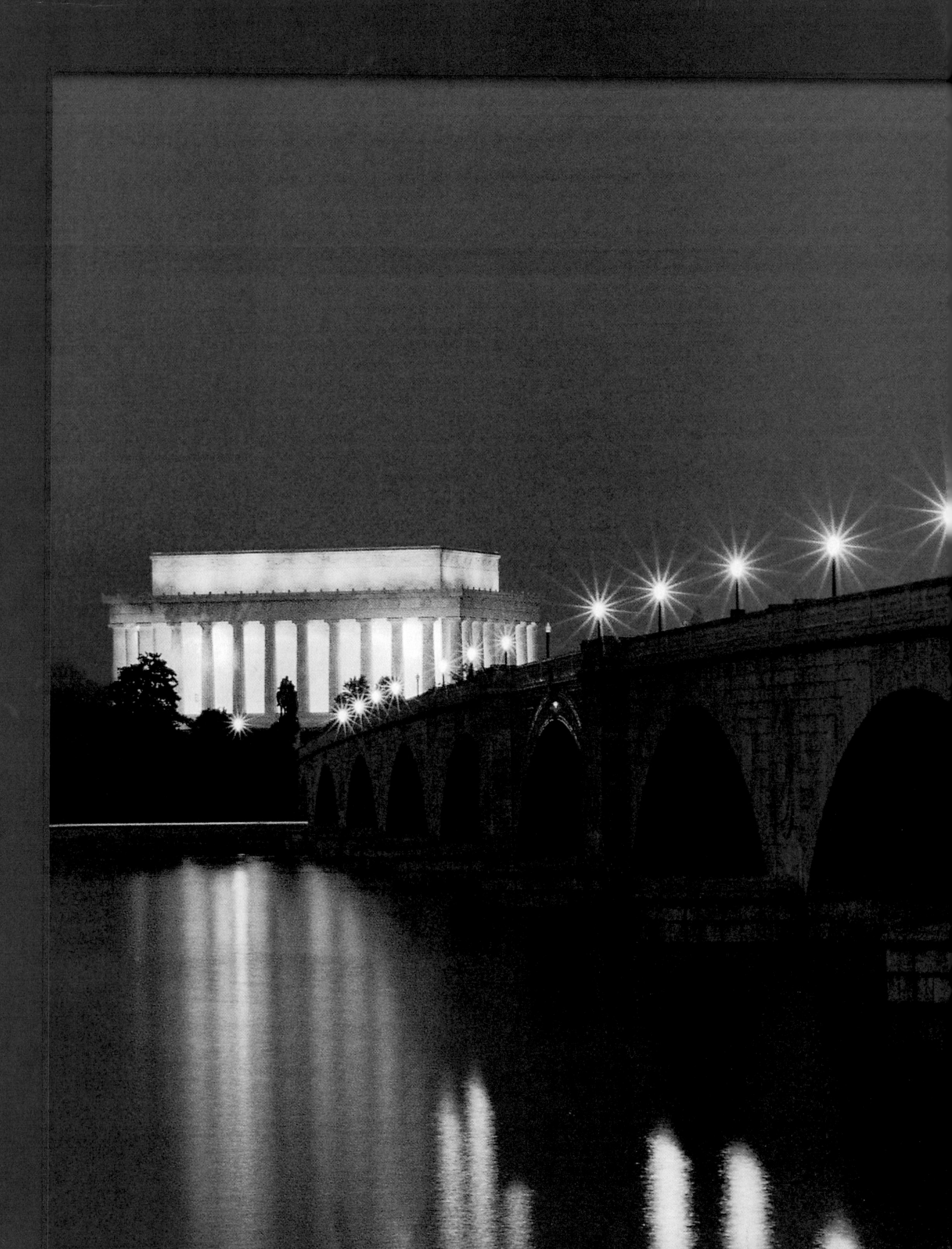

References

The United States of America: Political

ATLAS

CANADA
WASHINGTON
Seattle
Tacoma
Olympia
Spokane
Puget Sound
Franklin D. Roosevelt Lake
Pend Oreille
Portland
Columbia River
OREGON
Salem
Eugene
IDAHO
Boise
Sun Valley
Pocatello
Snake River
MONTANA
Flathead Lake
Great Falls
Helena
Billings
Missouri River
Fort Peck Lake
Yellowstone River
NORTH DAKOTA
Lake Sakakawea
Bismarck
SOUTH DAKOTA
Lake Oahe
Pierre
Rapid City
WYOMING
Yellowstone Lake
Cheyenne
NEBRASKA
Platte River
CALIFORNIA
Cape Mendocino
Goose Lake
Shasta Lake
Sacramento River
Sacramento
Berkeley
Oakland
San Francisco
San Francisco Bay
San Jose
Monterey Bay
San Joaquin River
Fresno
Santa Barbara
Ventura
Los Angeles
Long Beach
Riverside
Anaheim
Palm Springs
Santa Ana
San Diego
Salton Sea
Channel Islands
NEVADA
Pyramid Lake
Reno
Carson City
Lake Tahoe
Las Vegas
Lake Mead
UTAH
Great Salt Lake
Ogden
Salt Lake City
Provo
Utah Lake
Lake Powell
COLORADO
Boulder
Vail
Denver
Aspen
Colorado Springs
Pueblo
Arkansas River
KANSAS
OKLAHOMA
Canadian River
Oklahoma City
Lawton
ARIZONA
Colorado River
Flagstaff
Phoenix
Gila River
Casa Grande
Tucson
NEW MEXICO
Taos
Santa Fe
Albuquerque
Las Cruces
TEXAS
El Paso
Amarillo
Lubbock
Abilene
Fort Worth
Midland
Odessa
Austin
San Antonio
Corpus Christi
Laredo
Padre Island
Amistad Reservoir
MEXICO
Gulf of California
PACIFIC OCEAN
45°N
40°N
35°N
30°N
125°W
120°W

To understand the relative locations of Alaska and Hawaii, as well as the vast distances separating them from the rest of the United States, see the world map.

HAWAII
Kauai
Niihau
Oahu
Honolulu
Molokai
Maui
Lanai
Kahoolawe
Hilo
Hawaii
PACIFIC OCEAN
22°N
19°N
160°W
155°W
0 75 150 Miles
0 75 150 Kilometers
Projection: Mercator

ALASKA
ARCTIC OCEAN
RUSSIA
Bering Strait
Arctic Circle
Nome
Yukon River
St. Lawrence Island
St. Matthew Island
Nunivak Island
Fairbanks
CANADA
Bering Sea
Attu Island
Anchorage
Valdez
Skagway
Juneau
Gulf of Alaska
Kodiak Island
Alexander Archipelago
PACIFIC OCEAN
55°N
50°N
170°E
180°
170°W
160°W
150°W
140°W
0 250 500 Miles
0 250 500 Kilometers
Projection: Albers Equal Area

CANADA

MINNESOTA
Grand Forks
Fargo
Red River
Duluth
Superior
Minnesota River
Minneapolis
St. Paul
Sioux Falls

WISCONSIN
Green Bay
Madison
Milwaukee
Mississippi River
Lake Superior
Marquette
Sault Ste. Marie

MICHIGAN
Lake Michigan
Lake Huron
Saginaw
Grand Rapids
Lansing
Detroit
Ann Arbor

IOWA
Sioux City
Cedar Rapids
Davenport
Des Moines
Omaha
Lincoln
Missouri River

ILLINOIS
Rockford
Chicago
Peoria
Springfield
Illinois River
East St. Louis

INDIANA
Gary
South Bend
Fort Wayne
Indianapolis
Evansville

OHIO
Toledo
Cleveland
Youngstown
Akron
Columbus
Dayton
Cincinnati
Lake Erie
Erie

NEW YORK
Lake Ontario
Buffalo
Rochester
Syracuse
Albany
Hudson R.
Lake Champlain
St. Lawrence River

PENNSYLVANIA
Susquehanna River
Pittsburgh
Harrisburg
Allentown
Philadelphia

VT
Burlington
Montpelier
NH
Concord
Manchester
MAINE
Augusta
Portland
Connecticut R.
MA
Boston
Worcester
Springfield
Cape Cod
RI
Providence
CT
Hartford
New Haven
Bridgeport
Long Island Sound
Long Island
Yonkers
New York City
Jersey City
Newark
NJ
Trenton
Camden
Atlantic City
DE
Dover
Delaware Bay
MD
Baltimore
Annapolis
Washington, D.C.
Chesapeake Bay

ATLANTIC OCEAN

MISSOURI
Kansas City
Kansas City
Topeka
Jefferson City
St. Louis
Springfield
Lake of the Ozarks
Wichita
Keystone Lake
Tulsa
Eufaula Lake
Lake Texoma

WEST VIRGINIA
Charleston
VIRGINIA
Richmond
Newport News
Norfolk
Virginia Beach

KENTUCKY
Louisville
Frankfort
Lexington
Ohio River
Lake Barkley
Kentucky Lake

TENNESSEE
Nashville
Knoxville
Chattanooga
Memphis

NORTH CAROLINA
Winston-Salem
Greensboro
Durham
Raleigh
Asheville
Charlotte
Cape Hatteras

SOUTH CAROLINA
Greenville
Columbia
Charleston
Savannah River
Sea Islands

ARKANSAS
Fayetteville
Little Rock
Pine Bluff
Mississippi River

MISSISSIPPI
Vicksburg
Jackson
Meridian
Biloxi

ALABAMA
Huntsville
Birmingham
Montgomery
Mobile

GEORGIA
Atlanta
Macon
Columbus
Savannah
Chattahoochee R.

LOUISIANA
Shreveport
Red River
Toledo Bend Reservoir
Baton Rouge
New Orleans
Chandeleur Islands
Dallas
Waco
Beaumont
Houston
Galveston

FLORIDA
Pensacola
Tallahassee
Jacksonville
Gainesville
Orlando
Cape Canaveral
Tampa
St. Petersburg
Lake Okeechobee
Fort Myers
Fort Lauderdale
Miami
Cape Sable
Florida Keys
Straits of Florida

Gulf of Mexico
THE BAHAMAS

N
E
S
W

40°N
35°N
30°N
25°N
25°N
70°W
75°W
80°W
85°W
90°W
95°W

National capital
State capitals
Other cities
0 100 200 Miles
0 100 200 Kilometers
Projection: Albers Equal Area

The United States of America: Physical

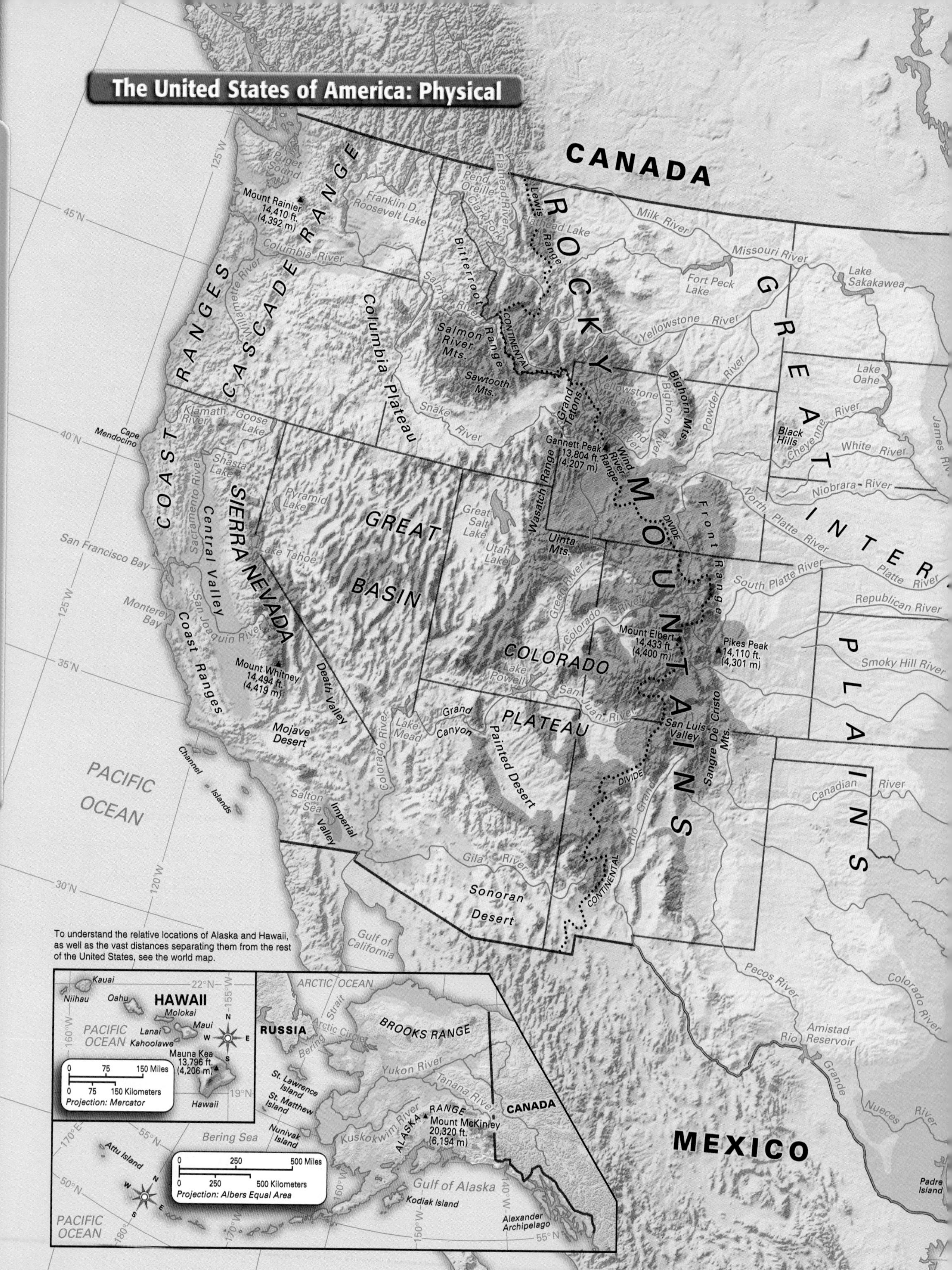

CANADA
ROCKY MOUNTAINS
GREAT PLAINS
INTERIOR PLAINS
CASCADE RANGE
COAST RANGES
SIERRA NEVADA
GREAT BASIN
COLORADO PLATEAU
Columbia Plateau
Puget Sound
Mount Rainier 14,410 ft. (4,392 m)
Franklin D. Roosevelt Lake
Pend Oreille
Flathead River
Clark Fork
Lewis Range
Flathead Lake
Milk River
Missouri River
Lake Sakakawea
Fort Peck Lake
Columbia River
Willamette River
Bitterroot Range
Salmon River
Salmon River Mts.
Sawtooth Mts.
Snake River
Yellowstone River
Yellowstone Lake
Bighorn Mts.
Bighorn River
Powder River
Lake Oahe
Cheyenne River
Black Hills
White River
Niobrara River
James River
Grand Tetons
Gannett Peak 13,804 ft. (4,207 m)
Wind River Range
Wasatch Range
Uinta Mts.
CONTINENTAL DIVIDE
Front Range
North Platte River
South Platte River
Platte River
Republican River
Smoky Hill River
Klamath River
Goose Lake
Cape Mendocino
Shasta Lake
Sacramento River
Central Valley
Pyramid Lake
Lake Tahoe
Great Salt Lake
Utah Lake
Green River
Colorado River
San Francisco Bay
Monterey Bay
San Joaquin River
Coast Ranges
Mount Whitney 14,494 ft. (4,419 m)
Death Valley
Mojave Desert
Mount Elbert 14,433 ft. (4,400 m)
Pikes Peak 14,110 ft. (4,301 m)
Lake Powell
San Juan River
Lake Mead
Grand Canyon
Painted Desert
San Luis Valley
Sangre De Cristo Mts.
Rio Grande
Canadian River
Channel Islands
PACIFIC OCEAN
Salton Sea
Imperial Valley
Gila River
Sonoran Desert
Gulf of California
Pecos River
Amistad Reservoir
Nueces River
Padre Island
MEXICO
45°N
40°N
35°N
30°N
125°W
120°W

To understand the relative locations of Alaska and Hawaii, as well as the vast distances separating them from the rest of the United States, see the world map.

HAWAII
Kauai
Niihau
Oahu
Molokai
Maui
Lanai
Kahoolawe
Mauna Kea 13,796 ft. (4,206 m)
Hawaii
PACIFIC OCEAN
22°N
19°N
160°W
155°W
0 75 150 Miles
0 75 150 Kilometers
Projection: Mercator

ARCTIC OCEAN
RUSSIA
Bering Strait
Arctic Circle
BROOKS RANGE
Yukon River
Tanana River
St. Lawrence Island
St. Matthew Island
Nunivak Island
Bering Sea
Kuskokwim River
ALASKA RANGE
Mount McKinley 20,320 ft. (6,194 m)
CANADA
Attu Island
Gulf of Alaska
Kodiak Island
Alexander Archipelago
PACIFIC OCEAN
55°N
50°N
170°E
180°
170°W
160°W
150°W
140°W
0 250 500 Miles
0 250 500 Kilometers
Projection: Albers Equal Area

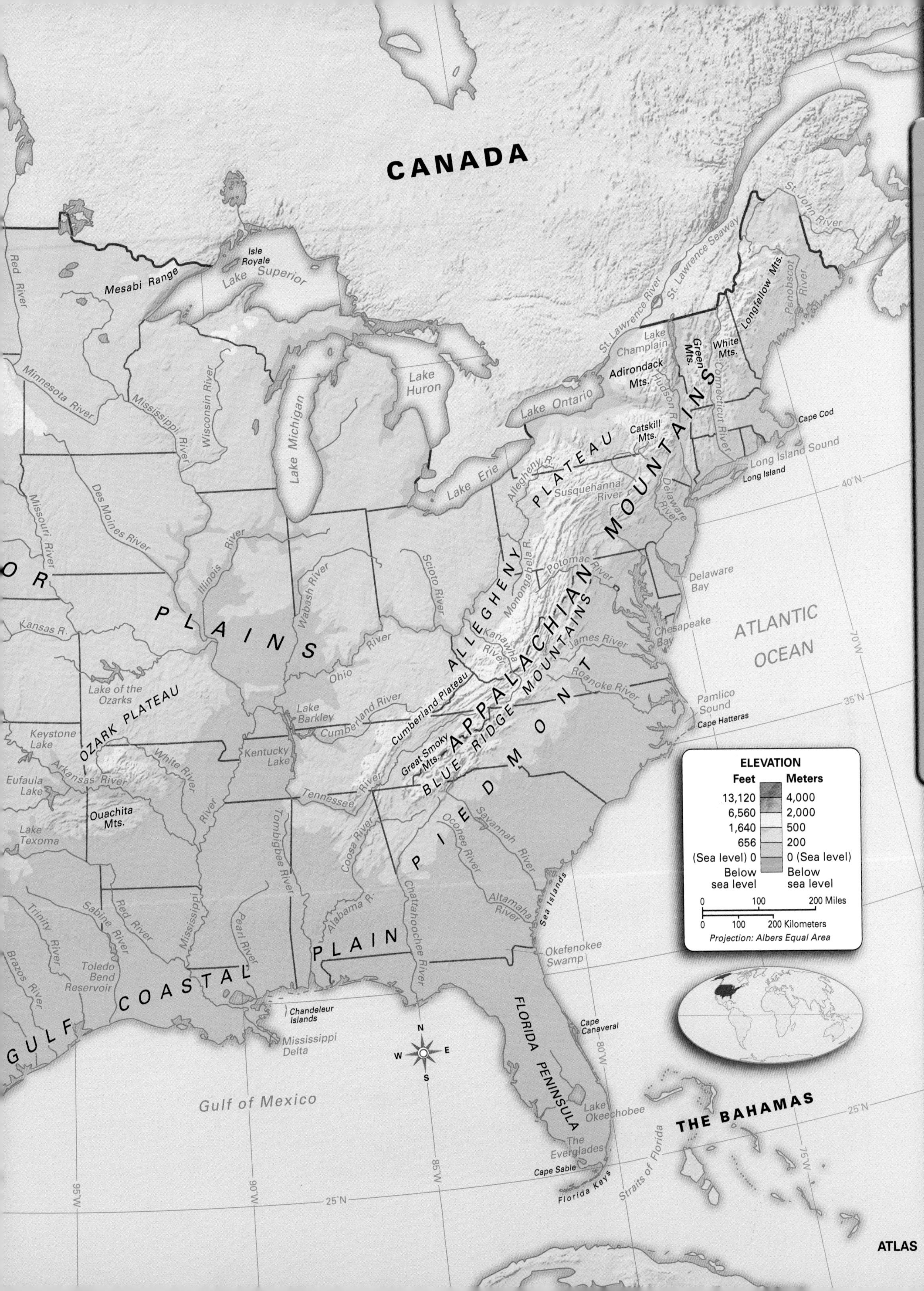

CANADA

Isle Royale
Lake Superior
Mesabi Range
Red River
Minnesota River
Mississippi River
Wisconsin River
Lake Michigan
Lake Huron
Lake Ontario
Lake Erie
St. Lawrence River
St. Lawrence Seaway
St. John River
Penobscot River
Longfellow Mts.
White Mts.
Green Mts.
Lake Champlain
Adirondack Mts.
Hudson R.
Connecticut River
Cape Cod
Long Island Sound
Long Island
Catskill Mts.
PLATEAU
Allegheny R.
Susquehanna River
Delaware River
MOUNTAINS
40°N
Missouri River
Des Moines River
Illinois River
Wabash River
Scioto River
Monongahela R.
Potomac River
ALLEGHENY
Delaware Bay
Chesapeake Bay
ATLANTIC OCEAN
70°W
OR PLAINS
Kansas R.
Ohio River
Kanawha River
APPALACHIAN
James River
Lake of the Ozarks
OZARK PLATEAU
Lake Barkley
Cumberland River
Cumberland Plateau
BLUE RIDGE MOUNTAINS
Roanoke River
Pamlico Sound
Cape Hatteras
35°N
Keystone Lake
Eufaula Lake
Arkansas River
White River
Kentucky Lake
Great Smoky Mts.
PIEDMONT
Tennessee River
Ouachita Mts.
River
Lake Texoma
Tombigbee River
Coosa River
Oconee River
Savannah River
Sea Islands
Alabama R.
Chattahoochee River
Altamaha River
Trinity River
Sabine River
Red River
Mississippi River
Pearl River
Brazos River
Toledo Bend Reservoir
COASTAL PLAIN
Okefenokee Swamp
GULF
Chandeleur Islands
Mississippi Delta
FLORIDA PENINSULA
Cape Canaveral
80°W
Gulf of Mexico
Lake Okeechobee
THE BAHAMAS
25°N
The Everglades
Cape Sable
Florida Keys
Straits of Florida
75°W
95°W
90°W
85°W
25°N
N
W
E
S

ELEVATION

Feet	Meters
13,120	4,000
6,560	2,000
1,640	500
656	200
(Sea level) 0	0 (Sea level)
Below sea level	Below sea level

0 100 200 Miles
0 100 200 Kilometers
Projection: Albers Equal Area

ATLAS

World: Political

	COUNTRY	CAPITAL
1	Antigua and Barbuda	St. Johns
2	St. Kitts and Nevis	Basseterre
3	Dominica	Roseau
4	St. Lucia	Castries
5	St. Vincent and the Grenadines	Kingstown
6	Barbados	Bridgetown
7	Grenada	St. George's

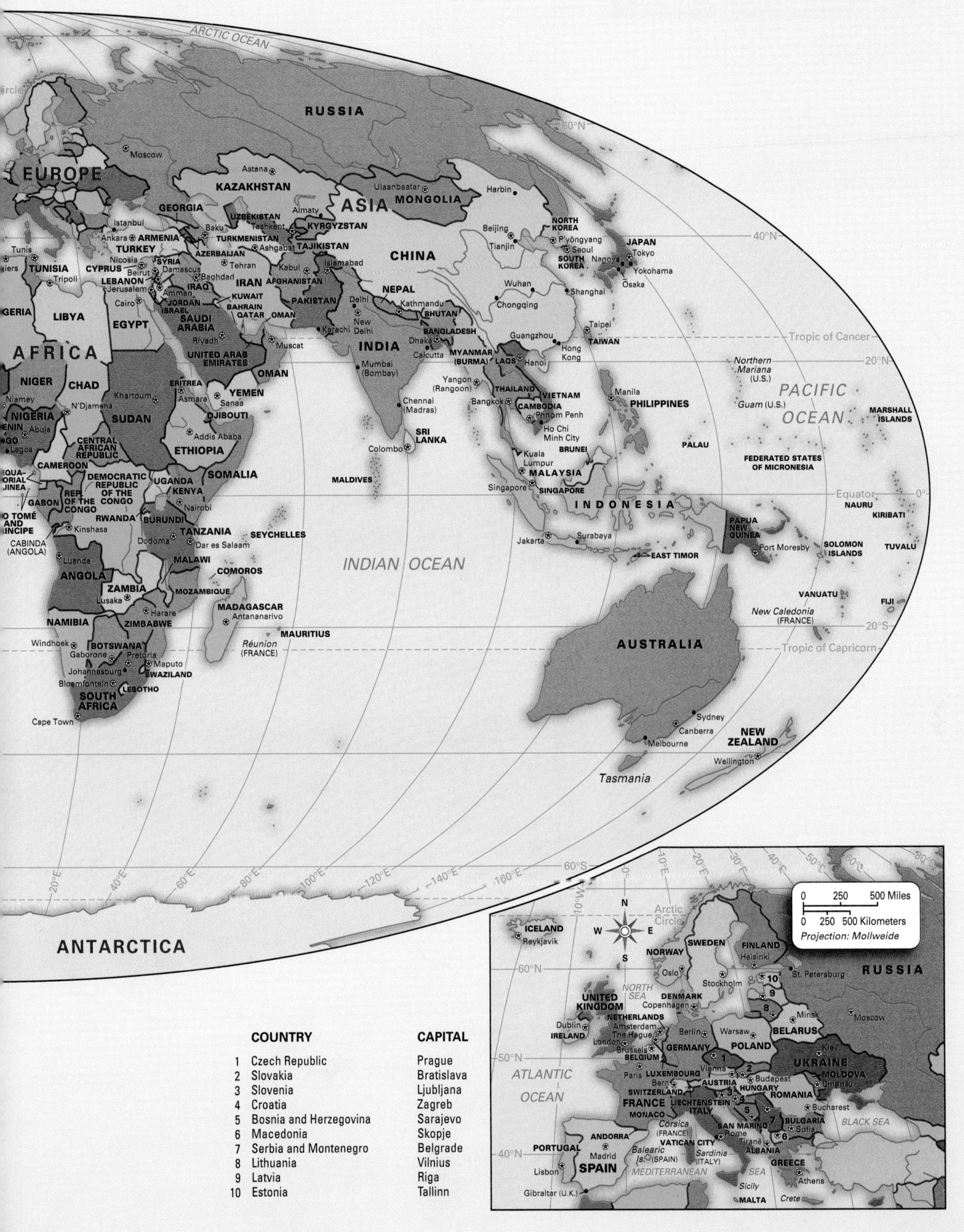

	COUNTRY	CAPITAL
1	Czech Republic	Prague
2	Slovakia	Bratislava
3	Slovenia	Ljubljana
4	Croatia	Zagreb
5	Bosnia and Herzegovina	Sarajevo
6	Macedonia	Skopje
7	Serbia and Montenegro	Belgrade
8	Lithuania	Vilnius
9	Latvia	Riga
10	Estonia	Tallinn

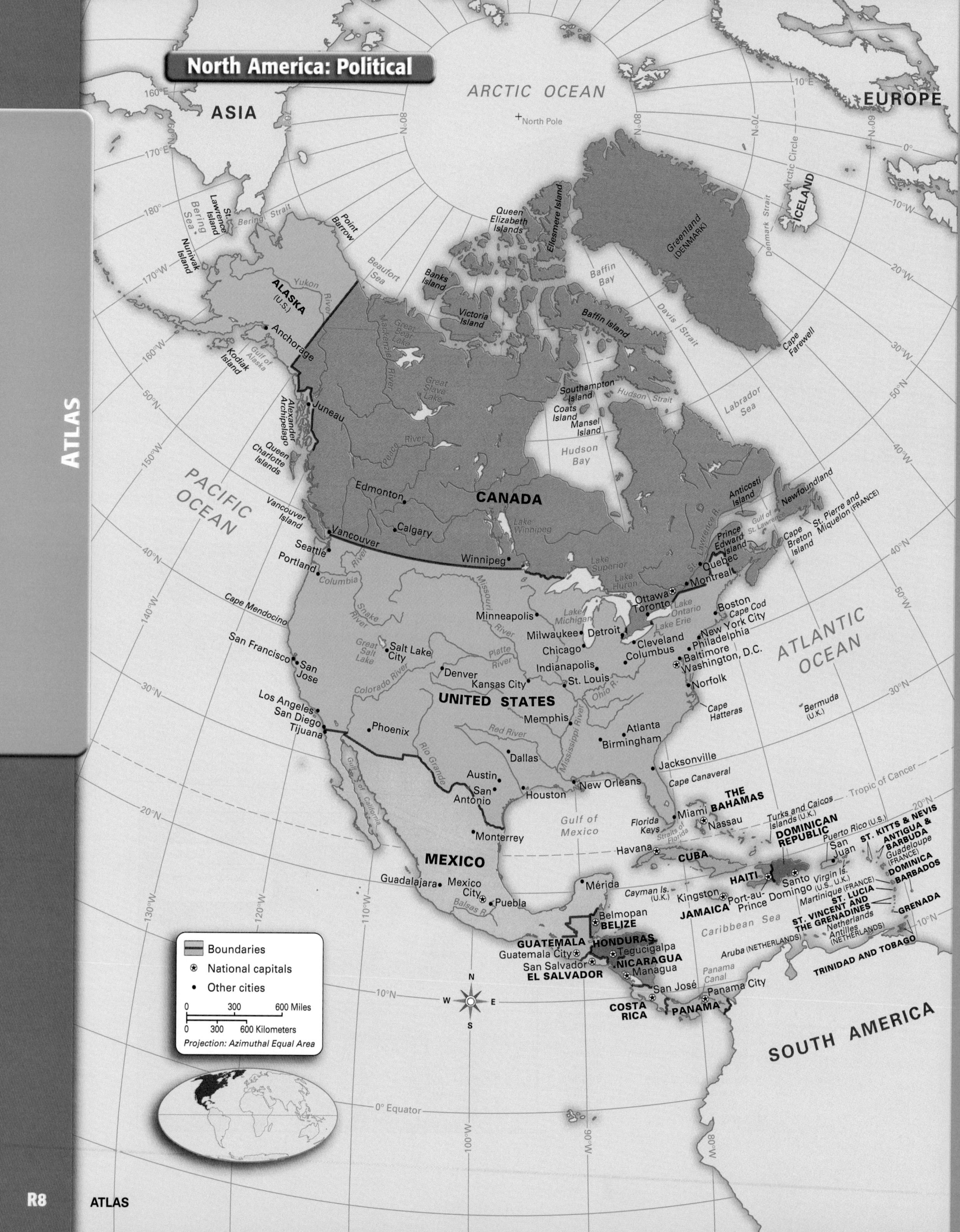
North America: Political
ARCTIC OCEAN
ASIA
EUROPE
North Pole
PACIFIC OCEAN
ATLANTIC OCEAN
SOUTH AMERICA
CANADA
UNITED STATES
MEXICO
ALASKA (U.S.)
Greenland (DENMARK)
ICELAND
Hudson Bay
Baffin Bay
Gulf of Mexico
Caribbean Sea
CUBA
HAITI
DOMINICAN REPUBLIC
JAMAICA
THE BAHAMAS
GUATEMALA
BELIZE
HONDURAS
EL SALVADOR
NICARAGUA
COSTA RICA
PANAMA
TRINIDAD AND TOBAGO
Boundaries
National capitals
Other cities
0 300 600 Miles
0 300 600 Kilometers
Projection: Azimuthal Equal Area

South America: Political

CENTRAL AMERICA
Caribbean Sea
ATLANTIC OCEAN
PACIFIC OCEAN
ATLANTIC OCEAN

VENEZUELA
Caracas
Lake Maracaibo
Orinoco River
Barranquilla
Cartagena
COLOMBIA
Medellín
Bogotá
Cali
Malpelo Island (COLOMBIA)
GUYANA
Georgetown
SURINAME
Paramaribo
FRENCH GUIANA (FRANCE)
Cayenne
ECUADOR
Quito
Guayaquil
Galápagos Islands (ECUADOR)
Rio Negro
Amazon River
Amazon River
Belém
PERU
Marañón River
Ucayali River
Trujillo
Callao
Lima
Arequipa
BRAZIL
Recife
São Francisco River
Salvador
Brasília
Belo Horizonte
Campinas
São Paulo
Rio de Janeiro
Curitiba
Pôrto Alegre
BOLIVIA
Lake Titicaca
La Paz
Lake Poopó
Sucre
Paraguay River
PARAGUAY
Asunción
Paraná River
Uruguay River
URUGUAY
Montevideo
Río de la Plata
CHILE
San Félix Island (CHILE)
San Ambrosio Island (CHILE)
Juan Fernández Islands (CHILE)
Valparaíso
Santiago
ARGENTINA
Córdoba
Rosario
Buenos Aires
Strait of Magellan
Tierra del Fuego
Falkland Islands (U.K.)
South Georgia Island (U.K.)

20°N
10°N
0° Equator
Equator 0°
10°S
20°S
Tropic of Capricorn
30°S
40°S
50°S
100°W
90°W
80°W
70°W
60°W
50°W
40°W
30°W
20°W

N
S
E
W

Boundaries
National capitals
Other cities
0 250 500 Miles
0 250 500 Kilometers
Projection: Azimuthal Equal Area

ATLAS

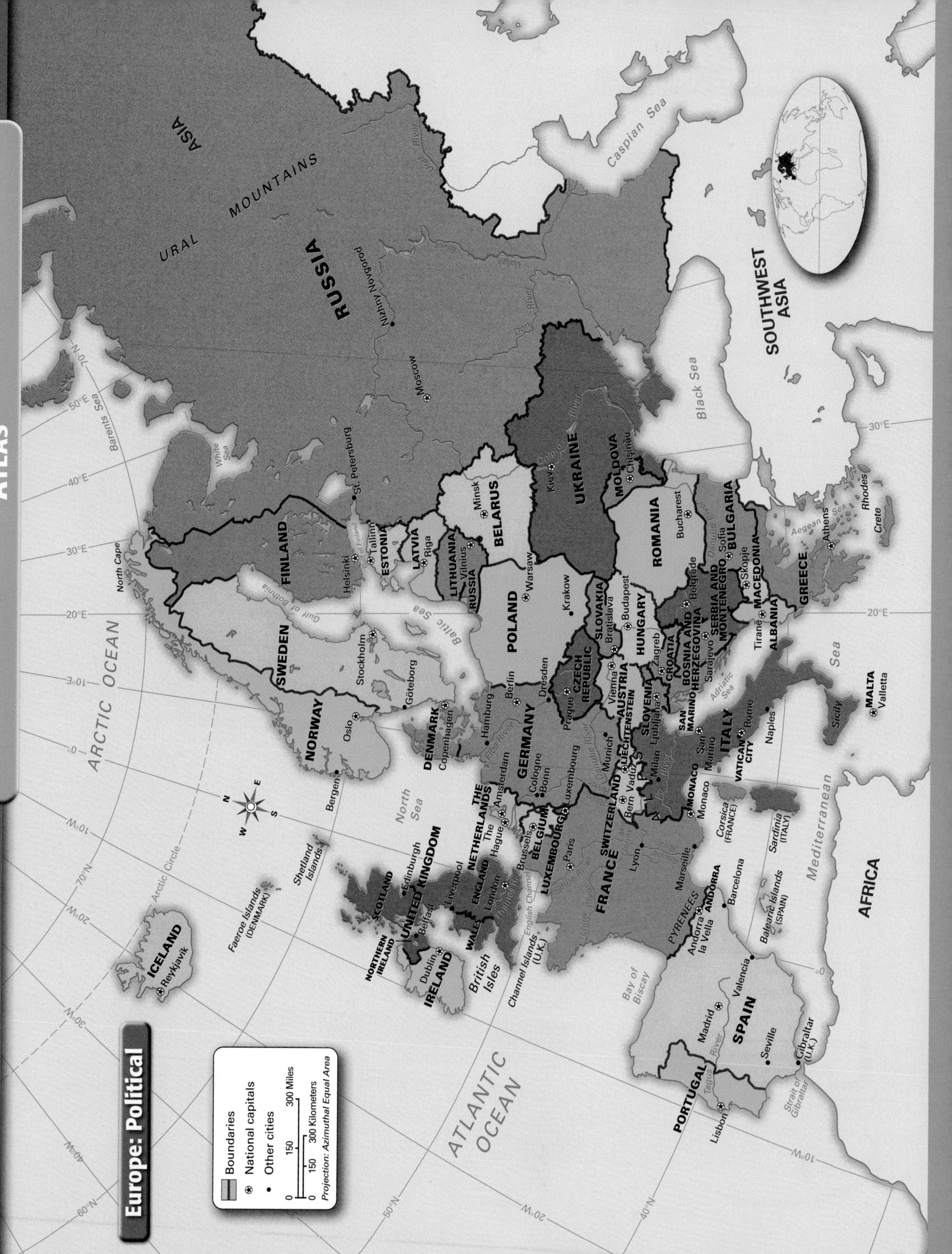

Europe: Political

Boundaries
National capitals
Other cities
0 150 300 Miles
0 150 300 Kilometers
Projection: Azimuthal Equal Area

ARCTIC OCEAN
Arctic Circle
North Cape
Barents Sea
White Sea
URAL MOUNTAINS
ASIA
ICELAND
Reykjavik
Faeroe Islands (DENMARK)
Shetland Islands
NORWAY
Bergen
Oslo
SWEDEN
Stockholm
Göteborg
Gulf of Bothnia
FINLAND
Helsinki
Gulf of Finland
St. Petersburg
RUSSIA
Nizhny Novgorod
Moscow
Ural River
Volga River
Don River
ESTONIA
Tallinn
LATVIA
Riga
LITHUANIA
Vilnius
RUSSIA
Baltic Sea
North Sea
DENMARK
Copenhagen
NORTHERN IRELAND
SCOTLAND
Edinburgh
UNITED KINGDOM
Belfast
IRELAND
Dublin
Liverpool
WALES
ENGLAND
London
Thames River
British Isles
ATLANTIC OCEAN
Channel Islands (U.K.)
English Channel
THE NETHERLANDS
The Hague
Amsterdam
Brussels
BELGIUM
LUXEMBOURG
Luxembourg
Hamburg
Elbe River
Berlin
GERMANY
Cologne
Bonn
Dresden
POLAND
Warsaw
Krakow
BELARUS
Minsk
UKRAINE
Kiev
Dnipro River
Paris
Seine River
Loire River
FRANCE
Lyon
Rhône River
Marseille
Bay of Biscay
PYRENEES
Andorra la Vella
ANDORRA
SWITZERLAND
Bern
Lake Geneva
Vaduz
LIECHTENSTEIN
Munich
Danube River
Prague
CZECH REPUBLIC
SLOVAKIA
Bratislava
Vienna
AUSTRIA
Budapest
HUNGARY
MOLDOVA
Chişinău
ROMANIA
Bucharest
Caspian Sea
Black Sea
SLOVENIA
Ljubljana
Zagreb
CROATIA
ALPS
Milan
Po River
MONACO
Monaco
SAN MARINO
San Marino
BOSNIA AND HERZEGOVINA
Sarajevo
Belgrade
SERBIA AND MONTENEGRO
Sofia
BULGARIA
Skopje
MACEDONIA
Tiranë
ALBANIA
GREECE
Athens
Aegean Sea
Rhodes
Crete
Adriatic Sea
ITALY
VATICAN CITY
Rome
Naples
Sicily
MALTA
Valletta
Corsica (FRANCE)
Sardinia (ITALY)
PORTUGAL
Lisbon
Tagus River
Madrid
SPAIN
Valencia
Barcelona
Seville
Gibraltar (U.K.)
Strait of Gibraltar
Balearic Islands (SPAIN)
Mediterranean Sea
AFRICA
SOUTHWEST ASIA

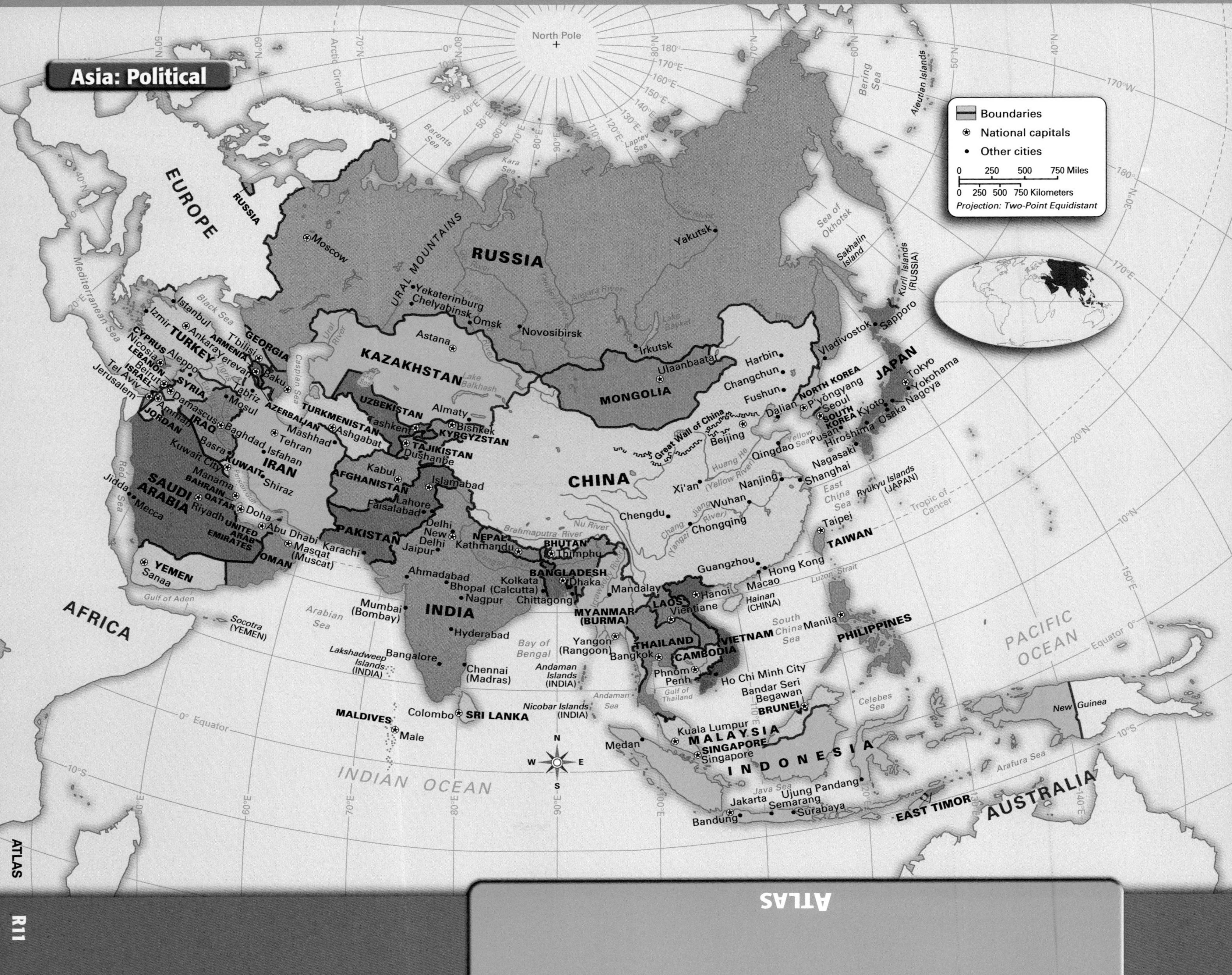

Asia: Political
Boundaries
National capitals
Other cities
0 250 500 750 Miles
0 250 500 750 Kilometers
Projection: Two-Point Equidistant
North Pole
EUROPE
RUSSIA
URAL MOUNTAINS
KAZAKHSTAN
MONGOLIA
CHINA
JAPAN
NORTH KOREA
SOUTH KOREA
TURKEY
GEORGIA
ARMENIA
AZERBAIJAN
CYPRUS
LEBANON
ISRAEL
SYRIA
JORDAN
IRAQ
IRAN
KUWAIT
BAHRAIN
QATAR
SAUDI ARABIA
UNITED ARAB EMIRATES
OMAN
YEMEN
TURKMENISTAN
UZBEKISTAN
KYRGYZSTAN
TAJIKISTAN
AFGHANISTAN
PAKISTAN
INDIA
NEPAL
BHUTAN
BANGLADESH
MYANMAR (BURMA)
LAOS
THAILAND
CAMBODIA
VIETNAM
TAIWAN
PHILIPPINES
MALAYSIA
SINGAPORE
BRUNEI
INDONESIA
EAST TIMOR
SRI LANKA
MALDIVES
AUSTRALIA
AFRICA
Moscow
Yekaterinburg
Chelyabinsk
Omsk
Novosibirsk
Astana
Irkutsk
Yakutsk
Ulaanbaatar
Harbin
Changchun
Fushun
Vladivostok
Sapporo
Tokyo
Yokohama
Kyoto
Osaka
Nagoya
Hiroshima
Nagasaki
P'yŏngyang
Seoul
Pusan
Dalian
Beijing
Qingdao
Nanjing
Shanghai
Xi'an
Wuhan
Chengdu
Chongqing
Guangzhou
Hong Kong
Macao
Hainan (CHINA)
Taipei
Manila
Hanoi
Vientiane
Bangkok
Phnom Penh
Ho Chi Minh City
Bandar Seri Begawan
Kuala Lumpur
Singapore
Medan
Jakarta
Bandung
Semarang
Surabaya
Ujung Pandang
Yangon (Rangoon)
Mandalay
Dhaka
Chittagong
Thimphu
Kathmandu
Kolkata (Calcutta)
Bhopal
Nagpur
Delhi
New Delhi
Jaipur
Ahmadabad
Mumbai (Bombay)
Hyderabad
Bangalore
Chennai (Madras)
Colombo
Male
Islamabad
Lahore
Faisalabad
Karachi
Kabul
Dushanbe
Tashkent
Bishkek
Almaty
Ashgabat
Mashhad
Tehran
Isfahan
Shiraz
Baku
T'bilisi
Yerevan
Tabriz
Mosul
Baghdad
Basra
Kuwait City
Manama
Doha
Abu Dhabi
Masqat (Muscat)
Riyadh
Mecca
Jidda
Sanaa
Istanbul
Ankara
Izmir
Aleppo
Nicosia
Beirut
Damascus
Amman
Tel Aviv
Jerusalem
Socotra (YEMEN)
Lakshadweep Islands (INDIA)
Andaman Islands (INDIA)
Nicobar Islands (INDIA)
Ryukyu Islands (JAPAN)
Kuril Islands (RUSSIA)
Sakhalin Island
Aleutian Islands
New Guinea
Great Wall of China
Mediterranean Sea
Black Sea
Caspian Sea
Red Sea
Persian Gulf
Gulf of Aden
Arabian Sea
Bay of Bengal
Andaman Sea
Gulf of Thailand
South China Sea
East China Sea
Yellow Sea
Java Sea
Celebes Sea
Arafura Sea
Sea of Okhotsk
Bering Sea
Barents Sea
Kara Sea
Laptev Sea
Lake Baykal
Lake Balkhash
PACIFIC OCEAN
INDIAN OCEAN
Ural River
Ob River
Irtysh River
Yenisey River
Angara River
Lena River
Amur River
Huang He (Yellow River)
Chang Jiang (Yangzi River)
Nu River
Brahmaputra River
Irrawaddy River
Tigris
Euphrates
Arctic Circle
Tropic of Cancer
Equator
Luzon Strait
N
S
E
W

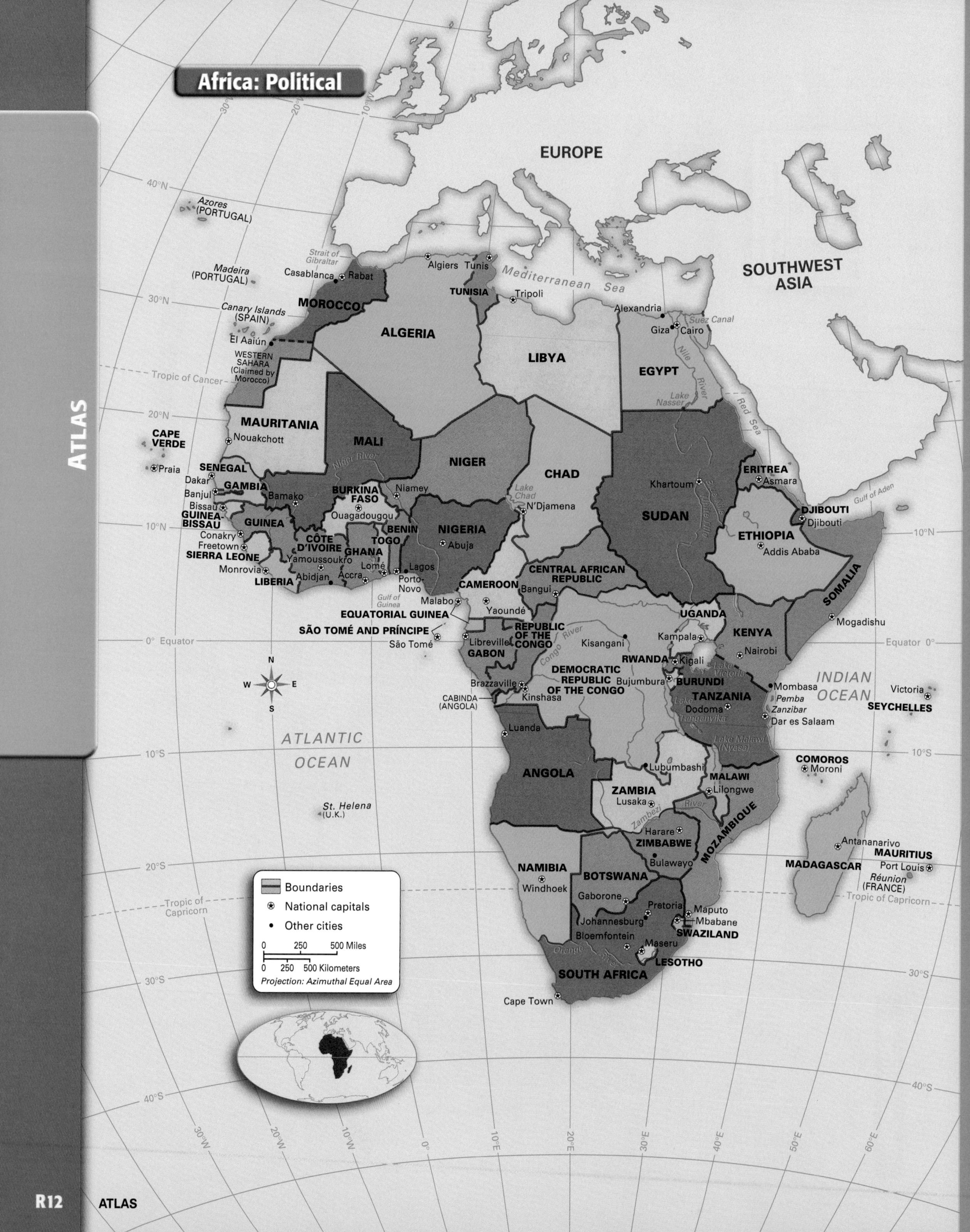

Africa: Political
ATLAS
EUROPE
SOUTHWEST ASIA
Azores (PORTUGAL)
Madeira (PORTUGAL)
Canary Islands (SPAIN)
Strait of Gibraltar
Mediterranean Sea
Red Sea
Gulf of Aden
Suez Canal
Nile River
Lake Nasser
Niger River
Lake Chad
Congo River
Lake Victoria
Lake Tanganyika
Lake Malawi (Nyasa)
Zambezi River
Orange River
Gulf of Guinea
ATLANTIC OCEAN
INDIAN OCEAN
Tropic of Cancer
Equator
Tropic of Capricorn
MOROCCO
Casablanca
Rabat
ALGERIA
Algiers
TUNISIA
Tunis
LIBYA
Tripoli
EGYPT
Alexandria
Giza
Cairo
El Aaiún
WESTERN SAHARA (Claimed by Morocco)
MAURITANIA
Nouakchott
CAPE VERDE
Praia
SENEGAL
Dakar
GAMBIA
Banjul
GUINEA-BISSAU
Bissau
GUINEA
Conakry
SIERRA LEONE
Freetown
LIBERIA
Monrovia
CÔTE D'IVOIRE
Yamoussoukro
Abidjan
MALI
Bamako
BURKINA FASO
Ouagadougou
GHANA
Accra
TOGO
Lomé
BENIN
Porto-Novo
NIGER
Niamey
NIGERIA
Abuja
Lagos
CHAD
N'Djamena
SUDAN
Khartoum
ERITREA
Asmara
DJIBOUTI
Djibouti
ETHIOPIA
Addis Ababa
SOMALIA
Mogadishu
CENTRAL AFRICAN REPUBLIC
Bangui
CAMEROON
Yaoundé
Malabo
EQUATORIAL GUINEA
SÃO TOMÉ AND PRÍNCIPE
São Tomé
GABON
Libreville
REPUBLIC OF THE CONGO
Brazzaville
DEMOCRATIC REPUBLIC OF THE CONGO
Kinshasa
Kisangani
Lubumbashi
CABINDA (ANGOLA)
UGANDA
Kampala
KENYA
Nairobi
Mombasa
RWANDA
Kigali
BURUNDI
Bujumbura
TANZANIA
Dodoma
Dar es Salaam
Pemba
Zanzibar
SEYCHELLES
Victoria
COMOROS
Moroni
ANGOLA
Luanda
ZAMBIA
Lusaka
MALAWI
Lilongwe
MOZAMBIQUE
Maputo
ZIMBABWE
Harare
Bulawayo
NAMIBIA
Windhoek
BOTSWANA
Gaborone
SOUTH AFRICA
Pretoria
Johannesburg
Bloemfontein
Cape Town
SWAZILAND
Mbabane
LESOTHO
Maseru
MADAGASCAR
Antananarivo
MAURITIUS
Port Louis
Réunion (FRANCE)
St. Helena (U.K.)
Boundaries
National capitals
Other cities
0 250 500 Miles
0 250 500 Kilometers
Projection: Azimuthal Equal Area
N
S
E
W
40°N
30°N
20°N
10°N
0°
10°S
20°S
30°S
40°S
30°W
20°W
10°W
0°
10°E
20°E
30°E
40°E
50°E
60°E

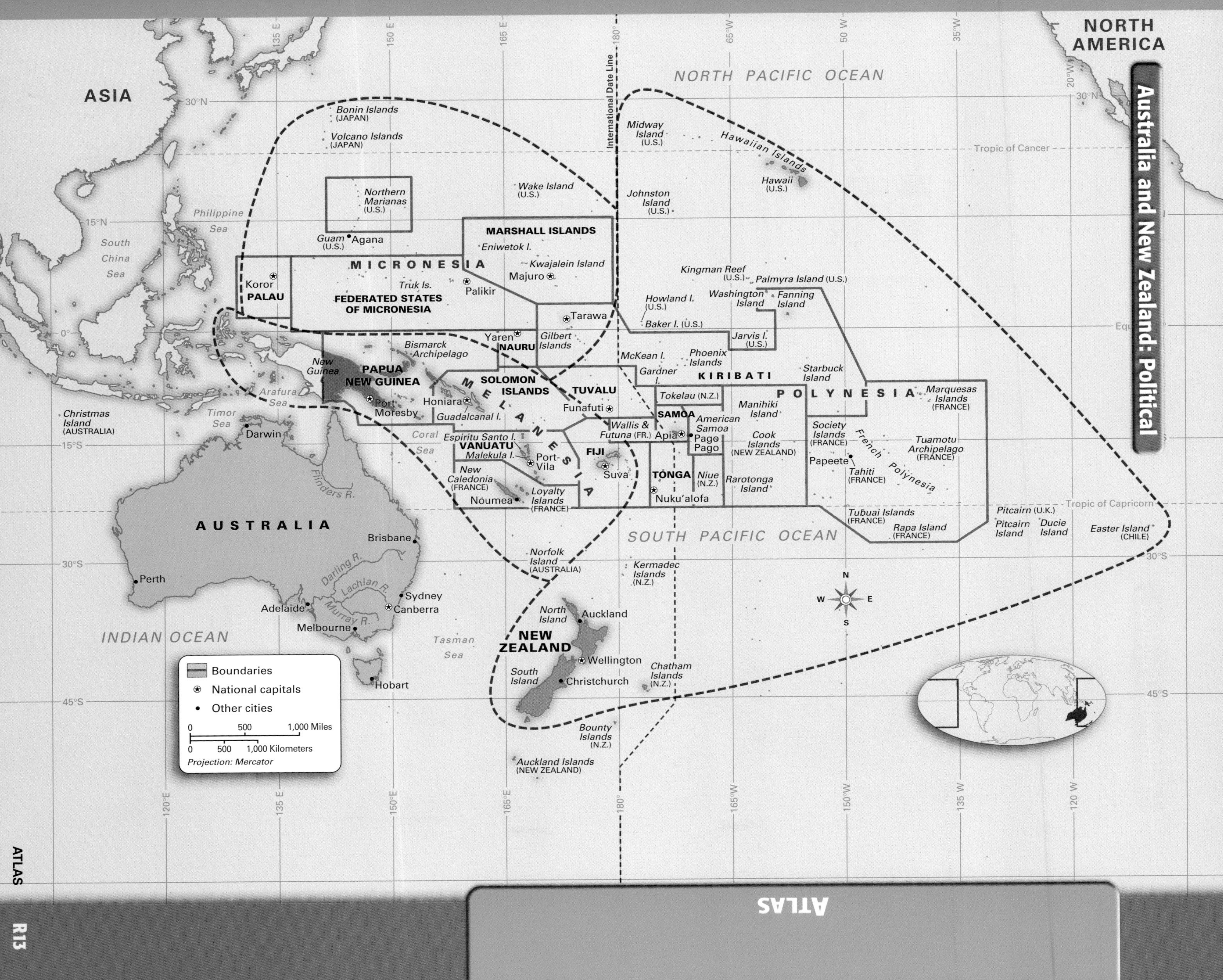

Australia and New Zealand: Political
ASIA
NORTH AMERICA
NORTH PACIFIC OCEAN
SOUTH PACIFIC OCEAN
INDIAN OCEAN
South China Sea
Philippine Sea
Timor Sea
Arafura Sea
Coral Sea
Tasman Sea
International Date Line
Tropic of Cancer
Tropic of Capricorn
Bonin Islands (JAPAN)
Volcano Islands (JAPAN)
Northern Marianas (U.S.)
Guam (U.S.)
Agana
Wake Island (U.S.)
Midway Island (U.S.)
Hawaiian Islands
Hawaii (U.S.)
Johnston Island (U.S.)
MARSHALL ISLANDS
Eniwetok I.
Kwajalein Island
Majuro
MICRONESIA
Koror
PALAU
Truk Is.
FEDERATED STATES OF MICRONESIA
Palikir
Tarawa
Kingman Reef (U.S.)
Palmyra Island (U.S.)
Howland I. (U.S.)
Washington Island
Fanning Island
Baker I. (U.S.)
Jarvis I. (U.S.)
Yaren
NAURU
Gilbert Islands
Bismarck Archipelago
McKean I.
Phoenix Islands
Gardner I.
KIRIBATI
Starbuck Island
New Guinea
PAPUA NEW GUINEA
Port Moresby
MELANESIA
SOLOMON ISLANDS
Honiara
Guadalcanal I.
TUVALU
Funafuti
Tokelau (N.Z.)
POLYNESIA
Marquesas Islands (FRANCE)
Manihiki Island
SAMOA
American Samoa
Apia
Pago Pago
Wallis & Futuna (FR.)
Cook Islands (NEW ZEALAND)
Society Islands (FRANCE)
French Polynesia
Tuamotu Archipelago (FRANCE)
Papeete
Tahiti (FRANCE)
Christmas Island (AUSTRALIA)
Darwin
Espiritu Santo I.
VANUATU
Malekula I.
Port-Vila
FIJI
Suva
TONGA
Nuku'alofa
Niue (N.Z.)
Rarotonga Island
New Caledonia (FRANCE)
Noumea
Loyalty Islands (FRANCE)
Tubuai Islands (FRANCE)
Rapa Island (FRANCE)
Pitcairn (U.K.)
Pitcairn Island
Ducie Island
Easter Island (CHILE)
Flinders R.
AUSTRALIA
Brisbane
Perth
Darling R.
Lachlan R.
Murray R.
Sydney
Canberra
Adelaide
Melbourne
Hobart
Norfolk Island (AUSTRALIA)
Kermadec Islands (N.Z.)
North Island
Auckland
NEW ZEALAND
Wellington
South Island
Christchurch
Chatham Islands (N.Z.)
Bounty Islands (N.Z.)
Auckland Islands (NEW ZEALAND)
N
E
S
W
Boundaries
National capitals
Other cities
0 500 1,000 Miles
0 500 1,000 Kilometers
Projection: Mercator
30°N
15°N
0°
15°S
30°S
45°S
120°E
135 E
150 E
165 E
180°
165°W
150°W
135 W
120 W

ATLAS

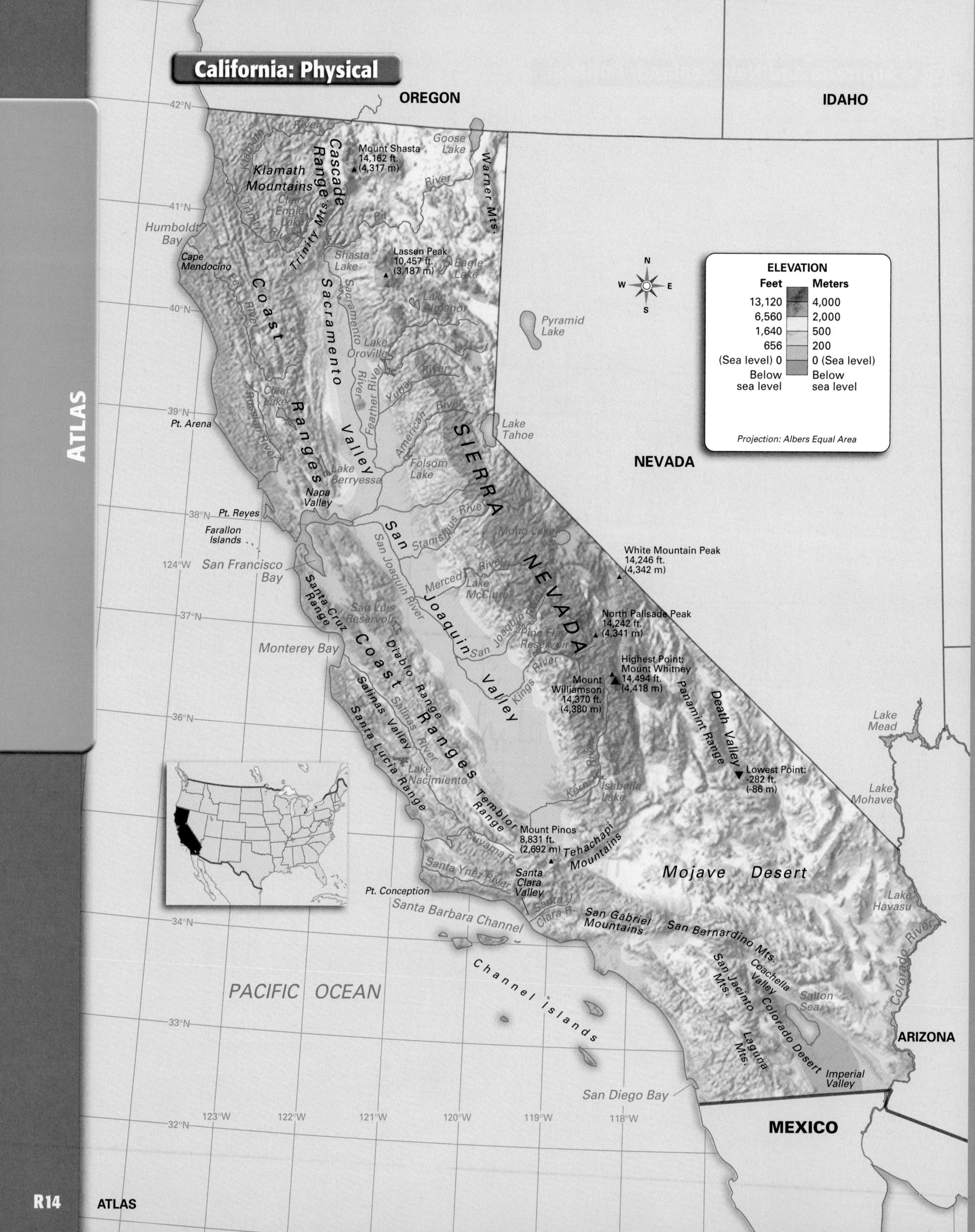

California: Physical
OREGON
IDAHO
NEVADA
ARIZONA
MEXICO
PACIFIC OCEAN
ATLAS
ELEVATION
Feet
Meters
13,120
4,000
6,560
2,000
1,640
500
656
200
(Sea level) 0
0 (Sea level)
Below sea level
Below sea level
Projection: Albers Equal Area
N
S
E
W
Mount Shasta 14,162 ft. (4,317 m)
Lassen Peak 10,457 ft. (3,187 m)
White Mountain Peak 14,246 ft. (4,342 m)
North Palisade Peak 14,242 ft. (4,341 m)
Highest Point: Mount Whitney 14,494 ft. (4,418 m)
Mount Williamson 14,370 ft. (4,380 m)
Lowest Point: -282 ft. (-86 m)
Mount Pinos 8,831 ft. (2,692 m)
Klamath Mountains
Cascade Range
Trinity Mts.
Warner Mts.
Coast Ranges
Sacramento Valley
SIERRA NEVADA
San Joaquin Valley
Diablo Range
Santa Cruz Range
Salinas Valley
Santa Lucia Range
Temblor Range
Tehachapi Mountains
Death Valley
Panamint Range
Mojave Desert
San Gabriel Mountains
San Bernardino Mts.
San Jacinto Mts.
Coachella Valley
Colorado Desert
Laguna Mts.
Imperial Valley
Santa Clara Valley
Napa Valley
Channel Islands
Santa Barbara Channel
Humboldt Bay
Cape Mendocino
Pt. Arena
Pt. Reyes
Farallon Islands
San Francisco Bay
Monterey Bay
Pt. Conception
San Diego Bay
Goose Lake
Clear Engle Lake
Shasta Lake
Eagle Lake
Lake Almanor
Pyramid Lake
Lake Oroville
Clear Lake
Lake Tahoe
Lake Berryessa
Folsom Lake
Mono Lake
Lake McClure
San Luis Reservoir
Pine Flat Reservoir
Lake Nacimiento
Isabella Lake
Lake Mead
Lake Mohave
Lake Havasu
Salton Sea
Klamath River
Trinity River
Pit River
Eel River
Russian River
Sacramento River
Feather River
Yuba River
American River
Stanislaus River
Merced River
San Joaquin River
Kings River
Kern River
Salinas River
Cuyama R.
Santa Ynez River
Santa Clara R.
Colorado River
42°N
41°N
40°N
39°N
38°N
37°N
36°N
34°N
33°N
32°N
124°W
123°W
122°W
121°W
120°W
119°W
118°W

California: Political
OREGON
IDAHO
NEVADA
ARIZONA
MEXICO
PACIFIC OCEAN
State boundary
International boundary
State capital
Other cities
0
50
100 Miles
0
50
100 Kilometers
Projection: Albers Equal Area
Crescent City
Yreka
Redwood National Park
Goose Lake
Alturas
Eureka
Weaverville
Redding
Shasta Lake
Lassen Volcanic Natl. Park
Susanville
Red Bluff
Sacramento River
Quincy
Chico
Fort Bragg
Willows
Downieville
Oroville
Grass Valley
Nevada City
Ukiah
Colusa
Truckee
Lakeport
Yuba City
Marysville
Lake Tahoe
South Lake Tahoe
Auburn
Placerville
Markleeville
Woodland
Santa Rosa
Sacramento
Sonoma
Napa
Jackson
Petaluma
Fairfield
San Andreas
Bridgeport
San Rafael
Concord
Stockton
Berkeley
Sonora
SAN FRANCISCO
Oakland
Yosemite National Park
Mono Lake
Redwood City
Hayward
Modesto
San Joaquin River
Sunnyvale
Mariposa
San Jose
Merced
Santa Cruz
Hollister
Madera
Kings Canyon Natl. Park
Independence
Salinas
Fresno
Monterey
Sequoia Natl. Park
Death Valley National Park
Hanford
Visalia
Tulare
Porterville
Atascadero
Ridgecrest
San Luis Obispo
Bakersfield
Santa Maria
Barstow
Needles
Lompoc
Santa Clarita
Palmdale
Santa Barbara
Ventura
Oxnard
Glendale
Pasadena
San Bernardino
LOS ANGELES
Riverside
Joshua Tree Natl. Park
Channel Islands Natl. Park
Anaheim
Long Beach
Santa Ana
Palm Springs
Blythe
Huntington Beach
Salton Sea
Colorado River
Oceanside
Escondido
SAN DIEGO
El Centro
42°N
41°N
40°N
39°N
38°N
37°N
36°N
34°N
33°N
32°N
124°W
123°W
122°W
121°W
120°W
119°W
118°W

ATLAS

California Governors

Peter Burnett (1849–1851)
John McDougall (1851–1852)
John Bigler (1852–1856)
J. Neeley Johnson (1856–1858)
John Weller (1858–1860)
Milton Latham (1860)
John Downey (1860–1862)
Leland Stanford (1862–1863)
Frederick Low (1863–1867)
Henry Haight (1867–1871)
Newton Booth (1871–1875)
Romualdo Pacheco (1875)
William Irwin (1875–1880)
George Perkins (1880–1883)
George Stoneman (1883–1887)
Washington Bartlett (1887)
Robert Waterman (1887–1891)
Henry Markham (1891–1895)
James Budd (1895–1899)
Henry Gage (1899–1903)
George Pardee (1903–1907)
James Gillett (1907–1911)
Hiram Johnson (1911–1917)
William Stephens (1917–1923)
Friend Richardson (1923–1927)
C. C. Young (1927–1931)
James Rolph (1931–1934)
Frank Merriam (1934–1939)
Culburt Olson (1939–1943)
Earl Warren (1943–1953)
Goodwin Knight (1953–1959)
Edmund G. "Pat" Brown (1959–1967)
Ronald Reagan (1967–1975)
Edmund G. "Jerry" Brown (1975–1983)
George Deukmejian (1983–1991)
Pete Wilson (1991–1999)
Gray Davis (1999–2003)
Arnold Schwarzenegger (2003–)

California Government

Executive Branch

Carries out the laws and policies of state government

The Governor

- Elected by voters to a four-year term
- Can serve two terms
- Appoints officials and some judges
- Can veto whole laws or items of laws passed by legislature

Lieutenant Governor

- Elected along with governor, but not as a running mate
- Various jobs include replacing governor should he or she leave office

The Cabinet

- Consists of officials appointed by governor
- Offers advice to governor on specific areas of knowledge

Legislative Branch

Makes state laws

Bicameral System

- Has two houses—State Senate and Assembly
- Both houses take part in law-making
- Legislature can override the governor's veto with a two-thirds vote in both houses

The State Senate

- 40 senators
- Serve four-year terms
- Limited to two terms

The Assembly

- 80 Assembly members
- Serve two-year terms
- Limited to three terms

Judicial Branch

Decides conflicts and questions about the law

Trial Courts

58 Superior Courts, one in each county

Appellate Courts

- Hear most appeals from lower courts
- Six district courts of appeals
- Have at least three justices:
  - Appointed by governor then confirmed by Commission on Judicial Appointments
  - Approved by voters in next election
  - Four-year terms

Supreme Court of California

- Hears appeals of criminal cases involving death penalty and cases where state laws or state constitution are found invalid
- Has seven justices:
  - Appointed by governor then confirmed by Commission on Judicial Appointments
  - Approved by voters in next election
  - 12-year terms

California Facts

State tree	California Redwood
State bird	California valley quail
State marine animal	Gray whale
State animal	Grizzly bear
State reptile	Desert tortoise
State flower	Golden Poppy
Capital	Sacramento
Year of Statehood	1850 (31st state)
Nickname	The Golden State
Motto	Eureka (I have found it.)
Song	"I Love You, California"
Highest Elevation	Mt. Whitney, 14,495 feet above sea level
Lowest Elevation	Death Valley, 282 feet below sea level
Total Area	163,707 sq. miles
National Rank in Land Area	3
Total Coastline	840 miles
Largest City	Los Angeles
Largest Lake	Lake Tahoe
Number of Counties	58
Longest River	Sacramento River
Population	35,484,453 (as of 2003)
National Rank in Population	1
Length (North to South)	770 miles
Width (East to West)	250 miles

Golden poppies

State flag

Death Valley, California

ATLAS

Gazetteer

A

Africa Second-largest continent. Lies in both the Northern and the Southern Hemispheres. p. 13

Alabama (AL) State in the southern United States. Admitted as a state in 1819. Capital: Montgomery. (33°N 87°W) p. 248

Alaska (AK) U.S. state in northwestern North America. Purchased from Russia in 1867. Became a territory in 1912. Admitted as a state in 1959. Capital: Juneau. (64°N 150°W) p. 8

Albany Capital of New York. (42°N 74°W). p. 92

Appalachian Mountains Mountain system in eastern North America that extends from Canada to central Alabama. p. 59

Arctic Region around the North Pole including Arctic Ocean, parts of Alaska, Canada, Russia and Scandinavian countries. (90°N 0°E) p. 8

Arizona (AZ) State in the southwestern United States. Organized into a territory in 1863. Admitted as a state in 1912. Capital: Phoenix. (34°N 113°W) p. 8

Arkansas (AR) State in the south-central United States. Admitted as a state in 1836. Capital: Little Rock. (35°N 93°W) p. 26

Asia Largest continent. Occupies the same land mass as Europe. p. 13

Atlanta Capital of Georgia. (33°N 84°W) p. 501

Atlantic Ocean Vast body of water separating North and South America from Europe and Africa. p. 7

B

Baltimore Maryland city northeast of Washington, D.C., on the Chesapeake Bay. (39°N 76°W) p. 248

Bering Land Bridge Land bridge that once connected what is now Alaska with Siberia. p. 6

Boston Capital of Massachusetts. (42°N 71°W) p. 44

Brazil Republic in eastern South America. Capital: Brasília. (10°S 55°W) p. 661

Buena Vista City in northeastern Mexico. (33°N 117°W) p. 321

Bull Run Creek in northeastern Virginia where the Confederates won two major battles during the Civil War. p. 479

Bunker Hill Hill in Boston, Massachusetts. Site of an early Revolutionary War battle. p. 79

C

California (CA) State in the western United States. Admitted as a state in 1850. Capital: Sacramento. (38°N 121°W) p. 10

Canada Country in northern North America. Capital: Ottawa. (50°N 100°W) p. 8

Cape of Good Hope Southern tip of Africa. p. 15

Caribbean Sea Arm of the Atlantic Ocean between North and South America. p. 55

Central America Region of land connecting North and South America. p. 22

Charleston Port city in southeastern South Carolina. Originally called Charles Town. (33°N 80°W) p. 97

Chesapeake Bay Inlet of the Atlantic Ocean in Virginia and Maryland. p. 37

Chicago Large U.S. City in northeastern Illinois on Lake Michigan. Major port (41°N 87°W) p. 358

China Country in East Asia with the world's largest population. Capital: Beijing. (Official name: People's Republic of China) p. 13

Colombia Republic in northwest South America. Capital: Bogotá. (4°N 72°W) p. 21

Columbia River River in northwestern United States and southwestern Canada. Forms part of boundary between Oregon and Washington. p. 238

Colorado (CO) State in the southwestern United States. Admitted as a state in 1876. Capital: Denver. (39°N 107°W) p. 8

Concord One of two northeastern Massachusetts towns (along with Lexington) where the first fighting of the American Revolution took place in 1775. (42°N 71°W) p. 77

Connecticut (CT) State in the northeastern United States. One of the original thirteen colonies. Admitted as a state in 1788. Capital: Hartford. (41°N 73°W) p. 46

Cuba Island-country in the Caribbean about 90 miles south of Florida. Capital: Havana. (22°N 79°W) p. 646

D

Delaware (DE) State in the eastern United States. One of the original thirteen colonies. Capital: Dover. (38°N 75°W) p. 76

District of Columbia Federal district between Maryland and Virginia where the capital of the United States is located. (39°N 77°W) p. 248

Ecuador Republic in northwest South America. Capital: Quito. (2°S 78°W) p. 8

England Region of the United Kingdom that makes up most of the southern part of the island of Great Britain. Capital: London. (51°N 1°W) p. 25

Erie Canal An early 1800s building project created a waterway between New York cities of Albany, the capital, and Buffalo, on Lake Erie. p. 264

Europe Continent occupying the same land mass as Asia. p. 12

Florida (FL) State in the southeastern United States. Organized as a territory in 1822. Admitted as a state in 1845. Capital: Tallahassee. (30°N 84°W) p. 22

Fort McHenry U.S. fort that guarded Baltimore, Maryland. The British attacked the fort in the War of 1812. p. 248

Fort Necessity Site where the French defeated British colonists in 1754, in what was the first battle of the French and Indian War. p. 58

Fort Sumter Fort on Charleston Harbor, South Carolina. Attack by Confederate forces here began the Civil War. p. 473

France Country in Western Europe. Capital: Paris. (46°N 0°W) p. 18

Georgia (GA) State in the southeastern United States. Admitted as a state in 1788. One of the original thirteen colonies. Capital: Atlanta. (32°N 84°W) p. 40

Germany Country in Western Europe. Capital: Berlin. (51°N 8°E) p. 24

Gettysburg Town in southern Pennsylvania. (40°N 77°W) p. 498

Great Basin Elevated region made up of parts of California, Idaho, Nevada, Oregon, Utah, and Wyoming that was home to many American Indian nations. p. 10

Great Britain Kingdom in western Europe that includes England, Scotland, and Wales. p. 54

Great Lakes Chain of lakes located in central North America and that extends across the U.S.-Canada border. Includes Lake Superior, Lake Michigan, Lake Huron, Lake Erie, and Lake Ontario. p. 18

Great Plains Region of central North America that lies between the Mississippi River and the Rocky Mountains p. 10

Gulf of Mexico Gulf on the southeastern coast of North America, bordered by the United States, Mexico, and Cuba. p. 7

Haiti Republic in the West Indies. Capital: Port-au-Prince. (19°N 72°W) p. 658

Hartford Capital of Connecticut. (41°N 72°W) p. 249

Hawaii (HI) U.S. state in the central Pacific Ocean that is made up of the Hawaiian Islands. Organized as a territory in 1900. Admitted as a state in 1959. Capital: Honolulu. (20°N 157°W) p. 642

Hispaniola Island that includes the countries of Haiti and the Dominican Republic. p. 17

Hudson Bay Inland sea in east-central Canada. Explored by Henry Hudson in 1610. p. 9

Hudson River River flowing from northeastern to southern New York. p. 27

Idaho (ID) State in the northwestern United States. Admitted as a state in 1890. Capital: Boise. (44°N 115°W) p. 324

Illinois (IL) State in the north-central United States. Admitted as a state in 1819. Capital: Springfield. (40°N 90°W) p. 95

India Large republic in southern Asia. Capital: New Delhi. (28°N 77°E) p. 14

Indiana (IN) State in the north-central United States. Admitted as a state in 1816 Capital: Indianapolis. (40°N 86°W) p. 115

Indian Ocean Vast body of water east of Africa, south of Asia, west of Australia, and north of Antarctica. p. 14

Iowa (IA) State in the north-central United States. Admitted as a state in 1846. Capital: Des Moines. (42°N 94°W) p. 239

Ireland Island in the British Isles. Divided into Northern Ireland (Capital: Belfast), and the Republic of Ireland (Capital: Dublin). (54°N 8°W) p. 400

Italy Country in southern Europe. Capital: Rome. (44°N 11°E) p. 12

Jamestown First successful English colony in America. Established in eastern Virginia in 1607. p. 36

Japan Country in the Western Pacific Ocean. Made up of a chain of islands. Capital: Tokyo. (37°N 134°E) p. 643

Kansas (KS) State in the central United States. Organized as a territory in 1854. Admitted as a state in 1861. Capital: Topeka. (38°N 99°W) p. 239

Kentucky (KY) State in the east-central United States. Admitted as a state in 1792. Capital: Frankfort. (37°N 87°W) p. 210

Lake Erie One of the Great Lakes. Located in the United States and Canada. p. 247

Latin America Spanish-speaking countries of North and South America that were once claimed by Spain and Portugal. p. 262

Lexington One of two northeastern Massachusetts towns (along with Concord) where the first fighting of the American Revolution took place in 1775. (42°N 71°W) p. 77

Liberia Country on the west coast of Africa. (6°N 10°W) p. 417

London Capital of the United Kingdom, in England. (52°N 0°W) p. 42

Los Angeles Large city in southern California. (34°N 118°W) p. 320

Louisiana (LA) State in the southeastern United States carved out of the Louisiana Territory. Admitted as a state in 1812. Capital: Baton Rouge. (31°N 92°W) p. 26

Maine (ME) State in the northeastern United States. Admitted as a state in 1820. Capital: Augusta. (45°N 70°W) p. 18

Manhattan Island Island at the north end of New York Bay. One of the five boroughs that make up New York City. p. 27

Maryland (MD) State in the east-central United States. One of the original thirteen colonies. Admitted as a state in 1788. Capital: Annapolis. (39°N 76°W) p. 39

Massachusetts (MA) State in the northeastern United States. One of the original thirteen colonies. Admitted as a state in 1788. Capital: Boston. (42°N 72°W) p. 44

Mediterranean Sea Large sea bordered by southern Europe, Southwest Asia, and northern Africa. p. 14

Mesoamerica Area from Mexico to North Central American during pre-Spanish culture. p. 8

Mexico Country in southern North America. Capital: Mexico City. (23°N 104°W) p. 8

Michigan (MI) State in the north-central United States. Admitted as a state in 1837. Capital: Lansing. (46°N 87°W) p. 115

Minnesota (MN) State in the north-central United States. Admitted as a state in 1858. Capital: St. Paul. (46°N 90°W) p. 239

Mississippi (MS) State in the southeastern United States. Admitted as a state in 1817. Capital: Jackson. (32°N 89°W) p. 261

Mississippi River River that flows from Minnesota south to the Gulf of Mexico. p. 8

Missouri (MO) State in the central United States. Admitted as a state in 1821. Capital: Jefferson City. (38°N 93°W) p. 239

Missouri River River that flows from southern Montana and joins the Mississippi River. p. 8

Montana (MT) State in the northwestern United States. Admitted as a state in 1889. Capital: Helena. (47°N 112°W) p. 239

Montreal City in southeastern Canada founded by the French in 1642. (46°N 74°W) p. 18

Nebraska (NE) State in the central United States. Admitted as a state in 1867. Capital: Lincoln. (41°N 101°W) p. 239

Netherlands Country in northwestern Europe. Capital: Amsterdam. (52°N 5°E) p. 27

Nevada (NV) State in the western United States. Organized as a territory in 1861. Admitted as a state in 1864. Capital: Carson City. (39°N 117°W) p. 318

New Amsterdam Dutch settlement on the island of Manhattan. Founded in 1626. p. 24

New England Northeastern section of the United States. Made up of Connecticut, Maine, Massachusetts, New Hampshire, Rhode Island, and Vermont. p. 42

New Hampshire (NH) State in the northeastern United States. One of the original thirteen colonies. Admitted as a state in 1788. Capital: Concord. (44°N 71°W) p. 44

New Jersey (NJ) State in the northeastern United States. One of the original thirteen colonies. Admitted as a state in 1787. Capital: Trenton. (40°N 75°W) p. 49

New Mexico (NM) State in the southwestern United States. Admitted as a state in 1912. Capital: Santa Fe. (34°N 107°W) p. 8

New Orleans Port city in southeastern Louisiana. (30°N 90°W) p. 26

New Spain Vast area of North America controlled by Spain. p. 22

New Sweden Swedish colony in North America that was located along the Delaware River. p. 27

New York (NY) State in the northeastern United States. One of the original thirteen colonies. Admitted as a state in 1788. Capital: Albany. (42°N 78°W) p. 18

New York City Largest city in the United States. (41°N 74°W) p. 51

Nicaragua Republic in Central America. Capital: Managua. (13°N 85°W) p. 657

North America Continent in the northern Western Hemisphere. p. 8

North Carolina (NC) State in the southeastern United States. One of the original thirteen colonies. Admitted as a state in 1789. Capital: Raleigh. (35°N 81°W) p. 18

North Dakota (ND) State in the north-central United States. Admitted as a state in 1889. Capital: Bismarck. (47°N 102°W) p. 239

Ohio (OH) State in the north-central United States. Originally part of the Northwest Territory. Admitted as a state in 1803. Capital: Columbus. (40°N 83°W) p. 59

Ohio River River that flows through Pennsylvania, Ohio, Indiana, and Illinois. p. 8

Oklahoma (OK) State in the south-central United States. Organized as a territory in 1890. Admitted as a state in 1907. Capital: Oklahoma City. (36°N 98°W) p. 239

Oregon (OR) State in the northwestern United States. Admitted as a state in 1859. Capital: Salem. (43°N 122°W) p. 317

Pacific Ocean Body of water extending from the Arctic Circle to Antarctica and from western North and South America to Australia, the Malay Archipelago, and East Asia. p. 7

Panama Country in southern Central America. Location of the Panama Canal. Capital: Panama City. (8°N 81°W) p. 652

Pennsylvania (PA) State in the eastern United States. One of the original thirteen colonies. Admitted as a state in 1787. Capital: Harrisburg. (41°N 78°W) p. 50

Peru Country in western South America. Capital: Lima (10°S 75°W) p. 22

Philadelphia City in southeastern Pennsylvania. Capital of the United States from 1790 to 1800. (40°N 75°W) p. 50

Philippines Country in the western Pacific Ocean. Made up of about 7,100 islands. Capital: Manila. (14°N 125°E) p. 647

Plymouth Site in Massachusetts where the Pilgrims first landed in North America in 1620. (42°N 70°W) p. 43

Portugal Country in southwestern Europe on the western Iberian Peninsula. (38°N 8°W) p. 14

Providence Capital of Rhode Island. (42°N 71°W) p. 46

Puerto Rico Island east of Cuba and southeast of Florida. A U.S. territory acquired in the Spanish American War. Capital: San Juan. (18°N 67°W) p. 649

R

Rhode Island (RI) State in the northeastern United States. One of the original thirteen colonies. Admitted as a state in 1790. Capital: Providence. (41°N 71°W) p. 46

Richmond Capital of Virginia. Capital of the Confederate States of America during the Civil War. (37°N 7°W) p. 381

Rio Grande Spanish for Great River. Forms the border between Texas and Mexico. p. 320

Roanoke Island Island off the coast of North Carolina. Site of Britain's first settlement in North America. p. 27

Rocky Mountains Mountain range in western North America that extends from Alaska south to New Mexico. p. 11

Russia Vast country that extends from Eastern Europe through northwestern Asia. Capital: Moscow. (61°N 60°E) p. 262

Sacramento River River in northwest California. Sacramento, capital of California sits at its head. (38°N 121°W) p. 326

San Antonio City in southern Texas. Site of the Mexican victory over Texas forces at the Alamo during the Texas Revolution. (29°N 99°W) p. 314

San Diego City in southern California. Located on San Diego Bay. (33°N 117°W) p. 320

San Francisco City in western California on a peninsula between the Pacific Ocean and San Francisco Bay. (37°N 122°W) p. 23

Santa Fe Capital of New Mexico. (35°N 106°W) p. 310

Saratoga Site in eastern New York of the Revolutionary War's Battle of Saratoga, the turning point of the war. p. 92

Savannah Port city in southeastern Georgia. Founded by James Oglethorpe in 1733. (32°N 81°W) p. 40

Seneca Falls Village in west-central New York State. Site of the first women's rights convention in the United States in 1848. (43°N 77°W) p. 426

Sierra Nevada Large mountain range in eastern California. p. 320

South America Continent in the southern Western Hemisphere. p. 6

South Carolina (SC) State in the southeastern United States. One of the original thirteen colonies. Admitted as a state in 1788. Capital: Columbia. (34°N 81°W) p. 40

South Dakota (SD) State in the north-central United States. Organized as part of the Dakota Territory in 1861. Admitted as a state in 1889. Capital: Pierre. (44°N 102°W) p. 239

Spain Country in southwestern Europe that occupies the greater part of the Iberian Peninsula. Capital: Madrid. (40°N 4°W) p. 12

Tennessee (TN) State in the south-central United States. Admitted as a state in 1796. Capital: Nashville. (36°N 88°W) p. 261

Tenochtitlán Aztec island-city that was located on the site what is now Mexico City. p. 20

Texas (TX) State in the south-central United States. Independent republic from 1836 to 1845. Admitted as a state in 1845. Capital: Austin. (31°N 101°W) p. 10

United States of America Country in central North America. Capital: Washington, D.C. (38°N 110°W) p. 7

Utah (UT) State in the western United States. Admitted as a state in 1896. Capital: Salt Lake City. (39°N 112°W) p. 8

Valley Forge Site in southeastern Pennsylvania where General George Washington and his troops spent the harsh winter of 1777–78. p. 94

Venezuela Republic in northern South America. Capital: Caracas. (8°N 66°W) p. 656

Vermont (VT) State in the northeastern United States. Admitted as a state in 1791. Capital: Montpelier. (44°N 73°W) p. 261

Vicksburg City in western Mississippi on the bluffs above the Mississippi River. (42°N 85°W) p. 484

Virginia (VA) State in the eastern United States. One of the original thirteen colonies. Admitted as a state in 1788. Capital: Richmond. (37°N 80°W) p. 27

Washington (WA) State in the northwestern United States. Admitted as a state in 1889. Capital: Olympia. (47°N 121°W) p. 324

Washington, D.C. Capital of the United States. Located on the Potomac River between Virginia and Maryland. (39°N 77°W) p. 204

West Virginia (WV) State in the east-central United States. Part of Virginia until the area refused to join the Confederacy in 1861. Admitted as a state in 1863. Capital: Charleston. (39°N 81°W) p. 474

Wisconsin (WI) State in the north-central United States. Became part of the Northwest Territory in 1787. Admitted as a state in 1848. Capital: Madison. (44°N 91°W) p. 115

Wyoming (WY) State in the northwestern United States. Admitted as a state in 1890. Capital: Cheyenne. (43°N 108°W) p. 239

GAZETTEER

Presidents

1 George Washington
Born: 1732 Died: 1799
Years in Office: 1789–97
Political Party: None
Home State: Virginia
Vice President:

2 John Adams
Born: 1735 Died: 1826
Years in Office: 1797–1801
Political Party: Federalist
Home State: Massachusetts
Vice President: Thomas Jefferson

3 Thomas Jefferson
Born: 1743 Died: 1826
Years in Office: 1801–09
Political Party: Republican*
Home State: Virginia
Vice Presidents: Aaron Burr, George Clinton

4 James Madison
Born: 1751 Died: 1836
Years in Office: 1809–17
Political Party: Republican
Home State: Virginia
Vice Presidents: George Clinton, Elbridge Gerry

5 James Monroe
Born: 1758 Died: 1831
Years in Office: 1817–25
Political Party: Republican
Home State: Virginia
Vice President: Daniel D. Tompkins

6 John Quincy Adams
Born: 1767 Died: 1848
Years in Office: 1825–29
Political Party: Republican
Home State: Massachusetts
Vice President: John C. Calhoun

7 Andrew Jackson
Born: 1767 Died: 1845
Years in Office: 1829–37
Political Party: Democratic
Home State: Tennessee
Vice Presidents: John C. Calhoun, Martin Van Buren

8 Martin Van Buren
Born: 1782 Died: 1862
Years in Office: 1837–41
Political Party: Democratic
Home State: New York
Vice President: Richard M. Johnson

* The Republican Party of the third through sixth presidents is not the party of Abraham Lincoln, which was founded in 1854.

9 William Henry Harrison
Born: 1773 **Died:** 1841
Years in Office: 1841
Political Party: Whig
Home State: Ohio
Vice President: John Tyler

10 John Tyler
Born: 1790 **Died:** 1862
Years in Office: 1841–45
Political Party: Whig
Home State: Virginia
Vice President: None

11 James K. Polk
Born: 1795 **Died:** 1849
Years in Office: 1845–49
Political Party: Democratic
Home State: Tennessee
Vice President: George M. Dallas

12 Zachary Taylor
Born: 1784 **Died:** 1850
Years in Office: 1849–50
Political Party: Whig
Home State: Louisiana
Vice President: Millard Fillmore

13 Millard Fillmore
Born: 1800 **Died:** 1874
Years in Office: 1850–53
Political Party: Whig
Home State: New York
Vice President: None

14 Franklin Pierce
Born: 1804 **Died:** 1869
Years in Office: 1853–57
Political Party: Democratic
Home State: New Hampshire
Vice President: William R. King

15 James Buchanan
Born: 1791 **Died:** 1868
Years in Office: 1857–61
Political Party: Democratic
Home State: Pennsylvania
Vice President: John C. Breckinridge

16 Abraham Lincoln
Born: 1809 **Died:** 1865
Years in Office: 1861–65
Political Party: Republican
Home State: Illinois
Vice Presidents: Hannibal Hamlin, Andrew Johnson

17 Andrew Johnson
Born: 1808 **Died:** 1875
Years in Office: 1865–69
Political Party: Republican
Home State: Tennessee
Vice President: None

18 Ulysses S. Grant
Born: 1822 **Died:** 1885
Years in Office: 1869–77
Political Party: Republican
Home State: Illinois
Vice Presidents: Schuyler Colfax, Henry Wilson

19 Rutherford B. Hayes
Born: 1822 **Died:** 1893
Years in Office: 1877–81
Political Party: Republican
Home State: Ohio
Vice President: William A. Wheeler

20 James A. Garfield
Born: 1831 **Died:** 1881
Years in Office: 1881
Political Party: Republican
Home State: Ohio
Vice President: Chester A. Arthur

21 Chester A. Arthur
Born: 1829 **Died:** 1886
Years in Office: 1881–85
Political Party: Republican
Home State: New York
Vice President: None

22 Grover Cleveland
Born: 1837 **Died:** 1908
Years in Office: 1885–89
Political Party: Democratic
Home State: New York
Vice President: Thomas A. Hendricks

23 Benjamin Harrison
Born: 1833 **Died:** 1901
Years in Office: 1889–93
Political Party: Republican
Home State: Indiana
Vice President: Levi P. Morton

24 Grover Cleveland
Born: 1837 **Died:** 1908
Years in Office: 1893–97
Political Party: Democratic
Home State: New York
Vice President: Adlai E. Stevenson

25 William McKinley
Born: 1843 **Died:** 1901
Years in Office: 1897–1901
Political Party: Republican
Home State: Ohio
Vice Presidents: Garret A. Hobart, Theodore Roosevelt

26 Theodore Roosevelt
Born: 1858 **Died:** 1919
Years in Office: 1901–09
Political Party: Republican
Home State: New York
Vice President: Charles W. Fairbanks

27 William Howard Taft
Born: 1857 **Died:** 1930
Years in Office: 1909–13
Political Party: Republican
Home State: Ohio
Vice President: James S. Sherman

28 Woodrow Wilson
Born: 1856 **Died:** 1924
Years in Office: 1913–21
Political Party: Democratic
Home State: New Jersey
Vice President: Thomas R. Marshall

29 Warren G. Harding
Born: 1865 **Died:** 1923
Years in Office: 1921–23
Political Party: Republican
Home State: Ohio
Vice President: Calvin Coolidge

30 Calvin Coolidge
Born: 1872 **Died:** 1933
Years in Office: 1923–29
Political Party: Republican
Home State: Massachusetts
Vice President: Charles G. Dawes

31 Herbert Hoover
Born: 1874 **Died:** 1964
Years in Office: 1929–33
Political Party: Republican
Home State: California
Vice President: Charles Curtis

32 Franklin D. Roosevelt
Born: 1882 **Died:** 1945
Years in Office: 1933–45
Political Party: Democratic
Home State: New York
Vice Presidents: John Nance Garner, Henry Wallace, Harry S Truman

33 Harry S Truman
Born: 1884 **Died:** 1972
Years in Office: 1945–53
Political Party: Democratic
Home State: Missouri
Vice President: Alben W. Barkley

34 Dwight D. Eisenhower
Born: 1890 **Died:** 1969
Years in Office: 1953–61
Political Party: Republican
Home State: Kansas
Vice President: Richard M. Nixon

35 John F. Kennedy
Born: 1917 **Died:** 1963
Years in Office: 1961–63
Political Party: Democratic
Home State: Massachusetts
Vice President: Lyndon B. Johnson

36 Lyndon B. Johnson
Born: 1908 **Died:** 1973
Years in Office: 1963–69
Political Party: Democratic
Home State: Texas
Vice President: Hubert H. Humphrey

37 Richard M. Nixon
Born: 1913 **Died:** 1994
Years in Office: 1969–74
Political Party: Republican
Home State: California
Vice Presidents: Spiro T. Agnew, Gerald R. Ford

38 Gerald R. Ford
Born: 1913
Years in Office: 1974–77
Political Party: Republican
Home State: Michigan
Vice President: Nelson A. Rockefeller

39 Jimmy Carter
Born: 1924
Years in Office: 1977–81
Political Party: Democratic
Home State: Georgia
Vice President: Walter F. Mondale

40 Ronald Reagan
Born: 1911
Years in Office: 1981–89
Political Party: Republican
Home State: California
Vice President: George Bush

41 George Bush
Born: 1924
Years in Office: 1989–93
Political Party: Republican
Home State: Texas
Vice President: J. Danforth Quayle

42 Bill Clinton
Born: 1946
Years in Office: 1993–2001
Political Party: Democratic
Home State: Arkansas
Vice President: Albert Gore Jr.

43 George W. Bush
Born: 1946
Years in Office: 2001–
Political Party: Republican
Home State: Texas
Vice President: Richard B. Cheney

Facts About the States

State	Year of Statehood	2003 Population	Area (Sq. Mi.)	Population Density (Sq Mi.)	Capital
Alabama	1819	4,500,752	50,744	88.7	Montgomery
Alaska	1959	648,818	571,951	1.1	Juneau
Arizona	1912	5,580,811	113,635	49.1	Phoenix
Arkansas	1836	2,725,714	52,068	52.3	Little Rock
California	1850	35,484,453	155,959	227.5	Sacramento
Colorado	1876	4,550,688	103,718	43.9	Denver
Connecticut	1788	3,483,372	4,845	719.0	Hartford
Delaware	1787	817,491	1,954	418.4	Dover
District of Columbia	—	563,384	61	9,235.8	—
Florida	1845	17,019,068	53,927	315.6	Tallahassee
Georgia	1788	8,684,715	57,906	150.0	Atlanta
Hawaii	1959	1,257,608	6,423	195.8	Honolulu
Idaho	1890	1,366,332	82,747	16.5	Boise
Illinois	1818	12,653,544	55,584	227.6	Springfield
Indiana	1816	6,195,643	35,867	172.7	Indianapolis
Iowa	1846	2,944,062	55,869	52.7	Des Moines
Kansas	1861	2,723,507	81,815	33.3	Topeka
Kentucky	1792	4,117,827	39,728	103.7	Frankfort
Louisiana	1812	4,496,334	43,562	103.2	Baton Rouge
Maine	1820	1,305,728	30,862	42.3	Augusta
Maryland	1788	5,508,909	9,774	563.6	Annapolis
Massachusetts	1788	6,433,422	7,840	820.6	Boston
Michigan	1837	10,079,985	56,804	177.5	Lansing
Minnesota	1858	5,059,375	79,610	63.6	St. Paul

State	Year of Statehood	2003 Population	Area (Sq. Mi.)	Population Density (Sq Mi.)	Capital
Mississippi	1817	2,881,281	46,907	61.4	Jackson
Missouri	1821	5,704,484	68,886	82.8	Jefferson City
Montana	1889	917,621	145,552	6.3	Helena
Nebraska	1867	1,739,291	76,872	22.6	Lincoln
Nevada	1864	2,241,154	109,826	20.4	Carson City
New Hampshire	1788	1,287,687	8,968	143.6	Concord
New Jersey	1787	8,638,396	7,417	1,164.7	Trenton
New Mexico	1912	1,874,614	121,356	15.4	Santa Fe
New York	1788	19,190,115	47,214	406.4	Albany
North Carolina	1789	8,407,248	48,711	172.6	Raleigh
North Dakota	1889	633,837	68,976	9.2	Bismarck
Ohio	1803	11,435,798	40,948	279.3	Columbus
Oklahoma	1907	3,511,532	68,667	51.1	Oklahoma City
Oregon	1859	3,559,596	95,997	37.1	Salem
Pennsylvania	1787	12,365,455	44,817	275.9	Harrisburg
Rhode Island	1790	1,076,164	1,045	1,029.8	Providence
South Carolina	1788	4,147,152	30,109	137.7	Columbia
South Dakota	1889	764,309	75,885	10.1	Pierre
Tennessee	1796	5,841,748	41,217	141.7	Nashville
Texas	1845	22,118,509	261,797	84.5	Austin
Utah	1896	2,351,467	82,144	28.6	Salt Lake City
Vermont	1791	619,107	9,250	66.9	Montpelier
Virginia	1788	7,386,330	39,594	186.6	Richmond
Washington	1889	6,131,445	66,544	92.1	Olympia
West Virginia	1863	1,810,354	24,078	75.2	Charleston
Wisconsin	1848	5,472,299	54,310	100.8	Madison
Wyoming	1890	501,242	97,100	5.2	Cheyenne

American Flag

The American flag is a symbol of the nation. It is recognized instantly, whether as a big banner waving in the wind or a tiny emblem worn on a lapel. The flag is so important that it is a major theme of the national anthem, "The Star-Spangled Banner." One of the most popular names for the flag is the Stars and Stripes. It is also known as Old Glory.

The Meaning of the Flag

The American flag has 13 stripes—7 red and 6 white. In the upper-left corner of the flag is the union—50 white five-pointed stars against a blue background.

The 13 stripes stand for the original 13 American states, and the 50 stars represent the states of the nation today. According to the U.S. Department of State, the colors of the flag also are symbolic:

Red stands for courage.

White symbolizes purity.

Blue is the color of vigilance, perseverance, and justice.

Displaying the Flag

It is customary not to display the American flag in bad weather. It is also customary for the flag to be displayed outdoors only from sunrise to sunset, except on certain occasions. In a few special places, however, the flag is always flown day and night. When flown at night, the flag should be illuminated.

Near a speaker's platform, the flag should occupy the place of honor at the speaker's right. When carried in a parade with other flags, the American flag should be on the marching right or in front at the center. When flying with the flags of the 50 states, the national flag must be at the center and the highest point. In a group of national flags, all should be of equal size and all should be flown from staffs, or flagpoles, of equal height.

The flag should never touch the ground or the floor. It should not be marked with any insignia, pictures, or words. Nor should it be used in any disrespectful way—as an advertising decoration, for instance. The flag should never be dipped to honor any person or thing.

Saluting the Flag

The United States, like other countries, has a flag code, or rules for displaying and honoring the flag. For example, all those present should stand at attention facing the flag and salute it when it is being raised or lowered or when it is carried past them in a parade or procession. A man wearing a hat should take it off and hold it with his right hand over his heart. All women and hatless men should stand with their right hands over their hearts to show their respect for the flag. The flag should also receive these honors during the playing of the national anthem and the reciting of the Pledge of Allegiance.

The Pledge of Allegiance

The Pledge of Allegiance was written in 1892 by Massachusetts magazine (*Youth's Companion*) editor Francis Bellamy. (Congress added the words "under God" in 1954.)

I pledge allegiance to the flag of the United States of America and to the republic for which it stands, one nation under God, indivisible, with liberty and justice for all.

Civilians should say the Pledge of Allegiance with their right hands placed over their hearts. People in the armed forces give the military salute. By saying the Pledge of Allegiance, we promise loyalty ("pledge allegiance") to the United States and its ideals.

"THE STAR-SPANGLED BANNER"

"The Star-Spangled Banner" is the national anthem of the United States. It was written by Francis Scott Key during the War of 1812. While being detained by the British aboard a ship on September 13–14, 1814, Key watched the British bombardment of Fort McHenry at Baltimore. The attack lasted 25 hours. The smoke was so thick that Key could not tell who had won. When the air cleared, Key saw the American flag that was still flying over the fort. "The Star-Spangled Banner" is sung to music written by British composer John Stafford Smith. In 1931 Congress designated "The Star-Spangled Banner" as the national anthem.

I

Oh, say, can you see, by the dawn's early light,
What so proudly we hailed at the twilight's last gleaming,
Whose broad stripes and bright stars through the perilous fight,
O'er the ramparts we watched were so gallantly streaming?
And the rockets' red glare, the bombs bursting in air,
Gave proof through the night that our flag was still there.
Oh, say, does that star-spangled banner yet wave
O'er the land of the free, and the home of the brave?

II

On the shore, dimly seen through the mists of the deep,
Where the foe's haughty host in dread silence reposes,
What is that which the breeze, o'er the towering steep,
As it fitfully blows, half conceals, half discloses?
Now it catches the gleam of the morning's first beam,
In full glory reflected, now shines on the stream.
'Tis the star-spangled banner; oh, long may it wave
O'er the land of the free, and the home of the brave!

III

And where is that band who so vauntingly swore
That the havoc of war and the battle's confusion
A home and a country should leave us no more?
Their blood has washed out their foul footsteps' pollution.
No refuge could save the hireling and slave
From the terror of flight, or the gloom of the grave:
And the star-spangled banner in triumph doth wave
O'er the land of the free, and the home of the brave!

IV

Oh! thus be it ever when freemen shall stand
Between their loved homes and the war's desolation!
Blest with victory and peace, may the heaven-rescued land
Praise the Power that hath made and preserved us a nation!
Then conquer we must, for our cause it is just,
And this be our motto: "In God is our trust!"
And the star-spangled banner in triumph shall wave,
O'er the land of the free, and the home of the brave!

Sheet music to the national anthem

"AMERICA, THE BEAUTIFUL"

One of the most beloved songs celebrating our nation is "America, the Beautiful." Katharine Lee Bates first wrote the lyrics to the song in 1893 after visiting Colorado. The version of the song we know today is set to music by Samuel A. Ward. The first and last stanzas of "America, the Beautiful" are shown below.

O beautiful for spacious skies,
For amber waves of grain,
For purple mountain majesties
Above the fruited plain!
America! America!
God shed his grace on thee
And crown thy good with brotherhood
From sea to shining sea!

O beautiful for patriot dream
That sees beyond the years
Thine alabaster cities gleam
Undimmed by human tears!
America! America!
God shed his grace on thee
And crown thy good with brotherhood
From sea to shining sea!

Supreme Court Decisions

Marbury v. *Madison,* (1803)

Significance: This ruling established the Supreme Court's power of judicial review,by which the Court decides whether laws passed by Congress are constitutional. This decision greatly increased the prestige of the Court and gave the judiciary branch a powerful check against the legislative and executive branches.

Background: William Marbury and several others were commissioned as judges by Federalist president John Adams during his last days in office. This act angered the new Democratic-Republican president, Thomas Jefferson. Jefferson ordered his secretary of state, James Madison, not to deliver the commissions. Marbury took advantage of a section in the Judiciary Act of 1789 that allowed him to take his case directly to the Supreme Court. He sued Madison, demanding the commission and the judgeship.

Decision: This case was decided on February 24, 1803, by a vote of 5 to 0. Chief Justice John Marshall spoke for the Court, which decided against Marbury. The court ruled that although Marbury's commission had been unfairly withheld, he could not lawfully take his case to the Supreme Court without first trying it in a lower court. Marshall said that the section of the Judiciary Act that Marbury had used was actually unconstitutional, and that the Constitution must take priority over laws passed by Congress.

McCulloch v. *Maryland,* (1819)

Significance: This ruling established that Congress had the constitutional power to charter a national bank. The case also established the principle of national supremacy, which states that the Constitution and other laws of the federal government take priority over state laws. In addition, the ruling reinforced the loose construction interpretation of the Constitution favored by many Federalists.

Background: In 1816 the federal government set up the Second Bank of the United States to stabilize the economy following the War of 1812. Many states were opposed to the competition provided by the new national bank. Some of these states passed heavy taxes on the Bank. The national bank refused to pay the taxes. This led the state of Maryland to sue James McCulloch, the cashier of the Baltimore, Maryland, branch of the national bank.

Decision: This case was decided on March 6, 1819, by a vote of 7 to 0. Chief Justice John Marshall spoke for the unanimous Court, which ruled that the national bank was constitutional because it helped the federal government carry out other powers granted to it by the Constitution. The Court declared that any attempt by the states to interfere with the duties of the federal government could not be permitted.

Gibbons v. *Ogden,* (1824)

Significance: This ruling was the first case to deal with the clause of the Constitution that allows Congress to regulate interstate and foreign commerce. This case was important because it reinforced both the authority of the federal government over the states and the division of powers between the federal government and the state governments.

Background: Steamboat operators who wanted to travel on New York waters had to obtain a state license. Thomas Gibbons had a federal license to travel along the coast, but not a state license for New York. He wanted the freedom to compete with state-licensed Aaron Ogden for steam travel between New Jersey and the New York island of Manhattan.

Decision: This case was decided on March 2, 1824, by a vote of 6 to 0. Chief Justice John Marshall spoke for the Court, which ruled in favor of Gibbons. The Court stated that the congressional statute (Gibbons's federal license) took priority over the state statute (Ogden's state-monopoly license). The ruling also defined commerce as more than simply the exchange of goods, broadening it to include the transportation of people and the use of new inventions (such as the steamboat).

Worcester v. *Georgia,* (1832)

Significance: This ruling made Georgia's removal of the Cherokee illegal. However, Georgia, with President Andrew Jackson's support, defied the Court's decision. By not enforcing the Court's ruling, Jackson violated his constitutional oath as president. As a result, the Cherokee and other American Indian tribes continued to be forced off of lands protected by treaties.

Supreme Court Building, Washington, D. C.

Background: The state of Georgia wanted to remove Cherokee Indians from lands they held by treaty. Samuel Worcester, a missionary who worked with the Cherokee Nation, was arrested for failing to take an oath of allegiance to the state and to obey a Georgia militia order to leave the Cherokee's lands. Worcester sued, charging that Georgia had no legal authority on Cherokee lands.

Decision: This case was decided on March 3, 1832, by a vote of 5 to 1 in favor of Worcester. Chief Justice John Marshall spoke for the Supreme Court, which ruled that the Cherokee were an independent political community. The Court decided that only the federal government, not the state of Georgia, had authority over legal matters involving the Cherokee people.

Scott v. *Sandford,* (1857)

Significance: This ruling denied enslaved African Americans U.S. citizenship and the right to sue in federal court. The decision also invalidated the Missouri Compromise, which had prevented slavery in territories north of the 36° 30' line of latitude. The ruling increased the controversy over the expansion of slavery in new states and territories.

Background: John Emerson, an army doctor, took his slave Dred Scott with him to live in Illinois and then Wisconsin Territory, both of which had banned slavery. In 1842 the two moved to Missouri, a slave state. Four years later, Scott sued for his freedom according to a Missouri legal principle of "once free, always free." The principle meant that a slave was entitled to freedom if he or she had once lived in a free state or territory.

Decision: This case was decided March 6–7, 1857, by a vote of 7 to 2. Chief Justice Roger B. Taney spoke for the Court, which ruled that slaves did not have the right to sue in federal courts because they were considered property, not citizens. In addition, the Court ruled that Congress did not have the power to abolish slavery in territories because that power was not strictly defined in the Constitution. Furthermore, the Court overturned the once-free, always-free principle.

Plessy v. *Ferguson,* (1896)

Significance: This case upheld the constitutionality of racial segregation by ruling that separate facilities for different races were legal as long as those facilities were equal to one another. This case provided a legal justification for racial segregation for nearly 60 years until it was overturned by *Brown* v. *Board of Education* in 1954.

Background: An 1890 Louisiana law required that all railway companies in the state use "separate-but-equal" railcars for white and African American passengers. A group of citizens in New Orleans banded together to challenge the law and chose Homer Plessy to test the law in 1892. Plessy took a seat in a whites-only coach, and when he refused

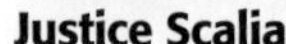
Justice Scalia

Justice Ginsberg

Justice Souter

Justice Rehnquist

Justice O'Connor

to move, he was arrested. Plessy eventually sought review by the U.S. Supreme Court, claiming that the Louisiana law violated his Fourteenth Amendment right to equal protection.

Decision: This case was decided on May 18, 1896, by a vote of 7 to 1. Justice Henry Billings Brown spoke for the Court, which upheld the constitutionality of the Louisiana law that segregated railcars. Justice John M. Harlan dissented, arguing that the Constitution should not be interpreted in ways that recognize class or racial distinctions.

Lochner v. *New York,* (1905)

Significance: This decision established the Supreme Court's role in overseeing state regulations. For more than 30 years *Lochner* was often used as a precedent in striking down state laws such as minimum-wage laws, child labor laws, and regulations placed on the banking and transportation industries.

Background: In 1895 the state of New York passed a labor law limiting bakers to working no more than 10 hours per day or 60 hours per week. The purpose of the law was to protect the health of bakers, who worked in hot and damp conditions and breathed in large quantities of flour dust. In 1902 Joseph Lochner, the owner of a small bakery in New York, claimed that the state law violated his Fourteenth Amendment rights by unfairly depriving him of the liberty to make contracts with employees. This case went to the U.S. Supreme Court.

Decision: This case was decided on April 17, 1905, by a vote of 5 to 4 in favor of Lochner. The Supreme Court judged that the Fourteenth Amendment protected the right to sell and buy labor, and that any state law restricting that right was unconstitutional. The Court rejected the argument that the limited workday and workweek were necessary to protect the health of bakery workers.

Muller v. *Oregon,* (1908)

Significance: A landmark for cases involving social reform, this decision established the Court's recognition of social and economic conditions (in this case, women's health) as a factor in making laws.

Background: In 1903 Oregon passed a law limiting workdays to 10 hours for female workers in laundries and factories. In 1905 Curt Muller's Grand Laundry was found guilty of breaking this law. Muller appealed, claiming that the state law violated his freedom of contract (the Supreme Court had upheld a similar claim that year in *Lochner* v. *New York*). When this case came to the Court, the National Consumers' League hired lawyer Louis D. Brandeis to present Oregon's argument. Brandeis argued that the Court had already defended the state's police power to protect its citizens' health, safety, and welfare.

Decision: This case was decided on February 24, 1908, by a vote of 9 to 0 upholding the Oregon law. The Court agreed that women's well-being was in the state's public interest and that the 10-hour law was a valid way to protect their well-being.

Korematsu v. *U.S.,* (1944)

Significance: This case addressed the question of whether government action that treats a racial group differently from other people violates the Equal Protection Clause of the Fourteenth Amendment. The ruling in the case held that distinctions based on race are "inherently suspect," and that laws and rules based on race must withstand "strict scrutiny" by the courts.

Justice Stevens

Justice Breyer

Justice Thomas

Justice Kennedy

Background: When the United States declared war on Japan in 1941, about 112,000 Japanese-Americans lived on the West Coast. About 70,000 of these Japanese-Americans were citizens. In 1942, the U.S. military was afraid that these people could not be trusted in wartime. They ordered most of the Japanese-Americans to move to special camps far from their homes. Fred Korematsu, a Japanese-American and an American citizen, did not go to the camps as ordered. He stayed in California and was arrested. He was sent to a camp in Utah. Korematsu then sued, claiming that the government acted illegally when it sent people of Japanese descent to camps.

Decision: By a 6-3 margin, the Supreme Court said the orders moving the Japanese-Americans into the camps were constitutional. Justice Hugo Black wrote the opinion for the Court. He said that the unusual demands of wartime security justified the orders. However, he made it clear that distinctions based on race are "inherently suspect," and that laws based on race must withstand "strict scrutiny" by the courts. Justice Robert H. Jackson dissented; he wrote that Korematsu was "convicted of an act not commonly a crime ... being present in the state [where] he is a citizen, near where he was born, and where all his life he has lived." Justice Frank Murphy, another dissenter, said the military order was based on racial prejudice. Though the case went against the Japanese, the Court still applies the "strict scrutiny" standard today to cases involving race and other groups.

Brown v. *Board of Education,* (1954)

Significance: This ruling reversed the Supreme Court's earlier position on segregation set by *Plessy* v. *Ferguson* (1896). The decision also inspired Congress and the federal courts to help carry out further civil rights reforms for African Americans.

Background: Beginning in the 1930s, the National Association for the Advancement of Colored People (NAACP) began using the courts to challenge racial segregation in public education. In 1952 the NAACP took a number of school segregation cases to the Supreme Court. These included the Brown family's suit against the school board of Topeka, Kansas, over its "separate-but-equal" policy.

Decision: This case was decided on May 17, 1954, by a vote of 9 to 0. Chief Justice Earl Warren spoke for the unanimous Court, which ruled that segregation in public education created inequality. The Court held that racial segregation in public schools was by nature unequal, even if the school facilities were equal. The Court noted that such segregation created feelings of inferiority that could not be undone. Therefore, enforced separation of the races in public education is unconstitutional.

Engel v. *Vitale,* (1962)

Significance: The case deals with the specific issue of organized prayer in schools and the broader issue of the proper relationship between government and religion under the First Amendment. The question in the case was whether a state violates the First Amendment when it composes a prayer that students must say at the beginning of each school day. This decision was—and still is—very controversial. Many people felt it was against religion. Attempts have been made to change the Constitution to permit prayer, but none have been successful.

Background: The state of New York recommended that public schools in the state begin the day by having students recite a prayer. In fact, the state wrote the prayer for students to say. A group of parents sued to stop the official prayer, saying that it was contrary to their beliefs and their children's beliefs. They said the law was unconstitutional.

This artist's sketch shows attorney Frank Dunham in front of the Supreme Court defending his client Yaser Hamdi on April 28, 2004.

The parents argued that the state prayer amounted to "establishing" (officially supporting) religion. Though students were permitted to remain silent, the parents claimed that there would always be pressure on students to pray. New York replied that no one was forced to pray, and that it didn't involve spending any tax dollars and it didn't establish religion.

Decision: By a 6-1 margin (two justices did not take part in the case), the Court agreed with the parents. It struck down the state law. Justice Hugo Black wrote for the majority. He pointed out that the prayer was clearly religious. He said that under the First Amendment, "it is no part of the business of government to compose official prayers for any group of American people to recite as part of a religious program carried on by government." Black, referring to Jefferson and Madison, said "These men knew that the First Amendment, which tried to put an end to governmental control of religion and prayer, was not written to destroy either."

Gideon v. *Wainwright,* (1963)

Significance: This ruling was one of several key Supreme Court decisions establishing free legal help for those who cannot otherwise afford representation in court.

Background: Clarence Earl Gideon was accused of robbery in Florida. Gideon could not afford a lawyer for his trial, and the judge refused to supply him with one for free. Gideon tried to defend himself and was found guilty. He eventually appealed to the U.S. Supreme Court, claiming that the lower court's denial of a court-appointed lawyer violated his Sixth and Fourteenth Amendment rights.

Decision: This case was decided on March 18, 1963, by a vote of 9 to 0 in favor of Gideon. The Court agreed that the Sixth Amendment (which protects a citizen's right to have a lawyer for his or her defense) applied to the states because it fell under the due process clause of the Fourteenth Amendment. Thus, the states are required to provide legal aid to those defendants in criminal cases who cannot afford to pay for legal representation.

Miranda v. *Arizona,* (1966)

Significance: This decision ruled that an accused person's Fifth Amendment rights begin at the time of arrest. The ruling caused controversy because it made the questioning of suspects and collecting evidence more difficult for law enforcement officers.

Background: In 1963 Ernesto Miranda was arrested in Arizona for a kidnapping. Miranda signed a confession and was later found guilty of the crime. The arresting police officers, however, admitted that they had not told Miranda of his right to talk with an attorney before his confession. Miranda appealed his conviction on the grounds that by not informing him of his legal rights the police had violated his Fifth Amendment right against self-incrimination.

Decision: This case was decided on June 13, 1966, by a vote of 5 to 4. Chief Justice Earl Warren spoke for the Court, which ruled in Miranda's favor. The Court decided that an accused person must be given four warnings after being taken into police custody: (1) the suspect has the right to remain silent, (2) anything the suspect says can and will be used against him or her, (3) the suspect has the right to consult with an attorney and to have an attorney present during questioning, and (4) if the suspect cannot afford a lawyer, one will be provided before questioning begins.

Tinker v. *Des Moines Independent Community School District,* (1969)

Significance: This ruling established the extent to which American public school students can take part in political protests in their schools. The question the case raised is whether, under the First Amendment, can school officials prohibit students from wearing armbands to symbolize political protest?

Background: Some students in Des Moines, Iowa, decided to wear black armbands to protest the Vietnam War. Two days before the protest, the school board created a new policy. The policy stated that any student who wore an armband to school and refused to remove it would be suspended. Three students wore armbands and were suspended. They said that their First Amendment right to freedom of speech had been violated. In 1969, the United States Supreme Court decided their case.

The Decision By a 7-2 margin, the Court agreed with the students. Justice Abe Fortas wrote for the majority. He said that students do not "shed their constitutional rights to freedom of speech...at the schoolhouse gate." Fortas admitted that school officials had the right to set rules. However, their rules must be consistent with the First Amendment. In this case, Des Moines school officials thought their rule was justified. They feared that the protest would disrupt learning. Fortas's opinion held that wearing an armband symbolizing political protest was a form of speech called symbolic speech. Symbolic speech is conduct that expresses an idea. Even though the protest did not involve spoken words, called pure speech, it did express an opinion. This expression is protected the same as pure speech is. Fortas wrote that student symbolic speech could be punished, but only if it really disrupts education. Fortas also noted that school officials allowed other political symbols, such as campaign buttons, to be worn in school.

Reed v. *Reed,* (1971)

Significance: This ruling was the first in a century of Fourteenth Amendment decisions to say that gender discrimination violated the equal protection clause. This case was later used to strike down other statutes that discriminated against women.

Background: Cecil and Sally Reed were separated. When their son died without a will, the law gave preference to Cecil to be appointed the administrator of the son's estate. Sally sued Cecil for the right to administer the estate, challenging the gender preference in the law.

Decision: This case was decided on November 22, 1971, by a vote of 7 to 0. Chief Justice Warren Burger spoke for the unanimous Supreme Court. Although the Court had upheld laws based on gender preference in the past, in this case it reversed its position. The Court declared that gender discrimination violated the equal protection clause of the Fourteenth Amendment and therefore could not be the basis for a law.

Texas v. *Johnson,* (1989)

Significance: This ruling answered the question of whether the First Amendment protects burning the U.S. flag as a form of symbolic speech. It deals with the limits of symbolic speech. This case is particularly important because it involves burning the flag, one of our national symbols.

Background: At the 1984 Republican National Convention in Texas, Gregory Lee Johnson doused a U.S. flag with kerosene. He did this during a demonstration, as a form of protest. Johnson was convicted of violating a Texas law that made it a crime to desecrate [treat disrespectfully] the national flag. He was sentenced to one year in prison and fined $2,000. The Texas Court of Criminal Appeals reversed the conviction because, it said, Johnson's burning of the flag was a form of symbolic speech protected by the First Amendment. Texas then appealed to the U.S. Supreme Court.

Decision: The Court ruled for Johnson, five to four. Justice William Brennan wrote for the majority. He said that Johnson was within his constitutional rights when he burned the U.S. flag in protest. As in Tinker v. Des Moines Independent Community School District (1969), the Court looked at the First Amendment and "symbolic speech." Brennan concluded that Johnson's burning the flag was a form of symbolic speech—like the students wearing armbands in Des Moines—is protected by the First Amendment. According to Brennan, "Government may not prohibit the expression of an idea [because it is] offensive." Chief Justice Rehnquist dissented. He said the flag is "the visible symbol embodying our Nation. It does not represent the views of any particular political party, and it does not represent any particular political philosophy. The flag is not simply another 'idea' or 'point of view' competing for recognition in the marketplace of ideas." Since this decision, several amendments banning flag burning have been proposed in Congress, but so far all have failed.

Bush v. *Gore,* (2000)

Significance: In effect, the Supreme Court picked which candidate was the next President of the United States. The question before the court was whether ballots that could not be read by voting machines should be recounted by hand. The broader issues were whether the Supreme Court can overrule of state court decisions on state laws, and whether an appointed judiciary can affect the result of democratic elections.

Background: The 2000 Presidential election between Democrat Gore and Republican Bush was very close. Who would be president would be determined by votes in the state of Florida. People in Florida voted by punching a hole in a ballot card. The votes were counted by a machine that detected these holes. According to that count, Bush won the state of Florida by a few hundred votes. Florida's Election Commission declared that Bush had won Florida. However, about 60,000 ballots were not counted because the machines could not detect a hole in the ballot. Gore argued in the Florida Supreme Court that these votes should be recounted by hand. The Florida Supreme Court ordered counties to recount all those votes. Bush appealed to the United States Supreme Court, which issued an order to stop the recounts while it made a decision.

The Decision: On December 12, 2000, the Supreme Court voted 5–4 to end the hand recount of votes ordered by the Florida Supreme Court. The majority said that the Florida Supreme Court had ordered a recount without setting standards for what was a valid vote. Different vote-counters might use different standards. The Court said that this inconsistency meant that votes were treated *arbitrarily* (based on a person's choice rather than on standards). This arbitrariness, said the Court, violated the Due Process Clause and the Equal Protection Clause of the Constitution. Also, the justices said that Florida law required the vote count to be finalized by December 12. The justices said that rules for recounts could not be made by that date, so they ordered election officials to stop re-counting votes.

Gratz. v. *Bollinger and Grutter* v. *Bollinger* (2003)

Significance: These cases considered whether a university violates the Constitution by using race as a factor for admitting students to its undergraduate school and its law school. The ruling affects use of affirmative action programs in higher education. The decisions gave colleges guidelines as to what is permitted and what is not. The decisions were limited to higher education and may not apply to other affirmative action programs such as getting a job or a government contract.

Background Jennifer Gratz and Barbara Grutter are both white. They challenged the University of Michigan's affirmative action admissions policies. Gratz said that the university violated the Constitution by considering race as a factor in its *undergraduate* admissions programs. Grutter claimed that the University of Michigan Law School also did so.

Decisions In *Gratz*, the Court ruled 6-3 that the undergraduate program—which gave each minority applicant an automatic 20 points toward admission—was unconstitutional. Chief Justice Rehnquist's opinion held that the policy violated the Equal Protection Clause because it did not consider each applicant individually. "The ... automatic distribution of 20 points has the effect of making 'the factor of race ... decisive' for virtually every minimally qualified underrepresented minority applicant." It was almost an automatic preference based on the minority status of the applicant. The result was different when the Court turned to the affirmative action policy of Michigan's Law School, which used race as one factor for admission. In *Grutter*, by a 5-4 margin, the Court held that this policy did not violate the Equal Protection Clause. Justice O'Connor wrote for the majority. "Truly individualized consideration demands that race be used in a flexible, nonmechanical way.... Universities can...consider race or ethnicity...as a 'plus' factor [when individually considering] each and every applicant." Thus, the law school policy was constitutional.

United States v. *American Library Association,* (2003)

Significance: This case deals with the constitutionality of a federal law called the Children's Internet Protection Act (CIPA). The law was designed to protect children from being exposed to pornographic Web sites while using computers in public libraries. The question before the court was does a public library violate the First Amendment by installing Internet filtering software on its public computers?

Background: The law, CIPA, applies to public libraries that accept federal money to help pay for Internet access. These libraries must install filtering software to block pornographic images. Some library associations sued to block these filtering requirements. They argued that by linking money and filters, the law required public libraries to violate the First Amendment's guarantees of free speech. The libraries argued that filters block some non-pornographic sites along with pornographic ones. That, they said, violates library patrons' First Amendment rights. CIPA does allow anyone to ask a librarian to unblock a specific website. It also allows adults to ask that the filter be turned off altogether. But, the libraries argued, people using the library would find these remedies embarrassing and impractical.

Decision: In this case, Chief Justice Rehnquist authored a plurality opinion. He explained that the law does not require any library to accept federal money. A library can choose to do without federal money. If the library makes that choice, they don't have to install Internet filters. And Rehnquist didn't think that filtering software's tendency to overblock non-pornographic sites was a constitutional problem. Adult patrons could simply ask a librarian to unblock a blocked site, or they have the filter disabled entirely.

The Dissents: Justice Stevens viewed CIPA "as a blunt nationwide restraint on adult access to an enormous amount of valuable" and often constitutionally protected speech. Justice Souter noted that he would have joined the plurality if the First Amendment interests raised in this case were those of children rather than those of adults.

Hamdi v. *Rumsfeld* and *Rasul* v. *Bush,* (2004)

Significance These cases addressed the balance between the government's powers to fight terrorism and the Constitution's promise of due process. Each case raised a slightly different question:

1. Can the government hold American citizens for an indefinite period as "enemy combatants" and not permit them to access to American courts, and
2. Whether foreigners captured overseas and jailed at Guantanamo Bay, Cuba, have the right to ask American courts to decide if they are being held legally?

Background **Detaining American Citizens:** In *Hamdi* v. *Rumsfeld*, Yaser Hamdi, an American citizen, was captured in Afghanistan in 2001. The U.S. military said Hamdi was an enemy combatant and claimed that "it has the authority to hold ... enemy combatants captured on the battlefield ... to prevent them from returning to the battle." Hamdi's attorney said that Hamdi deserved the due process rights that other Americans have, including a hearing in court to argue that he was not an enemy combatant.

Detaining Foreigners at Guantanamo Bay: The prisoners in *Rasul* v. *Bush* also claimed they were wrongly imprisoned. They wanted a court hearing, but Guantanamo Bay Naval Base is on Cuban soil. Cuba leases the base to the U.S. In an earlier case, the Court had ruled that "if an alien is outside the country's sovereign territory, then ... the alien is not permitted access to the courts of the United States to enforce the Constitution."

Decisions: In *Hamdi*, the Court ruled 6-3 that Hamdi had a right to a hearing. Justice O'Connor wrote that the Court has "made clear that a state of war is not a blank check for the president when it comes to the rights of the nation's citizens." The government decided not to prosecute Hamdi. In *Rasul*, also decided 6-3, Justice Stevens wrote that the prisoners had been held for more than two years in territory that the U.S. controls. Thus, even though the prisoners are not on U.S. soil, they can ask U.S. courts if their detention is legal. The *Rasul* cases were still pending when this book was printed.

Historical Documents

Magna Carta

England's King John angered many people with high taxes. In 1215 a group of English nobles joined the archbishop of Canterbury to force the king to agree to sign Magna Carta. This document stated that the king was subject to the rule of law, just as other citizens of England were. It also presented the ideas of a fair and speedy trial and due process of law. These principles are still a part of the U.S. Bill of Rights.

1. In the first place have granted to God, and by this our present charter confirmed for us and our heirs for ever that the English church shall be free, and shall have its rights undiminished and its liberties unimpaired . . . We have also granted to all free men of our kingdom, for ourselves and our heirs for ever, all the liberties written below, to be had and held by them and their heirs of us and our heirs.
2. If any of our earls or barons or others holding of us in chief by knight service dies, and at his death his heir be of full age and owe relief he shall have his inheritance on payment of the old relief, namely the heir or heirs of an earl 100 for a whole earl's barony, the heir or heirs of a baron 100 for a whole barony, the heir or heirs of a knight 100s, at most, for a whole knight's fee; and he who owes less shall give less according to the ancient usage of fiefs.
3. If, however, the heir of any such be under age and a ward, he shall have his inheritance when he comes of age without paying relief and without making fine.

40. To no one will we sell, to no one will we refuse or delay right or justice.
41. All merchants shall be able to go out of and come into England safely and securely and stay and travel throughout England, as well by land as by water, for buying and selling by the ancient and right customs free from all evil tolls, except in time of war and if they are of the land that is at war with us . . .
42. It shall be lawful in future for anyone, without prejudicing the allegiance due to us, to leave our kingdom and return safely and securely by land and water, save, in the public interest, for a short period in time of war—except for those imprisoned or outlawed in accordance with the law of the kingdom and natives of a land that is at war with us and merchants (who shall be treated as aforesaid).

62. And we have fully remitted and pardoned to everyone all the ill–will, indignation and rancour that have arisen between us and our men, clergy and laity, from the time of the quarrel. Furthermore, we have fully remitted to all, clergy and laity, and as far as pertains to us have completely forgiven, all trespasses occasioned by the same quarrel between Easter in the sixteenth year of our reign and the restoration of peace. And, besides, we have caused to be made for them letters testimonial patent of the lord Stephen archbishop of Canterbury, of the lord Henry archbishop of Dublin and of the aforementioned bishops and of master Pandulf about this security and the aforementioned concessions.
63. An oath, moreover, has been taken, as well on our part as on the part of the barons, that all these things aforesaid shall be observed in good faith and without evil disposition. Witness the above–mentioned and many others. Given by our hand in the meadow which is called Runnymede between Windsor and Staines on the fifteenth day of June, in the seventeenth year of our reign.

From "English Bill of Rights." Britannica Online. Vers. 99.1. 1994–1999. Encyclopedia Britannica.

The Mayflower Compact

In November 1620, the Pilgrim leaders aboard the Mayflower *drafted the Mayflower Compact. This was the first document in the English colonies to establish guidelines for self-government. This excerpt from the Mayflower Compact describes the principles of the Pilgrim colony's government.*

The Mayflower Compact

We whose names are underwritten, the loyal subjects of our dread Sovereign Lord King James, by the Grace of God of Great Britain, France and Ireland, King, Defender of the Faith, etc.

Having undertaken, for the Glory of God and advancement of the Christian Faith and Honour of our King and Country, a Voyage to plant the First Colony in the Northern Parts of Virginia, do by these presents solemnly and mutually in the presence of God and one of another, Covenant and Combine ourselves together into a Civil Body Politic, for our better ordering and preservation and furtherance of the ends aforesaid; and by virtue hereof to enact, constitute and frame such just and equal Laws, Ordinances, Acts, Constitutions and Offices, from time to time, as shall be thought most meet and convenient for the general good of the Colony, unto which we promise all due submission and obedience. In witness whereof we have hereunder subscribed our names at Cape Cod, the 11th of November, in the year of the reign of our Sovereign Lord King James, of England, France and Ireland the eighteenth, and of Scotland the fifty-fourth. Anno Domini 1620.

Source: *William Bradford, Of Plymouth Plantation, 1620–1647 (Samuel Eliot Morison, ed., 1952), 75–76*

Fundamental Orders of Connecticut

In January 1639, settlers in Connecticut led by Thomas Hooker drew up the Fundamental Orders of Connecticut—America's first written Constitution. It is essentially a compact among the settlers and a body of laws.

Forasmuch as it hath pleased the All-mighty God by the wise disposition of his divyne pruvidence so to Order and dispose of things that we the Inhabitants and Residents of Windsor, Harteford and Wethersfield are now cohabiting and dwelling in and uppon the River of Conectecotte and the Lands thereunto adioyneing; As also in our Civell Affaires to be guided and governed according to such Lawes, Rules, Orders and decrees as shall be made, ordered & decreed, as followeth:—

1. It is Ordered . . . that there shall be yerely two generall Assemblies or Courts, the one the second thursday in Aprill, the other the second thursday in September, following; the first shall be called the Courte of Election, wherein shall be yerely Chosen . . . soe many Magestrats and other publike Officers as shall be found requisitte: which choise shall be made by all that are admitted freemen and have taken the Oath of Fidelity, and doe cohabitte within this Jurisdiction, (having beene admitted Inhabitants by the major part of the Towne wherein they live,) or the major parte of such as shall be then present . . .

Source: *F. N. Thorpe, ed., Federal and State Constitutions, vol.1 (1909), 519.*

The English Bill of Rights

In 1689, after the Glorious Revolution, Parliament passed the English Bill of Rights, which ensured that Parliament would have supreme power over the monarchy. The bill also protected the rights of English citizens.

By assuming and exercising a power of dispensing with and suspending of laws and the execution of laws without consent of Parliament; . . .

By levying money for and to the use of the Crown by pretence of prerogative for other time and in other manner than the same was granted by Parliament;

By raising and keeping a standing army within this kingdom in time of peace without consent of Parliament, and quartering soldiers contrary to law; . . .

And excessive bail hath been required of persons committed in criminal cases to elude the benefit of the laws made for the liberty of the subjects;

And excessive fines have been imposed;

And illegal and cruel punishments inflicted;

And several grants and promises made of fines and forfeitures before any conviction or judgment against the persons upon whom the same were to be levied;

All which are utterly and directly contrary to the known laws and statutes and freedom of this realm . . .

From "English Bill of Rights." Britannica Online. Vers. 99.1. 1994–1999. Encyclopedia Britannica. Copyright © 1994–1999 Encyclopedia Britannica, Inc.

Virginia Statute for Religious Freedom

In 1777 Thomas Jefferson wrote the Virginia Statute for Religious Freedom. Jefferson hoped that by separating church and state, Virginians could practice their religion—whatever it might be—freely.

. . . to compel a man to furnish contributions of money for the propagation of opinions which he disbelieves, is sinful and tyrannical; that even the forcing him to support this or that teacher of his own religious persuasion, is depriving him of the comfortable liberty of giving his contributions to the particular pastor . . . that our civil rights have no dependence on our religious opinions, any more than our opinions in physics or geometry; that therefore the proscribing any citizen as unworthy the public confidence by laying upon him an incapacity of being called to offices of trust and emolument, unless he profess or renounce this or that religious opinion, is depriving him injuriously of those privileges and advantages to which in common with his fellow-citizens he has a natural right . . .

Be it enacted by the General Assembly, That no man shall be compelled to frequent or support any religious worship, place, or ministry whatsoever, nor shall be enforced, restrained, molested, or burthened in his body or goods, nor shall otherwise suffer on account of his religious opinions or belief; but that all men shall be free to profess, and by argument to maintain, their opinion in matters of religion, and that the same shall in no wise diminish enlarge, or affect their civil capacities.

. . . yet we are free to declare, and do declare, that the rights hereby asserted are of the natural rights of mankind, and that if any act shall be hereafter passed to repeal the present, or to narrow its operation, such act shall be an infringement of natural right.

Source: *W.W. Hening, ed., Statutes at Large of Virginia, vol. 12 (1823): 84–86.*

Objections to This Constitution of Government

George Mason played a behind-the-scenes role in the Revolutionary War and wrote Virginia's Declaration of Rights. He attended the Constitutional Convention in 1787. Mason criticized the proposed Constitution for allowing slavery, creating a strong central government, and lacking a bill of rights. As a result, he refused to sign the Constitution. In the following excerpt, Mason explains why he would not sign the Constitution.

There is no Declaration of Rights, and the laws of the general government being paramount to the laws and constitution of the several States, the Declarations of Rights in the separate States are no security. Nor are the people secured even in the enjoyment of the benefit of the common law.

In the House of Representatives there is not the substance but the shadow only of representation . . .

The Senate have the power of altering all money bills, and of originating appropriations of money, and the salaries of the officers of their own appointment, in conjunction with the president of the United States, although they are not the representatives of the people or amenable to them. . . .

The Judiciary of the United States is so constructed and extended, as to absorb and destroy the judiciaries of the several States; thereby rendering law as tedious, intricate and expensive, and justice as unattainable, by a great part of the community, as in England, and enabling the rich to oppress and ruin the poor.

The President of the United States has no Constitutional Council, a thing unknown in any safe and regular government. He will therefore be unsupported by proper information and advice, and will generally be directed by minions and favorites; or he will become a tool to the Senate . . .

The President of the United States has the unrestrained power of granting pardons for treason, which may be sometimes exercised to screen from punishment those whom he had secretly instigated to commit the crime, and thereby prevent a discovery of his own guilt. . . .

Washington's Farewell Address

In 1796 at the end of his second term as president, George Washington wrote his farewell address with the help of Alexander Hamilton and James Madison. In it he spoke of the dangers facing the young nation. He warned against the dangers of political parties and sectionalism, and he advised the nation against permanent alliances with other nations.

In contemplating the causes, which may disturb our Union, it occurs as matter of serious concern, that any ground should have been furnished for characterizing parties by geographical discriminations-Northern and Southern-Atlantic and Western . . .

No alliances, however strict, between the parts can be an adequate substitute; they must inevitably experience the infractions and interruptions which all alliances in all times have experienced . . .

The great rule of conduct for us, in regard to foreign nations, is, in extending our commercial relations, to have with them as little political connexion as possible. So far as we have already formed engagements, let them be fulfilled with perfect good faith. Here let us stop.

From Annals of Congress, 4th Congress, pp. 2869–2880. American Memory Library of Congress. 1999. Address

Jefferson's 1801 Inaugural Address

In 1800 Thomas Jefferson, representing the Democratic-Republican Party, ran against the Federalist candidate, President John Adams. Jefferson won the election and used his inaugural address to try to bridge the gap between the new political parties and to reach out to the Federalists.

March 4, 1801

Friends and Fellow–Citizens:

Called upon to undertake the duties of the first executive office of our country, I avail myself of the presence of that portion of my fellow–citizens which is here assembled to express my grateful thanks for the favor with which they have been pleased to look toward me, to declare a sincere consciousness that the task is above my talents, and that I approach it with those anxious and awful presentiments which the greatness of the charge and the weakness of my powers so justly inspire. A rising nation, spread over a wide and fruitful land, traversing all the seas with the rich productions of their industry, engaged in commerce with nations who feel power and forget right, advancing rapidly to destinies beyond the reach of mortal eye when I contemplate these transcendent objects, and see the honor, the happiness, and the hopes of this beloved country committed to the issue, and the auspices of this day, I shrink from the contemplation, and humble myself before the magnitude of the undertaking. . . .

I repair, then, fellow–citizens, to the post you have assigned me. With experience enough in subordinate offices to have seen the difficulties of this the greatest of all, I have learnt to expect that it will rarely fall to the lot of imperfect man to retire from this station with the reputation and the favor which bring him into it. Without pretensions to that high confidence you reposed in our first and greatest revolutionary character, whose preeminent services had entitled him to the first place in his country's love and destined for him the fairest page in the volume of faithful history, I ask so much confidence only as may give firmness and effect to the legal administration of your affairs.

From Inaugural Addresses of the Presidents of the United States. 1989. Bartleby Library.

John Quincy Adams's Fourth of July 1821 Address

John Quincy Adams made the following Fourth of July speech in 1821.

And now, friends and countrymen, if the wise and learned philosophers of the elder world, the first observers of nutation and aberration, the discoverers of maddening ether and invisible planets, the inventors of Congreve rockets and Shrapnel shells, should find their hearts disposed to enquire what has America done for the benefit of mankind?

Let our answer be this: America, with the same voice which spoke herself into existence as a nation, proclaimed to mankind the inextinguishable rights of human nature, and the only lawful foundations of government.

She has abstained from interference in the concerns of others, even when conflict has been for principles to which she clings, as to the last vital drop that visits the heart. . . .

[America's] glory is not *dominion*, but *liberty*. Her march is the march of the mind. She has a spear and a shield: but the motto upon her shield is, *Freedom, Independence, Peace*. This has been her Declaration: this has been, as far as her necessary intercourse with the rest of mankind would permit, her practice.

Monroe Doctrine

In 1823 President James Monroe proclaimed the Monroe Doctrine. Designed to end European influence in the Western Hemisphere, it became a cornerstone of U.S. foreign policy.

With the existing colonies or dependencies of any European power we have not interfered and shall not interfere. But with the governments who have declared their independence and maintained it, and whose independence we have, on great consideration and on just principles, acknowledged, we could not view any interposition for the purpose of oppressing them, or controlling in any other manner their destiny, by any European power in any other light than as the manifestation of an unfriendly disposition toward the United States. . . .

Our policy in regard to Europe, which was adopted at an early stage of the wars which have so long agitated that quarter of the globe, nevertheless remains the same, which is not to interfere in the internal concerns of any of its powers; to consider the government de facto as the legitimate government for us; to cultivate friendly relations with it, and to preserve those relations by a frank, firm, and manly policy, meeting in all instances the just claims of every power, submitting to injuries from none.

Seneca Falls Declaration of Sentiments

One of the first documents to express the desire for equal rights for women is the Declaration of Sentiments, issued in 1848 at the Seneca Falls Convention in Seneca Falls, New York. Led by Elizabeth Cady Stanton and Lucretia Mott, the delegates adopted a set of resolutions modeled on the Declaration of Independence.

When, in the course of human events, it becomes necessary for one portion of the family of man to assume among the people of the earth a position different from that which they have hitherto occupied, but one to which the laws of nature and of nature's God entitle them, a decent respect to the opinions of mankind requires that they should declare the causes that impel them to such a course.

We hold these truths to be self–evident: that all men and women are created equal; that they are endowed by their Creator with certain inalienable rights; that among these are life, liberty, and the pursuit of happiness; that to secure these rights governments are instituted, deriving their just powers from the consent of the governed. Whenever any form of government becomes destructive of these ends, it is the right of those who suffer from it to refuse allegiance to it, and to insist upon the institution of a new government, laying its foundation on such principles, and organizing its powers in such form, as to them shall seem most likely to effect their safety and happiness.

Denmark Vesey Document

Some enslaved African Americans struck back against the slave system in the South by using violence. Denmark Vesey, a free African American, planned a revolt in 1822. He was betrayed before the revolt began, and he and other people were executed. Included below is an excerpt from A Narrative of the Conspiracy and Intended Insurrection *by Denmark Vesey.*

Excerpts from A NARRATIVE OF THE Conspiracy and Intended Insurrection, AMONGST A PORTION OF THE Negroes in the State of South-Carolina, *In the Year 1822.*

At the head of this conspiracy stood Denmark Vesey, a free negro; with him the idea undoubtedly originated. For several years before he disclosed his intentions to any one, he appears to have been constantly and assiduously engaged in endeavoring to embitter the minds of the colored population against the white. He rendered himself perfectly familiar with all those parts of the Scriptures, which he thought he could pervert to his purpose; and would readily quote them, to prove that slavery was contrary to the laws of God; that slaves were bound to attempt their emancipation, however shocking and bloody might be the consequences, and that such efforts would not only be pleasing to the Almighty, but were absolutely enjoined, and their success predicted in the Scriptures. . . .

In the selection of his leaders, Vesey shewed great penetration and sound judgment. Rolla was plausible, and possessed uncommon self-possession; bold and ardent, he was not to be deterred from his purpose by danger. Ned's appearance indicated, that he was a man of firm nerves, and desperate courage. Peter was intrepid and resolute, true to his engagements, and cautious in observing secrecy where it was necessary; he was not to be daunted nor impeded by difficulties, and though confident of success, was careful in providing against any obstacles or casualties which might arise, and intent upon discovering every means which might be in their power if thought of before hand. Gullah Jack was regarded as a Sorcerer, and as such feared by the natives of Africa, who believe in witchcraft. He was not only considered invulnerable, but that he could make others so by his charms; and that he could and certainly would provide all his followers with arms. He was artful, cruel, bloody; his disposition in short was diabolical. His influence amongst the Africans was inconceiveable. Monday was firm, resolute, discreet and intelligent. . . .

As Vesey, from whom all orders emanated, and perhaps to whom only all important information was conveyed, died without confessing any thing, any opinion formed as to the numbers actually engaged in the plot, must be altogether conjectural; but enough has been disclosed to satisfy every reasonable mind, that considerable numbers were concerned. Indeed the plan of attack, which embraced so many points to be assailed at the same instant, affords sufficient evidence of the fact.

Lincoln's First Inaugural Address

After his election as president of the United States in 1860, Abraham Lincoln pledged that there would be no war unless the South started it. He discusses the disagreements that led to the nation's greatest crisis in the excerpt below from his first inaugural address.

March 4, 1861

Fellow–Citizens of the United States:

In compliance with a custom as old as the Government itself, I appear before you to address you briefly and to take in your presence the oath prescribed by the Constitution of the United States to be taken by the President "before he enters on the execution of this office." . . .

I have no purpose, directly or indirectly, to interfere with the institution of slavery in the States where it exists. I believe I have no lawful right to do so, and I have no inclination to do so.

Those who nominated and elected me did so with full knowledge that I had made this and many similar declarations and had never recanted them; and more than this, they placed in the platform for my acceptance, and as a law to themselves and to me, the clear and emphatic resolution which I now read:

. . . In any law upon this subject ought not all the safeguards of liberty known in civilized and humane jurisprudence to be introduced, so that a free man be not in any case surrendered as a slave? And might it not be well at the same time to provide by law for the enforcement of that clause in the Constitution which guarantees that "the citizens of each State shall be entitled to all privileges and immunities of citizens in the several States?" . . .

It follows from these views that no State upon its own mere motion can lawfully get out of the Union; that resolves and ordinances to that effect are legally void, and that acts of violence within any State or States against the authority of the United States are insurrectionary or revolutionary, according to circumstances.

I therefore consider that in view of the Constitution and the laws the Union is unbroken, and to the extent of my ability, I shall take care, as the Constitution itself expressly enjoins upon me, that the laws of the Union be faithfully executed in all the States. . . .

One section of our country believes slavery is right and ought to be extended, while the other believes it is wrong and ought not to be extended. This is the only substantial dispute.

Physically speaking, we can not separate. We can not remove our respective sections from each other nor build an impassable wall between them. A husband and wife may be divorced and go out of the presence and beyond the reach of each other, but the different parts of our country can not do this.

This country, with its institutions, belongs to the people who inhabit it. Whenever they shall grow weary of the existing Government, they can exercise their constitutional right of amending it or their revolutionary right to dismember or overthrow it. . . .

In your hands, my dissatisfied fellow–countrymen, and not in mine, is the momentous issue of civil war. The Government will not assail you. You can have no conflict without being yourselves the aggressors. You have no oath registered in heaven to destroy the Government, while I shall have the most solemn one to "preserve, protect, and defend it."

I am loath to close. We are not enemies, but friends. We must not be enemies. Though passion may have strained it must not break our bonds of affection. The mystic chords of memory, stretching from every battlefield and patriot grave to every living heart and hearthstone all over this broad land, will yet swell the chorus of the Union, when again touched, as surely they will be, by the better angels of our nature.

From Inaugural Addresses of the Presidents of the United States. 1989. Bartleby Library.

The Emancipation Proclamation

When the Union army won the Battle of Antietam, President Abraham Lincoln decided to issue the Emancipation Proclamation, which freed all enslaved people in states under Confederate control. The proclamation, which went into effect on January 1, 1863, was a step toward the Thirteenth Amendment (1865), which ended slavery in all of the United States.

That on the 1st day of January, in the year of our Lord 1863, all persons held as slaves within any state or designated part of a state, the people whereof shall then be in rebellion against the United States, shall be then, thenceforward, and forever free; and the executive government of the United States, including the military and naval authority thereof, will recognize and maintain the freedom of such persons and will do no act or acts to repress such persons, or any of them, in any efforts they may make for their actual freedom. . . .

And I further declare and make known that such persons of suitable condition will be received into the armed service of the United States to garrison forts, positions, stations, and other places, and to man vessels of all sorts in said service.

And upon this act, sincerely believed to be an act of justice, warranted by the Constitution upon military necessity, I invoke the considerate judgment of mankind and the gracious favor of Almighty God.

Lincoln's Gettysburg Address

On November 19, 1863, Abraham Lincoln addressed a crowd gathered to dedicate a cemetery at the Gettysburg battlefield. His short speech, which is excerpted below, reminded Americans of the ideals on which the Republic was founded.

FOUR SCORE AND SEVEN YEARS ago our fathers brought forth on this continent a new nation, conceived in liberty and dedicated to the proposition that all men are created equal.

Now we are engaged in a great civil war, testing whether that nation or any nation so conceived and so dedicated can long endure. We are met on a great battlefield of that war. We have come to dedicate a portion of that field as a final resting–place for those who here gave their lives that that nation might live. It is altogether fitting and proper that we should do this.

But in a larger sense, we cannot dedicate—we cannot consecrate—we cannot hallow—this ground. The brave men, living and dead, who struggled here have consecrated it far above our poor power to add or detract. The world will little note nor long remember what we say here, but it can never forget what they did here. It is for us, the living, rather, to be dedicated here to the unfinished work which they who fought here have thus far so nobly advanced.

It is rather for us to be here dedicated to the great task remaining before us—that from these honored dead we take increased devotion to that cause for which they gave the last full measure of devotion; that we here highly resolve that these dead shall not have died in vain; that this nation, under God, shall have a new birth of freedom; and that government of the people, by the people, for the people shall not perish from the earth.

Lincoln's Second Inaugural Address

On March 4, 1865, President Lincoln laid out his approach to Reconstruction in his second inaugural address. As the excerpt below shows, Lincoln hoped to peacefully reunite the nation and its people.

At this second appearing to take the oath of the Presidential office there is less occasion for an extended address than there was at the first. Then a statement somewhat in detail of a course to be pursued seemed fitting and proper. Now, at the expiration of four years, during which public declarations have been constantly called forth on every point and phase of the great contest which still absorbs the attention and engrosses the energies of the nation, little that is new could be presented. The progress of our arms, upon which all else chiefly depends, is as well known to the public as to myself, and it is, I trust, reasonably satisfactory and encouraging to all. With high hope for the future, no prediction in regard to it is ventured.

On the occasion corresponding to this four years ago all thoughts were anxiously directed to an impending civil war. All dreaded it, all sought to avert it. While the inaugural address was being delivered from this place, devoted altogether to saving the Union without war, urgent agents were in the city seeking to destroy it without war—seeking to dissolve the Union and divide effects by negotiation. Both parties deprecated war, but one of them would make war rather than let the nation survive, and the other would accept war rather than let it perish, and the war came. . . .

With malice toward none, with charity for all, with firmness in the right as God gives us to see the right, let us strive on to finish the work we are in, to bind up the nation's wounds, to care for him who shall have borne the battle and for his widow and his orphan, to do all which may achieve and cherish a just and lasting peace among ourselves and with all nations.

From Inaugural Addresses of the Presidents of the United States. 1989. Bartleby Library.

Declaration of the Rights of Women

Included below are excerpts from a speech made on July 4, 1876, by Susan B. Anthony in support of rights for women.

Susan B. Anthony, July 4, 1876

While the nation is buoyant with patriotism, and all hearts are attuned to praise, it is with sorrow we come to strike the one discordant note, on this one-hundredth anniversary of our country's birth. When subjects of kings, emperors, and czars from the old world join in our national jubilee, shall the women of the republic refuse to lay their hands with benedictions on the nation's head? . . . Yet we cannot forget, even in this glad hour, that while all men of every race, and clime, and condition, have been invested with the full rights of citizenship under our hospitable flag, all women still suffer the degradation of disfranchisement.

The history of our country the past one hundred years has been a series of assumptions and usurpations of power over woman, in direct opposition to the principles of just government, acknowledged by the United States as its foundations, which are:

First - the natural rights of each individual
Second - the equality of these rights
Third - that rights not delegated are retained by the individual
Fourth - that no person can exercise the rights of others without delegated authority
Fifth - that the non-use of rights does not destroy them

And for the violation of these fundamental principles of our government, we arraign our rulers on this Fourth day of July, 1876 . . .

These articles of impeachment against our rulers we now submit to the impartial judgment of the people. To all these wrongs and oppressions woman has not submitted in silence and resignation. From the beginning of the century, when Abigail Adams, the wife of one president and the mother of another, said, "We will not hold ourselves bound to obey laws in which we have no voice or representation," until now, woman's discontent has been steadily increasing, culminating nearly thirty years ago in a simultaneous movement among the women of the nation, demanding the right of suffrage. . . .

And now, at the close of a hundred years, as the hour hand of the great clock that marks the centuries points to 1876, we declare our faith in the principles of self-government; our full equality with man in natural rights . . . We ask of our rulers, at this hour, no special favors, no special privileges, no special legislation. We ask justice, we ask equality, we ask that all the civil and political rights that belong to citizens of the United States, be guaranteed to us and our daughters forever.

President Bush's Address to the Nation

On September 11, 2001, two passenger airplanes crashed into the World Trade Center in New York City. Terrorist hijackers had seized control of the planes and deliberately flown them into the buildings. Excerpts from President Bush's message to the nation in response to this terrorist attack follows.

THE PRESIDENT: Good evening. Today, our fellow citizens, our way of life, our very freedom came under attack in a series of deliberate and deadly terrorist acts. The victims were in airplanes, or in their offices; secretaries, businessmen and women, military and federal workers; moms and dads, friends and neighbors. Thousands of lives were suddenly ended by evil, despicable acts of terror.

The pictures of airplanes flying into buildings, fires burning, huge structures collapsing, have filled us with disbelief, terrible sadness, and a quiet, unyielding anger. These acts of mass murder were intended to frighten our nation into chaos and retreat. But they have failed; our country is strong.

A great people has been moved to defend a great nation. Terrorist attacks can shake the foundations of our biggest buildings, but they cannot touch the foundation of America. These acts shattered steel, but they cannot dent the steel of American resolve.

America was targeted for attack because we're the brightest beacon for freedom and opportunity in the world. And no one will keep that light from shining.

Today, our nation saw evil, the very worst of human nature. And we responded with the best of America—with the daring of our rescue workers, with the caring for strangers and neighbors who came to give blood and help in any way they could.

Immediately following the first attack, I implemented our government's emergency response plans. Our military is powerful, and it's prepared. Our emergency teams are working in New York City and Washington, D.C. to help with local rescue efforts.

Our first priority is to get help to those who have been injured, and to take every precaution to protect our citizens at home and around the world from further attacks.

The functions of our government continue without interruption. Federal agencies in Washington which had to be evacuated today are reopening for essential personnel tonight, and will be open for business tomorrow. Our financial institutions remain strong, and the American economy will be open for business, as well.

The search is underway for those who are behind these evil acts. I've directed the full resources of our intelligence and law enforcement communities to find those responsible and to bring them to justice. We will make no distinction between the terrorists who committed these acts and those who harbor them.

I appreciate so very much the members of Congress who have joined me in strongly condemning these attacks. And on behalf of the American people, I thank the many world leaders who have called to offer their condolences and assistance.

America and our friends and allies join with all those who want peace and security in the world, and we stand together to win the war against terrorism. Tonight, I ask for your prayers for all those who grieve, for the children whose worlds have been shattered, for all whose sense of safety and security has been threatened. And I pray they will be comforted by a power greater than any of us, spoken through the ages in Psalm 23: "Even though I walk through the valley of the shadow of death, I fear no evil, for You are with me."

This is a day when all Americans from every walk of life unite in our resolve for justice and peace. America has stood down enemies before, and we will do so this time. None of us will ever forget this day. Yet, we go forward to defend freedom and all that is good and just in our world.

Thank you. Good night, and God bless America.

END 8:35 P.M. EDT

Biographical Dictionary

A

Adams, John (1735–1826) American statesman, he was a delegate to the Continental Congress, a member of the committee that drafted the Declaration of Independence, vice president to George Washington, and was the second president of the United States. (p. 228)

Adams, John Quincy (1767–1848) Son of President John Adams and the secretary of state to James Monroe, he largely formulated the Monroe Doctrine. He was the sixth president of the United States and later became a representative in Congress. (p. 267)

Adams, Samuel (1722–1803) American revolutionary who led the agitation that led to the Boston Tea Party; he signed the Declaration of Independence. (p. 63)

Addams, Jane (1860–1935) American social worker and activist, she was the co-founder of Hull House, an organization that focused on the needs of immigrants. She helped found the American Civil Liberties Union and won the Nobel Peace Prize in 1931. (p. 597)

Aguinaldo (ahg-ee-NAHL-doh), **Emilio** (1869–1964) Filipino leader and commander of forces in rebellion against Spain, he led an insurrection against the authority of the United States. (p. 648)

Alcott, Louisa May (1832–1888) American novelist, her revised letters written as a Civil War nurse were published as *Hospital Sketches*. She is famed for the novel, *Little Women,* and its sequels. (p. 409)

Anthony, Susan B. (1820–1906) American social reformer, she was active in the temperance, abolitionist, and women's suffrage movements and was co-organizer and president of the National Woman Suffrage Association. (p. 427)

Arkwright, Richard (1732–1792) English inventor, he patented the water-powered spinning frame, improving the production of cotton thread. (p. 347)

Arthur, Chester A. (1829–1886) Vice-president of the United States in 1880, he became the twenty-first president of the United States upon the death of James Garfield. (p. 607)

Astor, John Jacob (1763–1848) American fur trader and financier, he founded the fur-trading post of Astoria and the American Fur Company. (p. 308)

Austin, Stephen F. (1793–1836) American colonizer in Texas, he was imprisoned for urging Texas statehood after Santa Anna suspended Mexico's constitution. After helping Texas win independence from Mexico, he became secretary of state for the Texas Republic. (p. 313)

B

Bagley, Sarah G. (d. 1847?) American mill worker and union activist, she advocated the 10-hour workday for private industry. She was elected vice president of the New England Working Men's Association, becoming the first woman to hold such high rank in the American labor movement. (p. 357)

Banneker, Benjamin (1731–1806) African American mathematician and astronomer, he was hired by Thomas Jefferson to help survey land for the new capital in Washington, D.C. (p. 202)

Barton, Clara (1821–1912) Founder of the American Red Cross, she obtained and administered supplies and care to the Union soldiers during the American Civil War. (p. 496)

Beecher, Catharine (1800–1878) American educator and the daughter of Lyman Beecher, she promoted education for women in such writings as *An Essay on the Education of Female Teachers*. She founded the first all-female academy. (p. 413)

Beecher, Lyman (1775–1863) American clergyman, he disapproved of the style of preaching of the Great Awakening ministers. He served as president of the Lane Theological Seminary and supported female higher education. (p. 411)

Bell, Alexander Graham (1847–1922) American inventor and educator, his interest in electrical and mechanical devices to aid the hearing-impaired led to the development and patent of the telephone. (p. 577)

Bidwell, Annie (1839–1918) American pioneer activist, she worked for social and moral causes and for women's suffrage. (p. 562)

Black Hawk (1767–1838) Native American leader of Fox and Sauk Indians, he resisted the U.S.-ordered removal of Indian nations from Illinois and raided settlements and fought the U.S. Army. (p. 297)

Bolívar, Simon (1783–1830) South American revolutionary leader who was nicknamed the Liberator, he fought many battles for independence, winning the support of many U.S. leaders. (p. 262)

Brandeis, Louis (1856–1941) Progressive lawyer and jurist, he was the first Jewish nominee to the Supreme Court and was appointed Associate Justice. (p. 629)

Brooks, Preston (1819–1857) American congressman, he assaulted and beat Senator Charles Sumner for his antislavery speeches and for insulting a pro-slavery relative. He was nicknamed Bully Brooks by northerners. (p. 449)

Brown, John (1800–1859) American abolitionist, he started the Pottawatomie Massacre in Kansas to revenge killings of abolitionists; he later seized the federal arsenal at Harpers Ferry, Virginia, to encourage a slave revolt. He was later tried and executed. (p. 455)

Bryan, William Jennings (1860–1925) American lawyer and Populist politician, he favored free silver coinage, an economic policy expected to help farmers. He was a Democratic nominee for president in 1896 and was defeated by William McKinley. (p. 564)

Buchanan, James (1791–1868) American politician and fifteenth president of the United States, he was chosen as the Democratic nominee for president in 1854 for being politically experienced and not offensive to slave states. (p. 450)

Bunau-Varilla, Philippe (1859–1940) French engineer, he served as minister from Panama to the United States and negotiated a treaty for U.S. control of the Panama Canal Zone. (p. 653)

Burns, Anthony (1834–1862) American enslaved African, he ran away and was arrested in Boston. His arrest became the center of violent protests by northern opponents of the Fugitive Slave Act. (p. 442)

C

Calhoun, John C. (1782–1850) American politician and supporter of slavery and states' rights, he served as vice president to Andrew Jackson and was instrumental in the South Carolina nullification crisis. (p. 285)

Carnegie, Andrew (1835–1919) American industrialist and humanitarian, he focused his attention on steelmaking and made a fortune through his vertical integration method. (pp. 580, 583)

Carranza, Venustiano (1859–1920) Mexican revolutionist, he led revolts against Huerta and became president of Mexico. He adopted programs of social and economic reform, but he faced revolts from other revolutionists. (p. 661)

Catt, Carrie Chapman (1859–1947) American educator and reformer, she led a successful fight to obtain suffrage for women and to secure the passage of the Nineteenth Amendment. (p. 621)

Chief Joseph (c.1840–1904) Chief of Nez Percé tribe, he led a resistance against white settlement in the Northwest. He eventually surrendered, but his eloquent surrender speech earned him a place in American history. (p. 559)

Clark, George Rogers (1752–1818) American Revolutionary soldier and frontier leader, he captured the British trading village of Kaskaskia during the Revolution and encouraged Indian leaders to remain neutral. (p. 95)

Clark, William (1770–1838) American soldier and friend of Meriwether Lewis, he was invited to explore the Louisiana Purchase and joined what became known as the Lewis and Clark expedition. (p. 236)

Clay, Henry (1777–1852) American politician from Kentucky, he was known as the Great Pacificator because of his support of the Missouri Compromise. He developed the Compromise of 1850 to try to avoid civil war. (pp. 264, 266)

Cleveland, Grover (1837–1908) Twenty-second and twenty-forth president of the United States, he promoted civil service reform and a merit system of advancement for government jobs. (p. 608)

Cole, Thomas (1801–1848) American painter, he was the founder of the Hudson River school, a group of artists who emphasized the beauty of the American landscape, especially the Hudson River valley. (p. 272)

Columbus, Christopher (1451–1506) Italian explorer, he was convinced that he could reach Asia by sailing westward across the Atlantic Ocean. He gained the support of Spain's monarchs and commanded a small fleet that reached the so-called New World, setting off a tide of European exploration of the area. (pp. 15, 17)

Cooper, James Fenimore (1789–1851) Well-known Early American novelist, he wrote the *Last of* *the Mohicans* and many stories about the West. (p. 271)

Cooper, Peter (1791–1883) American ironworks manufacturer who designed and built *Tom Thumb,* the first American locomotive. (p. 360)

Cortés, Hernán (1485–1547) Spanish conquistador, he conquered Mexico and brought about the fall of the Aztec Empire. (p. 20)

Crazy Horse (1842?–1877) Native American chief of Oglala Sioux, he took part in the Battle of the Little Bighorn, in which General Custer was surrounded and killed. He was killed after surrendering and resisting imprisonment. (p. 555)

Crittenden, John J. (1787–1863) Kentucky senator, he attempted to save the Union by reconciling differences between northern and southern states in the Senate proposal known as Crittenden's Compromise. (p. 459)

Custer, George Armstrong (1839–1876) American army officer in the Civil War, he became a Native American fighter in the West and was killed with his troops in the Battle of the Little Bighorn. (p. 556)

D

Davis, Jefferson (1808–1889) First and only president of the Confederate States of America after the election of President Abraham Lincoln in 1860 led to the secession of many southern states. (p. 458)

Deere, John (1804–1886) American industrialist; he developed a steel plow to ease difficulty of turning thick soil on the Great Plains. (p. 366)

Dewey, John (1859–1952) American educator, psychologist, and philosopher, he developed teaching methods that emphasized problem-solving skills over memorization and that became the model for progressive public education. (p. 612)

Díaz, Porfirio (1830–1915) Mexican general and politician, he was president and dictator of Mexico for a total of 30 years. He ruled the people of Mexico harshly but encouraged foreign investment. (p. 659)

Dickinson, Emily (1830–1886) American poet, she lived a reclusive life, and her poems were not widely acclaimed until after her death. (p. 407)

Dix, Dorothea (1802–1887) American philanthropist and social reformer, she helped change the prison system nationwide by advocating the development of state hospitals for treatment for the mentally ill instead of imprisonment. (p. 412)

Douglas, Stephen (1813–1861) American politician and pro-slavery nominee for president, he debated Abraham Lincoln about slavery during the Illinois senatorial race. He proposed the unpopular Kansas-Nebraska Act, and he established the Freeport Doctrine, upholding the idea of popular sovereignty. (p. 446)

Douglass, Frederick (1817–1895) American abolitionist and writer, he escaped slavery and became a leading African American spokesman and writer. He published his biography, *The Narrative of the Life of Frederick Douglass,* and founded the abolitionist newspaper, the *North Star.* (pp. 418, 422)

Du Bois, W. E. B. (1868–1963) African American educator, editor, and writer, he led the Niagara Movement, calling for economic and educational equality for African Americans. He helped found the National Association for the Advancement of Colored People (NAACP). (p. 622)

Frederick Douglass

E

Edison, Thomas Alva (1847–1931) American inventor of over 1,000 patents, he invented the lightbulb and established a power plant that supplied electricity to parts of New York City. (p. 576)

Edwards, Jonathan (1703–1758) Important and influential revivalist leader in the Great Awakening religious movement, he delivered dramatic sermons on the choice between salvation and damnation. (p. 58)

Emerson, Ralph Waldo (1803–1882) American essayist and poet, he was a supporter of the transcendentalist philosophy of self-reliance. (p. 405)

Equiano, Olaudah (c.1750–1797) African American abolitionist, he was an enslaved African who was eventually freed and became a leader of the abolitionist meovement and writer of *The Interesting Narrative of the Life of Olaudah Equiano.* (pp. 41, 57)

F

Farragut, David (1801–1870) American soldier, he was the first commissioned American admiral, and in the Civil War he captured New Orleans and maintained a blockade along the Gulf Coast against Confederate forces. (pp. 485, 487)

Finney, Charles Grandison (1792–1875) American clergyman and educator, he became influential in the Second Great Awakening after a dramatic religious experience and conversion. He led long revivals that annoyed conventional ministers. (p. 410)

Franklin, Benjamin (1706–1790) American statesman, he was a philosopher, scientist, inventor, writer, publisher, first U.S. postmaster, and member of the committee to draft the Constitution. He invented bifocals and the lightning rod and wrote *Poor Richard's Almanack.* (p. 131)

Frémont, John C. (1813–1890) American explorer, army officer, and politician, he was chosen as the first Republican candidate for president. He was against the spread of slavery, and he was rejected by all but the free states as a "single issue" candidate in the election of 1856. (p. 451)

Fulton, Robert (1765–1815) American engineer and inventor, he built the first commercially successful full-sized steamboat, the *Clermont,* which lead to the development of commercial steamboat ferry services for goods and people. (p. 359)

G

Gallaudet, Thomas (1787–1851) American educator, he studied techniques for instructing hearing-impaired people and established the first American school for the hearing impaired. (p. 413)

Gálvez, Bernardo de (1746–1786) Governor of Spanish Louisiana, he captured key cities from the British, greatly aiding the American Patriot movement and enabling the Spanish acquisition of Florida. (p. 95)

Garfield, James A. (1831–1881) Twentieth president of the United States, he was elected in 1880 but was assassinated only months after inauguration. (p. 607)

Garrison, William Lloyd (1805–1879) American journalist and reformer; he published the famous antislavery newspaper, the *Liberator,* and helped found the American Anti–Slavery Society, promoting immediate emancipation and racial equality. (p. 417)

Geronimo (1829–1909) Chiricahua Apache leader, he evaded capture for years and led an extraordinary opposition struggle against white settlements in the American Southwest until his eventual surrender. (p. 557)

Gompers, Samuel (1850–1924) American labor leader, he helped found the American Federation of Labor to campaign for workers' rights, such as the right to organize boycotts. (p. 585)

Grant, Ulysses S. (1822–1885) Eighteenth president of the United States, he received a field promotion to lieutenant general in charge of all Union forces after leading a successful battle. He accepted General Lee's surrender of Confederate forces at Appomattox Courthouse, ending the Civil War. (pp. 484, 489)

Grimké, Angelina (1805–1879) and **Sarah** (1792–1873) American sisters and reformers, they were the daughters of a slaveholding family from South Carolina who became antislavery supporters and lecturers for the American Anti-Slavery Society. They also took up the women's rights campaign. (p. 417)

H

Hamilton, Alexander (1755–1804) American statesman and member of the Continental Congress and the Constitutional Convention, he was an author of the *Federalist Papers,* which supported ratification of the Constitution. He was the first secretary of treasury under George Washington and developed the Bank of the United States. (p. 200)

Harrison, Benjamin (1833–1901) Twenty-third president of the United States, he was a general in the Civil War and helped pass the Sherman Antitrust Act, regulating monopolies. (p. 608)

Harrison, William Henry (1773–1841) American politician, he served as the governor of Indian Territory and fought Tecumseh in the Battle of Tippecanoe. He was the ninth president of the United States. (p. 293)

Hawthorne, Nathaniel (1804–1864) American writer, he is famous for his many stories and books, including *The Scarlet Letter,* and he is recognized as one of the first authors to write in a unique American style. (p. 406)

Hay, John (1838–1905) American diplomat, he was secretary of state in the Roosevelt administration, and he negotiated treaties providing for the United States' construction of the Panama Canal and put forth the Open Door policy with regard to China. (p. 653)

Hayes, Rutherford B. (1822–1893) Nineteenth president of the United States, he was a Civil War general and hero and, in the disputed presidential election of 1876, he was chosen president by a special electoral committee. (p. 607)

Hearst, William Randolph (1863–1951) American journalist, he was famed for sensational news stories, known as yellow journalism, that stirred feelings of nationalism and formed public opinion for the Spanish-American War. (p. 619)

Hidalgo y Costilla, Father Miguel (1753–1811) Mexican priest and revolutionist, he led a rebellion of about 80,000 impoverished Indians and *mestizos* against Spain in the hope of improving living conditions; though defeated, the rebellion eventually grew and helped lead to Mexican independence. (p. 312)

Huerta, Victoriano (1854–1916) Mexican general and politician, he overthrew Madero as Mexican president and faced revolts with many revolutionary leaders. His government was not recognized by the United States. (p. 661)

Hutchinson, Anne (1591–1643) Puritan leader who angered other Puritans by claiming that people's relationship to God did not need guidance from ministers; she was tried and convicted of undermining church authorities and was banished from Massachusetts colony; she later established the colony of Portsmouth in present-day Rhode Island. (pp. 46, 47)

I

Irving, Washington (1783–1859) Early American satirical writer, he was the first American writer to gain international acclaim. His works include *Rip Van Winkle* and *The Legend of Sleepy Hollow.* He often used American history and authentic American settings and characters. (p. 270)

J

Jackson, Andrew (1767–1845) Nicknamed Old Hickory, he was an American hero in the Battle of New Orleans. As commander of the Tennessee militia, he defeated the Creek Indians, securing 23 million acres of land. His election as the seventh president of the United States marked an era of democracy called Jeffersonian Democracy. (pp. 248, 287)

Jackson, Thomas "Stonewall" (1824–1863) American Confederate general, he led the Shenandoah Valley campaign and fought with Lee in the Seven Days' Battles and the First and Second Battles of Bull Run. (p. 478)

Jay, John (1745–1829) American statesman and member of the Continental Congress, he authored some of the *Federalist Papers* and negotiated Jay's Treaty with Great Britain to settle outstanding disputes. (p. 209)

Jefferson, Thomas (1743–1826) American statesman, and member of two Continental Congresses, chairman of the committee to draft the Declaration of Independence, the Declaration's main author and one of its signers, and the third president of the United States. (pp. 84, 233)

Johnson, Andrew (1808–1875) American politician and the seventeenth president of the United States upon the assassination of Lincoln, he was impeached for his unpopular ideas about Reconstruction. He held onto the office by a one-vote margin. (p. 517)

Jones, John Paul (1747–1792) American naval officer famed for bravery, his most famous victory was the defeat of the British warship *Serapis,* during which he declared, "I have not yet begun to fight!" (p. 97)

Jones, Mary Harris (1830–1930) Irish immigrant and American labor leader, she was known as Mother Jones and was a key speaker and organizer. She helped found the Industrial Workers of the World. (p. 586)

K

Kelley, Florence (1859–1932) American reformer, she was active in the settlement house movement and led progressive reforms in labor conditions for women and children. (p. 616)

L

Lafayette, Marquis de (1757–1834) French statesman and officer who viewed the American Revolution as important to the world, he helped finance the Revolution and served as major general. (p. 95)

La Follette, Robert M. (1855–1925) Progressive American politician, he was active in local Wisconsin issues and challenged party bosses. As governor, he began the reform program called the Wisconsin Idea to make state government more professional. (p. 614)

Las Casas, Bartolomé de (1474–1566) Spanish missionary and historian, he became the first ordained Catholic priest in the New World and advocated for the welfare and protection of Native Americans as well as preached against the slavery system. (p. 23)

Lee, Robert E. (1807–1870) American soldier, he refused Lincoln's offer to head the Union Army and agreed to lead Confederate forces. He successfully led several major battles until his defeat at Gettysburg, and he surrendered to the Union's commander General Grant at Appomattox Courthouse. (pp. 480, 481)

Lewis, Meriwether (1774–1809) Former army captain selected by President Jefferson to explore the Louisiana Purchase, he lead the expedition that became known as the Lewis and Clark expedition. (p. 236)

Liliuokalani (li-lee-uh-woh-kuh-LAHN-ee) (1838–1917) Queen of the Hawaiian Islands, she opposed annexation by the United States but lost power in a U.S.-supported revolt by planters that led to a new government. (p. 642)

Lincoln, Abraham (1809–1865) Sixteenth president of the United States, he promoted equal rights for African Americans in the famed Lincoln-Douglas debates. He issued the Emancipation Proclamation and set in motion the Civil War, but he was determined to preserve the Union. He was assassinated in 1865. (pp. 452, 477)

Little Turtle (c. 1752–1812) Miami chief who led a Native American alliance that raided settlements in the Northwest Territory, he was defeated and forced to sign the Treaty of Greenville, and he later became an advocate for peace. (p. 208)

Longfellow, Henry Wadsworth (1807–1882) American poet in the mid-nineteenth century, he is best known for his story-poems, such as "Paul Revere's Ride" in *Tales of a Wayside Inn* and *The Song of Hiawatha.* (p. 407)

Lowell, Francis Cabot (1775–1817) American industrialist who developed the Lowell system, a mill system that included looms that could both weave thread and spin cloth. He hired young women to live and work in his mill. (p. 354)

M

McClellan, George B. (1826–1885) American army general put in charge of Union troops and later removed by Lincoln for failure to press Lee's Confederate troops in Richmond. (p. 480)

McCormick, Cyrus (1809–1884) American inventor and industrialist, he invented the mechanical reaper and harvesting machine that quickly cut down wheat. (p. 366)

McKinley, William (1843–1901) Twenty-fifth president of the United States, he enacted protective tariffs in the McKinley Tariff Act of 1890 and acquired Cuba, Puerto Rico, Guam, and the Philippines during his administration. He was later assassinated. (p. 608)

Madero, Francisco (1873–1913) Mexican revolutionary leader, he called for the restoration of the Mexican constitution and planned an overthrow of Díaz. He became president of Mexico but was overthrown by Victoriano Huerta. (p. 660)

Madison, James (1751–1836) American statesman, he was a delegate to the Constitutional Convention, the fourth president of the United States, the author of some of the *Federalist Papers,* and is called the father of the Constitution for his proposals at the Constitutional Convention. He led the United States through the War of 1812. (pp. 126, 149)

Magellan (muh–jel–uhn), **Ferdinand** (1480–1521) Portuguese captain of a Spanish fleet that sought a western route to Asia via the "Southern Ocean", he found a passage through South America, now known as the Strait of Magellan, but died during the expedition. His crew of 18 people with one remaining ship successfully circumnavigated the world. (p. 71)

Mann, Horace (1796–1859) American educator, he is considered the father of American public education. He was a leader of the common-school movement, advocating education for all children. (pp. 412, 413)

Marion, Francis (1732?–1795) Revolutionary War commander of Marion's Brigade, a group of guerrilla soldiers in South Carolina that used surprise raids against British communications and supply lines. (p. 99)

Marshall, John (1755–1835) Federalist leader who served in the House of Representatives and as U.S. Secretary of State, he later became the Chief

Justice of the U.S. Supreme Court, establishing in *Marbury* v. *Madison* the Supreme Court's power of judicial review. (p. 232)

Marshall, Thurgood (1908–1993) First African American U.S. Supreme Court Justice, he represented as a lawyer the National Association for the Advancement of Colored People and fought racial segregation. (p. 148)

Meade, George G. (1815–1872) American army officer, he served as a Union general at major Civil War battles. He forced back General Lee's Confederate army at Gettysburg but failed to obtain a decisive victory. (p. 498)

Melville, Herman (1819–1891) American writer, he based his books on his own sailing experiences and is famous for *Moby-Dick*. (p. 407)

Moctezuma II (1466–1520) Emperor of Mexico's Aztec Empire, he welcomed explorer Cortés as a god but was taken prisoner by him. He was later killed, and the Aztec capital was destroyed during the following Aztec uprising. (p. 20)

Monroe, James (1758–1831) Leading Revolutionary figure and negotiator of the Louisiana Purchase, he was the fifth president of the United States. He put forth the Monroe Doctrine establishing the U.S. sphere of influence in the Western Hemisphere that became the foundation of U.S. foreign policy. (p. 261)

Morse, Samuel F. B. (1791–1872) American artist and inventor, he applied scientists' discoveries of electricity and magnetism to develop the telegraph, which soon sent messages all across the country. (pp. 364, 365)

Mott, Lucretia (1793–1880) American reformer, she planned the Seneca Falls Convention with Elizabeth Cady Stanton, the first organized meeting for women's rights in the United States. (p. 426)

O

O'Connor, Sandra Day (1930–) Associate justice of the U.S. Supreme Court, she was the first woman appointed to the Court. (p. 148)

Osceola (c.1804–1838) Florida Seminole leader, he resisted removal by the U.S. government despite an earlier treaty that Seminole leaders had been forced to sign. He was eventually captured and died in prison. (p. 297)

P

Paine, Thomas (1737–1809) American political philosopher and author, he urged an immediate declaration of independence from England in his anonymously and simply written pamphlet, *Common Sense*. (p. 83)

Paul, Alice (1885–1977) American social reformer, suffragist, and activist, she was the founder of the organization that became the National Woman's Party (NWP) that worked to obtain women's suffrage. (p. 622)

Penn, William (1644–1718) Quaker leader who founded a colony for Quakers in Pennsylvania; the colony provided an important example of representative self-government and became a model of freedom and tolerance. (p. 50)

Perry, Oliver Hazard (1785–1819) American naval captain who put together the fleet that defeated the British at the Battle of Lake Erie in the War of 1812. (p. 247)

Pershing, John J. (1860–1948) American army commander, he commanded the expeditionary force sent into Mexico to find Pancho Villa. He was the major general and commander in chief of the American Expeditionary Forces in World War I. (p. 661)

Pickett, George (1825–1875) American general in the Confederate army, he was famed for Pickett's Charge, a failed but heroic effort at Cemetery Ridge in the Battle of Gettysburg, often considered a turning point of the Civil War. (p. 499)

Pierce, Franklin (1804–1869) Democratic candidate for president in 1852 and the fourteenth president of the United States, he made the Gadsden Purchase, which opened the Northwest for settlement, and passed the unpopular Kansas-Nebraska Act. (p. 445)

Pike, Zebulon (1779–1813) Army officer sent on a mission to explore the West, he was ordered to find the headwaters of the Red River. He attempted to climb what is now known as Pikes Peak in Colorado. (p. 239)

Pizarro (puh-ZAHR-oh), **Francisco** (c. 1475–1541) Spanish conquistador who sailed with Balboa on the discovery of the Pacific Ocean, he later pursued rumors of golden cities in the Andes Mountains of South America and conquered the Inca Empire. (p. 21)

Pocahontas (c.1595–1617) American Indian princess, she saved the life of John Smith when he was captured and sentenced to death by the Powhatan. She was later taken prisoner by the English, converted to Christianity, and married colonist John Rolfe. (p. 37)

Poe, Edgar Allan (1809–1849) American writer, he is famed for his haunting poem, "The Raven," as well as many other chilling or romantic stories and poems. He is credited with creating the first detective story, *The Gold Bug*. (p. 407)

Polk, James K. (1795–1849) Eleventh president of the United States, he settled the Oregon boundary with Great Britain and successfully conducted the Mexican-American War. (p. 317)

Pontiac (c.1720–1769) Ottawa chief who united

the Great Lakes' Indians to try to halt the advance of European settlements, he attacked British forts in a rebellion known as Pontiac's Rebellion; he eventually surrendered in 1766. (p. 61)

Powderly, Terence V. (1849–1924) American labor leader for the Knights of Labor, he removed the secrecy originally surrounding the organization, leading to its becoming the first truly national American labor union. (p. 585)

Pulitzer, Joseph (1847–1911) American journalist and newspaper publisher, he established the Pulitzer Prize for public service and advancement of education. (p. 646)

R

Revels, Hiram (1822–1901) American clergyman, educator, and politician, he became the first African American in the U.S. Senate. (p. 525)

Rockefeller, John D. (1839–1937) American

industrialist and philanthropist, he made a fortune in the oil business and used vertical and horizontal integration to establish a monopoly on the steel business. (pp. 580, 583)

Roosevelt, Theodore (1858–1919) Twenty-sixth president of the United States after William McKinley was assassinated, he organized the first volunteer cavalry regiment known as the Rough Riders who fought in Cuba during the Spanish-American War. As President, he acquired the Panama Canal Zone, and announced the Roosevelt Corollary, making the United States the defender of the Western Hemisphere. (pp. 625, 655)

S

Sacagawea (sak–uh–juh–WEE–uh) (1786?–1812) Shoshone woman who, along with French fur trapper husband, accompanied and aided Lewis and Clark on their expedition. (p. 236)

Santa Anna, Antonio López de (1794–1876) Mexican general and politician, he was president of Mexico and became a dictator. He fought in the Texas Revolution and seized the Alamo but was defeated and captured by Sam Houston at San Jacinto. (p. 313)

Scott, Dred (1795?–1858) Enslaved African who filed suit for his freedom stating that his time living in a free state made him a free man; the Supreme Court ruling known as the *Dred Scott* decision upheld slavery and found the Missouri Compromise unconstitutional. (p. 451)

Scott, Winfield (1786–1866) American general, he served as commander in the Mexican War and used a two-part strategy against the South in the Civil War; he wanted to destroy the South's economy with a naval blockade and gain control of the Mississippi River. (p. 475)

Sequoya (between 1760 and 1770–1843) American Indian scholar and craftsman, he created a writing system for the Cherokee language and taught literacy to many Cherokee. (p. 295)

Serra (ser–rah), **Junípero** (hoo–nee–pay–roh) (1713–1784) Spanish Franciscan missionary to California, he planned or founded numerous missions all along the Pacific coast and founded San Francisco in an effort to spread Christianity. (p. 23)

Seward, William H. (1801–1872) American politician, who as Secretary of State was laughed at for "Seward's Folly," the purchase of Alaska from Russia for less than two cents an acre, which added approximately 600,000 square miles of land to the United States. (p. 641)

Shays, Daniel (1747?–1825) Revolutionary War officer who led Shays's Rebellion, an uprising of farmers in western Massachusetts that shut down the courts so that farmers would not lose their farms for tax debts. He was defeated and condemned to death, but pardoned. (p. 123)

Sherman, William Tecumseh (1820–1891) American Union army officer, his famous March to the Sea captured Atlanta, Georgia, marking an important turning point in the war. (p. 501)

Singer, Isaac (1811–1875) American inventor; he patented an improved sewing machine and by 1860, was the largest manufacturer of sewing machines in the country. (p. 367)

Sitting Bull (c.1831–1890) American Indian leader who became the head chief of the entire Sioux nation, he encouraged other Sioux leaders to resist government demands to buy lands on the Black Hills reservations. (p. 556)

Slater, Samuel (1768–1835) English industrialist who brought a design for a textile mill to America, he is considered the founder of the American cotton industry. (p. 348)

Smith, John (c.1580–1631) English colonist to the Americas who helped found Jamestown Colony and encouraged settlers to work harder and build better housing. (p. 36)

Squanto (?–1622) Patuxet Indian who was captured and enslaved in Spain but later escaped to England and then America; he taught the Pilgrims native farming methods and helped them establish relations with the Wampanoag, the Indians at the feast later known as Thanksgiving. (p. 43)

Stanford, Leland (1824–1893) American railroad builder and politician, he established the California Central Pacific Railroad and founded Stanford University. (pp. 581, 583)

Stanton, Elizabeth Cady (1815–1902) American woman suffrage leader, she organized the Seneca Falls Convention with Lucretia Mott. The convention was the first organized meeting for women's rights in the United States, which launched the suffrage movement. (pp. 426, 429)

Stevens, Thaddeus (1792–1868) American lawyer and politician, he was the leader of the Radical Republicans in the Reconstruction effort and was an opponent and critic of Andrew Johnson's policies. He sought economic justice for freedmen and poor southerners. (p. 520)

Stone, Lucy (1818–1893) American woman suffragist, she was a well-known and accomplished antislavery speaker who supported the women's rights movement. (p. 427)

Stowe, Harriet Beecher (1811–1896) American author and daughter of Lyman Beecher, she was an abolitionist and author of the famous antislavery novel, *Uncle Tom's Cabin* (p. 443)

Stuyvesant (STY–vuh–suhnt), **Peter** (c.1610–1672) Director general of the Dutch New Netherland colony, he was forced to surrender New Netherland to the English. (p. 50)

Sutter, John (1803–1880) American pioneer who built Sutter's Fort, a trading post on the California frontier; gold was discovered leading to the California gold rush. (p. 327)

T

Taft, William Howard (1857–1930) Twenty-seventh president of the United States, he angered progressives by moving cautiously toward reforms and by supporting the Payne-Aldrich Tariff, which did not lower tariffs very much. He lost Roosevelt's support and was defeated for a second term. (p. 627)

Taney (TAW–nee), **Roger B.** (1777–1864) U.S. Supreme Court Chief Justice he wrote the majority opinion in the *Dred Scott* decision, stating that African Americans were not citizens and that the Missouri Compromise was unconstitutional. (p. 452)

Taylor, Frederick W. (1856–1915) American efficiency engineer, he introduced the manufacturing system known as scientific management that viewed workers as mechanical parts of the production process, not as human beings. (p. 584)

Tecumseh (1768–1813) Shawnee chief who attempted to form an Indian confederation to resist white settlement in the Northwest Territory. (p. 242)

Thoreau, Henry David (1817–1862) American writer and transcendentalist philosopher, he studied nature and published a magazine article, "Civil Disobedience," as well as his famous book, *Walden Pond.* (p. 405)

Truth, Sojourner (c.1797–1883) American evangelist and reformer, she was born an enslaved African but was later freed and became a speaker for abolition and women's suffrage. (p. 418)

Tubman, Harriet (c.1820–1913) American abolitionist who escaped slavery and assisted other enslaved Africans to escape; she is the most famous Underground Railroad conductor and is known as the Moses of her people. (p. 420)

Turner, Nat (1800–1831) American slave leader, he claimed that divine inspiration had led him to end the slavery system. Called Nat Turner's Rebellion, the slave revolt was the most violent one in U.S. history; he was tried, convicted, and executed. (p. 390)

Tweed, William Marcy (1823–1878) American politician, he gained control of New York City's Tammany Hall political machine and became known as Boss Tweed. He was convicted of stealing from the New York City treasury. (p. 607)

V

Vallejo, Mariano Guadalupe (1808–1890) American soldier and politician, he increased settlement in northern California and became a rich cattleman. He helped in the effort to get statehood for California. (p. 319)

Van Buren, Martin (1782–1862) American politician and secretary of state under Andrew Jackson, he later became the eighth president of the United States. (p. 286)

Vesey, Denmark (c.1767–1822) American insurrectionist, he was brought to America as a slave but purchased his own freedom. He planned a large slave uprising in South Carolina and was tried and hanged along with 36 others accused of plotting the rebellion. (p. 390)

Villa, Francisco "Pancho" (1878–1923) Mexican bandit and revolutionary leader, he led revolts against Carranza and Huerta. He was pursued by the U.S. but evaded General Pershing. (p. 661)

Washington, Booker T. (1856–1915) African American educator and civil rights leader, he was born into slavery and later became head of the Tuskegee Institute for career training for African Americans. He was an advocate for conservative social change. (p. 622)

Washington, George (1732–1799) Revolutionary War hero and Patriot leader, he served as a representative to the Continental Congresses, commanded the Continental Army, and was unanimously elected to two terms as president of the United States. (pp. 80, 82)

Webster, Daniel (1782–1852) American lawyer and statesman, he spoke out against nullification and states' rights, believing that the country should stay unified. (p. 291)

Wells, Ida B. (1862–1931) African American journalist and anti-lynching activist, she was part owner and editor of the *Memphis Free Speech*. (p. 622)

Whitman, Walt (1819–1892) American poet, he gained recognition abroad and later at home for unrhymed works of poetry praising the United States, Americans, democracy, and individualism.(p. 407)

Whitney, Eli (1765–1825) American inventor whose cotton gin changed cotton harvesting procedures and enabled large increases in cotton production; he introduced the technology of mass production through the development of interchangeable parts in gun-making. (p. 349)

Wilder, Laura Ingalls (1867–1957) American writer and frontierswoman who wrote a well-known series of children's books based on her own experiences, including the classic, *Little House on the Prairie*. (p. 564)

Wilson, Woodrow (1856–1924) Twenty-eighth president of the United States, his reform legislation was given the name New Freedom, and it included three constitutional amendments: direct election of senators, prohibition, and women's suffrage. He created the Federal Reserve System, the Federal Trade Commission, and he enacted child labor laws. (p. 628)

Winnemucca, Sarah (1844–1891) Paiute Indian reformer, she was an activist for Indian rights and lectured specifically about the problems of the reservation system. (p. 558)

Winthrop, John (1588–1649) Leader of the Massachusetts Bay Colony who led Puritan colonists to Massachusetts to establish an ideal Christian community; he later became the colony's first governor. (p. 44)

Wright, Orville (1871–1948) and **Wilbur** (1867–1912) American pioneers of aviation, they went from experiments with kites and gliders to piloting the first successful gas-powered airplane flight and later founded the American Wright Company to manufacture airplanes. (p. 578)

Young, Brigham (1801–1877) American religious leader who headed the Mormon Church after the murder of Joseph Smith, he moved the community to Utah, leading thousands along what came to be known as the Mormon Trail to the main settlement at Salt Lake City. (p. 311)

Zapata, Emiliano (1879–1919) Mexican revolutionary, he was a guerrilla leader helping Madera overthrow Díaz. He was a champion of farmers and revolted against Carranza. (p. 661)

English and Spanish Glossary

MARK	AS IN	RESPELLING	EXAMPLE
a	alphabet	a	*AL-fuh-bet
ā	Asia	ay	AY-zhuh
ä	cart, top	ah	KAHRT, TAHP
e	let, ten	e	LET, TEN
ē	even, leaf	ee	EE-vuhn, LEEF
i	it, tip, British	i	IT, TIP, BRIT-ish
ī	site, buy, Ohio	y	SYT, BY, oh-HY-oh
	iris	eye	EYE-ris
k	card	k	KAHRD
ō	over, rainbow	oh	OH-vuhr, RAYN-boh
ù	book, wood	ooh	BOOHK, WOOHD
ò	all, orchid	aw	AWL, AWR-kid
òi	foil, coin	oy	FOYL, KOYN
àu	out	ow	OWT
ə	cup, butter	uh	KUHP, BUHT-uhr
ü	rule, food	oo	ROOL, FOOD
yü	few	yoo	FYOO
zh	vision	zh	VIZH-uhn

*A syllable printed in small capital letters receives heavier emphasis than the other syllable(s) in a word.

Phonetic Respelling and Pronunciation Guide

Many of the key terms in this textbook have been respelled to help you pronounce them. The letter combinations used in the respelling throughout the narrative are explained in the following phonetic respelling and pronunciation guide. The guide is adapted from *Webster's Tenth New College Dictionary, Merriam-Webster's New Geographical Dictionary, and Merriam-Webster's New Biographical Dictionary.*

A

ABC Powers Argentina, Brazil and Chile; nations that offered to negotiate a dispute between the United States and Mexico when unrest following the Mexican Revolution brought the two countries into conflict (p. 661)
potencias ABC Argentina, Brasil y Chile; naciones que se ofrecieron a resolver el desacuerdo entre Estados Unidos y México cuando el descontento posterior a la Revolución mexicana provocó un conflicto entre ambos países (pág. 661)

abolition an end to slavery (p. 416)
abolición fin de la esclavitud (pág. 416)

Adams-Onís Treaty (1819) an agreement in which Spain gave East Florida to the United States (p. 261)
tratado de Adams y Onís (1819) acuerdo en el que España cedió el territorio del este de Florida a Estados Unidos (pág. 261)

Alamo Spanish mission in San Antonio, Texas, that was the site of a famous battle of the Texas Revolution in 1836 (p. 314)
El Álamo misión española en San Antonio, Texas; escenario de una famosa batalla durante la Revolución texana de 1836 (pág. 314)

Alien and Sedition Acts (1798) laws passed by a Federalist-dominated Congress aimed at protecting the government from treasonous ideas, actions, and people (p. 215)
Leyes de No Intervención Extranjera (1798) leyes aprobadas por un Congreso mayormente federalista con el fin de proteger al gobierno de la influencia de ideas, acciones y personas desleales (pág. 215)

amendment official change, correction, or addition to a law or constitution (p. 135)
enmienda cambio, corrección o adición realizado de manera oficial a una ley o constitución (pág. 135)

American Federation of Labor an organization that united skilled workers into national unions for specific industries (p. 585)
Federación Estadounidense del Trabajo organización que agrupó obreros especializados en sindicatos nacionales definidos por industrias (pág. 585)

American System Henry Clay's plan for raising tariffs to pay for internal improvements such as better roads and canals (p. 264)
Sistema estadounidense plan de alza de impuestos creado por Henry Clay para realizar mejoras internas como la reparación de caminos y canales (pág. 264)

Antifederalists people who opposed ratification of the Constitution (p. 132)
antifederalistas personas que se oponían a la aprobación de la Constitución (pág. 132)

Anti-Imperialist League a group of citizens opposed to imperialism, and, specifically, to the peace treaty that gave the United States control of Cuba, Guam, Puerto Rico, and the Philippines (p. 650)
Liga Antiimperialista grupo de ciudadanos que se oponían al imperialismo y, más concretamente, al tratado de paz que otorgaba a Estados Unidos el control de Cuba, Guam, Puerto Rico y Filipinas (pág. 650)

American Anti-Slavery Society an organization started by William Lloyd Garrison whose members wanted immediate emancipation and racial equality for African Americans (p. 417)
Sociedad Americana contra la Esclavitud organización fundada por William Lloyd Garrison cuyos miembros pedían la emancipación inmediata y la igualdad racial de los afroamericanos (pág. 417)

Appomattox Courthouse Virginia town where General Robert E. Lee was forced to surrender, thus ending the Civil War (p. 502)
Appomattox Courthouse poblado de Virginia donde el general Robert E. Lee fue obligado a rendirse, dando fin a la Guerra Civil (pág. 502)

Articles of Confederation (1777) the document that created the first central government for the United States; was replaced by the Constitution in 1789 (p. 116)
Artículos de la Confederación (1777) documento que creó el primer gobierno central en Estados Unidos; fue reemplazado por la Constitución en 1789 (pág. 116)

B

Bacon's Rebellion (1676) an atttack led by Nathaniel Bacon against American Indians and the colonial government in Virginia (p. 38)
Rebelión de Bacon (1676) ataque encabezado por Nathaniel Bacon contra los indígenas norteamericanos y el gobierno colonial en Virginia (pág. 38)

Bank of the United States a national bank chartered by Congress in 1791 to provide security for the U.S. economy (p. 204)
Banco de Estados Unidos banco nacional constituido por el Congreso en 1791 para dar establidad a la economía de Estados Unidos (pág. 204)

Battle of Antietam (1862) a Union victory in the Civil War that marked the bloodiest single-day battle in U.S. military history (p. 481)
batalla de Antietam (1862) victoria del ejército de la Unión durante la Guerra Civil en la batalla de un solo día más sangrienta en la historia militar de Estados Unidos (pág. 481)

Battle of Bunker Hill (1775) a Revolutionary War battle in Boston that demonstrated that the colonists could fight well against the British army (p. 81)
batalla de Bunker Hill (1775) batalla de la Guerra de Independencia estadounidense que tuvo lugar en Boston; en ésta se demostró que los colonos podían luchar bien contra el ejército británico (pág. 81)

Battle of Fallen Timbers (1794) a battle between U.S. troops and an American Indian confederation that ended Indian efforts to halt white settlement in the Northwest Territory (p. 209)
batalla de Fallen Timbers (1794) batalla entre las tropas estadounidenses y una confederación de indígenas norteamericanos que puso fin a los intentos de los indígenas para detener la emigración de personas de raza blanca al Territorio del Noroeste (pág. 209)

Battle of Gettysburg (1863) a Union Civil War victory that turned the tide against the Confederates at Gettysburg, Pennsylvania (p. 498)
batalla de Gettysburg (1863) victoria del ejército de la Unión durante la Guerra Civil que cambió el curso de la guerra en contra de los confederados en Gettysburg, Pensilvania (pág. 498)

Battle of Lake Erie (1813) U.S. victory in the War of 1812, led by Oliver Hazard Perry; broke Britain's control of Lake Erie (p. 247)
batalla del lago Erie (1813) victoria en la Guerra de 1812 en la que el ejército estadounidense, comandado por Oliver Hazard Perry, puso fin al control británico del lago Erie (pág. 247)

Battle of New Orleans (1815) the greatest U.S. victory in the War of 1812; actually took place two weeks after a peace treaty had been signed ending the war (p. 248)
batalla de Nueva Orleáns (1815) la mayor victoria del ejército estadounidense en la Guerra de 1812; tuvo lugar dos semanas después de la firma de un tratado de paz en el que se declaraba el final de la guerra (pág. 248)

Battle of San Jacinto (1836) the final battle of the Texas Revolution; resulted in the defeat of the Mexican army and independence for Texas (p. 314)
batalla de San Jacinto (1836) batalla final de la Revolución texana en la que fue derrotado el ejército mexicano y Texas obtuvo su independencia (pág. 314)

Battle of Saratoga (1777) a Revolutionary War battle in New York that resulted in a major defeat of British troops; marked the Patriots' greatest victory up to that point in the war (p. 94)
batalla de Saratoga (1777) batalla de la Guerra de Independencia estadounidense que tuvo lugar en Nueva York y en la que las fuerzas británicas sufrieron una de sus mayores derrotas; los patriotas obtuvieron su mayor victoria hasta ese momento (pág. 94)

Battle of Shiloh (1862) a Civil War battle in Tennessee in which the Union army gained greater control over the Mississippi River valley (p. 485)
batalla de Shiloh (1862) batalla de la Guerra Civil en Tennessee en la que el ejército de la Unión adquirió mayor control sobre el valle del río Mississippi (pág. 485)

Battle of the Little Big Horn (1876) "Custer's Last Stand"; battle between U.S. soldiers, led by George Armstrong Custer, and Sioux warriors, led by Crazy Horse and Sitting Bull, that resulted in the worst defeat for the U.S. Army in the West (p. 556)
batalla de Little Big Horn (1876) última batalla del general Custer; esta batalla entre las tropas de George Armstrong Custer y los guerreros siux al mando de Caballo Loco y Toro Sentado produjo la mayor derrota del ejército estadounidense en el Oeste (pág. 556)

Battle of Tippecanoe (1811) U.S. victory over an Indian confederation that wanted to stop white settlement in the Northwest Territory; increased tensions between Great Britain and the United States (p. 244)
batalla de Tippecanoe (1811) victoria del ejército estadounidense sobre la confederación indígena que intentaba evitar el establecimiento de poblaciones de blancos en el Territorio del Noroeste; esta batalla aumentó las hostilidades entre Gran Bretaña y Estados Unidos (pág. 244)

Battle of Trenton (1776) a Revolutionary War battle in New Jersey in which Patriot forces captured more than 900 Hessian troops (p. 93)
batalla de Trenton (1776) batalla de la Guerra de Independencia estadounidense que tuvo lugar en Nueva Jersey; en esta batalla las fuerzas de los patriotas capturaron a más de 900 soldados mercenarios hessianos (pág. 93)

Battle of Yorktown (1781) the last major battle of the Revolutionary War; site of British general Charles Cornwallis's surrender to the Patriots in Virginia (p. 100)
batalla de Yorktown (1781) la última batalla importante de la Guerra de Independencia estadounidense; lugar donde se rindió el general británico Charles Cornwallis ante las tropas de los patriotas en Virginia (pág. 100)

Bear Flag Revolt (1846) a revolt against Mexico by American settlers in California who declared the territory an independent republic (p. 320)
Revuelta de Bear Flag (1846) rebelión iniciada por colonos estadounidenses en contra de México para declarar al territorio de California una república independiente (pág. 320)

benevolent society an aid organization formed by immigrant communities (p. 591)
sociedad de beneficencia organización de ayuda formada por comunidades de inmigrantes (pág. 591)

Bessemer process a process developed in the 1850s that led to faster, cheaper steel production (p. 575)
proceso de Bessemer proceso de producción de acero más económico y rápido, desarrollado en la década de 1850 (pág. 575)

Bill of Rights the first 10 amendments to the Constitution; ratified in 1791 (p. 135)
Declaración de Derechos primeras 10 enmiendas hechas a la Constitución; aprobada en 1791 (pág. 135)

Black Codes laws passed in the southern states during Reconstruction that greatly limited the freedom and rights of African Americans (p. 518)
códigos para negros decretos aprobados en los estados sureños en la época de la Reconstrucción que limitaron en gran medida la libertad y los derechos de los afroamericanos (pág. 518)

bond a certificate that represents money the government has borrowed from private citizens (p. 201)
bono certificado que representa dinero que el gobierno toma prestado de los ciudadanos (pág. 201)

boomtown a Western community that grew quickly because of the mining boom and often disappeared when the boom ended (p. 548)
pueblo de rápido crecimiento comunidad del Oeste que se desarrolló con gran rapidez debido a la fiebre del oro, pero que desapareció cuando los yacimientos se agotaron (pág. 548)

border states Delaware, Kentucky, Maryland, and Missouri; slave states that lay between the North and the South and did not join the Confederacy during the Civil War (p. 474)
estados fronterizos Delaware, Kentucky, Maryland y Missouri; estados ubicados entre el Norte y el Sur, que practicaban la esclavitud y que no se unieron a la Confederación durante la Guerra Civil (pág. 474)

Boston Massacre (1770) an incident in which British soldiers fired into a crowd of colonists, killing five people (p. 65)
matanza de Boston (1770) incidente en el que los soldados británicos dispararon entre una multitud de colonos, ocasionando la muerte a cinco personas (pág. 65)

Boston Tea Party (1773) a protest against the Tea Act in which a group of colonists boarded British tea ships and dumped more than 340 chests of tea into Boston Harbor (p. 66)
Motín del Té de Boston (1773) protesta en contra de la Ley del Té en la que un grupo de colonos abordó barcos británicos que transportaban té y arrojó al mar alrededor de 340 baúles con este producto en el puerto de Boston (pág. 66)

Boxer Rebellion (1900) a siege of a foreign settlement in Beijing by Chinese nationalists who were angry at foreign involvement in China (p. 645)
rebelión de los boxers (1900) asedio a un asentamiento extranjero en Beijing por parte de un grupo de nacionalistas chinos que estaban en desacuerdo con la participación extranjera en China (pág. 645)

Bureau of Indian Affairs a government agency created in the 1800s to oversee federal policy toward Native Americans (p. 294)
Oficina de Asuntos Indígenas agencia creada por el gobierno en el siglo XIX para encargarse de las políticas federales sobre los indígenas norteamericanos (pág. 294)

C

Californios Spanish colonists in California in the 1800s (p. 319)
californios colonos españoles que vivían en California en el siglo XIX (pág. 319)

capital money or property that is used to earn more money (p. 13)
capital dinero o propiedades usadas para ganar más dinero (pág. 13)

capitalism an economic system in which private businesses run most industries (p. 619)
capitalismo sistema económico en el que las empresas privadas controlan la mayoría de las industrias (pág. 619)

cattle drive a long journey on which cowboys herded cattle to northern markets or better grazing lands (p. 549)
arreo de ganado viaje largo en el que los vaqueros arreaban ganado para llevarlo a los mercados del Norte o a mejores pastizales (pág. 549)

Cattle Kingdom an area of the Great Plains on which many ranchers raised cattle in the late 1800s (p. 549)
Reino del Ganado área de las Grandes Planicies en la que muchos ganaderos se establecieron a finales de siglo XIX (pág. 549)

charter an official document that gives a person the right to establish a colony (p. 27)
carta de constitución documento legal que da a una persona el derecho de establecer una colonia (pág. 27)

checks and balances a system established by the Constitution that prevents any branch of government from becoming too powerful (p. 129)
pesos y contrapesos sistema establecido por la Constitución para evitar que cualquier poder del gobierno adquiera demasiada autoridad en relación con los demás (pág. 129)

Chinese Exclusion Act (1882) a law passed by Congress that banned Chinese from immigrating to the United States for 10 years (p. 593)
Ley de Exclusión de Chinos (1882) ley aprobada por el Congreso que prohibió la inmigración de chinos a Estados Unidos por un período de 10 años (pág. 593)

Chisholm Trail a trail that ran from San Antonio, Texas, to Abilene, Kansas, established by Jesse Chisholm in the late 1860s for cattle drives (p. 549)
Camino de Chisholm camino creado por Jesse Chisholm a finales de la década de 1860 que iba desde San Antonio, Texas hasta Abilene, Kansas, para realizar arreos de ganado (pág. 549)

Civil Rights Act of 1866 a law that gave African Americans legal rights equal to those of white Americans (p. 520)
Ley de Derechos Civiles de 1866 ley que daba a los afroamericanos derechos legales similares a los que tenían los ciudadanos de raza blanca (pág. 520)

Clermont the first full-sized U.S. commercial steamboat; developed by Robert Fulton and tested in 1807 (p. 359)
Clermont primer barco comercial de vapor de grandes dimensiones, diseñado por Robert Fulton y probado en 1807 (pág. 359)

collective bargaining a technique used by labor unions in which workers act collectively to change working conditions or wages (p. 586)
negociación colectiva método empleado por los sindicatos en el que los trabajadores actúan colectivamente para cambiar las condiciones laborales o los salarios (pág. 586)

Columbian Exchange the transfer of plants, animals, and diseases between the Americas and Europe, Asia, and Africa (p. 18)
intercambio colombino intercambio de plantas, animales y enfermedades entre América y Europa, Asia y África (pág. 18)

Committees of Correspondence committees created by the Massachusetts House of Representatives in the 1760s to help towns and colonies share information about resisting British laws (p. 63)
comités de correspondencia comités creados por la Cámara de Representantes de Massachusetts en la década de 1760 para que poblados y colonias compartieran información que los ayudara a resistirse a las leyes británicas (pág. 63)

common-school movement a social reform effort that began in the mid-1800s and promoted the idea of having all children educated in a common place regardless of social class or background (p. 412)
movimiento de escuelas comunes reforma social iniciada a mediados del siglo XIX para fomentar la idea de que todos los niños debían recibir educación en un mismo lugar sin importar su origen o clase social (pág. 412)

Common Sense (1776) a pamphlet written by Thomas Paine that criticized monarchies and convinced many American colonists of the need to break away from Britain (p. 83)
Sentido común (1776) folleto escrito por Thomas Paine en el que criticaba a las monarquías con el fin de convencer a los colonos estadounidenses de la necesidad de independizarse de Gran Bretaña (pág. 83)

Compromise of 1850 Henry Clay's proposed agreement that allowed California to enter the Union as a free state and divided the rest of the Mexican Cession into two territories where slavery would be decided by popular sovereignty (p. 441)
Acuerdo de 1850 acuerdo redactado por Henry Clay en que se permitía a California ingresar en la Unión como estado libre y se proponía la división del resto del territorio cedido por México en dos partes donde la esclavitud sería reglamentada por soberanía popular (pág. 441)

Compromise of 1877 an agreement to settle the disputed presidential election of 1876; Democrats agreed to accept Republican Rutherford B. Hayes as president in return for the removal of federal troops from the South (p. 527)
Acuerdo de 1877 acuerdo en el que se resolvió la disputa de las elecciones presidenciales de 1876; los demócratas aceptaron al republicano Rutherford B. Hayes como presidente a cambio del retiro de las tropas federales del Sur (pág. 527)

Comstock Lode Nevada gold and silver mine discovered by Henry Comstock in 1859 (p. 547)
veta de Comstock yacimiento de oro y plata descubierto en Nevada por Henry Comstock en 1859 (pág. 547)

Confederate States of America the nation formed by the southern states when they seceded from the Union; also known as the Confederacy (p. 458)
Estados Confederados de América nación formada por los estados del Sur cuando se separaron de la Unión; también conocida como Confederación (pág. 458)

conquistador a Spanish soldier and explorer who led military expeditions in the Americas and captured land for Spain (p. 20)
conquistador soldado y explorador español que encabezó expediciones militares en América y capturó territorios en nombre de España (pág. 20)

consul-general chief diplomat (p. 644)
cónsul general jefe diplomático (pág. 644)

constitution a set of basic principles that determines the powers and duties of a government (p. 115)
constitución conjunto de principios básicos que determina los poderes y las obligaciones de un gobierno (pág. 115)

Constitutional Convention (1787) a meeting held in Philadelphia at which delegates from the states wrote the Constitution (p. 126)
Convención Constitucional (1787) encuentro realizado en Filadelfia en el que delegados de los estados redactaron la Constitución (pág. 126)

Constitutional Union Party a political party formed in 1860 by a group of northerners and southerners who supported the Union, its laws, and the Constitution (p. 457)
Partido Constitucional por la Unión partido político formado en 1860 por habitantes del Norte y del Sur en apoyo de la Unión, sus leyes y la Constitución (pág. 457)

Continental Army the army created by the Second Continental Congress in 1775 to defend the American colonies from Britain (p. 80)
Ejército Continental ejército creado por el Segundo Congreso Continental en 1775 para defender las colonias estadounidenses del dominio británico (pág. 80)

contraband an escaped slave who joined the Union army during the Civil War (p. 493)
contrabando bienes introducidos en un país de forma ilegal; esclavo que escapó y que se unió al ejército de la Unión durante la Guerra Civil (pág. 493)

Convention of 1818 an agreement between the United States and Great Britain that settled fishing rights and established new North American borders (p. 260)
Convención de 1818 acuerdo entre Estados Unidos y Gran Bretaña para definir los derechos de pesca y establecer las nuevas fronteras norteamericanas (pág. 260)

Copperheads a group of northern Democrats who opposed abolition and sympathized with the South during the Civil War (p. 494)
copperheads grupo de demócratas del Norte que se oponían a la abolición de la esclavitud y simpatizaban con las creencias sureñas durante la Guerra Civil (pág. 494)

corporation a business that sells portions of ownership called stock shares (p. 579)
corporación compañía que vende partes de la misma llamadas acciones (pág. 579)

cotton belt a region stretching from South Carolina to east Texas where most U.S. cotton was produced during the mid-1800s (p. 379)
región algodonera zona que se extendía desde Carolina del Sur hasta el este de Texas, en la que se producía la mayor parte del algodón cosechado en Estados Unidos a mediados del siglo XIX (pág. 379)

cotton diplomacy Confederate efforts to use the importance of southern cotton to Britain's textile industry to persuade the British to support the Confederacy in the Civil War (p. 475)
diplomacia del algodón esfuerzos de la Confederación por aprovechar la influencia del algodón del Sur en la industria textil británica para convencer a Gran Bretaña de apoyar su causa durante la Guerra Civil (pág. 475)

cotton gin a machine invented by Eli Whitney in 1793 to remove seeds from short-staple cotton; revolutionized the cotton industry (p. 377)
desmotadora de algodón máquina inventada por Eli Whitney en 1793 para separar las fibras de algodón de las semillas; revolucionó la industria del algodón (pág. 377)

culture the common values and traditions of a society, such as language, government, and family relationships (p. 7)
cultura valores y tradiciones comunes de una sociedad, como el lenguaje, la forma de gobierno y las relaciones familiares (pág. 7)

Cumberland Road the first federal road project, construction of which began in 1815; ran from Cumberland, Maryland, to present-day Wheeling, West Virginia (p. 265)
camino de Cumberland primer proyecto federal de construcción de carreteras, iniciado en 1815 para crear un camino entre Cumberland, Maryland y el poblado que actualmente lleva el nombre de Wheeling, en Virginia Occidental (pág. 265)

D

Dawes General Allotment Act (1887) legislation passed by Congress that split up Indian reservation lands among individual Indians and promised them citizenship (p. 558)
Ley de Adjudicación General de Dawes (1887) ley aprobada por el Congreso que dividía el terreno de las reservaciones indígenas entre sus habitantes y les prometía otorgarles la ciudadanía estadounidense (pág. 558)

Declaration of Independence (1776) the document written to declare the colonies free from British rule (p. 84)
Declaración de Independencia (1776) documento redactado para declarar la independencia de las colonias del dominio británico (pág. 84)

Declaration of Sentiments (1848) a statement written and signed by women's rights supporters at the Seneca Falls Convention; detailed their beliefs about social injustice against women (p. 426)

Declaración de Sentimientos (1848) declaración redactada y firmada por una serie de personas en apoyo de los derechos de la mujer durante la Convención de Seneca Falls, en la que se describía con detalle su punto de vista sobre las injusticias sociales que afectaban a las mujeres (pág. 426)

deflation a decrease in money supply and overall lower prices (p. 564)
deflación reducción de la disponibilidad del dinero y baja general en los precios (pág. 564)

Democratic Party a political party formed by supporters of Andrew Jackson after the presidential election of 1824 (p. 285)
Partido Demócrata partido político formado por partidarios de Andrew Jackson después de las elecciones presidenciales de 1824 (pág. 285)

Democratic-Republican Party a political party founded in the 1790s by Thomas Jefferson, James Madison, and other leaders who wanted to preserve the power of the state governments and promote agriculture (p. 212)
Partido Demócrata Republicano partido político formado en la década de 1790 por Thomas Jefferson, James Madison y otros líderes políticos con el fin de preservar el poder de los gobiernos estatales y promover la agricultura (pág. 212)

department store giant retail shop (p. 596)
tiendas por departamenentos grandes comercios de venta al público (pág. 596)

deport to send an immigrant back to his or her country of origin (p. 184)
deportar enviar a un inmigrante de regreso a su país de origen (pág. 184)

depression a steep drop in economic activity combined with rising unemployment (p. 123)
depresión descenso considerable en la actividad económica, combinado con un alza en el desempleo (pág. 123)

direct primary a procedure for direct selection of candidates by voters instead of by party leaders (p. 613)
elecciones primarias método de elección en el que los votantes (y no los líderes de los partidos) eligen directamente a los candidatos (pág. 613)

dollar diplomacy President Taft's policy of influencing Latin America through economic rather than military intervention (p. 657)
diplomacia del dólar política creada por el presidente Taft para influir en los gobiernos de América Latina mediante la intervención económica en lugar de la militar (pág. 657)

Donner party a group of western travelers who were stranded in the Sierra Nevada during the winter of 1846–47; only 45 of the party's 87 members survived (p. 327)
grupo Donner grupo de viajeros del Oeste extraviados en la Sierra Nevada durante el invierno de 1846–47; sólo 45 de los 87 viajeros sobrevivieron (pág. 327)

double jeopardy the act of trying a person twice for the same crime (p. 180)
doble proceso acto de juzgar a una persona dos veces por el mismo delito (pág. 180)

draft a system of required service in the armed forces (p. 185)
conscripción sistema de servicio obligatorio en las fuerzas armadas (pág. 185)

Dred Scott (1857) a slave whose courtcase led to a U.S. Supreme Court ruling that declared African Americans were not U.S. citizens, that the Missouri Compromise's restriction on slavery was unconstitutional, and that Congress did not have the right to ban slavery in any federal territory (p. 451)
Dred Scott (1857) esclavo que fue encausado y cuyo juicio concluyó con una decisión de la Corte Suprema; en la que se declaraba que los afroamericanos no podían ser ciudadanos de Estados Unidos, que las restricciones de la esclavitud impuestas en el Acuerdo de Missouri eran inconstitucionales y que el Congreso no tenía derecho de abolir la esclavitud en ninguna parte del territorio federal (pág. 451)

dry farming a method of farming used by Plains farmers in the 1890s that shifted focus from water-dependent crops to more hardy crops (p. 561)
agricultura sin irrigación método de cultivo que usaban los agricultores de las Planicies en la década de 1890 que provocó un cambio de los cultivos que dependían del agua a otros más resistentes (pág. 561)

due process the fair application of the law (p. 180)
debido proceso aplicación justa de la ley (pág. 180)

E

Eighteenth Amendment (1919) a constitutional amendment that outlawed the production and sale of alcoholic beverages in the United States; repealed in 1933 (p. 623)
Decimoctava Enmienda (1919) enmienda constitucional que prohibía la producción y venta de bebidas alcohólicas en Estados Unidos; revocada en 1933 (pág. 623)

electoral college a group of people selected from each of the states to cast votes in presidential elections (p. 196)
colegio electoral grupo de personas elegido en cada estado para votar en las elecciones presidenciales (pág. 196)

emancipation freeing of the slaves (p. 491)
emancipación liberación de los esclavos (pág. 491)

Emancipation Proclamation (1862) an order issued by President Abraham Lincoln freeing the slaves in areas rebelling against the Union; took effect January 1, 1863 (p. 491)

Proclamación de Emancipación (1862) decreto emitido por el presidente Abraham Lincoln para liberar a los esclavos en las áreas que luchaban contra la Unión; entró en vigor el primero de enero de 1863 (pág. 491)

embargo the banning of trade with a country (p. 241)
embargo prohibición del comercio con un país (pág. 241)

Embargo Act (1807) a law that prohibited American merchants from trading with other countries (p. 241)
Ley de Embargo (1807) ley que prohibía a los comerciantes estadounidenses comerciar con otros países (pág. 241)

eminent domain the government's power to take personal property to benefit the public (p. 180)
derecho de expropiación poder otorgado al gobierno para tomar propiedades particulares por el bien común (pág. 180)

empresarios agents who were contracted by the Mexican republic to bring settlers to Texas in the early 1800s (p. 312)
empresarios personas contratadas por la República Mexicana para reclutar personas que desearan establecer poblaciones en Texas a principios del siglo XIX (pág. 312)

encomienda system a system in Spanish America that gave settlers the right to tax local Indians or to demand their labor in exchange for protecting them and converting them to Christianity (p. 22)
sistema de encomienda sistema adoptado en la América española que permitía a los colonos cobrar impuestos a los indígenas o exigirles trabajo a cambio de su protección y de convertirlos al cristianismo (pág. 22)

English Bill of Rights (1689) a shift of political power from the British monarchy to Parliament (pp. 55, 114)
Declaración de Derechos inglesa (1689) cambio del poder político de la monarquía británica al Parlamento inglés (págs. 55, 114)

Enlightenment the Age of Reason; movement that began in Europe in the 1700s as people began examining the natural world, society, and government (p. 59)
Ilustración Era de la Razón; movimiento iniciado en Europa en el siglo XVIII cuando las personas empezaron a adquirir más conocimientos sobre la naturaleza, la sociedad y el gobierno (pág. 59)

environment the climate and landscape that surrounds living things (p. 7)
medio ambiente el clima y paisaje donde habitan seres vivos (pág. 7)

Era of Good Feelings a period of peace, pride, and progress for the United States from 1815 to 1825 (p. 265)
Era de los buenos sentimientos período de paz, orgullo y progreso de los Estados Unidos de 1815 a 1825 (pág. 265)

Erie Canal the canal that runs from Albany to Buffalo, New York; completed in 1825 (p. 265)
canal de Erie canal que va de Albany a Búfalo, en el estado de Nueva York; completado en 1825 (pág. 265)

executive branch the division of the federal government that includes the president and the administrative departments; enforces the nation's laws (p. 129)
Poder Ejecutivo división del gobierno federal que incluye al presidente y a los departamentos administrativos; vigila el cumplimiento de las leyes de la nación (pág. 129)

executive orders nonlegislative directives issued by the U.S. president in certain circumstances; executive orders have the force of congressional law (p. 147)
órdenes ejecutivas órdenes no legislativas dictadas por el presidente de Estados Unidos en circunstancias específicas; tienen la misma validez que las leyes del Congreso (pág. 147)

Exodusters African Americans who settled western lands in the late 1800s (p. 561)
colonos del éxodo afroamericanos que se establecieron en el Oeste a finales del siglo XIX (pág. 561)

F

factor a crop broker who managed the trade between southern planters and their customers (p. 379)
comisionado intermediario que administraba el intercambio comercial entre las plantaciones del Sur y sus clientes (pág. 379)

federal system a system that divided powers between the states and the federal government (p. 144)
sistema federal sistema en el que se distribuye el poder entre los estados y el gobierno federal (pág. 144)

federalism U.S. system of government in which power is distributed between a central government and individual states (p. 129)
federalismo sistema de gobierno de Estados Unidos en el que el poder está distribuido entre una autoridad centralizada y varios estados (pág. 129)

Federalist Papers a series of essays that defended and explained the Constitution and tried to reassure Americans that the states would not be overpowered by the proposed national government (p. 133)
Federalist Papers serie de ensayos que defienden y explican la Constitución con el propósito de que los ciudadanos quedaran convencidos de que el gobierno nacional propuesto no tendría supremacía sobre el gobierno de los estados (pág. 133)

Federalist Party a political party created in the 1790s and influenced by Alexander Hamilton that wanted to strengthen the federal government and promote industry and trade (p. 212)
Partido Federalista partido político creado en la década de 1790 siguiendo las ideas de Alexander Hamilton para fortalecer al gobierno federal y fomentar la industria y el intercambio comercial (pág. 212)

Federalists people who supported ratification of the Constitution (p. 132)
federalistas personas que apoyaban la ratificación de la Constitución (pág. 132)

Fifteenth Amendment (1870) a constitutional amendment that gave African American men the right to vote (p. 523)
Decimoquinta Enmienda (1870) enmienda constitucional que otorgaba a los hombres afroamericanos el derecho al voto (pág. 523)

54th Massachusetts Infantry African American Civil War regiment that captured Fort Wagner in South Carolina (p. 493)
54° Batallón de Infantería de Massachusetts regimiento de la Guerra Civil formado por soldados afroamericanos que tomó el fuerte Wagner en Carolina del Sur (pág. 493)

First Battle of Bull Run (1861) the first major battle of the Civil War, resulting in a Confederate victory; showed that the Civil War would not be won easily (p. 479)
primera batalla de Bull Run (1861) primera batalla importante de la Guerra Civil, en la cual el ejército confederado obtuvo la victoria; en esta batalla se demostró que ninguno de los bandos ganaría la guerra con facilidad (pág. 479)

First Continental Congress (1774) a meeting of colonial delegates in Philadelphia to decide how to respond to the closing of Boston Harbor, increased taxes, and abuses of authority by the British government; delegates petitioned King George III, listing the freedoms they believed colonists should enjoy (p. 78)
Primer Congreso Continental (1774) encuentro de delegados de las colonias en Filadelfia para decidir cómo responderían al cierre del puerto de Boston, al alza de impuestos y a los abusos de la autoridad británica; los delegados hicieron una serie de peticiones al rey Jorge III, incluyendo los derechos que consideraban justos para los colonos (pág. 78)

folktale a story that often provides a moral lesson (p. 389)
cuento popular narración que con frecuencia ofrece una moraleja (pág. 389)

Fort Sumter a federal outpost in Charleston, South Carolina, that was attacked by the Confederates in April 1861, sparking the Civil War (p. 472)
fuerte Sumter puesto de avanzada federal en Charleston, Carolina del Sur, cuyo ataque por parte de los confederados en abril de 1861 dio origen a la Guerra Civil (pág. 472)

forty-niner a gold-seeker who moved to California during the gold rush (p. 327)
gambusino buscador de oro que emigró a California durante la fiebre del oro (pág. 327)

Fourteenth Amendment (1866) a constitutional amendment giving full rights of citizenship to all people born or naturalized in the United States, except for American Indians (p. 521)
Decimocuarta Enmienda (1866) enmienda constitucional que otorgaba derechos totales de ciudadanía a todas las personas nacidas en Estados Unidos o naturalizadas estadounidenses, con excepción de los indígenas (pág. 521)

Freedmen's Bureau an agency established by Congress in 1865 to help poor people throughout the South (p. 516)
Oficina de Esclavos Libertos oficina creada por el Congreso en 1865 para ayudar a los pobres del Sur del país (pág. 516)

Freeport Doctrine (1858) a statement made by Stephen Douglas during the Lincoln-Douglas debates that pointed out how people could use popular sovereignty to determine if their state or territory should permit slavery (p. 453)
Doctrina de Freeport (1858) declaración hecha por Stephen Douglas durante los debates Lincoln-Douglas que señalaba que el pueblo podía usar la soberanía popular para decidir si su estado o territorio debía permitir la esclavitud (pág. 453)

Free-Soil Party a political party formed in 1848 by antislavery northerners who left the Whig and Democratic parties because neither addressed the slavery issue (p. 439)
Partido Tierra Libre partido político formado en 1848 por abolicionistas de los estados del Norte que habían abandonado al Partido Whig y al Partido Demócrata porque ninguno de los dos apoyaba esta causa (pág. 439)

French Revolution French rebellion that began in 1789 in which the French people overthrew the monarchy and made their country a republic (p. 205)
Revolución francesa rebelión francesa iniciada en 1789 en la que la población francesa derrocó la monarquía y convirtió el país en una república (pág. 205)

frontier an undeveloped area (p. 546)
frontera área sin explotar (pág. 546)

Fugitive Slave Act (1850) a law that made it a crime to help runaway slaves; allowed for the arrest of escaped slaves in areas where slavery was illegal and required their return to slaveholders (p. 441)
Ley de Esclavos Fugitivos (1850) ley que calificaba como delito el ayudar a un esclavo a escapar de su amo, además de permitir la captura de esclavos fugitivos en zonas donde la esclavitud era ilegal para devolverlos a sus dueños (pág. 441)

G

Gadsden Purchase (1853) U.S. purchase of land from Mexico that included the southern parts of present-day Arizona and New Mexico (p. 323)
Compra de Gadsden (1853) compra por parte del gobierno de Estados Unidos de territorio mexicano que incluía la región ocupada actualmente por el sur de Arizona y Nuevo México (pág. 323)

Gettysburg Address (1863) a speech given by Abraham Lincoln in which he praised the bravery of Union soldiers and renewed his commitment to winning the Civil War (p. 500)
Discurso de Gettysburg (1863) discurso presentado por Abraham Lincoln en el que alababa la valentía de las tropas de la Unión y renovaba su compromiso de triunfar en la Guerra Civil (pág. 500)

Ghost Dance a religious movement among Native Americans that spread across the Plains in the 1880s (p. 558)
Danza de los Espíritus movimiento religioso de los indígenas norteamericanos que se extendió por la región de las Planicies en la década de 1880 (pág. 558)

Gibbons* v. *Ogden (1824) a Supreme Court ruling that reinforced the federal government's authority over the states (p. 359)
Gibbons* contra *Ogden (1824) decreto de la Corte Suprema que reforzó la autoridad del gobierno federal sobre los estados (pág. 359)

Great Awakening a religious movement that became widespread in the American colonies in the 1730s and 1740s (p. 58)
Gran Despertar movimiento religioso que tuvo gran popularidad en las colonias estadounidenses en las décadas de 1730 y 1740 (pág. 58)

Great Compromise (1787) an agreement worked out at the Constitutional Convention establishing that a state's population would determine representation in the lower house of the legislature, while each state would have equal representation in the upper house of the legislature (p. 127)
Gran Acuerdo (1787) acuerdo redactado durante la Convención Constitucional en el que se establece que la población de un estado debe determinar su representación en la cámara baja de la asamblea legislativa y que cada estado debe tener igual representación en la cámara alta de ésta (pág. 127)

habeas corpus the constitutional protection against unlawful imprisonment (p. 494)
hábeas corpus protección constitucional contra el encarcelamiento ilegal (pág. 494)

Hartford Convention (1815) a meeting of Federalists at Hartford, Connecticut, to protest the War of 1812 (p. 249)
Convención de Hartford (1815) encuentro de federalistas en Hartford, Connecticut, para protestar por la Guerra de 1812 (pág. 249)

Hay–Bunau-Varilla Treaty (1903) an identical treaty to the earlier Hay-Herrán Treaty except that it widened the Panama Canal zone to 10 miles (p. 655)
tratado de Hay-Bunau-Varilla (1903) tratado idéntico al anterior tratado Hay-Herrán, con la excepción de que amplió la zona del canal de Panamá a 10 millas (pág. 655)

Hay-Herrán Treaty (1903) an agreement that the United States would pay Colombia $10 million plus $250,000 a year for a 99-year lease on a strip of land across the Isthmus of Panama (p. 653)
tratado de Hay-Herrán (1903) acuerdo que estableció que Estados Unidos pagaría 10 millones de dólares más $250,000 al año a Colombia por una concesión de 99 años para operar en el terreno del canal que cruza el istmo de Panamá (pág. 653)

Haymarket Riot a riot that broke out at Haymarket Square in Chicago over the deaths of two strikers (p. 586)
Revuelta de Haymarket revuelta que se originó en la Plaza Haymarket de Chicago por la muerte de dos huelguistas (pág. 586)

Homestead Act (1862) a law passed by Congress to encourage settlement in the West by giving government-owned land to small farmers (p. 560)
Ley de Colonización de Tierras (1862) ley aprobada por el Congreso para fomentar la colonización del Oeste mediante la cesión de tierras gubernamentales a pequeños agricultores (pág. 560)

Homestead strike (1892) a labor-union strike at Andrew Carnegie's Homestead Steel factory in Pennsylvania that erupted in violence between strikers and private detectives (p. 587)
huelga de Homestead (1892) huelga sindical en la fábrica de acero de Andrew Carnegie en Homestead, Pensilvania, que originó brotes de violencia entre huelguistas y detectives privados (pág. 587)

horizontal integration owning all the businesses in a certain field (p. 581)
integración horizontal posesión de todas las empresas que realizan actividades comerciales en un campo específico (pág. 581)

Hudson River school a group of American artists in the mid-1800s whose paintings focused on the American landscape (p. 272)
Escuela del Río Hudson grupo de artistas norteamericanos a mediados del siglo XIX cuya obra muestra diversos paisajes del territorio estadounidense (pág. 272)

Hull House a settlement house founded by Jane Addams and Ellen Gates Starr in 1889 (p. 597)
Hull Casa casa de asistencia a la comunidad fundada por Jane Addams y Ellen Gates Starr en 1889 (pág. 597)

hunter-gatherer a person who hunts animals and gathers wild plants to provide for his or her needs (p. 6)
cazador y recolector persona que caza animales y recolecta plantas para satisfacer sus necesidades (pág. 6)

immigrant a person who moves to another country after leaving his or her homeland (pp. 42, 182)
inmigrante persona que abandona su país para establecerse en un país diferente (págs. 42, 182)

Immigration Restriction League a group founded in 1894 by nativists who made demands intended to reduce immigration (p. 593)
Liga de Restricción de Inmigración grupo fundado en 1894 por nativistas que exigían medidas dirigidas a la reducción de la inmigración (pág. 593)

impeach to bring charges against (p. 146)
someter a juicio político presentar cargos en contra de un funcionario (pág. 146)

impeachment the process used by a legislative body to bring charges of wrongdoing against a public official (p. 522)
juicio político proceso por el cual se presentan cargos en contra de un funcionario público (pág. 522)

imperialism the practice of extending a nation's power by gaining territories for a colonial empire (p. 640)
imperialismo práctica en la que una nación extiende su poder mediante la adquisición de territorios para un imperio colonial (pág. 640)

impressment the practice of forcing people to serve in the army or navy; led to increased tensions between Great Britain and the United States in the early 1800s (p. 241)
leva práctica que obligaba a las personas a servir en el ejército o la marina; aumentó las fricciones entre Gran Bretaña y Estados Unidos a principios del siglo XIX (pág. 241)

indentured servant a colonist who received free passage to North America in exchange for working without pay for a certain number of years (p. 38)
sirviente por contrato colono que recibía un pasaje gratuito a Norteamérica a cambio de trabajar sin salario por varios años (pág. 38)

Indian Removal Act (1830) a congressional act that authorized the removal of Native Americans who lived east of the Mississippi River (p. 294)
Ley de Expulsión de Indígenas (1830) ley redactada por el Congreso que autorizaba la expulsión de los indígenas norteamericanos que habitaban al este del río Mississippi (pág. 294)

Indian Territory an area covering most of present-day Oklahoma to which most Native Americans in the Southeast were forced to move in the 1830s (p. 294)
Territorio Indígena área que abarcaba la mayor parte del actual estado de Oklahoma a la que la mayoría de las tribus indígenas del sureste fueron obligadas a trasladarse durante la década de 1830 (pág. 294)

indict to formally accuse (p. 180)
procesar acusar formalmente (pág. 180)

Industrial Revolution a period of rapid growth in the use of machines in manufacturing and production that began in the mid-1700s (p. 347)
revolución industrial período de rápido desarrollo debido al uso de maquinaria en la fabricación y producción; comenzó a mediados del siglo XVIII (pág. 347)

Industrial Workers of the World (IWW) a union founded in 1905 by socialists and union leaders that included workers not welcomed in the AFL (p. 619)
Trabajadores Industriales del Mundo (IWW, por sus siglas en inglés) sindicato fundado en 1905 por socialistas y líderes sindicales que agrupaba a los obreros que no admitía la Federación Estadounidense del Trabajo (pág. 619)

inflation increased prices for goods and services combined with the reduced value of money (p. 25)
inflación alza en los precios de los bienes al mismo tiempo que se produce una devaluación del dinero (pág. 25)

initiative a method of allowing voters to propose a new law if enough signatures are collected on a petition (p. 613)
iniciativa método que permite a los votantes proponer una nueva ley mediante la recopilación de firmas para una petición (pág. 613)

interchangeable parts a process developed by Eli Whitney in the 1790s that called for making each part of a machine exactly the same (p. 349)
piezas intercambiables proceso desarrollado por Eli Whitney en la década de 1790 para que las piezas de todas las máquinas similares fueran exactamente iguales (pág. 349)

interest group a group of people who share common interests for political action (p. 186)
grupo de interés grupo de personas que comparten intereses comunes en lo que respecta a iniciativas políticas (pág. 186)

interstate commerce trade between two or more states (p. 122)
comercio interestatal intercambio comercial entre dos o más estados (pág. 122)

Intolerable Acts (1774) laws passed by Parliament to punish the colonists for the Boston Tea Party and to tighten government control of the colonies (p. 67)
Ley de Asuntos Intolerables (1774) serie de decretos aprobados por el Parlamento para castigar a los colonos que participaron en el Motín del Té de Boston y para aumentar su control sobre las colonias (pág. 67)

ironclad a warship that is heavily armored with iron (p. 482)
acorazado buque de guerra fuertemente protegido con hierro (pág. 482)

Iroquois League a political confederation of five northeastern Native American nations of the Seneca, Oneida, Mohawk, Cayuga, and Onondaga that made decisions concerning war and peace (p. 11)
Liga de Iroqueses confederación política formada por cinco naciones indígenas del noreste de Estados Unidos (los senecas, los oneidas, los mohawks, los cayugas y los onondagas) para tomar decisiones relacionadas con asuntos de guerra y de paz (pág. 11)

isolationism a national policy of avoiding involvement in other countries' affairs (p. 641)
aislacionismo política mediante la cual una nación evita involucrarse en los asuntos de otras naciones (pág. 641)

J

Jacksonian Democracy an expansion of voting rights during the popular Andrew Jackson administration (p. 285)
democracia jacksoniana ampliación del derecho al voto durante el popular gobierno del presidente Andrew Jackson (pág. 285)

Jamestown the first colony in America; set up in 1607 along the James River in Virginia (p. 36)

ENGLISH AND SPANISH GLOSSARY

Jamestown primera colonia estadounidense; fundada en 1607 a lo largo del río James en Virginia (pág. 36)

Jay's Treaty (1794) an agreement negotiated by John Jay to work out problems between Britain and the United States over northwestern lands, British seizure of U.S. ships, and U.S. debts owed to the British (p. 207)
Tratado de Jay (1794) acuerdo negociado por John Jay para resolver los problemas entre Gran Bretaña y Estados Unidos por los territorios del noroeste, por la incautación británica de barcos estadounidenses, y por las deudas estadounidenses con los británicos (pág. 207)

Jim Crow law a law that enforced segregation in the southern states (p. 528)
ley de Jim Crow ley que fomentaba la segregación en los estados del Sur (pág. 528)

John Brown's raid (1859) an incident in which abolitionist John Brown and 21 other men captured a federal arsenal in Harpers Ferry, Virginia, in hope of starting a slave rebellion (p. 455)
ataque de John Brown (1859) incidente en el que el abolicionista John Brown y otros 21 hombres se apropiaron de un arsenal federal en Harpers Ferry, Virginia, con la esperanza de iniciar una rebelión de esclavos (pág. 455)

joint-stock company a business formed by a group of people who jointly make an investment and share in the profits and losses (p. 13)
sociedad por acciones negocio formado por un grupo de personas que realizan una inversión conjuntamente y comparten las ganancias y las pérdidas (pág. 13)

judicial branch the division of the federal government that is made up of the national courts; interprets laws, punishes criminals, and settles disputes between states (p. 129)
Poder Judicial división del gobierno federal conformada por las cortes de justicia; interpreta las leyes, castiga a los delincuentes y resuelve las disputas entre estados (pág. 129)

judicial review the Supreme Court's power to declare acts of Congress unconstitutional (p. 232)
recurso de inconstitucionalidad poder de la Corte Suprema para declarar inconstitucionales las acciones del Congreso (pág. 232)

Judiciary Act of 1789 legislation passed by Congress that created the federal court system (p. 198)
Ley de Judicatura de 1789 decreto aprobado por el Congreso para crear el sistema federal de tribunales (pág. 198)

Kansas-Nebraska Act (1854) a law that allowed voters in Kansas and Nebraska to choose whether to allow slavery (p. 447)
Ley de Kansas y Nebraska (1854) ley que permitía a los votantes de Kansas y Nebraska decidir la aprobación o abolición de la esclavitud (pág. 447)

Kentucky and Virginia Resolutions (1798–99) Republican documents that argued that the Alien and Sedition Acts were unconstitutional (p. 215)
Resoluciones de Kentucky y Virginia (1798–99) documentos republicanos que argumentaban el carácter inconstitucional de las Leyes de No Intervención Extranjera (pág. 215)

Kitchen Cabinet President Andrew Jackson's group of informal advisers; so called because they often met in the White House kitchen (p. 286)
gabinete de la cocina grupo informal de consejeros del presidente Andrew Jackson; llamado así porque solían reunirse en la cocina de la Casa Blanca (pág. 286)

Knights of Labor secret society that became the first truly national labor union in the United States (p. 585)
Knights of Labor sociedad secreta que se convirtió en el primer sindicato verdaderamente nacional en Estados Unidos (pág. 585)

Know-Nothing Party a political organization founded in 1849 by nativists who supported measures making it difficult for foreigners to become citizens and to hold office (p. 402)
Partido de los Ignorantes organización política fundada en 1849 por un grupo de nativistas; apoyaba medidas que dificultaban a los inmigrantes de otros países la adquisición de la ciudadanía estadounidense y su nombramiento en cargos públicos (pág. 402)

Ku Klux Klan a secret society created by white southerners in 1866 that used terror and violence to keep African Americans from obtaining their civil rights (p. 526)
Ku Klux Klan sociedad secreta creada en 1866 por personas de raza blanca del Sur que usaba el terror y la violencia para impedir que los afroamericanos obtuvieran derechos civiles (pág. 526)

Land Ordinance of 1785 legislation passed by Congress authorizing surveys and the division of public lands in the western region of the country (p. 117)
Ordenanza de Territorios de 1785 decreto aprobado por el Congreso en el que se autorizaban las mediciones de terreno y la división de territorios públicos en el oeste del país (pág. 117)

legislative branch the division of the government that proposes bills and passes them into laws (p. 129)
Poder Legislativo división del gobierno federal que propone proyectos de ley y los somete a aprobación para convertirlos en leyes (pág. 129)

Lewis and Clark expedition an expedition led by Meriwether Lewis and William Clark that began in 1804 to explore the Louisiana Purchase (p. 237)
expedición de Lewis y Clark expedición encabezada por Meriwether Lewis y William Clark que partió en 1804 para explorar el territorio adquirido en la Compra de Louisiana (pág. 237)

Lincoln-Douglas debates a series of debates between Republican Abraham Lincoln and Democrat Stephen Douglas during the 1858 U.S. Senate campaign in Illinois (p. 453)
debates Lincoln-Douglas serie de debates entre el republicano Abraham Lincoln y el demócrata Stephen Douglas durante la campaña de 1858 para el Senado estadounidense en Illinois (pág. 453)

Lochner* v. *New York (1905) Supreme Court case that ruled that states could not restrict the rights of employers and workers to enter into any labor agreement they wished (p. 618)
Lochner* contra *Nueva York (1905) caso de la Corte Suprema que resolvió que los estados no podían restringir el derecho de los empleadores y los trabajadores de alcanzar el acuerdo laboral que quisieran (pág. 618)

Long Walk (1864) a 300-mile march made by Navajo captives to a reservation in Bosque Redondo, New Mexico, that led to the deaths of hundreds of Navajo (p. 557)
La Larga Marcha (1864) caminata de 300 millas que hizo un grupo de prisioneros navajos hasta una reservación indígena en Bosque Redondo, Nuevo México, en la que murieron cientos de ellos (pág. 557)

loose construction a way of interpreting the Constitution that allows the federal government to take actions that the Constitution does not specifically forbid it from taking (p. 204)
interpretación flexible interpretación de la Constitución que permite al gobierno federal tomar acciones que el mismo documento no prohíbe de manera específica (pág. 204)

Louisiana Purchase (1803) the purchase of French land between the Mississippi River and the Rocky Mountains that doubled the size of the United States (p. 236)
Compra de Luisiana (1803) adquisición del territorio francés localizado entre el río Mississippi y las montañas Rocallosas, que duplicó el tamaño del territorio de Estados Unidos (pág. 236)

Lowell system the use of waterpowered textile mills that employed young, unmarried women in the 1800s (p. 354)
sistema de Lowell el uso de molinos de agua en la industria textil, medida que dio empleo a muchas mujeres jóvenes solteras en el siglo XIX (pág. 354)

Loyalists colonists who sided with Britain in the American Revolution (p. 84)
leales colonos que apoyaron la causa británica durante la Guerra de Independencia estadounidense (pág. 84)

M

Magna Carta (1215) a charter of liberties agreed to by King John of England, it made the king obey the same laws as citizens (p. 114)
Carta Magna (1215) carta de libertades, firmada por el rey Juan de Inglaterra, que establecía que el rey debía obedecer las mismas leyes que el resto de los ciudadanos (pág. 114)

majority rule the idea that policies are decided by the greatest number of people (p. 178)
principio de la mayoría idea de que las políticas se adoptan en función de lo que decida el mayor número de personas (pág. 178)

manifest destiny a belief shared by many Americans in the mid-1800s that the United States should expand across the continent to the Pacific Ocean (p. 316)
destino manifiesto creencia de muchos ciudadanos estadounidenses a mediados del siglo XIX de que Estados Unidos debía expandirse por todo el continente hasta el océano Pacífico (pág. 316)

Marbury* v. *Madison (1803) U.S. Supreme Court case that established the principle of judicial review (p. 232)
Marbury* contra *Madison (1803) caso de la Corte Suprema que dio origen al recurso de inconstitucionalidad (pág. 232)

Massacre at Wounded Knee (1890) the U.S. Army's killing of approximately 150 Sioux at Wounded Knee Creek in South Dakota; ended U.S-Indian wars on the Plains (p. 557)
matanza de Wounded Knee (1890) matanza de aproximadamente 150 indios siux en Wounded Knee Creek, Dakota del Sur; dio por terminadas las guerras entre estadounidenses e indígenas en las Planicies (pág. 557)

mass culture leisure and cultural activities shared by many people (p. 595)
cultura de masas actividades de ocio y cultura populares entre mucha gente (pág. 595)

mass production the efficient production of large numbers of identical goods (p. 349)
producción en masa producción eficiente de grandes cantidades de productos idénticos (pág. 349)

mass transit public transportation (p. 595)
transporte colectivo transporte público (pág. 595)

Mayflower Compact (1620) a document written by the Pilgrims establishing themselves as a political society and setting guidelines for self-government (p. 43)
Pacto del Mayflower (1620) documento redactado por los peregrinos en el que se constituían en una sociedad política y establecían los principios para gobernarse a sí mismos (pág. 43)

McCulloch* v. *Maryland (1819) U.S. Supreme Court case that declared the Second Bank of the United States was constitutional and that Maryland could not interfere with it (p. 292)
McCulloch* contra *Maryland (1819) caso de la Corte Suprema que declaraba que el Segundo Banco de la Nación era constitucional y que Maryland no podía intervenir en sus operaciones (pág. 292)

mercenaries hired foreign soldiers (p. 92)
mercenarios soldados extranjeros a sueldo (pág. 92)

Mexican Revolution a revolution led by Francisco Madero in 1910 that eventually forced the Mexican dictator Díaz to resign (p. 660)

Revolución mexicana revolución iniciada en 1910 por Francisco Madero, que finalmente obligó al dictador mexicano Díaz a renunciar (pág. 660)

middle class the social and economic level between the wealthy and the poor (p. 402)
clase media nivel social y económico ubicado entre la clase rica y la clase pobre (pág. 402)

Middle Passage a voyage that brought enslaved Africans across the Atlantic Ocean to North America and the West Indies (p. 58)
Paso Central viaje a través del océano Atlántico para transportar esclavos africanos a Norteamérica y a las Antillas (pág. 58)

migration the movement of people from one region to another (p. 6)
migración desplazamiento de personas de una región a otra (pág. 6)

minutemen American colonial militia members ready to fight at a minute's notice (p. 79)
milicianos miembros de la milicia norteamericana en la época colonial que estaban preparados para combatir en cualquier momento si la situación lo requería (pág. 79)

Missouri Compromise (1820) an agreement proposed by Henry Clay that allowed Missouri to enter the Union as a slave state and Maine to enter as a free state and outlawed slavery in any territories or states north of 36°30´ latitude (p. 267)
Acuerdo de Missouri (1820) acuerdo redactado por Henry Clay en el que se aceptaba a Missouri en la Unión como estado esclavista y a Maine como estado libre, además de prohibir la esclavitud en los territorios o estados localizados al norte del paralelo 36°30´ (pág. 267)

Monroe Doctrine (1823) President James Monroe's statement forbidding further colonization in the Americas and declaring that any attempt by a foreign country to colonize would be considered an act of hostility (p. 262)
Doctrina Monroe (1823) declaración hecha por el presidente James Monroe en la que se prohibía la colonización adicional del continente americano a partir de entonces, considerando cualquier intento de colonización por parte de un país extranjero como inicio de hostilidades (pág. 262)

Mormon a member of the Church of Jesus Christ of Latter-day Saints (p. 310)
mormón miembro de la Iglesia de Jesucristo de los Santos de los Últimos Días (pág. 310)

Morrill Act (1862) a federal law passed by Congress that gave land to western states to encourage them to build colleges (p. 560)
Ley de Morrill (1862) ley federal aprobada por el Congreso para otorgar tierras a los estados del Oeste con el fin de fomentar la construcción de universidades (pág. 560)

Morse code a system developed by Alfred Lewis Vail for the telegraph that used a certain combination of dots and dashes to represent each letter of the alphabet (p. 365)
clave Morse sistema desarrollado por Alfred Lewis Vail para el telégrafo en el que una combinación de puntos y rayas representa cada letra del alfabeto (pág. 365)

mountain men men hired by eastern companies to trap animals for fur in the Rocky Mountains and other western regions of the United States (p. 308)
montañeses hombres contratados por compañías del este para atrapar animales y obtener sus pieles en las montañas Rocallosas y en otras regiones del oeste de Estados Unidos (pág. 308)

muckrakers a term coined for journalists who "raked up" and exposed corruption and problems of society (p. 610)
muckrakers término acuñado para denominar a los periodistas que se dedicaban a investigar y exponer la corrupción y los problemas de la sociedad (pág. 610)

N

National American Woman Suffrage Association (NAWSA) an organization founded by Elizabeth Cady Stanton and Susan B. Anthony in 1890 to obtain women's right to vote (p. 623)
Asociación Nacional Estadounidense para el Sufragio Femenino (NAWSA, por sus siglas en inglés) organización fundada en 1890 por Elizabeth Cady Stanton y Susan B. Anthony para obtener el derecho al voto de las mujeres (pág. 623)

National Association for the Advancement of Colored People (NAACP) an organization founded in 1909 by W. E. B. Du Bois and other reformers to bring attention to racial inequality (p. 625)
Asociación Nacional para el Progreso de la Gente de Color (NAACP, por sus siglas en inglés) organización fundada en 1909 por W. E. B. Du Bois y otros reformadores para llamar la atención sobre la desigualdad racial existente (pág. 625)

national debt the total amount of money owed by a country to its lenders (p. 200)
deuda pública cantidad de dinero que un país debe a sus acreedores (pág. 200)

National Grange a social and educational organization for farmers (p. 563)
National Grange organización social y educativa para los agricultores (pág. 563)

nationalism a sense of pride and devotion to a nation (p. 264)
nacionalismo sentimiento de orgullo y lealtad a una nación (pág. 264)

National Woman's Party (NWP) a women's suffrage organization that used more aggressive means than the National American Woman Suffrage Association to attain its goals (p. 624)
Partido Nacional de la Mujer (NWP, por sus siglas en inglés) organización a favor del sufragio femenino que empleaba medios más agresivos que la Asociación Nacional Estadounidense para el Sufragio Femenino para alcanzar sus objetivos (pág. 624)

nativists U.S. citizens who opposed immigration because they were suspicious of immigrants and feared losing jobs to them (p. 402)
nativistas ciudadanos estadounidenses que se oponían a la aceptación de inmigrantes porque sospechaban de ellos y temían que se apropiaran de sus empleos (pág. 402)

Nat Turner's Rebellion (1831) a rebellion in which Nat Turner led a group of slaves in Virginia in an unsuccessful attempt to overthrow and kill planter families (p. 390)
Rebelión de Nat Turner (1831) rebelión de un grupo de esclavos encabezados por Nat Turner en Virginia en un intento frustrado de derrocar y asesinar a los dueños de plantaciones y a sus familias (pág. 390)

naturalized citizen a person born in another country who has been granted citizenship in the United States (p. 184)
ciudadano naturalizado persona nacida en otro país que ha obtenido la ciudadanía estadounidense (pág. 184)

Neutrality Proclamation (1793) a statement made by President George Washington that the United States would not side with any of the nations at war in Europe following the French Revolution (p. 206)
Proclamación de Neutralidad (1793) declaración en la que el presidente George Washington anunció que Estados Unidos no sería aliado de ninguna de las naciones europeas en guerra después de la Revolución francesa (pág. 206)

new immigrant a term often used for an immigrant who arrived in the United States beginning in the 1880s (p. 588)
nuevo inmigrante término empleado a menudo para referirse a los inmigrantes que llegaron a Estados Unidos a partir de la década de 1880 (pág. 588)

New Jersey Plan a proposal to create a unicameral legislature with equal representation of states rather than representation by population; rejected at the Constitutional Convention (p. 127)
Plan de Nueva Jersey propuesta para la creación de un gobierno con una sola cámara que contara con la misma representación por parte de cada estado, sin basarse en el tamaño de su población; la propuesta fue rechazada en la Convención Constitucional (pág. 127)

Nineteenth Amendment (1920) a constitutional amendment that gave women the vote (p. 624)
Decimonovena Enmienda (1920) enmienda constitucional que otorgó a la mujer el derecho al voto (pág. 624)

nominating conventions a meeting at which a political party selects its presidential and vice presidential candidate; first held in the 1820s (p. 285)
convenciones de nominación encuentro en el que un partido político elige a sus candidatos a la presidencia y la vicepresidencia; se realizaron por primera vez en la década de 1820 (pág. 285)

Non-Intercourse Act (1809) a law that replaced the Embargo Act and restored trade with all nations except Britain, France, and their colonies (p. 242)
Ley de No Interacción (1809) ley que reemplazaba a la Ley de Embargo, restableciendo el intercambio comercial con todas las naciones, excepto Gran Bretaña, Francia y sus colonias (pág. 242)

Northwest Ordinance of 1787 legislation passed by Congress to establish a political structure for the Northwest Territory and create a system for the admission of new states (p. 117)
Ordenanza del Noroeste de 1787 ley aprobada por el Congreso para establecer una estructura política en el Territorio del Noroeste y crear un proceso de admisión de nuevos estados (pág. 117)

Northwest Passage a nonexistent path through North America that early explorers searched for that would allow ships to sail from the Atlantic to the Pacific Ocean (p. 17)
Pasaje del Noroeste ruta inexistente buscada por muchos exploradores a lo largo de Norteamérica para cruzar en barco del océano Atlántico al océano Pacífico (pág. 17)

Northwest Territory lands including present-day Illinois, Indiana, Michigan, Ohio, and Wisconsin; organized by the Northwest Ordinance of 1787 (p. 117)
Territorio del Noroeste organización del territorio que incluía los actuales estados de Illinois, Indiana, Michigan, Ohio y Wisconsin; creado por la Ordenanza del Noroeste de 1787 (pág. 117)

nullification crisis a dispute led by John C. Calhoun that said that states could ignore federal laws if they believed those laws violated the Constitution (p. 290)
crisis de anulación controversia iniciada por John C. Calhoun que argumentaba que los estados podían hacer caso omiso a las leyes federales si consideraban que dichas leyes violaban la Constitución (pág. 290)

O

old immigrant a term often used for an immigrant who arrived in the United States before the 1880s (p. 588)
antiguo inmigrante término empleado a menudo para referirse a los inmigrantes que llegaron a Estados Unidos antes de la década de 1880 (pág. 588)

Open Door Policy a policy established by the United States in 1899 to promote equal access for all nations to trade in China (p. 644)
política de puertas abiertas política establecida por Estados Unidos en 1899 para promover el acceso por igual a todas las naciones al intercambio comercial con China (pág. 644)

Oregon Trail a 2,000-mile trail stretching through the Great Plains from western Missouri to the Oregon Territory (p. 309)
Camino de Oregón ruta de 2,000 millas que cruzaba las Grandes Planicies desde el oeste de Missouri hasta el Territorio de Oregón (pág. 309)

Paleo-Indians the first Americans who crossed from Asia into North America sometime between 38,000 and 10,000 BC (p. 6)
paleoindígenas primeros habitantes de América que cruzaron de Asia a Norteamérica entre el 38,000 y el 10,000 a. C. (pág. 6)

Panama Canal an artificial waterway across the Isthmus of Panama; completed by the United States in 1914 (p. 655)
canal de Panamá canal artificial que atraviesa el istmo de Panamá; Estados Unidos completó su construcción en 1914 (pág. 655)

Panic of 1837 a financial crisis in the United States that led to an economic depression (p. 293)
Pánico de 1837 crisis financiera en Estados Unidos que provocó una depresión económica (pág. 293)

pardon freedom from punishment (p. 147)
indulto liberación de un castigo (pág. 147)

patent an exclusive right to make or sell an invention (p. 576)
patente derecho de exclusividad para la fabricación o venta de un invento (pág. 576)

Patriots American colonists who fought for independence from Great Britain during the Revolutionary War (p. 84)
patriotas colonos estadounidenses que lucharon para independizarse de Gran Bretaña durante la Guerra de Independencia estadounidense (pág. 84)

Pendleton Civil Service Act (1883) a law applying a merit system controlled by the Civil Service Commission to federal government jobs (p. 608)
Ley Pendleton de Administración Pública (1883) ley que estableció un sistema de méritos controlado por la Comisión de Administración Pública para otorgar empleos en el gobierno federal (pág. 608)

petition to make a formal request of the government (p. 179)
petición hacer una solicitud formal al gobierno (pág. 179)

Pickett's Charge (1863) a failed Confederate attack during the Civil War led by General George Pickett at the Battle of Gettysburg (p. 499)
ataque de Pickett (1863) ataque fallido del ejército confederado, al mando del general George Pickett, en la batalla de Gettysburg durante la Guerra Civil (pág. 499)

Pilgrim a member of a Puritan Separatist sect that left England in the early 1600s to settle in the Americas (p. 42)
peregrino miembro de una secta separatista puritana que emigró de Inglaterra a principios del siglo XVII para establecerse en América (pág. 42)

Pinckney's Treaty (1795) an agreement between the United States and Spain that changed Florida's border and made it easier for American ships to use the port of New Orleans (p. 207)
tratado de Pinckney (1795) acuerdo entre Estados Unidos y España que modificó los límites de Florida y facilitó a los barcos estadounidenses el uso del puerto de Nueva Orleáns (pág. 207)

placer miner a person who mines for gold by using pans or other devices to wash gold nuggets out of loose rock and gravel (p. 328)
buscador de oro con batea persona que busca oro con bateas u otros dispositivos similares para lavar las pepitas de oro y separarlas de las piedras y la gravilla del lecho de un río (pág. 328)

plantation a large farm that usually specialized in growing one kind of crop for profit (p. 23)
plantación gran finca que por lo general se especializa en un cultivo específico para obtener ganancias (pág. 23)

planter a large-scale farmer who held more than 20 slaves (p. 378)
hacendado agricultor a gran escala que tenía más de 20 esclavos (pág. 378)

Platt Amendment a part of the Cuban constitution drafted under the supervision of the United States that limited Cuba's right to make treaties, gave the U.S. the right to intervene in Cuban affairs, and required Cuba to sell or lease land to the U.S (p. 650)
Enmienda Platt parte de la constitución cubana cuyo borrador fue redactado bajo la supervisión de Estados Unidos y que limitaba el derecho de Cuba a firmar tratados, otorgaba a Estados Unidos el derecho de intervenir en los asuntos cubanos y exigía a Cuba vender o arrendar tierras a Estados Unidos (pág. 650)

Plessy* v. *Ferguson (1896) U.S. Supreme Court case that established the separate-but-equal doctrine for public facilities (p. 529)
Plessy* contra *Ferguson (1896) caso en el que la Corte Suprema estableció la doctrina de "separados pero iguales" en los lugares públicos (pág. 529)

political action committee (PAC) an organization that collects money to distribute to candidates who support the same issues as the contributors (p. 186)
comité de acción política (PAC, por sus siglas en inglés) organización que recolecta dinero para distribuirlo entre los candidatos que apoyan los mismos asuntos que los contribuyentes (pág. 186)

political machine a powerful organization that influenced city and county politics in the late 1800s (p. 606)
maquinaria política organización poderosa que influía en la política municipal y del condado a finales del siglo XIX (pág. 606)

political party a group of people who organize to help elect government officials and influence government policies (p. 212)
partido político grupo de personas que se organiza para facilitar la elección de los funcionarios del gobierno e influye en las políticas gubernamentales (pág. 212)

poll tax a special tax that a person had to pay in order to vote (p. 528)
impuesto electoral impuesto especial que debía pagar una persona para poder votar (pág. 528)

Pony Express a system of messengers that carried mail between relay stations on a route 2,000-miles long in 1860 and 1861 (p. 550)
Pony Express sistema de mensajeros que transportaba el correo entre estaciones de relevo a lo largo de una ruta de 2,000 millas entre 1860 y 1861 (pág. 550)

popular sovereignty the idea that political authority belongs to the people (pp. 129, 438)
soberanía popular idea de que la autoridad política pertenece al pueblo (págs. 129, 438)

Populist Party a political party formed in 1892 that supported free coinage of silver, work reforms, immigration restrictions, and government ownership of railroads and telegraph and telephone systems (p. 564)
Partido Populista partido político formado en 1892 que apoyaba la libre producción de monedas de plata, reformas laborales y restricciones inmigratorias, además de asignar al gobierno la propiedad de los sistemas ferroviario, telegráfico y telefónico (pág. 564)

Pottawatomie Massacre (1856) an incident in which abolitionist John Brown and seven other men murdered pro-slavery Kansans (p. 448)
matanza de Pottawatomie (1856) incidente en el que el abolicionista John Brown y siete hombres más asesinaron a habitantes de Kansas que apoyaban la esclavitud (pág. 448)

precedent an action or decision that later serves as an example (p. 197)
precedente acción o decisión que más tarde sirve de ejemplo (pág. 197)

printing press a machine that produces printed copies (p. 25)
imprenta máquina que produce copias impresas (pág. 25)

privateer a private ship authorized by a nation to attack its enemies (p. 206)
corsario barco privado autorizado por una nación para atacar a sus enemigos (pág. 206)

progressives a group of reformers who worked to improve social and political problems in the late 1800s (p. 610)
progresistas grupo de reformistas que trabajaban para resolver problemas sociales y políticos a finales del siglo XIX (pág. 610)

prospect to search for gold (p. 328)
catear buscar oro (pág. 328)

Protestant Reformation a religious movement begun by Martin Luther and others in 1517 to reform the Catholic Church (p. 25)
Reforma protestante movimiento religioso iniciado por Martín Lutero y otros en 1517 para reformar la Iglesia católica (pág. 25)

Protestants reformers who protested certain practices of the Catholic Church (p. 25)
protestantes reformistas que protestaban por ciertas prácticas de la Iglesia católica (pág. 25)

Pullman strike (1894) a railroad strike that ended when President Grover Cleveland sent in federal troops (p. 587)
huelga de Pullman (1894) huelga de los trabajadores del ferrocarril que finalizó cuando el presidente Grover Cleveland envió a tropas federales (pág. 587)

Puritans Protestants who wanted to reform the Church of England (p. 42)
puritanos protestantes que querían reformar la Iglesia anglicana (pág. 42)

Quakers Society of Friends; Protestant sect founded in 1640s in England whose members believed that salvation was available to all people (p. 50)
cuáqueros Sociedad de Amigos; secta protestante fundada en la década de 1640 en Inglaterra cuyos miembros creían que la salvación estaba al alcance de todos (pág. 50)

Radical Republicans members of Congress who felt that southern states needed to make great social changes before they could be readmitted to the Union (p. 519)
republicanos radicales integrantes del Congreso convencidos de que los estados del Sur necesitaban realizar grandes cambios sociales antes de volver a ser admitidos en la Unión (pág. 519)

ratification an official approval (p. 116)
ratificación aprobación formal (pág. 116)

recall a vote to remove an official from office (p. 613)
destitución votación para retirar a un funcionario de su cargo (pág. 613)

Reconstruction (1865–77) the period following the Civil War during which the U.S. government worked to reunite the nation and to rebuild the southern states (p. 512)
Reconstrucción (1865–77) período posterior a la Guerra Civil en el que el gobierno de Estados Unidos trabajó por lograr la unificación de la nación y la reconstrucción de los estados del Sur (pág. 512)

Reconstruction Acts (1867–68) the laws that put the southern states under U.S. military control and required them to draft new constitutions upholding the Fourteenth Amendment (p. 521)
Leyes de Reconstrucción (1867–68) leyes que declaraban a los estados del Sur territorio sujeto a control militar estadounidense y los obligaban a reformar sus constituciones, de manera que defendieran la Decimocuarta Enmienda (pág. 521)

Redcoats British soldiers who fought against the colonists in the American Revolution; so called because of their bright red uniforms (p. 80)
casacas rojas soldados británicos que lucharon contra los colonos en la Guerra de Independencia estadounidense, llamados así por el color rojo brillante de sus uniformes (pág. 80)

referendum a procedure that allows voters to approve or reject a law already proposed or passed by government (p. 613)

ENGLISH AND SPANISH GLOSSARY

referéndum medida que permite a los ciudadanos votar para aprobar o rechazar una ley previamente propuesta o aprobada por el gobierno (pág. 613)

Republican Party a political party formed in the 1850s to stop the spread of slavery in the West (p. 450)
Partido Republicano partido político formado en la década de 1850 para detener la expansión de la esclavitud en el Oeste (pág. 450)

reservations federal lands set aside for American Indians (p. 555)
reservaciones territorios federales apartados para los indígenas norteamericanos (pág. 555)

Rhode Island system a system developed by Samuel Slater in the mid-1800s in which whole families were hired as textile workers and factory work was divided into simple tasks (p. 353)
Sistema de Rhode Island sistema desarrollado por Samuel Slater a mediados del siglo XIX mediante el cual se contrataba a familias completas para trabajar en la industria textil y en el que el trabajo de las fábricas estaba dividido en tareas sencillas (pág. 353)

Roosevelt Corollary (1904) Theodore Roosevelt's addition to the Monroe Doctrine warning nations in the Americas that if they didn't pay their debts, the United States would get involved (p. 656)
Corolario de Roosevelt (1904) agregado del presidente Theodore Roosevelt a la Doctrina Monroe advirtiendo a las naciones de América que si no pagaban sus deudas, el gobierno de Estados Unidos intervendría (pág. 656)

Rush-Bagot Agreement (1817) an agreement that limited naval power on the Great Lakes for both the United States and British Canada (p. 260)
Acuerdo de Rush-Bagot (1817) acuerdo que limitaba el poder naval en los Grandes Lagos a embarcaciones de Estados Unidos y de la Canadá británica (pág. 260)

S

Santa Fe Trail an important trade trail west from Independence, Missouri, to Santa Fe, New Mexico (p. 310)
Camino de Santa Fe importante ruta comercial que va desde Independence, Missouri, hasta Santa Fe, Nuevo México (pág. 310)

search warrant a judge's order authorizing the search of a person's home or property to look for evidence of a crime (p. 180)
orden de cateo orden de un juez que permite registrar el hogar y las propiedades de una persona en busca de posibles pruebas de un delito (pág. 180)

secession the act of formally withdrawing from the Union (p. 458)
secesión acto de separarse formalmente de la Unión (pág. 458)

Second Battle of Bull Run (1862) a Civil War battle in which the Confederate army forced most of the Union army out of Virginia (p. 480)
segunda batalla de Bull Run (1862) batalla de la Guerra Civil en la que el ejército confederado obligó a gran parte de las tropas de la Unión a abandonar el territorio de Virginia (pág. 480)

Second Continental Congress (1775) a meeting of colonial delegates in Philadelphia to decide how to react to fighting at Lexington and Concord (p. 80)
Segundo Congreso Continental (1775) reunión de delegados coloniales realizada en Filadelfia para tomar decisiones acerca de la lucha en Lexington y Concord (pág. 80)

Second Great Awakening a period of religious evangelism that began in the 1790s and became widespread in the United States by the 1830s (p. 410)
Segundo Gran Despertar período de evangelización religiosa iniciado en la década de 1790 que se extendió por Estados Unidos para la década de 1830 (pág. 410)

Second Industrial Revolution a period of rapid growth in manufacturing and industry in the late 1800s (p. 575)
segunda revolución industrial período de gran crecimiento en la manufactura y en la industria, a finales del siglo XIX (pág. 575)

sectionalism a devotion to the interests of one geographic region over the interests of the country as a whole (pp. 266, 439)
regionalismo dedicación a los intereses de una región geográfica y no a los de un país (págs. 266, 439)

segregation the forced separation of people of different races in public places (p. 528)
segregación separación obligada de personas de diferentes razas en lugares públicos (pág. 528)

Seneca Falls Convention (1848) the first national women's rights convention at which the Declaration of Sentiments was written (p. 426)
Convención de Seneca Falls (1848) primera convención nacional a favor de los derechos de la mujer, en la cual se redactó la Declaración de Sentimientos (pág. 426)

settlement houses neighborhood centers staffed by professionals and volunteers for education, recreation, and social activities in poor areas (p. 597)
casas de la comunidad centros comunitarios atendidos por profesionales y voluntarios para ofrecer educación, esparcimiento y actividades sociales en zonas pobres (pág. 597)

Seven Days' Battles (1862) a series of Civil War battles in which Confederate army successes forced the Union army to retreat from Richmond, Virginia, the Confederate capital (p. 480)
batallas de los Siete Días (1862) serie de batallas de la Guerra Civil en las que las victorias del ejército confederado obligaron a las tropas de la Unión a retirarse de Richmond, Virginia, la capital confederada (pág. 480)

Seventeenth Amendment (1913) a constitutional amendment allowing American voters to directly elect U.S. senators (p. 613)
Decimoséptima Enmienda (1913) enmienda constitucional que permite a los votantes estadounidenses elegir directamente a los senadores de Estados Unidos (pág. 613)

sharecropping a system used on southern farms after the Civil War in which farmers worked land owned by someone else in return for a small portion of the crops (p. 529)
cultivo de aparceros sistema usado en las fincas sureñas después de la Guerra Civil en el que los agricultores trabajaban las tierras de otra persona a cambio de una pequeña porción de la cosecha (pág. 529)

Shays's Rebellion (1786–87) an uprising of Massachusetts's farmers, led by Daniel Shays, to protest high taxes, heavy debt, and farm foreclosures (p. 123)
Rebelión de Shays (1786–87) rebelión de los agricultores de Massachusetts, encabezados por Daniel Shays, para protestar por los altos impuestos, el aumento de sus deudas y la confiscación de las granjas (pág. 123)

Sherman Antitrust Act (1890) a law that made it illegal to create monopolies or trusts that restrained free trade (p. 582)
Ley Antimonopolio de Sherman (1890) ley que prohibía la creación de monopolios o consorcios que restringieran el libre comercio (pág. 582)

Siege of Vicksburg (1863) the Union army's six-week blockade of Vicksburg that led the city to surrender during the Civil War (p. 486)
Sitio de Vicksburg (1863) bloqueo de seis semanas realizado por el ejército de la Unión en Vicksburg para forzar la rendición de esa ciudad durante la Guerra Civil (pág. 486)

slave codes laws passed in the colonies to control slaves (p. 41)
códigos de esclavos leyes aprobadas por las colonias para el control de los esclavos (pág. 41)

social Darwinism a view of society based on Charles Darwin's scientific theory of natural selection (p. 658)
darwinismo social visión de la sociedad basada en la teoría científica de la selección natural de Charles Darwin (pág. 658)

socialism economic system in which government owns and operates a country's means of production (p. 619)
socialismo sistema económico en el que el gobierno controla y maneja los medios de producción de un país (pág. 619)

society a group of people who live together and share a culture (p. 7)
sociedad grupo de personas que viven juntas y comparten la misma cultura (pág. 7)

sodbusters the name given to Plains farmers who worked hard to break up the region's tough sod (p. 561)
sodbusters nombre dado a los agricultores de las Planicies que se esforzaron mucho para trabajar el duro terreno de la región (pág. 561)

Spanish Armada a large Spanish fleet defeated by England in 1588 (p. 25)
Armada española gran flota española que fue derrotada por las tropas de Inglaterra en 1588 (pág. 25)

speculator an investor who buys items at low prices in hope that their values will rise (p. 201)
especulador inversionista que compra artículos a precios bajos con la esperanza de que aumente su valor (pág. 201)

sphere of influence an area where foreign countries control trade or natural resources of another nation or area (p. 644)
esfera de influencia área de un país cuyos recursos naturales y comercio son controlados por otra nación o área (pág. 644)

spirituals emotional Christian songs sung by enslaved people in the South that mixed African and European elements and usually expressed slaves' religious beliefs (p. 389)
espirituales canciones religiosas cantadas con gran emotividad por los esclavos del Sur que combinaban elementos de origen africano y europeo y solían expresar sus creencias religiosas (pág. 389)

spoils system a politicians' practice of giving government jobs to his or her supporters (p. 286)
tráfico de influencias práctica de los políticos de ofrecer empleos a las personas que los apoyan (pág. 286)

Stamp Act of 1765 a law passed by Parliament that raised tax money by requiring colonists to pay for an official stamp whenever they bought paper items such as newspapers, licenses, and legal documents (p. 64)
Ley del Timbre de 1765 ley aprobada por el Parlamento para recaudar impuestos en la que se obligaba a los colonos a pagar un timbre oficial cada vez que compraran artículos de papel, como periódicos, licencias y documentos legales (pág. 64)

staple crop a crop that is continuously in demand (p. 51)
cultivo básico producto de demanda constante (pág. 51)

states' rights doctrine the belief that the power of the states should be greater than the power of the federal government (p. 290)
doctrina de los derechos estatales creencia de que el poder de los estados debe ser mayor que el del gobierno federal (pág. 290)

steerage the area on a ship in the lower levels where the steering mechanisms were located and where cramped quarters were provided for people who could only afford cheap passage (p. 588)
tercera clase área inferior del casco de un barco en la que se encontraban los mecanismos del timón y se ofrecían habitaciones muy reducidas para las personas que sólo podían comprar un pasaje barato (pág. 588)

strict construction a way of interpreting the Constitution that allows the federal government to take only those actions the Constitution specifically says it can take (p. 204)
interpretación estricta interpretación de la Constitución que sólo permite al gobierno federal realizar las acciones permitidas de manera específica en ella (pág. 204)

strike the refusal of workers to perform their jobs until employers meet their demands (p. 356)

huelga negativa de los empleados a trabajar hasta que sus empleadores satisfagan sus demandas (pág. 356)

subsidy a bonus payment (p. 642)
subsidio pago adicional (pág. 642)

suburb a neighborhood outside of a downtown area (p. 595)
suburbio vecindario residencial en las afueras de una ciudad (pág. 595)

suffrage voting rights (p. 115)
sufragio derecho al voto (pág. 115)

Tariff of Abominations (1828) the nickname given to a tariff by southerners who opposed it (p. 289)
Arancel de abominaciones (1828) sobrenombre dado a un nuevo impuesto por los habitantes del Sur que se oponían a éste (pág. 289)

tariff a tax on imports or exports (p. 121)
arancel impuestos pagados por los bienes importados o exportados (pág. 121)

Tea Act (1773) a law passed by Parliament allowing the British East India Company to sell its low-cost tea directly to the colonies, undermining colonial tea merchants; led to the Boston Tea Party (p. 66)
Tea Act/Ley del Té (1773) ley aprobada por el Parlamento británico que le permitía a la British East India Company vender té a bajo costo a las colonias sin intermediarios, afectando a los comerciantes locales de té; esta decisión dio origen al Motín del Té de Boston (pág. 66)

technology the tools used to produce goods or to do work (p. 349)
tecnología herramientas utilizadas para producir bienes o realizar un trabajo (pág. 349)

telegraph a machine perfected by Samuel F. B. Morse in 1832 that uses pulses of electric current to send messages across long distances through wires (p. 364)
telégrafo máquina perfeccionada por Samuel F. B. Morse en 1832 que emplea impulsos eléctricos transmitidos por cables para enviar mensajes a grandes distancias (pág. 364)

Teller Amendment (1898) a congressional resolution stating that the U.S. had no interest in taking control of Cuba (p. 647)
Enmienda Teller (1898) resolución del Congreso en la que Estados Unidos declaraba que no tenía intención de tomar el control de Cuba (pág. 647)

temperance movement a social reform effort begun in the mid-1800s to encourage people to drink less alcohol (p. 411)
movimiento de abstinencia movimiento de reforma social iniciado a mediados del siglo XIX para fomentar la disminución en el consumo de bebidas alcohólicas (pág. 411)

Ten Percent Plan President Abraham Lincoln's plan for Reconstruction; once 10 percent of voters in a former Confederate state took a U.S. loyalty oath, they could form a new state government and be readmitted to the Union (p. 513)
Plan del Diez por Ciento plan de Reconstrucción del presidente Abraham Lincoln; si el 10 por ciento de los votantes de un estado que había sido parte de la Confederación juraba lealtad a la nación, tenían derecho a formar un nuevo gobierno y ser readmitidos en la Unión (pág. 513)

tenements poorly built, overcrowded housing where many immigrants lived (p. 404)
barracas casas mal construidas donde vivían amontonados una gran cantidad de inmigrantes (pág. 404)

textile cloth (p. 347)
textil tela (pág. 347)

Thirteenth Amendment (1865) a constitutional amendment that outlawed slavery (p. 514)
Decimotercera Enmienda (1865) enmienda constitucional que abolió la esclavitud (pág. 514)

Three-Fifths Compromise (1787) an agreement worked out at the Constitutional Convention stating that enslaved people would be counted as three-fifths of a person when determining a state's population for representation in the lower house of Congress (p. 128)
Acuerdo de las Tres Quintas Partes (1787) acuerdo negociado durante la Convención Constitucional en el que se estableció que los esclavos contarían como tres quintas partes de una persona para determinar la representación de ese estado en el Congreso (pág. 128)

Toleration Act of 1649 a Maryland law that made restricting the religious rights of Christians a crime; the first law guaranteeing religious freedom to be passed in America (p. 39)
Ley de Tolerancia de 1649 ley de Maryland que calificaba como delito la restricción de los derechos religiosos de los cristianos; fue la primera ley que garantizó la libertad religiosa en América (pág. 39)

total war a type of war in which an army destroys its opponent's ability to fight by targeting civilian and economic as well as military resources (p. 502)
guerra total tipo de guerra en la que un ejército destruye la capacidad de lucha de su oponente mediante ataques a la población civil, la economía y los recursos militares (pág. 502)

totems images of ancestors or animal spirits; often carved onto tall, wooden poles by Native American peoples of the Pacific Northwest (p. 10)
tótems imágenes de antepasados o animales; a menudo talladas en troncos de árboles cortados por los indígenas de la costa noroeste del Pacífico (pág. 10)

town meeting a political meeting at which people make decisions on local issues; used primarily in New England (p. 55)
reunión del pueblo reunión política en la que los habitantes de una población toman decisiones sobre temas locales; se realizan principalmente en Nueva Inglaterra (pág. 55)

trade unions workers' organizations that try to improve working conditions (p. 356)
sindicatos organizaciones formadas por trabajadores para mejorar sus condiciones laborales (pág. 356)

Trail of Tears (1838–39) an 800-mile forced march made by the Cherokee from their homeland in Georgia to Indian Territory; resulted in the deaths of almost one-fourth of the Cherokee people (p. 296)
Ruta de las lágrimas (1838–39) marcha forzada de 800 millas que realizó la tribu cherokee desde su territorio natal en Georgia hasta el Territorio Indígena, y en la que perdió la vida casi una cuarta parte del pueblo cherokee (pág. 296)

transcendentalism the idea that people could rise above the material things in life; a popular movement among New England writers and thinkers in the mid-1800s (p. 405)
trascendentalismo creencia de que las personas podían prescindir de los objetos materiales en la vida; movimiento popular entre los escritores y pensadores de Nueva Inglaterra a mediados del siglo XIX (pág. 405)

transcontinental railroad a railroad system that crossed the continental United States; construction began in 1863 (p. 550)
ferrocarril transcontinental línea ferroviaria que cruzaba Estados Unidos de un extremo a otro; su construcción se inició en 1863 (pág. 550)

Transportation Revolution the rapid growth in the speed and convenience of transportation (p. 358)
revolución del transporte rápido crecimiento de la velocidad y comodidad ofrecida por los medios de transporte (pág. 358)

Treaty of Fort Jackson a treaty signed after the U.S. victory at the Battle of Horseshoe Bend; the Creek was forced to give up 23 million acres of their land (p. 248)
tratado del fuerte Jackson tratado que se firmó tras la victoria de Estados Unidos en la batalla de Horseshoe Bend; los indígenas creek se vieron obligados a ceder 23 millones de acres de su territorio (pág. 248)

Treaty of Fort Laramie (1851) a treaty signed in Wyoming by the United States and northern Plains nations (p. 554)
tratado del fuerte Laramie (1851) tratado firmado en Wyoming por Estados Unidos y las naciones indígenas de las Planicies del norte (pág. 554)

Treaty of Ghent (1814) a treaty signed by the United States and Britain ending the War of 1812 (p. 249)
tratado de Gante (1814) tratado firmado por Estados Unidos y Gran Bretaña para dar fin a la Guerra de 1812 (pág. 249)

Treaty of Greenville (1795) an agreement between Native American confederation leaders and the U.S. government that gave the United States Indian lands in the Northwest Territory and guaranteed that U.S. citizens could safely travel through the region (p. 209)
tratado de Greenville (1795) acuerdo entre los líderes de la confederación de indígenas norteamericanos y el gobierno estadounidense que otorgó a Estados Unidos parte del Territorio del Noroeste y garantizó la seguridad a los ciudadanos estadounidenses que viajaran por esas tierras (pág. 209)

Treaty of Guadalupe Hidalgo (1848) a treaty that ended the Mexican War and gave the United States much of Mexico's northern territory (p. 323)
tratado de Guadalupe Hidalgo (1848) tratado que daba por terminada la Guerra contra México y daba posesión a Estados Unidos de gran parte del norte del territorio mexicano (pág. 323)

Treaty of Medicine Lodge (1867) an agreement between the U.S. government and southern Plains Indians in which the Indians agreed to move onto reservations (p. 555)
tratado de Medicine Lodge (1867) acuerdo entre el gobierno de Estados Unidos y los indígenas de las Planicies del sur en el que éstos aceptaban reubicarse en el territorio reservado por el gobierno para ellos (pág. 555)

Treaty of Paris of 1783 a peace agreement that officially ended the Revolutionary War and established British recognition of the independence of the United States (p. 101)
tratado de París de 1783 acuerdo de paz que oficialmente daba por terminada la Guerra de Independencia estadounidense y en el que Gran Bretaña reconocía la soberanía de Estados Unidos (pág. 101)

Tredegar Iron Works a large iron factory that operated in Richmond, Virginia, in the early to mid-1800s (p. 379)
Tredegar Iron Works gran fábrica de acero que operaba a mediados del siglo XIX en Richmond, Virginia (pág. 379)

Triangle Shirtwaist Fire a factory fire that killed 146 workers trapped in the building; led to new safety standard laws (p. 618)
incendio de Triangle Shirtwaist incendio de una fábrica en la que murieron 146 trabajadores atrapados en el edificio; este suceso obligó a crear nuevos estándares legales de seguridad (pág. 618)

triangular trade trading networks in which goods and slaves moved among England, the American colonies, and Africa (p. 57)
comercio triangular redes de intercambio de esclavos y bienes entre Inglaterra, las colonias americanas y África (pág. 57)

trust a number of companies legally grouped under a single board of directors (p. 581)
consorcio varias compañías agrupadas legalmente bajo el mando de un solo consejo directivo (pág. 581)

U

Uncle Tom's Cabin (1852) an antislavery novel written by Harriet Beecher Stowe that showed northerners the violent reality of slavery and drew many people to the abolitionists' cause (p. 443)
La cabaña del tío Tom (1852) novela abolicionista escrita por Harriet Beecher Stowe que mostró a los habitantes del norte del país la cruda realidad de la esclavitud e hizo que muchos de ellos se unieran a la causa abolicionista (pág. 443)

ENGLISH AND SPANISH GLOSSARY

Underground Railroad a network of people who helped thousands of enslaved people escape to the North by providing transportation and hiding places (p. 418)
Tren Clandestino red de personas que ayudó a miles de esclavos a escapar al Norte ofreciéndoles transporte y lugares para ocultarse (pág. 418)

USS *Constitution* a large warship (p. 240)
USS *Constitution* gran buque de guerra (pág. 240)

utopian communities places where people worked to establish a perfect society; such communities were popular in the United States during the late 1700s and early to mid-1800s (p. 406)
comunidades utópicas lugares en los que un grupo de personas trabajaba para establecer una sociedad perfecta, como las que se popularizaron en Estados Unidos a finales del siglo XVIII y principios y mediados del XIX (pág. 406)

vaqueros Mexican cowboys in the West who tended cattle and horses (p. 549)
vaqueros arrieros mexicanos que vivían en el Oeste y se ganaban la vida arreando ganado y caballos (pág. 549)

vertical integration the business practice of owning all of the businesses involved in each step of a manufacturing process (p. 580)
integración vertical práctica empresarial de poseer todas las empresas implicadas en cada paso de un proceso de manufactura (pág. 580)

veto to cancel (p. 146)
vetar cancelar (pág. 146)

Virginia Plan (1787) the plan for government proposed at the Constitutional Convention in which the national government would have supreme power and a legislative branch would have two houses with representation determined by state population (p. 126)
Plan de Virginia (1787) plan del gobierno propuesto en la Convención Constitucional por el que el gobierno nacional tendría poder supremo y habría un Poder Legislativo con dos cámaras en las que la representación de cada estado sería determinada por su población (pág. 126)

Virginia Statute for Religious Freedom (1786) a document that gave people in Virginia freedom of worship and prohibited tax money from being used to fund churches (p. 115)
Estatuto de Virginia por la Libertad Religiosa (1786) documento que reconocía a los habitantes de Virginia la libertad de culto y prohibía utilizar el dinero procedente de impuestos para financiar iglesias (pág. 115)

War Hawks members of Congress who wanted to declare war against Britain after the Battle of Tippecanoe (p. 244)
halcones de guerra integrantes del Congreso que tenían la intención de declarar la guerra a Gran Bretaña tras la batalla de Tippecanoe (pág. 244)

Whig Party a political party formed in 1834 by opponents of Andrew Jackson and who supported a strong legislature (p. 292)
Partido Whig partido político formado en 1834 por oponentes de Andrew Jackson que apoyaba una asamblea legislativa con mucha autoridad (pág. 292)

Whiskey Rebellion (1794) a protest of small farmers in Pennsylvania against new taxes on whiskey (p. 209)
Rebelión del Whisky (1794) protesta de pequeños agricultores de Pensilvania contra los nuevos impuestos sobre la producción de whisky (pág. 209)

Wilderness Campaign (1864) a series of battles between Union and Confederate forces in northern and central Virginia that delayed the Union capture of Richmond (p. 500)
Campaña Wilderness (1864) serie de batallas entre la Unión y los confederados en el norte y el centro de Virginia que retrasaron la captura de Richmond por parte de la Unión (pág. 500)

Wilmot Proviso (1846) a proposal to outlaw slavery in the territory added to the United States by the Mexican Cession; passed in the House of Representatives but was defeated in the Senate (p. 438)
Condición de Wilmot (1846) propuesta de prohibir la esclavitud en el territorio adherido a Estados Unidos por la Cesión mexicana; aprobada por la Cámara de Representantes, pero rechazada por el Senado (pág. 438)

Wisconsin Idea a program of progressive reforms set forth by Robert M. La Follette to reduce the power of political machines and make state government more professional (p. 614)
idea de Wisconsin programa de reformas progresistas creado por Robert M. La Follette para reducir el poder de la maquinaria política y profesionalizar el gobierno de los estados (pág. 614)

Women's Christian Temperance Union (WCTU) a reform movement founded in 1874 to prohibit the production and sale of alcohol (p. 623)
Unión de Mujeres Cristianas por la Abstinencia (WCTU, por sus siglas en inglés) movimiento de reforma fundado en 1874 para prohibir la producción y venta de bebidas alcohólicas (pág. 623)

Worcester* v. *Georgia (1832) the Supreme Court ruling that stated that the Cherokee nation was a distinct territory over which only the federal government had authority; ignored by both President Andrew Jackson and the state of Georgia (p. 296)

Worcester **contra** *Georgia* (1832) resolución de la Corte Suprema que establecía que la nación cherokee era un territorio distinto sobre el que sólo el gobierno federal tenía autoridad; fue ignorada por el presidente Andrew Jackson y por el estado de Georgia (pág. 296)

workers' compensation laws laws which would guarantee a portion of lost wages to workers injured on the job (p. 618)
leyes de seguro de accidentes del trabajo leyes que garantizan que se les pague a los trabajadores una porción de su salario si se lesionan durante el desempeño de sus funciones laborales (pág. 618)

XYZ affair (1797) an incident in which French agents attempted to get a bribe and loans from U.S. diplomats in exchange for an agreement that French privateers would no longer attack American ships; it led to an undeclared naval war between the two countries (p. 214)
incidente XYZ (1797) incidente en el que funcionarios franceses intentaron obtener sobornos y préstamos de diplomáticos estadounidenses a cambio de un acuerdo por el cual sus barcos corsarios no atacarían más a los barcos estadounidenses; provocó una guerra no declarada entre las fuerzas navales de ambas naciones (pág. 214)

yellow journalism the reporting of exaggerated stories in newspapers to increase sales (p. 646)
prensa amarillista publicación de noticias exageradas en los periódicos para aumentar las ventas (pág. 646)

yeomen owners of small farms (p. 384)
pequeños terratenientes propietarios de granjas pequeñas (pág. 384)

Index

KEY TO INDEX

c = chart	*p* = photo
f = feature	*A* = Atlas
m = map	*R* = Reference

A

INDEX

G

H

INDEX

INDEX

Credits and Acknowledgments

For permission to reproduce copyrighted material, grateful acknowledgment is made to the following sources:

Norwegian-American Historical Association: From quote by Gro Svendsen from *Frontier Mother: The Letters of Gro Svendsen,* translated and edited by Pauline Farseth and Theodore C. Blegen. Copyright © 1950 Norwegian-American Historical Association.

Saint Martin's Press: Quote by Sarah G. Bagley from *The Belles of New England: The Women of the Textile Mills and the Families Whose Wealth They Wove* by William Moran. Copyright © 2002 by William Moran.

Sources Cited:

Quote by an Aztec messenger from *The Broken Spears: The Aztec Account of the Conquest of Mexico,* Expanded and Updated Edition, edited by Miguel León-Portilla. Published by Beacon Press, Boston, 1992.

From *Yesterday: A Memoir of a Russian Jewish Family* by Miram Shomer Zunser, edited by Emily Wortis Leider. Published by HarperCollins Publishers, New York, 1978.

Quote by a Hungarian immigrant from *This Was America* by Oscar Handlin. Published by Harvard University Press, Cambridge, Mass., 1949.

Chapter Opener Timelines (tl) Photodisc Green/ Getty Images; (bl) © Stockbyte.

Unit One. Chapter 1: Pages 2-3 (t), © Rebecca Marvil/Index Stock Imagery, Inc. ; 2 (b), The Art Archive/National Anthropological Museum Mexico/Dagli Orti; 3 (both), Scala/Art Resource, NY; 7 (t), Smithsonian Institution, Washington, DC. Photograph by Chip Clark # 90-14563; 7 (b), Getty Images; 8 (t), The Field Museum of Natural History, Neg. A108557-c, Photo by Ron Testa; 9 (tl), Ohio Historical Society; (tr), From the Collection of Gilcrease Museum, Tulsa; (bl), ©2000 The Art Institute of Chicago (detail); 10 (tl), ©Marilyn Wynn/Nativestock Pictures; (tr), The Granger Collection, New York; 13, Scala/Art Resource, NY; 17, Art Reference: AKG-Images; 21 ®, ©Robert Frerck/Woodfin Camp & Associates; 23, PRC Archive; 24 (l), Saint Bride Printing Library; 24-25, AKG-Images; 25 (r), Mary Evans Picture Library; 30, Sam Dudgeon/HRW. **Chapter 2:** Pages 32-33 (t), Ted Curtin for Plimoth Plantation; 32 (b), © David Ball/CORBIS; 33 (c), Courtesy of the Pilgrim Society, Plymouth, Massachusetts; 33 (bl), © SuperStock; 33 (br), © Culver Pictures, Inc.; 39 (b), Colonial Williamsburg Foundation; 46 (tl), Art Reference: PRC Archive; 49 (b), © SuperStock; 50 (bl), Art Reference: Historical Society of Pennsylvania; 57 (r), Art Reference: Royal Albert Memorial Museum, Exeter, Devon, UK/ Bridgeman Art Library; 57 (b), Private Collection/www.bridgeman.co.uk; 58 (t), National Portrait Library, London/Bridgeman Art Library; 61 (tr), Art Reference: Courtesy of the Burton Historical Collection, Detroit Public Library; 64-65 (t), Virginia Historical Society; 67, Peter Newark's American Pictures; 68, Courtesy of the Massachusetts Historical Society; 69 (tl), © Bettmann/CORBIS; 69 (tr), American Antiquarian Society. **Chapter 3:** Pages 74-75 (t), © James Lemass/Index Stock Imagery; 75 (cl), The Granger Collection, New York; 75 (c), North Wind Picture Archives; 75 (br), © Christie's Images ; 79, © Concord Museum/ Photograph by Chip Fanelli; 82 (l), (art reference) Phoenix Museum of Art, Arizona/ Bridgeman Art Library; 82 (b), © Robert Llewellyn/SuperStock; 84, © Bettmann/CORBIS; 91 (l), #1921.101, ©Collection of The New-York Historical Society; 91 (r), ©Collection of The New-York Historical Society, neg. 31665; 93 (t), © SuperStock; 94 (l), Saratoga National Historic Park; 94 (r), Chateau de Versailles, France/Giraudon/ Bridgeman Art Library; 95 (l), Falmouth Art Gallery, Cornwall, UK/Bridgeman Art Library; 95 (r), Hotel Galvez, Galveston, Texas; 96, Superstock; 99, The Granger Collection, New York.

Unit Two. Chapter 4: Pages 110-111 (t), Joe Marquette/AP/Wide World Photos; 110, Library of Congress/PRC Archive; 111 (c), Collection of the American Numismatic Society, New York; 111 (bl), © Nik Wheeler/CORBIS; 111 (bc), © Andrea Jemolo/CORBIS; 111 (br), Tokyo National Museum; 115, The Granger Collection, New York; 122-123, The Granger Collection, New York; 125, © Dennis Degnan/CORBIS; 126 (t), Hall of Representatives, Washington, DC/ Bridgeman Art Library; 126 (bl), Independence National Historical Park ; 126 (bc), Stock Montage; 126 (br), Portrait by Robert S. Susan, Collection of the Supreme Court of the United States; 127, © Alex Wong/Getty Images; 128 (l), South Carolina Legal History Collection; 128 (r), City of Bristol Museum and Art Gallery/Bridgeman Art Library; 131 (l), (art reference) Historical Society of Pennsylvania; 131 (br), American Antiquarian Society; 133 (l), Stock Montage, Inc.; 133 (r), © Bettmann/CORBIS. **Chapter 5:** 140-141 (t), Sam Dudgeon/HRW Photo; 141 (cl), PRC Archive; 141 (cr), © Tony Freeman/PhotoEdit; 141 (b), © Bettmannn/CORBIS; 149 (both), National Archives (NARA); 152 (br), Dennis Cook/AP/Wide World Photos; 154-155 (bc), © Mark Wilson/ Getty Images; 154, © Royalty-Free/CORBIS; 155, © Brooks Kraft/CORBIS; 166 (bl), © Yang Liu/CORBIS; (bc), Norm Detlaff, Las Cruces Sun-News/AP/Wide World Photos; 167 (bl), ©Alex Webb/Magnum Photos; (bc), © David Young-Wolff/PhotoEdit; (br), © Bettmann/CORBIS; 171, Library of Congress/PRC Archive; 173, Library of Congress; 175 (l), © Bettmann/CORBIS; 175 (r), © Oscar White/CORBIS; 176 (tl), Dr. Hector P. Garcia Papers, Special Collections & Archives, Texas A&M University-Corpus Christi, Bell Library; 176 (tr), ©1978 Matt Herron/TakeStock; 176 (tc), Texas State Library & Archives Commission; 179, © Daily News Pix; 181, © Spencer Grant/PhotoEdit; 182-183 (b), © Ariel Skelley/CORBIS; 185, © David Butow/CORBIS; 186 (tl), ©James Pickerell/The Image Works; 186 (tr), © Brownie Harris/CORBIS; 187 (tl), © Ariel Skelly/CORBIS; (tc), Janet Knott/The Boston Globe. Republished with permission of The Globe Newspaper Company, Inc.; (tr), © Jeff Greenberg/ PhotoEdit. **Chapter 6:** Pages 192-193 (t), © Miles Ertman/Masterfile; 192, © Christie's Images; 193 (bl), Giraudon/Art Resource, NY; 193 (r), Art Resource, NY; 196-197 (b), ©SuperStock; 197, Library of Congress/PRC Archive; 198-199 (t), © The New York Public Library, Miriam and Ira D. Wallch Division of Art, Prints and Photographs, Astor, Lenox and Tilden Foundations / Art Resource, NY; 199, (inset) (#1907.32) © Collection of The New-York Historical Society; 202 (c), Photo ©2004 Roger Foley; 202 (b), © Joseph Sohm; Chromosohm, Inc./CORBIS; 203 (l), Stock Montage, Inc.; 203 (r), Stock Montage/Getty Images; 205, Réunion des Musées Nationaux/Art Resource, NY; 206 (l), Chicago Historical Society, #i35980aa; 206 (r), Library of Congress/PRC Archive; 207, HRW Photo Research Library; 208, Courtesy Ohio Historical Society; 210, © Museum of the City of New York/CORBIS ; 213 (tl), ©The New York Historical Society, New York, NY/ Bridgeman Art Library; 213 (tc), The Art Archive/Chateau de Blernacourt/Dagli Orti; 213 (tr), ©The New-York Historical Society, New York, NY/ Bridgeman Art Library; 213 (bl), Independence National Historical Park Collection; 213 (bc), The Henry Luce III Center for the Study of American Culture/ SuperStock; 213 (br), National Portrait Gallery, Smithsonian Institution, Washington, DC/Art Resource, NY; 214, Library of Congress/PRC Archive.

Unit Three. Pages 222-223 (Art Ref) ©Tom Bean/CORBIS. **Chapter 7:** Pages 224-225 (t), Superstock; 224, The Granger Collection, New York; 225 (bl), New Haven Colony Historical Society, Gift of George W. Crawford, 1973. #1973.20.C; 225 (cl), Benninghoff Collection of the American Revolution; 225 (cr), Portrait of the Founder, Munetada Kurozumi. Image courtesy of Kurozumikyo Shinto; 225 (cr), Library of Congress, LC-USZC4-6466; 229 (l), The Art Archive/Chateau de Blernacourt/Dagli Orti; 229 (r), © Bettmann/CORBIS; 229 bkgd © Alan Schein Photography/CORBIS; 231 (b), Getty Images; 232 (t), Washington and Lee University; 239, © Terry W. Eggers/CORBIS; 242 (l), The Mariners Museum; (r), North Wind Picture Archives; 243 (t), North Wind Picture Archives; 243 (bl), The Granger Collection, New York; 243 (br), © 1993 Mickey Osterreischer/Black Star; 244 (l), ©The Field Museum, Neg #A93851.1c, Chicago.; 244 (r), National Portrait Gallery, Smithsonian Institution, Washington, DC; gift of Mrs. Herbert Lee Pratt, Jr.; 248 (b), ©Bettmann/ CORBIS; 248(inset) © New-York Historical Society/Bridgeman Art Library. **Chapter 8:** Pages 256-257 (t), © Lee Snider/Photo Images/CORBIS ; 256, National Portrait Gallery, Smithsonian Institution, Washington, DC/Art Resource, NY; 257 (tl), The Granger Collection, New York; 257 (tr), Library of Congress #LC-USZC4-5801; 257 (bl), The Granger Collection, New York; 257 (br), Courtesy PRC Archive; 265 (t), © Bettmann/ CORBIS; 265 (b), Maryland Historical Society, Baltimore, Maryland; 266 (cl), (Art Reference) Chicago Historical Society; 270 (l), Hampton University Museum, Hampton, Virginia.; 271 (tl), Library of Congress; 271 (bl), © Andre Jenny/Alamy Photos; 271 (tr), © Bettmann/ CORBIS; 271 (br), American Antiquarian Society; 272 (b), Smithsonian American Art Museum, Washington DC/Art Resource, NY; 273, © Francis G. Mayer/CORBIS; **Chapter 9:** Pages 280-281, Detroit Publishing Company Collection, from *Birth of A Century,* KEA Publishing Services Ltd.; 280 (b), The Granger Collection, New York; 281 (tl), Janice L. and David J. Frent Collection of Political Americana; 281 (tr), National Portrait Gallery, Smithsonian Institution/Art Resource, NY; 281 (bl), The Stapleton Collection, UK/ Bridgeman Art Library; 281 (br), The Art Archive; 285 (t), R.W. Norton Art Gallery, Shreveport, LA. Used by permission; 285 (b), David Young-Wolff/PhotoEdit; 286-287 (bl), (Art Reference) © Board of Trustees, National Gallery of Art, Washington; 287 (br), The Hermitage, Home of Andrew Jackson; 289 (l), The Fine Arts Museum of San Francisco, Gift of Eleanor Martin, 37566; (c), Christie's Images/ Bridgeman Art Library; (r), American Museum of Textile History; 296, © Collection of The New-York Historical Society; 299, Superstock. **Chapter 10:** Pages 304-305 (t), Seaver Center for Western History Research, Natural History Museum of Los Angeles County; 305 (tl), Used by permission, Utah State Historical Society, all rights reserved; 305 (tr), © The Oakland Museum, The City of Oakland; 305 (bl), Peter Newark's Western Americana; 305 (br), Library of Congress, LC-USZC4-1307/PRC Archive; 309, © Bettmann/CORBIS; 313, (both), Courtesy of *Texas Highways* Magazine; 314, Jack Lewis/TxDOT; 315, Texas State Library and Archives Commission; 317 (t), Janice L. and David J. Frent Collection of Political Americana; 317 (b), American Antiquarian Society; 318-319 (b), James Walker, *Vaqueros in a Horse Corral,* 1877, #0126.1480, From the Collection of Gilcrease Museum, Tulsa, Oklahoma.; 319 (br), (Art Reference) Courtesy The Bancroft Library, University of California, Berkeley; 321 (t), Society of California Pioneers; 322-323, Texas State Library and Archives Commission; 324, J. Griffiths Smith/TxDOT; 327, (both)Collection of Matthew Isenburg; 328 (t), Courtesy of the

California History Room, California State Library, Sacramento, California; 329 (tl), Seaver Center for Western History Research, Natural History Museum of Los Angeles County; 330, Library of Congress. #LC-USZC4-7421; 332-333, Courtesy Steve Pinkston; 333 (inset), Bob Burch/ Index Stock Imagery, Inc.

Unit Four. Chapter 11: Pages 342-343 (t), © Marilyn Root/Index Stock Imagery, Inc.; 342 (b), New York State Historical Association, Cooperstown; 343 (inset),George Eastman House; 343 (cl), PRC Archive; 343 (cr), © Southeast Museum; 343 (bl), NASA; 343 (br), © CORBIS; 348 (l), Samuel Finley Breese Morse, Eli Whitney (1765-1825), Yale University Art Gallery. Gift of George Hoadley, B.A. 1801; 348 (r), Museum of Connecticut History; 349 (l), Museum of Connecticut History; 349 (r), New Haven Colony Historical Society; 350, © Bob Krist/CORBIS ; 353, Rhode Island Historical Society; 354, Jack Naylor Collection; 359, Library of Congress, Detroit Publishing Company Collection; 364, Museum of Connecticut History; 365 (t), (Art Ref) Stock Montage, Inc.; 365 (bl), Smithsonian Institution, Washington, DC (Photograph by Charles Phillips); 365 (br), Courtesy John Deere & Company Archives; 366 (l), National Museum of American History, Smithsonian Institution, Washington, DC (#89-6626); 366 (r), The Granger Collection, New York. **Chapter 12:** 372-373, Penn School Papers, Southern Historical Collection, University of North Carolina at Chapel Hill, Wilson Library, #P.3615/0824(A); 372, National Museum of American History, Smithsonian Institution, Washington, DC. Photo by Kim Neilson, #83-2953; 373 (bc), © Hulton-Deutsch Collection/ CORBIS; 373 (br), Library of Congress; 384 (tl), The Valentine Museum; 384 (tr), Collection of the American Numismatic Society, New York; 387 (b), The J. Paul Getty Museum, Los Angeles; 388-389 (t), *Hauling the Whole Week's Pickings* by William Henry Brown, The Historic New Orleans Collection; 389 (tr), South Carolina Historical Society; 390, North Wind Picture Archives. **Chapter 13:** Pages 396-397 (t), The Metropolitan Museum of Art, Gift of I.N. Phelps Stokes, Edward S. Hawes, Alice Mary Hawes, Marion Augusta Hawes, 1937.[37.14.22]. All rights reserved, The Metropolitan Museum of Art.; 397 (cl), Courtesy of the Massachusetts Historical Society; 397 (cr), PRC Archive; 397 (bl), Photo © David Modica, courtesy American Printing House for the Blind Museum; 397 (br), Peter Newark's American Pictures; 401 (c), Wiliam B. Becker Collection/ American Museum of Photography; 405, © Royalty-Free/CORBIS; 406-407, Brooklyn Museum of Art, Gift of the Brooklyn Institute of Arts and Sciences/ Bridgeman Art Library; 411 (r), The Metropolitan Museum of Art; 413 (t), (Art Reference) Library of Congress, #LC-USZC4-7396; 414-415, Courtesy of Oberlin Archives; 415 (inset) Museum of Art, Rhode Island School of Design. Gift of Lucy T. Aldrich; 417 (t), Trustees of the Boston Public Library; 418, Library of Congress; 419 (t), Courtesy of the Levi Coffin House Association and Waynet; 419 (b), Courtesy of The Brooklyn Museum of Art [40.59]; 420, Library of Congress; 421 (c), Courtesy of the Massachusetts Historical Society; 422 (l), (art reference) PRC Archive; 422 (r), Library of Congress, Manuscript Division; 424 (l), Courtesy of the Massachusetts Historical Society; 424 (r), The Granger Collection, New York; 425 (l), Courtesy of the Susan B. Anthony House, Rochester, NY; 425 (r), Library of Congress/PRC Archive; 427, Stock Montage, Inc.; 428, © Bettmann/CORBIS; 429 (bl), (Art Reference) Susan B. Anthony House; 429 (r), © 1973 Historical Documents Co. Harcourt Photo by Maria Paraskevas; 435 (bl), The Art Archive/ Private Collection/Dagli Orti; **Chapter 14:** Pages 434-453 (t), © Dave G. Houser; 435 (bl) The Art Archive/Private Collection/Dagli Orti; 435 (br), India Office Library & Records, The British Library; 435 (cr), Chicago Historical Society; 435 (cl), Nancy Gewitz/Antique Textile Resources; 440, PRC Archive; 442, The J. Paul Getty Museum, Los Angeles.; 445, Library of Congress, LC-USZ62-92043; 448 (t), Kansas Museum of History; 448 (b), Kansas State Historical Society, Topeka, Kansas; 451, Getty Images; 452, Missouri Historical Society; 453, Library of Congress/PRC Archive; 454 (r), The Museum of American Political Life, University of Hartford, West Hartford, CT; 454 (tl), Picture History; 456 (t), Ohio Historical Society; 489, Naval Historical Center.

Unit Five. Chapter 15: Pages 466-467, Steve Stone w/special thanks to The American Civil War Society of the United Kingdom, 2nd Wisconsin Volunteer Infantry (esp. 1st Lt. Tom Reed & Private James Reed), and the 18th Virginia Infantry, Company G (esp. Stuart Colquitt). 468-469 (t), Library of Congress, Brady Civil War Photo Collection; 468 (b), Confederate Museum, United Daughters of the Confederacy; 469 (cl), © SuperStock; 469 (cr), © SuperStock; 469 (b), Chicago Historical Society, # i26736aa; 479 (t), © Medford Historical Society Collection/ CORBIS; 480, National Park Service; 481 (b), Library of Congress; 482, Library of Congress/ PRC Archive; 485 (b), © 1989, The Greenwich Workshop, Inc., Reproduced with the permission of the Greenwich Workshop, Inc., Shelton, CT; 489, Naval Historical Center; 490, SuperStock; 491, South Carolina Historical Society; 492 (l), Courtesy of the Massachusetts Historical Society; (r) Library of Congress; 494, © Bettmann/ CORBIS; 495 (t), National Museum of American History, Smithsonian Institution, Washington, DC (ID#84-9312); 495 (b), © REUTERS/Kai Pfaffenbach/CORBIS; 496, American Antiquarian Society; 502, © SuperStock; 503, © Topham / The Image Works; 504, 506, The Granger Collection, New York; **Chapter 16:** Pages 508-509 (t), © Paul Rocheleau; 508 (b), © Kean Collection/Getty Images; 509 (cl), The Granger Collection, New York; 509 (cr), Herbert F. Johnson Museum of Art, Cornell University; 509 (bl), © Michael Maslan Historic Photographs/ CORBIS; 512-513 (b), National Archives (NARA); 514 (t), Library of Congress; 514 (inset), Chicago Historical Society; 515, University of Texas at El Paso Library, Special Collections Department, Ada Tharp Photograph Collection; 516, © William Gladstone Collection; 519, Library of Congress; 520 (l), Library of Congress; 520 (r), ©CORBIS; 522, North Wind Picture Archives; 525 (both), Library of Congress; 526, The Granger Collection, New York; 527, Tennessee State Museum Collection. Photography by June Dorman; 528, Getty Images; 529 (b), North Wind Picture Archives; 530, Courtesy of The Charleston Renaissance Gallery, Robert M. Hicklin, Jr. Inc., Charleston, South Carolina; 531, © Bettmann/CORBIS. **Chapter 17:** Pages 542-543 (t), © James L. Amos/CORBIS; 542 (b), Courtesy Wells Fargo Bank; 543 (cl), Southern Pacific Lines/PRC Archive; 543 (cr), © CORBIS; 543 (bl), The Art Archive /Musée d'Orsay Paris/ Dagli Orti; 543 (br), The Granger Collection, New York; 548 (l), Denver Public Library, Western History Collection; 548-549 (r), Nebraska State Historical Society, Photograph Collections; 549, Bob Boze Bell, *True West* Magazine; 550, © James L. Amos/CORBIS; 551, Library of Congress/PRC Archive; 552, The Granger Collection, New York; 553, SuperStock; 555, George Lane/AP/Wide World Photos; 556-557, © Bettmann/CORBIS; 557, Western History Division, National Museum of American History/Smithsonian Institution, Washington, DC; 558, The Granger Collection, New York; 559 (r) Janice & David Frent Collection of Political Americana; 561, Western History Collections, University of Oklahoma; 562 (t), Elias Carr Papers, East Carolina Manuscript Collection, J.Y. Joyner Library, East Carolina University, Greenville, NC. Photo by Dewane Frutiger; 562 (bl), Library of Congress; 562 (br), Courtesy of the Northern Indiana Center for History; 563 (l), Culver Pictures; 565, © CORBIS **Chapter 18:** Pages 570-571 (t), PRC Archive; 571 (c), George Meany Memorial Archives; 571 (bl), ©Bettmann/ CORBIS; 571 (br), Archives Larousse, Paris, France/Bridgeman Art Library; 574-575, Library of Congress; 576 (r), [neg. #40578] © Collection of The New York Historical Society; 577 (l), Property of AT&T Archives. Printed with permission of AT&T; (r), © Hulton Archive/ Getty Images; 578 (l), © CORBIS; (r), Library of Congress/PRC Archive; 579, Montgomery County Historical Society; 580, © CORBIS; 580 (inset), Courtesy of the Rockefeller Archive Center; 581, [#71880T] © Collection of The New-York Historical Society; 583 (l), (Art Ref) AP/Wide World Photos & © Bettmann/CORBIS; 583 (c), (Art Ref) AP/Wide World Photos; 583 (r), (Art Reference) Photo courtesy Union Pacific Historical Collection; 585 (t), Brown Brothers; 585 (b), (Art Ref) © Bettmann/CORBIS; 589 (l), Copyright The New York Public Library/Art Resource, NY; (r), © Joseph Sohm, Chromosohm, Inc./CORBIS; 590 (l), National Archives, #90-G-152-2038; (r), Shades of L.A. Archives/Los Angeles Public Library; 591 (l), © CORBIS; 591 (r), Col. Ernest Swanson Papers, Swenson Swedish Immigration Research Center, Augustana College, Rock Island, IL; 592 (r), © A. Ramey/PhotoEdit; 595, Chicago Historical Society; 596 (l), Jane Addams Memorial Collection (JAMC neg 227), Special Collections, University Library, University of Illinois at Chicago; 596 (r), Curt Teich Postcard Archives, Lake County, IL Museum; 599, ©Bettmann/CORBIS. **Chapter 19:** Pages 602-603 (t), Elizabeth Cady Stanton Trust; 603 (cl, cr), Janice L. and David J. Frent Collection of Political Americana; 603 (b), The Granger Collection, New York; 608-609, PRC Archive; 609 (r), The Granger Collection, New York; 612, Museum of the City of New York, Jacob Riis Collection 502; 613, LifeCare Alliance/Ohio Historical Society; 615, National Archives; 616, Library of Congress; 618, Courtesy of Steve Latham; 623, © Bettmann/ CORBIS; 625, Seaver Center for Western History Research, Natural History Museum of Los Angeles County; 626, Dr. Ching Collection/ PRC Archive; 628, Leroy Radanovich/Yosemite Museum; 628-629, © W. Perry Conway/CORBIS; 630, Stock Montage, Inc.; 635, Library of Congress. **Chapter 20:** Pages 636-637 (t), © Bettmann/CORBIS; 636 (b), © Charles Sleicher; 637 (c), Denver Public Library, Western History Collection; 637 (bl), Press Information Bureau of India; 641, Naval Parade, held in honor of commander George Dewey (1837-1917) 1898 (oil on canvas) by Fred Pansing (1854-1912) Museum of the City of New York, USA / Bridgeman Art Library; 642, © CORBIS; 643, National Portrait Gallery, Smithsonian Institution/ Art Resource, NY; 644, Trustees of the British Museum; 647 (t), PRC Archive; 647 (b), © Bettmann/CORBIS; 648, National Archives/PRC Archive; 649, Courtesy Frederic Remington Art Museum, Ogdensburg, New York; 650, Keystone-Mast Collection (KU58458)/University of California at Riverside/ California Museum of Photography; 654, © Danny Lehman/CORBIS; 656, The Granger Collection, New York; 659, 660, © Bettmann/ CORBIS; **Back Matter.** Pages R1-R5, White House Historical Association (White House Collection); R5 (last) The White House, photo by Eric Draper.

Staff Credits. The people who contributed to ***Holt California Social Studies: United States History, Independence to 1914*** are listed below. They represent editorial, design, intellectual property resources, production, emedia, and permissions.

Lissa B. Anderson, Melanie Baccus, Charles Becker, Jessica Bega, Ed Blake, Gillian Brody, Shirley Cantrell, Erin Cornett, Rose Degollado, Chase Edmond, Mescal Evler, Rhonda Fariss, Marsh Flournoy, Leanna Ford, Bob Fullilove, Matthew Gierhart, Janet Harrington, Rhonda Haynes, Rob Hrechko, Wilonda Ieans, Cathy Jenevinein, Kadonna Knape, Cathy Kuhles, Debbie Lofland, Bob McClellan, Joe Melomo, Richard Metzger, Cynthia Munoz, Karl Pallmeyer, Chanda Pearmon, Shelly Ramos, Désirée Reid, Curtis Riker, Marleis Roberts, Diana Rodriguez, Gene Rumann, Annette Saunders, Kay Selke, Ken Shepardson, Michele Shukers, Chris Smith, Elaine Tate, Jeannie Taylor, Joni Wackwitz, Ken Whiteside